W9-CGP-513

Mathematics: Applications and Concepts Features and Benefits

		See page(s):
Curriculum and Instructional Strategies	. . . deliver sound mathematics based on sound research. • Chapters grouped by units provide for depth of content. • Relevant real-life, problem-based learning format enhances contextual learning. • The series is vertically aligned to eliminate gaps and redundancies; it is horizontally aligned for consistency from level to level.	iii
Student Support	. . . is provided throughout the text to help all students achieve success in mathematics. • **Foldables**™ Study Organizers help students focus on the organization and analysis of main ideas and vocabulary. • **Study Skills** help students organize, understand, and retain course information. • **How to Use Your Math Textbook** helps students understand how to get the most value out of the Student Edition. • **Homework Help** in the exercise sets links homework exercises to corresponding examples within the lesson.	313 16, 81 xxiii–1 118
Reading and Writing In Mathematics	. . . strategies and activities are essential for student success in mathematics. • **Reading Math** tips help students learn and use the language of mathematics. • **Practice** in vocabulary usage in each lesson and at the end of each chapter builds reading and writing skills. • **Writing Math** questions allow students to define, describe, and explain mathematical concepts. • **Reading in the Content Area** links appear in each chapter to help students read and analyze key lessons. • **Noteables™: Interactive Study Notebook with Foldables™** guides students in taking notes throughout each chapter.	315 125, 146 317, 392 62 206
Daily Intervention	. . . opportunities are provided throughout the program. • **Prerequisite Skills** at the beginning of each chapter and in each lesson help you assess student readiness. • The **Student Handbook** contains review and practice of prerequisite skills. • **Daily Intervention** features in the Teacher Wraparound Edition provide suggestions for addressing various learning styles and helping students who are having difficulty. • A variety of **Online Study Tools** are readily accessible to students.	115, 136 589–659 117, 397 msmath3.net
Test Preparation and Assessment	. . . are comprehensive to address local, state, and national tests. • Each lesson has two **Standardized Test Practice** questions. • Each Mid-Chapter Practice Test and Chapter Practice Test also has Standardized Test Practice questions. • Standardized Test Practice **Examples** help students learn how to approach test questions. • **Standardized Test Practice** at the end of each chapter include multiple-choice, short response/grid in, and extended response questions. • **Preparing for Standardized Tests** in the Student Handbook provides practice for the types of questions and concepts commonly seen on standardized tests. • **Interactive Standardized Test Practice** is available in the Online Study Tools.	387 327 394, 413 150–151 660–677 msmath3.net
Staff Development "Sticky Notes" in Chapter 1 provide a "walk-through" of key features. pp. 4–59	. . . features are available to assist new teachers and those teaching outside their primary subject area. • **Continuity of Instruction** and **Mathematical Background** provides an overview of the mathematics in the chapter and links prior knowledge to future topics. • **Tips for New Teachers** provide helpful suggestions for classroom management, teaching strategies, intervention, and more. • McGraw-Hill Professional Development products provide professional learning opportunities in mathematics instruction; correlation to the standards-based program *Mathematics, YES!*	4C–4D 77, 138 T19, 4D
Education Partnership	. . . strengthens the relevance of applications, projects, and assessment. • **USA TODAY Snapshots**® provide current topics and data in graphs, charts, and tables.	127

GLENCOE MATHEMATICS

Mathematics

Applications and Concepts

Course 3

Teacher Wraparound Edition

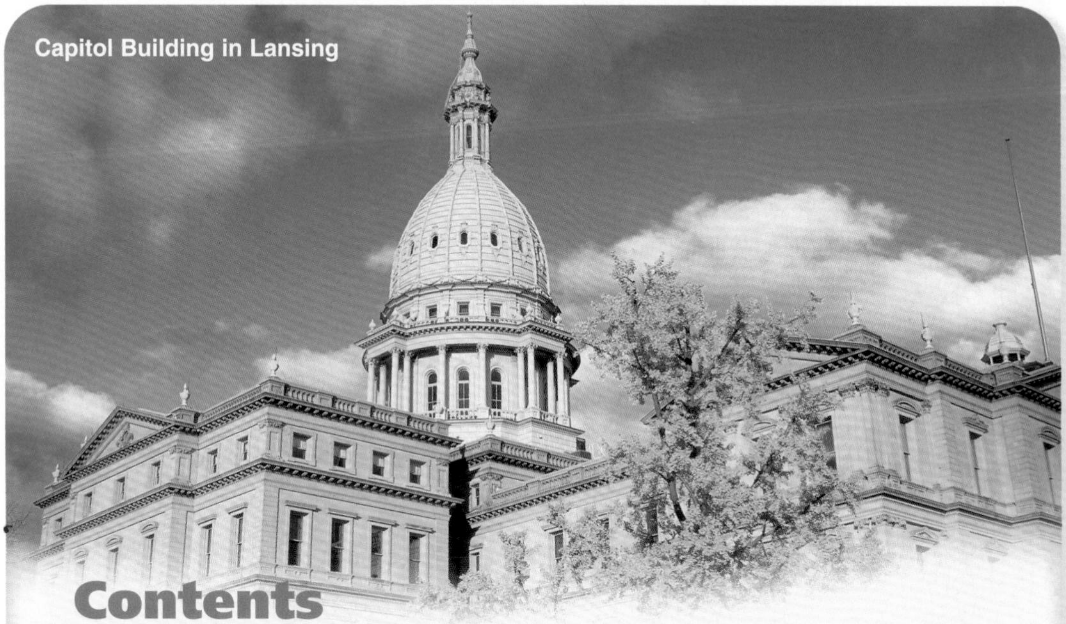

Capitol Building in Lansing

Contents

ISBN: 0-07-869349-7 *(Michigan Student Edition)* 0-07-869352-7 *(Michigan Teacher Wraparound Edition)*

4 5 6 7 8 9 10 043/127 12 11 10 09 08 07 06

Mathematics

Applications and Concepts

Course 3

Features of the Michigan Teacher Wraparound Edition

Exclusively from Glencoe

Additional Michigan Resources

Exclusively from Glencoe

- **Mastering the GLCEs: Diagnose-Prescribe-Practice Workbook, Grade 7** Diagnose student weaknesses, prescribe specific MEAP practice worksheets, and practice problems similar to those on the MEAP test.
- **Preparing for the Michigan Tests CD-ROM** Includes questions that can help your students prepare for success on Michigan tests.
- **Michigan TeacherWorks™** An all-in-one lesson planner and resource center that helps you customize lesson plans and reproduce classroom resources quickly and easily.
- **Michigan StudentWorks™** This backpack solution CD-ROM allows students instant access to the Student Edition, lesson worksheet pages, and web resources.
- **Michigan Middle School Guide to Daily Intervention** A lesson-by-lesson guide to available resources to reach students in need of intervention/remediation.
- **Exam*View*® Pro** A customizable testmaker with built-in Michigan curriculum correlations.
- **Correlation** Michigan Content Standards and Working Benchmarks for Middle School, Correlated to *Glencoe Mathematics: Applications and Concepts,* Course 3 online at **www.mi.msmath3.net**

Michigan Teacher Reviewers and Field Test School

- **Mary H. Jones, Reviewer** Math Curriculum Coordinator, Grand Rapids Public Schools, Grand Rapids
- **Katie Davidson, National Teacher Advisory Board** Mathematics Teacher, Legg Middle School, Coldwater
- **Field Test School** Legg Middle School, Coldwater

For more information, visit: www.mi.msmath3.net

Michigan Teacher Advisory Board

Photo Credits: MI i Joseph Sohm; ChromoSohm Inc./CORBIS, **MI iv** Dietrick Floeter/Travel Michigan, **MI ix** Getty Images, **MI xvi** Travel Michigan, **MI 16** Conrad Zobel/CORBIS

Detroit Skyline

Contents in Brief

Authors

Rhonda Bailey
Mathematics Consultant
Mathematics by Design
DeSoto, Texas

Roger Day, Ph.D.
Associate Professor
Illinois State University
Normal, Illinois

Patricia Frey
Director of Staffing and Retention
Buffalo City Schools
Buffalo, New York

Arthur C. Howard
Mathematics Teacher
Houston Christian High School
Houston, Texas

Deborah T. Hutchens, Ed.D.
Assistant Principal
Great Bridge Middle School
Chesapeake, Virginia

Kay McClain, Ed.D.
Assistant Professor
Vanderbilt University
Nashville, Tennessee

Beatrice Moore-Harris
Mathematics Consultant
League City, Texas

Jack M. Ott, Ph.D.
Distinguished Professor of Secondary Education Emeritus
University of South Carolina
Columbia, South Carolina

Ronald Pelfrey, Ed.D.
Mathematics Specialist
Appalachian Rural Systemic Initiative
Lexington, Kentucky

Jack Price, Ed.D.
Professor Emeritus
California State Polytechnic University
Pomona, California

Kathleen Vielhaber
Mathematics Specialist
Parkway School District
St. Louis, Missouri

Teri Willard, Ed.D.
Assisstant Professor of Mathematics Education
Central Washington University
Ellensburg, Washington

Contributing Authors

USA TODAY
The USA TODAY Snapshots®, created by USA TODAY®, help students make the connection between real life and mathematics.

FOLDABLES™ **Dinah Zike**
Educational Consultant
Dinah-Might Activities, Inc.
San Antonio, Texas

Content Consultants

Each of the Content Consultants reviewed every chapter and gave suggestions for improving the effectiveness of the mathematics instruction.

Mathematics Consultants

L. Harvey Almarode
Curriculum Supervisor, Mathematics K–12
Augusta County Public Schools
Fishersville, VA

Claudia Carter, MA, NBCT
Mathematics Teacher
Mississippi School for Mathematics and Science
Columbus, MS

Carol E. Malloy, Ph.D.
Associate Professor, Curriculum Instruction, Secondary Mathematics
The University of North Carolina at Chapel Hill
Chapel Hill, NC

Melissa McClure, Ph.D.
Mathematics Instructor
University of Phoenix On-Line
Fort Worth, TX

Robyn R. Silbey
School-Based Mathematics Specialist
Montgomery County Public Schools
Rockville, MD

Leon L. "Butch" Sloan, Ed.D.
Secondary Mathematics Coordinator
Garland ISD
Garland, TX

Barbara Smith
Mathematics Instructor
Delaware County Community College
Media, PA

Reading Consultant

Lynn T. Havens
Director
Project CRISS
Kalispell, MT

ELL Consultants

Idania Dorta
Mathematics Educational Specialist
Miami–Dade County Public Schools
Miami, FL

Frank de Varona, Ed.S.
Visiting Associate Professor
Florida International University College of Education
Miami, FL

Teacher Reviewers

Each Teacher Reviewer reviewed at least two chapters of the Student Edition, giving feedback and suggestions for improving the effectiveness of the mathematics instruction.

Royallee Allen
Teacher, Math Department Head
Eisenhower Middle School
San Antonio, TX

Dennis Baker
Mathematics Department Chair
Desert Shadows Middle School
Scottsdale, AZ

Rosie L. Barnes
Teacher
Fairway Middle School–KISD
Killeen, TX

Charlie Bialowas
Math Curriculum Specialist
Anaheim Union High School District
Anaheim, CA

Stephanie R. Boudreaux
Teacher
Fontainebleau Jr. High School
Mandeville, LA

Dianne G. Bounds
Teacher
Nettleton Junior High School
Jonesboro, AR

Susan Peavy Brooks
Math Teacher
Louis Pizitz Middle School
Vestavia Hills, AL

Karen Sykes Brown
Mathematics Educator
Riverview Middle School
Grundy, VA

Kay E. Brown
Teacher, 7th Grade
North Johnston Middle School
Micro, NC

Renee Burgdorf
Middle Grades Math Teacher
Morgan Co. Middle
Madison, GA

Kelley Summers Calloway
Teacher
Baldwin Middle School
Montgomery, AL

Carolyn M. Catto
Teacher
Harney Middle School
Las Vegas, NV

Claudia M. Cazanas
Math Department Chair
Fairmont Junior High
Pasadena, TX

David J. Chamberlain
Secondary Math Resource Teacher
Capistrano Unified School District
San Juan Capistrano, CA

David M. Chioda
Supervisor Math/Science
Marlboro Township Public Schools
Marlboro, NJ

Carrie Coate
7th Grade Math Teacher
Spanish Fort School
Spanish Fort, AL

Toinette Thomas Coleman
Secondary Mathematics Teacher
Caddo Middle Career & Technology School
Shreveport, LA

Linda M. Cordes
Math Department Chairperson
Paul Robeson Middle School
Kansas City, MO

Polly Crabtree
Teacher
Hendersonville Middle School
Hendersonville, NC

Dr. Michael T. Crane
Chairman Mathematics
B.M.C. Durfee High School
Fall River, MA

Tricia Creech, Ph.D.
Curriculum Facilitator
Southeast Guilford Middle School
Greensboro, NC

Lyn Crowell
Math Department Chair
Chisholm Trail Middle School
Round Rock, TX

B. Cummins
Teacher
Crestdale Middle School
Matthews, NC

Debbie Davis
8th Grade Math Teacher
Max Bruner, Jr. Middle School
Ft. Walton Beach, FL

Diane Yendell Day
Math Teacher
Moore Square Museums Magnet Middle School
Raleigh, NC

Wendysue Dodrill
Teacher
Barboursville Middle School
Barboursville, WV

Judith F. Duke
Math Teacher
Cranford Burns Middle School
Mobile, AL

Carol Fatta
Math/Computer Instructor
Chester Jr. Sr. M.S.
Chester, NY

Cynthia Fielder
Mathematics Consultant
Atlanta, GA

Georganne Fitzgerald
Mathematics Chair
Crittenden Middle School
Mt. View, CA

Jason M. Fountain
7th Grade Mathematics Teacher
Bay Minette Middle School
Bay Minette, AL

Sandra Gavin
Teacher
Highland Junior High School
Cowiche, WA

Ronald Gohn
8th Grade Mathematics
Dover Intermediate School
Dover, PA

Larry J. Gonzales
Math Department Chairperson
Desert Ridge Middle School
Albuquerque, NM

Shirley Gonzales
Math Teacher
Desert Ridge Middle School
Albuquerque, NM

Paul N. Hartley, Jr.
Mathematics Instructor
Loudoun County Public Schools
Leesburg, VA

Deborah L. Hewitt
Math Teacher
Chester High School
Chester, NY

Steven J. Huesch
Mathematics Teacher/Department Chair
Cortney Jr. High
Las Vegas, NV

Sherry Jarvis
8th Grade Math/Algebra 1 Teacher
Flat Rock Middle School
East Flat Rock, NC

Teacher Reviewers *continued*

Mary H. Jones
Math Curriculum Coordinator
Grand Rapids Public Schools
Grand Rapids, MI

Vincent D.R. Kole
Math Teacher
Eisenhower Middle School
Albuquerque, NM

Ladine Kunnanz
Middle School Math Teacher
Sequoyah Middle School
Edmond, OK

Barbara B. Larson
Math Teacher/Department Head
Andersen Middle School
Omaha, NE

Judith Lecocq
7th Grade Teacher
Murphysboro Middle School
Murphysboro, IL

Paula C. Lichiello
7th Grade Math and Pre-Algebra Teacher
Forest Middle School
Forest, VA

Michelle Mercier Maher
Teacher
Glasgow Middle School
Baton Rouge, LA

Jeri Manthei
Math Teacher
Millard North Middle School
Omaha, NE

Albert H. Mauthe, Ed.D.
Supervisor of Mathematics (Retired)
Norristown Area School District
Norristown, PA

Karen M. McClellan
Teacher & Math Department Chair
Harper Park Middle
Leesburg, VA

Ken Montgomery
Mathematics Teacher
Tri-Cities High School
East Point, GA

Helen M. O'Connor
Secondary Math Specialist
Harrison School District Two
Colorado Springs, CO

Cindy Ostrander
8th Grade Math Teacher
Edwardsville Middle School
Edwardsville, IL

Michael H. Perlin
8th Grade Mathematics Teacher
John Jay Middle School
Cross River, NY

Denise Pico
Mathematics Teacher
Jack Lund Schofield Middle School
Las Vegas, NV

Ann C. Raymond
Teacher
Oak Ave. Intermediate School
Temple City, CA

M.J. Richards
Middle School Math Teacher
Davis Middle School
Dublin, OH

Linda Lou Rohleder
Math Teacher, Grades 7 & 8
Jasper Middle School
Jasper, IN

Dana Schaefer
Pre-Algebra & Algebra I Teacher
Coachman Fundamental Middle School
Clearwater, FL

Donald W. Scheuer, Jr.
Coordinator of Mathematics
Abington School District
Abington, PA

Angela Hardee Slate
Teacher, 7th Grade Math/Algebra
Martin Middle School
Raleigh, NC

Mary Ferrington Soto
7th Grade Math
Calhoun Middle School-Ouachita Parish Schools
Calhoun, LA

Diane Stilwell
Mathematics Teacher/Technology Coordinator
South Middle School
Morgantown, WV

Pamela Ann Summers
K–12 Mathematics Coordinator
Lubbock ISD–Central Office
Lubbock, TX

Marnita L. Taylor
Mathematics Teacher/Department Chairperson
Tolleston Middle School
Gary, IN

Susan Troutman
Teacher
Dulles Middle School
Sugar Land, TX

Barbara C. VanDenBerg
Math Coordinator, K–8
Clifton Board of Education
Clifton, NJ

Mollie VanVeckhoven-Boeving
7th Grade Math and Algebra Teacher
White Hall Jr. High School
White Hall, AR

Mary A. Voss
7th Grade Math Teacher
Andersen Middle School
Omaha, NE

Christine Waddell
Teacher Specialist
Jordan School District
Sandy, UT

E. Jean Ware
Supervisor
Caddo Parish School Board
Shreveport, LA

Karen Y. Watts
9th Grade Math Teacher
Douglas High School
Douglas, AL

Lu Wiggs
Supervisor
I.S. 195
New York, NY

Teacher Advisory Board and Field Test Schools

Teacher Advisory Board

Glencoe/McGraw-Hill wishes to thank the following teachers for their feedback on *Mathematics: Applications and Concepts*. They were instrumental in providing valuable input toward the development of this program.

Katie Davidson
Legg Middle School
Coldwater, MI

Lynanne Gabriel
Bradley Middle School
Huntersville, NC

Kathleen M. Johnson
New Albany-Plain Local Middle School
New Albany, OH

Ronald C. Myer
Indian Springs Middle School
Columbia City, IN

Mike Perlin
John Jay Middle School
Cross River, NY

Reema Rahaman
Brentwood Middle School
Brentwood, MO

Diane T. Scheuber
Elizabeth Middle School
Elizabeth, CO

Deborah Sykora
Hubert H. Humphrey Middle School
Bolingbrook, IL

DeLynn Woodside
Roosevelt Middle School,
Oklahoma City Public Schools
Oklahoma City, OK

Field Test Schools

Glencoe/McGraw-Hill wishes to thank the following schools that field-tested pre-publication manuscript during the 2002–2003 school year. They were instrumental in providing feedback and verifying the effectiveness of this program.

Knox Community Middle School
Knox, IN

Roosevelt Middle School
Oklahoma City, OK

Brentwood Middle School
Brentwood, MO

Elizabeth Middle School
Elizabeth, CO

Legg Middle School
Coldwater, MI

Great Hollow Middle School
Nesconset, NY

Student Advisory Board

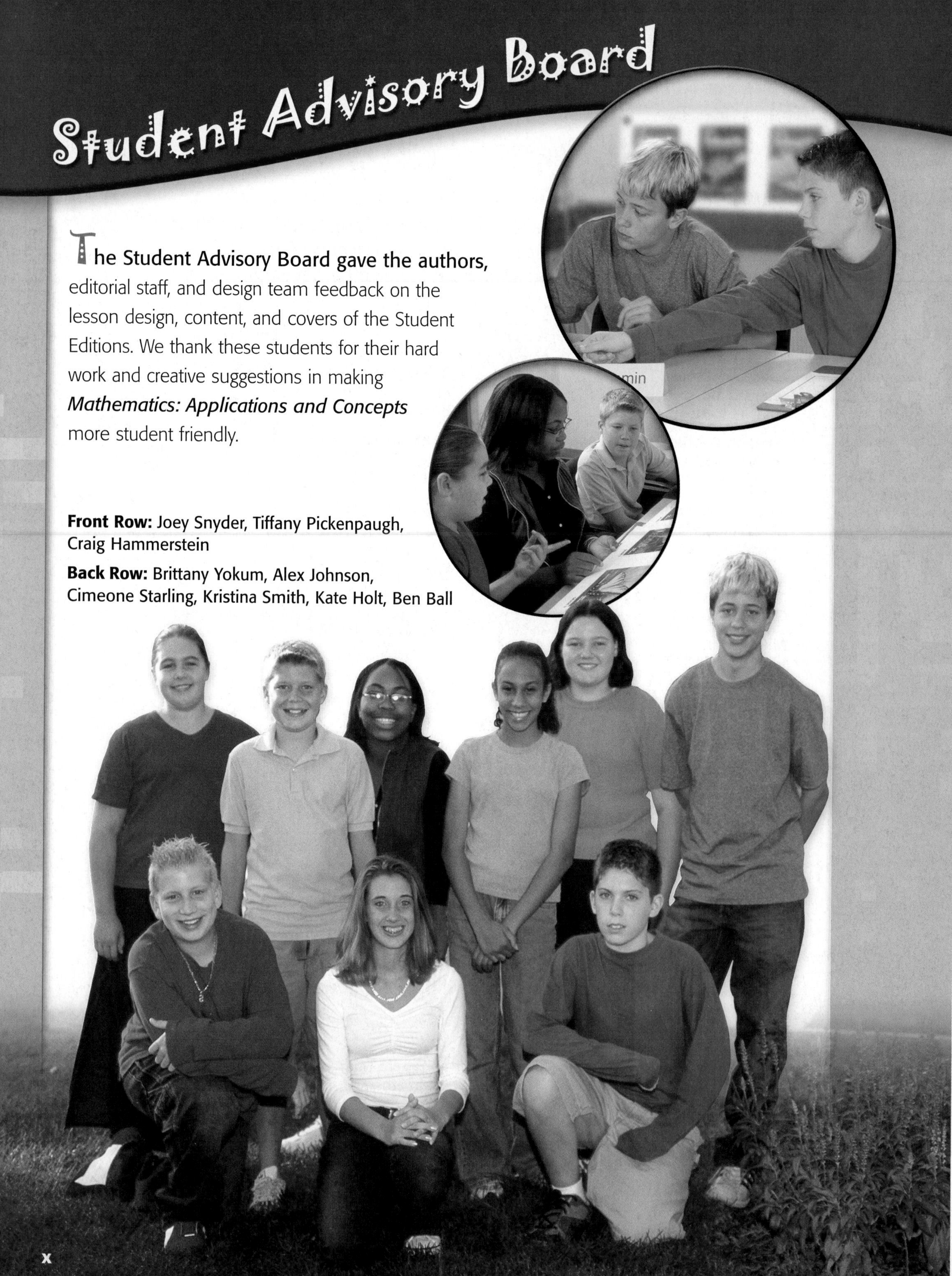

The Student Advisory Board gave the authors, editorial staff, and design team feedback on the lesson design, content, and covers of the Student Editions. We thank these students for their hard work and creative suggestions in making ***Mathematics: Applications and Concepts*** more student friendly.

Front Row: Joey Snyder, Tiffany Pickenpaugh, Craig Hammerstein

Back Row: Brittany Yokum, Alex Johnson, Cimeone Starling, Kristina Smith, Kate Holt, Ben Ball

Michigan Grade Level Content Expectations: Grade 7, Correlated to Glencoe *Mathematics: Applications and Concepts,* Grade 7

Grade Level Content Expectations		Student Edition Lesson(s)		
		Introduce	Develop/ Master	Extend
STRAND N NUMBER AND OPERATIONS				
Understand derived quantities				
N.ME.07.01	Understand derived quantities such as density, velocity, and weighted averages.	2-3, 2-4	2-3, 2-4, 4-1	4-1
N.FL.07.02	Solve problems involving derived quantities.	2-3, 2-4	2-3, 2-4	2-8a
Understand and solve problems involving rates, ratios, and proportions				
N.FL.07.03	Calculate rates of change including speed.	4-1	4-2	4-2b, 4-3
N.MR.07.04	Convert ratio quantities between different systems of units such as feet per second to miles per hour.	4-1	4-1	4-1
N.FL.07.05	Solve simple proportion problems using such methods as unit rate, scaling, finding equivalent fractions, and solving the proportion equation $\frac{a}{b} = \frac{c}{d}$; know how to see patterns about proportional situations in tables.	4-4	4-4, 4-5a, 4-5, 4-5b, 4-6, 4-7	4-8
Recognize irrational numbers				
N.MR.07.06	Understand the concept of square root and cube root, and estimate using calculators.	3-1, 3-2	3-1, 3-2, 3-3, 3-4, 3-5	3-4, 3-5, 3-5b, 3-6
Compute with rational numbers				
N.FL.07.07	Solve problems involving operations with integers.	1-1, 1-2, 1-3, 1-3b	1-4, 1-5, 1-6	1-8a, 1-8, 1-9
N.FL.07.08	Add, subtract, multiply and divide negative rational numbers.	2-3, 2-4, 2-5, 2-6	2-3, 2-4, 2-5, 2-6	2-7, 2-8a
N.FL.07.09	Estimate results of computations with rational numbers.	PS1	2-5	

PS = Prerequisite Skill Lessons (pp. 600–615)

Grade Level Content Expectations		Student Edition Lesson(s)		
		Introduce	Develop/ Master	Extend
STRAND A ALGEBRA				
Understand and apply directly proportional relationships and relate to linear relationships				
A.PA.07.01	Recognize when information given in a table, graph, or formula suggests a proportional or linear relationship.	4-2b, 4-3, 11-3a	11-3a, 11-3	11-3, 12-1
A.RP.07.02	Represent directly proportional and linear relationships using verbal descriptions, tables, graphs, and formulas, and translate among these representations.	4-2b, 4-3, 4-4, 11-2, 11-3a	11-3, 11-5	11-7
A.PA.07.03	Given a directly proportional or linear situation, graph and interpret the slope and intercept(s) in terms of the original situation; evaluate $y = kx$ for specific x values, given k, e.g., weight vs. volume of water, base cost plus cost per unit.	4-3, 4-4, 11-3a	11-3, 11-5a, 11-5	11-6a
A.PA.07.04	For directly proportional or linear situations, solve applied problems using graphs and equations, e.g., the heights and volume of a container with uniform cross-section, height of water in a tank being filled at a constant rate, degrees Celsius and degrees Fahrenheit, distance and time under constant speed.	4-2b, 4-3, 4-4	11-3a, 11-3, 11-4, 11-5	11-6a, 11-7
A.PA.07.05	Understand and use directly proportional relationships of the form $y = mx$, and distinguish from linear relationships of the form $y = mx + b$, b non-zero; understand that in a directly proportional relationship between two quantities one quantity is a constant multiple of the other quantity.	11-3	11-3, 11-5a, 11-5	11-7
Understand and represent linear functions				
A.PA.07.06	Calculate the slope from the graph of a linear function as the ratio of "rise/run" for a pair of points on the graph, and express the answer as a fraction and a decimal; understand that linear functions have slope that is a constant rate of change.	4-3, 11-4	4-3, 11-4	11-5a, 11-5

PS = Prerequisite Skill Lessons (pp. 600–615)

Grade Level Content Expectations		Student Edition Lesson(s) Introduce	Develop/ Master	Extend
A.PA.07.07	Represent linear functions in the form $y = x + b$, $y = mx$, and $y = mx + b$, and graph, interpreting slope and *y*-intercept.	11-2	11-3, 11-5a, 11-5	11-6, 11-7
A.FO.07.08	Know that the solution to a linear equation corresponds to the point at which its graph crosses the *x*-axis.	Beyond the scope of this textbook	Beyond the scope of this textbook	Beyond the scope of this textbook
Understand and solve problems about inversely proportional relationships				
A.PA.07.09	Recognize inversely proportional relationships in contextual situations; know that quantities are inversely proportional if their product is constant, e.g., the length and width of a rectangle with fixed area, and that an inversely proportional relationship is of the form $y = \frac{k}{x}$ where *k* is some non-zero number.	12-1	*Glencoe Algebra 1:* 12-1	*Glencoe Algebra 1:* 12-1
A.RP.07.10	Know that the graph of $y = \frac{k}{x}$ is not a line; know its shape; and know that it crosses neither the *x* nor the *y*-axis.	12-1	12-1	*Glencoe Algebra 1:* 12-1
Apply basic properties of real numbers in algebraic contexts				
A.PA.07.11	Understand and use basic properties of real numbers: additive and multiplicative identities, additive and multiplicative inverses, commutativity, associativity, and the distributive property of multiplication over addition.	1-2, 1-4	1-2, 1-4, 2-4	10-1, 12-3, 12-4, 12-5, 12-6, 12-7
Combine algebraic expressions and solve equations				
A.FO.07.12	Add, subtract, and multiply simple algebraic expressions of the first degree, e.g., $(92x + 8y) - 5x + y$, or $-2x\,(5x - 4)$, and justify using properties of real numbers.	10-1, 10-4a, 10-4, 12-3	12-4, 12-5	12-4, 12-5, 12-6
A.FO.07.13	From applied situations, generate and solve linear equations of the form $ax + b = c$ and $ax + b = cx + d$, and interpret solutions.	10-2, 10-3, 10-4	10-2, 10-3, 10-4	10-2, 10-3, 10-4, 10-4b

PS = Prerequisite Skill Lessons (pp. 600–615)

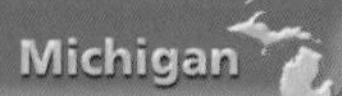

Grade Level Content Expectations		Student Edition Lesson(s) Introduce	Develop/ Master	Extend
STRAND G GEOMETRY				
Draw and construct geometric objects				
G.SR.07.02	Use compass and straightedge to perform basic geometric constructions: the perpendicular bisector of a segment, an equilateral triangle, and the bisector of an angle; understand informal justifications.	6-1b	6-2b, 6-3b	6-5b
Understand the concept of similar polygons, and solve related problems				
G.TR.07.03	Understand that in similar polygons, corresponding angles are congruent and the ratios of corresponding sides are equal; understand the concepts of similar figures and scale factor.	4-5, 4-6	4-5, 4-6, 4-7	4-8
G.TR.07.04	Solve problems about similar figures and scale drawings.	4-5, 4-6	4-5, 4-6, 4-7	4-7, 4-8
G.TR.07.05	Show that two triangles are similar using the criteria: corresponding angles are congruent (AAA similarity); the ratios of two pairs of corresponding sides are equal and the included angles are congruent (SAS similarity); ratios of all pairs of corresponding sides are equal (SSS similarity); use these criteria to solve problems and to justify arguments.	4-5	4-5	4-5
G.TR.07.06	Understand and use the fact that when two triangles are similar with scale factor of r, their areas are related by a factor of r^2.	4-5	4-5	4-5
STRAND D DATA AND PROBABILITY				
Represent data and interpret				
D.RE.07.01	Represent and interpret data using circle graphs, stem and leaf plots, histograms, and box-and-whisker plots, and select appropriate representation to address specific questions.	PS2, 9-1, 9-1b, 9-2	9-1, 9-1b, 9-2, 9-3, 9-6	9-7
D.AN.07.02	Create and interpret scatter plots and find line of best fit and use an estimated line of best fit to answer questions about the data.	11-6a	11-6, 11-6b	11-6, 11-6b

PS = Prerequisite Skill Lessons (pp. 600–615)

Grade Level Content Expectations		Student Edition Lesson(s) Introduce	Develop/ Master	Extend
Compute statistics about data sets				
D.AN.07.03	Calculate and interpret relative frequencies and cumulative frequencies for given data sets.	9-1a	*Glencoe Pre-Algebra:* 12-4	*Glencoe Pre-Algebra:* 12-4
D.AN.07.04	Find and interpret the median, quartiles, and interquartile range of a given set of data.	9-4, 9-4b	9-5, 9-6	9-7

PS = Prerequisite Skill Lessons (pp. 600–615)

State Tree
White Pine

Grade 7 Pacing Chart

Bold indicates the benchmark most directly addressed by the lesson.
Pacing is given in school calendar days.

Lesson	Grade 7 GLCE	Grades 5–8 Curriculum Framework	Michigan Pacing	
			Regular Schedule	Block Schedule
Countdown to MEAP	In addition to the lessons assigned in the next 5 days, complete the problems on pages MI 6–MI 7.			
1-1	N.FL.07.07		1	0.5
1-2	N.FL.07.07, A.PA.07.11	MS.IV.1.3, **MS.V.1.3,** MS.V.1.4, MS.V.2.1	1	0.5
1-3	N.FL.07.07	**MS.IV.1.1,** MS.IV.2.1, MS.IV.3.1	1	0.5
1-3b	N.FL.07.07	MS.III.3.4, **MS.III.3.5**	1	0.5
1-4	N.FL.07.07, A.PA.07.11	MS.IV.1.4, MS.IV.2.5, **MS.V.1.1,** MS.V.1.4, MS.VI.2.5	1	0.5
Countdown to MEAP	In addition to the lessons assigned in the next 5 days, complete the problems on pages MI 8–MI 9.			
1-5	N.FL.07.07	MS.IV.1.4, MS.IV.2.5, MS.V.1.1, **MS.V.1.4,** MS.VI.2.5	1	0.5
1-6	N.FL.07.07	MS.IV.1.4, MS.IV.2.5, MS.V.1.3, **MS.V.1.4,** MS.VI.2.5	1	0.5
1-7		MS.IV.2.5, **MS.V.2.1**	1	0.5
1-8a	N.FL.07.07	MS.IV.3.5, **MS.V.1.2,** MS.V.2.5	1	0.5
1-8	N.FL.07.07	**MS.IV.2.5**	1	0.5
Countdown to MEAP	In addition to the lessons assigned in the next 5 days, complete the problems on pages MI 10–MI 11.			
1-9	N.FL.07.07	**MS.IV.2.5**	1	1
Chapter 1 Review and Testing			2	1
2-1		**MS.IV.1.1,** MS.IV.2.2	1	0.5
2-2		MS.IV.2.2, **MS.IV.3.1**	1	0.5
Countdown to MEAP	In addition to the lessons assigned in the next 5 days, complete the problems on pages MI 12–MI 13.			
2-3	N.ME.07.01, N.FL.07.02, N.FL.07.08	MS.IV.1.4, MS.IV.2.5, **MS.V.1.4,** MS.VI.2.5	1	0.5
2-4	N.ME.07.01, N.FL.07.02, N.FL.07.08, A.PA.07.11	**MS.IV.1.3,** MS.IV.1.4, MS.IV.2.5, MS.V.1.1, MS.V.1.4, MS.VI.2.5	1	0.5
2-5	N.FL.07.08, N.FL.07.09	MS.IV.1.4, MS.IV.2.5, **MS.V.1.4,** MS.VI.2.5	1	1
2-6	N.FL.07.08	MS.IV.1.4, MS.IV.2.5, **MS.V.1.4,** MS.VI.2.5	1	0.5
2-7	N.FL.07.08	**MS.IV.1.4,** MS.IV.2.5	1	0.5

Lesson	Grade 7 GLCE	Grades 5–8 Curriculum Framework	Michigan Pacing	
			Regular Schedule	Block Schedule
Countdown to MEAP	In addition to the lessons assigned in the next 5 days, complete the problems on pages MI 14–MI 15.			
2-8a	N.FL.07.02, N.FL.07.08	MS.I.1.1, MS.I.1.3, MS.I.1.4, **MS.I.1.5,** MS.IV.3.5, MS.V.1.2, MS.V.2.5	1	0.5
2-8		MS.IV.1.4, **MS.IV.3.4**	1	0.5
2-8b			0	0
2-9		**MS.IV.1.2,** MS.IV.1.4	1	1
Chapter 2 Review and Testing			2	1
3-1	N.MR.07.06	MS.IV.2.1, **MS.IV.3.4**	1	0.5
3-2	N.MR.07.06	**MS.IV.2.4**	1	0.5
3-3a		**MS.VI.2.5,** MS.IV.3.5, MS.V.2.5	1	0.5
3-3	N.MR.07.06	MS.IV.2.1, **MS.IV.2.3**	1	0.5
3-4	N.MR.07.06	**MS.II.1.7**	1	0.5
3-5	N.MR.07.06		1	0.5
3-5b	N.MR.07.06		0	0
3-6	N.MR.07.06	**MS.II.2.1,** MS.II.2.4, MS.II.2.5	1	1
Chapter 3 Review and Testing			2	1
4-1	N.ME.07.01, N.FL.07.03, N.MR.07.04	**MS.IV.3.2**	1	1
4-2	N.FL.07.03	**MS.I.2.1,** MS.I.2.4	1	0.5
4-2b	N.FL.07.03, A.PA.07.01, A.RP.07.02, A.PA.07.04	**MS.I.2.3**	1	0.5
4-3	N.FL.07.03, A.PA.07.01, A.RP.07.02, A.PA.07.03, A.PA.07.04, A.PA.07.06	MS.I.2.1, **MS.I.2.4,** MS.II.2.1	1	0.5
4-4	N.FL.07.05, A.RP.07.02, A.PA.07.03, A.PA.07.04	**MS.II.3.5**	1	0.5
4-5a	N.FL.07.05	MS.IV.3.5, **MS.V.2.5**	1	0.5
4-5	N.FL.07.05, G.TR.07.03, G.TR.07.04, G.TR.07.05, G.TR.07.06	**MS.II.3.5**	1	0.5
4-5b	N.FL.07.05		1	0
4-6	N.FL.07.05, G.TR.07.03, G.TR.07.04	**MS.II.3.5**	1	1
4-7	N.FL.07.05, G.TR.07.03, G.TR.07.04	**MS.II.3.5**	1	0.5

Lesson	Grade 7 GLCE	Grades 5–8 Curriculum Framework	Michigan Pacing	
			Regular Schedule	Block Schedule
4-7b		**MS.II.1.7**	1	0
4-8	N.FL.07.05, G.TR.07.03, G.TR.07.04	MS.II.2.1, **MS.II.2.3**	1	0.5
Chapter 4 Review and Testing			2	1
5-1		**MS.IV.2.1**	1	0.5
5-2		**MS.IV.2.2**	1	0.5
5-3			1	0.5
5-4		**MS.IV.2.4**	1	0.5
5-5a		**MS.IV.2.4,** MS.IV.3.5, MS.V.2.5	1	0.5
5-5		**MS.IV.2.4**	1	0.5
5-6			1	0.5
5-7		MS.I.2.1, **MS.I.2.4**	1	0.5
5-8			1	0.5
5-8b		MS.V.2.5, **MS.VI.2.4**	1	0.5
Chapter 5 Review and Testing			2	1
6-1		MS.II.1.6, MS.II.2.2, **MS.II.3.2,** MS.II.3.6	1	0.5
6-1b	G.SR.07.02	**MS.II.1.6**	1	0.5
6-2	G.SR.07.01	MS.II.1.1, MS.II.1.2, **MS.II.1.3,** MS.II.1.7	1	0.5
6-2b	G.SR.07.02		1	0.5
6-3	G.SR.07.01	MS.II.1.2, MS.II.1.3, MS.II.1.7, **MS.II.3.6**	1	0.5
6-3b	G.SR.07.02	**MS.II.1.6,** MS.II.2.2	1	0.5
6-4	G.SR.07.01	**MS.II.1.1,** MS.II.1.2, MS.II.1.3, MS.II.1.7	1	0.5
6-4b		**MS.IV.3.5,** MS.V.2.5	1	0.5
6-5a	G.SR.07.01		1	0
6-5	G.SR.07.01	**MS.II.1.6,** MS.II.1.7	1	0.5
6-5b	G.SR.07.01, G.SR.07.02	**MS.II.1.4,** MS.II.1.6	1	0.5
6-6		MS.I.1.4, MS.II.1.7, **MS.II.2.2,** MS.II.2.5	1	0.5
6-7		MS.II.1.5, MS.II.2.1, MS.II.2.2, **MS.II.2.3,** MS.II.2.4, MS.II.2.5	1	0.5
6-8		MS.II.1.5, MS.II.2.1, MS.II.2.2, MS.II.2.3, **MS.II.2.4,** MS.II.2.5	1	1

Lesson	Grade 7 GLCE	Grades 5–8 Curriculum Framework	Michigan Pacing	
			Regular Schedule	Block Schedule
6-9		MS.II.1.5, MS.II.2.1, MS.II.2.2, MS.II.2.3, MS.II.2.4, **MS.II.2.5**	1	0.5
6-9b		**MS.II.1.5**	1	0.5
Chapter 6 Review and Testing			2	1
7-1	G.SR.07.01	MS.II.1.7, MS.II.3.2, **MS.II.3.6**	1	0.5
7-2		MS.II.1.7, MS.II.3.2, **MS.II.3.6**	1	0.5
7-3a		**MS.IV.3.5,** MS.V.2.5	1	0.5
7-3		**MS.II.1.5,** MS.II.1.7, MS.II.3.2, MS.II.3.6	1	0.5
7-4a		**MS.II.1.4**	1	0.5
7-4		**MS.II.1.1**	1	0.5
7-5		MS.II.1.7, MS.II.3.2, MS.II.3.4, **MS.II.3.6**	1	0.5
7-6	G.SR.07.01	MS.II.1.7, MS.II.3.2, **MS.II.3.4,** MS.II.3.6	1	0.5
7-7a		**MS.II.1.4**	1	0.5
7-7		MS.II.1.7, **MS.II.3.6**	1	0.5
7-8		MS.II.1.7, **MS.II.3.6**	1	0.5
7-8b		MS.I.2.6, **MS.II.1.6**	1	0.5
7-9		**MS.II.3.3,** MS.II.3.6, MS.IV.2.3	1	1
Chapter 7 Review and Testing			2	1
8-1		**MS.VI.1.1, MS.VI.1.2**	1	1
8-2a		**MS.IV.3.5,** MS.V.2.5	1	0.5
8-2		MS.III.1.4, **MS.VI.2.1**	1	0.5
8-3		**MS.VI.2.1**	1	1
8-4		**MS.VI.2.1**	1	0.5
8-4b		**MS.III.2.5, MS.III.3.1,** MS.VI.1.2	1	0.5
8-5		**MS.VI.1.3**	1	1
8-6		MS.III.1.1, MS.III.3.2, MS.III.3.3, MS.VI.1.2, MS.VI.1.3, **MS.VI.1.4,** MS.VI.1.5	1	0.5
8-6b		MS.III.1.1, MS.III.2.5, **MS.III.3.2,** MS.III.3.3, **MS.III.3.5,** MS.V.2.5, MS.VI.1.3, MS.VI.1.4, **MS.VI.1.5**	1	0.5
8-7		**MS.III.1.1,** MS.III.2.1, **MS.III.2.4, MS.III.3.2, MS.III.3.4,** MS.III.3.5	1	1
Chapter 8 Review and Testing			2	1
9-1a	D.AN.07.03	MS.III.1.2, MS.III.1.3, **MS.III.1.4,** MS.IV.3.5, MS.V.2.5	1	0.5

Lesson	Grade 7 GLCE	Grades 5–8 Curriculum Framework	Michigan Pacing	
			Regular Schedule	Block Schedule
9-1	D.RE.07.01	**MS.III.1.2,** MS.III.1.3, MS.III.2.1, **MS.III.2.3**	1	0.5
9-1b	D.RE.07.01	**MS.III.1.2,** MS.III.1.3	1	0
9-2	D.RE.07.01	**MS.III.1.2,** MS.III.1.3, MS.III.2.1, **MS.III.2.3**	1	0.5
9-3	D.RE.07.01	**MS.III.1.3**	1	0.5
9-3b		**MS.III.1.2,** MS.III.1.3, MS.III.2.3	1	0
9-4	D.AN.07.04	MS.III.2.1, **MS.III.2.2,** MS.III.2.3	1	0.5
9-4b	D.AN.07.04	**MS.III.2.2,** MS.V.2.5	1	0.5
9-5	D.AN.07.04	MS.III.2.1, **MS.III.2.2,** MS.III.2.3	1	0.5
9-6	D.RE.07.01, D.AN.07.04	MS.III.1.2, MS.III.1.3, **MS.III.2.1, MS.III.2.3**	1	0.5
9-7	D.RE.07.01, D.AN.07.04	MS.III.1.3, MS.III.2.1, MS.III.2.3, **MS.III.2.4, MS.III.3.3**	1	0.5
9-8			0	0.5
Chapter 9 Review and Testing			2	1
10-1a		**MS.V.2.2**	1	0.5
10-1	A.PA.07.11, A.FO.07.12		1	0.5
10-2	A.FO.07.13		1	0.5
10-3	A.FO.07.13	**MS.V.2.2**	1	0.5
10-4a	A.FO.07.12	**MS.V.2.2**	0.5	0.5
10-4	A.FO.07.12, A.FO.07.13		0.5	0.5
10-4b	A.FO.07.13	**MS.IV.3.5,** MS.V.2.5	1	0
10-5			1	0.5
10-6		**MS.VI.2.2,** MS.VI.2.6	1	0.5
10-7		**MS.VI.2.2,** MS.VI.2.6	1	1
Chapter 10 Review and Testing			2	1
11-1		**MS.I.1.1,** MS.I.1.2, MS.I.1.3, **MS.I.1.4,** MS.I.1.5, MS.I.2.2	1	0.5
11-1b		MS.I.1.1, MS.I.1.2, **MS.I.1.3,** MS.I.1.4	1	0.5
11-2	A.RP.07.02, A.PA.07.07	MS.I.1.2, **MS.I.2.2,** MS.I.2.4, MS.I.2.6	1	1
11-3a	A.PA.07.01, A.RP.07.02, A.PA.07.03, A.PA.07.04	MS.I.1.1, MS.I.1.2, MS.I.1.3, MS.I.1.4, MS.I.2.3, MS.I.2.4, **MS.I.2.6,** MS.III.3.4, MS.III.3.5	1	0.5
11-3	A.PA.07.01, A.RP.07.02, A.PA.07.03, A.PA.07.04, A.PA.07.05, A.PA.07.07	**MS.I.1.4,** MS.I.1.5, MS.I.2.3, MS.I.2.4, MS.I.2.6, MS.V.2.1, **MS.V.2.4**	1	0.5

Lesson	Grade 7 GLCE	Grades 5–8 Curriculum Framework	Michigan Pacing	
			Regular Schedule	Block Schedule
11-4	A.PA.07.04, A.PA.07.06	MS.I.2.1, **MS.I.2.4**	1	1
11-5a	A.PA.07.03, A.PA.07.04, A.PA.07.05, A.PA.07.06, A.PA.07.07		1	0.5
11-5	A.RP.07.02, A.PA.07.03, A.PA.07.04, A.PA.07.05, A.PA.07.06, A.PA.07.07	MS.V.2.1, **MS.V.2.4**	1	0.5
11-6a	A.PA.07.03, A.PA.07.04, D.AN.07.02	MS.III.2.1, **MS.III.2.3,** MS.IV.3.5, MS.V.2.5	1	0.5
11-6	A.PA.07.07, D.AN.07.02	**MS.I.2.1,** MS.I.2.2, MS.I.2.3, **MS.I.2.4,** MS.I.2.6, MS.II.1.1, MS.III.1.2, MS.III.1.3, MS.III.2.1, MS.III.2.3, MS.III.3.4, MS.III.3.5	0.5	0.5
11-6b	D.AN.07.02		0.5	0
11-7	A.RP.07.02, A.PA.07.04, A.PA.07.05, A.PA.07.07	**MS.V.2.3,** MS.V.2.4	1	0.5
11-8		MS.V.2.1, MS.V.2.3, **MS.VI.2.6**	1	0.5
Chapter 10 Review and Testing			2	1
12-1	A.PA.07.01, A.PA.07.09, A.RP.07.10	MS.I.1.4, MS.I.2.2, MS.I.2.3, MS.I.2.4, **MS.I.2.5**	1	0.5
12-2a			0.5	0
12-2		**MS.I.1.5**	0.5	0.5
12-3a		**MS.V.2.2**	1	0.5
12-3	A.PA.07.11, A.FO.07.12	**MS.V.2.2**	1	0.5
12-4	A.PA.07.11, A.FO.07.12		1	0.5
12-5	A.PA.07.11, A.FO.07.12		1	0.5
12-6	A.PA.07.11, A.PA.07.11		1	1
12-7a		MS.IV.3.5, MS.V.2.5, **MS.VI.2.3**	1	0.5
12-7	A.PA.07.11		1	0.5
Chapter 12 Review and Testing			2	1
PS1	N.FL.07.09		1	0.5
PS2	D.RE.07.01	**MS.III.1.3**	1	0.5
PS3		MS.II.3.1, MS.II.3.2, **MS.II.3.6,** MS.IV.2.3	1	1
PS4		MS.II.3.1, MS.II.3.2, **MS.II.3.6,** MS.IV.2.3	1	0.5
PS5		**MS.IV.3.3**	1	0.5
PS6		**MS.IV.3.3**	1	0.5
PS7		**MS.IV.3.3**	1	0.5

Lesson	Grade 7 GLCE	Grades 5–8 Curriculum Framework	Michigan Pacing	
			Regular Schedule	Block Schedule
PS8		MS.IV.2.2	1	0.5
PS9		MS.IV.3.3	1	0.5
PS10		MS.II.3.2	1	0.5
PS11			0	0
PS12		MS.II.3.1	1	0.5
Total Days of Instruction			165	89

Mackinac Bridge

How To...

Prepare for the MEAP

Countdown to MEAP

Pages MI 6–MI 15 of this text include a section called **Countdown to MEAP**. The MEAP is the Michigan Educational Assessment Program. The mathematics portion of the MEAP test assesses the concepts and skills from the Michigan Grade Level Content Expectations. A list of these can be found on pages MI 3 and MI 4 of this textbook.

Counting Down to MEAP
Each set of problems "counts down" to the week of the MEAP test. You should plan to complete one two-page spread each week to help you prepare for the test.

One-a-Day
Plan to spend a few minutes each day working on the MEAP test problem(s) for that day unless your teacher asks you to do otherwise.

Variety
The problems are similar to those on the MEAP test.
- Monday and Tuesday, constructed response
- Wednesday through Friday, selected response (multiple-choice)

Record Answers
Your teacher can provide you with an answer sheet to record your work and your answers for each week. A printable answer sheet is also available at mi.msmath3.net. At the end of the week, your teacher may want you to turn in the answer sheet.

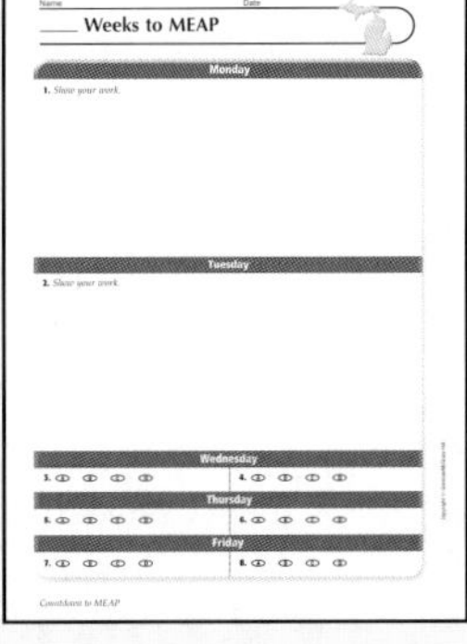

Countdown to MEAP

Mastering the GLCEs: Diagnose–Prescribe–Practice Workbook, Grade 7

The **Mastering the GLCEs: Diagnose–Prescribe–Practice Workbook, Grade 7,** contains a diagnostic test, practice for each of the Grade 7 Michigan Grade Level Content Expectations, and a sample test.

As students practice and master each Grade Level Content Expectation, they can record their progress in the Student Recording Chart in the workbook.

The Teacher's Annotated Edition of this workbook also contains a Class recording Chart to monitor the progress of all of your students.

Answer Sheet

The answer sheet pictured is also available in the Teacher Annotated Edition of the **Mastering the GLCEs: Diagnose–Prescribe–Practice Workbook, Grade 7**.

Pacing

This Countdown to MEAP is to be used the first five weeks of your school calendar to review for the MEAP test given in October.

Additional Correlation

A correlation of this textbook to the Michigan Mathematics Content Standards: Middle School is available online at **www.mi.msmath3.net.**

Countdown to MEAP

Grade Level Content Expectations

This problem set covers the following Michigan Grade Level Content Expectations.

N.ME.06.05 Order rational numbers and place them on the number line. *(Question 1)*

N.ME.06.06 Represent rational numbers as fractions or terminating decimals when possible, and translate between these representations. *(Question 1)*

N.FL.06.12 Calculate part of a number given the percentage and the number. *(Question 1)*

D.PR.06.01 Express probabilities as fractions, decimals or percentages between 0 and 1; know that 0 probability means an event will not occur and that probability 1 means an event will occur. *(Question 2)*

A.PA.06.01 Solve applied problems involving rates including speed, e.g., if a car is going 50 mph, how far will it go in $3\frac{1}{2}$ hours? *(Question 3)*

G.GS.06.01 Understand and apply basic properties of lines, angles, and triangles, including:
—triangle inequality
—relationships of vertical angles, complementary angles, supplementary angles

5 Weeks to MEAP

Monday

1. Kevin surveyed his class to find where they would most like to vacation. The following table shows the outcome.

Destinaton	Fraction of Class
ocean	$\frac{1}{10}$
national park	$\frac{2}{5}$
amusement park	$\frac{1}{2}$

A. Where would most of his class like to go? Explain your answer. *(N.ME.06.05)*

B. What percent of the class wants to go to a national park? Explain your answer. *(N.ME.06.06)*

C. If 40 students are in Kevin's class, how many would want to go to the ocean? Explain your answer. *(N.FL.06.12)*
4; Sample answer: $\frac{1}{10}$ of the class chose the ocean. Find $\frac{1}{10}$ of 40, which is $\frac{1}{10} \times 40$, or 4.

1A. Amusement park; Sample answer: Using the least common denominator of 10, the fractions are $\frac{1}{10}, \frac{2}{5} = \frac{4}{10}$, and $\frac{1}{2} = \frac{5}{10}$. Since $\frac{5}{10}$ is the greatest fraction, more students chose an amusement park than the other destinations.

1B. 40%; Sample answer: $\frac{2}{5}$ of the class chose a national park, so this fraction written as a decimal is $2 \div 5$, which is 0.4. Multiply 0.4 by 100 to find the percent, which is 40%.

Tuesday

2. Michigan borders five states as shown on the map. Minnesota and Illinois are included as water border states. *(D.PR.06.01)*

A. If a state is chosen at random from all 50 states, what is the probability that it borders Michigan? Explain your answer.

B. Sara is planning to use her frequent flyer miles to travel in the United States. If she chooses to fly to a state that borders Michigan, what is the probability that the name of the state will begin with the letter C? Explain your answer.

2A. $\frac{1}{10}$; Sample answer: There are 5 possible states out of 50 states total. This probability is $\frac{5}{50}$, which is $\frac{1}{10}$ in simplest form.

2A. 0; Sample answer: There are no states bordering Michigan that begin with the letter C, so the probability is 0.

Countdown to MEAP

Wednesday

3. Carter can run at a rate of 5 miles per hour. How many miles can he run in 3 hours? ***(A.PA.06.01)*** **C**
   - (A) 1.7 miles
   - (B) 8 miles
   - (C) 15 miles
   - (D) 60 miles

4. In the Ferris wheel, which two angles form vertical angles? ***(G.GS.06.01)*** **B**

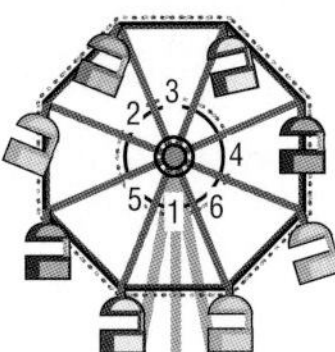

   - (A) ∠1 and ∠2
   - (B) ∠2 and ∠6
   - (C) ∠3 and ∠4
   - (D) ∠1 and ∠6

Thursday

5. Maryn is building a model of a dinosaur for her science project. The ratio of the length to height is 12 inches to 18 inches. Which ratio is *not* the same as this ratio? ***(N.ME.06.11)*** **D**
   - (A) $\frac{6}{9}$
   - (B) $\frac{2}{3}$
   - (C) $\frac{24}{36}$
   - (D) $\frac{1}{2}$

6. The Hoover Dam on the Colorado River is made of 4,360,000 cubic yards of concrete. How many cubic feet is this? ***(M.UN.06.01)*** **A**
   - (A) 117,720,000 cu ft
   - (B) 39,240,000 cu ft
   - (C) 13,080,000 cu ft
   - (D) 1,453,333 cu ft

Friday

7. Which equation and solution represent the verbal sentence below?

   The product of 4 and a number plus three is 19. ***(A.FO.06.06, A.FO.06.11)*** **C**
   - (A) $4m + 3 = 19; 5.5$
   - (B) $4(m + 3) = 19; 4$
   - (C) $4m + 3 = 19; 4$
   - (D) $\frac{4}{m} + 3 = 19; 5.5$

8. On the diagram, Cedar St. and Pine St. are parallel. Which angles are congruent? ***(G.GS.06.01)*** **C**

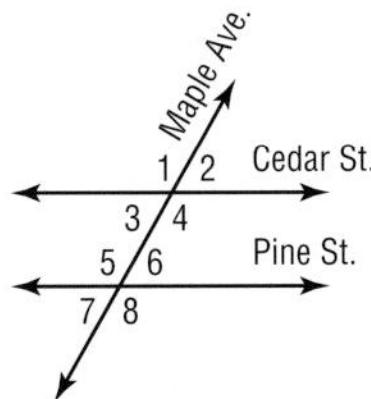

   - (A) ∠1 and ∠3
   - (B) ∠4 and ∠7
   - (C) ∠3 and ∠6
   - (D) ∠2 and ∠4

Countdown to MEAP

—congruence of corresponding and alternate interior angles when parallel lines are cut by a transversal, and that such congruencies imply parallel lines

—locate interior and exterior angles of any triangle, and use the property that an exterior angle of a triangle is equal to the sum of the remote (opposite) interior angles

—know that the sum of the exterior angles of a convex polygon is 360°. *(Questions 4, 8)*

N.ME.06.11 Find equivalent ratios by scaling up or scaling down. *(Question 5)*

M.UN.06.01 Convert between basic units of measurement within a single measurement system, e.g., square inches to square feet. *(Question 6)*

A.FO.06.06 Represent information given in words using algebraic expressions and equations. *(Question 7)*

A.FO.06.11 Relate simple linear equations with integer coefficients to particular contexts, and solve, e.g., $3x = 8$ or $x + 5 = 10$. *(Question 7)*

Countdown to

MEAP

Grade Level Content Expectations

This problem set covers the following Michigan Grade Level Content Expectations.

A.FO.06.11 **Relate simple linear equations with integer coefficients to particular contexts, and solve, e.g., $3x = 8$ or $x + 5 = 10$. *(Question 1)***

G.TR.06.03 **Understand the basic rigid motions in the plane (reflections, rotations, translations), relate these to congruence, and apply them to solve problems. *(Question 2)***

N.FL.06.04 **Multiply and divide any two fractions, including mixed numbers, fluently. *(Question 3)***

D.PR.06.01 **Express probabilities as fractions, decimals or percentages between 0 and 1; know that 0 probability means an event will not occur and that probability 1 means an event will occur. *(Questions 4, 5)***

4 Weeks to MEAP

Monday

1. Aidan bought shoes and a T-shirt at the local sports store. The cost of the shoes was \$75. He spent a total of \$94. ***(A.FO.06.11)***

A. Let C represent the cost of the T-shirt. Write an equation that represents the total cost of the items. Explain your answer. **Sample answer: $94 = C + 75$; The total, \$94, is equal to the sum of the cost of the T-shirt *C*, plus the cost of the shoes, \$75.**

B. Solve the equation to find the cost of the T-shirt.

$$94 = C + 75$$
$$94 - 75 = C + 75 - 75$$
$$19 = C$$

The cost of the T-shirt is \$19.

Tuesday

2. Use the figure to answer the following questions. ***(G.TR.06.03)***

A. What types of transformations are shown in the figure? Explain your answer..

2A. Sample answer: Reflections, translations, and rotations; Each white triangle is a reflection of another white triangle, each gray triangle is a translation of a black triangle, and one fourth of the entire square is rotated three times to complete the figure.

B. Which shapes are similar? Explain your answer. **Sample answer: They all appear to be similar because they are 45°–45°–90° triangles.**

C. Which shapes are congruent? Explain your answer. **Sample answer: The white triangles are congruent because they are reflections of each other. All gray and black triangles are congruent because they are translations. Reflections and translations do not change the dimensions of a figure, therefore, corresponding angle measures and corresponding sides are the same, and the figures are congruent.**

Wednesday

3. Mrs. Collins is forming an all-star swimming team. She first chooses $\frac{1}{3}$ of her entire swim team. She then chooses $\frac{1}{2}$ of this group to form the all-star team. What fraction of the entire swim team will be on the all-star team? *(N.MR.06.04)* **A**

   (A) $\frac{1}{6}$ (B) $\frac{1}{5}$
   (C) $\frac{1}{2}$ (D) $\frac{2}{3}$

4. Marcus wrote each of the letters in the word *Michigan* on a card. If Marcus chooses one card at random, what is the probability that he chooses an *r*? *(D.PR.06.01)* **D**

M	I	C	H	I	G	A	N

   (A) 1 (B) $\frac{1}{2}$
   (C) $\frac{1}{8}$ (D) 0

Thursday

5. Kyle spins the spinner below. What is the probability that the spinner will land on red? *(D.PR.06.01)* **C**

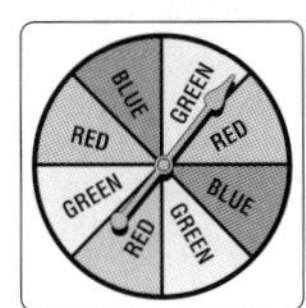

   (A) 1 (B) $\frac{1}{2}$ (C) $\frac{3}{8}$ (D) $\frac{1}{8}$

6. A thread snake is one of the world's smallest animals. It measures about 4 inches. How many feet is this? *(M.UN.06.01)* **A**

   (A) $\frac{1}{3}$ ft
   (B) $\frac{1}{2}$ ft
   (C) 3 ft
   (D) 48 ft

Friday

7. The line graph shows the distance traveled by a lion after a certain number of hours. Which function represents the graph? *(A.RP.06.10)* **B**

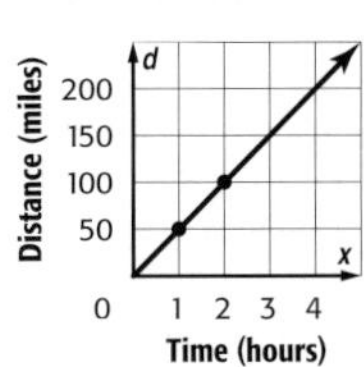

   (A) $y = 50x + 50$ (B) $y = 50x$
   (C) $y = 5x$ (D) $y = x$

8. Keeli wants to buy a CD that costs $15. The sales tax is 6%. If the CD is the only thing that Keeli buys, what will be the sales tax? *(N.FL.06.13)* **D**

   (A) $15.90
   (B) $9.00
   (C) $2.50
   (D) $0.90

Countdown to MEAP

M.UN.06.01 **Convert between basic units of measurement within a single measurement system, e.g., square inches to square feet.** ***(Question 6)***

A.RP.06.10 **Represent simple relationships between quantities using verbal descriptions, formulas or equations, tables, and graphs, e.g., perimeter-side relationship for a square, distance-time graphs, and conversions such as feet to inches.** ***(Question 7)***

N.FL.06.13 **Solve word problems involving percentages in such contexts as sales taxes and tips, and involving positive rational numbers.** ***(Question 8)***

Michigan Mathematics: Applications and Concepts, Grade 7 MI9

Countdown to

MEAP

Grade Level Content Expectations

This problem set covers the following Michigan Grade Level Content Expectations.

M.UN.06.01 Convert between basic units of measurement within a single measurement system, e.g., square inches to square feet. *(Questions 1, 2)*

N.FL.06.04 Multiply and divide any two fractions, including mixed numbers, fluently. *(Questions 1, 2)*

G.TR.06.03 Understand the basic rigid motions in the plane (reflections, rotations, translations), relate these to congruence, and apply them to solve problems. *(Question 3)*

G.GS.06.01 Understand and apply basic properties of lines, angles, and triangles, including:

—triangle inequality
—relationships of vertical angles, complementary angles, supplementary angles
—congruence of corresponding and alternate interior angles when parallel lines are cut by a transversal, and that such congruencies imply parallel lines

3 Weeks to MEAP

Monday

1. Petra is making a giant Michigan state flag to hang in her school gymnasium. The final dimensions of the flag will be 12 feet wide by 18 feet long.

A. What will be the area of the flag in square feet? Explain your answer. ***(Prerequisite Skill)*** **216 sq ft; Sample answer: Multiply the length times the width to find the area. $12 \times 18 = 216$ sq ft.**

B. How many square yards of fabric will she need? Explain your answer. ***(M.UN.06.01)*** **24 sq yd; Sample answer: One square yard is equal to 3 feet times 3 feet, or 9 square feet. So, divide the total number of square feet by 9 to find the square yards, $216 \div 9 = 24$ sq yd.**

C. The wingspan of the eagle on the flag is $\frac{3}{16}$ the length of the entire flag. How long will the wingspan of the eagle on Petra's flag be in feet? Explain your answer. ***(N.FL.06.04)*** **$3\frac{3}{8}$ ft; Sample answer: To find the length of the wingspan multiply the length of the flag by $\frac{3}{16}$. $18 \times \frac{3}{16} = 9 \times \frac{3}{8} = \frac{27}{8} = 3\frac{3}{8}$ ft**

Tuesday

2. Payton made 60 cups of fruit juice for a class picnic.

A. Payton stored the juice in gallon containers. How many gallon containers did she use? Explain your answer. ***(M.UN.06.01)*** **4; Sample answer; Divide 60 by 4 to convert cups to quarts, $60 \div 4 = 15$ quarts. Then divide by 4 again to convert quarts to gallons, $15 \div 4 = 3.75$ gallons of juice, so Payton used 4 gallon containers.**

B. If each student had $2\frac{1}{2}$ cups of juice, and there was no juice left over, how many students were in the class? Explain your answer. ***(N.FL.06.04)*** **24; Sample answer: Divide the total number of cups by $2\frac{1}{2}$ to find the number of students. $60 \div 2\frac{1}{2} = 60 \div \frac{5}{2} = 60 \times \frac{2}{5} = \frac{120}{5} = 24$**

MI 10 *Michigan Mathematics: Applications and Concepts,* Grade 7

Wednesday

3. Which graph shows the reflection of the letter *A*? *(G.TR.06.03)* **B**

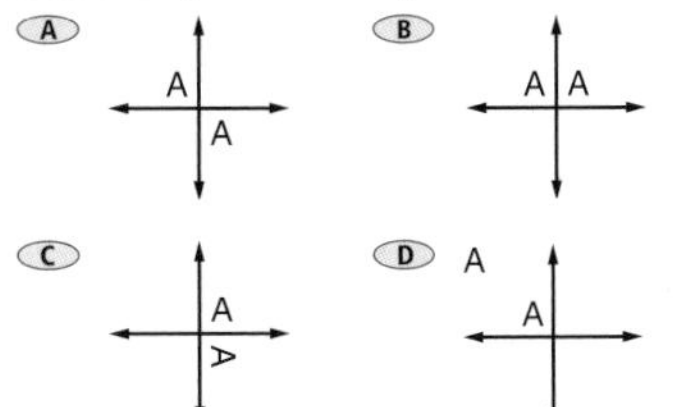

4. In the diagram, $\angle 1$ and $\angle 2$ are supplementary. If $\angle 1$ measures 120°, what is the measure of $\angle 2$? *(G.GS.06.01)* **B**

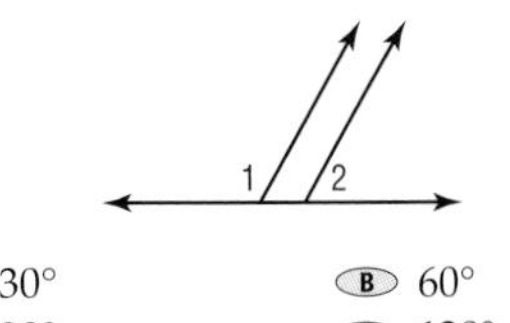

Ⓐ 30° Ⓑ 60°
Ⓒ 90° Ⓓ 120°

Thursday

5. If $a = 1\frac{1}{8}$ and $b = 1\frac{1}{4}$, what is the value of $a \div b$? *(A.FO.06.07)* **D**

Ⓐ $\frac{45}{32}$
Ⓑ $\frac{10}{9}$
Ⓒ 1
Ⓓ $\frac{9}{10}$

6. What are the coordinates of point *K* on the graph? *(A.RP.06.02)* **C**

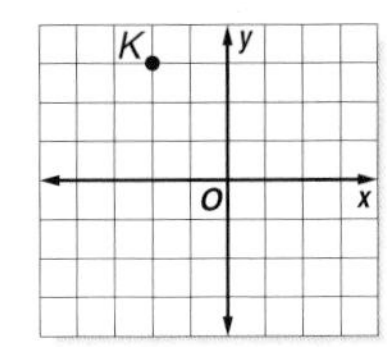

Ⓐ (3, −2) Ⓑ (2, 3)
Ⓒ (−2, 3) Ⓓ (−3, 2)

Friday

7. The Larson's have three children. What is the probability that they have only one girl? *(D.PR.06.02)* **B**

Ⓐ $\frac{1}{3}$
Ⓑ $\frac{3}{8}$
Ⓒ $\frac{1}{2}$
Ⓓ 1

8. What is the volume of the box? *(M.TE.06.03)* **D**

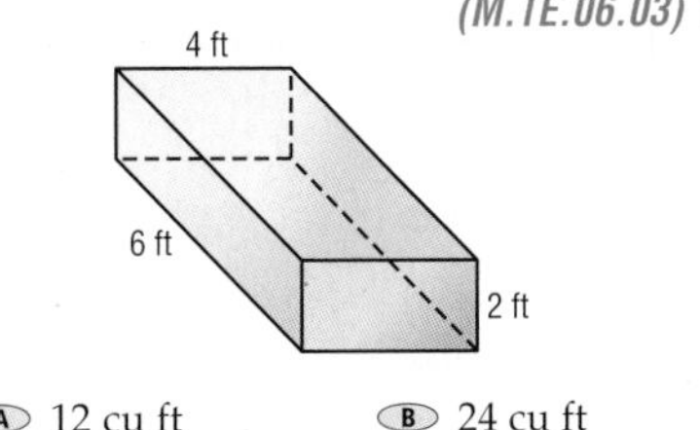

Ⓐ 12 cu ft Ⓑ 24 cu ft
Ⓒ 36 cu ft Ⓓ 48 cu ft

Countdown to MEAP

—locate interior and exterior angles of any triangle, and use the property that an exterior angle of a triangle is equal to the sum of the remote (opposite) interior angles

—know that the sum of the exterior angles of a convex polygon is 360°. *(Question 4)*

A.FO.06.06 Represent information given in words using algebraic expressions and equations. *(Question 5)*

A.RP.06.02 Plot ordered pairs of integers and use ordered pairs of integers to identify points in all four quadrants of the coordinate plane. *(Question 6)*

D.PR.06.02 Compute probabilities of events from simple experiments with equally likely outcomes, e.g., tossing dice, flipping coins, spinning spinners, by listing all possibilities and finding the fraction that meets given conditions. *(Question 7)*

M.TE.06.03 Compute the volume and surface area of cubes and rectangular prisms given the lengths of their sides using formulas. *(Question 8)*

Countdown to MEAP

Grade Level Content Expectations

This problem set covers the following Michigan Grade Level Content Expectations.

M.TE.06.03 Compute the volume and surface area of cubes and rectangular prisms given the lengths of their sides using formulas. *(Question 1)*

N.MR.06.08 Understand integer subtraction as the inverse of integer addition; add and subtract integers using integers from 10 to −10. *(Question 2)*

G.GS.06.02 Understand that for polygons, congruence means corresponding sides and angles have equal measures. *(Question 3)*

G.GS.06.01 Understand and apply basic properties of lines, angles, and triangles, including:
- —triangle inequality
- —relationships of vertical angles, complementary angles, supplementary angles
- —congruence of corresponding and alternate interior angles when parallel lines are cut by a transversal, and that such congruencies imply parallel lines

2 Weeks to MEAP

Monday

1. Brian is building a set for the school play. He is painting the box below to use as a bench in the play. *(M.TE.06.03)*

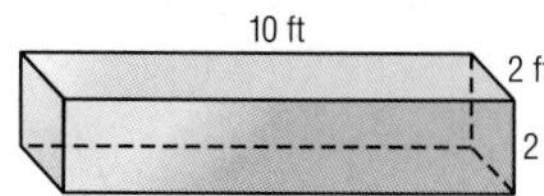

A. All sides of the box need to be painted. What is the surface area that needs to be painted? Explain your answer.

B. If one can of paint will cover 50 square feet, how many cans of paint will be needed to cover the box? Explain your answer. **2; Sample answer: Divide the area to be painted by 50 to find the number of cans. $88 \div 50 = 1.76$ cans, so Brian needs to buy 2 cans.**

1A. 88 sq ft; Sample answer: To find the surface area, add the area of all 6 faces. $2(10 \times 2) + 2(2 \times 2) + 2(2 \times 10) = 40 + 8 + 40 = 88$ sq ft

Tuesday

2. On Sunday morning, the temperature was −3 degrees Fahrenheit. It rose 10 degrees by 6 P.M. It then fell 4 degrees by midnight. *(N.MR.06.08)*

A. Write an addition statement representing this situation. Explain your answer.

B. What was the temperature at midnight? Explain your answer. **3°; $-3 + 10 + (-4) = -3 + 10 - 4 = 7 - 4 = 3°$**

2A. $-3 + 10 + (-4)$; Sample answer: The beginning temperature was −3 degrees. Add 10 because the temperature increased by 10 degrees. Then add −4 because the temperature decreased 4 degrees.

Wednesday

3. If triangle ABC is congruent to triangle XYZ, which of the following statements is true? ***(G.GS.06.02)*** **C**

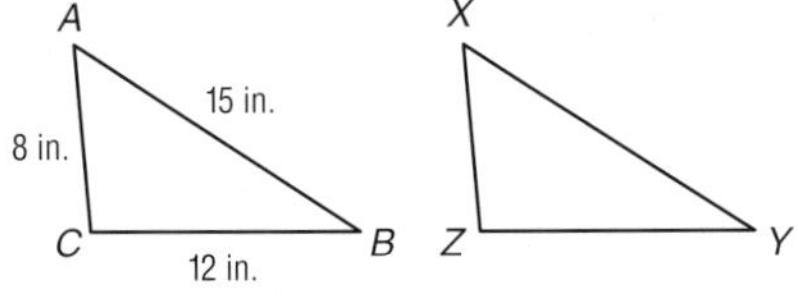

(A) $YZ = 30$
(B) $XZ = 12$
(C) $XY = 15$
(D) $YZ = 8$

4. What is the measure of $\angle B$ in the figure? ***(G.GS.06.01)*** **A**

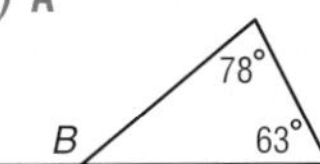

(A) 141°
(B) 95°
(C) 78°
(D) 63°

Thursday

5. Karla needs to choose a representative from her sports club to be on the student council. In the sports club, there are 6 swim team members, 4 soccer players, and 8 basketball players. What is the probability that she chooses a swim team member? ***(D.PR.06.02)*** **A**

(A) $\frac{1}{3}$ (B) $\frac{1}{2}$
(C) $\frac{2}{3}$ (D) 1

6. In the equation $\frac{1}{9}y = -4$, what is the value of y? ***(A.FO.06.13)*** **A**

(A) -36
(B) $-\frac{4}{9}$
(C) $\frac{4}{9}$
(D) 36

Friday

7. The population of Michigan in 2003 was 10,079,985. What is this number written in scientific notation? ***(N.ME.06.16)*** **D**

(A) 100.79985×10^5
(B) 10.079985×10^6
(C) 1.0079985×10^6
(D) 1.0079985×10^7

8. Which statement represents the algebraic expression below? ***(A.FO.06.05)*** **C**

$$3x + 4$$

(A) three times "a number plus four"
(B) three times four plus a number
(C) three times a number plus four
(D) a number plus four times three

Countdown to MEAP

—locate interior and exterior angles of any triangle, and use the property that an exterior angle of a triangle is equal to the sum of the remote (opposite) interior angles

—know that the sum of the exterior angles of a convex polygon is 360°. *(Question 4)*

D.PR.06.02 Compute probabilities of events from simple experiments with equally likely outcomes, e.g., tossing dice, flipping coins, spinning spinners, by listing all possibilities and finding the fraction that meets given conditions. *(Question 5)*

A.FO.06.13 Understand that multiplying or dividing both sides of an equation by the same non-zero number creates a new equation that has the same solutions. *(Question 6)*

N.ME.06.16 Understand and use integer exponents, excluding powers of negative numbers; express numbers in scientific notation. *(Question 7)*

A.FO.06.05 Use standard conventions for writing algebraic expressions, e.g., $2x + 1$ means "two times x, plus 1" and $2(x + 1)$ means "two times the quantity $(x + 1)$." *(Question 8)*

Countdown to MEAP

Grade Level Content Expectations

This problem set covers the following Michigan Grade Level Content Expectations.

A.RP.06.09 Graph and write equations for linear functions of the form $y = mx$, and solve related problems, e.g., given n chairs, the "leg function" is $f(n) = 4n$; if you have 5 chairs, how many legs?; if you have 12 legs, how many chairs? *(Question 1)*

G.TR.06.03 Understand the basic rigid motions in the plane (reflections, rotations, translations), relate these to congruence, and apply them to solve problems. *(Question 2)*

N.FL.06.15 Solve applied problems that use the four operations with appropriate decimal numbers. *(Question 3)*

D.PR.06.01 Express probabilities as fractions, decimals or percentages between 0 and 1; know that 0 probability means an event will not occur and that probability 1 means an event will occur. *(Question 4)*

1 Week to MEAP

Monday

1. Caroline owns a mowing and landscaping business. She charges \$7.50 per hour to mow lawns and \$10.50 per hour to landscape. ***(A.PA.06.09)***

   A. Mr. Peterson wants to hire Caroline to mow the lawn outside his office building. Write the function rule for Caroline's salary for mowing lawns. Explain your answer. **7.50*h*; Sample answer: Her salary is the cost per hour, \$7.50, times the number of hours, *h*.**

   B. Mr. Peterson decides he also wants to hire Caroline to landscape. Write a function rule for Caroline's salary to landscape. Explain your answer. **10.50*h*; Sample answer: Her salary is the cost per hour, \$10.50, times the number of hours, *h*.**

   C. How much will Caroline make if she landscapes for 5 hours? Explain your answer. **\$52.50; Sample answer: Use 10.50*h*, and substitute 5 for *h*, 10.50(5) = \$52.50.**

Tuesday

2. The American Robin is the state bird of Michigan. Some drawing software use a coordinate system to locate objects in the drawing. ***(G.TR.06.03)***

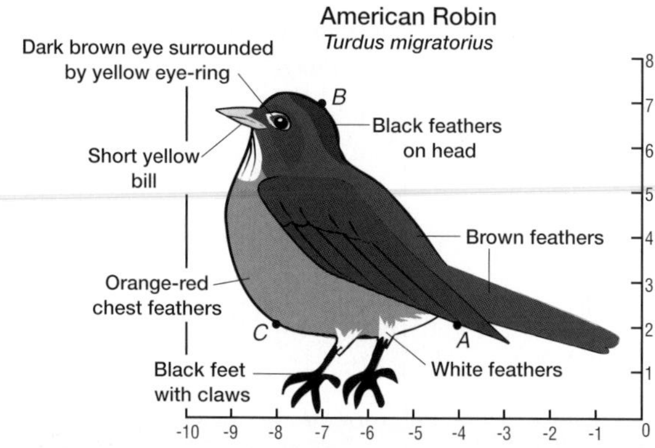

   A. What are the coordinates of points *A*, *B*, and *C* labeled on the bird? Explain your answer. **A(−4, 2), B(−7, 7), C(−8, 2); Sample answer: Find the *x*-value of each point then find the *y*-value of each point.**

   B. What will be the coordinates of the three points after the bird is moved 3 units to the right? Explain your answer. **A(−1, 2), B(−4, 7), C(−5, 2); Sample answer: Each *x*-value increases by 3, and each *y*-value remains the same.**

   C. Is the new picture of the bird congruent to the original? Explain your answer. **Yes; Sample answer: The bird was translated 3 units to the right, so the dimensions did not change, and the new figure is congruent to the original.**

MI 14 *Michigan Mathematics: Applications and Concepts,* Grade 7

Countdown to MEAP

A.PA.06.09 Graph and write equations for linear functions of the form $y = mx$, and solve related problems, e.g., given n chairs, the "leg function" is $f(n) = 4n$; if you have 5 chairs, how many legs?; if you have 12 legs, how many chairs? *(Question 5)*

N.ME.06.05 Order rational numbers and place them on the number line. *(Question 6)*

N.ME.06.17 Locate negative rational numbers (including integers) on the number line; know that numbers and their negatives add to 0, and are on opposite sides and at equal distance from 0 on a number line. *(Question 6)*

M.PS.06.02 Draw patterns (of faces) for a cube and rectangular prism that, when cut, will cover the solid exactly (nets). *(Question 7)*

G.GS.06.02 Understand that for polygons, congruence means corresponding sides and angles have equal measures. *(Question 8)*

Wednesday

3. Jake is planning a barbeque. He needs 10 packages of hot dogs and 8 packages of hamburgers. Hot dogs cost \$5.25 per package, and hamburgers cost \$6.50 per package. Which expression shows the total cost for the hot dogs and the hamburgers? ***(N.FL.06.15)*** **D**
   - A $C = (5.25 + 6.50) \times (10 + 8)$
   - B $C = (5.25 \times 8) + (6.50 \times 10)$
   - C $C = (5.25 \times 6.50) + (10 \times 8)$
   - D $C = (5.25 \times 10) + (6.50 \times 8)$

4. For which spinner will the probability of spinning green be 0? **B**

A
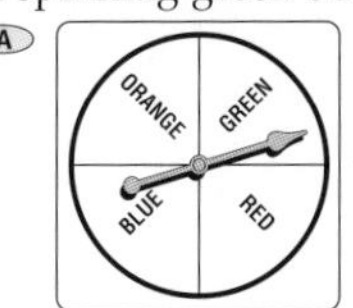

B
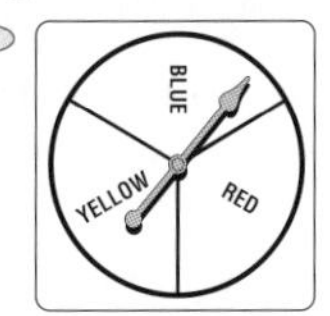

C
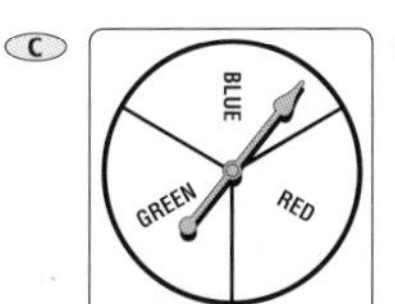

D
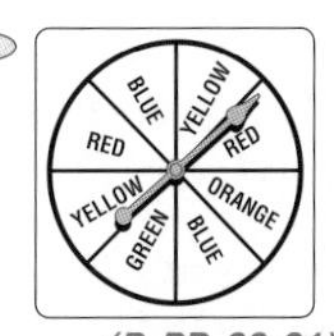

(D.PR.06.01)

Thursday

5. The formula for the area of a triangle is given by $A = \frac{1}{2}bh$. What is the length of the base of the triangle below? ***(A.PA.06.09)*** **B**

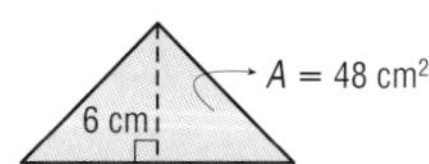

   - A 12 cm
   - B 16 cm
   - C 24 cm
   - D 144 cm

6. Which net will make a cube? ***(M.PS.06.02)*** **C**

A
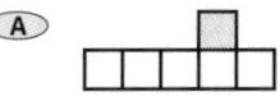

B

C

D
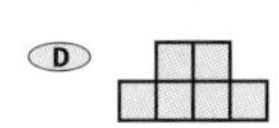

Friday

7. Which number line shows −9, 6, 4, 0, and −2 ordered correctly from least to greatest?

A −10 −8 −6 −4 −2 0 2 4 6 8 10 12

B −10 −8 −6 −4 −2 0 2 4 6 8 10 12

C −10 −8 −6 −4 −2 0 2 4 6 8 10 12

D −10 −8 −6 −4 −2 0 2 4 6 8 10 12

(N.ME.06.05, N.ME.06.17) **A**

8. Triangle LMN and triangle RST are congruent. Which statement is true about the triangles? ***(G.GS.06.02)*** **A**

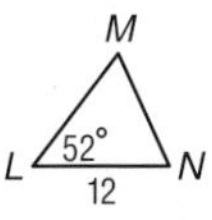

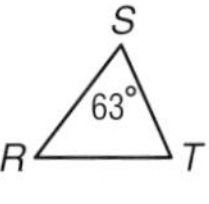

   - A $\angle R = 52°$, $RT = 12$
   - B $\angle M = 52°$, $MN = 18$
   - C $\angle M = 63°$, $MN = 12$
   - D $\angle R = 63°$, $RT = 18$

Michigan Mathematics: Applications and Concepts, Grade 7 MI 15

MEAP Test-taking Guidelines

- Make sure you have **only** No. 2 pencils.
- All answers **must** be recorded in your test booklet.
- Always read each question carefully. Be sure to think about the answer.
- For each selected response test item, choose the best answer by **circling** the letter in your test booklet.
- If you erase an answer on a selected response item, make sure you erase the first letter circled completely.
- If an answer space is provided in your test booklet, be sure to show all your work. Write your answer clearly and neatly in the space provided.
- If you do not know the answer to a question, go on to the next question. You can return to that question later.
- If you finish a section of the test early, be sure to go back and check your work in that section of the test. Do **not** look at the questions in other sections of the test.
- When you come to the word **STOP** in your test booklet, do **not** turn the page.

Pictured Rock
National Lakeshore

Teacher Wraparound Edition

GLENCOE MATHEMATICS

Mathematics

Applications and Concepts

Course 3

Bailey
Day
Frey
Howard
Hutchens
McClain
Moore-Harris
Ott
Pelfrey
Price
Vielhaber
Willard

Teacher Handbook

McGraw Hill Glencoe

New York, New York Columbus, Ohio Chicago, Illinois Peoria, Illinois Woodland Hills, California

About the Cover
On the cover of this book, you will find the word *circumference* and the formula for calculating circumference, $C = 2\pi r$. When an object drops in water, circular rings are formed on the surface of the water. These rings are concentric circles, as they share a common center. You will learn more about circles and circumference in Chapter 7.

The McGraw-Hill Companies

Send all inquiries to:
Glencoe/McGraw-Hill
8787 Orion Place
Columbus, OH 43240-4027

ISBN: 0-07-865265-0 (Student Edition)
ISBN: 0-07-865266-9 (Teacher Wraparound Edition)

2 3 4 5 6 7 8 9 10 043/071 13 12 11 10 09 08 07 06 05

Teacher Handbook

Table of Contents

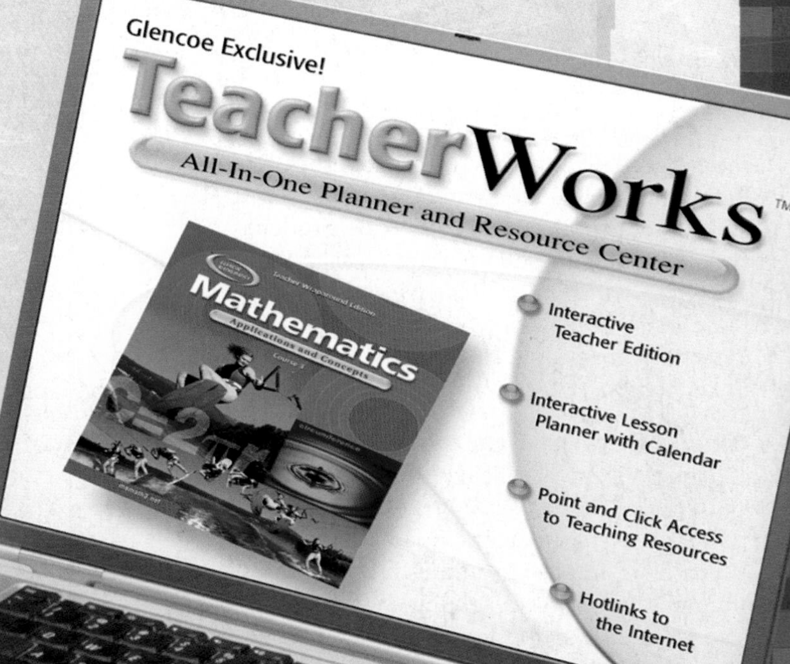

Designed to be in more

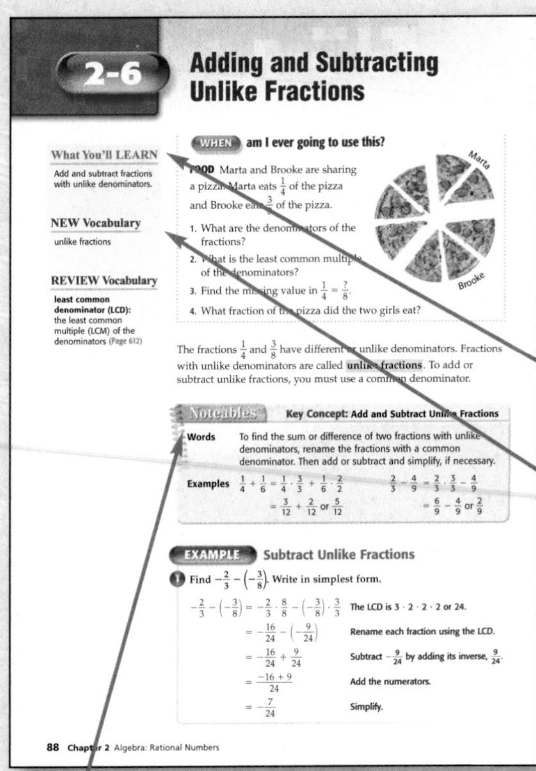

The consistent instructional design of the lessons strengthens student learning—from the very beginning of each lesson where students see "What You'll Learn," to the very end of each lesson where they have a chance to prepare for the next lesson.

What You'll Learn previews the topics to come, and engaging questions incorporate problem-based learning in your classroom.

New and Review Vocabulary terms are listed at the beginning of each lesson for easy reference. New terms are also highlighted in yellow as they appear in the lesson. **Link to Reading** features relate mathematical terms to everyday meanings. **Math Symbols** are listed in the lesson in which they are introduced.

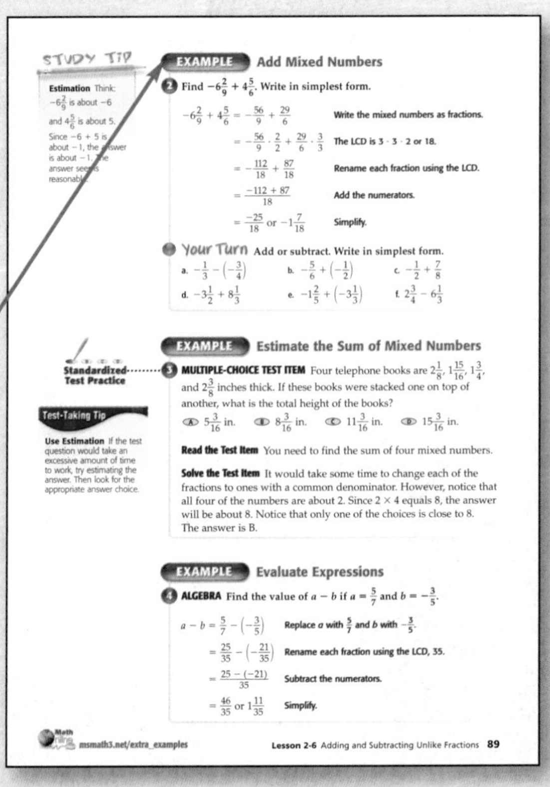

Key Concept boxes use words, symbols, and models to illustrate new rules, properties, and definitions, so students can build their reading skills as they build their math skills. Students should include these important ideas in their *Noteables™: Interactive Study Notebook with Foldables™*, or their notebooks. **Concept Summary** boxes provide a concise overview of key topics.

Completely worked-out examples with clear explanations are paralleled by the Guided Practice and Practice and Applications exercises that follow. Your Turn exercises are included as appropriate after skill examples. Examples often include strategies for problem-solving and mastering standardized test questions.

effective, ways than one.

Skill and Concept Check

You can use this portion of the exercises in class to ensure that all students understand the concepts.

- **Writing Math** exercises give students opportunities to define, describe, and explain the mathematical concepts they've just learned.
- **Guided Practice** presents a representative sample of the exercises in the Practice and Applications section. A key is provided in the Teacher Wraparound Edition that correlates the exercises with appropriate examples.
- **Application** problems give students the opportunity to use the skills they have learned in a real-world setting.

Practice and Applications

- **Skill Exercises** correspond to the Guided Practice exercises and are structured so that students practice the same concepts whether they are assigned odd- or even-numbered problems. *Homework Help* refers students to examples as they complete these exercises.
- **Applications** give students frequent opportunities to apply concepts to both real-life and mathematical situations.
- **Critical Thinking** exercises in each lesson require students to explain, make conjectures, and prove mathematical relationships.

Spiral Review with Standardized Test Practice

- **Standardized Test Practice** questions provide students with ongoing opportunities to sharpen their test-taking skills.
- **Spiral Review** includes spiraled, cumulative exercises from the two previous lessons as well as earlier lessons.
- **Getting Ready for the Next Lesson** exercises give students the chance to review prerequisite skills for the coming lesson. A reference is provided should students need additional help.

Skill and Concept Check

1. Writing Math Describe the first step in adding unlike fractions.
2. **OPEN ENDED** Write a subtraction problem with unlike fractions with a least common denominator of 12. Find the answer.
3. **NUMBER SENSE** Without doing the computation, determine whether $\frac{4}{7} + \frac{5}{9}$ is greater than, less than, or equal to 1. Explain.

GUIDED PRACTICE

Add or subtract. Write in simplest form.

4. $\frac{3}{4} + \frac{1}{6}$ 5. $\frac{7}{8} - \frac{3}{4}$ 6. $-\frac{1}{7} - \left(-\frac{4}{5}\right)$
7. $-\frac{2}{5} + \left(-\frac{5}{6}\right)$ 8. $3\frac{5}{8} - 1\frac{1}{3}$ 9. $-4\frac{2}{3} - \left(-3\frac{4}{5}\right)$

10. **MUSIC** A waltz is written in $\frac{3}{4}$ time. This means the quarter note gets one beat and the total value of each measure is $\frac{3}{4}$. What type of note must be used to finish the last measure of the waltz below?

Practice and Applications

Add or subtract. Write in simplest form.

11. $\frac{3}{8} + \frac{5}{6}$ 12. $\frac{7}{8} + \frac{3}{12}$ 13. $\frac{3}{4} - \frac{1}{6}$
14. $\frac{4}{5} - \frac{2}{15}$ 15. $-\frac{6}{7} - \left(-\frac{1}{3}\right)$ 16. $-\frac{4}{5} - \left(-\frac{2}{3}\right)$
17. $8\frac{3}{7} - \left(-6\frac{1}{2}\right)$ 18. $7\frac{3}{4} - \left(-1\frac{1}{8}\right)$ 19. $-4\frac{3}{4} - 5\frac{5}{8}$ 20. $-8\frac{1}{3} - 4\frac{5}{6}$
21. $9\frac{1}{6} - 4\frac{1}{2}$ 22. $9\frac{1}{3} - 2\frac{1}{2}$ 23. $3\frac{1}{5} + \left(-8\frac{1}{2}\right)$ 24. $1\frac{1}{6} + \left(-6\frac{2}{3}\right)$
25. $-15\frac{5}{8} + 11\frac{2}{3}$ 26. $-22\frac{2}{5} + 15\frac{5}{6}$ 27. $\frac{65}{187} - \frac{9}{136}$ 28. $\frac{45}{152} - \frac{13}{209}$
29. Subtract $-6\frac{1}{4}$ from 9. 30. What is $2\frac{3}{8}$ less than $-8\frac{1}{5}$?
31. What is the sum of −5/[illegible] and −1/[illegible]? 32. Find the sum of −4/[illegible] and −2/[illegible].

HOMEWORK HELP

For Exercises	See Examples
11–32, 35	1–3
33–34	4

Extra Practice See pages 620, 649.

35. **HISTORY** In the 1824 presidential election, Andrew Jackson, John Quincy Adams, Henry Clay, and William H. Crawford received electoral votes. Use the information at the right to determine what fraction of the votes William H. Crawford received.

Candidate	Fraction of Vote
Andrew Jackson	$\frac{3}{8}$
John Quincy Adams	$\frac{1}{3}$
Henry Clay	$\frac{1}{7}$

Source: *The World Almanac*

WATER MANAGEMENT For Exercises 36–40, use the following information.
Suppose a bucket is placed under two faucets.

36. If one faucet is turned on alone, the bucket will be filled in 5 minutes. Write the fraction of the bucket that will be filled in 1 minute.
37. If the other faucet is turned on alone, the bucket will be filled in 3 minutes. Write the fraction of the bucket that will be filled in 1 minute.
38. Write the fraction of the bucket that will be filled in 1 minute if both faucets are turned on.
39. Divide 1 by the sum in Exercise 38 to determine the number of minutes it will take to fill the bucket if both faucets are turned on.
40. How many seconds will it take to fill the bucket if both faucets are turned on?
41. **CRITICAL THINKING** Write an expression for each statement. Then find the answer.
    a. $\frac{3}{4}$ of $\frac{2}{3}$ b. $\frac{3}{4}$ more than $\frac{2}{3}$
    c. $\frac{3}{4}$ less than $\frac{2}{3}$ d. $\frac{3}{4}$ divided into $\frac{2}{3}$

Spiral Review with Standardized Test Practice

42. **MULTIPLE CHOICE** Teresa worked on homework $\frac{2}{3}$ of an hour on Monday and $1\frac{1}{2}$ hours on Tuesday. How much more time did she spend working on homework on Tuesday than on Monday?
    (A) $\frac{1}{6}$ h (B) $\frac{1}{4}$ h (C) $\frac{5}{6}$ h (D) $\frac{13}{6}$ h
43. **SHORT RESPONSE** Show each step in finding $5\frac{1}{6} + 4\frac{2}{9}$.

Add or subtract. Write in simplest form. (Lesson 2-5)

44. $-\frac{7}{11} + \frac{5}{11}$ 45. $-\frac{7}{15} - \frac{4}{15}$ 46. $5\frac{4}{5} - 7\frac{1}{5}$
47. **ALGEBRA** Find $a \div b$ if $a = 3\frac{1}{2}$ and $b = -\frac{7}{8}$. (Lesson 2-4)

GETTING READY FOR THE NEXT LESSON

PREREQUISITE SKILL Solve each equation. Check your solution. (Lessons 1-8 and 1-9)

48. $d - 13 = -44$ 49. $-18t = 270$ 50. $-34 = y + 22$ 51. $-5 = \frac{a}{16}$

Math Online msmath3.net/self_check_quiz

Lesson 2-6 Adding and Subtracting Unlike Fractions 91

Accomplish more

***Glencoe Mathematics: Applications and Concepts* provides so many resources for lesson planning and teaching that you can create a complete, customized course in mathematics quickly … and easily.**

This is where you start.

In addition to teaching suggestions, additional examples, and answers, the **Teacher Wraparound Edition** provides a guide for all of the materials available for each lesson.

FAST FILE *Chapter Resource Masters* contain all of the core supplements you'll need to begin teaching a chapter of *Glencoe Mathematics: Applications and Concepts.* Each chapter booklet features convenient tabs for easy filing.

FAST FILE

- The **Family Letter** and **Family Activity** inform families of the requirements of the chapter and helps them understand how the mathematics applies to real life.
- **Vocabulary Builder** helps students locate and define key vocabulary words from the chapter.
- **Study Guide and Intervention** summarizes key concepts and provides practice.
- **Practice: Skills** exercises help students develop computational skills, lesson by lesson.
- **Practice: Word Problems** mimics the verbal problems in each lesson at an average level.
- **Reading to Learn Mathematics** provides students with various reading strategies to master the mathematics presented in each lesson.
- **Enrichment** activities extend students' knowledge and widen their appreciation of how mathematics relates to the world around them.
- **Assessment** options for each chapter include six forms of chapter tests, assessment tasks, quizzes, mid-chapter test, cumulative review, and standardized test practice.

Reading and Writing

FOLDABLES™ Study Organizer

Teaching Mathematics with Foldables™ offers guidelines for using Foldables interactive study organizers in your class.

Noteables™

Interactive Study Notebook with Foldables™ is a helpful note-taking guide for students.

WebQuests, Projects, and Interdisciplinary Investigations include teaching notes and answers for the long-term projects.

Reading and Writing in the Mathematics Classroom features suggestions for including reading as an integral part of the mathematics curriculum as well as differentiated approaches for English learning and inclusion.

More information on options for reading and writing is available on pages T6–T7.

Applications

Classroom Math Games include Game Zone tools and additional games to help students improve their problem solving, logic, and computational skills. (available online)

Calculator and Spreadsheet Masters include activities to incorporate technology into your mathematics classroom.

Science and Mathematics Lab Manual includes activity masters for integrating science into your mathematics classroom. (available online)

What's Math Got To Do With It? Telly award-winning videos connect mathematics to real life. (also available on one Super DVD combined with MindJogger Videoquizzes)

Real-Life Career Masters features activities that relate mathematics to various careers.

than you'd ever imagine

in less time than you'd ever believe

Transparencies with Standardized Test Practice for each lesson evaluates what students learned in the previous lesson. Each transparency also includes a standardized test practice question.

Key Teaching Transparencies provide key concepts and worked-out examples for key lessons.

Closing the Gap for Absent Students provides an easy-to-use summary of all the materials you have covered in the chapter in a format that can be posted or distributed to students who have missed class.

Guide to Daily Intervention offers suggestions for daily assessment and tips on how to help students succeed.

Math Skills Maintenance includes worksheets to review basic mathematics skills.

Technology Support for Teachers

TeacherWorks **All-in-One Lesson Planner and Resource Center** CD-ROM includes a lesson planner and interactive Teacher Edition, so you can customize lesson plans and reproduce classroom resources quickly and easily.

Answer Key Maker with Solutions Manual software allows you to customize answer keys for your assignments from the Student Edition exercises.

Interactive Chalkboard CD-ROM includes fully worked-out examples, 5-Minute Check Transparencies, and Your Turn exercises in a customizable Microsoft® PowerPoint® format.

And more... *Additional technology products and Internet resources for students, teachers, and parents are discussed on pages T6–T7, T11, T16, and T22.*

Staff Development

Answer Key Transparencies provide answers to Student Edition exercises.

Solutions Manual includes completely worked-out solutions for all exercises in the Student Edition.

Using the Internet in the Mathematics Classroom provides guidelines for using the Internet as well as resources that are available on the Internet.

Teaching Mathematics with Manipulatives features activities and teaching suggestions to help you present mathematics concepts with manipulatives and hands-on materials.

HELP your students become fluent

Glencoe Mathematics: Applications and Concepts **makes it easy for you to incorporate constructive reading and writing strategies into every class you teach.**

Student Edition

Foldables™ Study Organizers at the beginning of each chapter provide students with tools for organizing what they are reading and studying.

Reading Math tips appear throughout each chapter to help students learn and use the language of math.

Link to Reading margin features connect mathematics terms with the meanings of commonly used words and phrases.

Study Skill activities include strategies that provide students with a variety of methods to read, study, and comprehend the mathematics they are learning.

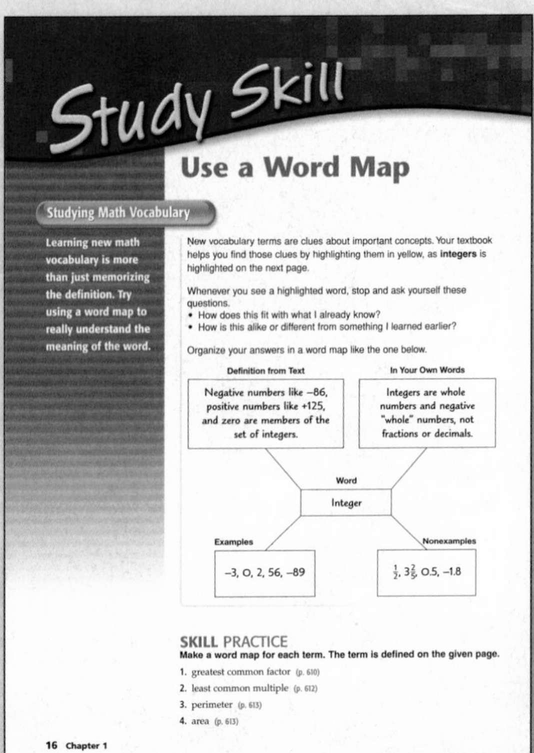

Study Skill

Use a Word Map

Studying Math Vocabulary

Learning new math vocabulary is more than just memorizing the definition. Try using a word map to really understand the meaning of the word.

New vocabulary terms are clues about important concepts. Your textbook helps you find those clues by highlighting them in yellow, as **integers** is highlighted on the next page.

Whenever you see a highlighted word, stop and ask yourself these questions.

- How does this fit with what I already know?
- How is this alike or different from something I learned earlier?

Organize your answers in a word map like the one below.

SKILL PRACTICE

Make a word map for each term. The term is defined on the given page.

1. greatest common factor (p. 610)
2. least common multiple (p. 612)
3. perimeter (p. 613)
4. area (p. 613)

16 Chapter 1

Noteables™ Interactive Study Notebook with Foldables™ is designed to help students take organized notes as they study each chapter.

Writing Math questions give students opportunities to define, describe, and explain the mathematical concepts they've just learned.

New Vocabulary terms are listed at the beginning of each lesson and highlighted when defined.

Review Vocabulary terms are defined in the appropriate lessons.

The **Vocabulary and Concept Check** in each Study Guide and Review summarizes and reviews key terms.

Key Concepts are illustrated using **Words, Symbols,** and **Models** as appropriate. This approach improves reading comprehension by using multiple representations.

WebQuest Interdisciplinary Projects give students the chance to work through long-term projects to develop their research and creative writing skills.

Teacher Wraparound Edition

Foldables™ Follow-Up provide suggestions to help students create Foldables that are thorough and effective.

Modeling, Speaking, and **Writing** activities in the Assess step require students to summarize what they have learned by responding to open-ended prompts.

in the Language of MATHEMATICS.

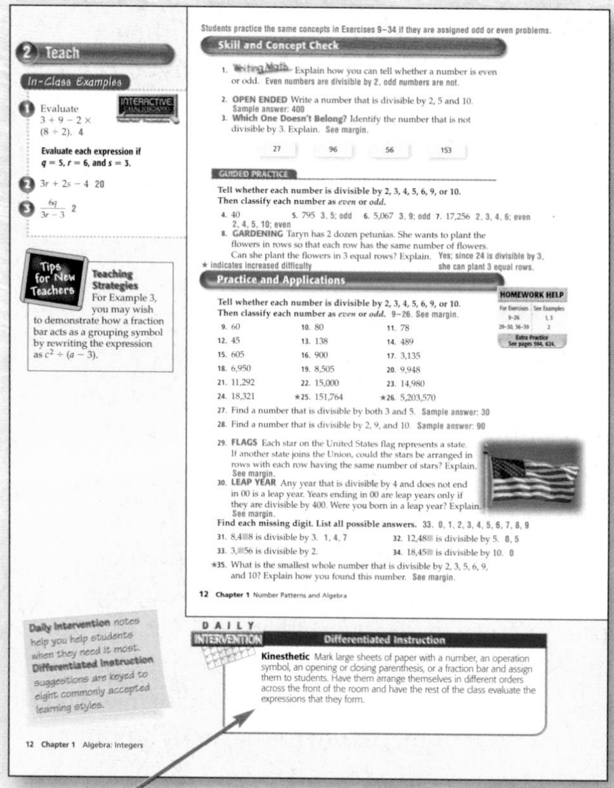

Differentiated Instruction features help students at all points on the learning spectrum develop their reading, writing, and comprehension skills.

Unlocking Misconceptions features point out preconceived ideas that students may have that are not necessarily true. Often, you can head off a global misconception that students may have.

Flexible Grouping features outline opportunities for using heterogeneous groups for instruction or intervention.

Recommended Outside Reading provides suggestions for both fiction and nonfiction literature that relates to the mathematics in each chapter.

ELL English Language Learners Strategies suggest lesson activities that help English Language Learners grasp content.

For more information on teaching to English Language Learners, see p. T8.

Technology Support

StudentWorks includes the entire text, formatted like the hardbound book, so students can study from just about anywhere. With StudentWorks, students can also access six different worksheets for each lesson as well as online study tools and *Noteables™: Interactive Study Notebook with Foldables™*.

Math Online msmath3.net/vocabulary_review is a Glencoe site that provides online study tools for reviewing the vocabulary of each chapter. www.math.glencoe.com/multilingual_glossary contains a multilingual glossary. For a list of languages, see page 692.

Reading in the Content Area links appear in each chapter to help students read and analyze key lessons.

Vocabulary PuzzleMaker software creates crossword, jumble, and word search puzzles online using vocabulary lists that you can customize.

for Middle School Mathematics CD-ROM provides interactive problem-based learning activities that help students explore the main concepts of each chapter in a real-world setting.

Additional Resources

Chapter Resource Masters

- Vocabulary Builder
- Reading to Learn Mathematics

Teaching Mathematics With Foldables™

Reading and Writing in the Mathematics Classroom

WebQuests, Projects, and Interdisciplinary Investigations

For more information on these products, see pp. T4–T5.

Give students control,

so that they leave your classroom

As an educator, you know that each student has his or her own unique style of learning. The challenge is to develop a curriculum that meets the needs of *every* student and ensures that everyone in your class, including special needs and inclusion students, has the same chance at success. *Glencoe Mathematics: Applications and Concepts* provides you with a wide range of tools to help you reach every student you teach.

Student Edition

Prerequisite Skills at the beginning of each chapter and end of each lesson assess student readiness. In the Student Handbook at the back of the Student Edition, you can also find a built-in workbook of prerequisite skills review.

Foldables™, Noteables™: Interactive Study Notebook with Foldables™, Hands-On Labs, and **Mini Labs** are hands-on study organizers and activities to accommodate the visual/spatial learner.

Key Concepts and **Concept Summaries** focus students on key mathematical concepts in each lesson. Multiple representations—words, symbols, and models—reach students of all learning styles.

The **Spiral Review** in each lesson allows students to use skills taught in previous chapters.

Teacher Wraparound Edition

Assignment Guides are organized by three different levels, making it easy to assign homework.

> *Assignment Guide*
> **Basic:** 41–51 odd, 52–73
>
> **Average:** 19–51 odd, 52–73
>
> **Enriched:** 18–50 even, 51–52, 54–69 (Optional: 70–73)

Differentiated Instruction strategies focus on eight learning styles: verbal/linguistic, logical, visual/spatial, auditory/musical, kinesthetic, interpersonal, intrapersonal, and naturalist.

ELL English Language Learners (ELL) may need specialized help in overcoming a language barrier to grasp mathematical content. The activities, features, and strategies listed below are particularly helpful to ELL students. Suggestions like these appear in the interleaf of the Teacher Wraparound Edition.

- hands-on activities
- modeling
- working in flexible groups
- vocabulary building activities

PROJECT CRISS℠ Study Skill

Project CRISS℠ is a research-based staff development program created to help students better organize, understand, and retain course information. **Project CRISS Study Skills** were developed to facilitate the teaching of each chapter of *Glencoe Mathematics: Applications and Concepts*. These strategies appear in the interleaf of the Teacher Wraparound Edition.

For more information on Project CRISS℠, visit www.projectcriss.com.

CReating Independence Through Student-Owned Strategies

with *knowledge and power* over their *own learning.*

Teacher Classroom Resources

Glencoe's **Leveled Worksheets** are helpful for meeting the needs of every student in a variety of ways. These worksheets, many of which are found in the **FAST FILE Chapter Resource Masters,** are shown in the chart below.

Technology

MathPASS: Tutorial Plus is a CD-ROM that provides step-by-step, self paced instruction correlated to *Glencoe Mathematics: Applications and Concepts.*

TeacherWorks CD-ROM includes an Interactive Teacher Edition enabling you to customize an entire course of study to meet the specific needs of your students.

An **Online Multilingual Glossary,** which includes 11 languages in addition to English, can be found at www.math.glencoe.com/multilingual_glossary.

Online Study Tools at msmath3.net include Extra Examples, Self-Check Quizzes, and Vocabulary Review.

Leveled Worksheets

9 Different Options

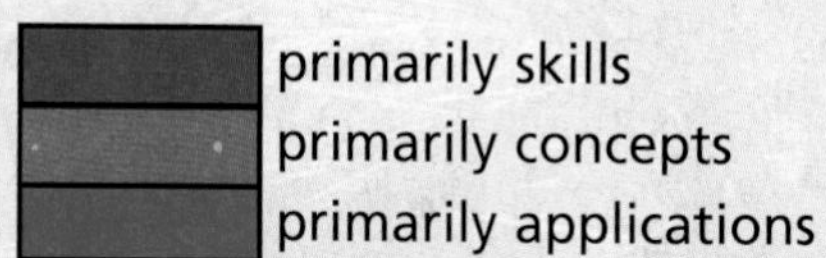

BASIC	AVERAGE	ADVANCED

❶ Math Skills Maintenance

❷ Study Guide and Intervention

❸ Reading to Learn Mathematics

❹ Noteables™: Interactive Study Notebook with Foldables™

❺ Practice: Skills

❻ Practice: Word Problems

❼ Vocabulary Builder

❽ Parent and Student Study Guide (online)

❾ Enrichment

With these TOOLS, you'll always know

Whether you need daily intervention resources integrated right into the program, or supplemental materials for after school and summer school programs, *Glencoe Mathematics: Applications and Concepts* puts it all right at your fingertips!

Diagnose Readiness

Placement Tests

Glencoe's *Diagnostic and Placement Tests* help you identify the key mathematical objectives that students are struggling with so you can make course placement decisions more effectively. A list of intervention resources is provided for each Glencoe program, including *Glencoe Mathematics: Applications and Concepts.*

Prerequisite Skills

Students often struggle in mathematics because they have not mastered the prerequisite skills needed to be successful. *Glencoe Mathematics: Applications and Concepts* provides several opportunities to check student skills and determine if they need additional review and practice.

- The **Prerequisite Skills** at the beginning of every chapter help students identify and practice skills they'll need for each new concept.
- Additional **prerequisite skills** practice is provided at the end of each lesson and includes page references to help students get extra review whenever they need it. More prerequisite skills practice appears in the Student Handbook section at the back of the Student Edition.
- The **Math Skills Maintenance** masters provide extra practice on basic skills needed for success in mathematics.

Daily Intervention Opportunities

Guide to Daily Intervention offers suggestions for using *Glencoe Mathematics: Applications and Concepts* and *Glencoe MathScape™* to intercept students who are having difficulties and prescribes a system of reinforcement to promote student success.

The **Chapter Resource Masters** include several types of worksheets that can be used for daily intervention in each lesson.

- **Study Guide and Intervention*** masters provide worked-out examples as well as practice problems.
- **Practice: Skills*** masters allow students who are progressing at a slower pace to practice the concept using easier problems.
- **Practice: Word Problems*** masters provide word problems for students who are moving at a regular or faster pace.
- **Reading to Learn Mathematics** provides various reading strategies to help students master the mathematics presented in each lesson.

Each of these types of worksheets is available as a* ***consumable workbook* *in both English and Spanish.*

The **Student Edition** contains additional problems in the Student Handbook to help students master each lesson.

- **Extra Practice** provides additional, immediate practice with the concepts from each lesson.
- **Mixed Problem Solving** includes numerous verbal problems for students to reinforce their problem-solving skills.

who needs EXTRA HELP.

And you'll be able to *DELIVER* it.

Technology Resources

Glencoe offers a variety of timesaving technology tools to help students build their math skills more effectively.

MathPASS: Tutorial Plus CD-ROM provides an interactive, self-paced tutorial for a complete middle school mathematics curriculum. The lessons are correlated directly to *Glencoe Mathematics: Applications and Concepts*. Each lesson, or concept, includes a pretest, tutorial, guided practice, and posttest. Students' answers to the pretests automatically determine whether they need the tutorial for each concept, so students can take responsibility for their own learning—without taking teacher time for grading.

Math Online **Study Tools** at msmath3.net include comprehensive review and intervention tools that are available anytime. Self-check quizzes are available for every lesson, and immediate feedback helps students check their progress and find specific pages and examples in the Student Edition whenever they need extra review. These Online Study Tools also include extra examples, chapter tests, standardized test practice, and vocabulary review.

Students' achievement in mathematics was shown to improve when teachers received weekly summaries of their performances (Fuchs, et al., 1994). **Yearly ProgressPro** is an online instructional, assessment, and intervention tool that provides detailed diagnostic information weekly on students' academic progress. For more information, visit mhdigitallearning.com.

Additional Teacher Resources

The following materials are available to help you determine which students need intervention and allow you to develop strategies for giving students the help they need. For a description of each feature, see page T5.

- **5-Minute Check Transparencies with Standardized Test Practice**
- **Daily Intervention** features in the Teacher Wraparound Edition
- **Closing the Gap for Absent Students**

Give ASSESSMENT

***Glencoe Mathematics: Applications and Concepts* gives you all the tools you need to prepare students for success—including Standardized Test Practice in every lesson and the powerful ExamView® Pro CD-ROM.**

Student Edition

Each chapter begins with a **Getting Started** section on **Prerequisite Skills** to help diagnose student readiness.

Standardized Test Practice questions appear in every lesson. Every chapter contains a completely worked-out standardized test example as well as two full pages of Standardized Test Practice with Test-Taking Tips. A Student Recording Answer Sheet and a sample scoring rubric are available in the Teacher Wraparound Edition.

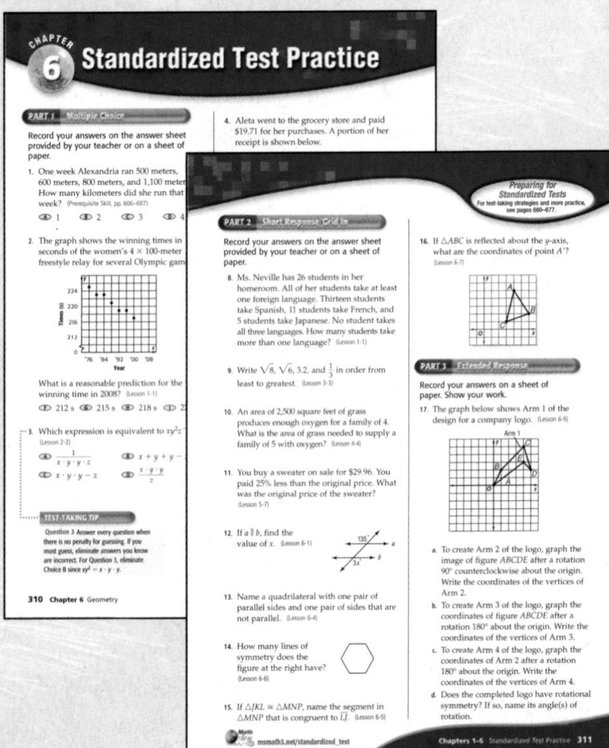

Chapter Study Guide and Review provides Vocabulary and Concept review and Lesson-by-Lesson Exercises and Examples, all at the point of use for students.

A **Mid-Chapter Practice Test** and a **Practice Test** for each chapter provide the variety of practice questions students need to succeed on tests.

Preparing for Standardized Tests is designed to help your students become better test-takers. Included are examples and practice for the types of questions and concepts commonly seen on standardized tests. The short-response and extended-response sections contain sample rubrics, as well as sample solutions:

- full credit solutions
- partial credit solutions
- no credit solutions

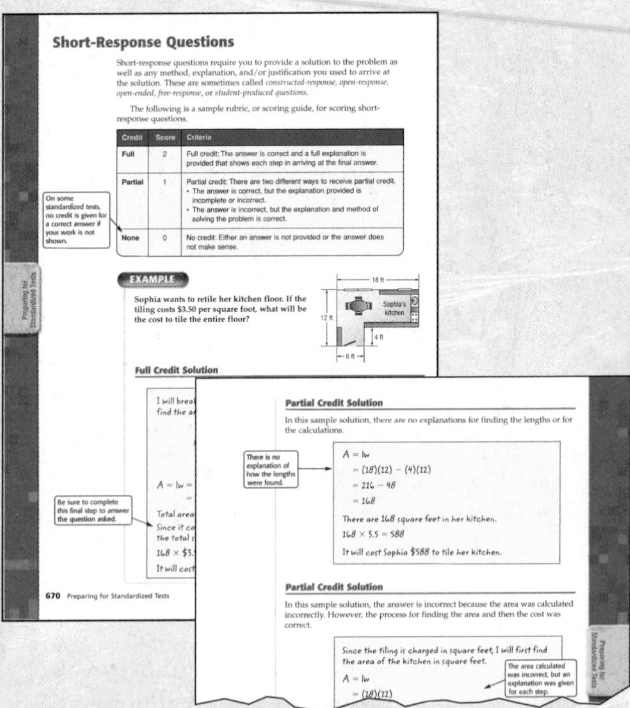

Teacher Wraparound Edition

An **Open-Ended Assessment** activity is provided in each lesson in the margin of the Teacher Wraparound Edition. These activities involve speaking, writing, modeling, and higher-level thinking.

Opportunities to **Assess** students' work appear in every Hands-On Lab in the Teacher Wraparound Edition.

the extra attention it deserves, without the extra prep time.

Teacher Classroom Resources

5-Minute Check Transparencies with Standardized Test Practice provide full-size transparencies with questions covering the previous lesson or chapter. Standardized Test Practice Questions are also included. (also available on Interactive Chalkboard CD-ROM)

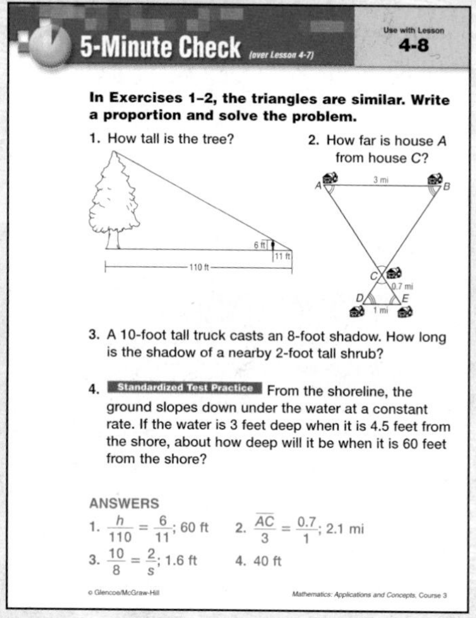
5-Minute Check *(over Lesson 4-7)* Use with Lesson 4-8

In Exercises 1–2, the triangles are similar. Write a proportion and solve the problem.

1. How tall is the tree?
2. How far is house *A* from house *C*?

3. A 10-foot tall truck casts an 8-foot shadow. How long is the shadow of a nearby 2-foot tall shrub?
4. **Standardized Test Practice** From the shoreline, the ground slopes down under the water at a constant rate. If the water is 3 feet deep when it is 4.5 feet from the shore, about how deep will it be when it is 60 feet from the shore?

ANSWERS

1. $\frac{h}{110} = \frac{6}{11}$; 60 ft
2. $\frac{\overline{AC}}{3} = \frac{0.7}{1}$; 2.1 mi
3. $\frac{10}{8} = \frac{2}{s}$; 1.6 ft
4. 40 ft

© Glencoe/McGraw-Hill — *Mathematics: Applications and Concepts, Course 3*

Assessment Options in the Chapter Resource Masters

These assessment resources are available for each chapter in *Glencoe Mathematics: Applications and Concepts.*

- 6 Chapter Tests
- Open-Ended Assessment with Scoring Rubric
- Vocabulary Test and Review **Glencoe Exclusive!**
- 4 Quizzes
- Mid-Chapter Test
- Cumulative Review
- 2-page Standardized Test Practice

Unit Tests, Semester Tests, and a **Final Test** are also available at point of use in the Chapter Resource Masters.

Technology Support

Use the networkable **ExamView® Pro** to:

- Create **multiple versions** of tests.
- Create **modified** tests for inclusion students.
- **Insert** art into your tests using files from the **math art folder.**
- Use built-in **state curriculum correlations** to create tests aligned with state standards.
- Change **English** tests to **Spanish** with one mouse click and vice versa.

MindJogger Videoquizzes present chapter-by-chapter review sessions in a game show format to make review more interesting and active to students—especially great for reluctant readers. Available on VHS or on one Super DVD with What's Math Got To Do With It? Real-Life Math Videos.

Math Online Study Tools

- Extra Examples
- Self-Check Quizzes
- Vocabulary Review
- Chapter Test Practice
- Standardized Test Practice

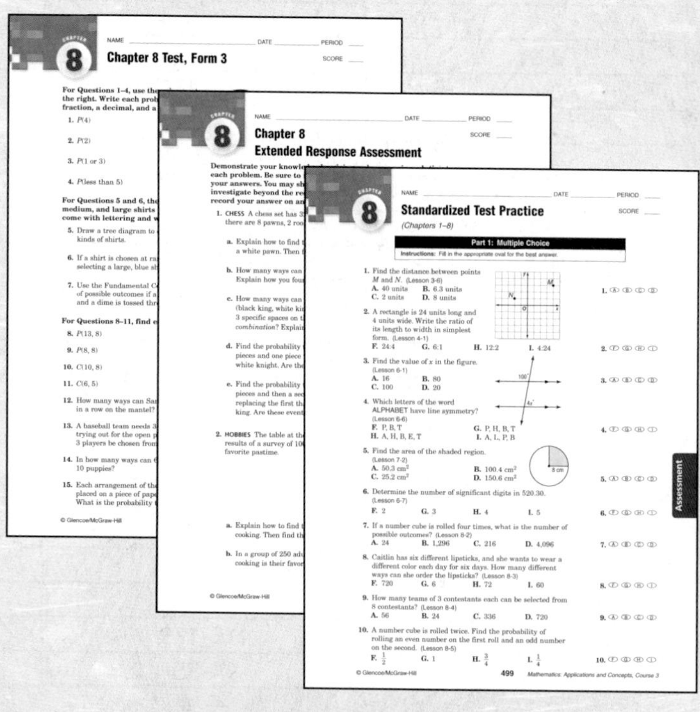
Chapter 8 Test, Form 3

Chapter 8 Extended Response Assessment

Standardized Test Practice (Chapters 1–8)

Part 1: Multiple Choice

A Comprehensive, research-based curriculum

NSF ***MathScape*™ is an NSF-funded, standards-based mathematics curriculum. This unique, comprehensive program encourages students to learn mathematics by doing mathematics, by using and connecting mathematical ideas, and by communicating about mathematics through writing and discussion.**

New for 2005!

MathScape

SEEING AND THINKING MATHEMATICALLY

MATH X-ING

Core Principles

- *MathScape* combines classroom strategies, group activities, cooperative learning situations, and homework.
- Seven units in each of grade levels 6–8 contain rigorous mathematics in engaging projects and investigations. These investigations are designed to get your students to think critically and creatively about mathematical topics.
- Using *MathScape* is an effective way to enhance chapters in *Glencoe Mathematics: Applications and Concepts.*

The chart shows how the lessons in *Glencoe Mathematics: Applications and Concepts* correlate to the units in *MathScape*. The interleaf pages of the Teacher Wraparound Edition offer specific suggestions for how to use *MathScape* with the lessons in the chart that are in **bold**.

Mathematics: Applications and Concepts, Course 3	MathScape, Course 3	Mathematics: Applications and Concepts, Course 3	MathScape, Course 3
Lessons	Pages	Lessons	Pages
1-1	50–89	**7-7**	98–101, 104, 106, 108–109, 111
1-2	182–185	7-8	114, 120–121, 131
1-4	192–193	**8-2**	28–29
1-5	192–193	**8-3**	30–33
2-8	296	8-5	27
2-9	300–301	8-6	26
3-4	236–237	**9-2**	6–7
3-5	238–239	**9-4**	8–13
4-1	50–57, 74	**10-1**	182–183, 194–195
4-2	60–73, 75–77	**10-4**	204–209
4-4	244–245	11-1	138–165
4-6	120–121, 229, 231, 238, 252–255	**11-2**	272
4-7	231	11-3	274–275
4-7b	250–251	**11-4**	280–281
5-1	246–247	11-5	282–285
5-2	250–251	11-6	18–23
6-2	16–17	**12-1**	273, 276–277, 296–297
6-3	250–251	**12-2**	288–293
7-3	110	12-3	182–183, 194–195
7-4	96–97	12-5	196, 202–203
7-5	105, 107	12-6	298–299
7-6	115–119	12-7	186–189, 197–199
7-7a	94–95		

that *engages* students and builds mathematical understanding.

Student Benefits

Through *MathScape*, students develop mathematical understanding and proficiency by exploring mathematics that is used in everyday activities.

The long-term investigations in each unit include a list of ways in which the activities may be adapted or modified to benefit special needs students.

Implementing MathScape

You can use a *MathScape* activity in a variety of ways, depending on your objective.

- **Introduce** → Use the activity *before* teaching a lesson in *Glencoe Mathematics: Applications and Concepts.*
- **Reinforce and Enrich** → Use the activity *after* teaching a lesson in *Glencoe Mathematics: Applications and Concepts.*
- **Shift the Focus** → To respond to students' needs, use the activity *in place of* a lesson in *Glencoe Mathematics: Applications and Concepts.*

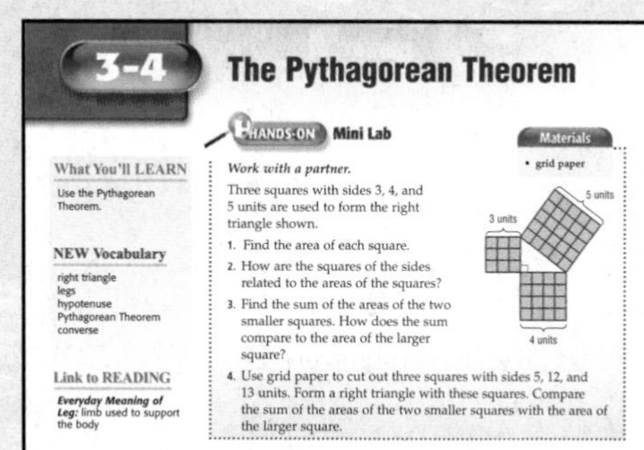

3-4 The Pythagorean Theorem

HANDS-ON Mini Lab

What You'll LEARN
Use the Pythagorean Theorem.

NEW Vocabulary
right triangle
legs
hypotenuse
Pythagorean Theorem
converse

Link to READING
Everyday Meaning of Leg: limb used to support the body

Materials
- grid paper

Work with a partner.

Three squares with sides 3, 4, and 5 units are used to form the right triangle shown.

1. Find the area of each square.
2. How are the squares of the sides related to the areas of the squares?
3. Find the sum of the areas of the two smaller squares. How does the sum compare to the area of the larger square?
4. Use grid paper to cut out three squares with sides 5, 12, and 13 units. Form a right triangle with these squares. Compare the sum of the areas of the two smaller squares with the area of the larger square.

…with one right angle. A right angle is an

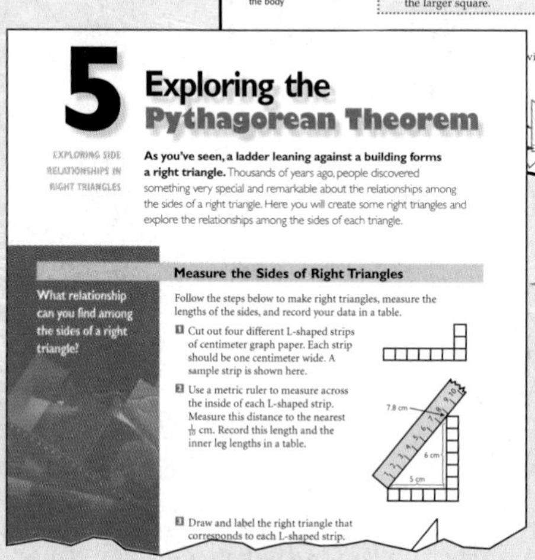

5 Exploring the Pythagorean Theorem

EXPLORING SIDE RELATIONSHIPS IN RIGHT TRIANGLES

As you've seen, a ladder leaning against a building forms a right triangle. Thousands of years ago, people discovered something very special and remarkable about the relationships among the sides of a right triangle. Here you will create some right triangles and explore the relationships among the sides of each triangle.

What relationship can you find among the sides of a right triangle?

Measure the Sides of Right Triangles

Follow the steps below to make right triangles, measure the lengths of the sides, and record your data in a table.

1. Cut out four different L-shaped strips of centimeter graph paper. Each strip should be one centimeter wide. A sample strip is shown here.
2. Use a metric ruler to measure across the inside of each L-shaped strip. Measure this distance to the nearest $\frac{1}{10}$ cm. Record this length and the inner leg lengths in a table.
3. Draw and label the right triangle that corresponds to each L-shaped strip.

Use *MathScape* …

… to enhance *Glencoe Mathematics: Applications and Concepts.*

Teacher's Guide

Each Teacher's Guide contains all the tools you need for effectively implementing *MathScape.*

- **Lesson Plans** with a pacing guide and suggestions for alternative plans

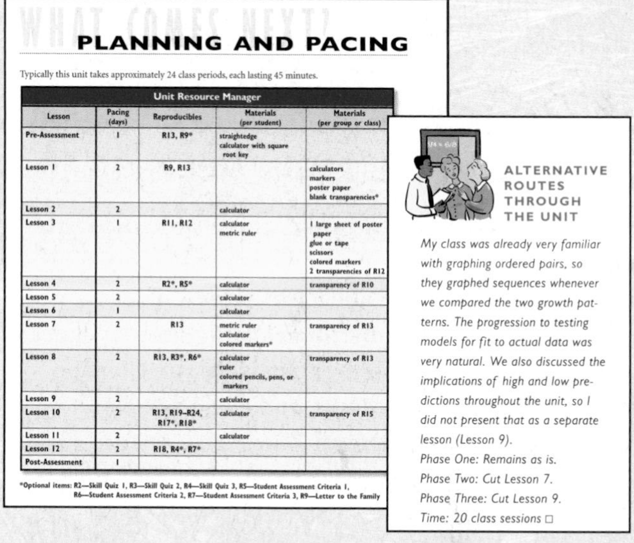

WHAT COMES NEXT?

PLANNING AND PACING

Typically this unit takes approximately 24 class periods, each lasting 45 minutes.

Unit Resource Manager				
Lesson	Pacing (days)	Reproducibles	Materials (per student)	Materials (per group or class)
Pre-Assessment	1	R13, R9*	straightedge calculator with square root key	
Lesson 1	2	R9, R13		calculators markers poster paper blank transparencies*
Lesson 2	2		calculator	
Lesson 3	1	R11, R12	calculator metric ruler	1 large sheet of poster paper glue or tape scissors colored markers 2 transparencies of R12
Lesson 4	2	R2*, R5*	calculator	transparency of R10
Lesson 5	2		calculator	
Lesson 6	1		calculator	
Lesson 7	2	R13	metric ruler calculator colored markers*	transparency of R13
Lesson 8	2	R13, R3*, R6*	calculator ruler colored pencils, pens, or markers	transparency of R13
Lesson 9	2		calculator	
Lesson 10	2	R13, R19–R24, R17*, R18*	calculator	transparency of R15
Lesson 11	2		calculator	
Lesson 12	2	R18, R4*, R7*		
Post-Assessment	1			

*Optional items: R2—Skill Quiz 1, R3—Skill Quiz 2, R4—Skill Quiz 3, R5—Student Assessment Criteria 1, R6—Student Assessment Criteria 2, R7—Student Assessment Criteria 3, R9—Letter to the Family

ALTERNATIVE ROUTES THROUGH THE UNIT

My class was already very familiar with graphing ordered pairs, so they graphed sequences whenever we compared the two growth patterns. The progression to testing models for fit to actual data was very natural. We also discussed the implications of high and low predictions throughout the unit, so I did not present that as a separate lesson (Lesson 9).

Phase One: Remains as is.

Phase Two: Cut Lesson 7.

Phase Three: Cut Lesson 9.

Time: 20 class sessions □

- **Assessment Tools** including What To Look For, Assessment Rubric, and Skill Check
- **Reproducible Masters**
- **Technology Options** for incorporating graphing calculators, computer software, and the Internet

Research-Based

MathScape was developed by the Seeing and Thinking Mathematically Project at the Education Development Center (EDC). Extensive and formative research activities that were conducted, along with extensive field testing, helped to develop materials that are mathematically clear and pedagogically effective with diverse populations of students.

The *MathScape* curriculum aligns to the NCTM Standards for grades 5–8. Each of the units is designed to fully address current standards and recommendations for teaching middle school mathematics.

DISCOVER how a simple sheet of paper can CHANGE the way your students THINK about math... forever.

Students love Foldables™ because they're fun. Teachers love them because they're effective.

Foldables are easy-to-make, three-dimensional interactive graphic organizers that students create out of simple sheets of paper. These unique hands-on tools for learning and reviewing were created exclusively for *Glencoe Mathematics: Applications and Concepts* by teaching specialist Dinah Zike.

Building Prereading Skills

At the beginning of each chapter, students construct one of a variety of Foldables. Each Foldable helps students create an interactive strategy for organizing what they read and observe. As they work through each chapter, students add more detail to their Foldable until they have created a comprehensive, interactive snapshot of the key concepts and vocabulary of the chapter. Instructions for making and using Foldables are also included in the *Noteables™: Interactive Study Notebook with Foldables™*.

Reading and Writing

Each foldable helps students practice basic reading and writing skills, find and report main ideas, organize information, review key vocabulary terms, and more.

Review and Reinforcement

The completed Foldable is a comprehensive overview of the chapter concepts—perfect for preparing for chapter, unit, and even end-of-course tests.

Assessment

Foldables present an ideal opportunity to probe the depth of your students' understanding of chapter concepts. You'll get detailed feedback on what your students know and any misconceptions they have.

Staff Development

Teaching Mathematics with Foldables™ equips teachers to extend the use of Foldables in their classrooms by exploring the different Foldable formats and providing suggestions for using them throughout the mathematics curriculum.

Introducing our partner

USA TODAY® Education

In an exclusive partnership with Glencoe/McGraw-Hill, USA TODAY® Education has brought its powerful one-of-a-kind perspective and dynamic content to the pages of *Glencoe Mathematics: Applications and Concepts.*

USA TODAY Snapshots®

Visit USA TODAY® K–12 Education's website at www.education.usatoday.com to find resources and interactive features connected to each day's newspaper.

- *Experience TODAY* is a daily lesson plan that provides instruction for integrating USA TODAY® graphics and key editorial features into your mathematics classroom.
- Real-world problems require students to interpret USA TODAY Snapshots® and analyze the data.
- *Math TODAY* activities, which are correlated to NCTM Standards, engage students in current, relevant information. Reproducible pages, teaching suggestions, and prerequisite skills are provided for each activity.
- Free online educational math resources integrate USA TODAY® content with graphing calculator technology.
- By completing the Professional Development Training Program, teachers can earn credit while learning how to use USA TODAY® as a resource in the classroom to meet state standards.

For more information, visit www.education.usatoday.com or contact USA TODAY® at 1-800-757-TEACH.

25. **MONEY MATTERS** Generation X (Gen Xers) are people who were born in the late 1960s or the early 1970s. According to the graphic at the right, most Gen Xers would invest an unexpected $50,000. Suppose someone invested this money at a simple interest rate of 4.5%. How much money would they have at the end of 10 years?

26. **INVESTMENTS** Booker earned $1,200 over the summer. He invested the money in stocks. To his surprise, the stocks increased in value to $1,335 in only 9 months. Find the simple interest rate for the investment.

27. **CRITICAL THINKING** Ethan's bank account listed a balance of $328.80. He originally opened the account with a $200 deposit and a simple interest rate of 4.6%. If there were no deposits or withdrawals, how long ago was the account opened?

Spiral Review with Standardized Test Practice

28. **MULTIPLE CHOICE** Suppose Mr. and Mrs. Owens placed $1,500 in a college savings account with a simple interest rate of 4% when Lauren was born...

29. SH...

30. SAL...

Solve e...

31. Wh...

REAL-LIFE CAREERS

How Does a Navigator Use Math?

Navigators use math to calculate the course of a ship. They sometimes use lighthouses as landmarks in their navigating.

Math Online Research

For information about a career as a navigator, visit: msmath3.net/careers

EXAMPLE Use Real Numbers

7 **LIGHTHOUSES** On a clear day, the number of miles a person can see to the horizon is about 1.23 times the square root of his or her distance from the ground, in feet. Suppose Domingo is at the top of the lighthouse at Cape Hatteras and Jewel is at the top of the lighthouse at Cape Lookout. How much farther can Domingo see than Jewel?

USA TODAY Snapshots®

Tallest lighthouses

The U.S. Lighthouse Society announced last month it will convert the former U.S. Lighthouse Service headquarters on New York's Staten Island into a national lighthouse museum. Tallest of the estimated 850 U.S. lighthouses:

Cape Hatteras, N.C.	Cape Charles, Va.	Pensacola, Fla.	Cape May, N.J.	Absecon, N.J.	Cape Lookout, N.C.
196 ft.	191 ft.	171 ft.	170 ft.	170 ft.	169 ft.

Source: U.S. Lighthouse Society, San Francisco

By Anne R. Carey and Sam Ward, USA TODAY

Use a calculator to approximate the distance each person can see.

Domingo: $1.23\sqrt{196} = 17.22$ Jewel: $1.23\sqrt{169} = 15.99$

Domingo can see about 17.22 − 15.99 or 1.23 miles farther than Jewel.

It's Staff Development,

As professional development continues to take on greater importance for educators across the country, teachers are constantly looking for easy-to-use tools to help them stay abreast of current trends and issues. At Glencoe, we know how valuable your time is, so we've developed a variety of staff development tools to help you meet your district's requirements.

Teacher Wraparound Edition

Continuity of Instruction and Mathematical Background found at the beginning of each chapter gives you an overview of the mathematics in each lesson. Information about prior knowledge as well as future connections lets you see the how the mathematics your students are learning fits into the whole of their education.

Tips for New Teachers offers helpful suggestions for such things as classroom management, assessment, teaching techniques, and more.

Teaching Tips can be found on the reduced student pages at point of use.

What the Research Says describes educational research strategies that are incorporated in each chapter.

Teacher Classroom Resources

Glencoe Mathematics Staff Development Series allows you to stay current with issues that affect your teaching effectiveness. The series is intended to help you implement new mathematics strategies and enhance your classroom performance.

Print Resources

- *Using the Internet in the Mathematics Classroom*
- *Reading and Writing in the Mathematics Classroom*
- *Teaching Math with Manipulatives*
- *Teaching Mathematics with Foldables™*

Technology Support

At math.glencoe.com, you'll find:

- *Key Concepts: Mathematical Background and Teaching Notes*
- *Graphing Calculators in the Mathematics Classroom*
- *Cooperative Learning in the Mathematics Classroom*
- *Alternative Assessment in the Mathematics Classroom*
- *Involving Parents and the Community in the Mathematics Classroom*
- a Staff Development site that addresses current issues in education
- a Bulletin Board that allows teachers to discuss issues and ideas with colleagues
- a State and National Resources site that links to math and math education resources

made convenient.

McGraw-Hill Professional Development

Glencoe and McGraw-Hill Professional Development offer a suite of professional development products, designed to enrich content knowledge and develop a greater mastery of teaching strategies and techniques in mathematics instruction. These programs provide professional learning opportunities in various formats, which are described below.

***Mathematics: Applications and Concepts* Implementation Workshop** introduces teachers to the content and instructional strategies of the Teacher Wraparound Edition, plus an overview of the additional resources for lesson planning and teaching.

Innovative Math for Innovative Teachers is a hands-on workshop that provides a motivational introduction to key mathematical concepts found in *Mathematics: Applications and Concepts*. Teachers learn grade-level-appropriate mathematical concepts and activities through games, small groups, manipulative activities, and classroom video.

Mathematics, YES! Videos* with *Video Workshop Facilitator's Guide is a program of ten facilitator-led units. Teachers view video segments of a classroom lesson and hear mathematics experts discuss critical content and the teaching strategies that can be used. Teachers then evaluate what they have seen and discuss how the strategies can be implemented in their classrooms.

Units from ***Mathematics, YES!***

- Number Relations
- Patterns and Functions
- Integers and Order of Operations
- Fractions, Decimals, and Percentages
- Coordinate Pairs and Graphing
- Ratio and Proportional Reasoning
- Solving Equations and Inequalities
- Geometry and Measurement of Plane Figures
- Geometry and Measurement of Solid Figures
- Statistics, Data Analysis, and Probability

Mathematics, YES! Online is comprised of ten units that may be used individually or combined to develop custom courses. During the online experience, users watch and listen to video clips of a classroom lesson delivered over the Web with the use of a CD. Through video and interactive learning activities, each online unit emphasizes the strategies and techniques used to teach mathematics. University credit is available.

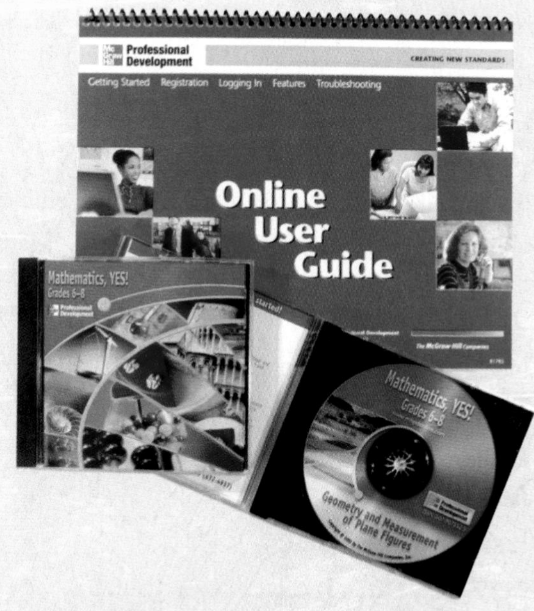

For more information on *Mathematics, YES! Online*, visit mhpdonline.com or contact McGraw-Hill Professional Development at 1-866-501-6997 or by e-mail at mhpd@mcgraw-hill.com.

Mathematics, YES! Trainer's Package includes materials for teachers to participate in trainer-led, hand-on activities that emphasize the acquisition of content knowledge. Participants see teaching strategies modeled by the trainer and watch video of real classroom teachers. Each unit is 6 to 8 hours of instruction time and comes with a trainer's guide, video, reproducible transparency files, and game cards. University credit is available.

Glencoe Mathematics Programs—Research-Based and

Glencoe's mathematics programs are the product of ongoing classroom and educational research activities involving students, teachers, curriculum supervisors, administrators, parents, and college-level mathematics educators, mathematicians, and researchers.

The *No Child Left Behind Act of 2001* requires that schools implement education programs and practices that have been clearly demonstrated to be effective through rigorous scientific research. The latest research studies on best practices in mathematics education were incorporated in every step in the development of *Glencoe Mathematics: Applications and Concepts* to ensure that all students succeed.

Research-Based Instructional Strategies

Glencoe Mathematics: Applications and Concepts is specifically designed to utilize several important research-based instructional strategies to reinforce the high goals set by *No Child Left Behind* and the *Principles and Standards for School Mathematics.*

Nine proven instructional strategies that are embedded throughout Glencoe's mathematics programs, described in Marzano's *Classroom Instruction that Works*, are listed below.

Proven Instructional Strategies

1. Identifying Similarities and Differences
2. Summarizing and Notetaking
3. Reinforcing Effort and Providing Recognition
4. Homework and Practice
5. Nonlinguistic Representations
6. Cooperative Learning
7. Setting Objectives and Providing Feedback
8. Generating and Testing Hypotheses
9. Cues, Questions, and Advance Organizers

Source: Marzano, R. J., Pickering, D. J., & Pollock, J. E. (2001) *Classroom Instruction that Works: Research Based Strategies for Increasing Student Achievement*, Association for Supervision and Curriculum Development, Alexandria, VA.

Glencoe Pre-Development Research is a booklet that demonstrates Glencoe's commitment to provide research-based curriculum materials.

The **White Paper** for *Glencoe Mathematics: Applications and Concepts* shows how the program was specifically designed to utilize several important research-based instructional strategies.

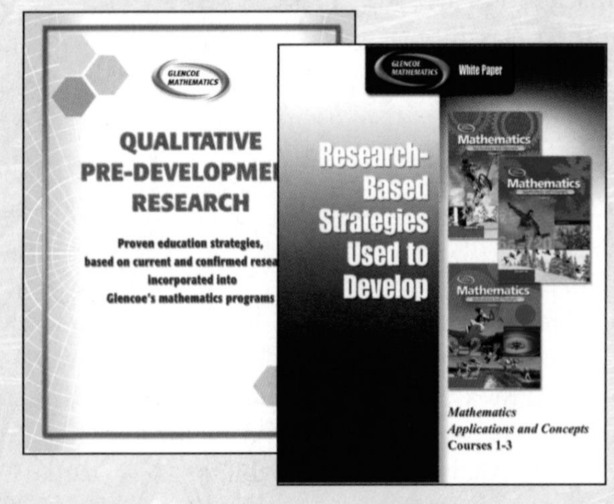

proven to ensure success.

Research-Based Evidence Portfolio

Glencoe Mathematics: Applications and Concepts is designed to help close the achievement gap in mathematics classrooms so that *all* students are proficient in mathematics. A portfolio of evidence supports the effectiveness of Glencoe mathematics programs.

Results with Mathematics: Applications and Concepts is a report that details the progress made in a variety of school districts that have implemented *Glencoe Mathematics: Applications and Concepts*. The results show that all have raised the academic performance of their student populations.

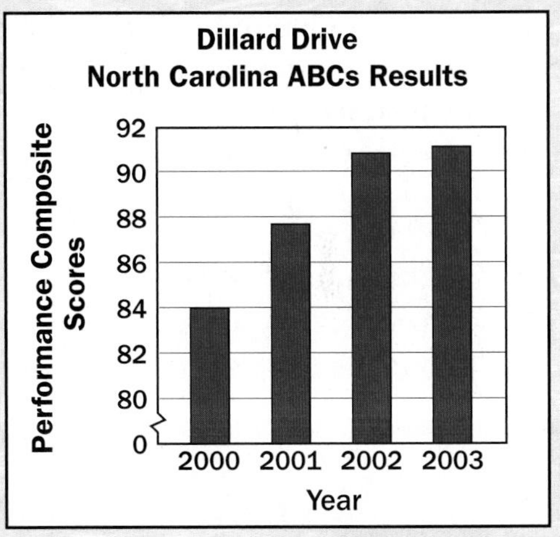

Source: *Results with Mathematics: Applications and Concepts*

NSF-Funded Program

Glencoe's **MathScape™: Seeing and Thinking Mathematically,** an NSF-funded program, can be used to enhance or replace selected lessons in *Glencoe Mathematics: Applications and Concepts.*

Proven Satisfaction

Glencoe's mathematics programs, currently used by millions of students and tens of thousands of teachers, have proven track records of success. The mix of authors and consultants, along with the incorporation of national trends and research results, contributes to a preferred rating among teachers and students.

Quasi-Experimental Design Research Studies provide strong support that the use of Glencoe's mathematics programs produce greater levels of achievement. Glencoe also conducts **Learner Verification Research** in which students and teachers use pre-publication manuscripts in the classroom. The results for *Mathematics: Applications and Concepts*, compiled by an independent contractor, are summarized below.

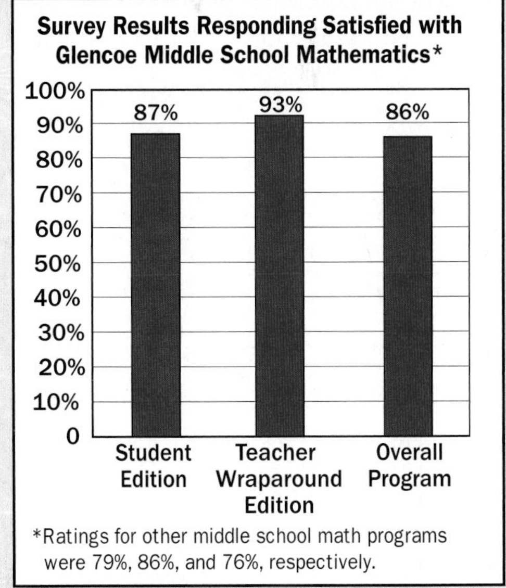

*Ratings for other middle school math programs were 79%, 86%, and 76%, respectively.

Source: *Results with Mathematics: Applications and Concepts*

Top-Line Results

- The research indicates that test scores significantly increased among students using *Mathematics: Applications and Concepts.*
- The program was equally effective with boys and girls, and with minority and non-minority students.
- Overall, the gap between the average pre-test score and a perfect score closed by 27%. On average, scores increased 29% after students used the Glencoe program.

For more details of Glencoe's research, please contact us at www.math.glencoe.com.

The INTERNET: One TOOL. Endless possibilities.

With *Glencoe Mathematics: Applications and Concepts*, your students can use the Internet to build their math skills. And you can access a wide variety of resources to help you plan classes, extend lessons, even meet professional development requirements.

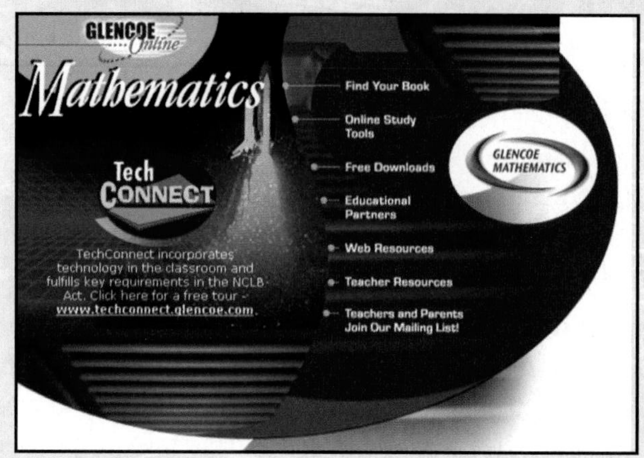

For Students

Online Study Tools, referenced on the Student Edition pages, are keyed specifically to *Glencoe Mathematics: Applications and Concepts.*

- msmath3.net/chapter_readiness lets students take a self-check quiz before beginning each chapter.
- msmath3.net/extra_examples features additional fully worked-out examples.
- msmath3.net/self_check_quiz allows students to check their progress in each lesson.
- msmath3.net/vocabulary_review lets students check their vocabulary comprehension.
- msmath3.net/chapter_test provides additional practice in test taking.
- msmath3.net/standardized_test simulates standardized and proficiency tests.

Other Online Resources

- msmath3.net/webquest offers an online research project.
- msmath3.net/data_update features links to updated statistical data presented in exercises.
- msmath3.net/reading provides strategies to help students read and analyze key lessons.
- msmath3.net/careers offers information about career opportunities.
- msmath3.net/other_calculator_keystrokes provides keystrokes for various calculators to accompany graphing calculator activities and exercises.
- www.math.glencoe.com/multilingual_glossary provides the glossary in 11 languages, in addition to English.

Using TechCONNECT, your students develop computer skills as they reinforce basic concepts in *Glencoe Mathematics: Applications and Concepts*. TechCONNECT provides a solution for incorporating technology in the classroom, as states and districts fulfill *No Child Left Behind* requirements.

Visit www.techconnect.glencoe.com for a FREE tour.

For Teachers

Powerful tools to make your job easier

- Game Zone: Classroom Math Games
- Science and Mathematics Lab Manual
- Real-Life Career Masters
- Family Letters and Family Activities, English and Spanish
- USA TODAY® K–12 Education daily lesson plans
- Activities, Games, Puzzles, and Software Links

Staff Development sites

- NCTM links
- Teaching Today link

For Parents

Help parents get involved with their child's learning

- Parent and Student Study Guide Online Worksheets
- Involving Parents and Community in the Mathematics Classroom

Planning YOUR Mathematics Course

Glencoe Mathematics: Applications and Concepts and the accompanying support materials allow you to create a mathematics course that meets the needs of each class of students. The charts shown below offer general suggestions for pacing your students through the book. Pacing for both standard class periods and block schedule class periods is given.

The total number of days in each level of pacing is less than the typical 180-day school year and 90-day semester to allow for flexibility in planning due to testing, school cancellation, or shortened class periods.

You may want to use one of the Chapter Test 2C provided in the *Chapter Resource Masters* as a pretest to determine how well your students are prepared for each chapter. If you find that they are well prepared, consider using the Study Guide and Review at the end of the chapter as a one-day lesson and proceed to the next chapter.

Year-Long Schedule
45–50-minute periods

Grading Period	Chapter	Days
1	1 2 3	13 13 10
2	4 5 6	14 12 18
3	7 8 9	15 12 14
4	10 11 12	12 15 12
	Total	160

Block Schedule
90-minute periods

Chapter	Days
1	7
2	7
3	5
4	7
5	6
6	9
7	8
8	6
9	7
10	6
11	8
12	6
Total	82

Daily Planning

TeacherWorks ***All in One Lesson Planner and Resource Center***

This CD-ROM includes a lesson planner and an Interactive Teacher Edition enabling you to customize an entire course of study to meet your specific needs.

NCTM Standards for School Mathematics

The Standards portion of the *NCTM Principles and Standards for School Mathematics* center upon ten areas of mathematics curriculum development. The number assigned to each standard is for easy reference and is not part of each standard's official title.

Instructional programs from pre-kindergarten through grade 12 should enable all students to—

1 Number and Operations

- Understand numbers, ways of representing numbers, relationships among numbers, and number systems
- Understand the meaning of operations and how they relate to each other
- Compute fluently and make reasonable estimates

Lessons: 1-2–1-6, 1-8, 1-9, 2-1–2-9, 3-1–3-6, 4-1–4-8, 5-1–5-8, 6-1–6-9, 7-1–7-9, 8-1–8-7, 9-1–9-8, 10-1–10-7, 11-1–11-8, 12-1–12-7

2 Algebra

- Understand patterns, relations, and functions
- Represent and analyze mathematical situations and structures using algebraic symbols
- Use mathematical models to represent and understand quantitative relationships
- Analyze change in various contexts

Lessons: 1-2, 1-3, 1-5–1-9, 2-1–2-3, 2-5–2-8, 3-1, 3-4–3-6, 4-2–4-8, 5-2, 5-3, 5-6–5-8, 6-1–6-9, 7-1–7-9, 8-6, 9-1–9-8, 10-1–10-7, 11-2–11-8, 12-2, 12-3, 12-6, 12-7

3 Geometry

- Analyze characteristics and properties of two- and three-dimensional geometric shapes and develop mathematical arguments about geometric relationships
- Specify locations and describe spatial relationships using coordinate geometry and other representational systems
- Apply transformations and use symmetry to analyze mathematical situations
- Use visualization, spatial reasoning, and geometric modeling to solve problems

Lessons: 3-4–3-6, 4-3, 4-5–4-8, 6-1–6-9, 7-1–7-9, 11-3–11-8

4 Measurement

- Understand measurable attributes of objects and the units, systems, and processes of measurement
- Apply appropriate techniques, tools, and formulas to detemine measurements

Lessons: 2-3, 2-4, 3-4–3-6, 4-5–4-7, 6-1–6-9, 7-1–7-9, 9-1–9-8

5 Data Analysis and Probability

- Formulate questions that can be addressed with data and collect, organize, and display relevant data to answer them
- Select and use appropriate statistical methods to analyze data
- Develop and evaluate inferences and predictions that are based on data
- Understand and apply basic concepts of probability

Lessons: 2-1–2-4, 2-9, 8-1–8-7, 9-1–9-8

Instructional programs from pre-kindergarten through grade 12 should enable all students to—

6 Problem Solving

- Build new mathematical knowledge through problem solving
- Solve problems that arise in mathematics and in other contexts
- Apply and adapt a variety of appropriate strategies to solve problems
- Monitor and reflect on the process of mathematical problem solving

Lessons: 1-1, 1-8, 2-3, 2-4, 2-6, 2-7, 2-9, 3-1–3-6, 4-1–4-8, 5-1–5-8, 6-1–6-9, 7-1–7-9, 8-1–8-7, 9-1–9-8, 10-1–10-7, 11-1–11-8, 12-1–12-7

7 Reasoning and Proof

- Recognize reasoning and proof as fundamental aspects of mathematics
- Make and investigate mathematical conjectures
- Develop and evaluate mathematical arguments and proofs
- Select and use various types of reasoning and methods of proof

Lessons: 1-1, 1-2, 3-1–3-6, 4-1–4-8, 5-1–5-8, 6-1–6-9, 7-1–7-9, 8-1–8-7, 9-1–9-8, 10-1–10-7, 11-1–11-8, 12-1–12-7

8 Communication

- Organize and consolidate their mathematical thinking through communication
- Communicate their mathematical thinking coherently and clearly to peers, teachers, and others
- Analyze and evaluate the mathematical thinking and strategies of others
- Use the language of mathematics to express mathematical ideas precisely

Lessons: 1-7, 3-1–3-6, 4-1–4-8, 8-2–8-7

9 Connections

- Recognize and use connections among mathematical ideas
- Understand how mathematical ideas build on one another to produce a coherent whole
- Recognize and apply mathematics in contexts outside of mathematics

Lessons: 1-3, 1-7, 3-1–3-6, 4-1–4-8, 5-3, 5-5–5-8, 6-2–6-9, 7-2–7-9, 8-1–8-7, 10-1–10-7, 11-3, 11-5–11-8, 12-3, 12-5–12-7

10 Representation

- Create and use representations to organize, record, and communicate mathematical ideas
- Select, apply, and translate among mathematical representations to solve problems
- Use representations to model and interpret physical, social, and mathematical phenomena

Lessons: 1-1–1-5, 1-8, 2-1–2-4, 2-8, 2-9, 3-1–3-6, 4-1–4-8, 5-1–5-8, 6-1–6-9, 7-1–7-9, 8-1–8-7, 9-1–9-8, 10-1–10-7, 11-1–11-8, 12-1–12-7

NAEP 2005 Standards

The National Assessment of Educational Progress (NAEP) is the leading national assessment of mathematics and many other academic subjects for American students. For a correlation to the standards to be tested on the NAEP 2005 test, see the interleaf pages in the Teacher Wraparound Edition for each chapter. For a listing of the NAEP 2005 standards, visit Teacher Resources at math.glencoe.com.

Scope and Sequence

Mathematics: Applications and Concepts is a comprehensive, well-balanced, three-course program that prepares middle school students for success in algebra and geometry. Through a carefully planned scope and sequence of mathematical topics, students encounter, practice, and extend their knowledge of mathematics to promote confidence and mastery.

The chart below shows the chapter titles for the three courses in *Mathematics: Applications and Concepts.* The following pages present a detailed chart describing the depth to which each topic is covered.

Chapter	Course 1	Course 2	Course 3
1	Number Patterns and Algebra	Decimal Patterns and Algebra	Algebra: Integers
2	Statistics and Graphs	Statistics: Analyzing Data	Algebra: Rational Numbers
3	Adding and Subtracting Decimals	Algebra: Integers	Algebra: Real Numbers and the Pythagorean Theorem
4	Multiplying and Dividing Decimals	Algebra: Linear Equations and Functions	Proportions, Algebra, and Geometry
5	Fractions and Decimals	Fractions, Decimals, and Percents	Percent
6	Adding and Subtracting Fractions	Applying Fractions	Geometry
7	Multiplying and Dividing Fractions	Ratios and Proportions	Geometry: Measuring Area and Volume
8	Algebra: Integers	Applying Percent	Probability
9	Algebra: Solving Equations	Probability	Statistics and Matrices
10	Ratio, Proportion, and Percent	Geometry	Algebra: More Equations and Inequalities
11	Probability	Geometry: Measuring Two-Dimensional Figures	Algebra: Linear Functions
12	Measurement	Geometry: Measuring Three-Dimensional Figures	Algebra: Nonlinear Functions and Polynomials
13	Geometry: Angles and Polygons		
14	Geometry: Measuring Area and Volume		

Key

Introduction · Development · Reinforcement · Implicit Use

Course	1	2	3
PROBLEM SOLVING			
Look for a Pattern	●	●	●
Solve a Simpler Problem	●	●	●
Use a simulation; act it out	●	●	●
Guess and check	●	●	●
Draw a diagram	●	●	●
Make a table (NAEP 8)	●		●
Work backward	●	●	●
Make a list	●	●	●
Eliminate possibilities		●	
Make a model (NAEP 8)	●	●	●
Use a graph	●	●	●
Use an equation	●		●
Use logical reasoning		●	●
Use a Venn diagram	◐	◐	●
Four-step plan	●	●	●
Conduct a poll or survey			◐
Use a matrix			●
Apply benchmarks (NAEP 8)	◐		
Use and evaluate formulas (NAEP 8)	◐	●	●
NUMBERS			
Number Relationships			
Decimals			
Model decimals	●		
Read and write decimals	●	●	
Place value (NAEP 8)	●	●	
Compare and order	●	●	○
Round decimals	●	●	●
Relate decimals and fractions	◐	◐	○
Relate decimals, ratios, and percents (NAEP 8)	◐	◐	○
Terminating and repeating decimals	◐	◐	◐
Scientific notation (NAEP 8)	●	◐	●
Powers of ten	◐	●	○
Fractions			
Model fractions	◐	○	
Mixed numbers and improper fractions	●		
Equivalent fractions	●	◐	●
Compare and order fractions	●	◐	○
Simplify fractions	●	◐	●
Least common denominator (LCD)	●	◐	○
Round and estimate fractions	●	◐	●
Relate fractions and decimals	●	◐	●
Relate fractions and percents	◐	◐	○
Represent probability using fractions, decimals, and percents (NAEP 8)	◐	●	●

Course	1	2	3
Proportional Reasoning			
Ratios			
Model ratios	●		○
Read and write ratios	◐	●	●
Simplify ratios	●	●	●
Use in problem situations (NAEP 8)	●	●	◐
Relate ratios and fractions (NAEP 8)	●	●	◐
Scale factor		◐	◐
Rate, direct variation (NAEP 8)	●	◐	◐
Unit rate	●	◐	◐
Dimensional analysis			●
Common ratio, geometric sequence			◐
Proportion			
Solve proportions (NAEP 8)	◐	●	●
Property of proportion (cross products)	●	●	●
Similar figures	◐	●	●
Indirect measurement		●	●
Percent			
Model percent	◐	◐	◐
Fractions and decimals as percents	◐	◐	●
Relate percent and ratio	◐	◐	●
Percent of a number	◐	●	●
Percent one number is of another		◐	●
Percent of change		◐	●
Percent proportion		◐	●
Percent equation		◐	●
Number Systems and Number Theory			
Whole Numbers			
Positive exponents	◐	●	○
Divisibility patterns (NAEP 8)	●	●	●
Prime and composite numbers (NAEP 8)	◐	●	●
Prime factorization (NAEP 8)	◐	●	●
Greatest common factor (GCF)	◐	●	●
Least common multiple (LCM)	◐	●	●
Factorials		◐	●
Perfect squares and roots		◐	◐
Integers			
Read and write integers	◐	●	●
Graph integers on a number line	◐	●	●
Compare and order integers	◐	●	●
Absolute value (NAEP 8)	●	●	◐
Negative-integer exponents			◐
Rational Numbers			
Identify and simplify		●	◐
Rational numbers and decimals (NAEP 8)		◐	◐
Compare and order (NAEP 8)		◐	◐

Course	1	2	3
NUMBERS (continued)			
Graph on a number line (NAEP 8)			●
Scientific notation (NAEP 8)		●	●
Irrational numbers			
Identify irrational numbers		●	●
Graph irrational numbers			●
Real numbers			
Identify and classify real numbers		●	●
Graph real numbers			●
Roots		●	●
Estimate square roots		●	●
Properties			
Associative, Commutative, and Distributive	●	●	○
Identity	●	●	●
Inverse		●	●
Closure, whole numbers			●
Closure, rational numbers		●	
Properties of equality	●		●
Addition, subtraction	●	●	●
Multiplication, division		●	●
Multiplicative Inverse		●	●
Properties of inequalities			●
OPERATIONS			
Computation			
Order of operations	●	●	○
Decimals			
Model decimal operations	●		
Add and subtract decimals	●	●	●
Multiply by a whole number	●	●	●
Multiply two decimals	●	●	●
Divide by a whole number	●	●	●
Divide by decimals	●	●	●
Powers of ten	●	●	●
Fractions			
Add and subtract fractions with like and unlike denominators	●	●	●
Multiply and divide fractions	●	●	●
Add and subtract mixed numbers	●	●	●
Multiply and divide mixed numbers	●	●	●
Integers			
Model integer addition, subtraction, multiplication, division	●	●	●
Add and subtract integers	●	●	●
Multiply and divide integers	●	●	●
Rational Numbers (NAEP 8)			
Add and subtract			●
Multiply and divide			●
Estimation (NAEP 8)			
Decimals			
Rounding	●	●	●

Course	1	2	3
Sums and differences	●	●	●
Products and quotients	●	●	●
Fractions			
Rounding	●	●	●
Sums and differences	●	●	●
Products and quotients	●	●	●
Percents	●	●	●
Square roots (NAEP 8)		●	●
Angle measure	●		
Area or volume (NAEP 8)	●		
Strategies for estimating			
Rounding	●	●	●
Compatible numbers	●	●	●
Clustering	●	●	●
Mental math			
Divisibility patterns	●	●	●
Solving equations mentally	●	●	
Multiply by powers of ten	●	●	
PATTERNS AND FUNCTIONS			
Discrete Patterns			
Sequences			
Arithmetic and geometric, informally	●	●	●
Fibonacci sequence			●
Pascal's Triangle		●	●
Arithmetic, definition		●	●
Geometric, definition		●	●
Functions and Relations			
Represent using function tables	●	●	●
Represent using graphs	●	●	●
Represent using rules and equations	●	●	●
Function machines	●	●	
Domain and range		●	●
Dependent and independent variables			●
$f(x)$ notation			●
Graphing linear functions			●
Slope		●	●
Intercepts			●
Graphing quadratic functions			●
ALGEBRA			
Equations and Expressions			
Basic Concepts			
Variable, expression, equation	●	●	○
Evaluate algebraic expressions (NAEP 8)	●	●	●
Write algebraic expressions, equations (NAEP 8)		●	●
Solution (solution set)	●	●	●
Multiple representations of expressions (NAEP 8)		●	●
Exponents			
Positive integer exponents	●	●	●

Course	1	2	3
ALGEBRA (continued)			
Negative integer exponents			●
Properties of exponents (powers)			●
Monomials and Polynomials			
Model monomials			●
Constants, coefficients, like terms			●
Multiply and divide monomials			●
Simplify polynomial expressions			●
Add and subtract polynomials			●
Multiply polynomials by monomials			●
Solve Equations (NAEP 8)			
Addition and subtraction equations	●	●	●
Multiplication and division equations	●	●	●
Multi-step (two-step) equations	●	●	●
Equations with variables on both sides			●
Use concrete methods (models)	●	●	●
Use informal methods	●	●	
Use formal methods	●	●	●
Solve Inequalities (NAEP 8)			
Write inequalities			●
Graph inequalities	●	●	●
Addition, subtraction inequalities	●	●	●
Multiplication, division inequalities		●	●
Multi-step inequalities		●	●
Graph a solution set on a number line		●	●
Linear Equations and Inequalities			
Find intercepts from an equation			●
Graph linear equations	●	●	●
With calculators			●
Slope of a line		●	●
Graph linear inequalities			●
Systems of linear equations			●
Solve systems by graphing and by substitution			●
Quadratic and Polynomial Equations			
Families of quadratic graphs			●
Graph quadratic equations			●
Parabolas, definition			●
Simplify radical expressions			●
GEOMETRY AND SPATIAL SENSE			
Constructions			
Congruent segments	●		
Congruent angles	●	●	
Segment bisectors	●		
Angle bisectors	●	●	●
Parallel lines (NAEP 8)		●	●
Perpendicular lines		●	●
Congruent triangles			●
Points, Lines, Planes			
Measuring segments	●		

Course	1	2	3
Perimeter (NAEP 8)	●	●	●
Parallel lines (NAEP 8)	●	●	●
Skew lines	●		●
Parallel lines and transversal, angles	●	●	●
Perpendicular lines	●	●	●
Angles and Polygons			
Classify and measure angles (degrees)	●	●	●
Angle relationships	●	●	●
Identify and classify polygons	●	●	●
Congruent figures	●	●	●
Angles of polygons	●	●	●
Tessellations	●	●	●
Area			
Rectangle	●	●	●
Parallelogram	●	●	○
Triangle	●	●	○
Rhombus, trapezoid	●	●	○
Regular polygons and circles	●	●	●
Square roots and area of squares		●	●
Triangles			
Classify triangles	●	●	●
Sum of angles in a triangle	●	●	●
Congruent triangles	●		●
Isosceles triangle properties		●	
Right triangles		●	●
Similar triangles, identify	●	●	●
Right Triangles and Trigonometry			
Special right triangles			●
Sine, cosine, tangent ratios			●
Pythagorean Theorem (NAEP 8)		●	●
Trigonometric ratios in right triangles			●
Angle of elevation and depression			●
Quadrilaterals			
Angles in quadrilaterals	●	●	●
Parallelograms and rectangles	●		●
Squares, rhombi, and trapezoids	●		●
Congruent figures	●		●
Similarity and Proportion			
Corresponding parts of similar figures	●	●	●
Similar figures	●	●	●
Similar polygons		●	●
Scale drawings (NAEP 8)	●	●	●
Golden rectangle			●
Sierpinski's Triangle	●		
Pascal's Triangle		●	●
Circles			
Radius, diameter, center	●	●	○
Circumference and area	●	●	○
Arcs and chords			●

GEOMETRY AND SPATIAL SENSE (continued)

Course	1	2	3
Solids and Space			
Draw three-dimensional figures	●	●	●
Cross sections (NAEP 8)			●
Identify three-dimensional figures (NAEP 8)	●		●
Nets	●	●	●
Surface area			
Prisms and cylinders	●	●	●
Pyramids and cones			●
Spheres			●
Volume			
Prisms and cylinders (NAEP 8)	●	●	●
Pyramids and cones			●
Spheres			●
Congruent and similar solids			●
Relating surface area and volume		●	●
Coordinate Geometry			
Coordinate plane	●	●	●
Graphing ordered pairs (NAEP 8)	●	●	●
Distance Formula			●
Transformations with coordinates	●	●	●
Lines			
Slope-intercept form of line			●
Slope of parallel, perpendicular lines			●
Fitted lines on scatter plots			●
Transformations and Symmetry			
Model transformations		●	●
Translations (NAEP 8)	●	●	●
Reflections and Rotations	●	●	●
Dilations		●	●
Symmetry (line and rotation) (NAEP 8)	●	●	●
Reasoning and Proof			
Inductive reasoning		●	●
Conjecturing			●
Venn diagrams	●	●	●
Deductive reasoning		●	●

MEASUREMENT

Course	1	2	3
Metric system			
Unit of length, capacity, and mass	●	○	●
Convert units within system (NAEP 8)	●	○	●
Customary system			
Units of length, capacity, and weight	●	●	●
Convert units within system (NAEP 8)	●	●	●
Time	●		●
Nonstandard units	●		
Compare measures of objects (NAEP 8)	●	●	●
Estimate the size of an object (NAEP 8)	●	●	●
Precision and significant digits	●	●	●

DATA ANALYSIS, STATISTICS, AND PROBABILITY

Course	1	2	3
Statistics			
Concepts and Techniques			
Organize data with a table	●		●
Use a data graph to solve problems	●	●	●
Frequency table	●	●	●
Samples and surveys	●	●	●
Constructing and Interpreting Graphs			
Choose an appropriate display			●
Bar graphs (NAEP 8)	●	●	●
Circle graphs (NAEP 8)	●	●	●
Line graphs (NAEP 8)	●	●	●
Stem-and-leaf plots (NAEP 8)	●	●	●
Box-and-whisker plots (NAEP 8)	●	●	●
Line plots		●	●
Histograms (NAEP 8)	●	●	●
Scatter plots (NAEP 8)		●	●
Positive, negative, no correlation			●
Fitted line (prediction equation) (NAEP 8)			●
Compare data sets (NAEP 8)	●	●	●
Interpreting Data			
Mean, median, and mode (NAEP 8)	●	●	●
Range (NAEP 8)	●	●	●
Quartiles, interquartile range	●	●	●
Outlier (NAEP 8)		●	●
Misleading Graphs and Statistics (NAEP 8)	●	●	●
Making Predictions			
From graphs	●	●	●
From a sample	●	●	●
Probability			
Outcomes and sample space (NAEP 8)	●	●	●
Probability of simple events (NAEP 8)	●	●	●
Complementary events	●	●	●
Independent events (NAEP 8)	●	●	●
Dependent events (NAEP 8)		●	●
Mutually exclusive or inclusive events		●	●
Odds	●	●	●
Experimental probability (NAEP 8)	●	●	●
Theoretical probability (NAEP 8)	●	●	●
Tree diagrams	●	●	●
Fundamental Counting Principle		●	●
Permutations and combinations	●	●	●
Probability and ratio	●	●	●
Fair and unfair games		●	
Simulations (NAEP 8)	●	●	●
Geometric probability (area models)	●	●	
Bias and random samples (NAEP 8)	●	●	●
Capture-recapture		●	

UNIT 1
Real Numbers and Algebra

Chapter 1 Algebra: Integers

Student Toolbox

Prerequisite Skills
- Diagnose Readiness 5
- Getting Ready for the Next Lesson 10, 15, 21, 27, 31, 38, 42, 49

Reading and Writing Mathematics
- Reading in the Content Area 11
- Reading Math 8, 35
- Writing Math 9, 14, 22, 26, 41, 47, 52

Standardized Test Practice
- Multiple Choice 10, 15, 21, 27, 31, 32, 38, 42, 44, 49, 53, 57, 58
- Short Response/Grid In 10, 32, 38, 42, 53, 59
- Extended Response 59
- Worked-Out Example 47

Interdisciplinary Connections
- WebQuest Math and Geography 3
- Art 9
- Geography 17, 30, 40
- Health 41
- History 10, 41
- Life Science 37, 41
- Music 42
- Science 21, 54

HANDS-ON **Mini Lab** 6, 11, 28, 45

Comparing Integers 33

USA TODAY **Snapshots** 8, 53

Lesson 1-7, p. 40

Algebra: Rational Numbers

Lesson 2-9, p. 107

Student Toolbox

Algebra: Real Numbers and the Pythagorean Theorem

Student Toolbox

Prerequisite Skills
- Diagnose Readiness 115
- Getting Ready for the Next Lesson 119, 122, 129, 136, 140

Reading and Writing Mathematics
- Link to Reading 132
- Reading in the Content Area 116
- Reading Math 117
- Writing Math 118, 138, 141

Standardized Test Practice
- Multiple Choice 119, 122, 124, 129, 130, 136, 140, 145, 149, 150
- Short Response/Grid In 119, 129, 136, 145, 151
- Extended Response 151
- Worked-Out Example 134

Interdisciplinary Connections
- WebQuest Math and Geography 145
- Art 121
- Geography 122, 136, 139
- Health 124
- History 117, 122
- Science 122, 124
- Technology 145

HANDS-ON **Mini Lab** 116, 120, 132

The Game Zone
Estimate Square Roots 131

USA TODAY **Snapshots** 127

Lesson 3-3, p. 127

UNIT 2
Proportional Reasoning

Chapter 4 Proportions, Algebra, and Geometry

Lesson 4-6, p. 187

Student Toolbox

Percent

Student Toolbox

Prerequisite Skills
- Diagnose Readiness 205
- Getting Ready for the Next Lesson 209, 214, 219, 223, 231, 235, 240

Reading and Writing Mathematics
- Link to Reading 216
- Reading in the Content Area 216
- Writing Math 218, 222, 230, 239, 243

Standardized Test Practice
- Multiple Choice 209, 214, 219, 223, 224, 227, 231, 235, 240, 244, 249, 250
- Short Response/Grid In 219, 223, 224, 240, 244, 251
- Extended Response 251
- Worked-Out Example 242

Interdisciplinary Connections
- WebQuest Math and Art 244
- Biology 230
- Ecology 227
- Geography 208, 209, 212, 228, 232
- Health 222
- History 217
- Music 208, 209
- Science 209
- Technology 206, 207

Mini Lab 216

The Game Zone
Equivalent Percents, Fractions, and Decimals 225

USA TODAY **Snapshots** 209, 214, 219, 244

Lesson 5-2, p. 210

UNIT 3
Geometry and Measurement

Geometry

Student Toolbox

CHAPTER 7 Geometry: Measuring Area and Volume

Student Toolbox

Prerequisite Skills
- Diagnose Readiness 313
- Getting Ready for the Next Lesson 318, 323, 329, 334, 339, 345, 351, 355

Reading and Writing Mathematics
- Link to Reading 330, 352
- Reading in the Content Area 326
- Reading Math 315
- Writing Math 317, 322, 328, 330, 337, 344, 346, 349, 354, 360

Standardized Test Practice
- Multiple Choice 318, 323, 325, 329, 334, 339, 340, 345, 351, 355, 362, 367, 368
- Short Response/Grid In 323, 334, 345, 351, 362, 369
- Extended Response 369
- Worked-Out Example 327

Interdisciplinary Connections
- WebQuest Math and Architecture 362
- Geography 318
- Health 325, 351
- History 352, 362
- Reading 325

HANDS-ON **Mini Lab** 314, 319, 335, 342, 347

The Game Zone
Three-Dimensional Figures 341

Snapshots 361

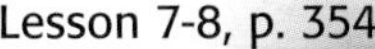

Lesson 7-8, p. 354

UNIT 4
Probability and Statistics

Probability

Lesson 8-5, p. 397

Student Toolbox

Chapter 9 Statistics and Matrices

Student Toolbox

Prerequisite Skills
- Diagnose Readiness 417
- Getting Ready for the Next Lesson 424, 429, 433, 438, 445, 449, 453

Reading and Writing Mathematics
- Link to Reading 442
- Reading in the Content Area 420
- Reading Math 421, 455
- Writing Math 428, 432, 434, 437, 448, 451

Standardized Test Practice
- Multiple Choice 419, 424, 429, 433, 438, 440, 445, 449, 453, 457, 461, 462
- Short Response/Grid In 429, 433, 440, 445, 449, 463
- Extended Response 463
- Worked-Out Example 447

Interdisciplinary Connections
- WebQuest Math and Science 457
- Civics 438
- Geography 419, 423, 436, 459
- History 421, 427, 429, 448
- Life Science 449
- Music 453

The Game Zone
Mean and Median 441

Snapshots 426, 433

Lesson 9-2, p. 428

UNIT 5
Algebra: Linear and Nonlinear Functions

Algebra: More Equations and Inequalities

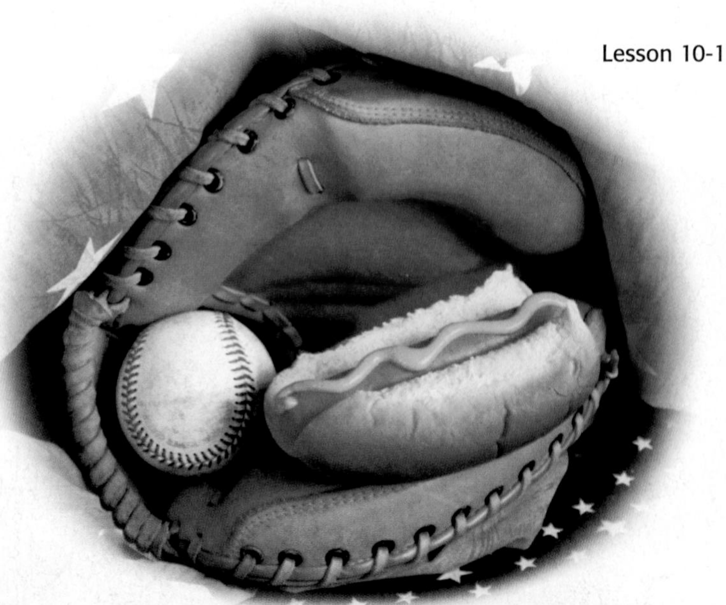
Lesson 10-1, p. 471

Student Toolbox

Chapter 11 Algebra: Linear Functions

Student Toolbox

Prerequisite Skills
- Diagnose Readiness 511
- Getting Ready for the Next Lesson 515, 520, 525, 529, 536, 542, 547

Reading and Writing Mathematics
- Link to Reading 533
- Reading in the Content Area 517
- Reading Math 513
- Writing Math 514, 516, 521, 524, 528, 535, 541

Standardized Test Practice
- Multiple Choice 515, 520, 525, 529, 530, 536, 538, 542, 547, 551, 555, 556
- Short Response/Grid In 520, 525, 529, 547, 557
- Extended Response 557
- Worked-Out Example 523

Interdisciplinary Connections
- Science 525
- Space Science 536
- Technology 538
- Zoology 538

HANDS-ON **Mini Lab** 512, 526, 533, 539

The Game Zone
Graphing Linear Functions 531

Snapshots 528

Lesson 11-7, p. 547

Chapter 12 Algebra: Nonlinear Functions and Polynomials

Student Handbook

Student Toolbox

HOW TO...

Use Your Math Book

Why do I need my math book?

Have you ever been in class and not understood all of what was presented? Or, you understood everything in class, but at home, got stuck on how to solve a couple of problems? Maybe you just wondered when you were ever going to use this stuff?

These next few pages are designed to help you understand everything your math book can be used for . . . besides homework problems!

BEFORE YOU READ

Have a Goal

- What information are you trying to find?
- Why is this information important to you?
- How will you use the information?

Have a Plan

- Read *What You'll Learn* at the beginning of the lesson.
- Look over photos, tables, graphs, and opening activities.
- Locate boldfaced words and read their definitions.
- Find Key Concept and Concept Summary boxes for a preview of what's important.
- Skim the example problems.

Have an Opinion

- Is this information what you were looking for?
- Do you understand what you have read?
- How does this information fit with what you already know?

HOW TO . . . Use Your Math Book is an inservice for students that guides them through the successful use of their textbook.

IN CLASS

During class is the opportunity to learn as much as possible about that day's lesson. Ask questions about things that you don't understand, and take notes to help you remember important information.

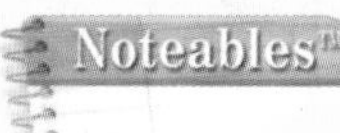

Each time you find this logo throughout your book, use your *Noteables™: Interactive Study Notebook with Foldables™* or your own notebook to take notes.

To help keep your notes in order, try making a Foldables Study Organizer. It's as easy as 1-2-3! Here's a Foldable you can use to keep track of the rules for addition, subtraction, multiplication, and division.

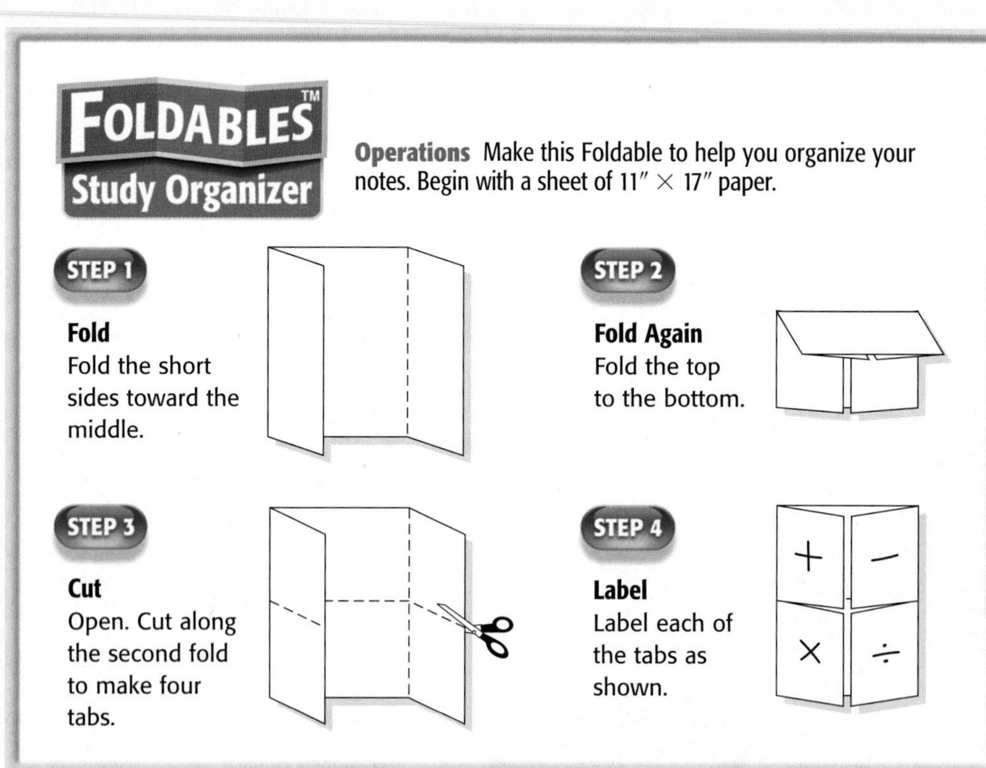

LOOK FOR...

on these pages:

5, 61, 115, 155, 205, 255, 313, 373, 417, 467, 511, and 559.

Need to Cover Your Book?

Inside the back cover are directions for a Foldable that you can use to cover your math book quickly and easily!

Regardless of how well you paid attention in class, by the time you arrive at home, your notes may no longer make any sense and your homework seems impossible. It's during these times that your book can be most useful.

- Each lesson has example problems, solved step-by-step, so you can review the day's lesson material.
- A Web site has extra examples to coach you through solving those difficult problems.
- Each exercise set has Homework Help boxes that show you which examples may help with your homework problems.
- Answers to the odd-numbered problems are in the back of the book. Use them to see if you are solving the problems correctly. If you have difficulty on an even problem, do the odd problem next to it. That should give you a hint about how to proceed with the even problem.

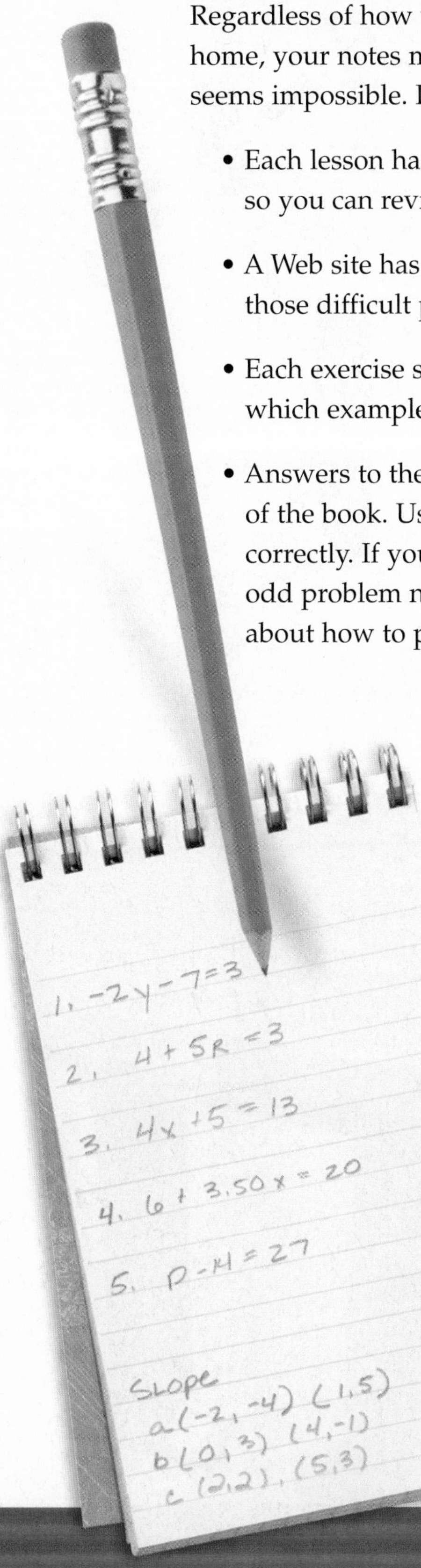

1. $-2y-7=3$
2. $4+5R=3$
3. $4x+5=13$
4. $6+3.50x=20$
5. $p-14=27$

Slope
a $(-2,-4)$ $(1,5)$
b $(0,3)$ $(4,-1)$
c $(2,2)$, $(5,3)$

LOOK FOR...

The Web site with extra examples on these pages in Chapter 1: 7, 13, 19, 25, 29, 35, 39, 47, and 51.

Homework Help boxes on these pages in Chapter 1: 9, 14, 20, 26, 30, 37, 41, 48, and 52.

Selected Answers starting on page 719.

BEFORE A TEST

Admit it! You think there is no way to study for a math test! However, there *are* ways to review before a test. Your book offers help with this also.

- Review all of the new vocabulary words and be sure you understand their definitions. These can be found on the first page of each lesson or highlighted in yellow in the text.
- Review the notes you've taken on your Foldable and write down any questions that you still need answered.
- Practice all of the concepts presented in the chapter by using the chapter Study Guide and Review. It has additional problems for you to try as well as more examples to help you understand. You can also take the Chapter Practice Test.
- Take the self-check quizzes from the Web site.

$<$ $3n - 8 = 7$ $+$ $y = x + 0.5$ π

LOOK FOR...

The Web site with self-check quizzes on these pages in Chapter 1: 9, 15, 21, 27, 31, 37, 41, 49, and 53.

The Study Guide and Review for Chapter 1 on page 54.

LET'S GET STARTED

To help you find the information you need quickly, use the Scavenger Hunt below to learn where things are located in each chapter.

2. Sample answer: There is a statement in the "What You'll Learn" section at the beginning of Lesson 1-1, in the left-hand column, that will tell me what I will learn in the lesson.

4. Sample answer: The lesson opener shows an example of how integers can be used to describe elevations and temperatures.

1. What is the title of Chapter 1? **Algebra: Integers**
2. How can you tell what you'll learn in Lesson 1-1?
3. What is the key concept presented in Lesson 1-2? **The key concept explains how to follow the order of operations.**
4. Sometimes you may ask "When am I ever going to use this?" Name a situation that uses the concepts from Lesson 1-3.
5. In Lesson 1-3, there is a paragraph that tells you that the absolute value of a number is not the same as the opposite of a number. What is the main heading above that paragraph? **Study Tip**
6. What is the web address where you could find extra examples? **msmath3.net/extra_examples**
7. List the new vocabulary words that are presented in Lesson 1-4. **opposites, additive inverse**
8. How many Examples are presented in Lesson 1-5? **6**
9. In Lesson 1-8, there is a problem presented that deals with the minimum wage. Where could you find information about the current minimum wage? **I can look online at msmath3.net/data_update.**
10. Suppose you're doing your homework on page 48 and you get stuck on Exercise 18. Where could you find help? **Sample answer: I can look at Examples 1 and 2 on page 46 for help.**
11. There is a Real-Life Career mentioned in Lesson 1-9. What is it? **Zoologist**
12. What is the web address that would allow you to take a self-check quiz to be sure you understand the lesson? **msmath3.net/self_check_quiz**
13. On what pages will you find the Study Guide and Review? **pages 54–56**
14. Suppose you can't figure out how to do Exercise 29 in the Study Guide on page 55. Where could you find help? **Sample answer: I can review Examples 1–8 in Lesson 1-4.**
15. You complete the Practice Test on page 57 to study for your chapter test. Where could you find another test for more practice? **I can look online at msmath3.net/chapter_test.**

UNIT 1 Notes

Introduction

In this unit, students will explore integers, rational numbers, and real numbers and how they are utilized in algebra. Students will learn to add, subtract, multiply, and divide integers and solve algebraic equations involving integers. In addition, students will study rational numbers and learn to compare, order, multiply, and divide them.

As students continue to explore algebra, they will learn how to add and subtract like and unlike fractions and how to solve equations involving rational numbers. Additionally, students will develop proficiency using powers, exponents, and scientific notation. Finally, students will examine square roots, the real number system, and the Pythagorean Theorem, and learn to find distances on the coordinate plane.

Assessment Options

Unit 1 Test Pages 183–184 of the *Chapter 3 Resource Masters* may be used as a test or a review for Unit 1. This assessment contains both multiple-choice and short-response items.

Yearly Progress Pro

An online, research-based, instructional, assessment, and intervention tool that provides specific feedback on student mastery of state and national standards, instant remediation, and a data management system to track performance. For more information, contact mhdigitallearning.com

UNIT 1

Real Numbers and Algebra

Chapter 1

Algebra: Integers

Chapter 2

Algebra: Rational Numbers

Chapter 3

Algebra: Real Numbers and the Pythagorean Theorem

Your study of math includes many different types of real numbers. In this unit, you will solve equations using integers, rational numbers, and irrational numbers.

Real-Life Math Videos engage students, showing them how math is used in everyday situations. Use Video 1 with this unit to discuss how square roots and the Pythagorean Theorem are used in rock climbing and kite flying. (also available on one Super DVD combined with MindJogger Videoquizzes)

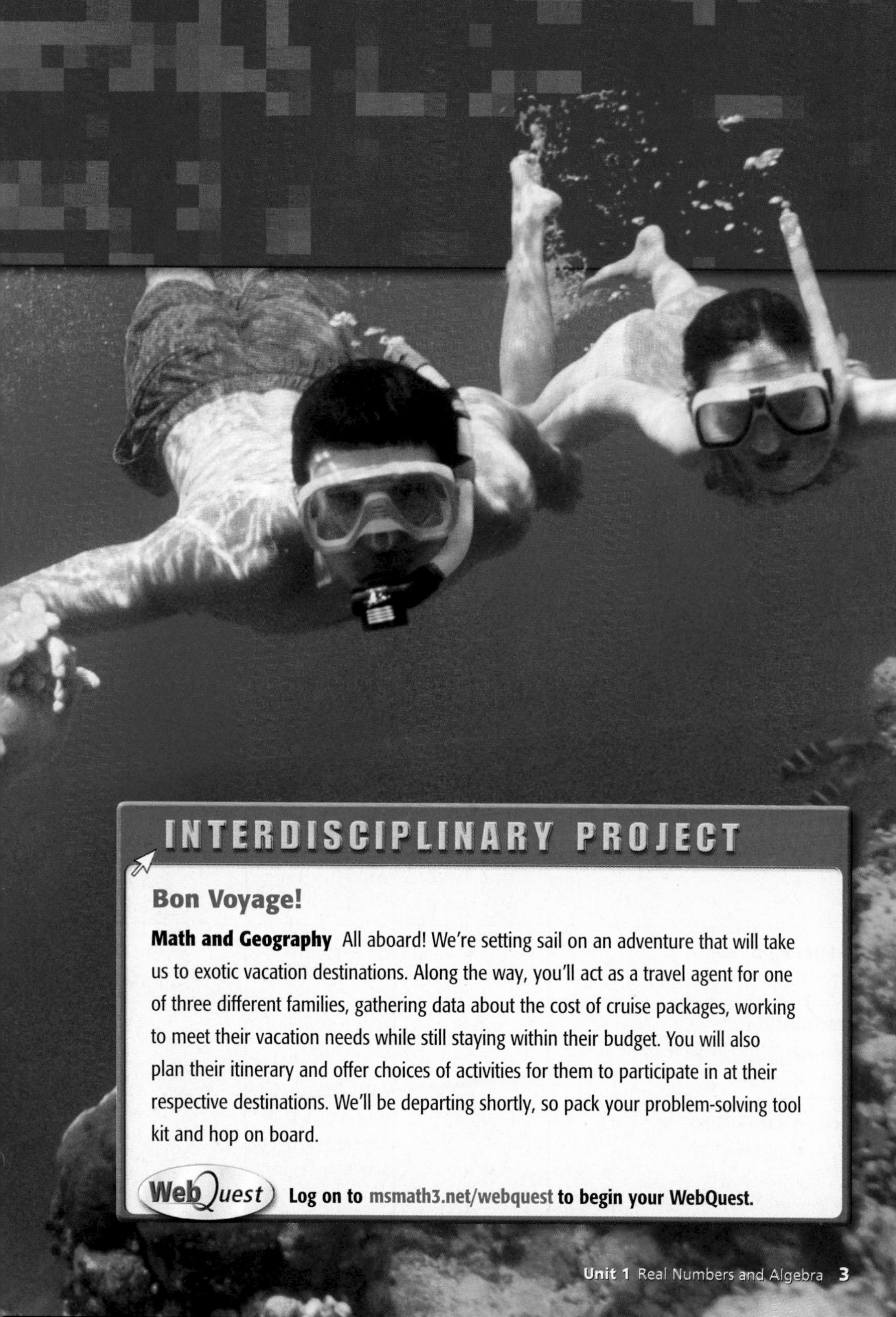

INTERDISCIPLINARY PROJECT

Bon Voyage!

A WebQuest is an online project in which students do research on the Internet, gather data, and make presentations using word processing, graphing, page-making, or presentation software. In each chapter, students advance to the next step in their WebQuest. At the end of Chapter 3, the project culminates with a presentation of their findings.

WebQuest Teaching suggestions and sample answers are available in the WebQuests, Projects, and Interdisciplinary Investigations.

Math and Geography You can use this WebQuest Interdisciplinary Project with your students' social studies teacher to make the connection from mathematics to the geography your students are studying.

More Interdisciplinary Connections

You may wish to share these suggestions with your students' other teachers.

Math and Life Skills

Research the foods popular in your clients' chosen vacation destinations. Prepare some suggested meal plans for each locale based on the FDA food pyramid. Include some suggestions for vegetarian diets and dairy-free diets.

Math and Social Studies

Research the history of navigation. What changes in navigation science occurred during the fifteenth century? How are longitude and latitude calculated? What historical events affected the locations of the prime meridian and the line of demarcation?

Chapter Overview

Algebra: Integers

*An electronic version of this chapter is available on **StudentWorks**™. This backpack solution CD-ROM allows students instant access to the Student Edition, lesson worksheet pages, and web resources.*

	LESSON OBJECTIVES	NCTM Standards	NAEP 2005	State/Local Objectives
1-1	**A Plan for Problem Solving** (pp. 6–10) • Solve problems by using the four-step plan.	6, 7, 10	A1a, D1a, G3c, N3g	
1-2	**Variables, Expressions, and Properties** (pp. 11–15) • Evaluate expressions and identify properties.	1, 2, 7, 10	A1a, A1b, A3b, N5a, N5e	
1-3	**Integers and Absolute Value** (pp. 17–22) • Graph integers on a number line and find absolute value. **1-3b Hands-On Lab:** Graph and interpret data.	1, 2, 9, 10	A1a, A2a, A2c, A3b, N1b, N1d, N1g, N1i, N1j, N5f	
1-4	**Adding Integers** (pp. 23–27) • Add integers.	1, 10	N1b, N1g, N3a, N3f, N3g, N5e, N5f	
1-5	**Subtracting Integers** (pp. 28–31) • Subtract integers.	1, 2, 10	A3b, N1b, N3a, N3f, N3g, N5a, N5e	
1-6	**Multiplying and Dividing Integers** (pp. 34–38) • Multiply and divide integers.	1, 2	A3b, D2a, N1b, N3a, N3f, N3g, N5a, N5e	
1-7	**Writing Expressions and Equations** (pp. 39–42) • Write algebraic expressions and equations from verbal phrases and sentences.	2, 8, 9	A1b, A2a, A3a, N3f	
1-8	**Solving Addition and Subtraction Equations** (pp. 43–49) **1-8a Problem-Solving Strategy:** Solve problems by using the work backward strategy. • Solve equations using the Subtraction and Addition Properties of Equality.	1, 2, 6, 10	A3a, A4a, A4b, A4c, N1b, N1g, N3f, N5e	
1-9	**Solving Multiplication and Division Equations** (pp. 50–53) • Solve equations by using the Division and Multiplication Properties of Equality.	1, 2	A3a, A4a, A4b, A4c, N3f, N5e	

Key to NCTM Standards:
1=Number & Operations, 2=Algebra, 3=Geometry, 4=Measurement, 5=Data Analysis & Probability, 6=Problem Solving, 7=Reasoning & Proof, 8=Communication, 9=Connections, 10=Representation

NAEP 2005 Standards: See Teacher Resources at math.glencoe.com

Pacing suggestions for the entire year can be found on page T23.

Chapter Resource Manager

CHAPTER 1 RESOURCE MASTERS

Study Guide and Intervention	Practice (Skills and Word Problems)	Reading to Learn Mathematics	Enrichment	Assessment	Applications*	Parent and Student Study Guide Online Worksheets	5-Minute Check Transparencies	Key Teaching Transparencies	MathPASS: Tutorial Plus (lessons)	Teaching Mathematics with Manipulatives	Noteables™: Interactive Study Notebook	Optional Materials
1	2–3	4	5			1-1	1-1	1	1, 2		1-1	
6	7–8	9	10		CS 13	1-2	1-2		3		1-2	toothpicks
11	12–13	14	15	61		1-3	1-3			33	1-3	cardboard, masking tape, metric measuring tape, tennis ball
16	17–18	19	20			1-4	1-4				1-4	
21	22–23	24	25	61, 63		1-5	1-5				1-5	
26	27–28	29	30		CM 1–4 RC 27	1-6	1-6		4		1-6	
31	32–33	34	35	62		1-7	1-7	2	5		1-7	
36	37–38	39	40		SM 45–48	1-8	1-8	3			1-8	
41	42–43	44	45	47–60, 62, 64–66	CS 14	1-9	1-9	4	6	34–35	1-9	

*** Key to Abbreviations:** *CS = Calculator and Spreadsheet Masters, RC = Real-Life Career Masters, CM = Classroom Math Games (online), SM = Science and Math Lab Manual (online)*

INTERACTIVE CHALKBOARD

PowerPoint® Presentations

This CD-ROM is a customizable Microsoft® PowerPoint® presentation that includes:

- In-Class Examples
- Links to Online Study Tools
- 5-Minute Check Transparencies
- Your Turn Exercises

Math Skills Maintenance

Use the Math Skills Maintenance Masters to keep your students' basic math skills fresh. Students can review skills one at a time or in a combined format. The Masters are also available online at msmath3.net/maintenance.

Mathematical Content and Teaching Strategies

Continuity of Instruction

Building on Prior Knowledge

Prior to this course, students should have mastered basic skills using nonnegative rational numbers and the mathematical operations of addition, subtraction, multiplication, and division. They should demonstrate basic knowledge of properties of operations such as the Commutative Property as well as expressions of inequality. They also should be able to represent and analyze patterns using words, models, and graphs.

Learning in This Chapter

Students use the four-step plan for problem solving and apply problem-solving strategies to real-life problems. They learn how to use variables to write algebraic expressions and equations. Students are introduced to integers and absolute value. They learn to add, subtract, multiply, and divide integers and to compare and order integers using a number line and counters. Students then apply their knowledge of integers to the evaluation of algebraic expressions and equations. Students also solve problems by working backward.

Making Future Connections

Students will use their knowledge of integers and mathematical operations throughout this course and in subsequent math courses, including algebra and statistics courses. Skill in problem solving will be necessary in future coursework–math and otherwise–and in everyday life. Knowing how to solve algebraic equations will aid student learning in science, engineering, and business classes.

Mathematical Background

1-1 A Plan for Problem Solving

The four-step plan for problem solving outlines the way that students can approach any mathematical problem. Students should become familiar with these steps and use them on each problem they solve in the remainder of their studies of mathematics.

Teacher to Teacher

Steven Huesch
Cortney Junior High
Las Vegas, NV

"Throughout the year I use the letters of the alphabet to help students to remember several math concepts. For example, remember the correct order of the coordinates in an ordered pair by noticing that *x* is before *y* in the alphabet. Encourage students to look for and invent this type of memory device."

Steven Huesch

1-2 Variables, Expressions, and Properties

At first, students may find using variables in mathematics intimidating. However, they have been using non-letter variables since elementary school. A problem like $\square + 6 = 8$ that they might have seen in an earlier course is now written with a variable as $x + 6 = 8$. Relating the algebraic notation they are learning to these previous experiences may help students overcome their anxiety.

1-3 Integers and Absolute Value

So far in their studies of mathematics, students have been working with positive integers. They have graphed numbers on number lines and compared numbers using inequality symbols. In this lesson, students will expand these concepts to include negative integers. They also study the concept of absolute value as it relates to the distance from a point to 0 on the number line.

1-4 Adding Integers

Adding integers in real-life problems can be modeled by imagining movement along a number line. A plane flying at 150 kph can be said to be moving in a positive direction. If it is flying into a 25-kph headwind (a negative direction), the velocity of the plane with respect to a person on the ground is 150 kph + (–25 kph) = 125 kph.

Team Teaching

Inform the other teachers on your team that your classes are studying integers. Suggestions for curriculum integration are:
Earth Science: temperature
Geography: elevation of mountains and oceanic trenches
Language Arts: synonyms and antonyms

1-5 Subtracting Integers

Not all subtraction problems can be determined with positive integers. The difference between the highest point in the United States (Mt. McKinley, 20,320 feet above sea level) and the lowest point (Death Valley, 282 feet below sea level) requires the use of negative integers: 20,320 – (–282) = 20,602.

1-6 Multiplying and Dividing Integers

Students will need to multiply and divide integers as they solve and graph equations. For example, the equation $y = (-3)x + 5$ can be graphed by substituting values for x and plotting these values against the resulting y values.

1-7 Writing Expressions and Equations

In the course of writing expressions and equations, students have already progressed from using words—3 plus what number equals seven?—to using mathematical symbols—$3 + x = 7$. In this lesson, students learn to extract information from verbal phrases and apply mathematical symbols to that information.

1-8 Solving Addition and Subtraction Equations

So far, students have substituted numbers for variables in algebraic expressions, and they have set up algebraic equations. This lesson introduces formal procedures for solving algebraic equations. If students are intimidated, remind them that they have intuitively answered similar problems. Even if they cannot walk through the formal solution of $7 - x = 3$, they will be able to say, "4 is the number you need to subtract from 7 to make 3."

1-9 Solving Multiplication and Division Equations

At this point, students will probably be getting used to manipulating equations, but might be intimidated by the increasing difficulty of word problems. Encourage students to read a word problem, write down all the given information in mathematical symbols, and make a sketch (if applicable) before trying to solve the problem.

What the Research Says

According to Kinzel in "Understanding Algebraic Notation from the Students' Perspective," using symbols and interpreting symbols should receive explicit attention in algebra instruction.

- **In Lesson 1-7, students use symbols to convert verbal phrases to algebraic expressions and equations.**

McGraw-Hill Professional Development

Mathematics, YES! is a self-paced, web-based professional development program. Units are based on major mathematical concepts and are standards-based. Actual classroom videos provide a springboard for discussion and activities. Units appropriate for this chapter:

- Number Relations
- Integers
- Solving Equations and Inequalities

Additional mathematical information and teaching notes are available at **msmath3.net/key_concepts**.

DAILY INTERVENTION and Assessment

* Key to Abbreviations:
TWE = Teacher Wraparound Edition, *CRM* = Chapter Resource Masters

	Type	Student Edition	Teacher Resources	Technology/Internet
INTERVENTION	Ongoing	Prerequisite Skills, pp. 5, 27, 42, 49 Mid-Chapter Practice Test, p. 32	5-Minute Check Transparencies Quizzes 1–4, *CRM*, pp. 61–62 Mid-Chapter Test, *CRM*, p. 63 Study Guide and Intervention, *CRM*, pp. 1, 6, 11, 16, 21, 26, 31, 36, 41	MathPASS: Tutorial Plus msmath3.net/self_check_quiz msmath3.net/extra_examples
	Mixed Review	pp. 10, 15, 21, 27, 31, 38, 42, 49, 53	Cumulative Review, *CRM*, p. 64	
	Error Analysis	Find the Error, pp. 30, 41	Find the Error, *TWE*, pp. 30, 41 Unlocking Misconceptions, *TWE*, pp. 18, 46 Tips for New Teachers, *TWE*, p. 7	
ASSESSMENT	Standardized Test Practice	pp. 10, 15, 21, 27, 31, 32, 38, 42, 44, 47, 49, 53, 57, 58–59	Standardized Test Practice, *CRM*, pp. 65–66	Standardized Test Practice CD-ROM msmath3.net/standardized_test
	Open-Ended Assessment	Writing Math, pp. 9, 14, 20, 22, 26, 30, 37, 41, 47, 52 Open-Ended, pp. 9, 14, 26, 41, 47, 52 Standardized Test, p. 59	Modeling: *TWE*, pp. 15, 49 Speaking: *TWE*, pp. 10, 16, 31 Writing: *TWE*, pp. 27, 42 Extended Response Assessment, *CRM*, p. 59	
	Chapter Assessment	Study Guide, pp. 54–56 Practice Test, p. 57	Multiple-Choice Tests (Forms 1, 2A, 2B), *CRM*, pp. 47–52 Free-Response Tests (Forms 2C, 2D, 3), *CRM*, pp. 53–58 Vocabulary Test/Review, *CRM*, p. 60	ExamView® Pro Testmaker (see below) MindJogger Videoquizzes msmath3.net/vocabulary_review msmath3.net/chapter_test

For more information on Yearly ProgressPro, see p. 2.

Glencoe Lesson	Yearly ProgressPro Skill Name
1-1	Plan for Problem Solving
1-2	Evaluate Algebraic Expression
1-3	Compare/Order Integers; Absolute Value
1-4	Add Three Integers
1-5	Subtracting Integers
1-6	Multiply Integers; Divide Integers
1-7	Writing Expressions and Equations
1-8	Solving Addition and Subtraction Equations
1-9	Solving Multiplication Equations Solving Equations with Division

ExamView® Pro

Use ExamView® Pro Testmaker CD-ROM to:

- Create multiple versions of tests.
- Create modified tests for inclusion students with one mouse click.
- Edit existing questions and add your own questions.
- Build tests aligned with state standards using built-in state curriculum correlations.
- Change English tests to Spanish with one mouse click and vice versa.

Reading and Writing in Mathematics

READING in the Content Area

This online worksheet provides strategies for reading and analyzing Lesson 1-2, Variables, Expressions, and Properties. Students are guided through questions about the main idea, subject matter, supporting details, conclusion, clarifying details, and vocabulary of the lesson.

Interactive Study Notebook With Foldables™ is a study organizer that provides helpful steps for students to follow to organize their notes for Chapter 1.

- Students use Noteables to record notes and to complete their Foldables as you present the material in Lessons 1-1 through 1-9.
- Noteables follow the *Teacher Wraparound Edition's* In-Class Examples and *Interactive Chalkboard CD-ROM.*

For more information on Reading and Writing in Mathematics, see pp. T6–T7.

Recommended Outside Reading for Students

Nonfiction

- Great Source Education Group Staff. *Algebra to Go: A Mathematics Handbook.* Great Source Education Group, ©2000.

  This book is designed as a reference for students in grades 8 and higher. In addition to explanations of topics in algebra, the book contains tips for solving problems, writing, taking tests, and using computers.

Fiction

- Connell, David D. *The Case of the Mystery Weekend*. Scientific American Books for Young Readers, ©1994.

  Written in the style of the old Dragnet series, this novel relates what happens when two young math detectives, heading for a mystery weekend, get lost and must use problem-solving and other math skills to solve a real mystery.

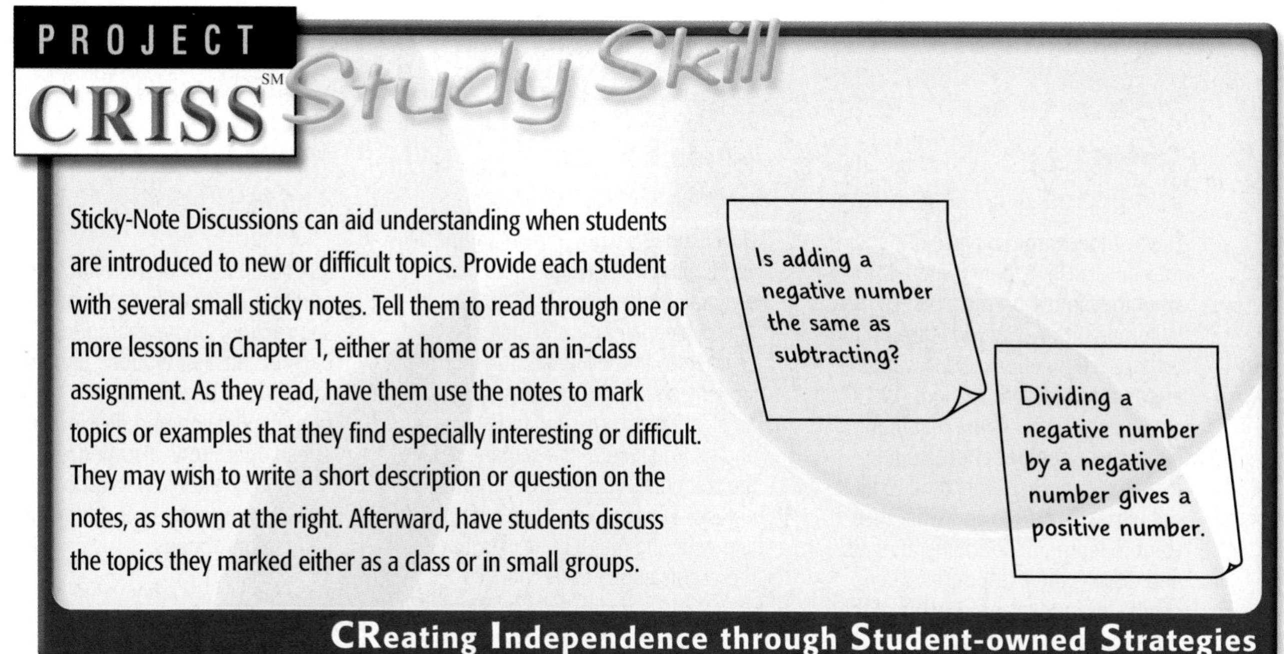

Sticky-Note Discussions can aid understanding when students are introduced to new or difficult topics. Provide each student with several small sticky notes. Tell them to read through one or more lessons in Chapter 1, either at home or as an in-class assignment. As they read, have them use the notes to mark topics or examples that they find especially interesting or difficult. They may wish to write a short description or question on the notes, as shown at the right. Afterward, have students discuss the topics they marked either as a class or in small groups.

For more information on Project CRISS, see p. T8.

Making Connections

School-To-Home

Parent and Student Study Guide

Parents and students may work together to reinforce the concepts and skills of this chapter. These online worksheets are available in English and Spanish at msmath3.net/parent_student. A sample lesson is shown below.

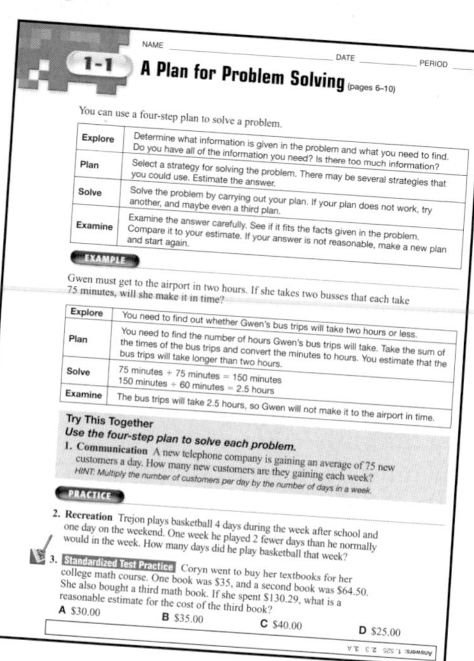

NAME ______ DATE ______ PERIOD ____

1-1 A Plan for Problem Solving (pages 6–10)

You can use a four-step plan to solve a problem.

Explore	Determine what information is given in the problem and what you need to find. Do you have all of the information you need? Is there too much information?
Plan	Select a strategy for solving the problem. There may be several strategies that you could use. Estimate the answer.
Solve	Solve the problem by carrying out your plan. If your plan does not work, try another, and maybe even a third plan.
Examine	Examine the answer carefully. See if it fits the facts given in the problem. Compare it to your estimate. If your answer is not reasonable, make a new plan and start again.

EXAMPLE

Gwen must get to the airport in two hours. If she takes two busses that each take 75 minutes, will she make it in time?

Explore	You need to find out whether Gwen's bus trips will take two hours or less.
Plan	You need to find the number of hours Gwen's bus trips will take. Take the sum of the times of the bus trips and convert the minutes to hours. You estimate that the bus trips will take longer than two hours.
Solve	75 minutes + 75 minutes = 150 minutes 150 minutes ÷ 60 minutes = 2.5 hours
Examine	The bus trips will take 2.5 hours, so Gwen will not make it to the airport in time.

Try This Together

Use the four-step plan to solve each problem.

1. **Communication** A new telephone company is gaining an average of 75 new customers a day. How many new customers are they gaining each week?
HINT: Multiply the number of customers per day by the number of days in a week.

PRACTICE

2. **Recreation** Trejon plays basketball 4 days during the week after school and one day on the weekend. One week he played 2 fewer days than he normally would in the week. How many days did he play basketball that week?
3. **Standardized Test Practice** Coryn went to buy her textbooks for her college math course. One book was \$35, and a second book was \$64.50. She also bought a third math book. If she spent \$130.29, what is a reasonable estimate for the cost of the third book?
A \$30.00 **B** \$35.00 **C** \$40.00 **D** \$25.00

Answers: 1. 525 2. 3 3. A

Family Letters and Activities

Send a letter and activity for this chapter home to encourage family members to become active participants in their students' learning. (English: *Chapter 1 Resource Masters*, pp. ix–x; Spanish: log on to msmath3.net/family_letters)

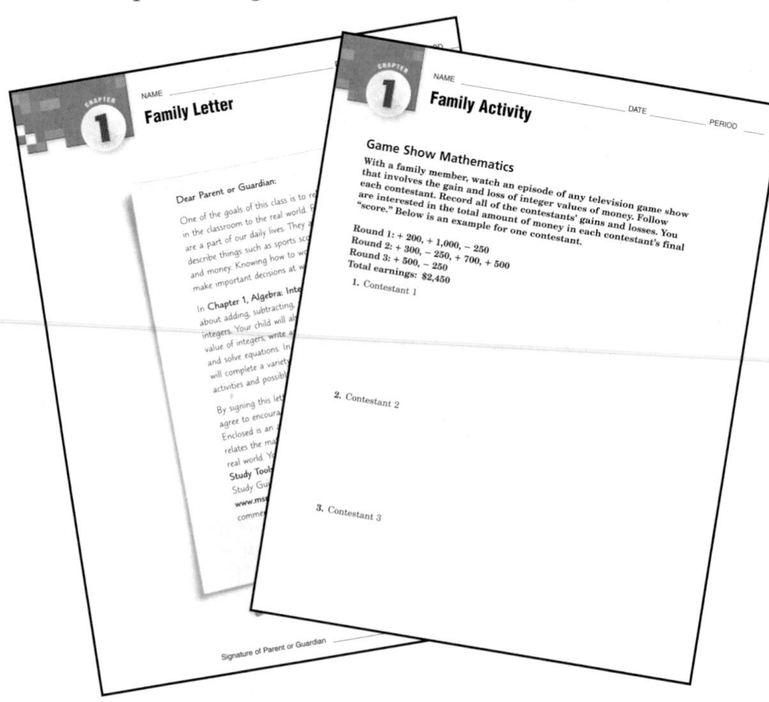

NAME ______

Family Letter

Dear Parent or Guardian:

Signature of Parent or Guardian ______

NAME ______ DATE ______ PERIOD ____

Family Activity

Game Show Mathematics

With a family member, watch an episode of any television game show that involves the gain and loss of integer values of money. Follow each contestant. Record all of the contestants' gains and losses. You are interested in the total amount of money in each contestant's final "score." Below is an example for one contestant.

Round 1: + 200, + 1,000, − 250
Round 2: + 300, − 250, + 700, + 500
Round 3: + 500, − 250
Total earnings: \$2,450

1. Contestant 1
2. Contestant 2
3. Contestant 3

English Language Learner ELL

Lesson 1-4
Building on Prior Knowledge

Have students fold a piece of paper into thirds. Have them write a K for what they know on the left section, a W for what they want to learn on the center section, and an L for what they learned on the right section. Ask students to list anything that they know or remember about adding integers. Allow students time to fill out what they know and what they want to learn about adding integers and discuss their responses. Then clarify, list, and give examples of the rules for adding integers.

Lesson 1-7
Peer Tutoring

Have students work in pairs to translate verbal phrases and sentences into algebraic expressions and equations. If possible, pair English Language Learners with a bilingual student. Help students to see the connection between an algebraic expression and a phrase, and an equation and a sentence. Have the students underline the key words or phrases in each expression or sentence and write the mathematical symbol it represents above each one.

Lesson 1-8
Language Experience Approach to Illustrations

Ask students what the opposite of addition is. What is the opposite of subtraction? Show examples of how each of these operations undoes the other. Ask students what the opposites of multiplication and division are. These operations also undo each other. Operations that undo each other are opposites and are called inverse operations.

MathScape™  This project was supported, in part, by the **National Science Foundation**

MathScape is a mathematics curriculum for grades 6–8 developed by the Seeing and Thinking Mathematically Project at the Education Development Center.

Writing and Solving Equations

Exploring the Unknown

How to Use *MathScape* with Chapter 1

The unit *Exploring the Unknown* can be used to enhance Lessons 1-2 and 1-5.

- **Enrich** → After you complete **Lesson 1-2,** you can introduce Lab Gear blocks and play "What's in the Bag?" on page 185.
- **Reinforce** → After you complete **Lesson 1-5,** you can help students who are still having difficulty with adding and subtracting integers by using the activities on pages 192–193.

For other lessons in Chapter 1 that correlate to *MathScape*, see the chart on page T14.

Online Lesson Planner

USA TODAY® Education's Online site offers resources and interactive features connected to each day's newspaper. *Experience Today,* USA TODAY's® daily lesson plan, is available on the site and delivered daily to subscribers. This plan provides instruction for integrating USA TODAY® graphics and key editorial features into your mathematics classroom. Log on to **education.usatoday.com.**

USA TODAY Snapshots® in Chapter 1	
Lesson	**Snapshot**
1-1	Americans work the most hours
1-9	Population grows by the hour

Quick Review Math Handbook

is Glencoe's mathematical handbook for students. The Hot Words section includes a glossary of terms while the Hot Topics section consists of explanations of key mathematical concepts. An exercise set is included to check students' understanding of the concepts. This valuable resource can be used as a reference in the classroom or for home study.

Lesson	Hot Topics Section	Lesson	Hot Topics Section
1-1	5-1	1-6	1-5
1-2	1-2, 1-3	1-7	6-1, 6-4
1-3	1-1, 1-5, 6-7	1-8	6-1, 6-4
1-4,1-5	1-5	1-9	6-1, 6-4

Notes

Key Chapter Objectives

Lesson 1-1 Solve problems by using the four-step plan.

Lesson 1-2 Evaluate expressions and identify properties.

Lessons 1-3 through 1-6 Graph integers on a number line and perform operations using integers.

Lesson 1-7 Write algebraic expressions and equations from verbal phrases and sentences.

Lessons 1-8 and 1-9 Solve equations using the Properties of Equality.

"How do you use math in scuba diving?"

Point out to students that this is only one of many applications of the math that they are studying. Others are provided in the introduction to each lesson.

Vocabulary Builder, pp. vii–viii — ELL

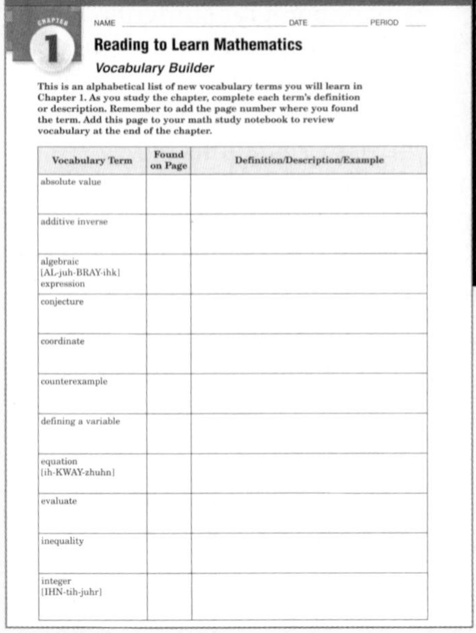

CHAPTER 1

NAME ______ DATE ______ PERIOD ____

Reading to Learn Mathematics

Vocabulary Builder

This is an alphabetical list of new vocabulary terms you will learn in Chapter 1. As you study the chapter, complete each term's definition or description. Remember to add the page number where you found the term. Add this page to your math study notebook to review vocabulary at the end of the chapter.

Vocabulary Term	Found on Page	Definition/Description/Example
absolute value		
additive inverse		
algebraic [AL-juh-BRAY-ihk] expression		
conjecture		
coordinate		
counterexample		
defining a variable		
equation [ih-KWAY-zhuhn]		
evaluate		
inequality		
integer [IHN-tih-juhr]		

CHAPTER 1 Algebra: Integers

"How do you use math in scuba diving?"

Recreational scuba divers dive no more than 130 feet below the water's surface. You can use the integer **−130** to describe this depth. In algebra, you will use integers to describe many real-life situations.

You will describe situations using integers in Lesson 1-3.

4 Chapter 1 Algebra: Integers

Vocabulary Builder

For a thorough vocabulary list with pronunciations of new words, give students the Vocabulary Builder worksheets from the *Chapter 1 Resource Masters*. Encourage them to complete the definition of each term as they progress through the chapter.

GETTING STARTED

▶ Diagnose Readiness

Take this quiz to see whether you are ready to begin Chapter 1.

Vocabulary Review

Choose the correct term to complete each sentence.

1. To find the product of two numbers, you must (add, multiply).
2. (Division, Addition) and subtraction are opposites because they undo each other.

Prerequisite Skills

Add.

3. 64 + 13 **77**
4. 10.3 + 4.7 **15**
5. 2.5 + 77 **79.5**
6. 38 + 156 **194**

Subtract.

7. 200 − 48 **152**
8. 59 − 26 **33**
9. 3.3 − 0.7 **2.6**
10. 73.5 − 0.87 **72.63**

Multiply.

11. 3 × 5 × 2 **30**
12. 2.8 × 5 **14**
13. 12 × 6 **72**
14. 4 × 9 × 3 **108**

Divide.

15. 244 ÷ 0.2 **1,220**
16. 72 ÷ 9 **8**
17. 96 ÷ 3 **32**
18. 100 ÷ 0.5 **200**
19. 2 ÷ 5 **0.4**
20. 0.36 ÷ 0.3 **1.2**

Replace each ● with <, >, or = to make a true sentence.

21. 13 ● 16 <
22. 5 ● 0.5 >
23. 25 ● 22 >
24. 3 ● 3.0 =

Integers and Equations Make this Foldable to organize your notes. Begin with a piece of 11" × 17" paper.

STEP 1 **Fold** Fold the paper in sixths lengthwise.

STEP 2 **Open and Fold** Fold a 4" tab along the short side. Then fold the rest in half.

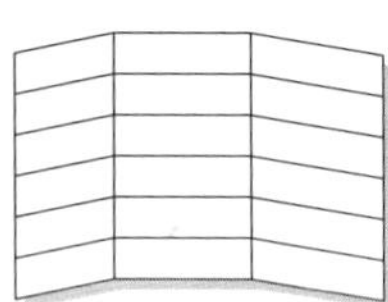

STEP 3 **Label** Draw lines along the folds and label as shown.

	Words	Example(s)
A Plan for Problem Solving		
+ & − of Integers		
× & ÷ of Integers		
Solving + & − Equations		
Solving × & ÷ Equations		

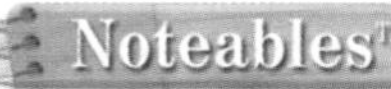

Chapter Notes Each time you find this logo throughout the chapter, use your *Noteables™: Interactive Study Notebook with Foldables™* or your own notebook to take notes. Begin your chapter notes with this Foldable activity.

Readiness To prepare yourself for this chapter with another quiz, visit **msmath3.net/chapter_readiness**

GETTING STARTED

Diagnose Readiness This section provides a review of the basic concepts needed before beginning Chapter 1. Page references are included for additional student help.

Prerequisite Skills review skills needed in this chapter.

Exercises	Needed for Lesson	Skill
3–6	1-4	Add Rational Numbers
7–10	1-5	Subtract Rational Numbers
11–14	1-6	Multiply Rational Numbers
15–20	1-6	Divide Rational Numbers
21–24	1-3	Compare and Order Positive Numbers

For more prerequisite skills, see:

- Getting Ready for the Next Lesson, at the end of each lesson
- Prerequisite Skills in the Student Handbook on pp. 600–615
- *Math Skills Maintenance Masters*

Each chapter opens with **Vocabulary Review** and **Prerequisite Skills** practice for lessons in the chapter. See the list above for more Prerequisite Skills practice.

FOLDABLES™ Study Organizer

For more information about Foldables, see *Teaching Mathematics with Foldables.*

After students make their Foldables, have them label the columns and rows as illustrated. Students use their Foldables to take notes, define terms, record concepts, and write examples. As students progress through the chapter, ask them to use their notes to write a descriptive paragraph about their learning experiences related to integers. For example, a student might descriptively write about how they find absolute value or solve multiplication equations.

Foldables™ are a unique way to enhance students' study skills.

1-1 Lesson Notes

Lesson Resources

Chapter 1 Resource Masters FAST FILE

- Study Guide and Intervention, p. 1
- Practice: Skills, p. 2
- Practice: Word Problems, p. 3
- Reading to Learn Mathematics, p. 4
- Enrichment, p. 5

Key Teaching Transparencies, 1

MathPASS Tutorial CD-ROM, 1, 11

Parent and Student Study Guide Online Worksheets, 1-1

Noteables™: Interactive Study Notebook with Foldables™, 1-1

1 Focus

5-Minute Check 1-1

Use as a quiz over prerequisite skills. (Also available as a transparency)

Bellringer

Communication Have students brainstorm ways to approach planning a trip. Ask them what they would need to consider, such as directions or gas expenses, and how to figure out each one. List the approaches on the chalkboard or on an overhead transparency.

Reading to Learn Mathematics, p. 4 **ELL**

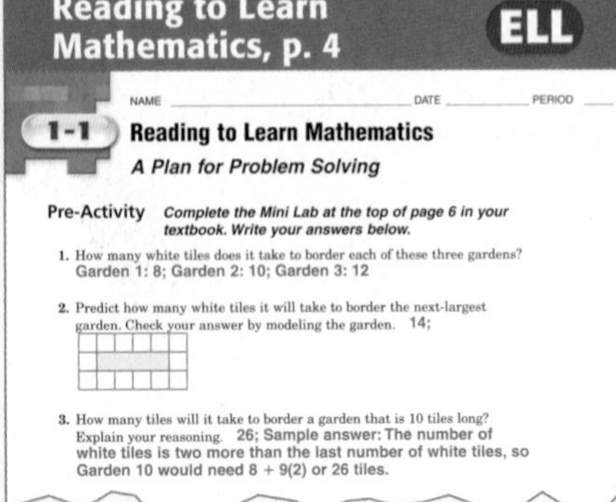

NAME ______ DATE ______ PERIOD ____

1-1 Reading to Learn Mathematics

A Plan for Problem Solving

Pre-Activity ***Complete the Mini Lab at the top of page 6 in your textbook. Write your answers below.***

1. How many white tiles does it take to border each of these three gardens? Garden 1: 8; Garden 2: 10; Garden 3: 12
2. Predict how many white tiles it will take to border the next-largest garden. Check your answer by modeling the garden. 14;
3. How many tiles will it take to border a garden that is 10 tiles long? Explain your reasoning. 26; Sample answer: The number of white tiles is two more than the last number of white tiles, so Garden 10 would need 8 + 9(2) or 26 tiles.

A Plan for Problem Solving

What You'll LEARN

Solve problems by using the four-step plan.

NEW Vocabulary

conjecture

HANDS-ON Mini Lab

Materials

- blue and white square tiles

Work with a partner.

Suppose you are designing rectangular gardens that are bordered by white tiles. The three smallest gardens you can design are shown below.

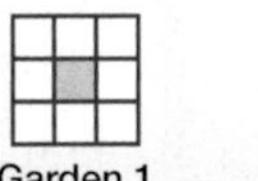

Garden 1

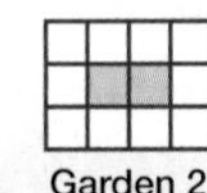

Garden 2

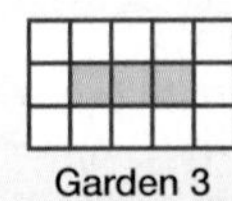

Garden 3

1. How many white tiles does it take to border each of these three gardens? **Garden 1: 8, Garden 2: 10, Garden 3: 12**
2. Predict how many white tiles it will take to border the next-largest garden. Check your answer by modeling the garden.
3. How many white tiles will it take to border a garden that is 10 tiles long? Explain your reasoning.

2. 14;

3. 26; Sample answer: The number of white tiles is two more than the last number of white tiles, so Garden 10 would need 8 + 9(2) or 26 tiles.

In this textbook, you will be solving many kinds of problems. Some, like the problem presented above, can be solved by using one or more problem-solving strategies.

No matter which strategy you use, you can always use the four-step plan to solve a problem.

Explore
- Determine what information is given in the problem and what you need to find.
- Do you have all the information you need?
- Is there too much information?

Plan
- Visualize the problem and select a strategy for solving it. There may be several strategies that you can use.
- Estimate what you think the answer should be.

Solve
- Solve the problem by carrying out your plan.
- If your plan doesn't work, try another.

Examine
- Examine your answer carefully.
- See if your answer fits the facts given in the problem.
- Compare your answer to your estimate.
- You may also want to check your answer by solving the problem again in a different way.
- If the answer is not reasonable, make a new plan and start again.

The **Lesson Resources** lists all of the resources available for the lesson, including workbooks, blackline masters, transparencies, and technology.

ELL notations indicate items that can assist English-Language Learners. Additional **ELL** strategies can be found at the beginning of each chapter.

STUDY TIP

Problem-Solving Strategies
- Make a model.
- Solve a simpler problem.
- Make an organized list.
- Make a table.
- Find a pattern.
- Work backward.
- Draw a graph.
- Guess and check.

Some problem-solving strategies require you to make an educated guess or **conjecture**.

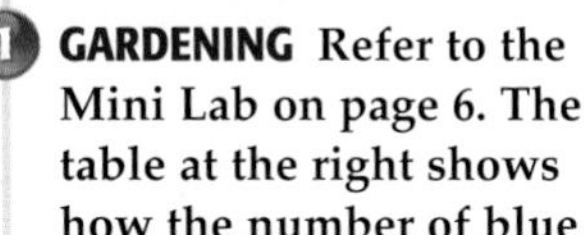

EXAMPLE Use the Four-Step Plan

1 GARDENING Refer to the Mini Lab on page 6. The table at the right shows how the number of blue tiles it takes to represent each garden is related to the number of white tiles needed to border the garden. How many white tiles will it take to border a garden that is 12 blue tiles long?

Blue Tiles	1	2	3	4	5	6
White Tiles	8	10	12	14	16	18

Explore You know the number of white tiles it takes to border gardens up to 6 tiles long. You need to determine how many white tiles it will take to border a garden 12 tiles long.

Plan You might make the conjecture that there is a pattern to the number of white tiles used. One method of solving this problem is to look for a pattern.

Solve First, look for the pattern.

Blue Tiles	1	2	3	4	5	6
White Tiles	8	10	12	14	16	18

+2 +2 +2 +2 +2

Next, extend the pattern.

Blue Tiles	6	7	8	9	10	11	12
White Tiles	18	20	22	24	26	28	30

+2 +2 +2 +2 +2 +2

It would take 30 white tiles to border a garden that was 12 blue tiles long.

Examine It takes 8 white tiles to border a garden that is 1 blue tile wide. As shown below, each additional blue tile added to the shape of the garden needs 2 white tiles to border it, one above and one below.

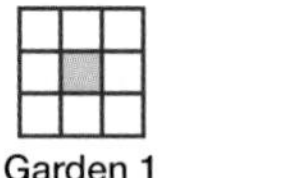

Garden 1 Garden 2

So, to border a garden 12 blue tiles long, it would take 8 white tiles for the first blue tile and 11×2 or 22 for the 11 additional tiles. Since $8 + 22 = 30$, the answer is correct.

Study Tips offer students helpful information about the topics they are studying.

STUDY TIP

Reasonableness Always check to be sure your answer is reasonable. If the answer seems unreasonable, solve the problem again.

Math Online msmath3.net/extra_examples

2 Teach

Noteables™

As you work the **In-Class Examples,** have students follow along in their *Noteables™: Interactive Study Notebook with Foldables™*, or have students work the examples in their notebooks.

In-Class Example

1 HOME IMPROVEMENT The Vorhees family plans to paint the walls in their family room. They need to cover 512 square feet with 2 coats of paint. If a one-gallon can of paint covers 220 square feet, how many one-gallon cans of paint should they purchase? **5 cans**

Intervention Students who consistently use the four-step plan will find word problems to be much easier to understand. Encourage students to write the four-step plan on a note card that they can have nearby while doing homework. They can refer to the card to make sure they do not skip a step.

New teachers, or teachers new to teaching mathematics, may especially appreciate the **Tips for New Teachers.**

DAILY INTERVENTION

Differentiated Instruction

Intrapersonal Have students write an analysis of their use of the four-step plan for problem solving in this lesson. Ask them to identify any areas needing further attention. Perhaps they rush through the Explore stage, missing key information. Or perhaps they need guidance in selecting the most effective strategy. Some students may find that they do not examine their answers carefully enough for errors and reasonableness.

In-Class Example

2 GEOGRAPHY Study the table. The five largest states in total area, which includes land and water, are shown. Of the five states shown, which one has the smallest area of water? **New Mexico**

Largest States in Area

State	Land Area (mi^2)	Total Area (mi^2)
Alaska	570,374	615,230
Texas	261,914	267,277
California	155,973	158,869
Montana	145,556	147,046
New Mexico	121,364	121,598

Source: U.S. Census Bureau

In-Class Examples, included for every example in the Student Edition, parallel the examples in the text.

READING Math

Word Problems It is important to read a problem more than once before attempting to solve it. You may discover important details that you overlooked when you read the problem the first time.

Reading Math features help students learn and use the language of mathematics.

TEACHING TIP

You could divide the yearly total for each country by 52 first. Then subtract to find the difference.

$1,877 \div 52 \approx 36.10$
$1,708 \div 52 \approx 32.85$
$36.10 - 32.85 = 3.25$

Some problems can be solved by adding, subtracting, multiplying, or dividing. Others can require a combination of these operations.

EXAMPLE Use the Four-Step Plan

2 WORK Refer to the graphic. On average, how many more hours per week did a person in the United States work in 2000 than a person in the United Kingdom?

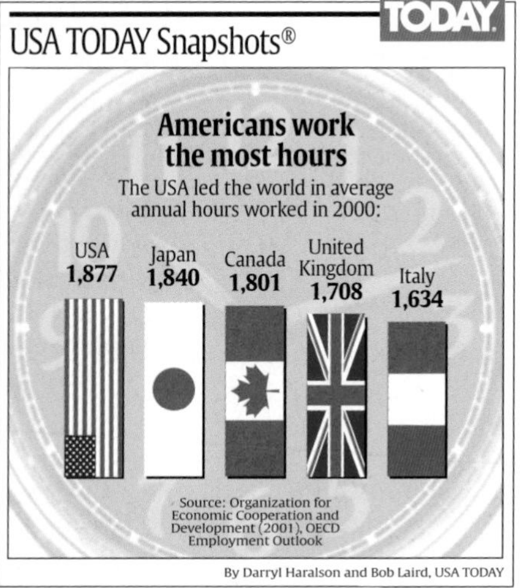

Explore *What do you know?*
You know the average number of hours worked in the year 2000 by a person in the United States, Japan, Canada, the United Kingdom, and Italy.

What are you trying to find?
You need to find the difference in the number of hours worked *per week* by a person in the United States and in the United Kingdom.

Plan Extra information is given. Use only the number of hours worked for the United States, 1,877, and the United Kingdom, 1,708.

Begin by subtracting to find the annual difference in the number of hours worked in each country. Then divide by the number of weeks in a year to find the weekly difference.

Estimate $1,900 - 1,700 = 200$ and $200 \div 50 = 4$
The number of hours is about 4.

Solve $1,877 - 1,708 = 169$ USA hours in 2000 – UK hours in 2000
$169 \div 52 = 3.25$ There are 52 weeks in a year.

On average, a person in the United States worked 3.25 hours more per week in 2000 than a person in the United Kingdom.

Examine Is your answer reasonable? The answer is close to the estimate, so the answer is reasonable.

Glencoe's exclusive partnership with USA TODAY® provides actual USA TODAY Snapshots® that illustrate mathematical concepts.

Students practice the same concepts in Exercises 8–15 if they are assigned odd or even problems.

Skill and Concept Check

1. **Writing Math** Explain each step in the four-step problem-solving plan. **1–2. See margin.**
2. **OPEN ENDED** Describe another method you could use to find the number of white tiles it takes to border a garden 12 green tiles long.
3. **NUMBER SENSE** Find a pattern in this list of numbers 4, 5, 7, 10, 14, 19. Then find the next number in the list. **The numbers increase by 1, 2, 3, and so on; 25.**

Writing Math identifies exercises in which students can practice their communication skills.

GUIDED PRACTICE

Use the four-step plan to solve each problem.

4. **SCHOOL SUPPLIES** At the school bookstore, a pen costs $0.45, and a small writing tablet costs $0.85. What combination of pens and tablets could you buy for exactly $2.15? **1 pen and 2 tablets**
5. **HOBBIES** Lucero put 4 pounds of sunflower seeds in her bird feeder on Sunday. On Friday, the bird feeder was empty, so she put 4 more pounds of seed in it. The following Sunday, the seeds were half gone. How many pounds of sunflower seeds were eaten that week? **6 lb**
6. **FIELD TRIP** Two 8th-grade teams, the Tigers and the Waves, are going to Washington, D.C. There are 123 students and 4 teachers on the Tiger team and 115 students and 4 teachers on the Waves team. If one bus holds 64 people, how many buses are needed for the trip? **4**

Practice and Applications

HOMEWORK HELP

For Exercises	See Examples
7–17	1, 2

Extra Practice See pages 616, 648.

Use the four-step plan to solve each problem.

7. **FOOD** Almost 90 million jars of a popular brand of peanut butter are sold annually. Estimate the number of jars sold every second. **almost 3 jars/s**

Draw the next two figures in each pattern.

8. 

9.

Year	Paintings Produced
1	59
2	34
3	91
4	20

ART For Exercises 10–12, use the following information.
The number of paintings an artist produced during her first four years as a professional is shown in the table at the right.

10. Estimate the total number of paintings the artist has produced. **200**
11. About how many more paintings did she produce in the last two years than in the first two years? **20**
12. About how many more paintings did she produce in the odd years than the even years? **100**

Math Online msmath3.net/self_check_quiz

3 Practice/Apply

FOLDABLES™ Follow-Up Encourage students to summarize the four-step problem-solving plan in words and symbols in the appropriate sections of their Foldables. Students might include an example of how they have used this plan to solve a problem.

NUMBER SENSE
In Exercise 3, have students consider different operations on the numbers in the series, such as adding, subtracting, multiplying, and dividing, to help them discern the pattern.

About the Exercises...

Guided Practice Key

Exercises	Examples
4–6	1, 2

Assignment Guide

Basic: 7–17 odd, 18–24

Average: 7–13 odd, 14, 15, 17–24

Enriched: 8–12 even, 13, 14, 16, 18–20 (Optional: 21–24)

Answers

1. Explore - Identify what information is given and what you need to find.
Plan - Estimate the answer and then select a strategy for solving.
Solve - Carry out the plan and solve.
Examine - Compare the answer to the estimate and determine if it is reasonable. If not, make a new plan.
2. Sample answer: The number of tiles above and below the garden is twice the garden's length. The number of tiles on either side always total 6. So a garden 12 tiles long would have $2 \times 12 + 6$ or 30 tiles bordering it.

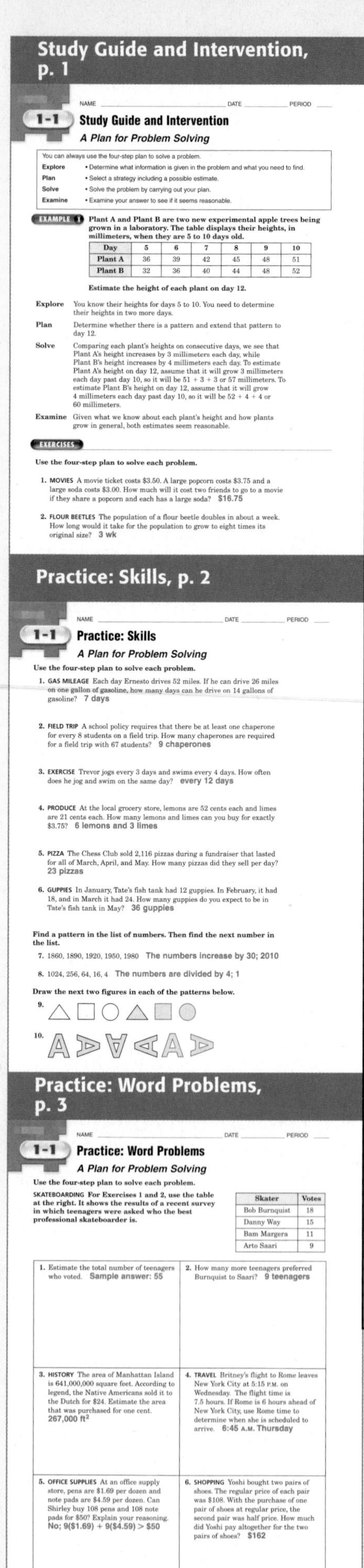
Study Guide and Intervention, p. 1

NAME ______________ DATE ________ PERIOD ____

1-1 Study Guide and Intervention
A Plan for Problem Solving

You can always use the four-step plan to solve a problem.

Explore	• Determine what information is given in the problem and what you need to find.
Plan	• Select a strategy including a possible estimate.
Solve	• Solve the problem by carrying out your plan.
Examine	• Examine your answer to see if it seems reasonable.

EXAMPLE 1 Plant A and Plant B are two new experimental apple trees being grown in a laboratory. The table displays their heights, in millimeters, when they are 5 to 10 days old.

Day	5	6	7	8	9	10
Plant A	36	39	42	45	48	51
Plant B	32	36	40	44	48	52

Estimate the height of each plant on day 12.

Explore You know their heights for days 5 to 10. You need to determine their heights in two more days.

Plan Determine whether there is a pattern and extend that pattern to day 12.

Solve Comparing each plant's heights on consecutive days, we see that Plant A's height increases by 3 millimeters each day, while Plant B's height increases by 4 millimeters each day. To estimate Plant A's height on day 12, assume that it will grow 3 millimeters each day past day 10, so it will be 51 + 3 + 3 or 57 millimeters. To estimate Plant B's height on day 12, assume that it will grow 4 millimeters each day past day 10, so it will be 52 + 4 + 4 or 60 millimeters.

Examine Given what we know about each plant's height and how plants grow in general, both estimates seem reasonable.

EXERCISES

Use the four-step plan to solve each problem.

1. MOVIES A movie ticket costs $3.50. A large popcorn costs $3.75 and a large soda costs $3.00. How much will it cost two friends to go to a movie if they share a popcorn and each has a large soda? **$16.75**

2. FLOUR BEETLES The population of a flour beetle doubles in about a week. How long would it take for the population to grow to eight times its original size? **3 wk**

Practice: Skills, p. 2

NAME ______________ DATE ________ PERIOD ____

1-1 Practice: Skills
A Plan for Problem Solving

Use the four-step plan to solve each problem.

1. GAS MILEAGE Each day Ernesto drives 52 miles. If he can drive 26 miles on one gallon of gasoline, how many days can he drive on 14 gallons of gasoline? **7 days**

2. FIELD TRIP A school policy requires that there be at least one chaperone for every 8 students on a field trip. How many chaperones are required for a field trip with 67 students? **9 chaperones**

3. EXERCISE Trevor jogs every 3 days and swims every 4 days. How often does he jog and swim on the same day? **every 12 days**

4. PRODUCE At the local grocery store, lemons are 52 cents each and limes are 21 cents each. How many lemons and limes can you buy for exactly $3.75? **6 lemons and 3 limes**

5. PIZZA The Chess Club sold 2,116 pizzas during a fundraiser that lasted for all of March, April, and May. How many pizzas did they sell per day? **23 pizzas**

6. GUPPIES In January, Tate's fish tank had 12 guppies. In February, it had 18, and in March it had 24. How many guppies do you expect to be in Tate's fish tank in May? **36 guppies**

Find a pattern in the list of numbers. Then find the next number in the list.

7. 1860, 1890, 1920, 1950, 1980 **The numbers increase by 30; 2010**

8. 1024, 256, 64, 16, 4 **The numbers are divided by 4; 1**

Draw the next two figures in each of the patterns below.

9.

10.

Practice: Word Problems, p. 3

NAME ______________ DATE ________ PERIOD ____

1-1 Practice: Word Problems
A Plan for Problem Solving

Use the four-step plan to solve each problem.

SKATEBOARDING For Exercises 1 and 2, use the table at the right. It shows the results of a recent survey in which teenagers were asked who the best professional skateboarder is.

Skater	Votes
Bob Burnquist	18
Danny Way	15
Bam Margera	11
Arto Saari	9

1. Estimate the total number of teenagers who voted. **Sample answer: 55**

2. How many more teenagers preferred Burnquist to Saari? **9 teenagers**

3. HISTORY The area of Manhattan Island is 641,000,000 square feet. According to legend, the Native Americans sold it to the Dutch for $24. Estimate the area that was purchased for one cent. **267,000 ft²**

4. TRAVEL Britney's flight to Rome leaves New York City at 5:15 P.M. on Wednesday. The flight time is 7.5 hours. If Rome is 6 hours ahead of New York City, use Rome time to determine when she is scheduled to arrive. **6:45 A.M. Thursday**

5. OFFICE SUPPLIES At an office supply store, pens are $1.69 per dozen and note pads are $4.59 per dozen. Can Shirley buy 108 pens and 108 note pads for $50? Explain your reasoning. **No; 9($1.69) + 9($4.59) > $50**

6. SHOPPING Yoshi bought two pairs of shoes. The regular price of each pair was $108. With the purchase of one pair of shoes at regular price, the second pair was half price. How much did Yoshi pay altogether for the two pairs of shoes? **$162**

HISTORY For Exercises 13 and 14, use the information below.
In 1803, the United States bought the Louisiana Territory from France for $15 million. The area of this purchase was 828,000 square miles.

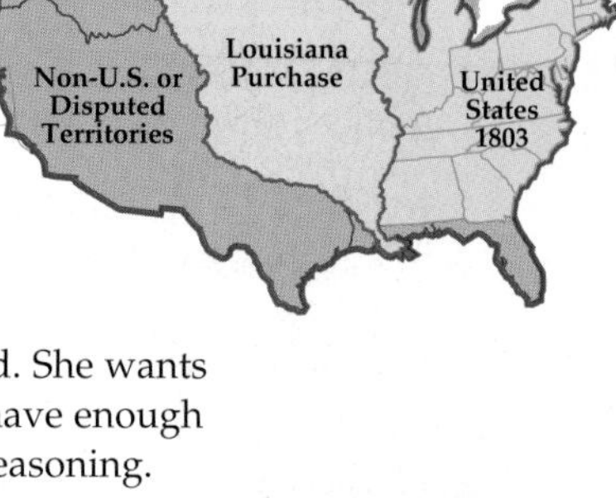

13. If one square mile is equal to 640 acres, how many acres of land did the United States acquire through the Louisiana Purchase? **529,920,000 acres**

14. About how much did the United States pay for the Louisiana Territory per acre? **about 3¢ per acre**

15. **BABY-SITTING** Kayla earned $30 baby-sitting last weekend. She wants to buy 3 CDs that cost $7.89, $12.25, and $11.95. Does she have enough money to purchase the CDs, including tax? Explain your reasoning. **No; $8 + $12 + $12 > $30**

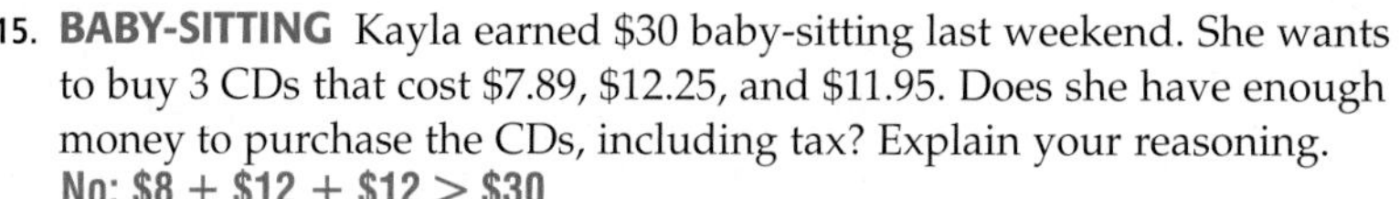

16. **TRAVEL** The table shows a portion of the bus schedule for the bus stop at the corner of Second Street and Elm Street. What is the earliest time that Tyler can catch the bus if he cannot make it to the bus stop before 9:30 A.M.? **9:40 A.M.**

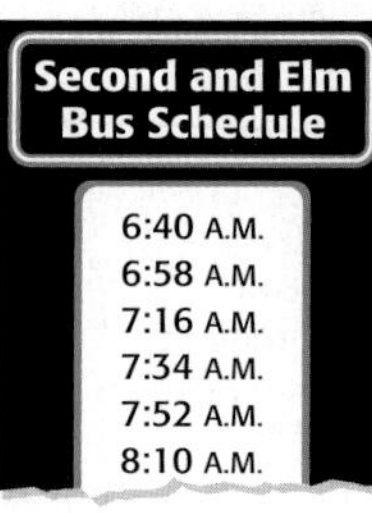

17. **SHOPPING** Miguel went to the store to buy jeans. Each pair costs $24. If he buys two pairs, he can get the second pair for half price. How much will he save per pair if he buys two pairs? **$6 per pair**

18. **CRITICAL THINKING** Draw the next figure in the pattern shown below. Then predict the number of tiles it will take to create the 10th figure in this pattern. Explain your reasoning. **See margin.**

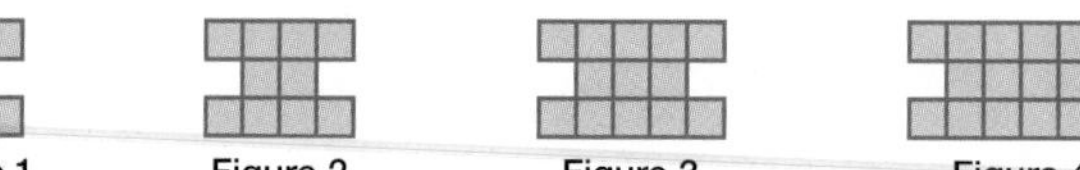

Spiral Review with Standardized Test Practice

19. **MULTIPLE CHOICE** Mrs. Acosta wants to buy 2 flag pins for each of the 168 band members for the Fourth of July Parade. Pins cost $0.09 each. Which is the best estimate of the cost of the pins? **C**

(A) $8 (B) $20 (C) $30 (D) $50

20. **GRID IN** John stocks the vending machines at Rose Hill Elementary School every 9 school days and Nassaux Intermediate School every 6 school days. In September, he stocked both schools on the 27th. How many school days earlier had he stocked the vending machines at both schools on the same day? **18**

GETTING READY FOR THE NEXT LESSON

BASIC SKILL Add, subtract, multiply, or divide.

21. 15 + 45 **60**
22. 1,287 − 978 **309**
23. 4 × 3.6 **14.4**
24. 280 ÷ 0.4 **700**

4 Assess

Open-Ended Assessment

Speaking Have students describe each step of the four-step problem-solving plan in their own words.

Answer

18. **34; Sample answer: Add 2 to the figure number and then multiply this answer by 2 to get the top and bottom rows in the figure. Then add the figure number to account for the middle row.**

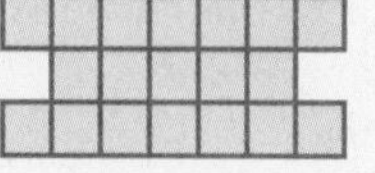

Variables, Expressions, and Properties

What You'll LEARN

Evaluate expressions and identify properties.

NEW Vocabulary

variable
algebraic expression
numerical expression
evaluate
order of operations
powers
equation
open sentence
property
counterexample

A **Reading in the Content Area** link appears in each chapter to help improve students' reading, as required by the No Child Left Behind Act.

HANDS-ON Mini Lab

Materials

- toothpicks

The figures at the right are formed using toothpicks. If each toothpick is a unit, then the perimeter of the first figure is 4 units.

Figure 1 Figure 2 Figure 3

1. Copy and complete the table below.

Figure Number	1	2	3	4	5	6
Perimeter	4	8	12	16	20	24

2. What would be the perimeter of Figure 10? **40**
3. What is the relationship between the figure number and the perimeter of the figure? **The perimeter is 4 times the figure number.**

You can use the variable n to represent the figure number in the Mini Lab above. A **variable** is a symbol, usually a letter, used to represent a number.

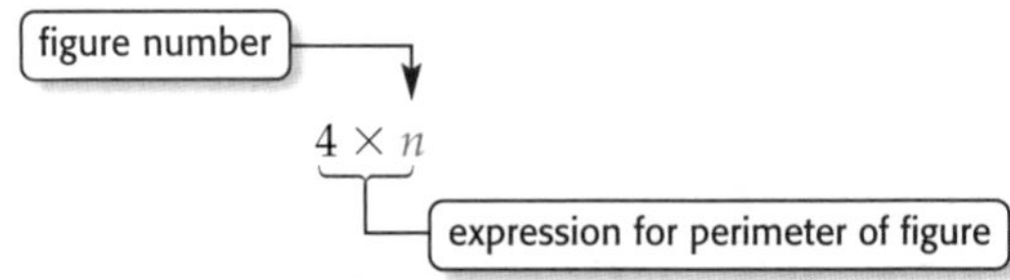

The expression $4 \times n$ is called an **algebraic expression** because it contains a variable, a number, and at least one operation symbol. When you substitute 10 for n, or replace n with 10, the algebraic expression $4 \times n$ becomes the **numerical expression** 4×10.

When you **evaluate** an expression, you find its numerical value. To avoid confusion, mathematicians have agreed on a set of rules called the **order of operations**.

TEACHING TIP

Grouping symbols include:
- parentheses ( ),
- brackets [ ], and
- fraction bars, as in $\frac{4+6}{5}$.

READING in the Content Area

For strategies in reading this lesson, visit **msmath3.net/reading**.

Noteables™ Key Concept: Order of Operations

1. Do all operations within grouping symbols first; start with the innermost grouping symbols.
2. Evaluate all powers before other operations.
3. Multiply and divide in order from left to right.
4. Add and subtract in order from left to right.

1-2 Lesson Notes

Lesson Resources

Chapter 1 Resource Masters FAST FILE
- Study Guide and Intervention, p. 6
- Practice: Skills, p. 7
- Practice: Word Problems, p. 8
- Reading to Learn Mathematics, p. 9
- Enrichment, p. 10

Calculator and Spreadsheet Masters, p. 13
MathPASS Tutorial CD-ROM, 4
Parent and Student Study Guide Online Worksheets, 1-2
Noteables™: Interactive Study Notebook with Foldables™, 1-2

Focus

5-Minute Check 1-2
Use as a quiz or review of Lesson 1-1. (Also available as a transparency)

Bellringer

Reading Mathematics The root word in the English word *evaluate* is the Latin word for *value,* which means worth. So, in everyday language, *evaluate* means to find out what something is worth. How does this relate to the mathematical meaning of *evaluate?*

NCLB NO CHILD LEFT BEHIND

The goals of the NCLB Act include a stronger emphasis on reading. The **Reading in the Content Area** link helps students become proficient readers.

TEACHING TIP

Grouping symbols include:
- parentheses ( ),
- brackets [ ], and
- fraction bars, as in $\frac{4+6}{5}$.

Reading to Learn Mathematics, p. 9 **ELL**

NAME ________ DATE ________ PERIOD ____

1-2 Reading to Learn Mathematics
Variables, Expressions, and Properties

Pre-Activity *Complete the Mini Lab at the top of page 11 in your textbook. Write your answers below.*

1. Complete the table below.

Figure Number	1	2	3	4	5	6
Perimeter	4	8	12	16	20	24

2. What would be the perimeter of Figure 10? 40
3. What is the relationship between the figure number and the perimeter of the figure? The perimeter is 4 times the figure number.

Reading the Lesson

4. Number the operations in the correct order for simplifying $2 + 4(9 - 6 \div 3)$. Then simplify the expression. 30

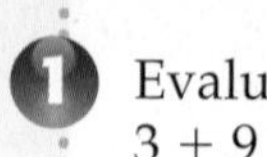

Teach

In-Class Examples

1 Evaluate $3 + 9 - 2 \times (8 \div 2)$. **4**

Evaluate each expression if $q = 5$, $r = 6$, and $s = 3$.

2 $3r + 2s - 4$ **20**

3 $\frac{6q}{3r - 3}$ **2**

Tips for New Teachers

Teaching Strategies For Example 3, you may wish to demonstrate how a fraction bar acts as a grouping symbol by rewriting the expression as $c^2 \div (a - 3)$.

STUDY TIP

Technology Enter $4 + 3 \times 2$ into your calculator. If it displays 10, then your calculator follows the order of operations. If it displays 14, then it does not.

EXAMPLE Evaluate a Numerical Expression

1 Evaluate $8 + 5 \times (12 - 6 \div 3)$.

$8 + 5 \times (12 - 6 \div 3) = 8 + 5 \times (12 - 2)$	Divide inside parentheses first.
$= 8 + 5 \times (10)$	Subtract inside parentheses next.
$= 8 + 50$ or 58	Multiply 5 and 10. Then add 8 and 50.

Your Turn **Evaluate each expression.**

a. $(9 + 6) \div 5 \times 4 + (3 - 2)$ **13** b. $2 + 3 \times (18 - 7)$ **35**

Algebra has special symbols that are used for multiplication.

Expressions such as 7^2 and 2^3 are called **powers** and represent repeated multiplication.

To evaluate an algebraic expression, replace the variable or variables with the known values and then use the order of operations.

EXAMPLES Evaluate Algebraic Expressions

Evaluate each expression if $a = 5$, $b = 4$, and $c = 8$.

2 $4a - 3b + 1$

$4a - 3b + 1 = 4(5) - 3(4) + 1$	Replace a with 5 and b with 4.
$= 20 - 12 + 1$	Do all multiplications first.
$= 8 + 1$ or 9	Add and subtract in order from left to right.

3 $\frac{c^2}{a - 3}$

The fraction bar is a grouping symbol. Evaluate the expressions in the numerator and denominator separately before dividing.

$\frac{c^2}{a-3} = \frac{8^2}{5-3}$	Replace c with 8 and a with 5.
$= \frac{64}{5-3}$	Evaluate the power in the numerator. $8^2 = 8 \cdot 8$ or 64
$= \frac{64}{2}$ or 32	Subtract in the denominator. Then divide.

STUDY TIP

Parentheses Parentheses around a single number do not necessarily mean that multiplication should be performed first. Remember to multiply or divide in order from left to right.

$20 \div 4(2) = 5(2)$ or 10

Your Turn **Evaluate each expression if $m = 9$, $n = 2$, and $p = 5$.**

c. $25 - 5p$ **0** d. $\frac{4 + 6m}{2p - 8}$ **29** e. $n^2 + 5n - 6$ **8**

DAILY INTERVENTION **Differentiated Instruction**

Kinesthetic Mark large sheets of paper with a number, an operation symbol, an opening or closing parenthesis, or a fraction bar and assign them to students. Have them arrange themselves in different orders across the front of the room and have the rest of the class evaluate the expressions that they form.

Daily Intervention notes help you help students when they need it most. Differentiated Instruction suggestions are keyed to eight commonly accepted learning styles.

A mathematical sentence that contains an equals sign (=) is called an **equation**. Some examples of equations are shown below.

$7 + 8 = 15$ $\quad$ $3(6) = 18$ $\quad$ $x + 2 = 5$

An equation that contains a variable is an **open sentence**. When a number is substituted for the variable in an open sentence, the sentence is true or false. Consider the equation $x + 2 = 5$.

Replace x with 2. $\quad 2 + 2 \stackrel{?}{=} 5$ ✗ $\quad$ This equation is false.

Replace x with 3. $\quad 3 + 2 \stackrel{?}{=} 5$ ✓ $\quad$ This equation is true.

Properties are open sentences that are true for any numbers.

Property	Algebra	Arithmetic
Commutative	$a + b = b + a$ $a \cdot b = b \cdot a$	$6 + 1 = 1 + 6$ $7 \cdot 3 = 3 \cdot 7$
Associative	$a + (b + c) = (a + b) + c$ $a \cdot (b \cdot c) = (a \cdot b) \cdot c$	$2 + (3 + 8) = (2 + 3) + 8$ $3 \cdot (4 \cdot 5) = (3 \cdot 4) \cdot 5$
Distributive	$a(b + c) = ab + ac$ $a(b - c) = ab - ac$	$4(6 + 2) = 4 \cdot 6 + 4 \cdot 2$ $3(7 - 5) = 3 \cdot 7 - 3 \cdot 5$
Identity	$a + 0 = a$ $a \cdot 1 = a$	$9 + 0 = 9$ $5 \cdot 1 = 5$
Transitive	If $a = b$ and $b = c$, then $a = c$.	If $2 + 4 = 6$ and $6 = 3 \cdot 2$, then $2 + 4 = 3 \cdot 2$.

STUDY TIP

Substitution Property Replacing a variable with a number demonstrates the *Substitution Property of Equality*. This property states that if two quantities are equal, then one quantity can be replaced by the other.

TEACHING TIP

Students will have more exposure to and practice using the Distributive Property in Chapter 10.

EXAMPLE Identify Properties

4 Name the property shown by the statement $2 \cdot (5 \cdot n) = (2 \cdot 5) \cdot n$.

The grouping of the numbers and variables changed. This is the Associative Property of Multiplication.

You may wonder whether each of the properties applies to subtraction. If you can find a counterexample, the property does not apply. A **counterexample** is an example that shows that a conjecture is false.

TEACHING TIP

Remind students that whole numbers include all the counting numbers, 1, 2, 3, . . . , as well as the number 0.

EXAMPLE Find a Counterexample

5 State whether the following conjecture is *true* or *false*. If *false*, provide a counterexample.

Division of whole numbers is commutative.

Write two division expressions using the Commutative Property, and then check to see whether they are equal.

$15 \div 3 \stackrel{?}{=} 3 \div 15$ $\quad$ State the conjecture.

$5 \neq \frac{1}{5}$ $\quad$ Divide.

We found a counterexample. That is, $15 \div 3 \neq 3 \div 15$. So, division is *not* commutative. The conjecture is false.

STUDY TIP

Counterexample It takes only one counterexample to prove that a statement is false.

Math Online msmath3.net/extra_examples

In-Class Examples

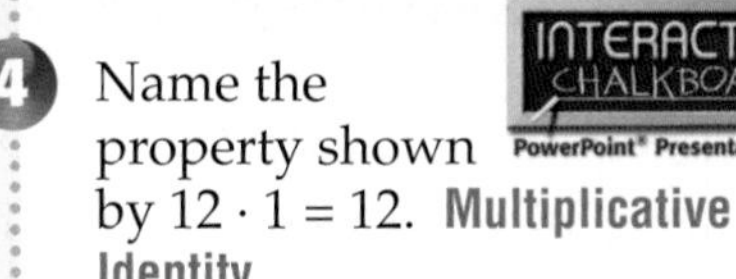

4 Name the property shown by $12 \cdot 1 = 12$. **Multiplicative Identity**

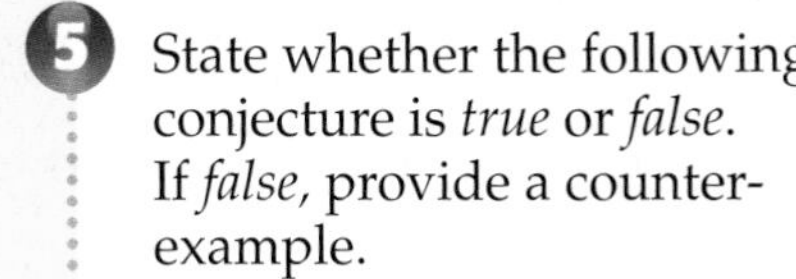

5 State whether the following conjecture is *true* or *false*. If *false*, provide a counterexample.

The sum of an odd number and an even number is always odd. **true**

3 Practice/Apply

About the Exercises...

Guided Practice Key

Exercises	Examples
4–6	1
7–9	2, 3
10, 11	4
12, 13	5

Assignment Guide

Basic: 15–47 odd, 51–55 odd, 56–63

Average: 15–55 odd, 56–63

Enriched: 14–40 even, 41, 42, 44–54 even, 56–63 (Optional: 60–63)

Alert! For Exercise 55, students will need to use the Internet or another resource.

About the Exercises and Assignment Guide help you plan to get the most from the exercise set. Many of the homework exercises are paired, so that students can do the odds one day and the evens the next day.

Answers

1. The everyday meaning of variable is something that is likely to change or vary, and the mathematical meaning of a variable is a placeholder for a value that can change or vary.
2. $3k + 9$ is an algebraic expression and $3k + 9 = 15$ is an equation.

Students practice the same concepts in Exercises 14–39 if they are assigned odd or even problems.

Skill and Concept Check

1. Writing Math Compare the everyday meaning of the term *variable* with its mathematical definition. **1–2. See margin.**
2. **Describe** the difference between $3k + 9$ and $3k + 9 = 15$.
3. **OPEN ENDED** Write an equation that illustrates the Commutative Property of Multiplication. **Sample answer: $4 \cdot 5 = 5 \cdot 4$**

GUIDED PRACTICE

Evaluate each expression.

4. $14 - 3 \cdot 2$ **8**
5. $4^2 - 2 \cdot 5 + (8 - 2)$ **12**
6. $\dfrac{28}{4^2 - 2}$ **2**

Evaluate each expression if $a = 2$, $b = 7$, and $c = 4$.

7. $6b - 5a$ **32**
8. $\dfrac{bc}{2}$ **14**
9. $b^2 - (8 + 3c)$ **29**

Name the property shown by each statement.

10. $3(2 + 5) = 3(2) + 3(5)$ **Dist.**
11. $3(12 \cdot 4) = (12 \cdot 4)3$ **Comm. (×)**

State whether each conjecture is *true* or *false*. If *false*, provide a counterexample.

12. Subtraction of whole numbers is associative. **false; $(8 - 5) - 3 \neq 8 - (5 - 3)$**
13. The sum of two different whole numbers is always greater than either addend. **false; $6 + 0 \not> 6$**

★ indicates increased difficulty

Practice and Applications

HOMEWORK HELP

For Exercises	See Examples
14–27	1
28–42	2, 3
43–48	4
51–54	5

Extra Practice See pages 616, 648.

Evaluate each expression. **21. 22 23. 20**

14. $12 \div 4 + 2$ **5**
15. $25 - 15 \div 5$ **22**
16. $3(7) - 4 \div 2$ **19**
17. $18 + 1(12) \div 6$ **20**
18. $16 - 6 + 5 \cdot 2^3$ **50**
19. $5^2 - 4 \cdot 6 \div 3$ **17**
20. $4^3 \div (16 - 12) \cdot 3$ **48**
21. $5^2 - 2 \cdot 4 + (7 - 2)$
22. $\dfrac{36}{3^2 - 3}$ **6**
23. $(14 - 8) \cdot 3 + \dfrac{31 - 9}{11}$
24. $\dfrac{(18 - 12)(21 + 4)}{3}$ **50**
25. $\dfrac{8 + 2(4 - 1)}{3^2 - 2}$ **2**
26. $2[18 - (5 + 3^2) \div 7]$ **32**
27. $4 - 3 + 7(12 - 2^2)$ **57**

Evaluate each expression if $w = 2$, $x = 6$, $y = 4$, and $z = 5$.

28. $2x + y$ **16**
29. $3z - 2w$ **11**
30. $9 + 7x - y$ **47**
31. $3y + z - x$ **11**
32. wx^2 **72**
33. $(wx)^2$ **144**
34. $x(3 + y) - z$ **37**
35. $2(xy - 9) \div z$ **6**
36. $\dfrac{x^2 - 3}{2z + 1}$ **3**
37. $\dfrac{wz^2}{y + 6}$ **5**
38. $3y^2 + 2y - 7$ **49**
39. $2z^2 - 4z + 5$ **35**
40. **INSECTS** The number of times a cricket chirps can be used to estimate the temperature in degrees Fahrenheit. Find the approximate temperature if a cricket chirps 140 times in a minute. Use the expression $c \div 4 + 37$, where c is the number of chirps per minute. **72°F**

PETS **For Exercises 41 and 42, use the information below.**
You can estimate the number of households with pets in your community using the expression $\frac{c}{n} \cdot p$, where c is the population of your community, n is the national number of people per household, and p is the national percent of households owning pets.

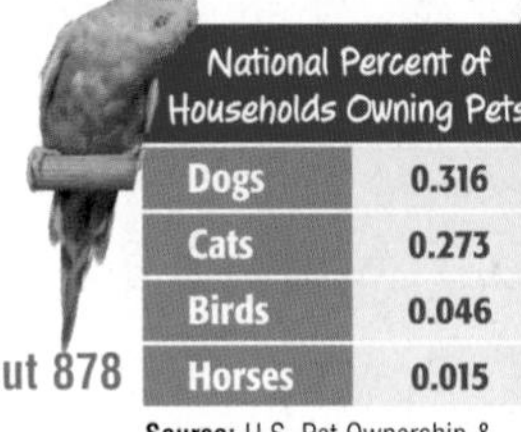

National Percent of Households Owning Pets	
Dogs	0.316
Cats	0.273
Birds	0.046
Horses	0.015

Source: U.S. Pet Ownership & Demographics Sourcebook

41. In 2000, the U.S. Census Bureau estimated that there were 2.62 people per household. Estimate the number of dog-owning households for a community of 50,000 people. **about 6,031**
42. Estimate the number of bird-owning households. **about 878**

Name the property shown by each statement.

43. $(6 + 3)2 = 6(2) + 3(2)$ **Dist.**
44. $1 \cdot 5abc = 5abc$ **Iden. (×)**
45. $5 + (8 + 12) = (8 + 12) + 5$ **Comm. (+)**
46. $(3 + 9) + 20 = 3 + (9 + 20)$ **Assoc. (+)**
47. $(5 + x) + 0 = 5 + x$ **Iden. (+)**
48. If $5 + 4 = 9$ and $9 = 3^2$, then $5 + 4 = 3^2$. **Trans.**

Rewrite each expression using the indicated property. **49. 6(4 + 3)**

★ 49. $6(4) + 6(3)$, Distributive Property
★ 50. x, Identity Property **$x \cdot 1$ or $x + 0$**

State whether each conjecture is *true* or *false*. If *false*, provide a counterexample.

51. The sum of two even numbers is always even. **true**
52. The sum of two odd numbers is always odd. **false; $7 + 3 = 10$**
53. Division of whole numbers is associative. **false; $(24 \div 4) \div 2 \neq 24 \div (4 \div 2)$**
54. Subtraction of whole numbers is commutative. **false; $10 - 4 \neq 4 - 10$**
55. **RESEARCH** Use the Internet or another resource to find out who first introduced a mathematical symbol such as the equals sign (=).
Sample answer: The equals sign was first introduced by Robert Recorde in 1557.
56. **CRITICAL THINKING** Decide whether $6 + 7 \cdot 2 + 5 = 55$ is *true* or *false*. If *false*, copy the equation and insert parentheses to make it true. **false; $6 + 7 \cdot (2 + 5) = 55$**

Spiral Review with Standardized Test Practice

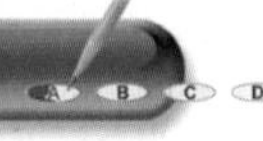

57. **MULTIPLE CHOICE** What is the value of $3^2 + 4 \cdot 2 - 6 \div 2$? **C**
Ⓐ 5.5 Ⓑ 10 Ⓒ 14 Ⓓ 26

58. **MULTIPLE CHOICE** Which is an example of the Associative Property? **I**
Ⓕ $4 \cdot 6 = 6 \cdot 4$
Ⓖ $5 + (4 + 1) = (4 + 1) + 5$
Ⓗ $7 + (3 + 2) = 7 + (2 + 3)$
Ⓘ $8(9 \cdot 2) = (8 \cdot 9)2$

59. **DINING** Kyung had \$17. His dinner cost \$5.62, and he gave the cashier a \$10 bill. How much change should he receive? (Lesson 1-1) **\$4.38**

Getting Ready for the Next Lesson exercises target specific skills students will need for the next lesson.

GETTING READY FOR THE NEXT LESSON

BASIC SKILL **Replace each ● with <, >, or = to make a true sentence.**

60. 4 ● 9 **<**
61. 7 ● 7 **=**
62. 8 ● 5 **>**
63. 3 ● 2 **>**

4 Assess

Open-Ended Assessment

Modeling Divide the chalkboard into 4 columns and label them with the property names. Have students write an example for each property and tape them in the correct column. Have students check all the examples to make sure they are in the correct column.

Study Guide and Intervention, p. 6

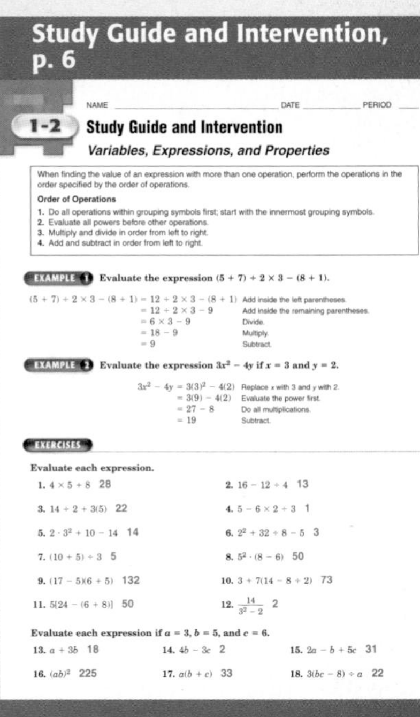

NAME ________ DATE ________ PERIOD ____

1-2 Study Guide and Intervention
Variables, Expressions, and Properties

When finding the value of an expression with more than one operation, perform the operations in the order specified by the order of operations.

Order of Operations
1. Do all operations within grouping symbols first; start with the innermost grouping symbols.
2. Evaluate all powers before other operations.
3. Multiply and divide in order from left to right.
4. Add and subtract in order from left to right.

EXAMPLE 1 **Evaluate the expression $(5 + 7) \div 2 \times 3 - (8 + 1)$.**

$(5 + 7) \div 2 \times 3 - (8 + 1) = 12 \div 2 \times 3 - (8 + 1)$ Add inside the left parentheses.
$= 12 \div 2 \times 3 - 9$ Add inside the remaining parentheses.
$= 6 \times 3 - 9$ Divide.
$= 18 - 9$ Multiply.
$= 9$ Subtract.

EXAMPLE 2 **Evaluate the expression $3x^2 - 4y$ if $x = 3$ and $y = 2$.**

$3x^2 - 4y = 3(3)^2 - 4(2)$ Replace x with 3 and y with 2.
$= 3(9) - 4(2)$ Evaluate the power first.
$= 27 - 8$ Do all multiplications.
$= 19$ Subtract.

EXERCISES

Evaluate each expression.

1. $4 \times 5 + 8$ 28
2. $16 - 12 \div 4$ 13
3. $14 \div 2 + 3(5)$ 22
4. $5 - 6 \times 2 \div 3$ 1
5. $2 \cdot 3^2 + 10 - 14$ 14
6. $2^2 + 32 \div 8 - 5$ 3
7. $(10 + 5) \div 3$ 5
8. $5^2 \cdot (8 - 6)$ 50
9. $(17 - 5)(6 + 5)$ 132
10. $3 + 7(14 - 8 \div 2)$ 73
11. $5[24 - (6 + 8)]$ 50
12. $\frac{14}{3^2 - 2}$ 2

Evaluate each expression if $a = 3$, $b = 5$, and $c = 6$.

13. $a + 3b$ 18
14. $4b - 3c$ 2
15. $2a - b + 5c$ 31
16. $(ab)^2$ 225
17. $a(b + c)$ 33
18. $3(bc - 8) \div a$ 22

Practice: Skills, p. 7

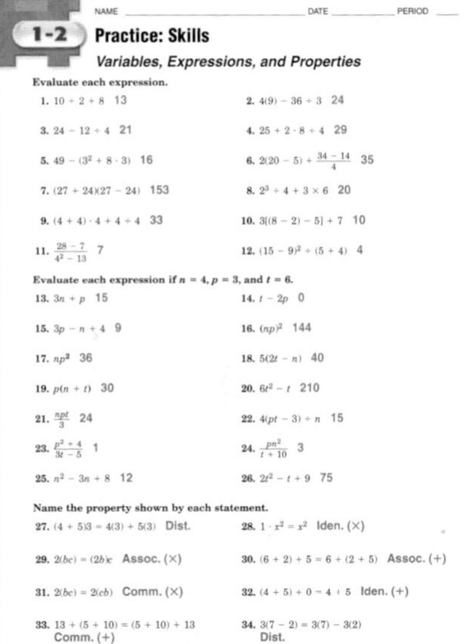

NAME ________ DATE ________ PERIOD ____

1-2 Practice: Skills
Variables, Expressions, and Properties

Evaluate each expression.

1. $10 \div 2 + 8$ 13
2. $4(9) - 36 \div 3$ 24
3. $24 - 12 \div 4$ 21
4. $25 + 2 \cdot 8 \div 4$ 29
5. $49 - (3^2 + 8 \cdot 3)$ 16
6. $2(20 - 5) + \frac{34 - 14}{4}$ 35
7. $(27 + 24)(27 - 24)$ 153
8. $2^3 \div 4 + 3 \times 6$ 20
9. $(4 + 4) \cdot 4 + 4 \div 4$ 33
10. $3[(8 - 2) - 5] + 7$ 10
11. $\frac{28 - 7}{4^2 - 13}$ 7
12. $(15 - 9)^2 \div (5 + 4)$ 4

Evaluate each expression if $n = 4$, $p = 3$, and $t = 6$.

13. $3n + p$ 15
14. $t - 2p$ 0
15. $3p - n + 4$ 9
16. $(np)^2$ 144
17. np^2 36
18. $5(2t - n)$ 40
19. $p(n + t)$ 30
20. $6t^2 - t$ 210
21. $\frac{npt}{3}$ 24
22. $4(pt - 3) \div n$ 15
23. $\frac{p^2 + 4}{3t - 5}$ 1
24. $\frac{pn^2}{t + 10}$ 3
25. $n^2 - 3n + 8$ 12
26. $2t^2 - t + 9$ 75

Name the property shown by each statement.

27. $(4 + 5)3 = 4(3) + 5(3)$ Dist.
28. $1 \cdot x^2 = x^2$ Iden. (×)
29. $2(bc) = (2b)c$ Assoc. (×)
30. $(6 + 2) + 5 = 6 + (2 + 5)$ Assoc. (+)
31. $2(bc) = 2(cb)$ Comm. (×)
32. $(4 + 5) + 0 = 4 + 5$ Iden. (+)
33. $13 + (5 + 10) = (5 + 10) + 13$ Comm. (+)
34. $3(7 - 2) = 3(7) - 3(2)$ Dist.

Practice: Word Problems, p. 8

NAME ________ DATE ________ PERIOD ____

1-2 Practice: Word Problems
Variables, Expressions, and Properties

FOOTBALL **For Exercises 1 and 2, use the table that shows statistics from the 2002 Super Bowl.**

Team	Touchdowns	Extra Points	Field Goals
New England	2	2	2
St. Louis	2	2	1

1. Each team's final score for a football game can be found using the expression $6t + e + 3f$, where t is the number of touchdowns, e is the number of extra points, and f is the number of field goals. Find New England's final score in the 2002 Super Bowl. 20
2. Use the expression $6t + e + 3f$ to find St. Louis's final score in the 2002 Super Bowl. 17
3. GEOMETRY The expression $6s^2$ can be used to find the surface area of a cube, where s is the lengh of an edge of the cube. Find the surface area of a cube with an edge of length 10 centimeters. 10 cm 600 cm²
4. VERTICAL MOTION The height of an object dropped from the top of a 300-foot tall building can be described by the expression $300 - 16t^2$, where t is the time, in seconds, after the ball is dropped. Find the height of the object 3 seconds after it is dropped. 156 ft
5. MOVIE RENTALS Mario intends to rent 10 movies for his birthday party. He can rent new releases for \$4 each, while older ones are \$2 each. If he rents n new releases, the total cost, in dollars, of the 10 movies is represented by the expression $4n + 2(10 - n)$. Evaluate the expression to find the total cost if he rents 7 new releases. \$34
6. CIRCULAR MOTION Pelipa is able to spin her yo-yo along a circular path. The yo-yo is kept in this path by a force which can be described by the expression $\frac{mv^2}{r}$. Evaluate the expression to find the force when $m = 12$, $v = 4$, and $r = 8$. 24

Objective Use a word map to understand vocabulary.

GETTING STARTED

Word Map A word map is a type of concept map. It allows students to list different aspects of the word in an organized manner. By listing different definitions, students are encouraged to truly understand the word rather than just memorize it.

You may want to have students work in pairs to develop their word maps.

TEACH

Word mapping suggestions for students:

- Read the paragraph containing the new word several times. Try to develop the meaning of the word from its context. How the word is used gives hints to its meaning.
- Include any examples that are provided in the text and add some of your own.
- If you do not understand the definition given in the text, use a standard dictionary. This may give you a nonmathematical definition.

ASSESS

Open-Ended Assessment

Speaking Have students take turns sharing their personal definitions with the rest of the class.

Study Skill

Use a Word Map

Studying Math Vocabulary

Learning new math vocabulary is more than just memorizing the definition. Try using a word map to really understand the meaning of the word.

Study Skill pages offer practical suggestions for taking notes, learning vocabulary, and reading word problems.

New vocabulary terms are clues about important concepts. Your textbook helps you find those clues by highlighting them in yellow, as **integers** is highlighted on the next page.

Whenever you see a highlighted word, stop and ask yourself these questions.

- How does this fit with what I already know?
- How is this alike or different from something I learned earlier?

Organize your answers in a word map like the one below.

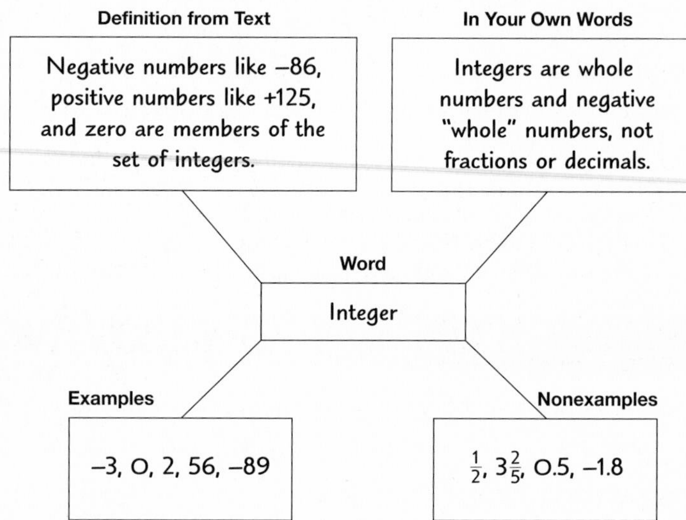

SKILL PRACTICE 1–4. See students' work.

Make a word map for each term. The term is defined on the given page.

1. greatest common factor (p. 610)
2. least common multiple (p. 612)
3. perimeter (p. 613)
4. area (p. 613)

16 Chapter 1

Integers and Absolute Value

What You'll LEARN

Graph integers on a number line and find absolute value.

NEW Vocabulary

negative number
integer
coordinate
inequality
absolute value

New Vocabulary words are listed at the beginning of the lesson and are highlighted in yellow at point of use.

TEACHING TIP

Remind students that the arrowheads on the number line indicate that the set of numbers continues indefinitely in each direction.

WHEN am I ever going to use this?

GEOGRAPHY Badwater, in Death Valley, California, is the lowest point in North America, while Mt. McKinley in Alaska, is the highest point. The graph shows their elevations and extreme temperatures.

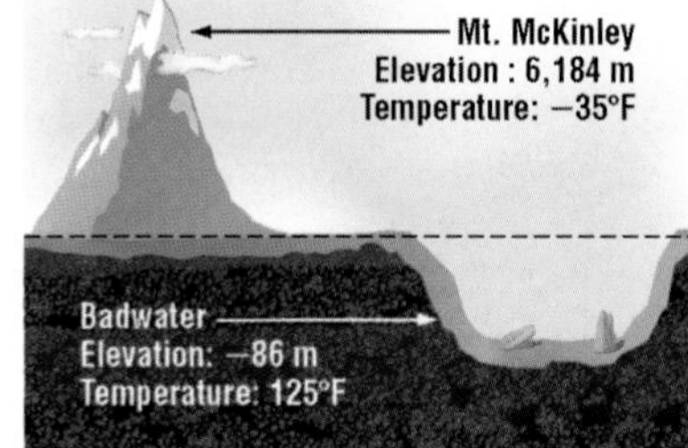

1. What does an elevation of −86 meters represent?
2. What does a temperature of −35° represent?

1. 86 meters below sea level 2. 35 degrees below zero F

With sea level as the starting point of 0, you can express 86 meters below sea level as 0 − 86, or −86. A **negative number** is a number less than zero.

Negative numbers like −86, positive numbers like +125, and zero are members of the set of **integers**. Integers can be represented as points on a number line.

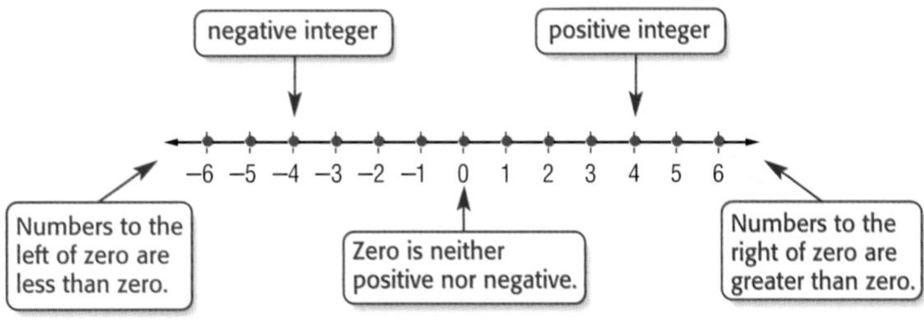

This set of integers can be written as {. . . , −3, −2, −1, 0, 1, 2, 3, . . .}, where . . . means *continues indefinitely*.

EXAMPLES Write Integers for Real-Life Situations

Write an integer for each situation.

1 **a 15-yard loss** The integer is −15.

2 **3 inches above normal** The integer is +3.

Your Turn **Write an integer for each situation.**

a. a gain of $2 a share +2 b. 10 degrees below zero −10

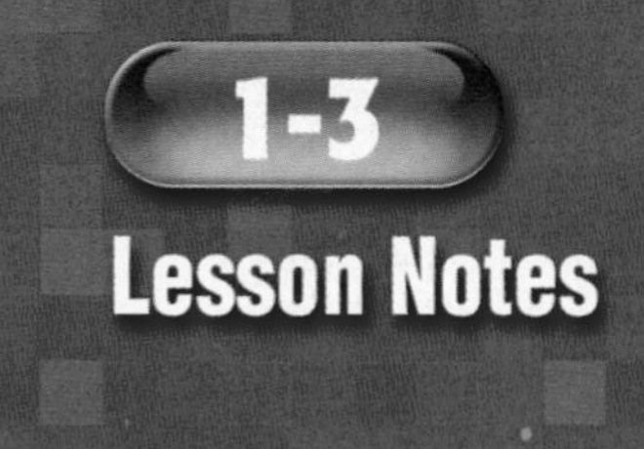

1-3 Lesson Notes

Lesson Resources

Chapter 1 Resource Masters
- Study Guide and Intervention, p. 11
- Practice: Skills, p. 12
- Practice: Word Problems, p. 13
- Reading to Learn Mathematics, p. 14
- Enrichment, p. 15

Parent and Student Study Guide Online Worksheets, 1-3

Noteables™: Interactive Study Notebook with Foldables™, 1-3

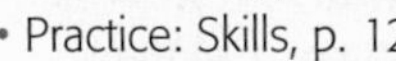

1 Focus

5-Minute Check 1-3

Use as a quiz or review of Lesson 1-2. (Also available as a transparency)

Bellringer

Hands-On Activity From the newspaper, collect several days of reports that show the high and low temperatures for cities across the country. Assign small groups of students a particular city and have them record the rise and fall of the days' high temperatures on a vertical number line.

Reading to Learn Mathematics, p. 14 **ELL**

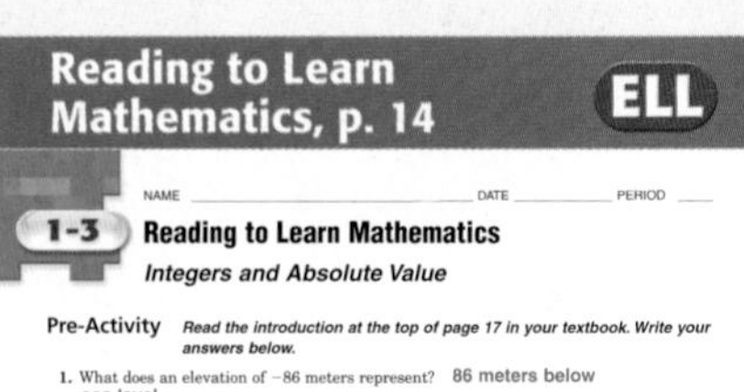

NAME DATE PERIOD

1-3 Reading to Learn Mathematics

Integers and Absolute Value

Pre-Activity *Read the introduction at the top of page 17 in your textbook. Write your answers below.*

1. What does an elevation of −86 meters represent? 86 meters below sea level
2. What does a temperature of −35° represent? 35 degrees below zero F

Reading the Lesson

The symbol ... is called an ellipsis.

3. Look on page 17 in your textbook to find the meaning of the ellipsis as it is used in the list 1, 4, 7, 10,... . The list continues indefinitely.
4. Use a dictionary to find the meaning of the ellipsis as it is used in the sentence *The marathon began...downtown.* Sample answer: A word or phrase has been omitted.
5. How can you explain the usage of the ellipsis in the list in Exercise 3 in terms of the meaning for the ellipsis in the sentence in Exercise 4?

2 Teach

In-Class Examples

Write an integer for each situation.

1. a 35¢ discount **−35**
2. a fever of 4 degrees above normal **+4**

Replace each ● with <, >, or = to make a true sentence. Use the integers graphed on the number line below.

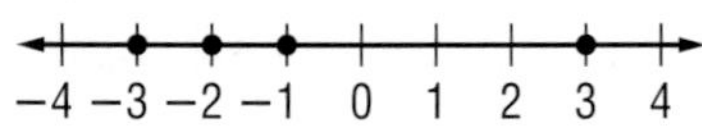

3. −3 ● 3 <
4. −2 ● −1 <
5. **FOOTBALL** The table below shows the number of yards rushing for several players on a football team during one game. Order these statistics from least to greatest.

Player	Yards Rushing
Marty	8
Autry	4
Shane	5
Brad	−10
Glyn	3
Jim	−19

−19, −10, 3, 4, 5, 8

Examples illustrate all of the concepts taught in the lesson and closely mirror the exercises in the Guided Practice and Applications sections.

Daily Intervention notes help you help students when they need it most. **Unlocking Misconceptions** suggestions help you analyze common errors so you can help students avoid these trouble spots.

To graph integers, locate the point named by the integers on a number line. The number that corresponds to a point is called the **coordinate** of that point.

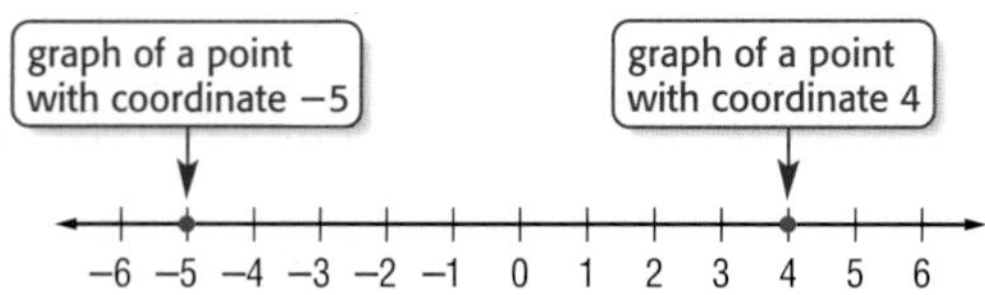

Notice that −5 is to the left of 4 on the number line. This means that −5 is less than 4. A sentence that compares two different numbers or quantities is called an **inequality**. They contain symbols like < and >.

−5 is less than 4. → $-5 < 4$ $4 > -5$ ← 4 is greater than −5.

EXAMPLES Compare Two Integers

Replace each ● with <, >, or = to make a true sentence. Use the integers graphed on the number line below.

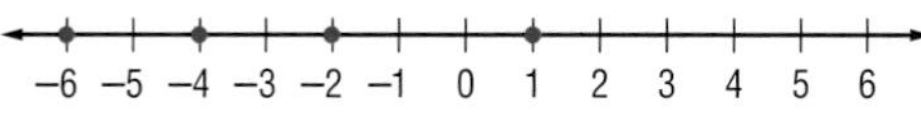

3. **1 ● −6** 1 is greater than −6, since it lies to the right of −6. Write $1 > -6$.

4. **−4 ● −2** −4 is less than −2, since it lies to the left of −2. Write $-4 < -2$.

Your Turn Replace each ● with <, >, or = to make a true sentence.

c. −3 ● 2 < d. −5 ● −6 > e. −1 ● 1 <

REAL-LIFE MATH

WEATHER A Celsius thermometer may be similar to a vertical number line. Negative temperatures on a Celsius thermometer are below the freezing point, 0°C.

Source: *The World Almanac*

Integers are used to compare numbers in many real-life situations.

EXAMPLE Order Integers

5. **WEATHER The table below shows the record low temperatures for selected states. Order these temperatures from least to greatest.**

State	AL	CA	GA	IN	KY	NC	TN	TX	VA
Temperature (°F)	−27	−45	−17	−36	−37	−34	−32	−23	−30

Graph each integer on a number line.

−46 −44 −42 −40 −38 −36 −34 −32 −30 −28 −26 −24 −22 −20 −18 −16

Write the numbers as they appear from left to right.

The temperatures −45°, −37°, −36°, −34°, −32°, −30°, −27°, −23°, and −17° are in order from least to greatest.

DAILY INTERVENTION — Unlocking Misconceptions

Absolute Value Some students may mistakenly believe that changing the sign of a number will find its absolute value. Stress that the absolute value of a number is its distance from zero on the number line. You may wish to illustrate this by placing one end of a string at zero on a number line and cutting the string where it falls on a particular number. The length of the string will never be negative.

On the number line, notice that −4 and 4 are on opposite sides of zero and that they are the same distance from zero. In mathematics, we say they have the same absolute value, 4.

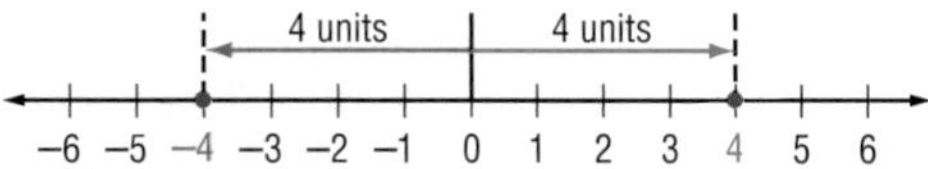

The **absolute value** of a number is the distance the number is from 0 on the number line. The symbol for absolute value is two vertical bars on either side of the number.

The absolute value of 4 is 4. → $|4| = 4$

$|-4| = 4$ ← The absolute value of −4 is 4.

Since distance cannot be negative, the absolute value of a number is always positive or zero.

EXAMPLES Expressions with Absolute Value

Evaluate each expression.

6 $|-7|$

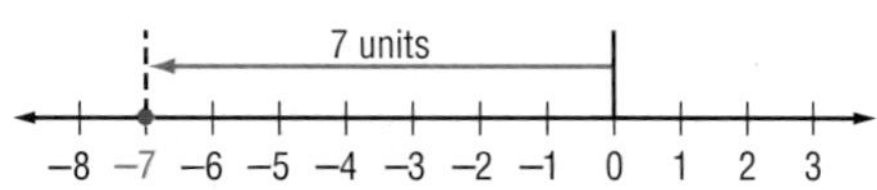

$|-7| = 7$ The graph of −7 is 7 units from 0 on the number line.

7 $|5| + |-6|$

$|5| + |-6| = 5 + |-6|$ The absolute value of 5 is 5.

$= 5 + 6$ The absolute value of −6 is 6.

$= 11$ Simplify.

Your Turn **Evaluate each expression.**

f. $|14|$ **14** g. $|-9| + |3|$ **12** h. $|-8| - |-2|$ **6**

Since variables represent numbers, you can use absolute value notation with algebraic expression involving variables.

EXAMPLE Expressions with Absolute Value

8 **Evaluate $8 + |n|$ if $n = -12$.**

$8 + |n| = 8 + |-12|$ Replace n with −12.

$= 8 + 12$ $|-12| = 12$

$= 20$ Simplify.

Your Turn **Evaluate each expression if $a = -5$ and $b = 3$.**

i. $|b| + 7$ **10** j. $|a| - 2$ **3** k. $4|a| + b$ **23**

STUDY TIP

Common Error
The absolute value of a number is *not* the same as the opposite of a number. Remember that the absolute value of a number cannot be negative.

Your Turn exercises allow students to practice concepts in a classroom setting.

In-Class Examples

Evaluate each expression.

6 $|5|$ **5**

7 $|6| - |-5|$ **1**

8 Evaluate $|x| + 13$ if $x = -4$. **17**

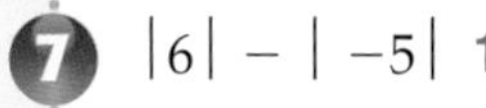

Teaching Strategies
Students may better understand absolute value by relating it to their distance from home to school. For example, two students can both live 3 minutes from school in opposite directions. Similarly $|3| = 3$ and $|-3| = 3$.

3 Practice/Apply

Which One Doesn't Belong?
In Exercise 2, have students change each phrase into mathematical notation to make the choice clearer.

About the Exercises...

Guided Practice Key

Exercises	Examples
3, 4	1, 2
6–8	3, 4
5	5
9–11	6, 7
12–14	8

Assignment Guide

Basic: 15–29 odd, 33–45 odd, 49–57 odd, 59–71

Average: 15–57 odd, 59–71

Enriched: 16–58 even, 59–67 (Optional: 68–71)

Answers

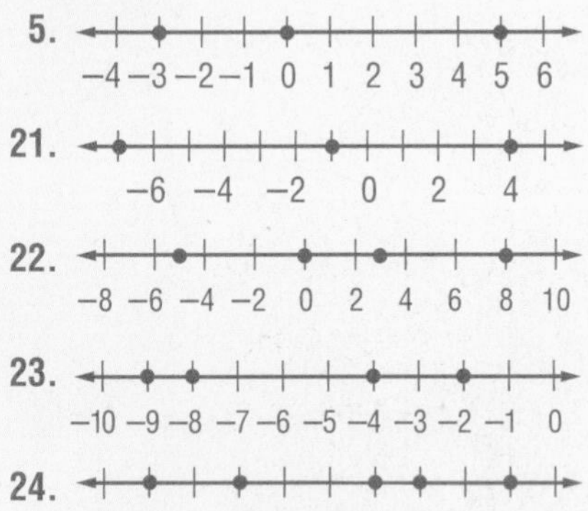

Every effort is made to show the **Answers** to exercises (1) on the Student Edition page, or (2) in the margin of the Teacher Wraparound Edition. Answers that do not fit can be found in the Answer Appendix at the end of each chapter.

Students practice the same concepts in Exercises 15–48 if they are assigned odd or even problems.

Skill and Concept Check

1. **OPEN ENDED** Write two inequalities using the same two integers. **Sample answer: $4 > -5$; $-5 < 4$**
2. **Which One Doesn't Belong?** Identify the phrase that cannot be described by the same integer as the other three. Explain your reasoning.

5° below normal	5 miles above sea level	a loss of 5 pounds	giving away $5

5 miles above sea level; the other phrases translate to the integer −5, but this phrase translates to 5.

GUIDED PRACTICE

Write an integer for each situation.

3. a 10-yard gain **+10**
4. 34 miles below sea level **−34**
5. Graph the set of integers {5, −3, 0} on a number line. **See margin.**

Replace each ● with <, >, or = to make a true sentence.

6. $-4 \bullet 3$ **<**
7. $-10 \bullet -12$ **>**
8. $7 \bullet -7$ **>**

Evaluate each expression.

9. $|-5|$ **5**
10. $|20| - |-3|$ **17**
11. $|-16| + |-12|$ **28**

Evaluate each expression if $x = -10$ and $y = 6$.

12. $3 + |x|$ **13**
13. $|x| - y$ **4**
14. $3|y|$ **18**

Skill and Concept Check exercises are intended to be completed in class to ensure that students understand the concepts in the lesson. The **Guided Practice** exercises are representative of the exercises used for homework or seatwork.

★ indicates increased difficulty

Practice and Applications

HOMEWORK HELP

For Exercises	See Examples
15–20, 50	1, 2
21–32, 52	3, 4
33–36, 49	5
37–48	6, 7
52–57	8

Extra Practice See pages 616, 648.

Write an integer for each situation. **15. −2**

15. a loss of 2 hours
16. earning $45 **+45**
17. a gain of 4 ounces **+4**
18. 13° below zero **−13**
19. a $60 deposit **+60**
20. spending $25 **−25**

Graph each set of integers on a number line. **21–24. See margin.**

21. {−1, 4, −7}
22. {0, −5, 3, 8}
23. {−2, −8, −4, −9}
24. {−4, 0, −6, −1, 2}

Replace each ● with <, >, or = to make a true sentence.

25. $-7 \bullet -2$ **<**
26. $-9 \bullet -10$ **>**
27. $-3 \bullet 0$ **<**
28. $0 \bullet 12$ **<**
29. $4 \bullet -11$ **>**
30. $-15 \bullet 14$ **<**
★31. $|-8| \bullet |8|$ **=**
★32. $|-13| \bullet |-6|$ **>**

Order the integers in each set from least to greatest. **33. {−37, −23, −12, 0, 45, 55}**

33. {45, −23, 55, 0, −12, −37}
34. {97, −46, −50, 38, −100}
35. {−17, −2, −5, −11, 6}
36. {21, 8, −47, 3, −1, 0}

34. {−100, −50, −46, 38, 97} 35. {−17, −11, −5, −2, 6} 36. {−47, −1, 0, 3, 8, 21}

Evaluate each expression.

37. $|-14|$ **14**
38. $|18|$ **18**
39. $|25|$ **25**
40. $|0|$ **0**
41. $|2| + |-13|$ **15**
42. $|-15| + |-6|$ **21**
43. $|-20| - |17|$ **3**
44. $|31| - |-1|$ **30**
45. $-|3|$ **−3**
46. $-|-10|$ **−10**
★47. $|5 + 9|$ **14**
★48. $|17 - 8|$ **9**

GOLF For Exercises 49 and 50, use the information below. In golf, a score of 0 is called *even par*. Two under par is written as −2. Two over par is written as +2.

Name	Second Round
Phillip Bryan	−4
James Sacheck	+1
Webb Simpson	+2
Adam Porzak	−1
Marc Gladson	−3
Todd Obergoenner	−1
Andy Winings	+5
Zen Brown	+1
Daniel Woltman	+4
Robbie Fillmore	+4

Source: www.pga.com

49. The second round scores of the top ten Boys' Division finishers in the 2003 Westfield Junior PGA Championship in Westfield Center, Ohio, are shown at the right. Order the scores from least to greatest.

50. Phillip Bryan of Mustang, Oklahoma, won the Championship, finishing 5 under par. Write an integer to describe Phillip Bryan's score. **−5**

49. −4, −3, −1, −1, +1, +1, +2, +4, +4, +5

51. **SCIENCE** Hydrogen freezes at about −435°F, and helium freezes at about −458°F. Which element has the lower freezing point? **helium**

Evaluate each expression if $a = 5$, $b = -8$, and $c = -3$.

52. $|b| + 7$ **15**
53. $a - |c|$ **2**
54. $|a| + |b|$ **13**
55. $|4a|$ **20**
56. $6|b|$ **48**
57. $|16 - a|$ **11**

58. **WRITE A PROBLEM** Write about a real-life situation that can be described by an integer. Then write the integer.
Sample answer: 2 inches shorter than average; −2

CRITICAL THINKING Determine whether the following statements are *always*, *sometimes*, or *never* true. Explain your reasoning. **59–61. See margin for explanation.**

59. The absolute value of a positive integer is a negative integer. **never**
60. The absolute value of a negative integer is a positive integer. **always**
61. If a and b are integers and $a > b$, then $|a| > |b|$. **sometimes**

Spiral Review with Standardized Test Practice

62. **MULTIPLE CHOICE** Which is in order from least to greatest? **A**

(A) −4, 2, 8 (B) 4, −1, −6 (C) −1, 2, −4 (D) 0, −1, −4

63. **MULTIPLE CHOICE** If $a = -3$ and $b = 3$, then which statement is false? **H**

(F) $|a| > 2$ (G) $|a| = |b|$ (H) $|b| < 2$ (I) $|a| = b$

Evaluate each expression. (Lesson 1-2)

64. $3[14 - (8 - 5)^2] + 20$ **35**
65. $6 \cdot (18 - 14) + \frac{22 - 4}{9}$ **26**
66. $\frac{45 - 9}{3^2 + 3}$ **3**

67. **CHARITY WALK** Krystal knows that she can walk about 1.5 meters per second. If she can maintain that pace, about how long should it take her to complete a 10-kilometer charity walk? (Lesson 1-1) **about 2 h**

GETTING READY FOR THE NEXT LESSON

BASIC SKILL Add or subtract.

68. 9 + 14 **23**
69. 100 − 57 **43**
70. 47 − 19 **28**
71. 18 + 34 + 13 **65**

msmath3.net/self_check_quiz

4 Assess

Higher-Level Thinking

Does −|−4| have the same value as 4? Explain your reasoning. **No; −|−4| = −4 because the absolute value of −4 is 4, and the opposite of 4 is −4.**

Answers

59. **Never; the absolute value of a positive number is always positive.**
60. **Always; the absolute value of a non-zero number is always positive.**
61. **Sometimes; 5 > −4 and |5| > |−4|, but −4 > −5 and |−4| ≯ |−5|.**

Study Guide and Intervention, p. 11

NAME ______ DATE ______ PERIOD ____

1-3 Study Guide and Intervention

Integers and Absolute Value

A number line can help you order a set of integers. When graphed on a number line, the smaller of two integers is always to the left of the greater integer.

EXAMPLE 1 **Order the set of integers {10, −3, −9, 4, 0} from least to greatest.**

Graph each integer on a number line.

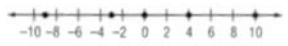

−10 −8 −6 −4 −2 0 2 4 6 8 10

The numbers from left to right are {−9, −3, 0, 4, 10}.

The absolute value of a number is the distance of that number from 0 on a number line.

EXAMPLE 2 **Evaluate the expression |−20| + |10|.**

|−20| + |10| = 20 + |10| The absolute value of −20 is 20.
= 20 + 10 The absolute value of 10 is 10.
= 30 Simplify.

EXERCISES

Order the integers in each set from least to greatest.

1. {3, 0, −5, 1, 4} **{−5, 0, 1, 3, 4}**
2. {−6, −8, 3, −1, −4} **{−8, −6, −4, −1, 3}**
3. {2, 13, −11, −21, 5} **{−21, −11, 2, 5, 13}**
4. {31, 0, −34, −9, 7} **{−34, −9, 0, 7, 31}**

Evaluate each expression.

5. |−13| **13**
6. |21| **21**
7. |−3| + |−5| **8**
8. |9| + |−8| **17**
9. |−13| + |15| **28**
10. |21 − 18| **3**
11. |−11| − |−5| **6**
12. |4| − |−4| **0**
13. |23 + 15| **38**

Evaluate each expression if $a = -6$, $b = 4$, and $c = 5$.

14. $|a| + 14$ **20**
15. $|c - b|$ **1**
16. $b + |c|$ **9**
17. $|3b|$ **12**
18. $2|a| + c$ **17**
19. $|2b + c|$ **13**

Practice: Skills, p. 12

NAME ______ DATE ______ PERIOD ____

1-3 Practice: Skills

Integers and Absolute Value

Write an integer for each situation.

1. 3 strokes below par **−3**
2. 10 strokes above par **+10**
3. a 6-yard loss **−6**
4. an 8-yard gain **+8**
5. 12 centimeters longer **+12**
6. 7 inches below normal **−7**
7. $5 off the original price **−5**
8. a gain of 6 hours **+6**
9. 2° above zero **+2**
10. a loss of 15 pounds **−15**
11. a $35 withdrawal **−35**
12. a $75 deposit **+75**
13. 1 mile above sea level **+1**
14. 20 fathoms below the surface **−20**

Replace ● with <, >, or = to make a true sentence.

15. −12 ● 4 **<**
16. −4 ● −5 **>**
17. −10 ● −8 **<**
18. 3 ● −13 **>**
19. |−6| ● |6| **=**
20. |−4| ● |−5| **<**

Order the integers in each set from least to greatest.

21. {0, −6, 7, 2, −4} **{−6, −4, 0, 2, 7}**
22. {−1, −2, −3, 3, 2, 1} **{−3, −2, −1, 1, 2, 3}**

Evaluate each expression.

23. |−8| **8**
24. |31| **31**
25. |−1| **1**
26. −|−256| **−256**
27. |3| + |−19| **22**
28. |−12| + |−13| **25**
29. |28| − |−26| **2**
30. |28| + |−26| **54**
31. |24| − |−15| **9**

Evaluate each expression if $a = 3$, $b = 8$, and $c = -5$.

32. $|a| + 5$ **8**
33. $|b| - 2$ **6**
34. $2|c| + b$ **18**
35. $a + |a|$ **6**
36. $|3b|$ **24**
37. $|a + 16|$ **19**

Practice: Word Problems, p. 13

NAME ______ DATE ______ PERIOD ____

1-3 Practice: Word Problems

Integers and Absolute Value

GOLF For Exercises 1 and 2, use the table that lists ten players and their scores in the 2002 Ladies Master Golf Tournament.

Player	Score	Player	Score
Brooky, Lynnette	−4	Neumann, Liselotte	0
Hjorth, Maria	−15	Park, Grace	−10
Jeong Jang	−5	Se Ri Pak	−14
King, Betsy	−8	Sorenstam, Annika	−19
Moodie, Janice	+5	Tinning, Iben	+3

1. Order the scores in the table from least to greatest. **−19, −15, −14, −10, −8, −5, −4, 0, +3, +5**

2. Who had the lowest score? **Annika Sorenstam**

3. **LONGITUDE** London, England, is located at 0° longitude. Write integers for the locations of New York City whose longitude is 74° west and Tokyo whose longitude is 140° east. Assume that east is the positive direction. **New York: −74; Tokyo: +140**

4. **STOCK MARKET** Your stock loses 53 points on Monday and 23 points on Tuesday, but gains 67 points on Wednesday. Write an integer for each day's change. **Monday: −53; Tuesday: −23; Wednesday: +67**

5. **SOLAR SYSTEM** The average temperature of Saturn is −218°F, while the average temperature of Jupiter is −162°F. Which planet has the lower average temperature? **Saturn**

6. **OCEAN TRENCHES** The elevation of the Puerto Rican Trench in the Atlantic Ocean is −8,605 meters, the elevation of the Mariana Trench in the Pacific Ocean is −10,924 meters, and the elevation of the Java Trench in the Indian Ocean is −7,125 meters. Which trench has the the lowest elevation? **Mariana Trench**

1-3b HANDS-ON LAB

Lesson Notes

Lesson Resources

Teaching Mathematics with Manipulatives
- student recording sheet 1-3b

Glencoe Mathematics Classroom Manipulative Kit
- metric measuring tape

GETTING STARTED

Teaching Tip You may want to have a setup already prepared for students to examine.

TEACH

- Have students tape the bottom of the chute at the 0-meter mark so that it doesn't slide when they are raising the chute.
- Make sure students slide the vertical meterstick forward as they raise the chute. Otherwise the height measurement will not be accurate.

ASSESS

Observe as students solve the **Writing Math** exercises. They should:
- graph ordered pairs on a coordinate grid,
- describe the appearance of the graphed points, and
- explain the relationship between raising the chute and the distance the ball travels.

1-3b HANDS-ON LAB

A Follow-Up of Lesson 1-3

Graphing Data

What You'll LEARN

Graph and interpret data.

Materials
- metric measuring tape
- masking tape
- cardboard
- 2 metersticks
- tennis ball

Hands-On Mini Labs and **Hands-On Labs** use manipulatives and models to help students learn key concepts.

INVESTIGATE *Work in groups of 4.*

In this Lab, you will investigate the relationship between the height of a chute and the distance an object travels as it leaves the chute.

STEP 1 Make a meter-long chute for the ball out of cardboard. Reinforce the chute by taping it to one of the metersticks.

STEP 2 Use the tape measure to mark off a distance of 3 meters on the floor. Make a 0-meter mark and a 3-meter mark using tape.

STEP 3 Place the end of your chute at the edge of the 0-meter mark. Raise the back of the chute to a height of 5 centimeters.

STEP 4 Let a tennis ball roll down the chute. When the ball stops, measure how far it is from the 3-meter mark.

STEP 5 Copy the table shown and record your results. If the ball stops short of the 3-meter mark, record the distance as a negative number. If the ball passes the 3-meter mark, record the distance as a positive number.

STEP 6 Raise the chute by 5 centimeters and repeat the experiment. Continue until the chute is 40 centimeters high.

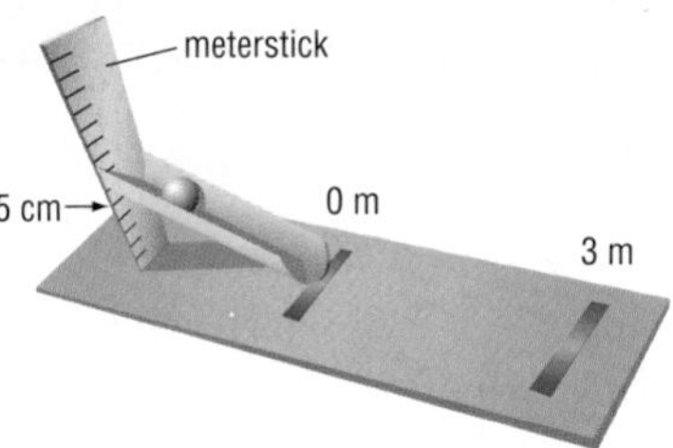

Height h of Chute (cm)	Distance d from 3-meter Mark (cm)
5	
10	
15	

Writing Math

Work with a partner.

1. **Graph** the ordered pairs (h, d) on a coordinate grid.
2. **Describe** how the points appear on your graph.
3. **Describe** how raising the chute affects the distance the ball travels.
4. Use your graph to **predict** how far the ball will roll when the chute is raised to the 50-centimeter mark. Then check your prediction.

1. See students' work.
2. See students' work.
3. See margin.
4. See students' work.

Answer

3. Raising the chute causes the ball to travel farther, until the chute reaches a certain height, after which the distance the ball travels will begin to decrease.

1-4 Adding Integers

What You'll LEARN

Add integers.

NEW Vocabulary

opposites
additive inverse

REVIEW Vocabulary

addend: numbers that are added together
sum: the result when two or more numbers are added together

Review Vocabulary lists terms and definitions presented earlier in the course.

1. Write an integer that describes the game show host's statement.
2. Write an addition sentence that describes this situation.

1. −13,200 2. −3,200 + (−7,400) + (−2,600) = −13,200

The equation $-3{,}200 + (-7{,}400) + (-2{,}600) = -13{,}200$ is an example of adding integers with the same sign. Notice that the sign of the sum is the same as the sign of each addend.

EXAMPLE Add Integers with the Same Sign

1 Find $-4 + (-2)$.

Method 1 Use a number line.
- Start at zero.
- Move 4 units left.
- From there, move 2 units left.

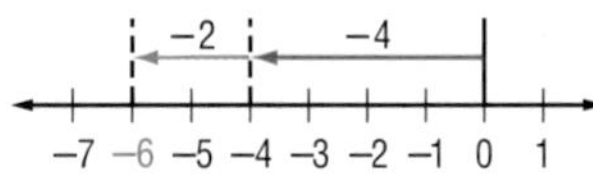

Method 2 Use counters.

−4 + (−2) −4 + (−2) = −6

So, $-4 + (-2) = -6$.

Your Turn Add using a number line or counters.

a. $-3 + (-2)$ **−5** b. $1 + 5$ **6** c. $-5 + (-4)$ **−9**

These examples suggest a rule for adding integers with the same sign.

Noteables™ Key Concept: Add Integers with the Same Sign

Words To add integers with the same sign, add their absolute values. Give the result the same sign as the integers.

Examples $-7 + (-3) = -10$ $5 + 4 = 9$

TEACHING TIP

When adding integers on a number line, students should always start at zero. Remind students to move right to model a positive integer and left to model a negative integer.

1-4 Lesson Notes

Lesson Resources

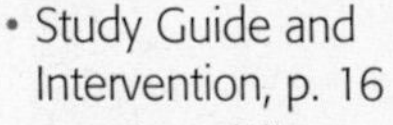

Chapter 1 Resource Masters FAST FILE
- Study Guide and Intervention, p. 16
- Practice: Skills, p. 17
- Practice: Word Problems, p. 18
- Reading to Learn Mathematics, p. 19
- Enrichment, p. 20

Parent and Student Study Guide Online Worksheets, 1-4
Noteables™: Interactive Study Notebook with Foldables™, 1-4
Virtual Activities CD-ROM, Adding Integers

1 Focus

5-Minute Check 1-4

Use as a quiz or review of Lesson 1-3. (Also available as a transparency)

Bellringer

Problem Solving Have students suggest ways to find the sum of 33 and –24. List the suggested methods on the board and try any feasible approaches as a class. **Possible methods: use a calculator; use a number line; subtract 24 from 33; use positive and negative counters and remove any zero pairs and count the remaining counters.**

(Continued in bottom margin.)

Ask students to make conjectures about how to add integers from this activity. You may wish to refer to this activity throughout the lesson to help students make connections.

Reading to Learn Mathematics, p. 19 ELL

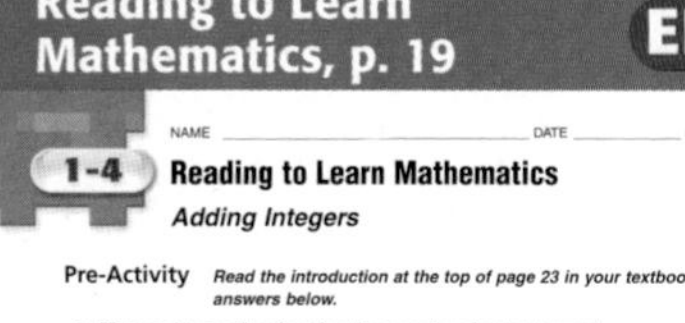

NAME ________ DATE ______ PERIOD ____

1-4 Reading to Learn Mathematics
Adding Integers

Pre-Activity *Read the introduction at the top of page 23 in your textbook. Write your answers below.*

1. Write an integer that describes the game show host's statement. −13,200
2. Write an addition sentence that describes this situation. −3,200 + (−7,400) + (−2,600) = −13,200

Reading the Lesson

3. Look at your answer for Exercise 2. Identify each number in the addition sentence as either an addend or a sum. −3,200: addend; −7,400: addend; −2,600: addend; −13,200: sum

Identify the number with the greater absolute value.

4. 4, 8 8
5. −3, 5 5
6. 9, −12 −12
7. −23, −16 −23

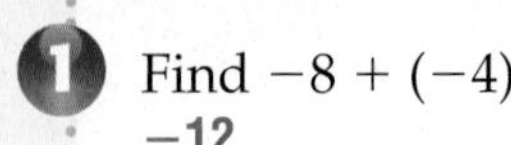

2 Teach

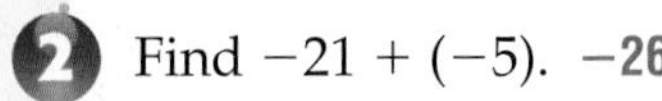

In-Class Examples

1. Find $-8 + (-4)$. **−12**
2. Find $-21 + (-5)$. **−26**
3. Find $4 + (-6)$. **−2**
4. Find $-5 + 9$. **4**

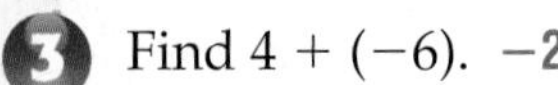

Tips for New Teachers

Using Applications Encourage students to think of real-life situations when they aren't sure they understand a problem. For example, $-4 + (-12) + 4$ could represent owing your sister \$4, then borrowing \$12 to buy a CD. Then you got your allowance and gave her \$4. You now owe her \$12.

TEACHING TIP

To explain why $-28 + 0 = -28$, remind students of the Addition Property of Zero. This property states that the sum of a number and zero is that same number.

EXAMPLE Add Integers with the Same Sign

2 **Find $-13 + (-18)$.**

$-13 + (-18) = -31$ Add $|-13|$ and $|-18|$. Both numbers are negative, so the sum is negative.

Your Turn **Add.**

d. $-43 + -11$ **−54** e. $15 + 22$ **37** f. $-28 + 0$ **−28**

Models can also help you add integers with different signs.

EXAMPLES Add Integers with Different Signs

STUDY TIP

Adding Integers on an Integer Mat When one positive counter is paired with one negative counter, the result is called a *zero pair*.

3 **Find $5 + (-2)$.**

Method 1 Use a number line.

- Start at zero.
- Move 5 units right.
- From there, move 2 units left.

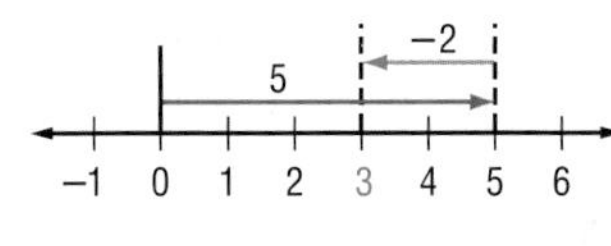

$5 + (-2) = 3$

Method 2 Use counters.

Remove zero pairs.

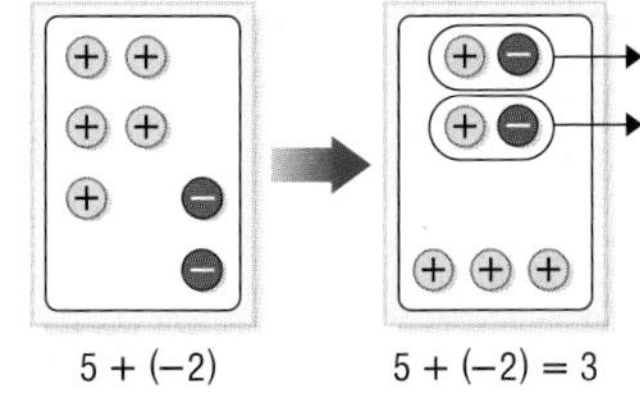

$5 + (-2)$ $5 + (-2) = 3$

4 **Find $-4 + 3$.**

Method 1 Use a number line.

- Start at zero.
- Move 4 units left.
- From there, move 3 units right.

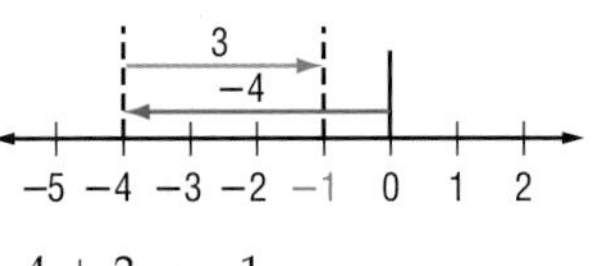

$-4 + 3 = -1$

Method 2 Use counters.

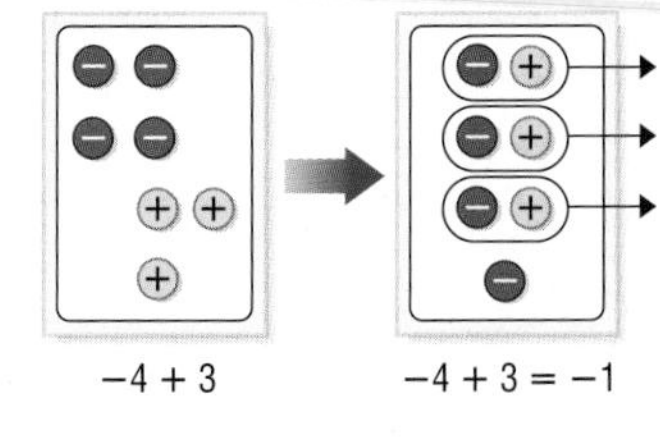

$-4 + 3$ $-4 + 3 = -1$

Your Turn **Add using a number line or counters.**

g. $7 + (-5)$ **2** h. $-6 + 4$ **−2** i. $-1 + 8$ **7**

These examples suggest a rule for adding integers with different signs.

Noteables™ **Key Concept: Add Integers with Different Signs**

Words To add integers with different signs, subtract their absolute values. Give the result the same sign as the integer with the greater absolute value.

Examples $8 + (-3) = 5$ $-8 + 3 = -5$

DAILY INTERVENTION **Differentiated Instruction**

Visual/Spatial Have the class track deposits and expenditures for a checking account using a number line. Give each student a chronological list of transactions rounded to the nearest dollar. Start students off with a balance of \$1,000 and have them track the account on a number line and as a running tally to find the balance after all transactions are recorded. Finally, the students should compare the final tally with the final position on the number line to check their work.

EXAMPLE Add Integers with Different Signs

5 **Find $-14 + 9$.**

$-14 + 9 = -5$ To find $-14 + 9$, subtract $|9|$ from $|-14|$. The sum is negative because $|-14| > |9|$.

Your Turn **Add.**

j. $-20 + 4$ **−16** k. $17 + (-6)$ **11** l. $-8 + 27$ **19**

Two numbers with the same absolute value but different signs are called **opposites**. For example, −2 and 2 are opposites. An integer and its opposite are also called **additive inverses**.

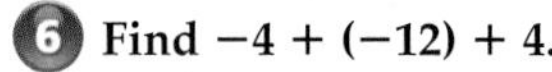

Noteables™ **Key Concept: Additive Inverse Property**

Words The sum of any number and its additive inverse is zero.

Symbols

Arithmetic	Algebra
$7 + (-7) = 0$	$x + (-x) = 0$

The Commutative, Associative, and Identity Properties, along with the Additive Inverse Property, can help you add three or more integers.

EXAMPLES Add Three or More Integers

6 **Find $-4 + (-12) + 4$.**

$-4 + (-12) + 4 = -4 + 4 + (-12)$	Commutative Property
$= 0 + (-12)$	Additive Inverse Property
$= -12$	Identity Property of Addition

7 **Find $-9 + 8 + (-2) + 16$.**

$-9 + 8 + (-2) + 16 = -9 + (-2) + 8 + 16$	Commutative Property
$= [-9 + (-2)] + (8 + 16)$	Associative Property
$= -11 + 24$ or 13	Simplify.

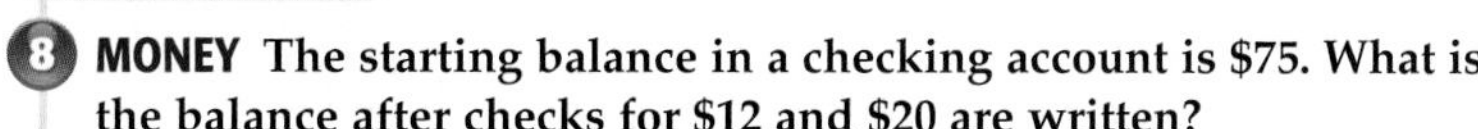

STUDY TIP

Mental Math

- One way to add a group of integers mentally is to look for addends that are opposites.
- Another way is to group the positive addends together and the negative addends together. Then add.

EXAMPLE Use Integers to Solve a Problem

8 **MONEY The starting balance in a checking account is \$75. What is the balance after checks for \$12 and \$20 are written?**

Writing a check *decreases* your account balance, so integers for this situation are −12 and −20. Add these integers to the starting balance to find the new balance.

$75 + (-12) + (-20) = 75 + [-12 + (-20)]$	Associative Property
$= 75 + (-32)$	$-12 + (-20) = -32$
$= 43$	Simplify.

The balance is now \$43.

Math Online msmath3.net/extra_examples

In-Class Examples

5 Find 33 + (–16). **17**

6 Find 2 + (–5) + (–3). **−6**

7 Find –17 + 6 + 17 + 20. **26**

8 **STOCKS** An investor owns 50 shares in a video game manufacturer. A broker purchases 30 shares more for the client on Tuesday. On Friday, the investor asks the broker to sell 65 shares. How many shares of this stock will the client own after these trades are completed? **15 shares**

3 Practice/Apply

FOLDABLES™ Follow-Up Remind students to use their Foldable tables to record in words and symbols what they learn about adding integers. For example, they might explain how to add integers with the same sign and how to add integers with different signs and compare the two procedures.

Foldables™ Follow-Ups remind you to encourage students to add to their Foldables as they work through the chapter and use them to review for the chapter test.

Which One Doesn't Belong? In Exercise 3, ask students what clues helped them determine that the third set of numbers was different. Point out that while the third pair of numbers is different because both numbers are positive, it is also the only pair for which the sum of the numbers is not zero.

About the Exercises...

Guided Practice Key

Exercises	Examples
4	1, 2
5–7	3–5
8, 9	6, 7
10	8

Assignment Guide

Basic: 11–43 odd, 45–58

Average: 11–43 odd, 44–58

Enriched: 12–42 even, 43–54 (Optional: 55–58)

Alert! The Data Update for Exercises 43–44 requires access to the Internet.

Students practice the same concepts in Exercises 11–42 if they are assigned odd or even problems.

Skill and Concept Check

1. *Writing Math* Explain how to add integers that have different signs. **See margin.**
2. **OPEN ENDED** Give an example of a positive and a negative integer whose sum is negative. Then find their sum. **Sample answer: 8 and −11; 8 + (−11) = −3**
3. **Which One Doesn't Belong?** Identify the pair of numbers that does not have the same characteristic as the other three. Explain your reasoning.

−16 and 16	22 and −22	45 and 54	−3 and 3

45 and 54; All of the other numbers are additive inverses.

GUIDED PRACTICE

Add.

4. $-4 + (-5)$ **−9**
5. $10 + (-6)$ **4**
6. $7 + (-18)$ **−11**
7. $-21 + 8$ **−13**
8. $11 + (-3) + 9$ **17**
9. $-14 + 2 + (-15) + 7$ **−20**
10. **GOLF** Suppose a player shot −5, +2, −3, and −2 in four rounds of a tournament. What was the player's final score? **−8 or 8 under par**

Practice and Applications

HOMEWORK HELP

For Exercises	See Examples
11–16, 25–26	1, 2
17–24, 27–28	3–5
33–38	6, 7
43–44	8

Extra Practice See pages 617, 648.

Add.

11. $-18 + (-8)$ **−26**
12. $7 + 16$ **23**
13. $14 + 8$ **22**
14. $-14 + (-6)$ **−20**
15. $-3 + (-12)$ **−15**
16. $-5 + (-31)$ **−36**
17. $20 + (-5)$ **15**
18. $-15 + 8$ **−7**
19. $45 + (-4)$ **41**
20. $-19 + 2$ **−17**
21. $-10 + 34$ **24**
22. $17 + (-18)$ **−1**
23. $13 + (-43)$ **−30**
24. $-21 + 30$ **9**
25. $-7 + (-25)$ **−32**
26. $-54 + (-14)$ **−68**
27. $36 + (-47)$ **−11**
28. $-41 + 33$ **−8**

Write an addition expression to describe each situation. Then find each sum.

29. **FOOTBALL** A team gains 8 yards on one play, then loses 5 yards on the next. **8 + (−5); 3**
30. **SCUBA DIVING** A scuba diver dives 125 feet. Later, she rises 46 feet. **−125 + 46; −79**
31. **ELEVATOR** You get on an elevator in the basement of a building, which is one floor below ground level. The elevator goes up 7 floors. **−1 + 7; 6**
32. **WEATHER** The temperature outside is −2°F. The temperature drops by 9°. **−2 + (−9); −11**

Add.

33. $8 + (-6) + 5$ **7**
34. $-7 + 2 + (-9)$ **−14**
35. $-5 + 11 + (-4)$ **2**
36. $3 + (-15) + 1$ **−11**
37. $-13 + 6 + (-8) + 13$ **−2**
38. $9 + (-4) + (-12) + (-9)$ **−16**

Evaluate each expression if $a = -5$, $b = 2$, and $c = -3$.

39. $8 + a$ **3**
40. $|b| + c$ **−1**
41. $a + b + c$ **−6**
42. $|a + b|$ **3**

Answers

1. **To add numbers with different signs, subtract the absolute values of the numbers. Then use the sign of the number with the greater absolute value.**

45. **If x and y have different signs, then $|x + y| \neq |x| + |y|$. If x and y have the same sign, then $|x + y| = |x| + |y|$.**

MUSIC TRENDS For Exercises 43 and 44, use the table below that shows the change in music sales to the nearest percent from 1998 to 2002.

Style of Music	Percent of Music Sold in 1998	Percent Change as of 2002
Rock	26	−1
Rap/Hip Hop	10	+4
Pop	10	−1
Country	14	−3

Source: Recording Industry Assoc. of America

43. What is the percent of music sold in 2002 for each of these musical categories?

44. What was the total percent change in the sale of these types of music? **−1**

43. Rock: 25, Rap/Hip Hop: 14, Pop: 9, Country: 11

Data Update What percent of music sold last year was rock, rap/hip hop, pop, or country? Visit msmath3.net/data_update to learn more.

45. **CRITICAL THINKING** Determine whether the following statement is *always*, *sometimes*, or *never* true. **See margin for explanation.**

If x and y are integers, then $|x + y| = |x| + |y|$. **sometimes**

Spiral Review with Standardized Test Practice

46. **MULTIPLE CHOICE** A stock on the New York Stock Exchange opened at $52 on Monday morning. The table shows the change in the value of the stock for each day that week. What was the stock worth at the close of business on Friday? **B**

Day	Change
Monday	−$2
Tuesday	+$1
Wednesday	+$3
Thursday	−$1
Friday	−$4

Ⓐ $41   Ⓑ $49   Ⓒ $57   Ⓓ $63

47. **MULTIPLE CHOICE** Simplify $-6 + |5| + (-3) + 4$. **F**

Ⓕ 0   Ⓖ −4   Ⓗ −10   Ⓘ −18

Replace each ● with <, >, or = to make a true sentence. (Lesson 1-3)

48. $-6 \bullet -11$ **>**   49. $5 \bullet -5$ **>**   50. $5 \bullet |8|$ **<**   51. $|-7| \bullet -7$ **>**

52. **WEATHER** The time *t* in seconds between seeing lightning and hearing thunder can be used to estimate a storm's distance in miles. How far away is a storm if this time is 15 seconds? Use the expression $\frac{t}{5}$. (Lesson 1-2) **3 mi**

TELEVISION For Exercises 53 and 54, use the information below and the graph at the right.
The graph shows the number of prime-time television viewers in millions for different age groups. (Lesson 1-1)

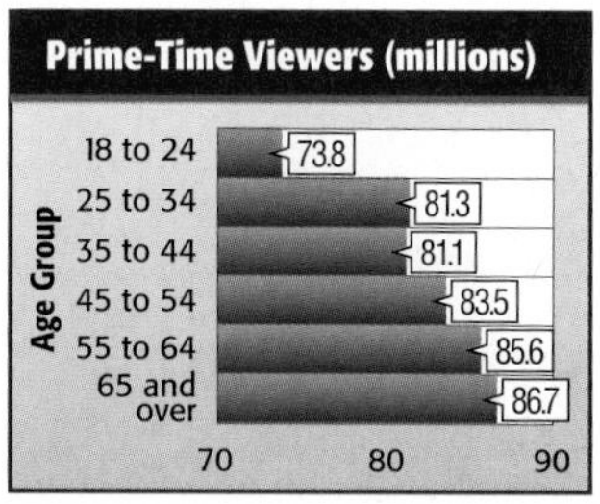

Prime-Time Viewers (millions)

Age Group	Viewers (millions)
18 to 24	73.8
25 to 34	81.3
35 to 44	81.1
45 to 54	83.5
55 to 64	85.6
65 and over	86.7

(Horizontal axis: 70, 80, 90)

53. Estimate the total number of viewers for all the age groups given. **Sample answer: about 500 million**

54. About how many more people 65 years and over watch prime-time television than 18 to 24-year-olds? **Sample answer: about 13 million**

GETTING READY FOR THE NEXT LESSON

PREREQUISITE SKILL Evaluate each expression if x = 3, y = 9, and z = 5. (Lesson 1-2)

55. $x + 14$ **17**   56. $z - 2$ **3**   57. $y - z$ **4**   58. $x + y - z$ **7**

msmath3.net/self_check_quiz

4 Assess

Open-Ended Assessment

Writing Have students write a paragraph that compares adding integers on a number line with adding integers using counters.

There is a Study Guide and Intervention, Practice: Skills, Practice: Word Problems, Reading to Learn Mathematics, and Enrichment Master for every lesson. These masters can be found in the Chapter Resource Masters.

Study Guide and Intervention, p. 16

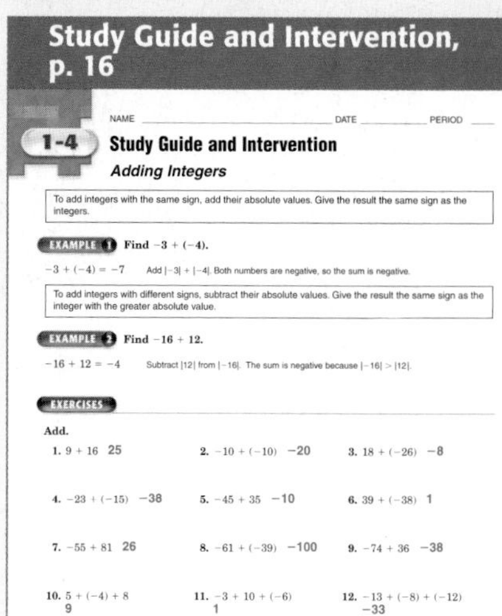

NAME ______ DATE ______ PERIOD ____

1-4 Study Guide and Intervention
Adding Integers

To add integers with the same sign, add their absolute values. Give the result the same sign as the integers.

EXAMPLE 1 **Find −3 + (−4).**

$-3 + (-4) = -7$ Add $|-3| + |-4|$. Both numbers are negative, so the sum is negative.

To add integers with different signs, subtract their absolute values. Give the result the same sign as the integer with the greater absolute value.

EXAMPLE 2 **Find −16 + 12.**

$-16 + 12 = -4$ Subtract $|12|$ from $|-16|$. The sum is negative because $|-16| > |12|$.

EXERCISES

Add.

1. $9 + 16$ **25**   2. $-10 + (-10)$ **−20**   3. $18 + (-26)$ **−8**
4. $-23 + (-15)$ **−38**   5. $-45 + 35$ **−10**   6. $39 + (-38)$ **1**
7. $-55 + 81$ **26**   8. $-61 + (-39)$ **−100**   9. $-74 + 36$ **−38**
10. $5 + (-4) + 8$ **9**   11. $-3 + 10 + (-6)$ **1**   12. $-13 + (-8) + (-12)$ **−33**
13. $3 + (-10) + (-16) + 11$ **−12**   14. $-17 + 31 + (-14) + 26$ **26**

Evaluate each expression if x = 4 and y = −3.

15. $11 + y$ **8**   16. $x + (-6)$ **−2**   17. $y + 2$ **−1**
18. $|x + y|$ **1**   19. $|x| + y$ **1**   20. $x + |y|$ **7**

Practice: Skills, p. 17

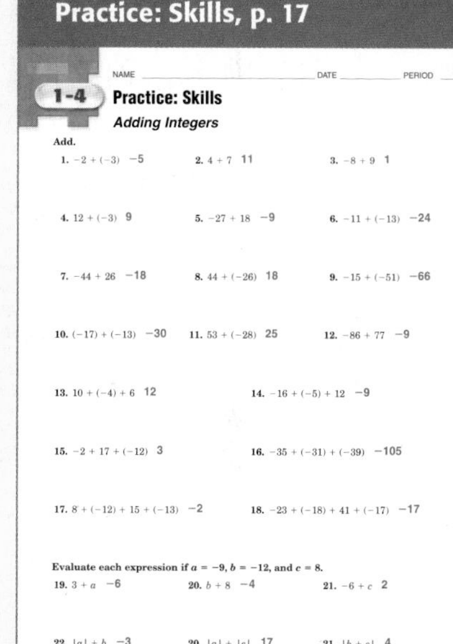

NAME ______ DATE ______ PERIOD ____

1-4 Practice: Skills
Adding Integers

Add.

1. $-2 + (-3)$ **−5**   2. $4 + 7$ **11**   3. $-8 + 9$ **1**
4. $12 + (-3)$ **9**   5. $-27 + 18$ **−9**   6. $-11 + (-13)$ **−24**
7. $-44 + 26$ **−18**   8. $44 + (-26)$ **18**   9. $-15 + (-51)$ **−66**
10. $(-17) + (-13)$ **−30**   11. $53 + (-28)$ **25**   12. $-86 + 77$ **−9**
13. $10 + (-4) + 6$ **12**   14. $-16 + (-5) + 12$ **−9**
15. $-2 + 17 + (-12)$ **3**   16. $-35 + (-31) + (-39)$ **−105**
17. $8 + (-12) + 15 + (-13)$ **−2**   18. $-23 + (-18) + 41 + (-17)$ **−17**

Evaluate each expression if a = −9, b = −12, and c = 8.

19. $3 + a$ **−6**   20. $b + 8$ **−4**   21. $-6 + c$ **2**
22. $|a| + b$ **−3**   20. $|a| + |c|$ **17**   21. $|b + c|$ **4**

Practice: Word Problems, p. 18

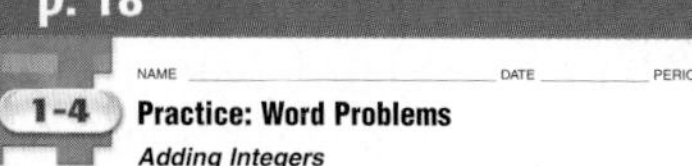

NAME ______ DATE ______ PERIOD ____

1-4 Practice: Word Problems
Adding Integers

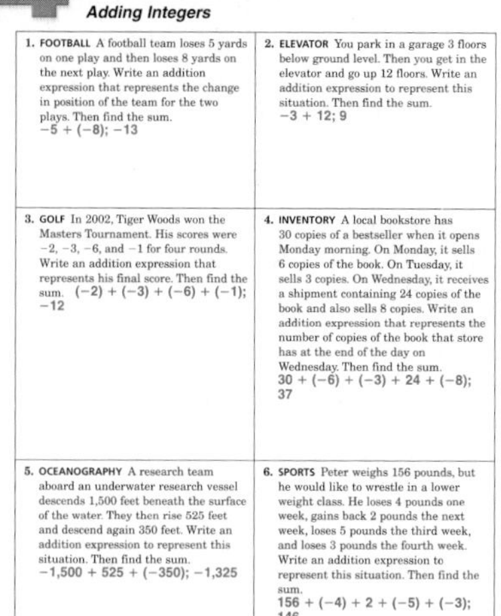

1. **FOOTBALL** A football team loses 5 yards on one play and then loses 8 yards on the next play. Write an addition expression that represents the change in position of the team for the two plays. Then find the sum. **−5 + (−8); −13**

2. **ELEVATOR** You park in a garage 3 floors below ground level. Then you get in the elevator and go up 12 floors. Write an addition expression to represent this situation. Then find the sum. **−3 + 12; 9**

3. **GOLF** In 2002, Tiger Woods won the Masters Tournament. His scores were −2, −3, −6, and −1 for four rounds. Write an addition expression that represents his final score. Then find the sum. **(−2) + (−3) + (−6) + (−1); −12**

4. **INVENTORY** A local bookstore has 30 copies of a bestseller when it opens Monday morning. On Monday, it sells 6 copies of the book. On Tuesday, it sells 3 copies. On Wednesday, it receives a shipment containing 24 copies of the book and also sells 8 copies. Write an addition expression that represents the number of copies of the book that store has at the end of the day on Wednesday. Then find the sum. **30 + (−6) + (−3) + 24 + (−8); 37**

5. **OCEANOGRAPHY** A research team aboard an underwater research vessel descends 1,500 feet beneath the surface of the water. They then rise 525 feet and descend again 350 feet. Write an addition expression to represent this situation. Then find the sum. **−1,500 + 525 + (−350); −1,325**

6. **SPORTS** Peter weighs 156 pounds, but he would like to wrestle in a lower weight class. He loses 4 pounds one week, gains back 2 pounds the next week, loses 5 pounds the third week, and loses 3 pounds the fourth week. Write an addition expression to represent this situation. Then find the sum. **156 + (−4) + 2 + (−5) + (−3); 146**

1-5 Lesson Notes

Lesson Resources

Chapter 1 Resource Masters
- Study Guide and Intervention, p. 21
- Practice: Skills, p. 22
- Practice: Word Problems, p. 23
- Reading to Learn Mathematics, p. 24
- Enrichment, p. 25

Parent and Student Study Guide Online Worksheets, 1-5

Noteables™: Interactive Study Notebook with Foldables™, 1-5

FAST FILE

Focus

5-Minute Check 1-5

Use as a quiz or review of Lesson 1-4. (Also available as a transparency)

Bellringer

Reading Mathematics The word *opposite* comes from Latin and means *across from* or *facing*. Relate the word to integers by asking students "What is the opposite of 3 steps up?" **3 steps down** "What is the opposite of 3 steps left?" **3 steps right** Then have two student volunteers stand on a number line drawn on the floor with tape. Each student starts at zero. One student steps 3 units left and, at the same time, the other one steps 3 units right. (Continued in bottom margin.)

Reading to Learn Mathematics, p. 24 ELL

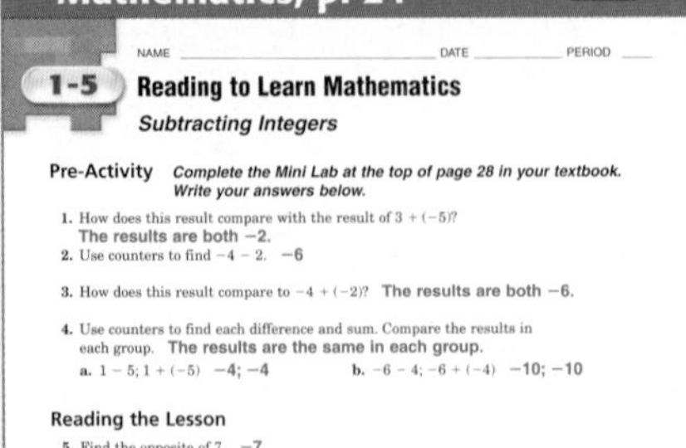
NAME ______ DATE ______ PERIOD ____

1-5 Reading to Learn Mathematics

Subtracting Integers

Pre-Activity *Complete the Mini Lab at the top of page 28 in your textbook. Write your answers below.*

1. How does this result compare with the result of $3 + (-5)$? The results are both -2.
2. Use counters to find $-4 - 2$. -6
3. How does this result compare to $-4 + (-2)$? The results are both -6.
4. Use counters to find each difference and sum. Compare the results in each group. The results are the same in each group.
   a. $1 - 5$; $1 + (-5)$ -4; -4 b. $-6 - 4$; $-6 + (-4)$ -10; -10

Reading the Lesson

5. Find the opposite of 7. -7
6. Find the additive inverse of 7. -7

1-5 Subtracting Integers

HANDS-ON Mini Lab

Materials
- counters
- integer mat

What You'll LEARN

Subtract integers.

Work with a partner.

You can also use counters to model the subtraction of two integers. Follow these steps to model $3 - 5$. Remember that subtract means *take away* or *remove*.

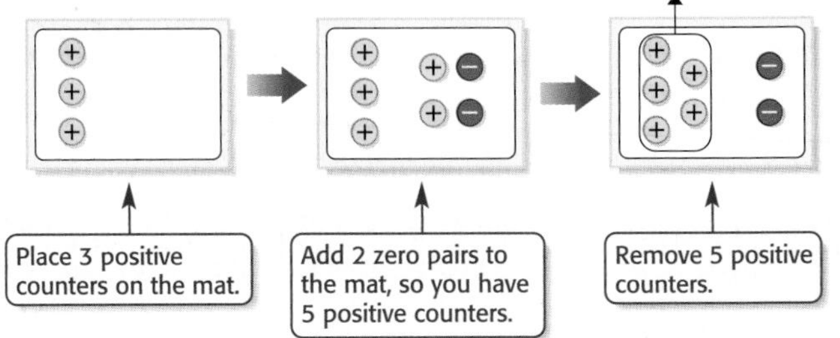

Since 2 negative counters remain, $3 - 5 = -2$. **1. The results are both -2.**

1. How does this result compare with the result of $3 + (-5)$?
2. Use counters to find $-4 - 2$. **-6** **3. The results are both -6.**
3. How does this result compare to $-4 + (-2)$?
4. Use counters to find each difference and sum. Compare the results in each group. **The results are the same in each group.**
   a. $1 - 5$; $1 + (-5)$ **-4; -4** b. $-6 - 4$; $-6 + (-4)$ **-10; -10**

When you subtract $3 - 5$, as you did using counters in the Mini Lab, the result is the same as adding $3 + (-5)$. When you subtract $-4 - 2$, the result is the same as adding $-4 + (-2)$.

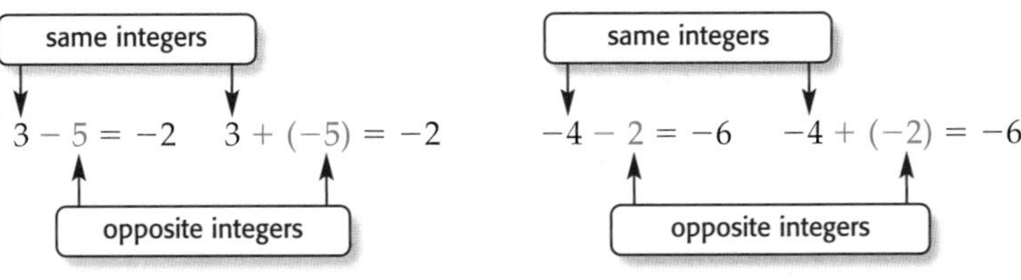

These and other examples suggest a method for subtracting integers.

TEACHING TIP

Be sure to tell students that $-b$ does not necessarily mean that the value of $-b$ is negative. For example, if $b = -4$, then its opposite, $-b$, is 4.

Noteables™ **Key Concept: Subtract Integers**

Words To subtract an integer, add its opposite or additive inverse.

Symbols

Arithmetic	Algebra
$4 - 7 = 4 + (-7)$ or -3	$a - b = a + (-b)$

The word *inverse* also comes from Latin and means turned *upside down*. Draw a vertical line on the chalkboard and hold a rigid, flat object such as a notebook against the chalkboard. Mark where the object crosses the line. Then flip the object down, making the pivot point zero. Mark the new point where the object crosses the line. The top and bottom points are opposites and additive inverses of one another.

EXAMPLES Subtract a Positive Integer

1 **Find 9 − 12.**

$9 - 12 = 9 + (-12)$ To subtract 12, add −12.

$= -3$ Add.

2 **Find −6 − 8.**

$-6 - 8 = -6 + (-8)$ To subtract 8, add −8.

$= -14$ Add.

Your Turn Subtract.

a. $3 - 8$ **−5** b. $-5 - 4$ **−9** c. $10 - 7$ **3**

In Examples 1 and 2, you subtracted a positive integer by adding its opposite, a negative integer. To subtract a negative integer, you also add its opposite, a positive integer.

EXAMPLES Subtract a Negative Integer

3 **Find 7 − (−15).**

$7 - (-15) = 7 + 15$ To subtract −15, add 15.

$= 22$ Add.

4 **Find −30 − (−20).**

$-30 - (-20) = -30 + 20$ To subtract −20, add 20.

$= -10$ Add.

Your Turn Subtract.

d. $6 - (-7)$ **13** e. $-5 - (-19)$ **14** f. $-14 - (-2)$ **−12**

Common Error In Example 5, a common error is to replace *b* with 8 instead of its correct value of −8. Prevent this error by inserting parentheses before replacing *b* with its value.

$14 - b = 14 - (\ \ )$
$= 14 - (-8)$

Use the rule for subtracting integers to evaluate expressions.

EXAMPLES Evaluate Algebraic Expressions

Evaluate each expression if $a = 9$, $b = -8$, and $c = -2$.

5 $14 - b$

$14 - b = 14 - (-8)$ Replace *b* with −8.

$= 14 + 8$ To subtract −8, add 8.

$= 22$ Add.

6 $c - a$

$c - a = -2 - 9$ Replace *c* with −2 and *a* with 9.

$= -2 + (-9)$ To subtract 9, add −9.

$= -11$ Add.

Your Turn Evaluate each expression if $x = -5$ and $y = 7$.

g. $x - (-8)$ **3** h. $-3 - y$ **−10** i. $y - x - 3$ **9**

msmath3.net/extra_examples

2 Teach

In-Class Examples

Subtract.

1. Find $2 - 6$. **−4**
2. Find $-7 - 5$. **−12**
3. Find $11 - (-8)$. **19**
4. Find $-6 - (-9)$. **3**

Evaluate each expression if $p = 6$, $q = -3$, and $r = -7$.

5. $12 - r$ **19**
6. $q - p$ **−9**

DAILY INTERVENTION — Flexible Grouping

Adding and Subtracting Integers Assign students to teams for an integer addition/subtraction tournament. First have team members prepare each other for the tournament. Then have students compete against members of other teams with similar abilities as determined by the teacher. The winner of each competition earns points for his or her team. After a pre-selected number of questions or amount of time, the team with the most points wins.

Daily Intervention notes help you help students when they need it most. **Flexible Grouping** suggestions provide a variety of grouping options.

3 Practice/Apply

FOLDABLES™ Follow-Up Remind students to use their Foldable tables to record in words and symbols what they learn about subtracting integers. For example, they might explain how to subtract integers using additive inverses.

DAILY INTERVENTION **FIND THE ERROR** In Exercise 2, reinforce the concept of subtracting the second integer from an existing, fixed quantity. Illustrate with a real-life example, such as when subtracting 3 oranges from 5 oranges, the original 5 oranges do not become negative or change in any way. Emphasize that the same is true when subtracting from a negative number; its sign does not change in any way.

About the Exercises...

Guided Practice Key

Exercises	Examples
3, 5	1
4	2
6	3
7, 8	4
9	5
10, 11	6

Assignment Guide

Basic: 13–27 odd, 31–45 odd, 46–57

Average: 13–45 odd, 46–57

Enriched: 12–44 even, 46–53 (Optional: 54–57)

Students practice the same concepts in Exercises 12–41 if they are assigned odd or even problems.

Skill and Concept Check

1. **OPEN ENDED** Write an expression involving the subtraction of a negative integer. Then write an equivalent addition expression. Sample answer: 7 − (−3); 7 + 3
2. **FIND THE ERROR** Anna and David are finding −5 − (−8). Who is correct? Explain.

Anna
−5 − (−8) = 5 + 8
= 13

David
−5 − (−8) = −5 + 8
= 3

David; only the second integer should be replaced with its opposite.

Find the Error exercises help students identify and address common errors before they occur.

GUIDED PRACTICE

Subtract.

3. 8 − 13 −5
4. −4 − 10 −14
5. 5 − 24 −19
6. 7 − (−3) 10
7. −2 − (−6) 4
8. −18 − (−7) −11

Evaluate each expression if $n = 10$, $m = -4$, and $p = -12$.

9. $n - 17$ −7
10. $m - p$ 8
11. $p + n - m$ 2

★ indicates increased difficulty

Practice and Applications

HOMEWORK HELP

For Exercises	See Examples
12–33, 42–44	1–4
34–41	5, 6

Extra Practice See pages 617, 648.

Subtract.

12. 5 − 9 −4
13. 1 − 8 −7
14. 12 − 15 −3
15. 4 − 16 −12
16. −6 − 3 −9
17. −8 − 8 −16
18. −3 − 14 −17
19. −7 − 13 −20
20. 2 − (−8) 10
21. 9 − (−5) 14
22. 10 − (−2) 12
23. 5 − (−11) 16
24. −5 − (−4) −1
25. −18 − (−7) −11
26. −3 − (−6) 3
27. −7 − (−14) 7
★28. 2 − |12| −10
★29. |−6| − |8| −2

GEOGRAPHY **For Exercises 30–33, use the table at the right.** 32. 342 m

30. How far below the surface is the deepest part of Lake Huron? 405 m
31. How far below the surface is the deepest part of Lake Superior? 589 m
32. Find the difference between the deepest part of Lake Erie and the deepest part of Lake Superior.
33. How does the deepest part of Lake Michigan compare with the deepest part of Lake Ontario? Lake Michigan is 37 m deeper than Lake Ontario.

Great Lake	Deepest Point (m)	Surface Elevation (m)
Erie	−64	174
Huron	−229	176
Michigan	−281	176
Ontario	−244	75
Superior	−406	183

Source: National Ocean Service

Evaluate each expression if $a = -3$, $b = 14$, and $c = -8$.

34. $b - 20$ −6
35. $a - c$ 5
36. $a - b$ −17
37. $c - 15$ −23
38. $a + b$ 11
39. $c + b$ 6
40. $b - a - c$ 25
41. $a - c - b$ −9

42. **SPACE** On Mercury, the temperatures range from 805°F during the day to −275°F at night. Find the drop in temperature from day to night. **1,080°F**

WEATHER For Exercises 43 and 44, use the following information and the table at the right.
The wind makes the outside temperature feel colder than the actual temperature.

Wind Chill Temperature				
	Wind (miles per hour)			
Temperature (F)	Calm	10	20	30
	20°	9°	4°	1°
	10°	−4°	−9°	−12°
	0°	−16°	−22°	−26°
	−10°	−28°	−35°	−39°

Source: National Weather Service

43. How much colder does a temperature of 0°F with a 30-mile-per-hour wind feel than the same temperature with a 10-mile-per-hour wind? **10°F**

44. How much warmer does 20°F feel than −10°F when there is a 30-mile-per-hour wind blowing? **40°F**

45. **WRITE A PROBLEM** Write a problem about a real-life situation involving subtraction of integers for which the answer is −4. **See margin.**

CRITICAL THINKING For Exercises 46 and 47, determine whether the statement is *true* or *false*. If *false*, give a counterexample.

46. If x is a positive integer and y is a positive integer, then $x - y$ is a positive integer. **false; $2 - 3 = -1$**

47. Subtraction of integers is commutative. **false; $3 - 2 \neq 2 - 3$**

Spiral Review with Standardized Test Practice

48. **MULTIPLE CHOICE** Use the thermometers at the right to determine how much the temperature increased between 8:00 A.M. and 12:00 P.M. **D**

Ⓐ 14°F Ⓑ 15°F Ⓒ 30°F Ⓓ 31°F

8:00 A.M. °F −8° 12:00 P.M. °F 23°

49. **MULTIPLE CHOICE** Find the distance between A and B. **I**

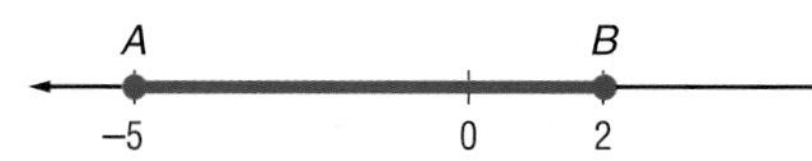

Ⓕ −7 units Ⓖ −3 units Ⓗ 3 units Ⓘ 7 units

50. **BASEBALL** The table at the right shows the money taken in (income) of several baseball teams in a recent year. What was the total income of all of these teams? (*Hint:* A gain is positive income and a loss is negative income.) (Lesson 1-4) **$3,555,000**

Team	Income (thousands)
Atlanta Braves	−$14,360
Chicago Cubs	$4,797
Florida Marlins	−$27,741
New York Yankees	$40,859

Source: www.mlb.com

Evaluate each expression. (Lesson 1-3)

51. $|-14| + |3|$ **17** 52. $|20| - |-5|$ **15**

53. Name the property shown by $12n = 12n + 0$. (Lesson 1-2) **Iden. (+)**

GETTING READY FOR THE NEXT LESSON

BASIC SKILL Multiply.

54. $4 \cdot 13$ **52** 55. $9 \cdot 15$ **135** 56. $2 \cdot 7 \cdot 6$ **84** 57. $3 \cdot 9 \cdot 4 \cdot 5$ **540**

Math Online msmath3.net/self_check_quiz

4 Assess

Open-Ended Assessment

Speaking Ask students to explain how to use addition to subtract an integer. Guide them to incorporate the concepts of opposite and additive inverses in their answers.

Answer

45. **Sample answer: You have $26 in your checking account. Find the balance in your account after you write a check for $30.**

Study Guide and Intervention, p. 21

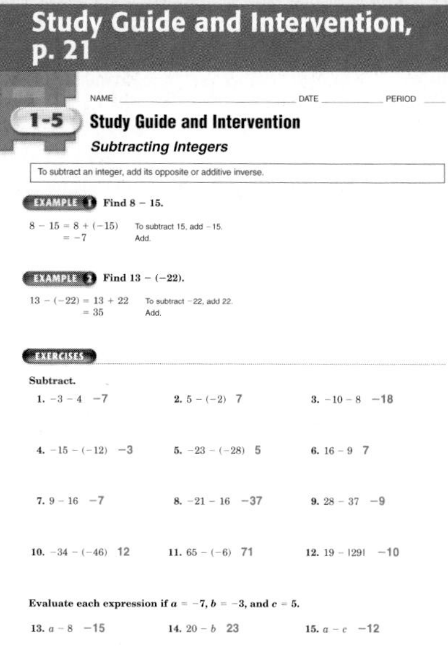

NAME ______ DATE ______ PERIOD ____

1-5 Study Guide and Intervention
Subtracting Integers

To subtract an integer, add its opposite or additive inverse.

EXAMPLE 1 Find 8 − 15.
8 − 15 = 8 + (−15) To subtract 15, add −15.
= −7 Add.

EXAMPLE 2 Find 13 − (−22).
13 − (−22) = 13 + 22 To subtract −22, add 22.
= 35 Add.

EXERCISES

Subtract.
1. −3 − 4 −7 2. 5 − (−2) 7 3. −10 − 8 −18
4. −15 − (−12) −3 5. −23 − (−28) 5 6. 16 − 9 7
7. 9 − 16 −7 8. −21 − 16 −37 9. 28 − 37 −9
10. −34 − (−46) 12 11. 65 − (−6) 71 12. 19 − (29) −10

Evaluate each expression if a = −7, b = −3, and c = 5.
13. a − 8 −15 14. 20 − b 23 15. a − c −12
16. c − b 8 17. b − a − c −1 18. c − b − a 15

Practice: Skills, p. 22

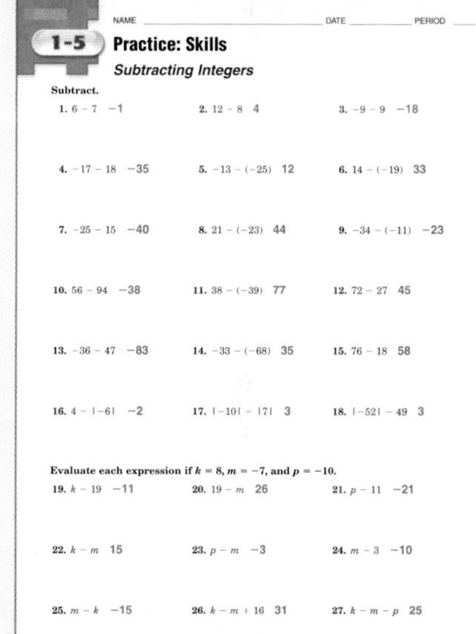

NAME ______ DATE ______ PERIOD ____

1-5 Practice: Skills
Subtracting Integers

Subtract.
1. 6 − 7 −1 2. 12 − 8 4 3. −9 − 9 −18
4. −17 − 18 −35 5. −13 − (−25) 12 6. 14 − (−19) 33
7. −25 − 15 −40 8. 21 − (−23) 44 9. −34 − (−11) −23
10. 56 − 94 −38 11. 38 − (−39) 77 12. 72 − 27 45
13. −36 − 47 −83 14. −33 − (−68) 35 15. 76 − 18 58
16. 4 − |−6| −2 17. |−10| − |7| 3 18. |−52| − 49 3

Evaluate each expression if k = 8, m = −7, and p = −10.
19. k − 19 −11 20. 19 − m 26 21. p − 11 −21
22. k − m 15 23. p − m −3 24. m − 3 −10
25. m − k −15 26. k − m + 16 31 27. k − m − p 25

Practice: Word Problems, p. 23

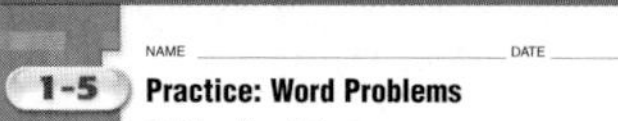

NAME ______ DATE ______ PERIOD ____

1-5 Practice: Word Problems
Subtracting Integers

GEOGRAPHY For Exercises 1 and 2, use the table. The table shows the elevations of several places on Earth.

Place	Elevation (feet)
Mt. McKinley	+20,320
Puerto Rican Trench	−28,232
Mt. Everest	+29,035
Dead Sea	−1,348
Death Valley	−282

1. Find the difference in elevation between the top of Mt. McKinley and the top of Mt. Everest. 8,715 ft

2. Find the difference in elevation between Death Valley and the Dead Sea. 1,066 ft

3. TEMPERATURE The highest recorded temperature on Earth was recorded in Africa at 136°F, while the lowest was −129°F in Antarctica. What is the range of temperatures recorded on Earth? 265°F

4. WEATHER If the overnight temperature at the Arctic Circle was −14°F, but the temperature rose to 8°F during the day, what was the difference between these high and low temperatures? 22°F

5. WATER The boiling point of water is 212°F, while −460°F is its absolute lowest temperature. Find the difference between these two temperatures. 672°F

6. STOCK MARKET During the course of one day, the price of a stock fluctuated between a high of $3 above the previous day's closing price and a low of $2 below the previous day's closing price. What was the difference between the high and low prices for that day? $5

Mid-Chapter Practice Test

Assessment Option

Mid-Chapter Test (Lessons 1-1 through 1-5) is available on p. 63 of the *Chapter 1 Resource Masters*.

ExamView® Pro

Use the networkable ExamView® Pro Testmaker CD-ROM to:

- Create **multiple versions** of tests.
- Create **modified** tests for **inclusion** students with one mouse click.
- **Edit** existing questions and **add** your own questions.
- Build tests aligned with state standards using built-in **state curriculum correlations.**
- Change **English** tests to **Spanish** with one mouse click and vice versa.

FOLDABLES™ Follow-Up Before students complete the Mid-Chapter Practice Test, encourage them to review the notes, definitions, concepts, and main ideas recorded in their Foldable tables.

Mid-Chapter Practice Test

Vocabulary and Concepts

1. **OPEN ENDED** Write an equation that illustrates the Associative Property of Addition. (Lesson 1-2) **Sample answer: $6 + (3 + x) = (6 + 3) + x$**
2. **Explain** how to determine the absolute value of a number. (Lesson 1-3) **Determine the distance that number is from 0 on a number line.**

Skills and Applications

3. **TRAVEL** A cruise ship has 148 rooms, with fifty on the two upper decks and the rest on the two lower decks. An upper deck room costs $1,100, and a lower deck room costs $900. Use the four-step plan to find the greatest possible room sales on one trip. (Lesson 1-1) **$143,200**
4. Evaluate $6 + 2(5 - 6 \div 2)$. (Lesson 1-2) **10**
5. Find the value of $x^2 + y^2 - z^2$ if $x = 3$, $y = 6$, and $z = 2$. (Lesson 1-2) **41**

The Mid-Chapter Practice Test reviews skills and concepts present in previous lessor

Replace each ● with <, >, or = to make a true sentence. (Lesson 1-3)

6. $-2 ● 3$ **<**
7. $5 ● -6$ **>**
8. $|-4| ● |4|$ **=**

Evaluate each expression if $x = -7$ and $y = 3$. (Lesson 1-3)

9. $|-2|$ **2**
10. $|3| + |-6|$ **9**
11. $5 + |x|$ **12**
12. $|x| + |y|$ **10**

Add or subtract. (Lessons 1-4 and 1-5)

13. $6 + (-1)$ **5**
14. $-5 + (-8)$ **−13**
15. $2 - 6$ **−4**
16. $-2 - 3$ **−5**
17. $-7 + 2$ **−5**
18. $-1 - 7$ **−8**

Standardized Test Practice

19. **GRID IN** You plant bushes in a row across the back and down two sides of a yard. A bush is planted at each of the four corners and every 4 meters. How many bushes are planted? (Lesson 1-1) **36**

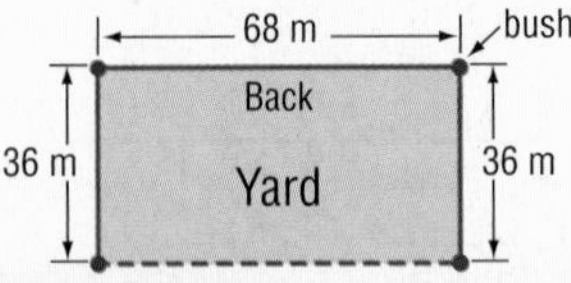

20. **MULTIPLE CHOICE** Naya recorded the low temperature for each of four days. Which list shows these temperatures in order from coldest to warmest? (Lesson 1-3) **D**

    Ⓐ −2.3°C, 1.4°C, −1.2°C, −0.7°C
    Ⓑ −0.7°C, −1.2°C, −2.3°C, 1.4°C
    Ⓒ −0.7°C, −1.2°C, 1.4°C, −2.3°C
    Ⓓ −2.3°C, −1.2°C, −0.7°C, 1.4°C

The Game Zone

A Place To Practice Your Math Skills

Math Skill
Comparing Integers

Absolutely!

GET READY!

Players: two
Materials: scissors, 14 index cards

GET SET!

- Cut each index card in half, making 28 cards.
- Copy the integers below, one integer onto each of 24 cards.

−17	−3	0	19	16	5	25	−10
3	−2	−8	−7	7	6	9	22
11	12	1	14	−20	−13	−16	−18

- Write "absolute value" on the 4 remaining cards and place these cards aside.
- Shuffle the integer cards and deal them facedown to each player. Each player gets 2 "absolute value" cards.

GO!

- Each player turns the top card from his or her pile faceup. The player with the greater card takes both cards and puts them facedown in a separate pile. When there are no more cards in the original pile, shuffle the cards in the second pile and use them.
- Twice during the game, each player can use an "absolute value" card after the two other cards have been played. When an absolute value card is played, players compare the absolute values of the integers on the cards. The player with the greater absolute value takes both cards. If there is a tie, continue play.
- **Who Wins?** The player who takes all of the cards is the winner.

Students will enjoy using **The Game Zone** math games to develop concepts, review, and utilize problem-solving strategies.

The Game Zone

Glencoe Mathematics Classroom Manipulative Kit

- scissors

GETTING READY

Objective Compare integers.

MANAGEMENT TIPS

Recommended Time
20 minutes

Tips

- Consider having the index cards precut, numbered, and packaged in sets to give to students at the beginning of the activity.
- You may wish to use standard playing cards in place of the numbered index cards. Remove the face cards and designate black cards as positive and red cards as negative.
- Another play option would be to have each student turn over the top 2 cards and find the sum. The student with the greatest (or least) sum takes the cards.
- You may wish to use the game as an assessment tool for the concepts in Lessons 1-1 through 1-5.

Math Online For an additional game for this chapter, visit: msmath3.net/gamezone

1-6 Lesson Notes

Lesson Resources

Chapter 1 Resource Masters

FAST FILE

- Study Guide and Intervention, p. 26
- Practice: Skills, p. 27
- Practice: Word Problems, p. 28
- Reading to Learn Mathematics, p. 29
- Enrichment, p. 30

Classroom Math Games, pp. 1–4
MathPASS Tutorial CD-ROM, 27
Parent and Student Study Guide Online Worksheets, 1-6
Real-Life Career Masters, p. 27
Noteables™: Interactive Study Notebook with Foldables™, 1-6

1 Focus

5-Minute Check 1-6

Use as a quiz or review of Lesson 1-5. (Also available as a transparency)

Bellringer

Hands-On Activity Have students use counters to solve the following problems.

3×-2 **−6** $\quad 9 \times -3$ **−27**

$-8 \div 4$ **−2** $\quad -12 \div 3$ **−4**

After students have worked the problems, ask them to make conjectures regarding the solutions to the problems that follow.

-3×2 **−6** $\quad -9 \times 3$ **−27**

$8 \div (-4)$ **−2** $\quad 12 \div (-3)$ **−4**

Reading to Learn Mathematics, p. 29 ELL

NAME ________ DATE ________ PERIOD ____

Reading to Learn Mathematics
Multiplying and Dividing Integers

Pre-Activity *Read the introduction at the top of page 34 in your textbook. Write your answers below.*

1. Write two different addition sentences that could be used to find the submersible's depth after 3 minutes. Then find their sum. Sample answers: −240 + (−120) or −120 + (−120) + (−120); −360
2. Write a multiplication sentence that could be used to find this same depth. Explain your reasoning. 3(−120); you are adding −120 three times.
3. Write a multiplication sentence that could be used to find the submersible's depth after 10 minutes. Then find the product. 10(−120); −1,200

Reading the Lesson

4. Identify each number in the multiplication sentence 3(−120) = −360 as either a factor or a product. 3: factor; −120: factor; −360: product

1-6 Multiplying and Dividing Integers

What You'll LEARN

Multiply and divide integers.

REVIEW Vocabulary

factor: numbers that are multiplied together

product: the result when two or more numbers are multiplied together

WHEN am I ever going to use this?

OCEANOGRAPHY A deep-sea submersible descends 120 feet each minute to reach the bottom of Challenger Deep in the Pacific Ocean. A descent of 120 feet is represented by −120. The table shows the submersible's depth after various numbers of minutes.

Time (min)	Depth (ft)
1	−120
2	−240
⋮	⋮
9	−1,080
10	−1,200

1. Write two different addition sentences that could be used to find the submersible's depth after 3 minutes. Then find their sums.
2. Write a multiplication sentence that could be used to find this same depth. Explain your reasoning. **1–3. See margin.**
3. Write a multiplication sentence that could be used to find the submersible's depth after 10 minutes. Then find the product.

Multiplication is repeated addition. So, 3(−120) means that −120 is used as an addend 3 times.

$$3(-120) = -120 + (-120) + (-120)$$
$$= -360$$

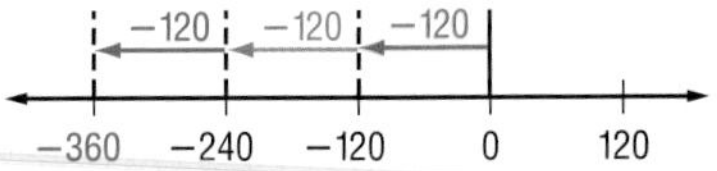

Number line: −360, −240, −120, 0, 120; arrows labeled −120, −120, −120.

By the Commutative Property of Multiplication, 3(−120) = −120(3). This example suggests the following rule.

Key Concept boxes highlight definitions, formulas, and other important ideas that students should include in their Noteables™ or their notebooks. Multiple representations—words, symbols, examples, models—reach students of all learning styles.

Noteables™ Key Concept: Multiply Integers with Different Signs

Words	The product of two integers with different signs is negative.	
Examples	2(−5) = −10	−5(2) = −10

EXAMPLES Multiply Integers with Different Signs

1 Find 6(−8).

6(−8) = −48 The factors have different signs. The product is negative.

2 Find −9(2).

−9(2) = −18 The factors have different signs. The product is negative.

Your Turn Multiply.

a. 5(−3) **−15** b. −8(6) **−48** c. −2(4) **−8**

Answers (When am I ever going to use this?)

1. Sample answers: −240 + (−120) or −120 + (−120) + (−120); −360
2. 3(−120); you are adding −120 three times.
3. 10(−120); −1,200

The product of two positive integers is positive. For example, $3 \cdot 2 = 6$. What is the sign of the product of two negative integers? Look for a pattern to find $-3 \cdot (-2)$.

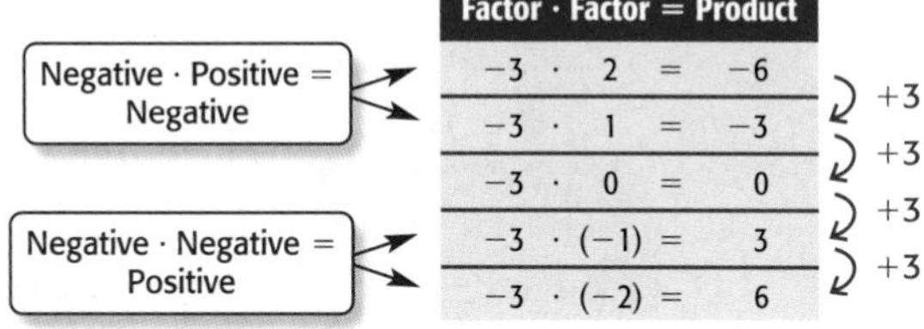

Factor · Factor = Product	
$-3 \cdot 2 = -6$	
$-3 \cdot 1 = -3$	+3
$-3 \cdot 0 = 0$	+3
$-3 \cdot (-1) = 3$	+3
$-3 \cdot (-2) = 6$	+3

This example suggests the following rule.

Noteables™ Key Concept: Multiply Integers with the Same Sign

Words The product of two integers with the same sign is positive.

Examples $2(5) = 10$ $-2(-5) = 10$

EXAMPLE Multiply Integers with the Same Sign

3 Find $-4(-3)$.

$-4(-3) = 12$ The factors have the same sign. The product is positive.

Your Turn **Multiply.**

d. $-3(-7)$ **21** e. $6(4)$ **24** f. $(-5)^2$ **25**

To multiply more than two integers, group factors using the Associative Property of Multiplication.

EXAMPLE Multiply More than Two Integers

4 Find $-2(3)(-9)$.

$-2(3)(-9) = [-2(3)](-9)$ Associative Property

$= -6(-9)$ $-2(3) = -6$

$= 54$ $-6(-9) = 54$

You know that multiplication and division are opposite operations. Examine the following multiplication sentences and their related division sentences.

Multiplication Sentence	Related Division Sentences	
$4(3) = 12$	$12 \div 3 = 4$	$12 \div 4 = 3$
$-4(3) = -12$	$-12 \div 3 = -4$	$-12 \div (-4) = 3$
$4(-3) = -12$	$-12 \div (-3) = 4$	$-12 \div 4 = -3$
$-4(-3) = 12$	$12 \div (-3) = -4$	$12 \div (-4) = -3$

These examples suggest that the rules for dividing integers are similar to the rules for multiplying integers.

Teaching Tips on the reduced student page offer practical suggestions for your lessons.

TEACHING TIP

When multiplying more than two integers, students may find it helpful to decide on the sign of the product before multiplying. If the number of negatives is *even* the product is positive. If the number of negatives is *odd* the product is negative.

READING Math

Division In a division sentence like $12 \div 3 = 4$, the number you are dividing, 12, is called the *dividend*. The number you are dividing by, 3, is called the *divisor*. The result is called the *quotient*.

msmath3.net/extra_examples

2 Teach

In-Class Examples

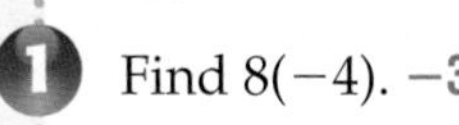

1 Find $8(-4)$. **−32**

2 Find $-5(7)$. **−35**

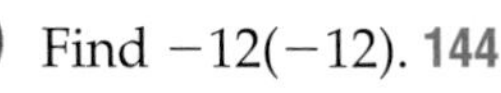

3 Find $-12(-12)$. **144**

4 Find $6(-2)(-4)$. **48**

DAILY INTERVENTION **Differentiated Instruction**

Logical Help students see the relationship between division, multiplication, and the signs of the integers by having them solve several problems following the format shown.

$24 \div (-6) = \blacksquare \rightarrow \blacksquare \cdot (-6) = 24$

Within a problem, the boxes must contain the same integer.

In-Class Examples

5 Find $30 \div (-5)$. **−6**

6 Find $\frac{-27}{9}$. **−3**

7 Evaluate $3x - (-4y)$ if $x = -10$ and $y = -4$. **−46**

8 **WEATHER** The table shows the low temperature for each month in McGrath, Alaska. Find the mean (average) of all 12 temperatures. **−9°C**

Average Low Temperatures

Month	Temperature (°C)
January	−27
February	−26
March	−19
April	−9
May	1
June	7
July	9
August	7
September	2
October	−8
November	−19
December	−26

Source: weather.com

Noteables™ **Key Concept: Divide Integers**

Words The quotient of two integers with different signs is negative. The quotient of two integers with the same sign is positive.

Examples $16 \div (-8) = -2$ $-16 \div (-8) = 2$

EXAMPLES Divide Integers

5 **Find $-24 \div 3$.** The dividend and the divisor have different signs.

$-24 \div 3 = -8$ The quotient is negative.

6 **Find $-30 \div (-15)$.** The signs are the same.

$-30 \div (-15) = 2$ The quotient is positive.

Your Turn Divide.

g. $-28 \div (-7)$ **4** h. $\frac{36}{-2}$ **−18** i. $\frac{-40}{8}$ **−5**

You can use all of the rules you have learned for adding, subtracting, multiplying, and dividing integers to evaluate algebraic expressions. Remember to follow the order of operations.

EXAMPLE Evaluate Algebraic Expressions

7 **Evaluate $-2a - b$ if $a = -3$ and $b = -5$.**

$-2a - b = -2(-3) - (-5)$ Replace a with −3 and b with −5.

$= 6 - (-5)$ The product of −2 and −3 is positive.

$= 6 + 5$ To subtract −5, add 5.

$= 11$ Add.

REAL-LIFE MATH

CARD GAMES In the game of *Hearts*, the object is to avoid scoring points. Each heart is worth one penalty point, the queen of spades is worth 13, and the other cards have no value.

Source: www.pagat.com

EXAMPLE Find the Mean of a Set of Integers

8 **CARD GAMES In a certain card game, you can gain or lose points with each round played. Atepa's change in score for each of five rounds is shown. Find Atepa's mean (average) point gain or loss per round.**

Atepa
−10
−30
−20
10
20

To find the mean of a set of numbers, find the sum of the numbers. Then divide the result by how many numbers there are in the set.

$\frac{-10 + (-30) + (-20) + 10 + 20}{5} = \frac{-30}{5}$ Find the sum of the set of numbers. Divide by the number in the set.

$= -6$ Simplify.

Atepa lost an average 6 points per round of cards.

36 Chapter 1 Algebra: Integers

Students practice the same concepts in Exercises 15–46 if they are assigned odd or even problems.

Skill and Concept Check

1. **State** whether each product or quotient is positive or negative.
   a. $-8(-6)$ **positive** b. $16 \div (-4)$ **negative** c. $5(-7)(9)$ **negative**
2. **OPEN ENDED** Name two integers whose quotient is -7. **Sample answer: -21 and 3**
3. **NUMBER SENSE** Find the sign of each of the following if n is a negative number. Explain your reasoning. **a–d. See margin.**
   a. n^2 b. n^3 c. n^4 d. n^5

Number Sense exercises help students with their mental math skills.

GUIDED PRACTICE

Multiply.

4. $-4 \cdot 5$ **-20** 5. $-2(-7)$ **14** 6. $(-3)^2$ **9** 7. $-4(5)(-7)$ **140**

Divide.

8. $-25 \div (-5)$ **5** 9. $-16 \div 4$ **-4** 10. $\frac{-49}{7}$ **-7** 11. $\frac{30}{-10}$ **-3**

Evaluate each expression if $a = -5$, $b = 8$, and $c = -12$.

12. $4a + 9$ **-11** 13. $\frac{b - c}{a}$ **-4** 14. $3b - a^2$ **-1**

★ indicates increased difficulty

Practice and Applications

HOMEWORK HELP	
For Exercises	See Examples
15–34	1–4
35–48	5, 6
49–56	7
57–60	8

Extra Practice See pages 617, 648.

Multiply.

15. $7(-8)$ **-56** 16. $-5 \cdot 8$ **-40** 17. $-4(-6)$ **24**
18. $-14(-2)$ **28** 19. $12 \cdot 5$ **60** 20. $-3(-9)$ **27**
21. $8(-9)$ **-72** 22. $4(7)$ **28** 23. $(-8)^2$ **64**
24. $(-7)^2$ **49** 25. $6(-2)(-7)$ **84** 26. $-3(-3)(-4)$ **-36**
27. $(-5)^3$ **-125** 28. $(-3)^3$ **-27** 29. $-2(4)(-3)(-10)$ **-240**
30. $-4(-8)(-2)(-5)$ **320** 31. $-2(-4)^2$ **-32** ★ 32. $(2)^2 \cdot (-6)^2$ **144**

33. **HIKING** For every 1-kilometer increase in altitude, the temperature drops 7°C. Find the temperature change for a 5-kilometer altitude increase. **-35°C**
34. **LIFE SCIENCE** Most people lose 100 to 200 hairs per day. If you were to lose 150 hairs per day for 10 days, what would be the change in the number of hairs you have? **$-1{,}500$**

Divide.

35. $50 \div (-5)$ **-10** 36. $28 \div 7$ **4** 37. $-60 \div 3$ **-20** 38. $-84 \div (-4)$ **21**
39. $45 \div 9$ **5** 40. $64 \div (-8)$ **-8** 41. $-34 \div (-2)$ **17** 42. $-72 \div 6$ **-12**
43. $\frac{-108}{12}$ **-9** 44. $\frac{-39}{-13}$ **3** 45. $\frac{-42}{-6}$ **7** 46. $\frac{121}{-11}$ **-11**

47. **WEATHER** A weather forecaster says that the temperature is changing at a rate of $-8°$ per hour. At that rate, how long will it take for the temperature change to be $-24°$? **3 h**

msmath3.net/self_check_quiz

3 Practice/Apply

FOLDABLES™ Follow-Up Remind students to use their Foldable tables to record in words and symbols what they learn about multiplying and dividing integers. For example, they might describe why the product of two integers with the same sign is positive and the product of two integers with different signs is negative.

NUMBER SENSE

For Exercise 3, suggest that students substitute a number into the expressions and write them as multiplication problems to help analyze the sign of each.

a. $-3(-3) = 9$
b. $(-3)(-3)(-3) = -27$
c. $(-3)(-3)(-3)(-3) = 81$
d. $(-3)(-3)(-3)(-3)(-3) = -243$

About the Exercises...

Guided Practice Key

Exercises	Examples
4	1, 2
5, 6	3
7	4
8–11	5, 6
12–14	7

Assignment Guide

Basic: 15–53 odd, 57–61 odd, 65–76

Average: 15–61 odd, 65–76 (Optional: 62–64)

Enriched: 16–60 even, 61–72 (Optional: 73–76)

Answers (pp. 37–38)

3a. Positive; the product of two negative numbers is always a positive number.
3b. Negative; the product of three negative numbers is always a negative number.
3c. Positive; the product of four negative numbers is always a positive number.
3d. Negative; the product of five negative numbers is always a negative number.
61. If the number of negative factors is odd, then the product is negative. If the number of negative factors is even, then the product is positive.
73. Sample answer: in all
74. Sample answer: difference
75. Sample answer: of
76. Sample answer: separated

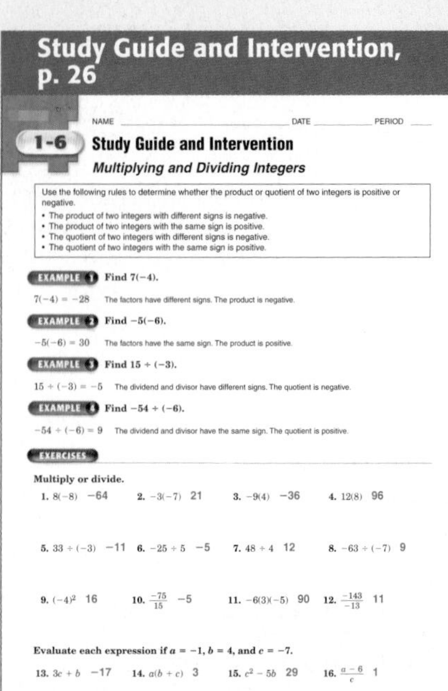

Study Guide and Intervention, p. 26

NAME ______ DATE ______ PERIOD ____

1-6 Study Guide and Intervention

Multiplying and Dividing Integers

Use the following rules to determine whether the product or quotient of two integers is positive or negative.

- The product of two integers with different signs is negative.
- The product of two integers with the same sign is positive.
- The quotient of two integers with different signs is negative.
- The quotient of two integers with the same sign is positive.

EXAMPLE 1 **Find 7(−4).**

7(−4) = −28 The factors have different signs. The product is negative.

EXAMPLE 2 **Find −5(−6).**

−5(−6) = 30 The factors have the same sign. The product is positive.

EXAMPLE 3 **Find 15 ÷ (−3).**

15 ÷ (−3) = −5 The dividend and divisor have different signs. The quotient is negative.

EXAMPLE 4 **Find −54 ÷ (−6).**

−54 ÷ (−6) = 9 The dividend and divisor have the same sign. The quotient is positive.

EXERCISES

Multiply or divide.

1. 8(−8) −64
2. −3(−7) 21
3. −9(4) −36
4. 12(8) 96
5. 33 ÷ (−3) −11
6. −25 ÷ 5 −5
7. 48 ÷ 4 12
8. −63 ÷ (−7) 9
9. $(-4)^2$ 16
10. $\frac{-75}{15}$ −5
11. −6(3)(−5) 90
12. $\frac{-143}{-13}$ 11

Evaluate each expression if $a = -1$, $b = 4$, and $c = -7$.

13. $3c + b$ −17
14. $a(b + c)$ 3
15. $c^2 - 5b$ 29
16. $\frac{a - 6}{c}$ 1

Practice: Skills, p. 27

NAME ______ DATE ______ PERIOD ____

1-6 Practice: Skills

Multiplying and Dividing Integers

Multiply.

1. −2 · 3 −6
2. 3(−3) −9
3. −4(−2) 8
4. 5 · 7 35
5. −9(−8) 72
6. −11 · 12 −132
7. 15(−3) −45
8. −7(−13) 91
9. −5(2)(−7) 70
10. $(-10)^2$ 100
11. 6(8)(−3) −144
12. $(-4)^3$ −64
13. $(-9)^2$ 81
14. −1(−3)(−4) −12
15. $(-10)^3$ −1,000
16. −3(−4)(−7) −84

Divide.

17. −15 ÷ 3 −5
18. 40 ÷ (−5) −8
19. −63 ÷ (−7) 9
20. 76 ÷ 4 19
21. $\frac{-56}{-4}$ 14
22. $\frac{-48}{16}$ −3
23. $\frac{-57}{-19}$ 3
24. $\frac{75}{-5}$ −15

Evaluate each expression if $a = -2$, $b = 5$, and $c = -6$.

25. abc 60
26. $2b + c$ 4
27. $\frac{2b - c}{a}$ −8
28. $ab - c$ −4
29. $\frac{c}{a + b}$ −2
30. $\frac{2a + c}{b}$ −2
31. $b^2 - 5a$ 35
32. $(-c)^2$ 36

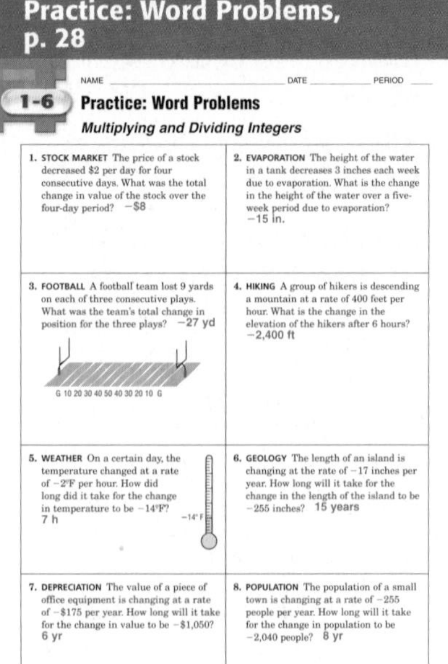

Practice: Word Problems, p. 28

NAME ______ DATE ______ PERIOD ____

1-6 Practice: Word Problems

Multiplying and Dividing Integers

1. STOCK MARKET The price of a stock decreased $2 per day for four consecutive days. What was the total change in value of the stock over the four-day period? −$8
2. EVAPORATION The height of the water in a tank decreases 3 inches each week due to evaporation. What is the change in the height of the water over a five-week period due to evaporation? −15 in.
3. FOOTBALL A football team lost 9 yards on each of three consecutive plays. What was the team's total change in position for the three plays? −27 yd

4. HIKING A group of hikers is descending a mountain at a rate of 400 feet per hour. What is the change in the elevation of the hikers after 6 hours? −2,400 ft
5. WEATHER On a certain day, the temperature changed at a rate of −2°F per hour. How did long did it take for the change in temperature to be −14°F? 7 h

6. GEOLOGY The length of an island is changing at the rate of −17 inches per year. How long will it take for the change in the length of the island to be −255 inches? 15 years
7. DEPRECIATION The value of a piece of office equipment is changing at a rate of −$175 per year. How long will it take for the change in value to be −$1,050? 6 yr
8. POPULATION The population of a small town is changing at a rate of −255 people per year. How long will it take for the change in population to be −2,040 people? 8 yr

48. **NUMBER SENSE** The absolute value of a given negative number is −1 times the number. Using this rule, evaluate the expression $|-5|$. Then justify your answer using a number line. **5; See students' work.**

Evaluate each expression if $w = -2$, $x = 3$, $y = -4$, and $z = -5$.

49. $x + 6y$ **−21**
50. $9 - wz$ **−1**
51. $\frac{w - x}{z}$ **1**
52. $\frac{8y}{x - 5}$ **16**
53. $\frac{6z}{x} - y$ **−6**
54. $\frac{-42}{y - x} + w$ **4**
55. ★ $-z^2$ **−25**
56. ★ $4(3w + 2)^2$ **64**

Find the mean of each set of integers.

57. −2, −7, −6, 5, −10 **−4**
58. −14, −17, −20, −16, −13 **−16**
59. −23, −21, −28, −27, −25, −26 **−25**
60. −15, 19, −13, 17, −12, 16 **2**

61. **CRITICAL THINKING** Explain how you can use the number of negative factors to determine the sign of the product when multiplying more than two integers. **See p. 37 margin.**

EXTENDING THE LESSON

The sum or product of any two whole numbers (0, 1, 2, 3, . . .) is always a whole number. So, the set of whole numbers is said to be *closed* under addition and multiplication. This is an example of the *Closure Property*. State whether each statement is *true* or *false*. If *false*, give a counterexample.

62. The set of whole numbers is closed under subtraction. **false; 3 − 5 = −5**
63. The set of integers is closed under multiplication. **true**
64. The set of integers is closed under division. **false; 1 ÷ 2 = 0.5**

Spiral Review with Standardized Test Practice

65. **MULTIPLE CHOICE** A glacier receded at a rate of 350 feet per day for two consecutive weeks. How much did the glacier's position change in all? **D**

    (A) −336 ft (B) −348 ft (C) −700 ft (D) −4,900 ft

66. **SHORT RESPONSE** On six consecutive days, the low temperature in a city was −5°C, −4°C, 6°C, 3°C, −1°C, and −8°C. What was the average low temperature for the six days? **−1.5°C**

Subtract. (Lesson 1-5)

67. 12 − 18 **−6**
68. −5 − (−14) **9**
69. −3 − 20 **−23**

Add. (Lesson 1-4)

70. −9 + 2 + (−8) **−15**
71. −24 + (−11) + 24 **−11**
72. −7 + 12 + (−3) + 6 **8**

GETTING READY FOR THE NEXT LESSON

BASIC SKILL Give an example of a word or phrase that could indicate each operation. **73–76. See p. 37 margin.**

Example: addition → the sum of

73. addition
74. subtraction
75. multiplication
76. division

4 Assess

Higher-Level Thinking

Ask students how they could use counters to show that the quotient of two integers with different signs is negative. Have them choose positive divisors.

Sample answer: Show that −9 ÷ 3 = −3 by dividing 9 negative counters into 3 sets. Each set will have 3 negative counters.

38 Chapter 1 Algebra: Integers

Writing Expressions and Equations

What You'll LEARN

Write algebraic expressions and equations from verbal phrases and sentences.

NEW Vocabulary

defining a variable

WHEN am I ever going to use this?

PARTY PLANNING It costs $8 per guest to hold a birthday party at the Community Center, as shown in the table.

Number of Guests	Party Cost
5	$5 \cdot 8$ or 40
7	$7 \cdot 8$ or 56
10	$10 \cdot 8$ or 80
12	$12 \cdot 8$ or 96
g	?

1. What is the relationship between the number of guests and the cost of the party?
2. Write an expression representing the cost of a party with g guests. **$8 \cdot g$ or $8g$**

1. The cost is equal to 8 times the number of guests.

An important skill in algebra is writing verbal expressions as algebraic expressions. The steps in this process are given below.

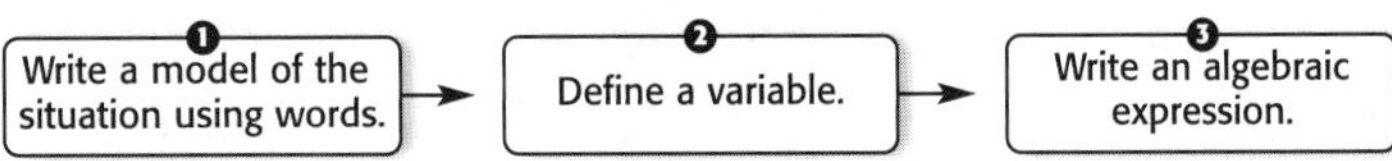

When you choose a variable and an unknown quantity for the variable to represent, this is called **defining a variable**. In the example above, g is defined as the *unknown number of guests*.

Algebraic expressions are made up of variables and operation symbols. The following table lists some common words and phrases that usually indicate the four operations.

Addition or Subtraction				Multiplication or Division			
plus	increased by	minus	subtract	times	each	divided	rate
sum	in all	less	decreased by	product	of	quotient	ratio
total	more than	less than	difference	multiplied	factors	an, in, or per	separate

STUDY TIP

Defining a Variable Any letter can be used as a variable, but it is often helpful to select letters that can be easily connected to the quantity they represent.

Example: age $\rightarrow a$

EXAMPLE Write an Algebraic Expression

1 Write *five years older than her brother* as an algebraic expression.

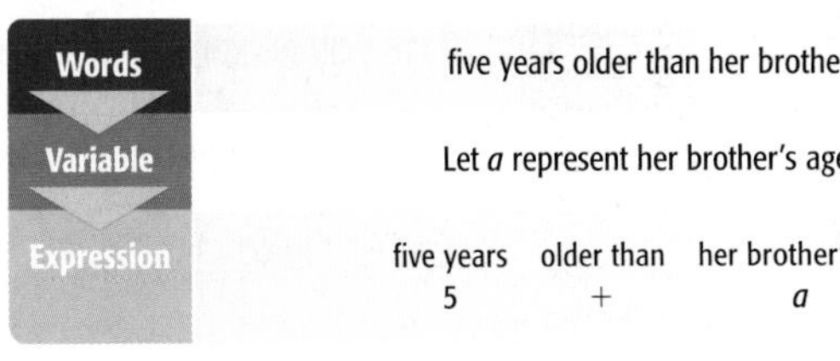

Words	five years older than her brother
Variable	Let a represent her brother's age.
Expression	five years (5) older than (+) her brother's age (a)

The expression is $5 + a$.

msmath3.net/extra_examples

1-7 Lesson Notes

Lesson Resources

Chapter 1 Resource Masters
- Study Guide and Intervention, p. 31
- Practice: Skills, p. 32
- Practice: Word Problems, p. 33
- Reading to Learn Mathematics, p. 34
- Enrichment, p. 35

Key Teaching Transparencies, 2
MathPASS Tutorial CD-ROM, 36
Parent and Student Study Guide Online Worksheets, 1-7
Noteables™: Interactive Study Notebook with Foldables™, 1-7

1 Focus

5-Minute Check 1-7

Use as a quiz or review of Lesson 1-6. (Also available as a transparency)

Bellringer

Communication Have students review translating algebraic expressions and equations into verbal phrases and sentences. Write several expressions and equations such as $\frac{x}{3} + 7 = y$ one at a time on the chalkboard, or cover a transparency with a sheet of paper and reveal one at a time. Encourage students to use everyday language. **When a number x, is divided by 3 and then that quotient is added to 7, the sum is equal to y.**

Reading to Learn Mathematics, p. 34 **ELL**

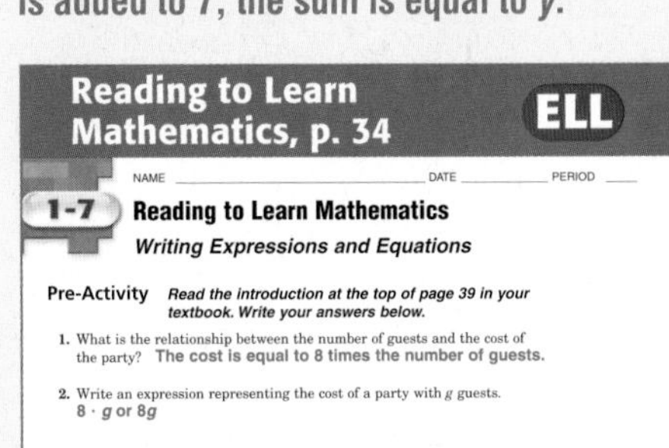
NAME ______ DATE ______ PERIOD ____

1-7 Reading to Learn Mathematics

Writing Expressions and Equations

Pre-Activity *Read the introduction at the top of page 39 in your textbook. Write your answers below.*

1. What is the relationship between the number of guests and the cost of the party? The cost is equal to 8 times the number of guests.
2. Write an expression representing the cost of a party with g guests. $8 \cdot g$ or $8g$

Reading the Lesson

Look at the table of common words and phrases on page 39. Then determine whether each situation requires *addition, subtraction, multiplication,* or *division.*

3. Find the difference between the cost of a gallon of premium gasoline and the cost of a gallon of regular gasoline. subtraction

2 Teach

In-Class Examples

Write each verbal phrase as an algebraic expression.

1. double the price of a loaf of bread **$2p$**
2. stalks of celery are divided into 4 portions **$\frac{c}{4}$**
3. Write *the price of the book plus \$5 shipping is \$29* as an algebraic equation. **$p + 5 = 29$**
4. **NUTRITION** A particular box of oatmeal contains 10 individual packages. If the box contains 30 grams of fiber, write an equation to find the amount of fiber in one package of oatmeal. **$10f = 30$**

Teaching Strategies You may wish to collect newspaper and magazine stories containing numerical information. Have students search through the stories for information to translate into algebraic expressions or equations. For example, the zoo added three camels to its Asian exhibit bringing the total to nine: $x + 3 = 9$.

TEACHING TIP

The letters *e*, *i*, and *o* are not usually used as variables because they might be confused with their meanings as real or imaginary numbers.

TEACHING TIP

In this book, the *difference of 5 and 3* means start with 5 and subtract 3, so the expression is $5 - 3$. Similarly, *the quotient of 8 and 4* means $8 \div 4$.

EXAMPLE Write an Algebraic Expression

2 **Write *six dollars an hour times the number of hours* as an algebraic expression.**

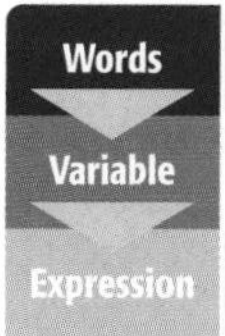

Words	six dollars an hour times the number of hours		
Variable	Let h represent the number of hours.		
Expression	six dollars an hour	times	the number of hours
	6	·	h

The expression is $6 \cdot h$ or $6h$.

You can also translate a verbal sentence into an equation. Some key words that indicate an equation are *equals* and *is*.

EXAMPLE Write an Algebraic Equation

3 **Write *a number less 8 is 22* as an algebraic equation.**

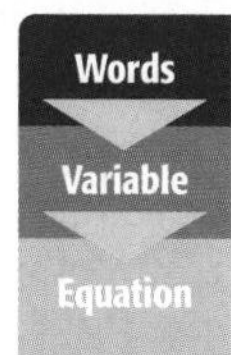

Words	A number less 8 is 22.		
Variable	Let n represent the number.		
Equation	A number less 8	is	22.
	$n - 8$	=	22

The equation is $n - 8 = 22$.

Your Turn **Write each verbal sentence as an algebraic equation.**

a. 4 inches shorter than Ryan's height is 58 inches **$h - 4 = 58$**

b. 30 is 6 times a number. **$30 = 6n$**

REAL-LIFE MATH

GEOGRAPHY More than 6 million cubic feet of water go over the crestline of Niagara Falls every minute during peak daytime tourist hours.

Source: www.infoniagara.com

EXAMPLE Write an Equation to Solve a Problem

4 **GEOGRAPHY** Niagara Falls is one of the most visited waterfalls in North America, but it is not the tallest. Yosemite Falls is 2,249 feet taller. If Yosemite Falls is 2,425 feet high, write an equation to find the height of Niagara Falls.

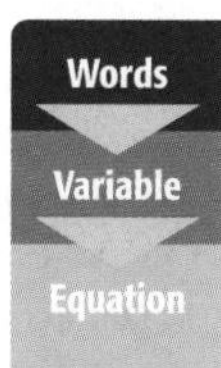

Words	Yosemite's height is 2,249 feet taller than Niagara's height.				
Variable	Let n represent the height of Niagara Falls.				
Equation	Yosemite's height	is	2,249 ft	taller than	Niagara's height.
	2,425	=	2,249	+	n

The equation is $2{,}425 = 2{,}249 + n$.

Words/Variable/Equation entries help students translate between word problems and equations.

DAILY INTERVENTION **Flexible Grouping**

Intervention Watch for students who have difficulty translating words into algebraic equations. Pair weaker students with stronger ones. Have each student write a verbal expression, then trade and translate the expression into an algebraic expression. After completing several turns, the pairs should work backward translating the algebraic expressions to verbal expressions. Pairs should compare their verbal expressions and discuss any discrepancies.

Students practice the same concepts in Exercises 8–17 and 25–30 if they are assigned odd or even problems.

Skill and Concept Check

1. Writing Math Write two different verbal phrases that could be represented by the algebraic expression $x + 4$. Sample answer: the sum of a number and 4; 4 more than a number.

2. **FIND THE ERROR** Regina and Kamilah are translating the verbal phrase *6 less than a number* into an algebraic expression. Who is correct? Explain.

Regina $n - 6$ | Kamilah $6 - n$

Regina; Kamilah's expression is the translation of *6 less n*, instead of 6 less than *n*.

GUIDED PRACTICE

Write each verbal phrase as an algebraic expression.

3. 18 seconds faster than Tina's time $t - 18$
4. the difference between 7 and a number $7 - n$
5. the quotient of a number and 9 $\frac{n}{9}$

Write each verbal sentence as an algebraic equation.

6. The sum of 6 and a number is 2. $6 + n = 2$
7. When the people are separated into 5 committees, there are 3 people on each committee. $p \div 5 = 3$

★ indicates increased difficulty

Practice and Applications

Write each verbal phrase as an algebraic expression. 9. $n - 6$

8. a $4 tip added to the bill $4 + b$
9. a number decreased by 6
10. half of Jessica's allowance $\frac{a}{2}$ or $\frac{1}{2}a$
11. the sum of a number and −9
12. 5 points less than the average
13. a number divided by −3 $\frac{n}{-3}$
14. 16 pounds more than his sister's weight $w + 16$
15. 20 fewer people than the number expected $n - 20$
16. 65 miles per hour for a number of hours $65h$
17. 4 more touchdowns than the other team scored $t + 4$

11. $n + (-9)$ 12. $a - 5$

18. **LIFE SCIENCE** An adult cat has 2 fewer teeth than an adult human. Define a variable and write an expression for the number of teeth in an adult cat. t = the number of teeth an adult human has; $t - 2$
19. **HISTORY** Tennessee became a state 4 years after Kentucky. Define a variable and write an expression for the year Tennessee became a state. k = the year Kentucky became a state; $k + 4$
20. **HEALTH** You count the number of times your heart beats in 15 seconds. Define a variable and write an expression for the number of times your heart beats in a minute. b = the number of beats in 15 seconds; $4b$
21. **TRAVEL** Define a variable and write an expression for the number of miles Travis's car gets per gallon of gasoline if he drives 260 miles. 21. g = gallons of gasoline; $\frac{260}{g}$

HOMEWORK HELP

For Exercises	See Examples
8–24	1, 2
25–30	3
31	4

Extra Practice
See pages 618, 648.

Math Online msmath3.net/self_check_quiz

3 Practice/Apply

DAILY INTERVENTION FIND THE ERROR In Exercise 2, point out that order may be misleading in verbal expressions. Remind students that $n - 6$ also can be written as $-6 + n$, and so the reference to 6 need not occur first in the algebraic version.

You may wish to suggest that students identify which term in the verbal expression is undergoing a change and which term in the expression is a factor of change. In this example, *a number* is being changed by the number 6, or *a number is being reduced by 6*, that is, $n - 6$.

About the Exercises...

Guided Practice Key

Exercises	Examples
3–5	1, 2
6, 7	3

Assignment Guide

Basic: 9–31 odd, 32–43

Average: 9–21 odd, 22, 23–31 odd, 32–43

Enriched: 8–32 even, 33–39 (Optional: 40–43)

Students can use **Homework Help** references when they complete the exercises at home. **Extra Practice** for every lesson and **Mixed Problem Solving** for every chapter are provided in the back of the book.

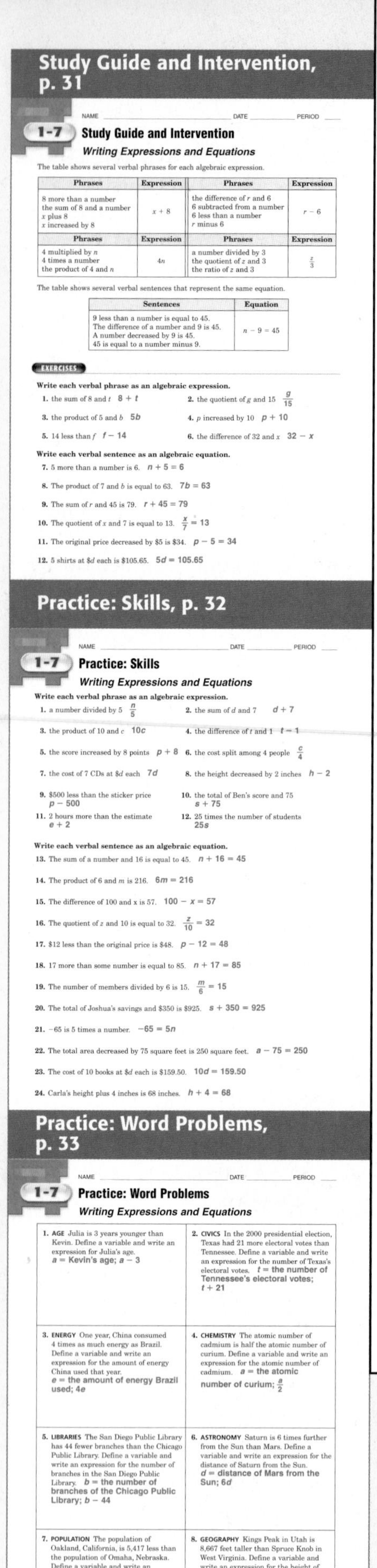

Study Guide and Intervention, p. 31

NAME ________________ DATE ________ PERIOD ____

1-7 Study Guide and Intervention

Writing Expressions and Equations

The table shows several verbal phrases for each algebraic expression.

Phrases	Expression	Phrases	Expression
8 more than a number the sum of 8 and a number x plus 8 x increased by 8	$x + 8$	the difference of r and 6 6 subtracted from a number 6 less than a number r minus 6	$r - 6$
Phrases	**Expression**	**Phrases**	**Expression**
4 multiplied by n 4 times a number the product of 4 and n	$4n$	a number divided by 3 the quotient of z and 3 the ratio of z and 3	$\frac{z}{3}$

The table shows several verbal sentences that represent the same equation.

Sentences	Equation
9 less than a number is equal to 45. The difference of a number and 9 is 45. A number decreased by 9 is 45. 45 is equal to a number minus 9.	$n - 9 = 45$

EXERCISES

Write each verbal phrase as an algebraic expression.

1. the sum of 8 and t $8 + t$
2. the quotient of g and 15 $\frac{g}{15}$
3. the product of 5 and b $5b$
4. p increased by 10 $p + 10$
5. 14 less than f $f - 14$
6. the difference of 32 and x $32 - x$

Write each verbal sentence as an algebraic equation.

7. 5 more than a number is 6. $n + 5 = 6$
8. The product of 7 and b is equal to 63. $7b = 63$
9. The sum of r and 45 is 79. $r + 45 = 79$
10. The quotient of x and 7 is equal to 13. $\frac{x}{7} = 13$
11. The original price decreased by \$5 is \$34. $p - 5 = 34$
12. 5 shirts at \$$d$ each is \$105.65. $5d = 105.65$

Practice: Skills, p. 32

NAME ________________ DATE ________ PERIOD ____

1-7 Practice: Skills

Writing Expressions and Equations

Write each verbal phrase as an algebraic expression.

1. a number divided by 5 $\frac{n}{5}$
2. the sum of d and 7 $d + 7$
3. the product of 10 and c $10c$
4. the difference of t and 1 $t - 1$
5. the score increased by 8 points $p + 8$
6. the cost split among 4 people $\frac{c}{4}$
7. the cost of 7 CDs at \$$d$ each $7d$
8. the height decreased by 2 inches $h - 2$
9. \$500 less than the sticker price $p - 500$
10. the total of Ben's score and 75 $s + 75$
11. 2 hours more than the estimate $e + 2$
12. 25 times the number of students $25s$

Write each verbal sentence as an algebraic equation.

13. The sum of a number and 16 is equal to 45. $n + 16 = 45$
14. The product of 6 and m is 216. $6m = 216$
15. The difference of 100 and x is 57. $100 - x = 57$
16. The quotient of z and 10 is equal to 32. $\frac{z}{10} = 32$
17. \$12 less than the original price is \$48. $p - 12 = 48$
18. 17 more than some number is equal to 85. $n + 17 = 85$
19. The number of members divided by 6 is 15. $\frac{m}{6} = 15$
20. The total of Joshua's savings and \$350 is \$925. $s + 350 = 925$
21. −65 is 5 times a number. $-65 = 5n$
22. The total area decreased by 75 square feet is 250 square feet. $a - 75 = 250$
23. The cost of 10 books at \$$d$ each is \$159.50. $10d = 159.50$
24. Carla's height plus 4 inches is 68 inches. $h + 4 = 68$

Practice: Word Problems, p. 33

NAME ________________ DATE ________ PERIOD ____

1-7 Practice: Word Problems

Writing Expressions and Equations

1. **AGE** Julia is 3 years younger than Kevin. Define a variable and write an expression for Julia's age. a = Kevin's age; $a - 3$
2. **CIVICS** In the 2000 presidential election, Texas had 21 more electoral votes than Tennessee. Define a variable and write an expression for the number of Texas's electoral votes. t = the number of Tennessee's electoral votes; $t + 21$
3. **ENERGY** One year, China consumed 4 times as much energy as Brazil. Define a variable and write an expression for the amount of energy China used that year. e = the amount of energy Brazil used; $4e$
4. **CHEMISTRY** The atomic number of cadmium is half the atomic number of curium. Define a variable and write an expression for the atomic number of cadmium. a = the atomic number of curium; $\frac{a}{2}$
5. **LIBRARIES** The San Diego Public Library has 44 fewer branches than the Chicago Public Library. Define a variable and write an expression for the number of branches in the San Diego Public Library. b = the number of branches of the Chicago Public Library; $b - 44$
6. **ASTRONOMY** Saturn is 6 times further from the Sun than Mars. Define a variable and write an expression for the distance of Saturn from the Sun. d = distance of Mars from the Sun; $6d$
7. **POPULATION** The population of Oakland, California, is 5,417 less than the population of Omaha, Nebraska. Define a variable and write an expression for the population of Oakland. p = population of Omaha; $p - 5{,}417$
8. **GEOGRAPHY** Kings Peak in Utah is 8,667 feet taller than Spruce Knob in West Virginia. Define a variable and write an expression for the height of Kings Peak. h = the height of Spruce Knob; $h + 8{,}667$

Write an algebraic expression that represents the relationship in each table.

22.

Age Now	Age in 12 years
5	17
8	20
12	24
16	28
a	■

$a + 12$

23.

Number of Servings	Total Calories
2	300
5	750
7	1,050
12	1,800
n	■

$150n$

★ 24.

Regular Price	Sale Price
\$8	\$6
\$12	\$9
\$16	\$12
\$20	\$15
\$$p$	■

$0.75p$

Write each verbal sentence as an algebraic equation.

25. 8 less than some number is equal to 15. $n - 8 = 15$
26. −30 is the product of −5 and a number. $-30 = -5n$
27. −14 is twice a number. $-14 = 2n$
28. 10 batches of cookies is 4 fewer than she made yesterday $10 = y - 4$
29. \$10 less the amount she spent is \$3.50. $10 - a = 3.50$
30. 3 pairs of jeans at \$$d$ each is \$106.50. $3d = 106.50$

31. **MUSIC** A musician cannot be inducted into the Rock and Roll Hall of Fame until 25 years after their first album debuted. If an artist was inducted this year, write an equation to find the latest year y the artist's first album could have debuted. **Sample answer: If the year is 2004, then the equation is $y + 25 = 2004$.**
32. **CRITICAL THINKING** Write an expression to represent *the difference of twice x and 3*. Then find the value of your expression if $x = -2$. $2x - 3$; -7

Spiral Review with Standardized Test Practice

33. **MULTIPLE CHOICE** Javier is 4 years older than his sister Rita. If Javier is y years old, which expression represents Rita's age? **B**

    (A) $y + 4$ (B) $y - 4$ (C) $4y$ (D) $y \div 4$

34. **SHORT RESPONSE** Write an expression for the perimeter of a figure in the pattern at the right that contains x triangles. The sides of each triangle are 1 unit in length. $x + 2$

    Figure 1 Figure 2 Figure 3

Multiply or divide. (Lesson 1-6)

35. $-9(10)$ -90
36. $-5(-14)$ 70
37. $34 \div (-17)$ -2
38. $\frac{-105}{-5}$ 21

39. **BUSINESS** The formula $P = I - E$ is used to find the profit P when income I and expenses E are known. One month, a business had income of \$18,600 and expenses of \$20,400. What was the business's profit that month? (Lesson 1-5) **−\$1,800**

GETTING READY FOR THE NEXT LESSON

PREREQUISITE SKILL **Add.** (Lesson 1-4)

40. $-11 + 11$ 0
41. $-14 + 5$ -9
42. $6 + (-23)$ -17
43. $-7 + (-20)$ -27

4 Assess

Open-Ended Assessment

Writing Ask students to write the steps they would follow to translate a verbal expression into an algebraic expression and provide an example.

Spiral Review With a Plan The first two exercises are Standardized Test Questions and are from the current lesson. The next two exercises or sets are from the previous two lessons. All lessons are covered proportionately throughout the book.

Problem-Solving Strategy

A Preview of Lesson 1-8

Work Backward

What You'll LEARN

Solve problems by using the work backward strategy.

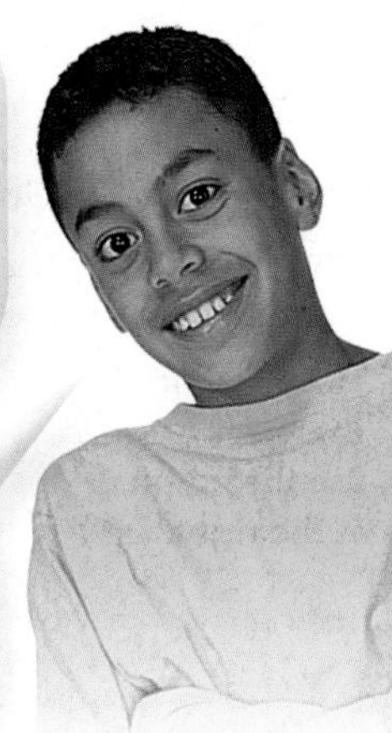

The closing day activities at the Junior Camp must be over by 2:45 P.M. We need $1\frac{1}{2}$ hours for field competitions, another 45 minutes for the awards ceremony, and an hour and 15 minutes for the cookout.

We also need an hour for room checkout. So how early do we need to get started? Let's **work backward** to figure it out.

Explore	We know the time that the campers must leave. We know the time it takes for each activity. We need to determine the time the day's activities should begin.	
Plan	Let's start with the ending time and work backward.	
Solve	The day is over at 2:45 P.M.	**2:45 P.M.**
	Go back 1 hour for checkout.	**1:45 P.M.**
	Go back 1 hour and 15 minutes for the cookout.	**12:30 A.M.**
	Go back 45 minutes for the awards ceremony.	**11:45 A.M.**
	Go back $1\frac{1}{2}$ hours for the field competitions.	**10:15 A.M.**
	So, the day's activities should start no later than 10:15 A.M.	
Examine	Assume that the day starts at 10:15 A.M. After $1\frac{1}{2}$ hours of field competitions, it is 11:45 A.M. After a 45-minute awards ceremony, it is 12:30 P.M. After the 1 hour and 15 minute cookout, it is 1:45 P.M., and after one hour for checkout, it is 2:45 P.M. So starting at 10:15 A.M. gives us enough time for all activities.	

The **Problem-Solving Strategy** lessons provide an opportunity for mixed problem solving.

Analyze the Strategy

1. **Tell** why the work backward strategy is the best way to solve this problem. **See margin.**
2. **Explain** how you can examine the solution when you solve a problem by working backward. **Work the problem forward and make sure the ending number is correct.**
3. **Write** a problem that could be solved by working backward. Then write the steps you would take to find the solution to your problem. **See p. 44 margin.**

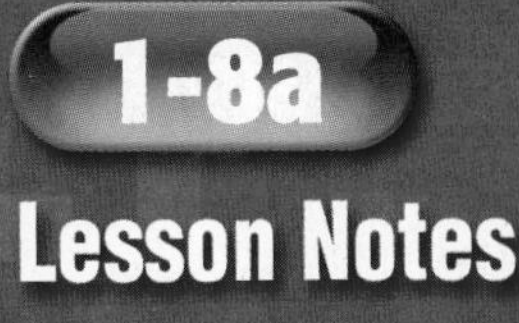

Lesson Notes

1 Focus

Bellringer Problem Solving Ask students how they would decide what food to buy for a party. What would they need to know first? **How many people will attend; what the menu will be; what ingredients are needed for the recipes; how much money is in the budget.** Then have students consider why shopping for food should not be the first step in planning the party.

2 Teach

In-Class Example

Solve. Use the work backward strategy.

SCHEDULING Wendie is meeting some friends for dinner and a movie. She needs to be finished with dinner by 7:30 P.M. to make it home by 8:00 P.M. The movie runs for 90 minutes, and she wants to have at least 1 hour for dinner. If it takes 20 minutes to get from the theater to the restaurant, what is the latest starting time she can choose for the movie she wants to see? **4:40 P.M.**

DAILY INTERVENTION — Differentiated Instruction

Auditory/Musical Read this example to students: *If I add 3 to a number, then divide by 6, the result is 2. Guess the number.* **9** Then have groups of students write several similar problems and then read them aloud for students in the other groups to solve. You may wish to have teams compete, scoring one point for the team for each correct answer.

Answer

1. **Sample answer: The students had an ending number and the operations that lead to that number. They need to work their way back to the beginning number.**

3 Practice/Apply

About the Exercises...

Problem-Solving Strategies
Exercises 6–14 are structured so that students have the opportunity to practice many different problem-solving strategies. You may wish to remind them of some of the strategies they have studied.

- use the four-step plan (p. 4)
- work backward ✓

Answers (pp. 43–44)

3. Sample answer: Jacob spent a third of his money as a deposit on a campsite. Then he bought sports equipment that cost $21. Finally, he spent $16 at the grocery store. How much money did Jacob have initially if he now has $3 left?
Start with 3 and add 16.
$\rightarrow 3 + 16 = 19$
Add 21.
$\rightarrow 19 + 21 = 40$
Divide by $\frac{2}{3}$.
$\rightarrow 40 \div \frac{2}{3} = 60$
Jacob started with $60.
6. Sample answer: Mr. Parker stopped the car.

Apply the Strategy

Solve. Use the work backward strategy.

4. **FAMILY** Mikal's great-grandmother was 6 years old when her family came to the United States, 73 years ago. If the year is 2003, when was her great-grandmother born? **1924**

5. **MONEY** The cash-in receipts in Brandon's cash drawer total $823.27, and his cash-out receipts total $734.87. If he currently has $338.40 in his drawer, what was his opening balance? **$250**

Mixed Problem Solving

Solve. Use any strategy.

TRAVEL For Exercises 6 and 7, use the graph at the right.

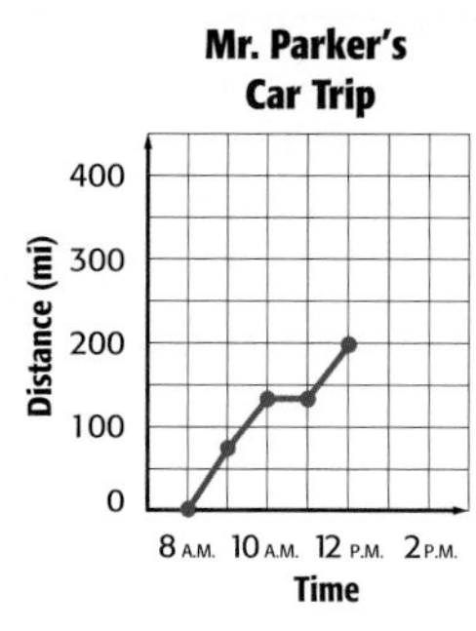

6. What may have happened between 10:00 A.M. and 11:00 A.M.? **See margin.**

7. Mr. Parker's total trip will cover 355 miles. If he maintains the speed set between 11:00 A.M. and noon, about what time should he reach his final destination? **2:00 P.M.**

8. **GRADES** Amelia wants to maintain an average of at least 90 in science class. So far her grades are 94, 88, 93, 85, and 91. What is the minimum grade she can make on her next assignment to maintain her average? **89**

9. **CARS** Ms. Calzada will pay $375 a month for five years in order to buy her new car. The bank loaned her $16,800 to pay for the car. How much extra will Ms. Calzada end up paying for the loan? **$5,700**

10. **USE A MODEL** Suppose you had 100 sugar cubes. What is the largest cube you could build with the sugar cubes? **4 by 4 by 4**

JEANS For Exercises 11 and 12, use the following information.
A store tripled the price it paid for a pair of jeans. After a month, the jeans were marked down $5. Two weeks later, the price was divided in half. Finally, the price was reduced by $3, and the jeans sold for $14.99. **11. $13.66**

11. How much did the store pay for the jeans?

12. Did the store make or lose money on the sale of the jeans? **The store made $1.33.**

13. Sample answer: 5 million

13. **SPORTS** The graph shows the number of injuries for the top seven summer recreational activities. About how many injuries were there in all for these activities?

Source: American Academy of Orthopedic Surgeons

14. **STANDARDIZED TEST PRACTICE**
Find the next three numbers in the pattern 5, 2, −1, −4 . . . . **B**
(A) −1, 2, 5 (B) −7, −10, −13
(C) −5, −6, −7 (D) −6, −8, −10

4 Assess

Higher-Level Thinking
Have students organize the situation on page 43 into a table like the one to the right. Discuss how this strategy can help solve such problems.

Event	Start Time	End Time
Field	10:15 A.M.	11:45 A.M.
Awards	11:45 A.M.	12:30 P.M.
Cookout	12:30 P.M.	1:45 P.M.
Checkout	1:45 P.M.	2:45 P.M.

1-8 Solving Addition and Subtraction Equations

What You'll LEARN

Solve equations using the Subtraction and Addition Properties of Equality.

NEW Vocabulary

solve
solution
inverse operations

HANDS-ON Mini Lab

Materials

- cups
- counters
- equation mat

Work with a partner.

When you **solve** an equation, you are trying to find the values of the variable that make the equation true. These values are called the **solutions** of the equation. You can use cups, counters, and an equation mat to solve $x + 4 = 6$.

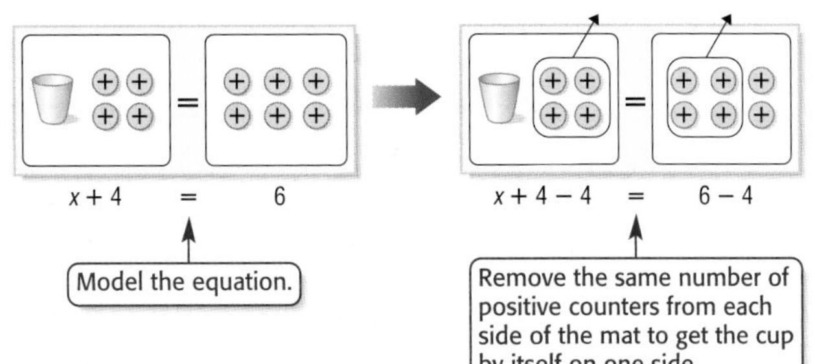

The number of positive counters remaining on the right side of the mat represents the value of x. So when $x = 2$, $x + 4 = 6$ is true.

Solve each equation using cups and counters.

1. $x + 1 = 4$ **3**
2. $x + 3 = 7$ **4**
3. $x + (-4) = -5$ **−1**

1–3. See margin for models.

4. Explain how you would find a value of x that makes $x + (-3) = -8$ true without using models. **Subtract −3 from each side.**

In the Mini Lab, you solved the equation $x + 4 = 6$ by *removing*, or subtracting, the same number of positive counters from each side of the mat. This suggests the **Subtraction Property of Equality**.

Noteables™ Key Concept: Subtraction Property of Equality

Words If you subtract the same number from each side of an equation, the two sides remain equal.

Symbols

Arithmetic	Algebra
$7 = 7$	$x + 4 = 6$
$7 - 3 = 7 - 3$	$x + 4 - 4 = 6 - 4$
$4 = 4$	$x = 2$

You can use this property to solve any addition equation. Remember to check your solution by substituting it back into the original equation.

1-8 Lesson Notes

Lesson Resources

Chapter 1 Resource Masters

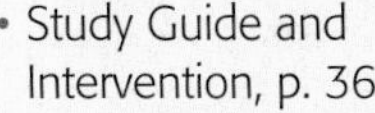

- Study Guide and Intervention, p. 36
- Practice: Skills, p. 37
- Practice: Word Problems, p. 38
- Reading to Learn Mathematics, p. 39
- Enrichment, p. 40

Key Teaching Transparencies, 3

Parent and Student Study Guide Online Worksheets, 1-8

Science and Math Lab Masters, pp. 45–48

Noteables™: Interactive Study Notebook with Foldables™, 1-8

1 Focus

5-Minute Check 1-8

Use as a quiz or review of Lesson 1-7. (Also available as a transparency)

Bellringer

Hands-On Activity Place equal weights on each side of a two-pan balance. Add weight to one pan and ask students what can be done to bring the scale back into balance. **Add the same weight to the other pan.**

Begin again with equal weights on each side. Remove weight from one side, and ask what can be done to bring the scale back into balance. **Remove an equal weight from the other pan.**

Reading to Learn Mathematics, p. 39 ELL

NAME ____ DATE ____ PERIOD ____

1-8 Reading to Learn Mathematics

Solving Addition and Subtraction Equations

Pre-Activity *Complete the Mini Lab at the top of page 45 in your textbook. Write your answers below.*

Solve each equation using cups and counters.

1. $x + 1 = 4$ 3
2. $x + 3 = 7$ 4
3. $x + (-4) = -5$ −1

4. Explain how you would find a value of x that makes $x + (-3) = -8$ true without using models. Subtract −3 from each side.

Reading the Lesson

Answers (Hands-On Mini Lab)

1.

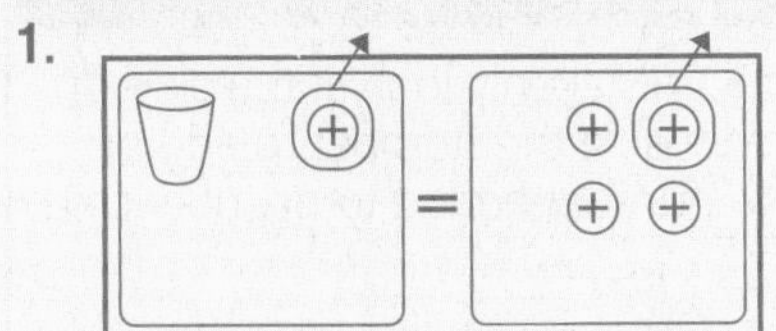

2.

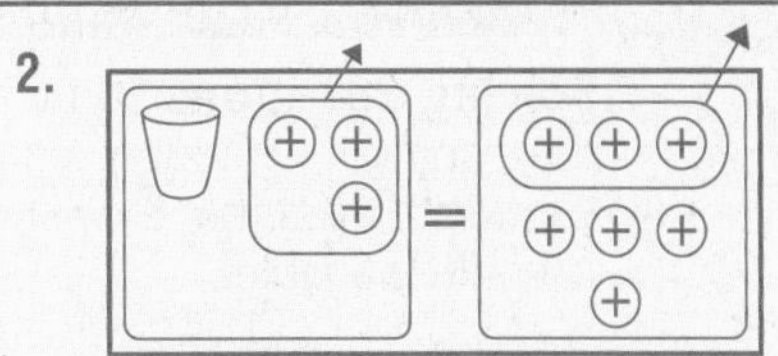

(Continued on page 46.)

2 Teach

In-Class Examples

1 Solve $7 = 15 + c$. Check your solution. **−8**

2 Solve $-5 = z - 16$. **11**

Answer (Hands-On Mini Lab)

3.

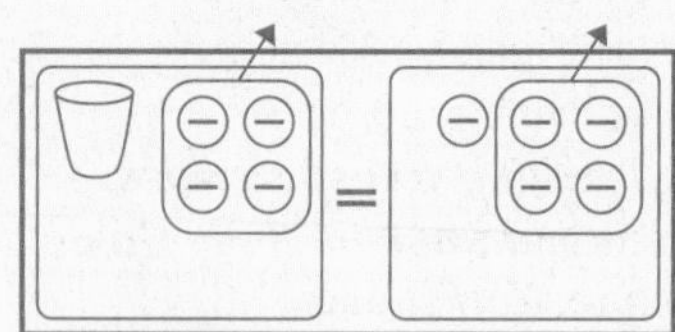

STUDY TIP

Isolating the Variable When trying to decide which value to subtract from each side of an addition equation, remember that your goal is to get the variable by itself on one side of the equal sign. This is called *isolating the variable*.

EXAMPLE Solve an Addition Equation

1 Solve $x + 5 = 3$. Check your solution.

Method 1 Vertical Method

$x + 5 = 3$	Write the equation.
$x + 5 = 3$	
$\underline{-5 = -5}$	Subtract 5 from each side.
$x = -2$	$5 - 5 = 0$ and $3 - 5 = -2$. x is by itself.

Method 2 Horizontal Method

$x + 5 = 3$

$x + 5 - 5 = 3 - 5$

$x = -2$

The solution is -2.

Check	$x + 5 = 3$	Write the original equation.
	$-2 + 5 \stackrel{?}{=} 3$	Replace x with -2. Is this sentence true?
	$3 = 3$ ✓	The sentence is true.

Your Turn **Solve each equation. Check your solution.**

a. $a + 6 = 2$ **−4** b. $y + 3 = -8$ **−11** c. $5 = n + 4$ **1**

Addition and subtraction are called **inverse operations** because they "undo" each other. For this reason, you can use the **Addition Property of Equality** to solve subtraction equations like $x - 7 = -5$.

Noteables™ **Key Concept: Addition Property of Equality**

Words If you add the same number to each side of an equation, the two sides remain equal.

Symbols	**Arithmetic**	**Algebra**
	$7 = 7$	$x - 5 = 6$
	$7 + 3 = 7 + 3$	$x - 5 + 5 = 6 + 5$
	$10 = 10$	$x = 11$

EXAMPLE Solve a Subtraction Equation

2 Solve $-6 = y - 7$.

Method 1 Vertical Method

$-6 = y - 7$	Write the equation.
$-6 = y - 7$	
$\underline{+7 = \;\; +7}$	Add 7 to each side.
$1 = y$	$-6 + 7 = 1$ and $-7 + 7 = 0$. y is by itself.

Method 2 Horizontal Method

$-6 = y - 7$

$-6 + 7 = y - 7 + 7$

$1 = y$

The solution is 1. Check the solution.

TEACHING TIP

Students can also solve a subtraction equation like $y - 7 = -6$ by first rewriting the expression as an addition expression. Then they would add the additive inverse to each side.

Your Turn **Solve each equation. Check your solution.**

d. $x - 8 = -3$ **5** e. $b - 4 = -10$ **−6** f. $7 = p - 12$ **19**

DAILY INTERVENTION **Unlocking Misconceptions**

Solving Equations Some students may mistakenly look at the side of the equation without a variable when choosing the number to add or subtract. Stress that they should use the number added to or subtracted from the variable.

Standardized Test Practice

EXAMPLE Write and Solve an Equation

3 **MULTIPLE-CHOICE TEST ITEM** What value of n makes the sum of n and 25 equal -18?

(A) -43 (B) -7 (C) 7 (D) 43

Test-Taking Tip

Backsolving In some instances, it may be easier to try each choice than to write and solve an equation.

Read the Test Item To find the value of n, write and solve an equation.

Solve the Test Item

The sum of n and 25	equals	-18.	
$n + 25$	$=$	-18	Write the equation.
$n + 25 - 25 = -18 - 25$			Subtract 25 from each side.
$n = -43$			$-18 - 25 = -18 + (-25)$

The answer is A.

Students practice the same concepts in Exercises 12–39 if they are assigned odd or even problems.

Skill and Concept Check

1. Writing Math Tell what you might say to the boy in the cartoon to explain why the solution is correct. See margin.

A Standardized Test Practice example is worked out for students.

"Hey, wait. That can't be right; yesterday we said x equals 3."

2. **OPEN ENDED** Write one addition equation and one subtraction equation that each have -3 as a solution. Sample answer: $n + 5 = 2$, $n - 6 = -9$

3. **Which One Doesn't Belong?** Identify the equation that cannot be solved using the same property of equality as the other three. Explain.

$g + 4 = 2$ $a + 5 = -3$ $m - 6 = 4$ $x + 1 = -7$

$m - 6 = 4$; see margin for explanation.

GUIDED PRACTICE

Solve each equation. Check your solution.

4. $a + 4 = 10$ 6
5. $z + 7 = 2$ -5
6. $x + 9 = -3$ -12
7. $y - 2 = 5$ 7
8. $n - 5 = -6$ -1
9. $d - 11 = -8$ 3

Write and solve an equation to find each number.

10. The sum of a number and 8 is 1. $n + 8 = 1$; -7
11. If you decrease a number by 20, the result is -14. $n - 20 = -14$; 6

Students practice comparing and contrasting when they identify Which One Doesn't Belong?

Math Online msmath3.net/extra_examples

In-Class Example

3 **MULTIPLE-CHOICE TEST ITEM** What value of y makes the difference of 30 and y equal to 12? C

A -42

B -18

C 18

D 28

3 Practice/Apply

About the Exercises...

Guided Practice Key

Exercises	Examples
4–6	1
7–9	2
10, 11	3

Assignment Guide

Basic: 13–29 odd, 33–45 odd, 46–55

Average: 13–45 odd, 46–55

Enriched: 12–46 even, 47–51 (Optional: 52–55)

Alert! The Data Update after Exercise 43 requires access to the Internet.

Which One Doesn't Belong?
In Exercise 3, students may quickly choose the third box because it is the only one with a minus sign. Check that they also understand which property of equality is involved in each box.

Answers

1. If you replace x with 4 in the equation $x + 3 = 7$, you get a true statement, $4 + 3 = 7$.
3. This equation can be solved using the Add. Prop. of Equality, and the others can be solved using the Sub. Prop. of Equality.

FOLDABLES™ Follow-Up Remind students to use their Foldable tables to record in words and symbols what they learn about solving addition and subtraction equations. For example, they might compare how they solve an equation involving whole numbers and an equation involving integers.

★ indicates increased difficulty

Practice and Applications

HOMEWORK HELP	
For Exercises	See Examples
12–31	1, 2
32–44	3

Extra Practice See pages 618, 648.

Solve each equation. Check your solution.

12. $x + 5 = 18$ **13**
13. $p + 11 = 9$ **−2**
14. $a + 7 = 1$ **−6**
15. $y + 12 = -3$ **−15**
16. $w + 8 = -6$ **−14**
17. $n + 3 = 20$ **17**
18. $g - 2 = -13$ **−11**
19. $m - 15 = 3$ **18**
20. $b - 9 = -8$ **1**
21. $r - 20 = -4$ **16**
22. $k - 4 = 17$ **21**
23. $t - 6 = -16$ **−10**
24. $28 + n = 34$ **6**
25. $52 + x = -7$ **−59**
26. $-49 = c - 18$ **−31**
27. $62 = f - 14$ **76**
28. $35 = -19 + d$ **54**
29. $-22 = -14 + q$ **−8**

★30. Find the value of x if $x + (-5) = -7$. **−2**

★31. If $a - (-2) = 10$, what is the value of a? **8**

Write and solve an equation to find each number.

32. If you increase a number by 12, the result is 7. **$n + 12 = 7$; −5**
33. If you decrease a number by 8, the result is −14. **$n - 8 = -14$; −6**
34. The difference of a number and 24 is −10. **$n - 24 = -10$; 14**
35. The sum of a number and 30 is 9. **$n + 30 = 9$; −21**

36. **GEOMETRY** Two angles are complementary if the sum of their measures is 90°. Angles A and B, shown at the right, are complementary. Write and solve an addition equation to find the measure of angle A. **$m + 37 = 90$; 53°**

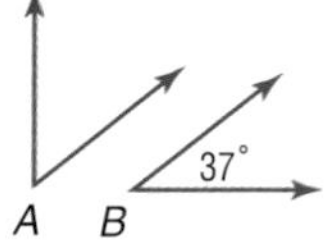

37. **BANKING** After you deposit \$50 into your savings account, the balance is \$124. Write and solve an addition equation to find your balance before this deposit. **$b + 50 = 124$; \$74**

38. **WEATHER** After falling 10°F, the temperature was −8°F. Write and solve a subtraction equation to find the starting temperature. **$t - 10 = -8$; 2°F**

39. **GOLF** After four rounds of golf, Lazaro's score was 5 under par or −5. Lazaro had improved his overall score during the fourth round by decreasing it by 6 strokes. Write and solve a subtraction equation to find Lazaro's score after the third round. **$s - 6 = -5$; 1 or 1 over par**

BASKETBALL For Exercises 40 and 41, use the information below and in the table.
Lauren Jackson averaged 0.7 point per game more than Chamique Holdsclaw during the 2003 WNBA regular season.

40. Write and solve an addition equation to find Chamique Holdsclaw's average points scored per game. **$p + 0.7 = 21.2$; 20.5**

41. Tina Thompson of the Houston Comets averaged 1.3 fewer points than Katie Smith that season. Write and solve an equation to find how many points Tina Thompson averaged per game. **$p = 18.2 - 1.3$; 16.9**

2003 WNBA Regular Season Points Leaders

Player (Team)	AVG
Lauren Jackson (Seattle Storm)	21.2
Chamique Holdsclaw (Washington Mystics)	?
Tamika Catchings (Indiana Fever)	19.7
Lisa Leslie (Los Angeles Sparks)	18.4
Katie Smith (Minnesota Lynx)	18.2

Source: wnba.com

48 Chapter 1 Algebra: Integers

MINIMUM WAGE For Exercises 42 and 43, use the information in the table.

Year	Action
1996	A subminimum wage of $4.25 an hour is established for employees under 20 years of age during their first 90 days of employment.
1997	Congress raises the minimum wage to $5.15 an hour.

42. Write and solve an addition equation to find the increase in pay a teenager who started out at the subminimum wage would receive after their first 90 days of work.

43. In 1997, the minimum wage was increased by $0.40 per hour. Write and solve an addition equation to find the minimum wage before this increase. $x + 0.40 = 5.15$; $4.75 per hour

Data Update What is the current minimum wage? Visit msmath3.net/data_update to learn more. 42. $4.25 + x = 5.15$; $0.90 per hour increase

44. **MULTI STEP** Suppose you buy a pencil for $1.25, a notebook for $6.49, and some paper. The total cost before tax is $8.79. Write an equation that can be used to find the cost c in dollars of the paper. Then solve your equation to find the cost of the paper. $1.25 + 6.49 + c = 8.79$; $1.05

45. **WRITE A PROBLEM** Write a problem about a real-life situation that can be answered by solving the equation $x + 60 = 20$. Then solve the equation to find the answer to your problem. See margin.

46. **CRITICAL THINKING** Solve $|x| + 5 = 7$. -2 or 2

Spiral Review with Standardized Test Practice

47. **MULTIPLE CHOICE** Dante paid $42 for a jacket, which included $2.52 in sales tax. Which equation could be used to find the price of the jacket before tax? B

(A) $x - 2.52 = 42$ (B) $x + 2.52 = 42$

(C) $x - 42 = 2.52$ (D) $x + 42 = 2.52$

48. **MULTIPLE CHOICE** The record low temperature for the state of Arkansas is 7°F warmer than the record low for Illinois. If the record low for Arkansas is −29°F, what is Illinois' record low? F

(F) −36°F (G) −22°F (H) 22°F (I) 36°F

Write each verbal phrase as an algebraic expression. (Lesson 1-7)

49. 7 inches per minute for a number of minutes $7m$

50. 5 degrees warmer than yesterday's high temperature $y + 5$

51. **MULTI STEP** Experts estimate that there may have been 100,000 tigers living 100 years ago. Now there are only about 6,000. Find the average change in the tiger population per year for the last 100 years. (Lesson 1-6) −940 tigers per year

GETTING READY FOR THE NEXT LESSON

PREREQUISITE SKILL Multiply. (Lesson 1-6)

52. 3(9) 27 53. −2(18) −36 54. −5(−11) 55 55. 4(−15) −60

msmath3.net/self_check_quiz

4 Assess

Open-Ended Assessment

Modeling Have students work in pairs using cups and counters to write and then solve equations similar to those solved in the Hands-On Mini Lab.

Answer

45. Sample answer: While playing a computer trivia game, you answer a question correctly and your score is increased by 60 points. If your score is now 20 points, what was your original score? Answer: −40

Study Guide and Intervention, p. 36

NAME ______ DATE ______ PERIOD ____

1-8 Study Guide and Intervention

Solving Addition and Subtraction Equations

You can use the following properties to solve addition and subtraction equations.
- *Addition Property of Equality* - If you add the same number to each side of an equation, the two sides remain equal.
- *Subtraction Property of Equality* - If you subtract the same number from each side of an equation, the two sides remain equal.

EXAMPLE 1 Solve $w + 19 = 45$. Check your solution.

	$w + 19 = 45$	Write the equation.
	$w + 19 - 19 = 45 - 19$	Subtract 19 from each side.
	$w = 26$	$19 - 19 = 0$ and $45 - 19 = 26$. w is by itself.
Check	$w + 19 = 45$	Write the original equation.
	$26 + 19 \stackrel{?}{=} 45$	Replace w with 26. Is this sentence true?
	$45 = 45$ ✓	$26 + 19 = 45$

EXAMPLE 2 Solve $h - 25 = -76$. Check your solution.

	$h - 25 = -76$	Write the equation.
	$h - 25 + 25 = -76 + 25$	Add 25 to each side.
	$h = -51$	$-25 + 25 = 0$ and $-76 + 25 = -51$. h is by itself.
Check	$h - 25 = -76$	Write the original equation.
	$-51 - 25 \stackrel{?}{=} -76$	Replace h with -51. Is this sentence true?
	$-76 = -76$ ✓	$-51 - 25 = -51 + (-25)$ or -76

EXERCISES

Solve each equation. Check your solution.

1. $s - 4 = 12$ 16 2. $d + 2 = 21$ 19 3. $h + 6 = 15$ 9

4. $x + 5 = -8$ −13 5. $b - 10 = -34$ −24 6. $f - 22 = -6$ 16

7. $17 + c = 41$ 24 8. $v - 36 = 25$ 61 9. $y - 29 = -51$ −22

10. $19 = z - 32$ 51 11. $13 + t = -29$ −42 12. $55 = 39 + k$ 16

13. $62 + b = 45$ −17 14. $x - 39 = -65$ −26 15. $-56 = -47 + n$ −9

Practice: Skills, p. 37

NAME ______ DATE ______ PERIOD ____

1-8 Practice: Skills

Solving Addition and Subtraction Equations

Solve each equation. Check your solution.

1. $x + 3 = 4$ 1 2. $y + 6 = 5$ −1 3. $t - 2 = 2$ 4

4. $z - 5 = 1$ 6 5. $a + 4 = -3$ −7 6. $h - 3 = -6$ −3

7. $u - 4 = -1$ 3 8. $8 + d = 14$ 6 9. $19 = x + 7$ 12

10. $17 = b - 8$ 25 11. $-19 = z - 21$ 2 12. $22 = y + 29$ −7

13. $16 = 24 + p$ −8 14. $-17 = 19 + x$ −36 15. $f - 25 = 35$ 60

16. $y + 37 = 59$ 22 17. $s + 46 = 72$ 26 18. $m + 65 = 11$ −54

19. $r + 53 = -19$ −72 20. $n - 75 = 42$ 117 21. $g - 35 = -62$ −27

22. $111 = x + 68$ 43 23. $-54 = -32 + w$ −22 24. $-27 + z = 47$ 74

Practice: Word Problems, p. 38

NAME ______ DATE ______

1-8 Practice: Word Problems

Solving Addition and Subtraction Equations

1. **AGE** Walter lived 2 years longer than his brother Martin. Walter was 79 at the time of his death. Write and solve an addition equation to find Martin's age at the time of his death. $a + 2 = 79$; 77 years old

2. **CIVICS** New York has 21 fewer members in the House of Representatives than California. New York has 33 representatives. Write and solve a subtraction equation to find the number of representatives. $r - 21 = 33$; 54 representatives

3. **GEOMETRY** Two angles are supplementary if the sum of their measures is 180°. Angles A and B are supplementary. If the measure of angle A is 78°, write and solve an addition equation to find the measure of angle B. $m + 78° = 180°$; 102°

180° m∠A = 78° B A

4. **BANKING** After you withdraw $40 from your checking account, the balance is $287. Write and solve a subtraction equation to find your balance before this withdrawal. $b - 40 = 287$; $327

5. **WEATHER** After the temperature had risen 12°F, the temperature was 7°F. Write and solve an addition equation to find the starting temperature. $t + 12 = 7$; −5°F

7°F

6. **CHEMISTRY** The atomic number of mercury is the sum of the atomic number of aluminum and 67. The atomic number of mercury is 80. Write and solve an addition equation to find the atomic number of aluminum. $a + 67 = 80$; 13

7. **ELEVATION** The lowest point in Louisiana is 543 feet lower than the highest point in Louisiana. The elevation of the lowest point is −8 feet. Write and solve a subtraction equation to find the elevation of the highest point in Louisiana. $h - 543 = -8$; 535 ft

8. **POPULATION** The population of Honduras is the population of Haiti decreased by 618,397. The population of Honduras is 6,249,598. Write and solve a subtraction equation to find the population of Haiti. $p - 618,397 = 6,249,598$; 6,867,995

1-9 Lesson Notes

Lesson Resources

Chapter 1 Resource Masters

FAST FILE

- Study Guide and Intervention, p. 41
- Practice: Skills, p. 42
- Practice: Word Problems, p. 43
- Reading to Learn Mathematics, p. 44
- Enrichment, p. 45

Calculator and Spreadsheet Masters, p. 14

Key Teaching Transparencies, 4

MathPASS Tutorial CD-ROM, 38

Parent and Student Study Guide Online Worksheets, 1-9

Teaching Mathematics with Manipulatives, pp. 34–35

Noteables™: Interactive Study Notebook with Foldables™, 1-9

Focus

5-Minute Check 1-9

Use as a quiz or review of Lesson 1-8. (Also available as a transparency)

Bellringer

Communication Ask students how the concept of inverse operations as discussed in Lesson 1-8 could be applied to solving $5x = 15$. Remind them that their goal is to find the value of x.

(Continued in bottom margin.)

Reading to Learn Mathematics, p. 44 ELL

NAME ______ DATE ______ PERIOD ___

1-9 Reading to Learn Mathematics

Solving Multiplication and Division Equations

Pre-Activity ***Read the introduction at the top of page 50 in your textbook. Write your answers below.***

1. If d represents the number of days the bamboo has been growing, write a multiplication equation you could use to find how long it would take for the bamboo to reach a height of 210 inches. $35d = 210$

Reading the Lesson

Complete each sentence.

2. To solve $3x = 51$, ______ each side by 3. divide
3. To solve $\frac{b}{-2} = 4$, ______ each side by −2. multiply
4. To [illegible] $65 = -5t$, ______ [illegible] side by −5. divide

Solving Multiplication and Division Equations

What You'll LEARN

Solve equations by using the Division and Multiplication Properties of Equality.

REVIEW Vocabulary

Identity Property (×): the product of a number and 1 is that same number

WHEN am I ever going to use this?

PLANTS Some species of a bamboo can grow 35 inches per day. That is as many inches as the average child grows in the first 10 years of his or her life!

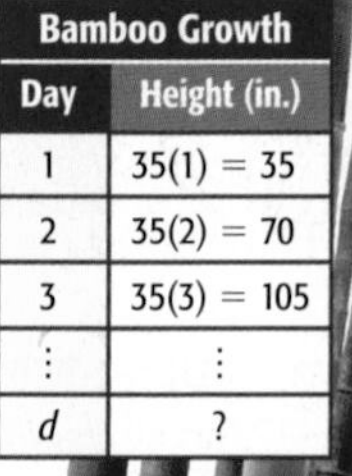

Bamboo Growth	
Day	**Height (in.)**
1	35(1) = 35
2	35(2) = 70
3	35(3) = 105
⋮	⋮
d	?

1. If d represents the number of days the bamboo has been growing, write a multiplication equation you could use to find how long it would take for the bamboo to reach a height of 210 inches. $35d = 210$

The equation $35d = 210$ models the relationship described above. To undo the multiplication of 35, divide each side of the equation by 35.

TEACHING TIP

Point out to students that Example 1 answers Exercise 1 posed in the opener. So, it would take 6 days for a bamboo plant to reach a height of 210 inches.

EXAMPLE Solve a Multiplication Equation

1 **Solve $35d = 210$.**

$35d = 210$ Write the equation.

$\frac{35d}{35} = \frac{210}{35}$ Divide each side of the equation by 35.

$1d = 6$ $35 \div 35 = 1$ and $210 \div 35 = 6$

$d = 6$ Identity Property; $1d = d$

The solution is 6. Check the solution.

STUDY TIP

Solving Equations When you solve a simple equation like $8x = 72$, you can mentally divide each side by 8.

Your Turn **Solve each equation. Check your solution.**

a. $8x = 72$ **9**
b. $-4n = 28$ **−7**
c. $-12 = -6k$ **2**

In Example 1, you used the **Division Property of Equality** to solve a multiplication equation.

Noteables™ **Key Concept: Division Property of Equality**

Words If you divide each side of an equation by the same nonzero number, the two sides remain equal.

Symbols

Arithmetic	Algebra
$12 = 12$	$5x = -60$
$\frac{12}{4} = \frac{12}{4}$	$\frac{5x}{5} = \frac{-60}{5}$
$3 = 3$	$x = -12$

Guide them to the following steps:

1. The variable x is being multiplied by 5.
2. Division is the inverse of multiplication.
3. Therefore, they could undo the multiplication by dividing by 5.

50 Chapter 1 Algebra: Integers

Division Expressions

Remember, $\frac{a}{-3}$ means *a divided by −3*.

You can use the **Multiplication Property of Equality** to solve division equations like $\frac{a}{-3} = -7$.

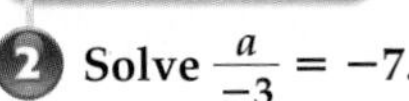

Key Concept: Multiplication Property of Equality

Words If you multiply each side of an equation by the same number, the two sides remain equal.

Symbols

Arithmetic	Algebra
$5 = 5$	$\frac{x}{2} = 8$
$5(-4) = 5(-4)$	$\frac{x}{2}(2) = 8(2)$
$-20 = -20$	$x = 16$

TEACHING TIP

When solving an equation like $\frac{a}{-3} = -7$, a common error is to multiply each side by 3 instead of −3. Caution students to multiply each side by the *integer* the variable is divided by, paying close attention to the sign of that integer.

EXAMPLE Solve a Division Equation

2 **Solve $\frac{a}{-3} = -7$.**

$\frac{a}{-3} = -7$	Write the equation.
$\frac{a}{-3}(-3) = -7(-3)$	Multiply each side by −3 to undo the division in $\frac{a}{-3}$.
$a = 21$	$-7 \cdot (-3) = 21$
The solution is 21	Check the solution.

Your Turn **Solve each equation. Check your solution.**

d. $\frac{y}{-4} = -8$ **32** e. $\frac{m}{5} = -9$ **−45** f. $30 = \frac{b}{-2}$ **−60**

REAL-LIFE CAREERS

How Does a Zoologist Use Math?

Zoologists use equations to predict the growth of animal populations.

Research For information about a career as a zoologist, visit: msmath3.net/careers

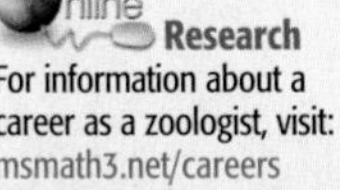

EXAMPLE Use an Equation to Solve a Problem

3 **REPTILES** A Nile crocodile grows to be 4,000 times as heavy as the egg from which it hatched. If an adult crocodile weighs 2,000 pounds, how much does a crocodile egg weigh?

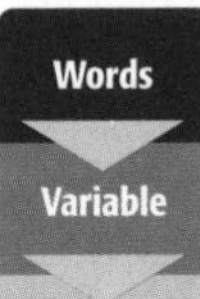

Words	The weight of an adult crocodile is 4,000 times as heavy as the weight of a crocodile egg.		
Variable	Let g = the weight of the crocodile egg.		
Equation	Weight of adult	is	4,000 times the egg's weight.
	2,000	=	$4{,}000g$

$2{,}000 = 4{,}000g$	Write the equation.
$\frac{2{,}000}{4{,}000} = \frac{4{,}000g}{4{,}000}$	Divide each side by 4,000.
$0.5 = g$	$2{,}000 \div 4{,}000 = 0.5$

The crocodile egg weighs 0.5 pound. Check this solution.

msmath3.net/extra_examples

2 Teach

1 Solve $7z = -49$. **−7**

2 Solve $\frac{c}{9} = -6$. **−54**

3 **SURVEYING** English mathematician Edmund Gunter lived around 1600. He invented the *chain*, which was used to measure land for maps and deeds. One chain equals 66 feet. If the south side of a property measures 330 feet, how many chains long is it? **5 chains**

DAILY INTERVENTION

Differentiated Instruction **ELL**

Verbal/Linguistic Have groups of students discuss how to solve equations with counters and how to solve equations using algebra. Then have each student summarize this comparison in a paragraph and include an example.

3 Practice/Apply

FOLDABLES Follow-Up Remind students to use their Foldable tables to record in words and symbols what they learn about solving multiplication and division equations. For example, they might explain how to solve multiplication equations using the multiplication properties of equality.

NUMBER SENSE
In Exercise 3, some questions students may consider include whether x is positive or negative, greater than or less than 25, greater than or less than 300, or zero. **positive; greater than 25; greater than 300; not zero** You also may wish to point out that 25 must divide evenly into x in order to get 300.

About the Exercises...

Guided Practice Key

Exercises	Examples
4–7	1
8–11	2
12, 13	3

Assignment Guide

Basic: 15–41 odd, 45–50

Average: 15–41 odd, 42, 43, 45–50

Enriched: 14–40 even, 42–50

Students practice the same concepts in Exercises 14–41 if they are assigned odd or even problems.

Skill and Concept Check

1. *Writing Math* State what property you would use to solve $-4a = 84$. Explain your reasoning. **Division Prop. of Equality; the inverse operation of multiplication is division.**
2. **OPEN ENDED** Write a division equation whose solution is -10. **Sample answer: $\frac{n}{5} = -2$**
3. **NUMBER SENSE** Without solving the equation, tell what you know about the value of x in the equation $\frac{x}{25} = 300$. **Sample answer: it is greater than 300.**

GUIDED PRACTICE

Solve each equation. Check your solution.

4. $5b = 40$ **8**
5. $-7k = 14$ **−2**
6. $-3n = -18$ **6**
7. $-20 = 4x$ **−5**
8. $\frac{p}{9} = 9$ **81**
9. $\frac{a}{12} = -3$ **−36**
10. $\frac{m}{-2} = -22$ **44**
11. $7 = \frac{z}{-8}$ **−56**

Write and solve an equation to find each number.

12. The product of -9 and a number is 45. **$-9n = 45$; −5**
13. When you divide a number by 4, the result is -16. **$\frac{n}{4} = -16$; −64**

★ **indicates increased difficulty**

Practice and Applications

HOMEWORK HELP

For Exercises	See Examples
14–31	1, 2
32–44	3

Extra Practice
See pages 618, 648.

Solve each equation. Check your solution.

14. $4c = 44$ **11**
15. $9b = 72$ **8**
16. $34 = -2x$ **−17**
17. $-36 = 18y$ **−2**
18. $-8d = 32$ **−4**
19. $-5n = -35$ **7**
20. $-52 = -4g$ **13**
21. $-90 = 6w$ **−15**
22. $\frac{k}{12} = 2$ **24**
23. $10 = \frac{m}{7}$ **70**
24. $6 = \frac{u}{-9}$ **−54**
25. $\frac{h}{-3} = 33$ **−99**
26. $\frac{c}{12} = -8$ **−96**
27. $\frac{r}{24} = -3$ **−72**
28. $\frac{q}{-5} = -20$ **100**
29. $\frac{t}{-4} = -15$ **60**
30. ★ $\frac{10}{x} = -5$ **−2**
31. ★ $\frac{-126}{a} = -21$ **6**

Write and solve an equation to find each number.

32. The product of a number and 8 is 56. **$8n = 56$; 7**
33. When you multiply a number by -3, the result is 39. **$-3n = 39$; −13**
34. When you divide a number by -5, the result is -10. **$\frac{n}{-5} = -10$; 50**
35. The quotient of a number and 7 is -14. **$\frac{n}{7} = -14$; −98**

MEASUREMENT For Exercises 36–39, refer to the table. Write and solve an equation to find each quantity.

Customary System Conversions (length)
1 foot = 12 inches
1 yard = 3 feet
1 yard = 36 inches
1 mile = 5,280 feet
1 mile = 1,760 yards

36. the number of yards in 18 feet **$3y = 18$; 6**
37. the number of feet in 288 inches **$12f = 288$; 24**
38. the number of yards in 540 inches **$36y = 540$; 15**
39. the number of miles in 26,400 feet **$5{,}280m = 26{,}400$; 5**

40. **LAWN SERVICE** Josh charges \$15 to mow an average size lawn in his neighborhood. Write and solve a multiplication equation to find how many of these lawns he needs to mow to earn \$600. **$15\ell = 600$; 40 lawns**

41. **ANIMALS** An African elephant can eat 500 pounds of vegetation per day. Write and solve a multiplication equation to find how many days a 3,000-pound supply of vegetation will last for one elephant. **$500d = 3,000$; 6 days**

POPULATION For Exercises 42–44 use the information in the graphic at the right.

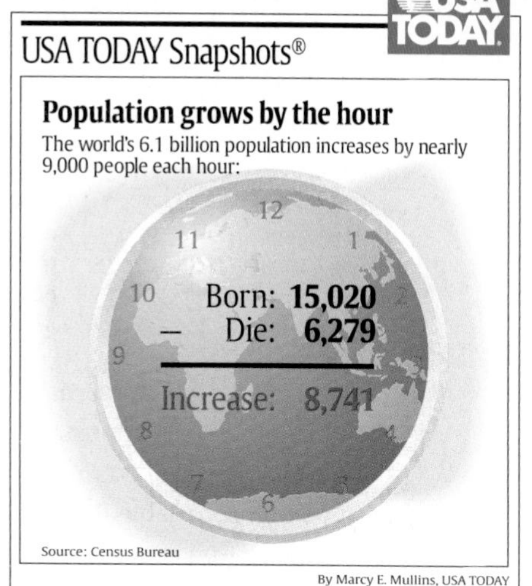

42. Write a multiplication equation that could be used to find how many hours it would take the world's population to increase by 1 million. **$8,741n = 1,000,000$**

43. Solve the equation. Round to the nearest hour. **about 114 h**

44. There are 24 hours in one day. Write and solve a multiplication equation to determine how many days it would take the world's population to increase by 1 million. Round to the nearest day. **$24d = 114$; about 5 days**

45. **CRITICAL THINKING** If an object is traveling at a rate of speed r, then the distance d the object travels after a time t is given by $d = rt$. Write an expression for the value of t. $\frac{d}{r}$

Spiral Review with Standardized Test Practice

46. **SHORT RESPONSE** The base B of a triangular prism has an area of 24 square inches. If the volume V of the prism is 216 cubic inches, use the formula $V = Bh$ to find the height of the prism in inches. **9 in.**

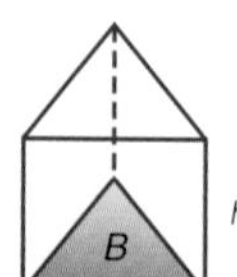

47. **MULTIPLE CHOICE** Luis ran 2.5 times the distance that Mark ran. If Mark ran 3 miles, which equation can be used to find the distance d in miles that Luis ran? **C**

(A) $d = 2.5 + 3$ (B) $d + 2.5 = 3$ (C) $d = 2.5(3)$ (D) $2.5d = 3$

48. **ARCHITECTURE** William G. Durant wanted the Empire State Building to be taller than the building being built by his competitor, Walter Chrysler. He secretly had a 185-foot spire built inside the building and then hoisted to the top of the building upon its completion. Write and solve an addition equation that could be used to find the height of the Empire State Building without its spire. (Lesson 1-8) **$x + 185 = 1,250$; 1,065 ft**

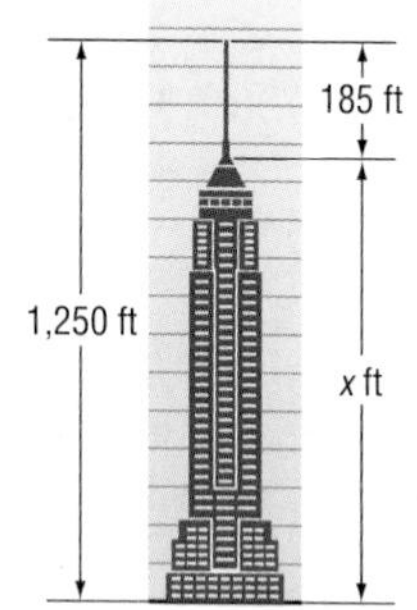

Write each verbal sentence as an algebraic equation. (Lesson 1-7)

49. A number increased by 10 is 4. **$x + 10 = 4$**

50. 8 feet longer than she jumped is 15 feet. **$8 + j = 15$**

Math Online msmath3.net/self_check_quiz

4 Assess

Higher-Level Thinking

Ask students to outline the steps needed to solve $10x - 2 = 28$. Remind them to consider the order of operations as discussed in Lesson 1-2.

Study Guide and Intervention, p. 41

NAME ________ DATE ________ PERIOD ____

1-9 Study Guide and Intervention

Solving Multiplication and Division Equations

You can use the following properties to solve multiplication and division equations.

- *Multiplication Property of Equality* - If you multiply each side of an equation by the same number, the two sides remain equal.
- *Division Property of Equality* - If you divide each side of an equation by the same nonzero number, the two sides remain equal.

EXAMPLE 1 **Solve $19w = 104$. Check your solution.**

$19w = 114$ Write the equation.

$\frac{19w}{19} = \frac{114}{19}$ Divide each side of the equation by 19.

$1w = 6$ $19 \div 19 = 1$ and $114 \div 19 = 6$.

$w = 6$ Identity Property; $1w = w$

Check $19w = 114$ Write the original equation.

$19(6) \stackrel{?}{=} 114$ Replace w with 6.

$114 = 114$ ✓ This sentence is true.

EXAMPLE 2 **Solve $\frac{d}{15} = -9$. Check your solution.**

$\frac{d}{15} = -9$

$\frac{d}{15}(15) = -9(15)$ Multiply each side of the equation by 15.

$d = -135$

Check $\frac{d}{15} = -9$ Write the original equation.

$\frac{-135}{15} \stackrel{?}{=} -9$ Replace d with -135.

$-9 = -9$ ✓ $-135 \div 15 = -9$

EXERCISES

Solve each equation. Check your solution.

1. $\frac{r}{5} = 6$ **30**
2. $2d = 12$ **6**
3. $7h = -21$ **−3**
4. $-8x = 40$ **−5**
5. $\frac{f}{8} = -6$ **−48**
6. $\frac{x}{-10} = -7$ **70**
7. $17c = -68$ **−4**
8. $\frac{h}{-11} = 12$ **−132**
9. $29t = -145$ **−5**
10. $125 = 5z$ **25**
11. $13t = -182$ **−14**
12. $117 = -39k$ **−3**

Practice: Skills, p. 42

NAME ________ DATE ________ PERIOD ____

1-9 Practice: Skills

Solving Multiplication and Division Equations

Solve each equation. Check your solution.

1. $\frac{u}{7} = 3$ **21**
2. $3c = 12$ **4**
3. $5x = -15$ **−3**
4. $-7z = 49$ **−7**
5. $\frac{n}{3} = -7$ **−21**
6. $\frac{a}{-9} = -11$ **99**
7. $-14g = -56$ **4**
8. $\frac{t}{-12} = 11$ **−132**
9. $18y = -144$ **−8**
10. $135 = 9z$ **15**
11. $11d = -143$ **−13**
12. $116 = -29k$ **−4**
13. $\frac{w}{9} = 17$ **153**
14. $-14 = \frac{y}{-7}$ **98**
15. $-112 = -8v$ **14**
16. $17c = 136$ **8**
17. $-21a = -126$ **6**
18. $\frac{s}{-19} = 9$ **−171**
19. $\frac{m}{-31} = -7$ **217**
20. $16q = 272$ **17**
21. $15 = \frac{z}{-14}$ **−210**
22. $\frac{g}{-22} = -23$ **506**
23. $\frac{y}{25} = 16$ **400**
24. $47k = 517$ **11**

Practice: Word Problems, p. 43

NAME ________ DATE ________ PERIOD ____

1-9 Practice: Word Problems

Solving Multiplication and Division Equations

1. **WAGES** Felipe earns \$9 per hour for helping his grandmother with her yard work. Write and solve a multiplication equation to find how many hours he must help his grandmother in order to earn \$54. **$9h = 54$; 6 h**

2. **SHOPPING** Chocolate bars are on sale for \$0.50 each. If Brad paid \$5 for chocolate bars, write and solve a multiplication equation to find how many bars he bought. **$0.50b = 5$; 10 bars**

3. **EXERCISE** Jasmine jogs 3 miles each day. Write and solve a multiplication equation to find how many days it will take her to jog 57 miles. **$3d = 57$; 19 days**

4. **TRAVEL** On a trip, the Rollins family drove at an average rate of 62 miles per hour. Write and solve a multiplication equation to find how long it took them to drive 558 miles. **$62h = 558$; 9 h**

5. **ROBOTS** The smallest robot can travel 20 inches per minute through a pipe. Write and solve a multiplication equation to find how long it will take this robot to travel through 10 *feet* of pipe. **$20m = 120$; 6 min**

6. **BANKING** Nate withdraws \$40 from his checking account each day. Write and solve a multiplication equation to find how long it will take him to withdraw \$680. **$-40w = -680$; 17 days**

7. **AGE** The product of Bart's age and 26 is 338. Write and solve a multiplication equation to find Bart's age. **$26a = 338$; 13 yr**

8. **POPULATION** The population of a small town is increasing at a rate of 325 people per year. Write and solve a multiplication equation to find how long it will take the population to increase by 6,825. **$325p = 6,825$; 21 yr**

Lesson 1-9 Solving Multiplication and Division Equations 53

Study Guide and Review

Vocabulary Assessment

- This alphabetical list of vocabulary terms in Chapter 1 includes a page reference where each term was introduced.
- A vocabulary review/test for Chapter 1 is available on p. 60 of the *Chapter 1 Resource Masters*.

Vocabulary PuzzleMaker

ELL The online Vocabulary PuzzleMaker improves students' mathematics vocabulary using four puzzle formats – crossword, scramble, word search using a word list, and word search using clues. Students can work on a computer screen or from a printed handout.

MindJogger Videoquizzes

ELL MindJogger Videoquizzes provide an alternative review of concepts presented in this chapter. Students work in teams in a game show format to gain points for correct answers. The questions are presented in three rounds.

Round 1 Concepts (5 questions)
Round 2 Skills (4 questions)
Round 3 Problem Solving (4 questions)

ExamView® Pro

Use the networkable ExamView® Pro Testmaker CD-ROM to:

- Create **multiple versions** of tests.
- Create **modified** tests for **inclusion** students with one mouse click.
- **Edit** existing questions and **add** your own questions.
- Build tests aligned with state standards using built-in **state curriculum correlations.**
- Change **English** tests to **Spanish** with one mouse click and vice versa.

Study Guide and Review

Vocabulary and Concept Check

absolute value (p. 19)	evaluate (p. 11)	order of operations (p. 11)
additive inverse (p. 25)	inequality (p. 18)	powers (p. 12)
algebraic expression (p. 11)	integer (p. 17)	property (p. 13)
conjecture (p. 7)	inverse operations (p. 46)	solution (p. 45)
coordinate (p. 18)	negative number (p. 17)	solve (p. 45)
counterexample (p. 13)	numerical expression (p. 11)	variable (p. 11)
defining a variable (p. 39)	open sentence (p. 13)	
equation (p. 13)	opposites (p. 25)	

Choose the letter of the term that best matches each statement or phrase.

1. an integer and its opposite e
2. a number less than zero i
3. value of the variable that makes the equation true h
4. a sentence that compares two different numbers j
5. contains a variable, a number, and at least one operation symbol a
6. to find the value of an expression b
7. a mathematical sentence that contains an equals sign d
8. an open sentence that is true for any number f
9. the distance a number is from zero c
10. operations that "undo" each other g

a. algebraic expression
b. evaluate
c. absolute value
d. equation
e. additive inverses
f. property
g. inverse operations
h. solution
i. negative number
j. inequality

Lesson-by-Lesson Exercises and Examples

1-1 A Plan for Problem Solving (pp. 6–10)

Use the four-step plan to solve each problem.

11. **SCIENCE** A chemist pours table salt into a beaker. If the beaker plus the salt has a mass of 84.7 grams and the beaker itself has a mass of 63.3 grams, what was the mass of the salt? 21.4 g
12. **SPORTS** In a basketball game, the Sliders scored five 3-point shots, seven 2-point shots, and 15 1-point shots. Find the total points scored. 44

Example 1 **At Smart's Car Rental, it costs $57 per day plus $0.10 per mile to rent a certain car. How much will it cost to rent the car for 1 day and drive 180 miles?**

Multiply the number of miles by the cost per mile. Then add the daily cost.

$\$0.10 \times 180 = \$18$

$\$18 + \$57 = \$75$

The cost is $75.

 msmath3.net/vocabulary_review

Key concepts from the lesson, one or two examples, and several practice problems are included in the **Lesson-by-Lesson Exercises and Examples.**

1-2 Variables, Expressions, and Properties (pp. 11–15)

Evaluate each expression.

13. $3^2 - 2 \cdot 3 + 5$ **8**
14. $4 + 2(5 - 2)$ **10**
15. $\frac{25}{6^2 - 11}$ **1**
16. $\frac{22 - 6}{4} + 10(2)$ **24**

Evaluate each expression if $a = 6$, $b = 2$, and $c = 1$.

17. $3a - 2b + c$ **15**
18. $\frac{(a + 2)^2}{bc}$ **32**

Example 2 **Evaluate $x^2 + yx - z^2$ if $x = 4$, $y = 2$, and $z = 1$.**

$x^2 + yx - z^2$ — Write the expression.
$= 4^2 + (2)(4) - (1)^2$ — $x = 4$, $y = 2$, and $z = 1$
$= 16 + (2)(4) - 1$ — Evaluate powers first.
$= 16 + 8 - 1$ — Multiply.
$= 23$ — Add and subtract.

1-3 Integers and Absolute Value (pp. 17–21)

19. **MONEY** Kara made an \$80 withdrawal from her checking account. Write an integer for this situation. **−80**

Replace each ● with <, >, or = to make a true sentence.

20. −8 ● 7 **<**
21. −2 ● −6 **>**
22. Order the set of integers {−7, 8, 0, −3, −2, 5, 6} from least to greatest. **{−7, −3, −2, 0, 5, 6, 8}**

Evaluate each expression.

23. |−5| **5**
24. |−12| − |4| **8**

Example 3 **Replace the ● in −3 ● −7 with <, >, or = to make a true sentence.**

Graph the integers on a number line.

−8 −7 −6 −5 −4 −3 −2 −1 0 1

−3 lies to the right of −7, so −3 > −7.

Example 4 **Evaluate |−3|.**

Since the graph of −3 is 3 units from 0 on the number line, the absolute value of −3 is 3.

1-4 Adding Integers (pp. 23–27)

Add.

25. −54 + 21 **−33**
26. 100 + (−75) **25**
27. −14 + (−20) **−34**
28. 38 + (−46) **−8**
29. −14 + 37 + (−20) + 2 **5**
30. **WEATHER** At 8:00 A.M., it was −5°F. By noon, it had risen 34°. Write an addition statement to describe this situation. Then find the sum. **−5 + 34; 29**

Example 5 **Find −16 + (−11).**

−16 + (−11) = −27 — Add |−16| and |−11|. Both numbers are negative, so the sum is negative.

Example 6 **Find −7 + 20.**

−7 + 20 = 13 — To find −7 + 20, subtract |−7| from |20|. The sum is positive because |20| > |−7|.

1-5 Subtracting Integers (pp. 28–31)

Subtract.

31. −2 − (−5) **3**
32. −30 − 13 **−43**
33. 11 − 15 **−4**
34. 25 − (−11) **36**

Example 7 **Find −27 − (−6).**

−27 − (−6) = −27 + 6 — To subtract −6, add 6.
= −21 — Add.

FOLDABLES™ Study Organizer

For more information about Foldables, see *Teaching Mathematics with Foldables.*

Have students look through the chapter to make sure they have included examples in their Foldables for each lesson or topic in the chapter.

Encourage students to refer to their Foldables while completing the Study Guide and Review and to use them in preparing for the Chapter Test.

Mixed Problem Solving
For mixed problem-solving practice, see page 648.

1-6 Multiplying and Dividing Integers (pp. 34–38)

Multiply or divide.

35. $-4(-25)$ **100**
36. $-7(3)$ **−21**
37. $-15(-4)(-1)$ **−60**
38. $180 \div (-15)$ **−12**
39. $-170 \div (-5)$ **34**
40. $-88 \div 8$ **−11**
41. **GOLF** José scored −2 on each of six golf holes. What was his overall score for these six holes? **−12**

Example 8 Find $3(-20)$.

$3(-20) = -60$ The factors have different signs. The product is negative.

Example 9 Find $-48 \div (-12)$.

$-48 \div (-12) = 4$ The dividend and the divisor have the same sign. The quotient is positive.

1-7 Writing Expressions and Equations (pp. 39–42)

Write each verbal phrase or sentence as an algebraic expression or equation.

42. Six divided by a number is $\frac{1}{2}$. $6 \div n = \frac{1}{2}$
43. the sum of a number and 7 $n + 7$
44. A number less 10 is 25. $n - 10 = 25$
45. Four times a number is 48. $4x = 48$

Example 10 Write *nine less than a number is 5* as an algebraic equation.

Let n represent the number.

Nine less than a number	is	5.
$n - 9$	$=$	5

The equation is $n - 9 = 5$.

1-8 Solving Addition and Subtraction Equations (pp. 45–49)

Solve each equation. Check your solution.

46. $n + 40 = 90$ **50**
47. $x - 3 = 10$ **13**
48. $c - 30 = -18$ **12**
49. $9 = a + 31$ **−22**
50. $d + 14 = -1$ **−15**
51. $27 = y - 12$ **39**
52. **CANDY** There are 75 candies in a bowl after you remove 37. Write and solve a subtraction equation to find how many candies were originally in the bowl. $c - 37 = 75$; **112**

Example 11 Solve $5 + k = 18$.

$5 + k = 18$ Write the equation.
$5 - 5 + k = 18 - 5$ Subtract 5 from each side.
$n = 13$ $18 - 5 = 13$

Example 12 Solve $n - 13 = -62$.

$n - 13 = -62$ Write the equation.
$n - 13 + 13 = -62 + 13$ Add 13 to each side.
$n = -49$ $-62 + 13 = -49$

1-9 Solving Multiplication and Division Equations (pp. 50–53)

Solve each equation. Check your solution.

53. $15x = -75$ **−5**
54. $-72 = -6f$ **12**
55. $-4x = 52$ **−13**
56. $\frac{s}{7} = 42$ **294**
57. $-3 = \frac{d}{24}$ **−72**
58. $\frac{y}{-10} = -15$ **150**

Example 13

Solve $60 = 5t$.

$60 = 5t$

$\frac{60}{5} = \frac{5t}{5}$

$12 = t$

Example 14

Solve $\frac{m}{-2} = 8$.

$\frac{m}{-2} = 8$

$\left(\frac{m}{-2}\right)(-2) = 8(-2)$

$m = -16$

Practice Test

Vocabulary and Concepts

1. **Determine** whether the following statement is *true* or *false*. Explain.
   The absolute value of a positive number is negative. **False; see margin.**
2. **Write** two different verbal phrases for the algebraic expression $8 - n$.
   Sample answer: 8 minus n; n less than 8

Skills and Applications

Evaluate each expression if $a = 3$, $b = 2$, and $c = 5$.

3. $a + 15 \div a$ **8**
4. $(2c + b) \div a - 3$ **1**
5. $4a^2 - 5a - 12$ **9**

Replace each ● with <, >, or = to make a true sentence.

6. $-6 \bullet 3$ **<**
7. $-8 \bullet -11$ **>**
8. $|8| \bullet -8$ **>**

9. Order the set of integers $\{-3, 0, -5, 1, -2\}$ from least to greatest. **$\{-5, -3, -2, 0, 1\}$**
10. Find the value of $|y| - |x|$ if $x = -4$ and $y = -9$. **5**

Add or subtract.

11. $-27 + 8$ **-19**
12. $-12 + 60$ **48**
13. $-9 + (-11)$ **-20**
14. $10 - 24$ **-14**
15. $-41 - 13$ **-54**
16. $-4 - (-35)$ **31**

Multiply or divide.

17. $-5(-13)$ **65**
18. $8(-9)$ **-72**
19. $7(-10)(-4)$ **280**
20. $-105 \div 15$ **-7**
21. $\frac{-70}{-5}$ **14**
22. $\frac{36}{-4}$ **-9**

Solve each equation. Check your solution.

23. $k - 10 = 65$ **75**
24. $x + 15 = -3$ **-18**
25. $-7 = a - 11$ **4**
26. $3d = 24$ **8**
27. $\frac{n}{-2} = 16$ **-32**
28. $-96 = 8y$ **-12**

29. **CARDS** After losing two rounds in a card game, Eneas' score was -40. After winning the third round, her score was 5. Write and solve an addition equation to find the number of points scored in the third round.
   $-40 + s = 5$; 45

Standardized Test Practice

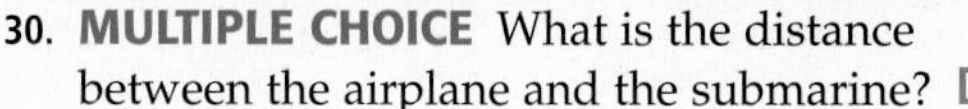

30. **MULTIPLE CHOICE** What is the distance between the airplane and the submarine? **D**

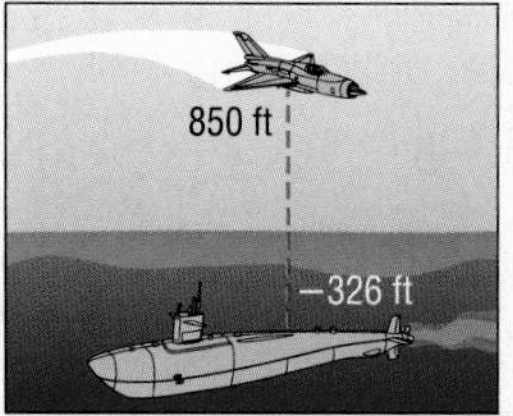

Ⓐ 524 ft Ⓑ 536 ft
Ⓒ 1,156 ft Ⓓ 1,176 ft

Math Online msmath3.net/chapter_test

Practice Test

Assessment Options

Vocabulary Test A vocabulary review/test for Chapter 1 can be found on p. 60 of the *Chapter 1 Resource Masters*.

Chapter Tests There are six Chapter 1 Tests and an Extended Response Assessment task available in the *Chapter 1 Resource Masters*.

Chapter 1 Tests			
Form	**Type**	**Level**	**Pages**
1	MC	basic	47–48
2A	MC	average	49–50
2B	MC	average	51–52
2C	FR	average	53–54
2D	FR	average	55–56
3	FR	advanced	57–58

MC = multiple-choice questions
FR = free-response questions

Extended Response Assessment

Extended Response tasks for Chapter 1 can be found on p. 59 of the *Chapter 1 Resource Masters.* A sample scoring rubric for these tasks appears on p. A31.

Assessment Options lists the tests that are available in the Chapter Resource Masters.

Portfolio Suggestion

Introduction The rules for operations on integers are fundamental to algebra as they apply to operations on variables as well.

Ask Students to include a summary of the rules for operations on integers. They should organize the information in the way that best suits them, such as in a table, on a Foldable, or in a paragraph.

Answer

1. The absolute value of a number is the distance that number is from 0 on the number line. Since distance is always positive, the absolute value of a positive number is always positive.

Standardized Test Practice

These two pages contain practice questions in the various formats that can be found on the most frequently given standardized tests.

A student recording sheet for these two pages can be found on page A1 of the *Chapter 1 Resource Masters.*

Standardized Test Practice Student Recording Sheet, p. A1

NAME ______ DATE ______ PERIOD ____

Standardized Test Practice SCORE ____

Student Recording Sheet *(Use with pages 58-59 of the Student Edition.)*

Part 1: Multiple Choice

Select the best answer from the choices given and fill in the corresponding oval.

1. Ⓐ Ⓑ Ⓒ Ⓓ
2. Ⓕ Ⓖ Ⓗ Ⓘ
3. Ⓐ Ⓑ Ⓒ Ⓓ
4. Ⓕ Ⓖ Ⓗ Ⓘ
5. Ⓐ Ⓑ Ⓒ Ⓓ
6. Ⓕ Ⓖ Ⓗ Ⓘ
7. Ⓐ Ⓑ Ⓒ Ⓓ
8. Ⓕ Ⓖ Ⓗ Ⓘ
9. Ⓐ Ⓑ Ⓒ Ⓓ

Part 2: Short Response/Grid in

Solve the problem and write your answer in the blank.

For grid in questions, also enter your answer by writing each number or symbol in a box. Then fill in the corresponding circle for that number of symbol.

10. ______
11. ______ (grid in)
12. ______ (grid in)
13. ______ (grid in)
14. ______
15. ______ (grid in)
16. ______ (grid in)

Part 3: Extended Response

Record your answers for Questions 17 and 18 on the back of this paper.

Additional Practice

See pp. 65–66 of the *Chapter 1 Resource Masters* for additional standardized test practice.

Standardized Test Practice exercises were created to closely parallel those on actual state proficiency tests. Rubrics are provided for assessment.

Chapter 1 Standardized Test Practice

PART 1 Multiple Choice

Record your answers on the answer sheet provided by your teacher or on a sheet of paper.

1. The table shows how much Miranda spent on her school lunch during one week.

Day	Amount
Monday	\$3.15
Tuesday	\$3.25
Wednesday	\$3.85
Thursday	\$2.95
Friday	\$4.05

Which of the following is a good estimate for the total amount Miranda spent on lunches that week? (Prerequisite Skill, p. 600) **C**

Ⓐ \$15 Ⓑ \$16
Ⓒ \$17 Ⓓ \$18

2. What is the order of operations for the expression $27 \div (4 + 5) \times 2$? (Lesson 1-2) **H**

Ⓕ $\div, +, \times$ Ⓖ $\div, \times, +$
Ⓗ $+, \div, \times$ Ⓘ $+, \times, \div$

3. Which of the following properties is illustrated by the equation $6 + (2 + 5) = (2 + 5) + 6$? (Lesson 1-2) **B**

Ⓐ Associative Property
Ⓑ Commutative Property
Ⓒ Distributive Property
Ⓓ Inverse Property

4. Find $-15 - (-9)$. (Lesson 1-5) **G**

Ⓕ -24 Ⓖ -6 Ⓗ 4 Ⓘ 6

5. Solve the equation $y = -8(-4)(-2)$. (Lesson 1-6) **A**

Ⓐ -64 Ⓑ -32 Ⓒ 32 Ⓓ 64

TEST-TAKING TIP

Question 6 Be careful when a question involves adding, subtracting, multiplying, or dividing negative integers. Check to be sure that you have chosen an answer with the correct sign.

6. What is -54 divided by -6? (Lesson 1-6) **I**

Ⓕ -60 Ⓖ -48 Ⓗ -9 Ⓘ 9

7. Which of these expresses the equation below in words? (Lesson 1-7) **C**

$$3(x - 4) = 7x + 5$$

Ⓐ Three times a number minus four is seven times that number plus five.
Ⓑ Three times a number minus four is seven times the sum of that number and five.
Ⓒ Three times the difference of a number and four is seven times that number plus five.
Ⓓ Three times the difference of a number and four is seven times the sum of that number and five.

8. Amy had 20 jellybeans. Tariq gave her 18 more. Amy ate the jellybeans as she walked home. When she got home, she had 13 left. Which equation shows how many jellybeans Amy ate? (Lesson 1-7) **I**

Ⓕ $20 + 18 + x = 13$
Ⓖ $(20 - 18) - x = 13$
Ⓗ $(20 - 18) + x = 13$
Ⓘ $(20 + 18) - x = 13$

9. If $x - 12 = -15$, find the value of $4 - x$. (Lesson 1-8) **D**

Ⓐ -13 Ⓑ -1 Ⓒ 1 Ⓓ 7

ExamView® Pro

Special banks of standardized test questions similar to those on the TIMSS and NAEP grade 8 tests can be found on this CD-ROM.

Preparing for Standardized Tests
For test-taking strategies and more practice, see pages 660–677.

PART 2 Short Response/Grid In

Record your answers on the answer sheet provided by your teacher or on a sheet of paper.

10. What is the area of the empty lot shown below in square feet? (Prerequisite Skill, p. 613) **1,058 ft²**

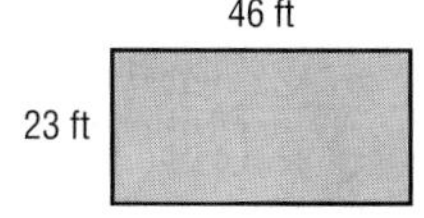

11. The graph shows the number of flat screen computer monitors sold during the last 6 months of the year at Marvel Computers.

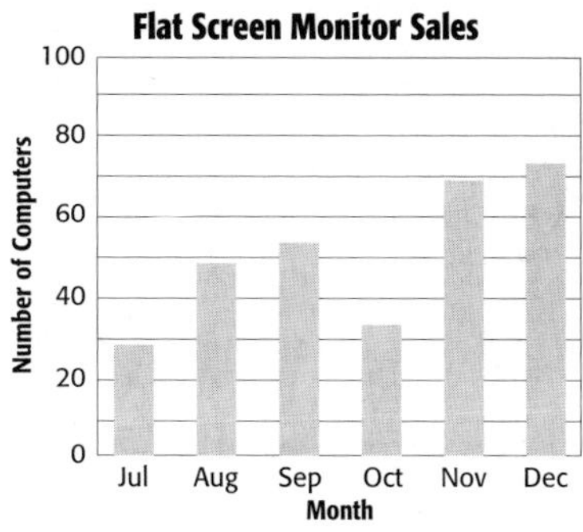

Estimate the average number of computers sold per month during the last 6 months to the nearest ten. (Prerequisite Skill, p. 602) **50**

12. One pound of coffee makes 100 cups. If 300 cups of coffee are served at each football game, how many pounds are needed for 7 games? (Lesson 1-1) **21**

13. What is the value of the following expression? (Lesson 1-2) **1/10 or .1**

$$\frac{5 - 3}{8 + 6 \div 2 \times 4}$$

14. Which points on the following number line have the same absolute value? (Lesson 1-3) ***M* and *P***

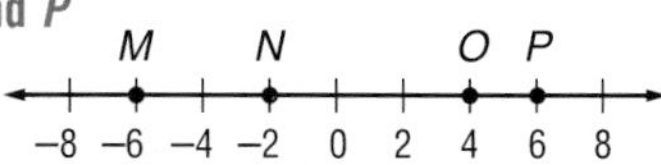

15. The table shows Mr. Carson's weight change during the first 3 months of his diet. If he started his diet at 245 pounds, how much did he weigh at the end of month 3? (Lesson 1-4) **224**

Month	1	2	3
Weight Change	−7	−9	−5

16. The eighth grade ordered 216 hot dogs for their end-of-the-year party. If 8 hot dogs come in a single package, how many packages did they buy? (Lesson 1-9) **27**

PART 3 Extended Response

Record your answers on a sheet of paper. Show your work.

17. To raise money for a charity, an 8th-grade science class asked a student group to perform a benefit concert in the school's 400-seat auditorium. Tickets for the 180 seats near the stage sold for $30 each. Tickets for other seats were sold at a lower price. The concert sold out, raising a total of $9,360. (Lesson 1-1)

a. How many seats are not in the section near the stage? **220**

b. Write an equation for the price p of each ticket in the section not near the stage. **$(180 \times 30) + 220p = 9{,}360$**

c. Find the price of the tickets in the section not near the stage. **$18**

18. In the table below, n, p, r, and t each represent a different integer. If $n = -4$ and $t \neq 1$, find each of the following values. Explain your reasoning using the properties of integers. (Lesson 1-2) **a–c. See margin.**

$$n \times p = n$$
$$t \times r = r$$
$$n + t = r$$

a. p b. r c. t

msmath3.net/standardized_test

Answers

18a. $p = 1$; **The Identity Property for Multiplication states that any number times one is that same number.**

18b. $r = 0$; **The Zero Product Property states that any number times zero is zero.**

18c. $t = 4$; **The Additive Inverse Property states that the sum of any number and its opposite is zero. Since $-4 + t = 0$, t must be the additive inverse of −4 or 4.**

Standardized Test Practice

Rubrics The following rubrics are sample scoring devices for short response and extended response questions.

Short Response

Points	Description
2	The student demonstrates a thorough understanding of the mathematics of the task. The response may contain minor flaws that do not detract from the demonstration of a thorough understanding.
1	The student has provided a response that is only partially correct.
0	The student has provided a completely incorrect solution or no response at all.

Extended Response

Points	Description
4	The student demonstrates a thorough understanding of the mathematics of the task. The response may contain minor flaws that do not detract from the demonstration of a thorough understanding.
3	The student demonstrates an understanding of the mathematics of the task. The response is essentially correct and demonstrates an essential but less than thorough understanding of the mathematics.
2	The student demonstrates only a partial understanding of the mathematics of the task. Although the student may have used the correct approach to a solution or may have provided a correct solution, the work lacks an essential understanding of the underlying mathematical concepts.
1	The student demonstrates a very limited understanding of the mathematics of the task. The response is incomplete and exhibits many flaws.
0	The student provides a completely incorrect solution or no response at all.

A more detailed 4-point rubric is provided on page A2 of the *Chapter 1 Resource Masters*.

Chapter Overview

Algebra: Rational Numbers

	LESSON OBJECTIVES	NCTM Standards	NAEP 2005	State/Local Objectives
2-1	**Fractions and Decimals** (pp. 62–66) • Express rational numbers as decimals and decimals as fractions.	1, 2, 5, 10	N1d, N1e, N3a, A1a, A2a, A3a	
2-2	**Comparing and Ordering Rational Numbers** (pp. 67–70) • Compare and order rational numbers.	1, 2, 5, 10	N1d, N1e, N1i, N1j, N5f	
2-3	**Multiplying Rational Numbers** (pp. 71–75) • Multiply fractions.	1, 2, 4, 5, 6, 10	N1d, N1b, N3a, N3g, A3b, A4e, N3d, N5b	
2-4	**Dividing Rational Numbers** (pp. 76–80) • Divide fractions.	1, 4, 5, 6, 10	N3a, N3g, N3f, N1d, A3b, N3d, N5b	
2-5	**Adding and Subtracting Like Fractions** (pp. 82–85) • Add and subtract fractions with like denominators.	1, 2	N1d, N3a, N3f, N3g, A3b, N5b	
2-6	**Adding and Subtracting Unlike Fractions** (pp. 88–91) • Add and subtract fractions with unlike denominators.	1, 2, 6	N1b, N1d, N3a, N3f, N3g, A3b, N5b	
2-7	**Equations with Rational Numbers** (pp. 92–95) • Solve equations involving rational numbers.	1, 2, 6	N1d, N3a, N3f, N5e, A4a, A4b, A3a, A4c	
2-8	**Powers and Exponents** (pp. 96–103) **2-8a Problem-Solving Strategy:** Solve problems using the look for a pattern strategy. • Use powers and exponents in expressions. **2-8b Hands-On Lab:** Use binary numbers.	1, 2, 10	N1d, N3f, A3b, A1a	
2-9	**Scientific Notation** (pp. 104–107) • Express numbers in scientific notation.	1, 5, 6, 10	N1f, N1d, N1i	

Key to NCTM Standards:

1=Number & Operations, 2=Algebra, 3=Geometry, 4=Measurement, 5=Data Analysis & Probability, 6=Problem Solving, 7=Reasoning & Proof, 8=Communication, 9=Connections, 10=Representation

NAEP 2005 Standards: See Teacher Resources at math.glencoe.com

Pacing suggestions for the entire year can be found on page T23.

StudentWorks

*An electronic version of this chapter is available on **StudentWorks™**. This backpack solution CD-ROM allows students instant access to the Student Edition, lesson worksheet pages, and web resources.*

Chapter Resource Manager

CHAPTER 2 RESOURCE MASTERS (FAST FILE)

Study Guide and Intervention	Practice (Skills and Word Problems)	Reading to Learn Mathematics	Enrichment	Assessment	Applications*	Parent and Student Study Guide Online Worksheets	5-Minute Check Transparencies	Key Teaching Transparencies	MathPASS: Tutorial Plus (lessons)	Teaching Mathematics with Manipulatives	Noteables™: Interactive Study Notebook	Optional Materials
67	68–69	70	71			2-1	2-1				2-1	
72	73–74	75	76			2-2	2-2	5	7, 8	37	2-2	
77	78–79	80	81	127	RC 28	2-3	2-3		9, 10		2-3	colored paper, colored pencils
82	83–84	85	86			2-4	2-4	6	11, 12		2-4	
87	88–89	90	91	127, 129		2-5	2-5			38	2-5	
92	93–94	95	96		CM 5–6	2-6	2-6	7	13–17		2-6	
97	98–99	100	101	128	CS 15	2-7	2-7				2-7	
102	103–104	105	106		CS 16	2-8	2-8	8		39	2-8	paper, pencil
107	108–109	110	111	113–126, 128, 130–132		2-9	2-9		18		2-9	

*** Key to Abbreviations:** *CS = Calculator and Spreadsheet Masters, RC = Real-Life Career Masters, CM = Classroom Math Games (online), SM = Science and Math Lab Manual (online)*

PowerPoint® Presentations

This CD-ROM is a customizable Microsoft® PowerPoint® presentation that includes:

- In-Class Examples
- Links to Online Study Tools
- 5-Minute Check Transparencies
- Your Turn Exercises

Math Skills Maintenance

Use the Math Skills Maintenance Masters to keep your students' basic math skills fresh. Students can review skills one at a time or in a combined format. The Masters are also available online at msmath3.net/maintenance.

Chapter 2 Mathematical Content and Teaching Strategies

Continuity of Instruction

Building on Prior Knowledge

Students have learned the basic principles of fractions, decimals, and exponents in previous courses. They can add and subtract mixed fractions by rewriting them as improper fractions. Students understand that an integer is a number from the set {. . . −3, −2, −1, 0, 1, 2, 3 . . .}, and they can solve simple algebraic equations. They can recognize simple patterns in sequences of numbers and geometric figures.

Learning in This Chapter

This chapter presents a more in-depth study of basic algebraic concepts. Students will add, subtract, multiply, and divide like and unlike fractions. They will learn to write equivalent fractions and decimals, and they will discover the difference between terminating and repeating decimals. The last two lessons in the chapter review properties of exponents and introduce students to scientific notation.

Making Future Connections

Students will use the basic algebra presented in this chapter in many everyday activities and in most science and mathematics classes they take. For example, when using recipes, students may perform operations on fractions to determine correct amounts of the ingredients. As students progress in math and science, they will use scientific notation to describe distances in space and will write rational expressions as improper fractions, rather than mixed numbers, in the formal study of algebra.

Mathematical Background

2-1 Fractions and Decimals

In this lesson, students become more familiar with expressing numbers as fractions and decimals and converting between fractions and decimals. Almost all scientific data are presented in decimal form, and the ability to understand fractions and decimals is an important everyday skill.

2-2 Comparing and Ordering Rational Numbers

Students initially overwhelmed by the comparison of fractions learn to use estimation for such problems. For example, realizing that $\frac{11}{21}$ is greater than $\frac{1}{2}$ and $\frac{3}{8}$ is less than $\frac{1}{2}$ makes it easier to find that $\frac{11}{21} > \frac{3}{8}$. Knowing a few decimal reference points, such as $\frac{1}{4} = 0.25$, $\frac{1}{2} = 0.5$, and $\frac{3}{4} = 0.75$ is also helpful.

Teacher to Teacher

Dennis Baker
Desert Shadows Middle School
Scottsdale, AZ

"In addition to the techniques in Example 1, I show students how to compare fractions by multiplying the means and extremes."

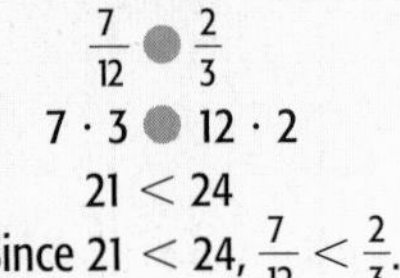

$\frac{7}{12} \bullet \frac{2}{3}$

$7 \cdot 3 \bullet 12 \cdot 2$

$21 < 24$

Since $21 < 24$, $\frac{7}{12} < \frac{2}{3}$.

Dennis Baker

2-3 Multiplying Rational Numbers

Dimensional analysis makes complex problems manageable. Have students write numbers and units in fraction form—20 meters per second as 20 m/s. Doing so will help students keep track of both numbers and units and will help them see how units divide out to arrive at the correct answer. Students will use dimensional analysis in chemistry and physics courses.

Multimedia

Have students watch the video *Fractions and All Their Parts* by Allied Video Corporation (1992). This 3-part series uses colorful animation to engage students in the study of fractions. Ask them to summarize the main points.

2-4 Dividing Rational Numbers

Any division problem can be written as a fraction or the product of fractions. Writing division problems as fractions or the product of fractions gives students practice in skills that are important in simplifying and solving algebraic expressions.

2-5 Adding and Subtracting Like Fractions

Students may be unsure whether to combine both numerators and denominators. Tell students that the numerator of a fraction gives the number of parts, and the denominator indicates the unit size of those parts. When you add and subtract, you are interested in the number of the parts, so you combine just the numerators.

2-6 Adding and Subtracting Unlike Fractions

In this lesson, students use renaming to combine unlike fractions. Again, it might be helpful for students to remember that the denominator of a fraction gives the unit size. Ask students whether adding 9 inches to 2 feet gives 11 feet (or 11 inches). Using a yardstick, show them that the correct answer is 33 inches.

2-7 Solving Equations with Rational Numbers

To solve equations with rational numbers, students must solve equations and manipulate fractions and decimals. Substituting an answer into the original equation will help them spot errors.

2-8 Powers and Exponents

Many scientific formulas use exponents. For instance, to find the amount of radioactive substance remaining after n half-lives, you divide the amount in the original sample by 2^n. As a link to dimensional analysis, point out that exponents can be applied to units. For example, a cube that is one centimeter on all sides has a volume of 1 cm × 1 cm × 1 cm, or 1 cm^3.

2-9 Scientific Notation

The ability to use scientific notation is critical for very small and very large numbers. In future lessons, students will need to use scientific notation to provide the appropriate number of significant digits. For example, 420 has two significant digits, and 420.0 has four. To report this number with three significant digits, you need to write 4.20×10^2.

Team Teaching

Inform the other teachers on your team that your classes are studying scientific notation. Suggestions for curriculum integration are:

Life Science: cell growth, cell size, bacteria counts
Earth Science: geologic timescale, pH of acid precipitation
Physical Science: atomic sizes, fundamental constants
Social Studies: population growth, government budgets

What the Research Says

According to a recent review by the National Reading Panel, repetition and multiple exposures to vocabulary words are effective in increasing student comprehension.

- **Students will find new vocabulary words listed in the beginning of the lesson, highlighted yellow in the text, and listed in the Study Guide and Review at the end of Chapter 2.**

McGraw-Hill Professional Development

Mathematics, YES! is a self-paced, web-based professional development program. Units are based on major mathematical concepts and are standards-based. Actual classroom videos provide a springboard for discussion and activities. Units appropriate for this chapter:

- Fractions, Decimals, and Percentages
- Solving Equations and Inequalities

Additional mathematical information and teaching notes are available at **msmath3.net/key_concepts**.

DAILY INTERVENTION and Assessment

* **Key to Abbreviations:**
TWE = Teacher Wraparound Edition, *CRM* = Chapter Resource Masters

	Type	Student Edition	Teacher Resources	Technology/Internet
INTERVENTION	Ongoing	Prerequisite Skills, pp. 61, 66, 70, 75, 80, 85, 91 Mid-Chapter Practice Test, p. 86	5-Minute Check Transparencies Quizzes 1–4, *CRM*, pp. 127–128 Mid-Chapter Test, *CRM*, p. 129 Study Guide and Intervention, *CRM*, pp. 67, 72, 77, 82, 87, 92, 97, 102, 107	MathPASS: Tutorial Plus msmath3.net/self_check_quiz msmath3.net/extra_examples
	Mixed Review	pp. 66, 70, 75, 80, 85, 91, 95, 101, 107	Cumulative Review, *CRM*, p. 130	
	Error Analysis	Find the Error, p. 74, 84	Find the Error, *TWE*, pp. 74, 84 Unlocking Misconceptions, *TWE*, pp. 93, 96, 105 Tips for New Teachers, *TWE*, p. 99	
	Standardized Test Practice	pp. 66, 70, 75, 80, 85, 86, 89, 91, 95, 97, 101, 107, 111, 112–113	Standardized Test Practice, *CRM*, pp. 131–132	Standardized Test Practice CD-ROM msmath3.net/standardized_test
ASSESSMENT	Open-Ended Assessment	Writing Math, pp. 69, 74, 79, 90, 103, 106 Open-Ended, pp. 65, 69, 74, 79, 84, 90, 94, 100, 106 Standardized Test, p. 113	Modeling: *TWE*, p. 85 Speaking: *TWE*, pp. 75, 81, 97 Writing: *TWE*, pp. 70, 107 Extended Response Assessment, *CRM*, p. 125	
	Chapter Assessment	Study Guide, pp. 108–110 Practice Test, p. 111	Multiple-Choice Tests (Forms 1, 2A, 2B), *CRM*, pp. 113–118 Free-Response Tests (Forms 2C, 2D, 3), *CRM*, pp. 119–124 Vocabulary Test/Review, *CRM*, p. 126	ExamView® Pro Testmaker (see below) MindJogger Videoquizzes msmath3.net/vocabulary_review msmath3.net/chapter_test

For more information on Yearly ProgressPro, see p. 2.

Glencoe Lesson	Yearly ProgressPro Skill Name
2-1	Fraction/Decimal/Percent Conversions: Level 2
2-2	Compare/Order Positive and Negative Rational Numbers
2-3, 2-4	Multiply and Divide Mixed Numbers
2-6	Add/Subtract Fractions with Unlike Denominators: Level 3
2-8	Evaluate Expressions with Exponents: Level 3; Negative Exponents
2-9	Scientific Notation: Level 1

ExamView® Pro

Use ExamView® Pro Testmaker CD-ROM to:

- **Create multiple versions of tests.**
- **Create modified tests for inclusion students with one mouse click.**
- **Edit existing questions and add your own questions.**
- **Build tests aligned with state standards using built-in state curriculum correlations.**
- **Change English tests to Spanish with one mouse click and vice versa.**

Reading and Writing in Mathematics

READING in the Content Area

This online worksheet provides strategies for reading and analyzing Lesson 2-1, Fractions and Decimals. Students are guided through questions about the main idea, subject matter, supporting details, conclusion, clarifying details, and vocabulary of the lesson.

Interactive Study Notebook With Foldables™ is a study organizer that provides helpful steps for students to follow to organize their notes for Chapter 2.

- Students use Noteables to record notes and to complete their Foldables as you present the material in Lessons 2-1 through 2-9.
- Noteables follow the *Teacher Wraparound Edition's* In-Class Examples and *Interactive Chalkboard CD-ROM.*

For more information on Reading and Writing in Mathematics, see pp. T6–T7.

Recommended Outside Reading for Students

Nonfiction

- Woods, Michael, and Woods, Mary. *Ancient Computing*. Runestone Press, ©2000.

  This book describes the clever calculation techniques used in early civilizations. Students will read about the origins of the base-10 number system and scientific notation. In addition, they learn that an Egyptian scribe wrote an algebra textbook more than 3,500 years ago.

Fiction

- Pappas, Theoni. *Fractals, Googols and Other Mathematical Tales.* Wide World Publishing/Tetra, ©1999, 1993.

  This collection of math stories and facts centers around Penrose the cat and his view of the history of mathematics. Sidebars supplement the tales. Topics include decimals, multiple dimensions, base-10 and base-12 number systems.

PROJECT CRISS℠ Study Skill

Most students already have some knowledge of the topics presented in Chapter 2. Help them build on this knowledge using a Know-Want to Learn-Learned (KWL) chart like the one at the right. Before starting the chapter, draw the chart on an overhead transparency. Name some topics covered in the chapter, such as fractions and exponents. Have students tell what they already know about the topics as you record their ideas. Next, have them list what they would like to know about the topics. After working through the chapter, again display the chart and have students fill in the last column, describing what they have learned.

Fractions		
Know	**Want to Learn**	**Learned**
If the denominators are alike, you can just add or subtract numerators.	How do you add and subtract fractions that have different denominators?	

CReating Independence through Student-owned Strategies

For more information on Project CRISS, see p. T8.

CHAPTER 2 Making Connections

School-To-Home

Parent and Student Study Guide

Parents and students may work together to reinforce the concepts and skills of this chapter. These online worksheets are available in English and Spanish at msmath3.net/parent_student. A sample lesson is shown below.

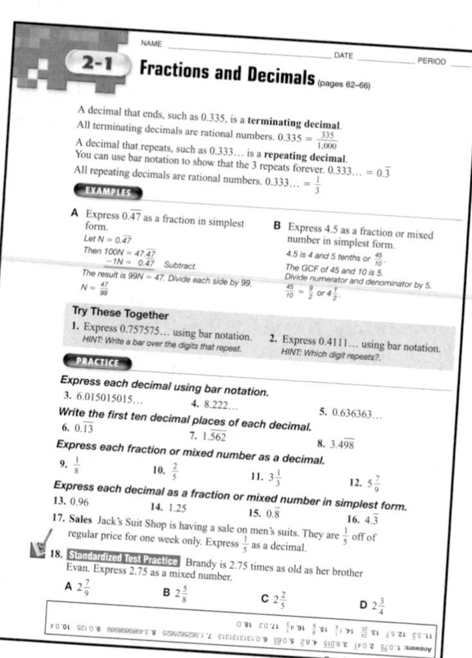

NAME ______ DATE ______ PERIOD ______

2-1 Fractions and Decimals (pages 62–66)

A decimal that ends, such as 0.335, is a **terminating decimal**. All terminating decimals are rational numbers. $0.335 = \frac{335}{1,000}$

A decimal that repeats, such as 0.333… is a **repeating decimal**. You can use bar notation to show that the 3 repeats forever. $0.333\ldots = 0.\overline{3}$ All repeating decimals are rational numbers. $0.333\ldots = \frac{1}{3}$

EXAMPLES

A Express $0.\overline{47}$ as a fraction in simplest form.

Let $N = 0.\overline{47}$

Then $100N = 47.\overline{47}$

$-1N = 0.\overline{47}$ *Subtract.*

The result is $99N = 47$. *Divide each side by 99.*

$N = \frac{47}{99}$

B Express 4.5 as a fraction or mixed number in simplest form.

4.5 is 4 and 5 tenths or $\frac{45}{10}$.

The GCF of 45 and 10 is 5.

Divide numerator and denominator by 5.

$\frac{45}{10} = \frac{9}{2}$ *or* $4\frac{1}{2}$.

Try These Together

1. Express 0.757575… using bar notation. *HINT: Write a bar over the digits that repeat.*
2. Express 0.4111… using bar notation. *HINT: Which digit repeats?.*

PRACTICE

Express each decimal using bar notation.

3. 6.015015015… 4. 8.222… 5. 0.636363…

Write the first ten decimal places of each decimal.

6. $0.\overline{13}$ 7. $1.5\overline{625}$ 8. $3.4\overline{98}$

Express each fraction or mixed number as a decimal.

9. $\frac{1}{8}$ 10. $\frac{2}{5}$ 11. $3\frac{1}{3}$ 12. $5\frac{7}{9}$

Express each decimal as a fraction or mixed number in simplest form.

13. 0.96 14. 1.25 15. $0.\overline{8}$ 16. $4.\overline{3}$

17. **Sales** Jack's Suit Shop is having a sale on men's suits. They are $\frac{1}{5}$ off of regular price for one week only. Express $\frac{1}{5}$ as a decimal.

18. **Standardized Test Practice** Brandy is 2.75 times as old as her brother Evan. Express 2.75 as a mixed number.

A $2\frac{7}{9}$ B $2\frac{5}{8}$ C $2\frac{2}{5}$ D $2\frac{3}{4}$

Answers: 1. $0.\overline{75}$ 2. $0.4\overline{1}$ 3. $6.\overline{015}$ 4. $8.\overline{2}$ 5. $0.\overline{63}$ 6. 0.1313131313 7. 1.5625625625 8. 3.4989898989 9. 0.125 10. 0.4 11. $3.\overline{3}$ 12. $5.\overline{7}$ 13. $\frac{24}{25}$ 14. $1\frac{1}{4}$ 15. $\frac{8}{9}$ 16. $4\frac{1}{3}$ 17. 0.2 18. D

Family Letters and Activities

Send a letter and activity for this chapter home to encourage family members to become active participants in their students' learning. (English: *Chapter 2 Resource Masters*, pp. ix–x; Spanish: log on to msmath3.net/family_letters)

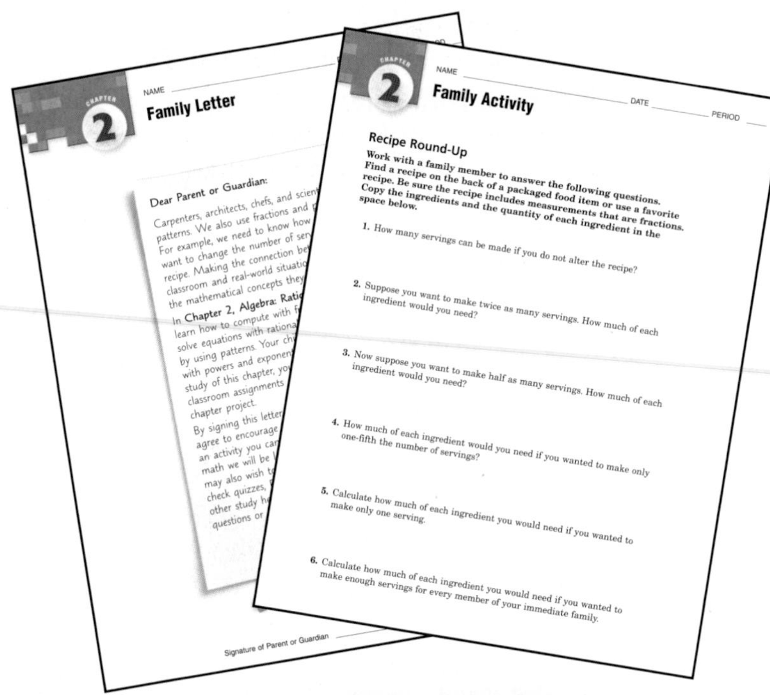

CHAPTER 2 NAME ______

Family Letter

Dear Parent or Guardian:

Carpenters, architects, chefs, and scien
patterns. We also use fractions and
For example, we need to know how
want to change the number of ser
recipe. Making the connection be
classroom and real-world situatio
the mathematical concepts they

In **Chapter 2, Algebra: Ratio**
learn how to compute with f
solve equations with rationa
by using patterns. Your ch
with powers and exponen
study of this chapter, yo
classroom assignments
chapter project.

By signing this letter
agree to encourage
an activity you can
math we will be
may also wish to
check quizzes,
other study h
questions or

Signature of Parent or Guardian ______

CHAPTER 2 NAME ______ DATE ______ PERIOD ______

Family Activity

Recipe Round-Up

Work with a family member to answer the following questions. Find a recipe on the back of a packaged food item or use a favorite recipe. Be sure the recipe includes measurements that are fractions. Copy the ingredients and the quantity of each ingredient in the space below.

1. How many servings can be made if you do not alter the recipe?
2. Suppose you want to make twice as many servings. How much of each ingredient would you need?
3. Now suppose you want to make half as many servings. How much of each ingredient would you need?
4. How much of each ingredient would you need if you wanted to make only one-fifth the number of servings?
5. Calculate how much of each ingredient you would need if you wanted to make only one serving.
6. Calculate how much of each ingredient you would need if you wanted to make enough servings for every member of your immediate family.

English Languaage Learners ELL

Lesson 2-2

Flexible Groups

Give groups of six students a set of six cards with rational numbers such as $1, -1, \frac{1}{2}, -3.75, 4\frac{3}{4}$, and so on. Have students order their numbers from least to greatest. Use masking tape to denote a number line showing zero, positive, and negative on a wall of the classroom. Have students come to the number line by group and position themselves in order along the number line. Have the groups check each other for accuracy.

Lesson 2-7

Building on Prior Knowledge

Students who know how to solve equations involving integers often have trouble solving equations with rational numbers because of the more complex computations. In order to help them with this transition, have students solve an equation with whole numbers, then with integers, and then integrate the rational numbers. When students need to perform an operation with the rational numbers, take the operation out of the problem or equation, perform it, and then let the variable equal the answer.

MathScape™  This project was supported, in part, by the **National Science Foundation**

MathScape is a mathematics curriculum for grades 6–8 developed by the Seeing and Thinking Mathematically Project at the Education Development Center.

Comparing Function Families
Family Portraits

How to Use *MathScape* with Chapter 2

The unit *Family Portraits* can be used to enhance Lessons 2-8 and 2-9.

- **Introduce** → Before you begin **Lesson 2-8,** you can introduce powers and exponents by using the activity on page 296.
- **Enrich** → After you complete **Lesson 2-9,** you can ask students to explore the limits of their calculators by using the activity at the top of page 301.

For other lessons in Chapter 2 that correlate to *MathScape,* see the chart on page T14.

Online Lesson Planner

USA TODAY® Education's Online site offers resources and interactive features connected to each day's newspaper. *Experience Today,* USA TODAY's® daily lesson plan, is available on the site and delivered daily to subscribers. This plan provides instruction for integrating USA TODAY® graphics and key editorial features into your mathematics classroom. Log on to **education.usatoday.com**.

USA TODAY Snapshots® in Chapter 2	
Lesson	**Snapshot**
2-7	Most popular national parks

Quick Review Math Handbook

is Glencoe's mathematical handbook for students. The Hot Words section includes a glossary of terms while the Hot Topics section consists of explanations of key mathematical concepts. An exercise set is included to check students' understanding of the concepts. This valuable resource can be used as a reference in the classroom or for home study.

Lesson	Hot Topics Section	Lesson	Hot Topics Section
2-1	2-1, 2-9	**2-6**	1-4, 2-3
2-2	1-1, 2-2	**2-7**	1-4, 2-3, 2-4
2-3, 2-4	2-4	**2-8**	3-1
2-5	1-4, 2-3	**2-9**	3-3

Key Chapter Objectives

Lesson 2-1 Express rational numbers as decimals and decimals as fractions.

Lesson 2-2 Compare and order rational numbers.

Lessons 2-3 through 2-7 Compute and solve equations with fractions and mixed numbers.

Lessons 2-8 and 2-9 Use powers and exponents in expressions and to write numbers in scientific notation.

"What do roller coasters have to do with math?"

Point out to students that this is only one of many applications of the math that they are studying. Others are provided in the introduction to each lesson.

Vocabulary Builder, pp. vii–viii ELL

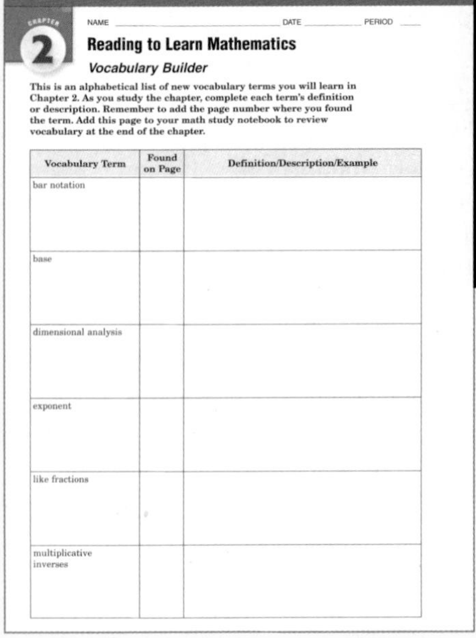

NAME ______________ DATE ________ PERIOD ______

2 Reading to Learn Mathematics

Vocabulary Builder

This is an alphabetical list of new vocabulary terms you will learn in Chapter 2. As you study the chapter, complete each term's definition or description. Remember to add the page number where you found the term. Add this page to your math study notebook to review vocabulary at the end of the chapter.

Vocabulary Term	Found on Page	Definition/Description/Example
bar notation		
base		
dimensional analysis		
exponent		
like fractions		
multiplicative inverses		

CHAPTER 2 Algebra: Rational Numbers

"What do roller coasters have to do with math?"

A ride on the roller coaster called *The Beast* takes 3 minutes and 40 seconds. You can write this time as $3\frac{40}{60}$ or $3\frac{2}{3}$ minutes. You can also write this mixed number as the decimal $3.\overline{6}$.

You will order fractions and mixed numbers by writing them as decimals in Lesson 2-2.

60 Chapter 2 Algebra: Rational Numbers

Vocabulary Builder

For a thorough vocabulary list with pronunciations of new words, give students the Vocabulary Builder worksheets from the *Chapter 2 Resource Masters.* Encourage them to complete the definition of each term as they progress through the chapter.

GETTING STARTED

▶ Diagnose Readiness

Take this quiz to see if you are ready to begin Chapter 2. Refer to the lesson or page number in parentheses for review.

Vocabulary Review

Complete each sentence.

1. Two numbers with the same absolute value but different signs are called __?__ or __?__ __?__. (Lesson 1-4) **1. opposites, additive inverses**
2. The value of a variable that makes an equation true is called the __?__ of the equation. (Lesson 1-8) **solution**

Prerequisite Skills

Add. (Lesson 1-4)

3. $-13 + 4$ **−9**
4. $28 + (-9)$ **19**
5. $-18 + 21$ **3**
6. $4 + (-16)$ **−12**

Subtract. (Lesson 1-5)

7. $-8 - 6$ **−14**
8. $23 - (-15)$ **38**
9. $-17 - 11$ **−28**
10. $-5 - (-10)$ **5**

Multiply or divide. (Lesson 1-6)

11. $6(-14)$ **−84**
12. $36 \div (-4)$ **−9**
13. $-86 \div (-2)$ **43**
14. $-3(-9)$ **27**

Solve each equation. (Lessons 1-8 and 1-9)

15. $-12x = 144$ **−12**
16. $a + 9 = 37$ **28**
17. $-18 = y - 42$ **24**
18. $25 = \frac{n}{5}$ **125**

Find the least common multiple (LCM) of each set of numbers. (Page 612)

19. 10, 5, 6 **30**
20. 3, 7, 9 **63**
21. 12, 16 **48**
22. 24, 9 **72**

Rational Numbers Make this Foldable to organize your notes. Begin with five sheets of $8\frac{1}{2}$" by 11" paper.

Stack Pages
Place 5 sheets of paper $\frac{3}{4}$ inch apart.

Roll Up Bottom Edges
All tabs should be the same size.

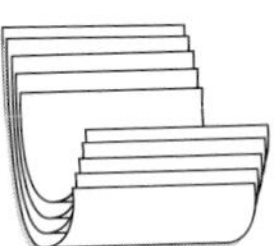

Crease and Staple
Staple along the fold.

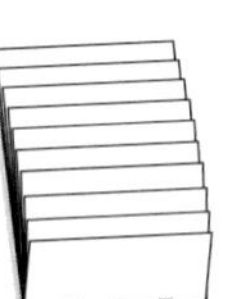

STEP 4 Label
Label the tabs with the lesson numbers.

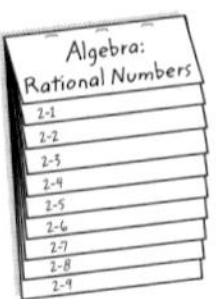

Chapter Notes Each time you find this logo throughout the chapter, use your *Noteables™: Interactive Study Notebook with Foldables™* or your own notebook to take notes. Begin your chapter notes with this Foldable activity.

Math Online **Readiness** To prepare yourself for this chapter with another quiz, visit **msmath3.net/chapter_readiness**

GETTING STARTED

Diagnose Readiness This section provides a review of the basic concepts needed before beginning Chapter 2. Page references are included for additional student help.

Prerequisite Skills review skills needed in this chapter.

Exercises	Needed for Lesson	Skill
3–6	2-5, 2-6	Add Integers
7–10	2-5, 2-6	Subtract Integers
11–14	2-3, 2-4	Multiply and Divide Integers
15–18	2-7	Solve Equations
19–22	2-6	Find the Least Common Multiple

For more prerequisite skills, see:

- Getting Ready for the Next Lesson, at the end of each lesson
- Prerequisite Skills in the Student Handbook on pp. 600–615
- *Math Skills Maintenance Masters*

FOLDABLES™ Study Organizer

For more information about Foldables, see *Teaching Mathematics with Foldables.*

Have students use Foldables to write about rational numbers. After students make their Foldables, have them label the tabs to correspond to the nine lessons in this chapter. As students read and work their way through the chapter, have them make annotations under the tabs of their Foldables. Annotations often include questions that arise, comments and reactions, short summaries, and key points highlighted or underlined. Make this a collaborative activity by having students work in small groups.

2-1 Lesson Notes

Lesson Resources

Chapter 2 Resource Masters

FAST FILE

- Study Guide and Intervention, p. 67
- Practice: Skills, p. 68
- Practice: Word Problems, p. 69
- Reading to Learn Mathematics, p. 70
- Enrichment, p. 71

Parent and Student Study Guide Online Worksheets, 2-1

Noteables™: Interactive Study Notebook with Foldables™, 2-1

5-Minute Check 2-1

Use as a quiz or review of Chapter 1.

(Also available as a transparency)

Bellringer

Hands-On Activity Have students read the definition of *rational numbers* on this page. Then use the Venn diagram in the bottom margin to show how rational numbers are related to whole numbers and integers. Have small groups graph the numbers on the diagram on a number line, using a different color of marker for each type of number. Be sure students realize that all three colors represent rational numbers.

(Continued in bottom margin.)

Reading to Learn Mathematics, p. 70 ELL

NAME ______________ DATE ________ PERIOD ____

2-1 Reading to Learn Mathematics

Fractions and Decimals

Pre-Activity ***Read the introduction at the top of page 62 in your textbook. Write your answers below.***

1. What fraction of the sites are in the United States? $\frac{1}{2}$
2. What fraction of the sites are in Canada? $\frac{1}{5}$
3. At what fraction of the sites might you see gray whales? $\frac{2}{5}$
4. What fraction of the humpback viewing sites are in Mexico? $\frac{1}{4}$

Reading the Lesson

5. Explain the difference in meaning between the expressions $4\frac{3}{4}$ and $4\left(\frac{3}{4}\right)$.
Sample answer: The expression $4\frac{3}{4}$ denotes addition, $4 + \frac{3}{4}$, ...

Fractions and Decimals

What You'll LEARN

Express rational numbers as decimals and decimals as fractions.

NEW Vocabulary

rational number
terminating decimal
repeating decimal
bar notation

Link to READING

Everyday Meaning of Terminate: to bring to an end

WHEN am I ever going to use this?

WHALE WATCHING The top ten places in the Northern Hemisphere to watch whales are listed below.

Viewing Site	Location	Type Seen
Sea of Cortez	Baja California, Mexico	Blue, Finback, Sei, Sperm, Minke, Pilot, Orca, Humpback, Gray
Dana Point	California	Gray
Monterey Bay	California	Gray
San Ignacio Lagoon	Baja California, Mexico	Gray
Churchill River Estuary	Manitoba, Canada	Beluga
Stellwagen Bank National Marine Sanctuary	Massachusetts	Humpback, Finback, Minke
Lahaina	Hawaii	Humpback
Silver Bank	Dominican Republic	Humpback
Mingan Island	Quebec, Canada	Blue
Friday Harbor	Washington	Orca, Minke

1. What fraction of the sites are in the United States? $\frac{1}{2}$
2. What fraction of the sites are in Canada? $\frac{1}{5}$
3. At what fraction of the sites might you see gray whales? $\frac{2}{5}$
4. What fraction of the humpback viewing sites are in Mexico? $\frac{1}{5}$

TEACHING TIP

Explain to students that rational numbers can be written as fractions.

Numbers such as $\frac{1}{2}, \frac{1}{5}, \frac{2}{5}$, and $\frac{1}{10}$ are called **rational numbers**.

Noteables™ **Key Concept: Rational Numbers**

Words A rational number is any number that can be expressed in the form $\frac{a}{b}$, where a and b are integers and $b \neq 0$.

READING in the Content Area

For strategies in reading this lesson, visit **msmath3.net/reading.**

Since -7 can be written as $\frac{-7}{1}$ and $2\frac{2}{3}$ can be written as $\frac{8}{3}$, -7 and $2\frac{2}{3}$ are rational numbers. All integers, fractions, and mixed numbers are rational numbers.

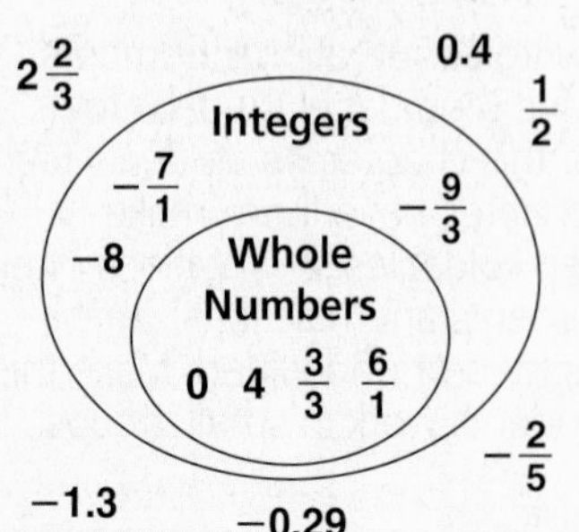

NCLB NO CHILD LEFT BEHIND

The goals of the NCLB Act include a stronger emphasis on reading. The **Reading in the Content Area** link helps students become proficient readers.

STUDY TIP

Mental Math It is helpful to memorize these commonly used fraction-decimal equivalencies.

$\frac{1}{2} = 0.5$ $\frac{1}{3} = 0.\overline{3}$

$\frac{1}{4} = 0.25$ $\frac{1}{5} = 0.2$

$\frac{1}{8} = 0.125$

$\frac{1}{10} = 0.1$

TEACHING TIP

Explain to students that a zero before the decimal point helps readers to see that the number is six hundred twenty-five thousandths, and not six hundred twenty-five.

Any fraction can be expressed as a decimal by dividing the numerator by the denominator.

EXAMPLE Write a Fraction as a Decimal

1 Write $\frac{5}{8}$ as a decimal.

$\frac{5}{8}$ means 5 ÷ 8.

```
    0.625
 8)5.000   Add a decimal point and zeros to the dividend: 5 = 5.000
   4 8
     20
     16
      40
      40
       0   Division ends when the remainder is 0.
```

You can also use a calculator. 5 [÷] 8 [ENTER] 0.625

The fraction $\frac{5}{8}$ can be written as 0.625.

A decimal like 0.625 is called a **terminating decimal** because the division ends, or terminates, when the remainder is 0.

EXAMPLE Write a Mixed Number as a Decimal

2 Write $1\frac{2}{3}$ as a decimal.

$1\frac{2}{3}$ means $1 + \frac{2}{3}$. To change $\frac{2}{3}$ to a decimal, divide 2 by 3.

```
    0.666...   The three dots means the six keeps repeating.
 3)2.000
   1 8
     20
     18
      20
      18
       2   The remainder after each step is 2.
```

You can also use a calculator. 2 [÷] 3 [ENTER] 0.666666667

The mixed number $1\frac{2}{3}$ can be written as 1 + 0.666... or 1.666... .

Your Turn **Write each fraction or mixed number as a decimal.**

a. $\frac{3}{4}$ **0.75** b. $-\frac{3}{5}$ **−0.6** c. $2\frac{1}{9}$ **2.111...** d. $5\frac{1}{6}$ **5.1666...**

STUDY TIP

Bar Notation The bar is placed above the repeating part. To write 8.636363... in bar notation, write $8.\overline{63}$, not $8.\overline{6}$ or $8.\overline{636}$. To write 0.3444... in bar notation, write $0.3\overline{4}$, not $0.\overline{34}$.

A decimal like 1.666... is called a **repeating decimal**. Since it is not possible to write all of the digits, you can use **bar notation** to show that the 6 repeats.

$$1.666... = 1.\overline{6}$$

Math Online msmath3.net/extra_examples

2 Teach

Noteables™

As you work the **In-Class Examples,** have students follow along in their *Noteables™: Interactive Study Notebook with Foldables™*, or have students work the examples in their notebooks.

In-Class Examples

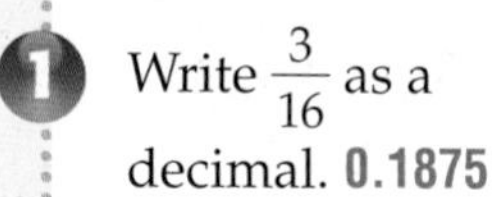

1 Write $\frac{3}{16}$ as a decimal. **0.1875**

2 Write $3\frac{2}{11}$ as a decimal. **3.1818. . .**

Teaching Strategies Students may memorize the procedure or formula for solving a math problem without understanding it. When students solve problems on the chalkboard, ask them questions about each step.

DAILY INTERVENTION **Differentiated Instruction**

Auditory/Musical Have a music student draw several measures of simple tunes on the chalkboard and explain how the notes relate to fractions. For example, the student could show that 8 sixteenth notes can be played in the same time as a half note. Have a student play the tunes on an instrument so the class can hear how fractions determine how the music sounds.

In-Class Examples

3 **AGRICULTURE** A Florida farmer lost the fruit on 8 of 15 orange trees because of unexpected freezing temperatures. Find the fraction of the orange trees that did not produce fruit. Express your answer as a decimal rounded to the nearest thousandth. **0.533**

4 Write 0.32 as a fraction. $\frac{8}{25}$

5 **ALGEBRA** Write $2.\overline{7}$ as a mixed number in simplest form. $2\frac{7}{9}$

REAL-LIFE CAREERS

How Does a Sports Statistician Use Math?

A baseball statistician uses decimal equivalents to determine batting averages and winning averages. A batting average is the number of hits divided by the number of times at bat.

Research
For information about a career as a sports statistician, visit: msmath3.net/careers

Repeating decimals often occur in real-life situations. However, they are usually rounded to a certain place-value position.

EXAMPLE Round a Repeating Decimal

3 **BASEBALL In a recent season, Kansas City pitcher Kris Wilson won 6 of the 11 games he started. To the nearest thousandth, find his winning average.**

To find his winning average, divide the number of wins, 6, by the number of games, 11.

6 [÷] 11 [ENTER] 0.5454545

Look at the digit to the right of the thousandths place. Round down since $4 < 5$.

Kris Wilson's winning average was 0.545.

Terminating and repeating decimals are also rational numbers because you can write them as fractions.

EXAMPLE Write a Terminating Decimal as a Fraction

4 **Write 0.45 as a fraction.**

$0.45 = \frac{45}{100}$ — 0.45 is 45 hundredths.

$= \frac{9}{20}$ — Simplify. Divide by the greatest common factor of 45 and 100, 5.

The decimal 0.45 can be written as $\frac{9}{20}$.

You can use algebra to change repeating decimals to fractions.

READING Math

Repeating Decimals Read $0.\overline{5}$ as *point five repeating.*

EXAMPLE Write a Repeating Decimal as a Fraction

5 **ALGEBRA Write $0.\overline{5}$ as a fraction in simplest form.**

Let $N = 0.\overline{5}$ or 0.555... . Then $10N = 5.555...$.

Multiply N by 10 because 1 digit repeats.

Subtract $N = 0.555...$ to eliminate the repeating part, 0.555... .

$10N = 5.555...$

$-1N = 0.555...$ — $N = 1N$

$9N = 5$ — $10N - 1N = 9N$

$\frac{9N}{9} = \frac{5}{9}$ — Divide each side by 9.

$N = \frac{5}{9}$ — Simplify.

The decimal $0.\overline{5}$ can be written as $\frac{5}{9}$.

TEACHING TIP

Explain to students that $10N - 1N = (10 - 1)N$, or $9N$.

Your Turn **Write each decimal as a fraction or mixed number in simplest form.**

e. -0.14 $-\frac{7}{50}$ f. 8.75 $8\frac{3}{4}$ g. $0.\overline{3}$ $\frac{1}{3}$ h. $-1.\overline{4}$ $-1\frac{4}{9}$

Students practice the same concepts in Exercises 14–39 if they are assigned odd or even problems.

Skill and Concept Check

1. **OPEN ENDED** Give an example of a repeating decimal where two digits repeat. Explain why your number is a rational number. **See margin.**

2. **Write** 5.321321321... using bar notation. $5.\overline{321}$

3. **Which One Doesn't Belong?** Identify the fraction that cannot be expressed as the same type of decimal as the other three. Explain.

$\frac{4}{11}$	$\frac{1}{2}$	$\frac{1}{9}$	$\frac{1}{3}$

$\frac{1}{2}$; It cannot be written as a repeating decimal.

GUIDED PRACTICE

Write each fraction or mixed number as a decimal.

4. $\frac{4}{5}$ **0.8**
5. $4\frac{3}{8}$ **4.375**
6. $-\frac{1}{3}$ $-0.\overline{3}$
7. $7\frac{5}{33}$ $7.\overline{15}$

Write each decimal as a fraction or mixed number in simplest form.

8. 0.6 $\frac{3}{5}$
9. −1.55 $-1\frac{11}{20}$
10. $-0.\overline{5}$ $-\frac{5}{9}$
11. $2.\overline{1}$ $2\frac{1}{9}$

BIOLOGY For Exercises 12 and 13, use the figure at the right.

12. Write the length of the ant as a fraction. $\frac{7}{8}$ **in.**
13. Write the length of the ant as a decimal. **0.875 in.**

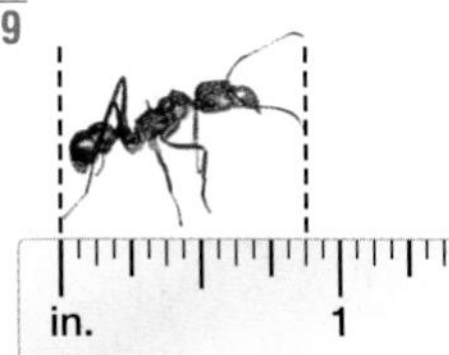

★ indicates increased difficulty

Practice and Applications

HOMEWORK HELP

For Exercises	See Examples
14–27	1, 2
28–33, 41–44	4
34–39	5
40	3

Extra Practice See pages 619, 649.

Write each fraction or mixed number as a decimal.

14. $\frac{1}{4}$ **0.25**
15. $\frac{1}{5}$ **0.2**
16. $-\frac{13}{25}$ **−0.52**
17. $-\frac{11}{50}$ **−0.22**
18. $2\frac{1}{8}$ **2.125**
19. $5\frac{5}{16}$ **5.3125**
20. $-\frac{5}{6}$ $-0.8\overline{3}$
21. $-\frac{2}{9}$ $-0.\overline{2}$
22. $-\frac{4}{33}$ $-0.\overline{12}$
23. $-\frac{6}{11}$ $-0.\overline{54}$
24. $6\frac{4}{11}$ $6.\overline{36}$
25. $7\frac{8}{33}$ $7.\overline{24}$
26. Write $\frac{10}{33}$ as a decimal using bar notation. $0.\overline{30}$
27. Write $\frac{2}{45}$ as a decimal using bar notation. $0.0\overline{4}$

Write each decimal as a fraction or mixed number in simplest form.

28. 0.4 $\frac{2}{5}$
29. 0.5 $\frac{1}{2}$
30. −0.16 $-\frac{4}{25}$
31. −0.35 $-\frac{7}{20}$
32. 5.55 $5\frac{11}{20}$
33. 7.32 $7\frac{8}{25}$
34. $-0.\overline{2}$ $-\frac{2}{9}$
35. $-0.\overline{4}$ $-\frac{4}{9}$
36. $3.\overline{6}$ $3\frac{2}{3}$
37. $2.\overline{7}$ $2\frac{7}{9}$
★ 38. $-4.\overline{21}$ $-4\frac{7}{33}$
★ 39. $-3.\overline{72}$ $-3\frac{8}{11}$

40. **BASEBALL** In a recent season, Sammy Sosa had 189 hits during his 577 at-bats. What was Sammy Sosa's batting average? Round to the nearest thousandth. **0.328**

msmath3.net/self_check_quiz

3 Practice/Apply

FOLDABLES™ Follow-Up Remind students to explain what they learn about identifying and working with rational numbers on the first tab of their Foldables. Encourage them to explain in their own words how to express rational numbers as decimals and decimals as fractions.

Which One Doesn't Belong? In Exercise 3, ask students to name the two types of decimals they have studied in this lesson. **terminating and repeating** When solving this problem, students should first write each fraction as a decimal and then compare the decimals.

About the Exercises...

Guided Practice Key

Exercises	Examples
4, 6, 12–13	1
5, 7	2
8–9	4
10–11	5

Assignment Guide

Basic: 15–37 odd, 43–47 odd, 48–58

Average: 15–47 odd, 48–58

Enriched: 14–44 even, 45–54 (Optional: 55–58)

Answer

1. Sample answer: $0.\overline{12}$; Since $0.\overline{12} = \frac{4}{33}$, it is a rational number.

★ 41. Write 0.38 and 0.383838 as fractions. $\frac{19}{50}$; $\frac{191,919}{500,000}$

BIOLOGY **For Exercises 42–44, use the information at the right.**

42. Write the weight of a queen bee as a fraction. $\frac{1}{250}$ oz
43. Write the weight of a hummingbird as a fraction. $\frac{11}{100}$ oz
44. Write the weight of a hamster as a mixed number. $3\frac{1}{2}$ oz

Animal	Weight (ounces)
Queen Bee	0.004
Hummingbird	0.11
Hamster	3.5

Source: *Animals as Our Companions*

THEATER **For Exercises 45 and 46, use the following information.** The Tony Award is given to exceptional plays and people involved in making them. The award weighs 1 pound 10 ounces.

45. Write the weight of the Tony Award in pounds using a mixed number in simplest form. $1\frac{5}{8}$ lb
46. Write the weight of the Tony Award in pounds using decimals. 1.625 lb
47. **CRITICAL THINKING** A *unit fraction* is a fraction that has 1 as its numerator.
   a. Write the four greatest unit fractions that are terminating decimals. Write each fraction as a decimal. $\frac{1}{2} = 0.5$, $\frac{1}{4} = 0.25$, $\frac{1}{5} = 0.2$, $\frac{1}{8} = 0.125$
   b. Write the four greatest unit fractions that are repeating decimals. Write each fraction as a decimal. $\frac{1}{3} = 0.\overline{3}$, $\frac{1}{6} = 0.1\overline{6}$, $\frac{1}{7} = 0.\overline{142857}$, $\frac{1}{9} = 0.\overline{1}$

Spiral Review with Standardized Test Practice

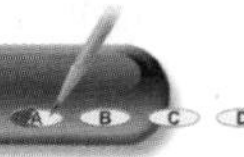

48. **MULTIPLE CHOICE** Janeth Arcain of the Houston Comets in the WNBA made 0.84 of her free throws in the 2003 season. Write this decimal as a fraction in simplest form. B

   (A) $\frac{17}{20}$ (B) $\frac{21}{25}$ (C) $\frac{8}{10}$ (D) $\frac{41}{50}$

49. **MULTIPLE CHOICE** A survey asked Americans to name the biggest problem with home improvement. The results are shown in the table. What decimal represents the fraction of people surveyed who chose procrastination? G

   (F) 0.15 (G) 0.32
   (H) 0.11 (I) 0.42

Reason	Fraction of Respondents
Lack of Time	$\frac{21}{50}$
Procrastination	$\frac{8}{25}$
Lack of Know-How	$\frac{3}{20}$
Lack of Tools	$\frac{11}{100}$

Source: Impulse Research for Ace Hardware

50. The product of two integers is 72. If one integer is −18, what is the other integer? (Lesson 1-9) −4

Solve each equation. Check your solution. (Lesson 1-8)

51. $t + 17 = -5$ −22
52. $a - 5 = 14$ 19
53. $5 = 9 + x$ −4
54. $m - 5 = -14$ −9

GETTING READY FOR THE NEXT LESSON

PREREQUISITE SKILL **Find the least common multiple for each pair of numbers.** (Page 612)

55. 15, 5 15
56. 6, 9 18
57. 8, 6 24
58. 3, 5 15

4 Assess

Higher-Level Thinking

Challenge students to develop a rule for predicting whether a fraction will be expressed as a terminating decimal or as a repeating decimal. To help students, encourage them to observe the decimal equivalents of different fractions, contrasting the denominators of fractions that form terminating decimals with those that form repeating ones. **Only fractions with denominators whose factors are 2s and 5s form terminating decimals.**

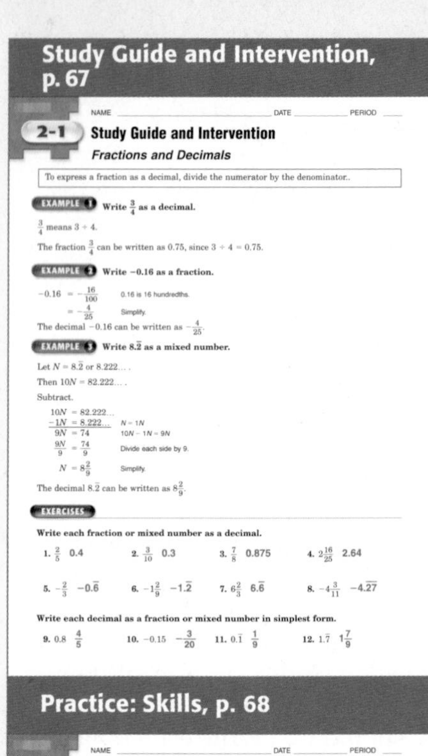

Study Guide and Intervention, p. 67

NAME ______ DATE ______ PERIOD ______

2-1 Study Guide and Intervention
Fractions and Decimals

To express a fraction as a decimal, divide the numerator by the denominator..

EXAMPLE 1 **Write $\frac{3}{4}$ as a decimal.**

$\frac{3}{4}$ means $3 \div 4$.

The fraction $\frac{3}{4}$ can be written as 0.75, since $3 \div 4 = 0.75$.

EXAMPLE 2 **Write −0.16 as a fraction.**

$-0.16 = -\frac{16}{100}$ 0.16 is 16 hundredths.
$= -\frac{4}{25}$ Simplify.

The decimal −0.16 can be written as $-\frac{4}{25}$.

EXAMPLE 3 **Write $8.\overline{2}$ as a mixed number.**

Let $N = 8.\overline{2}$ or 8.222... .
Then $10N = 82.222...$.
Subtract.

$10N = 82.222...$
$-1N = 8.222...$ $N = 1N$
$9N = 74$ $10N - 1N = 9N$
$\frac{9N}{9} = \frac{74}{9}$ Divide each side by 9.
$N = 8\frac{2}{9}$ Simplify.

The decimal $8.\overline{2}$ can be written as $8\frac{2}{9}$.

EXERCISES

Write each fraction or mixed number as a decimal.

1. $\frac{2}{5}$ 0.4
2. $\frac{3}{10}$ 0.3
3. $\frac{7}{8}$ 0.875
4. $2\frac{16}{25}$ 2.64
5. $-\frac{2}{3}$ $-0.\overline{6}$
6. $-1\frac{2}{9}$ $-1.\overline{2}$
7. $6\frac{2}{3}$ $6.\overline{6}$
8. $-4\frac{3}{11}$ $-4.\overline{27}$

Write each decimal as a fraction or mixed number in simplest form.

9. 0.8 $\frac{4}{5}$
10. −0.15 $-\frac{3}{20}$
11. $0.\overline{1}$ $\frac{1}{9}$
12. $1.\overline{7}$ $1\frac{7}{9}$

Practice: Skills, p. 68

NAME ______ DATE ______ PERIOD ______

2-1 Practice: Skills
Fractions and Decimals

Write each fraction or mixed number as a decimal.

1. $\frac{1}{10}$ 0.1
2. $\frac{1}{8}$ 0.125
3. $-\frac{3}{4}$ −0.75
4. $-\frac{4}{5}$ −0.8
5. $\frac{21}{50}$ 0.42
6. $-3\frac{9}{20}$ −3.45
7. $4\frac{9}{25}$ 4.36
8. $\frac{7}{9}$ $0.\overline{7}$
9. $1\frac{1}{6}$ $1.1\overline{6}$
10. $-2\frac{4}{15}$ $-2.2\overline{6}$
11. $\frac{5}{33}$ $0.\overline{15}$
12. $7\frac{3}{11}$ $7.\overline{27}$

Write each decimal as a fraction or mixed number in simplest form.

13. 0.9 $\frac{9}{10}$
14. 0.7 $\frac{7}{10}$
15. 0.84 $\frac{21}{25}$
16. 0.92 $\frac{23}{25}$
17. −1.12 $-1\frac{3}{25}$
18. −5.05 $-5\frac{1}{20}$
19. 2.35 $2\frac{7}{20}$
20. 8.85 $8\frac{17}{20}$
21. $-0.\overline{1}$ $-\frac{1}{9}$
22. $4.\overline{8}$ $4\frac{8}{9}$
23. $6.\overline{7}$ $6\frac{7}{9}$
24. $-8.\overline{4}$ $-8\frac{4}{9}$

Practice: Word Problems, p. 69

NAME ______ DATE ______ PERIOD ______

2-1 Practice: Word Problems
Fractions and Decimals

1. **ASTRONOMY** The pull of gravity on the surface of Mars is 0.38 that of Earth. Write 0.38 as a fraction in simplest form. $\frac{19}{50}$
2. **ENERGY** Nuclear power provided 76% of the energy used in France in 2000. Write 0.76 as a fraction in simplest form. $\frac{19}{25}$
3. **WEIGHTS AND MEASURES** One pint is about 0.55 liter. Write 0.55 liter as a fraction in simplest form. $\frac{11}{20}$ L
4. **WEIGHTS AND MEASURES** One inch is 25.4 millimeters. Write 25.4 millimeters as a mixed number in simplest form. $25\frac{2}{5}$ mm
5. **EDUCATION** A local middle school has 47 computers and 174 students. What is the number of students per computer at the school? Write your answer as both a mixed number in simplest form and a decimal rounded to the nearest tenth. $3\frac{33}{47}$ or 3.7 students per computer
6. **BASEBALL** In the 2002 season, the Atlanta Braves won 101 out of 162 games. What was the ratio of wins to total games? Write your answer as both a fraction in simplest form and a decimal rounded to the nearest thousandth. $\frac{101}{162}$ or 0.623 win per game
7. **COLLEGES AND UNIVERSITIES** Recently, a small college had an enrollment of 1,342 students and a total of 215 faculty. What was the student-faculty ratio for this college? Write your answer as both a mixed number in simplest form and a decimal rounded to the nearest hundredth. $6\frac{52}{215}$ or 6.24 students per faculty member
8. **BASKETBALL** In the 2000–2001 season, Shaquille O'Neal made 813 field goals out of 1,422 attempts. What was Shaquille O'Neal's ratio of successful field goals to attempts? Write your answer as both a fraction in simplest form and a decimal rounded to the nearest thousandth. $\frac{271}{474}$ or 0.572 success per attempt

Comparing and Ordering Rational Numbers

What You'll LEARN

Compare and order rational numbers.

MATH Symbols

$<$ less than
$>$ greater than

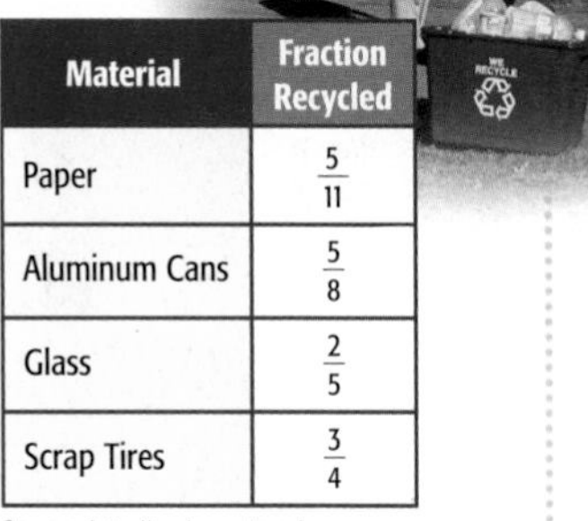

WHEN am I ever going to use this?

RECYCLING The table shows the portion of some common materials and products that are recycled.

Material	Fraction Recycled
Paper	$\frac{5}{11}$
Aluminum Cans	$\frac{5}{8}$
Glass	$\frac{2}{5}$
Scrap Tires	$\frac{3}{4}$

Source: http://envirosystemsinc.com

1. Do we recycle more or less than half of the paper we produce? Explain.
2. Do we recycle more or less than half of the aluminum cans? Explain.
3. Which items have a recycle rate less than one half? **paper, glass**
4. Which items have a recycle rate greater than one half?
5. Using this estimation method, can you order the rates from least to greatest?

1. Less, 5 is less than half of 11 or 5.5.
2. More; 5 is greater than half of 8 or 4.
4. aluminum cans, scrap tires
5. No; the numbers are being compared to $\frac{1}{2}$, not to each other.

Sometimes you can use estimation to compare rational numbers. Another method is to compare two fractions with common denominators. Or you can also compare decimals.

EXAMPLE Compare Rational Numbers

1 **Replace ● with <, >, or = to make $\frac{5}{8}$ ● $\frac{3}{4}$ a true sentence.**

Method 1 Write as fractions with the same denominator.

For $\frac{5}{8}$ and $\frac{3}{4}$, the least common denominator is 8.

$\frac{5}{8} = \frac{5 \cdot 1}{8 \cdot 1}$ or $\frac{5}{8}$

$\frac{3}{4} = \frac{3 \cdot 2}{4 \cdot 2}$ or $\frac{6}{8}$

Since $\frac{5}{8} < \frac{6}{8}$, $\frac{5}{8} < \frac{3}{4}$.

Method 2 Write as decimals.

Write $\frac{5}{8}$ and $\frac{3}{4}$ as decimals. Use a calculator.

5 [÷] 8 [ENTER] 0.625 | 3 [÷] 4 [ENTER] 0.75

$\frac{5}{8} = 0.625$ | $\frac{3}{4} = 0.75$

Since $0.625 < 0.75$, $\frac{5}{8} < \frac{3}{4}$.

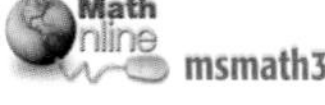

msmath3.net/extra_examples

2-2 Lesson Notes

Lesson Resources

Chapter 2 Resource Masters
- Study Guide and Intervention, p. 72
- Practice: Skills, p. 73
- Practice: Word Problems, p. 74
- Reading to Learn Mathematics, p. 75
- Enrichment, p. 76

FAST FILE

Key Teaching Transparencies, 5
MathPASS Tutorial CD-ROM, 5, 15
Parent and Student Study Guide Online Worksheets, 2-2
Teaching Mathematics with Manipulatives, p. 37
Noteables™: Interactive Study Notebook with Foldables™, 2-2

1 Focus

5-Minute Check 2-2

Use as a quiz or review of Lesson 2-1. (Also available as a transparency)

Bellringer

Hands-On Activity Separate students into pairs and make sure each pair has a ruler with inches divided into fourths and eighths. Then have each student mark off an inch on the edge of a piece of paper, cut out a short inch-wide strip, and fold the strip into thirds. The folds represent $\frac{1}{3}$-inch increments.
(Continued in bottom margin.)

Ask students to work with their partners to use the folded paper and the ruler to order the following from least to greatest:
$\frac{5}{8}, \frac{3}{4}, \frac{1}{2}, \frac{2}{3}, \frac{1}{8}, \frac{1}{3}, \frac{1}{4}$.
$\frac{1}{8}, \frac{1}{4}, \frac{1}{3}, \frac{1}{2}, \frac{5}{8}, \frac{2}{3}, \frac{3}{4}$

Reading to Learn Mathematics, p. 75 

NAME ______ DATE ______ PERIOD ____

2-2 Reading to Learn Mathematics
Comparing and Ordering Rational Numbers

Pre-Activity *Read the introduction at the top of page 67 in your textbook. Write your answers below.*

1. Do we recycle more or less than half of the paper we produce? Explain. Less; 5 is less than half of 11 or 5.5.
2. Do we recycle more or less than half of the aluminum cans? Explain. More; 5 is greater than half of 8 or 4.
3. Which items have a recycle rate less than one half? paper, glass
4. Which items have a recycle rate greater than one half? aluminum cans, scrap tires

2 Teach

In-Class Examples

INTERACTIVE CHALKBOARD PowerPoint® Presentations

1 Replace ● with <, >, or = to make $\frac{3}{7}$ ● $\frac{8}{13}$ a true sentence. $\frac{3}{7} < \frac{8}{13}$

2 Replace ● with <, >, or = to make -6.7 ● $-6\frac{3}{4}$ a true sentence. $-6.7 > -6\frac{3}{4}$

3 **CHEMISTRY** The values for the approximate densities of various substances are shown in the table below. Order the densities from least to greatest.

Substance	Density (g/cm^3)
aluminum	2.7
beryllium	1.87
brick	$1\frac{4}{5}$
crown glass	$2\frac{1}{4}$
fused silica	$2.\overline{2}$
marble	$2\frac{3}{5}$
nylon	1.1
pyrex glass	2.32
rubber neoprene	$1.\overline{3}$

Source: *CRC Handbook of Chemistry and Physics*

$1.1, 1.\overline{3}, 1\frac{4}{5}, 1.87, 2.\overline{2}, 2\frac{1}{4}, 2.32, 2\frac{3}{5}, 2.7$

EXAMPLE Compare Negative Rational Numbers

2 Replace ● with <, >, or = to make -5.2 ● $-5\frac{1}{4}$ a true sentence.

Write $-5\frac{1}{4}$ as a decimal.

$\frac{1}{4} = 0.25$, so $-5\frac{1}{4} = -5.25$.

Since $-5.2 > -5.25$, $-5.2 > -5\frac{1}{4}$.

Check Use a number line to check the answer.

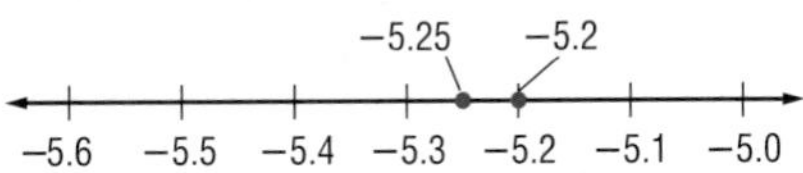

The answer is correct.

STUDY TIP

Number Lines A number to the left is always less than a number to the right.

Your Turn **Replace each ● with <, >, or = to make a true sentence.**

a. $\frac{5}{6}$ ● $\frac{7}{9}$ >

b. $-\frac{5}{7}$ ● -0.7 <

c. $2\frac{3}{5}$ ● $2.\overline{6}$ <

You can order rational numbers by writing any fractions as decimals. Then order the decimals.

EXAMPLE Order Rational Numbers

3 ROLLER COASTERS The ride times for nine roller coasters are shown in the table. Order the times from least to greatest.

Coaster	Ride Time (min)
Dragon Fire	$2\frac{1}{6}$
Mighty Canadian Minebuster	$2.\overline{6}$
Wilde Beast	2.5
Ghoster Coaster	$1\frac{5}{6}$
SkyRider	$2\frac{5}{12}$
Thunder Run	1.75
The Bat	$1\frac{5}{6}$
Vortex	1.75
Top Gun	$2\frac{5}{12}$

Source: Paramount

$2\frac{1}{6} = 2.1\overline{6}$ $\quad 1\frac{5}{6} = 1.8\overline{3}$ $\quad 2\frac{5}{12} = 2.41\overline{6}$

From least to greatest, the times are 1.75, 1.75, $1\frac{5}{6}$, $1\frac{5}{6}$, $2\frac{1}{6}$, $2\frac{5}{12}$, $2\frac{5}{12}$, 2.5, and $2.\overline{6}$. So, Vortex and Thunder Run have the shortest ride times, and Mighty Canadian Minebuster has the longest ride time.

REAL-LIFE MATH

ROLLER COASTERS The *Dragon Fire* is a double looping coaster with a corkscrew. The track is 2,160 feet long.

Source: Paramount

TEACHING TIP

Explain to students that each coaster must be represented. Therefore, they must list two 1.75s, $1\frac{5}{6}$s, and $2\frac{5}{12}$s.

DAILY INTERVENTION **Differentiated Instruction**

Logical Have students review the Study Tip box at the top of page 63. Then ask students to list ways to use these equivalencies to compare and order rational numbers. Elicit any other mental math techniques students may use.

Sample answer: $\frac{5}{8}$ and $\frac{5}{9}$ are both a bit more than $\frac{1}{2}$, since half of 8 is 4 and half of 9 is 4.5. Since $\frac{1}{9}$ is smaller than $\frac{1}{8}$, however, $\frac{5}{9}$ is less than $\frac{5}{8}$.

Students practice the same concepts in Exercises 12–31 if they are assigned odd or even problems.

Skill and Concept Check

1. *Writing Math* Explain why 0.28 is less than $0.\overline{28}$. **See margin.**

2. **OPEN ENDED** Name two fractions that are less than $\frac{1}{2}$ and two fractions that are greater than $\frac{1}{2}$. **Sample answers: $\frac{1}{3}, \frac{1}{4}$; $\frac{2}{3}, \frac{3}{4}$**

3. **NUMBER SENSE** Are the fractions $\frac{5}{11}, \frac{5}{12}, \frac{5}{13}$, and $\frac{5}{14}$ arranged in order from least to greatest or from greatest to least? Explain. **See margin.**

GUIDED PRACTICE

Replace each ● with <, >, or = to make a true sentence.

4. $\frac{3}{4}$ ● $\frac{7}{12}$ **>**
5. $-\frac{4}{5}$ ● $-\frac{7}{9}$ **<**
6. $3\frac{5}{8}$ ● 3.625 **=**
7. $-2\frac{4}{9}$ ● −2.42 **<**

Order each set of rational numbers from least to greatest. 8–10. See margin.

8. $\frac{4}{5}$, 0.5, $\frac{1}{3}$, 0.65
9. $-\frac{2}{3}$, 0.7, −0.68, $\frac{3}{4}$
10. $-1\frac{2}{3}$, −1.23, −1.45, $-1\frac{1}{2}$

11. **CARPENTRY** Rondell has some drill bits marked $\frac{7}{16}, \frac{3}{8}, \frac{5}{32}, \frac{9}{16}$, and $\frac{1}{4}$. If these are all measurements in inches, how should he arrange them if he wants them from least to greatest? **$\frac{5}{32}, \frac{1}{4}, \frac{3}{8}, \frac{7}{16}, \frac{9}{16}$**

★ indicates increased difficulty

Practice and Applications

Replace each ● with <, >, or = to make a true sentence.

12. $\frac{2}{3}$ ● $\frac{7}{9}$ **<**
13. $\frac{3}{5}$ ● $\frac{5}{8}$ **<**
14. $-\frac{3}{11}$ ● $-\frac{1}{3}$ **>**
15. $-\frac{8}{11}$ ● $-\frac{7}{9}$ **>**
16. −2.3125 ● $-2\frac{5}{16}$ **=**
17. −5.2 ● $-5\frac{3}{11}$ **>**
18. $0.\overline{38}$ ● $\frac{4}{11}$ **>**
19. $0.\overline{26}$ ● $\frac{4}{15}$ **<**
20. $-4.\overline{37}$ ● −4.37 **<**
21. $-3.1\overline{6}$ ● $-3.\overline{16}$ **<**
22. $\frac{3}{7}$ ● $0.\overline{42}$ **>**
23. $12\frac{5}{6}$ ● $12.8\overline{3}$ **=**

HOMEWORK HELP	
For Exercises	See Examples
12–23, 33	1, 2
24–32, 34–35	3

Extra Practice
See pages 619, 649.

Order each set of rational numbers from least to greatest. 24–29. See margin.

24. 1.8, 1.07, $1\frac{8}{9}$, $1\frac{1}{2}$
25. $7\frac{1}{5}$, 6.8, 7.6, $6\frac{3}{4}$
26. $\frac{1}{9}$, 0.1, $-\frac{1}{3}$, −0.25
27. $-\frac{3}{5}$, 0.45, −0.5, $\frac{4}{7}$
28. $-3\frac{2}{5}$, −3.68, −3.97, $-4\frac{3}{4}$
29. −2.9, −2.95, $-2\frac{9}{11}$, $-2\frac{13}{14}$

30. Which is least: $\frac{7}{11}$, 0.6, $\frac{2}{3}$, $0.6\overline{3}$, or $\frac{8}{13}$? **0.6**

31. Which is greatest: $\frac{3}{8}$, 0.376, 0.367, $\frac{2}{5}$, or $0.\overline{37}$? **$\frac{2}{5}$**

32. **STATISTICS** If you order a set of numbers from least to greatest, the middle number is the *median*. Find the median of 23.2, 22.45, 21.63, $22\frac{5}{8}$, and $21\frac{3}{5}$. **22.45**

msmath3.net/self_check_quiz

3 Practice/Apply

FOLDABLES™ Follow-Up Remind students to explain what they learn about comparing and ordering rational numbers expressed as fractions or decimals on the second tab of their Foldables. Encourage them to explain how they can compare two rational numbers by expressing them as decimals and comparing the decimals.

NUMBER SENSE
When students first encounter the ordering of fractions, they frequently think that a greater denominator means the fraction is greater. Use Exercise 3 to show that the opposite is true if the numerators are equal. Ask students to write other examples of fractions on the chalkboard that demonstrate this concept.

About the Exercises...

Guided Practice Key

Exercises	Examples
4–5	1
6–7	2
8–11	3

Assignment Guide

Basic: 13–33 odd, 36–47

Average: 13–35 odd, 36–47

Enriched: 12–36 even, 37–43 (Optional: 44–47)

Answers

1. Since 0.28 = 0.28000000 and $0.\overline{28}$ = 0.28282828…, 0.28 is less than $0.\overline{28}$.
3. Greatest to least; since the numerators are the same, the values of the fractions decrease as the denominators increase.
8. $\frac{1}{3}$, 0.5, 0.65, $\frac{4}{5}$
9. −0.68, $-\frac{2}{3}$, 0.7, and $\frac{3}{4}$
10. $-1\frac{2}{3}$, $-1\frac{1}{2}$, −1.45, −1.23
24. 1.07, $1\frac{1}{2}$, 1.8, $1\frac{8}{9}$
25. $6\frac{3}{4}$, 6.8, $7\frac{1}{5}$, 7.6
26. $-\frac{1}{3}$, −0.25, 0.1, $\frac{1}{9}$
27. $-\frac{3}{5}$, −0.5, 0.45, $\frac{4}{7}$
28. $-4\frac{3}{4}$, −3.97, −3.68, $-3\frac{2}{5}$
29. −2.95, $-2\frac{13}{14}$, −2.9, $-2\frac{9}{11}$

Lesson 2-2 Comparing and Ordering Rational Numbers 69

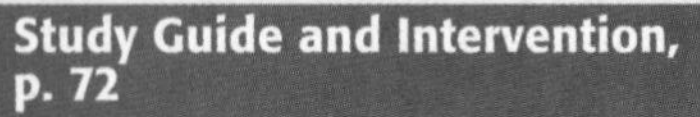

Study Guide and Intervention, p. 72

NAME ______________ DATE ________ PERIOD ____

2-2 Study Guide and Intervention

Comparing and Ordering Rational Numbers

When comparing two or more rational numbers, either write the numbers as fractions with the same denominator or write the numbers as decimals.

EXAMPLE 1 **Replace ● with <, >, or = to make $\frac{4}{5}$ ● $\frac{7}{10}$ a true sentence.**

Write as fractions with the same denominator. The least common denominator is 10.

$\frac{4}{5} = \frac{4 \cdot 2}{5 \cdot 2}$ or $\frac{8}{10}$

$\frac{7}{10} = \frac{7 \cdot 1}{10 \cdot 1}$ or $\frac{7}{10}$

Since $\frac{8}{10} > \frac{7}{10}$, $\frac{4}{5} > \frac{7}{10}$.

EXAMPLE 2 **Order the set of rational numbers -3.25, $-3\frac{1}{3}$, $-3\frac{2}{5}$, and $-3.2\overline{5}$ from least to greatest.**

Write $-3\frac{1}{3}$ and $-3\frac{2}{5}$ as decimals.

$\frac{1}{3} = 0.\overline{3}$, so $-3\frac{1}{3} = -3.\overline{3}$.

$\frac{2}{5} = 0.4$, so $-3\frac{2}{5} = -3.4$.

Since $-3.4 < -3.\overline{3} < -3.2\overline{5} < -3.25$, the numbers from least to greatest are $-3\frac{2}{5}$, $-3\frac{1}{3}$, $-3.2\overline{5}$, and -3.25.

EXERCISES

Replace each ● with <, >, or = to make a true sentence.

1. $\frac{5}{6}$ ● $\frac{2}{3}$ >
2. $\frac{4}{5}$ ● $\frac{13}{15}$ <
3. $\frac{1}{9}$ ● $\frac{1}{8}$ <
4. $-\frac{2}{3}$ ● $-\frac{7}{10}$ >
5. $3\frac{7}{10}$ ● $3\frac{4}{5}$ <
6. $-2\frac{3}{7}$ ● $-2\frac{4}{9}$ >
7. 2.6 ● $2\frac{5}{8}$ <
8. $4\frac{1}{6}$ ● $4.1\overline{6}$ =
9. $-4.5\overline{8}$ ● $-4.\overline{58}$ <

Order each set of rational numbers from least to greatest.

10. 0.5, 0.1, $\frac{1}{4}$, $\frac{2}{3}$
    0.1, $\frac{1}{4}$, 0.5, $\frac{2}{3}$
11. 2.4, $2\frac{4}{7}$, 2.13, $1\frac{9}{10}$
    $1\frac{9}{10}$, 2.13, 2.4, $2\frac{4}{7}$
12. $\frac{1}{5}$, -0.7, 0.25, $-\frac{3}{5}$
    -0.7, $-\frac{3}{5}$, $\frac{1}{5}$, 0.25
13. $1\frac{2}{9}$, $1\frac{2}{3}$, 1.45, 1.67
    $1\frac{2}{9}$, 1.45, $1\frac{2}{3}$, 1.67
14. $-2\frac{1}{4}$, -2.28, -2.7, $-2\frac{4}{5}$
    $-2\frac{4}{5}$, -2.7, -2.28, $-2\frac{1}{4}$
15. $4\frac{2}{3}$, $4\frac{5}{6}$, 4.6, 5.3
    4.6, $4\frac{2}{3}$, $4\frac{5}{6}$, 5.3

Practice: Skills, p. 73

NAME ______________ DATE ________ PERIOD ____

2-2 Practice: Skills

Comparing and Ordering Rational Numbers

Replace each ● with <, >, or = to make a true sentence.

1. $\frac{1}{2}$ ● $\frac{3}{4}$ <
2. $\frac{1}{3}$ ● $\frac{1}{6}$ >
3. $\frac{2}{5}$ ● $\frac{3}{10}$ >
4. $\frac{2}{9}$ ● $\frac{1}{3}$ <
5. $\frac{3}{4}$ ● $\frac{9}{12}$ =
6. $\frac{3}{8}$ ● $\frac{2}{5}$ <
7. $-\frac{5}{6}$ ● $-\frac{6}{7}$ >
8. $-\frac{4}{9}$ ● $-\frac{5}{11}$ >
9. $\frac{5}{9}$ ● 0.55 >
10. 4.72 ● $4\frac{10}{13}$ <
11. $-2\frac{7}{15}$ ● -2.45 <
12. 5.25 ● $5.\overline{25}$ <
13. -1.62 ● $-1\frac{5}{8}$ >
14. $11\frac{4}{9}$ ● $11.\overline{4}$ =
15. $-1.\overline{27}$ ● $-1.2\overline{7}$ >

Order each set of rational numbers from least to greatest.

16. 0.3, 0.2, $\frac{1}{3}$, $\frac{2}{9}$
    0.2, $\frac{2}{9}$, 0.3, $\frac{1}{3}$
17. $1\frac{2}{5}$, $1\frac{2}{3}$, 1.55, 1.67
    $1\frac{2}{5}$, 1.55, $1\frac{2}{3}$, 1.67
18. 2.7, $2\frac{1}{7}$, 3.13, $1\frac{9}{10}$
    $1\frac{9}{10}$, $2\frac{1}{7}$, 2.7, 3.13
19. $\frac{1}{4}$, -1.7, 0.2, $-1\frac{3}{4}$
    $-1\frac{3}{4}$, -1.7, 0.2, $\frac{1}{4}$
20. -2.21, -2.09, $-2\frac{1}{9}$, $-1\frac{10}{11}$
    -2.21, $-2\frac{1}{9}$, -2.09, $-1\frac{10}{11}$
21. -3.1, 2.75, $1\frac{7}{8}$, $-\frac{2}{3}$
    -3.1, $-\frac{2}{3}$, $1\frac{7}{8}$, 2.75
22. $6\frac{7}{8}$, $6\frac{15}{16}$, 6.9, 5.3
    5.3, $6\frac{7}{8}$, 6.9, $6\frac{15}{16}$
23. $-4\frac{1}{6}$, -4.19, -5.3, $-5\frac{1}{3}$
    $-5\frac{1}{3}$, -5.3, -4.19, $-4\frac{1}{6}$
24. $5\frac{9}{11}$, 5.93, $5\frac{7}{20}$, 5.81
    $5\frac{7}{20}$, 5.81, $5\frac{9}{11}$, 5.93
25. $-3\frac{1}{4}$, $-4\frac{1}{8}$, -3.65, $-3\frac{4}{11}$, -4.05
    $-4\frac{1}{8}$, -4.05, -3.65, $-3\frac{4}{11}$, $-3\frac{1}{4}$

Practice: Word Problems, p. 74

NAME ______________ DATE ________ PERIOD ____

2-2 Practice: Word Problems

Comparing and Ordering Rational Numbers

1. **BASKETBALL** In the last ten games, Percy made $\frac{7}{12}$ of his free throws. For the same period, Tariq made $\frac{4}{7}$ of his free throws. Which player has the better free throw record? Percy; $\frac{7}{12} > \frac{4}{7}$

2. **SPORTS** Central's baseball team won $\frac{53}{78}$ of its games last year, while Southern's team won $\frac{55}{81}$ of its games. Which team had the better record? Central

3. **MEASUREMENT** Beaker A contains $4\frac{1}{3}$ fluid ounces of water, while beaker B contains $4\frac{3}{10}$ fluid ounces of water. Which beaker has the smaller amount of water? Beaker B

4. **NATURE** The two trees in Opal's back yard have circumferences of $12\frac{5}{8}$ inches and $12\frac{3}{5}$ inches. Which circumference is larger? $12\frac{5}{8}$ in.

5. **EXERCISE** On Monday, Rob averaged 3.75 laps per minute. On Tuesday, he averaged $3\frac{4}{5}$ laps per minute. On which day did Rob run faster? Tuesday

6. **FOOD** Hector and Carla both gave apples to their teacher. Hector's apple weighed $6\frac{7}{12}$ ounces, while Carla's apple weighed 6.65 ounces. Which apple weighed more? Carla's

7. **SPORTS** Christina ran one lap in 83.86 seconds, while Della's time for one lap was $83\frac{7}{8}$ seconds. Which runner had the faster time? Christina

8. **STATISTICS** The median of a set of numbers can be found by first putting the numbers in order from least to greatest, then choosing the middle number. Find the median of 5.79, $5\frac{3}{4}$, $5\frac{7}{8}$, 5.9, and $5\frac{4}{5}$. $5\frac{4}{5}$

33. **PHOTOGRAPHY** The shutter time on Diego's camera is set at $\frac{1}{250}$ second. If Diego wants to increase the shutter time, should he set the time at $\frac{1}{500}$ second or $\frac{1}{125}$ second? $\frac{1}{125}$ **s**

★ 34. Match each number with a point on the number line.

a. 0.425 **R** b. $\frac{3}{8}$ **Q** c. $\frac{13}{16}$ **S** d. $0.\overline{15}$ **P**

★ 35. **MULTI STEP** The table shows the regular season records of five college baseball teams during a recent season. Which team had the best record?

Team	Games Won	Games Played
University of Alabama	48	61
University of Notre Dame	44	59
University of Southern California	34	56
Florida State University	56	68
Rice University	47	58

Florida State University

36. **CRITICAL THINKING** Are there any rational numbers between $0.\overline{2}$ and $\frac{2}{9}$? Explain. **No; $0.\overline{2} = \frac{2}{9}$.**

Spiral Review with Standardized Test Practice

37. **MULTIPLE CHOICE** Determine which statement is *not* true. **D**

Ⓐ $\frac{3}{4} < 0.\overline{7}$ Ⓑ $-\frac{2}{3} = -0.\overline{6}$ Ⓒ $0.81 > \frac{4}{5}$ Ⓓ $-0.58 > -\frac{5}{12}$

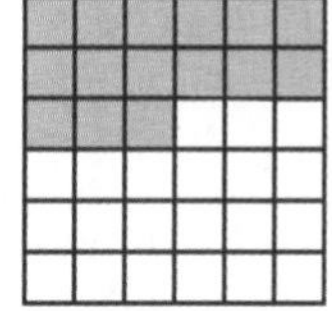

38. **SHORT RESPONSE** Is the fraction represented by the shaded part of the square at the right greater than, equal to, or less than 0.41? **Greater than; $\frac{15}{36} = 0.41\overline{6}$, which is greater than 0.41.**

39. **HISTORY** During the fourteenth and fifteenth centuries, printing presses used type cut from wood blocks. Each block was $\frac{7}{8}$ inch thick. Write this fraction as a decimal. (Lesson 2-1) **0.875 in.**

Solve each equation. Check your solution. (Lesson 1-9)

40. $\frac{y}{7} = 22$ **154** 41. $4p = -60$ **−15** 42. $20 = \frac{t}{15}$ **300** 43. $81 = -3d$ **−27**

GETTING READY FOR THE NEXT LESSON

PREREQUISITE SKILL Multiply. (Lesson 1-6)

44. $-4(-7)$ **28** 45. $8(-12)$ **−96** 46. $17(-3)$ **−51** 47. $-23(-5)$ **115**

4 Assess

Open-Ended Assessment

Writing Have each student choose a topic of personal interest and write a word problem that involves the comparison of rational numbers.

2-3 Multiplying Rational Numbers

HANDS-ON Mini Lab

Materials
- paper
- colored pencils

Work with a partner.

To multiply $\frac{1}{3}$ and $\frac{2}{5}$, you can use an area model to find $\frac{1}{3}$ of $\frac{2}{5}$.

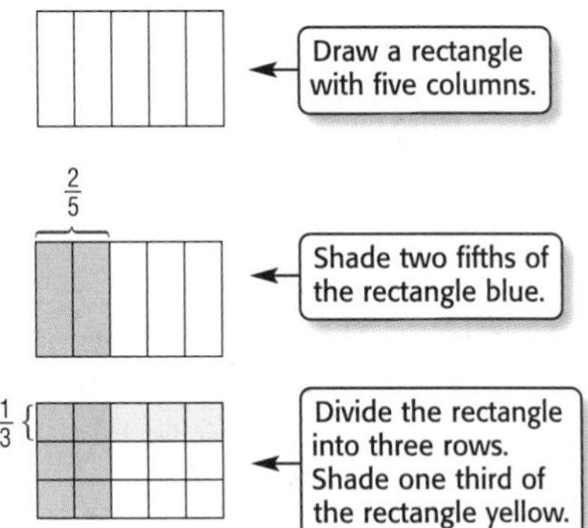

The overlapping green area represents the product of $\frac{1}{3}$ and $\frac{2}{5}$.

1. What is the product of $\frac{1}{3}$ and $\frac{2}{5}$? $\frac{2}{15}$
2. Use an area model to find each product. **a–d. See margin for area models.**
   a. $\frac{3}{4} \cdot \frac{1}{2}$ $\frac{3}{8}$ b. $\frac{2}{5} \cdot \frac{2}{3}$ $\frac{4}{15}$ c. $\frac{1}{4} \cdot \frac{3}{5}$ $\frac{3}{20}$ d. $\frac{2}{3} \cdot \frac{4}{5}$ $\frac{8}{15}$
3. What is the relationship between the numerators of the factors and the numerator of the product?
4. What is the relationship between the denominators of the factors and the denominator of the product?

What You'll LEARN
Multiply fractions.

NEW Vocabulary
dimensional analysis

REVIEW Vocabulary
greatest common factor (GCF): the greatest of the common factors of two or more numbers
(Page 610)

3. The product of the numerators of the factors equals the numerator of the product.
4. The product of the denominators of the factors equals the denominator of the product.

The Mini Lab suggests the rule for multiplying fractions.

Noteables™ Key Concept: Multiply Fractions

Words To multiply fractions, multiply the numerators and multiply the denominators.

Symbols

Arithmetic	Algebra
$\frac{2}{3} \cdot \frac{4}{5} = \frac{8}{15}$	$\frac{a}{b} \cdot \frac{c}{d} = \frac{ac}{bd}$, where $b \neq 0, d \neq 0$

2-3 Lesson Notes

Lesson Resources

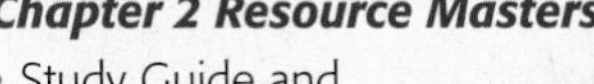

Chapter 2 Resource Masters
- Study Guide and Intervention, p. 77
- Practice: Skills, p. 78
- Practice: Word Problems, p. 79
- Reading to Learn Mathematics, p. 80
- Enrichment, p. 81

MathPASS Tutorial CD-ROM, 20, 21
Parent and Student Study Guide Online Worksheets, 2-3
Real-Life Career Masters, p. 28
Noteables™: Interactive Study Notebook with Foldables™, 2-3

1 Focus

5-Minute Check 2-3

Use as a quiz or review of Lesson 2-2. (Also available as a transparency)

Bellringer

Reading Mathematics Students may be confused to learn that multiplying by a fraction less than 1 decreases a number. Point out that multiplying a positive integer by a negative integer also results in a product that is less than the first integer. To reinforce this point, when multiplying by a fraction, have students read the multiplication sign as "of," so "$\frac{1}{2}$ times 4" equals "$\frac{1}{2}$ of 4."

Reading to Learn Mathematics, p. 80 **ELL**

NAME ______ DATE ______ PERIOD ____

2-3 Reading to Learn Mathematics
Multiplying Rational Numbers

Pre-Activity *Complete the Mini Lab at the top of page 71 in your textbook. Write your answers below.*

1. What is the product of $\frac{1}{3}$ and $\frac{2}{5}$? $\frac{2}{15}$
2. Use an area model to find each product.
   a. $\frac{3}{4} \cdot \frac{1}{2}$ $\frac{3}{8}$ b. $\frac{2}{5} \cdot \frac{2}{3}$ $\frac{4}{15}$ c. $\frac{1}{4} \cdot \frac{3}{5}$ $\frac{3}{20}$ d. $\frac{2}{3} \cdot \frac{4}{5}$ $\frac{8}{15}$
3. What is the relationship between the numerators of the factors and the numerator of the product? The product of the numerators of the factors equals the numerator of the product.
4. What is the relationship between the denominators of the factors and the denominator of the product? The product of the denominators of the factors equals the denominator of the product.

Reading the Lesson

Answers (Hands-On Mini Lab)

2a.

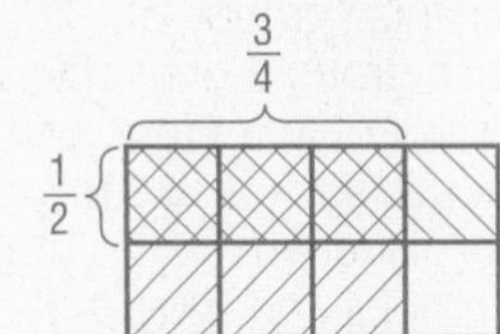

2b.

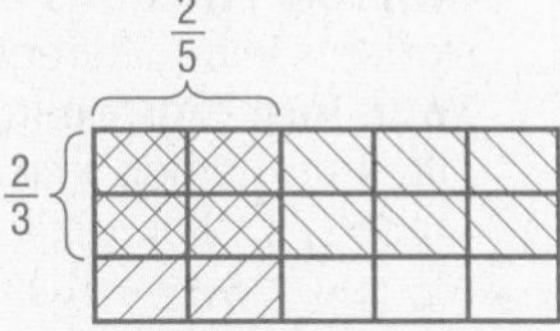

(Answers continued on page 72.)

2 Teach

In-Class Examples

1. Find $\frac{3}{7} \cdot \frac{8}{9}$. Write in simplest form. $\frac{8}{21}$

2. Find $-\frac{3}{4} \cdot \frac{7}{12}$. Write in simplest form. $-\frac{7}{16}$

3. Find $3\frac{1}{5} \cdot 1\frac{3}{4}$. Write in simplest form. $5\frac{3}{5}$

Answers (Hands-On Mini Lab, p. 71)

2c.

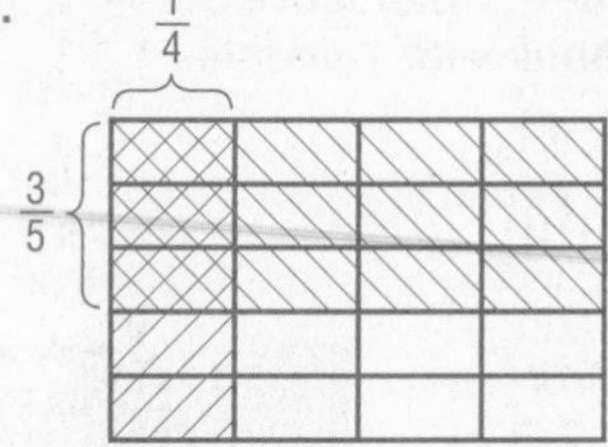

2d.

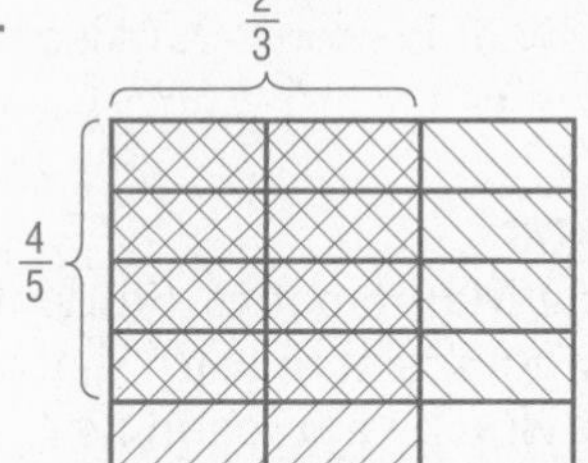

EXAMPLE Multiply Fractions

1 Find $\frac{4}{9} \cdot \frac{3}{5}$. Write in simplest form.

$\frac{4}{9} \cdot \frac{3}{5} = \frac{4}{\cancel{9}_3} \cdot \frac{\cancel{3}^1}{5}$ Divide 9 and 3 by their GCF, 3.

$= \frac{4 \cdot 1}{3 \cdot 5}$ ← Multiply the numerators. ← Multiply the denominators.

$= \frac{4}{15}$ Simplify.

Use the rules for multiplying integers to determine the sign of the product.

STUDY TIP

Negative Fractions $-\frac{5}{6}$ can be written as $\frac{-5}{6}$ or as $\frac{5}{-6}$.

EXAMPLE Multiply Negative Fractions

2 Find $-\frac{5}{6} \cdot \frac{3}{8}$. Write in simplest form.

$-\frac{5}{6} \cdot \frac{3}{8} = \frac{-5}{\cancel{6}_2} \cdot \frac{\cancel{3}^1}{8}$ Divide 6 and 3 by their GCF, 3.

$= \frac{-5 \cdot 1}{2 \cdot 8}$ ← Multiply the numerators. ← Multiply the denominators.

$= -\frac{5}{16}$ The fractions have different signs, so the product is negative.

Your Turn Multiply. Write in simplest form.

a. $\frac{8}{9} \cdot \frac{3}{4}$ $\frac{2}{3}$

b. $-\frac{3}{5} \cdot \frac{7}{9}$ $-\frac{7}{15}$

c. $\left(-\frac{1}{2}\right)\left(-\frac{6}{7}\right)$ $\frac{3}{7}$

To multiply mixed numbers, first rename them as improper fractions.

EXAMPLE Multiply Mixed Numbers

3 Find $4\frac{1}{2} \cdot 2\frac{2}{3}$. Write in simplest form.

TEACHING TIP

Encourage students to always divide out common factors before multiplying.

$4\frac{1}{2} \cdot 2\frac{2}{3} = \frac{9}{2} \cdot \frac{8}{3}$ $4\frac{1}{2} = \frac{9}{2}, 2\frac{2}{3} = \frac{8}{3}$

$= \frac{\cancel{9}^3}{\cancel{2}_1} \cdot \frac{\cancel{8}^4}{\cancel{3}_1}$ Divide out common factors.

$= \frac{3 \cdot 4}{1 \cdot 1}$ ← Multiply the numerators. ← Multiply the denominators.

$= \frac{12}{1}$ or 12 Simplify.

Check $4\frac{1}{2}$ is less than 5, and $2\frac{2}{3}$ is less than 3. Therefore, $4\frac{1}{2} \cdot 2\frac{2}{3}$ is less than $5 \cdot 3$ or 15. The answer is reasonable.

Your Turn Multiply. Write in simplest form.

d. $1\frac{1}{2} \cdot 1\frac{2}{3}$ $2\frac{1}{2}$

e. $\frac{5}{7} \cdot 1\frac{3}{5}$ $1\frac{1}{7}$

f. $\left(-2\frac{1}{6}\right)\left(-1\frac{1}{5}\right)$ $2\frac{3}{5}$

DAILY INTERVENTION Flexible Grouping

Multiply Fractions and Mixed Numbers Organize groups of students with different learning styles. Assign each group a different **Your Turn** exercise from this page. Have each student in a group use a different method to explain how to find the product, such as area models, fraction circles, a paragraph, a spoken explanation, or manipulatives such as straws. Then shuffle the groups and have the students share their explanations with their new groups.

EXAMPLE Evaluate an Algebraic Expression

4 **ALGEBRA** **Evaluate abc if $a = -\frac{1}{2}$, $b = \frac{3}{5}$, and $c = \frac{5}{9}$.**

$abc = -\frac{1}{2} \cdot \frac{3}{5} \cdot \frac{5}{9}$ — Replace a with $-\frac{1}{2}$, b with $\frac{3}{5}$, and c with $\frac{5}{9}$.

$= -\frac{1}{2} \cdot \frac{\overset{1}{\cancel{3}}}{\underset{1}{\cancel{5}}} \cdot \frac{\overset{1}{\cancel{5}}}{\underset{3}{\cancel{9}}}$ — Divide out common factors.

$= -\frac{1 \cdot 1 \cdot 1}{2 \cdot 1 \cdot 3}$ or $-\frac{1}{6}$ — Simplify.

Your Turn **Evaluate each expression if $a = \frac{3}{4}$, $b = -\frac{1}{2}$, and $c = \frac{2}{3}$.**

g. ac **$\frac{1}{2}$** h. ab **$-\frac{3}{8}$** i. abc **$-\frac{1}{4}$**

REAL-LIFE MATH

AIRCRAFT A 757 aircraft has a capacity of 242 passengers and a wingspan of 165 feet 4 inches.

Source: *Continental Traveler*

Dimensional analysis is the process of including units of measurement when you compute. You can use dimensional analysis to check whether your answers are reasonable.

EXAMPLE Use Dimensional Analysis

5 **AIRCRAFT** **Suppose a 757 aircraft is traveling at its cruise speed. How far will it travel in $1\frac{1}{3}$ hours?**

Aircraft	Cruise Speed (mph)
MD-80	505
DC-10	550
757	540
ATR-42	328

Source: *Continental Traveler*

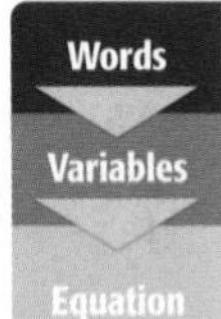

Words	Distance equals the rate multiplied by the time.
Variables	$d = r \cdot t$
Equation	d = 540 miles per hour · $1\frac{1}{3}$ hours

$d = \frac{540 \text{ miles}}{1 \text{ hour}} \cdot 1\frac{1}{3}$ hours — Write the equation.

$d = \frac{540 \text{ miles}}{1 \text{ hour}} \cdot \frac{4}{3}$ hours — $1\frac{1}{3} = \frac{4}{3}$

$d = \frac{\overset{180}{\cancel{540}} \text{ miles}}{1 \cancel{\text{hour}}} \cdot \frac{4}{\underset{1}{\cancel{3}}} \cancel{\text{hours}}$ — Divide by common factors and units.

$d = 720$ miles

At its cruising speed, a 757 will travel 720 miles in $1\frac{1}{3}$ hours.

Check The problem asks for the distance. When you divide the common units, the answer is expressed in miles. So, the answer is reasonable.

STUDY TIP

Mental Math

$\frac{1}{3}$ of 540 is 180. Using the Distributive Property, $1\frac{1}{3}$ of 540 should equal 540 + 180, or 720.

msmath3.net/extra_examples

In-Class Examples

4 **ALGEBRA** Evaluate prq if $p = \frac{2}{3}$, $r = -\frac{4}{5}$, and $q = \frac{7}{8}$. **$-\frac{7}{15}$**

5 **WATER USE** Low-flow showerheads use $2\frac{1}{2}$ gallons of water per minute. If family members shower a total of $2\frac{1}{3}$ hours per week, about how much water does the family use for showers each week? **about 350 gal**

3 Practice/Apply

Writing Math Have students model $\frac{1}{2} \cdot \frac{7}{8}$ as in the Hands-On Mini Lab if they have difficulty with Exercise 1.

DAILY INTERVENTION **FIND THE ERROR** In Exercise 3, students mistakenly answering "Matt" may be confusing the multiplication of mixed numbers with the addition of mixed numbers.

Show students the evaluations of $2\frac{1}{2} + 3\frac{1}{4}$ and $2\frac{1}{2} \cdot 3\frac{1}{4}$ and discuss their differences. Include in your discussion the Associative Property and order of operations.

About the Exercises...

Guided Practice Key

Exercises	Examples
4	1
5, 7	2
6	3
9	4
8	5

Assignment Guide

Basic: 11–21 odd, 25–31 odd, 35–45

Average: 11–31 odd, 35–45 (Optional: 32–34)

Enriched: 10–30 even, 31–41 (Optional: 42–45)

Alert! For Exercise 30, students will need to use the Internet or other resources.

Students practice the same concepts in Exercises 10–29 if they are assigned odd or even problems.

Skill and Concept Check

1. **Writing Math** Explain why the product of $\frac{1}{2}$ and $\frac{7}{8}$ is less than $\frac{1}{2}$. **See margin.**

2. **OPEN ENDED** Name two fractions whose product is greater than $\frac{1}{2}$ and less than 1. **Sample answer: $\frac{3}{4}, \frac{4}{5}$**

3. **FIND THE ERROR** Matt and Enrique are multiplying $2\frac{1}{2}$ and $3\frac{1}{4}$. Who is correct? Explain.

Matt

$2\frac{1}{2} \cdot 3\frac{1}{4} = 2 \cdot 3 + \frac{1}{2} \cdot \frac{1}{4}$
$= 6 + \frac{1}{8}$
$= 6\frac{1}{8}$

Enrique

$2\frac{1}{2} \cdot 3\frac{1}{4} = \frac{5}{2} \cdot \frac{13}{4}$
$= \frac{65}{8}$
$= 8\frac{1}{8}$

Enrique; to multiply mixed numbers, you must first rename them as fractions.

GUIDED PRACTICE

Multiply. Write in simplest form.

4. $\frac{3}{5} \cdot \frac{5}{7}$ **$\frac{3}{7}$**
5. $-\frac{1}{8} \cdot \frac{4}{9}$ **$-\frac{1}{18}$**
6. $1\frac{1}{3} \cdot 5\frac{1}{2}$ **$7\frac{1}{3}$**
7. $\left(-\frac{4}{5}\right)\left(-\frac{4}{5}\right)$ **$\frac{16}{25}$**

8. **FOOD** The nutrition label is from a can of green beans. How many cups of green beans does the can contain? **$1\frac{3}{4}$ c**

9. **ALGEBRA** Evaluate xy if $x = \frac{4}{5}$ and $y = \frac{1}{2}$. **$\frac{2}{5}$**

★ indicates increased difficulty

Practice and Applications

HOMEWORK HELP

For Exercises	See Examples
10–23	1–3
24–27	4
28–29	5

Extra Practice See pages 619, 649.

Multiply. Write in simplest form.

10. $\frac{3}{8} \cdot \frac{4}{5}$ **$\frac{3}{10}$**
11. $\frac{1}{12} \cdot \frac{4}{7}$ **$\frac{1}{21}$**
12. $-\frac{3}{8} \cdot \frac{4}{9}$ **$-\frac{1}{6}$**
13. $-\frac{9}{10} \cdot \frac{2}{3}$ **$-\frac{3}{5}$**
14. $-3\frac{3}{8} \cdot \left(-\frac{2}{3}\right)$ **$2\frac{1}{4}$**
15. $-\frac{5}{6} \cdot \left(-1\frac{4}{5}\right)$ **$1\frac{1}{2}$**
16. $3\frac{1}{3} \cdot 1\frac{1}{2}$ **5**
17. $2\frac{1}{2} \cdot 1\frac{2}{5}$ **$3\frac{1}{2}$**
18. $-3\frac{1}{3} \cdot 2\frac{1}{4}$ **$-7\frac{1}{2}$**
19. $-4\frac{1}{4} \cdot 3\frac{1}{3}$ **$-14\frac{1}{6}$**
20. $\left(-\frac{3}{7}\right)\left(-\frac{3}{7}\right)$ **$\frac{9}{49}$**
21. $\left(-\frac{2}{3}\right)\left(-\frac{2}{3}\right)$ **$\frac{4}{9}$**

★ 22. Find the product of $\frac{1}{3}$, $-\frac{3}{8}$, and $\frac{4}{5}$. **$-\frac{1}{10}$**

★ 23. What is one half of the product of $\frac{2}{5}$ and $\frac{3}{4}$? **$\frac{3}{20}$**

ALGEBRA Evaluate each expression if $r = -\frac{1}{4}$, $s = \frac{2}{5}$, $t = \frac{8}{9}$, and $v = -\frac{2}{3}$.

24. rs **$-\frac{1}{10}$**
25. rt **$-\frac{2}{9}$**
26. stv **$-\frac{32}{135}$**
27. rtv **$\frac{4}{27}$**

Answer

1. Since $\frac{1}{2} \cdot 1 = \frac{1}{2}$ and $\frac{7}{8}$ is less than 1, $\frac{1}{2} \cdot \frac{7}{8}$ is less than $\frac{1}{2}$.

28. **PHOTOGRAPHY** Minh-Thu has a square photograph that measures $3\frac{1}{2}$ inches on each side. She reduces it to $\frac{2}{3}$ of its size. What is the length of a side of the new photograph? **$2\frac{1}{3}$ in.**

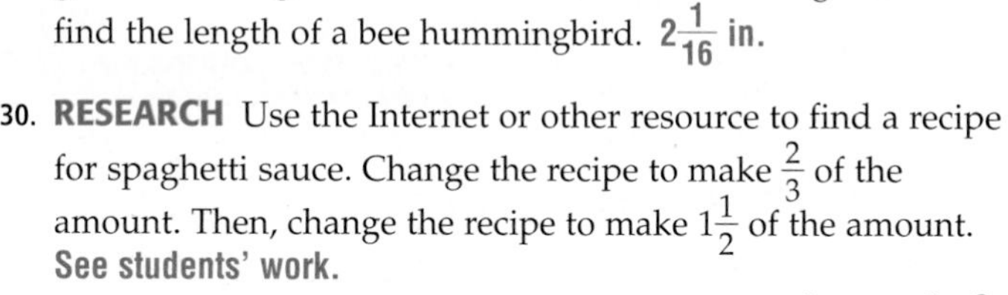

Giant Hummingbird

29. **BIOLOGY** The bee hummingbird of Cuba is the smallest hummingbird in the world. It is $\frac{1}{4}$ the length of the giant hummingbird. Use the information at the right to find the length of a bee hummingbird. **$2\frac{1}{16}$ in.**

30. **RESEARCH** Use the Internet or other resource to find a recipe for spaghetti sauce. Change the recipe to make $\frac{2}{3}$ of the amount. Then, change the recipe to make $1\frac{1}{2}$ of the amount. **See students' work.**

31. **CRITICAL THINKING** Find the missing fraction. $\frac{3}{4} \cdot ? = \frac{9}{14}$ **$\frac{6}{7}$**

EXTENDING THE LESSON

MENTAL MATH You can use number properties to simplify computations.

Example: $\frac{3}{4} \cdot \frac{3}{7} \cdot \frac{4}{3} = \left(\frac{3}{4} \cdot \frac{4}{3}\right) \cdot \frac{3}{7}$ Commutative and Associative Properties

$= 1 \cdot \frac{3}{7}$ or $\frac{3}{7}$ Identity Property of Multiplication

Use mental math to find each product.

32. $\frac{2}{5} \cdot \frac{1}{6} \cdot \frac{5}{2}$ **$\frac{1}{6}$**
33. $5 \cdot 3.78 \cdot \frac{1}{5}$ **3.78**
34. $\frac{2}{7} \cdot \frac{4}{9} \cdot \frac{3}{5} \cdot 0$ **0**

Spiral Review with Standardized Test Practice

35. **MULTIPLE CHOICE** Find the area of the triangle. Use the formula $A = \frac{1}{2}bh$. **C**

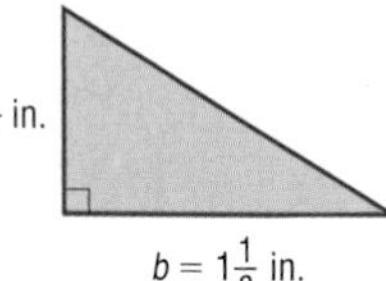

Ⓐ $\frac{3}{4}$ in^2 Ⓑ $\frac{5}{8}$ in^2 Ⓒ $\frac{3}{8}$ in^2 Ⓓ $\frac{1}{6}$ in^2

36. **MULTIPLE CHOICE** What number will make $\frac{3}{4} \cdot \frac{7}{8} = \frac{7}{8} \cdot n$ true? **G**

Ⓕ $\frac{4}{8}$ Ⓖ $\frac{3}{4}$ Ⓗ $\frac{10}{12}$ Ⓘ $\frac{7}{8}$

Replace each ● with <, >, or = to make a true sentence. (Lesson 2-2)

37. $\frac{1}{2}$ ● $\frac{4}{7}$ **<**
38. $\frac{2}{7}$ ● $0.\overline{28}$ **>**
39. -0.753 ● $-\frac{3}{4}$ **<**
40. $-\frac{4}{9}$ ● $-0.\overline{4}$ **=**

41. **HISTORY** In 1864, Abraham Lincoln won the presidential election with about 0.55 of the popular vote. Write this as a fraction in simplest form. (Lesson 2-1) **$\frac{11}{20}$**

GETTING READY FOR THE NEXT LESSON

PREREQUISITE SKILL **Divide.** (Lesson 1-6)

42. $51 \div (-17)$ **−3**
43. $-81 \div (-3)$ **27**
44. $-92 \div 4$ **−23**
45. $-105 \div (-7)$ **15**

Math Online msmath3.net/self_check_quiz

4 Assess

Open-Ended Assessment

Speaking Have students describe how to find the product of $\frac{5}{6}$ and $\frac{3}{5}$. **$\frac{1}{2}$**

Study Guide and Intervention, p. 77

NAME ________ DATE ________ PERIOD ____

2-3 Study Guide and Intervention

Multiplying Rational Numbers

To multiply fractions, multiply the numerators and multiply the denominators.

EXAMPLE 1 Find $\frac{3}{8} \cdot \frac{4}{11}$. Write in simplest form.

$\frac{3}{8} \cdot \frac{4}{11} = \frac{3}{\cancel{8}_2} \cdot \frac{\cancel{4}^1}{11}$ Divide 8 and 4 by their GCF, 4.

$= \frac{3 \cdot 1}{2 \cdot 11}$ Multiply the numerators and denominators.

$= \frac{3}{22}$ Simplify.

To multiply mixed numbers, first rewrite them as improper fractions.

EXAMPLE 2 Find $-2\frac{1}{3} \cdot 3\frac{3}{5}$. Write in simplest form.

$-2\frac{1}{3} \cdot 3\frac{3}{5} = -\frac{7}{3} \cdot \frac{18}{5}$ $-2\frac{1}{3} = -\frac{7}{3}$, $3\frac{3}{5} = \frac{18}{5}$

$= -\frac{7}{\cancel{3}_1} \cdot \frac{\cancel{18}^6}{5}$ Divide 18 and 3 by their GCF, 3.

$= -\frac{7 \cdot 6}{1 \cdot 5}$ Multiply the numerators and denominators.

$= -\frac{42}{5}$ Simplify.

$= -8\frac{2}{5}$ Write the result as a mixed number.

EXERCISES

Multiply. Write in simplest form.

1. $\frac{2}{3} \cdot \frac{3}{5}$ $\frac{2}{5}$
2. $\frac{4}{7} \cdot \frac{3}{4}$ $\frac{3}{7}$
3. $-\frac{1}{2} \cdot \frac{7}{9}$ $-\frac{7}{18}$
4. $\frac{9}{10} \cdot \frac{2}{3}$ $\frac{3}{5}$
5. $\frac{5}{8} \cdot \left(-\frac{4}{9}\right)$ $-\frac{5}{18}$
6. $-\frac{4}{7} \cdot \left(-\frac{2}{3}\right)$ $\frac{8}{21}$
7. $2\frac{2}{5} \cdot \frac{1}{6}$ $\frac{2}{5}$
8. $-3\frac{1}{3} \cdot 1\frac{1}{2}$ -5
9. $3\frac{3}{7} \cdot 2\frac{5}{8}$ 9
10. $-1\frac{7}{8} \cdot \left(-2\frac{2}{5}\right)$ $4\frac{1}{2}$
11. $-1\frac{3}{4} \cdot 2\frac{1}{5}$ $-3\frac{17}{20}$
12. $2\frac{2}{3} \cdot 2\frac{3}{7}$ $6\frac{10}{21}$

Practice: Skills, p. 78

NAME ________ DATE ________ PERIOD ____

2-3 Practice: Skills

Multiplying Rational Numbers

Multiply. Write in simplest form.

1. $\frac{1}{8} \cdot \frac{2}{3}$ $\frac{1}{12}$
2. $\frac{2}{9} \cdot \frac{7}{8}$ $\frac{7}{36}$
3. $\frac{5}{6} \cdot \frac{3}{11}$ $\frac{5}{22}$
4. $-\frac{4}{7} \cdot \frac{3}{10}$ $-\frac{6}{35}$
5. $\frac{2}{9} \cdot \left(-\frac{3}{8}\right)$ $-\frac{1}{12}$
6. $-\frac{3}{5} \cdot \left(-\frac{5}{9}\right)$ $\frac{1}{3}$
7. $1\frac{3}{4} \cdot \frac{2}{3}$ $1\frac{1}{6}$
8. $\frac{4}{5} \cdot 4\frac{3}{8}$ $3\frac{1}{2}$
9. $-\frac{2}{15} \cdot 5\frac{5}{6}$ $-\frac{7}{9}$
10. $-1\frac{3}{7} \cdot 1\frac{1}{5}$ $-1\frac{5}{7}$
11. $-2\frac{1}{4} \cdot 1\frac{2}{3}$ $-3\frac{3}{4}$
12. $1\frac{9}{16} \cdot 2\frac{4}{5}$ $4\frac{3}{8}$
13. $-3\frac{1}{7} \cdot \left(-1\frac{2}{11}\right)$ $3\frac{5}{7}$
14. $2\frac{2}{3} \cdot \left(-2\frac{1}{4}\right)$ -6
15. $\left(-\frac{4}{5}\right)\left(-\frac{4}{5}\right)$ $\frac{16}{25}$

ALGEBRA Evaluate each expression if $r = \frac{5}{6}$, $s = -\frac{1}{3}$, $t = \frac{4}{5}$, and $v = -\frac{3}{4}$.

16. rv $-\frac{5}{8}$
17. st $-\frac{4}{15}$
18. rs $-\frac{5}{18}$
19. stv $\frac{1}{5}$
20. rst $-\frac{2}{9}$
21. rtv $-\frac{1}{2}$

ALGEBRA Evaluate each expression if $a = -\frac{5}{9}$, $b = -\frac{1}{5}$, $c = \frac{2}{3}$, and $d = \frac{3}{4}$.

22. ad $-\frac{5}{12}$
23. bc $-\frac{2}{15}$
24. abc $\frac{2}{27}$

Practice: Word Problems, p. 79

NAME ________ DATE ________ PERIOD ____

2-3 Practice: Word Problems

Multiplying Rational Numbers

1. **NUTRITION** Maria's favorite candy bar has 230 Calories. The nutrition label states that $\frac{7}{8}$ of the Calories come from fat. How many Calories in the candy bar come from fat? $201\frac{1}{4}$ Calories	2. **ELECTIONS** In the last election, $\frac{3}{8}$ of the voters in Afton voted for the incumbent mayor. If 424 people voted in Afton in the last election, how many voted for the incumbent mayor? 159 people
3. **HOBBIES** Jerry is building a $\frac{1}{9}$ scale model of a race car. If the tires on the actual car are 33 inches in diameter, what is the diameter of the tires on the model? $3\frac{2}{3}$ in.	4. **COOKING** Enola's recipe for cookies calls for $2\frac{1}{2}$ cups of flour. If she wants to make $\frac{3}{4}$ of a batch of cookies, how much flour should she use? $1\frac{7}{8}$ c
5. **TRANSPORTATION** Hana's car used $\frac{3}{4}$ of a tank of gas to cross Arizona. The gas tank on her car holds $15\frac{1}{2}$ gallons. How many gallons of gas did it take to cross Arizona? $11\frac{5}{8}$ gal	6. **GEOMETRY** The area of a rectangle is found by multiplying its length times its width. What is the area of a rectangle with a length of $2\frac{1}{4}$ inches and a width of $1\frac{5}{9}$ inches? $3\frac{1}{2}$ in^2
7. **COOKING** A recipe for ice cream calls for $3\frac{1}{3}$ cups of heavy cream. If Steve wants to make $2\frac{1}{2}$ times the normal amount, how much heavy cream should he use? $8\frac{1}{3}$ c	8. **ADVERTISING** A jewelry advertisement shows a diamond at $6\frac{2}{7}$ times its actual size. If the actual diameter of the diamond is $5\frac{3}{10}$ millimeters, what is the diameter of the diamond in the photograph? $33\frac{11}{35}$ mm

2-4 Lesson Notes

Lesson Resources

Chapter 2 Resource Masters FAST FILE

- Study Guide and Intervention, p. 82
- Practice: Skills, p. 83
- Practice: Word Problems, p. 84
- Reading to Learn Mathematics, p. 85
- Enrichment, p. 86

Key Teaching Transparencies, 6

MathPASS Tutorial CD-ROM, 22, 23

Parent and Student Study Guide Online Worksheets, 2-4

Noteables™: Interactive Study Notebook with Foldables™, 2-4

Focus

5-Minute Check 2-4

Use as a quiz or review of Lesson 2-3. (Also available as a transparency)

Bellringer

Problem Solving Write the following problems on the chalkboard.

$216 \times \frac{1}{8}$ **27** $\quad$ $421 \times \frac{1}{5}$ **84.2**

$216 \div 8$ **27** $\quad$ $421 \div 5$ **84.2**

Have student volunteers solve them and discuss their results. Do students notice a pattern? Ask the class to make a conjecture about the quotient of $12 \div \frac{1}{4}$. **$12 \div \frac{1}{4} = 12 \cdot 4 = 48$**

Reading to Learn Mathematics, p. 85 **ELL**

NAME ______ DATE ______ PERIOD ______

2-4 Reading to Learn Mathematics

Dividing Rational Numbers

Pre-Activity *Read the introduction at the top of page 76 in your textbook. Write your answers below.*

1. Find the value of $110 \div 4$. 27.5
2. Find the value of $110 \cdot \frac{1}{4}$. $27\frac{1}{2}$
3. Compare the values of $110 \div 4$ and $110 \cdot \frac{1}{4}$. They are the same.
4. What can you conclude about the relationship between dividing by 4 and multiplying by $\frac{1}{4}$? They are the same.

Reading the Lesson

5. Describe the process for finding the multiplicative inverse of a mixed ... Sample an...

2-4 Dividing Rational Numbers

What You'll LEARN

Divide fractions.

NEW Vocabulary

multiplicative inverses
reciprocals

REVIEW Vocabulary

additive inverse: the sum of any number and its additive inverse is zero, $a + (-a) = 0$ (Lesson 1-5)

WHEN am I ever going to use this?

ANIMALS The world's longest snake is the reticulated python. It is approximately one-fourth the length of the blue whale.

World's Largest Animals		
Largest Animal	Blue Whale	110 feet long
Largest Reptile	Saltwater Crocodile	16 feet long
Largest Bird	Ostrich	9 feet tall
Largest Insect	Stick Insect	15 inches long

Source: *The World Almanac for Kids*

1. Find the value of $110 \div 4$. **27.5**
2. Find the value of $110 \cdot \frac{1}{4}$. **$27\frac{1}{2}$**
3. Compare the values of $110 \div 4$ and $110 \cdot \frac{1}{4}$. **They are the same.**
4. What can you conclude about the relationship between dividing by 4 and multiplying by $\frac{1}{4}$? **They are the same.**

In Chapter 1, you learned about additive inverses. A similar property applies to multiplication. Two numbers whose product is 1 are **multiplicative inverses**, or **reciprocals**, of each other. For example, 4 and $\frac{1}{4}$ are multiplicative inverses because $4 \cdot \frac{1}{4} = 1$.

Noteables™ Key Concept: Inverse Property of Multiplication

Words The product of a rational number and its multiplicative inverse is 1.

Symbols

Arithmetic	Algebra
$\frac{3}{4} \cdot \frac{4}{3} = 1$	$\frac{a}{b} \cdot \frac{b}{a} = 1$, where $a, b \neq 0$

EXAMPLE Find a Multiplicative Inverse

1 **Write the multiplicative inverse of $-5\frac{2}{3}$.**

$-5\frac{2}{3} = -\frac{17}{3}$ Write $-5\frac{2}{3}$ as an improper fraction.

Since $-\frac{17}{3}\left(-\frac{3}{17}\right) = 1$, the multiplicative inverse of $-5\frac{2}{3}$ is $-\frac{3}{17}$.

Your Turn **Write the multiplicative inverse of each number.**

a. $-2\frac{1}{3}$ **$-\frac{3}{7}$** $\quad$ b. $-\frac{5}{8}$ **$-\frac{8}{5}$** $\quad$ c. 7 **$\frac{1}{7}$**

Dividing by 4 is the same as multiplying by $\frac{1}{4}$, its multiplicative inverse. This is true for any rational number.

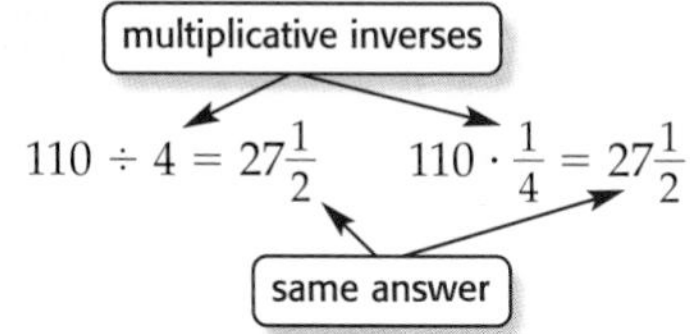

Noteables™ **Key Concept: Divide Fractions**

Words To divide by a fraction, multiply by its multiplicative inverse.

Symbols

Arithmetic	Algebra
$\frac{2}{5} \div \frac{3}{4} = \frac{2}{5} \cdot \frac{4}{3}$ or $\frac{8}{15}$	$\frac{a}{b} \div \frac{c}{d} = \frac{a}{b} \cdot \frac{d}{c}$, where $b, c, d \neq 0$

EXAMPLE Divide Fractions

2 **Find $\frac{7}{8} \div \frac{3}{4}$. Write in simplest form.**

$\frac{7}{8} \div \frac{3}{4} = \frac{7}{8} \cdot \frac{4}{3}$ Multiply by the multiplicative inverse of $\frac{3}{4}$, which is $\frac{4}{3}$.

$= \frac{7}{\cancel{8}_2} \cdot \frac{\cancel{4}^1}{3}$ Divide 8 and 4 by their GCF, 4.

$= \frac{7}{6}$ or $1\frac{1}{6}$ Simplify.

TEACHING TIP

In this book, improper fractions are written as mixed numbers. However in algebra, improper fractions are not changed to mixed numbers. Tell the students which form you prefer.

EXAMPLE Divide by a Whole Number

3 **Find $\frac{2}{5} \div 5$. Write in simplest form.**

$\frac{2}{5} \div 5 = \frac{2}{5} \div \frac{5}{1}$ Write 5 as $\frac{5}{1}$.

$= \frac{2}{5} \cdot \frac{1}{5}$ Multiply by the multiplicative inverse of 5, which is $\frac{1}{5}$.

$= \frac{2}{25}$ Simplify.

STUDY TIP

Dividing By a Whole Number When dividing by a whole number, always rename it as an improper fraction. Then multiply by its reciprocal.

EXAMPLE Divide Negative Fractions

4 **Find $-\frac{4}{5} \div \frac{6}{7}$. Write in simplest form.**

$-\frac{4}{5} \div \frac{6}{7} = -\frac{4}{5} \cdot \frac{7}{6}$ Multiply by the multiplicative inverse of $\frac{6}{7}$, which is $\frac{7}{6}$.

$= \frac{-\cancel{4}^2}{5} \cdot \frac{7}{\cancel{6}_3}$ Divide −4 and 6 by their GCF, 2.

$= -\frac{14}{15}$ The fractions have different signs, so the quotient is negative.

Your Turn Divide. Write in simplest form.

d. $\frac{3}{4} \div \frac{1}{2}$ $1\frac{1}{2}$ e. $\frac{3}{5} \div (6)$ $\frac{1}{10}$ f. $-\frac{2}{3} \div \left(-\frac{3}{5}\right)$ $1\frac{1}{9}$

Math Online msmath3.net/extra_examples

2 Teach

In-Class Examples

1 Write the multiplicative inverse of $-2\frac{4}{7}$. $-\frac{7}{18}$

2 Find $\frac{3}{10} \div \frac{2}{5}$. Write in simplest form. $\frac{3}{4}$

3 Find $\frac{6}{7} \div 12$. Write in simplest form. $\frac{1}{14}$

4 Find $\frac{2}{7} \div -\frac{8}{9}$. Write in simplest form. $-\frac{9}{28}$

Tips for New Teachers

Classroom Management Some students will not ask questions in class because they fear appearing unintelligent. Encourage students to write their questions in a journal. Review the journals frequently so you can answer the questions during class. Alternatively, you might consider setting up an e-mail account where students can submit questions from home or the library. Then answer questions individually or in class.

DAILY INTERVENTION **Differentiated Instruction**

Visual/Spatial On the chalkboard, show the problem and diagram at the right. Then, using different-colored chalk, shade three $\frac{1}{4}$ sections at a time to show that there are 3 complete sets of $\frac{3}{4}$. Have students use the same method to solve $3\frac{1}{2} \div \frac{1}{2}$. 7

$2\frac{1}{4} \div \frac{3}{4} = 3$

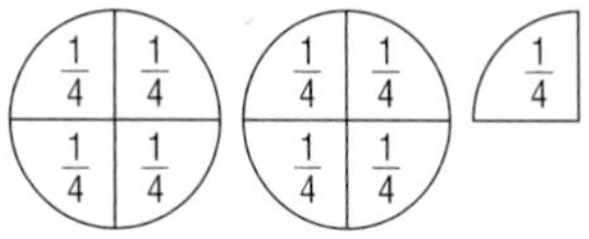

(Diagram: two circles divided into four sections each labeled $\frac{1}{4}$, and one quarter section labeled $\frac{1}{4}$.)

In-Class Examples

5 Find $3\frac{1}{4} \div \left(-2\frac{1}{8}\right)$. Write in simplest form. $-1\frac{9}{17}$

6 **MOVIES** One summer day, a cinema shows a hit action movie repeatedly for $12\frac{1}{2}$ hours. It takes about 150 minutes to run the movie and prepare for the next showing. How many times does the cinema show the movie that day? **5 times**

EXAMPLE Divide Mixed Numbers

5 **Find $4\frac{2}{3} \div \left(-3\frac{1}{2}\right)$. Write in simplest form.**

$4\frac{2}{3} \div \left(-3\frac{1}{2}\right) = \frac{14}{3} \div \left(-\frac{7}{2}\right)$ $\quad 4\frac{2}{3} = \frac{14}{3}, -3\frac{1}{2} = -\frac{7}{2}$

$= \frac{14}{3} \cdot \left(-\frac{2}{7}\right)$ $\quad$ The multiplicative inverse of $-\frac{7}{2}$ is $-\frac{2}{7}$.

$= \frac{\overset{2}{\cancel{14}}}{3} \cdot \left(-\frac{2}{\underset{1}{\cancel{7}}}\right)$ $\quad$ Divide 14 and 7 by their GCF, 7.

$= -\frac{4}{3}$ or $-1\frac{1}{3}$ $\quad$ Simplify.

Check Since $4\frac{2}{3}$ is about 5 and $-3\frac{1}{2}$ is about -4, you can estimate the answer to be about $5 \div (-4)$, which is $\frac{5}{-4}$ or $-1\frac{1}{4}$. The answer seems reasonable because $-1\frac{1}{3}$ is about $-1\frac{1}{4}$.

Your Turn Divide. Write in simplest form.

g. $2\frac{3}{4} \div \left(-2\frac{1}{5}\right)$ $-1\frac{1}{4}$ $\quad$ h. $1\frac{1}{2} \div 2\frac{1}{3}$ $\frac{9}{14}$ $\quad$ i. $-3\frac{1}{2} \div \left(-1\frac{1}{4}\right)$ $2\frac{4}{5}$

REAL-LIFE MATH

HOLIDAYS The first Flag Day was celebrated in 1877. It was the 100th anniversary of the day the Continental Congress adopted the Stars and Stripes as the official flag.

Source: *World Book*

You can use dimensional analysis to check for reasonable answers in division problems as well as multiplication problems.

EXAMPLE Use Dimensional Analysis

6 **HOLIDAYS Isabel and her friends are making ribbons to give to other campers at their day camp on Flag Day. They have a roll with 20 feet of ribbon. How many Flag Day ribbons as shown at the right can they make?**

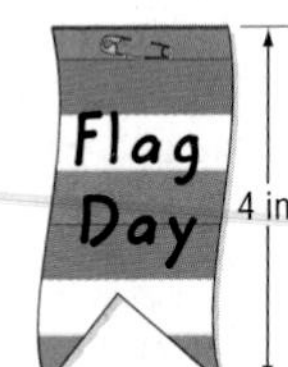

Since 4 inches equals $\frac{4}{12}$ or $\frac{1}{3}$ foot, divide 20 by $\frac{1}{3}$.

$20 \div \frac{1}{3} = \frac{20}{1} \div \frac{1}{3}$ $\quad$ Write 20 as $\frac{20}{1}$.

$= \frac{20}{1} \cdot \frac{3}{1}$ $\quad$ Multiply by the multiplicative inverse of $\frac{1}{3}$, which is 3.

$= \frac{60}{1}$ or 60 $\quad$ Simplify.

Isabel and her friends can make 60 Flag Day ribbons.

Check Use dimensional analysis to examine the units.

$\text{feet} \div \frac{\text{feet}}{\text{ribbon}} = \cancel{\text{feet}} \times \frac{\text{ribbon}}{\cancel{\text{feet}}}$ $\quad$ Divide out the units.

$= \text{ribbon}$ $\quad$ Simplify.

The result is expressed as ribbons. This agrees with your answer of 60 ribbons.

STUDY TIP

Mental Math
Isabel can make 3 ribbons for each foot. Since 3×20 is 60, Isabel can make 60 ribbons.

78 Chapter 2 Algebra: Rational Numbers

Students practice the same concepts in Exercises 12–37 if they are assigned odd or even problems.

Skill and Concept Check

1. **Writing Math** Explain how you know if two numbers are multiplicative inverses. **See margin.**
2. **Give a counterexample** to the statement *the quotient of two fractions between 0 and 1 is never a whole number.* **Sample answer: $\frac{3}{4} \div \frac{1}{4} = 3$**
3. **OPEN ENDED** Write a division problem that can be solved by multiplying a rational number by $\frac{6}{5}$. **Sample answer: $\frac{2}{3} \div \frac{5}{6}$**
4. **NUMBER SENSE** Which is greater: $30 \cdot \frac{3}{4}$ or $30 \div \frac{3}{4}$? Explain. **See margin.**

GUIDED PRACTICE

Write the multiplicative inverse of each number.

5. $\frac{5}{7}$ $\frac{7}{5}$
6. -12 $-\frac{1}{12}$
7. $-2\frac{3}{4}$ $-\frac{4}{11}$

Divide. Write in simplest form.

8. $\frac{2}{3} \div \frac{3}{4}$ $\frac{8}{9}$
9. $-5\frac{5}{6} \div 4\frac{2}{3}$ $-1\frac{1}{4}$
10. $-\frac{4}{5} \div (-8)$ $\frac{1}{10}$

11. **BIOLOGY** The 300-million-year-old fossil of a cockroach was recently found in eastern Ohio. The ancient cockroach is shown next to the common German cockroach found today. How many times longer is the ancient cockroach than the German cockroach? **7 times longer**

300-Million-Year-Old Cockroach

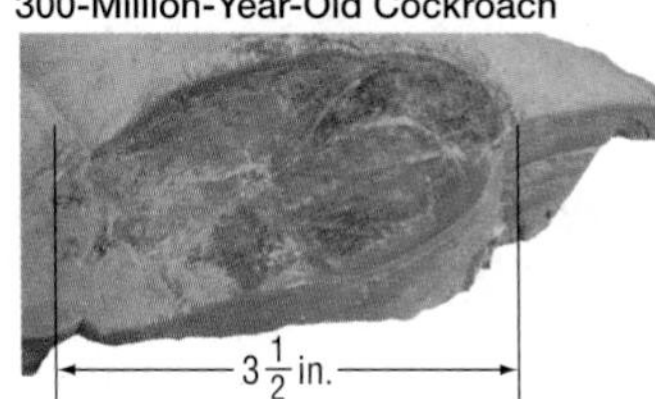

Common German Cockroach

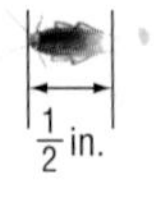

★ indicates increased difficulty

Practice and Applications

Write the multiplicative inverse of each number.

12. $-\frac{7}{9}$ $-\frac{9}{7}$
13. $-\frac{5}{8}$ $-\frac{8}{5}$
14. 15 $\frac{1}{15}$
15. 18 $\frac{1}{18}$
16. $\frac{6}{11}$ $\frac{11}{6}$
17. $\frac{7}{15}$ $\frac{15}{7}$
18. $3\frac{2}{5}$ $\frac{5}{17}$
19. $4\frac{1}{8}$ $\frac{8}{33}$

HOMEWORK HELP	
For Exercises	See Examples
12–19	1
20–35	2–5
36–39	6

Extra Practice
See pages 620, 649.

Divide. Write in simplest form.

20. $\frac{2}{5} \div \frac{3}{4}$ $\frac{8}{15}$
21. $\frac{3}{8} \div \frac{2}{3}$ $\frac{9}{16}$
22. $-\frac{3}{8} \div \frac{9}{10}$ $-\frac{5}{12}$
23. $-\frac{2}{3} \div \frac{5}{6}$ $-\frac{4}{5}$
24. $-5\frac{2}{5} \div \left(-2\frac{1}{10}\right)$ $2\frac{4}{7}$
25. $-3\frac{1}{4} \div \left(-8\frac{2}{3}\right)$ $\frac{3}{8}$
26. $3\frac{3}{4} \div 2\frac{1}{2}$ $1\frac{1}{2}$
27. $7\frac{1}{2} \div 2\frac{1}{10}$ $3\frac{4}{7}$
28. $\frac{4}{5} \div (-6)$ $-\frac{2}{15}$
29. $\frac{6}{7} \div (-4)$ $-\frac{3}{14}$
30. $-12\frac{1}{4} \div 4\frac{2}{3}$ $-2\frac{5}{8}$
31. $-10\frac{1}{5} \div 3\frac{3}{15}$ $-3\frac{3}{16}$
32. What is $\frac{7}{12}$ divided by $\frac{5}{6}$? $\frac{7}{10}$
33. Divide $\frac{5}{6}$ by $\frac{15}{16}$. $\frac{8}{9}$

★34. **ALGEBRA** Evaluate $x \div y$ if $x = -\frac{5}{12}$ and $y = \frac{5}{8}$. $-\frac{2}{3}$

★35. **ALGEBRA** Evaluate $a \div b$ if $a = \frac{3}{4}$ and $b = \frac{5}{6}$. $\frac{9}{10}$

msmath3.net/self_check_quiz

3 Practice/Apply

FOLDABLES Follow-Up Remind students to explain what they learn about dividing rational numbers on the fourth tab of their Foldables. Encourage them to use their own words and symbols so it will be more meaningful and memorable.

NUMBER SENSE
In Exercise 4, remind students that multiplication and division are inverse operations. Have them write $30 \div \frac{3}{4}$ as $30 \cdot \frac{4}{3}$ before comparing. Then it should be easier to see that multiplying by less than one $\left(\text{multiplying by } \frac{3}{4}\right)$ would result in a smaller product than multiplying by more than one $\left(\text{multiplying by } \frac{4}{3}\right)$.

About the Exercises...

Guided Practice Key

Exercises	Examples
5–7	1
8	2
9–10	3–5
11	6

Assignment Guide

Basic: 13–33 odd, 36, 41–54

Average: 13–39 odd, 41–54

Enriched: 12–40 even, 41–50 (Optional: 51–54)

Answers

1. If the product of the two numbers is 1, the two numbers are multiplicative inverses.
4. $30 \div \frac{3}{4}$; 30 times a number less than 1 will be less than 30. However, 30 divided by a number less than 1 will be greater than 30.

Study Guide and Intervention, p. 82

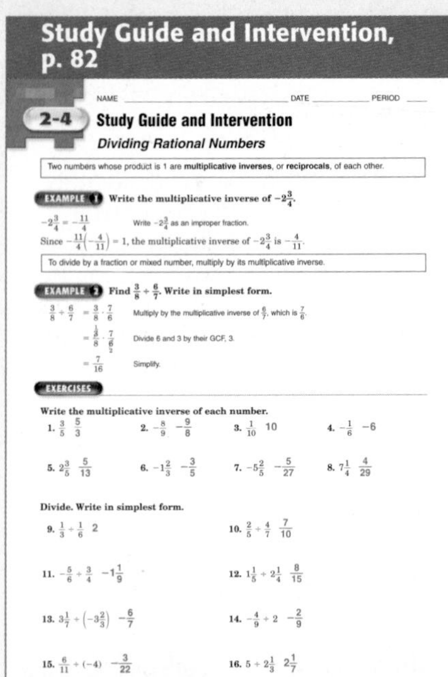

NAME ______________ DATE ________ PERIOD ____

2-4 Study Guide and Intervention

Dividing Rational Numbers

Two numbers whose product is 1 are **multiplicative inverses**, or **reciprocals**, of each other.

EXAMPLE 1 **Write the multiplicative inverse of $-2\frac{3}{4}$.**

$-2\frac{3}{4} = -\frac{11}{4}$ Write $-2\frac{3}{4}$ as an improper fraction.

Since $-\frac{11}{4}\left(-\frac{4}{11}\right) = 1$, the multiplicative inverse of $-2\frac{3}{4}$ is $-\frac{4}{11}$.

To divide by a fraction or mixed number, multiply by its multiplicative inverse.

EXAMPLE 2 **Find $\frac{3}{8} \div \frac{6}{7}$. Write in simplest form.**

$\frac{3}{8} \div \frac{6}{7} = \frac{3}{8} \cdot \frac{7}{6}$ Multiply by the multiplicative inverse of $\frac{6}{7}$, which is $\frac{7}{6}$.

$= \frac{\overset{1}{\cancel{3}}}{8} \cdot \frac{7}{\underset{2}{\cancel{6}}}$ Divide 6 and 3 by their GCF, 3.

$= \frac{7}{16}$ Simplify.

EXERCISES

Write the multiplicative inverse of each number.

1. $\frac{3}{5}$ $\frac{5}{3}$
2. $-\frac{8}{9}$ $-\frac{9}{8}$
3. $\frac{1}{10}$ 10
4. $-\frac{1}{6}$ -6
5. $2\frac{3}{5}$ $\frac{5}{13}$
6. $-1\frac{2}{3}$ $-\frac{3}{5}$
7. $-5\frac{2}{5}$ $-\frac{5}{27}$
8. $7\frac{1}{4}$ $\frac{4}{29}$

Divide. Write in simplest form.

9. $\frac{1}{3} \div \frac{1}{6}$ 2
10. $\frac{2}{5} \div \frac{4}{7}$ $\frac{7}{10}$
11. $-\frac{5}{6} \div \frac{3}{4}$ $-1\frac{1}{9}$
12. $1\frac{1}{5} \div 2\frac{1}{4}$ $\frac{8}{15}$
13. $3\frac{1}{7} \div \left(-3\frac{2}{3}\right)$ $-\frac{6}{7}$
14. $-\frac{4}{9} \div 2$ $-\frac{2}{9}$
15. $\frac{6}{11} \div (-4)$ $-\frac{3}{22}$
16. $5 \div 2\frac{1}{3}$ $2\frac{1}{7}$

Practice: Skills, p. 83

NAME ______________ DATE ________ PERIOD ____

2-4 Practice: Skills

Dividing Rational Numbers

Write the multiplicative inverse of each number.

1. $\frac{2}{3}$ $\frac{3}{2}$
2. $-\frac{4}{7}$ $-\frac{7}{4}$
3. $-\frac{1}{12}$ -12
4. 22 $\frac{1}{22}$
5. $\frac{9}{35}$ $\frac{35}{9}$
6. $-\frac{14}{17}$ $-\frac{17}{14}$
7. $1\frac{5}{7}$ $\frac{7}{12}$
8. $-1\frac{3}{13}$ $-\frac{13}{16}$
9. $2\frac{3}{7}$ $\frac{7}{17}$
10. $-3\frac{6}{11}$ $-\frac{11}{39}$
11. $4\frac{8}{15}$ $\frac{15}{68}$
12. $5\frac{3}{5}$ $\frac{5}{28}$

Divide. Write in simplest form.

13. $\frac{3}{7} \div \frac{3}{5}$ $\frac{5}{7}$
14. $\frac{2}{7} \div \frac{6}{7}$ $\frac{1}{3}$
15. $-\frac{5}{8} \div \frac{3}{4}$ $-\frac{5}{6}$
16. $\frac{7}{9} \div \left(-\frac{14}{15}\right)$ $-\frac{5}{6}$
17. $-\frac{4}{5} \div \frac{8}{9}$ $-\frac{9}{10}$
18. $\frac{2}{11} \div \frac{4}{9}$ $\frac{9}{22}$
19. $1\frac{3}{4} \div 2\frac{1}{2}$ $\frac{7}{10}$
20. $-2\frac{3}{5} \div 1\frac{3}{10}$ -2
21. $-3\frac{4}{7} \div \left(-1\frac{1}{14}\right)$ $3\frac{1}{3}$
22. $\frac{10}{11} \div 5$ $\frac{2}{11}$
23. $-4 \div \frac{3}{5}$ $-6\frac{2}{3}$
24. $3\frac{4}{15} \div 4\frac{2}{3}$ $\frac{7}{10}$
25. $9\frac{1}{3} \div 5\frac{3}{5}$ $1\frac{2}{3}$
26. $-12\frac{3}{4} \div \left(-2\frac{5}{6}\right)$ $4\frac{1}{2}$
27. $2\frac{4}{9} \div \left(-6\frac{2}{7}\right)$ $-\frac{7}{18}$
28. $-11\frac{1}{5} \div 3\frac{1}{9}$ $-3\frac{3}{5}$

Practice: Word Problems, p. 84

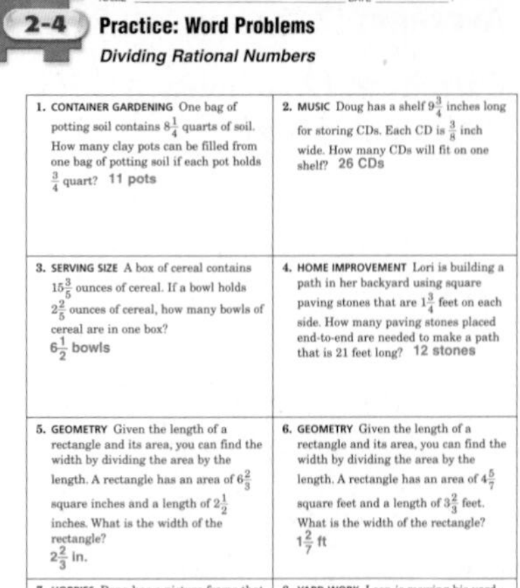

NAME ______________ DATE ________

2-4 Practice: Word Problems

Dividing Rational Numbers

1. **CONTAINER GARDENING** One bag of potting soil contains $8\frac{1}{4}$ quarts of soil. How many clay pots can be filled from one bag of potting soil if each pot holds $\frac{3}{4}$ quart? 11 pots

2. **MUSIC** Doug has a shelf $9\frac{3}{4}$ inches long for storing CDs. Each CD is $\frac{3}{8}$ inch wide. How many CDs will fit on one shelf? 26 CDs

3. **SERVING SIZE** A box of cereal contains $15\frac{3}{5}$ ounces of cereal. If a bowl holds $2\frac{2}{5}$ ounces of cereal, how many bowls of cereal are in one box? $6\frac{1}{2}$ bowls

4. **HOME IMPROVEMENT** Lori is building a path in her backyard using square paving stones that are $1\frac{3}{4}$ feet on each side. How many paving stones placed end-to-end are needed to make a path that is 21 feet long? 12 stones

5. **GEOMETRY** Given the length of a rectangle and its area, you can find the width by dividing the area by the length. A rectangle has an area of $6\frac{2}{3}$ square inches and a length of $2\frac{1}{2}$ inches. What is the width of the rectangle? $2\frac{2}{3}$ in.

6. **GEOMETRY** Given the length of a rectangle and its area, you can find the width by dividing the area by the length. A rectangle has an area of $4\frac{5}{7}$ square feet and a length of $3\frac{2}{3}$ feet. What is the width of the rectangle? $1\frac{2}{7}$ ft

7. **HOBBIES** Dena has a picture frame that is $13\frac{1}{2}$ inches wide. How many pictures that are $3\frac{3}{8}$ inches wide can be placed beside each other within the frame? 4 pictures

8. **YARD WORK** Leon is mowing his yard, which is $21\frac{2}{3}$ feet wide. His lawn mower makes a cut that is $1\frac{2}{3}$ feet wide on each pass. How many passes will Leon need to finish the lawn? 13 passes

36. **BIOLOGY** Use the information at the right. How many of the smallest grasshoppers need to be laid end-to-end to have the same length as the largest grasshoppers? **8 small grasshoppers**

★ 37. **ENERGY** Electricity costs $6\frac{1}{2}$¢ per kilowatt-hour. Of that cost, $3\frac{1}{4}$¢ goes toward the cost of the fuel. What fraction of the cost goes toward the fuel? $\frac{1}{2}$

GEOGRAPHY For Exercises 38 and 39, use the information at the right.

★ 38. About how many times larger is North America than South America? $1\frac{1}{3}$

★ 39. About how many times larger is Asia than North America? $1\frac{4}{5}$

Continent	Fraction of Earth's Landmass
North America	$\frac{1}{6}$
South America	$\frac{1}{8}$
Asia	$\frac{3}{10}$

Source: *The World Almanac*

40. **WRITE A PROBLEM** Write a real-life situation that can be solved by dividing fractions or mixed numbers. Solve the problem. **See margin.**

41. **CRITICAL THINKING** Use mental math to find each value.

a. $\frac{43}{594} \cdot \frac{641}{76} \div \frac{641}{594}$ $\frac{43}{76}$ b. $\frac{783}{241} \cdot \frac{241}{783} \div \frac{72}{53}$ $\frac{53}{72}$

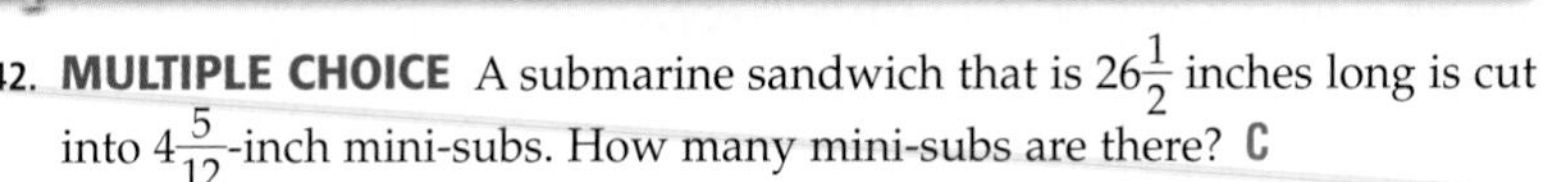

Spiral Review with Standardized Test Practice

42. **MULTIPLE CHOICE** A submarine sandwich that is $26\frac{1}{2}$ inches long is cut into $4\frac{5}{12}$-inch mini-subs. How many mini-subs are there? **C**

(A) 4 (B) 5 (C) 6 (D) 7

43. **SHORT RESPONSE** What is the multiplicative inverse of $-\frac{1}{a}$? $-a$

Multiply. Write in simplest form. (Lesson 2-3)

44. $\frac{1}{2} \cdot \frac{3}{4}$ $\frac{3}{8}$ 45. $\frac{7}{12} \cdot \frac{4}{7}$ $\frac{1}{3}$ 46. $1\frac{2}{3} \cdot 4\frac{1}{5}$ 7 47. $\frac{2}{3} \cdot 3\frac{1}{4}$ $2\frac{1}{6}$

48. **SCHOOL** In a survey of students at Centerburg Middle School, $\frac{13}{20}$ of the boys and $\frac{17}{25}$ of the girls said they rode the bus to school. Of those surveyed, do a greater fraction of boys or girls ride the bus? (Lesson 2-2) **girls**

49. **ALGEBRA** Write an algebraic expression to represent *eight million less than four times the population of Africa.* (Lesson 1-7) $4x - 8{,}000{,}000$

50. Write an integer to describe *10 candy bars short of his goal.* (Lesson 1-3) -10

GETTING READY FOR THE NEXT LESSON

PREREQUISITE SKILL Add or subtract. (Lessons 1-4 and 1-5)

51. $-7 + 15$ **8** 52. $-9 + (-4)$ -13 53. $-3 - 15$ -18 54. $12 - (-17)$ **29**

4 Assess

Higher-Level Thinking

Ask students to explain how the multiplicative inverse can be used to express the division of whole numbers as an improper fraction. For example, $4 \div 2$ can be written as $4 \cdot \frac{1}{2}$, or $\frac{4}{2}$.

Answer

40. Sample answer: John has $22\frac{1}{2}$ feet of rope. He wants to cut the rope into pieces that are $2\frac{1}{4}$ feet long. How many pieces will he have? 10 pieces

Study Skill

Use Two-Column Notes

Taking Good Notes

Have you ever written a step-by-step solution to a problem, but couldn't follow the steps later? Try using two-column notes. You may like this method of taking notes so well, you'll want to use it for your other classes.

To take two-column notes, first fold your paper lengthwise into two columns. Make the right-hand column about 3 inches wide.

When your teacher solves a problem in class, write all of the steps in the left-hand column. In the right-hand column, add notes in your own words that will help you remember how to solve the problem. Add a ★ by any step that you especially want to remember.

Here's a sample.

← 3 in. →

How to Divide Fractions	My Notes
$\frac{3}{4} \div 1\frac{1}{2} = \frac{3}{4} \div \frac{3}{2}$	Write $1\frac{1}{2}$ as a fraction.
$= \frac{3}{4} \cdot \frac{2}{3}$	★Use the inverse of the second fraction.
$= \frac{\cancel{3}^{1}}{\cancel{4}_{2}} \cdot \frac{\cancel{2}^{1}}{\cancel{3}_{1}}$	Then multiply. This is important.
$= \frac{1}{2}$	Cancel and multiply.

SKILL PRACTICE 1–4. See students' work.

Use the method above to write notes for each step-by-step solution.

1. $\frac{3}{4} \div 3 = \frac{3}{4} \div \frac{3}{1}$
   $= \frac{3}{4} \cdot \frac{1}{3}$
   $= \frac{\cancel{3}^{1}}{4} \cdot \frac{1}{\cancel{3}_{1}}$
   $= \frac{1}{4}$

2. $1\frac{1}{2} \cdot 1\frac{2}{3} = \frac{3}{2} \cdot \frac{5}{3}$
   $= \frac{\cancel{3}^{1}}{2} \cdot \frac{5}{\cancel{3}_{1}}$
   $= \frac{5}{2}$
   $= 2\frac{1}{2}$

3. $x + 8 = -6$
   $\underline{\quad -8 = -8}$
   $x \quad = -14$

4. $5 - 12 = 5 + (-12)$
   $= -7$

ASSESS

Open-Ended Assessment

Speaking Have students work with a partner. Students will take turns demonstrating on paper several problems from the chapter. As one student explains a problem, the other student takes two-column notes.

Study Skill

Objective Take two-column notes.

GETTING STARTED

Two-Column Notes Prepare a transparency in two-column format with a page's worth of content from Lesson 2-4. Write your information on the left, and then sample student comments on the right. You may wish to include information such as the Inverse Property of Multiplication in addition to sample problems.

TEACH

Give the following note-taking suggestions to students:

- Have several sheets of paper already divided into columns before class so you do not miss any part of the lesson.
- Pay close attention to any problem-solving steps you record to avoid making errors, which could hamper your studying later.
- Write neatly and allow yourself plenty of space on the page to make your notes easy to read later.
- You may want to record your notes in pencil first, and later in the day copy your notes in ink. This way you will not be slowed down during class worrying about appearance, and copying the notes will allow you to review what you have learned that day.

2-5 Lesson Notes

Lesson Resources

Chapter 2 Resource Masters

FAST FILE

- Study Guide and Intervention, p. 87
- Practice: Skills, p. 88
- Practice: Word Problems, p. 89
- Reading to Learn Mathematics, p. 90
- Enrichment, p. 91

Parent and Student Study Guide Online Worksheets, 2-5

Teaching Mathematics with Manipulatives, p. 38

Noteables™: Interactive Study Notebook with Foldables™, 2-5

1 Focus

5-Minute Check 2-5

Use as a quiz or review of Lesson 2-4. (Also available as a transparency)

Bellringer

Hands-On Activity Have students work in small groups to cut paper plates into various fractions and label each section. For example, one paper plate can be cut into a $\frac{5}{8}$ section and a $\frac{3}{8}$ section. Another can be cut into a $\frac{2}{3}$ section and a $\frac{1}{3}$ section. Students should demonstrate the addition and subtraction of fractions having the same denominator.

Reading to Learn Mathematics, p. 90 **ELL**

NAME ______ DATE ______ PERIOD ______

2-5 Reading to Learn Mathematics
Adding and Subtracting Like Fractions

Pre-Activity *Read the introduction at the top of page 82 in your textbook. Write your answers below.*

1. What is the sum of the whole-number parts of the amounts? 4 c
2. How many $\frac{1}{3}$ cups are there? 6
3. Since $\frac{1}{3}+\frac{1}{3}+\frac{1}{3}=1$, how many cups do all the $\frac{1}{3}$ cups make? 2 c
4. What is the total number of cups of the ingredients listed? 6 c

Reading the Lesson

5. Define *like fractions.* Like fractions are fractions with the same denominator.

2-5 Adding and Subtracting Like Fractions

What You'll LEARN

Add and subtract fractions with like denominators.

NEW Vocabulary

like fractions

WHEN am I ever going to use this?

BAKING A bread recipe calls for the ingredients at the right together with small amounts of sugar, oil, yeast, and salt.

Bread
$1\frac{1}{3}$ cups of whole wheat flour (sifted)
$2\frac{1}{3}$ cups of white flour (sifted)
$\frac{1}{3}$ cup oatmeal
$\frac{1}{3}$ cup apricots (diced)
$\frac{1}{3}$ cup hazelnuts (chopped)
$1\frac{1}{3}$ cups of warm water

1. What is the sum of the whole-number parts of the amounts? **4 c**
2. How many $\frac{1}{3}$ cups are there? **6**
3. Since $\frac{1}{3}+\frac{1}{3}+\frac{1}{3}=1$, how many cups do all the $\frac{1}{3}$ cups make? **2 c**
4. What is the total number of cups of the ingredients listed? **6 c**

The fractions above have like denominators. Fractions with like denominators are called **like fractions**.

Noteables™ **Key Concept: Add Like Fractions**

Words To add fractions with like denominators, add the numerators and write the sum over the denominator.

Symbols

Arithmetic	Algebra
$\frac{1}{3}+\frac{1}{3}=\frac{2}{3}$	$\frac{a}{c}+\frac{b}{c}=\frac{a+b}{c}$, where $c \neq 0$

You can use the rules for adding integers to determine the sign of the sum of fractions.

EXAMPLE Add Like Fractions

1 **Find $\frac{5}{8}+\left(-\frac{7}{8}\right)$. Write in simplest form.**

$\frac{5}{8}+\left(-\frac{7}{8}\right)=\frac{5+(-7)}{8}$ ← Add the numerators. ← The denominators are the same.

$=\frac{-2}{8}$ or $-\frac{1}{4}$ Simplify.

STUDY TIP

Look Back You can review **adding integers** in Lesson 1-4.

Your Turn **Add. Write in simplest form.**

a. $\frac{5}{9}+\frac{7}{9}$ $1\frac{1}{3}$

b. $-\frac{5}{6}+\frac{1}{6}$ $-\frac{2}{3}$

c. $-\frac{1}{6}+\left(-\frac{5}{6}\right)$ -1

82 Chapter 2 Algebra: Rational Numbers

Subtracting like fractions is similar to adding them.

Noteables™ **Key Concept: Subtract Like Fractions**

Words To subtract fractions with like denominators, subtract the numerators and write the difference over the denominator.

Symbols

Arithmetic: $\frac{5}{7} - \frac{3}{7} = \frac{5-3}{7}$ or $\frac{2}{7}$

Algebra: $\frac{a}{c} - \frac{b}{c} = \frac{a-b}{c}$, where $c \neq 0$

EXAMPLE Subtract Like Fractions

2 **Find $-\frac{8}{9} - \frac{7}{9}$. Write in simplest form.**

$-\frac{8}{9} - \frac{7}{9} = \frac{-8-7}{9}$ ←Subtract the numerators. ←The denominators are the same.

$= \frac{-15}{9}$ or $-1\frac{2}{3}$ Rename $\frac{-15}{9}$ as $-1\frac{6}{9}$ or $-1\frac{2}{3}$.

TEACHING TIP

Remind students to subtract a negative number by adding its opposite.

To add mixed numbers, add the whole numbers and the fractions separately. Then simplify.

EXAMPLE Add Mixed Numbers

3 **Find $5\frac{7}{9} + 8\frac{4}{9}$. Write in simplest form.**

$5\frac{7}{9} + 8\frac{4}{9} = (5 + 8) + \left(\frac{7}{9} + \frac{4}{9}\right)$ Add the whole numbers and fractions separately.

$= 13 + \frac{7+4}{9}$ Add the numerators.

$= 13\frac{11}{9}$ or $14\frac{2}{9}$ $\frac{11}{9} = 1\frac{2}{9}$

STUDY TIP

Alternative Method You can also add the mixed numbers vertically.

$$\begin{array}{r} 5\frac{7}{9} \\ +\ 8\frac{4}{9} \\ \hline 13\frac{11}{9} \text{ or } 14\frac{2}{9} \end{array}$$

One way to subtract mixed numbers is to write the mixed numbers as improper fractions.

EXAMPLE Subtract Mixed Numbers

4 **HEIGHTS Jasmine is $60\frac{1}{4}$ inches tall. Amber is $58\frac{3}{4}$ inches tall. How much taller is Jasmine than Amber?** **Estimate** 60 − 59 = 1

$60\frac{1}{4} - 58\frac{3}{4} = \frac{241}{4} - \frac{235}{4}$ Write the mixed numbers as improper fractions.

$= \frac{241 - 235}{4}$ ←Subtract the numerators. ←The denominators are the same.

$= \frac{6}{4}$ or $1\frac{1}{2}$ Rename $\frac{6}{4}$ as $1\frac{2}{4}$ or $1\frac{1}{2}$.

Jasmine is $1\frac{1}{2}$ inches taller than Amber.

msmath3.net/extra_examples

2 Teach

In-Class Examples

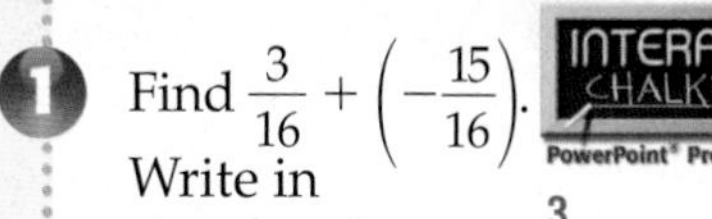

1 Find $\frac{3}{16} + \left(-\frac{15}{16}\right)$. Write in simplest form. $-\frac{3}{4}$

2 Find $-\frac{7}{10} - \frac{9}{10}$. Write in simplest form. $-1\frac{3}{5}$

3 Find $2\frac{5}{8} + 6\frac{1}{8}$. Write in simplest form. $8\frac{3}{4}$

4 **HEIGHTS** In the United States, the average height of a 9-year-old girl is $53\frac{4}{5}$ inches. The average height of a 16-year-old girl is $64\frac{1}{5}$ inches. How much does an average girl grow from age 9 to age 16? $10\frac{2}{5}$ in.

Teaching Strategies Help students remember not to add the denominators by relating them to units. For example, $\frac{1}{5} + \frac{3}{5}$ is 1 fifth + 3 fifths, or 4 fifths.

DAILY INTERVENTION **Differentiated Instruction**

Interpersonal Have students work in small groups to explore other ways to solve Example 4 in the Student Edition. Students may suggest changing $60\frac{1}{4}$ to $59\frac{5}{4}$. They then can subtract the integers and the fractions separately rather than changing the mixed numbers to improper fractions. Students may also suggest subtracting the mixed numbers vertically.

3 Practice/Apply

FOLDABLES™ Follow-Up Remind students to explain what they learn about adding and subtracting like fractions on the fifth tab of their Foldables. Encourage them to use their own words and symbols. Some students might choose to include models illustrating the addition and subtraction of two fractions with like denominators.

DAILY INTERVENTION FIND THE ERROR In Exercise 3, the incorrect method shown for adding like fractions is a common mistake. Working with a variety of math manipulatives will help students visualize this type of problem. You may wish to have them think about pouring water into a 2-cup measuring cup for liquids. For example, adding $\frac{1}{4}$ cup of water to $\frac{3}{4}$ cup of water makes $\frac{4}{4}$ or 1 cup, not $\frac{4}{8}$ or $\frac{1}{2}$ cup of water.

About the Exercises...

Guided Practice Key

Exercises	Examples
4, 5	1
7	2
6, 10	3
8, 9	4

Assignment Guide

Basic: 11–29 odd, 35, 37–48

Average: 11–35 odd, 37–48

Enriched: 12–36 even, 37–44 (Optional: 45–48)

Students practice the same concepts in Exercises 11–32 if they are assigned odd or even problems.

Skill and Concept Check

1. **Draw** a model to show the sum of $\frac{1}{5}$ and $\frac{3}{5}$. **See margin.**
2. **OPEN ENDED** Write a subtraction problem with a difference of $\frac{2}{9}$. **Sample answer: $\frac{7}{9} - \frac{5}{9} = \frac{2}{9}$**
3. **FIND THE ERROR** Allison and Wesley are adding $\frac{1}{7}$ and $\frac{3}{7}$. Who is correct? Explain.

Allison
$\frac{1}{7} + \frac{3}{7} = \frac{1+3}{7}$
$= \frac{4}{7}$

Wesley
$\frac{1}{7} + \frac{3}{7} = \frac{1+3}{7+7}$
$= \frac{4}{14}$ or $\frac{2}{7}$

Allison; to add like fractions, add the numerators and write the sum over the denominator.

GUIDED PRACTICE

Add or subtract. Write in simplest form.

4. $\frac{2}{5} + \frac{2}{5}$ $\frac{4}{5}$
5. $-\frac{3}{4} + \frac{1}{4}$ $-\frac{1}{2}$
6. $-5\frac{4}{9} + \left(-2\frac{2}{9}\right)$ $-7\frac{2}{3}$
7. $\frac{3}{8} - \frac{7}{8}$ $-\frac{1}{2}$
8. $8 - 6\frac{1}{6}$ $1\frac{5}{6}$
9. $-1\frac{3}{7} - \left(-2\frac{2}{7}\right)$ $\frac{6}{7}$

10. **SPORTS** One of the track and field events is the triple jump. In this event, the athlete takes a running start and makes three jumps without stopping. Find the total length of the 3 jumps for the athlete below. $57\frac{2}{3}$ **ft**

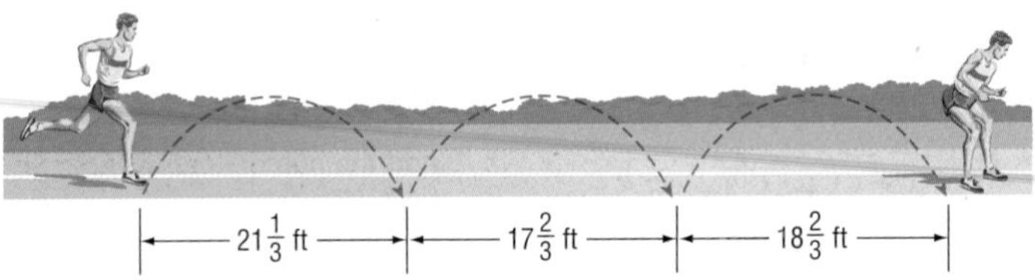

★ indicates increased difficulty

Practice and Applications

HOMEWORK HELP

For Exercises	See Examples
11–20, 32	1, 2
21–31, 34–36	3, 4

Extra Practice
See pages 620, 649.

Add or subtract. Write in simplest form.

11. $\frac{3}{7} + \frac{3}{7}$ $\frac{6}{7}$
12. $\frac{1}{9} + \frac{1}{9}$ $\frac{2}{9}$
13. $-\frac{5}{12} + \frac{7}{12}$ $\frac{1}{6}$
14. $-\frac{8}{9} + \frac{5}{9}$ $-\frac{1}{3}$
15. $-\frac{7}{8} + \left(-\frac{7}{8}\right)$
16. $-\frac{5}{9} + \left(-\frac{7}{9}\right)$
17. $\frac{1}{12} - \frac{7}{12}$ $-\frac{1}{2}$
18. $\frac{2}{9} - \frac{8}{9}$ $-\frac{2}{3}$
19. $-\frac{4}{5} - \frac{3}{5}$ $-1\frac{2}{5}$
20. $-\frac{2}{3} - \frac{2}{3}$ $-1\frac{1}{3}$
21. $3\frac{5}{8} + 7\frac{5}{8}$ $11\frac{1}{4}$
22. $9\frac{5}{9} + 4\frac{7}{9}$ $14\frac{1}{3}$
23. $8\frac{1}{10} - 2\frac{9}{10}$
24. $8\frac{5}{12} - 5\frac{11}{12}$
25. $-1\frac{5}{6} - 3\frac{5}{6}$
26. $-3\frac{3}{4} - 7\frac{3}{4}$ $-11\frac{1}{2}$
27. $7 - 5\frac{2}{5}$ $1\frac{3}{5}$
28. $9 - 6\frac{3}{7}$ $2\frac{4}{7}$
29. $-8 - \left(-3\frac{5}{8}\right)$
30. $-7 - \left(-2\frac{3}{5}\right)$ $-4\frac{2}{5}$

15. $-1\frac{3}{4}$ 16. $-1\frac{1}{3}$ 23. $5\frac{1}{5}$ 24. $2\frac{1}{2}$ 25. $-5\frac{2}{3}$ 29. $-4\frac{3}{8}$

★ 31. **ALGEBRA** Find $a - b$ if $a = 5\frac{1}{3}$ and $b = -2\frac{1}{3}$. $7\frac{2}{3}$

Answer

1.

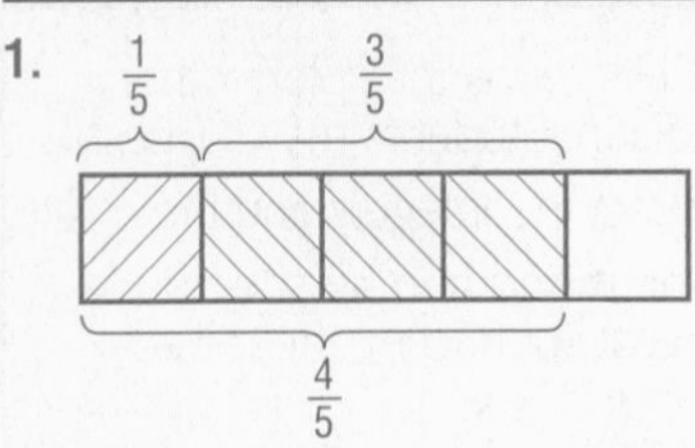

84 Chapter 2 Algebra: Rational Numbers

★ 32. **ALGEBRA** Find $x + y$ if $x = -\frac{5}{12}$ and $y = -\frac{1}{12}$. $-\frac{1}{2}$

★ 33. **MENTAL MATH** Explain how to use the Distributive Property to find $\frac{1}{2} \cdot \frac{3}{4} + \frac{1}{2} \cdot \frac{1}{4}$. **Since $\frac{1}{2} \cdot \frac{3}{4} + \frac{1}{2} \cdot \frac{1}{4} = \frac{1}{2}\left(\frac{3}{4} + \frac{1}{4}\right)$ or $\frac{1}{2}(1)$, the answer is $\frac{1}{2}$.**

34. **GEOMETRY** Find the perimeter of the rectangle at the right. **76 in.**

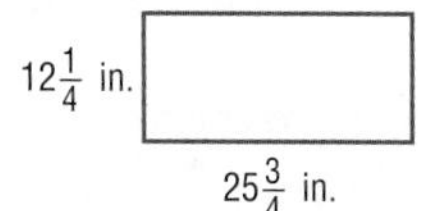

35. **CLOTHING** Hat sizes are determined by the distance across a person's head. How much wider is a person's head who wears a hat size of $7\frac{3}{4}$ inches than someone who wears a hat size of $6\frac{1}{4}$ inches? **$1\frac{1}{2}$ in.**

36. **MULTI STEP** Quoits was one of five original games in the ancient Greek Pentathlon. Find the distance across the hole of the quoit shown at the right. **$2\frac{3}{4}$ in.**

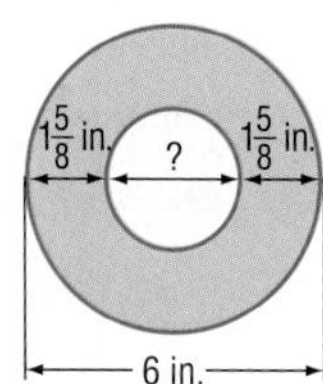

37. **CRITICAL THINKING** Explain how to use mental math to find the following sum. Then find the sum.

$$3\frac{2}{3} + 4\frac{2}{5} + 2\frac{1}{6} + 2\frac{5}{6} + 1\frac{1}{3} + \frac{3}{5}$$ **See margin.**

Spiral Review with Standardized Test Practice

38. **MULTIPLE CHOICE** Find $\frac{7}{8} - \left(-\frac{3}{8}\right)$. **D**

Ⓐ $-1\frac{1}{4}$ Ⓑ $-\frac{1}{2}$ Ⓒ $\frac{1}{2}$ Ⓓ $1\frac{1}{4}$

39. **MULTIPLE CHOICE** The equal-sized square tiles on a bathroom floor are set as shown. What is the width of the space between the tiles? **F**

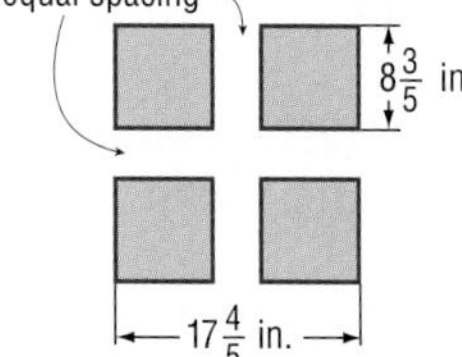

Ⓕ $\frac{3}{5}$ in. Ⓖ $\frac{1}{5}$ in.

Ⓗ $\frac{3}{10}$ in. Ⓘ $\frac{2}{5}$ in.

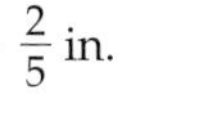

Divide. Write in simplest form. (Lesson 2-4)

40. $\frac{3}{5} \div \frac{6}{7}$ **$\frac{7}{10}$**

41. $\frac{7}{8} \div 2\frac{4}{5}$ **$\frac{5}{16}$**

42. $-3\frac{1}{4} \div 2\frac{1}{2}$ **$-1\frac{3}{10}$**

43. Find the product of $-\frac{7}{8}$ and $-\frac{6}{7}$. (Lesson 2-3) **$\frac{3}{4}$**

44. **FOOD** On a typical day, 2 million gallons of ice cream are produced in the United States. About how many gallons are produced each year? (Lesson 1-1) **about 360 × 2 or 720 million gallons**

GETTING READY FOR THE NEXT LESSON

PREREQUISITE SKILL Find the least common multiple (LCM) of each set of numbers. (Page 612)

45. 14, 21 **42**

46. 18, 9, 6 **18**

47. 6, 4, 9 **36**

48. 5, 10, 20 **20**

4 Assess

Open-Ended Assessment

Modeling Have students use a number line spanning −1 to 1 and marked off into eighths to model the addition and subtraction of fractions with denominators of 8.

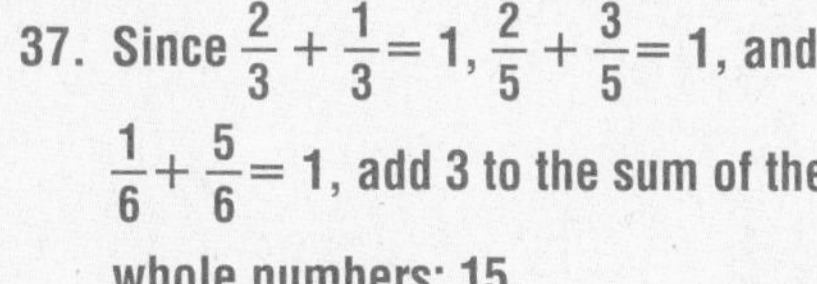

Answer

37. **Since $\frac{2}{3} + \frac{1}{3} = 1$, $\frac{2}{5} + \frac{3}{5} = 1$, and $\frac{1}{6} + \frac{5}{6} = 1$, add 3 to the sum of the whole numbers; 15.**

Study Guide and Intervention, p. 87

NAME ____________ DATE ________ PERIOD ____

2-5 Study Guide and Intervention

Adding and Subtracting Like Fractions

Fractions that have the same denominator are called **like fractions**. To add like fractions, add the numerators of the fractions and write the sum over the denominator.

EXAMPLE 1 **Find $\frac{1}{5} + \left(-\frac{4}{5}\right)$. Write in simplest form.**

$\frac{1}{5} + \left(-\frac{4}{5}\right) = \frac{1 + (-4)}{5}$ Add the numerators. The denominators are the same.

$= \frac{-3}{5}$ or $-\frac{3}{5}$ Simplify.

To subtract like fractions, subtract the numerators of the fractions and write the sum over the denominator.

EXAMPLE 2 **Find $-\frac{4}{9} - \frac{7}{9}$. Write in simplest form.**

$-\frac{4}{9} - \frac{7}{9} = \frac{-4 - 7}{9}$ Subtract the numerators. The denominators are the same.

$= \frac{-11}{9}$ or $-1\frac{2}{9}$ Rename $\frac{-11}{9}$ as $-1\frac{2}{9}$.

To add or subtract mixed numbers, first write the mixed numbers as improper fractions. Then add or subtract the improper fractions and simplify the result.

EXAMPLE 3 **Find $2\frac{3}{7} + 6\frac{5}{7}$. Write in simplest form.**

$2\frac{3}{7} + 6\frac{5}{7} = \frac{17}{7} + \frac{47}{7}$ Write the mixed numbers as improper fractions.

$= \frac{17 + 47}{7}$ Add the numerators. The denominators are the same.

$= \frac{64}{7}$ or $9\frac{1}{7}$ Rewrite $\frac{64}{7}$ as $9\frac{1}{7}$.

EXERCISES

Add or subtract. Write in simplest form.

1. $\frac{4}{7} + \frac{2}{7}$ **$\frac{6}{7}$**
2. $\frac{1}{10} + \frac{5}{10}$ **$\frac{3}{5}$**
3. $\frac{5}{9} + -\frac{1}{9}$ **$\frac{4}{9}$**
4. $\frac{1}{6} + -\frac{5}{6}$ **$-\frac{2}{3}$**
5. $-\frac{3}{8} + \frac{7}{8}$ **$\frac{1}{2}$**
6. $\frac{5}{11} - \left(-\frac{4}{11}\right)$ **$\frac{9}{11}$**
7. $-\frac{4}{5} - \frac{3}{5}$ **$-1\frac{2}{5}$**
8. $-\frac{9}{13} + \left(-\frac{6}{13}\right)$ **$-1\frac{2}{13}$**
9. $2\frac{1}{4} + 1\frac{1}{4}$ **$3\frac{1}{2}$**
10. $3\frac{5}{7} + 2\frac{3}{7}$ **$6\frac{1}{7}$**
11. $3\frac{5}{8} - 1\frac{3}{8}$ **$2\frac{1}{4}$**
12. $4\frac{3}{5} - 2\frac{4}{5}$ **$1\frac{4}{5}$**

Practice: Skills, p. 88

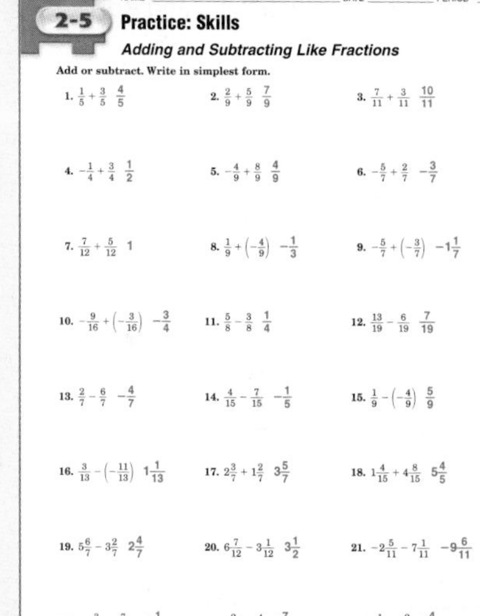

NAME ____________ DATE ________ PERIOD ____

2-5 Practice: Skills

Adding and Subtracting Like Fractions

Add or subtract. Write in simplest form.

1. $\frac{1}{5} + \frac{3}{5}$ **$\frac{4}{5}$**
2. $\frac{2}{9} + \frac{5}{9}$ **$\frac{7}{9}$**
3. $\frac{7}{11} + \frac{3}{11}$ **$\frac{10}{11}$**
4. $-\frac{1}{4} + \frac{3}{4}$ **$\frac{1}{2}$**
5. $-\frac{4}{9} + \frac{8}{9}$ **$\frac{4}{9}$**
6. $-\frac{5}{7} + \frac{2}{7}$ **$-\frac{3}{7}$**
7. $\frac{7}{12} + \frac{5}{12}$ **1**
8. $\frac{1}{9} + \left(-\frac{4}{9}\right)$ **$-\frac{1}{3}$**
9. $-\frac{5}{7} + \left(-\frac{3}{7}\right)$ **$-1\frac{1}{7}$**
10. $-\frac{9}{16} + \left(-\frac{3}{16}\right)$ **$-\frac{3}{4}$**
11. $\frac{5}{8} - \frac{3}{8}$ **$\frac{1}{4}$**
12. $\frac{13}{19} - \frac{6}{19}$ **$\frac{7}{19}$**
13. $\frac{2}{7} - \frac{6}{7}$ **$-\frac{4}{7}$**
14. $\frac{4}{15} - \frac{7}{15}$ **$-\frac{1}{5}$**
15. $\frac{1}{9} - \left(-\frac{4}{9}\right)$ **$\frac{5}{9}$**
16. $\frac{3}{13} - \left(-\frac{11}{13}\right)$ **$1\frac{1}{13}$**
17. $2\frac{3}{7} + 1\frac{2}{7}$ **$3\frac{5}{7}$**
18. $1\frac{4}{15} + 4\frac{8}{15}$ **$5\frac{4}{5}$**
19. $5\frac{6}{7} - 3\frac{2}{7}$ **$2\frac{4}{7}$**
20. $6\frac{7}{12} - 3\frac{1}{12}$ **$3\frac{1}{2}$**
21. $-2\frac{5}{11} - 7\frac{1}{11}$ **$-9\frac{6}{11}$**
22. $-4\frac{3}{8} - 2\frac{7}{8}$ **$-7\frac{1}{4}$**
23. $5\frac{2}{9} - 2\frac{4}{9}$ **$2\frac{7}{9}$**
24. $8\frac{1}{5} - 4\frac{2}{5}$ **$3\frac{4}{5}$**

Practice: Word Problems, p. 89

NAME ____________ DATE ________ PERIOD ____

2-5 Practice: Word Problems

Adding and Subtracting Like Fractions

1. **GEOMETRY** Find the perimeter of a rectangle with a length of $4\frac{2}{3}$ inches and a width of $3\frac{1}{3}$ inches. **16 in.**

2. **PETS** Pat wants to find out how much her dog Hunter weighs. Pat steps on the scale and reads her weight as $126\frac{3}{8}$ pounds. The combined weight of Pat and Hunter is $137\frac{7}{8}$ pounds. How much does Hunter weigh? **$11\frac{1}{2}$ lb**

3. **MEASUREMENTS** Tate fills a $13\frac{1}{3}$ ounce glass from a $21\frac{2}{3}$ ounce bottle of juice. How much juice is left in the bottle? **$8\frac{1}{3}$ oz**

4. **DECORATING** Jeri has two posters. One is $4\frac{7}{10}$ feet wide and the other is $5\frac{1}{10}$ feet wide. Will the two posters fit beside each other on a wall that is 10 feet wide? Explain. **Yes; $4\frac{7}{10} + 5\frac{1}{10} < 10$**

5. **AGE** Nida is $11\frac{1}{12}$ years old, while her sister Yoki is $8\frac{5}{12}$ years old. What is the sum of the ages of the sisters? **$19\frac{1}{2}$ years**

6. **GEOMETRY** A triangle has sides of $1\frac{1}{8}$ inches, $1\frac{3}{8}$ inches, and $1\frac{5}{8}$ inches. What is the perimeter of the triangle? **$4\frac{1}{8}$ in.**

7. **HUMAN BODY** Tom's right foot measures $10\frac{2}{5}$ inches, while Randy's right foot measures $9\frac{4}{5}$ inches. How much longer is Tom's foot than Randy's? **$\frac{3}{5}$ in.**

8. **COMPUTERS** Trey has two data files on his computer that he is going to combine. One file is $1\frac{4}{9}$ megabytes, while the other file is $3\frac{8}{9}$ megabytes. What will be the size of the resulting file? **$5\frac{1}{3}$ megabytes**

Assessment Option

Mid-Chapter Test (Lessons 2-1 through 2-5) is available on p. 129 of the *Chapter 2 Resource Masters.*

ExamView® Pro

Use the networkable ExamView® Pro Testmaker CD-ROM to:

- Create **multiple versions** of tests.
- Create **modified** tests for **inclusion** students with one mouse click.
- **Edit** existing questions and **add** your own questions.
- Build tests aligned with state standards using built-in **state curriculum correlations.**
- Change **English** tests to **Spanish** with one mouse click and vice versa.

FOLDABLES™ Follow-Up Before students complete the Mid-Chapter Practice Test, encourage them to review the notes, definitions, concepts, and main ideas they recorded on the first five tabs of their Foldables.

Answer

20. $12 \div \frac{1}{6}$; 72 candies

CHAPTER 2 Mid-Chapter Practice Test

Vocabulary and Concepts

1. **Name** three numbers that are between $\frac{1}{2}$ and $\frac{3}{4}$. (Lesson 2-2) **Sample answer: $\frac{9}{16}, \frac{5}{8}, \frac{11}{16}$**
2. **Define** reciprocals and give the reciprocal of $\frac{2}{3}$. (Lesson 2-4) **Reciprocals are two numbers whose product is 1; $\frac{3}{2}$.**
3. **OPEN ENDED** Write an addition problem with a sum of $2\frac{2}{3}$. (Lesson 2-5) **Sample answer: $1\frac{1}{3} + 1\frac{1}{3}$**

Skills and Applications

4. Write $-\frac{2}{9}$ as a decimal. (Lesson 2-1) **$-0.\overline{2}$**
5. Write -2.65 as a mixed number in simplest form. (Lesson 2-1) **$-2\frac{13}{20}$**
6. Write $0.\overline{5}$ as a fraction in simplest form. (Lesson 2-1) **$\frac{5}{9}$**

Replace each ● with <, >, or = to make a true sentence. (Lesson 2-2)

7. $\frac{1}{3}$ ● $\frac{1}{4}$ **>**
8. $-\frac{2}{5}$ ● $-\frac{3}{10}$ **<**
9. $0.\overline{12}$ ● $\frac{4}{33}$ **=**
10. $-\frac{5}{6}$ ● $-\frac{4}{5}$ **<**

Multiply, divide, add, or subtract. Write in simplest form. (Lessons 2-3, 2-4, and 2-5)

11. $-\frac{1}{3} \cdot \frac{2}{3}$ **$-\frac{2}{9}$**
12. $\frac{1}{2} \div \frac{3}{4}$ **$\frac{2}{3}$**
13. $-1\frac{1}{3} \div \left(-\frac{1}{4}\right)$ **$\frac{16}{3}$ or $5\frac{1}{3}$**
14. $2\frac{3}{4} \cdot \frac{1}{5}$ **$\frac{11}{20}$**
15. $\frac{3}{10} + \left(-\frac{7}{10}\right)$ **$-\frac{2}{5}$**
16. $-\frac{7}{9} - \frac{8}{9}$ **$-1\frac{2}{3}$**

17. **GEOMETRY** Find the area of the rectangle at the right. Use the formula $A = \ell w$. (Lesson 2-3) **$\frac{1}{6}$ units^2**

18. **CARPENTRY** A board that is $25\frac{1}{2}$ feet long is cut into equal pieces that are each $1\frac{1}{2}$ feet long. Into how many pieces is the board cut? (Lesson 2-4) **17 pieces**

Standardized Test Practice

19. **MULTIPLE CHOICE** One centimeter is about 0.392 inch. What fraction of an inch is this? (Lesson 2-1) **B**

Ⓐ $\frac{49}{500}$ in. Ⓑ $\frac{49}{125}$ in.

Ⓒ $\frac{98}{125}$ in. Ⓓ $\frac{392}{100}$ in.

20. **SHORT RESPONSE** A bag of candy weighs 12 ounces. Each individual piece of candy weighs $\frac{1}{6}$ ounce. Write a division problem that you could use to determine the number of candies in the bag. How many candies are in the bag? (Lesson 2-4) **See margin.**

A Place To Practice Your Math Skills

Plug It In

GET READY!

Players: two
Materials: 1 piece of paper, 9 index cards, scissors, marker

GET SET!

- Write the following fractions on a piece of paper.
  $-\frac{8}{9}, -\frac{7}{9}, -\frac{5}{9}, -\frac{4}{9}, -\frac{2}{9}, -\frac{1}{9}, \frac{1}{9}, \frac{2}{9}, \frac{4}{9}, \frac{5}{9}, \frac{7}{9}, \frac{8}{9}$
- Cut the index cards in half, making 18 cards.
- Write one of the following expressions on each of the cards.

$a + b$	$a - b$	$b - a$	ab	$\frac{1}{2}a$
$a \div b$	$b \div a$	$a + 1$	$b + 1$	$\frac{1}{2}b$
$1 - a$	$1 - b$	$a - 1$	$b - 1$	
a	b	$1 \div a$	$1 \div b$	

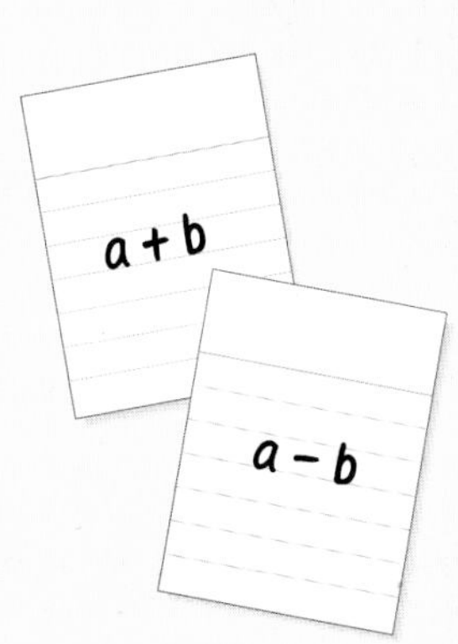

GO!

- The cards are shuffled and dealt facedown to each player.
- One player chooses the value for *a* from the list of fractions on the paper. The other player chooses the value for *b* from the same list.
- Each player turns over the top card from his or her pile and evaluates the expression. The person whose expression has the greatest value wins a point. If the values are equal, no points are awarded.
- The players choose new values for *a* and *b*. Each player turns over a new card. The play continues until all the cards are used.
- **Who Wins?** The person with the most points wins the game.

The Game Zone

Glencoe Mathematics Classroom Manipulative Kit
- scissors

GETTING READY

Objective Add, subtract, multiply, and divide fractions.

MANAGEMENT TIPS

Recommended Time
30 minutes

Tips
- For a variation of this game, begin by writing the fractions on index cards, too. Both players draw one expression card and one fraction card; the first fraction card chosen is the value for *a*, and the second is the value for *b*. Reuse the fraction cards as necessary, ending the game when all the expression cards have been used once.
- This game can be used after Lesson 2-4 by including only cards with expressions for multiplication and division.
- You may wish to use the game as an assessment tool for the concepts the students have been learning in Lessons 2-1 through 2-5.

Math Online For an additional game for this chapter, visit: msmath3.net/gamezone

2-6 Lesson Notes

Lesson Resources

Chapter 2 Resource Masters

- Study Guide and Intervention, p. 92
- Practice: Skills, p. 93
- Practice: Word Problems, p. 94
- Reading to Learn Mathematics, p. 95
- Enrichment, p. 96

FAST FILE

Classroom Math Games, pp. 5–6
Key Teaching Transparencies, 7
MathPASS Tutorial CD-ROM, 16–19, 24
Parent and Student Study Guide Online Worksheets, 2-6
Noteables™: Interactive Study Notebook with Foldables™, 2-6
Virtual Activities CD-ROM, Adding and Subtracting Fractions with Unlike Denominators

1 Focus

5-Minute Check 2-6
Use as a quiz or review of Lesson 2-5. (Also available as a transparency)

Bellringer
Hands-On Activity Have students use a ruler to model addition and subtraction of fractions with denominators of 2, 4, or 8. For example, to add $1\frac{1}{2} + \frac{5}{8}$, students should draw a (Continued in bottom margin.)

segment $1\frac{1}{2}$ inches long, extend it $\frac{5}{8}$ inch farther, and arrive at a final length of $2\frac{1}{8}$ inches.

Reading to Learn Mathematics, p. 95 **ELL**

NAME ________ DATE ________ PERIOD ____

2-6 Reading to Learn Mathematics
Adding and Subtracting Unlike Fractions

Pre-Activity *Read the introduction at the top of page 88 in your textbook. Write your answers below.*

1. What are the denominators of the fractions? *4, 8*
2. What is the least common multiple of the denominators? *8*
3. Find the missing value in $\frac{1}{4} = \frac{?}{8}$. *2*
4. What fraction of the pizza did the two girls eat? $\frac{5}{8}$

Reading the Lesson

5. What do *LCM* and *LCD* stand for? Give a definition for each. *LCM stands for least common multiple; the LCM of two or more numbers is the smallest number that is a multiple of each number; LCD stands for least common denominator; the LCD of two or more fractions is the LCM of the denominators of the fractions.*

2-6 Adding and Subtracting Unlike Fractions

What You'll LEARN
Add and subtract fractions with unlike denominators.

NEW Vocabulary
unlike fractions

REVIEW Vocabulary
least common denominator (LCD): the least common multiple (LCM) of the denominators (Page 612)

WHEN am I ever going to use this?

FOOD Marta and Brooke are sharing a pizza. Marta eats $\frac{1}{4}$ of the pizza and Brooke eats $\frac{3}{8}$ of the pizza.

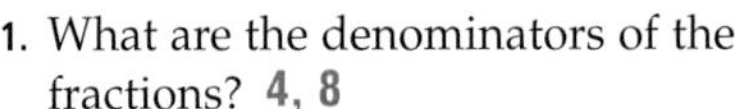
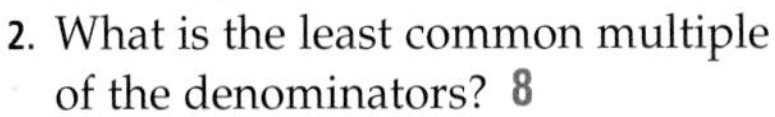
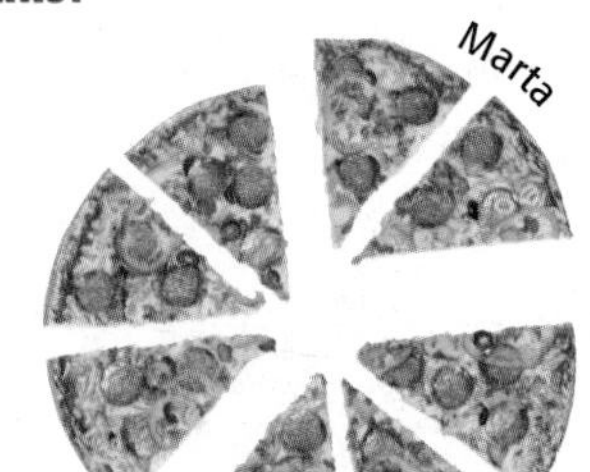
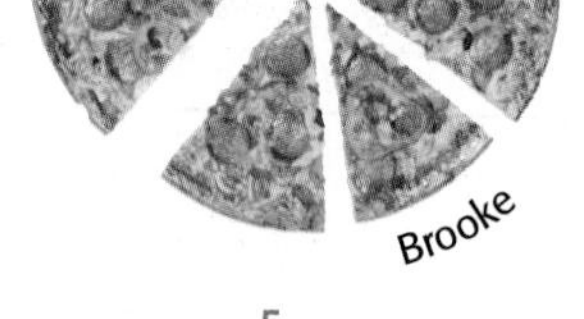

1. What are the denominators of the fractions? **4, 8**
2. What is the least common multiple of the denominators? **8**
3. Find the missing value in $\frac{1}{4} = \frac{?}{8}$. **2**
4. What fraction of the pizza did the two girls eat? $\frac{5}{8}$

The fractions $\frac{1}{4}$ and $\frac{3}{8}$ have different or unlike denominators. Fractions with unlike denominators are called **unlike fractions**. To add or subtract unlike fractions, you must use a common denominator.

Noteables™ Key Concept: Add and Subtract Unlike Fractions

Words To find the sum or difference of two fractions with unlike denominators, rename the fractions with a common denominator. Then add or subtract and simplify, if necessary.

Examples
$\frac{1}{4} + \frac{1}{6} = \frac{1}{4} \cdot \frac{3}{3} + \frac{1}{6} \cdot \frac{2}{2} = \frac{3}{12} + \frac{2}{12}$ or $\frac{5}{12}$

$\frac{2}{3} - \frac{4}{9} = \frac{2}{3} \cdot \frac{3}{3} - \frac{4}{9} = \frac{6}{9} - \frac{4}{9}$ or $\frac{2}{9}$

EXAMPLE Subtract Unlike Fractions

1 **Find $-\frac{2}{3} - \left(-\frac{3}{8}\right)$. Write in simplest form.**

$-\frac{2}{3} - \left(-\frac{3}{8}\right) = -\frac{2}{3} \cdot \frac{8}{8} - \left(-\frac{3}{8}\right) \cdot \frac{3}{3}$	The LCD is 3 · 2 · 2 · 2 or 24.
$= -\frac{16}{24} - \left(-\frac{9}{24}\right)$	Rename each fraction using the LCD.
$= -\frac{16}{24} + \frac{9}{24}$	Subtract $-\frac{9}{24}$ by adding its inverse, $\frac{9}{24}$.
$= \frac{-16 + 9}{24}$	Add the numerators.
$= -\frac{7}{24}$	Simplify.

STUDY TIP

Estimation Think: $-6\frac{2}{9}$ is about -6 and $4\frac{5}{6}$ is about 5. Since $-6 + 5$ is about -1, the answer is about -1. The answer seems reasonable.

EXAMPLE Add Mixed Numbers

2 **Find $-6\frac{2}{9} + 4\frac{5}{6}$. Write in simplest form.**

$$-6\frac{2}{9} + 4\frac{5}{6} = -\frac{56}{9} + \frac{29}{6} \quad \text{Write the mixed numbers as fractions.}$$

$$= -\frac{56}{9} \cdot \frac{2}{2} + \frac{29}{6} \cdot \frac{3}{3} \quad \text{The LCD is } 3 \cdot 3 \cdot 2 \text{ or } 18.$$

$$= -\frac{112}{18} + \frac{87}{18} \quad \text{Rename each fraction using the LCD.}$$

$$= \frac{-112 + 87}{18} \quad \text{Add the numerators.}$$

$$= \frac{-25}{18} \text{ or } -1\frac{7}{18} \quad \text{Simplify.}$$

Your Turn **Add or subtract. Write in simplest form.**

a. $-\frac{1}{3} - \left(-\frac{3}{4}\right)$ $\frac{5}{12}$
b. $-\frac{5}{6} + \left(-\frac{1}{2}\right)$ $-1\frac{1}{3}$
c. $-\frac{1}{2} + \frac{7}{8}$ $\frac{3}{8}$
d. $-3\frac{1}{2} + 8\frac{1}{3}$ $4\frac{5}{6}$
e. $-1\frac{2}{5} + \left(-3\frac{1}{3}\right)$ $-4\frac{11}{15}$
f. $2\frac{3}{4} - 6\frac{1}{3}$ $-3\frac{7}{12}$

Standardized Test Practice

EXAMPLE Estimate the Sum of Mixed Numbers

3 **MULTIPLE-CHOICE TEST ITEM** Four telephone books are $2\frac{1}{8}$, $1\frac{15}{16}$, $1\frac{3}{4}$, and $2\frac{3}{8}$ inches thick. If these books were stacked one on top of another, what is the total height of the books?

(A) $5\frac{3}{16}$ in. (B) $8\frac{3}{16}$ in. (C) $11\frac{3}{16}$ in. (D) $15\frac{3}{16}$ in.

Read the Test Item You need to find the sum of four mixed numbers.

Solve the Test Item It would take some time to change each of the fractions to ones with a common denominator. However, notice that all four of the numbers are about 2. Since 2×4 equals 8, the answer will be about 8. Notice that only one of the choices is close to 8. The answer is B.

Test-Taking Tip

Use Estimation If the test question would take an excessive amount of time to work, try estimating the answer. Then look for the appropriate answer choice.

TEACHING TIP

Explain to students that when several addends are approximately equal as in Example 3, they can estimate the sum by multiplying the number of addends by the rounded number. This technique is called *clustering*.

EXAMPLE Evaluate Expressions

4 **ALGEBRA Find the value of $a - b$ if $a = \frac{5}{7}$ and $b = -\frac{3}{5}$.**

$$a - b = \frac{5}{7} - \left(-\frac{3}{5}\right) \quad \text{Replace } a \text{ with } \tfrac{5}{7} \text{ and } b \text{ with } -\tfrac{3}{5}.$$

$$= \frac{25}{35} - \left(-\frac{21}{35}\right) \quad \text{Rename each fraction using the LCD, 35.}$$

$$= \frac{25 - (-21)}{35} \quad \text{Subtract the numerators.}$$

$$= \frac{46}{35} \text{ or } 1\frac{11}{35} \quad \text{Simplify.}$$

msmath3.net/extra_examples

2 Teach

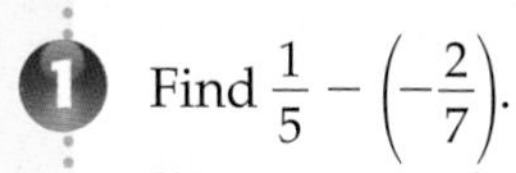

In-Class Examples

1 Find $\frac{1}{5} - \left(-\frac{2}{7}\right)$. Write in simplest form. $\frac{17}{35}$

2 Find $-4\frac{1}{8} + 2\frac{5}{12}$. Write in simplest form. $-1\frac{17}{24}$

3 **MULTIPLE-CHOICE TEST ITEM** During January, Nikki watched television $2\frac{1}{4}$ hours the first week, $2\frac{1}{8}$ hours the second week, $1\frac{3}{4}$ hours the third week, and $1\frac{1}{2}$ hours the fourth week. How much time did she watch television during the 4-week period? **B**

A $4\frac{5}{8}$ hours B $7\frac{5}{8}$ hours
C $10\frac{5}{8}$ hours D $12\frac{5}{8}$ hours

4 **ALGEBRA** Find the value of $p - q$ if $p = \frac{2}{5}$ and $q = -\frac{4}{9}$. $\frac{38}{45}$

DAILY INTERVENTION **Flexible Grouping**

Peer Tutoring Divide the class into groups of about 4 students each, and have each group work through the **Your Turn** exercises together. Be sure that students of diverse abilities are represented in each group, and encourage peer tutoring within the groups.

Students practice the same concepts in Exercises 11–34 if they are assigned odd or even problems.

3 Practice/Apply

FOLDABLES Follow-Up Remind students to explain what they learn about adding and subtracting unlike fractions on the sixth tab of their Foldables. Encourage them to find similiarites and differences between adding like and unlike fractions and subtracting like and unlike fractions.

NUMBER SENSE
In Exercise 3, suggest that students first try approximating both numbers as $\frac{1}{2}$, giving a sum of 1. Then they can fine tune the estimate by noticing that both numbers are greater than $\frac{1}{2}$, so the sum must be greater than 1.

About the Exercises...

Guided Practice Key

Exercises	Examples
4–7, 10	1
8–9	2

Assignment Guide

Basic: 11–23 odd, 29–35 odd, 41–51

Average: 11–35 odd, 36–51

Enriched: 12–34 even, 36–47 (Optional: 48–51)

Skill and Concept Check

1. Writing Math Describe the first step in adding unlike fractions. **See margin.**
2. **OPEN ENDED** Write a subtraction problem with unlike fractions with a least common denominator of 12. Find the answer. **Sample answer:** $\frac{3}{4} - \frac{1}{3} = \frac{5}{12}$
3. **NUMBER SENSE** Without doing the computation, determine whether $\frac{4}{7} + \frac{5}{9}$ is greater than, less than, or equal to 1. Explain. **See margin.**

GUIDED PRACTICE

Add or subtract. Write in simplest form.

4. $\frac{3}{4} + \frac{1}{6}$ $\frac{11}{12}$
5. $\frac{7}{8} - \frac{3}{4}$ $\frac{1}{8}$
6. $-\frac{1}{7} - \left(-\frac{4}{5}\right)$ $\frac{23}{35}$
7. $-\frac{2}{5} + \left(-\frac{5}{6}\right)$ $-1\frac{7}{30}$
8. $3\frac{5}{8} - 1\frac{1}{3}$ $2\frac{7}{24}$
9. $-4\frac{2}{3} - \left(-3\frac{4}{5}\right)$ $-\frac{13}{15}$
10. **MUSIC** A waltz is written in $\frac{3}{4}$ time. This means the quarter note gets one beat and the total value of each measure is $\frac{3}{4}$. What type of note must be used to finish the last measure of the waltz below? $\frac{1}{4}$

★ indicates increased difficulty

Practice and Applications

HOMEWORK HELP

For Exercises	See Examples
11–32, 35	1–3
33–34	4

Extra Practice See pages 620, 649.

Add or subtract. Write in simplest form.

11. $\frac{3}{8} + \frac{5}{6}$ $1\frac{5}{24}$
12. $\frac{7}{8} + \frac{3}{12}$ $1\frac{1}{8}$
13. $\frac{3}{4} - \frac{1}{6}$ $\frac{7}{12}$
14. $\frac{4}{5} - \frac{2}{15}$ $\frac{2}{3}$
15. $-\frac{6}{7} - \left(-\frac{1}{3}\right)$ $-\frac{11}{21}$
16. $-\frac{4}{5} - \left(-\frac{2}{3}\right)$ $-\frac{2}{15}$
17. $8\frac{3}{7} - \left(-6\frac{1}{2}\right)$ $14\frac{13}{14}$
18. $7\frac{3}{4} - \left(-1\frac{1}{8}\right)$ $8\frac{7}{8}$
19. $-4\frac{3}{4} - 5\frac{5}{8}$ $-10\frac{3}{8}$
20. $-8\frac{1}{3} - 4\frac{5}{6}$ $-13\frac{1}{6}$
21. $9\frac{1}{6} - 4\frac{1}{2}$ $4\frac{2}{3}$
22. $9\frac{1}{3} - 2\frac{1}{2}$ $6\frac{5}{6}$
23. $3\frac{1}{5} + \left(-8\frac{1}{2}\right)$ $-5\frac{3}{10}$
24. $1\frac{1}{6} + \left(-6\frac{2}{3}\right)$ $-5\frac{1}{2}$

★ 25. $-15\frac{5}{8} + 11\frac{2}{3}$ $-3\frac{23}{24}$
★ 26. $-22\frac{2}{5} + 15\frac{5}{6}$ $-6\frac{17}{30}$
★ 27. $\frac{65}{187} - \frac{9}{136}$ $\frac{421}{1,496}$
★ 28. $\frac{45}{152} - \frac{13}{209}$ $\frac{391}{1,672}$

29. Subtract $-6\frac{1}{4}$ from 9. $15\frac{1}{4}$
30. What is $2\frac{3}{8}$ less than $-8\frac{1}{5}$? $-10\frac{23}{40}$
31. What is the sum of $-\frac{5}{8}$ and $-\frac{1}{2}$? $-1\frac{1}{8}$
32. Find the sum of $-\frac{4}{9}$ and $-\frac{2}{3}$. $-1\frac{1}{9}$
33. **ALGEBRA** Evaluate $c - d$ if $c = -\frac{3}{4}$ and $d = -12\frac{7}{8}$. $12\frac{1}{8}$
34. **ALGEBRA** Evaluate $r - s$ if $r = -\frac{5}{8}$ and $s = 2\frac{5}{6}$. $-3\frac{11}{24}$

Answers

1. Rename the fractions so they have a common denominator.
3. Greater than; since both fractions are greater than $\frac{1}{2}$, the sum will be greater than $\frac{1}{2} + \frac{1}{2}$ or 1.

43. $5\frac{1}{6} + 4\frac{2}{9}$
$= (5 + 4) + \left(\frac{1}{6} + \frac{2}{9}\right)$
$= (5 + 4) + \left(\frac{3}{18} + \frac{4}{18}\right)$
$= 9 + \frac{7}{18}$
$= 9\frac{7}{18}$

35. **HISTORY** In the 1824 presidential election, Andrew Jackson, John Quincy Adams, Henry Clay, and William H. Crawford received electoral votes. Use the information at the right to determine what fraction of the votes William H. Crawford received. **about $\frac{25}{168}$**

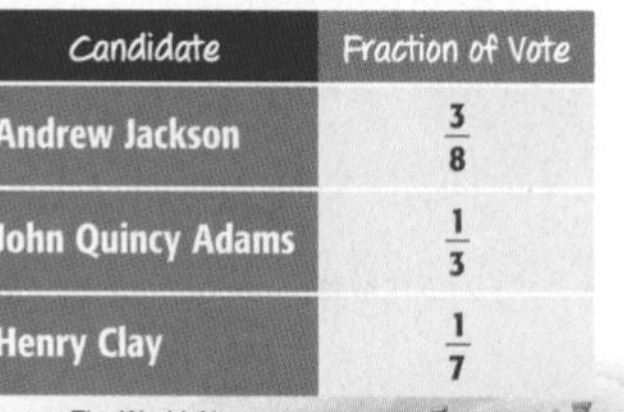

Candidate	Fraction of Vote
Andrew Jackson	$\frac{3}{8}$
John Quincy Adams	$\frac{1}{3}$
Henry Clay	$\frac{1}{7}$

Source: *The World Almanac*

WATER MANAGEMENT For Exercises 36–40, use the following information.
Suppose a bucket is placed under two faucets.

36. If one faucet is turned on alone, the bucket will be filled in 5 minutes. Write the fraction of the bucket that will be filled in 1 minute. **$\frac{1}{5}$**

37. If the other faucet is turned on alone, the bucket will be filled in 3 minutes. Write the fraction of the bucket that will be filled in 1 minute. **$\frac{1}{3}$**

38. Write the fraction of the bucket that will be filled in 1 minute if both faucets are turned on. **$\frac{8}{15}$**

39. Divide 1 by the sum in Exercise 38 to determine the number of minutes it will take to fill the bucket if both faucets are turned on. **$1\frac{7}{8}$ min**

40. How many seconds will it take to fill the bucket if both faucets are turned on? **$112\frac{1}{2}$ s**

41. **CRITICAL THINKING** Write an expression for each statement. Then find the answer.

a. $\frac{3}{4}$ of $\frac{2}{3}$ **$\frac{3}{4} \cdot \frac{2}{3} = \frac{1}{2}$**

b. $\frac{3}{4}$ more than $\frac{2}{3}$ **$\frac{2}{3} + \frac{3}{4} = 1\frac{5}{12}$**

c. $\frac{3}{4}$ less than $\frac{2}{3}$ **$\frac{2}{3} - \frac{3}{4} = -\frac{1}{12}$**

d. $\frac{3}{4}$ divided into $\frac{2}{3}$ **$\frac{2}{3} \div \frac{3}{4} = \frac{8}{9}$**

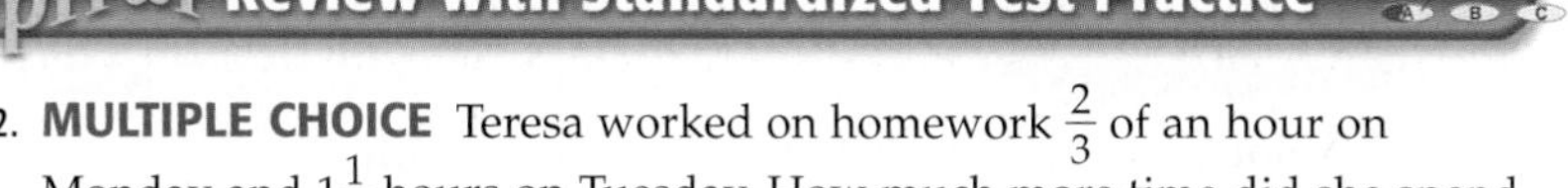

Spiral Review with Standardized Test Practice

42. **MULTIPLE CHOICE** Teresa worked on homework $\frac{2}{3}$ of an hour on Monday and $1\frac{1}{2}$ hours on Tuesday. How much more time did she spend working on homework on Tuesday than on Monday? **C**

Ⓐ $\frac{1}{6}$ h   Ⓑ $\frac{1}{4}$ h   Ⓒ $\frac{5}{6}$ h   Ⓓ $\frac{13}{6}$ h

43. **SHORT RESPONSE** Show each step in finding $5\frac{1}{6} + 4\frac{2}{9}$. **See margin.**

Add or subtract. Write in simplest form. (Lesson 2-5)

44. $-\frac{7}{11} + \frac{5}{11}$ **$-\frac{2}{11}$**

45. $-\frac{7}{15} - \frac{4}{15}$ **$-\frac{11}{15}$**

46. $5\frac{4}{5} - 7\frac{1}{5}$ **$-1\frac{2}{5}$**

47. **ALGEBRA** Find $a \div b$ if $a = 3\frac{1}{2}$ and $b = -\frac{7}{8}$. (Lesson 2-4) **-4**

GETTING READY FOR THE NEXT LESSON

PREREQUISITE SKILL Solve each equation. Check your solution. (Lessons 1-8 and 1-9)

48. $d - 13 = -44$ **-31**
49. $-18t = 270$ **-15**
50. $-34 = y + 22$ **-56**
51. $-5 = \frac{a}{16}$ **-80**

msmath3.net/self_check_quiz

4 Assess

Higher-Level Thinking

Have students use various colors of construction paper to create cutout models that demonstrate adding and subtracting unlike fractions. They should use the models to demonstrate the need to first find a common denominator.

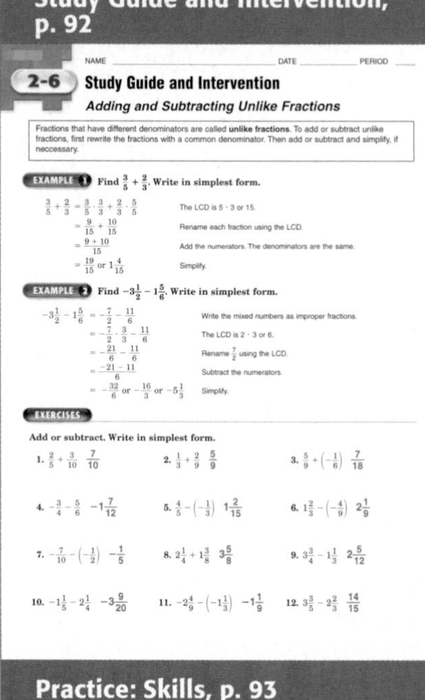

Study Guide and Intervention, p. 92

NAME ______ DATE ______ PERIOD ____

2-6 Study Guide and Intervention

Adding and Subtracting Unlike Fractions

Fractions that have different denominators are called **unlike fractions**. To add or subtract unlike fractions, first rewrite the fractions with a common denominator. Then add or subtract and simplify, if neccessary.

EXAMPLE 1 Find $\frac{3}{5} + \frac{2}{3}$. Write in simplest form.

$\frac{3}{5} + \frac{2}{3} = \frac{3}{5} \cdot \frac{3}{3} + \frac{2}{3} \cdot \frac{5}{5}$ The LCD is 5 · 3 or 15.

$= \frac{9}{15} + \frac{10}{15}$ Rename each fraction using the LCD.

$= \frac{9 + 10}{15}$ Add the numerators. The denominators are the same.

$= \frac{19}{15}$ or $1\frac{4}{15}$ Simplify.

EXAMPLE 2 Find $-3\frac{1}{2} - 1\frac{5}{6}$. Write in simplest form.

$-3\frac{1}{2} - 1\frac{5}{6} = -\frac{7}{2} - \frac{11}{6}$ Write the mixed numbers as improper fractions.

$= -\frac{7}{2} \cdot \frac{3}{3} - \frac{11}{6}$ The LCD is 2 · 3 or 6.

$= -\frac{21}{6} - \frac{11}{6}$ Rename $\frac{7}{2}$ using the LCD.

$= \frac{-21 - 11}{6}$ Subtract the numerators.

$= -\frac{32}{6}$ or $-\frac{16}{3}$ or $-5\frac{1}{3}$ Simplify.

EXERCISES

Add or subtract. Write in simplest form.

1. $\frac{2}{5} + \frac{3}{10}$ **$\frac{7}{10}$**
2. $\frac{1}{3} + \frac{2}{9}$ **$\frac{5}{9}$**
3. $\frac{5}{9} + \left(-\frac{1}{6}\right)$ **$\frac{7}{18}$**
4. $-\frac{3}{4} - \frac{5}{6}$ **$-1\frac{7}{12}$**
5. $\frac{4}{5} - \left(-\frac{1}{3}\right)$ **$1\frac{2}{15}$**
6. $1\frac{2}{3} - \left(-\frac{4}{9}\right)$ **$2\frac{1}{9}$**
7. $-\frac{7}{10} - \left(-\frac{1}{2}\right)$ **$-\frac{1}{5}$**
8. $2\frac{1}{4} + 1\frac{3}{8}$ **$3\frac{5}{8}$**
9. $3\frac{3}{4} - 1\frac{1}{3}$ **$2\frac{5}{12}$**
10. $-1\frac{1}{5} - 2\frac{1}{4}$ **$-3\frac{9}{20}$**
11. $-2\frac{4}{9} - \left(-1\frac{1}{3}\right)$ **$-1\frac{1}{9}$**
12. $3\frac{3}{5} - 2\frac{2}{3}$ **$\frac{14}{15}$**

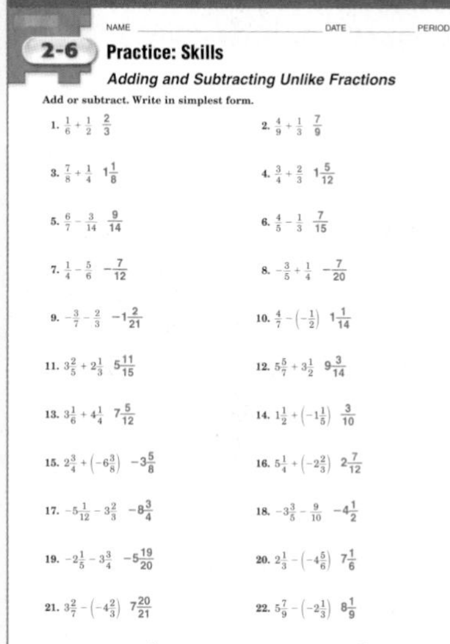

Practice: Skills, p. 93

NAME ______ DATE ______ PERIOD ____

2-6 Practice: Skills

Adding and Subtracting Unlike Fractions

Add or subtract. Write in simplest form.

1. $\frac{1}{6} + \frac{1}{2}$ **$\frac{2}{3}$**
2. $\frac{4}{9} + \frac{1}{3}$ **$\frac{7}{9}$**
3. $\frac{7}{8} + \frac{1}{4}$ **$1\frac{1}{8}$**
4. $\frac{3}{4} + \frac{2}{3}$ **$1\frac{5}{12}$**
5. $\frac{6}{7} - \frac{3}{14}$ **$\frac{9}{14}$**
6. $\frac{4}{5} - \frac{1}{3}$ **$\frac{7}{15}$**
7. $\frac{1}{4} - \frac{5}{6}$ **$-\frac{7}{12}$**
8. $-\frac{3}{5} + \frac{1}{4}$ **$-\frac{7}{20}$**
9. $-\frac{3}{7} - \frac{2}{3}$ **$-1\frac{2}{21}$**
10. $\frac{4}{7} - \left(-\frac{1}{2}\right)$ **$1\frac{1}{14}$**
11. $3\frac{2}{5} + 2\frac{1}{3}$ **$5\frac{11}{15}$**
12. $5\frac{5}{7} + 3\frac{1}{2}$ **$9\frac{3}{14}$**
13. $3\frac{1}{6} + 4\frac{1}{4}$ **$7\frac{5}{12}$**
14. $1\frac{1}{2} + \left(-1\frac{1}{5}\right)$ **$\frac{3}{10}$**
15. $2\frac{3}{4} + \left(-6\frac{3}{8}\right)$ **$-3\frac{5}{8}$**
16. $5\frac{1}{4} + \left(-2\frac{2}{3}\right)$ **$2\frac{7}{12}$**
17. $-5\frac{1}{12} - 3\frac{2}{3}$ **$-8\frac{3}{4}$**
18. $-3\frac{3}{5} - \frac{9}{10}$ **$-4\frac{1}{2}$**
19. $-2\frac{1}{5} - 3\frac{3}{4}$ **$-5\frac{19}{20}$**
20. $2\frac{1}{3} - \left(-4\frac{5}{6}\right)$ **$7\frac{1}{6}$**
21. $3\frac{2}{7} - \left(-4\frac{2}{3}\right)$ **$7\frac{20}{21}$**
22. $5\frac{7}{9} - \left(-2\frac{1}{3}\right)$ **$8\frac{1}{9}$**
23. $10\frac{2}{9} - \left(-3\frac{1}{3}\right)$ **$13\frac{5}{9}$**
24. $-2\frac{1}{3} - \left(-5\frac{4}{5}\right)$ **$3\frac{7}{15}$**

Practice: Word Problems, p. 94

NAME ______ DATE ______ PERIOD ____

2-6 Practice: Word Problems

Adding and Subtracting Unlike Fractions

1. **GEOMETRY** Two line segments have lengths of $3\frac{1}{4}$ inches and $1\frac{1}{3}$ inches. What is the sum of the lengths of the two line segments? **$4\frac{7}{12}$ in.**

2. **COMPUTERS** The biology class has created two data files on the computer. One file is $2\frac{1}{9}$ megabytes, while the other file is $4\frac{1}{2}$ megabytes. How much larger is the second file than the first? **$2\frac{7}{18}$ megabytes**

3. **HUMAN BODY** The index finger on Pablo's right hand measures $3\frac{3}{8}$ inches, while the index finger on his left hand measures $3\frac{5}{16}$ inches. Which hand has the longer index finger? How much longer is it? **Right hand; $\frac{1}{16}$ in.**

4. **DECORATING** Sugi has two pictures that she wants to put beside each other in a frame. One is $3\frac{1}{2}$ inches wide and the other is $5\frac{1}{8}$ inches wide. How wide must the frame be to fit both pictures? **$8\frac{5}{8}$ in.**

5. **PETS** Laura purchased two puppies from a litter. One of the puppies weighs $4\frac{5}{6}$ pounds and the other puppy weighs $5\frac{1}{2}$ pounds. How much more does the second puppy weigh than the first? **$\frac{2}{3}$ lb**

6. **AGE** Alma is $6\frac{3}{4}$ years old, while her brother David is $3\frac{5}{6}$ years old. What is the sum of the ages of Alma and David? **$10\frac{7}{12}$ years**

7. **MEASUREMENT** Ned pours $7\frac{2}{5}$ ounces of water from a beaker containing $10\frac{1}{4}$ ounces. How much water is left in the beaker? **$2\frac{17}{20}$ oz**

8. **GEOMETRY** A triangle has sides of $1\frac{1}{6}$ inches, $1\frac{1}{3}$ inches, and $1\frac{2}{3}$ inches. What is the perimeter of the triangle? **$4\frac{1}{6}$ in.**

2-7 Lesson Notes

Lesson Resources

Chapter 2 Resource Masters
- Study Guide and Intervention, p. 97
- Practice: Skills, p. 98
- Practice: Word Problems, p. 99
- Reading to Learn Mathematics, p. 100
- Enrichment, p. 101

Calculator and Spreadsheet Masters, p. 15

Parent and Student Study Guide Online Worksheets, 2-7

Noteables™: Interactive Study Notebook with Foldables™, 2-7

FAST FILE

1 Focus

5-Minute Check 2-7

Use as a quiz or review of Lesson 2-6. (Also available as a transparency)

Bellringer

Problem Solving Have the class apply the four-step plan for problem solving to the following: *About $\frac{3}{4}$ of Illinois's land is used for farming. If 27 million acres are farmland, about how many million acres of land does Illinois have?*

$\frac{3}{4}t = 27$ million; about 36 million acres

Reading to Learn Mathematics, p. 100 ELL

NAME ______ DATE ______ PERIOD ____

2-7 Reading to Learn Mathematics

Solving Equations with Rational Numbers

Pre-Activity *Read the introduction at the top of page 92 in your textbook. Write your answers below.*

1. Multiply each side of the equation by 6. Write the result. $150 = 5s$
2. Divide each side of the equation in Exercise 1 by 5. Write the result. $30 = s$
3. Multiply each side of the original equation $25 = \frac{5}{6}s$ by the multiplicative inverse of $\frac{5}{6}$. Write the result. $30 = s$
4. What is the speed of a grizzly bear? 30 mph
5. Which method of solving the equation seems most efficient? Explain. Multiplying by the multiplicative inverse; it only takes one step.

Reading the Lesson

2-7 Solving Equations with Rational Numbers

What You'll LEARN

Solve equations involving rational numbers.

REVIEW Vocabulary

equation: a mathematical sentence that contains an equals sign (Lesson 1-8)

WHEN am I ever going to use this?

BIOLOGY An elephant, which can run at a speed of 25 miles per hour, runs $\frac{5}{6}$ as fast as a grizzly bear. If s represents the speed of a grizzly bear, you can write the equation $25 = \frac{5}{6}s$.

1. Multiply each side of the equation by 6. Write the result. **$150 = 5s$**
2. Divide each side of the equation in Exercise 1 by 5. Write the result. **$30 = s$**
3. Multiply each side of the original equation $25 = \frac{5}{6}s$ by the multiplicative inverse of $\frac{5}{6}$. Write the result. **$30 = s$**
4. What is the speed of a grizzly bear? **30 mph**
5. Which method of solving the equation seems most efficient?

5. Multiplying by the multiplicative inverse; it only takes one step.

You used the Multiplication and Division Properties of Equality to solve $25 = \frac{5}{6}s$. You can also use the Addition and Subtraction Properties of Equality to solve equations with rational numbers.

EXAMPLES Solve by Using Addition or Subtraction

1 Solve $p - 7.36 = -2.84$. Check your solution.

$p - 7.36 = -2.84$	Write the equation.
$p - 7.36 + 7.36 = -2.84 + 7.36$	Add 7.36 to each side.
$p = 4.52$	Simplify.

2 Solve $\frac{1}{2} = t + \frac{3}{4}$.

$\frac{1}{2} = t + \frac{3}{4}$	Write the equation.
$\frac{1}{2} - \frac{3}{4} = t + \frac{3}{4} - \frac{3}{4}$	Subtract $\frac{3}{4}$ from each side.
$\frac{1}{2} - \frac{3}{4} = t$	Simplify.
$\frac{2}{4} - \frac{3}{4} = t$	Rename $\frac{1}{2}$.
$-\frac{1}{4} = t$	Simplify.

EXAMPLES Solve by Using Multiplication or Division

3 **Solve $\frac{4}{7}b = 16$. Check your solution.**

$\frac{4}{7}b = 16$	Write the equation.
$\frac{7}{4}\left(\frac{4}{7}b\right) = \frac{7}{4}(16)$	Multiply each side by $\frac{7}{4}$.
$b = 28$	Simplify.

Check

$\frac{4}{7}b = 16$	Write the original equation.
$\frac{4}{7}(28) \stackrel{?}{=} 16$	Replace b with 28.
$16 = 16$ ✓	Simplify.

4 **Solve $58.4 = -7.3m$.**

$58.4 = -7.3m$	Write the equation.
$\frac{58.4}{-7.3} = \frac{-7.3m}{-7.3}$	Divide each side by -7.3.
$-8 = m$	Simplify. Check the solution.

Your Turn **Solve each equation. Check your solution.** a. 12.13

a. $r - 7.81 = 4.32$ b. $7.2v = -36$ **−5** c. $-\frac{2}{3}n = -\frac{3}{5}$ $\frac{9}{10}$

REAL-LIFE MATH

BASKETBALL During her rookie season for the WNBA, Sue Bird's field goal average was 0.379, and she made 232 field goal attempts.

Source: WNBA.com

You can write equations with rational numbers to solve real-life problems.

EXAMPLE Write an Equation to Solve a Problem

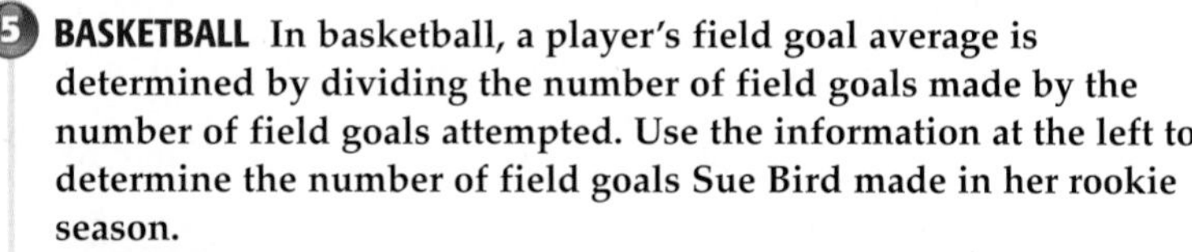

5 **BASKETBALL** **In basketball, a player's field goal average is determined by dividing the number of field goals made by the number of field goals attempted. Use the information at the left to determine the number of field goals Sue Bird made in her rookie season.**

Words	Field goal average equals goals divided by attempts.		
Variables	f	$=$	$\frac{g}{a}$
Equation	0.379	$=$	$\frac{g}{232}$

$0.379 = \frac{g}{232}$	Write the equation.
$232(0.379) = 232\left(\frac{g}{232}\right)$	Multiply each side by 232.
$87.928 = h$	Simplify.

Sue Bird made 88 field goals during her rookie season.

TEACHING TIP

Help students to estimate the answer for Example 5. 0.379 is about $\frac{1}{3}$, and 232 is about 240. So, $\frac{1}{3} = \frac{?}{240}$.

msmath3.net/extra_examples

2 Teach

In-Class Examples

1 Solve $g + 2.84 = 3.62$. Check your solution. **0.78**

2 Solve $-\frac{4}{5} = s - \frac{2}{3}$. $-\frac{2}{15}$

3 Solve $\frac{7}{11}c = -21$. Check your solution. **−33**

4 Solve $9.7t = -67.9$. **−7**

5 **PHYSICS** You can determine the rate an object is traveling by dividing the distance it travels by the time it takes to cover that distance $\left(r = \frac{d}{t}\right)$. If an object travels at a rate of 14.3 meters per second for 17 seconds, how far does it travel? **243.1 m**

DAILY INTERVENTION

Unlocking Misconceptions

Rounding Answers Students may mistakenly think that the answer to Example 5 in the Student Edition should be 87.928 rather than 88. Remind them to look at the context of the problem when determining whether to round the answer. In this case, the number of field goals must be a positive integer. The digits after the decimal are the result of rounding the field goal average to the thousandth place.

Lesson 2-7 Solving Equations with Rational Numbers **93**

3 Practice/Apply

FOLDABLES™ Follow-Up Remind students to explain what they learn about solving equations with rational numbers on the seventh tab of their Foldables. Encourage them to use their own words and symbols so it will be more meaningful and memorable.

Which One Doesn't Belong?
In Exercise 2, remind students that when they multiply a number by its multiplicative inverse, the result is 1. The multiplicative inverse of $-\frac{1}{3}$ is -3, not 3 or $\frac{1}{3}$. In addition, point out that $2 = \frac{2}{1}$.

About the Exercises...

Guided Practice Key

Exercises	Examples
3–4, 8	1, 2
5–7	3, 4
9–10	5

Assignment Guide

Basic: 11–23 odd, 29, 31, 34–47

Average: 11–31 odd, 32–47

Enriched: 12–30 even, 32–43 (Optional: 44–47)

Alert! In Exercises 25, 26, and 28, students will need to change mixed numbers to improper fractions.

Students practice the same concepts in Exercises 11–30 if they are assigned odd or even problems.

Skill and Concept Check

1. **OPEN ENDED** Write an equation with rational numbers that has a solution of $\frac{1}{4}$. **Sample answer: $x + \frac{3}{4} = 1$**

2. **Which One Doesn't Belong?** Identify the expression that does not have the same value as the other three. Explain your reasoning.

$\frac{4}{3}\left(\frac{3}{4}x\right)$	$-\frac{3}{2}\left(-\frac{2}{3}x\right)$	$2\left(\frac{1}{2}x\right)$	$-\frac{1}{3}\left(\frac{1}{3}x\right)$

$-\frac{1}{3}\left(\frac{1}{3}x\right)$; For all the other expressions equal x.

GUIDED PRACTICE

Solve each equation. Check your solution.

3. $t + 0.25 = -4.12$ **-4.37**
4. $a - \frac{3}{4} = -\frac{3}{8}$ **$\frac{3}{8}$**
5. $-45 = \frac{5}{6}d$ **-54**
6. $-26.5 = -5.3w$ **5**
7. $\frac{5}{8}z = \frac{2}{9}$ **$\frac{16}{45}$**
8. $p - (-0.03) = 3.2$ **3.17**

SPACE For Exercises 9 and 10, use the following information.
The planet Jupiter takes 11.9 years to make one revolution around the Sun.

9. Write a multiplication equation you can use to determine the number of revolutions Jupiter makes in 59.5 years. Let r represent the number of revolutions. **$11.9r = 59.5$**

10. How many revolutions does Jupiter make in 59.5 years? **5 revolutions**

★ **indicates increased difficulty**

Practice and Applications

HOMEWORK HELP

For Exercises	See Examples
11–30	1–4
31–33	5

Extra Practice See pages 621, 649.

Solve each equation. Check your solution.

11. $q + 0.45 = 1.29$ **0.84**
12. $a - 1.72 = 5.81$ **7.53**
13. $-\frac{1}{2} = m - \frac{2}{3}$ **$\frac{1}{6}$**
14. $-\frac{5}{9} = f + \frac{1}{3}$ **$-\frac{8}{9}$**
15. $-\frac{4}{7}b = 16$ **-28**
16. $-\frac{2}{9}p = -8$ **36**
17. $-1.92 = -0.32s$ **6**
18. $-8.4 = 1.2t$ **-7**
19. $\frac{3}{4}z = -\frac{5}{6}$ **$-1\frac{1}{9}$**
20. $-\frac{2}{5}d = \frac{4}{9}$ **$-1\frac{1}{9}$**
21. $g - (-1.5) = 2.35$ **0.85**
22. $-1.3 = n - (-6.12)$ **-7.42**
23. $\frac{t}{3.2} = -4.5$ **-14.4**
24. $-\frac{a}{1.6} = 7.5$ **-12**
★25. $-5\frac{3}{4} = -2\frac{1}{2}x$ **$2\frac{3}{10}$**
★26. $4\frac{1}{6} = -3\frac{1}{3}c$ **$-1\frac{1}{4}$**
★27. $3.5g = -\frac{7}{8}$ **$-\frac{1}{4}$**
★28. $-7.5r = -3\frac{1}{3}$ **$\frac{4}{9}$**

29. Find the solution of $v - \frac{2}{5} = -2$. **$-1\frac{3}{5}$**

30. What is the solution of $-4.2 = \frac{c}{7}$? **-29.4**

31. **MONEY** The currency of Egypt is called a pound. The equation $3\frac{3}{4}d = 21$ can be used to determine how many U.S. dollars d equal 21 Egyptian pounds. Solve the equation. **$5.60**

RECREATION For Exercises 32 and 33, use the graph.

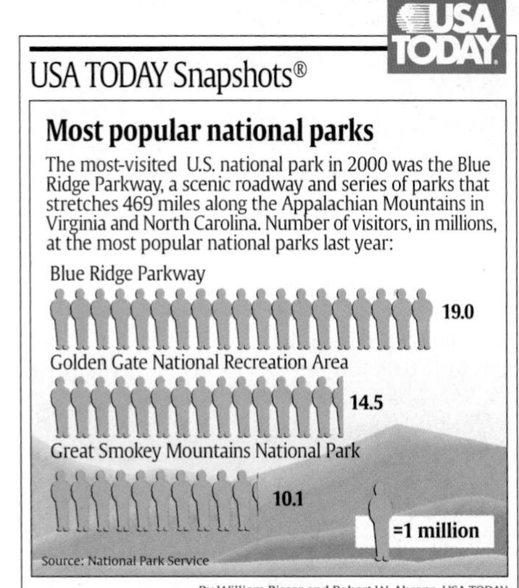

32. Let v equal the number of additional visitors that the Golden Gate National Recreation Area needed in the year 2000 to equal the number of visitors to the Blue Ridge Parkway. Write an addition equation to represent the situation. **$14.5 + v = 19.0$**

33. How many more visitors did the Golden Gate National Recreation Area need to equal the number of visitors to the Blue Ridge Parkway? **4.5 million visitors**

34. **CRITICAL THINKING** What is the solution of $\frac{1}{2}y + 3 = 15$? Check your solution. **24**

Spiral Review with Standardized Test Practice

35. **MULTIPLE CHOICE** Find the value of t in $t - (-4.36) = 7.2$. **A**

Ⓐ 2.84 Ⓑ 11.56 Ⓒ −2.84 Ⓓ −11.56

36. **MULTIPLE CHOICE** If the area of the rectangle at the right is $22\frac{3}{4}$ square inches, what is the width of the rectangle? **H**

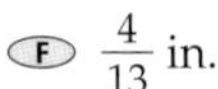

Ⓕ $\frac{4}{13}$ in. Ⓖ $2\frac{1}{2}$ in.

Ⓗ $3\frac{1}{4}$ in. Ⓘ $3\frac{3}{4}$ in.

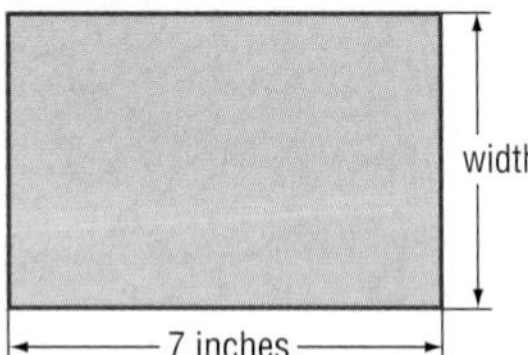

Add or subtract. Write in simplest form. (Lesson 2-6)

37. $\frac{1}{6} + \frac{1}{7}$ **$\frac{13}{42}$**

38. $\frac{7}{8} - \frac{1}{6}$ **$\frac{17}{24}$**

39. $-5\frac{1}{2} - 6\frac{4}{5}$ **$-12\frac{3}{10}$**

40. $2\frac{1}{2} + 5\frac{2}{3}$ **$8\frac{1}{6}$**

41. **SHIPPING** Plastic straps are often wound around large cardboard boxes to reinforce them during shipping. Suppose the end of the strap must overlap $\frac{7}{16}$ inch to fasten. How long is the plastic strap around the box at the right? (Lesson 2-5) **$106\frac{3}{16}$ in.**

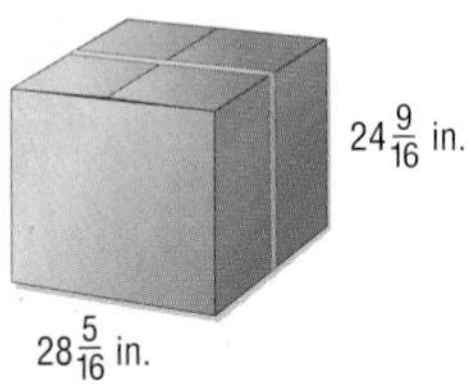

42. **ALGEBRA** The sum of two integers is 13. One of the integers is −5. Write an equation and solve to find the other integer. (Lesson 1-8) **$x + (-5) = 13$; 18**

43. **ALGEBRA** Write an expression for *17 more than p*. (Lesson 1-7) **$17 + p$**

GETTING READY FOR THE NEXT LESSON

BASIC SKILL Multiply.

44. $4 \cdot 4 \cdot 4$ **64**

45. $2 \cdot 2 \cdot 2 \cdot 2 \cdot 2$ **32**

46. $3 \cdot 3 \cdot 3 \cdot 3$ **81**

47. $5 \cdot 5 \cdot 5$ **125**

msmath3.net/self_check_quiz

4 Assess

Higher-Level Thinking

The equation $F = \frac{9}{5}C + 32$ can be used to convert Celsius degrees to Fahrenheit degrees. If the temperature is 60°F, what is the temperature in Celsius degrees? **about 15.6°C**

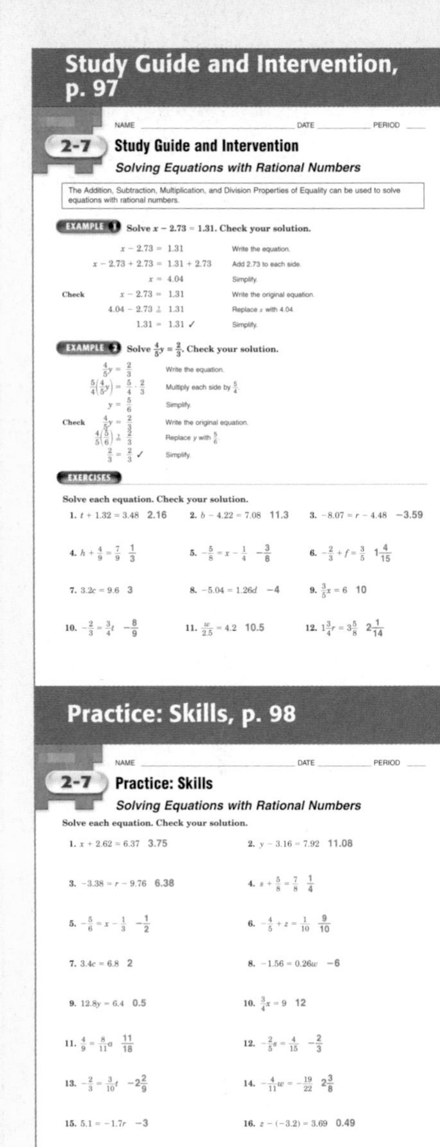

Study Guide and Intervention, p. 97

NAME ______ DATE ______ PERIOD ____

2-7 Study Guide and Intervention

Solving Equations with Rational Numbers

The Addition, Subtraction, Multiplication, and Division Properties of Equality can be used to solve equations with rational numbers.

EXAMPLE 1 Solve $x - 2.73 = 1.31$. Check your solution.

	$x - 2.73 = 1.31$	Write the equation.
	$x - 2.73 + 2.73 = 1.31 + 2.73$	Add 2.73 to each side.
	$x = 4.04$	Simplify.
Check	$x - 2.73 = 1.31$	Write the original equation.
	$4.04 - 2.73 \stackrel{?}{=} 1.31$	Replace x with 4.04.
	$1.31 = 1.31$ ✓	Simplify.

EXAMPLE 2 Solve $\frac{4}{5}y = \frac{2}{3}$. Check your solution.

	$\frac{4}{5}y = \frac{2}{3}$	Write the equation.
	$\frac{5}{4}\left(\frac{4}{5}y\right) = \frac{5}{4} \cdot \frac{2}{3}$	Multiply each side by $\frac{5}{4}$.
	$y = \frac{5}{6}$	Simplify.
Check	$\frac{4}{5}y = \frac{2}{3}$	Write the original equation.
	$\frac{4}{5}\left(\frac{5}{6}\right) \stackrel{?}{=} \frac{2}{3}$	Replace y with $\frac{5}{6}$.
	$\frac{2}{3} = \frac{2}{3}$ ✓	Simplify.

EXERCISES

Solve each equation. Check your solution.

1. $t + 1.32 = 3.48$ **2.16**
2. $b - 4.22 = 7.08$ **11.3**
3. $-8.07 = r - 4.48$ **−3.59**
4. $h + \frac{4}{9} = \frac{7}{9}$ **$\frac{1}{3}$**
5. $-\frac{5}{8} = x - \frac{1}{4}$ **$-\frac{3}{8}$**
6. $-\frac{2}{3} + f = \frac{3}{5}$ **$1\frac{4}{15}$**
7. $3.2c = 9.6$ **3**
8. $-5.04 = 1.26d$ **−4**
9. $\frac{3}{5}x = 6$ **10**
10. $-\frac{2}{3} = \frac{3}{4}t$ **$-\frac{8}{9}$**
11. $\frac{w}{2.5} = 4.2$ **10.5**
12. $1\frac{3}{4}r = 3\frac{5}{8}$ **$2\frac{1}{14}$**

Practice: Skills, p. 98

NAME ______ DATE ______ PERIOD ____

2-7 Practice: Skills

Solving Equations with Rational Numbers

Solve each equation. Check your solution.

1. $x + 2.62 = 6.37$ **3.75**
2. $y - 3.16 = 7.92$ **11.08**
3. $-3.38 = r - 9.76$ **6.38**
4. $s + \frac{5}{8} = \frac{7}{8}$ **$\frac{1}{4}$**
5. $-\frac{5}{6} = x - \frac{1}{3}$ **$-\frac{1}{2}$**
6. $-\frac{4}{5} + z = \frac{1}{10}$ **$\frac{9}{10}$**
7. $3.4c = 6.8$ **2**
8. $-1.56 = 0.26w$ **−6**
9. $12.8y = 6.4$ **0.5**
10. $\frac{3}{4}x = 9$ **12**
11. $\frac{4}{9} = \frac{8}{11}a$ **$\frac{11}{18}$**
12. $-\frac{2}{5}s = \frac{4}{15}$ **$-\frac{2}{3}$**
13. $-\frac{2}{3} = \frac{3}{10}t$ **$-2\frac{2}{9}$**
14. $-\frac{4}{11}w = -\frac{19}{22}$ **$2\frac{3}{8}$**
15. $5.1 = -1.7r$ **−3**
16. $z - (-3.2) = 3.69$ **0.49**
17. $-2.11 = w - (-5.81)$ **−7.92**
18. $\frac{w}{2.6} = 3.5$ **9.1**
19. $-\frac{x}{1.8} = 7.2$ **−12.96**
20. $2\frac{1}{4}y = 3\frac{3}{8}$ **$1\frac{1}{2}$**
21. $-2\frac{2}{5}f = -3\frac{1}{5}$ **$1\frac{1}{3}$**
22. $1.5d = \frac{3}{8}$ **$\frac{1}{4}$**
23. $-7.5g = -6\frac{2}{3}$ **$\frac{8}{9}$**
24. $-2\frac{1}{5} = c - \left(-\frac{4}{5}\right)$ **−3**

Practice: Word Problems, p. 99

NAME ______ DATE ______ PERIOD ____

2-7 Practice: Word Problems

Solving Equations with Rational Numbers

1. **NATURE** The height of a certain tree is 12.85 meters. The length ℓ of its longest branch can be found using the equation $\ell + 3.23 = 12.85$. Solve the equation. **9.62 m**	2. **SHOPPING** Kristen went shopping and spent \$84.63 on books and CDs. The equation $84.63 = b + 43.22$ can be used to determine the amount b that she spent on books. Solve the equation. **\$41.41**
3. **ENERGY PRICES** Suppose regular unleaded gasoline costs \$1.40 per gallon. The price p of premium gasoline can be found using the equation $\frac{p}{1.2} = 1.40$. What is the price of the premium gasoline? **\$1.68 per gallon**	4. **DRIVING TIME** Sam went for a drive last Sunday. His average speed was 46 miles per hour and he drove 115 miles. The equation $115 = 46t$ can be used to find the time t that he spent driving. Solve the equation. **2.5 h**
5. **AUTOMOBILES** The bed of Julian's truck is $2\frac{1}{3}$ yards long. The length ℓ of the truck can be found by solving the equation $\ell - 2\frac{4}{9} = 2\frac{1}{3}$. What is the length of the truck? **$4\frac{7}{9}$ yd**	6. **SPORTS** Leo and Ted both ran in a race. Leo's time was 9 minutes, which was $\frac{3}{4}$ of Ted's time. Using t for Ted's time, write a multiplication equation to represent the situation. **$\frac{3}{4}t = 9$**
7. **SPEED** Ella rode the bus to work today. The distance she traveled was $4\frac{1}{4}$ miles and the ride took $\frac{1}{3}$ of an hour. The equation $\frac{1}{3}s = 4\frac{1}{4}$ can be used to find the average speed s of the bus. What was the average speed of the bus? **$12\frac{3}{4}$ mph**	8. **GEOMETRY** A rectangle has area $6\frac{2}{3}$ square inches and length $2\frac{1}{2}$ inches. The equation $6\frac{2}{3} = 2\frac{1}{2}w$ can be used to find the width w of the rectangle. Solve the equation. **$2\frac{2}{3}$ in.**

2-8a Lesson Notes

1 Focus

Bellringer
Communication Write the following number sequences on the chalkboard.

a. 6, 8, 11, 15, 20, 26, 33
b. 4, 9, 19, 39, 79, 159
c. 5, 15, 45, 135, 405, 1,215
d. 2, 3, 5, 9, 17, 33

Have students work together to find patterns in the numbers. Periodically provide tips such as "Try finding the difference between each term" and "Does each term change by some common factor?" Explain that finding patterns can help them solve math problems. **Sample answers: a. Add 2, 3, 4, . . . ; b. multiply by 2 then add 1; c. multiply by 3; d. multiply by 2 then subtract 1.**

2 Teach

In-Class Example

Solve. Look for a pattern.

INTEREST The table below shows the amount of interest $3,000 would earn after 7 years at various interest rates. How much interest would $3,000 earn at 6 percent interest? **$1,260**

Interest Rate (%)	Interest Earned ($)
1	210
2	420
3	630
4	840
5	1,050

2-8a Problem-Solving Strategy

A Preview of Lesson 2-8

Look for a Pattern

What You'll LEARN
Solve problems using the look for a pattern strategy.

In science class, we dropped a ball from 48 inches above the ground. Each time it hit the ground, it bounced back up $\frac{1}{2}$ of the previous height.

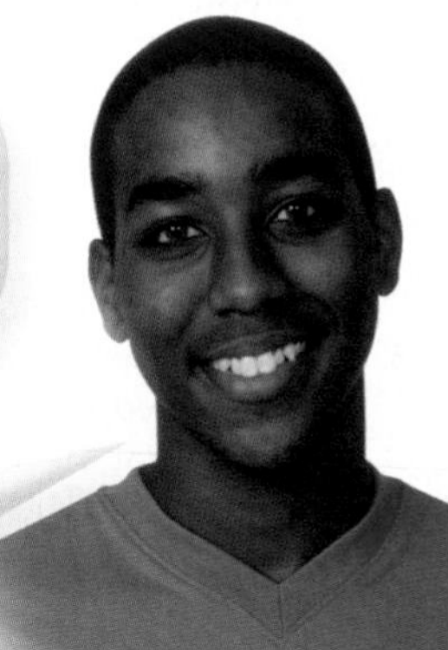

How many bounces occurred before the ball reached a height less than 5 inches?

Explore We know the original height of the ball. Each time the ball bounced, its height was $\frac{1}{2}$ of the previous height. We want to know the number of bounces before the ball reaches a height less than 5 inches.

Plan Use a pattern to determine when the ball will reach a height of less than 5 inches.

Solve

Bounce	Height (inches)
1	$\frac{1}{2} \cdot 48 = 24$
2	$\frac{1}{2} \cdot 24 = 12$
3	$\frac{1}{2} \cdot 12 = 6$
4	$\frac{1}{2} \cdot 6 = 3$

After the fourth bounce, the ball will reach a height less than 5 inches.

Examine Check your pattern to make sure the answer is correct.

Analyze the Strategy

1. **Explain** how Jerome and Haley determined the numbers in the first column. **1. Add 1 to each previous number.**
2. **Describe** how to continue the pattern in the second column. Find the fraction of the height after 7 bounces. **Multiply each previous number by $\frac{1}{2}$; $\frac{1}{128}$.**
3. **Write** a problem that can be solved by finding a pattern. Describe the pattern. **See margin.**

DAILY INTERVENTION — Unlocking Misconceptions

Patterns Finding patterns in number sequences is difficult for some students. They may mistakenly search only for patterns involving addition or subtraction. Remind students that they also should look for patterns involving multiplication or division, as well as combinations of the basic operations.

Apply the Strategy

Solve. Use the look for a pattern strategy.

4. **WATER MANAGEMENT** A tank is draining at a rate of 8 gallons every 3 minutes. If there are 70 gallons in the tank, when will the tank have just 22 gallons left? **in 18 min**

5. **MUSIC** The names of musical notes form a pattern. Name the next three notes in the following pattern. whole note, half note, quarter note **eighth note, sixteenth note, thirty-second note**

Mixed Problem Solving

Solve. Use any strategy.

6. **TRAVEL** Rafael is taking a vacation. His plane is scheduled to leave at 2:20 P.M. He must arrive at the airport at least 2 hours before his flight. It will take him 45 minutes to drive from his house to the airport. When is the latest he should plan to leave for the airport? **11:35 A.M.**

7. **GEOMETRY** What is the total number of rectangles, of any size, in the figure below? **21 rectangles**

8. **TECHNOLOGY** The price of calculators has been decreasing. A calculator sold for \$12.50 in 1990. A similar calculator sold for \$8.90 in 2000. If the price decrease continues at the same rate, what would be the price in 2020? **\$1.70**

9. **FUND-RAISING** Marissa is collecting donations for her 15-mile bike-a-thon. She is asking for pledges between \$1.50 and \$2.50 per mile. If she has 12 pledges, about how much could she expect to collect? **between \$270 and \$450**

10. **SCHOOL** Lawanda was assigned some math exercises for homework. She answered half of them in study period. After school, she answered 7 more exercises. If she still has 11 exercises to do, how many exercises were assigned? **36 exercises**

11. **SCIENCE** The Italian scientist Galileo discovered a relationship between the time of the back and forth swing of a pendulum and its length. How long is a pendulum with a swing of 5 seconds? **25 units**

Time of Swing	Length of Pendulum
1 second	1 unit
2 seconds	4 units
3 seconds	9 units
4 seconds	16 units

12. **MULTI STEP** Hiroshi is planning a party. He plans to order 4 pizzas, which cost \$12.75 each. If he has a coupon for \$1.50 off each pizza, find the total cost of the pizzas. **\$45.00**

13. **GEOMETRY** Draw the next two geometric figures in the pattern. **See margin.**

 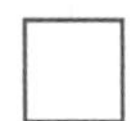  

14. **STANDARDIZED TEST PRACTICE**
Madeline rode her bicycle $\frac{1}{3}$ mile in 2 minutes. If she continues riding at the same rate, how far will she ride in 10 minutes? **A**

(A) $1\frac{2}{3}$ mi (B) $2\frac{1}{3}$ mi
(C) $2\frac{2}{3}$ mi (D) $3\frac{1}{3}$ mi

3 Practice/Apply

About the Exercises...

Problem-Solving Strategies
Exercises 6–14 are structured so that students have the opportunity to practice many different problem-solving strategies. You may wish to remind them of some of the strategies they have studied.

- four-step plan (p. 6)
- work backward (p. 45)
- look for a pattern ✓

Answers

3. **Sample answer: Sam has decided to start an exercise program. Each day of the first week, he did 10 sit-ups. Each day of the second week, he did 15 sit-ups. Each day of the third week, he did 20 sit-ups. If he continues this pattern, how many sit-ups will Sam do each day of the fifth week? To answer the problem, start with 10. Add 5 to each successive number. On the fifth week, Sam will do 30 sit-ups each day.**

13. 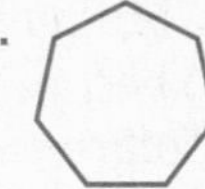 

4 Assess

Open-Ended Assessment

Speaking Have students work in small groups to create word problems involving patterns. Then have each group present a problem, including its solution, to the class.

2-8 Lesson Notes

Lesson Resources

Chapter 2 Resource Masters

- Study Guide and Intervention, p. 102
- Practice: Skills, p. 103
- Practice: Word Problems, p. 104
- Reading to Learn Mathematics, p. 105
- Enrichment, p. 106

Calculator and Spreadsheet Masters, p. 16

Key Teaching Transparencies, 8

Parent and Student Study Guide Online Worksheets, 2-8

Noteables™: Interactive Study Notebook with Foldables™, 2-8

1 Focus

5-Minute Check 2-8

Use as a quiz or review of Lesson 2-7. (Also available as a transparency)

Bellringer

Reading Mathematics Students may need some time to become familiar with the vocabulary in this lesson. Try using the following memory devices.

base Suggest that students visualize the base or foundation of a building, recipe, or idea on which to add floors of a building or variations on a recipe or theme.

(Continued in bottom margin.)

Reading to Learn Mathematics, p. 105 **ELL**

NAME ______ DATE ______ PERIOD ______

2-8 Reading to Learn Mathematics

Powers and Exponents

Pre-Activity *Read the introduction at the top of page 98 in your textbook. Write your answers below.*

1. How many 2s are multiplied to determine the number of great grandparents? 3
2. How many 2s would you multiply to determine the number of great-great grandparents? 4

Reading the Lesson

3. Define the terms *base, exponent,* and *power.* A *base* is a number that is multiplied. An *exponent* tells how many times the base appears as a factor. A *power* is a number expressed using an exponent.

For Ex... 4-6, identify the base, exponent, and power in each

2-8 Powers and Exponents

What You'll LEARN

Use powers and exponents in expressions.

NEW Vocabulary

base
exponent
power

REVIEW Vocabulary

evaluate: to find the value of an expression (Lesson 1-2)

WHEN am I ever going to use this?

FAMILY Every person has 2 biological parents. Study the family tree below.

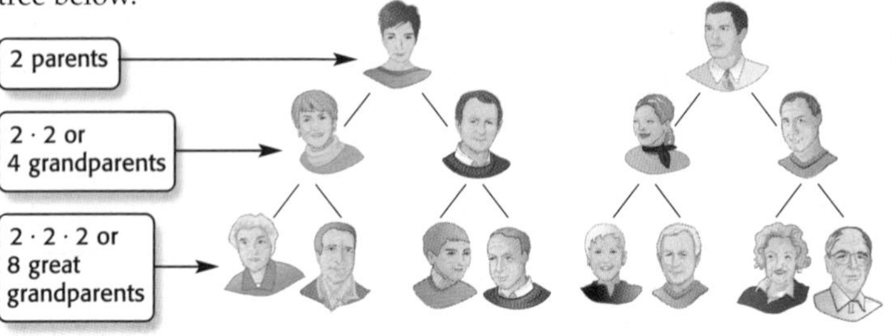

1. How many 2s are multiplied to determine the number of great grandparents? 3
2. How many 2s would you multiply to determine the number of great-great grandparents? 4

An expression like $2 \cdot 2 \cdot 2 \cdot 2$ can be written as the power 2^4.

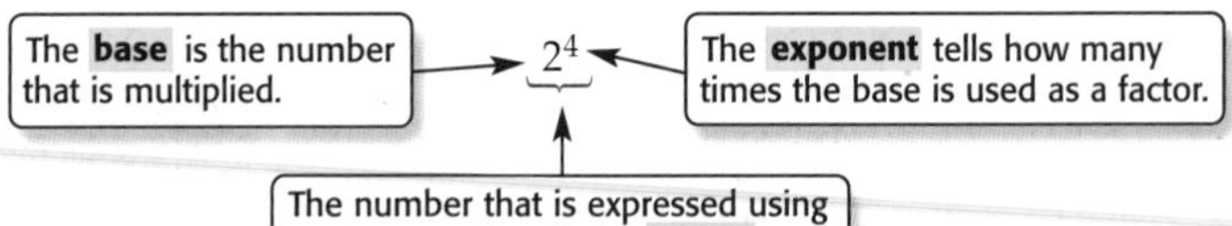

The table below shows how to write and read powers.

Powers	Words	Repeated Factors
2^1	2 to the first power	2
2^2	2 to the second power or 2 squared	$2 \cdot 2$
2^3	2 to the third power or 2 cubed	$2 \cdot 2 \cdot 2$
2^4	2 to the fourth power	$2 \cdot 2 \cdot 2 \cdot 2$
⋮	⋮	⋮
2^n	2 to the *n*th power	$\underbrace{2 \cdot 2 \cdot 2 \cdot \ldots \cdot 2}_{n \text{ factors}}$

EXAMPLE Write an Expression Using Powers

Write $a \cdot b \cdot b \cdot a \cdot b$ using exponents.

$a \cdot b \cdot b \cdot a \cdot b = a \cdot a \cdot b \cdot b \cdot b$	Commutative Property
$= (a \cdot a) \cdot (b \cdot b \cdot b)$	Associative Property
$= a^2 \cdot b^3$	Definition of exponents

exponent The word *exponent* has the same root as *expose,* which means to show or make visible. An exponent merely shows to what power the base has been raised.

You can also use powers to name numbers that are less than 1. Consider the pattern in the powers of 10.

$$10^3 = 10 \cdot 10 \cdot 10 \text{ or } 1{,}000$$
$1{,}000 \div 10 = 100$
$$10^2 = 10 \cdot 10 \text{ or } 100$$
$100 \div 10 = 10$
$$10^1 = 10$$
$10 \div 10 = 1$
$$10^0 = 1$$
$1 \div 10 = \frac{1}{10}$
$$10^{-1} = \frac{1}{10}$$
$\frac{1}{10} \div 10 = \frac{1}{10^2}$ or $\frac{1}{100}$
$$10^{-2} = \frac{1}{100}$$

STUDY TIP

Negative Exponents Remember that 10^{-2} equals $\frac{1}{10^2}$, *not* −20 or −100.

The pattern above suggests the following definitions for zero exponents and negative exponents.

Noteables™ Key Concept: Zero and Negative Exponents

Words Any nonzero number to the zero power is 1. Any nonzero number to the negative *n* power is 1 divided by the number to the *n*th power.

Symbols	Arithmetic	Algebra
	$5^0 = 1$	$x^0 = 1, x \neq 0$
	$7^{-3} = \frac{1}{7^3}$	$x^{-n} = \frac{1}{x^n}, x \neq 0$

EXAMPLES Evaluate Powers

2 **Evaluate 5^4.**

$5^4 = 5 \cdot 5 \cdot 5 \cdot 5$ Definition of exponents

$= 625$ Simplify.

Check using a calculator. 5 [^] 4 [ENTER] 625

3 **Evaluate 4^{-3}.**

$4^{-3} = \frac{1}{4^3}$ Definition of negative exponents

$= \frac{1}{64}$ Simplify.

4 **ALGEBRA Evaluate $a^2 \cdot b^4$ if $a = 3$ and $b = 5$.**

$a^2 \cdot b^4 = 3^2 \cdot 5^4$ Replace *a* with 3 and *b* with 5.

$= (3 \cdot 3) \cdot (5 \cdot 5 \cdot 5 \cdot 5)$ Definition of exponents

$= 9 \cdot 625$ Simplify.

$= 5{,}625$ Simplify.

Your Turn Evaluate each expression.

a. 15^3 **3,375** b. $2^5 \cdot 5^2$ **800** c. 5^{-4} $\frac{1}{625}$

TEACHING TIP

Remind students that according to the order of operations, they should always evaluate exponents before doing the other operations.

msmath3.net/extra_examples

2 Teach

In-Class Examples

1. Write $p \cdot p \cdot p \cdot q \cdot p \cdot q \cdot q$ using exponents. $p^4 q^3$
2. Evaluate 9^5. **59,049**
3. Evaluate 3^{-7}. $\frac{1}{2{,}187}$
4. **ALGEBRA** Evaluate $x^3 \cdot y^5$ if $x = 4$ and $y = 2$. **2,048**

Tips for New Teachers

Intervention Students who are learning to work with powers sometimes multiply the base and the exponent to evaluate. Stress that with powers, all of the factors are the same; the exponent tells how many factors there are.

$2^5 = 2 \cdot 2 \cdot 2 \cdot 2 \cdot 2$

$2^5 \neq 2 \cdot 5$

Intervention

Point out to students that 0^0 and 0 to negative powers are not defined.

DAILY INTERVENTION **Differentiated Instruction**

Kinesthetic Have students work in pairs to create patterns that model an exponential increase. Students may use beans, math cubes, or other manipulatives. Each pair of students should demonstrate their pattern to the class.

3 Practice/Apply

FOLDABLES™ Follow-Up Remind students to explain what they learn about powers and exponents on the eighth tab of their Foldables. Encourage them to compare how they reach the solution of an equation with positive exponents and the solution of an equation with negative exponents.

NUMBER SENSE
In Exercise 2, encourage students to think about whether each number is greater than 1, less than 1, or equal to 1. They should notice that the negative integer exponent makes 6^{-3} a fraction less than 1. The positive integer exponent makes 6^2 an integer greater than 1. Finally, the zero exponent means that 6^0 equals 1. Have students find the value of similar expressions to understand these properties.

About the Exercises...

Guided Practice Key

Exercises	Examples
3–5	1
6–8, 11–14	2
9	3
10	4

Assignment Guide

Basic: 15–35 odd, 39–43 odd, 45–56

Average: 15–43 odd, 45–56

Enriched: 16–44 even, 45–53 (Optional: 54–56)

Students practice the same concepts in Exercises 15–42 if they are assigned odd or even problems.

Skill and Concept Check

1. **OPEN ENDED** Write an expression with a negative exponent and explain what it means. **Sample answer:** 3^{-2}; $3^{-2} = \frac{1}{3^2}$ or $\frac{1}{9}$
2. **NUMBER SENSE** Without evaluating the powers, order 6^{-3}, 6^2, and 6^0 from least to greatest. 6^{-3}, 6^0, 6^2

GUIDED PRACTICE

Write each expression using exponents.

3. $3 \cdot 3 \cdot 3 \cdot 3 \cdot 3 \cdot 3$ 3^6
4. $2 \cdot 2 \cdot 2 \cdot 3 \cdot 3 \cdot 3$ $2^3 \cdot 3^3$
5. $r \cdot s \cdot r \cdot r \cdot s \cdot s \cdot r \cdot r$ $s^3 \cdot r^5$

Evaluate each expression.

6. 7^3 343
7. $2^3 \cdot 6^2$ 288
8. $4^2 \cdot 5^3$ 2,000
9. 6^{-3} $\frac{1}{216}$
10. **ALGEBRA** Evaluate $x^2 \cdot y^4$ if $x = 2$ and $y = 10$. 40,000

For Exercises 11–14, use the information at the right.

How Many Stars Can You See?	
Unaided Eye in Urban Area	$3 \cdot 10^2$ stars
Unaided Eye in Rural Area	$2 \cdot 10^3$ stars
With Binoculars	$3 \cdot 10^4$ stars
With Small Telescope	$2 \cdot 10^6$ stars

Source: *Kids Discover*

11. How many stars can be seen with unaided eyes in an urban area? 300 stars
12. How many stars can be seen with unaided eyes in a rural area? 2,000 stars
13. How many stars can be seen with binoculars? 30,000 stars
14. How many stars can be seen with a small telescope? 2,000,000 stars

★ indicates increased difficulty

Practice and Applications

HOMEWORK HELP

For Exercises	See Examples
15–26	1
27–38	2, 3
39–40	4

Extra Practice See pages 621, 649.

Write each expression using exponents. 19. $3^2 \cdot 4^3$

15. $8 \cdot 8 \cdot 8$ 8^3
16. $5 \cdot 5 \cdot 5 \cdot 5$ 5^4
17. $p \cdot p \cdot p \cdot p \cdot p \cdot p$ p^6
18. $d \cdot d \cdot d \cdot d \cdot d$ d^5
19. $3 \cdot 3 \cdot 4 \cdot 4 \cdot 4$
20. $2 \cdot 2 \cdot 2 \cdot 5 \cdot 5$ $2^3 \cdot 5^2$
21. $4 \cdot 7 \cdot 4 \cdot 4 \cdot 7 \cdot 7 \cdot 7 \cdot 7$ $4^3 \cdot 7^5$
22. $5 \cdot 5 \cdot 8 \cdot 8 \cdot 5 \cdot 8 \cdot 8$ $5^3 \cdot 8^4$
23. $a \cdot a \cdot b \cdot b \cdot a \cdot b \cdot b \cdot a$ a^4b^4
24. $x \cdot y \cdot y \cdot y \cdot x \cdot y \cdot y \cdot y$ $x^2 \cdot y^6$
25. Write the product $7 \cdot 7 \cdot 7 \cdot 15 \cdot 15 \cdot 7$ using exponents. $7^4 \cdot 15^2$
26. Write the product $5 \cdot 12 \cdot 12 \cdot 12 \cdot 5 \cdot 5 \cdot 5 \cdot 5$ using exponents. $5^5 \cdot 12^3$

Evaluate each expression.

27. 2^3 8
28. 3^4 81
29. 3^5 243
30. 9^3 729
31. $3^2 \cdot 5^2$ 225
32. $3^3 \cdot 4^2$ 432
33. $2^5 \cdot 5^3$ 4,000
34. $3^2 \cdot 7^3$ 3087
35. 5^{-4} $\frac{1}{625}$
36. 9^{-3} $\frac{1}{729}$
37. ★ $2^3 \cdot 7^{-2}$ $\frac{8}{49}$
38. ★ $5^2 \cdot 2^{-7}$ $\frac{25}{128}$
39. **ALGEBRA** Evaluate $g^5 \cdot h$ if $g = 2$ and $h = 7$. 224
40. **ALGEBRA** Evaluate $x^3 \cdot y^4$ if $x = 1$ and $y = 3$. 81
41. **BIOLOGY** Suppose a bacterium splits into two bacteria every 20 minutes. How many bacteria will there be in 2 hours? 64 bacteria

42. **LITERATURE** *The Rajah's Rice* is the story of a young girl named Chandra. She loved elephants and helped take care of the Rajah's elephants. The Rajah was pleased and wanted to reward her. She asked for the following reward.

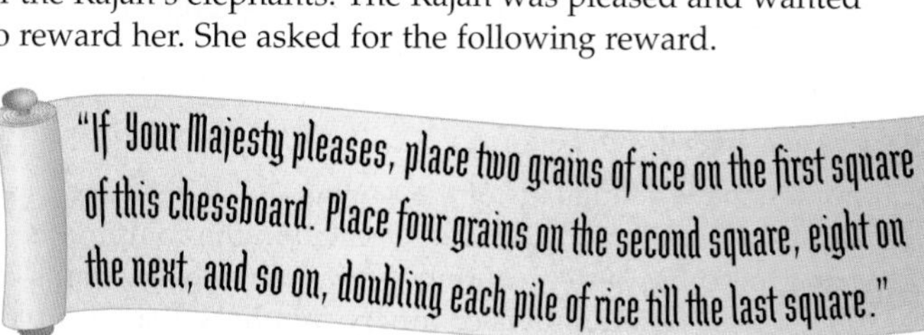

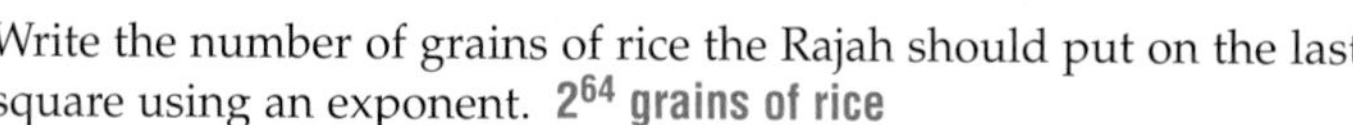

Write the number of grains of rice the Rajah should put on the last square using an exponent. **2^{64} grains of rice**

43. **GEOMETRY** To find the volume of a cube, multiply its length, its width, and its depth. Find the volume of each cube. **8 in^3; 216 in^3**

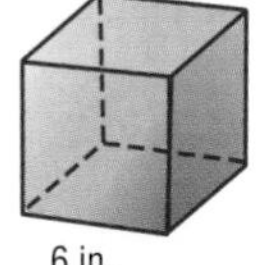

44. Continue the following pattern.
$3^4 = 81, 3^3 = 27, 3^2 = 9, 3^1 = 3,$
$3^0 = ?, 3^{-1} = ?, 3^{-2} = ?, 3^{-3} = ?$ **$1; \frac{1}{3}; \frac{1}{9}; \frac{1}{27}$**

45. **CRITICAL THINKING** Write each of the following as a power of 10 or the product of a whole number between 1 and 10 and a power of 10.

a. 100,000 **10^5**
b. fifty million **$5 \cdot 10^7$**
c. 3,000,000,000 **$3 \cdot 10^9$**
d. sixty thousand **$6 \cdot 10^4$**

Spiral Review with Standardized Test Practice

46. **MULTIPLE CHOICE** Write $5 \cdot 5 \cdot 7 \cdot 7 \cdot 7 \cdot q \cdot q$ using exponents. **B**

Ⓐ $5 \cdot 12^2 \cdot q^2$ Ⓑ $5^2 \cdot 7^3 \cdot q^2$ Ⓒ $35^2 \cdot q^2$ Ⓓ $70\,q^2$

47. **SHORT RESPONSE** Write $2^3 \cdot 6^2$ in expanded form. Then find its value. **$(2 \cdot 2 \cdot 2) \cdot (6 \cdot 6)$; 288**

48. **FOOD** Suppose hamburgers are cut in the shape of a square that is $2\frac{1}{2}$ inches on a side. Write a multiplication equation to determine how many hamburgers can fit across a grill that is 30 inches wide. Solve the equation. (Lesson 2-7) **$30 = 2\frac{1}{2}x$; 12 hamburgers**

Add or subtract. Write in simplest form. (Lesson 2-6)

49. $\frac{1}{6} + \frac{4}{9}$ **$\frac{11}{18}$**
50. $\frac{2}{5} - \frac{1}{4}$ **$\frac{3}{20}$**
51. $1\frac{1}{2} - \left(-\frac{7}{9}\right)$ **$2\frac{5}{18}$**
52. $-\frac{1}{8} + \frac{5}{6}$ **$\frac{17}{24}$**

53. **ALGEBRA** Write an algebraic expression for *12 more than a number.* (Lesson 1-7) **$x + 12$**

GETTING READY FOR THE NEXT LESSON

BASIC SKILL Write each number.

54. two million **2,000,000**
55. three hundred twenty **320**
56. twenty-six hundred **2,600**

msmath3.net/self_check_quiz

4 Assess

Higher-Level Thinking

Which of these numbers is greater: 5^{-p} or 5^{-q}? Assume that p and q are positive integers and $p > q$. Explain.

5^{-q}; Since $5^{-p} = 1/5^p$ and $5^{-q} = 1/5^q$, and since $p > q$, the denominator will be greater in $1/5^p$, resulting in a lesser fraction.

Study Guide and Intervention, p. 102

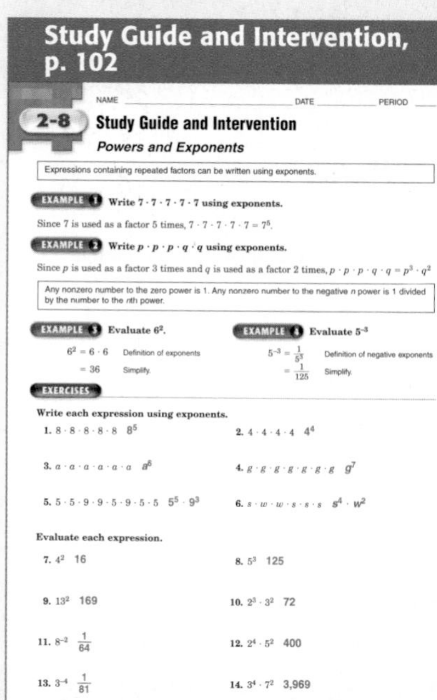

NAME ______ DATE ______ PERIOD ____

2-8 Study Guide and Intervention
Powers and Exponents

Expressions containing repeated factors can be written using exponents.

EXAMPLE 1 **Write $7 \cdot 7 \cdot 7 \cdot 7 \cdot 7$ using exponents.**

Since 7 is used as a factor 5 times, $7 \cdot 7 \cdot 7 \cdot 7 \cdot 7 = 7^5$.

EXAMPLE 2 **Write $p \cdot p \cdot p \cdot q \cdot q$ using exponents.**

Since p is used as a factor 3 times and q is used as a factor 2 times, $p \cdot p \cdot p \cdot q \cdot q = p^3 \cdot q^2$

Any nonzero number to the zero power is 1. Any nonzero number to the negative n power is 1 divided by the number to the nth power.

EXAMPLE 3 **Evaluate 6^2.**

$6^2 = 6 \cdot 6$ Definition of exponents
$= 36$ Simplify.

EXAMPLE 4 **Evaluate 5^{-3}**

$5^{-3} = \frac{1}{5^3}$ Definition of negative exponents
$= \frac{1}{125}$ Simplify.

EXERCISES

Write each expression using exponents.

1. $8 \cdot 8 \cdot 8 \cdot 8 \cdot 8$ 8^5
2. $4 \cdot 4 \cdot 4 \cdot 4$ 4^4
3. $a \cdot a \cdot a \cdot a \cdot a \cdot a$ a^6
4. $g \cdot g \cdot g \cdot g \cdot g \cdot g \cdot g$ g^7
5. $5 \cdot 5 \cdot 9 \cdot 9 \cdot 5 \cdot 9 \cdot 5 \cdot 5$ $5^5 \cdot 9^3$
6. $s \cdot w \cdot w \cdot s \cdot s \cdot s$ $s^4 \cdot w^2$

Evaluate each expression.

7. 4^2 16
8. 5^3 125
9. 13^2 169
10. $2^3 \cdot 3^2$ 72
11. 8^{-2} $\frac{1}{64}$
12. $2^4 \cdot 5^2$ 400
13. 3^{-4} $\frac{1}{81}$
14. $3^4 \cdot 7^2$ 3,969

Practice: Skills, p. 103

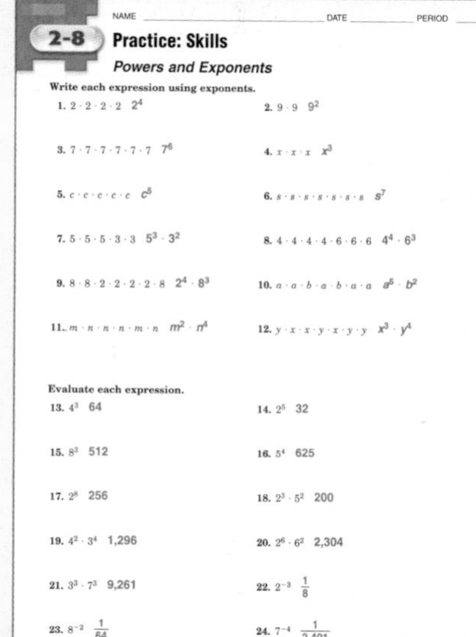

NAME ______ DATE ______ PERIOD ____

2-8 Practice: Skills
Powers and Exponents

Write each expression using exponents.

1. $2 \cdot 2 \cdot 2 \cdot 2$ 2^4
2. $9 \cdot 9$ 9^2
3. $7 \cdot 7 \cdot 7 \cdot 7 \cdot 7 \cdot 7$ 7^6
4. $x \cdot x \cdot x$ x^3
5. $c \cdot c \cdot c \cdot c \cdot c$ c^5
6. $s \cdot s \cdot s \cdot s \cdot s \cdot s \cdot s$ s^7
7. $5 \cdot 5 \cdot 5 \cdot 3 \cdot 3$ $5^3 \cdot 3^2$
8. $4 \cdot 4 \cdot 4 \cdot 4 \cdot 6 \cdot 6 \cdot 6$ $4^4 \cdot 6^3$
9. $8 \cdot 8 \cdot 2 \cdot 2 \cdot 2 \cdot 2 \cdot 8$ $2^4 \cdot 8^3$
10. $a \cdot a \cdot b \cdot a \cdot b \cdot a \cdot a$ $a^5 \cdot b^2$
11. $m \cdot n \cdot n \cdot n \cdot m \cdot n$ $m^2 \cdot n^4$
12. $y \cdot x \cdot x \cdot y \cdot x \cdot y \cdot y$ $x^3 \cdot y^4$

Evaluate each expression.

13. 4^3 64
14. 2^5 32
15. 8^3 512
16. 5^4 625
17. 2^8 256
18. $2^3 \cdot 5^2$ 200
19. $4^2 \cdot 3^4$ 1,296
20. $2^6 \cdot 6^2$ 2,304
21. $3^3 \cdot 7^3$ 9,261
22. 2^{-3} $\frac{1}{8}$
23. 8^{-2} $\frac{1}{64}$
24. 7^{-4} $\frac{1}{2{,}401}$

Practice: Word Problems, p. 104

NAME ______ DATE ______ F

2-8 Practice: Word Problems
Powers and Exponents

1. **SPORTS** In the first round of a local tennis tournament there are 2^5 matches. Find the number of matches. 32

2. **GEOMETRY** The volume of a box can be found by multiplying the length, width, and height of the box. If the length, width, and height of the box are all 5 inches, write the volume of the box using an exponent. 5^3 in^3

3. **MONEY** An apartment complex has 3 buildings. Each building has 3 apartments. There are 3 people living in each apartment, and each person pays 3 dollars per month for pool maintenance. The expression 3^4 denotes the amount paid each month for pool maintenance. Find this amount. $81

4. **ACTIVISM** A petition drive is being held in 10 cities. In each city, 10 people have collected 10 signatures each. The expression 10^3 denotes the number of signatures that have been collected altogether. Find this number. 1,000 signatures

5. **MEASUREMENT** There are 10^6 millimeters in a kilometer. Write the number of millimeters in a kilometer. 1,000,000 mm

6. **NATURE** Suppose a certain forest fire doubles in size every 12 hours. If the initial size of the fire was 1 acre, how many acres will the fire cover in 2 days? 16 acres

7. **BANKING** Suppose that a dollar placed into an account triples every 12 years. How much will be in the account after 60 years? $243

8. **BIOLOGY** Suppose a bacterium splits into two bacteria every 15 minutes. How many bacteria will there be in 3 hours? 4,096 bacteria

2-8b HANDS-ON LAB
Lesson Notes

Lesson Resources

Teaching Mathematics with Manipulatives
- student recording sheet 2-8b

GETTING STARTED

Teaching Tip Computers use several base systems, including binary, base 8, and base 16. Point out that most people have 10 fingers, which is most likely why we use the decimal system. Have students count to 20 on their fingers without using their thumbs to illustrate a base-8 system. Discuss how this would affect writing numbers using place-value columns. **There would be no digits for 8 and 9. Instead, a 1 carried to the next place value would stand in for powers of 8.**

TEACH

Activity 1
- Point out that each column in the decimal system represents a power of 10, just as each column in the binary system represents a power of 2. So 222 in base ten equals $(2 \times 10^2) + (2 \times 10^1) + (2 \times 10^0)$.

2-8b HANDS-ON LAB

A Follow-Up of Lesson 2-8

Binary Numbers

What You'll LEARN
Use binary numbers.

Materials
- paper and pencil
- grid paper

Computers have a language of their own. The digits 0 and 1, also called bits, translate into OFF and ON within the computer's electronic switches system. Numbers that use only the digits 0 and 1 are called **base two numbers** or **binary numbers**. For example, 101001_2 is a binary number. The small 2 after 101001_2 means the number is in base two.

INVESTIGATE

1. Copy and complete the table for the powers of 2.

Power of Two	2^5	2^4	2^3	2^2	2^1
Value	32	**16**	**8**	**4**	**2**

2. Use the pattern in the table to determine the value of 2^0. **1**

Find the value of each expression.

3. $2^3 + 2^2 + 2^0$ **13**
4. $2^4 + 2^2$ **20**
5. $2^5 + 2^3 + 2^2$ **44**
6. $2^5 + 2^2 + 2^0$ **37**
7. $2^4 + 2^3 + 2^2 + 2^1$ **30**
8. $2^5 + 2^4 + 2^1 + 2^0$ **51**

When using binary numbers, use the following rules.

- The digits 0 and 1 are the only digits used in base two.
- The digit 1 represents that the power of two is ON. The digit 0 represents the power is OFF.

Binary numbers can be written in our standard base ten system.

TEACHING TIP
Explain to students that base ten numbers are called decimal numbers.

ACTIVITY *Work with a partner.*

1 Write 10011_2 in base ten.

10011_2 is in base two. Each place value represents a power of 2.

1	0	0	1	1
ON	OFF	OFF	ON	ON
2^4 or 16	2^3 or 8	2^2 or 4	2^1 or 2	2^0 or 1

$$10011_2 = (1 \times 2^4) + (0 \times 2^3) + (0 \times 2^2) + (1 \times 2^1) + (1 \times 2^0)$$
$$= (1 \times 16) + (0 \times 8) + (0 \times 4) + (1 \times 2) + (1 \times 1)$$
$$= 16 + 0 + 0 + 2 + 1 \text{ or } 19$$

Therefore, 10011_2 is 19 in base ten.

Your Turn **Write each number in base ten.**

a. 10101_2 **21**
b. 1001_2 **9**
c. 110110_2 **54**

You can also reverse the process and write base ten numbers in base two.

ACTIVITY *Work with a partner.*

2 **Write 38 in base two.**

STEP 1 Make a base two place-value chart.

2^6 or 64	2^5 or 32	2^4 or 16	2^3 or 8	2^2 or 4	2^1 or 2	2^0 or 1

STEP 2 Find the greatest power of 2 that is less than or equal to 38. Place a 1 in that place value.

	1					
2^6 or 64	2^5 or 32	2^4 or 16	2^3 or 8	2^2 or 4	2^1 or 2	2^0 or 1

STEP 3 Since 38 − 32 = 6, find the greatest power of 2 that is less than or equal to 6. Place a 1 in that place value.

	1			1		
2^6 or 64	2^5 or 32	2^4 or 16	2^3 or 8	2^2 or 4	2^1 or 2	2^0 or 1

STEP 4 Since 6 − 4 = 2, find the greatest power of 2 that is less than or equal to 2. Place a 1 in that place value.

	1			1	1	
2^6 or 64	2^5 or 32	2^4 or 16	2^3 or 8	2^2 or 4	2^1 or 2	2^0 or 1

STEP 5 Since 2 − 2 = 0, place a 0 in any unfilled spaces.

0	1	0	0	1	1	0
2^6 or 64	2^5 or 32	2^4 or 16	2^3 or 8	2^2 or 4	2^1 or 2	2^0 or 1

The zero at the far left is not needed as a placeholder. Therefore, 38 in base ten is equal to 100110 in base two. Or, $38 = 100110_2$.

Your Turn **Write each number in base two.**

d. 46 **101110_2** e. 70 **1000110_2** f. 15 **1111_2**

★ **indicates increased difficulty**

Writing Math

1–2. See margin.

1. **Explain** how to determine the place value of each digit in base two.
★ 2. **Make** a place-value chart of the first four digits in base five.
3. **Identify** the digits you would use in base five. **0, 1, 2, 3, 4**
★ 4. **MAKE A CONJECTURE** Explain how to determine the place values for base *n*. What digits would you use for base *n*? **See margin.**

Activity 2

- If students find converting to base 2 difficult, try using sticks or toothpicks to represent the numbers. For example, if you have 13 toothpicks, ask "What is the largest power of 2 that you have enough sticks to show?"

Explain that since you could make 1 bundle of 8 or 2^3, you would put a 1 in the place-value column for 2^3. Now you have 5 sticks left, which is enough for 1 bundle of 4 or 2^2, so put a 1 in the place-value column for 2^2. Since $2^1 = 2$, and since you only have 1 stick left, put a 0 in the place-value column for 2^1. You have 1 stick remaining, enough to put a 1 in the place-value column for 2^0. So 13 in base ten equals $1{,}101_2$.

ASSESS

Observe as students solve the **Your Turn** exercises. They should:

- be able to convert binary numbers to base 10, and
- be able to convert decimal numbers to base 2.

Discuss the **Writing Math** exercises. Students should demonstrate an understanding of place value in any base system.

Answers

1. The first digit at the right is in the 2^0 or 1 place. As you move one place to the left, the place value is always equal to 2 times the value on the right.

2.

5^3 or 125	5^2 or 25	5^1 or 5	5^0 or 1

4. The first place on the right is n^0 or 1, the place one to the left is n^1, the place one more to the left is n^2, and so on. The digits used for base *n* are 0 to $n - 1$.

2-9 Lesson Notes

Lesson Resources

Chapter 2 Resource Masters FAST FILE
- Study Guide and Intervention, p. 107
- Practice: Skills, p. 108
- Practice: Word Problems, p. 109
- Reading to Learn Mathematics, p. 110
- Enrichment, p. 111

MathPASS Tutorial CD-ROM, 26
Parent and Student Study Guide Online Worksheets, 2-9
Noteables™: Interactive Study Notebook with Foldables™, 2-9

Focus

5-Minute Check 2-9

Use as a quiz or review of Lesson 2-8. (Also available as a transparency)

Bellringer
Problem Solving Have students solve the following problem.
In 1998, people in the United States used 80,060,000,000,000,000 Btus of fossil fuels. In 1960, they used 42,140,000,000,000,000 Btus of fossil fuels. What was the difference in Btu usage? **37,920,000,000,000,000 Btu**

Students may have noticed that most calculators will not handle such large numbers and in fact may return an incorrect answer.
(Continued in bottom margin.)

Reading to Learn Mathematics, p. 110 **ELL**

NAME ______________ DATE ________ PERIOD ____

2-9 Reading to Learn Mathematics
Scientific Notation

Pre-Activity *Read the introduction at the top of page 104 in your textbook. Write your answers below.*

1. All of the values contain 10^8. What is the value of 10^8? 100,000,000
2. How many people speak Mandarin as their native language? 874,000,000 people
3. How many people speak English as their native language? 341,000,000 people

Reading the Lesson

4. How can you tell that a number is in standard form?
There are no exponents.

Identif... positive numb... either very large or ve... small.

2-9 Scientific Notation

What You'll LEARN
Express numbers in scientific notation.

NEW Vocabulary
scientific notation

WHEN am I ever going to use this?

LANGUAGES The most frequently spoken languages are listed in the table. **1. 100,000,000**

1. All of the values contain 10^8. What is the value of 10^8?
2. How many people speak Mandarin as their native language?
3. How many people speak English as their native language?

Top Five Languages of the World

Language	Where Spoken	Number of Native Speakers
Mandarin	China, Taiwan	8.74×10^8
Hindi	India	3.66×10^8
English	U.S.A., Canada, Britain	3.41×10^8
Spanish	Spain, Latin America	3.22×10^8
Arabic	Arabian Peninsula	2.07×10^8

Source: *The World Almanac for Kids*

2. 874,000,000 people 3. 341,000,000 people

The number 8.74×10^8 is written in **scientific notation**. Scientific notation is often used to express very large or very small numbers.

Noteables™ **Key Concept: Scientific Notation**

A number is expressed in scientific notation when it is written as the product of a factor and a power of 10. The factor must be greater than or equal to 1 and less than 10.

Multiplying by a positive power of 10 moves the decimal point right. Multiplying by a negative power of 10 moves the decimal point left.

TEACHING TIP
Explain to students that 53,400 is in standard form because there are no exponents.

EXAMPLES Express Numbers in Standard Form

1 Write 5.34×10^4 in standard form.

$5.34 \times 10^4 = 5.34 \times 10{,}000$ $10^4 = 10 \cdot 10 \cdot 10 \cdot 10$ or 10,000
$= 53{,}400$ The decimal point moves 4 places to the right.

2 Write 3.27×10^{-3} in standard form.

$3.27 \times 10^{-3} = 3.27 \times \frac{1}{10^3}$ $10^{-3} = \frac{1}{10^3}$
$= 3.27 \times 0.001$ $\frac{1}{10^3} = \frac{1}{1{,}000}$ or 0.001
$= 0.00327$ The decimal point moves 3 places to the left.

Your Turn **Write each number in standard form.**

a. 7.42×10^5 **742,000** b. 6.1×10^{-2} **0.061** c. 3.714×10^2 **371.4**

Point out that while this problem is not difficult to solve by hand, doing calculations with many numbers of this size could quickly become unmanageable. Ask whether any students considered converting these figures to more manageable ones.

To write a number in scientific notation, place the decimal point after the first nonzero digit. Then find the power of 10. If a number is between 0 and 1, the power of ten is negative. Otherwise, the power of ten is positive.

STUDY TIP

Scientific Notation and Calculators To enter 3.725×10^6, use the following keystrokes.

3.725 [EE] 6

The screen will display **3.725E6**. This means 3.725×10^6.

EXAMPLES Write Numbers in Scientific Notation

3 Write 3,725,000 in scientific notation.

$3{,}725{,}000 = 3.725 \times 1{,}000{,}000$ The decimal point moves 6 places.

$= 3.725 \times 10^6$ The exponent is positive.

4 Write 0.000316 in scientific notation.

$0.000316 = 3.16 \times 0.0001$ The decimal point moves 4 places.

$= 3.16 \times 10^{-4}$ The exponent is negative.

Your Turn **Write each number in scientific notation.**

d. 14,140,000 e. 0.00876 **8.76×10^{-3}** f. 0.114 **1.14×10^{-1}**

d. 1.414×10^7

EXAMPLE Compare Numbers in Scientific Notation

REAL-LIFE MATH

TRAVEL In 2002, 5.455×10^{11} dollars were spent on travel expenditures in the United States.

Source: www.tia.org

5 TRAVEL The number of visitors from various countries to the United States in a recent year are listed in the table. Order the countries according to the number of visitors from greatest to least.

International Visitors to the U.S.A.	
Country	**Number of Visitors**
Canada	1.46×10^7
France	1.1×10^6
Germany	1.8×10^6
Japan	5.1×10^6
Mexico	1.03×10^7
United Kingdom	4.7×10^6

Source: International Trade Association

First, order the number according to their exponents. Then order the number with the same exponents by comparing the factors.

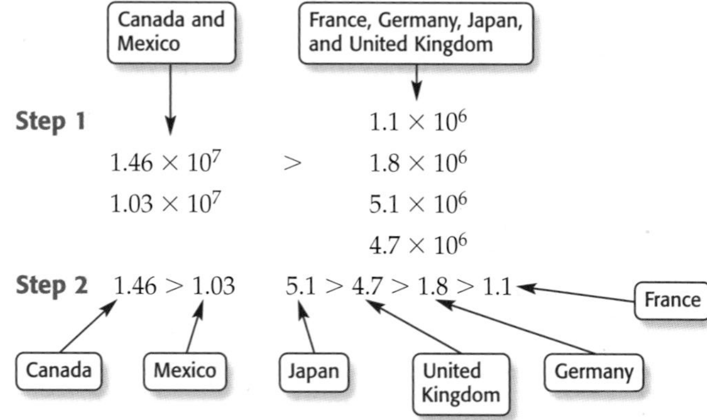

The countries in order are Canada, Mexico, Japan, United Kingdom, Germany, and France.

msmath3.net/extra_examples

2 Teach

In-Class Examples

1 Write 9.62×10^5 in standard form. **962,000**

2 Write 2.85×10^{-6} in standard form. **0.00000285**

3 Write 931,500,000 in scientific notation. **9.315×10^8**

4 Write 0.00443 in scientific notation. **4.43×10^{-3}**

5 **PLANETS** The following table lists the average radius at the equator for each of the planets in our solar system. Order the planets according to radius from largest to smallest.

Planet	Radius (km)
Earth	6.38×10^3
Jupiter	7.14×10^4
Mars	3.40×10^3
Mercury	2.44×10^3
Neptune	2.43×10^4
Pluto	1.5×10^3
Saturn	6.0×10^4
Uranus	2.54×10^4
Venus	6.05×10^3

Source: *CRC Handbook of Chemistry and Physics*

Jupiter, Saturn, Uranus, Neptune, Earth, Venus, Mars, Mercury, Pluto

DAILY INTERVENTION **Unlocking Misconceptions**

Scientific Notation When learning to write numbers in scientific notation, students may mistakenly think that a negative exponent indicates that the number is negative. Remind students of the meaning of a negative exponent. Have students solve several problems using the method shown in the following example. (*Hint:* Use a calculator for the last step.) $7.12 \times 10^{-6} = 7.12 \times \frac{1}{10^6} = \frac{7.12}{1{,}000{,}000} = 0.00000712$

3 Practice/Apply

FOLDABLES™ Follow-Up Remind students to explain what they learn about writing scientific notation on the ninth tab of their Foldables. Encourage them to collect examples of numbers they encounter in their daily life and write them in scientific notation.

NUMBER SENSE
In Exercise 3, point out to students that they will frequently use scientific notation in future science and mathematics courses. Encourage them to memorize the following facts.

1.0×10^3 = one thousand
1.0×10^6 = one million
1.0×10^9 = one billion
1.0×10^{-1} = one tenth
1.0×10^{-2} = one hundredth
1.0×10^{-3} = one thousandth

About the Exercises...

Guided Practice Key

Exercises	Examples
4–5	1
6–7	2
8–9, 12	3
10–11	4

Assignment Guide

Basic: 13–39 odd, 42–50

Average: 13–41 odd, 42–50

Enriched: 14–40 even, 42–50

Alert! The Data Update following Exercise 41 requires access to the Internet.

Answer

1. **Sometimes; if the decimal is greater than or equal to 1 and less than 10, the value is in scientific notation. If the decimal is less than 1 or greater than or equal to 10, the value is not in scientific notation.**

Students practice the same concepts in Exercises 13–40 if they are assigned odd or even problems.

Skill and Concept Check

1. Writing Math Determine whether a decimal times a power of 10 is *sometimes*, *always*, or *never* scientific notation. Explain. **See margin.**

2. **OPEN ENDED** Write a number in scientific notation that is less than 1 and greater than 0. Then write the number in standard form.
Sample answer: 1.2×10^{-2}; 0.012

3. **NUMBER SENSE** Is 1.2×10^5 or 1.2×10^6 closer to one million? Explain.
1.2×10^6; 1.2×10^5 is only 120,000, but 1.2×10^6 is just over one million.

GUIDED PRACTICE

Write each number in standard form.

4. 7.32×10^4 **73,200**
5. 9.931×10^5 **993,100**
6. 4.55×10^{-1} **0.455**
7. 6.02×10^{-4} **0.000602**

Write each number in scientific notation.

8. 277,000 **2.77×10^5**
9. 8,785,000,000 **8.785×10^9**
10. 0.00004955 **4.955×10^{-5}**
11. 0.524 **5.24×10^{-1}**

12. **CARTOONS** Use scientific notation to write the number of seconds in summer vacation according to the cartoon. **8.1216×10^6 s**

FoxTrot by Bill Amend

★ indicates increased difficulty **16. 4,265,000 19. 0.000873 20. 0.0000252**

Practice and Applications

HOMEWORK HELP

For Exercises	See Examples
13–26	1, 2
27–28, 41	5
29–39	3, 4

Extra Practice See pages 621, 649.

Write each number in standard form.

13. 2.08×10^2 **208**
14. 3.16×10^3 **3,160**
15. 7.113×10^7 **71,130,000**
16. 4.265×10^6
17. 7.8×10^{-3} **0.0078**
18. 1.1×10^{-4} **0.00011**
19. 8.73×10^{-4}
20. 2.52×10^{-5}
21. 1.046×10^6 **1,046,000**
22. 2.051×10^5 **205,100**
23. 6.299×10^{-6} **0.000006299**
24. 5.022×10^{-7} **0.0000005022**

25. **DINOSAURS** The Giganotosaurus weighed 1.4×10^4 pounds. Write this number in standard form. **14,000 lb**

26. **HEALTH** The diameter of a red blood cell is about 7.4×10^{-4} centimeter. Write this number using standard form. **0.00074 cm**

27. Which is greater: 6.3×10^5 or 7.1×10^4? **6.3×10^5**
28. Which is less: 4.1×10^3 or 3.2×10^7? **4.1×10^3**

Write each number in scientific notation. **31. 5.23×10^7 32. 1.47×10^8**

29. 6,700 **6.7×10^3**
30. 43,000 **4.3×10^4**
31. 52,300,000
32. 147,000,000
33. 0.037 **3.7×10^{-2}**
34. 0.0072 **7.2×10^{-3}**
35. 0.00000707 **7.07×10^{-6}**
36. 0.0000901 **9.01×10^{-5}**

37. **TIME** The smallest unit of time is the *yoctosecond*, which equals 0.000000000000000000000001 second. Write this number in scientific notation. **1×10^{-24} s**

38. **SPACE** The temperature of the Sun varies from 10,900°F on the surface to 27,000,000,000°F at its core. Write these temperatures in scientific notation. **(1.09×10^4)°F; (2.7×10^{10})°F**

39. **NUMBERS** A googol is a number written as a 1 followed by 100 zeros. Write a googol in scientific notation. **1×10^{100}**

40. **SCIENCE** An oxygen atom has a mass of 2.66×10^{-23} gram. Explain how to enter this number into a calculator. **2.66 [EE] [(–)] 23**

41. **BASEBALL** The following table lists five Major League Ballparks. List the ballparks from least capacity to greatest capacity.

Ballpark	Team	Capacity
H.H.H. Metrodome	Minnesota Twins	4.8×10^4
Network Associates Coliseum	Oakland Athletics	4.7×10^4
The Ballpark in Arlington	Texas Rangers	4.9×10^4
Wrigley Field	Chicago Cubs	3.9×10^4
Yankee Stadium	New York Yankees	5.5×10^4

Source: www.users.bestweb.net

41. Wrigley Field, Network Associates Coliseum, H.H.H. Metrodome, the Ballpark in Arlington, Yankee Stadium

Math Online **Data Update** What is the capacity of your favorite ballpark? Visit msmath3.net/data_update to learn more.

CRITICAL THINKING Compute and express each value in scientific notation. **42-43. See margin.**

42. $\dfrac{(130{,}000)(0.0057)}{0.0004}$

43. $\dfrac{(90{,}000)(0.0016)}{(200{,}000)(30{,}000)(0.00012)}$

Spiral Review with Standardized Test Practice

44. **MULTIPLE CHOICE** The distance from Milford to Loveland is 326 kilometers. If there are 1,000 meters in a kilometer, use scientific notation to write the distance from Milford to Loveland in meters. **D**

  Ⓐ 3.26×10^6 m
  Ⓑ 32.6×10^5 m
  Ⓒ 326×10^5 m
  Ⓓ 3.26×10^5 m

45. **SHORT RESPONSE** Name the Great Lake with the second greatest area. **Huron**

Great Lakes	
Lake	Area (square miles)
Erie	9.91×10^3
Huron	2.3×10^4
Michigan	2.23×10^4
Ontario	7.32×10^3
Superior	3.17×10^4

Source: *World Book*

46. **ALGEBRA** Evaluate $a^5 \cdot b^2$ if $a = 2$ and $b = 3$. (Lesson 2-8) **288**

ALGEBRA Solve each equation. Check your solution. (Lesson 2-7)

47. $t + 3\frac{1}{3} = 2\frac{1}{2}$ **$-\frac{5}{6}$**

48. $-\frac{2}{3}y = 14$ **-21**

49. $\frac{p}{1.3} = 2.4$ **3.12**

50. $-1\frac{3}{4} = n - 4\frac{1}{6}$ **$2\frac{5}{12}$**

msmath3.net/self_check_quiz

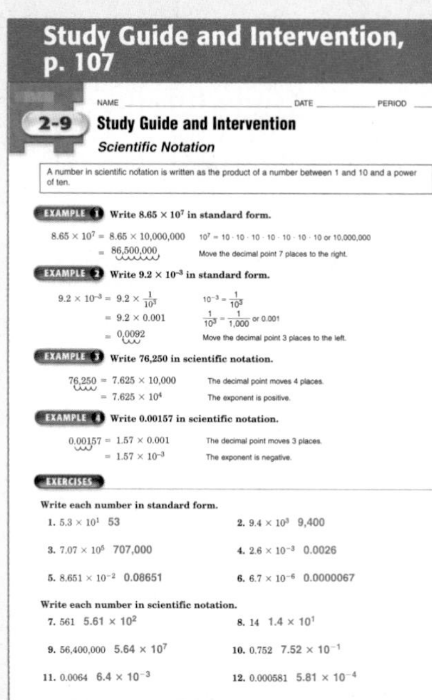

Study Guide and Intervention, p. 107

NAME ______ DATE ______ PERIOD ____

2-9 Study Guide and Intervention

Scientific Notation

A number in scientific notation is written as the product of a number between 1 and 10 and a power of ten.

EXAMPLE 1 **Write 8.65×10^7 in standard form.**

$8.65 \times 10^7 = 8.65 \times 10{,}000{,}000$ — $10^7 = 10 \cdot 10 \cdot 10 \cdot 10 \cdot 10 \cdot 10 \cdot 10$ or 10,000,000

$= 86{,}500{,}000$ — Move the decimal point 7 places to the right.

EXAMPLE 2 **Write 9.2×10^{-3} in standard form.**

$9.2 \times 10^{-3} = 9.2 \times \frac{1}{10^3}$ — $10^{-3} = \frac{1}{10^3}$

$= 9.2 \times 0.001$ — $\frac{1}{10^3} = \frac{1}{1{,}000}$ or 0.001

$= 0.0092$ — Move the decimal point 3 places to the left.

EXAMPLE 3 **Write 76,250 in scientific notation.**

$76{,}250 = 7.625 \times 10{,}000$ — The decimal point moves 4 places.

$= 7.625 \times 10^4$ — The exponent is positive.

EXAMPLE 4 **Write 0.00157 in scientific notation.**

$0.00157 = 1.57 \times 0.001$ — The decimal point moves 3 places.

$= 1.57 \times 10^{-3}$ — The exponent is negative.

EXERCISES

Write each number in standard form.

1. 5.3×10^1 53
2. 9.4×10^3 9,400
3. 7.07×10^5 707,000
4. 2.6×10^{-3} 0.0026
5. 8.651×10^{-2} 0.08651
6. 6.7×10^{-6} 0.0000067

Write each number in scientific notation.

7. 561 5.61×10^2
8. 14 1.4×10^1
9. 56,400,000 5.64×10^7
10. 0.752 7.52×10^{-1}
11. 0.0064 6.4×10^{-3}
12. 0.000581 5.81×10^{-4}

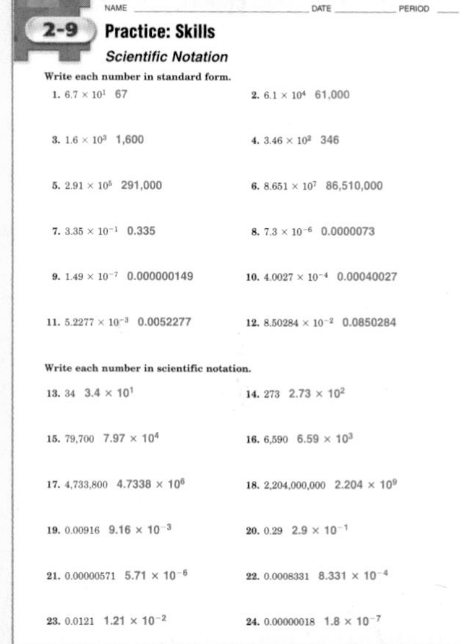

Practice: Skills, p. 108

NAME ______ DATE ______ PERIOD ____

2-9 Practice: Skills

Scientific Notation

Write each number in standard form.

1. 6.7×10^1 67
2. 6.1×10^4 61,000
3. 1.6×10^3 1,600
4. 3.46×10^2 346
5. 2.91×10^5 291,000
6. 8.651×10^7 86,510,000
7. 3.35×10^{-1} 0.335
8. 7.3×10^{-6} 0.0000073
9. 1.49×10^{-7} 0.000000149
10. 4.0027×10^{-4} 0.00040027
11. 5.2277×10^{-3} 0.0052277
12. 8.50284×10^{-2} 0.0850284

Write each number in scientific notation.

13. 34 3.4×10^1
14. 273 2.73×10^2
15. 79,700 7.97×10^4
16. 6,590 6.59×10^3
17. 4,733,800 4.7338×10^6
18. 2,204,000,000 2.204×10^9
19. 0.00916 9.16×10^{-3}
20. 0.29 2.9×10^{-1}
21. 0.00000571 5.71×10^{-6}
22. 0.0008331 8.331×10^{-4}
23. 0.0121 1.21×10^{-2}
24. 0.00000018 1.8×10^{-7}

Practice: Word Problems, p. 109

NAME ______ DATE ______ PERIOD ____

2-9 Practice: Word Problems

Scientific Notation

1. **MEASUREMENT** There are about 25.4 millimeters in one inch. Write this number in scientific notation. 2.54×10^1 mm

2. **POPULATION** In the year 2000, the population of Rahway, New Jersey, was 26,500. Write this number in scientific notation. 2.65×10^4

3. **MEASUREMENT** There are 5,280 feet in one mile. Write this number in scientific notation. 5.28×10^3 ft

4. **PHYSICS** The speed of light is about 1.86×10^5 miles per second. Write this number in standard notation. 186,000 mi per s

5. **COMPUTERS** A CD can store about 650,000,000 bytes of data. Write this number in scientific notation. 6.5×10^8 bytes

6. **SPACE** The diameter of the Sun is about 1.39×10^9 meters. Write this number in standard notation. 1,390,000,000 m

7. **ECONOMICS** The U.S. Gross Domestic Product in the year 2000 was 9.87×10^{12} dollars. Write this number in standard notation. 9,870,000,000,000 dollars

8. **MASS** The mass of planet Earth is about 5.98×10^{24} kilograms. Write this number in standard notation. 5,980,000,000,000,000,000,000,000 kg

4 Assess

Open-Ended Assessment

Writing Have students write a paragraph explaining how to use scientific notation. They should include at least two examples.

Answers

42. $\dfrac{(1.3 \times 10^5)(5.7 \times 10^{-3})}{4 \times 10^{-4}} = 1.8525 \times 10^6$

43. $\dfrac{(9 \times 10^4)(1.6 \times 10^{-3})}{(2 \times 10^5)(3 \times 10^4)(1.2 \times 10^{-4})} = 2 \times 10^{-4}$

CHAPTER 2 Study Guide and Review

Vocabulary Assessment

- This alphabetical list of vocabulary terms in Chapter 2 includes a page reference where each term was introduced.
- A vocabulary review/test for Chapter 2 is available on p. 126 of the *Chapter 2 Resource Masters*.

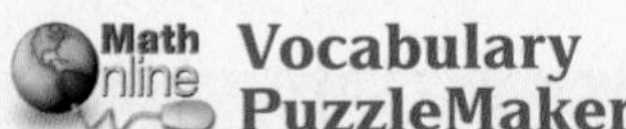

ELL The online Vocabulary PuzzleMaker improves students' mathematics vocabulary using four puzzle formats — crossword, scramble, word search using a word list, and word search using clues. Students can work on a computer screen or from a printed handout.

MindJogger Videoquizzes

ELL MindJogger Videoquizzes provide an alternative review of concepts presented in this chapter. Students work in teams in a game show format to gain points for correct answers. The questions are presented in three rounds.

Round 1 Concepts (5 questions)
Round 2 Skills (4 questions)
Round 3 Problem Solving (4 questions)

ExamView® Pro

Use the networkable ExamView® Pro Testmaker CD-ROM to:

- Create **multiple versions** of tests.
- Create **modified** tests for **inclusion** students with one mouse click.
- **Edit** existing questions and **add** your own questions.
- Build tests aligned with state standards using built-in **state curriculum correlations.**
- Change **English** tests to **Spanish** with one mouse click and vice versa.

CHAPTER 2 Study Guide and Review

Vocabulary and Concept Check

bar notation (p. 63)
base (p. 98)
dimensional analysis (p. 73)
exponent (p. 98)
like fractions (p. 82)
multiplicative inverses (p. 76)
power (p. 98)
rational number (p. 62)
reciprocals (p. 76)
repeating decimal (p. 63)
scientific notation (p. 104)
terminating decimal (p. 63)
unlike fractions (p. 88)

Choose the correct term to complete each sentence.

1. The (base, exponent) tells how many times a number is used as a factor.
2. Two numbers whose product is one are called (multiplicative inverses, rational numbers).
3. (Unlike fractions, Like fractions) have the same denominator.
4. A number that is expressed using an exponent is called a (power, base).
5. The (base, exponent) is the number that is multiplied.
6. The number 3.51×10^{-3} is written in (dimensional analysis, scientific notation).
7. The number $\frac{3}{4}$ is a (power, rational number).
8. Bar notation is used to represent a (terminating decimal, repeating decimal).

Lesson-by-Lesson Exercises and Examples

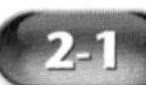

2-1 Fractions and Decimals (pp. 62–66)

Write each fraction or mixed number as a decimal.

9. $1\frac{1}{3}$ **$1.\overline{3}$**
10. $-\frac{5}{8}$ **-0.625**
11. $5\frac{13}{50}$ **5.26**
12. $-\frac{5}{6}$ **$-0.8\overline{3}$**
13. $-2\frac{3}{10}$ **-2.3**
14. $\frac{5}{9}$ **$0.\overline{5}$**

Write each decimal as a fraction or mixed number in simplest form.

15. 0.3 **$\frac{3}{10}$**
16. 3.56 **$3\frac{14}{25}$**
17. -2.75 **$-2\frac{3}{4}$**
18. -7.14 **$-7\frac{7}{50}$**
19. $4.\overline{3}$ **$4\frac{1}{3}$**
20. $-5.\overline{7}$ **$-5\frac{7}{9}$**

Example 1 Write $\frac{3}{5}$ as a decimal.

$\frac{3}{5}$ means $3 \div 5$.

$$\begin{array}{r} 0.6 \\ 5\overline{)3.0} \\ \underline{3\,0} \\ 0 \end{array}$$

The fraction $\frac{3}{5}$ can be written as 0.6.

Example 2 Write 0.25 as a fraction in simplest form.

$0.25 = \frac{25}{100}$ 0.25 is 25 hundredths.

$= \frac{1}{4}$ Simplify.

The decimal 0.25 can be written as $\frac{1}{4}$.

msmath3.net/vocabulary_review

For more information about Foldables, see *Teaching Mathematics with Foldables.*

Have students look through the chapter to make sure they have included examples in their Foldables for each lesson or topic in the chapter.

Encourage students to refer to their Foldables while completing the Study Guide and Review and to use them in preparing for the Chapter Test.

2-2 Comparing and Ordering Rational Numbers (pp. 67–70)

Replace each ● with <, >, or = to make a true sentence.

21. $\frac{2}{3}$ ● $\frac{8}{9}$ <

22. $-0.\overline{24}$ ● $-\frac{8}{33}$ =

23. $-\frac{1}{2}$ ● $-\frac{55}{110}$ =

24. $\frac{5}{6}$ ● $\frac{3}{4}$ >

25. Order $-\frac{1}{2}$, 0.75, $-\frac{3}{4}$, 0 from least to greatest. $-\frac{3}{4}, -\frac{1}{2}$, 0, 0.75

Example 3 Replace ● with <, >, or = to make $\frac{2}{5}$ ● 0.34 a true sentence.

$\frac{2}{5} = 0.4$

Since $0.4 > 0.34$, $\frac{2}{5} > 0.34$.

2-3 Multiplying Rational Numbers (pp. 71–75)

Multiply. Write in simplest form.

26. $\frac{3}{5} \cdot 1\frac{2}{3}$ 1

27. $-\frac{2}{3} \cdot \left(-\frac{2}{3}\right)$ $\frac{4}{9}$

28. $\frac{5}{6} \cdot \frac{3}{5}$ $\frac{1}{2}$

29. $\frac{1}{2} \cdot \frac{10}{11}$ $\frac{5}{11}$

30. **COOKING** Crystal is making $1\frac{1}{2}$ times a recipe. The original recipe calls for $3\frac{1}{2}$ cups of milk. How many cups of milk does she need? $5\frac{1}{4}$ c

Example 4 Find $\frac{2}{3} \cdot \frac{5}{7}$. Write in simplest form.

$\frac{2}{3} \cdot \frac{5}{7} = \frac{2 \cdot 5}{3 \cdot 7}$ ← Multiply the numerators. ← Multiply the denominators.

$= \frac{10}{21}$ Simplify.

2-4 Dividing Rational Numbers (pp. 76–80)

Divide. Write in simplest form.

31. $\frac{7}{9} \div \frac{1}{3}$ $2\frac{1}{3}$

32. $\frac{7}{12} \div \left(-\frac{2}{3}\right)$ $-\frac{7}{8}$

33. $-4\frac{2}{5} \div (-2)$ $2\frac{1}{5}$

34. $6\frac{1}{6} \div \left(-1\frac{2}{3}\right)$ $-3\frac{7}{10}$

Example 5 Find $-\frac{5}{6} \div \frac{3}{5}$. Write in simplest form.

$-\frac{5}{6} \div \frac{3}{5} = -\frac{5}{6} \cdot \frac{5}{3}$ Multiply by the multiplicative inverse.

$= -\frac{25}{18}$ or $-1\frac{7}{18}$ Simplify.

2-5 Adding and Subtracting Like Fractions (pp. 82–85)

Add or subtract. Write in simplest form.

35. $\frac{5}{11} + \frac{6}{11}$ 1

36. $\frac{1}{8} + \left(-\frac{3}{8}\right)$ $-\frac{1}{4}$

37. $\frac{1}{8} - \frac{7}{8}$ $-\frac{3}{4}$

38. $12\frac{4}{5} - 5\frac{3}{5}$ $7\frac{1}{5}$

Example 6 Find $\frac{1}{5} - \frac{3}{5}$. Write in simplest form.

$\frac{1}{5} - \frac{3}{5} = \frac{1-3}{5}$ ← Subtract the numerators. ← The denominators are the same.

$= \frac{-2}{5}$ or $-\frac{2}{5}$ Simplify.

Chapter 2 Study Guide and Review 109

Mixed Problem Solving
For mixed problem-solving practice, see page 649.

2-6 Adding and Subtracting Unlike Fractions (pp. 88–91)

Add or subtract. Write in simplest form.

39. $-\frac{2}{3} + \frac{3}{5}$ **$-\frac{1}{15}$**
40. $\frac{2}{3} + \frac{3}{4}$ **$1\frac{5}{12}$**
41. $-4\frac{1}{2} - 6\frac{2}{3}$ **$-11\frac{1}{6}$**
42. $5 - 1\frac{2}{5}$ **$3\frac{3}{5}$**
43. $7\frac{3}{4} + 3\frac{4}{5}$ **$11\frac{11}{20}$**
44. $5\frac{3}{5} - 12\frac{1}{2}$ **$-6\frac{9}{10}$**

Example 7 Find $\frac{3}{4} + \frac{1}{3}$. Write in simplest form.

$\frac{3}{4} + \frac{1}{3} = \frac{9}{12} + \frac{4}{12}$ Rename the fractions.

$= \frac{9+4}{12}$ Add the numerators.

$= \frac{13}{12}$ or $1\frac{1}{12}$ Simplify.

2-7 Solving Equations with Rational Numbers (pp. 92–95)

Solve each equation. Check your solution.

45. $d - (-0.8) = 4$ **3.2**
46. $\frac{x}{4} = -2.2$ **-8.8**
47. $\frac{3}{4}n = \frac{7}{8}$ **$1\frac{1}{6}$**
48. $-7.2 = \frac{r}{1.6}$ **-11.52**
49. **AGE** Trevor is $\frac{3}{8}$ of Maria's age. If Trevor is 15, how old is Maria? **40**

Example 8 Solve $t + \frac{1}{3} = \frac{5}{6}$.

$t + \frac{1}{3} = \frac{5}{6}$ Write the equation.

$t + \frac{1}{3} - \frac{1}{3} = \frac{5}{6} - \frac{1}{3}$ Subtract $\frac{1}{3}$ from each side.

$t = \frac{1}{2}$ Simplify.

2-8 Powers and Exponents (pp. 98–101)

Write each expression using exponents.

50. $3 \cdot 3 \cdot 3 \cdot 3 \cdot 3$ **3^5**
51. $2 \cdot 2 \cdot 5 \cdot 5 \cdot 5$ **$2^2 \cdot 5^3$**
52. $x \cdot x \cdot x \cdot x \cdot y$ **x^4y**
53. $4 \cdot 4 \cdot 9 \cdot 9$ **$4^2 \cdot 9^2$**

Evaluate each expression.

54. 5^4 **625**
55. $4^2 \cdot 3^3$ **432**
56. 5^{-3} **$\frac{1}{125}$**
57. $4^2 \cdot 2^3$ **128**

Example 9
Write $3 \cdot 3 \cdot 3 \cdot 7 \cdot 7$ using exponents.
$3 \cdot 3 \cdot 3 \cdot 7 \cdot 7 = 3^3 \cdot 7^2$

Example 10
Evaluate 7^3.
$7^3 = 7 \cdot 7 \cdot 7$ or 343

2-9 Scientific Notation (pp. 104–107)

Write each number in standard form.

58. 3.2×10^{-3} **0.0032**
59. 6.71×10^4 **67,100**
60. 1.72×10^5 **172,000**
61. 1.5×10^{-2} **0.015**

Write each number in scientific notation.

62. 0.000064 **6.4×10^{-5}**
63. 0.000351 **3.51×10^{-4}**
64. 87,500,000 **8.75×10^7**
65. 7,410,000 **7.41×10^6**

Example 11
Write 3.21×10^{-6} in standard form.
$3.21 \times 10^{-6} = 0.00000321$ Move the decimal point six places to the left.

110 Chapter 2 Algebra: Rational Numbers

Practice Test

Vocabulary and Concepts

1. **Explain** how to write a number in scientific notation. **See margin.**
2. **Write** $3 \cdot 3 \cdot 3 \cdot 3 \cdot 3$ using exponents. 3^5

Skills and Applications

Write each fraction or mixed number as a decimal.

3. $1\frac{2}{3}$ $1.\overline{6}$
4. $\frac{1}{8}$ 0.125
5. $-\frac{7}{20}$ -0.35

Write each decimal as a fraction or mixed number in simplest form.

6. 0.78 $\frac{39}{50}$
7. $0.\overline{1}$ $\frac{1}{9}$
8. 2.04 $2\frac{1}{25}$

Multiply, divide, add, or subtract. Write in simplest form.

9. $-\frac{2}{3} \cdot \frac{7}{8}$ $-\frac{7}{12}$
10. $-6 \div \frac{2}{3}$ -9
11. $-5\frac{1}{4} \cdot \left(-2\frac{1}{3}\right)$ $12\frac{1}{4}$
12. $\frac{1}{8} \div \frac{5}{6}$ $\frac{3}{20}$
13. $-\frac{5}{7} + \frac{3}{7}$ $-\frac{2}{7}$
14. $1\frac{1}{2} + \frac{2}{3}$ $2\frac{1}{6}$
15. $\frac{5}{6} - \frac{1}{2}$ $\frac{1}{3}$
16. $-\frac{7}{8} - \left(-\frac{1}{4}\right)$ $-\frac{5}{8}$

17. **BAKING** Madison needs $2\frac{3}{4}$ cups of flour. She has only $1\frac{1}{3}$ cups. How much does she need to borrow from her neighbor Raul? $1\frac{5}{12}$

18. **GEOMETRY** Find the perimeter of the rectangle. $2\frac{5}{6}$ units

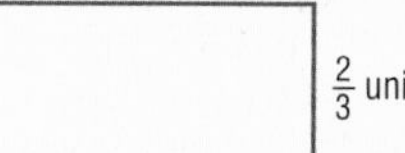

Solve each equation. Check your solution.

19. $x - \frac{5}{6} = \frac{1}{3}$ $1\frac{1}{6}$
20. $16 = \frac{2}{3}y$ 24

Write each expression using exponents.

21. $4 \cdot 4 \cdot 4 \cdot 4 \cdot 4 \cdot 5 \cdot 5 \cdot 5$ $4^5 \cdot 5^3$
22. $a \cdot a \cdot a \cdot a \cdot b \cdot b$ $a^4 \cdot b^2$

23. Write 8.83×10^{-7} in standard form. 0.000000883
24. Write 25,000 in scientific notation. 2.5×10^4

Standardized Test Practice

25. **MULTIPLE CHOICE** The table lists four movies and their running times. Which movie is the longest? **A**

    (A) Movie A (B) Movie B

    (C) Movie C (D) Movie D

Movie	Length (h)
Movie A	$2\frac{1}{4}$
Movie B	$2.1\overline{16}$
Movie C	$2\frac{1}{6}$
Movie D	$2.18\overline{3}$

Practice Test

Assessment Options

Vocabulary Test A vocabulary review/test for Chapter 2 can be found on p. 126 of the *Chapter 2 Resource Masters.*

Chapter Tests There are six Chapter 2 Tests and an Extended Response Assessment task available in the *Chapter 2 Resource Masters.*

Chapter 2 Tests			
Form	**Type**	**Level**	**Pages**
1	MC	basic	113–114
2A	MC	average	115–116
2B	MC	average	117–118
2C	FR	average	119–120
2D	FR	average	121–122
3	FR	advanced	123–124

MC = multiple-choice questions
FR = free-response questions

Extended Response Assessment

Extended Response tasks for Chapter 2 can be found on p. 125 of the *Chapter 2 Resource Masters.* A sample scoring rubric for these tasks appears on p. A31.

Answer

1. Write the number as a product of a power of 10 and a number greater or equal to 1 and less than 10.

Portfolio Suggestion

Introduction The rules for operations on integers studied in Chapter 1 are extended to rational numbers in this chapter, and will be extended to real numbers in the next chapter.

Ask Students to include an example of each of the following operations on rational numbers: multiplication, division, addition, and subtraction.

Standardized Test Practice

These two pages contain practice questions in the various formats that can be found on the most frequently given standardized tests.

A student recording sheet for these two pages can be found on page A1 of the *Chapter 2 Resource Masters.*

Standardized Test Practice Student Recording Sheet, p. A1

NAME ________ DATE ________ PERIOD ____

Standardized Test Practice SCORE ____

Student Recording Sheet (Use with pages 112–113 of the Student Edition.)

Part 1: Multiple Choice

Select the best answer from the choices given and fill in the corresponding oval.

1. Ⓐ Ⓑ Ⓒ Ⓓ 4. Ⓕ Ⓖ Ⓗ Ⓘ 7. Ⓐ Ⓑ Ⓒ Ⓓ 10. Ⓕ Ⓖ Ⓗ Ⓘ
2. Ⓕ Ⓖ Ⓗ Ⓘ 5. Ⓐ Ⓑ Ⓒ Ⓓ 8. Ⓕ Ⓖ Ⓗ Ⓘ
3. Ⓐ Ⓑ Ⓒ Ⓓ 6. Ⓕ Ⓖ Ⓗ Ⓘ 9. Ⓐ Ⓑ Ⓒ Ⓓ

Part 2: Short Response/Grid in

Solve the problem and write your answer in the blank.

For grid in questions, also enter your answer by writing each number or symbol in a box. Then fill in the corresponding circle for that number of symbol.

11. ________
12. ________
13. ________ (grid in)
14. ________ (grid in)
15. ________
16. ________
17. ________ (grid in)
18. ________

13. 14. 17.

Part 3: Extended Response

Record your answers for Questions 19 and 20 on the back of this paper.

Additional Practice

See pp. 131–132 of the *Chapter 2 Resource Masters* for additional standardized test practice.

Standardized Test Practice

PART 1 Multiple Choice

Record your answers on the answer sheet provided by your teacher or on a sheet of paper.

1. Sonia pours 8 ounces of water into a 12-ounce glass. Which of the following fractions represents how full the glass is? (Prerequisite Skill, p. 611) **B**

Ⓐ $\frac{3}{12}$ Ⓑ $\frac{2}{3}$ Ⓒ $\frac{8}{1}$ Ⓓ $\frac{12}{1}$

2. Which point is graphed at $|-3|$? (Lesson 1-3) **H**

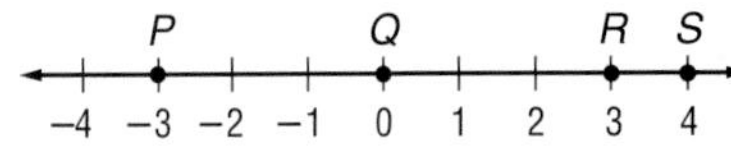

Ⓕ P Ⓖ Q Ⓗ R Ⓘ S

3. Which of the following is *not* equivalent to $(12)(-9)(-7)(5)$? (Lesson 1-6) **C**

Ⓐ $12[(-9)(-7)]5$

Ⓑ $[(12)(-9)](-7)(5)$

Ⓒ $[(12-9)](-7)(5)$

Ⓓ $[(12)(-9)][(-7)(5)]$

4. Which decimal can be written as the fraction $\frac{5}{9}$? (Lesson 2-1) **F**

Ⓕ $0.\overline{5}$ Ⓖ $0.\overline{59}$

Ⓗ 1.8 Ⓘ 9.500

5. If a whole number greater than one is multiplied by a fraction less than zero, which of the following describes the product? (Lesson 2-3) **B**

Ⓐ a number greater than the whole number

Ⓑ a negative number less than the fraction

Ⓒ a negative number greater than the fraction

Ⓓ zero

6. What is the length of the rectangle? (Lesson 2-7) **I**

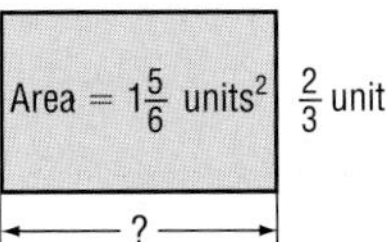

Ⓕ $\frac{4}{33}$ unit Ⓖ $\frac{4}{11}$ unit

Ⓗ $\frac{13}{9}$ units Ⓘ $\frac{11}{4}$ units

7. Which of the following represents the expression $12y^4$? (Lesson 2-8) **D**

Ⓐ $12 \cdot y \cdot 4$

Ⓑ $12 \cdot 12 \cdot y \cdot y$

Ⓒ $12 \cdot 12 \cdot 12 \cdot 12 \cdot y$

Ⓓ $12 \cdot y \cdot y \cdot y \cdot y$

8. What is the same as $(2 \cdot 2 \cdot 2)^3$? (Lesson 2-8) **H**

Ⓕ 3^2 Ⓖ 2^6 Ⓗ 8^3 Ⓘ 222^3

9. The populations of the three largest countries in the world in 2003 are given below.

Country	Population
China	1,304,000,000
India	1,065,000,000
United States	294,000,000

Source: *The World Almanac*

Which of the following does *not* express the population of the United States in another way? (Lesson 2-9) **C**

Ⓐ 2.94×10^8 Ⓑ 29.4×10^7

Ⓒ 29.4 million Ⓓ 294 million

10. What is the standard form of 4.673×10^{-5}? (Lesson 2-9) **F**

Ⓕ 0.00004673 Ⓖ 0.004673

Ⓗ 46,730 Ⓘ 467,300

ExamView® Pro

Special banks of standardized test questions similar to those on the TIMSS and NAEP grade 8 tests can be found on this CD-ROM.

Preparing for Standardized Tests
For test-taking strategies and more practice, see pages 660–677.

Standardized Test Practice

PART 2 Short Response/Grid In

Record your answers on the answer sheet provided by your teacher or on a sheet of paper. **11. Sample answers: $\frac{7}{10}, \frac{14}{20}$, 0.7**

11. Salvador has finished 28 of the 40 assigned math problems. Write this ratio in a different way. (Prerequisite Skill, p. 611)

12. At a golf tournament, a player scored 3, −4, −7, and −5. What was his total score? (Lesson 1-4) **−13**

13. Olivia made a coat rack with seven hooks. She found a board that was $31\frac{1}{2}$ inches long. She divided the board evenly, making the space at the ends of the rack the same as the space between the hooks. Each hook was $\frac{1}{2}$-inch in width. What was the space between each hook? (Lesson 2-5) **7/2**

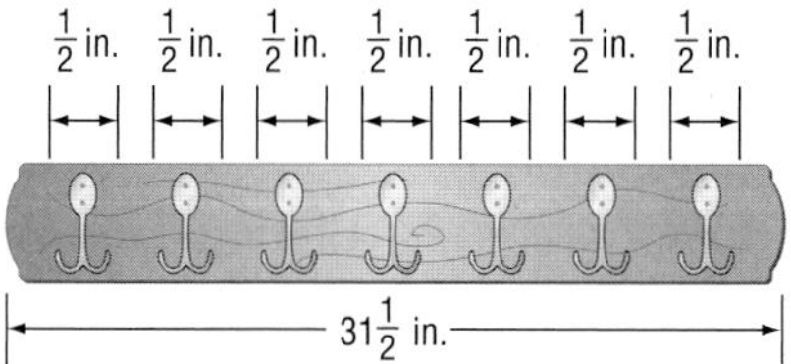

14. Logan was using 4 tiles of different lengths to make a mosaic. What is the length of the mosaic shown below? (Lesson 2-6) **39/4**

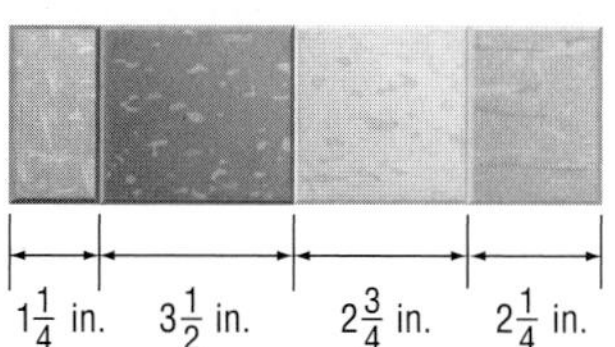

TEST-TAKING TIP

Questions 13 and 14 You cannot write mixed numbers, such as $2\frac{1}{2}$, on an answer grid. Answers such as these need to be written as improper fractions, such as 5/2, or as decimals, such as 2.5. Choose the method that you like best, so that you will avoid making unnecessary mistakes.

Math Online msmath3.net/standardized_test

15. During one week, Ms. Ito biked $1\frac{3}{8}$ miles, $1\frac{3}{4}$ miles, and $1\frac{1}{2}$ miles. What was the total distance she biked that week? (Lesson 2-6) **$4\frac{5}{8}$ mi**

16. Lindsey made $3\frac{3}{4}$ cups of chocolate milk. She poured $1\frac{1}{2}$ cups for her brother. How much did she have left? (Lesson 2-6) **$2\frac{1}{4}$ c**

17. Find the value of the expression $4^3 - 3^3$. (Lesson 2-8) **37**

18. Write an expression for the volume of the cube. (Lesson 2-8) **x^3 ft^3**

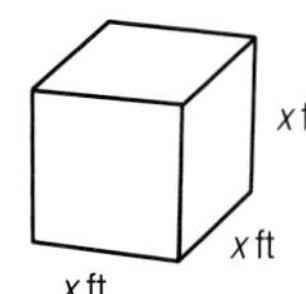

PART 3 Extended Response

Record your answers on a sheet of paper. Show your work.

19. Leo found the value of x in the equation $\frac{5x}{6} - 7 = 3$ to be 30. Is Leo correct or incorrect? Explain. (Lesson 2-7) **Incorrect; see margin.**

20. Masons are making large bricks. The container they are using is 9 inches by 9 inches by 9 inches. They have several boxes measuring 3 inches by 3 inches by 3 inches of cement that they will use to fill the large container. (Lesson 2-8)

    a. Describe how to determine the number of boxes of cement required to fill the container. **See margin.**

    b. Write and simplify an expression to solve the problem. **$\frac{9 \cdot 9 \cdot 9}{3 \cdot 3 \cdot 3} = 27$**

    c. How many boxes it will take? **27 boxes**

Rubrics The following rubrics are sample scoring devices for short response and extended response questions.

Short Response

Points	Description
2	The student demonstrates a <u>thorough understanding</u> of the mathematics of the task. The response may contain minor flaws that do not detract from the demonstration of a thorough understanding.
1	The student has provided a response that is only <u>partially correct</u>.
0	The student has provided a <u>completely incorrect</u> solution or no response at all.

Extended Response

Points	Description
4	The student demonstrates a <u>thorough understanding</u> of the mathematics of the task. The response may contain minor flaws that do not detract from the demonstration of a thorough understanding.
3	The student demonstrates an <u>understanding</u> of the mathematics of the task. The response is essentially correct and demonstrates an essential but less than thorough understanding of the mathematics.
2	The student demonstrates only a <u>partial understanding</u> of the mathematics of the task. Although the student may have used the correct approach to a solution or may have provided a correct solution, the work lacks an essential understanding of the underlying mathematical concepts.
1	The student demonstrates a <u>very limited understanding</u> of the mathematics of the task. The response is incomplete and exhibits many flaws.
0	The student provides a <u>completely incorrect</u> solution or no response at all.

A more detailed 4-point rubric is provided on page A2 of the *Chapter 2 Resource Masters*.

Answers

19. $$\frac{5x}{6} - 7 = 3$$
$$\frac{5(30)}{6} - 7 \stackrel{?}{=} 3$$
$$\frac{150}{6} - 7 \stackrel{?}{=} 3$$
$$25 - 7 \stackrel{?}{=} 3$$
$$18 \neq 3$$

20a. Find the volume of the large container, which is 9 · 9 · 9. Find the volume of a box, which is 3 · 3 · 3. Divide the volume of the large container by the volume of a box.

Chapter Overview

Algebra: Real Numbers and the Pythagorean Theorem

	LESSON OBJECTIVES	NCTM Standards	NAEP 2005	State/Local Objectives
3-1	**Square Roots** (pp. 116–119) • Find square roots of perfect squares.	1, 2, 6–10	A1a, A1b, N3f	
3-2	**Estimating Square Roots** (pp. 120–122) • Estimate square roots.	1, 6–10	A4e, N1b, N1j, N2d, N5f	
3-3	**The Real Number System** (pp. 123–129) **3-3a Problem-Solving Strategy:** Solve problems using a Venn diagram. • Identify and classify numbers in the real number system.	1, 6–10		
3-4	**The Pythagorean Theorem** (pp. 132–136) • Use the Pythagorean Theorem.	1–4, 6–10	G3c, G3d, M2a	
3-5	**Using the Pythagorean Theorem** (pp. 137–141) • Solve problems using the Pythagorean Theorem. **3-5b Hands-On Lab:** Graph irrational numbers.	1–4, 6–10	G3d, M2a	
3-6	**Geometry: Distance on the Coordinate Plane** (pp. 142–145) • Find the distance between points on the coordinate plane.	1–4, 6–10	A2c, A2d, G1a, G3d, G4a	

Key to NCTM Standards:

1=Number & Operations, 2=Algebra, 3=Geometry, 4=Measurement, 5=Data Analysis & Probability, 6=Problem Solving, 7=Reasoning & Proof, 8=Communication, 9=Connections, 10=Representation

NAEP 2005 Standards: See Teacher Resources at math.glencoe.com

Pacing suggestions for the entire year can be found on page T23.

*An electronic version of this chapter is available on **StudentWorks**™. This backpack solution CD-ROM allows students instant access to the Student Edition, lesson worksheet pages, and web resources.*

Chapter Resource Manager

Chapter 3 Resource Masters

FAST FILE

Study Guide and Intervention	Practice (Skills and Word Problems)	Reading to Learn Mathematics	Enrichment	Assessment	Applications*	Parent and Student Study Guide Online Worksheets	5-Minute Check Transparencies	Key Teaching Transparencies	MathPASS: Tutorial Plus (lessons)	Teaching Mathematics with Manipulatives	Noteables™: Interactive Study Notebook	Optional Materials
133	134–135	136	137		CS 17	3-1	3-1				3-1	
138	139–140	141	142	177	CS 18	3-2	3-2		19	42–43	3-2	
143	144–145	146	147	177, 179		3-3	3-3	9			3-3	
148	149–150	151	152		CM 7–11	3-4	3-4	10	20	44–45	3-4	
153	154–155	156	157	178	CS 19	3-5	3-5	11		46	3-5	compass, straightedge
158	159–160	161	162	163–176, 178, 180–182	CS 20 RC 29	3-6	3-6	12		47	3-6	

*** Key to Abbreviations:** *CS = Calculator and Spreadsheet Masters, RC = Real-Life Career Masters, CM = Classroom Math Games (online), SM = Science and Math Lab Manual (online)*

PowerPoint® Presentations

This CD-ROM is a customizable Microsoft® PowerPoint® presentation that includes:

- Step-by-step, dynamic solutions of each In-Class Example from the Teacher Wraparound Edition
- Additional, Your Turn exercises for each example
- 5-Minute Check Transparencies
- Hot links to Glencoe Online Study Tools

Math Skills Maintenance

Use the Math Skills Maintenance Masters to keep your students' basic math skills fresh. Students can review skills one at a time or in a combined format. The Masters are also available online at msmath3.net/maintenance.

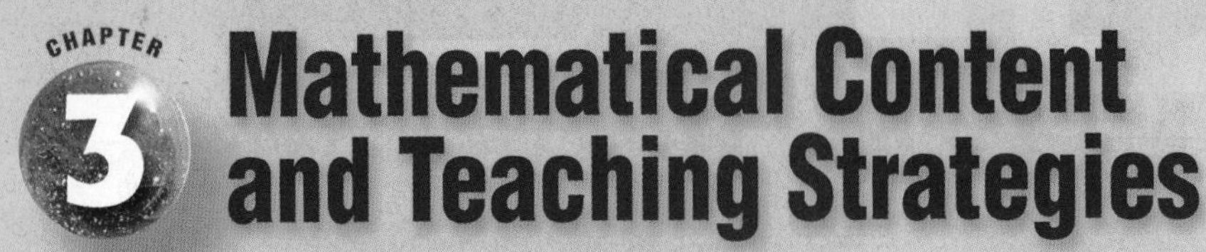

Continuity of Instruction

Building on Prior Knowledge

In Chapter 1, students learned to solve for variables algebraically by performing inverse operations to each side of an equation. In the previous chapter, students explored and compared rational numbers. Students also learned how to square numbers when they studied powers and exponents.

Learning in This Chapter

Students learn how to take the square roots of certain fractions, decimals, and perfect squares, and to estimate the square roots of whole numbers that are not perfect squares. They will discover the difference between rational and irrational numbers and compare these numbers using number lines. Students will use the Pythagorean Theorem to solve a variety of application and distance problems. They will use their knowledge of algebra to isolate and solve for variables while working with the Pythagorean Theorem.

Making Future Connections

Evaluating and estimating square roots is essential for solving quadratic equations and working with complex numbers in advanced algebra. Irrational numbers play an important role in geometry and trigonometry. The Pythagorean Theorem shows students how math can be used to solve geometric problems that arise in everyday life. It also helps prepare them for work with the distance formula in high school geometry courses.

Mathematical Background

3-1 Square Roots

Taking the square root of a number is the opposite of squaring it. The square root function has been in use since well before the 15th century and seems to have developed from the area equation for a square. Given the length of the side of a square, the area can be found by squaring the number. But, if you want a square of a given area, you need to find the length of the side. To find the exact square root of a number without a calculator takes more advanced math than that covered in this course.

3-2 Estimating Square Roots

Being able to estimate a square root is a good way to check answers. The calculator only gives an estimate of some square roots because calculators typically truncate a number after eight digits. Many equations in science and math involve squared values. Understanding the square root is important to the understanding of these equations.

3-3 The Real Number System

The real number system is made up of rational and irrational numbers. Rational numbers are numbers with decimals that terminate or repeat. Irrational numbers are numbers that cannot be expressed as fractions of integers. Many square roots are irrational numbers.

Teacher to Teacher

Diane Stilwell
South Middle School
Morgantown, WV

"I ask the students if they have ever noticed anyone behaving irrationally. After a discussion on irrational versus rational behavior, we note the *rational* behavior of rational numbers. In conclusion, real numbers are like real life—everyone, whether rational or irrational, is included."

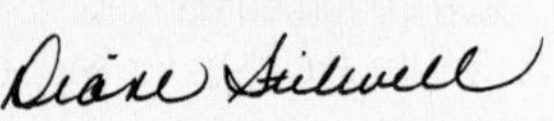

3-4 The Pythagorean Theorem

Pythagoras was born in 569 B.C. in Greece. He founded a group, the Brotherhood of Pythagoreans, which was devoted to the study of mathematics. This group discovered irrational numbers. However, they felt these numbers were "unutterable." Irrational numbers were not dealt with until 200 years later when Eudoxus, another Greek mathematician, developed a way to deal with these numbers.

Bulletin Board Starters

The second half of this chapter is centered around using the Pythagorean Theorem. Have students suggest a variety of ways to use the Pythagorean Theorem to solve problems involving right triangles. As they develop these real-life applications, ask students to illustrate their ideas using creative, colorful designs and post them on a bulletin board. They may wish to use pictures from newspapers or magazines that have right triangles in them. You may want to have a basic right triangle labeled appropriately in the center of the board.

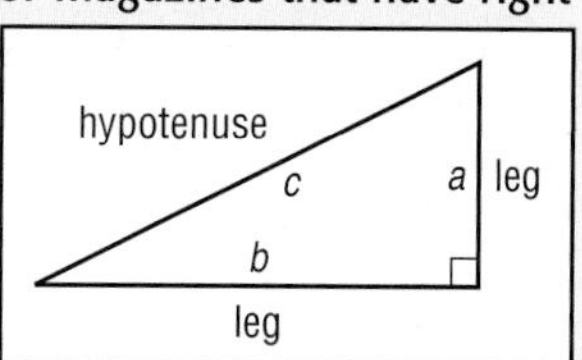

3-5 Using the Pythagorean Theorem

The Pythagorean Theorem shows the relationships among the legs of a right triangle. Knowing any two will lead you to the third. This theorem is used in math, science, astronomy, architecture, surveying, construction, and so on. Any field that uses measurements has the potential to use the Pythagorean Theorem.

3-6 Geometry: Distance on the Coordinate Plane

René Descartes developed the coordinate plane in the late 1500s. It is often called the Cartesian plane in his honor. This grid system is used in many areas such as map-making, surveying, town planning and development, and construction. Our use of latitude and longitude for mapping the world is based on the use of the Cartesian coordinate system.

In-Class Speaker

Architects design buildings using a multitude of line segments, planes, angles, rectangles, and triangles. Invite an architect to come in and speak to the class about areas, square footage, and applications of the Pythagorean Theorem.

What the Research Says

According to Marzano, Pickering, and Pollock in *Classroom Instruction that Works: Research Based Strategies for Increasing Student Achievement,* the mental operations of comparing and classifying are central to thinking.

- In Lesson 3-3, students use a Venn diagram and a web to classify the set of real numbers.

McGraw-Hill Professional Development

Mathematics, YES! is a a self-paced, web-based professional development program. Units are based on major mathematical concepts and are standards-based. Actual classroom videos provide a springboard for discussion and activities. Units appropriate for this chapter:

- Coordinate Pairs and Graphing
- Geometry and Measurement of Plane Figures

Additional mathematical information and teaching notes are available at **msmath3.net/key_concepts**.

DAILY INTERVENTION and Assessment

* **Key to Abbreviations:**
TWE = Teacher Wraparound Edition, *CRM* = Chapter Resource Masters

	Type	Student Edition	Teacher Resources	Technology/Internet
INTERVENTION	Ongoing	Prerequisite Skills, pp. 115, 119, 122, 129, 136, 140 Mid-Chapter Practice Test, p. 130	5-Minute Check Transparencies Quizzes 1–4, *CRM*, pp. 177–178 Mid-Chapter Test, *CRM*, p. 179 Study Guide and Intervention, *CRM*, pp. 133, 138, 143, 148, 153, 158	MathPASS: Tutorial Plus msmath3.net/self_check_quiz msmath3.net/extra_examples
	Mixed Review	pp. 119, 122, 129, 136, 140, 145	Cumulative Review, *CRM*, p. 180	
	Error Analysis	Find the Error, pp. 118, 121, 135	Find the Error, *TWE*, pp. 118, 121, 135 Unlocking Misconceptions, *TWE*, p. 117	
ASSESSMENT	Standardized Test Practice	pp. 119, 122, 124, 129, 130, 134, 136, 140, 145, 149, 150–151	Standardized Test Practice, *CRM*, pp. 181–182	Standardized Test Practice CD-ROM msmath3.net/standardized_test
	Open-Ended Assessment	Writing Math, pp. 118, 138, 141 Open-Ended, pp. 118, 121, 128, 135, 138, 144 Standardized Test, p. 151	Modeling: *TWE*, p. 136 Speaking: *TWE*, pp. 124, 129 Writing: *TWE*, p. 122 Extended Response Assessment, *CRM*, p. 175	
	Chapter Assessment	Study Guide, pp. 146–148 Practice Test, p. 149	Multiple-Choice Tests (Forms 1, 2A, 2B), *CRM*, pp. 163–168 Free-Response Tests (Forms 2C, 2D, 3), *CRM*, pp. 169–174 Vocabulary Test/Review, *CRM*, p. 176	ExamView® Pro Testmaker (see below) MindJogger Videoquizzes msmath3.net/vocabulary_review msmath3.net/chapter_test

For more information on Yearly ProgressPro, see p. 2.

Glencoe Lesson	Yearly ProgressPro Skill Name
3-1	Square Roots Solve Equations Using Square Roots
3-2	Estimating Square Roots
3-3	Classify Real Numbers
3-4	Pythagorean Theorem
3-5	Using the Pythagorean Theorem
3-6	Distance on the Coordinate Plane

ExamView® Pro

Use ExamView® Pro Testmaker CD-ROM to:

- Create multiple versions of tests.
- Create modified tests for inclusion students with one mouse click.
- Edit existing questions and add your own questions.
- Build tests aligned with state standards using built-in state curriculum correlations.
- Change English tests to Spanish with one mouse click and vice versa.

Reading and Writing in Mathematics

READING in the Content Area

This online worksheet provides strategies for reading and analyzing Lesson 3-1, Square Roots. Students are guided through questions about the main idea, subject matter, supporting details, conclusion, clarifying details, and vocabulary of the lesson.

Interactive Study Notebook With Foldables™ is a study organizer that provides helpful steps for students to follow to organize their notes for Chapter 3.

- Students use Noteables to record notes and to complete their Foldables as you present the material in Lessons 3-1 through 3-6.
- Noteables follow the *Teacher Wraparound Edition's* In-Class Examples and *Interactive Chalkboard CD-ROM*.

For more information on Reading and Writing in Mathematics, see pp. T6–T7.

Recommended Outside Reading for Students

Nonfiction

- Bunch, Bryan. *The Kingdom of Infinite Numbers*. W. H. Freeman and Company, ©2000.

  This book examines the relationships among real numbers as well as the properties and history of various real numbers. A great emphasis is placed on irrational numbers and perfect squares, which are topics students will study in Chapter 3.

Fiction

- Ellis, Julie. *Pythagoras Gets the Right Angle: A Math Adventure*. Charlesbridge Publishing, ©2003.

  This is a comical story about what Pythagoras might have been like as a child. The book recounts his adventures as he tries to discover the Pythagorean Theorem.

PROJECT CRISS℠ Study Skill

Encourage students to create frames to organize their notes. The math frame below describes the Pythagorean Theorem, which students learn in Lesson 3-4. Creating frames helps students understand topics by explaining them in their own words. Frames also allow students to quickly review information in the chapter.

Term/ Concept	Definition (in your own words)	Formula	Original Question with Answer
Pythagorean Theorem	In a right triangle, the square of the length of the hypotenuse is equal to the sum of the squares of the lengths of the legs.	$c^2 = a^2 + b^2$ 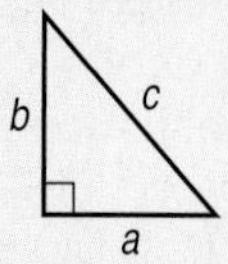 (right triangle with legs a, b and hypotenuse c)	A triangular tent has sides that are 5 feet long. If the distance from a side to the center is 3 feet, how tall is the tent? $3^2 + h^2 = 5^2$, $h = 4$ 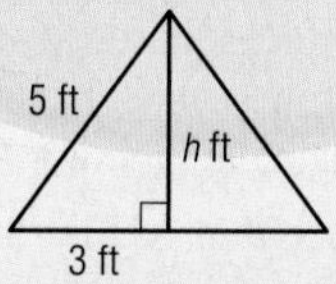 (figure labels: 5 ft, h ft, 3 ft)

CReating Independence through Student-owned Strategies

For more information on Project CRISS, see p. T8.

Making Connections

School-To-Home

Parent and Student Study Guide

Parents and students may work together to reinforce the concepts and skills of this chapter. These online worksheets are available in English and Spanish at msmath3.net/parent_student. A sample lesson is shown below.

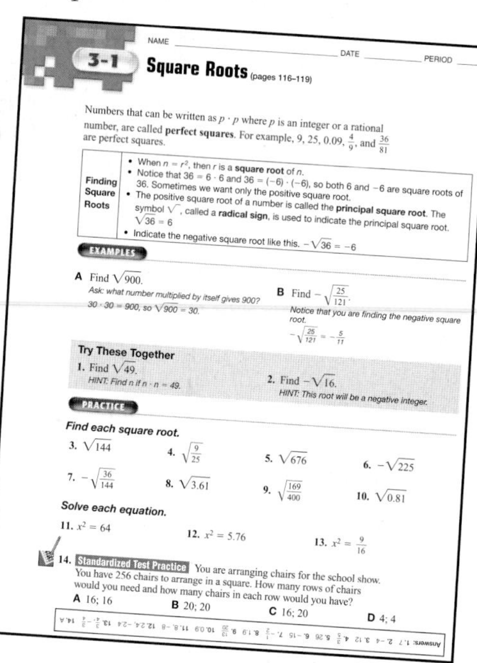

NAME ________________ DATE ________ PERIOD ____

3-1 Square Roots (pages 116–119)

Numbers that can be written as $p \cdot p$ where p is an integer or a rational number, are called **perfect squares**. For example, 9, 25, 0.09, $\frac{4}{9}$, and $\frac{36}{81}$ are perfect squares.

Finding Square Roots	• When $n = r^2$, then r is a **square root** of n. • Notice that $36 = 6 \cdot 6$ and $36 = (-6) \cdot (-6)$, so both 6 and −6 are square roots of 36. Sometimes we want only the positive square root. • The positive square root of a number is called the **principal square root**. The symbol $\sqrt{\ }$, called a **radical sign**, is used to indicate the principal square root. $\sqrt{36} = 6$ • Indicate the negative square root like this. $-\sqrt{36} = -6$

EXAMPLES

A Find $\sqrt{900}$.
Ask: what number multiplied by itself gives 900?
$30 \cdot 30 = 900$, so $\sqrt{900} = 30$.

B Find $-\sqrt{\frac{25}{121}}$.
Notice that you are finding the negative square root.
$-\sqrt{\frac{25}{121}} = -\frac{5}{11}$

Try These Together

1. Find $\sqrt{49}$.
HINT: Find n if $n \cdot n = 49$.

2. Find $-\sqrt{16}$.
HINT: This root will be a negative integer.

PRACTICE

Find each square root.

3. $\sqrt{144}$
4. $\sqrt{\frac{9}{25}}$
5. $\sqrt{676}$
6. $-\sqrt{225}$
7. $-\sqrt{\frac{36}{144}}$
8. $\sqrt{3.61}$
9. $\sqrt{\frac{169}{400}}$
10. $\sqrt{0.81}$

Solve each equation.

11. $x^2 = 64$
12. $x^2 = 5.76$
13. $x^2 = \frac{9}{16}$

14. **Standardized Test Practice** You are arranging chairs for the school show. You have 256 chairs to arrange in a square. How many rows of chairs would you need and how many chairs in each row would you have?
A 16; 16 **B** 20; 20 **C** 16; 20 **D** 4; 4

Answers: 1. 7 2. −4 3. 12 4. $\frac{3}{5}$ 5. 26 6. −15 7. $-\frac{1}{2}$ 8. 1.9 9. $\frac{13}{20}$ 10. 0.9 11. 8, −8 12. 2.4, −2.4 13. $\frac{3}{4}$, $-\frac{3}{4}$ 14. A

Family Letters and Activities

Send a letter and activity for this chapter home to encourage family members to become active participants in their students' learning. (English: *Chapter3 Resource Masters*, pp. ix–x; Spanish: log on to msmath3.net/family_letters)

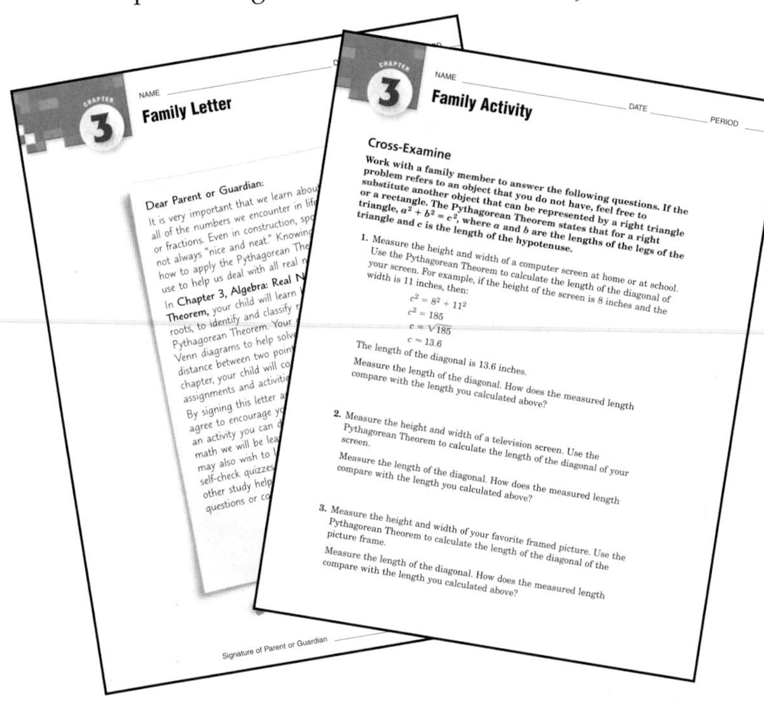

NAME ________________

Family Letter

Dear Parent or Guardian:
It is very important that we learn abou
all of the numbers we encounter in lif
or fractions. Even in construction, sp
not always "nice and neat." Knowin
how to apply the Pythagorean The
use to help us deal with all real n
In **Chapter 3, Algebra: Real N**
Theorem, your child will learn
roots, to identify and classify r
Pythagorean Theorem. Your
Venn diagrams to help solv
distance between two poin
chapter, your child will co
assignments and activiti
By signing this letter a
agree to encourage y
an activity you can d
math we will be lea
may also wish to
self-check quizzes
other study help
questions or co

Signature of Parent or Guardian ________________

NAME ________________ DATE ________ PERIOD ____

Family Activity

Cross-Examine

Work with a family member to answer the following questions. If the problem refers to an object that you do not have, feel free to substitute another object that can be represented by a right triangle or a rectangle. The Pythagorean Theorem states that for a right triangle, $a^2 + b^2 = c^2$, where a and b are the lengths of the legs of the triangle and c is the length of the hypotenuse.

1. Measure the height and width of a computer screen at home or at school. Use the Pythagorean Theorem to calculate the length of the diagonal of your screen. For example, if the height of the screen is 8 inches and the width is 11 inches, then:

$$c^2 = 8^2 + 11^2$$
$$c^2 = 185$$
$$c = \sqrt{185}$$
$$c \approx 13.6$$

The length of the diagonal is 13.6 inches.

Measure the length of the diagonal. How does the measured length compare with the length you calculated above?

2. Measure the height and width of a television screen. Use the Pythagorean Theorem to calculate the length of the diagonal of your screen.

Measure the length of the diagonal. How does the measured length compare with the length you calculated above?

3. Measure the height and width of your favorite framed picture. Use the Pythagorean Theorem to calculate the length of the diagonal of the picture frame.

Measure the length of the diagonal. How does the measured length compare with the length you calculated above?

English Language Learner ELL

Lesson 3-2a

Using Models

Have students make a list from 1 to 20 and multiply each number by itself. Using the list, have students find approximations of square roots of numbers that are not perfect squares. Model this by showing the students how to take the square root of 83. Have the students look on their list of perfect squares to see between which two perfect squares 83 lies. By looking at their list, students can see that $\sqrt{81} = 9$ and $\sqrt{100} = 10$, so $\sqrt{83}$ is between 9 and 10.

Lesson 3-3

Building on Prior Knowledge

Review whole numbers and integers. Then discuss rational numbers and irrational numbers. Have students use the information to design their own Venn diagram or semantic web. (Do not have the students look at the one provided in the lesson).

Lesson 3-5

Reading and Writing

Give groups of students a list of triples and have the students check to see whether the triples are Pythagorean triples. Also, have students write an explanation of why each triple is or is not a Pythagorean triple.

MathScape™  This project was supported, in part, by the **National Science Foundation**

MathScape is a mathematics curriculum for grades 6–8 developed by the Seeing and Thinking Mathematically Project at the Education Development Center.

Slopes, Angles, and Ratios
Roads and Ramps

How to Use *MathScape* with Chapter 3

The unit *Roads and Ramps* can be used to enhance Lessons 3-4 and 3-5.

- **Introduce** → Before you begin **Lesson 3-4,** you can introduce the Pythagorean Theorem by using the activity on page 236 and the writing activity at the top of page 237.
- **Reinforce** → After you complete **Lesson 3-5,** you can ask students to use the Pythagorean Theorem to complete the real-life activities on pages 238–239.

For other lessons in Chapter 3 that correlate to *MathScape*, see the chart on page T14.

Online Lesson Planner

USA TODAY® Education's Online site offers resources and interactive features connected to each day's newspaper. *Experience Today,* USA TODAY's® daily lesson plan, is available on the site and delivered daily to subscribers. This plan provides instruction for integrating USA TODAY® graphics and key editorial features into your mathematics classroom. Log on to **education.usatoday.com**.

USA TODAY Snapshots® in Chapter 3	
Lesson	**Snapshot**
3-3	Tallest lighthouses

Quick Review Math Handbook

is Glencoe's mathematical handbook for students. The Hot Words section includes a glossary of terms while the Hot Topics section consists of explanations of key mathematical concepts. An exercise set is included to check students' understanding of the concepts. This valuable resource can be used as a reference in the classroom or for home study.

Lesson	Hot Topics Section	Lesson	Hot Topics Section
3-1	3-2	**3-4**	3-2, 7-9
3-2	3-2	**3-5**	3-2, 7-9, 8-2
3-3	1-1	**3-6**	6-7, 8-2

Notes

Key Chapter Objectives

Lessons 3-1 and 3-2 Find square roots of perfect squares and estimate square roots.

Lessons 3-4 and 3-5 Use the Pythagorean Theorem and solve problems using it.

Lesson 3-6 Find the distance between points on the coordinate plane.

"How far can you see from a tall building?"

Point out to students that this is only one of many applications of the math that they are studying. Others are provided in the introduction to each lesson.

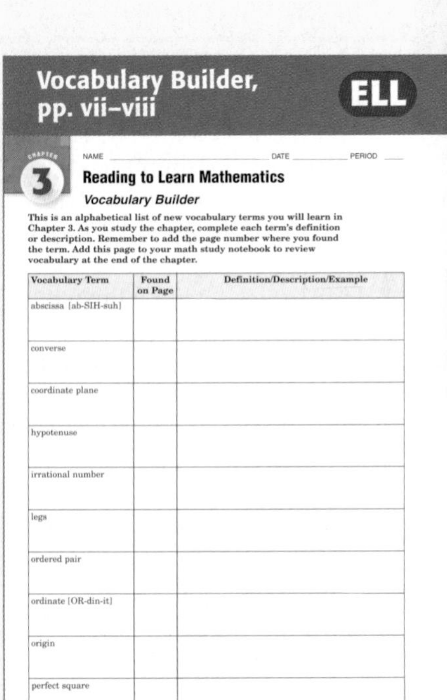

Vocabulary Builder, pp. vii–viii ELL

NAME ______ DATE ______ PERIOD ______

Reading to Learn Mathematics

Vocabulary Builder

This is an alphabetical list of new vocabulary terms you will learn in Chapter 3. As you study the chapter, complete each term's definition or description. Remember to add the page number where you found the term. Add this page to your math study notebook to review vocabulary at the end of the chapter.

Vocabulary Term	Found on Page	Definition/Description/Example
abscissa [ab-SIH-suh]		
converse		
coordinate plane		
hypotenuse		
irrational number		
legs		
ordered pair		
ordinate [OR-din-it]		
origin		
perfect square		

Chapter 3 Algebra: Real Numbers and the Pythagorean Theorem

"How far can you see from a tall building?"

The Sears Tower in Chicago is 1,450 feet high. You can determine approximately how far you can see from the top of the Sears Tower by multiplying 1.23 by $\sqrt{1,450}$. The symbol $\sqrt{1,450}$ represents the square root of 1,450.

You will solve problems about how far a person can see from a given height in Lesson 3-3.

Vocabulary Builder

For a thorough vocabulary list with pronunciations of new words, give students the Vocabulary Builder worksheets from the *Chapter 3 Resource Masters*. Encourage them to complete the definition of each term as they progress through the chapter.

GETTING STARTED

▶ Diagnose Readiness

Take this quiz to see if you are ready to begin Chapter 3. Refer to the lesson or page number in parentheses for review.

Vocabulary Review

State whether each sentence is *true* or *false*. If *false*, replace the underlined word to make a true sentence.

1. The number 0.6 is a rational number. (Lesson 2-1) **true**
2. In the number 3^2, the base is 2. (Lesson 2-8) **false; exponent**

Prerequisite Skills

Graph each point on a coordinate plane. (Page 614) **3–6. See margin.**

3. $A(-1, 3)$
4. $B(2, -4)$
5. $C(-2, -3)$
6. $D(-4, 0)$

Evaluate each expression. (Lesson 1-2)

7. $2^2 + 4^2$ **20**
8. $3^2 + 3^2$ **18**
9. $10^2 + 8^2$ **164**
10. $7^2 + 5^2$ **74**

Solve each equation. Check your solution. (Lesson 1-8)

11. $x + 13 = 45$ **32**
12. $56 + d = 71$ **15**
13. $101 = 39 + a$ **62**
14. $62 = 45 + m$ **17**

Express each decimal as a fraction in simplest form. (Lesson 2-1)

15. $0.\overline{6}$ $\frac{2}{3}$
16. 0.35 $\frac{7}{20}$
17. 0.375 $\frac{3}{8}$

Between which two of the following numbers does each number lie? 1, 4, 9, 16, 25, 36, 49, 64, 81 (Lesson 2-2)

18. 38 **36, 49**
19. 74 **64, 81**

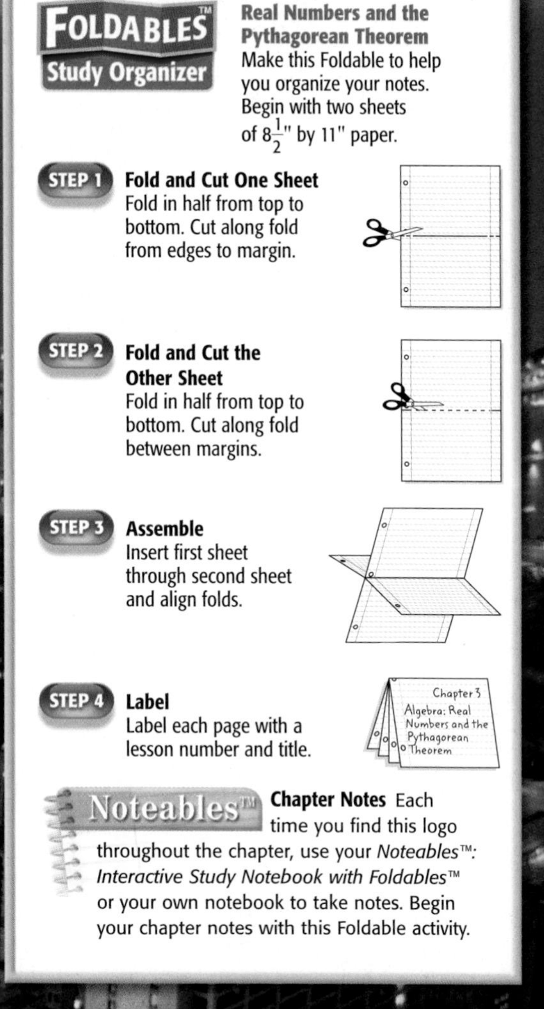

Math Online **Readiness** To prepare yourself for this chapter with another quiz, visit **msmath3.net/chapter_readiness**

GETTING STARTED

Diagnose Readiness This section provides a review of the basic concepts needed before beginning Chapter 3. Page references are included for additional student help.

Prerequisite Skills review skills needed in this chapter.

Exercises	Needed for Lesson	Skill
3–6	3-6	Graph Points
7–10	3-4	Evaluate Expressions
11–14	3-4, 3-5	Solve Equations
15–17	3-3	Express Decimals as Fractions
18–19	3-2	Order Whole Numbers

For more prerequisite skills, see:

- Getting Ready for the Next Lesson, at the end of each lesson
- Prerequisite Skills in the Student Handbook on pp. 600–615
- *Math Skills Maintenance Masters*

Answers

3–6.

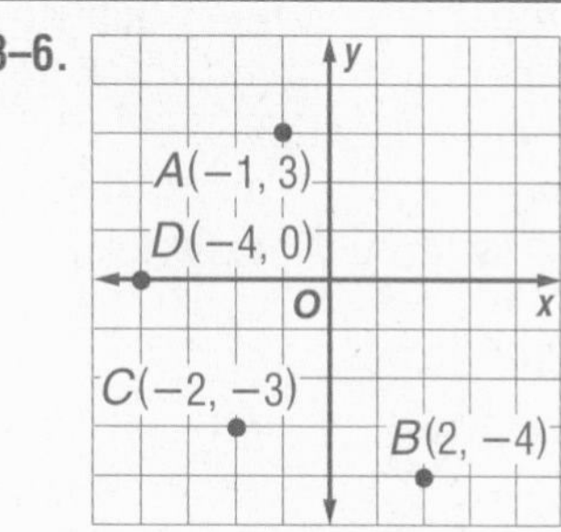

FOLDABLES™ Study Organizer

For more information about Foldables, see *Teaching Mathematics with Foldables.*

Students can use their Foldables to take notes, define terms, record concepts, and write examples. Writer's journals can also be used by students for the following: to record the direction and progress of learning, to describe positive and negative experiences during learning, to write about personal associations and experiences called to mind during learning, and to list examples of ways in which new knowledge has or will be used in their daily lives.

3-1 Lesson Notes

Lesson Resources

Chapter 3 Resource Masters
- Study Guide and Intervention, p. 133
- Practice: Skills, p. 134
- Practice: Word Problems, p. 135
- Reading to Learn Mathematics, p. 136
- Enrichment, p. 137

Calculator and Spreadsheet Masters, p. 17

Parent and Student Study Guide Online Worksheets, 3-1

Noteables™: Interactive Study Notebook with Foldables™, 3-1

FAST FILE

1 Focus

5-Minute Check 3-1

Use as a quiz or review of Chapter 2. (Also available as a transparency)

Bellringer

Problem Solving Have students list all factors of the following numbers: 4, 9, 10, 12, and 16. Which of these numbers has an odd number of factors? What do the numbers with an odd number of factors have in common? **4, 9, and 16 have an odd number of factors and are perfect squares.**

Reading to Learn Mathematics, p. 136 **ELL**

NAME ____________ DATE ________ PERIOD ____

3-1 Reading to Learn Mathematics

Square Roots

Pre-Activity *Complete the Mini Lab at the top of page 116 in your textbook. Write your answers below.*

1. Copy and complete the following table.

Tiles on a Side	1	2	3	4	5
Total Number of Tiles in the Square Arrangement	1	4	9	16	25

2. Suppose a square arrangement has 36 tiles. How many tiles are on a side? 6

3. What is the relationship between the number of tiles on a side and the number of tiles in the arrangement? The square of the number of tiles on a side is the number of tiles in the array.

3-1 Square Roots

What You'll LEARN

Find square roots of perfect squares.

NEW Vocabulary

perfect square
square root
radical sign
principal square root

REVIEW Vocabulary

exponent: tells the number of times the base is used as a factor (Lesson 1-7)

HANDS-ON Mini Lab

Materials
- color tiles

Work with a partner.

Look at the two square arrangements of tiles at the right. Continue this pattern of square arrays until you reach 5 tiles on each side.

1. Copy and complete the following table.

Tiles on a Side	1	2	3	4	5
Total Number of Tiles in the Square Arrangement	1	4	9	16	25

2. Suppose a square arrangement has 36 tiles. How many tiles are on a side? **6**
3. What is the relationship between the number of tiles on a side and the number of tiles in the arrangement?

3. The square of the number of tiles on a side is the number of tiles in the arrangement.

Numbers such as 1, 4, 9, 16, and 25 are called **perfect squares** because they are squares of whole numbers. The opposite of squaring a number is finding a **square root**.

Noteables™ **Key Concept: Square Root**

Words A square root of a number is one of its two equal factors.

Symbols **Arithmetic**

Since $3 \cdot 3 = 9$, a square root of 9 is 3.
Since $(-3)(-3) = 9$, a square root of 9 is -3.

Algebra

If $x^2 = y$, then x is a square root of y.

The symbol $\sqrt{}$, called a **radical sign**, is used to indicate the positive square root. The symbol $-\sqrt{}$ is used to indicate the negative square root.

READING in the Content Area

For strategies in reading this lesson, visit **msmath3.net/reading.**

EXAMPLE Find a Square Root

1 **Find $\sqrt{64}$.**

$\sqrt{64}$ indicates the *positive* square root of 64.

Since $8^2 = 64$, $\sqrt{64} = 8$.

NCLB *No Child Left Behind*

The goals of the NCLB Act include a stronger emphasis on reading. The **Reading in the Content Area** link helps students become proficient readers.

EXAMPLE Find the Negative Square Root

2 **Find $-\sqrt{121}$.**

$-\sqrt{121}$ indicates the *negative* square root of 121.

Since $(-11)(-11) = 121$, $-\sqrt{121} = -11$.

Your Turn **Find each square root.**

a. $\sqrt{49}$ **7** b. $-\sqrt{225}$ **−15** c. $-\sqrt{0.16}$ **−0.4**

READING Math

Square Roots A positive square root is called the principal square root.

Some equations that involve squares can be solved by taking the square root of each side of the equation. Remember that every positive number has both a positive and a negative square root.

EXAMPLE Use Square Roots to Solve an Equation

3 **ALGEBRA** **Solve $t^2 = \frac{25}{36}$.**

$t^2 = \frac{25}{36}$ — Write the equation.

$\sqrt{t^2} = \sqrt{\frac{25}{36}}$ or $-\sqrt{\frac{25}{36}}$ — Take the square root of each side.

$t = \frac{5}{6}$ or $-\frac{5}{6}$ — Notice that $\frac{5}{6} \cdot \frac{5}{6} = \frac{25}{36}$ and $\left(-\frac{5}{6}\right)\left(-\frac{5}{6}\right) = \frac{25}{36}$.

The equation has two solutions, $\frac{5}{6}$ and $-\frac{5}{6}$.

TEACHING TIP

Explain to students that since $t \cdot t = t^2$, $\sqrt{t^2} = t$.

Your Turn **Solve each equation.** **f. 0.3 or −0.3**

d. $y^2 = \frac{4}{25}$ **$\frac{2}{5}$ or $-\frac{2}{5}$** e. $196 = a^2$ **14 or −14** f. $m^2 = 0.09$

In real-life situations, a negative answer may not make sense.

EXAMPLE Use an Equation to Solve a Problem

4 **HISTORY** **The Great Pyramid of Giza has a square base with an area of about 567,009 square feet. Determine the length of each side of its base.**

Words	Area	is equal to	the square of the length of a side.
Variables	A	=	s^2
Equation	567,009	=	s^2

$567{,}009 = s^2$ — Write the equation.

$\sqrt{567{,}009} = \sqrt{s^2}$ — Take the square root of each side.

2nd $\sqrt{\ }$ 567009 ENTER — Use a calculator.

753 or $-753 = s$

The length of a side of the base of the Great Pyramid of Giza is about 753 feet since distance cannot be negative.

STUDY TIP

Rational Exponents Exponents can also be used to indicate the square root. $9^{\frac{1}{2}}$ means the same thing as $\sqrt{9}$. $9^{\frac{1}{2}}$ is read *nine to the one half power.* $9^{\frac{1}{2}} = 3$.

msmath3.net/extra_examples

2 Teach

Noteables™

As you work the **In-Class Examples,** have students follow along in their *Noteables™: Interactive Study Notebook with Foldables™*, or have students work the examples in their notebooks.

In-Class Examples

Find each square root.

1 $\sqrt{81}$ **9**

2 $-\sqrt{144}$ **−12**

3 **ALGEBRA** Solve $x^2 = \frac{49}{64}$. **$\frac{7}{8}, -\frac{7}{8}$**

4 **MUSIC** The art work on the square picture in a compact disc case is approximately 14,161 mm² in area. Find the length of each side of the square. **119 mm**

Teaching Strategies Sometimes students are confused by problems that include fractions. When students are presented with taking the square root of a fraction, make sure they apply the operation to the numerator and the denominator. For example, $\sqrt{\frac{36}{49}} = \frac{\sqrt{36}}{\sqrt{49}} = \frac{6}{7}$.

DAILY INTERVENTION **Unlocking Misconceptions**

Square Roots Some students may assume that $\sqrt{-9}$ is the same as $-\sqrt{9}$. Point out that it is impossible to square a real number and get −9, or any other negative number. Review the rules for multiplying negative numbers. Tell students that they will evaluate $\sqrt{-9}$ when they learn about *imaginary numbers* in later courses.

3 Practice/Apply

FOLDABLES™ Follow-Up Remind students to use their Foldable journals to record what they learn about square roots. For example, on the first page of their journals they might explain how to find the square root of a number and give an example.

DAILY INTERVENTION **FIND THE ERROR** In Exercise 4, ask students to examine both solutions carefully, substituting all possible values for x into the equation to determine which value or values are correct. Some calculators require students to place parentheses around negative numbers before squaring them.

About the Exercises...

Guided Practice Key

Exercises	Examples
5, 8	1
6, 7	2
9–13	3

Assignment Guide

Basic: 15–21 odd, 27–37 odd, 43, 45, 47–60

Average: 15–45 odd, 47–60

Enriched: 14–46 even, 47–56 (Optional: 57–60)

Answer

1. $\sqrt{16} = 4$, which is what golfers yell to warn other players that the ball is coming.

Students practice the same concepts in Exercises 14–45 if they are assigned odd or even problems.

Skill and Concept Check

1. *Writing Math* Explain the meaning of $\sqrt{16}$ in the cartoon. **See margin.**

FoxTrot by Bill Amend

2. **Write** the symbol for the negative square root of 25. $-\sqrt{25}$
3. **OPEN ENDED** Write an equation that can be solved by taking the square root of a perfect square. **Sample answer: $x^2 = 100$**
4. **FIND THE ERROR** Diana and Terrell are solving the equation $x^2 = 81$. Who is correct? Explain. **Terrell; both $9 \cdot 9 = 81$ and $(-9)(-9) = 81$.**

Diana	Terrell
$x^2 = 81$	$x^2 = 81$
$x = 9$	$x = 9$ or $x = -9$

GUIDED PRACTICE

Find each square root.

5. $\sqrt{25}$ **5**
6. $-\sqrt{100}$ **−10**
7. $-\sqrt{\frac{16}{81}}$ **$-\frac{4}{9}$**
8. 0.64 **0.8**

ALGEBRA Solve each equation.

9. $p^2 = 36$ **6 or −6**
10. $n^2 = 169$ **13 or −13**
11. $900 = r^2$ **30 or −30**
12. $t^2 = \frac{1}{9}$ **$\frac{1}{3}$ or $-\frac{1}{3}$**
13. **ALGEBRA** If $n^2 = 256$, find n. **16 or −16**

★ indicates increased difficulty

Practice and Applications

Find each square root.

14. $\sqrt{16}$ **4**
15. $\sqrt{81}$ **9**
16. $-\sqrt{64}$ **−8**
17. $-\sqrt{36}$ **−6**
18. $-\sqrt{196}$ **−14**
19. $-\sqrt{144}$ **−12**
20. $\sqrt{256}$ **16**
21. $\sqrt{324}$ **18**
22. ★ $-\sqrt{\frac{16}{25}}$ **$-\frac{4}{5}$**
23. ★ $-\sqrt{\frac{9}{49}}$ **$-\frac{3}{7}$**
24. ★ $\sqrt{0.25}$ **0.5**
25. ★ $\sqrt{1.44}$ **1.2**
26. Find the positive square root of 169. **13**
27. What is the negative square root of 400? **−20**

HOMEWORK HELP

For Exercises	See Examples
14–27	1, 2
28–41	3
42–45	4

Extra Practice See pages 622, 650.

118 Chapter 3 Algebra: Real Numbers and the Pythagorean Theorem

ALGEBRA **Solve each equation.**

28. $v^2 = 81$ **9 or −9**
29. $b^2 = 100$ **10 or −10**
30. $y^2 = 225$ **15 or −15**
31. $s^2 = 144$ **12 or −12**
32. $1{,}600 = a^2$ **40 or −40**
33. $2{,}500 = d^2$ **50 or −50**
34. $w^2 = 625$ **25 or −25**
35. $m^2 = 961$ **31 or −31**
36. $\frac{25}{81} = p^2$ $\frac{5}{9}$ **or** $-\frac{5}{9}$
37. $\frac{9}{64} = c^2$ $\frac{3}{8}$ **or** $-\frac{3}{8}$
★ 38. $r^2 = 2.25$ **1.5 or −1.5**
★ 39. $d^2 = 1.21$ **1.1 or −1.1**

★ 40. **ALGEBRA** Find a number that when squared equals 1.0404. **1.02 or −1.02**

★ 41. **ALGEBRA** Find a number that when squared equals 4.0401. **2.01 or −2.01**

42. **MARCHING BAND** A marching band wants to make a square formation. If there are 81 members in the band, how many should be in each row? **9 members**

GEOMETRY **The formula for the perimeter of a square is $P = 4s$, where s is the length of a side. Find the perimeter of each square.**

43. 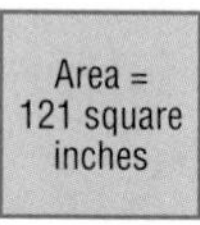

44 in.

44. 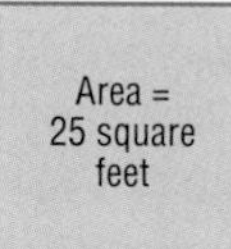

20 ft

45. 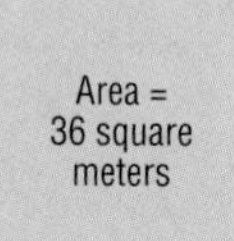

24 m

46. **MULTI STEP** Describe three different-sized squares that you could make at the same time out of 130 square tiles. How many tiles are left? **Sample answer: 10 in. by 10 in., 5 in. by 5 in., 2 in. by 2 in.; 1 tile**

47. **CRITICAL THINKING** Find each value.
a. $(\sqrt{36})^2$ **36**
b. $(\sqrt{81})^2$ **81**
c. $(\sqrt{21})^2$ **21**
d. $(\sqrt{x})^2$ **x**

48. **CRITICAL THINKING** *True* or *False*? $\sqrt{-25} = -5$. Explain. **False; $(-5)(-5) = 25$, not -25.**

Spiral Review with Standardized Test Practice

49. **MULTIPLE CHOICE** What is the solution of $a^2 = 49$? **C**
Ⓐ −7 Ⓑ 7 Ⓒ 7 or −7 Ⓓ 7 or 0 or −7

50. **SHORT RESPONSE** The area of each square is 4 square units. Find the perimeter of the figure. **24 units**

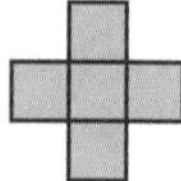

51. **SPACE** The Alpha Centauri stars are about 2.5×10^{13} miles from Earth. Write this distance in standard form. (Lesson 2-9) **25,000,000,000,000 mi**

Write each expression using exponents. (Lesson 2-8)

52. $6 \cdot 6 \cdot 6$ **6^3**
53. $2 \cdot 3 \cdot 3 \cdot 2 \cdot 2 \cdot 2$ **$2^4 \cdot 3^2$**
54. $a \cdot a \cdot a \cdot b$ **$a^3 \cdot b$**
55. $s \cdot t \cdot t \cdot s \cdot s \cdot t \cdot s$ **$s^4 \cdot t^3$**

56. What is the absolute value of −18? (Lesson 1-3) **18**

GETTING READY FOR THE NEXT LESSON

PREREQUISITE SKILL **Between which two perfect squares does each number lie?** (Lesson 2-2)

57. 57 **49, 64**
58. 68 **64, 81**
59. 33 **25, 36**
60. 40 **36, 49**

Math Online msmath3.net/self_check_quiz

Study Guide and Intervention, p. 133

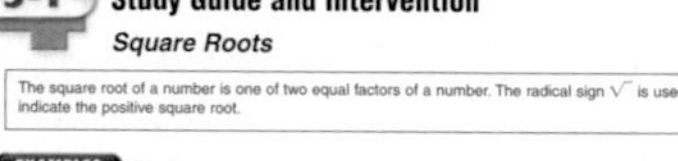

NAME ________ DATE ______ PERIOD ___

3-1 Study Guide and Intervention
Square Roots

The square root of a number is one of two equal factors of a number. The radical sign $\sqrt{\ }$ is used to indicate the positive square root.

EXAMPLES **Find each square root.**

1. $\sqrt{1}$ Since $1 \cdot 1 = 1$, $\sqrt{1} = 1$.
2. $-\sqrt{16}$ Since $4 \cdot 4 = 16$, $-\sqrt{16} = -4$.
3. $\sqrt{0.25}$ Since $0.5 \cdot 0.5 = 0.25$, $\sqrt{0.25} = 0.5$.
4. $\sqrt{\frac{25}{36}}$ Since $\frac{5}{6} \cdot \frac{5}{6} = \frac{25}{36}$, $\sqrt{\frac{25}{36}} = \frac{5}{6}$.

EXAMPLE 5 **Solve $a^2 = \frac{4}{9}$.**

$a^2 = \frac{4}{9}$ Write the equation.
$\sqrt{a^2} = \sqrt{\frac{4}{9}}$ Take the square root of each side.
$a = \frac{2}{3}$ or $-\frac{2}{3}$ Notice that $\frac{2}{3} \cdot \frac{2}{3} = \frac{4}{9}$ and $\left(-\frac{2}{3}\right)\left(-\frac{2}{3}\right) = \frac{4}{9}$.

The equation has two solutions, $\frac{2}{3}$ and $-\frac{2}{3}$.

EXERCISES

Find each square root.

1. $\sqrt{4}$ 2
2. $\sqrt{9}$ 3
3. $-\sqrt{49}$ −7
4. $-\sqrt{25}$ −5
5. $\sqrt{0.01}$ 0.1
6. $-\sqrt{0.64}$ −0.8
7. $\sqrt{\frac{9}{16}}$ $\frac{3}{4}$
8. $-\sqrt{\frac{1}{25}}$ $-\frac{1}{5}$

ALGEBRA **Solve each equation.**

9. $x^2 = 121$ 11 or −11
10. $a^2 = 3{,}600$ 60 or −60
11. $p^2 = \frac{81}{100}$ $\frac{9}{10}$ or $-\frac{9}{10}$
12. $t^2 = \frac{121}{196}$ $\frac{11}{14}$ or $-\frac{11}{14}$

Practice: Skills, p. 134

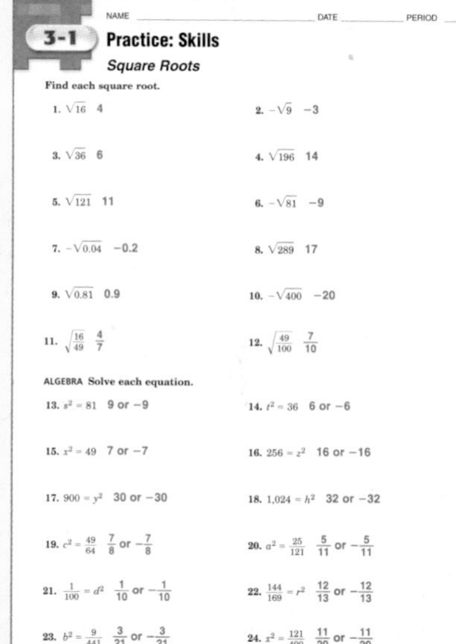

NAME ________ DATE ______ PERIOD ___

3-1 Practice: Skills
Square Roots

Find each square root.

1. $\sqrt{16}$ 4
2. $-\sqrt{9}$ −3
3. $\sqrt{36}$ 6
4. $\sqrt{196}$ 14
5. $\sqrt{121}$ 11
6. $-\sqrt{81}$ −9
7. $-\sqrt{0.04}$ −0.2
8. $\sqrt{289}$ 17
9. $\sqrt{0.81}$ 0.9
10. $-\sqrt{400}$ −20
11. $\sqrt{\frac{16}{49}}$ $\frac{4}{7}$
12. $\sqrt{\frac{49}{100}}$ $\frac{7}{10}$

ALGEBRA **Solve each equation.**

13. $s^2 = 81$ 9 or −9
14. $t^2 = 36$ 6 or −6
15. $x^2 = 49$ 7 or −7
16. $256 = z^2$ 16 or −16
17. $900 = y^2$ 30 or −30
18. $1{,}024 = h^2$ 32 or −32
19. $c^2 = \frac{49}{64}$ $\frac{7}{8}$ or $-\frac{7}{8}$
20. $a^2 = \frac{25}{121}$ $\frac{5}{11}$ or $-\frac{5}{11}$
21. $\frac{1}{100} = d^2$ $\frac{1}{10}$ or $-\frac{1}{10}$
22. $\frac{144}{169} = r^2$ $\frac{12}{13}$ or $-\frac{12}{13}$
23. $b^2 = \frac{9}{441}$ $\frac{3}{21}$ or $-\frac{3}{21}$
24. $x^2 = \frac{121}{400}$ $\frac{11}{20}$ or $-\frac{11}{20}$

Practice: Word Problems, p. 135

NAME ________ DATE ______ PERIOD ___

3-1 Practice: Word Problems
Square Roots

1. **PLANNING** Rosy wants a large picture window put in the living room of her new house. The window is to be square with an area of 49 square feet. How long should each side of the window be? 7 ft

2. **GEOMETRY** If the area of a square is 1 square meter, how many centimeters long is each side? 100 cm

3. **ART** A miniature portrait of George Washington is square and has an area of 169 square centimeters. How long is each side of the portrait? 13 cm

4. **BAKING** Len is baking a square cake for his friend's wedding. When served to the guests, the cake will be cut into square pieces 1 inch on a side. The cake should be large enough so that each of the 121 guests gets one piece. How long should each side of the cake be? 11 in.

5. **ART** Cara has 196 marbles that she is using to make a square formation. How many marbles should be in each row? 14 marbles

6. **GARDENING** Tate is planning to put a square garden with an area of 289 square feet in his back yard. What will be the length of each side of the garden? 17 ft

7. **HOME IMPROVEMENT** Al has 324 square paving stones that he plans to use to construct a square patio. How many paving stones wide will the patio be? 18 stones

8. **GEOMETRY** If the area of a square is 529 square inches, what is the length of a side of the square? 23 in.

4 Assess

Higher-Level Thinking

Suppose there are 40 lockers in a row and all are closed. One student opens every locker. A second student closes every second locker. A third student walks up to every third locker and closes the ones that are open and opens the ones that are closed. If this continues, which lockers will be open after the fortieth person walks through? **1, 4, 9, 16, 25, and 36; They have an odd number of factors and are opened or closed an odd number of times.**

3-2 Lesson Notes

Lesson Resources

Chapter 3 Resource Masters
- Study Guide and Intervention, p. 138
- Practice: Skills, p. 139
- Practice: Word Problems, p. 140
- Reading to Learn Mathematics, p. 141
- Enrichment, p. 142

Calculator and Spreadsheet Masters, p. 18
MathPASS Tutorial CD-ROM, 3
Parent and Student Study Guide Online Worksheets, 3-2
Teaching Mathematics with Manipulatives, pp. 42–43
Noteables™: Interactive Study Notebook with Foldables™, 3-2
Virtual Activities CD-ROM, Square Roots

FAST FILE

1 Focus

5-Minute Check 3-2

Use as a quiz or review of Lesson 3-1. (Also available as a transparency)

Bellringer
Hands-On Activity Hand out 30 small square tiles to each pair of students. First ask them to arrange the tiles into a 5×6 rectangle. Then have students remove as few tiles as possible to form a square and add as few tiles as possible to form another square. Between which two perfect squares does 30 lie? **25, 36**

Reading to Learn Mathematics, p. 141 **ELL**

NAME ______ DATE ______ PERIOD ______

3-2 Reading to Learn Mathematics
Estimating Square Roots

Pre-Activity *Complete the Mini Lab at the top of page 120 in your textbook. Write your answers below.*

1. How many squares are on each side of the largest possible square using no more than 40 small squares? 6 squares
2. How many squares are on each side of the smallest possible square using at least 40 small squares? 7 squares
3. The value of $\sqrt{40}$ is between two consecutive whole numbers. What are the numbers? 6 and 7

Use grid paper to determine between which two consecutive whole numbers each value is located.

4. $\sqrt{23}$ 4 and 5
5. $\sqrt{52}$ 7 and 8
6. $\sqrt{27}$ 5 and 6
7. $\sqrt{18}$ 4 and 5

3-2 Estimating Square Roots

What You'll LEARN
Estimate square roots.

MATH Symbols
$\approx$ about equal to

HANDS-ON Mini Lab

Materials
- grid paper

Work with a partner.

On grid paper, draw the largest possible square using no more than 40 small squares.

On grid paper, draw the smallest possible square using at least 40 small squares.

1. How many squares are on each side of the largest possible square using no more than 40 small squares? **6 squares**
2. How many squares are on each side of the smallest possible square using at least 40 small squares? **7 squares**
3. The value of $\sqrt{40}$ is between two consecutive whole numbers. What are the numbers? **6 and 7**

Use grid paper to determine between which two consecutive whole numbers each value is located.

4. $\sqrt{23}$ **4 and 5** 5. $\sqrt{52}$ **7 and 8** 6. $\sqrt{27}$ **5 and 6** 7. $\sqrt{18}$ **4 and 5**

Since 40 is not a perfect square, $\sqrt{40}$ is not a whole number.

The number line shows that $\sqrt{40}$ is between 6 and 7. Since 40 is closer to 36 than 49, the best whole number estimate for $\sqrt{40}$ is 6.

EXAMPLE Estimate Square Roots

Estimate to the nearest whole number.

1 $\sqrt{83}$

- The first perfect square less than 83 is 81.
- The first perfect square greater than 83 is 100.

$81 < 83 < 100$	Write an inequality.
$9^2 < 83 < 10^2$	$81 = 9^2$ and $100 = 10^2$
$\sqrt{9^2} < \sqrt{83} < \sqrt{10^2}$	Take the square root of each number.
$9 < \sqrt{83} < 10$	Simplify.

So, $\sqrt{83}$ is between 9 and 10. Since 83 is closer to 81 than 100, the best whole number estimate for $\sqrt{83}$ is 9.

TEACHING TIP
You may want students to make a list of perfect squares before they start estimating square roots.

Your Turn **Estimate to the nearest whole number.**

a. $\sqrt{35}$ **6** b. $\sqrt{170}$ **13** c. $\sqrt{14.8}$ **4**

DAILY INTERVENTION **Differentiated Instruction**

Visual/Spatial Have each student make a number line with the numbers 1 through 12 evenly spaced above the line and the squares of 1 through 12 evenly spaced below the line. Write a number between 1 and 144 on the chalkboard. Ask students to place the number in its approximate location below the number line and circle the closest square root to it. Repeat this using several different numbers.

EXAMPLE Estimate Square Roots

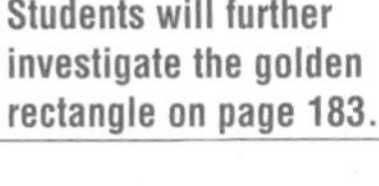

TEACHING TIP
Students will further investigate the golden rectangle on page 183.

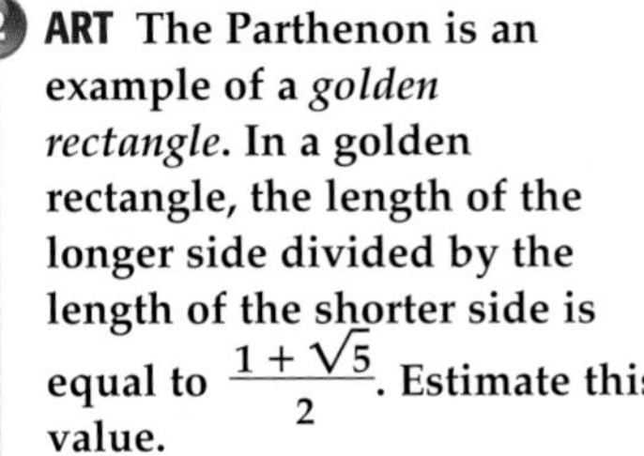

2 **ART** The Parthenon is an example of a *golden rectangle*. In a golden rectangle, the length of the longer side divided by the length of the shorter side is equal to $\frac{1 + \sqrt{5}}{2}$. Estimate this value.

STUDY TIP

Technology You can use a calculator to find a more accurate value of $\frac{1+\sqrt{5}}{2}$.

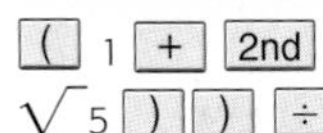

(1 + 2nd √ 5)) ÷ 2 ENTER 1.618033989

First estimate the value of $\sqrt{5}$.

$4 < 5 < 9$	4 and 9 are perfect squares.
$2^2 < 5 < 3^2$	$4 = 2^2$ and $9 = 3^2$
$2 < \sqrt{5} < 3$	Take the square root of each number.

Since 5 is closer to 4 than 9, the best whole number estimate for $\sqrt{5}$ is 2. Use this to evaluate the expression.

$$\frac{1 + \sqrt{5}}{2} \approx \frac{1 + 2}{2} \text{ or } 1.5$$

In a "golden rectangle," the length of the longer side divided by the length of the shorter side is about 1.5.

Students practice the same concepts in Exercises 10–33 if they are assigned odd or even problems.

Skill and Concept Check

1. Graph $\sqrt{78}$ on a number line. **See margin.**
2. **OPEN ENDED** Give two numbers that have square roots between 7 and 8. One number should have a square root closer to 7, and the other number should have a square root closer to 8. **Sample answers: 50; 60**
3. **FIND THE ERROR** Julia and Chun are estimating $\sqrt{50}$. Who is correct? Explain. **Julia; $7^2 = 49$ or about 50, but $25^2 = 625$.**

Julia	Chun
$\sqrt{50} \approx 7$	$\sqrt{50} \approx 25$

4. **NUMBER SENSE** Without a calculator, determine which is greater, $\sqrt{94}$ or 10. Explain your reasoning. **10; since 94 is less than 100, $\sqrt{94}$ is less than 10.**

GUIDED PRACTICE

Estimate to the nearest whole number.

5. $\sqrt{28}$ **5**
6. $\sqrt{60}$ **8**
7. $\sqrt{135}$ **12**
8. $\sqrt{13.5}$ **4**

9. **ALGEBRA** Estimate the solution of $t^2 = 78$ to the nearest whole number. **9 or −9**

Math Online msmath3.net/extra_examples

Answer

1.

2 Teach

In-Class Examples

Estimate to the nearest whole number.

1 $\sqrt{54}$ **7**

2 **FINANCE** If you were to invest \$100 in a bank account for two years, your money would earn interest daily and be worth more when you withdrew it. If you had \$120 after two years, the interest rate, written as a decimal, would be found using the expression $\frac{(\sqrt{120} - 10)}{10}$. Estimate this value. **0.10 or 10%**

3 Practice/Apply

DAILY INTERVENTION

FIND THE ERROR In Exercise 3, ask students how Chun may have reached his answer. They should recognize that Chun probably found the number that when multiplied by 2 equals 50.

NUMBER SENSE
For Exercise 4, have students use a number line to aid in the estimation.

About the Exercises...

Guided Practice Key

Exercises	Examples
5–8	1
9	2

Assignment Guide

Basic: 11–25 odd, 31, 35, 36–44

Average: 11–35 odd, 36–44

Enriched: 10–34 even, 36–40 (Optional: 41–44)

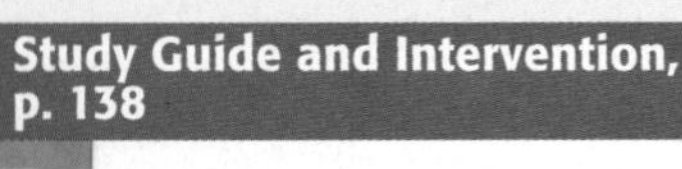

Study Guide and Intervention, p. 138

NAME ______ DATE ______ PERIOD ____

3-2 Study Guide and Intervention

Estimating Square Roots

Most numbers are not perfect squares. You can estimate square roots for these numbers.

EXAMPLE 1 Estimate $\sqrt{204}$ to the nearest whole number.

- The first perfect square less than 204 is 14.
- The first perfect square greater than 204 is 15.

$196 < 204 < 225$ Write an inequality.

$14^2 < 204 < 15^2$ $196 = 14^2$ and $225 = 15^2$

$14 < \sqrt{204} < 15$ Take the square root of each number.

So, $\sqrt{204}$ is between 14 and 15. Since 204 is closer to 196 than 225, the best whole number estimate for $\sqrt{204}$ is 14.

EXAMPLE 2 Estimate $\sqrt{79.3}$ to nearest whole number.

- The first perfect square less than 79.3 is 64.
- The first perfect square greater than 79.3 is 81.

$64 < 79.3 < 81$ Write an inequality.

$8^2 < 79.3 < 9^2$ $64 = 8^2$ and $81 = 9^2$

$8 < \sqrt{79.3} < 9$ Take the square root of each number.

So, $\sqrt{79.3}$ is between 8 and 9. Since 79.3 is closer to 81 than 64, the best whole number estimate for $\sqrt{79.3}$ is 9.

EXERCISES

Estimate to the nearest whole number.

1. $\sqrt{8}$ 3 2. $\sqrt{37}$ 6 3. $\sqrt{14}$ 4

4. $\sqrt{26}$ 5 5. $\sqrt{62}$ 8 6. $\sqrt{48}$ 7

7. $\sqrt{103}$ 10 8. $\sqrt{141}$ 12 9. $\sqrt{14.3}$ 4

10. $\sqrt{51.2}$ 7 11. $\sqrt{82.7}$ 9 12. $\sqrt{175.2}$ 13

Practice: Skills, p. 139

NAME ______ DATE ______ PERIOD ____

3-2 Practice: Skills

Estimating Square Roots

Estimate to the nearest whole number.

1. $\sqrt{5}$ 2 2. $\sqrt{18}$ 4 3. $\sqrt{10}$ 3

4. $\sqrt{34}$ 6 5. $\sqrt{53}$ 7 6. $\sqrt{80}$ 9

7. $\sqrt{69}$ 8 8. $\sqrt{99}$ 10 9. $\sqrt{120}$ 11

10. $\sqrt{77}$ 9 11. $\sqrt{171}$ 13 12. $\sqrt{230}$ 15

13. $\sqrt{147}$ 12 14. $\sqrt{194}$ 14 15. $\sqrt{290}$ 17

16. $\sqrt{440}$ 21 17. $\sqrt{578}$ 24 18. $\sqrt{730}$ 27

19. $\sqrt{1{,}010}$ 32 20. $\sqrt{1{,}230}$ 35 21. $\sqrt{8.42}$ 3

22. $\sqrt{17.8}$ 4 23. $\sqrt{11.5}$ 3 24. $\sqrt{37.7}$ 6

25. $\sqrt{23.8}$ 5 26. $\sqrt{59.4}$ 8 27. $\sqrt{97.3}$ 10

28. $\sqrt{118.4}$ 11 29. $\sqrt{84.35}$ 9 30. $\sqrt{45.92}$ 7

Practice: Word Problems, p. 140

NAME ______ DATE ______

3-2 Practice: Word Problems

Estimating Square Roots

1. GEOMETRY If the area of a square is 29 square inches, estimate the length of each side of the square to the nearest whole number. 5 in.	2. DECORATING Miki has an square rug in her living room that has an area of 19 square yards. Estimate the length of a side of the rug to the nearest whole number. 4 yd
3. GARDENING Ruby is planning to put a square garden with an area of 200 square feet in her back yard. Estimate the length of each side of the garden to the nearest whole number. 14 ft	4. ALGEBRA Estimate the solution of $c^2 = 40$ to the nearest integer. 6 or –6
5. ALGEBRA Estimate the solution of $x^2 = 138.2$ to the nearest integer. 12 or –12	6. ARITHMETIC The **geometric mean** of two numbers a and b can be found by evaluating $\sqrt{a \cdot b}$. Estimate the geometric mean of 5 and 10 to the nearest whole number. 7
7. GEOMETRY The radius r of a certain circle is given by $r = \sqrt{71}$. Estimate the radius of the circle to the nearest foot. 8 ft	8. GEOMETRY In a triangle whose base and height are equal, the base b is given by the formula $b = \sqrt{2A}$, where A is the area of the triangle. Estimate to the nearest whole number the base of this triangle if the area is 17 square meters. 6 m

★ indicates increased difficulty

Practice and Applications

HOMEWORK HELP

For Exercises	See Examples
10–31	1
34–35	2

Extra Practice
See pages 622, 650.

Estimate to the nearest whole number.

10. $\sqrt{11}$ **3** 11. $\sqrt{15}$ **4** 12. $\sqrt{44}$ **7** 13. $\sqrt{23}$ **5**

14. $\sqrt{113}$ **11** 15. $\sqrt{105}$ **10** 16. $\sqrt{82}$ **9** 17. $\sqrt{50}$ **7**

18. $\sqrt{15.6}$ **4** 19. $\sqrt{23.5}$ **5** 20. $\sqrt{85.1}$ **9** 21. $\sqrt{38.4}$ **6**

22. $\sqrt{200}$ **14** 23. $\sqrt{170}$ **13** 24. $\sqrt{150}$ **12** 25. $\sqrt{130}$ **11**

★26. $\sqrt{630}$ **25** ★27. $\sqrt{925}$ **30** ★28. $\sqrt{1{,}300}$ **36** ★29. $\sqrt{780}$ **28**

30. **ALGEBRA** Estimate the solution of $y^2 = 55$ to the nearest integer. **7 or −7**

31. **ALGEBRA** Estimate the solution of $d^2 = 95$ to the nearest integer. **10 or −10**

★32. Order 7, 9, $\sqrt{50}$, and $\sqrt{85}$ from least to greatest. **7, $\sqrt{50}$, 9, $\sqrt{85}$**

★33. Order $\sqrt{91}$, 7, 5, $\sqrt{38}$ from least to greatest. **5, $\sqrt{38}$, 7, $\sqrt{91}$**

34. **HISTORY** The Egyptian mathematician Heron created the formula $A = \sqrt{s(s-a)(s-b)(s-c)}$ to find the area A of a triangle. In this formula, a, b, and c are the measures of the sides, and s is one-half of the perimeter. Use this formula to estimate the area of the triangle. **about 12 cm²**

4 cm
6 cm
8 cm

35. **SCIENCE** The formula $t = \frac{\sqrt{h}}{4}$ represents the time t in seconds that it takes an object to fall from a height of h feet. If a ball is dropped from a height of 200 feet, estimate how long will it take to reach the ground. **about 3.5 s**

36. **CRITICAL THINKING** If $x^3 = y$, then x is the cube root of y. Explain how to estimate the cube root of 30. What is the cube root of 30 to the nearest whole number? **See margin.**

Spiral Review with Standardized Test Practice

37. **MULTIPLE CHOICE** Which is the best estimate of the value of $\sqrt{54}$? **B**

(A) 6 (B) 7 (C) 8 (D) 27

38. **MULTIPLE CHOICE** If $x^2 = 38$, then a value of x is approximately **G**

(F) 5. (G) 6. (H) 7. (I) 24.

39. **ALGEBRA** Find a number that, when squared, equals 8,100. (Lesson 3-1) **90 or −90**

40. **GEOGRAPHY** The Great Lakes cover about 94,000 square miles. Write this number in scientific notation. (Lesson 2-9) **9.4×10^4**

GETTING READY FOR THE NEXT LESSON

PREREQUISITE SKILL Express each decimal as a fraction in simplest form. (Lesson 2-1)

41. 0.15 $\frac{3}{20}$ 42. 0.8 $\frac{4}{5}$ 43. $0.\overline{3}$ $\frac{1}{3}$ 44. $0.\overline{4}$ $\frac{4}{9}$

msmath3.net/self_check_quiz

4 Assess

Open-Ended Assessment

Writing Have students write the steps for estimating a square root to the nearest whole number without including any numbers in their description.

Answer

36. Since 27 < 30 < 64, the cube root is between 3 and 4. Since 30 is closer to 27 than 64, the cube root of 30 is about 3.

Problem-Solving Strategy

A Preview of Lesson 3-3

Use a Venn Diagram

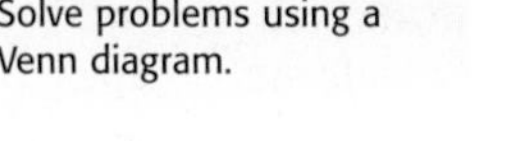

Solve problems using a Venn diagram.

Of the 12 students who ate lunch with me today, 9 are involved in music activities and 6 play sports. Four are involved in both music and sports.

How could we organize that information?

Explore	We know how many students are involved in each activity and how many are involved in both activities. We want to organize the information.
Plan	Let's use a **Venn diagram** to organize the information.
Solve	Draw two overlapping circles to represent the two different activities. Since 4 students are involved in both activities, place a 4 in the section that is part of both circles. Use subtraction to determine the number for each other section. 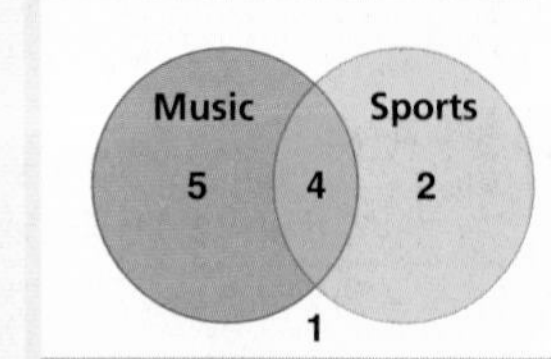 only music: $9 - 4 = 5$ only sports: $6 - 4 = 2$ neither music nor sports: $12 - 5 - 2 - 4 = 1$
Examine	Check each circle to see if the appropriate number of students is represented.

Analyze the Strategy

1. **Tell** what each section of the Venn diagram above represents and the number of students that belong to that category. **See margin.**
2. **Use** the Venn diagram above to determine the number of students who are in either music or sports but not both.
3. **Write** a situation that can be represented by the Venn diagram at the right. **See margin.**

2. 7 students

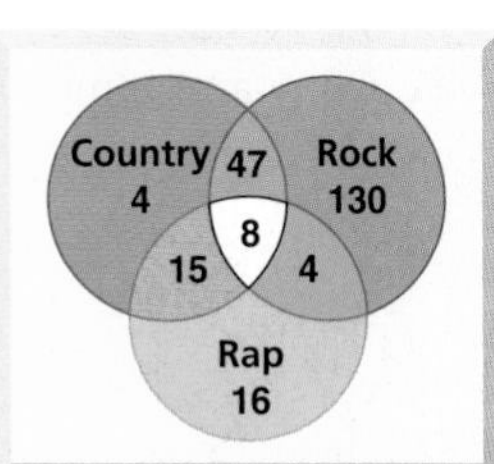

DAILY INTERVENTION

Differentiated Instruction ELL

Verbal/Linguistic Most Venn diagram problems at this level require students to work *inside out* as they organize the information given to them. Ask students to write about this method, describing in detail how it works. Students should explain which piece of information they will use to begin the diagram, and how they will use the rest of the information to complete the diagram.

3-3a Lesson Notes

1 Focus

Bellringer

Problem Solving When 24 atheletes were asked about their favorite sports, 14 said they liked softball, 18 liked basketball, and 8 liked both. Ask students how many athletes said they liked just softball and how many liked just basketball. Demonstrate the use of a Venn diagram to show the data. **6, 10**

2 Teach

In-Class Example

Solve. Use a Venn diagram.

LANGUAGES Of the 40 foreign exchange students attending a middle school, 20 speak French, 23 speak Spanish, and 22 speak Italian. Nine students speak French and Spanish, but not Italian. Six students speak French and Italian, but not Spanish. Ten students speak Spanish and Italian, but not French. Only 4 of the students speak all 3 languages. Use a Venn diagram to find how many exchange students do not speak any of these languages. **8**

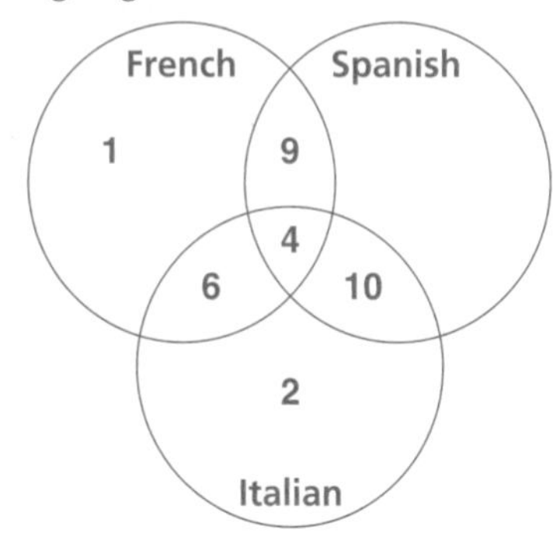

3 Practice/Apply

About the Exercises...

Problem-Solving Strategies
Exercises 6–12 are structured so that students have the opportunity to practice many different problem-solving strategies. You may wish to remind them of some of the strategies they have studied.

- use the four-step plan (p. 6)
- work backward (p. 43)
- look for a pattern (p. 96)
- use a Venn diagram ✓

4 Assess

Open-Ended Assessment

Speaking Have students explain how they would determine the number of people not falling into any of the given categories when organizing information into a Venn diagram.

Answers (pp. 123–124)

1. music only, 5; sports only, 2; music and sports, 4; neither music nor sports, 1
3. Sample answer: A survey asked 224 people if they like country, rock, and/or rap music. 74 people like country, 189 like rock, and 43 like rap. 55 people like rock and country, 12 like rock and rap, and 23 like rap and country. 8 people like all three types of music.
7. the $82.50 per 15-hour week job; $\$5.15 \cdot 15 = \$77.25$; $\$10.95 \cdot 5 = \$54.75$; Since $82.50 is greater than $77.25 and $54.75, the third job is the best paying job.
8.

6,300
60 · 105
4 · 15 · 5 · 21
2 · 2 · 3 · 5 · 5 · 7 · 3

Apply the Strategy

Solve. Use a Venn diagram.

4. **MARKETING** A survey showed that 83 customers bought wheat cereal, 83 bought rice cereal, and 20 bought corn cereal. Of those who bought exactly two boxes of cereal, 6 bought corn and wheat, 10 bought rice and corn, and 12 bought rice and wheat. Four customers bought all three. How many customers bought only rice cereal? **57 customers**

5. **FOOD** Napoli's Pizza conducted a survey of 75 customers. The results showed that 35 customers liked mushroom pizza, 41 liked pepperoni, and 11 liked both mushroom and pepperoni pizza. How many liked neither mushroom nor pepperoni pizza? **10 customers**

Mixed Problem Solving

Solve. Use any strategy.

6. **SCIENCE** Emilio created a graph of data he collected for a science project. If the pattern continues, about how far will the marble roll if the end of the tube is raised to an elevation of $3\frac{1}{2}$ feet? **about 19 ft**

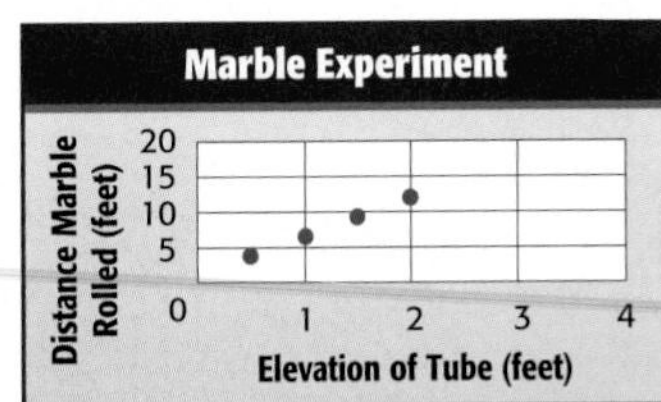

7. **MULTI STEP** Three after-school jobs are posted on the job board. The first job pays $5.15 per hour for 15 hours of work each week. The second job pays $10.95 per day for 2 hours of work, 5 days a week. The third job pays $82.50 for 15 hours of work each week. If you want to apply for the best-paying job, which job should you choose? Explain your reasoning. **See margin.**

8. **FACTOR TREE** Copy and complete the factor tree. **See margin.**

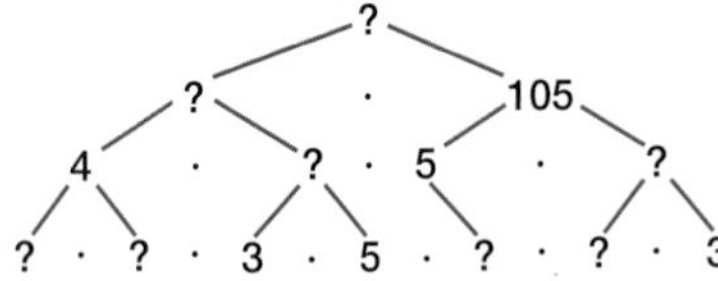

9. **NUMBER THEORY** A subset is a part of a set. The symbol ⊂ means "is a subset of." Consider the following two statements.

   integers ⊂ rational numbers
   rational numbers ⊂ integers

   Are both statements true? Draw a Venn diagram to justify your answer. **See margin.**

HEALTH For Exercises 10 and 11, use the following information.
Dr. Bagenstose is an allergist. Her patients had the following symptoms last week.

Symptom(s)	Number of Patients
runny nose	22
watery eyes	20
sneezing	28
runny nose and watery eyes	8
runny nose and sneezing	15
watery eyes and sneezing	12
runny nose, watery eyes, and sneezing	5

10. Draw a Venn diagram of the data. **See margin.**

11. How many patients had only watery eyes? **5 patients**

12. **STANDARDIZED TEST PRACTICE** Which value of x makes $7x - 10 = 9x$ true? **A**

    Ⓐ -5 Ⓑ -4 Ⓒ 4 Ⓓ 5

9. The first statement is true, but the second is not true.

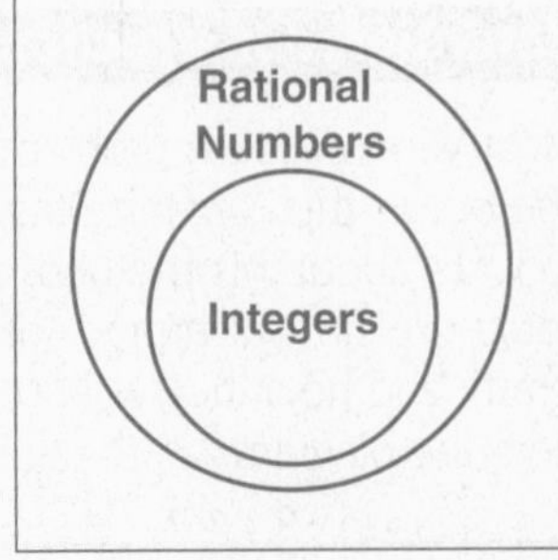

10.

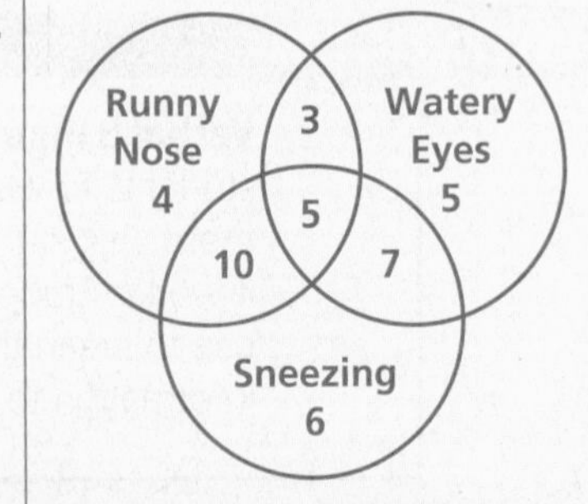

124 Chapter 3 Algebra: Real Numbers and the Pythagorean Theorem

3-3 The Real Number System

WHEN am I ever going to use this? 2. no; yes; $7\frac{1}{2} = \frac{15}{2}$

SPORTS Most sports have rules for the size of the field or court where the sport is played. A diagram of a volleyball court is shown.

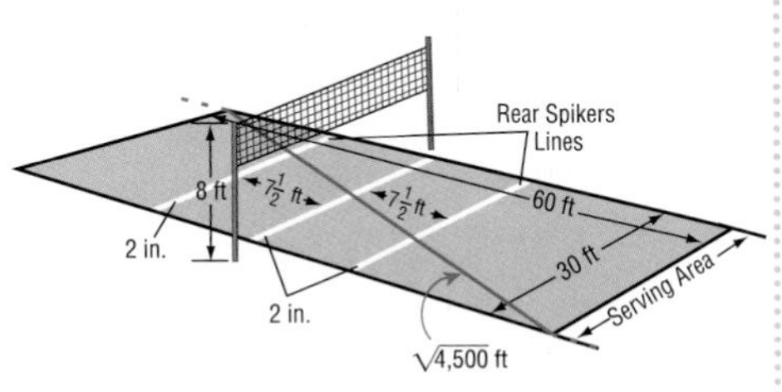

1. The length of the court is 60 feet. Is this number a whole number? Is it a rational number? Explain. **yes; yes; $60 = \frac{60}{1}$**
2. The distance from the net to the rear spikers line is $7\frac{1}{2}$ feet. Is this number a whole number? Is it a rational number? Explain.
3. The diagonal across the court is $\sqrt{4{,}500}$ feet. Can this square root be written as a whole number? a rational number? **no; no**

What You'll LEARN

Identify and classify numbers in the real number system.

NEW Vocabulary

irrational number
real number

REVIEW Vocabulary

rational number: any number that can be expressed in the form $\frac{a}{b}$, where a and b are integers and $b \neq 0$ (Lesson 2-1)

Use a calculator to find $\sqrt{4{,}500}$. $\sqrt{4{,}500} \approx 67.08203932...$

Although the decimal value of $\sqrt{4{,}500}$ continues on and on, it does not repeat. Since the decimal does not terminate or repeat, $\sqrt{4{,}500}$ is *not* a rational number. Numbers that are not rational are called **irrational numbers**. The square root of any number that is not a perfect square is irrational.

Noteables™ Key Concept: Irrational Numbers

Words An irrational number is a number that cannot be expressed as $\frac{a}{b}$, where a and b are integers and $b \neq 0$.

Symbols $\sqrt{2} \approx 1.414213562...$ $\sqrt{3} \approx 1.732050808...$

The set of rational numbers and the set of irrational numbers together make up the set of **real numbers**. Study the diagrams below.

Venn Diagram Real Numbers

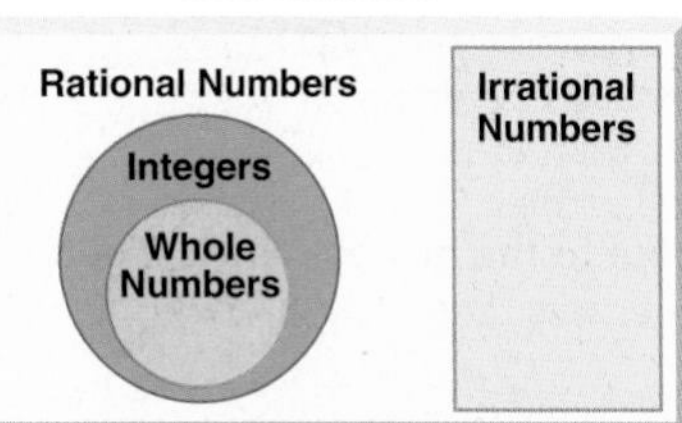

Web

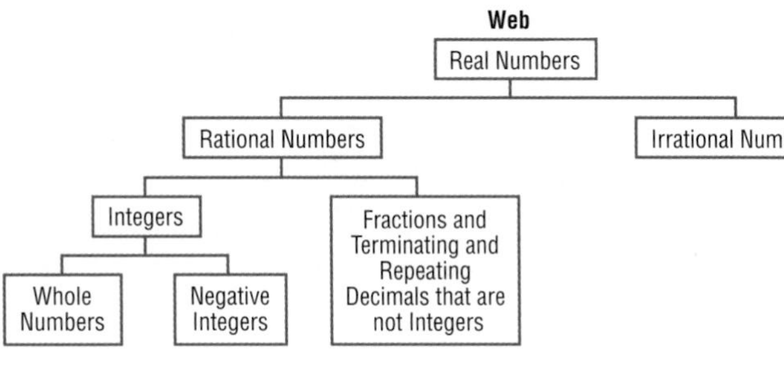

3-3 Lesson Notes

Lesson Resources

Chapter 3 Resource Masters

- Study Guide and Intervention, p. 143
- Practice: Skills, p. 144
- Practice: Word Problems, p. 145
- Reading to Learn Mathematics, p. 146
- Enrichment, p. 147

Key Teaching Transparencies, 9

Parent and Student Study Guide Online Worksheets, 3-3

Noteables™: Interactive Study Notebook with Foldables™, 3-3

1 Focus

5-Minute Check 3-3

Use as a quiz or review of Lesson 3-2. (Also available as a transparency)

Bellringer

Communication When students enter the room, have them draw three columns on a sheet of notebook paper and label the columns *whole numbers, integers*, and *rational numbers*. Ask them to place each one of the following numbers into all columns that describe it: $-4, 6.2, 20, 0.\overline{3}, -2\frac{1}{2}$, $\sqrt{64}$. Review the meanings of the column headings before they begin.

(Continued in bottom margin.)

Reading to Learn Mathematics, p. 146 **ELL**

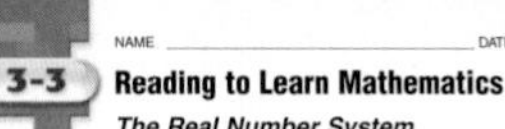

NAME ______ DATE ______ PERIOD ______

3-3 Reading to Learn Mathematics

The Real Number System

Pre-Activity *Read the introduction at the top of page 125 in your textbook. Write your answers below.*

1. The length of the court is 60 feet. Is this number a whole number? Is it a rational number? Explain.
yes; yes; $60 = \frac{60}{1}$
2. The distance from the net to the rear spikers line is $7\frac{1}{2}$ feet. Is this number a whole number? Is it a rational number? Explain.
no; yes; $7\frac{1}{2} = \frac{15}{2}$
3. The diagonal across the court is $\sqrt{4{,}500}$ feet. Can this square root be written as a whole number? a rational number? no; no

Reading the Lesson

4. What do rational and irrational numbers have in common? What is the ...

Whole Numbers	Integers	Rational Numbers
	-4	-4
		6.2
20	20	20
		$0.\overline{3}$
		$-2\frac{1}{2}$
$\sqrt{64}$	$\sqrt{64}$	$\sqrt{64}$

2 Teach

In-Class Examples

Name all sets of numbers to which each real number belongs.

1. 
$\sqrt{25}$ **whole, integer, rational**

2. 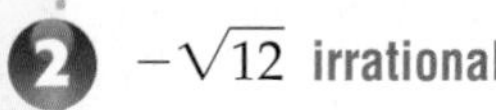
$-\sqrt{12}$ **irrational**

3. 
0.090909... **rational**

4. Estimate $\sqrt{8}$ and $-\sqrt{2}$ to the nearest tenth. Then graph $\sqrt{8}$ and $-\sqrt{2}$ on a number line.
$\sqrt{8} \approx 2.8$ and $-\sqrt{2} \approx -1.4$

Answers (Your Turn)

a. 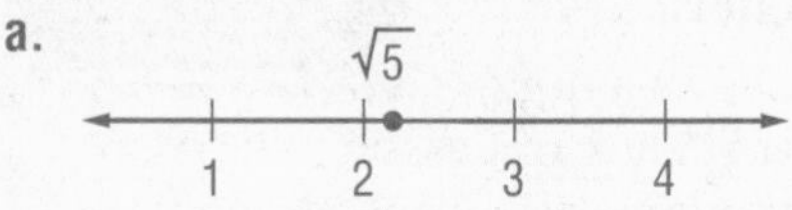

b. 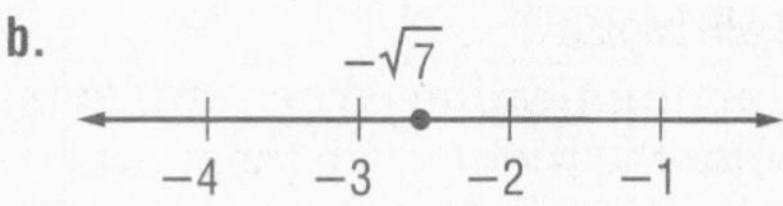

c. 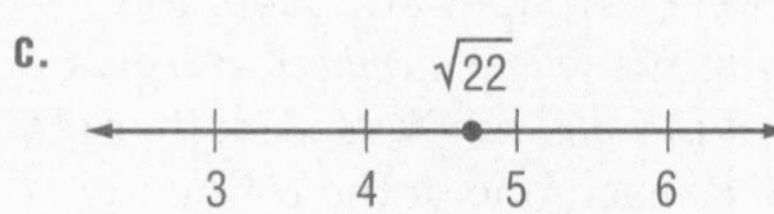

STUDY TIP

Classifying Numbers Always simplify numbers before classifying them.

EXAMPLES Classify Numbers

Name all sets of numbers to which each real number belongs.

1 0.252525... The decimal ends in a repeating pattern. It is a rational number because it is equivalent to $\frac{25}{99}$.

2 $\sqrt{36}$ Since $\sqrt{36} = 6$, it is a whole number, an integer, and a rational number.

3 $-\sqrt{7}$ $-\sqrt{7} \approx -2.645751311...$ Since the decimal does not terminate or repeat, it is an irrational number.

Real numbers follow the number properties that are true for whole numbers, integers, and rational numbers.

Concept Summary — **Real Number Properties**

Property	Arithmetic	Algebra
Commutative	$3.2 + 2.5 = 2.5 + 3.2$ $5.1 \cdot 2.8 = 2.8 \cdot 5.1$	$a + b = b + a$ $a \cdot b = b \cdot a$
Associative	$(2 + 1) + 5 = 2 + (1 + 5)$ $(3 \cdot 4) \cdot 6 = 3 \cdot (4 \cdot 6)$	$(a + b) + c = a + (b + c)$ $(a \cdot b) \cdot c = a \cdot (b \cdot c)$
Distributive	$2(3 + 5) = 2 \cdot 3 + 2 \cdot 5$	$a(b + c) = a \cdot b + a \cdot c$
Identity	$\sqrt{8} + 0 = \sqrt{8}$ $\sqrt{7} \cdot 1 = \sqrt{7}$	$a + 0 = a$ $a \cdot 1 = a$
Additive Inverse	$4 + (-4) = 0$	$a + (-a) = 0$
Multiplicative Inverse	$\frac{2}{3} \cdot \frac{3}{2} = 1$	$\frac{a}{b} \cdot \frac{b}{a} = 1$, where $a, b \neq 0$

The graph of all real numbers is the entire number line without any "holes."

TEACHING TIP

Point out that graphing real numbers using this method is an approximation. Students will learn to accurately graph real numbers in Lesson 3-5b.

EXAMPLE Graph Real Numbers

4 **Estimate $\sqrt{6}$ and $-\sqrt{3}$ to the nearest tenth. Then graph $\sqrt{6}$ and $-\sqrt{3}$ on a number line.**

Use a calculator to determine the approximate decimal values.

$\sqrt{6} \approx 2.449489743...$

$-\sqrt{3} \approx -1.7320508080...$

$\sqrt{6} \approx 2.4$ and $-\sqrt{3} \approx -1.7$. Locate these points on the number line.

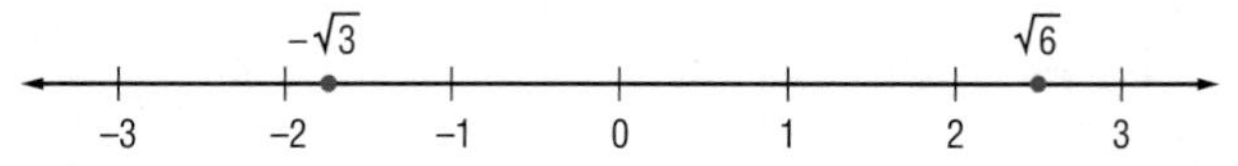

Your Turn **Estimate each square root to the nearest tenth. Then graph the square root on a number line.** **a–c. See margin for graphs.**

a. $\sqrt{5}$ **2.2** b. $-\sqrt{7}$ **−2.6** c. $\sqrt{22}$ **4.7**

DAILY INTERVENTION — **Differentiated Instruction**

Interpersonal Working in pairs, students should alternate giving their partners numbers and labeling the numbers as rational or irrational. The students who came up with the numbers should then state whether they agree or disagree and why.

Mental Math Remember that a negative number is always less than a positive number. Therefore, you can determine that $-\sqrt{3}$ is less than 1.7 without computation.

To compare real numbers, you can use a number line.

EXAMPLES Compare Real Numbers

Replace each ● with <, >, or = to make a true sentence.

5 $\sqrt{7}$ ● $2\frac{2}{3}$

Write each number as a decimal.

$\sqrt{7} \approx 2.645751311...$

$2\frac{2}{3} = 2.666666666...$

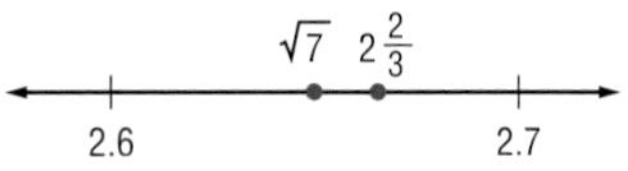

(Number line from 2.6 to 2.7 with points $\sqrt{7}$ and $2\frac{2}{3}$.)

Since 2.645751311. . . is less than 2.66666666. . . , $\sqrt{7} < 2\frac{2}{3}$.

6 $1.\bar{5}$ ● $\sqrt{2.25}$

Write $\sqrt{2.25}$ as a decimal.

$\sqrt{2.25} = 1.5$

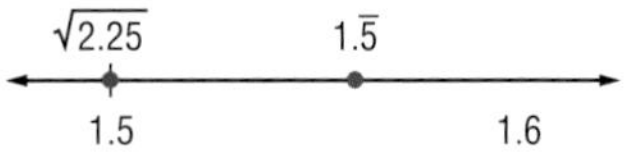

(Number line from 1.5 to 1.6 with points $\sqrt{2.25}$ and $1.\bar{5}$.)

Since $1.\bar{5}$ is greater than 1.5, $1.\bar{5} > \sqrt{2.25}$.

Your Turn Replace each ● with <, >, or = to make a true sentence.

d. $\sqrt{11}$ ● $3\frac{1}{3}$ < e. $\sqrt{17}$ ● 4.03 > f. $\sqrt{6.25}$ ● $2\frac{1}{2}$ =

How Does a Navigator Use Math?

Navigators use math to calculate the course of a ship. They sometimes use lighthouses as landmarks in their navigating.

Math Online Research For information about a career as a navigator, visit: msmath3.net/careers

EXAMPLE Use Real Numbers

7 **LIGHTHOUSES On a clear day, the number of miles a person can see to the horizon is about 1.23 times the square root of his or her distance from the ground, in feet. Suppose Domingo is at the top of the lighthouse at Cape Hatteras and Jewel is at the top of the lighthouse at Cape Lookout. How much farther can Domingo see than Jewel?**

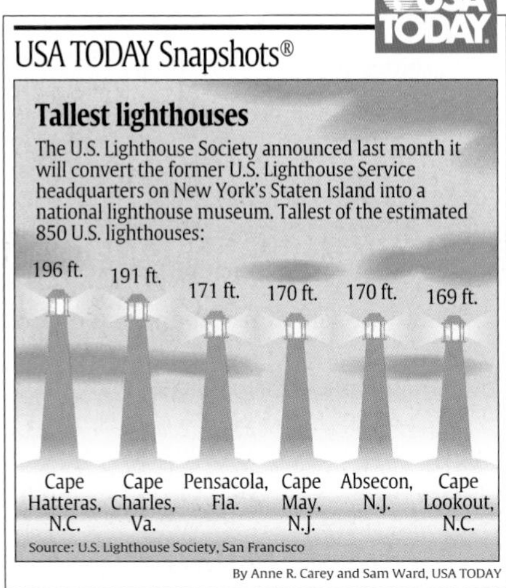

Use a calculator to approximate the distance each person can see.

Domingo: $1.23\sqrt{196} = 17.22$ Jewel: $1.23\sqrt{169} = 15.99$

Domingo can see about 17.22 − 15.99 or 1.23 miles farther than Jewel.

msmath3.net/extra_examples

In-Class Examples

Replace each ● with <, >, or = to make a true sentence.

5 $3\frac{7}{8}$ ● $\sqrt{15}$ >

6 $3.\bar{2}$ ● $\sqrt{10.4}$ <

7 **BASEBALL** The time in seconds that it takes an object to fall d feet is $0.25\sqrt{d}$. How many seconds would it take for a baseball that is hit 250 feet straight up in the air to fall from its highest point to the ground? **4 s**

3 Practice/Apply

FOLDABLES™ Follow-Up Remind students to use their Foldable journals to record what they learn about the real number system. On the third page of their journals, students might summarize the properties of the real number system.

Which One Doesn't Belong? For Exercise 3, point out that the only way for the square root of a whole number to be a rational number is if the whole number is a perfect square.

About the Exercises...

Guided Practice Key

Exercises	Examples
4–7	1–3
8–11	4
12–15	5, 6
16	7

Assignment Guide

Basic: 17–49 odd, 51–62

Average: 17–49 odd, 50–62

Enriched: 18–50 even, 51–58 (Optional: 59–62)

Answers

4. rational
5. integer, rational
6. irrational
7. rational
8.

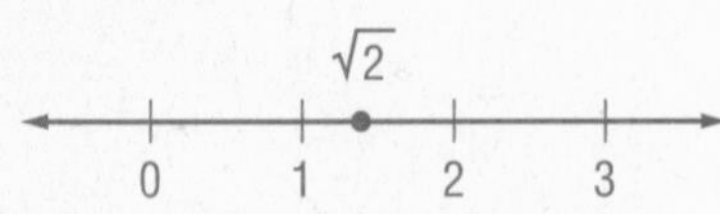

9.

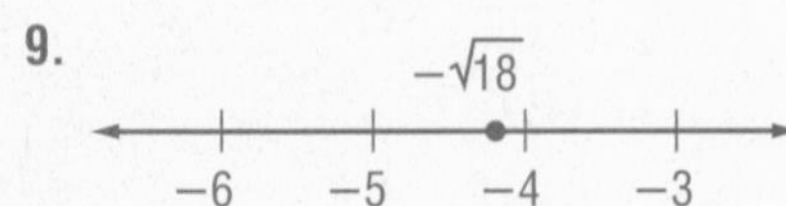

10.

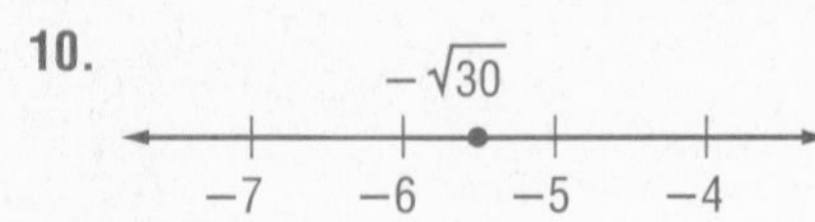

11.

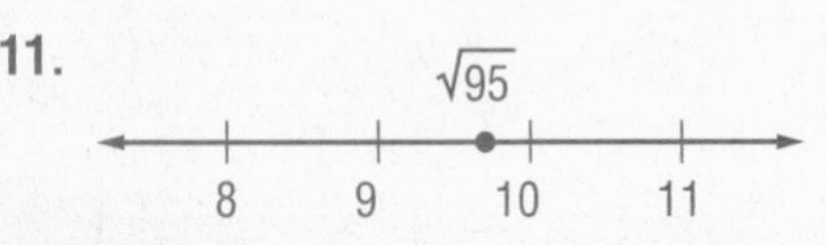

Students practice the same concepts in Exercises 17–48 if they are assigned odd or even problems.

Skill and Concept Check

1. **Give a counterexample** for the statement *all square roots are irrational numbers.* **Sample answer:** $\sqrt{4}$
2. **OPEN ENDED** Write an irrational number which would be graphed between 7 and 8 on the number line. **Sample answer:** $\sqrt{50}$
3. **Which One Doesn't Belong?** Identify the number that is not the same type as the other three. Explain your reasoning.

$\sqrt{7}$ $\sqrt{11}$ $\sqrt{25}$ $\sqrt{35}$

$\sqrt{25}$; since $\sqrt{25} = 5$, it is not an irrational number like the others.

GUIDED PRACTICE

Name all sets of numbers to which each real number belongs. 4–7. See margin.

4. 0.050505. . .
5. $-\sqrt{100}$
6. $\sqrt{17}$
7. $-3\frac{1}{4}$

Estimate each square root to the nearest tenth. Then graph the square root on a number line. 8–11. See margin for graphs.

8. $\sqrt{2}$ 1.4
9. $-\sqrt{18}$ −4.2
10. $-\sqrt{30}$ −5.5
11. $\sqrt{95}$ 9.7

Replace each ● with <, >, or = to make a true sentence.

12. $\sqrt{15}$ ● 3.5 >
13. $\sqrt{2.25}$ ● $1\frac{1}{2}$ =
14. $2.\overline{21}$ ● $\sqrt{5.2}$ <
15. Order $5.\overline{5}$, $\sqrt{30}$, $5\frac{1}{2}$, and 5.56 from least to greatest. $\sqrt{30}$, $5\frac{1}{2}$, $5.\overline{5}$, 5.56
16. **GEOMETRY** The area of a triangle with all three sides the same length is $\frac{s^2\sqrt{3}}{4}$, where s is the length of a side. Find the area of the triangle. about 15.6 in²

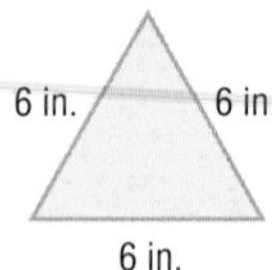

★ indicates increased difficulty   17–28. See margin.

Practice and Applications

Name all sets of numbers to which each real number belongs.

17. 14
18. $\frac{2}{3}$
19. $-\sqrt{16}$
20. $-\sqrt{20}$
21. 4.83
22. $7.\overline{2}$
23. $-\sqrt{90}$
24. $\frac{12}{4}$
25. $-0.\overline{182}$
26. −13
27. $5\frac{3}{8}$
28. −108.6
29. Are integers *always, sometimes,* or *never* rational numbers? Explain.
30. Are rational numbers *always, sometimes,* or *never* integers? Explain.

29–30. See margin.

HOMEWORK HELP

For Exercises	See Examples
17–30	1–3
31–38	4
39–48	5, 6
49–50	7

Extra Practice See pages 622, 650.

Estimate each square root to the nearest tenth. Then graph the square root on a number line. 31–38. See Ch. 3 Answer Appendix.

31. $\sqrt{6}$ 2.4
32. $\sqrt{8}$ 2.8
33. $-\sqrt{22}$ −4.7
34. $-\sqrt{27}$ −5.2
35. $\sqrt{50}$ 7.1
36. $-\sqrt{48}$ −6.9
37. $-\sqrt{105}$ −10.2
38. $\sqrt{150}$ 12.2

17. whole, integer, rational
18. rational
19. integer, rational
20. irrational
21. rational
22. rational
23. irrational
24. whole, integer, rational
25. rational
26. integer, rational
27. rational
28. rational

Replace each ● with <, >, or = to make a true sentence.

39. $\sqrt{10}$ ● 3.2 **<**
40. $\sqrt{12}$ ● 3.5 **<**
41. $6\frac{1}{3}$ ● $\sqrt{40}$ **>**
42. $2\frac{2}{5}$ ● $\sqrt{5.76}$ **=**
43. $5\frac{1}{6}$ ● $5.1\overline{6}$ **=**
44. $\sqrt{6.2}$ ● $2.\overline{4}$ **>**
45. Order $\sqrt{5}$, $\sqrt{3}$, 2.25, and $2.\overline{2}$ from least to greatest. **$\sqrt{3}$, $2.\overline{2}$, $\sqrt{5}$, 2.25**
46. Order 3.01, $3.\overline{1}$, $3.\overline{01}$, and $\sqrt{9}$ from least to greatest. **$\sqrt{9}$, 3.01, $3.\overline{01}$, $3.\overline{1}$**
47. Order −4.1, $\sqrt{17}$, $-4.\overline{1}$, and 4.01 from greatest to least. **$\sqrt{17}$, 4.01, −4.1, $-4.\overline{1}$**
48. Order $-\sqrt{5}$, $\sqrt{6}$, −2.5, and 2.5 from greatest to least. **2.5, $\sqrt{6}$, $-\sqrt{5}$, −2.5**
49. **LAW ENFORCEMENT** Traffic police can use the formula $s = 5.5\sqrt{0.75d}$ to estimate the speed of a vehicle before braking. In this formula, s is the speed of the vehicle in miles per hour, and d is the length of the skid marks in feet. How fast was the vehicle going for the skid marks at the right? **about 53.3 mph**

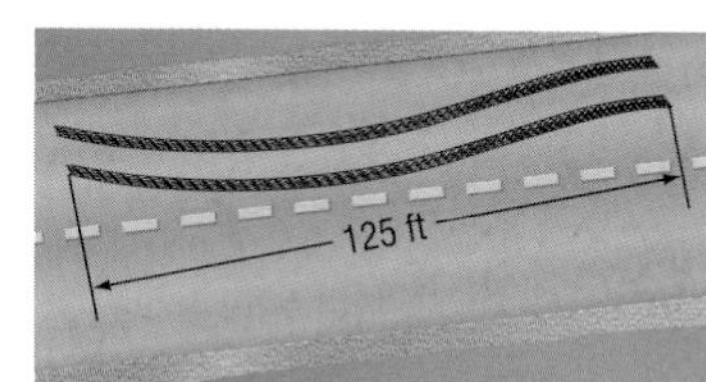

★ 50. **WEATHER** Meteorologists use the formula $t^2 = \frac{d^3}{216}$ to estimate the amount of time that a thunderstorm will last. In this formula, t is the time in hours, and d is the distance across the storm in miles. How long will a thunderstorm that is 8.4 miles wide last? **about 1.7 h**

51. **CRITICAL THINKING** Tell whether the following statement is *always*, *sometimes*, or *never* true.

The product of a rational number and an irrational number is an irrational number. **always**

Spiral Review with Standardized Test Practice

52. **MULTIPLE CHOICE** To which set of numbers does $-\sqrt{49}$ *not* belong? **A**

Ⓐ whole Ⓑ rational Ⓒ integers Ⓓ real

53. **SHORT RESPONSE** The area of a square playground is 361 square feet. What is the perimeter of the playground? **76 ft**

54. Order 7, $\sqrt{53}$, $\sqrt{32}$, and 6 from least to greatest. (Lesson 3-2) **$\sqrt{32}$, 6, 7, $\sqrt{53}$**

Solve each equation. (Lesson 3-1)

55. $t^2 = 25$ **5 or −5**
56. $y^2 = \frac{1}{49}$ **$\frac{1}{7}$ or $-\frac{1}{7}$**
57. $0.64 = a^2$ **0.8 or −0.8**

58. **ARCHAEOLOGY** Stone tools found in Ethiopia are estimated to be 2.5 million years old. That is about 700,000 years older than similar tools found in Tanzania. Write and solve an addition equation to find the age of the tools found in Tanzania. (Lesson 1-8) **2,500,000 = a + 700,000; 1.8 million years**

GETTING READY FOR THE NEXT LESSON

PREREQUISITE SKILL Evaluate each expression. (Lesson 1-2)

59. $3^2 + 5^2$ **34**
60. $6^2 + 4^2$ **52**
61. $9^2 + 11^2$ **202**
62. $4^2 + 7^2$ **65**

Math Online msmath3.net/self_check_quiz

4 Assess

Open-Ended Assessment

Speaking Have students name two numbers that are irrational, two that are rational but not integers, two that are integers but not whole numbers, and two whole numbers.

Answers

29. Always; an integer can always be written as the integer over 1, so an integer is always a rational number.
30. Sometimes; 3 or $\frac{3}{1}$ is a rational number and an integer, but $\frac{2}{3}$ is a rational number and not an integer.

Study Guide and Intervention, p. 143

NAME ______ DATE ______ PERIOD ____

3-3 Study Guide and Intervention
The Real Number System

Numbers may be classified by identifying to which of the following sets they belong.

Whole Numbers	0, 1, 2, 3, 4, ...
Integers	..., −2, −1, 0, 1, 2, ...
Rational Numbers	numbers that can be expressed in the form $\frac{a}{b}$, where a and b are integers and $b \neq 0$
Irrational Numbers	numbers that cannot be expressed in the form $\frac{a}{b}$, where a and b are integers and $b \neq 0$

EXAMPLES Name all sets of numbers to which each real number belongs.

1. 5 — whole number, integer, rational number
2. 0.666... — Decimals that terminate or repeat are rational numbers, since they can be expressed as fractions. $0.666... = \frac{2}{3}$
3. $-\sqrt{25}$ — Since $-\sqrt{25} = -5$, it is an integer and a rational number.
4. $-\sqrt{11}$ — $\sqrt{11} \approx 3.31662479...$ Since the decimal does not terminate or repeat, it is an irrational number.

To compare real numbers, write each number as a decimal and then compare the decimal values.

EXAMPLE 5 Replace ● with <, >, or = to make $2\frac{1}{4}$ ● $\sqrt{5}$ a true sentence.

Write each number as a decimal.

$2\frac{1}{4} = 2.25$

$\sqrt{5} \approx 2.236067...$

Since 2.25 is greater than 2.236067..., $2\frac{1}{4} > \sqrt{5}$.

EXERCISES

Name all sets of numbers to which each real number belongs.

1. 30 whole, integer, rational
2. −11 integer, rational
3. $5\frac{4}{7}$ rational
4. $\sqrt{21}$ irrational
5. 0 whole, integer, rational
6. $-\sqrt{9}$ integer, rational
7. $\frac{6}{3}$ whole, integer, rational
8. $-\sqrt{101}$ irrational

Replace each ● with <, >, or = to make a true sentence.

9. 2.7 ● $\sqrt{7}$ >
10. $\sqrt{11}$ ● $3\frac{1}{2}$ <
11. $4\frac{1}{6}$ ● $\sqrt{17}$ >
12. $3.\overline{8}$ ● $\sqrt{15}$ >

Practice: Skills, p. 144

NAME ______ DATE ______ PERIOD ____

3-3 Practice: Skills
The Real Number System

Name all sets of numbers to which each real number belongs.

1. 12 whole, integer, rational
2. −15 integer, rational
3. $1\frac{1}{2}$ rational
4. 3.18 rational
5. $\frac{8}{4}$ whole, integer, rational
6. $9.\overline{3}$ rational
7. $-2\frac{7}{9}$ rational
8. $\sqrt{25}$ whole, integer, rational
9. $\sqrt{3}$ irrational
10. $-\sqrt{64}$ integer, rational
11. $-\sqrt{12}$ irrational
12. $\sqrt{13}$ irrational

Estimate each square root to the nearest tenth. Then graph the square root on a number line.

13. $\sqrt{5}$ 2.2
14. $\sqrt{14}$ 3.7
15. $-\sqrt{6}$ −2.4
16. $-\sqrt{13}$ −3.6

Replace each ● with <, >, or = to make a true sentence.

17. 1.7 ● $\sqrt{3}$ <
18. $\sqrt{6}$ ● $2\frac{1}{2}$ <
19. $4\frac{2}{5}$ ● $\sqrt{19}$ >
20. $4.\overline{8}$ ● $\sqrt{24}$ <
21. $6\frac{1}{6}$ ● $\sqrt{38}$ >
22. $\sqrt{55}$ ● $7.4\overline{2}$ <
23. 2.1 ● $\sqrt{4.41}$ =
24. $2.\overline{7}$ ● $\sqrt{7.7}$ >

Practice: Word Problems, p. 145

NAME ______ DATE ______ PERIOD ____

3-3 Practice: Word Problems
The Real Number System

1. **GEOMETRY** If the area of a square is 33 square inches, estimate the length of a side of the square to the nearest tenth of an inch. 5.7 in.
2. **GARDENING** Hal has a square garden in his back yard with an area of 210 square feet. Estimate the length of a side of the garden to the nearest tenth of a foot. 14.5 ft
3. **ALGEBRA** Estimate the solution of $a^2 = 21$ to the nearest tenth. 4.6 or −4.6
4. **ALGEBRA** Estimate the solution of $b^2 = 67.5$ to the nearest tenth. 8.2 or −8.2
5. **ARITHMETIC** The **geometric mean** of two numbers a and b can be found by evaluating $\sqrt{a \cdot b}$. Estimate the geometric mean of 4 and 11 to the nearest tenth. 6.6
6. **ELECTRICITY** In a certain electrical circuit, the voltage V across a 20 ohm resistor is given by the formula $V = \sqrt{20P}$, where P is the power dissipated in the resistor, in watts. Estimate to the nearest tenth the voltage across the resistor if the power P is 4 watts. 8.9 volts
7. **GEOMETRY** The length s of a side of a cube is related to the surface area A of the cube by the formula $s = \sqrt{\frac{A}{6}}$. If the surface area is 27 square inches, what is the length of a side of the cube to the nearest tenth of an inch? 2.1 in.
8. **PETS** Alicia and Ella are comparing the weights of their pet dogs. Alicia's reports that her dog weighs $11\frac{1}{5}$ pounds, while Ella says that her dog weighs $\sqrt{125}$ pounds. Whose dog weighs more? Alicia's

Assessment Option

Mid-Chapter Test (Lessons 3-1 through 3-3) is available on p. 179 of the *Chapter 3 Resource Masters*.

ExamView® Pro

Use the networkable ExamView® Pro Testmaker CD-ROM to:

- Create **multiple versions** of tests.
- Create **modified** tests for **inclusion** students with one mouse click.
- **Edit** existing questions and **add** your own questions.
- Build tests aligned with state standards using built-in **state curriculum correlations.**
- Change **English** tests to **Spanish** with one mouse click and vice versa.

Follow-Up Before students complete the Mid-Chapter Practice Test, encourage them to review the notes, definitions, concepts, and main ideas they recorded in the first half of their Foldable journals.

Answer

1.

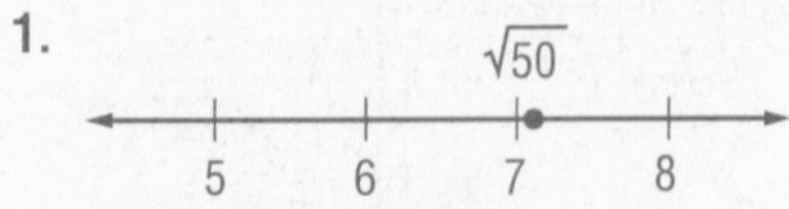

Chapter 3 Mid-Chapter Practice Test

Vocabulary and Concepts

1. **Graph** $\sqrt{50}$ on a number line. (Lesson 3-2) **See margin.**
2. **Write** an irrational number that would be graphed between 11 and 12 on a number line. (Lesson 3-3) **Sample answer: $\sqrt{122}$**
3. **OPEN ENDED** Give an example of a number that is an integer but not a whole number. (Lesson 3-3) **Sample answer: -3**

Skills and Applications

Find each square root. (Lesson 3-1)

4. $\sqrt{1}$ **1**
5. $-\sqrt{81}$ **-9**
6. $\sqrt{36}$ **6**
7. $-\sqrt{121}$ **-11**
8. $-\sqrt{\frac{1}{25}}$ **$-\frac{1}{5}$**
9. $\sqrt{0.09}$ **0.3**

10. **GEOMETRY** What is the length of a side of the square? (Lesson 3-1) **15 m**

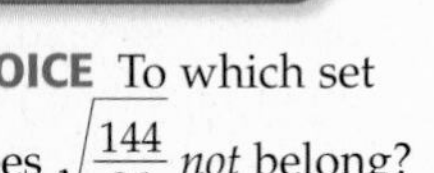

11. **ALGEBRA** Estimate the solution of $x^2 = 50$ to the nearest integer. (Lesson 3-2) **7 or -7**

Estimate to the nearest whole number. (Lesson 3-2)

12. $\sqrt{90}$ **9**
13. $\sqrt{28}$ **5**
14. $\sqrt{226}$ **15**
15. $\sqrt{17}$ **4**
16. $\sqrt{21}$ **5**
17. $\sqrt{75}$ **9**

Name all sets of numbers to which each real number belongs. (Lesson 3-3)

18. $\frac{2}{3}$ **rational**
19. $\sqrt{25}$ **whole, integer, rational**
20. $-\sqrt{15}$ **irrational**
21. $\sqrt{3}$ **irrational**
22. 10 **whole, integer, rational**
23. $-\sqrt{4}$ **integer, rational**

Standardized Test Practice

24. **MULTIPLE CHOICE** The area of a square checkerboard is 529 square centimeters. How long is each side of the checkerboard? (Lesson 3-1) **C**
    - Ⓐ 21 cm
    - Ⓑ 22 cm
    - Ⓒ 23 cm
    - Ⓓ 24 cm

25. **MULTIPLE CHOICE** To which set of numbers does $\sqrt{\frac{144}{36}}$ *not* belong? (Lesson 3-3) **I**
    - Ⓕ integers
    - Ⓖ rationals
    - Ⓗ wholes
    - Ⓘ irrationals

The Game Zone

A Place To Practice Your Math Skills

Math Skill: Estimate Square Roots

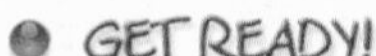

Players: four
Materials: 40 index cards, 4 markers

- Each player is given 10 index cards.
- Player 1 writes one of each of the whole numbers 1 to 10 on his or her cards. Player 2 writes the square of one of each of the whole numbers 1 to 10. Player 3 writes a different whole number between 11 and 50, that is not a perfect square. Player 4 writes a different whole number between 51 and 99, that is not a perfect square.

GO!

- Mix all 40 cards together. The dealer deals all of the cards.
- In turn, moving clockwise, each player lays down any pair(s) of a perfect square and its square root in his or her hand. The two cards should be laid down as shown at the right. If a player has no perfect square and square root pair, he or she skips a turn.

25 5

- After the first round, any player, during his or her turn may:
  (1) lay down a perfect square and square root pair, or
  (2) cover a card that is already on the table. The new card should form a square and *estimated* square root pair with the card next to it. A player makes as many plays as possible during his or her turn.
- After each round, each player passes one card left.
- **Who Wins?** The first person without any cards is the winner.

The Game Zone

GETTING READY

Objective Estimate square roots.

MANAGEMENT TIPS

Recommended Time
15 minutes

Tips

- If some groups finish early, have them begin a new game. When time is called, the player with the fewest cards remaining is the winner.
- If any group completes the game in less than ten minutes, you may want to ask them to make new cards for the numbers greater than 10 that are perfect squares and play another round.
- You may wish to use the game as an assessment tool for the concepts the students have been learning in Lessons 3-1 through 3-3.

Math Online For an additional game for this chapter, visit: msmath3.net/gamezone

3-4 Lesson Notes

Lesson Resources

Chapter 3 Resource Masters
- Study Guide and Intervention, p. 148
- Practice: Skills, p. 149
- Practice: Word Problems, p. 150
- Reading to Learn Mathematics, p. 151
- Enrichment, p. 152

Classroom Math Games, pp. 7–11
Key Teaching Transparencies, 10
MathPASS Tutorial CD-ROM, 47
Parent and Student Study Guide Online Worksheets, 3-4
Teaching Mathematics with Manipulatives, pp. 44–45
Noteables™: Interactive Study Notebook with Foldables™, 3-4

1 Focus

5-Minute Check 3-4

Use as a quiz or review of Lesson 3-3. (Also available as a transparency)

Bellringer
Reading Mathematics The term *square* is familiar to students from their work in geometry. Have students discuss the relationship between the meaning of this term as they have learned it in this chapter compared to its geometric meaning. Have them do the same for the phrase *perfect square.*

Reading to Learn Mathematics, p. 151 **ELL**

NAME ________ DATE ________ PERIOD ____

3-4 Reading to Learn Mathematics
The Pythagorean Theorem

Pre-Activity *Complete the Mini Lab at the top of page 132 in your textbook. Write your answers below.*

1. Find the area of each square. 9 units², 16 units², 25 units²
2. How are the squares of the sides related to the areas of the squares? They are the same.
3. Find the sum of the areas of the two smaller squares. How does the sum compare to the area of the larger square? 25 units²; They are equal.
4. Use grid paper to cut out three squares with sides 5, 12, and 13 units. Form a triangle with these squares. Compare the sum of the areas of the two smaller squares with the area of the larger square. They are the same.

Lesson

3-4 The Pythagorean Theorem

What You'll LEARN

Use the Pythagorean Theorem.

NEW Vocabulary

right triangle
legs
hypotenuse
Pythagorean Theorem
converse

Link to READING

Everyday Meaning of Leg: limb used to support the body

HANDS-ON Mini Lab 1. 9 units², 16 units², 25 units² 2. They are the same.

Materials
- grid paper

Work with a partner.

Three squares with sides 3, 4, and 5 units are used to form the right triangle shown.

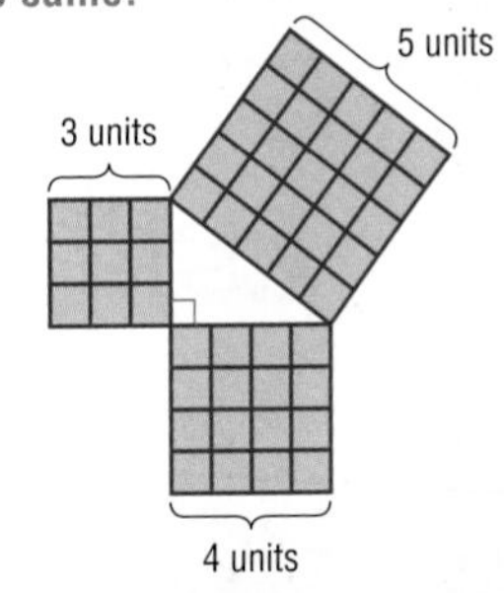

1. Find the area of each square.
2. How are the squares of the sides related to the areas of the squares?
3. Find the sum of the areas of the two smaller squares. How does the sum compare to the area of the larger square? **25 units²; They are equal.**
4. Use grid paper to cut out three squares with sides 5, 12, and 13 units. Form a right triangle with these squares. Compare the sum of the areas of the two smaller squares with the area of the larger square. **They are the same.**

A **right triangle** is a triangle with one right angle. A right angle is an angle with a measure of 90°.

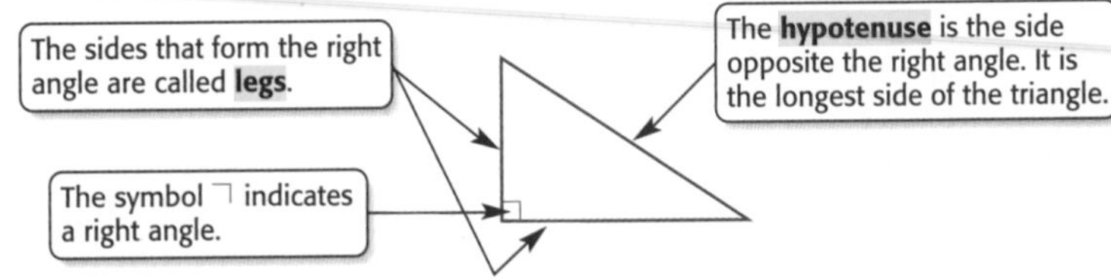

The **Pythagorean Theorem** describes the relationship between the lengths of the legs and the hypotenuse for *any* right triangle.

Noteables™ **Key Concept: Pythagorean Theorem**

Words In a right triangle, the square of the length of the hypotenuse is equal to the sum of the squares of the lengths of the legs.

Symbols	Arithmetic	Algebra	**Model**
	$5^2 = 3^2 + 4^2$	$c^2 = a^2 + b^2$	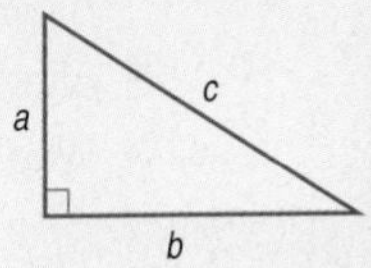 (right triangle with legs a, b and hypotenuse c)
	$25 = 9 + 16$		
	$25 = 25$		

You can use the Pythagorean Theorem to find the length of a side of a right triangle.

EXAMPLE Find the Length of the Hypotenuse

1 KITES Find the length of the kite string.

The kite string forms the hypotenuse of a right triangle. The vertical and horizontal distances form the legs.

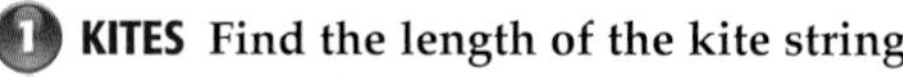

$c^2 = a^2 + b^2$	Pythagorean Theorem
$c^2 = 30^2 + 40^2$	Replace a with 30 and b with 40.
$c^2 = 900 + 1{,}600$	Evaluate 30^2 and 40^2.
$c^2 = 2{,}500$	Add 900 and 1,600.
$\sqrt{c^2} = \sqrt{2{,}500}$	Take the square root of each side.
$c = 50$ or -50	Simplify.

The equation has two solutions, 50 and −50. However, the length of the kite string must be positive. So, the kite string is 50 feet long.

Your Turn Find the length of each hypotenuse. Round to the nearest tenth if necessary.

a. 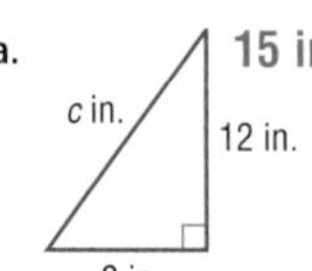

15 in.

b. 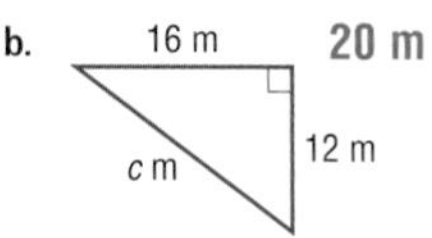

20 m

c. 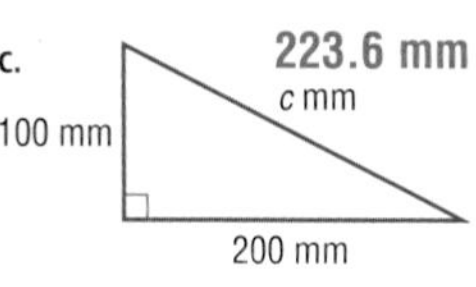

223.6 mm

REAL-LIFE MATH

KITES Some kites need as little as a 3-mile-per-hour breeze to fly. Others need a wind in excess of 10 miles per hour.

Source: *World Book*

EXAMPLE Find the Length of a Leg

2 The hypotenuse of a right triangle is 20 centimeters long and one of its legs is 17 centimeters. Find the length of the other leg.

$c^2 = a^2 + b^2$	Pythagorean Theorem
$20^2 = a^2 + 17^2$	Replace c with 20 and b with 17.
$400 = a^2 + 289$	Evaluate 20^2 and 17^2.
$400 - 289 = a^2 + 289 - 289$	Subtract 289 from each side.
$111 = a^2$	Simplify.
$\sqrt{111} = \sqrt{a^2}$	Take the square root of each side.
$10.5 \approx a$	Use a calculator.

The length of the other leg is about 10.5 centimeters.

Your Turn Write an equation you could use to find the length of the missing side of each right triangle. Then find the missing length. Round to the nearest tenth if necessary.

d. b, 9 ft; c, 12 ft   e. a, 3 m; c, 8 m   f. a, 15 in.; b, 18 in.

TEACHING TIP

Point out that the answer to Example 2 must be less than the length of the hypotenuse, 20 feet.

d. $12^2 = a^2 + 9^2$; 7.9 ft
e. $8^2 = 3^2 + b^2$; 7.4 m
f. $c^2 = 15^2 + 18^2$; 23.4 in.

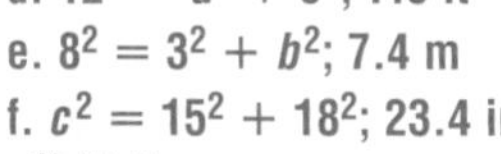

msmath3.net/extra_examples

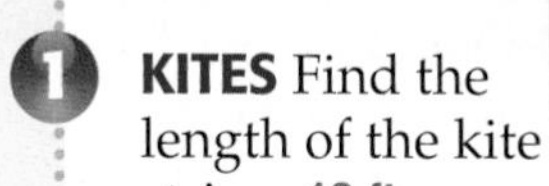

2 Teach

In-Class Examples

1 KITES Find the length of the kite string. **13 ft**

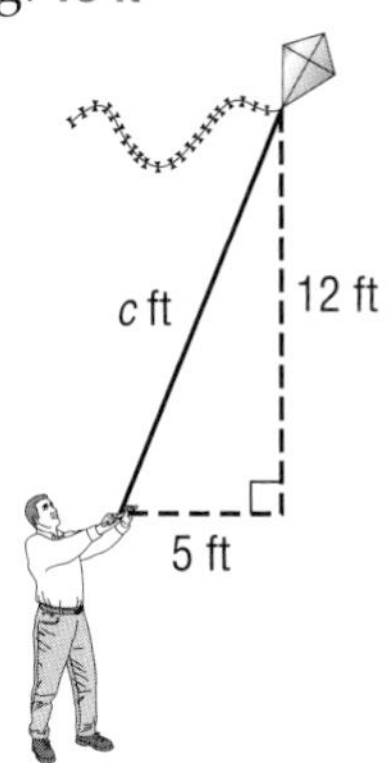

2 The hypotenuse of a right triangle is 33 centimeters long and one of its legs is 28 centimeters. Find the length of the other leg. **17.5 cm**

DAILY INTERVENTION

Differentiated Instruction

Logical Point out that the length of either leg of a right triangle may be substituted in for a and that the length of the other leg will be the value for b. Ask students to defend the fact that a and b are interchangeable by stating the property of real numbers that shows that $a^2 + b^2$ has the same sum as $b^2 + a^2$. **Commutative Property of Addition**

3 MULTIPLE-CHOICE TEST ITEM A 10-foot ramp is extended from the back of a truck to the ground to help movers load furniture onto the truck. If the ramp touches the ground at a point 9 feet behind the truck, how high off the ground is the top of the ramp? **B**

A about 1 foot

B about 4.4 feet

C about 13.5 feet

D about 19 feet

4 The measures of three sides of a triangle are 24 inches, 7 inches, and 25 inches. Determine whether the triangle is a right triangle. **yes**

Standardized Test Practice

Test-Taking Tip

Draw a Picture When solving a problem, it is sometimes helpful to draw a picture to represent the situation.

TEACHING TIP

Explain to students that the Pythagorean Theorem can be written as follows. "*If* a triangle is a right triangle, *then* the square of the hypotenuse is equal to the sum of the squares of the lengths of the legs."

EXAMPLE Use the Pythagorean Theorem

3 **MULTIPLE-CHOICE TEST ITEM** For safety reasons, the base of a 24-foot ladder should be at least 8 feet from the wall. How high can a 24-foot ladder safely reach?

Ⓐ about 16 feet Ⓑ about 22.6 feet

Ⓒ about 25.3 feet Ⓓ about 512 feet

Read the Test Item You know the length of the ladder and the distance from the base of the ladder to the side of the house. Make a drawing of the situation including the right triangle.

24 ft

8 ft

Solve the Test Item Use the Pythagorean Theorem.

$c^2 = a^2 + b^2$	Pythagorean Theorem
$24^2 = a^2 + 8^2$	Replace c with 24 and b with 8.
$576 = a^2 + 64$	Evaluate 24^2 and 8^2.
$576 - 64 = a^2 + 64 - 64$	Subtract 64 from each side.
$512 = a^2$	Simplify.
$\sqrt{512} = \sqrt{a^2}$	Take the square root of each side.
$22.6 \approx a$	Use a calculator.

The ladder can safely reach a height of 22.6 feet. The answer is B.

If you reverse the parts of the Pythagorean Theorem, you have formed its **converse**. The converse of the Pythagorean Theorem is also true.

Noteables™ **Key Concept: Converse of Pythagorean Theorem**

If the sides of a triangle have lengths a, b, and c units such that $c^2 = a^2 + b^2$, then the triangle is a right triangle.

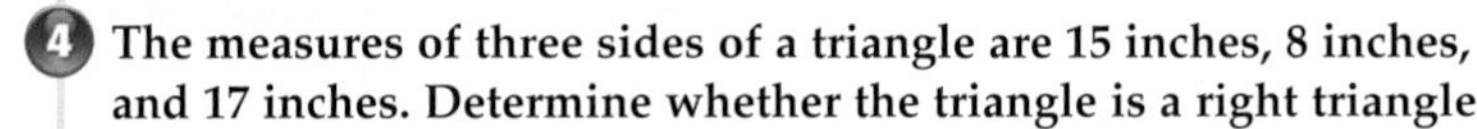

EXAMPLE Identify a Right Triangle

4 **The measures of three sides of a triangle are 15 inches, 8 inches, and 17 inches. Determine whether the triangle is a right triangle.**

$c^2 = a^2 + b^2$	Pythagorean Theorem
$17^2 \stackrel{?}{=} 15^2 + 8^2$	$c = 17, a = 15, b = 8$
$289 \stackrel{?}{=} 225 + 64$	Evaluate 17^2, 15^2, and 8^2.
$289 = 289$ ✓	Simplify.

The triangle is a right triangle.

STUDY TIP

Assigning Variables Remember that the longest side of a right triangle is the hypotenuse. Therefore, c represents the length of the longest side.

Your Turn **Determine whether each triangle with sides of given lengths is a right triangle.**

g. 18 mi, 24 mi, 30 mi **yes** h. 4 ft, 7 ft, 5 ft **no**

134 Chapter 3 Algebra: Real Numbers and the Pythagorean Theorem

Students practice the same concepts in Exercises 12–31 if they are assigned odd or even problems.

Skill and Concept Check

1. **Draw** a right triangle and label all the parts. **See margin.**
2. **OPEN ENDED** State three measures that could be the side measures of a right triangle. **Sample answer: 3, 4, 5**
3. **FIND THE ERROR** Catalina and Morgan are writing an equation to find the length of the third side of the triangle. Who is correct? Explain.

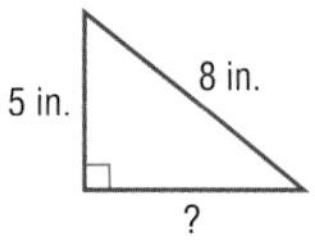

Catalina
$c^2 = 5^2 + 8^2$

Morgan
$8^2 = a^2 + 5^2$

Morgan; the hypotenuse (8) and a leg (5) are given. The correct equation to solve the problem is $8^2 = a^2 + 5^2$.

GUIDED PRACTICE

Write an equation you could use to find the length of the missing side of each right triangle. Then find the missing length. Round to the nearest tenth if necessary. **5. $12^2 = a^2 + 8^2$; 8.9 yd**

4.
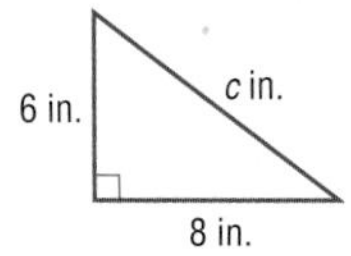

$c^2 = 6^2 + 8^2$; 10 in.

5.
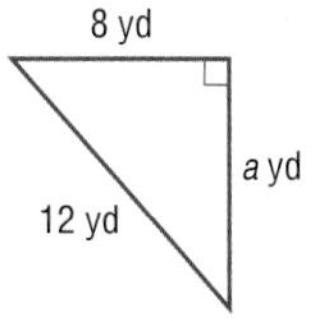

6.
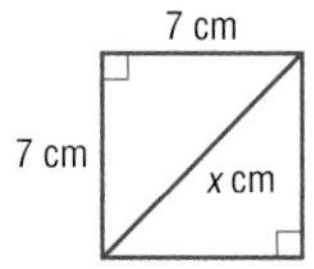

$x^2 = 7^2 + 7^2$; 9.9 cm

7. *a*, 5 ft; *c*, 6 ft **$6^2 = 5^2 + b^2$; 3.3 ft**
8. *a*, 9 m; *b*, 7 m **$c^2 = 9^2 + 7^2$; 11.4 m**
9. *b*, 4 yd; *c*, 10 yd **$10^2 = a^2 + 4^2$; 9.2 yd**

Determine whether each triangle with sides of given lengths is a right triangle.

10. 5 in., 10 in., 12 in. **no**
11. 9 m, 40 m, 41 m **yes**

★ indicates increased difficulty

Practice and Applications

Write an equation you could use to find the length of the missing side of each right triangle. Then find the missing length. Round to the nearest tenth if necessary. **14. $15^2 = a^2 + 10^2$; 11.2 cm**

HOMEWORK HELP	
For Exercises	See Examples
12–25, 32	1–3
26–31, 34	4

Extra Practice
See pages 623, 650.

12.
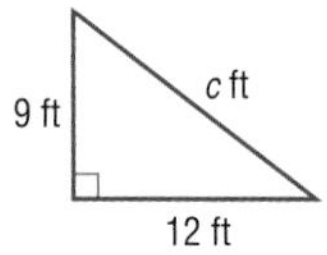

$c^2 = 9^2 + 12^2$; 15 ft

13.
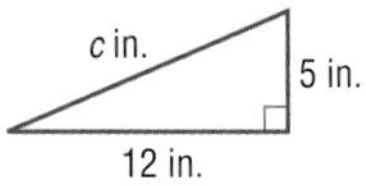

$c^2 = 5^2 + 12^2$; 13 in.

14.
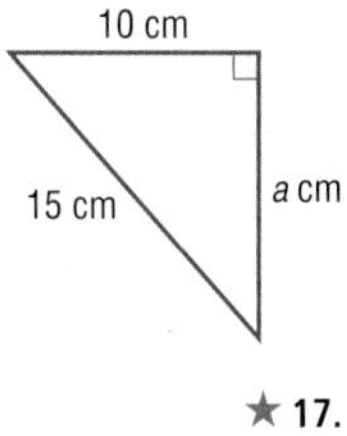

15.
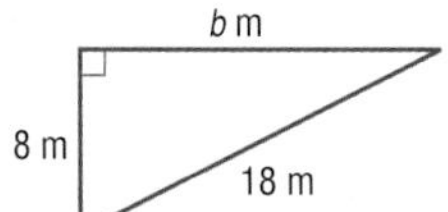

$18^2 = 8^2 + b^2$; 16.1 m

★ 16.
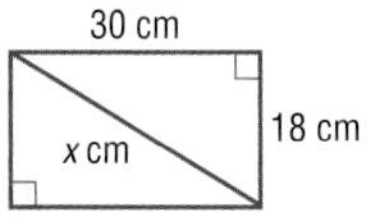

$x^2 = 30^2 + 18^2$; 35.0 cm

★ 17.
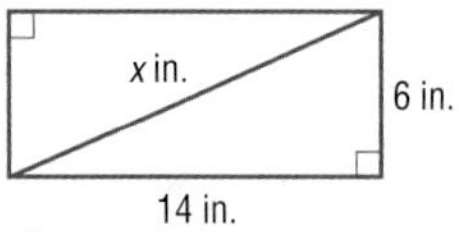

$x^2 = 14^2 + 6^2$; 15.2 in.

18. *b*, 99 mm; *c*, 101 mm
19. *a*, 48 yd; *b*, 55 yd
20. *a*, 17 ft; *c*, 20 ft
21. *a*, 23 in.; *b*, 18 in.
★ 22. *b*, 4.5 m; *c*, 9.4 m
★ 23. *b*, 5.1 m; *c*, 12.3 m

18–23. See margin.

Math Online **msmath3.net/self_check_quiz**

3 Practice/Apply

FOLDABLES™ Follow-Up Remind students to use their Foldable journals to record what they learn about the Pythagorean Theorem. For example, on the fourth page of their journals they might explain the Pythagorean Theorem and the converse of the Pythagorean Theorem in their own words and provide examples for each.

DAILY INTERVENTION **FIND THE ERROR** For Exercise 3, ask students to label the two legs of the right triangle *a* and *b* and to label the hypotenuse *c*. Point out that it is often helpful to write out the formula being used before replacing variables with numbers.

About the Exercises...

Guided Practice Key

Exercises	Examples
4, 6, 8	1
5, 7, 9	2
10–11	4

Assignment Guide

Basic: 13, 15, 19, 21, 25–33 odd, 35–46

Average: 13–33 odd, 35–46

Enriched: 12–34 even, 35–42 (Optional: 43–46)

Alert! Exercise 33 involves use of the Internet or another source of research.

Answers (pp. 135–136)

1.
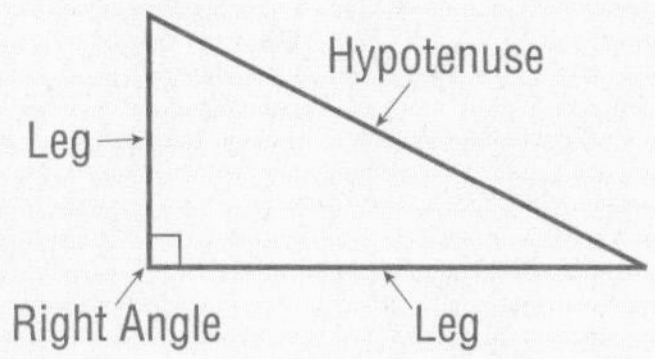

18. **$101^2 = a^2 + 99^2$; 20 mm**
19. **$c^2 = 48^2 + 55^2$; 73 yd**
20. **$20^2 = 17^2 + b^2$; 10.5 ft**
21. **$c^2 = 23^2 + 18^2$; 29.2 in.**
22. **$9.4^2 = a^2 + 4.5^2$; 8.3 m**
23. **$12.3^2 = a^2 + 5.1^2$; 11.2 m**

35. **at knots 3 and 7 from unstaked end**

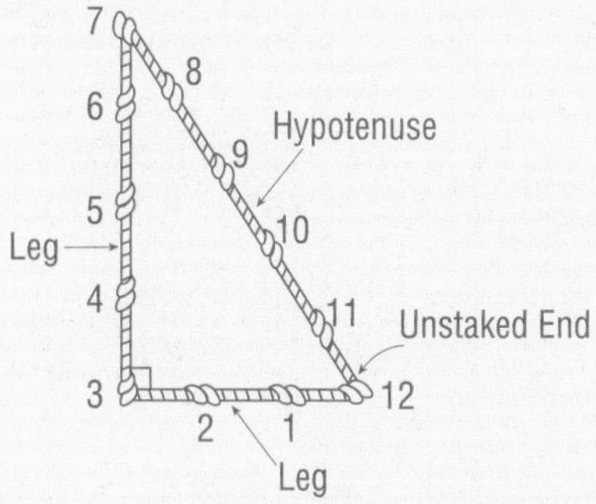

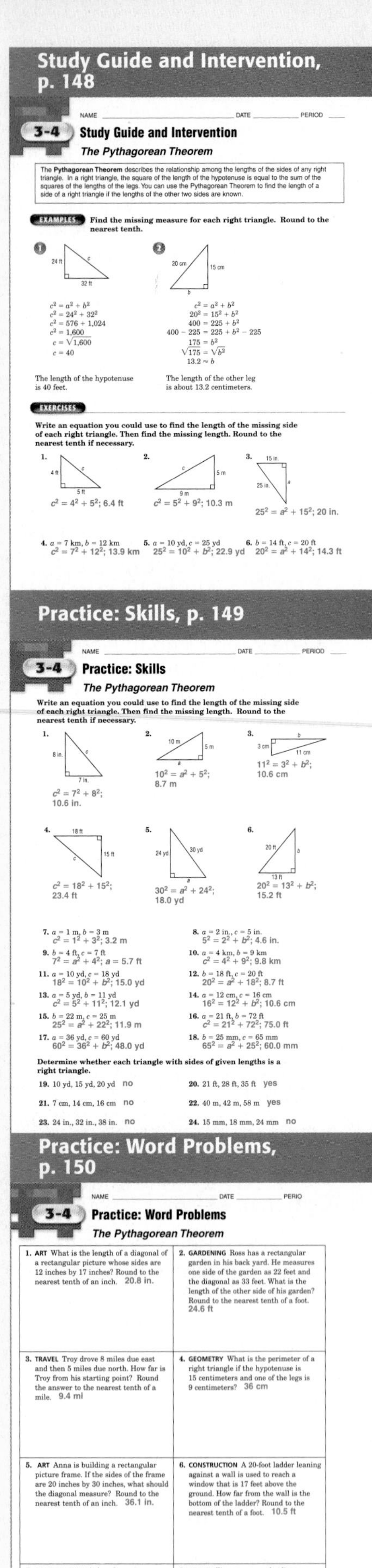

Study Guide and Intervention, p. 148

NAME ________________ DATE ________ PERIOD ____

3-4 Study Guide and Intervention

The Pythagorean Theorem

The **Pythagorean Theorem** describes the relationship among the lengths of the sides of any right triangle. In a right triangle, the square of the length of the hypotenuse is equal to the sum of the squares of the lengths of the legs. You can use the Pythagorean Theorem to find the length of a side of a right triangle if the lengths of the other two sides are known.

EXAMPLES **Find the missing measure for each right triangle. Round to the nearest tenth.**

1. (24 ft, 32 ft, c)

$c^2 = a^2 + b^2$
$c^2 = 24^2 + 32^2$
$c^2 = 576 + 1{,}024$
$c^2 = 1{,}600$
$c = \sqrt{1{,}600}$
$c = 40$

The length of the hypotenuse is 40 feet.

2. (20 cm, 15 cm, b)

$c^2 = a^2 + b^2$
$20^2 = 15^2 + b^2$
$400 = 225 + b^2$
$400 - 225 = 225 + b^2 - 225$
$175 = b^2$
$\sqrt{175} = \sqrt{b^2}$
$13.2 \approx b$

The length of the other leg is about 13.2 centimeters.

EXERCISES

Write an equation you could use to find the length of the missing side of each right triangle. Then find the missing length. Round to the nearest tenth if necessary.

1. (4 ft, 5 ft, c) $c^2 = 4^2 + 5^2$; 6.4 ft
2. (5 m, 9 m, c) $c^2 = 5^2 + 9^2$; 10.3 m
3. (15 in., 25 in., a) $25^2 = a^2 + 15^2$; 20 in.
4. $a = 7$ km, $b = 12$ km $c^2 = 7^2 + 12^2$; 13.9 km
5. $a = 10$ yd, $c = 25$ yd $25^2 = 10^2 + b^2$; 22.9 yd
6. $b = 14$ ft, $c = 20$ ft $20^2 = a^2 + 14^2$; 14.3 ft

Practice: Skills, p. 149

NAME ________________ DATE ________ PERIOD ____

3-4 Practice: Skills

The Pythagorean Theorem

Write an equation you could use to find the length of the missing side of each right triangle. Then find the missing length. Round to the nearest tenth if necessary.

1. (8 in., 7 in., c) $c^2 = 7^2 + 8^2$; 10.6 in.
2. (10 m, 5 m, a) $10^2 = a^2 + 5^2$; 8.7 m
3. (3 cm, 11 cm, b) $11^2 = 3^2 + b^2$; 10.6 cm
4. (18 ft, 15 ft, c) $c^2 = 18^2 + 15^2$; 23.4 ft
5. (24 yd, 30 yd, a) $30^2 = a^2 + 24^2$; 18.0 yd
6. (20 ft, 13 ft, b) $20^2 = 13^2 + b^2$; 15.2 ft
7. $a = 1$ m, $b = 3$ m $c^2 = 1^2 + 3^2$; 3.2 m
8. $a = 2$ in., $c = 5$ in. $5^2 = 2^2 + b^2$; 4.6 in.
9. $b = 4$ ft, $c = 7$ ft $7^2 = a^2 + 4^2$; $a = 5.7$ ft
10. $a = 4$ km, $b = 9$ km $c^2 = 4^2 + 9^2$; 9.8 km
11. $a = 10$ yd, $c = 18$ yd $18^2 = 10^2 + b^2$; 15.0 yd
12. $b = 18$ ft, $c = 20$ ft $20^2 = a^2 + 18^2$; 8.7 ft
13. $a = 5$ yd, $b = 11$ yd $c^2 = 5^2 + 11^2$; 12.1 yd
14. $a = 12$ cm, $c = 16$ cm $16^2 = 12^2 + b^2$; 10.6 cm
15. $b = 22$ m, $c = 25$ m $25^2 = a^2 + 22^2$; 11.9 m
16. $a = 21$ ft, $b = 72$ ft $c^2 = 21^2 + 72^2$; 75.0 ft
17. $a = 36$ yd, $c = 60$ yd $60^2 = 36^2 + b^2$; 48.0 yd
18. $b = 25$ mm, $c = 65$ mm $65^2 = a^2 + 25^2$; 60.0 mm

Determine whether each triangle with sides of given lengths is a right triangle.

19. 10 yd, 15 yd, 20 yd no
20. 21 ft, 28 ft, 35 ft yes
21. 7 cm, 14 cm, 16 cm no
22. 40 m, 42 m, 58 m yes
23. 24 in., 32 in., 38 in. no
24. 15 mm, 18 mm, 24 mm no

Practice: Word Problems, p. 150

NAME ________________ DATE ________ PERIO

3-4 Practice: Word Problems

The Pythagorean Theorem

1. ART What is the length of a diagonal of a rectangular picture whose sides are 12 inches by 17 inches? Round to the nearest tenth of an inch. 20.8 in.
2. GARDENING Ross has a rectangular garden in his back yard. He measures one side of the garden as 22 feet and the diagonal as 33 feet. What is the length of the other side of his garden? Round to the nearest tenth of a foot. 24.6 ft
3. TRAVEL Troy drove 8 miles due east and then 5 miles due north. How far is Troy from his starting point? Round the answer to the nearest tenth of a mile. 9.4 mi
4. GEOMETRY What is the perimeter of a right triangle if the hypotenuse is 15 centimeters and one of the legs is 9 centimeters? 36 cm
5. ART Anna is building a rectangular picture frame. If the sides of the frame are 20 inches by 30 inches, what should the diagonal measure? Round to the nearest tenth of an inch. 36.1 in.
6. CONSTRUCTION A 20-foot ladder leaning against a wall is used to reach a window that is 17 feet above the ground. How far from the wall is the bottom of the ladder? Round to the nearest tenth of a foot. 10.5 ft
7. CONSTRUCTION A door frame is 80 inches tall and 36 inches wide. What is the length of a diagonal of the door frame? Round to the nearest tenth of an inch. 87.7 in.
8. TRAVEL Tina measures the distances between three cities on a map. The distances between the three cities are 45 miles, 56 miles, and 72 miles. Do the positions of the three cities form a right triangle? no

24. The hypotenuse of a right triangle is 12 inches, and one of its legs is 7 inches. Find the length of the other leg. **about 9.7 in.**

25. If one leg of a right triangle is 8 feet and its hypotenuse is 14 feet, how long is the other leg? **about 11.5 ft**

Determine whether each triangle with sides of given lengths is a right triangle.

26. 28 yd, 195 yd, 197 yd **yes**
27. 30 cm, 122 cm, 125 cm **no**
28. 24 m, 143 m, 145 m **yes**
29. 135 in., 140 in., 175 in. **no**
30. 56 ft, 65 ft, 16 ft **no**
31. 44 cm, 70 cm, 55 cm **no**

32. **GEOGRAPHY** Wyoming's rectangular shape is about 275 miles by 365 miles. Find the length of the diagonal of the state of Wyoming. **about 457.0 mi**

33. **RESEARCH** Use the Internet or other resource to find the measurements of another state. Then calculate the length of a diagonal of the state. **See students' work.**

34. **TRAVEL** The Research Triangle in North Carolina is formed by Raleigh, Durham, and Chapel Hill. Is this triangle a right triangle? Explain. **No; $29^2 \neq 12^2 + 24^2$.**

35. **CRITICAL THINKING** About 2000 B.C., Egyptian engineers discovered a way to make a right triangle using a rope with 12 evenly spaced knots tied in it. They attached one end of the rope to a stake in the ground. At what knot locations should the other two stakes be placed in order to form a right triangle? Draw a diagram. **See margin.**

Spiral Review with Standardized Test Practice

36. **MULTIPLE CHOICE** A hiker walked 22 miles north and then walked 17 miles west. How far is the hiker from the starting point? **D**

Ⓐ 374 mi Ⓑ 112.6 mi Ⓒ 39 mi Ⓓ 27.8 mi

37. **SHORT RESPONSE** What is the perimeter of a right triangle if the lengths of the legs are 10 inches and 24 inches? **60 in.**

Replace each ● with <, >, or = to make each a true sentence. (Lesson 3-3)

38. $\sqrt{12}$ ● 3.5 **<**
39. $\sqrt{41}$ ● 6.4 **>**
40. $5.\overline{6}$ ● $\frac{17}{3}$ **=**
41. $\sqrt{55}$ ● $7.\overline{4}$ **<**

42. **ALGEBRA** Estimate the solution of $x^2 = 77$ to the nearest integer. (Lesson 3-2) **9 or −9**

GETTING READY FOR THE NEXT LESSON

PREREQUISITE SKILL Solve each equation. Check your solution. (Lesson 1-8)

43. $57 = x + 24$ **33**
44. $82 = 54 + y$ **28**
45. $71 = 35 + z$ **36**
46. $64 = a + 27$ **37**

4 Assess

Open-Ended Assessment

Modeling Have students create their own right triangles using geoboards and rubber bands. Ask them to use the Pythagorean Theorem to determine the length of the hypotenuse.

Using the Pythagorean Theorem

What You'll LEARN

Solve problems using the Pythagorean Theorem.

NEW Vocabulary

Pythagorean triple

WHEN am I ever going to use this?

GYMNASTICS In the floor exercises of women's gymnastics, athletes cross the diagonal of the mat flipping and twisting as they go. It is important that the gymnast does not step off the mat.

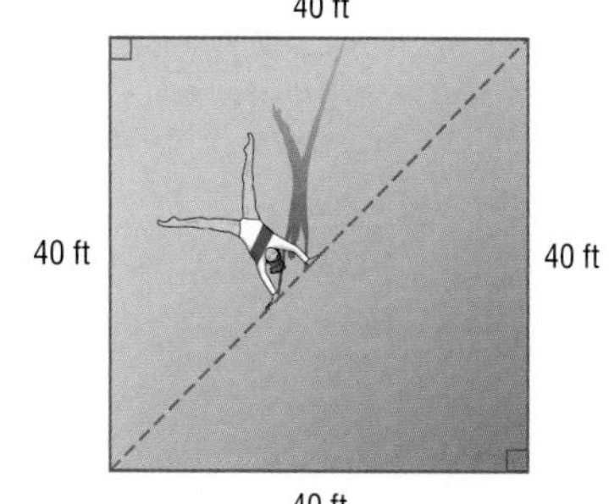

1. What type of triangle is formed by the sides of the mat and the diagonal? **right**
2. Write an equation that can be used to find the length of the diagonal. $d^2 = 40^2 + 40^2$

The Pythagorean Theorem can be used to solve a variety of problems.

EXAMPLE Use the Pythagorean Theorem

1 SKATEBOARDING Find the height of the skateboard ramp.

Notice the problem involves a right triangle. Use the Pythagorean Theorem.

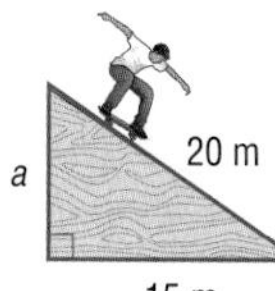

Words	The square of the hypotenuse	equals	the sum of the squares of the legs.
Variables	c^2	=	$a^2 + b^2$
Equation	20^2	=	$a^2 + 15^2$

$20^2 = a^2 + 15^2$	Write the equation.
$400 = a^2 + 225$	Evaluate 20^2 and 15^2.
$400 - 225 = a^2 + 225 - 225$	Subtract 225 from each side.
$175 = a^2$	Simplify.
$\sqrt{175} = \sqrt{a^2}$	Take the square root of each side.
$13.2 \approx a$	Simplify.

The height of the ramp is about 13.2 meters.

msmath3.net/extra_examples

3-5 Lesson Notes

Lesson Resources

Chapter 3 Resource Masters
- Study Guide and Intervention, p. 153
- Practice: Skills, p. 154
- Practice: Word Problems, p. 155
- Reading to Learn Mathematics, p. 156
- Enrichment, p. 157

Calculator and Spreadsheet Masters, p. 19

Key Teaching Transparencies, 11

Parent and Student Study Guide Online Worksheets, 3-5

Noteables™: Interactive Study Notebook with Foldables™, 3-5

1 Focus

5-Minute Check 3-5

Use as a quiz or review of Lesson 3-4. (Also available as a transparency)

Bellringer

Communication Draw a baseball diamond on the chalkboard. When students enter the classroom, have them write an equation that could be used to find the distance between home plate and second base, given that the distance between any two consecutive bases is 90 feet. $c^2 = 90^2 + 90^2$ Discuss how they know what to write. **Apply the Pythagorean Theorem.**

Reading to Learn Mathematics, p. 156 **ELL**

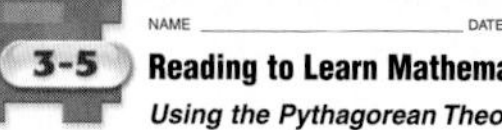

NAME ______ DATE ______ PERIOD ______

3-5 Reading to Learn Mathematics
Using the Pythagorean Theorem

Pre-Activity *Read the introduction at the top of page 137 in your textbook. Write your answers below.*

1. What type of triangle is formed by the sides of the mat and the diagonal? right
2. Write an equation that can be used to find the length of the diagonal. $d^2 = 40^2 + 40^2$

Reading the Lesson

Determine whether each of the following is a Pythagorean triple.

3. 13-84-85 yes
4. 11-60-61 yes
5. 21-23-29 no
6. 12-25-37 no
7. The triple 8-15-17 is a Pythagorean triple. Complete the table to find

2 Teach

In-Class Examples

INTERACTIVE CHALKBOARD
PowerPoint® Presentations

1 **RAMPS** A ramp to the entrance of a newly constructed building must be built according to accessibility guidelines stated in the Americans with Disabilities Act. If the ramp is 24.1 feet long and the top of the ramp is 2 feet off the ground, how far is the end of the ramp from the entrance? **about 24 ft**

2 Multiply the triple 5-12-13 by the numbers 2, 3, 4, 5, and 10 to find more Pythagorean triples. **10, 24, 26; 15, 36, 39; 20, 48, 52; 25, 60, 65; 50, 120, 130**

Using Applications There are many opportunities to use the Pythagorean Theorem to find various distances in the classroom. For example, have students work in small groups and rotate through stations in the room. Each station should require students to take measurements and calculate distances using the Pythagorean Theorem. Stations could include measuring the distance across the classroom from one corner to the far corner. You might also have students find the size of a TV screen, which is determined by the diagonal measurement.

TEACHING TIP

Explain to students that they could use any factor when determining other Pythagorean triples.

You know that a triangle with sides 3, 4, and 5 units is a right triangle because these numbers satisfy the Pythagorean Theorem. Such whole numbers are called **Pythagorean triples**. By using multiples of a Pythagorean triple, you can create additional triples.

EXAMPLE Write Pythagorean Triples

2 **Multiply the triple 3-4-5 by the numbers 2, 3, 4, and 10 to find more Pythagorean triples.**

You can organize your answers in a table. Multiply each Pythagorean triple entry by the same number and then check the Pythagorean relationship.

	a	b	c	Check: $c^2 = a^2 + b^2$
original	3	4	5	25 = 9 + 16 ✓
× 2	6	8	10	100 = 36 + 64 ✓
× 3	9	12	15	225 = 81 + 144 ✓
× 4	12	16	20	400 = 144 + 256 ✓
× 10	30	40	50	2,500 = 900 + 1,600 ✓

Students practice the same concepts in Exercises 8–15 if they are assigned odd or even problems.

Skill and Concept Check

1. *Writing Math* Explain why you can use any two sides of a right triangle to find the third side. **See margin.**
2. **OPEN ENDED** Write a problem that can be solved by using the Pythagorean Theorem. Then solve the problem. **See margin.**
3. **Which One Doesn't Belong?** Identify the set of numbers that are not Pythagorean triples. Explain your reasoning. **5-7-9; $9^2 \neq 5^2 + 7^2$**

5-12-13	10-24-26	5-7-9	8-15-17

GUIDED PRACTICE

Write an equation that can be used to answer the question. Then solve. Round to the nearest tenth if necessary.

4. How long is each rafter?

r, r, 9 ft, 12 ft, 12 ft

$r^2 = 9^2 + 12^2$; **15 ft**

5. How far apart are the planes?

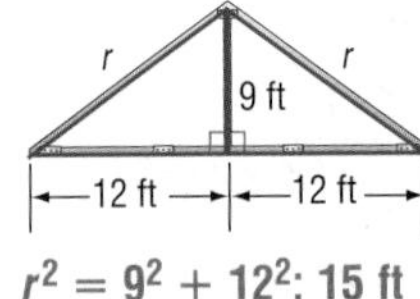

$d^2 = 7^2 + 10^2$; **12.2 mi**

6. How high does the ladder reach?

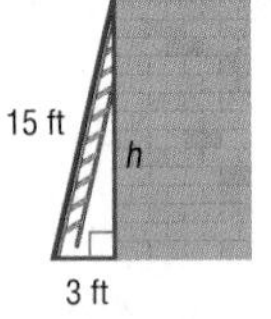

$15^2 = 3^2 + h^2$; **14.7 ft**

7. **GEOMETRY** An *isosceles* right triangle is a right triangle in which both legs are equal in length. If the leg of an isosceles triangle is 4 inches long, what is the length of the hypotenuse? **about 5.7 in.**

DAILY INTERVENTION — Flexible Grouping

Pythagorean Theorem Have each student in a group write a Pythagorean Theorem application problem on a sheet of paper and solve it on the back of the page. Each student should then pass his or her problem to the next student to the right to solve on a separate sheet of paper. Encourage students to check each other's work and to offer each other assistance. Students should continue passing problems to the right until all students in a group have solved all problems, or until time is up.

138 Chapter 3 Algebra: Real Numbers and the Pythagorean Theorem

★ indicates increased difficulty

Practice and Applications

HOMEWORK HELP	
For Exercises	See Examples
8–19	1, 2

Extra Practice See pages 623, 650.

Write an equation that can be used to answer the question. Then solve. Round to the nearest tenth if necessary.

8. How long is the kite string?

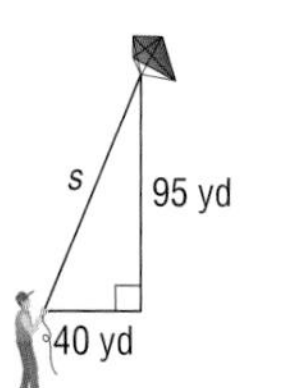

9. How far is the helicopter from the car?

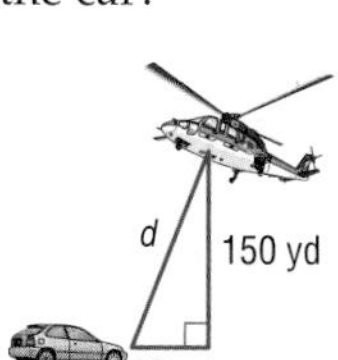

10. How high is the ski ramp?

8. $s^2 = 40^2 + 95^2$; 103.1 yd
9. $d^2 = 60^2 + 150^2$; 161.6 yd
10. $15^2 = 14^2 + h^2$; 5.4 ft

11. How long is the lake?

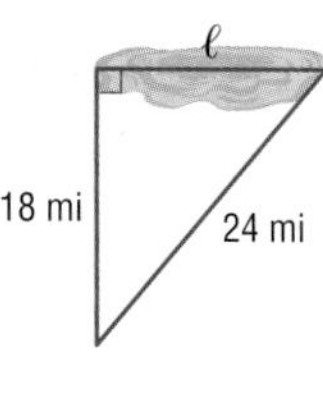

12. How high is the wire attached to the pole?

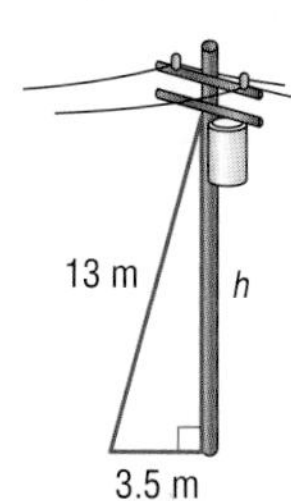

13. How high is the wheel chair ramp?

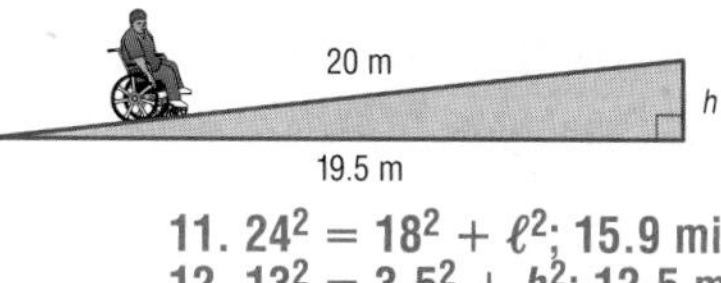

11. $24^2 = 18^2 + \ell^2$; 15.9 mi
12. $13^2 = 3.5^2 + h^2$; 12.5 m
13. $20^2 = 19.5^2 + h^2$; 4.4 m

14. **VOLLEYBALL** Two ropes and two stakes are needed to support each pole holding the volleyball net. Find the length of each rope. **about 8.7 ft**

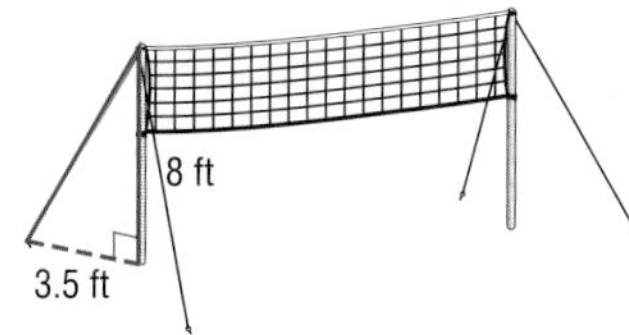

15. **ENTERTAINMENT** Connor loves to watch movies in the letterbox format on his television. He wants to buy a new television with a screen that is at least 25 inches by 13.6 inches. What diagonal size television meets Connor's requirements? **about 28.5 in.**

16. **GEOGRAPHY** Suppose Flint, Ann Arbor, and Kalamazoo, Michigan, form a right triangle. What is the distance from Kalamazoo to Ann Arbor? **about 96.9 mi**

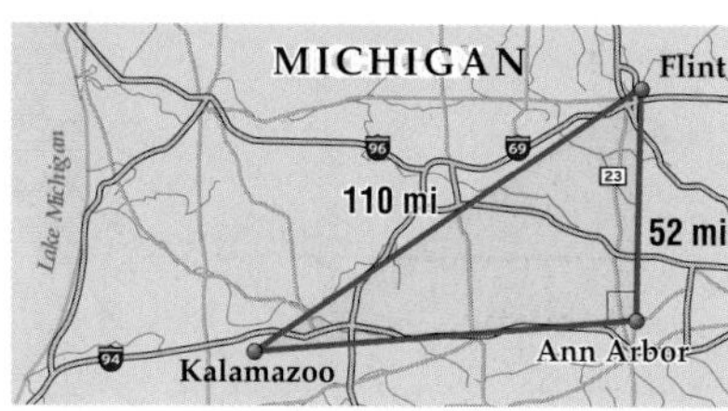
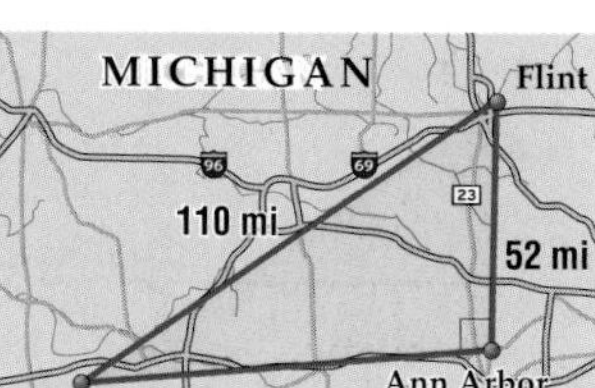

★ 17. **GEOMETRY** A line segment with endpoints on a circle is called a *chord*. Find the distance d from the center of the circle O to the chord $\overline{AB}$ in the circle below. **about 2.6 cm**

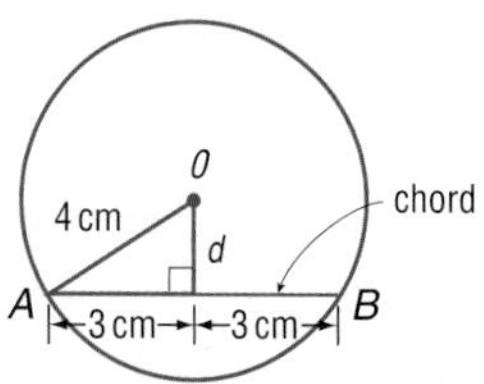

Math Online msmath3.net/self_check_quiz

3 Practice/Apply

FOLDABLES™ Follow-Up Remind students to use their Foldable journals to record what they learn about using the Pythagorean Theorem. For example, on the fifth page of their journals they might explain the Pythagorean Theorem in their own words and give an example of how it might be used in a real-life situation.

Which One Doesn't Belong?

For Exercise 3, ask students how to determine which number in the listed triples represents the length of the hypotenuse, or c in the equation. **The greatest number is always c, because it is the diagonal measure.** Does it matter which numbers are used for a and b? **No, since the squares of the numbers are added, the order doesn't matter.**

About the Exercises...

Guided Practice Key

Exercises	Example
4–7	1

Assignment Guide

Basic: 9–15 odd, 21–33

Average: 9–19 odd, 21–33

Enriched: 8–20 even, 21–29 (Optional: 30–33)

Answers

1. **The Pythagorean Theorem relates the lengths of the three sides of a right triangle. If you know the lengths of two sides of a right triangle, you can substitute the values into the Pythagorean Theorem and solve for the missing length.**
2. **Sample answer: Sam leaves his house. He walks 2 miles north, and then turns and walks 3 miles west. How far is Sam from his house? Sam is about 3.6 miles from his house.**

4 Assess

Higher-Level Thinking

Look at the figure. Start by finding the value for x_1, then for x_2, then x_3, and so on until you get the value for x_6. Write the lengths as square roots, as that makes it simpler. What is the value of x_6? **$\sqrt{7}$**

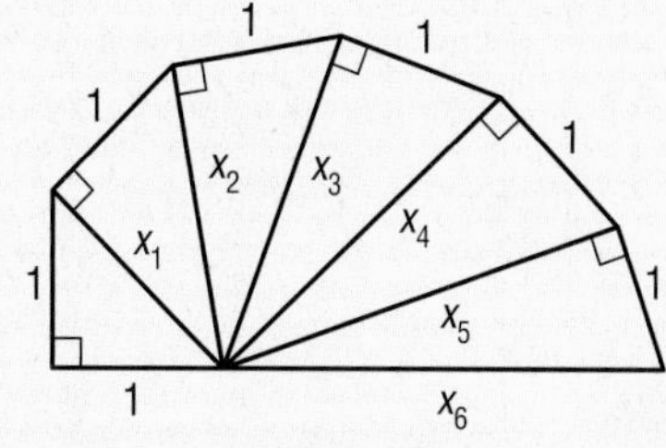

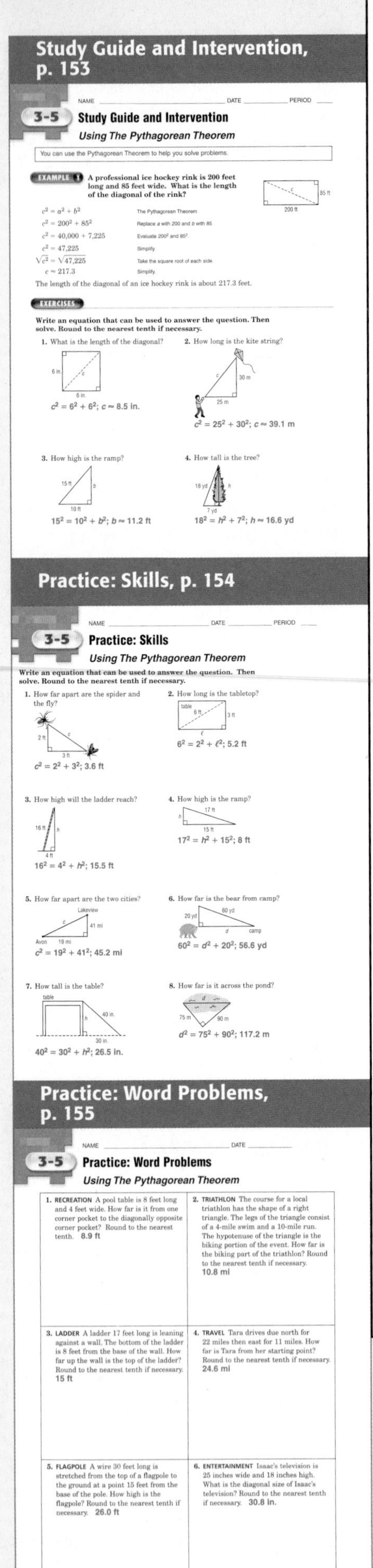

Study Guide and Intervention, p. 153

NAME ______ DATE ______ PERIOD ____

3-5 Study Guide and Intervention

Using The Pythagorean Theorem

You can use the Pythagorean Theorem to help you solve problems.

EXAMPLE 1 **A professional ice hockey rink is 200 feet long and 85 feet wide. What is the length of the diagonal of the rink?**

$c^2 = a^2 + b^2$	The Pythagorean Theorem
$c^2 = 200^2 + 85^2$	Replace *a* with 200 and *b* with 85
$c^2 = 40{,}000 + 7{,}225$	Evaluate 200^2 and 85^2.
$c^2 = 47{,}225$	Simplify.
$\sqrt{c^2} = \sqrt{47{,}225}$	Take the square root of each side.
$c \approx 217.3$	Simplify.

The length of the diagonal of an ice hockey rink is about 217.3 feet.

EXERCISES

Write an equation that can be used to answer the question. Then solve. Round to the nearest tenth if necessary.

1. What is the length of the diagonal? (6 in., 6 in., c) $c^2 = 6^2 + 6^2$; $c \approx 8.5$ in.
2. How long is the kite string? (c, 30 m, 25 m) $c^2 = 25^2 + 30^2$; $c \approx 39.1$ m
3. How high is the ramp? (15 ft, b, 10 ft) $15^2 = 10^2 + b^2$; $b \approx 11.2$ ft
4. How tall is the tree? (18 yd, h, 7 yd) $18^2 = h^2 + 7^2$; $h \approx 16.6$ yd

Practice: Skills, p. 154

NAME ______ DATE ______ PERIOD ____

3-5 Practice: Skills

Using The Pythagorean Theorem

Write an equation that can be used to answer the question. Then solve. Round to the nearest tenth if necessary.

1. How far apart are the spider and the fly? (2 ft, 3 ft, c) $c^2 = 2^2 + 3^2$; 3.6 ft
2. How long is the tabletop? (table, 6 ft, 3 ft, ℓ) $6^2 = 2^2 + \ell^2$; 5.2 ft
3. How high will the ladder reach? (16 ft, h, 4 ft) $16^2 = 4^2 + h^2$; 15.5 ft
4. How high is the ramp? (h, 17 ft, 15 ft) $17^2 = h^2 + 15^2$; 8 ft
5. How far apart are the two cities? (Lakeview, c, 41 mi, Avon, 19 mi) $c^2 = 19^2 + 41^2$; 45.2 mi
6. How far is the bear from camp? (20 yd, 60 yd, d, camp) $60^2 = d^2 + 20^2$; 56.6 yd
7. How tall is the table? (table, h, 40 in., 30 in.) $40^2 = 30^2 + h^2$; 26.5 in.
8. How far is it across the pond? (d, 75 m, 90 m) $d^2 = 75^2 + 90^2$; 117.2 m

Practice: Word Problems, p. 155

NAME ______ DATE ______

3-5 Practice: Word Problems

Using The Pythagorean Theorem

1. **RECREATION** A pool table is 8 feet long and 4 feet wide. How far is it from one corner pocket to the diagonally opposite corner pocket? Round to the nearest tenth. **8.9 ft**
2. **TRIATHLON** The course for a local triathlon has the shape of a right triangle. The legs of the triangle consist of a 4-mile swim and a 10-mile run. The hypotenuse of the triangle is the biking portion of the event. How far is the biking part of the triathlon? Round to the nearest tenth if necessary. **10.8 mi**
3. **LADDER** A ladder 17 feet long is leaning against a wall. The bottom of the ladder is 8 feet from the base of the wall. How far up the wall is the top of the ladder? Round to the nearest tenth if necessary. **15 ft**
4. **TRAVEL** Tara drives due north for 22 miles then east for 11 miles. How far is Tara from her starting point? Round to the nearest tenth if necessary. **24.6 mi**
5. **FLAGPOLE** A wire 30 feet long is stretched from the top of a flagpole to the ground at a point 15 feet from the base of the pole. How high is the flagpole? Round to the nearest tenth if necessary. **26.0 ft**
6. **ENTERTAINMENT** Isaac's television is 25 inches wide and 18 inches high. What is the diagonal size of Isaac's television? Round to the nearest tenth if necessary. **30.8 in.**

★ 18. **MULTI STEP** Home builders add corner bracing to give strength to a house frame. How long will the brace need to be for the frame below? **about 9.2 ft**

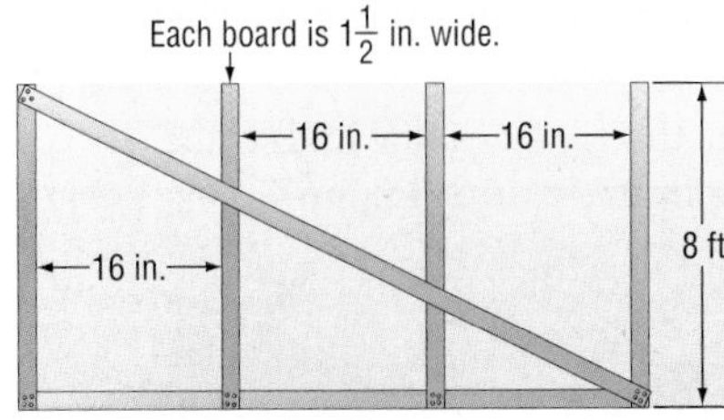

★ 19. **GEOMETRY** Find the length of the diagonal $\overline{AB}$ in the rectangular prism at the right. (*Hint:* First find the length of $\overline{BC}$.) **about 15.3 cm**

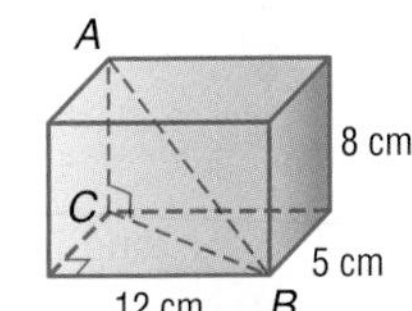

20. **MODELING** Measure the dimensions of a shoebox and use the dimensions to calculate the length of the diagonal of the box. Then use a piece of string and a ruler to check your calculation. **See students' work.**

21. **CRITICAL THINKING** Suppose a ladder 100 feet long is placed against a vertical wall 100 feet high. How far would the top of the ladder move down the wall by pulling out the bottom of the ladder 10 feet? **about 0.5 ft**

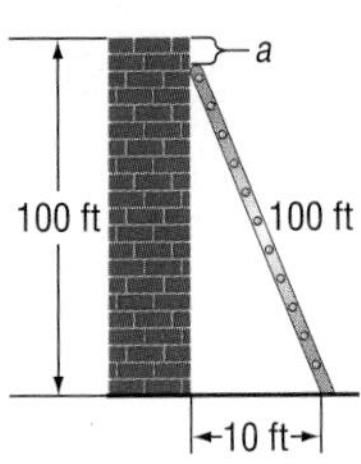

Spiral Review with Standardized Test Practice

22. **MULTIPLE CHOICE** What is the height of the tower? **B**

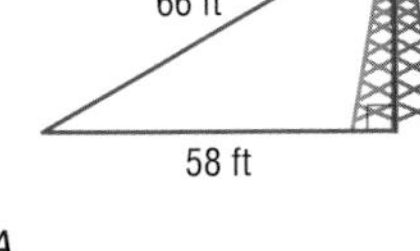

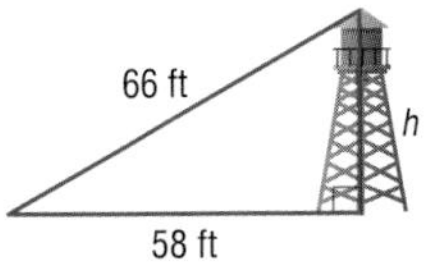

Ⓐ 8 feet Ⓑ 31.5 feet

Ⓒ 49.9 feet Ⓓ 992 feet

23. **MULTIPLE CHOICE** Triangle *ABC* is a right triangle. What is the perimeter of the triangle? **I**

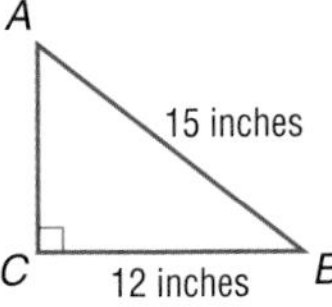

Ⓕ 3 in. Ⓖ 9 in.

Ⓗ 27 in. Ⓘ 36 in.

24. **GEOMETRY** Determine whether a triangle with sides 20 inches, 48 inches, and 52 inches long is a right triangle. (Lesson 3-4) **yes**

25. Order $\sqrt{45}$, $6.\overline{6}$, 6.75, and 6.7 from least to greatest. (Lesson 3-3) **$6.\overline{6}$, 6.7, $\sqrt{45}$, 6.75**

Evaluate each expression. (Lesson 2-8)

26. 2^4 **16**
27. 3^3 **27**
28. $2^3 \cdot 3^2$ **72**
29. $10^5 \cdot 4^2$ **1,600,000**

GETTING READY FOR THE NEXT LESSON **30–33. See Ch. 3 Answer Appendix.**

PREREQUISITE SKILL **Graph each point on a coordinate plane.** (Page 614)

30. $T(5, 2)$
31. $A(-1, 3)$
32. $M(-5, 0)$
33. $D(-2, -4)$

Answers, p. 141 (Your Turn)

a. $\sqrt{10}$ (number line −1 0 1 2 3 4 5)

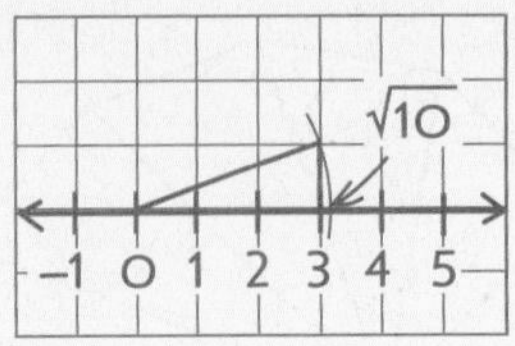

b.

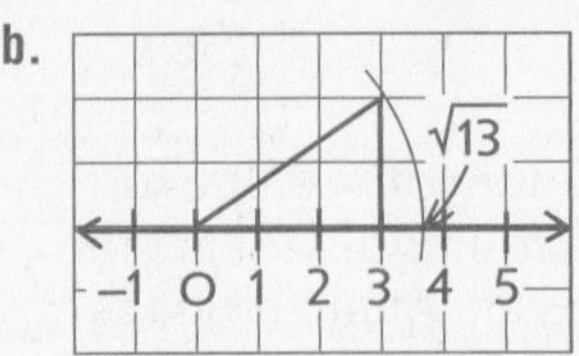

c.

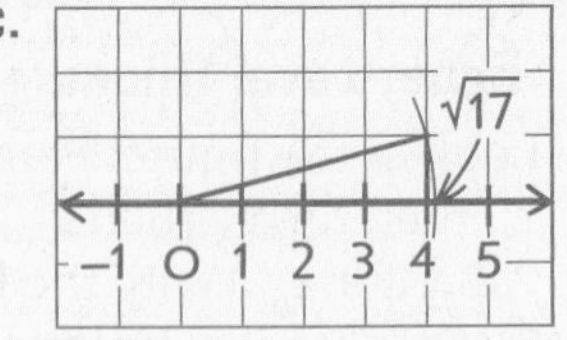

3-5b HANDS-ON LAB

A Follow-Up of Lesson 3-5

Graphing Irrational Numbers

What You'll LEARN

Graph irrational numbers.

In Lesson 3-3, you found approximate locations for irrational numbers on a number line. You can accurately graph irrational numbers.

Materials

- grid paper
- compass
- straightedge

TEACHING TIP

Point out that the triangle in Step 2 can be drawn in two different ways.

ACTIVITY *Work with a partner.*

Graph $\sqrt{34}$ on a number line as accurately as possible.

STEP 1 Find two numbers whose squares have a sum of 34.

$34 = 25 + 9$ The hypotenuse of a triangle with legs that
$34 = 5^2 + 3^2$ measure 5 and 3 units will measure $\sqrt{34}$ units.

STEP 2 Draw a number line on grid paper. Then draw a triangle whose legs measure 5 and 3 units.

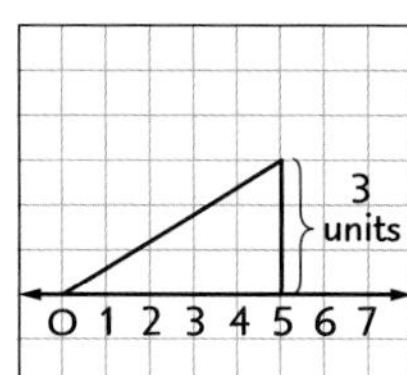

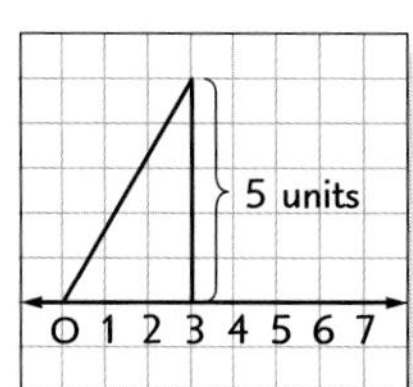

STEP 3 Adjust your compass to the length of the hypotenuse. Place the compass at 0, draw an arc that intersects the number line. The point of intersection is the graph of $\sqrt{34}$.

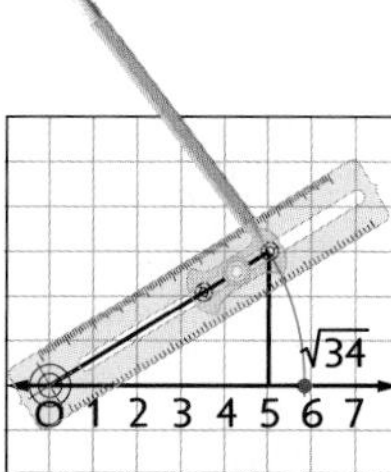

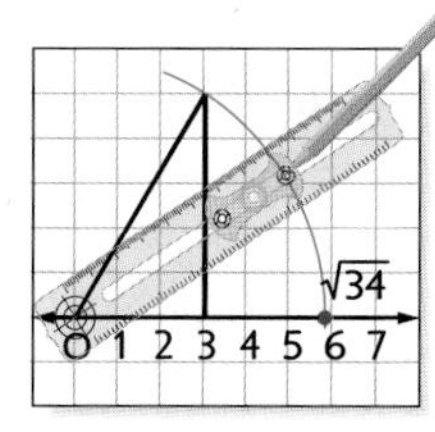

Your Turn **Accurately graph each irrational number.**

a. $\sqrt{10}$ b. $\sqrt{13}$ c. $\sqrt{17}$ d. $\sqrt{8}$

a–d. See margin.

Writing Math

1–3. See Ch. 3 Answer Appendix.

1. **Explain** how you decide what lengths to make the legs of the right triangle when graphing an irrational number.
2. **Explain** how the graph of $\sqrt{2}$ can be used to graph $\sqrt{3}$.
3. **MAKE A CONJECTURE** Do you think you could graph the square root of any whole number? Explain.

Answer (Your Turn)

d.

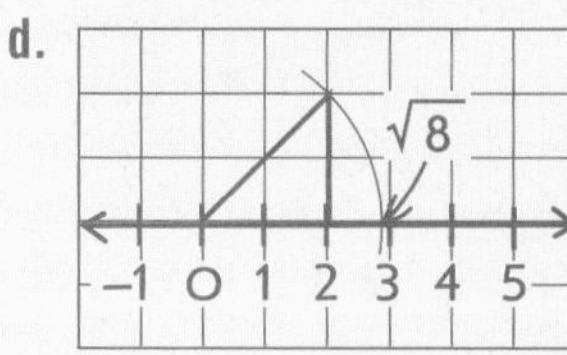

3-5b HANDS-ON LAB Lesson Notes

Lesson Resources

Teaching Mathematics with Manipulatives

FAST FILE

- quarter-inch grid, p. 10
- centimeter grid, p. 11
- student recording sheet 3-5b

Glencoe Mathematics Classroom Manipulative Kit

- compass

GETTING STARTED

Teaching Tip If students are unsure of how to use the compass, have them put a pin in a piece of string at the zero point and mark the string at the length of the hypotenuse. Bring the string down to the number line to find the length of the hypotenuse.

TEACH

- Point out that this method is very effective for graphing the square roots of some numbers, but less effective for numbers that are not the sum of two squares. Have students find one number that can be easily graphed using this technique and one that cannot. Ask students to justify their reasoning.

ASSESS

Observe as students solve the **Your Turn** exercises. They should:

- correctly determine lengths of legs of right triangles, and
- correctly graph irrational numbers.

Discuss the **Writing Math** exercises. You may wish to have students draw an example graph in their Foldables for Chapter 3.

3-6 Lesson Notes

Lesson Resources

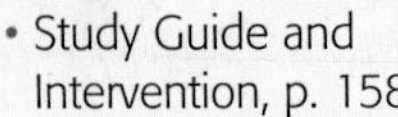

Chapter 3 Resource Masters
- Study Guide and Intervention, p. 158
- Practice: Skills, p. 159
- Practice: Word Problems, p. 160
- Reading to Learn Mathematics, p. 161
- Enrichment, p. 162

Calculator and Spreadsheet Masters, p. 20
Key Teaching Transparencies, 12
Parent and Student Study Guide Online Worksheets, 3-6
Real-Life Career Masters, p. 29
Teaching Mathematics with Manipulatives, p. 47
Noteables™: Interactive Study Notebook with Foldables™, 3-6

1 Focus

5-Minute Check 3-6

Use as a quiz or review of Lesson 3-5. (Also available as a transparency)

Bellringer
Hands-On Activity Draw a line segment diagonally between two points on a grid on an overhead transparency. Have students use geoboards to create right triangles that could be used to find the length of the segment. Ask them to explain how they would use their triangles to find the length of the segment.
(Continued in bottom margin.)

Reading to Learn Mathematics, p. 161 **ELL**

NAME ____ DATE ____ PERIOD ____

3-6 Reading to Learn Mathematics
Distance on the Coordinate Plane

Pre-Activity *Read the introduction at the top of page 142 in your textbook. Write your answers below.*

1. What type of triangle is formed by the blue and red lines? right
2. What is the length of the two red lines? 3 units, 2 units
3. Write an equation you could use to determine the distance d between the locations where the ring and necklace were found. $d^2 = 3^2 + 2^2$
4. How far apart were the ring and the necklace? about 3.6 units

Reading the Lesson

5. On the coordinate plane, what are the four sections determined by the axes called? quadrants

3-6 Geometry: Distance on the Coordinate Plane

What You'll LEARN

Find the distance between points on the coordinate plane.

NEW Vocabulary

coordinate plane
origin
y-axis
x-axis
quadrants
ordered pair
x-coordinate
abscissa
y-coordinate
ordinate

REVIEW Vocabulary

integers: whole numbers and their opposites (Lesson 1-3)

WHEN am I ever going to use this?

ARCHAEOLOGY Archaeologists keep careful records of the exact locations of objects found at digs. To accomplish this, they set up grids with string. Suppose a ring is found at (1, 3) and a necklace is found at (4, 5). The distance between the locations of these two objects is represented by the blue line. **3.** $d^2 = 3^2 + 2^2$

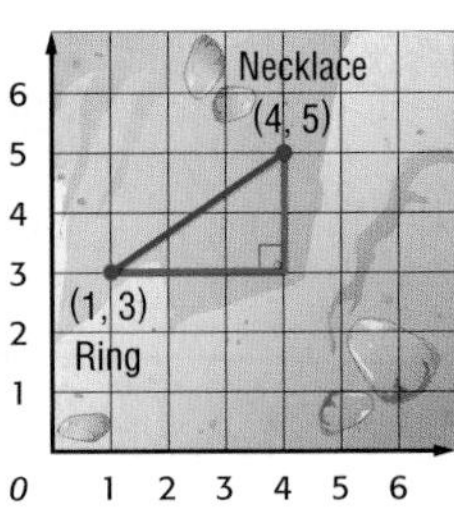

1. What type of triangle is formed by the blue and red lines? **right**
2. What is the length of the two red lines? **3 units, 2 units**
3. Write an equation you could use to determine the distance d between the locations where the ring and necklace were found.
4. How far apart were the ring and the necklace? **about 3.6 units**

In mathematics, you can locate a point by using a coordinate system similar to the grid system used by archaeologists. A **coordinate plane** is formed by two number lines that form right angles and intersect at their zero points.

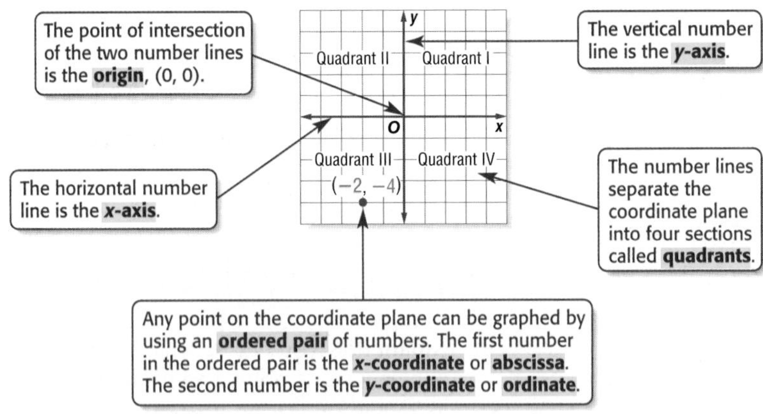

You can use the Pythagorean Theorem to find the distance between two points on the coordinate plane.

The line segment is the hypotenuse of the right triangle that was formed.

Answers (Your Turn)

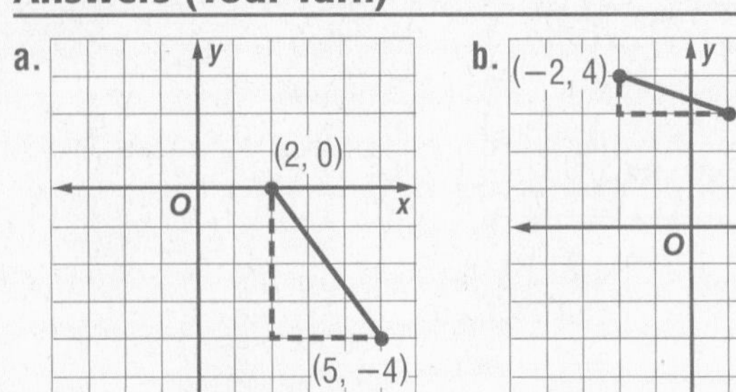

EXAMPLE Find Distance on the Coordinate Plane

TEACHING TIP

In this book, students are encouraged to draw right triangles to find the distance between two points on a coordinate plane. You may wish to challenge your better students by developing the distance formula.

1 **Graph the ordered pairs (3, 0) and (7, −5). Then find the distance between the points.**

Let c = the distance between the two points, $a = 4$, and $b = 5$.

$c^2 = a^2 + b^2$	Pythagorean Theorem
$c^2 = 4^2 + 5^2$	Replace a with 4 and b with 5.
$c^2 = 16 + 25$	Evaluate 4^2 and 5^2.
$c^2 = 41$	Add 16 and 25.
$\sqrt{c^2} = \sqrt{41}$	Take the square root of each side.
$c \approx 6.4$	Simplify.

The points are about 6.4 units apart.

Your Turn **Graph each pair of ordered pairs. Then find the distance between the points. Round to the nearest tenth if necessary.** **a–c. See margin for graphs.**

a. (2, 0), (5, −4)   b. (1, 3), (−2, 4)   c. (−3, −4), (2, −1)

a. 5 units
b. 3.2 units
c. 5.8 units

You can use this technique to find distances on a map.

REAL-LIFE MATH

TRAVEL Benjamin Banneker helped to survey and lay out Washington, D.C. He also made all the astronomical and tide calculations for the almanac he published.

Source: *World Book*

EXAMPLE Find Distance on a Map

2 **TRAVEL The Yeager family is visiting Washington, D.C. A unit on the grid of their map shown at the right is 0.05 mile. Find the distance between the Department of Defense at (−2, 9) and the Madison Building at (3, −3).**

Let c = the distance between the Department of Defense and the Madison Building. Then $a = 5$ and $b = 12$.

$c^2 = a^2 + b^2$	Pythagorean Theorem
$c^2 = 5^2 + 12^2$	Replace a with 5 and b with 12.
$c^2 = 25 + 144$	Evaluate 5^2 and 12^2.
$c^2 = 169$	Add 25 and 144.
$\sqrt{c^2} = \sqrt{169}$	Take the square root of each side.
$c = 13$	Simplify.

The distance between the Department of Defense and the Madison Building is 13 units on the map. Since each unit equals 0.05 mile, the distance between the two buildings is $0.05 \cdot 13$ or 0.65 mile.

msmath3.net/extra_examples

DAILY INTERVENTION **Differentiated Instruction**

Kinesthetic Using masking tape, mark a grid on the floor of the classroom. Have two students stand at different points. They can hold a piece of paper with their location on it. Then have another student explain to the rest of the class how to determine the distance between the two points. Have students trade off until all have taken part.

2 Teach

In-Class Examples

1 Graph the ordered pairs (0, –6) and (5, –1). Then find the distance between the points. **about 7.1 units**

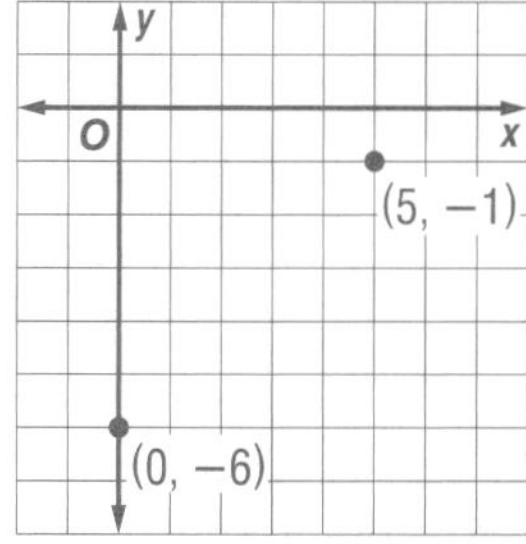

2 **TRAVEL** Melissa lives in Chicago. A unit on the grid of her map shown below is 0.08 mile. Find the distance between McCormickville at (−2, −1) and Lake Shore Park at (2, 2). **about 0.4 mi**

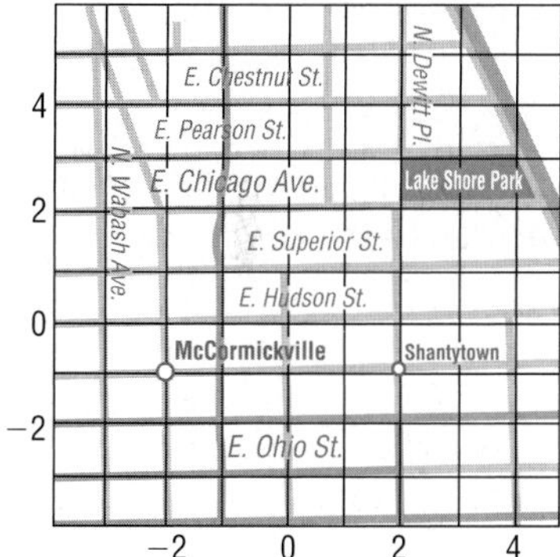

Answer (Your Turn)

c.

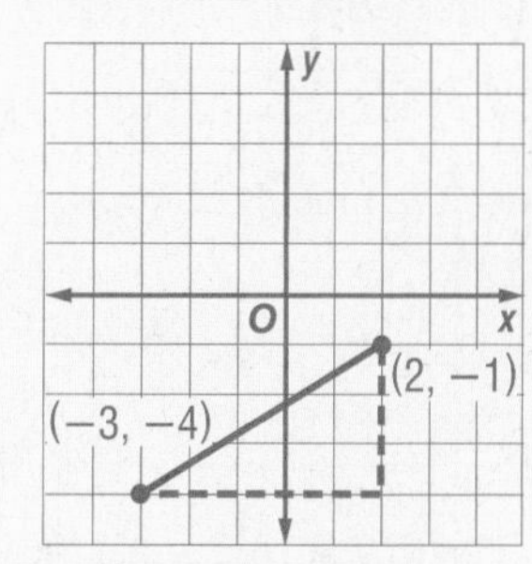

Practice/Apply

FOLDABLES™ Follow-Up Remind students to use their Foldable journals to record what they learn about finding the distance between points in the coordinate plane. Point out that students might explain in writing how to use ordered pairs to find the distance between two points.

About the Exercises...

Guided Practice Key

Exercises	Examples
7–9	1
4–6	2

Assignment Guide

Basic: 11–19 odd, 23–30

Average: 11–23 odd, 24–30

Enriched: 10–22 even, 24–30 (Optional: 61–64)

Alert! The Data Update following Exercise 23 requires access to the Internet.

Students practice the same concepts in Exercises 10–23 if they are assigned odd or even problems.

Skill and Concept Check

1. **Name** the theorem that is used to find the distance between two points on the coordinate plane. **Pythagorean Theorem**
2. **Draw** a triangle that you can use to find the distance between points at (−3, 2) and (−6, −4). **See margin.**
3. **OPEN ENDED** Give the coordinates of a line segment that is neither horizontal nor vertical and has a length of 5 units. **Sample answer: (1, 2) and (4, 6)**

GUIDED PRACTICE

Find the distance between each pair of points whose coordinates are given. Round to the nearest tenth if necessary. **4. 4.5 units 5. 5.7 units 6. 6.3 units**

4. 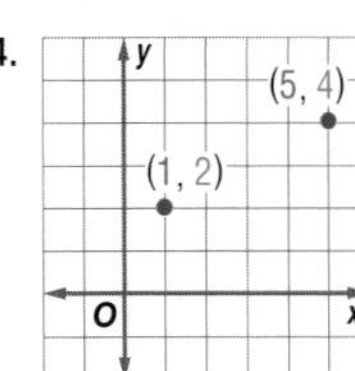

5. 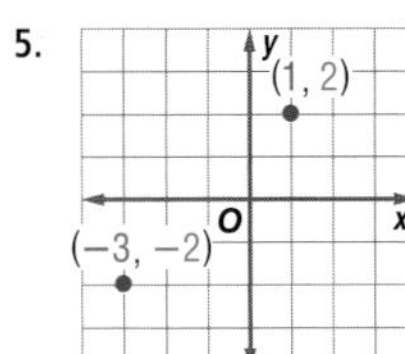

6. 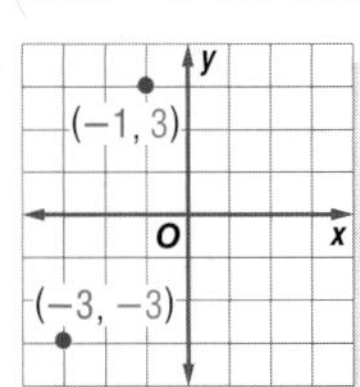

Graph each pair of ordered pairs. Then find the distance between the points. Round to the nearest tenth if necessary. **7–9. See margin for graphs.**

7. (1, 5), (3, 1) **4.5 units**
8. (−1, 0), (2, 7) **7.6 units**
9. (−5, −2), (2, 3) **8.6 units**

★ indicates increased difficulty

Practice and Applications

Find the distance between each pair of points whose coordinates are given. Round to the nearest tenth if necessary.

10. 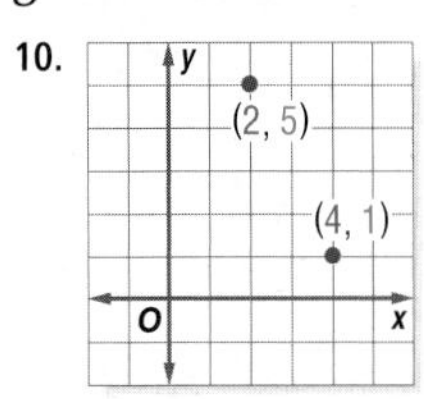

11. 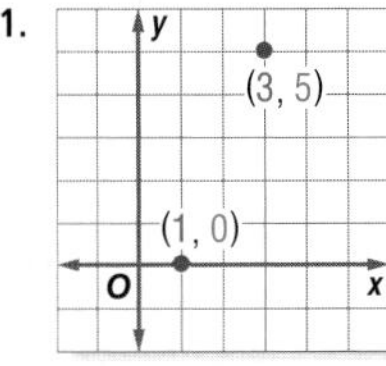

12. 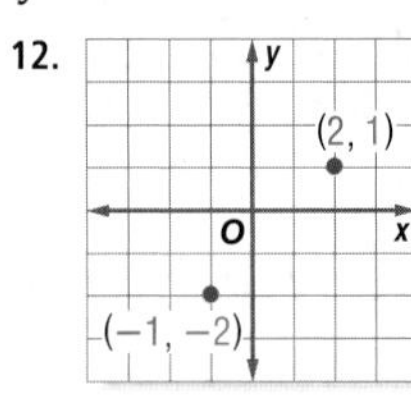

13. 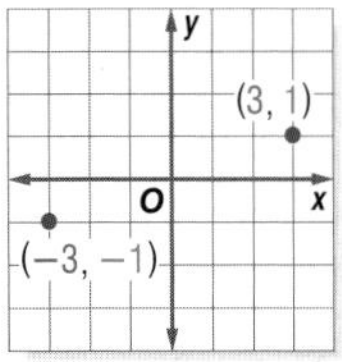 14. 15.

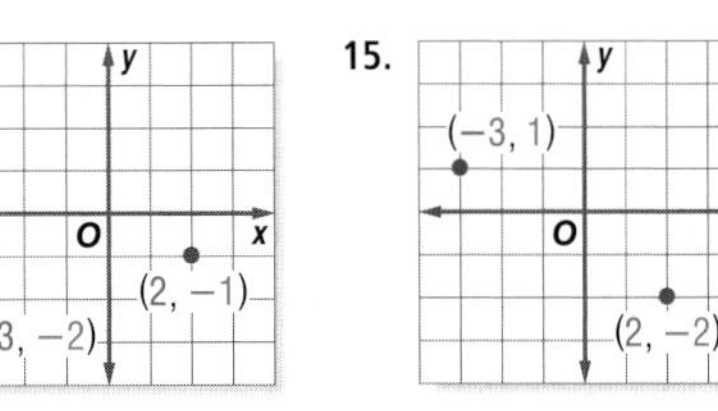

HOMEWORK HELP	
For Exercises	See Examples
10–21	1
22–23	2

Extra Practice See pages 623, 650.

10. 4.5 units
11. 5.4 units
12. 4.2 units
13. 6.3 units
14. 5.1 units
15. 5.8 units

Graph each pair of ordered pairs. Then find the distance between the points. Round to the nearest tenth if necessary. **16–21. See Ch. 3 Answer Appendix for graphs.**

16. (4, 5), (2, 2) **3.6 units**
17. (6, 2), (1, 0) **5.4 units**
18. (−3, 4), (1, 3) **4.1 units**
19. (−5, 1), (2, 4) **7.6 units**
★ 20. (2.5, −1), (−3.5, −5) **7.2 units**
★ 21. (4, −2.3), (−1, −6.3) **6.4 units**

Answers

2. 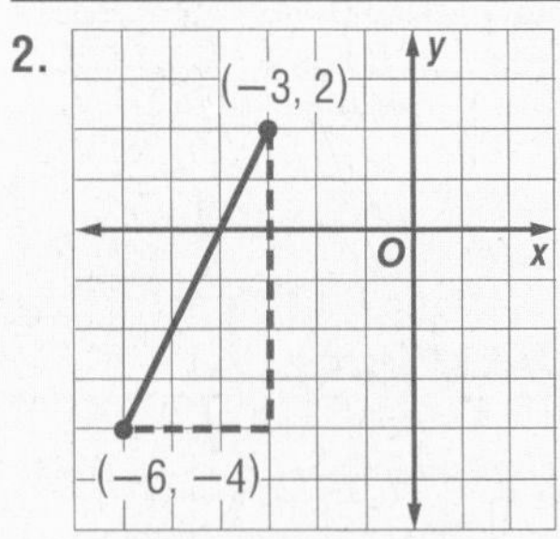

7. 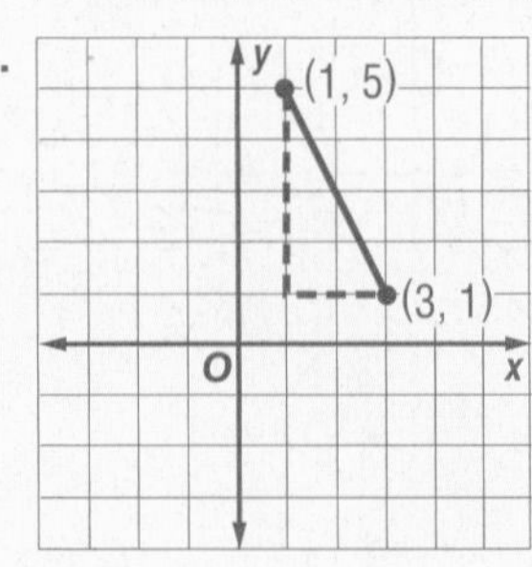

8. 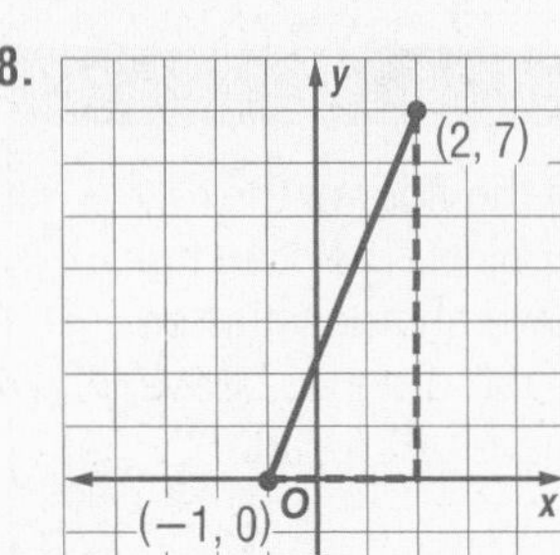

9. 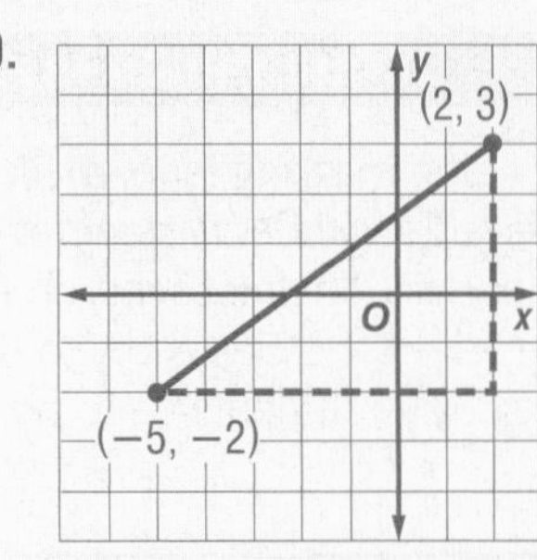

22. **TECHNOLOGY** A backpacker uses her GPS (Global Positioning System) receiver to find how much farther she needs to travel to get to her stopping point for the day. She is at the red dot on her GPS receiver screen and the blue dot shows her destination. How much farther does she need to travel? **about 7.2 mi**

2 mi.

23. **TRAVEL** Rochester, New York, has a longitude of 77° W and a latitude of 43° N. Pittsburgh, Pennsylvania, is located at 80° W and 40° N. At this longitude/latitude, each degree is about 53 miles. Find the distance between Rochester and Pittsburgh. **about 224.9 mi**

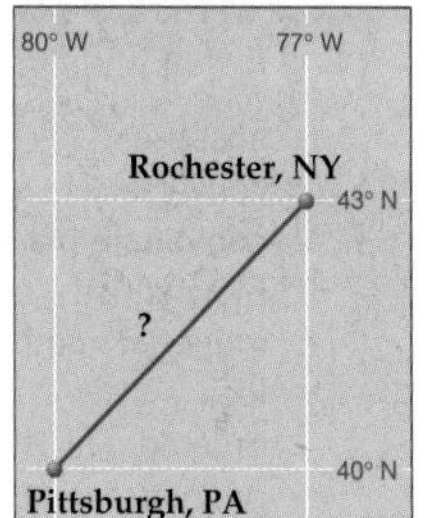

Data Update What is the distance between where you live and another place of your choice? Visit msmath3.net/data_update to find the longitude and latitude of each city.

24. **CRITICAL THINKING** The *midpoint* of a segment separates it into two parts of equal length. Find the midpoint of each horizontal or vertical line segment with coordinates of the endpoints given.

a. (5, 4), (5, 8) **(5, 6)** b. (3, 2), (3, −4) **(3, −1)** c. (−2, 5), (−2, −1) **(−2, 2)** d. $(a, 5), (b, 5)$ $\left(\frac{a+b}{2}, 5\right)$

25. **CRITICAL THINKING** Study your answers for Exercise 24. Write a rule for finding the midpoint of a horizontal or vertical line. **See CH. 3 Answer Appendix.**

Spiral Review with Standardized Test Practice

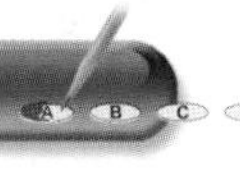

26. **MULTIPLE CHOICE** Find the distance between P and Q. **A**

Ⓐ 7.8 units Ⓑ 8.5 units

Ⓒ 9.5 units Ⓓ 9.0 units

27. **SHORT RESPONSE** Write an equation that can be used to find the distance between $M(-1, 3)$ and $N(3, 5)$. $c^2 = 4^2 + 2^2$

28. **HIKING** Hunter hikes 3 miles south and then turns and hikes 7 miles east. How far is he from his starting point? (Lesson 3-5) **7.6 mi**

Find the missing side of each right triangle. Round to the nearest tenth. (Lesson 3-4)

29. a, 15 cm; b, 18 cm **23.4 cm**

30. b, 14 in.; c, 17 in. **9.6 in.**

INTERDISCIPLINARY PROJECT

Bon Voyage!

Math and Geography It's time to complete your project. Use the information and data you have gathered about cruise packages and destination activities to prepare a video or brochure. Be sure to include a diagram and itinerary with your project.

 msmath3.net/webquest

 msmath3.net/self_check_quiz

4 Assess

Higher-Level Thinking

Try to write a general formula that could be used to find the distance between any two coordinates, (x_1, y_1) and (x_2, y_2). It may help to consider the Pythagorean Theorem. Draw a right triangle like the one shown and find the lengths of each leg.

$d = \sqrt{(x_2 - x_1)^2 + (y_2 - y_1)^2}$

Can your formula be used to find horizontal and vertical distances as well? **yes**

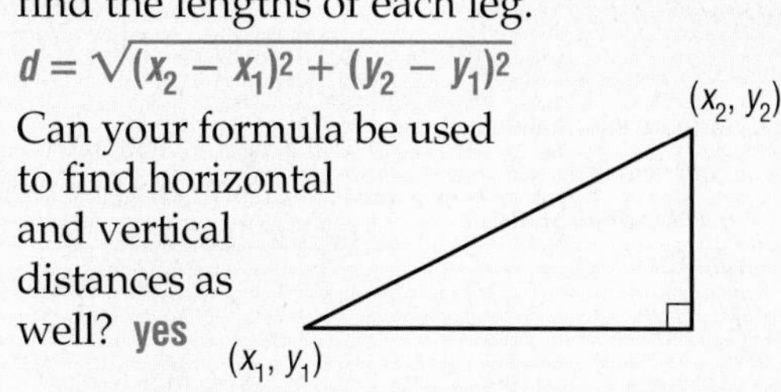

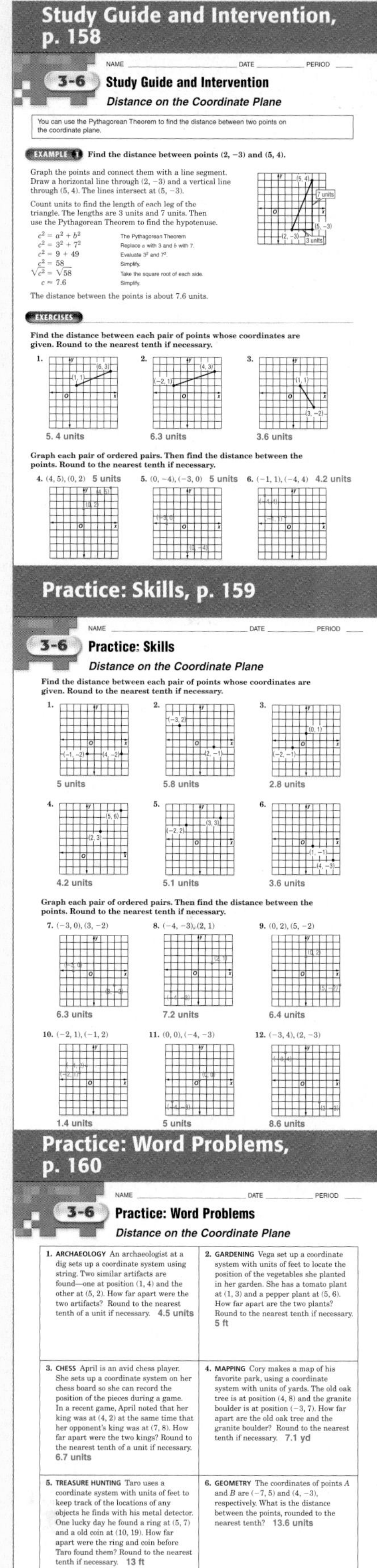

Study Guide and Intervention, p. 158

3-6 Study Guide and Intervention
Distance on the Coordinate Plane

You can use the Pythagorean Theorem to find the distance between two points on the coordinate plane.

EXAMPLE 1 Find the distance between points (2, −3) and (5, 4).

Graph the points and connect them with a line segment. Draw a horizontal line through (2, −3) and a vertical line through (5, 4). The lines intersect at (5, −3).

Count units to find the length of each leg of the triangle. The lengths are 3 units and 7 units. Then use the Pythagorean Theorem to find the hypotenuse.

$c^2 = a^2 + b^2$ The Pythagorean Theorem
$c^2 = 3^2 + 7^2$ Replace a with 3 and b with 7.
$c^2 = 9 + 49$ Evaluate 3^2 and 7^2.
$c^2 = 58$ Simplify.
$\sqrt{c^2} = \sqrt{58}$ Take the square root of each side.
$c \approx 7.6$ Simplify.

The distance between the points is about 7.6 units.

EXERCISES

Find the distance between each pair of points whose coordinates are given. Round to the nearest tenth if necessary.

1. 5.4 units 2. 6.3 units 3. 3.6 units

Graph each pair of ordered pairs. Then find the distance between the points. Round to the nearest tenth if necessary.

4. (4, 5), (0, 2) 5 units 5. (0, −4), (−3, 0) 5 units 6. (−1, 1), (−4, 4) 4.2 units

Practice: Skills, p. 159

3-6 Practice: Skills
Distance on the Coordinate Plane

Find the distance between each pair of points whose coordinates are given. Round to the nearest tenth if necessary.

1. 5 units 2. 5.8 units 3. 2.8 units

4. 4.2 units 5. 5.1 units 6. 3.6 units

Graph each pair of ordered pairs. Then find the distance between the points. Round to the nearest tenth if necessary.

7. (−3, 0), (3, −2) 6.3 units 8. (−4, −3), (2, 1) 7.2 units 9. (0, 2), (5, −2) 6.4 units

10. (−2, 1), (−1, 2) 1.4 units 11. (0, 0), (−4, −3) 5 units 12. (−3, 4), (2, −3) 8.6 units

Practice: Word Problems, p. 160

3-6 Practice: Word Problems
Distance on the Coordinate Plane

1. ARCHAEOLOGY An archaeologist at a dig sets up a coordinate system using string. Two similar artifacts are found—one at position (1, 4) and the other at (5, 2). How far apart were the two artifacts? Round to the nearest tenth of a unit if necessary. 4.5 units

2. GARDENING Vega set up a coordinate system with units of feet to locate the position of the vegetables she planted in her garden. She has a tomato plant at (1, 3) and a pepper plant at (5, 6). How far apart are the two plants? Round to the nearest tenth if necessary. 5 ft

3. CHESS April is an avid chess player. She sets up a coordinate system on her chess board so she can record the position of the pieces during a game. In a recent game, April noted that her king was at (4, 2) at the same time that her opponent's king was at (7, 8). How far apart were the two kings? Round to the nearest tenth of a unit if necessary. 6.7 units

4. MAPPING Cory makes a map of his favorite park, using a coordinate system with units of yards. The old oak tree is at position (4, 8) and the granite boulder is at position (−3, 7). How far apart are the old oak tree and the granite boulder? Round to the nearest tenth if necessary. 7.1 yd

5. TREASURE HUNTING Taro uses a coordinate system with units of feet to keep track of the locations of any objects he finds with his metal detector. One lucky day he found a ring at (5, 7) and a old coin at (10, 19). How far apart were the ring and coin before Taro found them? Round to the nearest tenth if necessary. 13 ft

6. GEOMETRY The coordinates of points A and B are (−7, 5) and (4, −3), respectively. What is the distance between the points, rounded to the nearest tenth? 13.6 units

7. GEOMETRY The coordinates of points A, B, and C are (5, 4), (−2, 1), and (4, −4), respectively. Which point, B or C, is closer to point A? B

8. THEME PARK Tom is looking at a map of the theme park. The map is laid out in a coordinate system. Tom is at (2, 3). The roller coaster is at (7, 8), and the water ride is at (9, 1). Is Tom closer to the roller coaster or the water ride? roller coaster

Vocabulary Assessment Check

- This alphabetical list of vocabulary terms in Chapter 3 includes a page reference where each term was introduced.
- A vocabulary review/test for Chapter 3 is available on p. 176 of the *Chapter 3 Resource Masters*.

Vocabulary PuzzleMaker

ELL The online Vocabulary PuzzleMaker improves students' mathematics vocabulary using four puzzle formats – crossword, scramble, word search using a word list, and word search using clues. Students can work on a computer screen or from a printed handout.

MindJogger Videoquizzes

ELL MindJogger Videoquizzes provide an alternative review of concepts presented in this chapter. Students work in teams in a game show format to gain points for correct answers. The questions are presented in three rounds.

Round 1 Concepts (5 questions)
Round 2 Skills (4 questions)
Round 3 Problem Solving (4 questions)

ExamView® Pro

Use the networkable ExamView® Pro Testmaker CD-ROM to:

- Create **multiple versions** of tests.
- Create **modified** tests for **inclusion** students with one mouse click.
- **Edit** existing questions and **add** your own questions.
- Build tests aligned with state standards using built-in **state curriculum correlations.**
- Change **English** tests to **Spanish** with one mouse click and vice versa.

Study Guide and Review

Vocabulary and Concept Check

abscissa (p. 142)	origin (p. 142)	right triangle (p. 132)
converse (p. 134)	perfect square (p. 116)	square root (p. 116)
coordinate plane (p. 142)	principal square root (p. 117)	*x*-axis (p. 142)
hypotenuse (p. 132)	Pythagorean Theorem (p. 132)	*x*-coordinate (p. 142)
irrational number (p. 125)	Pythagorean triple (p. 138)	*y*-axis (p. 142)
legs (p. 132)	quadrants (p. 142)	*y*-coordinate (p. 142)
ordered pair (p. 142)	radical sign (p. 116)	
ordinate (p. 142)	real number (p. 125)	

State whether each sentence is *true* or *false*. If *false*, replace the underlined word(s) or number(s) to make a true sentence.

1. An irrational number can be written as a fraction. **false; cannot**
2. The hypotenuse is the longest side of a right triangle. **true**
3. The set of numbers {3, 4, 5} is a Pythagorean triple. **true**
4. The number 11 is a perfect square. **false; sample answer: 25**
5. The horizontal axis is called the *y*-axis. **false; vertical axis**
6. In an ordered pair, the *y*-coordinate is the second number. **true**
7. The Pythagorean Theorem says that the sum of the squares of the lengths of the legs of a right triangle equals the square of the length of the hypotenuse. **true**
8. The coordinates of the origin are (0, 1). **false; (0, 0)**

Lesson-by-Lesson Exercises and Examples

3-1 Square Roots (pp. 116–119) **15. 17 rows of 17 trees in each row**

Find each square root.

9. $\sqrt{81}$ **9**
10. $\sqrt{225}$ **15**
11. $\sqrt{64}$ **8**
12. $-\sqrt{100}$ **−10**
13. $-\sqrt{\frac{4}{9}}$ $-\frac{2}{3}$
14. $\sqrt{6.25}$ **2.5**
15. **FARMING** Pecan trees are planted in square patterns to take advantage of land space and for ease in harvesting. For 289 trees, how many rows should be planted and how many trees should be planted in each row?

Example 1 Find $\sqrt{36}$.

$\sqrt{36}$ indicates the *positive* square root of 36.

Since $6^2 = 36$, $\sqrt{36} = 6$.

Example 2 Find $-\sqrt{169}$.

$-\sqrt{169}$ indicates the *negative* square root of 169.

Since $(-13)(-13) = 169$, $-\sqrt{169} = -13$.

msmath3.net/vocabulary_review

For more information about Foldables, see *Teaching Mathematics with Foldables.*

Have students look through the chapter to make sure they have included examples in their Foldables for each lesson or topic in the chapter.

Encourage students to refer to their Foldables while completing the Study Guide and Review and to use them in preparing for the Chapter Test.

3-2 Estimating Square Roots (pp. 120–122)

Estimate to the nearest whole number.

16. $\sqrt{32}$ 6
17. $\sqrt{42}$ 6
18. $\sqrt{230}$ 15
19. $\sqrt{96}$ 10
20. $\sqrt{150}$ 12
21. $\sqrt{8}$ 3
22. $\sqrt{50.1}$ 7
23. $\sqrt{19.25}$ 4
24. **ALGEBRA** Estimate the solution of $b^2 = 60$ to the nearest integer. 8 or −8

Example 3 **Estimate $\sqrt{135}$ to the nearest whole number.**

$121 < 135 < 144$	Write an inequality.
$11^2 < 135 < 12^2$	$121 = 11^2$ and $144 = 12^2$
$11 < \sqrt{135} < 12$	Take the square root of each number.

So, $\sqrt{135}$ is between 11 and 12. Since 135 is closer to 144 than to 121, the best whole number estimate is 12.

3-3 The Real Number System (pp. 125–129)

Name all sets of numbers to which each real number belongs. 28. integer, rational

25. $-\sqrt{19}$ irrational
26. $0.\overline{3}$ rational
27. 7.43 rational
28. −12
29. $\sqrt{32}$ irrational
30. 101

30. whole, integer, rational

Example 4 **Name all sets of numbers to which $-\sqrt{33}$ belongs.**

$-\sqrt{33} \approx -5.744562647$

Since the decimal does not terminate or repeat, it is an irrational number.

3-4 The Pythagorean Theorem (pp. 132–136)

Write an equation you could use to find the length of the missing side of each right triangle. Then find the missing length. Round to the nearest tenth if necessary.

31. 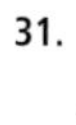
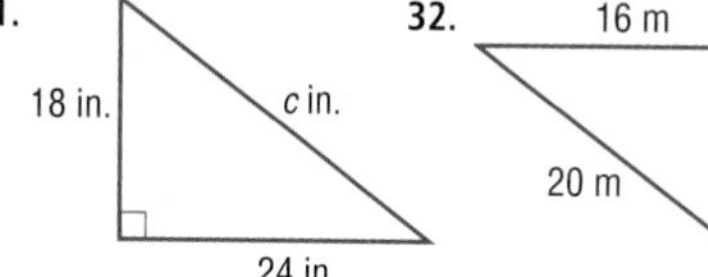

32.

$c^2 = 24^2 + 18^2$; 30 in. $20^2 = a^2 + 16^2$; 12 m

33. 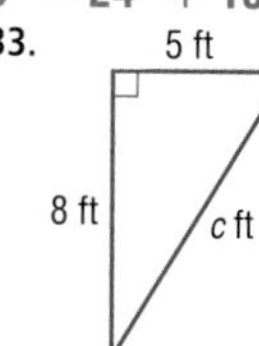

34.
9.5 m
4 m
b m

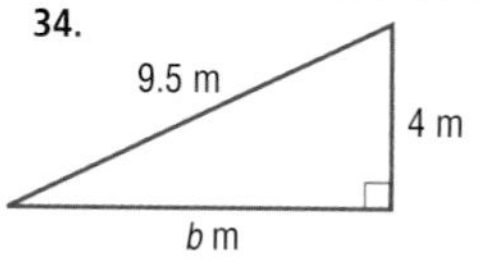

$c^2 = 8^2 + 5^2$; 9.4 ft $9.5^2 = 4^2 + b^2$; 8.6 m

35. a, 5 in.; c, 6 in.
36. a, 6 cm; b, 7 cm

$6^2 = 5^2 + b^2$; 3.3 in. $c^2 = 6^2 + 7^2$; 9.2 cm

Example 5 **Write an equation you could use to find the length of the hypotenuse of the right triangle. Then find the missing length.**

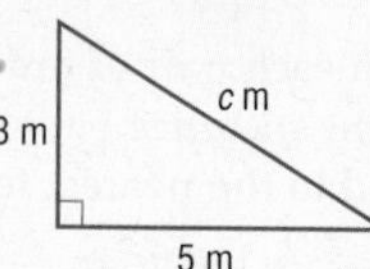

$c^2 = a^2 + b^2$	Pythagorean Theorem
$c^2 = 3^2 + 5^2$	Replace a with 3 and b with 5.
$c^2 = 9 + 25$	Evaluate 3^2 and 5^2.
$c^2 = 34$	Simplify.
$c = \sqrt{34}$	Take the square root of each side.
$c \approx 5.8$	Use a calculator.

The hypotenuse is about 5.8 meters long.

Answer (p. 148)

42. 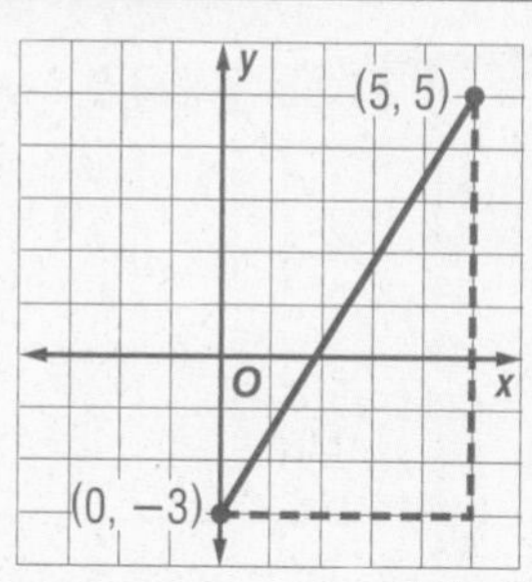

Answers

43. 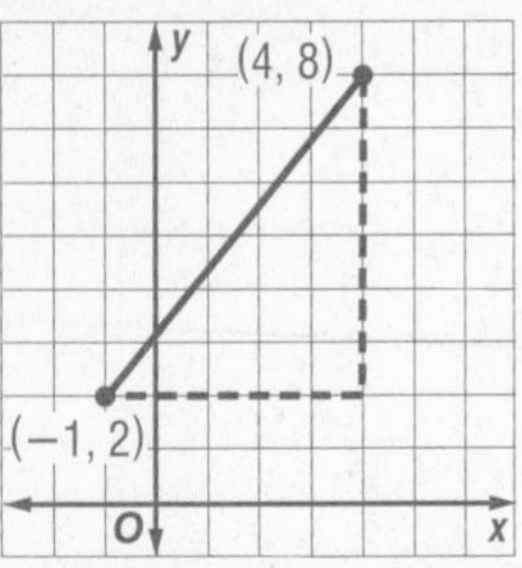

44. 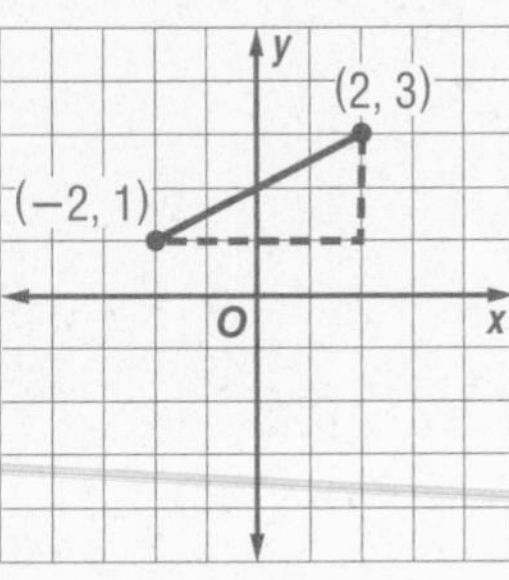

45. 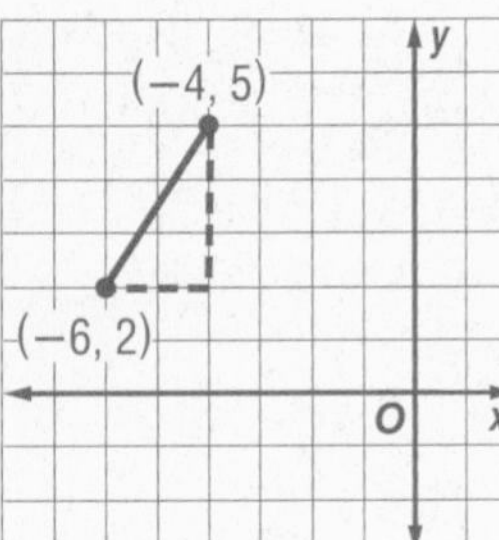

46. 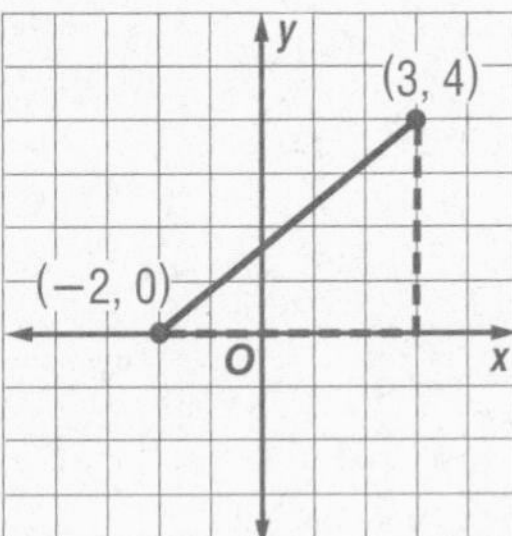

47. 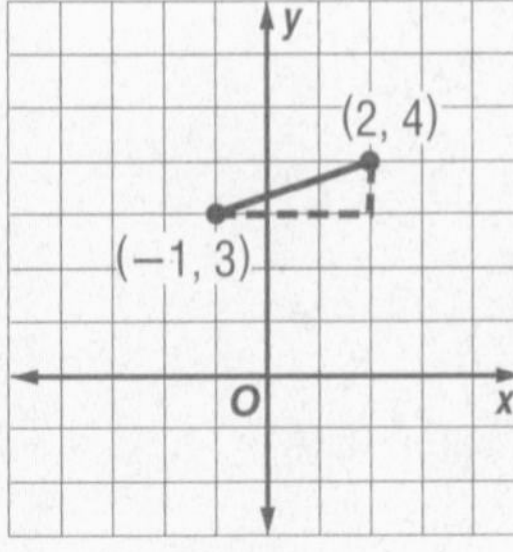

Mixed Problem Solving
For mixed problem-solving practice, see page 650.

3-5 Using the Pythagorean Theorem (pp. 137–140)

Write an equation that can be used to answer the question. Then solve. Round to the nearest tenth if necessary.

37. How tall is the light?

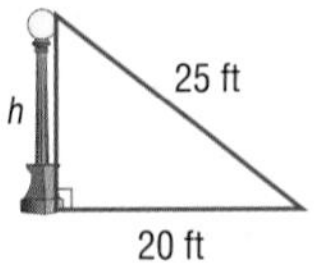

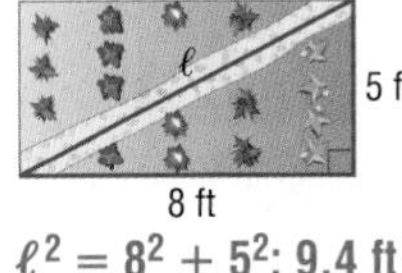

38. How wide is the window?

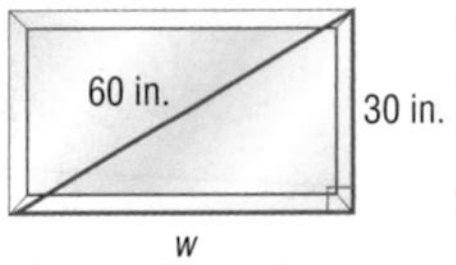

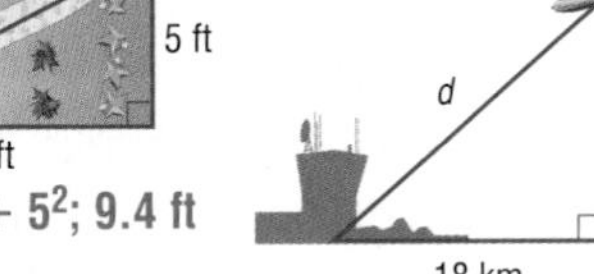

$60^2 = 30^2 + w^2$; 52.0 in.

39. How long is the walkway?

$\ell^2 = 8^2 + 5^2$; 9.4 ft

40. How far is the plane from the airport?

41. **GEOMETRY** A rectangle is 12 meters by 7 meters. What is the length of one of its diagonals? **about 13.9 m**

Example 6 **Write an equation that can be used to find the height of the tree. Then solve.**

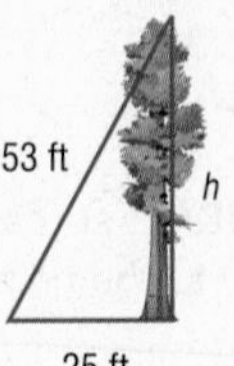

Use the Pythagorean Theorem to write the equation $53^2 = h^2 + 25^2$. Then solve the equation.

$53^2 = h^2 + 25^2$	Evaluate 53^2 and 25^2.
$2{,}809 = h^2 + 625$	
$2{,}809 - 625 = h^2 + 625 - 625$	Subtract 625.
$2{,}184 = h^2$	Simplify.
$\sqrt{2{,}184} = h$	Take the square root of each side.
$46.7 \approx h$	Use a calculator.

The height of the tree is about 47 feet.

37. $25^2 = 20^2 + h^2$; 15 ft
40. $d^2 = 10^2 + 18^2$; 20.6 km

3-6 Geometry: Distance on the Coordinate Plane (pp. 142–145)

Graph each pair of ordered pairs. Then find the distance between the points. Round to the nearest tenth if necessary.

42. (0, −3), (5, 5) **9.4**
43. (−1, 2), (4, 8) **7.8**
44. (−2, 1), (2, 3) **4.5**
45. (−6, 2), (−4, 5) **3.6**
46. (3, 4), (−2, 0) **6.4**
47. (−1, 3), (2, 4) **3.2**

42–47. See margin for graphs.

48. **GEOMETRY** The coordinates of points *R* and *S* are (4, 3) and (1, 6). What is the distance between the points? Round to the nearest tenth if necessary. **4.2 units**

Example 7 **Graph the ordered pairs (2, 3) and (−1, 1). Then find the distance between the points.**

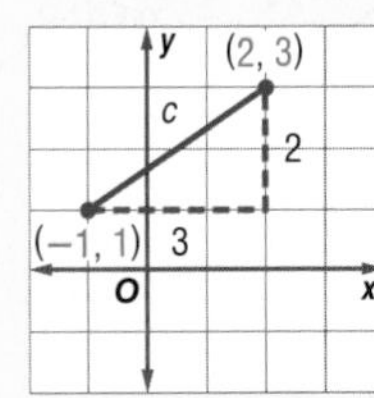

$c^2 = a^2 + b^2$
$c^2 = 3^2 + 2^2$
$c^2 = 9 + 4$
$c^2 = 13$
$c = \sqrt{13}$
$c \approx 3.6$

The distance is about 3.6 units.

Answers (Practice Test)

18. 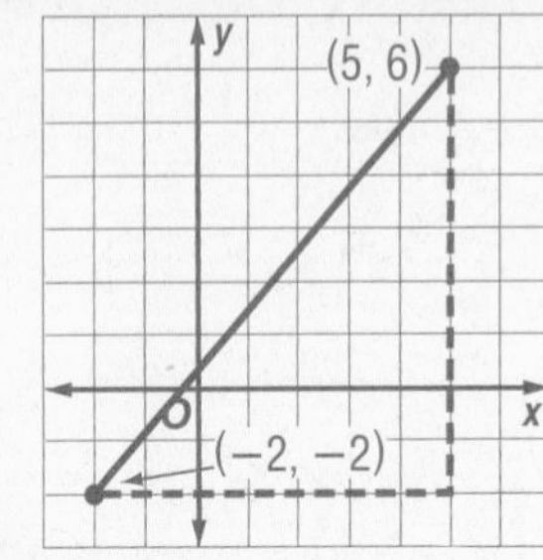

19. 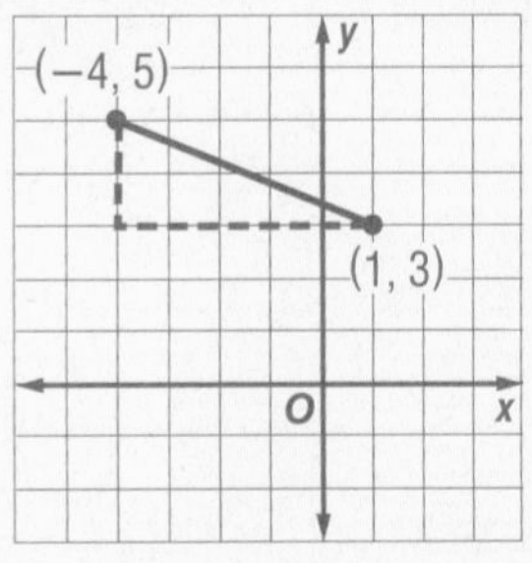

Practice Test

Vocabulary and Concepts

1. **OPEN ENDED** Write an equation that can be solved by taking the square root of a perfect square. **Sample answer: $x^2 = 25$**
2. **State** the Pythagorean Theorem. **$c^2 = a^2 + b^2$, where a and b are the legs and c is the hypotenuse of a right triangle.**

Skills and Applications

Find each square root.

3. $\sqrt{225}$ **15**
4. $-\sqrt{25}$ **−5**
5. $\sqrt{\frac{36}{49}}$ **$\frac{6}{7}$**

Estimate to the nearest whole number.

6. $\sqrt{67}$ **8**
7. $\sqrt{108}$ **10**
8. $\sqrt{82}$ **9**

Name all sets of numbers to which each real number belongs.

9. $-\sqrt{64}$ **integer, rational**
10. $6.\overline{13}$ **rational**
11. $\sqrt{14}$ **irrational**

Write an equation you could use to find the length of the missing side of each right triangle. Then find the missing length. Round to the nearest tenth if necessary.

12. a, 5 m; b, 5 m **$c^2 = 5^2 + 5^2$; 7.1 m**
13. b, 20 ft; c, 35 ft **$35^2 = a^2 + 20^2$; 28.7 ft**

Determine whether each triangle with sides of given lengths is a right triangle.

14. 12 in., 20 in., 24 in. **no**
15. 34 cm, 30 cm, 16 cm **yes**

16. **LANDSCAPING** To make a balanced landscaping plan for a yard, Kelsey needs to know the heights of various plants. How tall is the tree at the right? **about 18.7 ft**

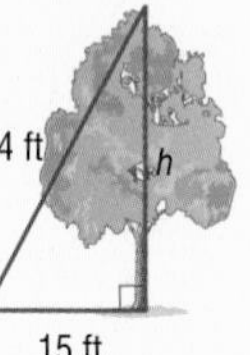

17. **GEOMETRY** Find the perimeter of a right triangle with legs of 10 inches and 8 inches. **about 30.8 in.**

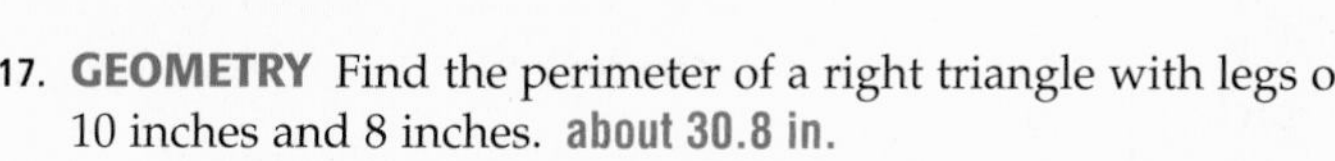

Graph each pair of ordered pairs. Then find the distance between points. Round to the nearest tenth if necessary. **18–19. See margin for graphs.**

18. (−2, −2), (5, 6) **10.6 units**
19. (1, 3), (−4, 5) **5.4 units**

Standardized Test Practice

20. **MULTIPLE CHOICE** If the area of a square is 40 square millimeters, what is the approximate length of one side of the square? **A**

Ⓐ 6.3 mm Ⓑ 7.5 mm Ⓒ 10 mm Ⓓ 20 mm

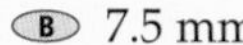

Math Online msmath3.net/chapter_test

Practice Test

Assessment Options

Vocabulary Test A vocabulary review/test for Chapter 3 can be found on p. 176 of the *Chapter 3 Resource Masters.*

Chapter Tests There are six Chapter 3 Tests and an Extended Response Assessment task available in the *Chapter 3 Resource Masters.*

Chapter 3 Tests			
Form	**Type**	**Level**	**Pages**
1	MC	basic	163–164
2A	MC	average	165–166
2B	MC	average	167–168
2C	FR	average	169–170
2D	FR	average	171–172
3	FR	advanced	173–174

MC = multiple-choice questions
FR = free-response questions

Extended Response Assessment

Extended Response tasks for Chapter 3 can be found on p. 175 of the *Chapter 3 Resource Masters.* A sample scoring rubric for these tasks appears on p. A23.

Unit 1 Test

A unit test/review can be found on pp. 183–184 of the *Chapter 3 Resource Masters.*

Portfolio Suggestion

Introduction Students will find that the Pythagorean Theorem is referred to frequently as they continue in math and science classes.

Ask Students to draw several right triangles on a page and show the process and solutions when solving for an unknown leg or the hypotenuse. Students may also wish to note several real-life situations for which the Pythagorean Theorem may be used.

CHAPTER 3 Standardized Test Practice

These two pages contain practice questions in the various formats that can be found on the most frequently given standardized tests.

A student recording sheet for these two pages can be found on page A1 of the *Chapter 3 Resource Masters.*

Standardized Test Practice Student Recording Sheet, p. A1

NAME ______ DATE ______ PERIOD ______

CHAPTER 3 **Standardized Test Practice** SCORE ______

Student Recording Sheet (Use with pages 150–151 of the Student Edition.)

Part 1: Multiple Choice

Select the best answer from the choices given and fill in the corresponding oval.

1. Ⓐ Ⓑ Ⓒ Ⓓ 4. Ⓕ Ⓖ Ⓗ Ⓘ 7. Ⓐ Ⓑ Ⓒ Ⓓ
2. Ⓕ Ⓖ Ⓗ Ⓘ 5. Ⓐ Ⓑ Ⓒ Ⓓ 8. Ⓕ Ⓖ Ⓗ Ⓘ
3. Ⓐ Ⓑ Ⓒ Ⓓ 6. Ⓕ Ⓖ Ⓗ Ⓘ

Part 2: Short Response/Grid In

Solve the problem and write your answer in the blank.

For grid in questions, also enter your answer by writing each number or symbol in a box. Then fill in the corresponding circle for that number of symbol.

9. ______
10. ______
11. ______
12. ______ (grid in)
13. ______
14. ______
15. ______

Part 3: Extended Response

Record your answers for Questions 16 and 17 on the back of this paper.

Additional Practice

See pp. 181–182 of the *Chapter 3 Resource Masters* for additional standardized test practice.

Answer

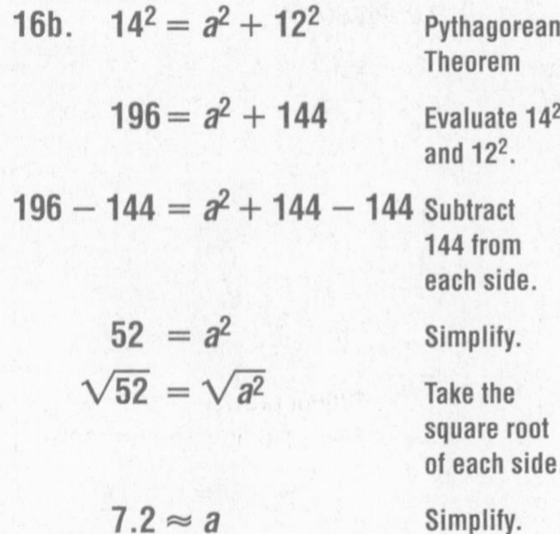

16b.	$14^2 = a^2 + 12^2$	Pythagorean Theorem
	$196 = a^2 + 144$	Evaluate 14^2 and 12^2.
	$196 - 144 = a^2 + 144 - 144$	Subtract 144 from each side.
	$52 = a^2$	Simplify.
	$\sqrt{52} = \sqrt{a^2}$	Take the square root of each side.
	$7.2 \approx a$	Simplify.

Standardized Test Practice

PART 1 Multiple Choice

Record your answers on the answer sheet provided by your teacher or on a sheet of paper.

1. Which of the following sets of ordered pairs represents two points on the line below? (Prerequisite Skill, p. 614) **C**

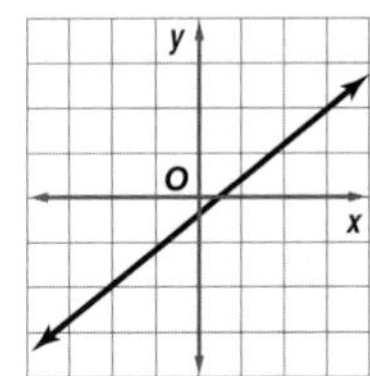

Ⓐ {(3, 1), (2, −1)} Ⓑ {(3, 2), (−1, −2)}
Ⓒ {(3, 2), (−2, −2)} Ⓓ {(3, 3), (−2, −3)}

2. The table below shows the income of several baseball teams in a recent year. What is the total revenue for all of these teams? (Lesson 1-4) **H**

Team	Income
Braves	−\$14,400,000
Orioles	\$1,500,000
Cubs	\$4,800,000
Tigers	\$500,000
Marlins	−\$27,700,000
Yankees	\$40,900,000
A's	−\$7,100,000
Pirates	−\$3,000,000

Source: www.mlb.com

Ⓕ \$99,900,000 Ⓖ \$4,500,000
Ⓗ −\$4,500,000 Ⓘ −\$99,900,000

3. Which of the following is equivalent to 0.64? (Lesson 2-1) **B**

Ⓐ $\frac{1}{64}$ Ⓑ $\frac{16}{25}$
Ⓒ $\frac{100}{64}$ Ⓓ $\frac{64}{10}$

4. Which of the following values are equivalent? (Lesson 2-2) **I**

$0.08, 0.8, \frac{1}{8}, \frac{4}{5}$

Ⓕ 0.08 and $\frac{1}{8}$ Ⓖ 0.8 and $\frac{1}{8}$
Ⓗ 0.08 and $\frac{4}{5}$ Ⓘ 0.8 and $\frac{4}{5}$

5. Between which two whole numbers is $\sqrt{56}$ located on a number line? (Lesson 3-2) **B**

Ⓐ 6 and 7 Ⓑ 7 and 8
Ⓒ 8 and 9 Ⓓ 9 and 10

6. Which of the points on the number line is the *best* representation of $-\sqrt{11}$? (Lesson 3-3) **G**

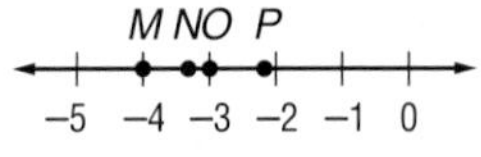

Ⓕ *M* Ⓖ *N* Ⓗ *O* Ⓘ *P*

7. What is the value of *x*? (Lesson 3-4) **B**

8 units
x units
11 units

Ⓐ $\sqrt{8 + 11}$
Ⓑ $\sqrt{8^2 + 11^2}$
Ⓒ $\frac{8^2 + 11^2}{2}$
Ⓓ $8^2 + 11^2$

8. Two fences meet in the corner of the yard. The length of one fence is 4 yards, and the other is 6 yards. What is the distance between the far ends of the fences? (Lesson 3-5) **G**

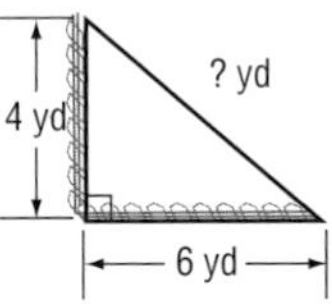

Ⓕ 6.3 yd Ⓖ 7.2 yd
Ⓗ 8.8 yd Ⓘ 9.5 yd

ExamView® Pro

Special banks of standardized test questions similar to those on the TIMSS and NAEP grade 8 tests can be found on this CD-ROM.

Preparing for Standardized Tests
For test-taking strategies and more practice, see pages 660–677.

PART 2 Short Response/Grid In

Record your answers on the answer sheet provided by your teacher or on a sheet of paper.

Wave Distance from Stick (inches)
+3
+5
−4
+2
+8
−6
−3
+7
−5
−4

9. Missy placed a stick near the edge of the water on the beach. If the sum of the distances from the stick is positive, the tide is coming in. If the sum of the distances is negative, the tide is going out. Determine whether the tide is coming in or going out for the readings at the right. (Lesson 1-4) **coming in**

10. Is the square root of 25 equal to 5, −5, or both? (Lesson 3-1) **both**

11. The value of $\sqrt{134}$ is between what two consecutive whole numbers? (Lesson 3-2) **11 and 12**

12. Find the value of x to the nearest tenth. (Lesson 3-4) **5.2**

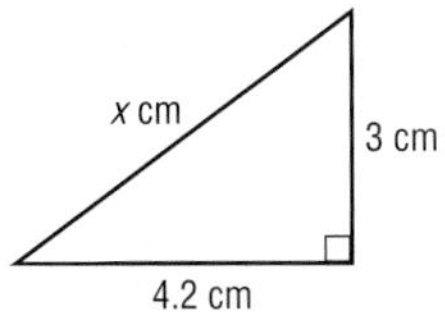

13. Lucas attaches a wire to a young oak tree 4 feet above the ground. The wire is anchored in the ground at an angle from the tree to help the tree stay upright as it grows. If the wire is 5 feet long, what is the distance from the base of the wire to the base of the tree? (Lesson 3-4) **3 ft**

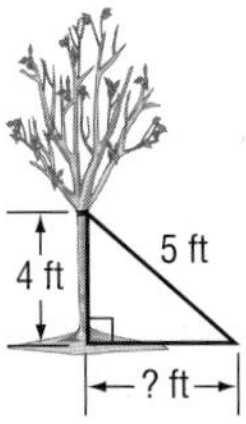

TEST-TAKING TIP

Questions 12 and 13 Remember that the hypotenuse of a right triangle is always opposite the right angle.

Math Online msmath3.net/standardized_test

14. A signpost casts a shadow that is 6 feet long. The top of the post is 10 feet from the end of the shadow. What is the height of the post? (Lesson 3-5) **8 ft**

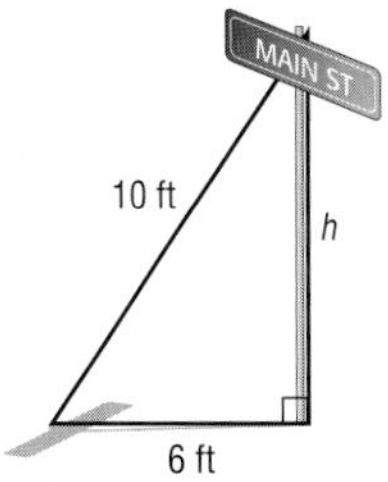

15. Find the distance between the points located on the graph below. Round to the nearest tenth. (Lesson 3-6) **2.8 units**

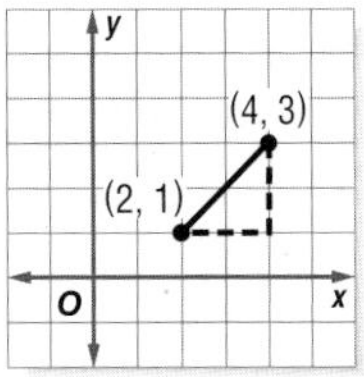

PART 3 Extended Response

Record your answers on a sheet of paper. Show your work.

16. Use the right triangle to answer the following questions. (Lesson 3-4)

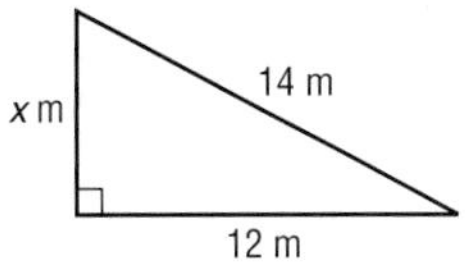

a. Write an equation that can be used to find the length of x. $14^2 = x^2 + 12^2$

b. Solve the equation. Justify each step.

c. What is the length of x? **about 7.2 m**

16b. 7.2; See margin.

17. Use a grid to graph and answer the following questions. (Lesson 3-6)

a. Graph the ordered pairs (3, 4) and (−2, 1). **a–b. See margin. c. about 5.8 units**

b. Describe how to find the distance between the two points.

c. Find the distance between the points.

Answers

17a.

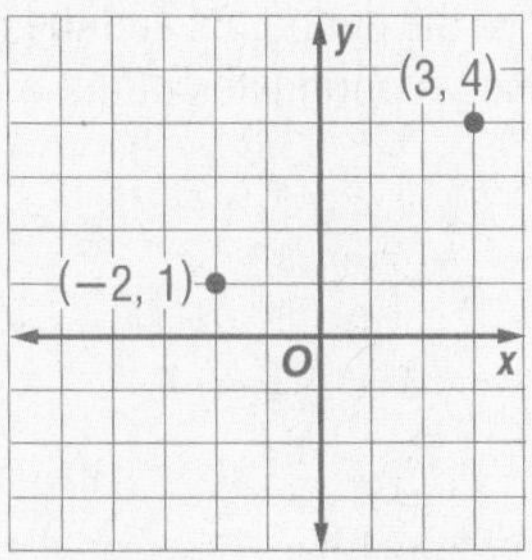

17b. Draw the line between the two points. Use the grid to draw a right triangle with the line between the two points as the hypotenuse. Determine the length of each leg of the triangle. Use the Pythagorean Theorem to determine the length of the hypotenuse. The length of the hypotenuse is the distance between the two points.

Standardized Test Practice

Rubrics The following rubrics are sample scoring devices for short response and extended response questions.

Short Response

Points	Description
2	The student demonstrates a thorough understanding of the mathematics of the task. The response may contain minor flaws that do not detract from the demonstration of a thorough understanding.
1	The student has provided a response that is only partially correct.
0	The student has provided a completely incorrect solution or no response at all.

Extended Response

Points	Description
4	The student demonstrates a thorough understanding of the mathematics of the task. The response may contain minor flaws that do not detract from the demonstration of a thorough understanding.
3	The student demonstrates an understanding of the mathematics of the task. The response is essentially correct and demonstrates an essential but less than thorough understanding of the mathematics.
2	The student demonstrates only a partial understanding of the mathematics of the task. Although the student may have used the correct approach to a solution or may have provided a correct solution, the work lacks an essential understanding of the underlying mathematical concepts.
1	The student demonstrates a very limited understanding of the mathematics of the task. The response is incomplete and exhibits many flaws.
0	The student provides a completely incorrect solution or no response at all.

A more detailed 4-point rubric is provided on page A2 of the *Chapter 3 Resource Masters*.

Page 128, Lesson 3-3

31.

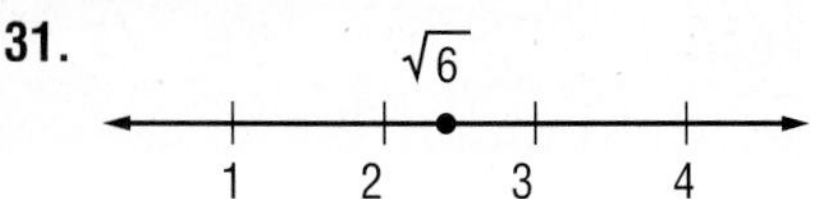

32. $\sqrt{8}$

1 2 3 4

33. $-\sqrt{22}$

−6 −5 −4 −3

34. $-\sqrt{27}$

−7 −6 −5 −4

35. $\sqrt{50}$

6 7 8 9

36. $-\sqrt{48}$

−8 −7 −6 −5

37. $-\sqrt{105}$

−12 −11 −10 −9

38. $\sqrt{150}$

11 12 13 14

Page 140, Lesson 3-5

30. y T (5, 2) O x

31.

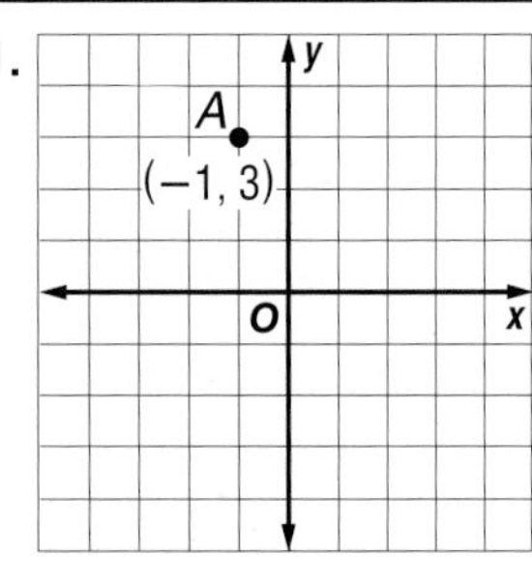

32.

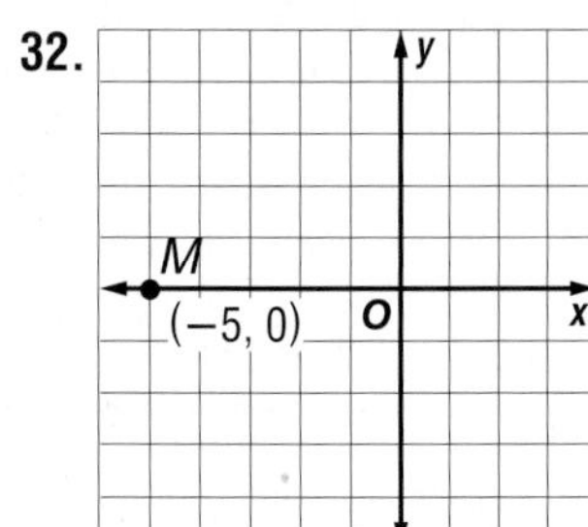

33.

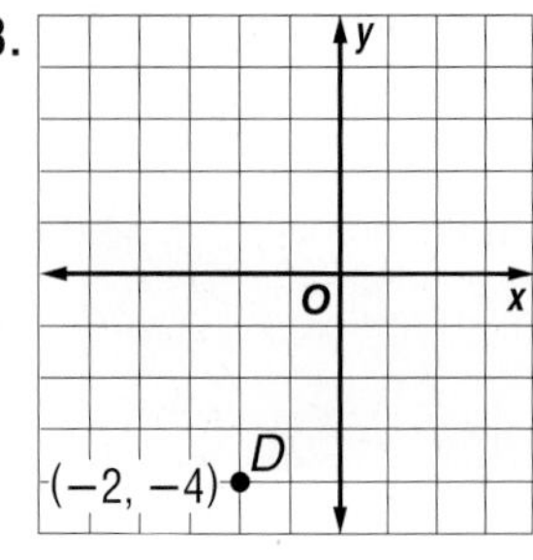

Page 141, Lesson 3-5b (Writing Math)

1. Sample answer: Try adding perfect squares that are less than the irrational number. When you find two perfect squares with a sum of the irrational number, use the square roots of the perfect squares as the lengths of the legs.
2. Sample answer: Since $(\sqrt{2})^2 + 1^2 = 3$, use $\sqrt{2}$ as one leg of a right triangle and 1 unit as the other leg. Then follow the procedure in the activity to locate the graph of $\sqrt{3}$.
3. Yes; for the square roots of numbers that are not the sum of perfect squares, you can graph other irrational numbers first. You can graph $\sqrt{1}$. For $\sqrt{2}$, you can use 1 for each leg. For $\sqrt{3}$, you can use $\sqrt{2}$ and 1 for the legs. You can graph $\sqrt{4}$. For $\sqrt{5}$, you can use 2 and 1 for the legs. For $\sqrt{6}$, you can use $\sqrt{5}$ and 1 for the legs, and so on.

Pages 144–145, Lesson 3-6

16.

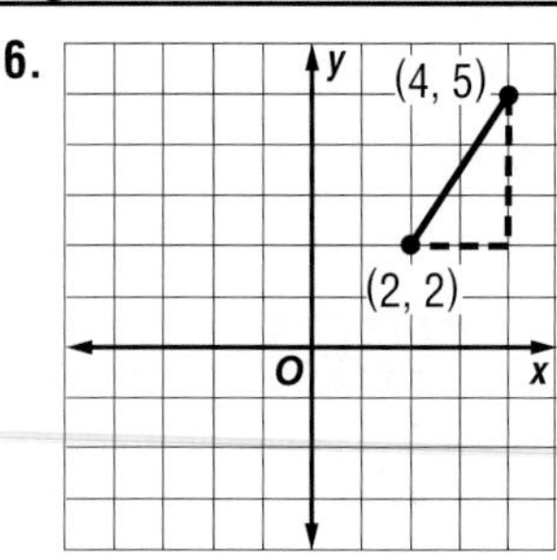

17.

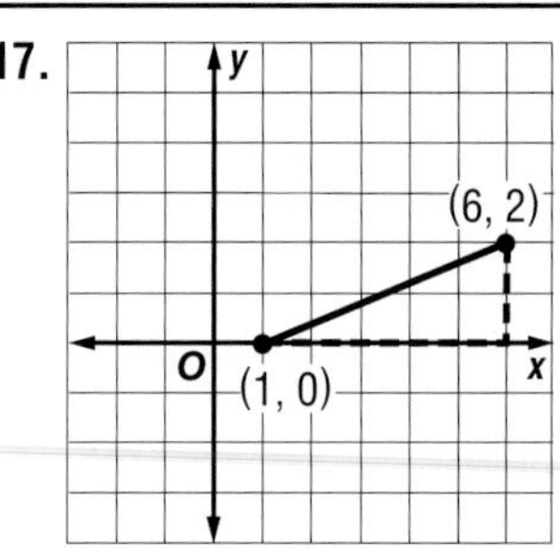

18.

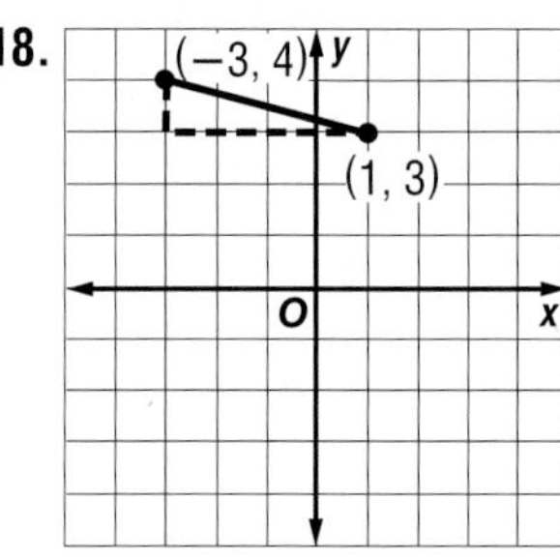

19.

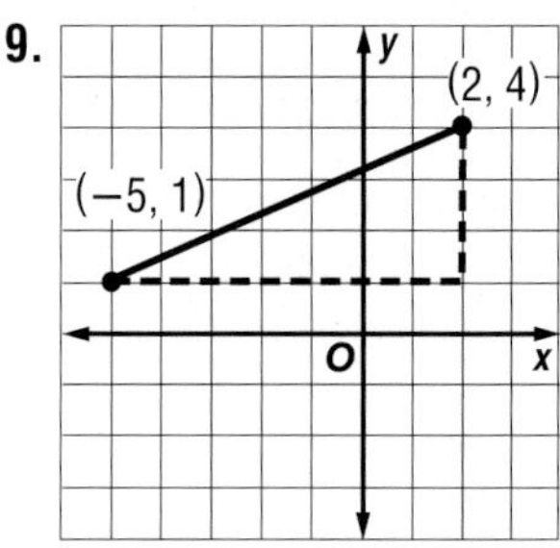

20.

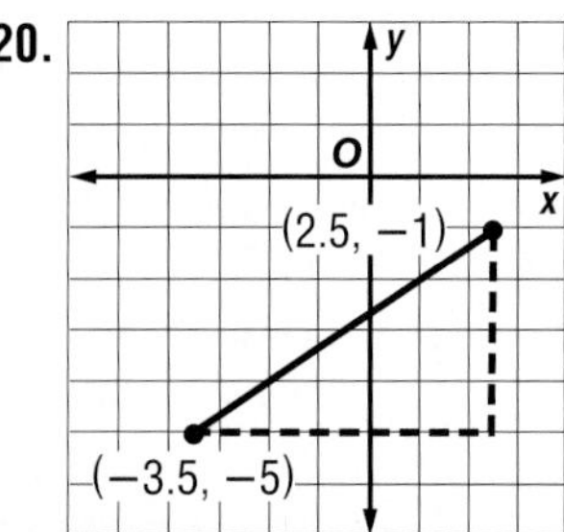

21.

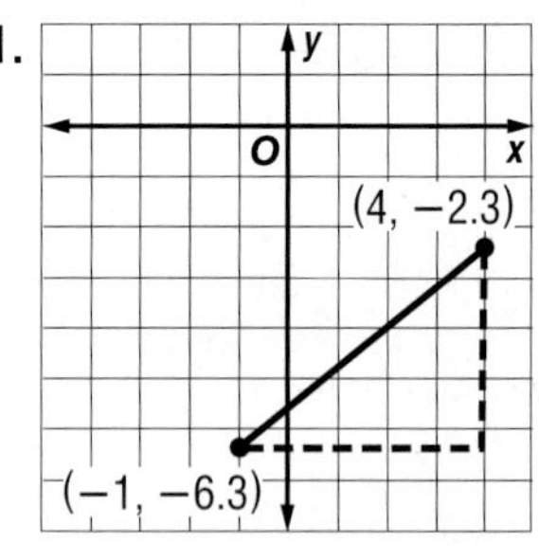

25. For horizontal lines, the *x*-coordinate is half the sum of the *x*-coordinates of the endpoints and the *y*-coordinate is the *y*-coordinate of the endpoints. For vertical lines, the *x*-coordinate is the *x*-coordinate of the endpoints and the *y*-coordinate is half the sum of the *y*-coordinates of the endpoints.

NOTES

UNIT 2 Notes

Introduction

In this unit, students are introduced to ratios and rate of change. They explore how to find the rate of change between two points on a graph by calculating slope. Students will apply their knowledge of ratios by solving proportions and constructing scale drawings and models. They also will investigate ratios and percents, and review the connections among fractions, decimals, and percents. In addition, students will learn to use the percent proportion to solve problems. Finally, students will explore how to estimate percents, use the percent equation, and calculate interest and the percent of change.

Assessment Options

Unit 2 Test Pages 305–306 of the *Chapter 5 Resource Masters* may be used as a test or a review for Unit 2. This assessment contains both multiple-choice and short-response items.

An online, research-based, instructional, assessment, and intervention tool that provides specific feedback on student mastery of state and national standards, instant remediation, and a data management system to track performance. For more information, contact mhdigitallearning.com

UNIT 2

Proportional Reasoning

Chapter 4

Proportions, Algebra, and Geometry

Chapter 5

Percent

Although they may seem unrelated, proportions, algebra, and geometry are closely related. In this unit, you will use proportions and algebra to solve problems involving geometry and percents.

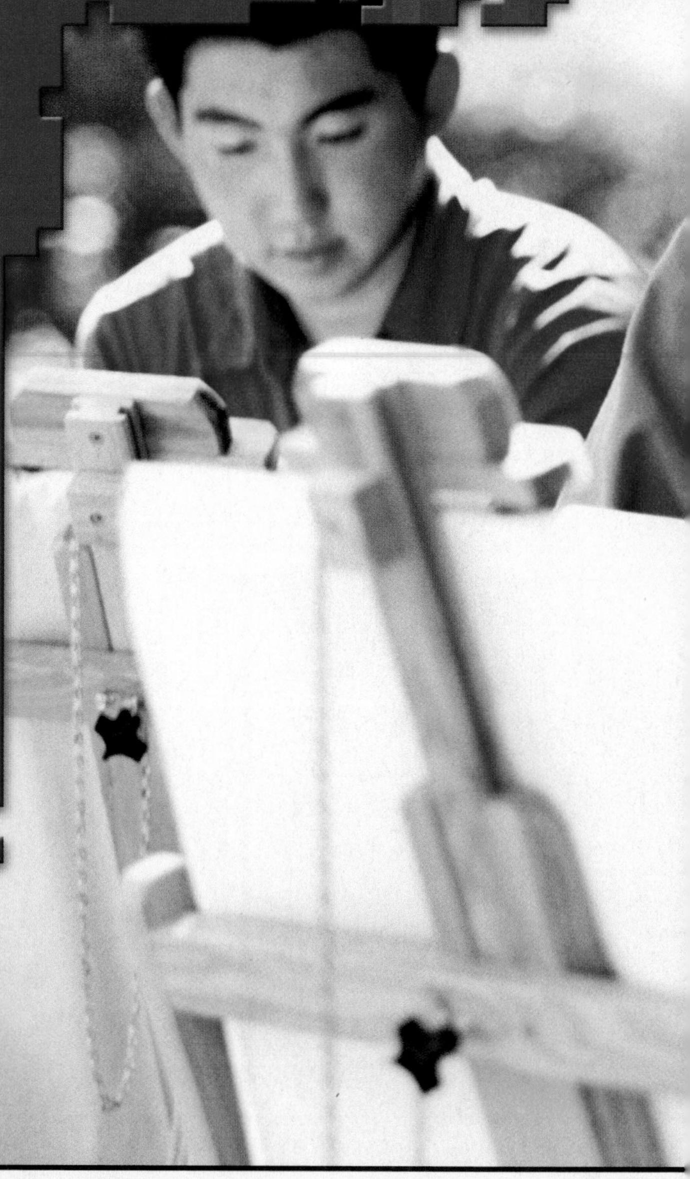

Real-Life Math Videos engage students, showing them how math is used in everyday situations. Use Video 2 with this unit to discuss how proportions, rate of change, and slope are used in construction, traffic control, and skateboarding. (also available on one Super DVD combined with MindJogger Videoquizzes)

INTERDISCIPLINARY PROJECT

It's a Masterpiece!

Math and Art Grab some canvas, paint, and paintbrushes. You're about to create a masterpiece! On this adventure, you'll learn about the art of painting the human face. Along the way, you'll research the methods of a master painter and learn about how artists use the Golden Ratio to achieve balance in their works. Don't forget to bring your math tool kit and a steady hand. This is an adventure you'll want to frame!

WebQuest **Log on to msmath3.net/webquest to begin your WebQuest.**

Unit 2 Proportional Reasoning 153

INTERDISCIPLINARY PROJECT

It's a Masterpiece!

A WebQuest is an online project in which students do research on the Internet, gather data, and make presentations using word processing, graphing, page-making, or presentation software. In each chapter, students advance to the next step in their WebQuest. At the end of Chapter 5, the project culminates with a presentation of their findings.

WebQuest Teaching suggestions and sample answers are available in the WebQuests, Projects, and Interdisciplinary Investigations.

Math and Art You can use this WebQuest Interdisciplinary Project with your students' art teacher to make the connection from mathematics to the art your students are studying.

More Interdisciplinary Connections

You may wish to share these suggestions with your students' other teachers.

Math and Technology Education

Experiment with scanning equipment and photo editing software to create a variety of portraits from photographs of faces. How does your own portrait change if you replace one side of your portrait with the mirror image of the other side?

Math and Health

Research what effects a healthy lifestyle has on the face. What foods are important to eat? What role does hygiene play? How do taking care of your teeth, getting enough rest and exercise, and not smoking affect how your face looks?

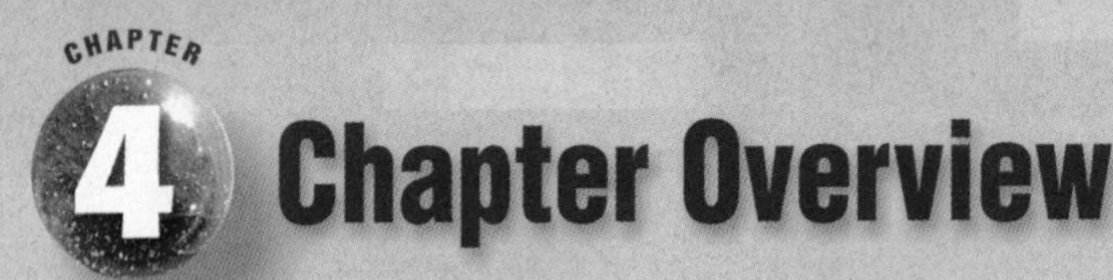

Chapter Overview

Proportions, Algebra, and Geometry

	LESSON OBJECTIVES	NCTM Standards	NAEP 2005	State/Local Objectives
4-1	**Ratios and Rates** (pp. 156–159) • Express ratios as fractions in simplest form and determine unit rates.	1, 6–10	N4a, N4b, N4c, M1l	
4-2	**Rate of Change** (pp. 160–165) • Find rates of change. **4-2b Spreadsheet Investigation:** Find rates of change using a spreadsheet.	1, 2, 6–10	A1a, A1f, A2a, A2b, A2c, D1a, G1f, M1l, N4c	
4-3	**Slope** (pp. 166–169) • Find the slope of a line.	1–3, 6–10	A1f, A2b, A2c, A2g, A4d	
4-4	**Solving Proportions** (pp. 170–173) • Use proportions to solve problems.	1, 2, 6–10	N4a, N4b, N4c, M1l, M2c	
4-5	**Similar Polygons** (pp. 176–183) **4-5a Problem-Solving Strategy:** Solve problems by using the draw a diagram strategy. • Identify similar polygons and find missing measures of similar polygons. **4-5b Hands-On Lab:** Find the value of the golden ratio.	1–4, 6–10	A1a, A1b, G2e, G2f, G3c, M1g, M1h, N4a, N4c	
4-6	**Scale Drawings and Models** (pp. 184–187) • Solve problems involving scale drawings.	1–4, 6–10	M2f, N4a, N4b, N4c, N5f	
4-7	**Indirect Measurement** (pp. 188–193) • Solve problems involving similar triangles. **4-7b Hands-On Lab:** Solve problems by using the trigonometric ratios of sine, cosine, and tangent.	1–4, 6–10	G1f, G2e, M1g, M1k, N4a, N4c	
4-8	**Dilations** (pp. 194–197) • Graph dilations on a coordinate plane.	1–3, 6–10	A2c, A2d, G2c, G4d, N4b, N4c	

Key to NCTM Standards:

1=Number & Operations, 2=Algebra, 3=Geometry, 4=Measurement, 5=Data Analysis & Probability, 6=Problem Solving, 7=Reasoning & Proof, 8=Communication, 9=Connections, 10=Representation

NAEP 2005 Standards: See Teacher Resources at math.glencoe.com

Pacing suggestions for the entire year can be found on page T23.

*An electronic version of this chapter is available on **StudentWorks™**. This backpack solution CD-ROM allows students instant access to the Student Edition, lesson worksheet pages, and web resources.*

Chapter Resource Manager

Chapter 4 Resource Masters												
Study Guide and Intervention	Practice (Skills and Word Problems)	Reading to Learn Mathematics	Enrichment	Assessment	Applications*	Parent and Student Study Guide Online Worksheets	5-Minute Check Transparencies	Key Teaching Transparencies	MathPASS: Tutorial Plus (lessons)	Teaching Mathematics with Manipulatives	Noteables™: Interactive Study Notebook	Optional Materials
185	186–187	188	189		SM 49–52 CS 21	4-1	4-1	13	21		4-1	
190	191–192	193	194	239		4-2	4-2				4-2	
195	196–197	198	199			4-3	4-3				4-3	
200	201–202	203	204	239, 241	CS 22	4-4	4-4	14	22		4-4	
205	206–207	208	209			4-5	4-5		23	50	4-5	tracing paper, centimeter ruler, scissors, calculator, tape measure
210	211–212	213	214	240	CS 23 CM 13–16	4-6	4-6			51	4-6	
215	216–217	218	219			4-7	4-7	15		52	4-7	metric ruler, calculator
220	221–222	223	224	225–238, 240, 242–244	RC 30 CS 24	4-8	4-8	16		53–54	4-8	ruler

*** Key to Abbreviations:** *CS = Calculator and Spreadsheet Masters, RC = Real-Life Career Masters, CM = Classroom Math Games (online), SM = Science and Math Lab Manual (online)*

PowerPoint® Presentations

This CD-ROM is a customizable Microsoft® PowerPoint® presentation that includes:

- In-Class Examples
- Links to Online Study Tools
- 5-Minute Check Transparencies
- Your Turn Exercises

Math Skills Maintenance

Use the Math Skills Maintenance Masters to keep your students' basic math skills fresh. Students can review skills one at a time or in a combined format. The Masters are also available online at msmath3.net/maintenance.

Mathematical Content and Teaching Strategies

Continuity of Instruction

Building on Prior Knowledge

In previous courses, students gained an understanding of various units of measurement and learned how to measure with those units. Also, students have worked with tables and graphs in Chapter 1 and in Courses 1 and 2 of *Mathematics: Applications and Concepts*. In Chapter 2, students performed operations with rational numbers. At the end of Chapter 3, students worked with the coordinate plane.

Learning in This Chapter

Students study ratios and rates. They apply the concept of rate to slopes of lines graphed on a coordinate grid. They solve proportions by using cross products and apply this skill to problems involving similar polygons, scale drawings, and indirect measurements. Students work with scale drawings. They use similar polygons to measure objects that are difficult to measure directly. Lastly, they investigate dilations, combining their knowledge of similar polygons with coordinate graphing.

Making Future Connections

An understanding of slope and rate of change is essential for further study in coordinate geometry. Proportions are used in numerous real-life situations. In particular, understanding how to create and read scale drawings will be essential to students in many careers, as well as in everyday activities, such as reading maps. Dilations help students further understand the numerical relationships among similar figures.

Mathematical Background

4-1 Ratios and Rates

Understanding and using ratios are necessary for the successful study of mathematics. Ratios involve simple division and are an important part of determining rates, finding slopes of lines, and solving a number of geometric applications.

4-2 Rate of Change

Students will recognize rates of change in miles per hour, miles per gallon, points per game, and so on, and learn to graph them. Understanding graphed trends is a valuable skill needed for future mathematics, social studies, and science courses.

4-3 Slope

Understanding slope involves understanding rate of change on a coordinate grid. Slope can be determined using the formula $\frac{\text{rise}}{\text{run}}$. Students will determine rise and run solely from looking at a graph. They also will make important connections among tables of data, graphs and slopes, and rate of change.

4-4 Solving Proportions

Proportions can be identified by confirming that the cross products of two ratios are equal. Students use the cross product to find the missing term of a proportion. A variety of disciplines, including science, use proportions.

Teacher to Teacher

Marla Timmerman
Berry Middle School
Lebanon, OH

"I use this lesson as an opportunity to talk about architecture. I give students a blueprint of a well-known building in town. Then they take measurements and use proportions to find the actual dimensions of the building."

4-5 Similar Polygons

Similar polygons have the same shape, but different sizes. Tell students to be careful when naming similar polygons; the corresponding parts of the figures should be written in the same order in each name. Using an understanding of proportion to solve for the unknown lengths of sides for similar polygons is an important early step in the study of geometry.

Building a Word Wall

Students may be familiar with the word *similar,* but not necessarily in a mathematical sense. Develop a word wall to clarify the concept and relate the mathematical meaning of *similar* to its meaning outside mathematics. Record the definitions on the wall.

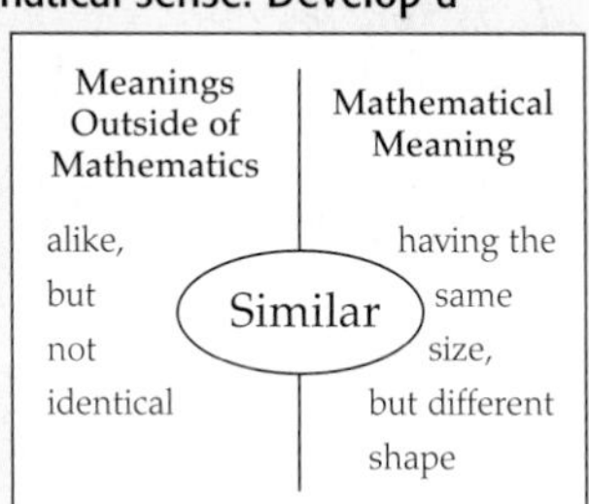

4-6 Scale Drawings and Models

Scale drawings and models are used to represent an object that is very large or very small. The scale factor is the ratio of a given model length to its corresponding actual length that can be used to find a length in an actual figure from a model or vice versa.

In-Class Speaker

Invite an architect to speak to the class. The architect can describe ways in which blueprints and scale drawings are used in architecture. If possible, ask the architect to bring examples of his or her work.

4-7 Indirect Measurements

Indirect measurement is a way to compute the measurement of difficult to measure lengths using the properties of similar polygons and proportions. Often the height of tall objects like trees or buildings is measured indirectly. Indirect measurement can also be used to compute the distance across a body of water.

4-8 Dilations

A dilation is a mathematical transformation. Dilation is the process of enlarging or reducing a figure. A figure and its dilation will always be similar. The coordinates of a dilation on a coordinate grid can be computed by multiplying each coordinate by the scale factor.

What the Research Says

According to Marzano, Pickering, and Pollock in *Classroom Instruction that Works: Research Based Strategies for Increasing Student Achievement,* practice is necessary for learning to occur.

- In Lessons 4-1, 4-2, 4-3, 4-4, 4-5, and 4-8, the Your Turn exercises allow students to practice concepts in a classroom setting.
- The Guided Practice exercises are representative of the exercises used for homework.

McGraw-Hill Professional Development

Mathematics, YES! a self-paced, web-based professional development program. Units are based on major mathematical concepts and are standards-based. Actual classroom videos provide a springboard for discussion and activities. Units appropriate for this chapter:

- Coordinate Pairs and Graphing
- Ratio and Proportional Reasoning
- Geometry and Measurement of Plane Figures

Additional mathematical information and teaching notes are available at msmath3.net/key_concepts.

DAILY INTERVENTION and Assessment

* **Key to Abbreviations:**
TWE = Teacher Wraparound Edition, *CRM* = Chapter Resource Masters

	Type	Student Edition	Teacher Resources	Technology/Internet
INTERVENTION	Ongoing	Prerequisite Skills, pp. 155, 159, 164, 169, 182, 187, 191 Mid-Chapter Practice Test, p. 174	5-Minute Check Transparencies Quizzes 1–4, *CRM*, pp. 239–240 Mid-Chapter Test, *CRM*, p. 241 Study Guide and Intervention, *CRM*, pp. 185, 190, 195, 200, 205, 210, 215, 220	MathPASS: Tutorial Plus msmath3.net/self_check_quiz msmath3.net/extra_examples
	Mixed Review	pp. 159, 164, 169, 173, 182, 187, 191, 197	Cumulative Review, *CRM*, p. 242	
	Error Analysis	Find the Error, pp. 168, 186	Find the Error, *TWE*, pp. 168, 186 Unlocking Misconceptions, *TWE*, pp. 171, 179 Tips for New Teachers, *TWE*, p. 171	
ASSESSMENT	Standardized Test Practice	pp. 159, 164, 169, 173, 174, 177, 180, 182, 187, 191, 197, 201, 202–203	Standardized Test Practice, *CRM*, pp. 243–244	Standardized Test Practice CD-ROM msmath3.net/standardized_test
	Open-Ended Assessment	Writing Math, pp. 158, 163, 181, 183, 193 Open-Ended, pp. 158, 163, 168, 172, 181, 186, 189, 196 Standardized Test, p. 203	Modeling: *TWE*, pp. 164, 182 Speaking: *TWE*, p. 173 Writing: *TWE*, p. 159 Extended Response Assessment, *CRM*, p. 237	
	Chapter Assessment	Study Guide, pp. 198–200 Practice Test, p. 201	Multiple-Choice Tests (Forms 1, 2A, 2B), *CRM*, pp. 225–230 Free-Response Tests (Forms 2C, 2D, 3), *CRM*, pp. 231–236 Vocabulary Test/Review, *CRM*, p. 238	ExamView® Pro Testmaker (see below) MindJogger Videoquizzes msmath3.net/vocabulary_review msmath3.net/chapter_test

For more information on Yearly ProgressPro, see p. 152.

Glencoe Lesson	Yearly ProgressPro Skill Name
4-1	Simple Ratios Rates
4-2	Rate of Change
4-3	Slope: Level 1
4-4	Identify Proportions Solve Proportions
4-5	Similar Figures
4-6	Scale Models
4-7	Indirect Measurement
4-8	Dilations

ExamView® Pro

Use ExamView® Pro Testmaker CD-ROM to:

- Create multiple versions of tests.
- Create modified tests for inclusion students with one mouse click.
- Edit existing questions and add your own questions.
- Build tests aligned with state standards using built-in state curriculum correlations.
- Change English tests to Spanish with one mouse click and vice versa.

Reading and Writing in Mathematics

READING in the Content Area

This online worksheet provides strategies for reading and analyzing Lesson 4-3, Slope. Students are guided through questions about the main idea, subject matter, supporting details, conclusion, clarifying details, and vocabulary of the lesson.

Noteables™ Interactive Study Notebook With Foldables™ is a study organizer that provides helpful steps for students to follow to organize their notes for Chapter 4.

- Students use Noteables to record notes and to complete their Foldables as you present the material in Lessons 4-1 through 4-8.
- Noteables follow the *Teacher Wraparound Edition's* In-Class Examples and *Interactive Chalkboard CD-ROM.*

For more information on Reading and Writing in Mathematics, see pp. T6–T7.

Recommended Outside Reading for Students

Nonfiction

- Dixon, Robert A. *Mathographics.* Dover Publications, ©1991.

  This book includes more than 100 classic mathematical drawings constructed with a compass or computer graphics. It includes exercises that students can use to create their own constructions. This book can be introduced in conjunction with Lesson 4-5b.

Fiction

- Pappas, Theoni. *The Adventures of Penrose, the Mathematical Cat.* Wide World Publishing, Tetra, ©1997.

  A cat named Penrose leads children on mathematical adventures. The book covers real-world concepts like fractals, infinity, and the golden ratio. This book reviews the content of Lessons 4-5b and 4-8b. The mathematical content is appropriate for 8th grade students.

PROJECT CRISS℠ Study Skill

Think-Pair-Share is a reading strategy that allows students to take an active part in the topics they study. Assign a lesson from the chapter for students to read. Have students think about what they have read and write a short summary. Next, divide the class into pairs and have students discuss the topic with their partners. Have students add information to their summary as they discuss the topic with their partner. Finally, encourage students to share their ideas and conclusions with the entire class.

CReating Independence through Student-owned Strategies

For more information on Project CRISS, see p. T8.

School-To-Home

Parent and Student Study Guide

Parents and students may work together to reinforce the concepts and skills of this chapter. These online worksheets are available in English and Spanish at msmath3.net/parent_student. A sample lesson is shown below.

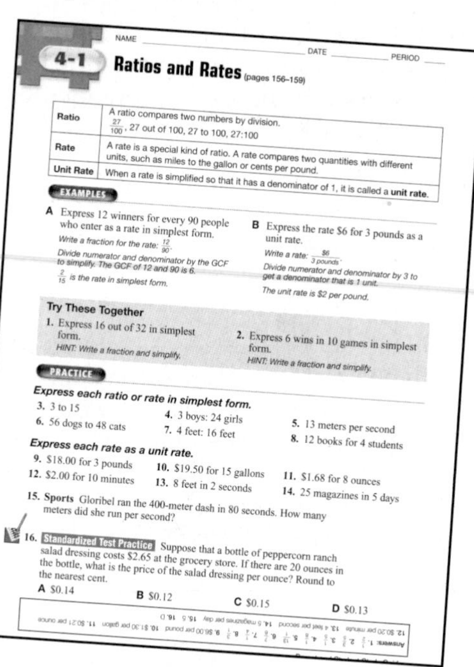

NAME ________ DATE ______ PERIOD ____

4-1 Ratios and Rates (pages 156–159)

Ratio	A ratio compares two numbers by division. $\frac{27}{100}$, 27 out of 100, 27 to 100, 27:100
Rate	A rate is a special kind of ratio. A rate compares two quantities with different units, such as miles to the gallon or cents per pound.
Unit Rate	When a rate is simplified so that it has a denominator of 1, it is called a **unit rate**.

EXAMPLES

A Express 12 winners for every 90 people who enter as a rate in simplest form.
Write a fraction for the rate: $\frac{12}{90}$.
Divide numerator and denominator by the GCF to simplify. The GCF of 12 and 90 is 6.
$\frac{2}{15}$ *is the rate in simplest form.*

B Express the rate \$6 for 3 pounds as a unit rate.
Write a rate: $\frac{\$6}{3 \text{ pounds}}$.
Divide numerator and denominator by 3 to get a denominator that is 1 unit.
The unit rate is \$2 per pound.

Try These Together

1. Express 16 out of 32 in simplest form. *HINT: Write a fraction and simplify.*
2. Express 6 wins in 10 games in simplest form. *HINT: Write a fraction and simplify.*

PRACTICE

Express each ratio or rate in simplest form.

3. 3 to 15
4. 3 boys: 24 girls
5. 13 meters per second
6. 56 dogs to 48 cats
7. 4 feet: 16 feet
8. 12 books for 4 students

Express each rate as a unit rate.

9. \$18.00 for 3 pounds
10. \$19.50 for 15 gallons
11. \$1.68 for 8 ounces
12. \$2.00 for 10 minutes
13. 8 feet in 2 seconds
14. 25 magazines in 5 days
15. **Sports** Gloribel ran the 400-meter dash in 80 seconds. How many meters did she run per second?
16. **Standardized Test Practice** Suppose that a bottle of peppercorn ranch salad dressing costs \$2.65 at the grocery store. If there are 20 ounces in the bottle, what is the price of the salad dressing per ounce? Round to the nearest cent.
A \$0.14 **B** \$0.12 **C** \$0.15 **D** \$0.13

Family Letters and Activities

Send a letter and activity for this chapter home to encourage family members to become active participants in their students' learning. (English: *Chapter 4 Resource Masters*, pp. ix–x; Spanish: log on to msmath3.net/family_letters)

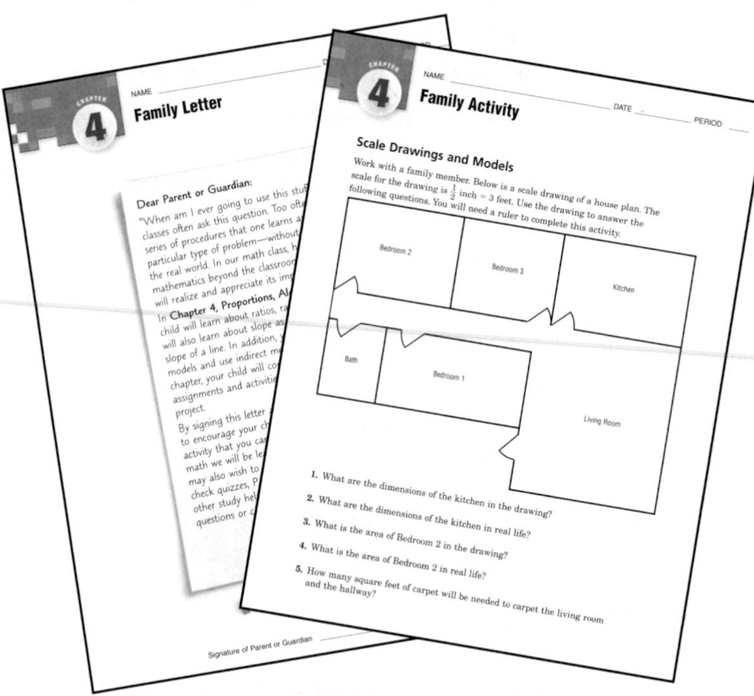

CHAPTER 4 **Family Letter**

NAME

Dear Parent or Guardian:

"When am I ever going to use this stuf... classes often ask this question. Too oft... series of procedures that one learns a... particular type of problem—without... the real world. In our math class, h... mathematics beyond the classroo... will realize and appreciate its imp...

In **Chapter 4, Proportions, Al...** child will learn about ratios, ra... will also learn about slope as... slope of a line. In addition, ... models and use indirect m... chapter, your child will co... assignments and activiti... project.

By signing this letter ... to encourage your ch... activity that you ca... math we will be le... may also wish to ... check quizzes, P... other study hel... questions or c...

Signature of Parent or Guardian ______

CHAPTER 4 **Family Activity**

NAME ________ DATE ______ PERIOD ____

Scale Drawings and Models

Work with a family member. Below is a scale drawing of a house plan. The scale for the drawing is $\frac{1}{2}$ inch = 3 feet. Use the drawing to answer the following questions. You will need a ruler to complete this activity.

1. What are the dimensions of the kitchen in the drawing?
2. What are the dimensions of the kitchen in real life?
3. What is the area of Bedroom 2 in the drawing?
4. What is the area of Bedroom 2 in real life?
5. How many square feet of carpet will be needed to carpet the living room and the hallway?

English Language Learners ELL

Lesson 4-3

Using Multisensory Activities

Have pairs of students use a graphing calculator. Show students how to input ordered pairs using the list function of the calculator. Once the calculator has graphed the data, ask students what they notice about the points. Use the connected graph feature to see what is formed when the points on the graph are connected. Also, you may wish to refer students to the menu on the calculator that will give them a linear regression equation for the data. Ask the students to write the linear equation and tell the slope and *y*-intercept of the equation.

Lesson 4-5

Higher-Level Thinking

Give groups of students a piece of grid paper and have them draw a square or rectangle. Ask students to label each side length by counting the squares on the grid. Then have students double each dimension and draw the new polygon on the same grid. Repeat, tripling each dimension of the original figure. Next, have students find the perimeter and area of each figure. What is the relationship between the perimeters and areas? Guide students to see that the perimeter of the second figure is twice that of the first and that the area is four times as that of the first. Then students can see how the perimeter and area of the third figure is related to the perimeter and area of the first. Ask students to explain these relationships.

MathScape™ This project was supported, in part, by the **National Science Foundation**

MathScape is a mathematics curriculum for grades 6–8 developed by the Seeing and Thinking Mathematically Project at the Education Development Center.

Slopes, Angles, and Ratios
Roads and Ramps

How to Use *MathScape* with Chapter 4

The unit *Roads and Ramps* can be used to enhance Lessons 4-4 and 4-6.

- **Reinforce** → After you complete **Lesson 4-4,** you can use the activities on pages 244–245 to provide a real-life problem involving slope and proportions.
- **Enrich** → After you complete **Lesson 4-6,** you can use the activities on pages 252–255 to extend scale drawings to three-dimensions.

For other lessons in Chapter 4 that correlate to *MathScape*, see the chart on page T14.

Online Lesson Planner

USA TODAY® Education's Online site offers resources and interactive features connected to each day's newspaper. *Experience Today,* USA TODAY's® daily lesson plan, is available on the site and delivered daily to subscribers. This plan provides instruction for integrating USA TODAY® graphics and key editorial features into your mathematics classroom. Log on to **education.usatoday.com.**

USA TODAY Snapshots® in Chapter 4	
Lesson	**Snapshot**
4-1	Earning top dollar
4-2	Food and drink sales up

Quick Review Math Handbook

is Glencoe's mathematical handbook for students. The Hot Words section includes a glossary of terms while the Hot Topics section consists of explanations of key mathematical concepts. An exercise set is included to check students' understanding of the concepts. This valuable resource can be used as a reference in the classroom or for home study.

Lesson	Hot Topics Section	Lesson	Hot Topics Section
4-1	6-5	4-5	6-5, 8-6
4-2	6-5, 9-4	4-6	6-5, 8-6
4-3	6-8	4-7	6-5, 7-10, 8-6
4-4	6-5	4-8	7-3

Key Chapter Objectives

Lesson 4-2 Find rates of change.

Lesson 4-3 Find the slope of a line.

Lesson 4-4 Use proportions to solve problems.

Lesson 4-7 Solve problems involving similar triangles.

"What do the planets have to do with math?"

Point out to students that this is only one of many applications of the math that they are studying. Others are provided in the introduction to each lesson.

Vocabulary Builder, pp. vii–viii **ELL**

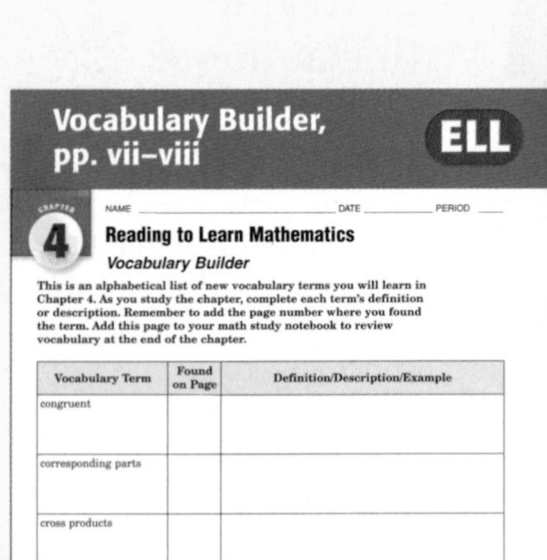

NAME ______________________ DATE __________ PERIOD ____

Chapter 4 Reading to Learn Mathematics

Vocabulary Builder

This is an alphabetical list of new vocabulary terms you will learn in Chapter 4. As you study the chapter, complete each term's definition or description. Remember to add the page number where you found the term. Add this page to your math study notebook to review vocabulary at the end of the chapter.

Vocabulary Term	Found on Page	Definition/Description/Example
congruent		
corresponding parts		
cross products		
dilation [deye-LAY-shuhn]		
indirect measurement		
polygon		
proportion		
rate		
rate of change		

CHAPTER 4 Proportions, Algebra, and Geometry

"What do the planets have to do with math?"

The circumference of Earth is about 40,000 kilometers. If you know the circumference of the other planets, you can use **proportions** to make a scale model of our solar system.

You will solve problems involving scale models in Lesson 4-6.

Vocabulary Builder

For a thorough vocabulary list with pronunciations of new words, give students the Vocabulary Builder worksheets from the *Chapter 4 Resource Masters*. Encourage them to complete the definition of each term as they progress through the chapter.

GETTING STARTED

▶ Diagnose Readiness

Take this quiz to see if you are ready to begin Chapter 4. Refer to the lesson or page number in parentheses for review.

Vocabulary Review

Complete each sentence.

1. A __?__ is a letter used to represent an unknown number. (Lesson 1-2) **variable**
2. The coordinate system includes a vertical number line called the __?__. (Lesson 3-6) **y-axis**
3. An __?__ names any given point on the coordinate plane with its x-coordinate and y-coordinate. (Lesson 3-6) **ordered pair**

Prerequisite Skills

Simplify each fraction. (Page 611)

4. $\frac{10}{24}$ **$\frac{5}{12}$**
5. $\frac{88}{104}$ **$\frac{11}{13}$**
6. $\frac{36}{81}$ **$\frac{4}{9}$**
7. $\frac{49}{91}$ **$\frac{7}{13}$**

Evaluate each expression. (Lesson 1-2)

8. $\frac{6-2}{5+5}$ **$\frac{2}{5}$**
9. $\frac{7-4}{8-4}$ **$\frac{3}{4}$**
10. $\frac{3-1}{1+9}$ **$\frac{1}{5}$**
11. $\frac{5+7}{8-6}$ **6**

Subtract. (Lesson 1-5)

12. $16 - 7$ **9**
13. $5 - 12$ **−7**
14. $-8 - 10$ **−18**
15. $4 - (-3)$ **7**

Solve each equation. (Lesson 1-9)

16. $5 \cdot 6 = x \cdot 2$ **15**
17. $c \cdot 1.5 = 3 \cdot 7$ **14**
18. $12 \cdot z = 9 \cdot 4$ **3**
19. $7 \cdot 2 = 8 \cdot g$ **1.75**
20. $3 \cdot 11 = 4 \cdot y$ **8.25**
21. $b \cdot 6 = 7 \cdot 9$ **10.5**

FOLDABLES™ Study Organizer

Using Proportions Make this Foldable to help you organize your notes. Begin with a plain sheet of 11" by 17" paper.

STEP 1 **Fold in thirds** Fold in thirds widthwise.

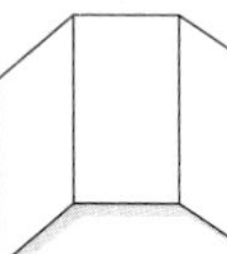

STEP 2 **Open and Fold Again** Fold the bottom to form a pocket. Glue edges.

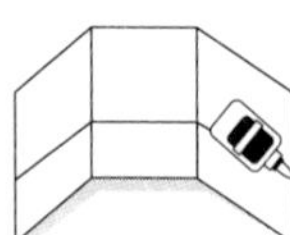

STEP 3 **Label** Label each pocket. Place index cards in each pocket.

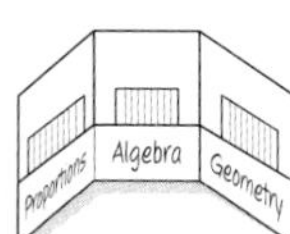

Noteables™ **Chapter Notes** Each time you find this logo throughout the chapter, use your *Noteables™: Interactive Study Notebook with Foldables™* or your own notebook to take notes. Begin your chapter notes with this Foldable activity.

Math Online **Readiness** To prepare yourself for this chapter with another quiz, visit **msmath3.net/chapter_readiness**

GETTING STARTED

Diagnose Readiness This section provides a review of the basic concepts needed before beginning Chapter 4. Page references are included for additional student help.

Prerequisite Skills review skills needed in this chapter.

Exercises	Needed for Lesson	Skill
4–7	4-1	Simplify Fractions
8–11	4-2	Evaluate Expressions
12–15	4-2	Subtract Integers
16–21	4-3	Solve Equations

For more prerequisite skills, see:

- Getting Ready for the Next Lesson, at the end of each lesson
- Prerequisite Skills in the Student Handbook on pp. 600–615
- *Math Skills Maintenance Masters*

FOLDABLES™ Study Organizer

For more information about Foldables, see *Teaching Mathematics with Foldables.*

Have students make and label their Foldables as illustrated. Students will need 3″ by 5″ index cards. As students learn about ratios and rates in Lesson 4-1, have them write examples on one side of their card and the verbal expression on the other side. Students sort their study cards into the appropriate pocket of their Foldables. Continue through the chapter using the study cards to take notes, solve equations, and record and define vocabulary words and concepts presented in each lesson.

4-1 Lesson Notes

Lesson Resources

Chapter 4 Resource Masters

- Study Guide and Intervention, p. 185
- Practice: Skills, p. 186
- Practice: Word Problems, p. 187
- Reading to Learn Mathematics, p. 188
- Enrichment, p. 189

Calculator and Spreadsheet Masters, p. 21
Key Teaching Transparencies, 13
MathPASS Tutorial CD-ROM, 28
Parent and Student Study Guide Online Worksheets, 4-1
Science and Math Lab Masters, pp. 49–52
Noteables™: Interactive Study Notebook with Foldables™, 4-1

1 Focus

5-Minute Check 4-1

Use as a quiz or review of Chapter 3. (Also available as a transparency)

Bellringer

Reading Mathematics Ask students to list expressions that are equivalent to *one out of five*. You can write the following phrases on the chalkboard for students to complete.

1. 2 out of _____ **10**
2. _____ out of 15 **3**
3. 5 out of _____ **25**

Reading to Learn Mathematics, p. 188 **ELL**

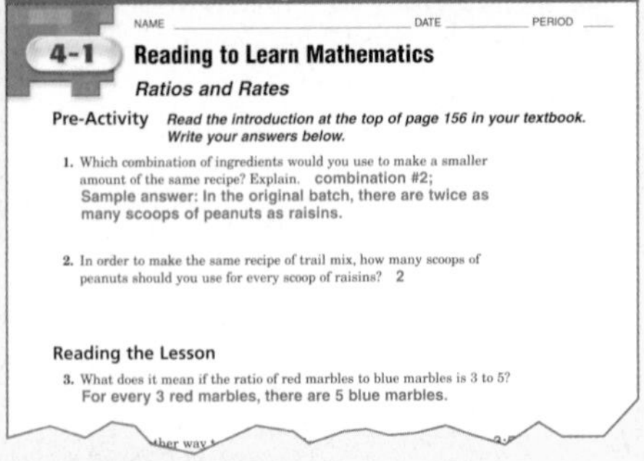

NAME _______ DATE _______ PERIOD _____

4-1 Reading to Learn Mathematics
Ratios and Rates

Pre-Activity *Read the introduction at the top of page 156 in your textbook. Write your answers below.*

1. Which combination of ingredients would you use to make a smaller amount of the same recipe? Explain. combination #2; Sample answer: In the original batch, there are twice as many scoops of peanuts as raisins.

2. In order to make the same recipe of trail mix, how many scoops of peanuts should you use for every scoop of raisins? 2

Reading the Lesson

3. What does it mean if the ratio of red marbles to blue marbles is 3 to 5? For every 3 red marbles, there are 5 blue marbles.

Ratios and Rates

What You'll LEARN

Express ratios as fractions in simplest form and determine unit rates.

NEW Vocabulary

ratio
rate
unit rate

MATH Symbols

≈ approximately equal to

WHEN am I ever going to use this?

TRAIL MIX The diagram shows a batch of trail mix that is made using 3 scoops of raisins and 6 scoops of peanuts.

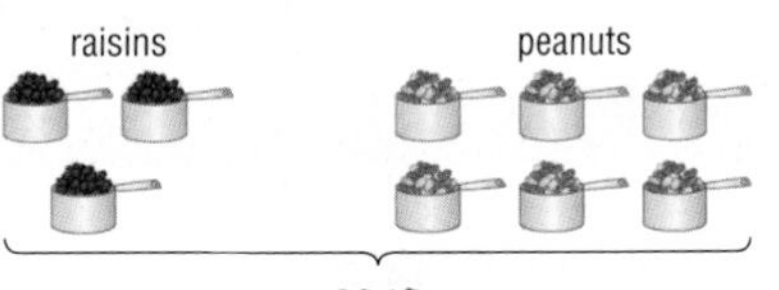

1. Which combination of ingredients below would you use to make a smaller amount of the same recipe? Explain. **See margin.**

Combination #1: raisins, peanuts
Combination #2: raisins, peanuts

2. In order to make the same recipe of trail mix, how many scoops of peanuts should you use for every scoop of raisins? **2**

A **ratio** is a comparison of two numbers by division. If a batch of trail mix contains 3 scoops of raisins and 6 scoops of peanuts, then the ratio comparing the raisins to the peanuts can be written as follows.

3 to 6   3:6 $\frac{3}{6}$

Since a ratio can be written as a fraction, it can be simplified.

EXAMPLES Write Ratios in Simplest Form

1 Express *8 Siamese cats out of 28 cats* in simplest form.

$\frac{8}{28} = \frac{2}{7}$ Divide the numerator and denominator by the greatest common factor, 4.

The ratio of Siamese cats to cats is $\frac{2}{7}$ or 2 out of 7.

READING Math

Ratios In Example 1, the ratio 2 out of 7 means that for every 7 cats, 2 are Siamese.

2 Express *10 ounces to 1 pound* in simplest form.

$\frac{10 \text{ ounces}}{1 \text{ pound}} = \frac{10 \text{ ounces}}{16 \text{ ounces}}$ Convert 1 pound to 16 ounces.

$= \frac{5 \text{ ounces}}{8 \text{ ounces}}$ Divide the numerator and the denominator by 2.

The ratio in simplest form is $\frac{5}{8}$ or 5:8.

Your Turn Express each ratio in simplest form.

a. 16 pepperoni pizzas out of 24 pizzas
b. 12 minutes to 2 hours

a. $\frac{2}{3}$ or 2:3
b. $\frac{1}{10}$ or 1:10

Answer (When am I ever going to use this?)

1. Combination #2; Sample answer: in the original batch, there are twice as many scoops of peanuts as raisins.

A **rate** is a special kind of ratio. It is a comparison of two quantities with different types of units. Here are two examples of rates.

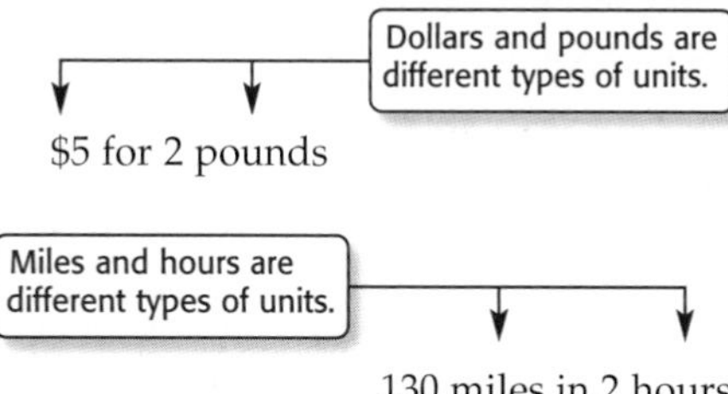

Miles and hours are different types of units.

130 miles in 2 hours

TEACHING TIP

Point out that a unit rate is another way of expressing the mean of a set of data.

When a rate is simplified so it has a denominator of 1, it is called a **unit rate**. An example of a unit rate is *$6.50 per hour*, which means *$6.50 per 1 hour*.

EXAMPLE Find a Unit Rate

3 TRAVEL On a trip from Nashville, Tennessee, to Birmingham, Alabama, Darrell drove 187 miles in 3 hours. What was Darrell's average speed in miles per hour?

Write the rate that expresses the comparison of miles to hours. Then find the average speed by finding the unit rate.

$\frac{187 \text{ miles}}{3 \text{ hours}} \approx \frac{62 \text{ miles}}{1 \text{ hour}}$ Divide the numerator and denominator by 3 to get a denominator of 1.

Darrell drove an average speed of about 62 miles per hour.

EXAMPLE Compare Unit Rates

4 CIVICS For the 2000 census, the population of Texas was about 20,900,000, and the population of Illinois was about 12,500,000. There were 30 members of the U.S. House of Representatives from Texas and 19 from Illinois. In which state did a member represent more people?

For each state, write a rate that compares the state's population to its number of representatives. Then find the unit rates.

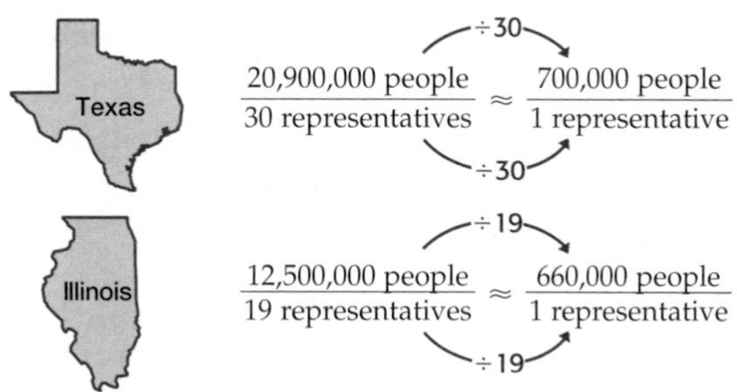

$\frac{20{,}900{,}000 \text{ people}}{30 \text{ representatives}} \approx \frac{700{,}000 \text{ people}}{1 \text{ representative}}$ (÷30)

$\frac{12{,}500{,}000 \text{ people}}{19 \text{ representatives}} \approx \frac{660{,}000 \text{ people}}{1 \text{ representative}}$ (÷19)

Therefore, in Texas, a member of the U.S. House of Representatives represented more people than in Illinois.

REAL-LIFE MATH

CIVICS In the U.S. House of Representatives, the number of representatives from each state is based on a state's population in the preceding census.

Source: www.house.gov

msmath3.net/extra_examples

DAILY INTERVENTION

Differentiated Instruction

Kinesthetic Have students work in pairs and take each other's pulse. Ask students to explain how a pulse is a ratio. **number of beats per minute** Have them write the pulse in simplest form. For more data, have students walk up and down stairs a couple of times and take their pulses again.

2 Teach

Noteables™

As you work the **In-Class Examples,** have students follow along in their *Noteables™: Interactive Study Notebook with Foldables™*, or have students work the examples in their notebooks.

In-Class Examples

Express each ratio in simplest form.

1. 12 blue marbles out of 18 marbles $\frac{2}{3}$
2. 10 inches to 2 feet $\frac{5}{12}$
3. **READING** Yi-Mei reads 141 pages in 3 hours. How many pages does she read per hour? **47 pages per hour**
4. **SHOPPING** Alex spends $12.50 for 2 pounds of almonds and $23.85 for 5 pounds of jelly beans. Which item costs less per pound? By how much? **Jelly beans by $1.48 per pound**

Using Applications

Encourage students to think about ratios and rates that apply to their own lives. They might think of the speed they walk or bike, or they might compare the ratio of the hours they spend on an activity to the hours in a week. As students develop ideas, have them share with other students. This will allow students of all levels to begin thinking of ratios in a practical manner. Also remind students that the order of the numbers in a ratio affects its meaning.

3 Practice/Apply

About the Exercises...

Guided Practice Key

Exercises	Examples
3–6	1, 2
7–8	3
9	4

Assignment Guide

Basic: 11–25 odd, 31, 33, 35–46

Average: 11–33 odd, 35–46

Enriched: 10–30 even, 31, 32, 34–42 (Optional: 43–46)

Answers

1. Sample answer: $\frac{16 \text{ yellow}}{10 \text{ red}}$; $\frac{8}{5}$; for every 8 yellow marbles, there are 5 red.

24. 21-oz box; the 21-oz box costs about 27.1¢/oz and the 17-oz box costs about 28.8¢/oz.

25. 6 cans for $1; 6 for $1 costs about 16.7¢/can and 10 for $1.95 costs about 19.5¢/can.

26. 1 lb 4 oz for $4.99; 1 lb 4 oz for $4.99 costs about 25.0¢/oz and 2 lbs 6 oz for $9.75 costs about 25.7¢/oz.

27. 2 liters for $1.39; 2 liters for $1.39 costs about 2.1¢/oz and 12 12-ounce cans for $3.49 costs about 2.4¢/oz.

32. Woods; Gordon earned about $185,000/win and Woods about $299,000/win.

34. Sample answer: Four out of 10 people surveyed preferred to eat in the cafeteria rather than bring their own lunch.

38. 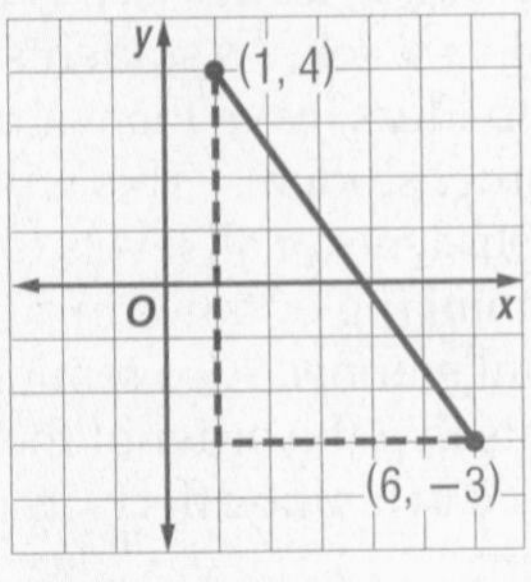

Students practice the same concepts in Exercises 10–29 if they are assigned odd or even problems.

Skill and Concept Check

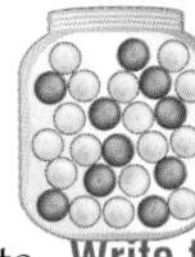

1. **OPEN ENDED** Write a ratio about the marbles in the jar. Simplify your ratio, if possible. Then explain the meaning of your ratio. **See margin.**

2. *Writing Math* Explain how to write a rate as a unit rate. **Write the rate as a fraction. Then divide the numerator and the denominator by the denominator.**

GUIDED PRACTICE

Express each ratio in simplest form. **3. 1:15**

3. 12 missed days in 180 school days
4. 12 wins to 18 losses **2:3**
5. 24 pints:1 quart **12 to 1**
6. 8 inches out of 4 feet $\frac{1}{6}$

Express each rate as a unit rate.

7. $50 for 4 days work **$12.50/day**
8. 3 feet of snow in 5 hours **0.6 ft/h**

9. **SHOPPING** You can buy 4 Granny Smith apples at Ben's Mart for $0.95. SaveMost sells the same quality apples 6 for $1.49. Which store has the better buy? Explain your reasoning. **9. Ben's Mart; the cost at Ben's Mart is about 23.8¢ per apple, while at SaveMost it is about 24.8¢.**

★ indicates increased difficulty

Practice and Applications

HOMEWORK HELP

For Exercises	See Examples
10–17, 31, 34	1, 2
18–23, 30, 33	3
24–27, 32	4

Extra Practice See pages 624, 651.

Express each ratio in simplest form. **10. 11:6** **12. 1 to 5**

10. 33 brown eggs to 18 white eggs
11. 56 boys to 64 girls **7:8**
12. 14 chosen out of 70 who applied
13. 28 out of 100 doctors $\frac{7}{25}$
14. 400 centimeters to 1 meter **4:1**
15. 6 feet : 9 yards **2 to 9**
16. 2 cups to 1 gallon $\frac{1}{8}$
17. 153 points in 18 games **17:2**

Express each rate as a unit rate. **20. 491 people/h** **21. 1,225 tickets/theater**

18. $22 for 5 dozen donuts **$4.40/dozen**
19. $73.45 in 13 hours **$5.65/h**
20. 1,473 people entered the park in 3 hours
21. 11,025 tickets sold at 9 theaters
22. 100 meters in 12.2 seconds **about 8.2 m/s**
23. 21.5 pounds in 12 weeks **about 1.8 lb/wk**

SHOPPING For Exercises 24–27, decide which is the better buy. Explain.

24. a 17-ounce box of cereal for $4.89 or a 21-ounce box for $5.69 **24–27. See margin.**
25. 6 cans of green beans for $1 or 10 cans for $1.95
★ 26. 1 pound 4 ounces of meat for $4.99 or 2 pounds 6 ounces for $9.75
★ 27. a 2-liter bottle of soda for $1.39 or a 12-pack of 12-ounce cans for $3.49 (*Hint*: 2 liters = 67.63 ounces)

Use ratios to convert the following rates.

★ 28. 60 mi/h = __?__ ft/s **88**
★ 29. 180 gal/h = __?__ oz/min **384**

30. **CARS** Gas mileage is the average number of miles you can drive a car per gallon of gasoline. A test of a new car resulted in 2,250 miles being driven using 125 gallons of gas. Find the car's gas mileage. **18 mi/gal**

39. 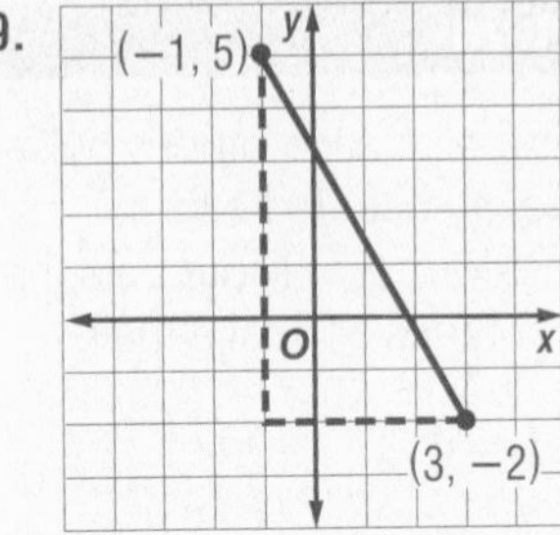

40. 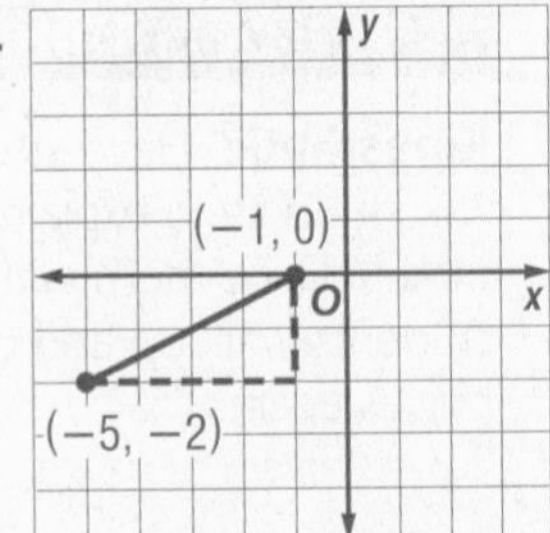

SPORTS For Exercises 31 and 32, use the graph at the right.

31. Write a ratio comparing the amount of money Jeff Gordon earned in the Winston Cup Series in 2001 to his number of wins that year. $\frac{1,662,269}{9}$

32. **MULTI STEP** On average, who earned more money per win in their sport in 2001, Jeff Gordon or Tiger Woods? Explain. **See margin.**

33. **ART** At an auction in New York City, a 2.55-square inch portrait of George Washington sold for \$1.2 million. About how much did the buyer pay per square inch for the portrait? **about \$471,000/in^2**

USA TODAY

USA TODAY Snapshots®

Earning top dollar

Biggest money winners in 2001 among athletes in individual sports (number of events in parentheses; endorsements not included)[1]:

Jeff Gordon NASCAR Winston Cup Series (36)	\$6,649,076
Tiger Woods PGA Tour (19)	\$5,687,777
Lleyton Hewitt ATP Tour (22)	\$3,770,618
Venus Williams WTA Tour (12)	\$2,662,610
Annika Sorenstam LPGA tour (26)	\$2,105,868

1 – Earnings do not reflect year-end bonuses.

Source: NASCAR

By Ellen J. Horrow and Bob Laird, USA TODAY

34. **WRITE A PROBLEM** Write about a real-life situation that can be represented by the ratio 2:5. **See margin.**

35. **CRITICAL THINKING** Luisa and Rachel have some trading cards. The ratio of their cards is 3:1. If Luisa gives Rachel 2 cards, the ratio will be 2:1. How many cards does Luisa have? **18**

Spiral Review with Standardized Test Practice

36. **MULTIPLE CHOICE** Which of the following cannot be written as a ratio? **B**

 (A) two pages for every one page he reads
 (B) three more chips than she has
 (C) half as many CDs as he has
 (D) twice as many pencils as she has

37. **SHORT RESPONSE** Three people leave at the same time from town A to town B. Sarah averaged 45 miles per hour for the first third of the distance, 55 miles per hour for the second third, and 75 miles per hour for the last third. Darnell averaged 55 miles per hour for the first half of the trip and 70 miles per hour for the second half. Megan drove at a steady speed of 60 miles per hour the entire trip. Who arrived first? **Darnell**

Graph each pair of ordered pairs. Then find the distance between the points. Round to the nearest tenth. (Lesson 3-6) **38–41. See margin for graphs.**

38. (1, 4), (6, −3) **8.6 units**
39. (−1, 5), (3, −2) **8.1 units**
40. (−5, −2), (−1, 0) **4.5 units**
41. (−2, −3), (3, 1) **6.4 units**

42. **GYMNASTICS** A gymnast is making a tumbling pass along the diagonal of a square floor exercise mat measuring 40 feet on each side. Find the measure of the diagonal. (Lesson 3-5) **56.6 ft**

GETTING READY FOR THE NEXT LESSON

PREREQUISITE SKILL Evaluate each expression. (Lesson 1-5)

43. $\frac{45 - 33}{10 - 8}$ **6**
44. $\frac{85 - 67}{2001 - 1995}$ **3**
45. $\frac{29 - 44}{55 - 50}$ **−3**
46. $\frac{18 - 19}{25 - 30}$ **0.2**

msmath3.net/self_check_quiz

4 Assess

Open-Ended Assessment

Writing Use United States census data to create a ratio comparing parts of the population, similar to Example 4. Then write a short paragraph explaining who might use the ratio.

Answer

41.

y
(3, 1)
O
x
(−2, −3)

Study Guide and Intervention, p. 185

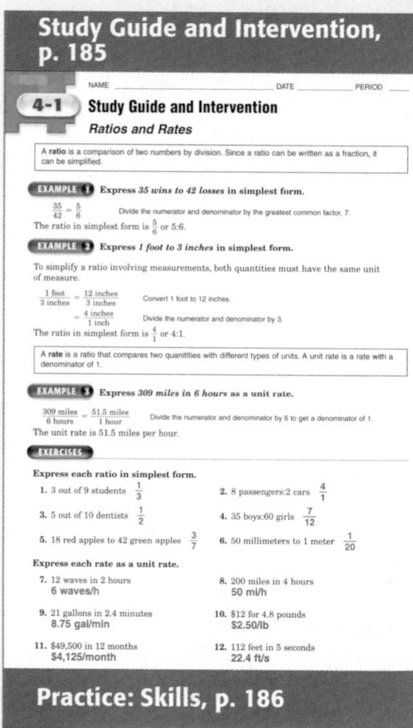

NAME ______ DATE ______ PERIOD ____

4-1 Study Guide and Intervention

Ratios and Rates

A **ratio** is a comparison of two numbers by division. Since a ratio can be written as a fraction, it can be simplified.

EXAMPLE 1 Express *35 wins to 42 losses* in simplest form.

$\frac{35}{42} = \frac{5}{6}$ Divide the numerator and denominator by the greatest common factor, 7.

The ratio in simplest form is $\frac{5}{6}$ or 5:6.

EXAMPLE 2 Express *1 foot to 3 inches* in simplest form.

To simplify a ratio involving measurements, both quantities must have the same unit of measure.

$\frac{1 \text{ foot}}{3 \text{ inches}} = \frac{12 \text{ inches}}{3 \text{ inches}}$ Convert 1 foot to 12 inches.

$= \frac{4 \text{ inches}}{1 \text{ inch}}$ Divide the numerator and denominator by 3.

The ratio in simplest form is $\frac{4}{1}$ or 4:1.

A **rate** is a ratio that compares two quanitities with different types of units. A unit rate is a rate with a denominator of 1.

EXAMPLE 3 Express *309 miles in 6 hours* as a unit rate.

$\frac{309 \text{ miles}}{6 \text{ hours}} = \frac{51.5 \text{ miles}}{1 \text{ hour}}$ Divide the numerator and denominator by 6 to get a denominator of 1.

The unit rate is 51.5 miles per hour.

EXERCISES

Express each ratio in simplest form.

1. 3 out of 9 students $\frac{1}{3}$
2. 8 passengers:2 cars $\frac{4}{1}$
3. 5 out of 10 dentists $\frac{1}{2}$
4. 35 boys:60 girls $\frac{7}{12}$
5. 18 red apples to 42 green apples $\frac{3}{7}$
6. 50 millimeters to 1 meter $\frac{1}{20}$

Express each rate as a unit rate.

7. 12 waves in 2 hours **6 waves/h**
8. 200 miles in 4 hours **50 mi/h**
9. 21 gallons in 2.4 minutes **8.75 gal/min**
10. \$12 for 4.8 pounds **\$2.50/lb**
11. \$49,500 in 12 months **\$4,125/month**
12. 112 feet in 5 seconds **22.4 ft/s**

Practice: Skills, p. 186

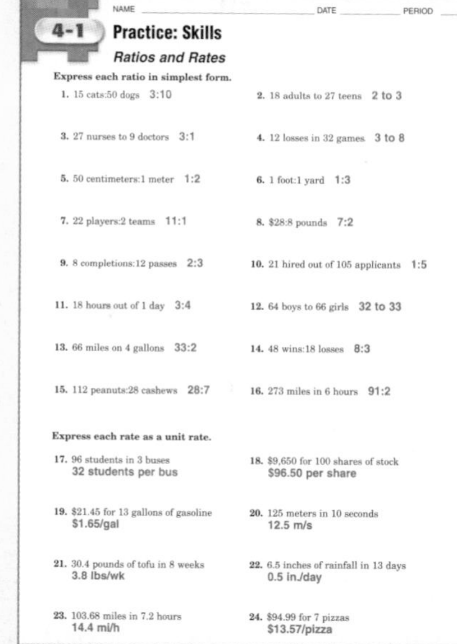

NAME ______ DATE ______ PERIOD ____

4-1 Practice: Skills

Ratios and Rates

Express each ratio in simplest form.

1. 15 cats:50 dogs **3:10**
2. 18 adults to 27 teens **2 to 3**
3. 27 nurses to 9 doctors **3:1**
4. 12 losses in 32 games **3 to 8**
5. 50 centimeters:1 meter **1:2**
6. 1 foot:1 yard **1:3**
7. 22 players:2 teams **11:1**
8. \$28:8 pounds **7:2**
9. 8 completions:12 passes **2:3**
10. 21 hired out of 105 applicants **1:5**
11. 18 hours out of 1 day **3:4**
12. 64 boys to 66 girls **32 to 33**
13. 66 miles on 4 gallons **33:2**
14. 48 wins:18 losses **8:3**
15. 112 peanuts:28 cashews **28:7**
16. 273 miles in 6 hours **91:2**

Express each rate as a unit rate.

17. 96 students in 3 buses **32 students per bus**
18. \$9,650 for 100 shares of stock **\$96.50 per share**
19. \$21.45 for 13 gallons of gasoline **\$1.65/gal**
20. 125 meters in 10 seconds **12.5 m/s**
21. 30.4 pounds of tofu in 8 weeks **3.8 lbs/wk**
22. 6.5 inches of rainfall in 13 days **0.5 in./day**
23. 103.68 miles in 7.2 hours **14.4 mi/h**
24. \$94.99 for 7 pizzas **\$13.57/pizza**

Practice: Word Problems, p. 187

NAME ______ DATE ______ PERIOD ____

4-1 Practice: Word Problems

Ratios and Rates

1. **COOKING** In a bread dough recipe, there are 3 eggs for every 9 cups of flour. Express this ratio in simplest form. **1:3**

2. **WILDLIFE** Dena counted 14 robins out of 150 birds. Express this ratio in simplest form. **7:75**

3. **INVESTMENTS** Josh earned dividends of \$2.16 on 54 shares of stock. Find the dividends per share. **\$0.04/share**

4. **TRANSPORTATION** When Denise bought gasoline, she paid \$18.48 for 11.2 gallons. Find the price of gasoline per gallon. **\$1.65/gal**

5. **WATER FLOW** Jacob filled his 60-gallon bathtub in 5 minutes. How fast was the water flowing? **12 gal/min**

6. **TRAVEL** On her vacation, Charmaine's flight lasted 4.5 hours. She traveled 954 miles. Find the average speed of the plane. **212 mi/h**

7. **HOUSING** Mr. And Mrs. Romero bought a 1,200 square-foot house for \$111,600. How much did they pay per square foot? **\$93/ft^2**

8. **SHOPPING** A breakfast cereal comes in two different sized packages. The 8-ounce box costs \$2.88, while the 12-ounce box costs \$3.60. Which box is the better buy? Explain your reasoning. **The 12-oz box at \$0.30/oz; the 8-oz box costs \$0.36 per oz, but the 12-oz box costs \$0.30 per oz.**

4-2 Lesson Notes

Lesson Resources

Chapter 4 Resource Masters
- Study Guide and Intervention, p. 190
- Practice: Skills, p. 191
- Practice: Word Problems, p. 192
- Reading to Learn Mathematics, p. 193
- Enrichment, p. 194

FAST FILE

Parent and Student Study Guide Online Worksheets, 4-2
Noteables™: Interactive Study Notebook with Foldables™, 4-2

1 Focus

5-Minute Check 4-2

Use as a quiz or review of Lesson 4-1. (Also available as a transparency)

Bellringer

Communication Ask students to explain (aloud or in writing) how they can use the graph in the opener to answer Exercise 2. They should determine that a steeper slope means a faster increase.

Reading to Learn Mathematics, p. 193 **ELL**

NAME ______ DATE ______ PERIOD ____

4-2 Reading to Learn Mathematics
Rate of Change

Pre-Activity *Read the introduction at the top of page 160 in your textbook. Write your answers below.*

1. By how many bears did Alicia's collection increase between 1997 and 1999? Between 1999 and 2002? 14;15

2. Between which years did Alicia's collection increase the fastest? between 1997 and 1999; Sample answer: While the increase between each time period is nearly the same, the first increase occurs over a shorter amount of time.

Reading the Lesson

3. What does a rate of change measure on a graph? Sample answer: ...

4-2 Rate of Change

WHEN am I ever going to use this?

What You'll LEARN
Find rates of change.

NEW Vocabulary
rate of change

HOBBIES Alicia likes to collect teddy bears. The graph shows the number of teddy bears in her collection between 2001 and 2006.

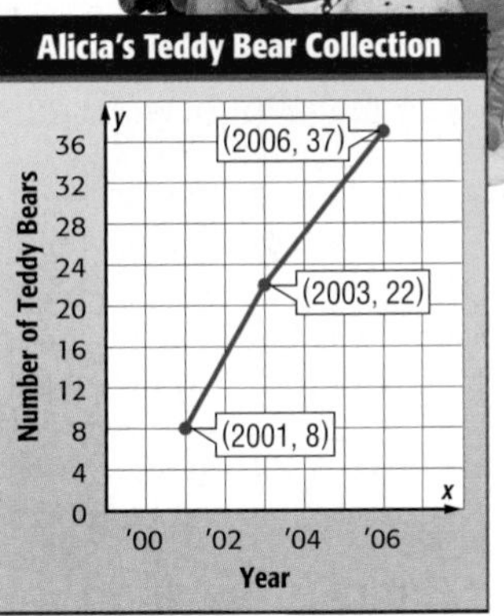

1. By how many bears did Alicia's collection increase between 2001 and 2003? Between 2003 and 2006? **14; 15**
2. Between which years did Alicia's collection increase the fastest? **2001–2003**

A **rate of change** is a rate that describes how one quantity changes in relation to another. In the example above, the rate of change in Alicia's teddy bear collection from 2001 to 2003 is shown below.

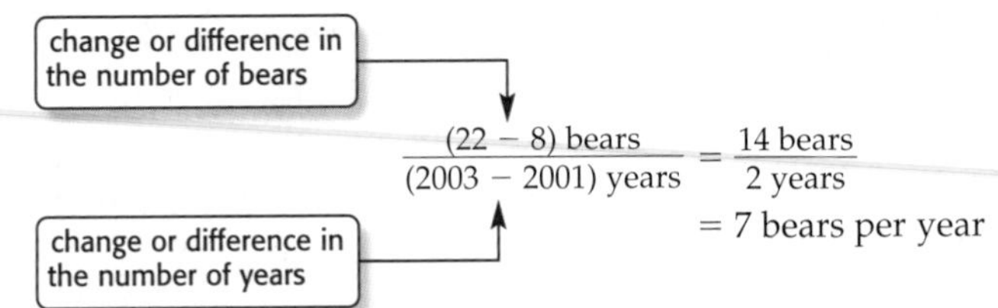

$$\frac{(22 - 8)\text{ bears}}{(2003 - 2001)\text{ years}} = \frac{14\text{ bears}}{2\text{ years}}$$
$$= 7\text{ bears per year}$$

EXAMPLE **Find a Rate of Change**

1 HEIGHTS **The table at the right shows Ramón's height in inches between the ages of 8 and 13. Find the rate of change in his height between ages 8 and 11.**

Age (yr)	8	11	13
Height (in.)	51	58	67

$$\frac{\text{change in height}}{\text{change in age}} = \frac{(58 - 51)\text{ inches}}{(11 - 8)\text{ years}}$$ Ramón grew from 51 to 58 inches tall from age 8 to age 11.

$$= \frac{7\text{ inches}}{3\text{ years}}$$ Subtract to find the change in heights and ages.

$$\approx \frac{2.3\text{ inches}}{1\text{ year}}$$ Express this rate as a unit rate.

Ramón grew an average of about 2.3 inches per year.

STUDY TIP

Mental Math
You can also find a unit rate by dividing the numerator by the denominator.

Your Turn **a. 4.5 in. per year**

a. Find the rate of change in his height between ages 11 and 13.

TEACHING TIP

Remind students to always read graphs from left to right, as they would read words on a page.

A graph of the data in Example 1 is shown at the right. The data points are connected by segments. On a graph, a rate of change measures how fast a segment goes up when the graph is read from left to right.

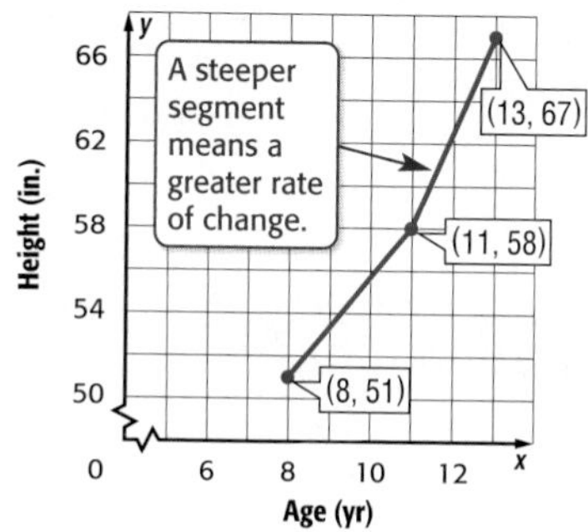

A formula for rate of change using data coordinates is given below.

READING Math

Subscripts Read x_1 as *x sub one* or *x one*.

Noteables™ **Key Concept: Rate of Change**

Words To find the rate of change, divide the difference in the y-coordinates by the difference in the x-coordinates.

Symbols The rate of change between (x_1, y_1) and (x_2, y_2) is $\frac{y_2 - y_1}{x_2 - x_1}$.

Rates of change can be positive or negative. This corresponds to an increase or decrease in the y-value between the two data points.

EXAMPLE Find a Negative Rate of Change

2 **MUSIC The graph shows cassette sales from 1994 to 2000. Find the rate of change between 1996 and 2000, and describe how this rate is shown on the graph.**

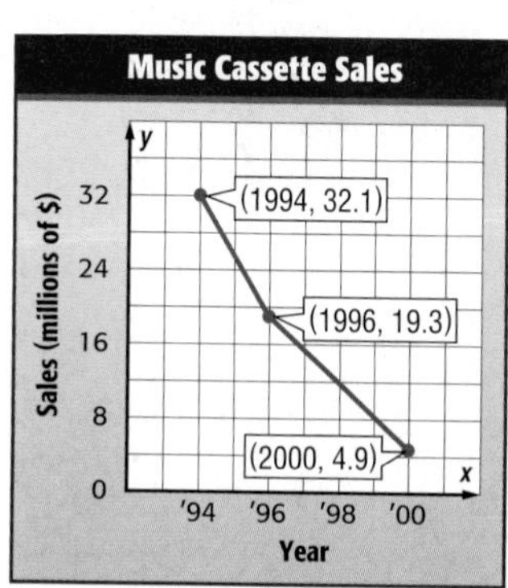

Source: Recording Industry Assoc. of America

Use the formula for the rate of change.

Let $(x_1, y_1) = (1996, 19.3)$ and $(x_2, y_2) = (2000, 4.9)$.

$\frac{y_2 - y_1}{x_2 - x_1} = \frac{4.9 - 19.3}{2000 - 1996}$ Write the formula for rate of change.

$= \frac{-14.4}{4}$ Simplify.

$= \frac{-3.6}{1}$ Express this rate as a unit rate.

The rate of change is −3.6 million dollars in sales per year. The rate is negative because between 1996 and 2000, the cassette sales *decreased*. This is shown on the graph by a line slanting downward from left to right.

Your Turn

b. In the graph above, find the rate of change between 1994 and 1996.

c. Describe how this rate is shown on the graph.

b. −6.4 million dollars in sales per year

c. as a line slanting downward from left to right

msmath3.net/extra_examples

DAILY INTERVENTION **Flexible Grouping**

Real-Life Application Have students work with a partner to locate two line graphs in a newspaper or on the Internet. Have the pair discuss and then write a summary of what changes have occurred in each. Students should alternate writing for the two paragraphs.

2 Teach

In-Class Examples

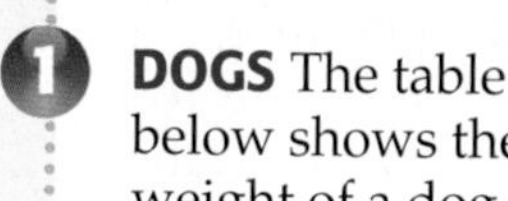

1 **DOGS** The table below shows the weight of a dog in pounds between 4 and 12 months old.

Age (mo.)	4	8	12
Weight (lb)	15	28	43

Find the rate of change in the dog's weight between 8 and 12 months of age. **3.75 pounds per month**

2 **SCHOOLS** The graph below shows the number of students in the 8th grade between 1998 and 2002. Find the rate of change between 2000 and 2002. **−13 students per year**

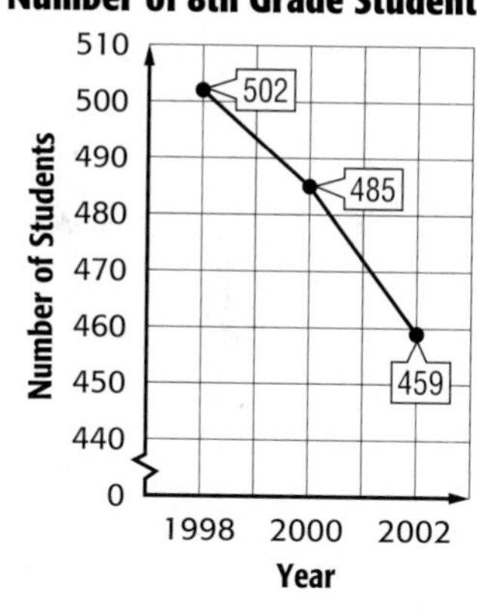

In-Class Examples

3 **TEMPERATURE** The graph shows the temperature measured on each hour from 10 A.M. to 3 P.M. Find a time period in which the temperature did not change. **1 P.M. to 2 P.M.**

Temperature Over Time

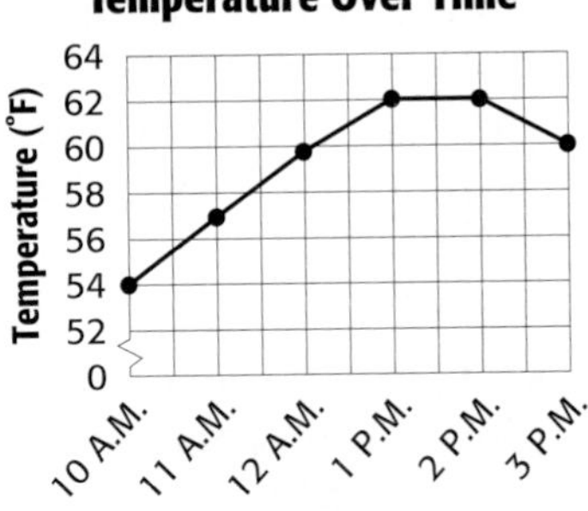

Time

4 **TEMPERATURE** Use the graph in In-Class Example 3. Find the rate of change from 1 P.M. to 2 P.M. **0**

Answers

1. Sample answer: cost of postage for a 1-oz letter over a period of 4 months in which the cost did not change
2. The rate of change is negative, since the height of the candle decreases over time.
5.

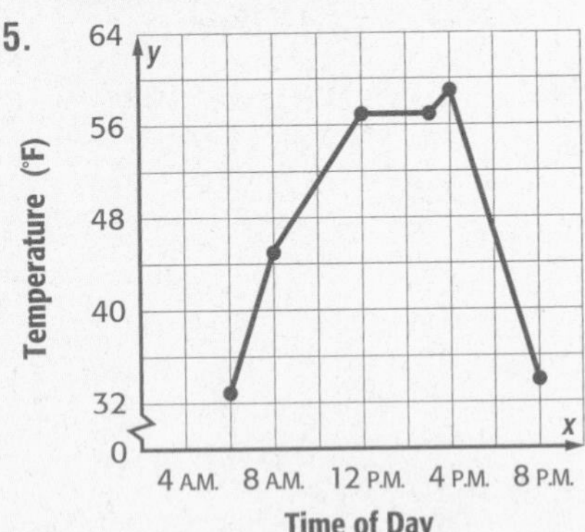

When a quantity does not change over a period of time, it is said to have a zero rate of change.

REAL-LIFE MATH

MAIL In 1847, it cost 5 cents per $\frac{1}{2}$ ounce to deliver mail to locations under 300 miles away and 10 cents per $\frac{1}{2}$ ounce to deliver it to locations over 300 miles away.

Source: www.stamps.org

EXAMPLES Zero Rates of Change

3 **MAIL** **The graph shows the cost in cents of mailing a 1-ounce first-class letter. Find a time period in which the cost of a first-class stamp did not change.**

Between 1996 and 1998, the cost of a first class stamp did not change. It remained 32¢. This is shown on the graph by a horizontal line segment.

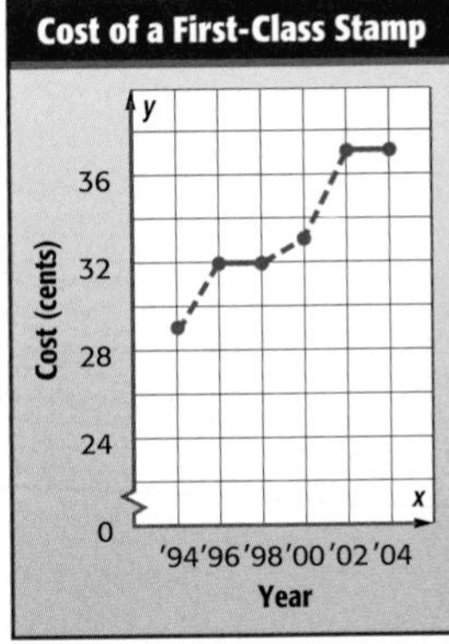

Source: www.stamps.org

4 **MAIL** **Find the rate of change from 2002 to 2004.**

Let $(x_1, y_1) = (2002, 37)$ and $(x_2, y_2) = (2004, 37)$.

$\frac{y_2 - y_1}{x_2 - x_1} = \frac{37 - 37}{2004 - 2002}$ Write the formula for rate of change.

$= \frac{0}{2}$ or 0 Simplify.

The rate of change in the cost of a first-class stamp between 2002 and 2004 is 0 cents per year.

Your Turn

d. Find the rate of change in the cost of a stamp between 2000 and 2002. **2¢ per year**

The table below summarizes the relationship between rates of change and their graphs.

Concept Summary — Rates of Change

Rate of Change	positive	zero	negative
Real-Life Meaning	increase	no change	decrease
Graph	slants upward	horizontal line	slants downward

162 Chapter 4 Proportions, Algebra, and Geometry

Students practice the same concepts in Exercises 7–18 if they are assigned odd or even problems.

Skill and Concept Check

1. **OPEN ENDED** Describe a situation involving a zero rate of change.
1–2. See margin.
2. **Writing Math** Does the height of a candle as it burns over time show a *positive*, *negative*, or *zero* rate of change? Explain your reasoning.

GUIDED PRACTICE

TEMPERATURE For Exercises 3–6, use the table at the right. It shows the outside air temperature at different times during one day.

Time	Temperature (°F)
6 A.M.	33
8 A.M.	45
12 P.M.	57
3 P.M.	57
4 P.M.	59
8 P.M.	34

3. Find the rate of temperature change in degrees per hour from 6 A.M. to 8 A.M. and from 4 P.M. and 8 P.M. **6°/h; about −6.3°/h**
4. Between which of these two time periods was the rate of change in temperature greater? **between 4 P.M. and 8 P.M.**
5. Make a graph of this data. **See margin.**
6. During which time period(s) was the rate of change in temperature positive? negative? 0° per hour? How can you tell this from your graph? **See margin.**

Practice and Applications

HOMEWORK HELP

For Exercises	See Examples
7–18	1–4

Extra Practice
See pages 624, 651.

ADVERTISING For Exercises 7–10, use the following information. Tanisha's job is to neatly fold flyers for the school play. She started folding at 12:55 P.M. The table below shows her progress.

Time	12:55	1:00	1:20	1:25	1:30
Flyers Folded	0	21	102	102	125

7. Find the rate of change in flyers per minute between 1:00 and 1:20. **4.1 flyers/min**
8. Find her rate of change between 1:25 and 1:30. **4.6 flyers/min**
9. During which time period did her folding rate increase the fastest? **between 1:25 and 1:30**
10. Find the rate of change from 1:20 to 1:25 and interpret its meaning.
0 flyers/min; it appears Tanisha stopped folding for 5 min.

BIRDS For Exercises 11–14, use the information below and at the right.
The graph shows the approximate number of American Bald Eagle pairs from 1963 to 1998.

11. Find the rate of change in the number of eagle pairs from 1974 to 1984. **100 eagle pairs/yr**
12. Find the rate of change in the number of eagle pairs from 1984 to 1994. **260 eagle pairs/yr**
13. During which of these two time periods did the eagle population grow faster? **between 1984 and 1994**
14. Find the rate of change in the population from 1994 to 1998. Then interpret its meaning. **See margin.**

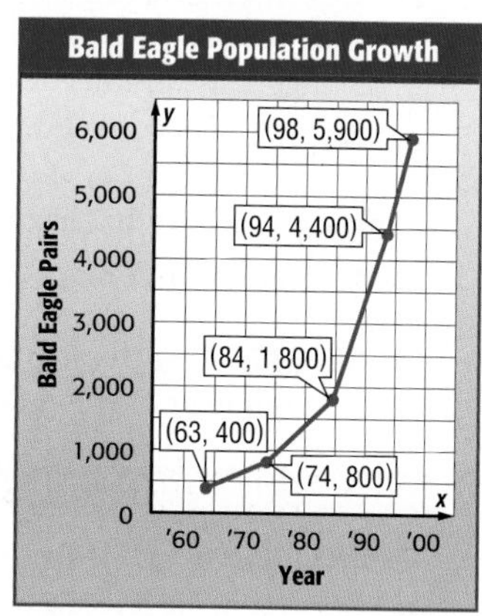

Source: birding.about.com

msmath3.net/self_check_quiz

3 Practice/Apply

FOLDABLES Follow-Up Remind students to record main ideas, definitions of vocabulary words, and other notes on study cards as they progress through the lesson. Students store their study cards from this lesson in the appropriate pocket of their Foldables.

Writing Math In Exercise 2, have students make some rough guesses as to how much a 10-inch taper candle would burn down over a period of several hours. They can then sketch a graph to demonstrate the rate of change.

About the Exercises...

Guided Practice Key

Exercises	Examples
3–5	1
6	2, 3

Assignment Guide

Basic: 7, 11–13, 15, 17, 19–28

Average: 7–9, 11–13, 15, 17, 19–28

Enriched: 7–24 (Optional: 25–28)

Alert! The Data Update following Exercises 17–18 requires access to the Internet.

6. Between 6 A.M. and 8 A.M., 8 P.M. and 12 P.M., 3 P.M. and 4 P.M., the line segment between these times slants upward; between 4 P.M. and 8 P.M., the line segment between these times slants downward; between 12 P.M. and 3 P.M., the line segment between these times is horizontal.

14. 375 eagle pairs/ yr; the eagle population increased at a rate of 375 eagle pairs per year.

FAST FOOD For Exercises 15 and 16, use the graph at the right.

15. During which time period was the rate of change in sales greatest? Explain. **See margin.**

16. Find the rate of change during that period. **$31.5 billion/yr**

CANDY For Exercises 17 and 18, use the following information. **17. $22 billion/yr**
According to the National Confectioners Association, candy sales during the winter holidays in 1995 totaled $1,342 billion. By 2001, this figure had risen to $1,474 billion.

17. Find the rate of change in candy sales during the winter holidays from 1995 to 2001.

18. If this rate of change were to continue, what would the total candy sales during the winter holidays be in 2005? **$1,562 billion**

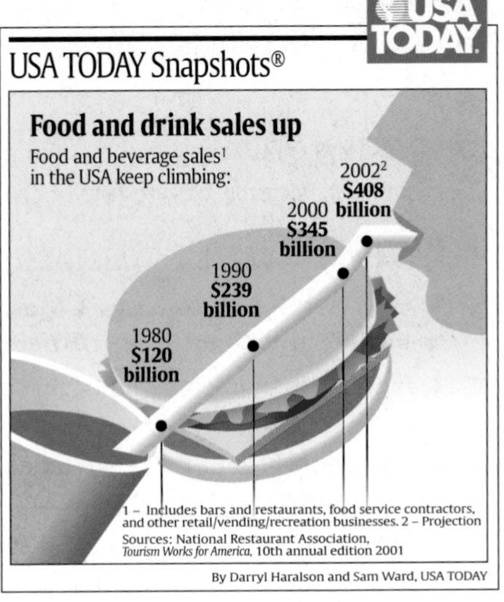

Data Update What were candy sales during the winter holidays last year? Visit msmath3.net/data_update to learn more.

19. **CRITICAL THINKING** The rate of change between point *A* and point *B* on the graph is 3 meters per day. Find the value of *y*. **18**

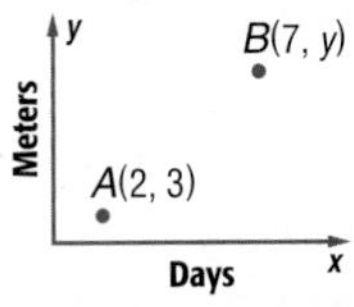

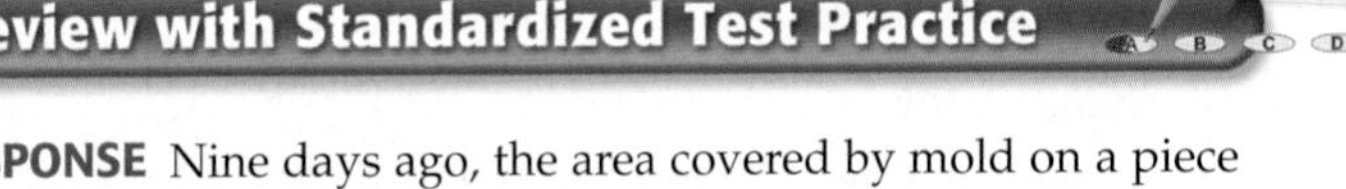

20. **SHORT RESPONSE** Nine days ago, the area covered by mold on a piece of bread was 3 square inches. Today the mold covers 9 square inches. Find the rate of change in the mold's area. **$\frac{2}{3}$ in²/day**

21. **MULTIPLE CHOICE** The graph shows the altitude of a falcon over time. Between which two points on the graph was the bird's rate of change in height negative? **B**

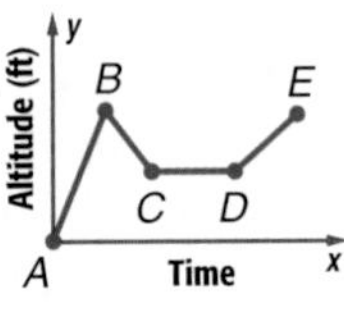

(A) A and B (B) B and C (C) C and D (D) D and E

Express each ratio in simplest form. (Lesson 4-1)

22. 42 red cars to 12 black cars **7:2**

23. 1,500 pounds to 2 tons **3 to 8**

24. **GEOMETRY** A triangle has vertices $A(-2, -5)$, $B(-2, 8)$, and $C(1, 4)$. Find the perimeter of triangle *ABC*. (Lesson 3-6) **about 27.5 units**

GETTING READY FOR THE NEXT LESSON

PREREQUISITE SKILL Evaluate each expression. (Lesson 1-2)

25. $\frac{8-5}{3-1}$ $\frac{3}{2}$

26. $\frac{3-7}{4-(-4)}$ $-\frac{1}{2}$

27. $\frac{-5-(-2)}{-1-8}$ $\frac{1}{3}$

28. $\frac{2-(-4)}{-2-(-3)}$ 6

Study Guide and Intervention, p. 190

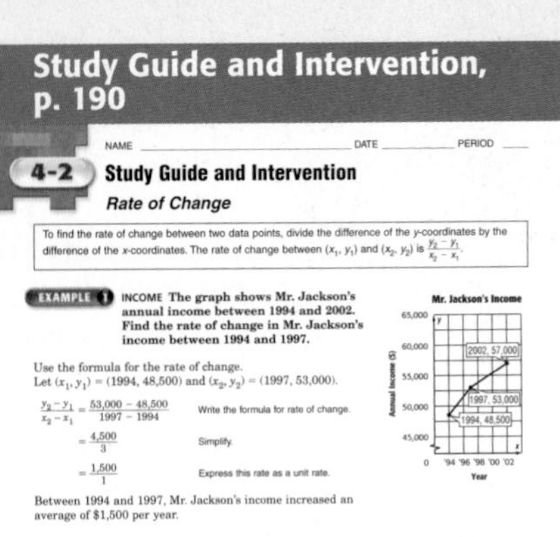

NAME ______ DATE ______ PERIOD ____

4-2 Study Guide and Intervention

Rate of Change

To find the rate of change between two data points, divide the difference of the *y*-coordinates by the difference of the *x*-coordinates. The rate of change between (x_1, y_1) and (x_2, y_2) is $\frac{y_2 - y_1}{x_2 - x_1}$.

EXAMPLE 1 INCOME **The graph shows Mr. Jackson's annual income between 1994 and 2002. Find the rate of change in Mr. Jackson's income between 1994 and 1997.**

Use the formula for the rate of change.
Let $(x_1, y_1) = (1994, 48{,}500)$ and $(x_2, y_2) = (1997, 53{,}000)$.

$\frac{y_2 - y_1}{x_2 - x_1} = \frac{53{,}000 - 48{,}500}{1997 - 1994}$ Write the formula for rate of change.

$= \frac{4{,}500}{3}$ Simplify.

$= \frac{1{,}500}{1}$ Express this rate as a unit rate.

Between 1994 and 1997, Mr. Jackson's income increased an average of $1,500 per year.

EXERCISES

SURF **For Exercises 1–3, use the graph that shows the average daily wave height as measured by an ocean buoy over a nine-day period.**

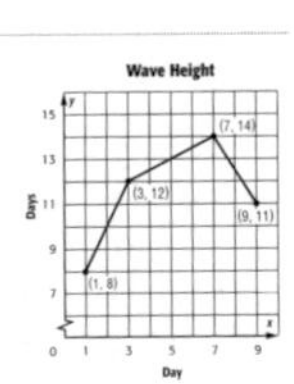

1. Find the rate of change in the average daily wave height between day 1 and day 3. 2 ft/day

2. Find the rate of change in the average daily wave height between day 3 and day 7. 0.5 ft/day

3. Find the rate of change in the average daily wave height between day 7 and day 9. −1.5 ft/day

Practice: Skills, p. 191

NAME ______ DATE ______ PERIOD ____

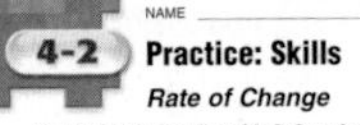

4-2 Practice: Skills

Rate of Change

TEMPERATURE **Use the table below that shows the high temperature of a city for the first part of August.**

Date	1	5	14	15
High Temperature (°F)	85	93	102	102

1. Find the rate of change in the high temperature between August 1 and August 5. 2°/day

2. Find the rate of change in the high temperature between August 5 and August 14. 1°/day

3. During which of these two time periods did the high temperature rise faster? between August 1 and August 5

4. Find the rate of change in the high temperature between August 14 and August 15. Then interpret its meaning. 0°/day; Between August 14 and August 15, the high temperature did not change.

COMPANY GROWTH **Use the graph that shows the number of employees at a company between 1994 and 2002.**

Company Growth

Year	Number of Employees
1994	18
1996	32
1999	41
2002	38

5. Find the rate of change in the number of employees between 1994 and 1996. 7 employees/yr

6. Find the rate of change in the number of employees between 1996 and 1999. 3 employees/yr

7. During which of these two time periods did the number of employees grow faster? between 1994 and 1996

8. Find the rate of change in the number of employees between 1999 and 2002. Then interpret its meaning. −1 employee/yr; Between 1999 and 2002, the number of employees decreased an average of 1 employee/yr.

Practice: Word Problems, p. 192

NAME ______ DATE ______

4-2 Practice: Word Problems

Rate of Change

ELECTIONS **For Exercises 1–3, use the table that shows the total number of people who had voted in District 5 at various times on election day.**

Time	8:00 A.M.	10:00 A.M.	1:00 P.M.	4:30 P.M.	7:00 P.M.
Number of Voters	141	351	798	1,008	1,753

1. Find the rate of change in the number of voters between 8:00 A.M. and 10:00 A.M. Then interpret its meaning. 105 voters/hr; Between 8:00 A.M. and 10:00 A.M., an average of 105 people voted each hour.

2. Find the rate of change in the number of voters between 10:00 A.M. and 1:00 P.M. Then interpret its meaning. 149 voters/hr; Between 10:00 A.M. and 1:00 P.M., an average of 149 people voted each hour.

3. During which of these two time periods did the number of people who had voted so far increase faster? Explain your reasoning. Between 10:00 A.M. and 1:00 P.M.; the rate of change is greater for this time period.

4. MUSIC At the end of 1999, Candace had 47 CDs in her music collection. At the end of 2002, she had 134 CDs. Find the rate of change in the number of CDs in Candace's collection between 1999 and 2002. 29 CDs/yr

5. FITNESS In 1992, the price of an annual membership at Mr. Jensen's health club was $225. In 2002, the price of the same membership was $319.50. Find the rate of change in the price of the annual membership between 1992 and 2002. $9.45/yr

6. HIKING Last Saturday Fumio and Kishi went hiking in the mountains. When they started back at 2:00 P.M., their elevation was 3,560 feet above sea level. At 6:00 P.M., their elevation was 2,390 feet. Find the rate of change of their elevation between 2:00 P.M. and 6:00 P.M. Then interpret its meaning. −292.5 ft/h; They descended at an average rate of 292.5 ft/h.

4 Assess

Open-Ended Assessment

Modeling Tell students that they are collecting recycled cans. Pick a number of cans collected in the first week, then draw a graph that shows an increase of 3 cans collected each week over the next 4 weeks.

Answer

15. Between 2000 and 2002; reading the graph from left to right, the segment connecting 2000 and 2002 is steeper than the segment connecting 1980 and 1990.

Constant Rates of Change

What You'll LEARN

Find rates of change using a spreadsheet.

You can calculate rates of change using a spreadsheet.

ACTIVITY

Andrew earns $18 per hour mowing lawns. Calculate the rate of change in the amount he earns between each consecutive pair of times. Then interpret your results.

Time (h)	Amount ($)
1	18
2	36
3	54
4	72

Set up a spreadsheet like the one shown below.

Lawn Earnings

	A	B	C
1	Time (h)	Amount ($)	Rate of Change
2	x	y	(change in y)/(change in x)
3	1	18	18
4	2	36	18
5	3	54	18
6	4	72	18

The rate of change between each consecutive pair of data is the same, or constant—$18 per hour.

EXERCISES

1. Graph the data given in the activity above. Then describe the figure formed when the points on the graph are connected. **See Ch. 4 Answer Appendix.**

PARKING **For Exercises 2–4, use the information in the table. It shows the charges for parking at a football stadium.**

Time (h)	Amount ($)
1	5
2	8
3	11
4	14

2. Use a spreadsheet to find the rate of change in the amount charged between each consecutive pair of times. **$3/h**
3. Interpret your results from Exercise 2.
4. Graph the data. Then describe the figure formed when the points on the graph are connected. **See Ch. 4 Answer Appendix.**

3. The stadium charges $5 for the first hour and then $3 for each additional hour for parking.

4-2b Spreadsheet Investigation

GETTING STARTED

Teaching Tip If students need to share computers, assign groups before going to the lab. Introduce the activity in advance so students will be prepared to work effectively.

TEACH

- Students should be able to apply the skills they learned in Lesson 4-2 to find the rate of change from a table and confirm that their spreadsheet results are accurate.
- Ask students how to use the constant rate of change to compute the amount earned in 6 hours. **$108**
- You may wish to have students use the spreadsheet's graphing tool to complete the graph for Exercise 1.
- As students work through the exercises, ask them to calculate the parking charge for 5 hours and to calculate the average rate of change from 1 to 5 hours. Have them compare this result to their answer for Exercise 2. **Since the rate of change is constant, the results are the same.**

ASSESS

Observe as students solve the **Exercises**. They should:

- graph both data sets and observe the straight line,
- create a spreadsheet that achieves accurate results, and
- understand what is meant by constant rate of change.

4-3 Lesson Notes

Lesson Resources

Chapter 4 Resource Masters

- Study Guide and Intervention, p. 195
- Practice: Skills, p. 196
- Practice: Word Problems, p. 197
- Reading to Learn Mathematics, p. 198
- Enrichment, p. 199

Parent and Student Study Guide Online Worksheets, 4-3

Noteables™: Interactive Study Notebook with Foldables™, 4-3

1 Focus

5-Minute Check 4-3

INTERACTIVE CHALKBOARD
PowerPoint® Presentations

Use as a quiz or review of Lesson 4-2. (Also available as a transparency)

Bellringer

Hands-On Activity Have students draw a coordinate grid on graph paper and plot any single point in Quadrant III. Tell them to roll one number cube and move that many units up from their point. Next, they should roll the number cube again and move that many units to the right, plotting this point as the second point on their graphs. Students should not roll again, but should plot two more points according to their previous rolls.

(Continued in bottom margin.)

Reading to Learn Mathematics, p. 198 ELL

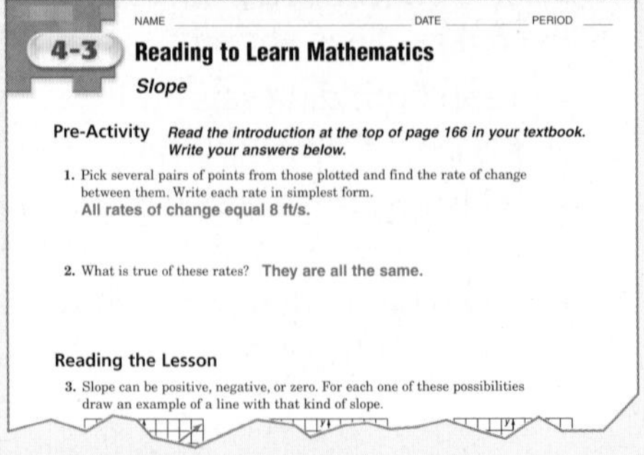

NAME ______ DATE ______ PERIOD ______

4-3 Reading to Learn Mathematics
Slope

Pre-Activity *Read the introduction at the top of page 166 in your textbook. Write your answers below.*

1. Pick several pairs of points from those plotted and find the rate of change between them. Write each rate in simplest form.
All rates of change equal 8 ft/s.

2. What is true of these rates? They are all the same.

Reading the Lesson

3. Slope can be positive, negative, or zero. For each one of these possibilities draw an example of a line with that kind of slope.

4-3 Slope

What You'll LEARN

Find the slope of a line.

NEW Vocabulary

slope
rise
run

WHEN am I ever going to use this?

EXERCISE As part of Cameron's fitness program, he tries to run every day. He knows that after he has warmed up, he can maintain a constant running speed of 8 feet per second. This is shown in the table and in the graph.

Time (s)	0	2	4	6	8
Distance (ft)	0	16	32	48	64

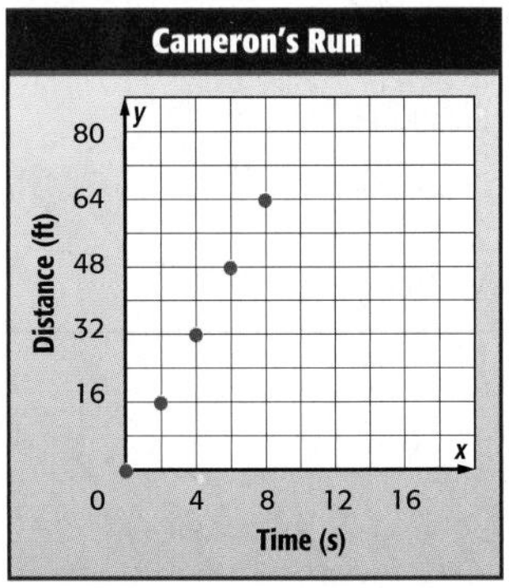

Cameron's Run

1. Pick several pairs of points from those plotted and find the rate of change between them. Write each rate in simplest form.
2. What is true of these rates? **They are all the same.**

1. All rates of change equal 8 ft/s.

In the graph above, the rate of change between any two points on a line is always the same. This constant rate of change is called the slope of the line. **Slope** is the ratio of the **rise**, or vertical change, to the **run**, or horizontal change.

$$\text{slope} = \frac{\text{rise}}{\text{run}}$$ ← vertical change between any two points ← horizontal change between the same two points

EXAMPLE Find Slope Using a Graph

1 Find the slope of the line.

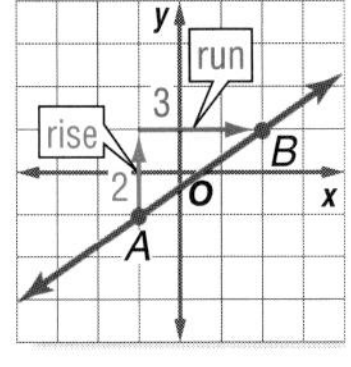

Choose two points on the line. The vertical change is 2 units while the horizontal change is 3 units.

$\text{slope} = \frac{\text{rise}}{\text{run}}$ Definition of slope

$= \frac{2}{3}$ rise = 2, run = 3

The slope of the line is $\frac{2}{3}$.

Your Turn Find the slope of each line.

a. $\frac{3}{4}$

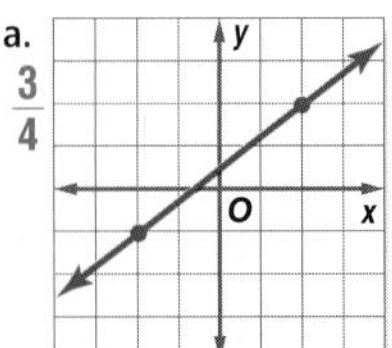

b. $-\frac{5}{2}$

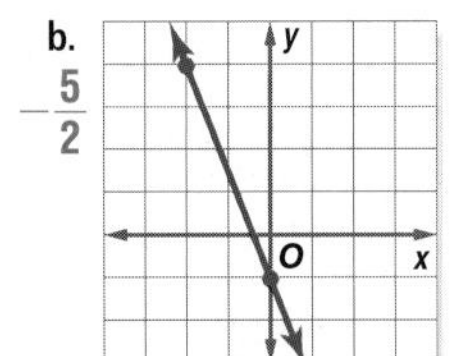

c. 0

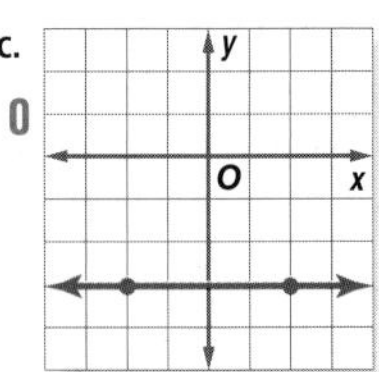

READING in the Content Area

For strategies in reading this lesson, visit **msmath3.net/reading.**

Have them connect the points on their graphs and describe the relationship between their moves as they plotted points and the rate of change between the points. You might also want to have students exchange graphs and reconstruct one another's rolls by looking at the graph.

NCLB NO CHILD LEFT BEHIND

The goals of the NCLB Act include a stronger emphasis on reading. The **Reading in the Content Area** link helps students become proficient readers.

STUDY TIP

Translating Rise and Run

up → positive
down → negative

right → positive
left → negative

TEACHING TIP

Students will learn about the slopes of vertical lines and the slope formula in Chapter 11.

Since slope is a rate of change, it can be positive (slanting upward), negative (slanting downward), or zero (horizontal).

EXAMPLE Find Slope Using a Table

2 **The points given in the table lie on a line. Find the slope of the line. Then graph the line.**

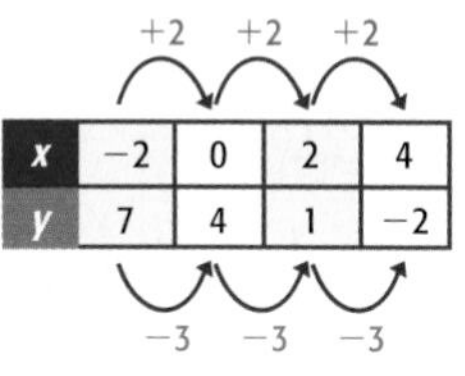

x	−2	0	2	4
y	7	4	1	−2

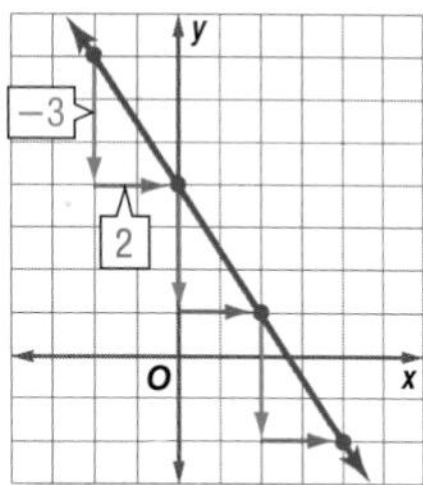

$\text{slope} = \frac{\text{rise}}{\text{run}}$ ← change in y / ← change in x

$= \frac{-3}{2} \text{ or } -\frac{3}{2}$

Your Turn **The points given in each table lie on a line. Find the slope of the line. Then graph the line.**

d.

x	−6	−2	2	6
y	−2	−1	0	1

$\frac{1}{4}$

e.

x	−1	0	1	2
y	−4	−4	−4	−4

0

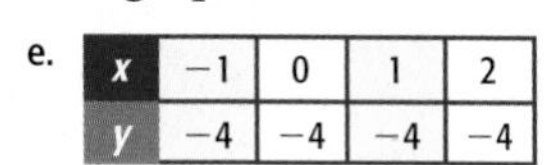

d–e. See Ch. 4 Answer Appendix for graphs.

Since slope is a rate of change, it can have real-life meaning.

EXAMPLES Use Slope to Solve a Problem

3 **LIBRARIES** **The graph shows the fines charged for overdue books per day at the Eastman Library. Find the slope of the line.**

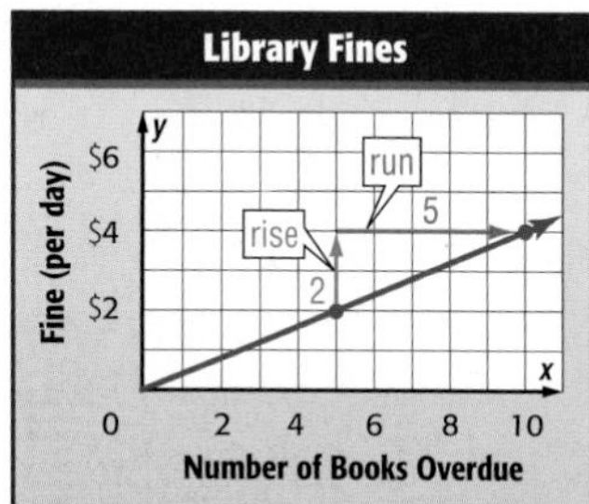

Count the units of vertical and horizontal change between any two points on the line.

$\text{slope} = \frac{\text{rise}}{\text{run}}$ Definition of slope

$= \frac{2}{5}$ rise = 2, run = 5

The slope of the line is $\frac{2}{5}$.

4 **Interpret the meaning of this slope as a rate of change.**

For this graph, a slope of $\frac{2}{5}$ means that the library fine increases $2 for every 5 overdue books. Written as a unit rate, $\frac{\$2}{5}$ is $\frac{\$0.40}{1}$. The fine is $0.40 per overdue book per day.

REAL-LIFE MATH

LIBRARIES With 85 branches, the New York Public Library is the world's largest public library. It has collections totaling 11.6 million items.

Source: www.nypl.org

msmath3.net/extra_examples

2 Teach

In-Class Examples

1 Find the slope of the line. **−2**

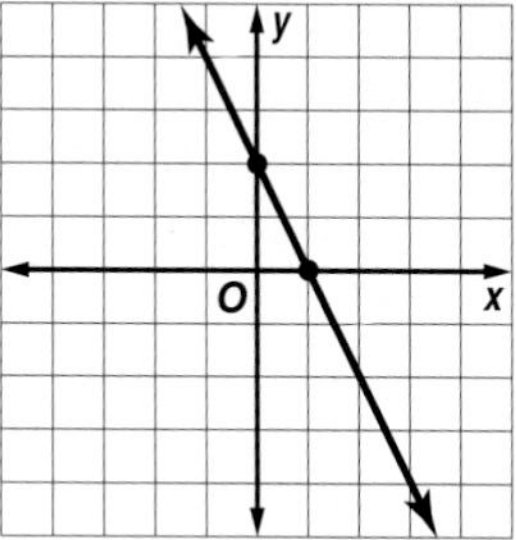

2 The points given in the table lie on a line. Find the slope of the line. Then graph the line. $-\frac{1}{2}$

x	5	3	1	−1
y	−1	0	1	2

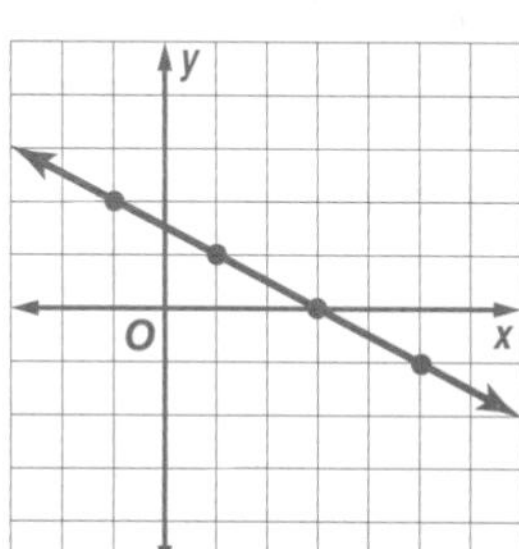

3 **TAXIS** The graph shows the cost of a taxi ride for the number of miles driven. Find the slope of the line. $\frac{4}{5}$

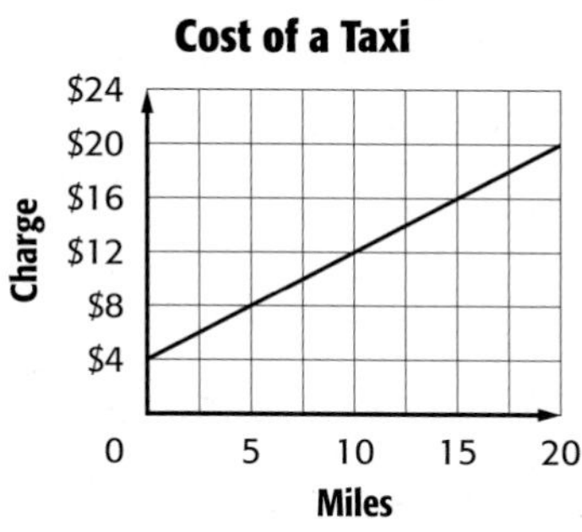

4 Interpret the meaning of the slope in In-Class Example 3 as a rate of change. **The charge increases $4 for every 5 miles driven, or $0.80 per mile.**

DAILY INTERVENTION

Differentiated Instruction

Logical Tell students that a graph has a slope of $-\frac{3}{2}$. Ask them to draw a line with that slope. Have students write the steps they took to draw their line.

3 Practice/Apply

DAILY INTERVENTION **FIND THE ERROR** In Exercise 2, remind students that we look at how lines change from left to right. Therefore, down is a negative rise, and it implies a negative number for that part of the fraction.

About the Exercises...

Guided Practice Key

Exercises	Examples
3–4	1
5	2

Assignment Guide

Basic: 7–17 odd, 18, 20–28

Average: 7–17 odd, 18–28

Enriched: 6–16 even, 18–24 (Optional: 25–28)

Answers

1.

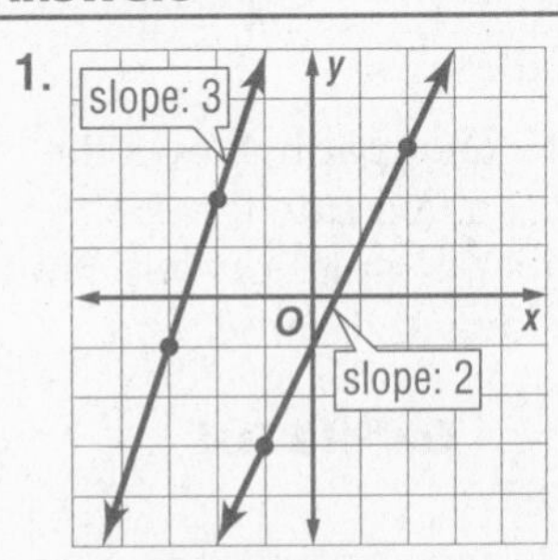

5.

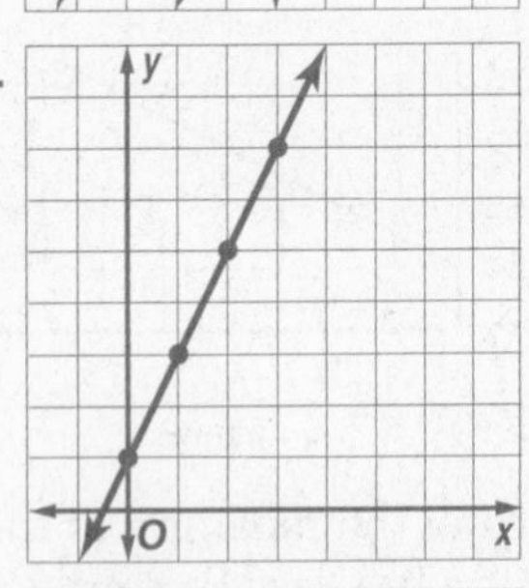

12.

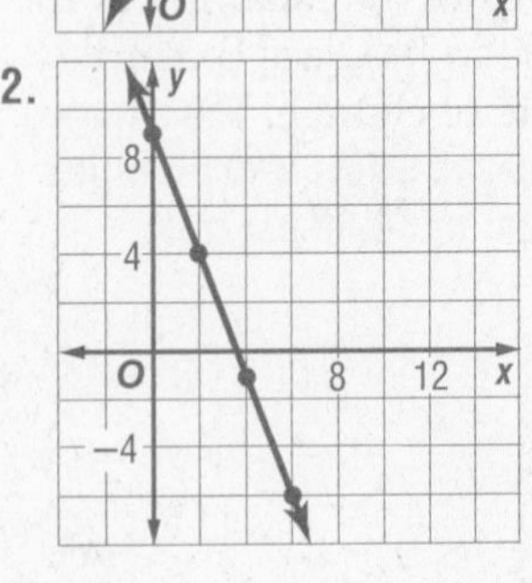

Students practice the same concepts in Exercises 6–11 if they are assigned odd or even problems.

Skill and Concept Check

1. **OPEN ENDED** Graph a line whose slope is 2 and another whose slope is 3. Which line is steeper? **See margin; the line with slope 3**

2. **FIND THE ERROR** Juan and Martina are finding the slope of the line graphed at the right. Who is correct? Explain.

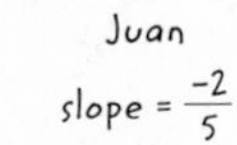

Martina

slope = $\frac{2}{5}$

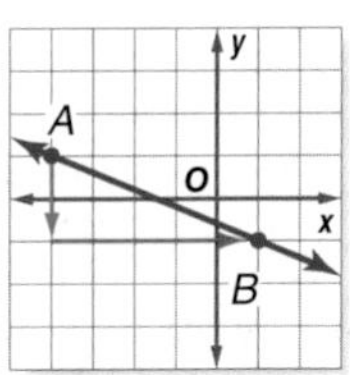

2. Juan; the vertical change from point *A* to point *B* is negative since the movement is downward.

GUIDED PRACTICE

Find the slope of each line.

3. 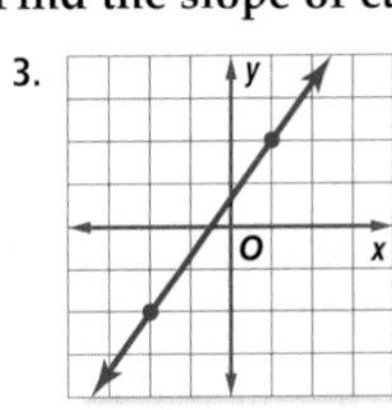 $\frac{4}{3}$

4. 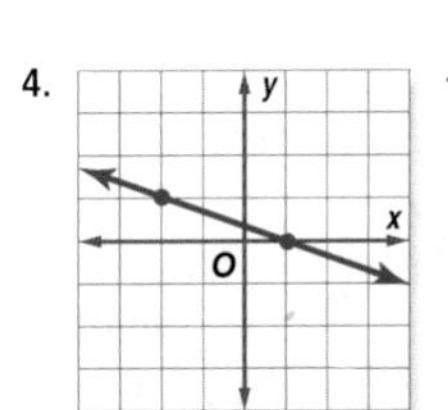 $-\frac{1}{3}$

5. The points given in the table at the right lie on a line. Find the slope of the line. Then graph the line. **2; See margin for graph.**

x	0	1	2	3
y	1	3	5	7

Practice and Applications

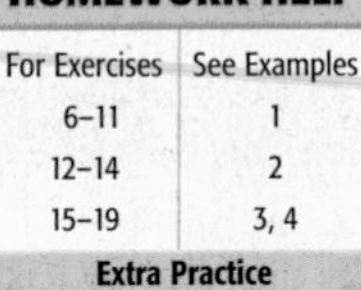

HOMEWORK HELP

For Exercises	See Examples
6–11	1
12–14	2
15–19	3, 4

Extra Practice See pages 624, 651.

Find the slope of each line. **6. $\frac{1}{2}$ 7. $-\frac{3}{4}$ 8. 0 9. 0 10. −3 11. $\frac{3}{2}$**

6. 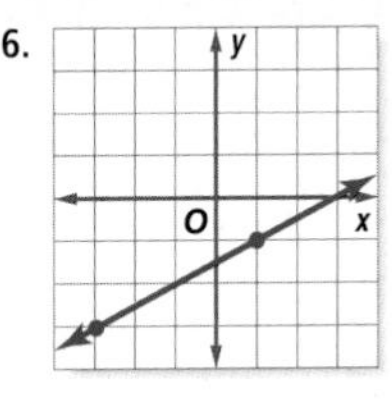

7. 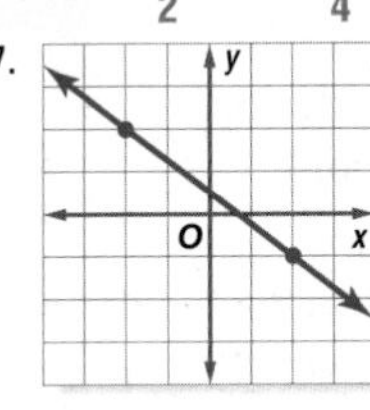

8. 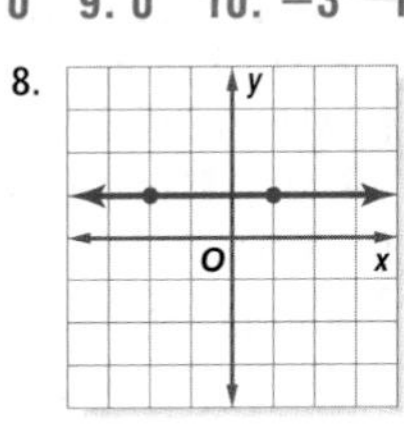

9. 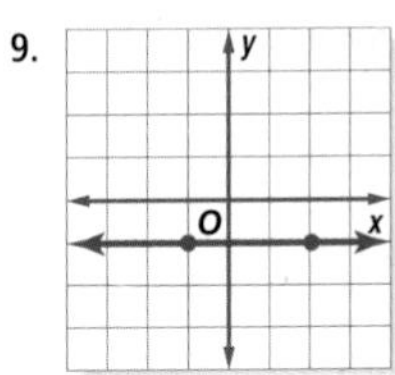

10. 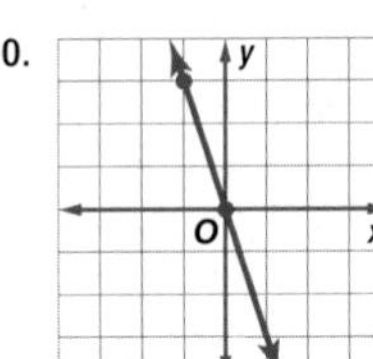

11. 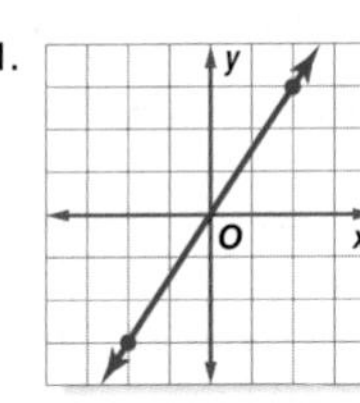

The points given in each table lie on a line. Find the slope of the line. Then graph the line. **12–14. See margin for graphs.**

12. $-\frac{5}{2}$

x	0	2	4	6
y	9	4	−1	−6

13. $\frac{2}{3}$

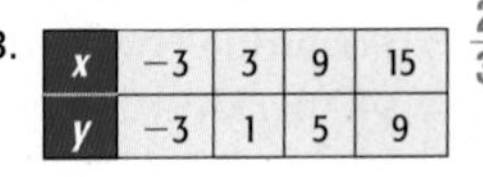

x	−3	3	9	15
y	−3	1	5	9

14. 0

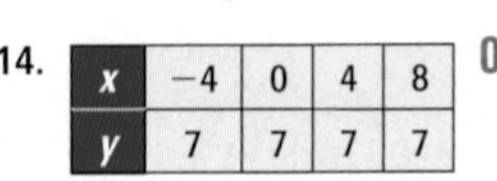

x	−4	0	4	8
y	7	7	7	7

13.

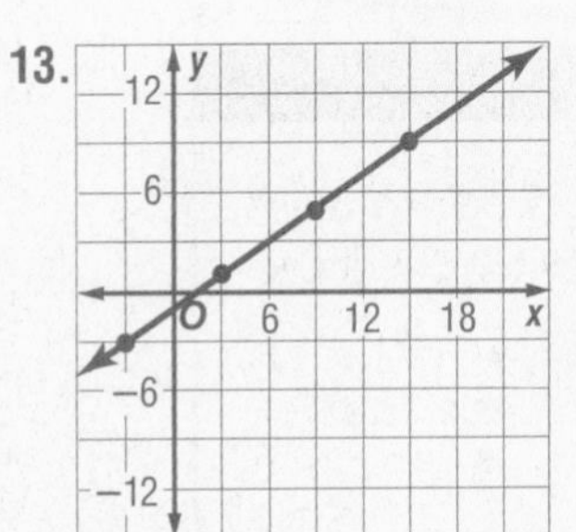

14.

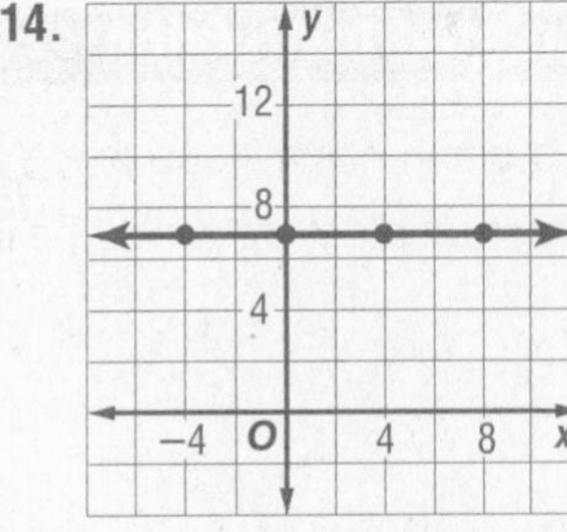

15. 10; \$10 increase in cost for each pizza delivered

16. −20; balance decreases by \$20 per payment.

17. $\frac{5}{11}$; pressure increases 5 lbs/in^2 for every 11 feet increase in depth.

19. Pedro; he is saving \$12.50 per week, while Jenna is only saving \$6 per week.

Find the slope of each line and interpret its meaning as a rate of change. **15–17. See margin.**

15\. 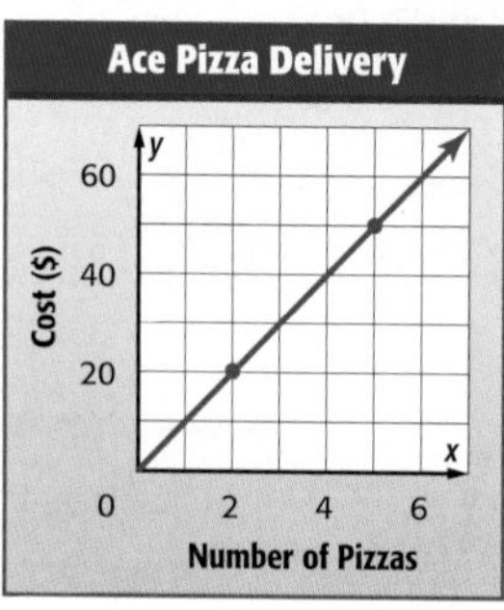

16\. 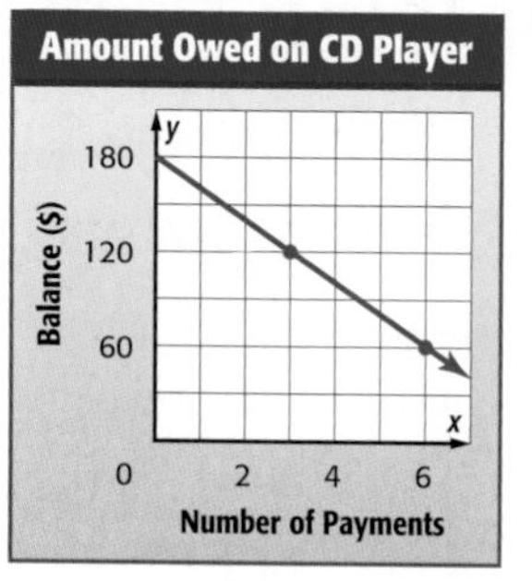

17\. 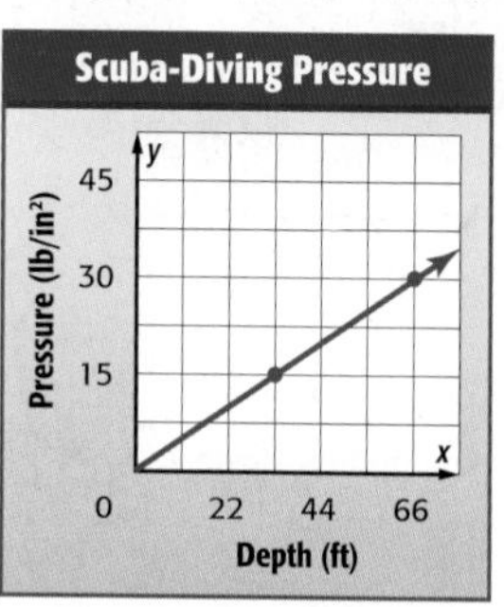

SAVINGS **For Exercises 18 and 19, use the following information.**

Pedro and Jenna are each saving money to buy the latest video game system. Their savings account balances over 7 weeks are shown in the graph at the right. **18. Pedro: $\frac{25}{2}$ or 12.5; Jenna: 6**

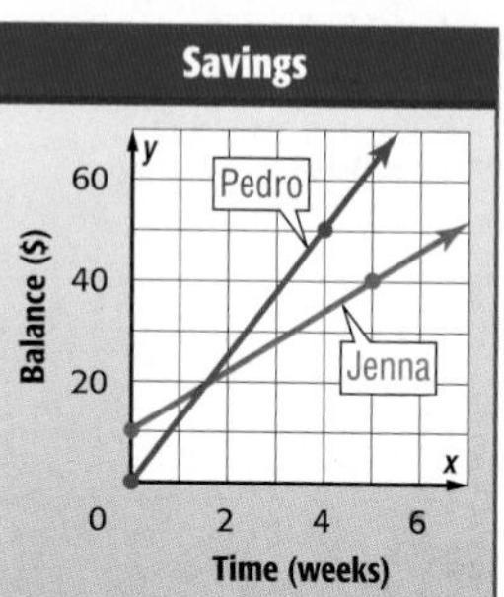

18\. Find the slope of each person's line.

19\. Who is saving more money each week? Explain. **See margin.**

20\. **CRITICAL THINKING** According to federal guidelines, wheelchair ramps for access to public buildings are allowed a maximum of one inch of rise for every foot of run. Would a ramp with a slope of $\frac{1}{10}$ comply with this guideline? Explain your reasoning. (*Hint*: Convert feet to inches.) **no; $\frac{1}{10} \not\leq \frac{1}{12}$**

Spiral Review with Standardized Test Practice

21\. **GRID IN** Find the slope of the roof shown. **2/3**

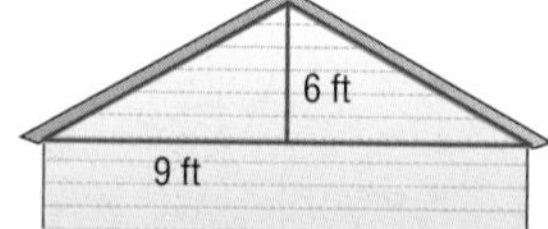

22\. **MULTIPLE CHOICE** The first major ski slope at a resort rises 8 feet vertically for every 48-foot run. The second rises 12 feet vertically for every 72-foot run. Which statement is true? **C**

- (A) The first slope is steeper than the second.
- (B) The second slope is steeper than the first.
- (C) Both slopes have the same steepness.
- (D) This cannot be determined from the information given.

23\. **POOL MAINTENANCE** After 15 minutes of filling a pool, the water level is at 2 feet. Twenty minutes later the water level is at 5 feet. Find rate of change in the water level between the first 15 minutes and the last 20 minutes in inches per minute. (Lesson 4-2) **1.8 in./min**

24\. Express *$25 for 10 disks* as a unit rate. (Lesson 4-1) **$2.50/disk**

GETTING READY FOR THE NEXT LESSON

PREREQUISITE SKILL **Solve each equation. Check your solution.** (Lesson 1-9)

25\. $5 \cdot x = 6 \cdot 10$ **12** 26. $8 \cdot 3 = 4 \cdot y$ **6** 27. $2 \cdot d = 3 \cdot 5$ **7.5** 28. $2.1 \cdot 7 = 3 \cdot a$ **4.9**

Math Online msmath3.net/self_check_quiz

4 Assess

Higher-Level Thinking

What is the slope of a horizontal line? Draw a graph and prove your answer.
The slope of a horizontal line is 0.

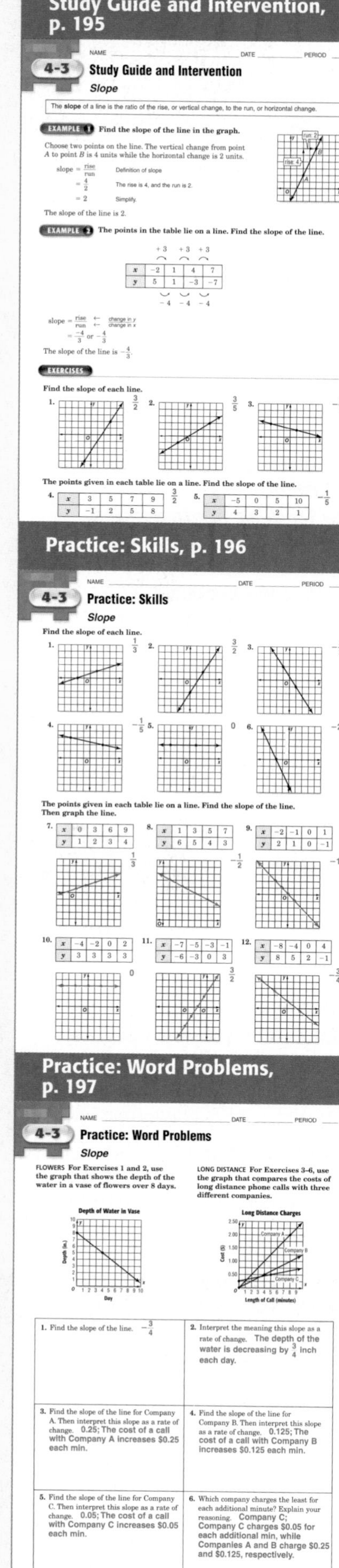

Study Guide and Intervention, p. 195

NAME ________ DATE ________ PERIOD ____

4-3 Study Guide and Intervention

Slope

The **slope** of a line is the ratio of the rise, or vertical change, to the run, or horizontal change.

EXAMPLE 1 **Find the slope of the line in the graph.**

Choose two points on the line. The vertical change from point A to point B is 4 units while the horizontal change is 2 units.

slope $= \frac{\text{rise}}{\text{run}}$ Definition of slope

$= \frac{4}{2}$ The rise is 4, and the run is 2.

$= 2$ Simplify.

The slope of the line is 2.

EXAMPLE 2 **The points in the table lie on a line. Find the slope of the line.**

+3 +3 +3

x	−2	1	4	7
y	5	1	−3	−7

−4 −4 −4

slope $= \frac{\text{rise}}{\text{run}} \leftarrow \frac{\text{change in } y}{\text{change in } x}$

$= \frac{-4}{3}$ or $-\frac{4}{3}$

The slope of the line is $-\frac{4}{3}$.

EXERCISES

Find the slope of each line.

1\. $\frac{3}{2}$ 2. $\frac{3}{5}$ 3. $-\frac{1}{4}$

The points given in each table lie on a line. Find the slope of the line.

4\. $\frac{3}{2}$

x	3	5	7	9
y	−1	2	5	8

5\. $-\frac{1}{5}$

x	−5	0	5	10
y	4	3	2	1

Practice: Skills, p. 196

NAME ________ DATE ________ PERIOD ____

4-3 Practice: Skills

Slope

Find the slope of each line.

1\. $\frac{1}{3}$ 2. $\frac{3}{2}$ 3. $-\frac{3}{2}$

4\. $-\frac{1}{5}$ 5. 0 6. −2

The points given in each table lie on a line. Find the slope of the line. Then graph the line.

7\. $\frac{1}{3}$

x	0	3	6	9
y	1	2	3	4

8\. $-\frac{1}{2}$

x	1	3	5	7
y	6	5	4	3

9\. −1

x	−2	−1	0	1
y	2	1	0	−1

10\. 0

x	−4	−2	0	2
y	3	3	3	3

11\. $\frac{3}{2}$

x	−7	−5	−3	−1
y	−6	−3	0	3

12\. $-\frac{3}{4}$

x	−8	−4	0	4
y	8	5	2	−1

Practice: Word Problems, p. 197

NAME ________ DATE ________ PERIOD ____

4-3 Practice: Word Problems

Slope

FLOWERS **For Exercises 1 and 2, use the graph that shows the depth of the water in a vase of flowers over 8 days.**

LONG DISTANCE **For Exercises 3–6, use the graph that compares the costs of long distance phone calls with three different companies.**

Depth of Water in Vase — Depth (in.), Day

Long Distance Charges — Cost ($), Length of Call (minutes), Company A, Company B, Company C

1\. Find the slope of the line. $-\frac{3}{4}$

2\. Interpret the meaning this slope as a rate of change. **The depth of the water is decreasing by $\frac{3}{4}$ inch each day.**

3\. Find the slope of the line for Company A. Then interpret this slope as a rate of change. **0.25; The cost of a call with Company A increases $0.25 each min.**

4\. Find the slope of the line for Company B. Then interpret this slope as a rate of change. **0.125; The cost of a call with Company B increases $0.125 each min.**

5\. Find the slope of the line for Company C. Then interpret this slope as a rate of change. **0.05; The cost of a call with Company C increases $0.05 each min.**

6\. Which company charges the least for each additional minute? Explain your reasoning. **Company C; Company C charges $0.05 for each additional min, while Companies A and B charge $0.25 and $0.125, respectively.**

4-4 Lesson Notes

Lesson Resources

Chapter 4 Resource Masters

FAST FILE

- Study Guide and Intervention, p. 200
- Practice: Skills, p. 201
- Practice: Word Problems, p. 202
- Reading to Learn Mathematics, p. 203
- Enrichment, p. 204

Calculator and Spreadsheet Masters, p. 22
Key Teaching Transparencies, 14
MathPASS Tutorial CD-ROM, 29
Parent and Student Study Guide Online Worksheets, 4-4
Noteables™: Interactive Study Notebook with Foldables™, 4-4
Virtual Activities CD-ROM, Solving Proportions

5-Minute Check 4-4

Use as a quiz or review of Lesson 4-3. (Also available as a transparency)

Bellringer

Hands-On Activity On graph paper, have students draw a rectangle whose length in units is a multiple of 5. Have them shade $\frac{3}{5}$ of this rectangle. Ask students to

(Continued in bottom margin.)

Solving Proportions

WHEN am I ever going to use this?

NUTRITION Part of the nutrition label from a granola bar is shown at the right.

1. Write a ratio that compares the number of Calories from fat to the total number of Calories. Write the ratio as a fraction in simplest form. $\frac{2}{11}$
2. Suppose you plan to eat two such granola bars. Write a ratio comparing the number of Calories from fat to the total number of Calories. $\frac{2}{11}$
3. Is the ratio of Calories the same for two granola bars as it is for one granola bar? Why or why not? **See margin.**

Nutrition Facts	
Serving Size 1 Bar (28g)	
Servings Per Container 10	
Amount Per Serving	
Calories 110 Calories from Fat 20	
	% Daily Value*
Total Fat 2g	**3%**
Saturated Fat 0.5g	**2%**
Cholesterol 0mg	**0%**
Sodium 70mg	**3%**

What You'll LEARN

Use proportions to solve problems.

NEW Vocabulary

proportion
cross products

In the example above, the ratio $\frac{20}{110}$ simplifies to $\frac{2}{11}$. The equation $\frac{20}{110} = \frac{2}{11}$ indicates that the two ratios are equivalent. This is an example of a **proportion**.

Noteables™ — Key Concept: Proportion

Words A proportion is an equation stating that two ratios are equivalent.

Symbols

Arithmetic	Algebra
$\frac{6}{8} = \frac{3}{4}$	$\frac{a}{b} = \frac{c}{d}, b \neq 0, d \neq 0$

STUDY TIP

Mental Math If both ratios simplify to the same fraction, they form a proportion.

$\frac{6}{15} = \frac{2}{5}$ and $\frac{8}{20} = \frac{2}{5}$.

So, $\frac{6}{15} = \frac{8}{20}$.

In a proportion, the two **cross products** are equal.

$$\frac{6}{8} = \frac{3}{4} \quad \rightarrow 8 \cdot 3 = 24, \quad \rightarrow 6 \cdot 4 = 24$$

The cross products are equal.

Noteables™ — Key Concept: Property of Proportions

Words The cross products of a proportion are equal.

Symbols If $\frac{a}{b} = \frac{c}{d}$, then $ad = bc$.

You can use cross products to determine whether a pair of ratios forms a proportion. If the cross products of two ratios are equal, then the ratios form a proportion. If the cross products are *not* equal, the ratios do *not* form a proportion.

Reading to Learn Mathematics, p. 203 ELL

NAME ______ DATE ______ PERIOD ____

4-4 Reading to Learn Mathematics
Solving Proportions

Pre-Activity *Read the introduction at the top of page 170 in your textbook. Write your answers below.*

1. Write a ratio that compares the number of Calories from fat to the total number of Calories. Write the ratio as a fraction in simplest form. $\frac{2}{11}$
2. Suppose you plan to eat two such granola bars. Write a ratio comparing the number of Calories from fat to the total number of Calories. $\frac{2}{11}$
3. Is the ratio of Calories the same for two granola bars as it is for one granola bar? Why or why not? **The ratios are equal because multiplying the numerator and denominator of a fraction by the same amount creates an equivalent fraction.**

write the fraction shaded as the number of square units shaded over the total number of square units in the rectangle. Write these fractions on the chalkboard. Point out that they are all equivalent.

Answer (When am I ever going to use this?)

3. The ratios are equal because multiplying the numerator and denominator of a fraction by the same amount creates an equivalent fraction.

EXAMPLE Identify a Proportion

1 **Determine whether the ratios $\frac{6}{9}$ and $\frac{8}{12}$ form a proportion.**

Find the cross products. $\frac{6}{9} \overset{?}{=} \frac{8}{12}$ $\rightarrow 9 \cdot 8 = 72$ $\rightarrow 6 \cdot 12 = 72$

Since the cross products are equal, the ratios form a proportion.

Your Turn **Determine whether the ratios form a proportion.**

a. $\frac{2}{5}, \frac{4}{10}$ **yes** b. $\frac{6}{16}, \frac{14}{56}$ **no** c. $\frac{30}{35}, \frac{12}{14}$ **yes**

TEACHING TIP
Point out that ratios are said to be *proportional* if they form a proportion.

You can also use cross products to *solve proportions* in which one of the terms is not known.

EXAMPLE Solve a Proportion

2 **Solve $\frac{x}{4} = \frac{9}{10}$.**

$\frac{x}{4} = \frac{9}{10}$	Write the equation.
$x \cdot 10 = 4 \cdot 9$	Find the cross products.
$10x = 36$	Multiply.
$\frac{10x}{10} = \frac{36}{10}$	Divide each side by 10.
$x = 3.6$	Simplify.

The solution is 3.6. Check the solution by substituting the value of x into the original proportion and checking the cross products.

Your Turn **Solve each proportion.**

d. $\frac{7}{d} = \frac{2}{3}$ **10.5** e. $\frac{2}{34} = \frac{5}{y}$ **85** f. $\frac{7}{3} = \frac{n}{2.1}$ **4.9**

TEACHING TIP
Point out to students that some proportions can be solved mentally by using equivalent fractions.

$\frac{4}{7} = \frac{20}{x}$

Think: $4 \times 5 = 20$
$7 \times 5 = 35$
So, $x = 35$.

Proportions can be used to make predictions.

EXAMPLE Use a Proportion to Solve a Problem

3 **LIFE SCIENCE** A microscope slide shows 37 red blood cells out of 60 blood cells. How many red blood cells would be expected in a sample of the same blood that has 925 blood cells?

Write a proportion. Let r represent the number of red blood cells.

red blood cells → $\frac{37}{60} = \frac{r}{925}$ ← red blood cells
total blood cells → ← total blood cells

$37 \cdot 925 = 60 \cdot r$	Find the cross products.
$34{,}225 = 60r$	Multiply.
$\frac{34{,}225}{60} = \frac{r}{60}$	Divide each side by 60.
$570.4 \approx r$	Simplify.

You would expect to find 570 or 571 red blood cells out of 925 blood cells.

REAL-LIFE CAREERS

How Does a Medical Technologist Use Math? Medical technologists use proportions in their analysis of blood samples.

Math Online **Research**
For information about a career as a medical technologist, visit: msmath3.net/careers

msmath3.net/extra_examples

2 Teach

In-Class Examples

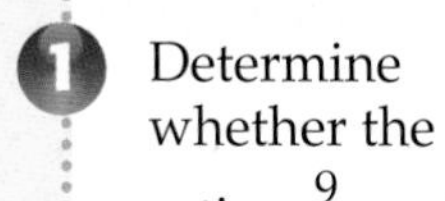

1 Determine whether the ratios $\frac{9}{12}$ and $\frac{18}{27}$ form a proportion. **no**

2 Solve $\frac{x}{4} = \frac{7}{20}$. **1.4**

3 **COOKING** A recipe serves 10 people and calls for 3 cups of flour. If you want to make the recipe for 15 people, how many cups of flour should you use? **4.5**

Tips for New Teachers

Intervention You can use the Multiplication Property of Equality to show students that the cross products of a proportion are equal.

$$\frac{a}{b} = \frac{c}{d}$$

$$\frac{a}{\cancel{b}_1} \cdot \cancel{b}^1 d = \frac{c}{\cancel{d}_1} \cdot b\cancel{d}^1$$

$$ad = cb$$

Ask students to explain why b and d cannot equal zero. **They are in the denominators of the fractions.**

DAILY INTERVENTION **Unlocking Misconceptions**

Equivalent Fractions Students often do not view proportions as equivalent fractions because the numbers are obvious multiples. Show students how the missing number can be found when treating the ratios as equivalent fractions. For example, in In-Class Example 2, $10 \div 4 = 2.5$, so $9 \div x$ must also equal 2.5. This means that $9 \div 2.5 = x$ or $x = 3.6$.

3 Practice/Apply

FOLDABLES™ Follow-Up Remind students to record main ideas, definitions of vocabulary words, and other notes on study cards as they progress through the lesson. Students store their study cards from this lesson in the appropriate pocket of their Foldables.

NUMBER SENSE
For Exercise 2, ask students why this sort of estimation is useful. They should note that such an estimate can be used as a quick check of their final answer. They might also recognize that sometimes a quick estimate is all that is needed.

About the Exercises...

Guided Practice Key

Exercises	Examples
3–5	1
6–8	2
9–10	3

Assignment Guide

Basic: 11–15 odd, 19–27 odd, 31–41 odd, 43–51

Average: 11–41 odd, 43–51

Enriched: 12–42 even, 43–48 (Optional: 49–51)

Answers

31. $\frac{6}{1} = \frac{96}{p}$

32. $\frac{2}{13} = \frac{25}{m}$

33. $\frac{3}{2{,}000} = \frac{x}{3{,}500}$

34. $\frac{n}{\frac{3}{4}} = \frac{1\frac{1}{2}}{\frac{1}{2}}$

39. $\frac{12}{x} = \frac{1}{2.54}$; 30.48

40. $\frac{20}{x} = \frac{1}{1.61}$; 32.2

41. $\frac{2}{x} = \frac{3.78}{1}$; 0.53

42. $\frac{45}{x} = \frac{0.454}{1}$; 99.12

43. Each statement can be written as a ratio equivalent to 3:2.

44. The second statement represents a difference comparison, not a ratio comparison, and so cannot be written as a ratio. Since a proportion is formed by two equal ratios, these statements do not have a proportional relationship.

Students practice the same concepts in Exercises 11–34 if they are assigned odd or even problems.

Skill and Concept Check

1. **OPEN ENDED** List four different ratios that form a proportion with $\frac{12}{40}$. Sample answer: $\frac{3}{10}, \frac{6}{20}, \frac{9}{30}, \frac{24}{80}$
2. **NUMBER SENSE** What would be a good estimate of the value of n in the equation $\frac{3}{5} = \frac{n}{11}$? Explain your reasoning. 6; 11 is about 5 × 2, so n is about 3 × 2 or 6.

GUIDED PRACTICE

Determine whether each pair of ratios form a proportion.

3. $\frac{8}{5}, \frac{40}{25}$ yes
4. $\frac{3}{5}, \frac{5}{8}$ no
5. $\frac{6}{16}, \frac{9}{24}$ yes

Solve each proportion.

6. $\frac{a}{13} = \frac{7}{1}$ 91
7. $\frac{41}{x} = \frac{5}{2}$ 16.4
8. $\frac{3.2}{9} = \frac{n}{36}$ 12.8

Write a proportion that could be used to solve for each variable. Then solve.

9. 18 heart beats in 15 seconds
b times in 60 seconds $\frac{18}{15} = \frac{b}{60}$; 72
10. 483 miles on 14 gallons of gas
600 miles on g gallons of gas $\frac{483}{14} = \frac{600}{g}$; about 17.4

★ indicates increased difficulty

Practice and Applications

HOMEWORK HELP

For Exercises	See Examples
11–18	1
19–30	2
31–42	3

Extra Practice See pages 625, 651.

Determine whether each pair of ratios form a proportion.

11. $\frac{8}{7}, \frac{10}{9}$ no
12. $\frac{12}{14}, \frac{6}{7}$ yes
13. $\frac{16}{12}, \frac{12}{9}$ yes
14. $\frac{3}{11}, \frac{55}{200}$ no
15. $\frac{42}{56}, \frac{3}{4}$ yes
16. $\frac{5}{18}, \frac{18}{65}$ no
★17. $\frac{0.4}{5}, \frac{0.6}{7.5}$ yes
★18. $\frac{1.5}{0.5}, \frac{2.1}{7}$ no

Solve each proportion.

19. $\frac{k}{7} = \frac{32}{56}$ 4
20. $\frac{44}{p} = \frac{11}{5}$ 20
21. $\frac{45}{y} = \frac{3}{8}$ 120
22. $\frac{x}{13} = \frac{18}{39}$ 6
23. $\frac{6}{25} = \frac{d}{30}$ 7.2
24. $\frac{48}{9} = \frac{72}{n}$ 13.5
25. $\frac{15}{2.1} = \frac{12}{c}$ 1.68
26. $\frac{2.5}{6} = \frac{h}{9}$ 3.75
27. $\frac{3.5}{8} = \frac{a}{3.2}$ 1.4
28. $\frac{2}{w} = \frac{0.4}{0.7}$ 3.5
★29. $\frac{2}{3} = \frac{18}{x+5}$ 22
★30. $\frac{m-4}{10} = \frac{7}{5}$ 18

Write a proportion that could be used to solve for each variable. Then solve. 31–34. See margin for proportions.

31. 6 Earth-pounds equals 1 moon-pound
96 Earth-pounds equals p moon-pounds 16
32. 2 pages typed in 13 minutes
25 pages typed in m minutes 162.5
33. 3 pounds of seed for 2,000 square feet
x pounds of seed for 3,500 square feet 5.25
★34. n cups flour used with $\frac{3}{4}$ cup sugar
$1\frac{1}{2}$ cups flour used with $\frac{1}{2}$ cup sugar $2\frac{1}{4}$

35. **LIFE SCIENCE** About 4 out of every 5 people are right-handed. If there are 30 students in a class, how many would you expect to be right-handed? 24

PEOPLE **For Exercises 36 and 37, use the following information.** Although people vary in size and shape, in general, people do not vary in proportion. The head height to overall height ratio for an adult is given in the diagram at the right. **36. 72 in. or 6 ft**

36. About how tall is an adult with a head height of 9.6 inches?

37. Find the average head height of an adult that is 64 inches tall. **about 8.5 in.**

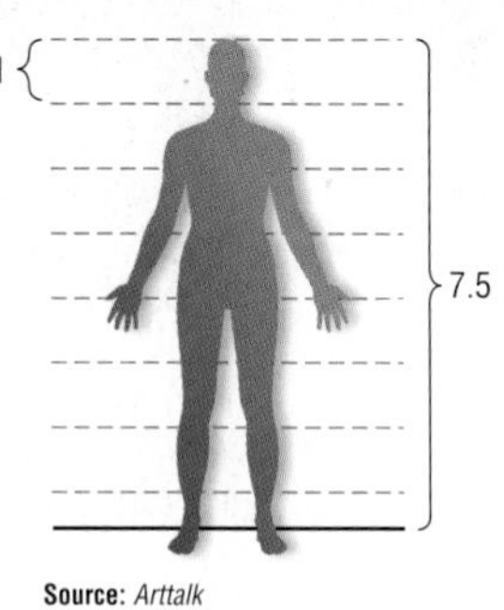

Source: *Arttalk*

38. **RECYCLING** The amount of paper recycled is directly proportional to the number of trees that recycling saves. If recycling 2,000 pounds of paper saves 17 trees, how many trees are saved when 5,000 pounds of paper are recycled? **42.5 trees**

MEASUREMENT **For Exercises 39–42, refer to the table. Write and solve a proportion to find each quantity.** **39–42. See margin.**

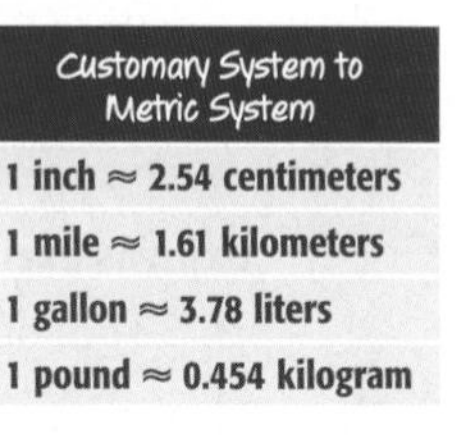

Customary System to Metric System
1 inch ≈ 2.54 centimeters
1 mile ≈ 1.61 kilometers
1 gallon ≈ 3.78 liters
1 pound ≈ 0.454 kilogram

39. 12 inches = ■ centimeters
40. 20 miles = ■ kilometers
41. 2 liters = ■ gallons
42. 45 kilograms = ■ pounds

CRITICAL THINKING **Classify the following pairs of statements as having a *proportional* or *nonproportional* relationship. Explain.**

43. You jump 63 inches and your friend jumps 42 inches. You jump 1.5 times the distance your friend jumps. **proportional** **43–44. See margin for explanation.**

44. You jump 63 inches and your friend jumps 42 inches. You jump 21 more inches than your friend jumps. **nonproportional**

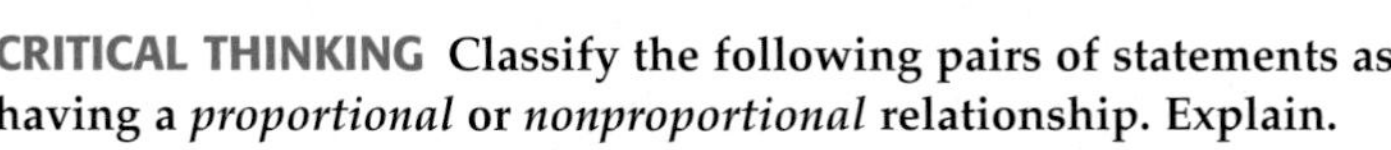

Spiral Review with Standardized Test Practice

45. **MULTIPLE CHOICE** At Northside Middle School, 30 students were surveyed about their favorite type of music. The results are graphed at the right. If there are 440 students at the middle school, predict how many prefer country music. **D**

Ⓐ 126 Ⓑ 128 Ⓒ 130 Ⓓ 132

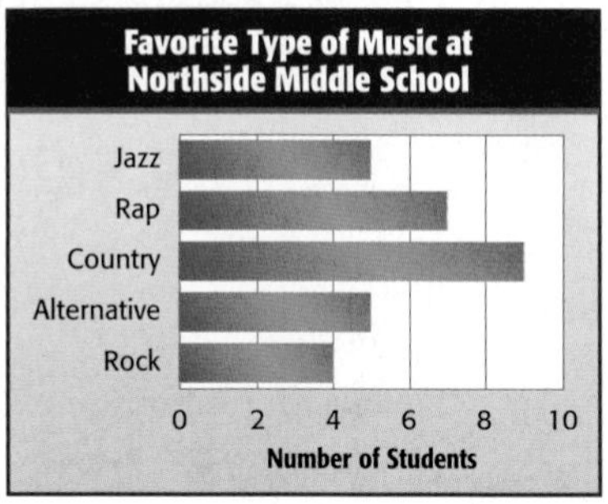

Favorite Type of Music at Northside Middle School

Jazz
Rap
Country
Alternative
Rock
0 2 4 6 8 10
Number of Students

46. **SHORT RESPONSE** Yutaka can run 3.5 miles in 40 minutes. About how many minutes would it take him to run 8 miles at this same rate? **91 min**

47. The points given in the table lie on a line. Find the slope of the line. Then graph the line. (Lesson 4-3) $\frac{8}{3}$; **See Ch. 4 Answer Appendix for graph.**

x	0	3	6	9
y	−10	−2	6	14

48. **GARDENING** Three years ago, an oak tree in Emily's back yard was 4 feet 5 inches tall. Today it is 6 feet 3 inches tall. How fast did the tree grow in inches per year? (Lesson 4-2) **about 7 in./yr**

GETTING READY FOR THE NEXT LESSON

BASIC SKILL **Name the sides of each figure.**

49. triangle *ABC* $\overline{AB}, \overline{BC}, \overline{CA}$
50. rectangle *DEFG* $\overline{DE}, \overline{EF}, \overline{FG}, \overline{GD}$
51. square *LMNP* $\overline{LM}, \overline{MN}, \overline{NP}, \overline{PL}$

Math Online msmath3.net/self_check_quiz

4 Assess

Open-Ended Assessment

Speaking Have students develop ratios based on the population in their class, such as blue eyes:brown eyes. Then have them explain how to set up a proportion to predict something about another class.

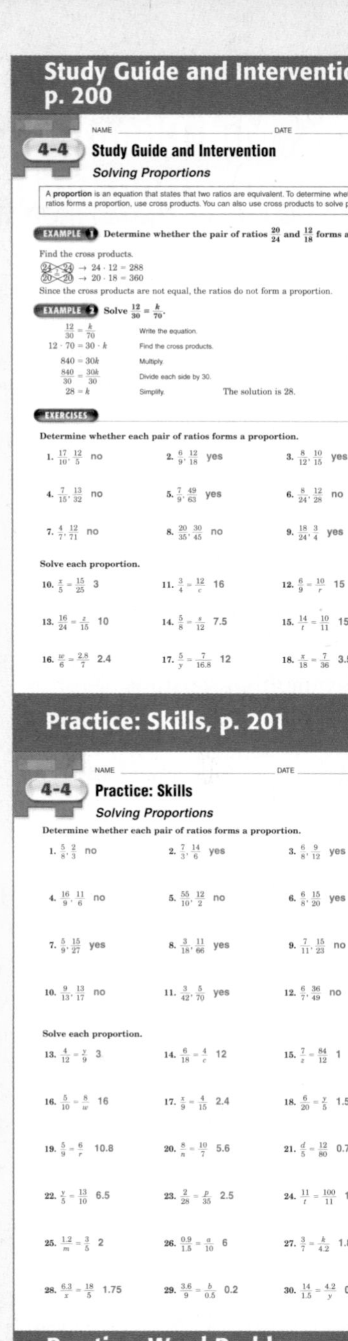

Study Guide and Intervention, p. 200

NAME ________ DATE ________ PERIOD ____

4-4 Study Guide and Intervention
Solving Proportions

A **proportion** is an equation that states that two ratios are equivalent. To determine whether a pair of ratios forms a proportion, use cross products. You can also use cross products to solve proportions.

EXAMPLE 1 **Determine whether the pair of ratios $\frac{20}{24}$ and $\frac{12}{18}$ forms a proportion.**

Find the cross products.

→ 24 · 12 = 288
→ 20 · 18 = 360

Since the cross products are not equal, the ratios do not form a proportion.

EXAMPLE 2 **Solve $\frac{12}{30} = \frac{k}{70}$.**

$\frac{12}{30} = \frac{k}{70}$ Write the equation.
$12 \cdot 70 = 30 \cdot k$ Find the cross products.
$840 = 30k$ Multiply.
$\frac{840}{30} = \frac{30k}{30}$ Divide each side by 30.
$28 = k$ Simplify. The solution is 28.

EXERCISES

Determine whether each pair of ratios forms a proportion.

1. $\frac{17}{10}, \frac{12}{5}$ no
2. $\frac{6}{9}, \frac{12}{18}$ yes
3. $\frac{8}{12}, \frac{10}{15}$ yes
4. $\frac{7}{15}, \frac{13}{32}$ no
5. $\frac{7}{9}, \frac{49}{63}$ yes
6. $\frac{8}{24}, \frac{12}{28}$ no
7. $\frac{4}{7}, \frac{12}{71}$ no
8. $\frac{20}{35}, \frac{30}{45}$ no
9. $\frac{18}{24}, \frac{3}{4}$ yes

Solve each proportion.

10. $\frac{x}{5} = \frac{15}{25}$ 3
11. $\frac{3}{4} = \frac{12}{c}$ 16
12. $\frac{6}{9} = \frac{10}{r}$ 15
13. $\frac{16}{24} = \frac{z}{15}$ 10
14. $\frac{5}{8} = \frac{s}{12}$ 7.5
15. $\frac{14}{t} = \frac{10}{11}$ 15.4
16. $\frac{w}{6} = \frac{2.8}{7}$ 2.4
17. $\frac{5}{y} = \frac{7}{16.8}$ 12
18. $\frac{x}{18} = \frac{7}{36}$ 3.5

Practice: Skills, p. 201

NAME ________ DATE ________ PERIOD ____

4-4 Practice: Skills
Solving Proportions

Determine whether each pair of ratios forms a proportion.

1. $\frac{5}{8}, \frac{2}{3}$ no
2. $\frac{7}{3}, \frac{14}{6}$ yes
3. $\frac{6}{8}, \frac{9}{12}$ yes
4. $\frac{16}{9}, \frac{11}{6}$ no
5. $\frac{55}{10}, \frac{12}{2}$ no
6. $\frac{6}{8}, \frac{15}{20}$ yes
7. $\frac{5}{9}, \frac{15}{27}$ yes
8. $\frac{3}{18}, \frac{11}{66}$ yes
9. $\frac{7}{11}, \frac{15}{23}$ no
10. $\frac{9}{13}, \frac{13}{17}$ no
11. $\frac{3}{42}, \frac{5}{70}$ yes
12. $\frac{6}{7}, \frac{36}{49}$ no

Solve each proportion.

13. $\frac{4}{12} = \frac{y}{9}$ 3
14. $\frac{6}{18} = \frac{4}{c}$ 12
15. $\frac{7}{z} = \frac{84}{12}$ 1
16. $\frac{5}{10} = \frac{8}{w}$ 16
17. $\frac{x}{9} = \frac{4}{15}$ 2.4
18. $\frac{6}{20} = \frac{y}{5}$ 1.5
19. $\frac{5}{9} = \frac{6}{r}$ 10.8
20. $\frac{8}{n} = \frac{10}{7}$ 5.6
21. $\frac{d}{5} = \frac{12}{80}$ 0.75
22. $\frac{y}{5} = \frac{13}{10}$ 6.5
23. $\frac{2}{28} = \frac{p}{35}$ 2.5
24. $\frac{11}{t} = \frac{100}{11}$ 1.21
25. $\frac{1.2}{m} = \frac{3}{5}$ 2
26. $\frac{0.9}{1.5} = \frac{a}{10}$ 6
27. $\frac{3}{7} = \frac{k}{4.2}$ 1.8
28. $\frac{6.3}{x} = \frac{18}{5}$ 1.75
29. $\frac{3.6}{9} = \frac{b}{0.5}$ 0.2
30. $\frac{14}{1.5} = \frac{4.2}{y}$ 0.45

Practice: Word Problems, p. 202

NAME ________ DATE ________ PERIOD ____

4-4 Practice: Word Problems
Solving Proportions

1. **USAGE** A 12-ounce bottle of shampoo lasts Enrique 16 weeks. How long would you expect an 18-ounce bottle of the same brand to last him? 24 wk

2. **COMPUTERS** About 13 out of 20 homes have a personal computer. On a street with 60 homes, how many would you expect to have a personal computer? 39 homes

3. **SNACKS** A 6-ounce package of fruit snacks contains 45 pieces. How many pieces would you expect in a 10-ounce package? 75 pieces

4. **TYPING** Ingrid types 3 pages in the same amount of time that Tanya types 4.5 pages. If Ingrid and Tanya start typing at the same time, how many pages will Tanya have typed when Ingrid has typed 11 pages? 16.5 pages

5. **SCHOOL** A grading machine can grade 48 multiple-choice tests in 1 minute. How long will it take the machine to grade 300 tests? 6.25 min

6. **AMUSEMENT PARKS** The waiting time to ride a roller coaster is 20 minutes when 150 people are in line. How long is the waiting time when 240 people are in line? 32 min

7. **PRODUCTION** A shop produces 39 wetsuits every 2 weeks. How long will it take the shop to produce 429 wetsuits? 22 wk

8. **FISH** Of the 50 fish that Jim caught from the lake, 14 were trout. The estimated population of the lake is 7,500 fish. About how many trout would you expect to be in the lake? 2,100 trout

Lesson 4-4 Solving Proportions 173

Assessment Option

Mid-Chapter Test (Lessons 4-1 through 4-4) is available on p. 241 of the *Chapter 4 Resource Masters.*

ExamView® Pro

Use the networkable ExamView® Pro Testmaker CD-ROM to:

- Create **multiple versions** of tests.
- Create **modified** tests for **inclusion** students with one mouse click.
- **Edit** existing questions and **add** your own questions.
- Build tests aligned with state standards using built-in **state curriculum correlations.**
- Change **English** tests to **Spanish** with one mouse click and vice versa.

FOLDABLES™ Follow-Up Before students complete the Mid-Chapter Practice Test, encourage them to review the notes, definitions, concepts, and main ideas they recorded and stored in the pockets of their Foldables.

CHAPTER 4 Mid-Chapter Practice Test

Vocabulary and Concepts

1. **Explain** the meaning of a rate of change of $-2°$ per hour. (Lesson 4-2)
2. **Describe** how to find the slope of a line given two points on the line. (Lesson 4-3) **See margin.**

1. The temperature is dropping 2° per hour.

Skills and Applications

Express each ratio in simplest form. (Lesson 4-1) **3. 8:25**

3. 32 out of 100 dentists
4. 12 chosen out of 60 **1:5**
5. 300 points in 20 games **15:1**
6. Express *\$420 for 15 tickets* as a unit rate. (Lesson 4-1) **\$28/ticket**

TEMPERATURE For Exercises 7 and 8, use the table at the right. (Lesson 4-2) **7. −13°/h; −2°/h**

7. Find the rate of the temperature change in degrees per hour from 1 P.M. to 3 P.M. and from 5 P.M. to 6 P.M.
8. Was the rate of change between 12 P.M. and 3 P.M. positive, negative, or zero? **negative**

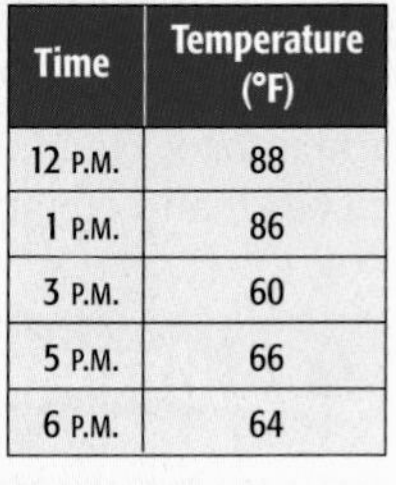

Time	Temperature (°F)
12 P.M.	88
1 P.M.	86
3 P.M.	60
5 P.M.	66
6 P.M.	64

Find the slope of each line. (Lesson 4-3) **9. $\frac{1}{4}$ 10. $-\frac{2}{3}$**

9. 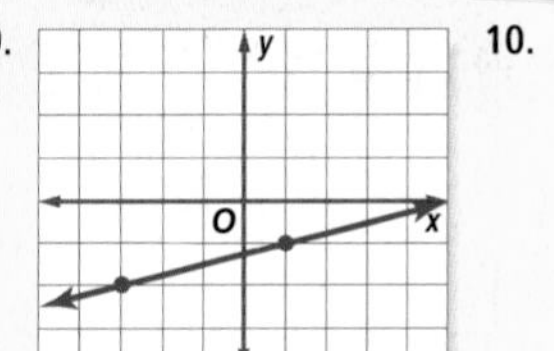
10. 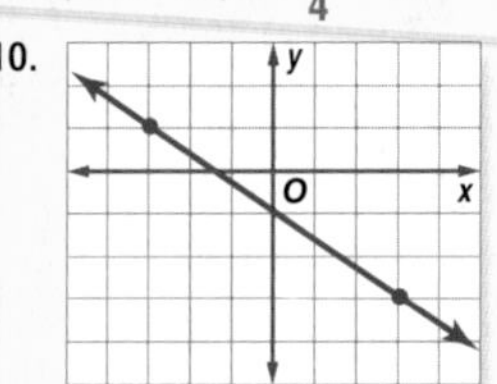
11. 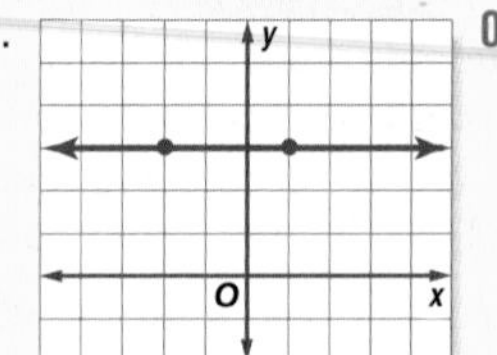 **0**

Solve each proportion. (Lesson 4-4)

12. $\frac{33}{r} = \frac{11}{2}$ **6**
13. $\frac{x}{36} = \frac{15}{24}$ **22.5**
14. $\frac{5}{9} = \frac{4.5}{a}$ **8.1**

Standardized Test Practice

15. **GRID IN** A typical 30-minute TV program in the United States has about 8 minutes of commercials. At that rate, how many commercial minutes are shown during a 2-hour TV movie? (Lesson 4-4) **32**

16. **MULTIPLE CHOICE** There are 2 cubs for every 3 adults in a certain lion pride. If the pride has 8 cubs, how many adults are there? (Lesson 4-4) **A**

   Ⓐ 12 Ⓑ 16
   Ⓒ 24 Ⓓ 48

Answer

2. **Count the units of vertical change and horizontal change between the two points. Then divide the vertical change by the horizontal change.**

The Game Zone

A Place To Practice Your Math Skills

Criss Cross

GET READY!

Players: two to four
Materials: paper; scissors; 24 index cards

GET SET!

- Each player should copy the game board shown onto a piece of paper.
- Cut each index card in half, making 48 cards.
- Copy the numbers below, one number onto each card.

1	1	1	1	2	2	2	3	3	3	4	4
4	5	5	5	6	6	6	7	7	7	8	8
8	9	9	9	10	10	11	11	12	12	13	13
14	14	15	15	16	16	18	18	20	22	24	25

- Deal 8 cards to each player. Place the rest facedown in a pile.

Criss Cross

=

GO!

- The player to the dealer's right begins by trying to form a proportion using his or her cards. If a proportion is formed, the player says, "Criss cross!" and displays the cards on his or her game board.
- If the cross products of the proportion are equal, the player forming the proportion is awarded 4 points and those cards are placed in a discard pile. If not that player loses his or her turn.
- If a player cannot form a proportion, he or she draws a card from the first pile. If the player cannot use the card, play continues to the right.
- When there are no more cards in the original pile, shuffle the cards in the discard pile and use them.
- **Who Wins?** The first player to reach 20 points wins the game.

The Game Zone

Resources

Math Online For an easy-to-make manipulative for this game, visit: msmath3.net/gamezone

Glencoe Mathematics Classroom Manipulative Kit

- scissors

GETTING READY

Objective Identify proportions.

MANAGEMENT TIPS

Recommended Time
25 minutes

Tips

- Prepare the index cards in advance.
- Select student groups in advance. You may want to pair students of different abilities in order to help those who are having difficulty and give the more advanced students a teaching opportunity.
- Students should observe the set of numbers that were copied onto the index cards. Tell them to use mental math to create a few proportions before play begins. After the game, have them discuss strategy and the importance of mental math skills.
- If the students get to play more than one game, have them switch groups.
- You may wish to use the game as an assessment tool for the concepts the students have been learning in Lessons 4-1 through 4-4.

Math Online For an additional game for this chapter, visit: msmath3.net/gamezone

4-5a Lesson Notes

1 Focus

Bellringer

Communication Ask each student to write a description of a room in their home. Allow one minute for this task. Then ask students to draw a picture of the room, again allowing them one minute. Ask which was easier and which provided more information about a room. Students should recognize that drawing a picture can provide much useful information.

2 Teach

In-Class Example

Solve. Use the draw a diagram strategy.

VOLUME A bathtub is being filled with water. After 4 minutes, $\frac{1}{5}$ of the bathtub is filled. How much longer will it take to completely fill the bathtub assuming the water rate is constant? **16 minutes**

Answer

1. **The problem involves physical elements that can be better visualized and understood by drawing a diagram.**

4-5a Problem-Solving Strategy

A Preview of Lesson 4-5

What You'll LEARN

Solve problems by using the draw a diagram strategy.

Draw a Diagram

Cleaning tanks for the city aquarium sure is hard work, and filling them back up seems to take forever. It's been 3 minutes and this 120-gallon tank is only at the 10-gallon mark!

I wonder how much longer it will take? Let's **draw a diagram** to help us picture what's happening.

Explore	The tank holds 120 gallons of water. After 3 minutes, the tank has 10 gallons of water in it. How many more minutes will it take to fill the tank?
Plan	Let's draw a diagram showing the water level after every 3 minutes.
Solve	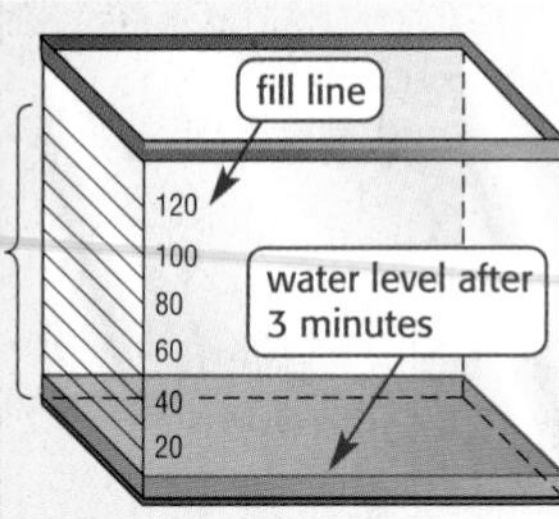 The tank will be filled after twelve 3-minute time periods. This is a total of 12×3 or 36 minutes.
Examine	The tank is filling at a rate of 10 gallons every 3 minutes, which is about 3 gallons per minute. So a 120-gallon tank will take about $120 \div 3$ or 40 minutes to fill. Our answer of 36 minutes seems reasonable.

Apply the Strategy

1. **Tell** how drawing a diagram helps solve this problem. **See margin.**
2. **Describe** another method the students could have used to find the number of 3-minute time periods it would take to fill the tank. **Divide 120 by 10.**
3. **Write** a problem that can be solved by drawing a diagram. Then draw a diagram and solve the problem. **See margin.**

DAILY INTERVENTION — **Flexible Grouping**

Drawing Pictures Have students work in small groups to draw pictures for each exercise. Put one student in charge of the shape of the picture, one student in charge of labeling, one student to write the expression to answer the problem, and one student to check the group's work. Have students switch responsibilities after each problem.

Apply the Strategy

Solve. Use the draw a diagram strategy.

4. **AQUARIUM** Angelina fills another 120-gallon tank at the same time Kyle is filling the first 120-gallon tank. After 3 minutes, her tank has 12 gallons in it. How much longer will it take Kyle to fill his tank than Angelina? **6 min**

5. **LOGGING** It takes 20 minutes to cut a log into 5 equally-sized pieces. How long will it take to cut a similar log into 3 equally-sized pieces? **10 min**

Mixed Problem Solving

Solve. Use any strategy.

6. **STORE DISPLAY** A stock clerk is stacking oranges in the shape of a square-based pyramid, as shown at the right. If the pyramid is to have 5 layers, how many oranges will he need? **55**

FOOD **For Exercises 7 and 8, use the following information.**
Of the 30 students in a life skills class, 19 like to cook main dishes, 15 prefer baking desserts, and 7 like to do both.

7. How many like to cook main dishes, but not bake desserts? **12**

8. How many do not like either baking desserts or making main dishes? **3**

9. **MOVIES** A section of a theater is arranged so that each row has the same number of seats. You are seated in the 5th row from the front and the 3rd row from the back. If your seat is 6th from the left and 2nd from the right, how many seats are in this section of the theater? **49**

10. **MONEY** Mi-Ling has only nickels in her pocket. Julián has only quarters in his and Aisha has only dimes in hers. Hannah approached all three for a donation for the school fund-raiser. What is the least each person could donate so that each one gives the same amount? **50 cents**

11. **TOURISM** An amusement park in Texas features giant statues of comic strip characters. If you multiply one character's height by 4 and add 1 foot, you will find the height of its statue. If the statue is 65 feet tall, how tall is the character? **16 ft**

TECHNOLOGY **For Exercises 12 and 13, use the diagram below and the following information.**
Seven closed shapes are used to make the digits 0 to 9 on a digital clock. (The number 1 is made using the line segments on the right side of the figure.)

12. In forming these digits, which line segment is used most often? **bottom right**

13. Which line segment is used the least? **bottom left**

14. **SPORTS** The width of a tennis court is ten more than one-third its length. If the court is 78 feet long, what is its perimeter? **228 ft**

15. **STANDARDIZED TEST PRACTICE** Three-inch square tiles that are 2 inches high are being packaged into boxes like the one at the right. If the tiles must be laid flat, how many will fit in one box? **A**

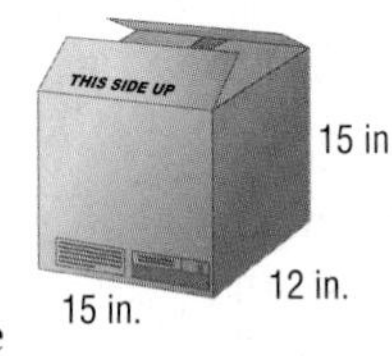

Ⓐ 140 Ⓑ 150 Ⓒ 450 Ⓓ 900

3 Practice/Apply

About the Exercises...

Problem-Solving Strategies
Exercises 6–15 are structured so that students have the opportunity to practice many different problem-solving strategies. You may wish to remind them of some of the strategies they have studied.

- work backward (p. 43)
- look for a pattern (p. 96)
- use a Venn diagram (p. 123)
- draw a diagram ✓

4 Assess

Higher-Level Thinking
Draw a diagram to help solve the following problem. Hilary, Ira, Jenny, and Ken live on the same street in houses 2, 4, 6, and 8. Ira does not live next to Jenny. Hilary lives two houses from Ken. Ken does not live in house 2. Jenny lives in house 8. Which house does each live in? **Hilary lives in 2, Ira lives in 4, Ken lives in 6, and Jenny lives in 8.**

Answer

3. **Sample answer: There are 8 people in a room. Each person shakes hands with each of the other people once and only once. How many handshakes are there? Continuing the pattern observed in the diagrams, there will be 7 + 6 + 5 + 4 + 3 + 2 + 1 + 0 or 28 handshakes.**

Person 1 shakes everyone's hand.

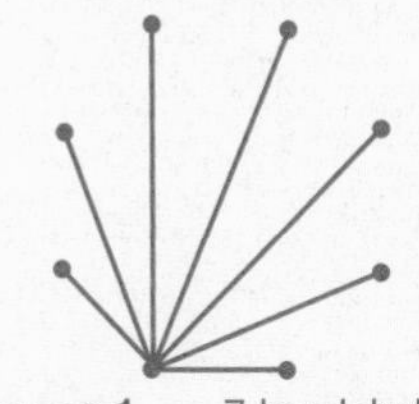

person 1 7 handshakes

Person 2 shakes everyone's hand, but not person 1's hand again.

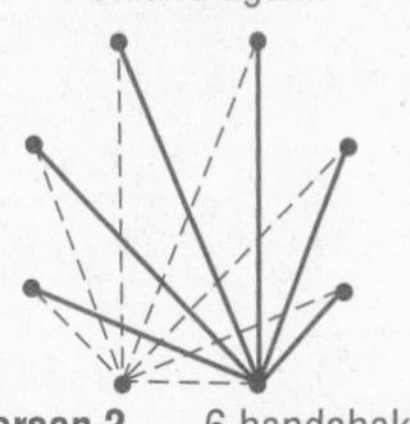

person 2 6 handshakes

Person 3 shakes everyone's hand, but not person 1 or 2's hand again.

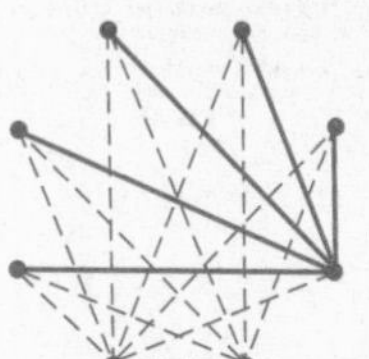

person 3 5 handshakes

4-5 Lesson Notes

Lesson Resources

Chapter 4 Resource Masters

FAST FILE

- Study Guide and Intervention, p. 205
- Practice: Skills, p. 206
- Practice: Word Problems, p. 207
- Reading to Learn Mathematics, p. 208
- Enrichment, p. 209

MathPASS Tutorial CD-ROM, 44

Parent and Student Study Guide Online Worksheets, 4-5

Noteables™: Interactive Study Notebook with Foldables™, 4-5

1 Focus

5-Minute Check 4-5

Use as a quiz or review of Lesson 4-4. (Also available as a transparency)

Bellringer

Hands-On Activity Have students work with a partner. Each student should create a shape on dot paper. Their partner should then redraw the shape with sides exactly twice as long. Have the class discuss the figures that were created.

Reading to Learn Mathematics, p. 208 ELL

NAME ______________ DATE ________ PERIOD ____

4-5 **Reading to Learn Mathematics**

Similar Polygons

Pre-Activity ***Complete the Mini Lab at the top of page 178 in your textbook. Write your answers below.***

1. Compare the angles of the triangles by matching them up. Identify the angle pairs that have equal measure. $m\angle D = m\angle L$, $m\angle E = m\angle J$, $m\angle F = m\angle K$

2. Express the ratios $\frac{DF}{LK}$, $\frac{EF}{JK}$, and $\frac{DE}{LJ}$ to the nearest tenth. 0.7; 0.7; 0.7

3. What do you notice about the ratios of the matching sides of matching triangles? They are approximately equal.

Readi... the Lesson

4-5 Similar Polygons

HANDS-ON Mini Lab

What You'll LEARN

Identify similar polygons and find missing measures of similar polygons.

NEW Vocabulary

polygon
similar
corresponding parts
congruent
scale factor

MATH Symbols

$\angle$	angle
$\overline{AB}$	segment AB
$\sim$	is similar to
$\cong$	is congruent to
AB	measure of $\overline{AB}$

Materials

- tracing paper
- centimeter ruler
- scissors

Work with a partner.

Follow the steps below to discover how the triangles at the right are related.

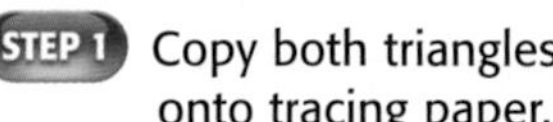

STEP 1 Copy both triangles onto tracing paper.

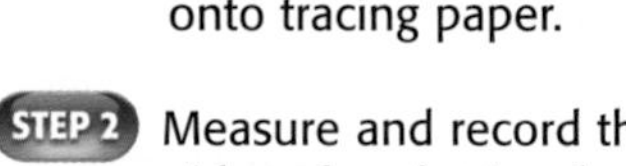

STEP 2 Measure and record the sides of each triangle.

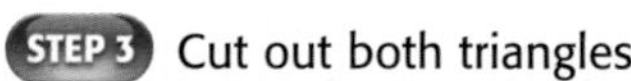

STEP 3 Cut out both triangles.

1. Compare the angles of the triangles by matching them up. Identify the angle pairs that have equal measure.
2. Express the ratios $\frac{DF}{LK}$, $\frac{EF}{JK}$, and $\frac{DE}{LJ}$ as decimals to the nearest tenth. **0.7; 0.7; 0.7**
3. What do you notice about the ratios of the matching sides of matching triangles? **They are approximately equal.**

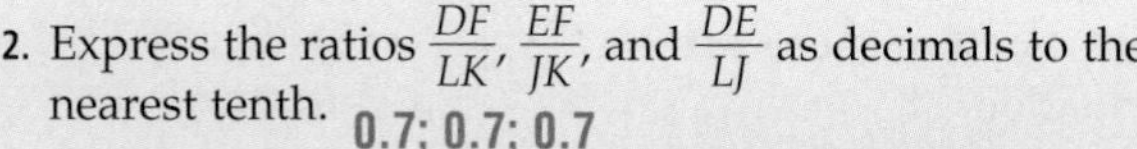

1. $m\angle D = m\angle L$, $m\angle E = m\angle J$, $m\angle F = m\angle K$

A simple closed figure in a plane formed by three or more line segments is called a **polygon**. Polygons that have the same shape are called **similar** polygons. In the figure below, polygon *ABCD* is similar to polygon *WXYZ*. This is written as polygon $ABCD \sim$ polygon $WXYZ$.

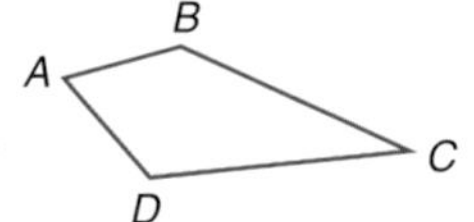

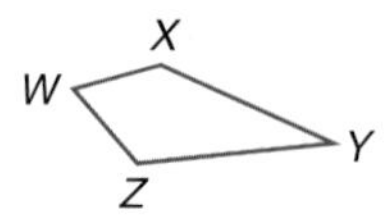

The parts of similar figures that "match" are called **corresponding parts**.

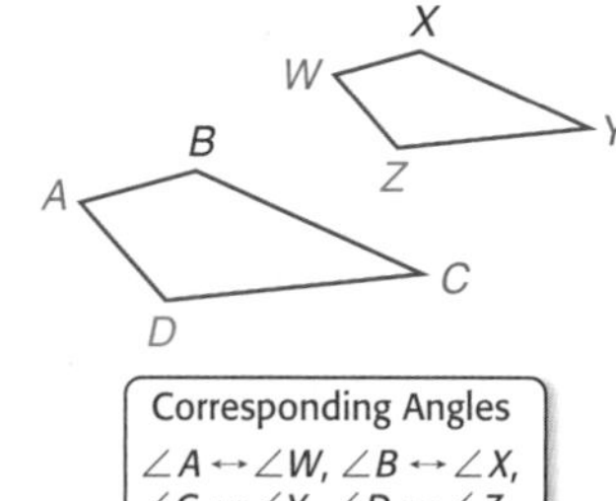

Corresponding Angles
$\angle A \leftrightarrow \angle W$, $\angle B \leftrightarrow \angle X$,
$\angle C \leftrightarrow \angle Y$, $\angle D \leftrightarrow \angle Z$

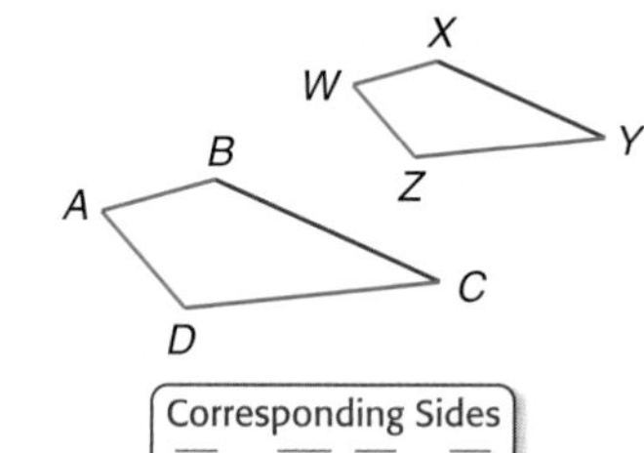

Corresponding Sides
$\overline{AB} \leftrightarrow \overline{WX}$, $\overline{BC} \leftrightarrow \overline{XY}$,
$\overline{CD} \leftrightarrow \overline{YZ}$, $\overline{DA} \leftrightarrow \overline{ZW}$

TEACHING TIP

Point out that similar polygons do not have to be the same size.

Congruence Arcs are used to show congruent angles.

TEACHING TIP

Students will learn more about congruence in Chapter 6.

The similar triangles in the Mini Lab suggest that the following properties are true for similar polygons.

Noteables™ **Key Concept: Similar Polygons**

Words If two polygons are similar, then
- their corresponding angles are **congruent**, or have the same measure, and
- their corresponding sides are proportional.

Models

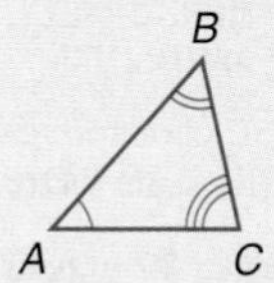

$\triangle ABC \sim \triangle XYZ$

Symbols $\angle A \cong \angle X, \angle B \cong \angle Y, \angle C \cong \angle Z$ and $\frac{AB}{XY} = \frac{BC}{YZ} = \frac{AC}{XZ}$

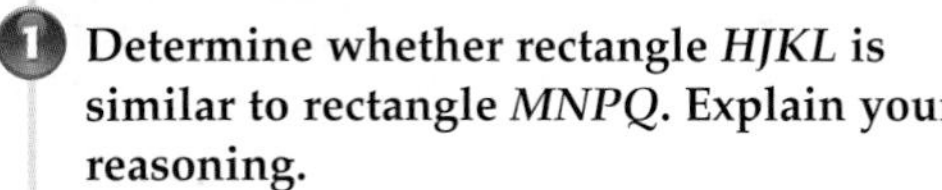

EXAMPLE Identify Similar Polygons

1 Determine whether rectangle *HJKL* is similar to rectangle *MNPQ*. Explain your reasoning.

First, check to see if corresponding angles are congruent.

Since the two polygons are rectangles, all of their angles are right angles. Therefore, all corresponding angles are congruent.

Next, check to see if corresponding sides are proportional.

$\frac{HJ}{MN} = \frac{7}{10}$ $\quad \frac{JK}{NP} = \frac{3}{6}$ or $\frac{1}{2}$ $\quad \frac{KL}{PQ} = \frac{7}{10}$ $\quad \frac{LH}{QM} = \frac{3}{6}$ or $\frac{1}{2}$

Since $\frac{7}{10}$ and $\frac{1}{2}$ are not equivalent ratios, rectangle *HJKL* is *not* similar to rectangle *MNPQ*.

Common Error Do not assume that two polygons are similar just because their corresponding angles are congruent. Their corresponding sides must also be proportional.

Your Turn

a. Determine whether these polygons are similar. Explain your reasoning.

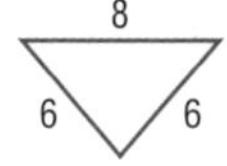

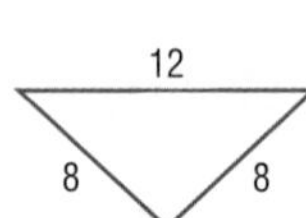

a. No; corresponding angles are not congruent and $\frac{2}{3} \neq \frac{3}{4}$.

The ratio of the lengths of two corresponding sides of two similar polygons is called the **scale factor**. The squares below are similar.

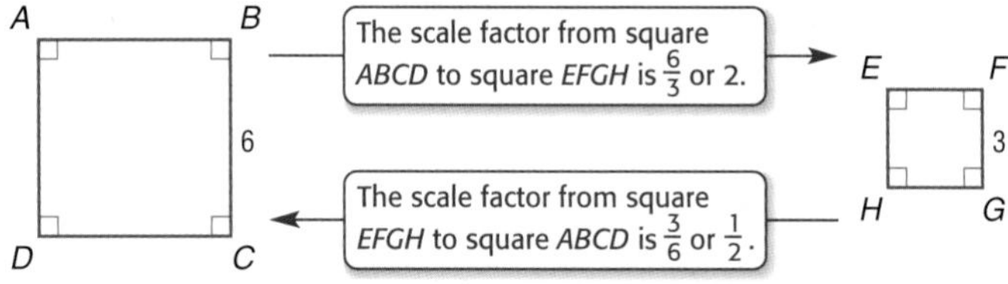

msmath3.net/extra_examples

2 Teach

In-Class Example

Determine whether triangle *DEF* is similar to triangle *HJK*. Explain your reasoning.

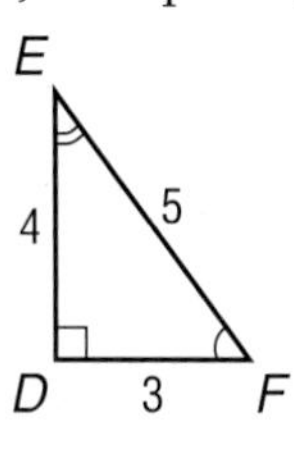

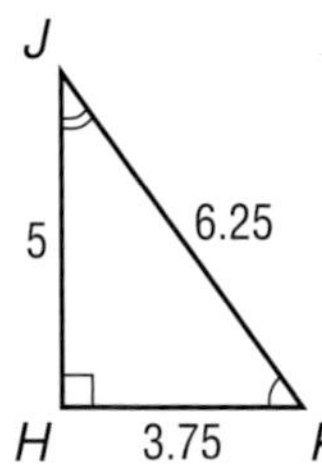

Yes; The corresponding angles are congruent and $\frac{4}{5} = \frac{5}{6.25} = \frac{3}{3.75}$.

Teaching Strategies When completing multiple-choice test items, encourage students to first look for answers that are obviously wrong and eliminate those answers from consideration. They can then concentrate more closely on those answers that may be correct.

DAILY INTERVENTION **Unlocking Misconceptions**

Setting Up Proportions Students often have difficulty placing the measures of a polygon's sides in the correct place when setting up proportions. Students may need to redraw the polygons so that they are oriented in the same direction. Then they should put a number from the first polygon on the top and the corresponding number from the second polygon on the bottom in order to create the appropriate proportion.

In-Class Examples

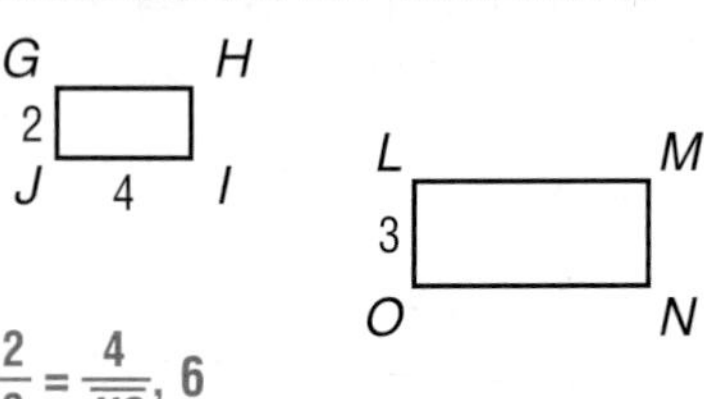

2 Given that rectangle $GHIJ \sim$ rectangle $LMNO$, write a proportion to find the measure of $\overline{NO}$. Then solve.

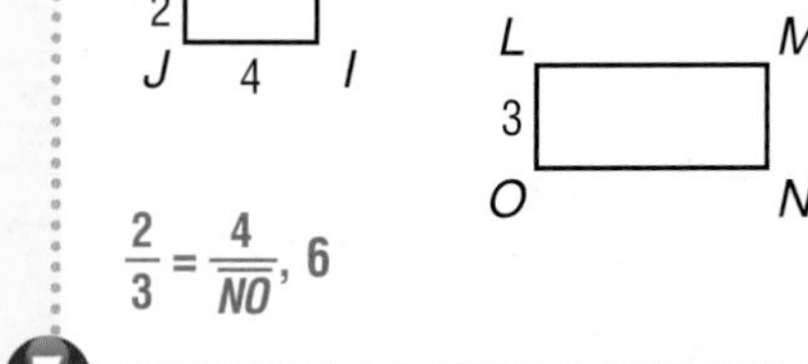

$\frac{2}{3} = \frac{4}{NO}$, 6

3 **MULTIPLE-CHOICE TEST ITEM** A polygon has sides 2.5 times as long as a similar polygon. The smaller polygon has a perimeter of 42 inches. What is the perimeter of the larger polygon? **D**

A 16.8 in.

B 45 in.

C 84 in.

D 105 in.

TEACHING TIP

Be sure students are able to use the arc symbols on the diagram to explain why $\overline{BC}$ corresponds to $\overline{XY}$ in Example 2.

EXAMPLE Find Missing Measures

2 **Given that polygon $ABCD \sim$ polygon $WXYZ$, write a proportion to find the measure of $\overline{XY}$. Then solve.**

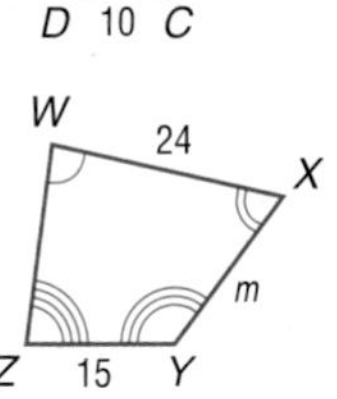

The scale factor from polygon $ABCD$ to polygon $WXYZ$ is $\frac{CD}{YZ}$, which is $\frac{10}{15}$ or $\frac{2}{3}$. Write a proportion with this scale factor. Let m represent the measure of $\overline{XY}$.

$\frac{BC}{XY} = \frac{2}{3}$ — $\overline{BC}$ corresponds to $\overline{XY}$. The scale factor is $\frac{2}{3}$.

$\frac{12}{m} = \frac{2}{3}$ — $BC = 12$ and $XY = m$

$12 \cdot 3 = m \cdot 2$ — Find the cross products.

$\frac{36}{2} = \frac{2m}{2}$ — Multiply. Then divide each side by 2.

$18 = m$ — Simplify.

Your Turn **Write a proportion to find the measure of each side above. Then solve.**

b. $\overline{WZ}$ $\frac{13}{WZ} = \frac{2}{3}$; 19.5

c. $\overline{AB}$ $\frac{AB}{24} = \frac{2}{3}$; 16

Standardized Test Practice

EXAMPLE Scale Factor and Perimeter

3 **MULTIPLE-CHOICE TEST ITEM** Triangle $LMN \sim \triangle PQR$. Each side of $\triangle LMN$ is $1\frac{1}{3}$ times longer than the corresponding sides of $\triangle PQR$.

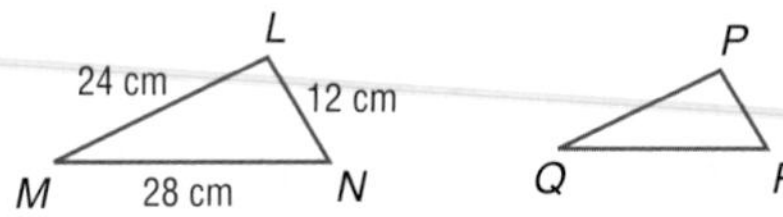

If the perimeter of $\triangle LMN$ is 64 centimeters, what is the perimeter of $\triangle PQR$?

(A) $5\frac{1}{3}$ cm (B) 16 cm (C) 48 cm (D) 61 cm

Test-Taking Tip

Use a Proportion
In similar figures, the ratio of the perimeters is the same as the ratio of corresponding sides. Use a proportion.

Read the Test Item Since each side of $\triangle LMN$ is $1\frac{1}{3}$ times longer than the corresponding sides of $\triangle PQR$, the scale factor from $\triangle LMN$ to $\triangle PQR$ is $1\frac{1}{3}$ or $\frac{4}{3}$.

Solve the Test Item Let x represent the perimeter of $\triangle PQR$. The ratio of the perimeters is equal to the ratio of the sides.

ratio of perimeters → $\frac{64}{x} = \frac{4}{3}$ ← ratio of sides

$64 \cdot 3 = x \cdot 4$ — Find the cross products.

$\frac{192}{4} = \frac{4x}{4}$ — Multiply. Then divide each side by 4.

$48 = x$ — Simplify.

The answer is C.

Answers

1. If 2 polygons have corresponding congruent angles and have corresponding sides that are in proportion, then the polygons are similar.
2. Sample answer:

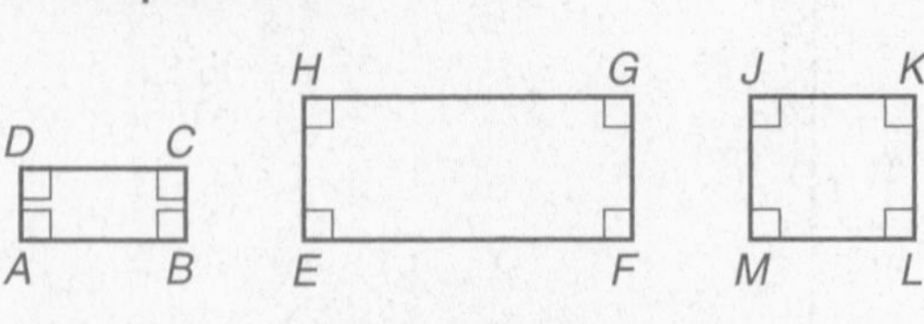

rectangle $ABCD \sim$ rectangle $EFGH$

3. $\frac{5}{3} \neq \frac{13}{5}$
4. The corresponding angles are congruent and $\frac{8}{6} = \frac{8}{6} = \frac{10}{7.5} = \frac{18}{13.5}$.
6. The corresponding angles are congruent, but $\frac{3}{7} \neq \frac{4}{8}$.
7. The corresponding angles are congruent and $\frac{3}{5} = \frac{3}{5}$.
8. The corresponding angles are congruent and $\frac{20}{15} = \frac{16}{12} = \frac{24}{18}$.
9. The corresponding angles are congruent, but $\frac{5}{4} \neq \frac{8}{6}$.

Students practice the same concepts in Exercises 6–13 if they are assigned odd or even problems.

Skill and Concept Check

1. **Writing Math** Explain how to determine if two polygons are similar. **See margin.**

2. **OPEN ENDED** Draw and label a pair of similar rectangles. Then draw a third rectangle that is not similar to the other two. **See margin.**

GUIDED PRACTICE

Determine whether each pair of polygons is similar. Explain your reasoning. **3–4. See margin for explanation.**

3. **no**

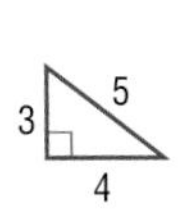

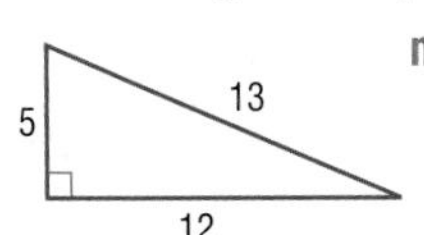

4. **yes**

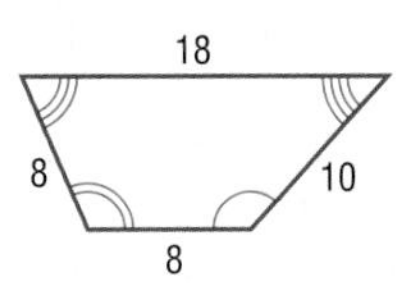

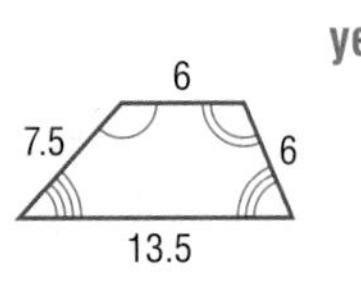

5. In the figure at the right, $\triangle FGH \sim \triangle KLJ$. Write a proportion to find each missing measure. Then solve. $\frac{x}{6} = \frac{2}{1}$; 12

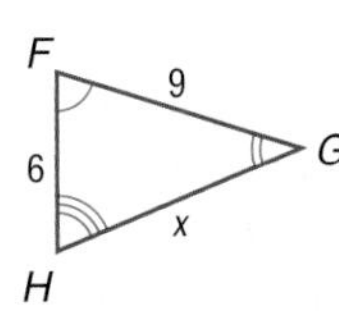

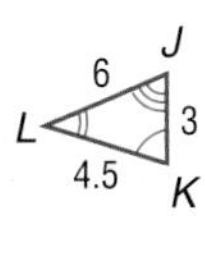

★ indicates increased difficulty

Practice and Applications

Determine whether each pair of polygons is similar. Explain your reasoning. **6–9. See margin for explanation.**

HOMEWORK HELP	
For Exercises	See Examples
6–9	1
10–16	2
17	3
Extra Practice	See pages 625, 651.

6. **no**

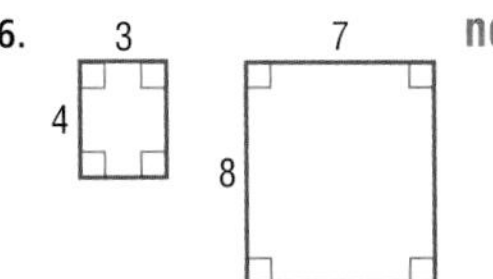

7. **yes**

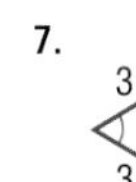

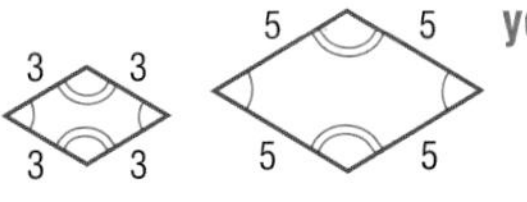

8. **yes**

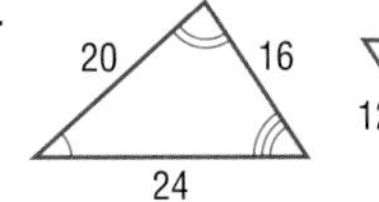

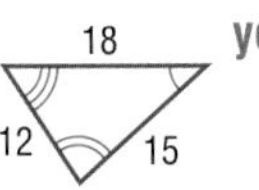

9. **no**

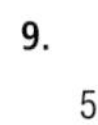

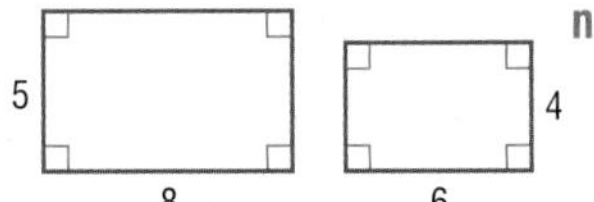

Each pair of polygons is similar. Write a proportion to find each missing measure. Then solve. **10–13. See margin for proportions.**

10. **2**

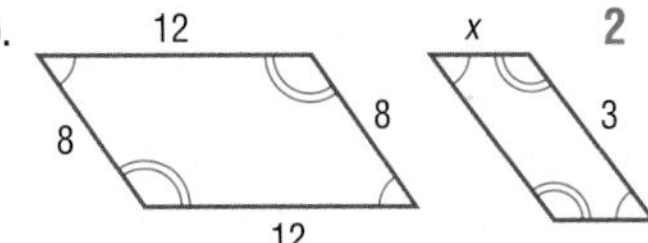

11. **6**

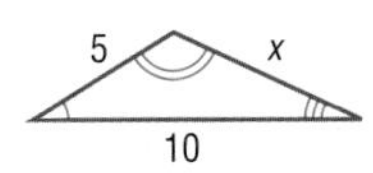

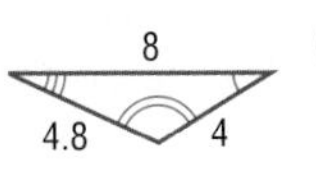

12. **20**

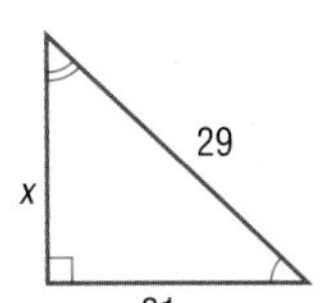

13. **16.25**

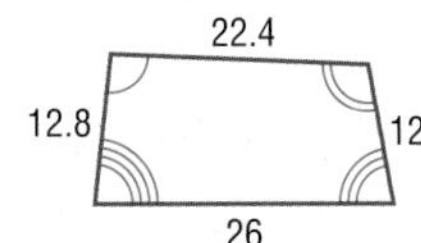

msmath3.net/self_check_quiz

3 Practice/Apply

About the Exercises...

Guided Practice Key

Exercises	Examples
3–4	1
5	2

Assignment Guide

Basic: 7–15 odd, 18–27

Average: 7–17 odd, 18–27

Enriched: 6–14 even, 15, 16, 18–25 (Optional: 26–27)

TEACHING TIP

Extending the Lesson
Two triangles are similar if:

- two pairs of corresponding angles are congruent (AA similarity),
- the ratios of two pairs of corresponding sides are equal and the included angles are congruent (SAS similarity), or
- the ratios of all pairs of corresponding sides are equal (SSS similarity).

10. $\frac{8}{x} = \frac{4}{1}$

11. $\frac{x}{4.8} = \frac{5}{4}$

12. $\frac{x}{10} = \frac{2}{1}$

13. $\frac{26}{x} = \frac{1.6}{1}$

18. Counterexample: All corresponding angles are congruent between the three rectangles. Rectangle *A* is similar to rectangle *C*, since $\frac{6}{9} = \frac{4}{6}$, but rectangle *A* is not similar to rectangle *B*, since $\frac{4}{4} \neq \frac{6}{12}$.

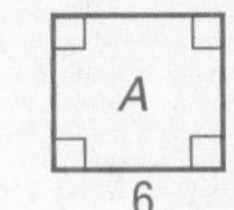

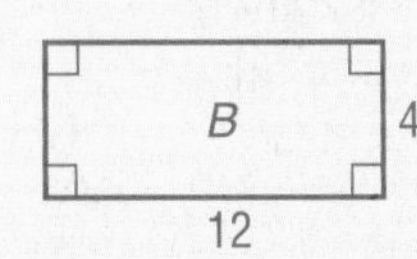

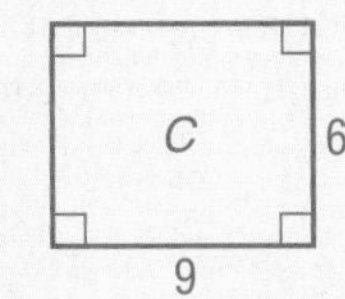

19. All corresponding angles between squares are congruent since all four angles in a square are right angles. In addition, all sides in a square are congruent. Therefore, all four ratios of corresponding sides are equal.

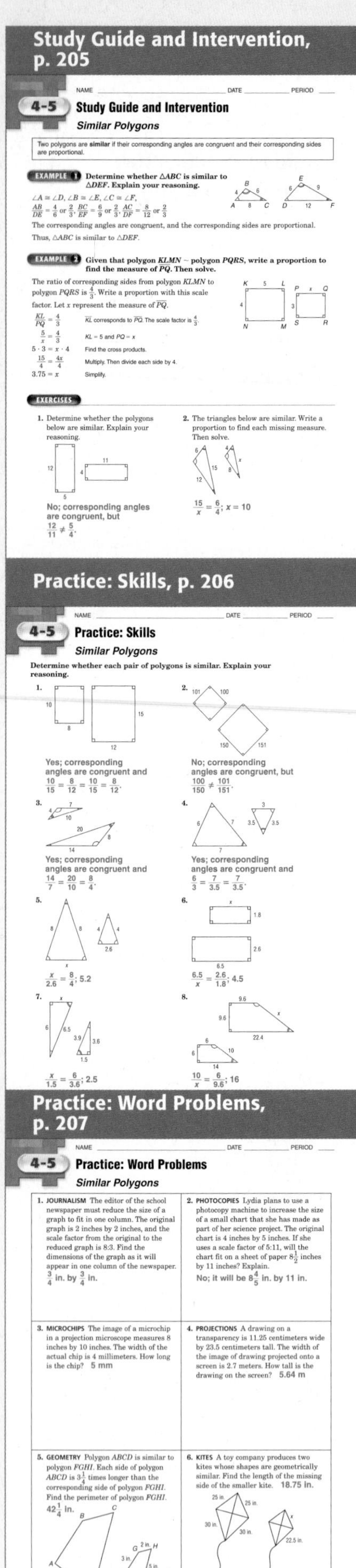
Study Guide and Intervention, p. 205

NAME ________ DATE ________ PERIOD ____

4-5 Study Guide and Intervention

Similar Polygons

Two polygons are **similar** if their corresponding angles are congruent and their corresponding sides are proportional.

EXAMPLE 1 **Determine whether $\triangle ABC$ is similar to $\triangle DEF$. Explain your reasoning.**

$\angle A \cong \angle D$, $\angle B \cong \angle E$, $\angle C \cong \angle F$,

$\frac{AB}{DE} = \frac{4}{6}$ or $\frac{2}{3}$, $\frac{BC}{EF} = \frac{6}{9}$ or $\frac{2}{3}$, $\frac{AC}{DF} = \frac{8}{12}$ or $\frac{2}{3}$

The corresponding angles are congruent, and the corresponding sides are proportional. Thus, $\triangle ABC$ is similar to $\triangle DEF$.

EXAMPLE 2 **Given that polygon $KLMN \sim$ polygon $PQRS$, write a proportion to find the measure of $\overline{PQ}$. Then solve.**

The ratio of corresponding sides from polygon $KLMN$ to polygon $PQRS$ is $\frac{4}{3}$. Write a proportion with this scale factor. Let x represent the measure of $\overline{PQ}$.

$\frac{KL}{PQ} = \frac{4}{3}$ — $\overline{KL}$ corresponds to $\overline{PQ}$. The scale factor is $\frac{4}{3}$.

$\frac{5}{x} = \frac{4}{3}$ — $KL = 5$ and $PQ = x$

$5 \cdot 3 = x \cdot 4$ — Find the cross products.

$\frac{15}{4} = \frac{4x}{4}$ — Multiply. Then divide each side by 4.

$3.75 = x$ — Simplify.

EXERCISES

1. Determine whether the polygons below are similar. Explain your reasoning.
No; corresponding angles are congruent, but $\frac{12}{11} \neq \frac{5}{4}$.

2. The triangles below are similar. Write a proportion to find each missing measure. Then solve.
$\frac{15}{x} = \frac{6}{4}$; $x = 10$

Practice: Skills, p. 206

NAME ________ DATE ________ PERIOD ____

4-5 Practice: Skills

Similar Polygons

Determine whether each pair of polygons is similar. Explain your reasoning.

1. Yes; corresponding angles are congruent and $\frac{10}{15} = \frac{8}{12} = \frac{10}{15} = \frac{8}{12}$.
2. No; corresponding angles are congruent, but $\frac{100}{150} \neq \frac{101}{151}$.
3. Yes; corresponding angles are congruent and $\frac{14}{7} = \frac{20}{10} = \frac{8}{4}$.
4. Yes; corresponding angles are congruent and $\frac{6}{3} = \frac{7}{3.5} = \frac{7}{3.5}$.
5. $\frac{x}{2.6} = \frac{8}{4}$; 5.2
6. $\frac{6.5}{x} = \frac{2.6}{1.8}$; 4.5
7. $\frac{x}{1.5} = \frac{6}{3.6}$; 2.5
8. $\frac{10}{x} = \frac{6}{9.6}$; 16

Practice: Word Problems, p. 207

NAME ________ DATE ________ PERIOD ____

4-5 Practice: Word Problems

Similar Polygons

1. **JOURNALISM** The editor of the school newspaper must reduce the size of a graph to fit in one column. The original graph is 2 inches by 2 inches, and the scale factor from the original to the reduced graph is 8:3. Find the dimensions of the graph as it will appear in one column of the newspaper. $\frac{3}{4}$ in. by $\frac{3}{4}$ in.
2. **PHOTOCOPIES** Lydia plans to use a photocopy machine to increase the size of a small chart that she has made as part of her science project. The original chart is 4 inches by 5 inches. If she uses a scale factor of 5:11, will the chart fit on a sheet of paper $8\frac{1}{2}$ inches by 11 inches? Explain. No; it will be $8\frac{4}{5}$ in. by 11 in.
3. **MICROCHIPS** The image of a microchip in a projection microscope measures 8 inches by 10 inches. The width of the actual chip is 4 millimeters. How long is the chip? 5 mm
4. **PROJECTIONS** A drawing on a transparency is 11.25 centimeters wide by 23.5 centimeters tall. The width of the image of drawing projected onto a screen is 2.7 meters. How tall is the drawing on the screen? 5.64 m
5. **GEOMETRY** Polygon $ABCD$ is similar to polygon $FGHI$. Each side of polygon $ABCD$ is $3\frac{1}{4}$ times longer than the corresponding side of polygon $FGHI$. Find the perimeter of polygon $FGHI$. $42\frac{1}{4}$ in.
6. **KITES** A toy company produces two kites whose shapes are geometrically similar. Find the length of the missing side of the smaller kite. 18.75 in.

14. **YEARBOOK** In order to fit 3 pictures across a page, the yearbook staff must reduce their portrait proofs using a scale factor of 8 to 5. Find the dimensions of the pictures as they will appear in the yearbook. **$2\frac{1}{2}$ in. by $3\frac{1}{8}$ in.**

MOVIES For Exercises 15 and 16, use the following information.
Film labeled 35-millimeter is film that is 35 millimeters wide.

15. When a frame of 35-millimeter movie film is projected onto a movie screen, the image from the film is 9 meters high and 6.75 meters wide. Find the height of the film. **46.67 mm**

16. If the image from this same film is projected so that it appears 8 meters high, what is the width of the projected image? **6 m**

★ 17. **GEOMETRY** Find the ratio of the area of rectangle A to the area of rectangle B for each of the following scale factors of corresponding sides. What can you conclude?
a. $\frac{1}{2}$ **$\frac{1}{4}$** b. $\frac{1}{3}$ **$\frac{1}{9}$** c. $\frac{1}{4}$ **$\frac{1}{16}$** d. $\frac{1}{5}$ **$\frac{1}{25}$**
The ratio of the areas is the square of the scale factor.

CRITICAL THINKING Determine whether each statement is *always*, *sometimes*, or *never* true. Explain your reasoning.

18. Two rectangles are similar. **sometimes**
19. Two squares are similar. **always**

18–19. See p. 181 margin for explanation.

Spiral Review with Standardized Test Practice

20. **MULTIPLE CHOICE** Which triangle is similar to $\triangle ABC$? **B**

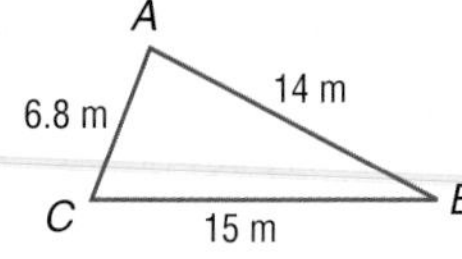

Ⓐ 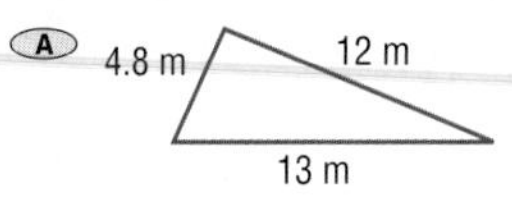

Ⓑ 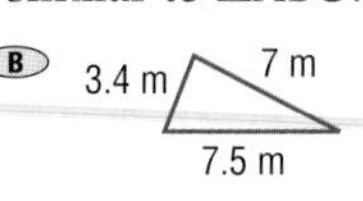

Ⓒ 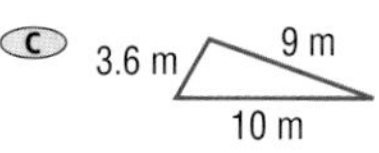

Ⓓ 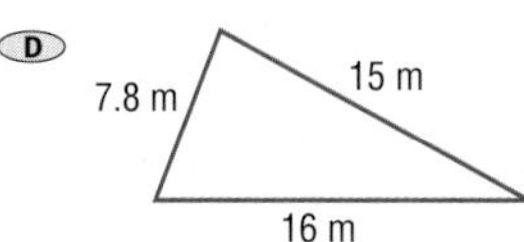

21. **SHORT RESPONSE** Polygon $JKLM \sim$ polygon $QRST$. If $JK = 2$ inches and $QR = 2\frac{1}{2}$ inches, find the measure of $\overline{ST}$ if $LM = 3$ inches. **$3\frac{3}{4}$ in.**

22. **BAKING** A recipe calls for 4 cups of flour for 64 cookies. How much flour is needed for 96 cookies? (Lesson 4-4) **6 c**

Graph each pair of points. Then find the slope of the line that passes through each pair of points. (Lesson 4-3) **23–25. See Ch. 4 Answer Appendix for graphs.**

23. $(-3, 9), (1, -5)$ **$-\frac{7}{2}$**
24. $(2, 4), (-6, 7)$ **$-\frac{3}{8}$**
25. $(3, -8), (-1, -8)$ **0**

GETTING READY FOR THE NEXT LESSON **26–27. See margin for proportions.**

PREREQUISITE SKILL Write a proportion and solve for x. (Lesson 4-4)

26. 3 cm is to 5 ft as x cm is to 9 ft **5.4**
27. 4 in. is to 5 mi as 5 in. is to x mi **6.25**

4 Assess

Open-Ended Assessment

Modeling Have students create and label three similar polygons. Ask them to explain the ratio of the sides of all three polygons.

Answers

26. $\frac{3}{5} = \frac{x}{9}$

27. $\frac{4}{5} = \frac{5}{x}$

4-5b HANDS-ON LAB

A Follow-Up of Lesson 4-5

The Golden Rectangle

What You'll LEARN

Find the value of the golden ratio.

Materials

- grid paper
- scissors
- calculator
- tape measure

INVESTIGATE *Work in groups of three.*

STEP 1 Cut a rectangle out of grid paper that measures 34 units long by 21 units wide. Using your calculator, find the ratio of the length to the width. Express it as a decimal to the nearest hundredth. Record your data in a table like the one below.

length	34	21	?	?	?
width	21	13	?	?	?
ratio	?	?	?	?	?
decimal	?	?	?	?	?

STEP 2 Cut this rectangle into two parts, in which one part is the largest possible square and the other part is a rectangle. Record the rectangle's length and width. Write the ratio of length to width. Express it as a decimal to the nearest hundredth and record in the table.

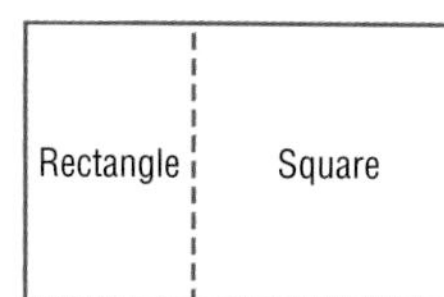

STEP 3 Repeat the procedure described in Step 2 until the remaining rectangle measures 3 units by 5 units. **See margin.**

Writing Math

1. **Describe** the pattern in the ratios you recorded. **All are about 1.6.**
2. If the rectangles you cut out are described as *golden rectangles*, **make a conjecture** as to what the value of the *golden ratio* is. **about 1.6**
3. **Write** a definition of *golden rectangle*. Use the word *ratio* in your definition. Then describe the shape of a golden rectangle. **See margin.**
4. **Determine** whether all golden rectangles are similar. Explain your reasoning. **Yes; all golden rectangles have the same shape.**
5. **RESEARCH** There are many examples of the golden rectangle in architecture. One is shown at the right. Use the Internet or another resource to find three places where the golden rectangle is used in architecture.

Taj Mahal, India

TEACHING TIP

The exact value of the golden ratio is equal to $\frac{1+\sqrt{5}}{2}$.

5. Sample answer: Pyramid of Khufu in Giza, Egypt; The Parthenon in Greece; The Lincoln Memorial in Washington, D.C.

4-5b HANDS-ON LAB Lesson Notes

Lesson Resources

Teaching Mathematics with Manipulatives

- quarter-inch grid, p.10
- centimeter grid, p.11
- student recording sheet 4-5b

Glencoe Mathematics Classroom Manipulative Kit

- scissors
- tape measure

GETTING STARTED

Teaching Tip Use an overhead to show students where they should cut and why. Allow them to continue the **Activity** on their own, but return to the overhead as needed.

TEACH

- The Golden Ratio is a naturally occurring ratio that is used frequently in architecture and art. It can be seen in the spiral of a shell or the curve of a fern and creates a feeling of order.

Answer (Steps 1–3)

length	34	21	13	8	5
width	21	13	8	5	3
ratio	$\frac{34}{21}$	$\frac{21}{13}$	$\frac{13}{8}$	$\frac{8}{5}$	$\frac{5}{3}$
decimal	1.62	1.62	1.63	1.60	1.67

Answer (Writing Math)

3. **Sample answer: A golden rectangle is a rectangle in which the ratio of the length to the width is 1.6. A golden rectangle is about 1 and a half times as long as it is wide.**

ASSESS

Discuss the **Writing Math** exercises.

- You may want students to redraw the different-sized rectangles and compare them. They should observe that the rectangles are nearly the same shape.
- After students research other examples of the golden ratio, have them share with the class.
- Ask the class to speculate why the golden ratio is used in art so often. **Because it is a naturally occurring ratio, art produced using the golden ratio has a natural feel to it.**

4-6 Lesson Notes

Lesson Resources

Chapter 4 Resource Masters
- Study Guide and Intervention, p. 210
- Practice: Skills, p. 211
- Practice: Word Problems, p. 212
- Reading to Learn Mathematics, p. 213
- Enrichment, p. 214

Calculator and Spreadsheet Masters, p. 23
Classroom Math Games, pp. 13–16
Parent and Student Study Guide Online Worksheets, 4-6
Teaching Mathematics with Manipulatives, p. 51
Noteables™: Interactive Study Notebook with Foldables™, 4-6

1 Focus

5-Minute Check 4-6
Use as a quiz or review of Lesson 4-5. (Also available as a transparency)

Bellringer
Communication Ask students to consider the following problem: *If you were to make a drawing of your classroom on a standard piece of paper, what size would you make it? How would you show relative sizes of furniture and doors and windows?*

Discuss students' answers as a class.

Reading to Learn Mathematics, p. 213 **ELL**

NAME ____ DATE ____ PERIOD ____

4-6 Reading to Learn Mathematics
Scale Drawings and Models

Pre-Activity *Read the introduction at the top of page 184 in your textbook. Write your answers below.*

1. How many units wide is the room? 9
2. The actual width of the room is 18 feet. Write a ratio comparing the drawing width to the actual width. 9 units:18 feet
3. Simplify the ratio you found and compare it to the scale shown at the bottom of the drawing. 2, 3. Both the ratio and the scale indicate that 1 unit on the drawing is equal to 2 feet in reality.

Reading the Lesson

4-6 Scale Drawings and Models

What You'll LEARN
Solve problems involving scale drawings.

NEW Vocabulary
scale drawing
scale model
scale

WHEN am I ever going to use this?

FLOOR PLANS The blueprint for a bedroom is given below.

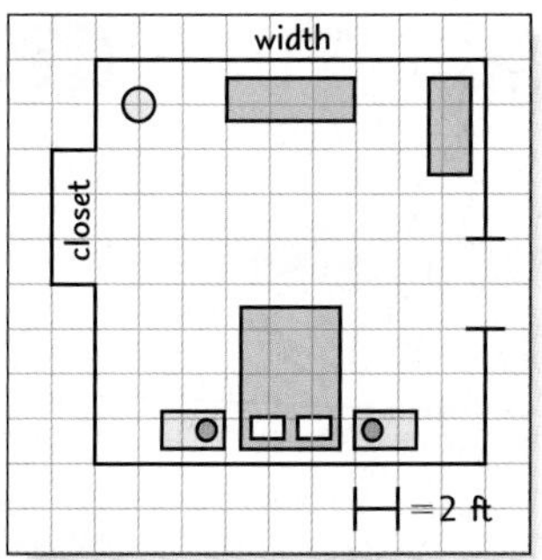

1. How many units wide is the room? **9**
2. The actual width of the room is 18 feet. Write a ratio comparing the drawing width to the actual width.
3. Simplify the ratio you found and compare it to the scale shown at the bottom of the drawing. **2, 3. See margin.**

A **scale drawing** or a **scale model** is used to represent an object that is too large or too small to be drawn or built at actual size. Examples are blueprints, maps, models of vehicles, and models of animal anatomy.

The **scale** is determined by the ratio of a given length on a drawing or model to its corresponding actual length. Consider the scales below.

1 inch = 4 feet   1 inch represents an actual distance of 4 feet.
1:30   1 unit represents an actual distance of 30 units.

Distances on a scale drawing are proportional to distances in real-life.

EXAMPLE Find a Missing Measurement

1 RECREATION The distance from the roller coaster to the food court on the map is 3.5 centimeters. Find the actual distance to the food court.

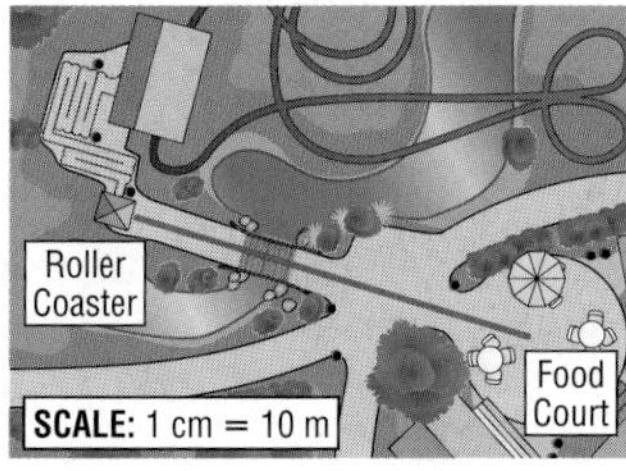

Let x represent the actual distance to the food court. Write and solve a proportion.

Map Scale → $\frac{1 \text{ cm}}{10 \text{ m}}$ ← map distance / actual distance; Actual Distance → $\frac{3.5 \text{ cm}}{x \text{ m}}$ ← map distance / actual distance

$$\frac{1 \text{ cm}}{10 \text{ m}} = \frac{3.5 \text{ cm}}{x \text{ m}}$$

$1 \cdot x = 10 \cdot 3.5$ Find the cross products.

$x = 35$ Simplify.

The actual distance to the food court is 35 meters.

STUDY TIP

Scales Scales and scale factors are always written so that the drawing length comes first in the ratio.

Answers (When am I ever going to use this?)

2. 9 units: 18 feet
3. Both the ratio and the scale indicate that one unit on the drawing is equal to 2 feet in reality.

To find the scale factor for scale drawings and models, write the ratio given by the scale in simplest form.

EXAMPLE Find the Scale Factor

2 **Find the scale factor for the map in Example 1.**

$\frac{1 \text{ cm}}{10 \text{ m}} = \frac{1 \cancel{\text{cm}}}{1{,}000 \cancel{\text{cm}}}$ Convert 10 meters to centimeters.

The scale factor is $\frac{1}{1{,}000}$ or 1:1,000. This means that each distance on the map is $\frac{1}{1{,}000}$ the actual distance.

EXAMPLE Find the Scale

3 **MODEL TRAINS** **A passenger car of a model train is 6 inches long. If the actual car is 80 feet long, what is the scale of the model?**

Write a ratio comparing the length of the model to the actual length of the train. Using x to represent the actual length of the train, write and solve a proportion to find the scale of the model.

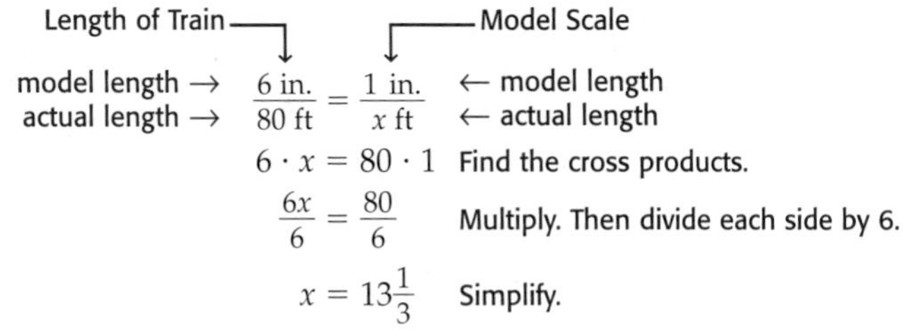

So, the scale is 1 inch = $13\frac{1}{3}$ feet.

REAL-LIFE MATH

MODEL TRAINS Some of the smallest model trains are built on the Z scale. Using this scale, models are $\frac{1}{220}$ the size of real trains.

Source: www.nmra.org

To construct a scale drawing of an object, find an appropriate scale.

EXAMPLE Construct a Scale Model

4 **SOCIAL STUDIES** **Each column of the Lincoln Memorial is 44 feet tall. Michaela wants the columns of her model to be no more than 12 inches tall. Choose an appropriate scale and use it to determine how tall she should make the model of Lincoln's 19-foot statue.**

Try a scale of 1 inch = 4 feet.

$\frac{1 \text{ in.}}{4 \text{ ft}} = \frac{x \text{ in.}}{44 \text{ ft}}$ ← model length ← actual length

$1 \cdot 44 = 4 \cdot x$ Find the cross products.

$44 = 4x$ Multiply.

$11 = x$ Divide each side by 4.

The columns are 11 inches tall.

Use this scale to find the height of the statue.

$\frac{1 \text{ in.}}{4 \text{ ft}} = \frac{y \text{ in.}}{19 \text{ ft}}$

$1 \cdot 19 = 4 \cdot y$

$19 = 4y$

$4\frac{3}{4} = y$

The statue is $4\frac{3}{4}$ inches tall.

TEACHING TIP

Show students other scales that would not have worked, such as 1 inch = 2 feet, which would have made the model 22 inches tall. Allowing more feet to represent 1 inch results in a smaller model. Thus, if a student's first guess resulted in a model that was too large, they should use a scale that allows for 1 inch to equal more feet.

msmath3.net/extra_examples

2 Teach

In-Class Examples

INTERACTIVE CHALKBOARD PowerPoint® Presentations

1 **MAPS** The distance from Bingston to Alanton is 1.5 inches on the map. Find the actual distance. **7.5 mi**

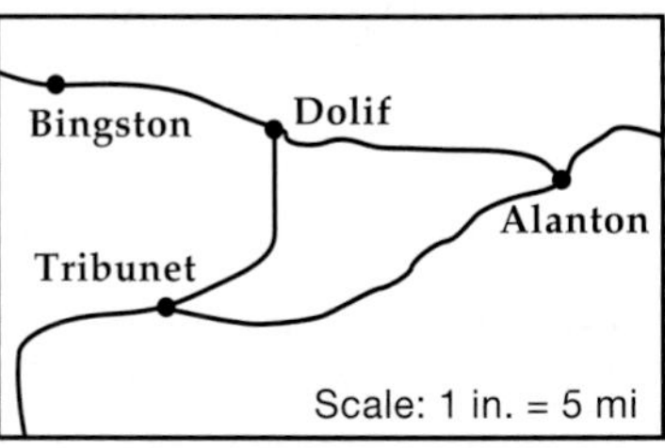

2 Find the scale factor for the map in In-Class Example 1 above. $\frac{1}{316{,}800}$ **or 1:316,800**

3 **SCALE DRAWINGS** A wall in a room is 15 feet long. On a scale drawing it is shown as 6 inches. What is the scale of the drawing? **1 inch = 2.5 feet**

4 **STATUE OF LIBERTY** Auguste Bartholdi created several smaller models of the Statue of Liberty before creating the 152-foot statue that stands in New York Harbor. One such model was only 21 inches tall. What is the scale of this model to the final version? Use the scale to determine the length of the statue's index finger on the model, which is 8 feet long on the actual statue. **Scale: 1 inch is about 7.2 feet; the finger in the model is about 1.1 inches long.**

DAILY INTERVENTION **Differentiated Instruction**

Interpersonal Have students work with a partner to create a scale drawing of the classroom. Provide pairs with tape measures or yard/metersticks. Partners may take turns measuring and recording the measurements. Make sure they include all major objects in the room. Have students include the scale factor they used.

Students practice the same concepts in Exercises 7–17 if they are assigned odd or even problems.

3 Practice/Apply

DAILY INTERVENTION **FIND THE ERROR** Use Exercise 2 as an opportunity to remind students to carefully note the units involved in a problem. Using incorrect units or converting incorrectly will lead to an incorrect answer.

About the Exercises...

Guided Practice Key

Exercises	Examples
3, 4	1
6	2
5	3

Assignment Guide

Basic: 7–17 odd, 21–30

Average: 7–17 odd, 18, 19, 21–30

Enriched: 8–16 even, 18–20, 22–28 (Optional: 29–30)

Using Applications In Exercises 3 and 4, students use a map's scale to calculate actual distances. Have students find an atlas in the library. They should use the maps in the atlas to calculate the distances from your city or area to places they would like to visit.

Answers

7. 12 ft
8. 18 ft
9. 8.4 ft
10. 12.6 ft
11. $13\frac{1}{2}$ ft
12. $6\frac{3}{4}$ ft

Skill and Concept Check

1. **OPEN ENDED** Choose an appropriate scale for a scale drawing of a bedroom 10 feet wide by 12 feet long. Identify the scale factor. **Sample answer: 1 in. = 10 ft; 1:120**
2. **FIND THE ERROR** On a map, 1 inch represents 4 feet. Jacob and Luna are finding the scale factor of the map. Who is correct? Explain.

Jacob	Luna
scale factor: 1:4	scale factor: 1:48

Luna; the scale is 1 in. = 4 ft or 1 in. = 48 in., which is 1:48.

GUIDED PRACTICE

On a map of the United States, the scale is 1 inch = 120 miles. Find the actual distance for each map distance.

	From	To	Map Distance	
3.	South Bend, Indiana	Enid, Oklahoma	6 inches	720 mi
4.	Atlanta, Georgia	Memphis, Tennessee	$2\frac{3}{4}$ inches	330 mi

MONUMENTS **For Exercises 5 and 6, use the following information.** At 555 feet tall, the Washington Monument is the highest all-masonry tower.

5. A scale model of the monument is 9.25 inches high. What is the model's scale? **1 in. = 60 ft**
6. What is the scale factor? **1:720**

★ indicates increased difficulty

Practice and Applications

The scale on a set of architectural drawings for a house is 0.5 inch = 3 feet. Find the actual length of each room. **7–12. See margin.**

	Room	Drawing Length
7.	Bed Room 2	2 inches
8.	Living Room	3 inches
9.	Kitchen	1.4 inches
10.	Dining Room	2.1 inches
11.	Master Bedroom	$2\frac{1}{4}$ inches
12.	Bath	$1\frac{1}{8}$ inches

HOMEWORK HELP

For Exercises	See Examples
7–12, 14	1
13, 21	2
15–16, 18	3
17, 19, 20	4

Extra Practice See pages 625, 651.

13. Refer to Exercises 7–12. What is the scale factor of these drawings? $\frac{1}{72}$

★14. **MULTI STEP** On the drawings for Exercises 7–12, the area of the living room is 15 square inches. What is the actual area of the living room? **540 ft²**

15. **LIFE SCIENCE** In the picture of a paramecium at the right, the length of the single celled organism is 4 centimeters. If the paramecium's actual size is 0.006 millimeter, what is the scale of the drawing? **1 cm = 0.0015 mm**

4 cm

16. **MOVIES** One of the models of the gorilla used in the filming of a 1933 movie was only 18 inches tall. In the movie, the gorilla was seen as 24 feet high. What was the scale used? **3 in. = 4 ft or 1 in. = $1\frac{1}{3}$ ft**

19. A tennis ball; if the circumference of the model is C, then $\frac{C}{11{,}000} = \frac{3}{4{,}000}$ so $C = 8.25$.

22. Measure the distance between two places on the map for which you already know the actual distance. Set up a ratio of the map distance to the known distance. Then simplify.

25. The corresponding angles are congruent, and $\frac{3}{4.8} = \frac{2}{3.2} = \frac{2}{3.2} = \frac{1.5}{2.4}$.

29. $\angle A \cong \angle D$, $\angle B \cong \angle E$, $\angle ACB \cong \angle DCE$

30. $\overline{AB} \leftrightarrow \overline{DE}$, $\overline{BC} \leftrightarrow \overline{EC}$, $\overline{CA} \leftrightarrow \overline{CD}$

17. **SPIDERS** A tarantula's body length is 5 centimeters. Choose an appropriate scale for a model of the spider that is to be just over 6 meters long. Use it to determine how long the tarantula's 9-centimeter legs should be. **Sample answer: 1 cm = 1.25 m; 11.25 m**

SPACE For Exercises 18 and 19, use the information in the table.

Astrological Body	Approximate Circumference
Earth	40,000 km
moon	11,000 km

18. You decide to use a basketball to represent Earth in a scale model of Earth and the moon. A basketball's circumference is about 30 inches. What is the scale of your model? **18. 3 in. = 4,000 km**

19. Which of the following should you use to represent the moon in your model? (The number in parentheses is the object's circumference.) Explain your reasoning. **See margin.**

    a. a soccer ball (28 in.)
    b. a tennis ball (8.25 in.)
    c. a golf ball (5.25 in.)
    d. a marble (4 in.)

20. **CONSTRUCT A SCALE DRAWING** Choose a large rectangular space such as the floor or wall of a room. Find its dimensions and choose an appropriate scale for a scale drawing of the space. Then construct a scale drawing and write a problem that uses your drawing. **See students' work.**

21. **NUMBER SENSE** One model of a building is built on a 1:75 scale. Another model of the same building is built on a 1:100 scale. Which model is larger? Explain your reasoning. **The model built on the 1:75 scale since $\frac{1}{75} > \frac{1}{100}$.**

22. **CRITICAL THINKING** Describe how you could find the scale of a map that did not have a scale printed on it. **See margin.**

Spiral Review with Standardized Test Practice

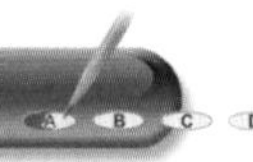

23. **MULTIPLE CHOICE** Using which scale would a scale model of a statue appear $\frac{1}{12}$ the size of the actual statue? **D**

    (A) 4 in. = 8 ft (B) 3 in. = 36 ft (C) 3 in. = 4 ft (D) 4 in. = 4 ft

24. **SHORT RESPONSE** The distance between San Antonio and Houston is $6\frac{3}{4}$ inches on a map with a scale of $\frac{1}{2}$ inch = 15 miles. About how long would it take to drive this distance going 60 miles per hour? **3 h 23 min**

25. Determine whether the polygons at the right are similar. Explain your reasoning. (Lesson 4-5) **Yes; see margin for explanation.**

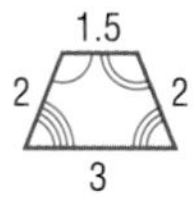

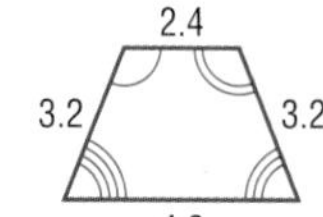

Solve each proportion. (Lesson 4-4)

26. $\frac{120}{b} = \frac{24}{60}$ **300**
27. $\frac{0.6}{5} = \frac{1.5}{n}$ **12.5**
28. $\frac{10}{6} = \frac{p}{26}$ **$43\frac{1}{3}$**

GETTING READY FOR THE NEXT LESSON

PREREQUISITE SKILL In the figure, $\triangle ABC \sim \triangle DEC$. (Lesson 4-5)

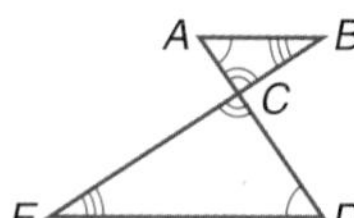

29. Identify the corresponding angles in the figure.
30. Identify the corresponding sides in the figure.

29–30. See margin.

msmath3.net/self_check_quiz

4 Assess

Higher-Level Thinking

When creating a scale drawing on a standard-sized piece of paper, what measurement should you use to determine your scale? Why?

Always begin with the longest measurement. That way you ensure you will have the appropriate space for the entire drawing.

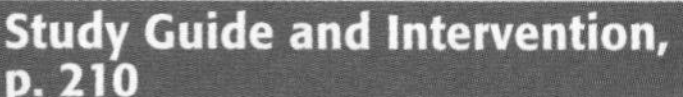

Study Guide and Intervention, p. 210

NAME ________ DATE ________ PERIOD ____

4-6 Study Guide and Intervention

Scale Drawings and Models

Distances on a scale drawing or model are proportional to real-life distances. The **scale** is determined by the ratio of a given length on a drawing or model to its corresponding actual length.

EXAMPLE 1 INTERIOR DESIGN **A designer has made a scale drawing of a living room for one of her clients. The scale of the drawing is 1 inch = $1\frac{1}{3}$ feet. On the drawing, the sofa is 6 inches long. Find the actual length of the sofa.**

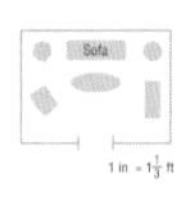

Let x represent the actual length of the sofa. Write and solve a proportion.

Drawing Scale → drawing distance → actual distance; Actual Length → drawing length → actual length

$\frac{1 \text{ in.}}{1\frac{1}{3} \text{ ft}} = \frac{6 \text{ in.}}{x \text{ ft}}$

$1 \cdot x = 1\frac{1}{3} \cdot 6$ Find the cross products.

$x = 8$ Simplify.

The actual length of the sofa is 8 feet.

To find the scale factor for scale drawings and models, write the ratio given by the scale in simplest form.

EXAMPLE 2 **Find the scale factor for the drawing in Example 1.**

Write the ratio of 1 inch to $1\frac{1}{3}$ feet in simplest form.

$\frac{1 \text{ in.}}{1\frac{1}{3} \text{ ft}} = \frac{1 \text{ in.}}{16 \text{ in.}}$ Convert $1\frac{1}{3}$ feet to inches.

The scale factor is $\frac{1}{16}$ or 1:16. This means that each distance on the drawing is $\frac{1}{16}$ the actual distance.

EXERCISES

LANDSCAPING **Yutaka has made a scale drawing of his yard. The scale of the drawing is 1 centimeter = 0.5 meter.**

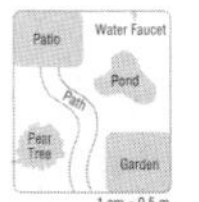

1. The length of the patio is 4.5 centimeters in the drawing. Find the actual length. **2.25 m**
2. The actual distance between the water faucet and the pear tree is 11.2 meters. Find the corresponding distance on the drawing. **22.4 cm**
3. Find the scale factor for the drawing. **$\frac{1}{50}$**

Practice: Skills, p. 211

NAME ________ DATE ________ PERIOD ____

4-6 Practice: Skills

Scale Drawings and Models

ARCHITECTURE **The scale on a set of architectural drawings for a house is 1.5 inches = 2 feet. Find the length of each part of the house.**

	Room	Drawing Length	Actual Length
1.	Living Room	15 inches	**20 ft**
2.	Dining Room	10.5 inches	**14 ft**
3.	Kitchen	$12\frac{3}{4}$ inches	**17 ft**
4.	Laundry Room	$8\frac{1}{4}$ inches	**11 ft**
5.	Hall	$13\frac{7}{8}$ inches	**18.5 ft**
6.	Garage	16.5 inches	**22 ft**

7. What is the scale factor of these drawings? **$\frac{1}{16}$**

TOWN PLANNING **For Exercises 8–11, use the following information.**

As part of a downtown renewal project, businesses have constructed a scale model of the town square to present to the city commission for its approval. The scale of the model is 1 inch = 7 feet.

8. The courthouse is the tallest building in the town square. If it is $5\frac{1}{2}$ inches tall in the model, how tall is the actual building? **$38\frac{1}{2}$ ft**
9. The business owners would like to install new lampposts that are each 12 feet tall. How tall are the lampposts in the model? **$1\frac{5}{7}$ in.**
10. In the model, the lampposts are $3\frac{3}{7}$ inches apart. How far apart will they be when they are installed? **24 ft**
11. What is the scale factor? **$\frac{1}{84}$**
12. MAPS On a map, two cities are $6\frac{1}{2}$ inches apart. The actual distance between the cities is 104 miles. What is the scale of the map? **1 in. = 16 mi**

Practice: Word Problems, p. 212

NAME ________ DATE ________ PERIOD ____

4-6 Practice: Word Problems

Scale Drawings and Models

CAMPUS PLANNING **For Exercises 1–3, use the following information.**

The local school district has made a scale model of the campus of Engels Middle School including a proposed new building. The scale of the model is 1 inch = 3 feet.

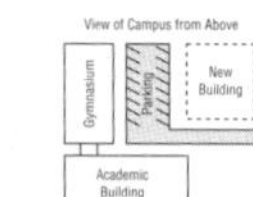

1. An existing gymnasium is 8 inches tall in the model. How tall is the actual gymnasium? **24 ft**
2. The new building is 22.5 inches from the gymnasium in the model. What will be the actual distance from the gymnasium to the new building if it is built? **67.5 ft**
3. What is the scale factor of the model? **$\frac{1}{36}$**
4. MAPS On a map, two cities are $5\frac{3}{4}$ inches apart. The scale of the map is $\frac{1}{2}$ inch = 3 miles. What is the actual distance between the towns? **$34\frac{1}{2}$ mi**
5. TRUCKS The bed of Jerry's pickup truck is 6 feet long. On a scale model of the truck, the bed is 8 inches long. What is the scale of the model? 6 ft **1 in. = $\frac{3}{4}$ ft**
6. HOUSING Marta is making a scale drawing of her apartment for a school project. The apartment is 28 feet wide. On her drawing, the apartment is 7 inches wide. What is the scale of Marta's drawing? **1 in. = 4 ft** 28 ft

4-7 Lesson Notes

Lesson Resources

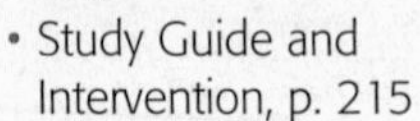

Chapter 4 Resource Masters
- Study Guide and Intervention, p. 215
- Practice: Skills, p. 216
- Practice: Word Problems, p. 217
- Reading to Learn Mathematics, p. 218
- Enrichment, p. 219

Key Teaching Transparencies, 15
Parent and Student Study Guide Online Worksheets, 4-7
Noteables™: Interactive Study Notebook with Foldables™, 4-7

1 Focus

5-Minute Check 4-7

Use as a quiz or review of Lesson 4-6. (Also available as a transparency)

Bellringer

Problem Solving Draw the similar triangles shown below on the chalkboard. Ask students to find $\overline{XY}$ by solving a proportion. **32 cm**

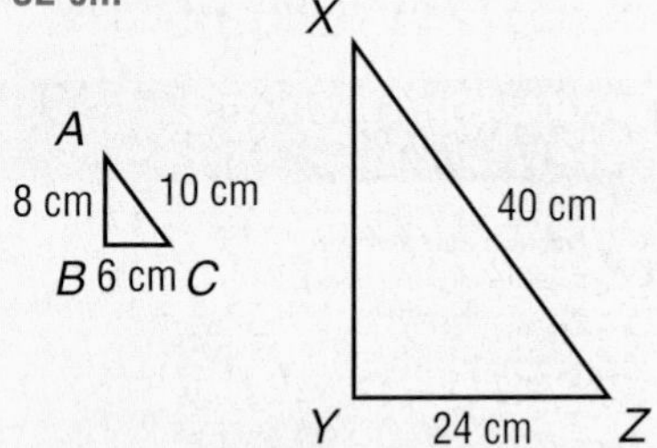

Reading to Learn Mathematics, p. 218 **ELL**

4-7 **Reading to Learn Mathematics**
Indirect Measurement

NAME ______ DATE ______ PERIOD ______

Pre-Activity *Read the introduction at the top of page 188 in your textbook. Write your answers below.*

1. How is the caveman measuring the distance to the Sun? **He is measuring the distance as if it were a flat surface directly in front of him.**

Reading the Lesson

2. Complete the following sentence.
When you solve a problem using shadow reckoning, the objects being compared and their shadows form two sides of ______. **similar triangles**

3. Su... that you are standi... near a building and you ... the shadows ...nd the h...

4-7 Indirect Measurement

WHEN am I ever going to use this?

COMICS The caveman is trying to measure the distance to the Sun.

1. How is the caveman measuring the distance to the Sun? **See margin.**

What You'll LEARN
Solve problems involving similar triangles.

NEW Vocabulary
indirect measurement

Distances or lengths that are difficult to measure directly can sometimes be found using the properties of similar polygons and proportions. This kind of measurement is called **indirect measurement**.

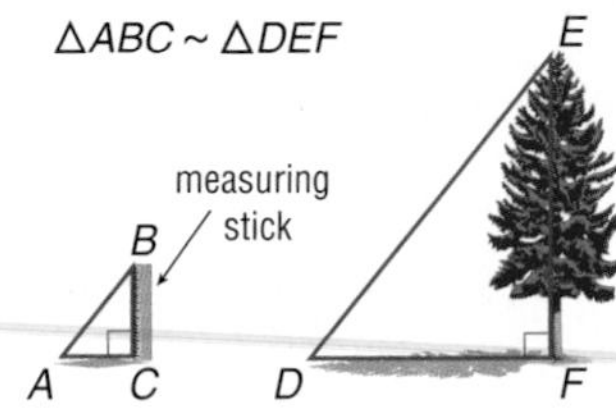

One type of indirect measurement is called *shadow reckoning*. Two objects and their shadows form two sides of similar triangles from which a proportion can be written.

$$\text{stick's shadow} \rightarrow \frac{AC}{DF} = \frac{BC}{EF} \leftarrow \text{stick's height}$$
$$\text{tree's shadow} \rightarrow \qquad\qquad \leftarrow \text{tree's height}$$

EXAMPLE **Use Shadow Reckoning**

1 **FLAGS** One of the tallest flagpoles in the U.S. is in Winsted, Minnesota. At the same time of day that Karen's shadow was about 0.8 meter, the flagpole's shadow was about 33.6 meters. If Karen is 1.5 meters tall, how tall is Winsted's flagpole?

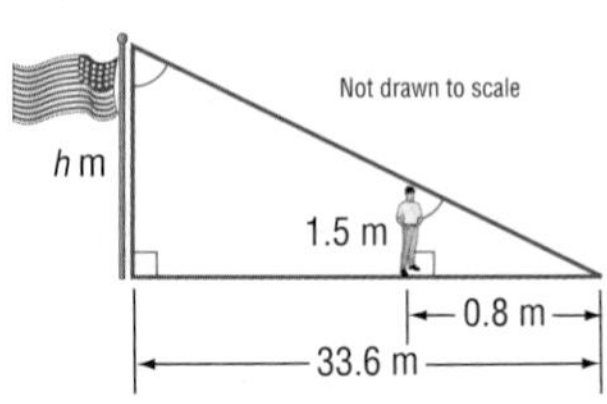

Karen's shadow → / flagpole's shadow → $\frac{0.8}{33.6} = \frac{1.5}{h}$ ← Karen's height / ← flagpole's height

$0.8h = 33.6 \cdot 1.5$ Find the cross products.

$0.8h = 50.4$ Multiply.

$\frac{0.8x}{0.8} = \frac{50.4}{0.8}$ Divide each side by 0.8

$x = 63$ Use a calculator.

The flagpole is 63 meters tall.

STUDY TIP

Mental Math
Karen's height is about 2 times her shadow's length. So the flagpole's height is about 2 times its shadow's length.

Answer (When am I ever going to use this?)

1. **He is measuring the distance as if it were a flat surface directly in front of him.**

Answer

1. $\frac{14}{5} = \frac{h}{6}$

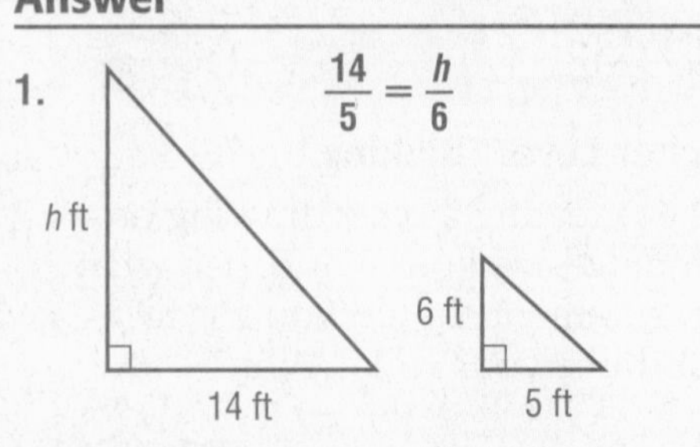

You can also use similar triangles that do not involve shadows to find missing measurements.

EXAMPLE Use Indirect Measurement

SURVEYING The two triangles shown in the figure are similar. Find the distance d across Coyote Ravine.

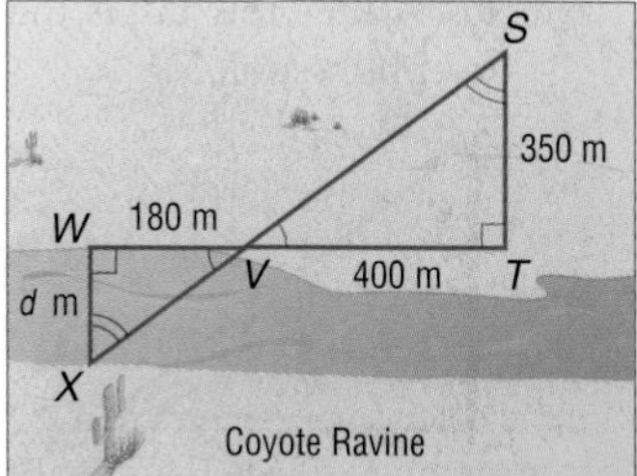

In the figure, $\triangle STV \sim \triangle XWV$. So, $\overline{ST}$ corresponds to $\overline{XW}$, and $\overline{TV}$ corresponds to $\overline{WV}$.

$\frac{ST}{XW} = \frac{TV}{WV}$ Write a proportion.

$\frac{350}{d} = \frac{400}{180}$ $ST = 350$, $XW = d$, $TV = 400$, and $WV = 180$

$350 \cdot 180 = d \cdot 400$ Find the cross products.

$\frac{63{,}000}{400} = \frac{400d}{400}$ Multiply. Then divide each side by 400.

$157.5 = d$ Use a calculator.

The distance across the ravine is 157.5 meters.

TEACHING TIP

Remind students to use the arc symbols in a diagram to match up the corresponding vertices of the triangles. Then write a statement of similarity.

Students practice the same concepts in Exercises 6–15 if they are assigned odd or even problems.

Skill and Concept Check

1. **Draw and label** similar triangles to illustrate the following problem. Then write an appropriate proportion. **See margin.**
A building's shadow is 14 feet long, and a street sign's shadow is 5 feet long. If the street sign is 6 feet tall, how tall is the building?

2. **OPEN ENDED** Write a problem that requires shadow reckoning. Explain how to solve the problem. **See margin.**

GUIDED PRACTICE

In Exercises 3 and 4, the triangles are similar. Write a proportion and solve the problem.

3. **ARCHITECTURE** How tall is the pyramid? $\frac{0.6}{56} = \frac{1.5}{h}$; **140 m**

Not drawn to scale

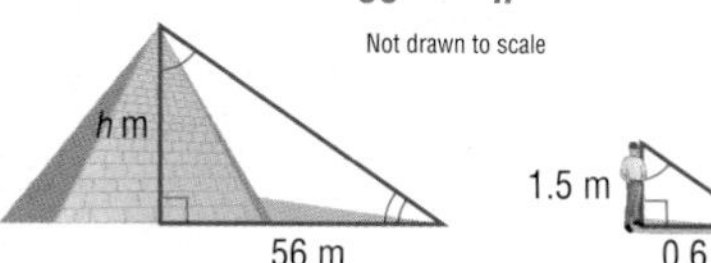

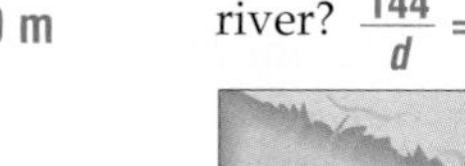

4. **BRIDGES** How far is it across the river? $\frac{144}{d} = \frac{150}{125}$; **120 ft**

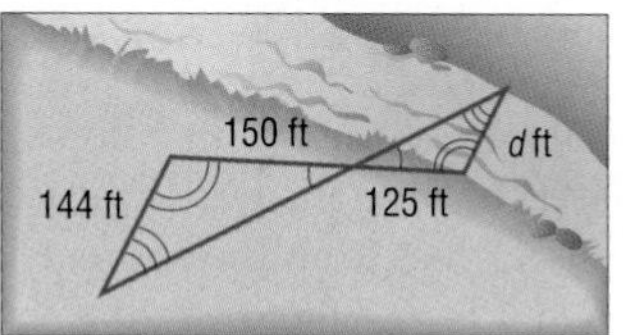

5. A building casts a 18.5-foot shadow. How tall is the building if a 10-foot tall sculpture nearby casts a 7-foot shadow? Draw a diagram of the situation. Then write a proportion and solve the problem. **See margin for diagram; $\frac{h}{18.5} = \frac{10}{7}$; about 26 ft.**

msmath3.net/extra_examples

2 Teach

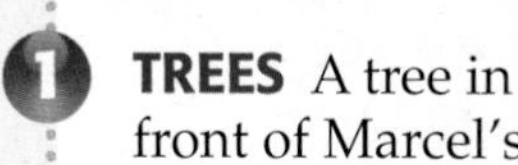

In-Class Examples

1. **TREES** A tree in front of Marcel's house has a shadow 12 feet long. At the same time, Marcel has a shadow 3 feet long. If Marcel is 5.5 feet tall, how tall is the tree? **22 ft**

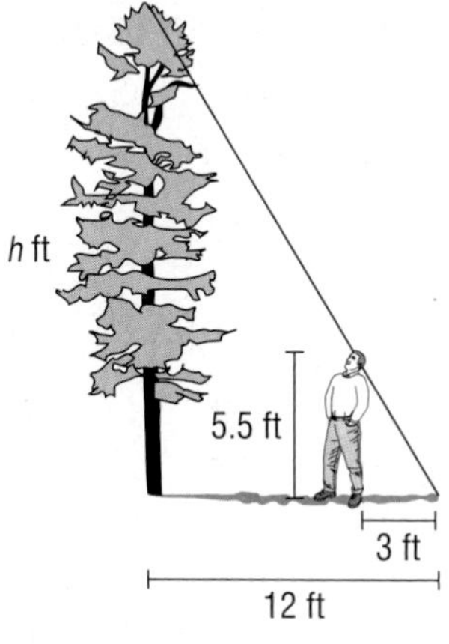

2. **SURVEYING** The two triangles shown in the figure are similar. Find the distance d across the stream. **16 m**

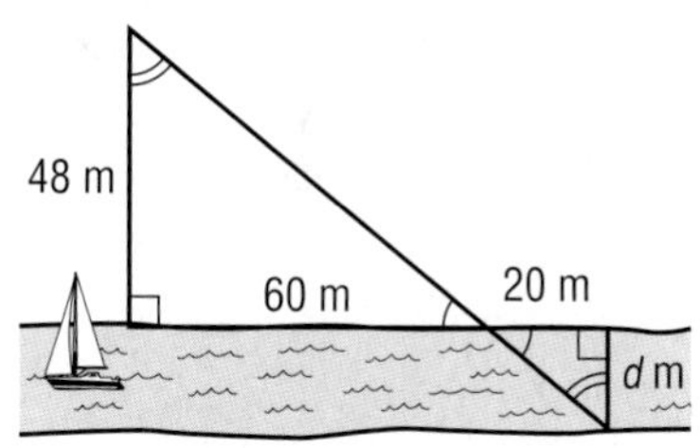

DAILY INTERVENTION

Differentiated Instruction

Naturalist Students may gain a better understanding of how to measure indirectly by going outside and measuring the heights of trees and buildings using *shadow reckoning*. To do this, they will need a meterstick or yardstick and a sunny day. Have them measure shadows and draw a diagram for their data as shown on page 188.

Answers

2. Sample answer: At the same time a baby giraffe casts a 3.2-foot shadow, a 15-foot adult giraffe casts an 8-foot shadow. How tall is the baby giraffe? Solving the proportion $\frac{x}{3.2} = \frac{15}{8}$ gives a height of 6 ft for the baby giraffe.

5. h ft, 18.5 ft; 10 ft, 7 ft

3 Practice/Apply

About the Exercises...

Guided Practice Key

Exercises	Examples
3, 5	1
4	2

Assignment Guide

Basic: 7, 11, 13, 16–37

Average: 7–15 odd, 16–37

Enriched: 6–14 even, 16–33 (Optional: 34–37)

Answers

10.

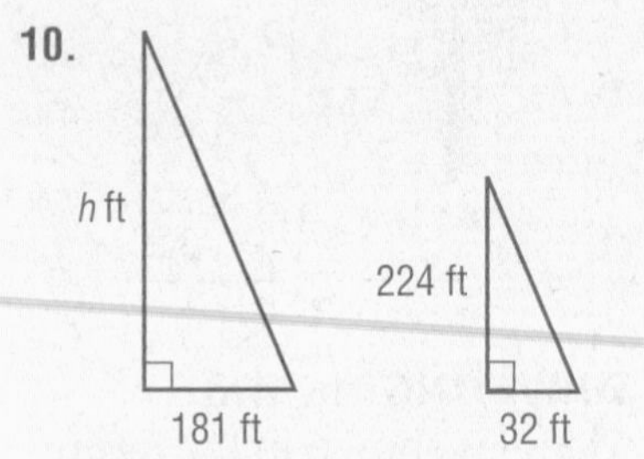

11.

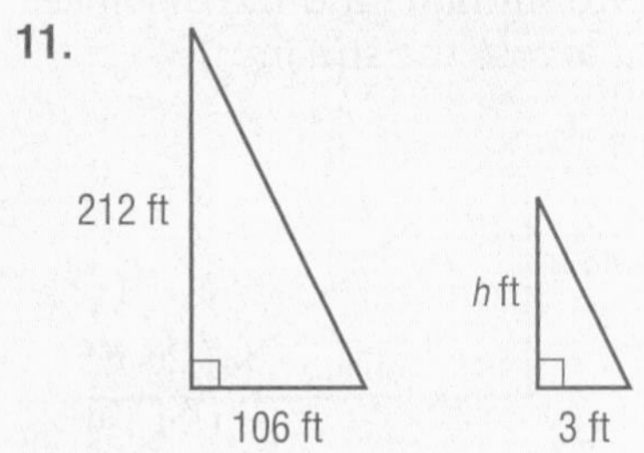

12.

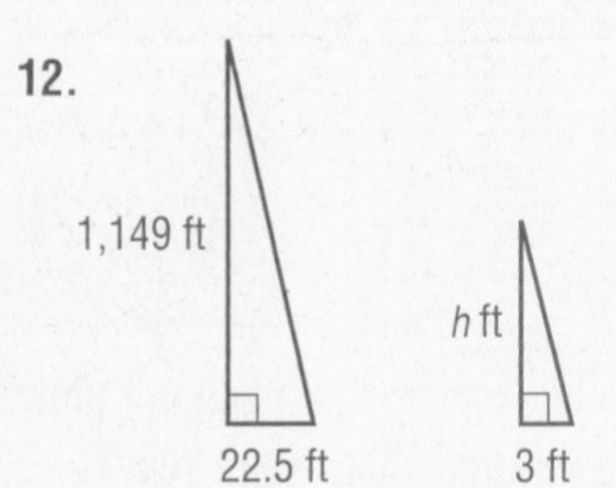

13.

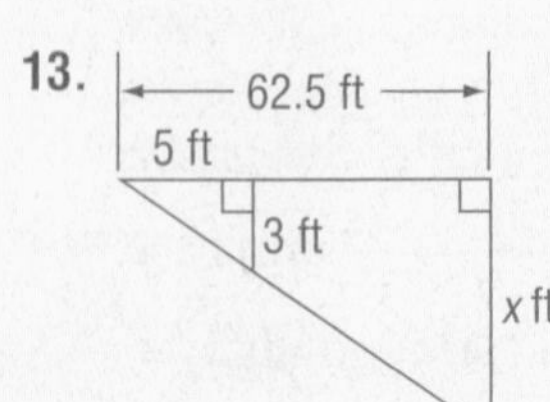

14.

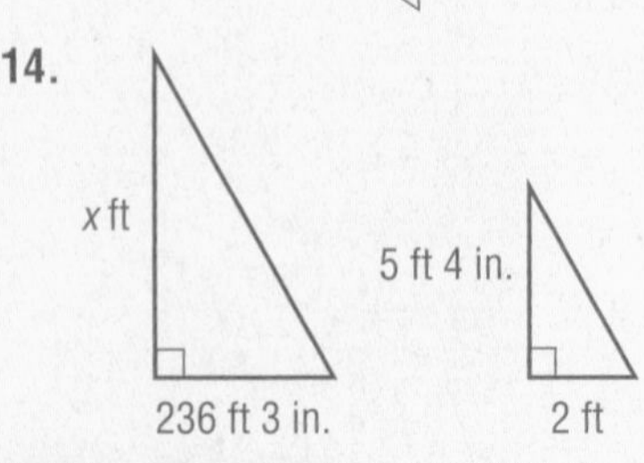

★ indicates increased difficulty

Practice and Applications

HOMEWORK HELP

For Exercises	See Examples
6–7, 10–12, 14	1
8–9, 13, 15	2

Extra Practice See pages 626, 651.

In Exercises 6–9, the triangles are similar. Write a proportion and solve the problem.

6. **REPAIRS** How tall is the telephone pole? $\frac{h}{2} = \frac{12.3}{3}$; 8.2 m

h m | 2 m | 12.3 m | 3 m

7. **LIGHTHOUSE** How tall is the house? $\frac{248}{h} = \frac{186}{9}$; 12 ft

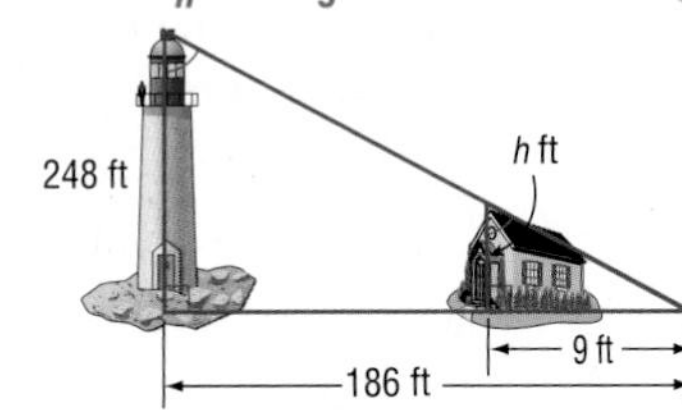

8. **ZOO** How far are the elephants from the aquarium? $\frac{68}{17} = \frac{x}{20}$; 80 m

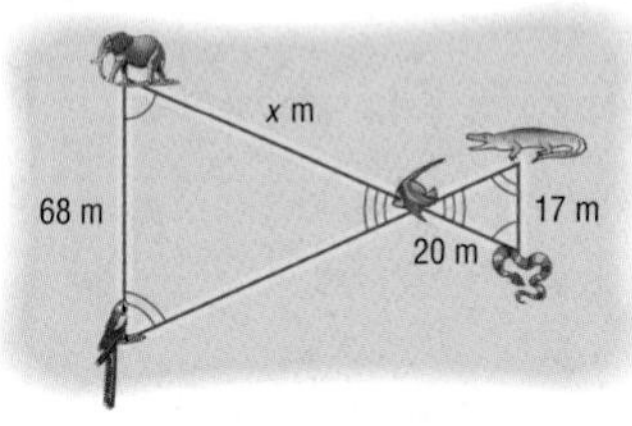

★9. **SURVEYING** How far is it across Mallard Pond? (*Hint*: $\triangle ABC \sim \triangle ADE$)

$\frac{135}{252} = \frac{204}{d}$; 380.8 ft

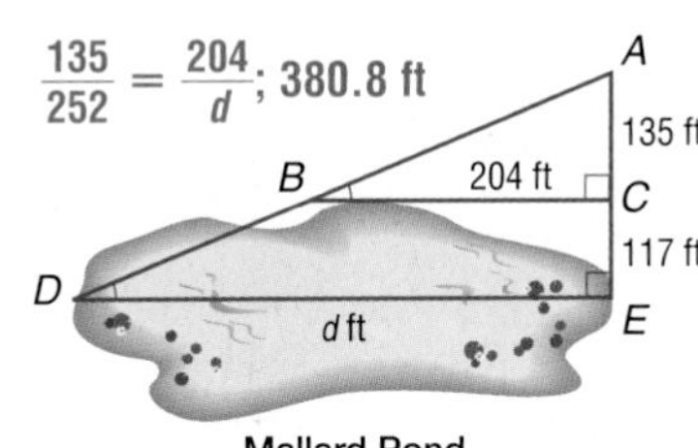

For Exercises 10–15, draw a diagram of the situation. Then write a proportion and solve the problem. 10–14. See margin for diagrams.

10. **NATIONAL MONUMENT** Devil's Tower in Wyoming was the United States' first national monument. At the same time this natural rock formation casts a 181-foot shadow, a nearby 224-foot tree casts a 32-foot shadow. How tall is the monument? $\frac{32}{181} = \frac{224}{h}$; 1,267 ft

11. **FAIR** Reaching 212 feet tall, the *Texas Star* at Fair Park in Dallas, Texas, is the tallest Ferris wheel in the United States. A man standing near this Ferris wheel casts a 3-foot shadow. At the same time, the Ferris wheel's shadow is 106 feet long. How tall is the man? $\frac{3}{106} = \frac{h}{212}$; 6 ft

12. **TOWER** The Stratosphere Tower in Las Vegas is the tallest free-standing observation tower in the United States. If the tower casts a 22.5-foot shadow, about how tall is a nearby flagpole that casts a 3-foot shadow? Use the information at the right. $\frac{22.5}{3} = \frac{1{,}149}{h}$; 153.2 ft

Stratosphere Hotel Facts

Floor 108 Indoor observation deck of 1,149-foot tall tower

Floor 112 World's highest roller coaster, the *High Roller*

Floor 113 *Big Shot* ride shoots riders 160 feet up tower mast in 2.5 seconds, allowing them to free-fall back to the launch pad

13. **LAKES** From the shoreline, the ground slopes down under the water at a constant incline. If the water is 3 feet deep when it is 5 feet from the shore, about how deep will it be when it is 62.5 feet from the shore?

13. $\frac{3}{x} = \frac{5}{62.5}$; 37.5 ft

★14. **LANDMARKS** The Gateway to the West Arch in St. Louis casts a shadow that is 236 foot 3 inches. At the same time, a 5 foot 4 inch tall tourist casts a 2-foot shadow. How tall is the arch? $\frac{236\frac{1}{4}}{2} = \frac{x}{5\frac{1}{3}}$; 630 ft

15.

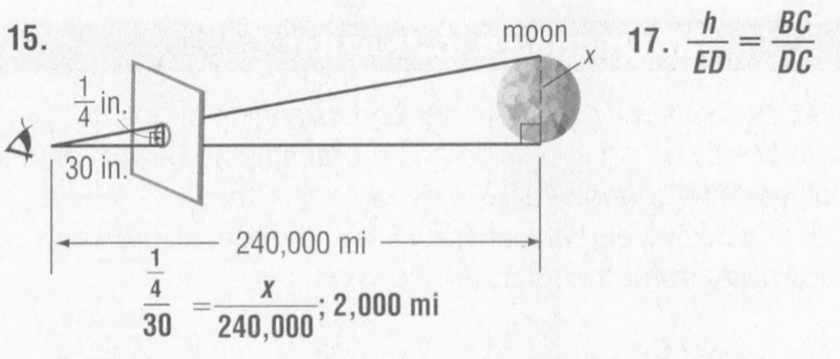

$\frac{\frac{1}{4}}{30} = \frac{x}{240{,}000}$; 2,000 mi

17. $\frac{h}{ED} = \frac{BC}{DC}$

★15. **SPACE SCIENCE** You cut a square hole $\frac{1}{4}$ inch wide in a piece of cardboard. With the cardboard 30 inches from your face, the moon fits exactly into the square hole. The moon is about 240,000 miles from Earth. Estimate the moon's diameter. Draw a diagram of the situation. Then write a proportion and solve the problem. **See margin.**

CRITICAL THINKING For Exercises 16–18, use the following information.

Another method of indirect measurement involves the use of a mirror as shown in the diagram at the right. The two triangles in the diagram are similar. **16. $\triangle ABC \sim \triangle EDC$**

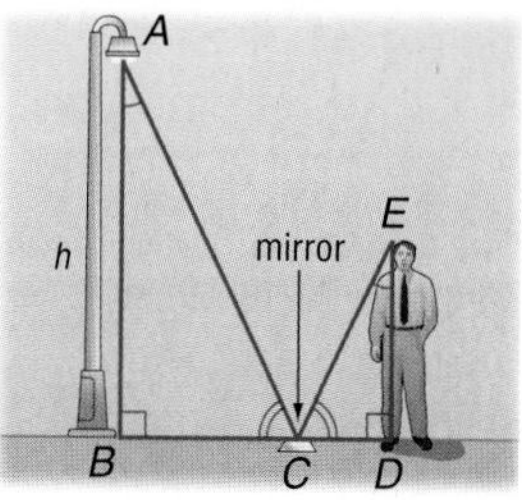

16. Write a statement of similarity between the two triangles.
17. Write a proportion that could be used to solve for the height h of the light pole. **See margin.**
18. What information would you need to know in order to solve this proportion? **The distance from the mirror to the person, the distance from the mirror to the base of the light pole, the height of the person's eyes.**

Spiral Review with Standardized Test Practice

19. **MULTIPLE CHOICE** A child $4\frac{1}{2}$ feet tall casts a 6-foot shadow. A nearby statue casts a 12-foot shadow. How tall is the statue? **B**

    (A) $8\frac{1}{4}$ ft (B) 9 ft (C) $13\frac{1}{2}$ ft (D) 24 ft

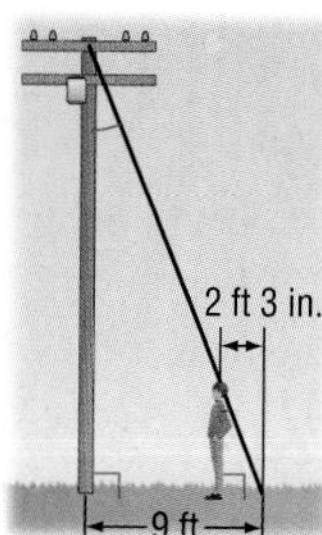

20. **GRID IN** A guy wire attached to the top of a telephone pole goes to the ground 9 feet from its base. When Jorge stands under the guy wire so that his head touches the wire, he is 2 feet 3 inches from where the wire goes into the ground. If Jorge is 5 feet tall, how tall in feet is the telephone pole? **20**

On a city map, the scale is 1 centimeter = 2.5 miles. Find the actual distance for each map distance. (Lesson 4-6)

21. 4 cm **10 mi** 22. 10 cm **25 mi** 23. 13 cm **32.5 mi** 24. 8.5 cm **21.25 mi**

25. The triangles at the right are similar. Write a proportion to find the missing measure. Then solve. (Lesson 4-5) **$\frac{4.5}{m} = \frac{3}{8}$; 12**

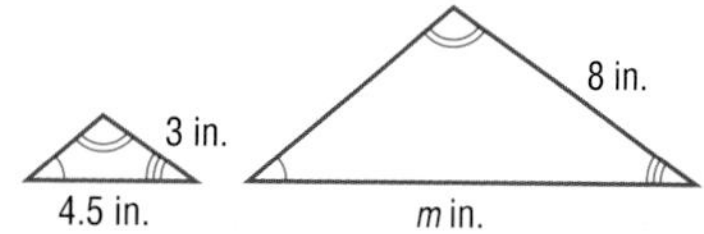

Solve each equation. Check your solution. (Lesson 2-7)

26. $\frac{2}{3}x + 4 = -6$ **−15** 27. $a - 2\frac{3}{5} = -6\frac{7}{10}$ **$-4\frac{1}{10}$** 28. $-2.3 = \frac{k}{-8}$ **18.4** 29. $-4\frac{1}{2}x = 6$ **$-1\frac{1}{3}$**

Express each number in scientific notation. (Lesson 2-9)

30. 0.0000236 **2.36×10^{-5}** 31. 4,300,000 **4.3×10^{6}** 32. 504,000 **5.04×10^{5}** 33. 0.0000002 **2.0×10^{-7}**

GETTING READY FOR THE NEXT LESSON

PREREQUISITE SKILL Graph each pair of ordered pairs. Then find the distance between the points. (Lesson 3-6) **34–37. See Ch. 4 Answer Appendix.**

34. (3, 4), (3, 8) 35. (−2, −1), (6, −1) 36. (1, 4), (5, 1) 37. (−1, −2), (4, 10)

msmath3.net/self_check_quiz

4 Assess

Higher-Level Thinking

When shadows are used for indirect measurement, both shadows must be measured at the same time. Explain why this is so.

Since the angle of the Sun determines the length of the shadow, the Sun must be in the same position and, therefore, at the same angle when measurements are taken.

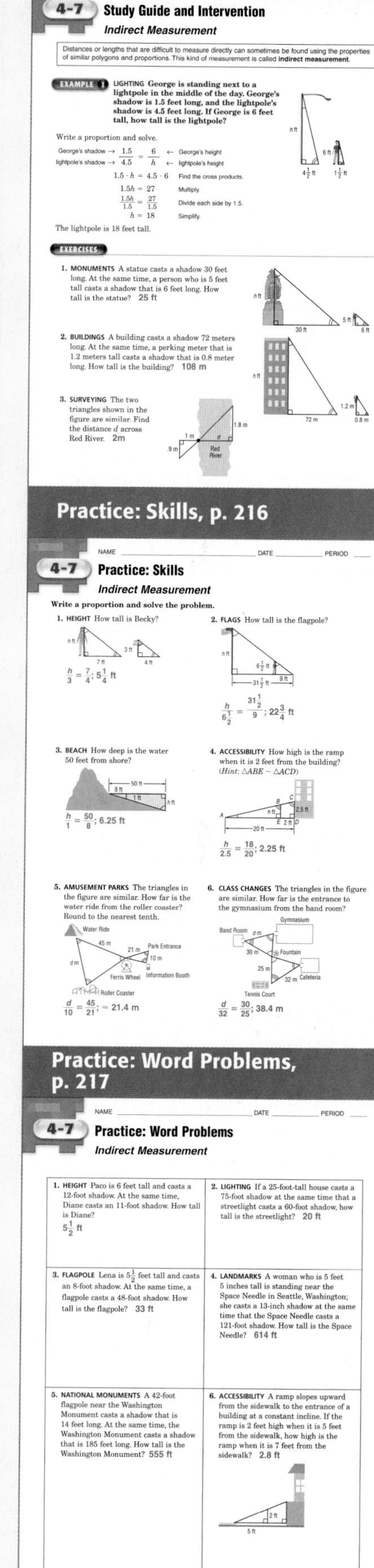

Study Guide and Intervention, p. 215

NAME ______ DATE ______ PERIOD ____

4-7 Study Guide and Intervention

Indirect Measurement

Distances or lengths that are difficult to measure directly can sometimes be found using the properties of similar polygons and proportions. This kind of measurement is called **indirect measurement**.

EXAMPLE 1 LIGHTING **George is standing next to a lightpole in the middle of the day. George's shadow is 1.5 feet long, and the lightpole's shadow is 4.5 feet long. If George is 6 feet tall, how tall is the lightpole?**

Write a proportion and solve.

George's shadow → $\frac{1.5}{4.5} = \frac{6}{h}$ ← George's height; lightpole's shadow → (denominator) ← lightpole's height

$1.5 \cdot h = 4.5 \cdot 6$ Find the cross products.

$1.5h = 27$ Multiply.

$\frac{1.5h}{1.5} = \frac{27}{1.5}$ Divide each side by 1.5.

$h = 18$ Simplify.

The lightpole is 18 feet tall.

EXERCISES

1. MONUMENTS A statue casts a shadow 30 feet long. At the same time, a person who is 5 feet tall casts a shadow that is 6 feet long. How tall is the statue? **25 ft**
2. BUILDINGS A building casts a shadow 72 meters long. At the same time, a perking meter that is 1.2 meters tall casts a shadow that is 0.8 meter long. How tall is the building? **108 m**
3. SURVEYING The two triangles shown in the figure are similar. Find the distance d across Red River. **2m**

Practice: Skills, p. 216

NAME ______ DATE ______ PERIOD ____

4-7 Practice: Skills

Indirect Measurement

Write a proportion and solve the problem.

1. HEIGHT How tall is Becky? **$\frac{h}{3} = \frac{7}{4}$; $5\frac{1}{4}$ ft**
2. FLAGS How tall is the flagpole? **$\frac{h}{6\frac{1}{2}} = \frac{31\frac{1}{2}}{9}$; $22\frac{3}{4}$ ft**
3. BEACH How deep is the water 50 feet from shore? **$\frac{h}{1} = \frac{50}{8}$; 6.25 ft**
4. ACCESSIBILITY How high is the ramp when it is 2 feet from the building? (*Hint*: $\triangle ABE \sim \triangle ACD$) **$\frac{h}{2.5} = \frac{18}{20}$; 2.25 ft**
5. AMUSEMENT PARKS The triangles in the figure are similar. How far is the water ride from the roller coaster? Round to the nearest tenth. **$\frac{d}{10} = \frac{45}{21}$; ≈ 21.4 m**
6. CLASS CHANGES The triangles in the figure are similar. How far is the entrance to the gymnasium from the band room? **$\frac{d}{32} = \frac{30}{25}$; 38.4 m**

Practice: Word Problems, p. 217

NAME ______ DATE ______ PERIOD ____

4-7 Practice: Word Problems

Indirect Measurement

1. HEIGHT Paco is 6 feet tall and casts a 12-foot shadow. At the same time, Diane casts an 11-foot shadow. How tall is Diane? **$5\frac{1}{2}$ ft**
2. LIGHTING If a 25-foot-tall house casts a 75-foot shadow at the same time that a streetlight casts a 60-foot shadow, how tall is the streetlight? **20 ft**
3. FLAGPOLE Lena is $5\frac{1}{2}$ feet tall and casts an 8-foot shadow. At the same time, a flagpole casts a 48-foot shadow. How tall is the flagpole? **33 ft**
4. LANDMARKS A woman who is 5 feet 5 inches tall is standing near the Space Needle in Seattle, Washington; she casts a 13-inch shadow at the same time that the Space Needle casts a 121-foot shadow. How tall is the Space Needle? **614 ft**
5. NATIONAL MONUMENTS A 42-foot flagpole near the Washington Monument casts a shadow that is 14 feet long. At the same time, the Washington Monument casts a shadow that is 185 feet long. How tall is the Washington Monument? **555 ft**
6. ACCESSIBILITY A ramp slopes upward from the sidewalk to the entrance of a building at a constant incline. If the ramp is 2 feet high when it is 5 feet from the sidewalk, how high is the ramp when it is 7 feet from the sidewalk? **2.8 ft**

4-7b HANDS-ON LAB

Lesson Notes

Lesson Resources

Teaching Mathematics with Manipulatives

- protractor, p. 21
- student recording sheet 4-7b

Glencoe Mathematics Classroom Manipulative Kit

- protractor
- ruler

GETTING STARTED

Teaching Tip You may want to create an overhead transparency for students to record their results for sine, cosine, and tangent. This will allow students to compare results easily.

TEACH

- Make sure students fully understand the terms *opposite* and *adjacent* before beginning the activity.
- If necessary, you should review with students how to draw with a protractor.
- If time is short, have half of the students complete the activity for a 30° angle and the other half complete it for a 60° angle.

TEACHING TIP

Students can learn more about trigonometry in the Student Handbook on pages 678–685.

4-7b HANDS-ON LAB

A Follow-Up of Lesson 4-7

Trigonometry

What You'll LEARN

Solve problems by using the trigonometric ratios of sine, cosine, and tangent.

Materials

- protractor
- metric rule
- calculator

INVESTIGATE *Work in groups of three.*

Trigonometry is the study of the properties of triangles. The word trigonometry means *triangle measure.* A **trigonometric ratio** is the ratio of the lengths of two sides of a right triangle.

In this Lab you will discover and apply the most common trigonometric ratios: *sine, cosine,* and *tangent.*

In any right triangle, the side **opposite** an angle is the side that is not part of the angle. In the triangle shown,

- side a is opposite $\angle A$,
- side b is opposite $\angle B$, and
- side c is opposite $\angle C$.

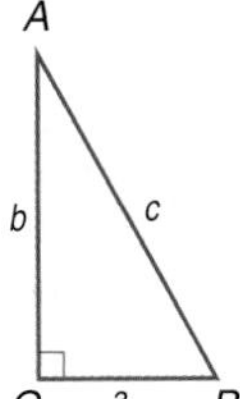

The side that is not opposite an angle and not the hypotenuse is called the **adjacent** side. In $\triangle ABC$,

- side b is adjacent to $\angle A$, and
- side a is adjacent to $\angle B$.

Each person in the group should complete steps 1–6.

STEP 1 Copy the table shown.

	30° angle	60° angle
Length (mm) of opposite leg		
Length (mm) of adjacent leg		
Length (mm) of hypotenuse		
sine		
cosine		
tangent		

STEP 2 Draw a right triangle XYZ so that $m\angle X = 30°$, $m\angle Y = 60°$, and $m\angle Z = 90°$.

STEP 3 Find the length to the nearest millimeter of the leg opposite the angle that measures 30°. Record the length.

STEP 4 Find the length of the leg adjacent to the 30° angle. Record the length.

STEP 5 Find the length of the hypotenuse. Record the length.

STEP 6 Use the measurements and a calculator to find each of the following ratios to the nearest hundredth. Notice that each of these ratios has a special name.

$$\textbf{sine} = \frac{\text{opposite}}{\text{hypotenuse}} \quad \textbf{cosine} = \frac{\text{adjacent}}{\text{hypotenuse}} \quad \textbf{tangent} = \frac{\text{opposite}}{\text{adjacent}}$$

STEP 7 Compare your ratios with the others in your group.

STEP 8 Repeat the procedure for the 60° angle. Record the results.

Writing Math

Work with your group.

1. **Make a conjecture** about the ratio of the sides of any 30°-60°-90° triangle.
2. **Repeat the activity** with a triangle whose angles measure 45°, 45°, and 90°. **See students' work.**
3. **Make a conjecture** about the ratio of the sides of any 45°-45°-90° triangle. **sin 45° = 0.707, cos 45° = 0.707, tan 45° = 1**

1. sin 30° = 0.5, cos 30° = 0.866, sin 60° = 0.866, cos 60° = 0.5, tan 30° = 0.577, tan 60° = 1.732

Use triangle *ABC* to find each of the following ratios to the nearest hundredth.

4. cosine of $\angle A$ **0.8**
5. sine of $\angle A$ **0.6**
6. tangent of $\angle A$ **0.75**

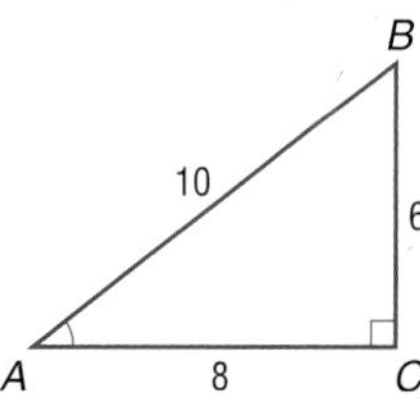

You can use a scientific calculator to find the sine SIN, cosine COS, or tangent TAN ratio for an angle with a given degree measure. Be sure your calculator is in *degree* mode. Find each value to the nearest thousandth.

7. sin 46° **0.719**
8. cos 63° **0.454**
9. tan 82° **7.115**
10. **SHADOWS** An *angle of elevation* is formed by a horizontal line and a line of sight above it. A flagpole casts a shadow 35 meters long when the angle of elevation of the Sun is 50°. How tall is the flagpole? (*Hint*: Use the tangent ratio.) **41.71 m**
11. **Describe** a triangle whose sine and cosine ratios are equal. **a 45°-45°-90° triangle**

line of sight

x m

50°

35 m

ASSESS

Discuss the **Writing Math** exercises. Students should recognize that the sine, cosine, and tangent of an angle will be the same regardless of the size of the triangle. If students have difficulty with Exercise 10, you may want to solve it as a group and create additional problems for them to solve on their own.

Lesson 4-7b Hands-On Lab: Trigonometry **193**

4-8 Lesson Notes

Lesson Resources

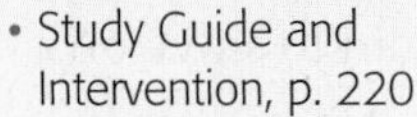

Chapter 4 Resource Masters
- Study Guide and Intervention, p. 220
- Practice: Skills, p. 221
- Practice: Word Problems, p. 222
- Reading to Learn Mathematics, p. 223
- Enrichment, p. 224

Calculator and Spreadsheet Masters, p. 24
Key Teaching Transparencies, 16
Parent and Student Study Guide Online Worksheets, 4-8
Real-Life Career Masters, p. 30
Teaching Math with Manipulatives, pp. 53–54
Noteables™: Interactive Study Notebook with Foldables™, 4-8
Virtual Activities CD-ROM, Dilations

1 Focus

5-Minute Check 4-8

Use as a quiz or review of Lesson 4-7. (Also available as a transparency)

Bellringer

Reading Mathematics Ask students how a scale factor can change a polygon. Then have them read the everyday meaning of the word *dilation* on this page and ask them to speculate about the relationships among polygons, scale factors, and dilations.

Reading to Learn Mathematics, p. 223 ELL

NAME ______ DATE ______ PERIOD ______

4-8 Reading to Learn Mathematics

Dilations

Pre-Activity *Complete the Mini Lab at the top of page 194 in your textbook. Write your answers below.*

1. Multiply each coordinate by 2 to find the coordinates of points A', B', and C'. **A′(0, 0), B′(2, 8), C′(8, 6)**
2. On the same coordinate plane, graph points A', B', and C'. Then draw $\triangle A'B'C'$.
3. Determine whether $\triangle ABC \sim \triangle A'B'C'$. Explain your reasoning. **Yes; corresponding sides of the two triangles are proportional.**

4-8 Dilations

What You'll LEARN

Graph dilations on a coordinate plane.

NEW Vocabulary

dilation

Link to READING

Everyday Meaning of dilation: the act of enlarging or expanding, as in dilating the pupils of your eyes

HANDS-ON Mini Lab

Materials
- graph paper
- ruler

Work with a partner.

Plot $A(0, 0)$, $B(1, 4)$, and $C(4, 3)$ on a coordinate plane. Then draw $\triangle ABC$.

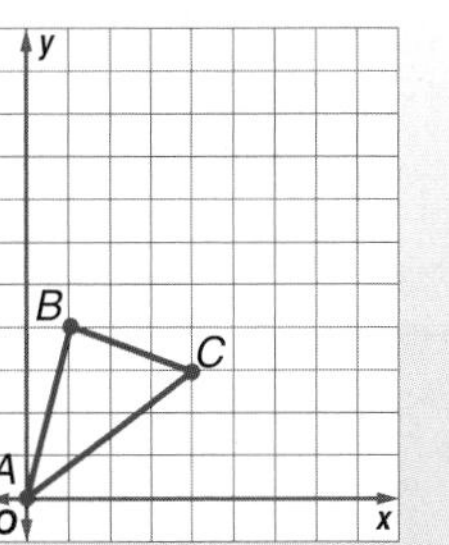

1. Multiply each coordinate by 2 to find the coordinates of points A', B', and C'. **A′(0, 0), B′(2, 8), C′(8, 6)**
2. On the same coordinate plane, graph points A', B', and C'. Then draw $\triangle A'B'C'$. **See margin.**
3. Determine whether $\triangle ABC \sim \triangle A'B'C'$. Explain your reasoning. **See margin.**

In mathematics, the image produced by enlarging or reducing a figure is called a **dilation**. In the Mini Lab, $\triangle A'B'C'$ has the same shape as $\triangle ABC$, so the two figures are similar. Recall that similar figures are related by a scale factor.

EXAMPLE Graph a Dilation

1 **Graph $\triangle JKL$ with vertices $J(3, 8)$, $K(10, 6)$, and $L(8, 2)$. Then graph its image $\triangle J'K'L'$ after a dilation with a scale factor of $\frac{1}{2}$.**

To find the vertices of the dilation, multiply each coordinate in the ordered pairs by $\frac{1}{2}$. Then graph both images on the same axes.

$J(3, 8) \rightarrow \left(3 \cdot \frac{1}{2}, 8 \cdot \frac{1}{2}\right) \rightarrow J'\left(\frac{3}{2}, 4\right)$

$K(10, 6) \rightarrow \left(10 \cdot \frac{1}{2}, 6 \cdot \frac{1}{2}\right) \rightarrow K'(5, 3)$

$L(8, 2) \rightarrow \left(8 \cdot \frac{1}{2}, 2 \cdot \frac{1}{2}\right) \rightarrow L'(4, 1)$

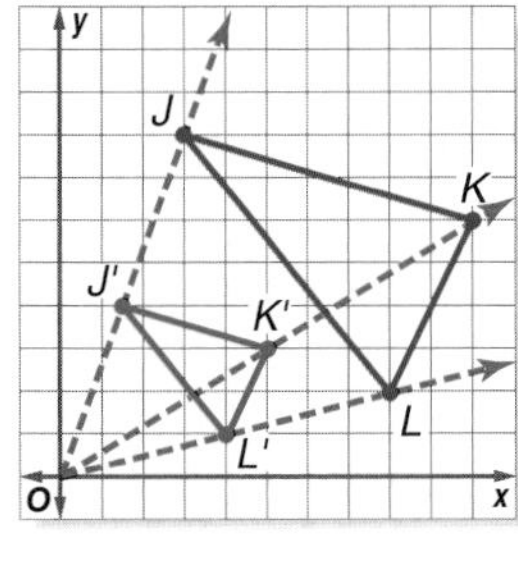

Check Draw lines through the origin and each of the vertices of the original figure. The vertices of the dilation should lie on those same lines.

STUDY TIP

Naming a Dilation A dilated image is usually named using the same letters as the original figure, but with primes, as in $\triangle JKL \sim \triangle J'K'L'$.

Your Turn **Find the coordinates of $\triangle JKL$ after a dilation with each scale factor.** **a. J′(6, 16), K′(20, 12), L′(16, 4)**

a. scale factor: 2

b. scale factor: $\frac{1}{3}$

b. $J'\left(1, 2\frac{2}{3}\right)$, $K'\left(3\frac{1}{3}, 2\right)$, $L'\left(2\frac{2}{3}, \frac{2}{3}\right)$

Answers (Hands-On Mini Lab)

2. See graph at the right.
3. Yes; corresponding sides of the two triangles are proportional.

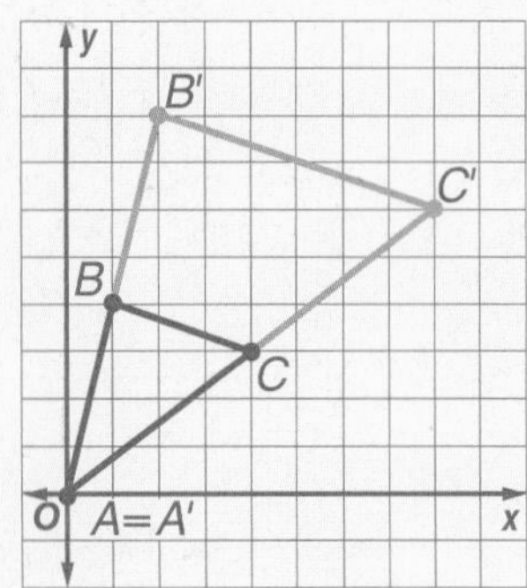

Notice that the dilation of $\triangle ABC$ in the Mini Lab is an *enlargement* of the original figure. The dilation of $\triangle JKL$ in Example 1 is a *reduction* of the original figure.

EXAMPLE Find and Classify a Scale Factor

2 Segment $V'W'$ is a dilation of segment VW. Find the scale factor of the dilation, and classify it as an enlargement or as a reduction.

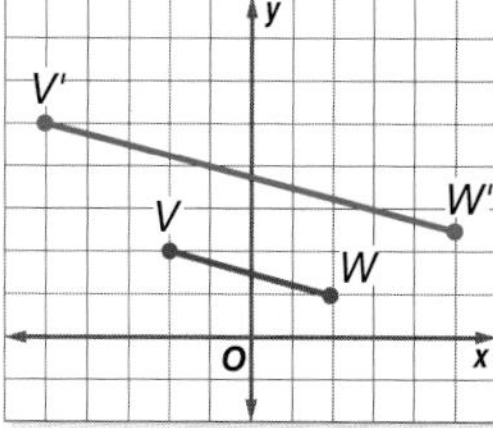

Write a ratio of the x- or y-coordinate of one vertex of the dilation to the x- or y-coordinate of the corresponding vertex of the original figure. Use the y-coordinates of $V(-2, 2)$ and $V'(-5, 5)$.

$$\frac{y\text{-coordinate of point } V'}{y\text{-coordinate of point } V} = \frac{5}{2}$$

The scale factor is $\frac{5}{2}$. Since the image is larger than the original figure, the dilation is an enlargement.

STUDY TIP

Scale Factors
- If the scale factor is between 0 and 1, the dilation is a reduction.
- If the scale factor is greater than 1, the dilation is an enlargement.
- If the scale factor is equal to 1, the dilation is the same size as the original figure.

Your Turn **Segment $A'B'$ is a dilation of segment AB. The endpoints of each segment are given. Find the scale factor of the dilation, and classify it as an *enlargement* or as a *reduction*.**

c. $A(4, -8)$, $B(12, -4)$ $\frac{3}{4}$; reduction
$A'(3, -6)$, $B'(9, -3)$

d. $A(-5, -7)$, $B(-3, 2)$
$A'(-10, -14)$, $B'(-6, 4)$

d. 2; enlargement

TEACHING TIP

Note that the method shown in Example 2 does not work for x- or y-coordinates that are zero. For coordinates that lie on the same horizontal or vertical line segment, students can find the scale factor of the dilation by writing the ratio of the length of the dilated segment to the original segment.

EXAMPLE Use a Scale Factor

3 EYES Carleta's optometrist uses medicine to dilate her pupils by a factor of $\frac{5}{3}$. The diagram shows the diameter of Carleta's pupil before dilation. Find the new diameter once her pupil is dilated.

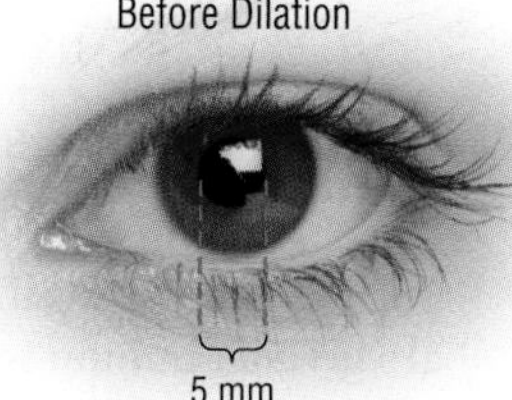

Write a proportion using the scale factor.

dilated eye → normal eye →	$\frac{x}{5} = \frac{5}{3}$	← dilated eye ← normal eye
	$x \cdot 3 = 5 \cdot 5$	Find the cross products.
	$\frac{3x}{3} = \frac{25}{3}$	Multiply. Then divide each side by 3.
	$x \approx 8.3$	Simplify.

Her pupil will be about 8.3 millimeters in diameter once dilated.

msmath3.net/extra_examples

2 Teach

In-Class Examples

INTERACTIVE CHALKBOARD PowerPoint® Presentations

1 Graph $\triangle MNO$ with vertices $M(3, -1)$, $N(2, -2)$, and $O(0, 4)$. Then graph its image $\triangle M'N'O'$ after a dilation with a scale factor of $\frac{3}{2}$.

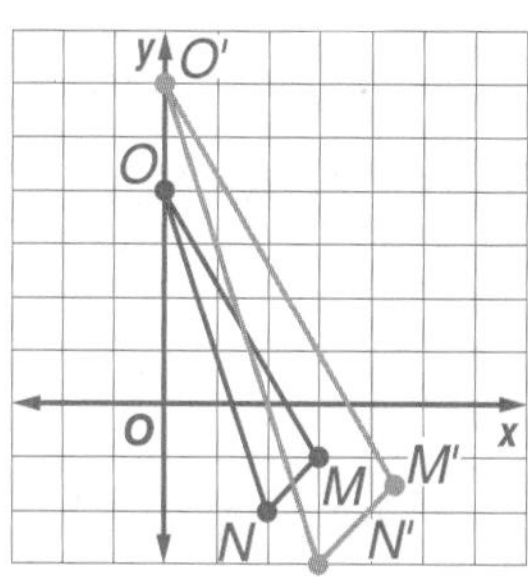

2 In the figure, segment $X'Y'$ is a dilation of segment XY. Find the scale factor of the dilation, and classify it as an *enlargement* or a *reduction*.

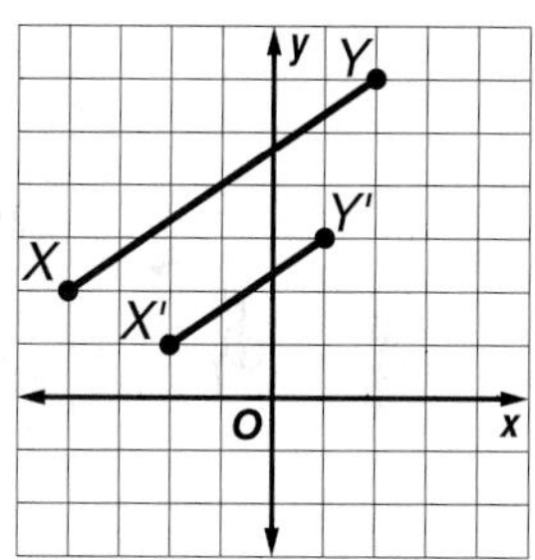

$\frac{1}{2}$, reduction

3 **EYES** The pupil of Josh's eye is 6 millimeters in diameter. His eye doctor uses medicine to dilate his pupils by a factor of $\frac{3}{2}$. Find the new diameter once his pupil is dilated. **9 mm**

DAILY INTERVENTION **Flexible Grouping**

Dilating Figures Count off so that students are in pairs. Have each student in the pair create a figure on the coordinate grid and decide on a scale factor. Partners should then exchange papers and create the described dilation.

3 Practice/Apply

Which One Doesn't Belong? For Exercise 2, have students explain how the coordinates for P' in the incorrect choice were calculated. **2 was added to each of the coordinates for *P*.** What would be the correct coordinates for P'? **(6, −2)**

About the Exercises...

Guided Practice Key

Exercises	Examples
3	1
4–5	2

Assignment Guide

Basic: 7–23 odd, 25–29

Average: 7–19 odd, 21–29

Enriched: 6–20 even, 21–29

Alert! Exercise 24 requires research on the Internet or another resource.

Answers

1. Sample answer:

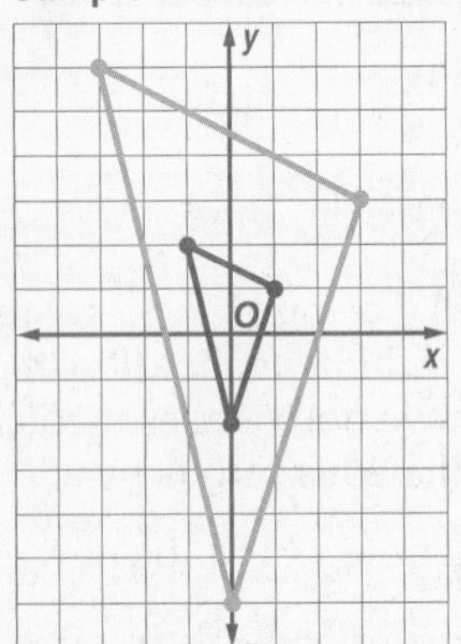

3. $A'(-1, 3)$, $B'\left[-\frac{1}{2}, -1\right]$, $C'\left[2, \frac{3}{2}\right]$

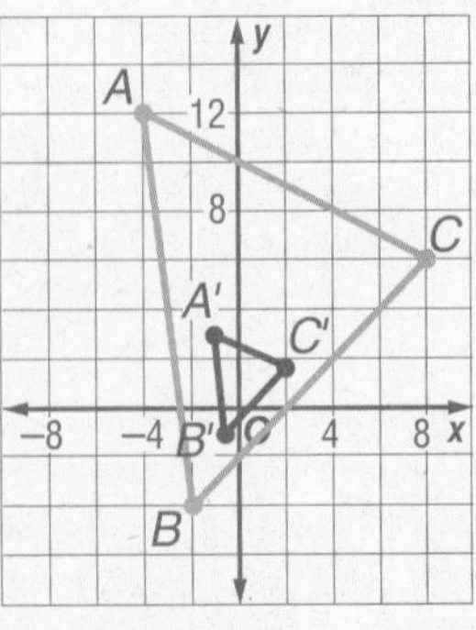

Students practice the same concepts in Exercises 6–9 and 11–20 if they are assigned odd or even problems.

Skill and Concept Check

1. **OPEN ENDED** Draw a triangle on the coordinate plane. Then graph its image after a dilation with a scale factor of 3. **See margin.**

2. **Which One Doesn't Belong?** Identify the pair of points that does not represent a dilation with a factor of 2. Explain your reasoning.

$P(3, -1)$, $P'(5, 1)$	$Q(4, 2)$, $Q'(8, 4)$	$R(-5, 3)$, $R'(-10, 6)$	$S(1, -7)$, $S'(2, -14)$

P and P'; $3 \cdot 2 \neq 5$ and $-1 \cdot 2 \neq 1$

GUIDED PRACTICE

3. Triangle ABC has vertices $A(-4, 12)$, $B(-2, -4)$, and $C(8, 6)$. Find the coordinates of $\triangle ABC$ after a dilation with a scale factor of $\frac{1}{4}$. Then graph $\triangle ABC$ and its dilation. **See margin.**

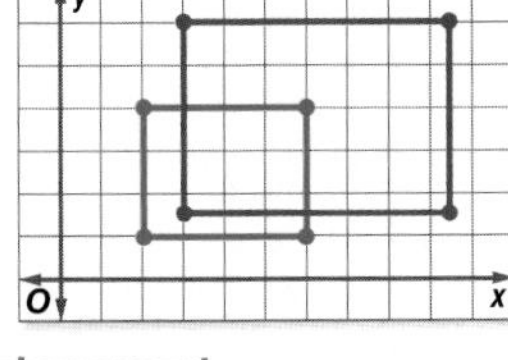

4. In the figure at the right, the green rectangle is a dilation of the blue rectangle. Find the scale factor and classify the dilation as an *enlargement* or as a *reduction*. **$\frac{2}{3}$; reduction**

5. Segment $C'D'$ with endpoints $C'(-3, 12)$ and $D'(6, -9)$ is a dilation of segment CD. If segment CD has endpoints $C(-2, 8)$ and $D(4, -6)$, find the scale factor of the dilation. Then classify the dilation as an *enlargement* or as a *reduction*. **$\frac{3}{2}$; enlargement**

★ **indicates increased difficulty**

Practice and Applications

HOMEWORK HELP	
For Exercises	See Examples
6–10, 15–16	1
11–14, 17–20	2
21–22	3
Extra Practice See pages 626, 651.	

Find the coordinates of the vertices of polygon $H'J'K'L'$ after polygon $HJKL$ is dilated using the given scale factor. Then graph polygon $HJKL$ and its dilation. **6–9. See Ch. 4 Answer Appendix.**

6. $H(-1, 3)$, $J(3, 2)$, $K(2, -3)$, $L(-2, -2)$; scale factor 2
7. $H(0, 2)$, $J(3, 1)$, $K(0, -4)$, $L(-2, -3)$; scale factor 3
8. $H(-6, 2)$, $J(4, 4)$, $K(7, -2)$, $L(-2, -4)$; scale factor $\frac{1}{2}$
9. $H(-8, 4)$, $J(6, 4)$, $K(6, -4)$, $L(-8, -4)$; scale factor $\frac{3}{4}$

★10. Write a general rule for finding the new coordinates of any ordered pair (x, y) after a dilation with a scale factor of k. **See margin.**

Segment $P'Q'$ is a dilation of segment PQ. The endpoints of each segment are given. Find the scale factor of the dilation, and classify it as an *enlargement* or as a *reduction*.

11. $P(0, -10)$ and $Q(5, -15)$
$P'(0, -6)$ and $Q'(3, -9)$ **$\frac{3}{5}$; reduction**

12. $P(-1, 2)$ and $Q(3, -3)$
$P'(-3, 6)$ and $Q'(9, -9)$ **3; enlargement**

13. $P(-3, -9)$ and $Q(6, -3)$
$P'(-4, -12)$ and $Q'(8, -4)$ **$\frac{4}{3}$; enlargement**

14. $P(-5, 6)$ and $Q(4, 3)$
$P'(-2.5, 3)$ and $Q'(2, 1.5)$ **$\frac{1}{2}$; reduction**

For Exercises 15 and 16, graph each figure on dot paper. **15–16. See margin.**

15. a square and its image after a dilation with a scale factor of 4
16. a right triangle and its image after a dilation with a scale factor of 0.5.

10. Multiply each number of the ordered pair (x, y) by the scale factor k. The new coordinates are (kx, ky).

15. Sample answer:

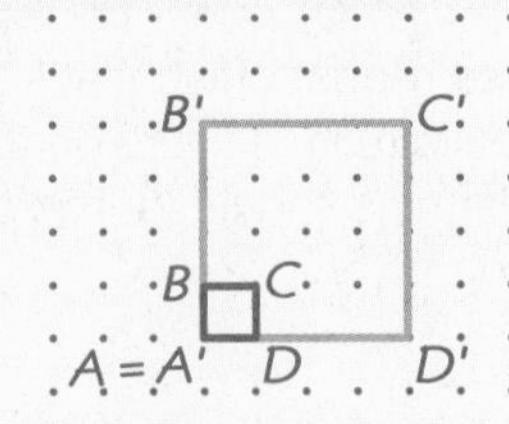

16. Sample answer:

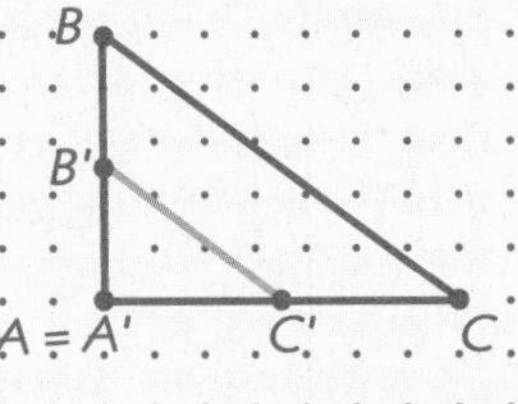

In each figure, the green figure is a dilation of the blue figure. Find the scale factor of each dilation and classify as an *enlargement* or as a *reduction*.

17. 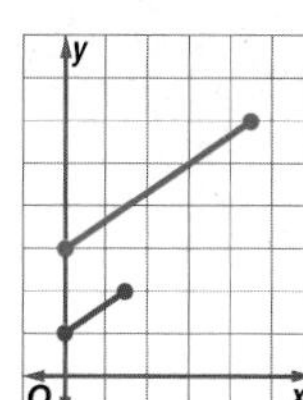

18. 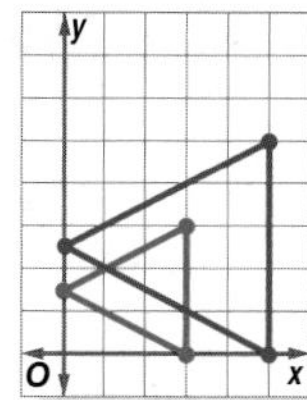

19. 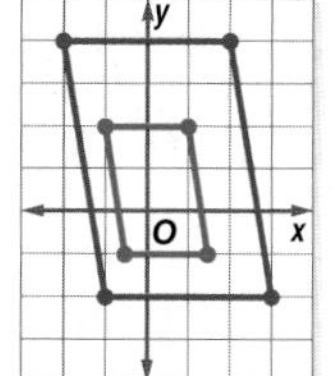

20. 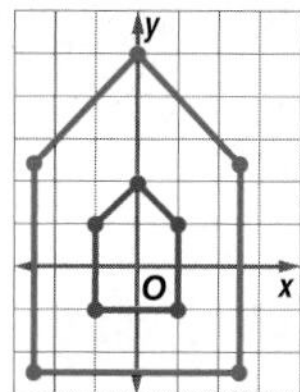

17. 3; enlargement
18. $\frac{3}{5}$; reduction
19. $\frac{1}{2}$; reduction
20. $\frac{5}{2}$; enlargement

DESIGN For Exercises 21 and 22, use the following information.
Simone designed a logo for her school. The logo, which is 5 inches wide and 8 inches long, will be enlarged and used on a school sweatshirt. On the sweatshirt, the logo will be $12\frac{1}{2}$ inches wide.

21. What is the scale factor for this enlargement? **2.5**
22. How long will the logo be on the sweatshirt? **20 in.**

ART For Exercises 23 and 24, use the painting at the right and the following information.
Painters use dilations to create the illusion of distance and depth. To create this illusion, the artist establishes a *vanishing point* on the horizon line. Objects are drawn using intersecting lines that lead to the vanishing point.

Skiffs by Gustave Caillebotte

23. Find the vanishing point in this painting. **See margin.**
24. **RESEARCH** Use the Internet or other reference to find examples of other paintings that use dilations. Identify the vanishing point in each painting. **See students' work.**
25. **CRITICAL THINKING** Describe the image of a figure after a dilation with a scale factor of −2. **The figure is enlarged and rotated 180°.**

Spiral Review with Standardized Test Practice

26. **MULTIPLE CHOICE** Square *A* is a dilation of square *B*. What is the scale factor of the dilation? **C**

(A) $\frac{1}{7}$ (B) $\frac{3}{5}$ (C) $\frac{5}{3}$ (D) 7

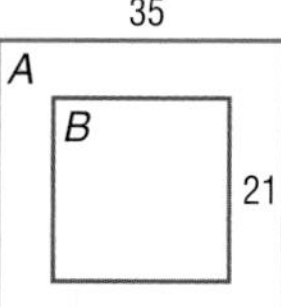

27. **MULTIPLE CHOICE** A photo is 8 inches wide by 10 inches long. You want to make a reduced color copy of the photo that is 5 inches wide for your scrapbook. What scale factor should you choose on the copy machine? **G**

(F) $\frac{1}{2}$ or 50% (G) $\frac{5}{8}$ or 62.5% (H) $\frac{8}{5}$ or 160% (I) 2 or 200%

28. **ARCHITECTURE** The Empire State Building casts a shadow 156.25 feet long. At the same time, a nearby building that is 84 feet high casts a shadow 10.5 feet long. How tall is the Empire State Building? (Lesson 4-7) **1,250 ft**
29. **HOBBIES** A model sports car is 10 inches long. If the actual car is 14 feet, find the scale of the model. (Lesson 4-6) **5 in. = 7 ft**

msmath3.net/self_check_quiz

4 Assess

Higher-Level Thinking

How would a negative scale factor affect a dilation? Use an example to explain. **A negative scale factor would reflect the figure over the origin or rotate it 180° in addition to changing its size.**

Answer

23. **The vanishing point is the spot at which the river banks converge with the horizon line of trees.**

Study Guide and Intervention, p. 220

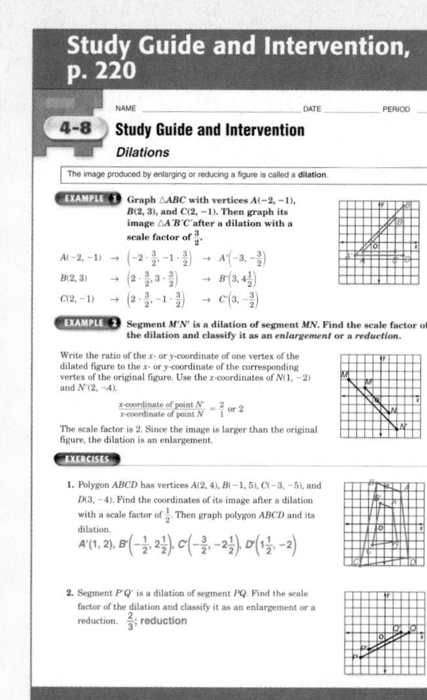

NAME ________ DATE ______ PERIOD ____

4-8 Study Guide and Intervention
Dilations

The image produced by enlarging or reducing a figure is called a **dilation**.

EXAMPLE 1 **Graph △*ABC* with vertices *A*(−2, −1), *B*(2, 3), and *C*(2, −1). Then graph its image △*A′B′C′* after a dilation with a scale factor of $\frac{3}{2}$.**

$A(-2,-1) \rightarrow \left(-2\cdot\frac{3}{2}, -1\cdot\frac{3}{2}\right) \rightarrow A'\left(-3, -\frac{3}{2}\right)$

$B(2,3) \rightarrow \left(2\cdot\frac{3}{2}, 3\cdot\frac{3}{2}\right) \rightarrow B'\left(3, 4\frac{1}{2}\right)$

$C(2,-1) \rightarrow \left(2\cdot\frac{3}{2}, -1\cdot\frac{3}{2}\right) \rightarrow C'\left(3, -\frac{3}{2}\right)$

EXAMPLE 2 **Segment *M′N′* is a dilation of segment *MN*. Find the scale factor of the dilation and classify it as an *enlargement* or a *reduction*.**

Write the ratio of the *x*- or *y*-coordinate of one vertex of the dilated figure to the *x*- or *y*-coordinate of the corresponding vertex of the original figure. Use the *x*-coordinates of *N*(1, −2) and *N′*(2, −4).

$\frac{x\text{-coordinate of point } N'}{x\text{-coordinate of point } N} = \frac{2}{1} \text{ or } 2$

The scale factor is 2. Since the image is larger than the original figure, the dilation is an enlargement.

EXERCISES

1. Polygon *ABCD* has vertices *A*(2, 4), *B*(−1, 5), *C*(−3, −5), and *D*(3, −4). Find the coordinates of its image after a dilation with a scale factor of $\frac{1}{2}$. Then graph polygon *ABCD* and its dilation.
$A'(1, 2), B'\left(-\frac{1}{2}, 2\frac{1}{2}\right), C'\left(-\frac{3}{2}, -2\frac{1}{2}\right), D'\left(1\frac{1}{2}, -2\right)$
2. Segment *P′Q′* is a dilation of segment *PQ*. Find the scale factor of the dilation and classify it as an enlargement or a reduction. $\frac{2}{3}$; reduction

Practice: Skills, p. 221

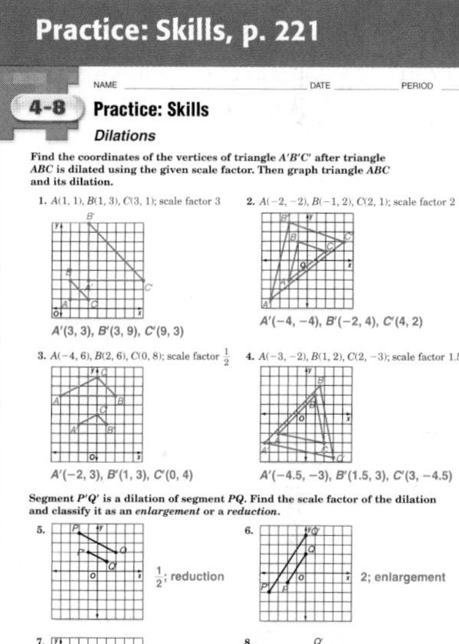

NAME ________ DATE ______ PERIOD ____

4-8 Practice: Skills
Dilations

Find the coordinates of the vertices of triangle *A′B′C′* after triangle *ABC* is dilated using the given scale factor. Then graph triangle *ABC* and its dilation.

1. *A*(1, 1), *B*(1, 3), *C*(3, 1); scale factor 3
A′(3, 3), *B′*(3, 9), *C′*(9, 3)
2. *A*(−2, −2), *B*(−1, 2), *C*(2, 1); scale factor 2
A′(−4, −4), *B′*(−2, 4), *C′*(4, 2)
3. *A*(−4, 6), *B*(2, 6), *C*(0, 8); scale factor $\frac{1}{2}$
A′(−2, 3), *B′*(1, 3), *C′*(0, 4)
4. *A*(−3, −2), *B*(1, 2), *C*(2, −3); scale factor 1.5
A′(−4.5, −3), *B′*(1.5, 3), *C′*(3, −4.5)

Segment *P′Q′* is a dilation of segment *PQ*. Find the scale factor of the dilation and classify it as an *enlargement* or a *reduction*.

5. $\frac{1}{2}$; reduction
6. 2; enlargement
7. $\frac{2}{3}$; reduction
8. $\frac{3}{2}$; enlargement

Practice: Word Problems, p. 222

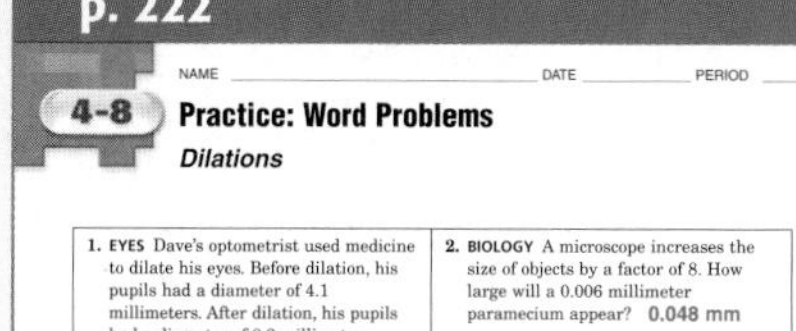

NAME ________ DATE ______ PERIOD ____

4-8 Practice: Word Problems
Dilations

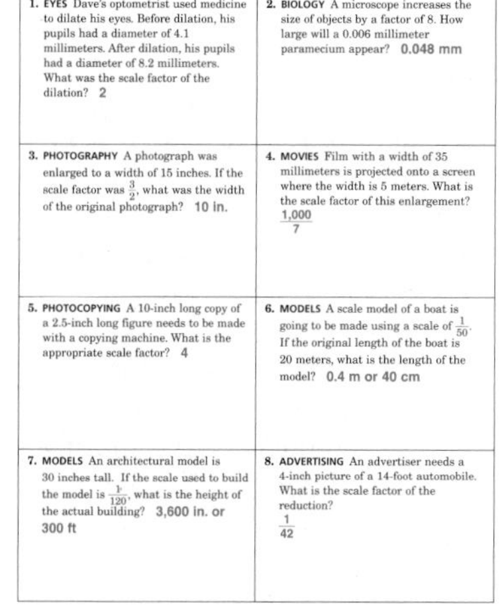

1. **EYES** Dave's optometrist used medicine to dilate his eyes. Before dilation, his pupils had a diameter of 4.1 millimeters. After dilation, his pupils had a diameter of 8.2 millimeters. What was the scale factor of the dilation? 2
2. **BIOLOGY** A microscope increases the size of objects by a factor of 8. How large will a 0.006 millimeter paramecium appear? 0.048 mm
3. **PHOTOGRAPHY** A photograph was enlarged to a width of 15 inches. If the scale factor was $\frac{3}{2}$, what was the width of the original photograph? 10 in.
4. **MOVIES** Film with a width of 35 millimeters is projected onto a screen where the width is 5 meters. What is the scale factor of this enlargement? $\frac{1{,}000}{7}$
5. **PHOTOCOPYING** A 10-inch long copy of a 2.5-inch long figure needs to be made with a copying machine. What is the appropriate scale factor? 4
6. **MODELS** A scale model of a boat is going to be made using a scale of $\frac{1}{50}$. If the original length of the boat is 20 meters, what is the length of the model? 0.4 m or 40 cm
7. **MODELS** An architectural model is 30 inches tall. If the scale used to build the model is $\frac{1}{120}$, what is the height of the actual building? 3,600 in. or 300 ft
8. **ADVERTISING** An advertiser needs a 4-inch picture of a 14-foot automobile. What is the scale factor of the reduction? $\frac{1}{42}$

Study Guide and Review

Vocabulary Assessment

- This alphabetical list of vocabulary terms in Chapter 4 includes a page reference where each term was introduced.
- A vocabulary review/test for Chapter 4 is available on p. 238 of the *Chapter 4 Resource Masters*.

Vocabulary PuzzleMaker

ELL The online Vocabulary PuzzleMaker improves students' mathematics vocabulary using four puzzle formats — crossword, scramble, word search using a word list, and word search using clues. Students can work on a computer screen or from a printed handout.

MindJogger Videoquizzes

ELL MindJogger Videoquizzes provide an alternative review of concepts presented in this chapter. Students work in teams in a game show format to gain points for correct answers. The questions are presented in three rounds.

Round 1 Concepts (5 questions)
Round 2 Skills (4 questions)
Round 3 Problem Solving (4 questions)

ExamView® Pro

Use the networkable ExamView® Pro Testmaker CD-ROM to:

- Create **multiple versions** of tests.
- Create **modified** tests for **inclusion** students with one mouse click.
- **Edit** existing questions and **add** your own questions.
- Build tests aligned with state standards using built-in **state curriculum correlations.**
- Change **English** tests to **Spanish** with one mouse click and vice versa.

Study Guide and Review

Vocabulary and Concept Check

congruent (p. 179)
corresponding parts (p. 178)
cross products (p. 170)
dilation (p. 194)
indirect measurement (p. 188)
polygon (p. 178)
proportion (p. 170)
rate (p. 157)
rate of change (p. 160)
ratio (p. 156)
rise (p. 166)
run (p. 166)
scale (p. 184)
scale drawing (p. 184)
scale factor (p. 179)
scale model (p. 184)
similar (p. 178)
slope (p. 166)
unit rate (p. 157)

Choose the letter of the term that best matches each statement or phrase.

1. polygons that have the same shape **f**
2. a rate with a denominator of one **e**
3. the constant rate of change between two points on a line **a**
4. a comparison of two numbers by division **g**
5. two equivalent ratios **d**
6. ratio of a length on a drawing to its actual length **h**
7. describes how one quantity changes in relation to another **b**
8. the enlarged or reduced image of a figure **c**

a. slope
b. rate of change
c. dilation
d. proportion
e. unit rate
f. similar
g. ratio
h. scale

Lesson-by-Lesson Exercises and Examples

4-1 Ratios and Rates (pp. 156–159)

Express each ratio in simplest form.

9. 7 chaperones for 56 students **1 for 8**
10. 12 peaches:8 pears **3:2**
11. 5 inches out of 5 feet **1 out of 12**

Example 1 **Express the ratio *10 milliliters to 8 liters* in simplest form.**

$$\frac{10 \text{ milliliters}}{8 \text{ liters}} = \frac{10 \text{ milliliters}}{8{,}000 \text{ milliliters}} \text{ or } \frac{1}{800}$$

4-2 Rate of Change (pp. 160–164)

12. **MONEY** The table below shows Victor's weekly allowance for different ages.

Age (yr)	4	6	8	10	12	15
$ per week	0.25	1.00	2.00	2.00	3.00	5.00

Find the rate of change in his allowance between ages 12 and 15. **$0.67/yr**

Example 2 **At 5 A.M., it was 54°F. At 11 A.M., it was 78°F. Find the rate of temperature change in degrees per hour.**

$$\frac{\text{change in temperature}}{\text{change in hours}} = \frac{(78-54)^\circ}{(11-5) \text{ hours}}$$

$$= \frac{24^\circ}{6 \text{ hours}} \text{ or } \frac{4^\circ}{1 \text{ hour}}$$

msmath3.net/vocabulary_review

FOLDABLES™ Study Organizer

For more information about Foldables, see *Teaching Mathematics with Foldables.*

Have students look through the chapter to make sure they have included examples in their Foldables for each lesson or topic in the chapter.

Encourage students to refer to their Foldables while completing the Study Guide and Review and to use them in preparing for the Chapter Test.

4-3 Slope (pp. 166–169)

Find the slope of each line graphed at the right.

13. $\overline{AB}$ $\frac{5}{2}$
14. $\overline{CD}$ -4
15. The points in the table lie on a line. Find the slope of the line. Then graph the line.

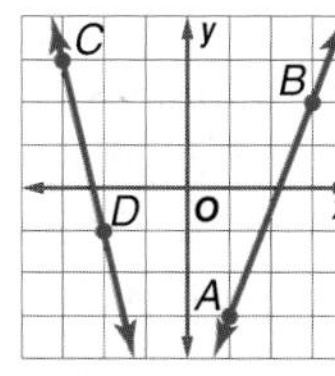

x	−6	−2	2
y	5	2	−1

15. $\frac{-3}{4}$; See margin.

Example 3 **Find the slope of the line.**

The vertical change from point J to point K is −5 units while the horizontal change is 4 units.

$\text{slope} = \frac{\text{rise}}{\text{run}}$ Definition of slope

$= \frac{-5}{4}$ or $-\frac{5}{4}$ rise = −5, run = 4

4-4 Solving Proportions (pp. 170–173)

Solve each proportion.

16. $\frac{3}{r} = \frac{6}{8}$ 4
17. $\frac{7}{4} = \frac{n}{2}$ 3.5
18. $\frac{k}{5} = \frac{72}{8}$ 45
19. $\frac{8}{3.8} = \frac{6}{x}$ 2.85
20. **ANIMALS** A turtle can move 5 inches in 4 minutes. How far will it travel in 10 minutes? 12.5 in.

Example 4 **Solve $\frac{9}{x} = \frac{4}{18}$.**

$\frac{9}{x} = \frac{4}{18}$ Write the equation.

$9 \cdot 18 = x \cdot 4$ Find the cross products.

$162 = 4x$ Multiply.

$\frac{162}{4} = \frac{4x}{4}$ Divide each side by 10.

$40.5 = x$ Simplify.

4-5 Similar Polygons (pp. 178–182)

Each pair of polygons is similar. Write a proportion to find each missing measure. Then solve.

21. 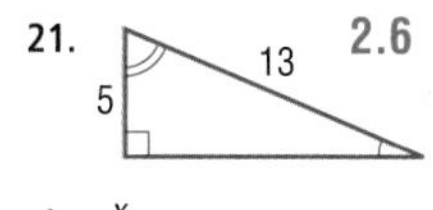 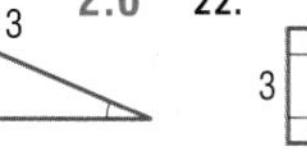 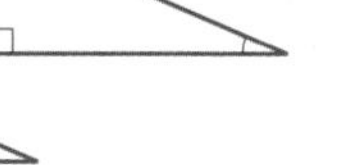

2.6

22. 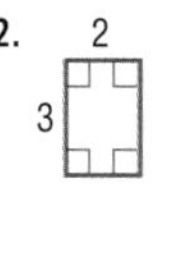 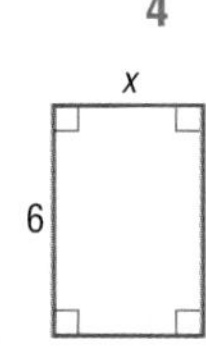

4

21–22. See margin for proportions.

23. **PARTY PLANNING** For your birthday party, you make a map to your house on a 3-inch wide by 5-inch long index card. How long will your map be if you use a copier to enlarge it so that it is 8 inches wide? $13\frac{1}{3}$ in.

Example 5 **Rectangle $GHJK$ is similar to rectangle $PQRS$. Find the value of x.**

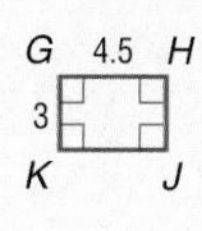

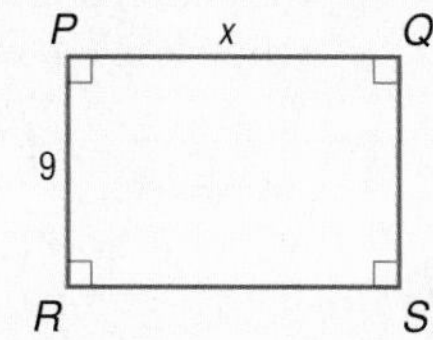

The scale factor from $GHJK$ to $PQSR$ is $\frac{GK}{PR}$, which is $\frac{3}{9}$ or $\frac{1}{3}$.

$\frac{GH}{PQ} = \frac{1}{3}$ Write a proportion.

$\frac{4.5}{x} = \frac{1}{3}$ $GH = 4.5$ and $PQ = y$

$13.5 = x$ Find the cross products. Simplify.

Answers

15.

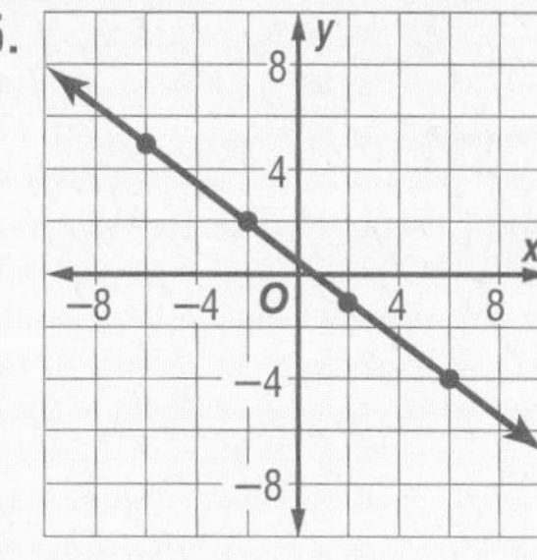

21. $\frac{13}{x} = \frac{5}{1}$

22. $\frac{2}{x} = \frac{1}{2}$

Mixed Problem Solving
For mixed problem-solving practice, see page 651.

4-6 Scale Drawings and Models (pp. 184–187)

The scale on a map is 2 inches = 5 miles. Find the actual distance for each map distance. 24. 30 mi 25. 22.5 mi 26. 6.25 mi

24. 12 in. 25. 9 in. 26. 2.5 in.

27. **HOBBIES** Mia's sister's dollhouse is a replica of their townhouse. The outside dimensions of the dollhouse are 25 inches by 35 inches. If the actual outside dimensions of the townhouse are 25 feet by 35 feet, what is the scale of the dollhouse?

27. 1 in. = 12 in. or 1 in. = 1 ft

Example 6 **The scale on a model is 3 centimeters = 45 meters. Find the actual length for a model distance of 5 centimeters.**

model length → / actual length → $\frac{3 \text{ cm}}{45 \text{ m}} = \frac{5 \text{ cm}}{x \text{ m}}$ ← model length / ← actual length

$3 \cdot x = 45 \cdot 5$

$3x = 225$

$x = 75$

The actual length is 75 meters.

4-7 Indirect Measurement (pp. 188–191) 28. $\frac{18}{234} = \frac{4}{x}$; 52 ft

Write a proportion. Then determine the missing measure.

28. **MAIL** A mailbox casts an 18-inch shadow. A tree casts a 234-inch shadow. If the mailbox is 4 feet tall, how tall is the tree?

29. **WATER** From the shoreline, the ground slopes down under the water at a constant incline. If the water is $5\frac{1}{2}$ feet deep when it is $2\frac{1}{4}$ feet from the shore, about how deep will it be when it is 6 feet from the shore?

29. $\frac{5.5}{x} = \frac{2.25}{6}$; $14\frac{2}{3}$ ft

Example 7 **A house casts a shadow that is 5 meters long. A tree casts a shadow that is 2.5 meters long. If the house is 20 meters tall, how tall is the tree?**

house's shadow → / tree's shadow → $\frac{5}{2.5} = \frac{20}{x}$ ← house's height / ← tree's height

$5 \cdot x = 20 \cdot 2.5$

$5x = 50$

$x = 10$

The tree is 10 meters tall.

4-8 Dilations (pp. 194–197) 30. 4; enlargement 31. $\frac{2}{5}$; reduction

Segment $C'D'$ is a dilation of segment CD. The endpoints of each segment are given. Find the scale factor of the dilation, and classify it as an *enlargement* or as a *reduction*.

30. $C(-2, 5)$, $D(1, 4)$; $C'(-8, 20)$, $D'(4, 16)$

31. $C(-5, 10)$, $D(0, 5)$; $C'(-2, 4)$, $D'(0, 2)$

Example 8 **Segment XY has endpoints $X(-4, 1)$ and $Y(8, -2)$. Find the coordinates of its image for a dilation with a scale factor of $\frac{3}{4}$.**

$X(-4, 1) \rightarrow \left(-4 \cdot \frac{3}{4}, 1 \cdot \frac{3}{4}\right) \rightarrow X'\left(-3, \frac{3}{4}\right)$

$Y(8, -2) \rightarrow \left(8 \cdot \frac{3}{4}, -2 \cdot \frac{3}{4}\right) \rightarrow Y'\left(6, -1\frac{1}{2}\right)$

200 Chapter 4 Proportions, Algebra, and Geometry

Practice Test

Vocabulary and Concepts

1. **OPEN ENDED** List four different ratios that form a proportion with $\frac{8}{12}$. **See margin.**
2. **Describe** a reasonable scale for a scale drawing of your classroom. **Sample answer: 1 in. = 2 ft**

Skills and Applications

3. Express *15 inches to 1 foot* in simplest form. **5:4**
4. Express *$1,105 for 26 jerseys* as a unit rate. **$42.50/jersey**

BUSINESS For Exercises 5 and 6, use the table at the right.

5. Find the rate of change in new customers per hour between 4 P.M. and 5 P.M. **17 people/h**
6. Find the rate of change in new customers per hour between 12 P.M. and 2 P.M. Then interpret its meaning. **−12 people/h; the number of new customers decreased at a rate of 12 people per hour.**

Lucky Diner	
Time	New Customers
12 P.M.	30
2 P.M.	6
4 P.M.	15
5 P.M.	32

Find the slope of each line graphed at the right.

7. $\overline{AB}$ $\frac{1}{7}$
8. $\overline{CD}$ -5

Solve each proportion.

9. $\frac{5}{3} = \frac{20}{y}$ **12**
10. $\frac{x}{2} = \frac{5}{8}$ **1.25**

Each pair of polygons is similar. Write a proportion to find each missing measure. Then solve.

11. 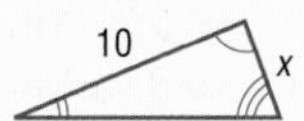 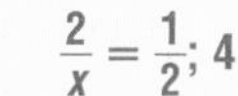 $\frac{2}{x} = \frac{1}{2}$; 4

12. 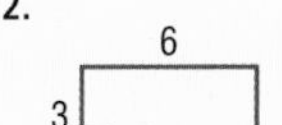 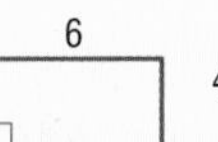 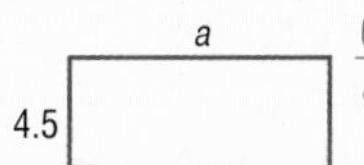 $\frac{6}{a} = \frac{3}{4.5}$; 9

13. **GEOMETRY** Graph triangle *FGH* with vertices $F(-4, -2)$, $G(-1, 2)$, and $H(3, 0)$. Then graph its image after a dilation with a scale factor of $\frac{3}{2}$. **See margin.**
14. On a map, 1 inch = 7.5 miles. How many miles does 2.5 inches represent? **18.75 mi**

Standardized Test Practice

15. **GRID IN** If it costs an average of $102 to feed a family of three for one week, on average, how much will it cost in dollars to feed a family of five for one week? **170**
16. **MULTIPLE CHOICE** A 36-foot flagpole casts a 9-foot shadow at the same time a building casts a 15-foot shadow. How tall is the building? **B**

Ⓐ 21.6 ft Ⓑ 60 ft
Ⓒ 135 ft Ⓓ 375 ft

msmath3.net/chapter_test

Portfolio Suggestion

Introduction Students frequently do not understand similar figures. Have them draw a figure, take it to the copier, and enlarge it.

Ask Students why enlarging on the copier is making a similar figure. Have them include their figures and explanations in their Portfolios.

Practice Test

Assessment Options

Vocabulary Test A vocabulary review/test for Chapter 4 can be found on p. 238 of the *Chapter 4 Resource Masters.*

Chapter Tests There are six Chapter 4 Tests and an Extended Response Assessment task available in the *Chapter 4 Resource Masters.*

Chapter 4 Tests			
Form	Type	Level	Pages
1	MC	basic	225–226
2A	MC	average	227–228
2B	MC	average	229–230
2C	FR	average	231–232
2D	FR	average	233–234
3	FR	advanced	235–236

MC = multiple-choice questions
FR = free-response questions

Extended Response Assessment

Extended Response tasks for Chapter 4 can be found on p. 237 of the *Chapter 4 Resource Masters.* A sample scoring rubric for these tasks appears on p. A28.

Answers

1. Sample answer: $\frac{2}{3}, \frac{10}{15}, \frac{6}{9}, \frac{12}{18}$
13. $F'(-6, -3)$, $G'(-1.5, 3)$, and $H'(4.5, 0)$

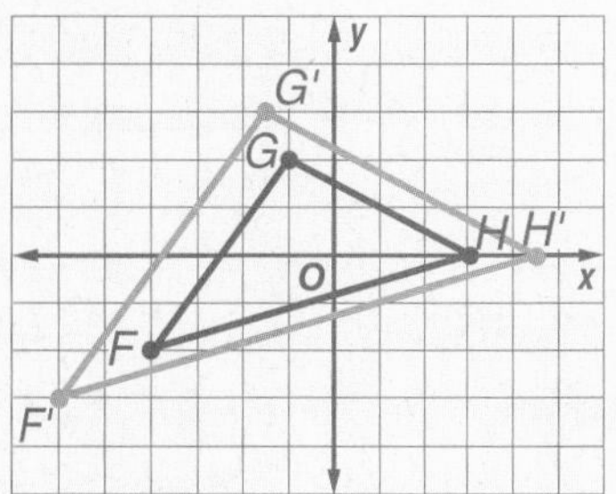

Standardized Test Practice

These two pages contain practice questions in the various formats that can be found on the most frequently given standardized tests.

A student recording sheet for these two pages can be found on page A1 of the *Chapter 4 Resource Masters.*

Standardized Test Practice Student Recording Sheet, p. A1

NAME ______ DATE ______ PERIOD ______

Standardized Test Practice SCORE ______

Student Recording Sheet (Use with pages 202-203 of the Student Edition.)

Part 1: Multiple Choice

Select the best answer from the choices given and fill in the corresponding oval.

1. Ⓐ Ⓑ Ⓒ Ⓓ 3. Ⓐ Ⓑ Ⓒ Ⓓ 5. Ⓐ Ⓑ Ⓒ Ⓓ

2. Ⓕ Ⓖ Ⓗ Ⓘ 4. Ⓕ Ⓖ Ⓗ Ⓘ 6. Ⓕ Ⓖ Ⓗ Ⓘ

Part 2: Short Response/Grid In

Solve the problem and write your answer in the blank.

For grid in questions, also enter your answer by writing each number or symbol in a box. Then fill in the corresponding circle for that number of symbol.

7. ______
8. ______ (grid in)
9. ______ (grid in)
10. ______ (grid in)
11. ______ (grid in)
12. ______ (grid in)
13. ______ (grid in)
14. ______
15. ______

Part 3: Extended Response

Record your answers for Questions 16 and 17 on the back of this paper.

Additional Practice

See pp. 243–244 of the *Chapter 4 Resource Masters* for additional standardized test practice.

Chapter 4 Standardized Test Practice

PART 1 Multiple Choice

Record your answers on the answer sheet provided by your teacher or on a sheet of paper.

1. Which of the numbers below is *not* a prime number? (Prerequisite Skill, p. 609) **B**

   Ⓐ 23 Ⓑ 49 Ⓒ 59 Ⓓ 61

2. One floor of a house is divided into two apartments as shown below.

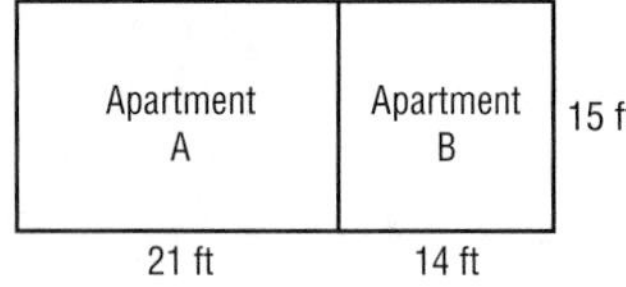

   How much larger is the area of apartment A than the area of apartment B? (Lesson 1-1) **H**

   Ⓕ 90 ft^2 Ⓖ 100 ft^2

   Ⓗ 105 ft^2 Ⓘ 115 ft^2

3. Which of the following numbers could replace the variable n to make the inequality true? (Lesson 2-2) **D**

$$\frac{4}{9} < n < 0.72$$

   Ⓐ $\frac{1}{3}$ Ⓑ $\frac{6}{8}$ Ⓒ $\frac{3}{2}$ Ⓓ $\frac{4}{6}$

4. Which of the following could *not* be the side lengths of a right triangle? (Lesson 3-4) **F**

   Ⓕ 2, 3, 5 Ⓖ 6, 10, 8

   Ⓗ 8, 15, 17 Ⓘ 13, 5, 12

TEST-TAKING TIP

Question 3 It will save you time to memorize the decimal equivalents or approximations of some common fractions.

$\frac{3}{4} = 0.75$ $\frac{1}{3} \approx 0.33$ $\frac{2}{3} \approx 0.66$ $\frac{3}{2} = 1.5$

5. Last week, Caleb traveled from home to his grandmother's house. The graph below shows the relationship between his travel time and the distance he traveled.

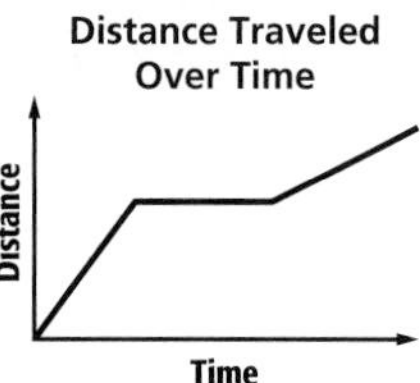

   Which best describes his trip? (Lesson 4-2) **D**

   Ⓐ He drove on a high-speed highway, then slowly on a dirt road, and finished his trip on a high-speed highway.

   Ⓑ He drove slowly on a dirt road, stopped for lunch, and then got on a high-speed highway for the rest of his trip.

   Ⓒ He drove slowly on a dirt road, then on a high-speed highway, and finished his trip on a dirt road.

   Ⓓ He started on a high-speed highway, stopped for lunch, and then got on a dirt road for the rest of his trip.

6. You are making a scale model of the car shown below. If your model is to be $\frac{1}{25}$ of car's actual size, which proportion could be used to find the measure ℓ of the model's length? (Lesson 4-6) **H**

   Ⓕ $\frac{\ell}{14} = \frac{25}{1}$ Ⓖ $\frac{14}{\ell} = \frac{1}{25}$

   Ⓗ $\frac{\ell}{14} = \frac{1}{25}$ Ⓘ $\frac{14}{25} = \frac{1}{\ell}$

ExamView® Pro

Special banks of standardized test questions similar to those on the TIMSS and NAEP grade 8 tests can be found on this CD-ROM.

Preparing for Standardized Tests
For test-taking strategies and more practice, see pages 660-677.

PART 2 Short Response/Grid In

Record your answers on the answer sheet provided by your teacher or on a sheet of paper.

7. The temperature at 9:00 A.M. was $-20°F$. If the temperature rose 15° from 9:00 A.M. to 12:00 noon, what was the temperature at noon? (Lesson 1-4) **$-5°F$**

8. Suppose you made fruit punch for a party using $3\frac{1}{2}$ cups of apple juice, 2 cups of orange juice, and $2\frac{1}{2}$ cups of cranberry juice. How many *quarts* of juice did you make? (Lesson 2-5) **2**

9. Estimate the value of $\sqrt{47}$ to the nearest whole number. (Lesson 3-2) **7**

10. A swan laid 5 eggs. Only 4 of the eggs hatched, and only 3 of these swans grew to become adults. Write the ratio of swans that grew to adulthood to the number of eggs that hatched as a fraction. (Lesson 4-1) **3/4**

11. Find the slope of the line graphed at the right. (Lesson 4-3) **5/3**

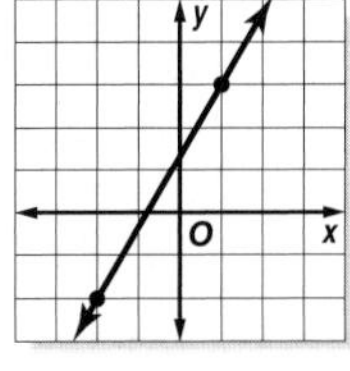

12. A truck used 6.3 gallons of gasoline to travel 107 miles. How many gallons of gasoline would it need to travel an additional 250 miles? (Lesson 4-4) **14.7**

13. Triangle FGH is similar to triangle JKL. The perimeter of triangle FGH is 30 centimeters.

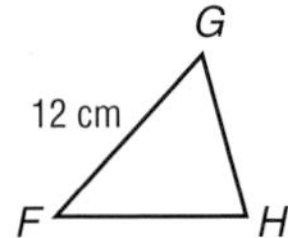

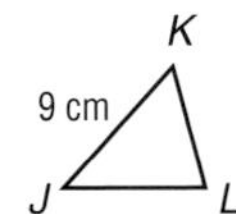

What is the perimeter of triangle JKL in centimeters? (Lesson 4-5) **22.5**

14. The distance between Jasper and Cartersville on a map is 3.8 centimeters. If the actual distance between these two cities is 209 miles, what is the scale for this map? (Lesson 4-6) **1 cm = 55 mi**

15. A 6-foot tall man casts a shadow that is 8 feet long. At the same time, a nearby crane casts a 20-foot long shadow. How tall is the crane? (Lesson 4-7) **15 ft**

PART 3 Extended Response

Record your answers on a sheet of paper. Show your work.

16. The table below shows how much Susan earns for different amounts of time she works at a fast food restaurant. (Lesson 4-3)

Time (h)	2	4	6	8
Wages ($)	9	18	27	36

a. Graph the data from the table and connect the points with a line.
b. Find the slope of the line. **$\frac{9}{2}$**
c. What is Susan's rate of pay? **$4.50/h**
d. If Susan continues to be paid at this rate, how much money will she make for working 10 hours? **$45**

16a. See Ch. 4 Answer Appendix.

17. Triangle ABC has vertices $A(-6, 3)$, $B(3, 6)$, and $C(6, -9)$. (Lesson 4-8)

a. Find the coordinates of the vertices of $\triangle A'B'C'$ after $\triangle ABC$ is dilated using a scale factor of $\frac{2}{3}$. **a–b. See Ch. 4 Answer Appendix.**
b. Graph $\triangle ABC$ and its dilation.
c. Name a scale factor that would result in $\triangle ABC$ being enlarged. **Sample answer: 2**
d. Find the coordinates of the vertices of $\triangle A'B'C'$ after this enlargement. **See Ch. 4 Answer Appendix.**

msmath3.net/standardized_test

Standardized Test Practice

Rubrics The following rubrics are sample scoring devices for short response and extended response questions.

Short Response

Points	Description
2	The student demonstrates a **thorough understanding** of the mathematics of the task. The response may contain minor flaws that do not detract from the demonstration of a thorough understanding.
1	The student has provided a response that is only **partially correct**.
0	The student has provided a **completely incorrect** solution or no response at all.

Extended Response

Points	Description
4	The student demonstrates a **thorough understanding** of the mathematics of the task. The response may contain minor flaws that do not detract from the demonstration of a thorough understanding.
3	The student demonstrates an **understanding** of the mathematics of the task. The response is essentially correct and demonstrates an essential but less than thorough understanding of the mathematics.
2	The student demonstrates only a **partial understanding** of the mathematics of the task. Although the student may have used the correct approach to a solution or may have provided a correct solution, the work lacks an essential understanding of the underlying mathematical concepts.
1	The student demonstrates a **very limited understanding** of the mathematics of the task. The response is incomplete and exhibits many flaws.
0	The student provides a **completely incorrect** solution or no response at all.

A more detailed 4-point rubric is provided on page A2 of the *Chapter 4 Resource Masters*.

Page 165, Lesson 4-2b

1. a line

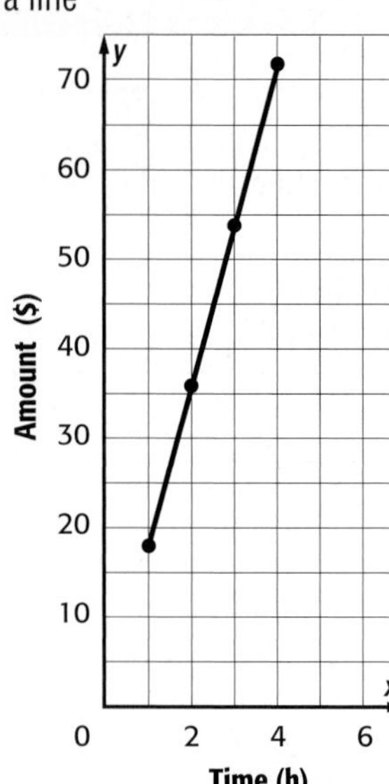

4. a line

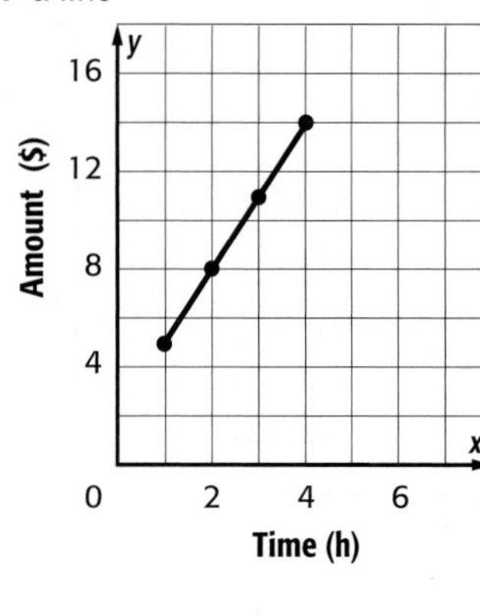

Page 167, Lesson 4-3 (Your Turn)

d.

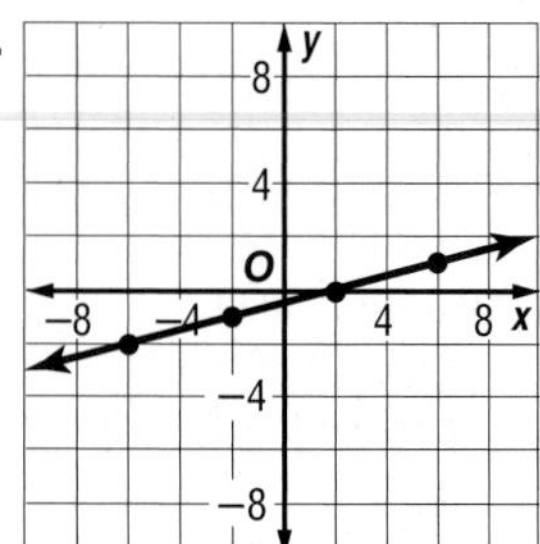

e.

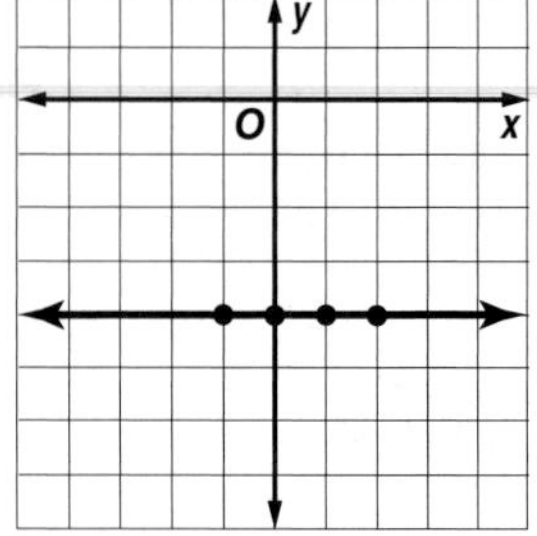

Page 173, Lesson 4-4

47.

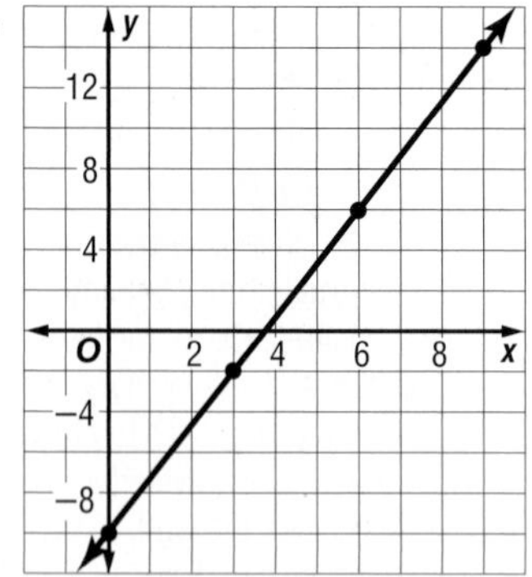

Page 182, Lesson 4-5

23.

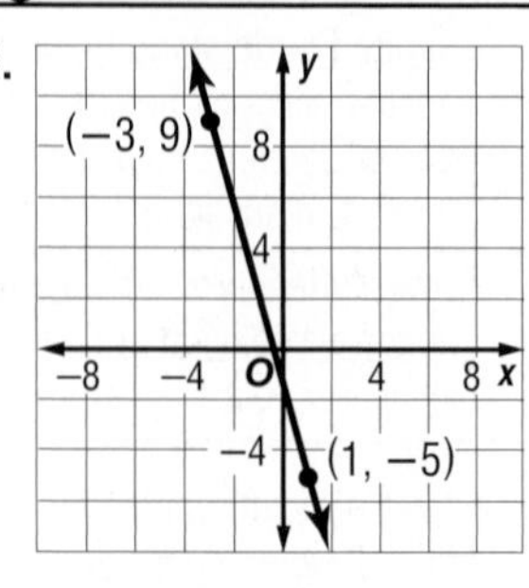

24.

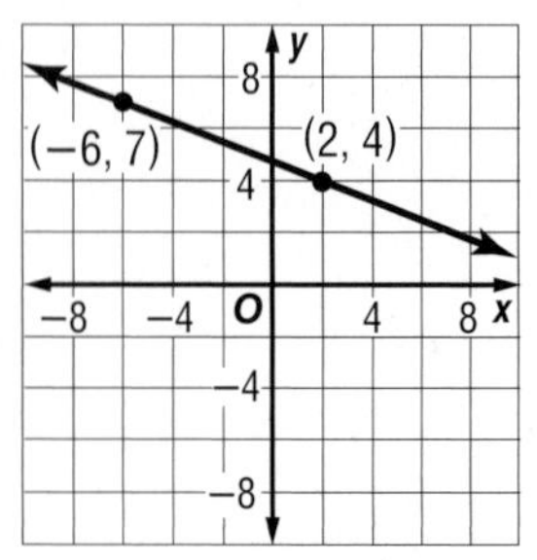

25.

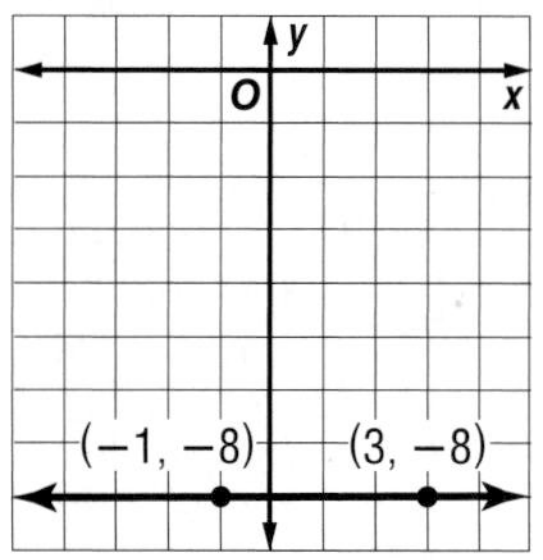

Page 191, Lesson 4-7

34. 4 units

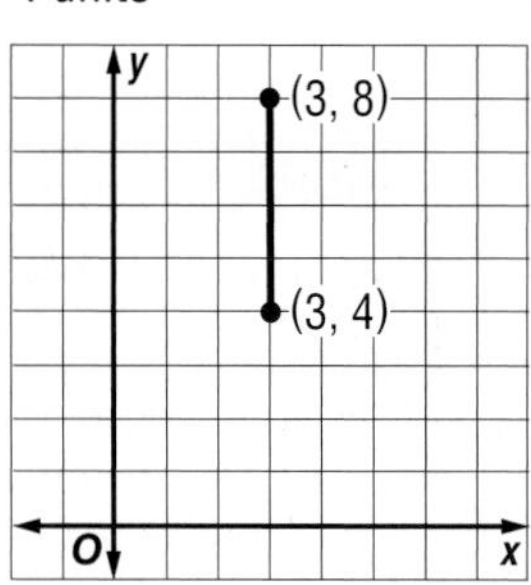

35. 8 units

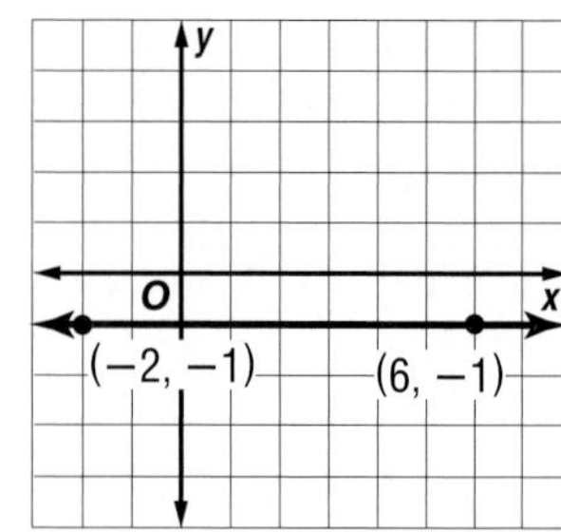

36. 5 units

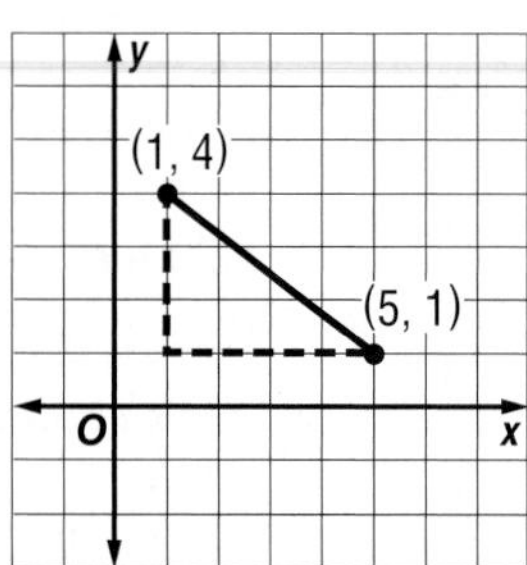

37. 13 units

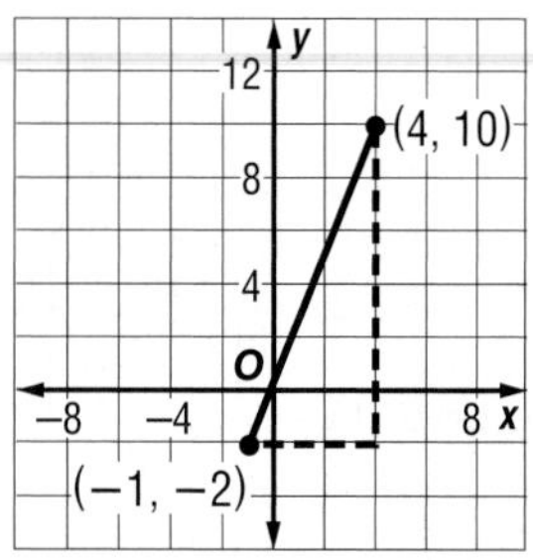

Page 196, Lesson 4-8

6. $H'(-2, 6)$, $J'(6, 4)$, $K'(4, -6)$, $L'(-4, -4)$

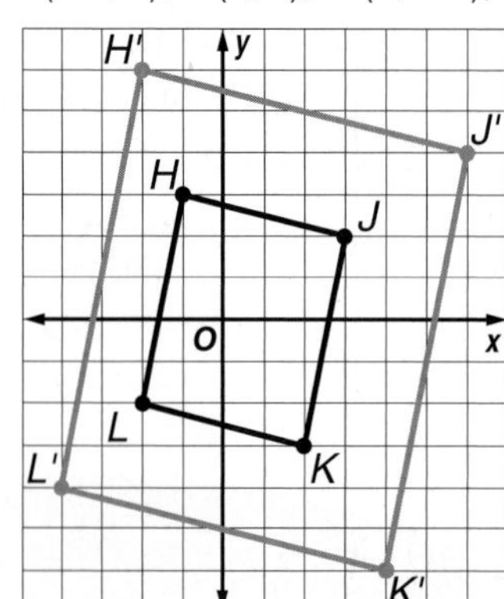

7. $H'(0, 6)$, $J'(9, 3)$, $K'(0, -12)$, $L'(-6, -9)$

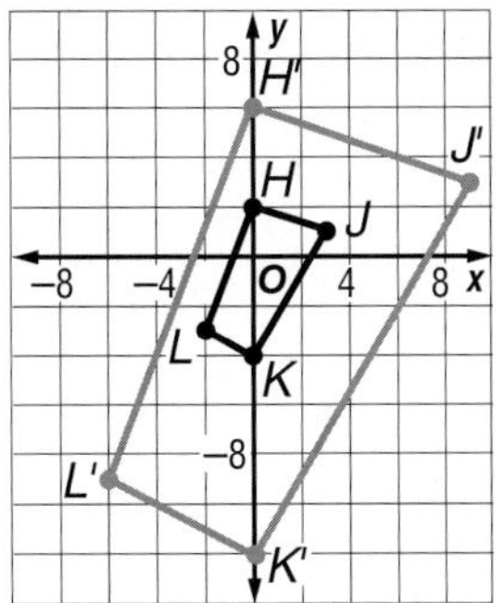

8. $H'(-3, 1)$, $J'(2, 2)$, $K'\left[3\frac{1}{2}\ -1\right]$, $L'(-1, -2)$

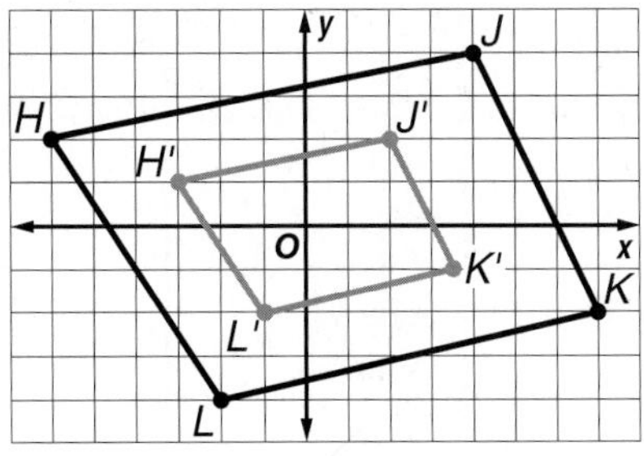

9. $H'(-6, 3)$, $J'\left[4\frac{1}{2}, 3\right]$, $K'\left[4\frac{1}{2}, -3\right]$, $L'(-6, -3)$

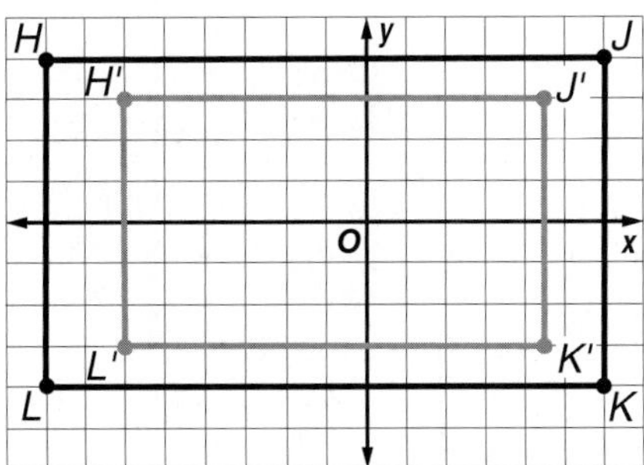

Page 203, Standardized Test Practice

16a.

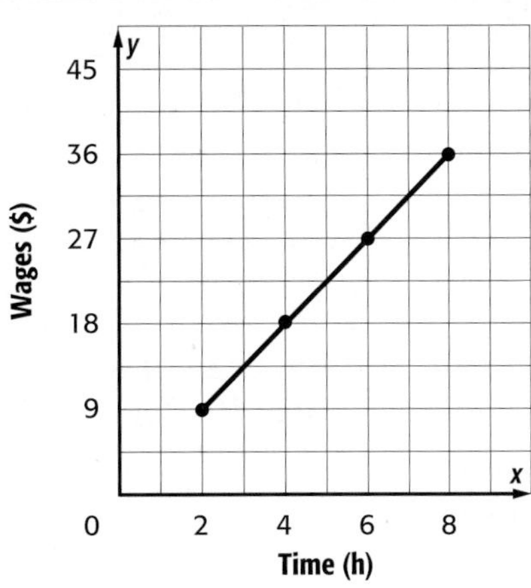

17a. $A'(-4, 2)$, $B'(2, 4)$, $C'(4, -6)$

17b.

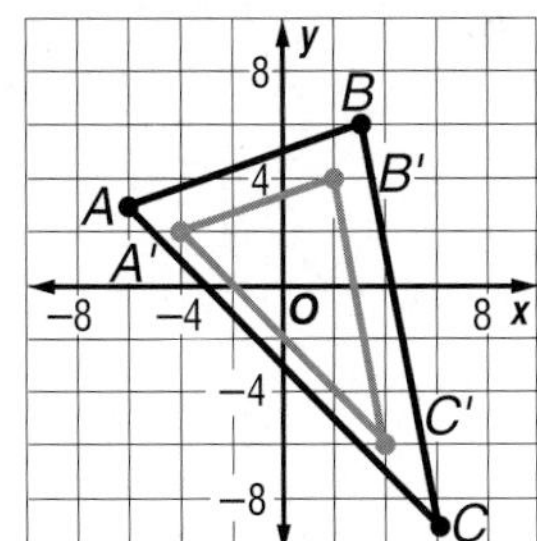

17d. $A'(-12, 6)$, $B'(6, 12)$, and $C'(12, -18)$

Chapter 5 Chapter Overview

Percent

LESSON OBJECTIVES	NCTM Standards	NAEP 2005	State/Local Objectives
5-1 **Ratios and Percents** (pp. 206–209) • Write ratios as percents and vice versa.	1, 6, 7, 10	N1d, N1e, N4a	
5-2 **Fractions, Decimals, and Percents** (pp. 210–214) • Write percents as fractions and decimals and vice versa.	1, 2, 6, 7, 10	N1e, N1j, N3a, N4c	
5-3 **Algebra: The Percent Proportion** (pp. 216–219) • Solve problems using the percent proportion.	1, 2, 6, 7, 9, 10	N1b, N4b, N4d, N5f	
5-4 **Finding Percents Mentally** (pp. 220–223) • Compute mentally with percents.	1, 6, 7, 10	N1b, N1e, N3a, N5f	
5-5 **Percent and Estimation** (pp. 226–231) **5-5a Problem-Solving Strategy:** Solve problems using the reasonable answer strategy. • Estimate by using equivalent fractions, decimals, and percents.	1, 6, 7, 9, 10	N1e, N2b, N3a, N3d, N3g	
5-6 **Algebra: The Percent Equation** (pp. 232–235) • Solve problems using the percent equation.	1, 2, 6, 7, 9, 10	A3a, A4a, A4c, N1e, N2c, N4a, N5f	
5-7 **Percent Change** (pp. 236–240) • Find and use the percent of increase or decrease.	1, 2, 6, 7, 9, 10	N4a, N4b, N4d, N3p	
5-8 **Simple Interest** (pp. 241–245) • Solve problems involving simple interest. **5-8b Spreadsheet Investigation:** Find compound interest.	1, 2, 6, 7, 9, 10	N4d, N4e, N5f	

Key to NCTM Standards:

1=Number & Operations, 2=Algebra, 3=Geometry, 4=Measurement, 5=Data Analysis & Probability, 6=Problem Solving, 7=Reasoning & Proof, 8=Communication, 9=Connections, 10=Representation

NAEP 2005 Standards: See Teacher Resources at math.glencoe.com

Pacing suggestions for the entire year can be found on page T23.

*An electronic version of this chapter is available on **StudentWorks**™. This backpack solution CD-ROM allows students instant access to the Student Edition, lesson worksheet pages, and web resources.*

Chapter Resource Manager

Chapter 5 Resource Masters

Study Guide and Intervention	Practice (Skills and Word Problems)	Reading to Learn Mathematics	Enrichment	Assessment	Applications*	Parent and Student Study Guide Online Worksheets	5-Minute Check Transparencies	Key Teaching Transparencies	MathPASS: Tutorial Plus (lessons)	Teaching Mathematics with Manipulatives	Noteables™: Interactive Study Notebook	Optional Materials
245	246–247	248	249			5-1	5-1	17		56–57	5-1	
250	251–252	253	254	299	CM 17–19 RC 31 CS 25	5-2	5-2	18	24, 25	58	5-2	markers
255	256–257	258	259			5-3	5-3		26		5-3	
260	261–262	263	264	299, 301		5-4	5-4				5-4	
265	266–267	268	269		SM 53–56, 89–92	5-5	5-5				5-5	
270	271–272	273	274	300	CS 26	5-6	5-6	19	27, 28		5-6	
275	276–277	278	279		CS 27	5-7	5-7	20		59	5-7	
280	281–282	283	284	285–298, 300, 302–304	CS 28	5-8	5-8		29		5-8	

* **Key to Abbreviations:** *CS = Calculator and Spreadsheet Masters, RC = Real-Life Career Masters, CM = Classroom Math Games (online), SM = Science and Math Lab Manual (online)*

PowerPoint® Presentations

This CD-ROM is a customizable Microsoft® PowerPoint® presentation that includes:

- In-Class Examples
- Links to Online Study Tools
- 5-Minute Check Transparencies
- Your Turn Exercises

Math Skills Maintenance

Use the Math Skills Maintenance Masters to keep your students' basic math skills fresh. Students can review skills one at a time or in a combined format. The Masters are also available online at msmath3.net/maintenance.

CHAPTER 5

Mathematical Content and Teaching Strategies

Continuity of Instruction

Building on Prior Knowledge

In previous courses, students studied a variety of estimation techniques. In Chapter 1, students worked with expressions and equations. They learned how to solve simple linear equations. In Chapter 2, students reviewed fractions. Specifically, they reviewed fraction/decimal conversions, comparing fractions, and operations with fractions. They further used fractions in ratios and proportions in the previous chapter.

Learning in This Chapter

Students study percents in a variety of situations. They investigate the relationships among fractions, decimals, ratios, and percents. They discover how to compute percents mentally, as well as how to estimate with percents. They apply their knowledge of equations to solving problems with percents. The chapter concludes with a study of percent of change and simple interest.

Making Future Connections

Students see percents in numerous real-life situations. The examples in this chapter illustrate many of these situations, such as retail pricing, taxes, banking, population, and so on. In particular, an understanding of interest will help students make wise financial decisions. Being able to compute percents easily and being able to manipulate them algebraically will be essential life skills.

Mathematical Background

5-1 Ratios and Percents

A percent is a standardized ratio comparing a number to 100. In order to apply ratios to a variety of situations, students must be able to convert a ratio to a percent. In this lesson, students work with terminating decimals. The concepts are expanded to include repeating decimals in Lesson 8-2.

5-2 Fractions, Decimals, and Percents

Percents can be converted to decimals or fractions to ease problem solving. Students need to understand the relationships among decimals, percents, and fractions so that they can compare numbers by converting the numbers into the same form.

5-3 Algebra: The Percent Proportion

Setting up a proportion is one way to solve problems involving percents. Students determine what information goes into the proportion and where it is placed. Proportions are used to compare two ratios. By using the proportion, students can keep track of the parts of the problem easily.

5-4 Finding Percents Mentally

While many percents are easily converted into fractions, there are some more common percent-fraction equivalents that students are encouraged to know. The ability to easily compute percents is important in a variety of real-life situations, such as retail pricing, tipping, and banking.

5-5 Percent and Estimation

Compatible numbers can be used when the exact percent is not required, for example, when estimating. When shopping, it is a good idea to have an estimated total to ensure that sale items are rung correctly.

5-6 Algebra: The Percent Equation

The percent equation is used to find the percent of a number. The equation can be manipulated to find whichever variable is missing. This equation is the algebraically simplified percent proportion. Students are able to use the algebraic form to quickly solve a problem involving percents.

Teacher to Teacher

Tricia Creech
Southeast Middle School
Greensboro, NC

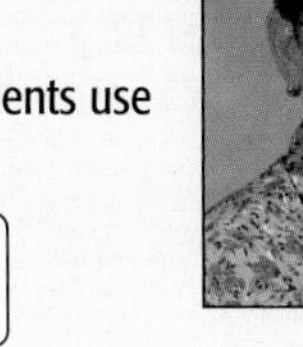

"I use a triangle to help students use the percent equation.

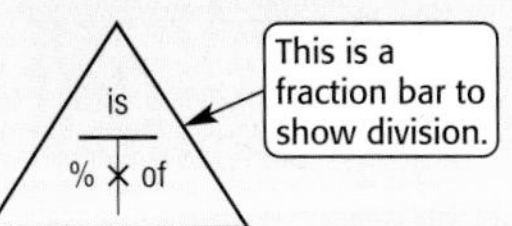

By filling in the appropriate numbers for a problem, students know whether to multiply or divide to solve."

Tricia Creech

5-7 Percent of Change

Any time two numbers are compared, the percent of change can be determined. This can be either an increase or decrease. Percent of change is frequently used when talking about population increases.

Team Teaching

Inform the other teachers on your team that your classes are studying percents and percent of change. Suggestions for curriculum integration are:

Physical Education: computing the percent of free throws made by the class in basketball, before and after practice

Science: change in mass of a substance, quantifying by computing the percent of change

5-8 Simple Interest

Although investing is rarely done using simple interest, it is a basis for understanding compound interest. Compound interest is simple interest performed frequently.

In-Class Speaker

Invite a banker or investment specialist to speak to the class. Have him or her discuss how interest is used in different types of accounts and loans. The speaker also can explain simple interest and compound interest.

What the Research Says

According to Musthafa in *Learning from Texts and Reading Instruction,* reading word problems requires special skills: understanding the problem situation, identifying the main idea, and extracting relevant information.

- The Study Skill activity on page 215 shows students how to read math problems by identifying key terms.
- The Problem-Solving Strategy lesson on page 226 provides two pages of exercises so that students can practice reading and solving word problems.

McGraw-Hill Professional Development

Mathematics, YES! is a self-paced, web-based professional development program. Units are based on major mathematical concepts and are standards-based. Actual classroom videos provide a springboard for discussion and activities. Unit appropriate for this chapter:

- Fractions, Decimals, and Percentages

Additional mathematical information and teaching notes are available at msmath3.net/key_concepts.

DAILY INTERVENTION and Assessment

* **Key to Abbreviations:**
TWE = Teacher Wraparound Edition, *CRM* = Chapter Resource Masters

	Type	Student Edition	Teacher Resources	Technology/Internet
INTERVENTION	Ongoing	Prerequisite Skills, pp. 205, 209, 214, 231, 235, 240 Mid-Chapter Practice Test, p. 224	5-Minute Check Transparencies Quizzes 1–4, *CRM*, pp. 299–300 Mid-Chapter Test, *CRM*, p. 301 Study Guide and Intervention, *CRM*, pp. 245, 250, 255, 260, 265, 270, 275, 280	MathPASS: Tutorial Plus msmath3.net/self_check_quiz msmath3.net/extra_examples
INTERVENTION	Mixed Review	pp. 209, 214, 219, 223, 231, 235, 240, 244	Cumulative Review, *CRM*, p. 302	
INTERVENTION	Error Analysis	Find the Error, pp. 212, 218, 222, 239	Find the Error, *TWE*, pp. 212, 218, 222, 239 Unlocking Misconceptions, *TWE*, pp. 221, 242 Tips for New Teachers, *TWE*, p. 211	
ASSESSMENT	Standardized Test Practice	pp. 209, 214, 219, 223, 224, 227, 231, 235, 240, 242, 244, 249, 250–251	Standardized Test Practice, *CRM*, pp. 303–304	Standardized Test Practice CD-ROM msmath3.net/standardized_test
ASSESSMENT	Open-Ended Assessment	Writing Math, pp. 218, 222, 230, 239, 243 Open-Ended, pp. 208, 212, 218, 222, 230, 234, 239, 243 Standardized Test, p. 251	Modeling: *TWE*, p. 231 Speaking: *TWE*, pp. 209, 244 Writing: *TWE*, pp. 214, 223, 227 Extended Response Assessment, *CRM*, p. 297	
ASSESSMENT	Chapter Assessment	Study Guide, pp. 246–248 Practice Test, p. 249	Multiple-Choice Tests (Forms 1, 2A, 2B), *CRM*, pp. 285–290 Free-Response Tests (Forms 2C, 2D, 3), *CRM*, pp. 291–296 Vocabulary Test/Review, *CRM*, p. 298	ExamView® Pro Testmaker (see below) MindJogger Videoquizzes msmath3.net/vocabulary_review msmath3.net/chapter_test

For more information on Yearly ProgressPro, see p. 152.

Glencoe Lesson	Yearly ProgressPro Skill Name
5-1	Ratios and Percents
5-2	Fraction/Decimal/Percent Conversions: Level 2
5-3	Percent Proportion and Equation
5-4	Finding Percents Mentally
5-5	Percent and Estimation
5-6	Percent Proportion and Equation
5-7	Percent of Change
5-8	Simple Interest

ExamView® Pro

Use ExamView® Pro Testmaker CD-ROM to:

- **Create multiple versions of tests.**
- **Create modified tests for inclusion students with one mouse click.**
- **Edit existing questions and add your own questions.**
- **Build tests aligned with state standards using built-in state curriculum correlations.**
- **Change English tests to Spanish with one mouse click and vice versa.**

Reading and Writing in Mathematics

READING in the Content Area

This online worksheet provides strategies for reading and analyzing Lesson 5-3, The Percent Proportion. Students are guided through questions about the main idea, subject matter, supporting details, conclusion, clarifying details, and vocabulary of the lesson.

Interactive Study Notebook With Foldables™ is a study organizer that provides helpful steps for students to follow to organize their notes for Chapter 5.

- Students use Noteables to record notes and to complete their Foldables as you present the material in Lessons 5-1 through 5-8.
- Noteables follow the *Teacher Wraparound Edition's* In-Class Examples and *Interactive Chalkboard CD-ROM.*

For more information on Reading and Writing in Mathematics, see pp. T6–T7.

Recommended Outside Reading for Students

Nonfiction

- Dewdney, A. K. *200 Percent of Nothing: An Eye-Opening Tour Through The Twists and Turns of Math Abuse and Innumeracy.* John Wiley and Sons, ©1993.

  This book examines how math is misused in every day contexts. It will help students recognize what to look out for when observing math in real life. Many of the examples include percents.

Fiction

- Ritchie, Alan. *Erin McEwan, Your Days Are Numbered.* Alfred Knopf, ©1990.

  Erin McEwan will have to repeat sixth grade if she doesn't improve her math grades. Against her parents' wishes, she gets a job. She ends up learning math at work.

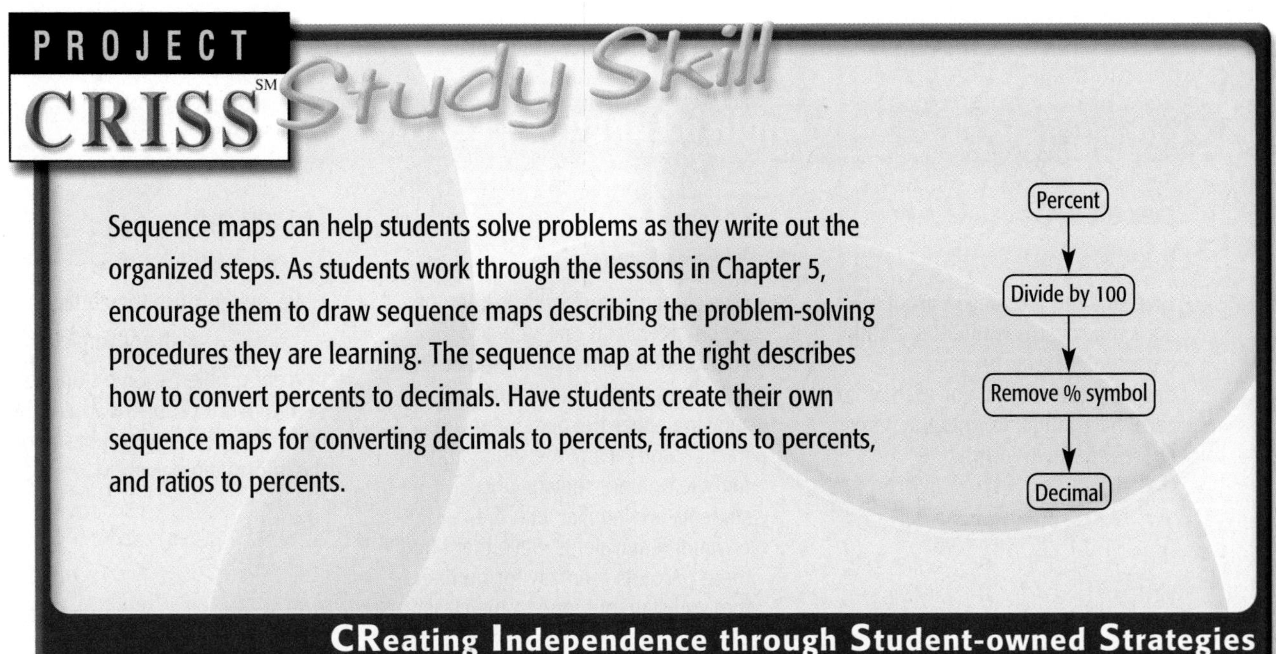

Sequence maps can help students solve problems as they write out the organized steps. As students work through the lessons in Chapter 5, encourage them to draw sequence maps describing the problem-solving procedures they are learning. The sequence map at the right describes how to convert percents to decimals. Have students create their own sequence maps for converting decimals to percents, fractions to percents, and ratios to percents.

For more information on Project CRISS, see p. T8.

CHAPTER 5 Making Connections

School-To-Home

Parent and Student Study Guide

Parents and students may work together to reinforce the concepts and skills of this chapter. These online worksheets are available in English and Spanish at msmath3.net/parent_student. A sample lesson is shown below.

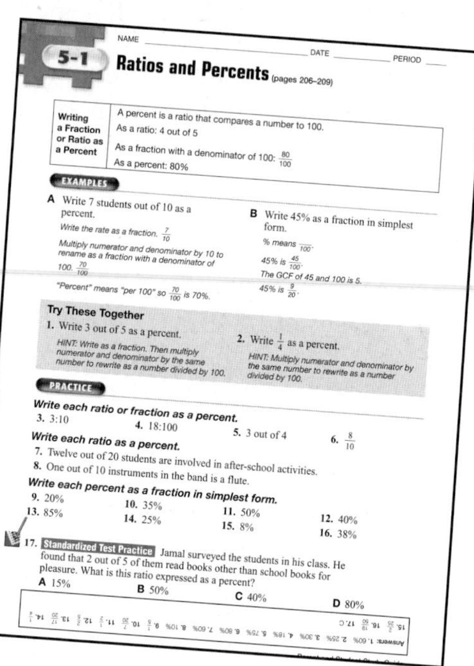

5-1 NAME ______ DATE ______ PERIOD ______

Ratios and Percents (pages 206–209)

Writing a Fraction or Ratio as a Percent	A percent is a ratio that compares a number to 100. As a ratio: 4 out of 5 As a fraction with a denominator of 100: $\frac{80}{100}$ As a percent: 80%

EXAMPLES

A Write 7 students out of 10 as a percent.
Write the rate as a fraction. $\frac{7}{10}$
Multiply numerator and denominator by 10 to rename as a fraction with a denominator of 100. $\frac{70}{100}$
"Percent" means "per 100" so $\frac{70}{100}$ is 70%.

B Write 45% as a fraction in simplest form.
% means $\frac{}{100}$.
45% is $\frac{45}{100}$.
The GCF of 45 and 100 is 5.
45% is $\frac{9}{20}$.

Try These Together

1. Write 3 out of 5 as a percent.
HINT: Write as a fraction. Then multiply numerator and denominator by the same number to rewrite as a number divided by 100.

2. Write $\frac{1}{4}$ as a percent.
HINT: Multiply numerator and denominator by the same number to rewrite as a number divided by 100.

PRACTICE

Write each ratio or fraction as a percent.
3. 3:10 4. 18:100 5. 3 out of 4 6. $\frac{8}{10}$

Write each ratio as a percent.
7. Twelve out of 20 students are involved in after-school activities.
8. One out of 10 instruments in the band is a flute.

Write each percent as a fraction in simplest form.
9. 20% 10. 35% 11. 50% 12. 40%
13. 85% 14. 25% 15. 8% 16. 38%

17. Standardized Test Practice Jamal surveyed the students in his class. He found that 2 out of 5 of them read books other than school books for pleasure. What is this ratio expressed as a percent?
A 15% B 50% C 40% D 80%

Family Letters and Activities

Send a letter and activity for this chapter home to encourage family members to become active participants in their students' learning. (English: *Chapter 5 Resource Masters*, pp. ix–x; Spanish: log on to msmath3.net/family_letters)

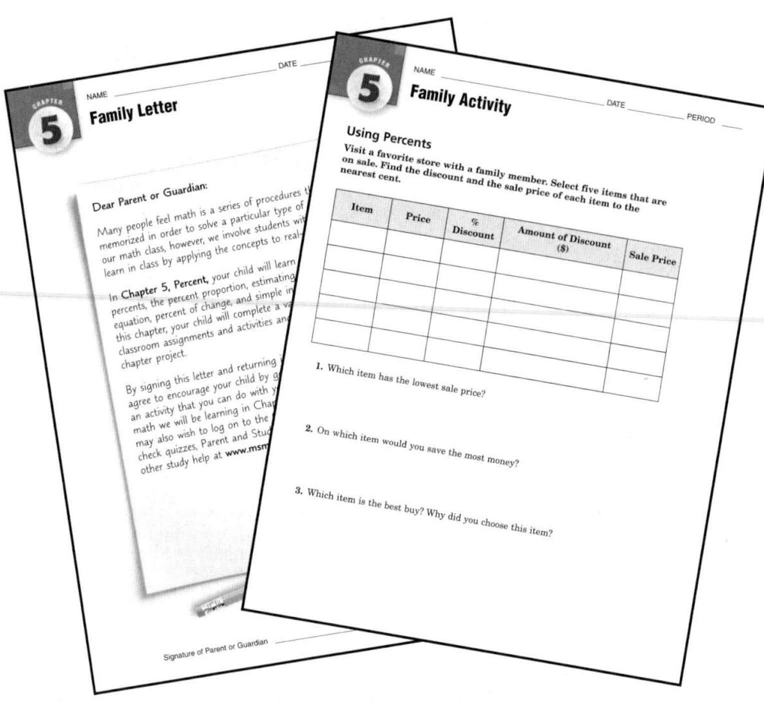

CHAPTER 5 NAME ______ DATE ______

Family Letter

Dear Parent or Guardian:

Many people feel math is a series of procedures t… memorized in order to solve a particular type of… our math class, however, we involve students wi… learn in class by applying the concepts to real…

In Chapter 5, Percent, your child will learn… percents, the percent proportion, estimating… equation, percent of change, and simple in… this chapter, your child will complete a va… classroom assignments and activities an… chapter project.

By signing this letter and returning… agree to encourage your child by g… an activity that you can do with y… math we will be learning in Cha… may also wish to log on to the… check quizzes, Parent and Stu… other study help at www.msm…

Signature of Parent or Guardian ______

CHAPTER 5 NAME ______ DATE ______ PERIOD ______

Family Activity

Using Percents

Visit a favorite store with a family member. Select five items that are on sale. Find the discount and the sale price of each item to the nearest cent.

Item	Price	% Discount	Amount of Discount ($)	Sale Price

1. Which item has the lowest sale price?

2. On which item would you save the most money?

3. Which item is the best buy? Why did you choose this item?

English Language Learner ELL

Lesson 5-1

Reading and Writing

Give students working in groups or pairs index cards with either a ratio, a percent, or a verbal phrase describing a percent. For each index card, have students write the percent in the other two forms.

Lesson 5-4

Peer Tutoring

Give students cards with commonly used percents on one side and the equivalent fractions on the other. In pairs, have students take turns showing either the percent or the fraction and having the other student find the one not shown. Once students are familiar with the common equivalents, have them find these percents mentally for numbers that you state out loud to the class.

Lesson 5-6

Using Applications

Have students use the equation $\frac{\%}{100} = \frac{\text{part}}{\text{whole}}$ as they complete percent problems. Give students several word problems where they can set up the equation based on the information given.

MathScape™

This project was supported, in part, by the **National Science Foundation**

MathScape is a mathematics curriculum for grades 6–8 developed by the Seeing and Thinking Mathematically Project at the Education Development Center.

Slopes, Angles, and Ratios

Roads and Ramps

How to Use *MathScape* with Chapter 5

The unit *Roads and Ramps* can be used to enhance Lessons 5-1 and 5-2.

- **Enrich** → After you complete **Lesson 5-1,** you can use the activities on pages 246–247 to relate slope ratios to percent grade.
- **Enrich** → After you complete **Lesson 5-2,** you can use the activities on pages 250–251 to relate the slope ratio to the tangent ratio written as a decimal.

For other lessons in Chapter 5 that correlate to *MathScape*, see the chart on page T14.

Online Lesson Planner

USA TODAY® Education's Online site offers resources and interactive features connected to each day's newspaper. *Experience Today,* USA TODAY's® daily lesson plan, is available on the site and delivered daily to subscribers. This plan provides instruction for integrating USA TODAY® graphics and key editorial features into your mathematics classroom. Log on to **education.usatoday.com**.

USA TODAY Snapshots® in Chapter 5	
Lesson	**Snapshot**
5-1	Radio is strong influence on music buying
5-2	Parents make the grade
5-3	Turtles are right at home
5-8	Generation X wants to invest

Quick Review Math Handbook

is Glencoe's mathematical handbook for students. The Hot Words section includes a glossary of terms while the Hot Topics section consists of explanations of key mathematical concepts. An exercise set is included to check students' understanding of the concepts. This valuable resource can be used as a reference in the classroom or for home study.

Lesson	Hot Topics Section	Lesson	Hot Topics Section
5-1	2-7, 2-9	5-5	2-8
5-2	2-5, 2-7, 2-9	5-6	2-8
5-3	2-8, 6-5	5-7	2-8, 6-5
5-4	2-8	5-8	2-8, 9-4

Key Chapter Objectives

Lesson 5-2 Write percents as fractions and decimals and vice versa.

Lessons 5-3 and 5-4 Solve problems and compute mentally with percents.

Lesson 5-7 Find and use the percent of increase or decrease.

Lesson 5-8 Solve problems involving simple interest.

"What does baseball have to do with math?"

Point out to students that this is only one of many applications of the math that they are studying. Others are provided in the introduction to each lesson.

Vocabulary Builder, pp. vii–viii ELL

NAME ______________ DATE ________ PERIOD ____

5 Reading to Learn Mathematics

Vocabulary Builder

This is an alphabetical list of new vocabulary terms you will learn in Chapter 5. As you study the chapter, complete each term's definition or description. Remember to add the page number where you found the term. Add this page to your math study notebook to review vocabulary at the end of the chapter.

Vocabulary Term	Found on Page	Definition/Description/Example
base		
compatible numbers		
discount		
interest		
markup		
part		
percent		

CHAPTER 5 Percent

"What does baseball have to do with math?"

Fans and people involved with baseball often track the ratio of a player's hits to his times at bat. This ratio can be written as a decimal or as a percent.

You will solve problems about baseball and other sports in Lesson 5-1.

Vocabulary Builder

For a thorough vocabulary list with pronunciations of new words, give students the Vocabulary Builder worksheets from the *Chapter 5 Resource Masters.* Encourage them to complete the definition of each term as they progress through the chapter.

GETTING STARTED

▶ Diagnose Readiness

Take this quiz to see if you are ready to begin Chapter 5. Refer to the lesson number in parentheses for review.

Vocabulary Review

Choose the correct term to complete each sentence.

1. 2 + 3 = 5 is an (equation, expression). (Lesson 1-7)
2. A (product, ratio) is a comparison of two numbers by division. (Lesson 4-1)
3. Two or more equal ratios can be written to form a (relation, proportion). (Lesson 4-4)

Prerequisite Skills

Compute each product mentally.

4. $\frac{1}{3} \cdot 303$ **101**
5. $644 \cdot \frac{1}{2}$ **322**
6. $0.1 \cdot 550$ **55**
7. $64 \cdot 0.5$ **32**

Write each fraction as a decimal. (Lesson 2-1)

8. $\frac{2}{5}$ **0.4**
9. $\frac{7}{8}$ **0.875**
10. $\frac{3}{4}$ **0.75**
11. $\frac{3}{8}$ **0.375**

Solve each equation. (Lesson 2-7)

12. $0.25d = 130$ **520**
13. $48r = 12$ **0.25**
14. $0.4m = 22$ **55**
15. $0.02n = 9$ **450**
16. $96 = y \cdot 30 \cdot 4$ **0.8**
17. $f \cdot 5 \cdot 12 = 21$ **0.35**

Solve each proportion. (Lesson 4-4)

18. $\frac{x}{10} = \frac{3}{5}$ **6**
19. $\frac{4}{9} = \frac{14}{b}$ **31.5**
20. $\frac{7}{23} = \frac{s}{46}$ **14**
21. $\frac{6}{z} = \frac{5}{13}$ **15.6**

Percent Make this Foldable to help you organize your notes. Begin with four sheets of $8\frac{1}{2}$" × 11" paper.

STEP 1 Draw a Circle Draw a large circle on one of the sheets of paper.

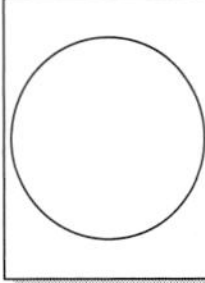

STEP 2 Stack and Cut Stack the sheets of paper. Place the one with the circle on top. Cut all four sheets in the shape of a circle.

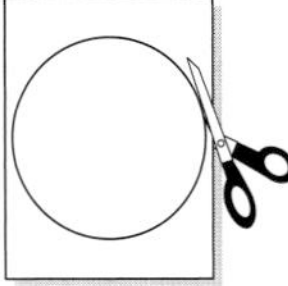

STEP 3 Staple and Label Staple the circles on the left side. Write the first four lesson numbers on each circle.

STEP 4 Turn and Label Turn the circles to the back side so that the staples are still on the left. Write the last four lesson numbers on each circle.

Chapter Notes Each time you find this logo throughout the chapter, use your *Noteables™: Interactive Study Notebook with Foldables™* or your own notebook to take notes. Begin your chapter notes with this Foldable activity.

Math Online **Readiness** To prepare yourself for this chapter with another quiz, visit **msmath3.net/chapter_readiness**

GETTING STARTED

Diagnose Readiness This section provides a review of the basic concepts needed before beginning Chapter 5. Page references are included for additional student help.

Prerequisite Skills review skills needed in this chapter.

Exercises	Needed for Lesson	Skill
4–7	5-4	Compute Products Mentally
8–11	5-2	Write Fractions as Decimals
12–17	5-6	Solve Equations
18–21	5-3	Solve Proportions

For more prerequisite skills, see:

- Getting Ready for the Next Lesson, at the end of each lesson
- Prerequisite Skills in the Student Handbook on pp. 600–615
- *Math Skills Maintenance Masters*

FOLDABLES™ Study Organizer

For more information about Foldables, see *Teaching Mathematics with Foldables.*

Use this Foldable study guide to help students understand the language and concepts of percent, and to use visuals and graphics to depict what they learn. You may wish to have students use a compass to draw neat circles for their Foldables. Encourage students to design visuals that present the information introduced in the lesson in a concrete, easy-to-study format. Ask students to clearly label their visuals and write captions when needed.

5-1 Lesson Notes

Lesson Resources

Chapter 5 Resource Masters
- Study Guide and Intervention, p. 245
- Practice: Skills, p. 246
- Practice: Word Problems, p. 247
- Reading to Learn Mathematics, p. 248
- Enrichment, p. 249

Key Teaching Transparencies, 17
Parent and Student Study Guide Online Worksheets, 5-1
Teaching Mathematics with Manipulatives, pp. 56–57
Noteables™: Interactive Study Notebook with Foldables™, 5-1

FAST FILE

1 Focus

5-Minute Check 5-1

Use as a quiz or review of Chapter 4. (Also available as a transparency)

Bellringer

Communication Take a survey of the class to answer questions such as the following.

1. How many students are wearing watches?
2. How many students are left-handed?
3. How many students have brown eyes?

Ask students whether they have any ideas of how to write the answers as comparisons.

Reading to Learn Mathematics, p. 248 **ELL**

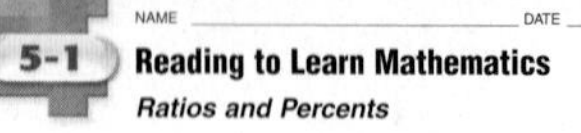

NAME ______________ DATE ________ PERIOD ____

5-1 Reading to Learn Mathematics
Ratios and Percents

Pre-Activity *Read the introduction at the top of page 206 in your textbook. Write your answers below.*

1. Name two states from the table that have ratios in which the second numbers are the same. **Hawaii and Utah**
2. Of the two states you named in Exercise 1, which state has a greater ratio of people under 18 to total population? Explain. **Utah; $6 < 8$**
3. Describe how to determine which of the four states has the greater ratio of people under 18 to total population. **Write the ratios as decimals or change the ratios so they are compared to the same number.**

Reading the Lesson

4. How is *percent* defined on page 206 of your textbook? **a ratio that compares a number to 100**

5-1 Ratios and Percents

What You'll LEARN

Write ratios as percents and vice versa.

NEW Vocabulary

percent

REVIEW Vocabulary

ratio: a comparison of two numbers by division (Lesson 4-1)

WHEN am I ever going to use this?

POPULATION The table shows the ratio of people under 18 years of age to the total population for various states. **2. Utah; $6 < 8$**

State	Ratio of People Under 18 to Total Population
Arkansas	1 out of 4
Hawaii	6 out of 25
Mississippi	27 out of 100
Utah	8 out of 25

Source: *Time Almanac*

1. Name two states from the table that have ratios in which the second numbers are the same. **Hawaii and Utah**
2. Of the two states you named in Exercise 1, which state has a greater ratio of people under 18 to total population? Explain.
3. Describe how to determine which of the four states has the greater ratio of people under 18 to total population.

3. Write the ratios as decimals or change the ratios so they are compared to the same number.

Ratios such as 27 out of 100 or 8 out of 25 can be written as **percents**.

Noteables™ **Key Concept: Percent**

A percent is a ratio that compares a number to 100.

Ratio 27 out of 100
Symbols 27%
Words twenty-seven percent

Model

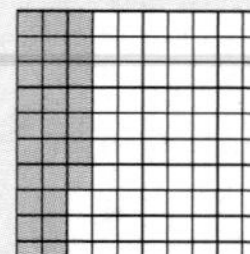

EXAMPLES Write Ratios as Percents

Write each ratio as a percent.

1 **POPULATION** **According to the 2000 U.S. Census, 26 out of every 100 people living in Illinois were younger than 18.**

26 out of 100 = 26%

2 **SPORTS** **At a recent triathlon, 180 women competed for every 100 women who competed ten years earlier.**

180 out of 100 = 180%

STUDY TIP

Large Percents Notice that some percents, such as 180%, are greater than 100%.

Your Turn **Write each ratio as a percent.**

a. **BASEBALL** During his baseball career, Babe Ruth had a base hit about 34 out of every 100 times he came to bat. **34%**

b. **TECHNOLOGY** In a recent year, 41.5 out of 100 households in the United States had access to the Internet. **41.5%**

DAILY INTERVENTION **Differentiated Instruction**

Intrapersonal Have students look at the table at the beginning of the lesson. Have them write in their journals about comparing ratios and comparing percents. Which do they find easier? Would they rather read an article with information in ratios or percents? Why?

REAL-LIFE MATH

CARS The first law regulating the speed of cars was passed in the state of New York in 1904. It stated that the maximum speed in populated areas was 10 miles per hour and the maximum speed in the country was 20 miles per hour.

Source: *The World Almanac*

One way to write a fraction or a ratio as a percent is by finding an equivalent fraction with a denominator of 100.

EXAMPLES Write Ratios and Fractions as Percents

Write each ratio or fraction as a percent.

3 CARS About 1 out of 5 luxury cars manufactured in the United States is white.

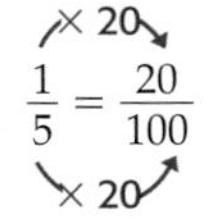

$$\frac{1}{5} = \frac{20}{100} \quad (\times 20)$$

So, 1 out of 5 equals 20%.

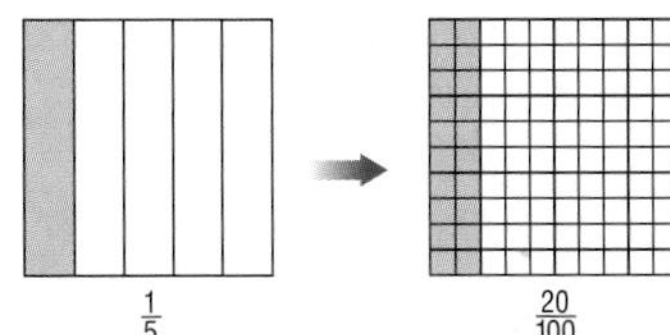

4 TRAVEL About $\frac{1}{200}$ of travelers use scheduled buses.

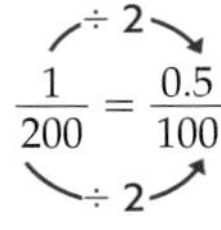

$$\frac{1}{200} = \frac{0.5}{100} \quad (\div 2)$$

So, 1 out of 200 equals 0.5%.

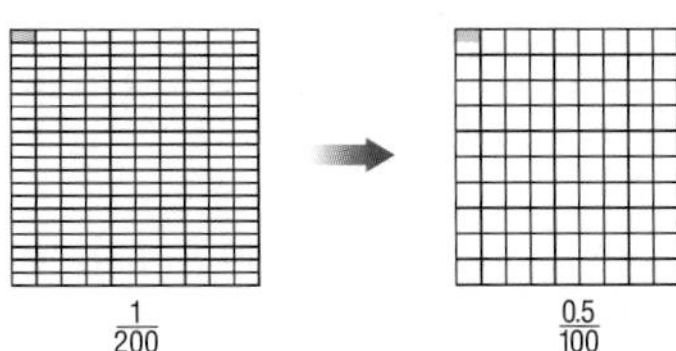

Your Turn **Write each ratio or fraction as a percent.**

c. **TECHNOLOGY** In Finland, almost 3 out of 5 people have cell phones. **60%**

d. **ANIMALS** About $\frac{1}{4}$ of the mammals in the world are bats. **25%**

STUDY TIP

Small Percents In Example 4, notice that 0.5% is less than 1%.

You can express a percent as a fraction by writing it as a fraction with a denominator of 100. Then write the fraction in simplest form.

EXAMPLE Write Percents as Fractions

5 ENVIRONMENT The circle graph shows an estimate of the percent of each type of trash in landfills. Write the percents for paper and for plastic as a fraction in simplest form.

Paper: $30\% = \frac{30}{100}$ or $\frac{3}{10}$

Plastic: $24\% = \frac{24}{100}$ or $\frac{6}{25}$

Trash in Landfills

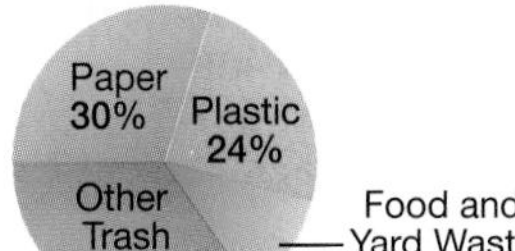

Source: Franklin Associates, Ltd.

TEACHING TIP

Tell students that the sum of the percents in a circle graph is 100%.

Your Turn **Write the percent for each of the following as a fraction in simplest form.**

e. food and yard waste $\frac{11}{100}$ f. other trash $\frac{7}{20}$

msmath3.net/extra_examples

2 Teach

Noteables™

As you work the **In-Class Examples,** have students follow along in their *Noteables™: Interactive Study Notebook with Foldables™*, or have students work the examples in their notebooks.

In-Class Examples

Write each ratio or fraction as a percent.

1 **POPULATION** According to the 2000 U.S. Census, 13 out of every 100 people living in Delaware were 65 or older. **13%**

2 **BASEBALL** In 2001, Manny Ramirez got on base 40.5 times for every 100 times he was at bat. **40.5%**

3 **TRANSPORTATION** About 4 out of 5 commuters in the United States drive or carpool to work. **80%**

4 **INTERNET** In 2000, about $\frac{3}{200}$ of the population in Peru used the Internet. **1.5%**

5 **SCHEDULE** The circle graph shows an estimate of the percent of his day that Peter spends on each activity. Write the percents for eating and sleeping as fractions in simplest form. **eat: $\frac{1}{20}$; sleep: $\frac{7}{20}$**

How Peter Spends His Day

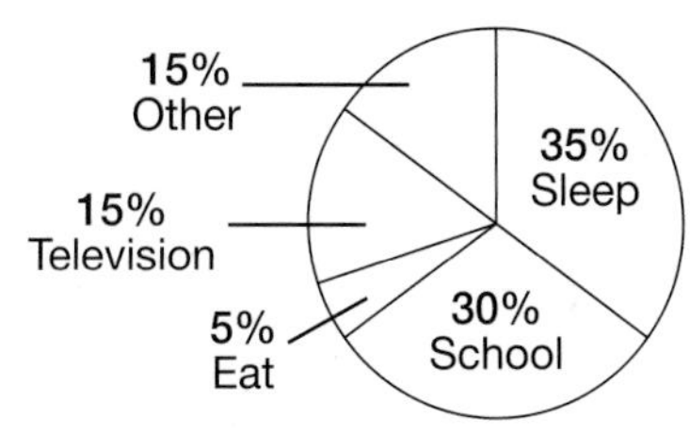

Tips for New Teachers

Classroom Management Often students who quickly understand a concept can help explain it to other students. Have them make up examples or problems to share.

3 Practice/Apply

FOLDABLES™ Follow-Up Remind students to use their Foldables to record in words and symbols what they learn about expressing percents as ratios and ratios as percents. Students might give examples of what they have learned, or they could record new terms that they need to learn. Encourage students to use grid paper to express a ratio as a percent and glue their examples in their Foldables.

Which One Doesn't Belong? Students should recognize that there are several ways to solve Exercise 3. They can convert the three fractions to percents, or convert 40% to a fraction and reduce all the fractions to simplest form.

About the Exercises...

Guided Practice Key

Exercises	Examples
4–7, 12	1–4
8–11	5

Assignment Guide

Basic: 13–33 odd, 39, 41, 47–56

Average: 13–43 odd, 44–56

Enriched: 14–42 even, 44–52 (Optional: 53–56)

Students practice the same concepts in Exercises 13–40 if they are assigned odd or even problems.

Skill and Concept Check

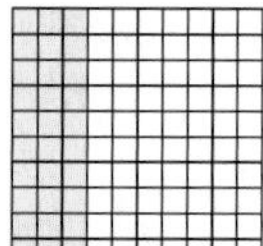

1. **Write** the percent and the fraction in simplest form for the model shown at the right. **30%; $\frac{3}{10}$**
2. **OPEN ENDED** Write a percent that is between $\frac{1}{2}$ and $\frac{3}{4}$. **Sample answer: 60%**
3. **Which One Doesn't Belong?** Identify the number that does not have the same value as the other three. Explain your reasoning.

$\frac{2}{5}$	40%	$\frac{20}{100}$	$\frac{10}{25}$

3. $\frac{20}{100}$; All the other numbers equal 40%.

GUIDED PRACTICE

Write each ratio or fraction as a percent.

4. 17 out of 100 **17%**
5. 237 out of 100 **237%**
6. 7:10 **70%**
7. $\frac{9}{20}$ **45%**

Write each percent as a fraction in simplest form.

8. 19% **$\frac{19}{100}$**
9. 50% **$\frac{1}{2}$**
10. 18% **$\frac{9}{50}$**
11. 0.4% **$\frac{1}{250}$**

12. **TRAVEL** One out of every 50 travelers visiting the United States is from France. Write this ratio as a percent. **2%**

★ indicates increased difficulty

Practice and Applications

HOMEWORK HELP

For Exercises	See Examples
13–16	1, 2
17–20, 25–26	3
21–24	4
27–41	5

Extra Practice See pages 626, 652.

Write each ratio or fraction as a percent.

13. 23 out of 100 **23%**
14. 9 out of 100 **9%**
15. 0.3 out of 100 **0.3%**
16. 0.7 out of 100 **0.7%**
17. 3:5 **60%**
18. 9:10 **90%**
19. 8:25 **32%**
20. 17:20 **85%**
21. $\frac{17}{50}$ **34%**
22. $\frac{7}{20}$ **35%**
★23. $\frac{39}{20}$ **195%**
★24. $\frac{47}{25}$ **188%**

25. **PETS** Three out of 25 households in the United States have both a dog and a cat. Write this ratio as a percent. **12%**

26. **MUSIC** Eleven out of 25 Americans like rock music. Write this ratio as a percent. **44%**

Write each percent as a fraction in simplest form.

27. 29% **$\frac{29}{100}$**
28. 43% **$\frac{43}{100}$**
29. 40% **$\frac{2}{5}$**
30. 70% **$\frac{7}{10}$**
31. 45% **$\frac{9}{20}$**
32. 28% **$\frac{7}{25}$**
33. 64% **$\frac{16}{25}$**
34. 65% **$\frac{13}{20}$**
★35. 125% **$1\frac{1}{4}$**
★36. 240% **$2\frac{2}{5}$**
★37. 0.2% **$\frac{1}{500}$**
★38. 0.8% **$\frac{1}{125}$**

39. **ENERGY** Germany uses about 4% of the world's energy. Write this percent as a fraction. **$\frac{1}{25}$**

40. **GEOGRAPHY** About 30% of Minnesota is forested. Write this percent as a fraction. **$\frac{3}{10}$**

41. **MUSIC** The influences in the purchases of CDs or cassettes are shown in the graphic at the right. Write each percent as a fraction in simplest form. **$\frac{9}{20}$; $\frac{3}{20}$; $\frac{1}{10}$; $\frac{2}{25}$; $\frac{7}{100}$**

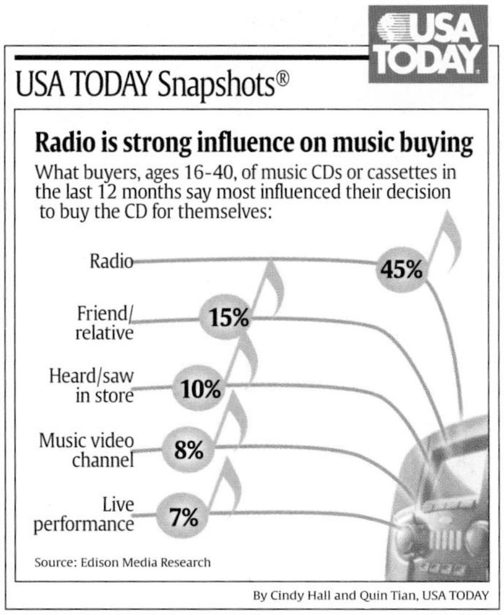

★ 42. Which is less, $\frac{1}{4}$ or 30%? **$\frac{1}{4}$**

★ 43. Which is less, $\frac{2}{5}$ or 37%? **37%**

USA TODAY Snapshots®

Radio is strong influence on music buying

What buyers, ages 16-40, of music CDs or cassettes in the last 12 months say most influenced their decision to buy the CD for themselves:

Radio	45%
Friend/relative	15%
Heard/saw in store	10%
Music video channel	8%
Live performance	7%

Source: Edison Media Research

By Cindy Hall and Quin Tian, USA TODAY

SCIENCE For Exercises 44–46, use the following information.

In 2000, 5 Tyrannosaurus Rex skeletons were found in Montana. In the previous 100 years, only 15 such skeletons had been found.

44. Write a ratio in simplest form to compare the number of Tyrannosaurus Rex skeletons found in 2000 to the total number of skeletons found during the 101 years. **$\frac{1}{4}$**

45. Write the ratio in Exercise 44 as a percent. **25%**

46. What percent of the skeletons where found in the previous 100 years? **75%**

47. **CRITICAL THINKING** Explain how a student can receive a 86% on a test with 50 questions. **See margin.**

Spiral Review with Standardized Test Practice

48. **MULTIPLE CHOICE** What percent of the circle at the right is shaded? **D**

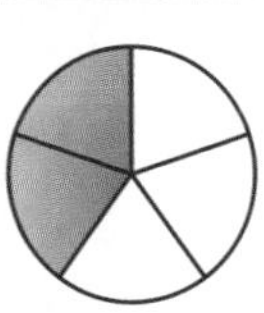

Ⓐ 10% Ⓑ 20%

Ⓒ 30% Ⓓ 40%

49. **MULTIPLE CHOICE** Which value is *not* equal to the other values? **H**

Ⓕ $\frac{14}{25}$ Ⓖ 56% Ⓗ 40:75 Ⓘ 28 out of 50

Segment $P'Q'$ is a dilation of segment PQ. The endpoints of each segment are given. Find the scale factor of the dilation, and classify it as an *enlargement* or as a *reduction*. (Lesson 4-8)

50. $P(0, 6)$ and $Q(3, -9)$
$P'(0, 4)$ and $Q'(2, -6)$ **$\frac{2}{3}$; reduction**

51. $P(-1, 2)$ and $Q(-3, 3)$
$P'(-4, 8)$ and $Q'(-12, 12)$ **4; enlargement**

52. **GEOGRAPHY** The Pyramid of the Sun near Mexico City casts a shadow 13.3 meters long. At the same time, a 1.83-meter tall tourist casts a shadow 0.4 meter long. How tall is the Pyramid of the Sun? (Lesson 4-7) **60.8475 m**

GETTING READY FOR THE NEXT LESSON

PREREQUISITE SKILL Write each fraction as a decimal. (Lesson 2-1)

53. $\frac{3}{5}$ **0.6**

54. $\frac{3}{4}$ **0.75**

55. $\frac{5}{8}$ **0.625**

56. $\frac{1}{3}$ **$0.\overline{3}$**

msmath3.net/self_check_quiz

4 Assess

Open-Ended Assessment

Speaking Have students talk with their other teachers to find out how ratios and percents are used in the different subject areas. Students can share their findings with the class.

Answer

47. Since $\frac{43}{50} = \frac{86}{100}$, a student would receive an 86% on the test if he or she answered 43 out of the 50 questions correctly.

Study Guide and Intervention, p. 245

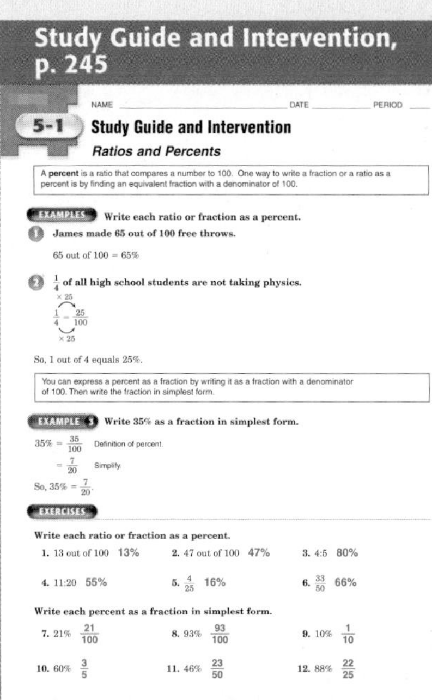

NAME DATE PERIOD

5-1 Study Guide and Intervention

Ratios and Percents

A **percent** is a ratio that compares a number to 100. One way to write a fraction or a ratio as a percent is by finding an equivalent fraction with a denominator of 100.

EXAMPLES Write each ratio or fraction as a percent.

1 James made 65 out of 100 free throws.

65 out of 100 = 65%

2 $\frac{1}{4}$ of all high school students are not taking physics.

$\frac{1}{4} = \frac{25}{100}$ (× 25)

So, 1 out of 4 equals 25%.

You can express a percent as a fraction by writing it as a fraction with a denominator of 100. Then write the fraction in simplest form.

EXAMPLE 3 Write 35% as a fraction in simplest form.

$35\% = \frac{35}{100}$ Definition of percent.

$= \frac{7}{20}$ Simplify.

So, $35\% = \frac{7}{20}$.

EXERCISES

Write each ratio or fraction as a percent.

1. 13 out of 100 13%
2. 47 out of 100 47%
3. 4:5 80%
4. 11:20 55%
5. $\frac{4}{25}$ 16%
6. $\frac{33}{50}$ 66%

Write each percent as a fraction in simplest form.

7. 21% $\frac{21}{100}$
8. 93% $\frac{93}{100}$
9. 10% $\frac{1}{10}$
10. 60% $\frac{3}{5}$
11. 46% $\frac{23}{50}$
12. 88% $\frac{22}{25}$

Practice: Skills, p. 246

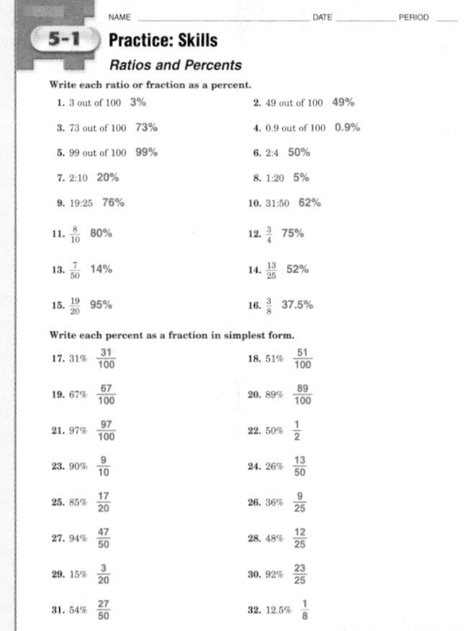

NAME DATE PERIOD

5-1 Practice: Skills

Ratios and Percents

Write each ratio or fraction as a percent.

1. 3 out of 100 3%
2. 49 out of 100 49%
3. 73 out of 100 73%
4. 0.9 out of 100 0.9%
5. 99 out of 100 99%
6. 2:4 50%
7. 2:10 20%
8. 1:20 5%
9. 19:25 76%
10. 31:50 62%
11. $\frac{8}{10}$ 80%
12. $\frac{3}{4}$ 75%
13. $\frac{7}{50}$ 14%
14. $\frac{13}{25}$ 52%
15. $\frac{19}{20}$ 95%
16. $\frac{3}{8}$ 37.5%

Write each percent as a fraction in simplest form.

17. 31% $\frac{31}{100}$
18. 51% $\frac{51}{100}$
19. 67% $\frac{67}{100}$
20. 89% $\frac{89}{100}$
21. 97% $\frac{97}{100}$
22. 50% $\frac{1}{2}$
23. 90% $\frac{9}{10}$
24. 26% $\frac{13}{50}$
25. 85% $\frac{17}{20}$
26. 36% $\frac{9}{25}$
27. 94% $\frac{47}{50}$
28. 48% $\frac{12}{25}$
29. 15% $\frac{3}{20}$
30. 92% $\frac{23}{25}$
31. 54% $\frac{27}{50}$
32. 12.5% $\frac{1}{8}$

Practice: Word Problems, p. 247

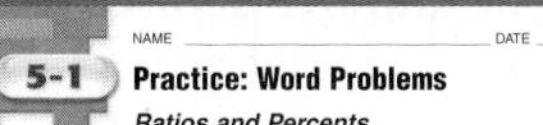

NAME DATE PERIOD

5-1 Practice: Word Problems

Ratios and Percents

1. PETS Three out of every 20 dogs in the U.S. are Golden Retrievers. Write this ratio as a percent. 15%

2. GEOGRAPHY About 29% of the world's surface is covered by land. Write this percent as a fraction. $\frac{29}{100}$

3. BASKETBALL Shaquille O'Neal of the L.A. Lakers hit 11 out of 20 free throws in a 5-game series. Write this number as a percent. 55%

4. EDUCATION In 2000, about 44% of 21-year-olds in the United States were enrolled in school. Write this percent as a fraction. $\frac{11}{25}$

5. HEALTH CARE In 2000, 14% of Americans did not have health insurance. Write this percent as a fraction. $\frac{7}{50}$

6. ENERGY In 2001, Japan accounted for about 8% of the world's petroleum consumption. Write this percent as a fraction. $\frac{2}{25}$

7. GEOGRAPHY The federal government owns about $\frac{13}{20}$ of the land in the state of Utah. Write this fraction as a percent. 65%

8. POPULATION In 2000, 11 out of every 50 people in the United States were age 65 or older. Write this ratio as a percent. 22%

5-2 Lesson Notes

Lesson Resources

Chapter 5 Resource Masters

- Study Guide and Intervention, p. 250
- Practice: Skills, p. 251
- Practice: Word Problems, p. 252
- Reading to Learn Mathematics, p. 253
- Enrichment, p. 254

FAST FILE

Calculator and Spreadsheet Masters, p. 25

Classroom Math Games, pp. 17–19

Key Teaching Transparencies, 18

MathPASS Tutorial CD-ROM, 30

Parent and Student Study Guide Online Worksheets, 5-2

Real-Life Career Masters, p. 31

Teaching Mathematics with Manipulatives, p. 58

Noteables™: Interactive Study Notebook with Foldables™, 5-2

1 Focus

5-Minute Check 5-2

Use as a quiz or review of Lesson 5-1. (Also available as a transparency)

Bellringer

Problem Solving Have students look at their homework or quiz scores as ratios. To determine their percentage on each item, they can convert the ratio to a percent.

(Continued in bottom margin.)

Reading to Learn Mathematics, p. 253 **ELL**

NAME ______ DATE ______ PERIOD ____

5-2 Reading to Learn Mathematics

Fractions, Decimals, and Percents

Pre-Activity *Read the introduction at the top of page 210 in your textbook. Write your answers below.*

1. Write each percent as a fraction. Do not simplify the fractions. $\frac{39}{100}, \frac{34}{100}, \frac{12}{100}, \frac{7}{100}, \frac{5}{100}$
2. Write each fraction in Exercise 1 as a decimal. 0.39; 0.34; 0.12; 0.07; 0.05
3. How could you write a percent as a decimal without writing the percent as a fraction first? Divide each percent by 100 and remove the percent symbol.

Reading the Lesson

Complete each sentence.

4. To write a decimal as a percent, ______ by 100 and add the percent symbol. multiply

5-2 Fractions, Decimals, and Percents

What You'll LEARN

Write percents as fractions and decimals and vice versa.

WHEN am I ever going to use this?

PETS The table gives the percent of households with various pets.

Households with Pets	
Pet	**Percent of Households**
dog	39%
cat	34%
freshwater fish	12%
bird	7%
small animal	5%

Source: American Pet Products Manufacturers Association

1. Write each percent as a fraction. Do not simplify the fractions.
2. Write each fraction in Exercise 1 as a decimal.
3. How could you write a percent as a decimal without writing the percent as a fraction first?

1. $\frac{39}{100}$; $\frac{34}{100}$; $\frac{12}{100}$; $\frac{7}{100}$; $\frac{5}{100}$
2. 0.39; 0.34; 0.12; 0.07; 0.05
3. Divide each percent by 100 and remove the percent symbol.

Fractions, percents, and decimals are all different ways to represent the same number.

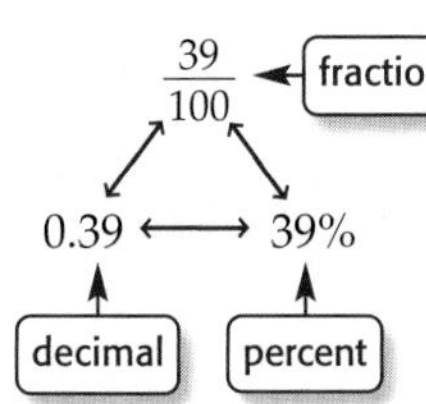

Remember that *percent* means *per hundred*. In Lesson 5-1, you wrote percents as fractions with 100 in the denominator. Similarly, you can write percents as decimals by dividing by 100.

Noteables™ **Key Concept: Decimals and Percents**

- To write a percent as a decimal, divide by 100 and remove the percent symbol.

  39% = 39% = 0.39

- To write a decimal as a percent, multiply by 100 and add the percent symbol.

  0.39 = 0.39 = 39%

EXAMPLES Percents as Decimals

Write each percent as a decimal.

1 **35%**

35% = 35% Divide by 100 and remove the percent symbol.
= 0.35

2 **115%**

115% = 115% Divide by 100 and remove the percent symbol.
= 1.15

Ask students why it is useful to be able to write numbers in different forms. **Sample answers: it is easier to add decimals than fractions; it is easier to write a quiz grade as a fraction.**

STUDY TIP

Mental Math To multiply by 100, move the decimal point two places to the right. To divide by 100, move the decimal point two places to the left.

EXAMPLES Decimals as Percents

Write each decimal as a percent.

3 **0.2**

$0.2 = 0.20$ Multiply by 100 and add the percent symbol.

$= 20\%$

4 **1.66**

$1.66 = 1.66$ Multiply by 100 and add the percent symbol.

$= 166\%$

You have learned to write a fraction as a percent by finding an equivalent fraction with a denominator of 100. This method works well if the denominator is a factor of 100. If the denominator is *not* a factor of 100, you can solve a proportion or you can write the fraction as a decimal and then write the decimal as a percent.

STUDY TIP

Look Back You can review **writing fractions as decimals** in Lesson 2-1.

EXAMPLES Fractions as Percents

Write each fraction as a percent.

5 $\frac{3}{8}$

Method 1 Use a proportion.

$\frac{3}{8} = \frac{x}{100}$

$3 \cdot 100 = 8 \cdot x$

$300 = 8x$

$\frac{300}{8} = \frac{8x}{8}$

$37.5 = x$

Method 2 Write as a decimal.

$\frac{3}{8} = 0.375$

$= 37.5\%$

$$\begin{array}{r} 0.375 \\ 8\overline{)3.000} \\ \underline{2\,4} \\ 60 \\ \underline{56} \\ 40 \\ \underline{40} \\ 0 \end{array}$$

So, $\frac{3}{8}$ can be written as 37.5%.

TEACHING TIP

Encourage students to use whatever method they like best.

6 $\frac{2}{3}$

Method 1 Use a proportion.

$\frac{2}{3} = \frac{x}{100}$

$2 \cdot 100 = 3 \cdot x$

$200 = 3x$

$\frac{200}{3} = \frac{3x}{3}$

$66.\overline{6} = x$

Method 2 Write as a decimal.

$\frac{2}{3} = 0.66\overline{6}$

$= 66.\overline{6}\%$

$$\begin{array}{r} 0.66\ldots \\ 3\overline{)2.0} \\ \underline{1\,8} \\ 20 \\ \underline{18} \\ 2 \end{array}$$

So, $\frac{2}{3}$ can be written as $66.\overline{6}\%$.

Your Turn Write each decimal or fraction as a percent.

a. 0.8 **80%** b. 0.564 **56.4%** c. $\frac{3}{16}$ **18.75%** d. $\frac{1}{9}$ **$11.\overline{1}\%$**

msmath3.net/extra_examples

2 Teach

In-Class Examples

Write each percent as a decimal.

1. 52% **0.52**
2. 245% **2.45**

Write each decimal as a percent.

3. 0.3 **30%**
4. 0.71 **71%**

Write each fraction as a percent.

5. $\frac{3}{4}$ **75%**
6. $\frac{1}{6}$ **$16.\overline{6}\%$**

Tips for New Teachers

Intervention Many students have a hard time with word problems because they have not mastered the math concept behind the problem. For example, you may at first want to assess students' ability to convert between fractions, decimals, and percents in problems that contain numbers only. Point out that moving the decimal point to write a decimal as a percent works because the % symbol means hundredths. Once they show a good understanding of the math involved, move on to real-life word problems.

DAILY INTERVENTION **Flexible Grouping**

Fractions, Decimals, and Percents Have students work in groups of three. Each group member should choose decimals, fractions, or percents. Have one person name an amount of their type; for example, the percent person might begin with 80%. Then the other two should name the amount in their form of number. After each student has begun a round, students should switch roles.

In-Class Example

 **POLITICS** In Sun City, $\frac{9}{20}$ of voters are Democrats. In Moon Town, 48% of voters are Democrats. In which town is there a greater proportion of Democrats? **Moon Town**

3 Practice/Apply

FOLDABLES™ Follow-Up Remind students to use their Foldables to record in words and symbols what they learn about expressing percents as fractions and decimals and decimals as fractions and percents. Students might give examples of what they have learned, or they could record new terms that they need to learn. Encourage students to explain how fractions, percents, and decimals can be used interchangeably.

DAILY INTERVENTION **FIND THE ERROR** For students who have difficulty with Exercise 3, encourage them to write all decimals to two decimal places when converting to percents. For example, they can rewrite 0.7 as 0.70.

About the Exercises...

Guided Practice Key

Exercises	Examples
4–7	1, 2
8–11	3, 4
12–16	5, 6

Assignment Guide

Basic: 17–49 odd, 53–63 odd, 67, 69, 71–85

Average: 17–69 odd, 71–85

Enriched: 18–70 even, 71–81 (Optional: 82–85)

To compare fractions, percents, and decimals, it may be easier to write all of the numbers as percents or decimals.

EXAMPLE Compare Numbers

 **GEOGRAPHY About $\frac{3}{20}$ of the land of Earth is covered by desert. North America is about 16% of the total land surface of Earth. Is the area of the deserts on Earth more or less than the area of North America?**

Write $\frac{3}{20}$ as a percent.

$\frac{3}{20} = 0.15$ $\quad$ $3 \div 20 = 0.15$

$= 15\%$ $\quad$ Multiply by 100 and add the percent symbol.

Since 15% is less than 16%, the area of the deserts on Earth is just slightly less than the area of North America.

Students practice the same concepts in Exercises 17–62 if they are assigned odd or even problems.

Skill and Concept Check

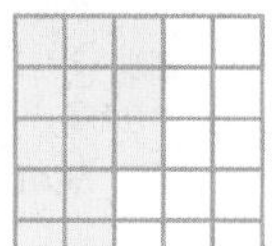

1. **Write** a fraction, a percent, and a decimal to represent the shaded part of the rectangle at the right. **$\frac{13}{25}$; 52%; 0.52**
2. **OPEN ENDED** Write a fraction that could be easily changed to a percent by using equivalent fractions. Then write a fraction that could *not* be easily changed to a percent by using equivalent fractions. Write each fraction as a percent. **Sample answer: $\frac{1}{4} = 25\%$; $\frac{1}{3} = 33.\overline{3}\%$**
3. **FIND THE ERROR** Kristin and Aislyn are changing 0.7 to a percent. Who is correct? Explain.

Kristin	Aislyn
0.7 = 7%	0.7 = 70%

Aislyn; 0.7 is 7 tenths, not 7 hundredths.

GUIDED PRACTICE

Write each percent as a decimal.

4. 40% **0.4** 5. 16% **0.16** 6. 85% **0.85** 7. 0.3% **0.003**

Write each decimal as a percent.

8. 0.68 **68%** 9. 1.23 **123%** 10. 0.3 **30%** 11. 0.725 **72.5%**

Write each fraction as a percent.

12. $\frac{11}{25}$ **44%** 13. $\frac{7}{8}$ **87.5%** 14. $\frac{13}{40}$ **32.5%** 15. $\frac{5}{6}$ **$83.\overline{3}\%$**

16. **ANIMALS** There are 250 known species of sharks. Of that number, only 27 species have been involved in attacks on humans. What percent of known species of sharks have attacked humans? **10.8%**

★ indicates increased difficulty

Practice and Applications

HOMEWORK HELP	
For Exercises	See Examples
17–30, 66	1, 2
31–42	3, 4
43–56	5, 6
57–62, 67–68	7

Extra Practice
See pages 627, 652.

Write each percent as a decimal.

17. 90% **0.9** 18. 80% **0.8** 19. 15% **0.15** 20. 32% **0.32**

21. 172% **1.72** 22. 245% **2.45** 23. 27.5% **0.275** 24. 84.2% **0.842**

25. 7% **0.07** 26. 5% **0.05** 27. 8.2% **0.082** 28. 0.12% **0.0012**

29. **TELEVISION** About 55% of cable TV subscribers decide what program to watch by surfing the channels. Write this number as a decimal. **0.55**

30. **MOVIES** In 1936, 85% of movie theaters had double features. Write this number as a decimal. **0.85**

Write each decimal as a percent.

31. 0.54 **54%** 32. 0.62 **62%** 33. 0.375 **37.5%** 34. 0.632 **63.2%** 35. 0.007 **0.7%**

36. 0.009 **0.9%** 37. 0.4 **40%** 38. 0.9 **90%** 39. 2.75 **275%** 40. 1.38 **138%**

41. **CAMPING** If 0.21 of adults go camping, what percent of the adults camp? **21%**

42. **POPULATION** In 2010, about 0.25 of the U.S. population will be 55 years old or older. What percent of the population will be 55 or older? **25%**

Write each fraction as a percent.

43. $\frac{17}{20}$ **85%** 44. $\frac{12}{25}$ **48%** 45. $\frac{1}{40}$ **2.5%** 46. $\frac{3}{40}$ **7.5%** 47. $\frac{8}{5}$ **160%**

48. $\frac{7}{4}$ **175%** 49. $\frac{1}{200}$ **0.5%** 50. $\frac{1}{400}$ **0.25%** ★51. $\frac{4}{9}$ **44.$\overline{4}$%** ★52. $\frac{2}{3}$ **66.$\overline{6}$%**

53. **TIME** Research indicates that $\frac{8}{25}$ of Americans set their watches five minutes ahead. What percent of Americans set their watches five minutes ahead? **32%**

54. **FOOD** About $\frac{3}{20}$ of Americans prefer cold pizza over hot pizza. What percent of Americans prefer cold pizza? **15%**

ANIMALS For Exercises 55 and 56, use the information at the right.

55. What percent of a day does a lion spend resting? **83.$\overline{3}$%**

56. What percent of a day does a lion spend doing activities? **16.$\overline{6}$%**

A Day in the Life of a Lion
Activities: 4 hours
Resting: 20 hours

Replace each ● with $<$, $>$, or $=$ to make a true sentence.

57. $\frac{5}{9}$ ● 55% $>$ 58. $\frac{7}{10}$ ● 70% $=$ 59. 88% ● 8.8 $<$

60. 0.03 ● 30% $<$ 61. 0.5 ● 50% $=$ 62. 0.09 ● 1% $>$

63. **MULTI STEP** What percent of the area of the square at the right is shaded? **31.25%**

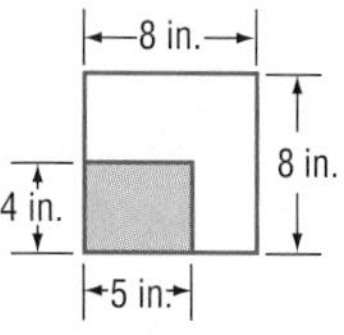

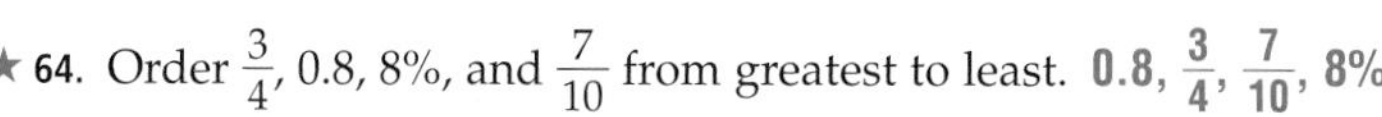

★ 64. Order $\frac{3}{4}$, 0.8, 8%, and $\frac{7}{10}$ from greatest to least. **0.8, $\frac{3}{4}$, $\frac{7}{10}$, 8%**

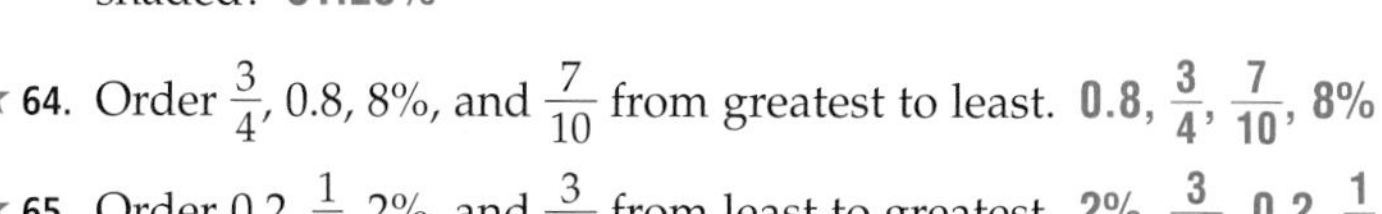

★ 65. Order 0.2, $\frac{1}{4}$, 2%, and $\frac{3}{20}$ from least to greatest. **2%, $\frac{3}{20}$, 0.2, $\frac{1}{4}$**

msmath3.net/self_check_quiz

Answer (p. 214)

78.

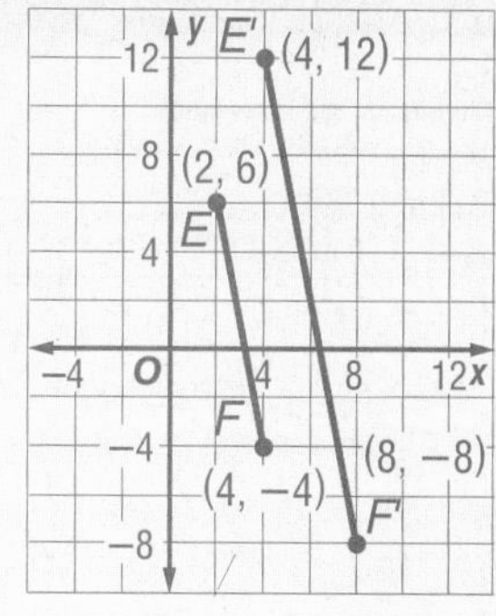

Study Guide and Intervention, p. 250

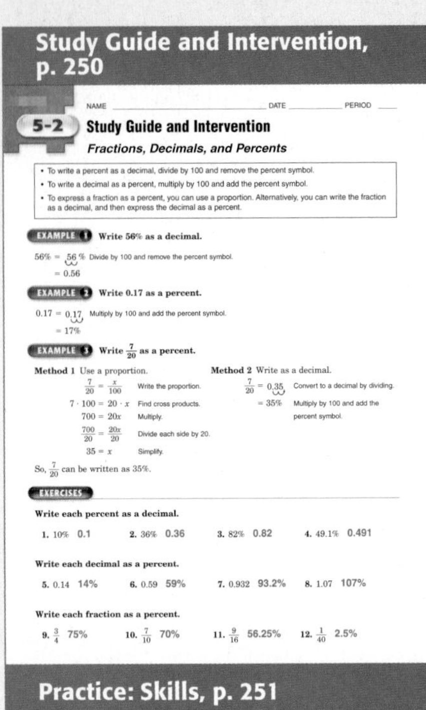
NAME ______ DATE ______ PERIOD ____

5-2 Study Guide and Intervention

Fractions, Decimals, and Percents

- To write a percent as a decimal, divide by 100 and remove the percent symbol.
- To write a decimal as a percent, multiply by 100 and add the percent symbol.
- To express a fraction as a percent, you can use a proportion. Alternatively, you can write the fraction as a decimal, and then express the decimal as a percent.

EXAMPLE 1 **Write 56% as a decimal.**

56% = 56% Divide by 100 and remove the percent symbol.
= 0.56

EXAMPLE 2 **Write 0.17 as a percent.**

0.17 = 0.17 Multiply by 100 and add the percent symbol.
= 17%

EXAMPLE 3 **Write $\frac{7}{20}$ as a percent.**

Method 1 Use a proportion.

$\frac{7}{20} = \frac{x}{100}$ Write the proportion.
$7 \cdot 100 = 20 \cdot x$ Find cross products.
$700 = 20x$ Multiply.
$\frac{700}{20} = \frac{20x}{20}$ Divide each side by 20.
$35 = x$ Simplify.

Method 2 Write as a decimal.

$\frac{7}{20} = 0.35$ Convert to a decimal by dividing.
$= 35\%$ Multiply by 100 and add the percent symbol.

So, $\frac{7}{20}$ can be written as 35%.

EXERCISES

Write each percent as a decimal.

1. 10% **0.1** 2. 36% **0.36** 3. 82% **0.82** 4. 49.1% **0.491**

Write each decimal as a percent.

5. 0.14 **14%** 6. 0.59 **59%** 7. 0.932 **93.2%** 8. 1.07 **107%**

Write each fraction as a percent.

9. $\frac{3}{4}$ **75%** 10. $\frac{7}{10}$ **70%** 11. $\frac{9}{16}$ **56.25%** 12. $\frac{1}{40}$ **2.5%**

Practice: Skills, p. 251

NAME ______ DATE ______ PERIOD ____

5-2 Practice: Skills

Fractions, Decimals, and Percents

Write each percent as a decimal.

1. 50% **0.5** 2. 13% **0.13** 3. 26% **0.26**
4. 41% **0.41** 5. 79% **0.79** 6. 9.1% **0.091**
7. 17.5% **0.175** 8. 33.4% **0.334** 9. 91.5% **0.915**
10. 122% **1.22** 11. 282% **2.82** 12. 331% **3.31**

Write each decimal as a percent.

13. 0.6 **60%** 14. 0.05 **5%** 15. 0.17 **17%**
16. 0.38 **38%** 17. 0.81 **81%** 18. 0.453 **45.3%**
19. 0.572 **57.2%** 20. 0.737 **73.7%** 21. 0.061 **6.1%**
22. 1.19 **119%** 23. 1.47 **147%** 24. 2.38 **238%**

Write each fraction as a percent.

25. $\frac{9}{20}$ **45%** 26. $\frac{2}{25}$ **8%** 27. $\frac{5}{16}$ **31.25%**
28. $\frac{33}{40}$ **82.5%** 29. $\frac{3}{80}$ **3.75%** 30. $\frac{13}{16}$ **81.25%**
31. $\frac{17}{40}$ **42.5%** 32. $\frac{59}{80}$ **73.75%** 33. $\frac{14}{10}$ **140%**
34. $\frac{28}{25}$ **112%** 35. $\frac{9}{4}$ **225%** 36. $\frac{33}{20}$ **165%**

Practice: Word Problems, p. 252

NAME ______ DATE ______ PERIOD ____

5-2 Practice: Word Problems

Fractions, Decimals, and Percents

1. **BASKETBALL** In the 2001–2002 season, Susan Bird of the WNBA team the Seattle Storm made 27% of her 3-point shots. Write this percent as a decimal. **0.27**	2. **POPULATION** From 1990 to 2000, the population of Las Vegas, Nevada, increased by 85%. Write this percent as a decimal. **0.85**
3. **BASEBALL** In the 2001 season, the Chicago White Sox had a team batting average of 0.268. Write this decimal as a percent. **26.8%**	4. **HEALTH** In 2000, 11.6% of Americans under the age of 18 were without health insurance. Write this percent as a decimal. **0.116**
5. **INTERNET** Internet access in the U.S. has increased dramatically in recent years. In 2000, 83 out of every 200 households had Internet access. What percent of households had Internet access? **41.5%**	6. **VOTING** The rate of voter turnout in the 1932 U.S. presidential election was 0.524. Write this decimal as a percent. **52.4%**
7. **ECONOMICS** Consumer prices in the U.S. rose at a rate of 0.034 from 1999 to 2000. Write this decimal as a percent. **3.4%**	8. **SPORTS** In the 2001 season, the WNBA Cleveland Rockets won $\frac{22}{32}$ of their games. Write this fraction as a percent. **68.75%**

SCHOOL For Exercises 66–68, use the graphic at the right.

66. Write the percent of parents who give themselves an A as a decimal. **0.38**

67. Did more or less than $\frac{2}{5}$ of the parents give themselves a B? **more**

68. Did more or less than $\frac{1}{5}$ of the parents give themselves a C? **less**

USA TODAY Snapshots®

Parents make the grade

The majority of parents give themselves A's or B's for involvement in their children's education. Parents assess their performance:

A (Superior)	38%
B (Above Average)	42%
C (Average)	17%
D (Below Average)	2%
F (Failing)	1%

Source: Opinion Research Corp.

By In-Sung Yoo and Adrienne Lewis, USA TODAY

TRAVEL For Exercises 69 and 70, use the following information.

The projected number of household trips in 2010 is 50,000,000. About 14,000,000 of these trips will involve air travel.

69. What fraction of the trips will involve air travel? $\frac{7}{25}$

70. What percent of the trips will involve air travel? **28%**

71. **CRITICAL THINKING** Write $1\frac{3}{5}$ as a percent. **160%**

Spiral Review with Standardized Test Practice

72. **MULTIPLE CHOICE** The graph at the right shows treats Americans prefer during the summer months. Which fraction is *not* equivalent to one of the percents in the graph? **B**

Ⓐ $\frac{7}{50}$ Ⓑ $\frac{11}{18}$ Ⓒ $\frac{16}{25}$ Ⓓ $\frac{3}{20}$

Favorite Summer Treat

	Percent
Ice Cream	64%
Italian Ice	15%
Popsicles	14%

Source: Opinion Research Corporation

73. **MULTIPLE CHOICE** Choose the fraction that is less than 35%. **H**

Ⓕ $\frac{2}{5}$ Ⓖ $\frac{3}{8}$ Ⓗ $\frac{1}{6}$ Ⓘ $\frac{5}{12}$

Write each ratio as a percent. (Lesson 5-1)

74. 27 out of 100 **27%**
75. 0.6 out of 100 **0.6%**
76. 9:20 **45%**
77. 33:50 **66%**

78. **GEOMETRY** Graph $\overline{EF}$ with endpoints $E(2, 6)$ and $F(4, -4)$. Then graph its image for a dilation with a scale factor of 2. (Lesson 4-8) **See p. 213 margin.**

Order the integers in each set from least to greatest. (Lesson 1-3)

79. $\{-12, 5, -5, 13, -1\}$ **$\{-12, -5, -1, 5, 13\}$**

80. $\{42, -56, -13, 101, 13\}$ **$\{-56, -13, 13, 42, 101\}$**

81. $\{64, -58, -65, 57, -61\}$ **$\{-65, -61, -58, 57, 64\}$**

GETTING READY FOR THE NEXT LESSON

PREREQUISITE SKILL Solve each proportion. (Lesson 4-4)

82. $\frac{5}{6} = \frac{x}{24}$ **20**
83. $\frac{a}{12} = \frac{2}{15}$ **1.6**
84. $\frac{2}{7} = \frac{5}{t}$ **17.5**
85. $\frac{3}{n} = \frac{10}{8}$ **2.4**

4 Assess

Open-Ended Assessment

Writing Have students discuss, in writing, a situation that would require the use of a fraction, a decimal, or a percent. They should fully outline the problem and explain why the suggested form is most appropriate for that example.

Study Skill

Compare Data

Reading Math Problems

Look for words such as *more than, times,* or *percent* in problems you are trying to solve. They give you a clue about what operation to use.

The table shows the final standings of the Women's United Soccer Association for the 2002 season.

Women's United Soccer Association					
Team	Games	Wins	Losses	Ties	Points
Carolina	21	12	5	4	40
Philadelphia	21	11	4	6	39
Washington	21	11	5	5	38
Atlanta	21	11	9	1	34
San Jose	21	8	8	5	29
Boston	21	6	8	7	25
San Diego	21	5	11	5	20
New York	21	3	17	1	10

You can compare the data in several ways.

▶**DIFFERENCES** Carolina won 7 more games than San Diego.
$12 - 5 = 7$

▶**RATIOS** Boston had 2.5 times more points than New York.
$25 \div 10 = 2.5$

▶**PERCENTS** Philadelphia lost about 19% of the games they played.
$(4 \div 21) \times 100 \approx 19$

SKILL PRACTICE

1. ratio; times more; 1.6   2. difference; more; 1
4. percent; percent; 57%

Determine whether each problem asks for a *difference, ratio,* or *percent.* Write out the key word or words in each problem. Solve each problem.

1. How many times more games did San Jose win than San Diego?
2. How many more games did Washington win than lose or tie?
3. How many fewer points did Atlanta have than Carolina? difference; fewer; 6
4. What percent of the time did Carolina win its games?
5. Write three statements comparing the data in the table. One comparison should be a difference, one should be a ratio, and one should be a percent. See students' work.

Study Skill

Objective Identify key terms in math problems.

GETTING STARTED

Slow Down Advise students to read math problems three times. They should skim over the problem the first time, read it slowly a second time, and then read it slowly again, checking that their understanding is consistent with the information printed on the page.

TEACH

- Encourage students to read the problem without the numbers and estimate whether the answer will be larger or smaller than what they start with. For example, for "Atlanta won more games than Boston," the number will be larger.

ASSESS

Open-Ended Assessment

Writing Have students write problems that ask for a difference, ratio, or percent. Have them trade problems and solve. Keep trading until everyone has written and solved a problem of each type.

5-3 Lesson Notes

Lesson Resources

Chapter 5 Resource Masters

- Study Guide and Intervention, p. 255
- Practice: Skills, p. 256
- Practice: Word Problems, p. 257
- Reading to Learn Mathematics, p. 258
- Enrichment, p. 259

MathPASS Tutorial CD-ROM, 31–32

Parent and Student Study Guide Online Worksheets, 5-3

Noteables™: Interactive Study Notebook with Foldables™, 5-3

1 Focus

5-Minute Check 5-3

Use as a quiz or review of Lesson 5-2. (Also available as a transparency)

Bellringer

Reading Mathematics Have students locate three uses of percent in everyday situations. You may want to provide students with newspapers to search. Students should be able to explain why using a percent is useful in those situations and what the percent means. For example, if 25% of school-aged children do not have a computer, that means that 25 out of 100 children do not have a computer.

Reading to Learn Mathematics, p. 258 ELL

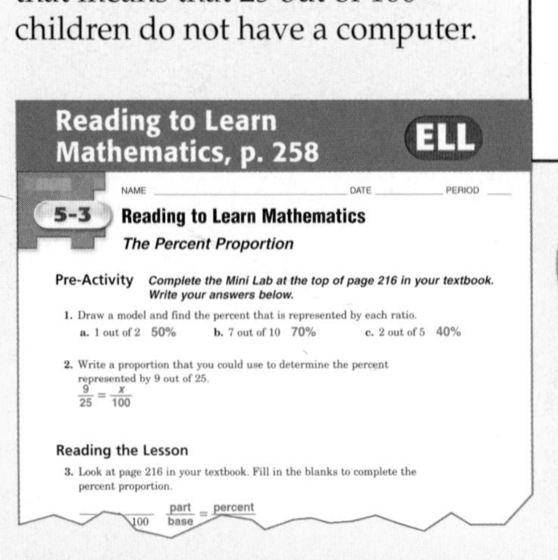

NAME ______ DATE ______ PERIOD ______

5-3 Reading to Learn Mathematics

The Percent Proportion

Pre-Activity *Complete the Mini Lab at the top of page 216 in your textbook. Write your answers below.*

1. Draw a model and find the percent that is represented by each ratio.
   a. 1 out of 2 50% b. 7 out of 10 70% c. 2 out of 5 40%
2. Write a proportion that you could use to determine the percent represented by 9 out of 25.
   $\frac{9}{25} = \frac{x}{100}$

Reading the Lesson

3. Look at page 216 in your textbook. Fill in the blanks to complete the percent proportion.
   $\frac{\text{part}}{\text{base}} = \frac{\text{percent}}{100}$

5-3 Algebra: The Percent Proportion

What You'll LEARN

Solve problems using the percent proportion.

NEW Vocabulary

percent proportion
part
base

Link to READING

Everyday Meaning of Base: the bottom of something considered to be its support

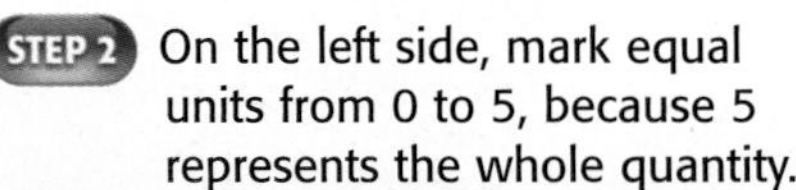

HANDS-ON Mini Lab

Materials
- grid paper
- markers

Work with a partner.

You can use proportion models to determine the percent represented by 3 out of 5.

STEP 1 Draw a 10-by-1 rectangle on grid paper. Label the units on the right from 0 to 100.

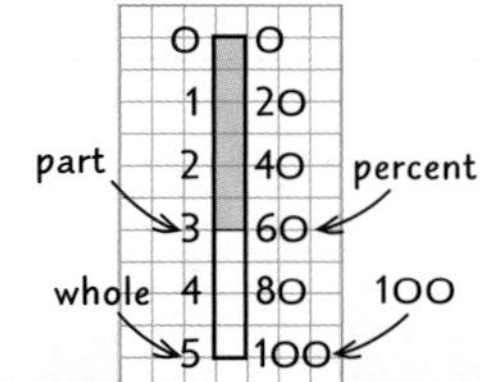

STEP 2 On the left side, mark equal units from 0 to 5, because 5 represents the whole quantity.

STEP 3 Draw a horizontal line from 3 on the left side of the model. The number on the right side is the percent.

1. Draw a model and find the percent that is represented by each ratio. **See margin for models.**
   a. 1 out of 2 **50%** b. 7 out of 10 **70%** c. 2 out of 5 **40%**
2. Write a proportion that you could use to determine the percent represented by 9 out of 25. $\frac{9}{25} = \frac{x}{100}$

In a **percent proportion**, one of the numbers, called the **part**, is being compared to the whole quantity, called the **base**. The other ratio is the percent, written as a fraction, whose base is 100.

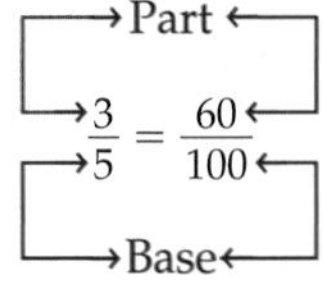

Noteables™ **Key Concept: Percent Proportion**

Words $\frac{\text{part}}{\text{base}} = \frac{\text{percent}}{100}$

Symbols $\frac{a}{b} = \frac{p}{100}$, where a is the part, b is the base, and p is the percent.

READING in the Content Area

For strategies in reading this lesson, visit **msmath3.net/reading.**

EXAMPLE Find the Percent

1 **22 is what percent of 110?**

Since 22 is being compared to 110, 22 is the part and 110 is the base. You need to find the percent.

NCLB NO CHILD LEFT BEHIND

The goals of the NCLB Act include a stronger emphasis on reading. The **Reading in the Content Area** link helps students become proficient readers.

Answers

1a. (model: left 0, 1, 2; right 0, 20, 40, 60, 80, 100)

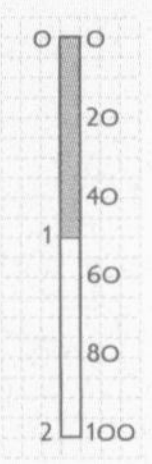

1b. (model: left 0–10; right 0, 20, 40, 60, 80, 100)

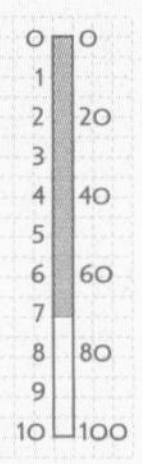

1c. (model: left 0–5; right 0, 20, 40, 60, 80, 100)

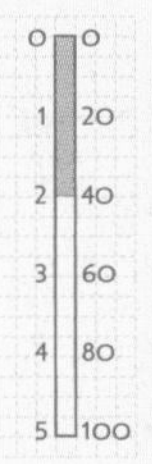

$$\frac{a}{b} = \frac{p}{100} \rightarrow \frac{22}{110} = \frac{p}{100}$$ Replace a with 22 and b with 110.

$22 \cdot 100 = 110 \cdot p$ Find the cross products.

$2{,}200 = 110p$ Multiply.

$\frac{2{,}200}{110} = \frac{110p}{110}$ Divide each side by 110.

$20 = p$ 22 is 20% of 110.

You can also use the percent proportion to find a missing part or base.

Concept Summary **Type of Percent Problems**

Type	Example	Proportion
Find the Percent	7 is what percent of 10? (percent)	$\frac{7}{10} = \frac{p}{100}$
Find the Part	What number is 70% of 10? (part)	$\frac{a}{10} = \frac{70}{100}$
Find the Base	7 is 70% of what number? (base)	$\frac{7}{b} = \frac{70}{100}$

TEACHING TIP
Tell students that the base usually follows the word *of*.

EXAMPLE Find the Part

2 What number is 80% of 500?

The percent is 80, and the base is 500. You need to find the part.

$\frac{a}{b} = \frac{p}{100} \rightarrow \frac{a}{500} = \frac{80}{100}$ Replace b with 500 and p with 80.

$a \cdot 100 = 500 \cdot 80$ Find the cross products.

$100a = 40{,}000$ Multiply.

$\frac{100a}{100} = \frac{40{,}000}{100}$ Divide each side by 100.

$a = 400$ 400 is 80% of 500.

REAL-LIFE MATH

HISTORY The members of the Lewis and Clark Expedition spent the winter of 1805–1806 in Oregon. They reported that it rained 94 days, which was about 89% of their days in Oregon.

Source: *Kids Discover*

EXAMPLE Find the Base

3 HISTORY Use the information at the left to determine how many days the Lewis and Clark Expedition spent in Oregon.

The percent is 89, and the part is 94. You need to find the base.

$\frac{a}{b} = \frac{p}{100} \rightarrow \frac{94}{b} = \frac{89}{100}$ Replace a with 94 and p with 89.

$94 \cdot 100 = b \cdot 89$ Find the cross products.

$9{,}400 = 89b$ Multiply.

$\frac{9{,}400}{89} = \frac{89b}{89}$ Divide each side by 89.

$105.6 \approx b$ Simplify.

The Lewis and Clark Expedition spent 106 days in Oregon.

Math Online msmath3.net/extra_examples

2 Teach

In-Class Examples

1. 34 is what percent of 136? **25%**

2. What number is 70% of 600? **420**

3. **BASEBALL** From 1999 to 2001, Derek Jeter had 11 hits with the bases loaded. This was about 30% of his at bats with the bases loaded. How many times was he at bat with the bases loaded? **37 times**

Tips for New Teachers

Teaching Strategies Students may find the memory device $\frac{\text{is}}{\text{of}} = \frac{\%}{100}$ helpful as they learn to use the percent proportion.

DAILY INTERVENTION **Differentiated Instruction**

Interpersonal Have students work in small groups to ask and answer percent questions about themselves, their homes, and their families. Examples include what percent of their time do they spend in school, what percent of the rooms in their house have telephones, or what percent of their family members are left-handed. **Sample question: Shaila spent 80% of her $12 allowance on makeup. How much did she spend? Answer: $9.60** Students should share their answers.

3 Practice/Apply

DAILY INTERVENTION **FIND THE ERROR**

In Exercise 3, point out that the number following the word "of" belongs on the bottom of the fraction. In this case, the variable is the denominator.

About the Exercises...

Guided Practice Key

Exercises	Examples
4, 7	1
5, 8	2
6, 9	3

Assignment Guide

Basic: 11–21 odd, 29–37 odd, 38–50

Average: 11–37 odd, 38–50

Enriched: 10–36 even, 38–46 (Optional: 47–50)

Alert! Exercise 37 uses the Internet or another source for research.

Students practice the same concepts in Exercises 10–27 if they are assigned odd or even problems.

Skill and Concept Check

1. *Writing Math* Explain why the value of p in $\frac{a}{b} = \frac{p}{100}$ represents a percent. **Percent means per 100 and p is the number out of 100.**
2. **OPEN ENDED** Write a real-life problem that could be solved using the proportion $\frac{a}{12} = \frac{25}{100}$. **See margin.**
3. **FIND THE ERROR** Roberto and Jamal are writing percent proportions to solve the following problem. Who is correct? Explain. **Roberto; the base b is unknown.**

95 is 25% of what number?

Roberto	Jamal
$\frac{95}{b} = \frac{25}{100}$	$\frac{a}{95} = \frac{25}{100}$

GUIDED PRACTICE

Write a percent proportion to solve each problem. Then solve. Round to the nearest tenth if necessary. **4–9. See margin for percent proportions.**

4. 70 is what percent of 280? **25%**
5. Find 60% of 90. **54**
6. 150 is 60% of what number? **250**
7. What percent of 49 is 7? **14.3%**
8. What is 72.5% of 200? **145**
9. 125 is 30% of what number? **416.7**

★ **indicates increased difficulty**

Practice and Applications

HOMEWORK HELP

For Exercises	See Examples
10–11, 16–17, 24–25, 28–30	1
12–13, 18–19, 22–23, 31–36	2
14–15, 20–21, 26–27	3

Extra Practice See pages 627, 652.

Write a percent proportion to solve each problem. Then solve. Round to the nearest tenth if necessary. **17. 33.3% 20. 4,833.3**

10. 3 is what percent of 15? **20%**
11. What percent of 64 is 16? **25%**
12. What is 15% of 60? **9**
13. Find 35% of 200. **70**
14. 18 is 45% of what number? **40**
15. 95 is 95% of what number? **100**
16. What percent of 56 is 8? **14.3%**
17. 120 is what percent of 360?
18. Find 12.4% of 150. **18.6**
19. What is 17.2% of 350? **60.2**
20. 725 is 15% of what number?
21. 225 is 95% of what number? **236.8**

★22. What is 2.5% of 95? **2.4**

★23. Find 5.8% of 42. **2.4**

★24. 17 is what percent of 55? **30.9%**

★25. What percent of 27 is 12? **44.4%**

★26. 98 is 22.5% of what number? **435.6**

★27. 57 is 13.5% of what number? **422.2**

10–27. See margin for percent proportions.

GAMES **For Exercises 28–30, use the following information.**
At the start of a game of chess, each player has the pieces listed at the right.

Chess Pieces
- 1 king
- 1 queen
- 2 bishops
- 2 knights
- 2 rooks
- 8 pawns

28. What percent of each player's pieces are pawns? **50%**
29. What percent of each player's pieces are knights? **12.5%**
30. What percent of each player's pieces are kings? **6.25%**

Answers

2. Sample answer: 25% of the marbles are blue. If there are 12 marbles, how many are blue?
4. $\frac{70}{280} = \frac{p}{100}$
5. $\frac{a}{90} = \frac{60}{100}$
6. $\frac{150}{b} = \frac{60}{100}$
7. $\frac{7}{49} = \frac{p}{100}$
8. $\frac{a}{200} = \frac{72.5}{100}$
9. $\frac{125}{b} = \frac{30}{100}$
10. $\frac{3}{15} = \frac{p}{100}$
11. $\frac{16}{64} = \frac{p}{100}$
12. $\frac{a}{60} = \frac{15}{100}$
13. $\frac{a}{200} = \frac{35}{100}$
14. $\frac{18}{b} = \frac{45}{100}$
15. $\frac{95}{b} = \frac{95}{100}$
16. $\frac{8}{56} = \frac{p}{100}$
17. $\frac{120}{360} = \frac{p}{100}$
18. $\frac{a}{150} = \frac{12.4}{100}$
19. $\frac{a}{350} = \frac{17.2}{100}$
20. $\frac{725}{b} = \frac{15}{100}$
21. $\frac{225}{b} = \frac{95}{100}$
22. $\frac{a}{95} = \frac{2.5}{100}$
23. $\frac{a}{42} = \frac{5.8}{100}$
24. $\frac{17}{55} = \frac{p}{100}$
25. $\frac{12}{27} = \frac{p}{100}$
26. $\frac{98}{b} = \frac{22.5}{100}$
27. $\frac{57}{b} = \frac{13.5}{100}$
31. 1,840,000 households
32. 880,000 households
33. 760,000 households
34. 720,000 households
35. 680,000 households
36. 200,000 households
38. Sample answer: Let the original number be 50. 10% of 50 is 5 and 5 + 50 is 55. 10% of 55 is 5.5 and 55 − 5.5 is 49.5. However, 49.5 ≠ 50.

ANIMALS **For Exercises 31–36, use the graphic at the right.** **31–36. See margin.**

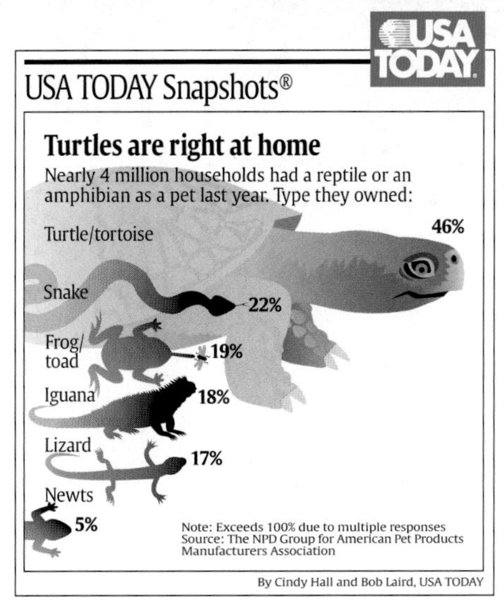

31. How many of the 4,000,000 households have turtles or tortoises?
32. How many households have snakes?
33. How many households have frogs or toads?
34. How many households have iguanas?
35. How many households have lizards?
36. How many households have newts?
37. **RESEARCH** Use the Internet or another source to find what percent of the total population of the United States is living in your state. **See students' work.**
38. **CRITICAL THINKING** Give a counterexample to show the following is *not* true.
10% of a number is added to the number. Then 10% of the sum is subtracted from the sum. The result is the original number. **See margin.**
39. **CRITICAL THINKING** Kwan made 56% of his free throws in the first half of the basketball season. If he makes 7 shots out of the next 13 attempts, will it help or hurt his average? Explain. **Hurt; 7 out of 13 is about 53.8% which is less than 56%.**

Spiral Review with Standardized Test Practice

40. **MULTIPLE CHOICE** The bar graph shows the number of wins for the Chicago Bulls from 1993 to 2003. If they play 82 games in a season, about what percent of games did they win in the 1997–1998 season? **A**

Ⓐ 76% Ⓑ 82%
Ⓒ 84% Ⓓ 88%

Chicago Bulls' Wins

Season	Number of Wins
1993–94	55
1994–95	47
1995–96	72
1996–97	69
1997–98	62
1998–99	13
1999–00	17
2000–01	15
2001–02	21
2002–03	30

Source: www.nba.com

41. **SHORT RESPONSE** Pure gold is 24-karat gold. In the United States, most jewelry is 18-karat gold. What percent of the 18-karat jewelry is gold? **75%**

Write each decimal as a percent. (Lesson 5-2)

42. 0.81 **81%**
43. 0.12 **12%**
44. 0.2 **20%**
45. 1.735 **173.5%**

46. Write 48% as a fraction in simplest form. (Lesson 5-1) $\frac{12}{25}$

GETTING READY FOR THE NEXT LESSON

BASIC SKILL **Compute each product mentally.**

47. $\frac{1}{2} \cdot 422$ **211**
48. $639 \cdot \frac{1}{3}$ **213**
49. $0.1 \cdot 722$ **72.2**
50. $0.5 \cdot 680$ **340**

Math Online msmath3.net/self_check_quiz

4 Assess

Higher-Level Thinking

Adam's soccer team won 15 of their games, or about 83%. How many games did they play? Explain why the first answer you find is not a whole number.

18 games played; The first answer found (about 18.07) is not a whole number because 83% is an estimate.

Study Guide and Intervention, p. 255

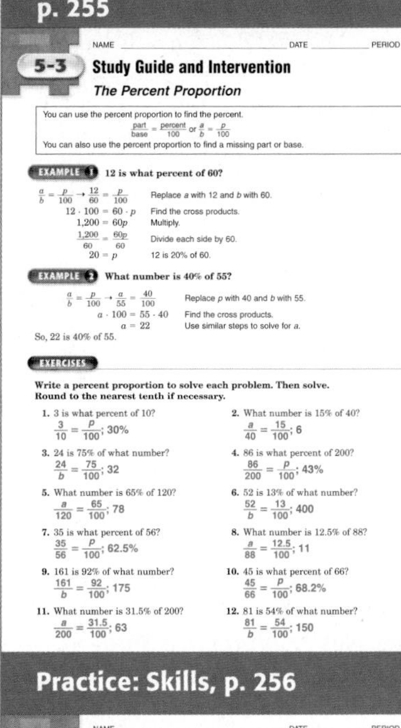
NAME ______ DATE ______ PERIOD ______

5-3 Study Guide and Intervention

The Percent Proportion

You can use the percent proportion to find the percent. $\frac{\text{part}}{\text{base}} = \frac{\text{percent}}{100}$ or $\frac{a}{b} = \frac{p}{100}$
You can also use the percent proportion to find a missing part or base.

EXAMPLE 1 **12 is what percent of 60?**

$\frac{a}{b} = \frac{p}{100} \rightarrow \frac{12}{60} = \frac{p}{100}$ Replace a with 12 and b with 60.
$12 \cdot 100 = 60 \cdot p$ Find the cross products.
$1{,}200 = 60p$ Multiply.
$\frac{1{,}200}{60} = \frac{60p}{60}$ Divide each side by 60.
$20 = p$ 12 is 20% of 60.

EXAMPLE 2 **What number is 40% of 55?**

$\frac{a}{b} = \frac{p}{100} \rightarrow \frac{a}{55} = \frac{40}{100}$ Replace p with 40 and b with 55.
$a \cdot 100 = 55 \cdot 40$ Find the cross products.
$a = 22$ Use similar steps to solve for a.
So, 22 is 40% of 55.

EXERCISES

Write a percent proportion to solve each problem. Then solve. Round to the nearest tenth if necessary.

1. 3 is what percent of 10? $\frac{3}{10} = \frac{p}{100}$; 30%
2. What number is 15% of 40? $\frac{a}{40} = \frac{15}{100}$; 6
3. 24 is 75% of what number? $\frac{24}{b} = \frac{75}{100}$; 32
4. 86 is what percent of 200? $\frac{86}{200} = \frac{p}{100}$; 43%
5. What number is 65% of 120? $\frac{a}{120} = \frac{65}{100}$; 78
6. 52 is 13% of what number? $\frac{52}{b} = \frac{13}{100}$; 400
7. 35 is what percent of 56? $\frac{35}{56} = \frac{p}{100}$; 62.5%
8. What number is 12.5% of 88? $\frac{a}{88} = \frac{12.5}{100}$; 11
9. 161 is 92% of what number? $\frac{161}{b} = \frac{92}{100}$; 175
10. 45 is what percent of 66? $\frac{45}{66} = \frac{p}{100}$; 68.2%
11. What number is 31.5% of 200? $\frac{a}{200} = \frac{31.5}{100}$; 63
12. 81 is 54% of what number? $\frac{81}{b} = \frac{54}{100}$; 150

Practice: Skills, p. 256

NAME ______ DATE ______ PERIOD ______

5-3 Practice: Skills

The Percent Proportion

Write a percent proportion to solve each problem. Then solve. Round to the nearest tenth if necessary.

1. 1 is what percent of 5? $\frac{1}{5} = \frac{p}{100}$; 20%
2. What number is 25% of 40? $\frac{a}{40} = \frac{25}{100}$; 10
3. 30 is 60% of what number? $\frac{30}{b} = \frac{60}{100}$; 50
4. What percent of 8 is 6? $\frac{6}{8} = \frac{p}{100}$; 75%
5. Find 15% of 20. $\frac{a}{20} = \frac{15}{100}$; 3
6. 33 is 33% of what number? $\frac{33}{b} = \frac{33}{100}$; 100
7. 15 is what percent of 150? $\frac{15}{150} = \frac{p}{100}$; 10%
8. What number is 30% of 140? $\frac{a}{140} = \frac{30}{100}$; 42
9. 90 is 60% of what number? $\frac{90}{b} = \frac{60}{100}$; 150
10. What percent of 60 is 42? $\frac{42}{60} = \frac{p}{100}$; 70%
11. Find 90% of 40. $\frac{a}{40} = \frac{90}{100}$; 36
12. 21 is 35% of what number? $\frac{21}{b} = \frac{35}{100}$; 60
13. 36 is what percent of 45? $\frac{36}{45} = \frac{p}{100}$; 80%
14. What number is 75% of 44? $\frac{a}{44} = \frac{75}{100}$; 33
15. 12 is 40% of what number? $\frac{12}{b} = \frac{40}{100}$; 30
16. What percent of 40 is 15? $\frac{15}{40} = \frac{p}{100}$; 37.5%
17. Find 5% of 80. $\frac{a}{80} = \frac{5}{100}$; 4
18. 45 is 60% of what number? $\frac{45}{b} = \frac{60}{100}$; 75
19. 46 is what percent of 69? $\frac{46}{69} = \frac{p}{100}$; 66.7%
20. Find 55% of 120. $\frac{a}{120} = \frac{55}{100}$; 66
21. 11 is 44% of what number? $\frac{11}{b} = \frac{44}{100}$; 25
22. 19 is what percent of 20? $\frac{19}{20} = \frac{p}{100}$; 95%
23. What number is 85% of 40? $\frac{a}{40} = \frac{85}{100}$; 34
24. 9 is 18% of what number? $\frac{9}{b} = \frac{18}{100}$; 50

Practice: Word Problems, p. 257

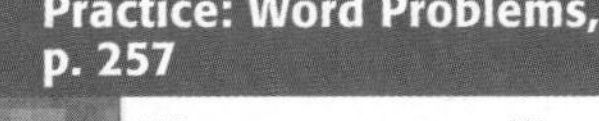
NAME ______ DATE ______ PERIOD ______

5-3 Practice: Word Problems

The Percent Proportion

1. **COMMUTING** On his trip across town, Mark was stopped by a red light at 9 out of 15 intersections. At what percent of intersections was Mark stopped by a red light? 60%
2. **CLIMATE** In Las Vegas, Nevada, the skies are clear on 92% of the days. How many days in the month of June would you expect the skies to be clear in Las Vegas? Round the answer to the nearest day. 28 days
3. **POLLING** A recent poll shows that 65% of adults are in favor of increased funding for education. The number of adults surveyed for the poll was 140. How many of the adults surveyed were in favor of increased funding for education? 91 adults
4. **FLOWERS** Mika's rose bush had 24 blooms in the first week of May. This was 80% as many blooms as Tammy's rose bush had during the same period. How many blooms did Tammy's rose bush have? 30 blooms
5. **SPORTS** In the 2002 regular season, the San Francisco Giants won 95 out of 161 games. What percent of their games did they win? Round to the nearest tenth if necessary. 59.0%
6. **GOLF** On a recent round of golf, Shana made par on 15 out of 18 holes. On what percent of holes did Shana make par? Round to the nearest tenth if necessary. 83.3%
7. **DRIVING TEST** On the written portion of her driving test, Sara answered 84% of the questions correctly. If Sara answered 42 questions correctly, how many questions were on the driving test? 50 questions
8. **EDUCATION** In a certain small town, 65% of the adults are college graduates. How many of the 240 adults living in the town are college graduates? 156 adults

5-4 Lesson Notes

Lesson Resources

Chapter 5 Resource Masters
- Study Guide and Intervention, p. 260
- Practice: Skills, p. 261
- Practice: Word Problems, p. 262
- Reading to Learn Mathematics, p. 263
- Enrichment, p. 264

Parent and Student Study Guide Online Worksheets, 5-4
Noteables™: Interactive Study Notebook with Foldables™, 5-4

1 Focus

5-Minute Check 5-4

Use as a quiz or review of Lesson 5-3. (Also available as a transparency)

Bellringer

Hands-On Activity Provide students with weekly retail store ads. Ask students how they determine the sale price of an item. How do they determine which store has the better price? What options do they have? **Sample answers may include carrying a calculator or a pad of paper to figure the percent. Encourage students to consider working the math mentally.**

Reading to Learn Mathematics, p. 263 ELL

NAME ______ DATE ______ PERIOD ____

5-4 Reading to Learn Mathematics
Finding Percents Mentally

Pre-Activity *Read the introduction at the top of page 220 in your textbook. Write your answers below.*

1. 50% of the eighth grade class are females. Write 50% as a fraction. $\frac{1}{2}$
2. Explain how you could find 50% of 104 without using a proportion. Multiply $\frac{1}{2}$ times 104.
3. Use mental math to find the number of females in the eighth grade class. $\frac{1}{2} \cdot 104 = 52$ females
4. 25% of the sixth grade class play intramural basketball. Write 25% as a fraction. $\frac{1}{4}$
5. Use mental math to find the number of students in the sixth grade who play intramural basketball. $\frac{1}{4} \cdot 84 = 21$ students

5-4 Finding Percents Mentally

What You'll LEARN

Compute mentally with percents.

WHEN am I ever going to use this?

SCHOOL The table below lists the enrollment at Roosevelt Middle School by grade level.

Roosevelt Middle School Enrollment	
Grade Level	**Number of Students**
Sixth	84
Seventh	93
Eighth	104

1. 50% of the eighth grade class are females. Write 50% as a fraction. $\frac{1}{2}$
2. Explain how you could find 50% of 104 without using a proportion. **Multiply $\frac{1}{2}$ times 104.**
3. Use mental math to find the number of females in the eighth grade class.
4. 25% of the sixth grade class play intramural basketball. Write 25% as a fraction. $\frac{1}{4}$
5. Use mental math to find the number of students in the sixth grade who play intramural basketball. $\frac{1}{4} \cdot 84 = 21$ **students**

3. $\frac{1}{2} \cdot 104 = 52$ **females**

When you compute with common percents like 50% or 25%, it may be easier to use the fraction form of the percent. This number line shows some fraction-percent equivalents.

0%	12.5%	25%	37.5%	50%	62.5%	75%	87.5%	100%
0	$\frac{1}{8}$	$\frac{1}{4}$	$\frac{3}{8}$	$\frac{1}{2}$	$\frac{5}{8}$	$\frac{3}{4}$	$\frac{7}{8}$	1

Some percents are used more frequently than others. So, it is a good idea to be familiar with these percents and their equivalent fractions.

Concept Summary — Percent-Fraction Equivalents

$25\% = \frac{1}{4}$	$20\% = \frac{1}{5}$	$16\frac{2}{3}\% = \frac{1}{6}$	$12\frac{1}{2}\% = \frac{1}{8}$	$10\% = \frac{1}{10}$
$50\% = \frac{1}{2}$	$40\% = \frac{2}{5}$	$33\frac{1}{3}\% = \frac{1}{3}$	$37\frac{1}{2}\% = \frac{3}{8}$	$30\% = \frac{3}{10}$
$75\% = \frac{3}{4}$	$60\% = \frac{3}{5}$	$66\frac{2}{3}\% = \frac{2}{3}$	$62\frac{1}{2}\% = \frac{5}{8}$	$70\% = \frac{7}{10}$
	$80\% = \frac{4}{5}$	$83\frac{1}{3}\% = \frac{5}{6}$	$87\frac{1}{2}\% = \frac{7}{8}$	$90\% = \frac{9}{10}$

EXAMPLES Use Fractions to Compute Mentally

STUDY TIP

Look Back You can review **multiplying fractions** in Lesson 2-3.

Compute mentally.

1 **20% of 45**

20% of 45 = $\frac{1}{5}$ of 45 or 9 Use the fraction form of 20%, which is $\frac{1}{5}$.

2 **$33\frac{1}{3}$% of 93**

$33\frac{1}{3}$% of 93 = $\frac{1}{3}$ of 93 or 31 Use the fraction form of $33\frac{1}{3}$%, which is $\frac{1}{3}$.

Your Turn Compute mentally.

a. 25% of 32 b. $12\frac{1}{2}$% of 160 c. 80% of 45

a. $\frac{1}{4} \cdot 32 = 8$
b. $\frac{1}{8} \cdot 160 = 20$
c. $\frac{4}{5} \cdot 45 = 36$

You can also use decimals to find percents mentally. Remember that 10% = 0.1 and 1% = 0.01.

EXAMPLES Use Decimals to Compute Mentally

STUDY TIP

Multiplying Decimals To multiply by 0.1, move the decimal point one place to the left. To multiply by 0.01, move the decimal point two places to the left.

Compute mentally.

3 **10% of 98**

10% of 98 = 0.1 of 98 or 9.8

4 **1% of 235**

1% of 235 = 0.01 of 235 or 2.35

Your Turn Compute mentally.

d. 10% of 65 **6.5** e. 1% of 450 **4.5** f. 30% of 22 **6.6**

TEACHING TIP

Encourage students to solve problems mentally whenever possible.

You can use either fractions or decimals to find percents mentally.

EXAMPLE Use Mental Math to Solve a Problem

5 **SCHOOL At Madison Middle School, 60% of the students voted in an election for student council officers. There are 1,500 students. How many students voted in the election?**

Method 1 Use a fraction.

60% of 1,500 = $\frac{3}{5}$ of 1,500 **THINK** $\frac{1}{5}$ of 1,500 is 300.

60% of 1,500 is 900. So, $\frac{3}{5}$ of 1,500 is $3 \cdot 300$ or 900.

Method 2 Use a decimal.

60% or 1,500 = 0.6 of 1,500 **THINK** 0.1 of 1,500 is 150.

60% of 1,500 is 900. So, 0.6 of 1,500 is $6 \cdot 150$ or 900.

There were 900 students who voted in the election.

Math Online msmath3.net/extra_examples

2 Teach

In-Class Examples

Compute mentally.

1 40% of 80 **32**

2 $66\frac{2}{3}$% of 75 **50**

3 10% of 65 **6.5**

4 1% of 304 **3.04**

5 **TECHNOLOGY** A company produces 2,500 of a particular printer. They later discover that 25% of the printers have defects. How many printers from this group have defects? **625**

Teaching Strategies To begin class, have students ask and answer questions that relate to the classroom. For example, *what percent of the class...?* Then solve the problems mentally. This will help students begin to focus on the topic in a manner that is interesting to them. By focusing students at the beginning, they will be more willing to participate in the entire lesson.

DAILY INTERVENTION Unlocking Misconceptions

Checking Mental Math Many students mistakenly feel that math is a set of arbitrary rules that they have to memorize for the test. However, truly understanding the concept is necessary, especially when doing mental math. Encourage students to check their mental math results by using a calculator.

3 Practice/Apply

FOLDABLES™ Follow-Up Remind students to use their Foldables to record how they find percents mentally. Students might give examples of what they have learned, or they could record new terms that they need to learn. Encourage students to write the steps they go through to compute mentally with percents.

DAILY INTERVENTION **FIND THE ERROR** If students have difficulty with Exercise 3, you may want to review place value. For 1%, 10%, and 100%, it may be helpful for students to immediately convert to decimals.

About the Exercises...

Guided Practice Key

Exercises	Examples
4–6	1, 2
7–9	3, 4
10	5

Assignment Guide

Basic: 11–25 odd, 29–37 odd, 41–53

Average: 11–37 odd, 38, 39, 41–53

Enriched: 12–38 even, 39–49 (Optional: 50–53)

Students practice the same concepts in Exercises 11–36 if they are assigned odd or even problems.

Skill and Concept Check

1. Writing Math Explain how to find 75% of 40 mentally. **1–2. See margin.**

2. **OPEN ENDED** Suppose you wish to find $33\frac{1}{3}\%$ of x. List two values of x for which you could do the computation mentally. Explain.

3. **FIND THE ERROR** Candace and Pablo are finding 10% of 95. Who is correct? Explain. **Candace; 10% of 95 = 0.1 · 95 or 9.5.**

Candace	Pablo
10% of 95 = 9.5	10% of 95 = 0.95

GUIDED PRACTICE

Compute mentally.

4. 50% of 120 **60**
5. $33\frac{1}{3}\%$ of 60 **20**
6. $37\frac{1}{2}\%$ of 72 **27**
7. 1% of 52 **0.52**
8. 10% of 350 **35**
9. 20% of 630 **126**

10. **PEOPLE** The average person has about 100,000 hairs on his or her head. However, if people with red hair are taken as a smaller group, they average only 90% of this number. What is the average number of hairs on the head of a person with red hair? **90,000 hairs**

★ indicates increased difficulty

Practice and Applications

HOMEWORK HELP

For Exercises	See Examples
11–18, 25–28	1, 2
19–24, 29–30	3, 4
37–39	5

Extra Practice
See pages 627, 652.

Compute mentally.

11. 25% of 44 **11**
12. 50% of 62 **31**
13. $12\frac{1}{2}\%$ of 64 **8**
14. $16\frac{2}{3}\%$ of 54 **9**
15. 40% of 35 **14**
16. 60% of 15 **9**
17. $66\frac{2}{3}\%$ of 120 **80**
18. $62\frac{1}{2}\%$ of 160 **100**
19. 10% of 57 **5.7**
20. 1% of 81 **0.81**
21. 1% of 28.3 **0.283**
22. 10% of 17.1 **1.71**
23. 3% of 130 **3.9**
24. 7% of 210 **14.7**
25. 150% of 80 **120**
26. 125% of 400 **500**
★27. $66\frac{2}{3}\%$ of 10.8 **7.2**
★28. $37\frac{1}{2}\%$ of 41.6 **15.6**
29. Find 1% of $42,200 mentally. **$422**
30. Find 10% of $17.40 mentally. **$1.74**

Replace each ● with <, >, or = to make a true sentence.

31. 7.5 ● 10% of 80 **<**
32. 75% of 80 ● 65 **<**
33. 1% of 150 ● 10% of 15 **=**
34. $66\frac{2}{3}\%$ of 18 ● 60% of 15 **>**
35. Which is greater, 25% of 16 or 5? **5**
36. Which is greater, 75% of 120 or 85? **75% of 120**

37. **HEALTH** Many health authorities recommend that a healthy diet contains no more than 30% of its Calories from fat. If Jennie consumes 1,500 Calories each day, what is the maximum number of Calories she should consume from fat? **450 Calories**

Answers

1. Since 75% equals $\frac{3}{4}$, find $\frac{3}{4}$ of 40. $\frac{1}{4}$ of 40 is 10. So $\frac{3}{4}$ of 40 is $3 \cdot 10$ or 30.
2. Sample answer: 30 and 300; Since $33\frac{1}{3}\% = \frac{1}{3}$, the numbers should be easily divisible by 3.

40. Sample answer: Pat has 50 marbles. 10% of his marbles are blue. How many of his marbles are blue? 10% of 50 equals 0.1 of 50 or 5. The answer is 5 marbles.

41. Sample answer: $a = 300$, $b = 100$; Since 10% is $\frac{1}{3}$ of 30%, a must equal $3b$.

42. Sample answer: Find 10% of the total bill and then find half of that. Add the two numbers together.

50. Sample answer: $\frac{1}{4}$ of 80 or 20

51. Sample answer: $\frac{2}{3}$ of 90 or 60

52. Sample answer: $\frac{4}{5}$ of 50 or 40

53. Sample answer: $\frac{2}{7}$ of 70 or 20

BASEBALL For Exercises 38 and 39, use the following information. The graphic shows the results of a survey asking women about their interest in Major League Baseball. Suppose 1,000 women were surveyed.

Women's Interest in Major League Baseball

Source: ESPN

38. How many women said they were interested in Major League Baseball? **300 women**

39. How many women said they were *not* interested in Major League Baseball? **700 women**

40. **WRITE A PROBLEM** Write and solve a real-life problem involving percents that uses mental math. **See margin.**

41. **CRITICAL THINKING** Find two numbers, a and b, such that 10% of a is the same as 30% of b. Explain. **See margin.**

42. **CRITICAL THINKING** Explain how to determine the 15% tip using mental math. **See margin.**

43. **MULTIPLE CHOICE** Alan and three of his coworkers ate lunch at Old Town Café. They plan to leave a 20% tip for the waiter. Two of his coworkers had turkey sandwiches, one had soup and salad, and Alan had pasta. What information is necessary to determine how much to leave for a tip? **B**

   (A) the cost of the pasta (B) the cost of the four meals

   (C) what day they had lunch (D) the soup of the day

44. **GRID IN** Find 10% of 23. **2.3**

45. **FOOTBALL** Eleven of the 48 members of the football team are on the field. What percent of the team members are playing? (Lesson 5-3) **about 22.9%**

Write each fraction as a percent. (Lesson 5-2)

46. $\frac{9}{20}$ **45%** 47. $\frac{7}{8}$ **87.5%** 48. $\frac{3}{500}$ **0.6%** 49. $\frac{2}{9}$ **$22.\overline{2}\%$**

GETTING READY FOR THE NEXT LESSON

BASIC SKILL Estimate. 50–53. See margin.

50. $\frac{1}{4}$ of 81 51. $\frac{2}{3}$ of 91 52. $\frac{4}{5}$ of 49 53. $\frac{2}{7}$ of 68

msmath3.net/self_check_quiz

4 Assess

Open-Ended Assessment

Writing Have students write out the process needed to compute 55% of a number using mental math. **First find half of the number (or 50%). Then find $\frac{1}{10}$ of that half (which is 5%). Add those two numbers.**

Study Guide and Intervention, p. 260

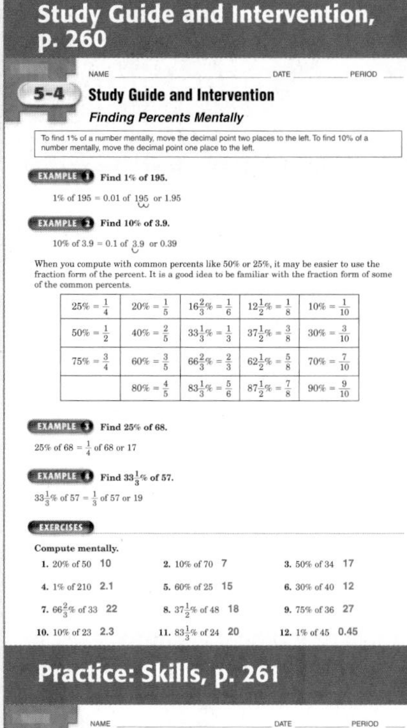

NAME ______ DATE ______ PERIOD ____

5-4 Study Guide and Intervention

Finding Percents Mentally

To find 1% of a number mentally, move the decimal point two places to the left. To find 10% of a number mentally, move the decimal point one place to the left.

EXAMPLE 1 **Find 1% of 195.**

1% of 195 = 0.01 of 195 or 1.95

EXAMPLE 2 **Find 10% of 3.9.**

10% of 3.9 = 0.1 of 3.9 or 0.39

When you compute with common percents like 50% or 25%, it may be easier to use the fraction form of the percent. It is a good idea to be familiar with the fraction form of some of the common percents.

$25\% = \frac{1}{4}$	$20\% = \frac{1}{5}$	$16\frac{2}{3}\% = \frac{1}{6}$	$12\frac{1}{2}\% = \frac{1}{8}$	$10\% = \frac{1}{10}$
$50\% = \frac{1}{2}$	$40\% = \frac{2}{5}$	$33\frac{1}{3}\% = \frac{1}{3}$	$37\frac{1}{2}\% = \frac{3}{8}$	$30\% = \frac{3}{10}$
$75\% = \frac{3}{4}$	$60\% = \frac{3}{5}$	$66\frac{2}{3}\% = \frac{2}{3}$	$62\frac{1}{2}\% = \frac{5}{8}$	$70\% = \frac{7}{10}$
	$80\% = \frac{4}{5}$	$83\frac{1}{3}\% = \frac{5}{6}$	$87\frac{1}{2}\% = \frac{7}{8}$	$90\% = \frac{9}{10}$

EXAMPLE 3 **Find 25% of 68.**

25% of 68 = $\frac{1}{4}$ of 68 or 17

EXAMPLE 4 **Find $33\frac{1}{3}$% of 57.**

$33\frac{1}{3}$% of 57 = $\frac{1}{3}$ of 57 or 19

EXERCISES

Compute mentally.

1. 20% of 50 10 2. 10% of 70 7 3. 50% of 34 17
4. 1% of 210 2.1 5. 60% of 25 15 6. 30% of 40 12
7. $66\frac{2}{3}$% of 33 22 8. $37\frac{1}{2}$% of 48 18 9. 75% of 36 27
10. 10% of 23 2.3 11. $83\frac{1}{3}$% of 24 20 12. 1% of 45 0.45

Practice: Skills, p. 261

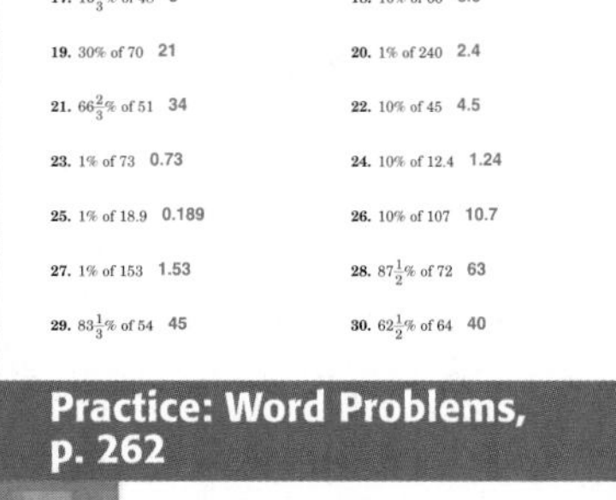

NAME ______ DATE ______ PERIOD ____

5-4 Practice: Skills

Finding Percents Mentally

Compute mentally.

1. 50% of 40 20 2. 25% of 36 9
3. 10% of 60 6 4. 1% of 100 1
5. 20% of 15 3 6. 40% of 30 12
7. $33\frac{1}{3}$% of 21 7 8. $12\frac{1}{2}$% of 32 4
9. 75% of 28 21 10. 10% of 230 23
11. 90% of 30 27 12. $83\frac{1}{3}$% of 18 15
13. 1% of 300 3 14. $62\frac{1}{2}$% of 24 15
15. 60% of 45 27 16. 70% of 50 35
17. $16\frac{2}{3}$% of 48 8 18. 10% of 66 6.6
19. 30% of 70 21 20. 1% of 240 2.4
21. $66\frac{2}{3}$% of 51 34 22. 10% of 45 4.5
23. 1% of 73 0.73 24. 10% of 12.4 1.24
25. 1% of 18.9 0.189 26. 10% of 107 10.7
27. 1% of 153 1.53 28. $87\frac{1}{2}$% of 72 63
29. $83\frac{1}{3}$% of 54 45 30. $62\frac{1}{2}$% of 64 40

Practice: Word Problems, p. 262

NAME ______ DATE ______ PERIOD ____

5-4 Practice: Word Problems

Finding Percents Mentally

1. **ELECTIONS** In a certain small town, 80% of the adults voted in the last election. How many of the 600 adults living in the town voted in the last election? **480 adults**

2. **FISH POPULATION** Fish and game managers have determined that 10% of the approximately 3,400 fish in Avondale Lake are catfish. How many catfish are there in Avondale Lake? **340 catfish**

3. **SURVEYS** In a recent survey, 1% of the people had no opinion on the topic. How many of the 1,100 people surveyed had no opinion on the topic? **11 people**

4. **BAND** In a local middle school, $33\frac{1}{3}$% of the students are in the band. There are 240 students in the school. How many middle school students are in the band? **80 students**

5. **AIR TRAVEL** At one large international airport in the U.S., 20% of the arriving flights are from other countries. On a recent day, 240 flights arrived at the airport. How many of these flights were from other countries? **48 flights**

6. **TELEPHONE** Ramona likes to keep track of her incoming calls. Last month, 25% of the 132 calls Ramona received were from telemarketers. How many calls did Ramona get from telemarketers last month? **33 calls**

7. **FARMING** Jake grows corn and soybeans on his farm. He has corn growing on $66\frac{2}{3}$% of his 330 acres. How many acres are being used for corn? **220 acres**

8. **ENERGY** The U.S. has 25% of the nuclear power plants in the world. How many of the world's 416 nuclear power plants are in the U.S.? **104 nuclear power plants**

Mid-Chapter Practice Test

Assessment Option

Mid-Chapter Test (Lessons 5-1 through 5-4) is available on p. 301 of the *Chapter 5 Resource Masters.*

ExamView® Pro

Use the networkable ExamView® Pro Testmaker CD-ROM to:

- Create **multiple versions** of tests.
- Create **modified** tests for **inclusion** students with one mouse click.
- **Edit** existing questions and **add** your own questions.
- Build tests aligned with state standards using built-in **state curriculum correlations.**
- Change **English** tests to **Spanish** with one mouse click and vice versa.

FOLDABLES™ Follow-Up

Before students complete the Mid-Chapter Practice Test, encourage them to review the notes, definitions, concepts, and main ideas they recorded on the first sections of their Foldables.

Answer

1. Method 1 Use a proportion.

$$\frac{5}{6} = \frac{x}{100}$$
$$5 \cdot 100 = 6 \cdot x$$
$$500 = 6x$$
$$\frac{500}{6} = \frac{6x}{6}$$
$$83.\overline{3} = x$$

Method 2 Write a decimal.

$$\frac{5}{6} = 0.83\overline{3}$$
$$= 83.\overline{3}\%$$

CHAPTER 5 Mid-Chapter Practice Test

Vocabulary and Concepts

1. **Show** two different ways to write $\frac{5}{6}$ as a percent. (Lesson 5-2) See margin.
2. **Explain** how to find 75% of 8 mentally. (Lesson 5-4)
   75% is $\frac{3}{4}$, $\frac{1}{4}$ of 8 is 2 and $\frac{3}{4}$ of 8 is $3 \cdot 2$ or 6.

Skills and Applications

Write each ratio or fraction as a percent. (Lesson 5-1)

3. 3 out of 20 15%
4. 15.2 out of 100 15.2%
5. $\frac{13}{25}$ 52%
6. $\frac{7}{20}$ 35%

Write each decimal or fraction as a percent. (Lesson 5-2)

7. 0.325 32.5%
8. $\frac{3}{50}$ 6%
9. $\frac{1}{5}$ 20%
10. 1.02 102%

Write a percent proportion to solve each problem. Then solve. Round to the nearest tenth if necessary. (Lesson 5-3)

11. 63 is what percent of 84?
12. Find 35% of 700. $\frac{a}{700} = \frac{35}{100}$; 245
13. 294 is 35% of what number? $\frac{294}{b} = \frac{35}{100}$; 840

11. $\frac{63}{84} = \frac{p}{100}$; 75%

Compute mentally. (Lesson 5-4)

14. 25% of 64 16
15. 50% of 150 75
16. 60% of 20 12
17. 3% of 600 18

18. **SCHOOL** Santos scored 87% on an English exam. Write this as a decimal. (Lesson 5-2) 0.87

Standardized Test Practice

19. **MULTIPLE CHOICE** Fifteen percent of the dogs at a show were Labrador retrievers. Which is *not* true? (Lesson 5-1) D
    - Ⓐ $\frac{3}{20}$ of the dogs were Labrador retrievers.
    - Ⓑ 15 out of every 100 dogs were Labrador retrievers.
    - Ⓒ 85% of the dogs were *not* Labrador retrievers.
    - Ⓓ 1 out of every 15 dogs were Labrador retrievers.

20. **SHORT RESPONSE** Use the graph below. Does Leah spend more of her day sleeping or at school? Explain. (Lesson 5-2)

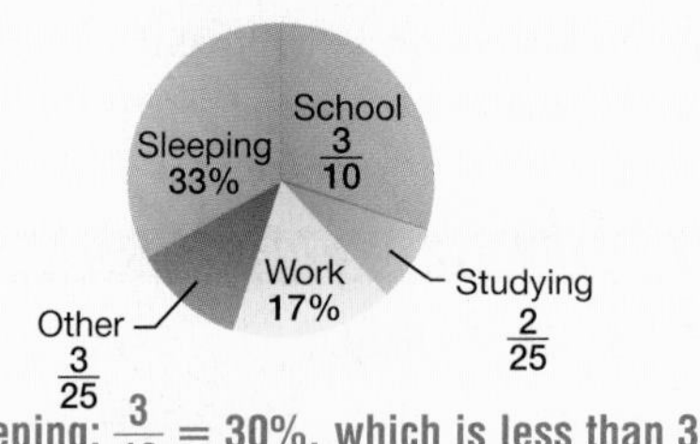

Sleeping; $\frac{3}{10}$ = 30%, which is less than 33%.

The Game Zone

A Place To Practice Your Math Skills

Per-Fraction

GET READY!

Players: two, three, or four
Materials: 38 index cards, scissors, markers

GET SET!

- Cut each index card in half, making 76 cards.
- Take four cards. On the first card, write a percent from the table on page 220. On the second card, write the corresponding fraction next to the percent. On the third card, write an equivalent fraction. On the fourth card, write the equivalent decimal.
- Repeat the steps until you have used all 19 percents from the table.

GO!

- Deal seven cards to each player. Place the remaining cards facedown on the table. Take the top card and place it faceup next to the deck, forming the discard pile.
- All players check their cards for scoring sets. A scoring set consists of three equivalent numbers.

60% $\frac{3}{5}$ $\frac{6}{10}$

Scoring Set

- The first player draws the top card from the deck or the discard pile. If the player has a scoring set, he or she should place it faceup on the table. The player may also build onto another player's scoring set by placing a card faceup on the table and announcing the set on which the player is building. The player's turn ends when he or she discards a card.
- **Who Wins?** The first person with no cards remaining wins.

The Game Zone

Glencoe Mathematics Classroom Manipulative Kit

- scissors

GETTING READY

Objective Find equivalent percents, fractions, and decimals.

MANAGEMENT TIPS

Recommended Time
40 minutes

Tips

- Consider having the index cards precut, numbered, and packaged in sets to give to students at the beginning of the activity.
- To make multiple decks to use again and again, use different colored index cards or mark the decks on the back. Then laminate the cards for durability.
- You may want to have weaker students work with partners. The pair can look for equivalent numbers together.
- You may wish to use the game as an assessment tool for the concepts in Lessons 5-1 through 5-4.

Math Online For an additional game for this chapter, visit: msmath3.net/gamezone

The Game Zone: Equivalent Percents, Fractions, and Decimals **225**

5-5a Lesson Notes

1 Focus

Bellringer

Communication Ask students to close their books. Show students the opening problem on a transparency or worksheet and have students suggest ways to solve it mentally. Jot down suggestions on the transparency or the chalkboard. **Sample answer: Some students may suggest finding 60 percent of $100 and then taking half of that: $\frac{1}{2}$ of $60 = $30.**

2 Teach

In-Class Example

Solve. Use the reasonable answer strategy.

SHOPPING Cara sees an advertisement for a pair of shoes she likes. One pair costs $34.99 plus 5 percent tax. She wants to buy a black pair and a brown pair. Cara has $75 saved in her clothing budget. Can she afford both pairs of shoes? **yes**

Answer

3. **Sample answer: Pat wants to buy items that cost $4.15, $11.97, and $8.27. He has $20. Does he have enough money to buy the items? He does not have enough since $4 + $12 + $8 = $24, which is greater than $20.**

5-5a Problem-Solving Strategy

A Preview of Lesson 5-5

Reasonable Answers

What You'll LEARN

Solve problems using the reasonable answer strategy.

Because I work at the Jean Shack, I can buy a $50 jacket there for 60% of its price.

Carla, will you have to pay more or less than $25?

Explore	We know the cost of the jacket. Carla can buy the jacket for 60% of the price. We want to know if the jacket will cost more or less than $25.
Plan	Use mental math to determine a reasonable answer.
Solve	THINK $\frac{25}{50} = \frac{1}{2}$ or 50% Since Carla will pay 60% of the cost, she will have to pay more than $25.
Examine	Find 60% of $50 60% of 50 = $\frac{3}{5}$ of 50 Since $\frac{1}{5}$ of 50 is 10, $\frac{3}{5}$ of 50 is 3×10 or 30. Carla will pay $30 which is more than $25.

Analyze the Strategy

1. **Explain** why determining a reasonable answer was an appropriate strategy for solving the above problem. **An exact cost was not needed.**
2. **Explain** why mental math skills are important when using the reasonable answer strategy. **Mental math skills can help estimate a solution.**
3. **Write** a problem where checking for a reasonable answer is appropriate. Explain how you would solve the problem. **See margin.**

DAILY INTERVENTION **Differentiated Instruction** **ELL**

Verbal/Linguistic Give students a variety of multiple-choice problems to solve. Have students explain ways of choosing the most reasonable answer for each.

Apply the Strategy

Solve. Use the reasonable answer strategy.

4. **SCHOOL** There are 750 students at Monroe Middle School. If 64% of the students have purchased yearbooks, would the number of yearbooks purchased be about 200, 480, or 700? **480 yearbooks**

5. **MONEY MATTERS** Spencer took $40 to the shopping mall. He has already spent $12.78. He wants to buy two items for $7.25 and $15.78. Does he have enough money with him to make these two purchases? **yes**

Mixed Problem Solving

Solve. Use any strategy.

6. **BAKING** Desiree spilled $1\frac{1}{2}$ cups of sugar, which she discarded. She then used half of the remaining sugar to make cookies. If she had $4\frac{1}{2}$ cups left, how much sugar did she have in the beginning? **$10\frac{1}{2}$ c**

7. **NUMBER THEORY** Study the pattern.

$1 \times 1 = 1$
$11 \times 11 = 121$
$111 \times 111 = 12{,}321$
$1111 \times 1111 = 1{,}234{,}321$

Without doing the multiplication, find 1111111×1111111. **1,234,567,654,321**

8. **FARMING** An orange grower harvested 1,260 pounds of oranges from one grove, 874 pounds from another, and 602 pounds from a third. The oranges will be placed in crates that hold 14 pounds oranges each. Should the orange grower order 100, 200, or 300 crates for the oranges? **200 crates**

9. **DESIGN** Juanita is designing isosceles triangular tiles for a mosaic. The sides of the larger triangle are $1\frac{1}{2}$ times larger than the sides of the triangle shown. What are the dimensions of the larger triangle?

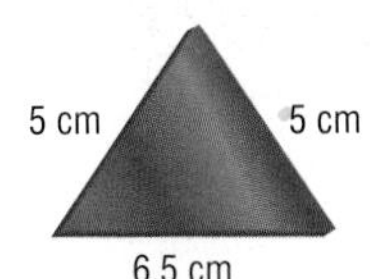

7.5 cm, 7.5 cm, 9.75 cm

10. **GEOMETRY** What percent of the large rectangle is blue? **25%**

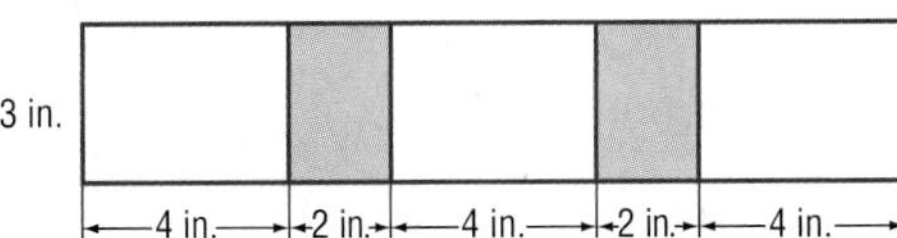

11. **MULTI STEP** Seth is saving for a down payment on a car. He wants to have a down payment of 10% for a car that costs $13,000. So far he has saved $850. If he saves $75 each week for the down payment, how soon can he buy the car? **6 weeks**

12. **ECOLOGY** In a survey of 1,413 shoppers, 6% said they would be willing to pay more for environmentally safe products. Is 8.4, 84, or 841 a reasonable estimate for the number of shoppers willing to pay more? **84 shoppers**

13. **BUILDING** The atrium of a new mega mall will need 2.3×10^5 square feet of ceramic tile. The tiles measure 2 feet by 2 feet and are sold in boxes of 24. How many boxes of tiles will be needed to complete the job? **2,396 boxes**

14. **STANDARDIZED TEST PRACTICE** In one month, the Shaffer family spent $121.59, $168.54, $98.67, and $141.78 on groceries. Which amount is a good estimate of the total cost of the groceries for the month? **B**

(A) $450 (B) $530
(C) $580 (D) $620

3 Practice/Apply

About the Exercises...

Problem-Solving Strategies
Exercises 6–14 are structured so that students have the opportunity to practice many different problem-solving strategies. You may wish to remind them of some of the strategies they have studied.

- use the four-step plan (p. 6)
- work backward (p. 43)
- look for a pattern (p. 96)
- reasonable answers ✓

4 Assess

Open-Ended Assessment

Writing Provide students with a local grocery store's newspaper section. Tell them they have $50. Give them 5 minutes to make a reasonable shopping list. Have students explain their choices in a short paragraph.

5-5 Lesson Notes

Lesson Resources

Chapter 5 Resource Masters

- Study Guide and Intervention, p. 265
- Practice: Skills, p. 266
- Practice: Word Problems, p. 267
- Reading to Learn Mathematics, p. 268
- Enrichment, p. 269

Science and Math Lab Masters, pp. 53–56, 89–92

Parent and Student Study Guide Online Worksheets, 5-5

Noteables™: Interactive Study Notebook with Foldables™, 5-5

Virtual Activities CD-ROM, Estimating Percent

FAST FILE

1 Focus

5-Minute Check 5-5

Use as a quiz or review of Lesson 5-4. (Also available as a transparency)

Bellringer

Problem Solving Ask students to round each of the following percents to a common equivalent fraction. (They should refer to the fractions and percents they learned in the previous lesson.)

1. 11% $\frac{1}{10}$ **2.** 34% $\frac{1}{3}$

3. 76% $\frac{3}{4}$ **4.** 87% $\frac{7}{8}$

Reading to Learn Mathematics, p. 268 

NAME ______ DATE ______ PERIOD ______

Reading to Learn Mathematics

Percent and Estimation

Pre-Activity *Read the introduction at the top of page 228 in your textbook. Write your answers below.*

1. Round the total area of Earth to the nearest hundred million square miles. 200,000,000 mi²
2. Round the percent of Earth that is land to the nearest ten percent. 30%
3. Use what you learned about mental math in Lesson 5-4 to estimate the area of the land on Earth. about 60,000,000 mi²

Reading the Lesson

5-5 Percent and Estimation

What You'll LEARN

Estimate by using equivalent fractions, decimals, and percents.

NEW Vocabulary

compatible numbers

MATH Symbols

≈ is approximately equal to

WHEN am I ever going to use this?

GEOGRAPHY The total area of Earth is 196,800,000 square miles. The graphic shows the percent of the area of Earth that is land and the percent that is water.

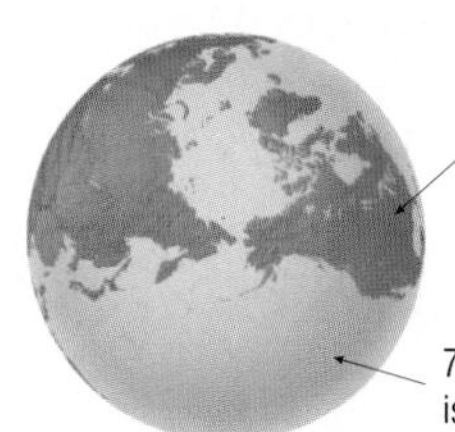

Source: *World Book*

1. Round the total area of Earth to the nearest hundred million square miles. **200,000,000 mi²**
2. Round the percent of Earth that is land to the nearest ten percent. **30%**
3. Use what you learned about mental math in Lesson 5-4 to estimate the area of the land on Earth. **about 60,000,000 mi²**

Sometimes an exact answer is not needed. One way to estimate a percent of a number is by using compatible numbers. **Compatible numbers** are two numbers that are easy to divide mentally.

EXAMPLES Estimate Percents of Numbers

Estimate.

1 19% of 30

19% is about 20% or $\frac{1}{5}$. $\frac{1}{5}$ and 30 are compatible numbers.

$\frac{1}{5}$ of 30 is 6.

So, 19% of 30 is about 6.

2 25% of 41

25% is $\frac{1}{4}$, and 41 is about 40. $\frac{1}{4}$ and 40 are compatible numbers.

$\frac{1}{4}$ of 40 is 10.

So, 25% of 41 is about 10.

3 65% of 76

65% is about $66\frac{2}{3}$% or $\frac{2}{3}$, and 76 is about 75. $\frac{1}{3}$ and 75 are compatible numbers.

$\frac{2}{3}$ of 75 is 50.

So, 65% of 76 is about 50.

You can use similar techniques to estimate a percent.

TEACHING TIP

Tell students that when estimating answers, different students may get slightly different answers.

EXAMPLES Estimate Percents

Estimate each percent.

4 **8 out of 25**

$\frac{8}{25} \approx \frac{8}{24}$ or $\frac{1}{3}$ 25 is about 24.

$\frac{1}{3} = 33\frac{1}{3}\%$

So, 8 out of 25 is about $33\frac{1}{3}\%$.

5 **14 out of 25**

$\frac{14}{25} \approx \frac{15}{25}$ or $\frac{3}{5}$ 14 is about 15.

$\frac{3}{5} = 60\%$

So, 14 out of 25 is about 60%.

6 **89 out of 121**

$\frac{89}{121} \approx \frac{90}{120}$ or $\frac{3}{4}$ 89 is about 90, and 121 is about 120.

$\frac{3}{4} = 75\%$

So, 89 out of 121 is about 75%.

Your Turn Estimate each percent.

a. 7 out of 57 b. 9 out of 25 c. 7 out of 79

a–c. Sample answers given.

a. $\frac{7}{57} \approx \frac{7}{56}$ **or** $12\frac{1}{2}\%$

b. $\frac{9}{25} \approx \frac{10}{25}$ **or 40%**

c. $\frac{7}{79} \approx \frac{8}{80}$ **or 10%**

Sometimes estimation is the best answer to a real-life problem.

REAL-LIFE MATH

FIREFIGHTING For many years, Smokey Bear has been the symbol for preventing forest fires. The real Smokey Bear was a 3-month-old cub when he was rescued from a fire in Lincoln National Forest in May, 1950.

Source: www.smokeybearstore.com

EXAMPLE Estimate Percent of an Area

7 **FIREFIGHTING Fire fighters use geometry and aerial photography to estimate how much of a forest has been damaged by fire. A grid is superimposed on a photograph of the forest. The gray part of the figure at the right represents the area damaged by a forest fire. Estimate the percent of the forest damaged by the fire.**

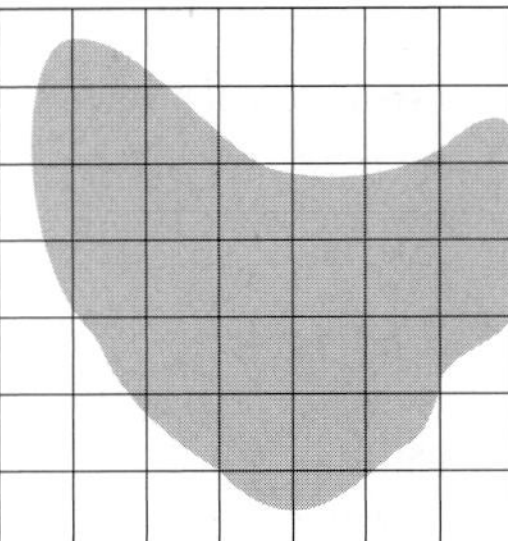

About 24 small squares out of 49 squares are shaded gray.

$\frac{24}{49} \approx \frac{25}{50}$ or $\frac{1}{2}$ 24 is about 25, and 49 is about 50.

$\frac{1}{2} = 50\%$

So, about 50% of the area has been damaged by the fire.

msmath3.net/extra_examples

2 Teach

In-Class Examples

Estimate.

1 48% of 70 **Sample answer:** $\frac{1}{2}$ **of 70 or 35**

2 75% of 98 **Sample answer:** $\frac{3}{4}$ **of 100 or 75**

3 12% of 81 **Sample answer:** $\frac{1}{8}$ **of 80 or 10**

Estimate each percent.

4 12 out of 47 **Sample answer:** $\frac{12}{47} \approx \frac{12}{48}$ **or 25%**

5 19 out of 31 **Sample answer:** $\frac{19}{31} \approx \frac{20}{30}$ **or** $66\frac{2}{3}\%$

6 41 out of 200 **Sample answer:** $\frac{41}{200} \approx \frac{40}{200}$ **or 20%**

7 **ART** An artist creates a design on a grid. Estimate the percent of the grid that has been painted so far.

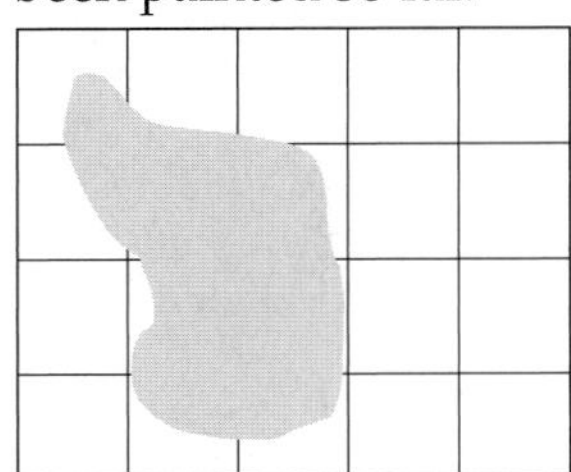

Sample answer: $\frac{6}{20}$ **or 30%**

Tips for New Teachers

Using Applications This is an excellent lesson to point out to students how math has real-life applications. The ability to do computations quickly and easily will be valuable in their lives.

DAILY INTERVENTION **Differentiated Instruction**

Naturalist Have students find pictures of natural landscapes and create a grid on them. From these grids, students can estimate the percent of the area that is covered by a certain type of land or plant. They might also look at county or local maps and use the grid supplied. They can determine how much of a county is parkland or green space.

Students practice the same concepts in Exercises 11–39 if they are assigned odd or even problems.

3 Practice/Apply

NUMBER SENSE
Use Exercise 3 to demonstrate the advantage of not just estimating an answer, but determining if that answer is "a little high" or "a little low."

About the Exercises...

Guided Practice Key

Exercises	Examples
4–6	1–3
7–9	4–6
10	7

Assignment Guide

Basic: 11–17 odd, 23–29 odd, 33, 35, 41–53

Average: 11–39 odd, 41–53

Enriched: 12–36 even, 37–49 (Optional: 50–53)

Skill and Concept Check

1. *Writing Math* Explain how you could use fractions and compatible numbers to estimate 26% of \$98.98. **See margin.**
2. **OPEN ENDED** Write a percent problem with an estimated answer of 10. **Sample answer: 9.9% of 99**
3. **NUMBER SENSE** Use mental math to determine which is greater: 24% of 240 or 51% of 120. Explain. **51% of 120; See margin.**

GUIDED PRACTICE

Estimate. 4–6. See margin.

4. 49% of 160
5. $66\frac{2}{3}$% of 20
6. 73% of 65

Estimate each percent. 7–9. See margin.

7. 6 out of 35
8. 8 out of 79
9. 17.5 out of 23

10. **BIOLOGY** The adult skeleton has 206 bones. Sixty of them are in the arms and hands. Estimate the percent of bones that are in the arms and hands. **Sample answer: $\frac{60}{206} \approx \frac{60}{200}$ or 30%**

★ indicates increased difficulty

Practice and Applications

Estimate. 11–22. See margin. 23. Sample answer: $\frac{1}{3}$ of 120 or 40

11. 29% of 50
12. 67% of 93
13. 20% of 76
14. 25% of 63
15. 21% of 71
16. 92% of 41
17. 48% of 159
18. 73% of 81
★19. 68% of 9.2
★20. 26.5% of 123
★21. 124% of 41
★22. 249% of 119

HOMEWORK HELP	
For Exercises	See Examples
11–24	1–3
25–32, 36–40	4–6
33–35	7

Extra Practice See pages 628, 652.

23. Estimate 34% of 121.
24. Estimate 21% of 348. **Sample answer: $\frac{1}{5}$ of 350 or 70**

Estimate each percent. 25–32. See margin.

25. 7 out of 29
26. 6 out of 59
27. 4 out of 21
28. 6 out of 35
29. 8 out of 13
30. 9 out of 23
★31. 150,078 out of 299,000
★32. 63,875 out of 245,000

Estimate the percent of the area shaded. 33–35. Sample answers given.

33. 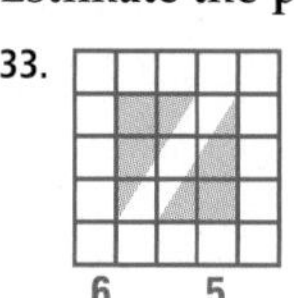
$\frac{6}{25} \approx \frac{5}{25}$ or 20%

34. 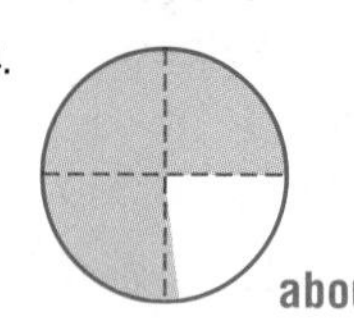
about 76%

35. 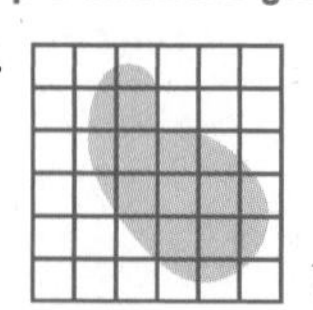
$\frac{13}{36} \approx \frac{12}{36}$ or $33\frac{1}{3}$%

36. **ANIMALS** In the year 2003, 1,072 species of animals were endangered or threatened. Of these species, 342 were mammals. Estimate the percent of endangered or threatened animals that were mammals. **Sample answer: $\frac{342}{1{,}072} \approx \frac{300}{1{,}000}$ or 30%**

Answers

1. 26% is about 25% or $\frac{1}{4}$. \$98.98 is about \$100. $\frac{1}{4}$ of 100 is 25. So, 26% of \$98.98 is about \$25.
3. 24% of 240 is less than $\frac{1}{4}$ of 240 or 60. 51% of 120 is greater than $\frac{1}{2}$ of 120 or 60.

4–32. Sample answers given.

4. $\frac{1}{2}$ of 160 or 80
5. $\frac{2}{3}$ of 21 or 14
6. $\frac{3}{4}$ of 64 or 48
7. $\frac{6}{35} \approx \frac{7}{35}$ or 20%
8. $\frac{8}{79} \approx \frac{8}{80}$ or 10%
9. $\frac{17.5}{23} \approx \frac{18}{24}$ or 75%
11. $\frac{3}{10}$ of 50 or 15
12. $\frac{2}{3}$ of 93 or 62
13. $\frac{1}{5}$ of 75 or 15
14. $\frac{1}{4}$ of 64 or 16
15. $\frac{1}{5}$ of 70 or 14
16. $\frac{9}{10}$ of 40 or 36
17. $\frac{1}{2}$ of 160 or 80
18. $\frac{3}{4}$ of 80 or 60
19. $\frac{2}{3}$ of 9 or 6
20. $\frac{1}{4}$ of 120 or 30
21. $1\frac{1}{4}$ of 40 or 50
22. $2\frac{1}{2}$ of 120 or 300
25. $\frac{7}{29} \approx \frac{7}{28}$ or 25%
26. $\frac{6}{59} \approx \frac{6}{60}$ or 10%
27. $\frac{4}{21} \approx \frac{4}{20}$ or 20%
28. $\frac{6}{35} \approx \frac{6}{36}$ or $16\frac{2}{3}$%
29. $\frac{8}{13} \approx \frac{8}{12}$ or $66\frac{2}{3}$%
30. $\frac{9}{23} \approx \frac{9}{24}$ or $37\frac{1}{2}$%
31. $\frac{150{,}078}{299{,}000} \approx \frac{150{,}000}{300{,}000}$ or 50%
32. $\frac{63{,}875}{245{,}000} \approx \frac{60{,}000}{240{,}000}$ or 25%
47. $\frac{7}{70} = \frac{p}{100}$; 10%
48. $\frac{a}{200} = \frac{65}{100}$; 130
49. $\frac{42}{b} = \frac{35}{100}$; 120

POPULATION For Exercises 37–40, use the following information.

2002 Population		
City	City Population	Entire State Population
New York, New York	8,084,316	19,134,293
Los Angeles, California	3,798,981	35,001,986
Chicago, Illinois	2,886,251	12,586,447

Source: U.S. Bureau of the Census

★ 37. Estimate what percent of the population of the entire state of New York live in New York City. **Sample answer:** $\frac{8{,}084{,}316}{19{,}134{,}293} \approx \frac{8{,}000{,}000}{20{,}000{,}000}$ **or 40%**

★ 38. Estimate what percent of the population of the entire state of California live in Los Angeles. **Sample answer:** $\frac{3{,}798{,}981}{35{,}001{,}986} \approx \frac{4{,}000{,}000}{36{,}000{,}000}$ **or 11.1%**

★ 39. Estimate what percent of the population of the entire state of Illinois live in Chicago. **Sample answer:** $\frac{2{,}886{,}251}{12{,}586{,}447} \approx \frac{3{,}000{,}000}{12{,}000{,}000}$ **or 25%**

40. Which city has the greatest percent of its state's population? **New York City**

CRITICAL THINKING Determine whether each statement about estimating percents of numbers is *sometimes*, *always*, or *never* true.

41. If both the percent and the number are rounded up, the estimate will be greater than the actual answer. **always**

42. If both the percent and the number are rounded down, the estimate will be less than the actual answer. **always**

43. If the percent is rounded up and the number is rounded down, the estimate will be greater than the actual answer. **sometimes**

Spiral Review with Standardized Test Practice

44. **MULTIPLE CHOICE** Rick took his father to dinner for his birthday. When the bill came, Rick's father reminded him that it is customary to tip the server 15% of the bill. If the bill was $19.60, a good estimate for the tip is **D**

Ⓐ $6. Ⓑ $5. Ⓒ $4. Ⓓ $3.

45. **MULTIPLE CHOICE** What is the best estimate of the percent represented by 12 out of 35? **G**

Ⓕ 20% Ⓖ $33\frac{1}{3}$% Ⓗ $37\frac{1}{2}$% Ⓘ 40%

46. Explain how to find 75% of 84 mentally. (Lesson 5-4) $\frac{3}{4}$ **of 84 = 63**

Write a percent proportion to solve each problem. Then solve. Round to the nearest tenth if necessary. (Lesson 5-3) **47–49. See margin.**

47. 7 is what percent of 70?

48. What is 65% of 200?

49. 42 is 35% of what number?

GETTING READY FOR THE NEXT LESSON

PREREQUISITE SKILL Solve each equation. (Lesson 2-7)

50. $0.2a = 7$ **35**

51. $20s = 8$ **0.4**

52. $0.35t = 140$ **400**

53. $30n = 3$ **0.1**

msmath3.net/self_check_quiz

4 Assess

Open-Ended Assessment

Modeling Have students draw five identical squares on grid paper. Without using a ruler, they should shade the following percents of each square: 20%, 25%, $33\frac{1}{3}$%, 50%, 75%.

Students should be able to explain how they determined how much of each square to shade.

Study Guide and Intervention, p. 265

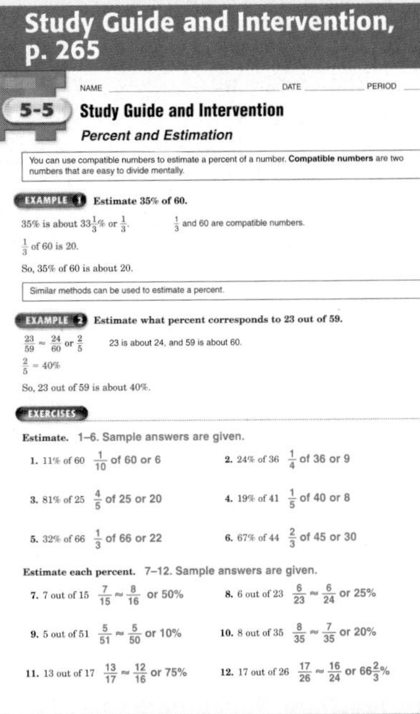

NAME ______ DATE ______ PERIOD ____

5-5 Study Guide and Intervention

Percent and Estimation

You can use compatible numbers to estimate a percent of a number. **Compatible numbers** are two numbers that are easy to divide mentally.

EXAMPLE 1 **Estimate 35% of 60.**

35% is about $33\frac{1}{3}$% or $\frac{1}{3}$. — $\frac{1}{3}$ and 60 are compatible numbers.

$\frac{1}{3}$ of 60 is 20.

So, 35% of 60 is about 20.

Similar methods can be used to estimate a percent.

EXAMPLE 2 **Estimate what percent corresponds to 23 out of 59.**

$\frac{23}{59} \approx \frac{24}{60}$ or $\frac{2}{5}$ — 23 is about 24, and 59 is about 60.

$\frac{2}{5} = 40\%$

So, 23 out of 59 is about 40%.

EXERCISES

Estimate. 1–6. Sample answers are given.

1. 11% of 60 $\frac{1}{10}$ of 60 or 6
2. 24% of 36 $\frac{1}{4}$ of 36 or 9
3. 81% of 25 $\frac{4}{5}$ of 25 or 20
4. 19% of 41 $\frac{1}{5}$ of 40 or 8
5. 32% of 66 $\frac{1}{3}$ of 66 or 22
6. 67% of 44 $\frac{2}{3}$ of 45 or 30

Estimate each percent. 7–12. Sample answers are given.

7. 7 out of 15 $\frac{7}{15} \approx \frac{8}{16}$ or 50%
8. 6 out of 23 $\frac{6}{23} \approx \frac{6}{24}$ or 25%
9. 5 out of 51 $\frac{5}{51} \approx \frac{5}{50}$ or 10%
10. 8 out of 35 $\frac{8}{35} \approx \frac{7}{35}$ or 20%
11. 13 out of 17 $\frac{13}{17} \approx \frac{12}{16}$ or 75%
12. 17 out of 26 $\frac{17}{26} \approx \frac{16}{24}$ or $66\frac{2}{3}$%

Practice: Skills, p. 266

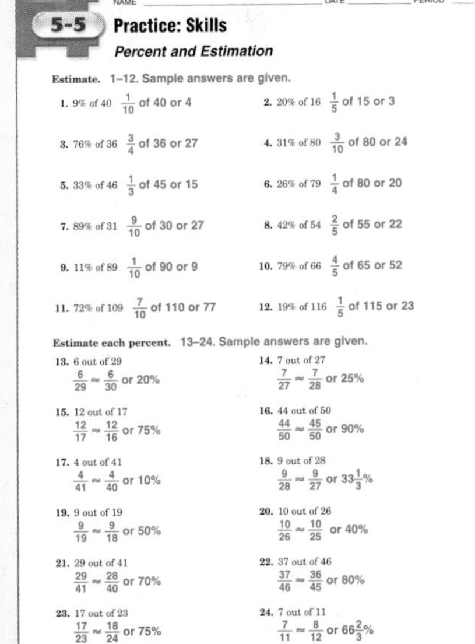

NAME ______ DATE ______ PERIOD ____

5-5 Practice: Skills

Percent and Estimation

Estimate. 1–12. Sample answers are given.

1. 9% of 40 $\frac{1}{10}$ of 40 or 4
2. 20% of 16 $\frac{1}{5}$ of 15 or 3
3. 76% of 36 $\frac{3}{4}$ of 36 or 27
4. 31% of 80 $\frac{3}{10}$ of 80 or 24
5. 33% of 46 $\frac{1}{3}$ of 45 or 15
6. 26% of 79 $\frac{1}{4}$ of 80 or 20
7. 89% of 31 $\frac{9}{10}$ of 30 or 27
8. 42% of 54 $\frac{2}{5}$ of 55 or 22
9. 11% of 89 $\frac{1}{10}$ of 90 or 9
10. 79% of 66 $\frac{4}{5}$ of 65 or 52
11. 72% of 109 $\frac{7}{10}$ of 110 or 77
12. 19% of 116 $\frac{1}{5}$ of 115 or 23

Estimate each percent. 13–24. Sample answers are given.

13. 6 out of 29 $\frac{6}{29} \approx \frac{6}{30}$ or 20%
14. 7 out of 27 $\frac{7}{27} \approx \frac{7}{28}$ or 25%
15. 12 out of 17 $\frac{12}{17} \approx \frac{12}{16}$ or 75%
16. 44 out of 50 $\frac{44}{50} \approx \frac{45}{50}$ or 90%
17. 4 out of 41 $\frac{4}{41} \approx \frac{4}{40}$ or 10%
18. 9 out of 28 $\frac{9}{28} \approx \frac{9}{27}$ or $33\frac{1}{3}$%
19. 9 out of 19 $\frac{9}{19} \approx \frac{9}{18}$ or 50%
20. 10 out of 26 $\frac{10}{26} \approx \frac{10}{25}$ or 40%
21. 29 out of 41 $\frac{29}{41} \approx \frac{28}{40}$ or 70%
22. 37 out of 46 $\frac{37}{46} \approx \frac{36}{45}$ or 80%
23. 17 out of 23 $\frac{17}{23} \approx \frac{18}{24}$ or 75%
24. 7 out of 11 $\frac{7}{11} \approx \frac{8}{12}$ or $66\frac{2}{3}$%

Practice: Word Problems, p. 267

NAME ______ DATE ______ PERIOD ____

5-5 Practice: Word Problems

Percent and Estimation

1. **FITNESS** At the office where Michael works, 8 out of 17 employees work out at least twice a week. Estimate the percent of employees that work out at least twice a week. **Sample answer:** $\frac{8}{17} \approx \frac{8}{16}$ **or 50%**

2. **PETS** Niki asked 25 of her classmates about what pets they have at home. Eleven of the 25 said they had both a cat and a dog. Estimate the percent of Niki's classmates that have both a cat and a dog. **Sample answer:** $\frac{11}{25} \approx \frac{10}{25}$ **or 40%**

3. **BOOKS** Jorge has read 19 novels this year, 4 of which were science fiction. Estimate the percent of novels that were science fiction. **Sample answer:** $\frac{4}{19} \approx \frac{4}{20}$ **or 20%**

4. **PARKS** The students in Kara's eighth grade science class determined that 9 out of 33 trees at a local park are pine trees. Estimate the percent of pine trees at the park. **Sample answer:** $\frac{9}{33} \approx \frac{8}{32}$ **or 25%**

5. **BAND** The marching band at Durango High School has 120 members. Of these, 18% are ninth-grade students. Estimate the number of ninth-grade students in the marching band. **Sample answer:** $\frac{1}{5}$ **of 120 or 24**

6. **RESTAURANTS** In one east-coast city, 35% of the restaurants in the city are on the bay. The city has 180 restaurants. Estimate the number of restaurants that are on the bay. **Sample answer:** $\frac{1}{3}$ **of 180 or 60**

7. **HOTELS** At the Westward Inn hotel, 48% of the rooms face the courtyard. The hotel has 91 rooms. Estimate the number of rooms that face the courtyard. **Sample answer:** $\frac{1}{2}$ **of 90 or 45**

8. **FARMING** Roy has planted soybeans on 68% of his farm this year. Roy's farm has 598 acres of land. Estimate the number of acres of soybeans that Roy has this year. **Sample answer:** $\frac{2}{3}$ **of 600 or 400 acres**

5-6 Lesson Notes

Lesson Resources

Chapter 5 Resource Masters
- Study Guide and Intervention, p. 270
- Practice: Skills, p. 271
- Practice: Word Problems, p. 272
- Reading to Learn Mathematics, p. 273
- Enrichment, p. 274

Calculator and Spreadsheet Masters, p. 26
Key Teaching Transparencies, 19
MathPASS Tutorial CD-ROM, 33–34
Parent and Student Study Guide Online Worksheets, 5-6
Noteables™: Interactive Study Notebook with Foldables™, 5-6

1 Focus

5-Minute Check 5-6

Use as a quiz or review of Lesson 5-5. (Also available as a transparency)

Bellringer

Communication Ask students to explain in a few short sentences how percents are related to decimals. **Percents express a part of a hundred. Two decimal places indicate hundredths or part of a hundred as well.**

Reading to Learn Mathematics, p. 273 **ELL**

NAME ____________ DATE ________ PERIOD ____

5-6 Reading to Learn Mathematics
The Percent Equation

Pre-Activity *Read the introduction at the top of page 232 in your textbook. Write your answers below.*

1. Use the percent proportion to find the area of water in Florida. 6,000 mi²
2. Express the percent for Florida as a decimal. Multiply the total area of Florida by this decimal. 0.10; 6,000
3. How are the answers for Exercises 1 and 2 related? They are the same.

Reading the Lesson

4. What is the *percent equation?* an equivalent form of the percent proportion in which the percent is written as a decimal

5-6 Algebra: The Percent Equation

What You'll LEARN

Solve problems using the percent equation.

NEW Vocabulary

percent equation

REVIEW Vocabulary

equation: a mathematical sentence that contains the equal sign (Lesson 1-8)

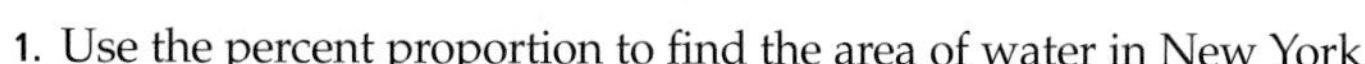

GEOGRAPHY The table shows New York's approximate area and the percent that is water.

New York	
Total Area (sq mi)	Percent of Area Occupied by Water
55,000	13%

1. Use the percent proportion to find the area of water in New York.
2. Express the percent for New York as a decimal. Multiply the total area of New York by this decimal. **0.13; 7,150** **1. 7,150 mi²**
3. How are the answers for Exercises 1 and 2 related?

3. They are the same.

The **percent equation** is an equivalent form of the percent proportion in which the percent is written as a decimal.

$\frac{\text{Part}}{\text{Base}} = \text{Percent}$ ← The percent is written as a decimal.

$\frac{\text{Part}}{\text{Base}} \cdot \text{Base} = \text{Percent} \cdot \text{Base}$ Multiply each side by the base.

$\text{Part} = \text{Percent} \cdot \text{Base}$ ← This form is called the percent equation.

TEACHING TIP

You may want to compare the Concept Summary on this page with the one on page 217.

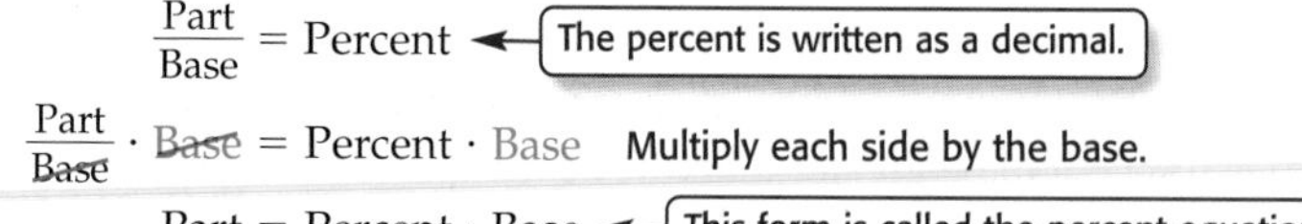

Concept Summary **The Percent Equation**

Type	Example	Equation
Find the Part	What number is 25% of 60? (part)	$n = 0.25(60)$
Find the Percent	15 is what percent of 60? (percent)	$15 = n(60)$
Find the Base	15 is 25% of what number? (base)	$15 = 0.25n$

EXAMPLE **Find the Part**

1 **Find 6% of 525.** **Estimate** 1% of 500 is 5. So, 6% of 500 is 6 · 5 or 30.

The percent is 6%, and the base is 525. Let n represent the part.

$n = 0.06(525)$ Write 6% as the decimal 0.06.

$n = 31.5$ Simplify.

So, 6% of 525 is 31.5. Compare to the estimate.

EXAMPLE Find the Percent

2 **420 is what percent of 600?** Estimate $\frac{420}{600} \approx \frac{400}{600}$ or $66\frac{2}{3}\%$

The part is 420, and the base is 600. Let n represent the percent.

$420 = n(600)$ Write the equation.

$\frac{420}{600} = \frac{600n}{600}$ Divide each side by 600.

$0.7 = n$ Simplify.

In the percent equation, the percent is written as a decimal. Since $0.7 = 70\%$, 420 is 70% of 600.

Your Turn **Solve each problem using the percent equation.**

a. What percent of 186 is 62? **$33\frac{1}{3}\%$** b. What percent of 90 is 180? **200%**

STUDY TIP

Look Back You can review **writing decimals as percents** in Lesson 5-2.

TEACHING TIP

Students have already learned to solve percent problems using the percent proportion in Lesson 5-3. Encourage students to use the percent equation when solving problems in this lesson. Once the students understand both methods, they can choose which method they prefer.

EXAMPLE Find the Base

3 **65 is 52% of what number?** Estimate 65 is 50% of 130.

The part is 65, and the percent is 52%. Let n represent the base.

$65 = 0.52n$ Write 52% as the decimal 0.52.

$\frac{65}{0.52} = \frac{0.52n}{0.52}$ Divide each side by 0.52.

$125 = n$ Simplify.

So, 65 is 52% of 125. Compare to the estimate.

Your Turn **Solve each problem using the percent equation.**

c. 210 is 75% of what number? **280** d. 18% of what number is 54? **300**

e. 0.2% of what number is 25? f. 7 is 2.5% of what number? **280**

e. 12,500

EXAMPLE Solve a Real-Life Problem

4 **SALES TAX** **A television costs $350. If a 7% tax is added, what is the total cost of the television?**

First find the amount of the tax t.

Words	What amount is 7% of $350?				
Symbols	part	=	percent	·	base
Equation	t	=	0.07	·	350

$t = 0.07 \cdot 350$ Write the equation.

$t = 24.5$ Simplify.

The amount of the tax is $24.50. The total cost of the television is $350.00 + $24.50 or $374.50.

msmath3.net/extra_examples

2 Teach

In-Class Examples

1 Find 30% of 450. **135**

2 102 is what percent of 150? **68%**

3 144 is 45% of what number? **320**

4 **SALES TAX** The price of a sweater is $75. The sales tax is $5\frac{3}{4}$ percent. What is the total price of the sweater? **$79.31**

DAILY INTERVENTION

Flexible Grouping

Peer Tutoring Have students complete Exercises 8–19 in groups of two or three. For each problem, they should identify whether it is the same type as Example 1, Example 2, or Example 3. Stronger students can help other students learn to identify the types of problems.

3 Practice/Apply

FOLDABLES™ Follow-Up Remind students to use their Foldables to record the percent equation in words and symbols. Students might give examples of what they have learned, or they could record new terms that they need to learn. Encourage students to explain why the rate in a percent equation is usually written as a decimal.

Which One Doesn't Belong? In Exercise 3, students might note that when dividing each of the equations by the number next to the variable, $\frac{80}{60}$ is the only one with a numerator larger than the denominator. That fact should signal that the equation is different from the other three.

About the Exercises...

Guided Practice Key

Exercises	Examples
4	1
5, 7	2
6	3

Assignment Guide

Basic: 9–19 odd, 27, 29, 30–41

Average: 9–29 odd, 30–41

Enriched: 8–28 even, 29–37 (Optional: 38–41)

Alert! The Data Update following Exercise 27 requires access to the Internet.

Answer

2. Sample answer: 5 is 10% of what number?

Proportion Equation

$\frac{a}{b} = \frac{p}{100} \rightarrow \frac{5}{b} = \frac{10}{100}$ Replace a with 5 and p with 10.

$5 \cdot 100 = b \cdot 10$ Find the cross products.

$500 = 10b$ Multiply.

$\frac{500}{10} = \frac{10b}{10}$ Divide each side by 10.

$50 = b$ Simplify.

Percent Equation

Let n represent the base.

Part = Percent · Base Percent equation

$5 = 0.1n$ Write 10% as 0.1.

$\frac{5}{0.1} = \frac{0.1n}{0.1}$ Divide each side by 0.1.

$50 = n$ Simplify.

The answer is 50. Both methods result in the same answer. Solving the problem using the percent equation uses fewer steps than solving the problem using the percent proportion.

Students practice the same concepts in Exercises 8–29 if they are assigned odd or even problems.

Skill and Concept Check

1. **Write** an equation you could use to find the percent of questions answered correctly if 32 out of 40 answers are correct. $32 = n(40)$

2. **OPEN ENDED** Write a percent problem in which you need to find the base. Solve the problem using the percent proportion and using the percent equation. Compare and contrast the two methods of solving the equation. See margin.

3. **Which One Doesn't Belong?** Identify the equation that does not have the same solution as the other three. Explain your reasoning.

$15 = n(20)$	$3 = n(4)$	$80 = n(60)$	$9 = n(12)$

$80 = n(60)$; The solution of $80 = n(60)$ is $1\frac{1}{3}$, while the solution of each of the others is $\frac{3}{4}$.

GUIDED PRACTICE

Solve each problem using the percent equation.

4. Find 85% of 920. 782
5. 25 is what percent of 625? 4%
6. 680 is 34% of what number? 2,000
7. 2 is what percent of 800? 0.25%

★ indicates increased difficulty

Practice and Applications

HOMEWORK HELP

For Exercises	See Examples
8–9, 16–17, 24–25	1
10–11, 14–15, 22–23	2
12–13, 18–21	3
26–29	4

Extra Practice See pages 628, 652.

Solve each problem using the percent equation. 20. $333\frac{1}{3}$ 22. $22\frac{2}{9}\%$

8. Find 60% of 30. 18
9. What is 40% of 90? 36
10. What percent of 90 is 36? 40%
11. 45 is what percent of 150? 30%
12. 75 is 50% of what number? 150
13. 15% of what number is 30? 200
14. 6 is what percent of 3,000? 0.2%
15. What percent of 5,000 is 6? 0.12%
16. What number is 130% of 52? 67.6
17. Find 240% of 84. 201.6
18. 3% of what number is 9? 300
19. 50 is 10% of what number? 500
★20. 8 is 2.4% of what number?
★21. 1.8% of what number is 40? $2,222\frac{2}{9}$
★22. What percent of 675 is 150?
★23. 360 is what percent of 270? $133\frac{1}{3}\%$
★24. Find 6.25% of 150. 9.375
★25. What is 12.5% of 92? 11.5

26. **REAL ESTATE** A *commission* is a fee paid to a salesperson based on a percent of sales. Suppose a real estate agent earns a 3% commission. How much commission would be earned for the sale of a $150,000 house? $4,500

27. **BASKETBALL** In a recent National Basketball Association season, Shaquille O'Neal made about 57.74% of his field-goal attempts. If he made 653 field goals, how many attempts did he take? 1,131 attempts

Data Update What percent of the field-goal attempts did your favorite player make last season? Visit msmath3.net/data_update to learn more.

28. **MULTI STEP** A sweater costs $45. If a 6.5% sales tax is added, what is the total cost of the sweater? $47.93

29. **ARCHITECTURE** Both the Guggenheim Museum in New York and the Guggenheim Museum in Bilbao, Spain, are known for their interesting architecture. Which museum uses the greater percent of space for exhibits? **New York**

Guggenheim Museum in New York	Guggenheim Museum in Bilbao
Total area: 79,600 square feet	Total area: 257,000 square feet
Exhibition space: 49,600 square feet	Exhibition space: 110,000 square feet

30. **CRITICAL THINKING** Determine whether $a\%$ of b is *sometimes*, *always*, or *never* equal to $b\%$ of a. Explain. **Always; $a\%$ of b is $\frac{a}{100} \cdot b$ or $\frac{ab}{100}$ and $b\%$ of a is $\frac{b}{100} \cdot a$ or $\frac{ab}{100}$.**

Spiral Review with Standardized Test Practice

31. **MULTIPLE CHOICE** Fifteen out of the 60 eighth-graders at Seabring Junior High are on the track team. What percent of the eighth-graders are on the track team? **B**

(A) 15% (B) 25% (C) 45% (D) 60%

32. **MULTIPLE CHOICE** The graph at the right shows the results of a recent survey asking Americans why we should explore Mars. About how many people were surveyed if 81 of them want to search Mars for a future home for the human race? **G**

(F) 100 (G) 125

(H) 150 (I) 175

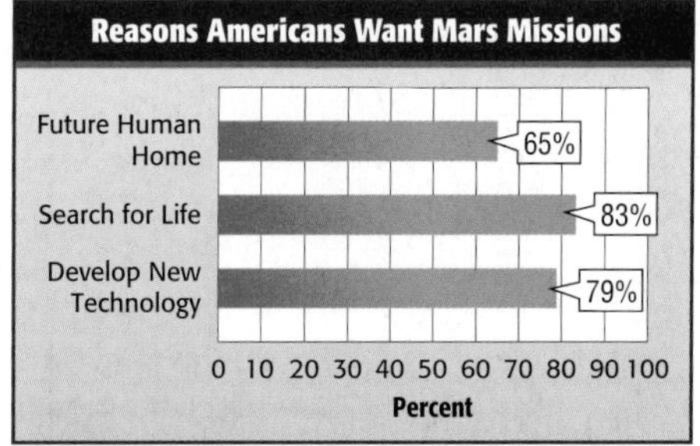

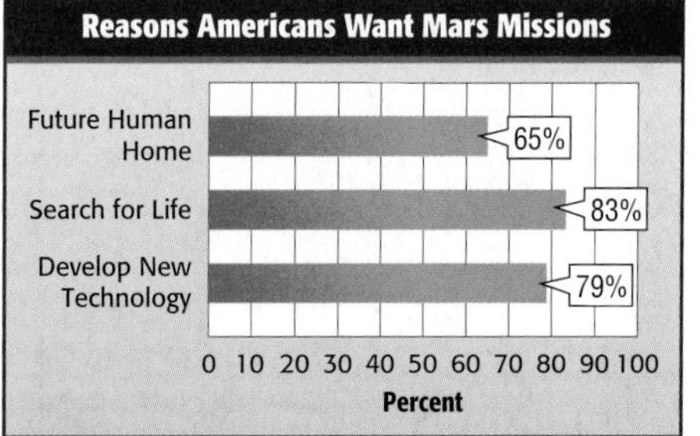

Source: SPACE.com/Harris Interactive

33. **FOOTBALL** A quarterback completed 19 out of 30 attempts to pass the football. Estimate his percent of completion. (Lesson 5-5) **Sample answer: $\frac{19}{30} \approx \frac{20}{30}$ or $66\frac{2}{3}\%$**

Compute mentally. (Lesson 5-4)

34. 15% of \$200 **\$30** 35. 62.5% of 96 **60** 36. 75% of 84 **63** 37. 60% of 150 **90**

GETTING READY FOR THE NEXT LESSON

PREREQUISITE SKILL Evaluate each expression. (Lesson 1-3)

38. $|17 - 24|$ **7** 39. $|340 - 253|$ **87** 40. $|531 - 487|$ **44** 41. $|352 - 581|$ **229**

Math Online msmath3.net/self_check_quiz

4 Assess

Higher-Level Thinking

Write the sentence "$a\%$ of b is c" as an equation. Then solve the equation for each variable. **$\frac{a}{100} \cdot b = c$; $a = \frac{100c}{b}$; $b = \frac{100c}{a}$; $c = \frac{ab}{100}$**

Study Guide and Intervention, p. 270

NAME ______ DATE ______ PERIOD ______

5-6 Study Guide and Intervention

The Percent Equation

The **percent equation** is an equivalent form of the percent proportion in which the percent is written as a decimal.

Part = Percent · Base.

EXAMPLE 1 **Find 22% of 245.**

The percent is 22%, and the base is 245. Let n represent the part.

$n = 0.22(245)$ Write 22% as the decimal 0.22.
$n = 53.9$ Simplify.

So, 22% of 245 is 53.9.

EXAMPLE 2 **600 is what percent of 750?**

The part is 600, and the base is 750. Let n represent the percent.

$600 = n(750)$ Write the equation.
$\frac{600}{750} = \frac{750n}{750}$ Divide each side by 750.
$0.8 = n$ Simplify.

Since 0.8 = 80%, 600 is 80% of 750.

EXAMPLE 3 **45 is 90% of what number?**

The part is 45, and the percent is 90%. Let n represent the base.

$45 = 0.90 \cdot n$ Write 90% as the decimal 0.90.
$\frac{45}{0.90} = \frac{0.90n}{0.90}$ Divide each side by 0.90.
$50 = n$ Simplify.

So, 45 is 90% of 50.

EXERCISES

Solve each problem using the percent equation.

1. Find 30% of 70. **21** 2. What is 80% of 65? **52**
3. What percent of 56 is 14? **25%** 4. 36 is what percent of 40? **90%**
5. 80 is 40% of what number? **200** 6. 65% of what number is 78? **120**
7. What percent of 2,000 is 8? **0.4%** 8. 12 is what percent of 4,000? **0.3%**
9. What percent of 3,000 is 18? **0.6%** 10. What is 110% of 80? **88**
11. Find 180% of 160. **288** 12. 4% of what number is 11? **275**

Practice: Skills, p. 271

NAME ______ DATE ______ PERIOD ______

5-6 Practice: Skills

The Percent Equation

Solve each problem using the percent equation.

1. Find 50% of 40. **20** 2. What is 90% of 20? **18**
3. What percent of 64 is 16? **25%** 4. 24 is what percent of 30? **80%**
5. Find 20% of 55. **11** 6. What is 60% of 45? **27**
7. 16 is 40% of what number? **40** 8. 70% of what number is 63? **90**
9. What percent of 84 is 63? **75%** 10. 9 is what percent of 30? **30%**
11. 35 is 10% of what number? **350** 12. 15% of what number is 24? **160**
13. What percent of 2,000 is 4? **0.2%** 14. 5 is what percent of 1,000? **0.5%**
15. What percent of 3,000 is 9? **0.3%** 16. 16 is what percent of 4,000? **0.4%**
17. What percent of 2,000 is 14? **0.7%** 18. What is 120% of 20? **24**
19. What percent of 5,000 is 20? **0.4%** 20. What is 140% of 60? **84**
21. Find 250% of 40. **100** 22. 2% of what number is 5? **250**
23. Find 175% of 28. **49** 24. 6% of what number is 21? **350**
25. 12 is 10% of what number? **120** 26. 5% of what number is 20? **400**
27. 75 is 20% of what number? **375** 28. 15% of what number is 42? **280**

Practice: Word Problems, p. 272

NAME ______ DATE ______ PERIOD ______

5-6 Practice: Word Problems

The Percent Equation

1. **DINING OUT** Trevor and Michelle's restaurant bill comes to \$35.50. They are planning to tip the waiter 20%. How much money should they leave for a tip? **\$7.10**

2. **CHESS** The local chess club has 60 members. Twenty-four of the members are younger than twenty. What percent of the members of the chess club are younger than twenty? **40%**

3. **TENNIS** In the city of Bridgeport, 75% of the parks have tennis courts. If 18 parks have tennis courts, how many parks does Bridgeport have altogether? **24 parks**

4. **COLLEGE** There are 175 students in twelveth grade at Silverado High School. A survey shows that 64% of them are planning to attend college. How many Silverado twelveth grade students are planning to attend college? **112 students**

5. **BASEBALL** In the 2001 season, the Chicago Cubs won 88 out of 162 games. What percent of games did the Cubs win? Round to the nearest tenth if necessary. **54.3%**

6. **HOUSING** In the Lakeview apartment complex, 35% of the apartments have one bedroom. If there are 63 one bedroom apartments, what is the total number of apartments at Lakeview? **180 apartments**

7. **FOOTBALL** In the 2000 season, quarterback Jeff Blake of the New Orleans Saints had 9 passes intercepted out of 302 attempts. What percent of Jeff Blake's passes were intercepted? Round to the nearest tenth if necessary. **3.0%**

8. **SPACE** On Mars, an object weighs 38% as much as on Earth. How much would a person who weighs 150 pounds on Earth weigh on Mars? **57 lb**

5-7 Lesson Notes

Lesson Resources

Chapter 5 Resource Masters
- Study Guide and Intervention, p. 275
- Practice: Skills, p. 276
- Practice: Word Problems, p. 277
- Reading to Learn Mathematics, p. 278
- Enrichment, p. 279

Calculator and Spreadsheet Masters, p. 27
Key Teaching Transparencies, 20
Parent and Student Study Guide Online Worksheets, 5-7
Teaching Mathematics with Manipulatives, p. 59
Noteables™: Interactive Study Notebook with Foldables™, 5-7

FAST FILE

Focus

5-Minute Check 5-7

Use as a quiz or review of Lesson 5-6. (Also available as a transparency)

Bellringer

Reading Mathematics Have students read retail store flyers. Have them find examples of cases where the sale price needs to be determined and where the sale price is given. Ask students why they think stores use both methods in their advertising.

Reading to Learn Mathematics, p. 278 **ELL**

NAME ______ DATE ______ PERIOD ____

5-7 Reading to Learn Mathematics
Percent of Change

Pre-Activity ***Read the introduction at the top of page 236 in your textbook. Write your answers below.***

1. How much did the price increase from 1930 to 1940? 5¢
2. Write the ratio $\frac{\text{amount of increase}}{\text{price in 1930}}$. Then write the ratio as a percent. $\frac{5}{10}$ or $\frac{1}{2}$; 50%
3. How much did the price increase from 1940 to 1950? Write the ratio $\frac{\text{amount of increase}}{\text{price in 1940}}$. Then write the ratio as a percent. 5¢; $\frac{5}{15}$ or $\frac{1}{3}$; $33\frac{1}{3}$%
4. How much did the price increase from 1950 to 1960? Write the ratio $\frac{\text{amount of increase}}{\text{price in 1950}}$. Then write the ratio as a percent. 5¢; $\frac{5}{20}$ or $\frac{1}{4}$; 25%
5. Compare the amount of increase for each ten-year period. The amount of increase for each ten-year period is the same.
6. Compare the percents in Exercises 2–4. The percents decrease.

5-7 Percent of Change

What You'll LEARN

Find and use the percent of increase or decrease.

NEW Vocabulary

percent of change
percent of increase
percent of decrease
markup
selling price
discount

WHEN am I ever going to use this?

MONEY MATTERS Over the years, some prices increase. Study the change in gasoline prices from 1930 to 1960.

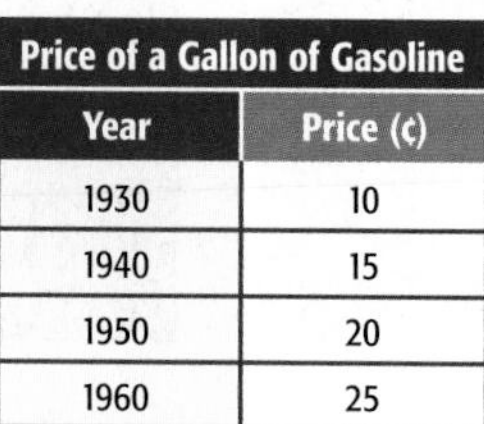

Price of a Gallon of Gasoline	
Year	Price (¢)
1930	10
1940	15
1950	20
1960	25

Source: Senior Living

1. How much did the price increase from 1930 to 1940? **5¢**
2. Write the ratio $\frac{\text{amount of increase}}{\text{price in 1930}}$. Then write the ratio as a percent. **$\frac{5}{10}$ or $\frac{1}{2}$; 50%**
3. How much did the price increase from 1940 to 1950? Write the ratio $\frac{\text{amount of increase}}{\text{price in 1940}}$. Then write the ratio as a percent.
4. How much did the price increase from 1950 to 1960? Write the ratio $\frac{\text{amount of increase}}{\text{price in 1950}}$. The write the ratio as a percent.
5. Compare the amount of increase for each ten-year period.
6. Compare the percents in Exercises 2–4. **The percents decrease.**
7. **Make a conjecture** about why the amounts of increase are the same but the percents are different.

3. 5¢; $\frac{5}{15}$ or $\frac{1}{3}$; $33\frac{1}{3}$%

4. 5¢; $\frac{5}{20}$ or $\frac{1}{4}$; 25%

5. The amount of increase for each ten-year period is the same.
7. The amounts are compared to different numbers.

TEACHING TIP

Ask students why the percents in this application decreased even though the amount of increase was the same.

In the above application, you expressed the amount of change as a percent of the original. This percent is called the **percent of change**.

Noteables™ **Key Concept: Percent of Change**

Words A percent of change is a ratio that compares the change in quantity to the original amount.

Symbols percent of change = $\frac{\text{amount of change}}{\text{original amount}}$

Example original: 12, new: 9

$\frac{12-9}{12} = \frac{3}{12} = \frac{1}{4}$ or 25%

When the new amount is greater than the original, the percent of change is a **percent of increase**.

STUDY TIP

Percent of Change When finding percent of change, always use the original amount as the base.

EXAMPLE Find the Percent of Increase

1 CLUBS The Science Club had 25 members. Now it has 30 members. Find the percent of increase.

Step 1 Subtract to find the amount of change. $30 - 25 = 5$

Step 2 Write a ratio that compares the amount of change to the original number of members. Express the ratio as a percent.

$\text{percent of change} = \frac{\text{amount of change}}{\text{original amount}}$	Definition of percent of change
$= \frac{5}{25}$	The amount of change is 5. The original amount is 25.
$= 0.2$ or 20%	Divide. Write as a percent.

The percent of increase is 20%.

Your Turn **Find each percent of increase. Round to the nearest tenth if necessary.**

a. original: 20
new: 23 **15%**

b. original: 50
new: 67 **34%**

c. original: 12
new: 20 **66.7%**

When the new amount is less than the original, the percent of change is called a **percent of decrease**.

EXAMPLE Find the Percent of Change

2 COMIC BOOKS Consuela had 20 comic books. She gave some to her friend. Now she has 13 comic books. Find the percent of change. State whether the percent of change is an *increase* or a *decrease*.

Step 1 Subtract to find the amount of change. $20 - 13 = 7$

Step 2 Write a ratio that compares the amount of change to the original number of comic books. Express the ratio as a percent.

$\text{percent of change} = \frac{\text{amount of change}}{\text{original amount}}$	Definition of percent of change
$= \frac{7}{20}$	The amount of change is 7. The original amount is 20.
$= 0.35$ or 35%	Divide. Write as a percent.

The percent of change is 35%. Since the new amount is less than the original, it is a percent of decrease.

Your Turn **Find each percent of change. Round to the nearest tenth if necessary. State whether the percent of change is an *increase* or a *decrease*.**

d. original: 10
new: 6 **40%; dec.**

e. original: 5
new: 6 **20%; inc.**

f. original: 80
new: 55 **31.3%; dec.**

Math Online msmath3.net/extra_examples

2 Teach

In-Class Examples

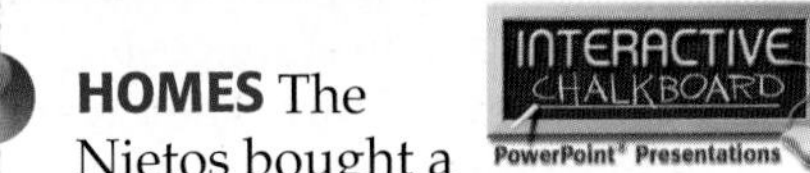

1 HOMES The Nietos bought a house several years ago for \$120,000. This year, they sold it for \$150,000. Find the percent of increase. **25%**

2 SCHOOLS Johnson Middle School had 240 students last year. This year, there are 192 students. Find the percent of change. State whether this percent of change is an *increase* or a *decrease*. **20%; decrease**

DAILY INTERVENTION

Differentiated Instruction

Visual/Spatial Using a national weather map, have students pick a city and note the high and low temperature for that day. Have students compute the percent of change. Post a map on a bulletin board and have students write in their answers. What cities had the greatest percent of change in temperature for the day?

In-Class Examples

INTERACTIVE CHALKBOARD PowerPoint® Presentations

3 **MARKUP** Shirts bought by a sporting goods store cost them $20 per shirt. They want to mark them up 40 percent. What will be the selling price? **$28**

4 **SHOPPING** A computer usually sells for $1,200. This week it is on sale for 30% off. What is the sale price? **$840**

A store sells an item for more than it paid for that item. The extra money is used to cover the expenses and to make a profit. The increase in the price is called the **markup**. The percent of markup is a percent of increase. The amount the customer pays is called the **selling price**.

STUDY TIP

Mental Math
To estimate the selling price, think $\frac{1}{4}$ of 36 is 9. The selling price should be about $35 + $9, or $44.

EXAMPLE Find the Selling Price

3 **MARKETING Shonny is selling some embroidered jackets on a Web site as shown in the photo. She wants to price the jackets 25% over her cost, which is $35. Find the selling price for a jacket.**

Method 1 Find the amount of the markup.

Find 25% of $35. Let m represent the markup.

$m = 0.25(35)$ Write 25% as a decimal. Multiply.

$m = 8.75$

Add the markup to the price Shonny paid for the jacket.

$35 + $8.75 = $43.75

Method 2 Find the total percent.

The customer will pay 100% of the price Shonny paid plus an extra 25% of the price. Find 100% + 25% or 125% of the price Shonny paid for the jacket. Let p represent the price.

$p = 1.25(35)$ Write 125% as a decimal. Multiply.

$p = 43.75$

The selling price of the jacket for the customer is $43.75.

TEACHING TIP

Remind students that they can use either the percent proportion or the percent equation to solve problems similar to Examples 3 and 4.

The amount by which a regular price is reduced is called the **discount**. The percent of discount is a percent of decrease.

STUDY TIP

Mental Math
To estimate the sale price of the snowskate, think 65% of 100 is 65. The sale price should be about $65.

EXAMPLE Find the Sale Price

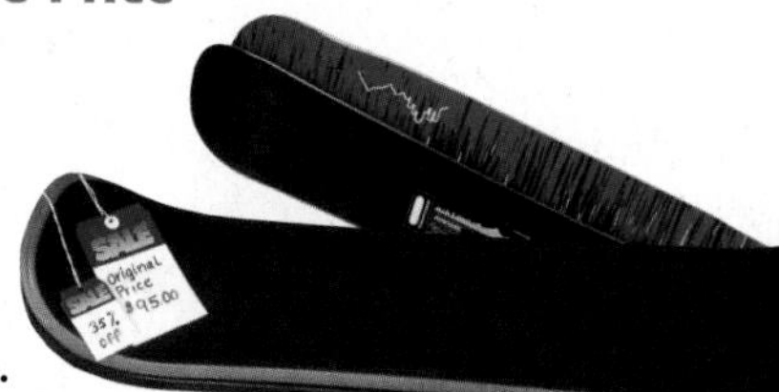

4 **SHOPPING The Sport Chalet is having a sale. The snowskate shown has an original price of $95. It is on sale for 35% off the original price. Find the sale price of the snowskate.**

Method 1 Find the amount of the discount.

Find 35% of $95. Let d represent the amount of the discount.

$d = 0.35(95)$

$d = 33.25$

Subtract the amount of the discount from the original price.

$95 − $33.25 = $61.75

Method 2 Find the percent paid.

If the amount of the discount is 35%, the percent paid is 100% − 35% or 65%. Find 65% of $95. Let s represent the sale price.

$s = 0.65(95)$

$s = 61.75$

The sale price of the snowskate is $61.75.

Students practice the same concepts in Exercises 12–29 if they are assigned odd or even problems.

Skill and Concept Check

1. **State** the first step in finding the percent of change. **Find the amount of change.**
2. *Writing Math* Explain how you know whether a percent of change is a percent of increase or a percent of decrease. **See margin.**
3. **OPEN ENDED** Write a percent of increase problem where the percent of increase is greater than 100%. **Sample answer: original: 10, new: 30; The percent of change is 200%.**
4. **FIND THE ERROR** Jared and Sydney are solving the following problem. *The price of a movie ticket rose from $5.75 to $6.25. What is the percent of increase for the price of a ticket?* Who is correct? Explain.

Jared

percent of change = $\frac{0.50}{5.75}$

≈ 0.087 or 8.7%

Sydney

percent of change = $\frac{0.50}{6.25}$

$= 0.08$ or 8%

Jared; the change must be compared to the original price $5.75, not the new price $6.25.

GUIDED PRACTICE

Find each percent of change. Round to the nearest tenth if necessary. State whether the percent of change is an *increase* or a *decrease*.

5. original: 40 new: 32 **20%; decrease**
6. original: 25 new: 32 **28%; increase**
7. original: 325 new: 400 **23.1%; increase**

Find the selling price for each item given the cost to the store and the markup.

8. roller blades: $60, 35% markup **$81.00**
9. coat: $87, $33\frac{1}{3}$% markup **$116.00**

Find the sale price of each item to the nearest cent.

10. CD: $14.50, 10% off **$13.05**
11. sweater: $39.95, 25% off **$29.96**

★ indicates increased difficulty

Practice and Applications

HOMEWORK HELP	
For Exercises	See Examples
12–17, 30, 32	1, 2
18–23	3
24–29	4

Extra Practice See pages 628, 652.

Find each percent of change. Round to the nearest tenth if necessary. State whether the percent of change is an *increase* or a *decrease*.

12. original: 6 new: 9 **50%; increase**
13. original: 80 new: 64 **20%; decrease**
14. original: 560 new: 420 **25%; decrease**
15. original: 68 new: 51 **25%; decrease**
16. original: 27 new: 39 **44.4%; increase**
17. original: 98 new: 150 **53.1%; increase**

Find the selling price for each item given the cost to the store and the markup.

18. computer: $700, 30% markup **$910.00**
19. CD player: $120, 20% markup **$144.00**
20. jeans: $25, 45% markup **$36.25**
21. video: $12, 48% markup **$17.76**
22. Find the markup rate on a $60 jacket that sells for $75. **25%**
23. What is the markup rate on a $230 game system that sells for $345? **50%**

msmath3.net/self_check_quiz

Answer

35. Sample answer:

$27.9 - 22.4 = 5.5$	Find the difference.
$\frac{a}{b} = \frac{p}{100} \rightarrow \frac{5.5}{22.4} = \frac{p}{100}$	Replace a with 5.5 and b with 22.4.
$5.5 \cdot 100 = 22.4 \cdot p$	Find the cross products.
$550 = 22.4p$	Multiply.
$\frac{550}{22.4} = \frac{22.4p}{22.4}$	Divide each side by 22.4.
$24.6 \approx p$	Simplify.

3 Practice/Apply

FOLDABLES™ Follow-Up Remind students to use their Foldables to record what they learn about expressing an increase or a decrease as a percent. Students might give examples of what they have learned, or they could record new terms that they need to learn. Encourage students to include at least one example of how they might use percent of change in their daily lives.

DAILY INTERVENTION **FIND THE ERROR** In Exercise 4, emphasize that the denominator is always the original amount when computing percent of change.

About the Exercises...

Guided Practice Key

Exercises	Examples
5–7	1, 2
8–9	3
10–11	4

Assignment Guide

Basic: 13–33 odd, 34–45

Average: 13–29 odd, 30, 31, 33–45

Enriched: 12–32 even, 34–41 (Optional: 42–45)

Answers (pp. 239–240)

2. If the new number is greater than the original number, it is a percent of increase. If the new number is less than the original number, it is a percent of decrease.
33. Sample answer: There were 25 students in the math class. Two more students enrolled in the class. What is the percent of change? Answer: 8%

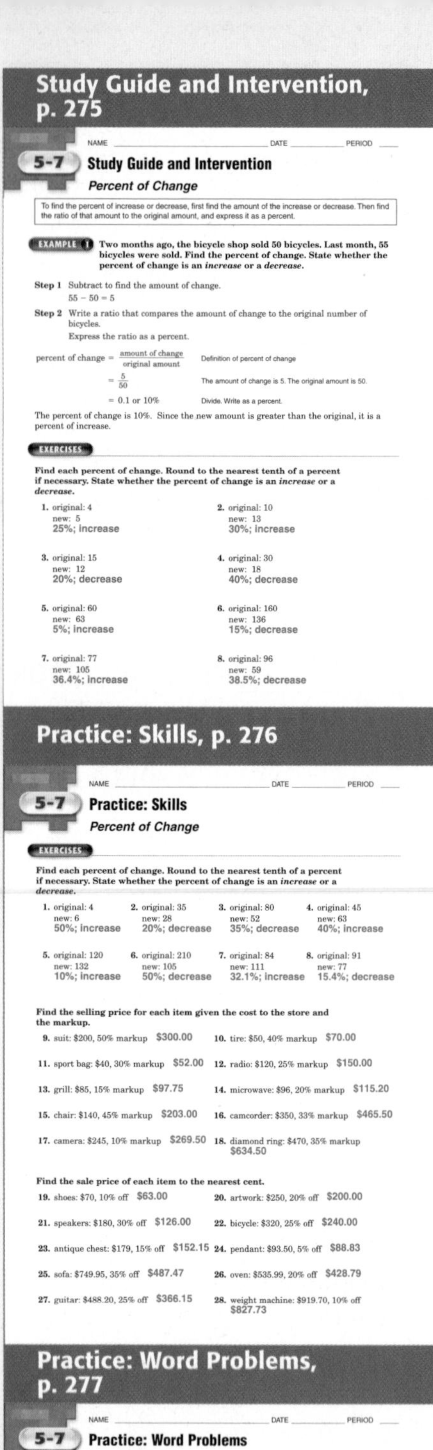
Study Guide and Intervention, p. 275

NAME ______ DATE ______ PERIOD ______

5-7 Study Guide and Intervention

Percent of Change

To find the percent of increase or decrease, first find the amount of the increase or decrease. Then find the ratio of that amount to the original amount, and express it as a percent.

EXAMPLE 1 **Two months ago, the bicycle shop sold 50 bicycles. Last month, 55 bicycles were sold. Find the percent of change. State whether the percent of change is an *increase* or a *decrease*.**

Step 1 Subtract to find the amount of change.
$55 - 50 = 5$

Step 2 Write a ratio that compares the amount of change to the original number of bicycles.
Express the ratio as a percent.

$\text{percent of change} = \frac{\text{amount of change}}{\text{original amount}}$ Definition of percent of change

$= \frac{5}{50}$ The amount of change is 5. The original amount is 50.

$= 0.1$ or 10% Divide. Write as a percent.

The percent of change is 10%. Since the new amount is greater than the original, it is a percent of increase.

EXERCISES

Find each percent of change. Round to the nearest tenth of a percent if necessary. State whether the percent of change is an *increase* or a *decrease*.

1. original: 4 new: 5 **25%; increase**
2. original: 10 new: 13 **30%; increase**
3. original: 15 new: 12 **20%; decrease**
4. original: 30 new: 18 **40%; decrease**
5. original: 60 new: 63 **5%; increase**
6. original: 160 new: 136 **15%; decrease**
7. original: 77 new: 105 **36.4%; increase**
8. original: 96 new: 59 **38.5%; decrease**

Practice: Skills, p. 276

NAME ______ DATE ______ PERIOD ______

5-7 Practice: Skills

Percent of Change

EXERCISES

Find each percent of change. Round to the nearest tenth of a percent if necessary. State whether the percent of change is an *increase* or a *decrease*.

1. original: 4 new: 6 **50%; increase**
2. original: 35 new: 28 **20%; decrease**
3. original: 80 new: 52 **35%; decrease**
4. original: 45 new: 63 **40%; increase**
5. original: 120 new: 132 **10%; increase**
6. original: 210 new: 105 **50%; decrease**
7. original: 84 new: 111 **32.1%; increase**
8. original: 91 new: 77 **15.4%; decrease**

Find the selling price for each item given the cost to the store and the markup.

9. suit: $200, 50% markup **$300.00**
10. tire: $50, 40% markup **$70.00**
11. sport bag: $40, 30% markup **$52.00**
12. radio: $120, 25% markup **$150.00**
13. grill: $85, 15% markup **$97.75**
14. microwave: $96, 20% markup **$115.20**
15. chair: $140, 45% markup **$203.00**
16. camcorder: $350, 33% markup **$465.50**
17. camera: $245, 10% markup **$269.50**
18. diamond ring: $470, 35% markup **$634.50**

Find the sale price of each item to the nearest cent.

19. shoes: $70, 10% off **$63.00**
20. artwork: $250, 20% off **$200.00**
21. speakers: $180, 30% off **$126.00**
22. bicycle: $320, 25% off **$240.00**
23. antique chest: $179, 15% off **$152.15**
24. pendant: $93.50, 5% off **$88.83**
25. sofa: $749.95, 35% off **$487.47**
26. oven: $535.99, 20% off **$428.79**
27. guitar: $488.20, 25% off **$366.15**
28. weight machine: $919.70, 10% off **$827.73**

Practice: Word Problems, p. 277

NAME ______ DATE ______ PERIOD ______

5-7 Practice: Word Problems

Percent of Change

1. CLUBS Last year the chess club had 20 members. This year the club has 15 members. Find the percent of change, and state whether the percent of change is an *increase* or a *decrease*. **25%; decrease**
2. READING During Todd's junior year in high school, he read 15 books. In his senior year, he read 18 books. Find the percent of change, and state whether the percent of change is an *increase* or a *decrease*. **20%; increase**
3. COMPUTERS The computer store pays $250 each for flat screen monitor. The store uses a 30% markup. Find the selling price for each flat screen monitor. **$325.00**
4. SHOES A popular brand of running shoes costs a local store $68 for each pair. Find the selling price for a pair of running shoes if the store has a markup of 75%. **$119.00**
5. CLOTHING Sandy's Clothing Shop has a markup of 45% on dresses. How much will Sandy's charge for a dress that costs the shop $48? **$69.60**
6. AUDIO The audio store is having a 20% off sale. What will be the sale price on a pair of speakers that normally sell for $280.00? **$224.00**
7. FURNITURE Leta is planning to buy a new sofa as soon as it goes on sale. The regular price for the sofa is $899.95. How much will the sofa cost if it goes on sale for 40% off? Round to the nearest cent. **$539.97**
8. AUTO REPAIR Don is getting a new set of tires for his car. The tires normally sell for $319.96, but they are on sale for 10% off. How much will Don pay for the new tires? Round to the nearest cent. **$287.96**

Find the sale price of each item to the nearest cent.

24. video game: $75, 25% off **$56.25**
25. trampoline: $399, 15% off **$339.15**
26. skateboard: $119.95, 30% off **$83.97**
27. television: $675.50, 35% off **$439.08**

28. Find the discount rate on a $24 watch that regularly sells for $32. **25%**
29. What is the discount rate on $294 skis that regularly sell for $420? **30%**

ANIMALS For Exercises 30 and 31, use the following information.
In 1937, a baby giraffe was born. It was 62 inches tall at birth and grew at the highly unusual rate of 0.5 inch per hour for x hours.

30. By what percent did the height of the giraffe increase in the first day? **about 19.4%**
31. **MULTI STEP** If the baby giraffe continued to grow at this amazing rate, how long would it take it to reach a height of 18 feet? **308 hours or 12 days and 20 hours**

★ 32. **MONEY MATTERS** The table gives the price of milk for various years. During which ten-year period did milk have the greatest percent of increase? **1980 to 1990**

Price of a Gallon of Milk

Year	Price ($)
1970	1.23
1980	1.60
1990	2.15
2000	2.78

Source: Senior Living

33. **WRITE A PROBLEM** Write and solve a real-life problem involving percent of change. **See margin.**
34. **CRITICAL THINKING** Blake bought a computer listed for $$x$ at a 15% discount. He also paid a 5% sales tax. After 6 months, he decided to sell the computer for $$y$, which was 55% of what he paid originally. Express y as a function of x. $y = 0.55[1.05(0.85x)] = 0.490875x$

35. **SHORT RESPONSE** Use the graph at the right to determine the percent of change in the average age of the U.S. Men's Olympic Track and Field Team from 1984 to 2000. Show your work. **About 24.6% increase; see p. 239 margin for work.**

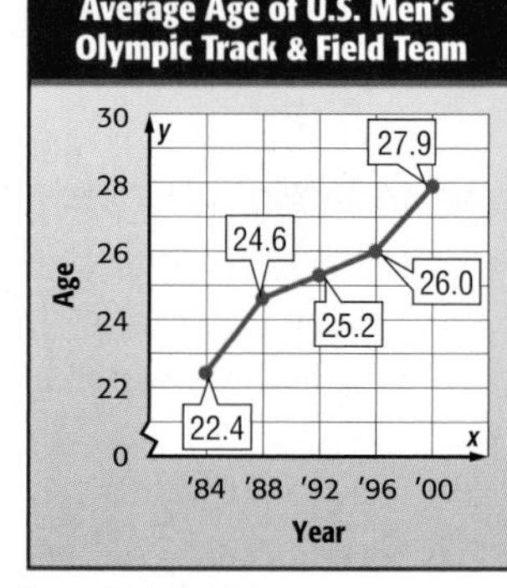

Source: *Sports Illustrated*

36. **MULTIPLE CHOICE** Find the amount of discount for a pair of $89 shoes that are on sale at a discount of 30%. **B**
    - Ⓐ $17.80
    - Ⓑ $26.70
    - Ⓒ $35.60
    - Ⓓ none of the above
37. **TAXES** An average of 40% of the cost of gasoline goes to state and federal taxes. If gasoline sells for $1.35 per gallon, how much goes to taxes? (Lesson 5-6) **about $0.54**

Estimate. (Lesson 5-5) **38–41. Sample answers given.**

38. 21% of 60 $\frac{1}{5}$ **of 60 or 12**
39. 25% of 83 $\frac{1}{4}$ **of 84 or 21**
40. 12% of 31 $\frac{1}{8}$ **of 32 or 4**
41. 34% of 95 $\frac{1}{3}$ **of 96 or 32**

GETTING READY FOR THE NEXT LESSON

PREREQUISITE SKILL Solve each equation. (Lesson 2-7)

42. $45 = 300 \cdot a \cdot 3$ **0.05**
43. $24 = 200 \cdot 0.04 \cdot y$ **3**
44. $21 = 60 \cdot m \cdot 5$ **0.07**
45. $18 = 90 \cdot b \cdot 5$ **0.04**

4 Assess

Higher-Level Thinking

If 100 is increased by 10% and then increased by 10% again, is the answer 120? Explain. **No; 10% of 100 is 10, so 10 is added to 100 the first time to reach 110. The second time, 10% of the new number, 110, is taken. 10% of 110 is 11, not 10, so the result is 110 + 11 or 121.**

Simple Interest

WHEN am I ever going to use this?

What You'll LEARN

Solve problems involving simple interest.

NEW Vocabulary

interest
principal

COLLEGE SAVINGS Hector received $1,000 from his grandparents. He plans to save it for college expenses. The graph shows rates for various investments for one year.

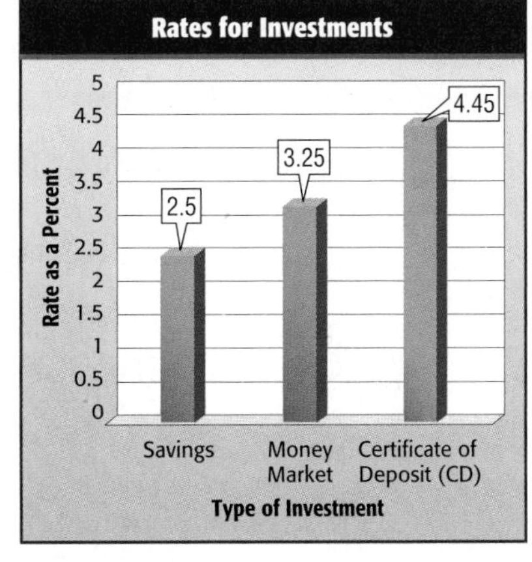

1. If Hector puts his money in a savings account, he will receive 2.5% of $1,000 in interest for one year. Find the interest Hector will receive. **$25**
2. Find the interest Hector will receive if he puts his money in a money market for one year. **$32.50**
3. Find the interest Hector will receive if he puts his money in a certificate of deposit for one year. **$44.50**

Interest is the amount of money paid or earned for the use of money. For a savings account, you earn interest from the bank. For a credit card, you pay interest to the bank. To solve problems involving simple interest, use the following formula.

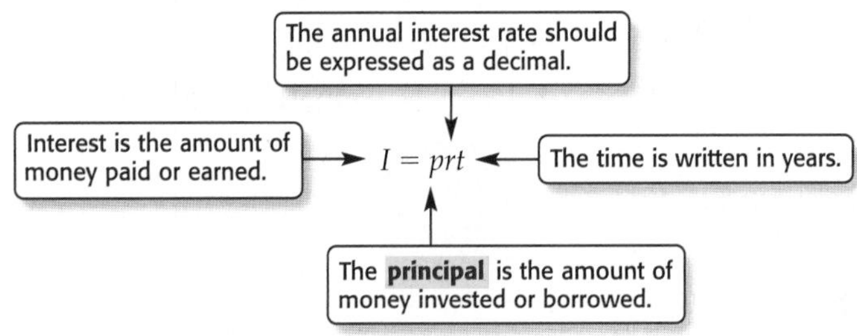

STUDY TIP

Reading Math
I = prt is read interest equals principal times rate times time.

EXAMPLE Find Simple Interest

1 Find the simple interest for $500 invested at 6.25% for 3 years.

$I = prt$	Write the simple interest formula.
$I = 500 \cdot 0.0625 \cdot 3$	Replace p with 500, r with 0.0625, and t with 3.
$I = 93.75$	The simple interest is $93.75.

5-8 Lesson Notes

Lesson Resources

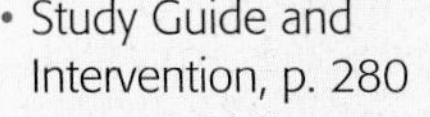

Chapter 5 Resource Masters
- Study Guide and Intervention, p. 280
- Practice: Skills, p. 281
- Practice: Word Problems, p. 282
- Reading to Learn Mathematics, p. 283
- Enrichment, p. 284

Calculator and Spreadsheet Masters, p. 28
MathPASS Tutorial CD-ROM, 35
Parent and Student Study Guide Online Worksheets, 5-8
Noteables™: Interactive Study Notebook with Foldables™, 5-8

1 Focus

5-Minute Check 5-8
Use as a quiz or review of Lesson 5-7. (Also available as a transparency)

Bellringer
Hands-On Activity Have students collect ads that involve interest. For example, car ads usually mention interest. Discuss when interest is charged or earned. **You are charged interest when you borrow money. You earn interest when you save money at an institution because they are borrowing money from you.**

Reading to Learn Mathematics, p. 283 **ELL**

NAME ______ DATE ______ PERIOD ______

5-8 Reading to Learn Mathematics
Simple Interest

Pre-Activity *Read the introduction at the top of page 241 in your textbook. Write your answers below.*

1. If Hector puts his money in a savings account, he will receive 2.5% of $1,000 in interest for one year. Find the interest Hector will receive. **$25**
2. Find the interest Hector will receive if he puts his money in a money market for one year. **$32.50**
3. Find the interest Hector will receive if he puts his money in a certificate of deposit for one year. **$44.50**

Reading the Lesson

4. Look up the word *interest* in a dictionary. Read some of the different definitions. Find and write a definition that seems to match the topic in ...

2 Teach

In-Class Examples

1 Find the simple interest for $2,000 invested at 5.5% for 4 years. **$440**

2 **GRID-IN TEST ITEM** Find the total dollar amount in an account where $80 is invested at 6% for 6 months. **82.40**

3 **LOANS** Gerardo borrowed $4,500 from his bank for home improvements. He will repay the loan by paying $120 a month for the next four years. Find the simple interest rate of the loan. **7%**

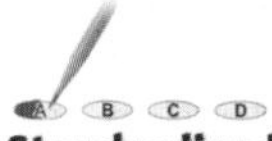

Standardized Test Practice

Test-Taking Tip

When answering grid-in questions, first fill in the answer on the top row. Then pencil in exactly one bubble under each number or symbol.

TEACHING TIP

Remind students that the *t* in the simple interest formula represents time in years. If months are given, they must change the time in months to time in years.

EXAMPLE Find the Total Amount

2 **GRID-IN TEST ITEM** Find the total amount of money in an account where $95 is invested at 7.5% for 8 months.

Read the Test Item

You need to find the total amount in an account. Notice that the time is given in months. Eight months is $\frac{8}{12}$ or $\frac{2}{3}$ year.

Solve the Test Item

$I = prt$

$I = 95 \cdot 0.075 \cdot \frac{2}{3}$

$I = 4.75$

The amount in the account is $95 + $4.75 or $99.75.

Fill in the Grid

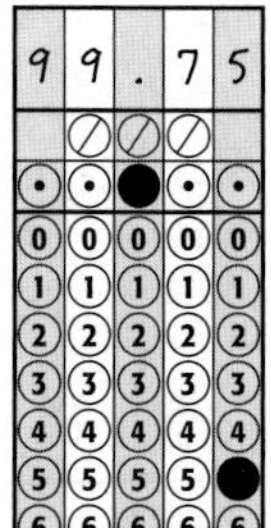

You can use the simple interest formula and what you know about solving equations to find the principal, the interest rate, or the amount of time.

EXAMPLE Find the Interest Rate

3 **CAR SALES Tonya borrowed $3,600 to buy a used car. She will be paying $131.50 each month for the next 36 months. Find the simple interest rate for her loan.**

First find the total amount of money Tonya will pay.

$131.50 · 36 = $4,734

Tonya will pay a total of $4,734.

She will pay $4,734 – $3,600 or $1,134 in interest.

The loan will be for 36 months or 3 years.

Use the simple interest formula to find the interest rate.

Words	Interest equals principal times rate times time.
Variables	$I = p \cdot r \cdot t$
Equation	$1{,}134 = 3{,}600 \cdot r \cdot 3$

$1{,}134 = 3{,}600 \cdot r \cdot 3$ Write the equation.

$1{,}134 = 10{,}800r$ Simplify.

$\frac{1{,}134}{10{,}800} = \frac{10{,}800r}{10{,}800}$ Divide each side by 10,800.

$0.105 = r$ Simplify.

The simple interest rate is 10.5%.

REAL-LIFE CAREERS

How Does a Car Salesperson Use Math?

A car salesperson must calculate the price of a car including any discounts, dealer preparation costs, and state taxes. They may also help customers by determining the amount of their car payments.

Math Online Research
For information about a career as a car salesperson, visit: msmath3.net/careers

DAILY INTERVENTION

Unlocking Misconceptions

Remind students to pay close attention to what is being asked for in a problem. The formula $I = prt$ computes interest. To compute the total amount in an account, the interest should be added to the original principal. Many students forget the extra step.

Students practice the same concepts in Exercises 9–26 if they are assigned odd or even problems.

Skill and Concept Check

1. Writing Math Explain what each variable in the simple interest formula represents. **See margin.**
2. **OPEN ENDED** Give a principal and interest rate where the amount of simple interest earned in two years would be $50. **Sample answer: $1,000 at 2.5%**
3. **NUMBER SENSE** Yoshiko needs to find the simple interest on a savings account of $600 at 7% interest for one-half year. She writes $I = 600 \cdot 0.035$. Will this equation give her the correct answer? Explain. (*Hint*: Use the Associative Property of Multiplication.) **Yes; Yoshiko will earn half of the interest which is 3.5% or 0.035.**

GUIDED PRACTICE

Find the simple interest to the nearest cent.

4. $300 at 7.5% for 5 years **$112.50**
5. $230 at 12% for 8 months **$18.40**

Find the total amount in each account to the nearest cent.

6. $660 at 5.25% for 2 years **$729.30**
7. $385 at 12.6% for 9 months **7. $421.38**
8. **HOUSING** After World War II, William Levitt and his family began to develop suburbs priced for the middle class. The prices of a ranch in Levittown, New York, are given at the right. Determine the simple interest rate for the investment of a ranch in Levittown from 1947 to 2000. **about 37.8%**

Price of Ranch in Levittown

Year	Price
1947	$9,500
2000	$200,000

Source: *Century of Change*

★ indicates increased difficulty

Practice and Applications

HOMEWORK HELP

For Exercises	See Examples
9–16	1
17–25	2
26–27	3

Extra Practice See pages 629, 652.

Find the simple interest to the nearest cent.

9. $250 at 6.5% for 3 years **$48.75**
10. $725 at 4.5% for 4 years **$130.50**
11. $834 at 7.25% for $1\frac{1}{2}$ years **$90.70**
12. $3,070 at 8.65% for $2\frac{1}{4}$ years **12. $597.50**
13. ★ $1,000 at 7.5% for 30 months **$187.50**
14. ★ $5,200 at 13.5% for 18 months **$1,053.00**
15. Suppose $1,250 is placed in a savings account for 2 years. Find the interest if the simple interest rate is 4.5%. **$112.50**
16. Suppose $580 is placed in a savings account at a simple interest rate of 5.5%. How much interest will the account earn in 3 years? **$95.70**

Find the total amount in each account to the nearest cent.

17. $2,250 at 5.5% for 3 years **$2,621.25**
18. $5,060 at 7.2% for 5 years **$6,881.60**
19. $575 at 4.25% for $2\frac{1}{2}$ years **$636.09**
20. $950 at 7.85% for $3\frac{2}{3}$ years **$1,223.44**
21. ★ $12,000 at 7.5% for 39 months **$14,925.00**
22. ★ $2,600 at 5.8% for 54 months **$3,278.60**
23. A savings account starts with $980. If the simple interest rate is 5%, find the total amount after 9 months. **$1,016.75**
24. Suppose $800 is deposited into a savings account with a simple interest rate of 6.5%. Find the total amount of the account after 15 months. **$865.00**

msmath3.net/self_check_quiz

3 Practice/Apply

FOLDABLES™ Follow-Up Remind students to use their Foldables to record what they have learned, or they could record new terms that they need to learn. Encourage students to explain the importance of knowing the formula for determining interest.

NUMBER SENSE
In Exercise 3, if students have difficulty seeing that this is the correct equation, have them rewrite the formula and plug in the numbers from the equation. They can compute the rate times time first. $I = 600 \cdot (0.07 \cdot 0.5) = 600 \cdot 0.035$.

About the Exercises...

Guided Practice Key

Exercises	Examples
4, 5	1
6, 7	2
8	3

Assignment Guide

Basic: 9, 11, 15–19 odd, 23, 25, 27–32

Average: 9–25 odd, 27–32

Enriched: 10–26 even, 27–32

Answer

1. In the formula $I = prt$, I represents the interest, p represents the principal, r represents the simple interest rate written as a decimal, and t represents the time in years.

Study Guide and Intervention, p. 280

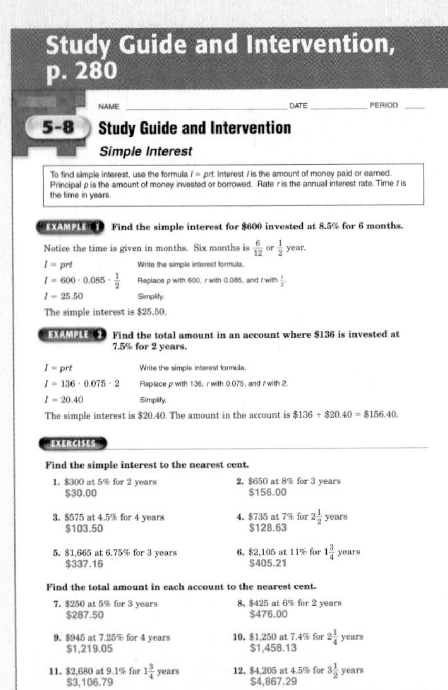

NAME ______________ DATE ________ PERIOD ____

5-8 Study Guide and Intervention

Simple Interest

To find simple interest, use the formula $I = prt$. Interest I is the amount of money paid or earned. Principal p is the amount of money invested or borrowed. Rate r is the annual interest rate. Time t is the time in years.

EXAMPLE 1 **Find the simple interest for $600 invested at 8.5% for 6 months.**

Notice the time is given in months. Six months is $\frac{6}{12}$ or $\frac{1}{2}$ year.

$I = prt$	Write the simple interest formula.
$I = 600 \cdot 0.085 \cdot \frac{1}{2}$	Replace p with 600, r with 0.085, and t with $\frac{1}{2}$.
$I = 25.50$	Simplify.

The simple interest is $25.50.

EXAMPLE 2 **Find the total amount in an account where $136 is invested at 7.5% for 2 years.**

$I = prt$	Write the simple interest formula.
$I = 136 \cdot 0.075 \cdot 2$	Replace p with 136, r with 0.075, and t with 2.
$I = 20.40$	Simplify.

The simple interest is $20.40. The amount in the account is $136 + $20.40 = $156.40.

EXERCISES

Find the simple interest to the nearest cent.

1. $300 at 5% for 2 years $30.00
2. $650 at 8% for 3 years $156.00
3. $575 at 4.5% for 4 years $103.50
4. $735 at 7% for $2\frac{1}{2}$ years $128.63
5. $1,665 at 6.75% for 3 years $337.16
6. $2,105 at 11% for $1\frac{3}{4}$ years $405.21

Find the total amount in each account to the nearest cent.

7. $250 at 5% for 3 years $287.50
8. $425 at 6% for 2 years $476.00
9. $945 at 7.25% for 4 years $1,219.05
10. $1,250 at 7.4% for $2\frac{1}{4}$ years $1,458.13
11. $2,680 at 9.1% for $1\frac{3}{4}$ years $3,106.79
12. $4,205 at 4.5% for $3\frac{1}{2}$ years $4,867.29

Practice: Skills, p. 281

NAME ______________ DATE ________ PERIOD ____

5-8 Practice: Skills

Simple Interest

Find the simple interest to the nearest cent.

1. $500 at 4% for 2 years $40.00
2. $800 at 9% for 4 years $288.00
3. $350 at 6.2% for 3 years $65.10
4. $280 at 5.5% for 4 years $61.60
5. $740 at 3.25% for 2 years $48.10
6. $1,150 at 7.6% for 5 years $437.00
7. $725 at 4.3% for $2\frac{1}{2}$ years $77.94
8. $266 at 5.2% for 3 years $41.50
9. $955 at 6.75% for $3\frac{1}{4}$ years $209.50
10. $1,245 at 5.4% for 4 years $268.92
11. $1,540 at 8.25% for 2 years $254.10
12. $2,180 at 7.7% for $2\frac{1}{2}$ years $419.65
13. $3,500 at 4.2% for $1\frac{3}{4}$ years $257.25
14. $2,650 at 3.65% for $4\frac{1}{2}$ years $435.26

Find the total amount in each account to the nearest cent.

15. $200 at 5% for 3 years $230.00
16. $700 at 6% for 2 years $784.00
17. $850 at 4% for 3 years $952.00
18. $350 at 8% for 2 years $406.00
19. $540 at 2.75% for 4 years $599.40
20. $360 at 4.5% for 5 years $441.00
21. $446 at 2.5% for 4 years $490.60
22. $780 at 3.6% for 3 years $864.24
23. $840 at 5.75% for $2\frac{1}{2}$ years $960.75
24. $530 at 7.25% for $1\frac{3}{4}$ years $597.24
25. $1,400 at 6.5% for 2 years $1,582.00
26. $1,880 at 4.3% for $3\frac{1}{2}$ years $2,162.94
27. $2,470 at 5.5% for 4 years $3,013.40
28. $3,200 at 9.75% for $1\frac{1}{2}$ years $3,668.00
29. $2,810 at 3.95% for $2\frac{1}{4}$ years $3,059.74
30. $4,340 at 8.12% for $3\frac{1}{4}$ years $5,485.33

Practice: Word Problems, p. 282

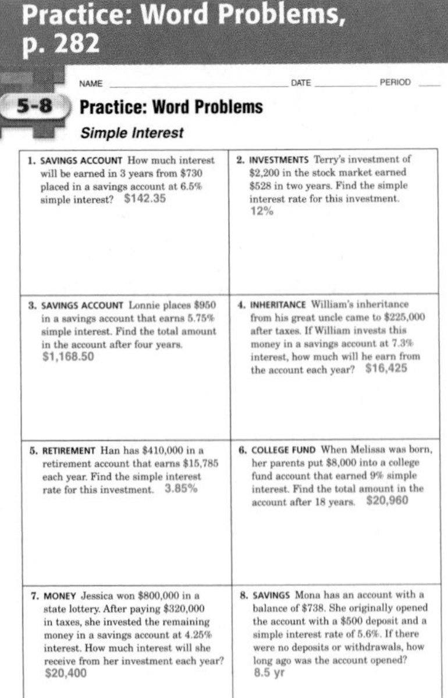

NAME ______________ DATE ________ PERIOD ____

5-8 Practice: Word Problems

Simple Interest

1. **SAVINGS ACCOUNT** How much interest will be earned in 3 years from $730 placed in a savings account at 6.5% simple interest? $142.35
2. **INVESTMENTS** Terry's investment of $2,200 in the stock market earned $528 in two years. Find the simple interest rate for this investment. 12%
3. **SAVINGS ACCOUNT** Lonnie places $950 in a savings account that earns 5.75% simple interest. Find the total amount in the account after four years. $1,168.50
4. **INHERITANCE** William's inheritance from his great uncle came to $225,000 after taxes. If William invests this money in a savings account at 7.3% interest, how much will he earn from the account each year? $16,425
5. **RETIREMENT** Han has $410,000 in a retirement account that earns $15,785 each year. Find the simple interest rate for this investment. 3.85%
6. **COLLEGE FUND** When Melissa was born, her parents put $8,000 into a college fund account that earned 9% simple interest. Find the total amount in the account after 18 years. $20,960
7. **MONEY** Jessica won $800,000 in a state lottery. After paying $320,000 in taxes, she invested the remaining money in a savings account at 4.25% interest. How much interest will she receive from her investment each year? $20,400
8. **SAVINGS** Mona has an account with a balance of $738. She originally opened the account with a $500 deposit and a simple interest rate of 5.6%. If there were no deposits or withdrawals, how long ago was the account opened? 8.5 yr

25. **MONEY MATTERS** Generation X (Gen Xers) are people who were born in the late 1960s or the early 1970s. According to the graphic at the right, most Gen Xers would invest an unexpected $50,000. Suppose someone invested this money at a simple interest rate of 4.5%. How much money would they have at the end of 10 years? **$72,500**

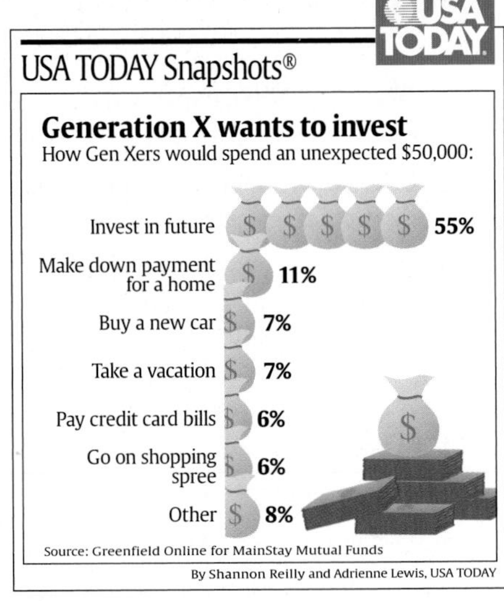

26. **INVESTMENTS** Booker earned $1,200 over the summer. He invested the money in stocks. To his surprise, the stocks increased in value to $1,335 in only 9 months. Find the simple interest rate for the investment. **15%**

27. **CRITICAL THINKING** Ethan's bank account listed a balance of $328.80. He originally opened the account with a $200 deposit and a simple interest rate of 4.6%. If there were no deposits or withdrawals, how long ago was the account opened? **14 yr**

Spiral Review with Standardized Test Practice

28. **MULTIPLE CHOICE** Suppose Mr. and Mrs. Owens placed $1,500 in a college savings account with a simple interest rate of 4% when Lauren was born. How much will be in the account in 18 years when Lauren is ready to go to college? Assume no more deposits or no withdrawals were made. **B**

    (A) $1,080 (B) $2,580 (C) $10,800 (D) $12,300

29. **SHORT RESPONSE** A $750 investment earned $540 in 6 years. Write an equation you can use to find the simple interest rate. Then find the simple interest rate. **$540 = 750 \cdot r \cdot 6$; 12%**

30. **SALES** What is the sale price of a $250 bicycle on sale at 10% off the regular price? (Lesson 5-7) **$225**

Solve each equation using the percent equation. (Lesson 5-6)

31. What percent of 70 is 17.5? **25%**
32. 18 is 30% of what number? **60**

INTERDISCIPLINARY PROJECT

It's a Masterpiece

Math and Art It's time to complete your project. Use the information and data you have gathered about your artist and the Golden Ratio to prepare a Web page or poster. Be sure to include your reports and calculations with your project.

WebQuest msmath3.net/webquest

244 Chapter 5 Percent

4 Assess

Open-Ended Assessment

Speaking Have students determine the total interest and the monthly payment for borrowing $4,500 at 6% for 4 years and $4,500 at 8% for 2 years. **$1,080, $116.25; $720, $217.50**

Have students describe when each option would be better for the person borrowing the money.

Spreadsheet Investigation

A Follow-Up of Lesson 5-8

What You'll LEARN

Find compound interest.

Compound Interest

Simple interest, which you studied in Lesson 5-8, is paid only on the initial principal of a savings account or a loan. *Compound interest* is paid on the initial principal and on interest earned in the past. You can use a spreadsheet to investigate the growth of compound interest.

ACTIVITY

SAVINGS Find the value of a $2,000 savings account after four years if the account pays 8% interest compounded semiannually.

8% interest compounded semiannually means that the interest is paid twice a year, or every 6 months. The interest rate is 8% ÷ 2 or 4%.

The interest rate is entered as a decimal.

The spreadsheet evaluates the formula A4 × B1.

The interest is added to the principal every 6 months. The spreadsheet evaluates the formula A4 + B4.

Compound Interest

	A	B	C	D
1	RATE	0.04		
2				
3	PRINCIPAL	INTEREST	NEW PRINCIPAL	TIME (YR)
4	$2000.00	$80.00	$2080.00	0.5
5	$2080.00	$83.20	$2163.20	1
6	$2163.20	$86.53	$2249.73	1.5
7	$2249.73	$89.99	$2339.72	2
8	$2339.72	$93.59	$2433.31	2.5
9	$2433.31	$97.33	$2530.64	3
10	$2530.64	$101.23	$2631.86	3.5
11	$2631.86	$105.27	$2737.14	4
12	$2737.14	$109.49	$2846.62	4.5
13	$2846.62	$113.86	$2960.49	5
14	$2960.49	$118.42	$3078.91	5.5
15	$3078.91	$123.16	$3202.06	6

Sheet1 Sheet2

The value of the savings account after four years is $2,737.14.

EXERCISES 2. $1,180; $1,194.05; $1,195.62

1. **Use a spreadsheet** to find the amount of money in a savings account if $2,000 is invested for four years at 8% interest compounded quarterly. **$2,745.57**
2. Suppose you leave $1,000 in each of three bank accounts paying 6% interest per year. One account pays simple interest, one pays interest compounded semiannually, and one pays interest compounded quarterly. Use a spreadsheet to find the amount of money in each account after three years.
3. **MAKE A CONJECTURE** How does the amount of interest change if the compounding occurs more frequently?

3. The amount of interest increases.

5-8b Spreadsheet Investigation

GETTING STARTED

Teaching Tip If you will be working in a computer lab where students need to share computers, have groups assigned before going to the lab. Make sure that each student has the opportunity to enter information into the spreadsheet.

TEACH

- Ask students to explain why compound interest is different from simple interest. They should recognize that the interest computed with each compounding is based on a different principal amount.
- Remind students to adjust the rate at the top of the spreadsheet for each new example.

ASSESS

Observe as students solve the **Exercises**. They should:

- create and adjust a spreadsheet to solve a problem, and
- be able to make conjectures based on their results as well as be able to explain their answer based on their understanding of compound interest.

Study Guide and Review

Vocabulary Assessment

- This alphabetical list of vocabulary terms in Chapter 5 includes a page reference where each term was introduced.
- A vocabulary review/test for Chapter 5 is available on p. 298 of the *Chapter 5 Resource Masters*.

Vocabulary PuzzleMaker

ELL The online Vocabulary PuzzleMaker improves students' mathematics vocabulary using four puzzle formats — crossword, scramble, word search using a word list, and word search using clues. Students can work on a computer screen or from a printed handout.

MindJogger Videoquizzes

ELL MindJogger Videoquizzes provide an alternative review of concepts presented in this chapter. Students work in teams in a game show format to gain points for correct answers. The questions are presented in three rounds.

Round 1 Concepts (5 questions)
Round 2 Skills (4 questions)
Round 3 Problem Solving (4 questions)

ExamView® Pro

Use the networkable ExamView® Pro Testmaker CD-ROM to:

- Create **multiple versions** of tests.
- Create **modified** tests for **inclusion** students with one mouse click.
- **Edit** existing questions and **add** your own questions.
- Build tests aligned with state standards using built-in **state curriculum correlations.**
- Change **English** tests to **Spanish** with one mouse click and vice versa.

Study Guide and Review

Vocabulary and Concept Check

base (p. 216)	part (p. 216)	percent of increase (p. 237)
compatible numbers (p. 228)	percent (p. 206)	percent proportion (p. 216)
discount (p. 238)	percent equation (p. 232)	principal (p. 241)
interest (p. 241)	percent of change (p. 236)	selling price (p. 238)
markup (p. 238)	percent of decrease (p. 237)	

Choose the correct term or number to complete each sentence.

1. A (proportion, percent) is a ratio that compares a number to 100.
2. In a percent proportion, the whole quantity is called a (part, base).
3. The proportion $\frac{1}{10} = \frac{p}{100}$ is an example of a (percent proportion, discount).
4. (Percents, Compatible numbers) are numbers that are easy to divide mentally.
5. A (markup, discount) is an increase in price.
6. A (markup, discount) is a decrease in price.
7. The (interest, principal) is the amount borrowed.
8. The (interest, principal) is the money paid for the use of money.
9. 25% of 16 is (4, 40).
10. The interest formula is ($I = prt$, $p = Irt$).

Lesson-by-Lesson Exercises and Examples

5-1 Ratios and Percents (pp. 206–209)

Write each ratio or fraction as a percent.

11. $\frac{4}{5}$ **80%**
12. $\frac{7}{5}$ **140%**
13. 16.5 out of 100 **16.5%**
14. 0.8 out of 100 **0.8%**
15. **WEATHER** There is a 1 in 5 chance of rain tomorrow. Write this as a percent. **20%**

Write each percent as a fraction in simplest form.

16. 90% $\frac{9}{10}$
17. 120% $1\frac{1}{5}$
18. **GAMES** 80% of students at Monroe Middle School play video games. Write this as a fraction in simplest form. $\frac{4}{5}$

Example 1 Write $\frac{1}{4}$ as a percent.

$\frac{1}{4} = \frac{25}{100}$ (× 25) So, $\frac{1}{4} = 25\%$.

Example 2 Write 35% as a fraction in simplest form.

$35\% = \frac{35}{100}$ Definition of percent

$= \frac{7}{20}$ Simplify.

So, $35\% = \frac{7}{20}$.

msmath3.net/vocabulary_review

FOLDABLES Study Organizer

For more information about Foldables, see *Teaching Mathematics with Foldables.*

Have students look through the chapter to make sure they have included examples in their Foldables for each lesson or topic in the chapter.

Encourage students to refer to their Foldables while completing the Study Guide and Review and to use them in preparing for the Chapter Test.

5-2 Fractions, Decimals, and Percents (pp. 210–214)

Write each percent as a decimal.

19. 4.3% **0.043**
20. 90% **0.9**
21. 13% **0.13**
22. 33.2% **0.332**
23. 147% **1.47**
24. 0.7% **0.007**

Write each decimal as a percent.

25. 0.655 **65.5%**
26. 0.35 **35%**
27. 0.7 **70%**
28. 0.38 **38%**
29. 0.015 **1.5%**
30. 2.55 **255%**

Write each fraction as a percent.

31. $\frac{7}{8}$ **87.5%**
32. $\frac{3}{40}$ **7.5%**
33. $\frac{24}{25}$ **96%**
34. $\frac{1}{6}$ **16.$\overline{6}$%**

Example 3 **Write 24% as a decimal.**

$24\% = 24\%$ Divide by 100 and remove the percent symbol.

$= 0.24$

Example 4 **Write 0.04 as a percent.**

$0.04 = 0.04$ Multiply by 100 and add the percent symbol.

$= 4\%$

Example 5 **Write $\frac{9}{25}$ as a percent.**

$\frac{9}{25} = 0.36$ Write as a decimal.

$= 36\%$ Change the decimal to a percent.

5-3 Algebra: The Percent Proportion (pp. 216–219)

35–37. See margin for proportions.

Write a percent proportion to solve each problem. Then solve. Round to the nearest tenth if necessary.

35. 15 is 30% of what number? **50**
36. Find 45% of 18. **8.1**
37. 75 is what percent of 250? **30%**
38. **SCHOOL** Hernando hired a band to play at the school dance. The band charges $3,000 and requires a 20% deposit. How much money does Hernando need for the deposit? **$600**

Example 6 **18 is what percent of 27? Round to the nearest tenth.**

$\frac{a}{b} = \frac{p}{100} \rightarrow \frac{18}{27} = \frac{p}{100}$ Percent proportion

$18 \cdot 100 = 27 \cdot p$ Find the cross products.

$1{,}800 = 27p$ Multiply.

$\frac{1{,}800}{27} = \frac{27p}{27}$ Divide each side by 27.

$66.7 \approx p$ Simplify.

So, 18 is 66.7% of 27.

5-4 Finding Percents Mentally (pp. 220–223)

Compute mentally.

39. 90% of 100 **90**
40. 10% of 18.3 **1.83**
41. $66\frac{2}{3}\%$ of 24 **16**
42. 20% of 60 **12**
43. 1% of 243 **2.43**
44. 6% of 200 **12**

Example 7 **Compute 50% of 42 mentally.**

50% of 42 = $\frac{1}{2}$ of 42 or 21 $50\% = \frac{1}{2}$

Answers

35. $\frac{15}{b} = \frac{30}{100}$
36. $\frac{a}{18} = \frac{45}{100}$
37. $\frac{75}{250} = \frac{p}{100}$

Answers

45. Sample answer: $\frac{1}{8}$ of 80 or 10
46. Sample answer: $\frac{2}{3}$ of 60 or 40
47. Sample answer: $\frac{2}{5}$ of 40 or 16
48. Sample answer: $\frac{1}{3}$ of 60 or 20
49. Sample answer: $\frac{33}{98} \approx \frac{33}{99}$ or $33\frac{1}{3}\%$
50. Sample answer: $\frac{19}{52} \approx \frac{20}{50}$ or 40%
55. 50%; increase
56. 25%; increase
57. 20%; decrease
58. 33.3%; decrease

Mixed Problem Solving
For mixed problem-solving practice, see page 652.

5-5 Percent and Estimation (pp. 228–231)

Estimate. 45–48. See margin.

45. 12.5% of 83
46. 67% of 60
47. 41% of 39
48. 34% of 61

Estimate each percent. 49–50. See margin.

49. 33 out of 98
50. 19 out of 52

Example 8 **Estimate 8% of 104.**

104 is about 100.
8% of 100 is 8.
So, 8% of 104 is about 8.

5-6 Algebra: The Percent Equation (pp. 232–235)

Solve each problem using the percent equation.

51. What is 66% of 7,000? **4,620**
52. 60 is what percent of 500? **12%**
53. Find 15% of 82. **12.3**
54. 25 is what percent of 125? **20%**

Example 9 **70 is 25% of what number?**

$70 = 0.25n$ Write 25% as the decimal 0.25.

$\frac{70}{0.25} = \frac{0.25n}{0.25}$ Divide each side by 0.25

$280 = n$ Simplify.

So, 70 is 25% of 280.

5-7 Percent of Change (pp. 236–240)

Find each percent of change. Round to the nearest tenth if necessary. State whether the percent of change is an *increase* or a *decrease*. 55–58. See margin.

55. original: 10
    new: 15
56. original: 8
    new: 10
57. original: 37.5
    new: 30
58. original: 18
    new: 12
59. **HOBBIES** Mariah collects comic books. Last year she had 50 comic books. If she now has 74 comic books, what is the percent of increase? **48%**

Example 10 **Find the percent of change if the original amount is 900 and the new amount is 725. Round to the nearest tenth.**

$900 - 725 = 175$ The amount of change is 175.

$\text{percent of change} = \frac{\text{amount of change}}{\text{original amount}}$

$= \frac{175}{900}$

≈ 0.194 or 19.4%

5-8 Simple Interest (pp. 241–244)

Find the simple interest to the nearest cent.

60. \$780 at 6% for 8 months **\$31.20**
61. \$100 at 8.5% for 2 years **\$17.00**
62. \$350 at 5% for 3 years **\$52.50**
63. \$260 at 17.5% for 18 months **\$68.25**

Example 11 **Find the simple interest for \$250 invested at 5.5% for 2 years.**

$I = prt$ Simple interest formula

$I = 250 \cdot 0.055 \cdot 2$ Write 5.5% as 0.055.

$I = 27.50$ Simplify.

The simple interest is \$27.50.

248 Chapter 5 Percent

Practice Test

Vocabulary and Concepts

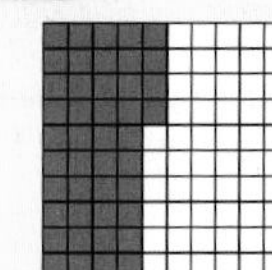

1. **Write** a percent, a decimal, and a fraction in simplest form for the model shown. 44%; 0.44; $\frac{11}{25}$
2. **Write** the percent proportion and the percent equation. Use a for the part, b for the base, and p for the percent. $\frac{a}{b} = \frac{p}{100}$; $a = pb$

Skills and Applications

Write each ratio or fraction as a percent. Round to the nearest tenth.

3. 7 out of 10 70%
4. 2:40 5%
5. $\frac{1}{6}$ 16.7%

Express each percent as a decimal.

6. 135% 1.35
7. 14.6% 0.146

Compute mentally.

8. 30% of 60 18
9. $33\frac{1}{3}$% of 90 30

Estimate.

10. 23% of 16 Sample answer: $\frac{1}{4}$ of 16 or 4
11. 9% of 81 Sample answer: 10% of 80 or 8

Solve each problem. Round to the nearest tenth.

12. What is 2% of 3,600? 72
13. 62 is 90% of what number? 68.9
14. Find 45% of 600. 270
15. 75 is what percent of 30? 250%

Find each percent of change. Round to the nearest tenth if necessary. State whether the percent of change is an *increase* or a *decrease*.

16. original: 15
    new: 12 20%; decrease
17. original: 40
    new: 55 37.5%; increase
18. **BUSINESS** A store prices items 30% over the price paid by the store. If the store purchases a tennis racket for $65, find the selling price of the racket. $84.50
19. **MONEY MATTERS** Find the simple interest if $300 is invested at 8% for 3 years. $72

Standardized Test Practice

20. **MULTIPLE CHOICE** Kevin opened a savings account with $125. The account earns 5.2% interest annually. If he does not deposit or withdraw any money for 18 months, how much will he have in his account? C

Ⓐ $9.75 Ⓑ $117 Ⓒ $134.75 Ⓓ $242

Chapter 5 Practice Test

Assessment Options

Vocabulary Test A vocabulary review/test for Chapter 5 can be found on p. 298 of the *Chapter 5 Resource Masters.*

Chapter Tests There are six Chapter 5 Tests and an Extended Response Assessment task available in the *Chapter 5 Resource Masters.*

Chapter 5 Tests			
Form	**Type**	**Level**	**Pages**
1	MC	basic	285–286
2A	MC	average	287–288
2B	MC	average	289–290
2C	FR	average	291–292
2D	FR	average	293–294
3	FR	advanced	295–296

MC = multiple-choice questions
FR = free-response questions

Extended Response Assessment

Extended Response tasks for Chapter 5 can be found on p. 297 of the *Chapter 5 Resource Masters.* A sample scoring rubric for these tasks appears on p. A28.

Unit 2 Test

A unit test/review can be found on pp. 305–306 of the *Chapter 5 Resource Masters.*

Portfolio Suggestion

Introduction Students will deal with percents in real life frequently. Sales, taxes, cost of living, raises, and population increases all involve percents.

Ask Students to find examples of percents in situations that weren't mentioned in the chapter. Have students summarize these in their portfolios for Chapter 5

Standardized Test Practice

These two pages contain practice questions in the various formats that can be found on the most frequently given standardized tests.

A student recording sheet for these two pages can be found on page A1 of the *Chapter 5 Resource Masters.*

Standardized Test Practice Student Recording Sheet, p. A1

NAME ________ DATE ________ PERIOD ____

Standardized Test Practice SCORE ____

Student Recording Sheet (Use with pages 250–251 of the Student Edition.)

Part 1: Multiple Choice

Select the best answer from the choices given and fill in the corresponding oval.

1. Ⓐ Ⓑ Ⓒ Ⓓ 4. Ⓕ Ⓖ Ⓗ Ⓘ 7. Ⓐ Ⓑ Ⓒ Ⓓ
2. Ⓕ Ⓖ Ⓗ Ⓘ 5. Ⓐ Ⓑ Ⓒ Ⓓ 8. Ⓕ Ⓖ Ⓗ Ⓘ
3. Ⓐ Ⓑ Ⓒ Ⓓ 6. Ⓕ Ⓖ Ⓗ Ⓘ 9. Ⓐ Ⓑ Ⓒ Ⓓ

Part 2: Short Response/Grid In

Solve the problem and write your answer in the blank.

For grid in questions, also enter your answer by writing each number or symbol in a box. Then fill in the corresponding circle for that number of symbol.

10. ________
11. ________
12. ________
13. ________ (grid in)
14. ________

Part 3: Extended Response

Record your answers for Questions 15 and 16 below or on the back of this paper.

Additional Practice

See pp. 303–304 of the *Chapter 5 Resource Masters* for additional standardized test practice.

Answer

15a. Sample answer: Since 1,497 is about 1,500 and 40% equals $\frac{2}{5}$, the number of people with type A blood is about $\frac{2}{5} \times 1{,}500$ or 600.

$n = 0.40(1{,}497)$ Write the percent equation.

$n = 598.8$ Simplify.

There are 599 people with type A blood, which is very close to the estimate.

Standardized Test Practice

PART 1 Multiple Choice

Record your answers on the answer sheet provided by your teacher or on a sheet of paper.

1. Which of these is the least number? (Basic Skill) **A**
   - Ⓐ three-thousandths
   - Ⓑ three and one-thousandth
   - Ⓒ three-hundredths
   - Ⓓ three and one-hundredth

2. When evaluating the following expression, which operation should be performed first? (Lesson 1-2) **I**

   $42 - 12 + [10(26 - 9)] \div 3$
   - Ⓕ Divide 9 by 3.
   - Ⓖ Subtract 12 from 42.
   - Ⓗ Multiply 10 times 26.
   - Ⓘ Subtract 9 from 26.

3. Charles made 8 cups of lemonade. He poured himself $1\frac{1}{2}$ cups, his sister $1\frac{1}{3}$ cups, his mother $2\frac{1}{4}$ cups, and his father $2\frac{5}{8}$ cups. How much did he have left? (Lesson 2-6) **A**
   - Ⓐ $\frac{7}{24}$ c
   - Ⓑ $\frac{5}{12}$ c
   - Ⓒ $\frac{7}{8}$ c
   - Ⓓ $1\frac{1}{12}$ c

4. What is the distance between the points in the graph below? (Lesson 3-6) **I**

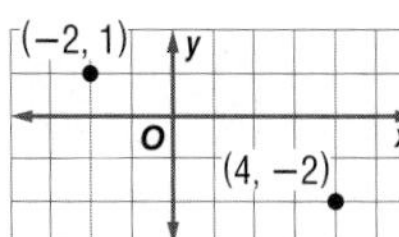

   - Ⓕ 3 units
   - Ⓖ 4.5 units
   - Ⓗ 6 units
   - Ⓘ 6.7 units

5. Which of the following percents is more than 2 out of 6 but less than 3 out of 5? (Lesson 5-1) **B**
   - Ⓐ 33%
   - Ⓑ 50%
   - Ⓒ 75%
   - Ⓓ 85%

6. Which of the following is the *best* estimate for the shaded portion of the rectangle below? (Lesson 5-2) **G**

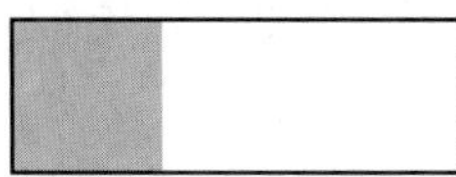

   - Ⓕ 10%
   - Ⓖ $\frac{1}{3}$
   - Ⓗ 0.60
   - Ⓘ 80%

7. Jesse got a 88% on his science test. How many questions did Jesse answer correctly? (Lesson 5-3) **D**
   - Ⓐ 88 questions
   - Ⓑ less than 88 questions
   - Ⓒ more than 88 questions
   - Ⓓ cannot be determined from the information

8. The pair of jeans is on sale for 25% off the regular price of \$47. How much money is discounted off the regular price? (Lesson 5-7) **H**
   - Ⓕ \$6.25
   - Ⓖ \$8.55
   - Ⓗ \$11.75
   - Ⓘ \$35.25

9. Ms. Katz took out a loan for \$1,200. The loan had a simple interest rate of 8.5%. If she paid off the loan in 6 months, which of the following expressions gives the total amount of interest she had to pay? (Lesson 5-8) **C**
   - Ⓐ $1{,}200 - 0.085 \times 0.6$
   - Ⓑ $1{,}200 \times 0.085 \div 6$
   - Ⓒ $1{,}200 \times 0.085 \times 0.5$
   - Ⓓ $1{,}200 \times 0.085 + 5$

ExamView® Pro

Special banks of standardized test questions similar to those on the TIMSS and NAEP grade 8 tests can be found on this CD-ROM.

Preparing for Standardized Tests
For test-taking strategies and more practice, see pages 660–677.

PART 2 Short Response/Grid In

Record your answers on the answer sheet provided by your teacher or on a sheet of paper.

10. The perimeter of the rectangular rug below is 42 feet. What is its length? (Lesson 1-1) **15 ft**

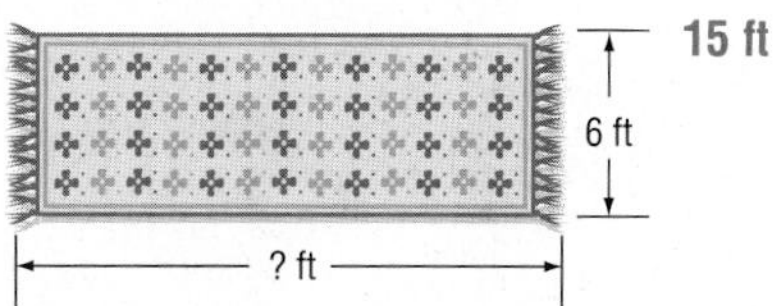

11. Find the length of the third side of the triangle. (Lesson 3-5) **13 in.**

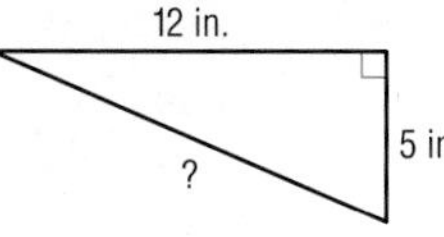

12. Which is less, 0.02% or $\frac{1}{7}$%? (Lesson 5-1) **0.02%**

13. Which is the greatest number? (Lesson 5-2) **1/4**

0.3%, 2%, $\frac{4}{26}$, $\frac{1}{4}$

14. Hakeem enlarged a photograph to 250% of its original size. If the length of the original photograph is indicated below, what is length of the copy of the photograph? (Lesson 5-4) **50 cm**

20 cm

TEST-TAKING TIP

Question 13 Use your ability to convert percents, decimals, and fractions to your advantage. For example, you may find Question 13 easiest to answer if you convert all of the answer choices to fractions.

msmath3.net/standardized_test

PART 3 Extended Response

Record your answers on a sheet of paper. Show your work.

15. A local health clinic found that 1,497 blood donors had a positive Rh factor. The following is the blood-type breakdown of these donors with a positive Rh factor. (Lessons 5-5 and 5-6) **a–b. See margin.**

Blood Type	Percent of Donors
O	45%
A	40%
B	10%
AB	5%

a. Explain how you could estimate the number of people with type A blood. Find the actual number of people with type A blood. Compare the actual number with your estimate.

b. Explain how you could estimate the number of people with type AB blood. Find the actual number of people with type AB blood. Compare the actual number with your estimate.

16. The Dow Jones Average is used to measure changes in stock values on the New York Stock Exchange. Three major drops in the Dow Jones Average for one day are listed below. (Lesson 5-7)

Date	Opening	Closing
October 29, 1929	261.07	230.07
October 19, 1987	2,246.74	1,738.74
September 17, 2001	9,605.51	8,920.70

Source: www.mdleasing.com

a. Which day had the greatest decrease in amount? **9/17/01**

b. Did this decrease represent the biggest percent of decrease of the three drops? Explain your reasoning. **See margin.**

Standardized Test Practice

Rubrics The following rubrics are sample scoring devices for short response and extended response questions.

Short Response

Points	Description
2	The student demonstrates a thorough understanding of the mathematics of the task. The response may contain minor flaws that do not detract from the demonstration of a thorough understanding.
1	The student has provided a response that is only partially correct.
0	The student has provided a completely incorrect solution or no response at all.

Extended Response

Points	Description
4	The student demonstrates a thorough understanding of the mathematics of the task. The response may contain minor flaws that do not detract from the demonstration of a thorough understanding.
3	The student demonstrates an understanding of the mathematics of the task. The response is essentially correct and demonstrates an essential but less than thorough understanding of the mathematics.
2	The student demonstrates only a partial understanding of the mathematics of the task. Although the student may have used the correct approach to a solution or may have provided a correct solution, the work lacks an essential understanding of the underlying mathematical concepts.
1	The student demonstrates a very limited understanding of the mathematics of the task. The response is incomplete and exhibits many flaws.
0	The student provides a completely incorrect solution or no response at all.

A more detailed 4-point rubric is provided on page A2 of the *Chapter 5 Resource Masters*.

Answers

15b. Sample answer: Since 1,497 is about 1,500 and 5% is half of 10%, the number of people with type AB blood is about half of 1,500 × 0.1 or 75.

$n = 0.05(1{,}497)$ **Write the percent equation.**

$n = 74.85$ **Simplify.**

There are 75 people with type AB blood, which is the same as the estimate.

16b. Sample answer: Although 9/17/01 was the greatest decrease in amount, the percent of decrease was only about 7.1%. On 10/29/29, the percent of decrease was 11.9%. The greatest percent of decrease was about 22.6% on 10/19/87, which would make that drop the most significant.

UNIT 3 Notes

Introduction

In this unit, students will investigate geometry and measurement. They will study relationships among lines and angles and learn to classify angles according to these relationships. They will find missing angles of triangles and special right triangles and classify quadrilaterals. Students also will examine congruence and symmetry of two-dimensional shapes and apply these concepts to transformations of shapes through reflections, translations, and rotations.

Students will then learn to find the circumference and area of circles as well as the surface area and volume of three-dimensional figures including prisms, cylinders, pyramids, and cones. Finally, they will study precision and the use of significant digits in measurement.

Assessment Options

Unit 3 Test Pages 443–444 of the *Chapter 7 Resource Masters* may be used as a test or a review for Unit 3. This assessment contains both multiple-choice and short-response items.

An online, research-based, instructional, assessment, and intervention tool that provides specific feedback on student mastery of state and national standards, instant remediation, and a data management system to track performance. For more information, contact mhdigitallearning.com

UNIT 3

Geometry and Measurement

Chapter 6

Geometry

Chapter 7

Geometry: Measuring Area and Volume

Our world is made up of lines, angles, and shapes, both two- and three-dimensional. In this unit, you will learn about the properties and measures of geometric figures.

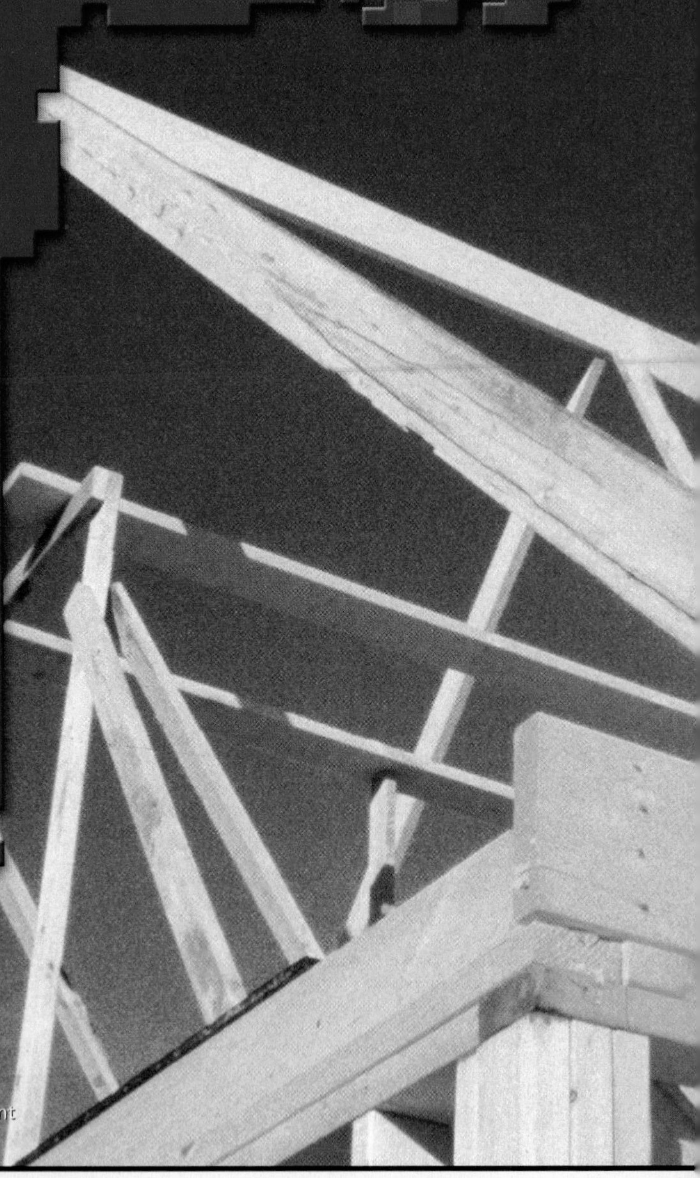

Real-Life Math Videos engage students, showing them how math is used in everyday situations. Use Video 3 with this unit to discuss how volume and symmetry are used in camping and car design. (also available on one Super DVD combined with Mindjogger Videoquizzes)

INTERDISCIPLINARY PROJECT

Under Construction

A WebQuest is an online project in which students do research on the Internet, gather data, and make presentations using word processing, graphing, page-making, or presentation software. In each chapter, students advance to the next step in their WebQuest. At the end of Chapter 7, the project culminates with a presentation of their findings.

WebQuest Teaching suggestions and sample answers are available in the WebQuests, Projects, and Interdisciplinary Investigations.

Math and Architecture You can use this WebQuest Interdisciplinary Project with your students' industrial education teacher to make the connection from mathematics to the architecture your students are studying.

More Interdisciplinary Connections

You may wish to share these suggestions with your students' other teachers.

Math and Social Studies

Research Mayan and Egyptian pyramids. What is known about how these structures were used? Calculate and compare the volumes of Mayan and Egyptian pyramids. How do their surface areas compare? Create a poster that shows your findings.

Math and Language Arts

Read a book or story in which a house portrays a central role and write a report on the house's character, mood, or symbolic meaning. Suggestions include *The House of the Seven Gables* by Nathaniel Hawthorne and *Little House on the Prairie* by Laura Ingalls Wilder.

Chapter Overview

Geometry

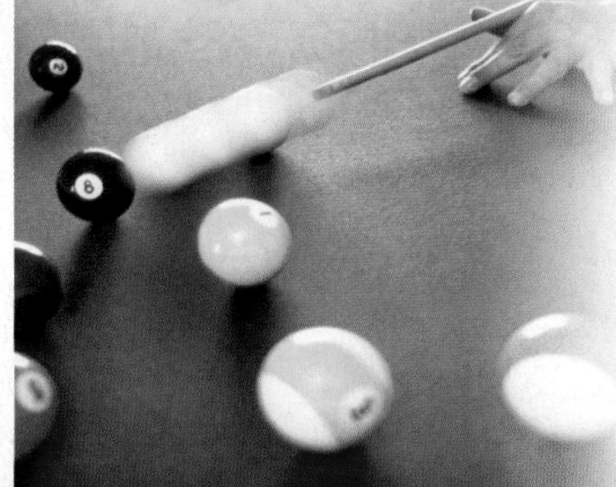

*An electronic version of this chapter is available on **StudentWorks**™. This backpack solution CD-ROM allows students instant access to the Student Edition, lesson worksheet pages, and web resources.*

	LESSON OBJECTIVES	NCTM Standards	NAEP 2005	State/Local Objectives
6-1	**Line and Angle Relationships** (pp. 256–261) • Identify special pairs of angles and relationships of angles formed by two parallel lines cut by a transversal. **6-1b Hands-On Lab:** Construct a line parallel to a given line.	1–4, 6, 7, 10	M1g, G3b, G3g, A3a, A4a, A4c, G1f	
6-2	**Triangles and Angles** (pp. 262–266) • Find missing angles in triangles and classify triangles by their angles and sides. **6-2b Hands-On Lab:** Bisect an angle.	1–4, 6, 7, 9, 10	G1f, G3b, G3f, A3a, A4a, A4c	
6-3	**Special Right Triangles** (pp. 267–271) • Find missing measures in 30°-60° right triangles and 45°-45° right triangles. **6-3b Hands-On Lab:** Construct a perpendicular bisector of a segment.	1–4, 6, 7, 9, 10	M1g, G3b, G3d, N4c, N3a, G1f	
6-4	**Classifying Quadrilaterals** (pp. 272–277) • Find missing angle measures in quadrilaterals and classify quadrilaterals. **6-4b Problem-Solving Strategy:** Solve problems using the logical reasoning strategy.	1–4, 6, 7, 9, 10	G1d, G1f, G3b, G3f, A3a, A4a	
6-5	**Congruent Polygons** (pp. 278–283) **6-5a Hands-On Lab:** Find the sum of the angle measures of polygons. • Identify congruent polygons. **6-5b Hands-On Lab:** Construct congruent triangles.	1–4, 6, 7, 9, 10	G2e, N5f, G1f	
6-6	**Symmetry** (pp. 286–289) • Identify line symmetry and rotational symmetry.	1–4, 6, 7, 9, 10	G2a	
6-7	**Reflections** (pp. 290–294) • Graph reflections on a coordinate plane.	1–4, 6, 7, 9, 10	G2c, A2c, A2d, G1p, G4d	
6-8	**Translations** (pp. 296–299) • Graph translations on a coordinate plane.	1–4, 6, 7, 9, 10	G2c, A2c, A2d, G1f, G4d	
6-9	**Rotations** (pp. 300–305) • Graph rotations on a coordinate plane. **6-9b Hands-On Lab:** Create Escher-like drawings using translations and rotations.	1–4, 6, 7, 9, 10	G2c, A2c, A2d, G1f, G4d, G2a, G2d	

Key to NCTM Standards:
1=Number & Operations, 2=Algebra, 3=Geometry, 4=Measurement, 5=Data Analysis & Probability, 6=Problem Solving, 7=Reasoning & Proof, 8=Communication, 9=Connections, 10=Representation

NAEP 2005 Standards: See Teacher Resources at math.glencoe.com

Pacing suggestions for the entire year can be found on page T23.

Chapter Resource Manager

Chapter 6 Resource Masters

Study Guide and Intervention	Practice (Skills and Word Problems)	Reading to Learn Mathematics	Enrichment	Assessment	Applications*	Parent and Student Study Guide Online Worksheets	5-Minute Check Transparencies	Key Teaching Transparencies	MathPASS: Tutorial Plus (lessons)	Teaching Mathematics with Manipulatives	Noteables™: Interactive Study Notebook	Optional Materials
307	308–309	310	311			6-1	6-1		30	64	6-1	straightedge, notebook paper, compass, paper
312	313–314	315	316			6-2	6-2			65	6-2	paper, scissors, straightedge, colored pencils, compass
317	318–319	320	321	367		6-3	6-3	21		66, 67	6-3	pencil, paper, scissors, ruler, compass, straightedge
322	323–324	325	326		CS 29	6-4	6-4	22		68, 69–70	6-4	paper, straightedge
327	328–329	330	331	367, 369	SM 73–76	6-5	6-5		31	71, 72	6-5	paper, straightedge, compass
332	333–334	335	336			6-6	6-6	23			6-6	tracing paper, transparency, pencil, overhead marker
337	338–339	340	341	368	CS 30	6-7	6-7			73–74	6-7	
342	343–344	345	346		RC 32	6-8	6-8		32	75	6-8	
347	348–349	350	351	353–366, 368, 370–372	CM 21–26	6-9	6-9	24		76	6-9	tracing paper, straightedge, tape, scissors, paper, index cards

*** Key to Abbreviations:** *CS = Calculator and Spreadsheet Masters, RC = Real-Life Career Masters, CM = Classroom Math Games (online), SM = Science and Math Lab Manual (online)*

CHAPTER 6

Mathematical Content and Teaching Strategies

Continuity of Instruction

Building on Prior Knowledge

Students have studied angles and their measures in previous courses. In Chapter 3, students learned the Pythagorean Theorem. They also studied the coordinate system, which will be applied to geometric figures in this chapter. In Chapter 4, students studied similar polygons and transformed polygons using dilations. Students encounter parallel and perpendicular lines in everyday life. In addition, they have some intuitive knowledge of symmetry and translations of figures through exposure to art and architectural works.

Learning in This Chapter

This chapter develops basic concepts in geometry. Students learn the classic methods of construction using a compass and a straightedge. They study the properties of parallel lines and the classification of triangles and quadrilaterals. Students discover the special relationships in 30°-60° and 45°-45° right triangles. They deepen their knowledge of geometric figures with the study of congruence and symmetry and the graphing of translations, reflections, and rotations. Students also solve problems using logical reasoning.

Making Future Connections

In Chapter 7, students will continue their study of geometry, learning how to find the area of figures other than rectangles and how to find the volume of three-dimensional figures. In future mathematics courses, students will relate algebra concepts to the geometry topics learned in this course. Students will use compass and straightedge constructions in drafting courses. Advanced skill in this area is the basis for computer-aided design used in building, architecture, and engineering.

Mathematical Background

6-1 Line and Angle Relationships

Much of present-day knowledge of lines and angles comes from the Greek mathematician Euclid (c. 325–265 B.C.). Euclid organized much ancient Egyptian, Babylonian, and Greek learning into *The Elements*—a collection of thirteen texts on various aspects of geometry. This, the first lesson of two chapters focusing on the study of geometry, classifies various types of angles and presents parallel and perpendicular lines.

In-Class Speaker

Have an architect visit the class and discuss how relationships among triangles and angles are used when producing building designs. Encourage the speaker to describe how symmetry affects the look of buildings. If possible, have the architect display some blueprints of buildings along with photographs showing the finished constructions.

6-2 Triangles and Angles

This lesson classifies triangles by their angle measures and number of congruent sides. The basic skills learned in this lesson will be added to in Lessons 6-3 through 6-5, which cover special right triangles, quadrilaterals, and congruent polygons.

6-3 Special Right Triangles

Both 30°-60° right triangles and 45°-45° right triangles have special relationships among their sides which students can use to find the measures of unknown side lengths. Students can then apply the Pythagorean Theorem studied in Chapter 3 to find the remaining side length.

6-4 Classifying Quadrilaterals

Students learn that more than one term can describe a quadrilateral, depending upon it's number of parallel or congruent sides and right angles. Students classify quadrilaterals from the most general to the most specific terms. For example, a square is also a rectangle, a rhombus, a parallelogram, and a quadrilateral.

Teacher to Teacher

Shirley Gonzales,
Desert Ridge Middle School
Albuquerque, NM

"When teaching quadrilaterals to students having difficulty, I copy the shapes onto cardstock. Students then cut out the shapes and label each one with its properties and all the names that describe it."

6-5 Congruent Polygons

Congruent polygons have congruent corresponding angles and their corresponding sides must also be congruent. Similar polygons have congruent corresponding angles, but their corresponding sides do not have to be congruent. Thus, similar polygons are not necessarily the same size. In contrast, congruent polygons are, by definition, the same size. Students learn to determine whether polygons are congruent and learn to use knowledge of congruence to find missing measures.

6-6 Symmetry

Students learn to classify types of symmetry. This lesson requires spatial reasoning. Geomirrors and tracing paper are very useful tools for teaching symmetry, which forms the basis for the study of reflections and rotations of figures in Lessons 6-7 and 6-9.

6-7 Reflections

In Chapter 4, students learned about one type of transformation called a *dilation.* This mapping produced an image similar but not congruent to the original figure. A *rigid* transformation does not change the shape *or size* of a figure. A *reflection* is one of three rigid transformations. Explain that this is the only transformation for which the orientation of the image is *different* from that of the original figure.

6-8 Translations

A second rigid transformation is a *translation.* Because the orientation of the image after a translation is the same as that of the original figure, and the image is not turned, most students will find this type of transformation easier to understand. Students should be encouraged to use the algorithmic approach suggested in this lesson for finding the vertices of the transformed image and then to check their results visually.

6-9 Rotations

The third rigid transformation is a *rotation.* The orientation of a figure after a rotation does not change, yet the figure is turned through an angle. To help students visualize the rotated image, have them use a protractor and a ruler to find its vertices. Ask visual/spatial students to find a rule giving the coordinates of the image after 90°-counterclockwise and 180° rotations.

What the Research Says

According to Miller and Mercer in "Educational Aspects of Mathematical Disabilities," students with learning disabilities benefit from activities-based, hands-on learning, as well as reasoning and problem-solving experiences.

- There are six Hands-On Labs and six Hands-On Mini Labs in Chapter 6. These activities help students discover and reinforce geometric concepts.

McGraw-Hill Professional Development

Mathematics, YES! is a self-paced, web-based professional development program. Units are based on major mathematical concepts and are standards-based. Actual classroom videos provide a springboard for discussion and activities. Unit appropriate for this chapter:

- Geometry and Measurement of Plane Figures

Additional mathematical information and teaching notes are available at msmath3.net/key_concepts.

DAILY INTERVENTION and Assessment

* **Key to Abbreviations:**
TWE = Teacher Wraparound Edition, *CRM* = Chapter Resource Masters

	Type	Student Edition	Teacher Resources	Technology/Internet
INTERVENTION	Ongoing	Prerequisite Skills, pp. 255, 260, 265, 270, 275, 289, 294, 299 Mid-Chapter Practice Test, p. 284	5-Minute Check Transparencies Quizzes 1–4, *CRM,* pp. 367–368 Mid-Chapter Test, *CRM,* p. 369 Study Guide and Intervention, *CRM,* pp. 307, 312, 317, 322, 327, 332, 337, 342, 347	MathPASS: Tutorial Plus msmath3.net/self_check_quiz msmath3.net/extra_examples
INTERVENTION	Mixed Review	pp. 260, 265, 270, 275, 282, 289, 294, 299, 303	Cumulative Review, *CRM,* p. 370	
INTERVENTION	Error Analysis	Find the Error, pp. 281, 302	Find the Error, *TWE,* pp. 281, 302 Unlocking Misconceptions, *TWE,* pp. 273, 291 Tips for New Teachers, *TWE,* p. 292	
ASSESSMENT	Standardized Test Practice	pp. 260, 265, 270, 275, 277, 282, 284, 289, 294, 297, 299, 303, 309, 310–311	Standardized Test Practice, *CRM,* pp. 371–372	Standardized Test Practice CD-ROM msmath3.net/standardized_test
ASSESSMENT	Open-Ended Assessment	Writing Math, pp. 261, 264, 266, 269, 271, 274, 278, 283, 292, 305 Open-Ended, pp. 259, 264, 269, 274, 281, 288, 292, 298, 302 Standardized Test, p. 311	Modeling: *TWE,* pp. 269, 289 Speaking: *TWE,* pp. 265, 282, 294, 295 Writing: *TWE,* pp. 275, 299 Extended Response Assessment, *CRM,* p. 365	
ASSESSMENT	Chapter Assessment	Study Guide, pp. 306–308 Practice Test, p. 309	Multiple-Choice Tests (Forms 1, 2A, 2B), *CRM,* pp. 353–358 Free-Response Tests (Forms 2C, 2D, 3), *CRM,* pp. 359–364 Vocabulary Test/Review, *CRM,* p. 366	ExamView® Pro Testmaker (see below) MindJogger Videoquizzes msmath3.net/vocabulary_review msmath3.net/chapter_test

For more information on Yearly ProgressPro, see p. 252.

Glencoe Lesson	Yearly ProgressPro Skill Name
6-1	Line and Angle Relationships
6-2	Types of Triangles Solve Problems with Unknown Angles
6-3	Special Right Triangles
6-4	Classifying Quadrilaterals
6-5	Congruent Polygons
6-6	Symmetry
6-7	Reflections
6-8	Translations
6-9	Rotations

ExamView® Pro

Use ExamView® Pro Testmaker CD-ROM to:

- **Create multiple versions of tests.**
- **Create modified tests for inclusion students with one mouse click.**
- **Edit existing questions and add your own questions.**
- **Build tests aligned with state standards using built-in state curriculum correlations.**
- **Change English tests to Spanish with one mouse click and vice versa.**

Reading and Writing in Mathematics

READING in the Content Area

This online worksheet provides strategies for reading and analyzing Lesson 6-3, Line and Angle Relationships. Students are guided through questions about the main idea, subject matter, supporting details, conclusion, clarifying details, and vocabulary of the lesson.

Interactive Study Notebook With Foldables™ is a study organizer that provides helpful steps for students to follow to organize their notes for Chapter 6.

- Students use Noteables to record notes and to complete their Foldables as you present the material in Lessons 6-1 through 6-9.
- Noteables follow the *Teacher Wraparound Edition's* In-Class Examples and *Interactive Chalkboard CD-ROM.*

For more information on Reading and Writing in Mathematics, see pp. T6–T7.

Recommended Outside Reading for Students

Nonfiction

- Smoothey, Marion. *Let's Investigate Quadrilaterals.* Benchmark Books, ©1992.

  This book describes hands-on activities, puzzles, and games that teach about quadrilaterals. It's a fun way for students to reinforce the geometry concepts they have learned. Topics include parallel lines, angles, tiling patterns, and symmetry.

Fiction

- Dodds, Doyle Ann. *The Shape of Things. Candlewick Press,* ©1996.

  Basic shapes are joined to make familiar objects in a story format.

PROJECT CRISS℠ Study Skill

Study cards can be a helpful study aid for students learning new definitions and relationships. The cards shown at the right describe some angle relationships that students learn in Lesson 6-1. A name and sketch is on the front of the card, and the relationship of the angles is on the back. As students work through the chapter, have them make study cards for other geometry concepts. They can use the cards to quiz themselves or each other when preparing for tests.

Front	Back
adjacent angles (A, B, C; angles 1, 2)	$\angle 1$ and $\angle 2$ are adjacent angles. $m\angle ABC = m\angle 1 + m\angle 2$
complementary angles (A, D, B, C; 50°, 40°)	$\angle ABD$ and $\angle DBC$ are complementary angles. $m\angle ABD + m\angle DBC = 90°$

CReating Independence through Student-owned Strategies

For more information on Project CRISS, see p. T8.

CHAPTER 6

Making Connections

School-To-Home

Parent and Student Study Guide

Parents and students may work together to reinforce the concepts and skills of this chapter. These online worksheets are available in English and Spanish at msmath3.net/parent_student. A sample lesson is shown below.

Family Letters and Activities

Send a letter and activity for this chapter home to encourage family members to become active participants in their students' learning. (English: *Chapter 6 Resource Masters*, pp. ix–x; Spanish: log on to msmath3.net/family_letters)

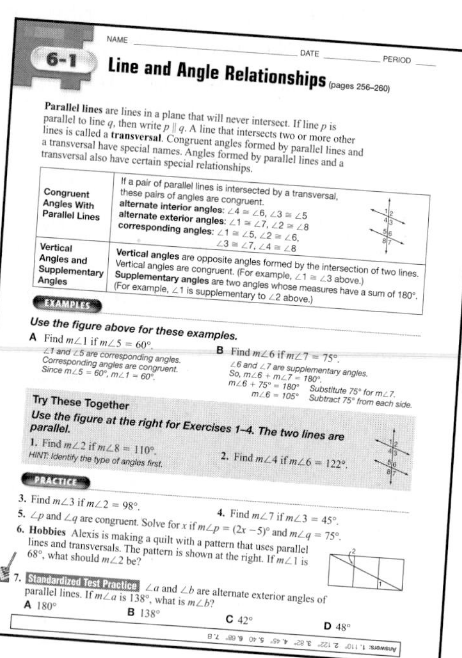

NAME ______ DATE ______ PERIOD ______

6-1 Line and Angle Relationships (pages 256–260)

Parallel lines are lines in a plane that will never intersect. If line p is parallel to line q, then write $p \parallel q$. A line that intersects two or more other lines is called a **transversal**. Congruent angles formed by parallel lines and a transversal have special names. Angles formed by parallel lines and a transversal also have certain special relationships.

Congruent Angles With Parallel Lines	If a pair of parallel lines is intersected by a transversal, these pairs of angles are congruent. **alternate interior angles:** $\angle 4 \cong \angle 6$, $\angle 3 \cong \angle 5$ **alternate exterior angles:** $\angle 1 \cong \angle 7$, $\angle 2 \cong \angle 8$ **corresponding angles:** $\angle 1 \cong \angle 5$, $\angle 2 \cong \angle 6$, $\angle 3 \cong \angle 7$, $\angle 4 \cong \angle 8$
Vertical Angles and Supplementary Angles	**Vertical angles** are opposite angles formed by the intersection of two lines. Vertical angles are congruent. (For example, $\angle 1 \cong \angle 3$ above.) **Supplementary angles** are two angles whose measures have a sum of 180°. (For example, $\angle 1$ is supplementary to $\angle 2$ above.)

EXAMPLES

Use the figure above for these examples.

A Find $m\angle 1$ if $m\angle 5 = 60°$.

$\angle 1$ and $\angle 5$ are corresponding angles. Corresponding angles are congruent. Since $m\angle 5 = 60°$, $m\angle 1 = 60°$.

B Find $m\angle 6$ if $m\angle 7 = 75°$.

$\angle 6$ and $\angle 7$ are supplementary angles. So, $m\angle 6 + m\angle 7 = 180°$.

$m\angle 6 + 75° = 180°$ Substitute 75° for $m\angle 7$.

$m\angle 6 = 105°$ Subtract 75° from each side.

Try These Together

Use the figure at the right for Exercises 1–4. The two lines are parallel.

1. Find $m\angle 2$ if $m\angle 8 = 110°$.
HINT: Identify the type of angles first.

2. Find $m\angle 4$ if $m\angle 6 = 122°$.

PRACTICE

3. Find $m\angle 3$ if $m\angle 2 = 98°$.
4. Find $m\angle 7$ if $m\angle 3 = 45°$.
5. $\angle p$ and $\angle q$ are congruent. Solve for x if $m\angle p = (2x - 5)°$ and $m\angle q = 75°$.
6. **Hobbies** Alexis is making a quilt with a pattern that uses parallel lines and transversals. The pattern is shown at the right. If $m\angle 1$ is 68°, what should $m\angle 2$ be?
7. **Standardized Test Practice** $\angle a$ and $\angle b$ are alternate exterior angles of parallel lines. If $m\angle a$ is 138°, what is $m\angle b$?
A 180° **B** 138° **C** 42° **D** 48°

Answers: 1. 110° 2. 122° 3. 82° 4. 45° 5. 40 6. 68° 7. B

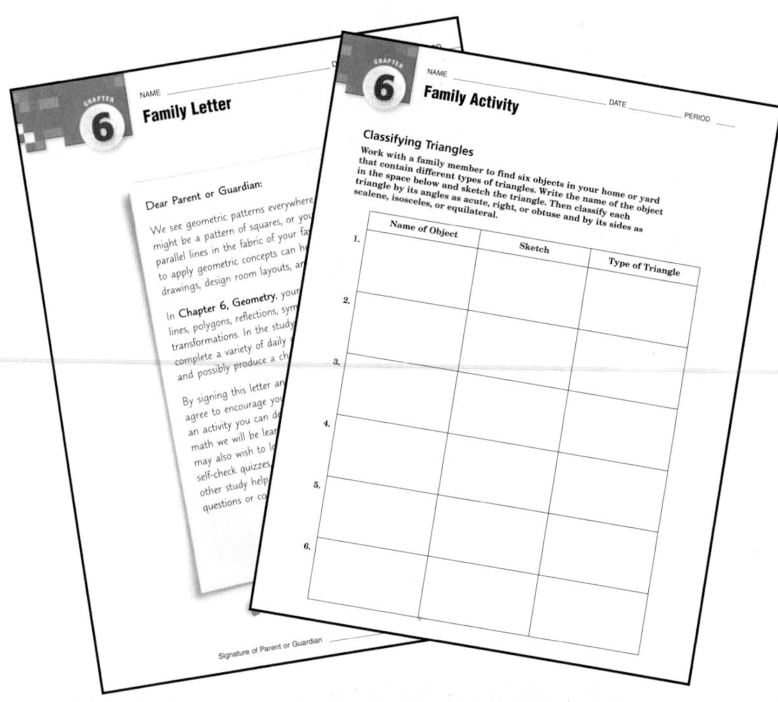

CHAPTER 6 NAME ______

Family Letter

Dear Parent or Guardian:

We see geometric patterns everywhere
might be a pattern of squares, or you
parallel lines in the fabric of your fa
to apply geometric concepts can he
drawings, design room layouts, an

In **Chapter 6, Geometry**, your
lines, polygons, reflections, sym
transformations. In the study
complete a variety of daily
and possibly produce a ch

By signing this letter an
agree to encourage yo
an activity you can d
math we will be lear
may also wish to l
self-check quizzes,
other study help
questions or co

Signature of Parent or Guardian ______

CHAPTER 6 NAME ______ DATE ______ PERIOD ______

Family Activity

Classifying Triangles

Work with a family member to find six objects in your home or yard that contain different types of triangles. Write the name of the object in the space below and sketch the triangle. Then classify each triangle by its angles as acute, right, or obtuse and by its sides as scalene, isosceles, or equilateral.

	Name of Object	Sketch	Type of Triangle
1.			
2.			
3.			
4.			
5.			
6.			

English Language Learner ELL

Lesson 6-1

Flexible Groups

Have groups of students create a concept map of all the new vocabulary listed in the lesson. Have students make their map in three columns: one with the term, the next with a pictorial representation of the term, and the last with the definition or explanation of the term. Give students chart paper on which to create and display their maps.

Lesson 6-1b

Using Manipulatives

Allow students the time to take a piece of paper and practice making arcs with their compasses. Many students have not used a compass before, and therefore, have difficulty making circles, arcs, and any kind of construction. After sufficient practice, allow students to work in pairs to complete the activity.

Lesson 6-3

Using Multisensory Activities

Have students use square dot paper and a straightedge to make a right triangle with both legs 8 units long. Have students use a protractor to verify that the triangle is a 45°-45° right triangle. Then, have students use triangular dot paper and a straightedge to make an equilateral triangle with sides 18 units long. Have them use a protractor to verify that the triangle is a 30°-60° right triangle. Ask students whether they notice any patterns.

MathScape™

This project was supported, in part, by the **National Science Foundation**

MathScape is a mathematics curriculum for grades 6–8 developed by the Seeing and Thinking Mathematically Project at the Education Development Center.

Slopes, Angles, and Ratios
Roads and Ramps

How to Use *MathScape* with Chapter 16

The unit *Roads and Ramps* can be used to enhance Lessons 6-2 and 6-3.

- **Introduce** → Before you begin **Lesson 6-2,** you can introduce angle relationships in right triangles by using the activity on pages 16–17.
- **Enrich** → After you complete **Lesson 6-3,** you can introduce trigonometry by using the activities on pages 250–251.

For other lessons in Chapter 6 that correlate to *MathScape,* see the chart on page T14.

Online Lesson Planner

USA TODAY® Education's Online site offers resources and interactive features connected to each day's newspaper. *Experience Today,* USA TODAY's® daily lesson plan, is available on the site and delivered daily to subscribers. This plan provides instruction for integrating USA TODAY® graphics and key editorial features into your mathematics classroom. Log on to **education.usatoday.com**.

USA TODAY Snapshots® in Chapter 6	
Lesson	**Snapshot**
6-9	Crafts are tops on this gift list

Quick Review Math Handbook

is Glencoe's mathematical handbook for students. The Hot Words section includes a glossary of terms while the Hot Topics section consists of explanations of key mathematical concepts. An exercise set is included to check students' understanding of the concepts. This valuable resource can be used as a reference in the classroom or for home study.

Lesson	Hot Topics Section	Lesson	Hot Topics Section
6-1,6-2	7-1, 9-3	**6-6**	7-3
6-3	7-1, 9-3	**6-7**	7-3
6-4	7-2	**6-8**	7-3
6-5	7-2, 9-3	**6-9**	7-3

Chapter 6 Notes

Key Chapter Objectives

Lessons 6-2 and 6-4 Find missing angles in triangles and quadrilaterals and classify them by their angles and sides.

Lesson 6-5 Identify congruent polygons.

Lesson 6-6 Identify line symmetry and rotational symmetry.

Lessons 6-7, 6-8, and 6-9 Graph reflections, translations, and rotations on a coordinate plane.

"How is geometry used in the game of pool?"

Point out to students that this is only one of many applications of the math that they are studying. Others are provided in the introduction to each lesson.

Vocabulary Builder, pp. vii–viii — ELL

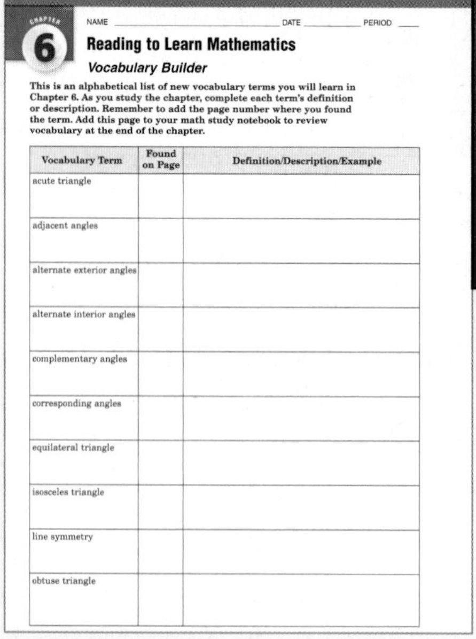

NAME ______ DATE ______ PERIOD ____

Chapter 6

Reading to Learn Mathematics

Vocabulary Builder

This is an alphabetical list of new vocabulary terms you will learn in Chapter 6. As you study the chapter, complete each term's definition or description. Remember to add the page number where you found the term. Add this page to your math study notebook to review vocabulary at the end of the chapter.

Vocabulary Term	Found on Page	Definition/Description/Example
acute triangle		
adjacent angles		
alternate exterior angles		
alternate interior angles		
complementary angles		
corresponding angles		
equilateral triangle		
isosceles triangle		
line symmetry		
obtuse triangle		

Chapter 6 Geometry

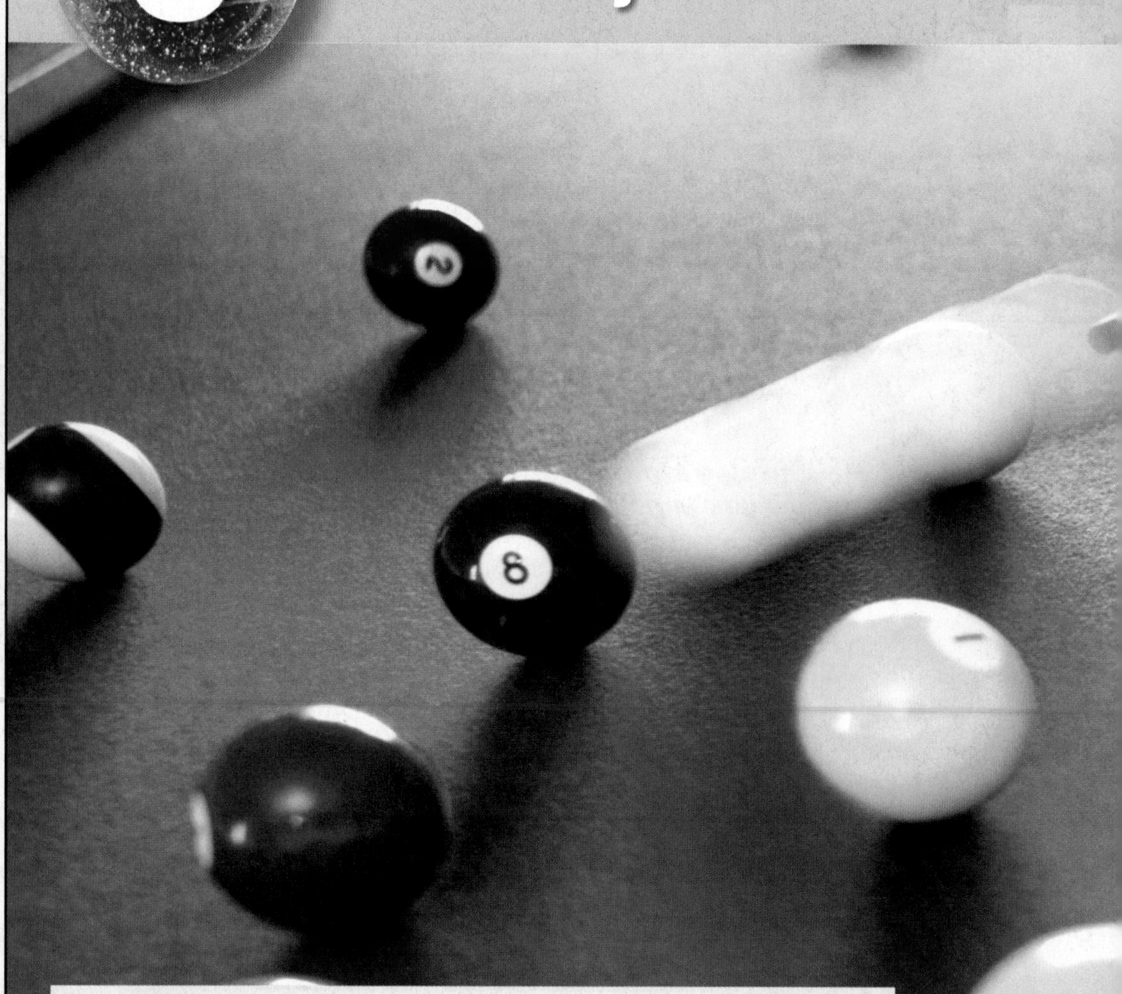

"How is geometry used in the game of pool?"

A billiard ball is struck so that it bounces off the cushion of a pool table and heads for a corner pocket. **The three angles created by the path of the ball and the cushion together form a straight angle that measures 180°.** Pool players use such angle relationships and the properties of reflections to make their shots.

You will solve problems about angle relationships in Lesson 6-1.

254 Chapter 6 Geometry

Vocabulary Builder

For a thorough vocabulary list with pronunciations of new words, give students the Vocabulary Builder worksheets from the *Chapter 6 Resource Masters.* Encourage them to complete the definition of each term as they progress through the chapter.

GETTING STARTED

▶ Diagnose Readiness

Take this quiz to see if you are ready to begin Chapter 6. Refer to the lesson number in parentheses for review.

Vocabulary Review

State whether each sentence is *true* or *false*. If *false*, replace the underlined word or number to make a true sentence.

1. For the right triangle shown, the Pythagorean Theorem states that $\underline{a^2 + c^2 = b^2}$. (Lesson 3-4)

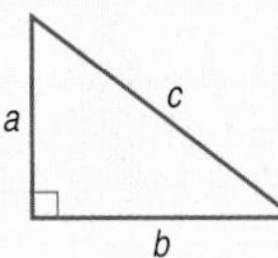

2. A rectangle is also a <u>polygon</u>. (Lesson 4-5) **true**

Prerequisite Skills **1. false; $a^2 + b^2 = c^2$**

Solve each equation. (Lesson 1-8)

3. $49 + b + 45 = 180$ **86**
4. $t + 98 + 55 = 180$ **27**
5. $15 + 67 + k = 180$ **98**

Find the missing side length of each right triangle. Round to the nearest tenth, if necessary. (Lesson 3-4) **7. 11.4 ft**

6. a, 8 m; b, 6 m **10 m**
7. b, 9 ft; a, 7 ft
8. a, 4 in.; c, 5 in. **3 in.**
9. c, 10 yd; a, 3 yd **9.5 yd**

Decide whether the figures are congruent. Write *yes* or *no* and explain your reasoning. (Lesson 4-5) **10–11. See margin.**

10.

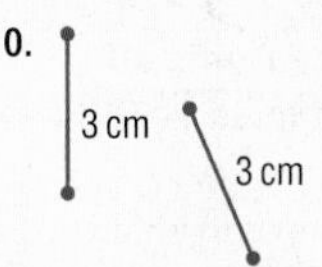

11.

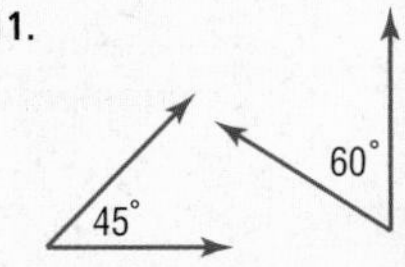

Geometry Make this Foldable to help you organize your notes. Begin with a plain piece of 11" × 17" paper.

STEP 1 **Fold** Fold the paper in fifths lengthwise.

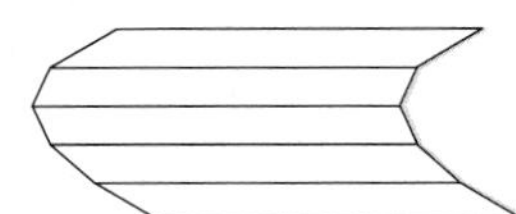

STEP 2 **Open and Fold** Fold a $2\frac{1}{2}$" tab along the short side. Then fold the rest in half.

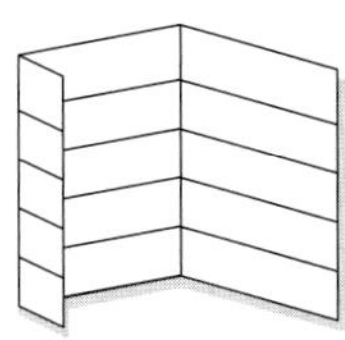

STEP 3 **Label** Draw lines along folds and label each section as shown.

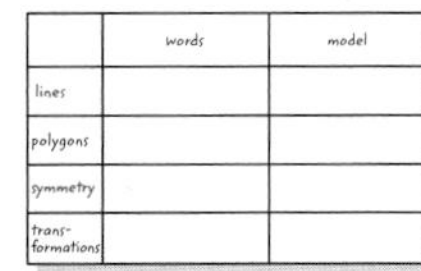

Chapter Notes Each time you find this logo throughout the chapter, use your *Noteables™: Interactive Study Notebook with Foldables™* or your own notebook to take notes. Begin your chapter notes with this Foldable activity.

Math Online **Readiness** To prepare yourself for this chapter with another quiz, visit **msmath3.net/chapter_readiness**

GETTING STARTED

Diagnose Readiness This section provides a review of the basic concepts needed before beginning Chapter 6. Page references are included for additional student help.

Prerequisite Skills review skills needed in this chapter.

Exercises	Needed for Lesson	Skill
3–5	6-2	Solve Equations
6–9	6-3	Find Missing Sides of Right Triangles
10–11	6-5	Determine Congruence

For more prerequisite skills, see:

- Getting Ready for the Next Lesson, at the end of each lesson
- Prerequisite Skills in the Student Handbook on pp. 600–615
- *Math Skills Maintenance Masters*

Answers

10. Yes; the segments have the same measure.
11. No; the angles do not have the same measure.

FOLDABLES Study Organizer

For more information about Foldables, see *Teaching Mathematics with Foldables.*

Use this Foldable table for student writing about geometry. After students make their Foldables, have them label the rows and columns as illustrated. Students use their Foldables to take notes, define terms, record concepts, and draw models. Discuss how the nine lessons in this chapter can be condensed into four general topics—lines, polygons, symmetry, and transformations. Have students select one thing that they included in their tables to share with the class as a mini-lesson review.

6-1 Lesson Notes

Lesson Resources

Chapter 6 Resource Masters
- Study Guide and Intervention, p. 307
- Practice: Skills, p. 308
- Practice: Word Problems, p. 309
- Reading to Learn Mathematics, p. 310
- Enrichment, p. 311

MathPASS Tutorial CD-ROM, 43

Parent and Student Study Guide Online Worksheets, 6-1

Noteables™: Interactive Study Notebook with Foldables™, 6-1

FAST FILE

1 Focus

5-Minute Check 6-1

Use as a quiz or review of Chapter 5. (Also available as a transparency)

Bellringer

Communication Draw a 90° angle with a right angle symbol on the chalkboard. Ask students whether they know the measure of the angle. Have them discuss the meaning of the right angle symbol. Next draw a line on the chalkboard. Ask students what kind of angle is represented. Discuss how the line can be defined as an angle with a measure of 180°.

Reading to Learn Mathematics, p. 310 ELL

NAME ______ DATE ______ PERIOD ______

6-1 Reading to Learn Mathematics

Line and Angle Relationships

Pre-Activity *Complete the Mini Lab at the top of page 256 in your textbook. Write your answers below.*

1. For each set of intersecting lines, identify the pairs of angles that have the same measure. ∠1 and ∠3, ∠2 and ∠4
2. What is true about the sum of the measures of the angles sharing a side? Their sum is 180°.

Reading the Lesson

3. Angles can be acute, right, obtuse, or straight. For each one of these possibilities draw an example of the angle.

acute angle Sample answer: | right angle Sample answer:

6-1 Line and Angle Relationships

What You'll LEARN

Identify special pairs of angles and relationships of angles formed by two parallel lines cut by a transversal.

NEW Vocabulary

acute angle
right angle
obtuse angle
straight angle
vertical angles
adjacent angles
complementary angles
supplementary angles
perpendicular lines
parallel lines
transversal

HANDS-ON Mini Lab

Materials
- straightedge
- protractor
- colored pencils
- notebook paper

Work with a partner.

STEP 1 Draw two different pairs of intersecting lines and label the angles formed as shown.

STEP 2 Find and record the measure of each angle.

STEP 3 Color angles that have the same measure.

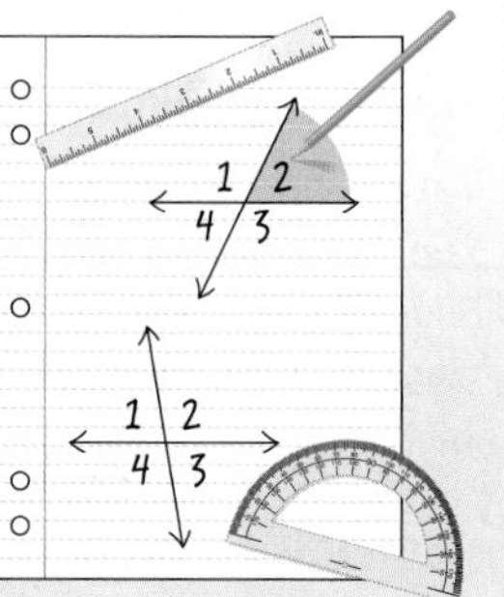

1. For each set of intersecting lines, identify the pairs of angles that have the same measure.
2. What is true about the sum of the measures of the angles sharing a side?

1. ∠1 and ∠3, ∠2 and ∠4 2. Their sum is 180°.

Angles can be classified by their measures.

- **Acute angles** have measures less than 90°.
- **Right angles** have measures equal to 90°.
- **Obtuse angles** have measures between 90° and 180°.
- **Straight angles** have measures equal to 180°.

Pairs of angles can be classified by their relationship to each other. Recall that angles with the same measure are congruent.

Noteables™ **Key Concept: Special Pairs of Angles**

Vertical angles are opposite angles formed by intersecting lines. Vertical angles are congruent.

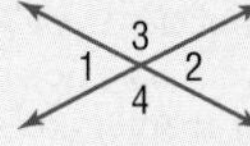

∠1 and ∠2 are vertical angles. ∠1 ≅ ∠2

Adjacent angles have the same vertex, share a common side, and do not overlap.

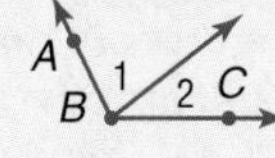

∠1 and ∠2 are adjacent angles. $m\angle ABC = m\angle 1 + m\angle 2$

The sum of the measures of **complementary angles** is 90°.

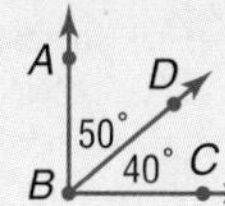

∠ABD and ∠DBC are complementary angles. $m\angle ABD + m\angle DBC = 90°$

The sum of the measures of **supplementary angles** is 180°.

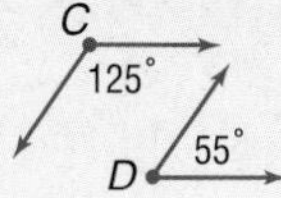

∠C and ∠D are supplementary angles. $m\angle C + m\angle D = 180°$

TEACHING TIP

Point out to students that complementary and supplementary angles may or may not be adjacent angles.

READING in the Content Area

For strategies in reading this lesson, visit **msmath3.net/reading.**

NCLB NO CHILD LEFT BEHIND

The goals of the NCLB Act include a stronger emphasis on reading. The **Reading in the Content Area** link helps students become proficient readers.

READING Math

Angle Measure Read *m∠1 as the measure of angle 1.*

EXAMPLES Classify Angles and Angle Pairs

Classify each angle or angle pair using all names that apply.

1 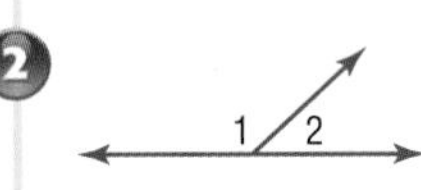

$m\angle 1$ is greater than 90°
So, ∠1 is an obtuse angle.

2 

∠1 and ∠2 are adjacent angles since they have the same vertex, share a common side, and do not overlap. Together, they form a straight angle measuring 180°. So, ∠1 and ∠2 are also supplementary angles.

Your Turn **Classify each angle or angle pair using all names that apply.** b. complementary

a. right

b. 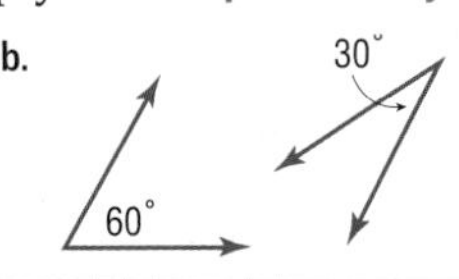

c. 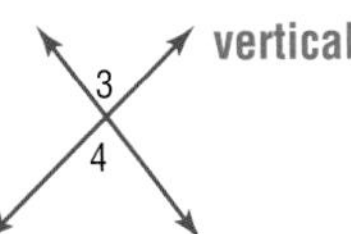

vertical

TEACHING TIP
Remind students that the symbol in Exercise a means that the angle is a right angle.

You can use the relationships between pairs of angles to find missing measures.

EXAMPLE Find a Missing Angle Measure

3 **In the figure, $m\angle ABC = 90°$. Find the value of x.**

$m\angle ABD + m\angle DBC =$	90	Write an equation.
$x + 65 =$	90	$m\angle ABD = x$ and $m\angle DBC = 65$
$-65 = -65$		Subtract 65 from each side.
$x =$	25	Simplify.

Your Turn **Find the value of x in each figure.**

d. 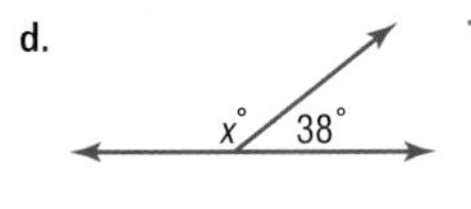

142

e. 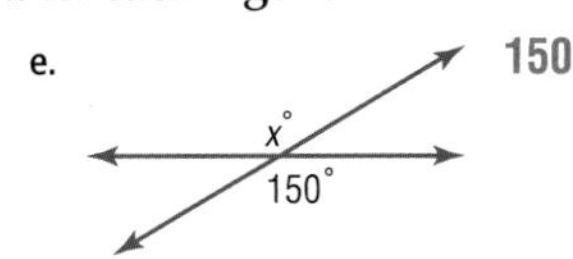

150

TEACHING TIP
Students will learn more about planes in Chapter 7.

Lines that intersect at right angles are called **perpendicular lines**. Two lines in a plane that never intersect or cross are called **parallel lines**.

A red right angle symbol indicates that lines *m* and *n* are perpendicular.

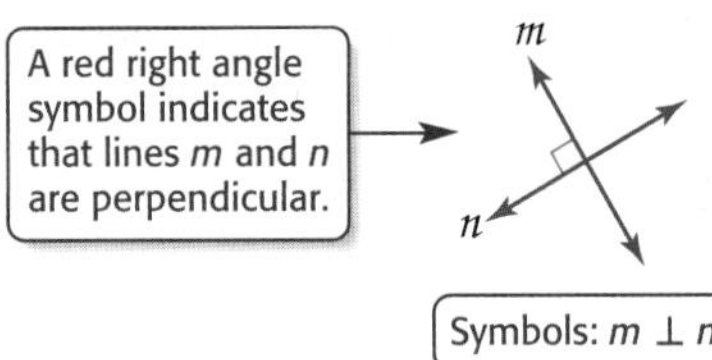

Symbols: $m \perp n$

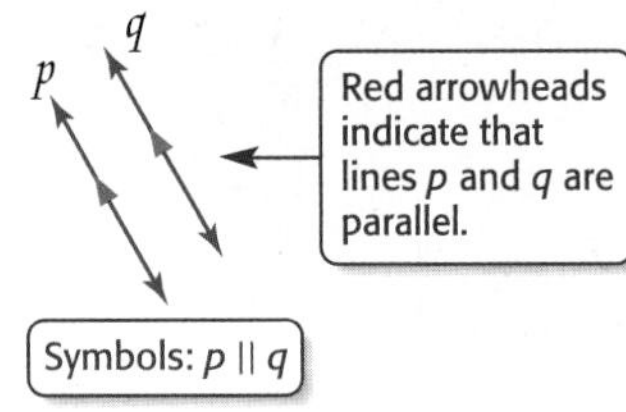

Red arrowheads indicate that lines *p* and *q* are parallel.

Symbols: $p \parallel q$

READING Math

Parallel and Perpendicular Lines
Read $m \perp n$ as *m is perpendicular to n*. Read $p \parallel q$ as *p is parallel to q*.

msmath3.net/extra_examples

2 Teach

Noteables™

As you work the **In-Class Examples,** have students follow along in their *Noteables™: Interactive Study Notebook with Foldables™*, or have students work the examples in their notebooks.

In-Class Examples

Classify each angle or angle pair using all names that apply.

1  acute

2 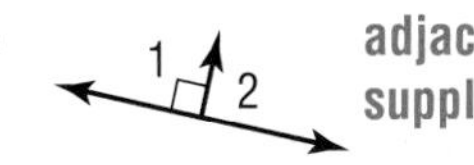 adjacent, supplementary

3 The two angles below are supplementary. Find the value of x. 25

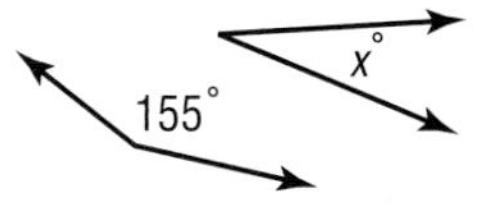

Using Manipulatives When using protractors, a small modification can be helpful. Drill a small hole at the cross hairs. Tie a string through the hole. When the knot is lined up over the cross hairs, the student can pull the string up along the angle side they are measuring and the string will indicate the correct number of degrees.

DAILY INTERVENTION Differentiated Instruction

Visual/Spatial Have students create a painting, drawing, or sculpture that demonstrates the relationships between vertical angles, adjacent angles, alternate interior angles, alternate exterior angles, or corresponding angles. Provide class time for them to display and describe their artwork to the other students.

In-Class Example

INTERACTIVE CHALKBOARD PowerPoint® Presentations

4 **BRIDGES** The sketch below shows a simple bridge design used in the 19th century. The top beam and floor of the bridge are parallel. If $m\angle 1 = 60°$ and $m\angle 3 = 45°$, find $m\angle 2$ and $m\angle 4$. **$m\angle 2 = 45°$ and $m\angle 4 = 75°$**

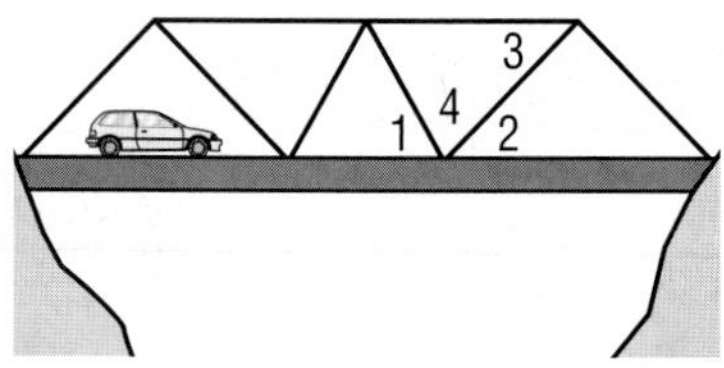

A line that intersects two or more other lines is called a **transversal**. When a transversal intersects two lines, eight angles are formed that have special names.

If the two lines cut by a transversal are *parallel*, then these special pairs of angles are congruent.

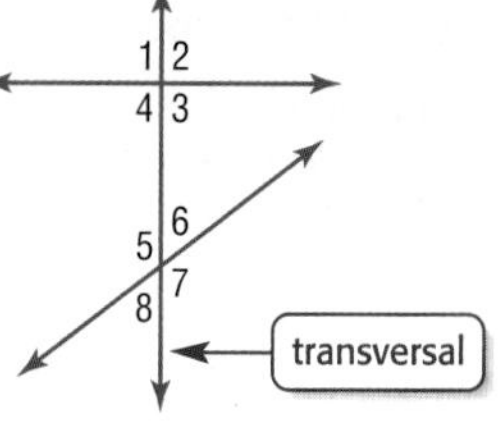

READING Math

Interior and Exterior Angles When two lines are cut by a transversal, the *interior angles* lie inside the two lines, and the *exterior angles* lie outside the two lines.

Noteables™ Key Concept: Parallel Lines

If two parallel lines are cut by a transversal, then the following statements are true.

- **Alternate interior angles**, those on opposite sides of the transversal and inside the other two lines, are congruent.
  Example: $\angle 2 \cong \angle 8$
- **Alternate exterior angles**, those on opposite sides of the transversal and outside the other two lines, are congruent.
  Example: $\angle 4 \cong \angle 6$
- **Corresponding angles**, those in the same position on the two lines in relation to the transversal, are congruent.
  Example: $\angle 3 \cong \angle 7$

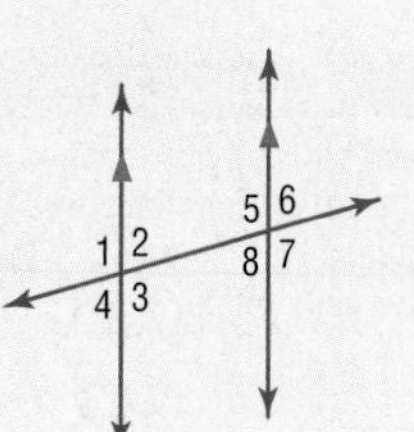

REAL-LIFE CAREERS

How Does a Carpenter Use Math?

Carpenters use angle relationships when cutting lumber to build anything from furniture to houses.

Math Online Research

For information about a career as a carpenter, visit: msmath3.net/careers

You can use congruent angle relationships to solve real-life problems.

EXAMPLE Find an Angle Measure

4 **CARPENTRY You are building a bench for a picnic table. The top of the bench will be parallel to the ground. If $m\angle 1 = 148°$, find $m\angle 2$ and $m\angle 3$.**

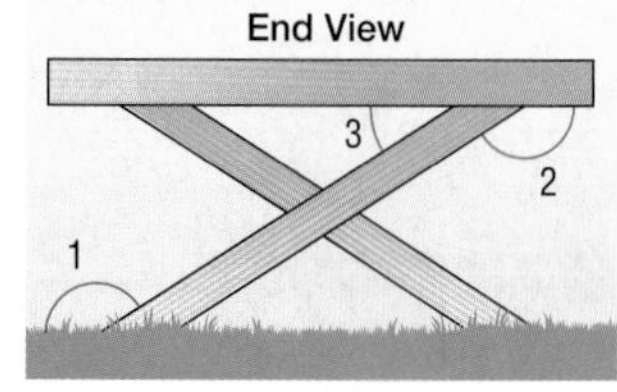

Since $\angle 1$ and $\angle 2$ are alternate interior angles, they are congruent. So, $m\angle 2 = 148°$.

Since $\angle 2$ and $\angle 3$ are supplementary, the sum of their measures is $180°$. Therefore, $m\angle 3 = 180° - 148°$ or $32°$.

Your Turn **For Exercises f–h, use the figure at the right.**

f. Find $m\angle 2$ if $m\angle 1 = 63°$. **63°**

g. Find $m\angle 3$ if $m\angle 8 = 100°$. **100°**

h. Find $m\angle 4$ if $m\angle 7 = 82°$. **98°**

258 Chapter 6 Geometry

Students practice the same concepts in Exercises 13–28 and 30–37 if they are assigned odd or even problems.

Skill and Concept Check

1. **OPEN ENDED** Draw a pair of complementary angles. **1–2. See margin.**
2. **Draw** a pair of parallel lines and a third line intersecting them. Choose one angle and mark it with a ✔. Then mark all other angles that are congruent to that angle with a ✔. Explain.

GUIDED PRACTICE

Classify each angle or angle pair using all names that apply.

3.  **straight**
4. 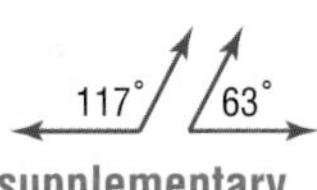

supplementary
5. 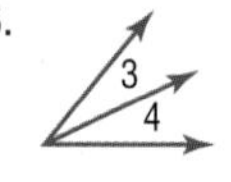

adjacent

Find the value of x in each figure.

6.  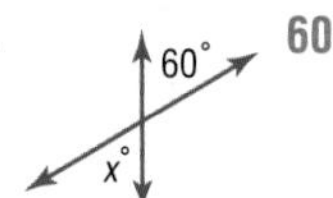

60
7. 

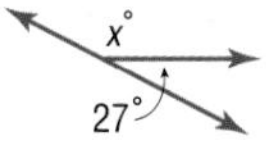

153
8. 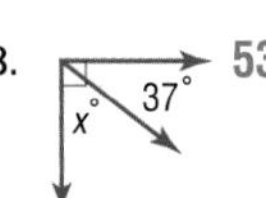

53

For Exercises 9–12, use the figure at the right.

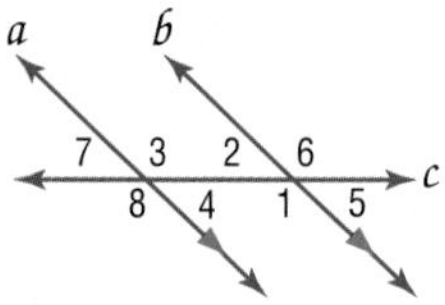

9. Find $m\angle 4$ if $m\angle 5 = 43°$. **43°**
10. Find $m\angle 1$ if $m\angle 3 = 135°$. **135°**
11. Find $m\angle 6$ if $m\angle 8 = 126°$. **126°**
12. Find $m\angle A$ if $m\angle B = 15°$ and $\angle A$ and $\angle B$ are supplementary. **165°**

★ indicates increased difficulty

Practice and Applications

Classify each angle or angle pair using all names that apply.

13. 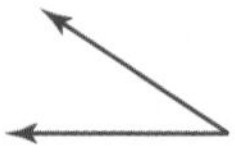 **acute**
14.  **obtuse**
15. 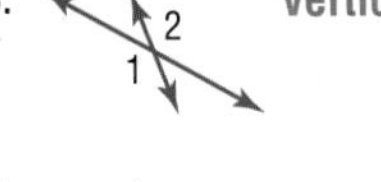

vertical
16. 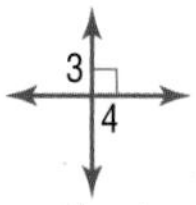 **vertical**
17. 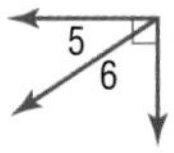 **adjacent, complementary**
18. 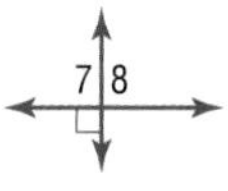 **adjacent, supplementary**

Find the value of x in each figure.

19. 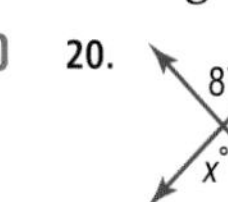

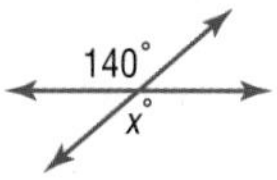

140
20. 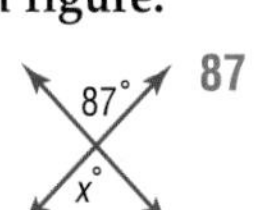

87
21. 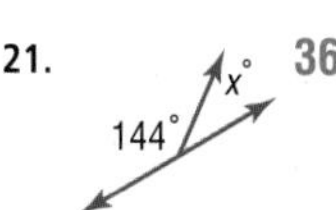

36
22. 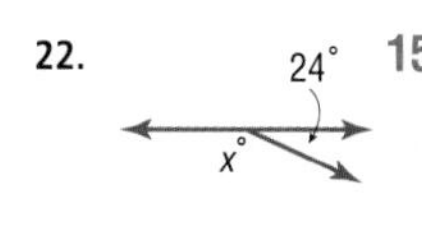

156
23. 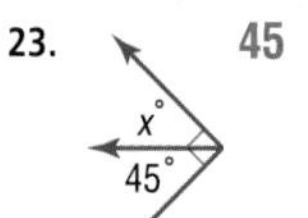

45
24. 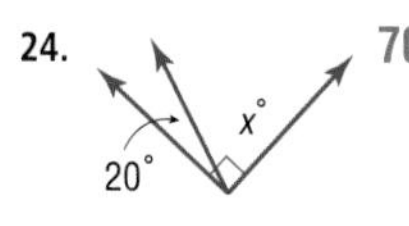

70
25. 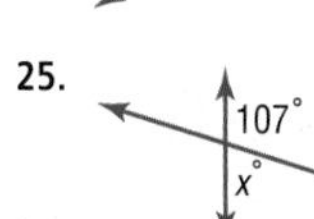

73
26. 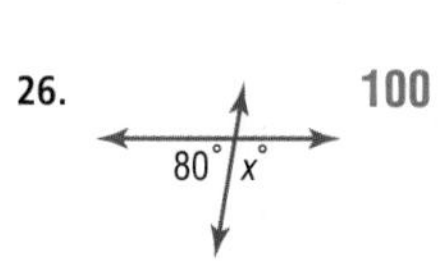

100

HOMEWORK HELP	
For Exercises	See Examples
13–18	1, 2
19–29	3
30–38	4

Extra Practice See pages 629, 653.

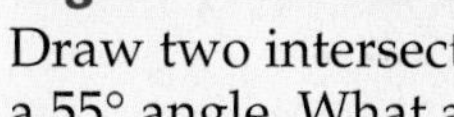

3 Practice/Apply

FOLDABLES™ Follow-Up Remind students to include information in words and symbols on what they learn about line and angle relationships in the "Lines" section of their Foldable tables.

About the Exercises...

Guided Practice Key

Exercises	Examples
3–5	1, 2
6–8	3
9–12	4

Assignment Guide

Basic: 13–25 odd, 29–37 odd, 39–49

Average: 13–37 odd, 39–49

Enriched: 14–38 even, 39–46 (Optional: 47–49)

Answers

1. 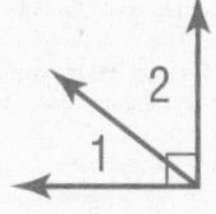

2. Sample answer:

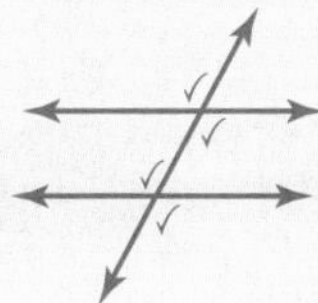

4 Assess

Higher-Level Thinking

Draw two intersecting lines that form a 55° angle. What are the measures of the other three angles formed by the lines? **55°, 125°, 125°** What is the sum of all four angles? **360°** Is this always the sum of four angles formed by two intersecting lines? **yes**

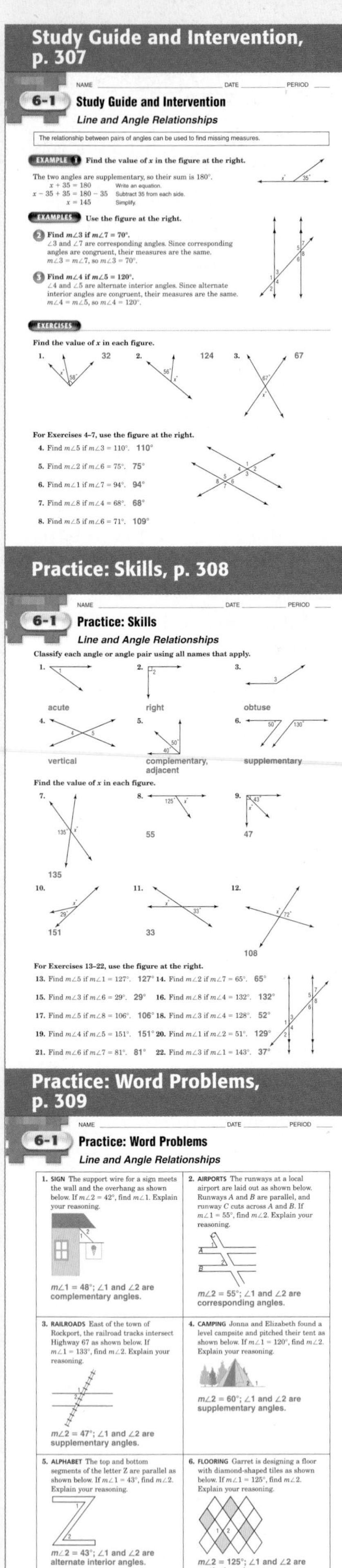

Study Guide and Intervention, p. 307

NAME ______ DATE ______ PERIOD ______

6-1 Study Guide and Intervention
Line and Angle Relationships

The relationship between pairs of angles can be used to find missing measures.

EXAMPLE 1 **Find the value of x in the figure at the right.**

The two angles are supplementary, so their sum is 180°.
$x + 35 = 180$ Write an equation.
$x - 35 + 35 = 180 - 35$ Subtract 35 from each side.
$x = 145$ Simplify.

EXAMPLES **Use the figure at the right.**

2 **Find $m\angle 3$ if $m\angle 7 = 70°$.**
$\angle 3$ and $\angle 7$ are corresponding angles. Since corresponding angles are congruent, their measures are the same. $m\angle 3 = m\angle 7$, so $m\angle 3 = 70°$.

3 **Find $m\angle 4$ if $m\angle 5 = 120°$.**
$\angle 4$ and $\angle 5$ are alternate interior angles. Since alternate interior angles are congruent, their measures are the same. $m\angle 4 = m\angle 5$, so $m\angle 4 = 120°$.

EXERCISES

Find the value of x in each figure.

1. 32
2. 124
3. 67

For Exercises 4–7, use the figure at the right.

4. Find $m\angle 5$ if $m\angle 3 = 110°$. 110°
5. Find $m\angle 2$ if $m\angle 6 = 75°$. 75°
6. Find $m\angle 1$ if $m\angle 7 = 94°$. 94°
7. Find $m\angle 8$ if $m\angle 4 = 68°$. 68°
8. Find $m\angle 5$ if $m\angle 6 = 71°$. 109°

Practice: Skills, p. 308

NAME ______ DATE ______ PERIOD ______

6-1 Practice: Skills
Line and Angle Relationships

Classify each angle or angle pair using all names that apply.

1. acute
2. right
3. obtuse
4. vertical
5. complementary, adjacent
6. supplementary

Find the value of x in each figure.

7. 135
8. 55
9. 47
10. 151
11. 33
12. 108

For Exercises 13–22, use the figure at the right.

13. Find $m\angle 5$ if $m\angle 1 = 127°$. 127°
14. Find $m\angle 2$ if $m\angle 7 = 65°$. 65°
15. Find $m\angle 3$ if $m\angle 6 = 29°$. 29°
16. Find $m\angle 8$ if $m\angle 4 = 132°$. 132°
17. Find $m\angle 5$ if $m\angle 8 = 106°$. 106°
18. Find $m\angle 3$ if $m\angle 4 = 128°$. 52°
19. Find $m\angle 4$ if $m\angle 5 = 151°$. 151°
20. Find $m\angle 1$ if $m\angle 2 = 51°$. 129°
21. Find $m\angle 6$ if $m\angle 7 = 81°$. 81°
22. Find $m\angle 3$ if $m\angle 1 = 143°$. 37°

Practice: Word Problems, p. 309

NAME ______ DATE ______ PERIOD ______

6-1 Practice: Word Problems
Line and Angle Relationships

1. **SIGN** The support wire for a sign meets the wall and the overhang as shown below. If $m\angle 2 = 42°$, find $m\angle 1$. Explain your reasoning.
$m\angle 1 = 48°$; $\angle 1$ and $\angle 2$ are complementary angles.

2. **AIRPORTS** The runways at a local airport are laid out as shown below. Runways *A* and *B* are parallel, and runway *C* cuts across *A* and *B*. If $m\angle 1 = 55°$, find $m\angle 2$. Explain your reasoning.
$m\angle 2 = 55°$; $\angle 1$ and $\angle 2$ are corresponding angles.

3. **RAILROADS** East of the town of Rockport, the railroad tracks intersect Highway 67 as shown below. If $m\angle 1 = 133°$, find $m\angle 2$. Explain your reasoning.
$m\angle 2 = 47°$; $\angle 1$ and $\angle 2$ are supplementary angles.

4. **CAMPING** Jonna and Elizabeth found a level campsite and pitched their tent as shown below. If $m\angle 1 = 120°$, find $m\angle 2$. Explain your reasoning.
$m\angle 2 = 60°$; $\angle 1$ and $\angle 2$ are supplementary angles.

5. **ALPHABET** The top and bottom segments of the letter Z are parallel as shown below. If $m\angle 1 = 43°$, find $m\angle 2$. Explain your reasoning.
$m\angle 2 = 43°$; $\angle 1$ and $\angle 2$ are alternate interior angles.

6. **FLOORING** Garret is designing a floor with diamond-shaped tiles as shown below. If $m\angle 1 = 125°$, find $m\angle 2$. Explain your reasoning.
$m\angle 2 = 125°$; $\angle 1$ and $\angle 2$ are vertical angles.

★ 27. **ALGEBRA** Angles P and Q are vertical angles. If $m\angle P = 45°$ and $m\angle Q = (x + 25)°$, find the value of x. **20**

★ 28. **ALGEBRA** Angles A and B are supplementary. If $m\angle A = 2x°$ and $m\angle B = 80°$, find the value of x. **50**

29. **POOL** Aaron is trying a complicated pool shot. He wants to hit the number 8 ball into the corner pocket. If Aaron knows the angle measures shown in the diagram, what angle x must the path of the ball take to go into the corner pocket? **70°**

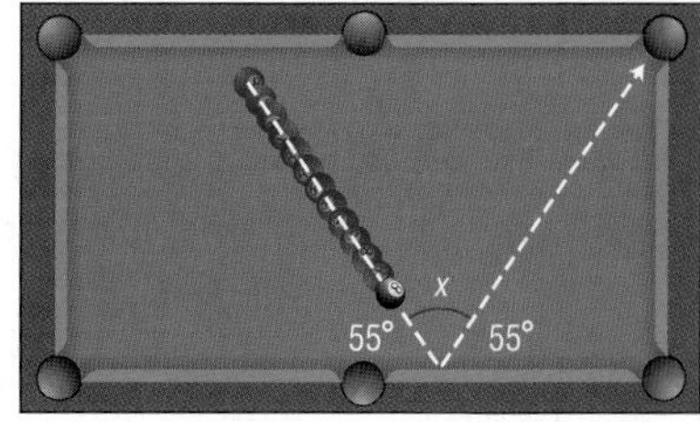

31. 111° 33. 63° 35. 59° 37. 82°

For Exercises 30–37, use the figure at the right.

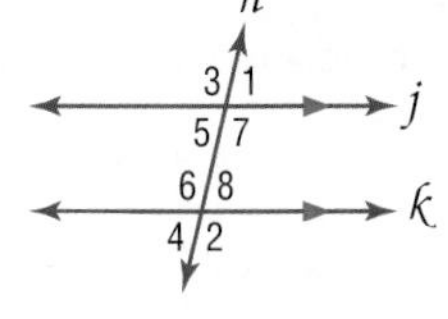

30. Find $m\angle 2$ if $m\angle 3 = 108°$. **108°**
31. Find $m\angle 6$ if $m\angle 7 = 111°$.
32. Find $m\angle 5$ if $m\angle 8 = 85°$. **85°**
33. Find $m\angle 8$ if $m\angle 1 = 63°$.
34. Find $m\angle 8$ if $m\angle 2 = 50°$. **130°**
35. Find $m\angle 4$ if $m\angle 1 = 59°$.
36. Find $m\angle 5$ if $m\angle 4 = 72°$. **72°**
37. Find $m\angle 5$ if $m\angle 7 = 98°$.

38. **PARKING** Engineers angled the parking spaces along a downtown street so that cars could park and back out easily. All of the lines marking the parking spaces are parallel. If $m\angle 1 = 55°$, find $m\angle 2$. Explain your reasoning.
55°; ∠1 and ∠2 are corresponding angles.

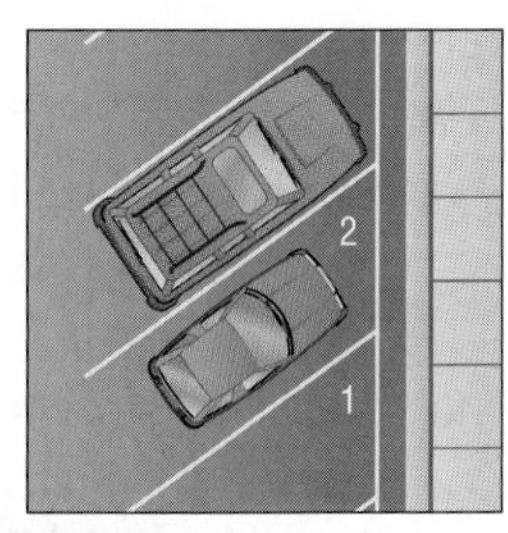

39. **CRITICAL THINKING** Suppose two parallel lines are cut by a transversal. How are the interior angles on the same side of the transversal related? Use a diagram to explain your reasoning. **See margin.**

Spiral Review with Standardized Test Practice

40. **SHORT RESPONSE** If $m\angle A = 81°$ and $\angle A$ and $\angle B$ are complementary, what is $m\angle B$? **9°**

41. **MULTIPLE CHOICE** Find the value of x in the figure at the right. **A**

Ⓐ 30 Ⓑ 40 Ⓒ 116 Ⓓ 124

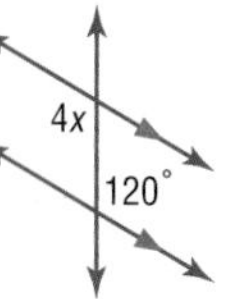

42. A savings account starts with $560. If the simple interest rate is 3%, find the total amount after 18 months. (Lesson 5-8) **$585.20**

Find each percent of change. Round to the nearest tenth if necessary. State whether the percent of change is an *increase* or a *decrease*. (Lesson 5-7)

43. original: 20
new: 27
35%; increase

44. original: 45
new: 18
60%; decrease

45. original: 620
new: 31
95%; decrease

46. original: 260
new: 299
15%; increase

GETTING READY FOR THE NEXT LESSON

PREREQUISITE SKILL Solve each equation. Check your solution. (Lesson 1-8)

47. $n + 32 + 67 = 180$ **81**
48. $45 + 89 + x = 180$ **46**
49. $180 = 120 + a + 15$ **45**

Answer

39. They are supplementary. Sample answer: In the diagram, ∠1 and ∠2 are supplementary. Since ∠1 and ∠3 are alternate interior angles, ∠1 ≅ ∠3. Therefore, replacing ∠1 with ∠3, ∠3 and ∠2 are supplementary.

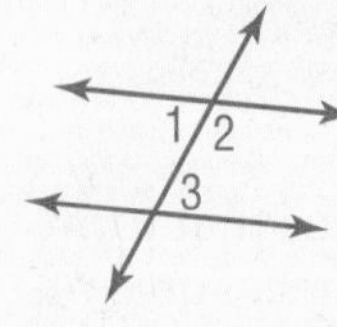

6-1b HANDS-ON LAB

A Follow-Up of Lesson 6-1

Constructing Parallel Lines

In this lab, you will construct a line parallel to a given line.

What You'll LEARN

Construct a line parallel to a given line.

Materials

- compass
- straightedge
- paper

ACTIVITY

STEP 1 Draw a line and label it p. Then draw and label a point A not on line p.

STEP 2 Draw a line through point A so that it intersects line p. Label the point of intersection point B.

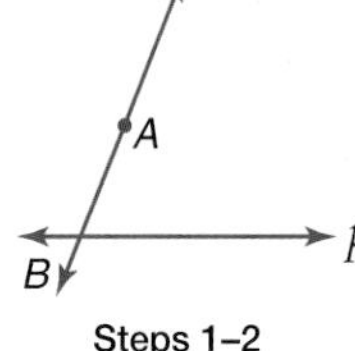

Steps 1–2

STEP 3 Place the compass at point B and draw a large arc. Label the point where the arc crosses line p as point C, and label where it crosses line AB as point D.

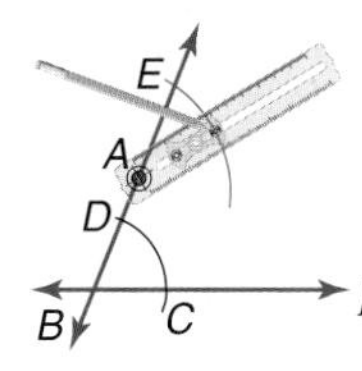

Steps 3–4

STEP 4 With the same compass opening, place the compass at point A and draw a large arc. Label the point of intersection with line AB as point E.

STEP 5 Use your compass to measure the distance between points D and C.

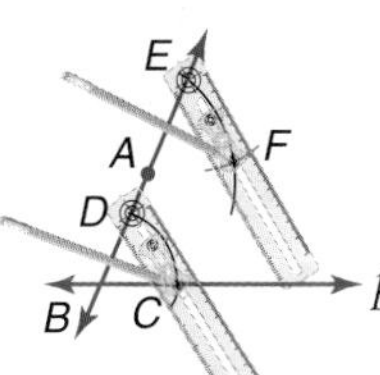

Steps 5–6

STEP 6 With the compass opened the same amount, place the compass at point E and draw an arc to intersect the arc already drawn. Label this point F.

STEP 7 Draw a line through points A and F. Label this line q. You have drawn $q \parallel p$.

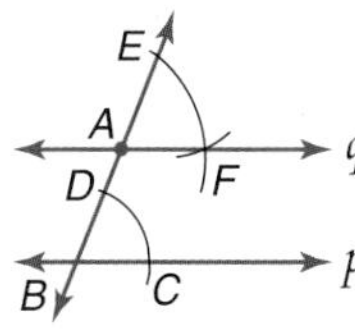

Step 7

Your Turn Draw a line. Then construct a line parallel to it. **See students' work.**

Writing Math

Work with a partner. Use the information in the activity above.

1. **Classify** $\angle DBC$ and $\angle FAE$ in relationship to lines p, q, and transversal AB. **corresponding angles**
2. **Explain** why you should expect $\angle ABC$ to be congruent to $\angle FAE$.

2. Corresponding angles formed by parallel lines and a transversal are congruent.

6-1b HANDS-ON LAB Lesson Notes

Lesson Resources

Teaching Mathematics with Manipulatives

- student recording sheet 6-1b

Glencoe Mathematics Classroom Manipulative Kit

- compass
- ruler (straightedge)

GETTING STARTED

Teaching Tip Students may be unfamiliar with using a compass. Observe as they practice using it before they start the lab.

TEACH

- Have students read through all steps of the lab and study the drawings carefully before they start the **Activity**. This will help them understand the reasons for the procedures.
- In Step 5, students are told to measure a distance. Explain that students do not need to determine a number value. They only need to be sure that the compass is opened to the distance between points D and C.

ASSESS

Observe as students solve the **Your Turn** exercise. They should:

- have the compass placed exactly on the angle's vertex when drawing the first arc,
- have the compass opened the correct distance when drawing the intersecting arcs, and
- draw the second line through the point of intersection of the arcs.

Discuss the **Writing Math** exercises. Refer students to the drawing in Step 7 of the **Activity** to answer these questions.

6-2 Lesson Notes

Lesson Resources

Chapter 6 Resource Masters

- Study Guide and Intervention, p. 312
- Practice: Skills, p. 313
- Practice: Word Problems, p. 314
- Reading to Learn Mathematics, p. 315
- Enrichment, p. 316

FAST FILE

Parent and Student Study Guide Online Worksheets, 6-2

Noteables™: Interactive Study Notebook with Foldables™, 6-2

1 Focus

5-Minute Check 6-2

Use as a quiz or review of Lesson 6-1. (Also available as a transparency)

Bellringer

Reading Mathematics Explain that the term *isosceles* comes from the Greek words *isos*, meaning "equal," and *skelos*, meaning "leg." Draw an isosceles triangle on the chalkboard. Have several students come up to measure the triangle's legs. Then discuss as a class why the name is appropriate. Encourage students to use a dictionary to research word parts whenever they are introduced to new mathematical terms.

Reading to Learn Mathematics, p. 315 ELL

NAME ______ DATE ______ PERIOD ____

6-2 Reading to Learn Mathematics

Triangles and Angles

Pre-Activity *Complete the Mini Lab at the top of page 262 in your textbook. Write your answers below.*

1. What do you think is the sum of the measures of the three angles of any triangle? Explain your reasoning. 180°; They form a straight line.

Reading the Lesson

2. How can you determine whether a triangle is a right triangle? Sample answer: If the triangle has a 90° angle, then it is a right triangle.
3. If one angle of a triangle is either right or obtuse, what must be true of the other two angles? They must both be acute.
4. Complete the table.

Type of Triangle	Number of Congruent Sides
[illegible]lene	[illegible]ngruent sides

6-2 Triangles and Angles

What You'll LEARN

Find missing angle measures in triangles and classify triangles by their angles and sides.

NEW Vocabulary

triangle
acute triangle
obtuse triangle
right triangle
scalene triangle
isosceles triangle
equilateral triangle

HANDS-ON Mini Lab

Materials

- paper
- straightedge
- colored pencils
- scissors

Work with a partner.

Investigate the relationship among the measures of the angles of a triangle.

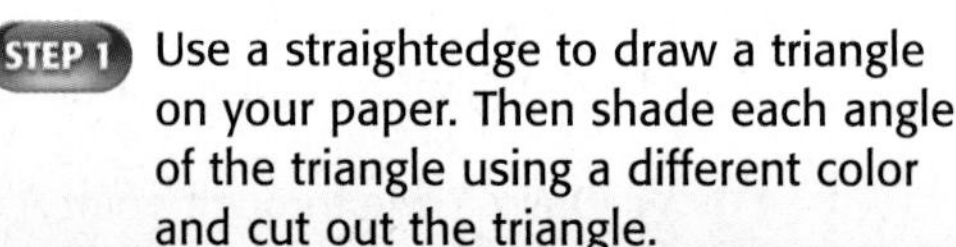

STEP 1 Use a straightedge to draw a triangle on your paper. Then shade each angle of the triangle using a different color and cut out the triangle.

STEP 2 Cut off each angle and arrange the pieces as shown so that the three angles are adjacent.

Repeat the steps above with several other triangles.

1. What do you think is the sum of the measures of the three angles of any triangle? Explain your reasoning.

1. 180°; They form a straight angle.

A **triangle** is a figure formed by three line segments that intersect only at their endpoints. Recall that triangles are named by the letters at their vertices.

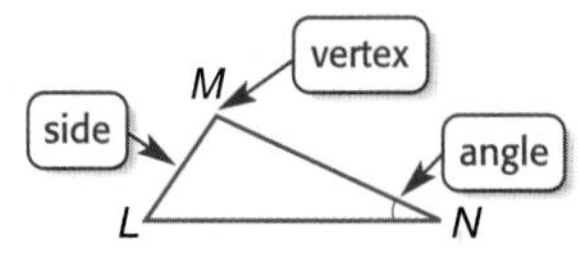

Triangle *LMN* is written $\triangle LMN$.

Noteables™ **Key Concept: Angles of a Triangle**

Words	The sum of the measures of the angles of a triangle is 180°.	**Model**
Symbols	$x + y + z = 180$	

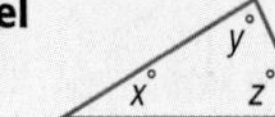

READING Math

Naming Triangles Read $\triangle RST$ as *triangle RST*.

EXAMPLE Find a Missing Angle Measure

1 **Find the value of x in $\triangle RST$.**

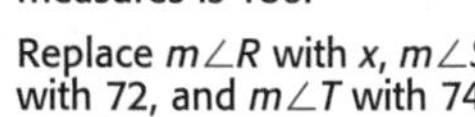

$m\angle R + m\angle S + m\angle T = 180$	The sum of the measures is 180.
$x + 72 + 74 = 180$	Replace $m\angle R$ with x, $m\angle S$ with 72, and $m\angle T$ with 74.
$x + 146 = 180$	Simplify.
$-146 = -146$	Subtract 146 from each side.
$x = 34$	The value of x is 34.

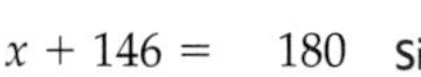

All triangles have at least two acute angles. Triangles can be classified by the measure of the third angle.

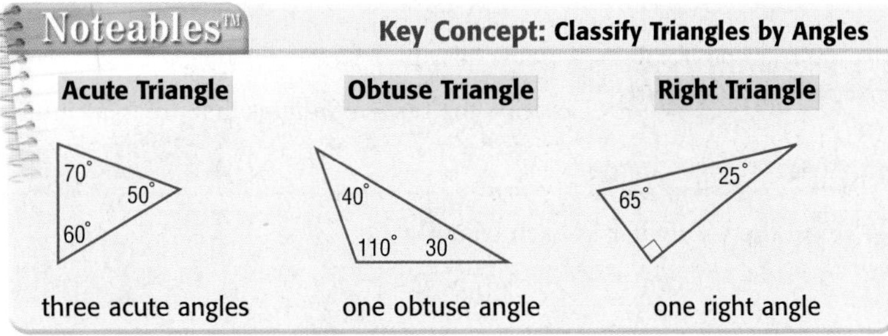

In an *equiangular* triangle, all angles have the same measure, 60°.

TEACHING TIP

Remind students that they should not assume that sides in a figure are congruent unless there are tick marks to indicate this.

Triangles can also be classified by the number of congruent sides. Congruent sides are often marked with tick marks.

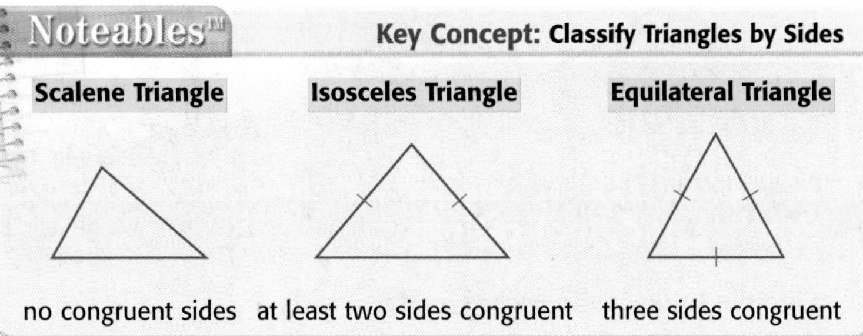

EXAMPLES Classify Triangles

Classify each triangle by its angles and by its sides.

STUDY TIP

Base Angles In Example 2, notice that the angles opposite the congruent sides are congruent. The congruent angles in an isosceles triangle are called the *base angles*.

2

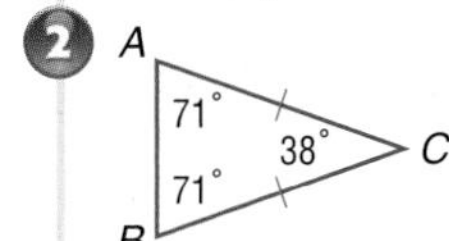

Angles $\triangle ABC$ has all acute angles.

Sides $\triangle ABC$ has two congruent sides.

So, $\triangle ABC$ is an acute isosceles triangle.

3

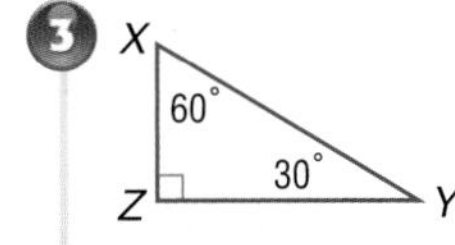

Angles $\triangle XYZ$ has one right angle.

Sides $\triangle XYZ$ has no congruent sides.

So, $\triangle XYZ$ is a right scalene triangle.

Your Turn **Classify each triangle by its angles and by its sides.**

a.

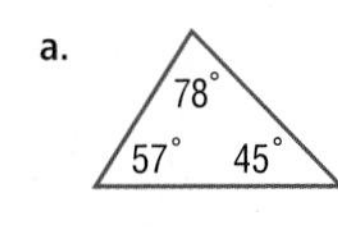

b.

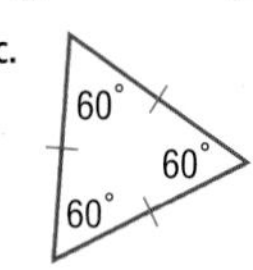

c.

60°, 60°, 60°

acute scalene | obtuse isosceles | acute equilateral

Math Online msmath3.net/extra_examples

2 Teach

In-Class Examples

1 Find the value of x in $\triangle PQR$. **117**

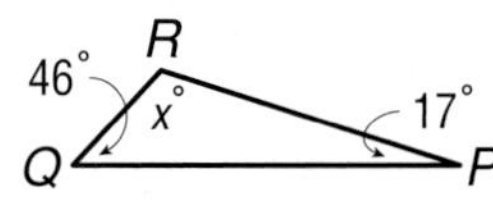

Classify each triangle by its angles and by its sides.

2

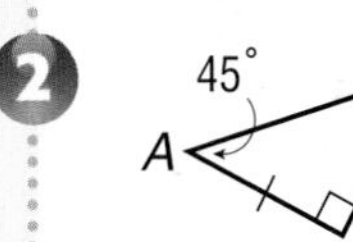

right isosceles

3

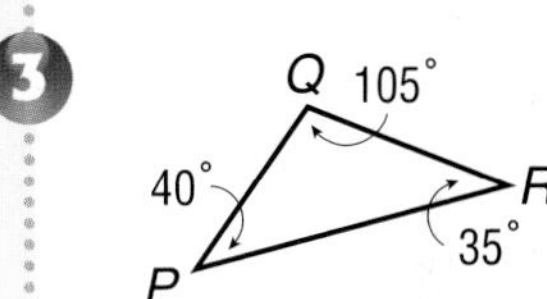

obtuse scalene

Tips for New Teachers

Using Applications Relating math to students' everyday life is important for maintaining their interest. For example, ask students to describe their favorite sports and activities. Look for ways to relate math to these sports and activities, either through word problems or in-class projects. For example, what angle does the kicker need to kick the football for it to go through the goal posts? This is especially important for students who have difficulty with math.

DAILY INTERVENTION **Flexible Grouping**

Triangles and Angles Students can work in pairs or small groups to look through magazines and find examples of triangles. Suggest that they look for photos showing triangles in nature, in artwork, or in buildings. Have them classify each triangle they find according to its angles and sides.

3 Practice/Apply

FOLDABLES™ Follow-Up Remind students to include information in words and symbols on what they learn about triangles and angles in the "Polygon" section of their Foldable tables.

About the Exercises...

Guided Practice Key

Exercises	Examples
3–5	1
6–9	2, 3

Assignment Guide

Basic: 11, 13, 17–31 odd, 33–44

Average: 11–31 odd, 33–44

Enriched: 10–32 even, 33–40 (Optional: 41–44)

Students practice the same concepts in Exercises 10–23 and 25–30 if they are assigned odd or even problems.

Skill and Concept Check

1. **OPEN ENDED** Name a real-life object that is shaped like an isosceles triangle. Explain. **Sample answer: a baseball pennant**
2. *Writing Math* Describe the types of angles that are in a right triangle. **See margin.**

GUIDED PRACTICE

Find the value of x in each triangle.

3. 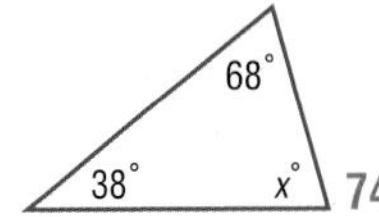

74

4. 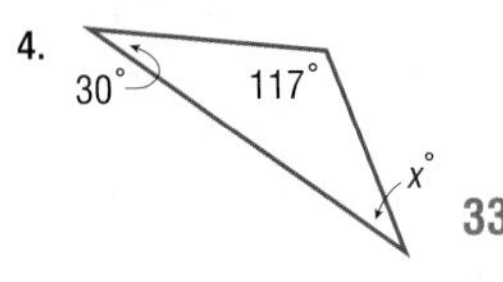

33

5. 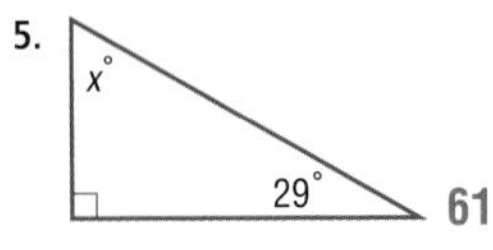

61

Classify each triangle by its angles and by its sides.

6. 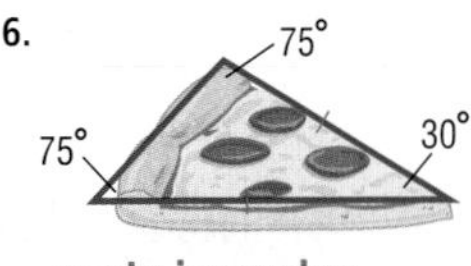

acute isosceles

7. 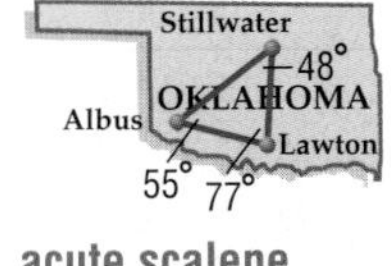

acute scalene

8. 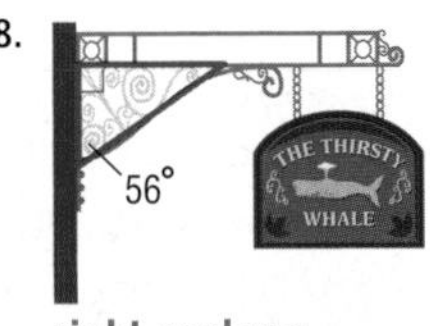

right scalene

9. 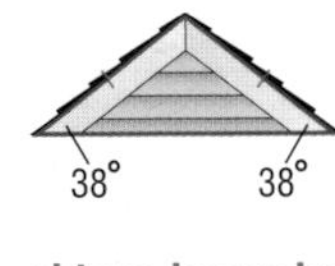

obtuse isosceles

★ indicates increased difficulty

Practice and Applications

HOMEWORK HELP	
For Exercises	See Examples
10–15	1
16–32	2, 3

Extra Practice See pages 629, 653.

Find the value of x in each triangle.

10. 11. 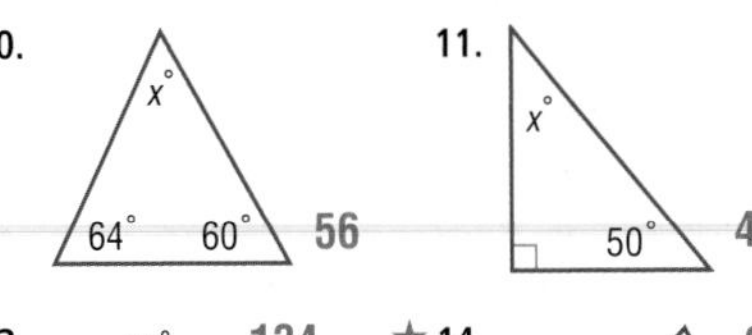

10. **56** 11. **40**

12. 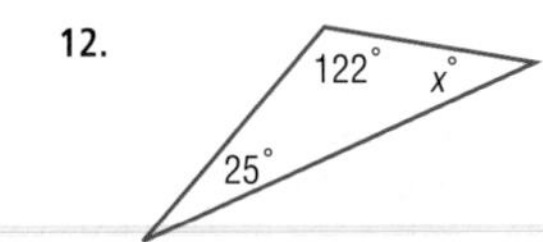

33

13. 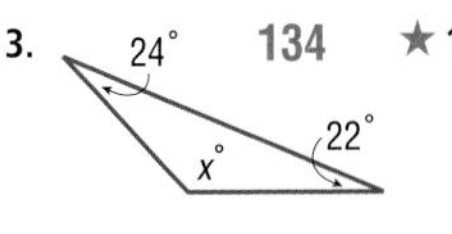

134

★14. 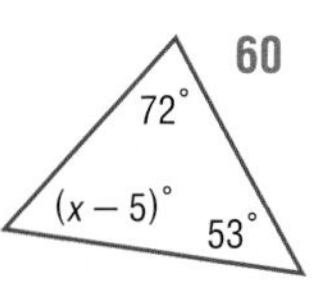

60

★15. 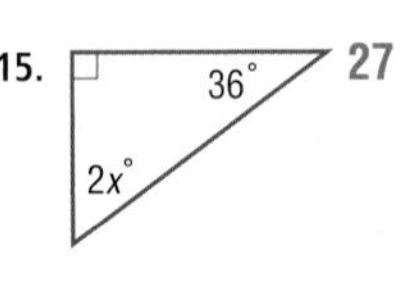

27

Classify each triangle by its angles and by its sides.

16. 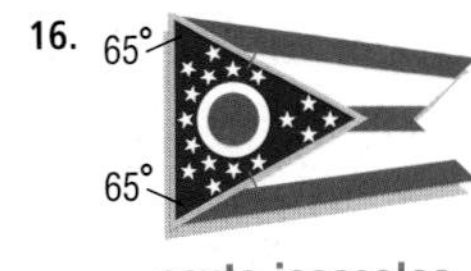

acute isosceles

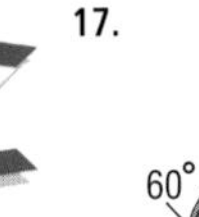

17. 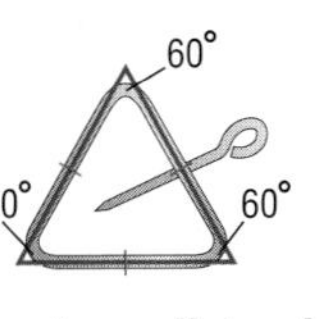

acute equilateral

18. 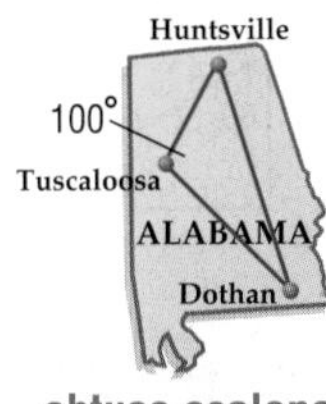

obtuse scalene

19. 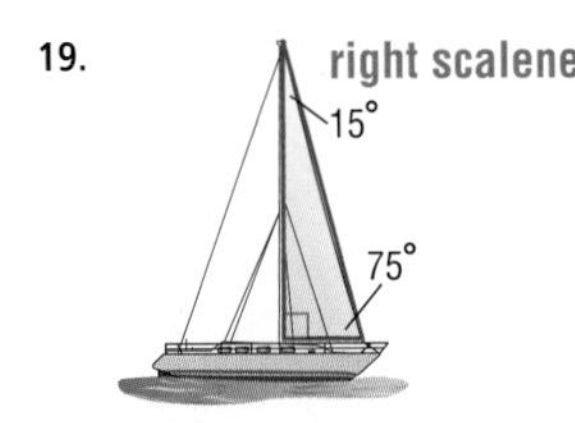

right scalene

20. 

acute equilateral

21. 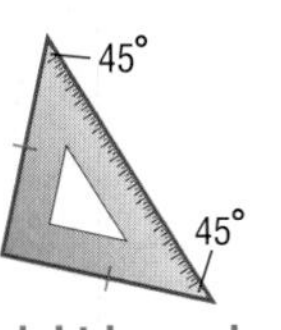

right isosceles

22. 80° **acute scalene**

23. 20° 20° **obtuse isosceles**

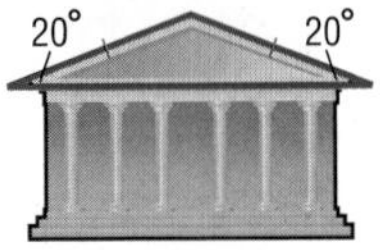

Answers

2. One angle is a 90° angle and the other two angles are each acute.

24. Sample answer: $\triangle ABN$, right isosceles; $\triangle NCL$, acute isosceles; $\triangle EJF$, acute scalene

25. 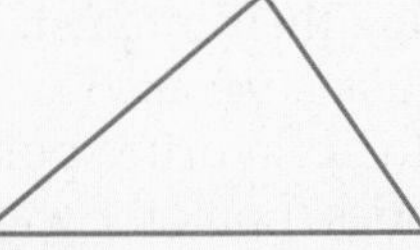

27. 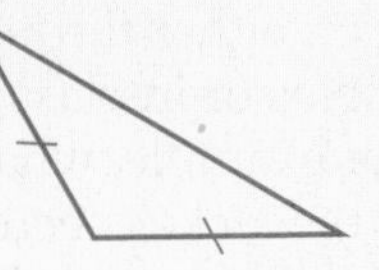

30. 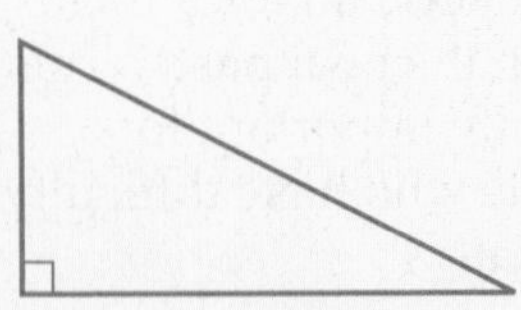

33. The sum of the measures of the angles of a triangle is 180°. If two of the angles of a triangle were greater than or equal to 90°, then the sum of these angles would already be greater than or equal to 180°.

41. 9.4 ft
42. 6.6 m
43. 11.5 in.
44. 9.9 yd

24. **BRIDGE BUILDING** At a Science Olympiad tournament, your team is to design and construct a bridge that will hold the most weight for a given span. Your team knows that triangles add stability to bridges. Below is a side view of your team's design. Name and classify three differently-shaped triangles in your design. **See margin.**

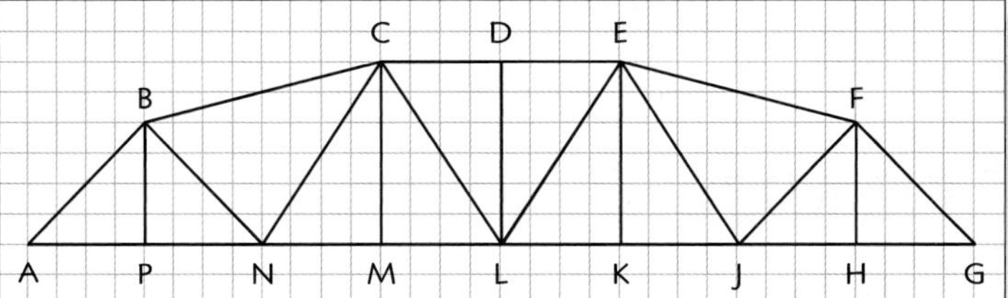

Draw each triangle. If it is not possible to draw the triangle, write *not possible*. **25, 27, 30. See margin.**

25. three acute angles
26. two obtuse angles **not possible**
27. obtuse isosceles with two acute angles
28. obtuse equilateral **not possible**
29. right equilateral **not possible**
30. right scalene

Determine whether each statement is *sometimes*, *always*, or *never* true.

31. Isosceles triangles are equilateral. **sometimes**
32. Equilateral triangles are isosceles. **always**
33. **CRITICAL THINKING** Explain why all triangles have at least two acute angles. **See margin.**

Spiral Review with Standardized Test Practice

34. **SHORT RESPONSE** Triangle ABC is isosceles. What is the value of x? **80°**

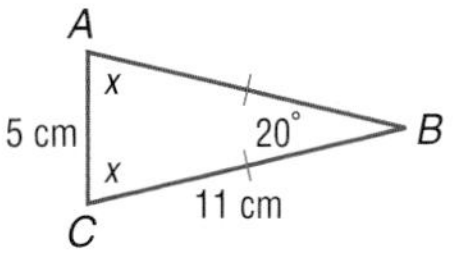

35. **MULTIPLE CHOICE** Which term describes the relationship between the two acute angles of a right triangle? **B**

Ⓐ adjacent
Ⓑ complementary
Ⓒ vertical
Ⓓ supplementary

Find the measure of each angle in the figure if $m \parallel n$ and $m\angle 7 = 95°$. (Lesson 6-1)

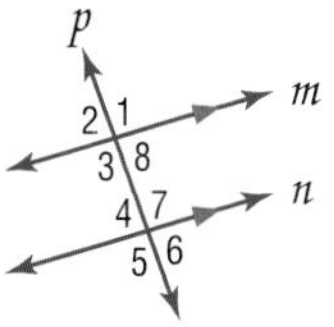

36. $\angle 4$ **85°**
37. $\angle 3$ **95°**
38. $\angle 1$ **95°**
39. $\angle 2$ **85°**

40. **SAVINGS** Shala's savings account earned \$4.56 in 6 months at a simple interest rate of 4.75%. How much was in her account at the beginning of that 6-month period? (Lesson 5-8) **\$192**

GETTING READY FOR THE NEXT LESSON

PREREQUISITE SKILL Find the missing side length of each right triangle. Round to the nearest tenth if necessary. (Lesson 3-4) **41–44. See margin.**

41. a, 5 ft; b, 8 ft
42. b, 10 m; c, 12 m
43. a, 6 in.; c, 13 in.
44. a, 7 yd; b, 7 yd

Math Online msmath3.net/self_check_quiz

4 Assess

Open-Ended Assessment

Speaking Ask students to explain why an equiangular triangle must also be an equilateral triangle. Encourage students to draw different sizes of equiangular triangles on the chalkboard as they discuss the question.

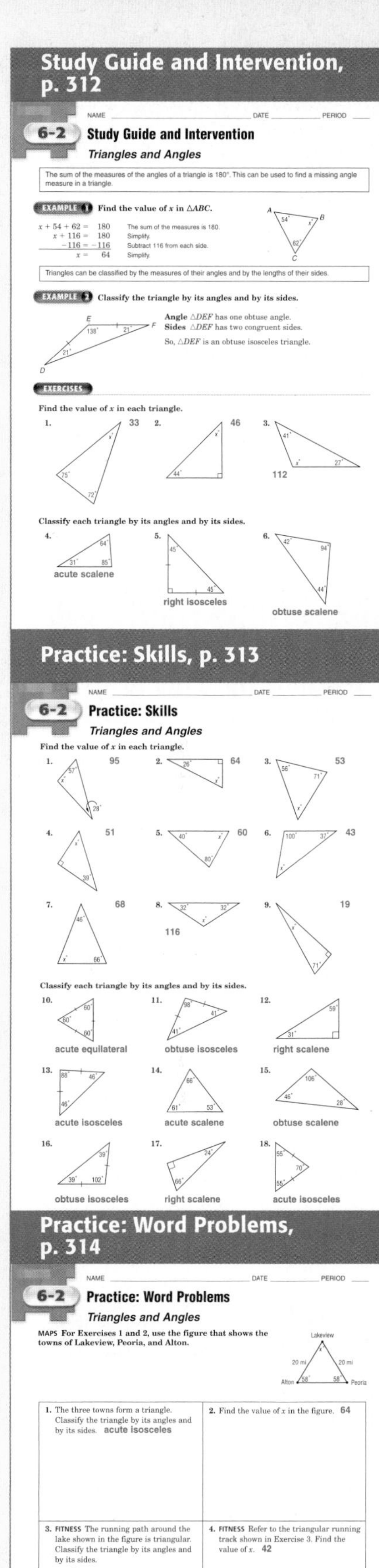

Study Guide and Intervention, p. 312

NAME ______ DATE ______ PERIOD ____

6-2 Study Guide and Intervention

Triangles and Angles

The sum of the measures of the angles of a triangle is 180°. This can be used to find a missing angle measure in a triangle.

EXAMPLE 1 Find the value of x in $\triangle ABC$.

$x + 54 + 62 = 180$ The sum of the measures is 180.
$x + 116 = 180$ Simplify.
$-116 = -116$ Subtract 116 from each side.
$x = 64$ Simplify.

Triangles can be classified by the measures of their angles and by the lengths of their sides.

EXAMPLE 2 Classify the triangle by its angles and by its sides.

Angle $\triangle DEF$ has one obtuse angle.
Sides $\triangle DEF$ has two congruent sides.
So, $\triangle DEF$ is an obtuse isosceles triangle.

EXERCISES

Find the value of x in each triangle.

1. 33
2. 46
3. 112

Classify each triangle by its angles and by its sides.

4. acute scalene
5. right isosceles
6. obtuse scalene

Practice: Skills, p. 313

NAME ______ DATE ______ PERIOD ____

6-2 Practice: Skills

Triangles and Angles

Find the value of x in each triangle.

1. 95
2. 64
3. 53
4. 51
5. 60
6. 43
7. 68
8. 116
9. 19

Classify each triangle by its angles and by its sides.

10. acute equilateral
11. obtuse isosceles
12. right scalene
13. acute isosceles
14. acute scalene
15. obtuse scalene
16. obtuse isosceles
17. right scalene
18. acute isosceles

Practice: Word Problems, p. 314

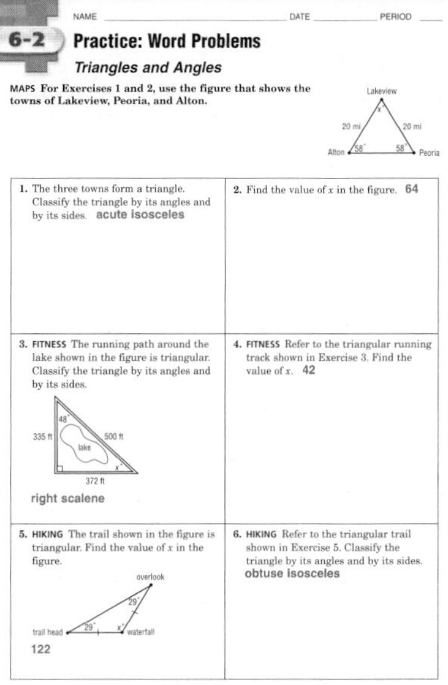

NAME ______ DATE ______ PERIOD ____

6-2 Practice: Word Problems

Triangles and Angles

MAPS For Exercises 1 and 2, use the figure that shows the towns of Lakeview, Peoria, and Alton.

1. The three towns form a triangle. Classify the triangle by its angles and by its sides. acute isosceles
2. Find the value of x in the figure. 64
3. **FITNESS** The running path around the lake shown in the figure is triangular. Classify the triangle by its angles and by its sides. right scalene
4. **FITNESS** Refer to the triangular running track shown in Exercise 3. Find the value of x. 42
5. **HIKING** The trail shown in the figure is triangular. Find the value of x in the figure. 122
6. **HIKING** Refer to the triangular trail shown in Exercise 5. Classify the triangle by its angles and by its sides. obtuse isosceles

6-2b HANDS-ON LAB

Lesson Notes

Lesson Resources

Teaching Mathematics with Manipulatives

- student recording sheet 6-2b

Glencoe Mathematics Classroom Manipulative Kit

- compass
- ruler (straightedge)

GETTING STARTED

Teaching Tip Prior to the lab, draw a bisected angle on the chalkboard. Be sure that students understand that *bisect* means *to divide into two equal parts*. Point out that the angle is bisected by the central ray.

TEACH

- Students must be careful not to change the setting of the compass after Step 3.
- After students complete the **Activity,** you may wish to have them use protractors to check that the angles' measures are equal.

ASSESS

Observe as students solve the **Your Turn** exercises. They should:

- place the compass exactly at the angle's vertex to make the first arc,
- draw the interior arcs accurately, and
- correctly draw the bisector from the angle's vertex to the intersection of the interior arcs.

6-2b HANDS-ON LAB

A Follow-Up of Lesson 6-2

Bisecting Angles

In this lab, you will learn to bisect an angle.

What You'll LEARN

Bisect an angle.

Link to READING

Everyday Meaning of Bisect: to divide into two equal parts

Materials

- compass
- straightedge
- paper

STUDY TIP

Symbols $\overrightarrow{KH}$ is read *ray KH.* A ray is a path that extends infinitely from one point in a certain direction.

ACTIVITY

STEP 1 Draw $\angle JKL$.

STEP 2 Place the compass at point K and draw an arc that intersects both sides of the angle. Label the intersections X and Y.

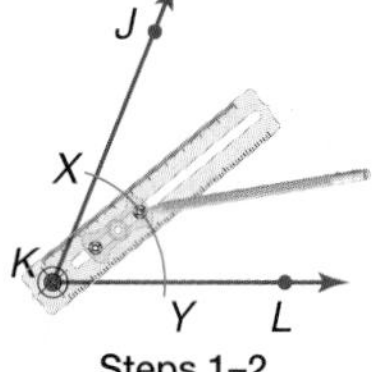

Steps 1–2

STEP 3 With the compass at point X, draw an arc in the interior of $\angle JKL$.

STEP 4 Using this setting, place the compass at point Y. Draw another arc.

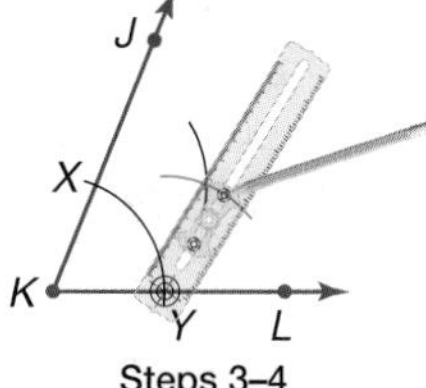

Steps 3–4

STEP 5 Label the intersection of these arcs H. Then draw $\overrightarrow{KH}$. $\overrightarrow{KH}$ is the **bisector** of $\angle JKL$.

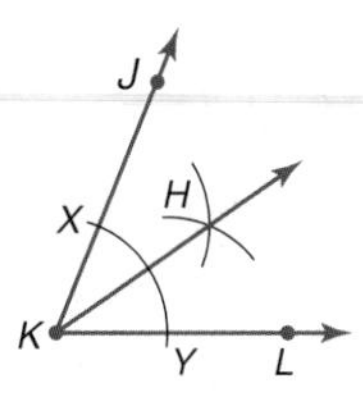

Step 5

Your Turn **Draw each kind of angle. Then bisect it.**

a. acute b. obtuse

a–b. See students' work.

Writing Math

Work with a partner. Use the information in the activity above.

1. **Describe** what is true about the measures of $\angle JKH$ and $\angle HKL$.
2. **Explain** why we say that $\overrightarrow{KH}$ is the bisector of $\angle JKL$.
3. The point where the bisectors of all three angles of a triangle meet is called the *incenter*. Draw a triangle. Then locate its incenter using only a compass and straightedge. **See margin.**

1. They are congruent.
2. It divides the angle into two congruent angles.

Discuss the **Writing Math** exercises. Use Exercise 3 to determine whether students realize that the three angle bisectors of a triangle always meet at only one point.

Answer (Writing Math)

3.

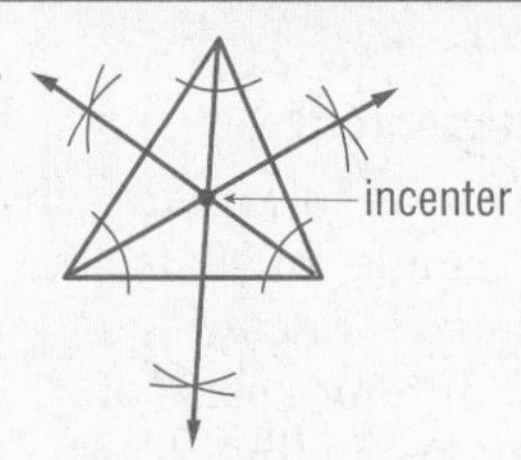

6-3 Special Right Triangles

What You'll LEARN

Find missing measures in 30°-60° right triangles and 45°-45° right triangles.

REVIEW Vocabulary

Pythagorean Theorem: in a right triangle, the square of the length of the hypotenuse is equal to the sum of the squares of the lengths of the legs
(Lesson 3-4)

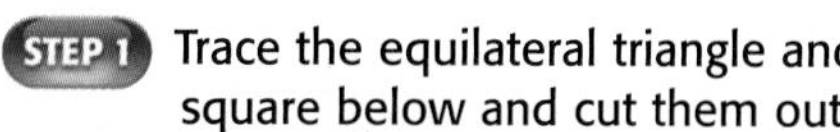

Materials

- pencil
- paper
- scissors
- ruler

Work with a partner.

 Trace the equilateral triangle and square below and cut them out.

 Measure each angle.

STEP 3 Fold the triangle so that one half matches the other. Fold the square in half along a diagonal.

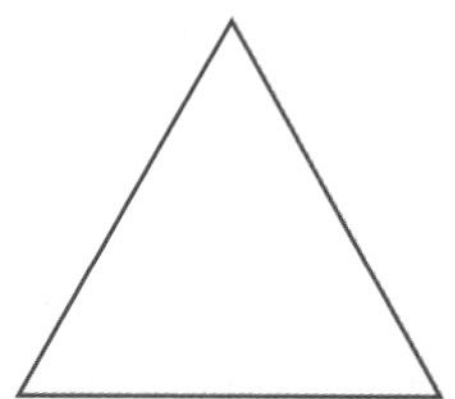

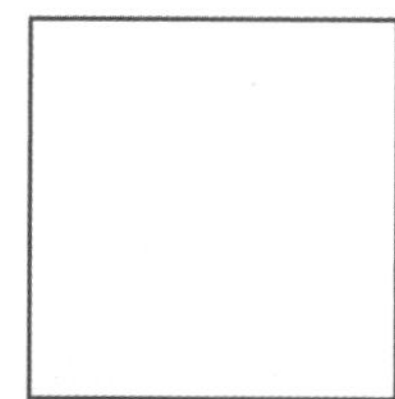

1. What type of triangles have you formed? **right**
2. What are the measures of the angles of the folded triangle?
3. Measure and describe the relationship between the shortest and longest sides of this triangle.
4. What are the measures of the angles of the triangle formed by folding the square? **90°, 45°, 45°**
5. Measure and describe the relationship between the legs of this triangle. **legs are the same length**

2. 90°, 60°, 30° 3. longest side is twice the length of shortest side

The sides of a triangle whose angles measure 30°, 60°, and 90° have a special relationship. The hypotenuse is always twice as long as the side opposite the 30° angle.

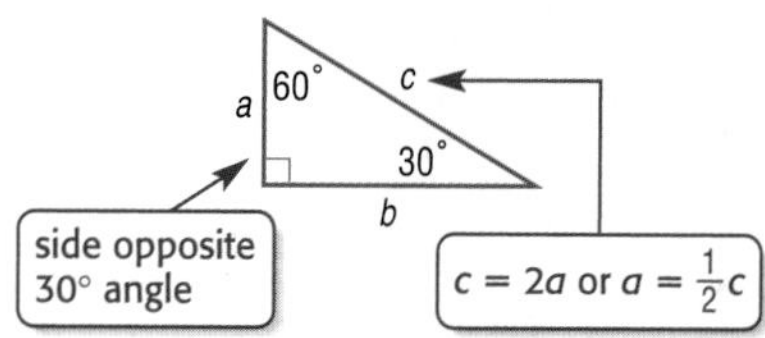

EXAMPLE Find Lengths of a 30°-60° Right Triangle

 **Find each missing length.**

Step 1 Find a.

$a = \frac{1}{2}c$ Write the equation.

$a = \frac{1}{2}(10)$ or 5 Replace c with 10.

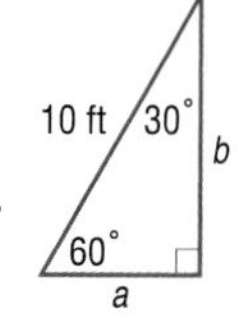

(continued on the next page)

msmath3.net/extra_examples

6-3 Lesson Notes

Lesson Resources

Chapter 6 Resource Masters

- Study Guide and Intervention, p. 317
- Practice: Skills, p. 318
- Practice: Word Problems, p. 319
- Reading to Learn Mathematics, p. 320
- Enrichment, p. 321

Key Teaching Transparencies, 21

Parent and Student Study Guide Online Worksheets, 6-3

Teaching Mathematics with Manipulatives, p. 66

Noteables™: Interactive Study Notebook with Foldables™, 6-3

1 Focus

5-Minute Check 6-3

Use as a quiz or review of Lesson 6-2. (Also available as a transparency)

Bellringer

Problem Solving Draw the triangles shown below on the chalkboard. Tell students that making careful observations is an important part of problem solving. Ask them to name ways the triangles are alike. Students will probably mention the similarities in the angles. They should also notice the relationships among the lengths of the sides.

(Continued in bottom margin.)

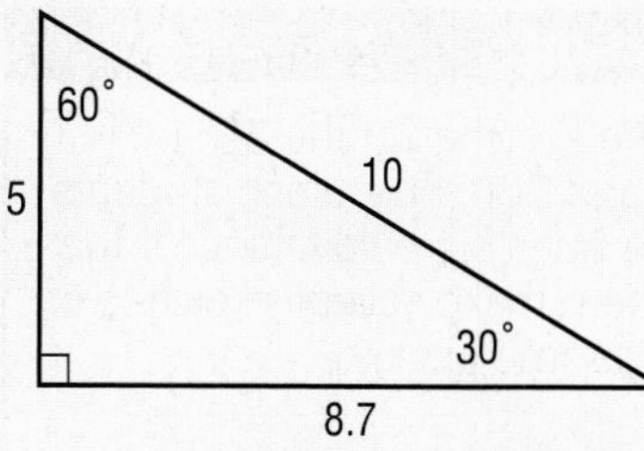

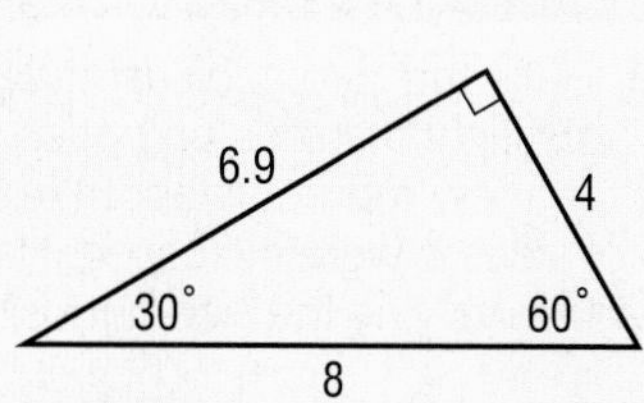

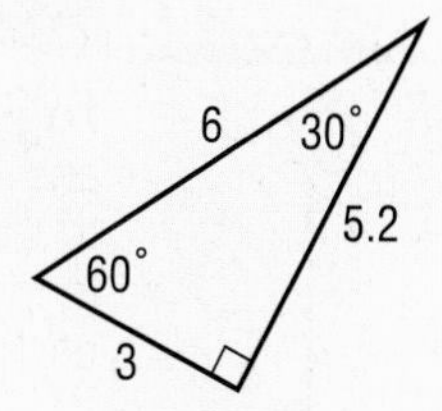

Reading to Learn Mathematics, p. 320 **ELL**

NAME ____ DATE ____ PERIOD ____

6-3 Reading to Learn Mathematics
Special Right Triangles

Pre-Activity *Complete the Mini Lab at the top of page 267 in your textbook. Write your answers below.*

1. What type of triangles have you formed? right
2. What are the measures of the angles of the folded triangle? 90°, 60°, 30°
3. Measure and describe the relationship between the shortest and longest sides of this triangle. longest side is twice the length of shortest side
4. What are the measures of the angles of the triangle formed by folding the square? 90°, 45°, 45°
5. Measure and describe the relationship between the legs of this triangle. legs are the same length

2 Teach

In-Class Examples

1 Find each missing length. Round to the nearest tenth if necessary.

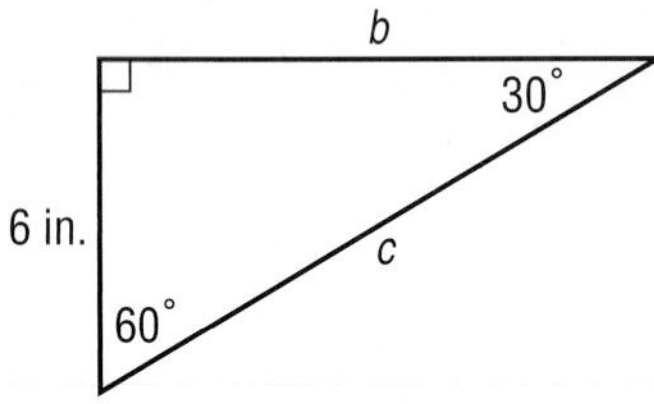

$b \approx 10.4$ in., $c = 12$ in.

2 **BASEBALL** The figure below shows the dimensions of a baseball diamond. The distance between home plate and first base is 90 feet. The area between first base, third base, and home plate forms a 45°-45° right triangle. What is the approximate distance between first base and third base? third base and home plate?

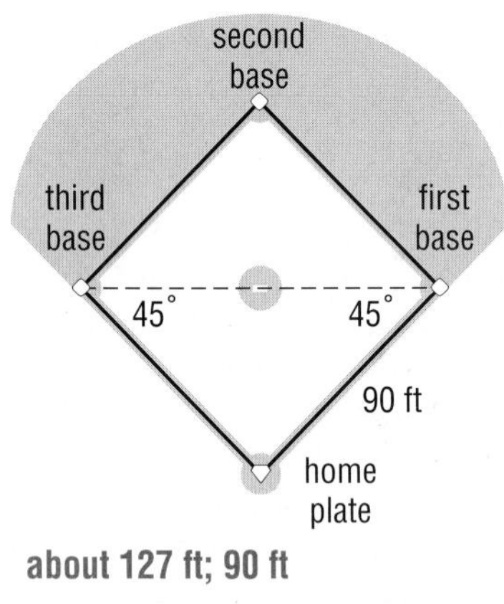

about 127 ft; 90 ft

TEACHING TIP

Remind students that 8.7 feet is only an approximation. The *exact* answer is $\sqrt{75}$ feet.

Step 2 Find b.

$c^2 = a^2 + b^2$	Pythagorean Theorem
$10^2 = 5^2 + b^2$	Replace c with 10 and a with 5.
$100 = 25 + b^2$	Evaluate 10^2 and 5^2.
$100 - 25 = 25 + b^2 - 25$	Subtract 25 from each side.
$75 = b^2$	Simplify.
$\sqrt{75} = \sqrt{b^2}$	Take the square root of each side.
$8.7 \approx b$	Use a calculator.

The length of a is 5 feet, and the length of b is about 8.7 feet.

Your Turn **Find each missing length. Round to the nearest tenth if necessary.**

a. 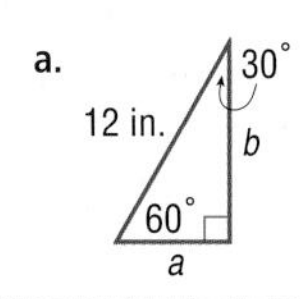

b. 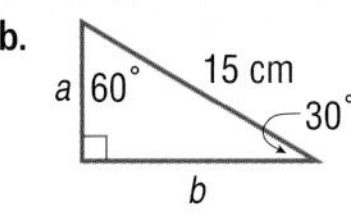

c. 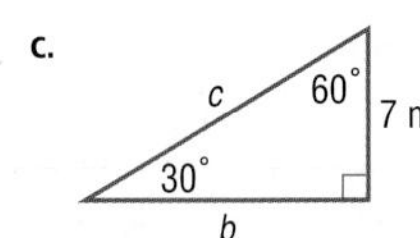

a. $a = 6$ in., $b \approx 10.4$ in.
b. $a = 7.5$ cm, $b \approx 13.0$ cm
c. $c = 14$ m, $b \approx 12.1$ m

A 45°-45° right triangle is also an isosceles triangle because two angle measures are the same. Thus, the legs are always congruent.

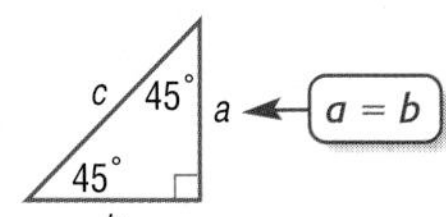

REAL-LIFE MATH

ART The Greek relief entitled *The Grave Stele of Hegeso* makes use of a 30°-60° right triangle.

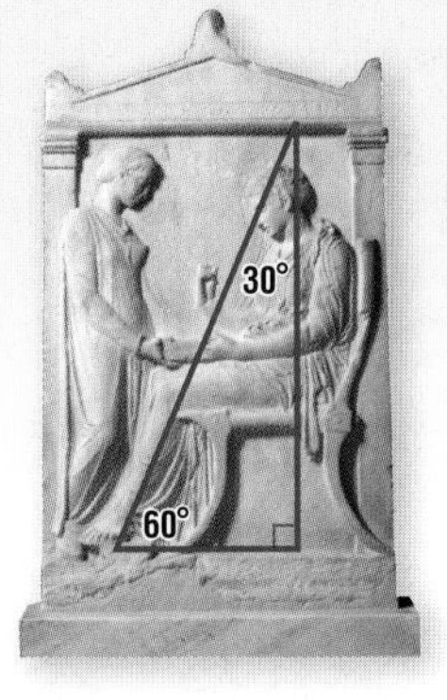

EXAMPLE Find Lengths of a 45°-45° Right Triangle

2 **ART The ancient Greeks sometimes used 45°-45° right triangles in their art. The sculpture on the right is based on such a triangle. Suppose the base of a reproduction of the sculpture shown is 15 feet long. Find each missing length.**

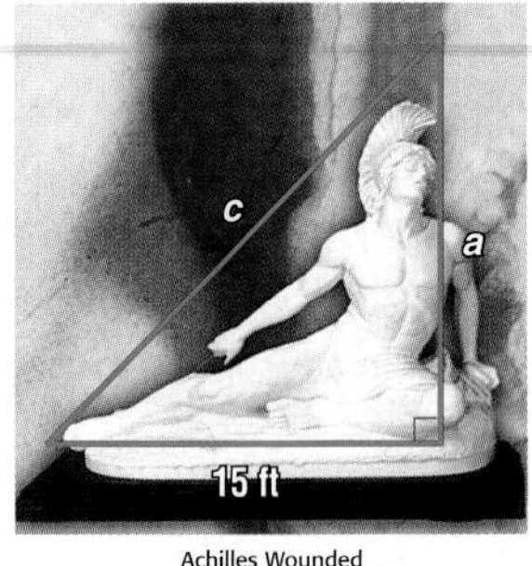

Achilles Wounded

Step 1 Find a.

Sides a and b are the same length. Since $b = 15$ feet, $a = 15$ feet.

Step 2 Find c.

$c^2 = a^2 + b^2$	Pythagorean Theorem
$c^2 = 15^2 + 15^2$	Replace a with 15 and b with 15.
$c^2 = 225 + 225$	Evaluate 15^2.
$c^2 = 450$	Add 225 and 225.
$\sqrt{c^2} = \sqrt{450}$	Take the square root of each side.
$c \approx 21.2$	Simplify.

DAILY INTERVENTION **Differentiated Instruction**

Logical Have the class look carefully at the sketches of the 30°-60° and 45°-45° right triangles on pages 267 and 268. Encourage students to think for a few moments about how the sides b would change if the lengths of sides a were increased. Have them make several sketches of each triangle, varying the size but using the same angles.

Students practice the same concepts in Exercises 6–15 if they are assigned odd or even problems.

Skill and Concept Check

1. **Writing Math** Write a sentence describing the relationship between the hypotenuse of a 30°-60° right triangle and the leg opposite the 30° angle. **See margin.**
2. **OPEN ENDED** Give a real-life example of a 45°-45° right triangle. **Sample answer: in baseball, the triangle formed by home plate, first base and second base**

GUIDED PRACTICE

Find each missing length. Round to the nearest tenth if necessary.

3. 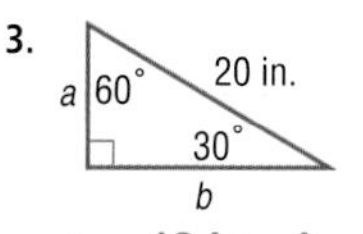
$a = 10$ in., $b \approx 17.3$ in.

4. 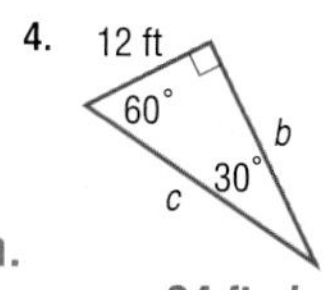
$c = 24$ ft, $b \approx 20.8$ ft

5. 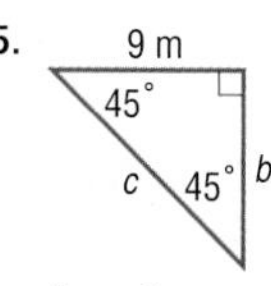
$b = 9$ m, $c \approx 12.7$ m

Practice and Applications

Find each missing length. Round to the nearest tenth if necessary.

6. 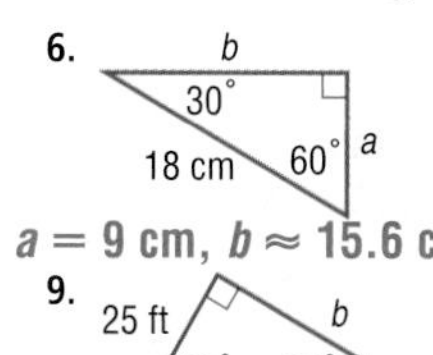
$a = 9$ cm, $b \approx 15.6$ cm

7. 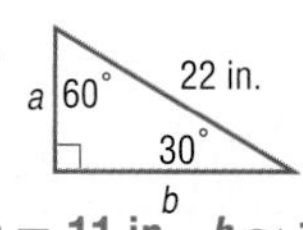
$a = 11$ in., $b \approx 19.1$ in.

8. 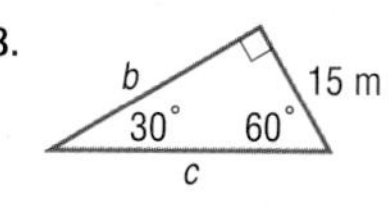
$c = 30$ m, $b \approx 26.0$ m

9. 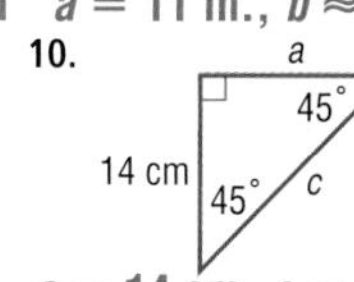
$c = 50$ ft, $b \approx 43.3$ ft

10. 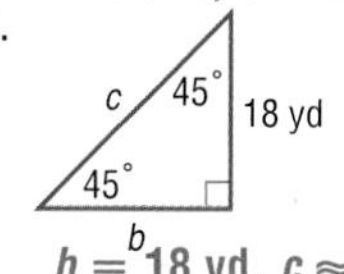
$a = 14$ cm, $c \approx 19.8$ cm

11. 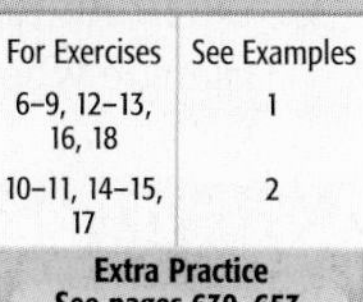
$b = 18$ yd, $c \approx 25.5$ yd

12. The length of the hypotenuse of a 30°-60° right triangle is 7.5 meters. Find the length of the side opposite the 30° angle. **3.75 m**
13. In a 30°-60° right triangle, the length of the side opposite the 30° angle is 5.8 centimeters. What is the length of the hypotenuse? **11.6 cm**
14. The length of one of the legs of a 45°-45° right triangle is 6.5 inches. Find the lengths of the other sides. **6.5 in., about 9.2 in.**
15. In a 45°-45° right triangle, the length of one leg is 7.5 feet. What are the lengths of the other sides? **7.5 ft, about 10.6 ft**
16. **HISTORY** Redan lines such as the one below were used at many battlefields in the Civil War. A *redan* is a triangular shape that goes out from the main line of defense. What is the distance h from the base of each redan to its farthest point? **about 52.0 yd**

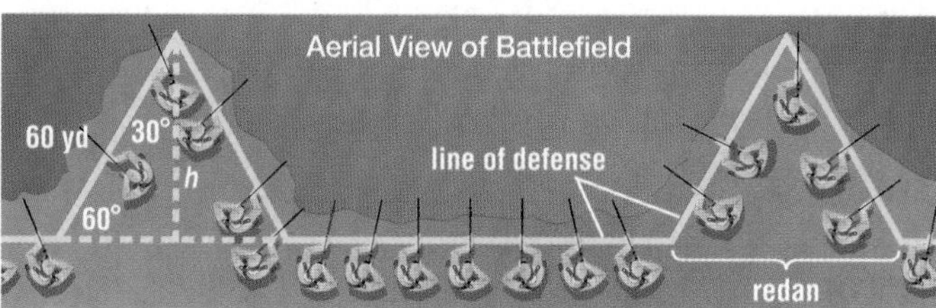

HOMEWORK HELP

For Exercises	See Examples
6–9, 12–13, 16, 18	1
10–11, 14–15, 17	2

Extra Practice
See pages 630, 653.

msmath3.net/self_check_quiz

3 Practice/Apply

FOLDABLES™ Follow-Up Remind students to include information on special right triangles in words and symbols in the "Polygons" section of their Foldable tables.

About the Exercises...

Guided Practice Key

Exercises	Examples
3–5	1, 2

Assignment Guide

Basic: 7–19 odd, 20–33

Average: 7–17 odd, 18–33

Enriched: 6–18 even, 20–31 (Optional: 32–33)

Answer

1. **The length of the hypotenuse is twice the length of the leg opposite the 30° angle.**

4 Assess

Open-Ended Assessment

Modeling Have students make a model of a 30°-60° right triangle or a 45°-45° right triangle. For example, they could use toothpicks or straws glued to construction paper. They should be careful to measure and label the angles and sides accurately. Share the models by posting them on a bulletin board.

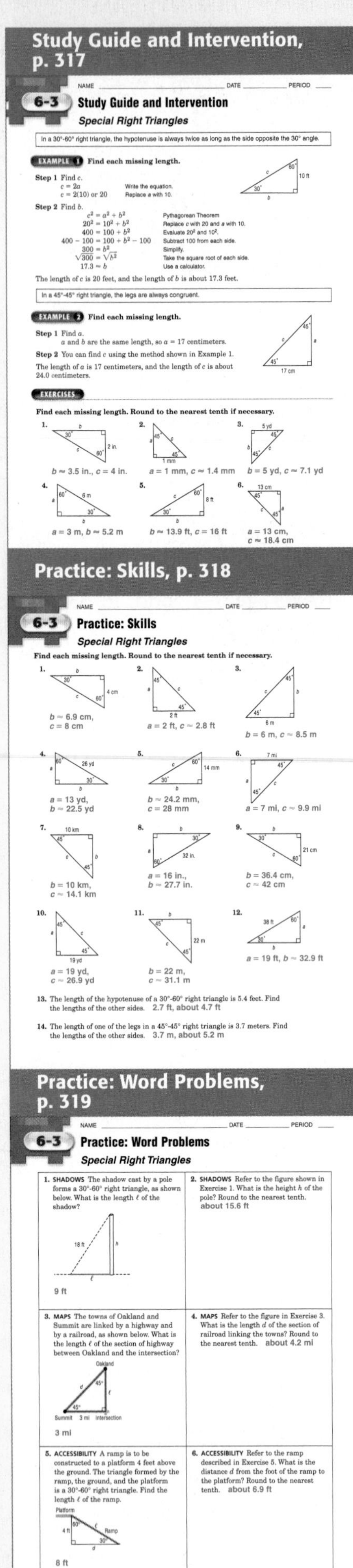

Study Guide and Intervention, p. 317

NAME ______ DATE ______ PERIOD ____

6-3 Study Guide and Intervention

Special Right Triangles

In a 30°-60° right triangle, the hypotenuse is always twice as long as the side opposite the 30° angle.

EXAMPLE 1 Find each missing length.

Step 1 Find c.

$c = 2a$	Write the equation.
$c = 2(10)$ or 20	Replace a with 10.

Step 2 Find b.

$c^2 = a^2 + b^2$	Pythagorean Theorem
$20^2 = 10^2 + b^2$	Replace c with 20 and a with 10.
$400 = 100 + b^2$	Evaluate 20^2 and 10^2.
$400 - 100 = 100 + b^2 - 100$	Subtract 100 from each side.
$300 = b^2$	Simplify.
$\sqrt{300} = \sqrt{b^2}$	Take the square root of each side.
$17.3 \approx b$	Use a calculator.

The length of c is 20 feet, and the length of b is about 17.3 feet.

In a 45°-45° right triangle, the legs are always congruent.

EXAMPLE 2 Find each missing length.

Step 1 Find a.
a and b are the same length, so $a = 17$ centimeters.

Step 2 You can find c using the method shown in Example 1.

The length of a is 17 centimeters, and the length of c is about 24.0 centimeters.

EXERCISES

Find each missing length. Round to the nearest tenth if necessary.

1. $b \approx 3.5$ in., $c = 4$ in.
2. $a = 1$ mm, $c \approx 1.4$ mm
3. $b = 5$ yd, $c \approx 7.1$ yd
4. $a = 3$ m, $b \approx 5.2$ m
5. $b \approx 13.9$ ft, $c = 16$ ft
6. $a = 13$ cm, $c \approx 18.4$ cm

Practice: Skills, p. 318

NAME ______ DATE ______ PERIOD ____

6-3 Practice: Skills

Special Right Triangles

Find each missing length. Round to the nearest tenth if necessary.

1. $b \approx 6.9$ cm, $c = 8$ cm
2. $a = 2$ ft, $c \approx 2.8$ ft
3. $b = 6$ m, $c \approx 8.5$ m
4. $a = 13$ yd, $b \approx 22.5$ yd
5. $b \approx 24.2$ mm, $c = 28$ mm
6. $a = 7$ mi, $c \approx 9.9$ mi
7. $b = 10$ km, $c \approx 14.1$ km
8. $a = 16$ in., $b \approx 27.7$ in.
9. $b = 36.4$ cm, $c \approx 42$ cm
10. $a = 19$ yd, $c \approx 26.9$ yd
11. $b = 22$ m, $c \approx 31.1$ m
12. $a = 19$ ft, $b \approx 32.9$ ft
13. The length of the hypotenuse of a 30°-60° right triangle is 5.4 feet. Find the lengths of the other sides. 2.7 ft, about 4.7 ft
14. The length of one of the legs in a 45°-45° right triangle is 3.7 meters. Find the lengths of the other sides. 3.7 m, about 5.2 m

Practice: Word Problems, p. 319

NAME ______ DATE ______ PERIOD ____

6-3 Practice: Word Problems

Special Right Triangles

1. **SHADOWS** The shadow cast by a pole forms a 30°-60° right triangle, as shown below. What is the length ℓ of the shadow? 9 ft
2. **SHADOWS** Refer to the figure shown in Exercise 1. What is the height h of the pole? Round to the nearest tenth. about 15.6 ft
3. **MAPS** The towns of Oakland and Summit are linked by a highway and by a railroad, as shown below. What is the length ℓ of the section of highway between Oakland and the intersection? 3 mi
4. **MAPS** Refer to the figure in Exercise 3. What is the length d of the section of railroad linking the towns? Round to the nearest tenth. about 4.2 mi
5. **ACCESSIBILITY** A ramp is to be constructed to a platform 4 feet above the ground. The triangle formed by the ramp, the ground, and the platform is a 30°-60° right triangle. Find the length ℓ of the ramp. 8 ft
6. **ACCESSIBILITY** Refer to the ramp described in Exercise 5. What is the distance d from the foot of the ramp to the platform? Round to the nearest tenth. about 6.9 ft

17. **QUILTING** Refer to the photograph at the right. Each triangle in the Flying Geese pattern is a 45°-45° right triangle. If the length of a leg is $2\frac{1}{2}$ inches, find the length of each hypotenuse. **about 3.5 in.**

18. **SKIING** A ski jump is constructed so that the length of the board necessary for the surface of the ramp is twice as long as the ramp is high h. If the ramp forms a right triangle, what is the measure of ∠1? Explain your reasoning. **30°; In a 30°-60° right triangle, the hypotenuse is always twice as long as the side opposite the 30° angle.**

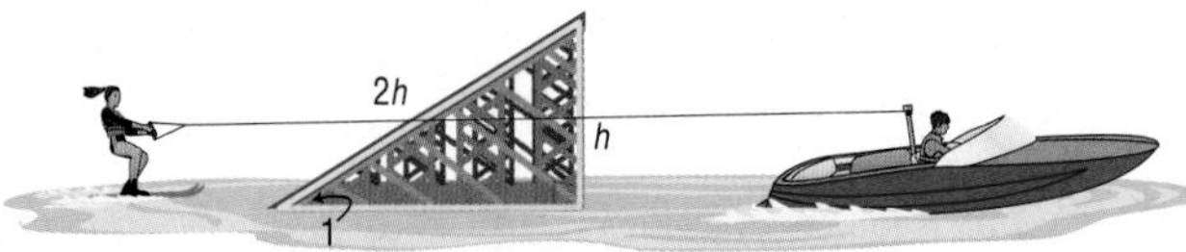

19. **WRITE A PROBLEM** Write a real-life problem involving a 30°-60° right triangle or a 45°-45° right triangle. Then solve the problem. **See margin.**

20. **CRITICAL THINKING** Find the length of each leg of a 45°-45° right triangle whose hypotenuse measures $\sqrt{162}$ centimeters. **9 cm, 9 cm**

Spiral Review with Standardized Test Practice

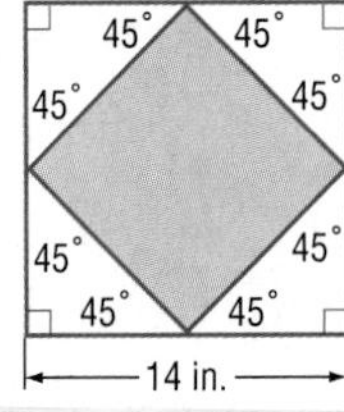

21. **MULTIPLE CHOICE** The midpoints of the sides of the square at the right are joined to form a smaller square. What is the area of the smaller square? **B**

    Ⓐ 196 in² Ⓑ 98 in² Ⓒ 49 in² Ⓓ 9.9 in²

22. **MULTIPLE CHOICE** Which values represent the sides of a 30°-60° right triangle? **H**

    Ⓕ 3 cm, 4 cm, 5 cm Ⓖ 8 cm, 8 cm, $\sqrt{128}$ cm
    Ⓗ 4 cm, 8 cm, $\sqrt{48}$ cm Ⓘ 5 cm, 12 cm, 13 cm

23. Two sides of a triangle are congruent. The angles opposite these sides each measure 70°. Classify the triangle by its angles and by its sides. (Lesson 6-2) **acute isosceles**

Classify each angle or angle pair using all names that apply. (Lesson 6-1)

24. 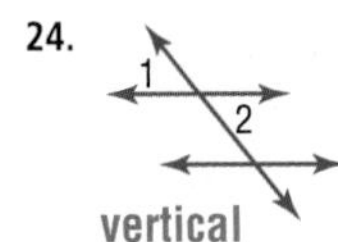

vertical

25. 
acute

26. 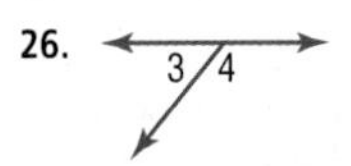

adj., supplementary

27.

alt. exterior

Multiply. Write in simplest form. (Lesson 2-3)

28. $\frac{2}{3} \cdot \frac{5}{8}$ **$\frac{5}{12}$**

29. $-\frac{2}{5} \cdot \frac{3}{4}$ **$-\frac{3}{10}$**

30. $-1\frac{1}{2}\left(-2\frac{1}{3}\right)$ **$3\frac{1}{2}$**

31. $2\frac{2}{3}\left(-2\frac{1}{4}\right)$ **-6**

GETTING READY FOR THE NEXT LESSON

PREREQUISITE SKILL Solve each equation. Check your solution. (Lesson 1-8)

32. $x + 90 + 50 + 100 = 360$ **120**

33. $45 + 150 + x + 85 = 360$ **80**

270 Chapter 6 Geometry

Answer

19. **Sample answer: A flowerbed is in the shape of a 45°-45° right triangle. The length of one leg is 6 feet. What is the length of the other two sides of the triangle? 6 ft and about 8.5 ft**

6-3b HANDS-ON LAB

A Follow-Up of Lesson 6-3

Constructing Perpendicular Bisectors

In this lab, you will learn to construct a line perpendicular to a segment so that it bisects that segment.

What You'll LEARN

Construct a perpendicular bisector of a segment.

Materials

- compass
- straightedge
- protractor
- paper

ACTIVITY

STEP 1 Draw $\overline{AB}$. Then place the compass at point A. Using a setting greater than one half the length of $\overline{AB}$, draw an arc above and below $\overline{AB}$.

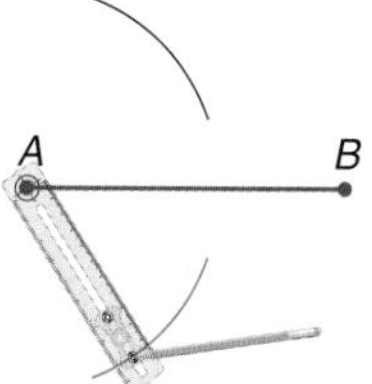

STEP 2 Using this setting, place the compass at point B. Draw another set of arcs above and below $\overline{AB}$ as shown.

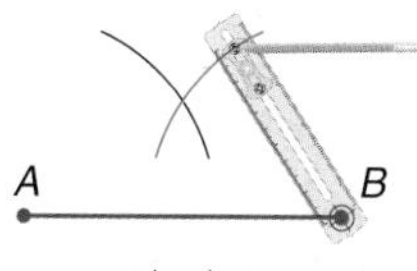

STEP 3 Label the intersection of these arcs X and Y as shown. Then draw $\overline{XY}$. $\overline{XY}$ is the **perpendicular bisector** of $\overline{AB}$. Label the intersection of $\overline{AB}$ and this new line segment M.

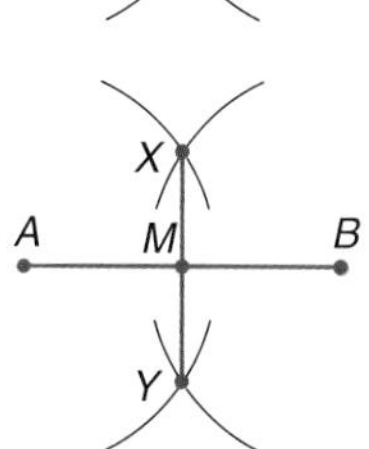

Your Turn

Draw a line segment. Then construct the perpendicular bisector of the segment.

See students' work.

Writing Math

Work with a partner. Use the information in the activity above.

1. **Describe** what is true about the measures of $\overline{AM}$ and $\overline{MB}$.
2. **Find** $m\angle XMB$. Then describe the relationship between $\overline{AB}$ and $\overline{XY}$. **90°; They are perpendicular.**
3. **Explain** how to construct a 45°-45° right triangle with legs half as long as the segment below. Then construct the triangle. **See Ch. 6 Answer Appendix.**

C ________________________________ D

TEACHING TIP

For Exercise 3, students will need to remember from their previous coursework how to construct a line segment congruent to a given line segment.

1. They are equal.

6-3b HANDS-ON LAB Lesson Notes

Lesson Resources

Teaching Mathematics with Manipulatives

- protractors, p. 21
- student recording sheet 6-3b

Glencoe Mathematics Classroom Manipulative Kit

- compass
- protractor
- ruler (straightedge)

GETTING STARTED

Teaching Tip Students will study precision of measurement in Lesson 7-9. Ask students to brainstorm cases in which bisecting a line segment exactly might be necessary. **Sample answer: When drawing up plans on paper for something larger such as a building or an airplane, tiny errors in miniature become quite large in real life.**

TEACH

- In Step 1 of the **Activity**, suggest that students set their compasses about halfway between the midpoint and the endpoints of $\overline{AB}$.
- Point out that the letters designating line segments and intersection points are completely arbitrary.

ASSESS

Observe as students solve the **Your Turn** exercise. They should:

- choose an appropriate compass setting and use it for both arcs, and
- clearly draw and label the perpendicular bisector.

Discuss the **Writing Math** exercises. For Exercise 3, ask students what they know about the legs of a 45°-45° right triangle. **They are congruent.**

6-4 Lesson Notes

Lesson Resources

Chapter 6 Resource Masters
- Study Guide and Intervention, p. 322
- Practice: Skills, p. 323
- Practice: Word Problems, p. 324
- Reading to Learn Mathematics, p. 325
- Enrichment, p. 326

FAST FILE

Calculator and Spreadsheet Masters, p. 29
Key Teaching Transparencies, 22
Parent and Student Study Guide Online Worksheets, 6-4
Teaching Mathematics with Manipulatives, pp. 68–70
Noteables™: Interactive Study Notebook with Foldables™, 6-4

1 Focus

5-Minute Check 6-4

Use as a quiz or review of Lesson 6-3. (Also available as a transparency)

Bellringer

Hands-On Activity Discuss the simple definition of *quadrilateral* with the class. Then have students find examples of quadrilaterals in the classroom. Have them make a drawing of each example and measure its sides and angles. Does everyone's example have the same shape?

(Continued in bottom margin.)

Reading to Learn Mathematics, p. 325 **ELL**

NAME ______________ DATE ________ PERIOD ____

6-4 Reading to Learn Mathematics

Classifying Quadrilaterals

Pre-Activity *Complete the Mini Lab at the top of page 272 in your textbook. Write your answers below.*

1. Name the shape of the figures formed when you drew the diagonal. How many figures were formed? **triangles; 2**
2. You know that the sum of the angle measures of a triangle is 180°. Use this fact to find the sum of the angle measures in a quadrilateral. Explain your reasoning. **360°; 2(180°) = 360°**
3. Find the measure of each angle of your quadrilateral. Compare the sum of these measures to the sum you found in Exercise 2. **See students' work. They are the same, 360°.**

Reading the Lesson

4. Explain what is done at each step in the following problem. Find the value of *y* in quadrilateral *ABCD*.

6-4 Classifying Quadrilaterals

What You'll LEARN

Find missing angle measures in quadrilaterals and classify quadrilaterals.

NEW Vocabulary

quadrilateral
trapezoid
parallelogram
rectangle
rhombus
square

Link to READING

Everyday meaning of prefix quadri-: four

HANDS-ON Mini Lab

Materials
- paper
- straightedge
- protractor

Work with a partner.

The polygon at the right is a **quadrilateral**, since it has four sides and four angles.

STEP 1 Draw a quadrilateral.

STEP 2 Pick one vertex and draw the diagonal to the opposite vertex.

1. Name the shape of the figures formed when you drew the diagonal. How many figures were formed? **triangles; 2**
2. You know that the sum of the angle measures of a triangle is 180°. Use this fact to find the sum of the angle measures in a quadrilateral. Explain your reasoning. **360°; 2(180°) = 360°**
3. Find the measure of each angle of your quadrilateral. Compare the sum of these measures to the sum you found in Exercise 2.

3. See students' work; They are the same, 360°.

The angles of a quadrilateral have a special relationship.

Noteables™ **Key Concept: Angles of a Quadrilateral**

Words The sum of the measures of the angles of a quadrilateral is 360°.

Model

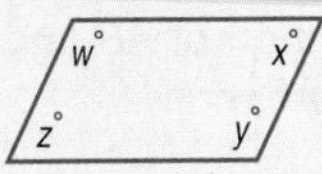

Symbols $w + x + y + z = 360$

EXAMPLE **Find a Missing Angle Measure**

1 **Find the value of *w* in quadrilateral *WXYZ*.**

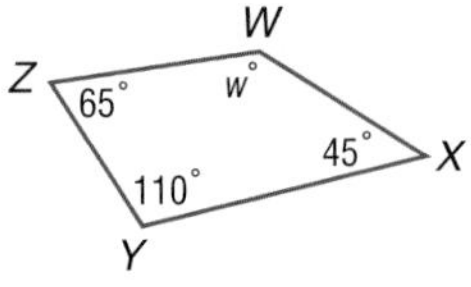

$m\angle W + m\angle X + m\angle Y + m\angle Z = 360$		The sum of the measures is 360.
$w + 45 + 110 + 65 = 360$		Let $m\angle W = w$, $m\angle X = 45$, $m\angle Y = 110$, and $m\angle Z = 65$.
$w + 220 = 360$		Simplify.
$-220 = -220$		Subtract 220 from each side.
$w = 140$		Simplify.

TEACHING TIP

Remind students that all polygons are named by the letters at their vertices in consecutive order. Thus, the figure in Example 1 could *not* be named quadrilateral *WYZX*.

What makes all of the shapes quadrilaterals even though they look different? **They have four sides and four angles.**

READING Math

Isosceles Trapezoid A trapezoid with one pair of opposite congruent sides is classified as an *isosceles* trapezoid.

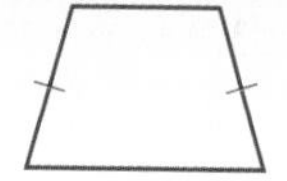

The concept map below shows how quadrilaterals are classified. Notice that the diagram goes from the most general type of quadrilateral to the most specific.

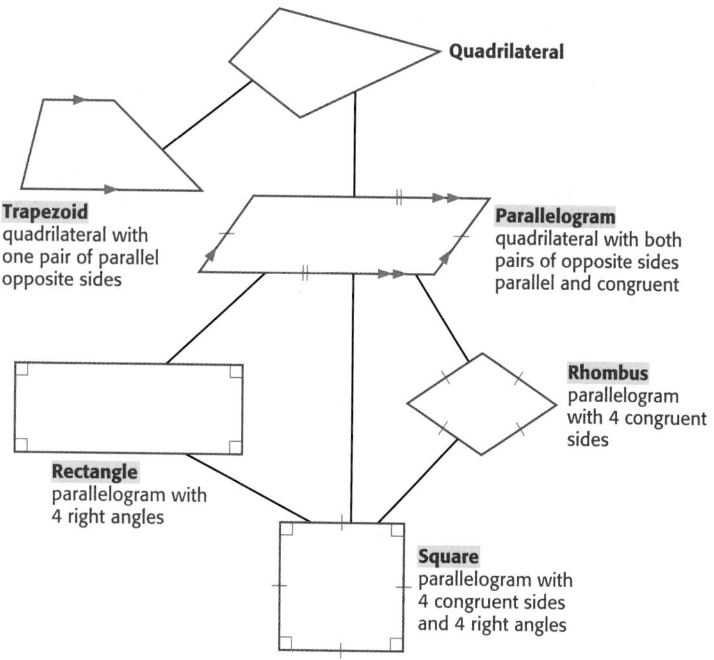

The best description of a quadrilateral is the one that is the most specific.

STUDY TIP

Classifying Quadrilaterals When classifying a quadrilateral, begin by counting the number of parallel lines. Then count the number of right angles and the number of congruent sides.

EXAMPLES Classify Quadrilaterals

Classify each quadrilateral using the name that *best* describes it.

2 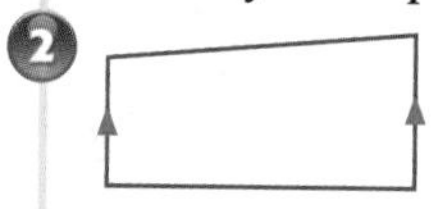

The quadrilateral has one pair of parallel sides. It is a trapezoid.

3 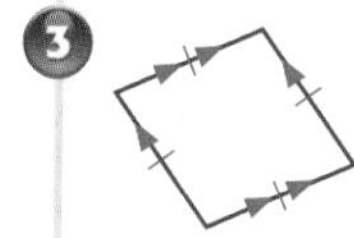

The quadrilateral is a parallelogram with four congruent sides. It is a rhombus.

Your Turn **Classify each quadrilateral using the name that *best* describes it.**

a. 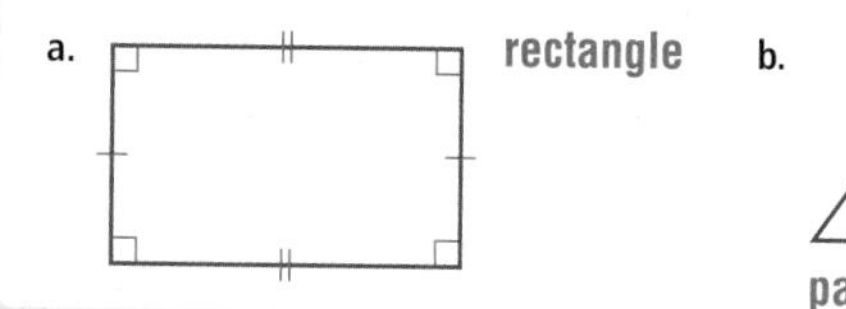 rectangle

b.  parallelogram

msmath3.net/extra_examples

2 Teach

In-Class Examples

INTERACTIVE CHALKBOARD PowerPoint® Presentations

1 Find the value of q in quadrilateral $PQRS$. **80**

S R P Q 120° 36° 124° q°

Classify each quadrilateral using the name that *best* describes it.

2 **quadrilateral**

3 **square**

DAILY INTERVENTION **Unlocking Misconceptions**

Classifying Quadrilaterals Students may not understand that quadrilaterals frequently can be identified by different names. For example, a square is also a parallelogram. Have students study the concept map on page 273 carefully. Discuss what is meant by the sentence, "The best description of a quadrilateral is the one that is the most specific."

3 Practice/Apply

FOLDABLES™ Follow-Up Remind students to include information on classifying quadrilaterals in words and symbols in the "Polygons" section of their Foldable tables.

Which One Doesn't Belong? If students have difficulty answering Exercise 3, suggest that they review the concept map on page 273. Encourage students to draw examples for each type.

About the Exercises...

Guided Practice Key

Exercises	Examples
4–6	1
7–9	2, 3

Assignment Guide

Basic: 11–23 odd, 27, 29, 31–44

Average: 11–29 odd, 31–44

Enriched: 10–30 even, 31–41 (Optional: 42–44)

Answers

27. trapezoid
28. parallelogram, rhombus, rectangle, square
29. rhombus, square
30. rectangle, square
33. 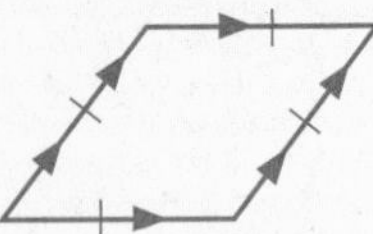
34. 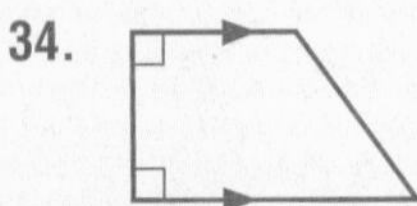
42. Yes, the segments have the same measure.

Students practice the same concepts in Exercises 10–23 and 25–34 if they are assigned odd or even problems.

Skill and Concept Check

1. *Writing Math* Explain why a square is a type of rhombus. **A square is a parallelogram with four congruent sides.**
2. **OPEN ENDED** Give a real-life example of a parallelogram. **Sample answer: a sheet of paper**
3. **Which One Doesn't Belong?** Identify the quadrilateral that does not belong with the other three. Explain your reasoning.

rhombus	rectangle	square	trapezoid

Trapezoid; the others are all examples of parallelograms.

GUIDED PRACTICE

Find the value of x in each quadrilateral.

4. 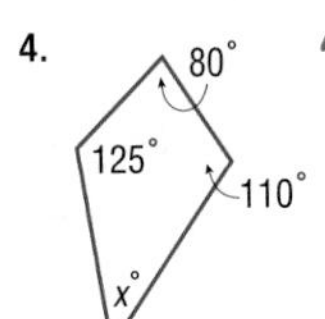

45

5. 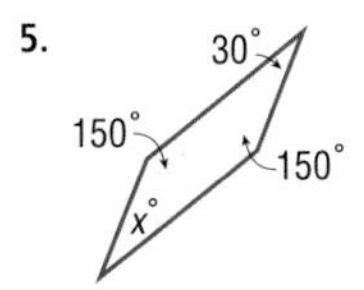

30

6. 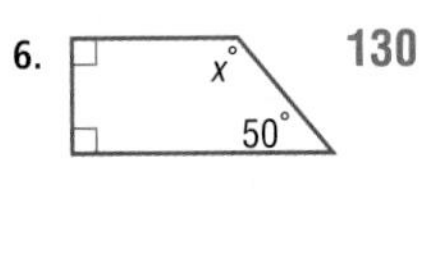

130

Classify each quadrilateral using the name that *best* describes it.

7. 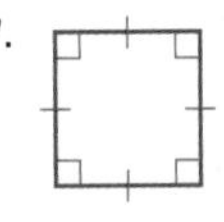 **square**

8. 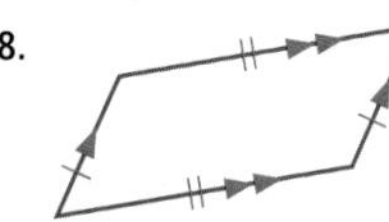 **parallelogram**

9. 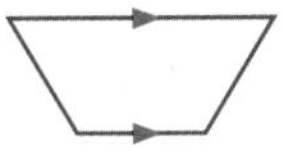  **trapezoid**

★ indicates increased difficulty

Practice and Applications

Find the value of x in each quadrilateral.

10. 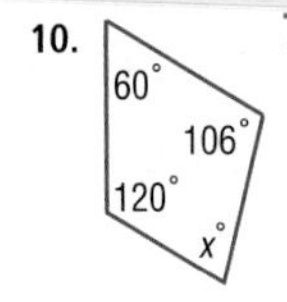

74

11. 95°, x°, 112°, 58° **95**

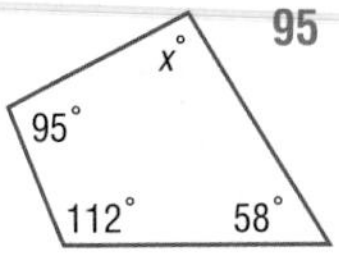

12. 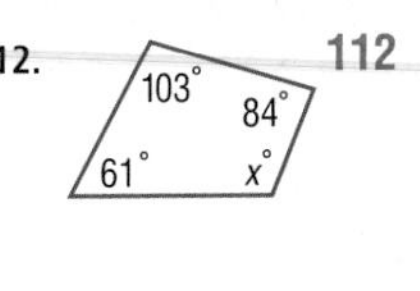

112

13. 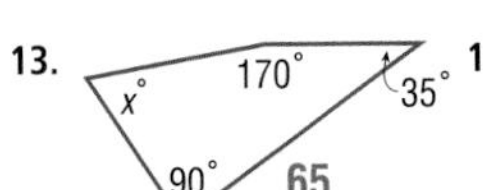

65

14. 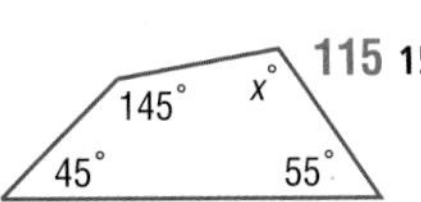

115

15. 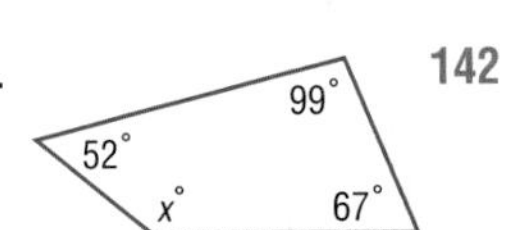

142

HOMEWORK HELP	
For Exercises	See Examples
10–15, 25–26	1
16–24, 27–30	2, 3

Extra Practice See pages 630, 653.

Classify each quadrilateral using the name that *best* describes it.

16. 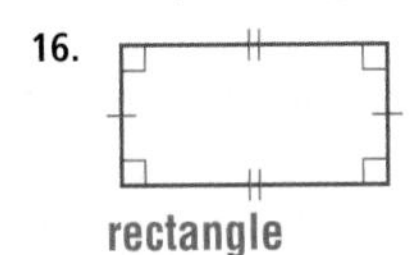 **rectangle**

17. 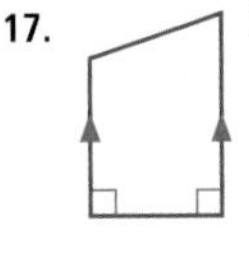 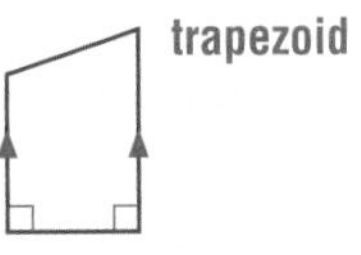 **trapezoid**

18. 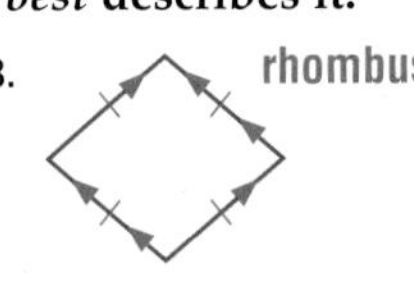 **rhombus**

19. 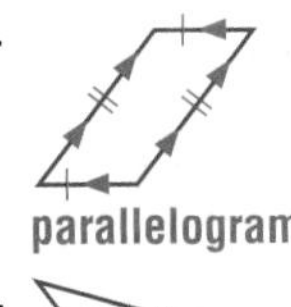 **parallelogram**

20.  **quadrilateral**

21. 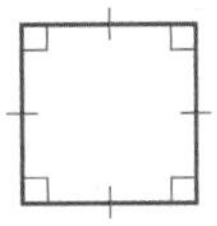 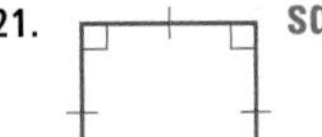 **square**

22. 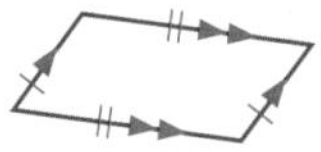 **parallelogram**

23. 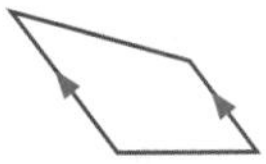 **trapezoid**

43. Yes, the angles have the same measure.
44. No, the segments do not have the same measure.

24. **INTERIOR DESIGN** The stained glass window shown is an example of how geometric figures can be used in decorating. Identify all of the quadrilaterals within the print. **Sample answer: parallelogram, rectangle, square, trapezoid**

★25. **ALGEBRA** In parallelogram $WXYZ$, $m\angle W = 45°$, $m\angle X = 135°$, $m\angle Y = 45°$, and $m\angle Z = (x + 15)°$. Find the value of x. **120**

★26. **ALGEBRA** In trapezoid $ABCD$, $m\angle A = 2a°$, $m\angle B = 40°$, $m\angle C = 110°$, and $m\angle D = 70°$. Find the value of a. **70**

27–30. See margin.

Name all quadrilaterals with the given characteristic.

27. only one pair of parallel sides
28. opposite sides congruent
29. all sides congruent
30. all angles are right angles

CRITICAL THINKING Determine whether each statement is *true* or *false*. If *false*, draw a counterexample.

31. All trapezoids are quadrilaterals. **true**
32. All squares are rectangles. **true**
33. All rhombi (plural of rhombus) are squares. **False; see margin.**
34. A trapezoid can have only one right angle. **False; see margin.**

Spiral Review with Standardized Test Practice

35. **MULTIPLE CHOICE** Which of the following does *not* describe the quadrilateral at the right? **C**

Ⓐ parallelogram Ⓑ square
Ⓒ trapezoid Ⓓ rhombus

36. **SHORT RESPONSE** In rhombus $WXYZ$, $m\angle Z = 70°$, $m\angle X = 70°$, and $m\angle Y = 110°$. Find the measure of $\angle W$. **110°**

37. The length of the hypotenuse of a 30°-60° right triangle is 16 feet. Find the length of the side opposite the 60° angle. Round to the nearest tenth. (Lesson 6-3) **13.9 ft**

38. The length of one of the legs of a 45°-45° right triangle is 8 meters. Find the length of the hypotenuse. Round to the nearest tenth. (Lesson 6-3) **11.3 m**

Classify each triangle by its angles and by its sides. (Lesson 6-2)

39. 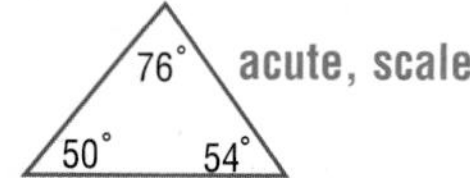

acute, scalene

40. 
right, isosceles

41. 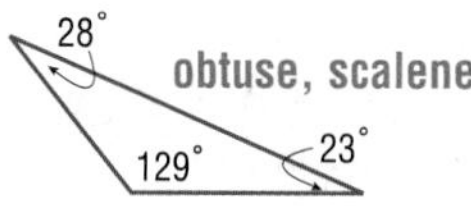

obtuse, scalene

GETTING READY FOR THE NEXT LESSON

PREREQUISITE SKILL Decide whether the figures are congruent. Write *yes* or *no* and explain your reasoning. (Lesson 4-5) **42–44. See margin.**

42. 

43. 

44. 

msmath3.net/self_check_quiz

4 Assess

Open-Ended Assessment

Writing Have students write a paragraph describing the relationships among quadrilaterals, trapezoids, parallelograms, rectangles, rhombuses, and squares.

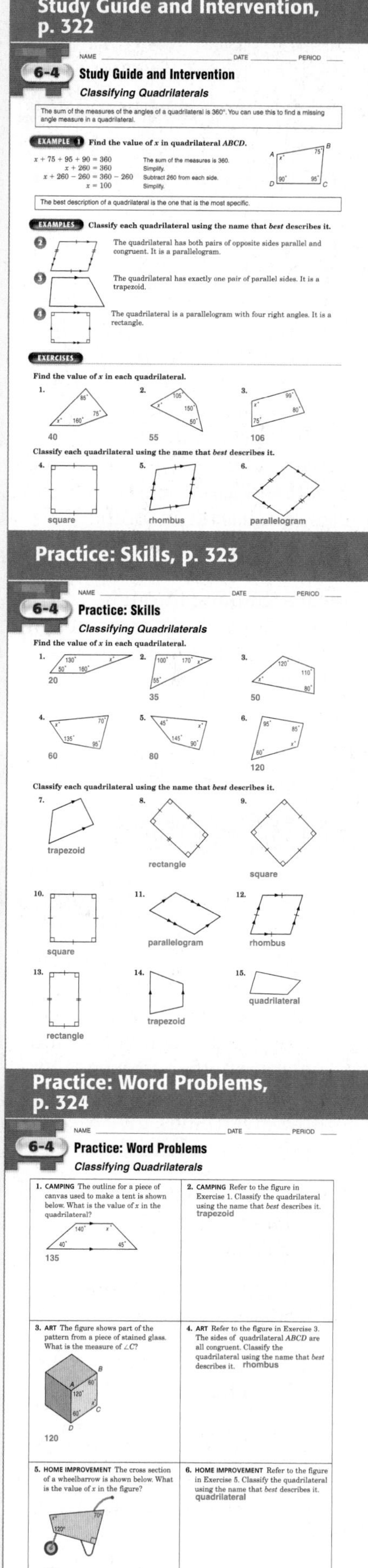

6-4b Lesson Notes

1 Focus

Bellringer

Reading Mathematics Students probably have heard the term *logical reasoning*, but they may not understand its meaning. Have students look up the words *logical* and *reasoning*. Then lead a class discussion about the meanings. Students should realize that logical reasoning means thinking through problems carefully, and reaching conclusions based on sound information or ideas.

2 Teach

In-Class Example

Solve. Use logical reasoning.

FOOD Mona, Sharon, Pat, and Dena each have a different favorite food. One likes pizza, another fish and chips, another chicken, and another hamburgers. From the given clues, give each person's favorite food.

- Pat does not like pizza, hamburgers, or fish and chips.
- Neither Mona nor Dena likes hamburgers.
- Mona does not like to eat fried food.

Mona, pizza; Sharon, hamburgers; Pat, chicken; Dena, fish and chips

6-4b Problem-Solving Strategy

A Follow-Up of Lesson 6-4

Use Logical Reasoning

What You'll LEARN

Solve problems using the logical reasoning strategy.

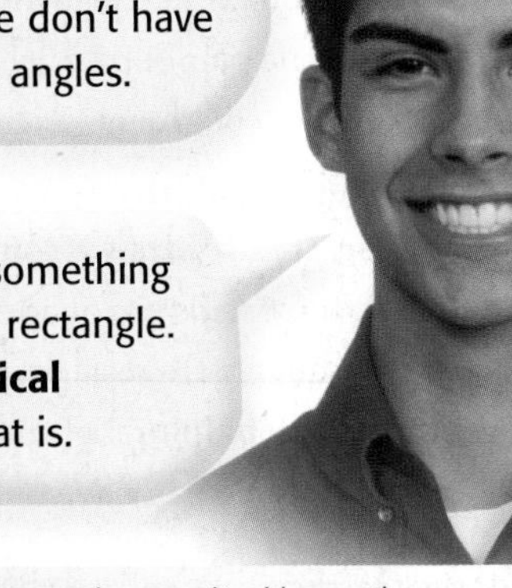

Jacy, how can we be sure this playing field we've marked out is a rectangle? We don't have anything we can use to measure its angles.

Someone told me that there is something special about the diagonals of a rectangle. Zach, let's see if we can **use logical reasoning** to figure out what that is.

Explore The playing field is a parallelogram because its opposite sides are the same length. Our math teacher said that means they are also parallel. We need to see what the relationship is between the diagonals of a rectangle.

Plan Let's draw several different rectangles, measure the diagonals, and see if there is a pattern.

Solve

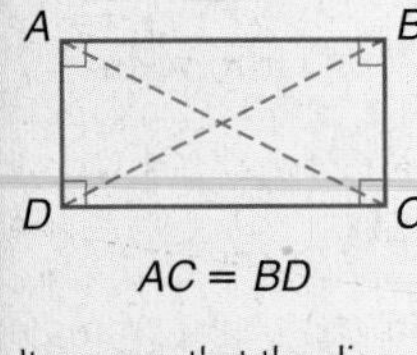

$AC = BD$

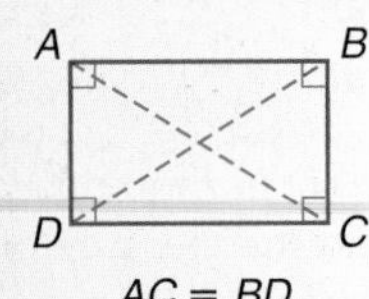

$AC = BD$

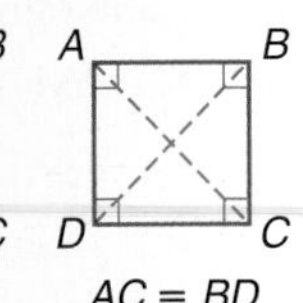

$AC = BD$

It appears that the diagonals of a rectangle are congruent. If the diagonals of our field are congruent, then we can reason that it is a rectangle.

Examine Do all parallelograms, not just rectangles, have congruent diagonals? The counterexample at the right suggests that this statement is false.

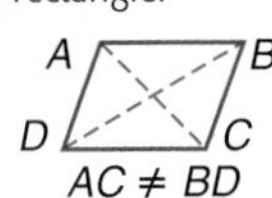

$AC \neq BD$

Apply the Strategy

1. *Deductive reasoning* uses an existing rule to make a decision. **Determine** where Zach and Jacy used deductive reasoning. Explain. **1–3. See margin.**
2. *Inductive reasoning* is the process of making a rule after observing several examples and using that rule to make a decision. **Determine** where Zach and Jacy used inductive reasoning. Explain.
3. **Write** about a situation in which you use inductive reasoning to solve a problem. Then solve the problem.

DAILY INTERVENTION — **Flexible Grouping**

Logical Reasoning Separate the class into groups of three or four students. Each group should write a word problem that can be solved using logical reasoning. Have the groups exchange problems and solve them. If there is sufficient class time, have a representative from each group describe to the rest of the class how the group's members solved their problem.

Apply the Strategy

Solve. Use logical reasoning.

4. **GEOMETRY** Draw several parallelograms and measure their angles. What can you conclude about opposite angles of parallelograms? Did you use deductive or inductive reasoning? **See margin.**

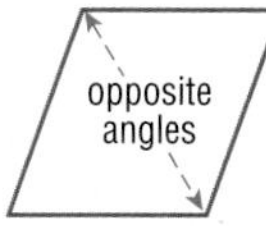

5. **SPORTS** Noah, Brianna, Mackenzie, Antoine, and Bianca were the first five finishers of a race. From the given clues, give the order in which they finished.
   - Noah passed Mackenzie just before the finish line.
   - Bianca finished 5 seconds ahead of Noah.
   - Brianna crossed the finish line after Mackenzie.
   - Antoine was fifth at the finish line.

   1st, Bianca; 2nd, Noah; 3rd, Mackenzie; 4th, Brianna; 5th, Antoine

Mixed Problem Solving

Solve. Use any strategy.

6. **GEOMETRY** If the sides of the pentagons shown are 1 unit long, find the perimeter of 8 pentagons arranged according to the pattern below. **26**

  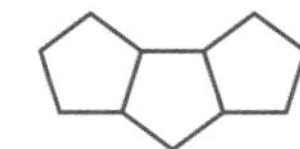

7. **MONEY** After a trip to the mall, Alex and Marcus counted their money to see how much they had left. Alex said, "If I had \$4 more, I would have as much as you." Marcus replied, "If I had \$4 more, I would have twice as much as you." How much does each boy have? **Alex, \$8; Marcus, \$12**

8. **WEATHER** Based on the data shown, what is a reasonable estimate for the difference in the July high and low temperatures in Statesboro? **Sample answer: 20°**

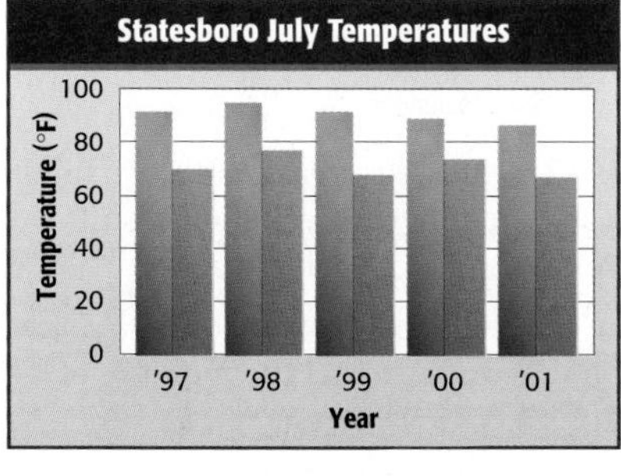

9. **MEASUREMENT** You have a large container of pineapple juice, an empty 4-pint container, and an empty 5-pint container. Explain how you can use these containers to measure 2 pints of juice for a punch recipe. **See Ch. 6 Answer Appendix.**

10. **LAUNDRY** You need two clothespins to hang one towel on a clothesline. One clothespin can be used on a corner of one towel and a corner of the towel next to it. What is the least number of clothespins you need to hang 8 towels? **9 clothespins**

11. **STANDARDIZED TEST PRACTICE** Vanessa and Ashley varied the length of a pendulum and measured the time it took for the pendulum to complete one swing back and forth. Based on their data, how long do you think a pendulum with a swing of 5 seconds is? **D**

Time (s)	1	2	3	4
Length (ft)	1	4	9	16

Ⓐ 21 ft Ⓑ 23 ft
Ⓒ 24 ft Ⓓ 25 ft

3 Practice/Apply

About the Exercises...

Problem-Solving Strategies
Exercises 6–11 are structured so that students have the opportunity to practice many different problem-solving strategies. You may wish to remind them of some of the strategies they have studied.

- work backward (p. 43)
- look for a pattern (p. 96)
- draw a diagram (p. 176)
- use logical reasoning ✓

4 Assess

Higher-Level Thinking
Alonso, Brenda, Claudia, and Darnell are different ages. They range in age from 11 to 14 years old. Brenda is older than Darnell but younger than Claudia. Darnell is not 12 years old. Alonso is one year older than Darnell. What are their ages? **Claudia, 14; Brenda, 13; Alonso, 12; Darnell, 11**

Answers

1. They used the rule their math teacher gave them that if opposite sides of a quadrilateral are congruent then they are also parallel to decide that their playing field was a parallelogram.
2. They observed that the diagonals of several different examples of rectangles were congruent to decide that the diagonals of all rectangles are congruent.
3. Sample answer: Tina wonders if she will have a quiz this Friday in her math class. She knows that her math teacher has given a quiz every Friday for the last four weeks. Using inductive reasoning, Tina should have a quiz this Friday.
4. See students' work; opposite angles in a parallelogram are congruent; inductive.

6-5a HANDS-ON LAB

Lesson Notes

Lesson Resources

Teaching Mathematics with Manipulatives

- student recording sheet 6-5a
- ruler (straightedge)

GETTING STARTED

Teaching Tip Provide each student with a large polygon printed on a piece of paper. You can make a variety of shapes using the drawing toolbar of word-processing software. Have students select one vertex of the shape and crease the paper from that vertex to another vertex. Repeat for all vertices. Ask what shapes were formed. **triangles**

TEACH

- Have students examine the sketch of the 5-sided figure in the table. They should note that all of the lines start at one vertex. Point out that any one vertex will work.

ASSESS

Observe as students complete the table. They should:

- correctly sketch each figure to match the number of sides stated in each row,
- correctly count the number of triangles in each figure, and
- correctly express the sum of angle measures for each figure as an equation.

Discuss the **Writing Math** exercises. For Exercise 3, remind students to examine the names of polygons when determining their number of sides. Use Exercise 4 to determine whether students have grasped the meaning of *regular polygon* and have learned how to express the sum of angle measures in polygons algebraically.

6-5a HANDS-ON LAB

A Preview of Lesson 6-5

What You'll LEARN

Find the sum of the angle measures of polygons.

REVIEW Vocabulary

polygon: a simple closed figure in a plane formed by three or more line segments (Lesson 4-5)

Materials

- paper
- straightedge

Angles of Polygons

In this lab, you will use the fact that the sum of the angle measures of a triangle is 180° to find the sum of the angle measures of any polygon.

INVESTIGATE *Work with a partner.*

Copy and complete the table below.

Number of Sides	Sketch of Figure	Number of Triangles	Sum of Angle Measures
3		1	1(180°) = 180°
4		2	2(180°) = 360°
5		3	3(180°) = 540°
6		4	4(180°) = 720°
7		5	5(180°) = 900°

See students' work for sketches.

Writing Math

1. 6; 1,080°; See margin for drawing.

1. **Predict** the number of triangles in an octagon and the sum of its angle measures. Check your prediction by drawing a figure.
2. **Write** an algebraic expression that tells the number of triangles in an n-sided polygon. Then write an expression for the sum of the angle measures in an n-sided polygon. $n - 2$; $(n - 2)180°$

REGULAR POLYGONS A **regular polygon** is one that is *equilateral* (all sides congruent) and *equiangular* (all angles congruent). Polygons that are not regular are said to be *irregular*.

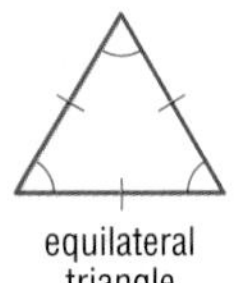
equilateral triangle

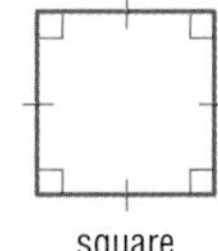
square

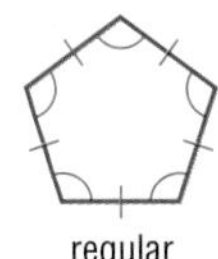
regular pentagon

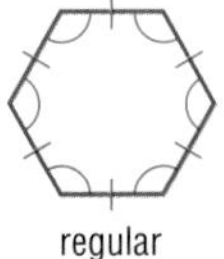
regular hexagon

3. Use your results from Exercise 2 to find the measure of each angle in the four regular polygons shown above. Check your results by using a protractor to measure one angle of each polygon.
4. **Write** an algebraic expression that tells the measure of each angle in an n-sided regular polygon. Use it to predict the measure of each angle in a regular octagon. $\frac{(n-2)180°}{n}$; 135°

3. equilateral triangle, 60°; square, 90°; regular pentagon, 108°; regular hexagon, 120°

TEACHING TIP

Using what they have learned in this lab, have students explain how they would draw a regular nonagon, or 9-sided figure, using a protractor and a ruler. Ask students to compare regular and irregular polygons.

Answer (Writing Math)

1.
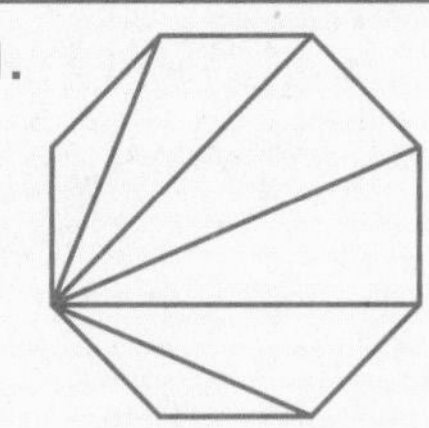

6-5 Congruent Polygons

What You'll LEARN

Identify congruent polygons.

NEW Vocabulary

congruent polygons

WHEN am I ever going to use this?

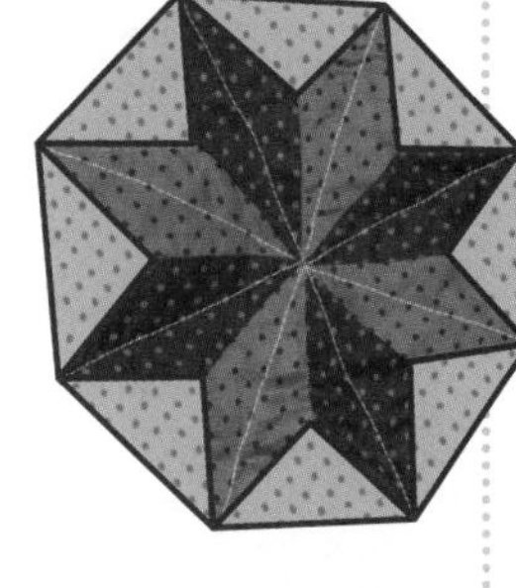

QUILTING A template, or pattern, for a quilt block contains the minimum number of shapes needed to create the pattern.

1. How many different kinds of triangles are shown in the *Winter Stars* quilt at the right? Explain your reasoning and draw each triangle.
2. Copy the quilt and label all matching triangles with the same number, starting with 1.

1. 2; All triangles in this pattern have the same shape and size as one of the two triangles below.

2. See Ch. 6 Answer Appendix.

Polygons that have the same size and shape are called **congruent polygons**. Recall that the parts of polygons that "match" are called *corresponding* parts.

Noteables™ **Key Concept: Congruent Polygons**

Words If two polygons are congruent, their corresponding sides are congruent and their corresponding angles are congruent.

Model

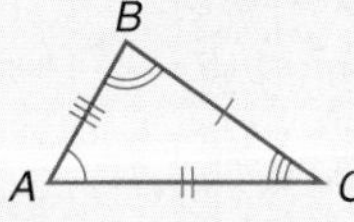

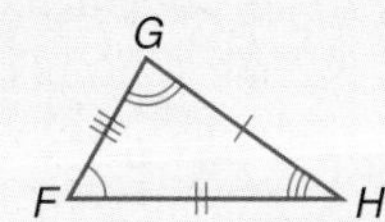

Symbols Congruent angles: $\angle A \cong \angle F$, $\angle B \cong \angle G$, $\angle C \cong \angle H$

Congruent sides: $\overline{BC} \cong \overline{GH}$, $\overline{AC} \cong \overline{FH}$, $\overline{AB} \cong \overline{FG}$

In a congruence statement, the letters identifying each polygon are written so that corresponding vertices appear in the same order. For example, for the diagram below, write $\triangle CBD \cong \triangle PQR$.

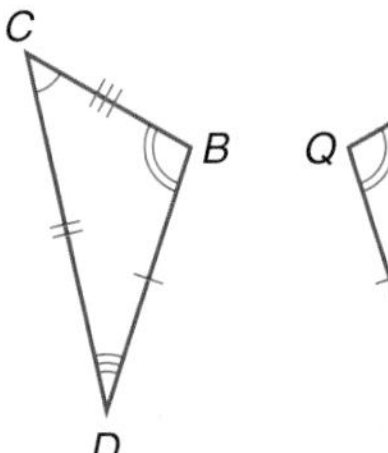

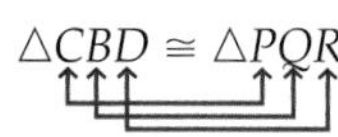

Vertex *C* corresponds to vertex *P*.
Vertex *B* corresponds to vertex *Q*.
Vertex *D* corresponds to vertex *R*.

Two polygons are congruent if all pairs of corresponding angles are congruent and all pairs of corresponding sides are congruent.

6-5 Lesson Notes

Lesson Resources

Chapter 6 Resource Masters
- Study Guide and Intervention, p. 327
- Practice: Skills, p. 328
- Practice: Word Problems, p. 329
- Reading to Learn Mathematics, p. 330
- Enrichment, p. 331

MathPASS Tutorial CD-ROM, 45

Parent and Student Study Guide Online Worksheets, 6-5

Science and Math Lab Masters, pp. 73–76

Noteables™: Interactive Study Notebook with Foldables™, 6-5

FAST FILE

1 Focus

5-Minute Check 6-5

Use as a quiz or review of Lesson 6-4. (Also available as a transparency)

Bellringer

Communication Draw the pairs of polygons shown in the bottom margin on the chalkboard. Ask students which pair has
- the same size and shape **b**
- the same shape but different sizes **a**
- neither the same size nor the same shape **c**

(Continued in bottom margin.)

Reading to Learn Mathematics, p. 330 **ELL**

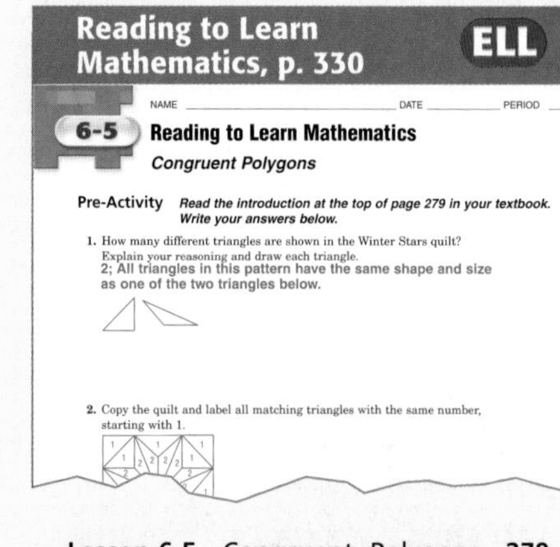

NAME ________ DATE ________ PERIOD ____

6-5 Reading to Learn Mathematics

Congruent Polygons

Pre-Activity *Read the introduction at the top of page 279 in your textbook. Write your answers below.*

1. How many different triangles are shown in the Winter Stars quilt? Explain your reasoning and draw each triangle.
2; All triangles in this pattern have the same shape and size as one of the two triangles below.

2. Copy the quilt and label all matching triangles with the same number, starting with 1.

a.

b.

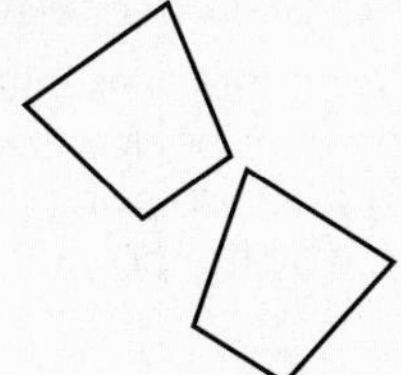

c.

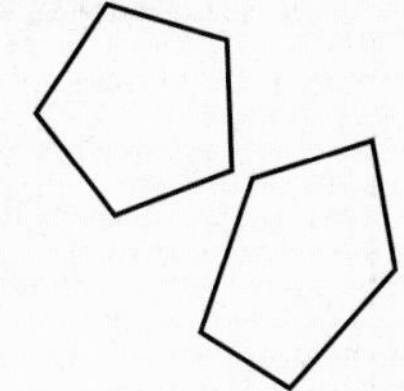

2 Teach

In-Class Examples

INTERACTIVE CHALKBOARD
PowerPoint® Presentations

1 Determine whether the trapezoids shown are congruent. If so, name the corresponding parts and write a congruence statement.

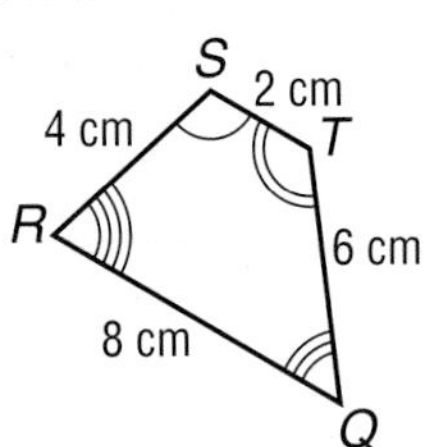

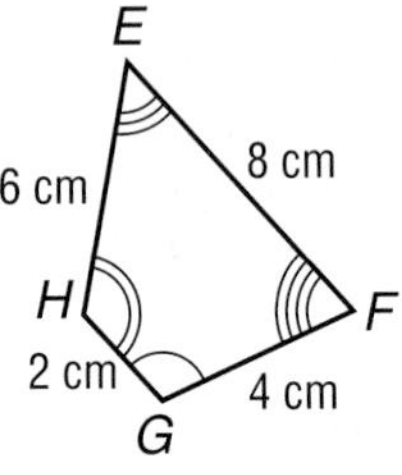

yes; $\angle Q \cong \angle E$, $\angle R \cong \angle F$, $\angle S \cong \angle G$, $\angle T \cong \angle H$, $\overline{QR} \cong \overline{EF}$, $\overline{RS} \cong \overline{FG}$, $\overline{ST} \cong \overline{GH}$, $\overline{TQ} \cong \overline{HE}$; trapezoid $EFGH \cong$ trapezoid $QRST$

In the figures shown below, $\triangle FGH \cong \triangle QRS$.

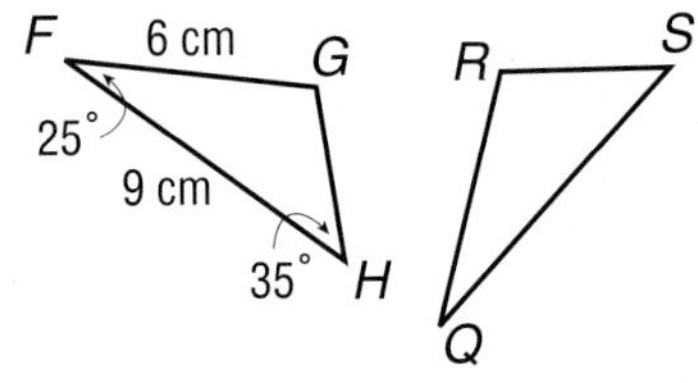

2 Find $m\angle S$. **35°**

3 Find QR. **6 cm**

TEACHING TIP

It may be easier for students to see the congruent parts if they redraw the triangles so that they have the same orientation.

STUDY TIP

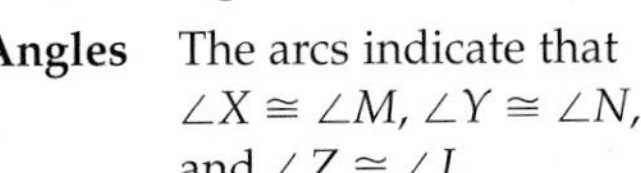

Congruence Statements Other possible congruence statements for Example 1 are $\triangle YZX \cong \triangle NLM$, $\triangle ZXY \cong \triangle LMN$, $\triangle YXZ \cong \triangle NML$, $\triangle XZY \cong \triangle MLN$, and $\triangle ZYX \cong \triangle LNM$.

a. yes; $\angle P \cong \angle C$, $\angle Q \cong \angle B$, $\angle R \cong \angle D$, $\overline{PQ} \cong \overline{CB}$, $\overline{QR} \cong \overline{BD}$, $\overline{PR} \cong \overline{CD}$; $\triangle PQR \cong \triangle CBD$

READING Math

Recall that symbols like RN refer to the measure of the segment with those endpoints.

EXAMPLE Identify Congruent Polygons

1 **Determine whether the triangles shown are congruent. If so, name the corresponding parts and write a congruence statement.**

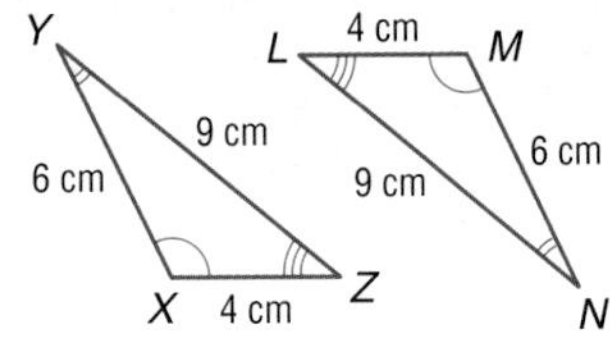

Angles The arcs indicate that $\angle X \cong \angle M$, $\angle Y \cong \angle N$, and $\angle Z \cong \angle L$.

Sides The side measures indicate that $\overline{XY} \cong \overline{MN}$, $\overline{YZ} \cong \overline{NL}$, and $\overline{XZ} \cong \overline{ML}$.

Since all pairs of corresponding angles and sides are congruent, the two triangles are congruent. One congruence statement is $\triangle XYZ \cong \triangle MNL$.

Your Turn **Determine whether the polygons shown are congruent. If so, name the corresponding parts and write a congruence statement.**

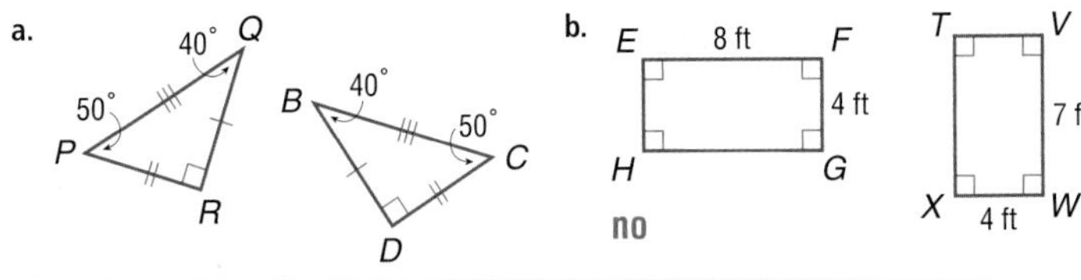

You can use corresponding parts to find the measures of an angle or side in a figure that is congruent to a figure with known measures.

EXAMPLES Find Missing Measures

In the figure, $\triangle AFH \cong \triangle QRN$.

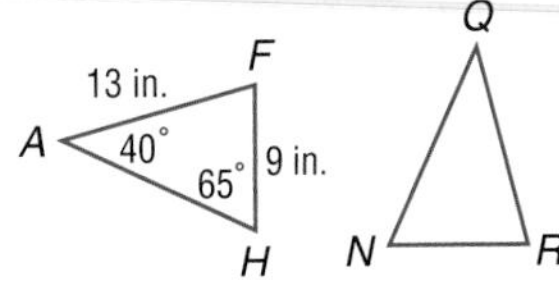

2 **Find $m\angle Q$.**

According to the congruence statement, $\angle A$ and $\angle Q$ are corresponding angles. So, $\angle A \cong \angle Q$. Since $m\angle A = 40°$, $m\angle Q = 40°$.

3 **Find RN.**

$\overline{FH}$ corresponds to $\overline{RN}$. So, $\overline{FH} \cong \overline{RN}$. Since $FH = 9$ inches, $RN = 9$ inches.

Your Turn **In the figure, quadrilateral $ABCD$ is congruent to quadrilateral $WXYZ$. Find each measure.**

c. $m\angle X$ **145°**

d. YX **4 m**

e. $m\angle Y$ **55°**

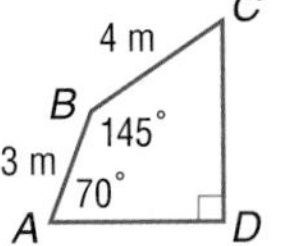

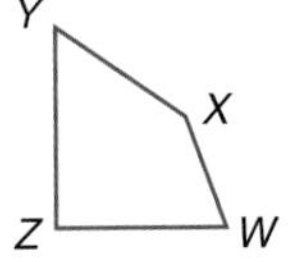

msmath3.net/extra_examples

DAILY INTERVENTION **Differentiated Instruction** **ELL**

Verbal/Linguistic Divide the class into small groups. Have each student draw two congruent polygons with sides and angles labeled. Students should take turns displaying their drawings and explaining to other group members why the polygons are congruent.

Students practice the same concepts in Exercises 9–12 and 14–21 if they are assigned odd or even problems.

Skill and Concept Check

1. **OPEN ENDED** Draw and label a pair of congruent polygons. Be sure to indicate congruent angles and sides on your drawing. **See margin.**

2. **FIND THE ERROR** Justin and Amanda are writing a congruence statement for the triangles at the right. Who is correct? Explain. **See margin.**

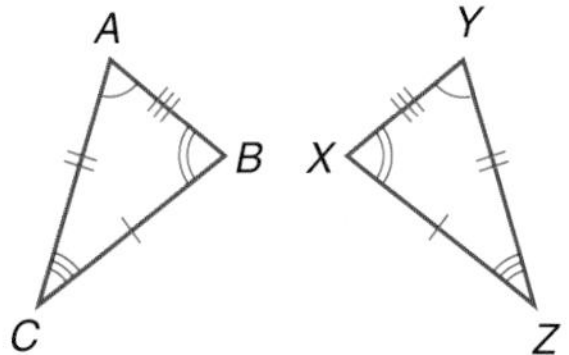

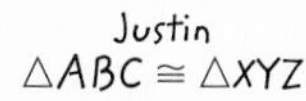

Amanda
△ABC ≅ △YXZ

GUIDED PRACTICE

Determine whether the polygons shown are congruent. If so, name the corresponding parts and write a congruence statement. 3–4. See margin.

3. 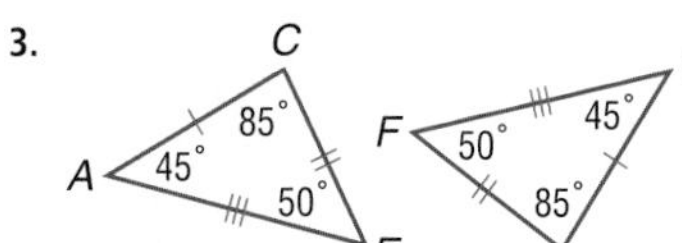

4. 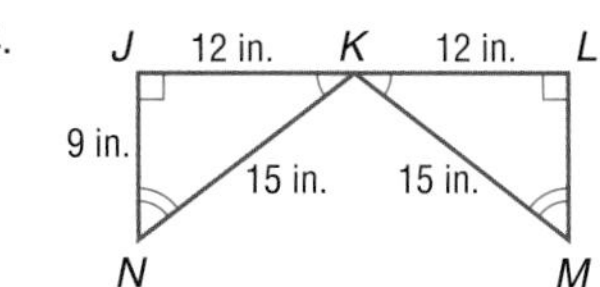

In the figure, △PQR ≅ △YWX. Find each measure.

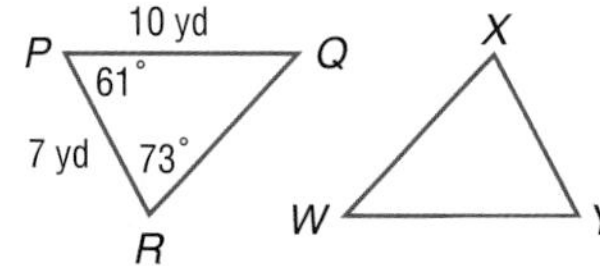

5. $m\angle X$ **73°**
6. YW **10 yd**
7. XY **7 yd**
8. $m\angle W$ **46°**

★ indicates increased difficulty

Practice and Applications

Determine whether the polygons shown are congruent. If so, name the corresponding parts and write a congruence statement.

HOMEWORK HELP	
For Exercises	See Examples
9–13	1
14–23	2, 3

Extra Practice See pages 630, 653.

9. yes

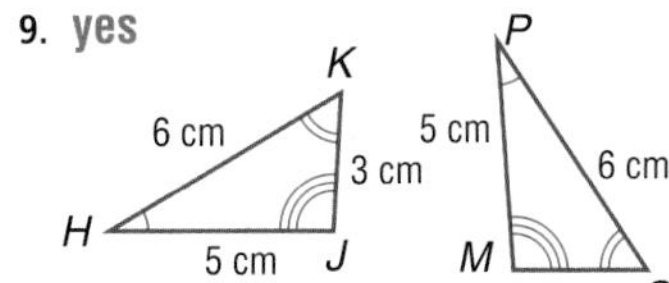

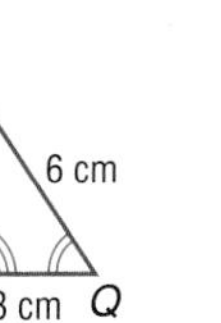

10. no

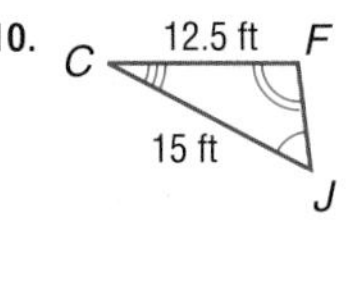

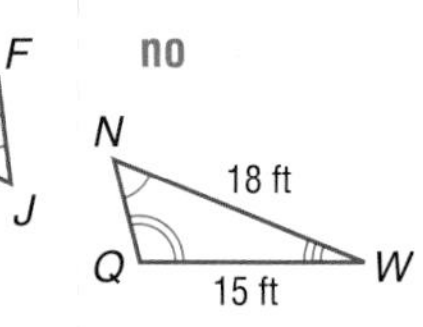

11. no

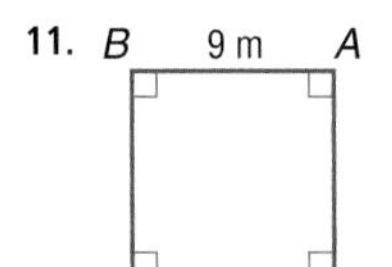

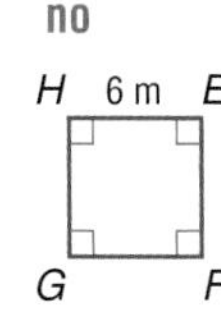

12. yes

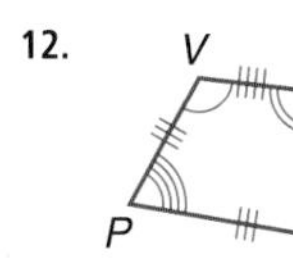

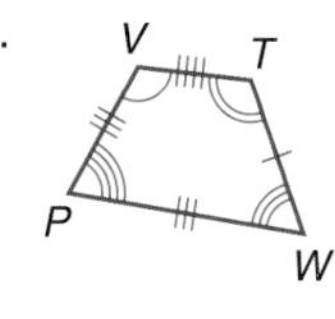

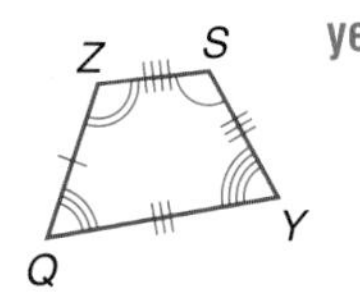

9–12. See Ch. 6 Answer Appendix for congruence statements.

13. **BIRDS** The wings of a hummingbird are shaped like triangles. Determine whether these triangles are congruent. If so, name the corresponding parts and write a congruence statement. **yes; ∠A ≅ ∠E, ∠B ≅ ∠D, ∠C ≅ ∠F, $\overline{AB} \cong \overline{ED}$, $\overline{BC} \cong \overline{DF}$, $\overline{AC} \cong \overline{EF}$; △ABC ≅ △EDF**

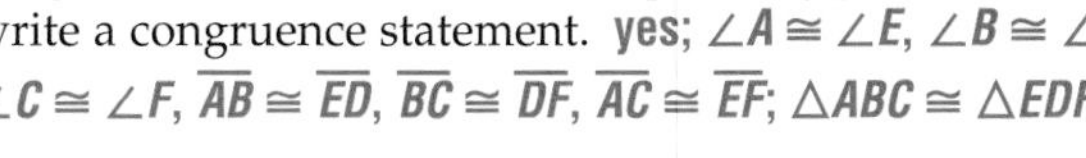

Math Online msmath3.net/self_check_quiz

Tips for New Teachers

Classroom Management When asking students to draw figures such as polygons on the chalkboard, remember that some students are more artistic than others. Some students may not wish to draw on the chalkboard for fear that other students will tease them. Allow students to use a ruler or meterstick as a straightedge when making drawings.

3 Practice/Apply

DAILY INTERVENTION FIND THE ERROR In Exercise 2, remind students that congruent figures are not always oriented in the same way. It may help to trace one figure on paper and then rotate the paper until the figures overlap. Then it is easy to see which angles and sides correspond.

About the Exercises...

Guided Practice Key

Exercises	Examples
3–4	1
5, 8	2
6–7	3

Assignment Guide

Basic: 9–23 odd, 24–32

Average: 9–21 odd, 22–32

Enriched: 10–22 even, 23–30 (Optional: 31–32)

Answers

1. Sample answer:

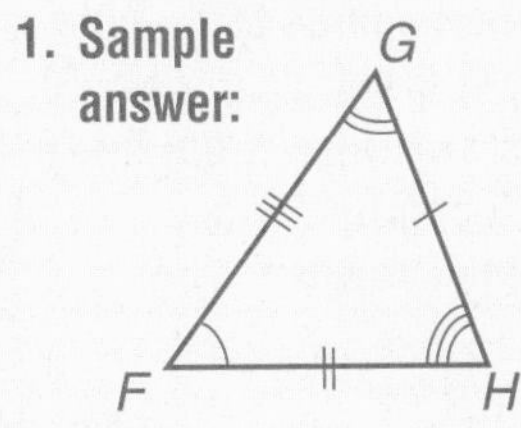

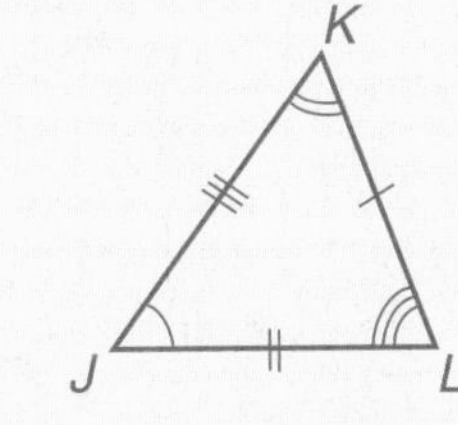

2. Amanda; corresponding vertices must be written in the same order. Vertex *A* corresponds to vertex *Y*, not to vertex *X*.

3. yes; ∠A ≅ ∠G, ∠C ≅ ∠H, ∠E ≅ ∠F, $\overline{AC} \cong \overline{GH}$, $\overline{CE} \cong \overline{HF}$, $\overline{AE} \cong \overline{GF}$; △ACE ≅ △GHF

4. yes; ∠J ≅ ∠L, ∠JKN ≅ ∠LKM, ∠N ≅ ∠M, $\overline{JK} \cong \overline{LK}$, $\overline{KN} \cong \overline{KM}$, $\overline{JN} \cong \overline{LM}$; △JKN ≅ △LKM

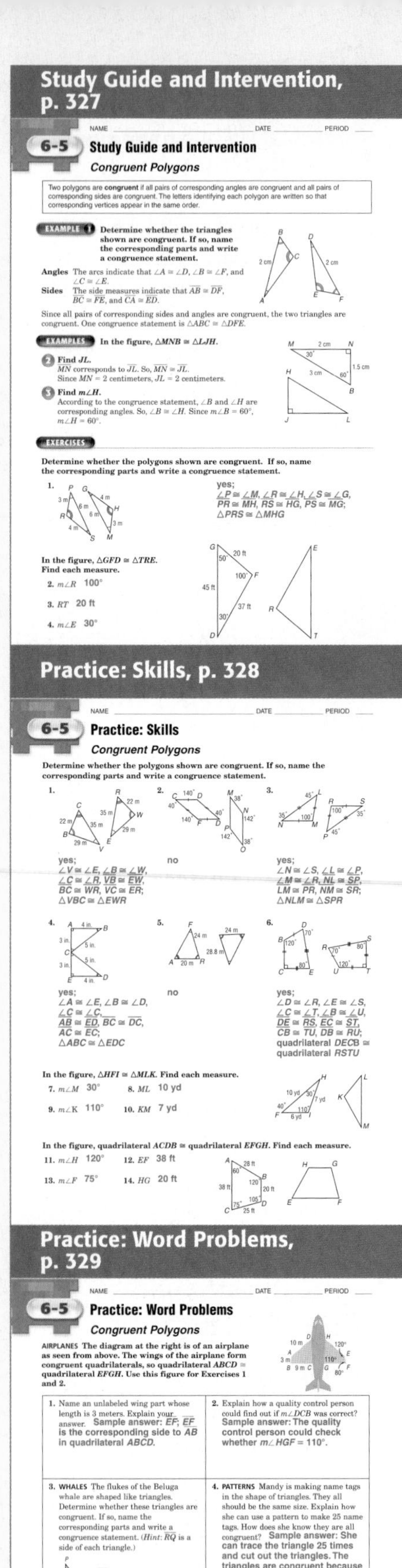
Study Guide and Intervention, p. 327

NAME ______ DATE ______ PERIOD ____

6-5 Study Guide and Intervention

Congruent Polygons

Two polygons are **congruent** if all pairs of corresponding angles are congruent and all pairs of corresponding sides are congruent. The letters identifying each polygon are written so that corresponding vertices appear in the same order.

EXAMPLE 1 **Determine whether the triangles shown are congruent. If so, name the corresponding parts and write a congruence statement.**

Angles The arcs indicate that $\angle A \cong \angle D$, $\angle B \cong \angle F$, and $\angle C \cong \angle E$.

Sides The side measures indicate that $\overline{AB} \cong \overline{DF}$, $\overline{BC} \cong \overline{FE}$, and $\overline{CA} \cong \overline{ED}$.

Since all pairs of corresponding sides and angles are congruent, the two triangles are congruent. One congruence statement is $\triangle ABC \cong \triangle DFE$.

EXAMPLES **In the figure, $\triangle MNB \cong \triangle LJH$.**

2 Find JL.
$\overline{MN}$ corresponds to $\overline{JL}$. So, $\overline{MN} \cong \overline{JL}$.
Since $MN = 2$ centimeters, $JL = 2$ centimeters.

3 Find $m\angle H$.
According to the congruence statement, $\angle B$ and $\angle H$ are corresponding angles. So, $\angle B \cong \angle H$. Since $m\angle B = 60°$, $m\angle H = 60°$.

EXERCISES

Determine whether the polygons shown are congruent. If so, name the corresponding parts and write a congruence statement.

1. yes; $\angle P \cong \angle M$, $\angle R \cong \angle H$, $\angle S \cong \angle G$, $\overline{PR} \cong \overline{MH}$, $\overline{RS} \cong \overline{HG}$, $\overline{PS} \cong \overline{MG}$; $\triangle PRS \cong \triangle MHG$

In the figure, $\triangle GFD \cong \triangle TRE$. Find each measure.

2. $m\angle R$ 100°
3. RT 20 ft
4. $m\angle E$ 30°

Practice: Skills, p. 328

NAME ______ DATE ______ PERIOD ____

6-5 Practice: Skills

Congruent Polygons

Determine whether the polygons shown are congruent. If so, name the corresponding parts and write a congruence statement.

1. yes; $\angle V \cong \angle E$, $\angle B \cong \angle W$, $\angle C \cong \angle R$, $\overline{VB} \cong \overline{EW}$, $\overline{BC} \cong \overline{WR}$, $\overline{VC} \cong \overline{ER}$; $\triangle VBC \cong \triangle EWR$
2. no
3. yes; $\angle N \cong \angle S$, $\angle L \cong \angle P$, $\angle M \cong \angle R$, $\overline{NL} \cong \overline{SP}$, $\overline{LM} \cong \overline{PR}$, $\overline{NM} \cong \overline{SR}$; $\triangle NLM \cong \triangle SPR$
4. yes; $\angle A \cong \angle E$, $\angle B \cong \angle D$, $\angle C \cong \angle C$, $\overline{AB} \cong \overline{ED}$, $\overline{BC} \cong \overline{DC}$, $\overline{AC} \cong \overline{EC}$; $\triangle ABC \cong \triangle EDC$
5. no
6. yes; $\angle D \cong \angle R$, $\angle E \cong \angle S$, $\angle C \cong \angle T$, $\angle B \cong \angle U$, $\overline{DE} \cong \overline{RS}$, $\overline{EC} \cong \overline{ST}$, $\overline{CB} \cong \overline{TU}$, $\overline{DB} \cong \overline{RU}$; quadrilateral $DECB \cong$ quadrilateral $RSTU$

In the figure, $\triangle HFI \cong \triangle MLK$. Find each measure.

7. $m\angle M$ 30°
8. ML 10 yd
9. $m\angle K$ 110°
10. KM 7 yd

In the figure, quadrilateral $ACDB \cong$ quadrilateral $EFGH$. Find each measure.

11. $m\angle H$ 120°
12. EF 38 ft
13. $m\angle F$ 75°
14. HG 20 ft

Practice: Word Problems, p. 329

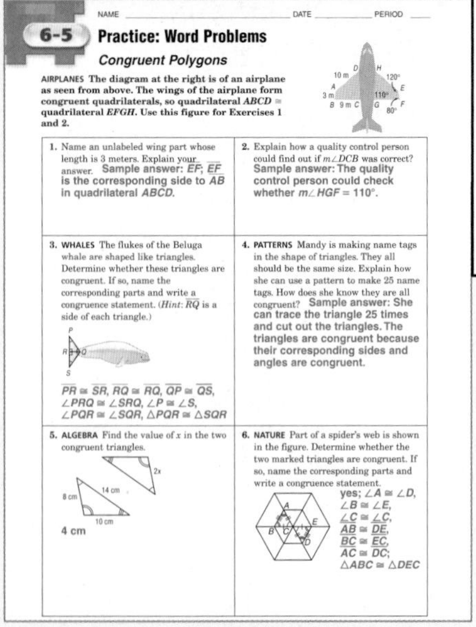

NAME ______ DATE ______ PERIOD ____

6-5 Practice: Word Problems

Congruent Polygons

AIRPLANES The diagram at the right is of an airplane as seen from above. The wings of the airplane form congruent quadrilaterals, so quadrilateral $ABCD \cong$ quadrilateral $EFGH$. Use this figure for Exercises 1 and 2.

1. Name an unlabeled wing part whose length is 3 meters. Explain your answer. Sample answer: $\overline{EF}$; $\overline{EF}$ is the corresponding side to $\overline{AB}$ in quadrilateral $ABCD$.
2. Explain how a quality control person could find out if $m\angle DCB$ was correct? Sample answer: The quality control person could check whether $m\angle HGF = 110°$.
3. WHALES The flukes of the Beluga whale are shaped like triangles. Determine whether these triangles are congruent. If so, name the corresponding parts and write a congruence statement. (*Hint*: $\overline{RQ}$ is a side of each triangle.) $\overline{PR} \cong \overline{SR}$, $\overline{RQ} \cong \overline{RQ}$, $\overline{QP} \cong \overline{QS}$, $\angle PRQ \cong \angle SRQ$, $\angle P \cong \angle S$, $\angle PQR \cong \angle SQR$, $\triangle PQR \cong \triangle SQR$
4. PATTERNS Mandy is making name tags in the shape of triangles. They all should be the same size. Explain how she can use a pattern to make 25 name tags. How does she know they are all congruent? Sample answer: She can trace the triangle 25 times and cut out the triangles. The triangles are congruent because their corresponding sides and angles are congruent.
5. ALGEBRA Find the value of x in the two congruent triangles. 4 cm
6. NATURE Part of a spider's web is shown in the figure. Determine whether the two marked triangles are congruent. If so, name the corresponding parts and write a congruence statement. yes; $\angle A \cong \angle D$, $\angle B \cong \angle E$, $\angle C \cong \angle C$, $\overline{AB} \cong \overline{DE}$, $\overline{BC} \cong \overline{EC}$, $\overline{AC} \cong \overline{DC}$; $\triangle ABC \cong \triangle DEC$

In the figure, $\triangle JKL \cong \triangle PNM$. Find each measure.

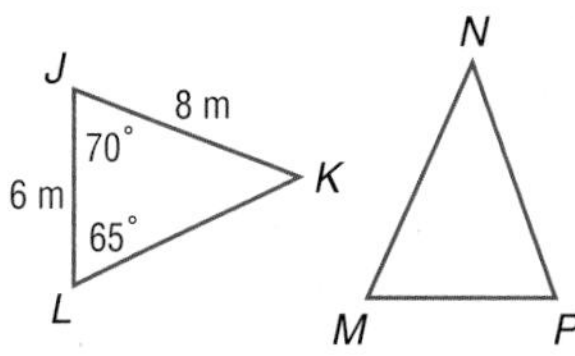

14. PN **8 m**
15. PM **6 m**
16. $m\angle P$ **70°**
17. $m\angle N$ **45°**

In the figure, quadrilateral $ABCD \cong$ quadrilateral $HEFG$. Find each measure.

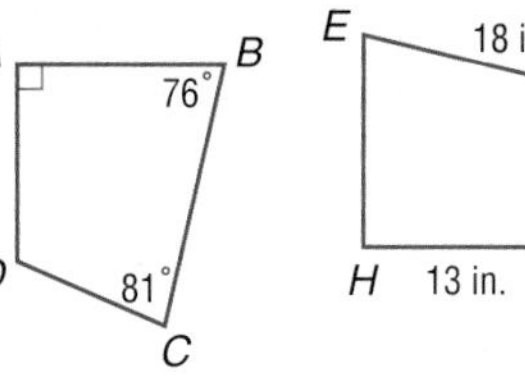

18. AD **13 in.**
19. $m\angle H$ **90°**
20. $m\angle G$ **113°**
21. CD **11 in.**

22. **ALGEBRA** Find the value of x in the two congruent triangles. **13**

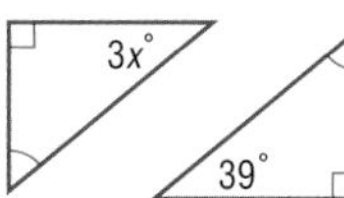

23. **TRAVEL** An overhead sign on an interstate highway is shown at the right. In the scaffolding, $\triangle ABC \cong \triangle DCB$, $AC = 2.5$ meters, $BC = 1$ meter, and $AB = 2.7$ meters. What is the length of $\overline{BD}$? **2.5 m**

24. **CRITICAL THINKING** Tell whether the following statement is *sometimes*, *always* or *never* true. Explain your reasoning.

If the perimeters of two triangles are equal, then the triangles are congruent. **Sometimes; see margin for explanation.**

Spiral Review with Standardized Test Practice

25. **SHORT RESPONSE** Which of the following polygons appear congruent? **a and d**

a. 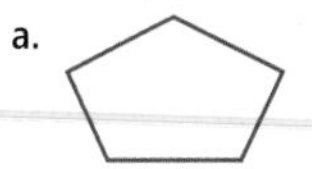
b. 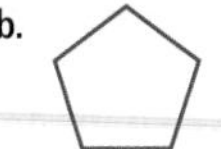
c. 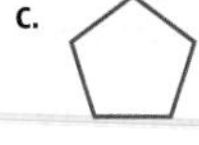
d. 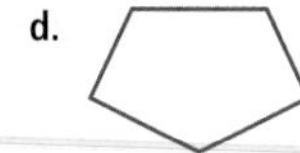

26. **MULTIPLE CHOICE** If $\triangle AFG \cong \triangle PQR$, which statement is *not* true? **G**

Ⓐ $\angle G \cong \angle R$ Ⓑ $\overline{AG} \cong \overline{PQ}$ Ⓒ $\angle P \cong \angle A$ Ⓓ $\overline{AG} \cong \overline{PR}$

Classify each quadrilateral using the name that *best* describes it. (Lesson 6-4)

27. 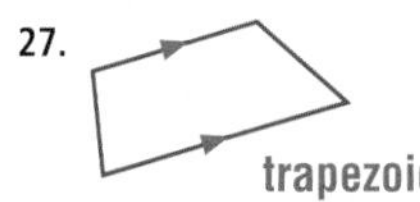 **trapezoid**
28.  **rhombus**
29. 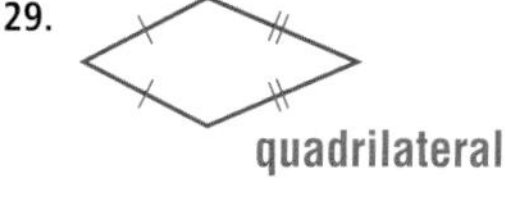 **quadrilateral**

30. The length of each leg of a 45°-45° right triangle is 14 feet. Find the length of the hypotenuse. (Lesson 6-3) **about 19.8 ft**

GETTING READY FOR THE NEXT LESSON

BASIC SKILL Which figure *cannot* be folded so one half matches the other?

31. **A**

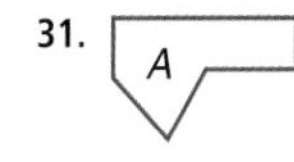

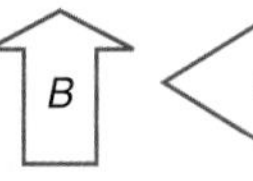

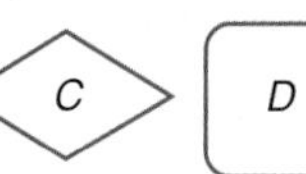

D

32. **D**

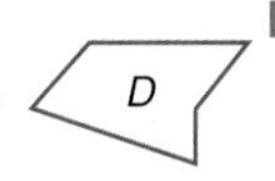

D

282 Chapter 6 Geometry

4 Assess

Open-Ended Assessment

Speaking Put pairs of polygons on the chalkboard and have students take turns explaining what parts are or are not congruent.

Answer

24. **A triangle with side lengths 5, 6, and 8 has the same perimeter as a triangle with side lengths 5, 7, and 7, but these triangles are not congruent since corresponding sides would not be congruent.**

6-5b HANDS-ON LAB

A Follow-Up of Lesson 6-5

Constructing Congruent Triangles

What You'll LEARN

Construct congruent triangles.

Materials

- compass
- straightedge
- protractor
- paper

ACTIVITY

STEP 1 Use a straightedge to draw a line. Put a point on it labeled *X*.

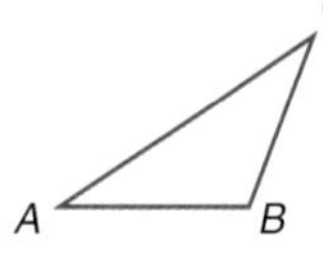

STEP 2 Open your compass to the same width as the length of $\overline{AB}$. Put the compass point at *X*. Draw an arc that intersects the line. Label this point of intersection *Y*.

STEP 3 Open your compass to the same width as the length of $\overline{AC}$. Place your compass point at *X* and draw an arc above the line.

STEP 4 Open your compass to the same width as the length of $\overline{BC}$. Place the compass point at *Y* and draw an arc above the line so that it intersects the arc drawn in Step 3. Label this point *Z*.

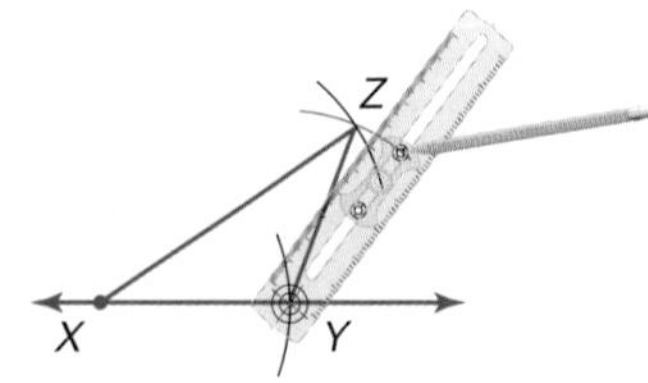

STEP 5 Draw $\overline{YZ}$ and $\overline{XZ}$. $\triangle ABC \cong \triangle XYZ$.

Writing Math

1. **Explain** why the corresponding sides of $\triangle ABC$ and $\triangle XYZ$ are congruent.
2. **Draw** three different triangles. Then construct a triangle that is congruent to each one. **See students' work.**

1. $\overline{XY} \cong \overline{AB}$ **since** $\overline{XY}$ **is a radius of the circle with radius** AB. $\overline{YZ} \cong \overline{BC}$ **since** $\overline{YZ}$ **is a radius of the circle with radius** BC. $\overline{XZ} \cong \overline{AC}$ **since** $\overline{XZ}$ **is a radius of the circle with radius** AC.

6-5b HANDS-ON LAB Lesson Notes

Lesson Resources

Teaching Mathematics with Manipulatives

- protractors, p. 21
- student recording sheet 6-5b

Glencoe Mathematics Classroom Manipulative Kit

- compass
- protractor
- ruler (straightedge)

GETTING STARTED

Teaching Tip Use a straightedge and chalk to draw a triangle on the chalkboard. Have students review Lessons 6-2b and 6-3b briefly. Ask them to brainstorm ways to draw an exact copy of the triangle elsewhere on the chalkboard without using a protractor or ruler.

TEACH

- Students may find it easier to trace $\triangle ABC$ onto their papers before beginning the **Activity**.
- Emphasize to students that the compass point must be at the right spot. You may want them to construct a triangle with the point a little bit off to see the results.
- Remind students of the importance of keeping their compasses open to the same width as the corresponding side on the original triangle.

ASSESS

Discuss the **Writing Math** exercises. Use Exercise 1 to determine whether students have understood the connection between the length of a triangle's side and the compass width used to draw an arc on a line.

Assessment Option

Mid-Chapter Test (Lessons 6-1 through 6-5) is available on p. 369 of the *Chapter 6 Resource Masters*.

ExamView® Pro

Use the networkable ExamView® Pro Testmaker CD-ROM to:

- Create **multiple versions** of tests.
- Create **modified** tests for **inclusion** students with one mouse click.
- **Edit** existing questions and **add** your own questions.
- Build tests aligned with state standards using built-in **state curriculum correlations.**
- Change **English** tests to **Spanish** with one mouse click and vice versa.

FOLDABLES™ Follow-Up Before students complete the Mid-Chapter Practice Test, encourage them to review the notes, definitions, concepts, and main ideas they recorded in their Foldable tables as they progressed through the first five lessons in this chapter.

Answers

1. scalene, no congruent sides; isosceles, at least 2 congruent sides; equilateral, 3 congruent sides
2. Sample answer: parallelogram, quadrilateral with both pairs of opposite sides parallel and congruent; trapezoid, quadrilateral with one pair of parallel opposite sides; rectangle, parallelogram with 4 right angles; rhombus, parallelogram with 4 congruent sides; square, parallelogram with 4 congruent sides and 4 right angles.

Chapter 6 Mid-Chapter Practice Test

Vocabulary and Concepts

1. **Describe** three ways to classify triangles by their sides. (Lesson 6-2)
2. **List and define** five types of quadrilaterals. (Lesson 6-4) **1–2. See margin.**

Skills and Applications

For Exercises 3–5, use the figure at the right. (Lesson 6-1)

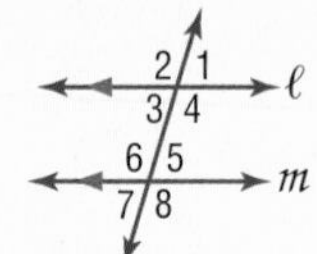

3. Find $m\angle 6$ if $m\angle 7 = 84°$. **96°**
4. Find $m\angle 5$ if $m\angle 1 = 35°$. **35°**

Find the value of x in each figure. (Lessons 6-2 and 6-4)

5. **65**

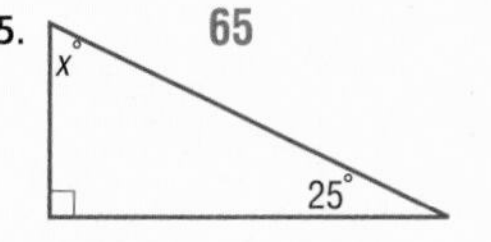

6. **142**

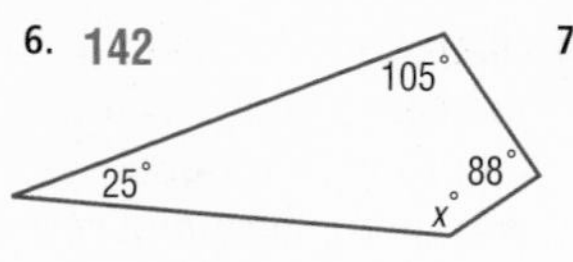

7. **42**

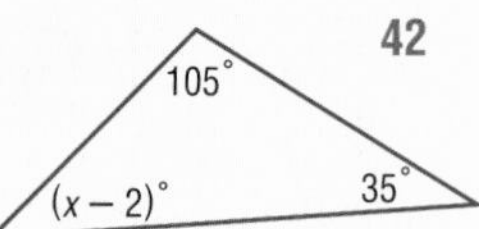

8. **FLAGS** The "Union Jack", a common name for the flag of the United Kingdom, is shown at the right. The blue portions of the flag are triangular. Determine whether the triangles indicated are congruent. If so, write a congruence statement. (Lesson 6-5)
yes; $\angle A \cong \angle H$, $\angle B \cong \angle G$, $\angle C \cong \angle F$, $\overline{AB} \cong \overline{HG}$, $\overline{BC} \cong \overline{GF}$, $\overline{AC} \cong \overline{HF}$; $\triangle ABC \cong \triangle HGF$

Standardized Test Practice

9. **MULTIPLE CHOICE** How many pairs of congruent triangles are formed by the diagonals of a rectangle? (Lesson 6-5) **C**
   - (A) 2
   - (B) 3
   - (C) 4
   - (D) 5

10. **GRID IN** Find the value of a and b. (Lesson 6-1) **$a = 13$ m, $b \approx 22.5$ m**

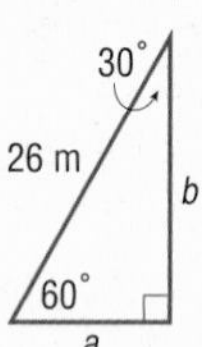

The Game Zone

A Place To Practice Your Math Skills

Math Skill

Classifying Polygons

Polygon Bingo

GET READY!

Players: two
Materials: 10 counters, 1 number cube, marker, 1 large red cube, 1 large blue cube, 2 square sheets of paper

GET SET!

- Write *quadrilateral*, *trapezoid*, *parallelogram*, *rectangle*, *rhombus*, and *square* on different faces of the red cube.
- In the same manner, write *scalene*, *isosceles*, *equilateral*, *acute*, *right*, and *obtuse* on different faces of the blue cube.
- Create two boards like the one shown by drawing a different polygon in each square. Use no shape more than once.

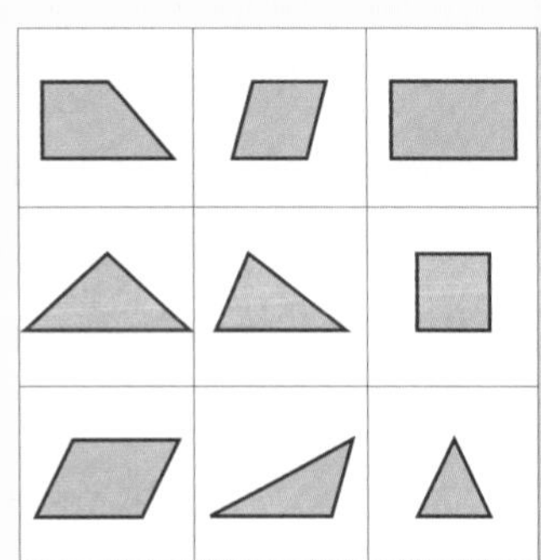

GO!

- The starting player rolls the number cube. If an even number is rolled, the player rolls the red cube. If an odd number is rolled, the player rolls the blue cube.
- The player covers with a counter any shape that matches the information on the top face of the cube. If a player cannot find a figure matching the information, he or she loses a turn.
- **Who Wins?** The first player to get three counters in a row wins.

The Game Zone

Glencoe Mathematics Classroom Manipulative Kit
- counters
- number cubes

GETTING READY

Objective Classify polygons.

MANAGEMENT TIPS

Recommended Time
20 minutes

Tips
- You may wish to make the game boards ahead of time so that each board has a variety of the shapes listed on the cube.
- Consider making labels for the large cubes ahead of time. You can use word-processing software to print onto standard business labels. You may also use masking tape and a marker to mark each side.
- Have students review the concept map of quadrilateral classification on page 273 before playing the game. You may wish to design a similar concept map for triangles.
- You may wish to use the game as an assessment tool for the concepts the students have been learning in Lessons 6-1 through 6-5.

Math Online For an additional game for this chapter, visit: msmath3.net/gamezone

6-6 Lesson Notes

Lesson Resources

Chapter 6 Resource Masters

FAST FILE

- Study Guide and Intervention, p. 332
- Practice: Skills, p. 333
- Practice: Word Problems, p. 334
- Reading to Learn Mathematics, p. 335
- Enrichment, p. 336

Key Teaching Transparencies, 23

Parent and Student Study Guide Online Worksheets, 6-6

Noteables™: Interactive Study Notebook with Foldables™, 6-6

Focus

5-Minute Check 6-6

Use as a quiz or review of Lesson 6-5. (Also available as a transparency)

Bellringer

Problem Solving Ask students what is meant when someone says that a figure is symmetrical. Draw each of the figures shown in the bottom margin on the chalkboard. Have students determine whether each figure is symmetrical. Encourage them to copy each figure onto a sheet of paper so that they can manipulate it before making their determinations. Then ask several students to explain their answers.

(Continued in bottom margin.)

Reading to Learn Mathematics, p. 335 **ELL**

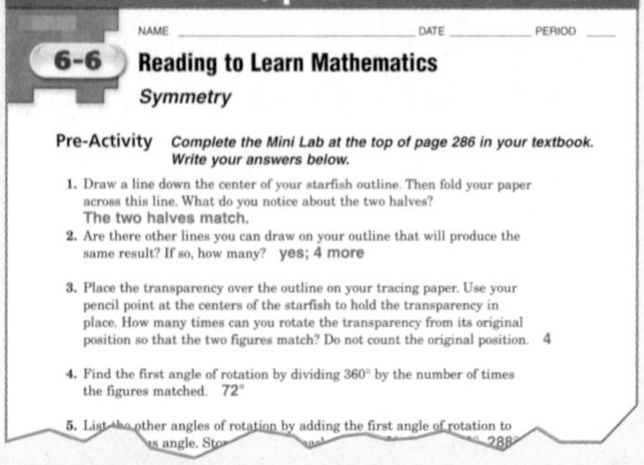

NAME ______________ DATE ________ PERIOD ____

6-6 Reading to Learn Mathematics

Symmetry

Pre-Activity ***Complete the Mini Lab at the top of page 286 in your textbook. Write your answers below.***

1. Draw a line down the center of your starfish outline. Then fold your paper across this line. What do you notice about the two halves? The two halves match.
2. Are there other lines you can draw on your outline that will produce the same result? If so, how many? yes; 4 more
3. Place the transparency over the outline on your tracing paper. Use your pencil point at the centers of the starfish to hold the transparency in place. How many times can you rotate the transparency from its original position so that the two figures match? Do not count the original position. 4
4. Find the first angle of rotation by dividing 360° by the number of times the figures matched. 72°
5. List the other angles of rotation by adding the first angle of rotation to ... angle. ... 288°

6-6 Symmetry

What You'll LEARN

Identify line symmetry and rotational symmetry.

NEW Vocabulary

line symmetry
line of symmetry
rotational symmetry
angle of rotation

HANDS-ON Mini Lab

Materials

- tracing paper
- transparency
- pencil
- overhead markers

Work with a partner.

Trace the outline of the starfish shown onto both a piece of tracing paper and a transparency.

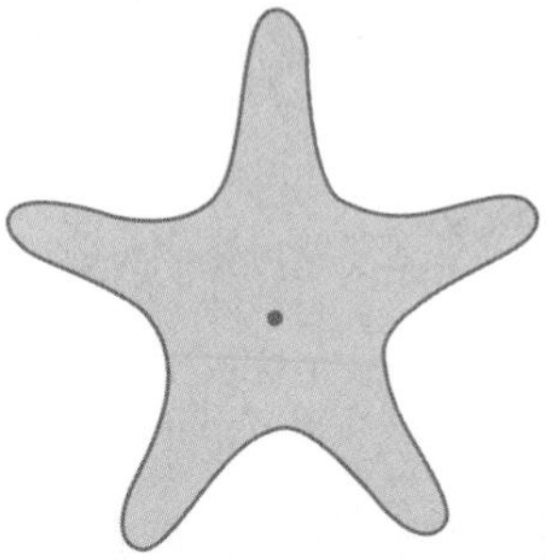

1. Draw a line down the center of your starfish outline. Then fold your paper across this line. What do you notice about the two halves?
2. Are there other lines you can draw on your outline that will produce the same result? If so, how many? **yes; 4 more**
3. Place the transparency over the outline on your tracing paper. Use your pencil point at the centers of the starfish to hold the transparency in place. How many times can you rotate the transparency from its original position so that the two figures match? Do not count the original position. **4**
4. Find the first angle of rotation by dividing 360° by the number of times the figures matched. **72°**
5. List the other angles of rotation by adding the first angle of rotation to the previous angle. Stop when you reach 360°.

1. The two halves match. 5. 72°, 144°, 216°, 288°

A figure has **line symmetry** if it can be folded over a line so that one half of the figure matches the other half. This fold line is called the **line of symmetry**.

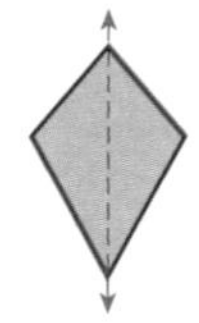

vertical line of symmetry

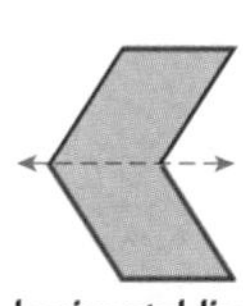

horizontal line of symmetry

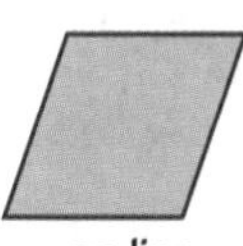

no line of symmetry

Some figures, such as the starfish in the Mini Lab above, have more than one line of symmetry. The figure at the right has one vertical, one horizontal, and two diagonal lines of symmetry.

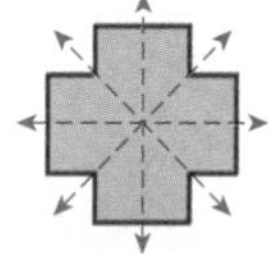

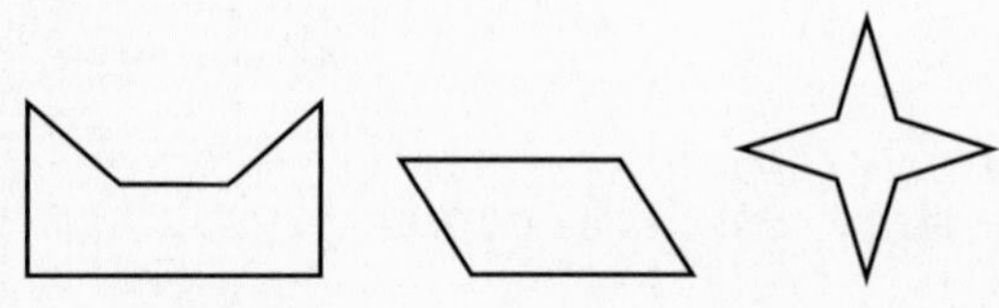

EXAMPLE Identify Line Symmetry

1 NATURE Determine whether the figure has line symmetry. If it does, trace the figure and draw all lines of symmetry. If not, write *none*.

This figure has one vertical line of symmetry.

TEACHING TIP

Remind students that one complete turn of a figure measures 360°. This is because there are 360° in a circle.

Your Turn **Determine whether each figure has line symmetry. If it does, trace the figure and draw all lines of symmetry. If not, write *none*.**

a. 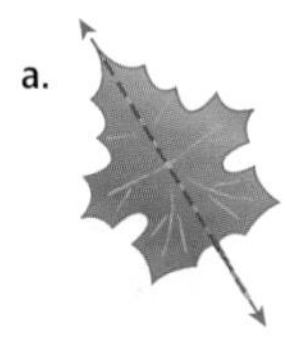

b. 

c. 
none

A figure has **rotational symmetry** if it can be rotated or turned less than 360° about its center so that the figure looks exactly as it does in its original position. The degree measure of the angle through which the figure is rotated is called the **angle of rotation**. Some figures have just one angle of rotation, while others, like the starfish, have several.

REAL-LIFE MATH

LOGOS Many companies and nonprofit groups use a logo so people can easily identify their products or services. They often design their logo to have line or rotational symmetry.

EXAMPLES Identify Rotational Symmetry

LOGOS Determine whether each figure has rotational symmetry. Write *yes* or *no*. If *yes*, name its angle(s) of rotation.

2 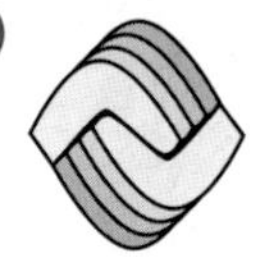

Yes, this figure has rotational symmetry. It will match itself after being rotated 180°.

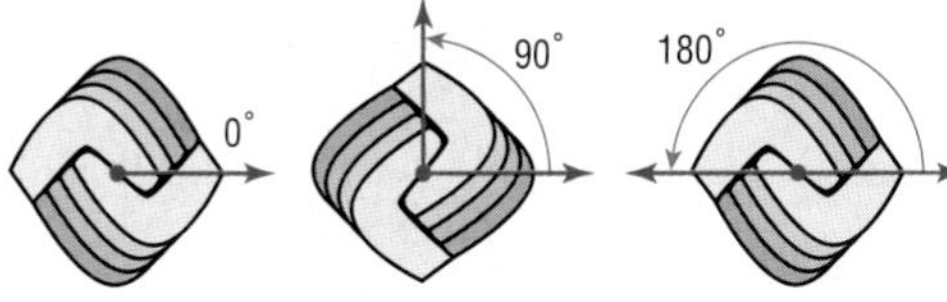

3 

Yes, this figure has rotational symmetry. It will match itself after being rotated 120° and 240°.

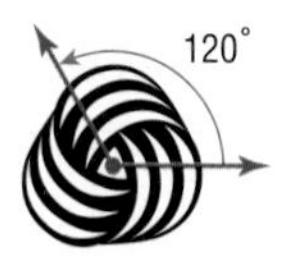

msmath3.net/extra_examples

2 Teach

In-Class Examples

1 TRILOBITES The trilobite is an animal that lived millions of years ago. Determine whether the figure has line symmetry. If it does, trace the figure and draw all lines of symmetry. If not, write *none*.

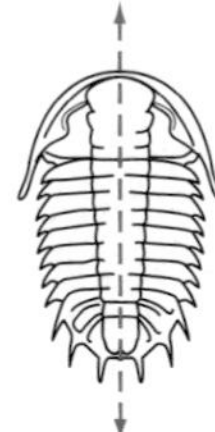

FLOWERS Determine whether each flower design shown below has rotational symmetry. Write *yes* or *no*. If *yes*, name its angle(s) of rotation.

yes; 90°, 180°, 270°

yes; 60°, 120°, 180°, 240°, 300°

DAILY INTERVENTION — **Differentiated Instruction**

Naturalist Ask students to think about symmetry in nature. Have them draw a plant or animal that shows symmetry. Allow class time for students to explain the symmetry in their drawings. If a plant or animal has rotational symmetry, the student should name its angles of rotation. If time allows, take the class outside and have students draw examples of symmetrical objects. The drawings should include lines of symmetry.

Students practice the same concepts in Exercises 7–14 if they are assigned odd or even problems.

Skill and Concept Check

1. **OPEN ENDED** Draw a figure that has rotational symmetry. **See margin.**

2. **Which One Doesn't Belong?** Identify the capital letter that does not have the same type of symmetry as the others. Explain your reasoning.

A	B	M	S

S; this letter has rotational symmetry and the other three have line symmetry.

GUIDED PRACTICE

SPORTS For Exercises 3–6, complete parts a and b for each figure. 3–6. See margin.

a. **Determine whether the logo has line symmetry. If it does, trace the figure and draw all lines of symmetry. If not, write *none*.**

b. **Determine whether the logo has rotational symmetry. Write *yes* or *no*. If yes, name its angle(s) of rotation.**

3. 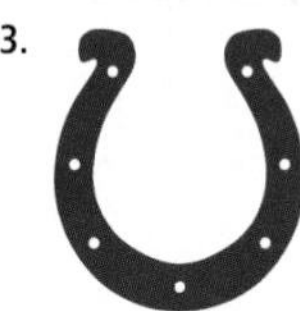
4. 
5. 
6. 

Practice and Applications

JAPANESE FAMILY CRESTS For Exercises 7–14, complete parts a and b for each figure. 7–14. See Ch. 6 Answer Appendix.

a. **Determine whether the figure has line symmetry. If it does, trace the figure and draw all lines of symmetry. If not, write *none*.**

b. **Determine whether the figure has rotational symmetry. Write *yes* or *no*. If *yes*, name its angle(s) of rotation.**

HOMEWORK HELP

For Exercises	See Examples
7–15, 17, 21	1
7–15, 16, 18	2, 3

Extra Practice
See pages 631, 653.

7. 
8. 
9. 
10. 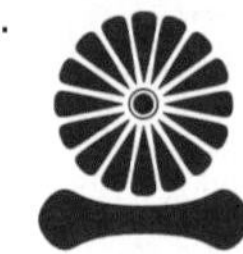
11.
12. 
13. 
14.  

15. **TRIANGLES** Which types of triangles—*scalene, isosceles, equilateral*—have line symmetry? Which have rotational symmetry? **Isosceles and equilateral triangles; equilateral triangles**

16. **ALPHABET** What capital letters of the alphabet produce the same letter after being rotated 180°? **H, I, N, O, S, X, Z**

3 Practice/Apply

Follow-Up Remind students to include information on symmetry in words and symbols in the "Symmetry" section of their Foldable tables.

Which One Doesn't Belong? For Exercise 2, some students may need to reproduce the letters on a sheet of paper to determine their symmetry. Suggest that they rotate the paper and observe how the appearance of the letters changes.

About the Exercises...

Guided Practice Key

Exercises	Examples
3a, 4a, 5a, 6a	1
3b, 4b, 5b, 6b	2, 3

Assignment Guide

Basic: 7–19 odd, 21–30

Average: 7–19 odd, 20–30

Enriched: 8–20 even, 21–26 (Optional: 27–30)

Alert! Exercise 19 requires research on the Internet or another source.

Answers

1. Sample answer:

3a. 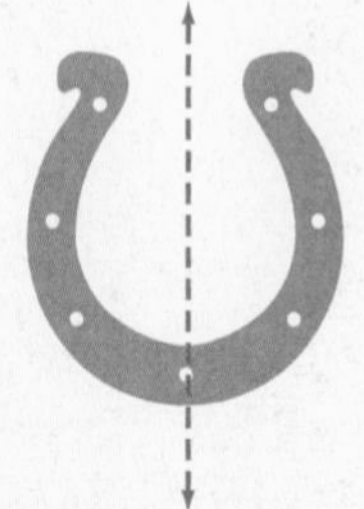

4a. 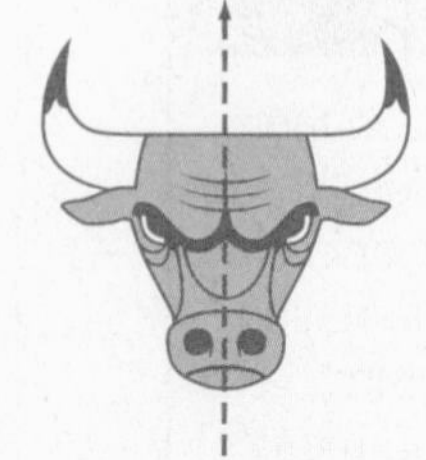

5a. 

6a. 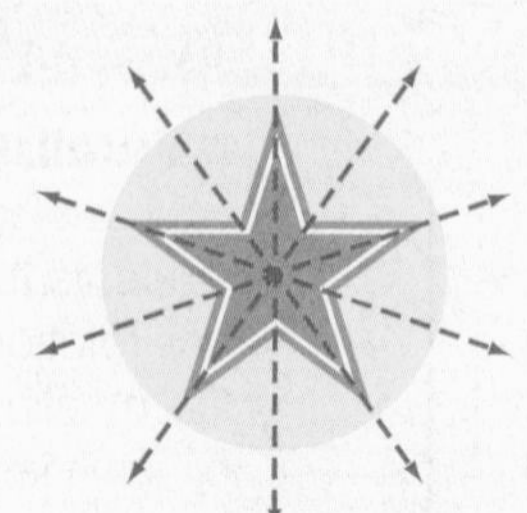

3b. no

4b. no

5b. no

6b. yes; 72°, 144°, 216°, 288°

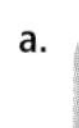

ROAD SIGNS **For Exercises 17 and 18, use the diagrams below.**

a.  b.  c.  d. 

17. Determine whether each sign has line symmetry. If it does, trace the sign and draw all lines of symmetry. If not, write *none*. **See Ch. 6 Answer Appendix.**

18. Which of the signs above could be rotated and still look the same? **b and d**

19. **RESEARCH** Use the Internet or other resource to find other examples of road signs that have line and/or rotational symmetry. **See Ch. 6 Answer Appendix.**

20. **ART** Artist Scott Kim uses reflections of words or names as part of his art. Patricia's reflected name is at the right. Create a reflection design for your name using tracing paper. **See students' work.**

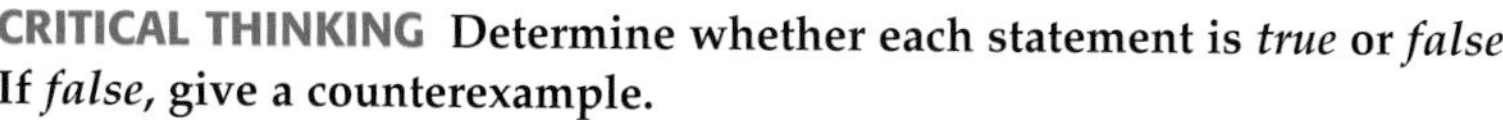

CRITICAL THINKING **Determine whether each statement is *true* or *false*. If *false*, give a counterexample.**

21. If a figure has one horizontal and one vertical line of symmetry, then it also has rotational symmetry. **true**

22. If a figure has rotational symmetry, it also has line symmetry. **false; See Ch. 6 Answer Appendix for counterexample.**

Spiral Review with Standardized Test Practice

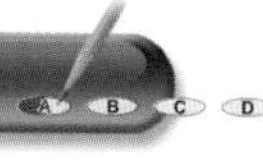

23. **MULTIPLE CHOICE** Which shape has *only* two lines of symmetry? **B**

Ⓐ 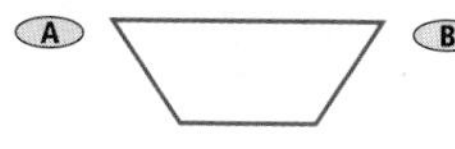 Ⓑ 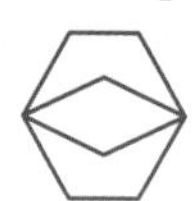 Ⓒ 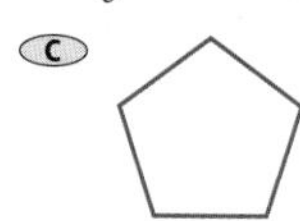 Ⓓ 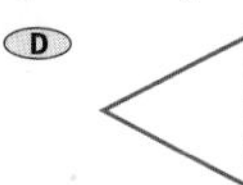

24. **SHORT RESPONSE** Copy the figure at the right. Then shade two squares so that the figure has rotational symmetry.

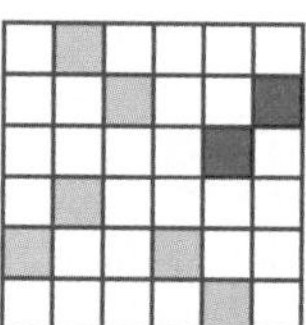

25. **DESIGN** The former symbol for the National Council of Teachers of Mathematics is shown at the right. Which triangles in the symbol appear to be congruent? (Lesson 6-5) **See Ch. 6 Answer Appendix.**

26. In parallelogram $ABCD$, $m\angle A = 55°$, $m\angle B = 125°$, $m\angle C = x°$, and $m\angle D = 125°$. Find the value of x. (Lesson 6-4) **55**

GETTING READY FOR THE NEXT LESSON

PREREQUISITE SKILL **Graph each point on a coordinate plane.** (Page 614)

27. $A(3, 2)$ 28. $B(-1, 4)$ 29. $C(-2, -1)$ 30. $D(0, 3)$

27–30. See Ch. 6 Answer Appendix.

Math Online msmath3.net/self_check_quiz

4 Assess

Open-Ended Assessment

Modeling Have students create some form of artwork, such as a painting, drawing, or sculpture, that has either line symmetry or rotational symmetry. Display the artwork in the classroom and have students explain the symmetry.

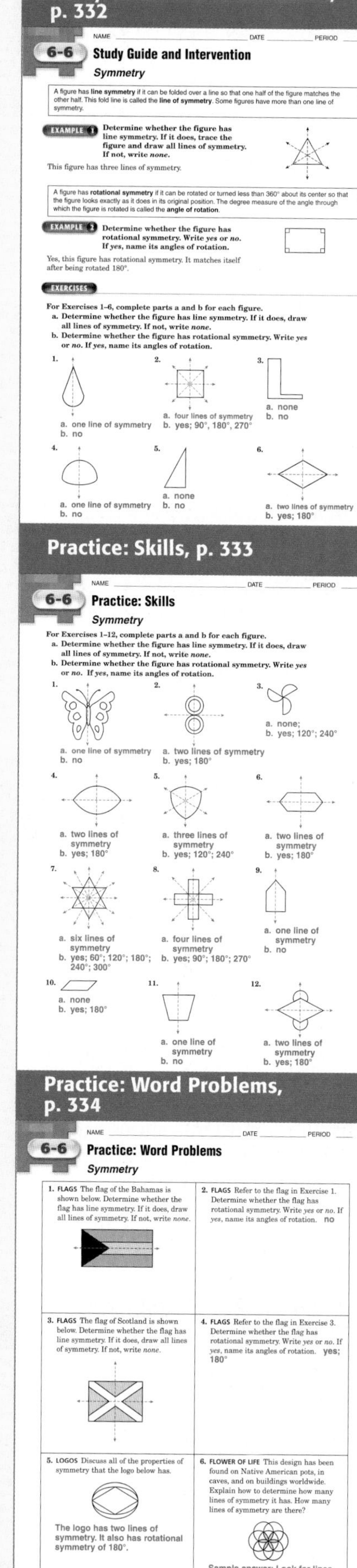

Study Guide and Intervention, p. 332

NAME ______ DATE ______ PERIOD ____

6-6 Study Guide and Intervention

Symmetry

A figure has **line symmetry** if it can be folded over a line so that one half of the figure matches the other half. This fold line is called the **line of symmetry**. Some figures have more than one line of symmetry.

EXAMPLE 1 **Determine whether the figure has line symmetry. If it does, trace the figure and draw all lines of symmetry. If not, write *none*.**

This figure has three lines of symmetry.

A figure has **rotational symmetry** if it can be rotated or turned less than 360° about its center so that the figure looks exactly as it does in its original position. The degree measure of the angle through which the figure is rotated is called the **angle of rotation**.

EXAMPLE 2 **Determine whether the figure has rotational symmetry. Write *yes* or *no*. If *yes*, name its angles of rotation.**

Yes, this figure has rotational symmetry. It matches itself after being rotated 180°.

EXERCISES

For Exercises 1–6, complete parts a and b for each figure.
a. Determine whether the figure has line symmetry. If it does, draw all lines of symmetry. If not, write *none*.
b. Determine whether the figure has rotational symmetry. Write *yes* or *no*. If *yes*, name its angles of rotation.

1. a. one line of symmetry b. no
2. a. four lines of symmetry b. yes; 90°, 180°, 270°
3. a. none b. no
4. a. one line of symmetry b. no
5. a. none b. no
6. a. two lines of symmetry b. yes; 180°

Practice: Skills, p. 333

NAME ______ DATE ______ PERIOD ____

6-6 Practice: Skills

Symmetry

For Exercises 1–12, complete parts a and b for each figure.
a. Determine whether the figure has line symmetry. If it does, draw all lines of symmetry. If not, write *none*.
b. Determine whether the figure has rotational symmetry. Write *yes* or *no*. If *yes*, name its angles of rotation.

1. a. one line of symmetry b. no
2. a. two lines of symmetry b. yes; 180°
3. a. none; b. yes; 120°; 240°
4. a. two lines of symmetry b. yes; 180°
5. a. three lines of symmetry b. yes; 120°; 240°
6. a. two lines of symmetry b. yes; 180°
7. a. six lines of symmetry b. yes; 60°; 120°; 180°; 240°; 300°
8. a. four lines of symmetry b. yes; 90°; 180°; 270°
9. a. one line of symmetry b. no
10. a. none b. yes; 180°
11. a. one line of symmetry b. no
12. a. two lines of symmetry b. yes; 180°

Practice: Word Problems, p. 334

NAME ______ DATE ______ PERIOD ____

6-6 Practice: Word Problems

Symmetry

1. **FLAGS** The flag of the Bahamas is shown below. Determine whether the flag has line symmetry. If it does, draw all lines of symmetry. If not, write *none*.

2. **FLAGS** Refer to the flag in Exercise 1. Determine whether the flag has rotational symmetry. Write *yes* or *no*. If *yes*, name its angles of rotation. **no**

3. **FLAGS** The flag of Scotland is shown below. Determine whether the flag has line symmetry. If it does, draw all lines of symmetry. If not, write *none*.

4. **FLAGS** Refer to the flag in Exercise 3. Determine whether the flag has rotational symmetry. Write *yes* or *no*. If *yes*, name its angles of rotation. **yes; 180°**

5. **LOGOS** Discuss all of the properties of symmetry that the logo below has.

The logo has two lines of symmetry. It also has rotational symmetry of 180°.

6. **FLOWER OF LIFE** This design has been found on Native American pots, in caves, and on buildings worldwide. Explain how to determine how many lines of symmetry it has. How many lines of symmetry are there?

Sample answer: Look for lines along which the design can be folded so that both sides have the same shape; 6.

6-7 Lesson Notes

Lesson Resources

Chapter 6 Resource Masters
- Study Guide and Intervention, p. 337
- Practice: Skills, p. 338
- Practice: Word Problems, p. 339
- Reading to Learn Mathematics, p. 340
- Enrichment, p. 341

Calculator and Spreadsheet Masters, p. 30
Parent and Student Study Guide Online Worksheets, 6-7
Teaching Mathematics with Manipulatives, pp. 73–74
Noteables™: Interactive Study Notebook with Foldables™, 6-7
Virtual Activities CD-ROM, Reflections

FAST FILE

1 Focus

5-Minute Check 6-7
Use as a quiz or review of Lesson 6-6. (Also available as a transparency)

Bellringer
Hands-On Activity Have students draw a polygon on one side of a sheet of tracing paper. Have them fold the paper so that its other side lies on top of the drawing. Students should then trace the figure and unfold the paper. Students can then measure from the fold to the corresponding points on the figure and its reflection.

Reading to Learn Mathematics, p. 340 ELL

NAME ______ DATE ______ PERIOD ____

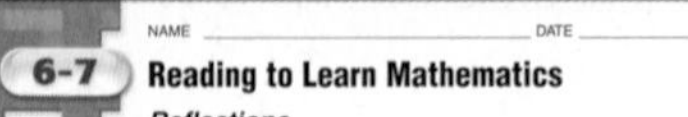

6-7 Reading to Learn Mathematics
Reflections

Pre-Activity *Read the introduction at the top of page 290 in your textbook. Write your answers below.*

1. Compare the shape and size of the bird to its image in the water. **The size and shape of the bird and its image appear to be the same.**
2. Compare the perpendicular distance from the water line to each of the points shown. What do you observe? **The distances from corresponding points on the bird and its image to the water line are equal.**
3. The points *A*, *B*, and *C* appear *counterclockwise* on the bird. How are these points oriented on the bird's image? **The points *A*, *B*, and *C* appear clockwise on the image of the bird.**

Reading the Lesson

For Exercises 4–7, read the Key Concept information on page 290 in your textbook and refer to the graph at the right that shows quadrilaterals *ABCD* and *A′B′C′D′* and a line.

4. Fi... distance of each ... from the given line. Are ... vertic...

6-7 Reflections

WHEN am I ever going to use this?

PHOTOGRAPHY The undisturbed surface of a pond acts like a mirror and can provide the subject for beautiful photographs.

1. Compare the shape and size of the bird to its image in the water. **1–3. See margin.**
2. Compare the perpendicular distance from the water line to each of the points shown. What do you observe?
3. The points A, B, and C appear *counterclockwise* on the bird. How are these points oriented on the bird's image?

What You'll LEARN
Graph reflections on a coordinate plane.

NEW Vocabulary
reflection
line of reflection
transformation

Link to READING
Everyday Meaning of reflection: the production of an image by or as if by a mirror

The mirror image produced by flipping a figure over a line is called a **reflection**. This line is called the **line of reflection**. A reflection is one type of **transformation** or mapping of a geometric figure.

Noteables™ Key Concept: Properties of Reflections

1. Every point on a reflection is the same distance from the line of reflection as the corresponding point on the original figure.
2. The image is congruent to the original figure, but the orientation of the image is *different* from that of the original figure.

Model
X, Y, Z original; line of reflection; X′, Y′, Z′ image

EXAMPLE Draw a Reflection

1 **Copy $\triangle JKL$ at the right on graph paper. Then draw the image of the figure after a reflection over the given line.**

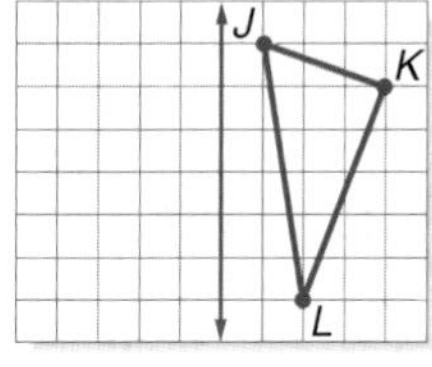

Step 1 Count the number of units between each vertex and the line of reflection.

Step 2 Plot a point for each vertex the same distance away from the line on the other side.

Step 3 Connect the new vertices to form the image of $\triangle JKL$, $\triangle J'K'L'$.

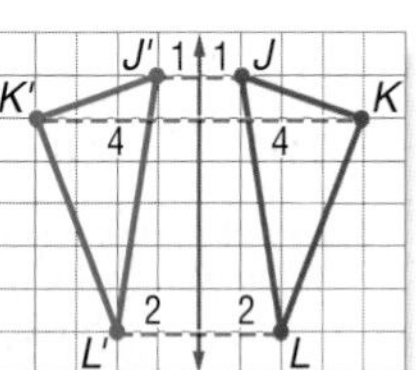

READING Math
Notation Read P' as *P prime*. It is the image of point P.

Answers (When am I ever going to use this?)

1. The size and shape of the bird and its image appear to be the same.
2. The distances from corresponding points on the bird and its image to the water line are equal.
3. No, the points A', B', and C' appear clockwise on the image of the bird.

EXAMPLE Reflect a Figure over the x-axis

TEACHING TIP
In this book, the image of a figure is shown in green.

2 **Graph $\triangle PQR$ with vertices $P(-3, 4)$, $Q(4, 2)$, and $R(-1, 1)$. Then graph the image of $\triangle PQR$ after a reflection over the x-axis, and write the coordinates of its vertices.**

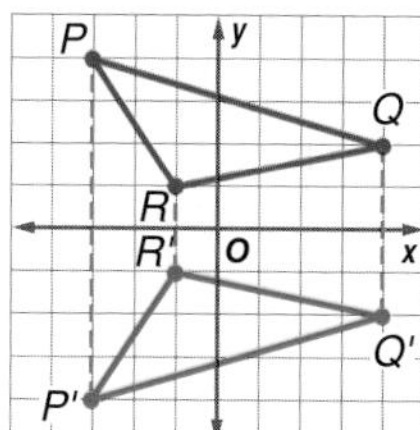

The coordinates of the vertices of the image are $P'(-3, -4)$, $Q'(4, -2)$, and $R'(-1, -1)$. Examine the relationship between the coordinates of each figure.

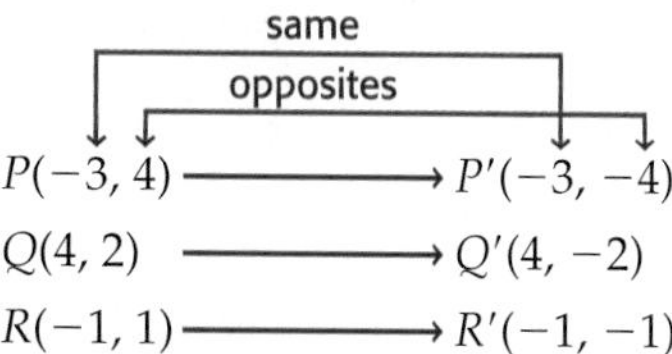

Notice that the y-coordinate of a point reflected over the x-axis is the opposite of the y-coordinate of the original point.

EXAMPLE Reflect a Figure over the y-axis

3 **Graph quadrilateral $ABCD$ with vertices $A(-4, 1)$, $B(-2, 3)$, $C(0, -3)$, and $D(-3, -2)$. Then graph the image of $ABCD$ after a reflection over the y-axis, and write the coordinates of its vertices.**

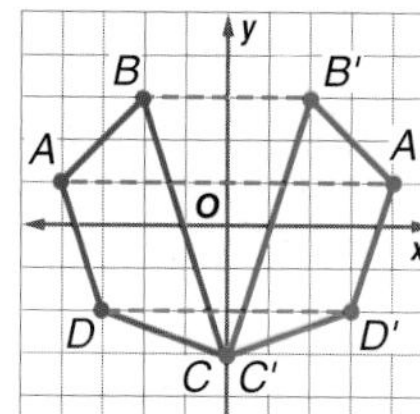

The coordinates of the vertices of the image are $A'(4, 1)$, $B'(2, 3)$, $C'(0, -3)$, and $D'(3, -2)$. Examine the relationship between the coordinates of each figure.

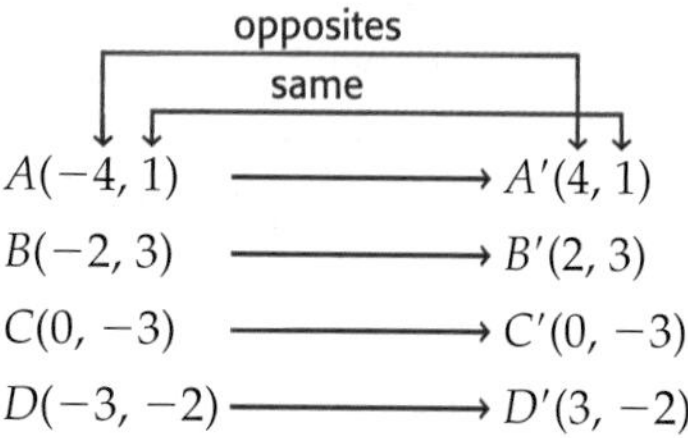

Notice that the x-coordinate of a point reflected over the y-axis is the opposite of the x-coordinate of the original point.

STUDY TIP

Points on Line of Reflection Notice that if a point lies on the line of reflection, the image of that point has the same coordinates as those of the point on the original figure.

Your Turn **Graph $\triangle FGH$ with vertices $F(1, -1)$, $G(5, -3)$, and $H(2, -4)$. Then graph the image of $\triangle FGH$ after a reflection over the given axis, and write the coordinates of its vertices.**

a. x-axis **$F'(1, 1)$, $G'(5, 3)$, $H'(2, 4)$** b. y-axis

a–b. See Ch. 6 Answer Appendix for graphs.
b. $F'(-1, -1)$, $G'(-5, -3)$, $H'(-2, -4)$

If a figure touches the line of reflection as it does in Example 3, then the figure and its image form a new figure that has line symmetry. The line of reflection is a line of symmetry.

msmath3.net/extra_examples

DAILY INTERVENTION **Unlocking Misconceptions**

Reflections When students are told to draw the reflection of a figure, a common misconception is that they think they should simply translate the figure across the x-axis or y-axis. Encourage students to determine the reflection of each point individually. They should also label each point and its coordinates to avoid confusion.

2 Teach

In-Class Examples

1 Copy trapezoid $STUV$ below on graph paper. Then draw the image of the figure after a reflection over the given line.

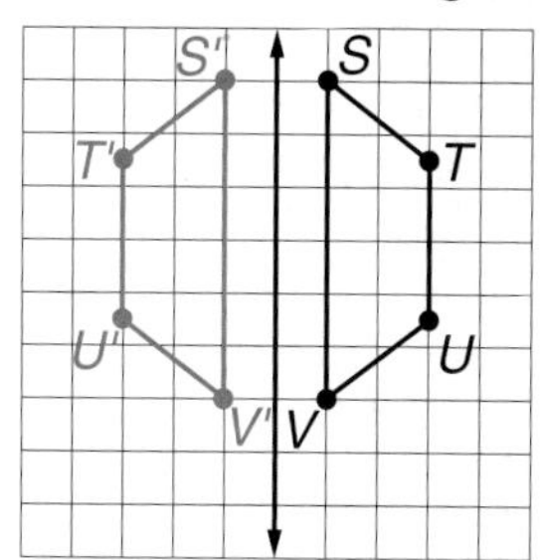

2 Graph quadrilateral $EFGH$ with vertices $E(-4, 4)$, $F(3, 3)$, $G(4, 2)$, and $H(-2, 1)$. Then graph the image of $EFGH$ after a reflection over the x-axis and write the coordinates of its vertices.
$E'(-4, -4)$, $F'(3, -3)$, $G'(4, -2)$, $H'(-2, -1)$

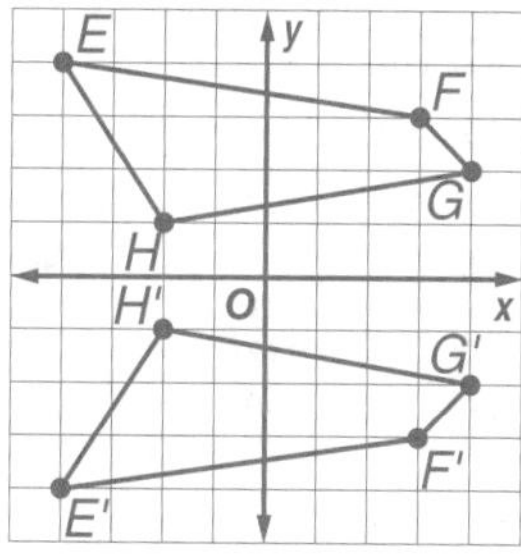

3 Graph trapezoid $ABCD$ with vertices $A(1, 3)$, $B(4, 0)$, $C(3, -4)$, and $D(1, -2)$. Then graph the image of $ABCD$ after a reflection over the y-axis and write the coordinates of its vertices.
$A'(-1, 3)$, $B'(-4, 0)$, $C'(-3, -4)$, $D'(-1, -2)$

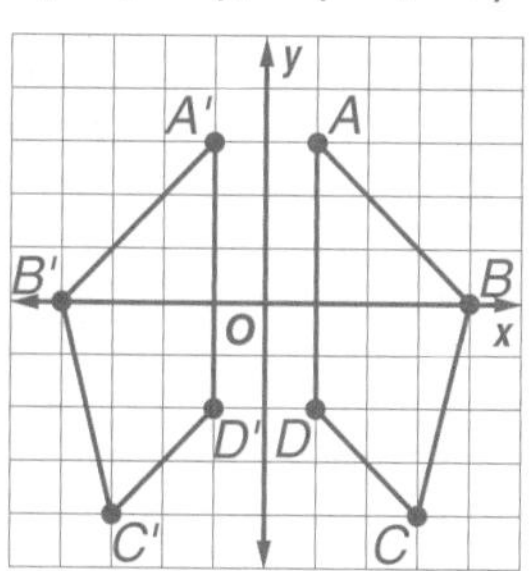

In-Class Example

4 ARCHITECTURE Copy and complete the office floor plan shown below so that the completed office has a horizontal line of symmetry.

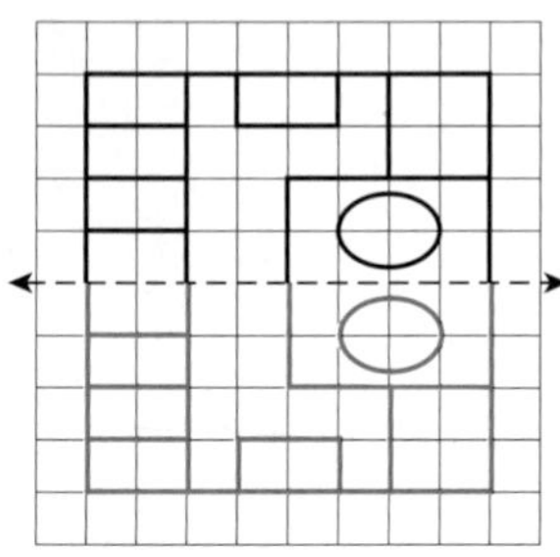

Intervention Students sometimes make errors because they do not fully understand the instructions. Ask specific questions to ascertain the problem with the instructions and determine a way to make them clearer.

3 Practice/Apply

Which One Doesn't Belong? When determining the reflection of a nonsymmetrical figure, students should choose several main points on the figure and determine their reflection. In Exercise 3, students might consider the reflection of points on the dog's tail, paw, and nose.

EXAMPLE Use a Reflection

4 MASKS Copy and complete the mask shown so that the completed figure has a vertical line of symmetry.

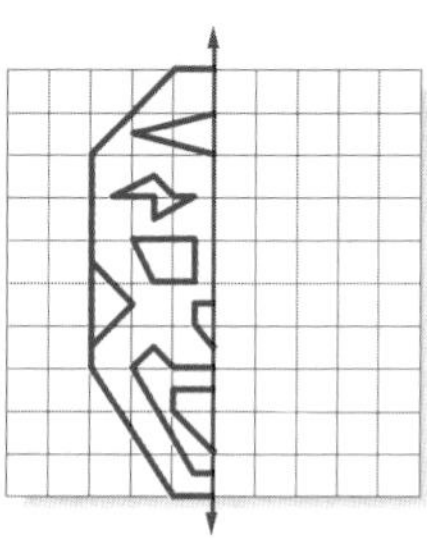

You can reflect the half of the mask shown over the indicated vertical line.

Find the distance from each vertex on the figure to the line of reflection.

Then plot a point that same distance away on the opposite side of the line. Connect vertices as appropriate.

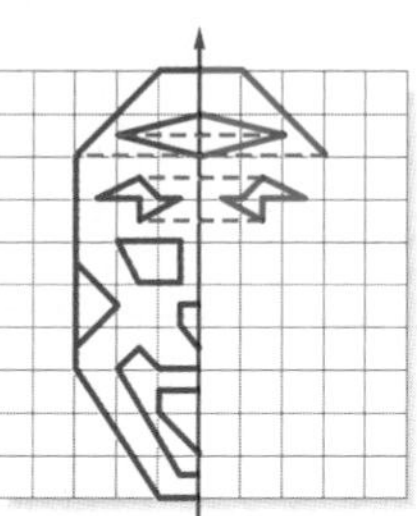

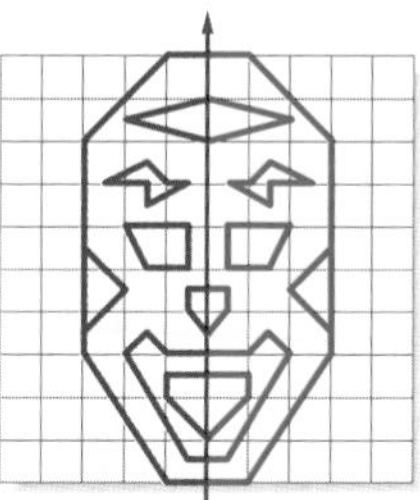

TEACHING TIP
You may wish to show students how they could use tracing paper to complete the image of the mask in Example 4.

Students practice the same concepts in Exercises 7–28 if they are assigned odd or even problems.

Skill and Concept Check

1. **OPEN ENDED** Draw a triangle on grid paper. Then draw a horizontal line below the triangle. Finally, draw the image of the triangle after it is reflected over the horizontal line. **1–3. See margin.**
2. Writing Math Explain how a reflection and line symmetry are related.
3. **Which One Doesn't Belong?** Identify the transformation that is not the same as the other three. Explain your reasoning.

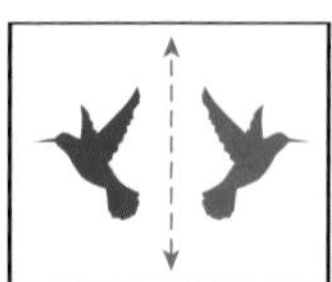 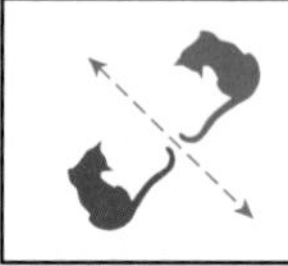 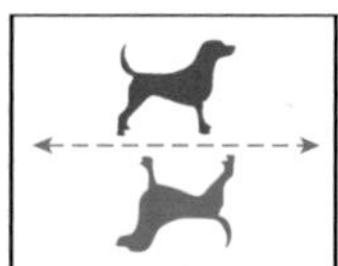 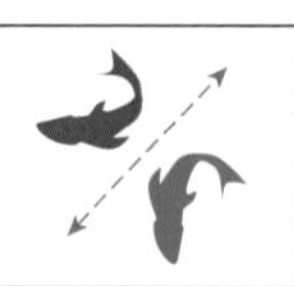

GUIDED PRACTICE

4. Copy the figure at the right on graph paper. Then draw the image of the figure after a reflection over the given line. **See margin.**

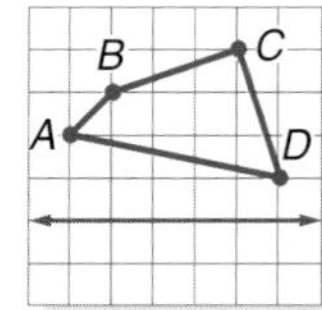

5–6. See margin for graphs.

Graph the figure with the given vertices. Then graph its image after a reflection over the given axis, and write the coordinates of its vertices.

5. parallelogram $QRST$ with vertices $Q(-3, 3)$, $R(2, 4)$, $S(3, 2)$, and $T(-2, 1)$; x-axis **$Q'(-3, -3)$, $R'(2, -4)$, $S'(3, -2)$, $T'(-2, -1)$**
6. triangle JKL with vertices $J(-2, 3)$, $K(-1, -4)$, and $L(-4, -2)$; y-axis **$J'(2, 3)$, $K'(1, -4)$, $L'(4, -2)$**

Answers

1. Sample answer:

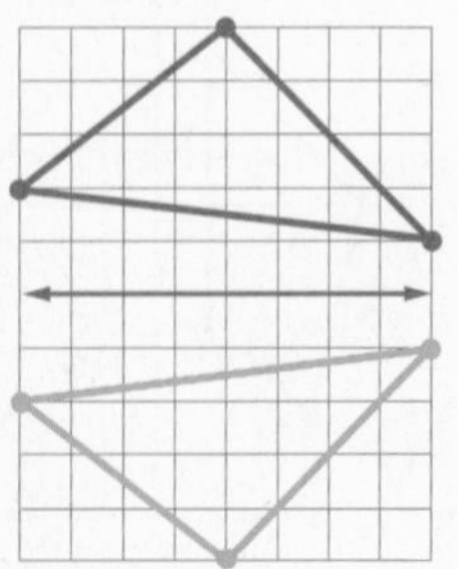

2. In line symmetry, half of the figure is the reflection of the other half.
3. The third transformation; all the transformations are reflections of the original figure about the given line. The image of the tip of the dog's tail is not directly across from the tip of the original dog's tail.
4. 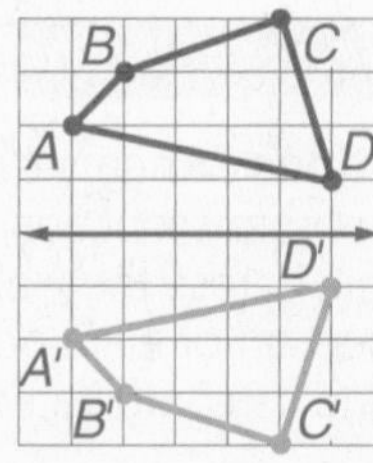

★ indicates increased difficulty

Practice and Applications

Copy each figure onto graph paper. Then draw the image of the figure after a reflection over the given line. 7–12. See margin.

HOMEWORK HELP	
For Exercises	See Examples
7–16, 27–28	1
17–24	2, 3
25–26	4

Extra Practice
See pages 631, 653.

7. 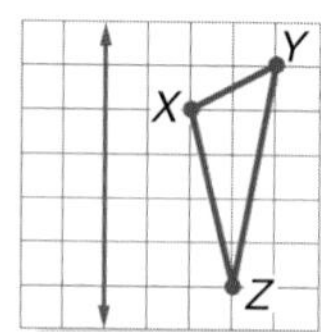
8. 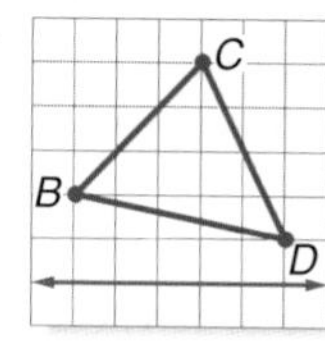
9. 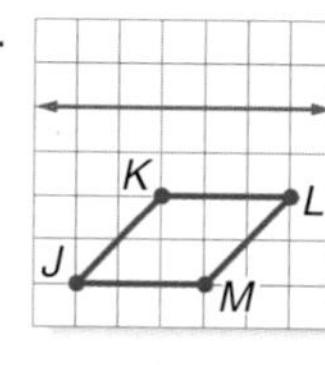
10. 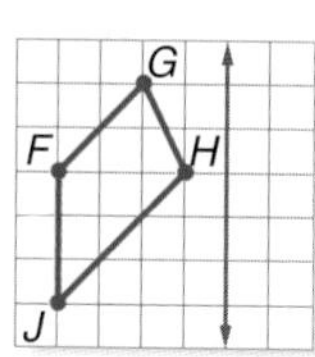
★11. 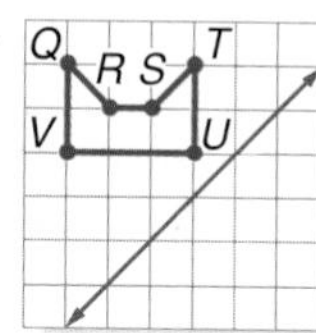
★12. 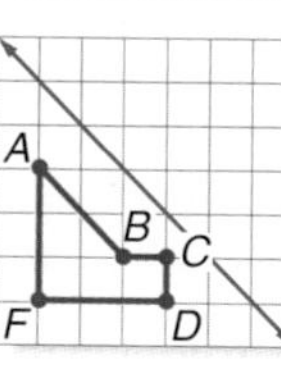

For Exercises 13–16, determine whether the figure in green is a reflection of the figure in blue over the line *n*. Write *yes* or *no*. Explain.

13. 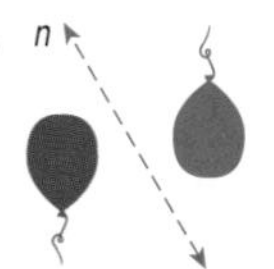 no
14. 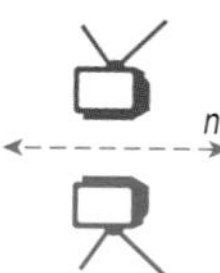 yes
15.  yes
16. 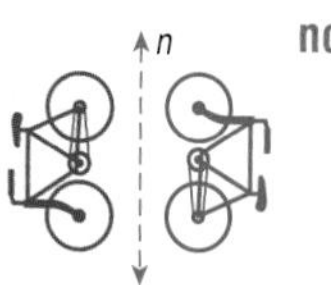 no

13–16. See Ch. 6 Answer Appendix for explanation.

Graph the figure with the given vertices. Then graph its image after a reflection over the given axis, and write the coordinates of its vertices. 17–20. See Ch. 6 Answer Appendix.

17. triangle ABC with vertices $A(-1, -1)$, $B(-2, -4)$, and $C(-4, -1)$; x-axis
18. triangle FGH with vertices $F(3, 3)$, $G(4, -3)$, and $H(2, 1)$; y-axis
19. square $JKLM$ with vertices $J(-2, 0)$, $K(-1, -2)$, $L(-3, -3)$, and $M(-4, -1)$; y-axis
20. quadrilateral $PQRS$ with vertices $P(1, 3)$, $Q(3, 5)$, $R(5, 2)$, and $S(3, 1)$; x-axis

Name the line of reflection for each pair of figures.

21. 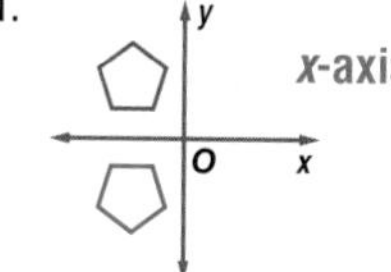 x-axis
22. 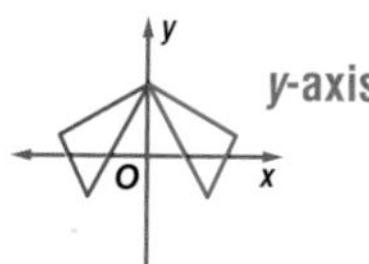 y-axis
23. 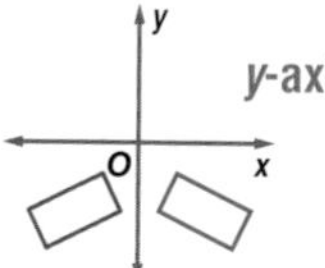 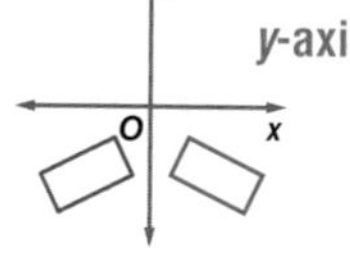 y-axis
24. 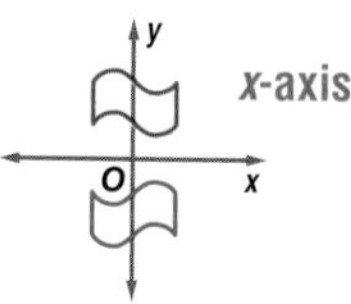 x-axis

25. **DESIGN** Does the rug below have line symmetry? If so, sketch the rug and draw the line(s) of symmetry. yes

26. **DESIGN** Copy and complete the rug pattern shown so that the completed figure has line symmetry.

Math Online msmath3.net/self_check_quiz

About the Exercises...

Guided Practice Key

Exercises	Examples
4	1
5	2
6	3

Assignment Guide

Basic: 7, 9, 13–27 odd, 29–41

Average: 7–27 odd, 29–41

Enriched: 8–28 even, 29–37 (Optional: 38–41)

Answers

8. 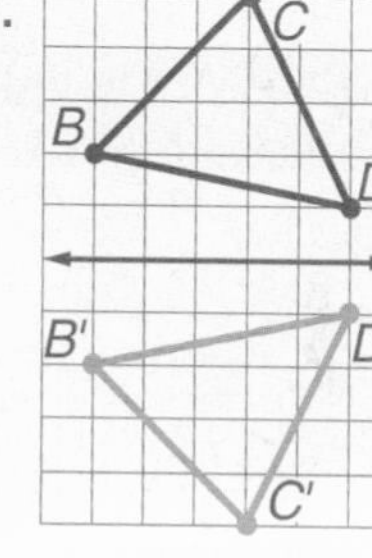
9. 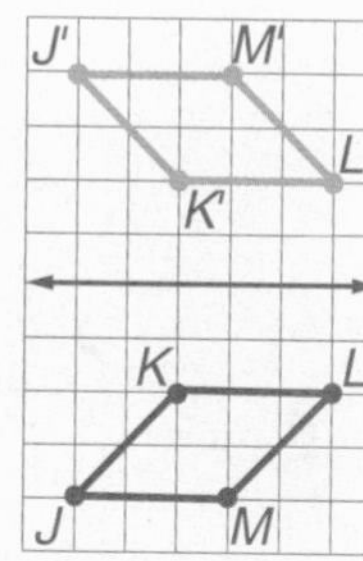
10. 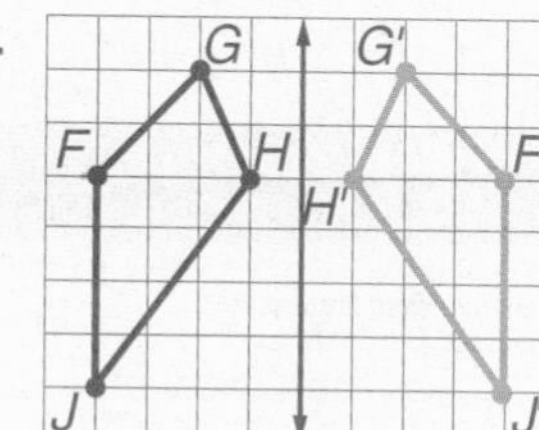
11. 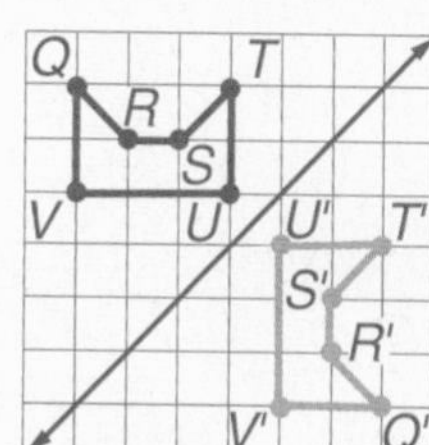
12. 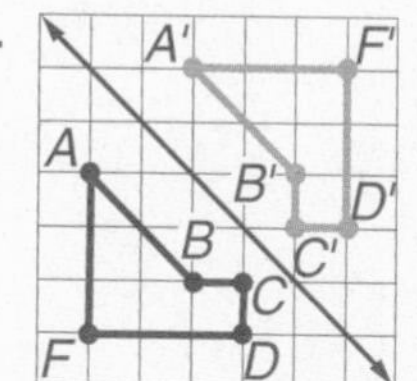
5. 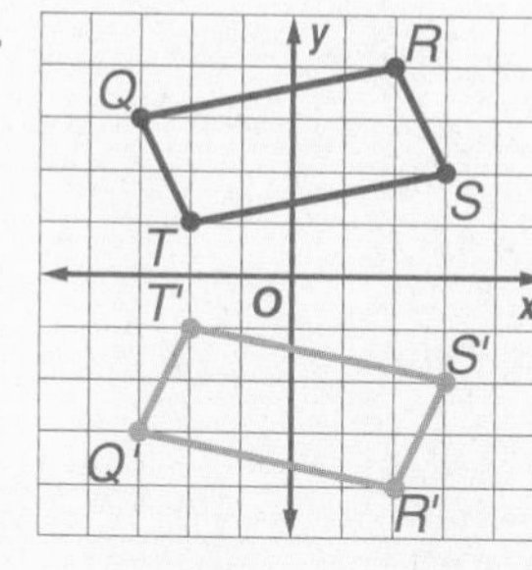
6. 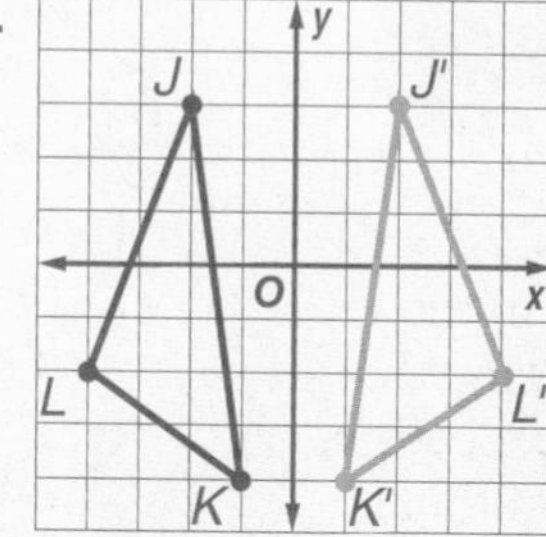
7. 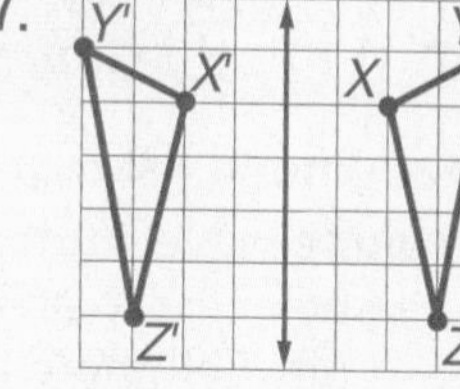

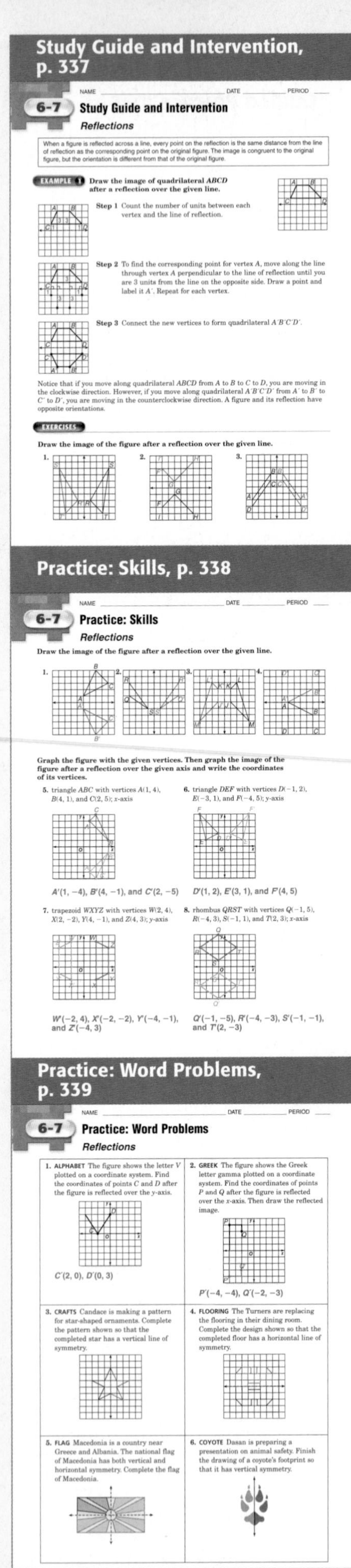
Study Guide and Intervention, p. 337

NAME ______ DATE ______ PERIOD ____

6-7 Study Guide and Intervention

Reflections

When a figure is reflected across a line, every point on the reflection is the same distance from the line of reflection as the corresponding point on the original figure. The image is congruent to the original figure, but the orientation is different from that of the original figure.

EXAMPLE 1 **Draw the image of quadrilateral $ABCD$ after a reflection over the given line.**

Step 1 Count the number of units between each vertex and the line of reflection.

Step 2 To find the corresponding point for vertex A, move along the line through vertex A perpendicular to the line of reflection until you are 3 units from the line on the opposite side. Draw a point and label it A'. Repeat for each vertex.

Step 3 Connect the new vertices to form quadrilateral $A'B'C'D'$.

Notice that if you move along quadrilateral $ABCD$ from A to B to C to D, you are moving in the clockwise direction. However, if you move along quadrilateral $A'B'C'D'$ from A' to B' to C' to D', you are moving in the counterclockwise direction. A figure and its reflection have opposite orientations.

EXERCISES

Draw the image of the figure after a reflection over the given line.

1\. 2\. 3\.

Practice: Skills, p. 338

NAME ______ DATE ______ PERIOD ____

6-7 Practice: Skills

Reflections

Draw the image of the figure after a reflection over the given line.

1\. 2\. 3\. 4\.

Graph the figure with the given vertices. Then graph the image of the figure after a reflection over the given axis and write the coordinates of its vertices.

5\. triangle ABC with vertices $A(1, 4)$, $B(4, 1)$, and $C(2, 5)$; x-axis

$A'(1, -4)$, $B'(4, -1)$, and $C'(2, -5)$

6\. triangle DEF with vertices $D(-1, 2)$, $E(-3, 1)$, and $F(-4, 5)$; y-axis

$D'(1, 2)$, $E'(3, 1)$, and $F'(4, 5)$

7\. trapezoid $WXYZ$ with vertices $W(2, 4)$, $X(2, -2)$, $Y(4, -1)$, and $Z(4, 3)$; y-axis

$W'(-2, 4)$, $X'(-2, -2)$, $Y'(-4, -1)$, and $Z'(-4, 3)$

8\. rhombus $QRST$ with vertices $Q(-1, 5)$, $R(-4, 3)$, $S(-1, 1)$, and $T(2, 3)$; x-axis

$Q'(-1, -5)$, $R'(-4, -3)$, $S'(-1, -1)$, and $T'(2, -3)$

Practice: Word Problems, p. 339

NAME ______ DATE ______ PERIOD ____

6-7 Practice: Word Problems

Reflections

1\. **ALPHABET** The figure shows the letter V plotted on a coordinate system. Find the coordinates of points C and D after the figure is reflected over the y-axis.

$C'(2, 0)$, $D'(0, 3)$

2\. **GREEK** The figure shows the Greek letter gamma plotted on a coordinate system. Find the coordinates of points P and Q after the figure is reflected over the x-axis. Then draw the reflected image.

$P'(-4, -4)$, $Q'(-2, -3)$

3\. **CRAFTS** Candace is making a pattern for star-shaped ornaments. Complete the pattern shown so that the completed star has a vertical line of symmetry.

4\. **FLOORING** The Turners are replacing the flooring in their dining room. Complete the design shown so that the completed floor has a horizontal line of symmetry.

5\. **FLAG** Macedonia is a country near Greece and Albania. The national flag of Macedonia has both vertical and horizontal symmetry. Complete the flag of Macedonia.

6\. **COYOTE** Dasan is preparing a presentation on animal safety. Finish the drawing of a coyote's footprint so that it has vertical symmetry.

ALPHABET For Exercises 27 and 28, use the figure at the right. It shows that the capital letter A looks the same after a reflection over a vertical line. It does not look the same after a reflection over a horizontal line.

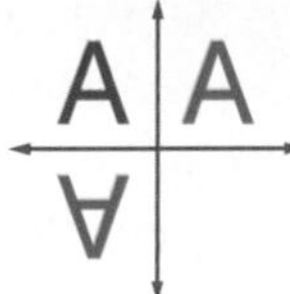

27\. What other capital letters look the same after a reflection over a vertical line? **H, I, M, O, T, U, V, W, X, Y**

28\. Which capital letters look the same after a reflection over a horizontal line? **B, C, D, E, H, I, K, O, X**

29\. **CRITICAL THINKING** Suppose a point P with coordinates $(-4, 5)$ is reflected so that the coordinates of its image are $(-4, -5)$. Without graphing, which axis was this point reflected over? Explain. **x-axis; The x-coordinates are the same, but the y-coordinates are opposites.**

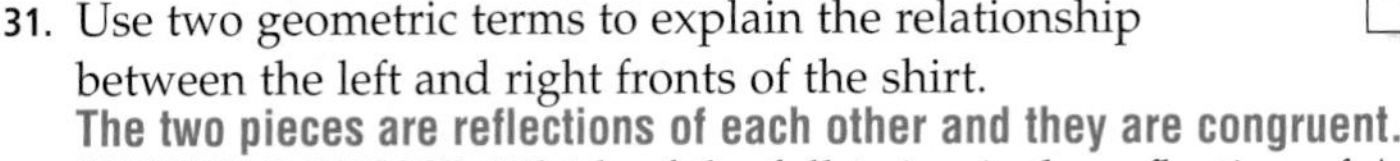

Spiral Review with Standardized Test Practice

SHORT RESPONSE For Exercises 30 and 31, use the drawing at the right.

Left Front

Right Front

30\. The drawing shows the pattern for the left half of the front of the shirt. Copy the pattern onto grid paper. Then draw the outline of the pattern after it has been flipped over a vertical line. Label it "Right Front."

31\. Use two geometric terms to explain the relationship between the left and right fronts of the shirt. **The two pieces are reflections of each other and they are congruent.**

32\. **MULTIPLE CHOICE** Which of the following is the reflection of $\triangle ABC$ with vertices $A(1, -1)$, $B(4, -1)$, and $C(2, -4)$ over the x-axis? **B**

Ⓐ
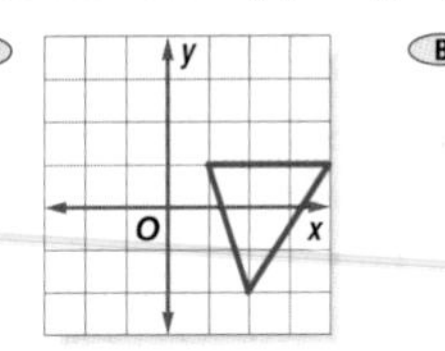

Ⓑ
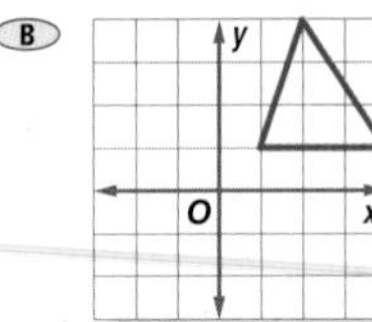

Ⓒ
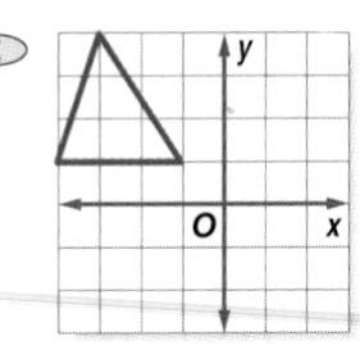

Ⓓ
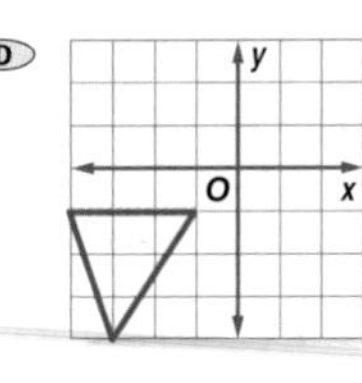

CARDS Determine whether each card has rotational symmetry. Write *yes* or *no*. If *yes*, name its angle(s) of rotation. (Lesson 6-6)

33\.  **yes; 180°**

34\. 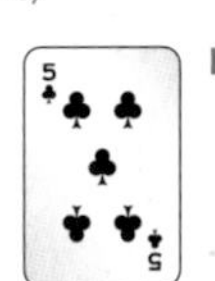 **no**

35\.  **no**

36\. **yes; 180°**

37\. Find the value of x if the triangles at the right are congruent. (Lesson 6-5) **20**

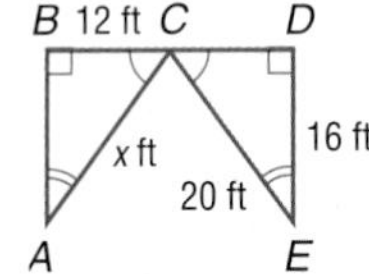

GETTING READY FOR THE NEXT LESSON

PREREQUISITE SKILL Add. (Lesson 1-4)

38\. $-4 + (-1)$ **−5**

39\. $-5 + 3$ **−2**

40\. $-1 + 4$ **3**

41\. $2 + (-2)$ **0**

4 Assess

Open-Ended Assessment

Speaking Have students hold a meterstick next to an object in the classroom. Tell them to imagine that the meterstick is an axis of reflection. Have students describe what the reflection of the object across this axis would look like.

Study Skill

Objective Use a definition map.

Use a Definition Map

Studying Math Vocabulary

Understanding a math term requires more than just memorizing a definition. Try completing a definition map to expand your understanding of a geometry vocabulary word.

A *definition map* can help you visualize the parts of a good definition. Ask yourself these questions about the vocabulary terms.

- What is it? (Category)
- What can it be compared to? (Comparisons)
- What is it like? (Properties)
- What are some examples? (Illustrations)

Here's a definition map for *reflection*.

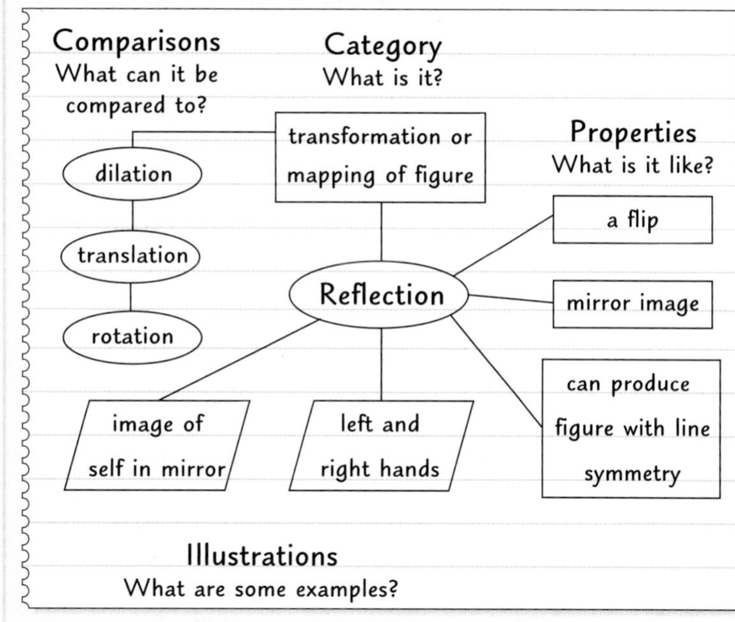

SKILL PRACTICE 1–4. See students' work.
Make a definition map for each term.

1. complementary angles (Page 256)
2. perpendicular lines (Page 257)
3. isosceles triangle (Page 263)
4. square (Page 273)

GETTING STARTED

Vocabulary Different students will find more success with different methods of studying vocabulary. Auditory learners will profit from reading words and their definitions out loud, particularly if they use mnemonic devices, rhythm, or rhyming. Verbal/linguistic learners will gain a lot by studying the meanings of root words and prefixes. Visual learners can study vocabulary by making flashcards with images or graphs of examples of the terms. They then can quiz themselves by trying to recall a word while looking at the image side of a card.

TEACH

Definition map suggestions to students:

- The number of comparisons, illustrations, or properties will vary for each term.
- Make drawings, graphs, or equations for the illustrations whenever possible.
- Do not limit yourself to the questions shown on this page. Other possible headings for mapping include symbols, standard equation, or root words and meanings.

ASSESS

Open-Ended Assessment

Speaking Have small groups of students work together to map the following terms. Have one students draw the map while all of the students in the group brainstorm answers to the questions for the map. Each student should take a turn as map recorder.

- obtuse angle (page 256)
- transversal (page 258)
- perpendicular bisector (page 271)
- rotational symmetry (page 287)

6-8 Translations

6-8 Lesson Notes

Lesson Resources

Chapter 6 Resource Masters
- Study Guide and Intervention, p. 342
- Practice: Skills, p. 343
- Practice: Word Problems, p. 344
- Reading to Learn Mathematics, p. 345
- Enrichment, p. 346

MathPASS Tutorial CD-ROM, 46
Parent and Student Study Guide Online Worksheets, 6-8
Real-Life Career Masters, p. 32
Teaching Mathematics with Manipulatives, p. 75
Noteables™: Interactive Study Notebook with Foldables™, 6-8

FAST FILE

1 Focus

5-Minute Check 6-8
Use as a quiz or review of Lesson 6-7. (Also available as a transparency)

Bellringer
Reading Mathematics Tell students that the Latin roots of *translate* mean *to bring across.* Discuss how the concept of translating words from one language to another relates to the concept of translating an object from one place to another. When you translate a sentence, each word maps to a word or phrase in the second language.

Reading to Learn Mathematics, p. 345 ELL

NAME ______________ DATE ________ PERIOD ____

6-8 Reading to Learn Mathematics
Translations

Pre-Activity *Read the introduction at the top of page 296 in your textbook. Write your answers below.*

1. Describe the motion involved in moving the knight. left two squares and up one square
2. Compare the shape, size, and orientation of the knight in its original position to that of the knight in its new position. They are the same.

Reading the Lesson

For Exercises 3-6, read the Key Concept information on page 296 in your textbook and refer to the graph at the right that shows quadrilaterals *ABCD* and *A'B'C'D'*.

3. Determine how many units up and to the right each vertex of quadrilateral ABCD has moved to get to the corresponding ...

What You'll LEARN
Graph translations on a coordinate plane.

NEW Vocabulary
translation

WHEN am I ever going to use this?

CHESS In chess, there are rules governing how many spaces and in what direction each game piece can be moved during a player's turn. The diagram at the right shows one legal move of a knight.

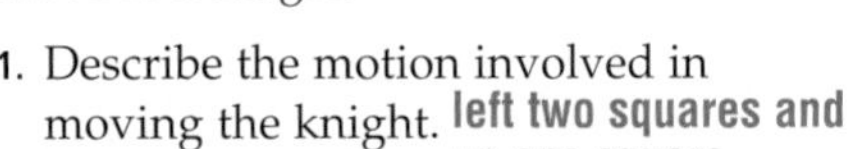

1. Describe the motion involved in moving the knight. **left two squares and up one square**

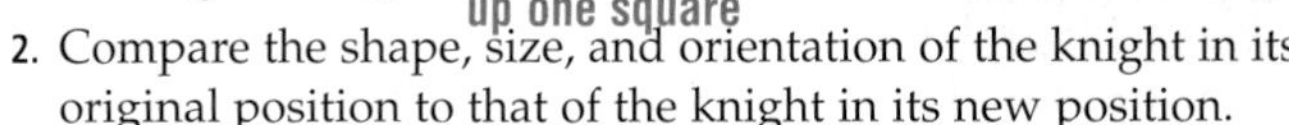

2. Compare the shape, size, and orientation of the knight in its original position to that of the knight in its new position.

2. They are the same.

A **translation** (sometimes called a *slide*) is the movement of a figure from one position to another without turning it.

Noteables™ **Key Concept: Properties of Translations**

1. Every point on the original figure is moved the same distance and in the same direction.
2. The image is congruent to the original figure, and the orientation of the image is *the same* as that of the original figure.

Model

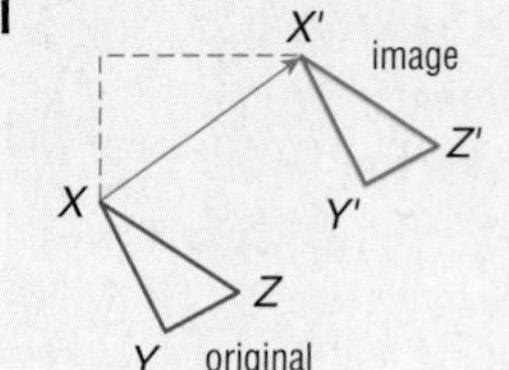

EXAMPLE **Draw a Translation**

1 **Copy trapezoid *WXYZ* at the right on graph paper. Then draw the image of the figure after a translation 4 units left and 2 units down.**

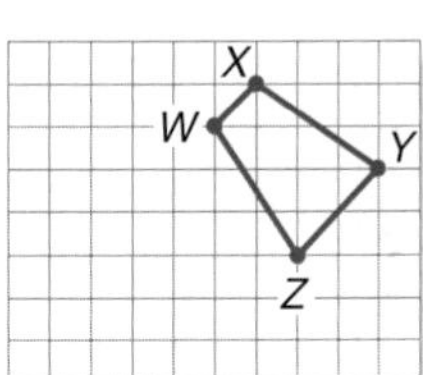

Step 1 Move each vertex of the trapezoid 4 units left and 2 units down.

Step 2 Connect the new vertices to form the image.

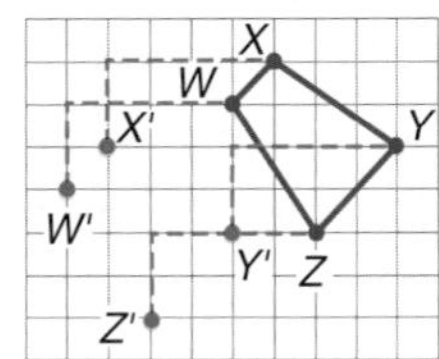

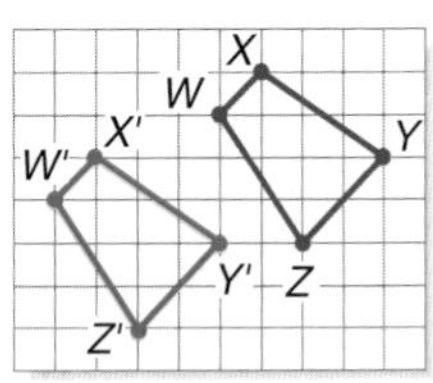

DAILY INTERVENTION **Differentiated Instruction**

Auditory/Musical Use the musical concept of octaves as an analogy for geometrical translations. Have a music student play a simple tune in one octave, and then repeat the tune in other octaves. Students should hear that the tune sounds the same, but it has been translated higher or lower. Give students copies of the sheet music used and have them determine the translation.

EXAMPLE Translation in the Coordinate Plane

2 **Graph $\triangle JKL$ with vertices $J(-3, 4)$, $K(1, 3)$, and $L(-4, 1)$. Then graph the image of $\triangle JKL$ after a translation 2 units right and 5 units down. Write the coordinates of its vertices.**

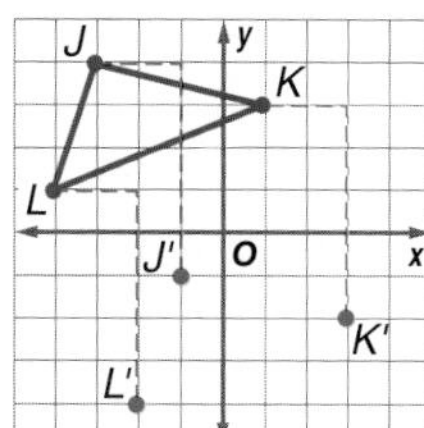

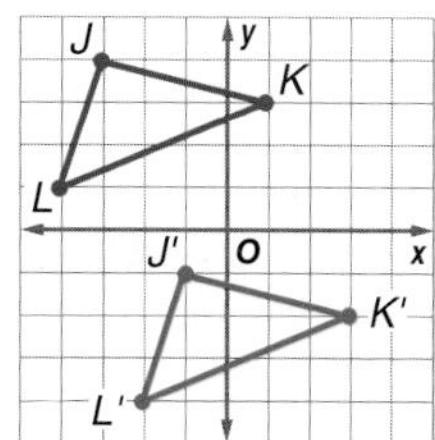

The coordinates of the vertices of the image are $J'(-1, -1)$, $K'(3, -2)$, and $L'(-2, -4)$. Notice that these vertices can also be found by adding 2 to the x-coordinates and -5 to the y-coordinates, or $(2, -5)$.

Original		Add (2, −5).		Image
$J(-3, 4)$	→	$(-3 + 2, 4 + (-5))$	→	$J'(-1, -1)$
$K(1, 3)$	→	$(1 + 2, 3 + (-5))$	→	$K'(3, -2)$
$L(-4, 1)$	→	$(-4 + 2, 1 + (-5))$	→	$L'(-2, -4)$

STUDY TIP

Translations In the coordinate plane, a translation can be described using an ordered pair. A translation *up* or to the *right* is positive. A translation *down* or to the *left* is negative. $(2, -5)$ means a translation 2 units right and 5 units down.

Your Turn **Graph $\triangle ABC$ with vertices $A(4, -3)$, $B(0, 2)$, and $C(5, 1)$. Then graph its image after each translation, and write the coordinates of its vertices.**

a. 2 units down

b. 4 units left and 3 units up

a. $A'(4, -5)$, $B'(0, 0)$, $C'(5, -1)$
b. $A'(0, 0)$, $B'(-4, 5)$, $C'(1, 4)$
a–b. See margin for graphs.

Standardized Test Practice

EXAMPLE Use a Translation

3 **MULTIPLE-CHOICE TEST ITEM** Point N is moved to a new location, N'. Which white shape shows where the shaded figure would be if it was translated in the same way?

 A  B  C  D

Read the Test Item

You are asked to determine which figure has been moved according to the same translation as Point N.

Solve the Test Item

Point N is translated 4 units left and 1 unit up. Identify the figure that is a translation of the shaded figure 4 units left and 1 unit up.

Figure A: 2 units left and 2 units up

Figure B: represents a turn, not a translation

Figure C: 4 units left and 1 unit up

The answer is C.

msmath3.net/extra_examples

Answers (Your Turn)

a.
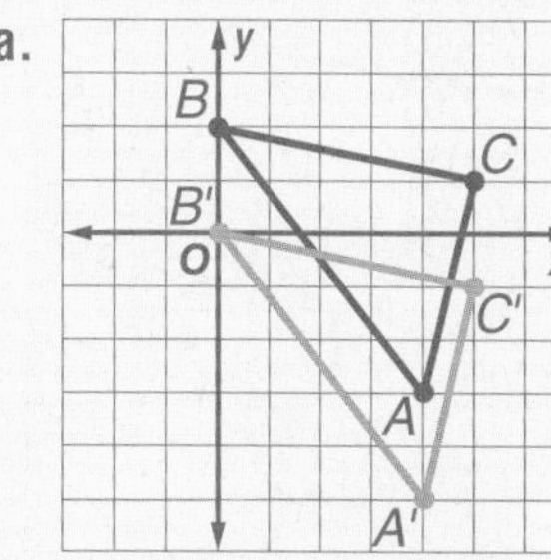

b.
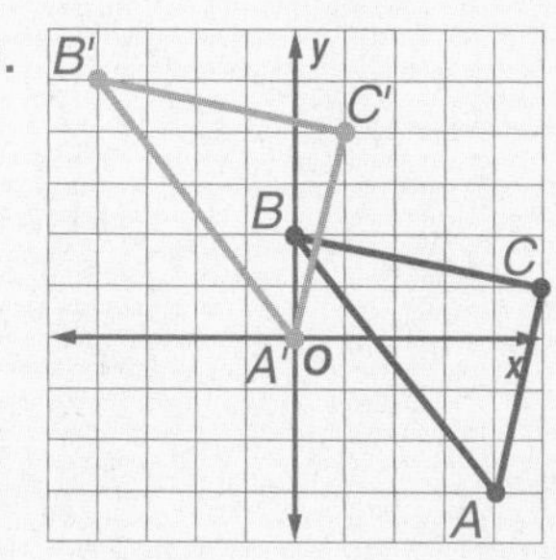

2 Teach

In-Class Examples

INTERACTIVE CHALKBOARD
PowerPoint® Presentations

1 Copy $\triangle EFG$ below on graph paper. Then draw the image of the figure after a translation 3 units right and 2 units up.

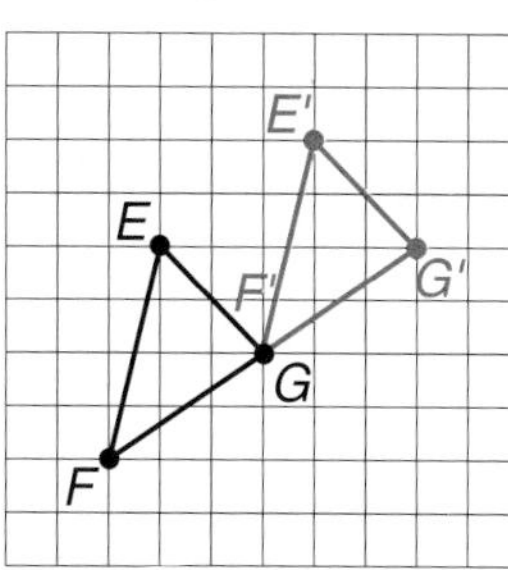

2 Graph $\triangle ABC$ with vertices $A(-2, 2)$, $B(3, 4)$, and $C(4, 1)$. Then graph the image of $\triangle ABC$ after a translation 2 units left and 5 units down. Write the coordinates of its vertices. **$A'(-4, -3)$, $B'(1, -1)$, $C'(2, -4)$**

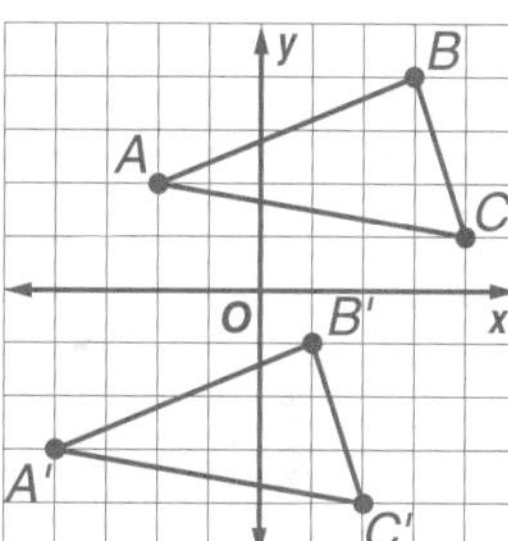

3 **MULTIPLE-CHOICE TEST ITEM** Point S is moved to a new location, S'. Which white shape shows where the shaded figure would be if it was translated in the same way? **B**

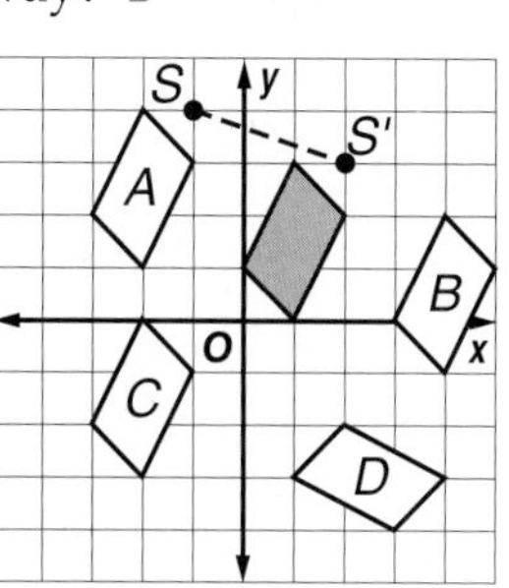

A A **C** C
B B **D** D

3 Practice/Apply

Which One Doesn't Belong?
In Exercise 1, students should realize that a translation is only a slide. The orientation of the figure does not change.

About the Exercises...

Guided Practice Key

Exercises	Examples
3	1
4–5	2

Assignment Guide

Basic: 7–13 odd, 15–24

Average: 7–13 odd, 14–24

Enriched: 6–12 even, 13–20 (Optional: 21–24)

Answers

1. The fourth transformation; the other transformations are translations, but in the fourth, the figure is turned, so it is not a translation.
2. Sample answer:

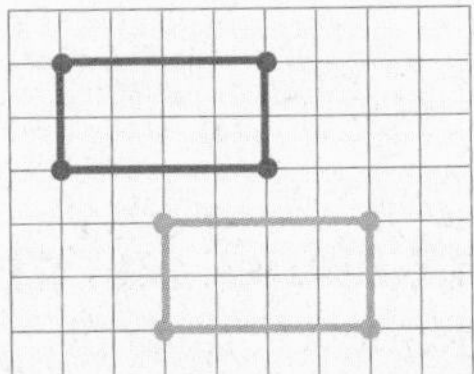

3.

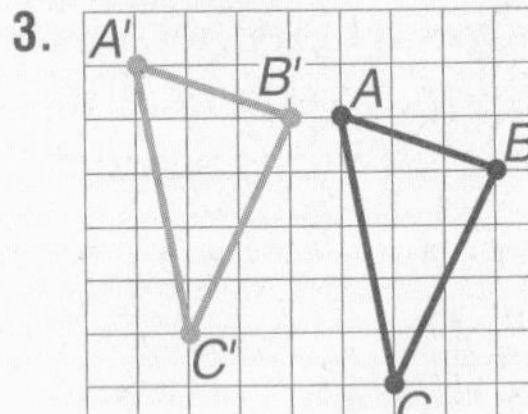

4.

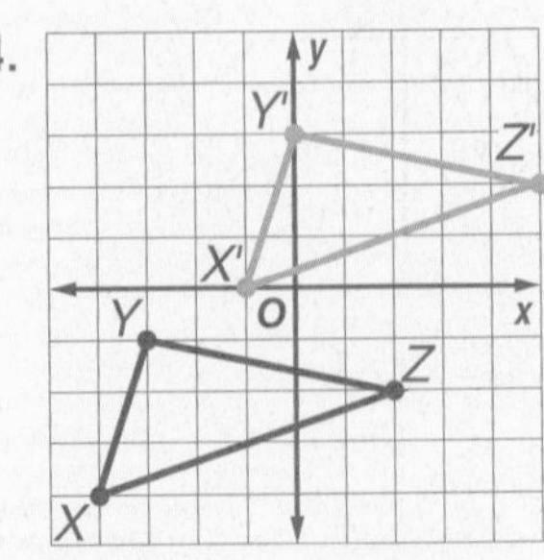

$X'(-1, 0)$, $Y'(0, 3)$, $Z'(5, 2)$

Students practice the same concepts in Exercises 6–11 if they are assigned odd or even problems.

Skill and Concept Check

1. **Which One Doesn't Belong?** Identify the transformation that is not the same as the other three. Explain your reasoning. See margin.

   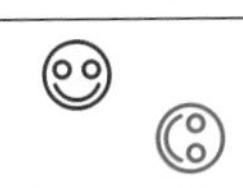

2. **OPEN ENDED** Draw a rectangle on grid paper. Then draw the image of the rectangle after a translation 2 units right and 3 units down. See margin.

GUIDED PRACTICE

3. Copy the figure at the right on graph paper. Then draw the image of the figure after a translation 4 units left and 1 unit up. See margin.

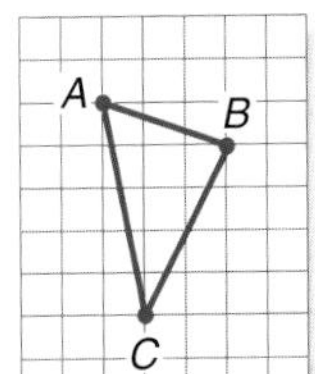

Graph the figure with the given vertices. Then graph the image of the figure after the indicated translation, and write the coordinates of its vertices. 4–5. See margin.

4. triangle XYZ with vertices $X(-4, -4)$, $Y(-3, -1)$, and $Z(2, -2)$ translated 3 units right and 4 units up
5. trapezoid $EFGH$ with vertices $E(0, 3)$, $F(3, 3)$, $G(4, 1)$, and $H(-2, 1)$ translated 2 units left and 3 units down

Practice and Applications

HOMEWORK HELP

For Exercises	See Examples
6–7	1
8–11	2
13–14	3

Extra Practice
See pages 631, 653.

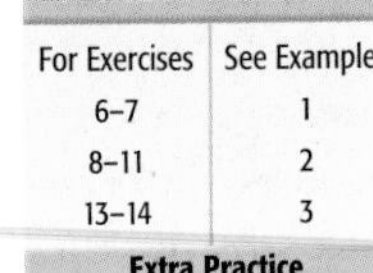

Copy each figure onto graph paper. Then draw the image of the figure after the indicated translation. 6–7. See margin.

6. 5 units right and 3 units up
7. 3 units right and 4 units down

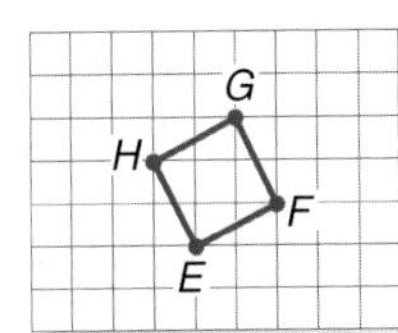

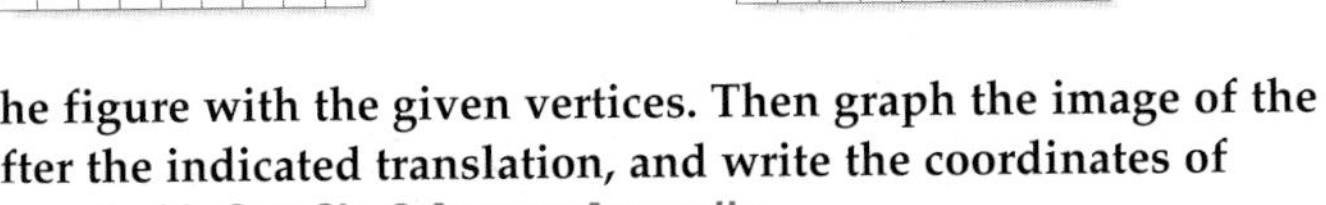

Graph the figure with the given vertices. Then graph the image of the figure after the indicated translation, and write the coordinates of its vertices. 8–11. See Ch. 6 Answer Appendix.

8. $\triangle ABC$ with vertices $A(1, 2)$, $B(3, 1)$, and $C(3, 4)$ translated 2 units left and 1 unit up
9. $\triangle RST$ with vertices $R(-5, -2)$, $S(-2, 3)$, and $T(2, -3)$ translated 1 unit left and 3 units down
10. rectangle $JKLM$ with vertices $J(-3, 2)$, $K(3, 5)$, $L(4, 3)$, and $M(-2, 0)$ translated by 1 unit right and 4 units down
11. parallelogram $ABCD$ with vertices $A(6, 3)$, $B(4, 0)$, $C(6, -2)$, and $D(8, 1)$ translated 3 units left and 2 units up

5.

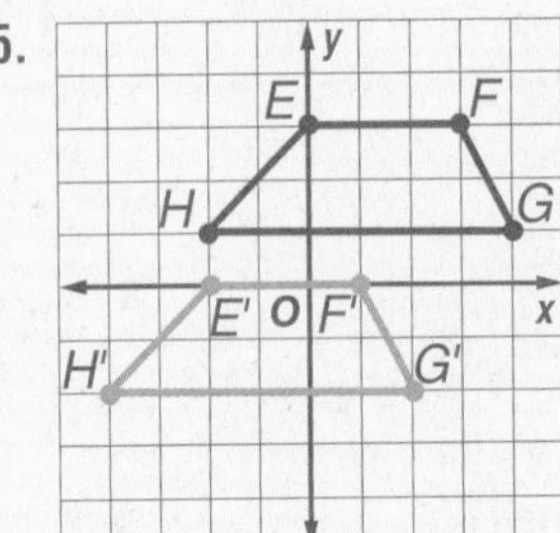

$E'(-2, 0)$, $F'(1, 0)$, $G'(2, -2)$, $H'(-4, -2)$

6.

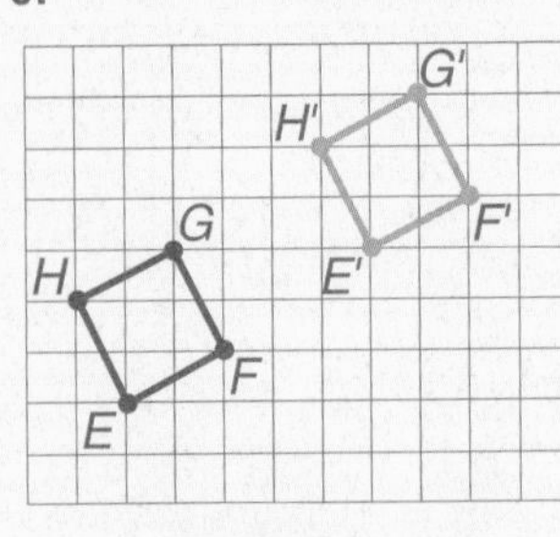

7.

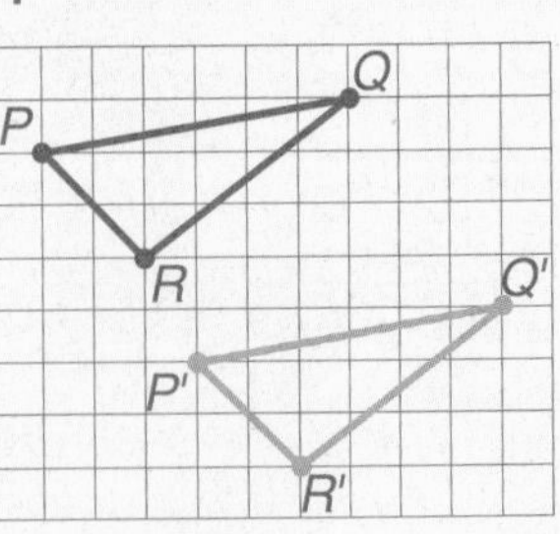

12. **ART** Explain why Andy Warhol's 1962 *Self Portrait*, shown at the right, is an example of an artist's use of translations. **See margin.**

MUSIC For Exercises 13 and 14, use the following information. The sound wave of a tuning fork is given below.

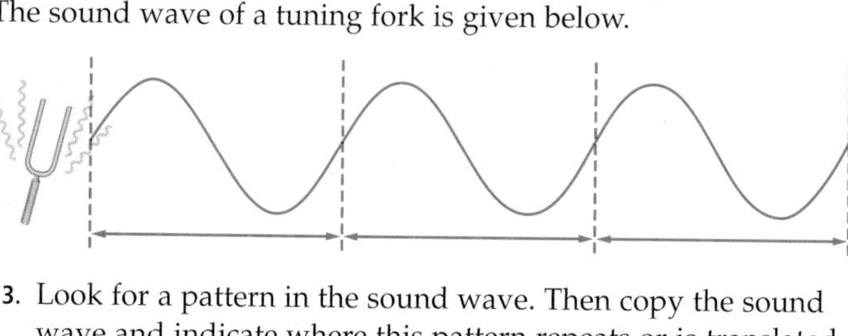

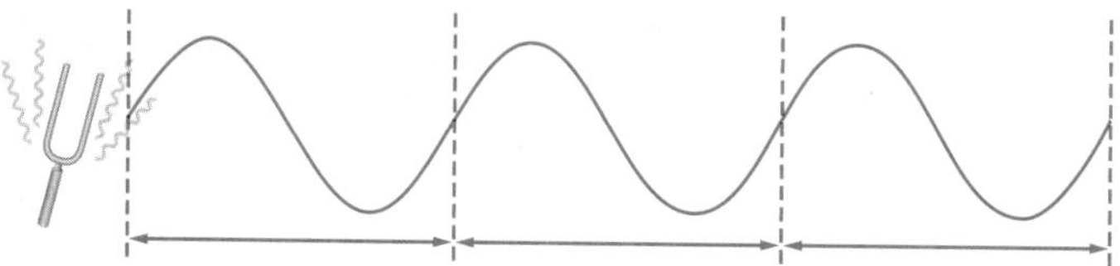

13. Look for a pattern in the sound wave. Then copy the sound wave and indicate where this pattern repeats or is translated.

14. How many translations of the original pattern are shown? **2**

15. **CRITICAL THINKING** Triangle *RST* has vertices $R(4, 2)$, $S(-8, 0)$, and $T(6, 7)$. When translated, R' has coordinates $(-2, 4)$. Find the coordinates of S' and T'. **$S'(-14, 2)$, $T'(0, 9)$**

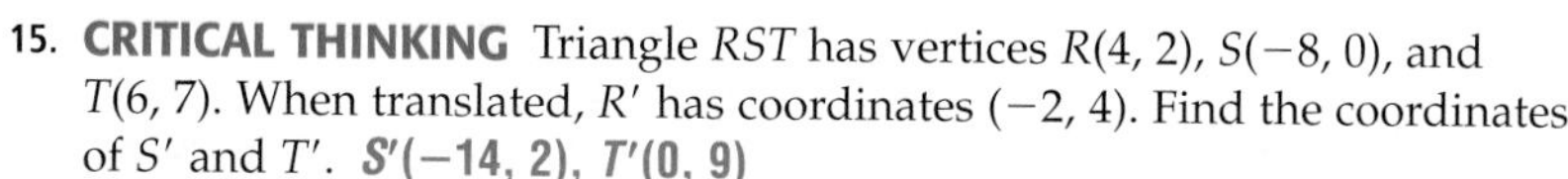

Spiral Review with Standardized Test Practice

16. **MULTIPLE CHOICE** Which of the following is a vertex of the figure shown at the right after a translation 4 units down? **A**

    Ⓐ $(1, -5)$ Ⓑ $(-6, -2)$ Ⓒ $(1, -3)$ Ⓓ $(-2, -2)$

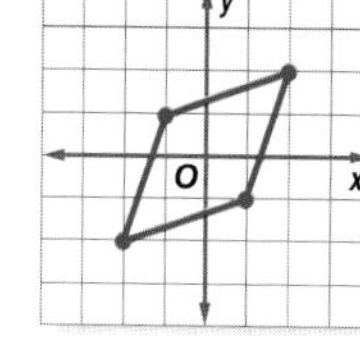

17. **SHORT RESPONSE** What are the coordinates of $W(-6, 3)$ after it is translated 2 units right and 1 unit down? **$(-4, 2)$**

18. Graph polygon *ABCDE* with vertices $A(-5, -3)$, $B(-2, 1)$, $C(-3, 4)$, $D(0, 2)$, and $E(0, -3)$. Then graph the image of the figure after a reflection over the y-axis, and write the coordinates of its vertices. (Lesson 6-7) **See Ch. 6 Answer Appendix.**

LIFE SCIENCE For Exercises 19 and 20, use the diagram of the diatom at the right. (Lesson 6-6)

19. Does the diatom have line symmetry? If so, trace the figure and draw any lines of symmetry. If not, write *none*. **yes**

20. Does the diatom have rotational symmetry? Write *yes* or *no*. If *yes*, name its angle(s) of rotation. **yes; 120°, 240°**

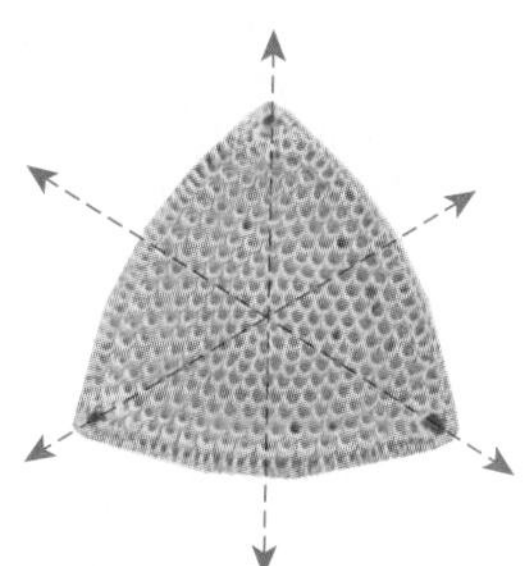

A *diatom* is a microscopic algae found in both marine and fresh water.

GETTING READY FOR THE NEXT LESSON

PREREQUISITE SKILL Determine whether each figure has rotational symmetry. Write *yes* or *no*. If *yes*, name its angles of rotation. (Lesson 6-6)

21. 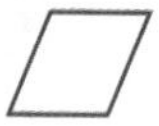 **yes; 180°**

22.  **yes; 120°, 240°**

23. 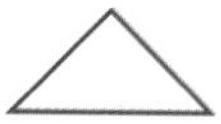 **no**

24.  **yes; 72°, 144°, 216°, 288°**

Math Online msmath3.net/self_check_quiz

4 Assess

Open-Ended Assessment

Writing Have students write a paragraph describing how the translation of a figure on a grid is different from a reflection of the figure. They should describe any changes in position or orientation.

Answer

12. The exact same picture of the man is shown in 4 different positions on the canvas without rotation.

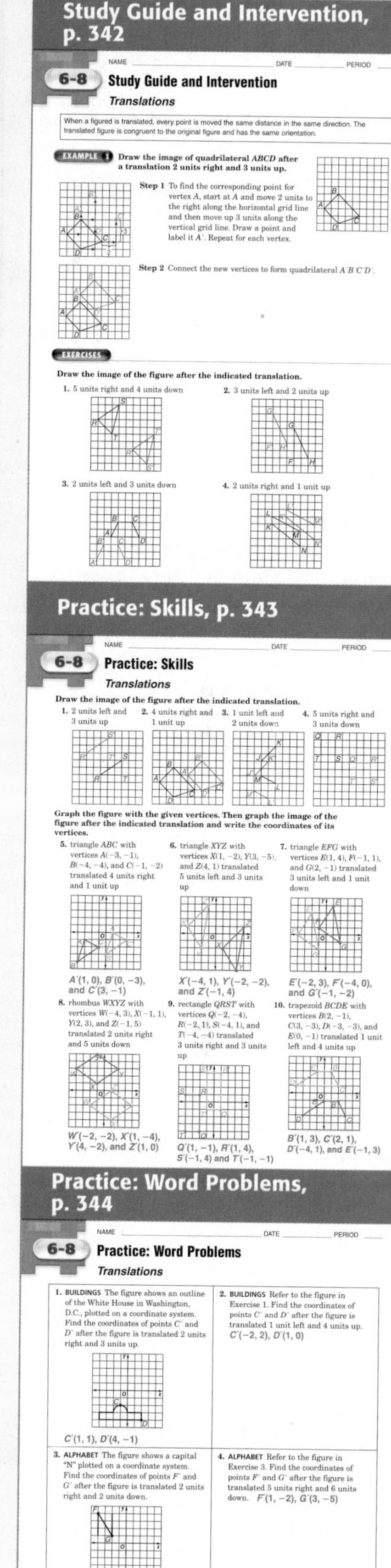

Study Guide and Intervention, p. 342

NAME ________ DATE ________ PERIOD ____

6-8 Study Guide and Intervention

Translations

When a figured is translated, every point is moved the same distance in the same direction. The translated figure is congruent to the original figure and has the same orientation.

EXAMPLE 1 **Draw the image of quadrilateral *ABCD* after a translation 2 units right and 3 units up.**

Step 1 To find the corresponding point for vertex *A*, start at *A* and move 2 units to the right along the horizontal grid line and then move up 3 units along the vertical grid line. Draw a point and label it *A*′. Repeat for each vertex.

Step 2 Connect the new vertices to form quadrilateral *A*′*B*′*C*′*D*′.

EXERCISES

Draw the image of the figure after the indicated translation.

1. 5 units right and 4 units down
2. 3 units left and 2 units up
3. 2 units left and 3 units down
4. 2 units right and 1 unit up

Practice: Skills, p. 343

NAME ________ DATE ________ PERIOD ____

6-8 Practice: Skills

Translations

Draw the image of the figure after the indicated translation.

1. 2 units left and 3 units up
2. 4 units right and 1 unit up
3. 1 unit left and 2 units down
4. 5 units right and 3 units down

Graph the figure with the given vertices. Then graph the image of the figure after the indicated translation and write the coordinates of its vertices.

5. triangle *ABC* with vertices $A(-3, -1)$, $B(-4, -4)$, and $C(-1, -2)$ translated 4 units right and 1 unit up
   $A'(1, 0)$, $B'(0, -3)$, and $C'(3, -1)$
6. triangle *XYZ* with vertices $X(1, -2)$, $Y(3, -5)$, and $Z(4, 1)$ translated 5 units left and 3 units up
   $X'(-4, 1)$, $Y'(-2, -2)$, and $Z'(-1, 4)$
7. triangle *EFG* with vertices $E(1, 4)$, $F(-1, 1)$, and $G(2, -1)$ translated 3 units left and 1 unit down
   $E'(-2, 3)$, $F'(-4, 0)$, and $G'(-1, -2)$
8. rhombus *WXYZ* with vertices $W(-4, 3)$, $X(-1, 1)$, $Y(2, 3)$, and $Z(-1, 5)$ translated 2 units right and 5 units down
   $W'(-2, -2)$, $X'(1, -4)$, $Y'(4, -2)$, and $Z'(1, 0)$
9. rectangle *QRST* with vertices $Q(-2, -4)$, $R(-2, 1)$, $S(-4, 1)$, and $T(-4, -4)$ translated 3 units right and 3 units up
   $Q'(1, -1)$, $R'(1, 4)$, $S'(-1, 4)$ and $T'(-1, -1)$
10. trapezoid *BCDE* with vertices $B(2, -1)$, $C(3, -3)$, $D(-3, -3)$, and $E(0, -1)$ translated 1 unit left and 4 units up
    $B'(1, 3)$, $C'(2, 1)$, $D'(-4, 1)$, and $E'(-1, 3)$

Practice: Word Problems, p. 344

NAME ________ DATE ________ PERIOD ____

6-8 Practice: Word Problems

Translations

1. **BUILDINGS** The figure shows an outline of the White House in Washington, D.C., plotted on a coordinate system. Find the coordinates of points *C*′ and *D*′ after the figure is translated 2 units right and 3 units up.
   $C'(1, 1)$, $D'(4, -1)$
2. **BUILDINGS** Refer to the figure in Exercise 1. Find the coordinates of points *C*′ and *D*′ after the figure is translated 1 unit left and 4 units up.
   $C'(-2, 2)$, $D'(1, 0)$
3. **ALPHABET** The figure shows a capital "N" plotted on a coordinate system. Find the coordinates of points *F*′ and *G*′ after the figure is translated 2 units right and 2 units down.
   $F'(-2, 2)$, $G'(0, -1)$
4. **ALPHABET** Refer to the figure in Exercise 3. Find the coordinates of points *F*′ and *G*′ after the figure is translated 5 units right and 6 units down. $F'(1, -2)$, $G'(3, -5)$
5. **QUILT** The beginning of a quilt is shown below. Look for a pattern in the quilt. Copy and translate the quilt square to finish the quilt. 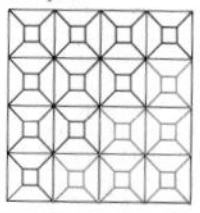
6. **BEACH** Tylia is walking on the beach. Copy and translate her footprints to show her path in the sand.

6-9 Lesson Notes

Lesson Resources

Chapter 6 Resource Masters FAST FILE
- Study Guide and Intervention, p. 347
- Practice: Skills, p. 348
- Practice: Word Problems, p. 349
- Reading to Learn Mathematics, p. 350
- Enrichment, p. 351

Classroom Math Games, pp. 21–26
Key Teaching Transparencies, 24
Parent and Student Study Guide Online Worksheets, 6-9
Noteables™: Interactive Study Notebook with Foldables™, 6-9
Virtual Activities CD-ROM, Rotations

1 Focus

5-Minute Check 6-9

Use as a quiz or review of Lesson 6-8. (Also available as a transparency)

Bellringer

Communication Hold a meterstick vertically against the chalkboard. Rotate the stick 45° clockwise and have students describe what you have done. Hold the stick vertically again and rotate it 45° counterclockwise. Again have students describe what you have done. Based on what they saw, have students explain why it is necessary to say whether a rotation is clockwise or counterclockwise.

Reading to Learn Mathematics, p. 350 ELL

NAME ______ DATE ______ PERIOD ______

6-9 Reading to Learn Mathematics
Rotations

Pre-Activity *Complete the Mini Lab at the top of page 300 in your textbook. Write your answers below.*

1. Measure the distances from points on the original figure and corresponding points on the image to the center of rotation. What do you observe? **These distances for corresponding points are equal.**
2. Measure the angles formed by connecting the center of rotation to pairs of corresponding points. What do you observe? **The angles all have the same measure.**

Reading the Lesson

For Exercises 3–6, read the Key Concept information on page 300 of your textbook and refer to the graph at the right that shows quadrilaterals *ABCD* and *A′B′C′D′* and a point.

3. Find the distance of each of the vertices *A*, *B*, *A′*, and *B′* from ...

Rotations

HANDS-ON Mini Lab

What You'll LEARN

Graph rotations on a coordinate plane.

NEW Vocabulary

rotation
center of rotation

REVIEW Vocabulary

angle of rotation: the degree measure of the angle through which a figure is rotated (Lesson 6-6)

Materials
- tracing paper
- straightedge
- tape
- protractor

A **rotation** is a transformation involving the turning or spinning of a figure around a fixed point called the **center of rotation**.

STEP 1 Draw a polygon, placing a dot at one vertex. Place a second dot, the center of rotation, in a nearby corner.

STEP 2 Form an angle of rotation by connecting the first dot, the center of rotation, and a point on the edge of the paper.

STEP 3 Place a second paper over the first and trace the figure, the dots, and the ray passing through the figure.

STEP 4 With your pencil on the center of rotation, turn the top paper until its ray lines up with the ray passing through the edge of the first paper. Tape the papers together.

Step 1

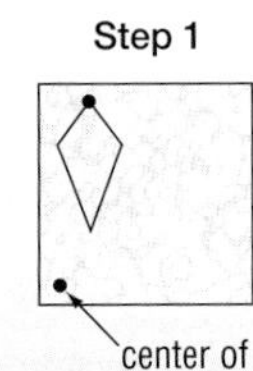

Step 2

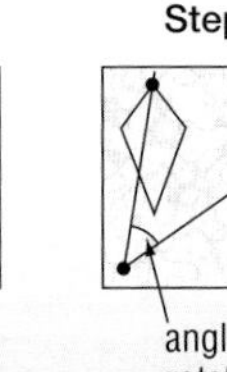

Step 3

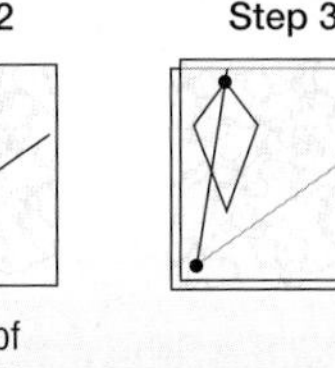

Step 4

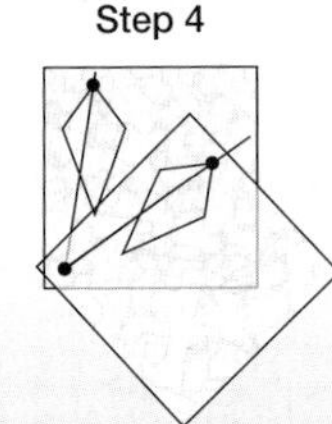

1. Measure the distances from points on the original figure and corresponding points on the image to the center of rotation. What do you observe?
2. Measure the angles formed by connecting the center of rotation to pairs of corresponding points. What do you observe?

1. These distances for corresponding points are equal.
2. The angles all have the same measure.

The Mini Lab suggests the following properties of rotations.

Noteables™ **Key Concept: Properties of Rotations**

1. Corresponding points are the same distance from *R*. The angles formed by connecting *R* to corresponding points are congruent.
2. The image is congruent to the original figure, and their orientations are *the same*.

Model

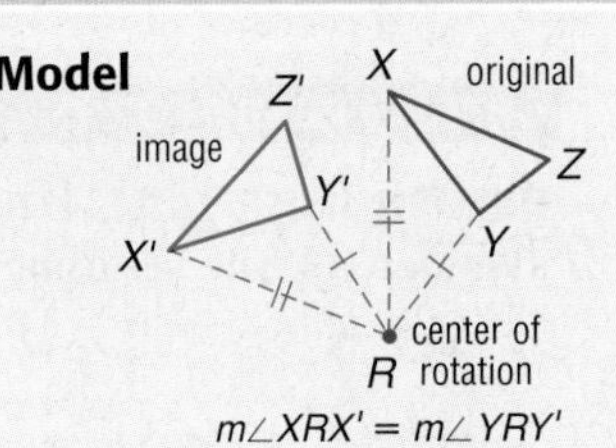

$m\angle XRX' = m\angle YRY'$

DAILY INTERVENTION **Flexible Grouping**

Rotations Divide the class into small groups. Have students cut out symmetrical shapes from construction paper. Next, have each group draw a grid on the chalkboard or on butcher paper taped to the floor. Tell them to place one shape at a time on the grid and observe rotations of 45°, 90°, 180°, and 270°.

STUDY TIP

Rotations About the Origin The center of rotation in Example 1 is the origin and the angle of rotation is 90° counterclockwise.

TEACHING TIP

Some students may need a protractor and a ruler for Example 1.

TEACHING TIP

Remind students that an angle measuring 180° is a straight line.

a–b. See margin for graphs.

a. $A'(2, 1)$, $B'(-1, 4)$, $C'(4, 3)$

b. $A'(-1, 2)$, $B'(-4, -1)$, $C'(-3, 4)$

REAL-LIFE MATH

FOLK ART The Pennsylvania Dutch, or Pennsylvania Germans, created signs that were painted on the sides of barns or houses. Many feature designs that have rotational symmetry.

Source: www.folkart.com

EXAMPLE Rotations in the Coordinate Plane

1 **Graph $\triangle XYZ$ with vertices $X(2, 2)$, $Y(4, 3)$, and $Z(3, 0)$. Then graph the image of $\triangle XYZ$ after a rotation 90° counterclockwise about the origin, and write the coordinates of its vertices.**

Step 1 Lightly draw a line connecting point X to the origin.

Step 2 Lightly draw $\overline{OX'}$ so that $m\angle X'OX = 90°$ and $OX' = OX$.

Step 3 Repeat steps 1–2 for points Y and Z. Then erase all lightly drawn lines and connect the vertices to form $\triangle X'Y'Z'$.

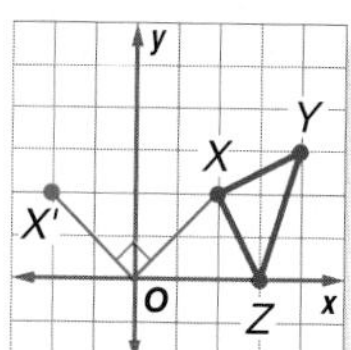

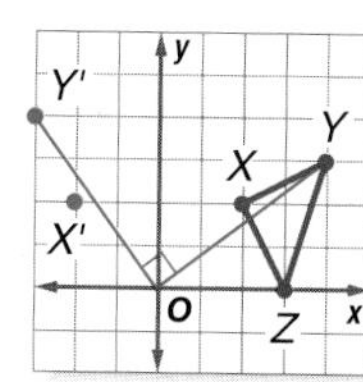

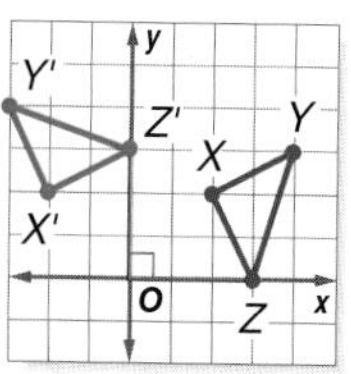

Triangle $X'Y'Z'$ has vertices $X'(-2, 2)$, $Y'(-3, 4)$, and $Z'(0, 3)$.

Your Turn **Graph $\triangle ABC$ with vertices $A(1, -2)$, $B(4, 1)$, and $C(3, -4)$. Then graph the image of $\triangle ABC$ after the indicated rotation about the origin, and write the coordinates of its vertices.**

a. 90° counterclockwise

b. 180° counterclockwise

If a figure touches its center of rotation, then one or more rotations of the figure can be used to create a new figure that has rotational symmetry.

EXAMPLE Use a Rotation

2 **FOLK ART Copy and complete the barn sign shown so that the completed figure has rotational symmetry with 90°, 180°, and 270° as its angles of rotation.**

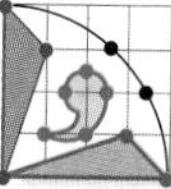

Use the procedure described above and the points indicated to rotate the figure 90°, 180°, and 270° counterclockwise. Use a 90° rotation *clockwise* to produce the same rotation as a 270° rotation counterclockwise.

90° counterclockwise

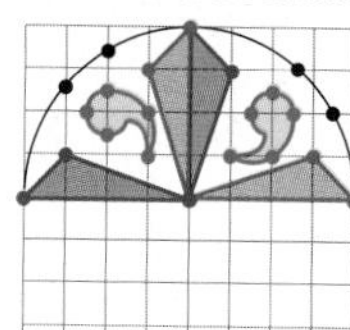

180° counterclockwise

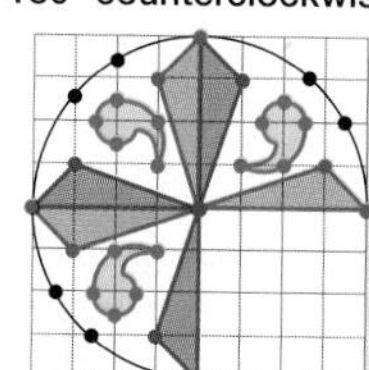

90° clockwise

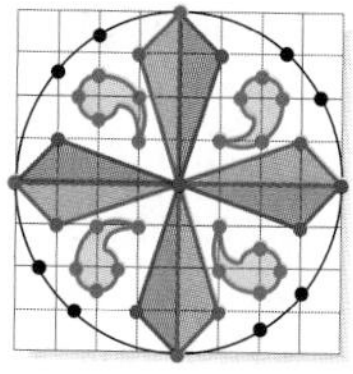

msmath3.net/extra_examples

Answers (Your Turn)

a.

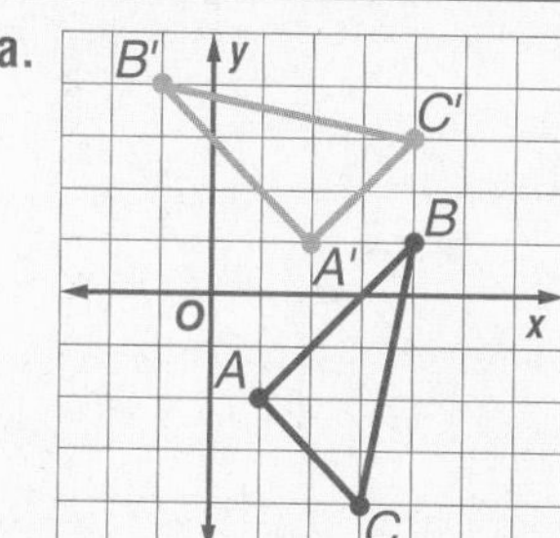

b.

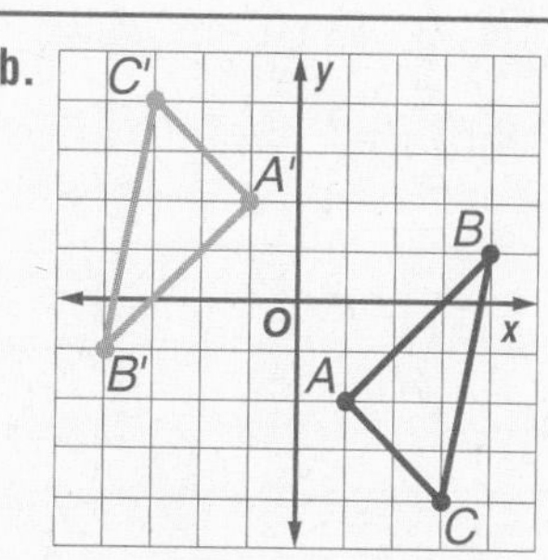

2 Teach

In-Class Examples

INTERACTIVE CHALKBOARD

PowerPoint® Presentations

1 Graph $\triangle QRS$ with vertices $Q(1, 1)$, $R(3, 4)$, and $S(4, 1)$. Then graph the image of $\triangle QRS$ after a rotation of 180° about the origin, and write the coordinates of its vertices. **$Q'(-1, -1)$, $R'(-3, -4)$, $S'(-4, -1)$**

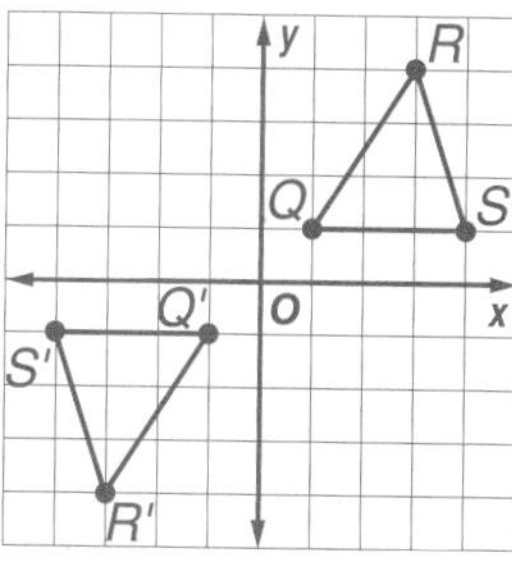

2 **QUILTS** Copy and complete the quilt piece shown below so that the completed figure has rotational symmetry with 90°, 180°, and 270° as its angles of rotation.

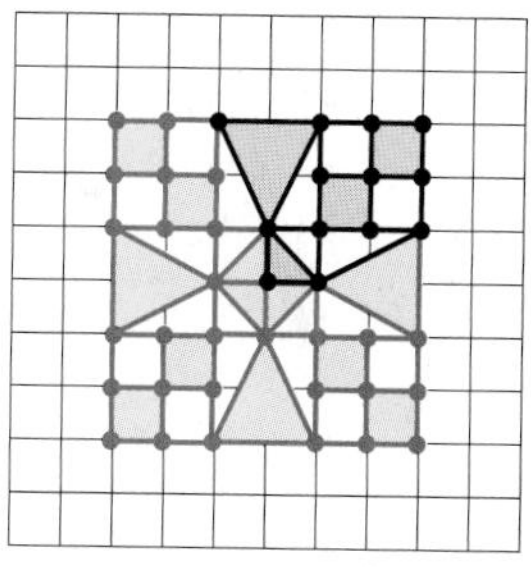

Answer (p. 302)

3. $A'(4, -2)$, $B'(1, 2)$, $C'(3, 4)$

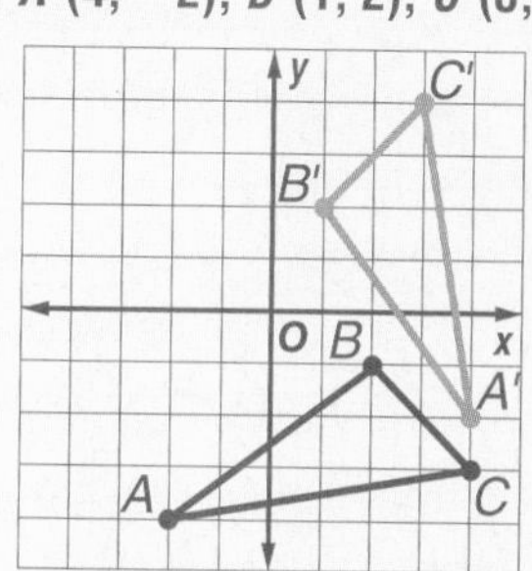

3 Practice/Apply

DAILY INTERVENTION **FIND THE ERROR** Students can solve Exercise 2 either by remembering the rule for switching coordinates after a 90° rotation or by sketching the triangle and its image on a coordinate plane.

About the Exercises...

Guided Practice Key

Exercises	Example
3–4	1

Assignment Guide

Basic: 5–13 odd, 14–25

Average: 5–13 odd, 14–25

Enriched: 6–12 even, 13–25

Answers

4. **D′(3, −2), F′(1, 0), G′(3, 4), H′(4, 2)**

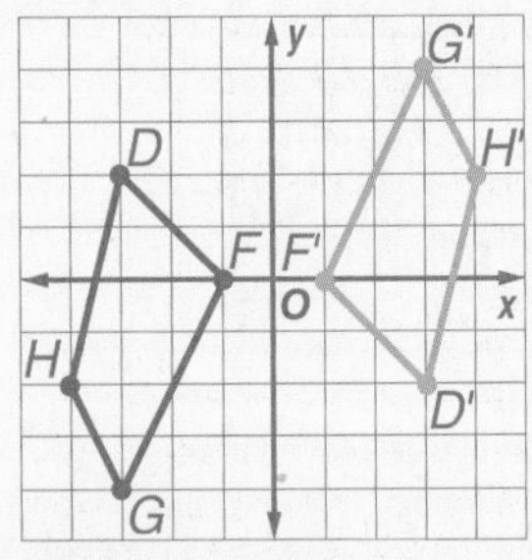

5. **V′(4, −2), W′(2, −4), X′(−2, −1)**

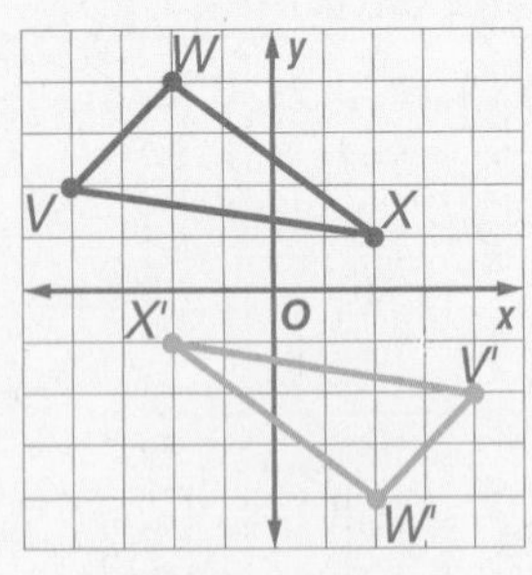

Students practice the same concepts in Exercises 5–12 if they are assigned odd or even problems.

Skill and Concept Check

1. **OPEN ENDED** Give three examples of rotating objects you see every day. **Sample answer: fan blade, Ferris wheel, car tire**

2. **FIND THE ERROR** Anita and Manuel are graphing $\triangle MNP$ with vertices $M(-3, 2)$, $N(-1, -1)$, and $P(-4, -2)$ and its image after a rotation 90° counterclockwise about the origin. Who is correct? Explain.

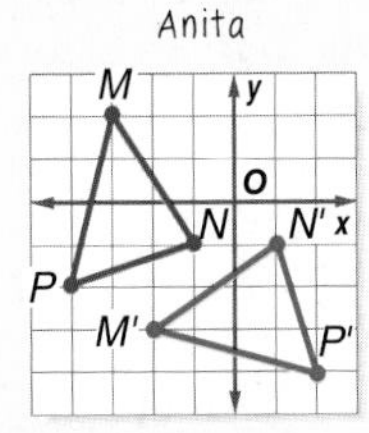

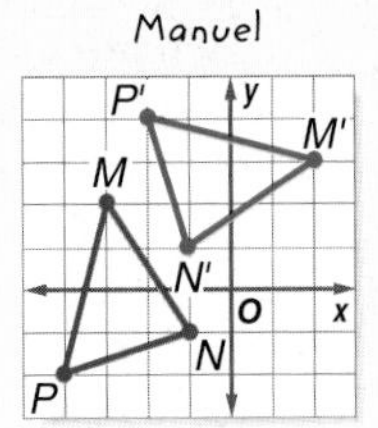

Anita; Manuel rotated the figure 90° *clockwise* instead of *counterclockwise*.

GUIDED PRACTICE

Graph the figure with the given vertices. Then graph the image of the figure after the indicated rotation about the origin, and write the coordinates of its vertices.

3. triangle ABC with vertices $A(-2, -4)$, $B(2, -1)$, and $C(4, -3)$; 90° counterclockwise **3–4. See margin.**

4. quadrilateral $DFGH$ with vertices $D(-3, 2)$, $F(-1, 0)$, $G(-3, -4)$, and $H(-4, -2)$; 180°

Practice and Applications

Graph the figure with the given vertices. Then graph the image of the figure after the indicated rotation about the origin, and write the coordinates of its vertices. **5–8. See margin.**

HOMEWORK HELP

For Exercises	See Examples
5–12	1
13	2

Extra Practice See pages 632, 653.

5. triangle VWX with vertices $V(-4, 2)$, $W(-2, 4)$, and $X(2, 1)$; 180°

6. triangle BCD with vertices $B(-5, 3)$, $C(-2, 5)$, and $D(-3, 2)$; 90° counterclockwise

7. trapezoid $LMNP$ with vertices $L(0, 3)$, $M(4, 3)$, $N(1, -3)$, and $P(-1, 1)$; 90° counterclockwise

8. quadrilateral $FGHJ$ with vertices $F(-5, 4)$, $G(-3, 4)$, $H(0, -1)$, and $J(-5, 2)$; 180°

Determine whether the figure in green is a rotation of the figure in blue about the origin. Write *yes* or *no*. Explain. **9–12. See Ch. 6 Answer Appendix for explanation.**

9. **yes**

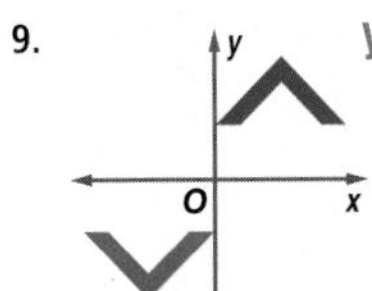

10. **yes**

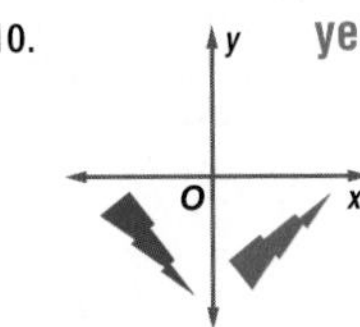

11. **no**

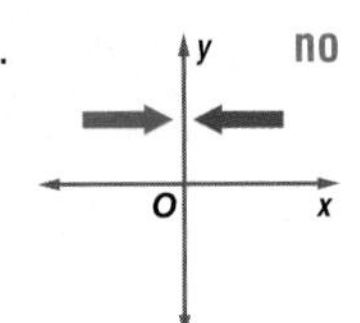

12. **no**

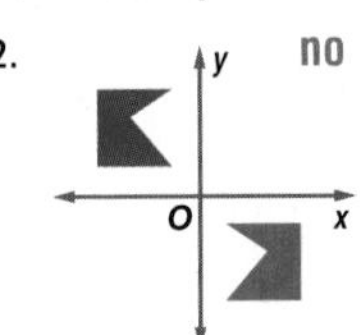

6. **B′(−3, −5), C′(−5, −2), D′(−2, −3)**

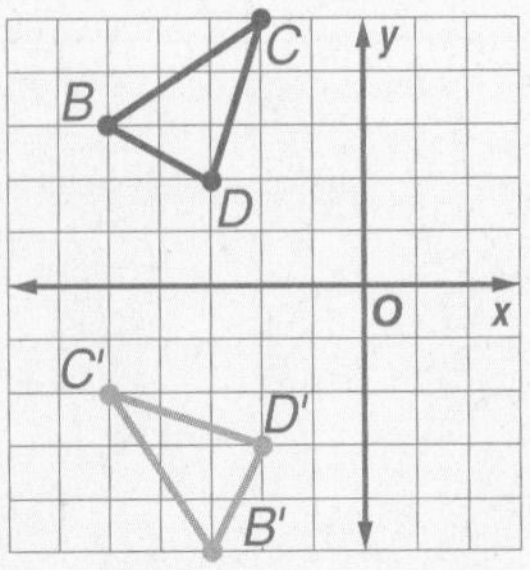

7. **L′(−3, 0), M′(−3, 4), N′(3, 1), P′(−1, −1)**

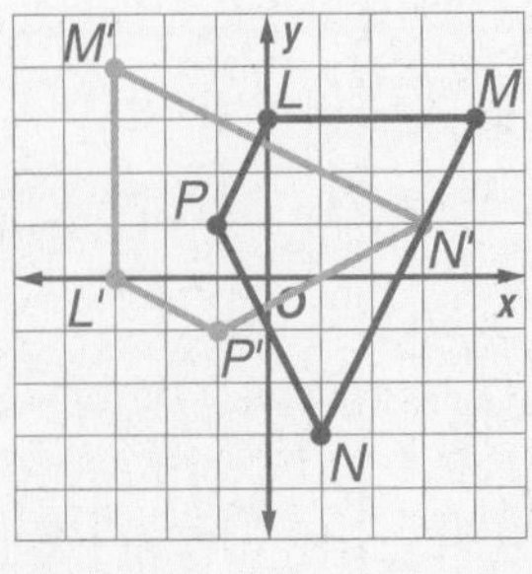

13. **FABRIC DESIGN** Copy and complete the handkerchief design at the right so that it has rotational symmetry. Rotate the figure 90°, 180°, and 270° counterclockwise about point C. **See Ch. 6 Answer Appendix.**

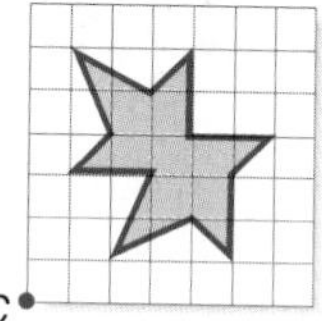

14. **CRITICAL THINKING** What are the new coordinates of a point at (x, y) after the point is rotated 90° counterclockwise? 180°? **$(-y, x)$; $(-x, -y)$**

C

Spiral Review with Standardized Test Practice

15. **SHORT RESPONSE** Draw a rectangle. Then draw the image of the rectangle after it has been translated 1.5 inches to the right and then rotated 90° counterclockwise about the bottom left vertex. Label this rectangle *I*. **See Ch. 6 Answer Appendix.**

16. **MULTIPLE CHOICE** Which illustration shows the figure at the right rotated 180°? **D**

Ⓐ  Ⓑ  Ⓒ 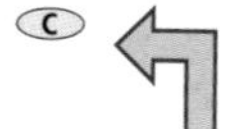 Ⓓ 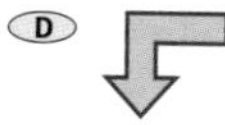

Identify each transformation as a *reflection*, a *translation*, or a *rotation*.
(Lessons 6-7, 6-8, and 6-9) **20. translation**

17. 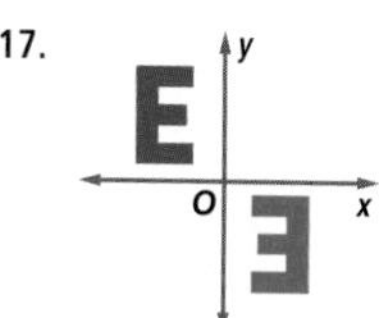

rotation

18. 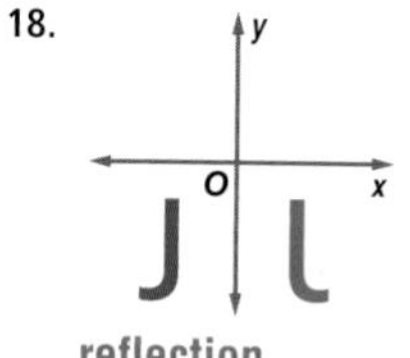

reflection

19. 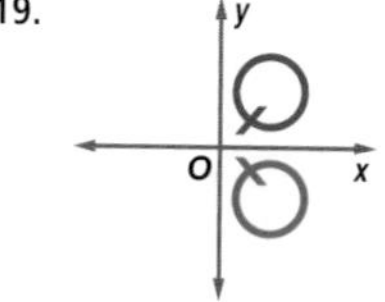

reflection

20. 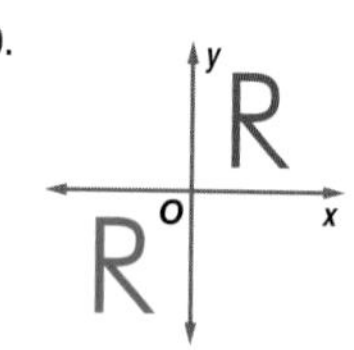

For Exercises 21–25, use the graphic at the right. **21–25. See Ch. 6 Answer Appendix.**

21. Describe a translation used in this graphic. (Lesson 6-8)

22. Trace at least two examples of figures or parts of figures in the graphic that appear to have line symmetry. Then draw all lines of symmetry. (Lesson 6-6)

23. Trace a figure or part of a figure used in the graphic that appears to have rotational symmetry. (Lesson 6-6)

24. Trace and then classify the quadrilateral that makes up the top portion of the collar on the shirt. (Lesson 6-4)

25. Trace the two triangles that make up the collar on the shirt. Classify each triangle by its angles and by its sides and then determine whether the two triangles are congruent. (Lessons 6-2 and 6-5)

Math Online msmath3.net/self_check_quiz

4 Assess

Higher-Level Thinking

Challenge students to develop a rule for finding the coordinates of the vertices of a figure after it has been rotated 180° about the origin. **Multiply both coordinates of each point in the original figure by −1.**

Answer

8. $F'(5, -4)$, $G'(3, -4)$, $H'(0, 1)$, $J'(5, -2)$

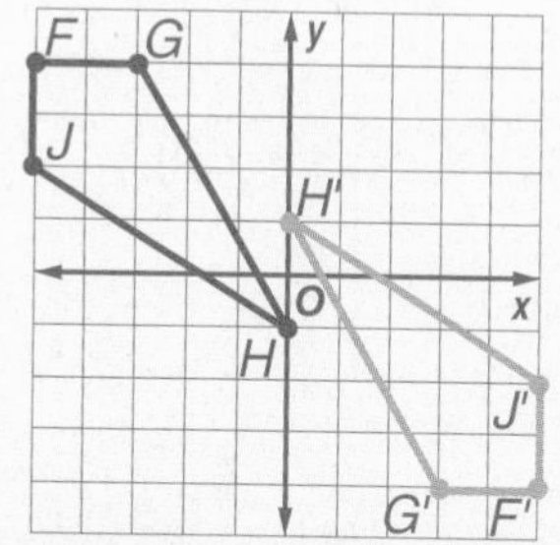

Study Guide and Intervention, p. 347

NAME ______ DATE ______ PERIOD ____

6-9 Study Guide and Intervention
Rotations

When a figure is rotated about a point, every point on the original figure has a corresponding point on the rotated image. A point and its corresponding point are the same distance from the center of rotation. The angles formed by connecting each point and its corresponding point to the center of rotation are all congruent. The rotated figure is congruent to the original figure and has the same orientation.

EXAMPLE 1 **Graph trapezoid $ABCD$ with vertices $A(1, 3)$, $B(4, 4)$, $C(4, 0)$, and $D(1, 1)$. Then graph the image of trapezoid $ABCD$ after a rotation 90° counterclockwise about the origin and write the coordinates of its vertices.**

Step 1 Graph trapezoid $ABCD$.

Step 2 To find the corresponding point for vertex A, draw a line segment between A and the origin. Then draw a second line segment starting at the origin that is the same length as the first segment and forms a 90° angle with the first segment. Draw a point at the end of the second segment and label it A'.

Step 3 Repeat for vertex B.

Step 4 Repeat for vertices C and D. Then connect the new vertices to form trapezoid $A'B'C'D'$.

EXERCISES

Graph the figure with the given vertices. Then graph the image of the figure after the indicated rotation about the origin and write the coordinates of its vertices.

1. triangle GHI with vertices $G(1, 0)$, $H(3, 1)$, and $I(2, 5)$; 90° counterclockwise
$G'(0, 1)$, $H'(-1, 3)$, and $I'(-5, 2)$

2. polygon $TUVW$ with vertices $T(2, -4)$, $U(3, -1)$, $V(-1, 0)$, and $W(-2, -3)$; 180°
$T'(-2, 4)$, $U'(-3, 1)$, $V'(1, 0)$, and $W'(2, 3)$

Practice: Skills, p. 348

NAME ______ DATE ______ PERIOD ____

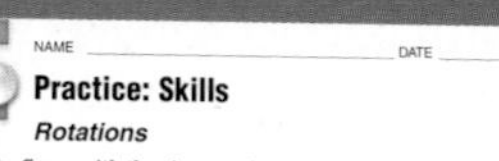

6-9 Practice: Skills
Rotations

Graph the figure with the given vertices. Then graph the image of the figure after the indicated rotation about the origin and write the coordinates of its vertices.

1. triangle ABC with vertices $A(1, 5)$, $B(3, 4)$, and $C(4, 0)$; 90° counterclockwise
$A'(-5, 1)$, $B'(-4, 3)$, and $C'(0, 4)$

2. triangle FGH with vertices $F(4, 2)$, $G(1, 1)$, and $H(1, 5)$; 180°
$F'(-4, -2)$, $G'(-1, -1)$, and $H'(-1, -5)$

3. triangle XYZ with vertices $X(4, -4)$, $Y(0, -5)$, and $Z(1, 2)$; 180°
$X'(-4, 4)$, $Y'(0, 5)$, and $Z'(-1, -2)$

4. triangle LMN with vertices $L(-1, -4)$, $M(-4, -3)$, and $N(-2, -1)$; 90° counterclockwise
$L'(4, -1)$, $M'(3, -4)$, and $N'(1, -2)$

5. square $DEFG$ with vertices $D(-4, 5)$, $E(-1, 5)$, $F(-1, 2)$, and $G(-4, 2)$; 90° counterclockwise
$D'(-5, -4)$, $E'(-5, -1)$, $F'(-2, -1)$, and $G'(-2, -4)$

6. quadrilateral $TUVW$ with vertices $T(-2, 1)$, $U(-1, 4)$, $V(-4, 4)$, and $W(-5, 0)$; 180°
$T'(2, -1)$, $U'(1, -4)$, $V'(4, -4)$, and $W'(5, 0)$

Practice: Word Problems, p. 349

NAME ______ DATE ______ PERIOD ____

6-9 Practice: Word Problems
Rotations

1. **ALPHABET** Draw a figure on the grid below so that the figure together with its image after a 180° rotation will form a letter of the alphabet.
Sample answer:

2. **ALPHABET** Draw a figure on the grid below so that the figure together with its images after 90°, 180°, and 270° counterclockwise rotations will form a letter of the alphabet.
Sample answer:

3. **QUILTS** Complete the pattern for a quilt square by rotating the design 180° about the given point. What does the completed figure resemble?
the numeral eight

4. **QUILTS** Complete the pattern for a quilt square by rotating the figure 90°, 180°, and 270° counterclockwise about the given point.

5. **SNOWFLAKE** Mr. Ai is cutting paper snowflakes to decorate his classroom. Complete the snowflake below so that the completed figure has symmetry with 90°, 180°, and 270° as its angles of rotation.

6. **LOGO** The local swimming pool is having a contest, and all students are welcome to enter. The pool officials want a new logo that has rotational symmetry with 120° and 240° as its angles of rotation. The student whose logo is chosen will win a one-year pass to the pool. In the space below, draw an entry for the contest. See students' work.

6-9b HANDS-ON LAB

Lesson Notes

Lesson Resources

Teaching Mathematics with Manipulatives

- student recording sheet 6-9b

Glencoe Mathematics Classroom Manipulative Kit

- scissors

GETTING STARTED

Teaching Tip Students must start with perfect squares and equilateral triangles in order to create their tessellations without overlaps or gaps. You may wish to cut these out ahead of time. Be sure the shapes are small enough to allow students to create a good pattern unit on the page.

Teaching Tip Share more examples of Escher's works with the class.

TEACH

Activity 1

- Point out that there should be no overlap of the original shape and the translated or rotated part.

Answers (Your Turn)

a.

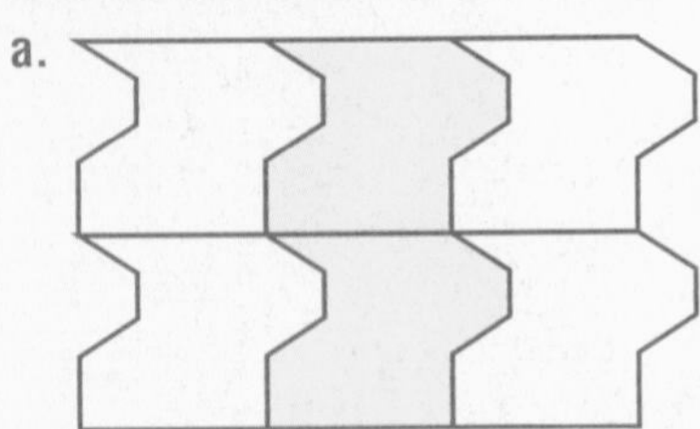

b.

c.

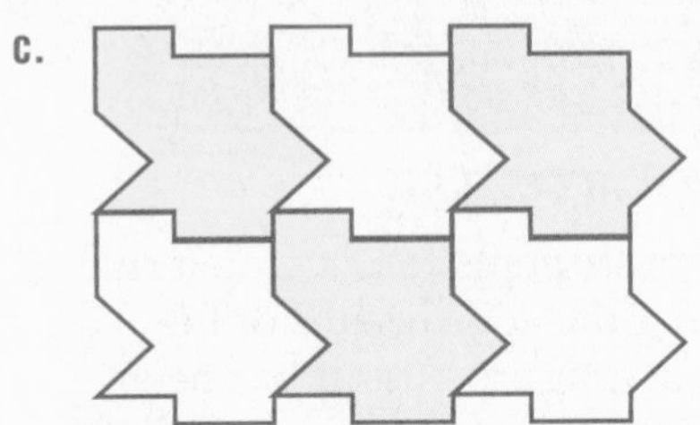

6-9b HANDS-ON LAB

A Follow-Up of Lesson 6-9

What You'll LEARN

Create Escher-like drawings using translations and rotations.

Materials

- index cards
- scissors
- tape
- paper

Tessellations

Symmetry drawing E70 by M.C. Escher. © 2002 Cordon Art-Baarn-Holland. All rights reserved.

Maurits Cornelis Escher (1898–1972) was a Dutch artist whose work used tessellations. A **tessellation** is a tiling made up of copies of the same shape or shapes that fit together without gaps and without overlapping. The sum of the angle measures where vertices meet in a tessellation must equal 360°. For this reason, equilateral triangles and squares will tessellate a plane.

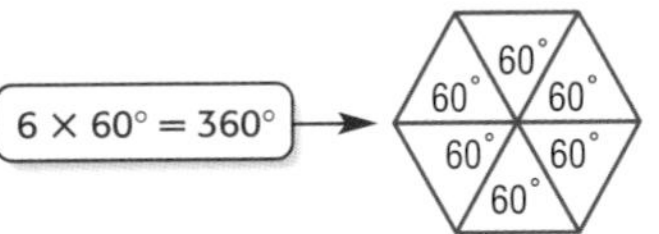

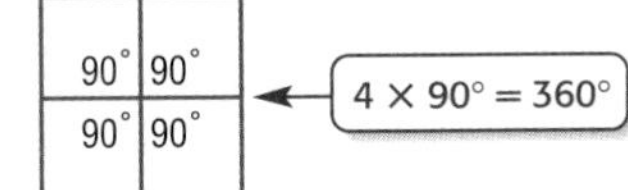

ACTIVITY

1 Create a tessellation using a translation.

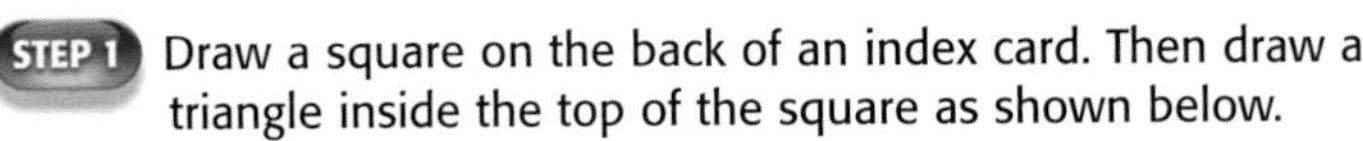

STEP 1 Draw a square on the back of an index card. Then draw a triangle inside the top of the square as shown below.

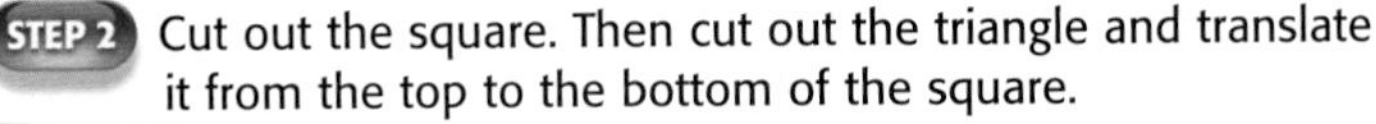

STEP 2 Cut out the square. Then cut out the triangle and translate it from the top to the bottom of the square.

STEP 3 Tape the triangle and square together to form a pattern.

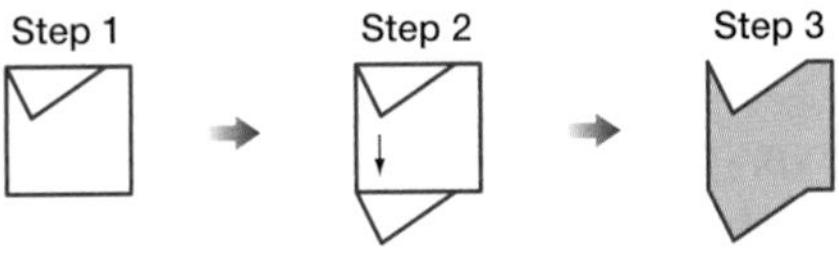

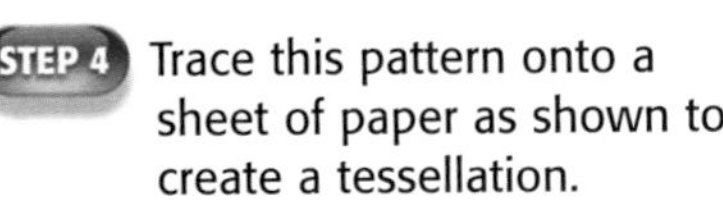

STEP 4 Trace this pattern onto a sheet of paper as shown to create a tessellation.

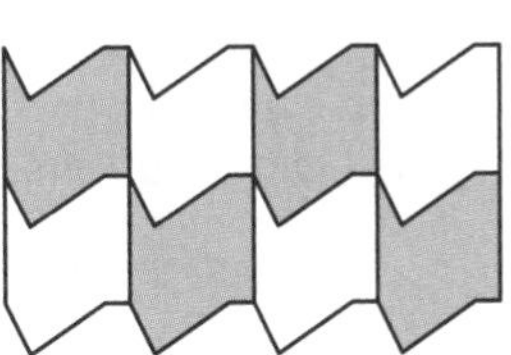

a–c. See margin.

Your Turn **Make an Escher-like drawing using each pattern.**

a. 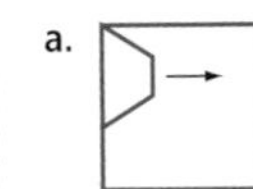

b. 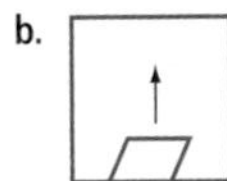

c. 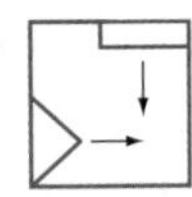

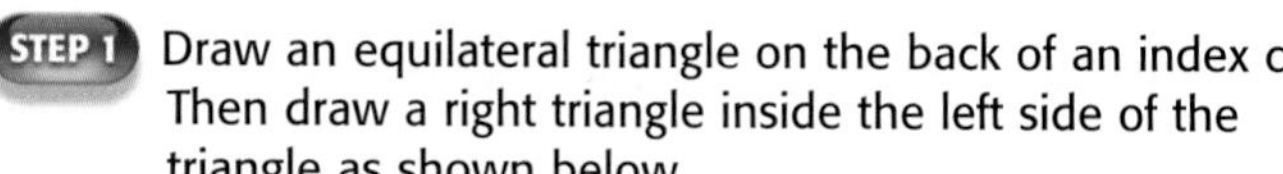

ACTIVITY

2 **Create a tessellation using a rotation.**

STEP 1 Draw an equilateral triangle on the back of an index card. Then draw a right triangle inside the left side of the triangle as shown below.

STEP 2 Cut out the equilateral triangle. Then cut out the right triangle and rotate it so that the right triangle is on the right side as indicated.

STEP 3 Tape the right triangle and equilateral triangle together to form a pattern unit.

STEP 4 Trace this pattern onto a sheet of paper as shown to create a tessellation.

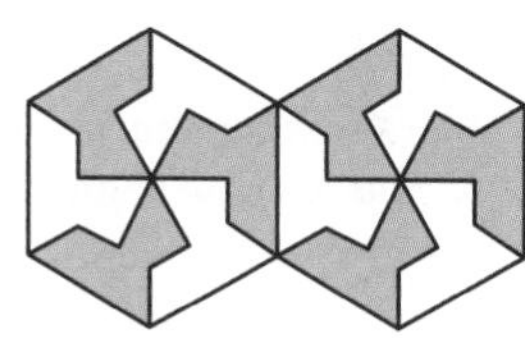

d–f. See margin.

Your Turn **Make an Escher-like drawing using each pattern.**

d. 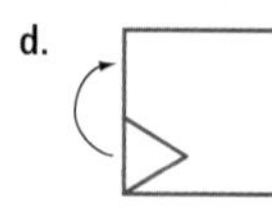

e. 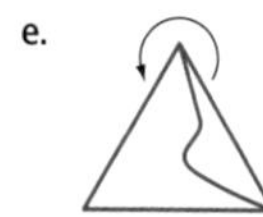

f. 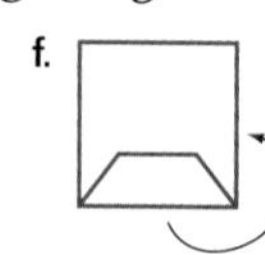

Writing Math

1–2. See students' work.

1. **Design and draw** a pattern for an Escher-like drawing.
2. **Describe** how to use your pattern to create a pattern unit for your tessellation. Then create a tessellation using your pattern.
3. **Name** another regular polygon other than an equilateral triangle or square that will tessellate a plane. Explain your reasoning.

Determine whether each of the following figures will tessellate a plane. Explain your reasoning.

4. 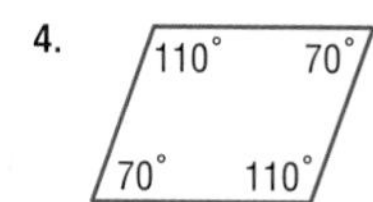

5. 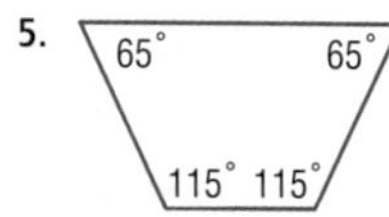

6. 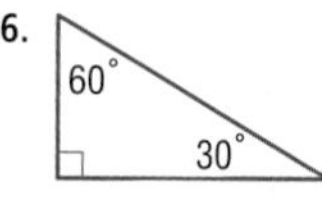

3. a regular hexagon; each angle measures 60°, so 6 regular hexagons should tessellate a plane since $6 \times 60° = 360°$.

4. yes; $110° + 70° + 110° + 70° = 360°$

5. yes; $65° + 115° + 65° + 115° = 360°$

6. yes; Sample answer: $90° + 90° + 90° + 90° = 360°$

Activity 2

- In Step 4 of **Activity 2**, students should fit the shapes together to form hexagons and fit the hexagons together to form a larger pattern.

ASSESS

Observe as students solve the **Your Turn** exercises. They should:

- carefully cut out and translate or rotate the shapes,
- trace the shapes together without overlaps or gaps, and
- recognize how translations and rotations are used to create tessellations.

Discuss the **Writing Math** exercises. Students may need to experiment with different shapes to answer Exercise 3.

d. 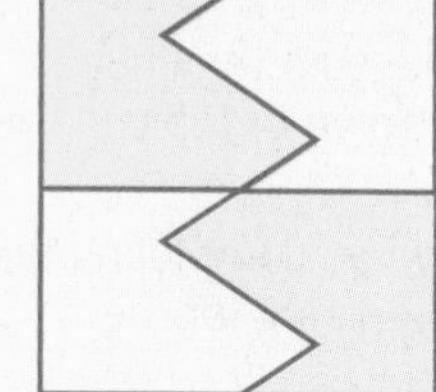

e. 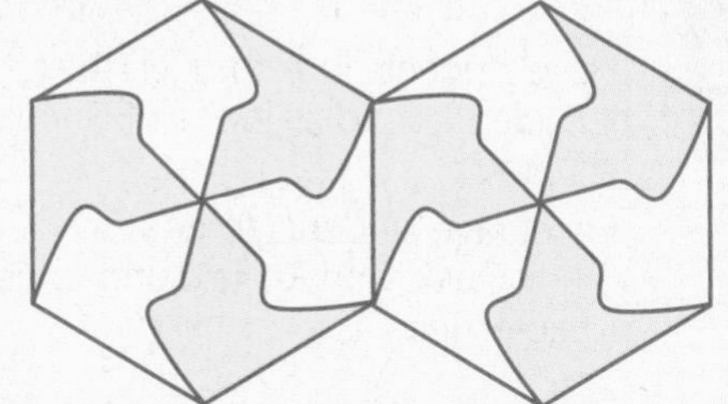

f. 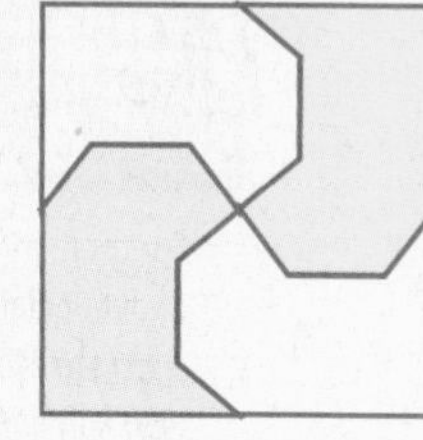

Vocabulary Assessment

- This alphabetical list of vocabulary terms in Chapter 6 includes a page reference where each term was introduced.
- A vocabulary review/test for Chapter 6 is available on p. 366 of the *Chapter 6 Resource Masters.*

Vocabulary PuzzleMaker

ELL The online Vocabulary PuzzleMaker improves students' mathematics vocabulary using four puzzle formats — crossword, scramble, word search using a word list, and word search using clues. Students can work on a computer screen or from a printed handout.

MindJogger Videoquizzes

ELL MindJogger Videoquizzes provide an alternative review of concepts presented in this chapter. Students work in teams in a game show format to gain points for correct answers. The questions are presented in three rounds.

Round 1 Concepts (5 questions)
Round 2 Skills (4 questions)
Round 3 Problem Solving (4 questions)

ExamView® Pro

Use the networkable ExamView® Pro Testmaker CD-ROM to:

- Create **multiple versions** of tests.
- Create **modified** tests for **inclusion** students with one mouse click.
- **Edit** existing questions and **add** your own questions.
- Build tests aligned with state standards using built-in **state curriculum correlations.**
- Change **English** tests to **Spanish** with one mouse click and vice versa.

Study Guide and Review

Vocabulary and Concept Check

acute angle (p. 256)
acute triangle (p. 263)
adjacent angles (p. 256)
alternate exterior angles (p. 258)
alternate interior angles (p. 258)
angle of rotation (p. 287)
center of rotation (p. 300)
complementary angles (p. 256)
congruent polygons (p. 279)
corresponding angles (p. 258)
equilateral triangle (p. 263)
isosceles triangle (p. 263)
line of reflection (p. 290)
line of symmetry (p. 286)
line symmetry (p. 286)
obtuse angle (p. 256)
obtuse triangle (p. 263)
parallel lines (p. 257)
parallelogram (p. 273)
perpendicular lines (p. 257)
quadrilateral (p. 272)
rectangle (p. 273)
reflection (p. 290)
rhombus (p. 273)
right angle (p. 256)
right triangle (p. 263)
rotation (p. 300)
rotational symmetry (p. 287)
scalene triangle (p. 263)
square (p. 273)
straight angle (p. 256)
supplementary angles (p. 256)
transformation (p. 290)
translation (p. 296)
transversal (p. 258)
trapezoid (p. 273)
triangle (p. 262)
vertical angles (p. 256)

State whether each sentence is *true* or *false*. If *false*, replace the underlined word to make a true sentence.

1. A(n) <u>acute</u> angle has a measure greater than 90° and less than 180°. **false; obtuse**
2. The sum of the measures of <u>supplementary</u> angles is 180°. **true**
3. <u>Parallel</u> lines intersect at a right angle. **false; perpendicular**
4. In a(n) <u>scalene</u> triangle, all three sides are congruent. **false; equilateral**
5. A(n) <u>rhombus</u> is a parallelogram with four congruent sides. **true**
6. An isosceles trapezoid has <u>rotational</u> symmetry. **false; line**
7. The orientations of a figure and its reflected image are <u>different</u>. **true**

Lesson-by-Lesson Exercises and Examples

6-1 Line and Angle Relationships (pp. 256–260)

Find the value of x in each figure.

8. (figure: 125°, x°) **125** 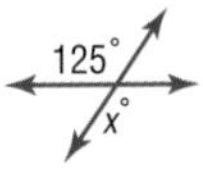
9. (figure: 43°, x°) **137**

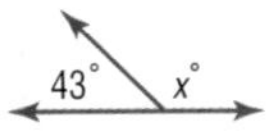

For Exercises 10 and 11, use the figure at the right.

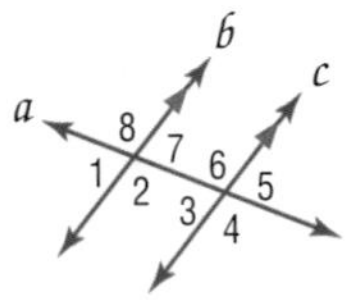

10. Find $m\angle 8$ if $m\angle 4 = 118°$. **118°**
11. Find $m\angle 6$ if $m\angle 2 = 135°$. **135°**

Example 1
If $m\angle 1 = 105°$, find $m\angle 3$, $m\angle 5$, and $m\angle 8$.

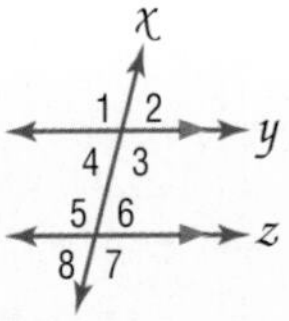

Since $\angle 1$ and $\angle 3$ are vertical angles $\angle 1 \cong \angle 3$. So, $m\angle 3 = 105°$.

Since $\angle 1$ and $\angle 5$ are corresponding angles, $\angle 1 \cong \angle 5$. Therefore, $m\angle 5 = 105°$.

Since $\angle 5$ and $\angle 8$ are supplementary, $m\angle 8 = 180° - 105°$ or $75°$.

msmath3.net/vocabulary_review

For more information about Foldables, see *Teaching Mathematics with Foldables.*

Have students look through the chapter to make sure they have included examples in their Foldables for each lesson or topic in the chapter.

Encourage students to refer to their Foldables while completing the Study Guide and Review and to use them in preparing for the Chapter Test.

6-2 Triangles and Angles (pp. 262–265)

Find the value of x in each triangle.

12. 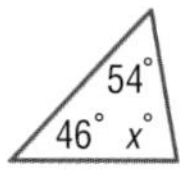 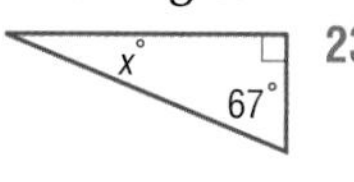 **80**

13. 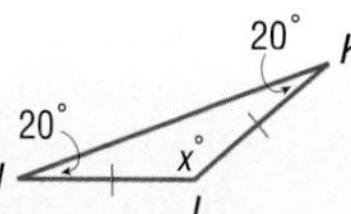 **23**

14. Classify the triangle in Exercise 13 by its angles and by its sides.

Example 2 **Find the value of x in $\triangle JKL$.**

$x + 20 + 20 = 180$

$x = 180 - (20 + 20)$ or 140

14. right, scalene

6-3 Special Right Triangles (pp. 267–270)

Find each missing length. Round to the nearest tenth if necessary.

15. 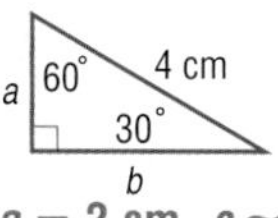
$a = 2$ cm, $c \approx 3.5$ cm

16. 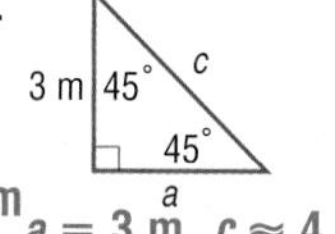
$a = 3$ m, $c \approx 4.2$ m

17. 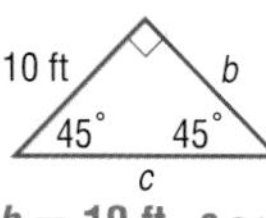
$b = 10$ ft, $c \approx 14.1$ ft

18. 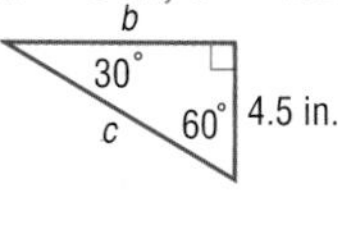

Example 3 **Find each missing length.**

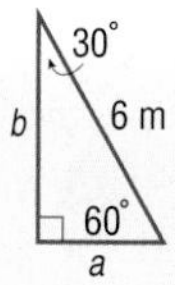

$a = \frac{1}{2}(6)$ or 3 m

To find b, use the Pythagorean Theorem.

$6^2 = 3^2 + b^2$ $c^2 = a^2 + b^2$

$36 = 9 + b^2$ Evaluate 6^2 and 3^2.

$27 = b^2$ Subtract 9 from each side.

$5.2 \approx b$ Take the square root of each side.

18. $c = 9$ in., $b \approx 7.8$ in.

6-4 Classifying Quadrilaterals (pp. 272–275)

19. In quadrilateral $JKLM$, $m\angle J = 123°$, $m\angle K = 90°$, and $m\angle M = 45°$. Find $m\angle L$. **102°**

20. Classify the quadrilateral shown using the name that *best* describes it. **trapezoid**

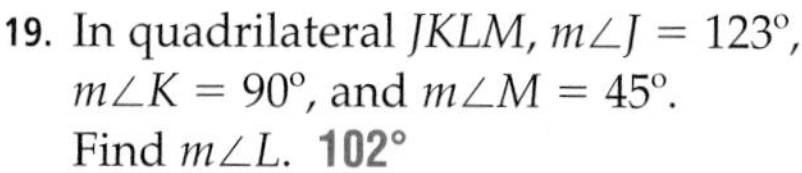

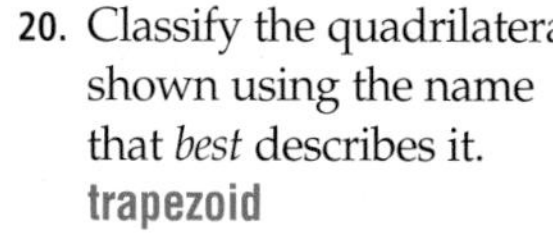

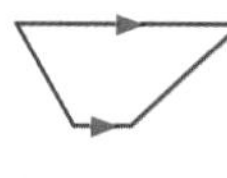

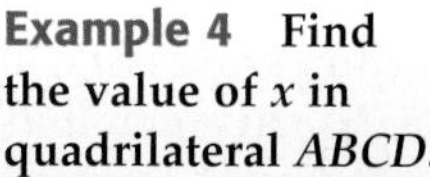

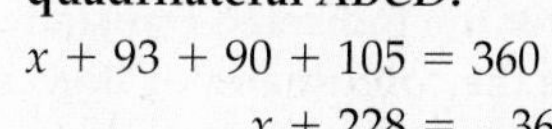

Example 4 **Find the value of x in quadrilateral $ABCD$.**

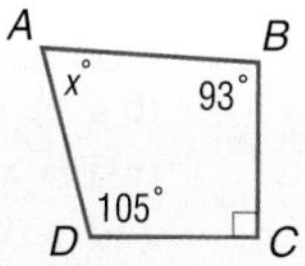

$x + 93 + 90 + 105 = 360$

$x + 228 = 360$

$-228 = -228$

$x = 72$

6-5 Congruent Polygons (pp. 279–282)

In the figure, $FGHJ \cong YXWZ$. Find each measure.

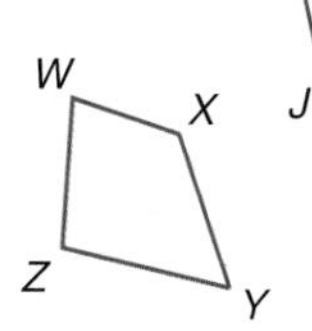

21. $m\angle X$ **124°**
22. WZ **10 cm**
23. YX **11 cm**
24. $m\angle Z$ **103°**

Example 5 **In the figure, $\triangle ABC \cong \triangle RPQ$. Find PQ.**

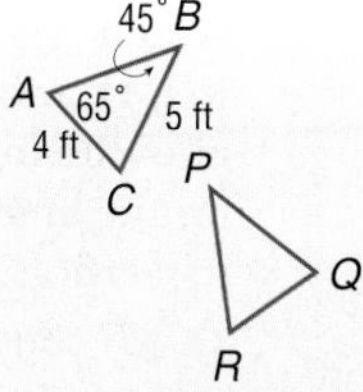

$\overline{PQ}$ corresponds to $\overline{BC}$. Since BC = 5 feet, PQ = 5 feet.

Study Guide and Review

Answers (p. 308)

30. $Q'(-2, 5)$, $R'(-4, 5)$, $S'(-3, 1)$, $T'(-1, 1)$

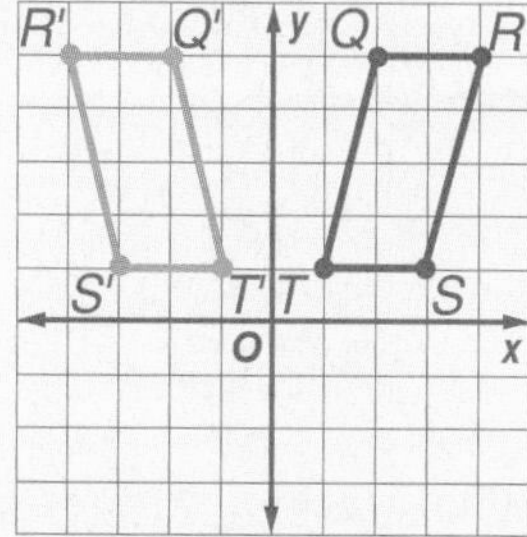

31. $A'(2, -4)$, $B'(3, -1)$, $C'(5, -3)$

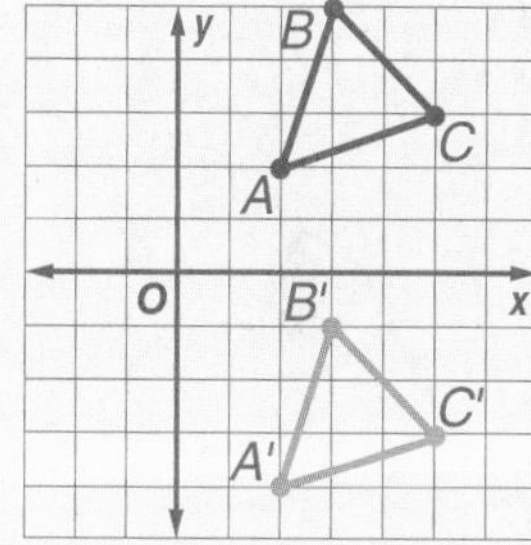

32. $A'(0, -2)$, $B'(1, 1)$, $C'(3, -1)$

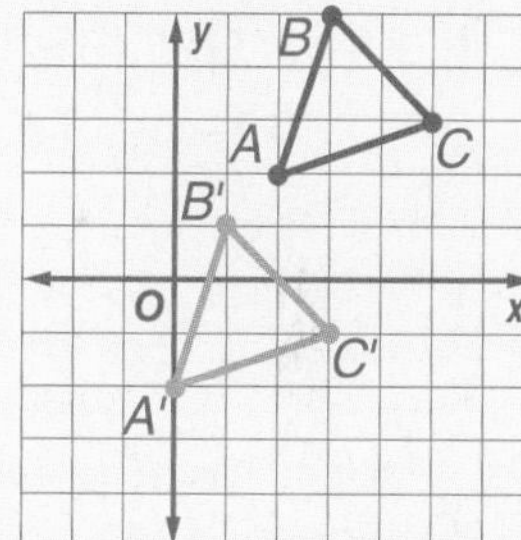

33. $J'(-3, -1)$, $K'(-1, 1)$, $L'(-4, 3)$

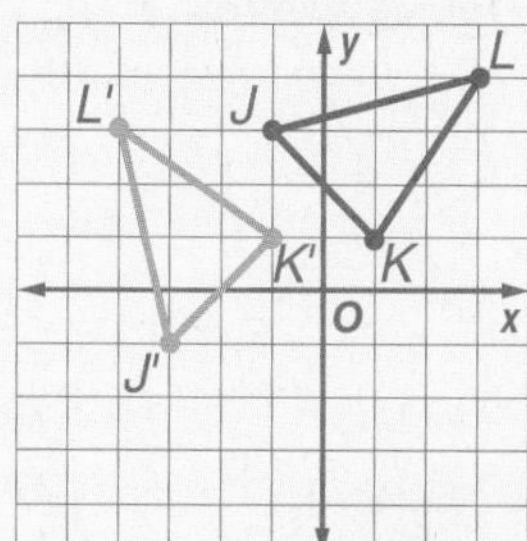

34. $J'(1, -3)$, $K'(-1, -1)$, $L'(-3, -4)$

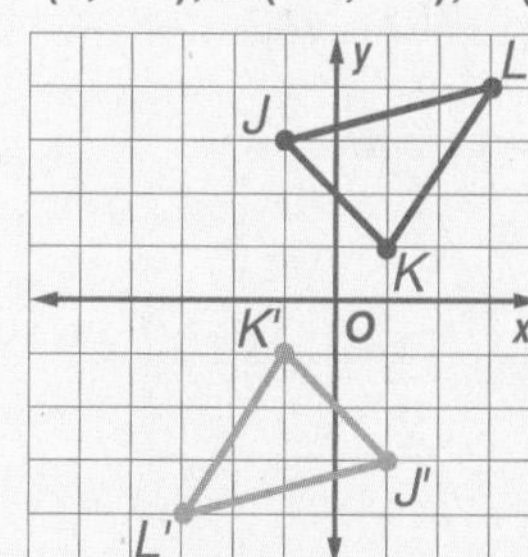

25. 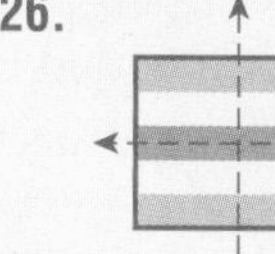

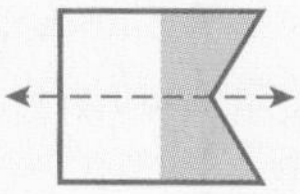

26. 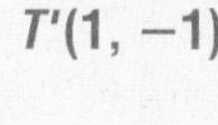

27. none

29. $Q'(2, -5)$, $R'(4, -5)$, $S'(3, -1)$, $T'(1, -1)$

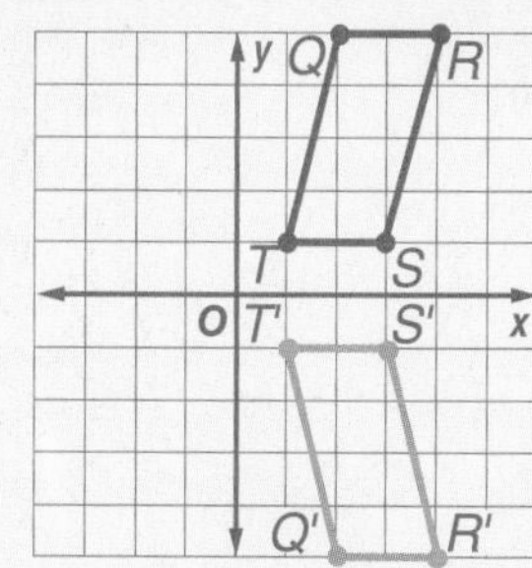

Answers (Practice Test)

1. Sample answer:

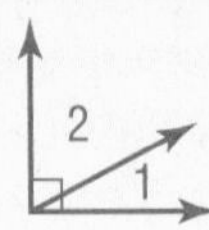

2. 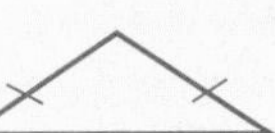

5. Sample answer: ∠2, ∠6

17. J′(2, −3), K′(−1, −4), L′(−3, 5)

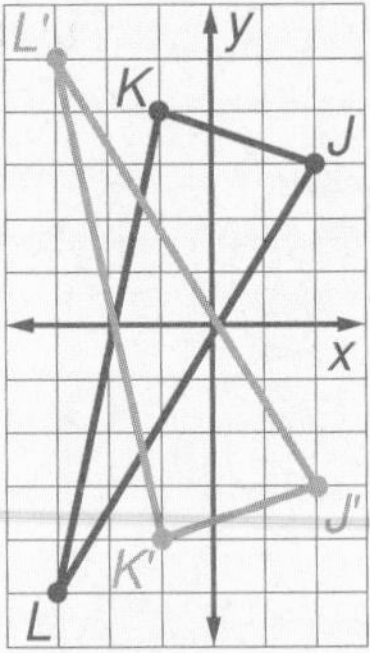

18. J′(0, 8), K′(−3, 9), L′(−5, 0)

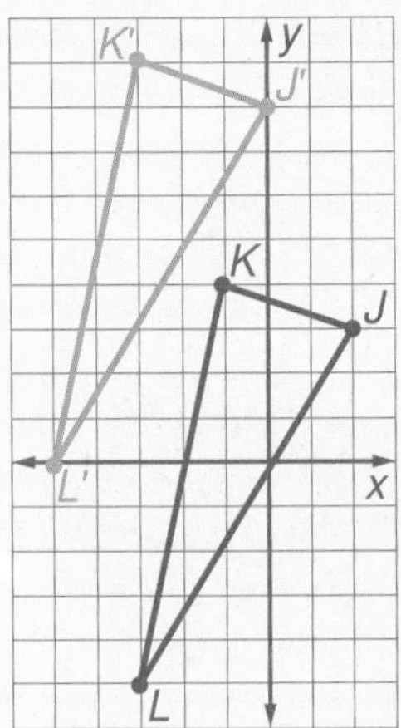

19. J′(−2, −3), K′(1, −4), L′(3, 5)

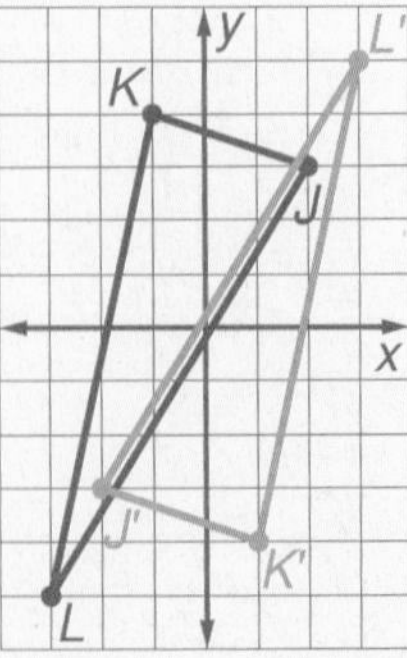

Mixed Problem Solving
For mixed problem-solving practice, see page 653.

6-6 Symmetry (pp. 286–289)

BOATING Determine whether each signal flag has line symmetry. If it does, trace the figure and draw all lines of symmetry. If not, write *none*. **25–27. See margin.**

25.  
26. 
27. 

28. Which of the figures above has rotational symmetry? Name the angle(s) of rotation.

28. The figures in Exercises 26 and 27; 180°

Example 6 Determine whether the logo at the right has rotational symmetry. If it does, name its angles of rotation.

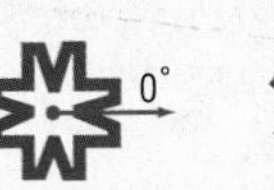

The logo has rotational symmetry. Its angles of rotation are 90°, 180°, and 270°.

6-7 Reflections (pp. 290–294)

Graph parallelogram *QRST* with vertices *Q*(2, 5), *R*(4, 5), *S*(3, 1), and *T*(1, 1). Then graph its image after a reflection over the given axis, and write the coordinates of its vertices. **29–30. See margin.**

29. *x*-axis
30. *y*-axis

Example 7 Graph △*FGH* with vertices *F*(1, −1), *G*(3, 1), and *H*(2, −3) and its image after a reflection over the *y*-axis.

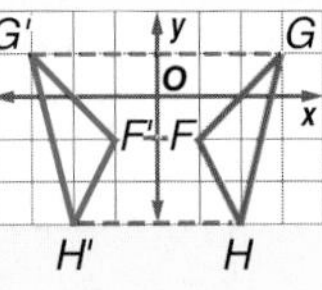

6-8 Translations (pp. 296–299)

Graph △*ABC* with vertices *A*(2, 2), *B*(3, 5), and *C*(5, 3). Then graph its image after the indicated translation, and write the coordinates of its vertices.

31. 6 units down
32. 2 units left and 4 units down

31–32. See margin.

Example 8 Graph △*XYZ* with vertices *X*(−3, −1), *Y*(−1, 0), and *Z*(−2, −3) and its image after a translation 4 units right and 1 unit up.

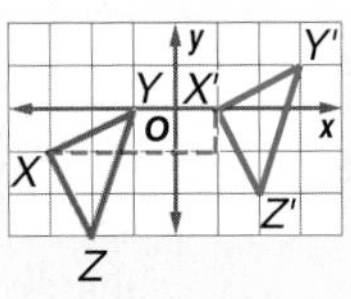

6-9 Rotations (pp. 300–303)

Graph △*JKL* with vertices *J*(−1, 3), *K*(1, 1), and *L*(3, 4). Then graph its image after the indicated rotation about the origin, and write the coordinates of its vertices.

33. 90° counterclockwise
34. 180° counterclockwise

33–34. See margin.

Example 9 Graph △*PQR* with vertices *P*(1, 3), *Q*(2, 1), and *R*(4, 2) and its image after a rotation of 90° counterclockwise about the origin.

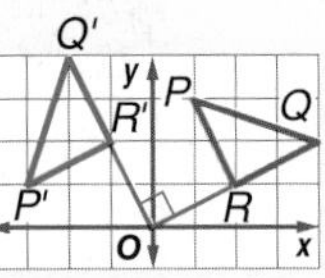

Practice Test

Vocabulary and Concepts

1. **Draw** a pair of complementary angles. Label the angles $\angle 1$ and $\angle 2$. **1–2. See margin.**
2. **OPEN ENDED** Draw an obtuse isosceles triangle.

Skills and Applications

For Exercises 3–5, use the figure at the right. **3. 120°**

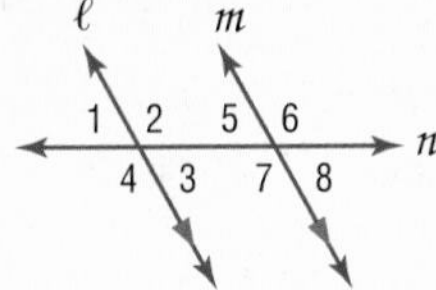

3. Find $m\angle 6$ if $m\angle 5 = 60°$.
4. Find $m\angle 8$ if $m\angle 1 = 82°$. **82°**
5. Name a pair of corresponding angles. **See margin.**

Find each missing measure. Round to the nearest tenth.

6. 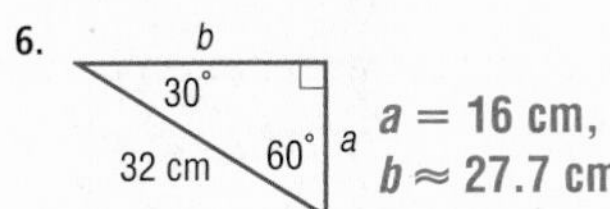

$a = 16$ cm, $b \approx 27.7$ cm

7. 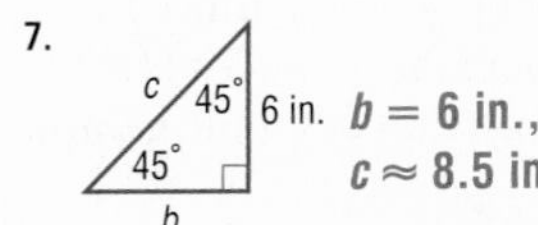

$b = 6$ in., $c \approx 8.5$ in.

DESIGN **Identify each quadrilateral in the stained glass window using the name that best describes it.**

8. A **rhombus**
9. B **square**
10. C **trapezoid**

In the figure at the right, $\triangle MNP \cong \triangle ZYX$. Find each measure.

11. ZY **6.3 m**
12. $\angle Z$ **117°**

MUSIC **Determine whether each figure has line symmetry. If it does, trace the figure and draw all lines of symmetry. If not, write *none*.**

13. 
14. 
15. 

16. Which of the figures in Exercises 13–15 has rotational symmetry? **The figure in Exercise 14, 45°, 90°, 135°, 180°, 225°, 270°, 315°**

Graph $\triangle JKL$ with vertices $J(2, 3)$, $K(-1, 4)$, and $L(-3, -5)$. Then graph its image, and write the coordinates of its vertices after each transformation.

17. reflection over the x-axis
18. translation by $(-2, 5)$
19. rotation 180°

17–19. See margin.

Standardized Test Practice

20. **MULTIPLE CHOICE** $\overline{WY}$ is a diagonal of rectangle $WXYZ$. Which angle is congruent to $\angle WYZ$? **D**

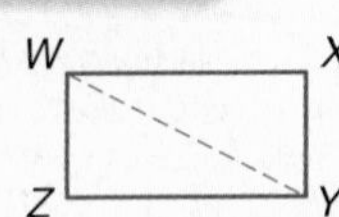

 $\angle WXY$  $\angle WYX$  $\angle ZWY$ Ⓓ $\angle XWY$

msmath3.net/chapter_test

Chapter 6 Practice Test

Assessment Options

Vocabulary Test A vocabulary review/test for Chapter 6 can be found on p. 366 of the *Chapter 6 Resource Masters.*

Chapter Tests There are six Chapter 6 Tests and an Extended Response Assessment task available in the *Chapter 6 Resource Masters*.

Chapter 6 Tests			
Form	**Type**	**Level**	**Pages**
1	MC	basic	353–354
2A	MC	average	355–356
2B	MC	average	357–358
2C	FR	average	359–360
2D	FR	average	361–362
3	FR	advanced	363–364

MC = multiple-choice questions
FR = free-response questions

Extended Response Assessment

Extended Response tasks for Chapter 6 can be found on p. 365 of the *Chapter 6 Resource Masters*. A sample scoring rubric for these tasks appears on p. A31.

First Semester Test

A first semester test can be found on pp. 373–376 of the *Chapter 6 Resource Masters.*

Portfolio Suggestion

Introduction Triangles are a very strong shape structurally. Force applied to the uppermost vertex is split by the two legs. Neither leg has to withstand as much force as a single vertical support would.

Ask Students to find examples of triangles used in architecture near their homes. Have them also look in books and on the computer for some unique architectural designs. Have them include sketches in their portfolios.

Standardized Test Practice

These two pages contain practice questions in the various formats that can be found on the most frequently given standardized tests.

A student recording sheet for these two pages can be found on p. A1 of the *Chapter 6 Resource Masters*.

Standardized Test Practice Student Recording Sheet, p. A1

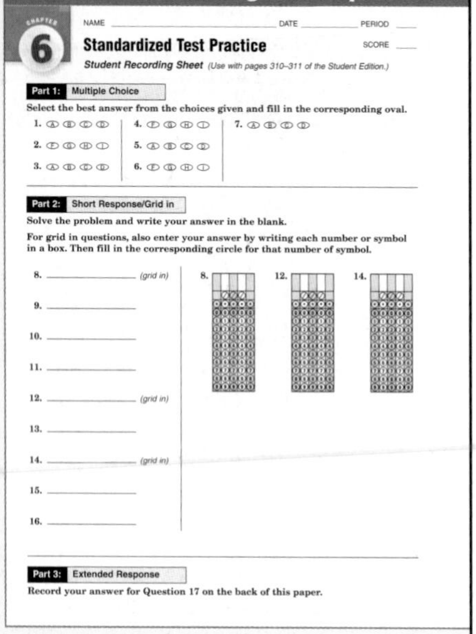

NAME ______ DATE ______ PERIOD ______

Standardized Test Practice SCORE ______

Student Recording Sheet (Use with pages 310–311 of the Student Edition.)

Part 1: Multiple Choice

Select the best answer from the choices given and fill in the corresponding oval.

1. Ⓐ Ⓑ Ⓒ Ⓓ 4. Ⓕ Ⓖ Ⓗ Ⓘ 7. Ⓐ Ⓑ Ⓒ Ⓓ
2. Ⓕ Ⓖ Ⓗ Ⓘ 5. Ⓐ Ⓑ Ⓒ Ⓓ
3. Ⓐ Ⓑ Ⓒ Ⓓ 6. Ⓕ Ⓖ Ⓗ Ⓘ

Part 2: Short Response/Grid In

Solve the problem and write your answer in the blank.

For grid in questions, also enter your answer by writing each number or symbol in a box. Then fill in the corresponding circle for that number of symbol.

8. ______ (grid in)
9. ______
10. ______
11. ______
12. ______ (grid in)
13. ______
14. ______ (grid in)
15. ______
16. ______

Part 3: Extended Response

Record your answer for Question 17 on the back of this paper.

Additional Practice

See pp. 371–372 in the *Chapter 6 Resource Masters* for additional standardized test practice.

Standardized Test Practice

PART 1 Multiple Choice

Record your answers on the answer sheet provided by your teacher or on a sheet of paper.

1. One week Alexandria ran 500 meters, 600 meters, 800 meters, and 1,100 meters. How many kilometers did she run that week? (Prerequisite Skill, pp. 606–607) **C**

   Ⓐ 1 Ⓑ 2 Ⓒ 3 Ⓓ 4

2. The graph shows the winning times in seconds of the women's 4 × 100-meter freestyle relay for several Olympic games.

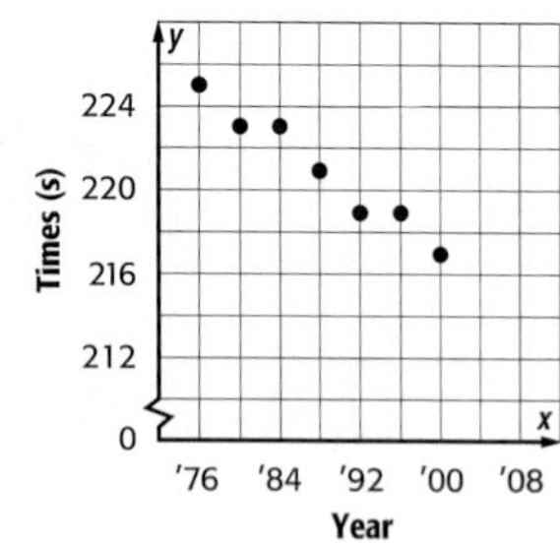

   What is a reasonable prediction for the winning time in 2008? (Lesson 1-1) **G**

   Ⓕ 212 s Ⓖ 215 s Ⓗ 218 s Ⓘ 221 s

3. Which expression is equivalent to xy^2z^{-1}? (Lesson 2-2) **D**

   Ⓐ $\frac{1}{x \cdot y \cdot y \cdot z}$ Ⓑ $x + y + y - z$

   Ⓒ $x \cdot y \cdot y - z$ Ⓓ $\frac{x \cdot y \cdot y}{z}$

TEST-TAKING TIP

Question 3 Answer every question when there is no penalty for guessing. If you must guess, eliminate answers you know are incorrect. For Question 3, eliminate Choice B since $xy^2 = x \cdot y \cdot y$.

4. Aleta went to the grocery store and paid \$19.71 for her purchases. A portion of her receipt is shown below.

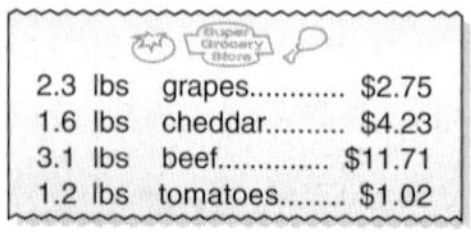

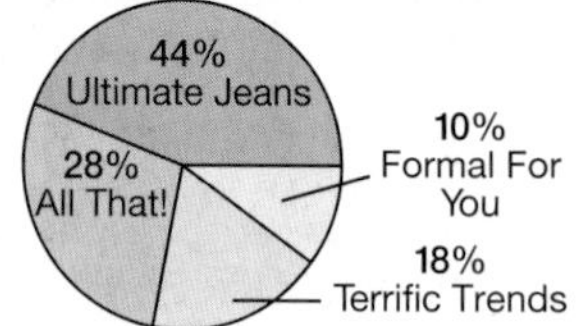

2.3 lbs	grapes............	\$2.75
1.6 lbs	cheddar..........	\$4.23
3.1 lbs	beef..............	\$11.71
1.2 lbs	tomatoes........	\$1.02

   About how much did the beef cost per pound? (Lesson 4-1) **H**

   Ⓕ \$2.60 Ⓖ \$3.34 Ⓗ \$3.80 Ⓘ \$4.25

5. Which of the stores represented in the circle graph is preferred by $\frac{7}{25}$ of the students? (Lesson 5-1) **B**

Preferred Clothing Stores

44% Ultimate Jeans

28% All That!

10% Formal For You

18% Terrific Trends

   Ⓐ Ultimate Jeans Ⓑ All That!

   Ⓒ Terrific Trends Ⓓ Formal For You

6. Which of the following could *not* be the measure of ∠*M*? (Lesson 6-4) **I**

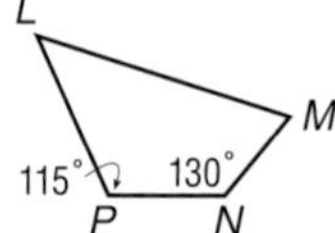

   Ⓕ 35° Ⓖ 50° Ⓗ 45° Ⓘ 116°

7. Which of the following figures is *not* a rotation of the figure at the right? (Lesson 6-9) **A**

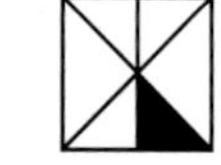

   Ⓐ 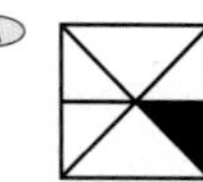 Ⓑ 

   Ⓒ Ⓓ 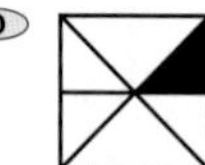

ExamView® Pro

Special banks of standardized test questions similar to those on the TIMSS and NAEP grade 8 tests can be found on this CD-ROM.

Preparing for Standardized Tests
For test-taking strategies and more practice, see pages 660–677.

PART 2 Short Response/Grid In

Record your answers on the answer sheet provided by your teacher or on a sheet of paper.

8. Ms. Neville has 26 students in her homeroom. All of her students take at least one foreign language. Thirteen students take Spanish, 11 students take French, and 5 students take Japanese. No student takes all three languages. How many students take more than one language? (Lesson 1-1) **3**

9. Write $\sqrt{8}$, $\sqrt{6}$, 3.2, and $\frac{1}{3}$ in order from least to greatest. (Lesson 3-3) **$\frac{1}{3}$, $\sqrt{6}$, $\sqrt{8}$, 3.2**

10. An area of 2,500 square feet of grass produces enough oxygen for a family of 4. What is the area of grass needed to supply a family of 5 with oxygen? (Lesson 4-4) **3,125 ft^2**

11. You buy a sweater on sale for $29.96. You paid 25% less than the original price. What was the original price of the sweater? (Lesson 5-7) **$39.95**

12. If $a \parallel b$, find the value of x. (Lesson 6-1) **45**

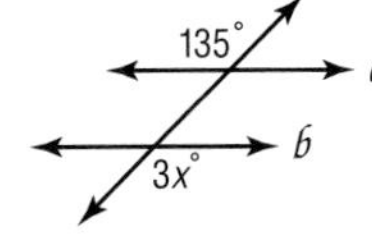

13. Name a quadrilateral with one pair of parallel sides and one pair of sides that are not parallel. (Lesson 6-4) **trapezoid**

14. How many lines of symmetry does the figure at the right have? (Lesson 6-6) **6**

15. If $\triangle JKL \cong \triangle MNP$, name the segment in $\triangle MNP$ that is congruent to $\overline{LJ}$. (Lesson 6-5) **$\overline{PM}$**

16. If $\triangle ABC$ is reflected about the y-axis, what are the coordinates of point A'? (Lesson 6-7) **(−4, 5)**

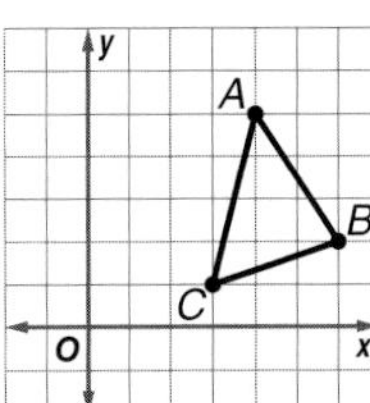

PART 3 Extended Response

Record your answers on a sheet of paper. Show your work.

17. The graph below shows Arm 1 of the design for a company logo. (Lesson 6-9)

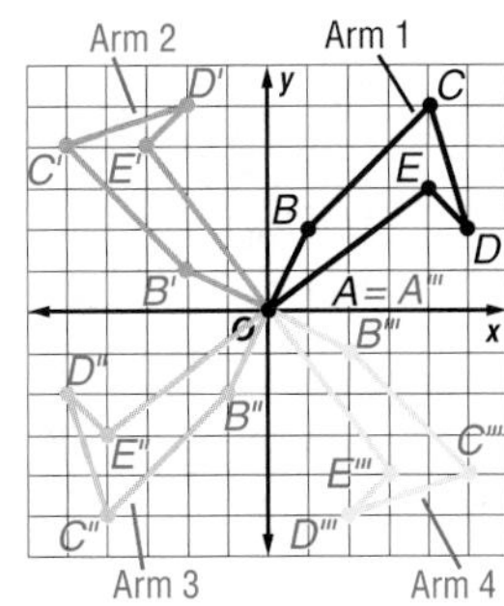

a. To create Arm 2 of the logo, graph the image of figure $ABCDE$ after a rotation 90° counterclockwise about the origin. Write the coordinates of the vertices of Arm 2. **a–c. See graph above.**

b. To create Arm 3 of the logo, graph the coordinates of figure $ABCDE$ after a rotation 180° about the origin. Write the coordinates of the vertices of Arm 3.

c. To create Arm 4 of the logo, graph the coordinates of Arm 2 after a rotation 180° about the origin. Write the coordinates of the vertices of Arm 4.

d. Does the completed logo have rotational symmetry? If so, name its angle(s) of rotation. **yes; 90°, 180°, 270°**

Math Online msmath3.net/standardized_test

Standardized Test Practice

Rubrics The following rubrics are sample scoring devices for short response and extended response questions.

Short Response

Points	Description
2	The student demonstrates a **thorough understanding** of the mathematics of the task. The response may contain minor flaws that do not detract from the demonstration of a thorough understanding.
1	The student has provided a response that is only **partially correct**.
0	The student has provided a **completely incorrect** solution or no response at all.

Extended Response

Points	Description
4	The student demonstrates a **thorough understanding** of the mathematics of the task. The response may contain minor flaws that do not detract from the demonstration of a thorough understanding.
3	The student demonstrates an **understanding** of the mathematics of the task. The response is essentially correct and demonstrates an essential but less than thorough understanding of the mathematics.
2	The student demonstrates only a **partial understanding** of the mathematics of the task. Although the student may have used the correct approach to a solution or may have provided a correct solution, the work lacks an essential understanding of the underlying mathematical concepts.
1	The student demonstrates a **very limited understanding** of the mathematics of the task. The response is incomplete and exhibits many flaws.
0	The student provides a **completely incorrect** solution or no response at all.

A more detailed 4-point rubric is provided on page A2 of the *Chapter 6 Resource Masters*.

Page 271, Lesson 6-3b (Writing Math)

3. Construct the perpendicular bisector of $\overline{CD}$. Label the point of intersection M. Then copy $\overline{CM}$ onto the perpendicular bisector to form $\overline{MN}$ with length CM. Then connect points N and D to form the 45°-45° right triangle NMD.

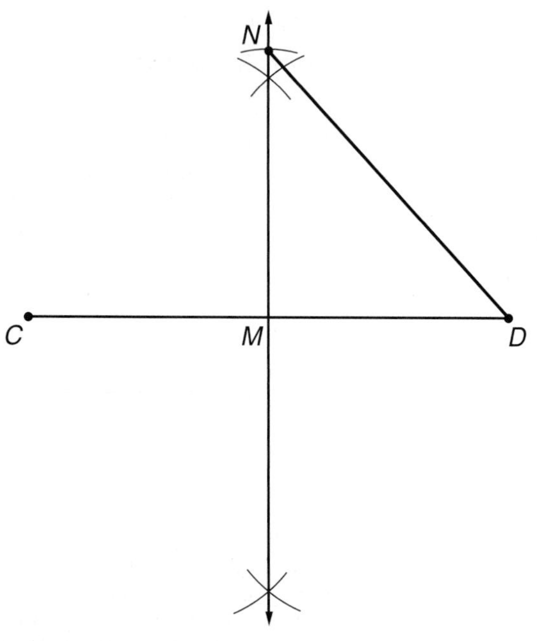

Page 277, Lesson 6-4b

9. Sample answer: Fill the 5-pint container and then use it to fill the 4-pint container, leaving 1 pint in the 5-pint container. Empty the 4-pint container and pour the 1 pint from the 5-pint container into the 4-pint container. Fill the 5-pint container and use it to fill the 4-pint container. This will require pouring 3 pints out of the 5-pint container, leaving exactly 2 pints in the 5-pint container.

Page 279, Lesson 6-5 (When am I ever going to use this?)

2.

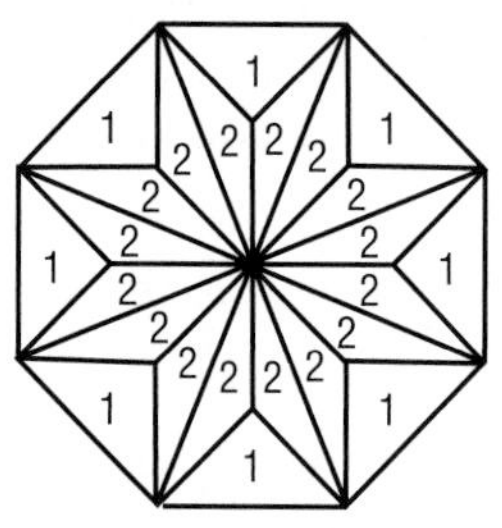

Page 281, Lesson 6-5

9. $\angle H \cong \angle P$, $\angle K \cong \angle Q$, $\angle J \cong \angle M$, $\overline{HK} \cong \overline{PQ}$, $\overline{KJ} \cong \overline{QM}$, $\overline{HJ} \cong \overline{PM}$; $\triangle HJK \cong \triangle PMQ$

12. $\angle V \cong \angle S$, $\angle T \cong \angle Z$, $\angle W \cong \angle Q$, $\angle P \cong \angle Y$ $\overline{VT} \cong \overline{SZ}$, $\overline{TW} \cong \overline{ZQ}$, $\overline{WP} \cong \overline{QY}$, $\overline{VP} \cong \overline{SY}$; quadrilateral $VTWP \cong$ quadrilateral $SZQY$

Pages 288–289, Lesson 6-6

7a.

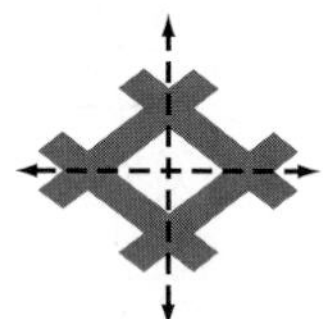

7b. yes; 180°

8a.

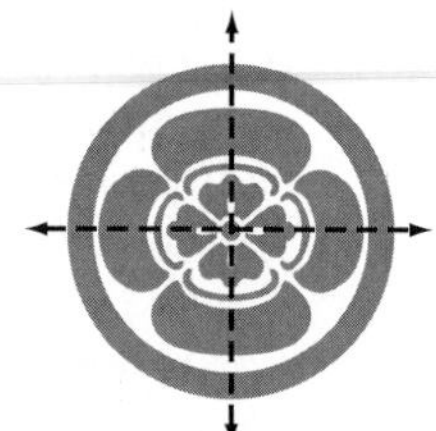

8b. yes; 180°

9a.

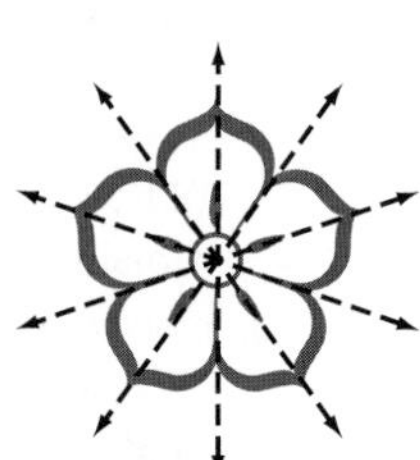

9b. yes; 72°, 144°, 216°, 288°

10a.

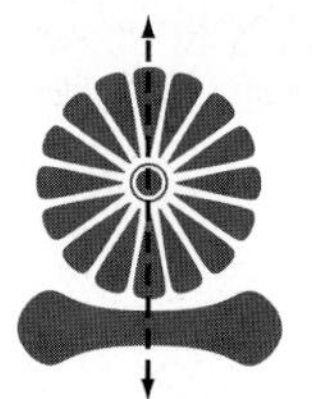

10b. no

11a.

11b. no

12a.

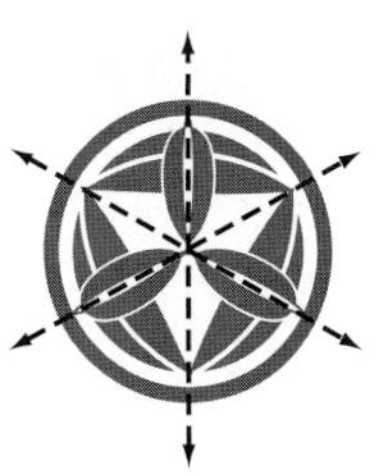

12b. yes; 120°, 240°

13a. none

13b. yes; 120°, 240°

14a. none

14b. no

17a.

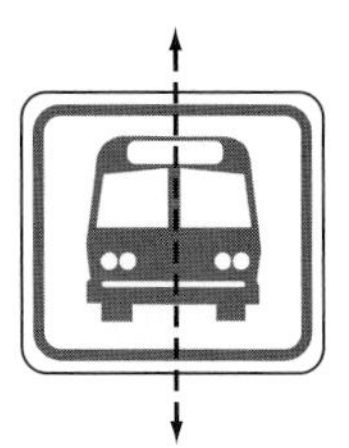

17b.

17c. none

17d. none

19. Sample answers:

line symmetry

line symmetry

line and rotational symmetry

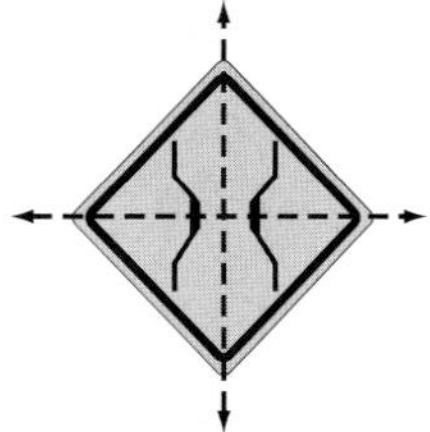

22.

25. The 4 triangles that form the large triangle in the center appear to be congruent. Three of these smaller triangles are divided into 3 smaller triangles. These smaller triangles appear to be congruent.

27.

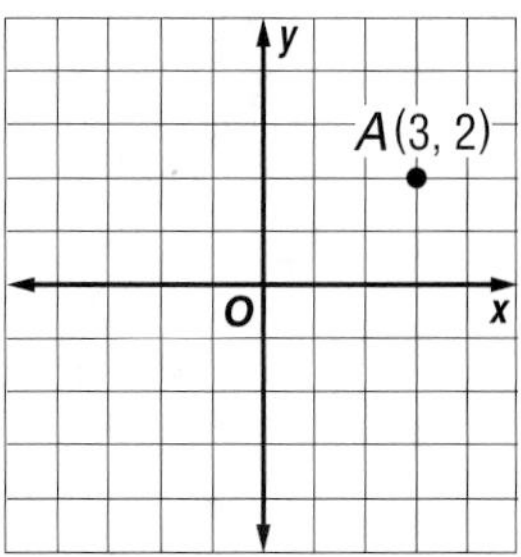

28.

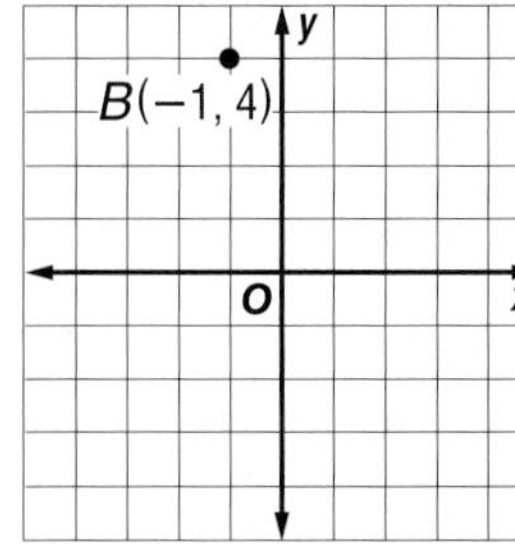

29.

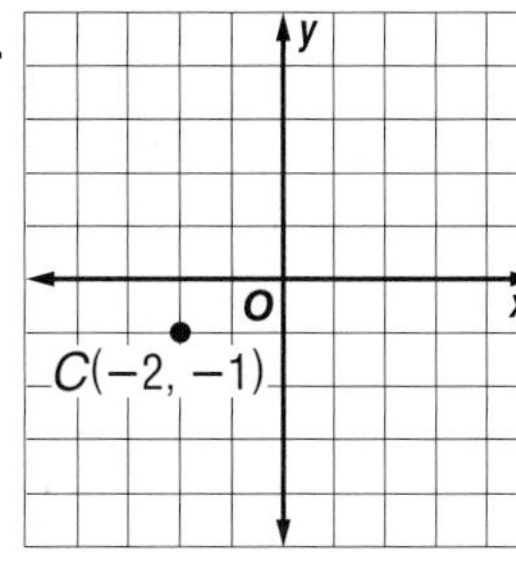

30.

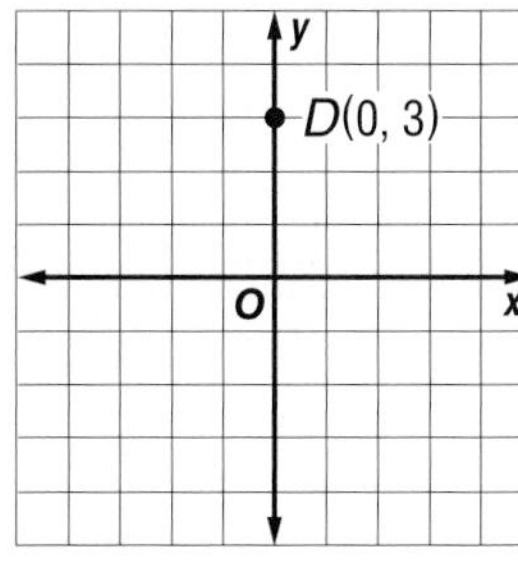

Page 291, Lesson 6-7 (Your Turn)

a.

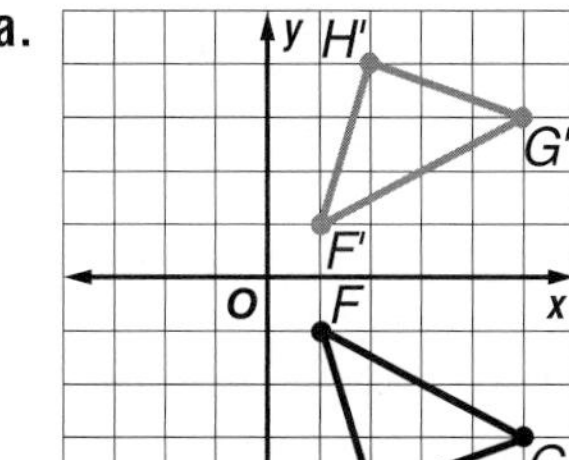

b.

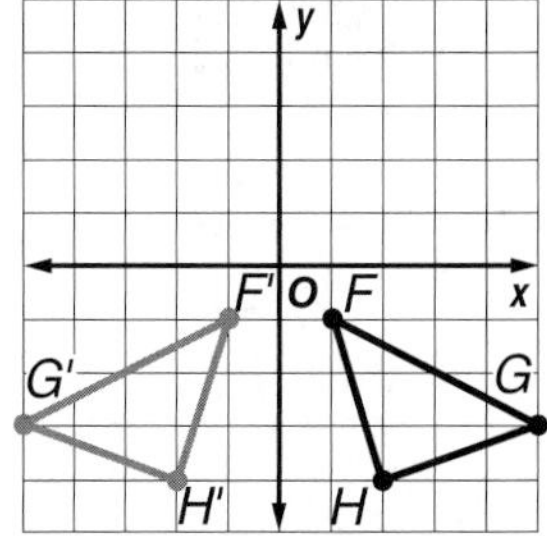

Pages 293–294, Lesson 6-7

13. The image of the tip of the balloon's tail is not directly across from the tip of the original balloon's tail.

14. Each point on the image of the TV is directly across from each corresponding point on the original TV.

15. Each point on the image of the cup is directly across from each corresponding point on the original cup.

16. The image of the handlebars of the bicycle is not directly across from the handlebars of the original bicycle.

17. $A'(-1, 1)$, $B'(-2, 4)$, $C'(-4, 1)$

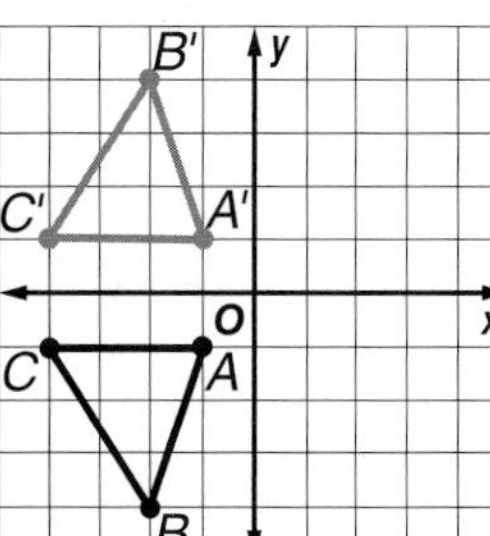

18. $F'(-3, 3)$, $G'(-4, -3)$, $H'(-2, 1)$

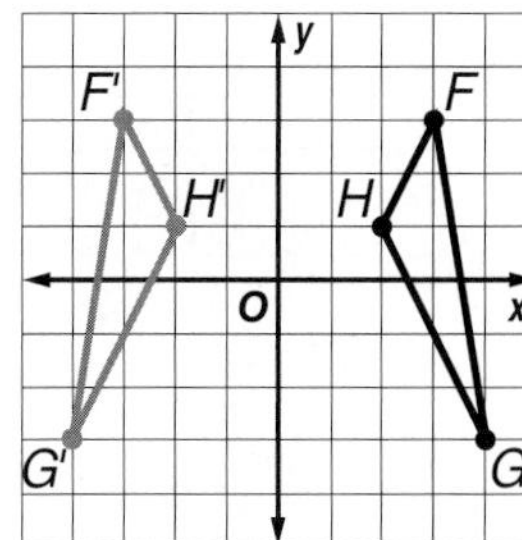

19. $J'(2, 0)$, $K'(1, -2)$, $L'(3, -3)$, $M'(4, -1)$

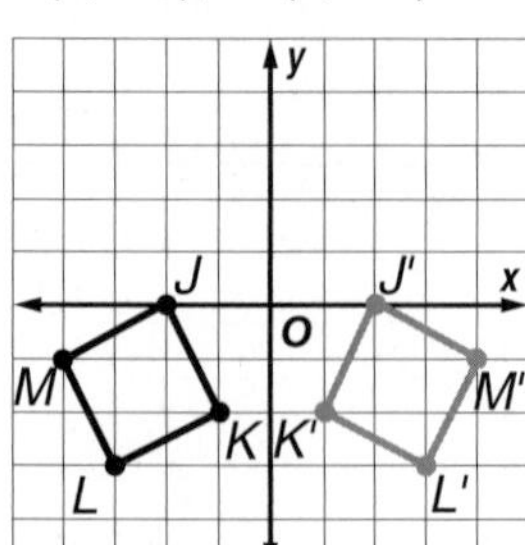

20. $P'(1, -3)$, $Q'(3, -5)$, $R'(5, -2)$, $S'(3, -1)$

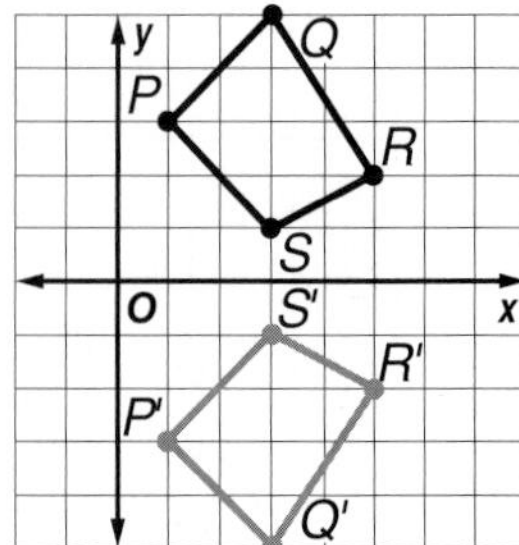

Pages 298–299, Lesson 6-8

8. $A'(-1, 3)$, $B'(1, 2)$, $C'(1, 5)$

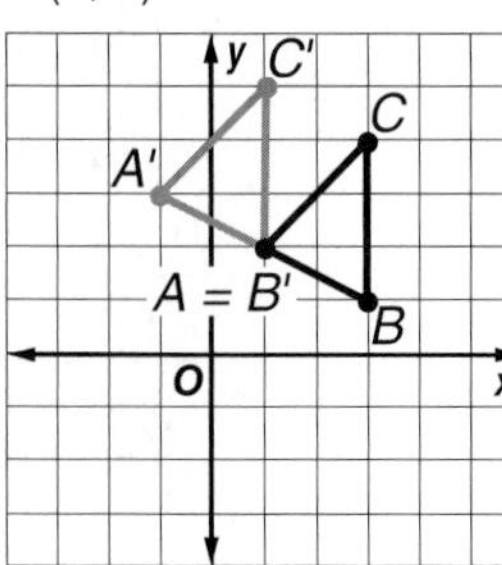

9. $R'(-6, -5)$, $S'(-3, 0)$, $T'(1, -6)$

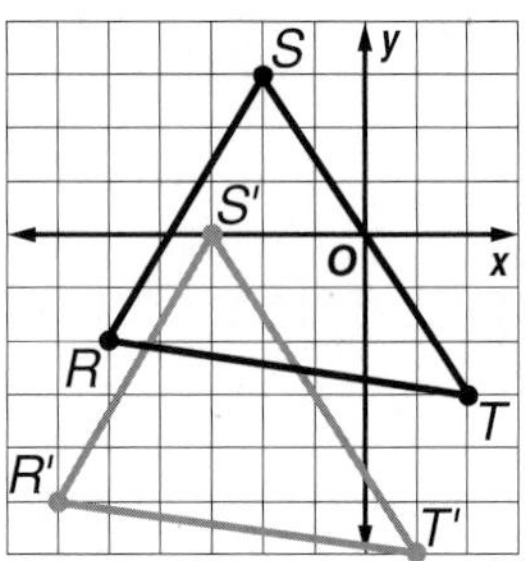

10. $J'(-2, -2)$, $K'(4, 1)$, $L'(5, -1)$, $M'(-1, -4)$

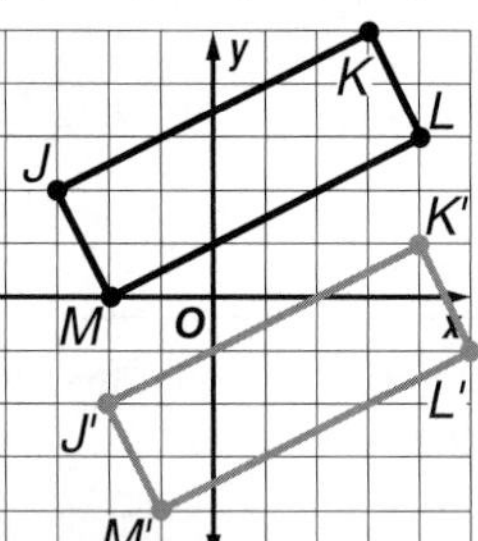

11. $A'(3, 5)$, $B'(1, 2)$, $C'(3, 0)$, $D'(5, 3)$

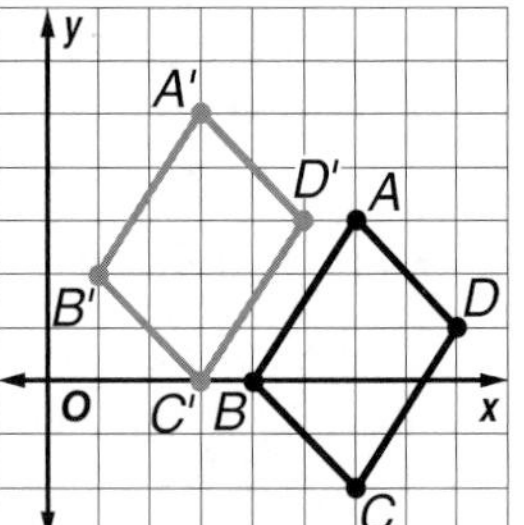

18. $A'(5, -3)$, $B'(2, 1)$, $C'(3, 4)$, $D'(0, 2)$, $E'(0, -3)$

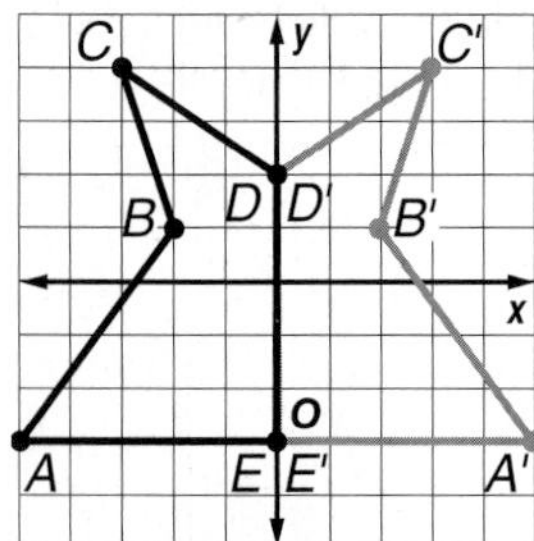

Pages 302–303, Lesson 6-9

9. The figure in green is a rotation of the figure in blue 180° about the origin.

10. The figure in green is a rotation of the figure in blue 90° about the origin.

11. The figure in green is a reflection of the figure in blue over the *y*-axis.

12. The figure in green is a reflection of the figure in blue over the *y*-axis that has then been translated down.

13.

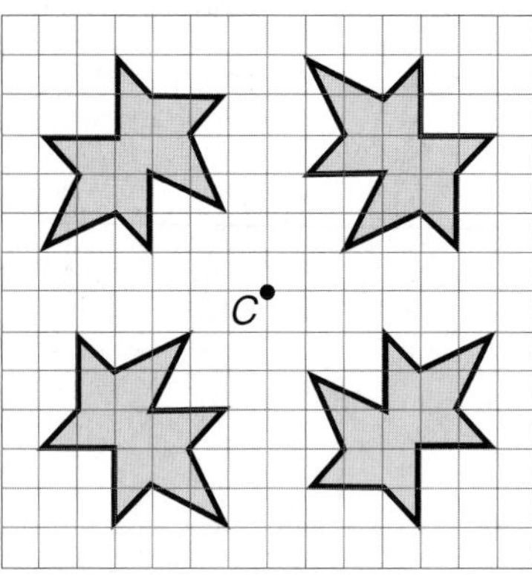

15.

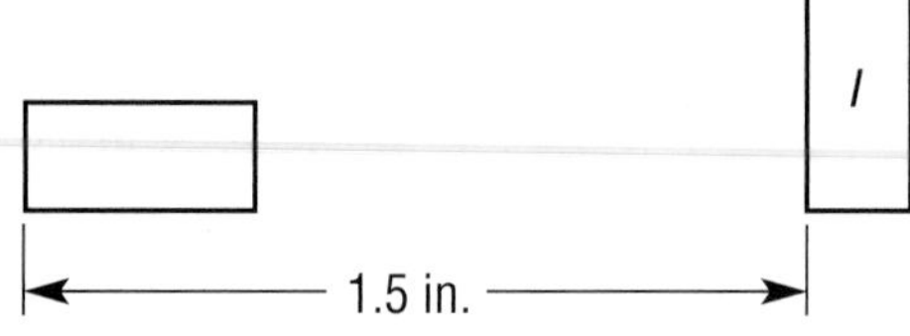

21. The 4 hearts at the bottom of the tie are translations of the first heart at the top of the tie.

22. Sample answers:

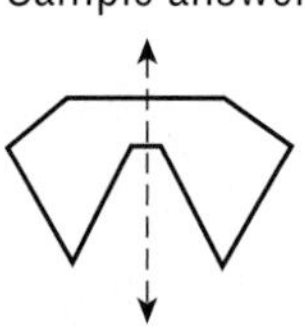

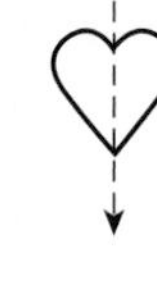

23.

24.

trapezoid

25.

acute equilateral; yes

CHAPTER 7

Chapter Overview

Geometry: Measuring Area and Volume

*An electronic version of this chapter is available on **StudentWorks™**. This backpack solution CD-ROM allows students instant access to the Student Edition, lesson worksheet pages, and web resources.*

	LESSON OBJECTIVES	NCTM Standards	NAEP 2005	State/Local Objectives
7-1	**Area of Parallelograms, Triangles, and Trapezoids** (pp. 314–318) • Find the areas of parallelograms, triangles, and trapezoids.	1–4, 6, 7, 10	G1f, G3b, G3f, A4e, M1h, M2a, N3a	
7-2	**Circumference and Area of Circles** (pp. 319–323) • Find the circumference and area of circles.	1–4, 6, 7, 9, 10	M1g, N3a, M1h, A4e, M2a, N2a	
7-3	**Area of Complex Figures** (pp. 324–329) **7-3a Problem-Solving Strategy**: Solve problems by solving a simpler problem. • Find the area of complex figures.	1–4, 6, 7, 9, 10	A4e, N3a, M1h, M2a, G3c, A1a	
7-4	**Three-Dimensional Figures** (pp. 330–334) **7-4a Hands-On Lab:** Build and draw three-dimensional figures. • Identify and draw three-dimensional figures.	1–4, 6, 7, 9, 10	G1c, G1f, G1e, G4a	
7-5	**Volume of Prisms and Cylinders** (p. 335–339) • Find the volumes of prisms and cylinders.	1–4, 6, 7, 9, 10	A1a, A1b, G1f, M1j, M2a, A4e, N3a, M2b	
7-6	**Volume of Pyramids and Cones** (pp. 342–345) • Find the volumes of pyramids and cones.	1–4, 6, 7, 9, 10	G1f, A4e, M1j, M2a, N3a, N2a	
7-7	**Surface Area of Prisms and Cylinders** (pp. 346–351) **7-7a Hands-On Lab:** Represent three-dimensional objects as nets. • Find the surface areas of prisms and cylinders.	1–4, 6, 7, 9, 10	A4e, M1j, M2a, N3a, G4c, N2a, G1f	
7-8	**Surface Area of Pyramids and Cones** (pp. 352–357) • Find the surface areas of pyramids and cones. **7-8b Spreadsheet Investigation:** Investigate the volume and surface area of similar solids.	1–4, 6, 7, 9, 10	A4e, M1j, M2a, N3a, N2a, M1j, N4c, G3b	
7-9	**Measurement: Precision and Significant Digits** (pp. 358–362) • Analyze measurements.	1–4, 6, 7, 9, 10	M2e, M2d	

Key to NCTM Standards:

1=Number & Operations, 2=Algebra, 3=Geometry, 4=Measurement, 5=Data Analysis & Probability, 6=Problem Solving, 7=Reasoning & Proof, 8=Communication, 9=Connections, 10=Representation

NAEP 2005 Standards: See Teacher Resources at math.glencoe.com

Pacing suggestions for the entire year can be found on page T23.

Chapter Resource Manager

Chapter 7 Resource Masters												
Study Guide and Intervention	Practice (Skills and Word Problems)	Reading to Learn Mathematics	Enrichment	Assessment	Applications*	Parent and Student Study Guide Online Worksheets	5-Minute Check Transparencies	Key Teaching Transparencies	MathPASS: Tutorial Plus (lessons)	Teaching Mathematics with Manipulatives	Noteables™: Interactive Study Notebook	Optional Materials
377	378–379	380	381			7-1	7-1			80, 81–82	7-1	
382	383–384	385	386		CS 31	7-2	7-2		33, 34	83–84	7-2	ruler, marker, objects like can or battery
387	388–389	390	391	437		7-3	7-3		35		7-3	
392	393–394	395	396		CM 27–29	7-4	7-4	25	36	85	7-4	
397	398–399	400	401	437, 439	SM 77–80 CS 32	7-5	7-5		37		7-5	
402	403–404	405	406		CS 33	7-6	7-6	26	38	86	7-6	construction paper, ruler, scissors, tape, rice
407	408–409	410	411	438	RC 33 CS 34	7-7	7-7		39	87	7-7	3 different-sized boxes, centimeter ruler, empty box with tuck in lid, scissors
412	413–414	415	416			7-8	7-8			88–89	7-8	
417	418–419	420	421	423–436, 438, 440–444		7-9	7-9	27	40		7-9	

*** Key to Abbreviations:** *CS = Calculator and Spreadsheet Masters, RC = Real-Life Career Masters, CM = Classroom Math Games (online), SM = Science and Math Lab Manual (online)*

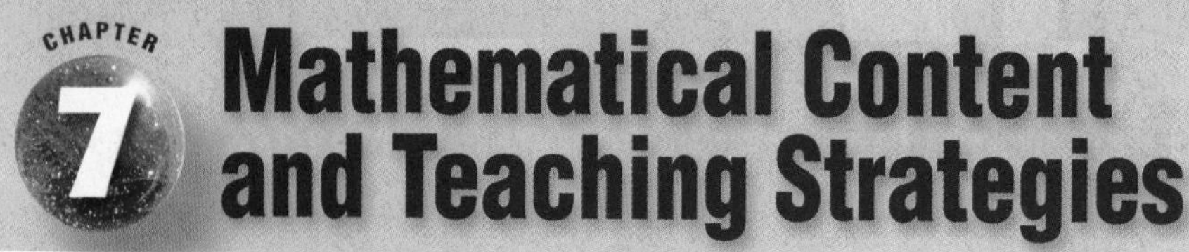

Mathematical Content and Teaching Strategies

Continuity of Instruction

Building on Prior Knowledge

In previous chapters, students performed basic operations with integers, fractions, and decimals as well as estimations. They have learned to evaluate algebraic expressions and solve algebraic equations involving integers, fractions, and decimals. Students have worked with polygons and have been introduced to area and perimeter. In Chapter 6, students developed skills in spatial visualization as they studied coordinate geometry and practiced transformations.

Learning in This Chapter

Students further their spatial sense as they study area and volume. They will study the area and perimeter of polygons and the surface area and volume of their corresponding solids. Students will apply the number sense that they developed while estimating in previous lessons to problems in this chapter. They will continue to evaluate algebraic expressions as they apply the formulas for surface area and volume. In this chapter, the concept of precision is introduced, and significant digits are studied for use with surface area and volume.

Making Future Connections

The ability to estimate and calculate area and volume are skills that students can apply to many situations in everyday life. They will continue to build on these skills and apply them to coursework in fine art, industrial arts, home economics, science, and social studies. Future mathematics courses, including geometry, algebra, trigonometry, and calculus, involve many applications that depend upon an understanding of the concepts learned in this chapter.

Mathematical Background

7-1 Area of Parallelograms, Triangles, and Trapezoids

One must know the size of an area in order to recover a floor, paint or wallpaper a wall, determine the size of a yard, and so on. Frequently the region in question is not a rectangle or a square. Other common figures include parallelograms, triangles, and trapezoids.

Bulletin Board Starters

Ask students to bring in photos from magazines, catalogs, or personal photo collections that show people working on activities, projects, and jobs involving calculations of area and volume. Cluster the photos around various headings, with Area and Volume as main headings, and group the different shapes and figures in their own regions surrounding the main headings.

7-2 Circumference and Area of Circles

The formula for the area of a circle includes a constant pi (π), which is an irrational number. 3.14 is a common approximation for π. Other equivalencies include $\frac{22}{7}$ and the calculator's pre-programmed key.

Teacher to Teacher

Ken Montgomery
Tri-Cities High School
East Point, GA

"The topic of circumference and area of circles is an excellent opportunity to incorporate multiculturalism and math history since many cultures discovered these formulas. An essay about this would enable teaching reading across the curriculum."

Ken Montgomery

7-3 Area of Complex Figures

Many objects, especially those found in architecture, are a combination of shapes. Finding the area of a complex figure is accomplished by dividing the original shape into basic shapes and finding the more familiar areas.

Team Teaching

Inform the other teachers on your team that your classes are studying the area of complex figures. Suggestions for curriculum integration are:

Social Studies: the area of states, countries, and bodies of water; population densities

Language Arts: the meanings of the prefixes of various polygons and polyhedra

Fine Arts, Home Economics: amounts of materials needed for various projects

Drama: calculations of area for building sets

7-4 Three-Dimensional Figures

The objects that make up our world are three-dimensional. Being able to identify and draw three-dimensional figures is useful in the arts, architecture, interior design, and so on.

7-5 Volume of Prisms and Cylinders

Food packages are one item that is labeled by volume. Being able to judge the size of container needed for storing leftovers or making juice requires an understanding of volume.

What the Research Says

According to Powel in "Capturing, Examining, and Responding to Mathematical Thinking through Writing," writing is effective in helping students learn mathematical concepts. It also gives teachers valuable information on student learning.

- Lessons 7-1, 7-2, 7-3, 7-4a, 7-5, 7-6, 7-7a, 7-8, and 7-9 contain Writing Math exercises so that students can practice communicating mathematical concepts.

7-6 Volume of Pyramids and Cones

The volume formulas for regular solids also apply to oblique solids. For example, when perfectly aligned, a deck of cards forms a right rectangular prism. Fanning the cards to one side forms an oblique prism. The number of cards in the deck stays the same, so its volume also stays the same.

7-7 Surface Areas of Prisms and Cylinders

The surface area of a present tells you how much paper it will take to wrap it. An object's surface area is the sum of the area of its faces.

7-8 Surface Area of Pyramids and Cones

Surface area also determines the area to be painted or covered in a remodeling project. The surface area of pyramids and cones is an extension of the surface area of prisms and cylinders.

7-9 Measurement: Precision and Significant Digits

Precision cutting is imperative in construction. Significant figures play an important role in finances and science. Significant figures can come into play when determining the area of a circle depending on what value is used for π. The more digits used, the more precise the answer.

McGraw-Hill Professional Development

Mathematics, YES! is a self-paced, web-based professional development program. Units are based on major mathematical concepts and are standards-based. Actual classroom videos provide a springboard for discussion and activities. Units appropriate for this chapter:

- Geometry and Measurement of Plane Figures
- Solid Geometry

Additional mathematical information and teaching notes are available at **msmath3.net/key_concepts**.

DAILY INTERVENTION and Assessment

* Key to Abbreviations:
TWE = Teacher Wraparound Edition, *CRM* = Chapter Resource Masters

	Type	Student Edition	Teacher Resources	Technology/Internet
INTERVENTION	Ongoing	Prerequisite Skills, pp. 313, 334, 339, 345, 351 Mid-Chapter Practice Test, p. 340	5-Minute Check Transparencies Quizzes 1–4, *CRM*, pp. 437–438 Mid-Chapter Test, *CRM*, p. 439 Study Guide and Intervention, *CRM*, pp. 377, 382, 387, 392, 397, 402, 407, 412, 417	MathPASS: Tutorial Plus msmath3.net/self_check_quiz msmath3.net/extra_examples
INTERVENTION	Mixed Review	pp. 318, 323, 329, 334, 339, 345, 351, 355, 362	Cumulative Review, *CRM*, p. 440	
INTERVENTION	Error Analysis	Find the Error, pp. 317, 337	Find the Error, *TWE*, pp. 317, 337 Unlocking Misconceptions, *TWE*, p. 320 Tips for New Teachers, *TWE*, p. 360	
ASSESSMENT	Standardized Test Practice	pp. 318, 323, 325, 327, 329, 334, 339, 340, 345, 351, 355, 362, 367, 368–369	Standardized Test Practice, *CRM*, pp. 441–442	Standardized Test Practice CD-ROM msmath3.net/standardized_test
ASSESSMENT	Open-Ended Assessment	Writing Math, pp. 317, 322, 328, 330, 337, 344, 346, 349, 354, 360 Open-Ended, pp. 317, 322, 328, 333, 337, 344, 349, 354, 360 Standardized Test, p. 369	Modeling: *TWE*, pp. 325, 334, 350 Speaking: *TWE*, pp. 338, 355 Writing: *TWE*, pp. 318, 362 Extended Response Assessment: *CRM*, p. 435	
ASSESSMENT	Chapter Assessment	Study Guide, pp. 363–366 Practice Test, p. 367	Multiple-Choice Tests (Forms 1, 2A, 2B), *CRM*, pp. 423–428 Free-Response Tests (Forms 2C, 2D, 3), *CRM*, pp. 429–434 Vocabulary Test/Review, *CRM*, p. 436	ExamView® Pro Testmaker (see below) MindJogger Videoquizzes msmath3.net/vocabulary_review msmath3.net/chapter_test

For more information on Yearly ProgressPro, see p. 252.

Glencoe Lesson	Yearly ProgressPro Skill Name
7-1	Area of Parallelograms Area of Triangles and Trapezoids
7-2	Area of Circles; Circumference of Circles
7-3	Area of Complex Figures
7-4	Three-Dimensional Figures
7-5	Volume of Triangular Prisms
7-6	Volume of Pyramids and Cones
7-7	Surface Area of Triangular Prisms
7-8	Surface Area of Pyramids and Cones
7-9	Precision and Measurement

ExamView® Pro

Use ExamView® Pro Testmaker CD-ROM to:

- **Create multiple versions of tests.**
- **Create modified tests for inclusion students with one mouse click.**
- **Edit existing questions and add your own questions.**
- **Build tests aligned with state standards using built-in state curriculum correlations.**
- **Change English tests to Spanish with one mouse click and vice versa.**

Reading and Writing in Mathematics

READING in the Content Area

This online worksheet provides strategies for reading and analyzing Lesson 7-3, Area of Complex Figures. Students are guided through questions about the main idea, subject matter, supporting details, conclusion, clarifying details, and vocabulary of the lesson.

Interactive Study Notebook With Foldables™ is a study organizer that provides helpful steps for students to follow to organize their notes for Chapter 7.

- Students use Noteables to record notes and to complete their Foldables as you present the material in Lessons 7-1 through 7-9.
- Noteables follow the *Teacher Wraparound Edition's* In-Class Examples and *Interactive Chalkboard CD-ROM.*

For more information on Reading and Writing in Mathematics, see pp. T6–T7.

Recommended Outside Reading for Students

Nonfiction

- Sheldrick Ross, Catherine. *Squares.* Kids Can Press, ©1997.

  Shapes have different forms and functions in nature, architecture, physics, and measurement. This book introduces students to squares through puzzles, riddles, and activities.

Fiction

- Murphy, Stuart. *Bigger, Better, Best!* HarperCollins Juvenile Books, ©2002.

  Three siblings and their parents move into a new house and can't decide who gets which bedroom. To determine the biggest room, they have to determine the area of each room. But is bigger always best?

PROJECT CRISS℠ Study Skill

Students can use frames to help them compare the area, surface area, and volume formulas of the various figures they learn in Chapter 7. Draw the frame shown at the right on the chalkboard. Have students copy the frame and add to it as they work through the chapter. They can make other frames to compare other types of formulas. Allow class time for students to discuss ways that the formulas are alike and ways that they are different.

Figure	Diagram	Area Formula
parallelogram		$A = bh$
triangle		$A = \frac{1}{2}bh$
trapezoid		$A = \frac{1}{2}h(b_1 + b_2)$

CReating Independence through Student-owned Strategies

For more information on Project CRISS, see p. T8.

Making Connections

School-To-Home

Parent and Student Study Guide

Parents and students may work together to reinforce the concepts and skills of this chapter. These online worksheets are available in English and Spanish at msmath3.net/parent_student. A sample lesson is shown below.

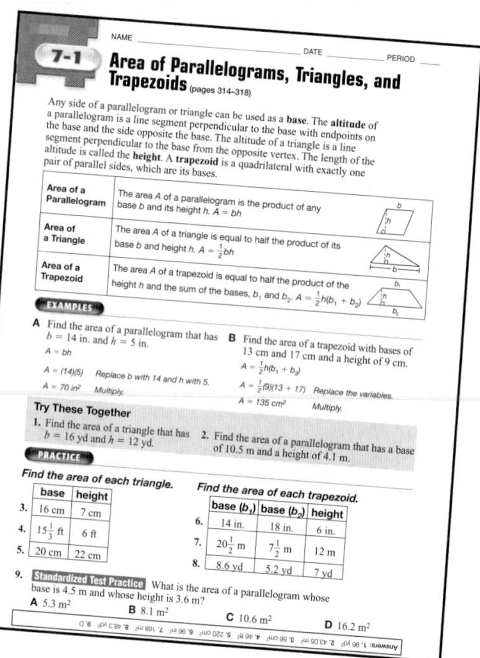

NAME ______ DATE ______ PERIOD ______

7-1 Area of Parallelograms, Triangles, and Trapezoids (pages 314–318)

Any side of a parallelogram or triangle can be used as a **base**. The **altitude** of a parallelogram is a line segment perpendicular to the base with endpoints on the base and the side opposite the base. The altitude of a triangle is a line segment perpendicular to the base from the opposite vertex. The length of the altitude is called the **height**. A **trapezoid** is a quadrilateral with exactly one pair of parallel sides, which are its bases.

Area of a Parallelogram	The area A of a parallelogram is the product of any base b and its height h. $A = bh$
Area of a Triangle	The area A of a triangle is equal to half the product of its base b and height h. $A = \frac{1}{2}bh$
Area of a Trapezoid	The area A of a trapezoid is equal to half the product of the height h and the sum of the bases, b_1 and b_2. $A = \frac{1}{2}h(b_1 + b_2)$

EXAMPLES

A Find the area of a parallelogram that has $b = 14$ in. and $h = 5$ in.

$A = bh$

$A = (14)(5)$ Replace b with 14 and h with 5.

$A = 70\ in^2$ Multiply.

B Find the area of a trapezoid with bases of 13 cm and 17 cm and a height of 9 cm.

$A = \frac{1}{2}h(b_1 + b_2)$

$A = \frac{1}{2}(9)(13 + 17)$ Replace the variables.

$A = 135\ cm^2$ Multiply.

Try These Together

1. Find the area of a triangle that has $b = 16$ yd and $h = 12$ yd.
2. Find the area of a parallelogram that has a base of 10.5 m and a height of 4.1 m.

PRACTICE

Find the area of each triangle.

	base	height
3.	16 cm	7 cm
4.	$15\frac{1}{3}$ ft	6 ft
5.	20 cm	22 cm

Find the area of each trapezoid.

	base (b_1)	base (b_2)	height
6.	14 in.	18 in.	6 in.
7.	$20\frac{1}{2}$ m	$7\frac{1}{2}$ m	12 m
8.	8.6 yd	5.2 yd	7 yd

9. **Standardized Test Practice** What is the area of a parallelogram whose base is 4.5 m and whose height is 3.6 m?
A 5.3 m² **B** 8.1 m² **C** 10.6 m² **D** 16.2 m²

Answers: 1. 96 yd² 2. 43.05 m² 3. 56 cm² 4. 46 ft² 5. 220 cm² 6. 96 in² 7. 168 m² 8. 48.3 yd² 9. D

Family Letters and Activities

Send a letter and activity for this chapter home to encourage family members to become active participants in their students' learning. (English: *Chapter 7 Resource Masters*, pp. ix–x; Spanish: log on to msmath3.net/family_letters)

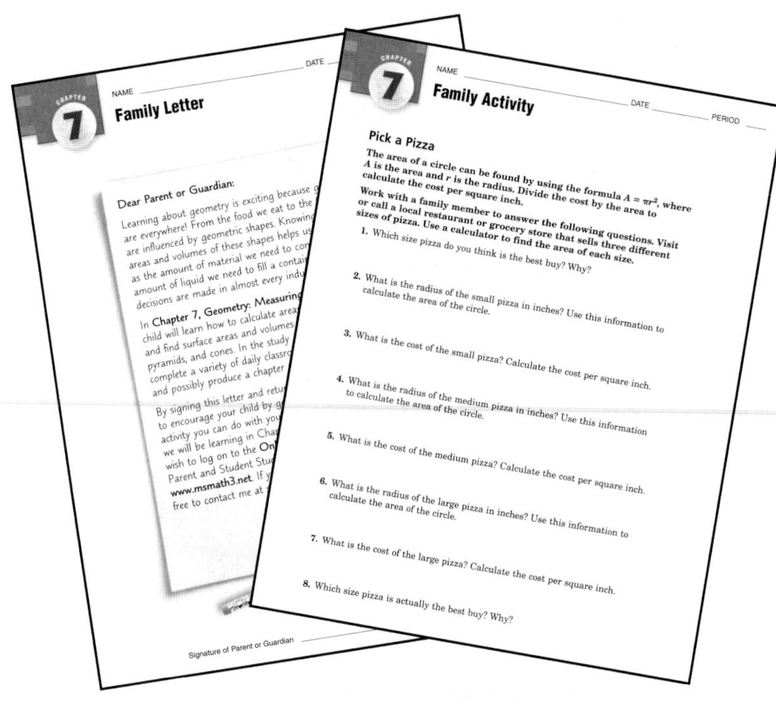

CHAPTER 7 NAME ______ DATE ______

Family Letter

Dear Parent or Guardian:

Learning about geometry is exciting because g
are everywhere! From the food we eat to the
are influenced by geometric shapes. Knowing
areas and volumes of these shapes helps us
as the amount of material we need to con
amount of liquid we need to fill a contai
decisions are made in almost every indu

In Chapter 7, Geometry: Measuring
child will learn how to calculate area
and find surface areas and volumes
pyramids, and cones. In the study
complete a variety of daily classro
and possibly produce a chapter

By signing this letter and retu
to encourage your child by g
activity you can do with you
we will be learning in Cha
wish to log on to the On
Parent and Student Stu
www.msmath3.net. If y
free to contact me at

Signature of Parent or Guardian ______

CHAPTER 7 NAME ______ DATE ______ PERIOD ______

Family Activity

Pick a Pizza

The area of a circle can be found by using the formula $A = \pi r^2$, where A is the area and r is the radius. Divide the cost by the area to calculate the cost per square inch.

Work with a family member to answer the following questions. Visit or call a local restaurant or grocery store that sells three different sizes of pizza. Use a calculator to find the area of each size.

1. Which size pizza do you think is the best buy? Why?
2. What is the radius of the small pizza in inches? Use this information to calculate the area of the circle.
3. What is the cost of the small pizza? Calculate the cost per square inch.
4. What is the radius of the medium pizza in inches? Use this information to calculate the area of the circle.
5. What is the cost of the medium pizza? Calculate the cost per square inch.
6. What is the radius of the large pizza in inches? Use this information to calculate the area of the circle.
7. What is the cost of the large pizza? Calculate the cost per square inch.
8. Which size pizza is actually the best buy? Why?

English Language Learner ELL

Lesson 7-2

Using Models

Draw a circle on the chalkboard. Have students come up to the chalkboard and draw and label each part of the circle they know. Have the students explain or define the term in their own words.

Lesson 7-4

Using Multisensory Activities

Discuss the key terms of the lesson: *polyhedron*, *face*, *vertex*, and *edge*. Give students in groups toothpicks and gumdrops. Build a triangle out of the toothpicks and gumdrops and show students that each gumdrop represents a vertex and each toothpick is an edge. Have the students build a variety of three-dimensional figures with these objects.

Lesson 7-5

Using Manipulatives

Give groups of students two sheets of paper, scissors, and tape. Have them tape the long edges of one sheet to make a cylinder. Have them tape the wide edges of the second sheet together. Ask students which cylinder has the greater volume. Then fill both cylinders with any uniform-sized objects to find which has the greater volume. Ask students why this is true.

MathScape™  This project was supported, in part, by the **National Science Foundation**

MathScape is a mathematics curriculum for grades 6–8 developed by the Seeing and Thinking Mathematically Project at the Education Development Center.

Thinking Three-Dimensionally

Shapes and Space

How to Use *MathScape* with Chapter 7

The unit *Shapes and Space* can be used to enhance Lessons 7-4 and 7-7.

- **Enrich** → After you complete **Lesson 7-4,** you can challenge students to think about cross sections of three-dimensional figures by using the activities on pages 96–97.
- **Enrich** → After you complete **Lesson 7-7,** you can encourage students to think about the relationship between surface area and volume by using the activities on pages 100–101.

For other lessons in Chapter 7 that correlate to *MathScape*, see the chart on page T14.

Online Lesson Planner

USA TODAY® Education's Online site offers resources and interactive features connected to each day's newspaper. *Experience Today,* USA TODAY's® daily lesson plan, is available on the site and delivered daily to subscribers. This plan provides instruction for integrating USA TODAY® graphics and key editorial features into your mathematics classroom. Log on to **education.usatoday.com**.

USA TODAY Snapshots® in Chapter 7	
Lesson	**Snapshot**
7-9	1 in 9 children are in private school

Quick Review Math Handbook

is Glencoe's mathematical handbook for students. The Hot Words section includes a glossary of terms while the Hot Topics section consists of explanations of key mathematical concepts. An exercise set is included to check students' understanding of the concepts. This valuable resource can be used as a reference in the classroom or for home study.

Lesson	Hot Topics Section	Lesson	Hot Topics Section
7-1	7-5, 8-3	7-6	7-7
7-2	7-8, 8-3	7-7	7-6
7-3	7-5, 8-3	7-8	6-5, 7-2, 7-6
7-4	7-2		8-6, 9-4
7-5	7-7	7-9	8-1

Key Chapter Objectives

Lessons 7-1 and 7-3 Find the areas of parallelograms, triangles, trapezoids, and complex figures.

Lesson 7-4 Identify and draw three-dimensional figures.

Lessons 7-6 and 7-8 Find the volumes and surface areas of pyramids and cones.

Lesson 7-9 Analyze measurements.

"How is math used in packaging candy?"

Point out to students that this is only one of many applications of the math that they are studying. Others are provided in the introduction to each lesson.

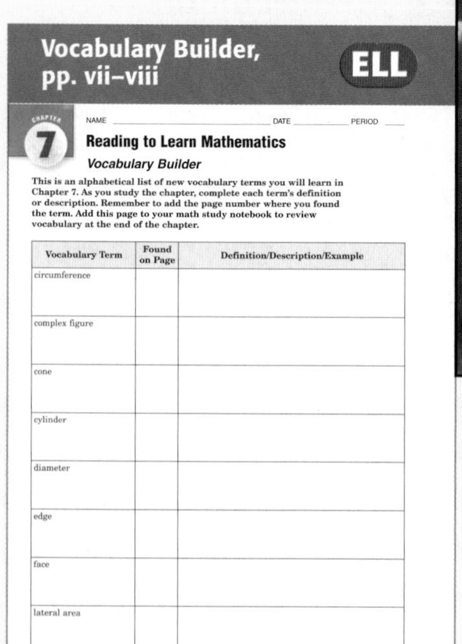

Vocabulary Builder, pp. vii–viii ELL

CHAPTER 7

NAME ____________ DATE ________ PERIOD ____

Reading to Learn Mathematics

Vocabulary Builder

This is an alphabetical list of new vocabulary terms you will learn in Chapter 7. As you study the chapter, complete each term's definition or description. Remember to add the page number where you found the term. Add this page to your math study notebook to review vocabulary at the end of the chapter.

Vocabulary Term	Found on Page	Definition/Description/Example
circumference		
complex figure		
cone		
cylinder		
diameter		
edge		
face		
lateral area		
lateral face		

CHAPTER 7

Geometry: Measuring Area and Volume

"How is math used in packaging candy?"

When marketing a product such as candy, how the product is packaged can be as important as how it tastes. A marketer must decide what shape container is best, how much candy the container should hold, and how much material it will take to make the chosen container. **To make these decisions, you must be able to identify three-dimensional objects, calculate their volumes, and calculate their surface areas.**

You will solve problems about packaging in Lesson 7-5.

312 Chapter 7 Geometry: Measuring Area and Volume

Vocabulary Builder

For a thorough vocabulary list with pronunciations of new words, give students the Vocabulary Builder worksheets from the *Chapter 7 Resource Masters.* Encourage them to complete the definition of each term as they progress through the chapter.

GETTING STARTED

▶ Diagnose Readiness

Take this quiz to see if you are ready to begin Chapter 7. Refer to the lesson number in parentheses for review.

Vocabulary Review

Choose the correct term to complete each sentence.

1. A quadrilateral with exactly one pair of parallel opposite sides is called a (parallelogram, trapezoid). (Lesson 6-4)
2. Polygons that have the same size and shape are called (congruent, similar) polygons. (Lesson 6-5)

Prerequisite Skills

Multiply. (Lesson 6-4)

3. $\frac{1}{3} \cdot 8 \cdot 12$ **32**
4. $\frac{1}{3} \cdot 4 \cdot 9^2$ **108**

Find the value of each expression to the nearest tenth.

5. $8.3 \cdot 4.1$ **34.0**
6. $9 \cdot 5.2$ **46.8**
7. $7.36 \div 4$ **1.8**
8. $12 \div 0.06$ **200**

Use the π key on a calculator to find the value of each expression. Round to the nearest tenth. **12. 283.5**

9. $\pi \cdot 15$ **47.1**
10. $2 \cdot \pi \cdot 3.2$ **20.1**
11. $\pi \cdot 7^2$ **153.9**
12. $\pi \cdot (19 \div 2)^2$

Classify each polygon according to its number of sides.

13.  **quadrilateral**
14.  **hexagon**

Area and Volume Make this Foldable to organize your notes. Begin with a piece of $8\frac{1}{2}$" × 11" paper.

STEP 1 Fold Fold in half widthwise.

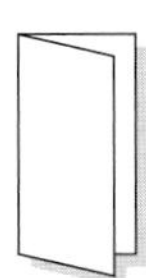

STEP 2 Open and Fold Again Fold the bottom to form a pocket. Glue edges.

STEP 3 Label Label each pocket. Place several index cards in each pocket.

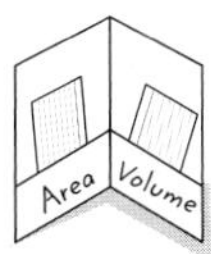

Noteables™ **Chapter Notes** Each time you find this logo throughout the chapter, use your *Noteables™: Interactive Study Notebook with Foldables™* or your own notebook to take notes. Begin your chapter notes with this Foldable activity.

Math Online **Readiness** To prepare yourself for this chapter with another quiz, visit **msmath3.net/chapter_readiness**

GETTING STARTED

Diagnose Readiness This section provides a review of the basic concepts needed before beginning Chapter 7. Page references are included for additional student help.

Prerequisite Skills review skills needed in this chapter.

Exercises	Needed for Lesson	Skill
3–4	7-6	Multiply Rational Numbers
5–8	7-9	Multiply and Divide Decimals
9–12	7-2	Multiply with π
13–14	7-4	Classify Polygons

For more prerequisite skills, see:

- Getting Ready for the Next Lesson, at the end of each lesson
- Prerequisite Skills in the Student Handbook on pp. 600–615
- *Math Skills Maintenance Masters*

FOLDABLES™ Study Organizer

For more information about Foldables, see *Teaching Mathematics with Foldables.*

Students will need 3″ × 5″ index cards, or sheets of notebook paper cut into quarter sections to use as study cards. As students learn how to measure area and volume, have them record examples of the process on one side and explain it in writing on the other side. Store these cards in the appropriate pocket of the Foldable. Continue through the chapter using the study cards to take notes, solve equations, and record and define vocabulary words and concepts presented in each lesson.

7-1 Lesson Notes

Lesson Resources

Chapter 7 Resource Masters
- Study Guide and Intervention, p. 377
- Practice: Skills, p. 378
- Practice: Word Problems, p. 379
- Reading to Learn Mathematics, p. 380
- Enrichment, p. 381

FAST FILE

Parent and Student Study Guide Online Worksheets, 7-1
Teaching Mathematics with Manipulatives, pp. 80–82
Noteables™: Interactive Study Notebook with Foldables™, 7-1

1 Focus

5-Minute Check 7-1

Use as a quiz or review of Chapter 6. (Also available as a transparency)

Bellringer

Communication Draw the figures below on the chalkboard. Ask students to label each as a parallelogram, trapezoid, or neither and to write a reason for their choice. Tell them to assume that the figures are drawn accurately.

a. 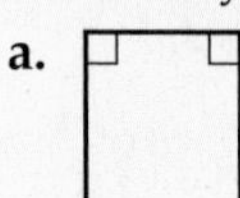 **Parallelogram; 4 sides, 2 sets of parallel sides**

(Continued in bottom margin.)

Reading to Learn Mathematics, p. 380 **ELL**

NAME ____ DATE ____ PERIOD ____

7-1 Reading to Learn Mathematics

Area of Parallelograms, Triangles, and Trapezoids

Pre-Activity *Complete the Mini Lab at the top of page 314 in your textbook. Write your answers below.*

1. What dimensions are the same in each figure? the base and height
2. Compare the areas of the three figures. What do you notice? The areas of the rectangle and parallelogram are the same. The area of the triangle is half the area of the rectangle and half the area of the parallelogram.

Reading the Lesson

3. If $A = \ell w$ is the formula for the area of a rectangle, make a conjecture about the formulas for the area of a parallelogram and triangle. parallelogram: $A = bh$, triangle: $A = \frac{1}{2}bh$

7-1 Area of Parallelograms, Triangles, and Trapezoids

What You'll LEARN

Find the areas of parallelograms, triangles, and trapezoids.

NEW Vocabulary

base
altitude

HANDS-ON Mini Lab

Materials
- grid paper

Work with a partner.

STEP 1 Draw a rectangle on grid paper.

STEP 2 Shift the top line 3 units right and draw a parallelogram.

STEP 3 Draw a line connecting two opposite vertices of the parallelogram and form two triangles.

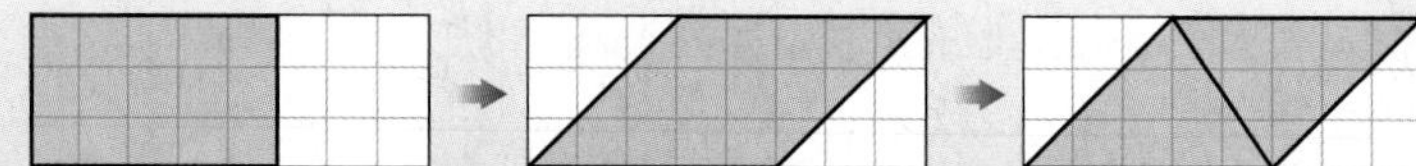

1. What dimensions are the same in each figure?
2. Compare the areas of the three figures. What do you notice?

1. the base and height 2. See margin.

The area of a parallelogram can be found by multiplying the measures of its base and its height.

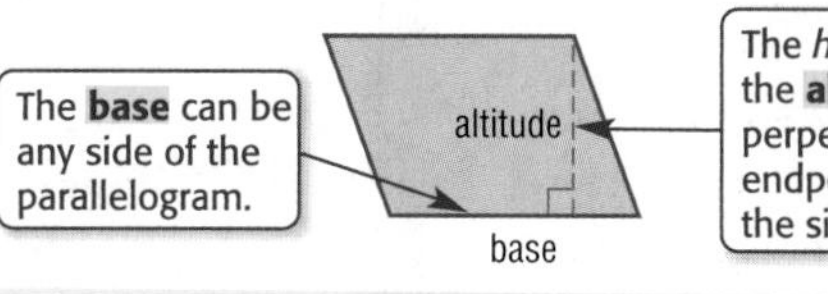

Noteables™ Key Concept: Area of a Parallelogram

Words The area A of a parallelogram is the product of any base b and its height h.

Symbols $A = bh$

Model

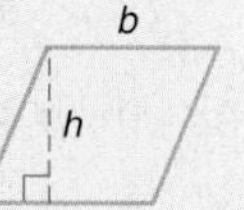

TEACHING TIP

Caution students about confusing the side of a quadrilateral for its height. Remind them that the height of a quadrilateral is the perpendicular distance from the figure's base to its opposite side.

EXAMPLE Find the Area of a Parallelogram

1 Find the area of the parallelogram.

The base is 5 feet. The height is 7 feet.

$A = bh$ Area of a parallelogram

$A = 5 \cdot 7$ Replace b with 5 and h with 7.

$A = 35$ Multiply.

The area is 35 square feet.

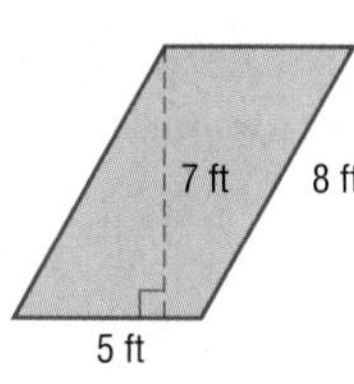

b. Neither; 4 sides, none is parallel

c. Trapezoid; 4 sides, 1 set of parallel sides

Answer (Hands-On Mini Lab)

2. The areas of the rectangle and parallelogram are the same. The area of the triangle is half the area of the parallelogram.

A diagonal of a parallelogram separates the parallelogram into two congruent triangles.

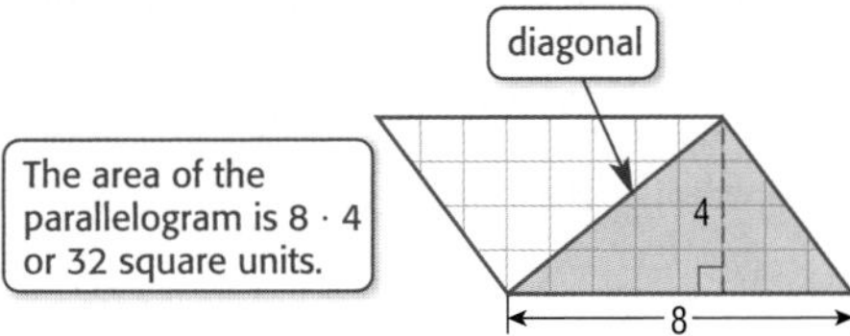

Using the formula for the area of a parallelogram, you can find the formula for the area of a triangle.

Noteables™ **Key Concept: Area of a Triangle**

Words The area A of a triangle is half the product of any base b and its height h.

Model

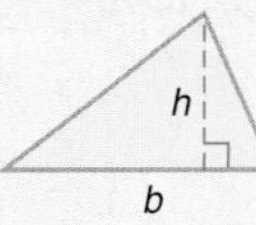

Symbols $A = \frac{1}{2}bh$

STUDY TIP

Altitudes An altitude can also be outside a figure.

EXAMPLE Find the Area of a Triangle

2 Find the area of the triangle.

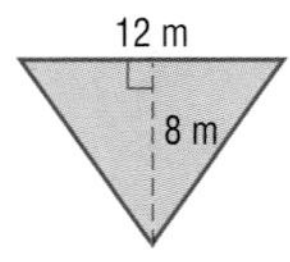

The base is 12 meters. The height is 8 meters.

$A = \frac{1}{2}bh$ Area of a triangle

$A = \frac{1}{2}(12)(8)$ Replace b with 12 and h with 8.

$A = \frac{1}{2}(96)$ Multiply. $12 \times 8 = 96$

$A = 48$ Multiply. $\frac{1}{2} \times 96 = 48$

The area is 48 square meters.

In Chapter 6, you learned that a trapezoid is a quadrilateral with exactly one pair of parallel sides. These parallel sides are its bases. A trapezoid can be separated into two triangles. Consider trapezoid $EFGH$.

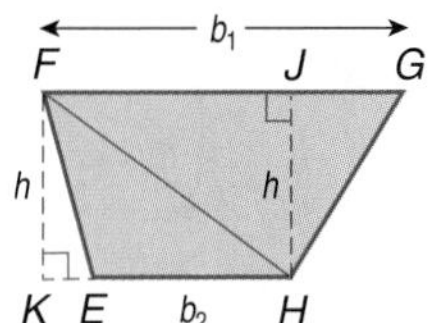

The triangles are $\triangle FGH$ and $\triangle EFH$.
The measure of a base of $\triangle FGH$ is b_1 units.
The measure of a base of $\triangle EFH$ is b_2 units.
The altitudes of the triangles, $\overline{FK}$ and $\overline{JH}$, are congruent. Both are h units long.

READING Math

Subscripts Read b_1 as *b sub 1* and b_2 as *b sub 2*. Even though the variables are the same, they represent different bases.

$$\text{area of trapezoid } EFGH = \underbrace{\text{area of } \triangle FGH}_{} + \underbrace{\text{area of } \triangle EFH}_{}$$
$$= \frac{1}{2}b_1h + \frac{1}{2}b_2h$$
$$= \frac{1}{2}h(b_1 + b_2) \quad \text{Distributive Property}$$

Math Online msmath3.net/extra_examples

2 Teach

Noteables™

As you work the **In-Class Examples,** have students follow along in their *Noteables™: Interactive Study Notebook with Foldables™*, or have students work the examples in their notebooks.

In-Class Examples

1 Find the area of the parallelogram. **14 cm²**

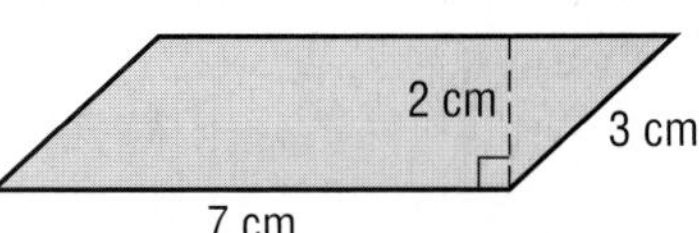

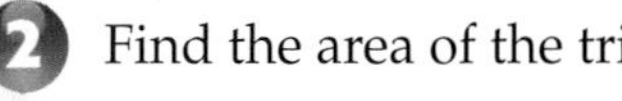

2 Find the area of the triangle.

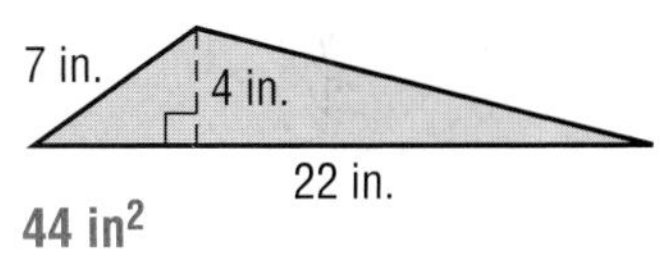

44 in²

Tips for New Teachers

Classroom Management

When students finish early, have them take measurements and find surface areas for various surfaces in the classroom, such as walls, desktops, bulletin boards, and windows. Keep a running list in the classroom of these measurements and use them for example problems, such as calculating the amount of paper needed to cover the bulletin board. Other calculations could include the number of $8\frac{1}{2}$ in. by 11 in. papers that can be posted on the bulletin board with 2 inches between each of the papers or the number of desks that will fit in a row with $2\frac{1}{2}$ feet between each of the desks.

DAILY INTERVENTION **Differentiated Instruction**

Naturalist Have students, in groups or as individuals, look up information on maps, the Internet, or in encyclopedias about National Wildlife Preserves, National and State Forests, and National Parks. Have them measure the dimensions of these wild areas, estimating for those that are not shaped exactly like quadrilaterals. Students should then find the areas of the preserves, forests, and parks. You may also wish to have students convert area to acreage. (1 square mile = 640 acres)

In-Class Examples

3 Find the area of the trapezoid. **10.2 yd^2**

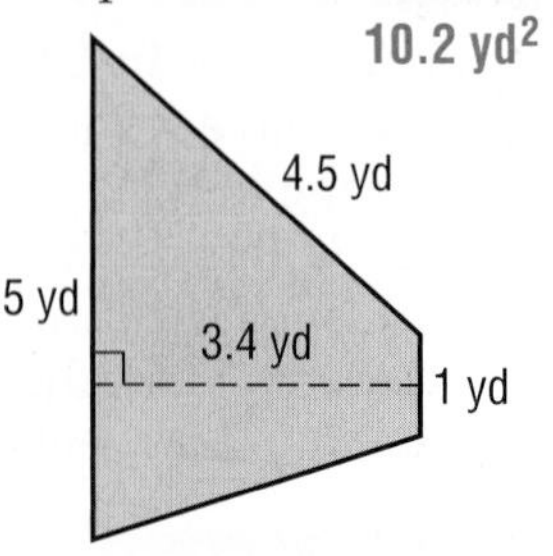

4 **PAINTING** A farmer plans to paint the triangular side of a large shed, shown below. Find the area to be painted. (Assume that no part of the window needs to be painted.) If a gallon of paint covers 350 square feet, how many gallons should the farmer buy? **378.5 ft^2; 2 gal**

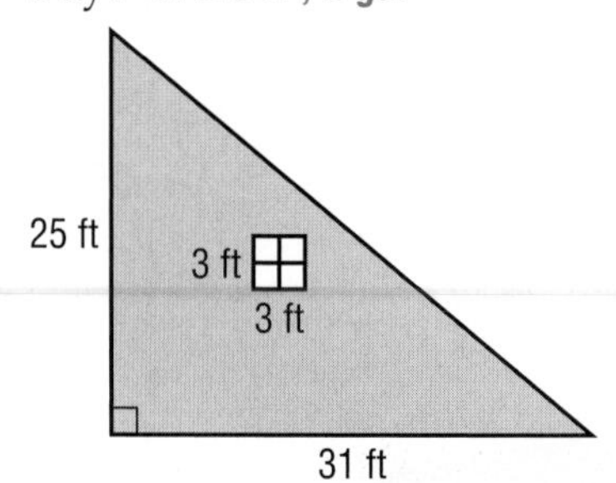

STUDY TIP

Bases The bases of a trapezoid are not always horizontal. To correctly identify the bases, remember to look for the sides that are parallel.

Noteables™ — Key Concept: Area of a Trapezoid

Words The area A of a trapezoid is half the product of the height h and the sum of the bases, b_1 and b_2.

Symbols $A = \frac{1}{2}h(b_1 + b_2)$

Model

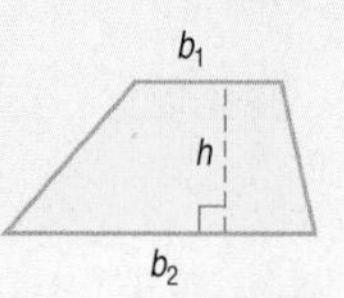

EXAMPLE Find the Area of a Trapezoid

3 **Find the area of the trapezoid.**

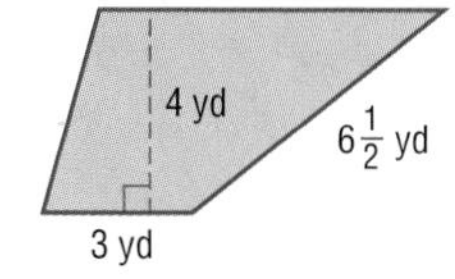

The height is 4 yards. The lengths of the bases are 7 yards and 3 yards.

$A = \frac{1}{2}h(b_1 + b_2)$ Area of a trapezoid

$A = \frac{1}{2}(4)(7 + 3)$ Replace h with 4, b_1 with 7, and b_2 with 3.

$A = \frac{1}{2}(4)(10)$ or 20 Simplify.

The area of the trapezoid is 20 square yards.

Your Turn **Find the area of each figure.**

a. **17.92 cm^2**

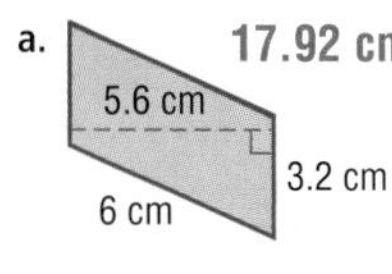

b. **$22\frac{1}{2}$ in^2**

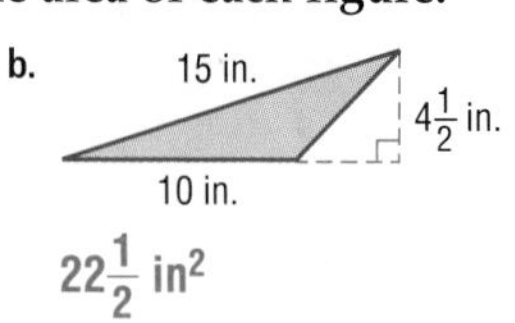

c. **24.8 cm^2**

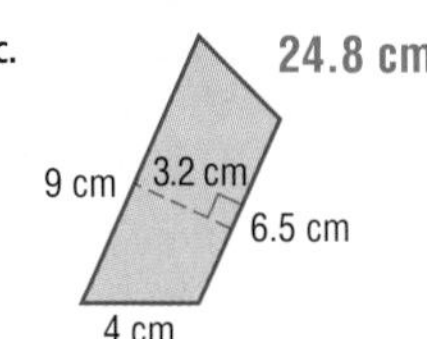

REAL-LIFE CAREERS

How Does a Landscape Architect Use Math?

Landscape architects must often calculate the area of irregularly shaped flowerbeds in order to know how much soil or ground covering to buy.

For information about a career as a landscape architect, visit: msmath3.net/careers

EXAMPLE Use Area to Solve a Real-Life Problem

4 **LANDSCAPING You are buying grass seed for the lawn surrounding three sides of an office building. If one bag covers 2,000 square feet, how many bags should you buy?**

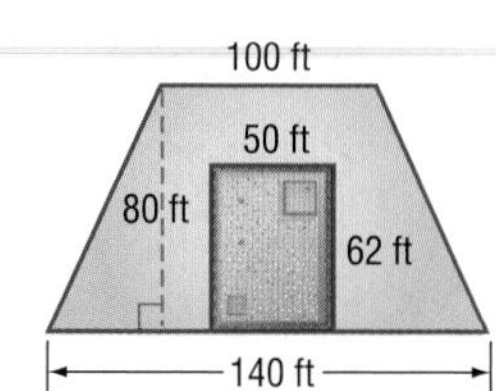

To find the area to be seeded, subtract the area of the rectangle from the area of the trapezoid.

Area of trapezoid

$A = \frac{1}{2}h(b_1 + b_2)$

$A = \frac{1}{2}(80)(100 + 140)$

$A = 9{,}600$

Area of rectangle

$A = \ell w$

$A = (50)(62)$

$A = 3{,}100$

The area to be seeded is 9,600 − 3,100 or 6,500 square feet. If one bag seeds 2,000 square feet, then you will need 6,500 ÷ 2,000 or 3.25 bags. Since you cannot buy a fraction of a bag, you should buy 4 bags.

Answers (pp. 317–318)

2. Sample answer:

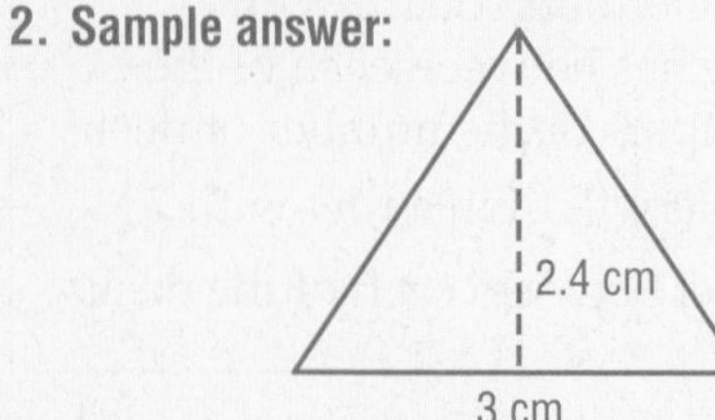

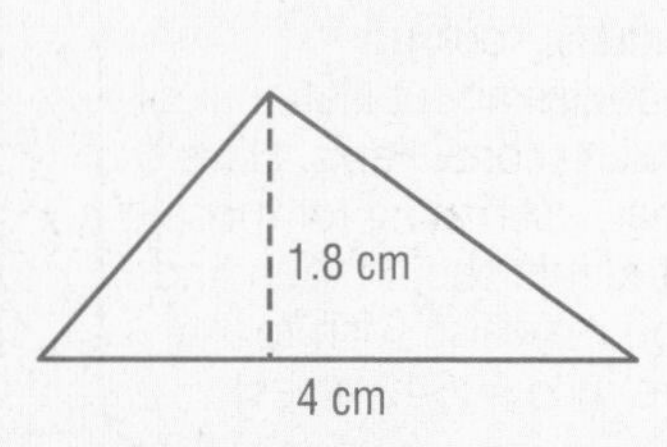

3. Malik; The area of a trapezoid is half the product of the height and the sum of the bases.

25. Tennessee: 109,158 km^2, Arkansas: 137,741 km^2, Virginia: 109,391 km^2, North Dakota: 183,123 km^2

Students practice the same concepts in Exercises 7–24 if they are assigned odd or even problems.

Skill and Concept Check

1. Writing Math Compare the formulas for the area of a rectangle and the area of a parallelogram. **They are the same; $A = bh$.**

2. **OPEN ENDED** Draw and label two different triangles that have the same area. **See margin.**

3. **FIND THE ERROR** Anthony and Malik are finding the area of the trapezoid at the right. Who is correct? Explain. **See margin.**

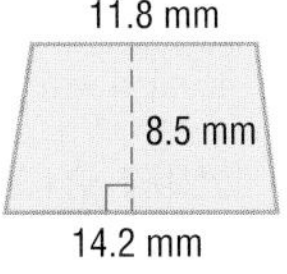

Anthony
$A = \frac{1}{2}(14.2)(8.5)$
$A = 60.35\ mm^2$

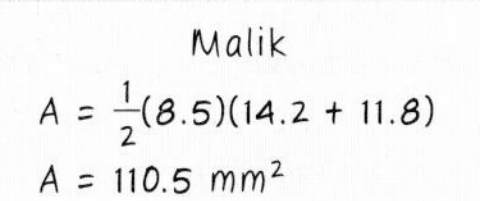

GUIDED PRACTICE

Find the area of each figure.

4. 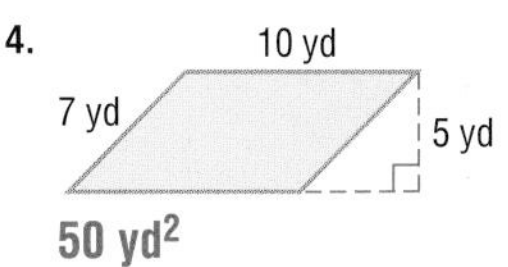

50 yd²

5. 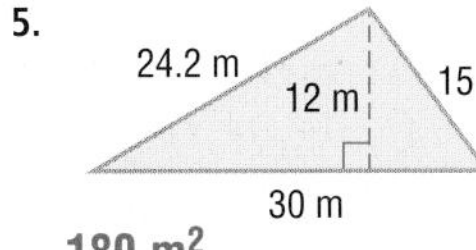

180 m²

6. 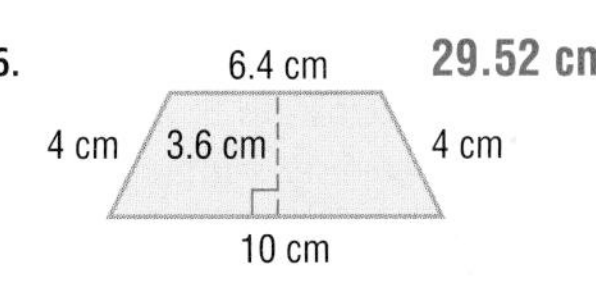

29.52 cm²

★ indicates increased difficulty

Practice and Applications

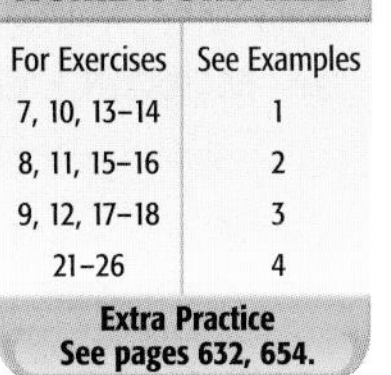

HOMEWORK HELP	
For Exercises	See Examples
7, 10, 13–14	1
8, 11, 15–16	2
9, 12, 17–18	3
21–26	4

Extra Practice See pages 632, 654.

Find the area of each figure.

7. 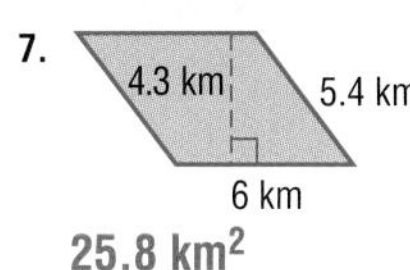

25.8 km²

8. 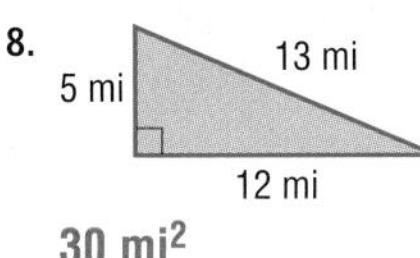

30 mi²

9. 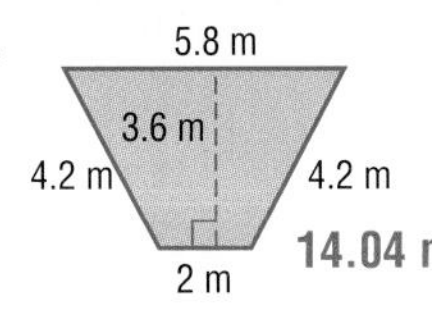

14.04 m²

10. $8\frac{1}{4}$ yd, 16 yd, $6\frac{1}{2}$ yd **104 yd²**

11. 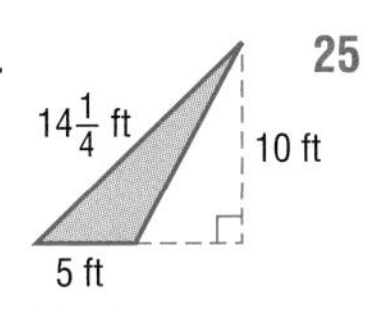

25 ft²

12. 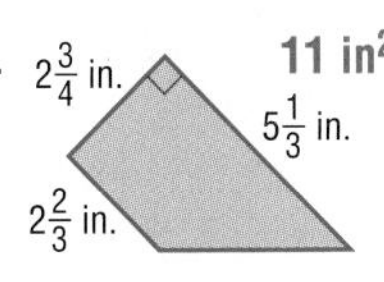

11 in²

13. 28 in² 14. 15.96 m²

13. parallelogram: base, $4\frac{2}{3}$ in.; height, 6 in.
14. parallelogram: base, 3.8 m; height, 4.2 m
15. triangle: base, 12 cm; height, 5.4 cm
16. triangle: base, $15\frac{3}{4}$ ft; height, $5\frac{1}{2}$ ft
17. trapezoid: height, 3.6 cm; bases, 2.2 cm and 5.8 cm **14.4 cm²**
18. trapezoid: height, 8 yd; bases, $10\frac{1}{2}$ yd and $15\frac{1}{3}$ yd **$103\frac{1}{3}$ yd²**

15. 32.4 cm² 16. $43\frac{5}{16}$ ft²

★ 19. **ALGEBRA** Find the height of a triangle with a base of 6.4 centimeters and an area of 22.4 square centimeters. **7 cm**

★ 20. **ALGEBRA** A trapezoid has an area of 108 square feet. If the lengths of the bases are 10 feet and 14 feet, find the height. **9 ft**

msmath3.net/self_check_quiz

3 Practice/Apply

DAILY INTERVENTION FIND THE ERROR

For Exercise 3, ask students to come up with a method to remember the difference between the formulas for the area of a triangle and the area of a trapezoid. Suggest that they think of which one has more sides (the trapezoid); this is also the one whose area formula includes more measurements.

About the Exercises...

Guided Practice Key

Exercises	Examples
4	1
5	2
6	3

Assignment Guide

Basic: 7–17 odd, 25, 27–37

Average: 7–25 odd, 27–37

Enriched: 8–26 even, 27–33 (Optional: 34–37)

Alert! In Exercises 4 and 11, students should understand that the altitudes are drawn outside of the figures.

Alert! Exercise 25 requires the use of the Internet or other research resources.

Answers (p. 318)

31. **$X'(-1, -1)$, $Y'(2, 2)$, $Z'(0, -5)$; See bottom margin.**
32. **$X'(-4, -1)$, $Y'(-1, -4)$, $Z'(-3, 3)$; See bottom margin.**
33. **$X'(4, -1)$, $Y'(1, -4)$, $Z'(3, 3)$; See bottom margin.**

31. Y, y, X, Y', O, x, X', Z, Z'

32. 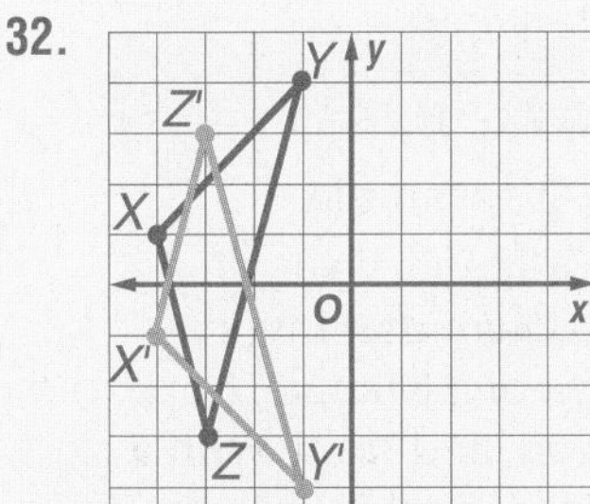

33. 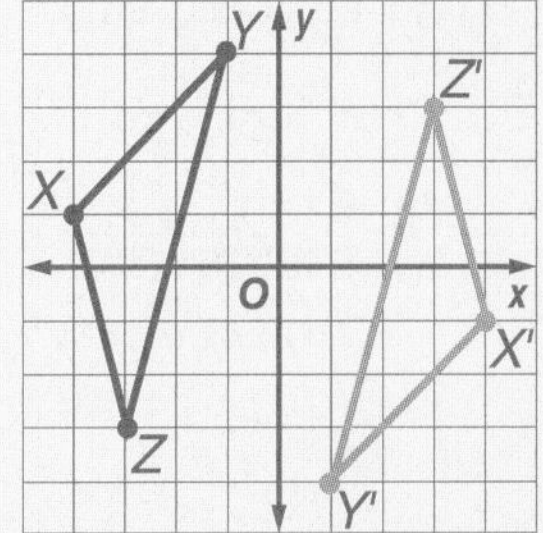

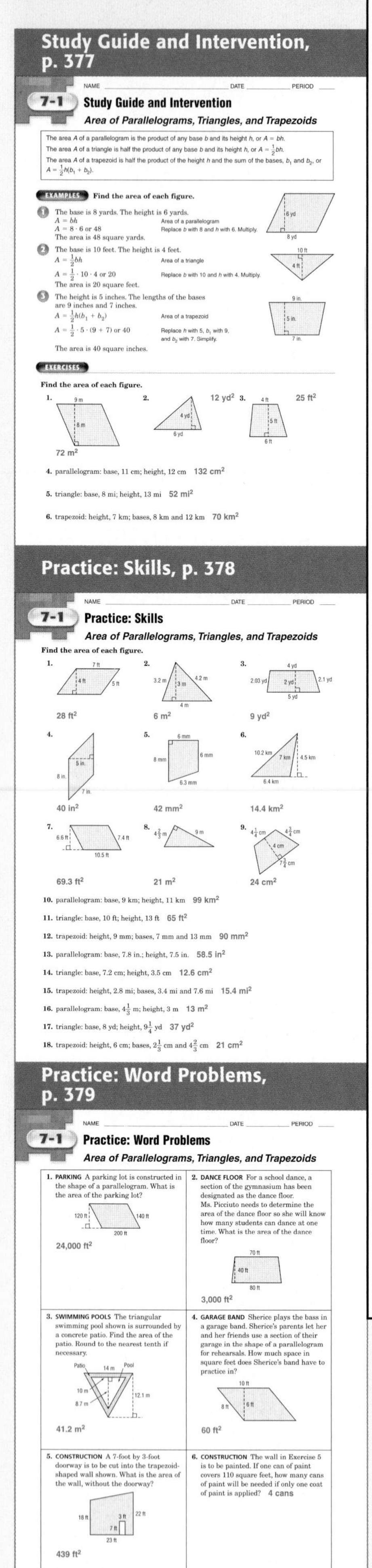

Study Guide and Intervention, p. 377

NAME ________________ DATE ________ PERIOD ____

7-1 Study Guide and Intervention

Area of Parallelograms, Triangles, and Trapezoids

The area A of a parallelogram is the product of any base b and its height h, or $A = bh$.
The area A of a triangle is half the product of any base b and its height h, or $A = \frac{1}{2}bh$.
The area A of a trapezoid is half the product of the height h and the sum of the bases, b_1 and b_2, or $A = \frac{1}{2}h(b_1 + b_2)$.

EXAMPLES **Find the area of each figure.**

1. The base is 8 yards. The height is 6 yards.
   $A = bh$ — Area of a parallelogram
   $A = 8 \cdot 6$ or 48 — Replace b with 8 and h with 6. Multiply.
   The area is 48 square yards.

2. The base is 10 feet. The height is 4 feet.
   $A = \frac{1}{2}bh$ — Area of a triangle
   $A = \frac{1}{2} \cdot 10 \cdot 4$ or 20 — Replace b with 10 and h with 4. Multiply.
   The area is 20 square feet.

3. The height is 5 inches. The lengths of the bases are 9 inches and 7 inches.
   $A = \frac{1}{2}h(b_1 + b_2)$ — Area of a trapezoid
   $A = \frac{1}{2} \cdot 5 \cdot (9 + 7)$ or 40 — Replace h with 5, b_1 with 9, and b_2 with 7. Simplify.
   The area is 40 square inches.

EXERCISES

Find the area of each figure.

1. 9 m; 8 m — **72 m²**
2. 4 yd; 6 yd — **12 yd²**
3. 4 ft; 5 ft; 6 ft — **25 ft²**
4. parallelogram: base, 11 cm; height, 12 cm **132 cm²**
5. triangle: base, 8 mi; height, 13 mi **52 mi²**
6. trapezoid: height, 7 km; bases, 8 km and 12 km **70 km²**

Practice: Skills, p. 378

NAME ________________ DATE ________ PERIOD ____

7-1 Practice: Skills

Area of Parallelograms, Triangles, and Trapezoids

Find the area of each figure.

1. 7 ft; 4 ft; 5 ft — **28 ft²**
2. 3.2 m; 4.2 m; 3 m; 4 m — **6 m²**
3. 4 yd; 2.03 yd; 2 yd; 2.1 yd; 5 yd — **9 yd²**
4. 5 in.; 8 in.; 7 in. — **40 in²**
5. 6 mm; 8 mm; 6 mm; 6.3 mm — **42 mm²**
6. 10.2 km; 7 km; 4.5 km; 6.4 km — **14.4 km²**
7. 6.6 ft; 7.4 ft; 10.5 ft — **69.3 ft²**
8. $4\frac{2}{3}$ m; 9 m — **21 m²**
9. $4\frac{1}{4}$ cm; $4\frac{3}{4}$ cm; 4 cm; $7\frac{3}{4}$ cm — **24 cm²**
10. parallelogram: base, 9 km; height, 11 km **99 km²**
11. triangle: base, 10 ft; height, 13 ft **65 ft²**
12. trapezoid: height, 9 mm; bases, 7 mm and 13 mm **90 mm²**
13. parallelogram: base, 7.8 in.; height, 7.5 in. **58.5 in²**
14. triangle: base, 7.2 cm; height, 3.5 cm **12.6 cm²**
15. trapezoid: height, 2.8 mi; bases, 3.4 mi and 7.6 mi **15.4 mi²**
16. parallelogram: base, $4\frac{1}{3}$ m; height, 3 m **13 m²**
17. triangle: base, 8 yd; height, $9\frac{1}{4}$ yd **37 yd²**
18. trapezoid: height, 6 cm; bases, $2\frac{1}{3}$ cm and $4\frac{2}{3}$ cm **21 cm²**

Practice: Word Problems, p. 379

NAME ________________ DATE ________ PERIOD ____

7-1 Practice: Word Problems

Area of Parallelograms, Triangles, and Trapezoids

1. **PARKING** A parking lot is constructed in the shape of a parallelogram. What is the area of the parking lot? (120 ft; 140 ft; 200 ft) **24,000 ft²**
2. **DANCE FLOOR** For a school dance, a section of the gymnasium has been designated as the dance floor. Ms. Picciuto needs to determine the area of the dance floor so she will know how many students can dance at one time. What is the area of the dance floor? (70 ft; 40 ft; 80 ft) **3,000 ft²**
3. **SWIMMING POOLS** The triangular swimming pool shown is surrounded by a concrete patio. Find the area of the patio. Round to the nearest tenth if necessary. (Patio; Pool; 14 m; 10 m; 8.7 m; 12.1 m) **41.2 m²**
4. **GARAGE BAND** Sherice plays the bass in a garage band. Sherice's parents let her and her friends use a section of their garage in the shape of a parallelogram for rehearsals. How much space in square feet does Sherice's band have to practice in? (10 ft; 8 ft; 6 ft) **60 ft²**
5. **CONSTRUCTION** A 7-foot by 3-foot doorway is to be cut into the trapezoid-shaped wall shown. What is the area of the wall, without the doorway? (18 ft; 3 ft; 22 ft; 7 ft; 23 ft) **439 ft²**
6. **CONSTRUCTION** The wall in Exercise 5 is to be painted. If one can of paint covers 110 square feet, how many cans of paint will be needed if only one coat of paint is applied? **4 cans**

GEOGRAPHY **For Exercises 21–24, estimate the area of each state using the scale given.** **21–24. Sample answers given.**

★21. 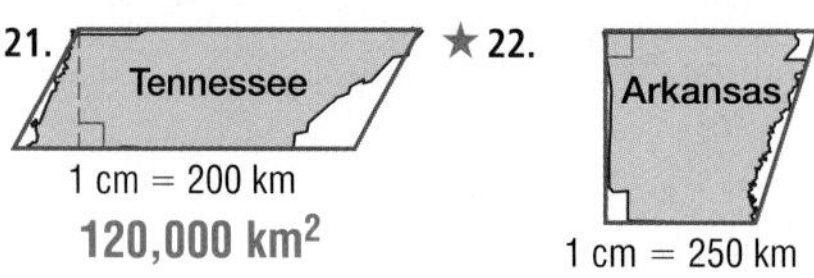

120,000 km²

★22. 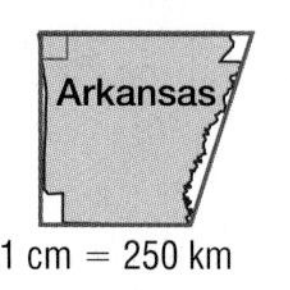

155,000 km²

★23. 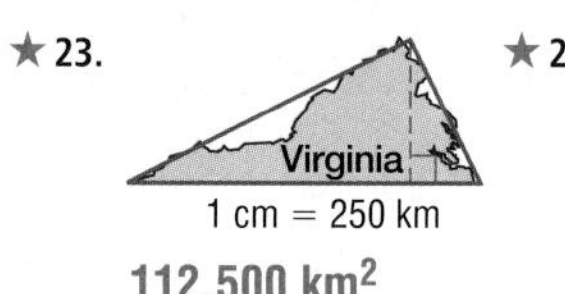

112,500 km²

★24. 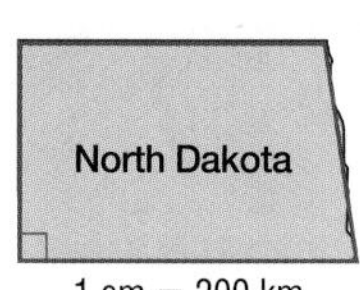

198,000 km²

25. **RESEARCH** Use the Internet or another reference to find the actual area of each state listed above. Compare to your estimate. **See margin.**

26. **MULTI STEP** A deck shown is constructed in the shape of a trapezoid, with a triangular area cut out for an existing oak tree. You want to waterproof the deck with a sealant. One can of sealant covers 400 square feet. Find the area of the deck. Then determine how many cans of sealant you should buy. **1,042 ft²; 3 cans**

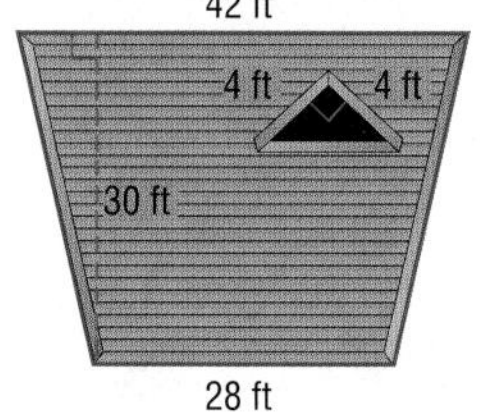

CRITICAL THINKING **For Exercises 27 and 28, decide how the area of each figure is affected.**

27. The height of a triangle is doubled, but the length of the base remains the same. **The area is doubled.**

28. The length of each base of a trapezoid is doubled and its height is also doubled. **The area is quadrupled.**

Spiral Review with Standardized Test Practice

29. **MULTIPLE CHOICE** Which figure does *not* have an area of 120 square feet? **A**

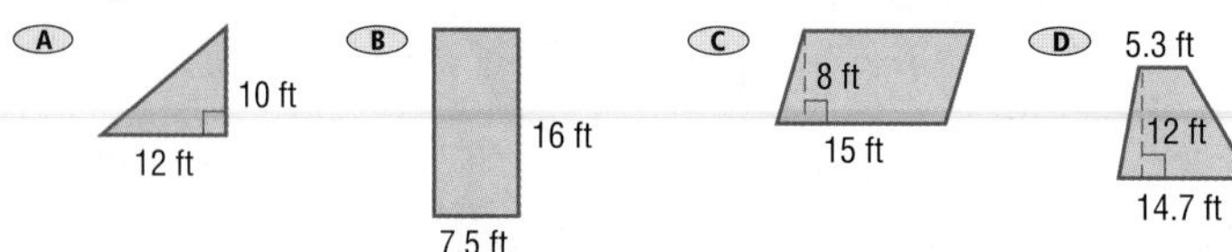

30. **MULTIPLE CHOICE** Which of the following is the best estimate of the area of the shaded region? **H**

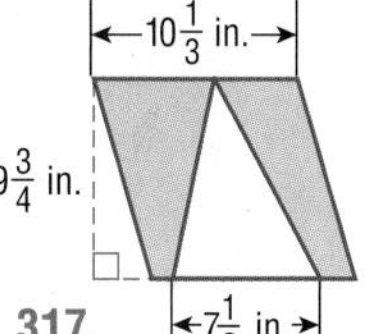

F 20 in² G 40 in² H 60 in² I 80 in²

For Exercises 31–33, use the following information. **31–33. See margin p. 317.** Triangle XYZ has vertices $X(-4, 1)$, $Y(-1, 4)$, and $Z(-3, -3)$. Graph $\triangle XYZ$. Then graph the image of $\triangle XYZ$ after the indicated transformation and write the coordinates of its vertices. (Lessons 6-7, 6-8, and 6-9)

31. translated by $(3, -2)$
32. reflected over the x-axis
33. rotated 180°

GETTING READY FOR THE NEXT LESSON

BASIC SKILL **Use the π key on a calculator to find the value of each expression. Round to the nearest tenth.**

34. $\pi \cdot 27$ **84.8**
35. $2 \cdot \pi \cdot 9.3$ **58.4**
36. $\pi \cdot 5^2$ **78.5**
37. $\pi \cdot (15 \div 2)^2$ **176.7**

4 Assess

Open-Ended Assessment

Writing Have students write an application problem that involves finding the area of a triangle, trapezoid, or parallelogram, and trade with a partner. Partners should work the problem, writing down the formula used, and showing all work. The writer of the problem should then check the answer.

Circumference and Area of Circles

What You'll LEARN

Find the circumference and area of circles.

NEW Vocabulary

circle
center
radius
diameter
circumference
pi

MATH Symbols

π pi
$\approx$ approximately equal to

HANDS-ON Mini Lab

Materials

- several different cylindrical objects like a can or battery
- ruler
- marker

Work with a partner.

STEP 1 Measure and record the distance *d* across the circular part of the object, through its center.

STEP 2 Place the object on a piece of paper. Mark the point where the object touches the paper on both the object and on the paper.

STEP 3 Carefully roll the object so that it makes one complete rotation. Then mark the paper again.

STEP 4 Finally, measure the distance *C* between the marks.

1. What distance does *C* represent? **distance around the object**
2. Find the ratio $\frac{C}{d}$ for this object.
3. Repeat the steps above for at least two other circular objects and compare the ratios of *C* to *d*. What do you observe?
4. Plot the data you collected as ordered pairs, (*d*, *C*). Then find the slope of a best-fit line through these points.

2. Answers will vary but should be about 3. 3. See margin.
4. See Ch. 7 Answer Appendix.

A **circle** is a set of points in a plane that are the same distance from a given point in the plane, called the **center**. The distance from the center to any point on the circle is called the **radius**. The distance across the circle through the center is its **diameter**. The distance around the circle is called the **circumference**.

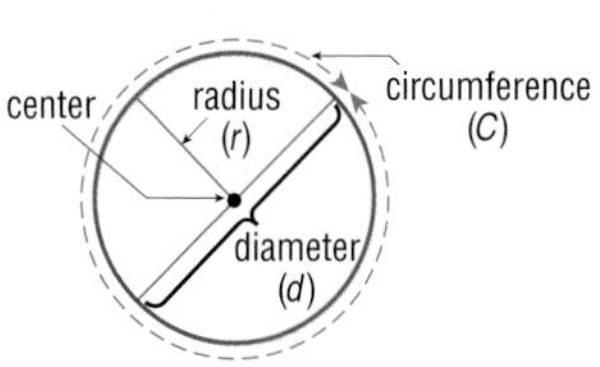

The diameter of a circle is twice its radius or $d = 2r$.

STUDY TIP

Pi The numbers 3.14 and $\frac{22}{7}$ are often used as approximations for π.

The relationship you discovered in the Mini Lab is true for all circles. The ratio of the circumference of a circle to its diameter is always 3.1415926…. The Greek letter **π (pi)** represents this number.

7-2 Lesson Notes

Lesson Resources

Chapter 7 Resource Masters FAST FILE

- Study Guide and Intervention, p. 382
- Practice: Skills, p. 383
- Practice: Word Problems, p. 384
- Reading to Learn Mathematics, p. 385
- Enrichment, p. 386

Calculator and Spreadsheet Masters, p. 31
MathPASS Tutorial CD-ROM, 49, 51
Parent and Student Study Guide Online Worksheets, 7-2
Teaching Mathematics with Manipulatives, pp. 83–84
Noteables™: Interactive Study Notebook with Foldables™, 7-2

1 Focus

5-Minute Check 7-2

Use as a quiz or review of Lesson 7-1. (Also available as a transparency)

Bellringer

Problem Solving Draw a circle inscribed in a square, as shown below. Ask students to use the area of the square to estimate the area of the circle. Point out that the portions that need to be subtracted are similar to triangles.

(Continued in bottom margin.)

Reading to Learn Mathematics, p. 385 ELL

NAME ______ DATE ______ PERIOD ______

7-2 Reading to Learn Mathematics
Circumference and Area of Circles

Pre-Activity *Complete the Mini Lab at the top of page 319 in your textbook. Write your answers below.*

1. What distance does *C* represent? **distance around the object**
2. Find the ratio $\frac{C}{d}$ for this object. **Answers will vary but should be about 3.**
3. Repeat the steps above for at least two other circular objects and compare the ratios of *C* to *d*. What do you observe? **The ratios are all about 3.**
4. Plot the data you collected as ordered pairs, (*d*, *C*). Then find the slope of a best-fit line through these points. **Sample answer:**

Answer (Hands-On Mini Lab)

3. The ratios are all about 3.

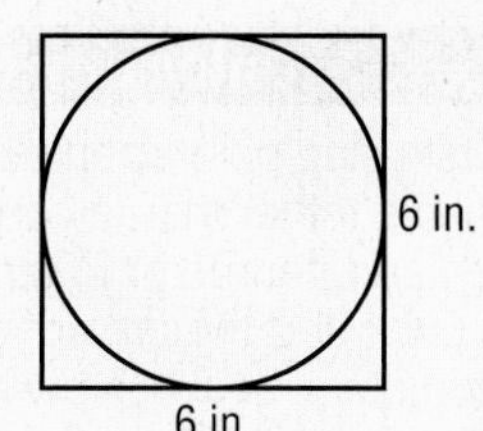

The area of the square is 36 in^2. Subtract about 2 in^2 for each corner to get about 28 in^2. The actual area is 9π, or 28.27 in^2.

Teach

In-Class Examples

Find the circumference of each circle. Round to the nearest tenth.

1 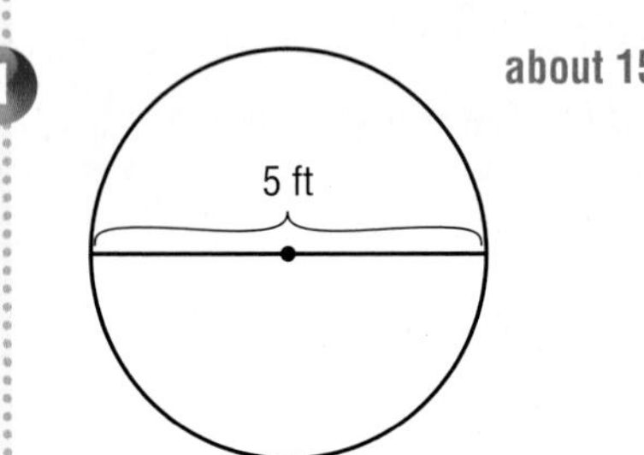

about 15.7 ft

2 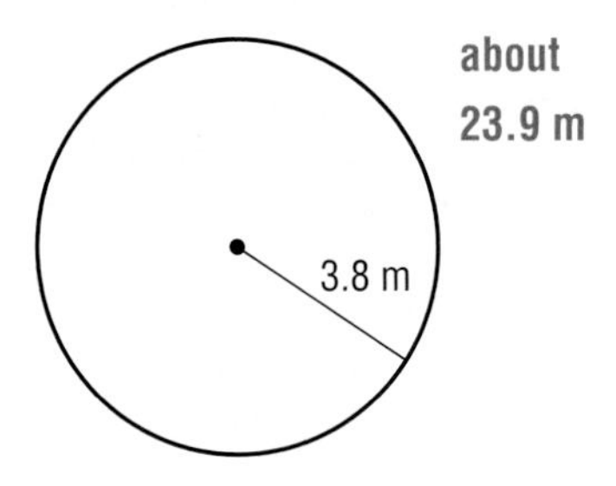

about 23.9 m

Using Manipulatives

As students read about the relationship between the area of a parallelogram and the area of a circle, have them try the exercise suggested in the text. They can use a compass to draw a circle and a protractor with a straightedge to draw the congruent wedge-like pieces. Tell students to begin by dividing the circle into 8 such pieces. After they cut out the pieces and assemble the parallelogram-shaped figure, tell them to cut the 8 pieces in half, making 16 congruent pieces. When they reassemble the figure, they should see it is a closer approximation of a parallelogram than was made with 8 pieces.

Noteables™ **Key Concept: Circumference of a Circle**

Words The circumference C of a circle is equal to its diameter d times π, or 2 times its radius r times π.

Symbols $C = \pi d$ or $C = 2\pi r$

Model

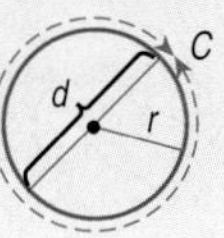

STUDY TIP

Calculating with Pi Unless otherwise specified, use the π key on a calculator to evaluate expressions involving π.

TEACHING TIP

In Example 2, point out to students that the equals sign is changed to an *approximately equals* sign ($\approx$) in the third step. This is because the value of C is no longer exact.

EXAMPLES Find the Circumferences of Circles

Find the circumference of each circle.

1 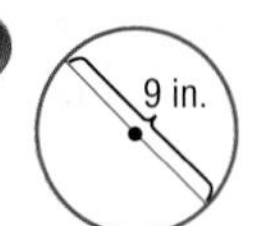

$C = \pi d$	Circumference of a circle
$C = \pi \cdot 9$	Replace d with 9.
$C = 9\pi$	This is the *exact* circumference.

Use a calculator to find 9π. 9 [×] [π] [ENTER] 28.27433388

The circumference is about 28.3 inches.

2 (Circle with radius 7.2 cm)

$C = 2\pi r$	Circumference of a circle
$C = 2 \cdot \pi \cdot 7.2$	Replace r with 7.2.
$C \approx 45.2$	Use a calculator.

The circumference is about 45.2 centimeters.

Finding the area of a circle can be related to finding the area of a parallelogram. A circle can be separated into congruent wedge-like pieces. Then the pieces can be rearranged to form the figure below.

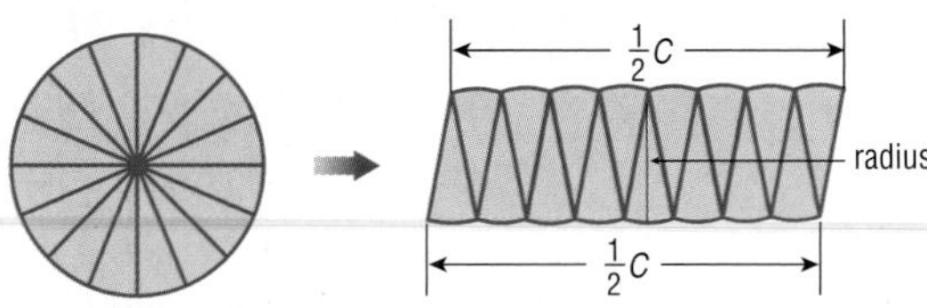

Since the circle has an area that is relatively close to the area of the parallelogram-shaped figure, you can use the formula for the area of a parallelogram to find the area of a circle.

$A = bh$	Area of a parallelogram
$A = \left(\frac{1}{2} \cdot C\right)r$	The base of the parallelogram is one-half the circumference and the height is the radius.
$A = \left(\frac{1}{2} \cdot 2\pi r\right)r$	Replace C with $2\pi r$.
$A = \pi \cdot r \cdot r$ or πr^2	Simplify.

Noteables™ **Key Concept: Area of a Circle**

Words The area A of a circle is equal to π times the square of the radius r.

Symbols $A = \pi r^2$

Model

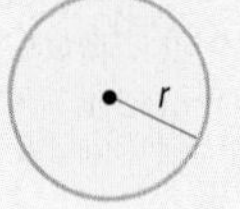

DAILY INTERVENTION **Unlocking Misconceptions**

When first using pi in algebraic expressions, students sometimes treat it as a variable rather than a constant. Give students some problems using total area and perimeter in terms of pi. For example, if the area of one circle is 6.8π and the area of another is 18π, ask students to find the combined area. **24.8π** Now ask them what the difference is between 24.8π, $24.8x$, and $24.8q$. **24.8π is a constant; you can simplify it on a calculator. For the other two, x and q are variables.**

STUDY TIP

Estimation To estimate the area of a circle, square the radius and then multiply by 3.

EXAMPLES Find the Areas of Circles

Find the area of each circle.

3

$A = \pi r^2$	Area of a circle
$A = \pi \cdot 8^2$	Replace r with 8.
$A = \pi \cdot 64$	Evaluate 8^2.
$A \approx 201.1$	Use a calculator.

The area is about 201.1 square kilometers.

4

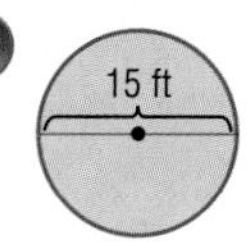

$A = \pi r^2$	Area of a circle
$A = \pi(7.5)^2$	Replace r with half of 15 or 7.5.
$A = \pi \cdot 56.25$	Evaluate 7.5^2.
$A \approx 176.7$	Use a calculator.

The area is about 176.7 square feet.

TEACHING TIP

Make sure students are aware that the unit of measure for the tree trunk in Example 5 is inches, but that the unit of measure for the protected zone is feet.

Your Turn **Find the circumference and area of each circle. Round to the nearest tenth.**

a. 11 cm — **69.1 cm; 380.1 cm²**

b. 5 mi — **15.7 mi; 19.6 mi²**

c. $2\frac{3}{4}$ in. — **17.3 in.; 23.8 in²**

REAL-LIFE MATH

TREES Trees should be planted so that they have plenty of room to grow. The planting site should have an area of at least 2 to 3 times the diameter of the circle the spreading roots of the maturing tree are expected to occupy.

Source: www.forestry.uga.edu

EXAMPLE Use Circumference and Area

5 **TREES During a construction project, barriers are placed around trees. For each inch of trunk diameter, the protected zone should have a radius of $1\frac{1}{2}$ feet. Find the area of this zone for a tree with a trunk circumference of 63 inches.**

d in. $1\frac{1}{2}d$ ft

First find the diameter of the tree.

$C = \pi d$	Circumference of a circle
$63 = \pi \cdot d$	Replace C with 63.
$\frac{63}{\pi} = d$	Divide each side by π.
$20.1 \approx d$	Use a calculator.

The diameter d of the tree is about 20.1 inches. The radius r of the protected zone should be $1\frac{1}{2}d$ feet. That is, $r = 1\frac{1}{2}(20.1)$ or 30.15 feet. Use this radius to find the area of the protected zone.

$A = \pi r^2$	Area of a circle
$A = \pi(30.15)^2$ or about 2,855.8	Replace r with 30.15 and use a calculator.

The area of the protected zone is about 2,855.8 square feet.

msmath3.net/extra_examples

In-Class Examples

Find the area of each circle. Round to the nearest tenth.

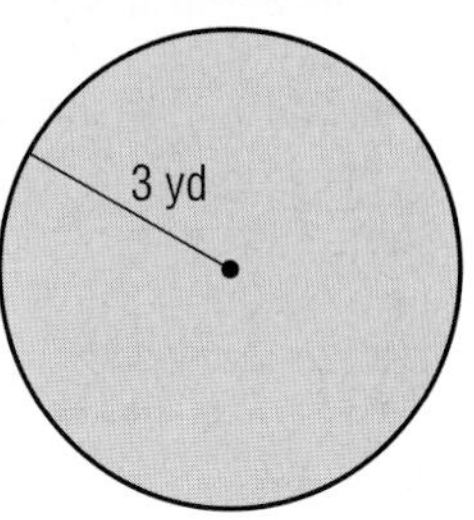

about 28.3 yd²

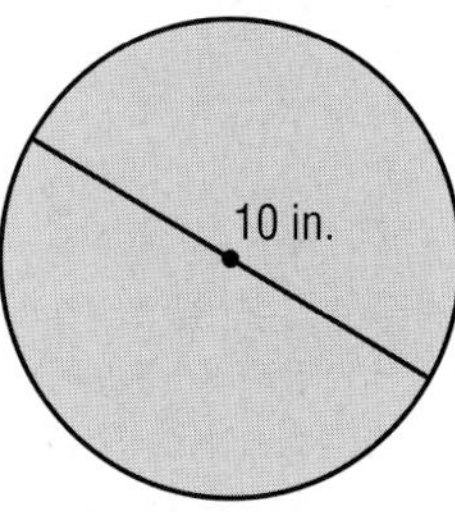

about 78.5 in²

Pools The Patels have a circular pool with a radius of 12 feet. They plan on installing a 4-foot-wide walkway around the pool. What will be the area of the walkway?

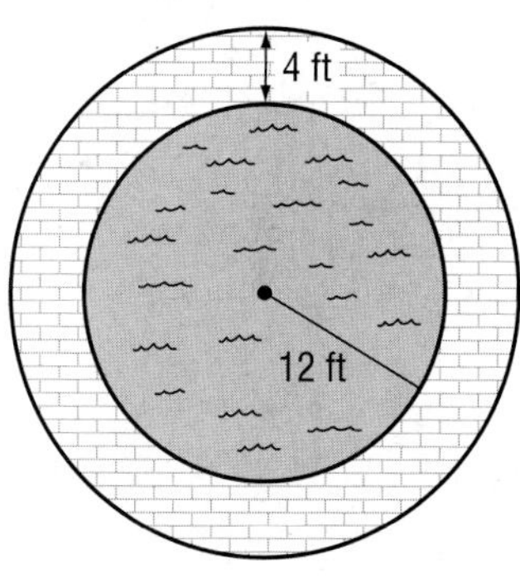

about 351.9 ft²

3 Practice/Apply

Follow-Up Remind students to record main ideas, definitions of vocabulary words, and other notes on study cards as they progress through the lesson. Students store their study cards from this lesson in the *Area* pocket of their Foldables.

Writing Math In Exercise 2, have students use examples to approach this problem. They can calculate the circumference of two circles, one whose radius is twice that of the other. Assign different radii to different students, so that they can see that the pattern holds with more than one circle. You may also wish to show the result algebraically.

Original circle, radius r: $C = 2\pi r$

Second circle, radius $2r$:
$C = 2\pi(2r) = 4\pi r$

$4\pi r = 2(2\pi r) = 2$(circumference of original circle)

So, the circumference is doubled.

About the Exercises...

Guided Practice Key

Exercises	Examples
3–8	1–4

Assignment Guide

Basic: 9–23 odd, 27–30, 33–41

Average: 9–25 odd, 27–30, 33–41 (Optional: 31–32)

Enriched: 10–22 even, 23, 24, 26–37 (Optional: 38–41)

Students practice the same concepts in Exercises 9–22 if they are assigned odd or even problems.

Skill and Concept Check

1. **OPEN ENDED** Draw and label a circle that has a circumference between 10 and 20 centimeters. **See margin for sample answer.**

2. *Writing Math* If the radius of a circle is doubled, how will this affect its circumference? its area? Explain your reasoning. **The circumference will double since $2\pi(2r) = 2(2\pi r)$; the area will quadruple since $\pi(2r)^2 = 4(\pi r^2)$.**

GUIDED PRACTICE

Find the circumference and area of each circle. Round to the nearest tenth.

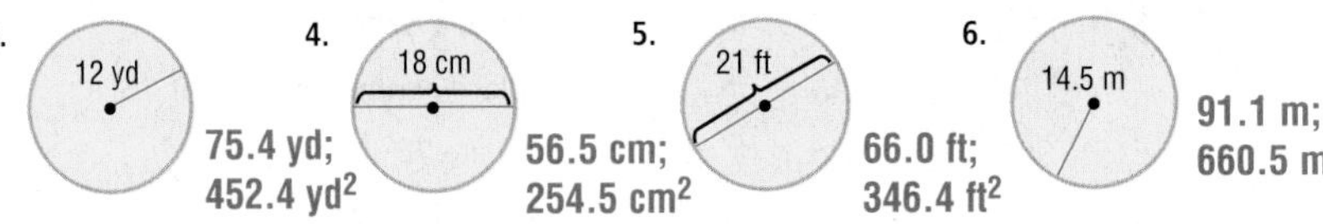

3. **75.4 yd; 452.4 yd^2**
4. **56.5 cm; 254.5 cm^2**
5. **66.0 ft; 346.4 ft^2**
6. **91.1 m; 660.5 m^2**

7. The diameter is 5.3 miles. **16.7 mi; 22.1 mi^2**
8. The radius is $4\frac{3}{4}$ inches. **29.8 in.; 70.9 in^2**

★ **indicates increased difficulty**

Practice and Applications

HOMEWORK HELP	
For Exercises	See Examples
9–18	1–4
19–24	5

Extra Practice See pages 632, 654.

Find the circumference and area of each circle. Round to the nearest tenth.

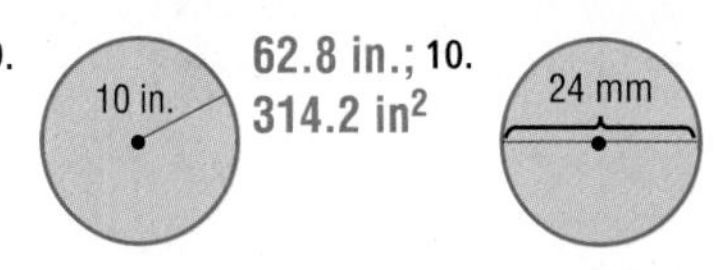

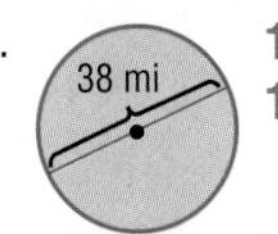

9. **62.8 in.; 314.2 in^2**
10. **75.4 mm; 452.4 mm^2**
11. **119.4 mi; 1,134.1 mi^2**
12. 17 km **106.8 km; 907.9 km^2**
13. 19.4 m **60.9 m; 295.6 m^2**
14. $7\frac{1}{4}$ ft **45.6 ft; 165.1 ft^2**

15. The radius is 3.5 centimeters. **22.0 cm; 38.5 cm^2**
16. The diameter is 8.6 kilometers. **27.0 km; 58.1 km^2**
17. The diameter is $10\frac{3}{8}$ feet. **32.6 ft; 84.5 ft^2**
18. The radius is $6\frac{2}{5}$ inches. **40.2 in.; 128.7 in^2**

19. **CARS** If the tires on a car each have a diameter of 25 inches, how far will the car travel in 100 rotations of its tires? **about 7,854 in. or 654.5 feet**

20. **SPORTS** Three tennis balls are packaged one on top of the other in a can. Which measure is greater, the can's height or circumference? Explain. **circumference; height = $3d$, $C = 3.14d$**

21. **ANIMALS** A California ground squirrel usually stays within 150 yards of its burrow. Find the area of a California ground squirrel's world. **about 70,686 yd^2**

★22. **LAWN CARE** The pattern of water distribution from a sprinkler is commonly a circle or part of a circle. A certain sprinkler is set to cover part of a circle measuring 270°. Find the area of the grass watered if the sprinkler reaches a distance of 15 feet. **530.1 ft^2**

Answers

1. **Sample answer:**

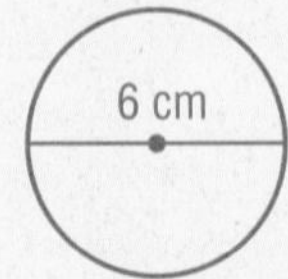

24. **1 large is about 4.7 cents/in^2, 2 mediums are about 3.9 cents/in^2, and 3 smalls are about 5.1 cents/in^2.**

31. **Sample answer:**

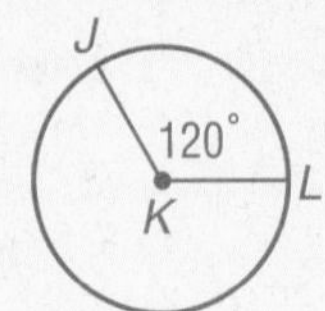

37.

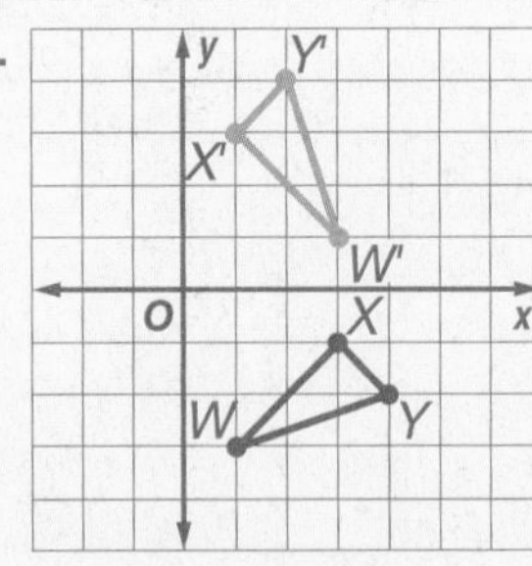

$W'(3, 1)$, $X'(1, 3)$, $Y'(2, 4)$

PIZZA For Exercises 23 and 24, use the diagram at the right. **23. 254.5 in^2; 153.9 in^2; 78.5 in^2**

HOLIDAY PIZZERIA

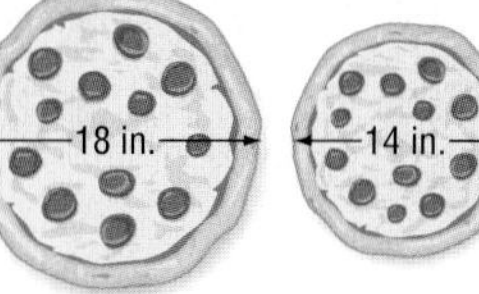
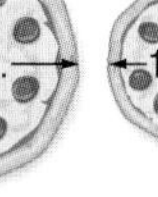

23. Find the area of each size pizza.

24. **MULTI STEP** The pizzeria has a special that offers one large, two medium, or three small pizzas for $12. Which offer is the best buy? Explain your reasoning. **2 medium pizzas for $12; See margin.**

ALGEBRA For Exercises 25 and 26, round to the nearest tenth.

★25. What is the diameter of a circle if its circumference is 41.8 feet? **13.3 ft**

★26. Find the radius of a circle if its area is 706.9 square millimeters. **15.0 mm**

CRITICAL THINKING Find the area of each shaded region.

27. 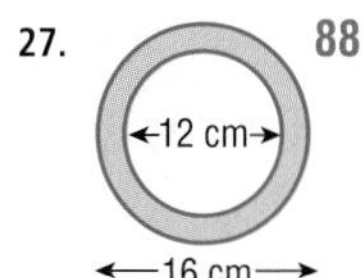

88.0 cm^2

28. 5 in. **21.5 in^2**

29. 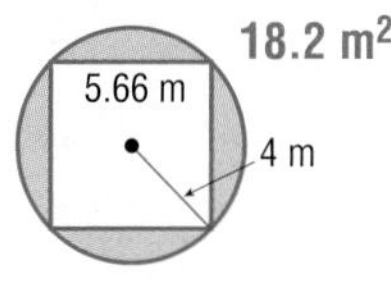

18.2 m^2

30. 6 ft, 3 ft, 10.39 ft **66.3 ft^3**

31. See margin for sample drawing; arc JL.

EXTENDING THE LESSON A *central angle* is an angle that intersects a circle in two points and has its vertex at the center of the circle. Central angles separate the circle into arcs. A *chord* is a line segment joining two points on a circle.

central angle ABC, D, A, B, arc AC, chord $\overline{DE}$, E, C

31. Draw and label a circle with a central angle JKL measuring 120°. Name the arc that corresponds to central angle JKL.

32. *True* or *False*? One side of a central angle can be a chord of the circle. Explain your reasoning. **False; both sides of a central angle are radii, not chords of the circle.**

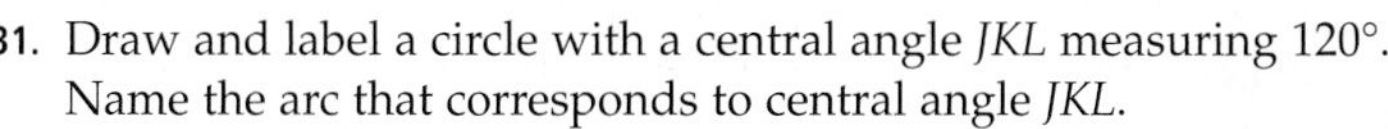

Spiral Review with Standardized Test Practice

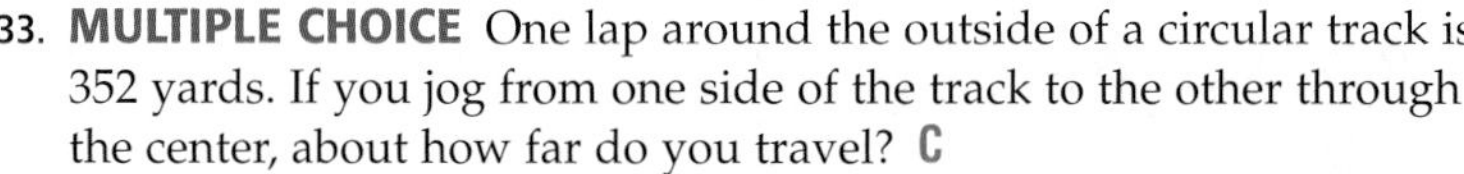

33. **MULTIPLE CHOICE** One lap around the outside of a circular track is 352 yards. If you jog from one side of the track to the other through the center, about how far do you travel? **C**

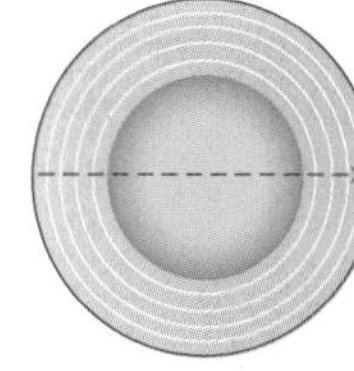

Ⓐ 11 yd Ⓑ 56 yd Ⓒ 112 yd Ⓓ 176 yd

34. **SHORT RESPONSE** The circumference of a circle is 16.5 feet. What is its area to the nearest tenth of a square foot? **21.7 ft^2**

Find the area of each figure described. (Lesson 7-1)

35. triangle: base, 4 cm
height, 8.7 cm **17.4 cm^2**

36. trapezoid: height, 4 in.
bases, 2.5 in. and 5 in. **15 in^2**

37. Graph $\triangle WXY$ with vertices $W(1, -3)$, $X(3, -1)$, and $Y(4, -2)$. Then graph its image after a rotation of 90° counterclockwise about the origin and write the coordinates of its vertices. (Lesson 6-9) **See margin.**

GETTING READY FOR THE NEXT LESSON

BASIC SKILL Add.

38. 450 + 210.5 **660.5** 39. 16.4 + 8.7 **25.1** 40. 25.9 + 134.8 **160.7** 41. 213.25 + 86.9 **300.15**

Math Online msmath3.net/self_check_quiz

4 Assess

Higher-Level Thinking

The wheels on a truck have a radius of 18 inches. How far will the truck have traveled after the wheels have made exactly 150 revolutions?

The truck will have traveled 150 times the circumference of the wheels, a total of about 16,964.6 inches, or 1,413.7 feet.

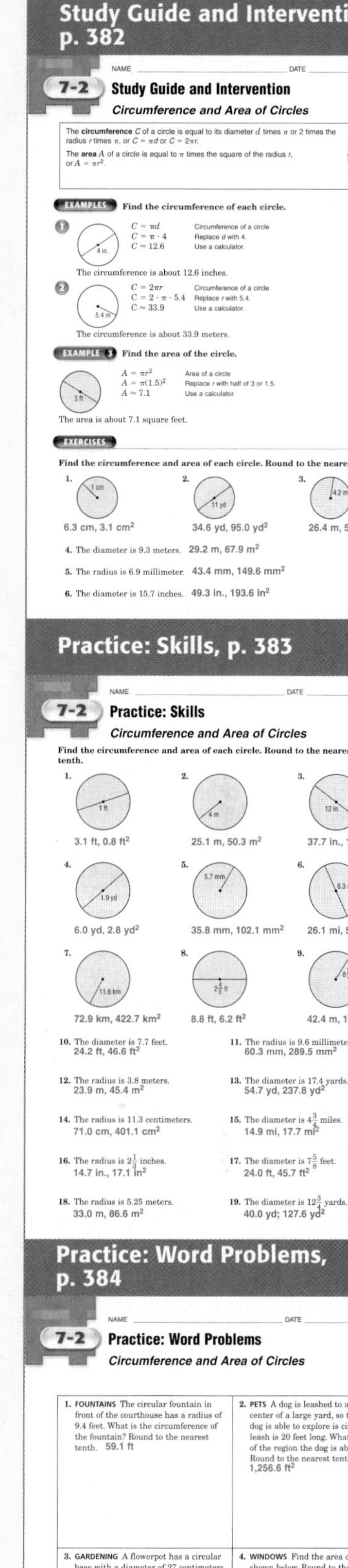

Study Guide and Intervention, p. 382

NAME ________ DATE ______ PERIOD ____

7-2 Study Guide and Intervention

Circumference and Area of Circles

The **circumference** C of a circle is equal to its diameter d times π or 2 times the radius r times π, or $C = \pi d$ or $C = 2\pi r$.

The **area** A of a circle is equal to π times the square of the radius r, or $A = \pi r^2$.

EXAMPLES Find the circumference of each circle.

1. 4 in.
$C = \pi d$ Circumference of a circle
$C = \pi \cdot 4$ Replace d with 4.
$C \approx 12.6$ Use a calculator.

The circumference is about 12.6 inches.

2. 5.4 m
$C = 2\pi r$ Circumference of a circle
$C = 2 \cdot \pi \cdot 5.4$ Replace r with 5.4.
$C \approx 33.9$ Use a calculator.

The circumference is about 33.9 meters.

EXAMPLE 3 Find the area of the circle.

3 ft
$A = \pi r^2$ Area of a circle
$A = \pi(1.5)^2$ Replace r with half of 3 or 1.5.
$A \approx 7.1$ Use a calculator.

The area is about 7.1 square feet.

EXERCISES

Find the circumference and area of each circle. Round to the nearest tenth.

1. 1 cm — 6.3 cm, 3.1 cm^2
2. 11 yd — 34.6 yd, 95.0 yd^2
3. 4.2 m — 26.4 m, 55.4 m^2
4. The diameter is 9.3 meters. 29.2 m, 67.9 m^2
5. The radius is 6.9 millimeter. 43.4 mm, 149.6 mm^2
6. The diameter is 15.7 inches. 49.3 in., 193.6 in^2

Practice: Skills, p. 383

NAME ________ DATE ______ PERIOD ____

7-2 Practice: Skills

Circumference and Area of Circles

Find the circumference and area of each circle. Round to the nearest tenth.

1. 1 ft — 3.1 ft, 0.8 ft^2
2. 4 m — 25.1 m, 50.3 m^2
3. 12 in. — 37.7 in., 113.1 in^2
4. 1.9 yd — 6.0 yd, 2.8 yd^2
5. 5.7 mm — 35.8 mm, 102.1 mm^2
6. 8.3 mi — 26.1 mi, 54.1 mi^2
7. 11.6 km — 72.9 km, 422.7 km^2
8. $2\frac{4}{5}$ ft — 8.8 ft, 6.2 ft^2
9. $6\frac{3}{4}$ m — 42.4 m, 143.1 m^2
10. The diameter is 7.7 feet. 24.2 ft, 46.6 ft^2
11. The radius is 9.6 millimeters. 60.3 mm, 289.5 mm^2
12. The radius is 3.8 meters. 23.9 m, 45.4 m^2
13. The diameter is 17.4 yards. 54.7 yd, 237.8 yd^2
14. The radius is 11.3 centimeters. 71.0 cm, 401.1 cm^2
15. The diameter is $4\frac{3}{4}$ miles. 14.9 mi, 17.7 mi^2
16. The radius is $2\frac{1}{3}$ inches. 14.7 in., 17.1 in^2
17. The diameter is $7\frac{5}{8}$ feet. 24.0 ft, 45.7 ft^2
18. The radius is 5.25 meters. 33.0 m, 86.6 m^2
19. The diameter is $12\frac{3}{4}$ yards. 40.0 yd; 127.6 yd^2

Practice: Word Problems, p. 384

NAME ________ DATE ______ PERIOD ____

7-2 Practice: Word Problems

Circumference and Area of Circles

1. **FOUNTAINS** The circular fountain in front of the courthouse has a radius of 9.4 feet. What is the circumference of the fountain? Round to the nearest tenth. 59.1 ft

2. **PETS** A dog is leashed to a point in the center of a large yard, so the area the dog is able to explore is circular. The leash is 20 feet long. What is the area of the region the dog is able to explore? Round to the nearest tenth. 1,256.6 ft^2

3. **GARDENING** A flowerpot has a circular base with a diameter of 27 centimeters. Find the circumference of the base of the flowerpot. Round to the nearest tenth. 84.8 cm

4. **WINDOWS** Find the area of the window shown below. Round to the nearest tenth.

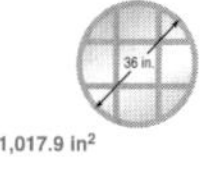

1,017.9 in^2

5. **BICYCLES** A bicycle tire has a radius of $13\frac{1}{4}$ inches. How far will the bicycle travel in 40 rotations of the tire? Round to the nearest tenth. ($13\frac{1}{4}$ in.) 3,330.1 in. or 277.5 ft

6. **LANDSCAPING** Joni has a circular garden with a diameter of $14\frac{1}{2}$ feet. If she uses 2 teaspoons of fertilizer for every 25 square feet of garden, how much fertilizer will Joni need for her entire garden? Round to the nearest tenth. 13.2 tsp

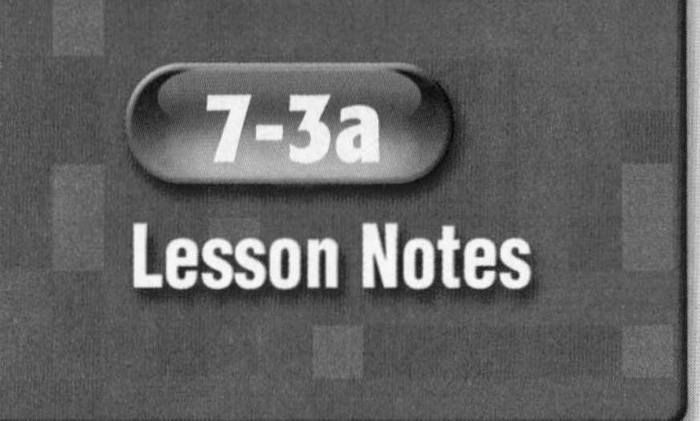

1 Focus

Bellringer

Problem Solving Separate students into groups of four and have them work together to solve the following problem: *How many 3-digit numbers between 100 and 500 have digits with a sum of 10?* Have each group find the pattern, report its findings to the class, and discuss the group's method. **There are 40 such numbers—10 in the 100s, 9 in the 200s, 8 in the 300s, and so on.**

2 Teach

In-Class Example

Solve. Use the solve a simpler problem strategy.

GARDENS A series of gardens framed by tiles is arranged such that each successive garden is one tile longer than the previous garden. The width of the gardens is four tiles. The first three gardens are shown below. How many tiles surround Garden 10? **28 tiles**

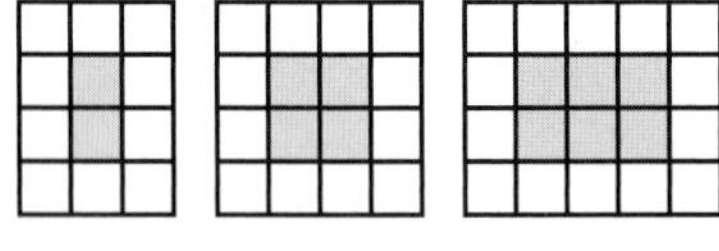

Garden 1 Garden 2 Garden 3

7-3a Problem-Solving Strategy

A Preview of Lesson 7-3

Solve a Simpler Problem

What You'll LEARN

Solve problems by solving a simpler problem.

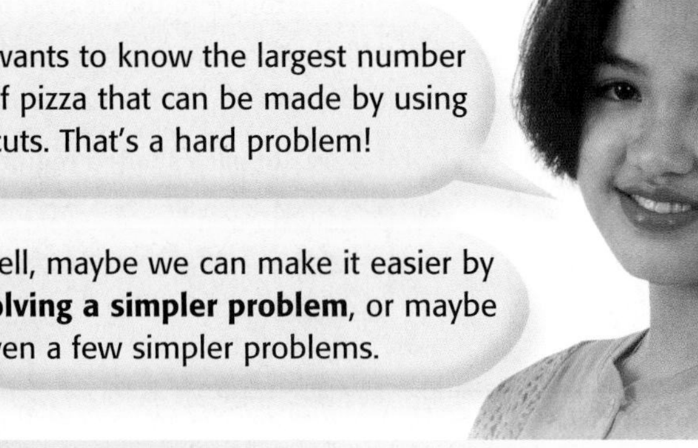

Explore Mr. Lewis said that a "cut" does not have to be along a diameter, but it must be from edge to edge. Also, the pieces do not have to be the same size.

Plan Let's draw diagrams to find the largest number of pieces formed by 1, 2, 3, and 4 cuts and then look for a pattern.

Solve

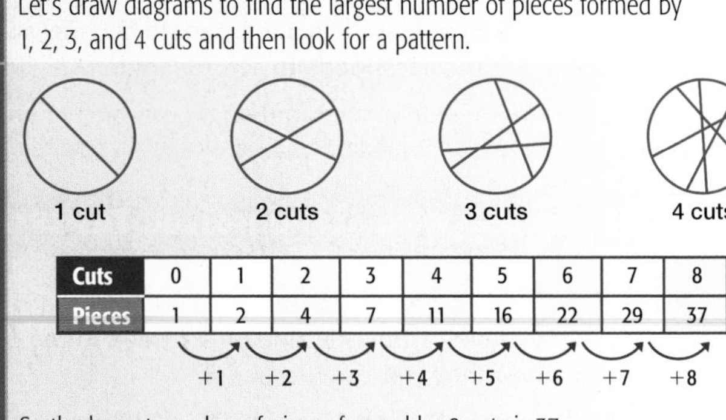

Cuts	0	1	2	3	4	5	6	7	8
Pieces	1	2	4	7	11	16	22	29	37

+1 +2 +3 +4 +5 +6 +7 +8

So the largest number of pieces formed by 8 cuts is 37.

Examine Two cuts formed $2 \cdot 2$ or 4 pieces, and 4 cuts formed about $3 \cdot 4$ or 12 pieces. It is reasonable to assume that 6 cuts would form about $4 \cdot 6$ or 24 pieces and 8 cuts about $5 \cdot 8$ or 40 pieces. Our answer is reasonable.

Apply the Strategy

1. **Explain** why it was helpful for Kimi and Paige to solve a simpler problem to answer Mr. Lewis' question. **1–3. See margin.**
2. **Explain** how you could use the solve a simpler problem strategy to find the thickness of one page in this book.
3. **Write** about a situation in which you might need to solve a simpler problem in order to find the solution to a more complicated problem. Then solve the problem.

Answers

1. The pieces of pizza would likely be difficult to see in a diagram showing 8 cuts.
2. Find the thickness of the entire book, not including the front and back covers, and divide that measure by the number of pages in the book, remembering that one page has two page numbers on it, one on the front side and one on the back side.
3. Sample answer: The bill for a meal comes to $18.60. How much tip should you add if you want the tip to be 15% of the cost of the meal? A simpler problem is to first find 10% of $18.60, which is $1.86. The other 5% of the bill is then found by taking half of $1.86, which is 0.93. The tip is then $1.86 + $0.93 or $2.79.

Apply the Strategy

Solve. Use the solve a simpler problem strategy.

4. **GEOMETRY** How many squares of any size are in the figure at the right? 55

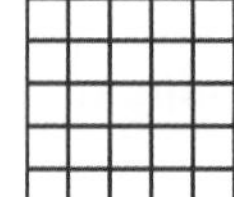

5. **TABLES** A restaurant has 25 square tables that can be pushed together to form one long table for a banquet. Each square table can seat only one person on each side. How many people can be seated at the banquet table? 52

Mixed Problem Solving

Solve. Use any strategy.

6. **PARTY SUPPLIES** Paper cups come in packages of 40 or 75. Monica needs 350 paper cups for the school party. How many packages of each size should she buy?
   5 packages of 40 and 2 packages of 75

7. **SOFT DRINKS** The graph represents a survey of 400 students. Determine the difference in the number of students who preferred cola to lemon-lime soda. 68

Soft Drink Preferences

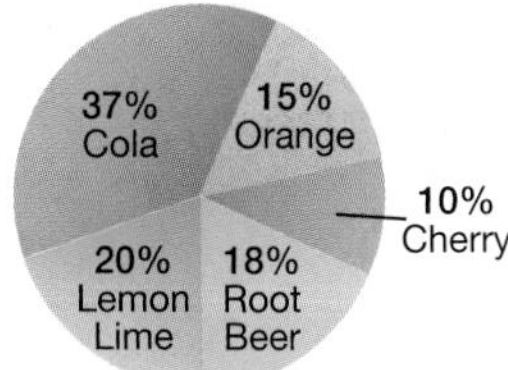

8. **GIFT WRAPPING** During the holidays, Tyler and Abigail earn extra money by wrapping gifts at a department store. Tyler wraps 8 packages an hour while Abigail wraps 10 packages an hour. Working together, about how long will it take them to wrap 40 packages? about 2 h 13 min

READING For Exercises 9 and 10, use the following information.
Carter Middle School has 487 fiction books and 675 nonfiction books. Of the nonfiction books, 84 are biographies. 9. See margin.

9. Draw a Venn diagram of this situation.
10. How many books are *not* biographies?
    1,078

11. **MONEY** Mario has \$12 to spend at the movies. After he pays the \$6.50 admission, he estimates that he can buy a tub of popcorn that costs \$4.25 and a medium drink that is \$2.50. Is this reasonable? Explain. no; $7 + 4 + 3 > 12$

12. **HEALTH** A human heart beats an average of 72 times in one minute. Estimate the number of times a human heart beats in one year. Sample answer: 37,800,000

13. **TRAVEL** When Mrs. Lopez started her trip from Jackson, Mississippi, to Atlanta, Georgia, her odometer read 35,400 miles. When she reached Atlanta, her odometer read 35,782 miles. If the trip took $6\frac{1}{2}$ hours, what was her average speed? 58.8 mph

14. **NUMBER SENSE** Find the sum of all the whole numbers from 1 to 40, inclusive. 820

15. **STANDARDIZED TEST PRACTICE**
    Three different views of a cube are shown. If the fish is currently faceup, what figure is facedown? A

Ⓐ heart Ⓑ lightning bolt
Ⓒ question mark Ⓓ tree

3 Practice/Apply

About the Exercises...

Problem-Solving Strategies
Exercises 6–15 are structured so that students have the opportunity to practice many different problem-solving strategies. You may wish to remind them of some of the strategies they have studied.

- work backward (p. 43)
- use a Venn diagram (p. 123)
- reasonable answers (p. 226)
- solve a simpler problem ✓

4 Assess

Open-Ended Assessment

Modeling Have students model the following problem by drawing a family tree on a piece of paper: Each couple in the Burns family has had three offspring every generation. How many children will the fourth generation produce if this pattern continues? Mother and Father Burns are the only members of the first generation. 81

Answer

9. Sample answer:

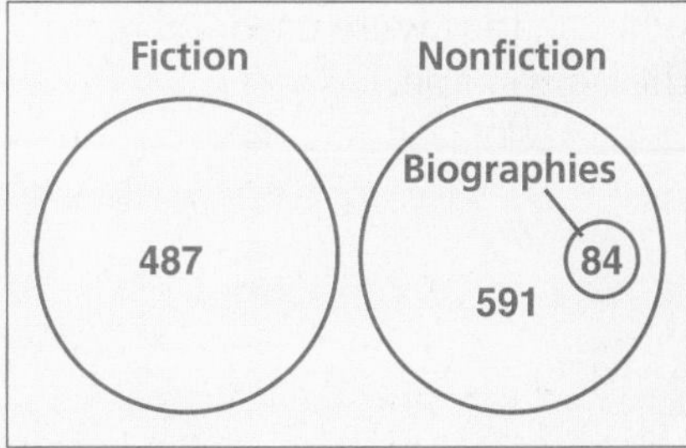

DAILY INTERVENTION **Flexible Grouping**

Place students into groups of 5 or 6. Within each group, students should figure out how many handshakes are needed for all members to shake hands exactly once. Students should start out by figuring out the handshakes needed for groups of 3, then 4. Next, have 2 groups form into 1 to expand the question. Using the same method, the students should figure out how many handshakes are needed for each student in the class to shake the hand of everyone else exactly once.

7-3 Lesson Notes

Lesson Resources

Chapter 7 Resource Masters
- Study Guide and Intervention, p. 387
- Practice: Skills, p. 388
- Practice: Word Problems, p. 389
- Reading to Learn Mathematics, p. 390
- Enrichment, p. 391

MathPASS Tutorial CD-ROM, 50

Parent and Student Study Guide Online Worksheets, 7-3

Noteables™: Interactive Study Notebook with Foldables™, 7-3

1 Focus

5-Minute Check 7-3

Use as a quiz or review of Lesson 7-2. (Also available as a transparency)

Bellringer

Hands-On Activity Give students tangram pieces and ask them to build new shapes with them. Sketch an outline of each new shape on paper or the overhead. Ask other students what shapes were used to create the new shape.

Reading to Learn Mathematics, p. 390 ELL

NAME ____ DATE ____ PERIOD ____

7-3 **Reading to Learn Mathematics**

Area of Complex Figures

Pre-Activity *Read the introduction at the top of page 326 in your textbook. Write your answers below.*

1. Identify some of the polygons that make up the family room, nook, and foyer area shown in this floor plan. **Sample answer: rectangles, trapezoids**

Reading the Lesson

2. What is a complex figure? **Sample answer: a figure made up of two or more shapes**

3. W... the first step in fin... the area of a complex fi... Sample... separate...

Area of Complex Figures

What You'll LEARN

Find the area of complex figures.

NEW Vocabulary

complex figure

WHEN am I ever going to use this?

CARPETING When carpeting, you must calculate the amount of carpet needed for the floor space you wish to cover. Sometimes the space is made up of several shapes.

1. Identify some of the polygons that make up the family room, nook, and foyer area shown in this floor plan.

Family Room
Nook
Foyer
Dining

1. Sample answer: rectangles, trapezoids

We have discussed the following area formulas.

Parallelogram	Triangle	Trapezoid	Circle
$A = bh$	$A = \frac{1}{2}bh$	$A = \frac{1}{2}h(b_1 + b_2)$	$A = \pi r^2$

You can use these formulas to help you find the area of complex figures. A **complex figure** is made up of two or more shapes.

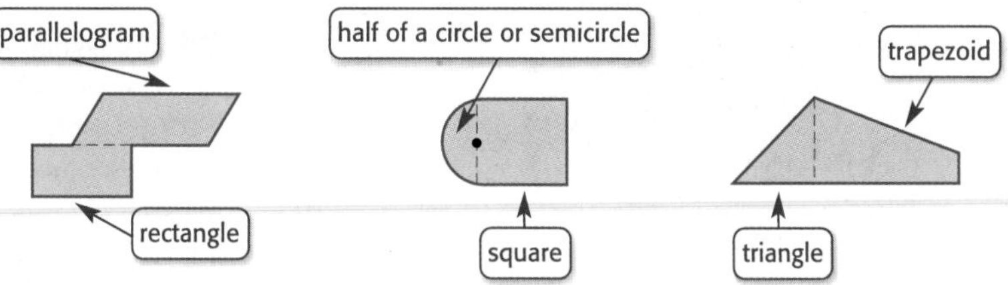

To find the area of a complex figure, separate the figure into shapes whose areas you know how to find. Then find the sum of these areas.

TEACHING TIP

Point out to students that there is often more than one way to separate a complex figure and that trying an alternate method is one way of checking their answer.

READING in the Content Area

For strategies in reading this lesson, visit **msmath3.net/reading.**

EXAMPLE Find the Area of a Complex Figure

1 Find the area of the complex figure.

4 ft
12 ft
15 ft

The figure can be separated into a rectangle and a triangle.

Area of rectangle	**Area of triangle**
$A = \ell w$	$A = \frac{1}{2}bh$
$A = 15 \cdot 12$	$A = \frac{1}{2} \cdot 15 \cdot 4$
$A = 180$	$A = 30$

The area of the figure is 180 + 30 or 210 square feet.

DAILY INTERVENTION

Differentiated Instruction

Visual/Spatial Take students on a tour of the school grounds. Have them work in groups to estimate the square footage of the floor space of the building, breaking it up into various pieces that are shaped like common polygons. Accurate measurements can also be made using tape measures. Check with the principal to determine the exact square footage of the school.

EXAMPLE Find the Area of a Complex Figure

2 **Find the area of the complex figure.**

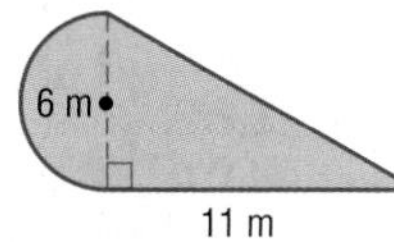

The figure can be separated into a semicircle and a triangle.

Area of semicircle

$A = \frac{1}{2}\pi r^2$

$A = \frac{1}{2} \cdot \pi \cdot 3^2$

$A \approx 14.1$

Area of triangle

$A = \frac{1}{2}bh$

$A = \frac{1}{2} \cdot 6 \cdot 11$

$A = 33$

The area of the figure is about 14.1 + 33 or 47.1 square meters.

Your Turn **Find the area of each figure. Round to the nearest tenth if necessary.** c. 482.5 in^2

a. 252 cm^2

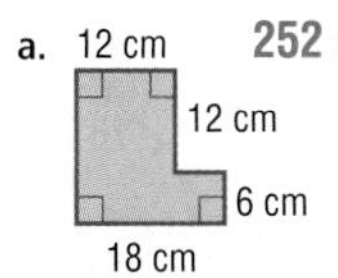

b. 193.4 m^2

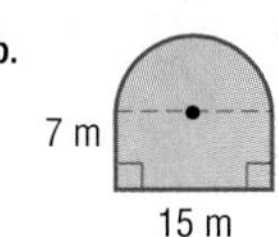

c.

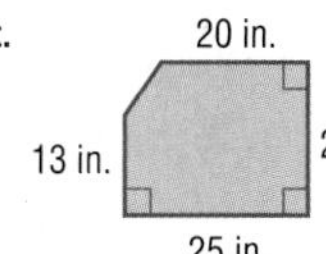

EXAMPLE Use the Area of a Complex Figure

Standardized Test Practice

3 **SHORT-RESPONSE TEST ITEM** The plans for one hole of a miniature golf course are shown. How many square feet of turf will be needed to cover the putting green if one square represents 1.5 square feet?

Read the Test Item You need to find the area of the putting green in square units and then multiply this result by 1.5 to find the area of the green in square feet.

Solve the Test Item Find the area of the green by dividing it into smaller areas.

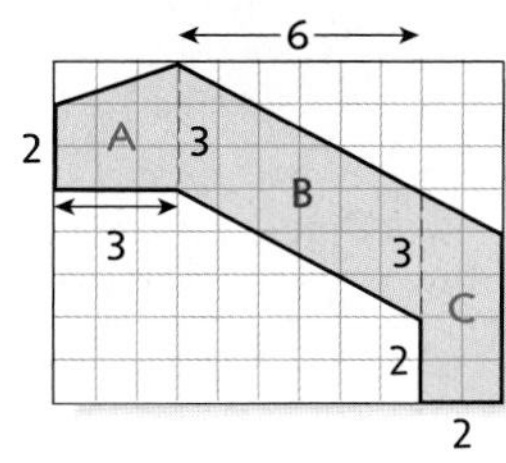

Region A Trapezoid

$A = \frac{1}{2}h(b_1 + b_2)$

$A = \frac{1}{2}(3)(2 + 3)$ or 7.5

Region B Parallelogram

$A = bh$

$A = 6 \cdot 3$ or 18

Region C Trapezoid

$A = \frac{1}{2}h(b_1 + b_2)$

$A = \frac{1}{2}(2)(4 + 5)$ or 9

The total area is 7.5 + 18 + 9 or 34.5 square units. So, 1.5(34.5) or 51.75 square feet of turf is needed to cover the green.

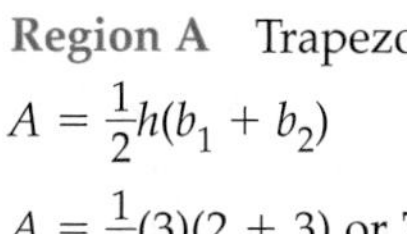

Test-Taking Tip

To check the reasonableness of your solution, estimate the area of the green. Count the *inner measure*, or the number of whole squares inside the figure. Then count the *outer measure*, which is the sum of the inner measure and any squares containing part of the figure. The mean of these two measures is an estimate of the area of the figure.

msmath3.net/extra_examples

2 Teach

In-Class Examples

1 Find the area of the complex figure. **45 in^2**

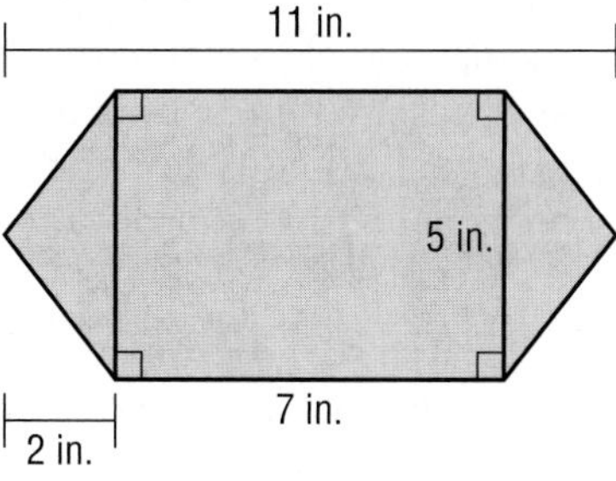

2 Find the area of the complex figure. Round to the nearest tenth. **100.3 cm^2**

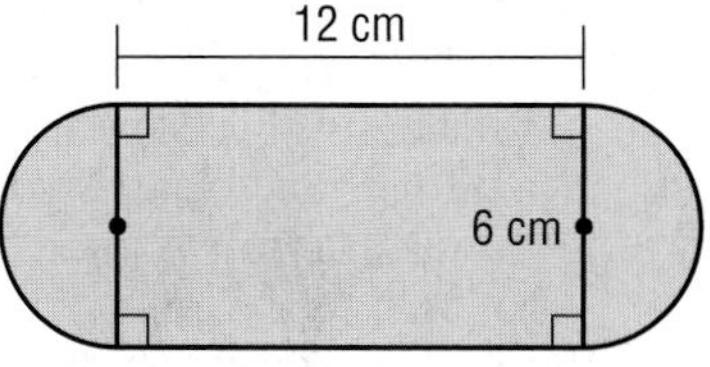

3 **SHORT-RESPONSE TEST ITEM** Below are the plans for the new deck on the Obwena's house. How many square feet of wood will be needed if one square represents two square feet?

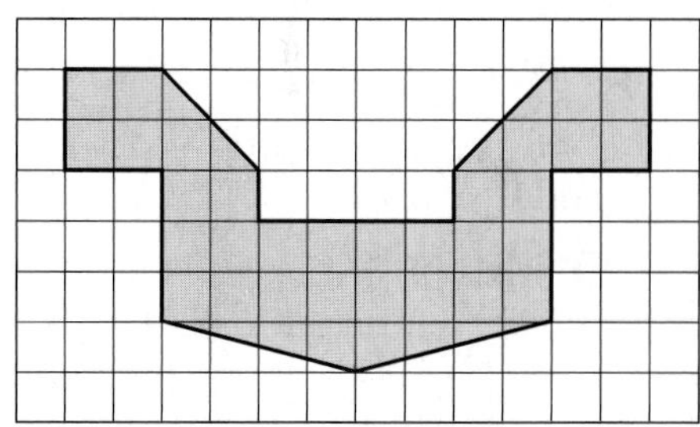

The area of the deck is 36 square units. You will need 2(36) or 72 ft^2 of wood to build the deck surface.

Tips for New Teachers

Teaching Strategies Challenge students to develop other methods for verifying their answers to Example 3 in the Student Edition. For example, after counting the inner measure of the figure, students might notice that Region A can be broken into a rectangle and a triangle, as can Region C. Determining the areas of these separate figures, combined with Region B (parallelogram), will give the overall area of the putting green.

Using Applications Magazines about building and architecture, which usually contain floor plans, can be used for activities such as identifying objects whose surfaces are represented by polygons and determining areas using formulas found in this section.

3 Practice/Apply

Remind students to record main ideas, definitions of vocabulary words, and other notes on study cards from this lesson in the *Area* pocket of their Foldables.

About the Exercises...

Guided Practice Key

Exercises	Examples
3–5	1, 2

Assignment Guide

Basic: 7–19 odd, 20–29

Average: 7–13 odd, 14, 15–19 odd, 20–29

Enriched: 6–12 even, 14–18, 20–25 (Optional: 26–29)

Students practice the same concepts in Exercises 6–13 if they are assigned odd or even problems.

Skill and Concept Check

1. **OPEN ENDED** Draw an example of a complex figure that can be separated into at least two different shapes whose area you know how to find. Then show how you would separate this figure to find its area. **See margin.**
2. *Writing Math* Explain at least two different ways of finding the area of the figure at the right. **Separate the figure horizontally into two trapezoids, find the area of each, and then find the sum of their areas; separate the figure vertically into two triangles and a square, find the area of each figure, then find the sum of their areas.**

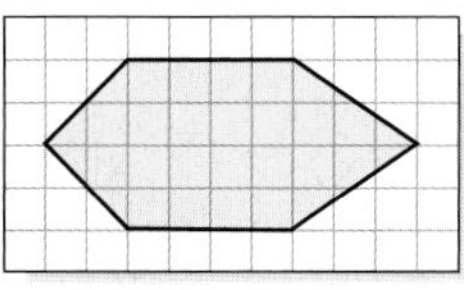

GUIDED PRACTICE

Find the area of each figure. Round to the nearest tenth if necessary.

3. **68 cm²**

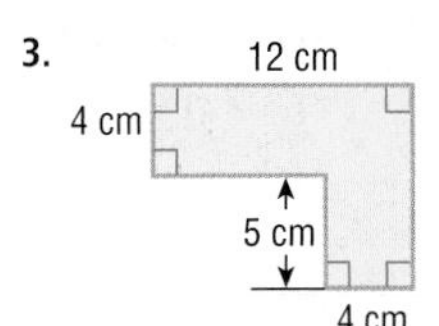

4. **78.1 yd²**

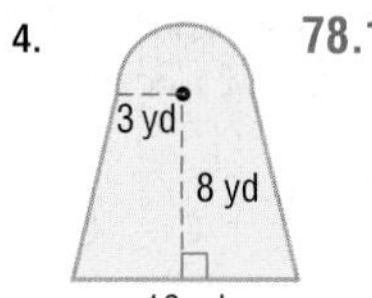
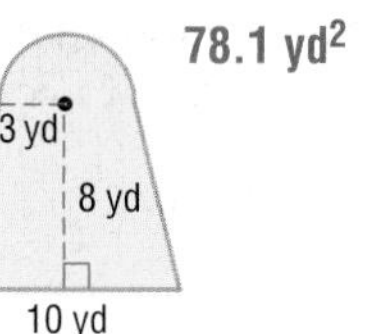

5. **216 in²**

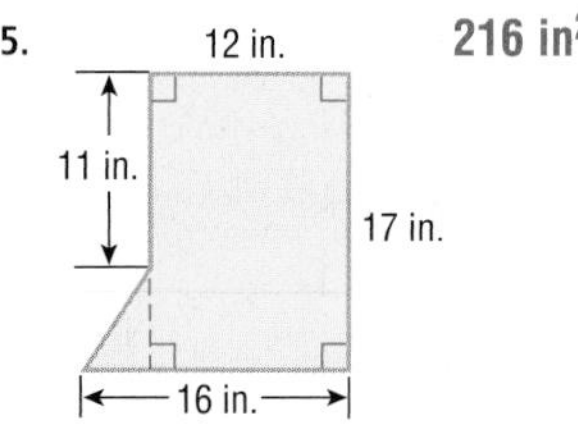

Practice and Applications

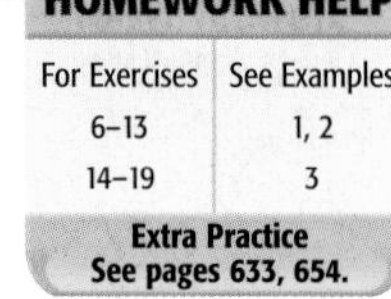

HOMEWORK HELP

For Exercises	See Examples
6–13	1, 2
14–19	3

Extra Practice See pages 633, 654.

Find the area of each figure. Round to the nearest tenth if necessary.

6. **220.5 cm²**

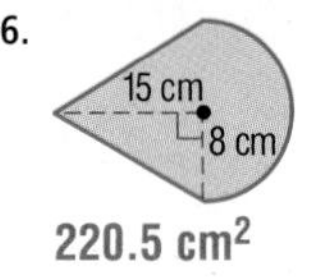

7. **240 yd²**

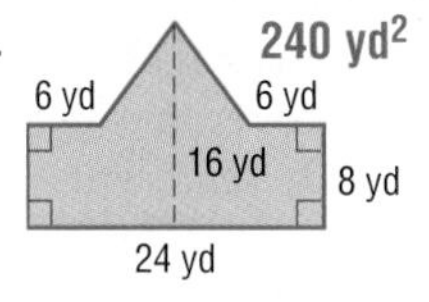

8. **142 in²**

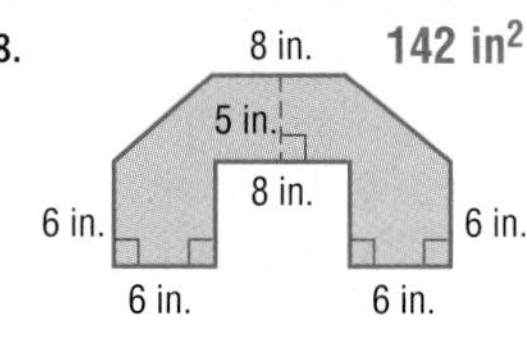

9. **87.5 m²**

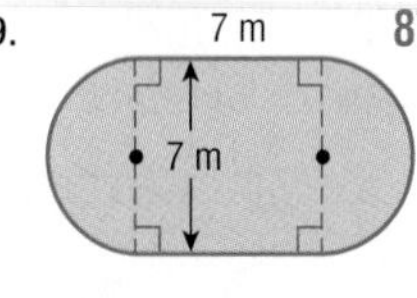

10. **38.6 ft²**

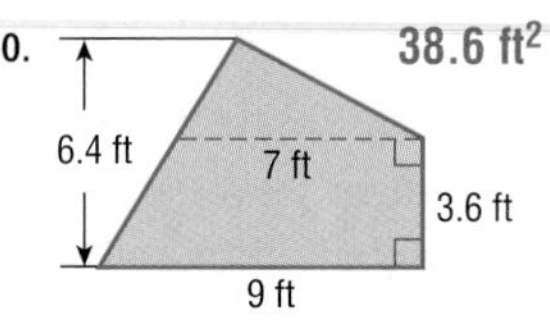

11. **121.2 cm²**

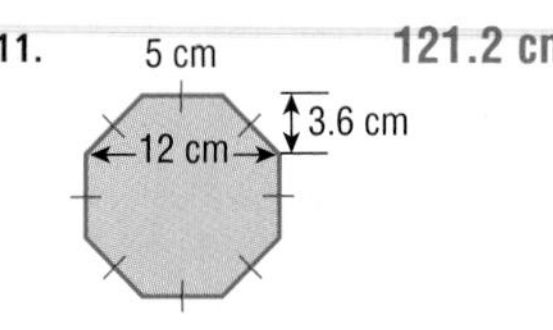

12. What is the area of a figure that is formed using a square with sides 15 yards and a triangle with a base of 8 yards and a height of 12 yards? **273 yd²**
13. What is the area of a figure that is formed using a trapezoid with one base of 9 meters, one base of 15 meters, and a height of 6 meters and a semicircle with a diameter of 9 meters? **103.8 m²**

FLAGS For Exercises 14–16, use the diagram of Ohio's state flag at the right. 14–15. See margin.

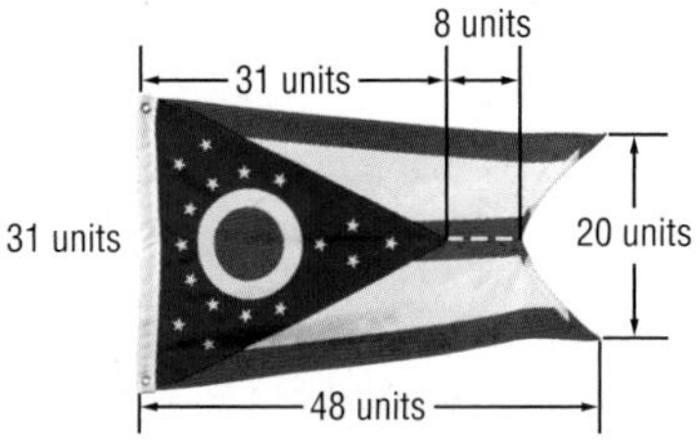

14. Find the area of the flag. Describe your method.
15. Find the area of the triangular region of the flag.
16. What percent of the total area of the flag is the triangular region? **about 42%**

8 units
31 units
31 units
20 units
48 units

Answers

1. Sample answer:

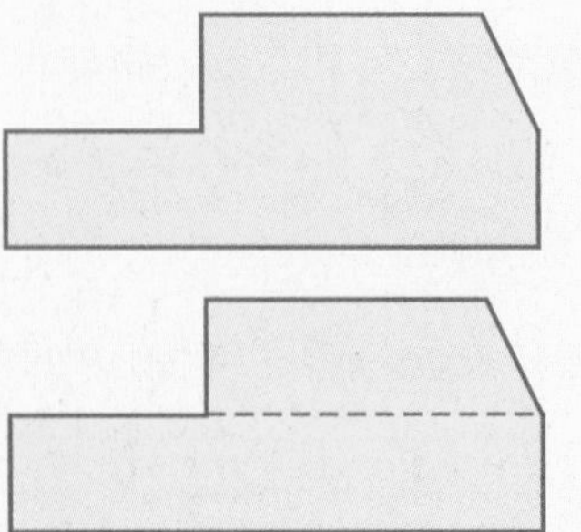

14. 1,134 units²; the flag is a trapezoid with bases 31 units and 20 units and a height of 48 units minus a triangle with a base of 20 units and a height of 48 − (31 + 8) units.
15. about 480.5 units²
17. The area to be painted is 857.5 ft², so 857.5 ÷ 350 or about 2.5 cans of paint are needed. Since you cannot buy half a can, you must buy 3 cans.
19. No, the area of the field is about 60,638.3 ft², so it will take 60,638.3 ÷ 1,750 or about 35 minutes to mow the field. The grounds crew only has 30 minutes.

HOME IMPROVEMENT For Exercises 17 and 18, use the diagram of one side of a house and the following information.
Suppose you are painting one side of your house. One gallon of paint covers 350 square feet and costs $21.95.

13 ft
18 ft
35 ft

17. If you are only planning to apply one coat of paint, how many cans should you buy? Explain your reasoning.
18. Find the total cost of the paint, not including tax. **$65.85**

17. 3 cans; See margin for explanation.

19. **MULTI STEP** A school's field, shown at the right, must be mowed before 10:00 A.M. on Monday. The maintenance crew says they can mow at a rate of 1,750 square feet of grass per minute. If the crew begins mowing at 9:30 that morning, will the field be mowed in time? Explain your reasoning. **See margin.**

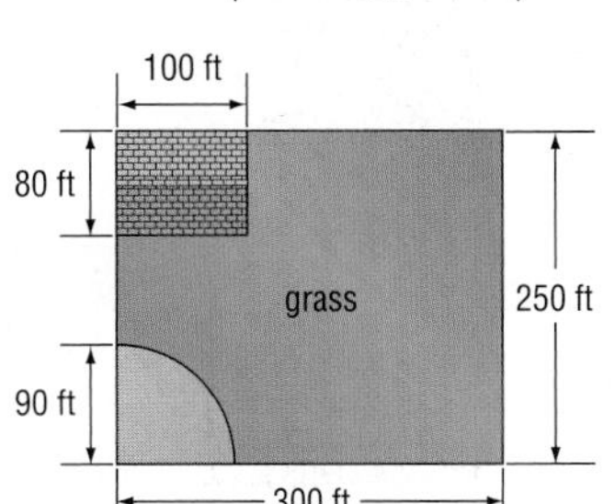

20. **CRITICAL THINKING** In the diagram at the right, a 3-foot wide wooden walkway surrounds a garden. What is the area of the walkway? **312 ft²**

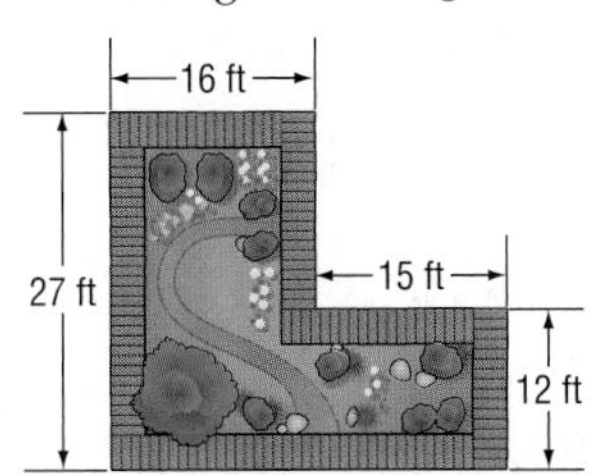

Spiral Review with Standardized Test Practice

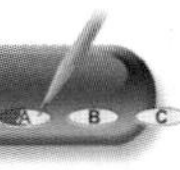

21. **MULTIPLE CHOICE** What is the area of the figure below? **C**

Ⓐ 17.5 m² Ⓑ 25.5 m² Ⓒ 437.5 m² Ⓓ 637.5 m²

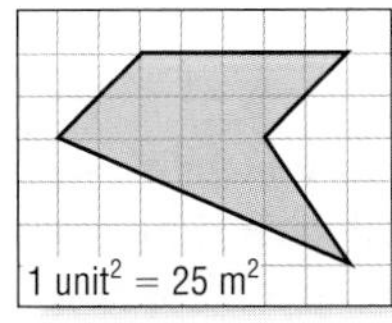

22. **MULTIPLE CHOICE** What is the best estimate for the area of the figure below? **G**

Ⓕ 36 units² Ⓖ 48 units² Ⓗ 54 units² Ⓘ 56 units²

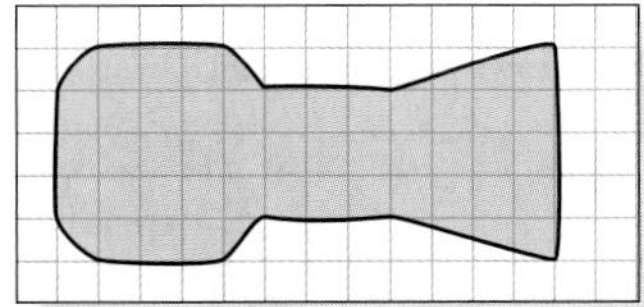

23. **MONUMENTS** Stonehenge is a circular array of giant stones in England. The diameter of Stonehenge is 30.5 meters. Find the approximate distance around Stonehenge. (Lesson 7-2) **95.8 m**

Find the area of each figure. (Lesson 7-1)

24. triangle: base, 4 mm
height, 3.5 mm **7 mm²**

25. trapezoid: height, 11 ft
bases, 17 ft and 23 ft **220 ft²**

GETTING READY FOR THE NEXT LESSON

BASIC SKILL Classify each polygon according to its number of sides.

26.  **triangle**

27.  **quadrilateral**

28.  **pentagon**

29. 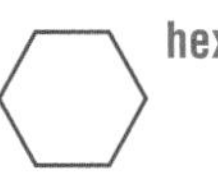 **hexagon**

Math Online msmath3.net/self_check_quiz

4 Assess

Higher-Level Thinking

Have students draw a complex figure and find the area of the figure in two different ways, writing about their methods in their journals. Ask students why it might be useful to see a problem two different ways.

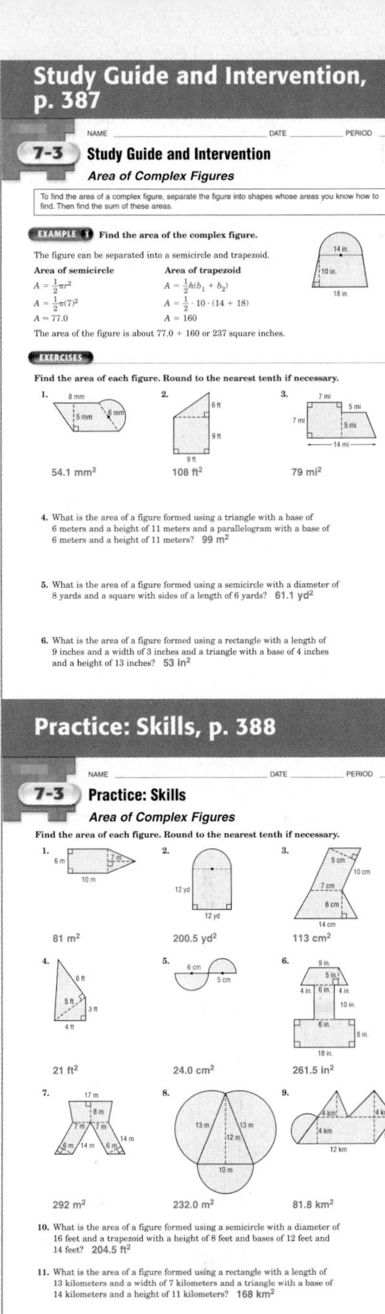

Study Guide and Intervention, p. 387

NAME ______ DATE ______ PERIOD ____

7-3 Study Guide and Intervention

Area of Complex Figures

To find the area of a complex figure, separate the figure into shapes whose areas you know how to find. Then find the sum of these areas.

EXAMPLE 1 Find the area of the complex figure.

The figure can be separated into a semicircle and trapezoid.

Area of semicircle	Area of trapezoid
$A = \frac{1}{2}\pi r^2$	$A = \frac{1}{2}h(b_1 + b_2)$
$A = \frac{1}{2}\pi(7)^2$	$A = \frac{1}{2} \cdot 10 \cdot (14 + 18)$
$A \approx 77.0$	$A = 160$

The area of the figure is about 77.0 + 160 or 237 square inches.

EXERCISES

Find the area of each figure. Round to the nearest tenth if necessary.

1. 54.1 mm²
2. 108 ft²
3. 79 mi²

4. What is the area of a figure formed using a triangle with a base of 6 meters and a height of 11 meters and a parallelogram with a base of 6 meters and a height of 11 meters? 99 m²

5. What is the area of a figure formed using a semicircle with a diameter of 8 yards and a square with sides of a length of 6 yards? 61.1 yd²

6. What is the area of a figure formed using a rectangle with a length of 9 inches and a width of 3 inches and a triangle with a base of 4 inches and a height of 13 inches? 53 in²

Practice: Skills, p. 388

NAME ______ DATE ______ PERIOD ____

7-3 Practice: Skills

Area of Complex Figures

Find the area of each figure. Round to the nearest tenth if necessary.

1. 81 m²
2. 200.5 yd²
3. 113 cm²
4. 21 ft²
5. 24.0 cm²
6. 261.5 in²
7. 292 m²
8. 232.0 m²
9. 81.8 km²

10. What is the area of a figure formed using a semicircle with a diameter of 16 feet and a trapezoid with a height of 8 feet and bases of 12 feet and 14 feet? 204.5 ft²

11. What is the area of a figure formed using a rectangle with a length of 13 kilometers and a width of 7 kilometers and a triangle with a base of 14 kilometers and a height of 11 kilometers? 168 km²

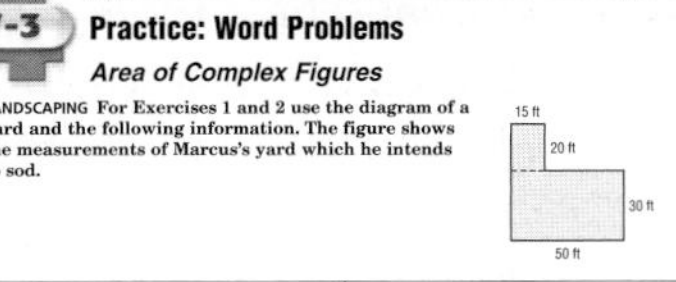

Practice: Word Problems, p. 389

NAME ______ DATE ______ PERIOD ____

7-3 Practice: Word Problems

Area of Complex Figures

LANDSCAPING For Exercises 1 and 2 use the diagram of a yard and the following information. The figure shows the measurements of Marcus's yard which he intends to sod.

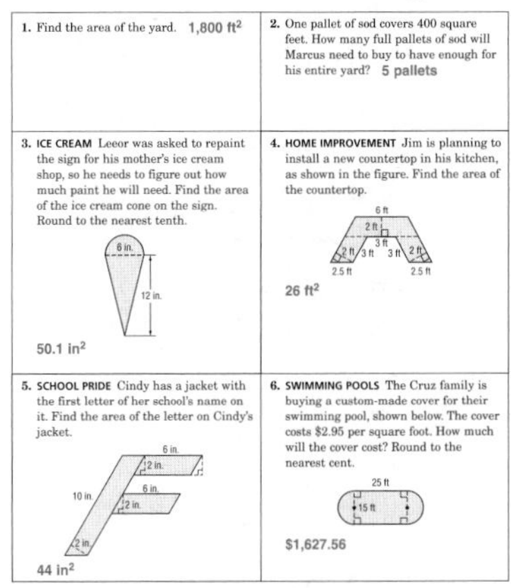

1. Find the area of the yard. 1,800 ft²	2. One pallet of sod covers 400 square feet. How many full pallets of sod will Marcus need to buy to have enough for his entire yard? 5 pallets
3. ICE CREAM Leeor was asked to repaint the sign for his mother's ice cream shop, so he needs to figure out how much paint he will need. Find the area of the ice cream cone on the sign. Round to the nearest tenth. 50.1 in²	4. HOME IMPROVEMENT Jim is planning to install a new countertop in his kitchen, as shown in the figure. Find the area of the countertop. 26 ft²
5. SCHOOL PRIDE Cindy has a jacket with the first letter of her school's name on it. Find the area of the letter on Cindy's jacket. 44 in²	6. SWIMMING POOLS The Cruz family is buying a custom-made cover for their swimming pool, shown below. The cover costs $2.95 per square foot. How much will the cover cost? Round to the nearest cent. $1,627.56

7-4a HANDS-ON LAB Lesson Notes

Lesson Resources

Teaching Mathematics with Manipulatives
- isometric dot paper, p. 13
- cube pattern, p. 23
- student recording sheet 7-4a

Glencoe Mathematics Classroom Manipulative Kit
- centimeter cubes
- isometric dot grid stamp
- ink pad

GETTING STARTED

Teaching Tip Model the **Activity** on an overhead as students follow along at their seats. You may wish to have students use colored pencils or crayons whose colors correspond to the cube colors to help them draw the cubes from the correct corner perspective.

TEACH

- Suggest that students build their figures on a piece of paper labeled correctly with *side* and *front*. Have them rotate the mat to view the sides and place the figure at a good angle for drawing.
- Have students count the number of blocks that they have used for the exercises, and compare their numbers with other groups. Ask whether they could add or remove blocks and still get the same front, top, and side views.

7-4a HANDS-ON LAB

A Preview of Lesson 7-4

Building Three-Dimensional Figures

What You'll LEARN

Build and draw three-dimensional figures.

Link to READING

Everyday Meaning of Perspective: the ability to view things in their true relationship or importance to one another.

Materials
- cubes
- isometric dot paper

Different views of a stack of cubes are shown in the activity below. A point of view is called a **perspective**. You can build or draw three-dimensional figures using different perspectives.

ACTIVITY *Work with a partner.*

The top, side, and front views of a three-dimensional figure are shown. Use cubes to build the figure. Then, draw your model on isometric dot paper.

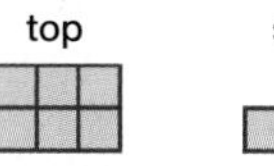

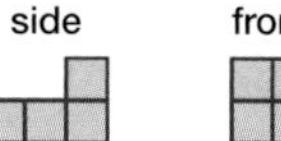

Build Base Using Top View

The base is a 2 by 3 rectangle.

Complete Figure Using Side View

The 1st and 2nd rows are 1 unit high.

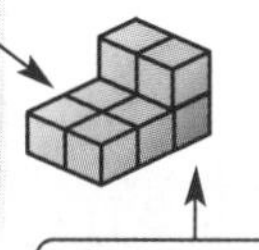

The 3rd row is 2 units high.

Check Figure Using Front View

The overall width is 2 units.

The overall height is 2 units.

Now draw your model on isometric dot paper as shown at the right. Label the front and the side of your figure.

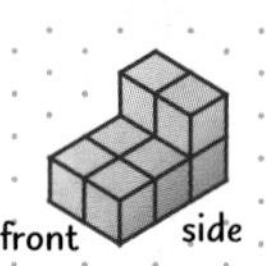

Your Turn **The top, side, and front views of three-dimensional figures are shown. Use cubes to build each figure. Then draw your model on isometric dot paper, labeling its front and side.**

a.

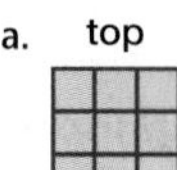

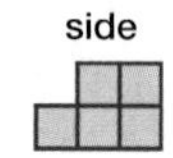

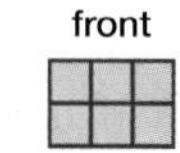

b.

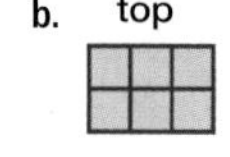

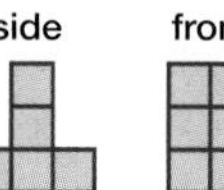

a–b. See Ch. 7 Answer Appendix.

Writing Math

1. **Determine** which view, *top*, *side*, or *front*, would show that a building has multiple heights. **side**
2. **Build** your own figure using up to 20 cubes and draw it on isometric dot paper. Then **draw** the figure's top, side, and front views. **Explain** your reasoning. **See Ch. 7 Answer Appendix.**

ASSESS

Observe as students solve the **Your Turn** exercises. They should:
- build figures with the indicated top, side, and front, and
- draw figures on isometric dot paper, labeling a side and front.

7-4 Three-Dimensional Figures

What You'll LEARN

Identify and draw three-dimensional figures.

NEW Vocabulary

plane
solid
polyhedron
edge
face
vertex
prism
base
pyramid

WHEN am I ever going to use this?

Amethyst

CRYSTALS A two-dimensional figure has two dimensions, length and width. A three-dimensional figure, like the Amethyst crystal shown at the right, has three dimensions, length, width, and depth (or height).

top

sides

bottom

1. Name the two-dimensional shapes that make up the sides of this crystal. **triangle, rectangle**
2. If you observed the crystal from directly above, what two-dimensional figure would you see? **hexagon**
3. How are two- and three-dimensional figures related?

A **plane** is a two-dimensional flat surface that extends in all directions. There are different ways that planes may be related in space.

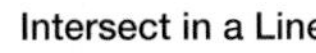

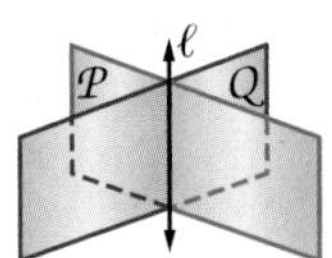

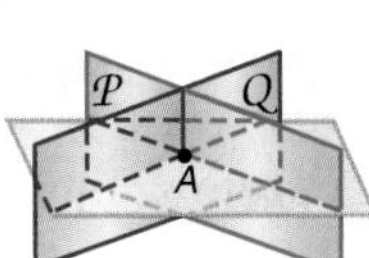

No Intersection

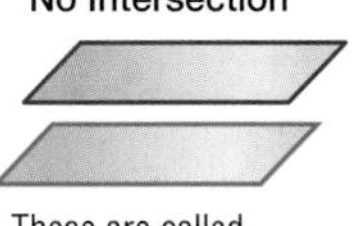

These are called *parallel planes.*

Intersecting planes can also form three-dimensional figures or **solids**. A **polyhedron** is a solid with flat surfaces that are polygons.

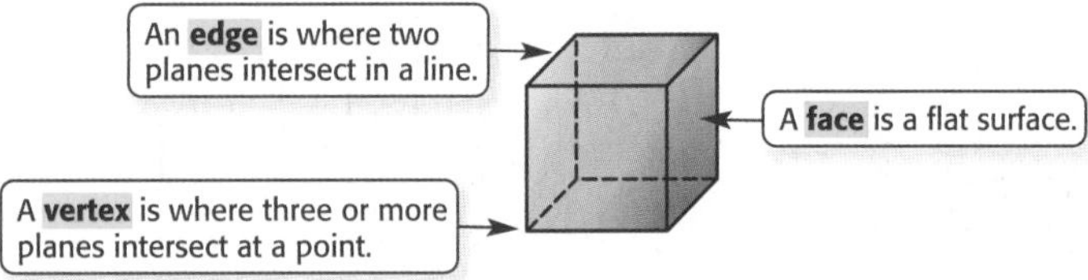

A **prism** is a polyhedron with two parallel, congruent faces called **bases**. A **pyramid** is a polyhedron with one base that is a polygon and faces that are triangles.

prism

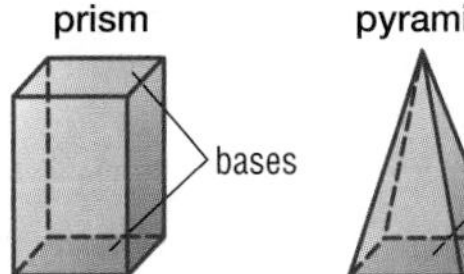

pyramid

base

Prisms and pyramids are named by the shape of their bases.

msmath3.net/extra_examples

7-4 Lesson Notes

Lesson Resources

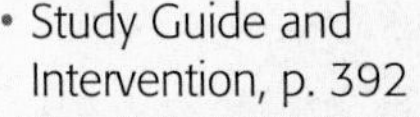

Chapter 7 Resource Masters
- Study Guide and Intervention, p. 392
- Practice: Skills, p. 393
- Practice: Word Problems, p. 394
- Reading to Learn Mathematics, p. 395
- Enrichment, p. 396

Classroom Math Games, pp. 27–29
Key Teaching Transparencies, 25
MathPASS Tutorial CD-ROM, 48
Parent and Student Study Guide Online Worksheets, 7-4
Noteables™: Interactive Study Notebook with Foldables™, 7-4

1 Focus

5-Minute Check 7-4

Use as a quiz or review of Lesson 7-3. (Also available as a transparency)

Bellringer

Reading Mathematics Write *hexagon, polygon, octagon, decagon,* and *pentagon* on the chalkboard. Have students look up the definitions of the prefixes. Discuss how they relate to the meaning of the words. Then ask students to come up with one or two more words that contain the same prefix.

Reading to Learn Mathematics, p. 395 ELL

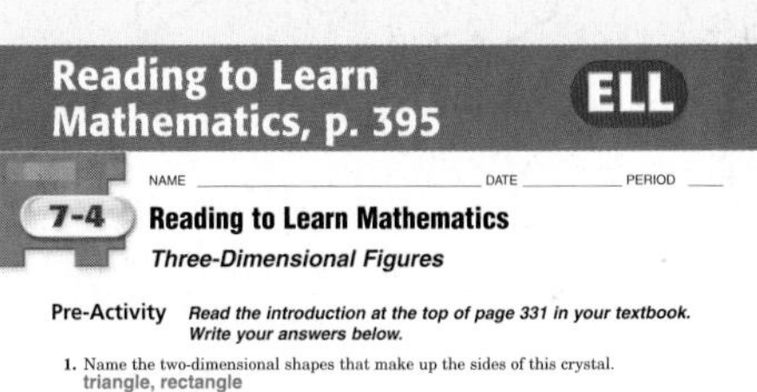
NAME DATE PERIOD

7-4 **Reading to Learn Mathematics**
Three-Dimensional Figures

Pre-Activity *Read the introduction at the top of page 331 in your textbook. Write your answers below.*

1. Name the two-dimensional shapes that make up the sides of this crystal. triangle, rectangle
2. If you observed the crystal from directly above, what two-dimensional figure would you see? hexagon
3. How are two- and three-dimensional figures related? Two-dimensional figures make up three-dimensional figures.

Reading the Lesson

4. A plane is a two-dimensional flat surface that extends in all directions. What is formed when two planes intersect? a line

DAILY INTERVENTION **Flexible Grouping**

Three-Dimensional Figures Separate students into groups of up to four, and have them use isometric dot paper to draw three-dimensional views of figures in the classroom that resemble polyhedra. Then have them trade drawings with their group members, who should draw the top, front, and side views.

2 Teach

In-Class Examples

INTERACTIVE CHALKBOARD PowerPoint® Presentations

Identify each solid. Name the number and shapes of the faces. Then name the number of edges and vertices.

1

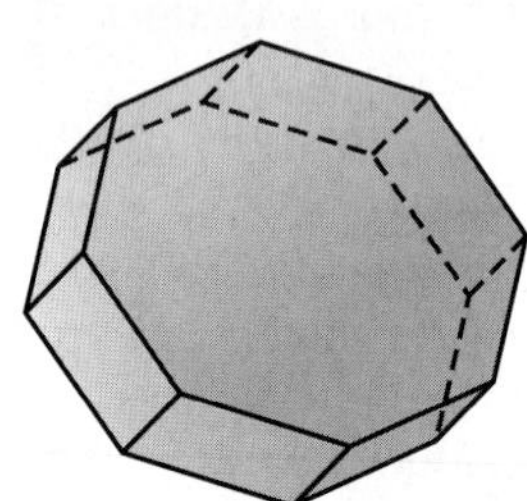

octagonal prism; 2 octagonal faces, 8 rectangular faces, 24 edges, 16 vertices

2

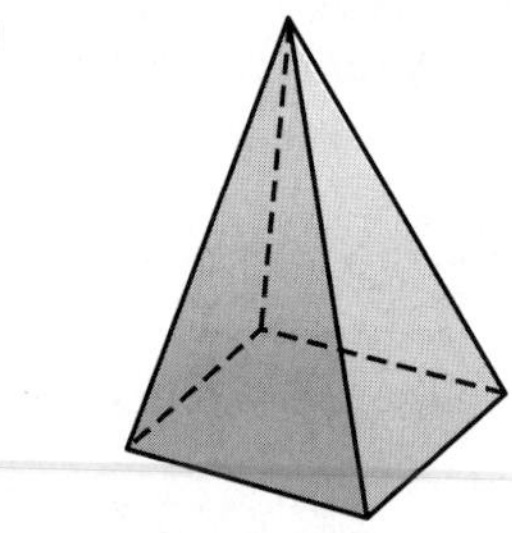

rectangular pyramid; 1 rectangular base, 4 triangular faces, 8 edges, 5 vertices

3 **ARCHITECTURE** The plans for a hotel fireplace are shown below. Each unit on the drawing represents 1.5 feet. Draw and label the top, front, and side views.

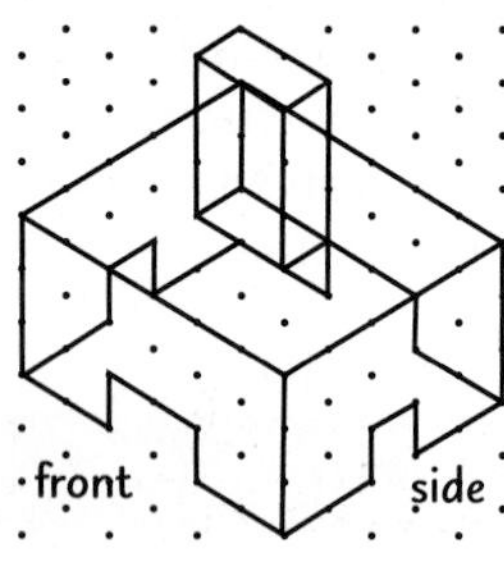

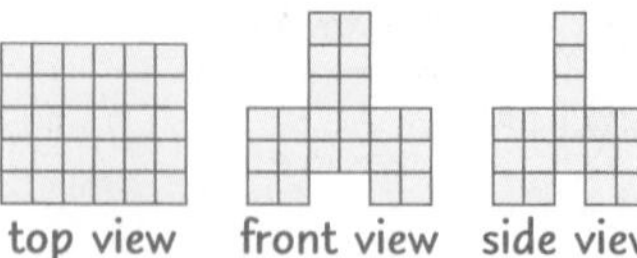

4 **ARCHITECTURE** Find the area of the floor covered by the fireplace. 67.5 ft^2

Noteables™ **Key Concept: Common Polyhedrons**

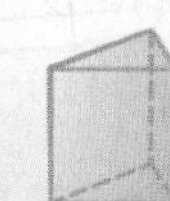
triangular prism

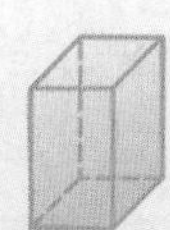
rectangular prism

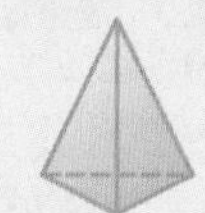
triangular pyramid

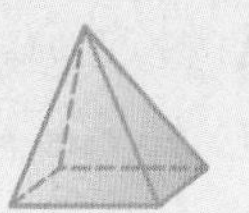
rectangular pyramid

STUDY TIP

Common Error In a rectangular prism, the bases do not have to be on the top and bottom. Any two parallel rectangles are bases. In a triangular pyramid, any face is a base.

EXAMPLES Identify Prisms and Pyramids

Identify each solid. Name the number and shapes of the faces. Then name the number of edges and vertices.

1 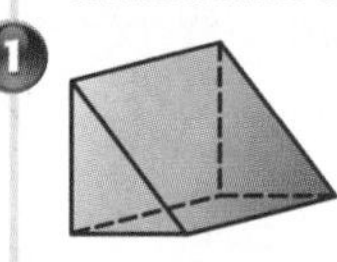

The figure has two parallel congruent bases that are triangles, so it is a triangular prism. The other three faces are rectangles. It has a total of 5 faces, 9 edges, and 6 vertices.

2 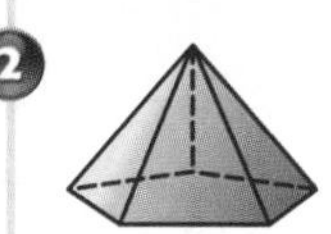

The figure has one base that is a pentagon, so it is a pentagonal pyramid. The other faces are triangles. It has a total of 6 faces, 10 edges, and 6 vertices.

Your Turn **Identify each solid. Name the number and shapes of the faces. Then name the number of edges and vertices.**

a. 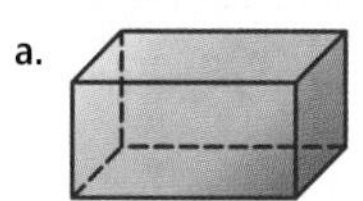

b. 

c. 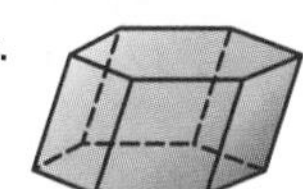

a. rectangular prism; 6 faces, all rectangles; 12 edges; 8 vertices
b. triangular pyramid; 4 faces, all triangles; 6 edges; 4 vertices
c. hexagonal prism; 8 faces, two hexagons and 6 parallelograms; 18 edges; 12 vertices

REAL-LIFE MATH

ARCHITECTURE Architects use computer aided design and drafting technology to produce their drawings.

EXAMPLES Analyze Real-Life Drawings

3 **ARCHITECTURE** **An artist's drawing shows the plans for a new office building. Each unit on the drawing represents 50 feet. Draw and label the top, front, and side views.**

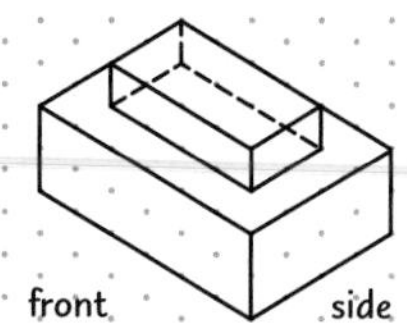

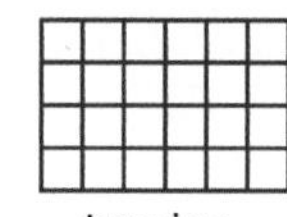
top view

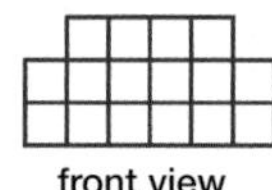
front view

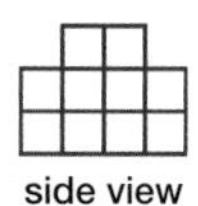
side view

4 **ARCHITECTURE** **Find the area of the top floor.**

You can see from the front and side views that the top floor is a rectangle that is 2 units wide by 4 units long. The actual dimensions are 4(50) feet by 2(50) feet or 200 feet by 100 feet.

$A = 200 \cdot 100$ $A = \ell \cdot w$

$A = 20{,}000$ Simplify.

The area of the top floor is 20,000 square feet.

Answers

1. a: vertex; b: face; c: base; d: edge
3. rectangular prism; 6 faces, all rectangles; 12 edges; 8 vertices
4. triangular prism; 5 faces, 2 triangles and 3 rectangles; 9 edges; 6 vertices
5. rectangular pyramid; 5 faces, 1 rectangle and 4 triangles; 8 edges; 5 vertices
6. Sample answer:

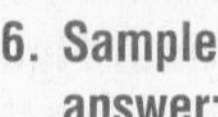

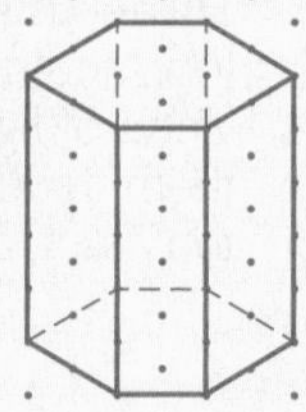

Students practice the same concepts in Exercises 7–12 if they are assigned odd or even problems.

Skill and Concept Check

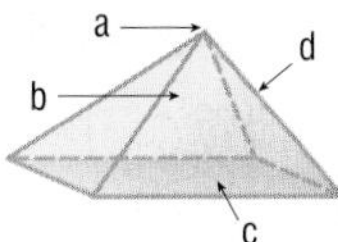

1. **Identify** the indicated parts of the polyhedron at the right. **See margin.**
2. **OPEN ENDED** Give a real-life example of three intersecting planes and describe their intersection. **Sample answer: two walls of a room intersect the floor in a point or corner.**

GUIDED PRACTICE

Identify each solid. Name the number and shapes of the faces. Then name the number of edges and vertices. **3–5. See margin.**

3. 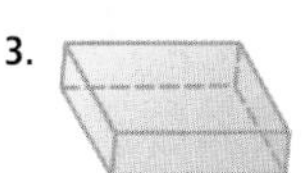
4. 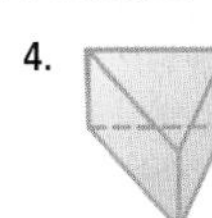
5. 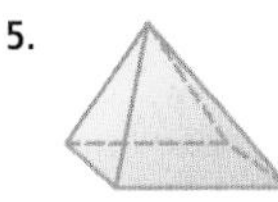

6. **PETS** Your pet lizard lives in an aquarium with a hexagonal base and a height of 5 units. Draw the aquarium using isometric dot paper. **See margin.**

Practice and Applications

Identify each solid. Name the number and shapes of the faces. Then name the number of edges and vertices. **7–10. See margin.**

7. 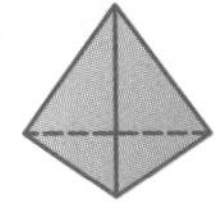
8. 
9. 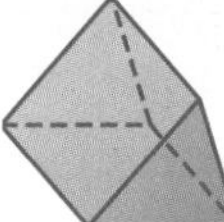
10. 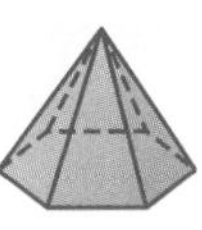

HOMEWORK HELP	
For Exercises	See Examples
7–10	1, 2
11–12, 16–18	3

Extra Practice See pages 633, 654.

ARCHITECTURE For Exercises 11 and 12, complete parts a–c for each architectural drawing. **11–12. See margin.**

a. **Draw and label the top, front, and side views.**
b. **Find the overall height of the solid in feet.**
c. **Find the area of the shaded region.**

11. Sculpture Pedestal

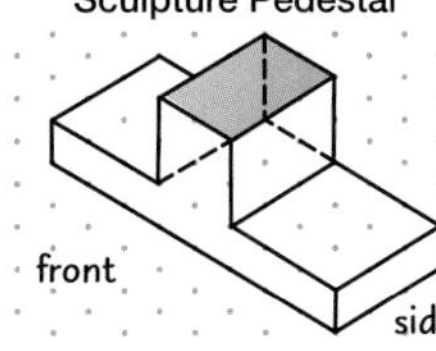

1 unit = 6 in.

12. Porch Steps

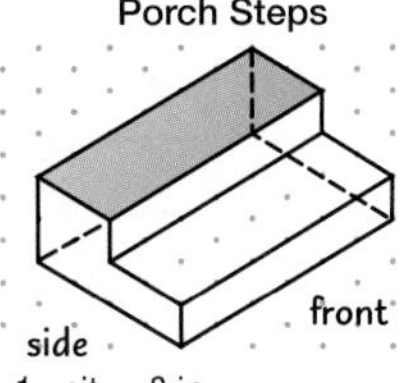

1 unit = 8 in.

Determine whether each statement is *sometimes*, *always*, or *never* true. Explain your reasoning.

13. Three planes do not intersect in a point. **Sometimes; see margin.**
14. A prism has two congruent bases. **always; definition of a prism**
15. A pyramid has five vertices. **Sometimes; see margin.**

msmath3.net/self_check_quiz

3 Practice/Apply

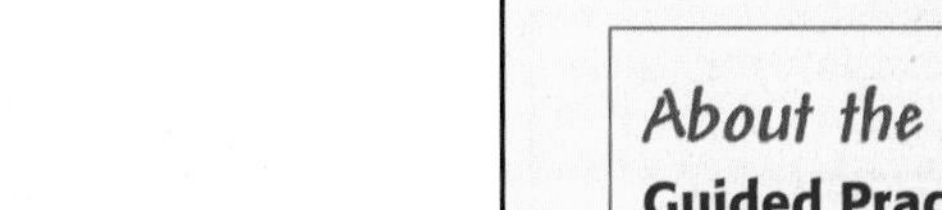

About the Exercises...

Guided Practice Key

Exercises	Examples
3–5	1, 2
6	3

Assignment Guide

Basic: 7–17 odd, 19, 23–31

Average: 7–17 odd, 19, 23–31 (Optional: 20–22)

Enriched: 8–18 even, 19–28 (Optional: 29–31)

Answers

7. triangular pyramid; 4 faces, all triangles; 6 edges; 4 vertices
8. rectangular prism; 6 faces, all rectangles; 12 edges; 8 vertices
9. triangular prism; 5 faces, 2 triangles and 3 rectangles; 9 edges; 6 vertices
10. hexagonal pyramid; 7 faces, 1 hexagon and 6 triangles; 12 edges; 7 vertices

11a. See bottom margin.

11b. $1\frac{1}{2}$ ft

11c. $1\frac{1}{2}$ ft^2

12a. See bottom margin.

12b. $1\frac{1}{3}$ ft

12c. $5\frac{1}{3}$ ft^2

13. Three planes can intersect in a line or not intersect at all if two or more are parallel.
15. A rectangular prism has 5 vertices, but a triangular prism has 4.

11a.

top view

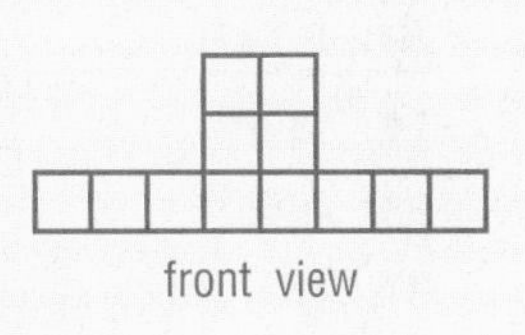

front view

side view

12a.

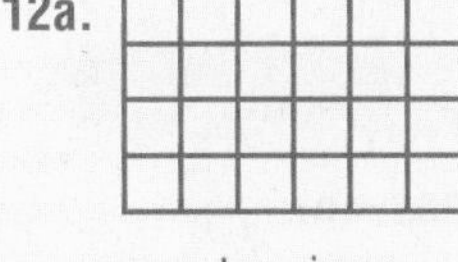

top view

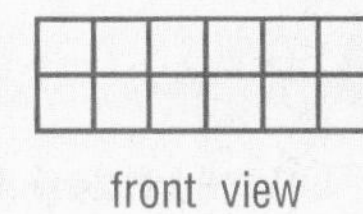

front view

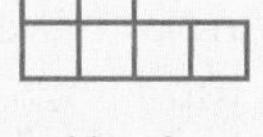

side view

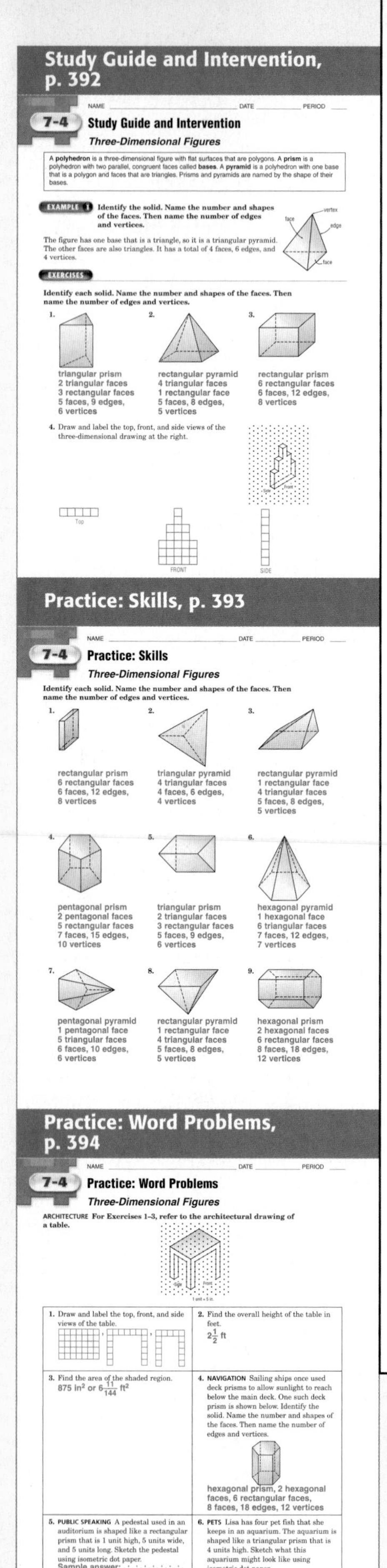
Study Guide and Intervention, p. 392

NAME ______ DATE ______ PERIOD ______

7-4 Study Guide and Intervention

Three-Dimensional Figures

A **polyhedron** is a three-dimensional figure with flat surfaces that are polygons. A **prism** is a polyhedron with two parallel, congruent faces called **bases**. A **pyramid** is a polyhedron with one base that is a polygon and faces that are triangles. Prisms and pyramids are named by the shape of their bases.

EXAMPLE 1 Identify the solid. Name the number and shapes of the faces. Then name the number of edges and vertices.

The figure has one base that is a triangle, so it is a triangular pyramid. The other faces are also triangles. It has a total of 4 faces, 6 edges, and 4 vertices.

EXERCISES

Identify each solid. Name the number and shapes of the faces. Then name the number of edges and vertices.

1. triangular prism, 2 triangular faces, 3 rectangular faces, 5 faces, 9 edges, 6 vertices
2. rectangular pyramid, 4 triangular faces, 1 rectangular face, 5 faces, 8 edges, 5 vertices
3. rectangular prism, 6 rectangular faces, 6 faces, 12 edges, 8 vertices
4. Draw and label the top, front, and side views of the three-dimensional drawing at the right.

Top FRONT SIDE

Practice: Skills, p. 393

NAME ______ DATE ______ PERIOD ______

7-4 Practice: Skills

Three-Dimensional Figures

Identify each solid. Name the number and shapes of the faces. Then name the number of edges and vertices.

1. rectangular prism, 6 rectangular faces, 6 faces, 12 edges, 8 vertices
2. triangular pyramid, 4 triangular faces, 4 faces, 6 edges, 4 vertices
3. rectangular pyramid, 1 rectangular face, 4 triangular faces, 5 faces, 8 edges, 5 vertices
4. pentagonal prism, 2 pentagonal faces, 5 rectangular faces, 7 faces, 15 edges, 10 vertices
5. triangular prism, 2 triangular faces, 3 rectangular faces, 5 faces, 9 edges, 6 vertices
6. hexagonal pyramid, 1 hexagonal face, 6 triangular faces, 7 faces, 12 edges, 7 vertices
7. pentagonal pyramid, 1 pentagonal face, 5 triangular faces, 6 faces, 10 edges, 6 vertices
8. rectangular pyramid, 1 rectangular face, 4 triangular faces, 5 faces, 8 edges, 5 vertices
9. hexagonal prism, 2 hexagonal faces, 6 rectangular faces, 8 faces, 18 edges, 12 vertices

Practice: Word Problems, p. 394

NAME ______ DATE ______ PERIOD ______

7-4 Practice: Word Problems

Three-Dimensional Figures

ARCHITECTURE For Exercises 1–3, refer to the architectural drawing of a table.

1. Draw and label the top, front, and side views of the table.
2. Find the overall height of the table in feet. $2\frac{1}{2}$ ft
3. Find the area of the shaded region. 875 in² or $6\frac{11}{144}$ ft²
4. NAVIGATION Sailing ships once used deck prisms to allow sunlight to reach below the main deck. One such deck prism is shown below. Identify the solid. Name the number and shapes of the faces. Then name the number of edges and vertices. hexagonal prism, 2 hexagonal faces, 6 rectangular faces, 8 faces, 18 edges, 12 vertices
5. PUBLIC SPEAKING A pedestal used in an auditorium is shaped like a rectangular prism that is 1 unit high, 5 units wide, and 5 units long. Sketch the pedestal using isometric dot paper. Sample answer:
6. PETS Lisa has four pet fish that she keeps in an aquarium. The aquarium is shaped like a triangular prism that is 4 units high. Sketch what this aquarium might look like using isometric dot paper. Sample answer:

CRYSTALS For Exercises 16–18, complete parts a and b for each crystal.

a. Identify the solid or solids that form the crystal. **16–18. See Ch. 7 Answer Appendix.**

b. Draw and label the top and one side view of the crystal.

16. 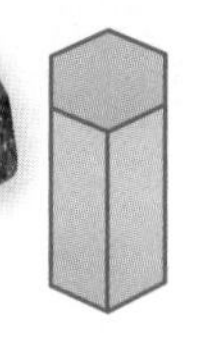

Emerald

17. 

Fluorite

18. 

Quartz

19. **CRITICAL THINKING** A pyramid with a triangular base has 6 edges and a pyramid with a rectangular base has 8 edges. Write a formula that gives the number of edges E for a pyramid with an n-sided base. $E = 2n$

EXTENDING THE LESSON *Skew lines* do not intersect, but are also not parallel. They lie in different planes. In the figure at the right, the lines containing $\overline{AD}$ and $\overline{CG}$ are skew. $\overline{BH}$ is a *diagonal* of this prism because it joins two vertices that have no faces in common.

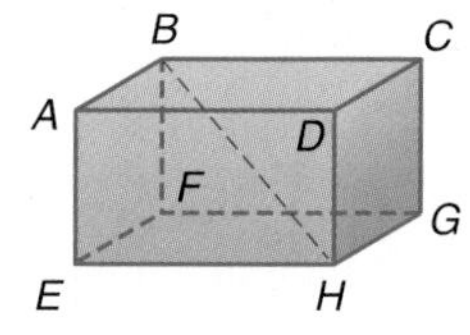

For Exercises 20–22, use the rectangular prism above.

20. Identify three other diagonals that could have been drawn. $\overline{FD}$, $\overline{EC}$, and $\overline{AG}$
21. Name two segments that are skew to $\overline{BH}$. $\overline{EF}$ and $\overline{AD}$
22. State whether $\overline{DH}$ and $\overline{CG}$ are *parallel, skew,* or *intersecting*. **parallel**

Spiral Review with Standardized Test Practice

For Exercises 23 and 24, use the figure at the right.

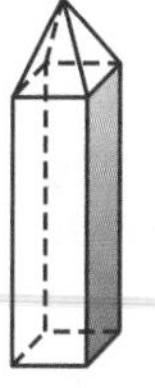

23. **SHORT RESPONSE** Identify the two polyhedrons that make up the figure. **top: rectangular pyramid; bottom: rectangular prism**
24. **MULTIPLE CHOICE** Identify the shaded part of the figure. **B**

    (A) edge (B) face (C) vertex (D) prism

Find the area of each figure. Round to the nearest tenth. (Lesson 7-3)

25. **146.3 ft²** 26. **81.9 m²** 27. **161.1 in²**

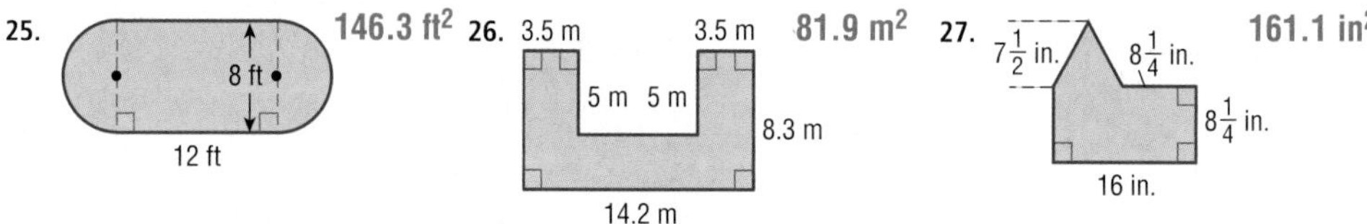

28. **MANUFACTURING** The label that goes around a jar of peanut butter overlaps itself by $\frac{3}{8}$ inch. If the diameter of the jar is 2 inches, what is the length of the label? (Lesson 7-2) **about 6.7 in.**

GETTING READY FOR THE NEXT LESSON

PREREQUISITE SKILL **Find the area of each triangle described.** (Lesson 7-1) **29–31. See margin.**

29. base, 3 in.; height, 10 in.
30. base, 8 ft; height, 7 feet
31. base, 5 cm; height, 11 cm

4 Assess

Open-Ended Assessment

Modeling Have students use their imaginations to build elaborate structures like the Eiffel Tower with cubes. Then have them draw the side, front, and top views of their towers.

Answers

29. 15 in²
30. 28 ft²
31. 27.5 cm²

Volume of Prisms and Cylinders

What You'll LEARN

Find the volumes of prisms and cylinders.

NEW Vocabulary

volume
cylinder
complex solid

HANDS-ON Mini Lab

Materials

- 12 cubes

The rectangular prism at the right has a volume of 12 cubic units.

 Model three other rectangular prisms with a volume of 12 cubic units.

 Copy and complete the following table.

Sample answers given.

Prism	Length (units)	Width (units)	Height (units)	Area of Base (units²)
A	4	1	3	4
B	2	3	2	6
C	6	1	2	6
D	12	1	1	12

1. Describe how the volume V of each prism is related to its length ℓ, width w, and height h. $V = \ell wh$
2. Describe how the area of the base B and the height h of each prism is related to its volume V. $V = Bh$

Volume is the measure of the space occupied by a solid. Standard measures of volume are cubic units such as cubic inches (in^3) or cubic feet (ft^3).

Noteables™ **Key Concept: Volume of a Prism**

Words The volume V of a prism is the area of the base B times the height h.

Models

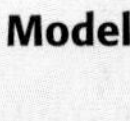

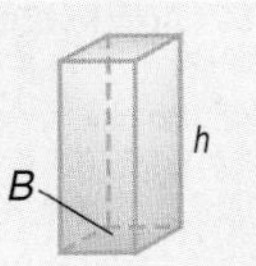

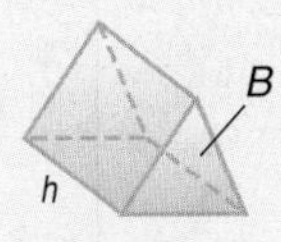

Symbols $V = Bh$

EXAMPLE Find the Volume of a Rectangular Prism

 **Find the volume of the prism.**

6.5 cm
5 cm
9 cm

$V = Bh$ Volume of a prism

$V = (\ell \cdot w)h$ The base is a rectangle, so $B = \ell \cdot w$.

$V = (9 \cdot 5)6.5$ $\ell = 9$, $w = 5$, $h = 6.5$

$V = 292.5$ Simplify.

The volume is 292.5 cubic centimeters.

TEACHING TIP

Point out to students that the formula for the volume of a prism is often written as $V = \ell wh$, since the area of the base B of a rectangular prism is always equal to ℓw.

7-5 Lesson Notes

Lesson Resources

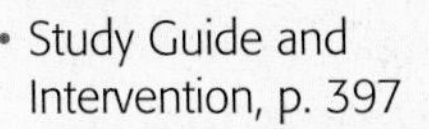

Chapter 7 Resource Masters FAST FILE
- Study Guide and Intervention, p. 397
- Practice: Skills, p. 398
- Practice: Word Problems, p. 399
- Reading to Learn Mathematics, p. 400
- Enrichment, p. 401

Calculator and Spreadsheet Masters, p. 32
MathPASS Tutorial CD-ROM, 52
Parent and Student Study Guide Online Worksheets, 7-5
Science and Math Lab Masters, pp. 77–80
Noteables™: Interactive Study Notebook with Foldables™, 7-5

1 Focus

5-Minute Check 7-5

Use as a quiz or review of Lesson 7-4. (Also available as a transparency)

Bellringer

Hands-On Activity Have students bring in objects from home that have the volume printed on the label, such as an empty milk jug or an empty jelly jar. Discuss what the volume measure means and compare the volumes of the different-sized containers. Find two containers

(Continued in bottom margin.)

Reading to Learn Mathematics, p. 400 **ELL**

NAME ______ DATE ______ PERIOD ____

Reading to Learn Mathematics
Volume of Prisms and Cylinders

Pre-Activity ***Complete the Mini Lab at the top of page 335 in your textbook. Write your answers below.***

1. Describe how the volume V of each prism is related to its length ℓ, width w, and height h. $V = \ell wh$
2. Describe how the area of the base B and the height h of each prism is related to its volume V. $V = Bh$

Reading the Lesson

3. What is another way to write the volume of a rectangular prism other than $V = Bh$? $V = \ell wh$
4. What does it mean if a figure has a volume of 120 cubic centimeters? Sample answer: The figure would be filled with 120 one-cubic-centimeter cubes.

that have the volume given in different units. Have students compare the volumes by filling one container with water and pouring the water into the second container. This procedure can be used to develop approximate conversion factors between different units of volume.

2 Teach

In-Class Examples

1 Find the volume of the prism. **385 in³**

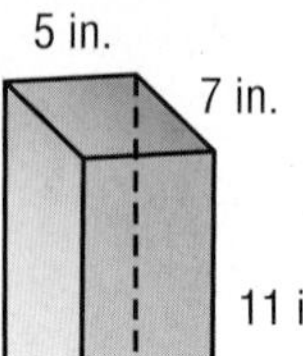

2 Find the volume of the prism. **270 ft³**

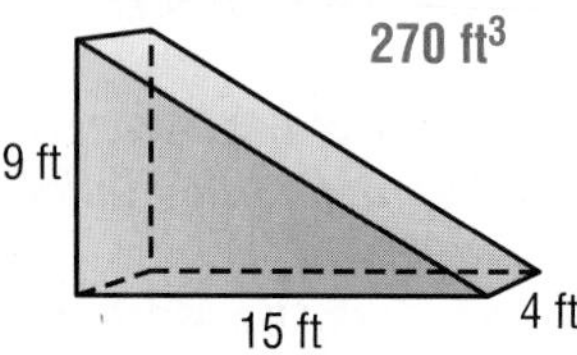

Find the volume of each cylinder. Round to the nearest tenth.

3 **339.3 cm³**

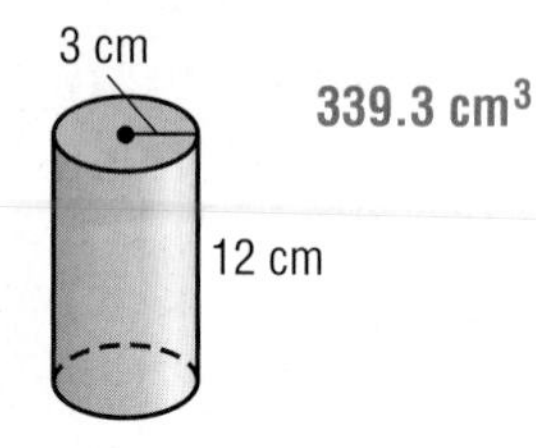

4 diameter of base, 18 yd; height, 25.4 yd **about 6,463.5 yd³**

Classroom Management Students who finish their assignments early can build cubes of different sizes using nets. Distribute templates for cube nets, and have the students trace the nets onto posterboard, taping the edges together with clear tape. Enlarging and reducing the size of the nets on a photocopy machine can make cubes of different sizes. Store the cubes and use them for lessons in spatial visualization and volume.

STUDY TIP

Common Error Remember that the bases of a triangular prism are triangles. In Example 2, these bases are not on the top and bottom of the figure, but on its sides.

EXAMPLE Find the Volume of a Triangular Prism

2 **Find the volume of the prism.**

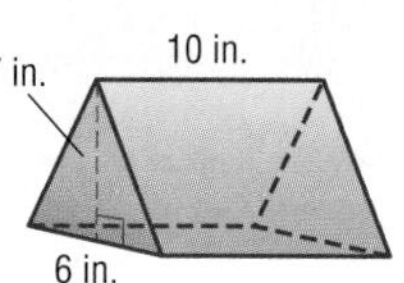

$V = Bh$ Volume of a prism

$V = \left(\frac{1}{2} \cdot 6 \cdot 7\right)h$ The base is a triangle, so $B = \frac{1}{2} \cdot 6 \cdot 7$.

$V = \left(\frac{1}{2} \cdot 6 \cdot 7\right)10$ The height of the prism is 10.

$V = 210$ Simplify.

The volume is 210 cubic inches.

TEACHING TIP

In this text, *cylinder* refers to a cylinder with a circular base.

A **cylinder** is a solid whose bases are congruent, parallel circles, connected with a curved side. You can use the formula $V = Bh$ to find the volume of a cylinder, where the base is a circle.

Noteables™ **Key Concept: Volume of a Cylinder**

Words The volume V of a cylinder with radius r is the area of the base B times the height h.

Symbols $V = Bh$ or $V = \pi r^2 h$, where $B = \pi r^2$

Model

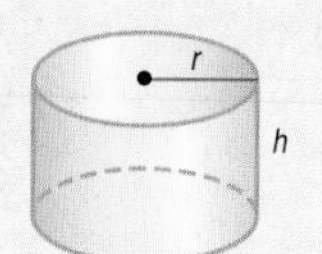

STUDY TIP

Estimation You can estimate the volume of the cylinder in Example 3 to be about $3 \cdot 6^2 \cdot 20$ or 2,160 ft³ to check the reasonableness of your result.

EXAMPLES Find the Volumes of Cylinders

Find the volume of each cylinder.

3

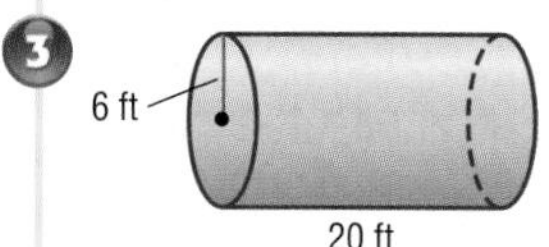

$V = \pi r^2 h$ Volume of a cylinder

$V = \pi \cdot 6^2 \cdot 20$ Replace r with 6 and h with 20.

$V \approx 2{,}261.9$ Simplify.

The volume is about 2,261.9 cubic feet.

4 **diameter of base, 13 m; height, 15.2 m**

Since the diameter is 13 meters, the radius is 6.5 meters.

$V = \pi r^2 h$ Volume of a cylinder

$V = \pi \cdot 6.5^2 \cdot 15.2$ Replace r with 6.5 and h with 15.2.

$V \approx 2{,}017.5$ Simplify.

The volume is about 2,017.5 cubic meters.

Your Turn **Find the volume of each solid. Round to the nearest tenth if necessary.**

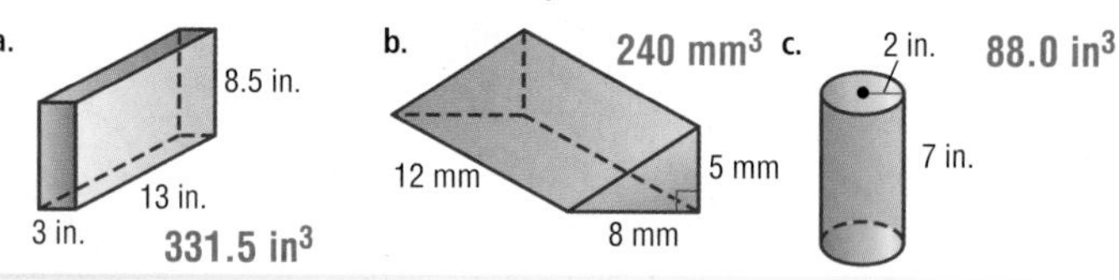

DAILY INTERVENTION **Differentiated Instruction**

Auditory/Musical Gather containers of uniform material construction, and bring them into the classroom. For example, you can bring in washed out food cans of different sizes and volumes. Turn out the lights and have students close their eyes. One at a time, strike the food containers with a drumstick or ruler and have students order the cans according to volume based on the sounds that they make. After you reveal the actual volumes, discuss how volume affects the sound.

Many objects in real-life are made up of more than one type of solid. Such figures are called **complex solids**. To find the volume of a complex solid, separate the figure into solids whose volumes you know how to find.

EXAMPLE Find the Volume of a Complex Solid

5 DISPENSERS Find the volume of the soap dispenser at the right.

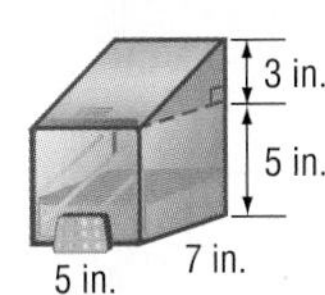

The dispenser is made of one rectangular prism and one triangular prism. Find the volume of each prism.

Rectangular Prism

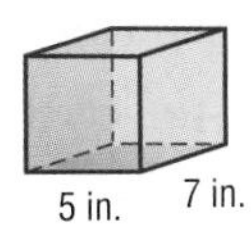

$V = Bh$

$V = (5 \cdot 7)5$ or 175

Triangular Prism

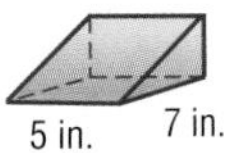

$V = Bh$

$V = \left(\frac{1}{2} \cdot 7 \cdot 3\right)5$ or 52.5

The volume of the dispenser is 175 + 52.5 or 227.5 cubic inches.

Students practice the same concepts in Exercises 8–23 if they are assigned odd or even problems.

Skill and Concept Check

1.  Writing Math Write another formula for the volume of a rectangular prism and explain how it is related to the formula $V = Bh$. **1–2. See margin.**

2. **FIND THE ERROR** Erin and Dulce are finding the volume of the prism shown at the right. Who is correct? Explain.

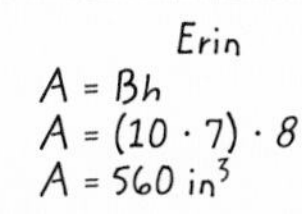

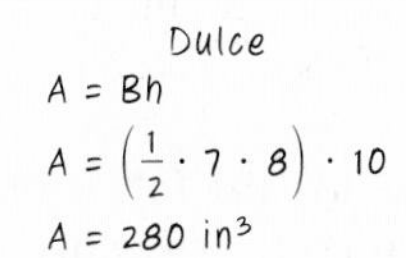

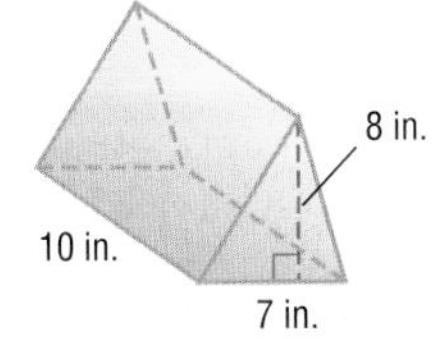

3. **OPEN ENDED** Find the volume of a can or other cylindrical object, being sure to include appropriate units. Explain your method. **See students' work.**

GUIDED PRACTICE

Find the volume of each solid. Round to the nearest tenth if necessary.

4. 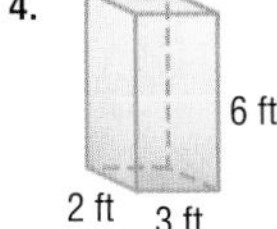

36 ft³

5. 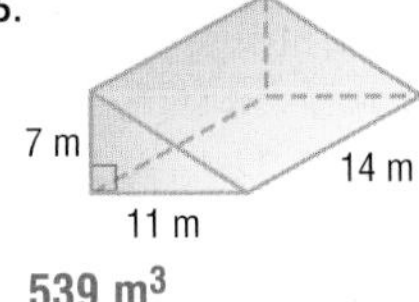

539 m³

6. 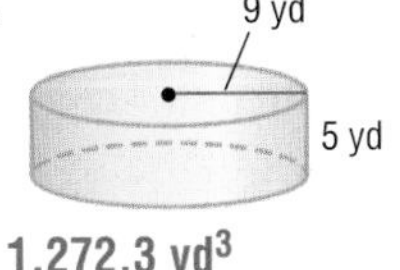

1,272.3 yd³

7. 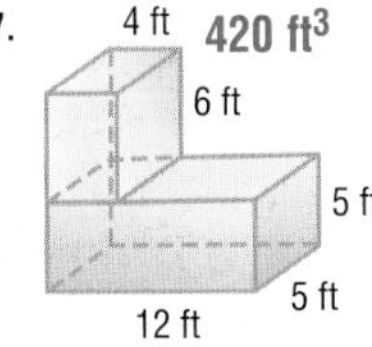

420 ft³

 msmath3.net/extra_examples

In-Class Example

5 **TOYS** A wooden block has a single hole drilled entirely through it. What is the volume of the block? Round to the nearest hundredth. **about 62.58 cm³**

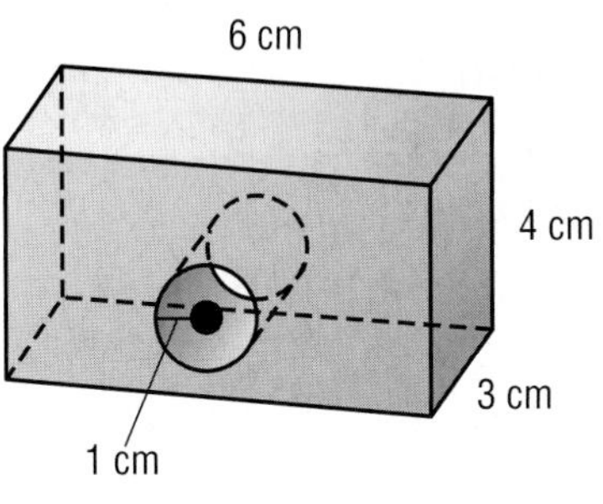

3 Practice/Apply

FOLDABLES™ Follow-Up Remind students to record main ideas, definitions of vocabulary words, and other notes on study cards as they progress through the lesson. Students store their study cards from this lesson in the *Volume* pocket of their Foldables.

DAILY INTERVENTION FIND THE ERROR When students are picking the base of the figure in Exercise 2, suggest that they think of the base as a polygon that can be stacked upon itself repeatedly to form the figure. In this case, the triangle can be stacked upon itself repeatedly to form the figure. If you tried the same with the rectangular surface, the figure would not be the one in the picture. You may want to have precut rectangles and triangles so that students can build the figure with these shapes.

Answers

1. The area of the base B of a rectangular prism equals the length ℓ times the width w. Replacing B with ℓw in the formula $V = Bh$, gives another formula for the volume of a rectangular prism, $V = (\ell w)h$ or $V = \ell wh$.

2. Dulce; the base of the prism is a triangle and the area of a triangle is one-half the product of the base times altitude of the triangle. The height of the prism is 10 in.

About the Exercises...

Guided Practice Key

Exercises	Examples
4	1
5	2
6	3, 4
7	5

Assignment Guide

Basic: 9–15 odd, 19–23 odd, 25–29 odd, 33–48

Average: 9–31 odd, 33–48

Enriched: 8–24 even, 25, 26–32 even, 33–44 (Optional: 45–48)

★ indicates increased difficulty

Practice and Applications

HOMEWORK HELP

For Exercises	See Examples
8–11, 14–15, 22, 25–26	1, 2
12–13, 16, 23	3, 4
18–21, 24	5

Extra Practice
See pages 633, 654.

Find the volume of each solid. Round to the nearest tenth if necessary.

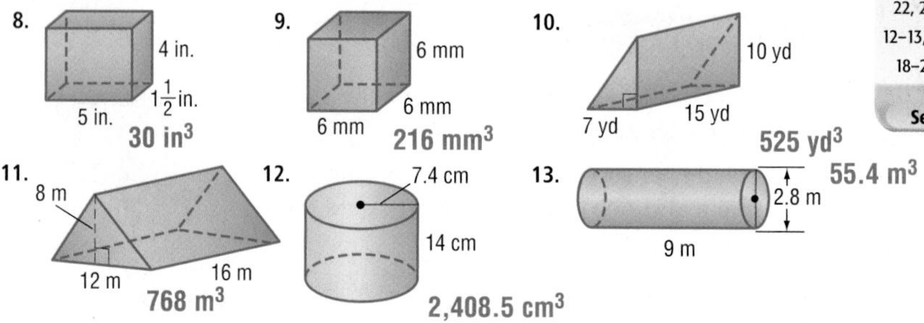

14. rectangular prism: length, 4 in.; width, 6 in.; height, 17 in. **408 in³**

15. triangular prism: base of triangle, 5 ft; altitude, 14 ft; height of prism, $8\frac{1}{2}$ft **297.5 ft³**

16. cylinder: diameter, 7.2 cm; height, 5.8 cm **236.1 cm³**

★17. hexagonal prism: base area 48 mm²; height, 12 mm **576 mm³**

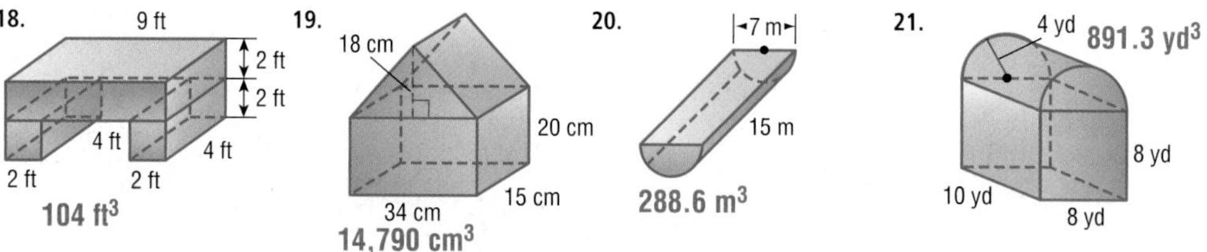

22. **ALGEBRA** Find the height of a rectangular prism with a length of 6.8 meters, a width of 1.5 meters, and a volume of 91.8 cubic meters. **9 m**

23. **ALGEBRA** Find the height of a cylinder with a radius of 4 inches and a volume of 301.6 cubic inches. **6 in.**

★24. Explain how you would find the volume of the hexagonal prism shown at the right. Then find its volume. **See margin.**

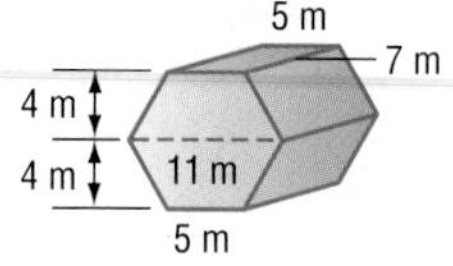

POOLS For Exercises 25 and 26, use the following information.
A wading pool is to be 20 feet long, 11 feet wide, and 1.5 feet deep.

25. Approximately how much water will the pool hold? **330 ft³**

26. The excavated dirt is to be hauled away by wheelbarrow. If the wheelbarrow holds 9 cubic feet of dirt, how many wheelbarrows of dirt must be hauled away from the site? **37**

CONVERTING UNITS OF MEASURE For Exercises 27–29, use the cubes at the right.
The volume of the left cube is 1 cubic yard. The right cube is the same size, but the unit of measure has been changed. So, 1 cubic yard = (3)(3)(3) or 27 cubic feet. Use a similar process to convert each measurement.

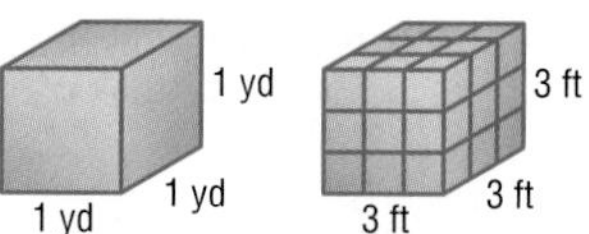

27. 1 ft³ = ■ in³ **1,728**

28. 1 cm³ = ■ mm³ **1,000**

29. 1 m³ = ■ cm³ **1,000,000**

4 Assess

Open-Ended Assessment

Speaking Ask students to define in their own words what volume means and how volume differs from area. Tell students to keep their answers general and to *not* include volume formulas.

Answer

24. The base of the prism is a hexagon, which can be separated into two congruent trapezoids. So the area of the base is $2 \cdot \frac{1}{2}(4)(11 + 5)$ or 64 m². The height of the prism is 7 m, so the volume of the prism is $64 \cdot 7$ or 448 m³.

★30. **PACKAGING** The Cooking Club is selling their own special blends of rice mixes. They can choose from the two containers at the right to package their product. Which container will hold more rice? Explain your reasoning. **See margin.**

★31. **FARMING** When filled to capacity, a silo can hold 8,042 cubic feet of grain. The circumference C of the silo is approximately 50.3 feet. Find the height h of the silo to the nearest foot. **40 ft**

32. **WRITE A PROBLEM** Write about a real-life problem that can be solved by finding the volume of a rectangular prism or a cylinder. Explain how you solved the problem. **See margin.**

CRITICAL THINKING For Exercises 33–36, describe how the volume of each solid is affected after the indicated change in its dimension(s).

33. You double one dimension of a rectangular prism. **volume doubles**
34. You double two dimensions of a rectangular prism. **volume quadruples**
35. You double all three dimensions of a rectangular prism. **volume is multiplied by 8**
36. You double the radius of a cylinder. **volume quadruples**

Spiral Review with Standardized Test Practice

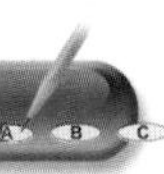

37. **MULTIPLE CHOICE** A bar of soap in the shape of a rectangular prism has a volume of 16 cubic inches. After several uses, it measures $2\frac{1}{4}$ inches by 2 inches by $1\frac{1}{2}$ inches. How much soap was used? **B**

(A) $6\frac{3}{4}$ in^3 (B) $9\frac{1}{4}$ in^3 (C) $10\frac{1}{4}$ in^3 (D) 108 in^3

38. **MULTIPLE CHOICE** Which is the best estimate of the volume of a cylinder that is 20 meters tall and whose diameter is 10 meters? **I**

(F) 200 m^3 (G) 500 m^3 (H) 600 m^3 (I) 1500 m^3

39. **PAINTING** You are painting a wall of this room red. Find the area of the red wall to the nearest square foot. (Lesson 7-3) **126 ft^2**

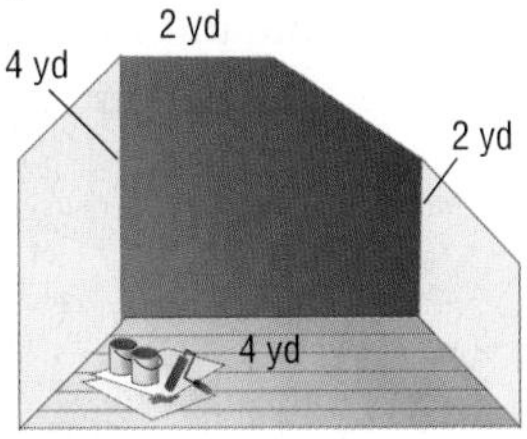

4 yd
2 yd
2 yd
4 yd

40. How many edges does an octagonal pyramid have? (Lesson 7-4) **16**

Write each percent as a fraction or mixed number in simplest form. (Lesson 5-1)

41. 0.12% $\frac{3}{2{,}500}$ 42. 225% $2\frac{1}{4}$ 43. 135% $1\frac{7}{20}$ 44. $\frac{3}{8}$% $\frac{3}{800}$

GETTING READY FOR THE NEXT LESSON

PREREQUISITE SKILL Multiply. (Lesson 2-5)

45. $\frac{1}{3} \cdot 6 \cdot 10$ **20** 46. $\frac{1}{3} \cdot 7 \cdot 15$ **35** 47. $\frac{1}{3} \cdot 4^2 \cdot 9$ **48** 48. $\frac{1}{3} \cdot 6^2 \cdot 20$ **240**

Math Online msmath3.net/self_check_quiz

Answers

30. The container A; the volume of container A is about 509 cm^3, while the volume of container B is 480 cm^3.

32. Sample answer: A flower box measures 5 feet long, 2 feet wide, and 2 feet deep. How many cubic feet of potting soil will the flower box hold? Find the volume of the flower box by multiplying the length times the width times the height of the box. Since $5 \cdot 2 \cdot 2 = 20$, the flower box will hold 20 cubic feet of potting soil.

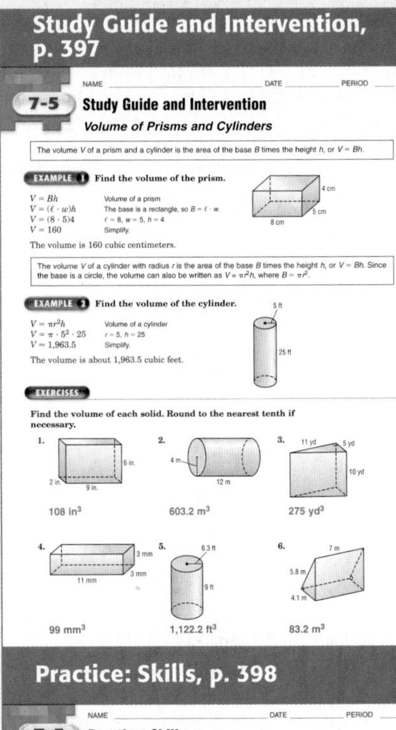

Study Guide and Intervention, p. 397

NAME ______ DATE ______ PERIOD ____

7-5 Study Guide and Intervention

Volume of Prisms and Cylinders

The volume V of a prism and a cylinder is the area of the base B times the height h, or $V = Bh$.

EXAMPLE 1 Find the volume of the prism.

$V = Bh$ Volume of a prism
$V = (\ell \cdot w)h$ The base is a rectangle, so $B = \ell \cdot w$.
$V = (8 \cdot 5)4$ $\ell = 8$, $w = 5$, $h = 4$
$V = 160$ Simplify.

The volume is 160 cubic centimeters.

The volume V of a cylinder with radius r is the area of the base B times the height h, or $V = Bh$. Since the base is a circle, the volume can also be written as $V = \pi r^2 h$, where $B = \pi r^2$.

EXAMPLE 2 Find the volume of the cylinder.

$V = \pi r^2 h$ Volume of a cylinder
$V = \pi \cdot 5^2 \cdot 25$ $r = 5$, $h = 25$
$V \approx 1{,}963.5$ Simplify.

The volume is about 1,963.5 cubic feet.

EXERCISES

Find the volume of each solid. Round to the nearest tenth if necessary.

1. 108 in^3 2. 603.2 m^3 3. 275 yd^3
4. 99 mm^3 5. 1,122.2 ft^3 6. 83.2 m^3

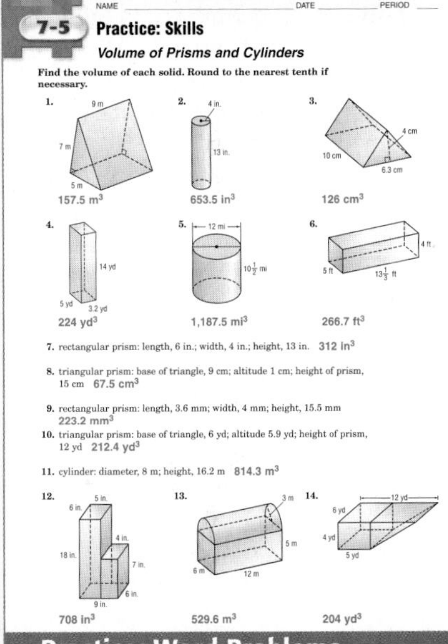

Practice: Skills, p. 398

NAME ______ DATE ______ PERIOD ____

7-5 Practice: Skills

Volume of Prisms and Cylinders

Find the volume of each solid. Round to the nearest tenth if necessary.

1. 157.5 m^3 2. 653.5 in^3 3. 126 cm^3
4. 224 yd^3 5. 1,187.5 mi^3 6. 266.7 ft^3

7. rectangular prism: length, 6 in.; width, 4 in.; height, 13 in. 312 in^3
8. triangular prism: base of triangle, 9 cm; altitude 1 cm; height of prism, 15 cm 67.5 cm^3
9. rectangular prism: length, 3.6 mm; width, 4 mm; height, 15.5 mm 223.2 mm^3
10. triangular prism: base of triangle, 6 yd; altitude 5.9 yd; height of prism, 12 yd 212.4 yd^3
11. cylinder: diameter, 8 m; height, 16.2 m 814.3 m^3

12. 708 in^3 13. 529.6 m^3 14. 204 yd^3

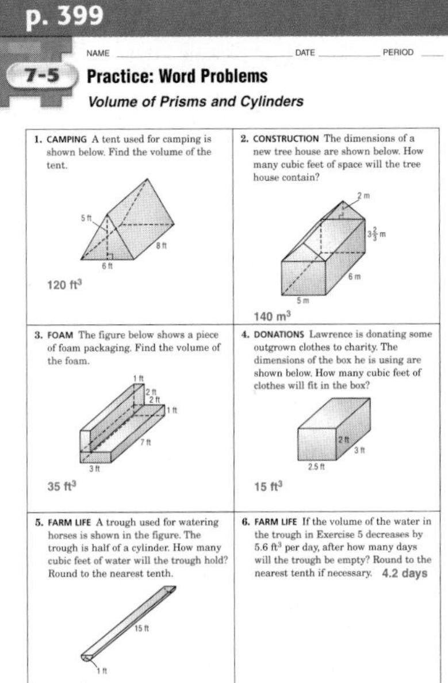

Practice: Word Problems, p. 399

NAME ______ DATE ______ PERIOD ____

7-5 Practice: Word Problems

Volume of Prisms and Cylinders

1. CAMPING A tent used for camping is shown below. Find the volume of the tent. 120 ft^3

2. CONSTRUCTION The dimensions of a new tree house are shown below. How many cubic feet of space will the tree house contain? 140 m^3

3. FOAM The figure below shows a piece of foam packaging. Find the volume of the foam. 35 ft^3

4. DONATIONS Lawrence is donating some outgrown clothes to charity. The dimensions of the box he is using are shown below. How many cubic feet of clothes will fit in the box? 15 ft^3

5. FARM LIFE A trough used for watering horses is shown in the figure. The trough is half of a cylinder. How many cubic feet of water will the trough hold? Round to the nearest tenth. 23.6 ft^3

6. FARM LIFE If the volume of the water in the trough in Exercise 5 decreases by 5.6 ft^3 per day, after how many days will the trough be empty? Round to the nearest tenth if necessary. 4.2 days

Mid-Chapter Practice Test

Assessment Option

Mid-Chapter Test (Lessons 7-1 through 7-5) is available on p. 439 of the *Chapter 7 Resource Masters*.

ExamView® Pro

Use the networkable ExamView® Pro Testmaker CD-ROM to:

- Create **multiple versions** of tests.
- Create **modified** tests for **inclusion** students with one mouse click.
- **Edit** existing questions and **add** your own questions.
- Build tests aligned with state standards using built-in **state curriculum correlations.**
- Change **English** tests to **Spanish** with one mouse click and vice versa.

FOLDABLES™ Follow-Up Before students complete the Mid-Chapter Practice Test, encourage them to review the notes, definitions, concepts, and main ideas recorded on the study cards stored in their Foldables.

CHAPTER 7 Mid-Chapter Practice Test

Vocabulary and Concepts

1. Draw and label a trapezoid with an area of 20 square centimeters. (Lesson 7-1)
2. **Compare and contrast** the characteristics of prisms and pyramids. (Lesson 7-4)

1–2. See margin.

Skills and Applications

3. Find the area of a triangle with a 30-meter base and 12-meter height. (Lesson 7-1) **180 m^2**
4. **SPORTS** A shot-putter must stay inside a circle with a diameter of 7 feet. What is the circumference and area of the region in which the athlete is able to move in this competition? Round to the nearest tenth. (Lesson 7-2) **22.0 ft, 38.5 ft^2**

Find the area of each figure. Round to the nearest tenth. (Lesson 7-3)

5. 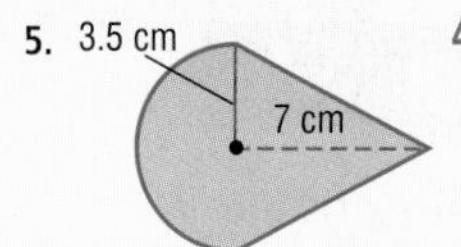

43.7 cm^2

6. 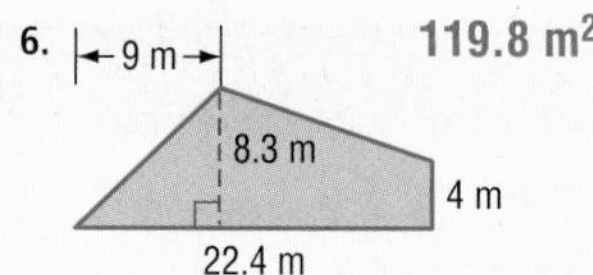

119.8 m^2

STORAGE For Exercises 7 and 8, use the diagram of the storage shed at the right.

7. Identify the solid. Name the number and shapes of the faces. Then name the number of edges and vertices. (Lesson 7-4) **See margin.**
8. Find the volume of this storage shed. (Lesson 7-5) **273 ft^3**

Find the volume of each solid. Round to the nearest tenth. (Lesson 7-5)

9. 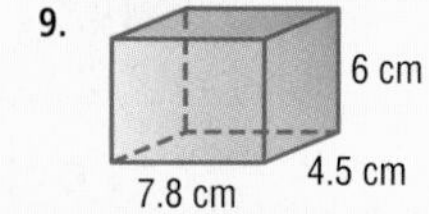

210.6 cm^3

10. 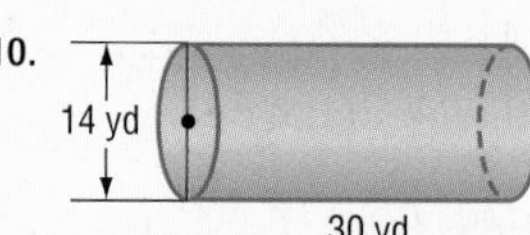

4,618.1 yd^3

Standardized Test Practice

11. **MULTIPLE CHOICE** Which of the following solids is *not* a polyhedron? (Lesson 7-4) **B**

   Ⓐ prism Ⓑ cylinder
   Ⓒ pyramid Ⓓ cube

12. **MULTIPLE CHOICE** Find the volume of a cube-shaped box with edges 15 inches long. (Lesson 7-5) **I**

   Ⓕ 225 in^3 Ⓖ 900 in^3
   Ⓗ 1,350 in^3 Ⓘ 3,375 in^3

Answers

1. Sample answer:

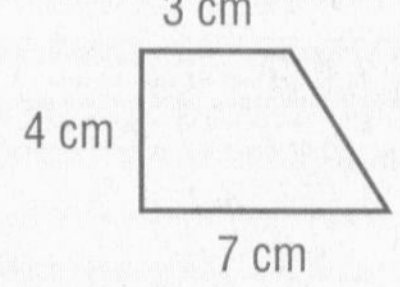

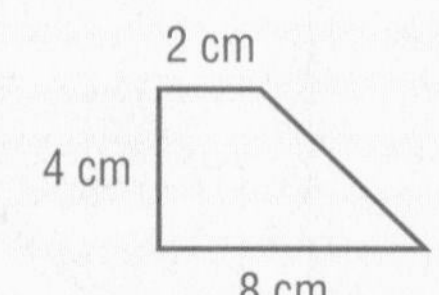

2. Prisms have two bases, while pyramids have one. Both are named by the shapes of their bases, which must be polygons. The faces of a prism are rectangles, while the faces of pyramids are triangles.

7. triangular prism; 5 faces; 2 triangles, 3 rectangles; 9 edges, 6 vertices

The Game Zone

A Place To Practice Your Math Skills

Math Skill
3-Dimensional Figures

Archi-test

GET READY!

Players: two
Materials: cubes, manila folders, index cards cut in half

- Players each receive 15 cubes and a manila folder.
- Each player designs a structure with some of his or her cubes, using the manila folder to hide the structure from the other player's view. The player then draws the top, front, back, and side views of the structure on separate index cards. The player also computes the structure's volume in cubic units, writing this on a fourth index card.

GO!

- Player A tries to guess Player B's structure. Player A does this by asking Player B for one of the index cards that shows one of the views of the structure. Player A tries to build Player B's structure.

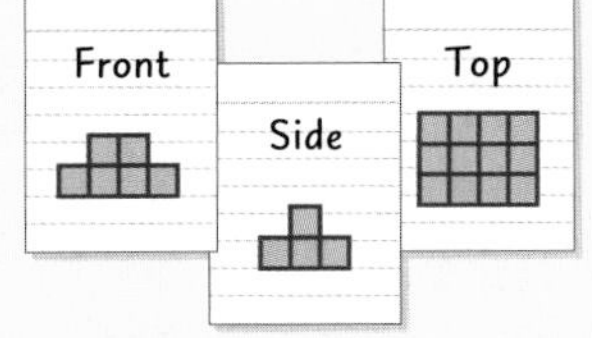

- Player A receives 4 points for correctly building Players B's structure after receiving only one piece of information, 3 points for correctly building after only two pieces of information, and so on.
- If Player A cannot build Player B's structure after receiving all 4 pieces of information, then Player B receives 2 points.
- Player B now tries to build Player A's structure.
- **Who Wins?** Play continues for an agreed-upon number of structures. The player with the most points at the end of the game wins.

The Game Zone

Glencoe Mathematics Classroom Manipulative Kit

- centimeter cubes

GETTING READY

Objective Find the volumes of three-dimensional figures.

MANAGEMENT TIPS

Recommended Time
20 minutes

Tips

- Have Player A build a structure first, so Player B can use his or her blocks to try to build Player A's structure. When that is completed, Player B builds a structure for Player A to try to build.
- Students may want to place their clues facedown and have the other player choose the clues randomly.
- You may wish to have students create more clues, such as the number of cubes in layer 1, the number in layer 2, and so on, to choose from.
- You may wish to use the game as an assessment tool for the concepts the students have been learning in Lessons 7-4 through 7-5.

Math Online For an additional game for this chapter, visit: msmath3.net/gamezone

The Game Zone: Three-Dimensional Figures 341

Volume of Pyramids and Cones

What You'll LEARN

Find the volumes of pyramids and cones.

NEW Vocabulary

cone

REVIEW Vocabulary

pyramid: a polyhedron with one base that is a polygon and faces that are triangles (Lesson 7-4)

HANDS-ON Mini Lab

Materials

- construction paper
- ruler
- scissors
- tape
- rice

Work with a partner.

In this Mini Lab, you will investigate the relationship between the volume of a pyramid and the volume of a prism with the same base area and height.

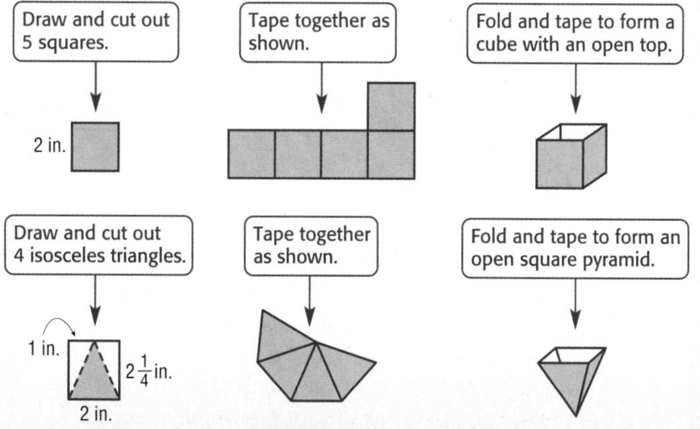

1. Compare the base areas and the heights of the two solids.
2. Fill the pyramid with rice, sliding a ruler across the top to level the amount. Pour the rice into the cube. Repeat until the prism is filled. How many times did you fill the pyramid in order to fill the cube? **3** **1. They are the same.**
3. What fraction of the cube's volume does one pyramid fill? $\frac{1}{3}$

The volume of a pyramid is one third the volume of a prism with the same base area and height.

Noteables™ **Key Concept: Volume of a Pyramid**

Words The volume V of a pyramid is one third the area of the base B times the height h.

Symbols $V = \frac{1}{3}Bh$

Model

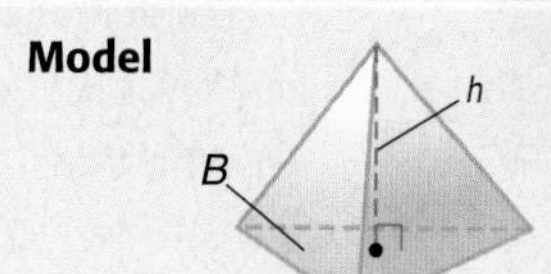

7-6 Lesson Notes

Lesson Resources

Chapter 7 Resource Masters
- Study Guide and Intervention, p. 402
- Practice: Skills, p. 403
- Practice: Word Problems, p. 404
- Reading to Learn Mathematics, p. 405
- Enrichment, p. 406

Calculator and Spreadsheet Masters, p. 33
Key Teaching Transparencies, 26
MathPASS Tutorial CD-ROM, 53
Parent and Student Study Guide Online Worksheets, 7-6
Teaching Mathematics with Manipulatives, p. 86
Noteables™: Interactive Study Notebook with Foldables™, 7-6

FAST FILE

1 Focus

5-Minute Check 7-6

Use as a quiz or review of Lesson 7-5. (Also available as a transparency)

Bellringer

Problem Solving Show students a square pyramid, a cylinder, and a cone, all of about the same height and all with open tops. Ask students which shape they would prefer as a container for popcorn at the movies. Discuss their responses if the price were the same for all three.

Reading to Learn Mathematics, p. 405 **ELL**

NAME ____________ DATE ________ PERIOD ____

7-6 Reading to Learn Mathematics
Volume of Pyramids and Cones

Pre-Activity *Complete the Mini Lab at the top of page 342 in your textbook. Write your answers below.*

1. Compare the base areas and the heights of the two solids. They are the same.
2. Fill the pyramid with rice, sliding a ruler across the top to level the amount. Pour the rice into the cube. Repeat until the prism is filled. How many times did you fill the pyramid in order to fill the cube? 3
3. What fraction of the cube's volume does one pyramid fill? $\frac{1}{3}$

Reading the Lesson

4. How is the volume of a cone related to that of a cylinder? The volume ... is one-thi...

Using Manipulatives In the Hands-On Mini Lab, unpopped popcorn can be substituted for the rice.

342 Chapter 7 Geometry: Measuring Area and Volume

STUDY TIP

Height of Cone or Pyramid The height of a pyramid or cone is the distance from the vertex, perpendicular to the base.

EXAMPLE Find the Volume of a Pyramid

1 **Find the volume of the pyramid.**

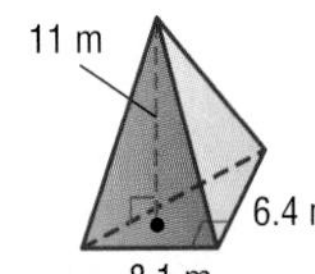

$V = \frac{1}{3}Bh$ Volume of a pyramid

$V = \frac{1}{3}\left(\frac{1}{2} \cdot 8.1 \cdot 6.4\right)11$ $B = \frac{1}{2} \cdot 8.1 \cdot 6.4, h = 11$

$V = 95.04$ Simplify.

The volume is about 95.0 cubic meters.

EXAMPLE Use Volume to Solve a Problem

2 **ARCHITECTURE The area of the base of the Pyramid Arena in Memphis, Tennessee, is 360,000 square feet. If its volume is 38,520,000 cubic feet, find the height of the structure.**

$V = \frac{1}{3}Bh$ Volume of a pyramid

$38{,}520{,}000 = \frac{1}{3} \cdot 360{,}000 \cdot h$ Replace V with 38,520,000 and B with 360,000.

$38{,}520{,}000 = 120{,}000 \cdot h$ Simplify.

$321 = h$ Divide each side by 120,000.

The height of the Pyramid Arena is 321 feet.

REAL-LIFE MATH

ARCHITECTURE The Pyramid Arena in Memphis, Tennessee, is the third largest pyramid in the world, seating over 20,000 people for sporting and entertainment events.

Source: www.pyramidarena.com

A **cone** is a three-dimensional figure with one circular base. A curved surface connects the base and the vertex. The volumes of a cone and a cylinder are related in the same way as those of a pyramid and prism.

Noteables™ **Key Concept: Volume of a Cone**

Words The volume V of a cone with radius r is one-third the area of the base B times the height h.

Model

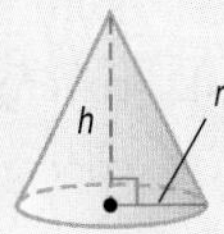

Symbols $V = \frac{1}{3}Bh$ or $V = \frac{1}{3}\pi r^2 h$

EXAMPLE Find the Volume of a Cone

3 **Find the volume of the cone.**

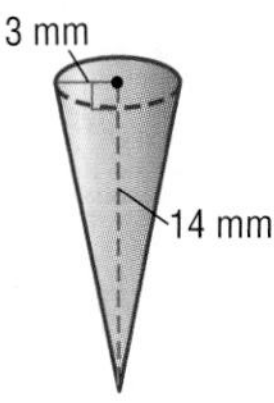

$V = \frac{1}{3}\pi r^2 h$ Volume of a cone

$V = \frac{1}{3} \cdot \pi \cdot 3^2 \cdot 14$ Replace r with 3 and h with 14.

$V \approx 131.9$ Simplify.

The volume is about 131.9 cubic millimeters.

Math Online msmath3.net/extra_examples

2 Teach

In-Class Examples

1 Find the volume of the pyramid. **140 cm^3**

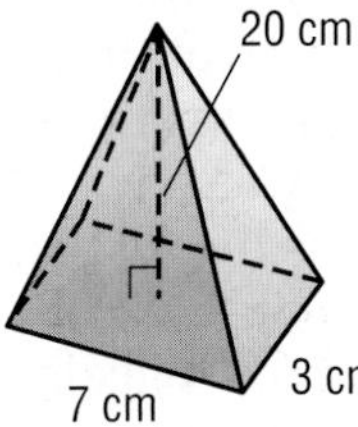

2 **SOUVENIRS** A novelty souvenir company wants to make snow "globes" shaped like a pyramid. It decides that the most cost-effective maximum volume of water for the pyramids is 12 cubic inches. If a pyramid globe measures 4 inches in height, find the area of its base. **9 in^2**

3 Find the volume of the cone. Round to the nearest tenth. **18.8 m^3**

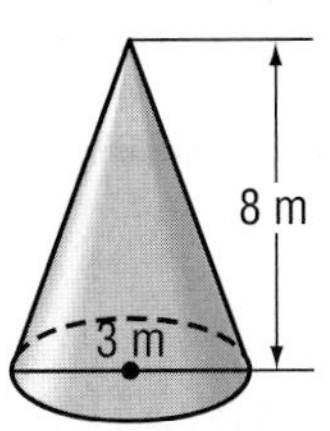

DAILY INTERVENTION **Differentiated Instruction**

Kinesthetic Have students construct pyramids based on the pyramids of ancient Egypt. One online source of measurements is www.ancient-egypt.org. Have students compare the volumes of the different pyramids. Ask students to research whether the volume of the pyramid was relative to the importance of the entombed.

3 Practice/Apply

Writing Math In Exercise 1, suggest that students choose an actual problem from the exercises and double the radius and the height, each in turn. Then have them compare the answers. You may also wish to have students use the formula for volume and substitute $2r$ for r and then $2h$ for h, again comparing the results. If students need help visualizing the changes, have them model or sketch each case.

About the Exercises...

Guided Practice Key

Exercises	Examples
4, 5	1
3	3

Assignment Guide

Basic: 7–15 odd, 21, 23, 24, 30–37

Average: 7–23 odd, 24, 30–37 (Optional: 25–29)

Enriched: 6–20 even, 21, 22, 24–33 (Optional: 34–37)

Answers

1. **Doubling its radius; doubling the radius means the volume of the cone is multiplied by 4, while doubling the height multiplies the volume of the cone by 2.**
2. **Sample answer:**

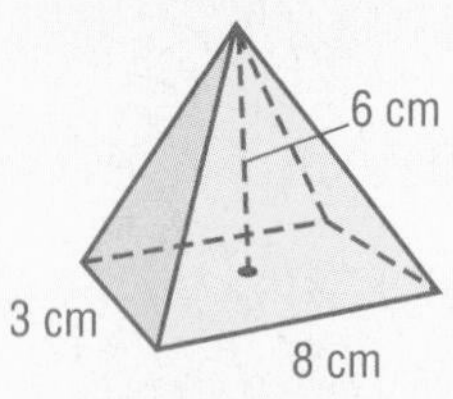

Students practice the same concepts in Exercises 6–19 if they are assigned odd or even problems.

Skill and Concept Check

1. *Writing Math* Which would have a greater effect on the volume of a cone, doubling its radius or doubling its height? Explain your reasoning.
2. **OPEN ENDED** Draw and label a rectangular pyramid with a volume of 48 cubic centimeters. **1–2. See margin.**

GUIDED PRACTICE

Find the volume of each solid. Round to the nearest tenth if necessary.

3. 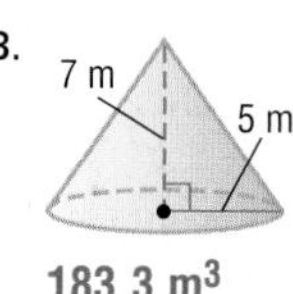

183.3 m³

4. 11 cm; 8 cm; 14 cm **410.7 cm³**

5. 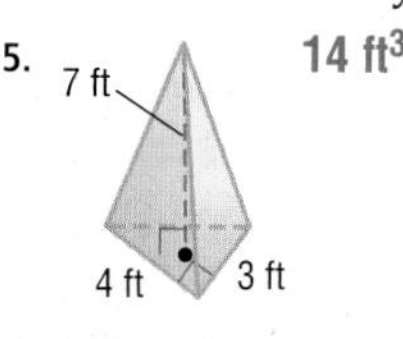

14 ft³

★ indicates increased difficulty

Practice and Applications

HOMEWORK HELP	
For Exercises	See Examples
8–11, 14–15	1
20–22	2
6–7, 12–13	3

Extra Practice See pages 634, 654.

Find the volume of each solid. Round to the nearest tenth if necessary.

6.–7. 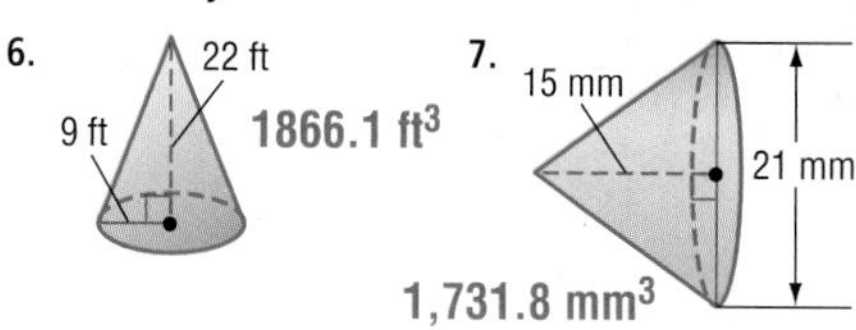

6. **1866.1 ft³** 7. **1,731.8 mm³**

8. 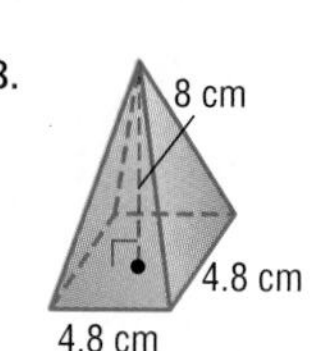

61.4 cm³

9. 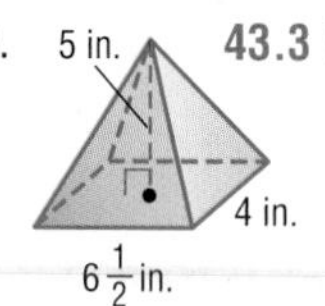

43.3 in³

10. 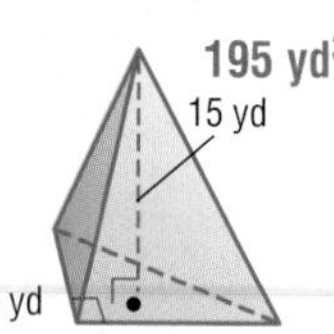

195 yd³

11. 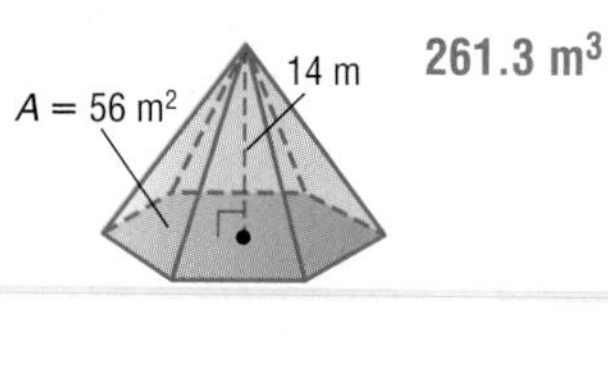

261.3 m³

12. cone: diameter, 12 mm; height, 5 mm **188.5 mm³**
13. cone: radius, $3\frac{1}{2}$ in.; height, 18 in. **230.9 in³**
14. octagonal pyramid: base area, 120 ft²; height, 19 ft **760 ft³**
15. triangular pyramid: triangle base, 10 cm; triangle height, 7 cm; prism height, 15 cm **175 cm³**

★16. 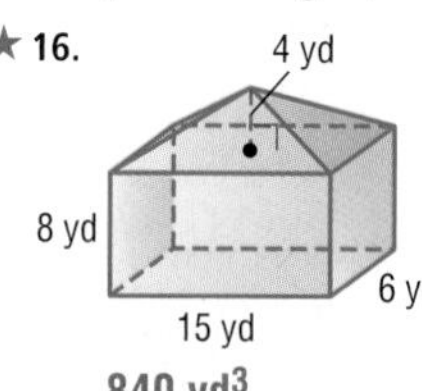

840 yd³

★17. 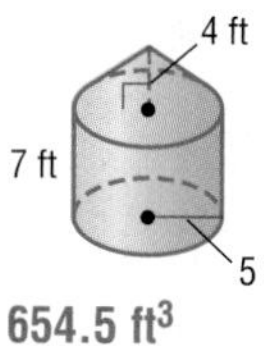

654.5 ft³

★18. 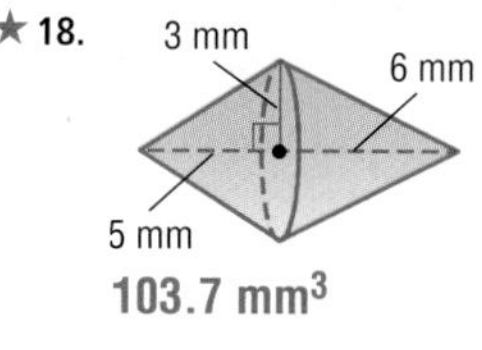

103.7 mm³

★19. 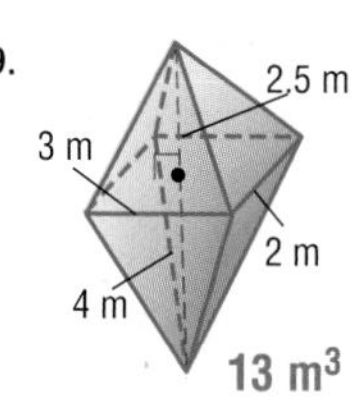

13 m³

20. **VOLCANO** A model of a volcano constructed for a science project is cone-shaped with a diameter of 10 inches. If the volume of the model is about 287 cubic inches, how tall is the model? **about 11 in.**

4 Assess

Higher-Level Thinking

Black Dragon's Caldron in Yellowstone National Park is approximately 80 feet by 200 feet with a depth of 36 feet. (Assume that the caldron's shape is similar to an inverted pyramid with a rectangular base.) If a cubic foot of fluid in the crater weighs 62 pounds, how much does the water in the crater weigh? **11.9 million lb**

344 Chapter 7 Geometry: Measuring Area and Volume

ICE CREAM For Exercises 21 and 22, use the diagram at the right and the following information.

You are filling cone-shaped glasses with frozen custard. Each glass is 8 centimeters wide and 15 centimeters tall.

21. Estimate the volume of custard each glass will hold assuming you fill each one level with the top of the glass. **Sample answer: 250 cm³**
22. One gallon is equivalent to about 4,000 cubic centimeters. Estimate how many glasses you can fill with one gallon of custard. **Sample answer: 16**
23. **WRITE A PROBLEM** Write about a real-life situation that can be solved by finding the volume of a cone. Then solve the problem. **See margin.**
24. **CRITICAL THINKING** How could you change the height of a cone so that its volume would remain the same when its radius was tripled? **Divide the height by 9.**

EXTENDING THE LESSON A *sphere* is the set of all points in space that are a given distance from a given point, called the center. The volume V of a sphere with radius r is given by the formula $V = \frac{4}{3}\pi r^3$.

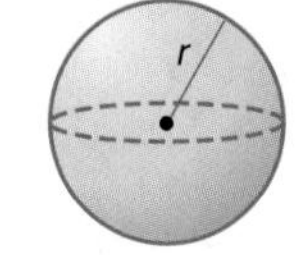

25. 113.1 in³ 26. 904.8 in³ 27. 523.6 m³ 28. 381.7 ft³

Find the volume of each sphere described. Round to the nearest tenth.

25. radius, 3 in.
26. radius, 6 in.
27. diameter, 10 m
28. diameter, 9 ft
29. How does doubling a sphere's radius affect its volume? Explain. **See margin.**

Spiral Review with Standardized Test Practice

30. **MULTIPLE CHOICE** If each of the following solids has a height of 8 centimeters, which has the greatest volume? **C**

Ⓐ 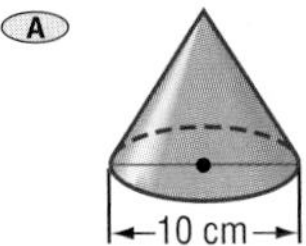

Ⓑ 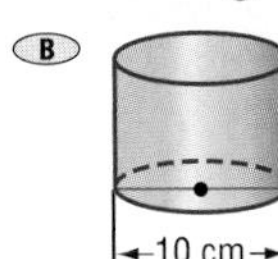

Ⓒ 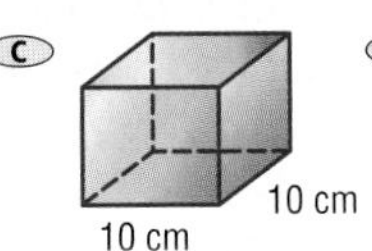

Ⓓ 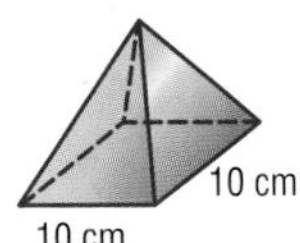

31. **SHORT RESPONSE** A triangular prism has a volume of 135 cubic centimeters. Find the volume in cubic centimeters of a triangular pyramid with the same base area and height as this prism. **45 cm³**
32. **PETS** Find the volume of a doghouse with a rectangular space that is 3 feet wide, 4 feet deep, and 5 feet high and has a triangular roof $1\frac{1}{2}$ feet higher than the walls of the house. (Lesson 7-5) **69 ft³**

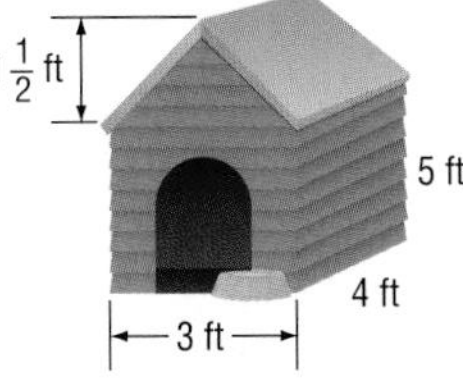

33. Name the number and shapes of the faces of a trapezoidal prism. Then name the number of edges and vertices. (Lesson 7-4) **trapezoidal prism; 6 faces, 2 trapezoids, 4 rectangles; 12 edges; 8 vertices**

GETTING READY FOR THE NEXT LESSON

PREREQUISITE SKILL Find the circumference of each circle. Round to the nearest tenth. (Lesson 7-2)

34. diameter, 9 in. **28.3 in.**
35. diameter, $5\frac{1}{2}$ ft **17.3 ft**
36. radius, 2 m **12.6 m**
37. radius, 3.8 cm **23.9 cm**

Math Online msmath3.net/self_check_quiz

Answers

23. Sample answer: A paper cup is shaped like a cone. If the cup is 6 cm wide and 10 cm tall, find the volume of water the cup will hold; 94.2 cm³.

29. It multiplies it by 8; replacing r with $2r$ in the formula for the volume of a sphere gives $\frac{4}{3}\pi(2r)^3$ or $8 \cdot \frac{4}{3}\pi r^3$.

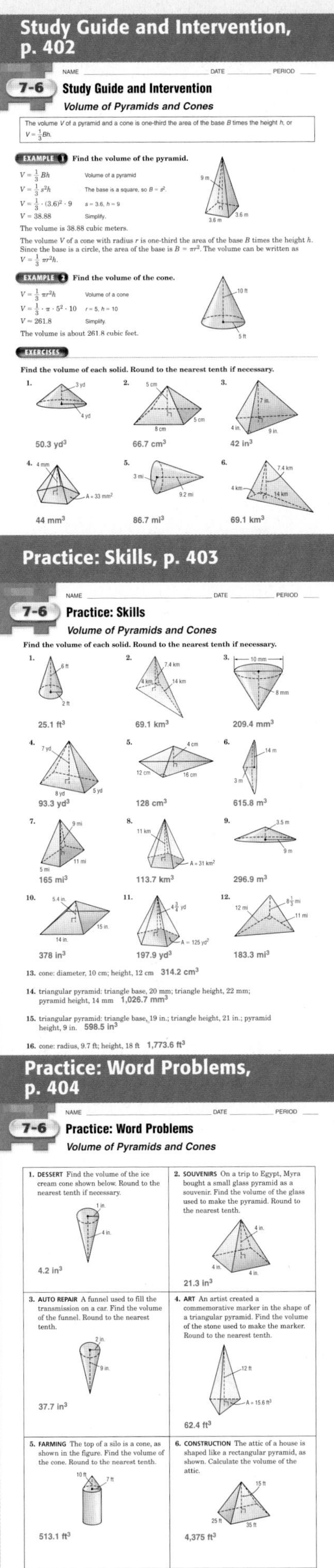

Study Guide and Intervention, p. 402

7-6 Study Guide and Intervention — Volume of Pyramids and Cones

The volume V of a pyramid and a cone is one-third the area of the base B times the height h, or $V = \frac{1}{3}Bh$.

EXAMPLE 1 Find the volume of the pyramid.

$V = \frac{1}{3}Bh$ Volume of a pyramid
$V = \frac{1}{3}s^2h$ The base is a square, so $B = s^2$.
$V = \frac{1}{3} \cdot (3.6)^2 \cdot 9$ $s = 3.6, h = 9$
$V = 38.88$ Simplify.
The volume is 38.88 cubic meters.

The volume V of a cone with radius r is one-third the area of the base B times the height h. Since the base is a circle, the area of the base is $B = \pi r^2$. The volume can be written as $V = \frac{1}{3}\pi r^2 h$.

EXAMPLE 2 Find the volume of the cone.

$V = \frac{1}{3}\pi r^2 h$ Volume of a cone
$V = \frac{1}{3} \cdot \pi \cdot 5^2 \cdot 10$ $r = 5, h = 10$
$V = 261.8$ Simplify.
The volume is about 261.8 cubic feet.

EXERCISES

Find the volume of each solid. Round to the nearest tenth if necessary.

1. 50.3 yd³ 2. 66.7 cm³ 3. 42 in³ 4. 44 mm³ 5. 86.7 mi³ 6. 69.1 km³

Practice: Skills, p. 403

7-6 Practice: Skills — Volume of Pyramids and Cones

Find the volume of each solid. Round to the nearest tenth if necessary.

1. 25.1 ft³ 2. 69.1 km³ 3. 209.4 mm³ 4. 93.3 yd³ 5. 128 cm³ 6. 615.8 m³ 7. 165 mi³ 8. 113.7 km³ 9. 296.9 m³ 10. 378 in³ 11. 197.9 yd³ 12. 183.3 mi³

13. cone: diameter, 10 cm; height, 12 cm 314.2 cm³
14. triangular pyramid: triangle base, 20 mm; triangle height, 22 mm; pyramid height, 14 mm 1,026.7 mm³
15. triangular pyramid: triangle base, 19 in.; triangle height, 21 in.; pyramid height, 9 in. 598.5 in³
16. cone: radius, 9.7 ft; height, 18 ft 1,773.6 ft³

Practice: Word Problems, p. 404

7-6 Practice: Word Problems — Volume of Pyramids and Cones

1. DESSERT Find the volume of the ice cream cone shown below. Round to the nearest tenth if necessary. 4.2 in³
2. SOUVENIRS On a trip to Egypt, Myra bought a small glass pyramid as a souvenir. Find the volume of the glass used to make the pyramid. Round to the nearest tenth. 21.3 in³
3. AUTO REPAIR A funnel used to fill the transmission on a car. Find the volume of the funnel. Round to the nearest tenth. 37.7 in³
4. ART An artist created a commemorative marker in the shape of a triangular pyramid. Find the volume of the stone used to make the marker. Round to the nearest tenth. 62.4 ft³
5. FARMING The top of a silo is a cone, as shown in the figure. Find the volume of the cone. Round to the nearest tenth. 513.1 ft³
6. CONSTRUCTION The attic of a house is shaped like a rectangular pyramid, as shown. Calculate the volume of the attic. 4,375 ft³

7-7a HANDS-ON LAB Lesson Notes

Lesson Resources

Teaching Mathematics with Manipulatives

- student recording sheet 7-7a

Glencoe Mathematics Classroom Manipulative Kit

- scissors

GETTING STARTED

Teaching Tip You may wish to have students use heavy construction paper or posterboard to make their figures. They can then save their figures for future work with three-dimensional figures.

TEACH

- At the front of the class, model the **Activity** with an enlarged copy of the net as students follow along at their seats.
- Before students begin the **Your Turn** exercises, show them copies of the solids they will construct. Have them match the net to the solid, explaining their reasoning in writing.
- You may also wish to have students draw the three-dimensional views of the figures on isometric dot paper.

ASSESS

Observe as students solve the **Your Turn** exercises. They should:

- use the nets to correctly build the indicated figures and
- draw and label accurate top, side, and front views of the constructed figures.

7-7a HANDS-ON LAB

A Preview of Lesson 7-7

Nets

What You'll LEARN

Represent three-dimensional objects as nets.

Materials

- empty box with tuck-in lid
- scissors

TEACHING TIP

You may wish to give students enlarged copies of the nets in this lab instead of having students copy the nets by hand.

Work with a partner.

Open the lid of a box and make 5 cuts as shown. Then open the box up and lay it flat. The result is a net. **Nets** are two-dimensional patterns of three-dimensional figures. You can use a net to build a three-dimensional figure.

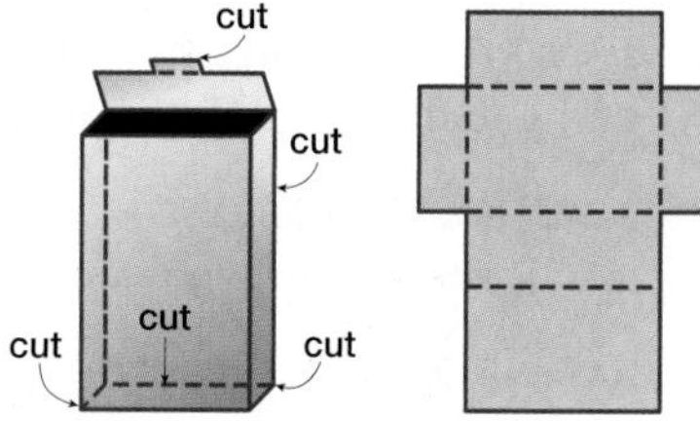

ACTIVITY

STEP 1 Copy the net onto a piece of paper, shading the base as shown.

STEP 2 Use scissors to cut out the net.

STEP 3 Fold on the dashed lines and tape the sides together.

STEP 4 Sketch the figure and draw its top, side, and front views.

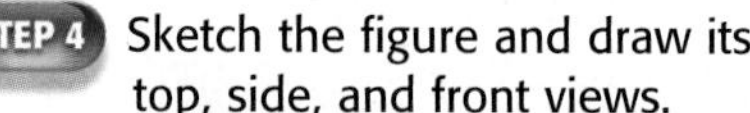

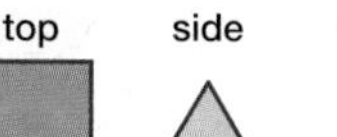

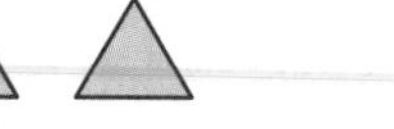

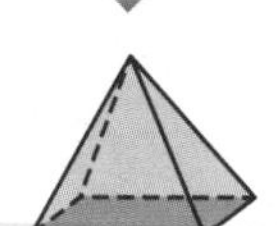

Your Turn **Use each net to build a figure. Then sketch the figure, and draw and label its top, side, and front views.**

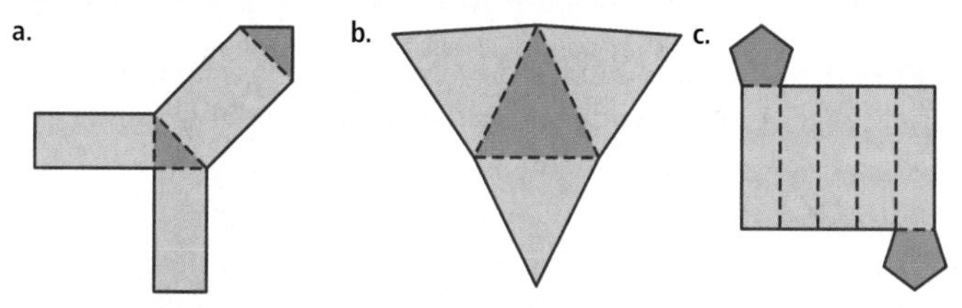

a–c. See Ch. 7 Answer Appendix.

Writing Math

1–2. See margin.

1. **Describe** each shape that makes up the three nets above.
2. **Identify** each of the solids formed by the three nets above.

Answers (Writing Math)

1. a: two congruent rectangles, one larger rectangle, and two congruent right triangles; b: two sets of congruent triangles; c: 5 congruent rectangles and two congruent pentagons
2. a: triangular prism; b: triangular pyramid; c: pentagonal prism

7-7 Surface Area of Prisms and Cylinders

What You'll LEARN

Find the surface areas of prisms and cylinders.

NEW Vocabulary

surface area

HANDS-ON Mini Lab

Materials
- 3 different-sized boxes
- centimeter ruler

The **surface area** of a solid is the sum of the areas of all its surfaces, or faces. In this lab, you will find the surface areas of rectangular prisms.

1. Estimate the area in square centimeters of each face for one of your boxes. Then find the sum of these six areas.
2. Now use your ruler to measure the sides of each face. Then find the area of each face to the nearest square centimeter. Find the sum of these areas and compare to your estimate.
3. Estimate and then find the surface areas of your other boxes.

1–3. See students' work.

One way to easily visualize all of the surfaces of a prism is to sketch a two-dimensional pattern of the solid, called a *net*, and label all its dimensions.

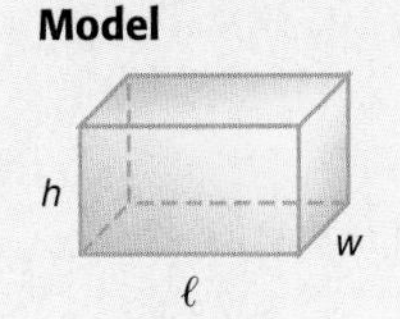

Faces	Area
top and bottom	$(\ell \cdot w) + (\ell \cdot w) = 2\ell w$
front and back	$(\ell \cdot h) + (\ell \cdot h) = 2\ell h$
two sides	$(w \cdot h) + (w \cdot h) = 2wh$
Sum of areas →	$2\ell w + 2\ell h + 2wh$

ℓ, h, back, h, w, side, bottom, side, h, front, w, top

Noteables™ Key Concept: Surface Area of a Rectangular Prism

Words The surface area S of a rectangular prism with length ℓ, width w, and height h is the sum of the areas of the faces.

Symbols $S = 2\ell w + 2\ell h + 2wh$

Model

EXAMPLE Surface Area of a Rectangular Prism

1 Find the surface area of the rectangular prism.

$S = 2\ell w + 2\ell h + 2wh$ Write the formula.

$S = 2(7)(3) + 2(7)(12) + 2(3)(12)$ Substitution

$S = 282$ Simplify.

The surface area is 282 square meters.

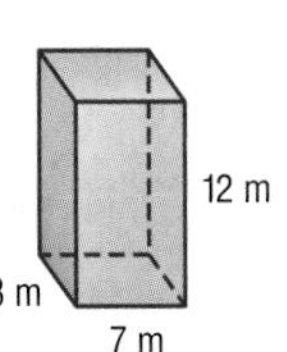

7-7 Lesson Notes

Lesson Resources

Chapter 7 Resource Masters
- Study Guide and Intervention, p. 407
- Practice: Skills, p. 408
- Practice: Word Problems, p. 409
- Reading to Learn Mathematics, p. 410
- Enrichment, p. 411

Calculator and Spreadsheet Masters, p. 34
MathPASS Tutorial CD-ROM, 54
Parent and Student Study Guide Online Worksheets, 7-7
Real-Life Career Masters, p. 33
Noteables™: Interactive Study Notebook with Foldables™, 7-7
Virtual Activities CD-ROM, Surface Area of Prisms

1 Focus

5-Minute Check 7-7

INTERACTIVE CHALKBOARD PowerPoint® Presentations

Use as a quiz or review of Lesson 7-6. (Also available as a transparency)

Bellringer

Hands-On Activity Bring in several different sizes of gift boxes and shipping tubes. Discuss with students how much wrapping paper would be needed to wrap the various containers and how they could measure them to determine the amount required.

Reading to Learn Mathematics, p. 410 ELL

NAME ____ DATE ____ PERIOD ____

7-7 Reading to Learn Mathematics
Surface Area of Prisms and Cylinders

Pre-Activity *Complete the Mini Lab at the top of page 347 in your textbook. Write your answers below.*

1. Estimate the area in square centimeters of each face for one of your boxes. Then find the sum of these six areas. See students' work.
2. Now use your ruler to measure the sides of each face. Then find the area of each face to the nearest square centimeter. Find the sum of all these areas and compare to your estimate. See students' work.
3. Estimate and then find the surface areas of your other boxes. See students' work.

Reading the Lesson

4. Complete the sentence with the correct numbers. When you draw a net of a triangular prism, there are ___ congruent triangular faces and ___ rect... 2; 3

Tips for New Teachers

Using Manipulatives Give students two nets with the same volume but different surface areas. For example, a rectangular prism with dimensions 10 inches by 3 inches by 3 inches and one with dimensions 30 inches by 3 inches by 1 inch meet this criterion. Have students measure the nets and calculate the volume and surface areas. Ask them why a manufacturer, such as a cereal producer, might prefer one box over the other. **The box with less surface area will be less expensive to produce.**

2 Teach

In-Class Examples

1 Find the surface area of the rectangular prism. **606 mm²**

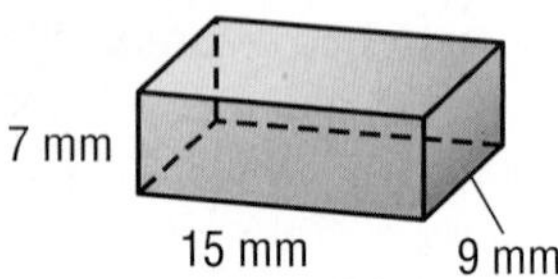

2 **CAMPING** A family wants to reinforce the fabric of its tent with a waterproofing treatment. Find the surface area, including the floor, of the tent below. **131.1 ft²**

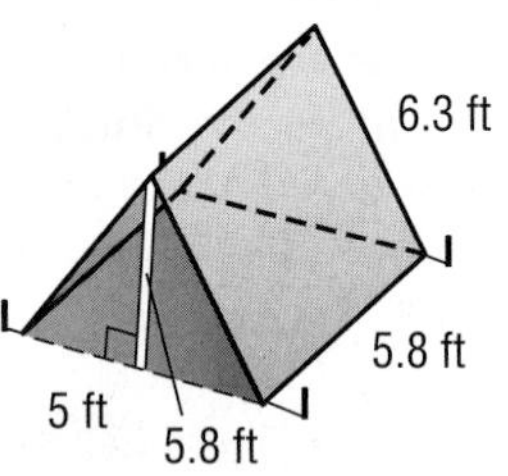

Tips for New Teachers

Intervention Students often make mistakes when using complicated formulas because they do not work step-by-step. Encourage students to show all of the steps in their assignments by offering full, or extra, credit when problems are shown in detail. The first step should be writing down the formula.

REAL-LIFE MATH

SKATEBOARDING Other types of skateboarding ramps include angled boxes, lo-banks, quarterpipes, and micro halfpipes. Kits for building ramps can include isometric drawings of side and rear views.

EXAMPLE Surface Area of a Triangular Prism

2 **SKATEBOARDING A skateboarding ramp called a *wedge* is built in the shape of a triangular prism. You plan to paint all surfaces of the ramp. Find the surface area to be painted.**

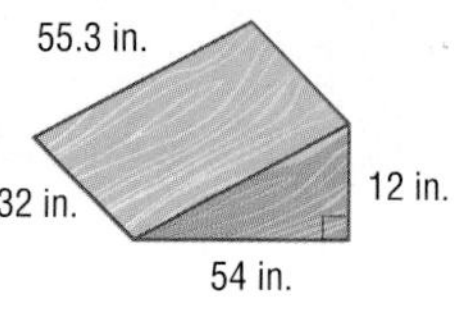

A triangular prism consists of two congruent triangular faces and three rectangular faces.

Draw and label a net of this prism. Find the area of each face.

bottom	$54 \cdot 32 = 1{,}728$
left side	$55.3 \cdot 32 = 1{,}769.6$
right side	$12 \cdot 32 = 384$
two bases	$2\left(\frac{1}{2} \cdot 54 \cdot 12\right) = 648$

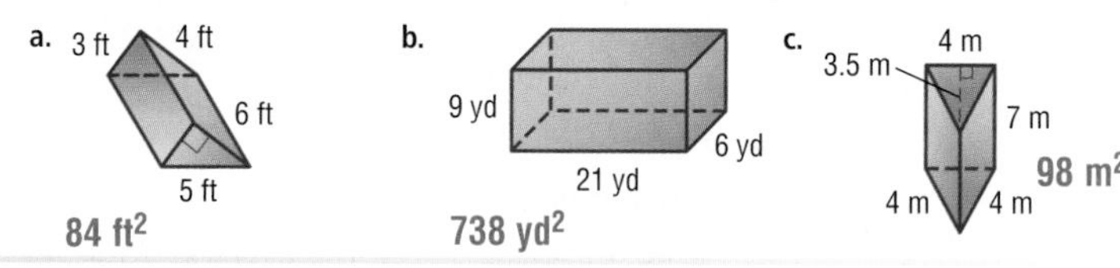

Add to find the total surface area.

$1{,}728 + 1{,}769.6 + 384 + 648 = 4{,}529.6$

The surface area of the ramp is 4,529.6 square inches.

Your Turn **Find the surface area of each prism.**

a. 3 ft, 4 ft, 6 ft, 5 ft **84 ft²**

b. 9 yd, 21 yd, 6 yd **738 yd²**

c. 3.5 m, 4 m, 7 m, 4 m, 4 m **98 m²**

You can find the surface area of a cylinder by finding the area of its two bases and adding the area of its curved side. If you unroll a cylinder, its net is two circles and a rectangle.

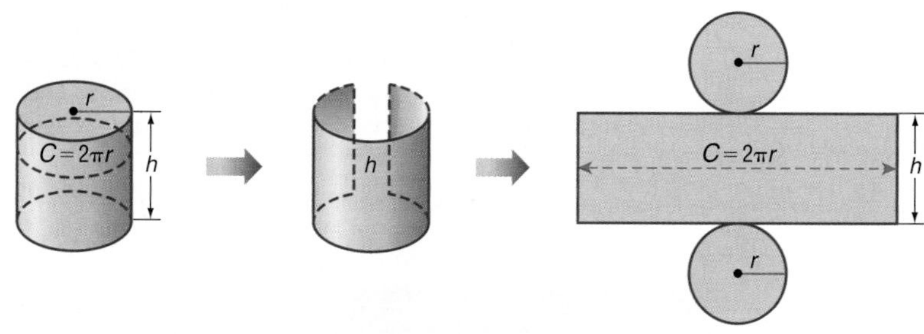

Model	Net	Area
2 circular bases	2 congruent circles with radius r	$2(\pi r^2)$ or $2\pi r^2$
1 curved surface	1 rectangle with width h and length $2\pi r$	$2\pi r \cdot h$ or $2\pi rh$

So, the surface area S of a cylinder is $2\pi r^2 + 2\pi rh$.

DAILY INTERVENTION **Differentiated Instruction**

Logical Have students predict the effect on the surface area of a cylinder if the height and radius are increased or decreased. Have students construct models to test their predictions.

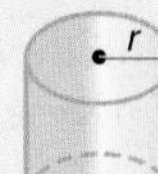

Noteables™ **Key Concept: Surface Area of a Cylinder**

Words The surface area S of a cylinder with height h and radius r is the area of the two bases plus the area of the curved surface.

Model

Symbols $S = 2\pi r^2 + 2\pi rh$

EXAMPLE Surface Area of a Cylinder

3 **Find the surface area of the cylinder. Round to the nearest tenth.**

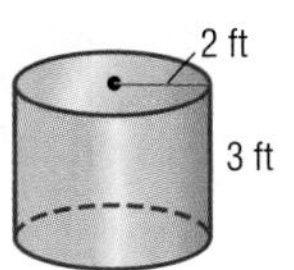

$S = 2\pi r^2 + 2\pi rh$ Surface area of a cylinder

$S = 2\pi(2)^2 + 2\pi(2)(3)$ Replace r with 2 and h with 3.

$S \approx 62.8$ Simplify.

The surface area is 62.8 square feet.

Your Turn **Find the surface area of each cylinder. Round to the nearest tenth.**

d. 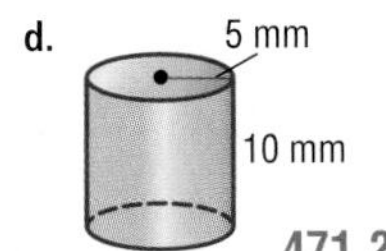 **471.2 mm²**

e. 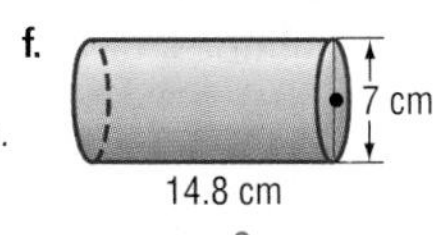 **428.8 in²**

f. 7 cm, 14.8 cm **402.4 cm²**

Students practice the same concepts in Exercises 9–22 if they are assigned odd or even problems.

Skill and Concept Check

1. **Determine** whether the following statement is *true* or *false*. If *false*, give a counterexample.

   If two rectangular prisms have the same volume, then they also have the same surface area. **False; see margin.**

2. Writing Math If you double the edge length of a cube, explain how this affects the surface area of the prism. **See margin.**

3. **OPEN ENDED** The surface area of a rectangular prism is 96 square feet. Name one possible set of dimensions for this prism. **Sample answer: 2 ft × 2 ft × 11 ft**

GUIDED PRACTICE

Find the surface area of each solid. Round to the nearest tenth if necessary.

4. 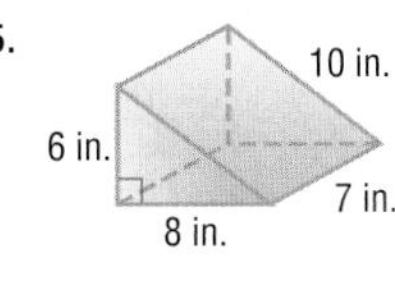
94 yd²

5. 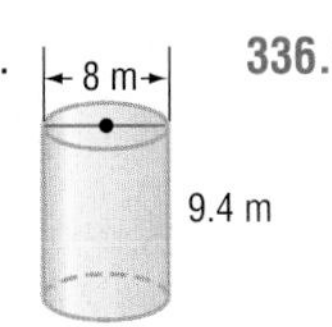
216 in²

6. 8 m, 9.4 m **336.8 m²**

7. rectangular prism: length, 12.2 cm; width, 4.8 cm; height, 10.3 cm **467.3 cm²**

8. cylinder: radius, 16 yd; height, 25 yd **4,121.8 yd²**

Math Online msmath3.net/extra_examples

In-Class Example

3 Find the surface area of the cylinder. Round to the nearest tenth. **70.7 m²**

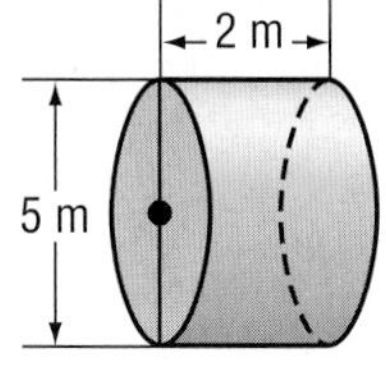

3 Practice/Apply

FOLDABLES™ Follow-Up Remind students to record main ideas, definitions of vocabulary words, and other notes on study cards as they progress through the lesson. Students store their study cards from this lesson in the *Area* pocket of their Foldables.

Writing Math In Exercise 2, you may wish to have students use actual cubes to figure out the effect of doubling one side of a prism. They can start with one cube and then attach others to simulate lengthening the sides of the prism.

About the Exercises...

Guided Practice Key

Exercises	Examples
4, 7	1
5	2
6, 8	3

Assignment Guide

Basic: 9–23 odd, 24–28, 33–41

Average: 9–23 odd, 24–28, 33–41 (Optional: 29–32)

Enriched: 10–22 even, 23–37 (Optional: 38–41)

Answers

1. A rectangular prism 2 ft long, 4 ft wide, and 6 ft high has the same volume as a prism 2 ft long, 2 ft wide, and 12 ft high, 48 ft³. The surface area of the first prism is 88 ft², but the surface area of the second prism is 104 ft².

2. It quadruples it; doubling the edge s of a square quadruples its area since $(2s)^2 = 4s^2$. Since all the faces of a cube are squares, this also quadruples the surface area of the cube.

4 Assess

Open-Ended Assessment

Modeling Have students create a prism or a cylinder with cubes or by drawing their own net. They should then trade with a partner who will find the surface area of the figure.

★ indicates increased difficulty

Practice and Applications

HOMEWORK HELP	
For Exercises	See Examples
9–10, 15, 18	1
11–12	2
13–14, 16–17	3

Extra Practice
See pages 634, 654.

Find the surface area of each solid. Round to the nearest tenth if necessary.

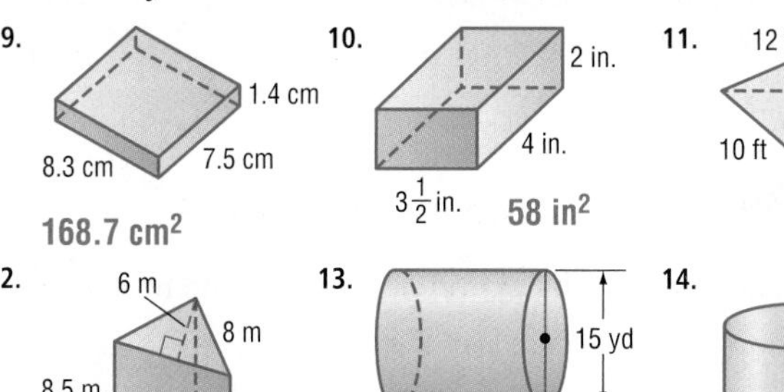

9. **168.7 cm²**
10. **58 in²**
11. 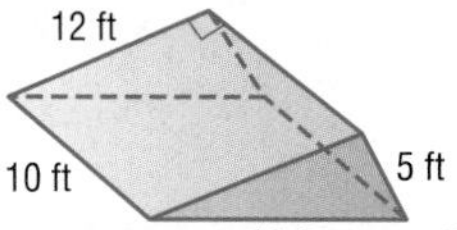 **360 ft²**

12. 6 m, 8 m, 8.5 m, 9.5 m, 11.2 m **330.4 m²**
13. 15 yd, 17 yd **1,154.5 yd²**
14. 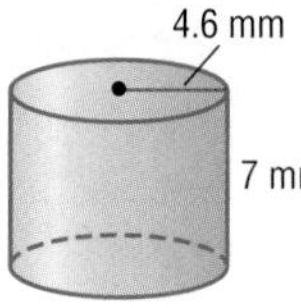 4.6 mm, 7 mm **335.3 mm²**

15. cube: edge length, 12 m **864 m²**
16. cylinder: diameter, 18 yd, height, 21 yd **1,696.5 yd²**
17. cylinder: radius, 7 in.; height, $9\frac{1}{2}$ in. **725.7 in²**
18. rectangular prism: length, $1\frac{1}{2}$ cm; width, $5\frac{3}{4}$ cm; height, $3\frac{1}{4}$ cm **64.4 cm²**

19. **POOL** A vinyl liner covers the inside walls and bottom of the swimming pool shown below. Find the area of this liner to the nearest square foot. **805 ft²**

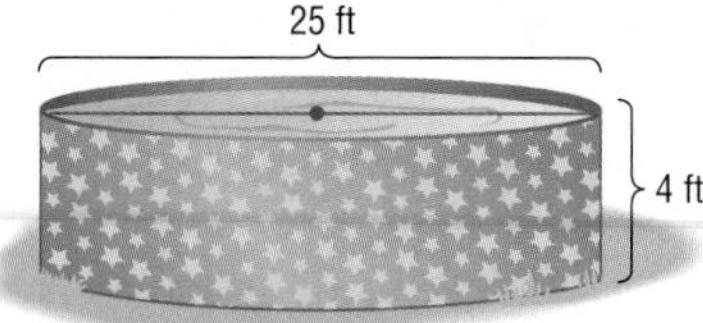

20. **GARDENING** The door of the greenhouse shown below has an area of 4.5 square feet. How many square feet of plastic are needed to cover the roof and sides of the greenhouse? **411.5 ft²**

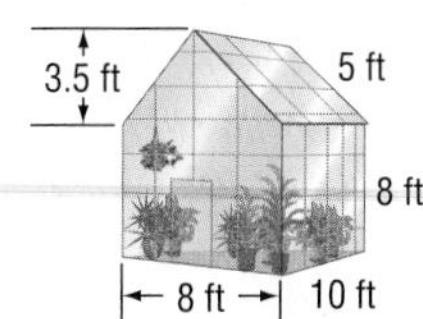

21. **MULTI STEP** An airport has changed the carrels used for public telephones. The old carrels consisted of four sides of a rectangular prism. The new carrels are half of a cylinder with an open top. How much less material is needed to construct a new carrel than an old carrel? **574.7 in²**

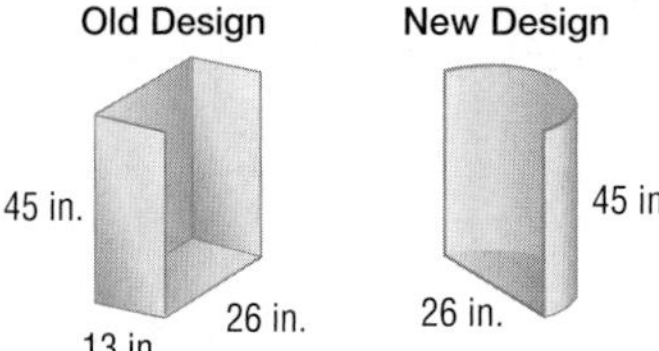

★ 22. **CAMPING** A camping club has designed a tent with canvas sides and floor as shown below. About how much canvas will the club members need to construct the tent? (*Hint:* Use the Pythagorean Theorem to find the height of the triangular base.) **about 21.5 yd²**

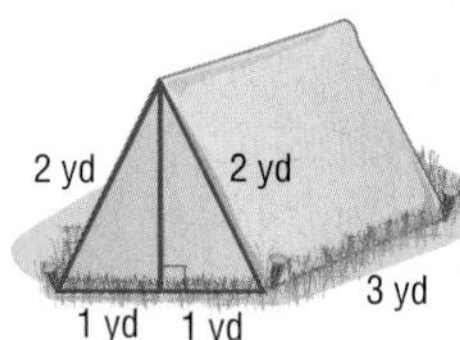

23. **CRITICAL THINKING** Will the surface area of a cylinder increase more if you double the height or double the radius? Explain your reasoning. **See margin.**

CRITICAL THINKING The length of each edge of a cube is 3 inches. Suppose the cube is painted and then cut into 27 smaller cubes that are 1 inch on each side.

24. How many of the smaller cubes will have paint on exactly three faces? **8**

25. How many of the smaller cubes will have paint on exactly two faces? **12**

26. How many of the smaller cubes will have paint on only one face? **6**

27. How many of the smaller cubes will have no paint on them at all? **1**

28. Find the answers to Exercises 24–27 if the cube is 10 inches on a side and cut into 1,000 smaller cubes. **3 faces: 8, 2 faces: 96, 1 face: 384; no faces: 512**

EXTENDING THE LESSON If you make cuts in a solid, different two-dimensional cross sections result, as shown at the right.

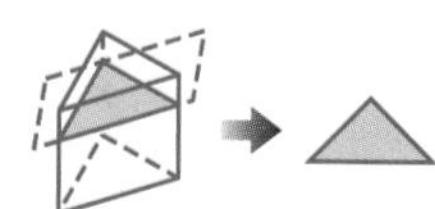

Describe the cross section of each figure cut below.

29. 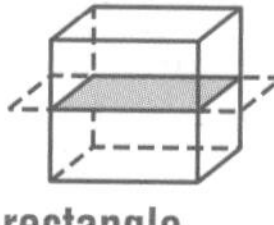
rectangle

30. 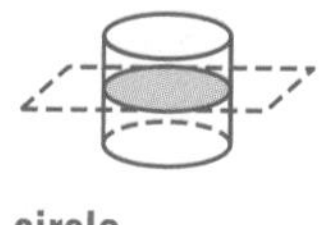
circle

31. 
triangle

32. 
pentagon

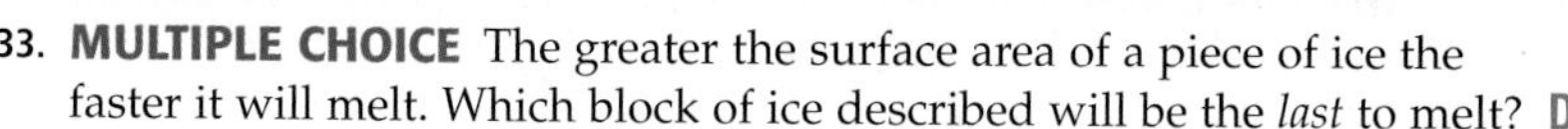

33. **MULTIPLE CHOICE** The greater the surface area of a piece of ice the faster it will melt. Which block of ice described will be the *last* to melt? **D**

Ⓐ 1 in. by 2 in. by 32 in. block
Ⓑ 4 in. by 8 in. by 2 in. block
Ⓒ 16 in. by 4 in. by 1 in. block
Ⓓ 4 in. by 4 in. by 4 in. block

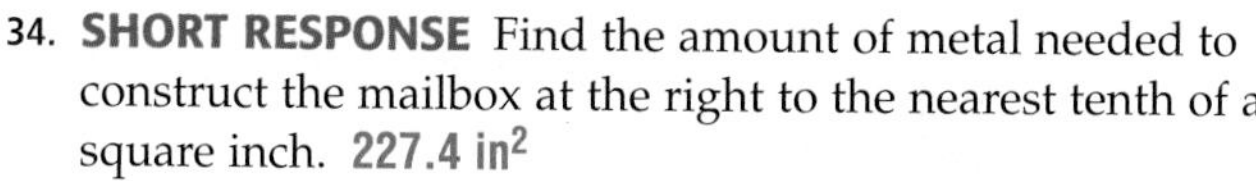

34. **SHORT RESPONSE** Find the amount of metal needed to construct the mailbox at the right to the nearest tenth of a square inch. **227.4 in^2**

Find the volume of each solid described. Round to the nearest tenth if necessary. (Lesson 7-6)

35. rectangular pyramid: length, 14 m; width, 12 m; height, 7 m **392 m^3**

36. cone: diameter 22 cm; height, 24 cm **3,041.1 cm^3**

37. **HEALTH** The inside of a refrigerator in a medical laboratory measures 17 inches by 18 inches by 42 inches. You need at least 8 cubic feet to refrigerate some samples from the lab. Is the refrigerator large enough for the samples? Explain. (Lesson 7-5) **No; the volume of the refrigerator is 12,852 in^3 or about 7.4 ft^3, which is less than 8 ft^3.**

GETTING READY FOR THE NEXT LESSON

PREREQUISITE SKILL Multiply. (Lesson 2-5)

38. $\frac{1}{2} \cdot 2.8$ **1.4**

39. $\frac{1}{2} \cdot 10 \cdot 23$ **115**

40. $\frac{1}{2} \cdot 2.5 \cdot 16$ **20**

41. $\frac{1}{2}\left(3\frac{1}{2}\right)(20)$ **35**

msmath3.net/self_check_quiz

Answer

23. Double the radius; consider the expression for the surface area of a cylinder, $2\pi r^2 + 2\pi rh$. If you double the height, you will double the second addend. If you double the radius, you will quadruple the first addend and double the second addend.

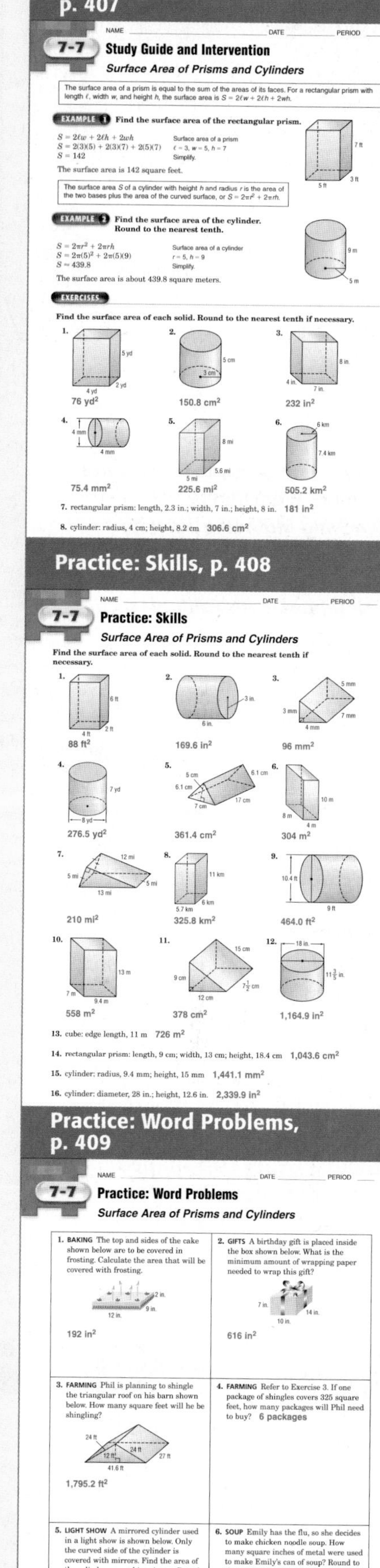

Study Guide and Intervention, p. 407

NAME ________ DATE ________ PERIOD ____

7-7 Study Guide and Intervention
Surface Area of Prisms and Cylinders

The surface area of a prism is equal to the sum of the areas of its faces. For a rectangular prism with length ℓ, width w, and height h, the surface area is $S = 2\ell w + 2\ell h + 2wh$.

EXAMPLE 1 Find the surface area of the rectangular prism.

$S = 2\ell w + 2\ell h + 2wh$ Surface area of a prism
$S = 2(3)(5) + 2(3)(7) + 2(5)(7)$ $\ell = 3, w = 5, h = 7$
$S = 142$ Simplify.

The surface area is 142 square feet.

The surface area S of a cylinder with height h and radius r is the area of the two bases plus the area of the curved surface, or $S = 2\pi r^2 + 2\pi rh$.

EXAMPLE 2 Find the surface area of the cylinder. Round to the nearest tenth.

$S = 2\pi r^2 + 2\pi rh$ Surface area of a cylinder
$S = 2\pi(5)^2 + 2\pi(5)(9)$ $r = 5, h = 9$
$S \approx 439.8$ Simplify.

The surface area is about 439.8 square meters.

EXERCISES

Find the surface area of each solid. Round to the nearest tenth if necessary.

1. 76 yd^2
2. 150.8 cm^2
3. 232 in^2
4. 75.4 mm^2
5. 225.6 mi^2
6. 505.2 km^2
7. rectangular prism: length, 2.3 in.; width, 7 in.; height, 8 in. **181 in^2**
8. cylinder: radius, 4 cm; height, 8.2 cm **306.6 cm^2**

Practice: Skills, p. 408

NAME ________ DATE ________ PERIOD ____

7-7 Practice: Skills
Surface Area of Prisms and Cylinders

Find the surface area of each solid. Round to the nearest tenth if necessary.

1. 88 ft^2
2. 169.6 in^2
3. 96 mm^2
4. 276.5 yd^2
5. 361.4 cm^2
6. 304 m^2
7. 210 mi^2
8. 325.8 km^2
9. 464.0 ft^2
10. 558 m^2
11. 378 cm^2
12. 1,164.9 in^2
13. cube: edge length, 11 m **726 m^2**
14. rectangular prism: length, 9 cm; width, 13 cm; height, 18.4 cm **1,043.6 cm^2**
15. cylinder: radius, 9.4 mm; height, 15 mm **1,441.1 mm^2**
16. cylinder: diameter, 28 in.; height, 12.6 in. **2,339.9 in^2**

Practice: Word Problems, p. 409

NAME ________ DATE ________ PERIOD ____

7-7 Practice: Word Problems
Surface Area of Prisms and Cylinders

1. **BAKING** The top and sides of the cake shown below are to be covered in frosting. Calculate the area that will be covered with frosting. **192 in^2**

2. **GIFTS** A birthday gift is placed inside the box shown below. What is the minimum amount of wrapping paper needed to wrap this gift? **616 in^2**

3. **FARMING** Phil is planning to shingle the triangular roof on his barn shown below. How many square feet will he be shingling? **1,795.2 ft^2**

4. **FARMING** Refer to Exercise 3. If one package of shingles covers 325 square feet, how many packages will Phil need to buy? **6 packages**

5. **LIGHT SHOW** A mirrored cylinder used in a light show is shown below. Only the curved side of the cylinder is covered with mirrors. Find the area of the cylinder covered in mirrors. Round to the nearest tenth. **2,073.5 cm^2**

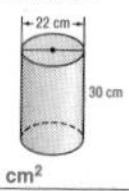

6. **SOUP** Emily has the flu, so she decides to make chicken noodle soup. How many square inches of metal were used to make Emily's can of soup? Round to the nearest tenth. **56.5 in^2**

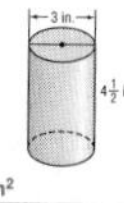

7-8 Lesson Notes

Lesson Resources

Chapter 7 Resource Masters
- Study Guide and Intervention, p. 412
- Practice: Skills, p. 413
- Practice: Word Problems, p. 414
- Reading to Learn Mathematics, p. 415
- Enrichment, p. 416

Parent and Student Study Guide Online Worksheets, 7-8
Teaching Mathematics with Manipulatives, pp. 88–89
Noteables™: Interactive Study Notebook with Foldables™, 7-8

FAST FILE

1 Focus

5-Minute Check 7-8

Use as a quiz or review of Lesson 7-7. (Also available as a transparency)

Bellringer

Hands-On Activity Ask students to describe the shapes of the faces of a pyramid. Then ask them to describe the shape of the face of a cone. Ask them to guess the shape of the curved part of a cone when it is unwrapped. Give them a water cup shaped like a cone and allow them to cut and unroll it. Then have them describe the shape.

Reading to Learn Mathematics, p. 415 ELL

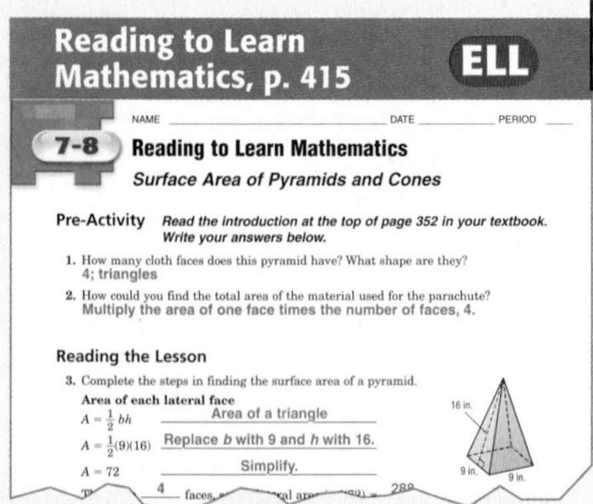

NAME ______ DATE ______ PERIOD ______

7-8 **Reading to Learn Mathematics**
Surface Area of Pyramids and Cones

Pre-Activity *Read the introduction at the top of page 352 in your textbook. Write your answers below.*

1. How many cloth faces does this pyramid have? What shape are they? 4; triangles
2. How could you find the total area of the material used for the parachute? Multiply the area of one face times the number of faces, 4.

Reading the Lesson

3. Complete the steps in finding the surface area of a pyramid.
Area of each lateral face
$A = \frac{1}{2}bh$ Area of a triangle
$A = \frac{1}{2}(9)(16)$ Replace b with 9 and h with 16.
$A = 72$ Simplify.

7-8 Surface Area of Pyramids and Cones

What You'll LEARN

Find the surface areas of pyramids and cones.

NEW Vocabulary

lateral face
slant height
lateral area

Link to READING

Everyday Meaning of lateral: situated on the side

WHEN am I ever going to use this?

HISTORY In 1485, Leonardo Da Vinci sketched a pyramid-shaped parachute in the margin of his notebook. In June 2000, using a parachute created with tools and materials available in medieval times, Adrian Nicholas proved Da Vinci's design worked by descending 7,000 feet.

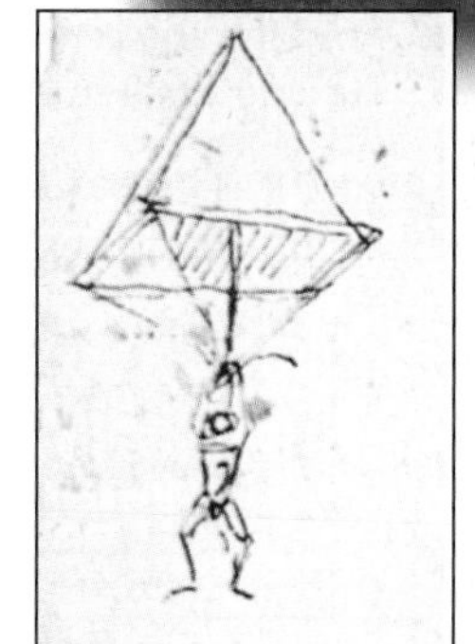

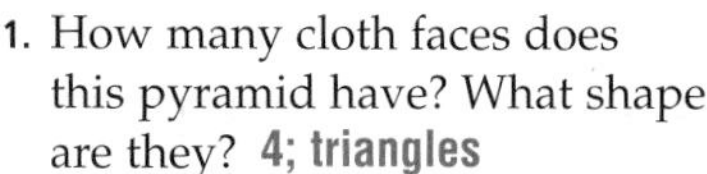

1. How many cloth faces does this pyramid have? What shape are they? **4; triangles**

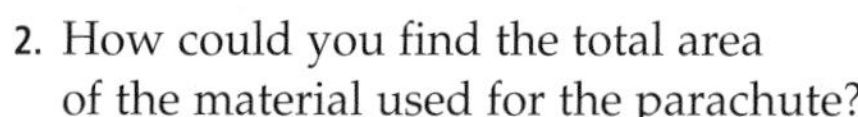

2. How could you find the total area of the material used for the parachute?

2. Multiply the area of one face times the number of faces, 4.

The triangular sides of a pyramid are called **lateral faces**. The triangles intersect at the vertex. The altitude or height of each lateral face is called the **slant height**.

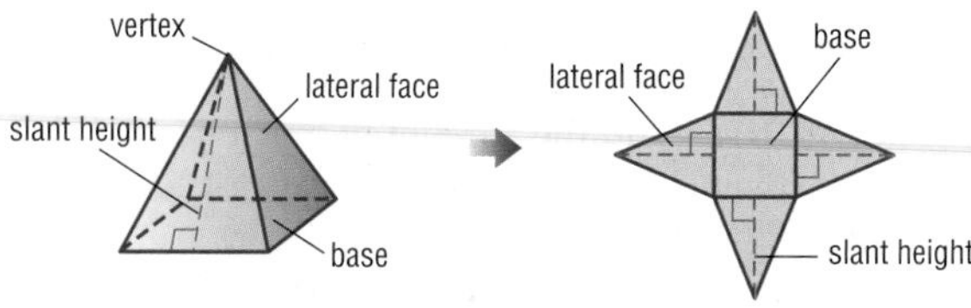

The sum of the areas of the lateral faces is the **lateral area**. The surface area of a pyramid is the lateral area plus the area of the base.

EXAMPLE Surface Area of a Pyramid

1 Find the surface area of the square pyramid.

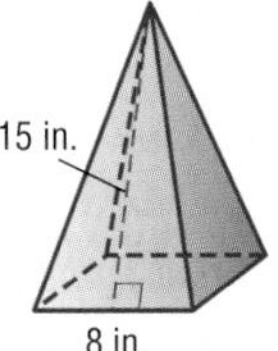

Find the lateral area and the area of the base.

Area of each lateral face

$A = \frac{1}{2}bh$ Area of a triangle

$A = \frac{1}{2}(8)(15)$ or 60 Replace b with 8 and h with 15.

There are 4 faces, so the lateral area is 4(60) or 240 square inches.

Area of base

$A = s^2$ Area of a square

$A = 8^2$ or 64 Replace s with 8.

The surface area of the pyramid is the sum of the lateral area and the area of the base, 240 + 64 or 304 square inches.

TEACHING TIP

The portion of the larger circle in the diagram at the right is called a *sector*. The area of the sector is proportional to the area of the larger circle. Similarly, the arc length of the sector is proportional to the circumference of the larger circle. Thus, $\frac{\text{sector area}}{\text{circle area}}$ equals $\frac{\text{arc length}}{\text{circle circumference}}$. In the diagram, the arc length of the sector of the circle forming the lateral surface of the cone is equal to the circumference of the base of the cone, $2\pi r$. Therefore, $\frac{\text{sector area}}{\pi \ell^2} = \frac{2\pi r}{2\pi \ell}$. Multiplying each side of the equation by $\pi \ell^2$, we find that the sector area is $\pi r \ell$.

You can find the surface area of a cone with radius r and slant height ℓ by finding the area of its bases and adding the area of its curved side. If you unroll a cone, its net is a circle and a portion of a larger circle.

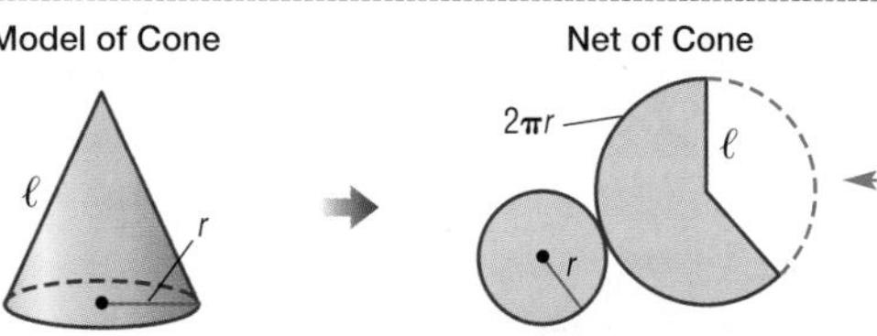

Model	Net	Area
lateral area	portion of circle with radius ℓ	$\pi r \ell$
circular base	circle with radius r	πr^2

So, the surface area S of a cone is $\pi r \ell + \pi r^2$.

Noteables™ Key Concept: Surface Area of a Cone

Words The surface area S of a cone with slant height ℓ and radius r is the lateral area plus the area of the base.

Symbols $S = \pi r \ell + \pi r^2$

Model

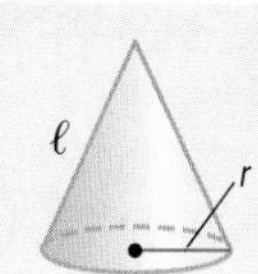

STUDY TIP

Slant Height Be careful not to use the height of a pyramid or cone in place of its slant height. Remember that a slant height lies along a cone or pyramid's lateral surface.

EXAMPLE Surface Area of a Cone

2 Find the surface area of the cone.

$S = \pi r \ell + \pi r^2$ Surface area of a cone

$S = \pi(7)(13) + \pi(7)^2$ Replace r with 7 and ℓ with 13.

$S \approx 439.8$ Simplify.

7 cm

13 cm

The surface area of the cone is about 439.8 square centimeters.

Your Turn Find the surface area of each solid. Round to the nearest tenth if necessary.

a. 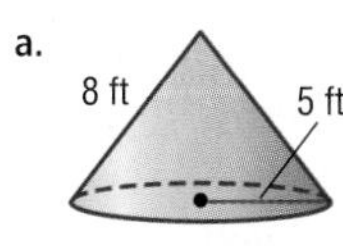

204.2 ft²

b. 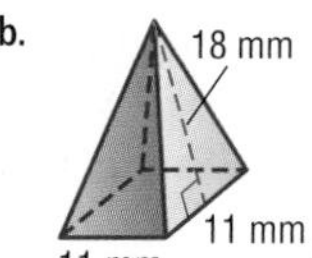

517 mm²

c. $3\frac{1}{2}$ in., 10 in. **148.4 in²**

msmath3.net/extra_examples

2 Teach

In-Class Examples

INTERACTIVE CHALKBOARD PowerPoint® Presentations

1 Find the surface area of the triangular pyramid. **70.8 in²**

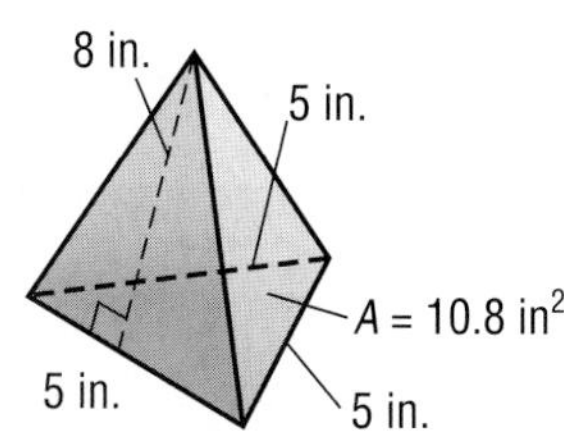

2 Find the surface area of the cone. Round to the nearest tenth. **about 28.3 m²**

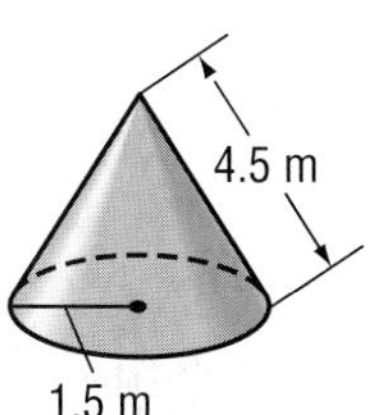

DAILY INTERVENTION Differentiated Instruction

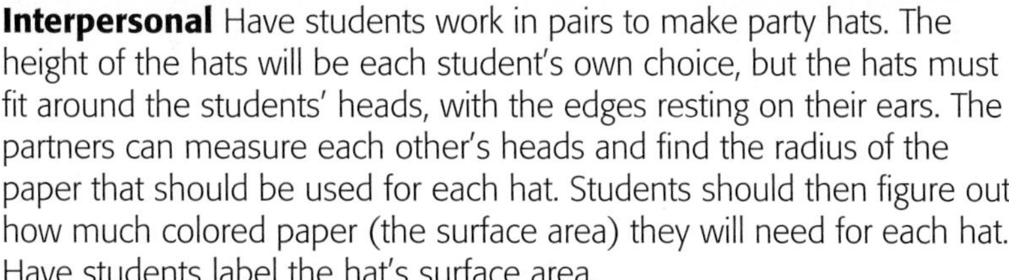

Interpersonal Have students work in pairs to make party hats. The height of the hats will be each student's own choice, but the hats must fit around the students' heads, with the edges resting on their ears. The partners can measure each other's heads and find the radius of the paper that should be used for each hat. Students should then figure out how much colored paper (the surface area) they will need for each hat. Have students label the hat's surface area.

3 Practice/Apply

FOLDABLES Follow-Up Remind students to record main ideas, definitions of vocabulary words, and other notes on study cards as they progress through the lesson. Students store their study cards from this lesson in the *Area* pocket of their Foldables.

About the Exercises...

Guided Practice Key

Exercises	Examples
3–4	1
5	2

Assignment Guide

Basic: 7–15 odd, 18–20, 25–32

Average: 7–17 odd, 18–20, 25–32 (Optional: 21–24)

Enriched: 6–16 even, 18–28 (Optional: 29–32)

Answers

1. The slant height is the height of each lateral face of the pyramid and the height is the perpendicular distance from the vertex to the base of the pyramid.
2. Sample answer:

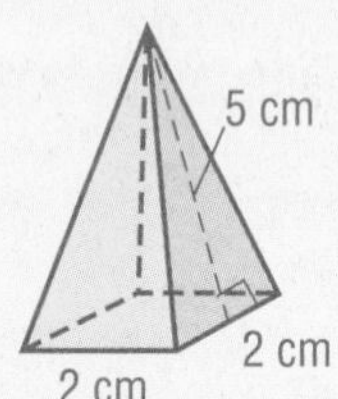

lateral area: 20 cm^2

15. 5; The surface area of the roof is 502.7 ft^2. $502.7 \div 120 \approx 4.2$. Since you cannot buy a fraction of a roll, 5 rolls of roofing material are needed.

Students practice the same concepts in Exercises 6–13 if they are assigned odd or even problems.

Skill and Concept Check

1. *Writing Math* Explain how the slant height and the height of a pyramid are different. See margin.
2. **OPEN ENDED** Draw a square pyramid, giving measures for its slant height and base side length. Then find its lateral area. See margin.

GUIDED PRACTICE

Find the surface area of each solid. Round to the nearest tenth if necessary.

3. 64 ft^2

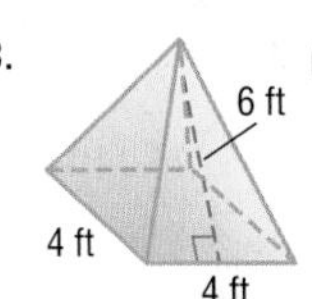

4. 332.4 m^2

12 m
15 m
62.4 m^2
12 m
12 m

5. 115.0 cm^2

9.2 cm
3 cm

★ indicates increased difficulty

Practice and Applications

HOMEWORK HELP

For Exercises	See Examples
6–9, 13, 16	1
10–12, 15, 17	2

Extra Practice See pages 634, 654.

Find the surface area of each solid. Round to the nearest tenth if necessary.

6. 18 in^2

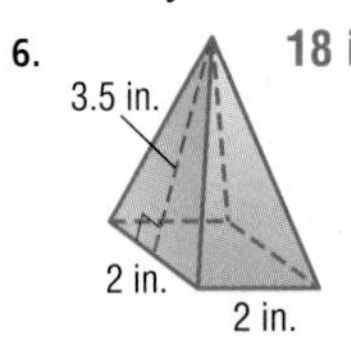

7. 47.3 ft^2

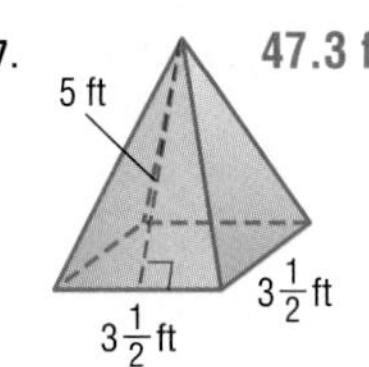

8. 90.3 m^2

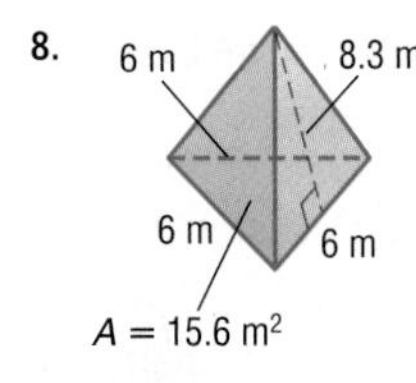

9. 140.4 mm^2

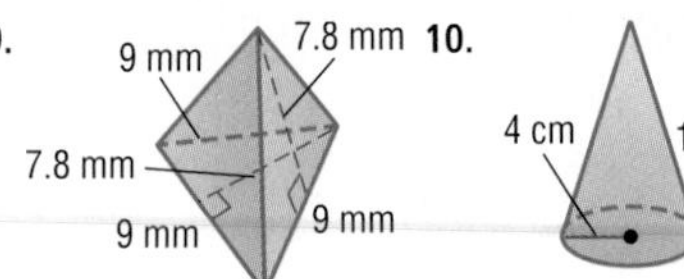

10. 204.8 cm^2

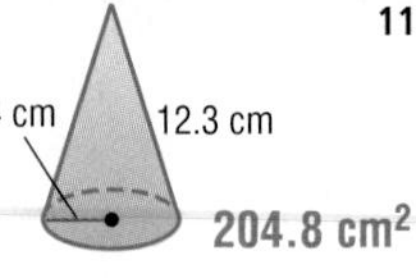

11. 659.6 yd^2

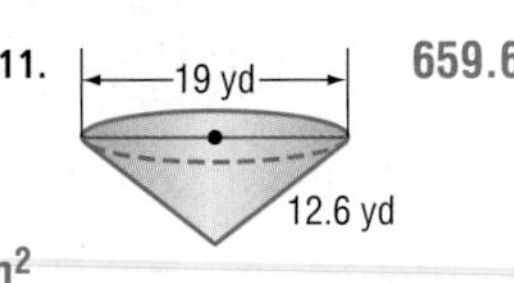

12. cone: diameter, 11.4 ft; slant height, 25 ft 549.7 ft^2
13. square pyramid: base side length, $6\frac{1}{2}$ cm; slant height $8\frac{1}{4}$ cm 149.5 cm^2

★ 14. Find the surface area of the complex solid at the right. Round to the nearest tenth. 207.3 m^2

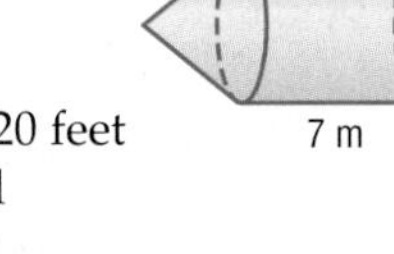

15. **ROOFS** A cone-shaped roof has a diameter of 20 feet and a slant height of 16 feet. If roofing material comes in 120 square-foot rolls, how many rolls will be needed to cover this roof? Explain. See margin.

★ 16. **GLASS** The Luxor Hotel in Las Vegas, Nevada, is a pyramid-shaped building standing 350 feet tall and covered with glass. Its base is a square with each side 646 feet long. Find the surface area of the glass on the Luxor. (*Hint*: Use the Pythagorean Theorem to find the pyramid's slant height ℓ.) 615,335.3 ft^2

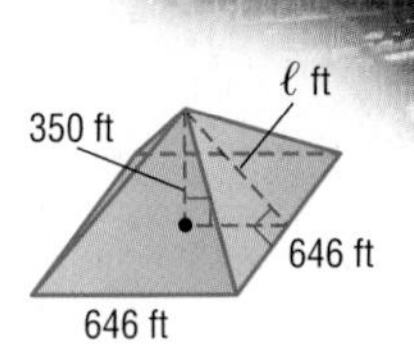

354 Chapter 7 Geometry: Measuring Area and Volume

★ 17. **GEOMETRY** A *frustum* is the part of a solid that remains after the top portion of the solid has been cut off by a plane parallel to the base. The lampshade at the right is a frustum of a cone. Find the surface area of the lampshade. **254.5 in^2**

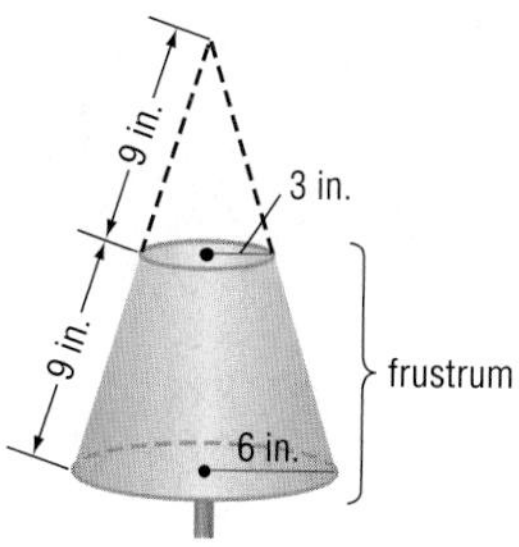

9 in. 3 in. 9 in. 6 in. frustrum

CRITICAL THINKING For Exercises 18–20, use the drawings of the pyramid below, whose lateral faces are equilateral triangles.

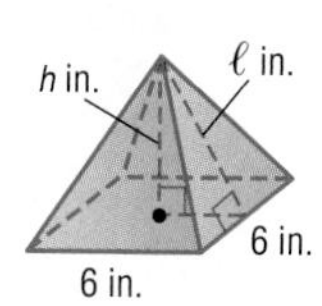

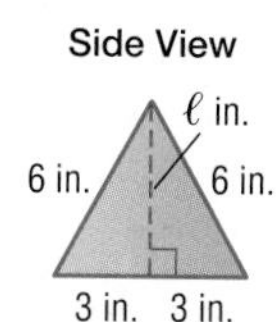

18. Find the exact measure of the slant height ℓ. **$\sqrt{27}$ in.**
19. Use the slant height to find the exact height h of the pyramid. **$\sqrt{18}$ in.**
20. Find the exact volume and surface area of the pyramid. **$\sqrt{2{,}592}$ in^3; $36 + \sqrt{3{,}888}$ in^2**

EXTENDING THE LESSON The surface area S of a sphere with radius r is given by the formula $S = 4\pi r^2$.

Find the surface area of each sphere to the nearest tenth.

21. 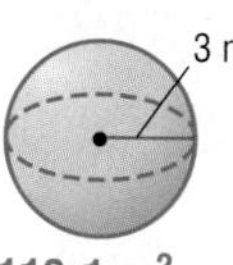

113.1 m^2

22. 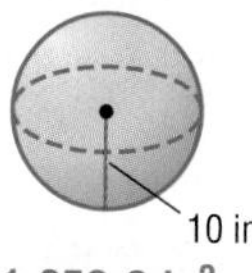

1,256.6 in^2

23. 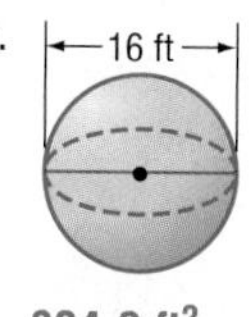

804.2 ft^2

24. 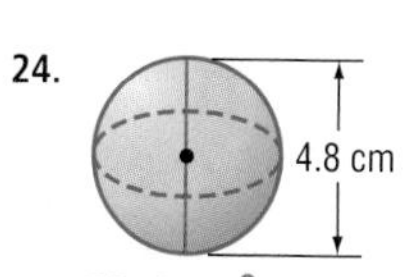

72.4 cm^2

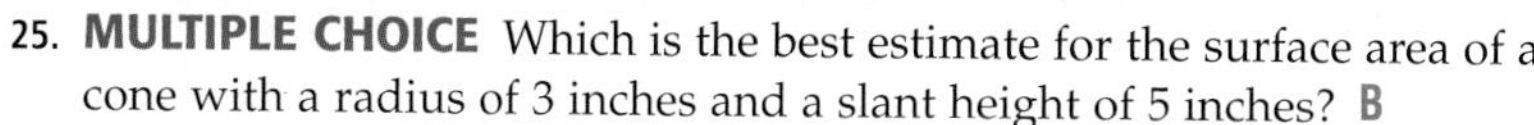

25. **MULTIPLE CHOICE** Which is the best estimate for the surface area of a cone with a radius of 3 inches and a slant height of 5 inches? **B**

Ⓐ 45 in^2 Ⓑ 72 in^2 Ⓒ 117 in^2 Ⓓ 135 in^2

26. **MULTIPLE CHOICE** What is the lateral area of the pentagonal pyramid at the right if the slant height is 9 centimeters? **H**

Ⓕ 18 cm^2 Ⓖ 72 cm^2 Ⓗ 90 cm^2 Ⓘ 180 cm^2

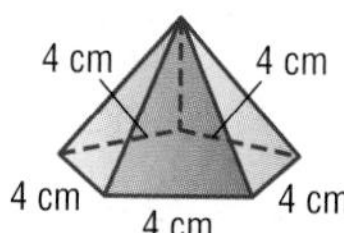

27. **GEOMETRY** Find the surface area of a cylinder whose diameter is 22 feet and whose height is 7.5 feet. (Lesson 7-7) **1,278.6 ft^2**

28. **MULTI STEP** The cylindrical air duct of a large furnace has a diameter of 30 inches and a height of 120 feet. If it takes 15 minutes for the contents of the duct to be expelled into the air, what is the volume of the substances being expelled each hour? (Lesson 7-5) **2,356.2 ft^3**

GETTING READY FOR THE NEXT LESSON

BASIC SKILL Find the value of each expression to the nearest tenth.

29. $8.35 + 54.2$ **62.6** 30. $7 - 2.89$ **4.1** 31. $4.2 \cdot 6.13$ **25.7** 32. $9.31 \div 5$ **1.9**

Math Online msmath3.net/self_check_quiz

4 Assess

Open-Ended Assessment

Speaking Have students explain how to find the surface area of an ice cream cone with a slant height of ten centimeters and a radius of three centimeters.

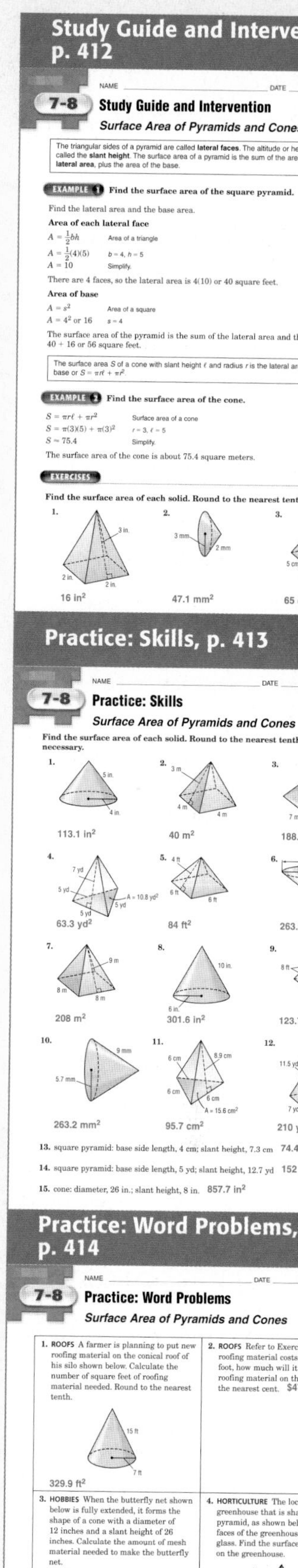

Study Guide and Intervention, p. 412

NAME DATE PERIOD

7-8 Study Guide and Intervention
Surface Area of Pyramids and Cones

The triangular sides of a pyramid are called **lateral faces**. The altitude or height of each lateral face is called the **slant height**. The surface area of a pyramid is the sum of the areas of the lateral faces, or **lateral area**, plus the area of the base.

EXAMPLE 1 Find the surface area of the square pyramid.

Find the lateral area and the base area.
Area of each lateral face
$A = \frac{1}{2}bh$ Area of a triangle
$A = \frac{1}{2}(4)(5)$ $b = 4, h = 5$
$A = 10$ Simplify.
There are 4 faces, so the lateral area is 4(10) or 40 square feet.
Area of base
$A = s^2$ Area of a square
$A = 4^2$ or 16 $s = 4$
The surface area of the pyramid is the sum of the lateral area and the area of the base, 40 + 16 or 56 square feet.

The surface area S of a cone with slant height ℓ and radius r is the lateral area plus the area of the base or $S = \pi r\ell + \pi r^2$.

EXAMPLE 2 Find the surface area of the cone.

$S = \pi r\ell + \pi r^2$ Surface area of a cone
$S = \pi(3)(5) + \pi(3)^2$ $r = 3, \ell = 5$
$S \approx 75.4$ Simplify.
The surface area of the cone is about 75.4 square meters.

EXERCISES

Find the surface area of each solid. Round to the nearest tenth if necessary.

1. 16 in^2 2. 47.1 mm^2 3. 65 cm^2

Practice: Skills, p. 413

NAME DATE PERIOD

7-8 Practice: Skills
Surface Area of Pyramids and Cones

Find the surface area of each solid. Round to the nearest tenth if necessary.

1. 113.1 in^2 2. 40 m^2 3. 188.5 mm^2
4. 63.3 yd^2 5. 84 ft^2 6. 263.9 cm^2
7. 208 m^2 8. 301.6 in^2 9. 123.7 ft^2
10. 263.2 mm^2 11. 95.7 cm^2 12. 210 yd^2

13. square pyramid: base side length, 4 cm; slant height, 7.3 cm 74.4 cm^2
14. square pyramid: base side length, 5 yd; slant height, 12.7 yd 152 yd^2
15. cone: diameter, 26 in.; slant height, 8 in. 857.7 in^2

Practice: Word Problems, p. 414

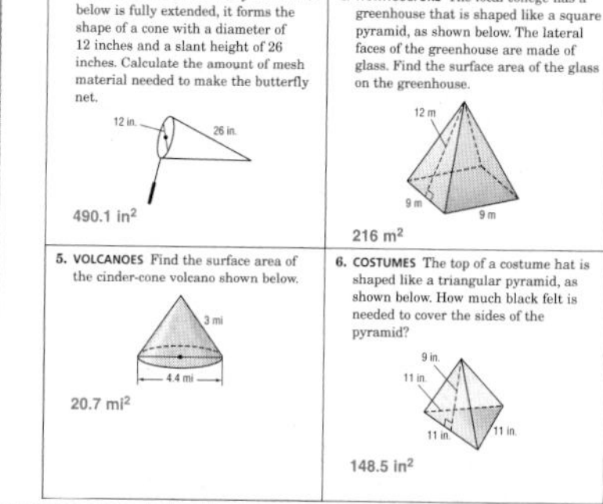

NAME DATE PERIOD

7-8 Practice: Word Problems
Surface Area of Pyramids and Cones

1. ROOFS A farmer is planning to put new roofing material on the conical roof of his silo shown below. Calculate the number of square feet of roofing material needed. Round to the nearest tenth. 329.9 ft^2

2. ROOFS Refer to Exercise 1. If the roofing material costs $1.45 per square foot, how much will it cost to put new roofing material on the silo? Round to the nearest cent. $478.36

3. HOBBIES When the butterfly net shown below is fully extended, it forms the shape of a cone with a diameter of 12 inches and a slant height of 26 inches. Calculate the amount of mesh material needed to make the butterfly net. 490.1 in^2

4. HORTICULTURE The local college has a greenhouse that is shaped like a square pyramid, as shown below. The lateral faces of the greenhouse are made of glass. Find the surface area of the glass on the greenhouse. 216 m^2

5. VOLCANOES Find the surface area of the cinder-cone volcano shown below. 20.7 mi^2

6. COSTUMES The top of a costume hat is shaped like a triangular pyramid, as shown below. How much black felt is needed to cover the sides of the pyramid? 148.5 in^2

7-8b Spreadsheet Investigation

GETTING STARTED

Teaching Tip Once students have the correct formula typed into cell F2, they can drag the formula and fill it into the rest of column F, or they can copy it and paste it into the rest of the column. They can repeat this procedure for the volume calculations in column G.

TEACH

Activity 1

- For each prism and cylinder, ask students to state the spreadsheet coordinates of the dimension that they are working with. For example, to find the volume of Prism B, multiply C3 × D3 × E3.
- As students study the spreadsheet, ask them whether the surface area or the volume is increasing at a faster rate. **volume**

7-8b Spreadsheet Investigation

A Follow-Up of Lesson 7-8

What You'll LEARN

Investigate the volume and surface area of similar solids.

REVIEW Vocabulary

proportion: an equation stating that two ratios are equivalent (Lesson 4-4)

Similar Solids

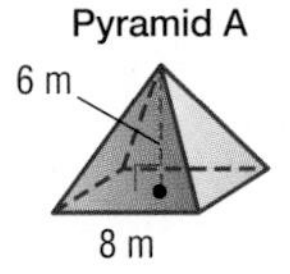

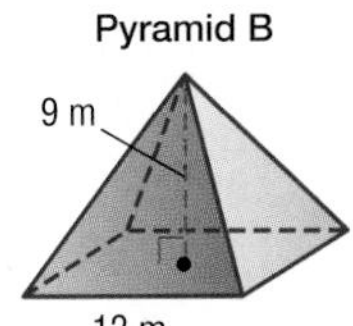

The pyramids are **similar solids**, because they have the same shape and their corresponding linear measures are proportional.

The number of times you increase or decrease the linear dimensions of a solid is called the **scale factor**. The heights of pyramid A and pyramid B are 6 meters and 9 meters, respectively. So the scale factor from pyramid A to pyramid B is $\frac{6}{9}$ or $\frac{2}{3}$.

ACTIVITY

Find the surface area and volume of the prism at the right. Then find the surface areas and volumes of similar prisms with scale factors of 2, 3, and 4.

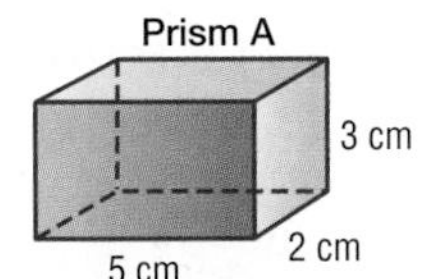

Similar Prisms

	A	B	C	D	E	F	G
1	Prism	Scale Factor	Length	Width	Height	Surface Area	Volume
2	A	1	5	2	3	62	30
3	B	2	10	4	6	248	240
4	C	3	15	6	9	558	810
5	D	4	20	8	12	992	1920

The spreadsheet evaluates the formula 2*C3*D3+2*C3*E3+2*D3*E3.

The spreadsheet evaluates the formula C5*D5*E5.

★ indicates increased difficulty

EXERCISES

1. How many times greater than the surface area of prism A is the surface area of prism B? prism C? prism D? **4; 9; 16**
2. How are the answers to Exercise 1 related to the scale factors?
3. How many times greater than the volume of prism A is the volume of prism B? prism C? prism D? **8; 27; 64**
4. How are the answers to Exercise 3 related to the scale factors?
5. ★ Considering the rectangular prism in the activity above, write expressions for the surface area and volume of a similar prism with scale factor x. **$62x^2$; $30x^3$**

2. Each number is the square of the scale factor for that prism.

4. Each number is the cube of the scale factor for that prism.

Find the surface area and volume of the cylinder at the right. Then find the surface areas and volumes of similar cylinders with scale factors of 2, 3, and 4.

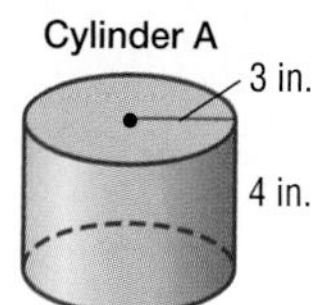

STUDY TIP

Spreadsheet Notation In Microsoft® Excel®, the expression PI() gives the value for π.

Similar Cylinders

	A	B	C	D	E	F	G
1	Cylinder	Scale Factor	Radius	Height	Surface Area	Volume	
2	A	1	3	4	131.9	113.1	
3	B	2	6	8	527.8	904.78	
4	C	3	9	12	1,187.5	3053.6	
5	D	4	12	16	2,111.2	7238.2	

The spreadsheet evaluates the formula 2*PI()*C3^2+2*PI()*C3*D3.

The spreadsheet evaluates the formula PI()*C5^2*D5.

STUDY TIP

Spreadsheet Notation The expression C5^2 squares the value in cell C5.

★ indicates increased difficulty

EXERCISES

6. How many times greater than the surface area of cylinder A is the surface area of cylinder B? cylinder C? cylinder D? **4; 9; 16**
7. How are the answers to Exercise 6 related to the scale factors of each cylinder?
8. How many times greater than the volume of cylinder A is the volume of cylinder B? cylinder C? cylinder D? **8; 27; 64**
9. How are the answers to Exercise 8 related to the scale factors of each cylinder?
★ 10. Considering the cylinder in the activity above, write expressions for the surface area and volume of a similar cylinder with scale factor x. **$131.9x^2$; $113.1x^3$**
★ 11. **Make a conjecture** about how the volume and surface area of a pyramid are affected when all edges of this solid are multiplied by a scale factor of x.

7. Each number is the square of the scale factor for that cylinder.

9. Each number is the cube of the scale factor for that cylinder.

11. The surface area is multiplied by x^2 and the volume is multiplied by x^3.

For Exercises 12 and 13, use the diagram of the two similar prisms at the right.

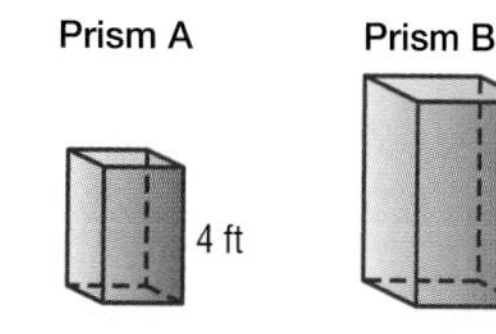

12. If the surface area of prism A is 52 square feet, find the surface area of prism B. **117 ft^2**
13. If the volume of prism A is 24 cubic feet, find the volume of prism B. **81 ft^3**

Activity 2

- Have students sketch cylinders A and B to help them get a sense of the changes in surface area and volume.
- For Exercise 11, have students compare their results for **Activities 1** and **2**. They should look for a pattern that can help them predict for a pyramid.

ASSESS

Observe as students solve the **Exercises**. They should:

- correctly determine the ratios of volumes and surface areas of figures with various scale factors,
- relate the ratios that they find to the scale factors, and
- translate the ratios to general expressions using variables.

7-9 Lesson Notes

Lesson Resources

Chapter 7 Resource Masters
- Study Guide and Intervention, p. 417
- Practice: Skills, p. 418
- Practice: Word Problems, p. 419
- Reading to Learn Mathematics, p. 420
- Enrichment, p. 421

Key Teaching Transparencies, 27
MathPASS Tutorial CD-ROM, 56
Parent and Student Study Guide Online Worksheets, 7-9
Noteables™: Interactive Study Notebook with Foldables™, 7-9

1 Focus

5-Minute Check 7-9

INTERACTIVE CHALKBOARD
PowerPoint® Presentations

Use as a quiz or review of Lesson 7-8. (Also available as a transparency)

Bellringer

Communication Ask students to state their age to the nearest year, month, day, and hour (if they know the hour of their birth). Ask which of these is the most precise statement of their ages. **Stating their ages to the nearest hour is the most precise statement of their ages.**

Reading to Learn Mathematics, p. 420 ELL

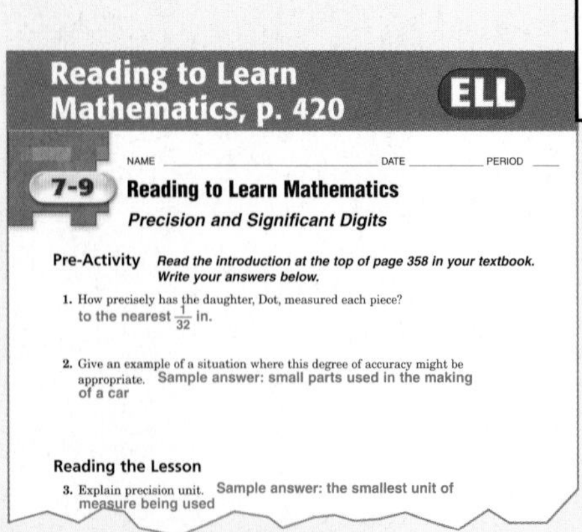

NAME ______ DATE ______ PERIOD ______

7-9 Reading to Learn Mathematics
Precision and Significant Digits

Pre-Activity *Read the introduction at the top of page 358 in your textbook. Write your answers below.*

1. How precisely has the daughter, Dot, measured each piece? to the nearest $\frac{1}{32}$ in.
2. Give an example of a situation where this degree of accuracy might be appropriate. Sample answer: small parts used in the making of a car

Reading the Lesson

3. Explain precision unit. Sample answer: the smallest unit of measure being used

7-9 Measurement: Precision and Significant Digits

What You'll LEARN

Analyze measurements.

NEW Vocabulary

precision
significant digits

WHEN am I ever going to use this?

CARTOONS Consider the cartoon below.

Hi & Lois

1. How precisely has the daughter, Dot, measured each piece?
2. Give an example of a situation where this degree of accuracy might be appropriate.

1. to the nearest $\frac{1}{32}$ in.
2. Sample answer: small parts used in the making of a car

The **precision** of a measurement is the exactness to which a measurement is made. Precision depends upon the smallest unit of measure being used, or the *precision unit*. A measurement is accurate to the nearest precision unit.

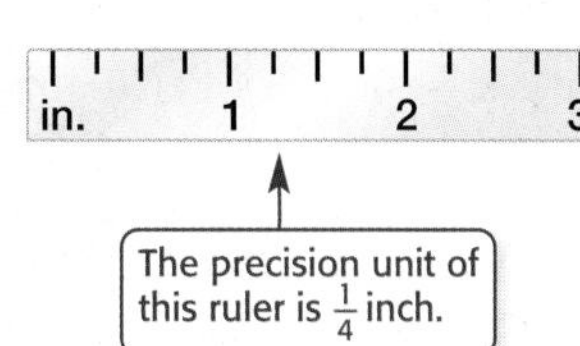

The precision unit of this ruler is $\frac{1}{4}$ inch.

EXAMPLE Identify Precision Units

1 Identify the precision unit of the flask.

There are two spaces between each 50 milliliter-mark, so the precision unit is $\frac{1}{2}$ of 50 milliliters or 25 milliliters.

Your Turn **Identify the precision unit of each measuring instrument.** **a. one tenth of a cm or 1 mm**

a.

b.

1 second

One way to record a measure is to estimate to the nearest precision unit. A more precise method is to include all of the digits that are actually measured, plus one estimated digit. The digits you record when you measure this way are called significant digits. **Significant digits** indicate the precision of the measurement.

STUDY TIP

Precision The precision unit of a measuring instrument determines the number of significant digits.

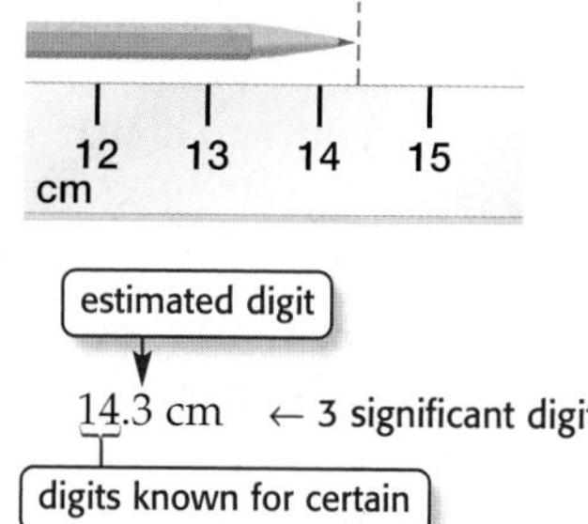

estimated digit

14.3 cm ← 3 significant digits

digits known for certain

precision unit: 1 cm
actual measure: 14–15 cm
estimated measure: 14.3 cm

12 13 14 15
cm

estimated digit

14.35 cm ← 4 significant digits

digits known for certain

precision unit: 0.1 cm
actual measure: 14.3–14.4 cm
estimated measure: 14.35

There are special rules for determining significant digits in a given measurement. Numbers are analyzed for significant digits by counting digits from left to right, starting with the first *nonzero* digit.

Number	Significant Digits	Rule
2.45	3	All nonzero digits are significant.
140.06	5	Zeros between two significant digits are significant.
0.013	2	Zeros used to show place value of the decimal are not significant.
120.0	4	In a number with a decimal point, all zeros to the right of a nonzero digit are significant.
350	2	In a number without a decimal point, any zeros to the right of the last nonzero digit are *not* significant.

EXAMPLES Identify Significant Digits

Determine the number of significant digits in each measure.

2 **10.25 g**
4 significant digits

3 **0.003 L**
1 significant digit

When adding or subtracting measurements, the sum or difference should have the *same precision* as the least precise measurement.

EXAMPLE Add Measurements

4 **LIFTING You are attempting to lift three packages that weigh 5.125 pounds, 6.75 pounds, and 4.6 pounds. Write the combined weight of the packages using the correct precision.**

6.75 ← 2 decimal places
5.125 ← 3 decimal places
+ 4.6 ← 1 decimal place
16.475

The least precise measurement has 1 decimal place, so round the sum to 1 decimal place.

The combined weight of the packages is about 16.5 pounds.

msmath3.net/extra_examples

2 Teach

In-Class Examples

1 Identify the precision unit of the thermometer.

130° 120° 110° 100° 90° 80° 70° 60° 50° 40° 30° 20° 10° 0° –10°
Fahrenheit

2 degrees

Determine the number of significant digits in each measure.

2 5,000 ft **1 significant digit**

3 315.05 oz **5 significant digits**

4 **MAIL** Venita took four packages to the post office. They weighed 1.27 pounds, 3.45 pounds, 0.524 pound, and 2.7 pounds. Write the combined weight of her mail using the correct precision. **7.9 lb**

DAILY INTERVENTION Differentiated Instruction

Intrapersonal Have students describe situations in their lives that involve measurements with varying precision. Have them write down the situations and indicate how the measurements could be more precise. To help them, you might give students one of the following examples: a student tells her mother that she will be home at about 6:00 or a parent pumps 4.56 gallons of gas into the gas tank.

In-Class Example

INTERACTIVE CHALKBOARD PowerPoint® Presentations

5 Use the correct number of significant digits to find the volume of the cylinder shown below. Use 3.14 for pi. **190 in^3**

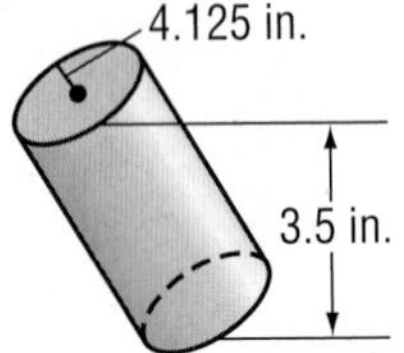

Intervention Students will often confuse accuracy and precision. Accuracy refers to the quality of a result, or how close it is to the true value. Precision refers to the quality of the operation by which the result is obtained; precise measurements cluster together repetition after repetition. A dartboard is the most common analogy for illustrating these concepts. Imagine the bullseye as representing the true value of a measurement. Shots that are randomly scattered are neither accurate nor precise; shots that cluster tightly on the edge of the board are precise but not accurate; and shots that cluster on the bullseye are both accurate and precise.

Answer

1. 5 lb is measured to the nearest pound, 74 oz is measured to the nearest ounce, and 74.8 oz is measured to the nearest 0.1 oz; therefore, 74.8 oz is most precise.

When multiplying or dividing measurements, the product or quotient should have the *same number of significant digits* as the measurement with the least number of significant digits.

EXAMPLE Multiply Measurements

5 GEOMETRY Use the correct number of significant digits to find the area of the parallelogram.

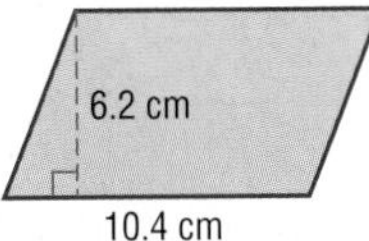

$$\begin{array}{rl} 10.4 & \leftarrow \text{3 significant digits} \\ \times\ 6.2 & \leftarrow \text{2 significant digits} \\ \hline 64.48 & \end{array}$$

This measurement has the least number of significant digits, 2.

Round the product, 64.48, so that it has 2 significant digits. The area of the parallelogram is about 64 square centimeters.

Your Turn

c. Find 3.48 liters − 0.2 liters using the correct precision. **3.3 L**

d. Use the correct number of significant digits to calculate 0.45 meter ÷ 0.8 meter. **0.6**

Students practice the same concepts in Exercises 14–37 if they are assigned odd or even problems.

Skill and Concept Check

1. **Writing Math** Determine which measurement of a bag of dog food would be the most precise: 5 pounds, 74 ounces, or 74.8 ounces. Explain. **74.8 oz; See margin.**
2. **OPEN ENDED** Write a 5-digit number with 3 significant digits. **Sample answer: 12,300**
3. **Which One Doesn't Belong?** Identify the number that does not have the same number of significant digits as the other three. Explain.

20.6	0.0815	4,260	375.0

375.0; all of the other numbers have 3 significant digits, while 375.0 has 4 significant digits.

GUIDED PRACTICE

Identify the precision of the unit of each measuring instrument.

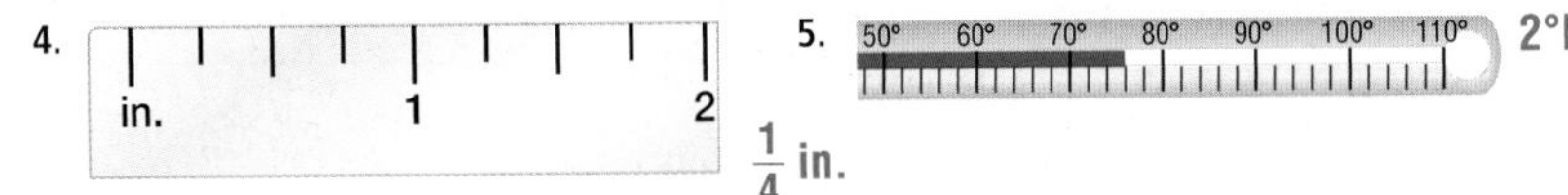

4. **$\frac{1}{4}$ in.** 5. **2°F**

Determine the number of significant digits in each measure.

6. 138.0 g **4**
7. 0.0037 mm **2**
8. 50 min **1**
9. 206.04 cm **5**

Find each sum or difference using the correct precision.

10. 45 in. + 12.7 in. **58 in.**
11. 7.38 m − 5.9 m **1.5 m**

Find each product or quotient using the correct number of significant digits.

12. 8.2 yd · 4.5 yd **37 yd^2**
13. 7.31 s ÷ 5.4 s **1.4**

360 Chapter 7 Geometry: Measuring Area and Volume

Practice and Applications

HOMEWORK HELP	
For Exercises	See Examples
14–17, 40	1
18–25, 41	2, 3
26–31, 38, 42	4
32–37, 39	5

Extra Practice
See pages 635, 654.

Identify the precision unit of each measuring instrument.

14. **0.5 cm**

15. $\frac{1}{8}$ **in.**

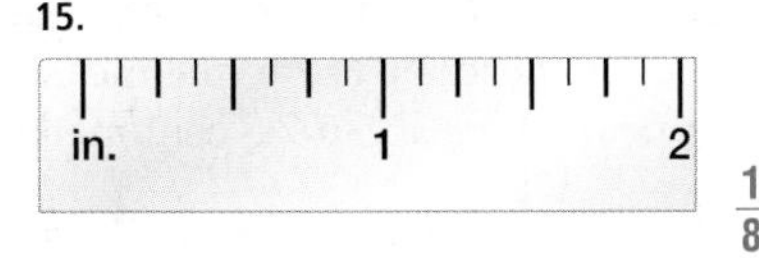

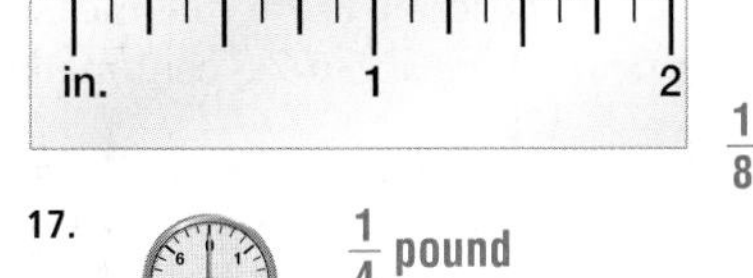

16. **0.5 mL**

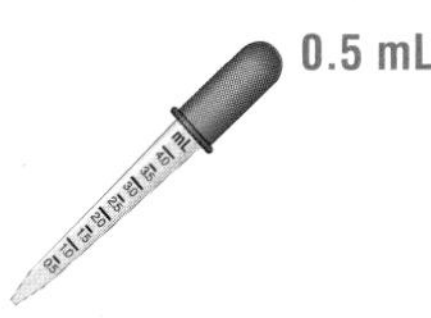

17. $\frac{1}{4}$ **pound**

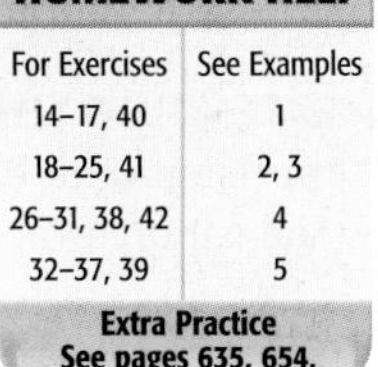

Determine the number of significant digits in each measure.

18. 0.025 mL **2**
19. 3,450 km **3**
20. 40.03 in. **4**
21. 7.0 kg **2**
22. 104.30 mi **5**
23. 3.06 s **3**
24. 0.009 mm **1**
25. 380 g **2**

Find each sum or difference using the correct precision.

26. 12.85 cm + 5.4 cm **18.3 cm**
27. 14.003 L − 4.61 L **9.39 L**
28. 34 g − 15.2 g **19 g**
29. 150 m + 44.7 m **190 m**
30. 100 mi + 63.7 mi **200 mi**
31. 14.37 s − 9.2 s **5.2 s**

Find each product or quotient using the correct number of significant digits.

32. 0.8 cm · 9.4 cm **8 cm^2**
33. 3.82 ft · 3.5 ft **13 ft^2**
34. 10 mi · 1.2 mi **10 mi^2**
35. 200 g ÷ 2.6 g **80**
36. 88.5 lb ÷ 0.05 lb **2,000**
37. 7.50 mL ÷ 0.2 mL **40**

38. **GEOMETRY** A triangle's sides measure 17.04 meters, 8.2 meters, and 7.375 meters. Write the perimeter using the correct precision. **32.6 m**

39. **SURVEYING** A surveyor measures the dimensions of a field and finds that the length is 122.5 meters and the width is 86.4 meters. What is the area of the field? Round to the correct number of significant digits. **10,600 m^2**

SCHOOL For Exercises 40–42, refer to the graphic at the right.

40. Are the numbers exact? Explain. **See margin.**
41. How many significant digits are used to describe the number of children enrolled in public school? **3**
42. Find the difference between public and private school enrollment using the correct precision. **See margin.**

msmath3.net/self_check_quiz

3 Practice/Apply

Which One Doesn't Belong?
In Exercise 3, remind students that zeros that show the place value of the decimal are not significant.

About the Exercises...

Guided Practice Key

Exercises	Examples
4–5	1
6–9	2, 3
10–11	4
12–13	5

Assignment Guide

Basic: 15–41 odd, 43, 45–52

Average: 15–41 odd, 43, 45–52 (Optional: 44)

Enriched: 14–38 even, 40–52

Answers

40. No; the numbers are rounded to the nearest 0.1 million.
42. 42 million or 42,000,000 children

Lesson 7-9 Measurement: Precision and Significant Digits 361

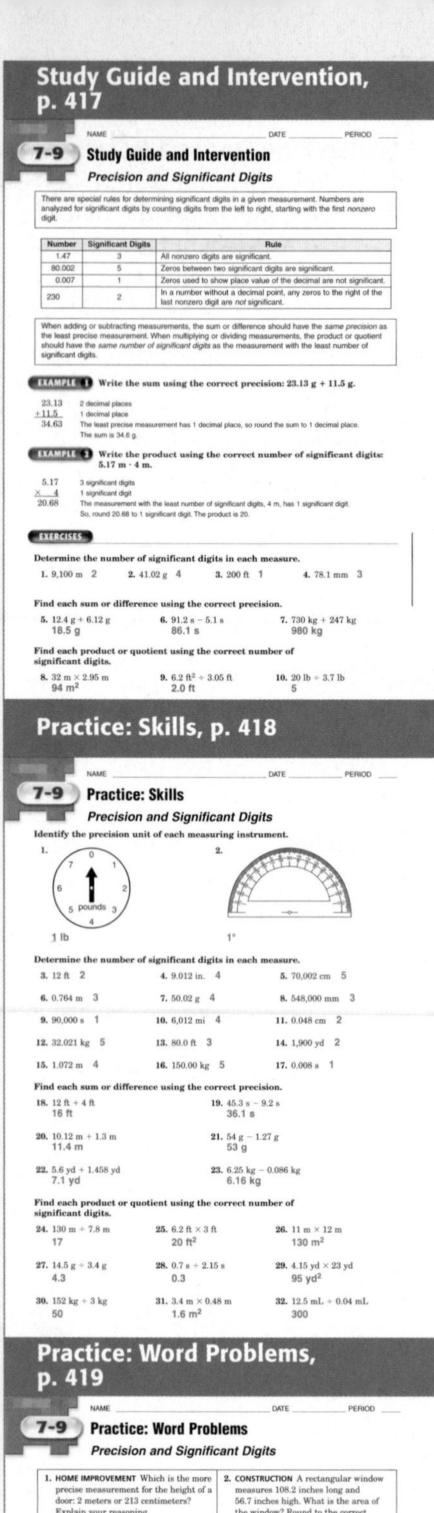

Study Guide and Intervention, p. 417

NAME ______________ DATE ________ PERIOD ____

7-9 Study Guide and Intervention

Precision and Significant Digits

There are special rules for determining significant digits in a given measurement. Numbers are analyzed for significant digits by counting digits from the left to right, starting with the first *nonzero* digit.

Number	Significant Digits	Rule
1.47	3	All nonzero digits are significant.
80.002	5	Zeros between two significant digits are significant.
0.007	1	Zeros used to show place value of the decimal are not significant.
230	2	In a number without a decimal point, any zeros to the right of the last nonzero digit are *not* significant.

When adding or subtracting measurements, the sum or difference should have the *same precision* as the least precise measurement. When multiplying or dividing measurements, the product or quotient should have the *same number of significant digits* as the measurement with the least number of significant digits.

EXAMPLE 1 Write the sum using the correct precision: 23.13 g + 11.5 g.

23.13 — 2 decimal places
+11.5 — 1 decimal place
34.63 — The least precise measurement has 1 decimal place, so round the sum to 1 decimal place. The sum is 34.6 g.

EXAMPLE 2 Write the product using the correct number of significant digits: 5.17 m · 4 m.

5.17 — 3 significant digits
× 4 — 1 significant digit
20.68 — The measurement with the least number of significant digits, 4 m, has 1 significant digit. So, round 20.68 to 1 significant digit. The product is 20.

EXERCISES

Determine the number of significant digits in each measure.

1. 9,100 m 2
2. 41.02 g 4
3. 200 ft 1
4. 78.1 mm 3

Find each sum or difference using the correct precision.

5. 12.4 g + 6.12 g 18.5 g
6. 91.2 s − 5.1 s 86.1 s
7. 730 kg + 247 kg 980 kg

Find each product or quotient using the correct number of significant digits.

8. 32 m × 2.95 m 94 m^2
9. $6.2 \text{ ft}^2 \div 3.05$ ft 2.0 ft
10. 20 lb ÷ 3.7 lb 5

Practice: Skills, p. 418

NAME ______________ DATE ________ PERIOD ____

7-9 Practice: Skills

Precision and Significant Digits

Identify the precision unit of each measuring instrument.

1. 1 lb
2. 1°

Determine the number of significant digits in each measure.

3. 12 ft 2
4. 9.012 in. 4
5. 70,002 cm 5
6. 0.764 m 3
7. 50.02 g 4
8. 548,000 mm 3
9. 90,000 s 1
10. 6,012 mi 4
11. 0.048 cm 2
12. 32.021 kg 5
13. 80.0 ft 3
14. 1,900 yd 2
15. 1.072 m 4
16. 150.00 kg 5
17. 0.008 s 1

Find each sum or difference using the correct precision.

18. 12 ft + 4 ft 16 ft
19. 45.3 s − 9.2 s 36.1 s
20. 10.12 m + 1.3 m 11.4 m
21. 54 g − 1.27 g 53 g
22. 5.6 yd + 1.458 yd 7.1 yd
23. 6.25 kg − 0.086 kg 6.16 kg

Find each product or quotient using the correct number of significant digits.

24. 130 m ÷ 7.8 m 17
25. 6.2 ft × 3 ft 20 ft^2
26. 11 m × 12 m 130 m^2
27. 14.5 g ÷ 3.4 g 4.3
28. 0.7 s ÷ 2.15 s 0.3
29. 4.15 yd × 23 yd 95 yd^2
30. 152 kg ÷ 3 kg 50
31. 3.4 m × 0.48 m 1.6 m^2
32. 12.5 mL ÷ 0.04 mL 300

Practice: Word Problems, p. 419

NAME ______________ DATE ________ PERIOD ____

7-9 Practice: Word Problems

Precision and Significant Digits

1. **HOME IMPROVEMENT** Which is the more precise measurement for the height of a door: 2 meters or 213 centimeters? Explain your reasoning. 213 cm; Centimeters are smaller units than meters.
2. **CONSTRUCTION** A rectangular window measures 108.2 inches long and 56.7 inches high. What is the area of the window? Round to the correct number of significant digits. $6{,}130 \text{ in}^2$
3. **PETS** Tara's two dogs, Cody and Tiger, weigh 34.4 pounds and 27.75 pounds, respectively. What is the difference in the weights of the two dogs? Write the difference using the correct precision. 6.7 lb
4. **GEOMETRY** A rectangle has a length of 34.913 centimeters and a width of 18.43 centimeters. Write the perimeter of the rectangle using the correct precision. 106.69 cm
5. **REAL ESTATE** An empty lot is rectangular in shape with a length of 62.4 feet and a width of 61.2 feet. Find the area of the lot. Round to the correct number of significant digits. $3{,}820 \text{ ft}^2$
6. **GEOMETRY** A rectangular prism is 3.48 inches long, 1.56 inches wide, and 2.1 inches tall. Find the volume of the prism. Round to the correct number of significant digits. 11 in^3
7. **HEALTH** Last night, Niki used an electronic thermometer to find out that her temperature was 100.34 degrees. This morning, she used a mercury thermometer and got a reading of 98.9 degrees. How much did Niki's fever go down overnight? Write the answer using the correct precision. 1.4°
8. **LIFTING** Andy is carrying three bags of groceries into the house. Individually the bags weigh 4.76 pounds, 7.4 pounds, and 9.12 pounds. What is the total weight that Andy is carrying? Write the answer using the correct precision. 21.3 lb

43. **CRITICAL THINKING** Find the surface area of the square pyramid at the right. Use the correct precision or number of significant digits as appropriate. **150 cm^2**

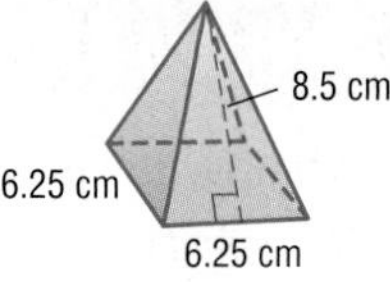

EXTENDING THE LESSON The *greatest possible error* is one-half the precision unit. It can be used to describe the actual measure.
The cotton swab below appears to be about 7.8 centimeters long.

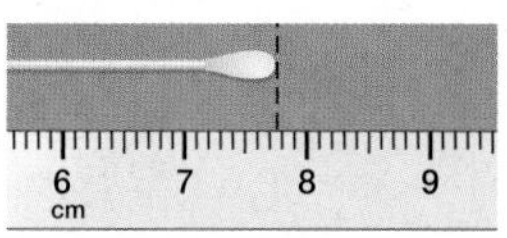

$$\text{greatest possible error} = \frac{1}{2} \cdot \text{precision unit}$$
$$= \frac{1}{2} \cdot 0.1 \text{ cm or } 0.05 \text{ cm}$$

The possible actual length of the cotton swab is 0.05 centimeter less than or 0.05 centimeter more than 7.8 centimeters. So, it is between 7.75 and 7.85 centimeters long.

44. **SPORTS** An Olympic swimmer won the gold medal in the 100-meter backstroke with a time of 61.19 seconds. Find the greatest possible error of the measurement and use it to determine between which two values is the swimmer's actual time. **0.005; between 61.185 and 61.195 s**

Spiral Review with Standardized Test Practice

45. **MULTIPLE CHOICE** Choose the measurement that is most precise. **D**

Ⓐ 54 kg Ⓑ 5.4 kg Ⓒ 54 g Ⓓ 54 mg

46. **GRID IN** Use the correct number of significant digits to find the volume of a cylinder in cubic feet whose radius is 4.0 feet and height is 10.2 feet. **510**

47. **DESSERT** Find the surface area of the waffle cone at the right. (Lesson 7-8) **74.6 cm^2**

5 cm

9.5 cm

48. **HISTORY** The great pyramid of Khufu in Egypt was originally 481 feet high, had a square base 756 feet on a side, and slant height of about 611.8 feet. What was its surface area, not including the base? Round to the nearest tenth. (Lesson 7-7) **$925{,}041.6 \text{ ft}^2$**

Solve each equation. Check your solution. (Lesson 2-9)

49. $x + 0.26 = -3.05$ **−3.31**
50. $\frac{3}{5} = a - \frac{1}{2}$ **$1\frac{1}{10}$**
51. $-\frac{1}{6} = -\frac{1}{4}n$ **$\frac{2}{3}$**
52. $\frac{y}{2.4} = -6.5$ **−15.6**

INTERDISCIPLINARY PROJECT

Under Construction

Math and Architecture It's time to complete your project. Use the information and data you have gathered about floor covering costs and loan rates to prepare a Web page or brochure. Be sure to include a labeled scale drawing with your project.

msmath3.net/webquest

4 Assess

Open-Ended Assessment

Writing Have students make a table describing the rules for determining significant digits and providing examples for each rule.

Study Guide and Review

Vocabulary and Concept Check

altitude (p. 314)	diameter (p. 319)	prism (p. 331)
base (pp. 314, 331)	edge (p. 331)	pyramid (p. 331)
center (p. 319)	face (p. 331)	radius (p. 319)
circle (p. 319)	lateral area (p. 352)	significant digits (p. 358)
circumference (p. 319)	lateral face (p. 352)	slant height (p. 352)
complex figure (p. 326)	pi (π) (p. 319)	solid (p. 331)
complex solid (p. 337)	plane (p. 331)	surface area (p. 347)
cone (p. 343)	polyhedron (p. 331)	vertex (p. 331)
cylinder (p. 336)	precision (p. 358)	volume (p. 335)

Choose the letter of the term that best matches each phrase.

1. a flat surface of a prism b
2. the measure of the space occupied by a solid a
3. a figure that has two parallel, congruent circular bases d
4. any three-dimensional figure f
5. the sides of a pyramid i
6. the distance around a circle h
7. the exactness to which a measurement is made c
8. any side of a parallelogram e
9. a solid figure with flat surfaces that are polygons g

a. volume
b. face
c. precision
d. cylinder
e. base
f. solid
g. polyhedron
h. circumference
i. lateral face

Lesson-by-Lesson Exercises and Examples

7-1 Area of Parallelograms, Triangles, and Trapezoids (pp. 314–318) **11.** $140\frac{1}{4}$ **in²**

Find the area of each figure.

10. 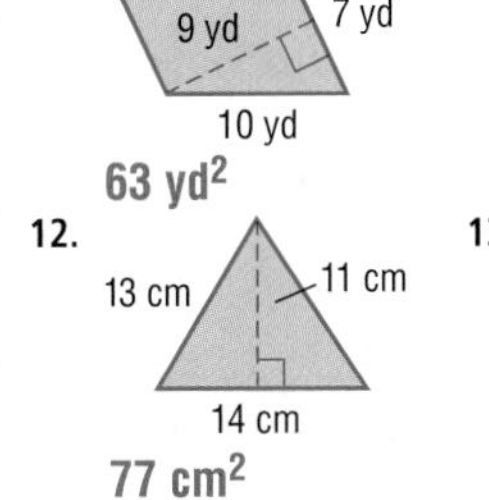

63 yd²

11. 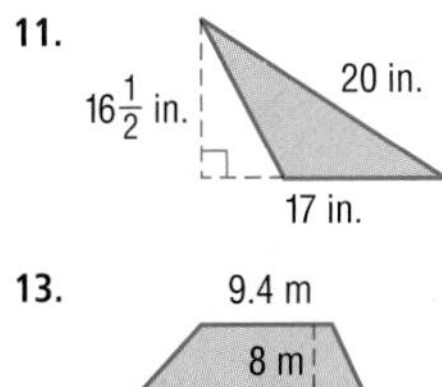

12. 13 cm, 11 cm, 14 cm

77 cm²

13. 9.4 m, 8 m, 17.2 m

106.4 m²

Example 1 **Find the area of the trapezoid.**

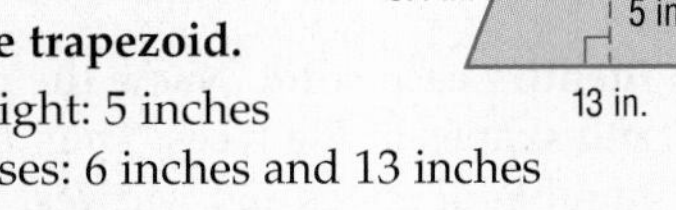

height: 5 inches
bases: 6 inches and 13 inches

$A = \frac{1}{2}h(b_1 + b_2)$ Area of a trapezoid

$A = \frac{1}{2}(5)(6 + 13)$ $h = 5, b_1 = 6, b_2 = 13$

$A = \frac{1}{2}(5)(19)$ or 47.5 Simplify.

The area is 47.5 square inches.

msmath3.net/vocabulary_review

FOLDABLES™ Study Organizer

For more information about Foldables, see *Teaching Mathematics with Foldables.*

Have students look through the chapter to make sure they have included examples in their Foldables for each lesson or topic in the chapter.

Encourage students to refer to their Foldables while completing the Study Guide and Review and to use them in preparing for the Chapter Test.

Chapter 7 Study Guide and Review

Vocabulary Assessment

- This alphabetical list of vocabulary terms in Chapter 7 includes a page reference where each term was introduced.
- A vocabulary review/test for Chapter 7 is available on p. 436 of the *Chapter 7 Resource Masters*.

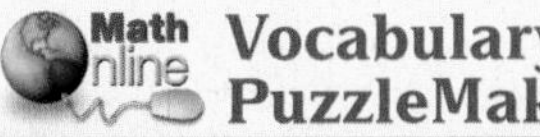

Vocabulary PuzzleMaker

ELL The online Vocabulary PuzzleMaker improves students' mathematics vocabulary using four puzzle formats — crossword, scramble, word search using a word list, and word search using clues. Students can work on a computer screen or from a printed handout.

MindJogger Videoquizzes

ELL MindJogger Videoquizzes provide an alternative review of concepts presented in this chapter. Students work in teams in a game show format to gain points for correct answers. The questions are presented in three rounds.

Round 1 Concepts (5 questions)
Round 2 Skills (4 questions)
Round 3 Problem Solving (4 questions)

ExamView® Pro

Use the networkable ExamView® Pro Testmaker CD-ROM to:

- Create **multiple versions** of tests.
- Create **modified** tests for **inclusion** students with one mouse click.
- **Edit** existing questions and **add** your own questions.
- Build tests aligned with state standards using built-in **state curriculum correlations.**
- Change **English** tests to **Spanish** with one mouse click and vice versa.

7-2 Circumference and Area of Circles (pp. 319–323)

Find the circumference and area of each circle. Round to the nearest tenth.

14. 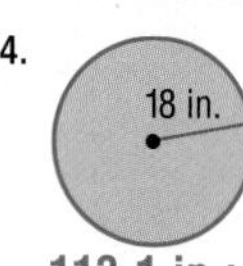

15. 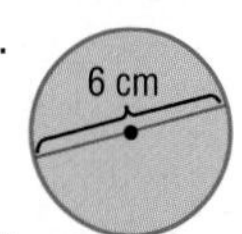

113.1 in.; 1,017.9 in^2 **18.8 cm; 28.3 cm^2**

16. The diameter is $4\frac{1}{3}$ feet. **13.6 ft; 14.7 ft^2**

17. The radius is 2.6 meters. **16.3 m; 21.2 m^2**

Example 2 **Find the circumference and area of the circle.**

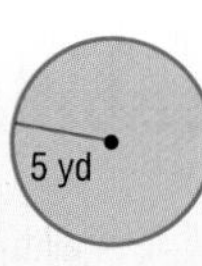

The radius of the circle is 5 yards.

$C = 2\pi r$	$A = \pi r^2$
$C = 2 \cdot \pi \cdot 5$	$A = \pi \cdot 5^2$
$C \approx 31.4$ yd	$A \approx 78.5$ yd^2

7-3 Area of Complex Figures (pp. 326–329)

Find the area of each figure. Round to the nearest tenth if necessary.

18. 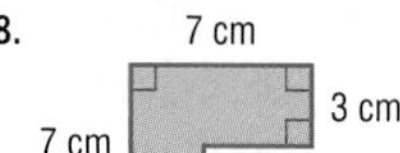

32.2 cm^2

19. 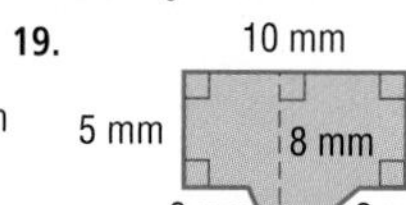

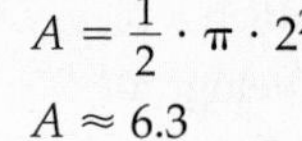

57.5 mm^2

20. 21. 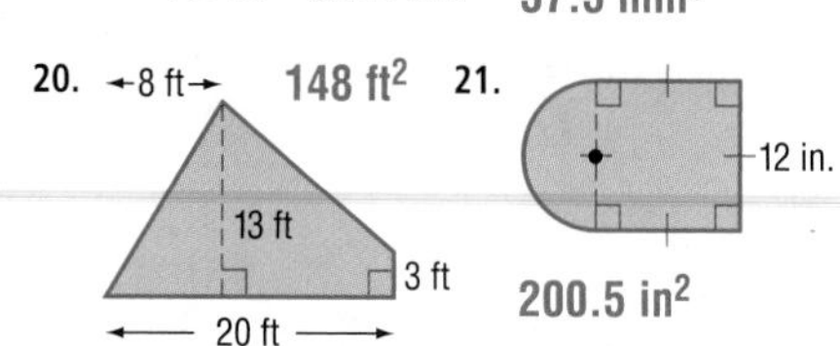

20. **148 ft^2** 21. **200.5 in^2**

Example 3 **Find the area of the complex figure.**

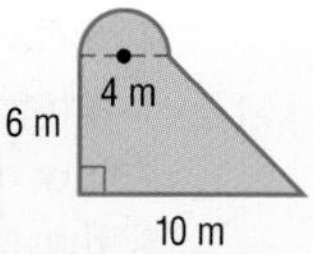

Figure labels: 4 m, 6 m, 10 m

Area of semicircle	Area of trapezoid
$A = \frac{1}{2} \cdot \pi \cdot 2^2$	$A = \frac{1}{2}(6)(4 + 10)$
$A \approx 6.3$	$A = 42$

The area is about 6.3 + 42 or 48.3 square meters.

22. triangular prism; 5 faces, two triangles and 3 rectangles; 9 edges; 6 vertices

7-4 Three-Dimensional Figures (pp. 331–334)

Identify each solid. Name the number and shapes of the faces. Then name the number of edges and vertices.

22. 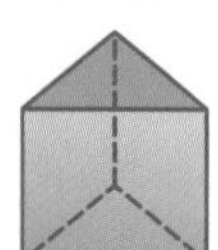

23. 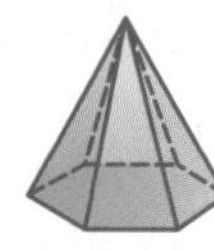

23. hexagonal pyramid; 7 faces, 1 hexagon and 6 triangles; 12 edges; 7 vertices

Example 4 **Name the number and shapes of the faces of a rectangular prism. Then name the number of edges and vertices.**

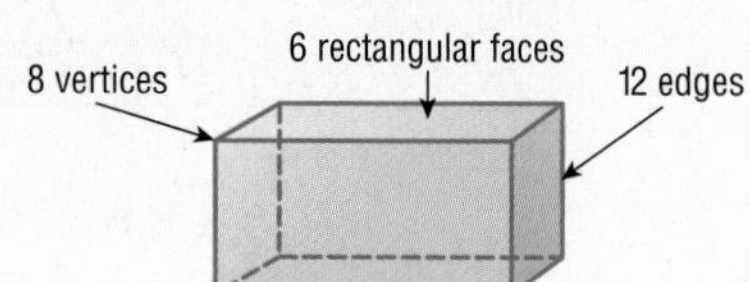

7-5 Volume of Prisms and Cylinders (pp. 335–339)

Find the volume of each solid.

24. **25.**

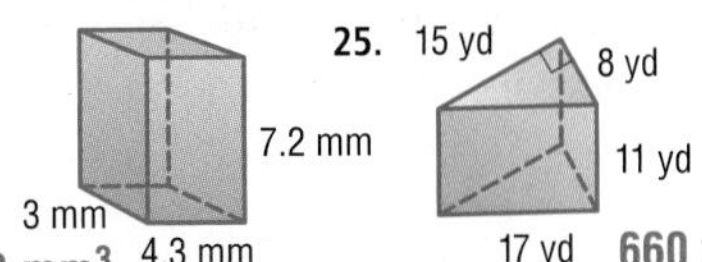

24. **92.88 mm³** 25. **660 yd³**

26. **FOOD** A can of green beans has a diameter of 10.5 centimeters and a height of 13 centimeters. Find its volume. **1,125.7 cm³**

Example 5 **Find the volume of the solid.**

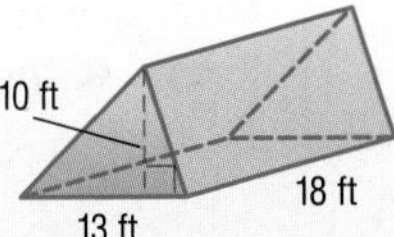

The base of this prism is a triangle.

$V = Bh$ B = area of base, h = height of prism

$V = \left(\frac{1}{2} \cdot 13 \cdot 10\right)18$

$V = 1{,}170 \text{ ft}^3$

7-6 Volume of Pyramids and Cones (pp. 342–345)

Find the volume of each solid. Round to the nearest tenth if necessary.

27. **28.**

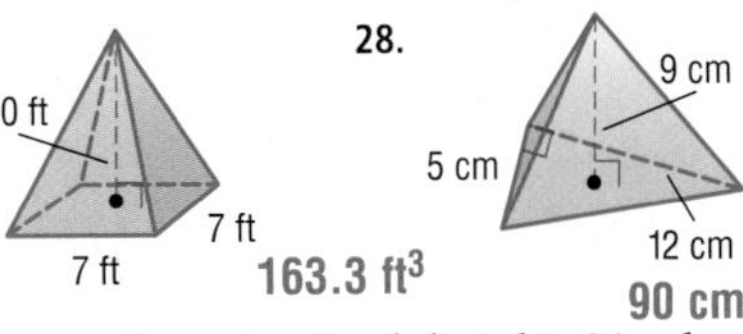

27. **163.3 ft³** 28. **90 cm³**

29. cone: diameter, 9 yd; height, 21 yd **445.3 yd³**

Example 6 **Find the volume of the pyramid.**

8 in.
6 in.
12 in.

The base B of the pyramid is a rectangle.

$V = \frac{1}{3}Bh$ Volume of pyramid or cone

$V = \frac{1}{3}(12 \cdot 6)8$

$V = 192 \text{ in}^3$

7-7 Surface Area of Prisms and Cylinders (pp. 347–351)

Find the surface area of each solid. Round to the nearest tenth if necessary.

30.

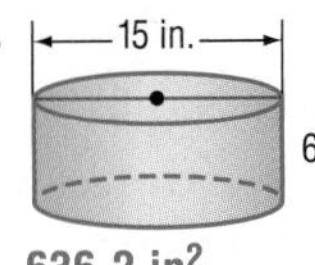

636.2 in²

31.

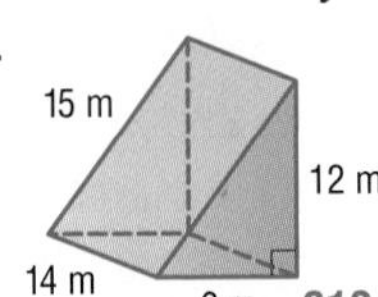

612 m²

32. **SET DESIGN** All but the bottom of a platform 15 feet long, 8 feet wide, and 3 feet high is to be painted for use in a play. Find the area of the surface to be painted. **258 ft²**

Example 7 **Find the surface area of the cylinder.**

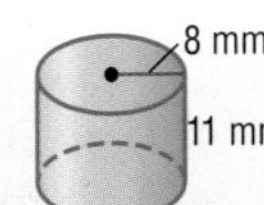

Find the area of the two circular bases and add the area of the curved surface.

$S = 2\pi r^2 + 2\pi rh$ Surface area of a cylinder

$S = 2\pi(8)^2 + 2\pi(8)(11)$ $r = 8$ and $h = 11$

$S \approx 955.0$ Use a calculator.

The surface area is about 955.0 square millimeters.

Chapter 7 Study Guide and Review 365

Answers (Practice Test)

1. Find the area of the base and multiply this by the height of the prism.
2. Find the area of each face and add to find the total surface area.
8. The area of the top of the cake is about 365 in^2, which is more than the area covered by one container but less than the area covered by 2 containers, 500 in^2.

Mixed Problem Solving
For mixed problem-solving practice, see page 654.

7-8 Surface Area of Pyramids and Cones (pp. 352–355)

Find the surface area of each solid. Round to the nearest tenth if necessary.

33. 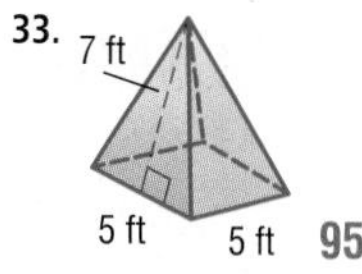

95 ft^2

34. 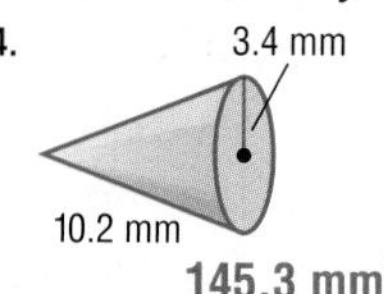

145.3 mm^2

35. 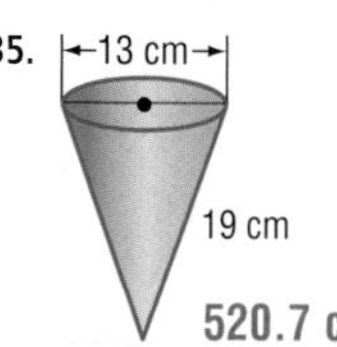

520.7 cm^2

36. 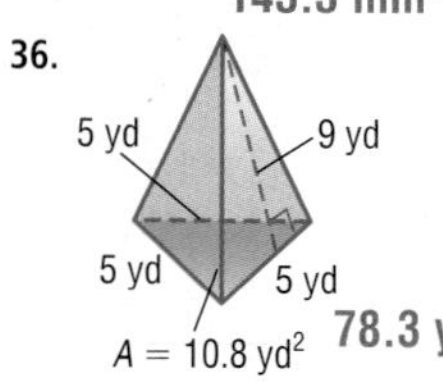

78.3 yd^2

37. **DECORATING** All but the underside of a 10-foot tall conical-shaped tree is to be covered with fake snow. The base of the tree has a radius of 5 feet, and its slant height is about 11.2 feet. How much area is to be covered with fake snow? **about 175.9 ft^2**

Example 8 **Find the surface area of the square pyramid.**

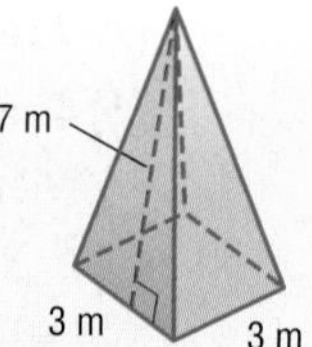

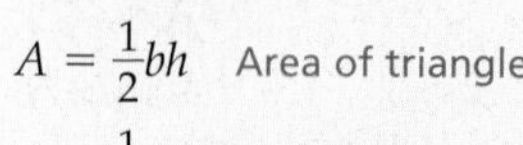

$A = \frac{1}{2}bh$ Area of triangle

$A = \frac{1}{2}(3)(7)$ or 10.5

The total lateral area is 4(10.5) or 42 square meters. The area of the base is 3(3) or 9 square meters. So the total surface area of the pyramid is 42 + 9 or 51 square meters.

Example 9 **Find the surface area of the cone.**

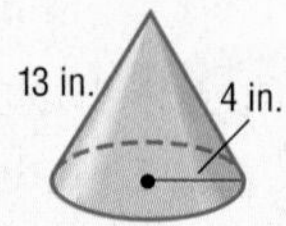

$S = \pi r\ell + \pi r^2$ Surface area of a cone

$S = \pi(4)(13) + \pi(4)^2$ $r = 4$ and $\ell = 13$

$S \approx 213.6$ Use a calculator.

The surface area is about 213.6 square inches.

7-9 Measurement: Precision and Significant Digits (pp. 358–362)

38. **MEASUREMENT** Order the following measures from least precise to most precise.
0.50 cm, 0.005 cm, 0.5 cm, 50 cm
50, 0.5, 0.50, 0.005

Determine the number of significant digits in each measure.

39. 0.14 ft **2**
40. 7.0 L **2**
41. 9.04 s **3**

Find each sum or difference using the correct precision.

42. 40 g + 15.7 g **60 g**
43. 45.3 lb − 0.02 lb **45.3 lb**

Find each product or quotient using the correct number of significant digits.

44. 6.4 yd · 2 yd **10 yd^2**
45. 200.8 m ÷ 12.0 m **16.7**

Example 10 **Determine the number of significant digits in a measure of 180 miles.**

In a number without a decimal point, any zeros to the right of the last nonzero digit are *not* significant. Therefore, 180 miles has 2 significant digits, 1 and 8.

Example 11 **Use the correct number of significant digits to find 701 feet · 0.04 feet.**

```
  701   ← 2 significant digits
× 0.04  ← 1 significant digit ← least number
 28.04
```

The product, rounded to 1 significant digit, is 30 square feet.

366 Chapter 7 Geometry: Measuring Area and Volume

Practice Test

Vocabulary and Concepts

1. **Explain** how to find the volume of any prism. **1–2. See margin.**
2. **Explain** how to find the surface area of any prism.

Skills and Applications

Find the area of each figure. Round to the nearest tenth if necessary.

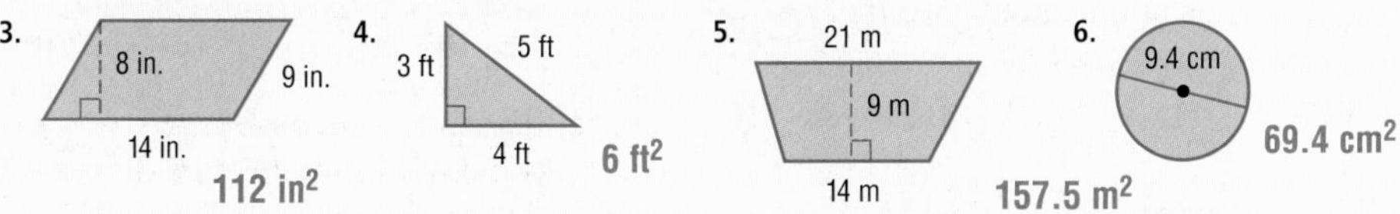

3. **112 in²**
4. **6 ft²**
5. **157.5 m²**
6. **69.4 cm²**

7. **CIRCUS** The elephants at a circus are paraded around the edge of the center ring two times. If the ring has a radius of 25 yards, about how far do the elephants walk during this part of the show? **about 314.2 yd**

8. **CAKE DECORATION** Mrs. Chávez designed the flashlight birthday cake shown at the right. If one container of frosting covers 250 square inches of cake, how many containers will she need to frost the top of this cake? Explain your reasoning. **2 containers; See margin for explanation.**

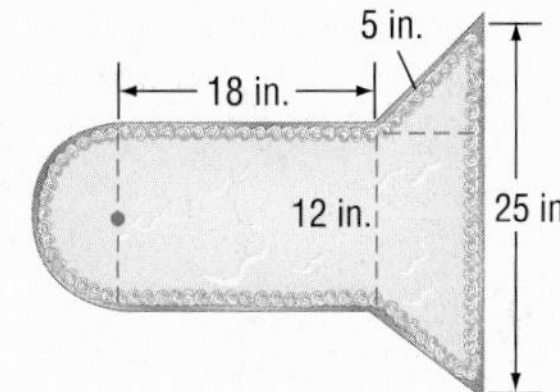

Find the volume and surface area of each solid. Round to the nearest tenth if necessary. **12. 553.7 mm³; 459.5 mm²**

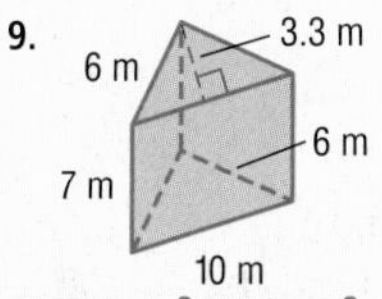

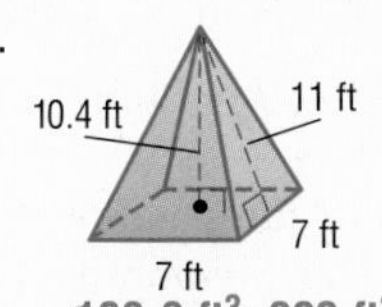

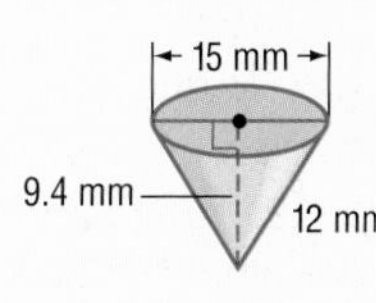

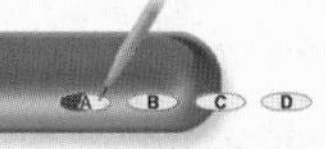

9. **115.5 m³; 187 m²**
10. **254.8 in³; 267.9 in²**
11. **169.9 ft³; 203 ft²**

13. Determine the number of significant digits in 0.089 milliliters. **2**
14. Find 18.2 milligrams − 7.34 milligrams using the correct precision. **10.9 mg**
15. Find 0.5 yards · 18.3 yards using the correct number of significant digits. **9 yd²**

Standardized Test Practice

16. **MULTIPLE CHOICE** Find the volume of the solid at the right. **A**

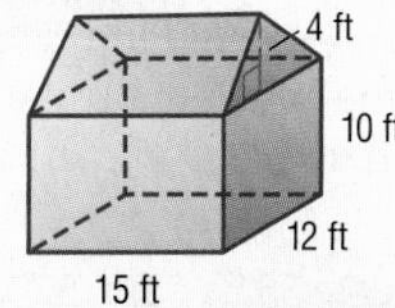

Ⓐ 2,160 ft³ Ⓑ 2,520 ft³
Ⓒ 3,600 ft³ Ⓓ 7,200 ft³

msmath3.net/chapter_test

Portfolio Suggestion

Introduction The size and shape of packaging is often changed to spark the interest of a new customer. Sometimes the packaging can determine whether or not a product is purchased.

Ask Students to investigate unusual packaging at their local grocery stores. Have them sketch the packages in their portfolios. Have them include a description of the types of figures that make up the overall shape and how they might determine each package's volume.

Practice Test

Assessment Options

Vocabulary Test A vocabulary review/test for Chapter 7 can be found on p. 436 of the *Chapter 7 Resource Masters.*

Chapter Tests There are six Chapter 7 Tests and an Extended Response Assessment task available in the *Chapter 7 Resource Masters.*

Chapter 7 Tests			
Form	**Type**	**Level**	**Pages**
1	MC	basic	423–424
2A	MC	average	425–426
2B	MC	average	427–428
2C	FR	average	429–430
2D	FR	average	431–432
3	FR	advanced	433–434

MC = multiple-choice questions
FR = free-response questions

Extended Response Assessment

Extended Response tasks for Chapter 7 can be found on p. 435 of the *Chapter 7 Resource Masters.* A sample scoring rubric for these tasks appears on p. A31.

Unit 3 Test

A unit test/review can be found on pp. 443–444 of the *Chapter 7 Resource Masters.*

Standardized Test Practice

These two pages contain practice questions in the various formats that can be found on the most frequently given standardized tests.

A student recording sheet for these two pages can be found on page A1 of the *Chapter 7 Resource Masters*.

Standardized Test Practice Student Recording Sheet, p. A1

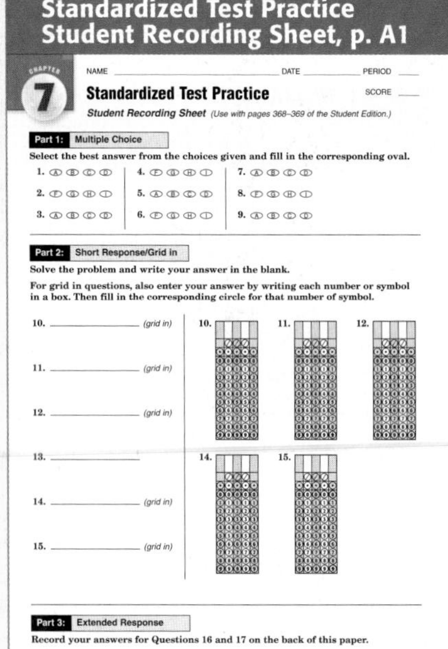

NAME ______ DATE ______ PERIOD ______

Standardized Test Practice SCORE ______

Student Recording Sheet (Use with pages 368–369 of the Student Edition.)

Part 1: Multiple Choice

Select the best answer from the choices given and fill in the corresponding oval.

1. Ⓐ Ⓑ Ⓒ Ⓓ 4. Ⓕ Ⓖ Ⓗ Ⓘ 7. Ⓐ Ⓑ Ⓒ Ⓓ
2. Ⓕ Ⓖ Ⓗ Ⓘ 5. Ⓐ Ⓑ Ⓒ Ⓓ 8. Ⓕ Ⓖ Ⓗ Ⓘ
3. Ⓐ Ⓑ Ⓒ Ⓓ 6. Ⓕ Ⓖ Ⓗ Ⓘ 9. Ⓐ Ⓑ Ⓒ Ⓓ

Part 2: Short Response/Grid in

Solve the problem and write your answer in the blank.

For grid in questions, also enter your answer by writing each number or symbol in a box. Then fill in the corresponding circle for that number of symbol.

10. ______ (grid in)
11. ______ (grid in)
12. ______ (grid in)
13. ______
14. ______ (grid in)
15. ______ (grid in)

Part 3: Extended Response

Record your answers for Questions 16 and 17 on the back of this paper.

Additional Practice

See pp. 441–442 of the *Chapter 7 Resource Masters* for additional standardized test practice.

CHAPTER 7 Standardized Test Practice

PART 1 Multiple Choice

Record your answers on the answer sheet provided by your teacher or on a sheet of paper.

1. Unleaded gasoline costs $\$1.49\frac{9}{10}$ per gallon. What is the best estimate of the cost of 8.131 gallons of unleaded gasoline? (Prerequisite Skill, pp. 600–601) **C**

   Ⓐ \$8 Ⓑ \$9 Ⓒ \$12 Ⓓ \$16

2. Which equation is equivalent to $n + 7 = -4$? (Lesson 1-8) **I**

   Ⓕ $n = 3$

   Ⓖ $n + 7 - 7 = -4 + 7$

   Ⓗ $n + 14 = -8$

   Ⓘ $n + 7 - 7 = -4 - 7$

3. Jamie started at point *F* and drove 28 miles due north to point *G*. He then drove due west to point *H*. He was then 35 miles from his starting point. What was the distance from point *G* to point *H*? (Lesson 3-5) **C**

   Ⓐ 7 mi Ⓑ 14 mi

   Ⓒ 21 mi Ⓓ 31.5 mi

4. In 1990, the population of Tampa, Florida, was about 281,000. In 2000, the population was about 303,000. What was the approximate percent of increase in population over this ten-year period? (Lesson 5-7) **G**

   Ⓕ 7% Ⓖ 8% Ⓗ 22% Ⓘ 93%

5. In the diagram, $\angle A \cong \angle B$. Find the measure of $\angle A$. (Lessons 6-1, 6-2) **A**

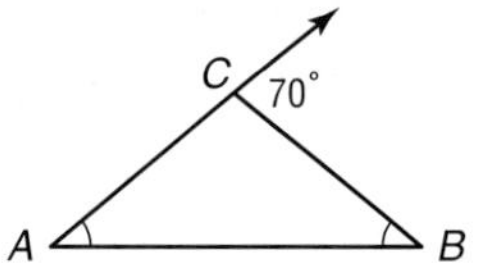

   C 70° A B

   Ⓐ 35° Ⓑ 55° Ⓒ 70° Ⓓ 110°

6. Keisha needed to paint a triangular wall that was 19 feet long and 8 feet tall. When she stopped to rest, she still had 25 square feet of wall unpainted. How many square feet of wall did she paint before she stopped to rest? (Lesson 7-1) **F**

   Ⓕ 51 ft^2 Ⓖ 76 ft^2

   Ⓗ 101 ft^2 Ⓘ 127 ft^2

7. If a circle's circumference is 28 yards, what is the *best* estimate of its diameter? (Lesson 7-2) **A**

   Ⓐ 9 yd Ⓑ 14 yd Ⓒ 21 yd Ⓓ 84 yd

8. The drawing shows a solid figure built with cubes. Which drawing represents a view of this solid from directly above? (Lesson 7-4) **G**

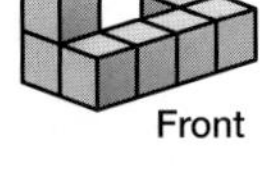

   Ⓕ

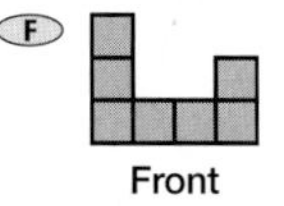

   Ⓖ

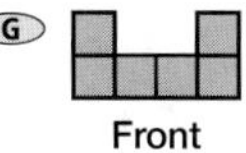

   Ⓗ

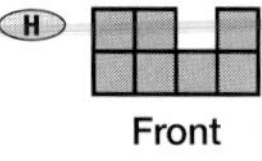

   Ⓘ

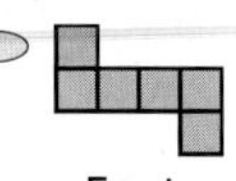

9. The volume of the pyramid at the right is 54 cubic meters. Find the height of the pyramid. (Lesson 7-6) **B**

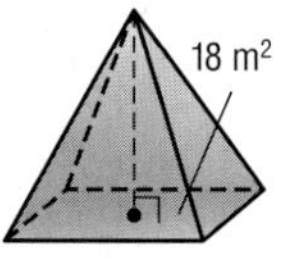

   Ⓐ 3 m Ⓑ 9 m Ⓒ 18 m Ⓓ 36 m

TEST-TAKING TIP

Question 9 Most standardized tests will include any commonly used formulas at the front of the test booklet, but it will save you time to memorize many of these formulas. For example, you should memorize that the volume of a pyramid is one-third the area of the base times the height of the pyramid.

368 Chapter 7 Geometry: Measuring Area and Volume

ExamView® Pro

Special banks of standardized test questions similar to those on the TIMSS and NAEP grade 8 tests can be found on this CD-ROM.

Preparing for Standardized Tests
For test-taking strategies and more practice, see pages 660–677.

PART 2 Short Response/Grid In

Record your answers on the answer sheet provided by your teacher or on a sheet of paper.

10. You need $1\frac{2}{3}$ cups of chocolate chips to make one batch of chocolate chip cookies. How many $\frac{1}{3}$-cups of chocolate chips is this? (Lesson 2-4) **5**

11. Four days ago, Evan had completed 5 pages of his term paper. Today he has completed a total of 15 pages. Find the rate of change in his progress in pages per day. (Lesson 4-2) **5/2**

12. A boy who is $5\frac{1}{2}$ feet tall casts a shadow 4 feet long. A nearby tree casts a shadow 10 feet long.

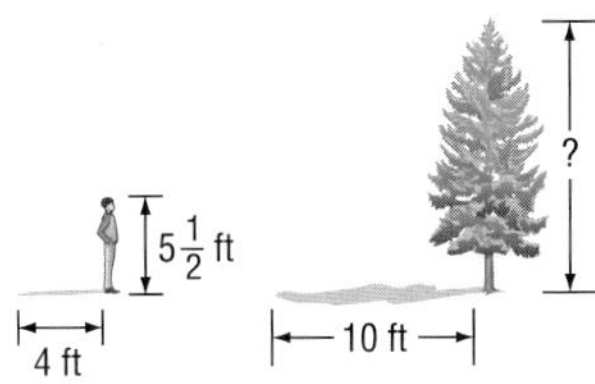

What is the height of the tree in feet? (Lesson 4-7) **13.75 or 55/4**

13. Find the area of the top of a compact disc if its diameter is 12 centimeters and the diameter of the hole is 1.5 centimeters. (Lesson 7-2) **111.3 cm^2**

14. Mr. Brauen plans to carpet the part of his house shown on the floor plan below. How many square feet of carpet does he need? (Lesson 7-3) **240**

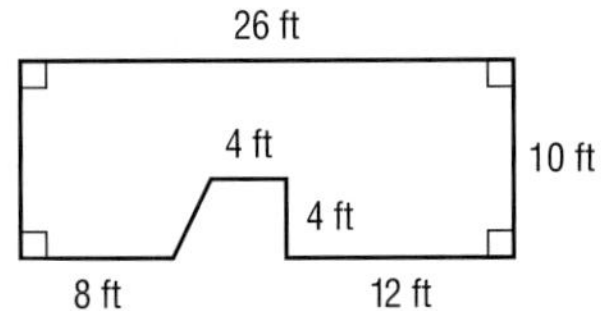

msmath3.net/standardized_test

15. The curved part of a can will be covered by a label. What is the area of the label to the nearest tenth of a square centimeter? (Lesson 7-7) **527.8**

PART 3 Extended Response

Record your answers on a sheet of paper. Show your work.

16. A prism with a triangular base has 9 edges, and a prism with a rectangular base has 12 edges.

9 edges

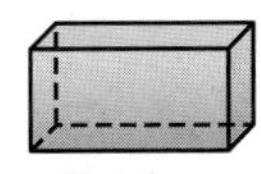
12 edges

Explain in words or symbols how to determine the number of edges for a prism with a 9-sided base. Be sure to include the number of edges in your explanation. (Lesson 7-4) **See margin.**

17. The diagrams show the design of the trashcans in the school cafeteria. (Lessons 7-5 and 7-7) **a. 10.8 ft^3**

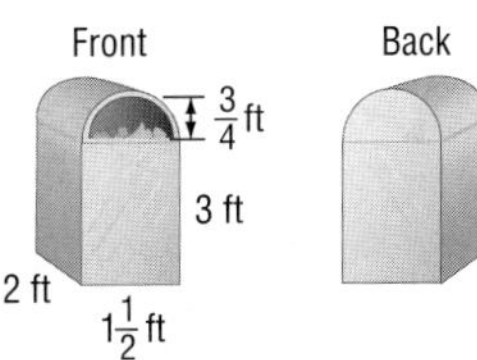

a. Find the volume of trash each can is designed to hold to the nearest tenth.

b. The top and sides of the cans need to be painted. Find the surface area of each can to the nearest tenth. **26.6 ft^2**

c. The paint used by the school covers 200 square feet per gallon. How many trashcans can be covered with 1 gallon of paint? **7**

Answer

16. Sample answer: the number of edges is 3 times the number of sides of the base of the prism; a prism with a 9-sided base would have 27 edges.

Standardized Test Practice

Rubrics The following rubrics are sample scoring devices for short response and extended response questions.

Short Response

Points	Description
2	The student demonstrates a thorough understanding of the mathematics of the task. The response may contain minor flaws that do not detract from the demonstration of a thorough understanding.
1	The student has provided a response that is only partially correct.
0	The student has provided a completely incorrect solution or no response at all.

Extended Response

Points	Description
4	The student demonstrates a thorough understanding of the mathematics of the task. The response may contain minor flaws that do not detract from the demonstration of a thorough understanding.
3	The student demonstrates an understanding of the mathematics of the task. The response is essentially correct and demonstrates an essential but less than thorough understanding of the mathematics.
2	The student demonstrates only a partial understanding of the mathematics of the task. Although the student may have used the correct approach to a solution or may have provided a correct solution, the work lacks an essential understanding of the underlying mathematical concepts.
1	The student demonstrates a very limited understanding of the mathematics of the task. The response is incomplete and exhibits many flaws.
0	The student provides a completely incorrect solution or no response at all.

A more detailed 4-point rubric is provided on page A2 of the *Chapter 7 Resource Masters*.

Page 319, Lesson 7-2 (Hands-On Mini Lab)

4. Sample answer:

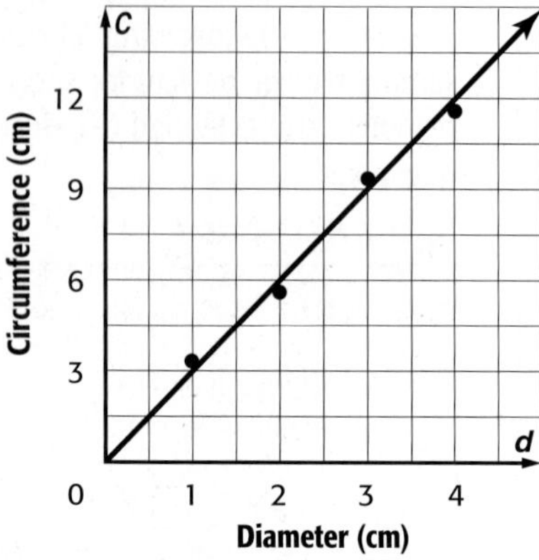

The slope of the line is about 3.

Page 330, Lesson 7-4a (Your Turn)

a. 

b. 

Page 330, Lesson 7-4a (Writing Math)

2. 

top

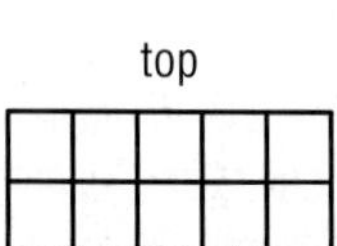

side

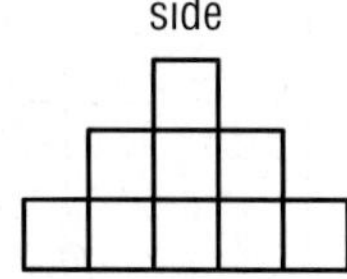

front

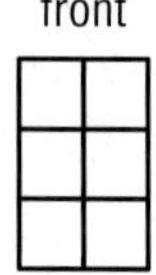

The base is a 2 by 5 rectangle. The 1st and 5th rows are 1 unit high, the 2nd and 4th rows are 2 units high, and the 3rd row is 3 units high. The overall width of the figure is 2 units and the overall height is 3 units.

Page 334, Lesson 7-4

16a. hexagonal prism

16b.

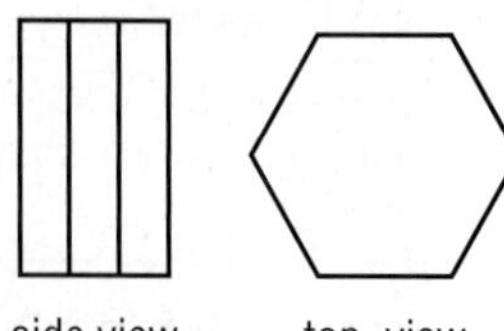

side view top view

17a. 2 square pyramids

17b.

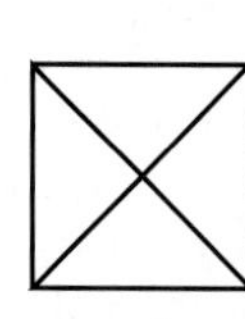

top view

side view

18a. 1 rectangular prism and 2 square pyramids

18b.

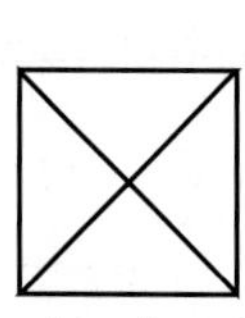

top view

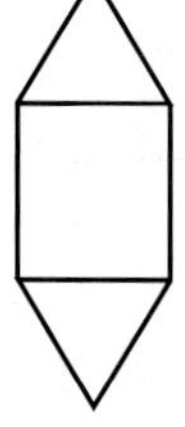

side view

Page 346, Lesson 7-7a (Your Turn)

a. 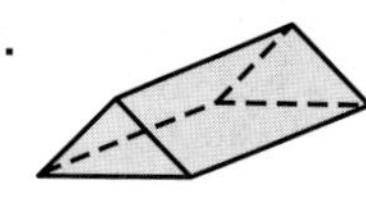 

b. 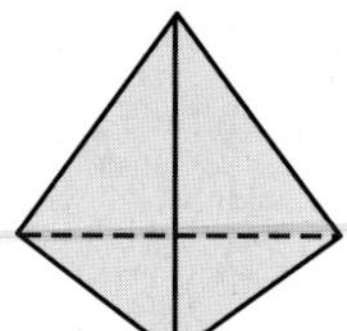

c. 

NOTES

UNIT 4 Notes

Introduction

In this unit, students will investigate probability and combinatorics and calculate outcomes, permutations, and combinations. They will also learn to distinguish dependent from independent events and study mutually exclusive events. Students will investigate how experimental probability differs from theoretical probability and the use of sampling to make predictions.

Students will then learn several tools for the display and analysis of statistical data and learn to choose an appropriate display. Students will also use measures of central tendency and measures of variation and determine whether graphs and statistics are misleading. Finally, they will learn to use matrices to organize and compare data.

Assessment Options

Unit 4 Test Pages 561–562 of the *Chapter 9 Resource Masters* may be used as a test or a review for Unit 4. This assessment contains both multiple-choice and short-response items.

An online, research-based, instructional, assessment, and intervention tool that provides specific feedback on student mastery of state and national standards, instant remediation, and a data management system to track performance. For more information, contact mhdigitallearning.com

UNIT 4

Probability and Statistics

Chapter 8

Probability

Chapter 9

Statistics and Matrices

People often base their decisions about the future on data they've collected. In this unit, you will learn how to make such predictions using probability and statistics.

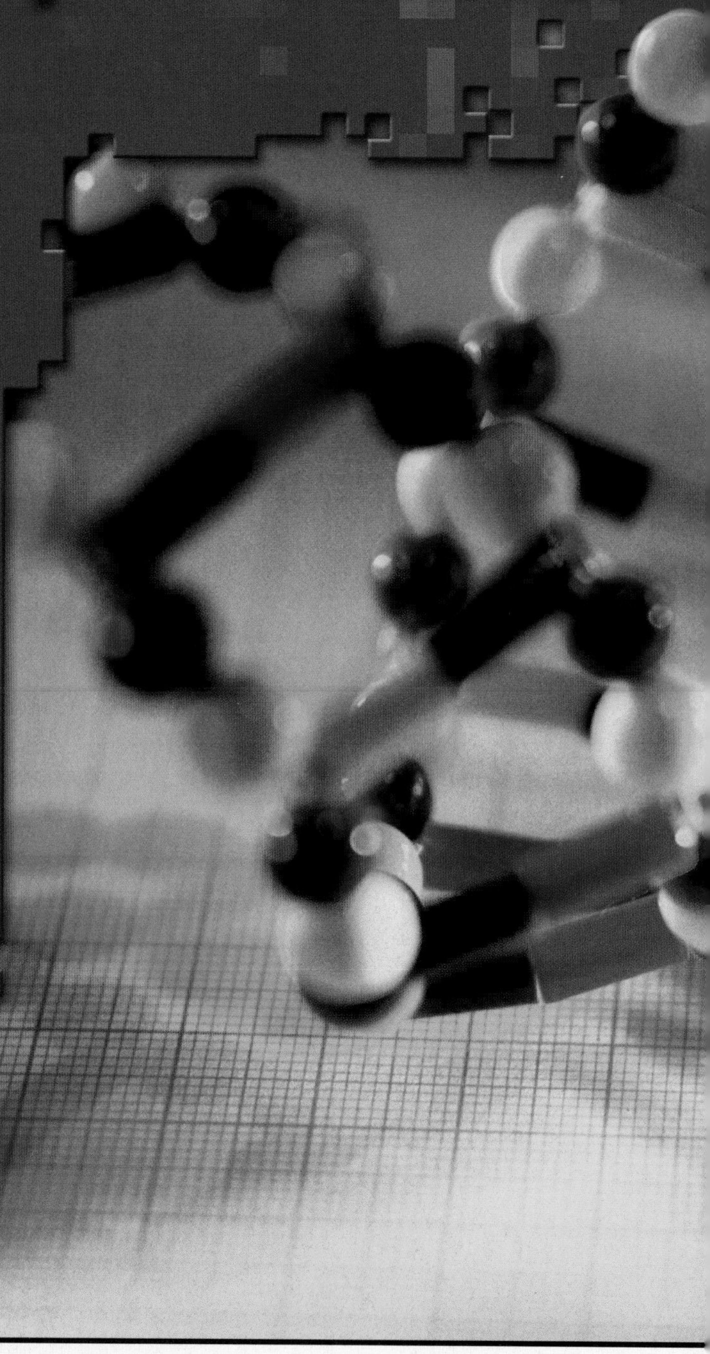

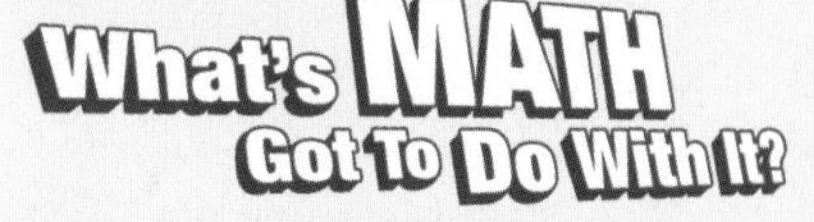

Real-Life Math Videos engage students, showing them how math is used in everyday situations. Use Video 4 with this unit to discuss how sampling, histograms, and variation are used in amusement parks and soccer. (also available on one Super DVD combined with MindJogger Videoquizzes)

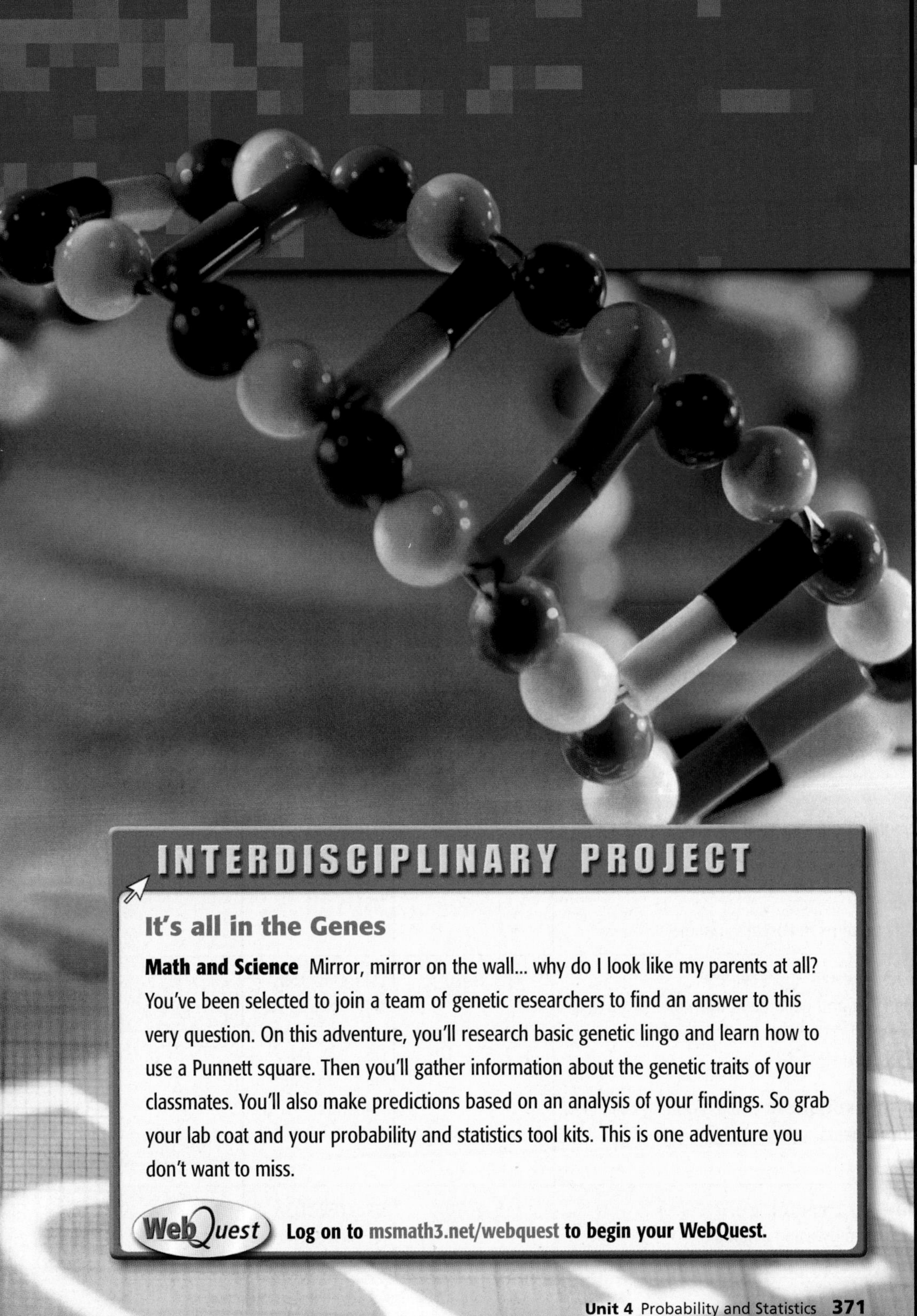

INTERDISCIPLINARY PROJECT

It's all in the Genes

Math and Science Mirror, mirror on the wall... why do I look like my parents at all? You've been selected to join a team of genetic researchers to find an answer to this very question. On this adventure, you'll research basic genetic lingo and learn how to use a Punnett square. Then you'll gather information about the genetic traits of your classmates. You'll also make predictions based on an analysis of your findings. So grab your lab coat and your probability and statistics tool kits. This is one adventure you don't want to miss.

WebQuest **Log on to msmath3.net/webquest to begin your WebQuest.**

Unit 4 Probability and Statistics 371

INTERDISCIPLINARY PROJECT

It's All in the Genes

A WebQuest is an online project in which students do research on the Internet, gather data, and make presentations using word processing, graphing, page-making, or presentation software. In each chapter, students advance to the next step in their WebQuest. At the end of Chapter 9, the project culminates with a presentation of their findings.

WebQuest Teaching suggestions and sample answers are available in the WebQuests, Projects, and Interdisciplinary Investigations.

Math and Science You can use this WebQuest Interdisciplinary Project with your students' science teacher to make the connection from mathematics to the science your students are studying.

More Interdisciplinary Connections

You may wish to share these suggestions with your students' other teachers.

Math and Language Arts

Write a fictional, humorous story about an "average" teenager who tires of being "middle-of-the-road." Describe the teenager's test scores and athletic performance as falling exactly on the mean, mode, or median. Describe the teenager's efforts to be an outlier.

Math and Science

Research the U.S. human genome project. How was it conducted and what did it map? In what ways will the results of this project change genetic and medical research and the treatment of diseases? Present a summary of your findings to the class.

Chapter Overview

Probability

LESSON OBJECTIVES		NCTM Standards	NAEP 2005	State/Local Objectives
8-1	**Probability of Simple Events** (pp. 374–377) • Find the probability of a simple event.	1, 5, 6, 7, 9, 10	D4a, D4b, D4g, D4j, N1d, N1e	
8-2	**Counting Outcomes** (pp. 378–383) **8-2a Problem-Solving Strategy:** Solve problems by making an organized list. • Count outcomes by using a tree diagram or the Fundamental Counting Principle.	1, 5, 6–10	D4e, D4f, D4g, N1e	
8-3	**Permutations** (pp. 384–387) • Find the number of permutations of objects.	1, 5, 6–10	D4e, D4f, D4g, N1e, N5f	
8-4	**Combinations** (pp. 388–393) • Find the number of combinations of objects. **8-4b Hands-On Lab:** Identify patterns in Pascal's Triangle.	1, 5, 6–10	A1a, A1b, D4e, N5f	
8-5	**Probability of Compound Events** (pp. 396–399) • Find the probability of independent and dependent events.	1, 5, 6–10	D4a, D4b, D4g, D4h	
8-6	**Experimental Probability** (pp. 400–405) • Find experimental probability. **8-6b Graphing Calculator Investigation:** Use a graphing calculator to simulate probability experiments.	1, 2, 5, 6–10	D4a, D4b, D4c, D4d, D4g, D4j, N4b, N4c	
8-7	**Statistics: Using Sampling to Predict** (pp. 406–409) • Predict the actions of a larger group by using a sample.	1, 5, 6–10	D3a, D3b, D3d, N1e, N3a, N4c	

Key to NCTM Standards:

1=Number & Operations, 2=Algebra, 3=Geometry, 4=Measurement, 5=Data Analysis & Probability, 6=Problem Solving, 7=Reasoning & Proof, 8=Communication, 9=Connections, 10=Representation

NAEP 2005 Standards: See Teacher Resources at math.glencoe.com

Pacing suggestions for the entire year can be found on page T23.

*An electronic version of this chapter is available on **StudentWorks**™. This backpack solution CD-ROM allows students instant access to the Student Edition, lesson worksheet pages, and web resources.*

Chapter Resource Manager

	Study Guide and Intervention	Practice (Skills and Word Problems)	Reading to Learn Mathematics	Enrichment	Assessment	Applications*	Parent and Student Study Guide Online Worksheets	5-Minute Check Transparencies	Key Teaching Transparencies	MathPASS: Tutorial Plus (lessons)	Teaching Mathematics with Manipulatives	Noteables™: Interactive Study Notebook	Optional Materials
	CHAPTER 8 RESOURCE MASTERS												
	445	446–447	448	449			8-1	8-1	28			8-1	
	450	451–452	453	454	495	CS 35	8-2	8-2	29		92–93	8-2	
	455	456–457	458	459		CS 36	8-3	8-3	30			8-3	4 different game pieces
	460	461–462	463	464	495, 497	CS 37, 38	8-4	8-4			94	8-4	paper, pencil
	465	466–467	468	469			8-5	8-5	31	41		8-5	
	470	471–472	473	474	496	SM 93–96	8-6	8-6	32		95, 96–97	8-6	paper bag, 10 colored marbles, graphing calculator, paper, pencil
	475	476–477	478	479	481–494, 496, 498–500	RC 34 CM 31–32	8-7	8-7	33			8-7	

*** Key to Abbreviations:** *CS = Calculator and Spreadsheet Masters, RC = Real-Life Career Masters, CM = Classroom Math Games (online), SM = Science and Math Lab Manual (online)*

PowerPoint® Presentations

This CD-ROM is a customizable Microsoft® PowerPoint® presentation that includes:

- In-Class Examples
- Links to Online Study Tools
- 5-Minute Check Transparencies
- Your Turn Exercises

Math Skills Maintenance

Use the Math Skills Maintenance Masters to keep your students' basic math skills fresh. Students can review skills one at a time or in a combined format. The Masters are also available online at msmath3.net/maintenance.

Mathematical Content and Teaching Strategies

Continuity of Instruction

Building on Prior Knowledge

In Chapter 2 and in previous courses, students learned how to compare, simplify, and multiply fractions. In Chapter 4, students solved proportions. Students changed fractions into decimals and percents in Chapter 5. In previous courses and in real life, students have worked with patterns and sequences of numbers.

Learning in This Chapter

Students find the probability of simple events and compare fractions to determine which events are more likely than others. They multiply fractions to find the probability of compound events. Students simplify fractions as they find permutations and combinations. They use proportions and percents while working with experimental probability and sampling.

Making Future Connections

Determining probabilities occurs in everyday life, as well as in algebra and other higher-level math courses. Counting outcomes is another everyday life skill and is essential in both high school and college coursework in combinatorics. Pascal's Triangle has applications in the study of advanced algebra. Experimental probability and sampling are used in statistics courses and have applications in numerous disciplines.

Mathematical Background

8-1 Probability of Simple Events

Simple events are events occurring by themselves, such as one number cube rolled once, one coin tossed once, or one spinner spun once. Students will study the probability of compound events in Lesson 8-5. Probability is used to determine insurance rates and monitor industrial quality, as well as in the study of genetics, quantum mechanics, and the kinetic theory of gases.

Teacher to Teacher

Ken Montgomery
Tri-Cities High School
East Point, GA

"Before introducing the formulas for $P(A \text{ or } B)$ and $P(A \text{ and } B)$, I help students' conceptual understanding by using Venn diagrams to show how the events are related."

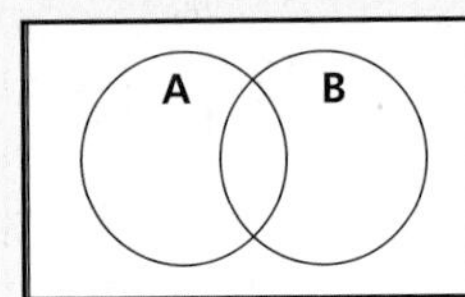

Ken Montgomery

8-2 Counting Outcomes

In this lesson, tree diagrams and other organized lists are used to count outcomes of events. Students also learn the Fundamental Counting Principle, which makes it possible to to find the number of possible outcomes for complex situations. Knowing the number of possible outcomes will be necessary in Lessons 8-3 and 8-4 to find the number of permutations and combinations of items.

8-3 Permutations

Permutations and combinations belong to the mathematical field of study known as combinatorics. Finding permutations involves finding how many ways a group of items can be arranged to fill a set number of positions in which the order of the arrangement matters. For example, how many ways can 3 out of 12 available students fill 3 leadership positions?

8-4 Combinations

Combinations are arrangements of objects where order is *not* important. For example, a club has 15 members and wants to elect four committee members. The order does not matter because the committee members are equal. Students first learn to find the number of combinations by making an organized list of all possible arrangements and then eliminating duplicates. For example, ABC, ACB, BAC, BCA, CAB, and CBA are six permutations but only one combination. Students then learn to find the number of possible combinations using combination notation.

8-5 Probability of Compound Events

Simple events may be combined to form compound events. These events may be independent or dependent. Dependent events influence one another. If one event occurs, it can change the outcome of the second event. For example, think of picking two socks out of a drawer. When the first sock is removed, one less sock is left from which to choose the next sock. Examples of independent events are rolling a number cube and tossing a coin.

8-6 Experimental Probability

In this lesson, students study experimental probability—the number of times an event actually occurs when trials are conducted. The theoretical probability as studied earlier in the chapter can be used to predict the outcome of an event. The more trials that are performed, the closer the experimental probability is likely to be to the theoretical probability.

8-7 Statistics: Using Sampling to Predict

Sampling is used to make mathematical predictions about entire populations. The lesson focuses on identifying several types of biased and unbiased samples, depending upon the method used to select the sample. Surveys often are used to predict trends in various industries. But whether the sample is selected randomly will affect the validity of the outcome. For example, predicting music sales based on a survey at the symphony would not take all music categories into account.

Team Teaching

Inform the other teachers on your team that your classes are studying the use of sampling in making predictions. Suggestions for curriculum integration are:

Science: taking a sample of a solid or a liquid to determine its properties, such as density or composition

Civics: use of sampling in election polls to predict voting patterns of entire populations

In-Class Speaker

Invite an actuary to speak about the use of probability in the insurance business. Actuaries use data based on past occurrences to determine the experimental probabilities of future occurrences, such as automobile accidents. They use these probabilities to analyze the risk associated with taking on various new clients and to determine the amount to charge these clients for insurance policies.

What the Research Says

According to Hopfsenberger, Kranendonk, and Schaeffer in *Data Driven Mathematics: Probability through Data*, an effective teaching strategy is to introduce students to probability through data.

- **Each lesson in Chapter 8 uses real-world data to help students learn probability concepts.**

McGraw-Hill Professional Development

Mathematics, YES! is a self-paced, web-based professional development program. Units are based on major mathematical concepts and are standards-based. Actual classroom videos provide a springboard for discussion and activities. Unit appropriate for this chapter:

- **Statistics, Data Analysis, and Probability**

Additional mathematical information and teaching notes are available at **msmath3.net/key_concepts**.

DAILY INTERVENTION and Assessment

* **Key to Abbreviations:**
TWE = Teacher Wraparound Edition, *CRM* = Chapter Resource Masters

	Type	Student Edition	Teacher Resources	Technology/Internet
INTERVENTION	Ongoing	Prerequisite Skills, pp. 373, 383, 387, 391, 399, 403 Mid-Chapter Practice Test, p. 394	5-Minute Check Transparencies Quizzes 1–4, *CRM*, pp. 495–496 Mid-Chapter Test, *CRM*, p. 497 Study Guide and Intervention, *CRM*, pp. 445, 450, 455, 460, 465, 470, 475	MathPASS: Tutorial Plus msmath3.net/self_check_quiz msmath3.net/extra_examples
INTERVENTION	Mixed Review	pp. 377, 383, 387, 391, 399, 403, 409	Cumulative Review, *CRM*, p. 498	
INTERVENTION	Error Analysis	Find the Error, pp. 376, 386, 398	Find the Error, *TWE*, pp. 376, 386, 398 Unlocking Misconceptions, *TWE*, pp. 397, 407	
ASSESSMENT	Standardized Test Practice	pp. 377, 379, 383, 385, 387, 391, 394, 399, 403, 409, 413, 414–415	Standardized Test Practice, *CRM*, pp. 499–500	Standardized Test Practice CD-ROM msmath3.net/standardized_test
ASSESSMENT	Open-Ended Assessment	Writing Math, pp. 382, 392, 393, 398, 402, 408 Open-Ended, pp. 376, 382, 386, 390, 398, 402, 408 Standardized Test, p. 415	Modeling: *TWE*, p. 377 Speaking: *TWE*, pp. 387, 409 Writing: *TWE*, pp. 383, 391 Extended Response Assessment, *CRM*, p. 493	
ASSESSMENT	Chapter Assessment	Study Guide, pp. 410–412 Practice Test, p. 413	Multiple-Choice Tests (Forms 1, 2A, 2B), *CRM*, pp. 481–486 Free-Response Tests (Forms 2C, 2D, 3), *CRM*, pp. 487–492 Vocabulary Test/Review, *CRM*, p. 494	ExamView® Pro Testmaker (see below) MindJogger Videoquizzes msmath3.net/vocabulary_review msmath3.net/chapter_test

For more information on Yearly ProgressPro, see p. 370.

Glencoe Lesson	Yearly ProgressPro Skill Name
8-1	Probability as Fractions: Level 2 Probability of Complementary Events
8-2	Tree Diagrams and the Fundamental Counting Principle
8-3	Permutations
8-4	Combinations
8-5	Probability of Compound Events
8-6	Experimental Probability
8-7	Using Sampling to Predict

ExamView® Pro

Use ExamView® Pro Testmaker CD-ROM to:

- **Create multiple versions of tests.**
- **Create modified tests for inclusion students with one mouse click.**
- **Edit existing questions and add your own questions.**
- **Build tests aligned with state standards using built-in state curriculum correlations.**
- **Change English tests to Spanish with one mouse click and vice versa.**

Reading and Writing in Mathematics

READING in the Content Area

This online worksheet provides strategies for reading and analyzing Lesson 8-3, Permutations. Students are guided through questions about the main idea, subject matter, supporting details, conclusion, clarifying details, and vocabulary of the lesson.

Interactive Study Notebook With Foldables™ is a study organizer that provides helpful steps for students to follow to organize their notes for Chapter 8.

- Students use Noteables to record notes and to complete their Foldables as you present the material in Lessons 8-1 through 8-7.
- Noteables follow the *Teacher Wraparound Edition's* In-Class Examples and *Interactive Chalkboard CD-ROM.*

For more information on Reading and Writing in Mathematics, see pp. T6–T7.

Recommended Outside Reading for Students

Nonfiction

- Seymour, Dale. *Visual Patterns in Pascal's Triangle.* Dale Seymour Publications, ©1997.

  This book examines many of the patterns found in Pascal's Triangle and relates them to topics such as probability, combinatorics, multiples, powers, and sequences. Students will learn about Pascal's Triangle's relationship to combinations and to the Fibonacci sequence, as described in the book in Chapter 8.

Fiction

- Bruce, Colin. *Conned Again, Watson! Cautionary Tales of Logic, Math, and Probability.* Perseus Publishing, ©2001.

  This collection includes Sherlock Holmes stories that involve math skills. Holmes uses his mathematical knowledge to unravel plots and save innocent people.

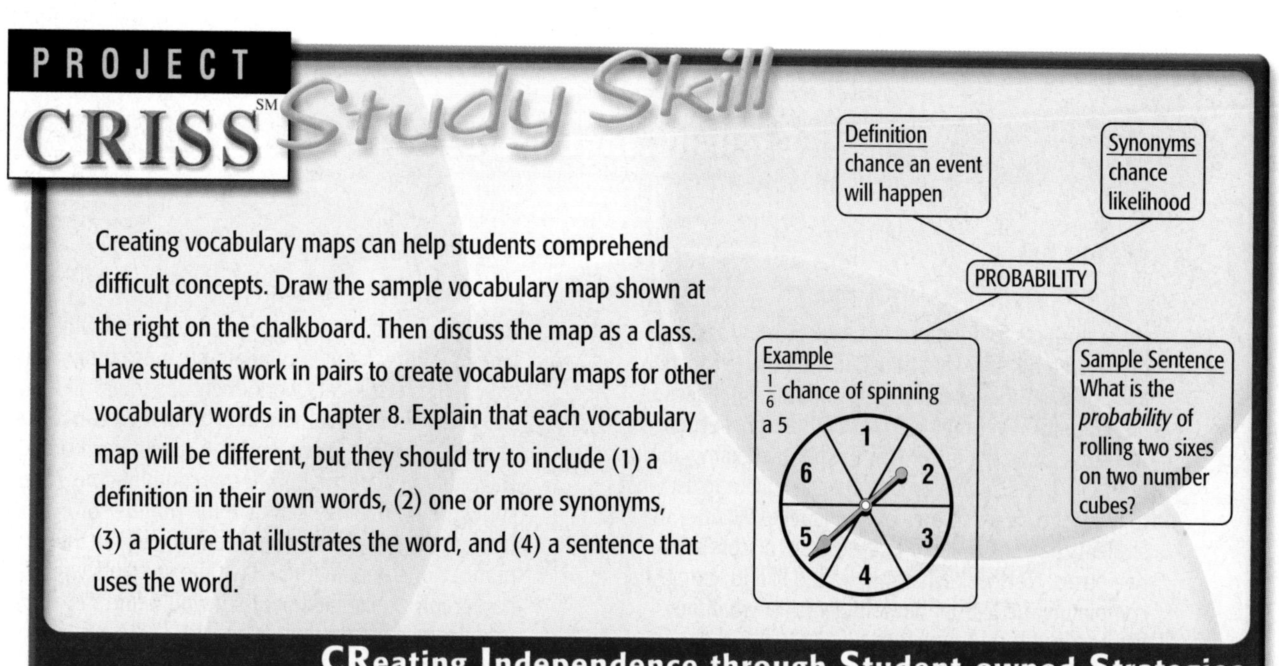

Creating vocabulary maps can help students comprehend difficult concepts. Draw the sample vocabulary map shown at the right on the chalkboard. Then discuss the map as a class. Have students work in pairs to create vocabulary maps for other vocabulary words in Chapter 8. Explain that each vocabulary map will be different, but they should try to include (1) a definition in their own words, (2) one or more synonyms, (3) a picture that illustrates the word, and (4) a sentence that uses the word.

For more information on Project CRISS, see p. T8.

Making Connections

School-To-Home

Parent and Student Study Guide

Parents and students may work together to reinforce the concepts and skills of this chapter. These online worksheets are available in English and Spanish at msmath3.net/parent_student. A sample lesson is shown below.

Family Letters and Activities

Send a letter and activity for this chapter home to encourage family members to become active participants in their students' learning. (English: *Chapter 8 Resource Masters*, pp. ix–x; Spanish: log on to msmath3.net/family_letters)

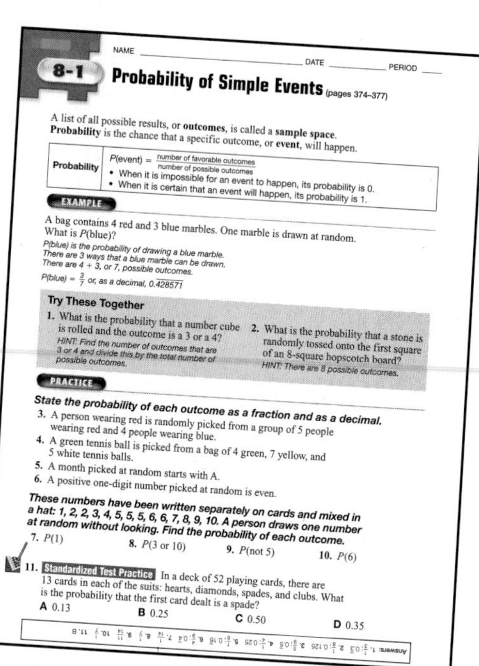

NAME ______________ DATE ________ PERIOD ____

8-1 Probability of Simple Events (pages 374–377)

A list of all possible results, or **outcomes**, is called a **sample space**. **Probability** is the chance that a specific outcome, or **event**, will happen.

Probability	$P(\text{event}) = \frac{\text{number of favorable outcomes}}{\text{number of possible outcomes}}$ • When it is impossible for an event to happen, its probability is 0. • When it is certain that an event will happen, its probability is 1.

EXAMPLE

A bag contains 4 red and 3 blue marbles. One marble is drawn at random. What is *P*(blue)?

P(blue) is the probability of drawing a blue marble.
There are 3 ways that a blue marble can be drawn.
There are 4 + 3, or 7, possible outcomes.
$P(\text{blue}) = \frac{3}{7}$ *or, as a decimal,* $0.\overline{428571}$

Try These Together

1. What is the probability that a number cube is rolled and the outcome is a 3 or a 4?
HINT: Find the number of outcomes that are 3 or 4 and divide this by the total number of possible outcomes.
2. What is the probability that a stone is randomly tossed onto the first square of an 8-square hopscotch board?
HINT: There are 8 possible outcomes.

PRACTICE

State the probability of each outcome as a fraction and as a decimal.

3. A person wearing red is randomly picked from a group of 5 people wearing red and 4 people wearing blue.
4. A green tennis ball is picked from a bag of 4 green, 7 yellow, and 5 white tennis balls.
5. A month picked at random starts with A.
6. A positive one-digit number picked at random is even.

These numbers have been written separately on cards and mixed in a hat: 1, 2, 2, 3, 4, 5, 5, 5, 6, 6, 7, 8, 9, 10. A person draws one number at random without looking. Find the probability of each outcome.

7. *P*(1) 8. *P*(3 or 10) 9. *P*(not 5) 10. *P*(6)

11. **Standardized Test Practice** In a deck of 52 playing cards, there are 13 cards in each of the suits: hearts, diamonds, spades, and clubs. What is the probability that the first card dealt is a spade?
A 0.13 **B** 0.25 **C** 0.50 **D** 0.35

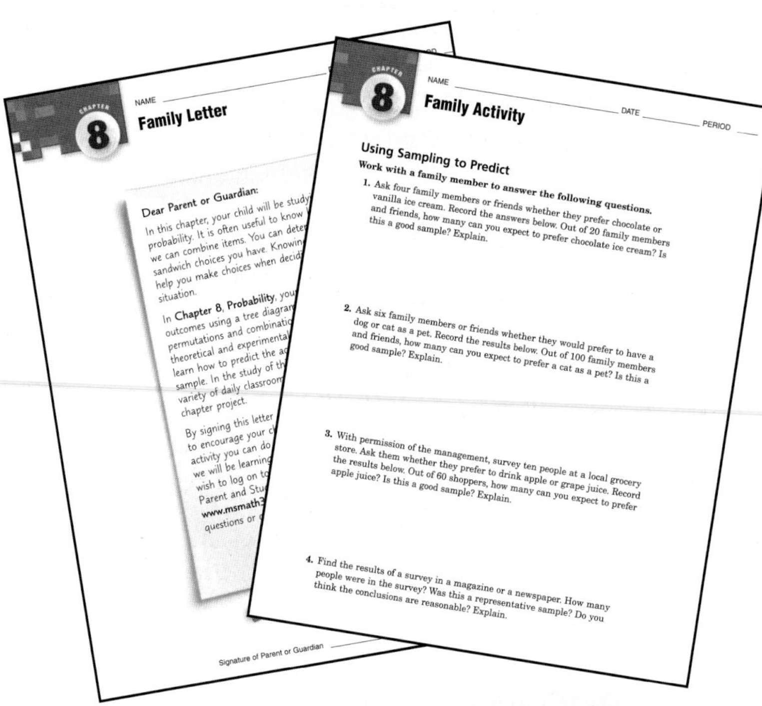

NAME ______________

Family Letter

Dear Parent or Guardian:

NAME ______________ DATE ________ PERIOD ____

Family Activity

Using Sampling to Predict

Work with a family member to answer the following questions.

1. Ask four family members or friends whether they prefer chocolate or vanilla ice cream. Record the answers below. Out of 20 family members and friends, how many can you expect to prefer chocolate ice cream? Is this a good sample? Explain.
2. Ask six family members or friends whether they would prefer to have a dog or cat as a pet. Record the results below. Out of 100 family members and friends, how many can you expect to prefer a cat as a pet? Is this a good sample? Explain.
3. With permission of the management, survey ten people at a local grocery store. Ask them whether they prefer to drink apple or grape juice. Record the results below. Out of 60 shoppers, how many can you expect to prefer apple juice? Is this a good sample? Explain.
4. Find the results of a survey in a magazine or a newspaper. How many people were in the survey? Was this a representative sample? Do you think the conclusions are reasonable? Explain.

English Language Learners ELL

Lesson 8-1

Building on Prior Knowledge

Have students fold a piece of paper into thirds. Have them write a K for what they know on the left section, a W for what they want to learn on the center section, and an L for what they learned on the right section. Ask students to list in column K what they know about probability and simple events. Then ask them to list what they want to learn in the column labeled W. After the students have completed this exercise, discuss their responses. Next, ask what they would like to learn. After completing the lesson, have students list what they learned in the column labeled L.

Lesson 8-2

Reading and Writing

Bring to class three types of bread, such as white, wheat, and rye; and two meats, such as bologna and salami. Have students work in groups to list all the possible sandwich combinations that they can make. Did they take one meat, and pair it with each bread? Have them count the number of combinations. Then show them how they can take the number of meats and multiply by the number of breads to get the total number of combinations. Have the students write a paragraph explaining how they would find the amount of outcomes of different examples.

MathScape™ This project was supported, in part, by the **National Science Foundation**

MathScape is a mathematics curriculum for grades 6–8 developed by the Seeing and Thinking Mathematically Project at the Education Development Center.

Correlations, Rankings, and Permutations

Looking Behind the Numbers

How to Use *MathScape* with Chapter 8

The unit *Looking Behind the Numbers* can be used to enhance Lessons 8-2 and 8-3.

- **Reinforce** → After you complete **Lesson 8-2,** you can use the activities on pages 28–29 to study a real-life situation involving counting outcomes.
- **Introduce** → Before you begin **Lesson 8-3,** you can introduce permutations by using the activities on pages 30–31.

For other lessons in Chapter 8 that correlate to *MathScape*, see the chart on page T14.

Online Lesson Planner

USA TODAY® Education's Online site offers resources and interactive features connected to each day's newspaper. *Experience Today,* USA TODAY's® daily lesson plan, is available on the site and delivered daily to subscribers. This plan provides instruction for integrating USA TODAY® graphics and key editorial features into your mathematics classroom. Log on to **education.usatoday.com**.

USA TODAY Snapshots® in Chapter 8	
Lesson	**Snapshot**
8-5	Now, where's that electric pan?

Quick Review Math Handbook

is Glencoe's mathematical handbook for students. The Hot Words section includes a glossary of terms while the Hot Topics section consists of explanations of key mathematical concepts. An exercise set is included to check students' understanding of the concepts. This valuable resource can be used as a reference in the classroom or for home study.

Lesson	Hot Topics Section	Lesson	Hot Topics Section
8-1	4-5, 4-6	**8-5**	4-6
8-2	4-5	**8-6**	4-6, 9-2
8-3, 8-4	4-5	**8-7**	4-1, 4-6

Notes

Key Chapter Objectives

Lesson 8-1 Find the probability of a simple event.

Lessons 8-3 and 8-4 Find the number of permutations and combinations of objects.

Lesson 8-5 Find the probability of independent and dependent events.

Lesson 8-7 Predict the actions of a larger group by using a sample.

"How are math and bicycles related?"

Point out to students that this is only one of many applications of the math that they are studying. Others are provided in the introduction to each lesson.

Vocabulary Builder, pp. vii–viii ELL

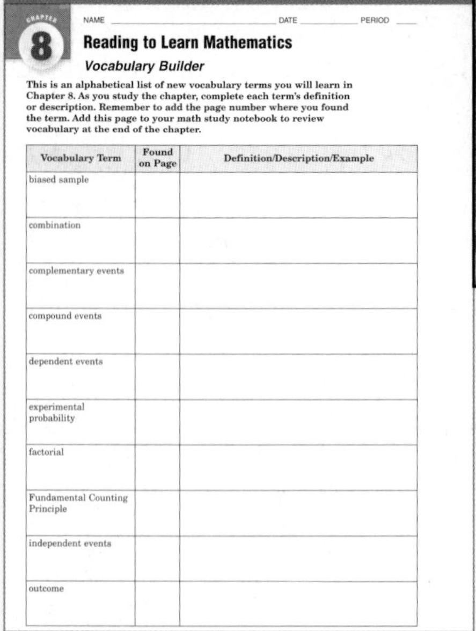

NAME ______ DATE ______ PERIOD ____

8 Reading to Learn Mathematics

Vocabulary Builder

This is an alphabetical list of new vocabulary terms you will learn in Chapter 8. As you study the chapter, complete each term's definition or description. Remember to add the page number where you found the term. Add this page to your math study notebook to review vocabulary at the end of the chapter.

Vocabulary Term	Found on Page	Definition/Description/Example
biased sample		
combination		
complementary events		
compound events		
dependent events		
experimental probability		
factorial		
Fundamental Counting Principle		
independent events		
outcome		

CHAPTER 8 Probability

"How are math and bicycles related?"

Bicycles come in many styles, colors, and sizes. **To find how many different types of bicycles a manufacturer makes, you can use a tree diagram or the Fundamental Counting Principle.**

You will solve problems about different types of bicycles in Lesson 8-2.

372 Chapter 8 Probability

Vocabulary Builder

For a thorough vocabulary list with pronunciations of new words, give students the Vocabulary Builder worksheets from the *Chapter 8 Resource Masters*. Encourage them to complete the definition of each term as they progress through the chapter.

GETTING STARTED

▶ Diagnose Readiness

Take this quiz to see if you are ready to begin Chapter 8. Refer to the lesson or page number in parentheses for review.

Vocabulary Review

Complete each sentence.

1. The equation $\frac{6}{15} = \frac{2}{5}$ is a __?__ because it contains two equivalent ratios. (Lesson 4-4) **proportion**
2. Percent is a ratio that compares a number to __?__. (Lesson 5-1) **100**

Prerequisite Skills

Write each fraction in simplest form. (Page 611)

3. $\frac{48}{72}$ **$\frac{2}{3}$**
4. $\frac{35}{60}$ **$\frac{7}{12}$**
5. $\frac{21}{99}$ **$\frac{7}{33}$**

Evaluate $x(x - 1)(x - 2)(x - 3)$ for each value of x. (Lesson 1-2)

6. $x = 11$ **7,920**
7. $x = 6$ **360**
8. $x = 9$ **3,024**
9. $x = 7$ **840**

Evaluate each expression. (Lesson 1-2)

10. $\frac{7 \cdot 6 \cdot 5}{3 \cdot 2 \cdot 1}$ **35**
11. $\frac{12 \cdot 11}{2 \cdot 1}$ **66**
12. $\frac{8 \cdot 7 \cdot 6 \cdot 5}{4 \cdot 3 \cdot 2 \cdot 1}$ **70**
13. $\frac{5 \cdot 4 \cdot 3}{3 \cdot 2 \cdot 1}$ **10**

Multiply. Write in simplest form. (Lesson 2-3)

14. $\frac{2}{3} \cdot \frac{3}{4}$ **$\frac{1}{2}$**
15. $\frac{4}{15} \cdot \frac{5}{7}$ **$\frac{4}{21}$**
16. $\frac{7}{8} \cdot \frac{4}{9}$ **$\frac{7}{18}$**
17. $\frac{3}{5} \cdot \frac{1}{6}$ **$\frac{1}{10}$**

Solve each problem. (Lessons 5-3 and 5-6)

18. Find 28% of 80. **22.4**
19. Find 55% of 34. **18.7**

Probability Make this Foldable to help you organize your notes. Begin with two sheets of $8\frac{1}{2}" \times 11"$ unlined paper.

STEP 1 **Fold in Quarters**
Fold each sheet in quarters along the width.

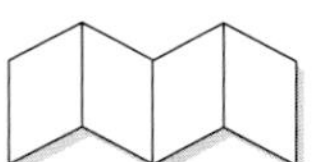

STEP 2 **Tape**
Unfold each sheet and tape to form one long piece.

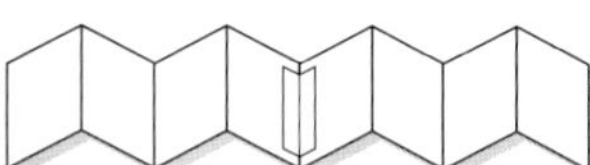

STEP 3 **Label**
Label each page with the lesson number as shown. Refold to form a booklet.

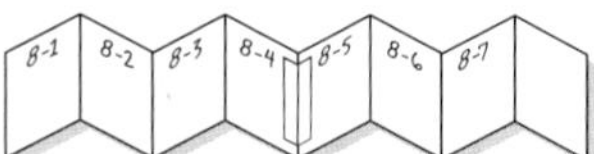

Chapter Notes Each time you find this logo throughout the chapter, use your *Noteables™: Interactive Study Notebook with Foldables™* or your own notebook to take notes. Begin your chapter notes with this Foldable activity.

Math Online **Readiness** To prepare yourself for this chapter with another quiz, visit **msmath3.net/chapter_readiness**

GETTING STARTED

Diagnose Readiness This section provides a review of the basic concepts needed before beginning Chapter 8. Page references are included for additional student help.

Prerequisite Skills review skills needed in this chapter.

Exercises	Needed for Lesson	Skill
3–5	8-1	Write Fractions in Simplest Form
6–9	8-3	Evaluate an Expression
10–13	8-4	Evaluate Expressions
14–17	8-5	Multiply Expressions
18–19	8-7	Solve Percent Problems

For more prerequisite skills, see:

- Getting Ready for the Next Lesson, at the end of each lesson
- Prerequisite Skills in the Student Handbook on pp. 600–615
- *Math Skills Maintenance Masters*

FOLDABLES™ Study Organizer

For more information about Foldables, see *Teaching Mathematics with Foldables.*

Use this Foldable for student writing about probability. After students make their Foldables, have them label the first seven sections to correspond to the seven lessons in this chapter. Have students use the last section for vocabulary words and definitions. Students use their Foldables to take notes, define terms, record concepts, and write examples. As students progress through the lessons, have them note the order in which concepts about probability are presented. They should include reasons for this sequence in their notes.

8-1 Lesson Notes

Lesson Resources

Chapter 8 Resource Masters

FAST FILE

- Study Guide and Intervention, p. 445
- Practice: Skills, p. 446
- Practice: Word Problems, p. 447
- Reading to Learn Mathematics, p. 448
- Enrichment, p. 449

Key Teaching Transparencies, 28

Parent and Student Study Guide Online Worksheets, 8-1

Noteables™: Interactive Study Notebook with Foldables™, 8-1

1 Focus

5-Minute Check 8-1

Use as a quiz or review of Chapter 7. (Also available as a transparency)

Bellringer

Hands-On Activity Have pairs of students roll two number cubes 25 times and record the sum and product of the two numbers. Then ask whether an even sum is more likely or less likely than an odd sum. Explain. **Half of the possibilities are even and half are odd.** Ask whether an even product is more likely or less likely than an odd product. Explain. **More likely; 3 out of 4 possible products are even.**

Reading to Learn Mathematics, p. 448 **ELL**

NAME ______ DATE ______ PERIOD ______

8-1 Reading to Learn Mathematics

Probability of Simple Events

Pre-Activity ***Read the introduction at the top of page 374 in your textbook. Write your answers below.***

1. Write the ratio that compares the number of double tiles to the total number of tiles. 7:28 or 1:4
2. What percent of the tiles are doubles? 25%
3. Write a fraction in simplest form that represents the part of the tiles that are doubles. $\frac{1}{4}$
4. Write a decimal that represents the part of the tiles that are doubles. 0.25
5. Suppose you pick a domino without looking at the spots. Would you be more likely to pick a tile that is a double or one that is not a double? Ex[...] One that is not a double; there are more tiles that [...]ubles th[...]

8-1 Probability of Simple Events

What You'll LEARN

Find the probability of a simple event.

NEW Vocabulary

outcome
sample space
random
simple event
probability
complementary events

REVIEW Vocabulary

percent: a ratio that compares a number to 100 (Lesson 5-1)

WHEN am I ever going to use this?

GAMES The game of double-six dominoes is played with 28 tiles. Seven of the tiles are called doubles.

Double

1. Write the ratio that compares the number of double tiles to the total number of tiles. **7:28 or 1:4**
2. What percent of the tiles are doubles? **25%**

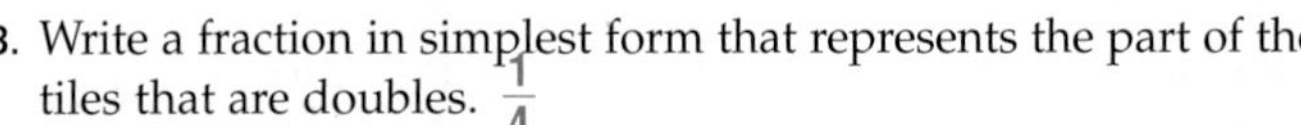

3. Write a fraction in simplest form that represents the part of the tiles that are doubles. $\frac{1}{4}$
4. Write a decimal that represents the part of the tiles that are doubles. **0.25**
5. Suppose you pick a domino without looking at the spots. Would you be more likely to pick a tile that is a double or one that is not a double? Explain.

5. One that is not a double; there are more tiles that are not doubles than there are doubles.

In the game of double-six dominoes, there are 28 tiles that can be picked. These tiles are called the **outcomes**. A list of all the tiles is called the **sample space**. If all outcomes occur by chance, the outcomes happen at **random**.

A **simple event** is a specific outcome or type of outcome. When picking dominoes, one event is picking a double. **Probability** is the chance that an event will happen.

Noteables™ **Key Concept: Probability**

Words The probability of an event is a ratio that compares the number of favorable outcomes to the number of possible outcomes.

Symbols $P(\text{event}) = \frac{\text{number of favorable outcomes}}{\text{number of possible outcomes}}$

Example $P(\text{doubles}) = \frac{7}{28}$ or $\frac{1}{4}$

The probability that an event will happen is between 0 and 1 inclusive. A probability can be expressed as a fraction, a decimal, or a percent.

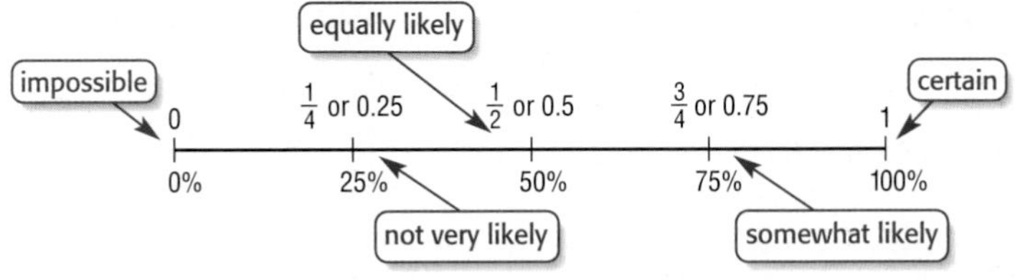

EXAMPLES Find Probabilities

A box contains 5 green pens, 3 blue pens, 8 black pens, and 4 red pens. A pen is picked at random.

1 What is the probability the pen is green?

There are 5 + 3 + 8 + 4 or 20 pens in the box.

$P(\text{green}) = \dfrac{\text{green pens}}{\text{total number of pens}}$ Definition of probability

$= \dfrac{5}{20}$ or $\dfrac{1}{4}$ There are 5 green pens out of 20 pens.

The probability the pen is green is $\frac{1}{4}$. The probability can also be written as 0.25 or 25%.

2 What is the probability the pen is blue or red?

$P(\text{blue or red}) = \dfrac{\text{blue pens} + \text{red pens}}{\text{total number of pens}}$ Definition of probability

$= \dfrac{3 + 4}{20}$ or $\dfrac{7}{20}$ There are 3 blue pens and 4 red pens.

The probability the pen is blue or red is $\frac{7}{20}$. The probability can also be written as 0.35 or 35%.

3 What is the probability the pen is gold?

Since there are no gold pens, the probability is 0.

READING Math

Probability *P*(green) is read *the probability of green.*

TEACHING TIP

Explain to the students that it is impossible to pick a gold pen, because there are no gold pens. Therefore, the probability of picking a gold pen is 0.

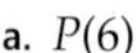

Your Turn **The spinner is used for a game. Write each probability as a fraction, a decimal, or a percent.**

a. $P(6)$ b. $P(\text{odd})$

c. $P(5 \text{ or even})$ d. $P(\text{a number less than } 7)$

a. $\frac{1}{6}$; $0.1\overline{6}$; $16.\overline{6}\%$

b. $\frac{1}{2}$; 0.5; 50%

c. $\frac{2}{3}$; $0.\overline{6}$; $66.\overline{6}\%$

d. 1; 1; 100%

Suppose you roll a number cube. The events of rolling a 6 and of *not* rolling a 6 are **complementary events**. The sum of the probabilities of complementary events is 1.

EXAMPLE Probability of a Complementary Event

4 PURCHASES A computer company manufactures 2,500 computers each day. An average of 100 of these computers are returned with defects. What is the probability that the computer you purchased is *not* defective?

2,500 − 100 or 2,400 computers were not defective.

$P(\text{not defective}) = \dfrac{\text{nondefective computers}}{\text{total number of computers}}$ Definition of probability

$= \dfrac{2{,}400}{2{,}500}$ or $\dfrac{24}{25}$ There are 2,400 nondefective computers.

The probability that your computer is *not* defective is $\frac{24}{25}$.

Mental Math The probability of a defective computer is $\frac{100}{2{,}500}$ or $\frac{1}{25}$. Since defective and nondefective computers are complementary events, the probability of a nondefective computer is $1 - \frac{1}{25}$ or $\frac{24}{25}$.

Math Online msmath3.net/extra_examples

2 Teach

Noteables™

As you work the **In-Class Examples,** have students follow along in their *Noteables™: Interactive Study Notebook with Foldables™*, or have students work the examples in their notebooks.

In-Class Examples

A bag contains 5 blue marbles, 10 red marbles, and 10 yellow marbles. A marble is picked at random.

1 What is the probability the marble is yellow? $\frac{2}{5}$

2 What is the probability the marble is blue or red? $\frac{3}{5}$

3 What is the probability the marble is white? 0

4 **PHONE LISTINGS** One town has 10,000 phone numbers in use. Of these, 500 are not listed in the local phone book. What is the probability that the phone number you are looking for is listed in the phone book? $\frac{19}{20}$

Using Manipulatives Try to have manipulatives available for students to use while they are learning probability. Spinners, playing cards, and counters of various colors can make learning probability more meaningful and fun.

DAILY INTERVENTION **Differentiated Instruction**

Visual/Spatial Ask students to design their own probability problems based on drawings. One student may choose to draw a square on grid paper and shade in a certain number of small squares within the larger square. Another student may wish to draw shapes of different colors and ask a probability question related to the number of shapes of each color that have been drawn. For example, "What is the probability that a raindrop falling within the grid will fall on a shaded square?"

3 Practice/Apply

DAILY INTERVENTION **FIND THE ERROR** In Exercise 3, ask students to think about whether the probability of getting every number on the number cube is the same or different.

About the Exercises...

Guided Practice Key

Exercises	Examples
4	1
5–6, 8–9	2
7	3
10	4

Assignment Guide

Basic: 11–17 odd, 21–27 odd, 31–41

Average: 11–27 odd, 31–41 (Optional: 28–30)

Enriched: 12–24 even, 25–37 (Optional: 38–41)

Alert! Exercise 23 requires research on the Internet or another resource.

Answers

1.

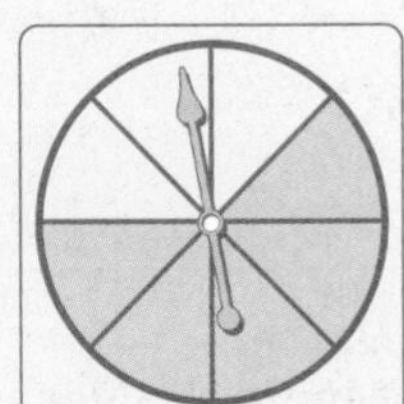

2. Sample answer: The probability that a one-digit number picked at random is less than 10.
3. A 2 is only 1 out of 6 possibilities when rolling a number cube. The probability is $\frac{1}{6}$.
4. $\frac{1}{8}$; 0.125; 12.5%
5. $\frac{1}{2}$; 0.5; 50%
6. $\frac{3}{8}$; 0.375; 37.5%
7. $\frac{7}{8}$; 0.875; 87.5%
8. 1; 1; 100%

Students practice the same concepts in Exercises 11–20 if they are assigned odd or even problems.

Skill and Concept Check

1. **Draw** a spinner where the probability of an outcome of white is $\frac{3}{8}$. **1–2. See margin.**
2. **OPEN ENDED** Give an example of an event with a probability of 1.
3. **FIND THE ERROR** Masao and Brian are finding the probability of getting a 2 when a number cube is rolled. Masao says it is $\frac{1}{6}$, and Brian says it is $\frac{2}{6}$. Who is correct? Explain. **Masao; see margin for explanation.**

GUIDED PRACTICE

The spinner is used for a game. Write each probability as a fraction, a decimal, and a percent. **4–9. See margin.**

4. $P(5)$
5. $P(\text{even})$
6. $P(\text{greater than } 5)$
7. $P(\text{not } 2)$
8. $P(\text{an integer})$
9. $P(\text{less than } 7)$
10. **GAMES** A card game has 25 red cards, 25 green cards, 25 yellow cards, 25 blue cards, and 8 wild cards. What is the probability that the first card dealt is a wild card? $\frac{2}{27}$

★ indicates increased difficulty

Practice and Applications

HOMEWORK HELP

For Exercises	See Examples
11–20, 24–25	1–3
21	4

Extra Practice See pages 635, 655.

A beanbag is tossed on the square at the right. It lands at random in a small square. Write each probability as a fraction, a decimal, and a percent.

11. $P(\text{red})$ **11–16. See margin.**
12. $P(\text{blue})$
13. $P(\text{white or yellow})$
14. $P(\text{blue or red})$
15. $P(\text{not green})$
16. $P(\text{brown})$
17. What is the probability that a month picked at random starts with J? $\frac{1}{4}$
18. What is the probability that a day picked at random is a Saturday? $\frac{1}{7}$
19. ★ A number cube is tossed. Are the events of rolling a number greater than 3 and a number less than 3 complementary events? Explain. **No; see margin.**
20. ★ A coin is tossed twice and shows heads both times. What is the probability that the coin will show a tail on the next toss? Explain. **See margin.**
21. **WEATHER** A weather reporter says that there is a 40% chance of rain. What is the probability of *no* rain? **60%**
22. **WRITE A PROBLEM** Write a real-life problem with a probability of $\frac{1}{6}$. **See margin.**
23. **RESEARCH** Use the Internet or other resource to find the probability that a person from your state picked at random will be from your city or community. **See students' work.**

9. $\frac{3}{4}$; 0.75; 75%
11. $\frac{6}{25}$; 0.24; 24%
12. $\frac{1}{5}$; 0.2; 20%
13. $\frac{14}{25}$; 0.56; 56%
14. $\frac{11}{25}$; 0.44; 44%
15. 1; 1; 100%
16. 0; 0; 0%
19. $P(\text{greater than } 3) = \frac{1}{2}$ and $P(\text{less than } 3) = \frac{1}{3}$, but $\frac{1}{2} + \frac{1}{3} \neq 1$.
20. $\frac{1}{2}$; Each time the coin is tossed, there are two equally likely events. The previous result does not affect the current result.

HISTORY For Exercises 24–26, use the table at the right and the information below. 25. 0.225

The U.S. Census Bureau divides the United States into four regions: Northeast, Midwest, South, and West.

U.S. Population (thousands)		
Region	1890	2000
Northeast	17,407	53,594
Midwest	22,410	64,393
South	20,028	100,237
West	3,134	63,198

Source: U.S. Census Bureau

24. Suppose a person living in the United States in 1890 was picked at random. What is the probability that the person lived in the West? Write as a decimal to the nearest thousandth. **0.050**

25. Suppose a person living in the United States in 2000 was picked at random. What is the probability that the person lived in the West? Write as a decimal to the nearest thousandth.

26. How has the population of the West changed? **See margin.**

27. **CRITICAL THINKING** A box contains 5 red, 6 blue, 3 green, and 2 yellow crayons. How many red crayons must be added to the box so that the probability of randomly picking a red crayon is $\frac{2}{3}$? **17 red crayons**

EXTENDING THE LESSON The *odds* of an event occurring is a ratio that compares the number of favorable outcomes to the number of unfavorable outcomes. Suppose a number cube is rolled.

Find the odds of each outcome.

28. a 6 **1:5**

29. not a 6 **5:1**

30. an even number **1:1**

Spiral Review with Standardized Test Practice

For Exercises 31 and 32, the following cards are put into a box.

2	6	7	5	8	9	8	4

31. **MULTIPLE CHOICE** Emma picks a card at random. The number on the card will *most likely* be **C**

Ⓐ a number greater than 6. Ⓑ a number less than 6.

Ⓒ an even number. Ⓓ an odd number.

32. **MULTIPLE CHOICE** What is the probability of *not* getting an 8? **I**

Ⓕ 25% Ⓖ 30% Ⓗ 50% Ⓘ 75%

Analyze each measurement. Give the precision, significant digits if appropriate, greatest possible error, and relative error to two significant digits. (Lesson 7-9) **33–36. See Ch. 8 Answer Appendix.**

33. 8 cm

34. 0.36 kg

35. 4.83 m

36. 410 cm

37. **GEOMETRY** Find the surface area of a cone with radius of 5 inches and slant height of 12 inches. (Lesson 7-8) **about 267 in^2**

GETTING READY FOR THE NEXT LESSON

BASIC SKILL Multiply.

38. $5 \cdot 6 \cdot 2$ **60**

39. $5 \cdot 5 \cdot 8$ **200**

40. $12 \cdot 5 \cdot 3$ **180**

41. $7 \cdot 8 \cdot 2$ **112**

Math Online msmath3.net/self_check_quiz

Study Guide and Intervention, p. 445

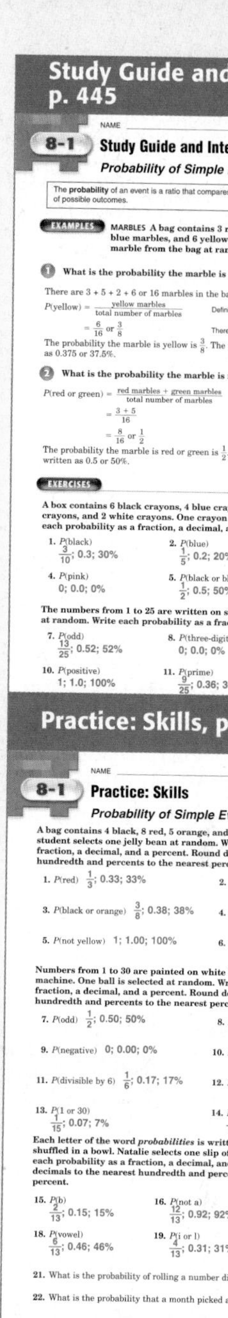

NAME ____ DATE ____ PERIOD ____

8-1 Study Guide and Intervention

Probability of Simple Events

The **probability** of an event is a ratio that compares the number of favorable outcomes to the number of possible outcomes.

EXAMPLES MARBLES A bag contains 3 red marbles, 5 green marbles, 2 blue marbles, and 6 yellow marbles. Evan picks one marble from the bag at random.

1. **What is the probability the marble is yellow?**

There are 3 + 5 + 2 + 6 or 16 marbles in the bag.

$P(\text{yellow}) = \frac{\text{yellow marbles}}{\text{total number of marbles}}$ Definition of probability

$= \frac{6}{16}$ or $\frac{3}{8}$ There are 6 yellow marbles out of 16 marbles.

The probability the marble is yellow is $\frac{3}{8}$. The probability can also be written as 0.375 or 37.5%.

2. **What is the probability the marble is red or green?**

$P(\text{red or green}) = \frac{\text{red marbles + green marbles}}{\text{total number of marbles}}$ Definition of probability

$= \frac{3+5}{16}$ There are 3 red marbles and 5 green marbles.

$= \frac{8}{16}$ or $\frac{1}{2}$ Simplify.

The probability the marble is red or green is $\frac{1}{2}$. The probability can also be written as 0.5 or 50%.

EXERCISES

A box contains 6 black crayons, 4 blue crayons, 5 red crayons, 3 yellow crayons, and 2 white crayons. One crayon is chosen at random. Write each probability as a fraction, a decimal, and a percent.

1. P(black) $\frac{3}{10}$; 0.3; 30%
2. P(blue) $\frac{1}{5}$; 0.2; 20%
3. P(not white) $\frac{9}{10}$; 0.9; 90%
4. P(pink) 0; 0.0; 0%
5. P(black or blue) $\frac{1}{2}$; 0.5; 50%
6. P(blue, red, or yellow) $\frac{3}{5}$; 0.6; 60%

The numbers from 1 to 25 are written on slips of paper and one is selected at random. Write each probability as a fraction, a decimal, and a percent.

7. P(odd) $\frac{13}{25}$; 0.52; 52%
8. P(three-digit number) 0; 0.0; 0%
9. P(not 4) $\frac{24}{25}$; 0.96; 96%
10. P(positive) 1; 1.0; 100%
11. P(prime) $\frac{9}{25}$; 0.36; 36%
12. P(greater than 19) $\frac{6}{25}$; 0.24; 24%

Practice: Skills, p. 446

NAME ____ DATE ____ PERIOD ____

8-1 Practice: Skills

Probability of Simple Events

A bag contains 4 black, 8 red, 5 orange, and 7 green jelly beans. A student selects one jelly bean at random. Write each probability as a fraction, a decimal, and a percent. Round decimals to the nearest hundredth and percents to the nearest percent.

1. P(red) $\frac{1}{3}$; 0.33; 33%
2. P(not green) $\frac{17}{24}$; 0.71; 71%
3. P(black or orange) $\frac{3}{8}$; 0.38; 38%
4. P(blue) 0; 0.00; 0%
5. P(not yellow) 1; 1.00; 100%
6. P(red, green, or orange) $\frac{5}{6}$; 0.83; 83%

Numbers from 1 to 30 are painted on white balls and mixed by a machine. One ball is selected at random. Write each probability as a fraction, a decimal, and a percent. Round decimals to the nearest hundredth and percents to the nearest percent.

7. P(odd) $\frac{1}{2}$; 0.50; 50%
8. P(one-digit number) $\frac{3}{10}$; 0.30; 30%
9. P(negative) 0; 0.00; 0%
10. P(ending in 0) $\frac{1}{10}$; 0.10; 10%
11. P(divisible by 6) $\frac{1}{6}$; 0.17; 17%
12. P(two-digit number) $\frac{7}{10}$; 0.70; 70%
13. P(1 or 30) $\frac{1}{15}$; 0.07; 7%
14. P(greater than 17 but less than 26) $\frac{4}{15}$; 0.27; 27%

Each letter of the word *probabilities* is written on a slip of paper and shuffled in a bowl. Natalie selects one slip of paper at random. Write each probability as a fraction, a decimal, and a percent. Round decimals to the nearest hundredth and percents to the nearest percent.

15. P(b) $\frac{2}{13}$; 0.15; 15%
16. P(not a) $\frac{12}{13}$; 0.92; 92%
17. P(u) 0; 0.00; 0%
18. P(vowel) $\frac{6}{13}$; 0.46; 46%
19. P(i or l) $\frac{4}{13}$; 0.31; 31%
20. P(not p or b) $\frac{10}{13}$; 0.77; 77%
21. What is the probability of rolling a number divisible by 2 on a number cube? $\frac{1}{2}$
22. What is the probability that a month picked a random ends with the letter y? $\frac{1}{3}$

Practice: Word Problems, p. 447

NAME ____ DATE ____ PERIOD ____

8-1 Practice: Word Problems

Probability of Simple Events

FOOD For Exercises 1 and 2, use the table that shows the results of a survey that asked students in a classroom to choose their favorite fruit.

Fruit	Orange	Apple	Banana	Strawberry	Other
Number of Students	3	8	11	6	4

1. Suppose a student in the classroom is picked at random. Explain how to find the probability that the student's favorite fruit is strawberry. Then find the probability. Write it as a decimal. Find the ratio of the number of students who preferred strawberries to the total number of students; 0.1875

2. Suppose a student in the classroom is picked at random. Explain how to find the probability that the student's favorite fruit is not an apple or a banana. Then find the probability. Write it as a decimal to the nearest thousandth. Add the numbers for orange, strawberry, and other, and divide this sum by the total number of students; 0.406

GAMES For Exercises 3 and 4, use the board game spinner that determines how many spaces to move during each player's turn.

3. Explain how to find the probability of spinning a number that is greater than or equal to 4. Then find the probability. There are 3 outcomes with numbers greater than or equal to 4 and 12 total spaces. Find the ratio of 3 to 12; $\frac{1}{4}$

4. What is the probability of spinning a number that is not a 2 or a 3? $\frac{1}{2}$

5. CARPENTRY Hiromi builds a wooden birdhouse that is shaped like a cube. She paints 2 sides red, 1 side green, and 3 sides black. If she picks a side at random for the front, what is the probability that she will *not* pick a red side? $\frac{2}{3}$

6. TRANSPORTATION In August 2002, 85% of an airline's flights arrived on time. What is the probability that one of its flights arrived late in August 2002? 15%

4 Assess

Open-Ended Assessment

Modeling Have each student model a probability problem using class manipulatives such as counters or spinners, and then ask a partner to solve it.

Answers

22. Sample answer: John is playing a game. He must roll a number cube and get a 6 to advance his game piece. What is the probability that he will advance his game piece on the next roll of the number cube?

26. The population of the West has increased and has become a larger part of the total population of the U.S.

8-2a Lesson Notes

1 Focus

Bellringer

Problem Solving Ask students to suggest steps for planning a project to build a backyard deck. Have them consider time, labor, materials, and expenses. **Students may suggest making a table, making a spreadsheet, or making lists of materials needed and tasks to complete.** Tell students that in this lesson, they will learn to solve problems by organizing lists that show all possible information needed to find a solution.

2 Teach

In-Class Example

Solve. Use the make an organized list strategy.

TENNIS Eight players compete in a tennis tournament. They are paired up for matches, and the winner of each match is paired up with the winner of another match. This continues until only one pair remains. How many matches are played in all? **7 matches**

Answer

3. **Sample answer: A deli makes sandwiches with ham or turkey and American or Swiss cheese on wheat or white bread. What sandwiches should they list on their menu? ham, American, wheat; ham, American, white; ham, Swiss, wheat; ham, Swiss, white; turkey, American, wheat; turkey, American, white; turkey, Swiss, wheat; turkey, Swiss, white**

8-2a Problem-Solving Strategy

A Preview of Lesson 8-2

Make an Organized List

What You'll LEARN

Solve problems by making an organized list.

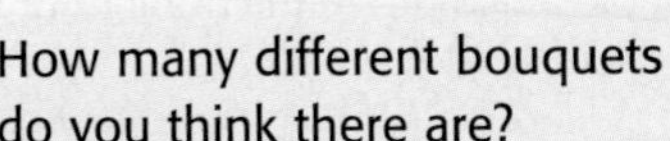

We have all the orders for the Valentine's Day bouquets. Each student could choose any combination of red, pink, white, or yellow carnations for their bouquets.

How many different bouquets do you think there are?

Explore	We want to know how many different bouquets can be made from four different colors of carnations.		
Plan	Let's make an organized list.		
Solve	Four-color bouquets:	red, pink, white, yellow	
	Three-color bouquets:	red, pink, white red, white, yellow	red, pink, yellow pink, white, yellow
	Two-color bouquets:	red, pink red, yellow pink, yellow	red, white pink, white white, yellow
	One-color bouquets:	red white	pink yellow
	There is 1 four-color bouquet, 4 three-color bouquets, 6 two-color bouquets, and 4 one-color bouquets. There are 1 + 4 + 6 + 4 or 15 bouquets.		
Examine	Check the list. Make sure that every color combination is listed and that no color combination is listed more than once.		

Analyze the Strategy

1. **Explain** why the list of possible bouquets was divided into four-color, three-color, two-color, and one-color bouquets. **to keep the list organized**
2. **Explain** why a red and white bouquet is the same as a white and red bouquet. **In the bouquet, the order of the colors is not significant.**
3. **Write** a problem that can be solved by making an organized list. Include the organized list you would use to solve the problem. **See margin.**

378 Chapter 8 Probability

DAILY INTERVENTION — Flexible Grouping

Make an Organized List Assign each student a partner of different math ability. Have students work together in pairs to discuss how they would use the make an organized list strategy to solve Exercises 4 and 5. Then have them work the exercises separately. Finally ask them to compare answers and explain their solutions to each other.

Apply the Strategy

Solve. Make an organized list.

4. **MONEY MATTERS** Destiny wants to buy a cookie from a vending machine. The cookie costs 45¢. If Destiny uses exact change, how many different combinations of nickels, dimes, and quarters can she use? **8 combinations**

5. **READING** Rosa checked out three books from the library. While she was at the library, she visited the fiction, nonfiction, and biography sections. What are the possible combinations of book types she could have checked out? **See margin.**

Mixed Problem Solving

Solve. Use any strategy.

6. **GAMES** Steven and Derek are playing a guessing game. Steven says he is thinking of two integers between −10 and 10 that have a product of −12. If Derek has one guess, what is the probability that he will guess the pair of numbers? $\frac{1}{4}$

7. **COOKING** The graph shows the number of types of outdoor grills sold. How does the number of charcoal grills compare to the number of gas grills? **See margin.**

Source: Barbecue Industry Association

BASEBALL For Exercises 8–10, use the following information.
In the World Series, two teams play each other until one team wins 4 games. **8. 4 games**

8. What is the least number of games needed to determine a winner of the World Series?

9. What is the greatest number of games needed to determine a winner? **7 games**

10. How many different ways can a team win the World Series in six games or less? (*Hint*: The team that wins the series must win the last game.) **15 ways**

11. **SLEEP** What is the probability that a person between the ages of 35 and 49 talks in his or her sleep? Write the probability as a fraction and as a decimal. $\frac{3}{20}$; **0.15**

Source: The Better Sleep Council

12. **MULTI STEP** At 2:00 P.M., Cody began writing the final draft of a report. At 3:30 P.M., he had written 5 pages. If he works at the same pace, when should he complete 8 pages? **4:24 P.M.**

13. **MONEY MATTERS** Rebecca is shopping for fishing equipment. She has $135 and has already selected items that total $98.50. If the sales tax is 8%, will she have enough to purchase a fishing net that costs $23? **yes**

14. **STANDARDIZED TEST PRACTICE** Which equation best identifies the pattern in the table? **C**

x	y
−2	2
−1	0.5
0	0
1	0.5
2	2

Ⓐ $y = x^2$
Ⓑ $y = 2x^2$
Ⓒ $y = 0.5x^2$
Ⓓ $y = -x^2$

3 Practice/Apply

About the Exercises...

Problem-Solving Strategies
Exercises 6–14 are structured so that students have the opportunity to practice many different problem-solving strategies. You may wish to remind them of some of the strategies they have studied.

- use the four-step plan (p. 6)
- look for a pattern (p. 96)
- draw a diagram (p. 176)
- reasonable answers (p. 226)
- make an organized list ✓

4 Assess

Higher-Level Thinking
Draw a four-unit by four-unit square on grid paper, and determine the total number of squares of all sizes within the square. **30 squares**

Answers

5. 1 fiction, 1 nonfiction, 1 biography; 2 fiction, 1 nonfiction; 2 fiction, 1 biography; 2 nonfiction, 1 fiction; 2 nonfiction, 1 biography; 2 biographies, 1 fiction; 2 biographies, 1 nonfiction; 3 fiction; 3 nonfiction; 3 biographies

7. Sample answer: There were almost twice as many charcoal grills sold as gas grills.

Lesson 8-2a Problem-Solving Strategy: Make an Organized List 379

8-2 Lesson Notes

Lesson Resources

Chapter 8 Resource Masters FAST FILE
- Study Guide and Intervention, p. 450
- Practice: Skills, p. 451
- Practice: Word Problems, p. 452
- Reading to Learn Mathematics, p. 453
- Enrichment, p. 454

Calculator and Spreadsheet Masters, p. 35

Key Teaching Transparencies, 29

Parent and Student Study Guide Online Worksheets, 8-2

Teaching Mathematics with Manipulatives, pp. 92–93

Noteables™: Interactive Study Notebook with Foldables™, 8-2

1 Focus

5-Minute Check 8-2
Use as a quiz or review of Lesson 8-1. (Also available as a transparency)

Bellringer
Communication Identify four different colored shirts and three different colored baseball caps on the chalkboard. Ask the students to describe all of the different pairs of shirts and caps that one could wear. Ask students for ideas on how to organize their choices. 12

Reading to Learn Mathematics, p. 453 ELL

NAME ______ DATE ______ PERIOD ______

8-2 Reading to Learn Mathematics
Counting Outcomes

Pre-Activity *Read the introduction at the top of page 380 in your textbook. Write your answers below.*

1. How many different styles are available? 2 styles
2. How many different colors are available? 3 colors
3. How many different sizes are available? 2 sizes
4. Make an organized list to determine how many different bicycles are available. 12 bicycles; mountain, red, 26 in. mountain, red, 28 in. mountain, black, 26 in. mountain, black, 28 in. mountain, green, 26 in. mountain, green, 28 in. 10-speed, red, 26 in. 10-speed, red, 28 in. 10-speed, black, 26 in. 10-speed, black, 28 in. 10-speed, green, 26 in. 10-speed, green, 28 in.

Reading the Lesson

5. Complete the tree diagram shown below for how many boys and how many girls are likely to be in a family of three children.

Child 2 Child 3 Sample Outcome

8-2 Counting Outcomes

What You'll LEARN
Count outcomes by using a tree diagram or the Fundamental Counting Principle.

NEW Vocabulary
tree diagram
Fundamental Counting Principle

WHEN am I ever going to use this?

BICYCLES Antonio wants to buy a Dynamo bicycle.

1. How many different styles are available? **2 styles**
2. How many different colors are available? **3 colors**
3. How many different sizes are available? **2 sizes**
4. Make an organized list to determine how many different bicycles are available. **See margin for organized list; 12 bicycles.**

Dynamo Bicycles are the Best!
Choose your Dynamo Today!
Styles: Mountain or 10-Speed
Colors: Red, Black, or Green
Sizes: 26-inch or 28-inch

An organized list can help you determine the number of possible combinations or outcomes. One type of organized list is a **tree diagram**.

EXAMPLE Use a Tree Diagram

1 BICYCLES **Draw a tree diagram to determine the number of different bicycles described in the real-life example above.**

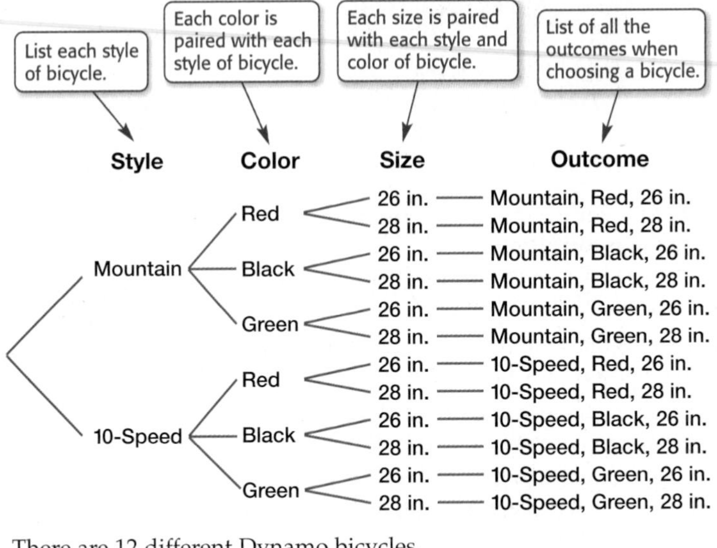

There are 12 different Dynamo bicycles.

Answer (When am I ever going to use this?)

4. Mountain, Red, 26 in.; Mountain, Red, 28 in.; Mountain, Black, 26 in.; Mountain, Black 28 in.; Mountain, Green, 26 in.; Mountain, Green, 28 in.; 10-speed, Red, 26 in.; 10-speed, Red, 28 in.; 10-speed, Black, 26 in.; 10-speed, Black, 28 in.; 10-speed, Green, 26 in.; 10-speed, Green, 28 in.

You can also find the total number of outcomes by multiplying. This principle is known as the **Fundamental Counting Principle**.

Noteables™ **Key Concept: Fundamental Counting Principle**

Words If event M can occur in m ways and is followed by event N that can occur in n ways, then the event M followed by the event N can occur in $m \cdot n$ ways.

Example If a number cube is rolled and a coin is tossed, there are $6 \cdot 2$ or 12 possible outcomes.

You can also use the Fundamental Counting Principle when there are more than two events.

EXAMPLE Use the Fundamental Counting Principle

2 COMMUNICATIONS In the United States, radio and television stations use call letters that start with K or W. How many different call letters with 4 letters are possible?

Use the Fundamental Counting Principle.

number of possible letters for the first letter	×	number of possible letters for the second letter	×	number of possible letters for the third letter	×	number of possible letters for the fourth letter	=	a total number of possible call letters
2	×	26	×	26	×	26	=	35,152

There 35,152 possible call letters.

Your Turn Use the Fundamental Counting Principle to find the number of possible outcomes.

a. A hair dryer has 3 settings for heat and 2 settings for fan speed.

b. A restaurant offers a choice of 3 types of pasta with 5 types of sauce. Each pasta entrée comes with or without a meatball.

a. 6 outcomes b. 30 outcomes

EXAMPLE Find Probability

3 GAMES What is the probability of winning a lottery game where the winning number is made up of three digits from 0 to 9 chosen at random?

First, find the number of possible outcomes. Use the Fundamental Counting Principle.

choices for the first digit	×	choices for the second digit	×	choices for the third digit	=	total number of outcomes
10	×	10	×	10	=	1,000

There are 1,000 possible outcomes. There is 1 winning number. So, the probability of winning with one ticket is $\frac{1}{1,000}$. This can also be written as a decimal, 0.001, or a percent, 0.1%.

REAL-LIFE MATH

COMMUNICATIONS On October 27, 1920, KDKA in Pittsburgh, Pennsylvania, became the first licensed radio station.

Source: *Time Almanac*

TEACHING TIP

Ask students how Example 3 would change if the first digit could not be 0.

msmath3.net/extra_examples

DAILY INTERVENTION **Differentiated Instruction**

Logical Ask students to use the Fundamental Counting Principle to find the probability of getting a 10 when rolling a pair of six-sided number cubes. **6×6 or 36 possible outcomes exist. There are 3 ways to make 10, so the probability of getting a 10 is $\frac{3}{36}$ or $\frac{1}{12}$.**

2 Teach

In-Class Examples

1 BOOKS A flea market vendor sells new and used books for adults and teens. Today she has fantasy novels and poetry collections to choose from. Draw a tree diagram to determine the number of categories of books. **8 outcomes**

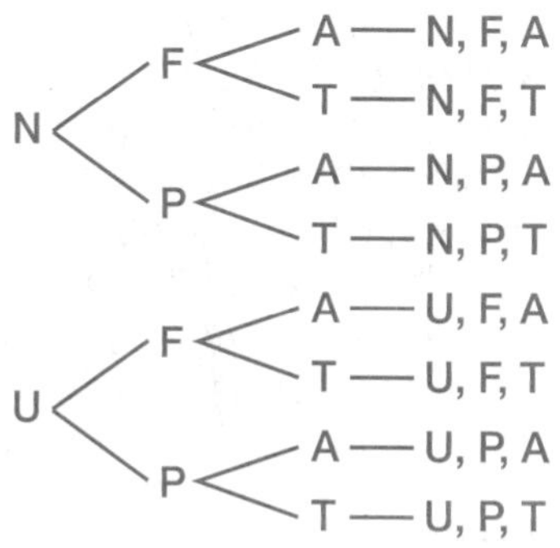

2 RESTAURANTS A manager assigns different codes to all the tables in a restaurant to make it easier for the wait staff to identify them. Each code consists of the vowel A, E, I, O, or U, followed by two digits from 0 through 9. How many codes could the manager assign using this method? **500**

3 COMPUTERS What is the probability that Liana will guess her friend's computer password on the first try if all she knows is that it consists of three letters? $\frac{1}{17,576}$

3 Practice/Apply

FOLDABLES™ Follow-Up Remind students to use the second section of their Foldables to record information on what they learn about counting outcomes by using a tree diagram or the Counting Principle, and to include examples of each. Encourage students to include the key terms and their definitions on the last section, or "Vocabulary" section, of their Foldables.

NUMBER SENSE
In Exercise 3, point out to students that they could make a tree diagram of the original situation with one color of pen. Then they can add a print blouse to the appropriate places in the diagram in another color. By counting the number of outcomes in the second color, they can find the answer.

About the Exercises...

Guided Practice Key

Exercises	Examples
4, 7	1
8	2
5–6	3

Assignment Guide

Basic: 9–23 odd, 24–35

Average: 9–21 odd, 22–35

Enriched: 10–16 even, 17–20, 22, 24–31 (Optional: 32–35)

Answers

1. With a tree diagram, you can see all the different outcomes. However, with the Fundamental Counting Principle, you only know how many outcomes there are.
2. Sample answer: Maria can choose from 5 flavors of ice cream and 3 different toppings. How many desserts can Maria make with one flavor of ice cream and one topping?

Students practice the same concepts in Exercises 9–16 if they are assigned odd or even problems.

Skill and Concept Check

1. *Writing Math* Describe a possible advantage for using a tree diagram rather than the Fundamental Counting Principle. **1–2. See margin.**
2. **OPEN ENDED** Give an example of a situation that has 15 outcomes.
3. **NUMBER SENSE** Whitney has a choice of a floral, plaid, or striped blouse to wear with a choice of a tan, black, navy, or white skirt. How many more outfits can she make if she buys a print blouse? **4 more outfits**

GUIDED PRACTICE **4. See Ch. 8 Answer Appendix for tree diagram; 9 outcomes.**

The spinner at the right is spun two times.

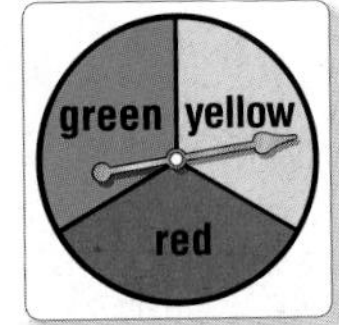

4. Draw a tree diagram to determine the number of outcomes.
5. What is the probability that both spins will land on red? $\frac{1}{9}$
6. What is the probability that the two spins will land on different colors? $\frac{2}{3}$
7. **FOOD** A pizza parlor has regular, deep-dish, and thin crust, 2 different cheeses, and 4 toppings. How many different one-cheese and one-topping pizzas can be ordered? **24 pizzas**
8. **GOVERNMENT** The first three digits of a social security number are a geographic code. The next two digits are determined by the year and the state where the number is issued. The final four digits are random numbers. How many possible ways can the last four digits be assigned? **10,000 ways**

9–12. See Ch. 8 Answer Appendix for tree diagrams.

Practice and Applications

HOMEWORK HELP

For Exercises	See Examples
9–12, 17	1
13–16, 22–23	2
18–21	3

Extra Practice See pages 635, 655.

Draw a tree diagram to determine the number of outcomes.

9. A penny, a nickel, and a dime are tossed. **8 outcomes**
10. A number cube is rolled and a penny is tossed. **12 outcomes**
11. A sweatshirt comes in small, medium, large, and extra large. It comes in white or red. **8 outcomes**
12. The Sweet Treats Shoppe has three flavors of ice cream: chocolate, vanilla, and strawberry; and two types of cones, regular and sugar. **6 outcomes**

Use the Fundamental Counting Principle to find the number of possible outcomes.

13. The day of the week is picked at random and a number cube is rolled. **42 outcomes**
14. A number cube is rolled 3 times. **216 outcomes**
15. There are 5 true-false questions on a history quiz. **32 outcomes**
16. There are 4 choices for each of 5 multiple-choice questions on a science quiz. **1,024 outcomes**

For Exercises 17–20, each of the spinners at the right is spun once.

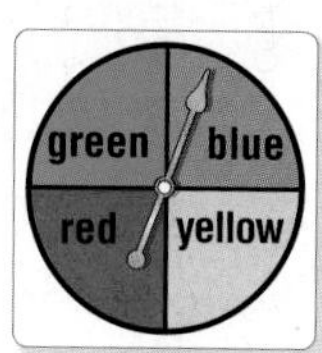

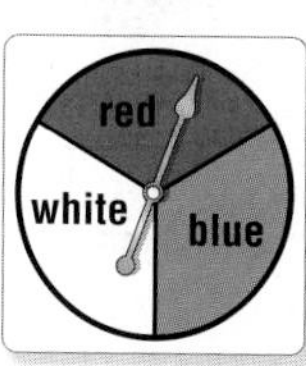

17. Draw a tree diagram to determine the number of outcomes. **See Ch. 8 Answer Appendix for tree diagram; 12 outcomes.**

18. What is the probability that both spinners land on the same color? $\frac{1}{6}$

19. What is the probability that at least one spinner lands on blue? $\frac{1}{2}$

20. What is the probability that at least one spinner lands on yellow? $\frac{1}{4}$

21. **PROBABILITY** What is the probability of winning a lottery game where the winning number is made up of five digits from 0 to 9 chosen at random? $\frac{1}{100,000}$

22. **SCHOOL** Doli can take 4 different classes first period, 3 different classes second period, and 5 different classes third period. How many different schedules can she have? **60 schedules**

23. **STATES** In 2003, Ohio celebrated its bicentennial. The state issued bicentennial license plates with 2 letters, followed by 2 numbers and then 2 more letters. How many bicentennial license plates could the state issue? **45,697,600 plates**

24. **CRITICAL THINKING** If x coins are tossed, write an algebraic expression for the number of possible outcomes. 2^x

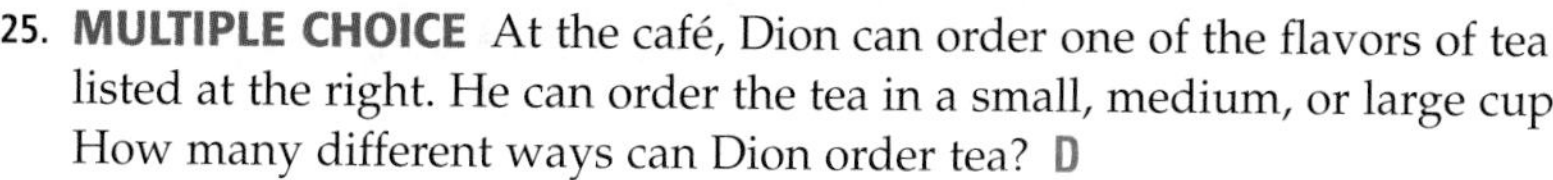

Spiral Review with Standardized Test Practice

25. **MULTIPLE CHOICE** At the café, Dion can order one of the flavors of tea listed at the right. He can order the tea in a small, medium, or large cup. How many different ways can Dion order tea? **D**

    Ⓐ 5 Ⓑ 8 Ⓒ 12 Ⓓ 15

Flavors of Tea
mint
orange
peach
raspberry
strawberry

26. **GRID IN** Felisa has a red and a white sweatshirt. Courtney has a black, a green, a red, and a white sweatshirt. Each girl picks a sweatshirt at random to wear to the picnic. What is the probability the girls will wear the same color sweatshirt? **1/4**

Each letter of the word *associative* is written on 11 identical slips of paper. A piece of paper is chosen at random. Find each probability. (Lesson 8-1)

27. $P(s)$ $\frac{2}{11}$ 28. $P(\text{vowel})$ $\frac{6}{11}$ 29. $P(\text{not } r)$ **1** 30. $P(d)$ **0**

31. **MEASUREMENT** How many significant digits are in the measurement 14.4 centimeters? (Lesson 7-9) **3 significant digits**

GETTING READY FOR THE NEXT LESSON

PREREQUISITE SKILL **Evaluate $n(n-1)(n-2)(n-3)$ for each value of n.** (Lesson 1-2)

32. $n = 5$ **120** 33. $n = 10$ **5,040** 34. $n = 12$ **11,880** 35. $n = 8$ **1,680**

Math Online msmath3.net/self_check_quiz

4 Assess

Open-Ended Assessment

Writing Ask students to select one of the exercises they solved using a tree diagram and one they solved using the Fundamental Counting Principle. Have them compare and contrast the two methods. Which one was easier for them to learn? Which one works better for more complex problems? **See students' work.**

Study Guide and Intervention, p. 450

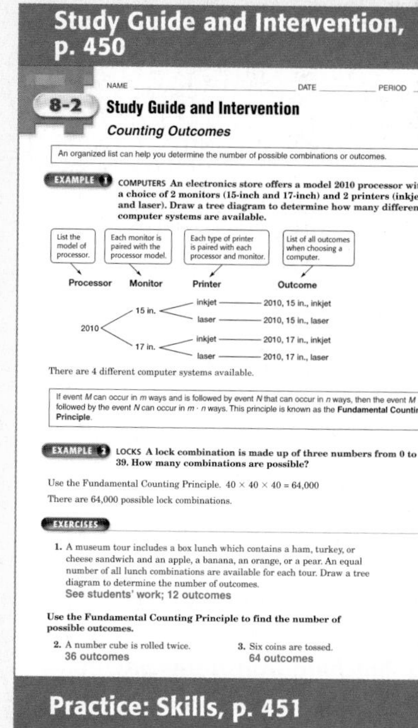

NAME ______ DATE ______ PERIOD ____

8-2 Study Guide and Intervention

Counting Outcomes

An organized list can help you determine the number of possible combinations or outcomes.

EXAMPLE 1 COMPUTERS **An electronics store offers a model 2010 processor with a choice of 2 monitors (15-inch and 17-inch) and 2 printers (inkjet and laser). Draw a tree diagram to determine how many different computer systems are available.**

There are 4 different computer systems available.

If event M can occur in m ways and is followed by event N that can occur in n ways, then the event M followed by the event N can occur in $m \cdot n$ ways. This principle is known as the **Fundamental Counting Principle**.

EXAMPLE 2 LOCKS **A lock combination is made up of three numbers from 0 to 39. How many combinations are possible?**

Use the Fundamental Counting Principle. $40 \times 40 \times 40 = 64,000$

There are 64,000 possible lock combinations.

EXERCISES

1. A museum tour includes a box lunch which contains a ham, turkey, or cheese sandwich and an apple, a banana, an orange, or a pear. An equal number of all lunch combinations are available for each tour. Draw a tree diagram to determine the number of outcomes.
   See students' work; 12 outcomes

Use the Fundamental Counting Principle to find the number of possible outcomes.

2. A number cube is rolled twice. 36 outcomes
3. Six coins are tossed. 64 outcomes

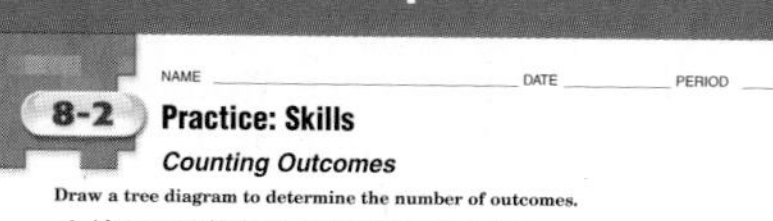

Practice: Skills, p. 451

NAME ______ DATE ______ PERIOD ____

8-2 Practice: Skills

Counting Outcomes

Draw a tree diagram to determine the number of outcomes.

1. A hat comes in black, red, or white, and medium or large.

Color	Size	Outcome
black	medium	black, medium
	large	black, large
red	medium	red, medium
	large	red, large
white	medium	white, medium
	large	white, large

6 outcomes

2. You have a choice of peach or vanilla yogurt topped with peanuts, granola, walnuts, or almonds.

Yogurt	Topping	Outcome
peach	peanuts	peach, peanuts
	granola	peach, granola
	walnuts	peach, walnuts
	almonds	peach, almonds
vanilla	peanuts	vanilla, peanuts
	granola	vanilla, granola
	walnuts	vanilla, walnuts
	almonds	vanilla, almonds

8 outcomes

Use the Fundamental Counting Principle to find the number of possible outcomes.

3. A test consists of 5 true-false questions. 32 outcomes
4. A number cube is rolled, and a dime and penny are tossed. 24 outcomes
5. Canned beans are packed in 3 sizes and 7 varieties. 21 outcomes
6. There are 5 choices for each of 6 multiple-choice questions on a history quiz. 15,625 outcomes

Practice: Word Problems, p. 452

NAME ______ DATE ______ PERIOD ____

8-2 Practice: Word Problems

Counting Outcomes

1. **RESTAURANT** An Italian restaurant offers mozzarella cheese, swiss cheese, sausage, ham, onions, and mushrooms for pizza toppings. For this week's special, you must choose one cheese, one meat, and one vegetable topping. On a separate sheet of paper, draw a tree diagram to find the number of possible outcomes. See students' work; 8 outcomes

2. **TOYS** Audra has a black and a white teddy bear. Cindy has a black, a white, a brown, and a pink teddy bear. Each girl picks a teddy bear at random to bring to a sleepover party. How many different combinations can the girls bring? 8 combinations

3. **FOOD** A candy maker offers milk, dark, or white chocolates with solid, cream, jelly, nut, fruit, or caramel centers. How many different chocolates can she make? Explain how you found your answer. 18 chocolates; using the Fundamental Counting Principle, multiply the number of types of chocolate, 3, by the number of different centers, 6.

4. **LOTTERY** In a lottery game, balls numbered 0 to 9 are placed in each of four chambers of a drawing machine. One ball is drawn from each chamber. How many four-number combinations are possible? 10,000 combinations

GAMES **Each of the spinners at the right is spun once to determine how a player's piece is moved in a board game.**

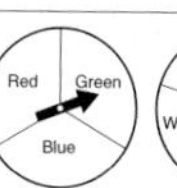

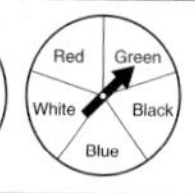

5. Jason needs to spin a red and a blue to move to the last square and win the game. What is the probability that Jason will win? Explain how you found your answer.
   $\frac{2}{15}$; There are 3 possible outcomes on one spinner and 5 on the other, so there are $3 \cdot 5$ or 15 possible outcomes. There are 2 ways to spin a red on one spinner and a blue on the other, so the probability is $\frac{2}{15}$.

6. If Jason spins a green or a white on either spinner, he will land on a "take an extra turn" square. What is the probability that Jason will get an extra turn?
   $\frac{3}{5}$

8-3 Lesson Notes

Lesson Resources

Chapter 8 Resource Masters

FAST FILE

- Study Guide and Intervention, p. 455
- Practice: Skills, p. 456
- Practice: Word Problems, p. 457
- Reading to Learn Mathematics, p. 458
- Enrichment, p. 459

Calculator and Spreadsheet Masters, p. 36

Key Teaching Transparencies, 30

Parent and Student Study Guide Online Worksheets, 8-3

Noteables™: Interactive Study Notebook with Foldables™, 8-3

1 Focus

5-Minute Check 8-3

Use as a quiz or review of Lesson 8-2. (Also available as a transparency)

Bellringer

Problem Solving Have students arrange the letters A, B, and C in as many different ways as they can. Have them record all of their arrangements and write down the number of ways they found. **6**

Reading to Learn Mathematics, p. 458 ELL

NAME ______ DATE ______ PERIOD ______

8-3 Reading to Learn Mathematics

Permutations

Pre-Activity *Complete the Mini Lab at the top of page 384 in your textbook. Write your answers below.*

1. How many different arrangements did you make? **12 arrangements**
2. How many different game pieces could you pick for the first place? **4 game pieces**
3. Once you pick the first-place game piece, how many game pieces could you pick for the second place? **3 game pieces**
4. Use the Fundamental Counting Principle to determine the number of arrangements for first and second places. **12 arrangements**
5. How do the numbers in Exercises 1 and 4 compare? **They are the same.**

8-3 Permutations

What You'll LEARN

Find the number of permutations of objects.

NEW Vocabulary

permutation
factorial

MATH Symbols

***P*(*a*, *b*)** the number of permutations of *a* things taken *b* at a time

! factorial

HANDS-ON Mini Lab

Materials
- four different game pieces

Work with a partner.

Suppose you are playing a game with 4 different game pieces. Show all of the ways the game pieces can be chosen first and second. Record each arrangement.

1. How many different arrangements did you make? **12 arrangements**
2. How many different game pieces could you pick for the first place? **4 game pieces**
3. Once you picked the first-place game piece, how many game pieces could you pick for the second place? **3 game pieces**
4. Use the Fundamental Counting Principle to determine the number of arrangements for first and second places.
5. How do the numbers in Exercises 1 and 4 compare?

4. 12 arrangements 5. They are the same.

When deciding who goes first and who goes second, order is important. An arrangement or listing in which order is important is called a **permutation**.

EXAMPLE Find a Permutation

1 **FOOD An ice cream shop has 31 flavors. Carlos wants to buy a three-scoop cone with three different flavors. How many cones can he buy if order is important?**

number of possible flavors for the first scoop	×	number of possible flavors for the second scoop	×	number of possible flavors for the third scoop	=	total number of possible cones
31	×	30	×	29	=	26,970

There are 26,970 different cones Carlos can order.

The symbol $P(31, 3)$ represents the number of permutations of 31 things taken 3 at a time.

Start with 31.

$$P(31, 3) = 31 \cdot 30 \cdot 29$$

Use three factors.

READING in the Content Area

For strategies in reading this lesson, visit **msmath3.net/reading**.

NCLB NO CHILD LEFT BEHIND

The goals of the NCLB Act include a stronger emphasis on reading. The **Reading in the Content Area** link helps students become proficient readers.

READING Math

Permutations $P(8, 3)$ can also be written $_8P_3$.

EXAMPLES Use Permutation Notation

Find each value.

2 $P(8, 3)$

$P(8, 3) = 8 \cdot 7 \cdot 6$ or 336 8 things taken 3 at a time.

3 $P(6, 6)$

$P(6, 6) = 6 \cdot 5 \cdot 4 \cdot 3 \cdot 2 \cdot 1$ or 720 6 things taken 6 at a time.

Your Turn Find each value.

a. $P(12, 2)$ **132** b. $P(4, 4)$ **24** c. $P(10, 5)$ **30,240**

In Example 3, $P(6, 6) = 6 \cdot 5 \cdot 4 \cdot 3 \cdot 2 \cdot 1$. The mathematical notation 6! also means $6 \cdot 5 \cdot 4 \cdot 3 \cdot 2 \cdot 1$. The symbol 6! is read *six* ***factorial***. n! means the product of all counting numbers beginning with n and counting backward to 1. We define 0! as 1.

EXAMPLE Find Probability

Standardized Test Practice

4 **MULTIPLE-CHOICE TEST ITEM** Consider all of the four-digit numbers that can be formed using the digits 1, 2, 3, and 4 where no digit is used twice. Find the probability that one of these numbers picked at random is between 1,000 and 2,000.

(A) $33\frac{1}{3}\%$ (B) 25% (C) 20% (D) 10%

Read the Test Item

You are considering all of the permutations of 4 digits taken 4 at a time. You wish to find the probability that one of these numbers picked at random is greater than 1,000, but less than 2,000.

Solve the Test Item

Find the number of possible four-digit numbers. $P(4, 4) = 4!$

In order for a number to be between 1,000 and 2,000, the thousands digit must be 1.

number of ways to pick the first digit	×	number of ways to pick the last three digits	=	number of permutations between 1,000 and 2,000
1	×	$P(3, 3)$	=	$P(3, 3)$ or 3!

P(between 1,000 and 2,000)

$= \frac{\text{number of permutations between 1,000 and 2,000}}{\text{total number of permutations}}$

$= \frac{3!}{4!}$ Substitute.

$= \frac{\overset{1}{\cancel{3}} \cdot \overset{1}{\cancel{2}} \cdot 1}{4 \cdot \underset{1}{\cancel{3}} \cdot \underset{1}{\cancel{2}} \cdot 1}$ Definition of factorial

$= \frac{1}{4}$ or 25% The probability is 25%, which is B.

Test-Taking Tip

Be Prepared
Before the day of the test, ask if you can use aids such as a calculator. Then come prepared on the day of the test. In Example 4, you could find the answer quickly by using the following keystrokes.

3 [PRB] [⇨] [⇨] [ENTER] [÷] 4 [PRB] [⇨] [⇨] [ENTER] [ENTER] 0.25

TEACHING TIP

Calculators use different keystrokes to find factorials. Help students determine how to find factorial on their calculators if the ones given above do not work.

msmath3.net/extra_examples

2 Teach

In-Class Examples

1 **SOFTBALL** There are 10 players on a softball team. In how many ways can the manager choose three players for first, second, and third base? **720**

Find each value.

2 $P(7, 2)$ **42**

3 $P(13, 7)$ **8,648,640**

4 **MULTIPLE-CHOICE TEST ITEM** Consider all of the five-digit numbers that can be formed using the digits 1, 2, 3, 4, and 5 where no digit is used twice. Find the probability that one of these numbers picked at random is an even number. **C**

A 20%

B 30%

C 40%

D 50%

Classroom Management Provide additional independent activities for students who finish a lesson's activities before the rest of the class. Possibilities include translating verbal expressions from the lessons in exercises to mathematical expressions and using classroom objects to model the lesson's content.

DAILY INTERVENTION Differentiated Instruction

Kinesthetic Have students work in groups of four, arranging themselves to sit in two available seats. Ask them to record all of their seating arrangements and to determine the number of permutations they find. **12**

3 Practice/Apply

FOLDABLES™ Follow-Up Remind students to use the third section of their Foldables to record information on what they learn about finding the number of permutations of objects in words and symbols, and to include an example of how they will use what they have learned. Encourage students to include the key terms and their definitions on the last section, or "Vocabulary" section, of their Foldables.

DAILY INTERVENTION **FIND THE ERROR** In Exercise 3, suggest that students think of $P(7, 3)$ as expressing the number of ways that seven people could be arranged to sit in three chairs.

About the Exercises...

Guided Practice Key

Exercises	Examples
8–10	1
4–7	2, 3

Assignment Guide

Basic: 11–25 odd, 29, 31, 33–46

Average: 11–31 odd, 33–46

Enriched: 12–32 even, 33–42 (Optional: 43–46)

Alert! The Data Update after Exercise 32 requires access to the Internet.

Answer

2. Sample answer: Seven friends are running a race. How many ways can they take first, second, and third place?

Students practice the same concepts in Exercises 11–28 if they are assigned odd or even problems.

Skill and Concept Check

1. **Tell** the difference between 9! and $P(9, 5)$. $9! = 9 \cdot 8 \cdot 7 \cdot 6 \cdot 5 \cdot 4 \cdot 3 \cdot 2 \cdot 1$ and $P(9, 5) = 9 \cdot 8 \cdot 7 \cdot 6 \cdot 5$
2. **OPEN ENDED** Write a problem that can be solved by finding the value of $P(7, 3)$. See margin.
3. **FIND THE ERROR** Daniel and Bailey are evaluating $P(7, 3)$. Who is correct? Explain. Bailey; $P(7, 3)$ means to start with 7 and use 3 factors.

Daniel
$P(7, 3) = 7 \cdot 6 \cdot 5 \cdot 4 \cdot 3$
$= 2,520$

Bailey
$P(7, 3) = 7 \cdot 6 \cdot 5$
$= 210$

GUIDED PRACTICE

Find each value.

4. $P(5, 3)$ 60
5. $P(7, 4)$ 840
6. 3! 6
7. 8! 40,320
8. In a race with 7 runners, how many ways can the runners end up in first, second, and third place? 210 ways
9. How many ways can you arrange the letters in the word *equals*? 720 ways
10. **SPORTS** There are 9 players on a baseball team. How many ways can the coach pick the first 4 batters? 3,024 ways

★ indicates increased difficulty

Practice and Applications

HOMEWORK HELP

For Exercises	See Examples
11–22	2, 3
23–26, 29–32	1
27–28	4

Extra Practice See pages 636, 655.

Find each value. 15. 240,240 16. 11,880 17. 303,600 18. 970,200

11. $P(6, 3)$ 120
12. $P(9, 2)$ 72
13. $P(5, 5)$ 120
14. $P(7, 7)$ 5,040
15. $P(14, 5)$
16. $P(12, 4)$
17. $P(25, 4)$
18. $P(100, 3)$
19. 2! 2
20. 5! 120
21. 11! 39,916,800
22. 12! 479,001,600
23. How many ways can the 4 runners on a relay team be arranged? 24 ways
24. **FLAGS** The flag of Mexico is shown at the right. How many ways could the Mexican government have chosen to arrange the three bar colors (green, white, and red) on the flag? 6 ways

25. A security system has a pad with 9 digits. How many four-number "passwords" are available if no digit is repeated? 3,024 passwords
26. Of the 10 games at the theater's arcade, Tyrone plans to play 3 different games. In how many orders can he play the 3 games? 720 orders
27. ★ **MULTI STEP** Each arrangement of the letters in the word *quilt* is written on a piece of paper. One paper is drawn at random. What is the probability that the word begins with *q*? $\frac{1}{5}$
28. ★ **MULTI STEP** Each arrangement of the letters in the word *math* is written on a piece of paper. One paper is drawn at random. What is the probability that the word ends with *th*? $\frac{1}{12}$

386 **Chapter 8** Probability

29. **SOCCER** The teams of the Eastern Conference of Major League Soccer are listed at the right. If there are no ties for placement in the conference, how many ways can the teams finish the season from first to last place? **120 ways**

Eastern Conference
Chicago Fire
Columbus Crew
D.C. United
MetroStars
New England Revolution

ENTERTAINMENT For Exercises 30–32, use the following information.

In the 2002 Tournament of Roses Parade, there were 54 floats, 23 bands, and 26 equestrian groups. **31. 15,600 ways**

30. In how many ways could the first 3 bands be chosen? **10,626 ways**

31. In how many ways could the first 3 equestrian groups be chosen?

★ 32. Two of the 54 floats were entered by the football teams competing in the Rose Bowl. If they cannot be first or second, how many ways can the first 3 floats be chosen? **137,904 ways**

Data Update How many floats, bands, and equestrian groups were in the last Tournament of Roses Parade? Visit msmath3.net/data_update to learn more.

33. **CRITICAL THINKING** If 9! = 362,880, use mental math to find 10! Explain. **3,628,800; 10! = 10 · 9!**

34. **CRITICAL THINKING** Compare $P(n, n)$ and $P(n, n - 1)$, where n is any whole number greater than one. Explain. **They are the same; see margin for explanation.**

Spiral Review with Standardized Test Practice

35. **MULTIPLE CHOICE** How many seven-digit phone numbers are available if a digit can only be used once and the first number cannot be 0 or 1? **B**

(A) 5,040 (B) 483,840 (C) 544,320 (D) 10,000,000

36. **MULTIPLE CHOICE** The school talent show is featuring 13 acts. In how many ways can the talent show coordinator order the first 5 acts? **H**

(F) 6,227,020,800 (G) 371,293 (H) 154,440 (I) 1,287

37. **SPORTS** The Silvercreek Ski Resort has 4 ski lifts up the mountain and 11 trails down the mountain. How many different ways can a skier take a ski lift up the mountain and then ski down? (Lesson 8-2) **44 different ways**

A number cube is rolled. Find each probability. (Lesson 8-1)

38. P(5 or 6) $\frac{1}{3}$ 39. P(odd) $\frac{1}{2}$ 40. P(less than 10) **1** 41. P(1 or even) $\frac{2}{3}$

42. Write an equation you could use to find the length of the missing side of the triangle at the right. Then find the missing length. (Lesson 3-4) $13^2 = a^2 + 5^2$; **12 ft**

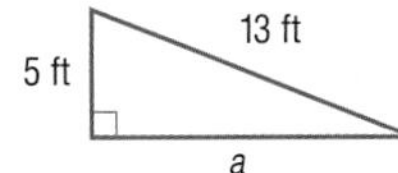

GETTING READY FOR THE NEXT LESSON

PREREQUISITE SKILL Evaluate each expression. (Lesson 1-2)

43. $\frac{6 \cdot 5 \cdot 4}{3 \cdot 2 \cdot 1}$ **20** 44. $\frac{10 \cdot 9 \cdot 8 \cdot 7}{4 \cdot 3 \cdot 2 \cdot 1}$ **210** 45. $\frac{20 \cdot 19}{2 \cdot 1}$ **190** 46. $\frac{6 \cdot 5 \cdot 4 \cdot 3 \cdot 2}{5 \cdot 4 \cdot 3 \cdot 2 \cdot 1}$ **6**

msmath3.net/self_check_quiz

4 Assess

Open-Ended Assessment

Speaking Have students explain how they would determine the number of different ways for all the students in the class to be arranged to sit in the seats that are currently being used.

Answer

34. $P(n, n) = n \cdot (n - 1) \cdot (n - 2) \cdot \ldots \cdot 2 \cdot 1$ and $P(n, n - 1) = n \cdot (n - 1) \cdot (n - 2) \cdot \ldots \cdot 2$, which are equal.

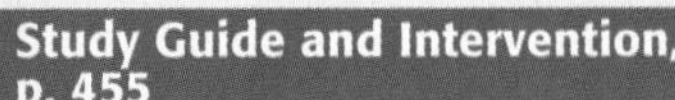

Study Guide and Intervention, p. 455

NAME ______ DATE ______ PERIOD ____

8-3 Study Guide and Intervention

Permutations

An arrangement or listing where order is important is called a **permutation**.

EXAMPLE 1 **SCHOOLS A school offers 23 different enrichment classes each semester. The students must list their three choices in order of preference. How many different ways can Lisa list her choices?**

Use the Fundamental Counting Principle. Once Lisa picks her first-choice class, there are only 22 classes that she can pick from for the second choice. Then there will be only 21 classes that Lisa can pick from for the third choice.

number of possible classes for the first choice	×	number of possible classes for the second choice	×	number of possible classes for the third choice	=	total number of ways students can list their choices
23	×	22	×	21	=	10,626

There are 10,626 different ways Lisa can list her enrichment class choices.

The symbol $P(23, 3)$ represents the number of permutations of 23 things taken 3 at a time.
$P(23, 3) = 23 \cdot 22 \cdot 21$

EXAMPLE 2 **Find $P(9, 4)$.**

$P(9, 4)$ represents the number of permutations of 9 things taken 4 at a time.

$P(9, 4) = 9 \cdot 8 \cdot 7 \cdot 6$ or 3,024

EXAMPLE 3 **Find 7!.**

$n!$ means the product of all counting numbers beginning with n and counting backward to 1.

$7! = 7 \cdot 6 \cdot 5 \cdot 4 \cdot 3 \cdot 2 \cdot 1 = 5{,}040$

EXERCISES

Find each value.

1. $P(5, 2)$ **20** 2. $P(6, 4)$ **360** 3. $P(8, 5)$ **6,720**

4. $P(15, 5)$ **360,360** 5. $P(24, 4)$ **255,024** 6. $P(101, 3)$ **999,900**

7. 6! **720** 8. 8! **40,320** 9. 10! **3,628,800**

10. How many ways can the three members of the debating team be arranged on the stage? **6 ways**

Practice: Skills, p. 456

NAME ______ DATE ______ PERIOD ____

8-3 Practice: Skills

Permutations

Find each value.

1. $P(5, 4)$ **120** 2. $P(9, 3)$ **504** 3. $P(8, 4)$ **1,680**

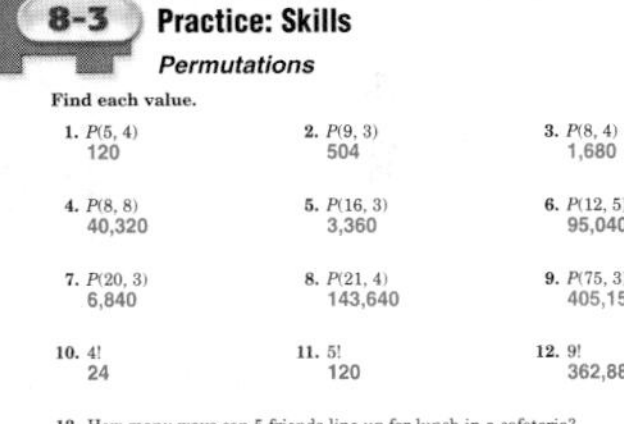

4. $P(8, 8)$ **40,320** 5. $P(16, 3)$ **3,360** 6. $P(12, 5)$ **95,040**

7. $P(20, 3)$ **6,840** 8. $P(21, 4)$ **143,640** 9. $P(75, 3)$ **405,150**

10. 4! **24** 11. 5! **120** 12. 9! **362,880**

13. How many ways can 5 friends line up for lunch in a cafeteria? **120 ways**

14. How many ways can you arrange the letters in the word *rainbow*? **5,040 ways**

15. Four employees of a company take a commuter van to work. In how many different orders can the driver pick up the four riders in the morning? **24 orders**

16. A bread recipe has 6 ingredients. How many ways can you place the first 4 ingredients in a bread maker? **360 ways**

17. How many ways can you arrange 8 books on a shelf? **40,320 ways**

18. Five students are finalists in a spelling bee. How many ways can they finish in first, second, and third place? **60 ways**

19. A flock of 9 pigeons lands on a telephone wire. How many ways can they be arranged on the wire? **362,880 ways**

20. How many even four-digit numbers can you form from the digits 1, 2, 3, and 5 where no digit is used twice? **6 numbers**

Practice: Word Problems, p. 457

NAME ______ DATE ______ PERIOD ____

8-3 Practice: Word Problems

Permutations

1. **LACROSSE** The United States Club Lacrosse Association has three divisions in the northeastern United States. The teams of the Empire Division are listed below.

Empire Division	
CNY Brine	Binghamton
Reebok	DeBeer
Zbonis	Tri-City

If there are no ties for placement in the division, how many ways can the teams finish the season from first to last place? **720 ways**

2. **GAMES** At lunchtime recess, 12 students race each other across the playground. In how many ways can students finish in first, second, third, and fourth places? **11,880 ways**

ENTERTAINMENT For Exercises 3 and 4, use the following information.

A music festival features 5 jazz bands, 9 rock bands, and 11 school bands. The bands play at various times over a long holiday weekend.

3. In how many ways can the first 4 rock bands be selected to play? **3,024 ways**

4. In how many ways can the first 3 school bands be selected to play? Explain how you found your answer. **990 ways; there are 11 school bands, so there are 11 bands for the first choice, 10 for the second, and 9 for the third. So there are 11 · 10 · 9 or 990 ways to select the first three bands.**

5. **FOOD** Latesha buys a small box of 12 different assorted chocolates. She lets her sister have her 2 favorite chocolates, and then she has just enough left to give one chocolate to each girl attending basketball practice. In how many ways can Latesha give out the chocolates to the basketball players? **3,628,800 ways**

6. **SCHEDULING** A plumber has 8 jobs to schedule in the next week. One of the jobs is high priority and must be done first. In how many ways can the next 4 jobs be scheduled? **840 ways**

8-4 Lesson Notes

Lesson Resources

Chapter 8 Resource Masters
- Study Guide and Intervention, p. 460
- Practice: Skills, p. 461
- Practice: Word Problems, p. 462
- Reading to Learn Mathematics, p. 463
- Enrichment, p. 464

FAST FILE

Calculator and Spreadsheet Masters, pp. 37–38
Parent and Student Study Guide Online Worksheets, 8-4
Noteables™: Interactive Study Notebook with Foldables™, 8-4

1 Focus

5-Minute Check 8-4

Use as a quiz or review of Lesson 8-3. (Also available as a transparency)

Bellringer
Reading Mathematics While the terms *permutation* and *combination* are closely related, the fact that the order of items selected is important for permutations but not for combinations makes them different. Have students look up the two words and compare the definitions.

Reading to Learn Mathematics, p. 463 ELL

NAME ______ DATE ______ PERIOD ____

8-4 Reading to Learn Mathematics
Combinations

Pre-Activity *Complete the Mini Lab at the top of page 388 in your textbook. Write your answers below.*

1. How many different handshakes did you record? 15 handshakes
2. Find $P(6, 2)$. 30
3. Is the number of handshakes equal to $P(6, 2)$? Explain. No; if x shakes y's hand, it is the same as y shaking x's hand.

Reading the Lesson

4. What is the difference between a permutation and a combination? Sample answer: For a combination, order is not important; whereas, for a permutation, order is important.

8-4 Combinations

What You'll LEARN
Find the number of combinations of objects.

NEW Vocabulary
combination

MATH Symbols
$C(a, b)$ the number of combinations of a things taken b at a time

HANDS-ON Mini Lab

Work in a group of 6.

Each member of the group should shake hands with every other member of the group. Make a list of each handshake.

1. How many different handshakes did you record? **15 handshakes**
2. Find $P(6, 2)$. **30**
3. Is the number of handshakes equal to $P(6, 2)$? Explain.

3. No; if x shakes y's hand, it is the same as y shaking x's hand.

In the Mini Lab, it did not matter whether you shook hands with your friend, or your friend shook hands with you. Order is not important. An arrangement or listing where order is not important is called a **combination**. Let's look at a simpler form of the handshake problem.

EXAMPLE Find a Combination

1 GEOMETRY Four points are located on a circle. How many line segments can be drawn with these points as endpoints?

Method 1

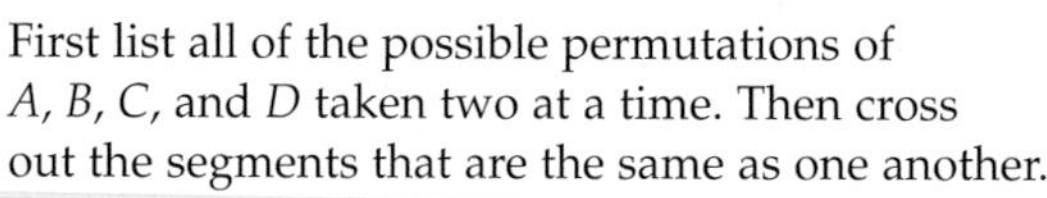

First list all of the possible permutations of A, B, C, and D taken two at a time. Then cross out the segments that are the same as one another.

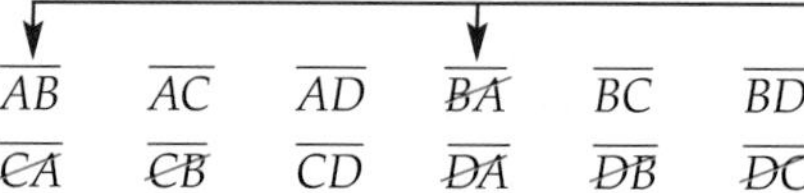

$\overline{AB}$ $\overline{AC}$ $\overline{AD}$ ~~$\overline{BA}$~~ $\overline{BC}$ $\overline{BD}$
~~$\overline{CA}$~~ ~~$\overline{CB}$~~ $\overline{CD}$ ~~$\overline{DA}$~~ ~~$\overline{DB}$~~ ~~$\overline{DC}$~~

There are only 6 different segments.

Method 2

Find the number of permutations of 4 points taken 2 at a time.

$P(4, 2) = 4 \cdot 3$ or 12

Since order is not important, divide the number of permutations by the number of ways 2 things can be arranged.

$\frac{12}{2!} = \frac{12}{2 \cdot 1}$ or 6

There are 6 segments that can be drawn.

Your Turn

a. If there are 8 people in a room, how many handshakes will occur if each person shakes hands with every other person? **28 handshakes**

The symbol C(4, 2) represents the number of combinations of 4 things taken 2 at a time.

$$C(4,2) = \frac{P(4,2)}{2!}$$

the number of combinations of 4 things taken 2 at a time → C(4, 2); P(4, 2) ← the number of permutations of 4 things taken 2 at a time; 2! ← the number of ways 2 things can be arranged

READING Math

Combinations C(7, 4) can also be written as ${}_7C_4$.

EXAMPLE Use Combination Notation

2 Find C(7, 4).

$C(7, 4) = \frac{P(7, 4)}{4!}$ Definition of C(7, 4)

$= \frac{7 \cdot \overset{1}{\cancel{\overset{2}{\cancel{6}}}} \cdot 5 \cdot \overset{1}{\cancel{4}}}{\underset{1}{\cancel{4}} \cdot \underset{1}{\cancel{3}} \cdot \underset{1}{\cancel{2}} \cdot 1}$ or 35 $P(7, 4) = 7 \cdot 6 \cdot 5 \cdot 4$ and $4! = 4 \cdot 3 \cdot 2 \cdot 1$

EXAMPLES Combinations and Permutations

MUSIC The makeup of a symphony is shown in the table at the right.

Makeup of the Symphony	
Instrument	**Number**
Strings	45
Woodwinds	8
Brass	8
Percussion	3
Harps	2

3 A group of 3 musicians from the strings section will talk to students at Madison Middle School. Does this represent a combination or a permutation? How many possible groups could talk to the students?

This is a combination problem since the order is not important.

$C(45, 3) = \frac{P(45, 3)}{3!}$ 45 musicians taken 3 at a time

$= \frac{\overset{15}{\cancel{45}} \cdot \overset{22}{\cancel{44}} \cdot 43}{\underset{1}{\cancel{3}} \cdot \underset{1}{\cancel{2}} \cdot 1}$ or 14,190 $P(45, 3) = 45 \cdot 44 \cdot 43$ and $3! = 3 \cdot 2 \cdot 1$

There are 14,190 different groups that could talk to the students.

REAL-LIFE MATH

MUSIC The harp is one of the oldest stringed instruments. It is about 70 inches tall and has 47 strings.

Source: *World Book*

4 One member from the strings section will talk to students at Brown Middle School, another to students at Oak Avenue Middle School, and another to students at Jefferson Junior High. Does this represent a combination or a permutation? How many possible ways can the strings members talk to the students?

Since it makes a difference which member goes to which school, order is important. This is a permutation.

$P(45, 3) = 45 \cdot 44 \cdot 43$ or 85,140 Definition of P(45, 3)

There are 85,140 ways for the members to talk to the students.

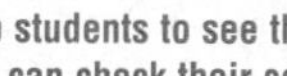

TEACHING TIP

Help students to see that they can check their computations by dividing the answer to Example 4 by 3! or 6. The quotient should be the answer to Example 3.

msmath3.net/extra_examples

2 Teach

In-Class Examples

1 **TOURNAMENTS** Five teams are playing each other in a tournament. If each team plays every other team once, how many games are played? **10**

2 Find C(8, 5). **56**

3 **SCHOOL** An eighth grade teacher needs to select 4 students from a class of 22 to help with sixth grade orientation. Does this represent a combination or a permutation? How many possible groups could be selected to help out the new students? **combination; 7,315 ways**

4 **SCHOOL** One eighth grade student will be assigned to sixth grade classes on the first floor, another student will be assigned to classes on the second floor, another student will be assigned to classes on the third floor, and still another student will be assigned to classes on the fourth floor. Does this represent a combination or a permutation? In how many possible ways can the eighth graders be assigned to help with the sixth grade orientation? **permutation; 175,560 ways**

DAILY INTERVENTION

Differentiated Instruction

Auditory/Musical Explain to the students that the white keys on a piano are represented by the letters A through G. Have them determine how many different pairs of seven white keys could be played at the same time if two keys with the same letter are not played together. **21**

Practice/Apply

FOLDABLES™ Follow-Up Remind students to use the fourth section of their Foldables to record information on what they learn about finding the number of combinations of objects, and to include an example that illustrates what they have learned. Encourage students to include the key terms and their definitions on the last section, or "Vocabulary" section, of their Foldables.

Which One Doesn't Belong?
In Exercise 2, remind students of the difference between combinations and permutations. Have students consider how order would affect each one. For example, would it matter in what order the toppings were placed on a pizza? **no** Would it matter which people chair which committees? **yes**

About the Exercises...

Guided Practice Key

Exercises	Examples
10	1
3–6	2
7–9	3, 4

Assignment Guide

Basic: 11–31 odd, 33–44

Average: 11–31 odd, 32–44

Enriched: 12–32 even, 33–40 (Optional: 41–44)

Alert! For Exercise 29, students will need to know that a standard deck of cards always includes 52 cards in 4 suits of 13 cards each.

Students practice the same concepts in Exercises 11–32 if they are assigned odd or even problems.

Skill and Concept Check

1. **OPEN ENDED** Give an example of a combination and an example of a permutation. **See margin.**

2. **Which One Doesn't Belong?** Identify the situation that is not the same as the other three. Explain your reasoning. **See margin.**

choosing 3 toppings for the pizzas to be served at the party	choosing 3 members for the decorating committee	choosing 3 people to chair 3 different committees	choosing 3 desserts to serve at the party

GUIDED PRACTICE

Find each value.

3. $C(6, 2)$ **15**
4. $C(10, 5)$ **252**
5. $C(7, 6)$ **7**
6. $C(8, 4)$ **70**

Determine whether each situation is a *permutation* or a *combination*.

7. writing a four-digit number using no digit more than once **permutation**
8. choosing 3 shirts to pack for vacation **combination**
9. How many different starting squads of 6 players can be picked from 10 volleyball players? **210 squads**
10. How many different combinations of 2 colors can be chosen as school colors from a possible list of 8 colors? **28 combinations**

Practice and Applications

Find each value.

11. $C(9, 2)$ **36**
12. $C(6, 3)$ **20**
13. $C(9, 8)$ **9**
14. $C(8, 7)$ **8**
15. $C(9, 5)$ **126**
16. $C(10, 4)$ **210**
17. $C(18, 4)$ **3,060**
18. $C(20, 3)$ **1,140**

Determine whether each situation is a *permutation* or a *combination*.

19. choosing a committee of 5 from the members of a class **combination**
20. choosing 2 co-captains of the basketball team **combination**
21. choosing the placement of 9 model cars in a line **permutation**
22. choosing 3 desserts from a dessert tray **combination**
23. choosing a chairperson and an assistant chairperson for a committee
24. choosing 4 paintings to display at different locations **permutation**

23. permutation

25. How many three-topping pizzas can be ordered from a list of toppings at the right? **220 pizzas**
26. **GEOMETRY** Eight points are located on a circle. How many line segments can be drawn with these points as endpoints? **28 segments**

HOMEWORK HELP

For Exercises	See Examples
11–18	2
19–24, 27–32	3, 4
25–26	1

Extra Practice See pages 636, 655.

Pizza Toppings

anchovies	sausage	onions
bacon	green peppers	black olives
ham	hot peppers	green olives
pepperoni	mushrooms	pineapple

Answers

1. Sample answers: selecting a committee of 5 people; selecting a president and vice president of a club
2. Choosing 3 people to chair 3 different committees; this is a permutation and the others are combinations.

27. There are 20 runners in a race. In how many ways can the runners take first, second, and third place? **6,840 ways**

28. How many ways can 7 people be arranged in a row for a photograph? **5,040 ways**

29. How many five-card hands can be dealt from a standard deck of 52 cards? **2,598,960 hands**

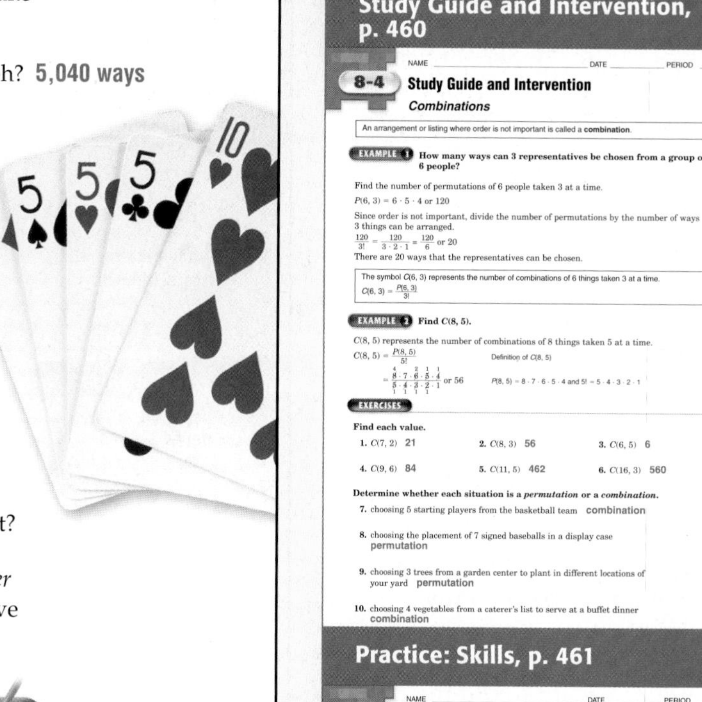

30. **GAMES** In the game of cribbage, a player gets 2 points for each combination of cards that totals 15. How many points for totals of 15 are in the hand at the right? **16 points**

ENTERTAINMENT For Exercises 31 and 32, use the following information.

An amusement park has 15 roller coasters. Suppose you only have time to ride 8 of the coasters.

31. How many ways are there to ride 8 coasters if order is important? **259,459,200 ways**

32. How many ways are there to ride 8 coasters if order is not important? **6,435 ways**

33. **CRITICAL THINKING** Is the value of $P(x, y)$ *sometimes*, *always*, or *never* greater than the value of $C(x, y)$? Explain. Assume x and y are positive integers and $x \geq y$. **Sometimes; they are equal if $y = 1$.**

Spiral Review with Standardized Test Practice

34. **MULTIPLE CHOICE** Which situation is represented by $C(8, 3)$? **B**
   - (A) the number of arrangements of 8 people in a line
   - (B) the number of ways to pick 3 out of 8 vegetables to add to a salad
   - (C) the number of ways to pick 3 out of 8 students to be the first, second, and third contestant in a spelling bee
   - (D) the number of ways 8 people can sit in a row of 3 chairs

35. **SHORT RESPONSE** The enrollment for Centerville Middle School is given at the right. How many different four-person committees could be formed from the students in the 8th grade? **4,249,575 committees**

Centerville Middle School

Class	Boys	Girls
6th grade	42	47
7th grade	55	49
8th grade	49	53

Find each value. (Lesson 8-3)

36. $P(7, 2)$ **42**
37. $P(15, 4)$ **32,760**
38. $10!$ **3,628,800**
39. $7!$ **5,040**

40. **SCHOOL** At the school cafeteria, students can choose from 4 entrees and 3 beverages. How many different lunches of one entree and one beverage can be purchased at the cafeteria? (Lesson 8-2) **12 lunches**

GETTING READY FOR THE NEXT LESSON

PREREQUISITE SKILL Multiply. Write in simplest form. (Lesson 2-3)

41. $\frac{4}{5} \cdot \frac{3}{8}$ **$\frac{3}{10}$**
42. $\frac{3}{10} \cdot \frac{5}{6}$ **$\frac{1}{4}$**
43. $\frac{7}{12} \cdot \frac{3}{14}$ **$\frac{1}{8}$**
44. $\frac{2}{3} \cdot \frac{9}{10}$ **$\frac{3}{5}$**

msmath3.net/self_check_quiz

4 Assess

Open-Ended Assessment

Writing Have students write a paragraph comparing and contrasting permutations and combinations, giving an example problem and solution for each.

Study Guide and Intervention, p. 460

NAME ______ DATE ______ PERIOD ______

8-4 Study Guide and Intervention

Combinations

An arrangement or listing where order is not important is called a **combination**.

EXAMPLE 1 **How many ways can 3 representatives be chosen from a group of 6 people?**

Find the number of permutations of 6 people taken 3 at a time.

$P(6, 3) = 6 \cdot 5 \cdot 4$ or 120

Since order is not important, divide the number of permutations by the number of ways 3 things can be arranged.

$\frac{120}{3!} = \frac{120}{3 \cdot 2 \cdot 1} = \frac{120}{6}$ or 20

There are 20 ways that the representatives can be chosen.

The symbol $C(6, 3)$ represents the number of combinations of 6 things taken 3 at a time.
$C(6, 3) = \frac{P(6, 3)}{3!}$

EXAMPLE 2 **Find C(8, 5).**

$C(8, 5)$ represents the number of combinations of 8 things taken 5 at a time.

$C(8, 5) = \frac{P(8, 5)}{5!}$ — Definition of $C(8, 5)$

$= \frac{8 \cdot 7 \cdot 6 \cdot 5 \cdot 4}{5 \cdot 4 \cdot 3 \cdot 2 \cdot 1}$ or 56 — $P(8, 5) = 8 \cdot 7 \cdot 6 \cdot 5 \cdot 4$ and $5! = 5 \cdot 4 \cdot 3 \cdot 2 \cdot 1$

EXERCISES

Find each value.

1. $C(7, 2)$ **21**
2. $C(8, 3)$ **56**
3. $C(6, 5)$ **6**
4. $C(9, 6)$ **84**
5. $C(11, 5)$ **462**
6. $C(16, 3)$ **560**

Determine whether each situation is a *permutation* or a *combination*.

7. choosing 5 starting players from the basketball team **combination**
8. choosing the placement of 7 signed baseballs in a display case **permutation**
9. choosing 3 trees from a garden center to plant in different locations of your yard **permutation**
10. choosing 4 vegetables from a caterer's list to serve at a buffet dinner **combination**

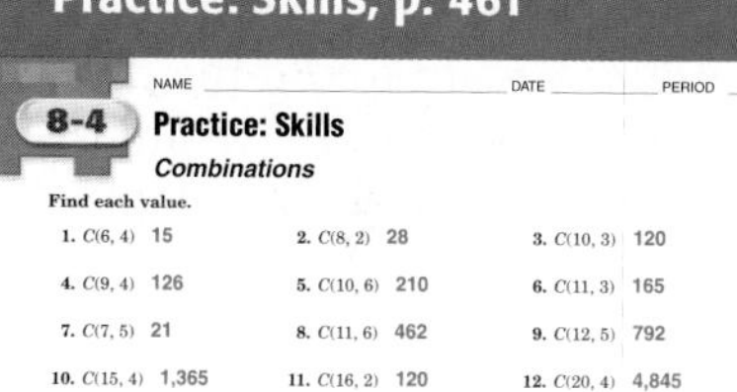

Practice: Skills, p. 461

NAME ______ DATE ______ PERIOD ______

8-4 Practice: Skills

Combinations

Find each value.

1. $C(6, 4)$ **15**
2. $C(8, 2)$ **28**
3. $C(10, 3)$ **120**
4. $C(9, 4)$ **126**
5. $C(10, 6)$ **210**
6. $C(11, 3)$ **165**
7. $C(7, 5)$ **21**
8. $C(11, 6)$ **462**
9. $C(12, 5)$ **792**
10. $C(15, 4)$ **1,365**
11. $C(16, 2)$ **120**
12. $C(20, 4)$ **4,845**

For Exercises 13–18, determine whether each situation is a *permutation* or a *combination*.

13. choosing the arrangement of 6 glass animals on a shelf **permutation**
14. choosing 3 Chinese dishes from a menu **combination**
15. choosing 5 friends to invite to a birthday party **combination**
16. choosing a president, vice-president, treasurer, and secretary from the members of the student council **permutation**
17. choosing 2 colors of paint from a paint chart to blend together for the walls in your room **combination**
18. choosing the order in which to watch 3 videotapes you rented from the video store **permutation**
19. How many ways can a coach choose the 6 starting players from a volleyball team of 13 players? **1,716 ways**
20. How many ways can 4 textbooks be chosen from 8 textbooks in a locker? **70 ways**
21. You have 7 clean shirts in a laundry basket. How many ways can you fold 4 shirts and stack them in a drawer? **840 ways**
22. How many ways can a delegation of 4 students be chosen from a class of 22 students? **7,315 ways**
23. On her birthday, Yolanda brings cupcakes to school for her 28 classmates. How many ways can she hand out cupcakes to the first 3 students returning from recess? **19,656 ways**
24. How many three-card hands can be dealt from a deck of 52 cards? **22,100 hands**

Practice: Word Problems, p. 462

NAME ______ DATE ______ PERIOD ______

8-4 Practice: Word Problems

Combinations

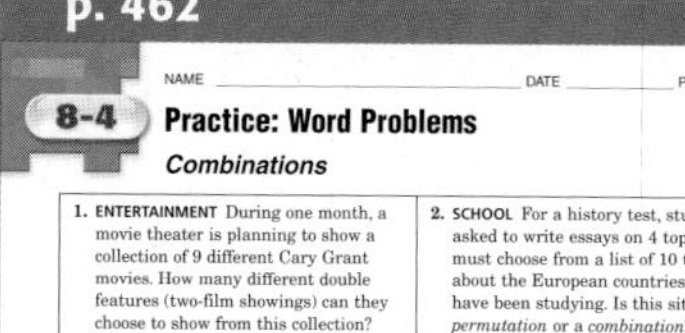

1. **ENTERTAINMENT** During one month, a movie theater is planning to show a collection of 9 different Cary Grant movies. How many different double features (two-film showings) can they choose to show from this collection? **36 double features**

2. **SCHOOL** For a history test, students are asked to write essays on 4 topics. They must choose from a list of 10 topics about the European countries they have been studying. Is this situation a *permutation* or a *combination*? Explain. How many ways can a student choose 4 topics? **Combination; the order of the topics is not important; 210 ways**

3. **MARKET RESEARCH** A taste test of 11 different soft drinks is held at a shopping mall. Each taster is randomly given 5 of the drinks to taste. How many combinations of soft drinks are possible? **462 combinations**

4. **BOOK FAIR** A school book fair is offering a package deal on the opening day. For a special price, students may purchase any 6 different paperback books from a list of 30 books that have won the Newbery Medal. How many packages are possible? **593,775 packages**

GARDENING For Exercises 5 and 6, use the shipping list at the right that shows the rosebushes Mrs. Lawson ordered for her front yard. She wants to plant 9 of them along the walkway from her driveway to her front porch.

Shipping List (1 each)

Aquarius	Purple Tiger	Candy Apple
Roundelay	Desert Dawn	Scarlet Knight
Fragrant Plum	Shining Hour	Golden Girl
Sonia Supreme	Linda Ann	Sundowner
Mount Shasta	Viceroy	Pink Parfait
Winifred		

5. How many ways can she plant the rosebushes along the walkway if order is not important? **11,440 ways**

6. How many ways can she plant the rosebushes along the walkway if order is important? **4,151,347,200 ways**

8-4b HANDS-ON LAB

A Follow-Up of Lesson 8-4

Combinations and Pascal's Triangle

What You'll LEARN

Identify patterns in Pascal's Triangle.

Materials

- paper
- pencil

For many years, mathematicians have been interested in a pattern called *Pascal's Triangle*.

Row										Sum
0					1					$1 = 2^0$
1				1		1				$2 = 2^1$
2			1		2		1			$4 = 2^2$
3		1		3		3		1		$8 = 2^3$
4	1		4		6		4		1	$16 = 2^4$

ACTIVITY *Work with a partner.*

1 **Find all possible outcomes if you toss a penny and a dime.**

STEP 1 Copy and complete the tree diagram shown below.

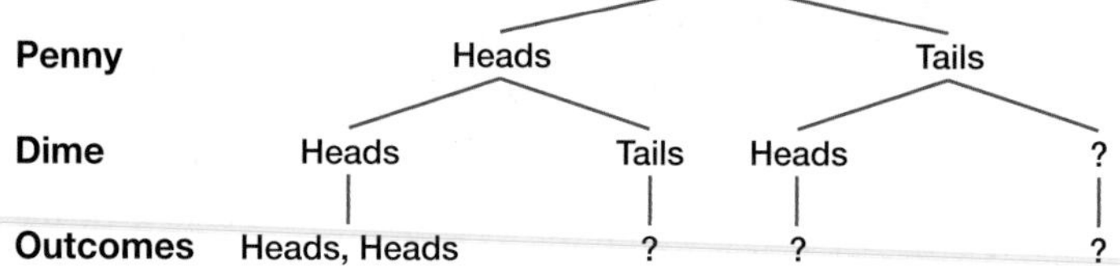

STEP 2 In the tree diagram above, how many outcomes have exactly no heads? one head? two heads? 1; 2; 1

STEP 3 Use a tree diagram to determine the outcomes of tossing a penny, a nickel, and a dime. How many outcomes have exactly no head, one head, two heads, three heads?

1; 3; 3; 1

Writing Math

3. See Ch. 8 Answer Appendix.

1. **Describe** the pattern in the numbers in Pascal's Triangle. Use the pattern to write the numbers in Rows 5, 6, and 7. **1–2. See margin.**
2. **Explain** how your tree diagrams are related to Pascal's Triangle.
3. Suppose you toss a penny, nickel, dime, and quarter. **Make a conjecture** about how many outcomes have exactly no head, one head, two heads, and so on. **Test your conjecture**.

8-4b HANDS-ON LAB Lesson Notes

Lesson Resources

Teaching Mathematics with Manipulatives

- student recording sheet 8-4b

GETTING STARTED

Teaching Tip If students have only made horizontal tree diagrams, they may need help with the vertical formation. You many want to put the tree diagram in **Activity 1** on an overhead and fill in the blanks as a class.

TEACH

Activity 1

- After students have completed their diagrams in Step 1, have them switch papers and proof the diagrams before proceeding to the rest of the activity.

Answers

1. The numbers down each side are ones. The inside numbers are the sums of the two numbers above the numbers. Row 5: 1, 5, 10, 10, 5, 1; Row 6: 1, 6, 15, 20, 15, 6, 1; Row 7: 1, 7, 21, 35, 35, 21, 7, 1
2. If the rows of Pascal's Triangle are numbered starting with 0, the number of combinations for each result for n coins are found in the nth row. The first number in the nth row gives the number of combinations for which no coins show heads. The second number in the nth row gives the number of combinations for which 1 coin shows heads. The third number in the nth row gives the number of combinations for which 2 coins show heads. The pattern continues until the last number, which represents the number of combinations for which n coins show heads.

392 Chapter 8 Probability

Pascal's Triangle can also be used to find probabilities of events for which there are only two possible outcomes, such as heads-tails, boy-girl, and true-false.

ACTIVITY *Work with a partner.*

In a five-item true-false quiz, what is the probability of getting exactly three right answers by guessing?

STEP 1 Since there are five items, look at Row 5.

Number Right	0	1	2	3	4	5
Row 5	1	5	10	10	5	1

There are 10 ways to get exactly three right answers.

STEP 2 Find the total possible outcomes.

$1 + 5 + 10 + 10 + 5 + 1 = 32$

STEP 3 Find the probability.

$$\frac{\text{number of ways to guess 3 right answers}}{\text{number of outcomes}} = \frac{10}{32} \text{ or } \frac{5}{16}$$

So, the probability of guessing exactly three right answers is $\frac{5}{16}$.

Writing Math

4. Suppose you guess on a five-item true-false test. What is the probability of getting all of the right answers? $\frac{1}{32}$
5. There are ten true-false questions on a quiz. What is the probability of guessing at least six correct answers and passing the quiz? $\frac{193}{512}$
6. If you toss eight coins, you would expect there to be four heads and four tails. What is the probability this will happen? $\frac{35}{128}$

For Exercises 7–9, use the following information. **9. 32 combinations**
The Band Boosters are selling pizzas. You can choose to add onions, pepperoni, mushrooms, and/or green pepper to the basic cheese pizza.

7. Find each number of combinations of toppings.
   a. C(4, 0) **1** b. C(4, 1) **4** c. C(4, 2) **6** d. C(4, 3) **4** e. C(4, 4) **1**
8. How many different combinations are there in all? **16 combinations**
9. Suppose the Boosters decide to offer hot peppers as an additional choice. How many combinations of pizzas are available?

Activity 2

- Point out that the first row of Pascal's Triangle is labeled Row 0. This numbering will be important when students examine the relationship between combinations and Pascal's Triangle.
- Make sure students remember to include the zero correct column when making their own tables.

ASSESS

Observe as students solve the **Writing Math** exercises. They should:

- accurately describe how to make Pascal's Triangle,
- be able to use Pascal's Triangle to find various combinations of tossing coins, and
- be able to apply Pascal's Triangle to other situations that have combinations.

Use Exercise 3 to determine whether students have progressed beyond mechanical calculations to grasp the mathematical connections between Pascal's Triangle and combinations.

Lesson 8-4b Hands-On Lab: Combinations and Pascal's Triangle **393**

Assessment Option

Mid-Chapter Test (Lessons 8-1 through 8-4) is available on p. 497 of the *Chapter 8 Resource Masters.*

ExamView® Pro

Use the networkable ExamView® Pro Testmaker CD-ROM to:

- Create **multiple versions** of tests.
- Create **modified** tests for **inclusion** students with one mouse click.
- **Edit** existing questions and **add** your own questions.
- Build tests aligned with state standards using built-in **state curriculum correlations.**
- Change **English** tests to **Spanish** with one mouse click and vice versa.

FOLDABLES™ Follow-Up Before students complete the Mid-Chapter Practice Test, encourage them to review the notes, definitions, concepts, and main ideas they recorded on the first four tabs of their Foldables.

Answers

1.

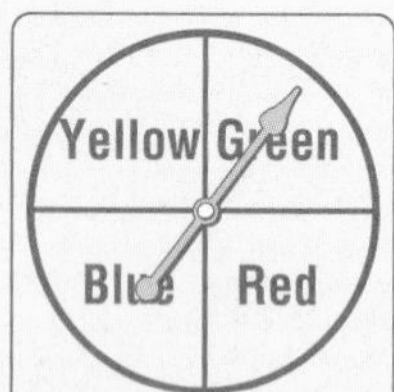

2. Sample answer: How many ways can 8 runners take first, second, and third place in the race?

6. $\frac{11}{20}$, 0.55, 55%

7. $\frac{9}{10}$, 0.9, 90%

CHAPTER 8 Mid-Chapter Practice Test

Vocabulary and Concepts

1. **Draw** a spinner where $P(\text{green})$ is $\frac{1}{4}$. (Lesson 8-1) **See margin.**
2. **Write** a problem that is solved by finding the value of $P(8, 3)$. (Lesson 8-3) **See margin.**

Skills and Applications

There are 6 purple, 5 blue, 3 yellow, 2 green, and 4 brown marbles in a bag. One marble is selected at random. Write each probability as a fraction, a decimal, and a percent. (Lesson 8-1) **6-7. See margin.**

3. $P(\text{purple})$ $\frac{3}{10}$, 0.3, 30%
4. $P(\text{blue})$ $\frac{1}{4}$, 0.25, 25%
5. $P(\text{not brown})$ $\frac{4}{5}$, 0.8, 80%
6. $P(\text{purple or blue})$
7. $P(\text{not green})$
8. $P(\text{blue or green})$ $\frac{7}{20}$, 0.35, 35%

For Exercises 9–11, a penny is tossed, and a number cube is rolled. (Lesson 8-2)

9. Draw a tree diagram to determine the number of outcomes. **See Ch. 8 Answer Appendix for tree diagram; 12 outcomes.**
10. What is the probability that the penny shows heads and the number cube shows a six? $\frac{1}{12}$
11. What is the probability that the penny shows heads and the number cube shows an even number? $\frac{1}{4}$

Find each value. (Lessons 8-3 and 8-4)

12. $P(5, 3)$ **60**
13. $P(6, 2)$ **30**
14. $P(5, 5)$ **120**
15. $C(5, 3)$ **10**
16. $C(6, 2)$ **15**
17. $C(5, 5)$ **1**
18. **SCHOOL** How many ways can 2 student council members be elected from 7 candidates? (Lesson 8-4) **21 ways**

Skills and Applications

19. **MULTIPLE CHOICE** A pizza shop advertises that it has 3 different crusts, 3 different meat toppings, and 5 different vegetables. If Carlotta wants a pizza with one meat and one vegetable, how many different pizzas can she order? (Lesson 8-2) **C**

    Ⓐ 11 Ⓑ 15
    Ⓒ 45 Ⓓ 90

20. **GRID IN** The spinner below is used for a game. Find the probability that the spinner will *not* land on yellow. (Lesson 8-1) **4/5**

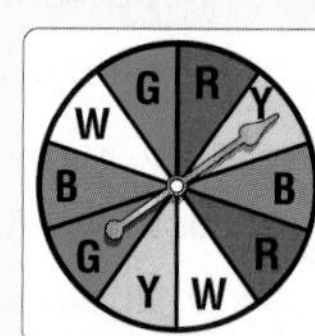

The Game Zone

A Place To Practice Your Math Skills

Math Skill

Probability

Winning Numbers

GET READY!

Players: three

Materials: 15 index cards, scissors, markers, 3 paper bags

GET SET!

- Cut each index card in half, making 30 cards.
- Give each player 10 cards.
- Each player writes one number from 0 to 9 on each card.
- Each player takes a different bag and places his or her cards in the bag.

0

1

GO!

- Each player writes down three numbers each between 0 and 9. Repeat numbers are allowed.
- Each player draws a card from his or her paper bag without looking. These are the winning numbers.
- Each player scores 2 points if one number matches, 16 points if two numbers match, and 32 points if all three numbers match. Order is not important.
- Replace the cards in the paper bags. Repeat the process.
- **Who Wins?** The first person to get a total of 100 points is the winner.

The Game Zone

Glencoe Mathematics Classroom Manipulative Kit

- scissors

GETTING READY

Objective Find the probability of compound events.

MANAGEMENT TIPS

Recommended Time

20 minutes

Tips

- To save time, consider having the index cards precut and packaged in sets to give to students at the beginning of the activity.
- After students have played the game, ask them what the probability should be of picking a 5 card out of the bag. $\frac{1}{10}$
- Ask students whether the results would change if the cards were not replaced after each turn. **yes**
- If you wish to make the game more difficult in later rounds, make the order of the numbers important.
- You may wish to use the game as an assessment tool for the concepts the students have been learning in Lessons 8-1 through 8-4.

Math Online For an additional game for this chapter, visit: msmath3.net/gamezone

8-5 Lesson Notes

Lesson Resources

Chapter 8 Resource Masters

FAST FILE

- Study Guide and Intervention, p. 465
- Practice: Skills, p. 466
- Practice: Word Problems, p. 467
- Reading to Learn Mathematics, p. 468
- Enrichment, p. 469

Key Teaching Transparencies, 31

MathPASS Tutorial CD-ROM, 59

Parent and Student Study Guide Online Worksheets, 8-5

Noteables™: Interactive Study Notebook with Foldables™, 8-5

Focus

5-Minute Check 8-5

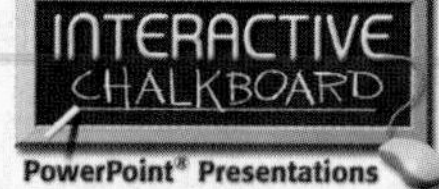

Use as a quiz or review of Lesson 8-4. (Also available as a transparency)

Bellringer

Communication Describe the following situation to students: *Elias tossed a coin nine times, getting tails each time.* Ask students what the probability is of getting heads on the next toss. $\frac{1}{2}$ Will the first nine tosses influence the tenth toss? **no**

Reading to Learn Mathematics, p. 468 **ELL**

NAME ______ DATE ______ PERIOD ____

8-5 Reading to Learn Mathematics

Probability of Compound Events

Pre-Activity *Read the introduction at the top of page 396 in your textbook. Write your answers below.*

1. A player rolls the number cube. What is P(odd)? $\frac{1}{2}$
2. The player spins the spinner. What is P(red)? $\frac{1}{3}$
3. What is the product of the probabilities in Exercises 1 and 2? $\frac{1}{6}$
4. On a separate piece of paper, draw a tree diagram to determine the probability that the player will get an odd number and red. See students' work; $\frac{1}{6}$
5. Compare your answers for Exercises 3 and 4. They are the same.

8-5 Probability of Compound Events

What You'll LEARN

Find the probability of independent and dependent events.

NEW Vocabulary

compound event
independent events
dependent events

WHEN am I ever going to use this?

GAMES A game uses a number cube and the spinner shown at the right.

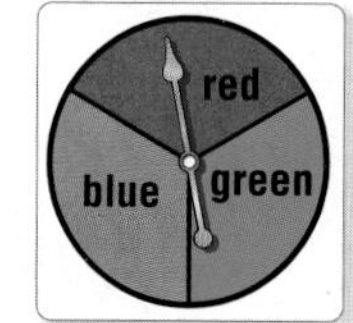

1. A player rolls the number cube. What is *P*(odd number)? $\frac{1}{2}$
2. The player spins the spinner. What is *P*(red)? $\frac{1}{3}$
3. What is the product of the probabilities in Exercises 1 and 2? $\frac{1}{6}$
4. Draw a tree diagram to determine the probability that the player will get an odd number and red.
5. Compare your answers for Exercises 3 and 4. **They are the same.**

4. See Answer Appendix for tree diagram; $\frac{1}{6}$.

The combined action of rolling a number cube and spinning a spinner is a compound event. In general, a **compound event** consists of two or more simple events.

The outcome of the spinner does not depend on the outcome of the number cube. These events are independent. For **independent events**, the outcome of one event does not affect the other event.

Noteables™ **Key Concept: Probability of Independent Events**

Words	The probability of two independent events can be found by multiplying the probability of the first event by the probability of the second event.
Symbols	$P(A \text{ and } B) = P(A) \cdot P(B)$

EXAMPLE Probability of Independent Events

The two spinners are spun. What is the probability that both spinners will show an even number?

$P(\text{first spinner is even}) = \frac{3}{7}$

$P(\text{second spinner is even}) = \frac{1}{2}$

$P(\text{both spinners are even}) = \frac{3}{7} \cdot \frac{1}{2} \text{ or } \frac{3}{14}$

REAL-LIFE MATH

POPULATION The population of the United States is getting older. In 2050, the fraction of the population 65 years and older is expected to be about $\frac{1}{5}$.

Source: U.S. Census Bureau

TEACHING TIP

Example 2 assumes that the age of the populations is distributed at the same rate in urban and rural areas.

EXAMPLE Use Probability to Solve a Problem

2 POPULATION Use the information in the table. In the United States, what is the probability that a person picked at random will be under the age of 18 and live in an urban area?

United States	
Demographic Group	Fraction of the Population
Under age 18	$\frac{1}{4}$
18 to 64 years old	$\frac{5}{8}$
65 years or older	$\frac{1}{8}$
Urban	$\frac{4}{5}$
Rural	$\frac{1}{5}$

Source: U.S. Census Bureau

$P(\text{younger than 18}) = \frac{1}{4}$

$P(\text{urban area}) = \frac{4}{5}$

$P(\text{younger than 18 and urban area})$

$= \frac{\overset{1}{\cancel{4}}}{\underset{1}{\cancel{4}}} \cdot \frac{4}{5}$ or $\frac{1}{5}$ Simplify.

The probability that the two events will occur is $\frac{1}{5}$.

If the outcome of one event affects the outcome of another event, the compound events are called **dependent events**.

Key Concept: Probability of Dependent Events

Words If two events, *A* and *B*, are dependent, then the probability of both events occurring is the product of the probability of *A* and the probability of *B* after *A* occurs.

Symbols $P(A \text{ and } B) = P(A) \cdot P(B \text{ following } A)$

EXAMPLE Probability of Dependent Events

3 There are 2 white, 8 red, and 5 blue marbles in a bag. Once a marble is selected, it is not replaced. Find the probability that two red marbles are chosen.

Since the first marble is not replaced, the first event affects the second event. These are dependent events.

$P(\text{first marble is red}) = \frac{8}{15}$ ← number of red marbles / ← total number of marbles

$P(\text{second marble is red}) = \frac{7}{14}$ ← number of red marbles after one red marble is removed / ← total number of marbles after one red marble is removed

$P(\text{two red marbles}) = \frac{\overset{4}{\cancel{8}}}{15} \cdot \frac{\overset{1}{\cancel{7}}}{\underset{\underset{1}{\cancel{7}}}{\cancel{14}}}$ or $\frac{4}{15}$

STUDY TIP

Mental Math You may wish to simplify $\frac{7}{14}$ to $\frac{1}{2}$ before multiplying the probabilities.

Your Turn Find each probability.

a. $P(\text{two blue marbles})$ $\frac{2}{21}$

b. $P(\text{a white marble and then a blue marble})$ $\frac{1}{21}$

Math Online msmath3.net/extra_examples

DAILY INTERVENTION

Unlocking Misconceptions

Independent Events and Mutually Exclusive Events Some students may mistakenly think that all independent events are mutually exclusive events, or may mistake one term for the other. Reinforce that the results of a second independent event do not depend on the results of the first, and that these two events can occur at the same time. On the other hand, mutually exclusive events cannot happen at the same time.

2 Teach

In-Class Examples

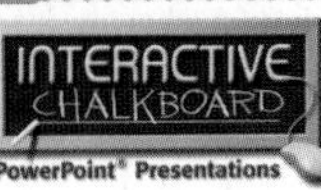

1 The two spinners below are spun.

What is the probability that both spinners will show a number greater than 6? $\frac{9}{100}$

2 POPULATION Use the information below. What is the probability that a student picked at random will be an eighth-grade girl? $\frac{1}{6}$

Cross River Middle School	
Demographic Group	Fraction of the Population
grade 6	$\frac{4}{10}$
grade 7	$\frac{3}{10}$
grade 8	$\frac{3}{10}$
boys	$\frac{4}{9}$
girls	$\frac{5}{9}$

3 There are 4 red, 8 yellow, and 6 blue socks in a drawer. Once a sock is selected, it is not replaced. Find the probability that two blue socks are chosen. $\frac{5}{51}$

3 Practice/Apply

FOLDABLES™ Follow-Up Remind students to use the fifth section of their Foldables to record what they learn about finding the probability of independent and dependent events, and to use what they have learned to determine how likely something is to happen. Encourage students to include the key terms and their definitions on the last section, or "Vocabulary" section, of their Foldables.

DAILY INTERVENTION FIND THE ERROR For Exercise 3, ask students to consider whether the spinner is changed in any way after the first spin. **no** Is this problem an example of a dependent or an independent event? **independent**

About the Exercises...

Guided Practice Key

Exercises	Examples
4–5	1
8	2
6–7	3

Assignment Guide

Basic: 9–19 odd, 23, 27–38

Average: 9–23 odd, 27–38 (Optional: 25–26)

Enriched: 10–24 even, 25–34 (Optional: 35–38)

Answers

1. Both independent events and dependent events are compound events. Independent events do not affect each other. Dependent events affect each other.
2. Sample answer: choosing two cards from a standard deck of 52 cards at random without replacement

Students practice the same concepts in Exercises 9–24 if they are assigned odd or even problems.

Skill and Concept Check

1. Writing Math Compare and contrast independent and dependent events.
2. **OPEN ENDED** Give an example of dependent events. **1–2. See margin.**
3. **FIND THE ERROR** The spinner at the right is spun twice. Evita and Tia are finding the probability that both spins will result in an odd number. Who is correct? Explain. **Evita; see margin.**

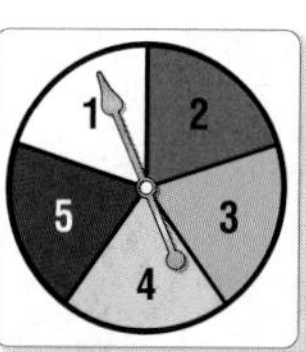

Evita

$\frac{3}{5} \cdot \frac{3}{5} = \frac{9}{25}$

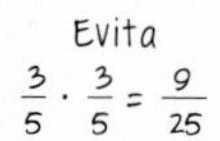

$\frac{3}{5} \cdot \frac{2}{4} = \frac{6}{20}$ or $\frac{3}{10}$

GUIDED PRACTICE

A penny is tossed, and a number cube is rolled. Find each probability.

4. P(tails and 3) $\frac{1}{12}$
5. P(heads and odd) $\frac{1}{4}$

Two cards are drawn from a deck of ten cards numbered 1 to 10. Once a card is selected, it is not returned. Find each probability.

6. P(two even cards) $\frac{2}{9}$
7. P(a 6 and then an odd number) $\frac{1}{18}$
8. **MARKETING** A discount supermarket has found that 60% of their customers spend more than \$75 each visit. What is the probability that the next two customers will spend more than \$75? **36%**

★ indicates increased difficulty

Practice and Applications

HOMEWORK HELP

For Exercises	See Examples
9–16	1
17–22	3
23–24	2

Extra Practice See pages 636, 655.

A number cube is rolled, and the spinner at the right is spun. Find each probability.

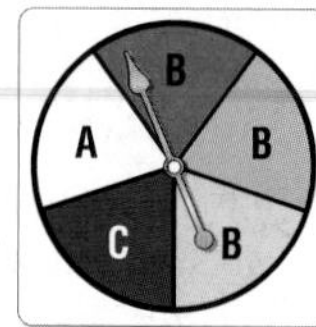

9. P(1 and A) $\frac{1}{30}$
10. P(3 and B) $\frac{1}{10}$
11. P(even and C) $\frac{1}{10}$
12. P(odd and B) $\frac{3}{10}$
13. P(greater than 2 and A) $\frac{2}{15}$
14. P(less than 3 and B) $\frac{1}{5}$
15. What is the probability of tossing a coin 3 times and getting heads each time? $\frac{1}{8}$
16. What is the probability of rolling a number cube 3 times and getting numbers greater than 4 each time? $\frac{1}{27}$

There are 3 yellow, 5 red, 4 blue, and 8 green candies in a bag. Once a candy is selected, it is not replaced. Find each probability.

17. P(two red candies) $\frac{1}{19}$
18. P(two blue candies) $\frac{3}{95}$
19. P(a yellow candy and then a blue candy) $\frac{3}{95}$
20. P(a green candy and then a red candy) $\frac{2}{19}$
21. ★ P(two candies that are not green) $\frac{33}{95}$
22. ★ P(two candies that are neither blue nor green) $\frac{14}{95}$

3. Spinning the spinner twice represents two independent events. The probability of getting an odd number is $\frac{3}{5}$ each time.

KITCHENS For Exercises 23 and 24, use the table at the right. Round to the nearest tenth of a percent.

23. What is the probability that a household picked at random will have both an electric frying pan and a toaster? **68.9%**

24. What is the probability that a household picked at random will use both a mixer and a drip coffee maker? **3.2%**

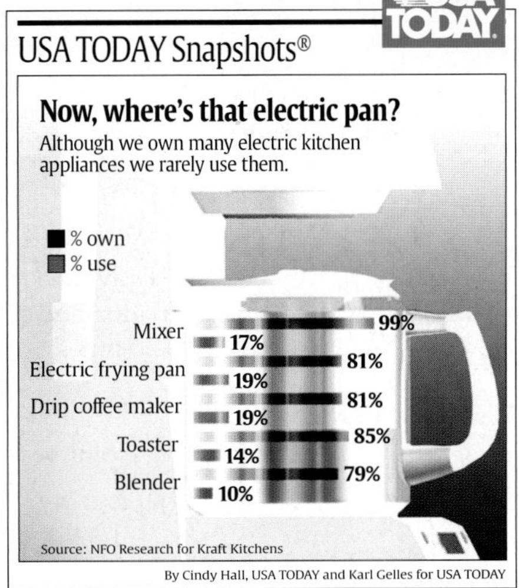

EXTENDING THE LESSON If two events cannot happen at the same time, they are said to be *mutually exclusive.* For example, suppose you randomly select a card from a standard deck of 52 cards. Getting a 5 or getting a 6 are mutually exclusive events. To find the probability of two mutually exclusive events, add the probabilities.

$$P(5 \text{ or } 6) = P(5) + P(6)$$
$$= \frac{1}{13} + \frac{1}{13} \text{ or } \frac{2}{13}$$

Consider a standard deck of 52 cards. Find each probability.

25. $P(\text{face card or an ace})$ $\frac{4}{13}$

26. $P(\text{club or a red card})$ $\frac{3}{4}$

27. **CRITICAL THINKING** There are 9 marbles in a bag having 3 colors of marbles. The probability of picking 2 red marbles at random and without replacement is $\frac{1}{6}$. How many red marbles are in the bag? **4**

Spiral Review with Standardized Test Practice

28. **MULTIPLE CHOICE** Jeremy tossed a coin and rolled a number cube. What is the probability that he will get tails and roll a multiple of 3? **D**

Ⓐ $\frac{1}{2}$ Ⓑ $\frac{1}{3}$ Ⓒ $\frac{1}{4}$ Ⓓ $\frac{1}{6}$

29. **GRID IN** Suppose you pick 3 cards from a standard deck of 52 cards without replacement. What is the probability all of the cards will be red? **2/17**

Find each value. (Lesson 8-4)

30. $C(8, 5)$ **56**

31. $C(7, 2)$ **21**

32. $C(6, 5)$ **6**

33. $C(9, 3)$ **84**

34. **SPORTS** There are 10 players on a softball team. How many ways can a coach pick the lineup of the first 3 batters? (Lesson 8-3) **720 ways**

GETTING READY FOR THE NEXT LESSON

PREREQUISITE SKILL Write each fraction in simplest form. (Page 611)

35. $\frac{52}{120}$ $\frac{13}{30}$

36. $\frac{33}{90}$ $\frac{11}{30}$

37. $\frac{49}{70}$ $\frac{7}{10}$

38. $\frac{24}{88}$ $\frac{3}{11}$

msmath3.net/self_check_quiz

4 Assess

Higher-Level Thinking

Suppose you are tossing a coin twice. Find the probabilities of getting two heads, two tails, and one of each. What is the sum of these probabilities? Is there a shorter way to determine the sum?

$\frac{1}{4} + \frac{1}{4} + \frac{1}{2} = 1$; **The sum must be 1 because the three possibilities are complementary—one of these cases must occur.**

Study Guide and Intervention, p. 465

NAME ______ DATE ______ PERIOD ____

8-5 Study Guide and Intervention

Probability of Compound Events

The probability of two independent events can be found by multiplying the probability of the first event by the probability of the second event.

EXAMPLE 1 **Two number cubes, one red and one blue, are rolled. What is the probability that the outcome of the red number cube is even and the outcome of the blue number cube is a 5?**

$P(\text{red number cube is even}) = \frac{1}{2}$

$P(\text{blue number cube is a 5}) = \frac{1}{6}$

$P(\text{red number cube is even and blue number cube is a 5}) = \frac{1}{2} \cdot \frac{1}{6}$ or $\frac{1}{12}$

The probability that the two events will occur is $\frac{1}{12}$.

If two events, *A* and *B*, are dependent, then the probability of both events occurring is the product of the probability of *A* and the probability of *B* after *A* occurs.

EXAMPLE 2 **There are 6 black socks and 4 white socks in a drawer. If one sock is taken out without looking and then a second is taken out, what is the probability that they both will be black?**

$P(\text{first sock is black}) = \frac{6}{10}$ or $\frac{3}{5}$ — 6 is the number of black socks; 10 is the total number of socks.

$P(\text{second sock is black}) = \frac{5}{9}$ — 5 is the number of black socks after one black sock is removed; 9 is the total number of socks after one black sock is removed.

$P(\text{two black socks}) = \frac{3}{5} \cdot \frac{5}{9}$ or $\frac{1}{3}$

The probability of choosing two black socks is $\frac{1}{3}$.

EXERCISES

A card is drawn from a deck of 10 cards numbered 1 through 10 and a number cube is rolled. Find each probability.

1. $P(\text{10 and 3})$ $\frac{1}{60}$
2. $P(\text{two even numbers})$ $\frac{1}{4}$
3. $P(\text{two prime numbers})$ $\frac{1}{5}$
4. $P(\text{9 and an odd number})$ $\frac{1}{20}$
5. $P(\text{two numbers less than 4})$ $\frac{3}{20}$
6. $P(\text{two numbers greater than 5})$ $\frac{1}{12}$

There are 4 red, 6 green, and 5 yellow pencils in a jar. Once a pencil is selected, it is not replaced. Find each probability.

7. $P(\text{red and then yellow})$ $\frac{2}{21}$
8. $P(\text{two green})$ $\frac{1}{7}$
9. $P(\text{green and then yellow})$ $\frac{1}{7}$
10. $P(\text{red and then green})$ $\frac{4}{35}$

Practice: Skills, p. 466

NAME ______ DATE ______ PERIOD ____

8-5 Practice: Skills

Probability of Compound Events

For Exercises 1–6, a number cube is rolled and the spinner at the right is spun. Find each probability.

1. $P(\text{1 and A})$ $\frac{1}{24}$
2. $P(\text{odd and B})$ $\frac{1}{8}$
3. $P(\text{prime and D})$ $\frac{1}{8}$
4. $P(\text{greater than 4 and C})$ $\frac{1}{12}$

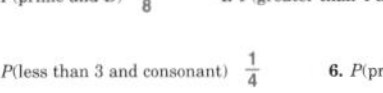

5. $P(\text{less than 3 and consonant})$ $\frac{1}{4}$
6. $P(\text{prime and consonant})$ $\frac{3}{8}$
7. What is the probability of spinning the spinner above 3 times and getting a vowel each time? $\frac{1}{64}$
8. What is the probability of rolling a number cube 3 times and getting a number less than 3 each time? $\frac{1}{27}$

Each spinner at the right is spun. Find each probability.

9. $P(\text{A and 2})$ $\frac{1}{15}$
10. $P(\text{vowel and even})$ $\frac{1}{5}$
11. $P(\text{consonant and 1})$ $\frac{1}{10}$
12. $P(\text{D and greater than 1})$ $\frac{1}{6}$

There are 3 red, 1 blue, and 2 yellow marbles in a bag. Once a marble is selected, it is not replaced. Find each probability.

13. $P(\text{red and then yellow})$ $\frac{1}{5}$
14. $P(\text{blue and then yellow})$ $\frac{1}{15}$
15. $P(\text{red and then blue})$ $\frac{1}{10}$
16. $P(\text{two yellow marbles})$ $\frac{1}{15}$
17. $P(\text{two red marbles in a row})$ $\frac{1}{5}$
18. $P(\text{three red marbles})$ $\frac{1}{20}$

The face cards are removed from a standard deck of 52 cards, and the rest are set aside. Two cards are drawn at random from the face cards. Once a card is selected, it is not replaced. Find each probability.

19. $P(\text{2 queens})$ $\frac{1}{11}$
20. $P(\text{jack and then king})$ $\frac{4}{33}$
21. $P(\text{black jack and then red queen})$ $\frac{1}{33}$
22. $P(\text{two black cards})$ $\frac{5}{22}$
23. $P(\text{black card and then red king})$ $\frac{1}{11}$
24. $P(\text{black jack and then black card})$ $\frac{5}{66}$

Practice: Word Problems, p. 467

NAME ______ DATE ______ PERIOD ____

8-5 Practice: Word Problems

Probability of Compound Events

1. **CHECKERS** In a game of checkers, there are 12 red game pieces and 12 black game pieces. Julio is setting up the board to begin playing. What is the probability that the first two checkers he pulls from the box at random will be two red checkers? $\frac{11}{46}$

2. **CHECKERS** What is the probability that the first two pieces are a red followed by a black? Explain how you found your answer. $\frac{6}{23}$; **on the first selection, there are 12 red out of 24 total, and on the second selection, there are 12 black out of 23 total. Multiply the probabilities** $\frac{12}{24}$ **and** $\frac{12}{23}$.

CHESS For Exercises 3 and 4, use the following information.

Ingrid keeps her white and black chess pieces in separate bags. For each color, there are 8 pawns, 2 rooks, 2 bishops, 2 knights, 1 queen, and 1 king.

3. Are the events of drawing a knight from the bag of white pieces and drawing a pawn from the bag of black pieces *dependent* or *independent* events? Explain. Find the probability of this compound event. **Independent; drawing a piece from one bag does not affect the pieces in the other bag;** $\frac{1}{16}$.

4. Are the events of drawing a bishop from the bag of white pieces and then drawing the queen from the same bag *dependent* or *independent* events? Explain. Find the probability of this compound event. **Dependent; once a bishop is drawn, there are fewer pieces in the bag from which to choose the second piece;** $\frac{1}{120}$.

5. **GAMES** A blackjack hand of 2 cards is randomly dealt from a standard deck of 52 cards. What is the probability that the first card is an ace and the second card is a face card? $\frac{4}{221}$

6. **SPORTS** During the 2002 soccer season, Maren Meinert of the Boston Breakers made approximately 2 goal points for every 5 of her shots on goal. What is the probability that Maren Meinert would make 2 goal points on two shots in a row during the 2002 season? $\frac{4}{25}$

8-6 Lesson Notes

Lesson Resources

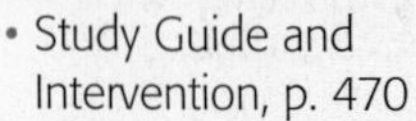

Chapter 8 Resource Masters
- Study Guide and Intervention, p. 470
- Practice: Skills, p. 471
- Practice: Word Problems, p. 472
- Reading to Learn Mathematics, p. 473
- Enrichment, p. 474

Key Teaching Transparencies, 32

Parent and Student Study Guide Online Worksheets, 8-6

Science and Mathematics Lab Masters, pp. 93–96

Teaching Mathematics with Manipulatives, pp. 95–97

Noteables™: Interactive Study Notebook with Foldables™, 8-6

Virtual Activities CD-ROM, Experimental Probability

1 Focus

5-Minute Check 8-6

INTERACTIVE CHALKBOARD PowerPoint® Presentations

Use as a quiz or review of Lesson 8-5. (Also available as a transparency)

Bellringer

Reading Mathematics Have students find the meaning of the Latin root for the words *experiment, experience,* and *expert.* **to try or learn by trying** Have them predict what *experimental probability* means. **probability that is determined by trying something, such as tossing a coin**

Reading to Learn Mathematics, p. 473 ELL

NAME ______ DATE ______ PERIOD ____

8-6 Reading to Learn Mathematics

Experimental Probability

Pre-Activity *Complete the Mini Lab at the top of page 400 in your textbook. Write your answers below.*

1. Compute the ratio $\frac{\text{number of times color was drawn}}{\text{total number of draws}}$ for each color of marble. **See students' work.**
2. Is it possible to have a certain color marble in the bag and never draw that color? **yes**
3. Open the bag and count the marbles. Find the ratio $\frac{\text{number of each color marble}}{\text{total number of marbles}}$ for each color of marble. **See students' work.**
4. Are the ratios in Exercises 1 and 3 the same? Explain why or why not. **See students' work.**

Reading the Lesson

8-6 Experimental Probability

What You'll LEARN

Find experimental probability.

NEW Vocabulary

experimental probability
theoretical probability

REVIEW Vocabulary

proportion: a statement of equality of two or more ratios, $\frac{a}{b} = \frac{c}{d}$, $b \neq 0, d \neq 0$ (Lesson 4-4)

HANDS-ON Mini Lab

Materials
- paper bag containing 10 colored marbles

Work with a partner.

Draw one marble from the bag, record its color, and replace it in the bag. Repeat this 50 times.

1. Compute the ratio $\frac{\text{number of times color was drawn}}{\text{total number of draws}}$ for each color of marble. **See students' work.**
2. Is it possible to have a certain color marble in the bag and never draw that color? **yes 3–4. See students' work.**
3. Open the bag and count the marbles. Find the ratio $\frac{\text{number of each color marble}}{\text{total number of marbles}}$ for each color of marble.
4. Are the ratios in Exercises 1 and 3 the same? Explain why or why not.

In the Mini Lab above, you determined a probability by conducting an experiment. Probabilities that are based on frequencies obtained by conducting an experiment are called **experimental probabilities**. Experimental probabilities usually vary when the experiment is repeated.

Probabilities based on known characteristics or facts are called **theoretical probabilities**. For example, you can compute the theoretical probability of picking a certain color marble from a bag. Theoretical probability tells you what *should* happen in an experiment.

EXAMPLES Experimental Probability

Michelle is conducting an experiment to find the probability of getting various sums when two number cubes are rolled. The results of her experiment are given at the right.

Results of Rolling Two Number Cubes

1 According to the experimental probability, is Michelle likely to get a sum of 12 on the next roll?

Based on the results of the rolls so far, a sum of 12 is not very likely.

2 How many possible outcomes are there for a pair of number cubes?

There are 6 · 6 or 36 possible outcomes.

DAILY INTERVENTION

Flexible Grouping

Experimental Probability Assign pairs of students of different math abilities a probability experiment that is possible to conduct in the classroom. Have one student determine the theoretical probability and the other student determine the experimental probability for the problem. How close were the answers? Have students switch roles and try a new problem.

400 Chapter 8 Probability

REAL-LIFE CAREERS

How Does a Marketing Manager Use Math?
A marketing manager uses information from surveys and experimental probability to help make decisions about changes in products and advertising.

For information about a career as a marketing manager, visit: msmath3.net/careers

EXAMPLE Theoretical Probability

3 What is the theoretical probability of rolling a double six?

The theoretical probability is $\frac{1}{6} \cdot \frac{1}{6}$ or $\frac{1}{36}$.

EXAMPLE Experimental Probability

4 MARKETING **Two hundred teenagers were asked whether they purchased certain items in the past year. What is the experimental probability that a teenager bought a photo frame in the last year?**

Item	Number Who Purchased the Item
candles	110
photo frames	95

There were 200 teenagers surveyed and 95 purchased a photo frame in the last year. The experimental probability is $\frac{95}{200}$ or $\frac{19}{40}$.

Your Turn a. $\frac{11}{20}$

a. What is the experimental probability that a teenager bought a candle in the last year?

TEACHING TIP
Some students may notice that 110 + 95 is not equal to 200. Point out that some teenagers may have purchased both candles and photo frames and some teenagers may have purchased neither item.

You can use past performance to predict future events.

EXAMPLES Use Probability to Predict

FARMING **Over the last 8 years, the probability that corn seeds planted by Ms. Diaz produced corn is $\frac{5}{6}$.**

5 Is this probability experimental or theoretical? Explain.

This is an experimental probability since it is based on what happened in the past.

6 If Ms. Diaz wants to have 10,000 corn-bearing plants, how many seeds should she plant?

This problem can be solved using a proportion.

5 out of 6 seeds should produce corn. → $\frac{5}{6} = \frac{10,000}{x}$ ← 10,000 out of x seeds should produce corn.

Solve the proportion.

$\frac{5}{6} = \frac{10,000}{x}$	Write the proportion.
$5 \cdot x = 6 \cdot 10,000$	Find the cross products.
$5x = 60,000$	Multiply.
$\frac{5x}{5} = \frac{60,000}{5}$	Divide each side by 5.
$x = 12,000$	Ms. Diaz should plant 12,000 seeds.

STUDY TIP

Mental Math
For every 5 corn bearing plants, Ms. Diaz must plant an extra seed. Think: 10,000 ÷ 5 = 2,000 Ms. Diaz must plant 2,000 extra seeds. She must plant a total of 10,000 + 2,000 or 12,000 seeds. The answer is correct.

msmath3.net/extra_examples

2 Teach

In-Class Examples

Nikki is conducting an experiment to find the probability of getting various results when three coins are tossed. The results of her experiment are given below.

Result	Number of Tosses
all heads	6
two heads	32
one head	30
no heads	12

1 According to the experimental probability, is Nikki more likely to get all heads or no heads on the next toss? **no heads**

2 How many possible outcomes are there for tossing three coins if order is important? **8**

3 Is the theoretical probability greater for tossing all heads or no heads? What is the theoretical probability of each? **The theoretical probabilities are the same; $\frac{1}{8}$.**

4 **MARKETING** Eight hundred adults were asked whether they were planning to stay home for winter vacation. Of those surveyed, 560 said that they were. What is the experimental probability that an adult planned to stay home for winter vacation? $\frac{7}{10}$

MATH TEAM **Over the past 3 years, the probability that the school math team would win a meet is $\frac{3}{5}$.**

5 Is this probability experimental or theoretical? Explain. **Experimental; it is based on actual results.**

6 If the team wants to win 12 more meets in the next 3 years, how many meets should the team enter? **20 meets**

3 Practice/Apply

FOLDABLES™ Follow-Up Remind students to use the sixth section of their Foldables to record what they learn about finding experimental probability, and to use what they have learned to compare and contrast experimental and theoretical probabilities. Encourage students to include the key terms and their definitions on the last section, or "Vocabulary" section, of their Foldables.

About the Exercises...

Guided Practice Key

Exercises	Examples
3	1
4	2
5	3
7	5
6, 8–9	6

Assignment Guide

Basic: 10, 11, 13, 15–19, 23–31

Average: 10, 11, 13, 15–21, 23–31

Enriched: 10–14, 16–28 (Optional: 29–31)

Alert! Have students assume that the samples for Exercises 13–14 and 16–17 were taken of random, representative populations.

Alert! Exercises 18–19 require two coins.

Answers

1. Each experimental probability will be different. Theoretical probability tells you approximately what should happen.
2. Sample answer:

Favorite Colors	
Color	Number of People
blue	100
red	70
green	50
other	30

Skill and Concept Check

1. *Writing Math* Explain why you would *not* expect the theoretical probability and the experimental probability of an event to always be the same. **1–2. See margin.**
2. **OPEN ENDED** Two hundred fifty people are surveyed about their favorite color. Make a possible table of results if the experimental probability that the favorite color is blue is $\frac{2}{5}$.

GUIDED PRACTICE

For Exercises 3–7, use the table that shows the results of tossing a coin.

Result	Number of Times
heads	26
tails	24

3. Based on your results, what is the probability of getting heads? $\frac{13}{25}$
4. Based on the results, how many heads would you expect to occur in 400 tries? **about 208 heads**
5. What is the theoretical probability of getting heads? $\frac{1}{2}$
6. Based on the theoretical probability, how many heads would you expect to occur in 400 tries? **about 200 heads**
7. Compare the theoretical probability to your experimental probability. **See margin.**

For Exercises 8 and 9, use the table at the right showing the results of a survey of cars that passed the school.

Cars Passing the School	
Color	Number of Cars
white	35
red	23
green	12
other	20

8. What is the probability that the next car will be white? $\frac{7}{18}$
9. Out of the next 180 cars, how many would you expect to be white? **about 70 cars**

Practice and Applications

HOMEWORK HELP	
For Exercises	See Examples
10, 12–13, 15–16, 18	1, 4, 5
11, 14, 17, 19	6
20–21	2, 3

Extra Practice See pages 637, 655.

SCHOOL For Exercises 10 and 11, use the following information. In keyboarding class, Cleveland made 4 typing errors in 60 words.

10. What is the probability that his next word will have an error? $\frac{1}{15}$
11. In a 1,000-word essay, how many errors would you expect Cleveland to make? **about 67 errors**
12. **SCHOOL** In the last 40 school days, Esteban's bus has been late 8 times. What is the experimental probability the bus will be late tomorrow? $\frac{1}{5}$

FOOD For Exercises 13 and 14, use the survey results at the right.

Favorite Snack While Watching Television	
Snack	Number
potato chips	55
corn chips	40
popcorn	35
pretzels	15
other	5

13. What is the probability that a person's favorite snack while watching television is corn chips? $\frac{4}{15}$
14. Out of 450 people, how many would you expect to have corn chips as their favorite snack with television? **about 120 people**
15. **SPORTS** In practice, Crystal made 80 out of 100 free throws. What is the experimental probability that she will make a free throw? $\frac{4}{5}$

7. The theoretical probability is about the same as the experimental probability.

25. The experimental probability is $\frac{15}{75}$ or $\frac{1}{5}$. The theoretical probability is $\frac{1}{4}$. The experimental probability is less than the theoretical probability.

Sports Participation by Teens	
Sport	**Number of Participants**
basketball	42
volleyball	26
soccer	24
football	16

SPORTS **For Exercises 16 and 17, use the results of a survey of 90 teens shown at the right.**

16. What is the probability that a teen plays soccer? $\frac{4}{15}$
17. Out of 300 teens, how many would you expect to play soccer? **about 80 teens**

For Exercises 18–22, toss two coins 50 times and record the results.

18. What is the experimental probability of tossing two heads?
19. Based on your results, how many times would you expect to get two heads in 800 tries? **18–19. See students' work.**
20. What is the theoretical probability of tossing two heads? $\frac{1}{4}$
21. Based on the theoretical probability, how many times would you expect to get two heads in 800 tries? **about 200 times**
22. Compare the theoretical and experimental probability. **See students' work.**

23. **CRITICAL THINKING** An inspector found that 15 out of 250 cars had a loose front door and that 10 out of 500 cars had headlight problems. What is the probability that a car has both problems? $\frac{3}{2{,}500}$

Spiral Review with Standardized Test Practice

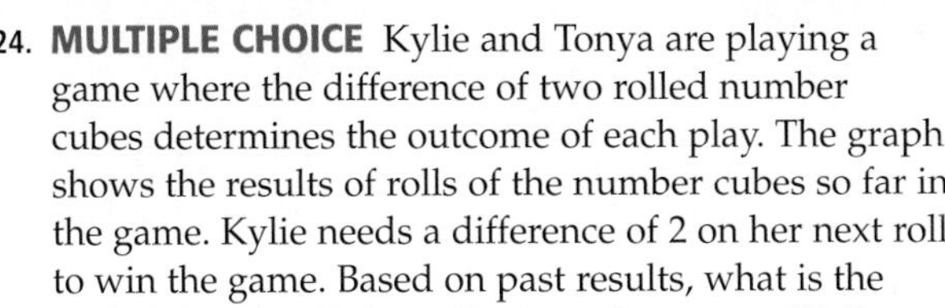

24. **MULTIPLE CHOICE** Kylie and Tonya are playing a game where the difference of two rolled number cubes determines the outcome of each play. The graph shows the results of rolls of the number cubes so far in the game. Kylie needs a difference of 2 on her next roll to win the game. Based on past results, what is the probability that Kylie will win on her next roll? **B**

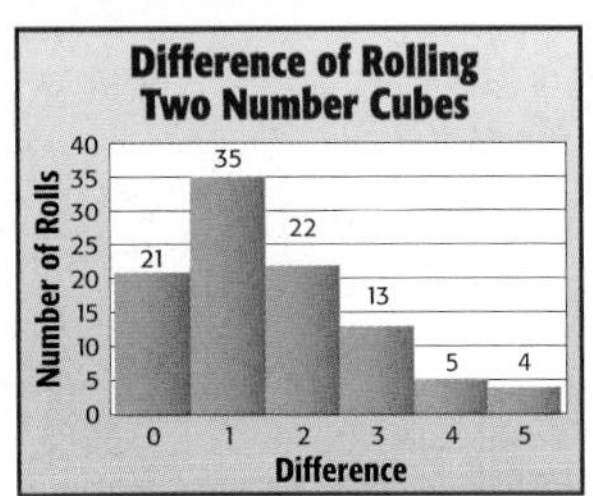

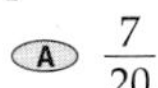 A $\frac{7}{20}$ 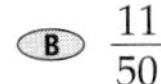 B $\frac{11}{50}$ C $\frac{1}{20}$ D $\frac{1}{25}$

25. **SHORT RESPONSE** A local video store has advertised that one out of every four customers will receive a free box of popcorn with their video rental. So far, 15 out of 75 customers have won popcorn. Compare the experimental and theoretical probability of getting popcorn. **See margin.**

There are 3 red marbles, 4 green marbles, and 5 blue marbles in a bag. Once a marble is selected, it is not replaced. Find the probability of each outcome. (Lesson 8-5)

26. 2 green marbles $\frac{1}{11}$
27. a blue marble and then a red marble $\frac{5}{44}$

28. **FOOD** Pepperoni, mushrooms, onions, and green peppers can be added to a basic cheese pizza. How many 2-item pizzas can be prepared? (Lesson 8-4) **6 pizzas**

GETTING READY FOR THE NEXT LESSON

PREREQUISITE SKILL **Solve each problem.** (Lessons 5-3 and 5-6)

29. Find 35% of 90. **31.5**
30. Find 42% of 340. **142.8**
31. What is 18% of 90? **16.2**

msmath3.net/self_check_quiz

4 Assess

Higher-Level Thinking

How often would you expect even numbers to come up when rolling a number cube? **about half the time** Roll a number cube 20 times. Do even numbers come up as often as you expect? Roll it 50 times, and then 100 times, recording the percent of the time that even numbers come up. Are these results getting closer to what you expected? Explain. **Yes; as the number of tries increases, the experimental probability will get closer to the theoretical probability.**

Study Guide and Intervention, p. 470

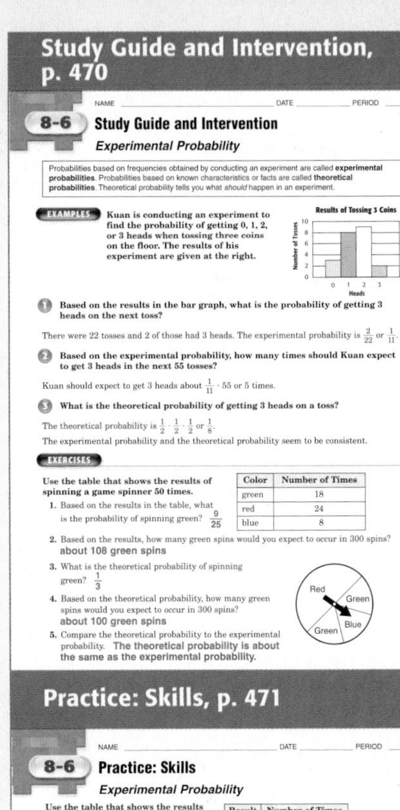

NAME ______ DATE ______ PERIOD ____

8-6 Study Guide and Intervention

Experimental Probability

Probabilities based on frequencies obtained by conducting an experiment are called **experimental probabilities**. Probabilities based on known characteristics or facts are called **theoretical probabilities**. Theoretical probability tells you what *should* happen in an experiment.

EXAMPLES **Kuan is conducting an experiment to find the probability of getting 0, 1, 2, or 3 heads when tossing three coins on the floor. The results of his experiment are given at the right.**

1. **Based on the results in the bar graph, what is the probability of getting 3 heads on the next toss?**

There were 22 tosses and 2 of those had 3 heads. The experimental probability is $\frac{2}{22}$ or $\frac{1}{11}$.

2. **Based on the experimental probability, how many times should Kuan expect to get 3 heads in the next 55 tosses?**

Kuan should expect to get 3 heads about $\frac{1}{11} \cdot 55$ or 5 times.

3. **What is the theoretical probability of getting 3 heads on a toss?**

The theoretical probability is $\frac{1}{2} \cdot \frac{1}{2} \cdot \frac{1}{2}$ or $\frac{1}{8}$.

The experimental probability and the theoretical probability seem to be consistent.

EXERCISES

Use the table that shows the results of spinning a game spinner 50 times.

Color	Number of Times
green	18
red	24
blue	8

1. Based on the results in the table, what is the probability of spinning green? $\frac{9}{25}$
2. Based on the results, how many green spins would you expect to occur in 300 spins? **about 108 green spins**
3. What is the theoretical probability of spinning green? $\frac{1}{3}$
4. Based on the theoretical probability, how many green spins would you expect to occur in 300 spins? **about 100 green spins**
5. Compare the theoretical probability to the experimental probability. **The theoretical probability is about the same as the experimental probability.**

Practice: Skills, p. 471

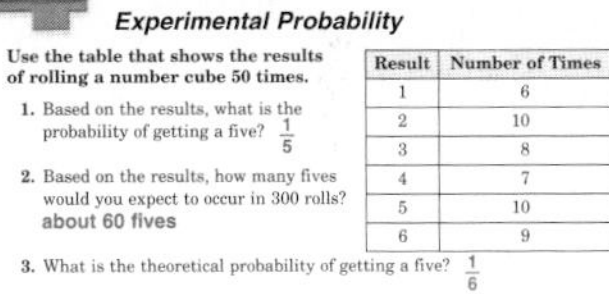

NAME ______ DATE ______ PERIOD ____

8-6 Practice: Skills

Experimental Probability

Use the table that shows the results of rolling a number cube 50 times.

Result	Number of Times
1	6
2	10
3	8
4	7
5	10
6	9

1. Based on the results, what is the probability of getting a five? $\frac{1}{5}$
2. Based on the results, how many fives would you expect to occur in 300 rolls? **about 60 fives**
3. What is the theoretical probability of getting a five? $\frac{1}{6}$
4. Based on the theoretical probability, how many fives would you expect to occur in 300 rolls? **about 50 fives**
5. Compare the theoretical probability to the experimental probability. **The theoretical probability is a little less than the experimental probability.**

ARCHERY **Use the following information.**

In archery class, Jocelyn missed the target 5 times in 40 shots.

6. What is the probability that her next shot will miss the target? $\frac{1}{8}$
7. In her next 160 shots, how many times would you expect Jocelyn to miss the target? **about 20 times**

PETS **For Exercises 8–11, use the results of a survey of 200 people shown at the right.**

First Pet	Number
bird	32
cat	56
dog	66
rabbit	19
other	27

8. What is the probability that a person says his or her first pet was a cat? $\frac{7}{25}$
9. Out of 500 people, how many would you expect to say a cat was his or her first pet? **about 140 people**
10. What is the probability that a person says his or her first pet was a bird? $\frac{4}{25}$
11. Out of 500 people, how many would you expect to say a bird was their first pet? **about 80 people**
12. FIGURE SKATING At figure skating practice, Michelle successfully landed 15 out of 18 attempts at a double axel. What is the experimental probability that she will successfully land a double axel? $\frac{5}{6}$

Practice: Word Problems, p. 472

NAME ______ DATE ______ PERIOD ____

8-6 Practice: Word Problems

Experimental Probability

ENTERTAINMENT **For Exercises 1 and 2, use the results of a survey of 120 eighth grade students shown at the right.**

Video Game Playing Time Per Week	
Hours	**Number of Participants**
0	18
1–3	43
3–6	35
more than 6	24

1. Explain how to find the probability that a student plays video games more than 6 hours per week. Then find the probability. **Find the ratio of the number of students who play video games more than 6 hours per week to the total number of students surveyed; $\frac{1}{5}$**
2. Out of 400 students, how many would you expect to play video games more than 6 hours per week? **about 80 students**
3. DINING Only 6 out of 100 Americans say they leave a tip of more than 20% for satisfactory service in a restaurant. Out of 1,500 restaurant customers, how many would you expect to leave a tip of more than 20%? **about 90 customers**
4. PLANTS Jason has a packet of tomato seeds left over from last year. He plants 36 of the seeds and only 8 sprout. What is the experimental probability that a tomato seed from this packet will sprout? $\frac{2}{9}$

SPORTS **For Exercises 5 and 6, use the results in the table at the right. In a survey, 102 people were asked to pick their favorite spectator sport.**

Favorite Spectator Sport	
Sport	**Number**
professional football	42
professional baseball	27
professional basketball	21
college football	12

5. What is the probability that a person's favorite spectator sport is professional baseball? Is this an *experimental* or a *theoretical* probability? Explain. **$\frac{9}{34}$; Experimental; it is based on frequencies obtained through a survey.**
6. Out of 10,000 people, how many would you expect to say that professional baseball is their favorite spectator sport? Round to the nearest person. **about 2,647 people**

8-6b Graphing Calculator Investigation

GETTING STARTED

Reading Tip Tell students that *simulate* is another word for imitate or model. They may be familiar with role-playing simulations. This lesson uses a TI-83 Plus calculator to simulate probability experiments such as when rolling a number cube or tossing a coin.

TEACH

Activity 1

- The graphing calculator has the capability of generating random numbers. Students must enter the lowest number (lower bound), the highest number (upper bound), and the quantity of numbers (trials) to be generated by the calculator.
- Some students' calculators may require different keystrokes than those supplied here. Have students refer to their user manuals for specific instructions on how to generate random numbers with their calculators.
- Suggest that students set up a frequency table with rows marked 1, 2, 3, 4, 5, and 6 to use when recording the numbers generated by their calculators.

Activity 2

- In **Your Turn**, some students may wish to record all of the numbers generated all 30 times in a large table. Remind them that they are simulating how likely it is that for every 12 boxes of cereal purchased, all eight cards will be obtained. So, for each time they repeat the simulation, students need only record whether or not all eight numbers are represented.

8-6b Graphing Calculator Investigation

A Follow-Up of Lesson 8-6

What You'll LEARN

Use a graphing calculator to simulate probability experiments.

Materials

- graphing calculator
- paper
- pencil

Simulations

A **simulation** is an experiment that is designed to act out a given situation. You can use items such as a number cube, a coin, a spinner, or a random number generator on a graphing calculator. From the simulation, you can calculate experimental probabilities.

ACTIVITY 1 *Work with a partner.*

Simulate rolling a number cube 50 times.

Use the random number generator on a TI-83/84 Plus graphing calculator. Enter 1 as the lower bound and 6 as the upper bound for 50 trials.

Keystrokes: MATH ◄ 5 1 , 6 , 50) ENTER

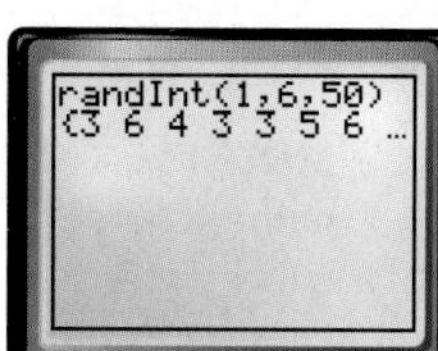

A set of 50 numbers ranging from 1 to 6 appears. Use the right arrow key to see the next number in the set. Record all 50 numbers on a separate sheet of paper.

Your Turn

a. Use the simulation to determine the experimental probability of each number showing on the number cube. **See students' work.**

b. Compare the experimental probabilities found in Step 2 to the theoretical probabilities. **See students' work.**

STUDY TIP

Simulations Repeating a simulation may result in different probabilities since the numbers generated are different each time.

ACTIVITY 2 *Work with a partner.*

A company is placing one of 8 different cards of action heroes in its boxes of cereal. If each card is equally likely to appear, what is the experimental probability that a person who buys 12 boxes of cereal will get all 8 cards?

Let the numbers 1 through 8 represent the cards. Use the random number generator on a graphing calculator. Enter 1 as the lower bound and 8 as the upper bound for 12 trials.

Keystrokes: MATH ◄ 5 1 , 8 , 12) ENTER

Record whether all of the numbers are represented.
See students' work.

msmath3.net/other_calculator_keystrokes

Your Turn

c. Repeat the simulation thirty times. **See students' work.**

d. Use the simulation to find the experimental probability that a person who buys 12 boxes of cereal will get all 8 cards.

d. See students' work.

EXERCISES

1. A *hypothesis* is a statement to be tested that describes what you expect to happen in a given situation. **State** your hypothesis as to the results of repeating the simulation in Activity 1 more than 50 times. Then test your hypothesis. **1–6. See margin.**
2. **Explain** how you could use a graphing calculator to simulate tossing a coin 40 times.
3. **CLOTHING** Rodolfo must wear a tie when he works at the mall on Friday, Saturday, and Sunday. Each day, he picks one of his 6 ties at random. Create a simulation to find the experimental probability that he wears a different tie each day of the weekend.
4. **TOYS** A fast food restaurant is putting 3 different toys in their children's meals. If the toys are placed in the meals at random, create a simulation to determine the experimental probability that a child will have all 3 toys after buying 5 meals.
5. **SCIENCE** Suppose a mouse is placed in the maze at the right. If each decision about direction is made at random, create a simulation to determine the probability that the mouse will find its way out before coming to a dead end or going out the In opening.

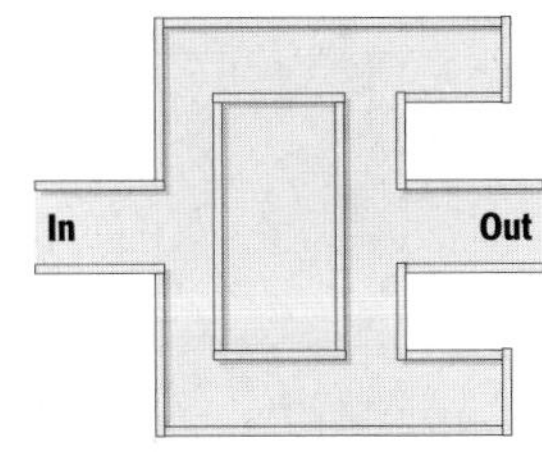

6. **WRITE A PROBLEM** Write a real-life problem that could be answered by using a simulation.

For Exercises 7–9, use the following information.
Suppose you play a game where there are three containers, each with 10 balls numbered 0 to 9. One number is randomly picked from each container. Pick three numbers each between 0 and 9. Then use the random number generator to simulate the game. Score 2 points if one number matches, 16 points if two numbers match, and 32 points if all three numbers match. Notice that numbers can appear more than once.

7. Play the game if the order of the numbers does *not* matter. Total your score for 10 simulations. **See students' work.**
8. Now play the game if order of the numbers does matter. Total your score for 10 simulations. **See students' work.**
9. With which game rules did you score more points? **Sample answer: the game where order does not matter**

TEACHING TIP

Notice that the simulation in Exercise 7 is the same as the game on page 395.

ASSESS

Observe as students solve the **Exercises**. They should:

- be able to use a graphing calculator to simulate a probability experiment,
- be able to calculate experimental probabilities, and
- be able to design simulations to determine probability.

Answers

1. Sample hypothesis: The experimental probability will become closer to the theoretical probability; see students' work.
2. Sample answer: Let 1 represent heads and 2 represent tails. Use the random number generator to randomly select 1s and 2s for 40 trials.
3. Sample answer: Assign a number from 1 to 6 to each tie. Use the random number generator to randomly select numbers from 1 to 6 three at a time. Record whether or not the same number appears twice. Repeat the process numerous times.
4. Sample answer: Assign a number from 1 to 3 to each toy. Use the random number generator to randomly select numbers from 1 to 3 five at a time. Record whether or not all numbers are represented. Repeat the process numerous times.
5. Sample answer: Use a coin to decide which way the mouse will go at each intersection. Record whether the mouse goes out the Out opening, goes out the In opening, or comes to a dead end. Repeat the experiment numerous times.
6. Sample answer: The basketball coach wants to know the probability that a player can make a shot from a certain location on the court.

8-7 Lesson Notes

Lesson Resources

FAST FILE

Chapter 8 Resource Masters
- Study Guide and Intervention, p. 475
- Practice: Skills, p. 476
- Practice: Word Problems, p. 477
- Reading to Learn Mathematics, p. 478
- Enrichment, p. 479

Classroom Math Games, pp. 31–32
Key Teaching Transparencies, 33
Parent and Student Study Guide Online Worksheets, 8-7
Real-Life Career Masters, p. 34
Noteables™: Interactive Study Notebook with Foldables™, 8-7

Focus

5-Minute Check 8-7
Use as a quiz or review of Lesson 8-6. (Also available as a transparency)

Bellringer

Reading Mathematics The terms *biased* and *unbiased* are important in studying probability and sampling at all levels of mathematics. Have students discuss the everyday uses of these terms and the dictionary definitions. Then tell them that in this lesson they will apply these terms to the collection of data for surveys.

Reading to Learn Mathematics, p. 478 **ELL**

NAME ______ DATE ______ PERIOD ____

8-7 Reading to Learn Mathematics
Using Sampling to Predict

Pre-Activity *Read the introduction at the top of page 406 in your textbook. Write your answers below.*

1. Suppose she decides to survey a group of people at a rock concert. Do you think the results would represent all of the people in the listening area? Explain. No; people who are at a rock concert will probably like rock.
2. Suppose she decides to survey students at your middle school. Do you think the results would represent all of the people in the listening area? Explain. No; middle school students will probably like different kinds of music than other age groups.
3. Suppose she decides to call every 100th household in the telephone book. Do you think the results would represent all of the people in the listening area? Explain. Yes; people of all ages and backgrounds are likely to be represented.

...e Lesson

Statistics: Using Sampling to Predict

What You'll LEARN

Predict the actions of a larger group by using a sample.

NEW Vocabulary

sample
population
unbiased sample
simple random sample
stratified random sample
systematic random sample
biased sample
convenience sample
voluntary response sample

WHEN am I ever going to use this?

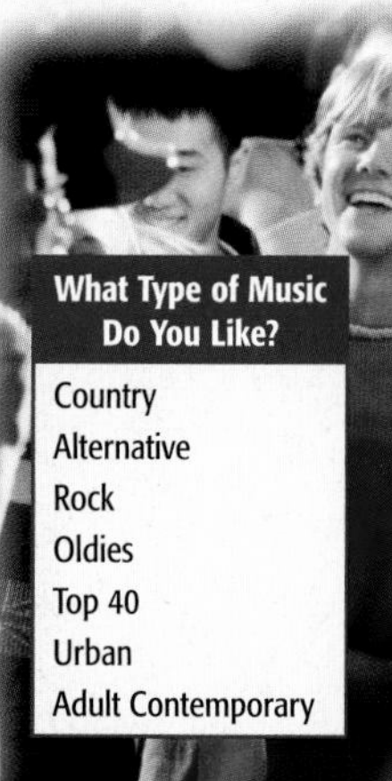

ENTERTAINMENT The manager of a radio station wants to conduct a survey to determine what type of music people like.

1. Suppose she decides to survey a group of people at a rock concert. Do you think the results would represent all of the people in the listening area? Explain.
2. Suppose she decides to survey students at your middle school. Do you think the results would represent all of the people in the listening area? Explain.
3. Suppose she decides to call every 100th household in the telephone book. Do you think the results would represent all of the people in the listening area? Explain.

1–3. See margin.

The manager of the radio station cannot survey everyone in the listening area. A smaller group called a **sample** is chosen. A sample is representative of a larger group called a **population**.

For valid results, a sample must be chosen very carefully. An **unbiased sample** is selected so that it is representative of the entire population. Three ways to pick an unbiased sample are listed below.

Concept Summary — **Unbiased Samples**

Type	Definition	Example
Simple Random Sample	A simple random sample is a sample where each item or person in the population is as likely to be chosen as any other.	Each student's name is written on a piece of paper. The names are placed in a bowl, and names are picked without looking.
Stratified Random Sample	In a stratified random sample, the population is divided into similar, non-overlapping groups. A simple random sample is then selected from each group.	Students are picked at random from each grade level at a school.
Systematic Random Sample	In a systematic random sample, the items or people are selected according to a specific time or item interval.	From an alphabetical list of all students attending a school, every 20th person is chosen.

Answers (When am I ever going to use this?)

1. No; people who are at a rock concert will probably like rock.
2. No; middle school students will probably like different kinds of music than other age groups.
3. Yes; people of all ages and backgrounds are likely to be represented.

In a **biased sample**, one or more parts of the population are favored over others. Two ways to pick a biased sample are listed below.

TEACHING TIP
Have students give examples of unbiased and biased samples.

Concept Summary — Biased Samples

Type	Definition	Example
Convenience Sample	A convenience sample includes members of a population that are easily accessed.	To represent all the students attending a school, the principal surveys the students in one math class.
Voluntary Response Sample	A voluntary response sample involves only those who want to participate in the sampling.	Students at a school who wish to express their opinion are asked to come to the office after school.

EXAMPLES Describe Samples

Describe each sample.

1 To determine what videos their customers like, every tenth person to walk into the video store is surveyed.

Since the population is the customers of the video store, the sample is a systematic random sample. It is an unbiased sample.

2 To determine what people like to do in their leisure time, the customers of a video store are surveyed.

The customers of a video store probably like to watch videos in their leisure time. This is a biased sample. The sample is a convenience sample since all of the people surveyed are in one location.

EXAMPLES Using Sampling to Predict

SCHOOL The school bookstore sells 3-ring binders in 4 different colors; red, green, blue, and yellow. The students who run the store survey 50 students at random. The colors they prefer are indicated at the right.

Color	Number
red	25
green	10
blue	13
yellow	2

3 What percent of the students prefer blue binders?

13 out of 50 students prefer blue binders.

$13 \div 50 = 0.26$ 26% of the students prefer blue binders.

4 If 450 binders are to be ordered to sell in the store, how many should be blue?

Find 26% of 450.

$0.26 \times 450 = 117$ About 117 binders should be blue.

STUDY TIP

Misleading Probabilities Probabilities based on biased samples can be misleading. If the students surveyed were all boys, the probabilities generated by the survey would not be valid, since both girls and boys purchase binders at the store.

msmath3.net/extra_examples

2 Teach

In-Class Examples

Describe each sample.

1 To determine which school lunches students like most, every twentieth student to walk into the cafeteria is surveyed. **This is an unbiased, systematic random sample.**

2 To determine what sports teenagers like, the student athletes on the girls' field hockey team are surveyed. **This is a biased sample, since the members of the population to be surveyed are chosen by convenience.**

BOOKS The student council is trying to decide what types of books to sell at its annual book fair to help raise money for the eighth-grade trip. It surveys 40 students at random. The books they prefer are in the table.

Book Type	Number of Students
mystery	12
adventure novel	9
sports	11
short stories	8

3 What percent of the students prefer mysteries? **30%**

4 If 220 books are to be sold at the book fair, how many should be mysteries? **66**

DAILY INTERVENTION — Unlocking Misconceptions

Unbiased Samples and Biased Samples Inform students that whether a sample is unbiased or biased depends in part on the purpose of the survey. For example, a sample chosen randomly from customers of a music store is unbiased if the survey is about the musical preferences of persons living near the store. In contrast, the same sample would be biased if the survey were about political views or about the musical preferences of all Americans.

Lesson 8-7 Statistics: Using Sampling to Predict 407

Using Applications Maintain a file of product surveys and opinion polls that you encounter in magazines, on television, and on the Internet. Students can classify the survey types, evaluate whether the surveys are biased, use bar graphs or circle graphs to display the results, or use them as models for their own surveys.

3 Practice/Apply

About the Exercises...

Guided Practice Key

Exercises	Examples
3–4	1, 2
5	3
6	4

Assignment Guide

Basic: 7–11 odd, 14, 15–19 odd, 21–26

Average: 7–13 odd, 14, 15–19 odd, 21–26

Enriched: 8–12 even, 14–16, 18–26

Answers

1. Taking a survey is one way to determine experimental probability.
2. Sample answer: A survey of middle school students about lowering the age to begin driving a car would not reflect the opinions of the majority of people.
3. This is a biased sample, since people in other states would spend much more than those in Arizona. The sample is a convenience sample since all the people are from the same state.
7. This is an unbiased, systematic random sample.
8. This is a biased sample, since only music students were surveyed. This is a convenience sample.
9. This is a biased sample, since only voluntary responses are used.
10. This is an unbiased, stratified random sample.
11. This is an unbiased, simple random sample.
12. This is a biased sample, since only the oranges on the top of the first crate are represented. This is a convenience sample.
13. Sample answer: Get a list of all the students in the school and contact every twentieth student on the list.
16. Yes; 350 out of 500 random customers agree. From this survey, you can predict that 70% of the customers would like a foreign food area, so the store should add such an area.

Students practice the same concepts in Exercises 7–12 if they are assigned odd or even problems.

Skill and Concept Check

1. *Writing Math* Compare taking a survey and finding an experimental probability. **1–2. See margin.**
2. **OPEN ENDED** Give a counterexample to the following statement. *The results of a survey are always valid.*

GUIDED PRACTICE

Describe each sample.

3. To determine how much money the average family in the United States spends to heat their home, a survey of 100 households from Arizona are picked at random. **See margin.**
4. To determine what benefits employees consider most important, one person from each department of the company is chosen at random. **This is an unbiased, stratified random sample.**

ELECTIONS For Exercises 5 and 6, use the following information. Three students are running for class president. Jonathan randomly surveyed some of his classmates and recorded the results at the right.

Candidate	Number
Luke	7
Della	12
Ryan	6

5. What percent said they were voting for Della? **48%**
6. If there are 180 students in the class, how many do you think will vote for Della? **about 86 students**

★ indicates increased difficulty

Practice and Applications

HOMEWORK HELP

For Exercises	See Examples
7–12, 19–20	1, 2
14–18	3, 4

Extra Practice See pages 637, 655.

Describe each sample. 7–12. See margin.

7. To evaluate the quality of their cell phones, a manufacturer pulls every 50th phone off the assembly line to check for defects.
8. To determine whether the students will attend a spring music concert at the school, Rico surveys her friends in the chorale.
9. To determine the most popular television stars, a magazine asks its readers to complete a questionnaire and send it back to the magazine.
10. To determine what people in Texas think about a proposed law, 2 people from each county in the state are picked at random.
11. To pick 2 students to represent the 28 students in a science class, the teacher uses the computer program to randomly pick 2 numbers from 1 to 28. The students whose names are next to those numbers in his grade book will represent the class.
12. To determine if the oranges in 20 crates are fresh, the produce manager at a grocery store takes 5 oranges from the top of the first crate off the delivery truck.

★ 13. **SCHOOL** Suppose you are writing an article for the school newspaper about the proposed changes to the cafeteria. Describe an unbiased way to conduct a survey of students. **See margin.**

SALES **For Exercises 14 and 15, use the following information.**
A random survey of shoppers shows that 19 prefer whole milk, 44 prefer low-fat milk, and 27 prefer skim milk.

14. What percent prefer skim milk? **30%**
15. If 800 containers of milk are ordered, how many should be skim milk? **about 240 containers**

16. **MARKETING** A grocery store is considering adding a world foods area. They survey 500 random customers, and 350 customers agree the world foods area is a good idea. Should the store add this area? Explain. **See margin.**

FOOD **For Exercises 17–20, conduct a survey of the students in your math class to determine whether they prefer hamburgers or pizza.**

17. What percent prefer hamburgers? **See students' work.**
18. Use your survey to predict how many students in your school prefer hamburgers. **See students' work.**
19. Is your survey a good way to determine the preferences of the students in your school? Explain. **No; the survey should be representative of the whole school.**
20. How could you improve your survey? **See margin.**

21. **CRITICAL THINKING** How could the wording of a question or the tone of voice of the interviewer affect a survey? Give at least two examples. **See Ch. 8 Answer Appendix.**

Spiral Review with Standardized Test Practice

22. **MULTIPLE CHOICE** The Star Theater records the number of food items sold at its concessions. If the manager orders 5,000 food items for next week, approximately how many trays of nachos should she order? **A**

Ⓐ 1,025 Ⓑ 850 Ⓒ 800 Ⓓ 400

Food Items Sold at Movie Concessions During the Past Week	
Item	**Number**
popcorn	620
nachos	401
candy	597
slices of pizza	336

23. **MULTIPLE CHOICE** Brett wants to conduct a survey about who stays for after-school activities at his school. Who should he ask? **I**

Ⓕ his friends on the bus Ⓖ members of the football team
Ⓗ community leaders Ⓘ every 10th student entering school

24. **MANUFACTURING** An inspector finds that 3 out of the 250 DVD players he checks are defective. What is the experimental probability that a DVD player is defective? (Lesson 8-6) $\frac{3}{250}$

Each spinner at the right is spun once. Find each probability. (Lesson 8-5)

25. P(3 and B) $\frac{1}{20}$ 26. P(even and consonant) $\frac{3}{10}$

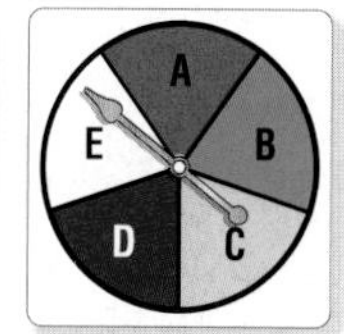

msmath3.net/self_check_quiz

4 Assess

Open-Ended Assessment

Speaking Have students work in pairs to give one example of a biased sample and one example of an unbiased sample. Ask them to specifically describe each type of sample they choose.

Answer

20. Sample answer: Ask every 10th student leaving the school which he or she prefers.

Study Guide and Intervention, p. 475

NAME ____________ DATE ________ PERIOD ____

8-7 **Study Guide and Intervention**
Using Sampling to Predict

Data gathered from a representative sample can be used to make predictions about a population. An **unbiased sample** is selected so that it is representative of the entire population. In a **biased sample**, one or more parts of the population are favored over others.

EXAMPLES **Describe each sample.**

1. **To determine the favorite dog breed of people who enter dog shows, every fifth person entering a dog show is surveyed.**
Since the people are selected according to a specific pattern, the sample is a systematic random sample. It is an unbiased sample.

2. **To determine what type of pet people prefer, the spectators at a dog show are surveyed.**
The spectators at a dog show probably prefer dogs. This is a biased sample. The sample is a convenience sample since all of the people surveyed are in one location.

EXAMPLES COOKIES **Students in the eighth grade surveyed 50 students at random about their favorite cookies. The results are in the table at the right.**

Flavor	Number
oatmeal	15
peanut butter	11
chocolate chip	16
sugar	8

3. **What percent of students prefer chocolate chip cookies?**

16 out of 50 students prefer chocolate chip cookies.
$16 \div 50 = 0.32$ 32% of the students prefer chocolate chip cookies.

4. **If the students order 500 boxes of cookie dough, how many boxes should be chocolate chip?**

Find 32% of 500.
$0.32 \times 500 = 160$ About 160 boxes of cookie dough should be chocolate chip.

EXERCISES

Describe the sample.

1. To determine if the tomatoes in 5 boxes stacked on a pallet are not spoiled, the restaurant manager checks 3 tomatoes from the top box. **This is a biased sample, since only tomatoes in the top box are represented. This is a convenience sample.**

A random survey of the students in eighth grade shows that 7 prefer hamburgers, 5 prefer chicken, and 3 prefer hot dogs.

2. What percent prefer hot dogs? **20%**
3. If 120 students will attend the eighth grade picnic, how many hot dogs should be ordered? **about 24 hot dogs**

Practice: Skills, p. 476

NAME ____________ DATE ________ PERIOD ____

8-7 **Practice: Skills**
Using Sampling to Predict

Describe each sample.

1. To evaluate the defect rate of its memory chips, an integrated circuit manufacturer tests every 100th chip off the production line. **This is an unbiased, systematic random sample.**
2. Students who wish to represent the school at a school board meeting are asked to stop by the office after lunch. **This is a biased sample since only students with strong opinions are likely to volunteer. This is a voluntary response sample.**
3. To determine if the class understood the homework assignment, the math teacher checks the top 3 papers in the pile of collected homework. **This is a biased sample, since only papers turned in and on top of the pile are represented. This is a convenience sample.**
4. To determine the representatives to the recess activities meeting, 2 students are selected at random from each homeroom. **This is an unbiased, stratified random sample.**
5. A member of the cafeteria staff asks every fifth student leaving the cafeteria to rank 5 vegetables from most favorite to least favorite. **This is an unbiased, systematic random sample.**
6. One bead for every member of the school orchestra is placed in a bag. All but 2 of the beads are white. Each member draws a bead from the bag, and the members who pick the non-white beads will represent the orchestra. **This is an unbiased, simple random sample.**
7. A real estate agent surveys people about their housing preferences at an open house for a luxury townhouse. **This is a biased sample since the people surveyed probably prefer townhouses. This is a convenience sample.**
8. To determine the most popular children's programs, a television station asks parents to call in and complete a phone survey. **This is a biased sample, since only parents with strong opinions are likely to call. This is a voluntary response sample.**
9. Two teachers from each school in the district are chosen at random to fill out a survey on classroom behavior. **This is an unbiased, stratified random sample.**
10. Airline boarding passes are marked with red stars at random to decide which passengers should have their carry-on luggage inspected. **This is an unbiased, simple random sample.**
11. To determine how often people eat out, every tenth person entering a fast-food restaurant is surveyed. **This is a biased sample, since the people surveyed are eating out. This is a convenience sample.**

Practice: Word Problems, p. 477

NAME ____________ DATE ________ PERIOD ____

8-7 **Practice: Word Problems**
Using Sampling to Predict

FUND-RAISING **For Exercises 1 and 2, use the survey results in the table at the right. Members of the Drama Club plan to sell popcorn as a fund-raiser for their Shakespeare production. They survey 75 students at random about their favorite flavors of popcorn.**

Flavor	Number
butter	33
cheese	15
caramel	27

1. What percent of the students prefer caramel popcorn? **36%**
2. If the club orders 400 boxes of popcorn to sell, how many boxes of caramel popcorn should they order? Explain how you found your answer. **about 144 boxes; multiply the percent who prefer caramel found through the survey by the total number of boxes.**

DINING OUT **For Exercises 3 and 4, use the following information. As people leave a restaurant one evening, 20 people are surveyed at random. Eight people say they usually order dessert when they eat out.**

3. What percent of those surveyed say they usually order dessert when they eat out? **40%**
4. If 130 people dine at the restaurant tomorrow, how many would you expect to order dessert? **about 52 people**

RECREATION **For Exercises 5 and 6, use the table at the right which shows the responses of 50 people who expect to purchase a bicycle next year.**

Bicycle Type	Number
mountain	11
touring	8
comfort	9
juvenile	19
other	3

5. What percent of those planning to buy a bicycle next year think they will buy a mountain bike? **22%**
6. If Mike's Bike shop plans to order 1,200 bicycles to sell next year, how many mountain bikes should be ordered? **about 264 mountain bikes**

Vocabulary Assessment

- This alphabetical list of vocabulary terms in Chapter 8 includes a page reference where each term was introduced.
- A vocabulary review/test for Chapter 8 is available on p. 494 of the *Chapter 8 Resource Masters*.

Vocabulary PuzzleMaker

ELL The online Vocabulary PuzzleMaker improves students' mathematics vocabulary using four puzzle formats — crossword, scramble, word search using a word list, and word search using clues. Students can work on a computer screen or from a printed handout.

MindJogger Videoquizzes

ELL MindJogger Videoquizzes provide an alternative review of concepts presented in this chapter. Students work in teams in a game show format to gain points for correct answers. The questions are presented in three rounds.

Round 1 Concepts (5 questions)
Round 2 Skills (4 questions)
Round 3 Problem Solving (4 questions)

ExamView® Pro

Use the networkable ExamView® Pro Testmaker CD-ROM to:

- Create **multiple versions** of tests.
- Create **modified** tests for **inclusion** students with one mouse click.
- **Edit** existing questions and **add** your own questions.
- Build tests aligned with state standards using built-in **state curriculum correlations.**
- Change **English** tests to **Spanish** with one mouse click and vice versa.

CHAPTER 8 Study Guide and Review

Vocabulary and Concept Check

biased sample (p. 407)
combination (p. 388)
complementary events (p. 375)
compound events (p. 396)
convenience sample (p. 407)
dependent events (p. 397)
experimental probability (p. 400)
factorial (p. 385)
Fundamental Counting Principle (p. 381)
independent events (p. 396)
outcome (p. 374)
permutation (p. 384)
population (p. 406)
probability (p. 374)
random (p. 374)
sample (p. 406)
sample space (p. 374)
simple event (p. 374)
simple random sample (p. 406)
stratified random sample (p. 406)
systematic random sample (p. 406)
theoretical probability (p. 400)
tree diagram (p. 380)
unbiased sample (p. 406)
voluntary response sample (p. 407)

Choose the correct term to complete each sentence.

1. A list of all the possible outcomes is called the (sample space, event).
2. (Outcome, Probability) is the chance that an event will happen.
3. The Fundamental Counting Principle says that you can find the total number of outcomes by (multiplying, dividing).
4. A (combination, permutation) is an arrangement where order matters.
5. A (combination, compound event) consists of two or more simple events.
6. For (independent events, dependent events), the outcome of one does not affect the other.
7. (Theoretical probability, Experimental probability) is based on known characteristics or facts.
8. A (simple random sample, convenience sample) is a biased sample.

Lesson-by-Lesson Exercises and Examples

8-1 Probability of Simple Events (pp. 374–377) 9–14. See margin.

A bag contains 6 white, 7 blue, 11 red, and 1 black marbles. A marble is picked at random. Write each probability as a fraction, a decimal, and a percent.

9. P(white)
10. P(blue)
11. P(not blue)
12. P(white or blue)
13. P(red or blue)
14. P(yellow)
15. If a month is picked at random, what is the probability that the month will start with M? $\frac{1}{6}$

Example 1 **A box contains 4 green, 7 blue, and 9 red pens. Write the probability that a pen picked at random is green.**

There are 4 + 7 + 9 or 20 pens in the box.

$$P(\text{green}) = \frac{\text{green pens}}{\text{total number of pens}}$$

$$= \frac{4}{20} \text{ or } \frac{1}{5}$$ There are 4 green pens out of 20 pens.

The probability the pen is green is $\frac{1}{5}$.

msmath3.net/vocabulary_review

FOLDABLES Study Organizer

For more information about Foldables, see *Teaching Mathematics with Foldables.*

Have students look through the chapter to make sure they have included examples in their Foldables for each lesson or topic in the chapter.

Encourage students to refer to their Foldables while completing the Study Guide and Review and to use them in preparing for the Chapter Test.

8-2 Counting Outcomes (pp. 380–383)

A penny is tossed and a 4 sided number cube with sides of 1, 2, 3, and 4 is rolled.

16. Draw a tree diagram to show the possible outcomes.
17. Find the probability of getting a head and a 3. $\frac{1}{8}$
18. Find the probability of getting a tail and an odd number. $\frac{1}{4}$
19. Find the probability of getting a head and a number less than 4. $\frac{3}{8}$
20. **FOOD** A restaurant offers 15 main menu items, 5 salads, and 8 desserts. How many meals of a main menu item, a salad, and a dessert are there?

20. 600 meals

Example 2 BUSINESS A car manufacturer makes 8 different models in 12 different colors. They also offer standard or automatic transmission. How many choices does a customer have?

number of models	×	number of colors	×	number of transmissions	=	total number of cars
8	×	12	×	2	=	192

The customer can choose from 192 cars.

16. See Ch. 8 Answer Appendix.

8-3 Permutations (pp. 384–387)

Find each value.

21. $P(6, 1)$ **6**
22. $P(4, 4)$ **24**
23. $P(5, 3)$ **60**
24. $P(7, 2)$ **42**
25. $P(10, 3)$ **720**
26. $P(4, 1)$ **4**

27. **NUMBER THEORY** How many 3-digit whole numbers can you write using the digits 1, 2, 3, 4, 5, and 6 if no digit can be used twice? **120 numbers**

Example 3 Find $P(4, 2)$.

$P(4, 2)$ represents the number of permutations of 4 things taken 2 at a time.

$P(4, 2) = 4 \cdot 3$ or 12

8-4 Combinations (pp. 388–391)

Find each value.

28. $C(5, 5)$ **1**
29. $C(4, 3)$ **4**
30. $C(12, 2)$ **66**
31. $C(9, 5)$ **126**
32. $C(3, 1)$ **3**
33. $C(7, 2)$ **21**

34. **PETS** How many different pairs of puppies can be selected from a litter of 8? **28 pairs**

Example 4 Find $C(4, 2)$.

$C(4, 2)$ represents the number of combinations of 4 things taken 2 at a time.

$C(4, 2) = \frac{P(4, 2)}{2!}$ Definition of $C(4, 2)$

$= \frac{\overset{2}{\cancel{4}} \cdot 3}{\underset{1}{\cancel{2}} \cdot 1}$ or 6 $P(4, 2) = 4 \cdot 3$ and $2! = 2 \cdot 1$

Answers

9. $\frac{6}{25}$; 0.24; 24%
10. $\frac{7}{25}$; 0.28; 28%
11. $\frac{18}{25}$; 0.72; 72%
12. $\frac{13}{25}$; 0.52; 52%
13. $\frac{18}{25}$; 0.72; 72%
14. 0; 0; 0%

Answers

46. This is a biased sample, since only voluntary responses are used.
47. This is a biased sample, since only people leaving a concert are surveyed. This is a convenience sample.

Mixed Problem Solving
For mixed problem-solving practice, see page 655.

8-5 Probability of Compound Events (pp. 396–399) 35. $\frac{1}{12}$ 36. $\frac{1}{4}$ 37. $\frac{1}{6}$ 38. $\frac{1}{4}$

A number cube is rolled, and a penny is tossed. Find each probability.

35. P(2 and heads) 36. P(even and heads)
37. P(1 or 2 and tails) 38. P(odd and tails)
39. P(divisible by 3 and tails) $\frac{1}{6}$
40. P(less than 7 and heads) $\frac{1}{2}$
41. **GAMES** A card is picked from a standard deck of 52 cards and is not replaced. A second card is picked. What is the probability that both cards are red? $\frac{25}{102}$

Example 5 **A bag of marbles contains 7 white and 3 blue marbles. Once selected, the marble is not replaced. What is the probability of choosing 2 blue marbles?**

$P(\text{first marble is blue}) = \frac{3}{10}$

$P(\text{second marble is blue}) = \frac{2}{9}$

$P(\text{two blue marbles}) = \frac{3}{10} \cdot \frac{2}{9}$

$= \frac{6}{90} \text{ or } \frac{1}{15}$

8-6 Experimental Probability (pp. 400–403)

A spinner has four sections. Each section is a different color. In the last 30 spins, the pointer landed on red 5 times, blue 10 times, green 8 times, and yellow 7 times. Find each experimental probability.

42. P(red) $\frac{1}{6}$ 43. P(green) $\frac{4}{15}$
44. P(red or blue) $\frac{1}{2}$ 45. P(not yellow) $\frac{23}{30}$

Example 6 **In an experiment, 3 coins are tossed 50 times. Five times no tails were showing. Find the experimental probability of no tails.**

Since no tails were showing 5 out of the 50 tries, the experimental probability is $\frac{5}{50}$ or $\frac{1}{10}$.

8-7 Statistics: Using Sampling to Predict (pp. 406–409)

Station WXYZ is taking a survey to determine how many people would attend a rock festival. 46–47. See margin.

46. Describe the sample if the station asks listeners to call the station.
47. Describe the sample if the station asks people coming out of a rock concert.
48. If 12 out of 80 people surveyed said they would attend the festival, what percent said they would attend? 15%
49. Use the result in Exercise 48 to determine how many out of 800 people would be expected to attend the festival. about 120 people

Example 7 **In a survey, 25 out of 40 students in the school cafeteria preferred chocolate to white milk.**

a. **What percent preferred chocolate milk?**

$25 \div 40 = 0.625$

62.5% of the students prefer chocolate milk.

b. **How much chocolate milk should the school buy for 400 students?**

Find 62.5% of 400.

$0.625 \times 400 = 250$

About 250 cartons of chocolate milk should be ordered.

412 Chapter 8 Probability

Practice Test

Vocabulary and Concepts

1. **Write** a probability problem that involves dependent events. See margin.
2. **Describe** the difference between biased and unbiased samples. Biased samples are not representative of the entire population, while unbiased samples are representative.

Skills and Applications

In a bag, there are 12 red, 3 blue, and 5 green candies. One is picked at random. Write each probability as a fraction, a decimal, and a percent.

3. $P(\text{red})$ $\frac{3}{5}$; 0.6; 60%
4. $P(\text{no green})$ $\frac{3}{4}$; 0.75; 75%
5. $P(\text{red or green})$ $\frac{17}{20}$; 0.85; 85%

Find each value.

6. $C(10, 5)$ 252
7. $P(6, 3)$ 120
8. $P(5, 2)$ 20
9. $C(7, 4)$ 35
10. In how many ways can 6 students stand in a line? 720 ways
11. How many teams of 5 players can be chosen from 15 players? 3,003 teams

There are 4 blue, 3 red, and 2 white marbles in a bag. Once selected, the marble is not replaced. Find each probability.

12. $P(\text{2 blue})$ $\frac{1}{6}$
13. $P(\text{red, then white})$ $\frac{1}{12}$
14. $P(\text{white, then blue})$ $\frac{1}{9}$
15. Are these events in Exercises 12–14 dependent or independent? dependent
16. **FOOD** Students at West Middle School can purchase a box lunch to take on their field trip. They choose one item from each category. How many lunches can be ordered? 36 lunches

Sandwich	Fruit	Cookie
ham	apple	chocolate
roast beef	banana	oatmeal
tuna	orange	sugar
turkey		

Two coins are tossed 20 times. No tails were tossed 4 times, one tail was tossed 11 times, and 2 tails were tossed 5 times.

17. What is the experimental probability of no tails? $\frac{1}{5}$
18. Draw a tree diagram to show the outcomes of tossing two coins. See Ch. 8 Answer Appendix.
19. Use the tree diagram in Exercise 18 to find the theoretical probability of getting no tails when two coins are tossed. $\frac{1}{4}$

Standardized Test Practice

20. **MULTIPLE CHOICE** A school board wants to know if it has community support for a new school. How should they conduct a valid survey? C
    - (A) Ask parents at a school open house.
    - (B) Ask people at the Senior Center.
    - (C) Call every 50th number in the phone book.
    - (D) Ask people to call with their opinions.

msmath3.net/chapter_test

Practice Test

Assessment Options

Vocabulary Test A vocabulary review/test for Chapter 8 can be found on p. 494 of the *Chapter 8 Resource Masters.*

Chapter Tests There are six Chapter 8 Tests and an Extended Response Assessment task available in the *Chapter 8 Resource Masters.*

Chapter 8 Tests			
Form	**Type**	**Level**	**Pages**
1	MC	basic	481–482
2A	MC	average	483–484
2B	MC	average	485–486
2C	FR	average	487–488
2D	FR	average	489–490
3	FR	advanced	491–492

MC = multiple-choice questions
FR = free-response questions

Extended Response Assessment

Extended Response tasks for Chapter 8 can be found on p. 493 of the *Chapter 8 Resource Masters.* A sample scoring rubric for these tasks appears on p. A26.

Answer

1. Sample answer: There are 5 fiction and 5 nonfiction books on the shelf. One book is chosen at random and is not replaced. Then a second book is chosen at random. What is the probability that both books are fiction? $\frac{2}{9}$

Portfolio Suggestion

Introduction Probability is used in weather forecasting. Since forecasters must predict future events, they have to make predictions based on data from instruments and on past activity.

Ask Students to find other careers that use probability. They may ask family members or neighbors for ideas. Have them include descriptions of how probability is used in different careers.

CHAPTER 8

Standardized Test Practice

These two pages contain practice questions in the various formats that can be found on the most frequently given standardized tests.

A student recording sheet for these two pages can be found on page A1 of the *Chapter 8 Resource Masters.*

Standardized Test Practice Student Recording Sheet, p. A1

NAME ____________ DATE ________ PERIOD ____

CHAPTER 8 **Standardized Test Practice** SCORE ____

Student Recording Sheet (Use with pages 414–415 of the Student Edition.)

Part 1: Multiple Choice

Select the best answer from the choices given and fill in the corresponding oval.

1. Ⓐ Ⓑ Ⓒ Ⓓ
4. Ⓕ Ⓖ Ⓗ Ⓘ
7. Ⓐ Ⓑ Ⓒ Ⓓ
2. Ⓕ Ⓖ Ⓗ Ⓘ
5. Ⓐ Ⓑ Ⓒ Ⓓ
3. Ⓐ Ⓑ Ⓒ Ⓓ
6. Ⓕ Ⓖ Ⓗ Ⓘ

Part 2: Short Response/Grid In

Solve the problem and write your answer in the blank.

8. ________
9. ________
10. ________
11. ________
12. ________
13. ________

Part 3: Extended Response

Record your answers for Questions 14 and 15 on the back of this paper.

Additional Practice

See pp. 499–500 of the *Chapter 8 Resource Masters* for additional standardized test practice.

CHAPTER 8

Standardized Test Practice

PART 1 Multiple Choice

Record your answers on the answer sheet provided by your teacher or on a sheet of paper.

1. Which of these would be the next number in the following pattern? (Lesson 1-1) **D**

   4, 12, 22, 34, …

   Ⓐ 40 Ⓑ 44
   Ⓒ 46 Ⓓ 48

2. Ms. Yeager asked the students in math class to tell one thing they did during the summer.

Activity	Number of Students
traveled with family	12
went to camp	6
worked on a summer job	10
other	2

   What fraction of the class said they went to camp or worked a summer job? (Lesson 2-1) **G**

   Ⓕ $\frac{2}{5}$ Ⓖ $\frac{8}{15}$
   Ⓗ $\frac{11}{15}$ Ⓘ $\frac{6}{5}$

3. Find the length of side FH. (Lesson 3-4) **B**

   Ⓐ 14 m
   Ⓑ 16 m
   Ⓒ 17 m
   Ⓓ 18 m

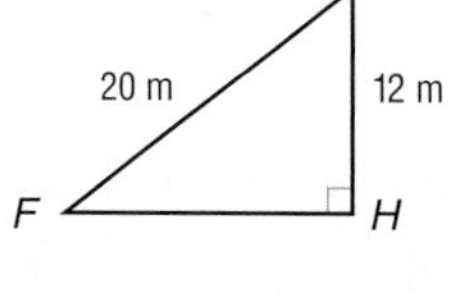

4. What is the area of the circle? (Lesson 7-2) **H**

   Ⓕ 540 in^2
   Ⓖ 907.5 in^2
   Ⓗ 1,017.9 in^2
   Ⓘ 1,105.1 in^2

18 in.

5. In the spinner below, what color should the blank portion of the spinner be so that the probability of landing on this color is $\frac{3}{8}$? (Lesson 8-1) **C**

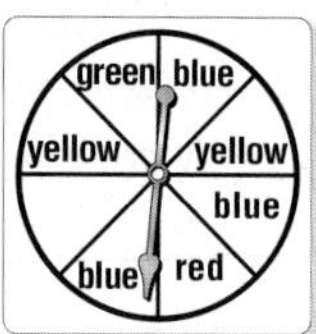

   Ⓐ red Ⓑ blue
   Ⓒ yellow Ⓓ green

6. Ed, Lauren, Sancho, James, Sofia, Tamara, and Haloke are running for president, vice-president, secretary, and recorder of the student council. Each of them would be happy to take any of the 4 positions, and none of them can take more than one position. How many ways can the offices be filled? (Lesson 8-3) **H**

   Ⓕ 28 Ⓖ 210
   Ⓗ 840 Ⓘ 2,520

7. Alonso surveyed people leaving a pizza parlor to determine whether people in his area like pizza. Explain why this might *not* have been a valid survey. (Lesson 8-7) **C**

   Ⓐ The survey is biased because Alonso should have asked people coming out of an ice cream parlor.
   Ⓑ Alonso should have mailed survey questionnaires to people.
   Ⓒ The survey is biased because Alonso was asking only people who had chosen to eat pizza.
   Ⓓ Alonso should have conducted the survey on a weekend.

ExamView® Pro

Special banks of standardized test questions similar to those on the TIMSS and NAEP grade 8 tests can be found on this CD-ROM.

Preparing for Standardized Tests
For test-taking strategies and more practice, see pages 660–677.

PART 2 Short Response/Grid In

Record your answers on the answer sheet provided by your teacher or on a sheet of paper.

8. The first super computer, the Cray-1, was installed in 1976. It was able to perform 160 million different operations in a second. Use scientific notation to represent the number of operations the Cray-1 could perform in one day. (Lesson 2-9) **1.3824×10^{13}**

9. What is the value of x if x is a whole number? (Lesson 5-5) **10 or 11**

$34\frac{1}{3}\%$ of $27 < x < 75\%$ of 16

10. Find the coordinates of the fourth vertex of the parallelogram in Quadrant IV. (Lesson 6-4) **(1, −2)**

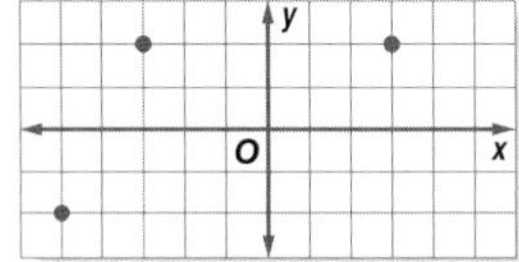

11. Ling knows the circumference of a circle and wants to find its radius. After she divides the circumference by π, what should she do next? (Lesson 7-2) **divide by 2**

12. The eighth-grade graduation party is being catered. The caterers offer 4 appetizers, 3 salads, and 2 main courses for each eighth-grade student to choose for dinner. If the caterers would like 48 different combinations of dinners, how many desserts should they offer? (Lesson 8-2) **2 desserts**

13. There are 15 glass containers of different flavored jellybeans in the candy store. If Jordan wants to try 4 different flavors, how many different combinations of flavors can he try? (Lesson 8-4) **1,365 combinations**

PART 3 Extended Response

Record your answers on a sheet of paper. Show your work.

14. A red number cube and a blue number cube are tossed. (Lesson 8-2) **b. See margin.**
   a. Make a tree diagram to show the outcomes. **See Ch. 8 Answer Appendix.**
   b. Use the Fundamental Counting Principle to determine the number of outcomes. What are the advantages of using the Fundamental Counting Principle? of using a tree diagram?
   c. What is the probability that the sum of the two number cubes is 8? **$\frac{5}{36}$**

15. Tiffany has a bag of 10 yellow, 10 red, and 10 green marbles. Tiffany picks two marbles at random and gives them to her sister. (Lesson 8-5)
   a. What is the probability of choosing 2 yellow marbles? **$\frac{3}{29}$**
   b. Of the marbles left, what is the probability of choosing a green marble next? **$\frac{5}{14}$**
   c. Of the marbles left, what color has a probability of $\frac{1}{3}$ of being picked? Explain how you determined your answer. **Green; see margin for explanation.**

TEST-TAKING TIP

Question 15 Extended response questions often involve several parts. When one part of the question involves the answer to a previous part of the question, make sure you check your answer to the first part before moving on. Also, remember to show all of your work. You may be able to get partial credit for your answers, even if they are not entirely correct.

msmath3.net/standardized_test

Standardized Test Practice

Rubrics The following rubrics are sample scoring devices for short response and extended response questions.

Short Response

Points	Description
2	The student demonstrates a <u>thorough understanding</u> of the mathematics of the task. The response may contain minor flaws that do not detract from the demonstration of a thorough understanding.
1	The student has provided a response that is only <u>partially correct</u>.
0	The student has provided a <u>completely incorrect</u> solution or no response at all.

Extended Response

Points	Description
4	The student demonstrates a <u>thorough understanding</u> of the mathematics of the task. The response may contain minor flaws that do not detract from the demonstration of a thorough understanding.
3	The student demonstrates an <u>understanding</u> of the mathematics of the task. The response is essentially correct and demonstrates an essential but less than thorough understanding of the mathematics.
2	The student demonstrates only a <u>partial understanding</u> of the mathematics of the task. Although the student may have used the correct approach to a solution or may have provided a correct solution, the work lacks an essential understanding of the underlying mathematical concepts.
1	The student demonstrates a <u>very limited understanding</u> of the mathematics of the task. The response is incomplete and exhibits many flaws.
0	The student provides a <u>completely incorrect</u> solution or no response at all.

A more detailed 4-point rubric is provided on page A2 of the *Chapter 8 Resource Masters*.

Answers

14b. $6 \cdot 6 = 36$; The Counting Principle is faster. The tree diagram gives all of the outcomes, not just how many outcomes.

15c. Two yellow marbles and one green marble have been removed. Therefore, the bag now contains 8 yellow, 10 red, and 9 green marbles. The total number of marbles is $8 + 10 + 9$ or 27. Since $\frac{9}{27} = \frac{1}{3}$, the probability of picking a green marble is $\frac{1}{3}$.

Page 377, Lesson 8-1

33. The measurement is to the nearest centimeter. There is 1 significant digit. The greatest possible error is 0.5 cm, and the relative error is $\frac{0.5}{8}$ or about 0.063.

34. The measurement is to the nearest 0.01 kg. There are 2 significant digits. The greatest possible error is 0.005 kg, and the relative error is $\frac{0.005}{0.36}$ or about 0.014.

35. The measurement is to the nearest 0.01 m. There are 3 significant digits. The greatest possible error is 0.005 m, and the relative error is $\frac{0.005}{4.83}$ or about 0.0010.

36. The measure is to the nearest 10 cm. There are 2 significant digits. The greatest possible error is 5 cm, and the relative error is $\frac{5}{410}$ or about 0.012.

Page 382, Lesson 8-2

4.

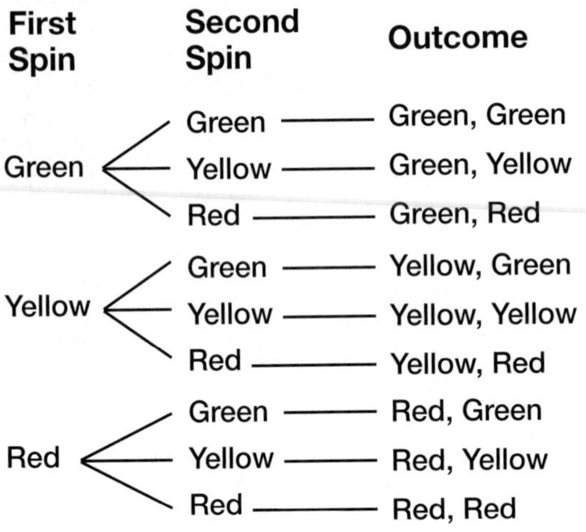

First Spin	Second Spin	Outcome
Green	Green	Green, Green
	Yellow	Green, Yellow
	Red	Green, Red
Yellow	Green	Yellow, Green
	Yellow	Yellow, Yellow
	Red	Yellow, Red
Red	Green	Red, Green
	Yellow	Red, Yellow
	Red	Red, Red

9.

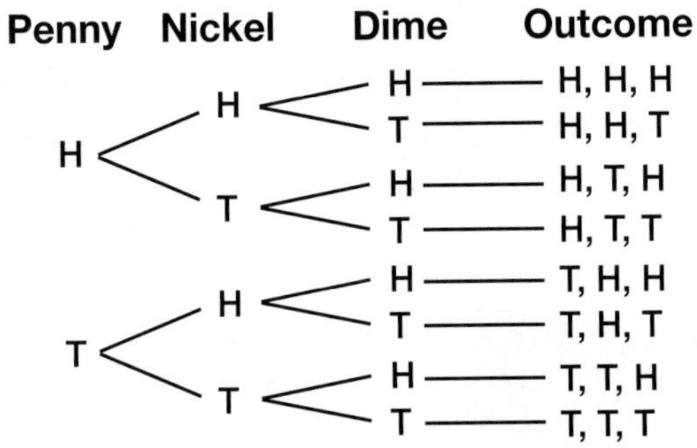

Penny	Nickel	Dime	Outcome
H	H	H	H, H, H
		T	H, H, T
	T	H	H, T, H
		T	H, T, T
T	H	H	T, H, H
		T	T, H, T
	T	H	T, T, H
		T	T, T, T

H = Heads

T = Tails

10.

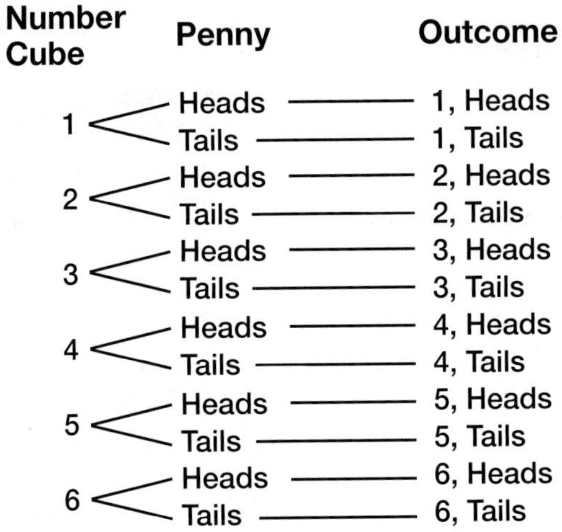

Number Cube	Penny	Outcome
1	Heads	1, Heads
	Tails	1, Tails
2	Heads	2, Heads
	Tails	2, Tails
3	Heads	3, Heads
	Tails	3, Tails
4	Heads	4, Heads
	Tails	4, Tails
5	Heads	5, Heads
	Tails	5, Tails
6	Heads	6, Heads
	Tails	6, Tails

11.

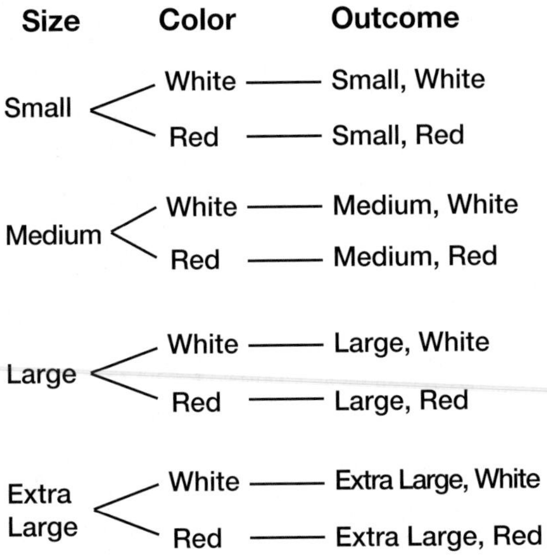

Size	Color	Outcome
Small	White	Small, White
	Red	Small, Red
Medium	White	Medium, White
	Red	Medium, Red
Large	White	Large, White
	Red	Large, Red
Extra Large	White	Extra Large, White
	Red	Extra Large, Red

12.

Flavor	Cone	Outcome
Chocolate	Regular	Chocolate, Regular
	Sugar	Chocolate, Sugar
Vanilla	Regular	Vanilla, Regular
	Sugar	Vanilla, Sugar
Strawberry	Regular	Strawberry, Regular
	Sugar	Strawberry, Sugar

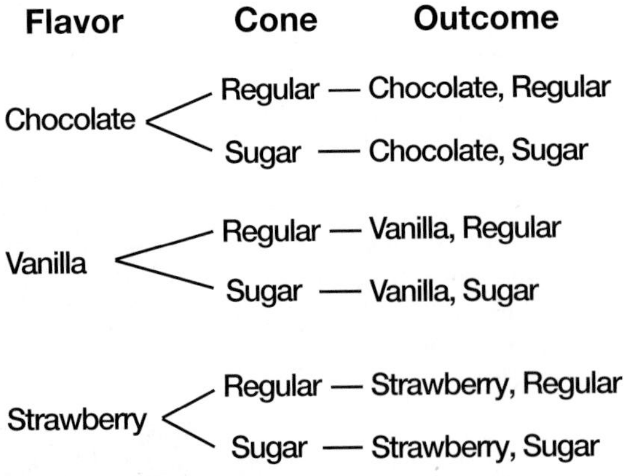

Page 382, Lesson 8-2

17.

First Spinner	Second Spinner	Outcome
Green	Red	Green, Red
	Blue	Green, Blue
	White	Green, White
Blue	Red	Blue, Red
	Blue	Blue, Blue
	White	Blue, White
Yellow	Red	Yellow, Red
	Blue	Yellow, Blue
	White	Yellow, White
Red	Red	Red, Red
	Blue	Red, Blue
	White	Red, White

Page 392, Lesson 8-4b

3. no heads: 1 outcome, one head: 4 outcomes, two heads: 6 outcomes, three heads: 4 outcomes, four heads: 1 outcome

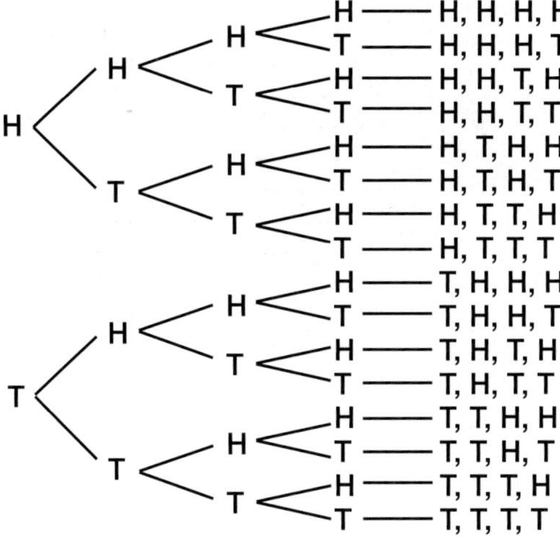

H = Heads

T = Tails

Page 394, Mid-Chapter Practice Test

9.

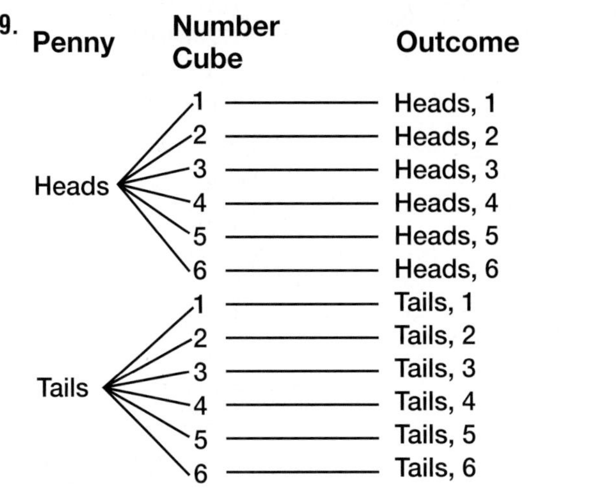

Page 396, Lesson 8-5 (When am I ever going to use this?)

4.

Number Cube	Spinner	Outcome
1	Red	1, Red
	Green	1, Green
	Blue	1, Blue
2	Red	2, Red
	Green	2, Green
	Blue	2, Blue
3	Red	3, Red
	Green	3, Green
	Blue	3, Blue
4	Red	4, Red
	Green	4, Green
	Blue	4, Blue
5	Red	5, Red
	Green	5, Green
	Blue	5, Blue
6	Red	6, Red
	Green	6, Green
	Blue	6, Blue

Page 409, Lesson 8-7

21. Sample answer: If the questions are not asked in a neutral manner, the people may not give their true opinion. For example, the question "You really don't like Brand X, do you?" might not get the same answer as the question "Do you prefer Brand X or Brand Y?" Also, the question "Why would anyone like rock music?" might not get the same answer as the question "What do you think about rock music?"

Page 411, Study Guide and Review

16.

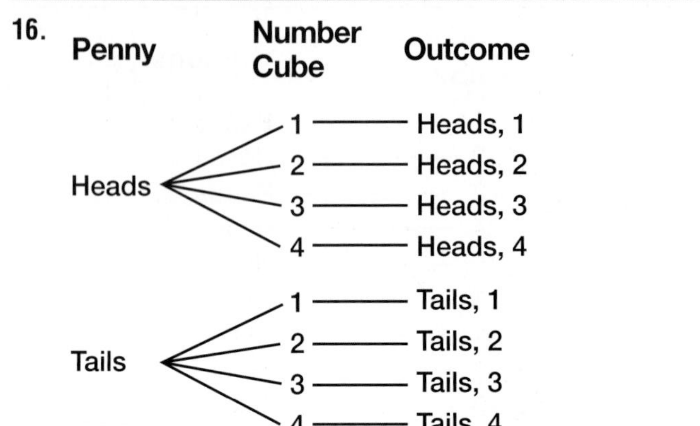

Page 413, Practice Test

18.

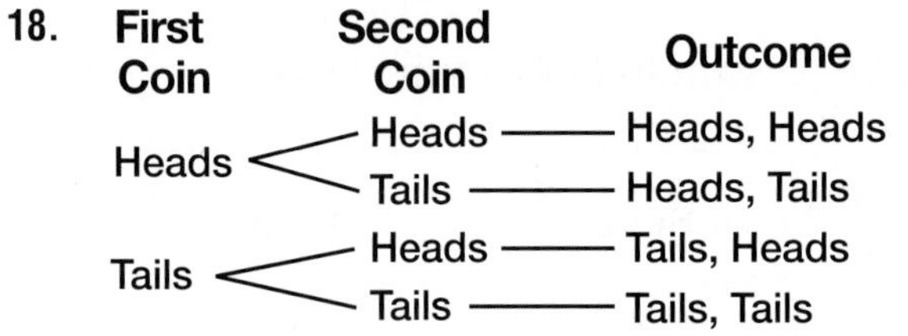

Page 415, Standardized Test Practice

14a.

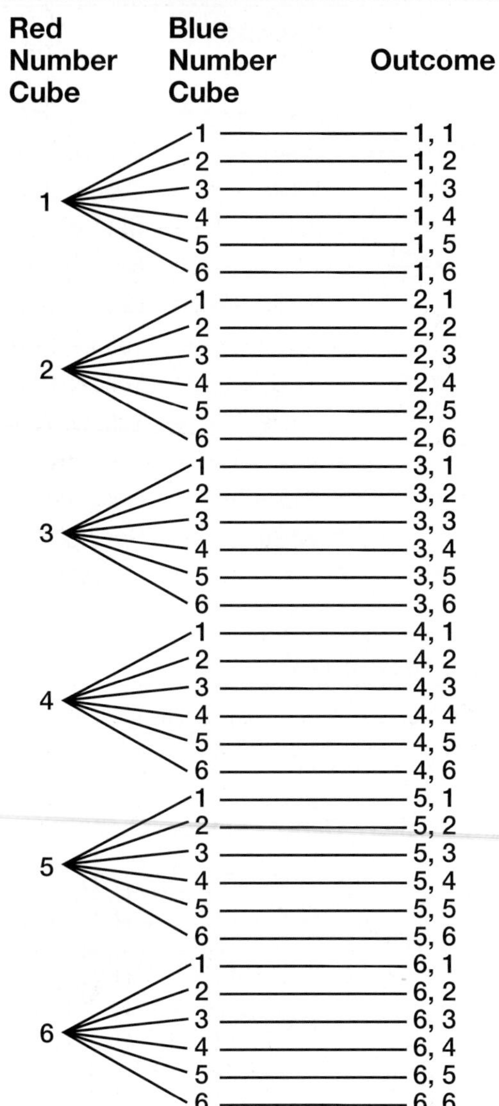

NOTES

CHAPTER 9

Chapter Overview

Statistics and Matrices

LESSON OBJECTIVES	NCTM Standards	NAEP 2005	State/Local Objectives
9-1 **Histograms** (pp. 418–425) **9-1a Problem-Solving Strategy:** Solve problems using the make a table strategy. • Construct and interpret histograms. **9-1b Graphing Calculator Investigation:** Use a graphing calculator to make histograms.	1, 2, 4, 5, 6, 7, 10	D1a, D1b, D1c, D1d, D1e	
9-2 **Circle Graphs** (pp. 426–429) • Construct and interpret circle graphs.	1, 2, 4, 5, 6, 7, 10	D1a, D1b, M1g, N1e, N3a, D1e	
9-3 **Choosing an Appropriate Display** (pp. 430–434) • Choose an appropriate display for a set of data. **9-3b Hands-On Lab:** Show statistics on maps.	1, 2, 4, 5, 6, 7, 10	D1a, D1d, D1e	
9-4 **Measures of Central Tendency** (pp. 435–439) • Find the mean, median, and mode of a set of data. **9-4b Spreadsheet Investigation:** Use a spreadsheet to find mean, median, and mode.	1, 2, 4, 5, 6, 7, 10	D2a, D2b, D2c, D2d	
9-5 **Measures of Variation** (pp. 442–445) • Find the range and quartiles of a set of data.	1, 2, 4, 5, 6, 7, 10	D1a, D1c, D2a, D2b, D2c	
9-6 **Box-and-Whisker Plots** (pp. 446–449) • Display and interpret data in a box-and-whisker plot.	1, 2, 4, 5, 6, 7, 10	D1a, D2a, D1c	
9-7 **Misleading Graphs and Statistics** (pp. 450–453) • Recognize when graphs and statistics are misleading.	1, 2, 4, 5, 6, 7, 10	D1a, D1d, D1e, D2a, D1b	
9-8 **Matrices** (pp. 454–457) • Use matrices to organize data.	1, 2, 4, 5, 6, 7, 10	D1a	

Key to NCTM Standards:

1=Number & Operations, 2=Algebra, 3=Geometry, 4=Measurement, 5=Data Analysis & Probability, 6=Problem Solving, 7=Reasoning & Proof, 8=Communication, 9=Connections, 10=Representation

NAEP 2005 Standards: See Teacher Resources at math.glencoe.com

Pacing suggestions for the entire year can be found on page T23.

*An electronic version of this chapter is available on **StudentWorks**[TM]. This backpack solution CD-ROM allows students instant access to the Student Edition, lesson worksheet pages, and web resources.*

Chapter Resource Manager

Chapter 9 Resource Masters

Study Guide and Intervention	Practice (Skills and Word Problems)	Reading to Learn Mathematics	Enrichment	Assessment	Applications*	Parent and Student Study Guide Online Worksheets	5-Minute Check Transparencies	Key Teaching Transparencies	MathPASS: Tutorial Plus (lessons)	Teaching Mathematics with Manipulatives	Noteables™: Interactive Study Notebook	Optional Materials
501	502–503	504	505		CS 39	9-1	9-1				9-1	graphing calculator
506	507–508	509	510	555		9-2	9-2	34		99, 100	9-2	
511	512–513	514	515			9-3	9-3	35		101	9-3	outline map of USA, colored pencils
516	517–518	519	520	555, 557	RC 35, CS 40 SM 81–84, 85–88	9-4	9-4	36			9-4	
521	522–523	524	525			9-5	9-5	37			9-5	
526	527–528	529	530	556	CM 33–34 CS 41	9-6	9-6		42		9-6	
531	532–533	534	535			9-7	9-7		43		9-7	
536	537–538	539	540	541–554, 556, 558–562	CS 42	9-8	9-8	38			9-8	

*** Key to Abbreviations:** *CS = Calculator and Spreadsheet Masters, RC = Real-Life Career Masters, CM = Classroom Math Games (online), SM = Science and Math Lab Manual (online)*

PowerPoint® Presentations

This CD-ROM is a customizable Microsoft® PowerPoint® presentation that includes:

- In-Class Examples
- Links to Online Study Tools
- 5-Minute Check Transparencies
- Your Turn Exercises

Math Skills Maintenance

Use the Math Skills Maintenance Masters to keep your students' basic math skills fresh. Students can review skills one at a time or in a combined format. The Masters are also available online at msmath3.net/maintenance.

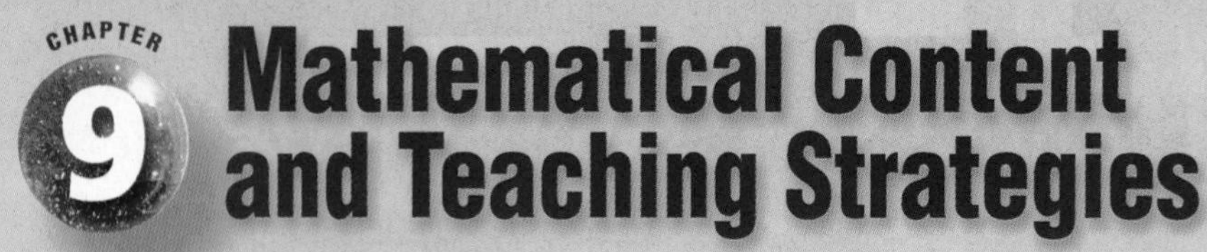

Chapter 9 Mathematical Content and Teaching Strategies

Continuity of Instruction

Building on Prior Knowledge

Students have learned about frequency tables and other types of data tables in previous courses. They understand how to make tally charts and how to use the data to create simple graphs. Students have had an introduction to the concepts of central tendency, such as mean, median, and mode.

Learning in This Chapter

This chapter begins with an introduction to histograms. Students learn to choose an appropriate display, depending on the type of data. They explore how mean, median, mode, and quartiles show trends in the data. Students compare different graphs to discover how certain graphing techniques can present data in a misleading way. In the last section, students are introduced to the addition and subtraction of matrices.

Making Future Connections

Students will benefit from the graphing skills they learn in this course by applying them in everyday life. Bar graphs, histograms, and circle graphs are common methods used to convey information in newspapers, magazines, and workplace documents. The statistical concepts students learn are often used to describe trends in figures such as test scores or company sales and manufacturing data. In algebra courses, students will learn more about matrices and how they can be applied to solve systems of equations.

Mathematical Background

9-1 Histograms

In this lesson, students apply previous knowledge of bar graphs and frequency tables to make and interpret histograms, a special type of bar graph with data organized into equal intervals. Histograms will be one choice available to students in Lesson 9-3 as they choose an appropriate display for data. In Lesson 9-7, students will learn how to recognize when histograms and other statistics can be misleading.

9-2 Circle Graphs

In Chapter 5, students learned about percent. In Chapters 6 and 7, they learned about angles and circles. They will apply these skills in this lesson to make and interpret circle graphs. Watch that students accurately translate data to percents and to the angles of a circle, and that data are mutually exclusive and represent 100 percent when totaled.

Team Teaching

Inform the other teachers on your team that your students are studying circle graphs.

Suggestions for curriculum integration are:

Geography: population distribution

Earth Science: land resources

Health: distribution of Calories in a healthful diet

Physical Science: composition of a chemical solution

9-3 Choosing an Appropriate Display

Prior to this lesson, students have learned to create various types of graphs and data displays. They explore the advantages and disadvantages of a particular type of display for particular types of situations. Depending upon what students wish to show about a set of data, they may choose different data displays.

In-Class Speaker
Ask a representative from an advertising firm to speak to the class about how statistics are used and displayed in advertising. If possible, have the representative bring brochures that show different data displays.

9-4 Measures of Central Tendency

In this lesson, students learn to find the mean, median, and mode. Be sure students understand when it is most useful to use each measure. This concept will be important in Lesson 9-7, when they will learn how measures of central tendency can be used to mislead.

9-5 Measures of Variation

In this lesson, students will divide data into quartiles and learn to find the range and interquartile range of the data. Such measures of variation describe how data are distributed throughout the set.

9-6 Box-and-Whisker Plots

Students learn how to display measures of variation visually in this lesson. By plotting the median, quartiles, extremes, and any outliers above a number line, students can create box-and-whisker plots that will help them interpret the data.

9-7 Misleading Graphs and Statistics

Graphs and statistics are often used to persuade an audience to buy a particular product or vote a particular way. Students apply their knowledge of statistics and graphs to learn to spot such misleading tactics. Students should pay close attention to the scales when evaluating graphs.

Teacher to Teacher
Sherry Jarvis
Flat Rock Middle School
East Flat Rock, NC

"Have students find a misleading graph in a newspaper, magazine, or on the Internet. Ask them to explain why the graph is misleading, then redraw the graph to make it an accurate representation of the data."

Sherry Jarvis

9-8 Matrices

A matrix is a rectangular arrangement of numbers, similar to a table. Each item of data occupies one cell of a matrix. Matrices can be added, subtracted, and multiplied to solve problems involving large data sets. Students will learn more about matrices in future math courses, particularly linear algebra courses.

What the Research Says

According to Konold and Higgins in "Reasoning About Data," many students misuse the mode when the median or mean is more appropriate.

- **In Lesson 9-4, students learn how to choose the appropriate measure of central tendency to describe a set of data.**

McGraw-Hill Professional Development

Mathematics, YES! is a self-paced, web-based professional development program. Units are based on major mathematical concepts and are standards-based. Actual classroom videos provide a springboard for discussion and activities. Unit appropriate for this chapter:

- **Statistics, Data Analysis, and Probability**

Additional mathematical information and teaching notes are available at msmath3.net/key_concepts.

DAILY INTERVENTION and Assessment

* Key to Abbreviations:
TWE = Teacher Wraparound Edition, *CRM* = Chapter Resource Masters

	Type	Student Edition	Teacher Resources	Technology/Internet
INTERVENTION	Ongoing	Prerequisite Skills, pp. 417, 424, 429, 433, 438, 445, 449, 453 Mid-Chapter Practice Test, p. 440	5-Minute Check Transparencies Quizzes 1–4, *CRM*, pp. 555–556 Mid-Chapter Test, *CRM*, p. 557 Study Guide and Intervention, *CRM*, pp. 501, 506, 511, 516, 521, 526, 531, 536	MathPASS: Tutorial Plus msmath3.net/self_check_quiz msmath3.net/extra_examples
	Mixed Review	pp. 424, 429, 433, 438, 445, 449, 453, 457	Cumulative Review, *CRM*, p. 558	
	Error Analysis	Find the Error, pp. 437, 448	Find the Error, *TWE*, pp. 437, 448 Unlocking Misconceptions, *TWE*, pp. 421, 454 Tips for New Teachers, *TWE*, pp. 444, 446	
ASSESSMENT	Standardized Test Practice	pp. 419, 424, 429, 433, 438, 440, 445, 447, 449, 453, 457, 461, 462–463	Standardized Test Practice, *CRM*, pp. 559–560	Standardized Test Practice CD-ROM msmath3.net/standardized_test
	Open-Ended Assessment	Writing Math, pp. 428, 432, 434, 437, 448, 451 Open-Ended, pp. 422, 428, 432, 437, 444, 448, 451, 456 Standardized Test, p. 463	Modeling: *TWE*, pp. 429, 453 Speaking: *TWE*, pp. 424, 449 Writing: *TWE*, pp. 419, 437 Extended Response Assessment, *CRM*, p. 553	
	Chapter Assessment	Study Guide, pp. 458–460 Practice Test, p. 461	Multiple-Choice Tests (Forms 1, 2A, 2B), *CRM*, pp. 541–546 Free-Response Tests (Forms 2C, 2D, 3), *CRM*, pp. 547–552 Vocabulary Test/Review, *CRM*, p. 554	ExamView® Pro Testmaker (see below) MindJogger Videoquizzes msmath3.net/vocabulary_review msmath3.net/chapter_test

For more information on Yearly ProgressPro, see p. 370.

Glencoe Lesson	Yearly ProgressPro Skill Name
9-1	Histograms: Level 1
9-2	Circle Graphs
9-3	Choosing an Appropriate Display
9-4	Mean: Level 2; Median: Level 2; Mode: Level 2; Range: Level 2
9-5	Measures of Variation
9-6	Box-and-Whisker Plots
9-7	Misleading Statistics
9-8	Matrices

ExamView® Pro

Use ExamView® Pro Testmaker CD-ROM to:

- Create multiple versions of tests.
- Create modified tests for inclusion students with one mouse click.
- Edit existing questions and add your own questions.
- Build tests aligned with state standards using built-in state curriculum correlations.
- Change English tests to Spanish with one mouse click and vice versa.

Reading and Writing in Mathematics

READING in the Content Area

This online worksheet provides strategies for reading and analyzing Lesson 9-1, Histograms. Students are guided through questions about the main idea, subject matter, supporting details, conclusion, clarifying details, and vocabulary of the lesson.

Interactive Study Notebook With Foldables™ is a study organizer that provides helpful steps for students to follow to organize their notes for Chapter 9.

- Students use Noteables to record notes and to complete their Foldables as you present the material in Lessons 9-1 through 9-8.
- Noteables follow the *Teacher Wraparound Edition's* In-Class Examples and *Interactive Chalkboard CD-ROM.*

For more information on Reading and Writing in Mathematics, see pp. T6–T7.

Recommended Outside Reading for Students

Nonfiction

- Gonick, Larry, and Smith, Woollcott. *The Cartoon Guide to Statistics.* HarperCollins, ©1994.

  This book uses a story presented in a humorous cartoon strip format to engage students' interest in the subject of statistics. Topics are presented in the context of real-life problems that are related to statistical methods. This book explains, in an easygoing manner, topics that may otherwise seem very dry.

Fiction

- Southgate, Merrie Koester. *Agnes Pflumm and the Stonecreek Science Fair.* Showboard, Inc., ©1998.

  In this novel, seven students, guided by their teacher, Agnes Pflumm, collect data from science investigations and decide on the best way to display them.

PROJECT CRISS℠ Study Skill

Writing a one-sentence summary by using a frame can help students better understand newly introduced material. The completed frame shown at the right gives a short description of *mean*. Have students read through several lessons in Chapter 9 and write one-sentence summaries about the topics. Students may create a number of different types of one-sentence summary frames, such as compare/contrast, sequences, problem/solution, and cause/effect. You may wish to have students fill in one of the frames with what they know about a topic before they read the lesson. Then, have them review and revise the frame after completing the lesson.

A *mean* **is a kind of** measure of central tendency **found by dividing** the sum of the data by the number of items in the data set.

CReating Independence through Student-owned Strategies

For more information on Project CRISS, see p. T8.

Making Connections

School-To-Home

Parent and Student Study Guide

Parents and students may work together to reinforce the concepts and skills of this chapter. These online worksheets are available in English and Spanish at msmath3.net/parent_student. A sample lesson is shown below.

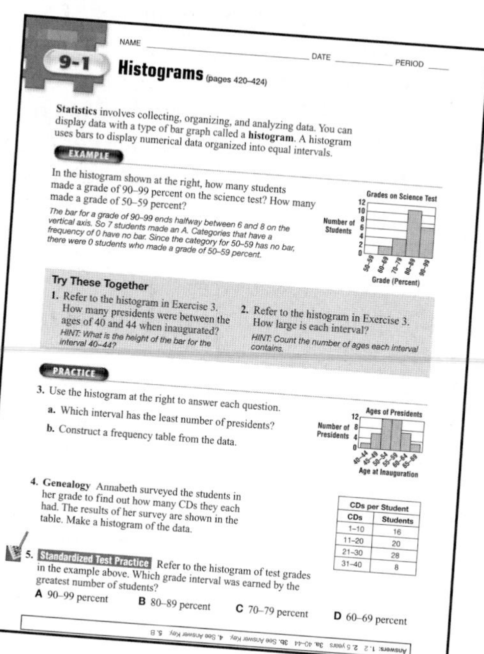

NAME ______ DATE ______ PERIOD ____

9-1 Histograms (pages 420–424)

Statistics involves collecting, organizing, and analyzing data. You can display data with a type of bar graph called a **histogram**. A histogram uses bars to display numerical data organized into equal intervals.

EXAMPLE

In the histogram shown at the right, how many students made a grade of 90–99 percent on the science test? How many made a grade of 50–59 percent?

The bar for a grade of 90–99 ends halfway between 6 and 8 on the vertical axis. So 7 students made an A. Categories that have a frequency of 0 have no bar. Since the category for 50–59 has no bar, there were 0 students who made a grade of 50–59 percent.

Try These Together

1. Refer to the histogram in Exercise 3. How many presidents were between the ages of 40 and 44 when inaugurated?
HINT: What is the height of the bar for the interval 40–44?

2. Refer to the histogram in Exercise 3. How large is each interval?
HINT: Count the number of ages each interval contains.

PRACTICE

3. Use the histogram at the right to answer each question.
   a. Which interval has the least number of presidents?
   b. Construct a frequency table from the data.

4. **Genealogy** Annabeth surveyed the students in her grade to find out how many CDs they each had. The results of her survey are shown in the table. Make a histogram of the data.

CDs per Student	
CDs	Students
1–10	16
11–20	20
21–30	28
31–40	8

5. **Standardized Test Practice** Refer to the histogram of test grades in the example above. Which grade interval was earned by the greatest number of students?
A 90–99 percent **B** 80–89 percent **C** 70–79 percent **D** 60–69 percent

Answers: 1. 2 2. 5 years 3a. 40–44 3b. See Answer Key. 4. See Answer Key. 5. B

Family Letters and Activities

Send a letter and activity for this chapter home to encourage family members to become active participants in their students' learning. (English: *Chapter 9 Resource Masters*, pp. ix–x; Spanish: log on to msmath3.net/family_letters)

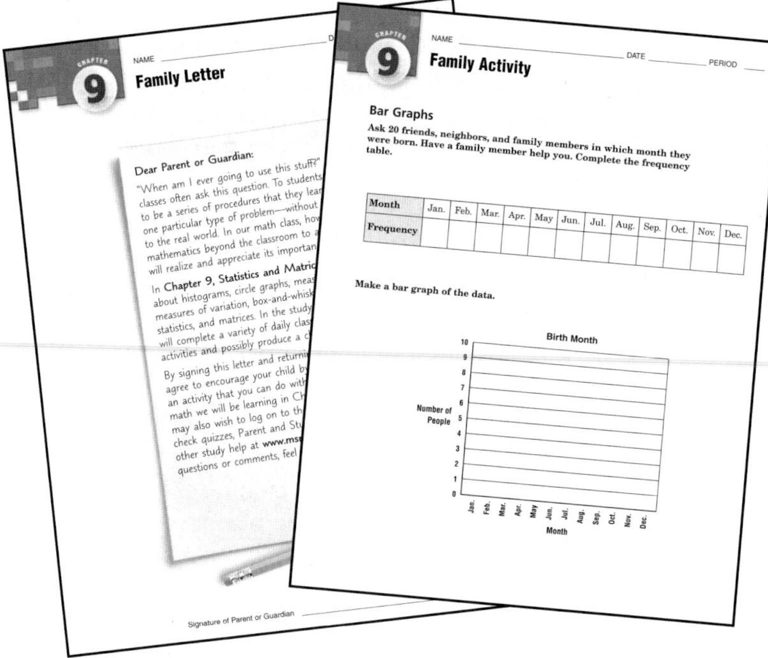

CHAPTER 9

NAME ______ D

Family Letter

Dear Parent or Guardian:

"When am I ever going to use this stuff?" ... classes often ask this question. To students ... to be a series of procedures that they lear ... one particular type of problem—without ... to the real world. In our math class, how ... mathematics beyond the classroom to a ... will realize and appreciate its importan...

In **Chapter 9, Statistics and Matric...** about histograms, circle graphs, meas... measures of variation, box-and-whisk... statistics, and matrices. In the study... will complete a variety of daily clas... activities and possibly produce a c...

By signing this letter and returni... agree to encourage your child by... an activity that you can do with... math we will be learning in Ch... may also wish to log on to th... check quizzes, Parent and Stu... other study help at **www.ms...** questions or comments, feel ...

Signature of Parent or Guardian ______

CHAPTER 9

NAME ______ DATE ______ PERIOD ____

Family Activity

Bar Graphs

Ask 20 friends, neighbors, and family members in which month they were born. Have a family member help you. Complete the frequency table.

Month	Jan.	Feb.	Mar.	Apr.	May	Jun.	Jul.	Aug.	Sep.	Oct.	Nov.	Dec.
Frequency												

Make a bar graph of the data.

English Language Learner ELL

Lesson 9-1

Reading and Writing

After completing the lesson, have students write similarities and differences between a bar graph and a histogram. Then have the students display these on a Venn diagram.

Lesson 9-3

Peer Tutoring

Give pairs of students index cards with different sets of real-world data copied from newspapers or magazines. Have them write how they would display the data for each situation.

Lesson 9-6

Flexible Groups

First have groups of students find the median and the quartiles of a set of data. Then, show students how they would use the data and measures they found to do a box-and-whisker plot. Have students use rulers and chart paper to construct a box-and-whisker plot.

MathScape™  This project was supported, in part, by the **National Science Foundation**

MathScape is a mathematics curriculum for grades 6–8 developed by the Seeing and Thinking Mathematically Project at the Education Development Center.

Correlations, Rankings, and Permutations
Looking Behind the Numbers

How to Use *MathScape* with Chapter 9

The unit *Looking Behind the Numbers* can be used to enhance Lessons 9-2 and 9-4.

- **Introduce** → Before you begin **Lesson 9-2,** you can introduce circle graphs by using the activities on pages 6–7.
- **Enrich** → After you complete **Lesson 9-4,** you can challenge students to apply their knowledge of mean, median, and mode to complete the activities on pages 8–13.

For other lessons in Chapter 9 that correlate to *MathScape*, see the chart on page T14.

Online Lesson Planner

USA TODAY® Education's Online site offers resources and interactive features connected to each day's newspaper. *Experience Today,* USA TODAY's® daily lesson plan, is available on the site and delivered daily to subscribers. This plan provides instruction for integrating USA TODAY® graphics and key editorial features into your mathematics classroom. Log on to **education.usatoday.com**.

USA TODAY Snapshots® in Chapter 9	
Lesson	**Snapshot**
9-2	Counties own the most roads
9-3	Online shoppers want a real store, too

Quick Review Math Handbook

is Glencoe's mathematical handbook for students. The Hot Words section includes a glossary of terms while the Hot Topics section consists of explanations of key mathematical concepts. An exercise set is included to check students' understanding of the concepts. This valuable resource can be used as a reference in the classroom or for home study.

Lesson	Hot Topics Section	Lesson	Hot Topics Section
9-1	4-2, 9-2	9-5	4-4
9-2	4-2	9-6	4-2
9-3	4-2, 4-3	9-7	4-1
9-4	4-2, 4-3, 4-4, 9-4	9-8	4-1, 4-2

Chapter 9 Notes

Key Chapter Objectives

Lessons 9-1 and 9-2 Construct and interpret histograms and circle graphs.

Lessons 9-4 and 9-5 Find the mean, median, mode, range, and quartiles of a set of data.

Lesson 9-7 Recognize when graphs and statistics are misleading.

Lesson 9-8 Use matrices to organize data.

"What does football have to do with math?"

Point out to students that this is only one of many applications of the math that they are studying. Others are provided in the introduction to each lesson.

Vocabulary Builder, pp. vii–viii — ELL

Chapter 9 NAME ______ DATE ______ PERIOD ______

Reading to Learn Mathematics

Vocabulary Builder

This is an alphabetical list of new vocabulary terms you will learn in Chapter 9. As you study the chapter, complete each term's definition or description. Remember to add the page number where you found the term. Add these pages to your math study notebook to review vocabulary at the end of the chapter.

Vocabulary Term	Found on Page	Definition/Description/Example
box-and-whisker plot		
circle graph		
column		
dimensions		
element		
histogram		
interquartile range		
lower quartile		
matrix (MAE-triks)		

Chapter 9 Statistics and Matrices

"What does football have to do with math?"

Many numbers, or data, are recorded during football games. These numbers include passing yards, running yards, interceptions, points scored, and distance of punts. These data can be represented by different types of graphs or by different measures of central tendency.

You will solve problems about football in Lesson 9-1.

416 Chapter 9 Statistics and Matrices

Vocabulary Builder

For a thorough vocabulary list with pronunciations of new words, give students the Vocabulary Builder worksheets from the *Chapter 9 Resource Masters*. Encourage them to complete the definition of each term as they progress through the chapter.

GETTING STARTED

▶ Diagnose Readiness

Take this quiz to see if you are ready to begin Chapter 9. Refer to the lesson or page number in parentheses for review.

Vocabulary Review 1. false; biased

State whether each sentence is *true* or *false*. If *false*, replace the underlined word or number to make a true sentence.

1. If one or more parts of a population are favored over others in a sample, then the sample is unbiased. (Lesson 8-7)
2. A line plot is a graph that uses an X above a number line to represent each number in a set of data. (Page 602) **true**

Prerequisite Skills

Graph each set of points on a number line. (Lesson 1-3) **3–6. See margin.**

3. {7, 8, 10, 15, 16}
4. {15, 20, 21, 25, 30}
5. {1, 4, 6, 10, 13}
6. {5, 7, 9, 13, 17}

Add or subtract. (Lessons 1-4 and 1-5)

7. $-4 + (-8)$ **−12**
8. $-5 + 2$ **−3**
9. $7 + (-3)$ **4**
10. $1 - (-5)$ **6**

Order each set of rational numbers from least to greatest. (Lesson 2-2)

11. 0.23, 2.03, 0.32 **0.23, 0.32, 2.03**
12. 5.4, 5.64, 5.46, 5.6 **5.4, 5.46, 5.6, 5.64**
13. 0.01, 1.01, 0.10, 1.10 **0.01, 0.10, 1.01, 1.10**

Solve each problem. (Lessons 5-3 and 5-6)

14. Find 52% of 360. **187.2**
15. What is 36% of 360? **129.6**
16. Find 14% of 360. **50.4**

Statistics and Matrices Make this Foldable to help you organize your notes. Begin with four pieces of $8\frac{1}{2}$" by 11" paper.

Stack Pages
Place 4 sheets of paper $\frac{3}{4}$ inch apart.

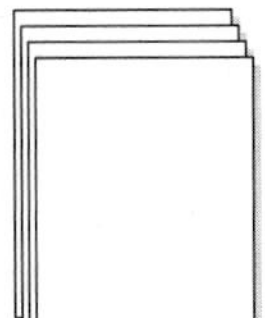

Roll Up Bottom Edges
All tabs should be the same size.

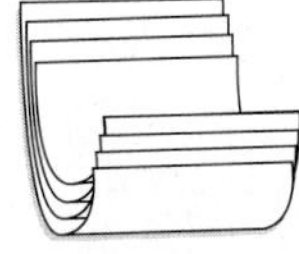

Crease and Staple
Staple along the fold.

Label
Label the tabs with topics from the chapter.

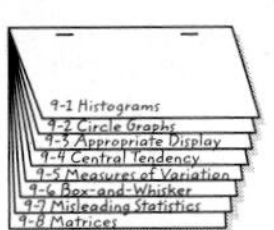

Chapter Notes Each time you find this logo throughout the chapter, use your *Noteables™: Interactive Study Notebook with Foldables™* or your own notebook to take notes. Begin your chapter notes with this Foldable activity.

Readiness To prepare yourself for this chapter with another quiz, visit **msmath3.net/chapter_readiness**

GETTING STARTED

Diagnose Readiness This section provides a review of the basic concepts needed before beginning Chapter 9. Page references are included for additional student help.

Prerequisite Skills review skills needed in this chapter.

Exercises	Needed for Lesson	Skill
3–6	9-6	Graph Points on a Number Line
7–10	9-8	Add or Subtract Integers
11–13	9-5	Order Rational Numbers
14–16	9-2	Solve Percent Problems

For more prerequisite skills, see:

- Getting Ready for the Next Lesson at the end of each lesson
- Prerequisite Skills in the Student Handbook on pp. 600–615
- *Math Skills Maintenance Masters*

Answers

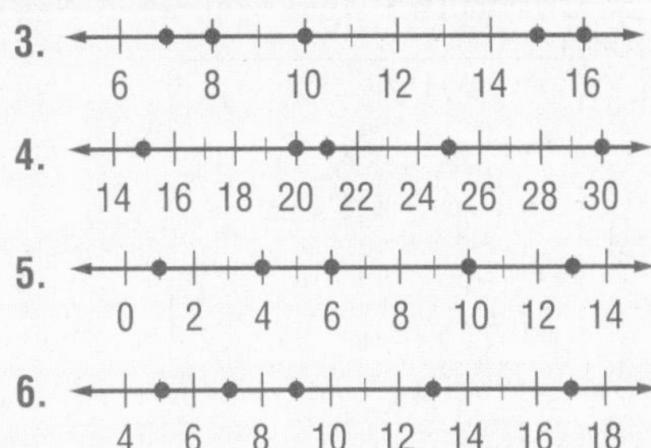

FOLDABLES™ Study Organizer

For more information about Foldables, see *Teaching Mathematics with Foldables.*

Use this Foldable for student writing about statistics. After students make their Foldables, have them label the tabs to correspond to the eight lessons in this chapter. Students use their Foldables to take notes, define terms, record concepts, and write examples. On the back of the Foldable, have students record examples of statistics they see in everyday print. Note how writers use statistics to prove or disprove points of view, and discuss the ethical responsibilities writers have when using statistics.

9-1a Lesson Notes

1 Focus

Bellringer

Hands-On Activity Have students take a class poll to determine favorite television shows. Before they start, have them write a list of step-by-step procedures they should follow when conducting the poll. Ask students how they could organize the results most efficiently.

2 Teach

In-Class Example

Solve. Use the make a table strategy.

The list shows the ages of 25 persons selected at random from the audience of a recent showing of a comedy movie. Make a frequency table of the ages using intervals 17–24, 25–32, 33–40, 41–48, and 49–56. What is the most common interval of attendance ages? **17–24**

26	42	22	26	24
21	27	35	28	18
19	25	46	31	29
17	56	19	41	23
38	20	21	25	22

Age (yr)	Tally	Frequency
17–24	𝍸 𝍸 I	11
25–32	𝍸 III	8
33–40	II	2
41–48	III	3
49–56	I	1

9-1a Problem-Solving Strategy

A Preview of Lesson 9-1

Make a Table

What You'll LEARN

Solve problems using the make a table strategy.

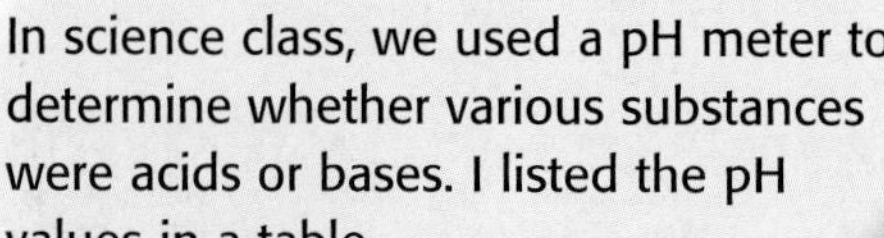

In science class, we used a pH meter to determine whether various substances were acids or bases. I listed the pH values in a table.

Substances with numbers less than 7 are acids, and substances with numbers greater than 7 are bases. Substances with the number 7 are neutral. How many acids, bases, and neutral substances did we test?

Explore We have a list of the numbers shown on the pH meter. We need to know how many substances have a pH number of less than 7, greater than 7, and equal to 7.

7	8	4	3
8	7	9	7
5	2	3	7
4	6	8	5
9	9	8	6

Plan Let's make a frequency table.

Solve

pH number	Tally	Frequency
Less than 7	𝍸 IIII	9
7	IIII	4
Greater than 7	𝍸 II	7

We tested 9 acids, 7 bases, and 4 neutral substances.

Examine The students tested 9 + 4 + 7 or 20 substances. Since there are 20 numbers listed, the table seems reasonable.

Analyze the Strategy

1. **Tell** an advantage and disadvantage of listing the values in a table. **1–3. See margin.**
2. **Describe** two types of information you have seen recorded in a table.
3. **Write** a problem that can be answered using a table.

DAILY INTERVENTION

Flexible Grouping

Make a Table Have students work in small groups to conduct a poll and make a table of the results. Students should begin by determining what question they want to answer, such as how many hours per week students study. Then they should decide on the type of poll and where they wish to conduct it. They may wish to poll students from other classes for the information. Have students analyze the results of their polls.

Apply the Strategy

Solve. Use the make a table strategy.

4. **FORESTS** What percent of the tree diameters below are from 4 to 9.9 inches? **about 73.9%**

Sample Tree Diameters from Cumberland National Forest		
Diameter (in.)	Tally	Frequency
2.0–3.9	𝍸 I	6
4.0–5.9	𝍸 𝍸 𝍸 𝍸 𝍸 𝍸	30
6.0–7.9	𝍸 𝍸 𝍸 𝍸 𝍸 III	28
8.0–9.9	𝍸 𝍸 𝍸 𝍸 IIII	24
10.0–11.9	𝍸 𝍸 𝍸 IIII	19
12.0–13.9	IIII	4

5. **ALLOWANCES** The list shows weekly allowances.

$2.50	$3.00	$3.75	$4.25	$4.25
$4.50	$4.75	$4.75	$5.00	$5.00
$5.00	$5.00	$5.50	$5.50	$5.75
$5.80	$6.00	$6.00	$6.00	$6.50
$6.75	$7.00	$8.50	$10.00	$10.00

a. Organize the data in a table using intervals $2.00–$2.99, $3.00–$3.99, $4.00–$4.99, and so on. **See margin.**

b. What is the most common interval of allowance amounts? **$5.00–$5.99**

Mixed Problem Solving

Solve. Use any strategy.

6. **MULTI STEP** The oldest magazine in the United States was first published in 1845. If 12 issues were published each year, how many issues would be published through 2005? **1,932 issues**

7. **SPORTS** In a recent survey of 120 students, 50 students said they play baseball, and 60 said they play soccer. If 20 play both sports, how many students do not play either baseball or soccer? **30 students**

8. **GEOGRAPHY** Name three countries that have a combined area of forests approximately equal to the area of forest in Russia. **Indonesia, Brazil, U.S.A.**

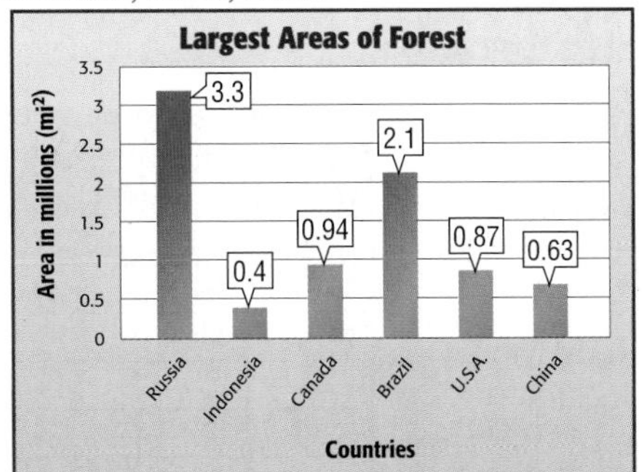

Source: *Top Ten Things*

9. **CARS** Dexter's brother wants to buy a used car. The list shows the model year of the cars listed in the classified ads. Which year is listed most frequently? **1999**

1998	2000	1999	1999	2001	2001
2002	1998	2000	2000	1997	2001
1998	1999	2001	2001	1999	2000
2000	1997	1999	1998	2002	1997
2000	1999	2000	2001	1999	1999

10. **BASKETBALL** The average salary of an NBA player is $4.5 million per season. The average salary of a WNBA player is $43,000 per season. About what percent of the NBA player's salary is the WNBA player's salary? **about 1%**

11. **STANDARDIZED TEST PRACTICE** What are the dimensions of the rectangle? **A**

Area = 24 m²

Perimeter = 22 m

Ⓐ 8 m by 3 m Ⓑ 6 m by 4 m
Ⓒ 12 m by 2 m Ⓓ 24 m by 1 m

3 Practice/Apply

About the Exercises...

Problem-Solving Strategies

Exercises 6–11 are structured so that students have the opportunity to practice many different problem-solving strategies. You may wish to remind them of some of the strategies they have studied.

- use the four-step plan (p. 6)
- use a Venn diagram (p. 123)
- reasonable answers (p. 226)
- make a table ✓

Answers

1. Sample answer: An advantage is that it organizes the data into classes; a disadvantage is that individual values of data are lost.
2. Sample answer: votes for candidates running for president, number of students in each grade in a school district
3. Sample answer: Pat is recording the color of cars as they pass his house. How many of each color car passed his house? red, green, black, red, red, green, white, red, white, black, green, red, white, black, red, blue, green, white, red, red, green, black, black, red, green

5a.

Allowances		
Amount	Tally	Frequency
$2.00–$2.99	I	1
$3.00–$3.99	II	2
$4.00–$4.99	𝍸	5
$5.00–$5.99	𝍸 III	8
$6.00–$6.99	𝍸	5
$7.00–$7.99	I	1
$8.00–$8.99	I	1
$9.00–$9.99		0
$10.00–$10.99	II	2

4 Assess

Open-Ended Assessment

Writing Have students list several types of data that could be recorded in a frequency table, and several types of data for which a frequency table would not be suitable. Have them explain their choices.

TEACHING TIP

Extending the Lesson In a frequency table, ***cumulative frequencies*** are the sums of all preceding frequencies. The ***relative frequency*** of a category in a frequency table is the fraction of the data that falls in that class.

9-1 Lesson Notes

Lesson Resources

Chapter 9 Resource Masters
- Study Guide and Intervention, p. 501
- Practice: Skills, p. 502
- Practice: Word Problems, p. 503
- Reading to Learn Mathematics, p. 504
- Enrichment, p. 505

Calculator and Spreadsheet Masters, p. 39

Parent and Student Study Guide Online Worksheets, 9-1

Noteables™: Interactive Study Notebook with Foldables™, 9-1

FAST FILE

1 Focus

5-Minute Check 9-1

Use as a quiz or review of Chapter 8. (Also available as a transparency)

Bellringer

Communication Show students the tables below. Ask students to compare the tables. Discuss the intervals used in each table. Make sure students understand that one table has even intervals and the other does not.

Students' Eye Colors	
blue	5
brown	11
green	4

(Continued in bottom margin.)

Weekly Television Viewing		
Number of Hours	Tally	Frequency
0–2	𝍸	5
3–5	𝍸 IIII	9
6–8	𝍸 III	8

Reading to Learn Mathematics, p. 504 ELL

NAME ______ DATE ______ PERIOD ____

9-1 Reading to Learn Mathematics
Histograms

Pre-Activity *Read the introduction at the top of page 420 in your textbook. Write your answers below.*

1. What do you notice about the price intervals? **The intervals are equal.**
2. What does each tally mark represent? **one concert**
3. How is the frequency for each price range determined? **by counting the tallies**

Reading the Lesson

4. Explain the difference between a bar graph and a histogram. **A histogram is a type of bar graph with the data organized into equal intervals and with no spaces between bars.**
5. What does a histogram display? **Sample answer: numerical data that have been organized into equal intervals**

9-1 Histograms

What You'll LEARN

Construct and interpret histograms.

NEW Vocabulary

histogram

REVIEW Vocabulary

bar graph: a graphic form using bars to make comparisons of statistics (page 602)

TEACHING TIP

Point out that histograms are useful for showing large data sets.

WHEN am I ever going to use this?

CONCERTS The table shows the number of concerts with an average ticket price in each price range.

Average Ticket Prices of Top 20 Money Earning Concerts		
Price	Tally	Frequency
$25.00–$49.99	𝍸 IIII	9
$50.00–$74.99	𝍸 II	7
$75.00–$99.99	I	1
$100.00–$124.99	II	2
$125.00–$149.99		0
$150.00–$174.99	I	1

Source: Pollstar

1. What do you notice about the price intervals?
2. What does each tally mark represent? **one concert**
3. How is the frequency for each price range determined? **by counting the tallies**

1. The intervals are equal.

Data from a frequency table, such as the one above, can be displayed as a histogram. A **histogram** is a type of bar graph used to display numerical data that have been organized into equal intervals.

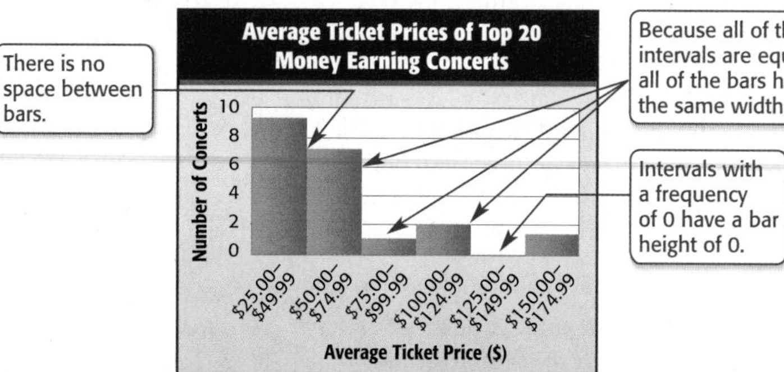

READING in the Content Area

For strategies in reading this lesson, visit **msmath3.net/reading.**

EXAMPLE Draw a Histogram

1 FOOD The frequency table at the right shows the number of Calories in certain soup-in-a-cup products. Draw a histogram to represent the data.

Calories of Soup-in-a-Cup		
Calories	Tally	Frequency
100–149	II	2
150–199	𝍸 II	7
200–249	𝍸 III	8
250–299	I	1
300–349	I	1
350–399	I	1

Step 1 Draw and label a horizontal and vertical axis. Include a title.

NCLB *No Child Left Behind*

The goals of the NCLB Act include a stronger emphasis on reading. The **Reading in the Content Area** link helps students become proficient readers.

Step 2 Show the intervals from the frequency table on the horizontal axis.

Step 3 For each Calorie interval, draw a bar whose height is given by the frequencies.

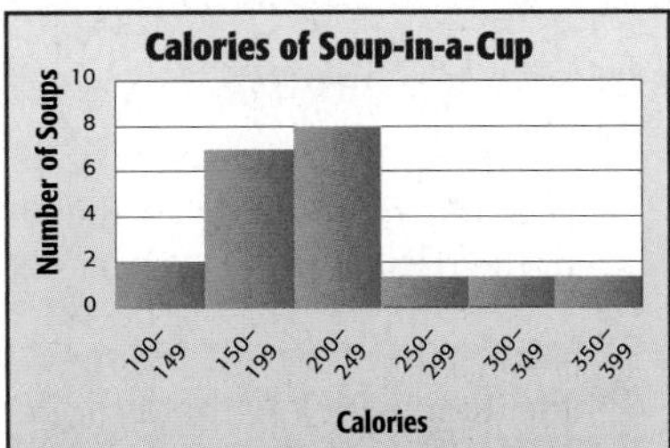

EXAMPLE Interpret Data

2 HISTORY How many presidents were younger than 50 when they were first inaugurated?

Two presidents were 40–44 years old, and six presidents were 45–49 years old. Therefore, 2 + 6 or 8 presidents were younger than 50 when they were first inaugurated.

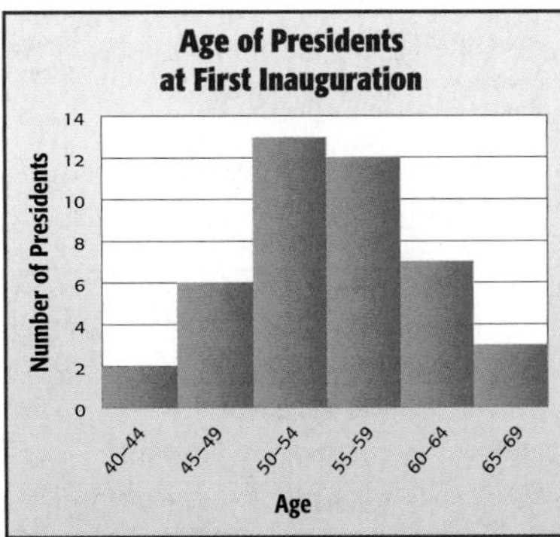

Source: *The World Almanac*

READING Math

At Least Recall that at least means *greater than or equal to.*

EXAMPLE Compare Two Sets of Data

3 FOOTBALL Determine which bowl game below has had a winning team score of at least 40 points more often.

Scores of Winning Teams through 2002

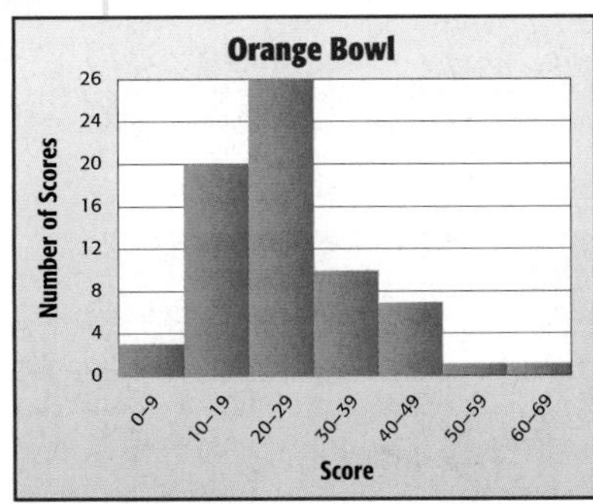

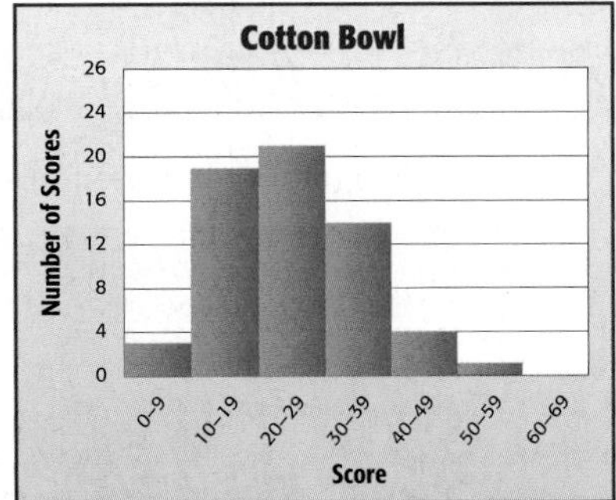

Source: *The World Almanac*

In the Orange Bowl, 7 + 1 + 1 or 9 winning teams scored at least 40 points. In the Cotton Bowl, 4 + 1 + 0 or 5 winning teams scored at least 40 points. The winning teams in the Orange Bowl scored 40 points more often than the winning teams in the Cotton Bowl.

TEACHING TIP

When comparing two histograms, encourage students to first check to make sure the scales and intervals are the same.

msmath3.net/extra_examples

2 Teach

In-Class Examples

1 FOOD The frequency table below shows the amount of caffeine in certain types of tea. Draw a histogram to represent the data.

Caffeine Content of Certain Types of Tea		
Caffeine (mg)	**Tally**	**Frequency**
1–20	卌 II	7
21–40	卌 III	8
41–60	II	2
61–80		0
81–100	II	2

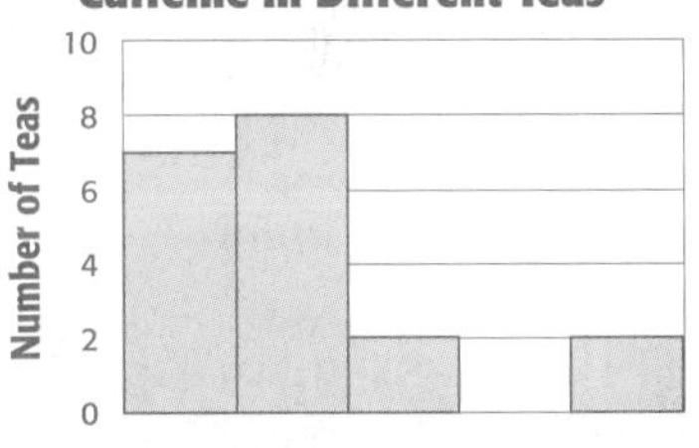

2 WEATHER How many months had six or more days of rain? **4**

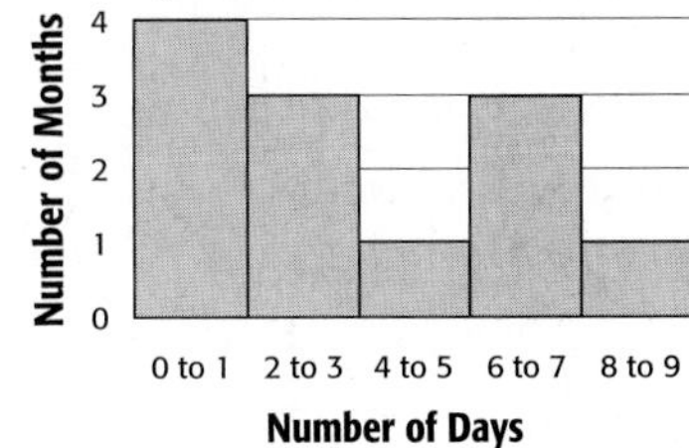

DAILY INTERVENTION **Unlocking Misconceptions**

Histograms Students may mistakenly think that all bar graphs are histograms. Explain that regular bar graphs are drawn with space between the columns. Unlike histograms, regular bar graphs do not have to be organized into equal intervals of data. Histograms display only continuous data. Bar graphs are for discrete data or continuous data.

Classroom Management Prepare a list of typical errors students have made on a quiz. Allow class time to discuss the errors and explain how the problems should be solved.

In-Class Example

INTERACTIVE CHALKBOARD
PowerPoint® Presentations

GRADES Determine which test had the greater number of students scoring 86 or higher. **test #2**

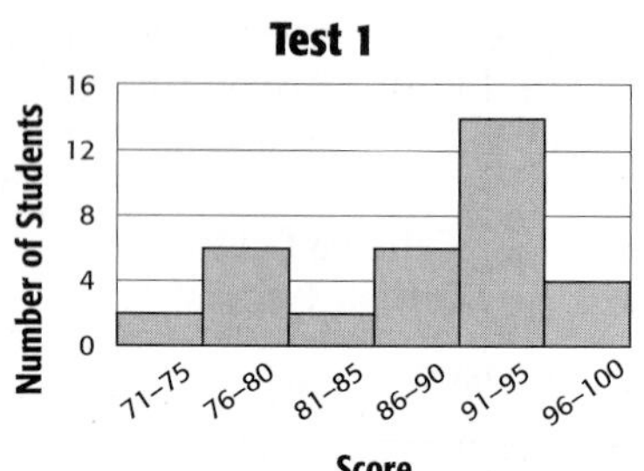

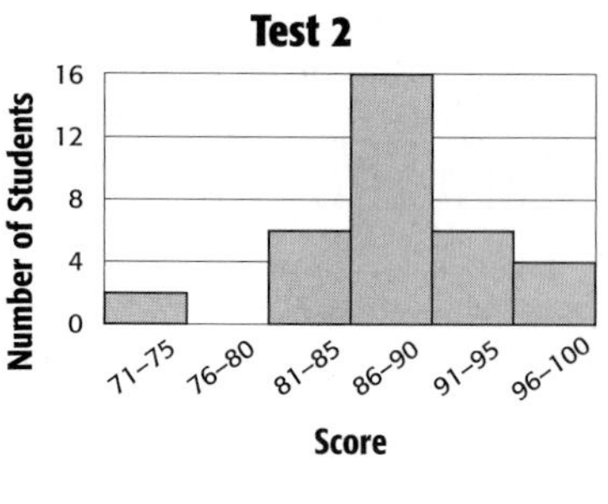

3 Practice/Apply

Which One Doesn't Belong?
In Exercise 2, remind students that data must be organized into equal intervals on frequency tables and histograms.

About the Exercises...

Guided Practice Key

Exercises	Examples
3	1
4	2

Assignment Guide

Basic: 5, 9–21 odd, 22–38

Average: 5–21 odd, 22–38

Enriched: 6–22 even, 23–35 (Optional: 36–38)

Alert! Exercise 23 requires research on the Internet or another source.

Students practice the same concepts in Exercises 5–12 and 14–17 if they are assigned odd or even problems.

Skill and Concept Check

1. **OPEN ENDED** Give a set of data that could be represented by the histogram at the right. **Sample answer: 2, 3, 5, 6, 7, 8, 9, 10, 11, 12, 13, 15, 16, 17**

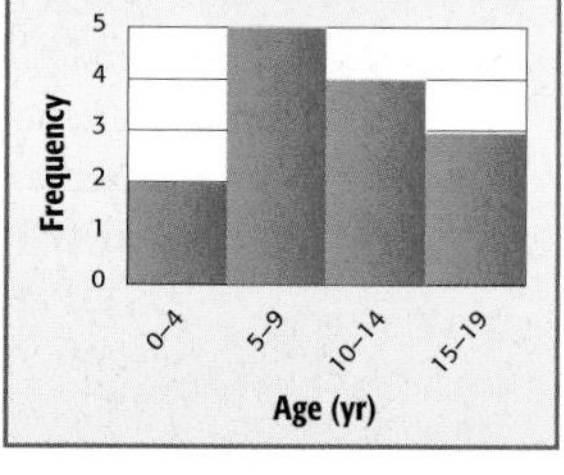

2. **Which One Doesn't Belong?** Identify the interval below that is not equal to the other three. Explain your reasoning.

40–45; all the other intervals represent 5 whole numbers.

GUIDED PRACTICE

3. **WEATHER** Draw a histogram to represent the data below. **See margin.**

Record High Temperatures for Each State		
Temperature (°F)	**Tally**	**Frequency**
100–104	III	3
105–109	~~IIII~~ III	8
110–114	~~IIII~~ ~~IIII~~ ~~IIII~~ II	17
115–119	~~IIII~~ ~~IIII~~ II	12
120–124	~~IIII~~ II	7
125–129	II	2
130–134	I	1

Source: National Climatic Data Center

4. **AUTO RACING** How many races had winning average speeds that were at least 150 miles per hour? **28 races**

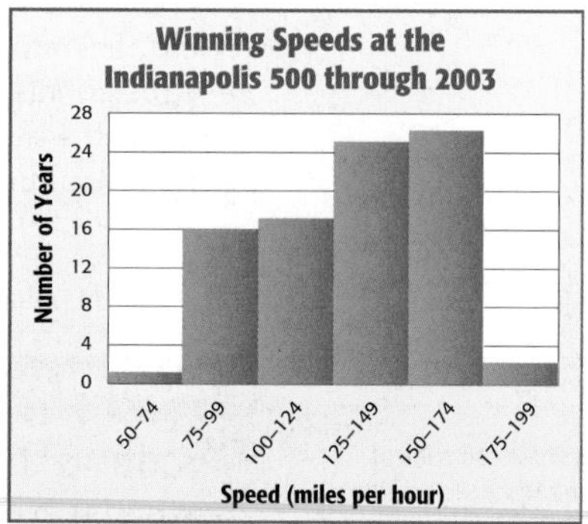

Source: *The World Almanac*

★ indicates increased difficulty

Practice and Applications

HOMEWORK HELP

For Exercises	See Examples
5–8	1
9–18	2
19–21	3

Extra Practice
See pages 637, 656.

Draw a histogram to represent each set of data. 5–6. See margin.

5.

New Broadway Productions for Each Year from 1960 to 2003		
Number of Shows	**Tally**	**Frequency**
20–29	II	2
30–39	~~IIII~~ ~~IIII~~ IIII	14
40–49	~~IIII~~ IIII	9
50–59	~~IIII~~ ~~IIII~~	10
60–69	~~IIII~~ III	8
70–79	I	1

Source: The League of American Theatres and Producers

6.

National League's Greatest Number of Individual Strikeouts from 1960 to 2003		
Strikeouts	**Tally**	**Frequency**
150–199	II	2
200–249	~~IIII~~ ~~IIII~~ II	12
250–299	~~IIII~~ ~~IIII~~ ~~IIII~~ II	17
300–349	~~IIII~~ ~~IIII~~	10
350–399	III	3

Source: *The World Almanac*

Answer

3. **Record High Temperatures for Each State**

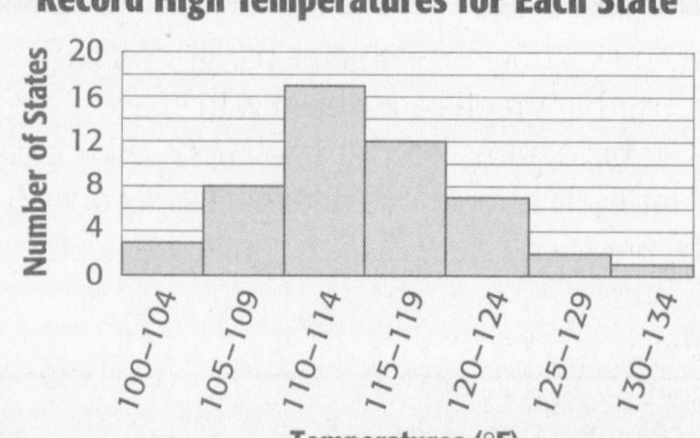

422 **Chapter 9** Statistics and Matrices

★ 7. Calories of various types of frozen bars **7–8. See margin.**
25, 35, 200, 280, 80, 80, 90, 40, 45, 50, 50, 60, 90, 100, 120, 40, 45, 60, 70, 350

★ 8. maximum height in feet of various species of trees in the United States
278, 272, 366, 302, 163, 161, 147, 223, 219, 216, 177

LIBRARIES For Exercises 9–13, use the histogram at the right. **10. cannot be determined**

9. Which interval represents the most number of states? **200–399**
10. Which state has the most public libraries?
11. How many states have at least 600 public libraries? **7 states**
12. How many states have between 400 and 800 public libraries? **11 states**
13. How many states have less than 400 public libraries? **37 states**

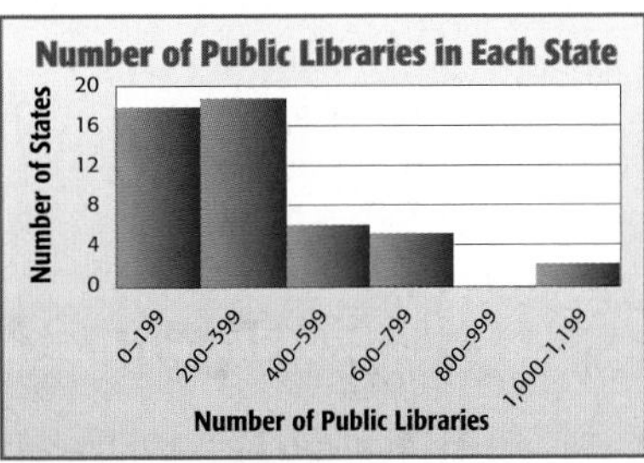

Source: Public Libraries Survey

BASKETBALL For Exercises 14–18, use the histogram at the right.

14. Which interval represents the most number of courts? **19,000–19,999**
15. How many courts have less than 19,000 seats? **8 courts**
16. Which court has the least number of seats? **cannot be determined**
17. How many courts have between 18,000 and 19,999 seats? **16 courts**
18. How many courts have at least 20,000 seats? **9 courts**

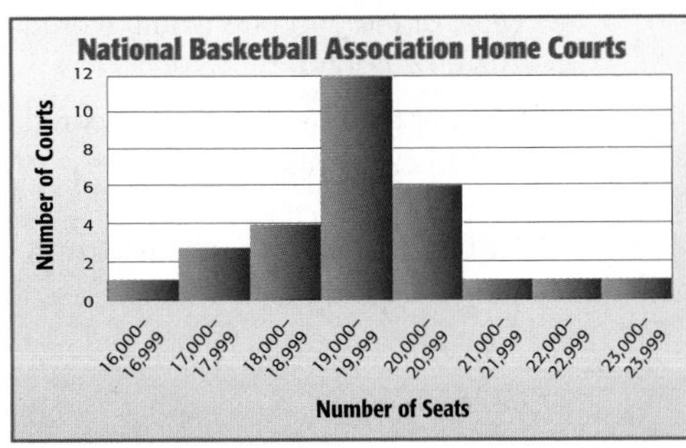

Source: *The World Almanac*

GEOGRAPHY For Exercises 19–21, use the histograms.

Land Area of Counties

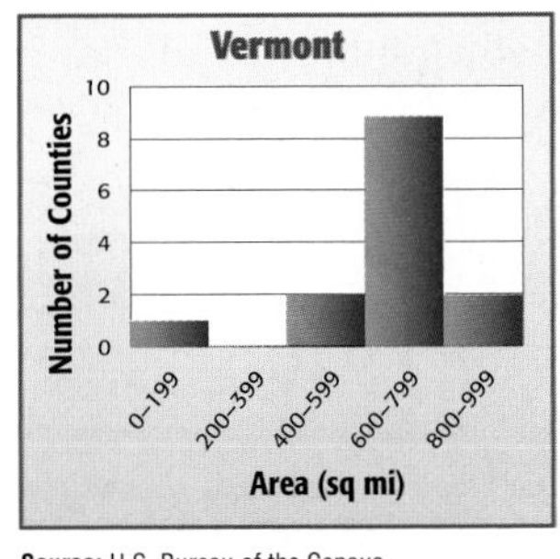

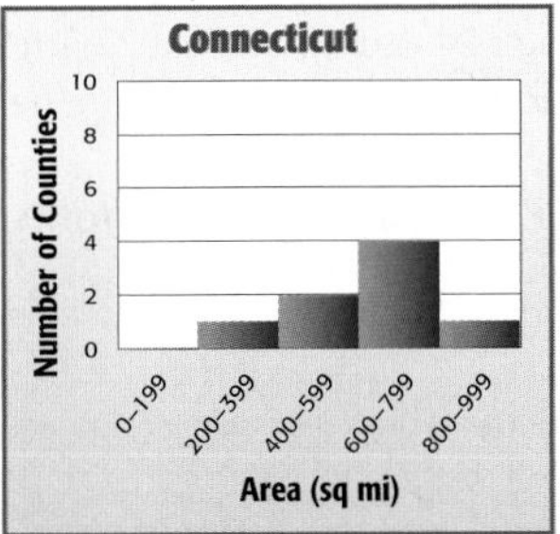

Source: U.S. Bureau of the Census

19. Which state has the smallest county by area? **Vermont**
20. Which state has more counties? **Vermont**
21. How many counties in the two states have less than 600 square miles? **6 counties**

Answers

5.
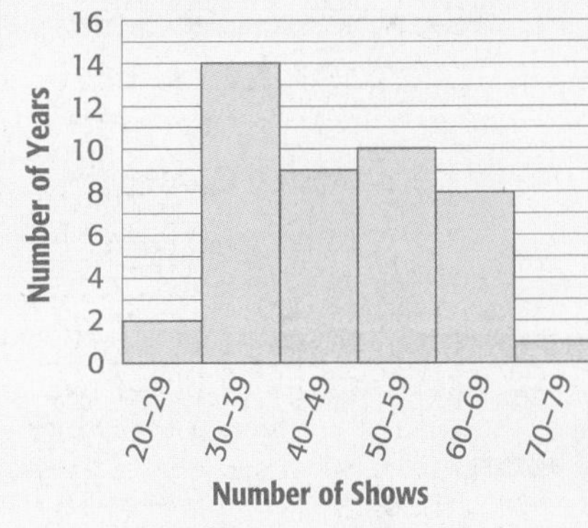

6.
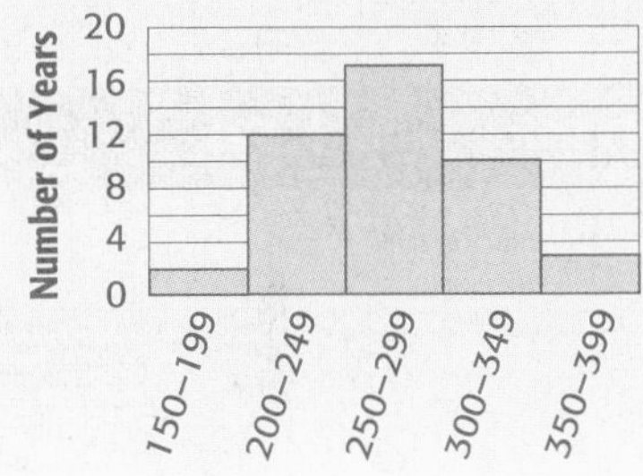

7. Sample answer:

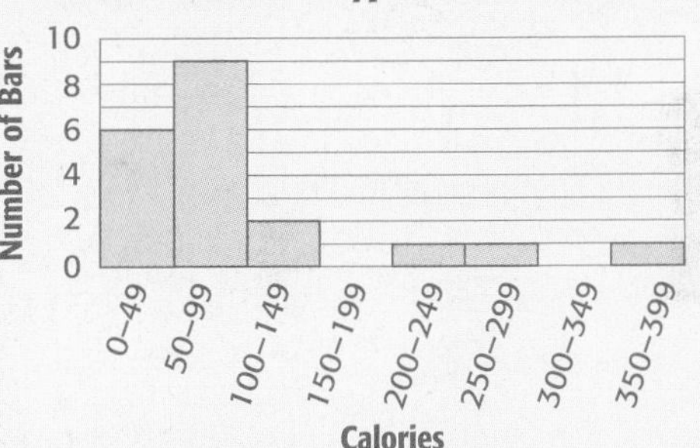

8. Sample answer:

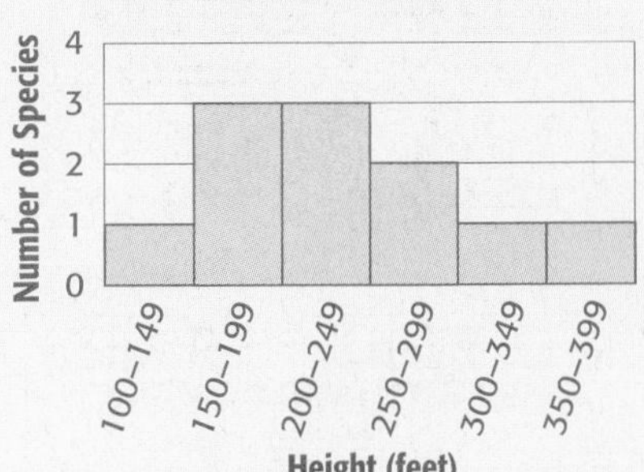

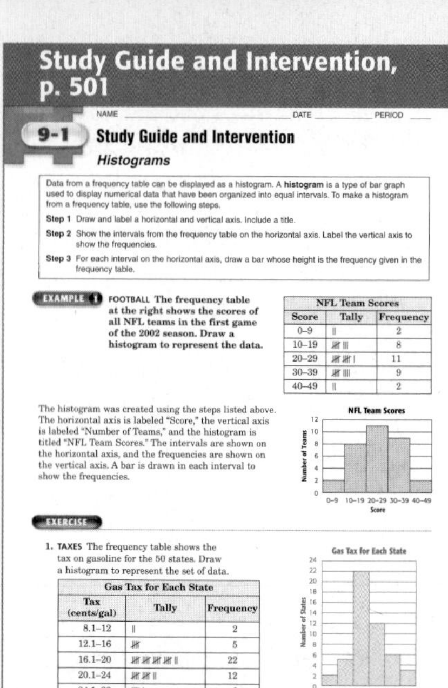

Study Guide and Intervention, p. 501

NAME ______________ DATE ________ PERIOD ____

9-1 Study Guide and Intervention

Histograms

Data from a frequency table can be displayed as a histogram. A **histogram** is a type of bar graph used to display numerical data that have been organized into equal intervals. To make a histogram from a frequency table, use the following steps.

Step 1 Draw and label a horizontal and vertical axis. Include a title.

Step 2 Show the intervals from the frequency table on the horizontal axis. Label the vertical axis to show the frequencies.

Step 3 For each interval on the horizontal axis, draw a bar whose height is the frequency given in the frequency table.

EXAMPLE 1 FOOTBALL **The frequency table at the right shows the scores of all NFL teams in the first game of the 2002 season. Draw a histogram to represent the data.**

NFL Team Scores		
Score	Tally	Frequency
0–9	||	2
10–19	𝍸 |||	8
20–29	𝍸 𝍸 |	11
30–39	𝍸 ||||	9
40–49	||	2

The histogram was created using the steps listed above. The horizontal axis is labeled "Score," the vertical axis is labeled "Number of Teams," and the histogram is titled "NFL Team Scores." The intervals are shown on the horizontal axis, and the frequencies are shown on the vertical axis. A bar is drawn in each interval to show the frequencies.

EXERCISE

1. TAXES The frequency table shows the tax on gasoline for the 50 states. Draw a histogram to represent the set of data.

Gas Tax for Each State		
Tax (cents/gal)	Tally	Frequency
8.1–12	||	2
12.1–16	𝍸	5
16.1–20	𝍸 𝍸 𝍸 𝍸 ||	22
20.1–24	𝍸 𝍸 ||	12
24.1–28	𝍸 |	6
28.1–32	|||	3

Practice: Skills, p. 502

NAME ______________ DATE ________ PERIOD ____

9-1 Practice: Skills

Histograms

1. BASKETBALL The frequency table at the right shows the average points per game for all NBA teams for the 2001–2002 season. Draw a histogram to represent the set of data.

Average Points per Game for NBA Teams, 2001–2002 Regular Season		
Points	Tally	Frequency
87–90.9	|||	3
91–94.9	𝍸 ||||	9
95–98.9	𝍸 𝍸 ||	12
99–102.9	|||	3
103–106.9	||	2

2. GOLF The frequency table at the right shows the score of the winner of the Masters golf tournament for the years 1950–2002. Draw a histogram to represent the set of data.

Score of the Winner of the Masters from 1950–2002		
Score	Tally	Frequency
265–270	|	1
271–275	𝍸 ||	7
276–280	𝍸 𝍸 𝍸 𝍸 𝍸 ||	27
281–285	𝍸 𝍸 |	11
286–290	𝍸 |	6

3. RAINFALL The frequency table at the right shows the average annual precipitation for the 50 states. Draw a histogram to represent the set of data.

Average Annual Precipitation for the 50 States		
Precipitation (in.)	Tally	Frequency
0–11.9	||||	4
12–23.9	𝍸 ||||	9
24–35.9	𝍸 |||	8
36–47.9	𝍸 𝍸 𝍸 𝍸 ||	22
48–59.9	||||	4
60–71.9	|||	3

Practice: Word Problems, p. 503

NAME ______________ DATE ________ PERIOD ____

9-1 Practice: Word Problems

Histograms

EXAMS **For Exercises 1–3, use the histogram below that shows data about scores on a history test.**

MOVIES **For Exercises 4–6, use the histogram below that shows data about movie revenues in 2000.**

1. How many students scored at least 81 on the test? Explain how you found your answer. **18; Add the heights of the bars for the intervals 81–90 and 91–100.**

2. How many students scored less than 81 on the exam? Explain how you found your answer. **15; Add the heights of the bars for the intervals 51–60, 61–70, and 71–80.**

3. Can you determine the highest grade from the histogram? Explain. **No; you can only tell that the highest grade is between 91 and 100.**

4. How many movies grossed at least \$141 million? Explain how you found your answer. **9; Add the heights of the bars for the intervals 141–180, 181–220, and 221–260.**

5. How many movies grossed between \$61 million and \$180 million? Explain how you found your answer. **22; Add the heights of the bars for the intervals 61–100, 101–140, and 141–180.**

6. Can you determine how many movies grossed between \$121 and \$140 million from the histogram? Explain. **No; you can only determine the number of movies within the intervals given on the histogram.**

22. **CRITICAL THINKING** Describe what is wrong with the histogram at the right. **The intervals are not equal.**

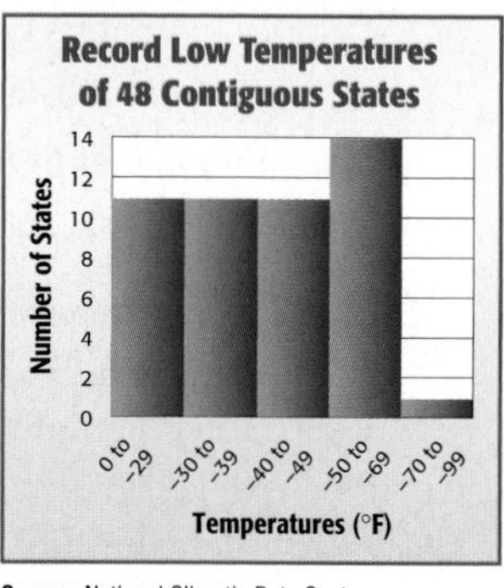

Source: National Climatic Data Center

23. **RESEARCH** Use the Internet or other resource to find the populations of each county, census division, or parish in your state. Make a histogram using your data. How does your county, census division, or parish compare with others in your state? **See students' work.**

Review with Standardized Test Practice

24. **MULTIPLE CHOICE** Which statement can be concluded for the histogram at the right? **D**
    - (A) The lowest winning score was 10.
    - (B) The highest winning score was 59.
    - (C) Most of the winning teams scored between 10 and 29 points.
    - (D) Most of the winning teams scored between 20 and 39 points.

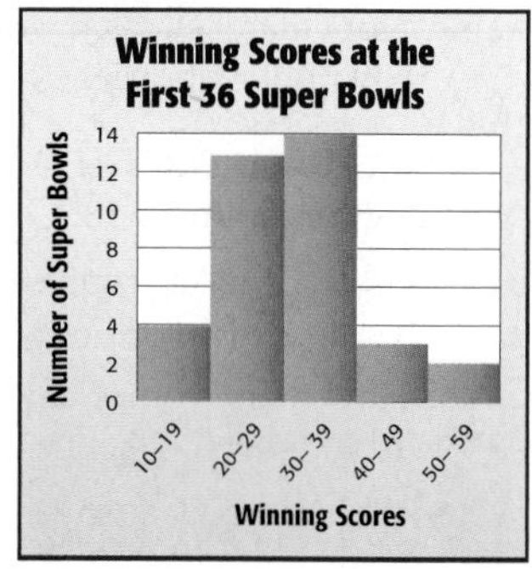

Source: *The World Almanac*

25. **MULTIPLE CHOICE** Use the histogram to determine how many winning teams scored less than 30 points. **G**
    - (F) 31 teams
    - (G) 17 teams
    - (H) 14 teams
    - (I) 13 teams

26. **ELECTIONS** Would a survey of your neighborhood be a good indication of who will be elected governor of your state? Explain. (Lesson 8-7) **No; one neighborhood would not be representative of a whole state.**

27. **GOLF** Tamika is practicing her putting from a certain place on the green. If she made 24 out of her last 32 attempts, what is the experimental probability that she will make her next putt? (Lesson 8-6) $\frac{3}{4}$

Write each percent as a fraction in simplest form. (Lesson 5-1)

28. 24% $\frac{6}{25}$
29. 55% $\frac{11}{20}$
30. 29% $\frac{29}{100}$
31. 66% $\frac{33}{50}$

Solve each proportion. (Lesson 4-4)

32. $\frac{t}{7} = \frac{12}{42}$ **2**
33. $\frac{8}{m} = \frac{96}{60}$ **5**
34. $\frac{3}{7} = \frac{36}{x}$ **84**
35. $\frac{9}{5} = \frac{a}{7}$ **12.6**

GETTING READY FOR THE NEXT LESSON

PREREQUISITE SKILL Solve each problem. (Lessons 5-3 and 5-6)

36. Find 26% of 360. **93.6**
37. What is 53% of 360? **190.8**
38. Find 73% of 360. **262.8**

424 Chapter 9 Statistics and Matrices

4 Assess

Open-Ended Assessment

Speaking Have students explain the process of grouping data into even intervals to obtain a frequency table that can be used to make a histogram.

Graphing Calculator Investigation

A Follow-Up of Lesson 9-1

What You'll LEARN

Use a graphing calculator to make histograms.

Histograms

You can make a histogram using a TI-83/84 Plus graphing calculator.

Mr. Yamaguchi's second period class has listed the distance each student lives from the school. Make a histogram.

Distance from School (miles)											
4	2	6	1	10	3	19	5	20	1	1	9
22	15	2	4	12	8	1	4	16	3	6	7

Enter the data.

Clear any existing data in list L1.

Keystrokes: [STAT] [ENTER] [▲] [CLEAR] [ENTER]

Then enter the data into L1. Input each number and press [ENTER].

Format the graph.

Turn on the statistical plot.

Keystrokes: [2nd] [STAT PLOT] [ENTER] [ENTER]

Select the histogram and L1 as the Xlist.

Keystrokes: [▼] [▶] [▶] [ENTER] [▼] [2nd] L1 [ENTER]

Graph the histogram.

Set the viewing window to be [0, 25] scl: 5 by [0, 12] scl: 1. Then graph.

Keystrokes:
[WINDOW] 0 [ENTER] 25
[ENTER] 5 [ENTER] 0 [ENTER]
12 [ENTER] 1 [ENTER] [GRAPH]

2. It contains all the possible distances in intervals of 5.

EXERCISES

1. Press [TRACE]. Find the frequency of each interval using the right arrow keys. **11; 6; 2; 3; 2**
2. Discuss why the domain is from 0 to 25 for this data set.
3. Make a histogram on the graphing calculator of your classmates' heights in inches. **See students' work.**

msmath3.net/other_calculator_keystrokes

9-1b Graphing Calculator Investigation

GETTING STARTED

Teaching Tip If an overhead projector graphing calculator is available, use it to demonstrate the steps in the **Activity**. An overhead transparency of the graphing calculator's keypad could also be used to help students locate the keys used in the **Activity**.

TEACH

- Students may be confused when entering data because it first appears in a command line near the bottom of the screen. Point out that the data will become part of the list when they press [ENTER] or press the down arrow key. Students should understand that the order of data entry is unimportant.
- Encourage students to work in pairs to proofread **L1** when they finish entering data. They can correct any mistake by moving the cursor over the incorrect number. Then, have them press [DEL] to delete the number or press [2nd] [INS] to type over the number.

ASSESS

Observe as students solve the **Exercises**. They should:

- determine the frequency of each interval on the graph,
- understand how to choose a domain for displaying data, and
- be able to apply the steps in the **Activity** to create histograms using other data.

9-2 Lesson Notes

Lesson Resources

Chapter 9 Resource Masters

FAST FILE

- Study Guide and Intervention, p. 506
- Practice: Skills, p. 507
- Practice: Word Problems, p. 508
- Reading to Learn Mathematics, p. 509
- Enrichment, p. 510

Key Teaching Transparencies, 34

Parent and Student Study Guide Online Worksheets, 9-2

Teaching Mathematics with Manipulatives, pp. 99–100

Noteables™: Interactive Study Notebook with Foldables™, 9-2

Virtual Activities CD-ROM, Making Circle Graphs

1 Focus

5-Minute Check 9-2

Use as a quiz or review of Lesson 9-1. (Also available as a transparency)

Bellringer

Reading Mathematics Draw the circle graph below on the chalkboard. Ask students if they can tell how many students in the school are taking geometry. **no** Point out that 16% does not mean that 16 students are taking geometry. The circle graph gives only percents.

(Continued in bottom margin.)

Reading to Learn Mathematics, p. 509 **ELL**

NAME ______ DATE ______ PERIOD ______

9-2 Reading to Learn Mathematics

Circle Graphs

Pre-Activity *Read the introduction at the top of page 426 in your textbook. Write your answers below.*

1. What percent of the public roads are owned by the counties? 45%
2. What government owns 19.6% of the public roads? states
3. How do you know that all types of government have been accounted for? The percents add to 100.

Reading the Lesson

4. Complete the sentence: A circle graph compares ______ to the ______. parts; whole
5. When drawing a circle graph from given percents, explain how the de... for each section are determined. Sample answer: Multiply ...cent by th...

9-2 Circle Graphs

What You'll LEARN

Construct and interpret circle graphs.

NEW Vocabulary

circle graph

REVIEW Vocabulary

line plot: a graph that uses an X above a number on a number line each time that number occurs in a set of data (page 602)

WHEN am I ever going to use this?

ROADS The graphic shows who owns the public roads in the United States.

1. What percent of the public roads are owned by the counties? **45%**
2. What government owns 19.6% of the public roads? **states**
3. How do you know that all types of government have been accounted for?

3. The percents add to 100.

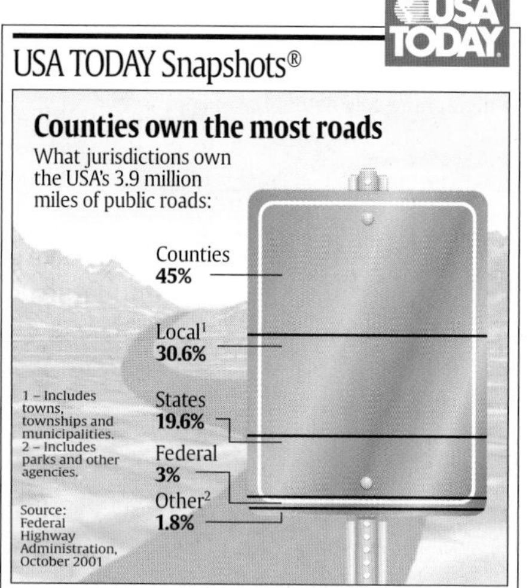

The graphic above compares parts of a set of data to the whole set. A **circle graph** also compares parts to the whole.

EXAMPLE Draw a Circle Graph

1 ROADS **Make a circle graph using the information above.**

Step 1 There are 360° in a circle. So, multiply each percent by 360 to find the number of degrees for each section of the graph.

Counties:	45% of 360° = 0.45 · 360 or 162°
Local:	30.6% of 360° = 0.306 · 360 or about 110°
States:	19.6% of 360° = 0.196 · 360 or about 71°
Federal:	3% of 360° = 0.03 · 360 or about 11°
Other:	1.8% of 360° = 0.018 · 360 or about 6°

Step 2 Use a compass to draw a circle and a radius. Then use a protractor to draw a 162° angle. This section represents county roads. From the new radius, draw the next angle. Repeat for each of the remaining angles. Label each section. Then give the graph a title.

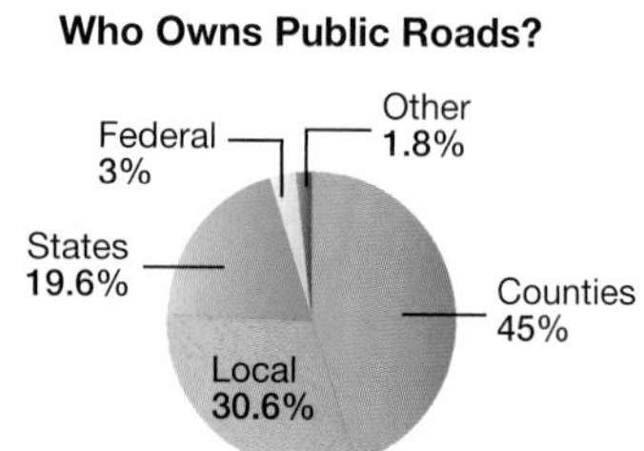

Based on the information given in the graph, it is impossible to tell how many students are taking each subject.

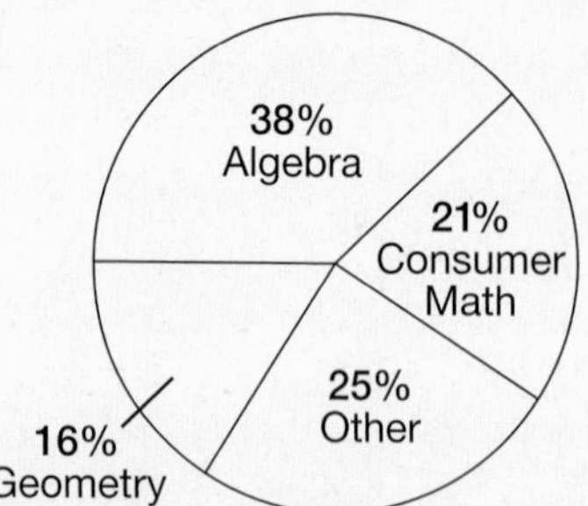

When percents are not known, you must first determine what part of the whole each item represents.

EXAMPLES Use Circle Graphs to Interpret Data

2 **HISTORY** **Make a circle graph using the information in the histogram at the right.**

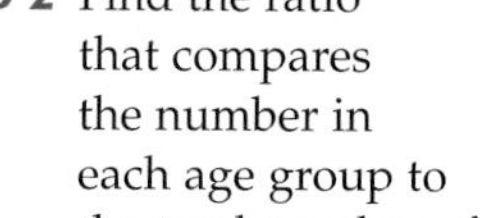

Ages of the Signers of the Declaration of Independence

Source: *The World Almanac*

Step 1 Find the total number of signers of the Declaration of Independence.

$3 + 17 + 19 + 10 + 6 + 1 = 56$

Step 2 Find the ratio that compares the number in each age group to the total number of signers. Round to the nearest hundredth.

20 to 29: $3 \div 56 \approx 0.05$	50 to 59: $10 \div 56 \approx 0.18$
30 to 39: $17 \div 56 \approx 0.30$	60 to 69: $6 \div 56 \approx 0.11$
40 to 49: $19 \div 56 \approx 0.34$	70 to 79: $1 \div 56 \approx 0.02$

Step 3 Use these ratios to find the number of degrees of each section. Round to the nearest degree if necessary.

20 to 29: $0.05 \cdot 360 = 18$

30 to 39: $0.30 \cdot 360 = 108$

40 to 49: $0.34 \cdot 360 = 122.4$ or about 122

50 to 59: $0.18 \cdot 360 = 64.8$ or about 65

60 to 69: $0.11 \cdot 360 = 39.6$ or about 40

70 to 79: $0.02 \cdot 360 = 7.2$ or about 7

Step 4 Use a compass and a protractor to draw a circle and the appropriate sections. Label each section and give the graph a title. Write the ratios as percents.

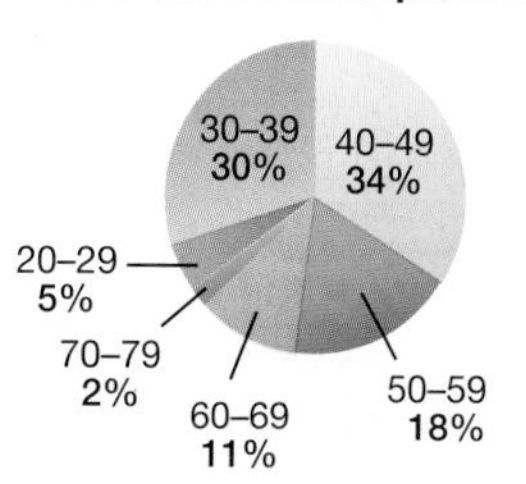

3 **Use the circle graph to describe the makeup of the ages of the signers of the Declaration of Independence.**

More signers of the Declaration of Independence were in their 40s than any other age group. Over $\frac{3}{4}$ of the signers were between 30 and 59.

REAL-LIFE MATH

HISTORY Ben Franklin was the oldest signer of the Declaration of Independence. He was 70 years old.

Source: *The World Almanac*

TEACHING TIP

Encourage students to find other descriptions of the makeup of the ages of the signers of the Declaration of Independence. For example, about half of the signers were between the ages of 40 and 59.

msmath3.net/extra_examples

DAILY INTERVENTION **Differentiated Instruction**

Auditory/Musical Being able to recognize notes is an important part of learning music. Have students listen several times to the first five notes of a scale (C, D, E, F, G). Next, play 25 notes, randomly chosen from the five, as students make a frequency table of what they hear. Have students make a circle graph of their results and compare their graphs with those of other students. Repeat the exercise several times to see whether students' ability to recognize notes improves.

2 Teach

In-Class Examples

1 **TORNADOES** The table shows when tornadoes occurred in the United States from 1999 to 2001. Make a circle graph using this information.

Tornadoes in the United States, 1999–2001	
January–March	15%
April–June	53%
July–September	21%
October–December	11%

Source: spc.noaa.gov/

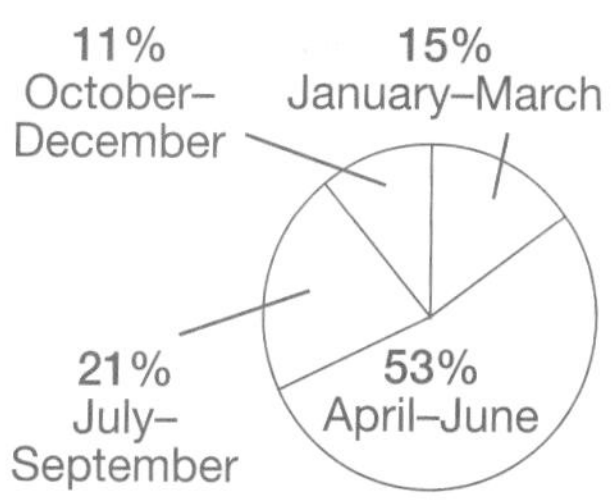

2 **BASKETBALL** Make a circle graph using the information in the histogram below.

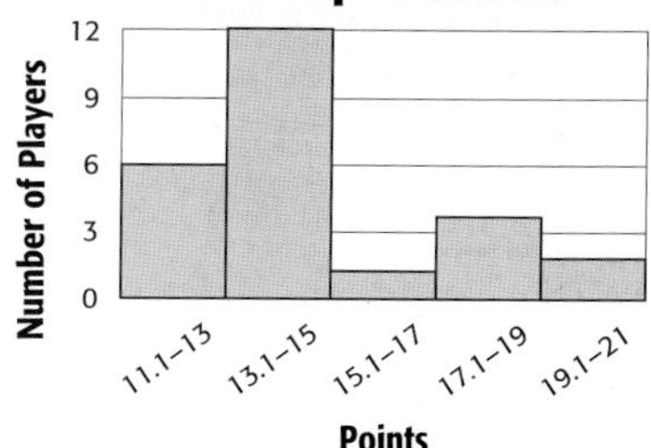

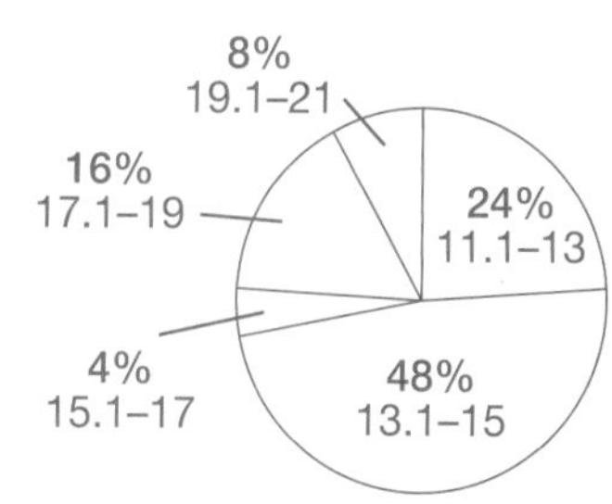

In-Class Example

3 Use the circle graph from In-Class Example 2 to describe the makeup of the average game scores of the 25 top-scoring basketball players. **Sample answer: Almost $\frac{3}{4}$ of the players had average game scores between 11.1 and 15 points. Fewer than $\frac{1}{4}$ had average game scores greater than 17 points.**

3 Practice/Apply

NUMBER SENSE
In Exercise 2, students should be able to recognize the primary divisions of a circle graph, such as 50% and 25%. Point out that half of 25% is 12.5%. Students also should be able to recognize divisions of $\frac{1}{3}$ ($33.\overline{3}\%$) and $\frac{2}{3}$ ($66.\overline{6}\%$). Knowing these divisions without having to calculate the number of degrees will enable students to sketch some circle graphs quickly.

About the Exercises...

Guided Practice Key

Exercises	Examples
4	1
5	2

Assignment Guide

Basic: 7–11 odd, 12–18

Average: 7–11 odd, 12–18

Enriched: 6–12 even, 13–16 (Optional: 17, 18)

Students practice the same concepts in Exercises 6–9 if they are assigned odd or even problems.

Skill and Concept Check

1. *Writing Math* Compare and contrast the histogram and the circle graph in Example 2 on page 427. **See margin.**
2. **NUMBER SENSE** What percent of the circle graph is represented by Section A? by Section B? by Section C? **50%; 25%; 12.5%**

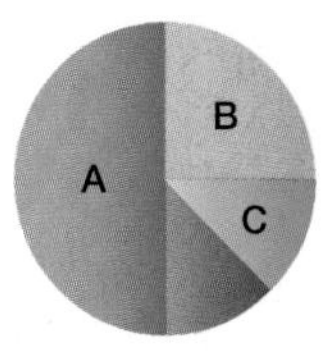

3. **OPEN ENDED** Make a circle graph with five categories showing how you spend 24 hours for a typical weekday. **See margin.**

GUIDED PRACTICE

Make a circle graph for each set of data. **4–5. See Ch. 9 Answer Appendix.**

4.

How Often Teens Borrow a CD from Their Parents	
frequently	11%
occasionally	34%
never/rarely	55%

Source: *USA WEEKEND*

5.

Area (square miles) of the Five Counties of Hawaii	
Hawaii	4,028
Honolulu	600
Kalawao	13
Kauai	623
Maui	1,159

Source: U.S. Department of Commerce

Practice and Applications

Make a circle graph for each set of data. **6–9. See Ch. 9 Answer Appendix.**

HOMEWORK HELP	
For Exercises	See Examples
6–7	1
8–10	2
11	3

Extra Practice
See pages 638, 657.

6.

Major Influences for Teens on Music Choices	
radio	43%
friends	30%
television	16%
parents	7%
concerts	3%
magazines	1%

Source: *USA WEEKEND*

7.

Types of Flowers and Plants Purchased for Mother's Day	
garden plants	37%
cut flowers	36%
flowering plants	18%
green plants	9%

Source: California Cut Flower Commission

8.

Acres (millions) Planted in Cotton	
Texas	6.2
Georgia	1.5
Mississippi	1.2
Arkansas	1.0
North Carolina	0.9
Other	4.1

Source: U.S. Department of Agriculture

9.

U.S. Population (millions) by Age	
0–19 years	78.8
20–39 years	78.1
40–59 years	75.2
60–79 years	36.5
80+ years	9.5

Source: U.S. Census Bureau

Answers

1. **Both graphs show how the ages of the signers of the Declaration of Independence were distributed. The bar graph shows how many were in each age interval. The circle graph shows what percent of the signers were in each age interval.**

3. **Sample answer:**

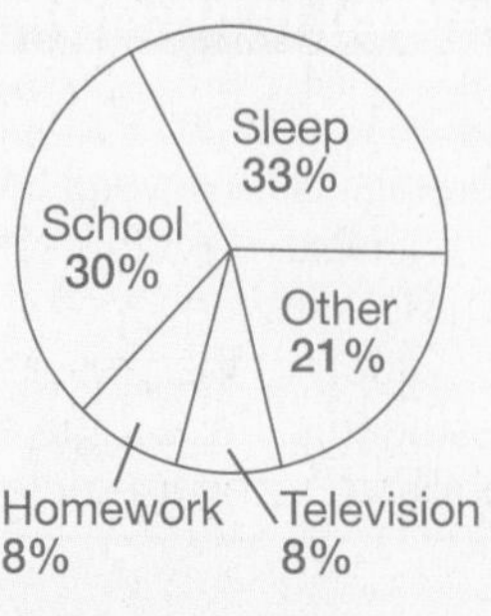

10. **HISTORY** The table shows the birthplaces of the signers of the Declaration of Independence. Make a circle graph of the data.

Location	Signers	Location	Signers	Location	Signers
Connecticut	5	Massachusetts	9	Rhode Island	2
Delaware	2	New York	3	South Carolina	4
Maine	1	New Jersey	3	United Kingdom	8
Maryland	5	Pennsylvania	5	Virginia	9

Source: *The World Almanac*

10. See Ch. 9 Answer Appendix.

11. **ENERGY** Use the circle graph to describe how we heat our homes. **See Ch. 9 Answer Appendix.**

Type of Fuel Used to Heat Homes

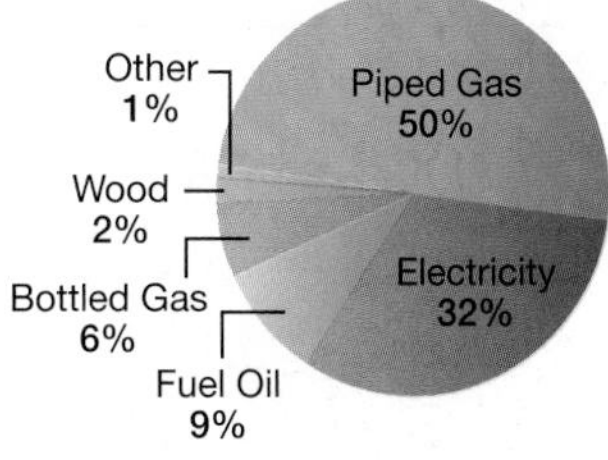

Source: U.S. Census Bureau

12. **CRITICAL THINKING** Make a circle graph using the data in the table. **See Ch. 9 Answer Appendix.**

Favorite NBA Team	
Los Angeles Lakers	12%
Chicago Bulls	6.3%
Philadelphia 76ers	3.7%
New York Knicks	3.3%
Boston Celtics	2.1%
None	56%

Source: ESPN

Spiral Review with Standardized Test Practice

13. **MULTIPLE CHOICE** Which statement *cannot* be determined from the graph at the right? **C**

    (A) Most adults want to live to 100.

    (B) Nearly one third of adults do not want to live to 100.

    (C) Five people who were surveyed "don't know."

    (D) One twentieth of the adults "don't know."

Do You Want to See Your 100th Birthday?

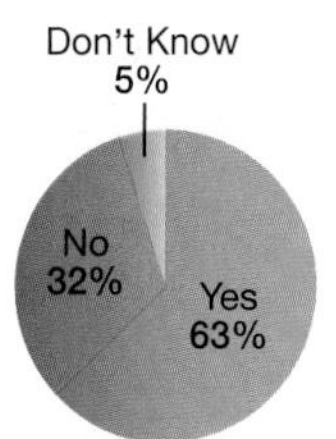
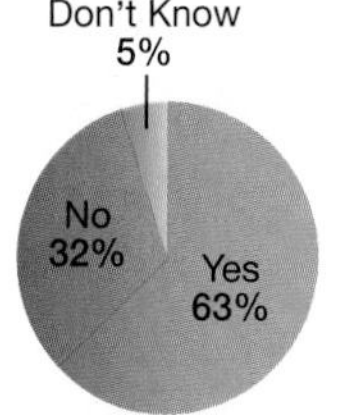

Source: Alliance for Aging

14. **GRID IN** Find the measure in degrees of the angle of the "no" section of the circle graph. **115.2**

15. **FOOD** The number of Calories in single serving, frozen pizzas are listed below. Make a histogram of the data. (Lesson 9-1)

    200, 270, 290, 300, 310, 320, 330, 350,
    360, 380, 380, 390, 390, 420, 440, 450 **See Ch. 9 Answer Appendix.**

16. **RADIO LISTENING** A radio station asks listeners to call in and state their favorite band. Explain why this is a biased sample. (Lesson 8-7) **See Ch. 9 Answer Appendix.**

GETTING READY FOR THE NEXT LESSON

PREREQUISITE SKILL Make a line plot for each set of data. (Page 602)

17. 2, 5, 9, 8, 2, 6, 2, 5, 8, 10

18. 14, 12, 9, 7, 12, 10, 14, 7, 8, 12

17–18. See Ch. 9 Answer Appendix.

Math Online msmath3.net/self_check_quiz

4 Assess

Open-Ended Assessment

Modeling Provide each student with two paper plates. Have them work in pairs to create a frequency table on any topic that can be represented by a circle graph. Then have students cut out and color sections of one paper plate to represent the sections of the graph. They can paste the sections on the other paper plate to model the circle graph.

Study Guide and Intervention, p. 506

NAME ______ DATE ______ PERIOD ____

9-2 Study Guide and Intervention

Circle Graphs

A **circle graph** compares parts to the whole. The whole is represented as a circle, and the parts are shown as sections of the circle.

EXAMPLE 1 BASEBALL **Make a circle graph using the information in the table at the right.**

Batting in Major League Baseball, 2002 Season	
Handedness	**Percent of Batters**
Right-Handed	53%
Left-Handed	29%
Switch Hitter	18%

Step 1 There are 360° in a circle. So, multiply each percent by 360 to find the number of degrees for each section of the graph. Use a calculator.
Right-Handed: 53% of 360 = 0.53 · 360 or about 191°
Left-Handed: 29% of 360 = 0.29 · 360 or about 104°
Switch Hitter: 18% of 360 = 0.18 · 360 or about 65°

Step 2 Use a compass to draw a circle and a radius. Then use a protractor to draw a 191° angle. This section represents right-handed hitters.

Step 3 From the new radius, draw a 104° angle. This section represents left-handed hitters. The remaining section represents switch hitters. Now label each section. Then give the graph a title.

Batting in Major League Baseball, 2002 Season
18% Switch-Hitter; 29% Left-Handed; 53% Right-Handed

When the percents are not given, you must first determine what part of the whole each item represents.

EXERCISES

Make a circle graph for each set of data.

1.

U.S. Car Sales by Vehicle Size and Type, 2000	
Size and Type	**Percent**
Luxury	17%
Large	7%
Midsize	48%
Small	28%

U.S. Car Sales by Vehicle Size and Type, 2000
28% Small; 17% Luxury; 7% Large; 48% Midsize

2.

Medals Won by the U.S. in the 2000 Summer Olympic Games	
Type	**Number**
Gold	40
Silver	24
Bronze	33

Medals Won by the U.S. in the 2000 Summer Olympic Games
34% Bronze; 41% Gold; 25% Silver

Practice: Skills, p. 507

NAME ______ DATE ______ PERIOD ____

9-2 Practice: Skills

Circle Graphs

Make a circle graph for each set of data.

1.

U.S. Energy Consumption, 2000	
Type	**Percent**
Commercial and Industrial	51%
Transportation	27%
Residential	20%
Other	2%

U.S. Energy Consumption, 2000
2% Other; 20% Residential; 51% Commercial and Industrial; 27% Transportation

2.

Color of Trucks Sold in U.S., 2000	
Color	**Percent**
White	23%
Silver	14%
Blue	11%
Black	11%
Red	15%
Other	26%

Color of Trucks Sold in U.S., 2000
26% Other; 23% White; 14% Silver; 11% Blue; 11% Black; 15% Red

3.

Davis Cup Winner, 1981–2000	
Country	**Wins**
Australia	3
France	2
Germany	3
Spain	1
Sweden	6
U.S.	5

Davis Cup Winner, 1981–2000
25% U.S.; 15% Australia; 10% France; 15% Germany; 5% Spain; 30% Sweden

4.

Top 5 Largest American Indian Tribes	
Tribe	**Number (thousands)**
Cherokee	369
Navajo	225
Sioux	107
Chippewa	106
Choctaw	86

Top 5 Largest American Indian Tribes
10% Choctaw; 12% Chippewa; 12% Sioux; 25% Navajo; 41% Cherokee

Practice: Word Problems, p. 508

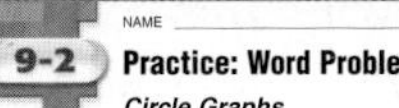

NAME ______ DATE ______ PERIOD ____

9-2 Practice: Word Problems

Circle Graphs

MUSIC **For Exercises 1 and 2, use the circle graph below that shows data about music sales in 2001.**

Music Sales, 2001

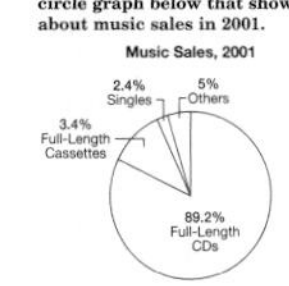

INVESTMENTS **For Exercises 3–6, use the table below that shows how Mr. Broussard has invested his money.**

Investments	
Savings Account	$60,000
Money Market Account	$100,000
Mutual Funds	$140,000
Stocks	$500,000
Bonds	$200,000

1. What angle corresponds to the sector labeled "Others" in the circle graph? Explain how you found your answer. **18°; Multiply 360° by 5% or 0.05.**

2. Use the circle graph to describe music sales in 2001. **Sample answer: Full-length CDs account for nearly all music sales. Other types only account for about 10% of sales.**

3. Explain how a circle graph could help you visualize the data in the table. **Sample answer: You could see how each part compares to the whole.**

4. Determine the percent of Mr. Broussard's total investments that each type of investment represents. **savings account: 6%; money market account: 10%; mutual funds: 14%; stocks: 50%; bonds: 20%**

5. Draw a circle graph to represent the data.

Mr. Broussard's Investments
14% Mutual Funds; 10% Money Market; 6% Saving Account; 20% Bonds; 50% Stocks

6. Use the circle graph you made in Exercise 5 to describe Mr. Broussard's investments. **Sample answer: Mr. Broussard has invested half of his money in stocks. The other half is invested in a combination of savings accounts, money market accounts, mutual funds, and bonds.**

9-3 Lesson Notes

Lesson Resources

Chapter 9 Resource Masters

FAST FILE

- Study Guide and Intervention, p. 511
- Practice: Skills, p. 512
- Practice: Word Problems, p. 513
- Reading to Learn Mathematics, p. 514
- Enrichment, p. 515

Key Teaching Transparencies, 35

Parent and Student Study Guide Online Worksheets, 9-3

Noteables™: Interactive Study Notebook with Foldables™, 9-3

Focus

5-Minute Check 9-3

Use as a quiz or review of Lesson 9-2. (Also available as a transparency)

Bellringer

Problem Solving Tell students you want to create a graph or display that shows what percent of students like hamburgers, chicken sandwiches, tacos, or pizza the most. Ask them which types of display listed in the concept summary would not be suitable for showing this data. **histogram, line graph, line plot, stem-and-leaf plot** Explain that eliminating answers you know are incorrect is often a good first step in problem solving.

Reading to Learn Mathematics, p. 514 **ELL**

NAME ____________ DATE ________ PERIOD ____

9-3 Reading to Learn Mathematics

Choosing an Appropriate Display

Pre-Activity *Read the introduction at the top of page 430 in your textbook. Write your answers below.*

1. Which display(s) show all of the individual test scores? **stem-and-leaf, line plot**
2. Do any of the displays allow you to find the test score of a certain student? If not, what type of display would show this type of information? **No; a table with names and scores would show an individual student's score.**

Reading the Lesson

3. Name three different ways to display data. **Sample answers: bar graph, circle graph, histogram, line graph, line plot, pictograph, stem-and-leaf plot, table**
4. What two questions should you ask yourself when determining which type of display to use? **Sample answer: What type of information do I have, and what do I want my display to show?**

9-3 Choosing an Appropriate Display

What You'll LEARN

Choose an appropriate display for a set of data.

REVIEW Vocabulary

line graph: a type of statistical graph using lines to show how values change over a period of time (page 602)

WHEN am I ever going to use this?

SCHOOL The following are four different ways a teacher can display the grades on a test.

Stem-and-Leaf Plot

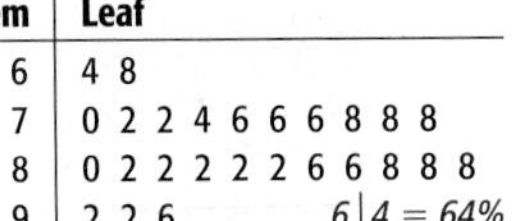

Line Plot

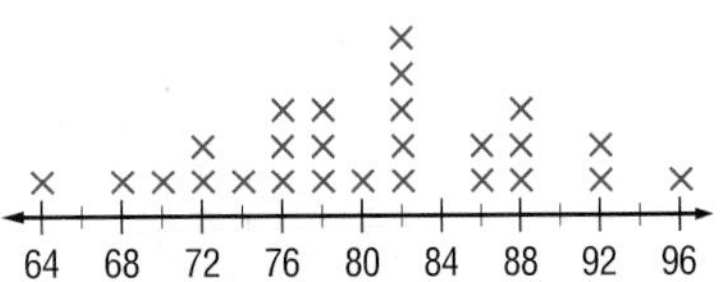

Histogram

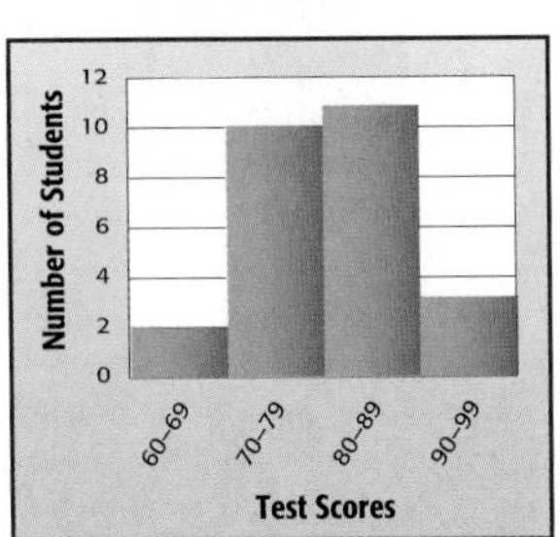

Circle Graph

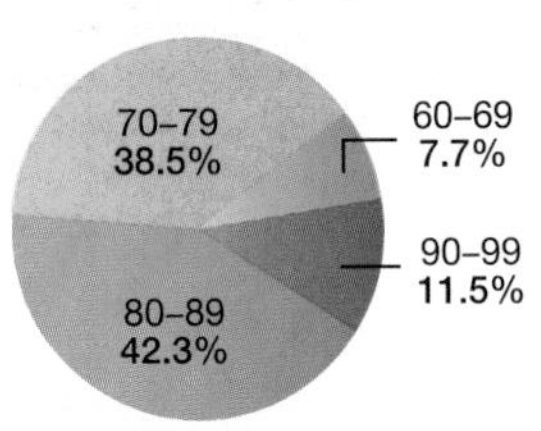

1. Which display(s) show all of the individual test scores?
2. Do any of the displays allow you to find the test score of a certain student? If not, what type of display would show this type of information?

1. stem-and-leaf, line plot

2. No; a table with names and scores would show an individual student's score.

Some of the ways to display data and their uses are listed below.

Concept Summary — **Statistical Displays**

Display	Use
Bar Graph	shows the number of items in specific categories
Circle Graph	compares parts of the data to the whole
Histogram	shows the frequency of data that has been organized into equal intervals
Line Graph	shows change over a period of time
Line Plot	shows how many times each number occurs in the data
Pictograph	shows the number of items in specific categories
Stem-and-Leaf Plot	lists all individual numerical data in a condensed form
Table	may list all the data individually or by groups

DAILY INTERVENTION — **Differentiated Instruction** **ELL**

Verbal/Linguistic Have students work on Exercises 12–14 in small groups. Each group should describe in writing why each of the possible displays listed in the concept summary on this page would or would not be appropriate for the data.

As you decide what type of display to use, ask the following questions.

- What type of information is this?
- What do I want my graph or display to show?

REAL-LIFE MATH

CELLULAR PHONES Cell phones are sophisticated radios. A cell phone carrier usually gets 832 radio frequencies to use across a city.

Source: www.howstuffworks.com

EXAMPLES Choose an Appropriate Display

Choose an appropriate type of display for each situation. Then make a display.

1 CELLULAR PHONES The table shows cellular phone subscribers.

Cellular Phones					
Year	Subscribers (millions)	Year	Subscribers (millions)	Year	Subscribers (millions)
1995	91	1998	319	2001	900
1996	145	1999	471	2002	1,155
1997	214	2000	650	2003	1,329

Source: International Telecommunication Union

This data deals with change over time. A line graph would be a good way to show the change over time.

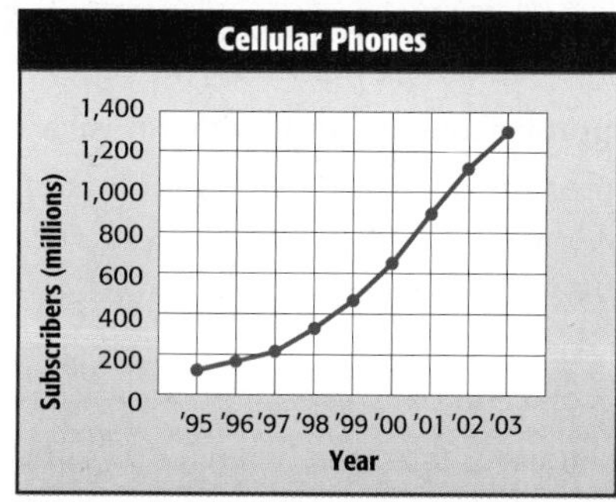

TEACHING TIP

Make sure students understand that there may be more than one way to display data.

2 BICYCLES The results of a survey of students asked to give their favorite bicycle color are given at the right.

Red	𝍸 𝍸 𝍸 I
Blue	𝍸 III
Silver	𝍸 𝍸 𝍸 𝍸
Black	𝍸 𝍸 III

In this case, there are specific categories. If you want to show the specific number, use a bar graph or a pictograph. If you want to show how each part is related to the whole, use a circle graph.

Favorite Bicycle Color

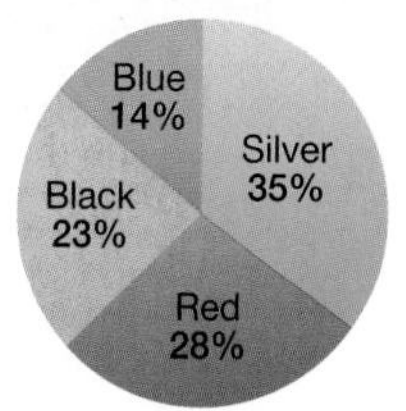

msmath3.net/extra_examples

2 Teach

In-Class Examples

Choose an appropriate type of display for each situation. Then make a display.

1 FARMS The table shows farm acres in Maine.

Farms in Maine by Size	
1–99 acres	46.8%
100–499 acres	43.8%
500–999 acres	6.9%
1,000 or more acres	2.5%

Source: ers.usda.gov

Sample answer: circle graph

Farms in Maine by Size

2 SCHOOL The results of a survey of a group of students asked to give their favorite school subject are shown below.

Favorite School Subject	
math	𝍸 𝍸 𝍸 II
history	𝍸 III
science	𝍸 𝍸 II
English	𝍸 II
other	𝍸 I

Sample answer: bar graph

Favorite School Subject

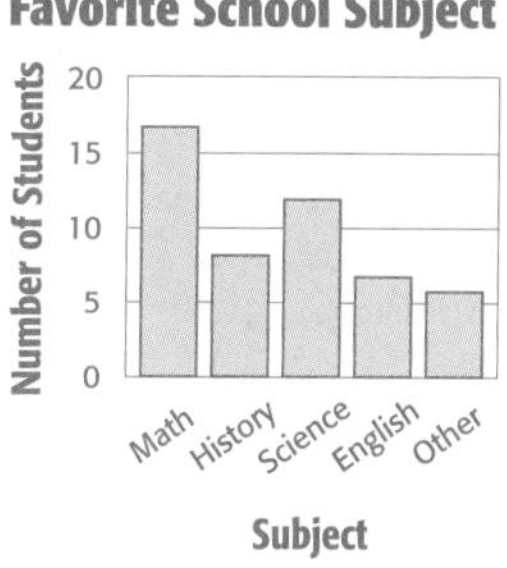

Tips for New Teachers

Using Applications To increase students' interest in math topics, have them focus on a certain job in the community. For example, they might choose to relate the math they are studying to a business that produces bicycles. Students could then produce sample data tables and graphs that relate to manufacturing, sales, or employee issues. You could also have a representative of a company visit the class to discuss how math skills are used in the company.

3 Practice/Apply

About the Exercises...

Guided Practice Key

Exercises	Examples
3–5	1, 2

Assignment Guide

Basic: 7–13 odd, 14, 16–21

Average: 7–13 odd, 14–21

Enriched: 6–14 even, 15–18 (Optional: 19–21)

Alert! Exercise 15 requires research on the Internet or another source.

Answers

1. Both bar graphs and histograms use bars to show how many things are in each category. A histogram shows the frequency of data that has been organized into equal intervals. There is no space between the bars in a histogram.
2. Sample answer:

Profits of ABC Corporation	
Year	Profit (million dollars)
1998	1.2
1999	1.5
2000	1.7
2001	1.6
2002	1.5
2003	1.8
2004	2.1

5. 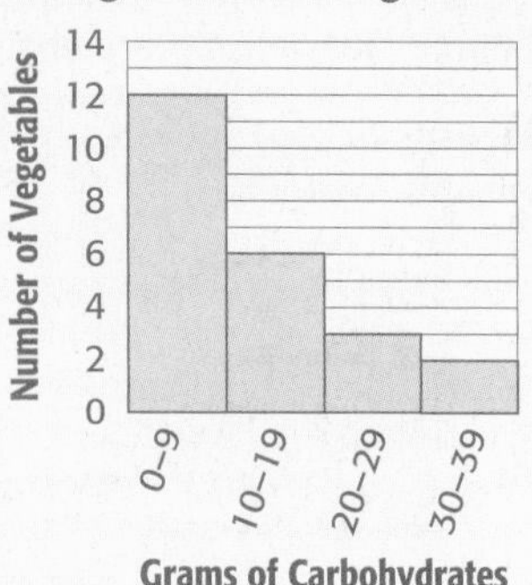

Students practice the same concepts in Exercises 6–13 if they are assigned odd or even problems.

Skill and Concept Check

1. *Writing Math* Compare and contrast bar graphs and histograms. **1–2. See margin.**
2. **OPEN ENDED** Give an example of data that could be represented using a line graph.

GUIDED PRACTICE

Choose an appropriate type of display for each situation.

3. the parts of a landfill used for various types of trash **circle graph**
4. plant height measurements made every 2 days in a science fair report **line graph**
5. **FOOD** Choose an appropriate type of display for the following situation. Then make a display.

Grams of Carbohydrates in a Serving of Various Vegetables											
3	8	10	4	7	6	1	5	19	6	1	2
3	12	23	34	17	37	10	28	7	28	11	

Sample answer: Histogram; see margin.

Practice and Applications

Choose an appropriate type of display for each situation.

6. points scored by individual members of a basketball team compared to the team total **circle graph**
7. numbers of Americans whose first language is Spanish, Mandarin, or Hindi **table, bar graph, or pictograph**
8. the profits of a company every year for the last ten years **line graph**
9. the populations of the states arranged by intervals **histogram**
10. the number of students who wish to order each size of T-shirt
11. the price of an average computer for the last twenty years **line graph**

10. table, bar graph, or pictograph

Choose an appropriate type of display for each situation. Then make a display.

12.

Americans Studying in Selected Countries	
Country	Number
United Kingdom	27,720
Spain	12,292
Italy	11,281
France	10,479

Source: Open Doors 2000

13.

Average Height of Girls	
Age (years)	Height (inches)
2	35
3	39
4	42
5	44
6	46
7	48
8	51
9	53
10	56

Source: www.babybag.com

12. Sample answer: Bar graph; see margin.
13. Sample answer: Line graph; see margin.

HOMEWORK HELP

For Exercises	See Examples
6–13	1, 2

Extra Practice See pages 638, 656.

12. 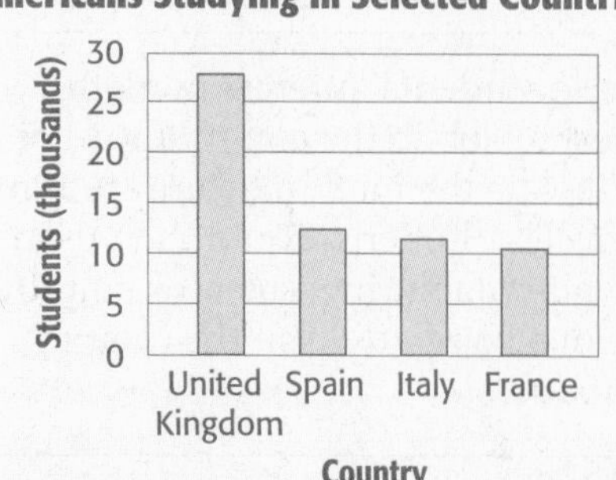

13. 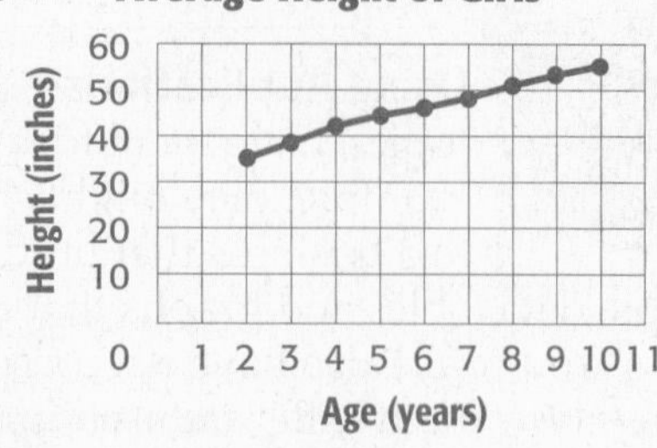

14. **CRITICAL THINKING** Display the data from the bar graph at the right using another type of display. Compare the displays. **See Ch. 9 Answer Appendix.**

15. **RESEARCH** Find a display of data in a newspaper or on the Internet. Do you think the most appropriate type of display was used? **See students' work.**

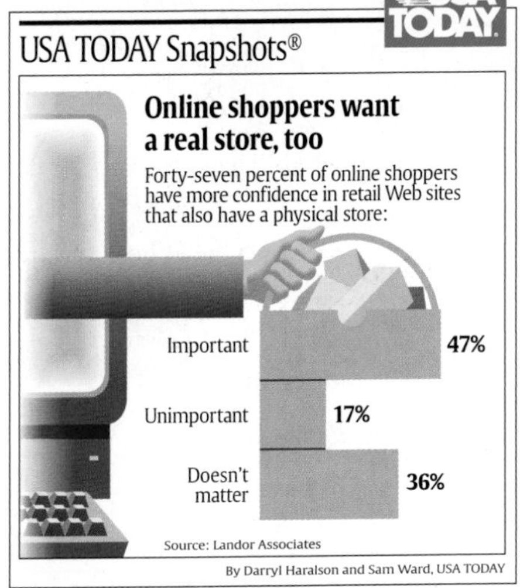

Spiral Review with Standardized Test Practice

16. **MULTIPLE CHOICE** All of the students in Mrs. Gomez's first period class walk to school. The line plot shows the time students take to walk to school. The data is labeled with "M" for male and "F" for female. Which statement is supported by the information in the graph? **C**

Time it Takes to Walk to School (min)

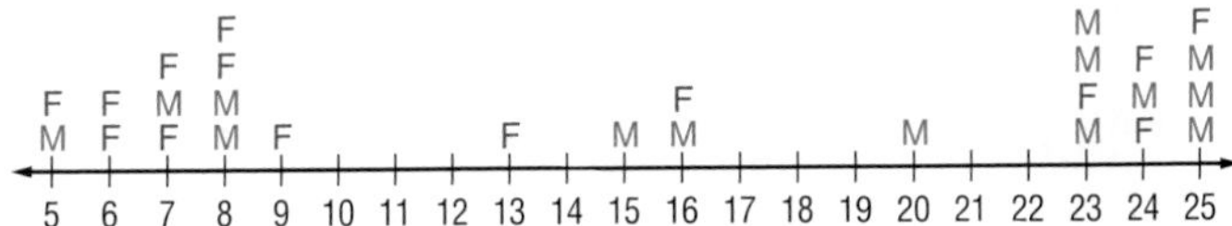

Ⓐ The majority of females live more than 15 minutes away.

Ⓑ Most of the students live more than 18 minutes away.

Ⓒ Most of the students live less than 10 minutes or more than 22 minutes away.

Ⓓ There are 25 students in the class.

17. **SHORT RESPONSE** Make a histogram of the data in the above line plot. **See Ch. 9 Answer Appendix.**

18. **NATIONAL PARKS** Yellowstone National Park has 3,159 square miles in Wyoming, 264 square miles in Montana, and 49 square miles in Idaho. Make a circle graph to show what part of Yellowstone National Park is in each state. (Lesson 9-2) **See Ch. 9 Answer Appendix.**

GETTING READY FOR THE NEXT LESSON

PREREQUISITE SKILL Evaluate each expression. (Lesson 1-2)

19. $\frac{14 + 22 + 18 + 28}{4}$ **20.5**

20. $\frac{23 + 19 + 2 + 8 + 18}{5}$ **14**

21. $\frac{7 + 9 + 2 + 1 + 14 + 6}{6}$ **6.5**

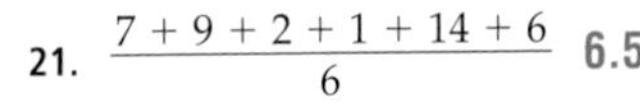

msmath3.net/self_check_quiz

4 Assess

Higher-Level Thinking

A class took a poll to determine students' favorite pets. They found that 32% liked dogs, 13% liked fish, 28% liked cats, 1% liked snakes, 8% liked birds, 19% liked gerbils, and 4% liked guinea pigs. Explain why these data could not be used in a circle graph. **Some students may have given more then one animal as their favorite pet. The percents totaled more than 100%.**

Study Guide and Intervention, p. 511

NAME ____________ DATE ________ PERIOD ____

9-3 Study Guide and Intervention

Choosing an Appropriate Display

There are many different ways to display data. Some of these displays and their uses are listed below.

Display	Use
Bar Graph	shows the number of items in specific categories using bars
Circle Graph	compares parts of the data to the whole
Histogram	shows the frequency of data in equal intervals
Line Graph	shows change over a period of time
Line Plot	shows how many times each number occurs in the data
Pictograph	shows the number of items in specific categories using symbols to represent a quantity
Stem-and-Leaf Plot	lists all numerical data in a condensed form
Table	may list all data individually or by groups

As you decide what type of display to use, ask the following questions.

- What type of information is this?
- What do I want my graph or display to show?

Remember, all data sets can be displayed in more than one way. And there is often more than one appropriate way to display a given set of data.

EXAMPLES **Choose an appropriate type of display for each situation.**

1 **The change in the winning times for the Kentucky Derby for the last 15 years**

This data does not deal with categories or intervals. It deals with the change of a value over time. A line graph is a good way to show changes over time.

2 **Energy usage in the U.S., categorized by the type of user**

In this case, there are specific categories. If you want to show the specific amount of energy used in each category, use a bar graph. If you want to show how each category is related to the whole, use a circle graph.

EXERCISES

Choose an appropriate type of display for each situation.

1. the cost of homeowners insurance over the past 10 years **line graph or bar graph**

2. the amount of federally owned land in each state, arranged in intervals **histogram**

Practice: Skills, p. 512

Choose an appropriate type of display for each situation.

1. energy usage in your home for the past year, categorized by month **bar or line graph**

2. exam scores for a whole class, arranged in intervals **histogram**

3. sales of a leading brand of toothpaste for the last 10 years **line graph**

4. average weight of a pet dog, categorized by breed **bar graph or table**

5. runs scored by individual members of a baseball team, as compared to the team total **circle graph**

6. ages of all 40 employees of a small company **line plot or stem-and-leaf plot**

Choose an appropriate type of display for each situation. Then make a display.

7.

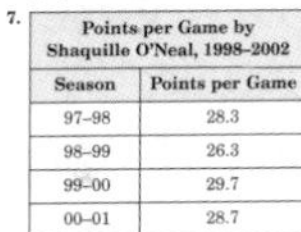

Points per Game by Shaquille O'Neal, 1998–2002	
Season	**Points per Game**
97–98	28.3
98–99	26.3
99–00	29.7
00–01	28.7
00–02	27.2

Sample answer: line graph

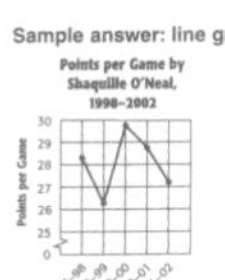

8.

Share of Workers by Commute Time, 2000	
Commute Time	**Percent of Workers**
Less than 15 min	30%
15–29 min	36%
30–39 min	16%
40–59 min	11%
60 min or more	7%

Sample answer: circle graph

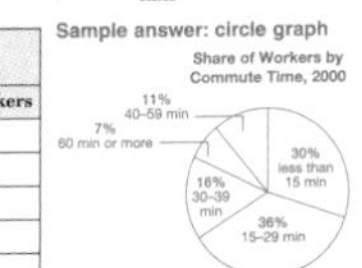

Practice: Word Problems, p. 513

NAME ____________ DATE ________ PERIOD ____

9-3 Practice: Word Problems

Choosing an Appropriate Display

AGE For Exercises 1–4, use the following information. Cosmic, Inc. is a software company with 30 employees. The ages of the employees are displayed below using both a histogram and a stem-and-leaf plot.

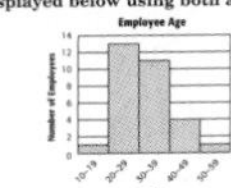

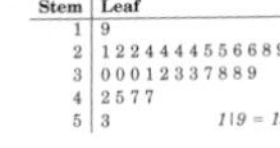

Stem	Leaf
1	9
2	1 2 2 4 4 4 4 5 5 6 6 8 9
3	0 0 0 1 2 3 3 7 8 8 9
4	2 5 7 7
5	3

1 | 9 = 19

1. Can you tell from the stem-and-leaf plot how many employees are between the ages of 20 and 29? If so, how many are there? If not, explain your reasoning. **yes; 13**

2. Can you tell from the histogram how many employees are between the ages of 30 and 39? If so, how many are there? If not, explain your reasoning. **yes; 11**

3. Can you tell from the stem-and-leaf plot how many employees are between the ages of 36 and 43? If so, how many are there? If not, explain your reasoning. **yes; 5**

4. Can you tell from the histogram how many employees are between the ages of 36 and 43? If so, how many are there? If not, explain your reasoning. **No; with the histogram, you do not know the actual employee ages. You know only the number within the intervals.**

5. **CARS** What percent of compact/sports cars sold in the year 2000 were red, white, or blue? Explain how you found your answer.

Colors of Compact/Sports Cars Sold in the U.S., 2000			
Color	**Percent**	**Color**	**Percent**
Silver	22%	Red	16%
Black	14%	Blue	7%
White	11%	Others	30%

34%; Add the percents for red, white, and blue.

6. **CARS** Make a circle graph using the data in the table in question 5. What benefit does the circle graph have? **The circle graph shows how each color compares to the whole.**

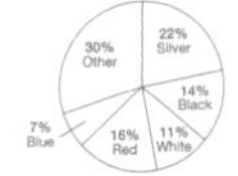

9-3b Hands-On Lab Lesson Notes

Lesson Resources

Teaching Mathematics with Manipulatives

- student recording sheet 9-3b

GETTING STARTED

Teaching Tip Obtain a clear outline map of the United States that is appropriate for this **Activity**. Be sure the map includes the state abbreviations. Make copies for each student.

TEACH

- Some students may have difficulty locating some of the states on the map. Encourage them to work together.
- Students may find it easier to color-code the state abbreviations on the list prior to coloring the map. You may wish to provide them with a photocopy of the table for this purpose.
- Exercise 3 requires research on the Internet or another source.

ASSESS

Discuss the **Writing Math** exercises. Students should demonstrate an understanding of how to find natural breaks in data in order to organize data into categories. Use Exercise 3 to determine whether students have grasped how data categories can be manipulated to support particular viewpoints.

9-3b Hands-On Lab

A Follow-Up of Lesson 9-3

What You'll LEARN

Show statistics on maps.

Materials

- outline of map of the United States
- markers

MAPS AND STATISTICS

Follow the steps below to make a map using data from the table.

Average Number of Tornadoes Each Year

State	No.	State	No.	State	No.	State	No.	State	No.
AL	22	HI	1	MA	3	NM	9	SD	29
AK	0	ID	3	MI	19	NY	6	TN	12
AZ	4	IL	27	MN	20	NC	15	TX	139
AR	20	IN	20	MS	26	ND	21	UT	2
CA	5	IA	36	MO	26	OH	15	VT	1
CO	26	KS	40	MT	6	OK	47	VA	6
CT	1	KY	10	NE	37	OR	1	WA	2
DE	1	LA	28	NV	1	PA	10	WV	2
FL	53	ME	2	NH	2	RI	0	WI	21
GA	21	MD	3	NJ	3	SC	10	WY	12

Source: National Severe Storm Forecast Center

STEP 1 Make a line plot of the data using the state abbreviations instead of ×s.

STEP 2 Find natural breaks in the data and organize the data into fewer than 7 categories.

STEP 3 Color each state according to its category. Include a key.

Writing Math

1. **Explain** how you could change the categories to show that a greater number of states have many tornadoes. How could you change the categories to show that only a few states have many tornadoes? **See margin.**
2. What information is obvious in the map that would not be found in a table? **See margin.**
3. **RESEARCH** Use the Internet or another source to find data about the 50 states. Make two different maps of the data showing two different points of view.

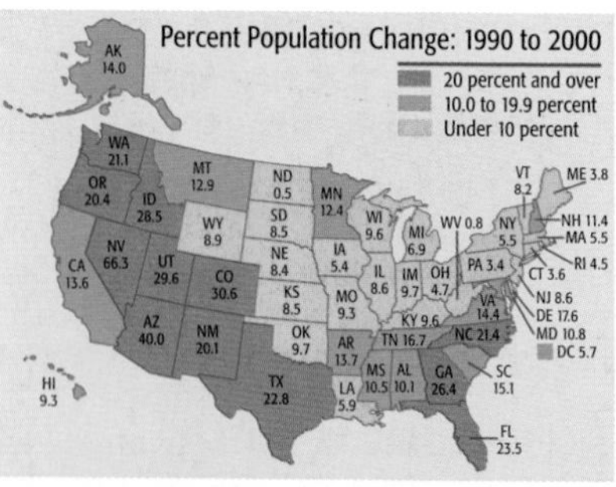

Source: U.S. Bureau of the Census

TEACHING TIP

Because the intervals are chosen to support a point of view, they are often not equal as they are in a histogram.

3. See students' work.

Answers (Writing Math)

1. To make it seem that a greater number of states have many tornadoes, increase the interval of the top category and make the other intervals smaller. To make it seem that only a few states have many tornadoes, decrease the interval of the top category and make the other intervals larger.
2. The greatest percent of change occurred in the western and southern states.

434 Chapter 9 Statistics and Matrices

Measures of Central Tendency

What You'll LEARN

Find the mean, median, and mode of a set of data.

NEW Vocabulary

measures of central tendency
mean
median
mode

WHEN am I ever going to use this?

VACATION DAYS Use the table to answer each question. **1. about 29**

Average Number of Vacation Days Per Year for Selected Countries	
Country	**Vacation Days**
Brazil	34
Canada	26
France	37
Germany	35
Italy	42
Japan	25
Korea	25
United Kingdom	28
United States	13

Source: World Tourism Organization

1. What is the *average* number of days for these nine countries?
2. Order the numbers from least to greatest. What is the middle number in your list? **28**
3. What number(s) appear more than once? **25**
4. Which of the number or numbers from Exercises 1–3 might be representative of the set of data? Explain.

4. Sample answer: 28 and 29 seem to be in the center of the data and could be used to represent the data.

Measures of central tendency are numbers that describe a set of data. The most common measures are **mean**, **median**, and **mode**.

Concept Summary — **Measures of Central Tendency**

Measure	Description
mean	the sum of the data divided by the number of items in the data set
median	the middle number of the data ordered from least to greatest, or the mean of the middle two numbers
mode	the number or numbers that occur most often

EXAMPLE Find Measures of Central Tendency

1 Find the mean, median, and mode of the set of data.
22, 18, 24, 32, 24, 18

Mean $\frac{22 + 18 + 24 + 32 + 24 + 18}{6} = \frac{138}{6}$

$= 23$ The mean is 23.

Median Arrange the numbers in order from least to greatest.

18 18 22 24 24 32

$\frac{22 + 24}{2} = 23$ The median is 23.

Mode The data has two modes, 18 and 24.

TEACHING TIP

Point out that the mean, median, and mode describe the center or middle of the data.

9-4 Lesson Notes

Lesson Resources

Chapter 9 Resource Masters FAST FILE

- Study Guide and Intervention, p. 516
- Practice: Skills, p. 517
- Practice: Word Problems, p. 518
- Reading to Learn Mathematics, p. 519
- Enrichment, p. 520

Calculator and Spreadsheet Masters, p. 40
Key Teaching Transparencies, 36
Parent and Student Study Guide Online Worksheets, 9-4
Real-Life Career Masters, p. 35
Science and Math Lab Masters, pp. 81–88
Noteables™: Interactive Study Notebook with Foldables™, 9-4

1 Focus

5-Minute Check 9-4

Use as a quiz or review of Lesson 9-3. (Also available as a transparency)

Bellringer

Hands-On Activity Have students work in small groups. Provide each group with 60 index cards. Each card should have one number, 1 to 20, and each number should appear on three cards.

(Continued in bottom margin.)

Reading to Learn Mathematics, p. 519

NAME ________ DATE ________ PERIOD ____

9-4 Reading to Learn Mathematics
Measures of Central Tendency

Pre-Activity *Read the introduction at the top of page 435 in your textbook. Write your answers below.*

1. What is the *average* number of days for these nine countries? about 29
2. Order the numbers from least to greatest. What is the middle number in your list? 28
3. What number(s) appear more than once? 25
4. Which of the number or numbers from Exercises 1–3 might be representative of the set of data? Explain. Sample answer: 28 and 29 seem to be in the center of the data and could be used to represent the data.

Students should mix the cards, then randomly choose 9 cards. Have them order the numbers from least to greatest and identify the middle card and its number. Tell students that in this lesson they will learn how to use numbers such as the middle number to describe a set of data.

2 Teach

In-Class Examples

1 Find the mean, median, and mode of the set of data.
4, 16, 32, 19, 27, 32 **21.7; 23; 32**

OLYMPICS Use the table below to answer each question.

Gold Medals Won by the United States at the Winter Olympics, 1924–2002	
Event	**Gold Medals**
alpine skiing	10
bobsleigh	6
cross country	0
figure skating	13
freestyle skiing	4
ice hockey	3
luge	2
short track speed skating	3
skeleton	3
ski jumping	0
snowboarding	2
speed skating	26

2 What is the mean, median, and mode of the data?
6; 3; 3

3 Which measure of central tendency is most representative of the data?
The median and the mode; The mean is affected by the extreme value of 26. The mode is the same as the median. So, both the median and the mode are good choices.

REAL-LIFE MATH

GEOGRAPHY Although no one actually resides on Antarctica, about 1,000 scientists live at over 30 scientific stations during the summer. Some scientists even stay through the winter, when the temperatures can drop to −94°F. Icy winds make the temperature seem even colder.

Source: *World Book*

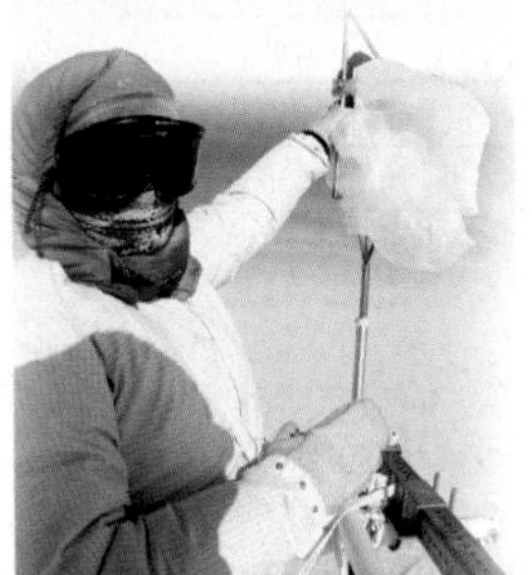

Sometimes one or two measures of central tendency are more representative of the data than the other measure(s).

EXAMPLES Using Appropriate Measures

GEOGRAPHY Use the table to answer each question.

Population of the Seven Continents	
Content	**Population (millions)**
North America	481
South America	347
Europe	729
Asia	3,688
Africa	805
Australia and Oceania	31
Antarctica	0

Source: *The World Almanac for Kids*

2 **What is the mean, median, and mode of the data?**

Mean $\frac{481 + 347 + 729 + 3{,}688 + 805 + 31 + 0}{7} = \frac{6{,}081}{7}$

≈ 868.7

The mean is about 868.7 million.

Median Arrange the numbers from least to greatest.

0, 31, 347, 481, 729, 805, 3,688

The median is the middle number or 481 million.

Mode Since each number only occurs once, there is no mode.

3 **Which measure of central tendency is most representative of the data?**

Since there is no mode, you must decide whether the mean, 868.7 million, or the median, 481 million, is more representative of the data.

Notice that the extremely large population of Asia greatly affected the mean. In fact, the only continent with a population greater than the mean is Asia.

The best representation of the data is the median, 481 million.

Different circumstances determine which of the measures of central tendency are most useful.

TEACHING TIP

Make sure the students understand how each measure of central tendency is determined, as well as when it is most useful.

Concept Summary — Using Mean, Median, and Mode

Measure	Most Useful When . . .
mean	• the data has no extreme values
median	• the data has extreme values • there are no big gaps in the middle of the data
mode	• data has many identical numbers

msmath3.net/extra_examples

DAILY INTERVENTION — Flexible Grouping

Measures of Central Tendency Divide the class into groups of 8 to 10 students. Have each student write his or her age in months on a sheet of paper, and place it where everyone in the group can easily see it. Next, have everyone in the group determine the mean, median, and mode for the set of numbers. Students should compare their answers and discuss any differences.

Students practice the same concepts in Exercises 8–15 if they are assigned odd or even problems.

Skill and Concept Check

1. *Writing Math* Determine whether all measures of central tendency must be members of the set of data. Explain. **See margin.**

2. **OPEN ENDED** Construct a set of data that has a mode of 4 and a median of 3. **Sample answer: 1, 2, 3, 4, 4**

3. **FIND THE ERROR** Tobias and Erica are finding the median of 93, 90, 94, 99, 92, 93, and 100. Who is correct? Explain.

Tobias	Erica
93, 90, 94, <u>99</u>, 92, 93, 100 The median is 99.	90, 92, 93, <u>93</u>, 94, 99, 100 The median is 93.

Erica; you must first order the numbers from least to greatest.

GUIDED PRACTICE

Find the mean, median, and mode of each set of data. Round to the nearest tenth if necessary.

4. 19, 21, 18, 17, 18, 22, 46 **23; 19; 18**
5. 10, 3, 17, 1, 8, 6, 12, 15 **9; 9; no mode**

FOOTBALL For Exercises 6 and 7, use the graphic. **6. about 37.7; 31; 27**

6. Find the mean, median, and mode of the data.
7. Which measure of central tendency is most representative of the data? Explain. **The median; the mean is affected by the extreme value of 74, and the mode is the least number in the set of data.**

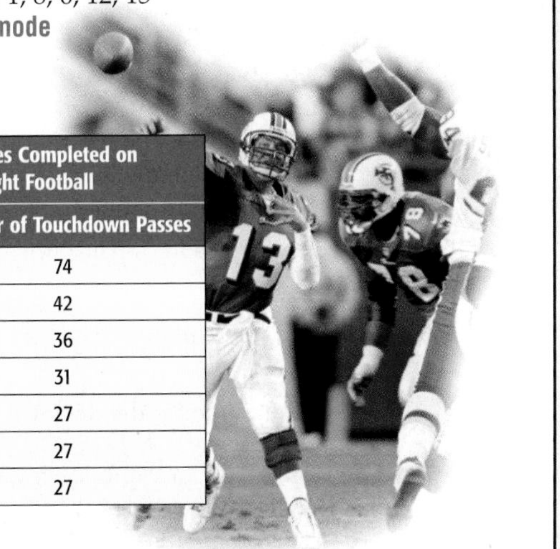

Touchdown Passes Completed on Monday Night Football

Quarterback	Number of Touchdown Passes
Dan Marino	74
Steve Young	42
Joe Montana	36
Jim Kelly	31
Brett Favre	27
Ken Stabler	27
Danny White	27

Source: NFL

★ indicates increased difficulty

Practice and Applications

Find the mean, median, and mode of each set of data. Round to the nearest tenth if necessary. **10. 79.3; 79.5; 84** **11. 34; 34; 34**

8. 9, 8, 15, 8, 20 **12; 9; 8**
9. 23, 16, 5, 6, 14 **12.8; 14, no mode**
10. 78, 80, 75, 73, 84, 81, 84, 79
11. 36, 38, 33, 34, 32, 30, 34, 35
12. 8.5, 8.7, 6.9, 7.5, 7, 9.8, 5.4, 8.9, 6.5, 8.2, 8, 9.4 **7.9; 8.1; no mode**
13. 1.2, 1.78, 1.73, 1.9, 1.19, 1.8, 1.24, 1.92, 1.54, 1.7, 1.42, 1 **1.5; 1.6; no mode**

★14.

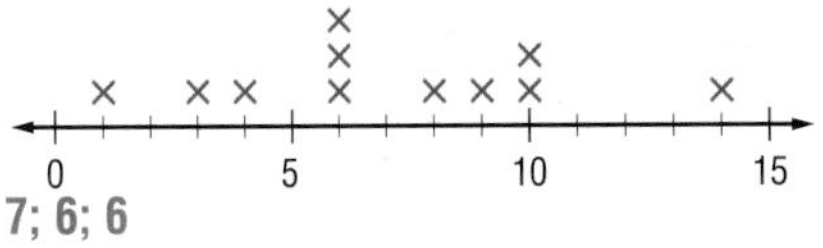

7; 6; 6

★15.

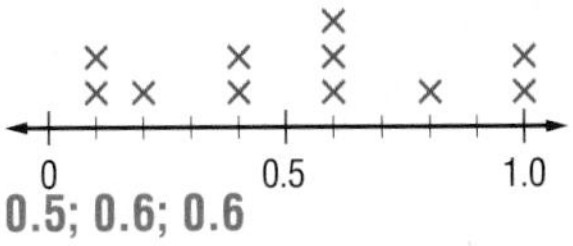

0.5; 0.6; 0.6

HOMEWORK HELP

For Exercises	See Examples
8–16	1, 2
17	3

Extra Practice See pages 638, 656.

Math Online msmath3.net/self_check_quiz

3 Practice/Apply

FOLDABLES™ Follow-Up Remind students to use their Foldables to record what they learn about finding the mean, median, and mode of a set of data. Encourage students to explain in their own words the vocabulary words introduced and give examples of each.

DAILY INTERVENTION **FIND THE ERROR** In Exercise 3, remind students that the order of numbers is unimportant when finding the mean and mode. When finding the median, however, they must first order the numbers from least to greatest.

About the Exercises...

Guided Practice Key

Exercises	Examples
4–5	1
6	2
7	3

Assignment Guide

Basic: 9–13 odd, 16, 17, 19–27

Average: 9–15 odd, 16, 17, 19–27

Enriched: 8–14 even, 16–24 (Optional: 25–27)

Answer

1. **No; the mode must always be a member of the set of data, but the mean and median may or may not be a member of the set of data.**

4 Assess

Open-Ended Assessment

Writing Have students write a short instructional booklet that describes mean, median, and mode. The writing could be aimed at younger children who know how to divide. Ask students to include possible uses for finding the mean, median, and mode.

Study Guide and Intervention, p. 516

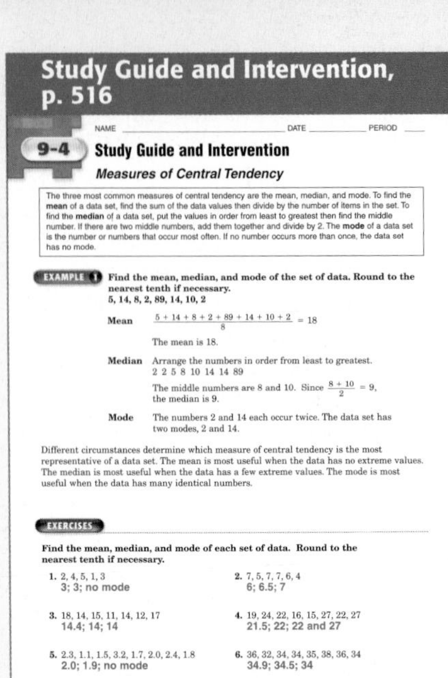

NAME ______ DATE ______ PERIOD ____

9-4 Study Guide and Intervention

Measures of Central Tendency

The three most common measures of central tendency are the mean, median, and mode. To find the **mean** of a data set, find the sum of the data values then divide by the number of items in the set. To find the **median** of a data set, put the values in order from least to greatest then find the middle number. If there are two middle numbers, add them together and divide by 2. The **mode** of a data set is the number or numbers that occur most often. If no number occurs more than once, the data set has no mode.

EXAMPLE 1 **Find the mean, median, and mode of the set of data. Round to the nearest tenth if necessary.**
5, 14, 8, 2, 89, 14, 10, 2

Mean $\frac{5 + 14 + 8 + 2 + 89 + 14 + 10 + 2}{8} = 18$

The mean is 18.

Median Arrange the numbers in order from least to greatest.
2 2 5 8 10 14 14 89

The middle numbers are 8 and 10. Since $\frac{8 + 10}{2} = 9$, the median is 9.

Mode The numbers 2 and 14 each occur twice. The data set has two modes, 2 and 14.

Different circumstances determine which measure of central tendency is the most representative of a data set. The mean is most useful when the data has no extreme values. The median is most useful when the data has a few extreme values. The mode is most useful when the data has many identical numbers.

EXERCISES

Find the mean, median, and mode of each set of data. Round to the nearest tenth if necessary.

1. 2, 4, 5, 1, 3
   3; 3; no mode
2. 7, 5, 7, 7, 6, 4
   6; 6.5; 7
3. 18, 14, 15, 11, 14, 12, 17
   14.4; 14; 14
4. 19, 24, 22, 16, 15, 27, 22, 27
   21.5; 22; 22 and 27
5. 2.3, 1.1, 1.5, 3.2, 1.7, 2.0, 2.4, 1.8
   2.0; 1.9; no mode
6. 36, 32, 34, 34, 35, 38, 36, 34
   34.9; 34.5; 34
7. 30, 29, 30, 31, 30
   30; 30; 30
8. 4.2, 5.2, 2.3, 4.0, 4.6, 6.0, 2.3, 5.3
   4.2; 4.4; 2.3

Practice: Skills, p. 517

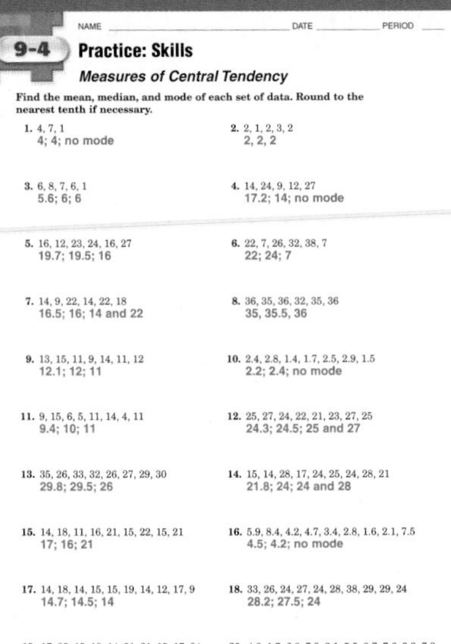

NAME ______ DATE ______ PERIOD ____

9-4 Practice: Skills

Measures of Central Tendency

Find the mean, median, and mode of each set of data. Round to the nearest tenth if necessary.

1. 4, 7, 1
   4; 4; no mode
2. 2, 1, 2, 3, 2
   2, 2, 2
3. 6, 8, 7, 6, 1
   5.6; 6; 6
4. 14, 24, 9, 12, 27
   17.2; 14; no mode
5. 16, 12, 23, 24, 16, 27
   19.7; 19.5; 16
6. 22, 7, 26, 32, 38, 7
   22; 24; 7
7. 14, 9, 22, 14, 22, 18
   16.5; 16; 14 and 22
8. 36, 35, 36, 32, 35, 36
   35, 35.5, 36
9. 13, 15, 11, 9, 14, 11, 12
   12.1; 12; 11
10. 2.4, 2.8, 1.4, 1.7, 2.5, 2.9, 1.5
    2.2; 2.4; no mode
11. 9, 15, 6, 5, 11, 14, 4, 11
    9.4; 10; 11
12. 25, 27, 24, 22, 21, 23, 27, 25
    24.3; 24.5; 25 and 27
13. 35, 26, 33, 32, 26, 27, 29, 30
    29.8; 29.5; 26
14. 15, 14, 28, 17, 24, 25, 24, 28, 21
    21.8; 24; 24 and 28
15. 14, 18, 11, 16, 21, 15, 22, 15, 21
    17; 16; 21
16. 5.9, 8.4, 4.2, 4.7, 3.4, 2.8, 1.6, 2.1, 7.5
    4.5; 4.2; no mode
17. 14, 18, 14, 15, 15, 19, 14, 12, 17, 9
    14.7; 14.5; 14
18. 33, 26, 24, 27, 24, 28, 38, 29, 29, 24
    28.2; 27.5; 24
19. 17, 25, 15, 19, 14, 21, 21, 15, 17, 24
    18.8; 18; 15, 17, and 21
20. 4.2, 1.7, 6.8, 7.3, 2.1, 5.5, 8.7, 7.6, 3.3, 7.3
    5.5; 6.2; 7.3

Practice: Word Problems, p. 518

NAME ______ DATE ______ PERIOD ____

9-4 Practice: Word Problems

Measures of Central Tendency

ANIMALS **For Exercises 1–4, use the information in the table below that shows the lifespan of selected mammals. Round to the nearest tenth if necessary.**

Average Lifespan for Mammals	
Mammal	**Average Lifespan**
Baboon	20 yr
Camel	12 yr
Chimpanzee	20 yr
Cow	15 yr
Goat	8 yr
Gorilla	20 yr
Moose	12 yr
Pig	10 yr

FOOTBALL **For Exercises 5 and 6, use the information in the table below. Round to the nearest tenth if necessary.**

2001 NFL Season, Games Won	
Team	**Games Won**
Atlanta	7
Carolina	1
Denver	8
Kansas City	6
New Orleans	7
Oakland	10
St. Louis	14
San Diego	5
San Francisco	12
Seattle	9

1. Explain how to find the mean of the lifespans listed in the table. Then find the mean. Sample answer: Add the lifespans together, and then divide by 8, the number of animals; 14.6 yr.
2. Explain how to find the median of the set of data. Then find the median. Sample answer: List the data from least to greatest and then find the mean of the middle two values; 13.5 yr.
3. Explain how to find the mode of the set of data. Then find the mode. Sample answer: Look for the most frequent value; 20 yr.
4. Which measure of central tendency is most representative of the data? Explain. Mean or median; the mode is the largest number in the data set.
5. What are the mean, median, and mode of the number of games won by the teams in the table? 7.9; 7.5; 7
6. Which measure of central tendency is most representative of the data? Explain. Mean, median or mode; all three are representative.

CIVICS **For Exercises 16 and 17, use the stem-and-leaf plot. It shows the number of members in the House of Representatives for each state.**

Stem	Leaf
0	1 1 1 1 1 1 1 2 2 2 2 2 3 3 3 3 3 4 4
	4 5 5 5 5 6 6 7 7 7 8 8 8 8 9 9 9 9
1	0 1 3 3 3 5 8 9 9
2	5 9
3	2
4	
5	3

$5|3 = 53$ members

Source: *The World Almanac*

16. Find the mean, median, and mode of the data. **about 8.7; 6; 1**
17. Which measure of central tendency is most representative of the data? Explain. **See margin.**

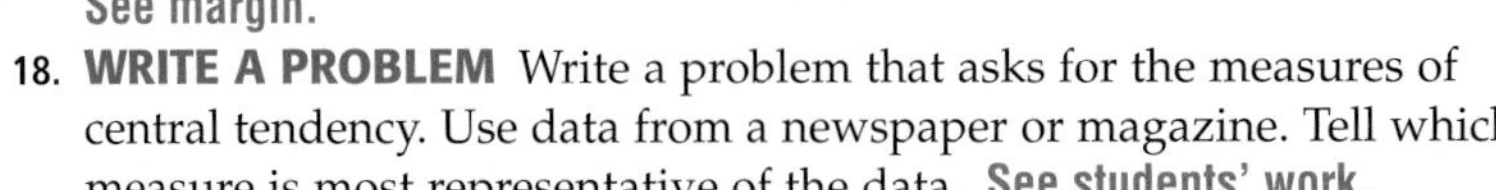

18. **WRITE A PROBLEM** Write a problem that asks for the measures of central tendency. Use data from a newspaper or magazine. Tell which measure is most representative of the data. **See students' work.**
19. **CRITICAL THINKING** Give a counterexample to show that the following statement is false. **Sample answer: 1, 1, 1, 1, 14, 15, 18**
    The median is always representative of the data.

Spiral Review with Standardized Test Practice

20. **MULTIPLE CHOICE** A consumer group tested several brands of headphones and compared their ratings (G-good, P-poor) with their price. Which statement is *not* supported by the information in the graph? **A**

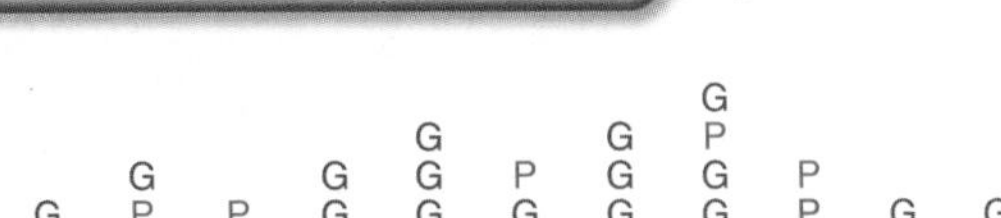

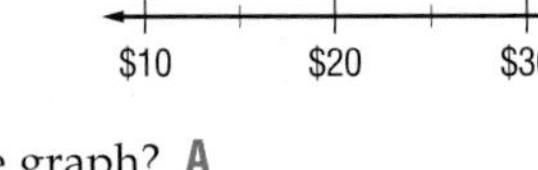

Ⓐ The mean price for a pair of headphones is $40.
Ⓑ There are 16 headphones that are rated good.
Ⓒ There is 1 headphone that is rated good and one that is rated poor for $35.
Ⓓ $45 is the mode for the data set.

21. **MULTIPLE CHOICE** In the following list of data, which number is the median? 27, 13, 26, 26, 17, 14, 15, 26, 16 **G**

Ⓕ 16 Ⓖ 17 Ⓗ 20 Ⓘ 26

Choose an appropriate type of display for each situation. (Lesson 9-3)

22. the amount of each flavor of ice cream sold relative to the total sales **circle graph**
23. the intervals of ages of the people attending the fair **histogram**
24. **TENNIS** Of the Americans who play tennis, 63% play at public parks, 26% play at private clubs, 6% play at apartment or condo complexes, and 5% play at other places. Make a circle graph of the data. (Lesson 9-2) **See margin.**

GETTING READY FOR THE NEXT LESSON

PREREQUISITE SKILL **Order each set of rational numbers from least to greatest.** (Lesson 2-2)

25. 3.1, 3.25, 3.2, 2.9, 2.89
    2.89, 2.9, 3.1, 3.2, 3.25
26. 91.3, 93.1, 94.7, 93.11, 93
    91.3, 93, 93.1, 93.11, 94.7
27. 17.4, 16.8, 16.79, 15.01, 15.1
    15.01, 15.1, 16.79, 16.8, 17.4

438 Chapter 9 Statistics and Matrices

Answers

17. Median; the mode is the least number in the set of data and the mean is affected by the very large number 53.

24.

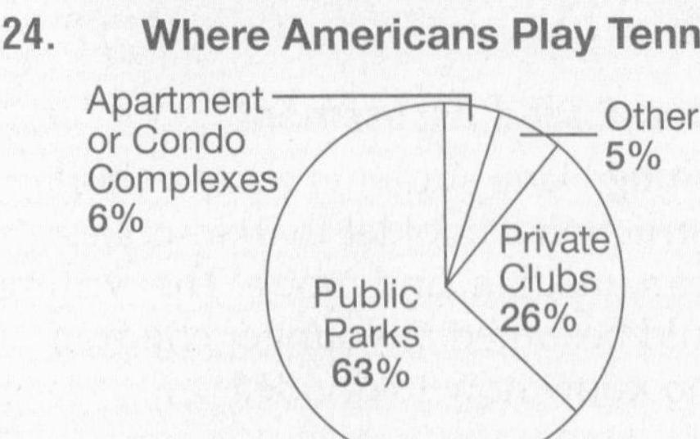

Spreadsheet Investigation

A Follow-Up of Lesson 9-4

What You'll LEARN

Use a spreadsheet to find mean, median, and mode.

Mean, Median, and Mode

You can use a spreadsheet to find the mean, median, and mode of data.

The following is a list of the top ten salaries of quarterbacks in the NFL in a recent year. Make a spreadsheet for the data.

Top Ten Salaries of Quarterbacks in the NFL				
$8,851,198	$6,942,399	$6,020,000	$5,552,250	$4,414,285
$8,485,333	$6,931,191	$5,859,691	$5,483,986	$4,260,000

Source: NFL Players Association

Use = AVERAGE(A2:A11) to find the mean.

Use = MEDIAN(A2:A11) to find the median.

Use = MODE(A2:A11) to find the mode.

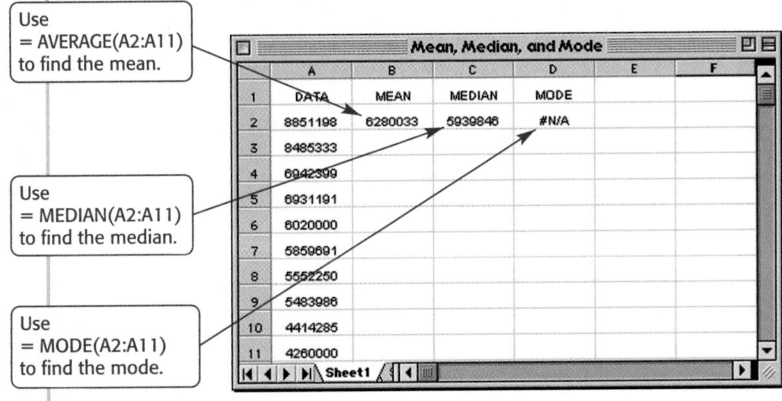

EXERCISES

For Exercises 1–3, use the following tables.

Top Ten Salaries of Running Backs in the NFL	
$8,455,125	$4,400,000
$5,000,000	$4,300,000
$4,962,703	$4,066,666
$4,800,000	$3,334,718
$4,783,600	$2,928,571

Top Ten Salaries of Defensive Ends in the NFL	
$8,750,000	$4,535,500
$5,249,411	$4,445,833
$5,050,000	$4,259,166
$4,843,666	$4,163,674
$4,600,000	$3,850,000

1. Use spreadsheets to find the mean, median, and mode of the top ten salaries for each position.
2. Compare the highest salary for the three positions.
3. Compare the mean and median of the three positions.

1. Running backs: $4,703,138; $4,591,800; none
Defensive ends: $4,974,725; $4,567,750; none
2–3. See margin.

9-4b Spreadsheet Investigation

GETTING STARTED

Teaching Tip Prior to the **Activity**, demonstrate how students should open and use the spreadsheet program. Review briefly the concept of cells and how they are labeled. The spreadsheet shown is in Microsoft Excel®.

TEACH

- Be sure that students realize that they are typing salary values into the DATA column. In the other columns, they are typing in formulas that allow the computer to determine the mean, median, and mode.
- Remind students that their formulas should begin with equal marks and that they should not key spaces in the formulas.
- Explain that #N/A appears in column D because there are no modes in the data set.

ASSESS

Observe as students solve the **Exercises**. They should:

- correctly enter data into cells,
- correctly use spreadsheet formulas, and
- be able to interpret the values generated by the formulas.

Answers

2. The highest paid quarterback has the greatest salary. The highest paid defensive end has the next greatest salary. The highest paid running back is less than the highest salary of a quarterback and a defensive end, as well as the second highest salary of a quarterback. All of the highest salaries are within $400,000 of each other.
3. The greatest mean is the mean of quarterback salaries. This is followed by the mean of defensive end salaries and then the mean of running back salaries. The means are more than $1,500,000 apart. The greatest median is the median of quarterback salaries. This is followed by the median of running back salaries and then the median of defensive end salaries. The medians are more than $1,300,000 apart.

Assessment Option

Mid-Chapter Test (Lessons 9-1 through 9-4) is available on p. 557 of the *Chapter 9 Resource Masters.*

ExamView® Pro

Use the networkable ExamView® Pro Testmaker CD-ROM to:

- Create **multiple versions** of tests.
- Create **modified** tests for **inclusion** students with one mouse click.
- **Edit** existing questions and **add** your own questions.
- Build tests aligned with state standards using built-in **state curriculum correlations.**
- Change **English** tests to **Spanish** with one mouse click and vice versa.

FOLDABLES™ Follow-Up Before students complete the Mid-Chapter Practice Test, encourage them to review the notes, definitions, concepts, and main ideas they recorded on the first four sections of their Foldables.

Answers

1. **Both bar graphs and histogram visually show data using bars. A histogram is a bar graph that displays numerical data that have been organized into equal intervals.**

3. **Sugar in Cereal**

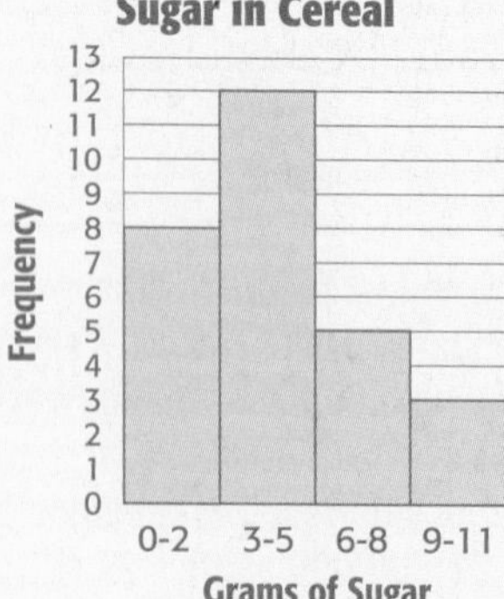

CHAPTER 9 Mid-Chapter Practice Test

Vocabulary and Concepts

1. **Compare and contrast** a bar graph and a histogram. (Lesson 9-1) **See margin.**
2. **OPEN ENDED** Give an example of data that could be displayed using a pictograph. (Lesson 9-3)
Sample answer: the color of school T-shirts ordered by the students

Skills and Applications

FOOD The frequency table shows the grams of sugar per serving in 28 cereals made for adults.

3. Use the intervals 0–2, 3–5, 6–8, and 9–11 to make a histogram of the data. (Lesson 9-1) **See margin.**
4. Make a circle graph of the data. (Lesson 9-2) **See margin.**

Sugar in Cereal		
Grams	Tally	Frequency
0	𝍸	5
1		0
2	III	3
3	𝍸 I	6
4	I	1
5	𝍸	5
6	IIII	4
7	I	1
8		0
9	I	1
10	I	1
11	I	1

Choose an appropriate type of display for each situation. (Lesson 9-3) **5. circle graph**

5. percent of students in each grade level in a school
6. prices of different brands of ice cream by intervals **histogram**

Find the mean, median, and mode of each set of data. Round to the nearest tenth if necessary. (Lesson 9-4)

7. 7, 3, 8, 6, 2 **5.2; 6; no mode**
8. 73, 78, 71, 95, 86, 88, 86 **82.4; 86; 86**

Standardized Test Practice

For Exercises 9 and 10, use the graph.

Nevada's Budget

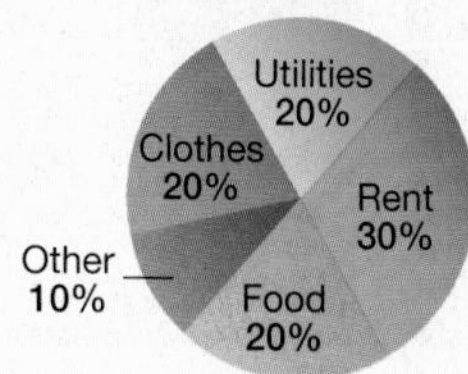

9. **GRID IN** If Nevada makes $1,200 per month, how much does she budget in dollars for rent? (Lesson 9-2) **360**

10. **MULTIPLE CHOICE** Which statement cannot be determined from the graph? (Lesson 9-2) **D**

Ⓐ Nevada budgets half of her money for rent and food.

Ⓑ Nevada budgets the same amount of money for clothes as food.

Ⓒ Nevada budgets more money for food and clothes than rent.

Ⓓ Nevada does not spend any money on going to the movies.

4. **Sugar in Cereal (grams)**

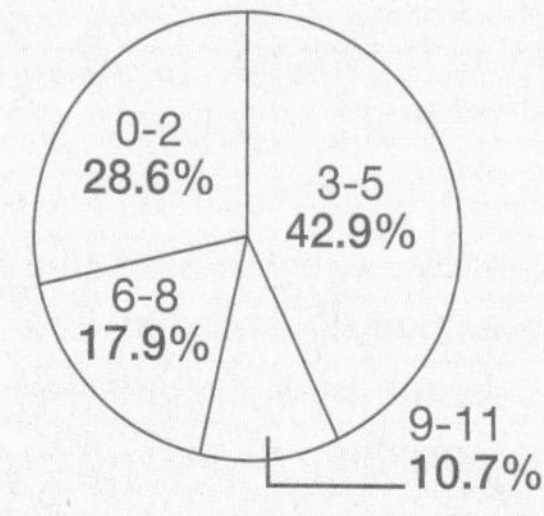

The Game Zone

A Place To Practice Your Math Skills

What's the Average?

GET READY!

Players: four
Materials: 4 index cards, 2 spinners

GET SET!

- Each player should write five whole numbers on an index card. The numbers should be from 1 through 10.
- Label a spinner that has two equal regions with the words *mean* and *median*.

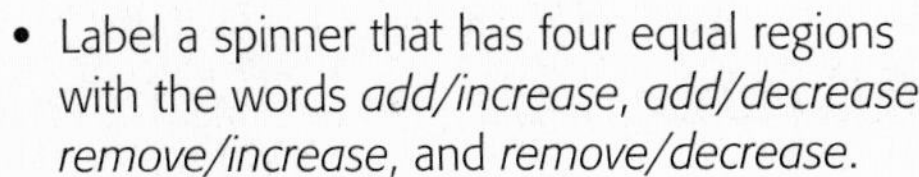

- Label a spinner that has four equal regions with the words *add/increase*, *add/decrease*, *remove/increase*, and *remove/decrease*.

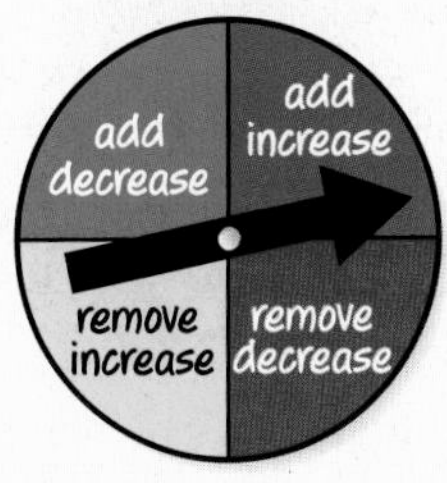

GO!

- Mix the index cards and turn them facedown.
- The first player randomly selects a card and spins each spinner once. Then the player adjusts the data set as instructed. For example, if the player gets *mean* and *add/decrease*, the player must add a piece of data to the data set so the mean decreases. If the player gets *median* and *remove/increase*, the player must remove a piece of data from the data set so the median of the set increases.
- The other players then check his or her work.
- A player scores two points for each correct solution and loses one point for each incorrect solution.
- **Who Wins?** The first player to get 10 points is the winner.

The Game Zone

Resources

Math Online For an easy-to-make manipulative for this game, visit: msmath3.net/gamezone

Glencoe Mathematics Classroom Manipulative Kit

- spinners

GETTING READY

Objective Find the mean and median of a set of numbers.

MANAGEMENT TIPS

Recommended Time
15 minutes

Tips

- If spinners are unavailable, you could use labeled cards that students can pick, without looking, from a box. Put 10 cards labeled "mean" and 10 cards labeled "median" in Box 1. In Box 2, place 5 cards for each of the 4 labels for the second spinner.
- Before students play the game, demonstrate what they should do if their spinner lands on add/decrease, add/increase, remove/increase, or remove/decrease.
- You may wish to use the game as an assessment tool for the concepts the students have been learning in Lessons 9-1 through 9-4.

Math Online For an additional game for this chapter, visit: msmath3.net/gamezone

9-5 Lesson Notes

Lesson Resources

Chapter 9 Resource Masters

FAST FILE

- Study Guide and Intervention, p. 521
- Practice: Skills, p. 522
- Practice: Word Problems, p. 523
- Reading to Learn Mathematics, p. 524
- Enrichment, p. 525

Key Teaching Transparencies, 37

Parent and Student Study Guide Online Worksheets, 9-5

Noteables™: Interactive Study Notebook with Foldables™, 9-5

1 Focus

Check 9-5

Use as a quiz or review of Lesson 9-4. (Also available as a transparency)

Bellringer

Reading Mathematics This lesson introduces many new mathematical terms and uses many terms introduced in Lesson 9-4. Have students copy the table in the bottom margin into their notebooks, leaving plenty of room to write. Before beginning the lesson, have students fill in what they already have learned. Then have them complete the remaining sections as they work this lesson.

(Continued in bottom margin.)

Reading to Learn Mathematics, p. 524 ELL

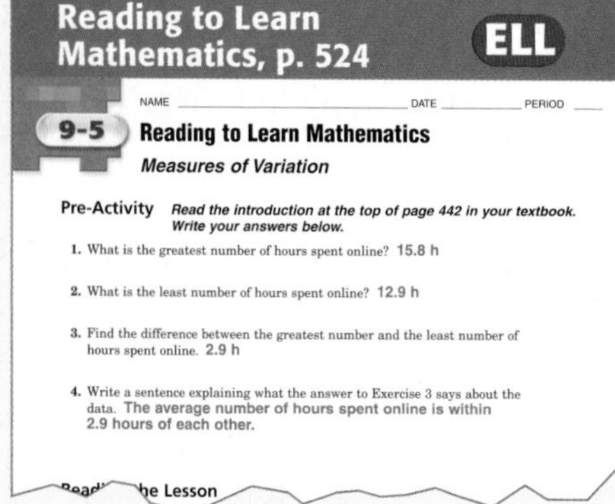

NAME ________ DATE ________ PERIOD ____

9-5 **Reading to Learn Mathematics**

Measures of Variation

Pre-Activity ***Read the introduction at the top of page 442 in your textbook. Write your answers below.***

1. What is the greatest number of hours spent online? 15.8 h
2. What is the least number of hours spent online? 12.9 h
3. Find the difference between the greatest number and the least number of hours spent online. 2.9 h
4. Write a sentence explaining what the answer to Exercise 3 says about the data. The average number of hours spent online is within 2.9 hours of each other.

Readi... the Lesson

9-5 Measures of Variation

What You'll LEARN

Find the range and quartiles of a set of data.

NEW Vocabulary

measures of variation
range
quartiles
lower quartile
upper quartile
interquartile range
outlier

Link to READING

Everyday Meaning of Quart: one fourth of a gallon

WHEN am I ever going to use this?

ONLINE TIME The average number of hours that teens in various cities spend online is given in the table.

Average Number of Hours Teens Spend Online Each Week	
City	**Hours Online**
Pittsburgh	15.8
New York	14.9
Cleveland	14.9
San Diego	14.4
Miami	14.2
Hartford	13.4
Los Angeles	13.3
Detroit	13.1
Philadelphia	12.9
Milwaukee	12.9

Source: Digital Marketing Services

1. What is the greatest number of hours spent online? **15.8 h**
2. What is the least number of hours spent online? **12.9 h**
3. Find the difference between the greatest number and the least number of hours spent online. **2.9 h**
4. Write a sentence explaining what the answer to Exercise 3 says about the data.

4. The average number of hours spent online is within 2.9 hours of each other.

Measures of variation are used to describe the distribution of the data. One measure of variation is the range. The **range** indicates how "spread out" the data are.

Noteables™ **Key Concept: Range**

The range of a set of data is the difference between the greatest and the least numbers in the set.

Quartiles are the values that divide the data into four equal parts. Recall that the median separates the data in two equal parts.

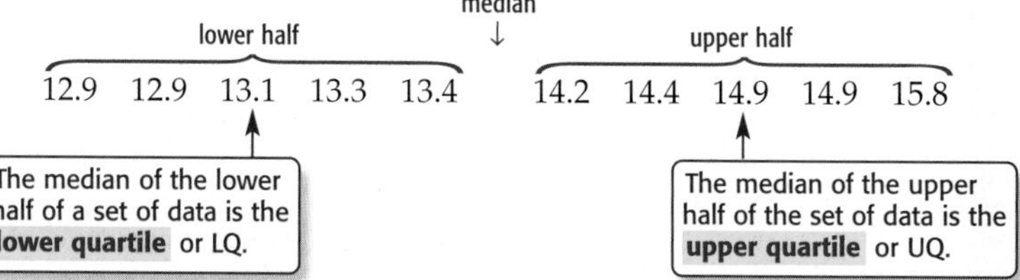

So, one half of the data lie between the lower quartile and the upper quartile. Another measure of variation is the **interquartile range**.

Noteables™ **Key Concept: Interquartile Range**

The interquartile range is the range of the middle half of the data. It is the difference between the upper quartile and the lower quartile.

Measures of Central Tendency		Measures of Variation	
Term	**Description**	**Term**	**Description**
mean		range	
		quartiles	
median		lower quartile	
		upper quartile	
mode		interquartile range	
		outlier	

EXAMPLES Find Measures of Variation

FOOD Use the table at the right.

Calories in a Serving of Juice	
Juice	**Calories**
Apple	120
Carrot	80
Grape	170
Grapefruit	100
Orange	120
Pineapple	110
Prune	180
Tomato	35

Source: Center for Science in the Public Interest

1 Find the range of the Calories.

The greatest number of Calories is 180. The least number of Calories is 35. The range is 180 − 35 or 145 Calories.

2 Find the median and the upper and lower quartiles.

Arrange the numbers in order from least to greatest.

lower quartile ↓ median ↓ upper quartile ↓

35 80 100 110 120 120 170 180

$\frac{80+100}{2} = 90$ $\frac{110+120}{2} = 115$ $\frac{120+170}{2} = 145$

The median is 115, the lower quartile is 90, and the upper quartile is 145.

3 Find the interquartile range.

Interquartile Range = 145 − 90 or 55

TEACHING TIP

When there is an odd number of data, the median is not included when finding the lower quartile and the upper quartile.

STUDY TIP

Interpreting Interquartile Range A small interquartile range means that the data in the middle of the set are close in value. A large interquartile range means that the data in the middle are spread out.

Data that are more than 1.5 times the value of the interquartile range beyond the quartiles are called **outliers**.

EXAMPLE Find Outliers

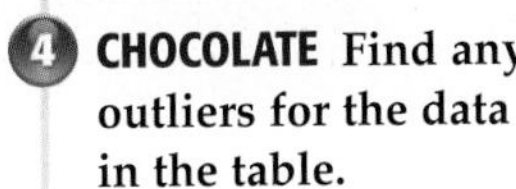

4 CHOCOLATE **Find any outliers for the data in the table.**

	Annual Chocolate Sales	
	Country	**Sales (billion dollars)**
	United States	16.6
upper quartile →	United Kingdom	6.5
	Germany	5.1
median →	Russia	4.9
	Japan	3.2
lower quartile →	France	2.1
	Brazil	2.0

Source: Euromonitor

Interquartile Range = 6.5 − 2.1 or 4.4

Multiply the interquartile range, 4.4, by 1.5. $4.4 \times 1.5 = 6.6$

Find the limits for the outliers.

Subtract 6.6 from the lower quartile. $2.1 - 6.6 = -4.5$

Add 6.6 to the upper quartile. $6.5 + 6.6 = 13.1$

The limits for the outliers are −4.5 and 13.1. The only outlier is 16.6.

Math Online msmath3.net/extra_examples

2 Teach

In-Class Examples

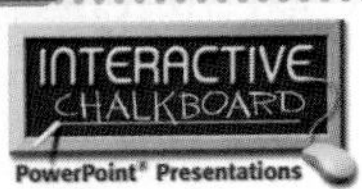

BASKETBALL **Use the table below.**

Points Scored by Top Ten Teams During the NBA Playoffs, 2002	
Team	**Points Scored**
Dallas	109
Minnesota	102
Sacramento	101.1
L.A. Lakers	97.8
Charlotte	96.1
New Jersey	95.4
Orlando	93.8
Indiana	91.6
Boston	91.3
Portland	91.3

Source: nba.com

1 Find the range of the scores. **17.7 points**

2 Find the median and the upper and lower quartiles. **95.75; 101.1; 91.6**

3 Find the interquartile range. **9.5**

4 **CONCESSION SALES** Find any outliers for the data in the table below. **196**

Items Sold at Football Game Concession Stand	
Item	**Number Sold**
colas	196
diet colas	32
water	46
coffee	18
candy bars	39
hotdogs	23
hamburgers	16
chips	41
popcorn	24

DAILY INTERVENTION **Differentiated Instruction**

Kinesthetic Have all the students arrange themselves by height from shortest to tallest. By comparison, have them determine the median, upper quartile, lower quartile, and interquartile range. They also should decide whether there are any outliers in the measurements. Instead of using numbers, represent the values with student names.

Students practice the same concepts in Exercises 11–16 if they are assigned odd or even problems.

Skill and Concept Check

1. **OPEN ENDED** Write a list of data with at least eight numbers that has an interquartile range of 20 and one outlier. Sample answer: {1, 50, 50, 60, 60, 70, 70, 80}
2. **Which One Doesn't Belong?** Identify the statistical value that is not the same as the other three. Explain your reasoning.

mean	median	range	mode

Range; the others are measures of central tendency.

GUIDED PRACTICE

Find the range, median, upper and lower quartiles, interquartile range, and any outliers for each set of data.

3. 54, 58, 58, 59, 60, 62, 63
   9; 59; 62, 58; 4; no outliers
4. 9, 0, 2, 8, 19, 5, 3, 2
   19; 4; 8.5, 2; 6.5; 19

POPULATION For Exercises 5–10, use the graphic at the right.

5. Find the range of the data. 41.1 million
6. Find the median of the data. 15.9 million
7. Find the upper and lower quartile of the data. 33.0 million, 9.1 million
8. Find the interquartile range of the data.
9. Find any outliers of the data. no outliers
10. Use the information in Exercises 5–9 to describe the data. See margin.

8. 23.9 million

Top Ancestral Origins of Americans

Country	Number (millions)
Germany	46.5
Ireland	33.0
England	28.3
Italy	15.9
France	9.8
Poland	9.1
Scotland	5.4

Source: Census 2000 Supplementary Survey

★ indicates increased difficulty

Practice and Applications

Find the range, median, upper and lower quartiles, interquartile range, and any outliers for each set of data. 11–14. See margin.

11. 43, 55, 49, 49, 53, 48, 57, 60, 57, 60, 47, 51, 59, 22
12. 55, 76, 104, 65, 62, 79, 63, 57, 52, 72, 57, 73, 55, 60, 80, 53
13. 19.8, 16.6, 19, 15.5, 14.6, 18.4, 13.5, 18, 14.5
14. 2.3, 2.3, 3.8, 2.6, 3.7, 2.9, 6.1, 2.3, 2.9, 2.5, 3.5

★15. (line plot; axis 0, 0.5, 1.0)
0.7; 0.55; 0.65, 0.25; 0.4; no outliers

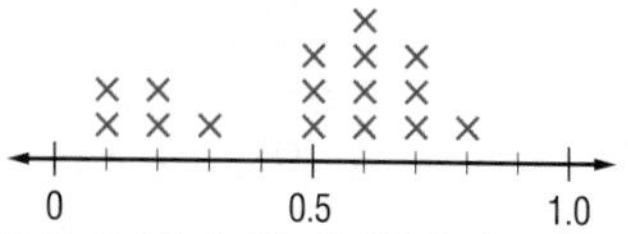

★16. (line plot; axis 2.0, 2.5, 3.0)
0.9; 2.4; 2.5, 2.3; 0.2; 3.0

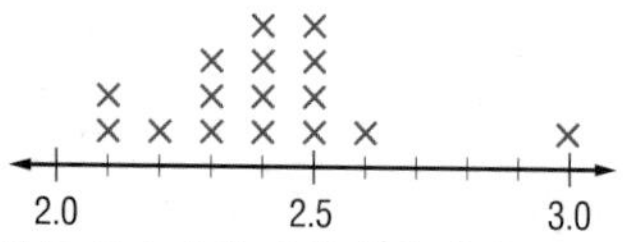

HOMEWORK HELP	
For Exercises	See Examples
11–23	1–4

Extra Practice
See pages 639, 656.

MOVIES For Exercises 17 and 18, use the stem-and-leaf plot at the right showing the ages of the Best Actress Academy Award winners from 1976 to 2003. 17. 38; 44, 30

17. Find the median and upper and lower quartiles of the data.
18. Between what two ages were the middle half of the actresses when they won the award? 30 and 44

Stem	Leaf
2	1 6 7 8 9 9
3	0 1 3 3 4 5 8 8
4	1 1 2 2 3 4 9
5	2 5
6	1
7	4
8	0 2|1 = 21 years old

Source: *The World Almanac*

Intervention Incorporating board games into math instruction is a great way to maintain students' interest, particularly if they have difficulty with a topic. For example, students may play a modified version of a board game that requires them to solve math problems related to topics they are currently studying.

3 Practice/Apply

FOLDABLES™ Follow-Up Remind students to use their Foldables to record what they learn about finding the range and quartiles of a set of data. They might use the information collected under the tabs of their Foldables to compare and contrast measures of variation and measures of central tendency.

Which One Doesn't Belong? If students have difficulty answering Exercise 2, suggest that they list the values that are measures of central tendency and the values that are measures of variation.

About the Exercises...

Guided Practice Key

Exercises	Examples
3–4, 10	1–4
5	1
6–7	2
8	3
9	4

Assignment Guide

Basic: 11, 13, 17–21 odd, 25–34

Average: 11–17 odd, 19–23, 25–34

Enriched: 12–16 even, 17–30, 31–34

Answers

10. Sample answer: There are no extreme values. The range of the middle half of the data is about half of the range of all of the data. The median is closer to the lower values than the higher values.
11. 38; 52; 57, 48; 9; 22
12. 52; 62.5; 74.5, 56; 18.5; 104
13. 6.3; 16.6; 18.7, 14.55; 4.15; no outliers
14. 3.8; 2.9; 3.7, 2.3; 1.4; 6.1
22. The median average temperature of San Francisco is only slightly greater than the median average temperature of Philadelphia.

WEATHER **For Exercises 19–23, use the table at the right.**

19. Which city has a greater range of temperatures?
20. Find the median and upper and lower quartile ranges of the average temperatures for San Francisco.
21. Find the median and upper and lower quartile ranges of the average temperatures for Philadelphia.
22. Compare the medians of the average temperatures.
23. Compare the interquartile ranges of the average temperatures. **22–23. See margin.**

19. Philadelphia 20. 57; 62.5; 52.5 21. 54; 70; 39

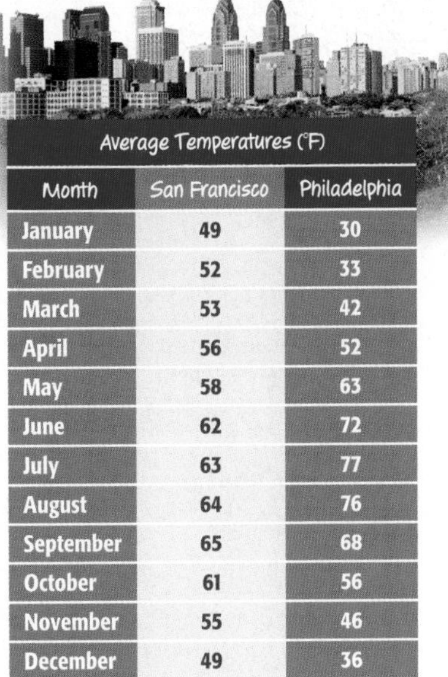

Average Temperatures (°F)		
Month	San Francisco	Philadelphia
January	49	30
February	52	33
March	53	42
April	56	52
May	58	63
June	62	72
July	63	77
August	64	76
September	65	68
October	61	56
November	55	46
December	49	36

Source: *The World Almanac*

24. **WRITE A PROBLEM** Write a real-life problem that asks for the interquartile range. **See margin.**

25. See Ch. 9 Answer Appendix.

25. **CRITICAL THINKING** Create two different sets of data that meet the following conditions.
    a. the same range, different interquartile ranges
    b. the same median and quartiles, but different ranges

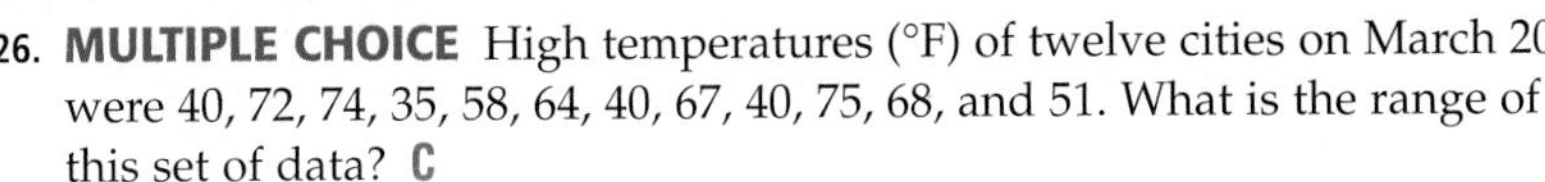

Spiral Review with Standardized Test Practice

26. **MULTIPLE CHOICE** High temperatures (°F) of twelve cities on March 20 were 40, 72, 74, 35, 58, 64, 40, 67, 40, 75, 68, and 51. What is the range of this set of data? **C**

    Ⓐ 75°F　Ⓑ 51°F　Ⓒ 40°F　Ⓓ 11°F

27. **GRID IN** Find the interquartile range of the data in the stem-and-leaf plot. **1.35**

Stem	Leaf
4	2 3 3 7
5	0 1 1 5 8 9
6	
7	2 3　*4 | 2 = 4.2 meters*

Find the mean, median, and mode for each set of data. Round to the nearest tenth if necessary. (Lesson 9-4)

28. 6, 4, 6, 12, 10, 8, 7, 12, 11, 9 **8.5; 8.5; 6 and 12**
29. 14, 3, 6, 8, 11, 9, 3, 2, 7 **7; 7; 3**

30. **RADIO LISTENING** Choose an appropriate display for the data. Then make a display. (Lesson 9-3)

Adult Audience of Oldies Radio					
Age	18 to 24	25 to 34	35 to 44	45 to 54	55 or older
Percent of Audience	10%	14%	29%	33%	14%

Source: Interep Research Division

See Ch. 9 Answer Appendix.

GETTING READY FOR THE NEXT LESSON **31–34. See Ch. 9 Answer Appendix.**

PREREQUISITE SKILL **Graph each set of points on a number line.** (Lesson 1-3)

31. {3, 5, 8, 9, 10}
32. {13, 15, 20, 27, 31}
33. {9, 13, 16, 17, 21}
34. {3, 9, 10, 15, 19}

Math Online msmath3.net/self_check_quiz

4 Assess

Higher-Level Thinking

Explain why you could not easily use a bar graph to display data that have an outlier. **Any range for the graph that would clearly display all of the data in columns would be quite large.**

Answers

23. **The interquartile range for San Francisco is only 10°F, while the interquartile range for Philadelphia is 31.**
24. **Sample answer: The heights of five children are 41 in., 39 in., 45 in., 50 in., and 38 in. Find the interquartile range of the heights. 9 in.**

Study Guide and Intervention, p. 521

NAME ________ DATE ________ PERIOD ____

9-5 Study Guide and Intervention

Measures of Variation

The **range** of a set of data is the difference between the greatest and least numbers in the set. The **lower quartile** is the median of the lower half of a set of data. The **upper quartile** is the median of the upper half of a set of data. The **interquartile range** is the difference between the upper quartile and the lower quartile.

EXAMPLE 1 **Find the range, median, upper and lower quartiles, and interquartile range for the following set of data.**
13, 20, 18, 12, 21, 2, 18, 17, 15, 10, 14

The greatest number in the data set is 21. The least number is 2. The range is 21 − 2 or 19.

To find the quartiles, arrange the numbers in order from least to greatest.
2 10 12 13 14 15 17 18 18 20 21

The median is 15. The numbers below 15 are 2, 10, 12, 13, and 14. The median of the numbers below 15 is 12, so the lower quartile is 12. The numbers above 15 are 17, 18, 18, 20, and 21. The median of the numbers above 15 is 18, so the upper quartile is 18. The interquartile range is 18 − 12 or 6.

In some data sets, a few of the values are much greater than or less than the rest of the data. Data that are more than 1.5 times the interquartile range less than the lower quartile or greater than the upper quartile are called **outliers**.

EXAMPLE 2 **Find any outliers for the set of data given in Example 1.**

The interquartile range is 8 − 12 or 6.
Multiply the interquartile range by 1.5. $6 \times 1.5 = 9$

Any data more than 9 above the upper quartile or below the lower quartile are outliers. Find the limits of the outliers.

Subtract 9 from the lower quartile. $12 - 9 = 3$
Add 9 to the upper quartile. $18 + 9 = 27$

The limits of the outliers are 3 and 27. The only data point outside this range is 2, so the only outlier is 2.

EXERCISES

Find the range, median, upper and lower quartiles, interquartile range, and any outliers for each set of data.

1. 14, 16, 18, 24, 19, 15, 13 **11; 16; 19, 14; 5; no outliers**
2. 29, 27, 24, 28, 30, 51, 28 **27; 28; 30, 27; 3; 51**
3. 57, 60, 43, 55, 46, 43, 62, 31 **31; 50.5; 58.5, 43; 15.5; no outliers**
4. 91, 92, 88, 89, 93, 95, 65, 85, 91 **30; 91; 92.5, 86.5; 6; 65**
5. 104, 116, 111, 108, 113, 127, 109, 122, 115, 105 **23; 112; 116, 108; 8; no outliers**

Practice: Skills, p. 522

NAME ________ DATE ________ PERIOD ____

9-5 Practice: Skills

Measures of Variation

Find the range, median, upper and lower quartiles, interquartile range, and any outliers for each set of data.

1. 15, 17, 10, 12, 19, 20, 16 **10; 16; 19, 12; 7; no outliers**
2. 52, 72, 89, 21, 58, 42, 75 **68; 58; 75, 42; 33; no outliers**
3. 20, 23, 18, 21, 4, 17, 15 **19; 18; 21, 15; 6; 4**
4. 24, 37, 32, 39, 35, 42, 44, 28 **20; 36; 40.5, 30; 10.5; no outliers**
5. 48, 56, 72, 47, 43, 36, 47, 14 **58; 47; 52, 39.5; 12.5; 14 and 72**
6. 116, 107, 105, 113, 112, 123, 115, 108 **18; 112.5; 115.5, 107.5; 8; no outliers**
7. 2.2, 2.6, 2.5, 3.6, 2.9, 2.8, 2.2, 2.4 **1.4; 2.55; 2.85, 2.3; 0.55; no outliers**
8. 59, 72, 57, 51, 62, 77, 73, 64, 54 **26; 62; 72.5, 55.5; 17; no outliers**
9. 81, 79, 88, 67, 89, 87, 85, 83, 83 **22; 83; 87.5, 80; 7.5; 67**
10. 132, 116, 108, 113, 126, 120, 131, 112, 126 **24; 120; 128.5, 112.5; 16; no outliers**
11. 6.3, 6.7, 6.2, 4.9, 6.7, 6.6, 5.3, 6.3, 6.4 **1.8; 6.3; 6.65, 5.75; 0.9; no outliers**
12. 22, 27, 25, 11, 29, 28, 41, 26, 28, 23 **30; 26.5; 28, 23; 5; 11 and 41**
13. 90, 88, 72, 85, 92, 95, 93, 86, 92, 91 **23; 90.5; 92, 86; 6; 72**
14. 107, 114, 124, 108, 117, 106, 107, 109, 117, 115 **18; 111.5; 117, 107; 10; no outliers**
15. 8.3, 8.5, 9.5, 8.7, 8.9, 8.3, 8.6, 8.8, 8.9, 8.7 **1.2; 8.7; 8.9, 8.5; 0.4; no outliers**
16. 42, 36, 58, 47, 34, 43, 54, 49, 48, 41, 38 **24; 43; 49, 38; 11; no outliers**
17. 8.3, 9.0, 8.1, 9.5, 8.2, 8.9, 9.4, 7.9, 8.3, 8.4, 8.0 **1.6; 8.3; 9.0, 8.1; 0.9; no outliers**
18. 15, 16, 18, 9, 18, 17, 19, 19, 10, 12, 15, 13, 16 **10; 16; 18, 12.5; 5.5; no outliers**

Practice: Word Problems, p. 523

NAME ________ DATE ________ PERIOD ____

9-5 Practice: Word Problems

Measures of Variation

FOOTBALL **For Exercises 1–4, use the table below that shows the winning scores in the Super Bowl from 1994 through 2003.**

Winning Super Bowl Scores, 1994–2003									
1994	1995	1996	1997	1998	1999	2000	2001	2002	2003
30	49	27	35	31	34	23	23	20	48

1. Explain how to find the range of the data. Then find the range. **Sample answer: Subtract the smallest score, 20, from the largest score, 49; 29.**
2. Find the median, the upper and lower quartiles, and the interquartile range of the winning scores. **30.5; 35, 23; 12**
3. Describe how to find the limits for outliers. Then find the limits. **Sample answer: Subtract 1.5 times the interquartile range from the lower quartile and add 1.5 times the interquartile range to the upper quartile; 5, 53.**
4. Are there any outliers among the winning Super Bowl scores? If so, what are they? Explain. **No; all values are between 5 and 53.**

GRADES **For Exercises 5 and 6, use the stem-and-leaf plot at the right showing the scores on the midterm exam in English.**

Stem	Leaf
7	5 7
8	0 1 4 5 6 8 9 9
9	7　*7 | 5 = 75*

5. Find the range, median, upper and lower quartiles, and the interquartile range of the exam scores. **22; 85; 89, 80; 9**
6. Are there any outliers in this data? Explain. **No; there are no scores below 66.5 or above 102.5.**

Lesson 9-5 Measures of Variation **445**

9-6 Lesson Notes

Lesson Resources

Chapter 9 Resource Masters
- Study Guide and Intervention, p. 526
- Practice: Skills, p. 527
- Practice: Word Problems, p.528
- Reading to Learn Mathematics, p. 529
- Enrichment, p. 530

Calculator and Spreadsheet Masters, p. 41
Classroom Math Games, pp. 33–34
MathPASS Tutorial CD-ROM, 58
Parent and Student Study Guide Online Worksheets, 9-6
Noteables™: Interactive Study Notebook with Foldables™, 9-6

1 Focus

5-Minute Check 9-6

Use as a quiz or review of Lesson 9-5. (Also available as a transparency)

Bellringer

Problem Solving Tell students that one visual tool used in math is a number line. Write the following numbers on the chalkboard: 27, 18, 5, 16, 33, 21, 29, 51, 12, 25. Have students draw a number line and plot the points on the line. Ask them to describe any interesting details they notice from the line. **Students should point out that the numbers 5 and 51 are far from the rest of the numbers.**

Reading to Learn Mathematics, p. 529 **ELL**

NAME ____ DATE ____ PERIOD ____

9-6 Reading to Learn Mathematics
Box-and-Whisker Plots

Pre-Activity *Read the introduction at the top of page 446 in your textbook. Write your answers below.*

1. What is the least value in the data? 343
2. What is the lower quartile of the data? 1,209
3. What is the median of the data? 1,489
4. What is the upper quartile of the data? 3,011
5. What is the greatest value in the data? 7,668
6. Name any outliers. 7,668

Reading the Lesson

7. Explain the parts of the box-and-whisker plot in your own words.
Sample answer: The box ... around the quartile values, ... whiskers ...

9-6 Box-and-Whisker Plots

What You'll LEARN

Display and interpret data in a box-and-whisker plot.

NEW Vocabulary

box-and-whisker plot

WHEN am I ever going to use this?

WILDFIRES The table gives the number of wildfires for various states.

1. What is the least value in the data? **451**
2. What is the lower quartile of the data? **1,373**
3. What is the median of the data? **1,936**
4. What is the upper quartile of the data? **2,326**
5. What is the greatest value in the data? **9,116**
6. Name any outliers. **9,116**

Wildfires in 2003

State	Number of Fires
Alaska	451
Nevada	797
Washington	1,373
Utah	1,630
Idaho	1,845
Colorado	2,027
Florida	2,118
Montana	2,326
Kansas	3,205
California	9,116

Source: National Interagency Fire Center

A **box-and-whisker plot** uses a number line to show the distribution of a set of data. The *box* is drawn around the quartile values, and the *whiskers* extend from each quartile to the extreme data points that are not outliers.

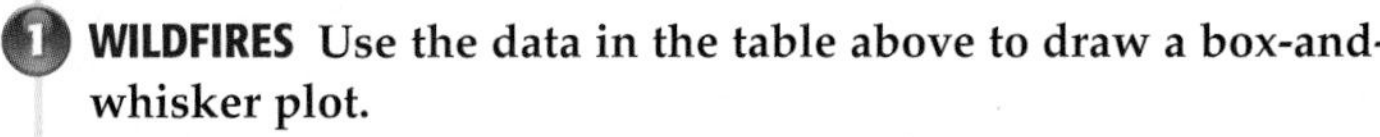

EXAMPLE Draw a Box-and-Whisker Plot

1 WILDFIRES Use the data in the table above to draw a box-and-whisker plot.

Step 1 Draw a number line that includes the least and greatest number in the data.

Step 2 Mark the extremes, the median, and the upper and lower quartile above the number line. Since the data have an outlier, mark the greatest value that is not an outlier.

Step 3 Draw the box and the whiskers.

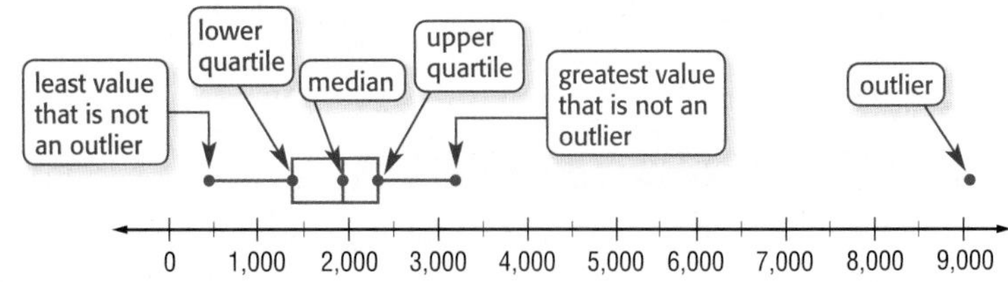

Intervention Point out to students that if there are outliers on one side of a box-and-whisker plot, they and the whisker on that side represent $\frac{1}{4}$ of the data.

TEACHING TIP

Help students to understand that each part of the box or each whisker represents the same number of data values.

REAL-LIFE CAREERS

How Does a Dietitian Use Math?

Dietitians keep track of Calories, fat, salt, and nutrients in food. They use this information to help people maintain an appropriate diet.

Research

For information about a career as a dietitian, visit: msmath3.net/careers

Standardized Test Practice

Test-Taking Tip

Study the Graphic

When answering a test question involving a graphic, always study the graphic and its labels carefully. Ask yourself, "What information is the graphic telling me?"

Box-and-whisker plots separate data into four parts. Although the parts usually differ in length, each part contains one fourth of the data.

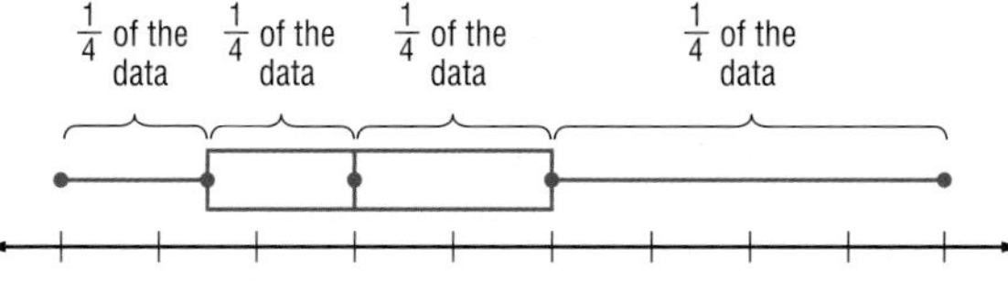

A long whisker or box indicates that the data in that quartile or quartiles have a greater range. A short whisker or box indicates the data in that quartile or quartiles have a lesser range.

EXAMPLE Interpret Data

2 **DIET** **What does the length of the box-and-whisker plot tell you about the data?**

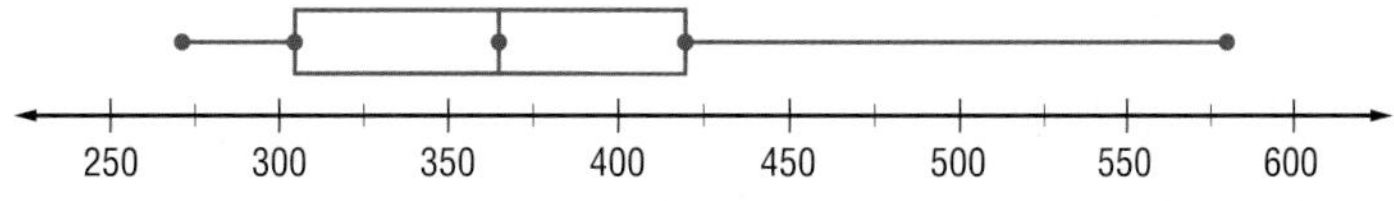

The median line seems to divide the box into two approximately equal parts, so data in the second and third quartiles are similarly spread out. The whisker at the right is longer than the other parts of the plot, so the data in the fourth quartile are more spread out.

A double box-and-whisker plot can be used to compare data.

EXAMPLE Compare Data

3 **MULTIPLE-CHOICE TEST ITEM** Use the box-and-whisker plots below to determine which statement is *not* true.

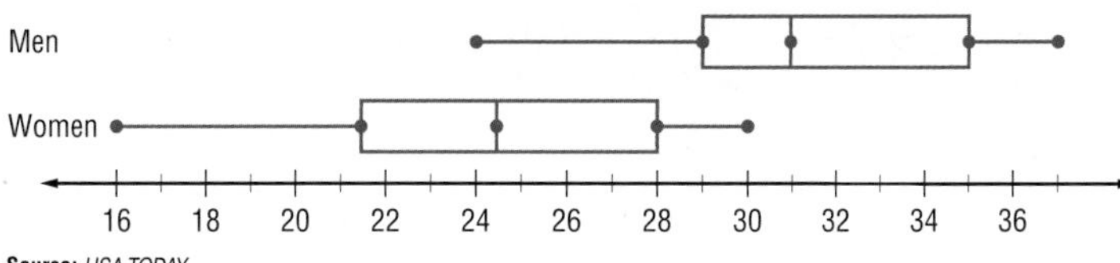

Source: *USA TODAY*

A The women's ages have a greater range than the men's ages.

B The women's ages were all less than the men's median age.

C The men's ages were all greater than the women's median age.

D Most of the men were 29 or older.

Read the Test Item You need to study the box-and-whisker plot.

Solve the Test Item The ages of the men were not all greater than the median age of the women. The answer is C.

Check to make sure A, B, and D are true.

msmath3.net/extra_examples

2 Teach

In-Class Examples

1 **POPULATION** Use the data in the table below to draw a box-and-whisker plot.

World's Most Populous Cities

City	Population (millions)
Tokyo	34.8
New York	20.2
Seoul	19.9
Mexico City	19.8
Sao Paulo	17.9
Bombay	17.9
Osaka	17.9
Los Angeles	16.2
Cairo	14.4
Manila	13.5

Source: *Time Almanac*

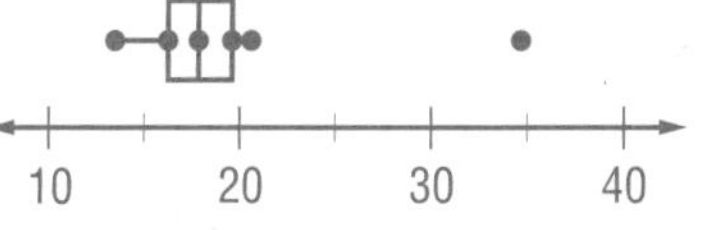

2 **WATERFALLS** What does the length of the box-and-whisker plot below tell you about the data?

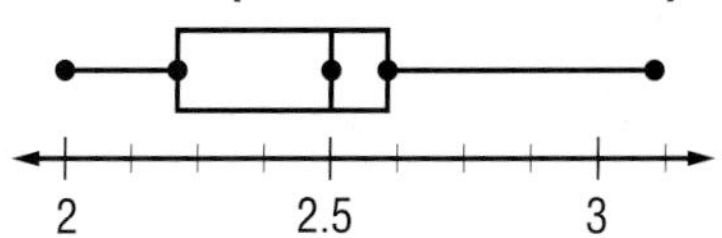

Source: *Time Almanac*

Data in the second quartile are slightly more spread out than data in the third quartile. You can see that data in the fourth quartile are the most spread out because the whisker is longer than other parts of the plot.

DAILY INTERVENTION **Flexible Grouping**

Box-and-Whisker Plots Assign students to work in small groups to explore how including or excluding certain data points in a display can alter the impression the data display makes. Ask students to create a data set about a topic of their choice. Then, have them create a box-and-whisker plot for the data. Next, have them eliminate the two lowest numbers and create another box-and-whisker plot. Students should discuss how the overall impression given by the data display changed.

In-Class Example

3 MULTIPLE-CHOICE TEST ITEM Use the box-and-whisker plots to determine which statement is *not* true. **C**

Average High Temperatures (°C)

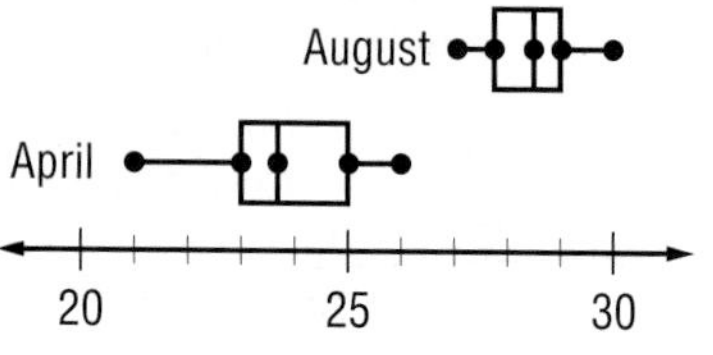

A August temperatures were greater than those in April.

B The temperatures were more spread out in April than in August.

C Most April temperatures were above 25°C.

D Most August temperatures were above 28°C.

Students practice the same concepts in Exercises 8–13 if they are assigned odd or even problems.

Skill and Concept Check

1. *Writing Math* Describe the meaning of the box in a box-and-whisker plot. **The box represents the spread of the middle half of the data.**
2. **OPEN ENDED** Write a set of data that could be represented by the box-and-whisker at the right. **Sample answer: 5, 6, 7, 8, 8, 8, 9, 10, 11, 12, 12**

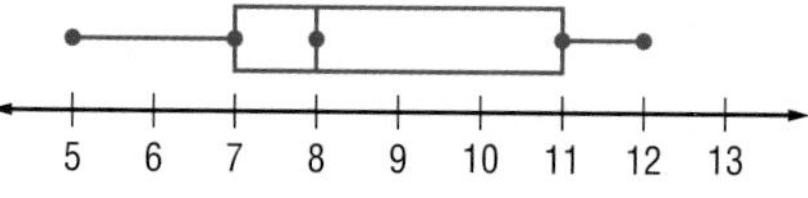

3. **FIND THE ERROR** Chapa and Joseph are making a box-and-whisker plot for the following set of data. Who is correct? Explain. **Joseph; 64 is an outlier.**

22, 23, 27, 30, 34, 38, 39, 40, 41, 47, 64

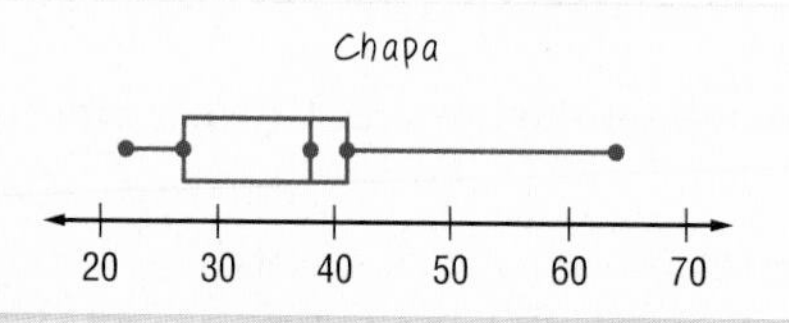

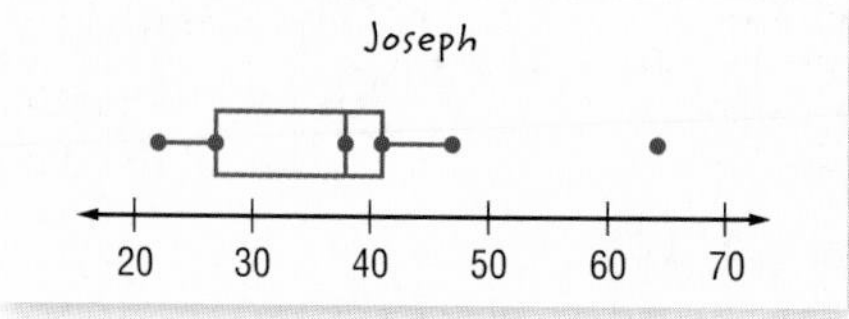

GUIDED PRACTICE

Draw a box-and-whisker plot for each set of data. **4–5. See margin.**

4. 38, 43, 36, 37, 32, 37, 29, 51
5. 100, 70, 70, 90, 50, 90, 50, 90, 100, 50, 90, 100, 90, 50, 25, 80

FOOD **For Exercises 6–8, use the following box-and-whisker plot.**

Calories in Fast Food Muffins

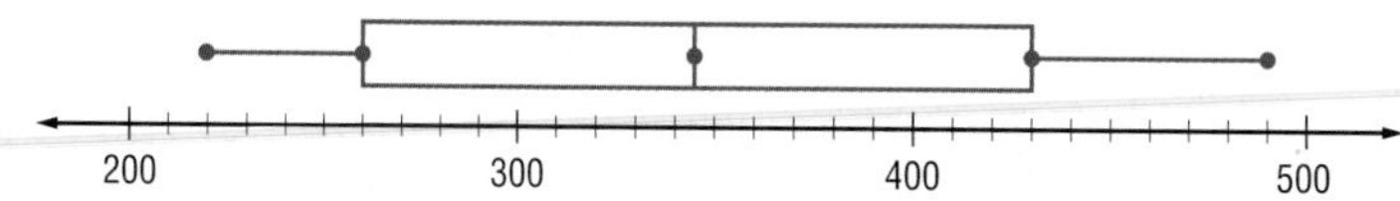

6. What is the interquartile range of the data? **170**
7. Three fourths of the muffins have at least how many Calories? **260**

★ indicates increased difficulty

Practice and Applications

Draw a box-and-whisker plot for each set of data. **8–13. See Ch. 9. Answer Appendix.**

8. 49, 45, 55, 32, 28, 53, 26, 38, 35, 35, 51
9. 77, 85, 72, 76, 95, 90, 73, 82, 82, 80, 73
10. 540, 460, 520, 350, 500, 480, 475, 525, 450, 515
11. 225, 245, 220, 270, 350, 280, 230, 240, 225, 270
12. 42, 38, 42, 45, 43, 80, 55, 50, 34, 36, 40, 35
13. 52, 58, 67, 63, 47, 44, 52, 15, 49, 65, 52, 59

★ 14. **HISTORY** The population in thousands of the American colonies in 1770 are listed below. Make a box-and-whisker plot of the data.

31.3, 62.4, 10.0, 235.3, 58.2, 183.9, 162.9, 117.4, 240.1, 35.5, 202.6, 447.0, 197.2, 124.2, 23.4, 15.7, 1.0 **See Ch. 9 Answer Appendix.**

HOMEWORK HELP

For Exercises	See Examples
8–14	1
15–18	2, 3

Extra Practice
See pages 639, 656.

3 Practice/Apply

DAILY INTERVENTION **FIND THE ERROR** In Exercise 3, remind students to plot the outliers separately. Including them in the whiskers gives the impression that the data set is more spread out than it is.

About the Exercises...

Guided Practice Key

Exercises	Examples
4–5	1
6–7	2, 3

Assignment Guide

Basic: 9–17 odd, 19–26

Average: 9–15 odd, 16–26

Enriched: 8–14 even, 15–24 (Optional: 25, 26)

Alert! The Data Update after Exercise 18 requires access to the Internet.

Answers

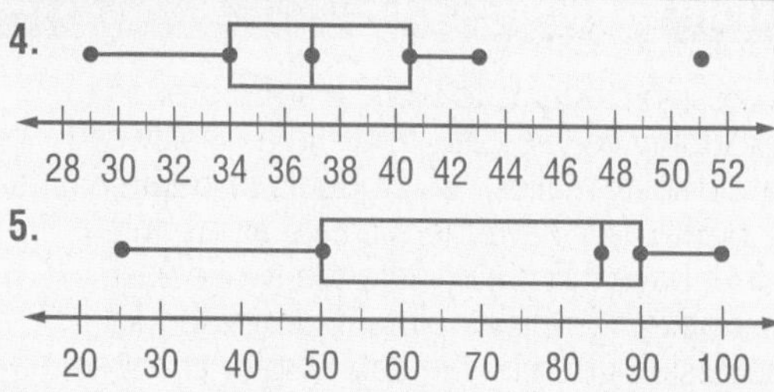

GAS MILEAGE For Exercises 15–18, use the following box-and-whisker plot.

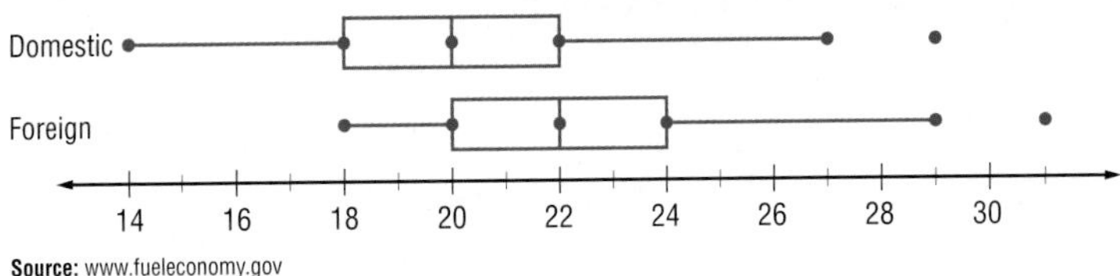

Source: www.fueleconomy.gov

15. Which set of data has a greater range? **domestic**
16. What percent of these domestic SUVs get at least 20 miles per gallon? **50%**
17. What percent of these foreign SUVs get at least 20 miles per gallon? **75%**
18. In general, do domestic two-wheel-drive SUVs get more or less gas mileage than the foreign ones? Explain. **Less; see margin.**

Data Update What is the gas mileage of current SUVs? Visit msmath3.net/data_update to learn more.

19. **CRITICAL THINKING** Write a set of data that could be represented by the box-and-whisker plot at the right. **Sample answer: {20, 20, 20, 30, 35, 40, 50, 60, 70, 70, 70}**

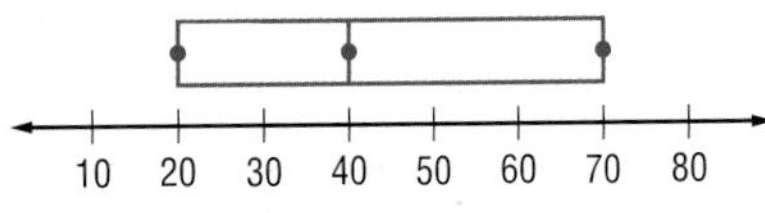

Spiral Review with Standardized Test Practice

For Exercises 20 and 21, use the box-and-whisker plot.

50 60 70 80 90 100

20. **MULTIPLE CHOICE** Twenty-five percent of the data are found between what two values? **D**

    Ⓐ 55 and 75 Ⓑ 60 and 80 Ⓒ 75 and 95 Ⓓ 60 and 75

21. **SHORT RESPONSE** What is the range of the data? **40**

Find the range, median, upper and lower quartiles, interquartile range, and any outliers for each set of data. (Lesson 9-5)

22. 73, 52, 31, 54, 46, 28, 47, 49, 58 **45; 49; 56, 38.5; 17.5; no outliers**
23. 87, 63, 84, 94, 89, 74, 50, 85, 91, 78, 99, 81, 77, 86, 65, 81, 74 **49; 81; 88, 74; 14; 50**

24. **LIFE SCIENCE** Find the mean, median, and mode of the plant heights 22, 4, 1, 12, 5, 22, 5, 25, 25, 19, 23, 24, 11, 16, 3, and 22 inches. (Lesson 9-4) **about 14.9 in.; 17.5 in.; 22 in.**

GETTING READY FOR THE NEXT LESSON

PREREQUISITE SKILL Describe each sample as *biased* or *unbiased*. Explain. (Lesson 8-7) **25–26. See Ch. 9 Answer Appendix.**

25. To determine how the neighborhood park should be improved, a survey is taken of every other house in the neighborhood.
26. To determine who will be elected governor, a survey is taken of every other house in one neighborhood.

msmath3.net/self_check_quiz

4 Assess

Open-Ended Assessment

Speaking Have a student study a box-and-whisker plot. It can be either one they have created or one found in this section. Then, have them describe how to interpret the plot.

Answer

18. **Only 50% of domestic vehicles get at least 20 miles per gallon, while 75% of the foreign vehicles get at least 20 miles per gallon. In general, the box-and-whisker plot of the foreign vehicles is shifted to the right of the box-and-whisker plot of the domestic vehicles.**

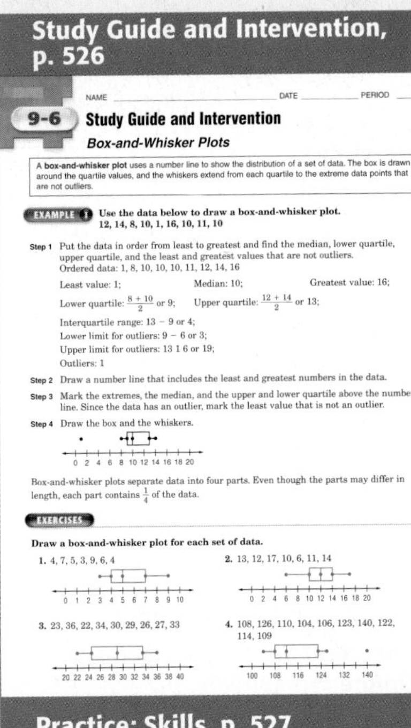

Study Guide and Intervention, p. 526

NAME ____ DATE ____ PERIOD ____

9-6 Study Guide and Intervention

Box-and-Whisker Plots

A **box-and-whisker plot** uses a number line to show the distribution of a set of data. The box is drawn around the quartile values, and the whiskers extend from each quartile to the extreme data points that are not outliers.

EXAMPLE 1 **Use the data below to draw a box-and-whisker plot.**
12, 14, 8, 10, 1, 16, 10, 11, 10

Step 1 Put the data in order from least to greatest and find the median, lower quartile, upper quartile, and the least and greatest values that are not outliers.
Ordered data: 1, 8, 10, 10, 10, 11, 12, 14, 16

Least value: 1; Median: 10; Greatest value: 16;

Lower quartile: $\frac{8 + 10}{2}$ or 9; Upper quartile: $\frac{12 + 14}{2}$ or 13;

Interquartile range: 13 − 9 or 4;
Lower limit for outliers: 9 − 6 or 3;
Upper limit for outliers: 13 1 6 or 19;
Outliers: 1

Step 2 Draw a number line that includes the least and greatest numbers in the data.

Step 3 Mark the extremes, the median, and the upper and lower quartile above the number line. Since the data has an outlier, mark the least value that is not an outlier.

Step 4 Draw the box and the whiskers.

0 2 4 6 8 10 12 14 16 18 20

Box-and-whisker plots separate data into four parts. Even though the parts may differ in length, each part contains $\frac{1}{4}$ of the data.

EXERCISES

Draw a box-and-whisker plot for each set of data.

1. 4, 7, 5, 3, 9, 6, 4
2. 13, 12, 17, 10, 6, 11, 14
3. 23, 36, 22, 34, 30, 29, 26, 27, 33
4. 108, 126, 110, 104, 106, 123, 140, 122, 114, 109

Practice: Skills, p. 527

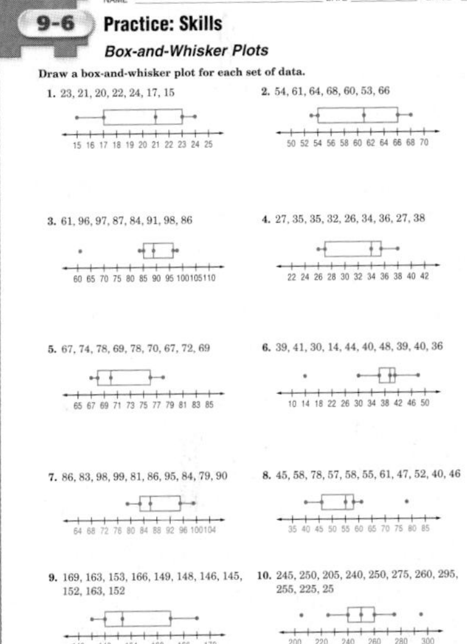

NAME ____ DATE ____ PERIOD ____

9-6 Practice: Skills

Box-and-Whisker Plots

Draw a box-and-whisker plot for each set of data.

1. 23, 21, 20, 22, 24, 17, 15
2. 54, 61, 64, 68, 60, 53, 66
3. 61, 96, 97, 87, 84, 91, 98, 86
4. 27, 35, 35, 32, 26, 34, 36, 27, 38
5. 67, 74, 78, 69, 78, 70, 67, 72, 69
6. 39, 41, 30, 14, 44, 40, 48, 39, 40, 36
7. 86, 83, 98, 99, 81, 86, 95, 84, 79, 90
8. 45, 58, 78, 57, 58, 55, 61, 47, 52, 40, 46
9. 169, 163, 153, 166, 149, 148, 146, 145, 152, 163, 152
10. 245, 250, 205, 240, 250, 275, 260, 295, 255, 225, 25

Practice: Word Problems, p. 528

NAME ____ DATE ____ PERIOD ____

9-6 Practice: Word Problems

Box-and-Whisker Plots

U.S. SENATE **For Exercises 1–4, use the box-and-whisker plot at the right.**

Ages of U.S. Senators, 2002

40 45 50 55 60 65 70 75 80 85 90 95 100

1. Explain how to determine from the box-and-whisker plot whether there are any outliers in the data. Then identify any outliers. **Outliers are represented by points not connected to the rest of the graph by whiskers; 100.**
2. Describe the distribution of the data. What can you say about the ages of U.S. senators? **Sample answer: The lower three quarters are fairly evenly distributed. The upper quarter is more spread out.**
3. What percent of U.S. senators are at least 54 years old? Explain how you found your answer. **75%; The lower quartile is 54, and 75% of the data is above the lower quartile.**
4. Can you determine from the box-and-whisker plot whether there are any U.S. Senators exactly 65 years old? Explain. **No; the only exact ages you can determine from the box-and-whisker plot are the extreme values and outliers.**

HOCKEY **For Exercises 5 and 6, use the box-and-whisker plot at the right.**

Goals Made by the Top 10 All-Time NHL Scorers

300 400 500 600 700 800 900

5. Identify any outliers in the data. **none**
6. Describe the distribution of the data. What can you say about the number of goals made by the top 10 all-time leading NHL scorers? **Sample answer: The upper half and lower half are evenly distributed. The second quarter is more spread out than the third quarter. The number of goals they made is evenly spread out.**

9-7 Lesson Notes

Lesson Resources

Chapter 9 Resource Masters
- Study Guide and Intervention, p. 531
- Practice: Skills, p. 532
- Practice: Word Problems, p. 533
- Reading to Learn Mathematics, p. 534
- Enrichment, p. 535

MathPASS Tutorial CD-ROM, 57
Parent and Student Study Guide Online Worksheets, 9-7
Noteables™: Interactive Study Notebook with Foldables™, 9-7

1 Focus

5-Minute Check 9-7

Use as a quiz or review of Lesson 9-6. (Also available as a transparency)

Bellringer

Communication Show students the table below. Ask them:

- What type of data display would you choose to show these data? **sample answer: line graph**
- What interval would you choose for the years? Explain. **Answers will vary. The data are not organized into equal intervals.**

(Continued in bottom margin.)

Reading to Learn Mathematics, p. 534 **ELL**

NAME ______ DATE ______ PERIOD ____

9-7 Reading to Learn Mathematics
Misleading Graphs and Statistics

Pre-Activity *Read the introduction at the top of page 450 in your textbook. Write your answers below.*

1. Do both graphs show the same data? yes
2. Which graph seems to show the greater increase in spending? Why? Graph B; the break in Graph B essentially starts the vertical axis with $28. Then each of the remaining intervals represent $2.

Reading the Lesson

3. Give an example of how a graph could be misleading. Sample answers: No title, no labels on scales, divisions are not equal on axis, drawings not proportional.
4. When writing an employment ad for an automotive dealership, would it ...

9-7 Misleading Graphs and Statistics

What You'll LEARN

Recognize when graphs and statistics are misleading.

REVIEW Vocabulary

biased sample: a sample where one or more parts of the population are favored over others (Lesson 8-7)

WHEN am I ever going to use this?

MOVIES Study the graphs.

Graph A

Source: Veronis, Schler and Associates, Inc.

Graph B

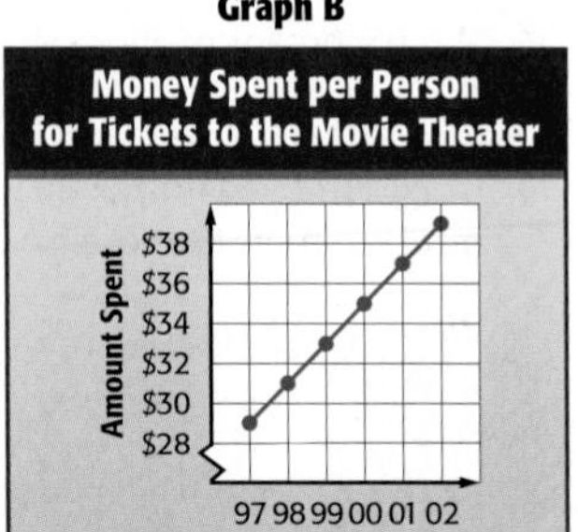

1. Do both graphs show the same data? **yes**
2. Which graph seems to show a greater increase in spending? Why?

2. Graph B; the break in Graph B essentially starts the vertical axis with $28. Then each of the remaining intervals represent $2.

When dealing with statistics, you must interpret the information carefully. The scale in Graph B above may make people think the increase is greater than the actual increase.

STUDY TIP

Statistics A graph should have a title and labels on both scales.

EXAMPLE Identify a Misleading Graph

1 CARS Which graph could be used to indicate a greater increase in sales of automotive equipment? Explain.

Graph A

Graph B

Source: Speciality Equipment Market Association

Both graphs show the amount of sales of specialty automotive equipment has about doubled. The ratio of the areas of the bars in Graph A is about 1 : 2. The ratio of the areas of the cars in Graph B is about 1 : 4. Graph B seems to show a greater increase in sales.

Value of Sales of Recording Media in the United States, 1982–2000 ($ million)

Year	CDs	Tapes	Vinyl Albums	Year	CDs	Tapes	Vinyl Albums
1982	N/A	1,384.5	1,925.1	1997	9,915.1	1,522.7	33.3
1985	389.5	2,411.5	1,280.5	1998	11,416.0	1,419.9	34.0
1990	3,451.6	3,472.4	86.5	1999	12,816.3	1,061.6	31.8
1995	9,377.4	2,303.6	25.1	2000	13,214.5	626.0	27.7
1996	9,934.7	1,905.3	36.8				

REAL-LIFE MATH

ROLLER COASTERS The world's longest roller coaster is the Steel Dragon in Mie, Japan. It is 8,133 feet long.

Source: *The World Almanac for Kids*

Recall that there are three different measures of central tendency or types of averages. They are mean, median, and mode. These different values can be used to show different points of view.

EXAMPLES Identify Different Uses of Statistics

ROLLER COASTERS The ride times of the roller coasters at an amusement park are 220, 150, 150, 150, 120, 90, 90, and 52 seconds.

2 Find the mean, median, and mode of the ride times.

Mean $\frac{\text{sum of values}}{\text{number of values}} = \frac{1{,}022}{8}$ or 127.75

Median $\frac{150 + 120}{2} = \frac{270}{2}$ or 135

Mode 150

The mean is 127.75 seconds, the median is 135 seconds, and the mode is 150 seconds.

3 Which average would the amusement park use to encourage people who like roller coasters to come to the park? Explain.

People who like roller coasters would probably enjoy longer rides. Therefore, the amusement park would use the mode since it is the greatest of the averages.

Students practice the same concepts in Exercises 5–6 if they are assigned odd or even problems.

Skill and Concept Check

1. Writing Math List two ways a graph can be misleading. See p. 452 margin.
2. **OPEN ENDED** Write a set of data in which the mean is not representative. Sample answer: 1, 2, 3, 4, 5, 20

GUIDED PRACTICE

3. Which graph would you use to indicate that Norway had many more medals than the Soviet Union? Explain. Graph B; see p. 452 margin.

Graph A

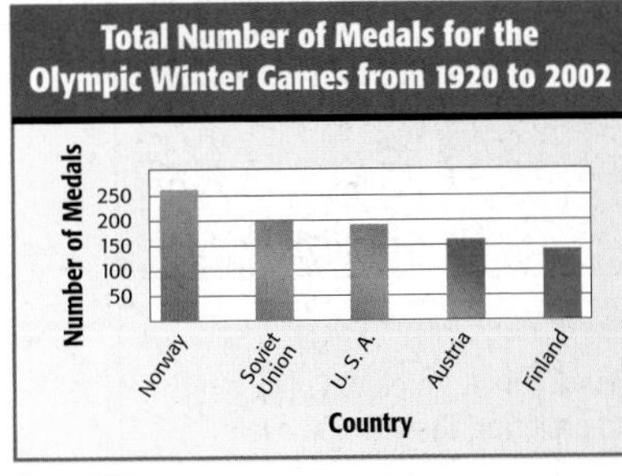

Graph B

Source: IOC

4. **SCHOOL** Drew received a 75% on his history test. If the mean of the test scores is 80%, the median is 78%, and the mode is 70%. Which average might Drew use when describing his score to his parents? Explain. Mode; his score is greater than the mode.

Math Online msmath3.net/extra_examples

2 Teach

In-Class Examples

1 TELEVISIONS Which graph below could be used to indicate a greater difference in number of televisions? Explain.

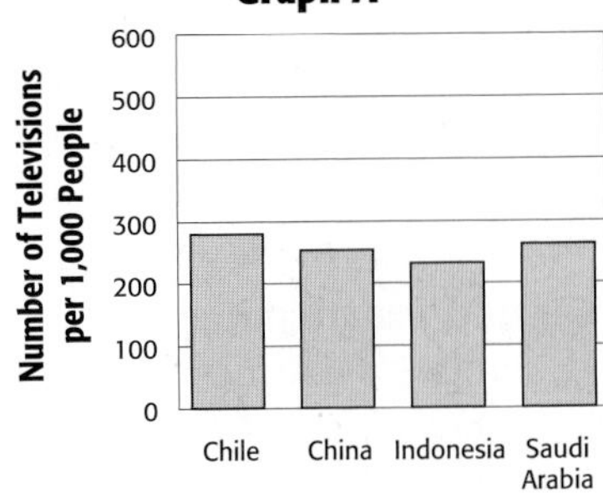

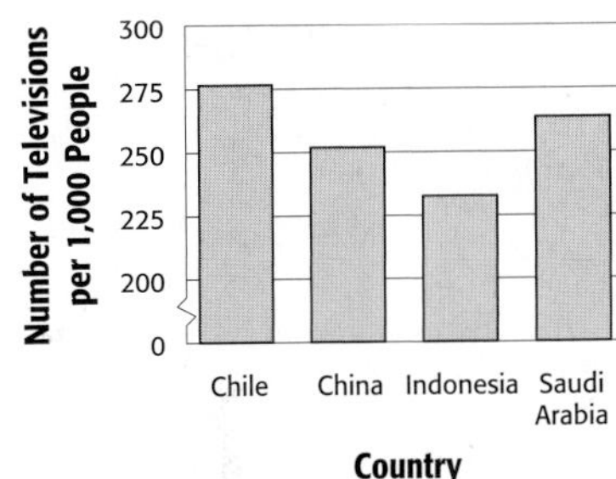

Graph B: the intervals in Graph B represent 200 to 300 instead of 0 to 600.

GYMNASTICS The scores for girls on a team competing on vault at a meet are 8.3, 8.5, 8.5, 8.8, 9.0, and 9.2.

2 Find the mean, median, and mode of the vault scores. 8.72; 8.65; 8.5

3 Which average would the team use to make its results look the best? Explain. Mean; it shows a higher event score.

DAILY INTERVENTION

Differentiated Instruction

Intrapersonal Ask students to think about situations in their everyday lives in which the mean, median, or mode would best show a particular point of view. Have each student write a description of one situation for each type of average. Ask them to include sample data and any useful data displays.

3 Practice/Apply

FOLDABLES™ Follow-Up Remind students to use their Foldables to record what they learn about recognizing misleading statistics or graphs. Encourage students to collect examples of misleading statistics or graphs in print, glue or tape them into their Foldables, and explain how and why they are misleading.

About the Exercises...

Guided Practice Key

Exercises	Examples
3	1
4	3

Assignment Guide

Basic: 5, 7–9, 13–26

Average: 5, 7–11, 13–26

Enriched: 6, 8–22 (Optional: 23–26)

Answers (pp. 451–453)

1. The scale may have a break or may have different sized intervals. The graph may show a larger area than the actual increase.
3. Since there is a break in the vertical scale, the number of medals for Norway appears to be much greater than the number of medals for the Soviet Union.
5. The area of the house indicates a much greater median income for the male householder than a female householder.
6. Since there is a break in the vertical scale, the number of American Indians living in California appears to be much greater than the number of American Indians living in Oklahoma.
7. The advertising is not false. In the last survey, 3 out of 4 people liked Tasty Treats better than Groovy Goodies. However, it is misleading, because combining all the survey results shows only half of the people liked Tasty Treats better than Groovy Goodies.
9. Mean; it is greater than the median and they will want to appear to pay more money.
11. Mean; it is greater than the median and they will want to appear to pay more money.
12. Sample answer: Based on salaries alone, you would choose Company B. More than half of the salaries are at or above all but one of the Company A salaries and all of Company B's salaries are greater than all but two of Company A's salaries.

Practice and Applications

HOMEWORK HELP

For Exercises	See Examples
5–6	1
8–12	2, 3

Extra Practice
See pages 639, 656.

5. Which graph would you use to indicate that a male householder has a much greater median income than a female householder? Explain. **Graph B; see margin.**

Graph A

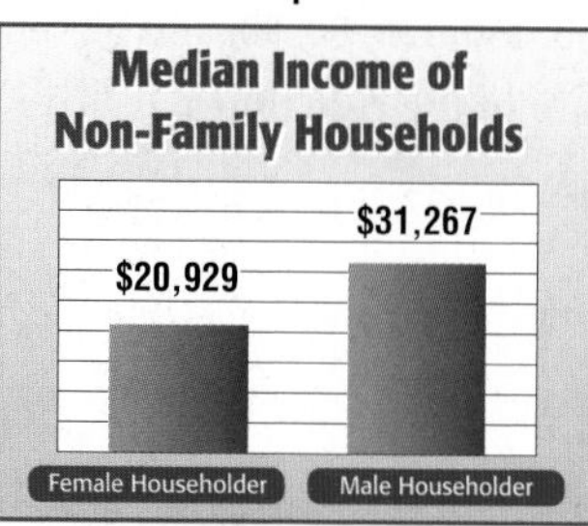

Graph B

Source: U.S. Bureau of the Census

6. Which graph would you use to indicate that there are many more American Indians living in California than Oklahoma? Explain. **Graph A; see margin.**

Graph A

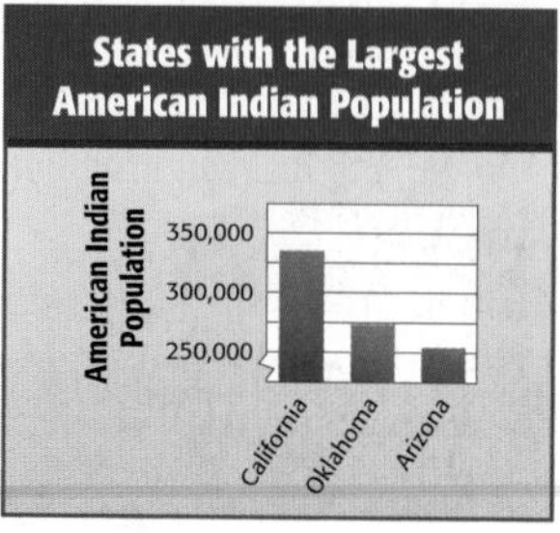

Graph B

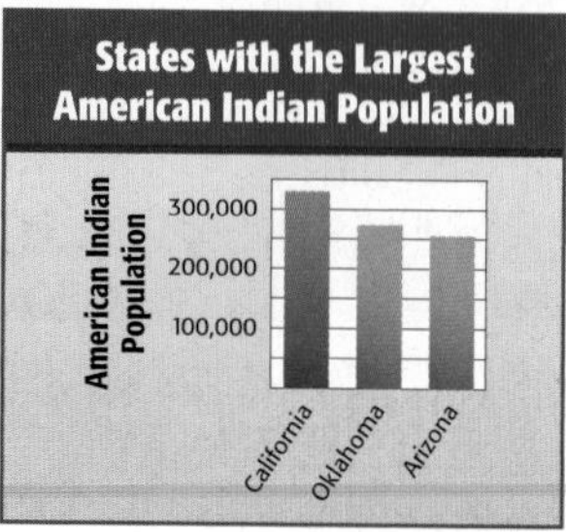

Source: U.S. Bureau of the Census

7. **ADVERTISING** Study the situation below. Is the advertisement false? Is it misleading? Explain. **See margin.**

SALARIES For Exercises 8–12, use the table. It compares the salaries of the employees of two small manufacturing companies.

Salaries	
Company A	Company B
\$69,800	\$25,100
\$21,500	\$23,650
\$18,000	\$23,600
\$17,600	\$23,100
\$17,400	\$21,750
\$17,300	\$21,600
\$16,150	\$21,500
\$16,050	\$20,680
\$15,100	\$19,670
\$14,900	\$19,450

8. What is the mean, median, and mode of the salaries of the employees of Company A? **\$22,380; \$17,350; none**
9. What average would Company A use to try to encourage someone to work for them? Explain. **See margin.**
10. What is the mean, median, and mode of the salaries of the employees of Company B? **\$22,010; \$21,675; none**
11. What average would Company B use to encourage someone to work for them? Explain. **See margin.**
12. If you were choosing to work for Company A or Company B, which might you choose? Explain. **See margin.**
13. **CRITICAL THINKING** The number of admissions to movie theaters went from 1.14 billion in 1991 to 1.49 billion in 2001.
    a. Make a graph that shows a small change in admissions.
    b. Make a graph that shows a large change in admissions. **See Ch. 9 Answer Appendix.**

Spiral Review with Standardized Test Practice

For Exercises 14 and 15, use the data in the table.

Borders of the United States			
Border	**Miles**	**Border**	**Miles**
Mainland/Canada	3,987	Gulf of Mexico Coast	1,631
Alaska/Canada	1,538	Pacific Coast	7,623
Mexican	1,933	Arctic Coast	1,060
Atlantic Coast	2,069		

Source: *The World Almanac for Kids*

14. **MULTIPLE CHOICE** Which value is the most misleading average of the data? **A**

    Ⓐ mean　Ⓑ median　Ⓒ mode　Ⓓ none of the averages

15. **MULTIPLE CHOICE** Which value is the most representative of the data? **G**

    Ⓕ mean　Ⓖ median　Ⓗ mode　Ⓘ none of the averages

Draw a box-and-whisker plot for each set of data. (Lesson 9-6)

16. 55, 63, 72, 52, 55, 68, 64, 61, 58 **16–17. See margin.**
17. 53, 49, 43, 5, 28, 38, 34, 45, 51, 45
18. **MUSIC** The numbers of pages in a magazine in the last nine issues were 196, 188, 184, 200, 168, 176, 192, 160, and 180. Find the median, upper quartile, and lower quartile of this data. (Lesson 9-5) **184; 194; 172**

Write each number in scientific notation. (Lesson 2-9)

19. 70,200 **7.02×10^4**
20. 0.000081 **8.1×10^{-5}**
21. 0.000456 **4.56×10^{-4}**
22. 620,000,000 **6.2×10^8**

GETTING READY FOR THE NEXT LESSON

PREREQUISITE SKILL Add or subtract. (Lessons 1-4 and 1-5)

23. $8 + (-5)$ **3**
24. $-7 + (-4)$ **−11**
25. $-6 - (-4)$ **−2**
26. $-7 - 8$ **−15**

msmath3.net/self_check_quiz

4 Assess

Open-Ended Assessment

Modeling Have students make two graphs using the same selection of data from the Bellringer table. Ask them to make one of the graphs misleading. As a class, discuss the graphs students produce.

Answers

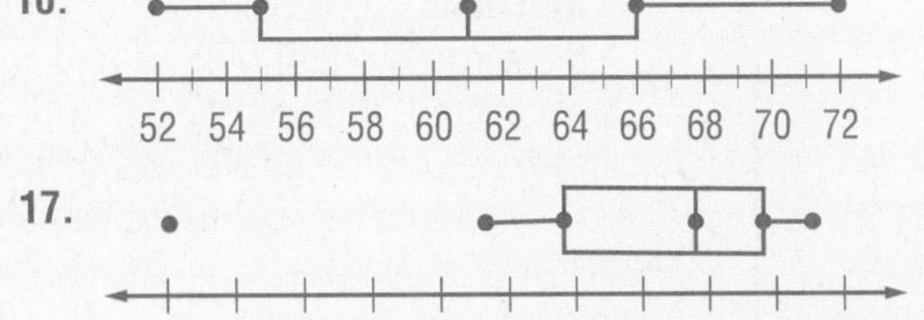

Study Guide and Intervention, p. 531

NAME ____ DATE ____ PERIOD ____

9-7 Study Guide and Intervention

Misleading Graphs and Statistics

When dealing with statistics, you must be careful that the information is presented in a straightforward manner. Graphs should be constructed to present the data in the correct proportions. If a graph is not properly constructed, the data may be misinterpreted. Be careful to identify when statistics are presented in a misleading way.

EXAMPLE 1 **Which graph below could be used to indicate a greater increase in the percent of Americans that are divorced?**

Graph A: Percent of Americans Divorced — Graph B: Percent of Americans Divorced

Both graphs show that the percent of Americans that are divorced rose from 8.3% to 9.8% during the period 1990 to 2000. The ratio of the heights of the bars in Graph A is about 4 to 5, while the ratio of the heights of the bars in Graph B is about 1 to 2. Graph B seems to show a greater increase in the divorce rate.

EXERCISE

1. Which graph would you use to indicate a greater increase in the average price of a new car purchased in the U.S.? Explain.

   Graph A: Average Price of a New Car — Graph B: Average Price of a New Car

   Both graphs show that the price rose from \$20,355 to \$21,605. But Graph B seems to show a greater increase in the price of new cars.

Practice: Skills, p. 532

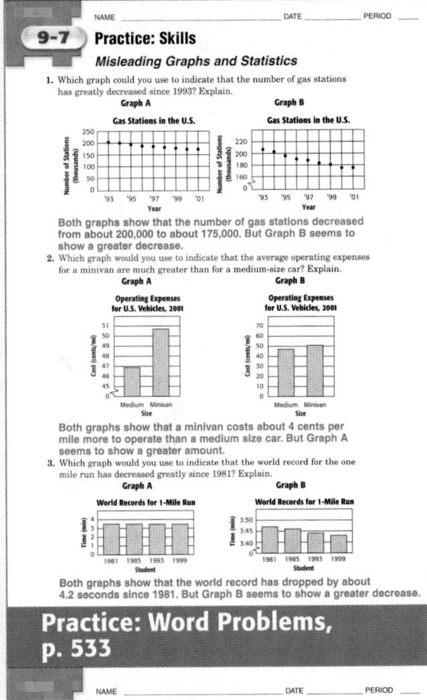

NAME ____ DATE ____ PERIOD ____

9-7 Practice: Skills

Misleading Graphs and Statistics

1. Which graph could you use to indicate that the number of gas stations has greatly decreased since 1993? Explain.

   Graph A: Gas Stations in the U.S. — Graph B: Gas Stations in the U.S.

   Both graphs show that the number of gas stations decreased from about 200,000 to about 175,000. But Graph B seems to show a greater decrease.

2. Which graph would you use to indicate that the average operating expenses for a minivan are much greater than for a medium-size car? Explain.

   Graph A: Operating Expenses for U.S. Vehicles, 2001 — Graph B: Operating Expenses for U.S. Vehicles, 2001

   Both graphs show that a minivan costs about 4 cents per mile more to operate than a medium size car. But Graph A seems to show a greater amount.

3. Which graph would you use to indicate that the world record for the one mile run has decreased greatly since 1981? Explain.

   Graph A: World Records for 1-Mile Run — Graph B: World Records for 1-Mile Run

   Both graphs show that the world record has dropped by about 4.2 seconds since 1981. But Graph B seems to show a greater decrease.

Practice: Word Problems, p. 533

NAME ____ DATE ____ PERIOD ____

9-7 Practice: Word Problems

Misleading Graphs and Statistics

1. **AMUSEMENT PARKS** The average wait times for the 10 different rides at an amusement park are 44, 37, 22, 11, 17, 25, 34, 17, 21, and 28 minutes. Find the mean, median, and mode of the average wait times for the rides. Round to the nearest tenth if necessary. **25.6 min; 23.5 min; 17 min**
2. Use the data in Exercise 1. Which measure of central tendency would the amusement park use to encourage people to come the park? Explain. **People do not enjoy waiting in line at the park. Therefore, the park would use the mode, since it is the least of the measures.**
3. Use the data in Exercise 1. Which measure or measures of central tendency would be more representative of the data? **Sample answer: Since the mode is the next-to-least of the 10 values, it is not as representative of the data as the mean or median.**
4. **CALORIES** The number of Calories in one serving of 7 different kinds of breakfast cereal made by one food company are 80, 120, 190, 240, 100, 130, and 190. Find the mean, median, and mode of the number of Calories in one serving of each kind of cereal. Round to the nearest tenth if necessary. **150; 130; 190**
5. Use the data in Exercise 4. Which measure of central tendency would the food company use to encourage people on a diet to try their cereal? Explain. **People on a diet will be looking for a cereal that is low in Calories. Therefore, the food company will use the median, since it is the least of the measures.**
6. Use the data in Exercise 4. Which measure or measures of central tendency would be more representative of the data? **Sample answer: Since the mode is the next-to-greatest number, it is not as representative of the data as the mean and median. The mean is perhaps the most representative.**

9-8 Lesson Notes

Lesson Resources

Chapter 9 Resource Masters
- Study Guide and Intervention, p. 536
- Practice: Skills, p. 537
- Practice: Word Problems, p. 538
- Reading to Learn Mathematics, p. 539
- Enrichment, p. 540

FAST FILE

Calculator and Spreadsheet Masters, p. 42
Key Teaching Transparencies, 38
Parent and Student Study Guide Online Worksheets, 9-8
Noteables™: Interactive Study Notebook with Foldables™, 9-8

Focus

5-Minute Check 9-8

Use as a quiz or review of Lesson 9-7. (Also available as a transparency)

Bellringer

Communication Draw the following grids on the chalkboard. Have students give the row-by-column dimensions of each. Which two have the same dimensions? **A, D**

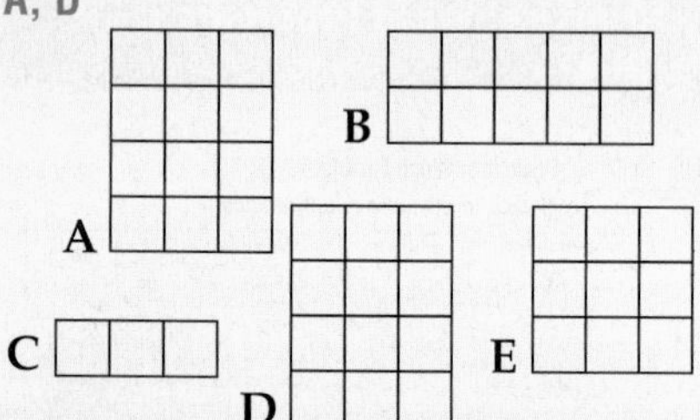

Reading to Learn Mathematics, p. 539 ELL

NAME ______ DATE ______ PERIOD ______

9-8 Reading to Learn Mathematics
Matrices

Pre-Activity *Read the introduction at the top of page 454 in your textbook. Write your answers below.*

1. How many continents are listed? 7
2. How many temperatures are given for each continent? 2
3. What does the number −129 represent? the lowest temperature in Antarctica
4. What does the number 136 represent? the highest temperature in Africa

Reading the Lesson

5. Describe the matrix in terms of its dimensions. 4 by 2

9-8 Matrices

What You'll LEARN

Use matrices to organize data.

NEW Vocabulary

matrix
row
column
element
dimensions

WHEN am I ever going to use this?

WEATHER The record temperatures for each continent are listed in the table below.

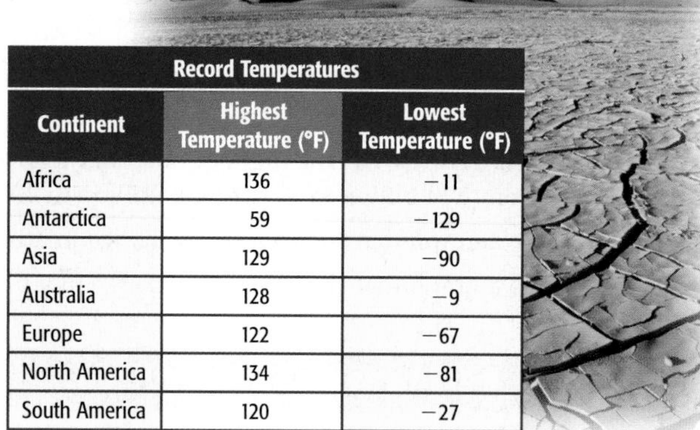

Record Temperatures		
Continent	**Highest Temperature (°F)**	**Lowest Temperature (°F)**
Africa	136	−11
Antarctica	59	−129
Asia	129	−90
Australia	128	−9
Europe	122	−67
North America	134	−81
South America	120	−27

Source: *The World Almanac for Kids*

1. How many continents are listed? **7**
2. How many temperatures are given for each continent? **2**
3. What does the number −129 represent?
4. What does the number 136 represent?

3. the lowest temperature in Antarctica
4. the highest temperature in Africa

The table above has rows and columns of data. A rectangular arrangement of numerical data is called a **matrix**.

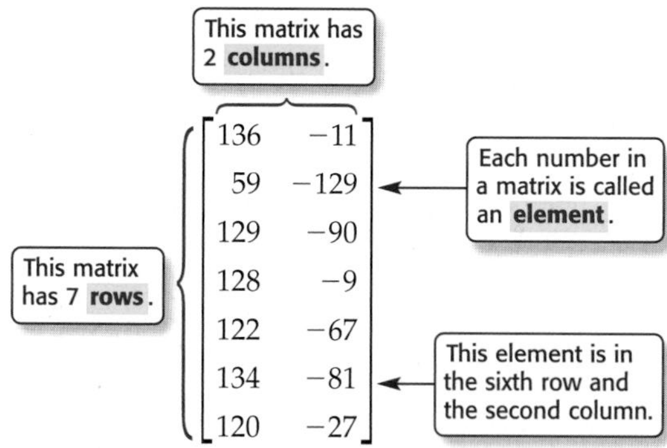

$$\begin{bmatrix} 136 & -11 \\ 59 & -129 \\ 129 & -90 \\ 128 & -9 \\ 122 & -67 \\ 134 & -81 \\ 120 & -27 \end{bmatrix}$$

A matrix is described by its **dimensions**, or the number of rows and columns, with the number of rows stated first. The dimensions of this matrix are 7 by 2.

DAILY INTERVENTION

Unlocking Misconceptions

Matrices Students may not understand that two matrices must have the same number of rows and columns in order to be added or subtracted. To reinforce this concept, have them draw examples of matrices on the chalkboard that can or cannot be added or subtracted. They should be able to explain the difference.

EXAMPLE Identify Dimensions and Elements

1 **State the dimensions of $\begin{bmatrix} -3 & 6 & \textcircled{9} & 3 \\ -5 & 8 & 4 & 0 \end{bmatrix}$. Then identify the position of the circled element.**

The matrix has 2 rows and 4 columns. The dimensions of the matrix are 2 by 4.

The circled element is in the first row and the third column.

Your Turn **State the dimensions of each matrix. Then identify the position of the circled element.**

a. $[7 \quad -8 \quad \textcircled{5}]$ b. $\begin{bmatrix} 14 & 17 \\ \textcircled{27} & 8 \end{bmatrix}$ c. $\begin{bmatrix} -5 & -7 & 3 & 2 \\ 9 & -3 & -10 & -1 \\ 2 & \textcircled{4} & 9 & -4 \end{bmatrix}$

a. 1 by 3; first row, third column
b. 2 by 2; second row, first column
c. 3 by 4; third row, second column

READING Math

Matrices The plural of matrix is *matrices*. It is pronounced MAY tra cees.

If two matrices have the same dimensions, you can add or subtract them. To do this, add or subtract corresponding elements of the two matrices.

EXAMPLES Add and Subtract Matrices

Add or subtract. If there is no sum or difference, write *impossible*.

2 $\begin{bmatrix} 4 & 3 & 2 \\ 7 & -1 & 5 \end{bmatrix} + \begin{bmatrix} 0 & 2 & -1 \\ 12 & 5 & 6 \end{bmatrix}$

$$\begin{bmatrix} 4 & 3 & 2 \\ 7 & -1 & 5 \end{bmatrix} + \begin{bmatrix} 0 & 2 & -1 \\ 12 & 5 & 6 \end{bmatrix} = \begin{bmatrix} 4+0 & 3+2 & 2+(-1) \\ 7+12 & -1+5 & 5+6 \end{bmatrix}$$

$$= \begin{bmatrix} 4 & 5 & 1 \\ 19 & 4 & 11 \end{bmatrix}$$

3 $[-7 \quad 8 \quad 4 \quad -9] - [-5 \quad -6 \quad 3 \quad 10]$

$[-7 \quad 8 \quad 4 \quad -9] - [-5 \quad -6 \quad 3 \quad 10]$

$= [-7-(-5) \quad 8-(-6) \quad 4-3 \quad -9-10]$

$= [-2 \quad 14 \quad 1 \quad -19]$

4 $\begin{bmatrix} 7 & -8 \\ 4 & -6 \end{bmatrix} - \begin{bmatrix} 8 & -19 \\ 22 & 4 \\ -8 & 12 \end{bmatrix}$

The first matrix has 2 rows and 2 columns. The second matrix has 3 rows and 2 columns. Since the matrices do not have the same dimensions, it is impossible to subtract them.

TEACHING TIP

Explain to students that matrices with different dimensions cannot be added or subtracted because there would be no way to pair the elements.

Your Turn **Add or subtract. If there is no sum or difference, write *impossible*.**

d. $\begin{bmatrix} 6 & -8 \\ 5 & 4 \end{bmatrix} - \begin{bmatrix} 5 & 8 \\ -10 & -3 \end{bmatrix}$ e. $\begin{bmatrix} 5 & -9 \\ 6 & 7 \\ -8 & -2 \end{bmatrix} + \begin{bmatrix} -1 & 5 & -6 \\ 4 & 7 & -3 \end{bmatrix}$ impossible

d. $\begin{bmatrix} 1 & -16 \\ 15 & 7 \end{bmatrix}$

msmath3.net/extra_examples

2 Teach

In-Class Examples

1 State the dimensions of $\begin{bmatrix} -3 & 2 & 8 \\ \textcircled{1} & -6 & 5 \\ 6 & -1 & 12 \end{bmatrix}$. Then identify the position of the circled element. **3 by 3; second row, first column**

Add or subtract. If there is no sum or difference, write *impossible*.

2 $\begin{bmatrix} -5 & -2 & -1 \\ 8 & 1 & -3 \end{bmatrix} + \begin{bmatrix} 2 & 3 & -2 \\ -2 & 7 & 9 \end{bmatrix}$ $\begin{bmatrix} -3 & 1 & -3 \\ 6 & 8 & 6 \end{bmatrix}$

3 $\begin{bmatrix} -3 & -3 \\ 8 & 2 \end{bmatrix} - [96]$ **impossible**

4 $\begin{bmatrix} 3 & 2 & -8 & 6 \\ 5 & 12 & 4 & -2 \\ 7 & -3 & 8 & 2 \\ 6 & 1 & 1 & -6 \end{bmatrix} - \begin{bmatrix} 2 & 1 & 7 & 2 \\ -2 & -3 & 2 & 5 \\ 4 & 1 & 6 & -2 \\ 2 & 9 & 12 & -4 \end{bmatrix}$ $\begin{bmatrix} 1 & 1 & -15 & 4 \\ 7 & 15 & 2 & -7 \\ 3 & -4 & 2 & 4 \\ 4 & -8 & -11 & -2 \end{bmatrix}$

3 Practice/Apply

About the Exercises...

Guided Practice Key

Exercises	Examples
3–5	1
6	2
7	3, 4

Assignment Guide

Basic: 9–17 odd, 18, 20–26

Average: 9–17 odd, 18–26

Enriched: 8–16 even, 18–26 (Optional: 39–42)

Answers

1. A 3-by-2 matrix has 3 rows and 2 columns, and a 2-by-3 matrix has 2 rows and 3 columns.
3. 3 by 1; third row, first column
4. 3 by 3; first row, third column
5. 2 by 5; second row, fourth column
6. $\begin{bmatrix} 4 & -11 & 11 \\ 2 & -3 & 1 \end{bmatrix}$
7. $\begin{bmatrix} -2 & 13 & -8 \\ 11 & 3 & -18 \\ -5 & -8 & 8 \end{bmatrix}$
8. 3 by 1; second row, first column
9. 1 by 3; first row, third column
10. 2 by 2; second row, second column
11. 3 by 3; third row, first column
12. 2 by 4; first row, fourth column
13. 3 by 4; third row, second column
18. $\begin{bmatrix} 6 & 5 & 4 \\ 10 & 10 & 5 \\ 6 & 3 & 4 \end{bmatrix}; \begin{bmatrix} 6 & 3 & 8 \\ 11 & 7 & 6 \\ 10 & 13 & 11 \end{bmatrix}$
19. $\begin{bmatrix} 12 & 8 & 12 \\ 21 & 17 & 11 \\ 16 & 16 & 15 \end{bmatrix}$

23. **Calories Burned Working Fairly Hard**

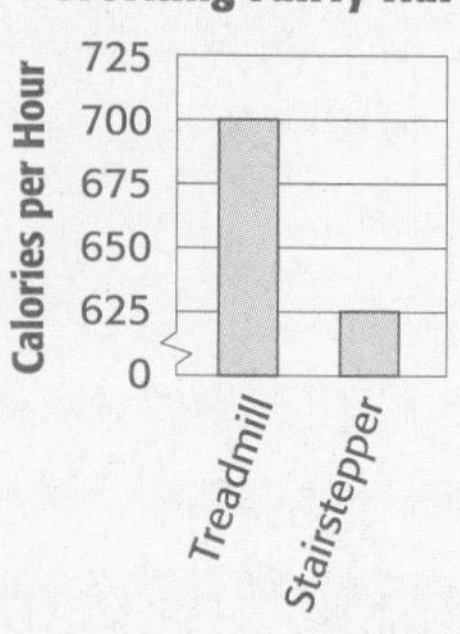

Students practice the same concepts in Exercises 8–17 if they are assigned odd or even problems.

Skill and Concept Check

1. **Describe** the difference between a 3-by-2 matrix and a 2-by-3 matrix. See margin.
2. **OPEN ENDED** Write two matrices whose sum is $\begin{bmatrix} 3 & 8 & -2 \\ -1 & 0 & 6 \end{bmatrix}$. Sample answer: $\begin{bmatrix} 2 & 5 & -1 \\ -7 & -6 & 4 \end{bmatrix}, \begin{bmatrix} 1 & 3 & -1 \\ 6 & 6 & 2 \end{bmatrix}$

GUIDED PRACTICE

State the dimensions of each matrix. Then identify the position of the circled element. 3–5. See margin.

3. $\begin{bmatrix} 5 \\ -7 \\ \textcircled{4} \end{bmatrix}$
4. $\begin{bmatrix} 8 & 5 & \textcircled{-6} \\ 10 & 18 & -5 \\ -10 & 14 & 7 \end{bmatrix}$
5. $\begin{bmatrix} 12 & 6 & 18 & 14 & 0 \\ 9 & 5 & 22 & \textcircled{16} & 25 \end{bmatrix}$

Add or subtract. If there is no sum or difference, write *impossible*. 6–7. See margin.

6. $\begin{bmatrix} 5 & -8 & 4 \\ -2 & 6 & 3 \end{bmatrix} + \begin{bmatrix} -1 & -3 & 7 \\ 4 & -9 & -2 \end{bmatrix}$
7. $\begin{bmatrix} 5 & 9 & -6 \\ 4 & -2 & -8 \\ 7 & -1 & 0 \end{bmatrix} - \begin{bmatrix} 7 & -4 & 2 \\ -7 & -5 & 10 \\ 12 & 7 & -8 \end{bmatrix}$

Practice and Applications

HOMEWORK HELP

For Exercises	See Examples
8–13	1
14–17, 19	2–4

Extra Practice See pages 640, 656.

State the dimensions of each matrix. Then identify the position of the circled element. 8–13. See margin.

8. $\begin{bmatrix} 5 \\ \textcircled{-6} \\ 2 \end{bmatrix}$
9. $\begin{bmatrix} 7 & -9 & \textcircled{5} \end{bmatrix}$
10. $\begin{bmatrix} 9 & -7 \\ 4 & \textcircled{3} \end{bmatrix}$
11. $\begin{bmatrix} 7 & -9 & 3 \\ -4 & 2 & 0 \\ \textcircled{18} & 12 & -6 \end{bmatrix}$
12. $\begin{bmatrix} 6 & -8 & 5 & \textcircled{9} \\ -3 & -2 & 0 & 0 \end{bmatrix}$
13. $\begin{bmatrix} 12 & -4 & 3 & 7 \\ -5 & -2 & 0 & 1 \\ 14 & \textcircled{11} & 25 & -9 \end{bmatrix}$

Add or subtract. If there is no sum or difference, write *impossible*.

14. $\begin{bmatrix} 2 & 1 \\ 3 & 0 \\ 5 & -4 \end{bmatrix} + \begin{bmatrix} 6 & 0 \\ 2 & -3 \\ 5 & 8 \end{bmatrix}$ $\begin{bmatrix} 8 & 1 \\ 5 & -3 \\ 10 & 4 \end{bmatrix}$
15. $\begin{bmatrix} 8 & 1 & 9 \\ 2 & 0 & 7 \\ 3 & -2 & 4 \end{bmatrix} - \begin{bmatrix} 6 & 0 & 7 \\ -1 & 5 & 8 \\ 2 & 6 & -4 \end{bmatrix}$ $\begin{bmatrix} 2 & 1 & 2 \\ 3 & -5 & -1 \\ 1 & -8 & 8 \end{bmatrix}$
16. $\begin{bmatrix} 4 & -2 \\ 3 & 1 \end{bmatrix} - \begin{bmatrix} 1 & 5 & 7 \\ 3 & -2 & 1 \\ 0 & 4 & 11 \end{bmatrix}$ impossible
17. $\begin{bmatrix} 1 \\ 2 \\ 9 \end{bmatrix} + \begin{bmatrix} -5 & -2 & -7 \end{bmatrix}$ impossible

18–19. See margin.

SPORTS For Exercises 18 and 19, use the following information.

1998 Winter Olympics Medals

Country	Gold	Silver	Bronze
Canada	6	5	4
Norway	10	10	5
U.S.A.	6	3	4

Source: *The World Almanac*

2002 Winter Olympics Medals

Country	Gold	Silver	Bronze
Canada	6	3	8
Norway	11	7	6
U.S.A.	10	13	11

Source: *USA TODAY*

18. Make a matrix for the information on each of the Olympics.
19. Use addition of matrices to find the total number of each type of medals won by the countries in the two Olympics. Write as a matrix.

24.
25.

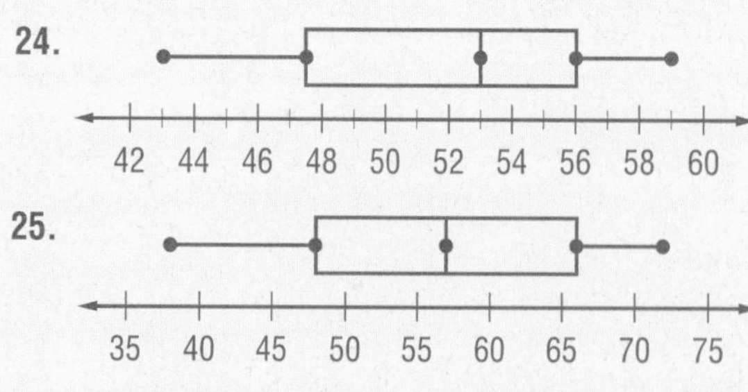

20. **CRITICAL THINKING** Find the values of a, b, c, and d if $\begin{bmatrix} 1 & 4 \\ 3 & -2 \end{bmatrix} + \begin{bmatrix} a & b \\ c & d \end{bmatrix} = \begin{bmatrix} -1 & 7 \\ 5 & -2 \end{bmatrix}$. **−2; 3; 2; 0**

Spiral Review with Standardized Test Practice

For Exercises 21 and 22, use the table below. It shows the attendance for four school concerts.

	Fall	Holiday	Winter	Spring
Friday Night	112	100	95	99
Saturday Night	101	103	75	60
Sunday Matinee	89	88	90	86

21. **MULTIPLE CHOICE** Choose the matrix that correctly displays the attendance. **C**

Ⓐ $\begin{bmatrix} 89 & 101 & 112 \\ 88 & 103 & 100 \\ 90 & 75 & 95 \\ 86 & 60 & 99 \end{bmatrix}$ Ⓑ $\begin{bmatrix} 112 & 101 & 89 & 100 \\ 103 & 88 & 95 & 75 \\ 90 & 99 & 60 & 86 \end{bmatrix}$

Ⓒ $\begin{bmatrix} 112 & 100 & 95 & 99 \\ 101 & 103 & 75 & 60 \\ 89 & 88 & 90 & 86 \end{bmatrix}$ Ⓓ $\begin{bmatrix} 112 & 101 & 89 \\ 100 & 103 & 88 \\ 95 & 75 & 90 \\ 99 & 60 & 86 \end{bmatrix}$

22. **MULTIPLE CHOICE** Which concert had the greatest attendance? **F**

Ⓕ Fall Ⓖ Holiday Ⓗ Winter Ⓘ Spring

23. **EXERCISE** A person working fairly hard on a treadmill will burn about 700 Calories per hour. A person working fairly hard on a stairstepper will burn about 625 Calories per hour. Make a graph of the data showing the treadmill is much better than the stairstepper in burning Calories. (Lesson 9-7) **See margin.**

Draw a box-and-whisker plot for each set of data. (Lesson 9-6) **24–25. See margin.**

24. 43, 47, 48, 50, 53, 54, 56, 56, 59

25. 37, 40, 56, 57, 57, 64, 68, 72

26. What is the probability that a month picked at random ends in *–ber*? (Lesson 8-1) $\frac{1}{3}$

INTERDISCIPLINARY PROJECT

It's all in the Genes

Math and Science It's time to complete your project. Use the information and data you have gathered about genetics and the traits of your classmates to prepare a Web page or poster. Be sure to include a chart displaying your data with your project.

msmath3.net/webquest

msmath3.net/self_check_quiz

4 Assess

Higher-Level Thinking

Matrices can also be multiplied. Suppose that a matrix shows the prices for a restaurant's weekly food order. Find the cost for each item for 8 weeks. Write a 4-by-4 matrix, then multiply it by the number 8 by multiplying each element by 8, forming a new matrix—a product matrix.

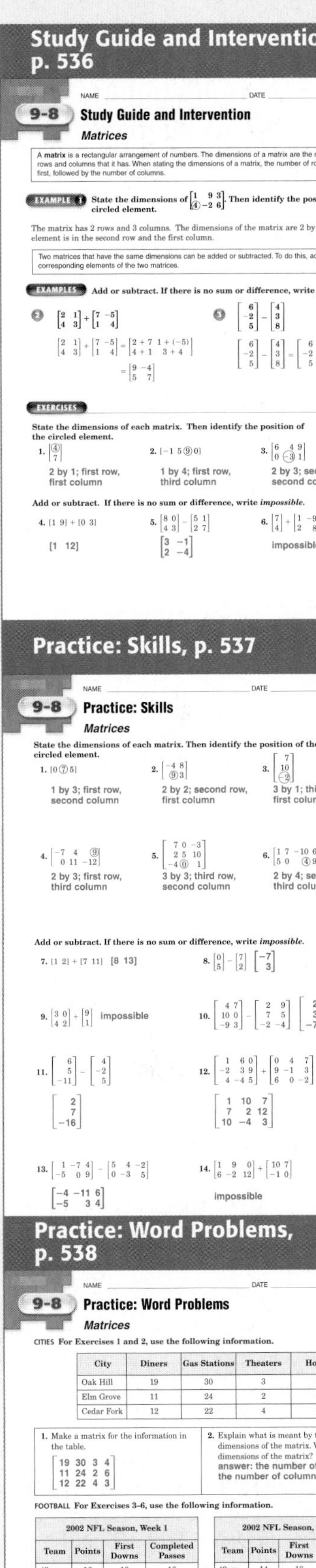

Study Guide and Intervention, p. 536

NAME ______ DATE ______ PERIOD ____

9-8 Study Guide and Intervention

Matrices

A **matrix** is a rectangular arrangement of numbers. The dimensions of a matrix are the number of rows and columns that it has. When stating the dimensions of a matrix, the number of rows is stated first, followed by the number of columns.

EXAMPLE 1 **State the dimensions of $\begin{bmatrix} 1 & 9 & 3 \\ \textcircled{4} & -2 & 6 \end{bmatrix}$. Then identify the position of the circled element.**

The matrix has 2 rows and 3 columns. The dimensions of the matrix are 2 by 3. The circled element is in the second row and the first column.

Two matrices that have the same dimensions can be added or subtracted. To do this, add or subtract corresponding elements of the two matrices.

EXAMPLES **Add or subtract. If there is no sum or difference, write *impossible*.**

2. $\begin{bmatrix} 2 & 1 \\ 4 & 3 \end{bmatrix} + \begin{bmatrix} 7 & -5 \\ 1 & 4 \end{bmatrix}$

$\begin{bmatrix} 2 & 1 \\ 4 & 3 \end{bmatrix} + \begin{bmatrix} 7 & -5 \\ 1 & 4 \end{bmatrix} = \begin{bmatrix} 2+7 & 1+(-5) \\ 4+1 & 3+4 \end{bmatrix} = \begin{bmatrix} 9 & -4 \\ 5 & 7 \end{bmatrix}$

3. $\begin{bmatrix} 6 \\ -2 \\ 5 \end{bmatrix} - \begin{bmatrix} 4 \\ 3 \\ 8 \end{bmatrix}$

$\begin{bmatrix} 6 \\ -2 \\ 5 \end{bmatrix} - \begin{bmatrix} 4 \\ 3 \\ 8 \end{bmatrix} = \begin{bmatrix} 6-4 \\ -2-3 \\ 5-8 \end{bmatrix} = \begin{bmatrix} 2 \\ -5 \\ -3 \end{bmatrix}$

EXERCISES

State the dimensions of each matrix. Then identify the position of the circled element.

1. $\begin{bmatrix} \textcircled{4} \\ 7 \end{bmatrix}$ 2 by 1; first row, first column

2. $\begin{bmatrix} -1 & 5 & \textcircled{9} & 0 \end{bmatrix}$ 1 by 4; first row, third column

3. $\begin{bmatrix} 6 & 4 & 9 \\ 0 & \textcircled{-3} & 1 \end{bmatrix}$ 2 by 3; second row, second column

Add or subtract. If there is no sum or difference, write *impossible*.

4. $[1\ 9] + [0\ 3]$ [1 12]

5. $\begin{bmatrix} 8 & 0 \\ 4 & 3 \end{bmatrix} - \begin{bmatrix} 5 & 1 \\ 2 & 7 \end{bmatrix}$ $\begin{bmatrix} 3 & -1 \\ 2 & -4 \end{bmatrix}$

6. $\begin{bmatrix} 7 \\ 4 \end{bmatrix} + \begin{bmatrix} 1 & -9 \\ 2 & 8 \end{bmatrix}$ impossible

Practice: Skills, p. 537

NAME ______ DATE ______ PERIOD ____

9-8 Practice: Skills

Matrices

State the dimensions of each matrix. Then identify the position of the circled element.

1. $[0\ \textcircled{7}\ 5]$ 1 by 3; first row, second column

2. $\begin{bmatrix} -4 & 8 \\ \textcircled{9} & 3 \end{bmatrix}$ 2 by 2; second row, first column

3. $\begin{bmatrix} 7 \\ 10 \\ \textcircled{-2} \end{bmatrix}$ 3 by 1; third row, first column

4. $\begin{bmatrix} -7 & 4 & \textcircled{9} \\ 0 & 11 & -12 \end{bmatrix}$ 2 by 3; first row, third column

5. $\begin{bmatrix} 7 & 0 & -3 \\ 2 & 5 & 10 \\ -4 & \textcircled{0} & 1 \end{bmatrix}$ 3 by 3; third row, second column

6. $\begin{bmatrix} 1 & 7 & -10 & 6 \\ 5 & 0 & \textcircled{4} & 9 \end{bmatrix}$ 2 by 4; second row, third column

Add or subtract. If there is no sum or difference, write *impossible*.

7. $[1\ 2] + [7\ 11]$ [8 13]

8. $\begin{bmatrix} 0 \\ 5 \end{bmatrix} - \begin{bmatrix} 7 \\ 2 \end{bmatrix}$ $\begin{bmatrix} -7 \\ 3 \end{bmatrix}$

9. $\begin{bmatrix} 3 & 0 \\ 4 & 2 \end{bmatrix} + \begin{bmatrix} 9 \\ 1 \end{bmatrix}$ impossible

10. $\begin{bmatrix} 4 & 7 \\ 10 & 0 \\ -9 & 3 \end{bmatrix} - \begin{bmatrix} 2 & 9 \\ 7 & 5 \\ -2 & -4 \end{bmatrix}$ $\begin{bmatrix} 2 & -2 \\ 3 & -5 \\ -7 & 7 \end{bmatrix}$

11. $\begin{bmatrix} 6 \\ 5 \\ -11 \end{bmatrix} - \begin{bmatrix} 4 \\ -2 \\ 5 \end{bmatrix}$ $\begin{bmatrix} 2 \\ 7 \\ -16 \end{bmatrix}$

12. $\begin{bmatrix} 1 & 6 & 0 \\ -2 & 3 & 9 \\ 4 & -4 & 5 \end{bmatrix} + \begin{bmatrix} 0 & 4 & 7 \\ 9 & -1 & 3 \\ 6 & 0 & -2 \end{bmatrix}$ $\begin{bmatrix} 1 & 10 & 7 \\ 7 & 2 & 12 \\ 10 & -4 & 3 \end{bmatrix}$

13. $\begin{bmatrix} 1 & -7 & 4 \\ -5 & 0 & 9 \end{bmatrix} - \begin{bmatrix} 5 & 4 & -2 \\ 0 & -3 & 5 \end{bmatrix}$ $\begin{bmatrix} -4 & -11 & 6 \\ -5 & 3 & 4 \end{bmatrix}$

14. $\begin{bmatrix} 1 & 9 & 0 \\ 6 & -2 & 12 \end{bmatrix} + \begin{bmatrix} 10 & 7 \\ -1 & 0 \end{bmatrix}$ impossible

Practice: Word Problems, p. 538

NAME ______ DATE ______

9-8 Practice: Word Problems

Matrices

CITIES **For Exercises 1 and 2, use the following information.**

City	Diners	Gas Stations	Theaters	Hotels
Oak Hill	19	30	3	4
Elm Grove	11	24	2	6
Cedar Fork	12	22	4	3

1. Make a matrix for the information in the table. $\begin{bmatrix} 19 & 30 & 3 & 4 \\ 11 & 24 & 2 & 6 \\ 12 & 22 & 4 & 3 \end{bmatrix}$

2. Explain what is meant by the dimensions of the matrix. What are the dimensions of the matrix? Sample answer: the number of rows and the number of columns; 3 by 4

FOOTBALL **For Exercises 3–6, use the following information.**

2002 NFL Season, Week 1

Team	Points	First Downs	Completed Passes
49ers	16	13	16
Giants	13	21	28
Vikings	23	19	16
Bears	27	20	20

2002 NFL Season, Week 2

Team	Points	First Downs	Completed Passes
49ers	14	18	27
Giants	26	16	22
Vikings	39	31	25
Bears	14	13	12

3. Make a matrix for the information for the first game of the 2002 season. $\begin{bmatrix} 16 & 13 & 16 \\ 13 & 21 & 28 \\ 23 & 19 & 16 \\ 27 & 20 & 20 \end{bmatrix}$

4. Make a matrix for the information for the second game of the 2002 season. $\begin{bmatrix} 14 & 18 & 27 \\ 26 & 16 & 22 \\ 39 & 31 & 25 \\ 14 & 13 & 12 \end{bmatrix}$

5. Explain the conditions necessary to be able to add two matrices. The number of rows and the number of columns must be the same.

6. Use the addition of matrices to find the totals in each category for each team in the two games. Write as a matrix. $\begin{bmatrix} 30 & 31 & 43 \\ 39 & 37 & 50 \\ 62 & 50 & 41 \\ 41 & 33 & 32 \end{bmatrix}$

Study Guide and Review

Vocabulary Assessment

- This alphabetical list of vocabulary terms in Chapter 9 includes a page reference where each term was introduced.
- A vocabulary review/test for Chapter 9 is available on p. 554 of the *Chapter 9 Resource Masters*.

Vocabulary PuzzleMaker

ELL The online Vocabulary PuzzleMaker improves students' mathematics vocabulary using four puzzle formats – crossword, scramble, word search using a word list, and word search using clues. Students can work on a computer screen or from a printed handout.

MindJogger Videoquizzes

ELL MindJogger Videoquizzes provide an alternative review of concepts presented in this chapter. Students work in teams in a game show format to gain points for correct answers. The questions are presented in three rounds.

Round 1 Concepts (5 questions)
Round 2 Skills (4 questions)
Round 3 Problem Solving (4 questions)

ExamView® Pro

Use the networkable ExamView® Pro Testmaker CD-ROM to:

- Create **multiple versions** of tests.
- Create **modified** tests for **inclusion** students with one mouse click.
- **Edit** existing questions and **add** your own questions.
- Build tests aligned with state standards using built-in **state curriculum correlations.**
- Change **English** tests to **Spanish** with one mouse click and vice versa.

Study Guide and Review

Vocabulary and Concept Check

box-and-whisker plot (p. 446)
circle graph (p. 426)
column (p. 454)
dimensions (p. 454)
element (p. 454)
histogram (p. 420)
interquartile range (p. 442)
lower quartile (p. 442)
matrix (p. 454)
mean (p. 435)
measures of central tendency (p. 435)
measures of variation (p. 442)
median (p. 435)
mode (p. 435)
outlier (p. 443)
quartiles (p. 442)
range (p. 442)
row (p. 454)
upper quartile (p. 442)

State whether each sentence is *true* or *false*. If *false*, replace the underlined word or number to make a true sentence.

1. A histogram is a bar graph that shows the frequency of data in intervals. **true**
2. The range is one of the measures of central tendency. **false; measures of variation**
3. The mean is the sum of the data divided by the number of pieces of data. **true**
4. If you want to show how the parts compare to the whole, use a circle graph. **true**
5. The mode is the middle number of a set of data. **false; median**
6. A matrix is a rectangular arrangement of numbers. **true**
7. A matrix is described by its rows. **false; dimensions**
8. Each number in a matrix is called an element. **true**

Lesson-by-Lesson Exercises and Examples

9-1 Histograms (pp. 420–424)

For Exercises 9–10, use the histogram at the right.

9. How many students received a score of at least 80? **10 students**
10. How many students received a score less than 70? **5 students**
11. **ANIMALS** The following is a list of years various types of animals are expected to live. Draw a histogram to represent the data. **See margin.**
    1, 3, 5, 5, 6, 7, 8, 8, 10, 10, 10, 12, 12, 12, 12, 15, 15, 15, 15, 16, 18, 20, 20, 25, 35

Example 1

Make a histogram to represent the following English test scores.

56, 87, 87, 74, 87, 84, 94, 80, 72, 58, 87, 90, 68, 90, 70, 73, 74, 82, 68, 64

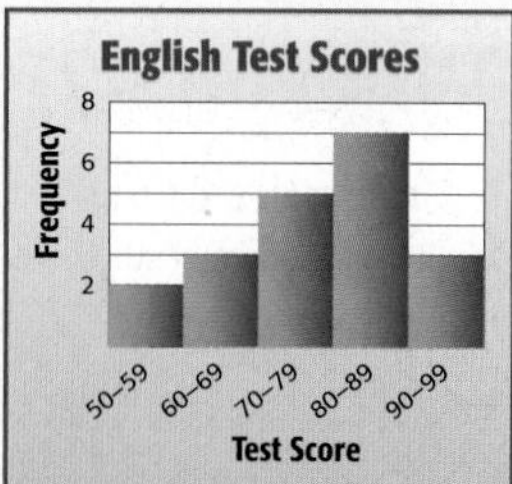

Math Online msmath3.net/vocabulary_review

FOLDABLES™ Study Organizer

For more information about Foldables, see *Teaching Mathematics with Foldables.*

Have students look through the chapter to make sure they have included examples in their Foldables for each lesson or topic in the chapter.

Encourage students to refer to their Foldables while completing the Study Guide and Review and to use them in preparing for the Chapter Test.

9-2 Circle Graphs (pp. 426–429)

12. **GEOGRAPHY** Lake Erie is 9,910 square miles, Lake Huron is 23,010 square miles, Lake Michigan is 22,300 square miles, Lake Ontario is 7,540 square miles, and Lake Superior is 31,700 square miles. Make a circle graph showing what percent of the total area of the Great Lakes is represented by each lake. **See margin.**

Example 2

CARS Which country made the same amount of motor vehicles as Canada and Japan?

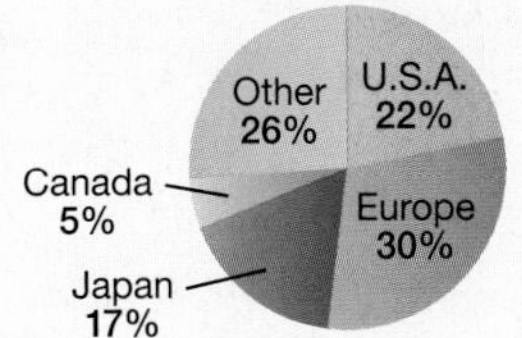

5% + 17% = 22%, so the answer is the U.S.A.

9-3 Choosing an Appropriate Display (pp. 430-433)

Choose an appropriate type of display for each situation. **13. circle graph**

13. percent of income people spend on different expenses each month
14. populations of counties in Pennsylvania arranged by intervals **histogram**

Example 3

Choose an appropriate display for the number of students who prefer each color.

An appropriate display would be a table, bar graph, or pictograph.

9-4 Measures of Central Tendency (pp. 435–438)

Find the mean, median, and mode for each set of data. Round to the nearest tenth if necessary.

15. 13, 15, 15, 15, 18, 19, 20 **16.4, 15, 15**
16. 5.6, 6.5, 6.8, 9.6, 10.1 **7.7, 6.8, no mode**
17. 5, 6, 7, 7, 8, 8, 8, 9, 9, 10 **7.7, 8, 8**

Example 4

Find the mean, median, and mode for the data 8, 8, 9, 9, 9, 13, 14.

$$\text{mean} = \frac{8 + 8 + 9 + 9 + 9 + 13 + 14}{7} \text{ or } 10$$

median = 9 mode = 9

9-5 Measures of Variation (pp. 442–445)

Find the range, median, upper and lower quartiles, interquartile range, and any outliers for each set of data.

18. 0, 5, 7, 11, 13, 13, 13, 14, 15
19. 1, 2, 2, 3, 3, 3, 4, 4, 5, 6, 12
20. 3, 5, 7, 7, 7, 8, 8, 9
21. 8, 9, 5, 10, 7, 6, 2, 4

18–21. See margin.

Example 5

Find the range, median, upper and lower quartiles, and interquartile range.

2, 3, 4, 5, 6, 9, 9, 9, 9, 9, 10

range = 10 − 2 or 8 median = 9

lower quartile = 4 upper quartile = 9

interquartile range = 9 − 4 or 5

Answers

11.

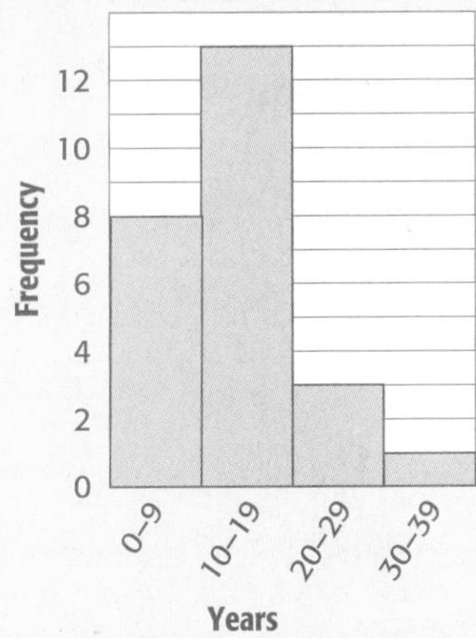

12.

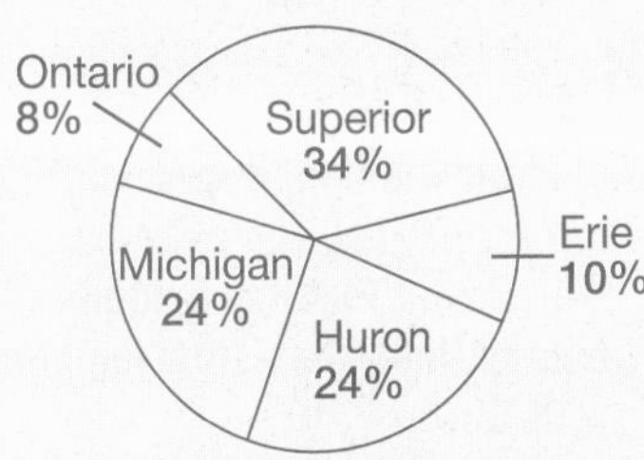

18. 15; 13; 13.5, 6; 7.5; no outliers
19. 11; 3; 5, 2; 3; 12
20. 6; 7; 8; 6; 2; no outliers
21. 8; 6.5; 8.5, 4.5; 4; no outliers

Study Guide and Review

Answers (Study Guide)

22. See bottom margin.

23.

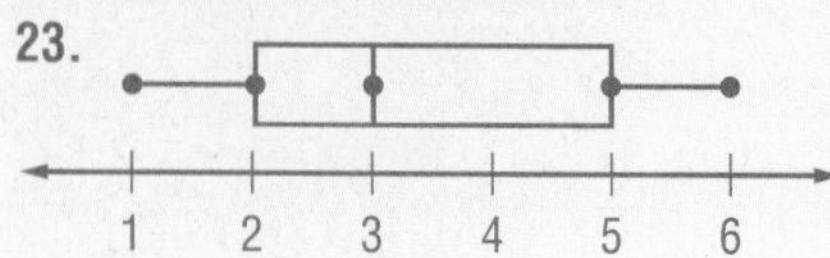

24. See bottom margin.

25.

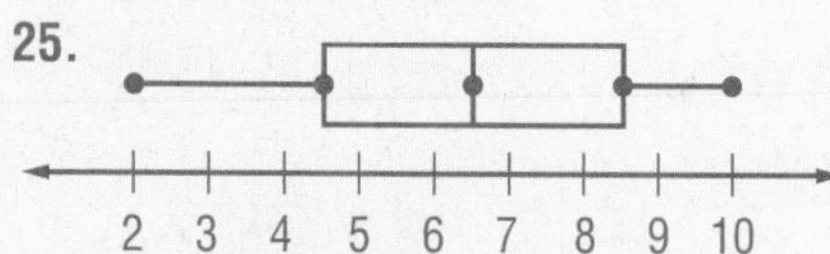

30. Although the medians are the same, Group A has a much lower mean and a much lower mode than Group B. In general, Group B did better than Group A.

Answers (Practice Test)

1. Find the median, upper quartile, lower quartile, and extremes of a set of data. Plot these numbers on a number line, then draw the box and whiskers.
2. A 4 by 2 has 4 rows and 2 columns. The second has 2 rows and 4 columns.

5.

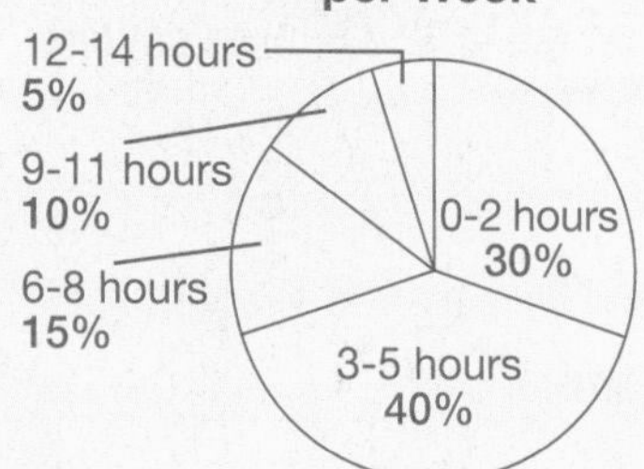

Mixed Problem Solving
For mixed problem-solving practice, see page 656.

9-6 Box-and-Whisker Plots (pp. 446–449)

Draw a box-and-whisker plot for each set of data. 22–25. See margin.

22. 0, 5, 7, 11, 13, 13, 13, 14, 15
23. 1, 2, 2, 3, 3, 3, 4, 4, 5, 6, 6
24. 2, 5, 7, 7, 7, 8, 8, 9
25. 8, 9, 5, 10, 7, 6, 2, 4

Example 6
Draw a box-and-whisker plot for the set of data.

2, 3, 4, 5, 6, 7, 9, 9, 9, 9, 10

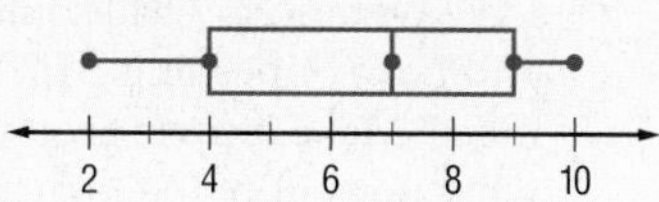

9-7 Misleading Graphs and Statistics (pp. 450–453)

SCHOOL For Exercises 26–30, use the list of test grades for two group of students.

Group A: 100, 95, 90, 89, 88, 45, 42, 40, 40
Group B: 99, 98, 93, 89, 88, 85, 85, 75, 72

26. What is the mean, median, and mode of the grades of Group A? **69.9; 88; 40**
27. What average is most favorable for Group A? **median**
28. What is the mean, median, and mode of the grades for Group B? **87.1; 88; 85**
29. What average is most favorable for Group B? **median**
30. Since both groups have the same median, did both groups do as well on the test? Explain. **No; see margin.**

Example 7
Which graph makes Program E appear to be much more popular than Program A? Explain.

Graph X makes Program E appear to be much more popular than Program A, because the scale does not start with 0.

Graph X

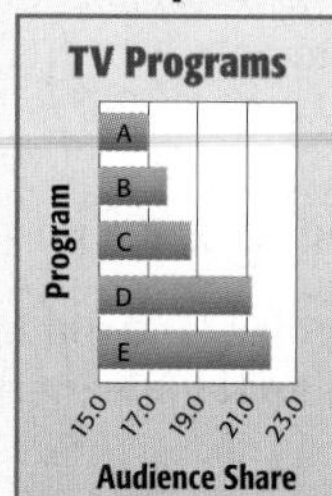

Graph Y

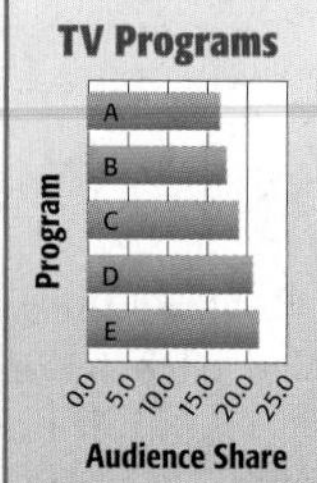

9-8 Matrices (pp. 454–457)

Add or subtract. If there is no sum or difference, write *impossible*.

31. $\begin{bmatrix} 6 & 5 \\ -2 & 1 \end{bmatrix} - \begin{bmatrix} -3 & -2 \\ 0 & -1 \end{bmatrix}$ $\begin{bmatrix} 9 & 7 \\ -2 & 2 \end{bmatrix}$

32. $\begin{bmatrix} 2 & -1 \\ -3 & 9 \end{bmatrix} + \begin{bmatrix} 10 & -3 \\ 8 & -3 \end{bmatrix}$ $\begin{bmatrix} 12 & -4 \\ 5 & 6 \end{bmatrix}$

33. $\begin{bmatrix} 3 & -2 \\ 4 & -1 \end{bmatrix} + \begin{bmatrix} -3 & 8 \\ 0 & 6 \\ -4 & 2 \end{bmatrix}$ **impossible**

Example 8
Add. If there is no sum, write *impossible*.

$\begin{bmatrix} 3 & 5 \\ -2 & 1 \end{bmatrix} + \begin{bmatrix} -2 & -1 \\ -3 & 5 \end{bmatrix}$

$= \begin{bmatrix} 3 + (-2) & 5 + (-1) \\ -2 + (-3) & 1 + 5 \end{bmatrix}$

$= \begin{bmatrix} 1 & 4 \\ -5 & 6 \end{bmatrix}$

22.

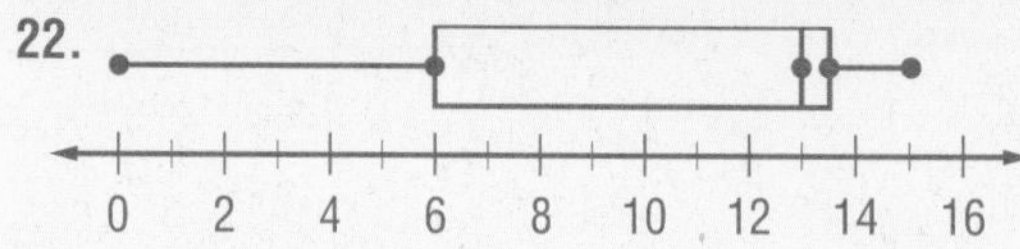

24.

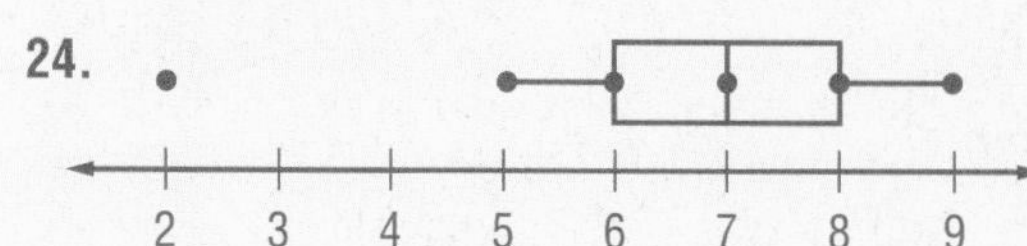

Practice Test

Vocabulary and Concepts

1. **Explain** how to draw a box-and-whisker plot. See margin.
2. **Describe** the difference between a 4 by 2 matrix and a 2 by 4 matrix. See margin.

Skills and Applications

EXERCISE For Exercises 3–5, use the histogram.

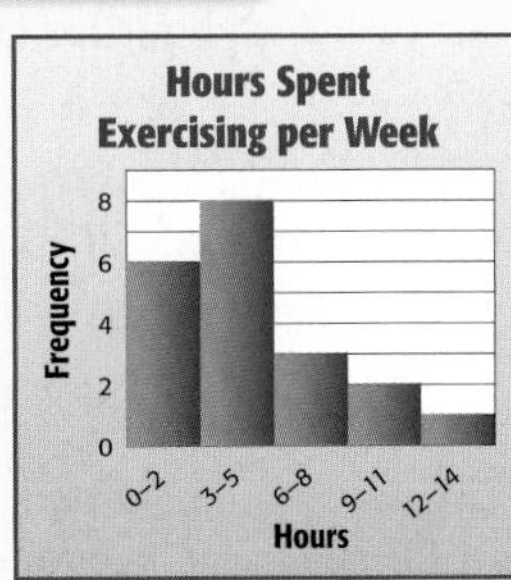

3. How many people were surveyed? 20 people
4. How many people spend more than 8 hours per week exercising? 3 people
5. Make a circle graph of the data. See margin.
6. **SPORTS** Toni made a survey about students' favorite sports. What type of graph should she use to show the percent of students who picked each sport? circle graph

For Exercises 7–12, use the following list of the ages of 13 people.

45, 36, 27, 16, 19, 46, 40, 38, 22, 23, 25, 40, 17.

7. Find the mean. about 30.3 years old
8. What is the median? 27 years old
9. Find the range. 30
10. Find the upper and lower quartile.
11. What is the interquartile range? 19.5
12. Draw a box-and-whisker plot. See Ch. 9 Answer Appendix.

10. 40 years old; 20.5 years old

13. **SCHOOL** Which graph indicates that there are many more eighth grade students that have a B average or better than students in the sixth grade with the same average? Explain. Graph A; the intervals are smaller.

Graph A

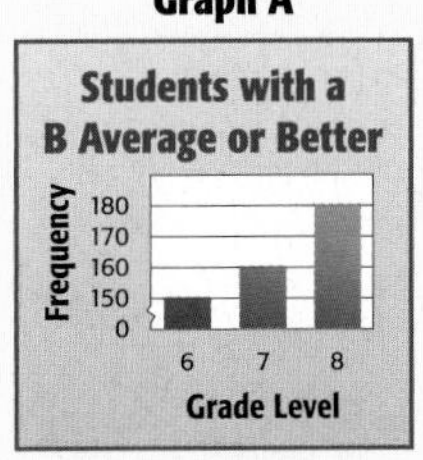

Graph B

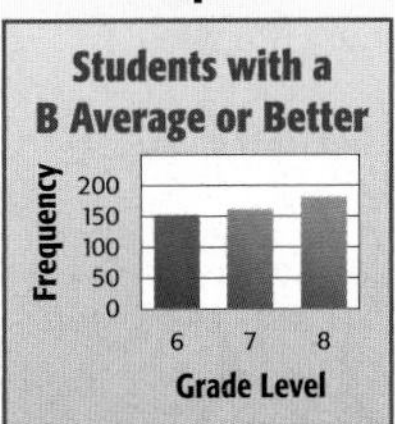

Add or subtract. If no sum or difference exists, write *impossible*.

14. $\begin{bmatrix} 3 & 2 \\ -2 & 5 \end{bmatrix} - \begin{bmatrix} -2 & -1 \\ 0 & 5 \end{bmatrix}$ $\begin{bmatrix} 5 & 3 \\ -2 & 0 \end{bmatrix}$

15. $\begin{bmatrix} 2 & 5 \\ 6 & 1 \end{bmatrix} + \begin{bmatrix} 2 & 5 & 0 \\ 3 & 1 & 2 \end{bmatrix}$ impossible

Standardized Test Practice

16. **MULTIPLE CHOICE** Alma's monthly earnings were $540, $450, $800, $560, $350, $400, $350, $380, $500, $450, $600, and $200. How much more would Alma have needed to earn to have an average monthly income of $500? C

Ⓐ 0 Ⓑ $220 Ⓒ $420 Ⓓ $500

msmath3.net/chapter_test

Assessment Options

Vocabulary Test A vocabulary review/test for Chapter 9 can be found on p. 554 of the *Chapter 9 Resource Masters.*

Chapter Tests There are six Chapter 9 Tests and an Extended Response Assessment task available in the *Chapter 9 Resource Masters.*

Chapter 9 Tests			
Form	Type	Level	Pages
1	MC	basic	541–542
2A	MC	average	543–544
2B	MC	average	545–546
2C	FR	average	547–548
2D	FR	average	549–550
3	FR	advanced	551–552

MC = multiple-choice questions
FR = free-response questions

Extended Response Assessment

Extended Response tasks for Chapter 9 can be found on p. 553 of the *Chapter 9 Resource Masters.* A sample scoring rubric for these tasks appears on p. A28.

Unit 4 Test

A unit test/review can be found on pp. 561–562 of the *Chapter 9 Resource Masters.*

Portfolio Suggestion

Introduction Statistical displays and matrices make it easy to see data and their relationships. Each type of display has particular advantages.

Ask Students to include a frequency table, a histogram, a circle graph, a box-and-whisker plot, and a matrix from their homework answers. Next to each example, have them write a sentence explaining how that display makes the data easier to understand.

Chapter 9 Standardized Test Practice

These two pages contain practice questions in the various formats that can be found on the most frequently given standardized tests.

A student recording sheet for these two pages can be found on p. A1 of the *Chapter 9 Resource Masters*.

Standardized Test Practice Student Recording Sheet, p. A1

NAME ______ DATE ______ PERIOD ______

9 Standardized Test Practice SCORE ______

Student Recording Sheet (Use with pages 462-463 of the Student Edition.)

Part 1: Multiple Choice

Select the best answer from the choices given and fill in the corresponding oval.

1. Ⓐ Ⓑ Ⓒ Ⓓ 4. Ⓕ Ⓖ Ⓗ Ⓘ 7. Ⓐ Ⓑ Ⓒ Ⓓ

2. Ⓕ Ⓖ Ⓗ Ⓘ 5. Ⓐ Ⓑ Ⓒ Ⓓ 8. Ⓕ Ⓖ Ⓗ Ⓘ

3. Ⓐ Ⓑ Ⓒ Ⓓ 6. Ⓕ Ⓖ Ⓗ Ⓘ 9. Ⓐ Ⓑ Ⓒ Ⓓ

Part 2: Short Response/Grid In

Solve the problem and write your answer in the blank.

Also enter your answer by writing each number or symbol in a box. Then fill in the corresponding oval for that number or symbol.

10. ______ 16.
11. ______
12. ______
13. ______
14. ______
15. ______
16. ______ (grid in)

Part 3: Extended Response

Record your answer for Questions 17 and 18 on the back of this paper.

Additional Practice

See pp. 559–560 of the *Chapter 9 Resource Masters* for additional standardized test practice.

Standardized Test Practice

PART 1 Multiple Choice

Record your answers on the answer sheet provided by your teacher or on a sheet of paper.

1. Federico counted the number of bacteria in one dish each hour for four hours.

   2, 4, 8, 16

   If the pattern continues, how many bacteria will there be in the fifth hour? (Lesson 2-8) **C**

   Ⓐ 20 bacteria Ⓑ 24 bacteria
   Ⓒ 32 bacteria Ⓓ 64 bacteria

2. Trina is planning a rectangular garden. She would like to make a diagonal walking path through the garden with stone tiles. If each tile is a 6-inch square, how many tiles will she need? (Lesson 3-5) **H**

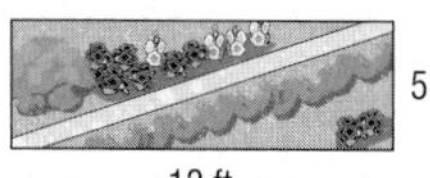

   Ⓕ 12 tiles Ⓖ 13 tiles
   Ⓗ 26 tiles Ⓘ 78 tiles

3. Describe the triangles. (Lesson 4-5) **B**

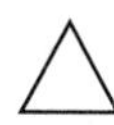

   Ⓐ right Ⓑ similar
   Ⓒ congruent Ⓓ corresponding

4. In the figure below, lines M and N are parallel, and lines O and P are parallel. Find the measure of $\angle 1$. (Lesson 6-1) **H**

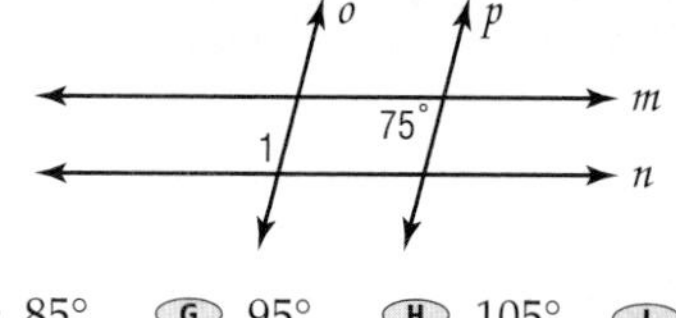

   Ⓕ 85° Ⓖ 95° Ⓗ 105° Ⓘ 125°

5. Samuel is setting up his tent for the night. What is the area of the canvas needed to form the front of his tent? (Lesson 7-1) **C**

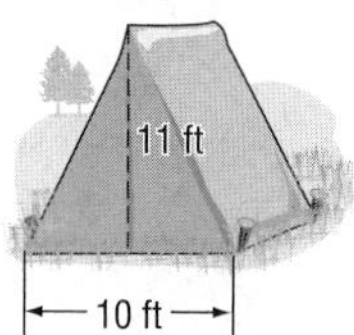

   Ⓐ 25 ft² Ⓑ $27\frac{1}{2}$ ft²
   Ⓒ 55 ft² Ⓓ 110 ft²

6. Alyssa is making a beaded bracelet. She has 12 red beads, 18 blue beads, 8 yellow beads, and 10 green beads. If she randomly chooses a bead from the bag, what is the probability that she will select a blue bead? (Lesson 8-1) **G**

   Ⓕ $\frac{1}{4}$ Ⓖ $\frac{3}{8}$
   Ⓗ $\frac{5}{12}$ Ⓘ $\frac{9}{19}$

7. Which of the following would best display the information in a frequency table that has been divided into intervals? (Lesson 9-1) **D**

   Ⓐ circle graph
   Ⓑ stem-and-leaf plot
   Ⓒ double bar graph
   Ⓓ histogram

8. Which of the following would best display data about different types of activities offered by a summer camp and the percent of time spent on each activity? (Lesson 9-3) **I**

   Ⓕ histogram Ⓖ line plot
   Ⓗ bar graph Ⓘ circle graph

9. The following is a list of the number of minutes Melanie spent on math homework each night. What is the lower quartile of the set of data? (Lesson 9-5) **B**

   26, 19, 45, 32, 40, 15,
   34, 12, 37, 25, 43, 21

   Ⓐ 19 Ⓑ 20 Ⓒ 21 Ⓓ 22

ExamView® Pro

Special banks of standardized test questions similar to those on the TIMSS and NAEP grade 8 tests can be found on this CD-ROM.

Preparing for Standardized Tests
For test-taking strategies and more practice, see pages 660–677.

PART 2 Short Response/Grid In

Record your answers on the answer sheet provided by your teacher or on a sheet of paper.

10. Hunter deposited \$450 in a savings account that receives 4.5% simple interest. Marina deposited \$550 in a savings account that receives 2.8% simple interest. Who will earn the greater amount of interest after 18 months? (Lesson 5-8) **Hunter**

11. The triangle at the right is translated 2 units up and 2 units to the left. What are the vertices of the translated triangle? (Lesson 6-8)
$A'(-1, -1)$, $B'(0, 1)$, $C'(2, 0)$

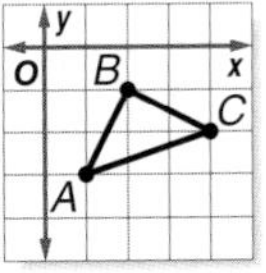

12. Curtis wants to cover the box at the right with decorative paper. How much paper will he need to cover the box? (Lesson 7-7) **972 cm^2**

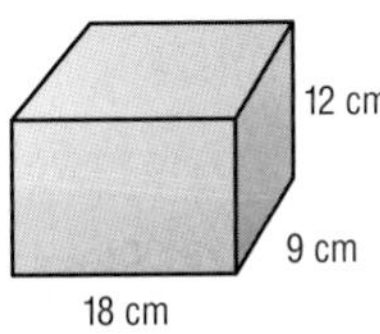

13. In Springwood Middle School, there are 50 students in the eighth grade. The class will elect 4 students as different class officers. If no student can hold more than one of these offices, how many different ways can the positions be filled? (Lesson 8-3) **5,527,200 ways**

14. Mr. Francis has told his students that he will remove the lowest exam score for each student at the end of the grading period. Seki received grades of 43, 78, 84, 85, 88, and 90 on her exams. What will be the difference between the mean of her original grades and the mean of her five grades after Mr. Francis removes one grade? (Lesson 9-4) **7 points**

15. The number of students who attended science club for each meeting last semester are listed.

    21, 33, 38, 12, 47, 18, 42, 51, 17, 35, 46

    Is the number 39 the upper quartile, the lower quartile, or the range of the set of numbers? (Lesson 9-5) **range**

16. Alfonso's bowling scores are listed below. What is the interquartile range? (Lesson 9-5) **34**

    125, 142, 167, 138, 176, 102, 156, 130, 142

PART 3 Extended Response

Record your answers on a sheet of paper. Show your work.

17. A pet store has 8 black dogs, 10 brown dogs, 2 white dogs, 6 spotted dogs, and 5 multicolored dogs. (Lesson 9-3)
    a. Make a graph that shows the number of each type of coloring the pet store has.
    b. Make a graph that shows what part of the total number of dogs is represented by each type of coloring.
    c. Describe an advantage of each type of graph you drew.
    a–c. See Ch. 9 Answer Appendix.

18. The price of a CD increased from \$12 to \$14. (Lesson 9-7)
    a. Make a graph to indicate that the increase in price was not too much.
    b. Make a graph to indicate that the increase in price is too much.
    a–b. See Ch. 9 Answer Appendix.

TEST-TAKING TIP

Question 16 Review any terms that you have learned before you take a test. For example, for a test on data and statistics, be sure that you understand such terms as *mean, median, mode, range, upper quartile, lower quartile,* and *interquartile range.*

msmath3.net/standardized_test

Standardized Test Practice

Rubrics The following rubrics are sample scoring devices for short response and extended response questions.

Short Response

Points	Description
2	The student demonstrates a <u>thorough understanding</u> of the mathematics of the task. The response may contain minor flaws that do not detract from the demonstration of a thorough understanding.
1	The student has provided a response that is only <u>partially correct</u>.
0	The student has provided a <u>completely incorrect</u> solution or no response at all.

Extended Response

Points	Description
4	The student demonstrates a <u>thorough understanding</u> of the mathematics of the task. The response may contain minor flaws that do not detract from the demonstration of a thorough understanding.
3	The student demonstrates an <u>understanding</u> of the mathematics of the task. The response is essentially correct and demonstrates an essential but less than thorough understanding of the mathematics.
2	The student demonstrates only a <u>partial understanding</u> of the mathematics of the task. Although the student may have used the correct approach to a solution or may have provided a correct solution, the work lacks an essential understanding of the underlying mathematical concepts.
1	The student demonstrates a <u>very limited understanding</u> of the mathematics of the task. The response is incomplete and exhibits many flaws.
0	The student provides a <u>completely incorrect</u> solution or no response at all.

A more detailed 4-point rubric is provided on page A2 of the *Chapter 9 Resource Masters*.

Pages 428–429, Lesson 9-2

4. **Borrowing a CD from Parents**

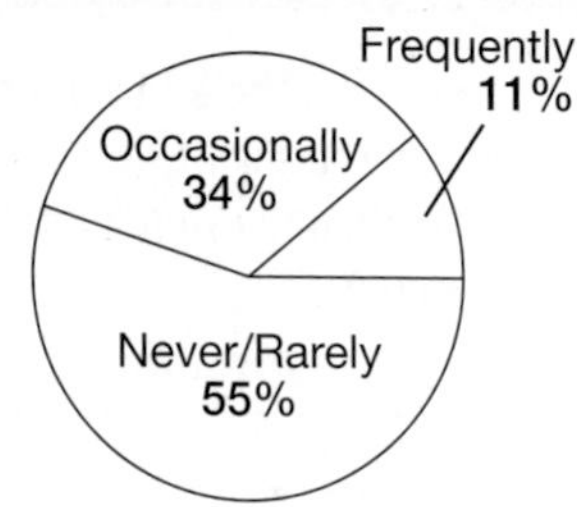

5. **Hawaiian Counties**

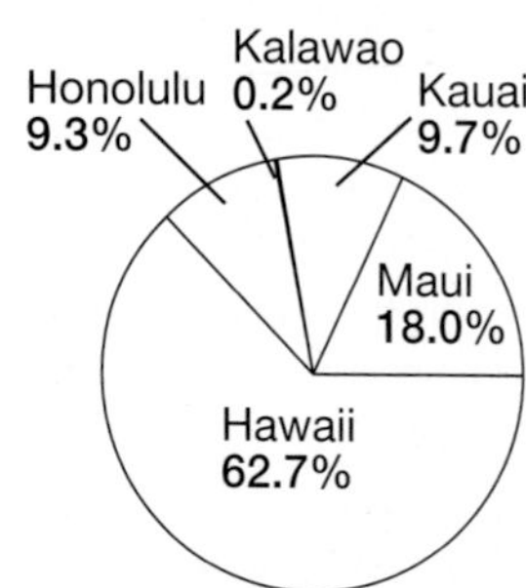

6. **Major Influence for Teens on Music Choices**

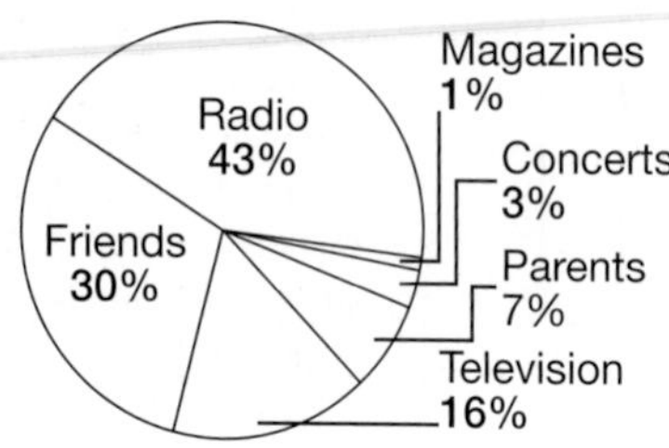

7. **Flowers and Plants Purchased for Mother's Day**

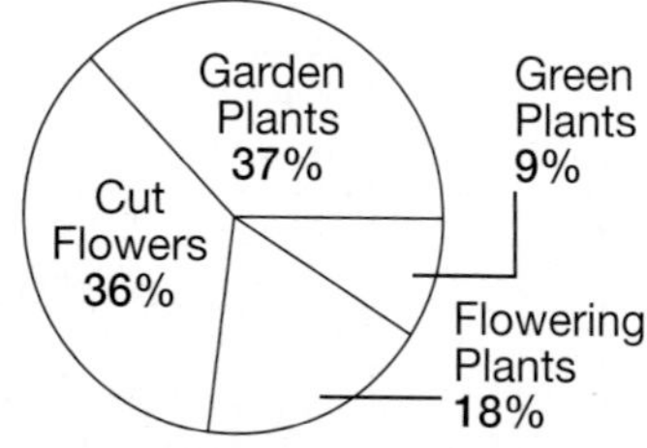

8. **Cotton Production**

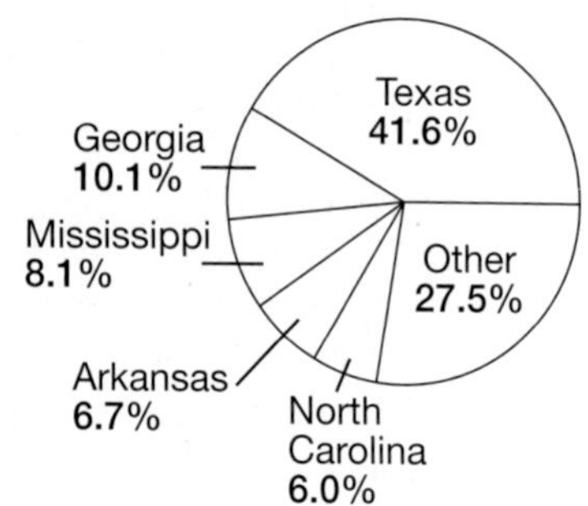

9. **U.S. Population by Age**

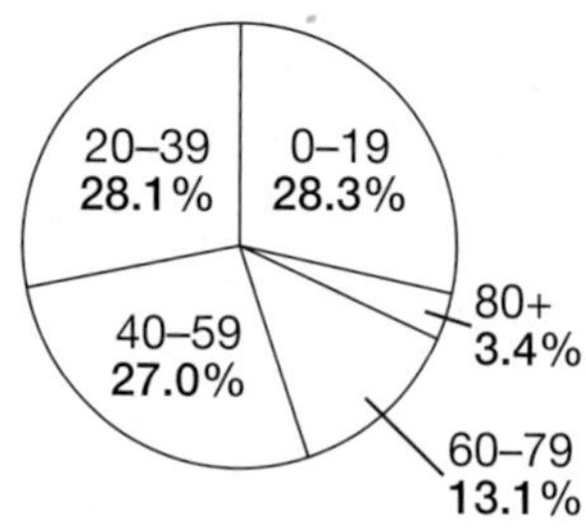

10. **Declaration Signers**

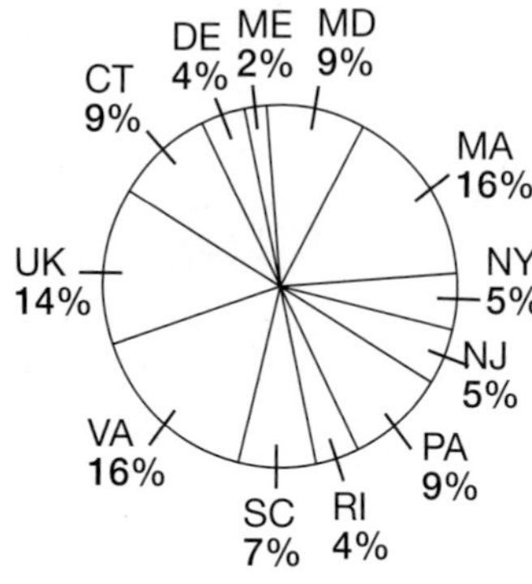

11. Half of the homes are heated with piped gas. About a third of the homes are heated with electricity. The rest of the homes are heated with fuel oil, bottled gas, wood, or something else.

12. **Favorite NBA Team**

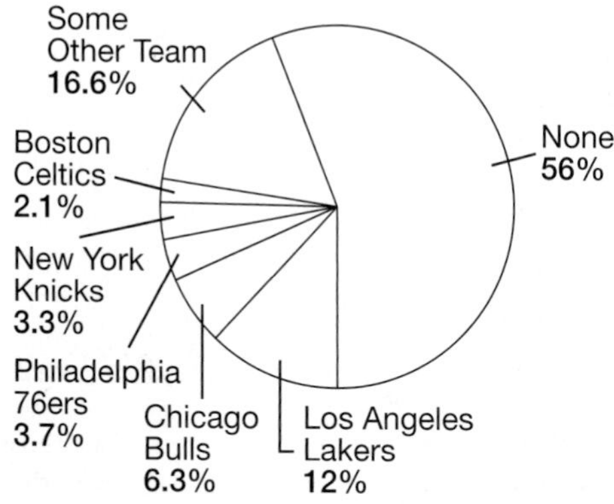

15. Sample answer:

Calories of Single Serving, Frozen Pizzas

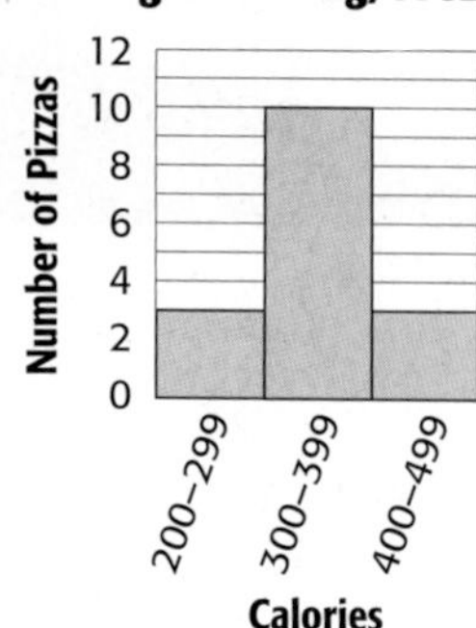

16. Only the listeners with a strong opinion will call into the radio station. If the radio station plays a certain type of music, those types of bands would probably be favored.

17.

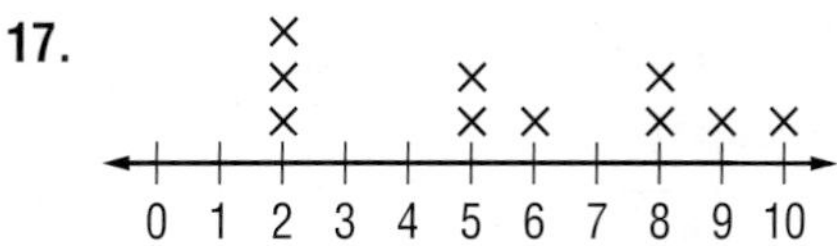

18.

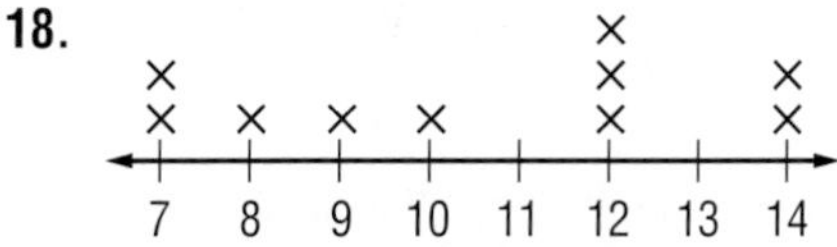

Page 433, Lesson 9-3

14. Sample answer:

The Importance of a Real Store to Online Shoppers

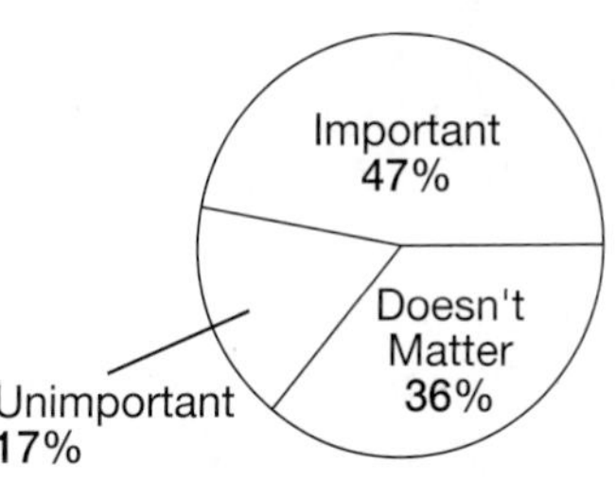

Both displays show which answer received the greatest response and which received the least response. The circle graph better shows how the responses compared to the whole.

17. Sample answer:

Time Needed to Walk to School

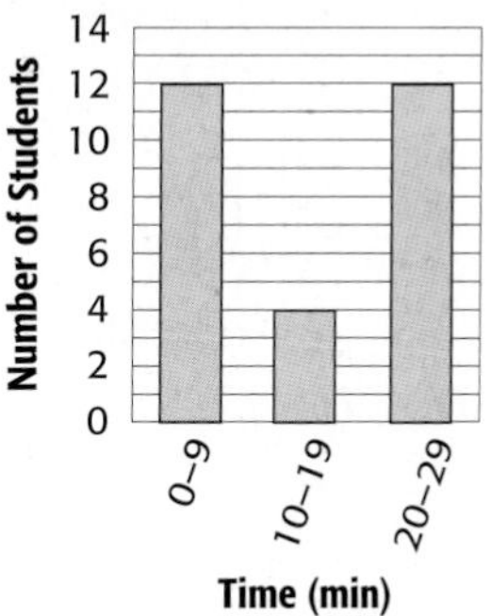

18. **Yellowstone National Park**

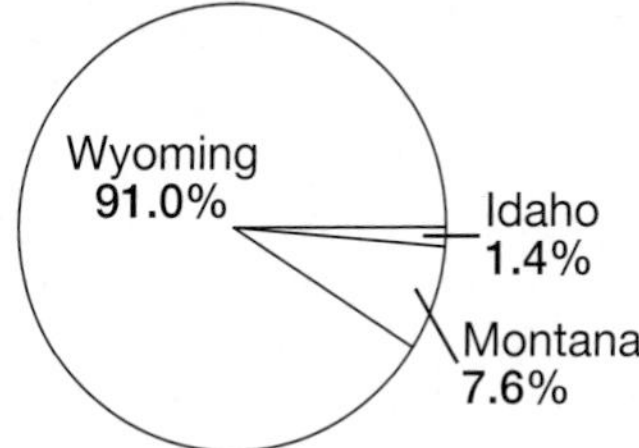

Page 445, Lesson 9-5

25a. Sample answer: {1, 1, 2, 2, 2, 5, 9, 9, 9, 10, 10} and {1, 4, 4, 4, 4, 5, 5, 5, 9, 10, 10}

25b. Sample answer: {1, 2, 5, 7, 9, 10, 12, 14, 15, 17, 22} and {0, 2, 5, 7, 9, 10, 12, 14, 15, 17, 27}

30. Sample answer: circle graph

Adult Audience of Oldies Radio by Age

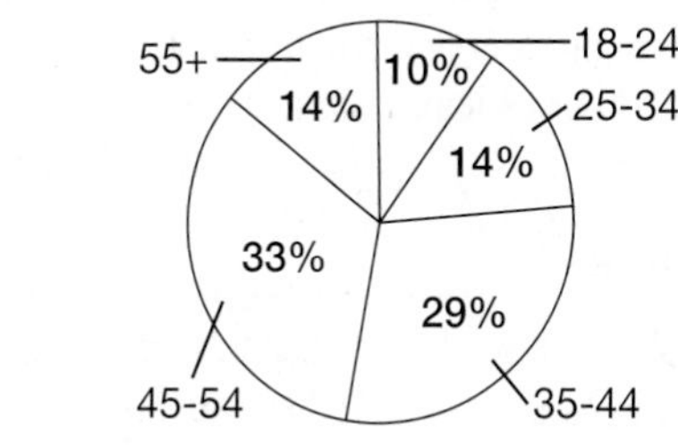

31. 0 1 2 3 4 5 6 7 8 9 10

32. 14 16 18 20 22 24 26 28 30

33. 8 10 12 14 16 18 20 22

34. 2 4 6 8 10 12 14 16 18 20

Pages 448–449, Lesson 9–6

8.

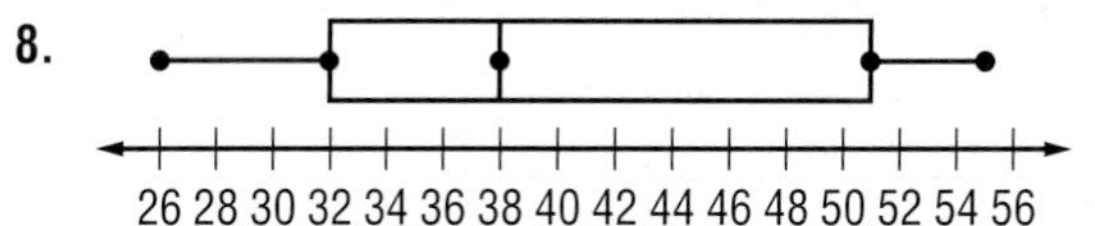

9.

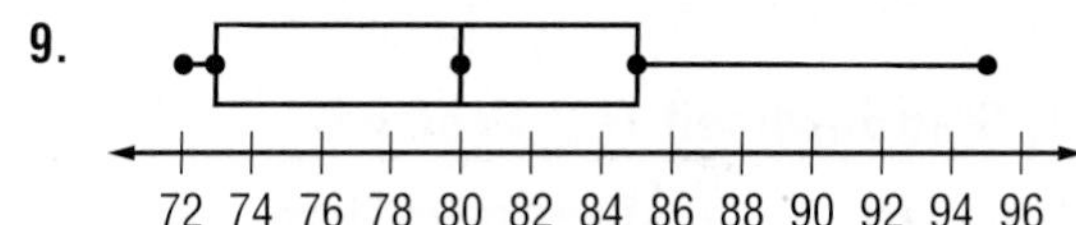

10.

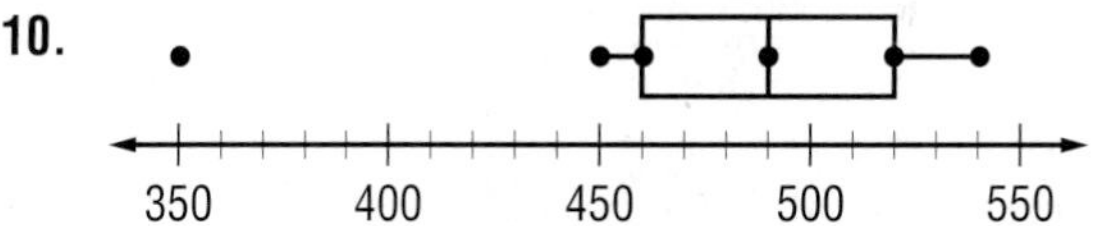

11.

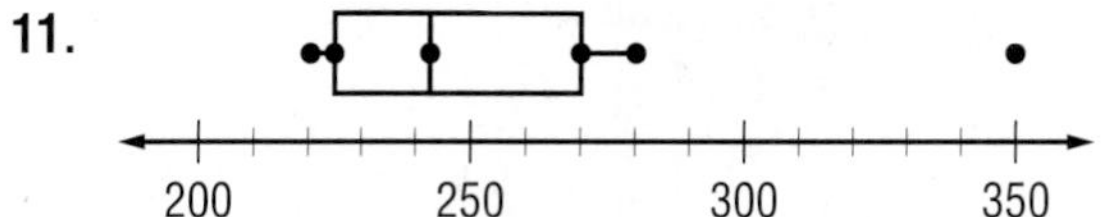

12.

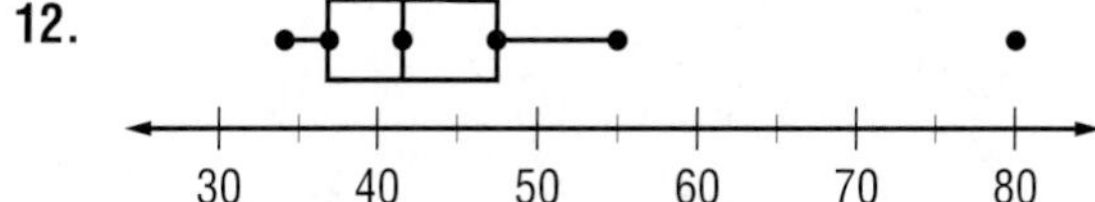

13.

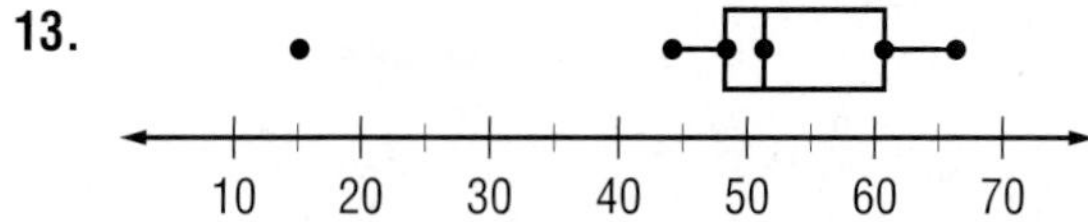

14. **Population of American Colonies in 1770**

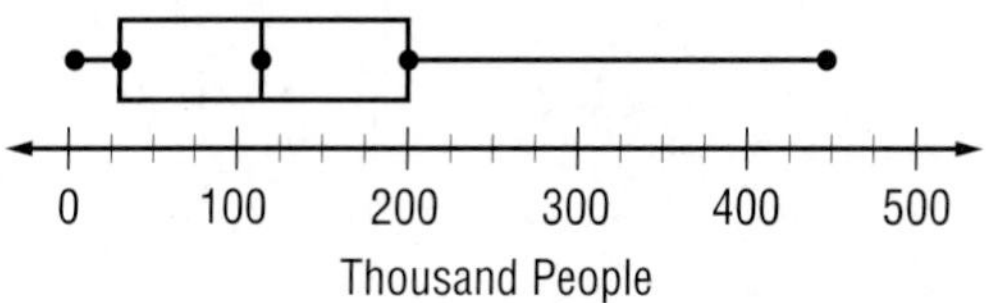

25. Since this is a systematic random sample of the entire population concerned with the park, it is an unbiased sample.

26. Since this is a sample of only a small area of the whole state, it is a biased convenience sample.

Page 453, Lesson 9-7

13a.

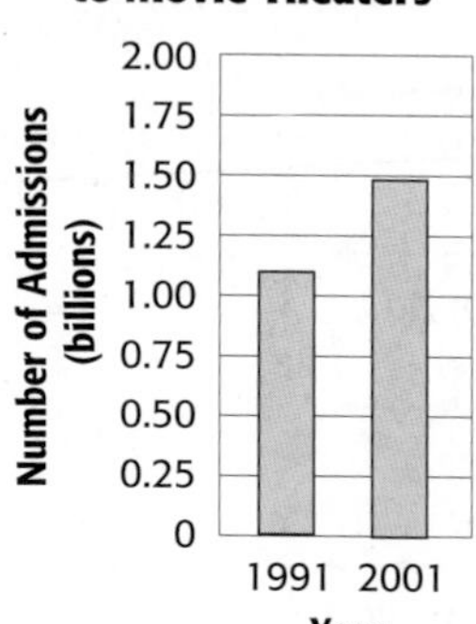

13b.

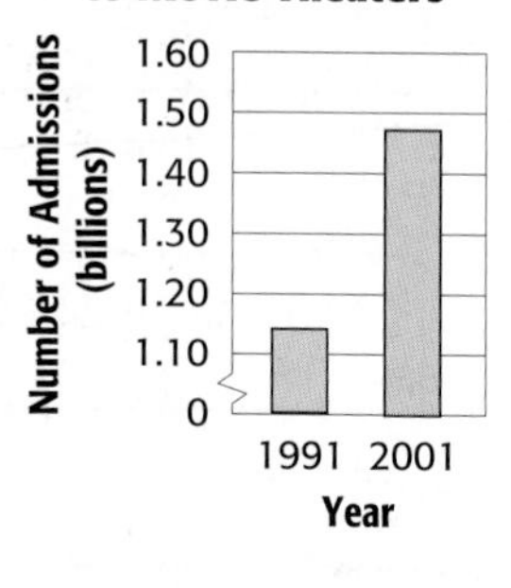

Page 461, Practice Test

12.

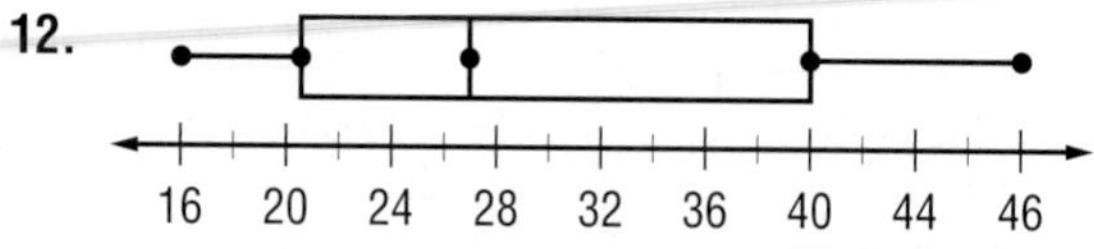

Page 463, Standardized Test Practice

17a. Sample answer:

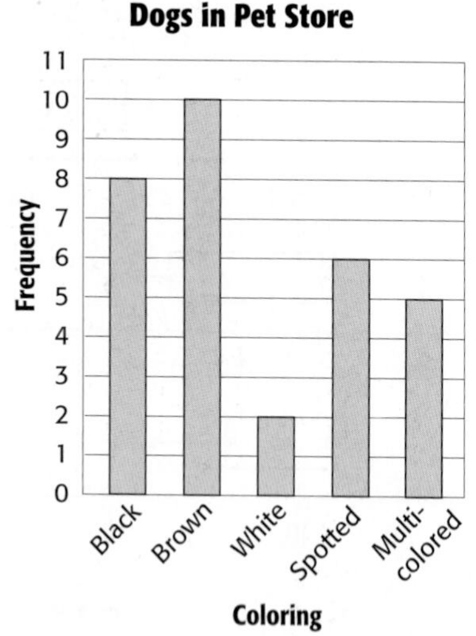

17b. Sample answer:

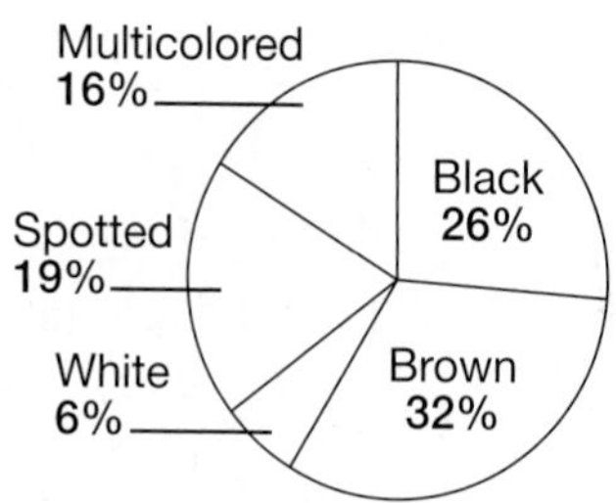

17c. Sample answer: The bar graph shows the actual number of each color of dog in the pet store. The circle graph shows what part of the total number of dogs is represented by each color. For example, a little more than $\frac{1}{4}$ of the dogs are black.

18a. Sample answer:

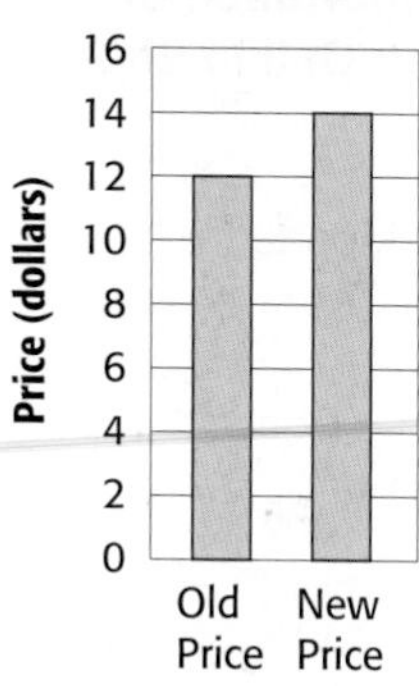

18b. Sample answer:

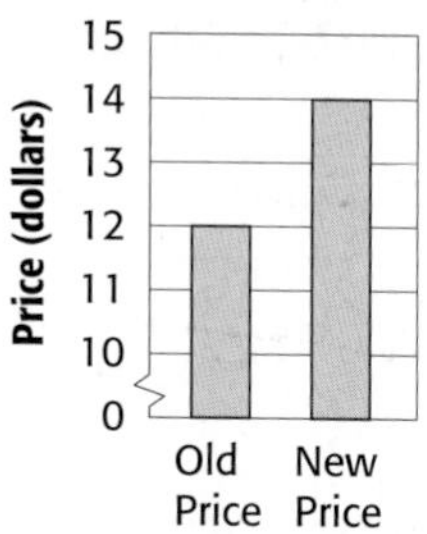

NOTES

UNIT 5 Notes

Introduction

In this unit, students will explore the use of algebraic equations to represent functions. They will learn to simplify equations and to write and solve two-step equations. Students also will solve inequalities.

In addition, students will learn how to identify and graph functions, calculate the slope of a line using the coordinates of points on the line, and use the slope-intercept form of linear equations to find the slope and the y-intercept. Students will also learn to distinguish linear from nonlinear functions, and graph scatter plots of data, systems of equations, linear inequalities, and quadratic functions. Students will then multiply and divide monomials, simplify polynomials, add and subtract polynomials, and multiply monomials with polynomials.

Assessment Options

Unit 5 Test Pages 735–736 of the *Chapter 12 Resource Masters* may be used as a test or a review for Unit 5. This assessment contains both multiple-choice and short-response items.

An online, research-based, instructional, assessment, and intervention tool that provides specific feedback on student mastery of state and national standards, instant remediation, and a data management system to track performance. For more information, contact mhdigitallearning.com

UNIT 5

Algebra: Linear and Nonlinear Functions

Chapter 10

Algebra: More Equations and Inequalities

Chapter 11

Algebra: Linear Functions

Chapter 12

Algebra: Nonlinear Functions and Polynomials

In this unit, you will build on your understanding of algebra to solve problems involving linear and nonlinear functions.

Real-Life Math Videos engage students, showing them how math is used in everyday situations. Use Video 5 with this unit to discuss how linear functions and scatter plots are used in animal care and the music industry. (also available on one Super DVD combined with MindJogger Videoquizzes)

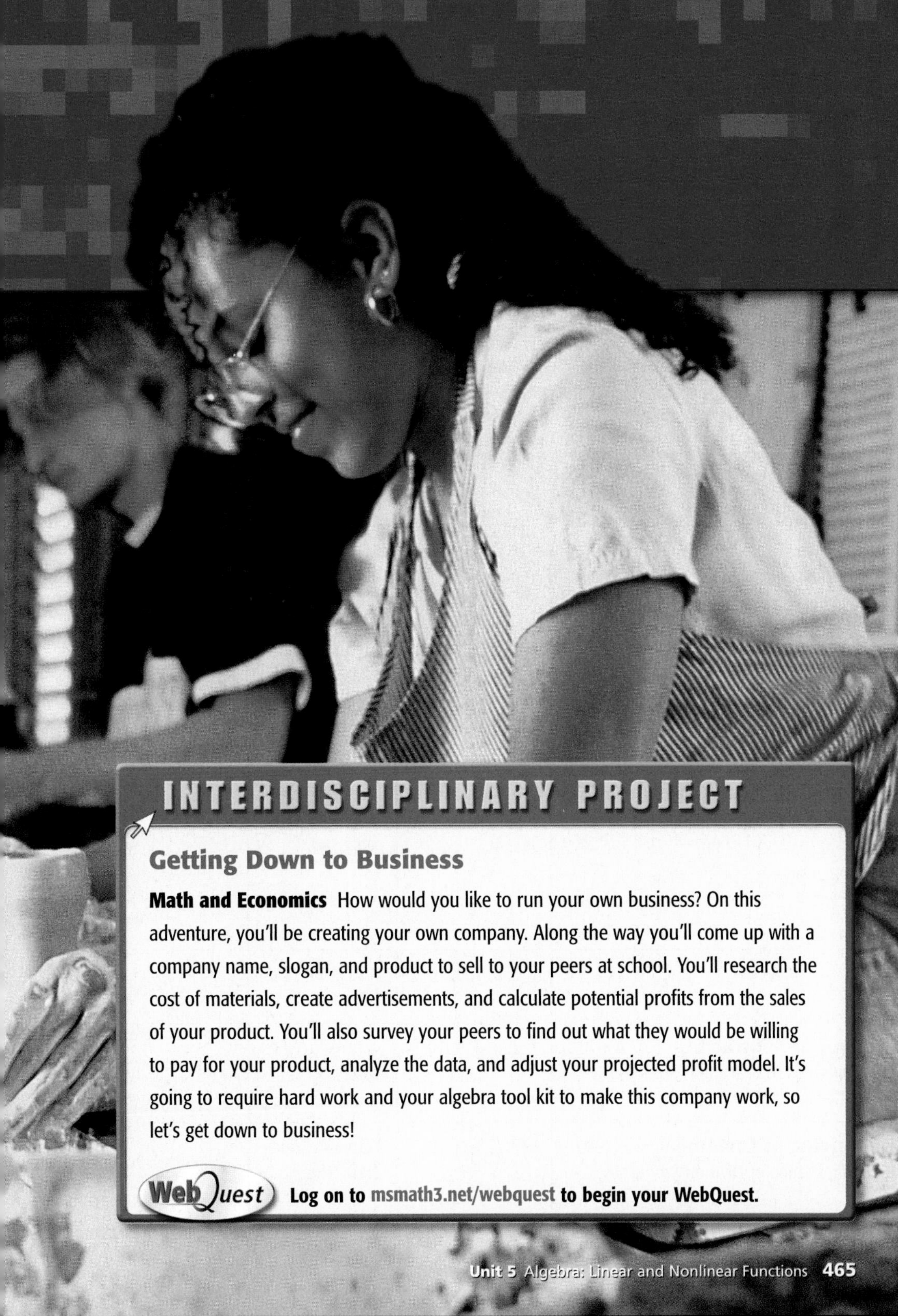

INTERDISCIPLINARY PROJECT

Getting Down to Business

Math and Economics How would you like to run your own business? On this adventure, you'll be creating your own company. Along the way you'll come up with a company name, slogan, and product to sell to your peers at school. You'll research the cost of materials, create advertisements, and calculate potential profits from the sales of your product. You'll also survey your peers to find out what they would be willing to pay for your product, analyze the data, and adjust your projected profit model. It's going to require hard work and your algebra tool kit to make this company work, so let's get down to business!

WebQuest **Log on to msmath3.net/webquest to begin your WebQuest.**

INTERDISCIPLINARY PROJECT

Getting Down to Business

A WebQuest is an online project in which students do research on the Internet, gather data, and make presentations using word processing, graphing, page-making, or presentation software. In each chapter, students advance to the next step in their WebQuest. At the end of Chapter 12, the project culminates with a presentation of their findings.

WebQuest Teaching suggestions and sample answers are available in the WebQuests, Projects, and Interdisciplinary Investigations.

Math and Economics You can use this WebQuest Interdisciplinary Project with your students' social studies teacher to make the connection from mathematics to the economics your students are studying.

More Interdisciplinary Connections

You may wish to share these suggestions with your students' other teachers.

Math and Language Arts

Write a step-by-step guide describing how to use your company's product. Direct your guide to a consumer who has never used the product. Include illustrations, but give enough written information to make your guide understandable without them.

Math and Music

Use your company's slogan to create an advertising jingle. Then set your jingle to a variety of musical styles to target different market shares. For example, an ad to appear during a daytime drama would look and sound different from one on a music video station.

Chapter Overview

Algebra: More Equations and Inequalities

	LESSON OBJECTIVES	NCTM Standards	NAEP 2005	State/Local Objectives
10-1	**Simplifying Algebraic Expressions** (pp. 468–473) **10-1a Hands-On Lab:** Model and solve equations using algebra tiles. • Use the Distributive Property to simplify algebraic expressions.	1, 2, 6, 7, 9, 10	N1b, A3b, N5e, A3a, M1h, N5f, A4a, A4b	
10-2	**Solving Two-Step Equations** (pp. 474–477) • Solve two-step equations.	1, 2, 6, 7, 9, 10	N1b, A4a, A4b, N5e, N3f	
10-3	**Writing Two-Step Equations** (pp. 478–481) • Write two-step equations that represent real-life situations.	1, 2, 6, 7, 9, 10	A3a, A4a, A4b, A4c, N3f	
10-4	**Solving Equations with Variables on Each Side** (pp. 482–489) **10-4a Hands-On Lab:** Solve equations with variables on each side using algebra tiles. • Solve equations with variables on each side. **10-4b Problem-Solving Strategy:** Solve problems using the guess and check strategy.	1, 2, 6, 7, 9, 10	A4a, A4b, A3b, A4c, N5e, N1b, N2b, N3g	
10-5	**Inequalities** (pp. 492–495) • Write and graph inequalities.	1, 2, 6, 7, 9, 10	A3a, A4a, N1b, N4f	
10-6	**Solving Inequalities by Adding or Subtracting** (pp. 496–499) • Solve inequalities by using the Addition or Subtraction Properties of Inequality.	1, 2, 6, 7, 9, 10	A3a, A4a, N5e, A4c, N5f	
10-7	**Solving Inequalities by Multiplying or Dividing** (pp. 500–504) • Solve inequalities by using the Multiplication or Division Properties of Inequality.	1, 2, 6, 7, 9, 10	A3a, A4a, A4c, N1b, N5e	

Key to NCTM Standards:

1=Number & Operations, 2=Algebra, 3=Geometry, 4=Measurement, 5=Data Analysis & Probability, 6=Problem Solving, 7=Reasoning & Proof, 8=Communication, 9=Connections, 10=Representation

NAEP 2005 Standards: See Teacher Resources at math.glencoe.com

Pacing suggestions for the entire year can be found on page T23.

*An electronic version of this chapter is available on **StudentWorks™**. This backpack solution CD-ROM allows students instant access to the Student Edition, lesson worksheet pages, and web resources.*

Chapter Resource Manager

FAST FILE

	Chapter 10 Resource Masters: Study Guide and Intervention	Practice (Skills and Word Problems)	Reading to Learn Mathematics	Enrichment	Assessment	Applications*	Parent and Student Study Guide Online Worksheets	5-Minute Check Transparencies	Key Teaching Transparencies	MathPASS: Tutorial Plus (lessons)	Teaching Mathematics with Manipulatives	Noteables™: Interactive Study Notebook	Optional Materials
	563	564–565	566	567			10-1	10-1			103	10-1	
	568	569–570	571	572	613	CM 35–36	10-2	10-2	39	44	104–105	10-2	
	573	574–575	576	577		CS 43	10-3	10-3				10-3	
	578	579–580	581	582	613, 615		10-4	10-4			106	10-4	
	583	584–585	586	587		RC 36 CS 44	10-5	10-5				10-5	
	588	589–590	591	592	614		10-6	10-6				10-6	
	593	594–595	596	597	599–612, 614, 616–618		10-7	10-7	40	45		10-7	

*** Key to Abbreviations:** *CS = Calculator and Spreadsheet Masters, RC = Real-Life Career Masters, CM = Classroom Math Games (online), SM = Science and Math Lab Manual (online)*

PowerPoint® Presentations

This CD-ROM is a customizable Microsoft® PowerPoint® presentation that includes:

- In-Class Examples
- Links to Online Study Tools
- 5-Minute Check Transparencies
- Your Turn Exercises

Math Skills Maintenance

Use the Math Skills Maintenance Masters to keep your students' basic math skills fresh. Students can review skills one at a time or in a combined format. The Masters are also available online at msmath3.net/maintenance.

CHAPTER 10 Mathematical Content and Teaching Strategies

Continuity of Instruction

Building on Prior Knowledge

Students began studying integers in Chapter 1 and have had much practice with the addition, subtraction, multiplication, and division of integers. They have used their knowledge of integers and variables to solve simple, one-step algebraic equations. In *Mathematics: Applications and Concepts*, Course 1, students used cups and counters to model algebraic equations. In Course 2, students used symbols to solve equations.

Learning in This Chapter

In this chapter, students simplify algebraic expressions using the Distributive Property, a skill required in later lessons. They continue by solving and writing two-step equations, and then, equations with the variable on each side. Students also begin to use algebra tiles to solve equations. In the second half of the chapter, students work with inequalities. They discover the similarities and differences between solving inequalities and solving equations.

Making Future Connections

Understanding equations and inequalities is essential for algebra and more advanced mathematics. In subsequent math courses, students will work with equations with more than one variable and will learn to solve systems of equations using various algebraic methods. Skill in writing and solving inequalities allows students to work with many numbers in real life that are a range rather than an absolute. For example, the ideal weight for an animal is usually between two numbers, not equal to a number.

Mathematical Background

10-1 Simplifying Algebraic Expressions

Algebraic expressions consist of one or more numbers and variables along with one or more arithmetic operations. Algebraic expressions can be simplified by applying the Distributive Property and by combining like terms. Since simplifying is often a first step in solving equations, this skill is crucial to success in the remainder of the chapter.

Teacher to Teacher

Lyn Crowell
Stony Point 9th Grade Center
Round Rock, TX

"When adding like terms, I encourage students to think of objects for the variables. For example, $2y + 3z$ could be 2 yo-yos and 3 zebras. Since yo-yos can't be combined with zebras, we know that the expression is simplified."

Lyn Crowell

10-2 Solving Two-Step Equations

A two-step equation involves two operations that must be undone in order to reach the solution. This reinforces student understanding of the order of operations. It is also an important skill since these types of equations are some of the most common students will see, both in math class and in everyday situations.

In-Class Speaker

Invite a crime investigator to speak to the class. Ask the speaker to describe ways in which algebra is used in his/her profession. Examples may include determining the time of an event or speed of a car. Encourage the speaker to bring examples for the students to solve.

10-3 Writing Two-Step Equations

In order to apply their knowledge of solving two-step equations in real-life situations, students need to be able to translate those situations into solvable equations. Recognizing key phrases will help students to write equations.

10-4 Solving Equations with Variables on Each Side

Some situations will dictate that a variable be part of the expressions on each side of the equation. Solving these equations can be a true test of student understanding of equation manipulation. In particular, this will confirm the principle that whatever operation is performed on one side of the equation must also be done to the other side.

10-5 Inequalities

An inequality is any mathematical sentence containing $>$ (greater than), $<$ (less than), $\geq$ (greater than or equal to), or $\leq$ (less than or equal to). Many everyday situations illustrate inequalities. For a better understanding of solutions, the solutions to inequalities can be graphed on a number line.

Building a Word Wall

Students may have heard the word *inequality* in nonmath contexts. If not, discuss the fact that *inequality* also means *not equal.* Develop a word wall to clarify the concept. Have students volunteer uses of the word *inequality* outside of mathematics. Record the real-life and mathematical meanings in the word wall.

10-6 Solving Inequalities by Adding or Subtracting

Inequalities with addition or subtraction are solved in the same manner as equations. Terms are added or subtracted from each side of an inequality to undo an operation. The solutions are then graphed on a number line.

10-7 Solving Inequalities by Multiplying or Dividing

Inequalities with multiplication and division are solved in the same manner as equations with one exception—when each side is multiplied or divided by a negative number, the direction of the inequality sign is reversed.

What the Research Says

According to Grouws and Cebulla in *Improving Student Achievement in Mathematics*, focusing on number sense encourages students to use problem-solving strategies that reflect number sense.

- **In Lessons 10-3 and 10-5, students use number sense to solve problems involving two-step equations and inequalities.**

McGraw-Hill Professional Development

Mathematics, YES! is a self-paced, web-based professional development program. Units are based on major mathematical concepts and are standards-based. Actual classroom videos provide a springboard for discussion and activities. Unit appropriate for this chapter:

- Solving Equations and Inequalities

Additional mathematical information and teaching notes are available at **msmath3.net/key_concepts**.

DAILY INTERVENTION and Assessment

* **Key to Abbreviations:**
TWE = Teacher Wraparound Edition, *CRM* = Chapter Resource Masters

	Type	Student Edition	Teacher Resources	Technology/Internet
INTERVENTION	Ongoing	Prerequisite Skills, pp. 467, 473, 477, 481, 487, 495, 499 Mid-Chapter Practice Test, p. 490	5-Minute Check Transparencies Quizzes 1–4, *CRM*, pp. 613–614 Mid-Chapter Test, *CRM*, p. 615 Study Guide and Intervention, *CRM*, pp. 563, 568, 573, 578, 583, 588, 593	MathPASS: Tutorial Plus msmath3.net/self_check_quiz msmath3.net/extra_examples
	Mixed Review	pp. 473, 477, 481, 487, 495, 499, 504	Cumulative Review, *CRM*, p. 616	
	Error Analysis	Find the Error, pp. 476, 503	Find the Error, *TWE*, pp. 476, 503 Unlocking Misconceptions, *TWE*, pp. 485, 496 Tips for New Teachers, *TWE*, p. 479	
ASSESSMENT	Standardized Test Practice	pp. 473, 477, 481, 485, 487, 489, 490, 495, 499, 504, 507, 508–509	Standardized Test Practice, *CRM*, pp. 617–618	Standardized Test Practice CD-ROM msmath3.net/standardized_test
	Open-Ended Assessment	Writing Math, pp. 472, 476, 482, 483, 498 Open-Ended, pp. 472, 476, 480, 486, 494, 498, 503 Standardized Test, p. 509	Modeling: *TWE*, p. 504 Speaking: *TWE*, pp. 481, 489 Writing: *TWE*, p. 477 Extended Response Assessment, *CRM*, p. 611	
	Chapter Assessment	Study Guide, pp. 505–506 Practice Test, p. 507	Multiple-Choice Tests (Forms 1, 2A, 2B), *CRM*, pp. 599–604 Free-Response Tests (Forms 2C, 2D, 3), *CRM*, pp. 605–610 Vocabulary Test/Review, *CRM*, p. 612	Exam View® Pro Testmaker (see below) MindJogger Videoquizzes msmath3.net/vocabulary_review msmath3.net/chapter_test

For more information on Yearly ProgressPro, see p. 464.

Glencoe Lesson	Yearly ProgressPro Skill Name
10-1	Simplifying Algebraic Expressions
10-2	Solving Two-Step Equations
10-3	Writing Two-Step Equations
10-4	Solving Equations with a Variable on Each Side
10-5	Inequalities
10-6	Solve Simple Inequalities Problem Solving with Inequalities
10-7	Solve Simple Inequalities Problem Solving with Inequalities

ExamView® Pro

Use ExamView® Pro Testmaker CD-ROM to:

- **Create multiple versions of tests.**
- **Create modified tests for inclusion students with one mouse click.**
- **Edit existing questions and add your own questions.**
- **Build tests aligned with state standards using built-in state curriculum correlations.**
- **Change English tests to Spanish with one mouse click and vice versa.**

Reading and Writing in Mathematics

READING in the Content Area

This online worksheet provides strategies for reading and analyzing Lesson 10-1, Simplifying Algebraic Expressions. Students are guided through questions about the main idea, subject matter, supporting details, conclusion, clarifying details, and vocabulary of the lesson.

Interactive Study Notebook With Foldables™ is a study organizer that provides helpful steps for students to follow to organize their notes for Chapter 10.

- Students use Noteables to record notes and to complete their Foldables as you present the material in Lessons 10-1 through 10-7.
- Noteables follow the *Teacher Wraparound Edition's* In-Class Examples and *Interactive Chalkboard CD-ROM.*

For more information on Reading and Writing in Mathematics, see pp. T6–T7.

Recommended Outside Reading for Students

Nonfiction

- Guillen, Michael. *Five Equations That Changed the World.* Fine Communications, ©2000.

  These five equations are pulled from the history of science and equated by this author to a great discovery. Each scientist is studied in a biographical sketch. How they came to their discovery and a few of the subsequent effects also are included.

Fiction

- Farlow, Jerry. *The Girl Who Ate Equations for Breakfast.* Aardvark Press, ©1997.

  The Girl Who Ate Equations for Breakfast is a collection of short stories with a mathematics theme. Students will enjoy the humor as well as learn some math through them. The title story involves an eighth grade Math Bee. Students will enjoy solving problems along with the contestants while they relate to the reactions of the characters involved.

PROJECT CRISS℠ Study Skill

Before beginning this chapter, demonstrate how students can use two-column notes like those for simplifying algebraic expressions shown at the right. Explain that the left column should contain each of the topics presented in the chapter. The right column should be short summaries of the steps needed to solve the problems. Students may also wish to include other notes about the topics that they feel are helpful.

Topic	Notes
simplifying algebraic expressions	**1.** can use Distributive Property **2.** combine like terms

CReating **I**ndependence through **S**tudent-owned **S**trategies

For more information on Project CRISS, see p. T8.

CHAPTER 10 Making Connections

School-To-Home

Parent and Student Study Guide

Parents and students may work together to reinforce the concepts and skills of this chapter. These online worksheets are available in English and Spanish at msmath3.net/parent_student. A sample lesson is shown below.

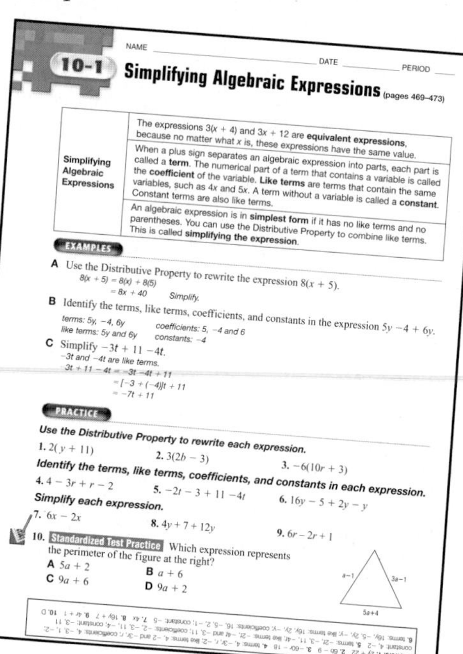

NAME ______ DATE ______ PERIOD ______

10-1 Simplifying Algebraic Expressions (pages 469–473)

Simplifying Algebraic Expressions	The expressions $3(x + 4)$ and $3x + 12$ are **equivalent expressions**, because no matter what x is, these expressions have the same value.
	When a plus sign separates an algebraic expression into parts, each part is called a **term**. The numerical part of a term that contains a variable is called the **coefficient** of the variable. **Like terms** are terms that contain the same variables, such as $4x$ and $5x$. A term without a variable is called a **constant**. Constant terms are also like terms.
	An algebraic expression is in **simplest form** if it has no like terms and no parentheses. You can use the Distributive Property to combine like terms. This is called **simplifying the expression**.

EXAMPLES

A Use the Distributive Property to rewrite the expression $8(x + 5)$.

$8(x + 5) = 8(x) + 8(5)$

$= 8x + 40$ *Simplify.*

B Identify the terms, like terms, coefficients, and constants in the expression $5y - 4 + 6y$.

terms: 5y, −4, 6y *coefficients: 5, −4 and 6*

like terms: 5y and 6y *constants: −4*

C Simplify $-3t + 11 - 4t$.

−3t and −4t are like terms.

$-3t + 11 - 4t = -3t - 4t + 11$

$= [-3 + (-4)]t + 11$

$= -7t + 11$

PRACTICE

Use the Distributive Property to rewrite each expression.

1. $2(y + 11)$ 2. $3(2b - 3)$ 3. $-6(10r + 3)$

Identify the terms, like terms, coefficients, and constants in each expression.

4. $4 - 3r + r - 2$ 5. $-2t - 3 + 11 - 4t$ 6. $16y - 5 + 2y - y$

Simplify each expression.

7. $6x - 2x$ 8. $4y + 7 + 12y$ 9. $6r - 2r + 1$

10. **Standardized Test Practice** Which expression represents the perimeter of the figure at the right?

A $5a + 2$ B $a + 6$

C $9a + 6$ D $9a + 2$

Family Letters and Activities

Send a letter and activity for this chapter home to encourage family members to become active participants in their students' learning. (English: *Chapter 10 Resource Masters*, pp. ix–x; Spanish: log on to msmath3.net/family_letters)

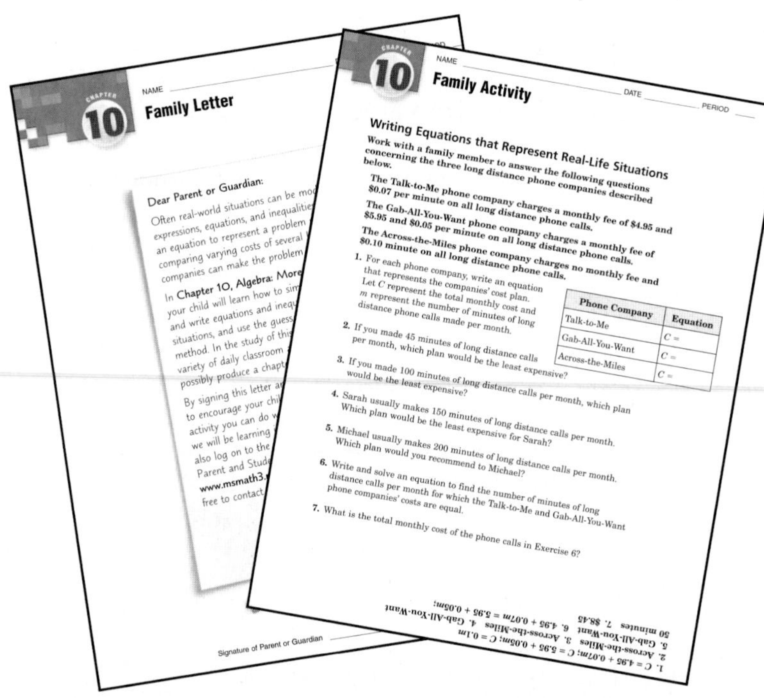

Family Letter

Dear Parent or Guardian:

Signature of Parent or Guardian ______

NAME ______ DATE ______ PERIOD ______

CHAPTER 10 Family Activity

Writing Equations that Represent Real-Life Situations

Work with a family member to answer the following questions concerning the three long distance phone companies described below.

The Talk-to-Me phone company charges a monthly fee of \$4.95 and \$0.07 per minute on all long distance phone calls.

The Gab-All-You-Want phone company charges a monthly fee of \$5.95 and \$0.05 per minute on all long distance phone calls.

The Across-the-Miles phone company charges no monthly fee and \$0.10 minute on all long distance phone calls.

1. For each phone company, write an equation that represents the companies' cost plan. Let C represent the total monthly cost and m represent the number of minutes of long distance phone calls made per month.

Phone Company	Equation
Talk-to-Me	$C =$
Gab-All-You-Want	$C =$
Across-the-Miles	$C =$

2. If you made 45 minutes of long distance calls per month, which plan would be the least expensive?
3. If you made 100 minutes of long distance calls per month, which plan would be the least expensive?
4. Sarah usually makes 150 minutes of long distance calls per month. Which plan would be the least expensive for Sarah?
5. Michael usually makes 200 minutes of long distance calls per month. Which plan would you recommend to Michael?
6. Write and solve an equation to find the number of minutes of long distance calls per month for which the Talk-to-Me and Gab-All-You-Want phone companies' costs are equal.
7. What is the total monthly cost of the phone calls in Exercise 6?

1. $C = 4.95 + 0.07m$; $C = 5.95 + 0.05m$; $C = 0.1m$ 2. Across-the-Miles 3. Across-the-Miles 4. Gab-All-You-Want 5. Gab-All-You-Want 6. $4.95 + 0.07m = 5.95 + 0.05m$; 50 minutes 7. \$8.45

English Language Learner ELL

Lesson 10-2
Using Modeling

Model solving a two-step equation by showing students how to isolate the variable. To solve $3x + 2 = 11$, cover the coefficient to show the students $x + 2 = 11$. Ask them to solve by subtracting 2 from each side. Next, ask students to solve $3x = 9$ for x. This method allows students to see that two steps are involved; addition or subtraction occurs first, followed by multiplication or division. Work several examples until students see a pattern and make a conjecture about how to solve two-step equations.

Lesson 10-3
Peer Tutoring

Write the words *addition, subtraction, multiplication,* and *division* on the chalkboard. Have the students come to the chalkboard and write words that signify each operation. Allow for and correct spelling/grammatical errors. Help students with the translation between verbal sentences and mathematical sentences by writing a verbal sentence on the chalkboard and highlighting text and translating each piece until they have formed the equation.

Lesson 10-7
Using Modeling

Show students an inequality such as $3 > -1$. Multiply each term by $+3$ and enter the correct inequality symbol.

$3(+3)$ _____ $-1(+3)$

$+9$ _____ -1

Now repeat the steps, multiplying the same inequality by -3.

$3(-3)$ _____ $-1(-3)$

-9 _____ $+3$

The inequality symbol changed direction. Show students several examples so they see that it happens every time.

MathScape™ — This project was supported, in part, by the **National Science Foundation**

MathScape is a mathematics curriculum for grades 6–8 developed by the Seeing and Thinking Mathematically Project at the Education Development Center.

Writing and Solving Equations

Exploring the Unknown

How to Use *MathScape* with Chapter 10

The unit *Exploring the Unknown* can be used to enhance Lessons 10-1 and 10-4.

- **Introduce** → Before you begin **Lesson 10-1,** you can introduce combining like terms by using the activities on pages 182–183.
- **Enrich** → After you complete **Lesson 10-4,** you can relate solving equations with a "break-even" point by using the activities on pages 208–209.

For other lessons in Chapter 10 that correlate to *MathScape*, see the chart on page T14.

Online Lesson Planner

USA TODAY® Education's Online site offers resources and interactive features connected to each day's newspaper. *Experience Today,* USA TODAY's® daily lesson plan, is available on the site and delivered daily to subscribers. This plan provides instruction for integrating USA TODAY® graphics and key editorial features into your mathematics classroom. Log on to **education.usatoday.com**.

USA TODAY Snapshots® in Chapter 10	
Lesson	**Snapshot**
10-5	TV commands kids' time
10-7	On the road

Quick Review Math Handbook

is Glencoe's mathematical handbook for students. The Hot Words section includes a glossary of terms while the Hot Topics section consists of explanations of key mathematical concepts. An exercise set is included to check students' understanding of the concepts. This valuable resource can be used as a reference in the classroom or for home study.

Lesson	Hot Topics Section	Lesson	Hot Topics Section
10-1	6-2	**10-4**	6-4
10-2	6-4	**10-5**	6-6
10-3	6-4	**10-6,10-7**	6-6

Key Chapter Objectives

Lesson 10-2 Solve two-step equations.

Lesson 10-4 Solve equations with variables on each side.

Lesson 10-5 Write and graph inequalities.

Lessons 10-6 and 10-7 Solve inequalities by using the Addition, Subtraction, Multiplication, or Division Properties of Inequality.

"How is math used in skiing competitions?"

Point out to students that this is only one of many applications of the math that they are studying. Others are provided in the introduction to each lesson.

Vocabulary Builder, pp. vii–viii ELL

NAME ______________ DATE ________ PERIOD ____

10 Reading to Learn Mathematics

Vocabulary Builder

This is an alphabetical list of new vocabulary terms you will learn in Chapter 10. As you study the chapter, complete each term's definition or description. Remember to add the page number where you found the term. Add this page to your math study notebook to review vocabulary at the end of the chapter.

Vocabulary Term	Found on Page	Definition/Description/Example
coefficient		
constant		
equivalent expressions		
like terms		
simplest form		
simplifying the expression		
term		
two-step equation		

"How is math used in skiing competitions?"

In aerial skiing competitions, the total judges score is multiplied by a *degree of difficulty* factor and then added to the skier's current score to obtain the final score. If you know your current score, the leader's final score, and your jump's degree of difficulty, you can solve a two-step equation to determine what score you need to win a competition.

You will solve a problem about aerial skiing in Lesson 10-3.

Vocabulary Builder

For a thorough vocabulary list with pronunciations of new words, give students the Vocabulary Builder worksheets from the *Chapter 10 Resource Masters*. Encourage them to complete the definition of each term as they progress through the chapter.

GETTING STARTED

▶ Diagnose Readiness

Take this quiz to see if you are ready to begin Chapter 10. Refer to the lesson number in parentheses for review.

Vocabulary Review

Complete each sentence.

1. A(n) __?__ expression contains a variable, a number, and at least one operation symbol. (Lesson 1-2) **algebraic**
2. A sentence that compares two numbers or quantities is called a(n) __?__. (Lesson 1-3) **inequality**

Prerequisite Skills

Determine whether each statement is *true* or *false*. (Lesson 1-3)

3. $10 > 4$ **true**
4. $3 < -3$ **false**
5. $-7 < -8$ **false**
6. $-1 < 0$ **true**

Write an algebraic equation for each verbal sentence. (Lesson 1-7)

7. Ten increased by a number is -8. **$10 + x = -8$**
8. The difference of -5 and $3x$ equals 32. **$-5 - 3x = 32$**
9. Twice a number decreased by 4 is 26. **$2x - 4 = 26$**
10. The sum of 9 and a number is 14. **$9 + x = 14$**

Solve each equation. Check your solution. (Lessons 1-8 and 1-9)

11. $n + 8 = -9$ **-17**
12. $4 = m + 19$ **-15**
13. $-4 + c = 15$ **19**
14. $z - 6 = -10$ **-4**
15. $p - 12 = 2$ **14**
16. $21 = y - (-3)$ **18**
17. $3c = -18$ **-6**
18. $-42 = -6b$ **7**
19. $\frac{w}{4} = -8$ **-32**
20. $12 = \frac{r}{-7}$ **-84**

Equations and Inequalities Make this Foldable to help you organize your notes. Begin with a plain sheet of 11" × 17" paper.

STEP 1 Fold Fold in half lengthwise.

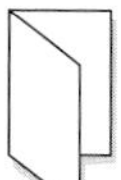

STEP 2 Fold Again Fold the top to the bottom.

STEP 3 Cut Open and cut along the second fold to make two tabs.

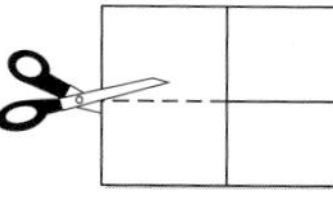

STEP 4 Label Label each tab as shown.

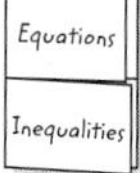

Noteables™ **Chapter Notes** Each time you find this logo throughout the chapter, use your *Noteables™: Interactive Study Notebook with Foldables™* or your own notebook to take notes. Begin your chapter notes with this Foldable activity.

Readiness To prepare yourself for this chapter with another quiz, visit **msmath3.net/chapter_readiness**

GETTING STARTED

Diagnose Readiness This section provides a review of the basic concepts needed before beginning Chapter 10. Page references are included for additional student help.

Prerequisite Skills review skills needed in this chapter.

Exercises	Needed for Lesson	Skill
3–6	10-5	Evaluate Inequalities
7–10	10-3	Write Equations from Verbal Sentences
11–20	10-2	Solve Equations

For more prerequisite skills, see:

- Getting Ready for the Next Lesson, at the end of each lesson
- Prerequisite Skills in the Student Handbook on pp. 600–615
- *Math Skills Maintenance Masters*

FOLDABLES™ Study Organizer

For more information about Foldables, see *Teaching Mathematics with Foldables.*

Use this Foldable for student writing about equations and inequalities. Students use their Foldables to take notes, define terms, record concepts, and write examples. At the end of each lesson, ask students to use their notes to orally summarize the lesson, or explain what the lesson was about. Summaries are useful for condensing data. Or, have students paraphrase something presented in the chapter, such as how to use the Distributive Property to simplify algebraic expressions.

10-1a Hands-On Lab Lesson Notes

Lesson Resources

Teaching Mathematics with Manipulatives
- algebra tiles, p. 29
- student recording sheet 10-1a

Glencoe Mathematics Classroom Manipulative Kit
- algebra tiles

GETTING STARTED

Teaching Tip Model the **Activity** on an overhead projector and complete it as a class. You may wish to have students complete the **Your Turn** exercises in pairs.

TEACH

- Explain to students that they are solving by adding a negative number, rather than subtracting a positive number. When the equation involves subtraction, students will need to add positive tiles to each side.
- Encourage students to check their answers by substituting their solution for x into the original equation.

ASSESS

Observe as students solve the **Your Turn** exercises. They should:
- model each equation with algebra tiles,
- manipulate the tiles to solve each equation, and
- check their solutions.

10-1a Hands-On Lab

A Preview of Lesson 10-1

What You'll LEARN

Model and solve equations using algebra tiles.

Materials
- algebra tiles

TEACHING TIP

Students are asked to use algebra tiles instead of cups and counters to solve equations in order to make the transition to Algebra 1 topics easier.

Algebra Tiles

In Chapter 1, you used cups and counters to model equations. In this lab and throughout the rest of this book, you will use **algebra tiles**. The table below shows how these two types of models are related.

Type of Model	Variable x	Integer 1	Integer −1
Cups and Counters	(cup)	(+)	(−)
Algebra Tiles	x	1	−1

You will use an equation mat to model and solve equations using algebra tiles in the same way as you did with cups and counters.

ACTIVITY *Work with a partner.*

Use algebra tiles to model and solve $x + 3 = -2$.

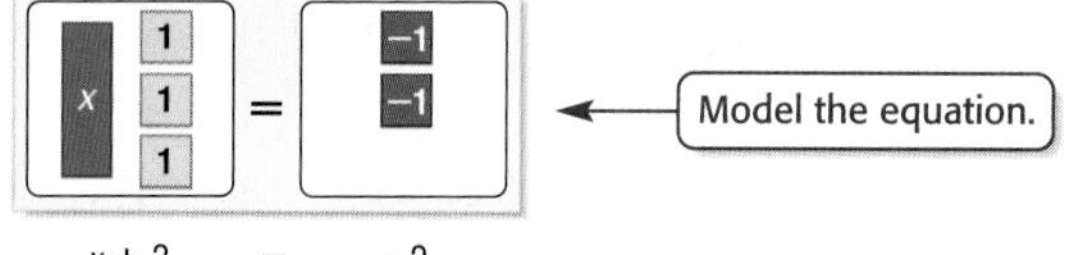

$x + 3 = -2$

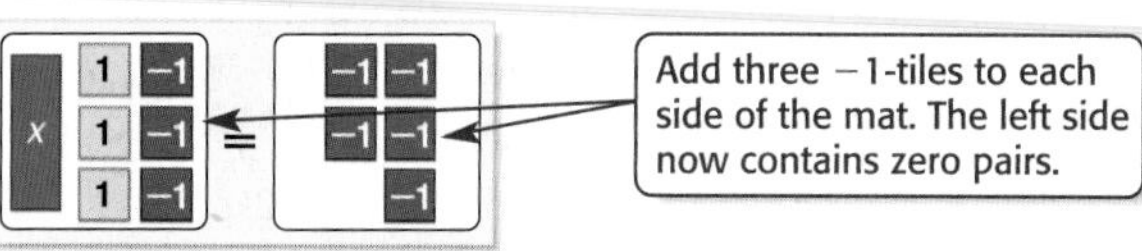

$x + 3 + (-3) = -2 + (-3)$

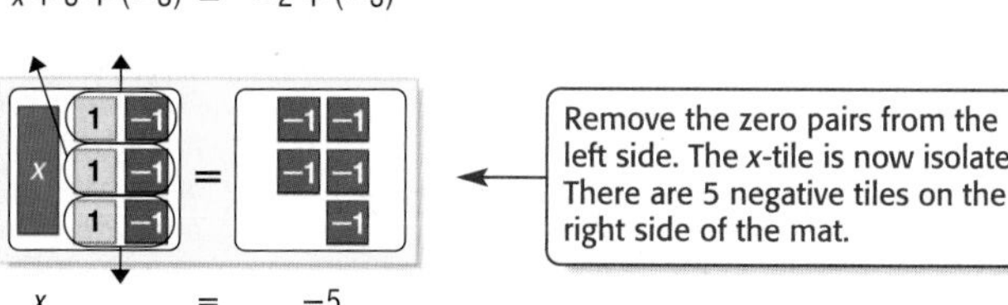

$x = -5$

Therefore, $x = -5$. Since $-5 + 3 = -2$, the solution is correct.

a–h. See Ch. 10 Answer Appendix for models. c. −3 d. −7

Your Turn **Use algebra tiles to model and solve each equation.**

a. $x + 2 = 3$ **1** b. $4 + x = 6$ **2** c. $x + 2 = -1$ d. $-4 = x + 3$

e. $x - 3 = 2$ **5** f. $x - 1 = -3$ **−2** g. $2x = -4$ **−2** h. $3 = 3x$ **1**

468 Chapter 10 Algebra: More Equations and Inequalities

NCLB No Child Left Behind

The goals of the NCLB Act include a stronger emphasis on reading. The **Reading in the Content Area** link helps students become proficient readers.

Simplifying Algebraic Expressions

What You'll LEARN

Use the Distributive Property to simplify algebraic expressions.

NEW Vocabulary

equivalent expressions
term
coefficient
like terms
constant
simplest form
simplifying the expression

Link to READING

Everyday Meaning of Constant: unchanging

1. See students' work; the expressions have the same value when evaluated for the same value of x.

HANDS-ON Mini Lab

Materials

- algebra tiles

You can use algebra tiles to rewrite the algebraic expression $2(x + 3)$.

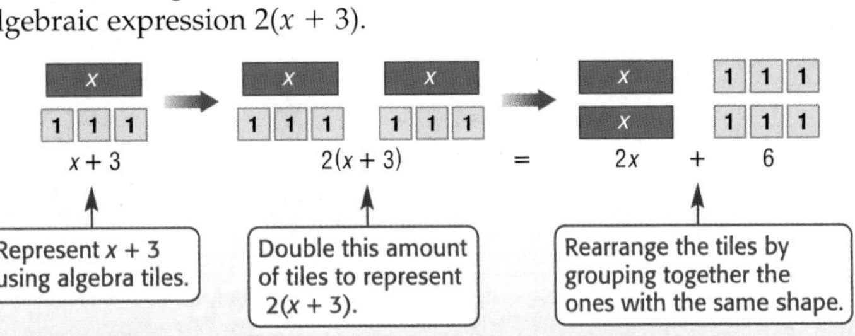

1. Choose two positive and one negative value for x. Then evaluate $2(x + 3)$ and $2x + 6$ for each of these values. What do you notice?
2. Use algebra tiles to rewrite the expression $3(x - 2)$. (*Hint:* Use one green x-tile and 2 red -1-tiles to represent $x - 2$.)

2. $3x - 6$; See margin for drawing.

In Chapter 1, you learned that expressions like $2(4 + 3)$ can be rewritten using the Distributive Property and then simplified.

$2(4 + 3) = 2(4) + 2(3)$ Distributive Property

$= 8 + 6$ or 14 Multiply. Then add.

The Distributive Property can also be used to simplify an algebraic expression like $2(x + 3)$.

$2(x + 3) = 2(x) + 2(3)$ Distributive Property

$= 2x + 6$ Multiply.

The expressions $2(x + 3)$ and $2x + 6$ are **equivalent expressions**, because no matter what x is, these expressions have the same value.

EXAMPLES Write Equivalent Expressions

Use the Distributive Property to rewrite each expression.

1 $4(x + 7)$

$4(x + 7) = 4(x) + 4(7)$

$= 4x + 28$ Simplify.

2 $(y + 2)5$

$(y + 2)5 = y \cdot 5 + 2 \cdot 5$

$= 5y + 10$ Simplify.

 **Your Turn** **Use the Distributive Property to rewrite each expression.**

a. $6(a + 4)$ $6a + 24$ b. $(n + 3)8$ $8n + 24$ c. $-2(x + 1)$ $-2x - 2$

READING in the Content Area

For strategies in reading this lesson, visit **msmath3.net/reading.**

Answer (Hands-On Mini Lab)

2.

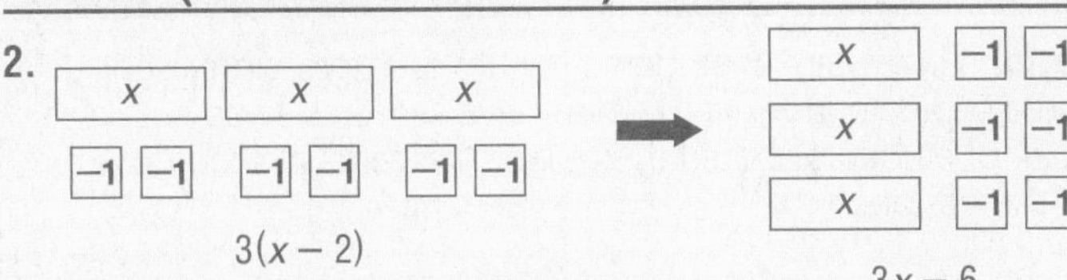

10-1 Lesson Notes

Lesson Resources

Chapter 10 Resource Masters

- Study Guide and Intervention, p. 563
- Practice: Skills, p. 564
- Practice: Word Problems, p. 565
- Reading to Learn Mathematics, p. 566
- Enrichment, p. 567

Parent and Student Study Guide Online Worksheets, 10-1

Noteables™: Interactive Study Notebook with Foldables™, 10-1

1 Focus

5-Minute Check 10-1

Use as a quiz or review of Chapter 9. (Also available as a transparency)

Bellringer

Problem Solving Have students write algebraic expressions using objects around the room, for example 3 books + 2 desks + 4 books + 1 desk. Students should simplify the expression by adding like terms. 7 books + 3 desks Since books and desks are different, there are two terms in the simplified expression.

Reading to Learn Mathematics, p. 566 

NAME ______ DATE ______ PERIOD ______

10-1 Reading to Learn Mathematics

Simplifying Algebraic Expressions

Pre-Activity *Do the Mini Lab at the top of page 469 in your textbook. Write your answers below.*

1. Choose two positive and one negative value for x. Then evaluate $2(x + 3)$ and $2x + 6$ for each of these values. What do you notice? See students' work; the expressions have the same value when evaluated for the same value of x.
2. Use algebra tiles to rewrite the expression $3(x - 2)$. (*Hint:* Use one green x-tile and 2 red 1-tiles to represent $x - 2$.) $3x - 6$

Reading the Lesson

3. When is the Distributive Property used to simplify an algebraic expression? Sample answer: when the expression contains two or more terms inside parentheses multiplied by a number

2 Teach

Noteables™

As you work the **In-Class Examples,** have students follow along in their *Noteables™: Interactive Study Notebook with Foldables™*, or have students work the examples in their notebooks.

In-Class Examples

Use the Distributive Property to rewrite each expression.

1. $3(x + 5)$ **$3x + 15$**
2. $(a + 4)7$ **$7a + 28$**
3. $(q - 3)9$ **$9q - 27$**
4. $-3(z - 7)$ **$-3z + 21$**
5. Identify the terms, like terms, coefficients, and constants in the expression $3x - 5 + 2x - x$. **The terms are $3x$, -5, $2x$, and $-x$. The like terms are $3x$, $2x$, and $-x$. The coefficients are 3, 2, and -1. The constant is -5.**

Teaching Strategies Remind students that adding terms with different variables is like adding apples and oranges—they cannot be combined since they are different.

STUDY TIP

Look Back You can review **multiplying integers** in Lesson 1-6.

EXAMPLES Write Expressions with Subtraction

Use the Distributive Property to rewrite each expression.

3 $6(p - 5)$

$6(p - 5) = 6[p + (-5)]$	Rewrite $p - 5$ as $p + (-5)$.
$= 6(p) + 6(-5)$	Distributive Property
$= 6p + (-30)$	Simplify.
$= 6p - 30$	Definition of subtraction

4 $-2(x - 8)$

$-2(x - 8) = -2[x + (-8)]$	Rewrite $x - 8$ as $x + (-8)$.
$= -2(x) + (-2)(-8)$	Distributive Property
$= -2x + 16$	Simplify.

Your Turn Use the Distributive Property to rewrite each expression. **e. $-7w + 28$ f. $-9n + 18$**

d. $3(y - 10)$ **$3y - 30$** e. $-7(w - 4)$ f. $(n - 2)(-9)$

When a plus sign separates an algebraic expression into parts, each part is called a **term**. The numerical factor of a term that contains a variable is called the **coefficient** of the variable.

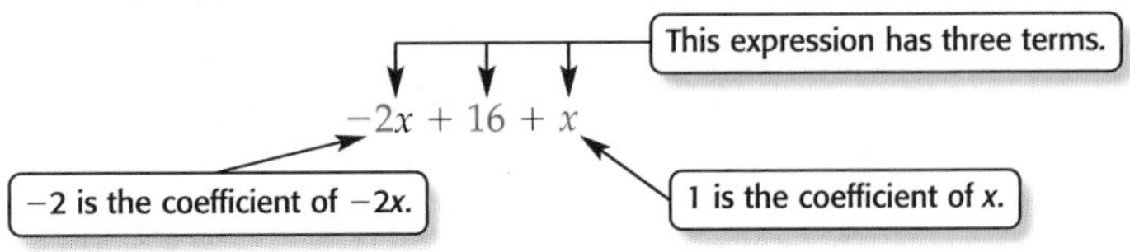

Like terms contain the same variables, such as $2x$ and x. A term without a variable is called a **constant**. Constant terms are also like terms.

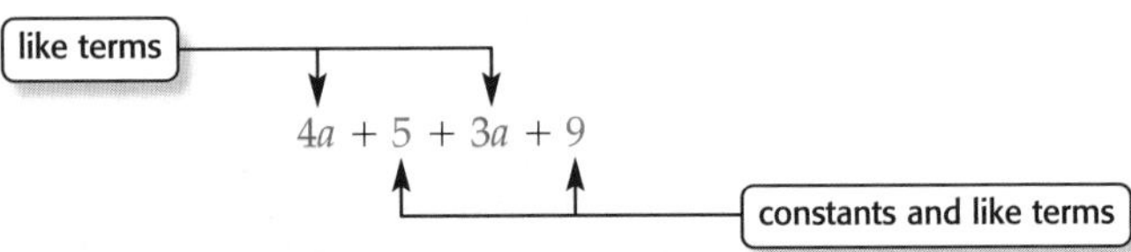

Rewriting a subtraction expression using addition will help you identify the like terms of an expression that contains subtraction.

EXAMPLE Identify Parts of an Expression

5 **Identify the terms, like terms, coefficients, and constants in the expression $6n - 7n - 4 + n$.**

$6n - 7n - 4 + n = 6n + (-7n) + (-4) + n$	Definition of subtraction
$= 6n + (-7n) + (-4) + 1n$	Identity Property; $n = 1n$

The terms are $6n$, $-7n$, -4, and n. The like terms are $6n$, $-7n$, and n. The coefficients are 6, -7, and 1. The constant is -4.

TEACHING TIP

Some students will incorrectly identify $7n$ as a term of the expression in Example 5. Remind them that terms are separated by a plus sign.

DAILY INTERVENTION Differentiated Instruction

Visual/Spatial Have pairs of students rewrite an expression, listing each step on a separate index card. Then have students swap sets of cards. The pair of students should then place the cards in order to simplify the expressions.

470 Chapter 10 Algebra: More Equations and Inequalities

An algebraic expression is in **simplest form** if it has no like terms and no parentheses. You can use the Distributive Property to combine like terms. This is called **simplifying the expression**.

EXAMPLES Simplify Algebraic Expressions

STUDY TIP

Equivalent Expressions To check whether $3y + y$ and $4y$ are equivalent expressions, substitute any value for y and see whether the expressions have the same value.

Simplify each expression.

6 $3y + y$

$3y$ and y are like terms.

$3y + y = 3y + 1y$	Identity Property; $y = 1y$
$= (3 + 1)y$	Distributive Property
$= 4y$	Simplify.

7 $-9k + 4 + 9k$

$-9k$ and $9k$ are like terms.

$-9k + 4 + 9k = -9k + 9k + 4$	Commutative Property
$= (-9 + 9)k + 4$	Distributive Property
$= 0k + 4$	$-9 + 9 = 0$
$= 0 + 4$ or 4	$0k = 0 \cdot k$ or 0

8 $5x - 2 - 7x + 6$

$5x$ and $-7x$ are like terms. -2 and 6 are also like terms.

$5x - 2 - 7x + 6 = 5x + (-2) + (-7x) + 6$	Definition of subtraction
$= 5x + (-7x) + (-2) + 6$	Commutative Property
$= [5 + (-7)]x + (-2) + 6$	Distributive Property
$= -2x + 4$	Simplify.

Your Turn Simplify each expression. h. $6 - 5n$

g. $4z - z$ $3z$ h. $6 + 3n - 8n$ i. $2g - 3 + 11 - 2g$ 8

REAL-LIFE MATH

FOOD In a recent year, Americans were expected to eat 26.3 million hot dogs in major league ballparks. This is enough to stretch from Dodgers' Stadium in Los Angeles to the Pirate's PNC Stadium in Pittsburgh.

Source: www.hot-dog.org

EXAMPLE Translate Phrases into Expressions

9 **FOOD At a baseball game, you buy some hot dogs that cost \$3 each and the same number of soft drinks for \$2.50 each. Write an expression in simplest form that represents the total amount of money spent on food and drinks.**

If x represents the number of hot dogs you buy, then x also represents the number of drinks you buy. To find the total amount spent, multiply the cost of each item by the number of items purchased. Then add the expressions.

$3x + 2.50x = (3 + 2.50)x$	Distributive Property
$= 5.50x$	Simplify.

The expression $\$5.50x$ represents the total amount of money spent on food and drink, where x is the number of hot dogs or drinks.

Math Online msmath3.net/extra_examples

In-Class Examples

Simplify each expression.

6 $6n - n$ **$5n$**

7 $5s + 3 - 12s$ **$-7s + 3$**

8 $8z + z - 5 - 9z + 2$ **-3**

9 **THEATER** Tickets for the school play cost \$5 for adults and \$3 for children. A family has the same number of adults as children. Write an expression in simplest form that represents the total amount of money spent on tickets. **$8x$**

3 Practice/Apply

Which One Doesn't Belong? By simplifying each expression in Exercise 3, students will easily see which one is different. Have them follow the steps shown in the examples if needed.

About the Exercises...

Guided Practice Key

Exercises	Examples
4–6	1–4
7–9	5
10–15	6–8

Assignment Guide

Basic: 17–27 odd, 33–51 odd, 54–66

Average: 17–53 odd, 54–66

Enriched: 16–52 even, 54–62 (Optional: 63–66)

Students practice the same concepts in Exercises 16–53 if they are assigned odd or even problems.

Skill and Concept Check

1. Writing Math Define *like terms*. **terms that contain the same variable or are constants**
2. **OPEN ENDED** Write an expression that has four terms and simplifies to $3n + 2$. Identify the coefficient(s) and constant(s) in your expression. **Sample answer: $5n - 2n + 8 - 6$; coefficients: 5, −2; constants: 8, −6**
3. **Which One Doesn't Belong?** Identify the expression that is not equivalent to the other three. Explain your reasoning. **$5(x - 3)$; See margin.**

$x - 3 + 4x$	$5(x - 3)$	$6 + 5x - 9$	$5x - 3$

GUIDED PRACTICE

Use the Distributive Property to rewrite each expression.

4. $5(x + 4)$ **$5x + 20$**
5. $-3(a + 9)$ **$-3a - 27$**
6. $-6(g - 2)$ **$-6g + 12$**

Identify the terms, like terms, coefficients, and constants in each expression. **7–9. See margin.**

7. $8a + 4 - 6a$
8. $7 - 3d - 8 + d$
9. $5n - n + 3 - 2n$

Simplify each expression.

10. $5x + 2x$ **$7x$**
11. $8n + n$ **$9n$**
12. $10y - 17y$ **$-7y$**
13. $12c - c$ **$11c$**
14. $4p - 7 + 6p$ **$10p - 7$**
15. $11x - 12 - 6x + 9$ **$5x - 3$**

★ indicates increased difficulty

Practice and Applications

HOMEWORK HELP

For Exercises	See Examples
16–31	1–4
32–37	5
38–49	6–8
50–53	9

Extra Practice See pages 640, 657.

Use the Distributive Property to rewrite each expression.

16. $3(x + 8)$ **$3x + 24$**
17. $7(m + 6)$ **$7m + 42$**
18. $-8(b + 5)$ **$-8b - 40$**
19. $-7(n + 2)$
20. $-4(k + 8)$
21. $(c - 8)(-8)$ **$-8c + 64$**
22. $-5(a - 9)$
23. $(x - 6)(-4)$
24. $2(a + b)$ **$2a + 2b$**
25. $4(x - y)$ **$4x - 4y$**
26. $3(2y + 1)$ **$6y + 3$**
27. $-4(3x + 5)$ **$-12x - 20$**

19. $-7n - 14$ 20. $-4k - 32$ 22. $-5a + 45$ 23. $-4x + 24$

GEOMETRY Write two equivalent expressions for the area of each figure.

★28. 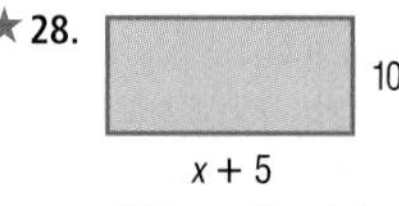

$10(x + 5)$; $10x + 50$

★29. 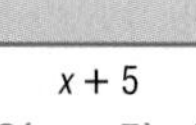 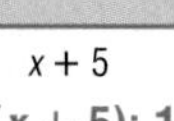

$12(x - 7)$; $12x - 84$

★30. 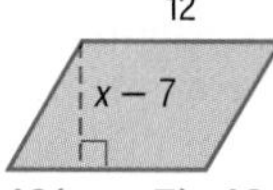

$8(x + 4)$; $8x + 32$

★31. 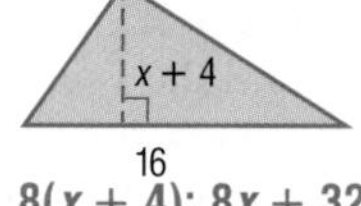 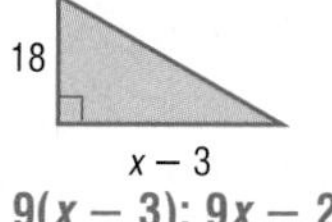

$9(x - 3)$; $9x - 27$

Identify the terms, like terms, coefficients, and constants in each expression. **32–37. See margin.**

32. $2 + 3a + 9a$
33. $7 - 5x + 1$
34. $4 + 5y - 6y + y$
35. $n + 4n - 7n - 1$
36. $-3d + 8 - d - 2$
37. $9 - z + 3 - 2z$

Simplify each expression. **46. $-6m + 5$ 48. $-2y + 3$ 49. -8**

38. $4y + 7y$ **$11y$**
39. $n + 5n$ **$6n$**
40. $12x - 5x$ **$7x$**
41. $4k - 7k$ **$-3k$**
42. $10k - k$ **$9k$**
43. $5x + 4 + 9x$ **$14x + 4$**
44. $2 + 3d + d$ **$2 + 4d$**
45. $6 - 4c + c$ **$6 - 3c$**
46. $2m + 5 - 8m$
47. $3r + 7 - 3r$ **7**
48. $9y - 4 - 11y + 7$
49. $3x + 2 - 10 - 3x$

Answers

3. $5(x - 3)$ is equivalent to $5x - 15$, while the other three expressions are equivalent to $5x - 3$.
7. terms: $8a$, 4, $-6a$; like terms: $8a$ and $-6a$; coefficients: 8, −6; constant: 4
8. terms: 7, $-3d$, −8, d; like terms: $-3d$ and d, 7 and −8; coefficients: −3, 1; constants: 7, −8
9. terms: $5n$, $-n$, 3, $-2n$; like terms: $5n$, $-n$, and $-2n$; coefficients: 5, −1, −2; constant: 3
32. terms: 2, $3a$, $9a$; like terms: $3a$, $9a$; coefficients: 3, 9; constant: 2
33. terms: 7, $-5x$, 1; like terms: 7, 1; coefficients: −5; constants: 7, 1
34. terms: 4, $5y$, $-6y$, y; like terms: $5y$, $-6y$, y; coefficients: 5, −6, 1; constant: 4
35. terms: n, $4n$, $-7n$, −1; like terms: n, $4n$, $-7n$; coefficients: 1, 4, −7; constant: −1
36. terms: $-3d$, 8, $-d$, −2; like terms: $-3d$ and $-d$, 8 and −2; coefficients: −3, −1; constants: 8, −2
37. terms: 9, $-z$, 3, $-2z$; like terms: 9 and 3, $-z$ and $-2z$; coefficients: −1, −2; constants: 9, 3
57. 1 by 2; first row, first column
58. 2 by 2; first row, second column
59. 3 by 1; third row, first column
60. 2 by 3; second row, third column

For Exercises 50–53, write an expression in simplest form that represents the total amount in each situation.

50. **MOVIES** You buy 2 drinks that each cost x dollars, a large bag of popcorn for \$3.50, and a chocolate bar for \$1.50. **$2x + 5$**

51. **PHYSICAL EDUCATION** Each lap around the school track is a distance of y yards. You ran 2 laps on Monday, $3\frac{1}{2}$ laps on Wednesday, and 100 yards on Friday. **$5\frac{1}{2}y + 100$**

52. **SHOPPING** You buy x shirts that each cost \$15.99, the same number of jeans for \$34.99 each, and a pair of sneakers for \$58.99. **$50.98x + 58.99$**

★53. **FUND-RAISING** You have sold t tickets for a school fund-raiser. Your friend has sold 24 more than you. **$2t + 24$**

54. **CRITICAL THINKING** Is $2(x - 1) + 3(x - 1) = 5(x - 1)$ a true statement? If so, explain your reasoning. If not, give a counterexample. **True; $2(x - 1) + 3(x - 1) = 2x - 2 + 3x - 3$ or $5x - 5$ which is equivalent to $5(x - 1)$.**

Spiral Review with Standardized Test Practice

55. **SHORT RESPONSE** Write an expression in simplest form for the perimeter of the figure. **$12x + 6$**

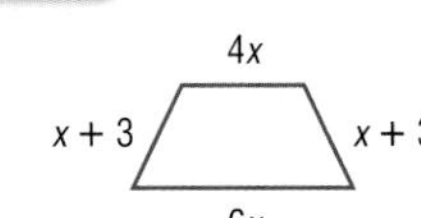

56. **MULTIPLE CHOICE** Dustin is 3 years younger than his older sister. If his older sister is y years old, which expression represents the sum of their ages? **A**

(A) $2y - 3$ (B) $y - 3$ (C) $y^2 - 3$ (D) $2y + 3$

State the dimensions of each matrix. Then identify the position of the circled element. (Lesson 9-8) **57–60. See margin.**

57. $\begin{bmatrix} \textcircled{3} & -2 \end{bmatrix}$ 58. $\begin{bmatrix} -4 & \textcircled{5} \\ 0 & 2 \end{bmatrix}$ 59. $\begin{bmatrix} 4 \\ -2 \\ \textcircled{7} \end{bmatrix}$ 60. $\begin{bmatrix} 9 & 3 & 5 \\ -4 & 7 & \textcircled{1} \end{bmatrix}$

TECHNOLOGY For Exercises 61 and 62, refer to the graphs at the right. (Lesson 9-7)

61. Which graph gives the impression that the number of DVD players sold in 2001 was more than 5 times the amount sold in 1999? **Graph B**

62. About how many times more DVD's were sold in 2001 than in 1999? **about 3 times as many**

Graph A

Graph B

GETTING READY FOR THE NEXT LESSON

PREREQUISITE SKILL Solve each equation. Check your solution. (Lessons 1-8 and 1-9)

63. $x + 8 = 2$ **-6** 64. $y - 5 = -9$ **-4** 65. $32 = -4n$ **-8** 66. $\frac{a}{3} = -15$ **-45**

msmath3.net/self_check_quiz

4 Assess

Higher-Level Thinking

In Jerome's backpack, he has 3 notebooks that weigh the same amount; 2 textbooks, each of which weighs 3 times as much as a notebook; and $1\frac{1}{2}$ pounds of other materials. Write an expression in simplest form for the total weight of the items in his backpack. **$9x + 1\frac{1}{2}$ lb**

Study Guide and Intervention, p. 563

NAME ____________ DATE ________ PERIOD ____

10-1 Study Guide and Intervention

Simplifying Algebraic Expressions

The **Distributive Property** can be used to simplify algebraic expressions.

EXAMPLES Use the Distributive Property to rewrite each expression.

1. $3(a + 5)$

$3(a + 5) = 3(a) + 3(5)$ Distributive Property
$= 3a + 15$ Simplify.

2. $-2(d - 3)$

$-2(d - 3) = -2[d + (-3)]$ Rewrite $d - 3$ as $d + (-3)$.
$= -2(d) + (-2)(-3)$ Distributive Property
$= -2(d) + 6$ Simplify.

When a plus sign separates an algebraic expression into parts, each part is called a **term**. In terms that contain a variable, the numerical part of the term is called the **coefficient** of the variable. A term without a variable is called a **constant. Like terms** contain the same variables, such as $3x$ and $2x$.

EXAMPLE 3 Identify the terms, like terms, coefficients, and constants in the expression $7x - 5 + x - 3x$.

$7x - 5 + x - 3x = 7x + (-5) + x + (-3x)$ Definition of subtraction
$= 7x + (-5) + 1x + (-3x)$ Identity Property; $x = 1x$

The terms are $7x$, -5, x, and $-3x$. The like terms are $7x$, x, and $-3x$. The coefficients are 7, 1, and -3. The constant is -5.

An algebraic expression is in **simplest form** if it has no like terms and no parentheses.

EXAMPLE 4 Simplify the expression $-2m + 5 + 6m - 3$.

$-2m$ and $6m$ are like terms. 5 and -3 are also like terms.

$-2m + 5 + 6m - 3 = -2m + 5 + 6m + (-3)$ Definition of subtraction
$= -2m + 6m + 5 + (-3)$ Commutative Property
$= (-2 + 6)m + 5 + (-3)$ Distributive Property
$= 4m + 2$ Simplify.

EXERCISES

Use the Distributive Property to rewrite each expression.

1. $2(c + 6)$ $2c + 12$ 2. $-4(w + 6)$ $-4w - 24$ 3. $(b - 4)(-3)$ $-3b + 12$

4. Identify the terms, like terms, coefficients, and constants in the expression $4m - 2 + 3m + 5$. terms: $4m$, -2, $3m$, 5; like terms: $4m$, $3m$ and -2, 5; coefficients: 4, 3; constants: -2, 5

Simplify each expression.

5. $3d + 6d$ $9d$ 6. $2 + 5s - 4$ $5s - 2$ 7. $2z + 3 + 9z - 8$ $11z - 5$

Practice: Skills, p. 564

NAME ____________ DATE ________ PERIOD ____

10-1 Practice: Skills

Simplifying Algebraic Expressions

Use the Distributive Property to rewrite each expression.

1. $4(j + 4)$ $4j + 16$ 2. $5(n + 2)$ $5n + 10$ 3. $(c + 9)3$ $3c + 27$
4. $2(w - 8)$ $2w - 16$ 5. $(s - 7)7$ $7s - 49$ 6. $-4(e + 6)$ $-4e - 24$
7. $(b + 3)(-7)$ $-7b - 21$ 8. $-8(v - 7)$ $-8v + 56$ 9. $(2n + 3)6$ $12n + 18$
10. $5(c + d)$ $5c + 5d$ 11. $-7(3x - 1)$ $-21x + 7$ 12. $(e - f)3$ $3e - 3f$
13. $2(-3m + 1)$ $-6m + 2$ 14. $(2b - 3)(-9)$ $-18b + 27$ 15. $-5(s + 7)$ $-5s - 35$
16. $(t + 7)3$ $3t + 21$ 17. $6(-2v + 4)$ $-12v + 24$ 18. $(m - n)(-3)$ $-3m + 3n$

Identify the terms, like terms, coefficients, and constants in each expression.

19. $4e + 7e + 5$ terms: $4e$, $7e$, 5; like terms: $4e$, $7e$; coefficients: 4, 7; constant: 5
20. $5 - 4x - 8$ terms: 5, $-4x$, -8; like terms: 5, -8; coefficients: -4; constants: 5, -8
21. $-3h - 2h + 6h + 9$ terms: $-3h$, $-2h$, $6h$, 9; like terms: $-3h$, $-2h$, $6h$; coefficients: -3, -2, 6; constant: 9
22. $7 - 5y + 2 + 1$ terms: 7, $-5y$, 2, 1; like terms: 7, 2, 1; coefficients: -5; constants: 7, 2, 1
23. $9k + 7 - k + 4$ terms: $9k$, 7, $-k$, 4; like terms: $9k$, $-k$ and 7, 4; coefficients: 9, -1; constants: 7, 4
24. $4z + 3 - 2z - z$ terms: $4z$, 3, $-2z$, $-z$; like terms: $4z$, $-2z$, $-z$; coefficients: 4, -2, -1; constant: 3

Simplify each expression.

25. $3t + 6t$ $9t$ 26. $4r + r$ $5r$ 27. $7f - 2f$ $5f$
28. $9a - 8a$ a 29. $5c + 8c$ $13c$ 30. $2g - 5g$ $-3g$
31. $8k + 3 + 4k$ $12k + 3$ 32. $7m - 5m - 6$ $2m - 6$ 33. $9 - 6x + 5$ $-6x + 14$
34. $7p - 1 - 9p + 5$ $-2p + 4$ 35. $-b - 3b + 8b + 4$ $4b + 4$ 36. $5h - 6 - 8 + 7h$ $12h - 14$
37. $8b + 6 - 8b + 1$ 7 38. $t - 5 - 2t + 5$ $-t$ 39. $4w - 5w + w$ 0
40. $6m - 7 + 2m + 7$ $8m$ 41. $5f - 7f + f$ $-f$ 42. $12y - 8 + 4y + y$ $17y - 8$
43. $9a + 5 - 7a - 2a$ 5 44. $6g - 7g + 13$ $-g + 13$ 45. $7x + 6 - 9x - 3$ $-2x + 3$

Practice: Word Problems, p. 565

NAME ____________ DATE ________ PERIOD ____

10-1 Practice: Word Problems

Simplifying Algebraic Expressions

1. **GAMES** At the Beltway Outlet store, you buy x computer games for \$13 each and a magazine for \$4. Write an expression in simplest form that represents the total amount of money you spend. $13x + 4$

2. **TENNIS** Two weeks ago James bought 3 cans of tennis balls. Last week he bought 4 cans of tennis balls. This week he bought 2 cans of tennis balls. The tennis balls cost d dollars per can. Write an expression in simplest form that represents the total amount that James spent. $9d$

3. **AMUSEMENT PARKS** Sari and her friends are going to play miniature golf. There are p people in the group. Each person pays \$5 for a round of golf and together they spend \$9 on snacks. Write an expression in simplest form that represents the total amount that Sari and her friends spent. $5p + 9$

4. **BICYCLING** The bicycle path at the park is a loop that covers a distance of m miles. Jorge biked 2 loops each on Monday and Wednesday and 3 loops on Friday. On Sunday Jorge biked 10 miles. Write an expression in simplest form that represents the total distance that Jorge biked this week. $7m + 10$

5. **GEOMETRY** Write an expression in simplest form for the perimeter of the triangle below.

2x
2x + 3
4x − 2

$8x + 1$

6. **SIBLINGS** Mala is y years old. Her sister is 4 years older than Mala. Write an expression in simplest form that represents the sum of the ages of the sisters. $2y + 4$

10-2 Lesson Notes

Lesson Resources

Chapter 10 Resource Masters

- Study Guide and Intervention, p. 568
- Practice: Skills, p. 569
- Practice: Word Problems, p. 570
- Reading to Learn Mathematics, p. 571
- Enrichment, p. 572

Classroom Math Games, pp. 35–36
Key Teaching Transparencies, 39
MathPASS Tutorial CD-ROM, 39
Parent and Student Study Guide Online Worksheets, 10-2
Teaching Mathematics with Manipulatives, pp. 104–105
Noteables™: Interactive Study Notebook with Foldables™, 10-2

FAST FILE

1 Focus

5-Minute Check 10-2

Use as a quiz or review of Lesson 10-1. (Also available as a transparency)

Bellringer

Communication Have students explain in words how to solve the following problem using the work backward strategy.

I'm thinking of a number. If you multiply it by 4 and add 7, the answer is 19.

Subtract 7 from 19. Then divide the answer, 12, by 4. The number is 3.

Reading to Learn Mathematics, p. 571 ELL

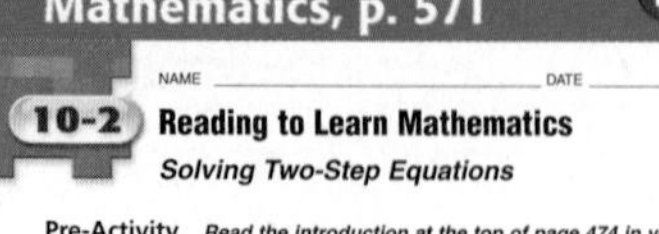

NAME ______ DATE ______ PERIOD ____

10-2 Reading to Learn Mathematics
Solving Two-Step Equations

Pre-Activity *Read the introduction at the top of page 474 in your textbook. Write your answers below.*

1. Explain how you could use the work backward strategy to find the cost of each hardback book. Then find the cost. Subtract the cost of the paperback book from the total paid, then divide the remaining cost by 3 to find the cost of each hardback book. So 7 − 1 = 6 and 6 ÷ 3 = 2. The cost of each hardback book was $2.

Reading the Lesson

2. Define *two-step equation.* A two-step equation is an equation that contains two operations.

10-2 Solving Two-Step Equations

What You'll LEARN
Solve two-step equations.

NEW Vocabulary
two-step equation

WHEN am I ever going to use this?

BOOK SALE Linda bought four books at a book sale benefiting a local charity. The handwritten receipt she received was missing the cost for the hardback books she purchased.

1. Explain how you could use the work backward strategy to find the cost of each hardback book. Then find the cost. **See margin.**

The solution to this problem can also be found by solving the equation $3x + 1 = 7$, where x is the cost per hardback book. This equation can be modeled using algebra tiles.

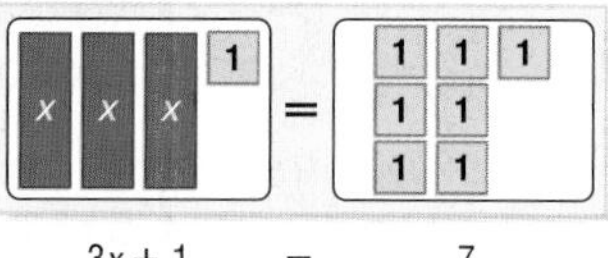

A **two-step equation** contains two operations. In the equation $3x + 1 = 7$, x is multiplied by 3 and then 1 is added. To solve two-step equations, undo each operation in reverse order.

EXAMPLE Solve a Two-Step Equation

1 **Solve $3x + 1 = 7$.**

Method 1 Use a model.

Remove one 1-tile from the mat.

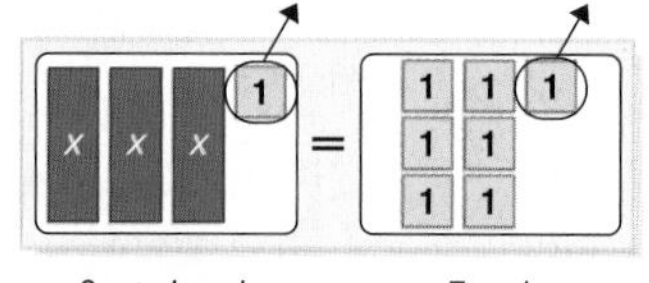

Separate the remaining tiles into 3 equal groups.

x = 1 1
x = 1 1
x = 1 1
3x = 6

There are 2 tiles in each group.

The solution is 2.

Method 2 Use symbols.

Use the Subtraction Property of Equality.

$$\begin{aligned} 3x + 1 &= 7 && \text{Write the equation.} \\ -1 &= -1 && \text{Subtract 1 from each side.} \\ \hline 3x &= 6 \end{aligned}$$

Use the Division Property of Equality.

$3x = 6$

$\frac{3x}{3} = \frac{6}{3}$ Divide each side by 3.

$x = 2$ Simplify.

Answer (When am I ever going to use this?)

1. **Subtract the cost of the paperback book from the total paid, then divide the remaining cost by 3 to find the cost of each hardback book. So 7 − 1 = 6 and 6 ÷ 3 = 2. The cost of each hardback book was $2.**

EXAMPLES Solve Two-Step Equations

Solve each equation. Check your solution.

2 $4x - 3 = 25$

Method 1 Vertical Method

$4x - 3 = 25$	Write the equation.
$4x - 3 = 25$	
$\underline{\quad + 3 = + 3}$	Add 3 to each side.
$4x = 28$	Simplify.
$\frac{4x}{4} = \frac{28}{4}$	Divide each side by 4.
$x = 7$	

Method 2 Horizontal Method

$4x - 3 = 25$

$4x - 3 + 3 = 25 + 3$

$4x = 28$

$\frac{4x}{4} = \frac{28}{4}$

$x = 7$

Check	$4x - 3 = 25$	Write the equation.
	$4(7) - 3 \stackrel{?}{=} 25$	Replace *x* with 7 and check to see if the sentence is true.
	$25 = 25$ ✔	The sentence is true.

The solution is 7.

3 $-1 = \frac{1}{2}m + 9$

$-1 = \frac{1}{2}m + 9$	Write the equation.
$-1 - 9 = \frac{1}{2}m + 9 - 9$	Subtract 9 from each side.
$-10 = \frac{1}{2}m$	Simplify.
$2(-10) = 2 \cdot \frac{1}{2}m$	Multiply each side by 2.
$-20 = m$	Simplify.
The solution is -20.	Check this solution.

TEACHING TIP

Some students may have difficulty solving a two-step equation that has the variable to the right of the equals sign. Show these students how to write an equivalent equation in which the variable is to the left of the equals sign. Students will be making use of the Reflexive Property of Equality, which states that for any numbers *a* and *b*, if $a = b$, then $b = a$.

$-1 = \frac{1}{2}m + 9$

$\rightarrow \frac{1}{2}m + 9 = -1$

Some two-step equations have a term with a negative coefficient.

EXAMPLE Equations with Negative Coefficients

4 **Solve $6 - 3x = 21$.**

$6 - 3x = 21$	Write the equation.
$6 + (-3x) = 21$	Definition of subtraction
$6 - 6 + (-3x) = 21 - 6$	Subtract 6 from each side.
$-3x = 15$	Simplify.
$\frac{-3x}{-3} = \frac{15}{-3}$	Divide each side by -3.
$x = -5$	Simplify.
The solution is -5.	Check this solution.

STUDY TIP

Common Error A common mistake when solving the equation in Example 4 is to divide each side by 3 instead of -3. Remember that you are dividing by the coefficient of the variable, which in this instance is a negative number.

Your Turn Solve each equation. Check your solution.

a. $\frac{n}{-3} - 2 = -18$ **48** b. $19 = 3x - 2$ **7** c. $5 - 2n = -1$ **3**

msmath3.net/extra_examples

2 Teach

In-Class Examples

1 Solve $5y + 1 = 26$. **5**

Solve each equation. Check your solution.

2 $2n - 8 = 34$ **21**

3 $-4 = \frac{1}{3}z + 2$ **−18**

4 Solve $8 - 3x = 14$. **−2**

DAILY INTERVENTION

Flexible Grouping

Solving Two-Step Equations Have students work in groups to illustrate how to solve a variety of equations with algebra tiles. Point out that students will need to use positive and negative tiles to solve many examples in this lesson. Have each group present one equation to the class. Groups may create posters or large-scale tiles or use an overhead projector, if available, to present their problems.

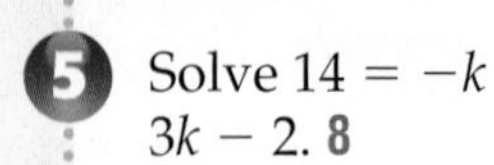

5 Solve $14 = -k + 3k - 2$. **8**

3 Practice/Apply

FOLDABLES™ Follow-Up Remind students to record main ideas, definitions of vocabulary words, and other notes under the "Equations" tab of their Foldables as they learn how to solve two-step equations. Encourage students to recall what they have learned about equations and self-check their responses by reviewing their notes under the tab.

DAILY INTERVENTION **FIND THE ERROR** Use Exercise 3 to review the order of operations. Discuss how the order is critical in arriving at a correct answer.

About the Exercises...

Guided Practice Key

Exercises	Examples
4–7	1–3
8–11	4
12	5

Assignment Guide

Basic: 13–41 odd, 45–54

Average: 13–43 odd, 45–54

Enriched: 14–44 even, 45–52 (Optional: 53, 54)

Answer

1. **You identify the order in which operations would be performed on the variable, then you undo each operation using its inverse operation in reverse order.**

Sometimes it is necessary to combine like terms before solving an equation.

EXAMPLE Combine Like Terms Before Solving

TEACHING TIP

In Example 5, students might also multiply both sides of the equation $-y = 16$ to find that $y = -16$.

5 **Solve $-2y + y - 5 = 11$. Check your solution.**

$-2y + y - 5 = 11$	Write the equation.
$-2y + 1y - 5 = 11$	Identity Property; $y = 1y$
$-y - 5 = 11$	Combine like terms; $-2y + 1y = (-2 + 1)y$ or $-y$.
$-y - 5 + 5 = 11 + 5$	Add 5 to each side.
$-y = 16$	Simplify.
$\frac{-1y}{-1} = \frac{16}{-1}$	$-y = -1y$; divide each side by -1.
$y = -16$	Simplify.

Check

$-2y + y - 5 = 11$	Write the equation.
$-2(-16) + (-16) - 5 \stackrel{?}{=} 11$	Replace y with -16.
$32 + (-16) - 5 \stackrel{?}{=} 11$	Multiply.
$11 = 11$ ✓	The statement is true.

The solution is -16.

Your Turn **Solve each equation. Check your solution.**

d. $x + 4x = 45$ **9** e. $10 = 2a + 13 - a$ **−3** f. $-3 = 6 - 5w + 2w$ **3**

Students practice the same concepts in Exercises 13–44 if they are assigned odd or even problems.

Skill and Concept Check

1. *Writing Math* Explain how you can use the work backward problem-solving strategy to solve a two-step equation. **See margin.**

2. **OPEN ENDED** Write a two-step equation that can be solved by using the Addition and Division Properties of Equality. **Sample answer: $7x - 4 = 10$**

3. **FIND THE ERROR** Alexis and Tomás are solving the equation $2x + 7 = 16$. Who is correct? Explain.

Alexis	Tomás
$2x + 7 = 16$	$2x + 7 = 16$
$\frac{2x}{2} + 7 = \frac{16}{2}$	$2x + 7 - 7 = 16 - 7$
$x + 7 = 8$	$2x = 9$
$x + 7 - 7 = 8 - 7$	$\frac{2x}{2} = \frac{9}{2}$
$x = 1$	$x = 4.5$

Tomás; Alexis did not undo the operations in reverse order.

GUIDED PRACTICE

Solve each equation. Check your solution.

4. $6x + 5 = 29$ **4**
5. $9m - 11 = -2$ **1**
6. $1 = 2p + 13$ **−6**
7. $10 = \frac{a}{4} + 3$ **28**
8. $\frac{c}{-2} - 4 = 3$ **−14**
9. $3 - 5y = -37$ **8**
10. $4 - d = 11$ **−7**
11. $7 = -2n + 1$ **−3**
12. $6k - 10k = 16$ **−4**

476 Chapter 10 Algebra: More Equations and Inequalities

★ indicates increased difficulty

Practice and Applications

HOMEWORK HELP

For Exercises	See Examples
13–26	1–3
27–34	4
35–44	5

Extra Practice See pages 640, 657.

Solve each equation. Check your solution.

13. $2h + 9 = 21$ **6**
14. $11 = 2b + 17$ **−3**
15. $5 = 4a - 7$ **3**
16. $6p - 5 = -17$ **−2**
17. $2g - 3 = -19$ **−8**
18. $16 = 5x - 9$ **5**
19. $3 + 8c = 35$ **4**
20. $13 + 3d = -8$ **−7**
21. $13 = \frac{g}{3} + 4$ **27**
22. $5 + \frac{y}{8} = -3$ **−64**
23. $-\frac{1}{2}x - 7 = -11$ **8**
24. $-\frac{1}{4}w + 15 = 28$ **−52**

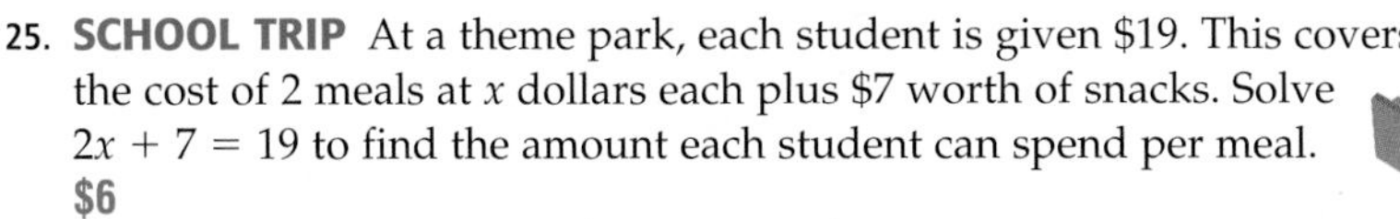

25. **SCHOOL TRIP** At a theme park, each student is given \$19. This covers the cost of 2 meals at x dollars each plus \$7 worth of snacks. Solve $2x + 7 = 19$ to find the amount each student can spend per meal. **\$6**
26. **SHOPPING** You receive a \$75 online gift to a music site. You want to purchase CDs that cost \$14 each. There is a \$5 shipping and handling fee. Solve $14n + 5 = 75$ to find the number of CDs you can purchase. **5**

Solve each equation. Check your solution.

27. $5 - 3c = 14$ **−3**
28. $9 - 5y = 19$ **−2**
29. $-6 = 4 - 2x$ **5**
30. $2 = 18 - 4d$ **4**
31. $8 - k = 17$ **−9**
32. $-7 - p = -15$ **8**
33. $12 = 6 - x$ **−6**
34. $-2 = 4 - t$ **6**
35. $5w - 8w = -12$ **4**
36. $28 = 3m - 7m$ **−7**
37. $y + 5y + 11 = 35$ **4**
38. $3 - 6x + 8x = 9$ **3**
39. $-21 = 9a - 15 - 3a$ **−1**
40. $26 = g + 10 - 3g$ **−8**
41. $8x + 5 - x = -2$ **−1**
42. $6h + 5 + h = -30$ **−5**
★43. $-n + 9 - 2n - 1 = -13$ **7**
★44. $10 = 6a + 4 - 9a + a$ **−3**
45. **CRITICAL THINKING** Work backward to write a two-step equation whose solution is −5. **Sample answer: $4x + 3 = -17$**

Spiral Review with Standardized Test Practice

46. **MULTIPLE CHOICE** If $3x + 10 = 4$, what is the value of $2 + 5x$? **B**

Ⓐ −14 Ⓑ −8 Ⓒ −2 Ⓓ 12

47. **SHORT RESPONSE** Write an equation for the given diagram. Then find the value of x. **$13 + 3x = 25$; 4**

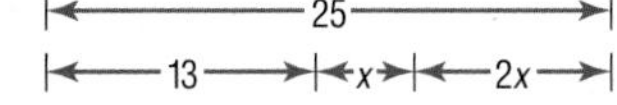

Use the Distributive Property to rewrite each expression. (Lesson 10-1)

48. $6(a + 6)$ **$6a + 36$**
49. $-3(x + 5)$ **$-3x - 15$**
50. $(y - 8)4$ **$4y - 32$**
51. $-8(p - 7)$ **$-8p + 56$**
52. Find $[6 \quad 3 \quad -1] - [2 \quad 8 \quad 9]$. If there is no difference, write *impossible*. (Lesson 9-8) **See margin.**

GETTING READY FOR THE NEXT LESSON

PREREQUISITE SKILL Write an algebraic equation for each verbal sentence. (Lesson 1-7) **53. $4n + 5 = 17$ 54. $2n - 8 = 10$**

53. Four times a number increased by 5 is 17.
54. 8 less than twice a number equals 10.

msmath3.net/self_check_quiz

4 Assess

Open-Ended Assessment

Writing Have students describe in a paragraph how to use the order of operations when solving an equation such as $4x - 3 = 17$.

Answer

52. $[4 \quad -5 \quad -10]$

Study Guide and Intervention, p. 568

NAME ______ DATE ______ PERIOD ____

10-2 Study Guide and Intervention

Solving Two-Step Equations

A **two-step equation** contains two operations. To solve a two-step equation, work backward using inverse operations to undo each operation in reverse order.

EXAMPLE 1 **Solve $-2a + 6 = 14$. Check your solution.**

Method 1 Vertical Method

$-2a + 6 = 14$	Write the equation.
$-6 = -6$	Subtract 6 from each side.
$-2a = 8$	Simplify.
$\frac{-2a}{-2} = \frac{8}{-2}$	Divide each side by −2.
$a = -4$	Simplify.

Method 2 Horizontal Method

$-2a + 6 = 14$
$-2a + 6 - 6 = 14 - 6$
$-2a = 8$
$\frac{-2a}{-2} = \frac{8}{-2}$
$a = -4$

Check

$-2a + 6 = 14$	Write the equation.
$-2(-4) + 6 \stackrel{?}{=} 14$	Replace *a* with −4 to see if the sentence is true.
$14 = 14$ ✓	The sentence is true.

The solution is −4.

Sometimes it is necessary to combine like terms before solving an equation.

EXAMPLE 2 **Solve $5 = 8x - 2x - 7$. Check your solution.**

$5 = 8x - 2x - 7$	Write the equation.
$5 = 6x - 7$	Combine like terms.
$5 + 7 = 6x - 7 + 7$	Add 7 to each side.
$12 = 6x$	Simplify.
$\frac{12}{6} = \frac{6x}{6}$	Divide each side by 6.
$2 = x$	Simplify.
The solution is 2.	Check this solution.

EXERCISES

Solve each equation. Check your solution.

1. $2d + 7 = 9$ 1
2. $11 = 3z + 5$ 2
3. $2s - 4 = 6$ 5
4. $-12 = 5r + 8$ −4
5. $-6p - 3 = 9$ −2
6. $-14 = 3x + x - 2$ −3
7. $5c + 2 - 3c = 10$ 4
8. $3 + 7n + 2n = 21$ 2
9. $21 = 6r + 5 - 7r$ −16
10. $8 - 5b = -7$ 3
11. $-10 = 6 - 4m$ 4
12. $-3t + 4 = 19$ −5
13. $2 + \frac{a}{6} = 5$ 18
14. $-\frac{1}{3}q - 7 = -3$ −12
15. $4 - \frac{v}{5} = 0$ 20

Practice: Skills, p. 569

NAME ______ DATE ______ PERIOD ____

10-2 Practice: Skills

Solving Two-Step Equations

Solve each equation. Check your solution.

1. $3n + 4 = 7$ 1
2. $9 = 2s + 1$ 4
3. $4c - 6 = 2$ 2
4. $-4 = 2t - 2$ −1
5. $3f - 12 = -3$ 3
6. $8 = 4v + 12$ −1
7. $5d - 6 = 9$ 3
8. $2k + 12 = -4$ −8
9. $-5 = 3m - 14$ 3
10. $0 = 8z + 8$ −1
11. $9a - 2 = -2$ 0
12. $-8 + 4s = -16$ −2
13. $-1 = 4 - 5x$ 1
14. $5 = 9 - 2x$ 2
15. $-2x + 12 = 14$ −1
16. $1 - x = 8$ −7
17. $-2 = -x + 4$ 6
18. $11 = 2 - 3x$ −3
19. $12 - 3x = 6$ 2
20. $-6x + 5 = 17$ −2
21. $13 = 18 - 5x$ 1
22. $4x + 2x + 2 = 26$ 4
23. $-18 = 9y - 5y + 10$ −7
24. $-24 = 6a - 15 - 5a$ −9
25. $3z - 17 + 2z = 13$ 6
26. $22 = 4 + 8e - 2e$ 3
27. $-15 = 9r + 1 - 7r$ −8
28. $8k - 8 + k = 10$ 2
29. $-27 = 2c - 7 - 6c$ 5
30. $11 = 18 + 3f + 4f$ −1

Practice: Word Problems, p. 570

NAME ______ DATE ______ PERIOD ____

10-2 Practice: Word Problems

Solving Two-Step Equations

1. **SHOPPING** Jenna bought 5 reams of paper at the store for a total of \$21. The tax on her purchase was \$1. Solve $5x + 1 = 21$ to find the price for each ream of paper. \$4
2. **CARS** It took Lisa 85 minutes to wash three cars. She spent x minutes on each car and 10 minutes putting everything away. Solve $3x + 10 = 85$ to find how long it took to wash each car. 25 min
3. **EXERCISE** Rick jogged the same distance on Tuesday and Friday, and 8 miles on Sunday, for a total of 20 miles for the week. Solve $2x + 8 = 20$ to find the distance Rick jogged on Tuesday and Friday. 6 mi
4. **MOVING** Heather has a collection of 26 mugs. When packing to move, she put the same number of mugs in each of the first 4 boxes and 2 mugs in the last box. Solve $4x + 2 = 26$ to find the number of mugs in each of the first four boxes. 6 mugs
5. **TELEVISION** Burt's parents allow him to watch a total of 10 hours of television per week. This week Burt is planning to watch several two-hour movies and four hours of sports. Solve $2x + 4 = 10$ to find the number of movies Burt is planning to watch this week. 3 movies
6. **TRAVEL** Lawrence drives the same distance Monday through Friday commuting to work. Last week Lawrence drove 25 miles on the weekend, for a total of 60 miles for the week. Solve $5x + 25 = 60$ to find the distance Lawrence drives each day commuting to work. 7 mi
7. **MONEY** McKenna had \$32 when she got to the carnival. After riding 6 rides, she had \$20 left. Solve $32 - 6x = 20$ to find the price for each ride. \$2
8. **GARDENING** Jack has 15 rosebushes. He has the same number of yellow, red, and pink bushes, and 3 multicolored bushes. Solve $3x + 3 = 15$ to find the number of yellow rosebushes Jack has. 4 yellow rosebushes

10-3 Lesson Notes

Lesson Resources

Chapter 10 Resource Masters
- Study Guide and Intervention, p. 573 **FAST FILE**
- Practice: Skills, p. 574
- Practice: Word Problems, p. 575
- Reading to Learn Mathematics, p. 576
- Enrichment, p. 577

Calculator and Spreadsheet Masters, p. 43

Parent and Student Study Guide Online Worksheets, 10-3

Noteables™: Interactive Study Notebook with Foldables™, 10-3

1 Focus

5-Minute Check 10-3

Use as a quiz or review of Lesson 10-2. (Also available as a transparency)

Bellringer

Reading Mathematics Have students translate each of the following phrases into a verbal sentence.

$n + 5$ **5 more than a number**

$3n$ **3 times a number**

$12 - n$ **n less than 12**

Reading to Learn Mathematics, p. 576 **ELL**

NAME ____ DATE ____ PERIOD ____

10-3 Reading to Learn Mathematics

Writing Two-Step Equations

Pre-Activity *Read the introduction at the top of page 478 in your textbook. Write your answers below.*

1. Let n represent the number of payments. Write an expression that represents the amount of the loan paid after n payments. $125 + 25n$
2. Write and solve an equation to find the number of payments you will have to make in order to pay off your loan. $125 + 25n = 600$; 19
3. What type of equation did you write for Exercise 2? Explain your reasoning. Two-step equation; it will take two operations, subtraction and then division, to solve this equation.

Reading the Lesson

Jennifer bought 3 CDs, each having the same price. Her total for the purchase was $51.84, which includes $3.84 in sales tax. Find the price

Writing Two-Step Equations

What You'll LEARN

Write two-step equations that represent real-life situations.

WHEN am I ever going to use this?

HOME ENTERTAINMENT Your parents offer to loan you the money to buy a $600 sound system. You give them $125 as a down payment and agree to make monthly payments of $25 until you have repaid the loan.

Payments	Amount Paid
0	$125 + 25(0) = \$125$
1	$125 + 25(1) = \$150$
2	$125 + 25(2) = \$175$
3	$125 + 25(3) = \$200$
⋮	⋮

1. Let n represent the number of payments. Write an expression that represents the amount of the loan paid after n payments.
2. Write and solve an equation to find the number of payments you will have to make in order to pay off your loan.
3. What type of equation did you write for Exercise 2? Explain your reasoning.

1. $125 + 25n$ 2. $125 + 25n = 600$; 19

3. Two-step equation; it will take two operations, subtraction and then division, to solve this equation.

In Chapter 1, you learned how to write verbal sentences as one-step equations. Some verbal sentences translate to two-step equations.

The sum of 125 and 25 times a number is 600.

Let n = the number.

The sum of 125 and 25 times a number is 600.

$125 + 25n = 600$

EXAMPLES Translate Sentences into Equations

Translate each sentence into an equation.

	Sentence	Equation
1	Eight less than three times a number is −23.	$3n - 8 = -23$
2	Thirteen is 7 more than twice a number.	$13 = 2n + 7$
3	The quotient of a number and 4, decreased by 1, is equal to 5.	$\frac{n}{4} - 1 = 5$

Your Turn **Translate each sentence into an equation.**

a. Fifteen equals three more than six times a number. **$15 = 6n + 3$**

b. If 10 is increased by the quotient of a number and 6, the result is 5. **$10 + \frac{n}{6} = 5$**

c. The difference between 12 and twice a number is 18. **$12 - 2n = 18$**

478 Chapter 10 Algebra: More Equations and Inequalities

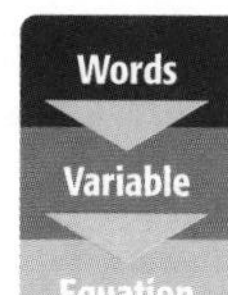

STUDY TIP

Look Back You can review writing expressions and equations in Lesson 1-7.

EXAMPLE Translate and Solve an Equation

4 **Nine more than four times a number is 21. Find the number.**

Words	Nine more than four times a number is 21.
Variable	Let n = the number.
Equation	$4n + 9 = 21$

$4n + 9 = 21$	Write the equation.
$4n + 9 - 9 = 21 - 9$	Subtract 9 from each side.
$4n = 12$	Simplify.
$n = 3$	Mentally divide each side by 4.

Therefore, the number is 3.

TEACHING TIP

Students may see that Example 5 can be solved by working backward and wonder why they need to learn how to write an equation. Explain that by using algebra to solve simpler problems, they will develop the skills needed to solve more complicated real-life problems.

In many real-life situations, you start with a given amount and then increase it at a certain rate. These situations can be represented by two-step equations.

EXAMPLE Write and Solve a Two-Step Equation

5 **FUND-RAISING Your Class Council needs \$600 for the Spring Dance. With only \$210 in their treasury, the Council decides to raise the rest by selling donuts for a profit of \$1.50 per dozen. How many dozen donuts will they need to sell?**

The council already has \$210 and will sell donuts for a profit of \$1.50 per dozen until they have \$600. Organize the data for the first few dozen donuts sold into a table and look for a pattern.

Dozens	Amount
0	210 + 1.50(0) = 210.00
1	210 + 1.50(1) = 211.50
2	210 + 1.50(2) = 213.00
3	210 + 1.50(3) = 214.50

Write an equation to represent the situation. Let d represent the number of dozens.

amount already in treasury	plus	d dozen sold at a profit of \$1.50 per dozen	equals	\$600
210	+	$1.50d$	=	600

$210 + 1.50d = 600$	Write the equation.
$210 - 210 + 1.50d = 600 - 210$	Subtract 210 from each side.
$1.50d = 390$	Simplify.
$\frac{1.50d}{1.50} = \frac{390}{1.50}$	Divide each side by 1.50.
$d = 260$	Simplify.

They need to sell 260 dozen donuts.

How Does a Fund-Raising Professional Use Math?

Fund-raising professionals use equations to help set and meet fund-raising goals.

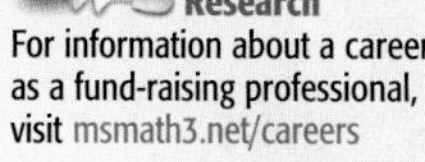

Research For information about a career as a fund-raising professional, visit msmath3.net/careers

Math Online msmath3.net/extra_examples

2 Teach

In-Class Examples

Translate each sentence into an equation.

1. Three more than half a number is 15. $\frac{1}{2}n + 3 = 15$
2. Nineteen is two more than five times a number. $19 = 5n + 2$
3. Eight less than twice a number is –35. $2n - 8 = -35$
4. Two more than $\frac{1}{3}$ of a number is 6. Find the number. $\frac{1}{3}n + 2 = 6$; 12
5. **TRANSPORTATION** A taxi ride costs \$3.50 plus \$2 for each mile traveled. If Jan pays \$11.50 for the ride, how many miles did she travel? **4 mi**

Intervention While solving a given equation may present no problem for most students, some may have great difficulty when translating a written description into an equation. Provide such students with extra practice, perhaps allowing them to write out simple mathematical expressions as sentences.

DAILY INTERVENTION

Differentiated Instruction

Interpersonal Explain to students the definitions of fixed and variable costs and their relationship to business. Then place students in small groups to create a business selling an item of their choice. They should decide, in very simple terms, what their fixed and variable costs will be each month and then create an expression for these expenses. They can use estimated or researched numbers. Have them determine how much they would need to sell in order to break even.

3 Practice/Apply

FOLDABLES™ Follow-Up Remind students to record main ideas, definitions of vocabulary words, and other notes under the "Equations" tab of their Foldables as they learn how to write two-step equations. Encourage students to recall what they have learned about equations and self-check their responses by reviewing their notes under the tab.

NUMBER SENSE
For Exercise 1, have students develop similar phrases, such as *three times* and *one third.*

About the Exercises...

Guided Practice Key

Exercises	Examples
3–5	1–4
6	5

Assignment Guide

Basic: 7–19 odd, 21–37

Average: 7–19 odd, 20–37

Enriched: 8–20 even, 21–33 (Optional: 34–37)

Answers

11. $\frac{n}{3} + 9 = 14$; 15
12. $\frac{n}{-7} - 4 = -11$; 49

Students practice the same concepts in Exercises 7–18 if they are assigned odd or even problems.

Skill and Concept Check

1. **NUMBER SENSE** Identify the operation indicated by the word *twice*. **multiplication by 2**
2. **OPEN ENDED** Write two different statements that translate into the same two-step equation. **Sample answer: 2 less than 5 times a number is 8; 5 times a number decreased by 2 is equal to 8.**

GUIDED PRACTICE

Translate each sentence into an equation. Then find each number.

3. One more than three times a number is 7. $3n + 1 = 7$; 2
4. Seven less than twice a number is -1. $2n - 7 = -1$; 3
5. The quotient of a number and 5, less 10, is 3. $\frac{n}{5} - 10 = 3$; 65
6. **FINES** You return a book that is 5 days overdue. Including a previous unpaid overdue balance of \$1.30, your new balance is \$2.05. Write and solve an equation to find the fine for a book that is one day overdue. $5f + 1.30 = 2.05$; \$0.15

Practice and Applications

HOMEWORK HELP

For Exercises	See Examples
7–14	1–4
15–19	5

Extra Practice
See pages 641, 657.

Translate each sentence into an equation. Then find each number.

7. Four less than five times a number is equal to 11. $5n - 4 = 11$; 3
8. Fifteen more than twice a number is 9. $2n + 15 = 9$; -3
9. Eight more than four times a number is -12. $4n + 8 = -12$; -5
10. Six less than seven times a number is equal to -20. $7n - 6 = -20$; -2
11. Nine more than the quotient of a number and 3 is 14. **See margin.**
12. The quotient of a number and -7, less 4, is -11. **See margin.**
13. The difference between three times a number and 10 is 17. $3n - 10 = 17$; 9
14. The difference between twice a number and 1 is -21. $2n - 1 = -21$; -10

Solve each problem by writing and solving an equation.

15. **VACATION** While on vacation, you purchase 4 identical T-shirts for some friends and a watch for yourself, all for \$75. You know that the watch cost \$25. How much did each T-shirt cost? $4x + 25 = 75$; \$12.50 each
16. **PERSONAL FITNESS** Angelica joins a local gym called *Fitness Solutions*. If she sets aside \$1,000 in her annual budget for gym costs, use the ad at the right to determine how many hours she can spend with a personal trainer. $720 + 35h = 1{,}000$; 8 h

17. **PHONE SERVICE** A telephone company advertises long distance service for 7¢ per minute plus a monthly fee of \$3.95. If your bill one month was \$12.63, find the number of minutes you used making long distance calls. $0.07m + 3.95 = 12.63$; 124 min
18. **GAMES** You and two friends share the cost of renting a video game system for 5 nights. Each person also rents one video game for \$6.33. If each person pays \$11.33, what is the cost of renting the system? $\frac{c}{3} + 6.33 = 11.33$; \$15

19. **SKIING** In aerial skiing competitions, the total judges score is multiplied by the jump's *degree of difficulty* and then added to the skier's current score to obtain their final score. The table shows the first-round scores of a competition. After her second jump, Toshiro's final score is 216.59. The degree of difficulty for Martin's second jump is 4.45. Write and solve an equation to find what the judge's score for Martin's jump must be in order for her to tie Toshiro for first.
$4.45s + 100.23 = 216.59$; 26.1

Skier	Score
Martin, S.	100.23
Toshiro, M.	105.34
Moseley, K.	93.99
Long, A.	87.50
Cruz, P.	80.63
Thompson, L.	75.23

20. **WRITE A PROBLEM** Write about a real-life situation that can be solved using a two-step equation. Then write the equation and solve the problem. **See margin.**

21. **CRITICAL THINKING** Student Council has a total of $200 to divide among the top class finishers in a used toy drive. Second place will receive twice as much as third place. First place will receive $15 more than second place. Write and solve an equation to find how much each winning class will receive.
$n + 2n + (2n + 15) = 200$; $37, $74, $89

Spiral Review with Standardized Test Practice

22. **MULTIPLE CHOICE** Ms. Anderson receives a weekly base salary of $325 plus 7% of her weekly sales. At the end of one week, she earned $500. Which equation can be used to find her sales *s* for that week? **D**

   (A) $325s + 0.07 = 500$ (B) $325 + 7s = 500$
   (C) $325 + 0.7s = 500$ (D) $325 + 0.07s = 500$

23. **GRID IN** Find the value of *x* in the parallelogram at the right. **46**

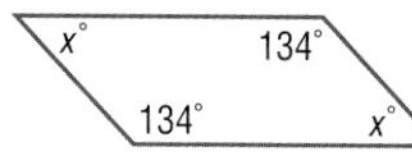

SHORT RESPONSE For Exercises 24 and 25, use the following information.
In a basketball game, 2 points are awarded for making a regular basket, and 1 point is awarded for making a foul shot. Emeril scored 21 points during one game. Three of those points were for foul shots. The rest were for regular goals.

24. Write an equation to find the number of regular baskets *b* Emeril made during the game. **$2b + 3 = 21$**

25. Solve the equation to find the number of regular baskets he made. **9**

Solve each equation. Check your solution. (Lesson 10-2)

26. $5x + 2 = 17$ **3**
27. $-7b + 13 = 27$ **−2**
28. $\frac{n}{8} + 1 = -6$ **−56**
29. $-15 = -4p + 9$ **6**

Determine the number of significant digits in each measure. (Lesson 7-9)

30. 140 ft **2**
31. 7.0 L **2**
32. 9.04 s **3**
33. 1,000.2 mi **5**

GETTING READY FOR THE NEXT LESSON

PREREQUISITE SKILL Simplify each expression. (Lesson 10-1)

34. $5x + 6 - x$ **$4x + 6$**
35. $8 - 3n + 3n$ **8**
36. $7a - 7a - 9$ **−9**
37. $3 - 4y + 9y$ **$3 + 5y$**

msmath3.net/self_check_quiz

4 Assess

Open-Ended Assessment

Speaking Have students explain to a partner how to determine what the variable represents in a word problem. Students can choose a few examples from the lesson to illustrate their explanations.

Answer

20. **Sample answer: At a gardening store, Tina bought an equal number of red, yellow, and purple tulip bulbs. She also bought 4 ferns. If she bought 22 plants in all, how many red tulip bulbs did she buy? $3x + 4 = 22$; 6**

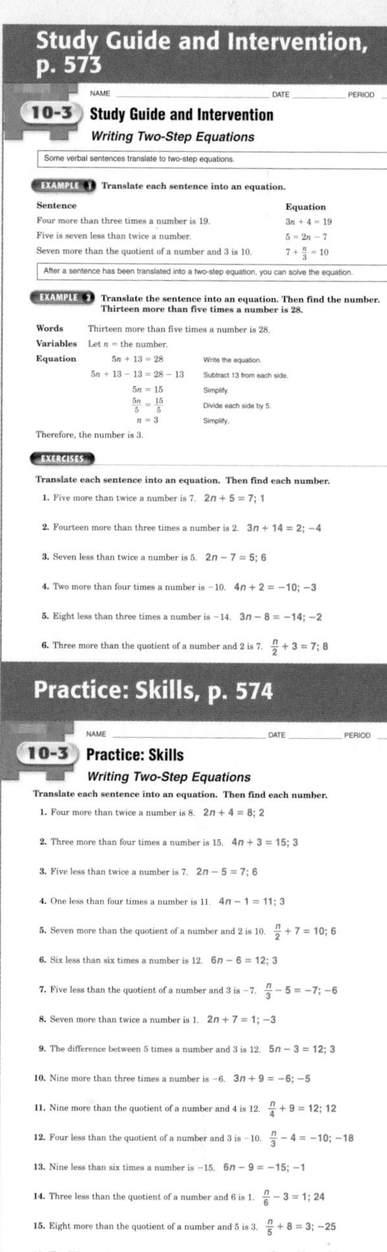

Study Guide and Intervention, p. 573

NAME ______ DATE ______ PERIOD ____

10-3 Study Guide and Intervention
Writing Two-Step Equations

Some verbal sentences translate to two-step equations.

EXAMPLE 1 **Translate each sentence into an equation.**

Sentence	Equation
Four more than three times a number is 19.	$3n + 4 = 19$
Five is seven less than twice a number.	$5 = 2n - 7$
Seven more than the quotient of a number and 3 is 10.	$7 + \frac{n}{3} = 10$

After a sentence has been translated into a two-step equation, you can solve the equation.

EXAMPLE 2 **Translate the sentence into an equation. Then find the number. Thirteen more than five times a number is 28.**

Words Thirteen more than five times a number is 28.
Variables Let n = the number.
Equation

$5n + 13 = 28$ Write the equation.
$5n + 13 - 13 = 28 - 13$ Subtract 13 from each side.
$5n = 15$ Simplify.
$\frac{5n}{5} = \frac{15}{5}$ Divide each side by 5.
$n = 3$ Simplify.

Therefore, the number is 3.

EXERCISES

Translate each sentence into an equation. Then find each number.

1. Five more than twice a number is 7. $2n + 5 = 7$; 1
2. Fourteen more than three times a number is 2. $3n + 14 = 2$; −4
3. Seven less than twice a number is 5. $2n - 7 = 5$; 6
4. Two more than four times a number is −10. $4n + 2 = -10$; −3
5. Eight less than three times a number is −14. $3n - 8 = -14$; −2
6. Three more than the quotient of a number and 2 is 7. $\frac{n}{2} + 3 = 7$; 8

Practice: Skills, p. 574

NAME ______ DATE ______ PERIOD ____

10-3 Practice: Skills
Writing Two-Step Equations

Translate each sentence into an equation. Then find each number.

1. Four more than twice a number is 8. $2n + 4 = 8$; 2
2. Three more than four times a number is 15. $4n + 3 = 15$; 3
3. Five less than twice a number is 7. $2n - 5 = 7$; 6
4. One less than four times a number is 11. $4n - 1 = 11$; 3
5. Seven more than the quotient of a number and 2 is 10. $\frac{n}{2} + 7 = 10$; 6
6. Six less than six times a number is 12. $6n - 6 = 12$; 3
7. Five less than the quotient of a number and 3 is −7. $\frac{n}{3} - 5 = -7$; −6
8. Seven more than twice a number is 1. $2n + 7 = 1$; −3
9. The difference between 5 times a number and 3 is 12. $5n - 3 = 12$; 3
10. Nine more than three times a number is −6. $3n + 9 = -6$; −5
11. Nine more than the quotient of a number and 4 is 12. $\frac{n}{4} + 9 = 12$; 12
12. Four less than the quotient of a number and 3 is −10. $\frac{n}{3} - 4 = -10$; −18
13. Nine less than six times a number is −15. $6n - 9 = -15$; −1
14. Three less than the quotient of a number and 6 is 1. $\frac{n}{6} - 3 = 1$; 24
15. Eight more than the quotient of a number and 5 is 3. $\frac{n}{5} + 8 = 3$; −25
16. The difference between twice a number and 11 is −23. $2n - 11 = -23$; −6

Practice: Word Problems, p. 575

NAME ______ DATE ______ PERIOD ____

10-3 Practice: Word Problems
Writing Two-Step Equations

Solve each problem by writing and solving an equation.

1. **CONSTRUCTION** Carlos is building a screen door. The height of the door is 1 foot more than twice its width. What is the width of the door if it is 7 feet high? $2x + 1 = 7$; 3 ft

2. **GEOMETRY** A rectangle has a width of 6 inches and a perimeter of 26 inches. What is the length of the rectangle? $2x + 12 = 26$; 7 in.

3. **EXERCISE** Ella swims four times a week at her club's pool. She swims the same number of laps on Monday, Wednesday, and Friday, and 15 laps on Saturday. She swims a total of 51 laps each week. How many laps does she swim on Monday? $3x + 15 = 51$; 12 laps

4. **SHOPPING** While at the music store, Drew bought 5 CDs, all at the same price. The tax on his purchase was $6, and the total was $61. What was the price of each CD? $5x + 6 = 61$; $11

5. **STUDYING** Over the weekend, Koko spent 2 hours on an assignment, and she spent equal amounts of time studying for 4 exams for a total of 16 hours. How much time did she spend studying for each exam? $4x + 2 = 16$; 3.5 h

6. **FOOD** At the market, Meyer buys a bunch of bananas for $0.35 per pound and a frozen pizza for $4.99. The total for his purchase was $6.04, without tax. How many pounds of bananas did Meyer buy? $0.35x + 4.99 = 6.04$; 3 lb

7. **HOME IMPROVEMENT** Laura is making a patio in her backyard using paving stones. She buys 44 paving stones and a flowerpot worth $7 for a total of $73. How much did each paving stone cost? $44x + 7 = 73$; $1.50

8. **TAXI** A taxi service charges you $1.50 plus $0.60 per minute for a trip to the airport. The distance to the airport is 10 miles, and the total charge is $13.50. How many minutes did the ride to the airport take? $0.60x + 1.50 = 13.50$; 20 min

Lesson 10-3 Writing Two-Step Equations 481

10-4a HANDS-ON LAB

Lesson Notes

Lesson Resources

Teaching Mathematics with Manipulatives
- algebra tiles, p. 29
- equation mat, p. 9
- student recording sheet 10-4a

Glencoe Mathematics Classroom Manipulative Kit
- algebra tiles
- equation mat

GETTING STARTED

Teaching Tip Model **Activity 1** on an overhead projector. Have students follow along using their algebra tiles.

TEACH

Activity 1

- Students should recognize that these examples are solved with the same methods as those used to solve equations with variables on only one side.
- Remind students that any operation they perform on one side of the equation must be performed on the other side. This ensures the equation remains in balance.

10-4a HANDS-ON LAB

A Preview of Lesson 10-4

Equations with Variables on Each Side

What You'll LEARN

Solve equations with variables on each side using algebra tiles.

Materials
- algebra tiles

You can also use algebra tiles to solve equations that have variables on each side of the equation.

ACTIVITY *Work with a partner.*

1 Use algebra tiles to model and solve $3x + 1 = x + 5$.

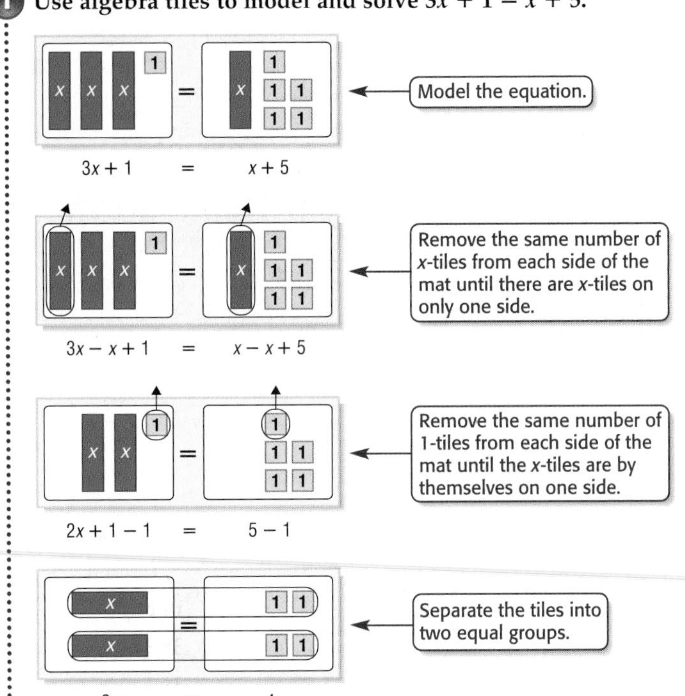

Therefore, $x = 2$. Since $3(2) + 1 = 2 + 5$, the solution is correct.

Your Turn Use algebra tiles to model and solve each equation.

a. $x + 2 = 2x + 1$ **1**
b. $2x + 7 = 3x + 4$ **3**
c. $2x - 5 = x - 7$ **−2**
d. $8 + x = 3x$ **4**
e. $4x = x - 6$ **−2**
f. $2x - 8 = 4x - 2$ **−3**

a–f. See margin for models.

Writing Math

1. **Identify** the property of equality that allows you to remove a 1-tile or −1-tile from each side of an equation mat.
2. **Explain** why you can remove an x-tile from each side of the mat.

1. Subtraction Property of Equality
2. The value of x is the same on each side of the mat.

Answers (Your Turn)

a.
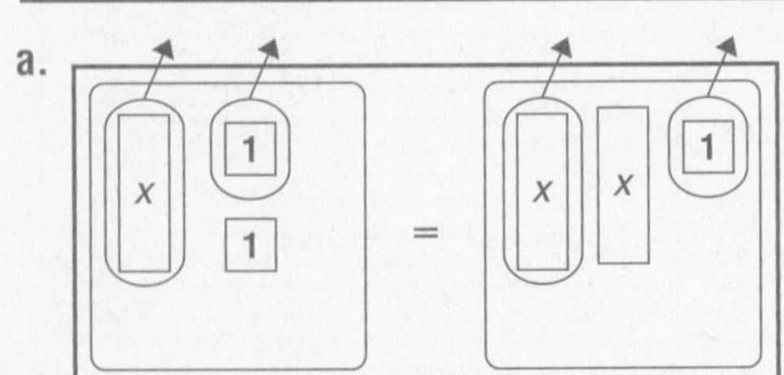

b.
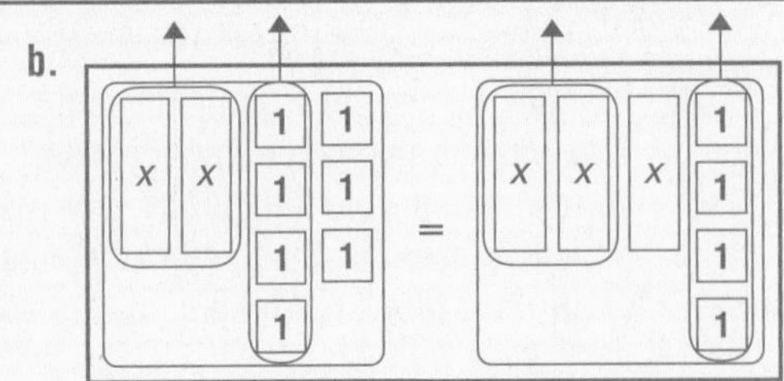

c.
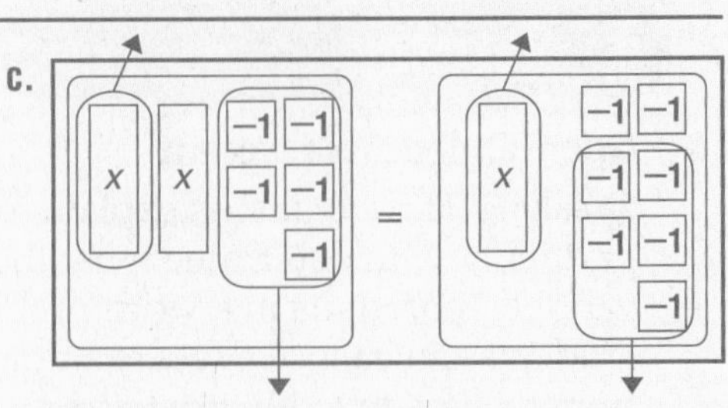

ACTIVITY *Work with a partner.*

2 **Use algebra tiles to model and solve $x - 4 = 2x + 2$.**

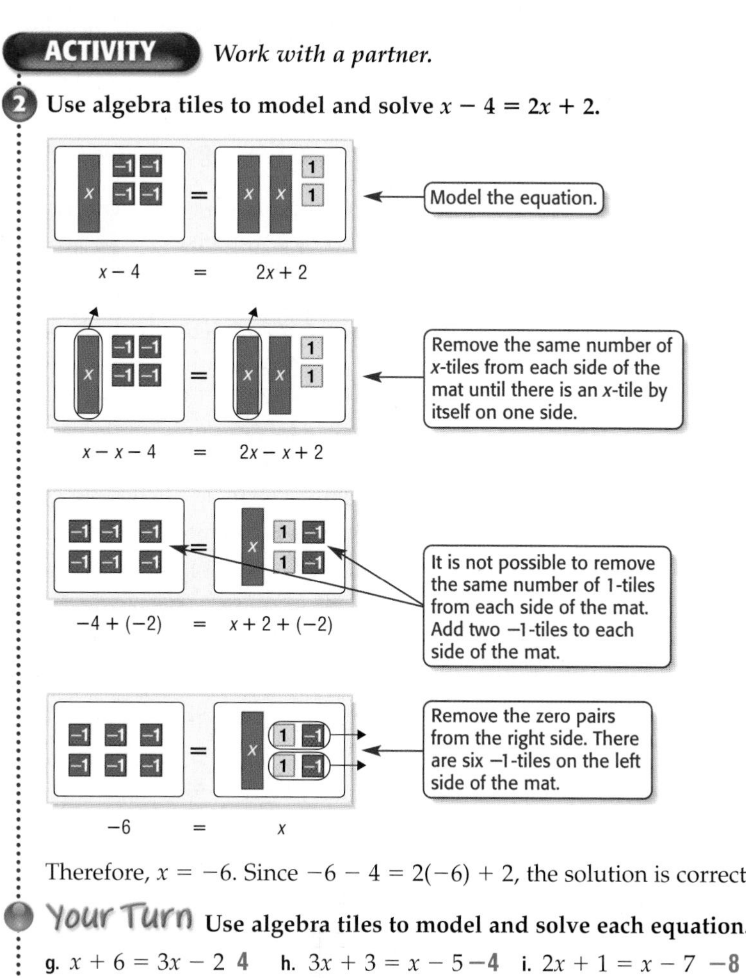

Therefore, $x = -6$. Since $-6 - 4 = 2(-6) + 2$, the solution is correct.

Your Turn **Use algebra tiles to model and solve each equation.**

g. $x + 6 = 3x - 2$ **4** h. $3x + 3 = x - 5$ **−4** i. $2x + 1 = x - 7$ **−8**

j. $x - 4 = 2x + 5$ **−9** k. $3x - 2 = 2x + 3$ **5** l. $2x + 5 = 4x - 1$ **3**

g–l. See Ch. 10 Answer Appendix for models.

3. You can remove either tile first. The order in which you add quantities to each side of an equation does not affect its solution. However, it may be more convenient to isolate the variable first.

4. Add 3 x-tiles to each side. Then add one 1-tile to each side. So, $x = 5$.

Writing Math

3. Solve $x + 4 = 3x - 4$ by removing 1-tiles first. Then solve the equation by removing x-tiles first. Does it matter whether you remove x-tiles or 1-tiles first? Is one way more convenient? Explain.

4. In the set of algebra tiles, $-x$ is represented by [−x tile]. **Make a conjecture** and explain how you could use $-x$-tiles and other algebra tiles to solve $-3x + 4 = -2x - 1$.

Activity 2

- You may want to remind students that the goal is to have only one type of algebra tile on each side of the equation mat, whether those are x-tiles or 1- or −1-tiles.

d.

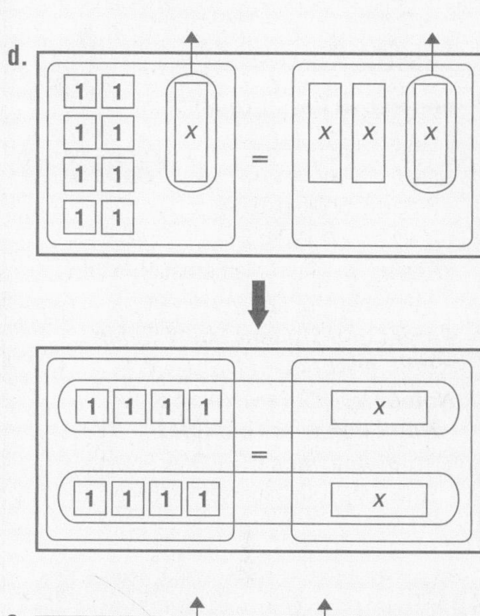

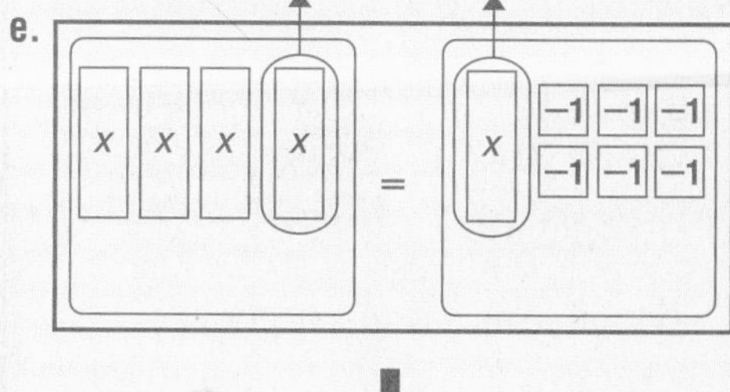

e.

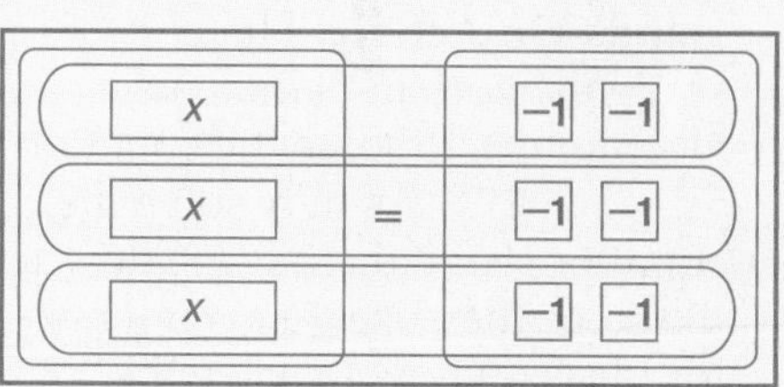

f.

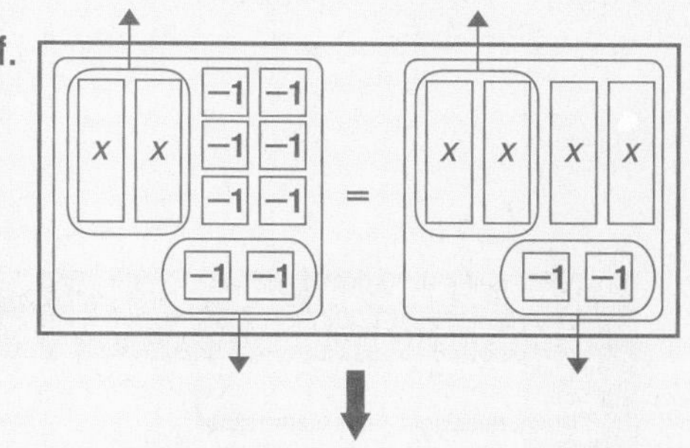

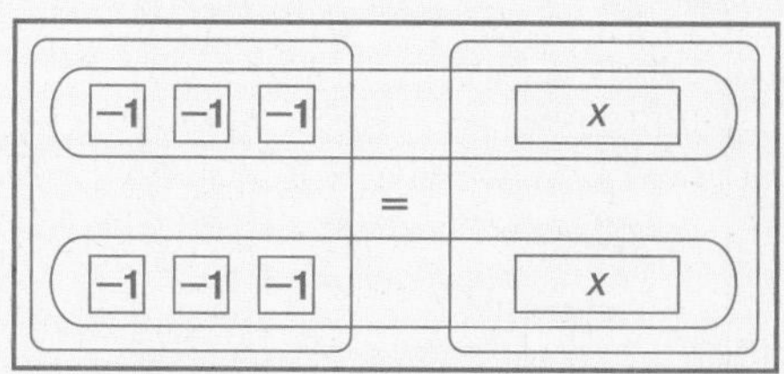

ASSESS

Observe as students solve the **Your Turn** exercises. They should:

- model an equation using algebra tiles,
- manipulate algebra tiles to solve equations, and
- check their solutions in the original equation.

Discuss the **Writing Math** exercises. You may wish to have students work in pairs on Exercise 4. Discuss students' conjectures as a class.

10-4 Lesson Notes

Lesson Resources

Chapter 10 Resource Masters
- Study Guide and Intervention, p. 578
- Practice: Skills, p. 579
- Practice: Word Problems, p. 580
- Reading to Learn Mathematics, p. 581
- Enrichment, p. 582

Parent and Student Study Guide Online Worksheets, 10-4
Noteables™: Interactive Study Notebook with Foldables™, 10-4
Virtual Activities CD-ROM, Solving Equations with Variables on Each Side

1 Focus

5-Minute Check 10-4

Use as a quiz or review of Lesson 10-3. (Also available as a transparency)

Bellringer

Hands-On Activity Have students work in pairs to use algebra tiles to solve the equation $5x = 3 + 2x$. 1 As they solve the equation, have them write down the steps they use. Ask students for ideas on how to solve this equation without algebra tiles.

Reading to Learn Mathematics, p. 581 ELL

NAME ______ DATE ______ PERIOD ____

10-4 Reading to Learn Mathematics
Solving Equations with Variables on Each Side

Pre-Activity *Read the introduction at the top of page 484 in your textbook. Write your answers below.*

1. Use the table. Continue filling in rows to find how long it will take you to catch up to your friend. If necessary, continue the table on another piece of paper. 15 s
2. Write an expression for your distance after x seconds. $6x$
3. Write an expression for your friend's distance after x seconds. $15 + 5x$
4. What is true about the distances you and your friend have gone when you catch up to your friend? They are equal.

Time (s)	Friend's Distance (m)	Your Distance (m)
0	$15 + 5(0) = 15$	$6(0) = 0$
1	$15 + 5(1) = 20$	$6(1) = 6$
2	$15 + 5(2) = 25$	$6(2) = 12$
3	$15 + 5(3) = 30$	$6(3) = 18$

10-4 Solving Equations with Variables on Each Side

What You'll LEARN

Solve equations with variables on each side.

WHEN am I ever going to use this?

SPORTS You and your friend are having a race. You give your friend a 15-meter head start. During the race, you average 6 meters per second and your friend averages 5 meters per second.

Time (s)	Friend's Distance (m)	Your Distance (m)
0	$15 + 5(0) = 15$	$6(0) = 0$
1	$15 + 5(1) = 20$	$6(1) = 6$
2	$15 + 5(2) = 25$	$6(2) = 12$
3	$15 + 5(3) = 30$	$6(3) = 18$
⋮	⋮	⋮

1. Copy the table. Continue filling in rows to find how long it will take you to catch up to your friend. **15 s**
2. Write an expression for your distance after x seconds. $6x$
3. Write an expression for your friend's distance after x seconds.
4. What is true about the distances you and your friend have gone when you catch up to your friend? **They are equal.**
5. Write an equation that could be used to find how long it will take for you to catch up to your friend. $15 + 5x = 6x$

3. $15 + 5x$

Some equations, like $15 + 5x = 6x$, have variables on each side of the equals sign. To solve these equations, use the Addition or Subtraction Property of Equality to write an equivalent equation with the variables on one side of the equals sign. Then solve the equation.

EXAMPLE Equations with Variables on Each Side

1 Solve $15 + 5x = 6x$. Check your solution.

$15 + 5x = 6x$ Write the equation.

$15 + 5x - 5x = 6x - 5x$ Subtract $5x$ from each side.

$15 = x$ Simplify by combining like terms.

Subtract $5x$ from the left side of the equation to isolate the variable.

Subtract $5x$ from the right side of the equation to keep it balanced.

To check your solution, replace x with 15 in the original equation.

Check $5x + 15 = 6x$ Write the equation.

$5(15) + 15 \stackrel{?}{=} 6(15)$ Replace x with 15.

$90 = 90$ ✓ The sentence is true.

The solution is 15.

484 Chapter 10 Algebra: More Equations and Inequalities

TEACHING TIP

The problem in Example 2 could have also been solved by first subtracting $6n$ from each side.

$$\begin{array}{rcl} 6n - 1 &=& 4n - 5 \\ -6n & & = -6n \\ \hline -1 &=& -2n - 5 \end{array}$$

Notice that this method results in a term with a negative coefficient, but the solution is the same.

EXAMPLE Equations with Variables on Each Side

2 **Solve $6n - 1 = 4n - 5$.**

$6n - 1 = 4n - 5$	Write the equation.
$6n - 4n - 1 = 4n - 4n - 5$	Subtract $4n$ from each side.
$2n - 1 = -5$	Simplify.
$2n - 1 + 1 = -5 + 1$	Add 1 to each side.
$2n = -4$	Simplify.
$n = -2$	Mentally divide each side by 2.

The solution is -2. Check this solution.

Your Turn **Solve each equation. Check your solution.** **b. -6**

a. $8a = 5a + 21$ **7** b. $3x - 7 = 8x + 23$ c. $7g - 12 = 3 + 2g$ **3**

EXAMPLE Use an Equation to Solve a Problem

Standardized Test Practice

3 **GRID-IN TEST ITEM** Find the value of x so that the polygons have the same perimeter.

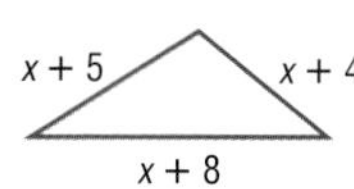

(Rectangle: $2x + 3$, $x + 5$, $x + 5$, $2x + 3$)

Read the Test Item You need to find the value of x that will make the perimeter of the triangle equal to the perimeter of the rectangle.

Solve the Test Item Write expressions for the perimeter of each figure. Then set the two expressions equal to each other and solve for x.

Triangle

$(x + 5) + (x + 4) + (x + 8) = 3x + 17$

Rectangle

$(2x + 3) + (2x + 3) + (x + 5) + (x + 5) = 6x + 16$

$$\underbrace{\text{Perimeter of Triangle}} = \underbrace{\text{Perimeter of Rectangle}}$$

$$3x + 17 = 6x + 16$$

$$3x - 3x + 17 = 6x - 3x + 16$$

$$17 = 3x + 16$$

$$17 - 16 = 3x + 16 - 16$$

$$1 = 3x$$

$$\frac{1}{3} = \frac{3x}{3}$$

$$\frac{1}{3} = x$$

Fill in the Grid

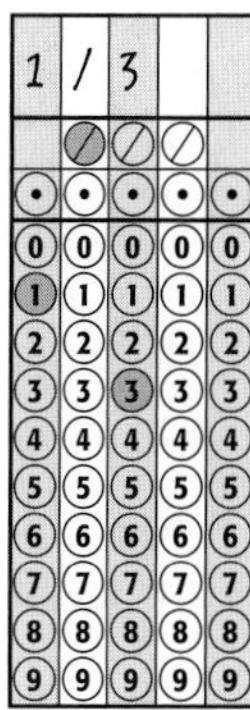

Test-Taking Tip

Fractions
To grid in a fraction, grid in the numerator, then a slash, then the denominator. To grid in an answer that is a mixed number, you must first rewrite your answer as an improper fraction.

TEACHING TIP

Students can also grid-in the answer as follows.

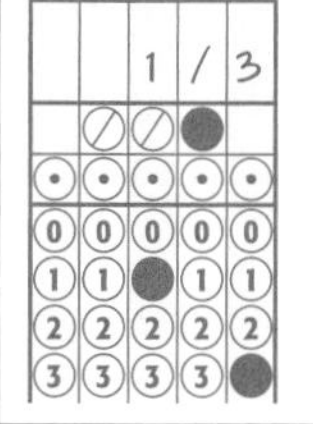

Math Online msmath3.net/extra_examples

2 Teach

In-Class Examples

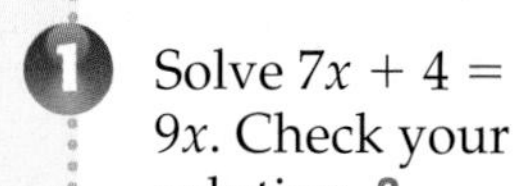

1 Solve $7x + 4 = 9x$. Check your solution. **2**

2 Solve $3x - 2 = 8x + 13$. Check your solution. **-3**

3 **GRID-IN TEST ITEM**
Find the value of x so that the polygons have the same perimeter. **8**

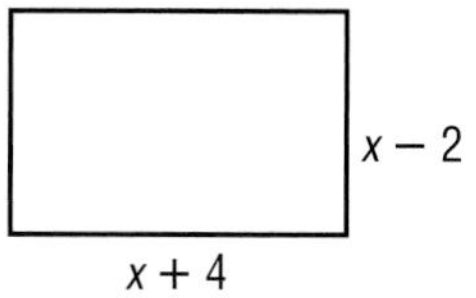

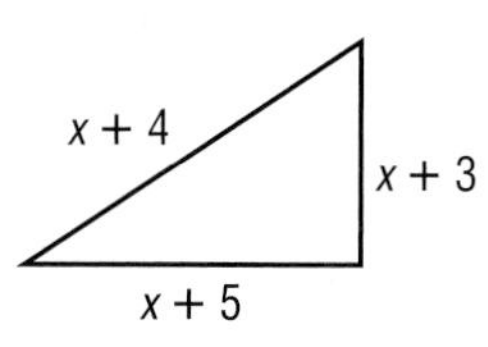

Tips for New Teachers

Teaching Strategies Encourage students to try different options for solving equations. For example, in Example 1, the explanation shows $5x$ being subtracted from each side. Instead, students could subtract $6x$ from each side. They would then have $15 - 1x = 0$. Add $1x$ to both sides to get $15 = 1x$.

DAILY INTERVENTION **Unlocking Misconceptions**

Solving Equations with Variables on Each Side Have students examine an equation such as $3x = x + 6$. Ask students what coefficient belongs in front of x on the right side of the equation. For students who have difficulty manipulating equations, it may be helpful for them to rewrite the equation as $3x = 1x + 6$ before solving.

3 Practice/Apply

About the Exercises...

Guided Practice Key

Exercises	Examples
3–5	1
6–8	2
9	3

Assignment Guide

Basic: 11–23 odd, 29, 31, 36–48

Average: 11–35 odd, 36–48

Enriched: 10–34 even, 36–44 (Optional: 45–48)

Students practice the same concepts in Exercises 10–33 if they are assigned odd or even problems.

Skill and Concept Check

1. **Name** the property of equality that allows you to add $3x$ to each side of the equation $1 - 3x = 5x - 7$. **Addition Property of Equality**

2. **OPEN ENDED** Write an equation that has variables on each side. Then list the steps you would use to isolate the variable. **Sample answer: $10x + 3 = 4x + 9$; subtract $4x$ from each side, then subtract 3 from each side.**

GUIDED PRACTICE

Solve each equation. Check your solution. **9. n = number; $3n - 18 = 2n$; 18**

3. $5n + 9 = 2n$ **−3**
4. $3k + 14 = k$ **−7**
5. $10x = 3x - 28$ **−4**
6. $7y - 8 = 6y + 1$ **9**
7. $2a + 21 = 8a - 9$ **5**
8. $-4p - 3 = 2 + p$ **−1**

9. Eighteen less than three times a number is twice the number. Define a variable, write an equation, and solve to find the number.

★ indicates increased difficulty

Practice and Applications

HOMEWORK HELP

For Exercises	See Examples
10–13, 20–21	1
14–19, 22–27	2
30–31	3

Extra Practice
See pages 641, 657.

Solve each equation. Check your solution.

10. $7a + 10 = 2a$ **−2**
11. $11x = 24 + 8x$ **8**
12. $9g - 14 = 2g$ **2**
13. $m - 18 = 3m$ **−9**
14. $5p + 2 = 4p - 1$ **−3**
15. $8y - 3 = 6y + 17$ **10**
16. $15 - 3n = n - 1$ **4**
17. $3 - 10b = 2b - 9$ **1**
18. $-6f + 13 = 2f - 11$ **3**
19. $2z - 31 = -9z + 24$ **5**
20. $2.5h - 15 = 4h$ **−10**
21. $21.6 - d = 5d$ **3.6**
22. $1 - 3c = 9c + 7$ **−0.5**
23. $7k + 12 = 8 - 9k$ **−0.25**

★ 24. $13.4w + 17 = 5w - 4$ **−2.5**

★ 25. $8.1a + 2.3 = 5.1a - 3.1$ **−1.8**

★ 26. $\frac{2}{3}x + 5 = \frac{1}{3}x + 14$ **27**

★ 27. $\frac{1}{2}a - 3 = 7 - \frac{3}{4}a$ **8**

28. n = number; $2n = 5n - 42$; 14

Define a variable and write an equation to find each number. Then solve.

28. Twice a number is 42 less than five times a number. What is the number?

29. Two more than 4 times a number is the number less 7. What is the number? **n = number; $4n + 2 = n - 7$; −3**

Write an equation to find the value of x so that each pair of polygons has the same perimeter. Then solve. **31. $60x = 8x + 26$; 0.5**

30.

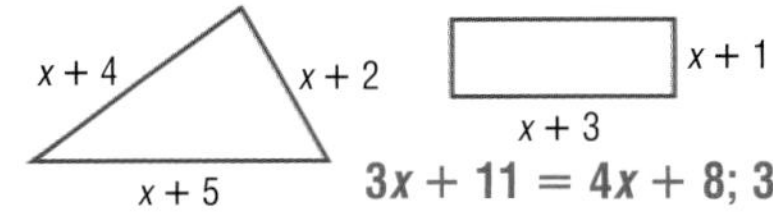

$3x + 11 = 4x + 8$; 3

31.

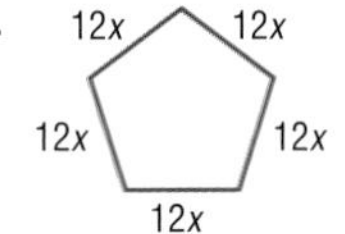

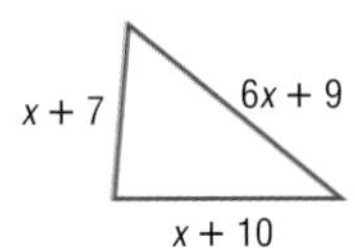

32. **MOVIES** For an annual fee of \$30, you can join a movie club that will allow you to purchase tickets for \$5.50 each at your local theater. The regular price of a ticket is \$8. Write and solve an equation to determine how many movie tickets you will have to buy through the movie club for the cost to equal that of buying regularly priced tickets. **$30 + 5.50x = 8x$; 12 tickets**

486 Chapter 10 Algebra: More Equations and Inequalities

★ 33. **DISCOUNTS** Band members are selling the coupons shown at the right for \$14 each. Write and solve an equation to determine how much money you would have to spend on food and drinks for the cost to equal that of buying the concessions without the discount. **$14 + 0.8x = x$; \$70**

Band Booster Plus Card

20% off on all food and drink at the Lions' Concession Stand

Good this season only

34. **FOOD DRIVES** The seventh graders at your school have collected 345 cans for the canned food drive and are averaging 115 cans per day. The eighth graders have collected 255 cans, but vow to win the contest by collecting an average of 130 cans per day. If both grades continue collecting at these rates, after how many days will the number of cans they have collected be equal? **$345 + 115x = 255 + 130x$; 6 days**

★ 35. **CRAFT FAIRS** The Art Club is selling handcrafted mugs at a local craft fair. Vendors at the fair must pay \$5 for a booth plus 10% of their sales. It costs \$8 in materials to make each mug. If the club sells each mug for \$10, write and solve an equation to find how many mugs they must sell to break even. (*Hint:* Total cost must equal total income.) **$5 + 0.10(10x) + 8x = 10x$; 5 mugs**

36. **CRITICAL THINKING** Find the area of the parallelogram at the right. **45 units^2**

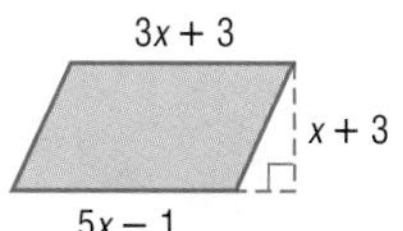

Spiral Review with Standardized Test Practice

37. **MULTIPLE CHOICE** Phone company A charges \$28.25 a month plus 18¢ per minute for local calls. Company B charges \$19.85 per month plus 32¢ per minute for local calls. Which equation can be used to find the number of minutes for which the companies' plans cost the same? **C**

   Ⓐ $28.25x + 0.18 = 19.85x + 0.32$ Ⓑ $28.25 + 0.32x = 19.85 + 0.18x$

   Ⓒ $28.25 + 0.18x = 19.85 + 0.32x$ Ⓓ $(28.25 + 0.18)x = (19.85 + 0.32)x$

38. **SHORT RESPONSE** Find the value of x so that the two figures at the right have the same area. **20**

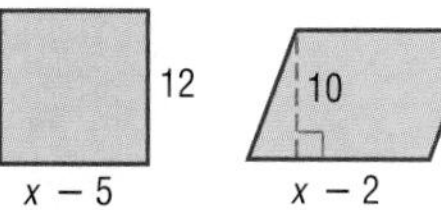

Translate each sentence into an equation. Then find each number. (Lesson 10-3)

39. Eight more than four times a number is 60. **$4n + 8 = 60$; 13**

40. Five less than the quotient of a number and 3 equals −9. **$\frac{n}{3} - 5 = -9$; −12**

Solve each equation. Check your solution. (Lesson 10-2)

41. $7r + 10 = -11$ **−3** 42. $3g - 7 = 8$ **5** 43. $8 - p = -10$ **18** 44. $2 + \frac{a}{-5} = 6$ **−20**

GETTING READY FOR THE NEXT LESSON

PREREQUISITE SKILL Determine whether each statement is *true* or *false*. (Lesson 1-3)

45. $8 > 11$ **false** 46. $3 \geq -6$ **true** 47. $-5 \geq -5$ **true** 48. $-2 < -9$ **false**

msmath3.net/self_check_quiz

4 Assess

Higher-Level Thinking

Store A is selling all items for 20% off. Store B is selling all items for 10% off plus another \$5 off. At what price will the discount on an item be equal at either store? Write an equation to represent this situation and solve the problem using the equation. **$0.2x = 0.1x + 5$; \$50**

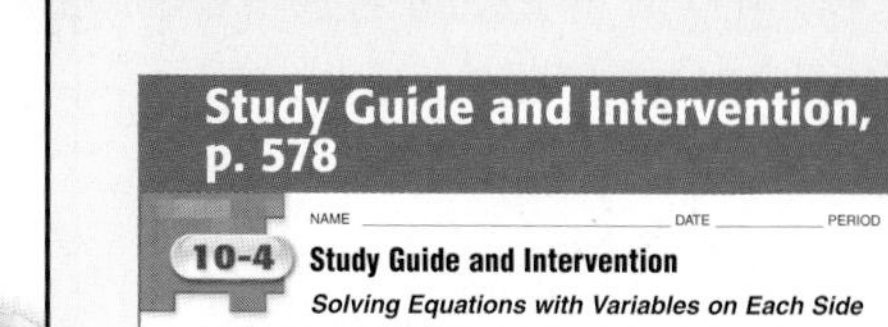

Study Guide and Intervention, p. 578

NAME ______ DATE ______ PERIOD ____

10-4 Study Guide and Intervention

Solving Equations with Variables on Each Side

Some equations, like $3x - 9 = 6x$, have variables on each side of the equals sign. Use the Addition or Subtraction Properties of Equality to write an equivalent equation with the variables on one side of the equals sign. Then solve the equation.

EXAMPLE 1 **Solve $3x - 9 = 6x$. Check your solution.**

$3x - 9 = 6x$	Write the equation.
$3x - 3x - 9 = 6x - 3x$	Subtract $3x$ from each side.
$-9 = 3x$	Simplify.
$-3 = x$	Mentally divide each side by 3.

To check your solution, replace x with −3 in the original equation.

Check $3x - 9 = 6x$	Write the equation.
$3(-3) - 9 \stackrel{?}{=} 6(-3)$	Replace x with −3.
$-18 = -18$ ✓	The sentence is true.

The solution is −3.

EXAMPLE 2 **Solve $4a - 7 = 5 - 2a$.**

$4a - 7 = 5 - 2a$	Write the equation.
$4a + 2a - 7 = 5 - 2a + 2a$	Add $2a$ to each side.
$6a - 7 = 5$	Simplify.
$6a - 7 + 7 = 5 + 7$	Add 7 to each side.
$6a = 12$	Simplify.
$a = 2$	Mentally divide each side by 6.
The solution is 2.	Check this solution.

EXERCISES

Solve each equation. Check your solution.

1. $6s - 10 = s$ **2** 2. $8r = 4r - 16$ **−4** 3. $25 - 3u = 2u$ **5**
4. $14t - 8 = 6t$ **1** 5. $k + 20 = 9k - 4$ **3** 6. $11m + 13 = m + 23$ **1**
7. $-4b - 5 = 3b + 9$ **−2** 8. $6y - 1 = 27 - y$ **4** 9. $1.6h - 72 = 4h - 30$ **−17.5**
10. $8.5 - 3z = -8z$ **−1.7** 11. $10x + 8 = 5x - 3$ **−2.2** 12. $16 - 7d = -3d + 2$ **3.5**

Practice: Skills, p. 579

NAME ______ DATE ______ PERIOD ____

10-4 Practice: Skills

Solving Equations with Variables on Each Side

Solve each equation. Check your solution.

1. $3w + 6 = 4w$ **6** 2. $a + 18 = 7a$ **3**
3. $8c = 5c + 21$ **7** 4. $11d + 10 = 6d$ **−2**
5. $2e = 4e - 16$ **8** 6. $7v = 2v - 20$ **−4**
7. $4n - 6 = 10n$ **−1** 8. $2y + 27 = 5y$ **9**
9. $8h = 6h - 14$ **−7** 10. $18 - 2g = 4g$ **3**
11. $4x - 9 = 6x - 13$ **2** 12. $5c - 15 = 2c + 6$ **7**
13. $t + 10 = 7t - 14$ **4** 14. $8z + 6 = 7z + 4$ **−2**
15. $2e - 12 = 7e + 8$ **−4** 16. $9k + 6 = 8k + 13$ **7**
17. $2d + 10 = 6d - 10$ **5** 18. $-2a - 9 = 6a + 15$ **−3**
19. $8 - 3k = 3k + 2$ **1** 20. $7t - 4 = 10t + 14$ **−6**
21. $3c - 15 = 17 - c$ **8** 22. $14 + 3n = 5n - 6$ **10**
23. $3y + 5.2 = 2 - 5y$ **−0.4** 24. $10b - 2 = 7b - 7.4$ **−1.8**
25. $2m - 2 = 6m - 4$ **0.5** 26. $3g + 5 = 7g + 4$ **0.25**
27. $4s - 1 = 8 - 2s$ **1.5** 28. $9w + 3 = 4w - 9$ **−2.4**
29. $6z - 7 = 2z - 2$ **1.25** 30. $3 - a = 4a + 12$ **−1.8**

Practice: Word Problems, p. 580

NAME ______ DATE ______ PERIOD ____

10-4 Practice: Word Problems

Solving Equations with Variables on Each Side

Solve each problem by writing and solving an equation.

1. **PLUMBING** A1 Plumbing Service charges \$35 per hour plus a \$25 travel charge for a service call. Good Guys Plumbing Repair charges \$40 per hour for a service call with no travel charge. How long must a service call be for the two companies to charge the same amount? **$35t + 25 = 40t$; 5 h**

2. **EXERCISE** Mike's Fitness Center charges \$30 per month for a membership. All-Day Fitness Club charges \$22 per month plus an \$80 initiation fee for a membership. After how many months will the total amount paid to the two fitness clubs be the same? **$30t = 22t + 80$; 10 months**

3. **SHIPPING** The Lone Star Shipping Company charges \$14 plus \$2 a pound to ship an overnight package. Discount Shipping Company charges \$20 plus \$1.50 a pound to ship an overnight package. For what weight is the charge the same for the two companies? **$14 + 2x = 20 + 1.50x$; 12 lb**

4. **MONEY** Julia and Lise are playing games at the arcade. Julia started with \$15, and the machine she is playing costs \$0.75 per game. Lise started with \$13, and her machine costs \$0.50 per game. After how many games will the two girls have the same amount of money remaining? **$15 - 0.75x = 13 - 0.50x$; 8 games**

5. **MONEY** The Wayside Hotel charges its guests \$1 plus \$0.80 per minute for long distance calls. Across the street, the Blue Sky Hotel charges its guests \$2 plus \$0.75 per minute for long distance calls. Find the length of a call for which the two hotels charge the same amount. **$1 + 0.80x = 2 + 0.75x$; 20 min**

6. **COLLEGE** Jeff is a part-time student at Horizon Community College. He currently has 22 credits, and he plans to take 6 credits per semester until he is finished. Jeff's friend Kila is also a student at the college. She has 4 credits and plans to take 12 credits per semester. After how many semesters will Jeff and Kila have the same number of credits? **$6x + 22 = 12x + 4$; 3 semesters**

10-4b Lesson Notes

1 Focus

Bellringer

Hands-On Activity Put several pennies and nickels in a bag. Tell the class their total value. Ask students to guess how many of each could be in the bag. After students have settled on a reasonable guess, have a volunteer count the coins to see whether the guess was correct.

2 Teach

In-Class Example

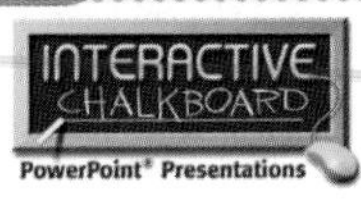

Solve. Use the guess and check strategy.

THEATER 120 tickets were sold for the school play. Adult tickets were sold for \$8 each and child tickets were sold for \$5 each. The total earned from ticket sales was \$840. How many tickets of each type were sold? **80 adult tickets and 40 child tickets**

Answers

1. **Sample answer: Make a guess. Check your guess. If it results in an answer that is too high or too low, adjust your guess appropriately and try again. Continue this process until you arrive at a correct solution.**
2. **Sample answer: You need to keep track of what numbers you have already guessed, so that you do not make the same guess twice. You also need to know what numbers produce answers that are too large or too small, so you can make better guesses.**

10-4b Problem-Solving Strategy

A Follow-Up of Lesson 10-4

Guess and Check

What You'll LEARN

Solve problems using the guess and check strategy.

Wow! The Fall Carnival was really a success! We collected 150 tickets at the Balloon Pop and Bean-Bag Toss booths alone.

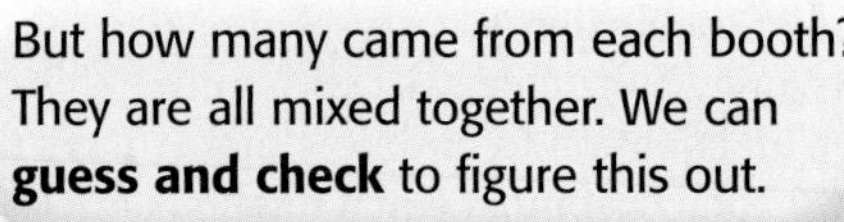

Explore	The Bean-Bag Toss was 3 tickets, and the Balloon Pop was 2 tickets. The person running the Bean-Bag Toss said 10 more games were played at her booth than at the Balloon Pop.
Plan	Let's make a guess and check to see if it is correct. Remember, the number we guess for the Bean-Bag Toss must be 10 more than the number we guess for the Balloon Pop.
Solve	We need to find the combination that gives us 150 total tickets. In our list, p is the number of Balloon Pop games, and t is the number of Bean-Bag Toss games.
Examine	36 Balloon Pop games is 10 more than 26 Bean-Bag Toss games. Since 78 tickets plus 72 tickets is 150 tickets, the guess is correct.

p	t	$3p + 2t$	Check
12	22	$3(12) + 2(22) = 80$	too low
30	40	$3(30) + 2(40) = 170$	too high
28	38	$3(28) + 2(38) = 160$	still too high
26	36	$3(26) + 2(36) = 150$	correct

So 3(26) or 78 tickets were from the Balloon Pop and 2(36) or 72 tickets were from the Bean-Bag Toss.

Analyze the Strategy

1. **Describe** how to solve a problem using the guess and check strategy. **1–3. See margin.**
2. **Explain** why it is important to make an organized list of your guesses and their results when using the guess and check strategy.
3. **Write** a problem that could be solved by guessing and checking. Then write the steps you would take to find the solution to your problem.

3. **Sample answer: The product of two whole numbers is 120. The sum of the numbers is 29. Find the numbers.**
   We know their product is 120.
   Make a guess:
   $2 \cdot 60 = 120$ and $2 + 60 = 62$ (too high)
   $6 \cdot 20 = 120$ and $6 + 20 = 26$ (too low)
   $5 \cdot 24 = 120$ and $5 + 24 = 29$
   So, the two numbers are 5 and 24.

Apply the Strategy

Solve. Use the guess and check strategy.

4. **NUMBER THEORY** The product of a number and its next two consecutive whole numbers is 60. Find the number. **3**

5. **MONEY MATTERS** Adam has exactly \$2 in quarters, dimes, and nickels. If he has 12 coins, how many of each coin does he have? **6 quarters, 4 dimes, 2 nickels**

Mixed Problem Solving

Solve. Use any strategy.

6. **DESIGN** Edu-Toys is designing a new package to hold a set of 30 *alphabet blocks* like the one shown. Give two possible dimensions for the box. **See margin.**

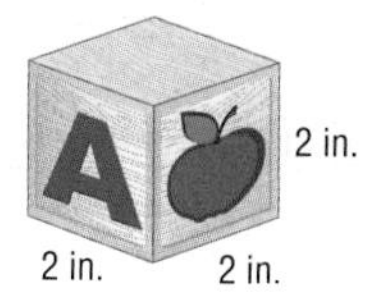

7. **RECREATION** During a routine, ballet dancers are evenly spaced in a circle. If the sixth person is directly opposite the sixteenth person, how many people are in the circle? **20**

8. **TECHNOLOGY** The average Internet user spends $6\frac{1}{2}$ hours online each week. What percent of the week does the average user spend online? **3.9%**

9. **READING** Terrence is reading a 255-page book. He needs to read twice as many pages as he has already read to finish the book. How many pages has he read so far? **85**

10. **DINING** The cost of your meal comes to \$8.25. If you want to leave a 15% tip, would it be more reasonable to expect the tip to be about \$1.25 or about \$1.50? **\$1.25**

11. **GEOMETRY** The length ℓ of the rectangle below is longer than its width w. List the possible whole number dimensions for the rectangle, and identify the possibility that gives the smallest perimeter. **See margin.**

$A = 84 \text{ in}^2$, w, ℓ

FOOD For Exercises 12 and 13, use the following information.
The school cafeteria surveyed 36 students about their dessert preference. The results are listed below.

Number of Students	Preference of Students
25	cake
20	ice cream
15	pie
2	all three
1	no desserts
15	cake or ice cream
8	pie or cake
3	ice cream only

12. How many students prefer only pie? **5**

13. How many prefer either pie or ice cream? **4**

14. **NUMBER SENSE** Find the product of $1 - \frac{1}{2}$, $1 - \frac{1}{3}$, $1 - \frac{1}{4}$, ..., $1 - \frac{1}{48}$, $1 - \frac{1}{49}$, and $1 - \frac{1}{50}$. $\mathbf{\frac{1}{50}}$

15. **STANDARDIZED TEST PRACTICE** At a souvenir shop, a mug costs \$3, and a pin costs \$2. Chase bought either a mug or a pin for each of his 11 friends. If he spent \$30 on these gifts and bought at least one of each type of souvenir, how many of each did he buy? **B**

 (A) 7 mugs, 4 pins
 (B) 8 mugs, 3 pins
 (C) 9 mugs, 2 pins
 (D) 10 mugs, 1 pin

3 Practice/Apply

About the Exercises...

Problem-Solving Strategies
Exercises 6–15 are structured so that students have the opportunity to practice many different problem-solving strategies. You may wish to remind them of some of the strategies they have studied.

- look for a pattern (p. 96)
- use logical reasoning (p. 276)
- make an organized list (p. 378)
- guess and check ✓

4 Assess

Open-Ended Assessment

Speaking Have students present the problems they wrote in Exercise 3 to the class. Have each student lead the class through solving the problem by guessing. Students should justify why each answer is too high or too low.

Answers

6. Sample answer: 10 in. by 6 in. by 4 in. or 10 in. by 12 in. by 2 in.

11. $\ell = 84$, $w = 1$; $\ell = 42$, $w = 2$; $\ell = 28$, $w = 3$; $\ell = 21$, $w = 4$; $\ell = 14$, $w = 6$; $\ell = 12$, $w = 7$; A length of 12 in. and a width of 7 in. give the smallest perimeter.

DAILY INTERVENTION — **Flexible Grouping**

Guess and Check Strategy Have students work in groups of two or three to complete Exercises 4 and 5. For each problem, one student should take the role of recorder to record all guesses made. After each guess, the group should assess how to change its guess to be closer to the answer.

Lesson 10-4b Problem-Solving Strategy: Guess and Check **489**

Chapter 10 Mid-Chapter Practice Test

Assessment Option

Mid-Chapter Test (Lessons 10-1 through 10-4) is available on p. 615 of the *Chapter 10 Resource Masters*.

ExamView® Pro

Use the networkable ExamView® Pro Testmaker CD-ROM to:

- Create **multiple versions** of tests.
- Create **modified** tests for **inclusion** students with one mouse click.
- **Edit** existing questions and **add** your own questions.
- Build tests aligned with state standards using built-in **state curriculum correlations.**
- Change **English** tests to **Spanish** with one mouse click and vice versa.

FOLDABLES™ Follow-Up

Before students complete the Mid-Chapter Practice Test, encourage them to review the notes, definitions, concepts, and main ideas they recorded under the "Equations" tab of their Foldables.

Answers

1. **Like terms are terms that contain the same variables. Sample answer: $6p$ and $-2p$ are like terms, $3x$ and $5y$ are not like terms.**
6. **terms: 5, $-4x$, x, -3; like terms: $-4x$ and x, 5 and -3; coefficients: -4, 1; constants: 5, -3**

Chapter 10 Mid-Chapter Practice Test

Vocabulary and Concepts

1. **Explain** what is meant by *like terms*. Then give an example of two terms that are considered like terms and two that are not. (Lesson 10-1) **See margin.**
2. **OPEN ENDED** Write a two-step equation whose solution is 12. (Lesson 10-2) **Sample answer: $\frac{x}{3} + 2 = 6$**

Skills and Applications

Use the Distributive Property to rewrite each expression. (Lesson 10-1)

3. $3(x + 2)$ **$3x + 6$**
4. $-2(a - 3)$ **$-2a + 6$**
5. $5(3c - 7)$ **$15c - 35$**
6. Identify the terms, like terms, coefficients, and constants in the expression $5 - 4x + x - 3$. (Lesson 10-1) **See margin.**

Simplify each expression. (Lesson 10-1)

7. $2a - 13a$ **$-11a$**
8. $6b + 5 - 6b$ **5**
9. $7x + 2 - 8x + 5$ **$-x + 7$**

Solve each equation. Check your solution. (Lessons 10-2 and 10-4)

10. $3m + 5 = 14$ **3**
11. $11 = \frac{1}{3}a + 2$ **27**
12. $-2k + 7 = -3$ **5**
13. $3x + 7 = 2x$ **-7**
14. $7p - 6 = 4p$ **2**
15. $3y - 5 = 5y + 7$ **-6**
16. Two less than 5 times a number is 23. Write and solve an equation to find the number. (Lesson 10-3) **$5n - 2 = 23$; 5**
17. **CAR RENTALS** A rental car company charges \$52 per day and \$0.32 per mile to rent a car. Ms. Misel was charged \$202.40 for a 3-day rental. Write and solve an equation to determine how many miles she drove. (Lesson 10-3) **$3(52) + 0.32x = \$202.40$; 145 mi**
18. **GEOMETRY** Write and solve an equation to find the value of x so that the polygons have the same perimeter. (Lesson 10-4)

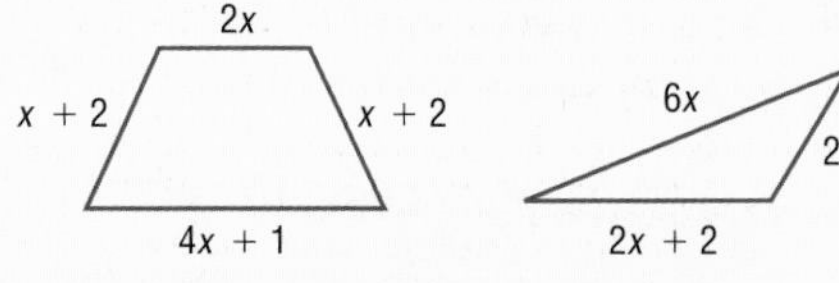

$8x + 5 = 10x + 2$; 1.5

Standardized Test Practice

19. **MULTIPLE CHOICE** Which expression is equivalent to $2(3x + 1 - x - 5)$? (Lesson 10-1) **B**
    - (A) $6x - 8$
    - (B) $4x - 8$
    - (C) $4x - 4$
    - (D) $7x - 4$
20. **SHORT RESPONSE** The length of a rectangular room is 3 feet more than twice its width. If the perimeter of the room is 78 feet, find its width. (Lesson 10-2) **12 ft**

A Place To Practice Your Math Skills

Math Skill
Solving Two-Step Equations

Math-O

GET READY!

Players: two, three, or four
Materials: 52 index cards and 4 different colored markers

GET SET!

- Make a set of four cards by using the markers to put a different-colored stripe at the top of each card.
- Then write a different two-step equation on each card. The solution of each equation should be 1.
- Continue to make sets of four cards having equations with solutions of 2, 3, 4, 5, 6, −1, −2, −3, −4, −5 and −6.
- Mark the remaining set of four cards "Wild".

$2x - 3 = 5$

$-5x + 8 = 3$

GO!

- The dealer shuffles the cards and deals five to each person. The remaining cards are placed in a pile facedown in the middle of the table. The dealer turns the top card faceup.
- The player to the left of the dealer plays a card with the same color or solution as the faceup card. Wild cards can be played any time. If the player cannot play a card, he or she takes a card from the pile and plays it, if possible. If it is not possible to play, the player places the card in his or her hand, and it is the next player's turn.
- **Who Wins?** The first person to play all cards in his or her hand is the winner.

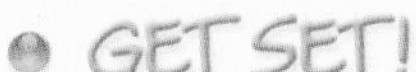

GETTING READY

Objective Solve two-step equations.

MANAGEMENT TIPS

Recommended Time
20 minutes

Tips

- Prepare the index cards in advance by writing equations and coloring the cards accordingly. Have them packaged in sets of 52.
- Group students by ability. This will allow slower students to practice solving equations without being rushed.
- You may wish to use the game as an assessment tool for the concepts the students have been learning in Lessons 10-1 through 10-4.

Math Online For an additional game for this chapter, visit: msmath3.net/gamezone

10-5 Lesson Notes

Lesson Resources

Chapter 10 Resource Masters FAST FILE
- Study Guide and Intervention, p. 583
- Practice: Skills, p. 584
- Practice: Word Problems, p. 585
- Reading to Learn Mathematics, p. 586
- Enrichment, p. 587

Calculator and Spreadsheet Masters, p. 44
Parent and Student Study Guide Online Worksheets, 10-5
Real-Life Career Masters, p. 36
Noteables™: Interactive Study Notebook with Foldables™, 10-5

Focus

5-Minute Check 10-5
Use as a quiz or review of Lesson 10-4. (Also available as a transparency)

Bellringer
Communication Ask students to think of situations in which the words *minimum* or *maximum* are used. Have them name a number that fits the situation and a number that does not apply. For example, if the minimum height to ride a roller coaster is 48 inches, someone who is 48 inches tall may ride, but someone with a height of 45 inches may not.

Reading to Learn Mathematics, p. 586 ELL

NAME ______ DATE ______ PERIOD ______

10-5 Reading to Learn Mathematics
Inequalities

Pre-Activity *Read the introduction at the top of page 492 in your textbook. Write your answers below.*

1. Name three truck heights that can safely pass on a road where the first sign is posted. Can a truck that is 10 feet 6 inches tall pass? Explain. **10'3", 10'4", 10'5"; Yes, 10'6" is not over 10'6".**
2. Name three speeds that are legal according to the second sign. Is a car traveling at 45 miles per hour driving at a legal speed? Explain. **25, 35, 40; Yes; 45 mph is equal to 45 mph or less.**

Reading the Lesson

3. Complete the table by providing the symbol used to represent each phrase.

Phrase	Symbol	Phrase	Symbol
is greater than	>	is at most	≤

10-5 Inequalities

What You'll LEARN
Write and graph inequalities.

MATH Symbols
≤ less than or equal to
≥ greater than or equal to

WHEN am I ever going to use this?

SIGNS The first highway sign at the right indicates that trucks *more than* 10 feet 6 inches tall cannot pass. The second sign indicates that a speed of 45 miles per hour *or less* is legal.

1. Name three truck heights that can safely pass on a road where the first sign is posted. Can a truck that is 10 feet 6 inches tall pass? Explain.
2. Name three speeds that are legal according to the second sign. Is a car traveling at 45 miles per hour driving at a legal speed? Explain. **Sample answer: 25, 35, 40; Yes; 45 mph is equal to 45 mph or less.**

1. Sample answer: 10' 3", 10' 4", 10' 5"; Yes, 10' 6" is not over 10' 6".

In Chapter 1, you learned that a mathematical sentence that contains > or < is called an inequality. When used to compare a variable and a number, inequalities can describe a range of values.

EXAMPLES Write Inequalities with < or >

Write an inequality for each sentence.

1 SAFETY A package must weigh less than 80 pounds.

Let w = package's weight.

$w < 80$

2 AGE You must be over 55 years old to join.

Let a = person's age.

$a > 55$

Some inequalities use the symbols ≤ or ≥. They are combinations of the symbol < or > with part of the equals sign. The symbol ≤ is read *is less than or equal to,* while the symbol ≥ is read *is greater than or equal to.*

EXAMPLES Write Inequalities with ≤ or ≥

Write an inequality for each sentence.

3 VOTING You must be 18 years of age or older to vote.

Let a = person's age.

$a \geq 18$

4 DRIVING Your speed must be 65 miles per hour or less.

Let s = car's speed.

$s \leq 65$

492 Chapter 10 Algebra: More Equations and Inequalities

DAILY INTERVENTION

Differentiated Instruction

Intrapersonal Have students write three or four inequalities that apply to their own lives. Examples include the number of hours they sleep each night, the number of hours of television they watch each week, and the number of people who can sleep comfortably in their homes.

492 Chapter 10 Algebra: More Equations and Inequalities

TEACHING TIP
Be sure that students know that this table gives some but not all phrases that suggest each inequality.

Inequalities				
Words	• is less than • is fewer than	• is greater than • is more than • exceeds	• is less than or equal to • is no more than • is at most	• is greater than or equal to • is no less than • is at least
Symbols	$<$	$>$	$\leq$	$\geq$

Inequalities with variables are open sentences. When the variable in an open sentence is replaced with a number, the inequality may be true or false.

STUDY TIP
Symbols Read $7 \not> 8$ as *7 is not greater than 8.*

EXAMPLES Determine the Truth of an Inequality

For the given value, state whether each inequality is *true* or *false*.

5 $a + 2 > 8, a = 5$

$a + 2 > 8$ Write the inequality.

$5 + 2 \overset{?}{>} 8$ Replace *a* with 5.

$7 \not> 8$ Simplify.

Since 7 is not greater than 8, $7 > 8$ is false.

6 $10 \leq 7 - x, x = -3$

$10 \leq 7 - x$ Write the inequality.

$10 \overset{?}{\leq} 7 - (-3)$ Replace *x* with -3.

$10 \leq 10$ Simplify.

While $10 < 10$ is false, $10 = 10$ is true, so $10 \leq 10$ is true.

TEACHING TIP
Remind students that $10 \leq 10$ is read as *10 is less than or equal to 10.* The word *or* indicates that only one condition must be met for the statement to be true.

Your Turn For the given value, state whether each inequality is *true* or *false*. **a. true b. false c. false**

a. $n - 6 < 15, n = 18$ b. $-3p \geq 24, p = 8$ c. $-2 > 5y - 7, y = 1$

Inequalities can be graphed on a number line. Since it is impossible to show all the values that make an inequality true, an open or closed circle is used to indicate where these values begin, and an arrow to the left or to the right is used to indicate that they continue in the indicated direction.

EXAMPLES Graph an Inequality

Graph each inequality on a number line.

7 $n < 3$

Place an open circle at 3. Then draw a line and an arrow to the left.

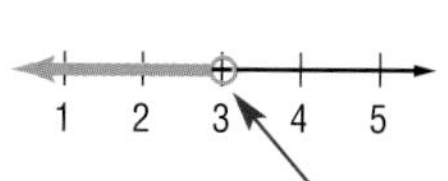

The open circle means the number 3 is *not* included in the graph.

8 $n \geq 3$

Place a closed circle at 3. Then draw a line and an arrow to the right.

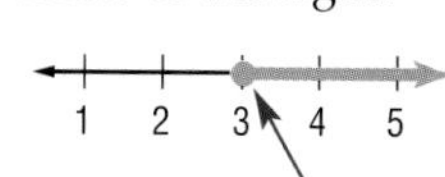

The closed circle means the number 3 *is* included in the graph.

Your Turn Graph each inequality on a number line.

d. $x > 2$ e. $x < 1$ f. $x \leq 5$ g. $x \geq -4$

d–g. See margin.

Math Online msmath3.net/extra_examples

2 Teach

In-Class Examples

Write an inequality for each sentence.

1 **SPORTS** Members of the little league team must be under 14 years old. **$a < 14$**

2 **CONSTRUCTION** The ladder must be over 30 feet tall to reach the top of the building. **$b > 30$**

3 **POLITICS** The president of the United States must be at least 35. **$a \geq 35$**

4 **CAPACITY** A theater can hold a maximum of 300 people. **$p \leq 300$**

For the given value, state whether each inequality is *true* or *false*.

5 $x - 4 < 6; x = 0$ **true**

6 $3x \geq 4; x = 1$ **false**

Graph each inequality on a number line.

7 $n \leq -1$

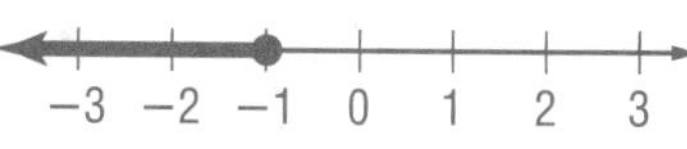

8 $n > -1$

Tips for New Teachers

Teaching Strategies If students have difficulty deciding on the correct symbol for an inequality, they should test numbers to see which fit the situation. Use "Children under 12 eat free" as an example. Can 12-year-olds eat free? No, they are too old. The situation requires a less than sign.

Answers (Your Turn)

d.

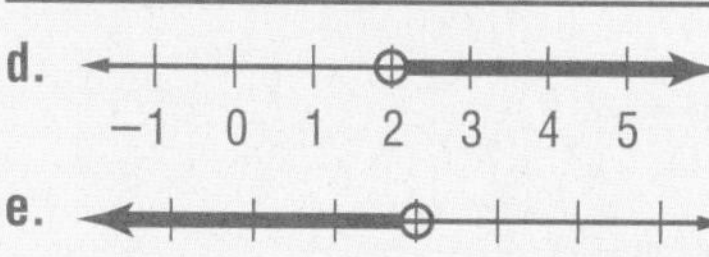

e.

f.

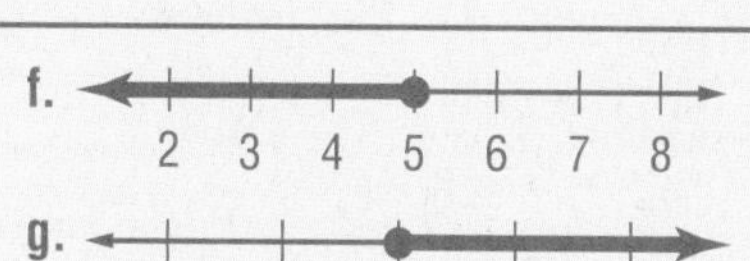

g.

Practice/Apply

FOLDABLES™ Follow-Up Remind students to record main ideas, definitions of vocabulary words, and other notes under the "Inequalities" tab of their Foldables as they progress through the lesson. Encourage students to recall what they have learned about inequalities and self-check their responses by reviewing their notes under the tab.

NUMBER SENSE
For Exercise 2, students may want to use a number line to visualize the inequality.

About the Exercises...

Guided Practice Key

Exercises	Examples
3	1, 2
4	3, 4
5–7	5, 6
8–11	7, 8

Assignment Guide

Basic: 13–31 odd, 39–43 odd, 44–55

Average: 13–43 odd, 44–55

Enriched: 12–42 even, 44–51 (Optional: 52–55)

Alert! Exercise 43 requires the use of the Internet or another source for research.

Students practice the same concepts in Exercises 12–37 if they are assigned odd or even problems.

Skill and Concept Check

1. **OPEN ENDED** Write an inequality using $\leq$ or $\geq$. Then give a situation that can be represented by the inequality. **Sample answer: $n \geq 9$; you will earn at least \$9.**
2. **NUMBER SENSE** Integers that are greater than or equal to zero are classified as what types of numbers? Represent this classification of numbers using an inequality. **whole numbers; $x \geq 0$**

GUIDED PRACTICE

Write an inequality for each sentence.

3. **RESTAURANTS** Children under the age of 6 eat free. **$a < 6$**
4. **TESTING** You are allowed a maximum of 45 minutes to complete one section of a standardized test. **$m \leq 45$**

For the given value, state whether each inequality is *true* or *false*.

5. $x - 11 < 9, x = 20$ **false**
6. $42 \geq 6a, a = 8$ **false**
7. $\frac{n}{3} + 1 \leq 6; n = 15$ **true**

Graph each inequality on a number line. **8–11. See margin.**

8. $n > 4$
9. $p \leq 2$
10. $x \geq 0$
11. $a < 7$

★ **indicates increased difficulty**

Practice and Applications

HOMEWORK HELP

For Exercises	See Examples
12–17	1–4
18–23	5, 6
24–33	7, 8

Extra Practice See pages 641, 657.

Write an inequality for each sentence. **12. $a < 13$ 13. $s > 100$**

12. **MOVIES** Children under 13 are not permitted without an adult.
13. **SHOPPING** You must spend more than \$100 to receive a discount.
14. **ELEVATORS** An elevator's maximum load is 3,400 pounds. **$w \leq 3,400$**
15. **FITNESS** You must run at least 4 laps around the track. **$\ell \geq 4$**
16. **GRADES** A grade of no less than 70 is considered passing. **$g \geq 70$**
17. **MONEY** The cost can be no more than \$25. **$c \leq 25$**

For the given value, state whether each inequality is *true* or *false*.

18. $12 + a < 20, a = 9$ **false**
19. $15 - k > 6, k = 8$ **true**
20. $-3y < 21; y = 8$ **true**
21. $32 \leq 2x, x = 16$ **true**
22. $\frac{n}{4} \geq 5, n = 12$ **false**
23. $\frac{-18}{x} > 9, x = -2$ **false**

Graph each inequality on a number line. **24–33. See margin.**

24. $x > 6$
25. $a > 0$
26. $y < 8$
27. $h < 2$
28. $w \leq 3$
29. $p \geq 7$
30. $n \geq 1$
31. $d \leq 4$
★32. $-5 > b$
★33. $-3 \leq y$

Write an inequality for each sentence.

★34. A number increased by 5 is at most 15. **$n + 5 \leq 15$**
★35. Eight times a number is no less than 24. **$8n \geq 24$**
★36. Sixteen is more than the quotient of number and 2. **$16 > \frac{n}{2}$**
★37. Four less than a number is less than 12. **$n - 4 < 12$**

Answers

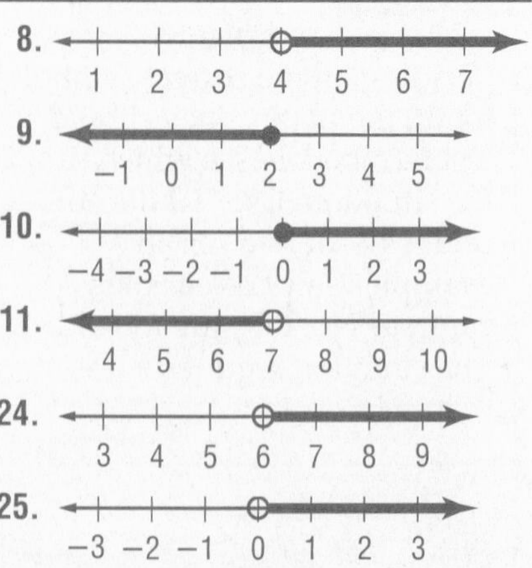

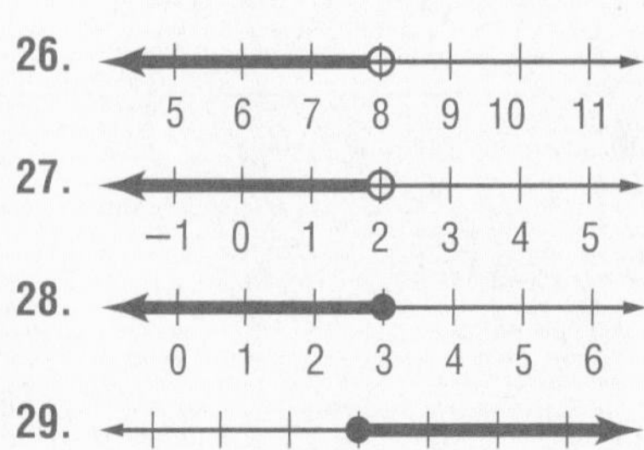

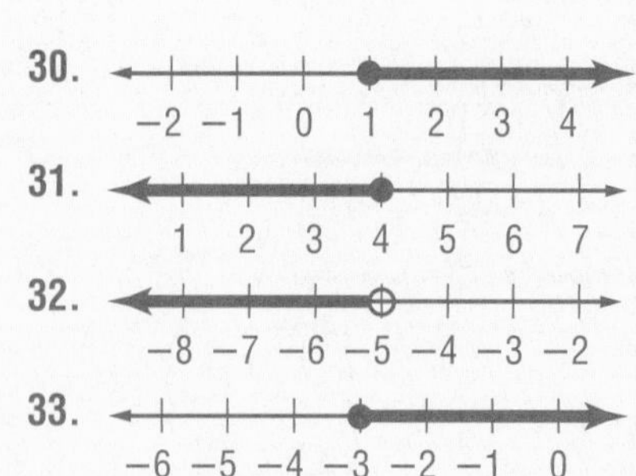

TELEVISION **For Exercises 38 and 39, use the information in the graphic.**

38. Rashid decides that he spends at least 100 more hours than the average time spent by kids watching television each year. Write an inequality for Rashid's TV viewing time. **$t - 1{,}023 \geq 100$ or $t \geq 1{,}123$**

39. Gabriela determines that she spends at most the same amount of time watching TV each year as the average amount of time kids spend attending school. Write an inequality to represent Gabriela's TV viewing time. **$t \leq 900$**

USA TODAY Snapshots®

TV commands kids' time

Average amount of time kids spend annually:

Watching TV	In school
1,023 hours	900 hours

Source: TV-Turnoff Network

By Cindy Hall and Robert W. Ahrens, USA TODAY

EQUIVALENT INEQUALITIES **The inequality $3 < x$ is equivalent to $x > 3$. Write an equivalent inequality for each of the following.**

40. $14 \leq a$ **$a \geq 14$**
41. $-2 > n$ **$n < -2$**
42. $-5 \geq y$ **$y \leq -5$**

43. **RESEARCH** Use the Internet or another resource to find who first used the symbols $<$ for *less than* and $>$ for *greater than*. **See margin.**

44. **CRITICAL THINKING** Determine whether the following statement is *sometimes*, *always*, or *never* true. Explain your reasoning. *If x is a real number, then $x \geq x$.* **Always; x is always equal to x.**

Spiral Review with Standardized Test Practice

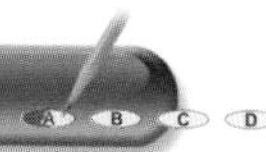

45. **MULTIPLE CHOICE** What inequality is graphed below? **D**

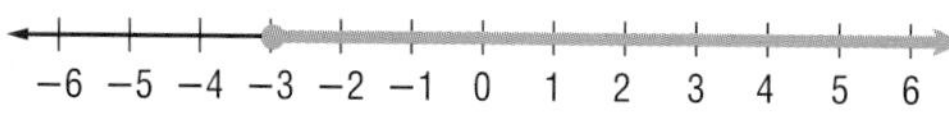

Ⓐ $x < -3$ Ⓑ $x \leq -3$ Ⓒ $x > -3$ Ⓓ $x \geq -3$

46. **MULTIPLE CHOICE** Which inequality represents *a number is at least 24*? **F**

Ⓕ $n \geq 24$ Ⓖ $n < 24$ Ⓗ $n \leq 24$ Ⓘ $n > 24$

Solve each equation. Check your solution. (Lesson 10-4)

47. $2x + 16 = 6x$ **4**
48. $5y - 1 = 3y + 11$ **6**
49. $4a - 9 = 7a + 6$ **−5**
50. $n + 0.8 = -n + 1$ **0.1**

51. **WEATHER** The temperature is −3°F. It is expected to rise 6° each hour for the next several hours. Write and solve an equation to find in how many hours the temperature will be 21°F. (Lesson 10-3) **$-3 + 6h = 21$; 4 h**

GETTING READY FOR THE NEXT LESSON

PREREQUISITE SKILL **Solve each equation.** (Lesson 1-8)

52. $y + 15 = 31$ **16**
53. $n + 4 = -7$ **−11**
54. $a - 8 = 25$ **33**
55. $-12 = x - 3$ **−9**

Math Online msmath3.net/self_check_quiz

4 Assess

Higher-Level Thinking

A teacher suggests studying between 30 and 45 minutes for a test. Write this as one inequality, then graph it on a number line. **$30 < m < 45$**

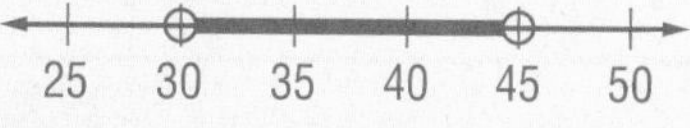

Answer

43. **Sample answer: These symbols were introduced by the editor of Thomas Harriot's work *Artis Analyticae Praxis ad Aequationes Algebraicas Resolvendas*.**

Study Guide and Intervention, p. 583

NAME ________ DATE ________ PERIOD ____

10-5 Study Guide and Intervention

Inequalities

A mathematical sentence that contains $<$ or $>$ is called an **inequality**. When used to compare a variable and a number, inequalities can describe a range of values. Some inequalities use the symbols $\leq$ or $\geq$. The symbol $\leq$ is read *is less than or equal to*. The symbol $\geq$ is read *is greater than or equal to*.

EXAMPLES **Write an inequality for each sentence.**

1. **SHOPPING** Shipping is free on orders of more than $100.
Let c = the cost of the order.
$c > 100$

2. **RESTAURANTS** The restaurant seats a maximum of 150 guests.
Let g = the number of guests.
$g \leq 150$

Inequalities can be graphed on a number line. An open or closed circle is used to show where the solutions start, and an arrow pointing either left or right indicates the rest of the solutions. An open circle is used with inequalities having $>$ or $<$. A closed circle is used with inequalities having $\leq$ or $\geq$.

EXAMPLES **Graph each inequality on a number line.**

3. $d \leq -2$
Place a closed circle at −2. Then draw a line and an arrow to the left.
−4 −3 −2 −1 0 1 2 3 4

4. $d > -2$
Place an open circle at −2. Then draw a line and an arrow to the right.
−4 −3 −2 −1 0 1 2 3 4

EXERCISES

Write an inequality for each sentence.

1. **FOOD** Our delivery time is guaranteed to be less than 30 minutes. $t < 30$
2. **DRIVING** Your speed must be at least 45 miles per hour on the highway. $s \geq 45$

Graph each inequality on a number line.

3. $r > 7$
0 1 2 3 4 5 6 7 8

4. $x \leq -1$
−4 −3 −2 −1 0 1 2 3 4

Practice: Skills, p. 584

NAME ________ DATE ________ PERIOD ____

10-5 Practice: Skills

Inequalities

Write an inequality for each sentence.

1. **SPORTS** You need to score at least 30 points to take the lead. $s \geq 30$
2. **SEASONS** There are less than 12 hours of daylight each day in winter. $h < 12$
3. **TRAVEL** The bus seats at most 60 people. $p \leq 60$
4. **MONEY** The coupon is good for any item that costs less than $10. $c < 10$
5. **TESTS** A score of at least 92 on the test is considered an "A." $s \geq 92$
6. **HEALTH** The baby weighed more than 7 pounds at birth. $w > 7$
7. **DRIVING** Victor drives less than 12,000 miles per year. $m < 12{,}000$
8. **TRAVEL** Your waiting time will be 18 minutes or less. $t \leq 18$
9. **SCHOOL TRIPS** At least 15 students must sign up for the school trip. $s \geq 15$

For the given value, state whether each inequality is *true* or *false*.

10. $y + 2 < 8, y = 3$ true
11. $12 > u - 1, u = 14$ false
12. $p + 5 \geq -6, p = 1$ true
13. $-6 < a - 3, a = -1$ true
14. $4s \leq 15, s = 4$ false
15. $-5 > 1 - d, d = -9$ false
16. $-2 - g \geq -7, g = 5$ true
17. $\frac{k}{3} > 4, k = 12$ false
18. $4 < \frac{-10}{z}, z = -2$ true
19. $\frac{12}{m} \geq 3, m = 4$ true

Graph each inequality on a number line.

20. $v \geq 3$
−4 −3 −2 −1 0 1 2 3 4

21. $b > 5$
0 1 2 3 4 5 6 7 8

22. $n \leq -3$
−4 −3 −2 −1 0 1 2 3 4

23. $w < 4$
0 1 2 3 4 5 6 7 8

24. $r > -1$
−4 −3 −2 −1 0 1 2 3 4

25. $h \geq -7$
−10 −9 −8 −7 −6 −5 −4 −3 −2

Practice: Word Problems, p. 585

NAME ________ DATE ________ PERIOD ____

10-5 Practice: Word Problems

Inequalities

1. **SPORTS** Colin's time in the 400-meter run was 62 seconds. Alvin was at least 4 seconds ahead of Colin. Write an inequality for Alvin's time in the 400-meter run. $t + 4 \leq 62$ or $t \leq 58$

2. **RESTAURANTS** Before Valerie and her two friends left Mel's Diner, there were more than 25 people seated. Write an inequality for the number of people seated at the diner after Valerie and her two friends left. $p + 3 \geq 25$ or $p \geq 22$

3. **FARM LIFE** Reggie has 4 dogs on his farm. One of his dogs, Lark, is about to have puppies. Write an inequality for the number of dogs Reggie will have if Lark has fewer than 4 puppies. $d - 4 < 4$ or $d < 8$

4. **MONEY** Alicia had $25 when she arrived at the fair. She bought some ride tickets and she spent $6.50 on games. Write an inequality for the amount of money Alicia had when she left the fair. $m + 6.50 < 25$ or $m < 18.50$

5. **HEALTH** Marcus was in the waiting room for 26 minutes before being called. He waited at least another 5 minutes before the doctor entered the examination room. Write an inequality for the amount of time Marcus waited before seeing the doctor. $t - 26 \geq 5$ or $t \geq 31$

6. **POPULATION** The population of Ellisville was already less than 250 before Bob and Ann Tyler and their three children moved away. Write an inequality for the population of Ellisville after the Tyler family left. $p + 5 < 250$ or $p < 245$

7. **HOMEWORK** Nova spent one hour on Thursday, one hour on Saturday, and more than 2 hours on Sunday working on her writing assignment. Write an inequality for the amount of time she worked on the assignment. $t - 2 > 2$ or $t > 4$

8. **YARD WORK** Harold was able to mow more than $\frac{3}{4}$ of his lawn on Saturday night. Write an inequality for the fraction of the lawn that Harold will mow on Sunday. $m + \frac{3}{4} < 1$ or $m < \frac{1}{4}$

10-6 Lesson Notes

Lesson Resources

Chapter 10 Resource Masters

FAST FILE

- Study Guide and Intervention, p. 588
- Practice: Skills, p. 589
- Practice: Word Problems, p. 590
- Reading to Learn Mathematics, p. 591
- Enrichment, p. 592

Parent and Student Study Guide Online Worksheets, 10-6

Noteables™: Interactive Study Notebook with Foldables™, 10-6

1 Focus

5-Minute Check 10-6

Use as a quiz or review of Lesson 10-5. (Also available as a transparency)

Bellringer

Problem Solving Show a double pan scale with 8 weights on one side and 3 on the other. Ask students to describe which side weighs more. Have them predict which side will weigh more after 2 weights are removed from each side. Repeat using different weight combinations.

Reading to Learn Mathematics, p. 591 ELL

NAME ______________ DATE ________ PERIOD ____

10-6 Reading to Learn Mathematics

Solving Inequalities by Adding or Subtracting

Pre-Activity ***Read the introduction at the top of page 496 in your textbook. Write your answers below.***

1. Add 10 to each side of the inequality $13 < 16$. Write the resulting inequality and decide whether it is *true* or *false*. $23 < 26$; true

2. Was Victoria's dad younger or older than Victoria's mom 13 years ago? Explain your reasoning using an inequality. older; $43 - 13 > 41 - 13$

Reading the Lesson

3. How are solving an inequality and solving an equation similar? Sample answer: Properties such as the Addition and Subtraction Properties are used to solve both inequalities and equations.

10-6 Solving Inequalities by Adding or Subtracting

What You'll LEARN

Solve inequalities by using the Addition or Subtraction Properties of Inequality.

WHEN am I ever going to use this?

FAMILY The table shows the age of each member of Victoria's family. Notice that Victoria is younger than her brother, since $13 < 16$. Will this be true 10 years from now?

Family Member	Age
Dad	43
Mom	41
Brother	16
Victoria	13

1. Add 10 to each side of the inequality $13 < 16$. Write the resulting inequality and decide whether it is *true* or *false*. **$23 < 26$; true**
2. Was Victoria's dad younger or older than Victoria's mom 13 years ago? Explain your reasoning using an inequality.

2. older; $43 - 13 > 41 - 13$

The examples above demonstrate properties of inequality.

Noteables™ **Key Concept: Properties of Inequality**

Words When you add or subtract the same number from each side of an inequality, the inequality remains true.

Symbols For all numbers a, b, and c,

1. if $a > b$, then $a + c > b + c$ and $a - c > b - c$.
2. if $a < b$, then $a + c < b + c$ and $a - c < b - c$.

Examples

$$2 > -3 \qquad\qquad 3 < 8$$
$$2 + 5 > -3 + 5 \qquad\qquad 3 - 4 < 8 - 4$$
$$7 > 2 \checkmark \qquad\qquad -1 < 4 \checkmark$$

These properties are also true for $a \geq b$ and $a \leq b$.

Solving an inequality means finding values for the variable that make the inequality true.

EXAMPLE **Solve an Inequality Using Addition**

Solve $n - 8 < 15$. Check your solution.

$n - 8 < 15$	Write the inequality.
$n - 8 + 8 < 15 + 8$	Add 8 to each side.
$n < 23$	Simplify.
Check $n - 8 < 15$	Write the inequality.
$22 - 8 \stackrel{?}{<} 15$	Replace n with a number less than 23, such as 22.
$14 < 15 \checkmark$	This statement is true.

Any number less than 23 will make the statement true, so the solution is $n < 23$.

TEACHING TIP

You might also suggest to students that they check the solution to Example 1 by replacing n with 23 and a number *greater* than 23. Both values should result in a false statement.

DAILY INTERVENTION

Unlocking Misconceptions

Solving Inequalities by Adding or Subtracting Some students may try to reverse the inequality sign when they add or subtract. Emphasize to them that adding or subtracting on each side does not change the equation.

STUDY TIP

Equivalent Inequalities If -11 is greater than or equal to a, then a is less than or equal to -11.

EXAMPLE Solve an Inequality Using Subtraction

2 **Solve $-4 \geq a + 7$. Check your solution.**

$-4 \geq a + 7$	Write the inequality.
$-4 - 7 \geq a + 7 - 7$	Subtract 7 from each side.
$-11 \geq a$ or $a \leq -11$	Simplify.

Check Replace a in the original inequality with -11 and then with a number less than -11.

The solution is $a \leq -11$.

TEACHING TIP

In Example 2, point out to students that by checking with -11, they are checking the equation $-4 = a + 7$. By checking with a number less than -11, they are checking the inequality, $-4 > a + 7$.

EXAMPLE Graph the Solutions of an Inequality

3 **Solve $y - \frac{1}{3} \leq 5$. Then graph the solution on a number line.**

$y - \frac{1}{3} \leq 5$

$y - \frac{1}{3} + \frac{1}{3} \leq 5 + \frac{1}{3}$

$y \leq 5\frac{1}{3}$

The solution is $y \leq 5\frac{1}{3}$.

Graph the solution.

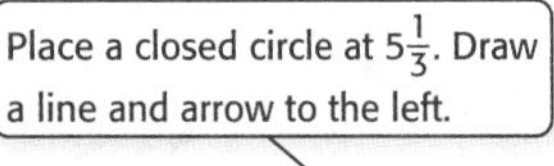

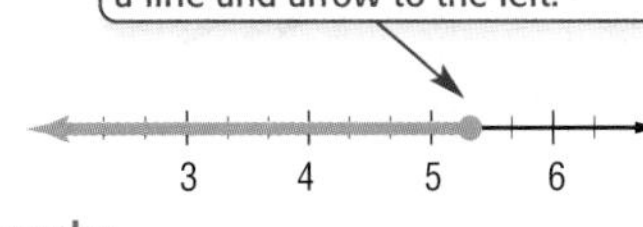

Your Turn **Solve each inequality and check your solution. Then graph the solution on a number line.** a–c. See margin for graphs.

a. $t + 3 > 12$ $t > 9$ b. $2 > p - 5$ $p < 7$ c. $n + \frac{1}{2} \geq 4$ $n \geq 3\frac{1}{2}$

REAL-LIFE MATH

ANIMALS The South American manatee can weigh up to 1,300 pounds.

Source: Kids Discover

EXAMPLE Use an Inequality to Solve a Problem

4 **ANIMALS** **Suppose a South American manatee weighs 968 pounds. Use the information at the left to determine how much more weight this manatee might gain.**

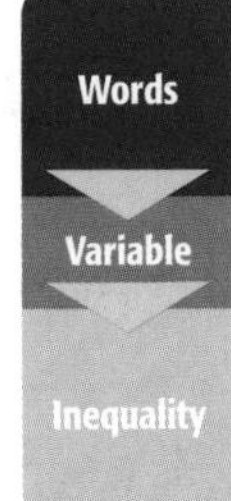

Words: The phrase *up to* means *less than or equal to*. So, the manatee's current weight plus any weight gained must be less than or equal to 1,300 pounds.

Variable: Let w = weight gained by the manatee.

Inequality:

manatee's current weight	plus	weight gained	must be less than or equal to	1,300 pounds
968	+	w	$\leq$	1,300

$968 + w \leq 1{,}300$	Write the inequality.
$968 - 968 + w \leq 1{,}300 - 968$	Subtract 968 from each side.
$w \leq 332$	Simplify.

The manatee might gain up to 332 more pounds.

Math Online msmath3.net/extra_examples

2 Teach

In-Class Examples

1 Solve $n - 4 > 6$. Check your solution. $n > 10$

2 Solve $x + 8 \leq -7$. Check your solution. $x \leq -15$

3 Solve $s - \frac{3}{4} < 2$. Then graph the solution on a number line.

$s < 2\frac{3}{4}$

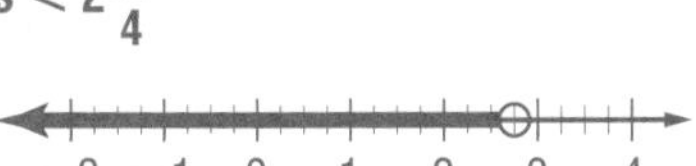

4 **TOWING CAPACITY** A pickup truck is towing a trailer that weighs 3,525 pounds. The maximum towing capacity of the truck is 4,700 pounds. Determine how much more weight can be added to the trailer and still be towed by the truck. Up to 1,175 more pounds can be added to the trailer.

Answers (Your Turn)

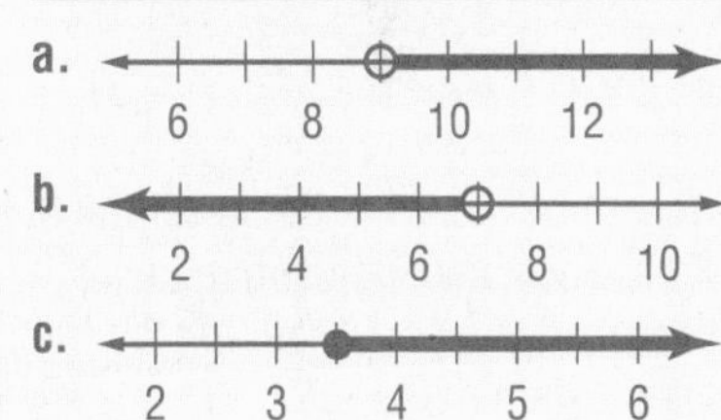

3 Practice/Apply

FOLDABLES™ Follow-Up Remind students to record main ideas, definitions of vocabulary words, and other notes under the "Inequalities" tab of their Foldables as they learn to solve inequalities by adding or subtracting. Encourage students to recall what they have learned about inequalities and self-check their responses by reviewing their notes under the tab.

About the Exercises...

Guided Practice Key

Exercises	Examples
3–5	2
6–8	1
9–11	3

Assignment Guide

Basic: 13–23 odd, 31–41 odd, 47, 49, 51–63

Average: 13–49 odd, 51–63

Enriched: 12–50 even, 51–59 (Optional: 60–63)

Answers

1. The same quantity can be subtracted from each side of the equation or inequality without changing the truth of the statement.

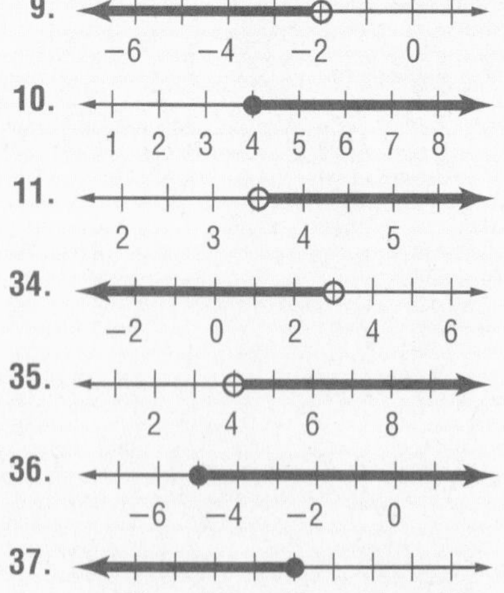

Students practice the same concepts in Exercises 12–47 if they are assigned odd or even problems.

Skill and Concept Check

1. Writing Math Explain how solving an inequality by using subtraction is similar to solving an equation by using subtraction. **See margin.**
2. **OPEN ENDED** Write an inequality whose solution is $n > 5$ that can be solved by using the Addition or Subtraction Property of Equality. **Sample answer: $n + 8 > 13$**

GUIDED PRACTICE

Solve each inequality. Check your solution.

3. $b + 5 > 9$ **$b > 4$**
4. $12 + n \leq 4$ **$n \leq -8$**
5. $-6 \leq 7 + g$ **$g \geq -13$**
6. $x - 4 < 10$ **$x < 14$**
7. $k - 9 \geq -2$ **$k \geq 7$**
8. $8 > y - 8$ **$y < 16$**

Solve each inequality and check your solution. Then graph the solution on a number line. **9–11. See margin for graphs.**

9. $c + 9 < 7$ **$c < -2$**
10. $m - 1 \geq 3$ **$m \geq 4$**
11. $a - \frac{1}{2} > 3$ **$a > 3\frac{1}{2}$**

★ indicates increased difficulty

Practice and Applications

HOMEWORK HELP	
For Exercises	See Examples
12–33	1, 2
34–45	3
46–49	4

Extra Practice See pages 642, 657.

Solve each inequality. Check your solution.

12. $a + 7 < 21$ **$a < 14$**
13. $5 + x \leq 18$ **$x \leq 13$**
14. $10 + n \geq -2$
15. $-4 < k + 6$ **$k > -10$**
16. $3 < y + 8$ **$y > -5$**
17. $c + 10 < 9$ **$c < -1$**
18. $r - 9 \leq 7$ **$r \leq 16$**
19. $g - 4 \geq 13$ **$g \geq 17$**
20. $-2 < b - 6$ **$b > 4$**
21. $s - 12 \leq -5$ **$s \leq 7$**
22. $t - 3 < -9$ **$t < -6$**
23. $-17 \leq w - 15$ **$w \geq -2$**
24. ★ $2 + m \geq 3.5$
25. ★ $q + 0.8 \leq -0.5$
26. ★ $v - 6 > 2.7$ **$v > 8.7$**
27. ★ $p - 4.8 > -6$
28. ★ $d - \frac{2}{3} \leq \frac{1}{2}$ **$d \leq 1\frac{1}{6}$**
29. ★ $5 > f + 1\frac{1}{4}$ **$f < 3\frac{3}{4}$**

14. $n \geq -12$ 24. $m \geq 1.5$ 25. $q \leq -1.3$ 27. $p > -1.2$

Write an inequality and solve each problem.

30. Five more than a number is at least 13. **$n + 5 \geq 13$; $n \geq 8$**
31. The difference between a number and 11 is less than 8. **$n - 11 < 8$; $n < 19$**
32. Nine less than a number is more than 4. **$n - 9 > 4$; $n > 13$**
33. The sum of a number and 17 is no more than 6. **$n + 17 \leq 6$; $n \leq -11$**

Solve each inequality and check your solution. Then graph the solution on a number line. **34–45. See margin for graphs.**

34. $c + 1 < 4$ **$c < 3$**
35. $n + 8 > 12$ **$n > 4$**
36. $2 \leq 7 + p$ **$p \geq -5$**
37. $-10 \geq x + 6$ **$x \leq -16$**
38. $a - 3 \leq 5$ **$a \leq 8$**
39. $-11 > g - 4$ **$g < -7$**
40. $-12 < k - 9$ **$k > -3$**
41. $h - 6 \geq -4$ **$h \geq 2$**
42. ★ $y - 1.5 < 2$ **$y < 3.5$**
43. ★ $b - 0.75 \leq 7$ **$b \leq 7.75$**
44. ★ $t + \frac{2}{3} > 8$ **$t > 7\frac{1}{3}$**
45. ★ $w + 5\frac{1}{3} < 10$ **$w < 4\frac{2}{3}$**

46. **INSECTS** There are more than 250,000 species of beetles. A science museum has a collection representing 320 of these species. Write and solve an inequality to find how many beetle species are not represented. **$320 + s > 250{,}000$; $s > 249{,}680$; more than 249,680 species**

38.
0 2 4 6 8 10

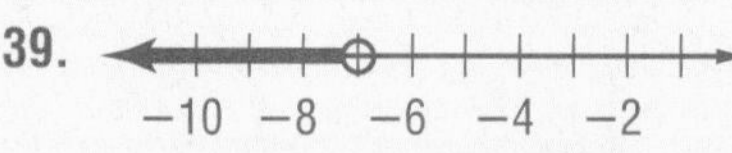

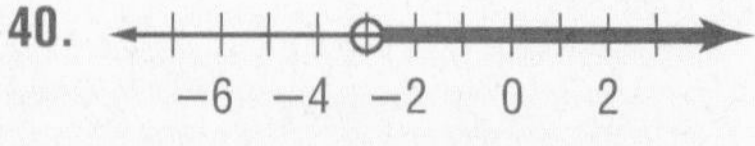

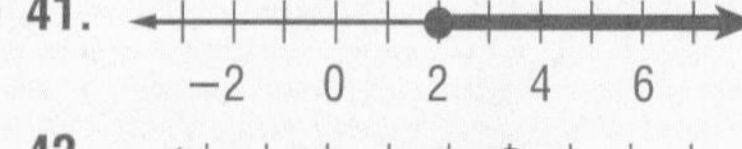

42.
1 2 3 4 5

43.
5 6 7 8 9

44.
6 7 8 9

45.
3 4 5 6

47. **$99.2 + t > 101$; $t > 1.8$; more than 1.8°F**

HEALTH For Exercises 47 and 48, use the diagram at the right.

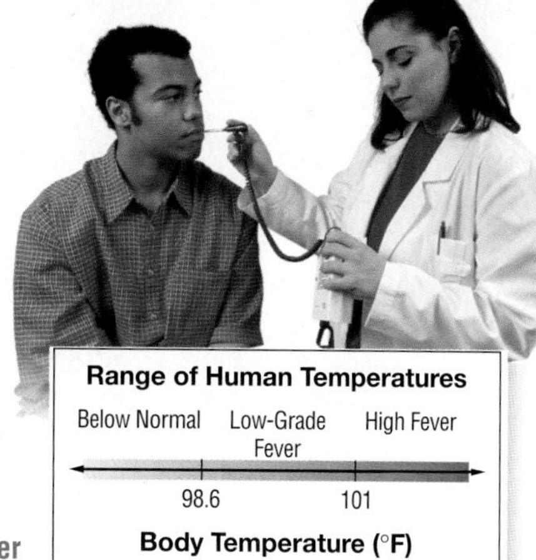

47. An adult is considered to have a high fever if his or her temperature goes above 101°F. Suppose Mr. Herr has a temperature of 99.2°F. Write and solve an inequality to find how much his temperature must increase before he is considered to have a high fever. **See margin.**

★ 48. *Hypothermia* occurs when a person's body temperature falls below 95°F. Write and solve an inequality that describes how much lower the body temperature of a person with hypothermia will be than a person with a normal body temperature of 98.6°F. **$98.6 - t < 95$; $t > 3.6$; more than 3.6° lower**

49. **GEOMETRY** The base of the rectangle shown is greater than its height. Write and solve an inequality to find the possible values of x. **$15 > x - 3$; $x < 18$; x is less than 18 cm**

50. **WRITE A PROBLEM** Write about a real-life situation that can be solved by using an addition inequality. Then write an inequality and solve the problem. **See margin.**

51. **CRITICAL THINKING** Is it *sometimes*, *always*, or *never* true that $x > x + 1$? Explain your reasoning. **Never; subtracting x from each side gives $0 > 1$, which is never true.**

Spiral Review with Standardized Test Practice

52. **MULTIPLE CHOICE** Adriana has \$30 to spend on food and rides at a carnival. She has already spent \$12 on food. Which inequality represents how much money she can spend on rides? **B**

Ⓐ $m < 18$ Ⓑ $m \leq 18$ Ⓒ $m > 18$ Ⓓ $m \geq 18$

53. **MULTIPLE CHOICE** If $x - 6 > 17$, then x could be which of the following values? **I**

Ⓕ 11 Ⓖ 22 Ⓗ 23 Ⓘ 24

For the given value, state whether each inequality is *true* or *false*. (Lesson 10-5)

54. $18 - n > 4$, $n = 11$ **true**
55. $13 + x < 21$, $x = 8$ **false**
56. $34 \leq 5p$, $p = 7$ **true**
57. $\frac{a}{-4} \geq 3$, $a = -12$ **true**

58. **CAR RENTAL** Suppose you can rent a car for either \$35 a day plus \$0.40 a mile or for \$20 a day plus \$0.55 per mile. Write and solve an equation to find the number of miles that results in the same cost for one day. (Lesson 10-4) **$35 + 0.40x = 20 + 0.55x$; 100 mi**

59. If $\angle F$ and $\angle G$ are supplementary and $m\angle G = 47°$, find $m\angle F$. (Lesson 6-1) **133°**

GETTING READY FOR THE NEXT LESSON

PREREQUISITE SKILL Solve each equation. (Lesson 1-9)

60. $3y = -15$ **−5**
61. $-18 = -2a$ **9**
62. $\frac{w}{4} = 12$ **48**
63. $20 = \frac{x}{-5}$ **−100**

msmath3.net/self_check_quiz

4 Assess

Higher-Level Thinking

Is it *always*, *never*, or *sometimes* true that $x + 2 < 8 + x - 1$? Explain your answer. **It is always true. Simplify the right side to $x + 7$. Subtract x from both sides. This leaves $2 < 7$, which is always true.**

Answer

50. **Sample answer: Tom is saving money for a class trip. His goal is to save at least \$150, but so far he has only saved \$81.50. How much more does Tom need to save to reach his goal? $81.50 + x \geq 150$; $x \geq 68.50$; at least \$68.50**

Study Guide and Intervention, p. 588

NAME ____________ DATE ________ PERIOD ____

10-6 Study Guide and Intervention

Solving Inequalities by Adding or Subtracting

Solving an inequality means finding values for the variable that make the inequality true. You can use the Addition and Subtraction Properties of Inequality to help solve an inequality. When you add or subtract the same number from each side of an inequality, the inequality remains true.

EXAMPLES **Solve each inequality. Check your solution. Then graph the solution on a number line.**

1. $9 < r + 5$ Write the inequality.
$9 - 5 < r + 5 - 5$ Subtract 5 from each side.
$4 < r$ or $r > 4$ Simplify.

Check Solutions to the inequality should be greater than 4. Check this result by replacing r in the original inequality with two different numbers greater than 4. Both replacements should give true statements.

To graph the solution, place an open circle at 4 and draw a line and arrow to the right.

0 1 2 3 4 5 6 7 8

2. $x - 7 \geq 24$ Write the inequality.
$x - 7 + 7 \geq -4 + 7$ Add 7 to each side.
$x \geq 3$ Simplify.

Check Replace x in the original inequality with 3 and then with a number greater than 3. The solution is $x \geq 3$.

To graph the solution, place a closed circle at 3 and draw a line and arrow to the right.

0 1 2 3 4 5 6 7 8

EXERCISES

Solve each inequality. Check your solution.

1. $t - 4 > 2$ $t > 6$
2. $b + 5 \leq 9$ $b \leq 4$
3. $8 < r - 7$ $r > 15$
4. $6 < p - 6$ $p > 12$
5. $2 > a + 7$ $a < -5$
6. $4 + m \geq -6$ $m \geq -10$

Solve each inequality and check your solution. Then graph the solution on a number line.

7. $s + 8 < 10$ $s < 2$
0 1 2 3 4 5 6 7 8
8. $-11 \leq d - 3$ $d \geq -8$
−10 −9 −8 −7 −6 −5 −4 −3 −2

Practice: Skills, p. 589

NAME ____________ DATE ________ PERIOD ____

10-6 Practice: Skills

Solving Inequalities by Adding or Subtracting

Solve each inequality. Check your solution.

1. $r + 5 < 6$ $r < 1$
2. $e - 3 > 2$ $e > 5$
3. $-8 \geq k - 5$ $k \leq -3$
4. $y + 6 > 5$ $y > -1$
5. $n - 4 \geq 6$ $n \geq 10$
6. $-4 > g - 10$ $g < 6$
7. $-1 \leq m + 8$ $m \geq -9$
8. $t + 1 \leq 6$ $t \leq 5$
9. $-17 > u - 2$ $u < -15$
10. $5 + x \leq -7$ $x \leq -12$
11. $10 > p + 9$ $p < 1$
12. $-4 + z < -12$ $z < -8$
13. $5 \leq q + 8$ $q \geq -3$
14. $k - 6 > -5$ $k > 1$
15. $s + 7 \leq -13$ $s \leq -20$

Write an inequality and solve each problem.

16. Two more than a number is less than eleven. $n + 2 < 11$; $n < 9$
17. Five less than a number is at least −2. $n - 5 \geq -2$; $n \geq 3$
18. The difference between a number and 6 is no more than 5. $n - 6 \leq 5$; $n \leq 11$
19. The sum of a number and 7 is more than 1. $n + 7 > 1$; $n > -6$
20. The difference between a number and ten is greater than 9. $n - 10 > 9$; $n > 19$
21. Four less than a number is less than 11. $n - 4 < 11$; $n < 15$

Solve each inequality and check your solution. Then graph the solution on a number line.

22. $9 < p - 6$ $p > 15$
11 12 13 14 15 16 17 18 19
23. $w + 4 \geq -3$ $w \geq -7$
−10 −9 −8 −7 −6 −5 −4 −3 −2
24. $1 > z + 5$ $z < -4$
−6 −5 −4 −3 −2 −1 0 1 2
25. $-6 \leq s - 7$ $s \geq 1$
−4 −3 −2 −1 0 1 2 3 4
26. $b - 3 \leq 7$ $b \leq 10$
6 7 8 9 10 11 12 13 14
27. $v + 9 > 23$ $v > 14$
10 11 12 13 14 15 16 17 18
28. $4 + v \geq 5$ $v \geq 1$
−4 −3 −2 −1 0 1 2 3 4
29. $m + 7 < 11$ $m < 4$
−4 −3 −2 −1 0 1 2 3 4

Practice: Word Problems, p. 590

NAME ____________ DATE ________ PERIOD ____

10-6 Practice: Word Problems

Solving Inequalities by Adding or Subtracting

1. **DRIVING** Michael is driving from Lakeview to Dodge City, a distance of more than 250 miles. After driving 60 miles, Michael stops for gas. Write and solve an inequality to find how much farther Michael has to drive to reach Dodge City. $d + 60 > 250$; $d > 190$; more than 190 mi

2. **ENTERTAINMENT** David and Marsha are going to dinner and a movie this evening. David wants to have at least \$70 cash in his wallet. He currently has \$10. Write and solve an inequality to find how much cash David should withdraw from the bank. $c + 10 \geq 70$; $c \geq 60$; at least \$60

3. **CLUBS** The charter for the Spartan Club limits the membership to 85. Currently the club has 47 members. Write and solve an inequality to find how many more members can be recruited. $m + 47 \leq 85$; $m \leq 38$; no more than 38 new members

4. **GROWTH** Akira hopes that he will someday be more than 71 inches tall. He is currently 63 inches tall. Write and solve an inequality to find how much more Akira must grow to fulfill his wish. $h + 63 > 71$; $h > 8$; more than 8 inches

5. **MUSIC** Jamie is preparing to burn a music CD. The CD holds at most 70 minutes of music. Jamie has 52 minutes of music already selected. Write and solve an inequality to find how many more minutes of music Jamie can select. $t + 52 \leq 70$; $t \leq 18$; no more than 18 minutes

6. **TELEVISION** Dario limits his TV watching to no more than 11 hours a week. This week, he has already watched 6 hours of TV. Write and solve an inequality to find how much more time Dario can spend watching TV this week. $t + 6 \leq 11$; $t \leq 5$; no more than 5 hours

7. **CARS** At the gas station, Elena bought a quart of oil for \$1.50, and she filled her car with gas. Her total was less than \$20. Write and solve an inequality to find how much she spent on gas. $g + 1.50 < 20$; $g < 18.50$; less than \$18.50

8. **HOMEWORK** Peter must write an essay with more than 500 words for his English class. So far, he has written 245 words. Write and solve an inequality to find how many more words Peter needs to write for his essay. $w + 245 > 500$; $w > 255$; more than 255 words

10-7 Lesson Notes

Lesson Resources

Chapter 10 Resource Masters
- Study Guide and Intervention, p. 593
- Practice: Skills, p. 594
- Practice: Word Problems, p. 595
- Reading to Learn Mathematics, p. 596
- Enrichment, p. 597

Key Teaching Transparencies, 40
MathPASS Tutorial CD-ROM, 40
Parent and Student Study Guide Online Worksheets, 10-7
Noteables™: Interactive Study Notebook with Foldables™, 10-7

FAST FILE

Focus

5-Minute Check 10-7

Use as a quiz or review of Lesson 10-6. (Also available as a transparency)

Bellringer

Reading Mathematics Ask students to read the following problems and to indicate whether each statement is true or false.

$3 < 5$ **true**

$2(3) < 2(5)$ **true**

$-2(3) < -2(5)$ **false**

$-2(3) > -2(5)$ **true**

$-1 < 2$ **true**

$3(-1) < 3(2)$ **true**

$-3(-1) > -3(2)$ **true**

Reading to Learn Mathematics, p. 596 **ELL**

NAME ______ DATE ______ PERIOD ____

Reading to Learn Mathematics

Solving Inequalities by Multiplying or Dividing

Pre-Activity ***Read the introduction at the top of page 500 in your textbook. Write your answers below.***

1. Divide each side of the inequality $80 < 150$ by 2. Write the resulting inequality and decide whether it is *true* or *false*. $40 < 75$; true
2. Would the cost of three pairs of basketball shoes be greater or less than the cost of three pairs of running shoes all sold at the regular price? Explain your reasoning using an inequality. greater; $3(120) > 3(100)$

Reading the Lesson

What is the first step in solving each inequality? How is the inequality symbol affected by this first step? Explain.

3. $\frac{x}{3} > 2$ Multiply each side by 3; the direction of the inequality symbol stays the same because you are multiplying by a positive number.
Divide ea...

10-7 Solving Inequalities by Multiplying or Dividing

What You'll LEARN

Solve inequalities by using the Multiplication or Division Properties of Inequality.

WHEN am I ever going to use this?

SHOPPING The table shows the prices of the same brand name of shoes at a sports apparel store. Notice that walking shoes cost less than cross-training shoes, since $80 < 150$. Will this inequality be true if the store sells both pairs of shoes at half price?

Shoe Style	Regular Price ($)
athletic sandal	60
walking	80
running	100
basketball	120
cross training	150

1. Divide each side of the inequality $80 < 150$ by 2. Write the resulting inequality and decide whether it is *true* or *false*. **$40 < 75$; true**
2. Would the cost of three pairs of basketball shoes be greater or less than the cost of three pairs of running shoes all sold at the regular price? Explain your reasoning using an inequality. **2. greater; $3(120) > 3(100)$**

The examples above demonstrate additional properties of inequality.

Noteables™ **Key Concept: Properties of Inequality**

Words When you multiply or divide each side of an inequality by a positive number, the inequality remains true.

Symbols For all numbers a, b, and c, where $c > 0$,

1. if $a > b$, then $ac > bc$ and $\frac{a}{c} > \frac{b}{c}$.

2. if $a < b$, then $ac < bc$ and $\frac{a}{c} < \frac{b}{c}$.

Examples

$5 < 8$	$2 > -10$
$4(5) < 4(8)$	$\frac{2}{2} > \frac{-10}{2}$
$20 < 32$	$1 > -5$

These properties also hold true for $a \geq b$ and $a \leq b$.

EXAMPLE **Divide by a Positive Number**

Solve $7y > -42$. Check your solution.

$7y > -42$ Write the inequality.

$\frac{7y}{7} > \frac{-42}{7}$ Divide each side by 7.

$y > -6$ Simplify.

The solution is $y > -6$. You can check this solution by substituting numbers greater than -6 into the inequality.

DAILY INTERVENTION **Differentiated Instruction**

Logical Explain how to solve an inequality like $-3x > 6$ or $-2n + 1 < 5$ without multiplying or dividing by a negative number. Use this to explain why multiplying or dividing by a negative number reverses the direction of the inequality sign. **You can solve those inequalities by adding $3x$ or $2n$ to each side of the equation. This places the variable on the other side of the inequality sign, which effectively reverses the sign.**

EXAMPLE Multiply by a Positive Number

2 **Solve $\frac{1}{3}x \leq 8$ and check your solution. Then graph the solution on a number line.**

$\frac{1}{3}x \leq 8$ Write the inequality.

$3\left(\frac{1}{3}x\right) \leq 3(8)$ Multiply each side by 3.

$x \leq 24$ Simplify.

The solution is $x \leq 24$. You can check this solution by substituting 24 and a number less than 24 into the inequality.

Graph the solution, $x \leq 24$.

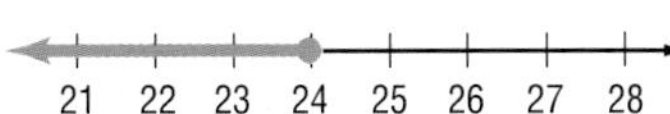

Your Turn **Solve each inequality and check your solution. Then graph the solution on a number line.**

a. $3a \geq 45$ $a \geq 15$ b. $\frac{n}{4} < -16$ $n < -64$ c. $81 \leq 9p$ $p \geq 9$

a–c. See margin for graphs.

What happens when each side of an inequality is multiplied or divided by a negative number?

Graph 3 and 5 on a number line.

−5 −4 −3 −2 −1 0 1 2 3 4 5

Since 3 is to the left of 5, $3 < 5$.

Multiply each number by −1.

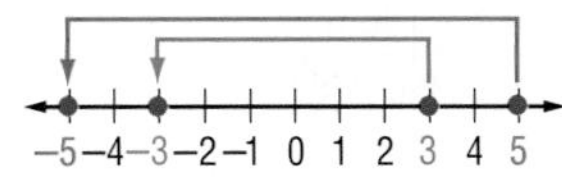

Since −3 is to the right of −5, $-3 > -5$.

TEACHING TIP

You may wish to present the following examples on a number line in the same manner as presented here.
$3 > 2 \rightarrow -2(3) < -2(2)$
$-3 \leq 1 \rightarrow -1(-3) \geq -1(1)$

Notice that the numbers being compared switched positions as a result of being multiplied by a negative number. In other words, their order reversed. These and other examples suggest the following properties.

STUDY TIP

Common Error Do not reverse the inequality symbol just because there is a negative sign in the inequality, as in Example 1. Only reverse the inequality symbol when you *multiply* or *divide* each side by a negative number.

Noteables™ Key Concept: Properties of Inequality

Words When you multiply or divide each side of an inequality by a negative number, the direction of the inequality symbol must be reversed for the inequality to remain true.

Symbols For all numbers *a*, *b*, and *c*, where $c < 0$,

1. if $a > b$, then $ac < bc$ and $\frac{a}{c} < \frac{b}{c}$.

2. if $a < b$, then $ac > bc$ and $\frac{a}{c} > \frac{b}{c}$.

Examples

$8 > 5$ $\qquad$ $-3 < 9$

$-1(8) < -1(5)$ Reverse the inequality symbols. $\frac{-3}{-3} > \frac{9}{-3}$

$-8 < -5$ $\qquad$ $1 > -3$

These properties also hold true for $a \geq b$ and $a \leq b$.

msmath3.net/extra_examples

2 Teach

In-Class Examples

1 Solve $6x < -30$. Check your solution. $x < -5$

2 Solve $\frac{1}{2}p \geq 9$ and check your solution. Then graph the solution on a number line. $p \geq 18$

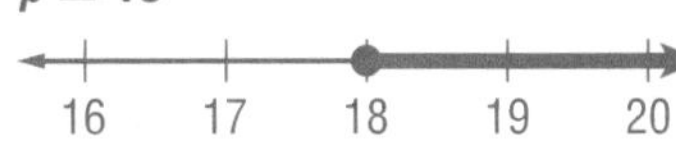

Answers (Your Turn)

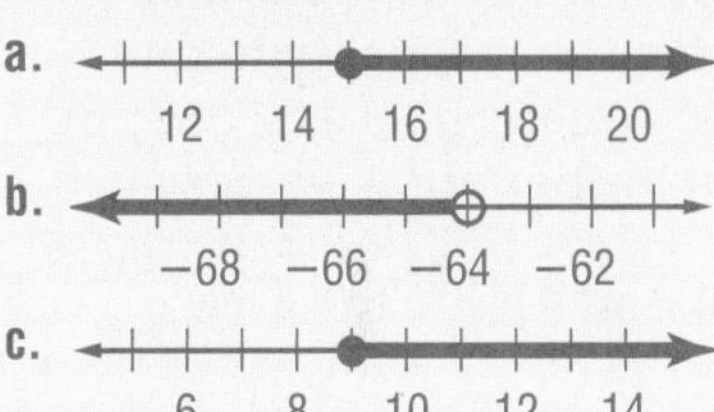

In-Class Examples

3 Solve $\frac{b}{-4} \leq 5$. Check your solution. $b \geq -20$

4 Solve $-60 < -4n$. Then graph the solution on a number line. $n < 15$

5 **PACKAGES** A box weighs 1 pound. It is filled with books that weigh 2 pounds each. Jesse can carry at most 20 pounds. Assuming space is not an issue, write and solve an inequality to find how many books he can put in the box and still carry it. $1 + 2p \leq 20$; $p \leq 9.5$. He can put at most 9 books in the box.

Answers (Your Turn)

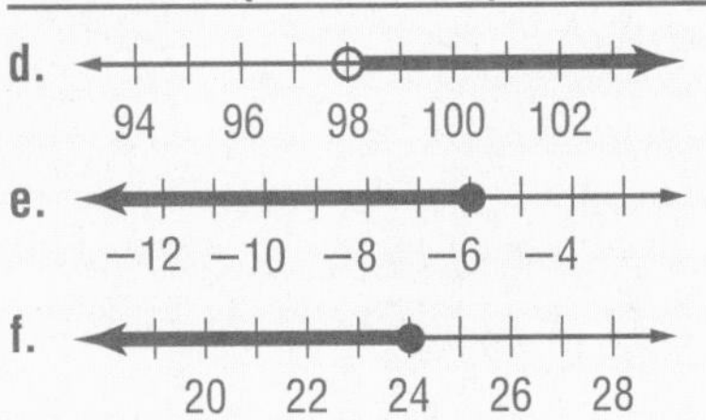

Answers

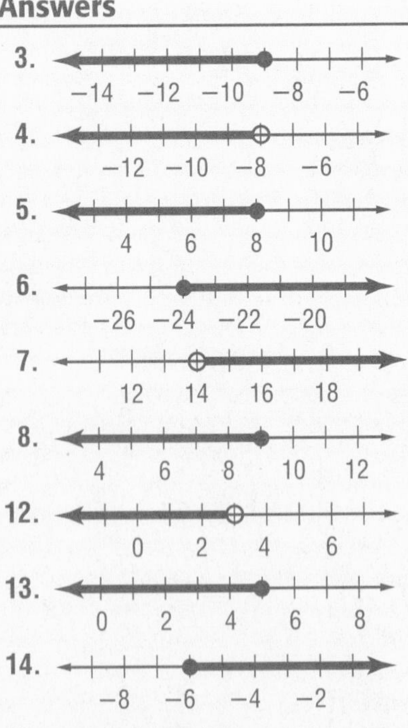

EXAMPLES Multiply or Divide by a Negative Number

3 **Solve $\frac{a}{-2} \geq 8$. Check your solution.**

$\frac{a}{-2} \geq 8$	Write the inequality.
$-2\left(\frac{a}{-2}\right) \leq -2(8)$	Multiply each side by −2 and reverse the inequality symbol.
$a \leq -16$	Simplify.

The solution is $a \leq -16$. You can check this solution by replacing a in the original inequality with −16 and a number less than −16.

4 **Solve $-24 > -6n$. Then graph the solution on a number line.**

$-24 > -6n$	Write the inequality.
$\frac{-24}{-6} < \frac{-6n}{-6}$	Divide each side by −6 and reverse the inequality symbol.
$4 < n$ or $n > 4$	Check this result.

Graph the solution, $n > 4$.

−2 −1 0 1 2 3 4 5 6 7 8 9

Your Turn **Solve each inequality and check your solution. Then graph the solution on a number line.**

d. $\frac{c}{-7} < -14$ $c > 98$ e. $-5d \geq 30$ $d \leq -6$ f. $-3 \leq \frac{w}{-8}$ $w \leq 24$

d–f. See margin for graphs.

REAL-LIFE MATH

WORK If you are 14 or 15 and have a part-time job, you can work no more than 3 hours on a school day, 18 hours in a school week, 8 hours on a nonschool day, or 40 hours in a nonschool week.

Source: www.youthrules.dol.gov

Some inequalities involve more than one operation. To solve, work backward to undo the operations as you did in solving two-step equations.

EXAMPLE Solve a Two-Step Inequality

5 **WORK Jason wants to earn at least \$30 this week to go to the state fair. His dad will pay him \$12 to mow the lawn. For washing their cars, his neighbors will pay him \$8 per car. If Jason mows the lawn, write and solve an inequality to find how many cars he needs to wash to earn at least \$30.**

The phrase *at least* means *greater than or equal to*. Let c = the number of cars he needs to wash. Then write an inequality.

\$12	plus	\$8 per car	is greater than or equal to	\$30.
12	+	8c	≥	30

$12 + 8c \geq 30$	Write the inequality.
$12 - 12 + 8c \geq 30 - 12$	Subtract 12 from each side.
$8c \geq 18$	Simplify.
$\frac{8c}{8} \geq \frac{18}{8}$	Divide each side by 8.
$c \geq 2.25$	Simplify.

Since he will not get paid for washing a fourth of a car, Jason must wash at least 3 cars.

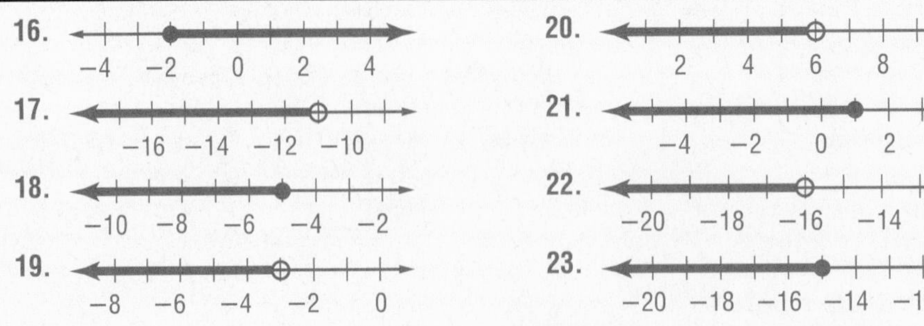

Students practice the same concepts in Exercises 12–45 if they are assigned odd or even problems.

Skill and Concept Check

1. **OPEN ENDED** Write an inequality that can be solved using the Multiplication Property of Equality where the inequality symbol needs to be reversed. **Sample answer: $\frac{x}{-6} > 3$**

2. **FIND THE ERROR** Olivia and Lakita each solved $8a \leq -56$. Who is correct? Explain.

Olivia	Lakita
$8a \leq -56$	$8a \leq -56$
$\frac{8a}{8} \geq \frac{-56}{8}$	$\frac{8a}{8} \leq \frac{-56}{8}$
$a \geq -7$	$a \leq -7$

Lakita; when dividing by a positive number, do not reverse the inequality symbol.

GUIDED PRACTICE

Solve each inequality and check your solution. Then graph the solution on a number line. **3–8. See margin for graphs.**

3. $8x \leq -72$ **$x \leq -9$**
4. $-4y > 32$ **$y < -8$**
5. $-56 \leq -7p$ **$p \leq 8$**
6. $\frac{h}{4} \geq -6$ **$h \geq -24$**
7. $\frac{g}{-2} < -7$ **$g > 14$**
8. $\frac{d}{-3} \geq -3$ **$d \leq 9$**

Solve each inequality. Check your solution.

9. $2a - 8 < -24$ **$a < -8$**
10. $-4k + 3 > -13$ **$k < 4$**
11. $\frac{m}{-3} + 7 \leq -2$ **$m \geq 27$**

★ indicates increased difficulty

Practice and Applications

HOMEWORK HELP	
For Exercises	See Examples
12–33	1–4
34–45	5

Extra Practice
See pages 642, 657.

Solve each inequality and check your solution. Then graph the solution on a number line. **12–29. See margin for graphs.**

12. $5x < 15$ **$x < 3$**
13. $9n \leq 45$ **$n \leq 5$**
14. $14k \geq -84$ **$k \geq -6$**
15. $-12 > 3g$ **$g < -4$**
16. $-100 \leq 50p$ **$p \geq -2$**
17. $2y < -22$ **$y < -11$**
18. $-4w \geq 20$ **$w \leq -5$**
19. $-3r > 9$ **$r < -3$**
20. $-72 < -12h$ **$h < 6$**
21. $-6c \geq -6$ **$c \leq 1$**
22. $\frac{v}{-4} > 4$ **$v < -16$**
23. $\frac{a}{-3} \geq 5$ **$a \leq -15$**
24. $\frac{x}{9} \leq -3$ **$x \leq -27$**
25. $\frac{n}{7} < -14$ **$n < -98$**
26. $\frac{m}{-2} < -7$ **$m > 14$**
27. $\frac{t}{-5} \leq -2$ **$t \geq 10$**
28. ★ $-8 \leq \frac{y}{0.2}$ **$y \geq -1.6$**
29. ★ $-\frac{1}{2}k > -10$ **$k < 20$**

30. **BUS TRAVEL** A city bus company charges $2.50 per trip. They also offer a monthly pass for $85.00. Write and solve an inequality to find how many times a person should use the bus so that the pass is less expensive than buying individual tickets. **$85 < 2.50t$; $t > 34$; more than 34 times**

31. **BABY-SITTING** You want to buy a pair of $42 inline skates with the money you make baby-sitting. If you charge $5.25 an hour, write and solve an inequality to find how many whole hours you must baby-sit to buy the skates. **$5.25c \geq 42$; $c \geq 8$; at least 8 h**

msmath3.net/self_check_quiz

3 Practice/Apply

FOLDABLES™ Follow-Up Remind students to record main ideas, definitions of vocabulary words, and other notes under the "Inequalities" tab of their Foldables as they learn to solve inequalities by multiplying or dividing.

DAILY INTERVENTION **FIND THE ERROR** For Exercise 2, remind students that the sign of the divisor or multiplier determines whether the direction of the inequality sign changes.

About the Exercises...

Guided Practice Key

Exercises	Examples
3, 6	1, 2
4, 5, 7, 8	3, 4
9–11	5

Assignment Guide

Basic: 13–27 odd, 31, 35–39 odd, 43, 45–54

Average: 13–45 odd, 46–54

Enriched: 12–44 even, 46–54

Alert! The Data Update after Exercise 33 requires access to the Internet.

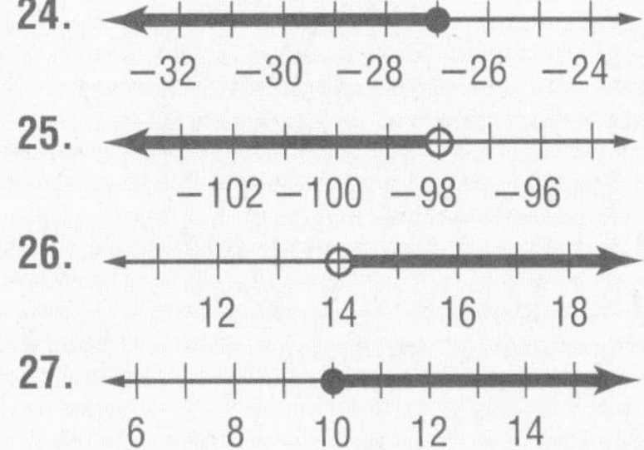

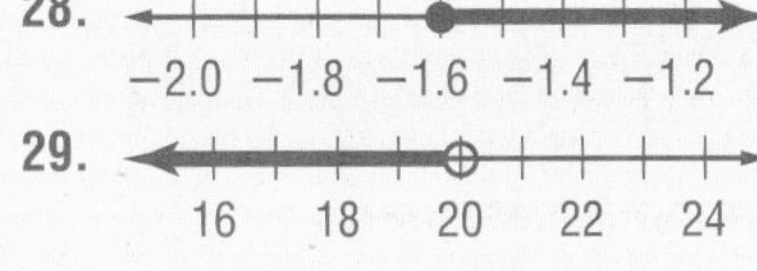

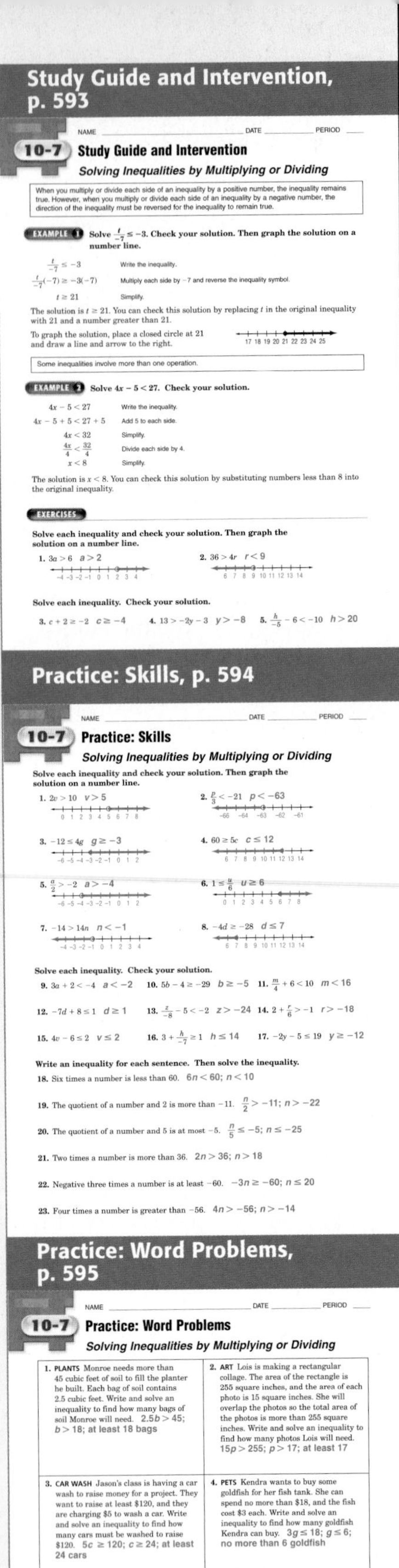

Study Guide and Intervention, p. 593

NAME ______ DATE ______ PERIOD ______

10-7 Study Guide and Intervention

Solving Inequalities by Multiplying or Dividing

When you multiply or divide each side of an inequality by a positive number, the inequality remains true. However, when you multiply or divide each side of an inequality by a negative number, the direction of the inequality must be reversed for the inequality to remain true.

EXAMPLE 1 Solve $\frac{t}{-7} \le -3$. Check your solution. Then graph the solution on a number line.

$\frac{t}{-7} \le -3$ Write the inequality.

$\frac{t}{-7}(-7) \ge -3(-7)$ Multiply each side by −7 and reverse the inequality symbol.

$t \ge 21$ Simplify.

The solution is $t \ge 21$. You can check this solution by replacing t in the original inequality with 21 and a number greater than 21.

To graph the solution, place a closed circle at 21 and draw a line and arrow to the right.

Some inequalities involve more than one operation.

EXAMPLE 2 Solve $4x - 5 < 27$. Check your solution.

$4x - 5 < 27$ Write the inequality.

$4x - 5 + 5 < 27 + 5$ Add 5 to each side.

$4x < 32$ Simplify.

$\frac{4x}{4} < \frac{32}{4}$ Divide each side by 4.

$x < 8$ Simplify.

The solution is $x < 8$. You can check this solution by substituting numbers less than 8 into the original inequality.

EXERCISES

Solve each inequality and check your solution. Then graph the solution on a number line.

1. $3a > 6$ $a > 2$
2. $36 > 4r$ $r < 9$

Solve each inequality. Check your solution.

3. $c + 2 \ge -2$ $c \ge -4$
4. $13 > -2y - 3$ $y > -8$
5. $\frac{h}{-5} - 6 < -10$ $h > 20$

Practice: Skills, p. 594

NAME ______ DATE ______ PERIOD ______

10-7 Practice: Skills

Solving Inequalities by Multiplying or Dividing

Solve each inequality and check your solution. Then graph the solution on a number line.

1. $2v > 10$ $v > 5$
2. $\frac{p}{3} < -21$ $p < -63$
3. $-12 \le 4g$ $g \ge -3$
4. $60 \ge 5c$ $c \le 12$
5. $\frac{a}{2} > -2$ $a > -4$
6. $1 \le \frac{u}{6}$ $u \ge 6$
7. $-14 > 14n$ $n < -1$
8. $-4d \ge -28$ $d \le 7$

Solve each inequality. Check your solution.

9. $3a + 2 < -4$ $a < -2$
10. $5b - 4 \ge -29$ $b \ge -5$
11. $\frac{m}{4} + 6 < 10$ $m < 16$
12. $-7d + 8 \le 1$ $d \ge 1$
13. $\frac{z}{-8} - 5 < -2$ $z > -24$
14. $2 + \frac{r}{6} > -1$ $r > -18$
15. $4v - 6 \le 2$ $v \le 2$
16. $3 + \frac{h}{-7} \ge 1$ $h \le 14$
17. $-2y - 5 \le 19$ $y \ge -12$

Write an inequality for each sentence. Then solve the inequality.

18. Six times a number is less than 60. $6n < 60$; $n < 10$
19. The quotient of a number and 2 is more than −11. $\frac{n}{2} > -11$; $n > -22$
20. The quotient of a number and 5 is at most −5. $\frac{n}{5} \le -5$; $n \le -25$
21. Two times a number is more than 36. $2n > 36$; $n > 18$
22. Negative three times a number is at least −60. $-3n \ge -60$; $n \le 20$
23. Four times a number is greater than −56. $4n > -56$; $n > -14$

Practice: Word Problems, p. 595

NAME ______ DATE ______ PERIOD ______

10-7 Practice: Word Problems

Solving Inequalities by Multiplying or Dividing

1. PLANTS Monroe needs more than 45 cubic feet of soil to fill the planter he built. Each bag of soil contains 2.5 cubic feet. Write and solve an inequality to find how many bags of soil Monroe will need. $2.5b > 45$; $b > 18$; at least 18 bags
2. ART Lois is making a rectangular collage. The area of the rectangle is 255 square inches, and the area of each photo is 15 square inches. She will overlap the photos so the total area of the photos is more than 255 square inches. Write and solve an inequality to find how many photos Lois will need. $15p > 255$; $p > 17$; at least 17
3. CAR WASH Jason's class is having a car wash to raise money for a project. They want to raise at least \$120, and they are charging \$5 to wash a car. Write and solve an inequality to find how many cars must be washed to raise \$120. $5c \ge 120$; $c \ge 24$; at least 24 cars
4. PETS Kendra wants to buy some goldfish for her fish tank. She can spend no more than \$18, and the fish cost \$3 each. Write and solve an inequality to find how many goldfish Kendra can buy. $3g \le 18$; $g \le 6$; no more than 6 goldfish
5. PIZZA Trent and three of his friends are ordering a pizza. They plan to split the cost, and they want to spend at most \$3.50 per person. Write and solve an inequality to find the cost of the pizza they should order. $\frac{c}{4} \le 3.50$; $c \le 14$; \$14 or less
6. GEOMETRY You are asked to draw a rectangle with a length of 6 inches and an area less than 30 square inches. Write and solve an inequality to find the width of the rectangle. $6w < 30$; $w < 5$; less than 5 in. wide
7. CONSTRUCTION Melinda wants to have a picture window in the shape of a regular hexagon in her new home. She wants the perimeter of the hexagon to be at least 9 feet. Write and solve an inequality to find the length of each side of the hexagon. $6s \ge 9$; $s \ge 1.5$; at least 1.5 ft
8. COOKING Len wants to make several batches of cookies. He is starting with less than 2 cups of raisins, and each batch takes $\frac{1}{3}$ of a cup. Write and solve an inequality to find how many batches of cookies Len can make. $\frac{1}{3}b < 2$; $b < 6$; less than 6 batches

ROADS For Exercises 32 and 33, use the information in the graphic at the right.

★ 32. Write and solve an inequality to find the approximate circumference of Earth.

★ 33. Write and solve an inequality to find the approximate distance from Earth to the moon and back. **32–33. See margin.**

USA TODAY Snapshots®

On the road

The 4 million miles of public roads in the United States would:

Circle the globe more than **157 times.**

Reach to the moon and back more than **eight times.**

Source: Bureau of Transportation Statistics

By William Risser and Bob Laird, USA TODAY

Data Update What is the circumference of Earth? the distance from Earth to the moon and back? Visit msmath3.net/data_update to learn more.

Solve each inequality. Check your solution.

34. $5y - 2 > 13$ **$y > 3$**
35. $8k + 3 \le -5$ **$k \le -1$**
36. $-3g + 8 \ge -4$
37. $7 + \frac{n}{3} < 4$ **$n < -9$**
38. $\frac{w}{8} - 4 \le -5$
39. $\frac{c}{-4} + 8 < 1$ **$c > 28$**

★ 40. $3a - 8 < 5a$

★ 41. $10 - 3x \ge 25 + 2x$ **$x \le -3$**

36. $g \le 4$ 38. $w \le -8$ 40. $a > -4$

Write an inequality for each sentence. Then solve the inequality.

42. Three times a number is less than −60. **$3n < -60$; $n < -20$**
43. The quotient of a number and −5 is at most 7. **$\frac{n}{-5} \le 7$; $n \ge -35$**
44. The quotient of a number and 3 is at least −12. **$\frac{n}{3} \ge -12$; $n \ge -36$**
45. The product of −2 and a number is greater than −18. **$-2n > -18$; $n < 9$**
46. **CRITICAL THINKING** You have scores of 88, 92, 85, and 87 on four tests. What number of points must you get on your fifth test to have a test average of at least 90? **98 or more points**

Spiral Review with Standardized Test Practice

47. **MULTIPLE CHOICE** Which number is a possible base length of the triangle if its area is greater than 45 square yards? **D**

Ⓐ 3 Ⓑ 4 Ⓒ 5 Ⓓ 6

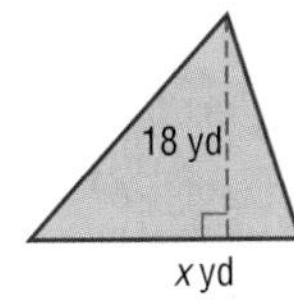

48. **MULTIPLE CHOICE** As a salesperson, you are paid \$60 per week plus \$5 per sale. This week you want your pay to be at least \$120. Which inequality can be used to find the number of sales you must make this week? **F**

Ⓕ $60 + 5x \ge 120$ Ⓖ $60x + 5 \ge 120$

Ⓗ $60 + 5x \le 120$ Ⓘ $60x + 5 \le 120$

Solve each inequality. Check your solution. (Lesson 10-6)

49. $y + 7 < 9$ **$y < 2$**
50. $a - 5 \le 2$ **$a \le 7$**
51. $j - 8 \ge -12$ **$j \ge -4$**
52. $-14 > 8 + n$ **$n < -22$**

Write an inequality for each sentence. (Lesson 10-5)

53. **HEALTH** Your heart beats over 100,000 times a day. **$b > 100{,}000$**
54. **BIRDS** A peregrine falcon can spot a pigeon up to 8 kilometers away. **$d \le 8$**

4 Assess

Open-Ended Assessment

Modeling Have students use grid paper to find the dimensions of a rectangle with a maximum area of 100 squares. Have them test their answers using the inequality $\ell \times w \le 100$.

Answers

32. $4{,}000{,}000 > 157c$; $c < 25{,}478$; less than 25,478 mi
33. $4{,}000{,}000 > 8d$; $d < 500{,}000$; less than 500,000 mi

Study Guide and Review

Vocabulary and Concept Check

coefficient (p. 470)
constant (p. 470)
equivalent expressions (p. 469)
like terms (p. 470)
simplest form (p. 471)
simplifying the expression (p. 471)
term (p. 470)
two-step equation (p. 474)

Choose the letter of the term that best matches each statement or phrase.

1. terms that contain the same variables **d**
2. an equation that contains two operations **c**
3. a term without a variable **a**
4. the parts of an algebraic expression separated by a plus sign **e**
5. an algebraic expression that has no like terms and no parentheses **f**
6. the numerical part of a term that contains a variable **b**

a. constant
b. coefficient
c. two-step equation
d. like terms
e. term
f. simplest form

Lesson-by-Lesson Exercises and Examples

10-1 Simplifying Algebraic Expressions (pp. 469–473)

Use the Distributive Property to rewrite each expression. **8. $-6x - 42$**

7. $4(a + 3)$ **$4a + 12$**
8. $-6(x + 7)$
9. $(n - 5)(-7)$ **$-7n + 35$**
10. $-2(6x - 3)$ **$-12x + 6$**

Simplify each expression. **12. $13b + 2$**

11. $p + 6p$ **$7p$**
12. $6b + 7b - 3 + 5$

Example 1 **Use the Distributive Property to rewrite $-8(x - 9)$.**

$-8(x - 9)$	Write the expression.
$= -8[x + (-9)]$	$x - 9 = x + (-9)$
$= -8(x) + (-8)(-9)$	Distributive Property
$= -8x + 72$	Simplify.

10-2 Solving Two-Step Equations (pp. 474–477)

Solve each equation. Check your solution.

13. $2x + 5 = 17$ **6**
14. $3d + 20 = 2$ **-6**
15. $10 = 3 - g$ **-7**
16. $4 = -3y - 2$ **-2**
17. $\frac{c}{5} + 2 = 9$ **35**
18. $a + 6a + 11 = 39$ **4**

Example 2 **Solve $5h + 8 = -12$.**

$5h + 8 = -12$	Write the equation.
$5h + 8 - 8 = -12 - 8$	Subtract 8.
$5h = -20$	$-12 - 8 = -12 + (-8)$
$\frac{5h}{5} = \frac{-20}{5}$	Divide each side by 5.
$h = -4$	Simplify.
The solution is -4.	Check this solution.

msmath3.net/vocabulary_review

FOLDABLES™ Study Organizer

For more information about Foldables, see *Teaching Mathematics with Foldables.*

Have students look through the chapter to make sure they have included examples in their Foldables for each lesson or topic in the chapter.

Encourage students to refer to their Foldables while completing the Study Guide and Review and to use them in preparing for the Chapter Test.

Chapter 10 Study Guide and Review

Vocabulary Assessment

- This alphabetical list of vocabulary terms in Chapter 10 includes a page reference where each term was introduced.
- A vocabulary review/test for Chapter 10 is available on p. 612 of the *Chapter 10 Resource Masters.*

Vocabulary PuzzleMaker

ELL The online Vocabulary PuzzleMaker improves students' mathematics vocabulary using four puzzle formats — crossword, scramble, word search using a word list, and word search using clues. Students can work on a computer screen or from a printed handout.

MindJogger Videoquizzes

ELL MindJogger Videoquizzes provide an alternative review of concepts presented in this chapter. Students work in teams in a game show format to gain points for correct answers. The questions are presented in three rounds.

Round 1 Concepts (5 questions)
Round 2 Skills (4 questions)
Round 3 Problem Solving (4 questions)

ExamView® Pro

Use the networkable ExamView® Pro Testmaker CD-ROM to:

- Create **multiple versions** of tests.
- Create **modified** tests for **inclusion** students with one mouse click.
- **Edit** existing questions and **add** your own questions.
- Build tests aligned with state standards using built-in **state curriculum correlations.**
- Change **English** tests to **Spanish** with one mouse click and vice versa.

Answers (Study Guide)

27.–28.

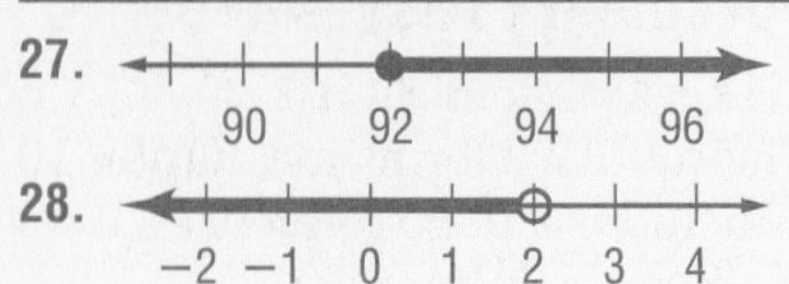

Answers (Practice Test)

13.–19.

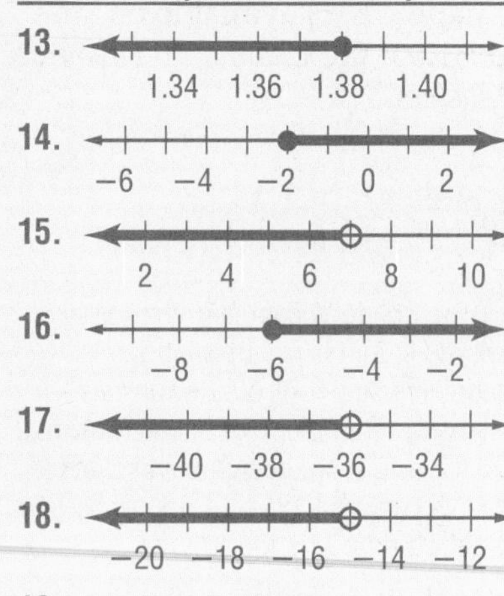

Mixed Problem Solving
For mixed problem-solving practice, see page 657.

10-3 Writing Two-Step Equations (pp. 478–481) 19. $2n + 6 = -4; -5$

Translate each sentence into an equation. Then find the number.

19. Six more than twice a number is −4.
20. Three less than 2 times a number equals 11. $2x - 3 = 11; 7$
21. The quotient of a number and 8, less 2, is 5. $\frac{x}{8} - 2 = 5; 56$

Example 3 Translate the following sentence into an equation.

6 less than 4 times a number is 10.

$$\underbrace{\text{6 less than}}\ \underbrace{\text{4 times a number}}\ \underbrace{\text{is}}\ \underbrace{10.}$$
$$4n - 6 = 10$$

10-4 Solving Equations with Variables on Each Side (pp. 484–487)

Solve each equation. Check your solution.

22. $11x = 20x + 18$ -2
23. $4n + 13 = n - 8$ -7
24. $3a + 5 = 2a + 7$ 2
25. $7b - 3 = -2b + 24$ 3
26. $9 - 2y = 8y - 6$ 1.5

Example 4 Solve $7x + 5 = 6x - 19$.

$$7x + 5 = 6x - 19$$
$$7x - 6x + 5 = 6x - 6x - 19$$
$$x + 5 = -19$$
$$x + 5 - 5 = -19 - 5$$
$$x = -24$$

10-5 Inequalities (pp. 492–495)

Write an inequality. Then graph the inequality on a number line. 27. $g \geq 92$

27. **GRADES** a grade of 92 or better
28. **SPORTS** qualifying time must be less than 2 minutes $t < 2$

27–28. See margin for graphs.

Example 5 Graph $a < -4$.

Place an open circle at −4. Then draw a line and an arrow to the left.

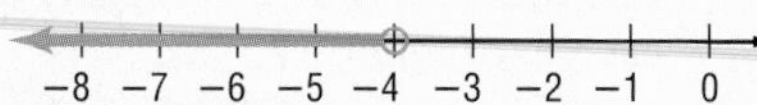

10-6 Solving Inequalities by Adding or Subtracting (pp. 496–499)

Solve each inequality. Check your solution.

29. $y + 7 \leq 5$ $y \leq -2$
30. $x - 2 < 7$ $x < 9$
31. $18 < 4 + d$ $d > 14$
32. $a - 6 > -2$ $a > 4$

Example 6 Solve $k + 2 > -5$.

$k + 2 > -5$	Write the inequality.
$k + 2 - 2 > -5 - 2$	Subtract 2.
$k > -7$	Simplify.

10-7 Solving Inequalities by Multiplying or Dividing (pp. 500–504)

Solve each inequality. Check your solution. 33. $c \leq -2$ 35. $m < -3$

33. $13c \leq -26$
34. $-2a \geq -10$ $a \leq 5$
35. $-6m > 18$
36. $22 \geq -3x - 2$ $x \geq -8$

Example 7 Solve $-9n < 54$.

$-9n < 54$	Write the inequality.
$\frac{-9n}{-9} > \frac{54}{-9}$	Divide each side by −9 and reverse the inequality symbol.
$n > -6$	Simplify. Check this result.

Practice Test

Vocabulary and Concepts

1. **Explain** how you determine whether or not an expression is in simplest form. **An expression is in simplest form when it has no like terms and no parentheses.**
2. **Give** three examples of phrases that indicate the inequality symbol $\leq$. **Sample answer: is less than or equal to; is no greater than; is at most**

Skills and Applications

3. Use the Distributive Property to rewrite the expression $-7(x - 10)$. $\mathbf{-7x + 70}$
4. Simplify the expression $9a - a + 15 - 10a - 6$. $\mathbf{-2a + 9}$

Solve each equation. Check your solution.

5. $3n + 18 = 6$ $\mathbf{-4}$
6. $\frac{k}{2} - 11 = 5$ $\mathbf{32}$
7. $-23 = 3p + 5 + p$ $\mathbf{-7}$
8. $4x - 6 = 5x$ $\mathbf{-6}$
9. $-3a - 2 = 2a + 3$ $\mathbf{-1}$
10. $-2y + 5 = y - 1$ $\mathbf{2}$
11. Translate *the quotient of a number and 6, plus 3, is 11* into an equation. Then find the number. $\mathbf{\frac{n}{6} + 3 = 11; 48}$
12. **FUND-RAISER** The band buys coupon books for a one-time fee of \$60 plus \$5 per book. If they sell the books for \$10 each, write and solve an equation to find how many books they must sell to break even. $\mathbf{60 + 5x = 10x; 12}$
13. **COMPUTERS** A disk can hold at most 1.38 megabytes of data. Write an inequality. Then graph the inequality on a number line. $\mathbf{m \leq 1.38}$**; See margin for graph.**

Solve each inequality and check the solution. Then graph the solution on a number line. 14–19. See margin for graphs.

14. $x + 5 \geq 3$ $\mathbf{x \geq -2}$
15. $5 > a - 2$ $\mathbf{a < 7}$
16. $-3d \leq 18$ $\mathbf{d \geq -6}$
17. $-4 > \frac{c}{9}$ $\mathbf{c < -36}$
18. $-2g + 15 > 45$ $\mathbf{g < -15}$
19. $\frac{m}{-5} + 4 \geq 1$ $\mathbf{m \leq 15}$

Standardized Test Practice

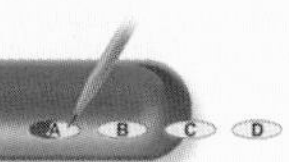

20. **MULTIPLE CHOICE** The perimeter of the parallelogram at the right is no more than 44 inches. Which of the following inequalities represents all possible values for x? **A**

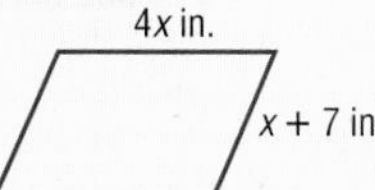

Ⓐ $x \leq 3$
Ⓑ $x \geq 3$
Ⓒ $x \leq 7.4$
Ⓓ $x \geq 7.4$

Assessment Options

Vocabulary Test A vocabulary review/test for Chapter 10 can be found on p. 612 of the *Chapter 10 Resource Masters.*

Chapter Tests There are six Chapter 10 Tests and an Extended Response Assessment task available in the *Chapter 10 Resource Masters.*

Chapter 10 Tests			
Form	**Type**	**Level**	**Pages**
1	MC	basic	599–600
2A	MC	average	601–602
2B	MC	average	603–604
2C	FR	average	605–606
2D	FR	average	607–608
3	FR	advanced	609–610

MC = multiple-choice questions
FR = free-response questions

Extended Response Assessment

Extended Response tasks for Chapter 10 can be found on p. 611 of the *Chapter 10 Resource Masters.* A sample scoring rubric for these tasks appears on p. A26.

Portfolio Suggestion

Introduction Many news stories have information that could be written as equations or inequalities. For example, the growth of a company could be written as an equation or a tuition cap could be written as an inequality.

Ask Students to use news sources to write examples of equations and inequalities. Have them solve the equations and graph the inequalities in their portfolios.

CHAPTER 10 Standardized Test Practice

These two pages contain practice questions in the various formats that can be found on the most frequently given standardized tests.

A student recording sheet for these two pages can be found on page A1 of the *Chapter 10 Resource Masters.*

Standardized Test Practice Student Recording Sheet, p. A1

CHAPTER 10 NAME ______ DATE ______ PERIOD ______

Standardized Test Practice SCORE ______

Student Recording Sheet (Use with pages 508–509 of the Student Edition.)

Part 1: Multiple Choice

Select the best answer from the choices given and fill in the corresponding oval.

1. Ⓐ Ⓑ Ⓒ Ⓓ 4. Ⓕ Ⓖ Ⓗ Ⓘ 7. Ⓐ Ⓑ Ⓒ Ⓓ
2. Ⓕ Ⓖ Ⓗ Ⓘ 5. Ⓐ Ⓑ Ⓒ Ⓓ
3. Ⓐ Ⓑ Ⓒ Ⓓ 6. Ⓕ Ⓖ Ⓗ Ⓘ

Part 2: Short Response/Grid in

Solve the problem and write your answer in the blank.

For grid in questions, also enter your answer by writing each number or symbol in a box. Then fill in the corresponding circle for that number of symbol.

8. ______ (grid in)
9. ______
10. ______ (grid in)
11. ______
12. ______
13. ______ (grid in)
14. ______

Part 3: Extended Response

Record your answers for Questions 15–19 on the back of this paper.

Additional Practice

See pp. 617–618 of the *Chapter 10 Resource Masters* for additional standardized test practice.

Answer

9. 

CHAPTER 10 Standardized Test Practice

PART 1 Multiple Choice

Record your answers on the answer sheet provided by your teacher or on a sheet of paper.

1. On Saturday Jennifer rode her bike to Robert's house. They then biked together to the library. Finally, Jennifer rode home alone from the library. If each unit on the grid represents 1 mile, what was the total distance that Jennifer biked on Saturday? (Lesson 3-6) **D**

Robert's House, Jennifer's House, Library

Ⓐ about 3.5 mi Ⓑ about 8.5 mi
Ⓒ about 15.5 mi Ⓓ about 20.5 mi

2. The data below was collected from four different remote-controlled car tests.

Car	Distance Traveled (ft)	Time (s)
Speedster	45	9
Turbo	31	5
Cruiser	33	6
Hurricane	51	$8\frac{1}{2}$

Which car traveled at the fastest rate? (Lesson 4-1) **G**

Ⓕ Speedster Ⓖ Turbo
Ⓗ Cruiser Ⓘ Hurricane

TEST-TAKING TIP

Question 2 You can often use estimation to eliminate incorrect answers. In Question 2, the Turbo's rate of speed is about 30 ÷ 5 or 6 feet per second, and the Cruiser's is about 30 ÷ 6 or 5 feet per second. Thus, the Cruiser can be eliminated since the Turbo's speed is faster.

3. In 1990, the number of students attending a school was 865. In 2000, the number was 680. By what percent did the number decrease from 1990 to 2000? (Lesson 5-7) **B**

Ⓐ 20% Ⓑ 21% Ⓒ 43% Ⓓ 79%

4. What is the volume of paint in a can that has a diameter of 10 inches and a height of 12 inches? (Lesson 7-5) **H**

Ⓕ 188.4 in^3 Ⓖ 376.8 in^3
Ⓗ 942 in^3 Ⓘ 1,884 in^3

5. The graph shows the results of the election for club president. Which statement is supported by the information on the graph? (Lesson 9-2) **B**

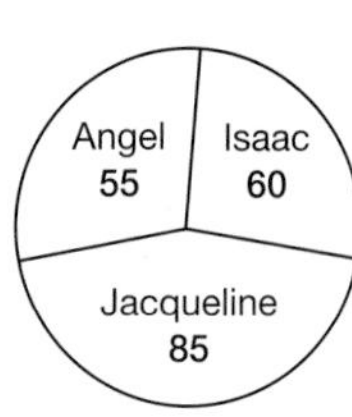

Ⓐ The total number of votes was 190.
Ⓑ Isaac received 30% of the votes.
Ⓒ The ratio of Angel's votes to Isaac's votes was 5 to 6.
Ⓓ Jacqueline received half the votes.

6. Find the value of x so that the isosceles trapezoid at the right has a perimeter of 200 inches. (Lesson 10-3) **G**

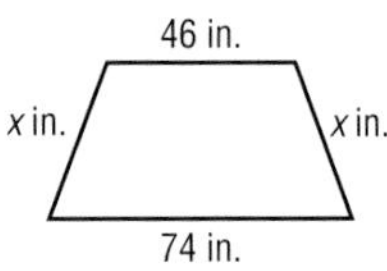

Ⓕ 35 Ⓖ 40 Ⓗ 55 Ⓘ 80

7. The number line below is the graph of which inequality? (Lesson 10-7) **A**

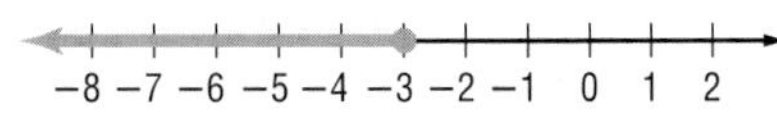

Ⓐ $4y \leq -12$ Ⓑ $-5y \leq 15$
Ⓒ $5y > -15$ Ⓓ $-4y > 12$

ExamView® Pro

Special banks of standardized test questions similar to those on the TIMSS and NAEP grade 8 tests can be found on this CD-ROM.

Preparing for Standardized Tests
For test-taking strategies and more practice, see pages 660–677.

PART 2 Short Response/Grid In

Record your answers on the answer sheet provided by your teacher or on a sheet of paper.

8. You are serving soup to 7 people. Each serving is $\frac{3}{4}$ of a cup. If each can of soup contains $2\frac{1}{2}$ cups, how many cans do you need in order to give every person a full serving? (Lessons 2-3 and 2-4) **3**

9. Draw the figure that results from rotating the figure at the right 90° counterclockwise about its center and then reflecting it over the indicated vertical axis. (Lessons 6-7 and 6-9) **See margin.**

10. Santiago is running the duck pond at the youth carnival. Each duck has a number on the bottom indicating the level of the prize awarded. The table shows how many ducks of each prize level are currently in the pond.

Prize Level	1	2	3	4
Number of Ducks	4	6	8	?

How many prize-level-4 ducks should Santiago place in the pond so that the chances of randomly selecting one of these ducks is $\frac{1}{2}$? (Lesson 8-1) **18**

11. The statistics below were listed on the board at the end of the grading period for a class of 9 students.

mean: 87
median: 88
range: 15

Sample answer: 78, 80, 86, 87, 88, 89, 90, 92, 93

List a possible set of grades for the students in this class. (Lesson 9-4)

12. Write an expression with four terms, two of which are constants. The other terms should be like terms, one with a coefficient of −2 and the other with a coefficient of 6. Then simplify your expression. (Lesson 10-1) **Sample answer: $5 - 2x + 6x + 1$; $4x + 6$**

13. If $8 + 5w = 11$, find the value of $2w$. (Lesson 10-2) **1.2 or 6/5**

14. A restaurant has s small tables that will seat 4 people each. They also have ℓ large tables that will seat 10 people each. Write an inequality representing the number of people p that can be seated at this restaurant. (Lesson 10-5) $p \leq 4s + 10\ell$

PART 3 Extended Response

Record your answers on a sheet of paper. Show your work.

The table below gives prices for two different bowling alleys in your area. (Lessons 10-4 and 10-5)

Bowling Alley	Shoe Rental	Cost per Game
X	$2.50	$4.00
Y	$3.50	$3.75

15. Write an equation to find the number of games g for which the total cost to bowl at each alley would be equal. $2.50 + 4g = 3.50 + 3.75g$

16. Explain how you would solve the equation you wrote in Question 15. **See margin.**

17. How many games would you have to play for the cost to bowl at each alley to be equal? **4**

18. Write an inequality giving the number of games g for which Bowling Alley X would be cheaper. $g < 4$

19. Write an inequality giving the number of games g for which Bowling Alley Y would be cheaper. $g > 4$

msmath3.net/standardized_test

Standardized Test Practice

Rubrics The following rubrics are sample scoring devices for short response and extended response questions.

Short Response

Points	Description
2	The student demonstrates a thorough understanding of the mathematics of the task. The response may contain minor flaws that do not detract from the demonstration of a thorough understanding.
1	The student has provided a response that is only partially correct.
0	The student has provided a completely incorrect solution or no response at all.

Extended Response

Points	Description
4	The student demonstrates a thorough understanding of the mathematics of the task. The response may contain minor flaws that do not detract from the demonstration of a thorough understanding.
3	The student demonstrates an understanding of the mathematics of the task. The response is essentially correct and demonstrates an essential but less than thorough understanding of the mathematics.
2	The student demonstrates only a partial understanding of the mathematics of the task. Although the student may have used the correct approach to a solution or may have provided a correct solution, the work lacks an essential understanding of the underlying mathematical concepts.
1	The student demonstrates a very limited understanding of the mathematics of the task. The response is incomplete and exhibits many flaws.
0	The student provides a completely incorrect solution or no response at all.

A more detailed 4-point rubric is provided on page A2 of the *Chapter 10 Resource Masters*.

Answer

16.
$2.50 + 4g - 3.75g = 3.50 + 3.75g - 3.75g$ — Subtract $3.75g$ from each side. $4g - 3.75g = 0.25g$
$2.50 + 0.25g = 3.50$
$2.50 - 2.50 + 0.25g = 3.50 - 2.50$ — Subtract 2.50 from each side. $3.50 - 2.50 = 1$
$0.25g = 1$
$\frac{0.25g}{0.25} = \frac{1}{0.25}$ — Divide each side by 0.25.
$g = 4$ — $1 \div 0.25 = 4$

Page 468, Lesson 10-1a (Your Turn)

a.

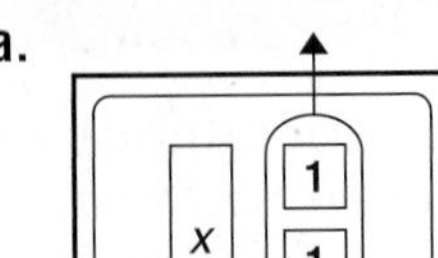
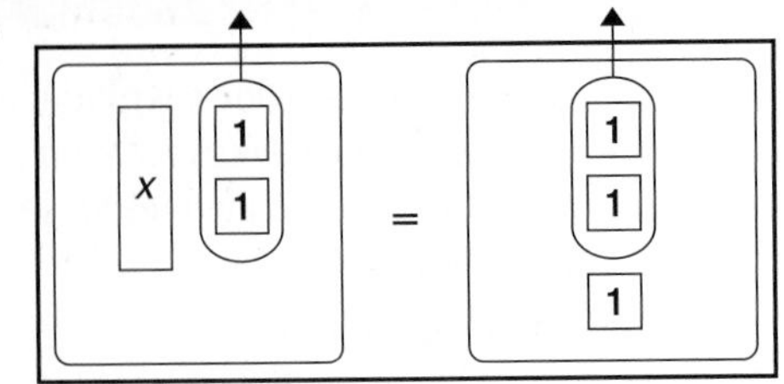

b.

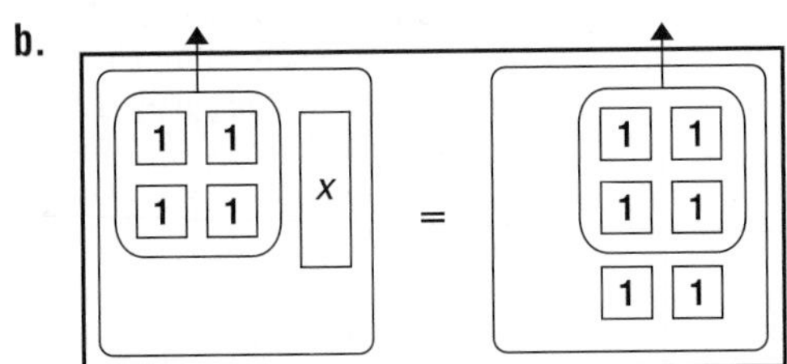

c.

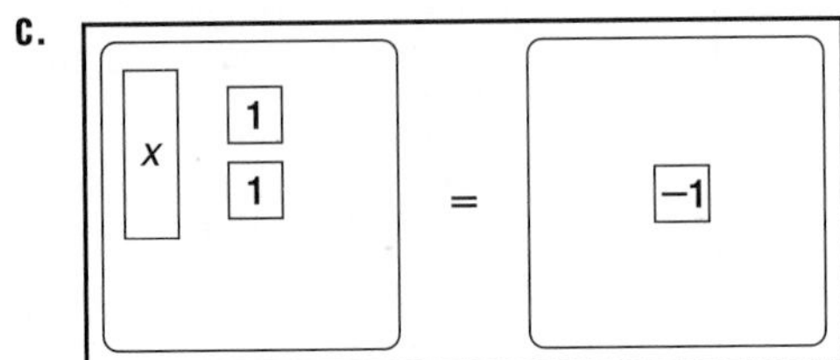

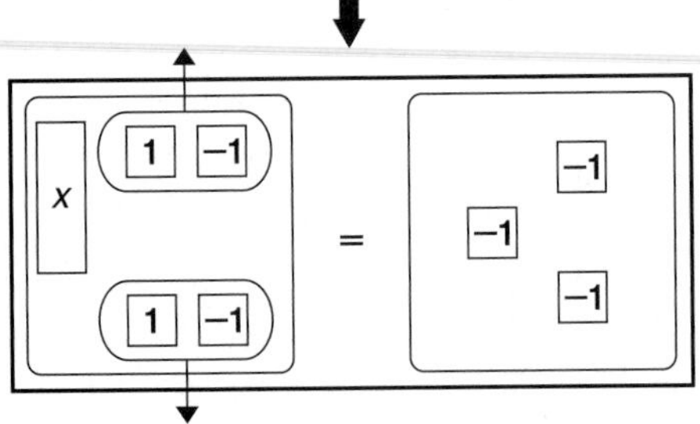

d.

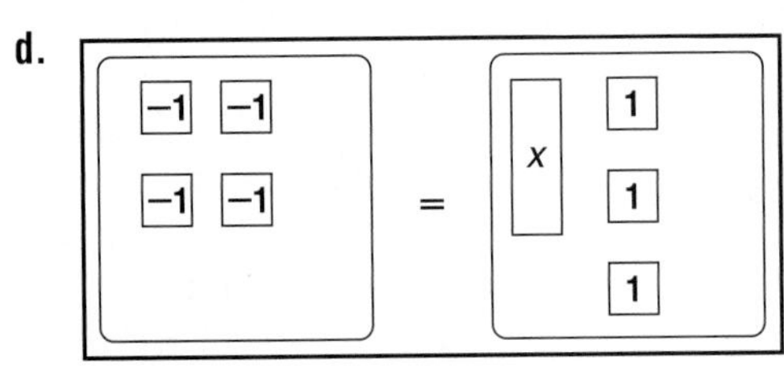

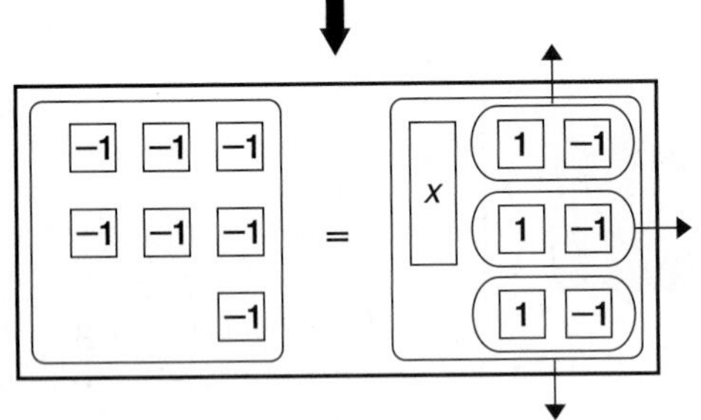

e.

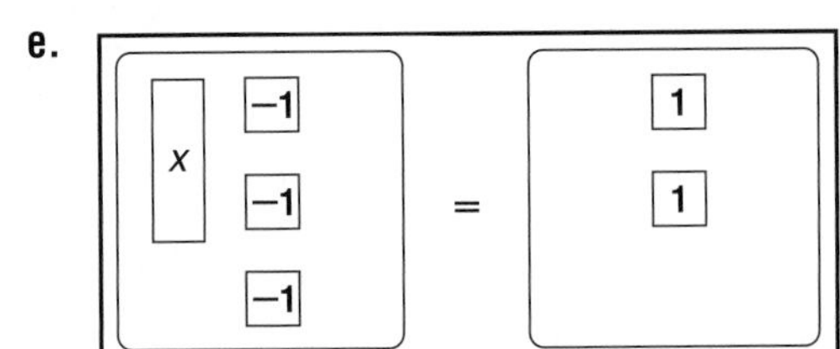

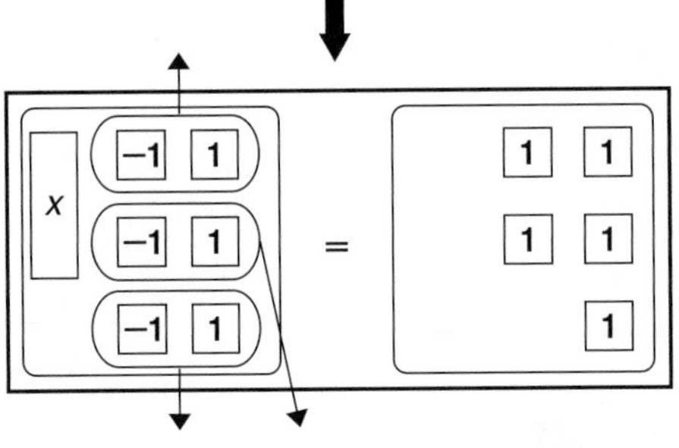

f.

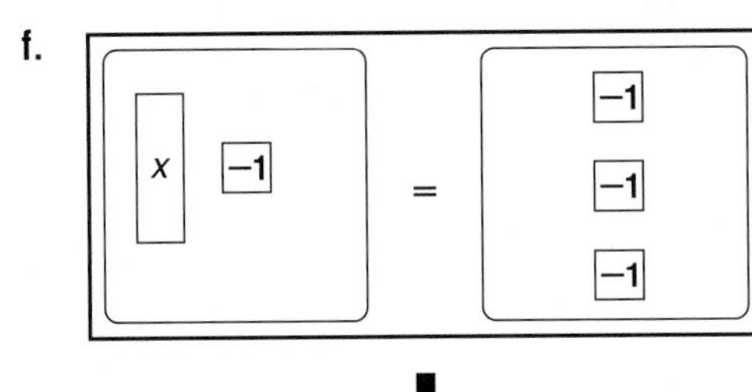

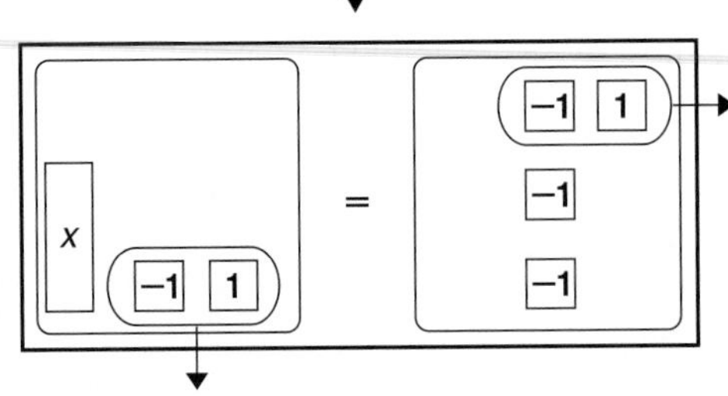

g.

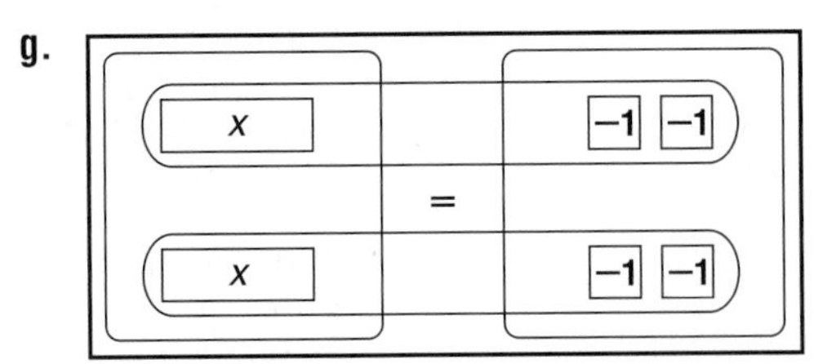

h.

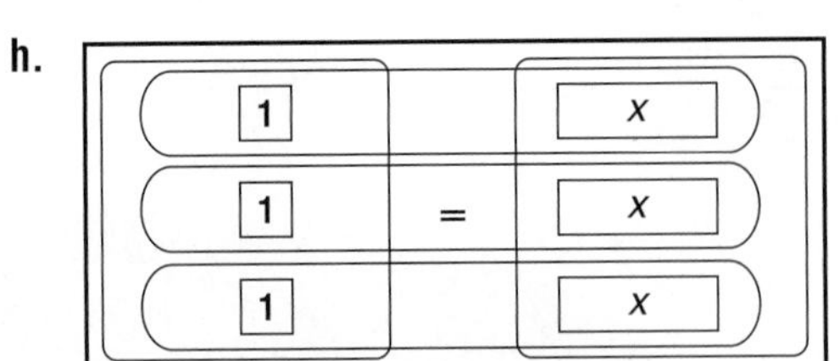

Page 483, Lesson 10-4a (Your Turn)

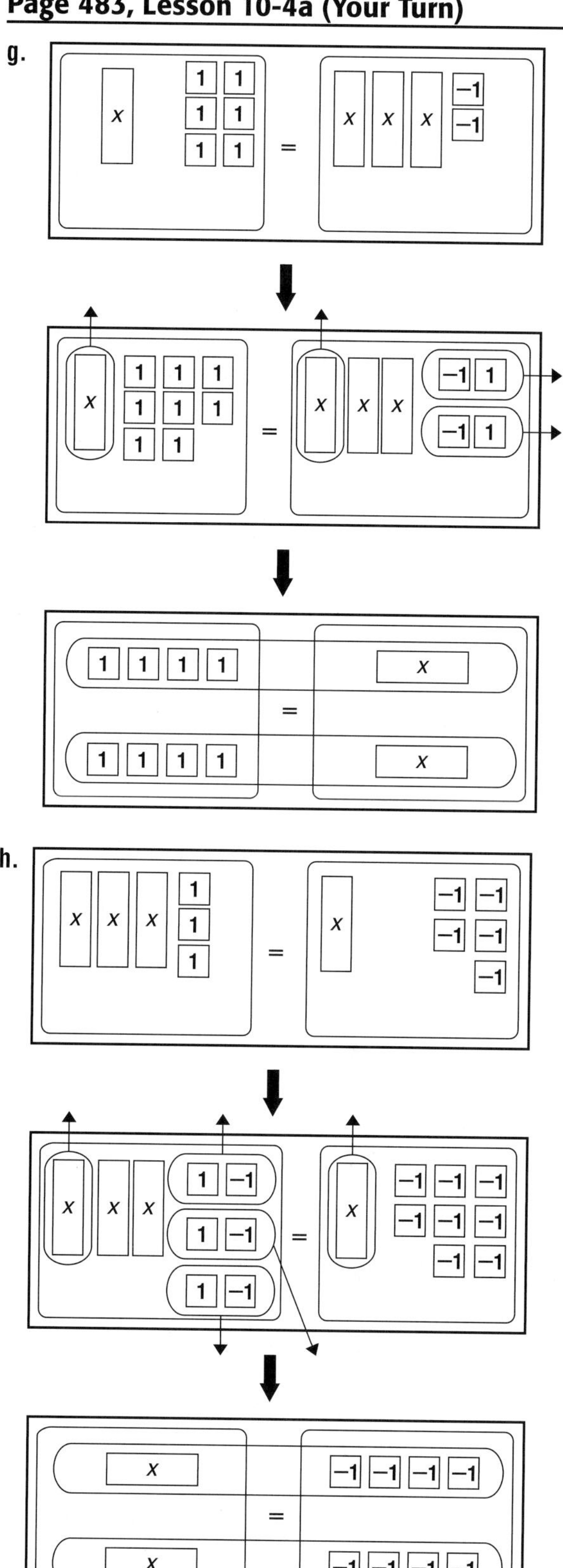

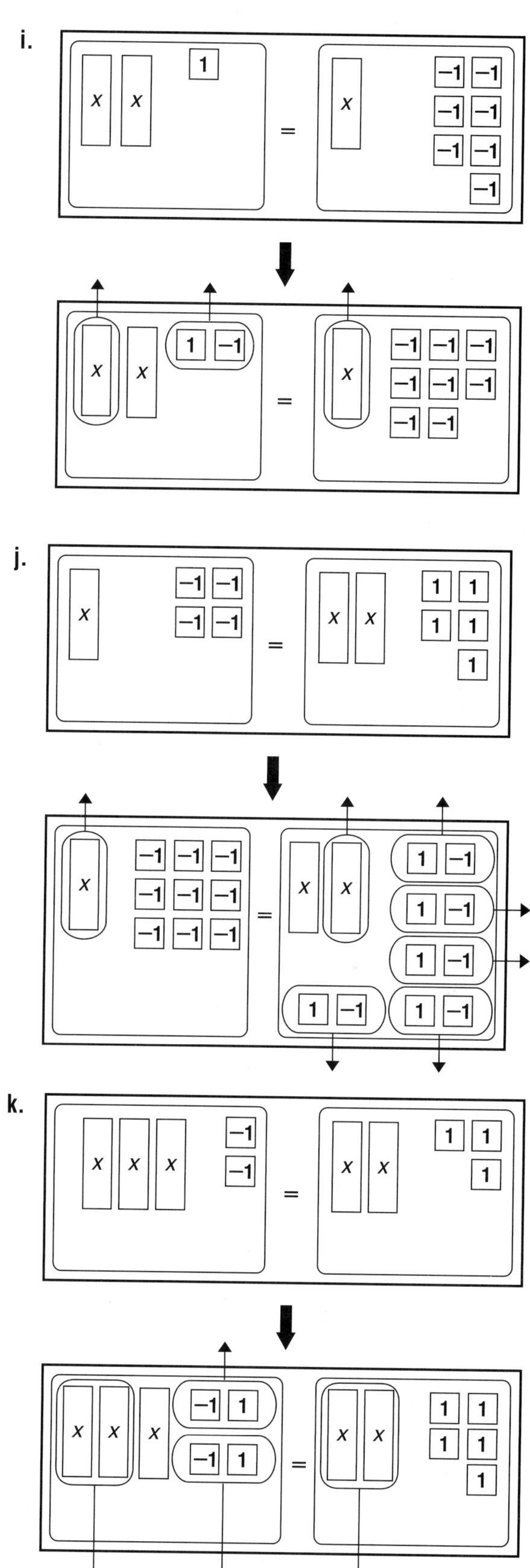

l.

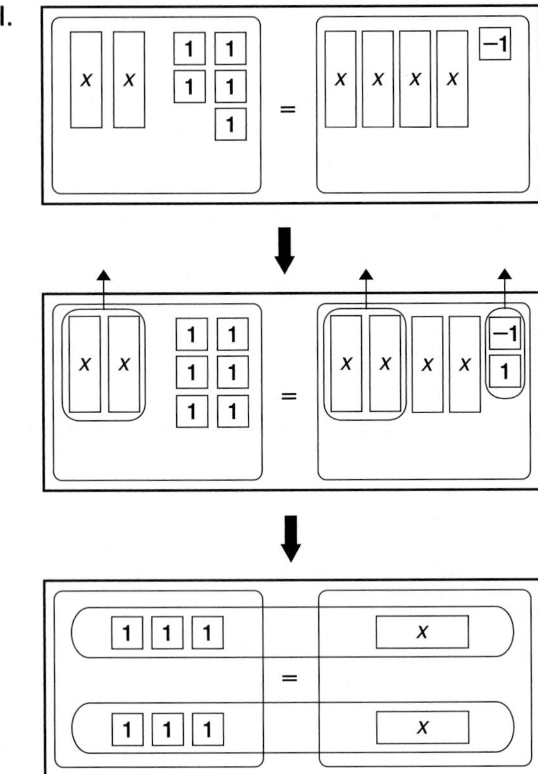

Additional Answers for Chapter 10

NOTES

Chapter Overview

Algebra: Linear Functions

	LESSON OBJECTIVES	NCTM Standards	NAEP 2005	State/Local Objectives
11-1	**Sequences** (pp. 512–516) • Recognize and extend arithmetic and geometric sequences. **11-1b Hands-On Lab:** Determine numbers that make up the Fibonacci Sequence.	1, 6, 7, 10	A1a, A1b, A1c	
11-2	**Functions** (pp. 517–520) • Complete function tables.	1, 2, 6, 7, 10	A1a, A1b, A1c, A2a, A2g	
11-3	**Graphing Linear Functions** (pp. 521–525) **11-3a Hands-On Lab:** Graph relationships. • Graph linear functions by using function tables and plotting points.	1, 2, 3, 6, 7, 9, 10	A1c, A2c, A1e, A2a, A4d, G4d, A1a, D2e, N4a	
11-4	**The Slope Formula** (pp. 526–529) • Find the slope of a line using the slope formula.	1, 2, 3, 6, 7, 10	A4d, A1f, A2c, G4d	
11-5	**Slope-Intercept Form** (pp. 532–536) **11-5a Graphing Calculator Investigation:** Use a graphing calculator to graph families of lines. • Graph linear equations using the slope and y-intercept.	1, 2, 3, 6, 7, 9, 10	A4d, A2a, A2c, A4c, A1f, A2e, A2b	
11-6	**Statistics: Scatter Plots** (pp. 537–543) **11-6a Problem-Solving Strategy:** Solve problems by using graphs. • Construct and interpret scatter plots. **11-6b Graphing Calculator Investigation:** Use a graphing calculator to make a scatter plot.	1, 2, 3, 6, 7, 9, 10	M1g, A2c, D1b, D2e, A2a, A1f, A4d, D1a, D1c	
11-7	**Graphing Systems of Equations** (pp. 544–547) • Solve systems of linear equations by graphing.	1, 2, 3, 6, 7, 9, 10	A2a, A4c, A3a	
11-8	**Graphing Linear Inequalities** (pp. 548–551) • Graph linear inequalities.	1, 2, 3, 6, 7, 9, 10	A2a, A4c	

Key to NCTM Standards:

1=Number & Operations, 2=Algebra, 3=Geometry, 4=Measurement, 5=Data Analysis & Probability, 6=Problem Solving, 7=Reasoning & Proof, 8=Communication, 9=Connections, 10=Representation

NAEP 2005 Standards: See Teacher Resources at math.glencoe.com

Pacing suggestions for the entire year can be found on page T23.

StudentWorks

*An electronic version of this chapter is available on **StudentWorks™**. This backpack solution CD-ROM allows students instant access to the Student Edition, lesson worksheet pages, and web resources.*

Chapter Resource Manager

	Chapter 11 Resource Masters: Study Guide and Intervention	Practice (Skills and Word Problems)	Reading to Learn Mathematics	Enrichment	Assessment	Applications*	Parent and Student Study Guide Online Worksheets	5-Minute Check Transparencies	Key Teaching Transparencies	MathPASS: Tutorial Plus (lessons)	Teaching Mathematics with Manipulatives	Noteables™: Interactive Study Notebook	Optional Materials
	619	620–621	622	623			11-1	11-1	41	46	108	11-1	colored pencils
	624	625–626	627	628	673	CM 37–38 CS 45	11-2	11-2	42			11-2	
	629	630–631	632	633		RC 37 CS 46	11-3	11-3		47	109	11-3	pencil, 2 paper clips, paper cup, large rubber band, tape, ruler, 10 pennies
	634	635–636	637	638	673, 675		11-4	11-4				11-4	
	639	640–641	642	643			11-5	11-5				11-5	
	644	645–646	647	648	674	SM 57–60 CS 47	11-6	11-6	43		110	11-6	tape measure
	649	650–651	652	653		CS 48	11-7	11-7	44			11-7	
	654	655–656	657	658	659–672, 674, 676–678		11-8	11-8				11-8	

* **Key to Abbreviations:** *CS = Calculator and Spreadsheet Masters, RC = Real-Life Career Masters, CM = Classroom Math Games (online), SM = Science and Math Lab Manual (online)*

PowerPoint® Presentations

This CD-ROM is a customizable Microsoft® PowerPoint® presentation that includes:

- In-Class Examples
- Links to Online Study Tools
- 5-Minute Check Transparencies
- Your Turn Exercises

Math Skills Maintenance

Use the Math Skills Maintenance Masters to keep your students' basic math skills fresh. Students can review skills one at a time or in a combined format. The Masters are also available online at msmath3.net/maintenance.

Mathematical Content and Teaching Strategies

Continuity of Instruction

Building on Prior Knowledge

Students have studied sequences of shapes and colors in earlier math courses. They are familiar with the coordinate plane through graphing ordered pairs, such as (3, 5). In Course 1 and Course 2 of *Glencoe Mathematics: Applications and Concepts,* their exposure to functions was primarily determining input and output values on a table. They can graph functions of this form, and they can graph simple inequalities, such as $x \leq 6$.

Learning in This Chapter

Students shift from visual sequences, such as shapes and colors, to sequences formed by adding or multiplying numbers. They are introduced to functions using the $f(x)$ notation. They extend their ability to graph on a coordinate plane from plotting ordered pairs to graphing linear functions, such as $f(x) = 3x - 2$. They also learn that an equivalent way of writing this is $y = 3x - 2$. Near the end of this chapter, students learn to graph systems of equations and linear inequalities.

Making Future Connections

In future math courses, students will learn about more advanced sequences. For example, a sequence may be formed by squaring a number then adding an integer. Students will apply more advanced functions to everyday situations. They will learn about direct and indirect variation of functions, such as $y = -5x$. Given a function of the form $f(x)$, students will be able determine, for example, $f(q + 3)$. Students will explore equations in point-slope form and recognize corresponding graphs.

Mathematical Background

11-1 Sequences

The ability to recognize patterns is an important problem-solving skill. A sequence is an ordered list of numbers. In arithmetic sequences, a number is added or subtracted to obtain the next term. In geometric sequences, a number is multiplied or divided to obtain the next term.

11-2 Functions

A function is a relationship in which one thing depends upon another. For example, the function $f(x) = x + 3$ shows that the output $f(x)$ is determined by adding 3 to the input x. Functions are important because they are what enable mathematics to describe and often explain the world around us.

11-3 Graphing Linear Functions

A function in which the graph of the solutions forms a line is a linear function. These are written in the form $y = mx + b$. Linear functions are graphed by determining possible values for x and y, plotting them, and connecting them to form a line.

Team Teaching

Tell other teachers on your team that your students are learning to graph linear equations, systems of equations, and linear inequalities. Ask them to incorporate these skills whenever possible in their classes.

Physical Science: graph motion

Earth Science: graph temperature changes or movement of tectonic plates

Social Studies: graph economic supply and demand

Bulletin Board Starters

Have students create a bulletin board showing a variety of the graphs they study in this chapter. Students might begin the bulletin board as they study graphing linear equations in Lesson 11-3. Other graphs to be included are scatter plots; systems of equations with one, infinite, or no solutions; and inequalities with a $\leq, \geq, <$, or $>$ sign.

11-4 The Slope Formula

Slope can be determined using the formula $m = \frac{y_2 - y_1}{x_2 - x_1}$, where $x_2 \neq x_1$. Using the graph of a line, the slope can be found by determining how much the y value changes for each change in the x value.

Using the Media

Bring to class several USA TODAY Snapshots® that show data that changed over time. Have groups of students find the rates of change between several consecutive years. What do the rates of change represent? Have each group present their findings.

11-5 Slope-Intercept Form

An equation of a line written as $y = mx + b$ is in the slope-intercept form. In this equation, m is the slope, and b is the y-intercept, or the value of y at the point where the line crosses the y-axis. By writing a linear equation in the slope-intercept form, the line can easily be graphed using the y-intercept and slope.

11-6 Statistics: Scatter Plots

Data written as ordered pairs can be plotted on a scatter plot. If all the data points are plotted and the points seem to cluster around a line, the data can be described as showing a relationship. If the points are scattered randomly, there is no relationship between the data points.

Teacher to Teacher

Sherry Jarvis
Flat Rock Middle School
East Flat Rock, NC

"I illustrate best-fit lines by laying a piece of thin dry spaghetti very close to the data. This works well as a student activity or as modeled by the teacher using an overhead projector."

Sherry Jarvis

11-7 Graphing Systems of Equations

Two or more equations are called a system of equations. Some everyday problems require finding an ordered pair that solves a system of equations. If on a graph of a system of equations, the lines intersect at just one point, those x and y values are the only ones that solve both equations. If the lines are parallel, there are no x and y values that solve both equations. If the lines are the same, the equations have an infinite number of points in common.

11-8 Graphing Linear Inequalities

If the equal sign in a linear equation is replaced by $<$, $>$, $\geq$, or $\leq$, the equation is a linear inequality. Linear inequalities are graphed the same as linear equations and then an area is shaded to show the range of solutions. Linear inequalities can be based on word problems, and the answers solved for by graphing.

What the Research Says

According to O'Callaghan in "Computer-Intensive Algebra and Students' Conceptual Knowledge of Functions," student understanding is increased when functions are used to model concrete situations and when they are expressed in various representations.

- In Lessons 11-2 through 11-8, functions are used to represent real-life situations.
- In Chapter 11, functions are expressed using equations, tables, and graphs.

McGraw-Hill Professional Development

Mathematics, YES! is a self-paced, web-based professional development program. Units are based on major mathematical concepts and are standards-based. Actual classroom videos provide a springboard for discussion and activities. Units appropriate for this chapter:

- Patterns and Functions
- Coordinate Pairs and Graphing
- Solving Equations and Inequalities

Additional mathematical information and teaching notes are available at msmath3.net/key_concepts.

DAILY INTERVENTION and Assessment

* **Key to Abbreviations:**
TWE = Teacher Wraparound Edition, *CRM* = Chapter Resource Masters

	Type	Student Edition	Teacher Resources	Technology/Internet
INTERVENTION	Ongoing	Prerequisite Skills, pp. 511, 515, 520, 525, 529, 536, 542, 547 Mid-Chapter Practice Test, p. 530	5-Minute Check Transparencies Quizzes 1–4, *CRM,* pp. 673–674 Mid-Chapter Test, *CRM,* p. 675 Study Guide and Intervention, *CRM,* pp. 619, 624, 629, 634, 639, 644, 649, 654	MathPASS: Tutorial Plus msmath3.net/self_check_quiz msmath3.net/extra_examples
	Mixed Review	pp. 515, 520, 525, 529, 536, 542, 547, 551	Cumulative Review, *CRM,* p. 676	
	Error Analysis	Find the Error, pp. 519, 528, 550	Find the Error, *TWE,* pp. 519, 528, 550 Unlocking Misconceptions, *TWE,* pp. 534, 540, 549 Tips for New Teachers, *TWE,* pp. 513, 518	
ASSESSMENT	Standardized Test Practice	pp. 515, 520, 523, 525, 529, 530, 536, 538, 542, 547, 551, 555, 556–557	Standardized Test Practice, *CRM,* pp. 677–678	Standardized Test Practice CD-ROM msmath3.net/standardized_test
	Open-Ended Assessment	Writing Math, pp. 514, 516, 521, 524, 528, 535, 541 Open-Ended, pp. 514, 519, 524, 528, 535, 541, 546, 550 Standardized Test, p. 557	Modeling: *TWE,* pp. 515, 529 Speaking: *TWE,* pp. 519, 542 Writing: *TWE,* pp. 525, 538, 551 Extended Response Assessment, *CRM,* p. 671	
	Chapter Assessment	Study Guide, pp. 552–554 Practice Test, p. 555	Multiple-Choice Tests (Forms 1, 2A, 2B), *CRM,* pp. 659–664 Free-Response Tests (Forms 2C, 2D, 3), *CRM,* pp. 665–670 Vocabulary Test/Review, *CRM,* p. 672	ExamView® Pro Testmaker (see below) MindJogger Videoquizzes msmath3.net/vocabulary_review msmath3.net/chapter_test

For more information on Yearly ProgressPro, see p. 464.

Glencoe Lesson	Yearly ProgressPro Skill Name
11-1	Sequences
11-2	Functions
11-3	Graphing Linear Functions
11-4	Slope: Level 1
11-5	Slope-Intercept Form
11-6	Scatter Plots
11-7	Graphing Systems of Equations
11-8	Graphing Inequalities

ExamView® Pro

Use ExamView® Pro Testmaker CD-ROM to:

- Create multiple versions of tests.
- Create modified tests for inclusion students with one mouse click.
- Edit existing questions and add your own questions.
- Build tests aligned with state standards using built-in state curriculum correlations.
- Change English tests to Spanish with one mouse click and vice versa.

Reading and Writing in Mathematics

READING in the Content Area

This online worksheet provides strategies for reading and analyzing Lesson 11-2, Functions. Students are guided through questions about the main idea, subject matter, supporting details, conclusion, clarifying details, and vocabulary of the lesson.

Interactive Study Notebook With Foldables™ is a study organizer that provides helpful steps for students to follow to organize their notes for Chapter 11.

- Students use Noteables to record notes and to complete their Foldables as you present the material in Lessons 11-1 through 11-8.
- Noteables follow the *Teacher Wraparound Edition's* In-Class Examples and *Interactive Chalkboard CD-ROM.*

For more information on Reading and Writing in Mathematics, see pp. T6–T7.

Recommended Outside Reading for Students

Nonfiction

- Flansburg, Scott. *Math Magic for Your Kids.* HarperCollins, © 1998.
  Using entertaining games and tricks, this book helps kids develop a positive foundation of math skills. Activities can be done independently or with family assistance.

Fiction

- Guedj, Denis. *The Parrot's Theorem: A Novel.* St. Martin's Press, © 2001.
  This book features mathematical history disguised as a murder mystery. This story follows three children as they discover math history on their way to solving the murder.

PROJECT CRISS℠ Study Skill

Capsule Vocabulary is a teaching strategy that helps students verbally review important terms. After students have studied Lesson 11-1, write the vocabulary words at the right on the chalkboard. Discuss sequences with the class, including the vocabulary words in your discussion. Divide the class into pairs. Have students talk about sequences with their partners. Each student should make sure his or her partner uses all of the words. Afterward, have students write a short summary about sequences.

Sequences Vocabulary
- term
- arithmetic sequence
- geometric sequence
- common ratio

CReating Independence through Student-owned Strategies

For more information on Project CRISS, see p. T8.

CHAPTER 11 Making Connections

School-To-Home

Parent and Student Study Guide

Parents and students may work together to reinforce the concepts and skills of this chapter. These online worksheets are available in English and Spanish at msmath3.net/parent_student. A sample lesson is shown below.

Family Letters and Activities

Send a letter and activity for this chapter home to encourage family members to become active participants in their students' learning. (English: *Chapter 11 Resource Masters*, pp. ix–x; Spanish: log on to msmath3.net/family_letters)

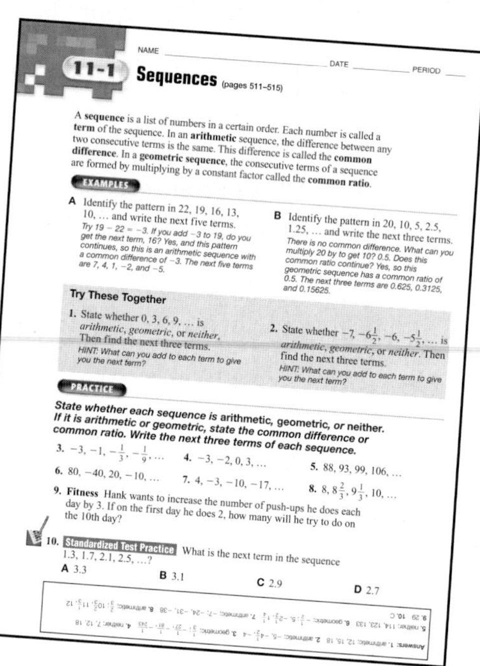

NAME ______ DATE ______ PERIOD ______

11-1 Sequences (pages 511–515)

A **sequence** is a list of numbers in a certain order. Each number is called a **term** of the sequence. In an **arithmetic** sequence, the difference between any two consecutive terms is the same. This difference is called the **common difference**. In a **geometric sequence**, the consecutive terms of a sequence are formed by multiplying by a constant factor called the **common ratio**.

EXAMPLES

A Identify the pattern in 22, 19, 16, 13, 10, … and write the next five terms.
Try 19 − 22 = −3. If you add −3 to 19, do you get the next term, 16? Yes, and this pattern continues, so this is an arithmetic sequence with a common difference of −3. The next five terms are 7, 4, 1, −2, and −5.

B Identify the pattern in 20, 10, 5, 2.5, 1.25, … and write the next three terms.
There is no common difference. What can you multiply 20 by to get 10? 0.5. Does this common ratio continue? Yes, so this geometric sequence has a common ratio of 0.5. The next three terms are 0.625, 0.3125, and 0.15625.

Try These Together

1. State whether 0, 3, 6, 9, … is *arithmetic*, *geometric*, or *neither*. Then find the next three terms.
HINT: What can you add to each term to give you the next term?

2. State whether $-7, -6\frac{1}{2}, -6, -5\frac{1}{2}, \ldots$ is *arithmetic*, *geometric*, or *neither*. Then find the next three terms.
HINT: What can you add to each term to give you the next term?

PRACTICE

State whether each sequence is arithmetic, geometric, or neither. If it is arithmetic or geometric, state the common difference or common ratio. Write the next three terms of each sequence.

3. $-3, -1, -\frac{1}{3}, -\frac{1}{9}, \ldots$
4. $-3, -2, 0, 3, \ldots$
5. 88, 93, 99, 106, …
6. 80, −40, 20, −10, …
7. 4, −3, −10, −17, …
8. $8, 8\frac{2}{3}, 9\frac{1}{3}, 10, \ldots$
9. **Fitness** Hank wants to increase the number of push-ups he does each day by 3. If on the first day he does 2, how many will he try to do on the 10th day?
10. **Standardized Test Practice** What is the next term in the sequence 1.3, 1.7, 2.1, 2.5, …?
A 3.3 **B** 3.1 **C** 2.9 **D** 2.7

Answers: 1. arithmetic; 12, 15, 18 2. arithmetic; $-5, -4\frac{1}{2}, -4$ 3. geometric; $\frac{1}{3}$; $-\frac{1}{27}, -\frac{1}{81}, -\frac{1}{243}$ 4. neither; 7, 12, 18 5. neither; 114, 123, 133 6. geometric; $-\frac{1}{2}$; $5, -2\frac{1}{2}, 1\frac{1}{4}$ 7. arithmetic; −7; −24, −31, −38 8. arithmetic; $\frac{2}{3}$; $10\frac{2}{3}, 11\frac{1}{3}, 12$ 9. 29 10. C

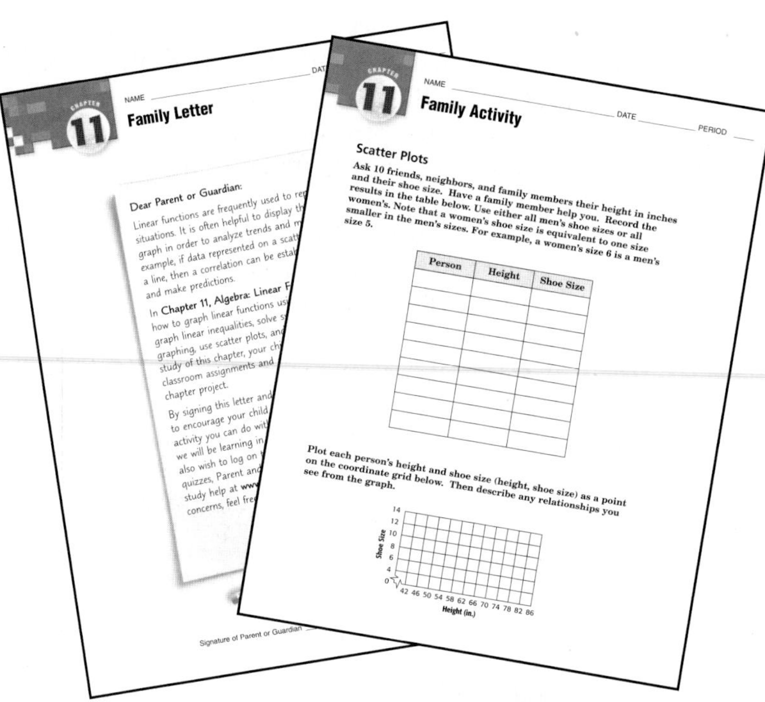

CHAPTER 11

NAME ______ DAT

Family Letter

Dear Parent or Guardian:

Linear functions are frequently used to rep
situations. It is often helpful to display th
graph in order to analyze trends and m
example, if data represented on a scatt
a line, then a correlation can be estab
and make predictions.

In **Chapter 11, Algebra: Linear F**
how to graph linear functions usi
graph linear inequalities, solve s
graphing, use scatter plots, an
study of this chapter, your ch
classroom assignments and
chapter project.

By signing this letter and
to encourage your child
activity you can do wit
we will be learning in
also wish to log on
quizzes, Parent and
study help at **www**
concerns, feel fre

Signature of Parent or Guardian ______

CHAPTER 11

NAME ______ DATE ______ PERIOD ______

Family Activity

Scatter Plots

Ask 10 friends, neighbors, and family members their height in inches and their shoe size. Have a family member help you. Record the results in the table below. Use either all men's shoe sizes or all women's. Note that a women's shoe size is equivalent to one size smaller in the men's sizes. For example, a women's size 6 is a men's size 5.

Person	Height	Shoe Size

Plot each person's height and shoe size (height, shoe size) as a point on the coordinate grid below. Then describe any relationships you see from the graph.

English Language Learner ELL

Lesson 11-1
Higher-Level Thinking

Give students in groups several index cards with sequences. Have them find the next term for each sequence. Then have them explain what kind of sequence each one is, find the common ratio or difference, and explain their reasoning.

Lesson 11-2
Building on Prior Knowledge

Give students an example of evaluating an expression. For example, $2x - 3$, where $x = 4$.

$$2x - 3 = 2(4) - 3$$
$$= 8 - 3$$
$$= 5$$

Then, show students the concept of evaluating a function for a specified value. Have the students note the similarities in the procedures.

Lesson 11-6
Using Multisensory Activities

To determine a line of best fit, bring in a box of spaghetti. Have students graph a set of data and use the spaghetti to model the line of best fit. Using the spaghetti helps students determine a positive or negative relationship for the given values. Once they have agreed on a best line for a set of data, they can find the slope and *y*-intercept for the line.

MathScape™  This project was supported, in part, by the **National Science Foundation**

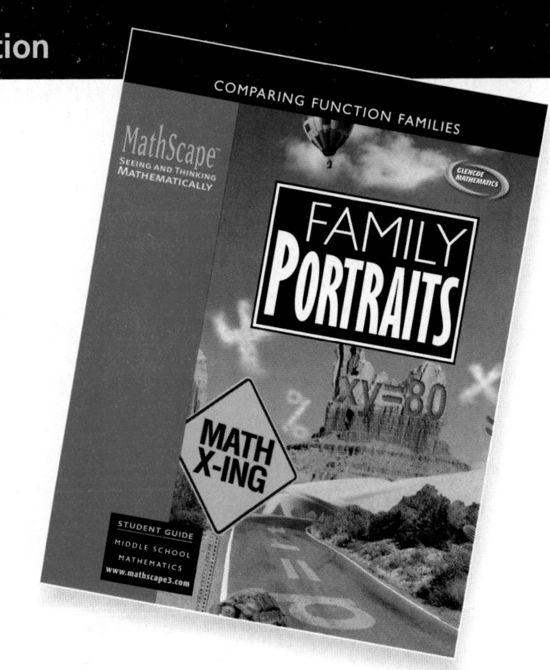

MathScape is a mathematics curriculum for grades 6–8 developed by the Seeing and Thinking Mathematically Project at the Education Development Center.

Comparing Function Families
Family Portraits

How to Use *MathScape* with Chapter 11

The unit *Family Portraits* can be used to enhance Lessons 11-2 and 11-4.

- **Enrich** → After you complete **Lesson 11-2,** you can challenge students to write function rules by using the activity on page 272.
- **Introduce** → Before you begin **Lesson 11-4,** you can introduce the slope of a line by using the activity on page 280.

For other lessons in Chapter 11 that correlate to *MathScape*, see the chart on page T14.

Online Lesson Planner

USA TODAY® Education's Online site offers resources and interactive features connected to each day's newspaper. *Experience Today,* USA TODAY's® daily lesson plan, is available on the site and delivered daily to subscribers. This plan provides instruction for integrating USA TODAY® graphics and key editorial features into your mathematics classroom. Log on to **education.usatoday.com.**

USA TODAY Snapshots® in Chapter 11	
Lesson	**Snapshot**
11-4	No place like home – both of them

Quick Review Math Handbook

is Glencoe's mathematical handbook for students. The Hot Words section includes a glossary of terms while the Hot Topics section consists of explanations of key mathematical concepts. An exercise set is included to check students' understanding of the concepts. This valuable resource can be used as a reference in the classroom or for home study.

Lesson	Hot Topics Section	Lesson	Hot Topics Section
11-1	1-4	**11-5**	6-8, 9-2
11-2	6-8	**11-6**	4-3, 6-7, 6-8, 9-2
11-3	6-8	**11-7**	6-8
11-4	6-8	**11-8**	6-8

Key Chapter Objectives

Lesson 11-2 Complete function tables.

Lesson 11-3 Graph linear functions by using function tables.

Lesson 11-5 Graph linear equations using the slope and y-intercept.

Lesson 11-8 Graph linear inequalities.

"What does mountain climbing have to do with math?"

Point out to students that this is only one of many applications of the math that they are studying. Others are provided in the introduction to each lesson.

Vocabulary Builder, pp. vii–viii ELL

CHAPTER 11

NAME ________________ DATE ________ PERIOD ____

Reading to Learn Mathematics

Vocabulary Builder

This is an alphabetical list of new vocabulary terms you will learn in Chapter 11. As you study the chapter, complete each term's definition or description. Remember to add the page number where you found the term. Add this page to your math study notebook to review vocabulary at the end of the chapter.

Vocabulary Term	Found on Page	Definition/Description/Example
arithmetic sequence [air-ith-MEH-tik]		
best-fit line		
boundary		
common difference		
common ratio		
dependent variable		
domain		
function		
function table		
geometric sequence [je-o-MET-rik]		
half plane		

CHAPTER 11

Algebra: Linear Functions

"What does mountain climbing have to do with math?"

As mountain climbers ascend the mountain, the temperature becomes colder. So, the temperature *depends* on the altitude. **In mathematics, you say that the temperature is a function of the altitude.**

You will solve problems about temperature changes and climbing mountains in Lesson 11-3.

Vocabulary Builder

For a thorough vocabulary list with pronunciations of new words, give students the Vocabulary Builder worksheets from the *Chapter 11 Resource Masters*. Encourage them to complete the definition of each term as they progress through the chapter.

GETTING STARTED

▶ Diagnose Readiness

Take this quiz to see if you are ready to begin Chapter 11. Refer to the lesson or page number in parentheses for review.

Vocabulary Review

State whether each sentence is *true* or *false*. If *false*, replace the underlined word or number to make a true sentence.

1. In terms of slope, the rise is the <u>horizontal</u> change. (Lesson 4-3) **false; vertical**
2. $y \geq x + 4$ is an example of an <u>inequality</u>. (Lesson 4-3) **true**

Prerequisite Skills

Graph each point on the same coordinate plane. (Page 614) **3–6. See margin.**

3. $A(-3, -4)$
4. $B(2, -1)$
5. $C(0, -2)$
6. $D(-4, 3)$

Evaluate each expression if $x = 6$. (Lesson 1-2)

7. $3x$ **18**
8. $4x - 9$ **15**
9. $2x + 8$ **20**
10. $5 + x$ **11**

Solve each equation. (Lesson 1-8)

11. $14 = n + 9$ **5**
12. $z - 3 = 8$ **11**
13. $-17 = b - 21$ **4**
14. $23 + r = 16$ **−7**

Find the slope of each line. (Lesson 4-3)

15. 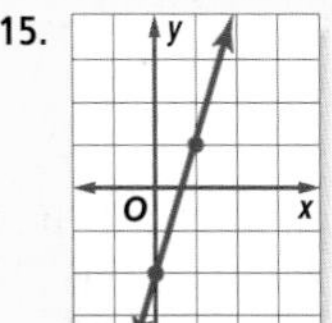

3

16. 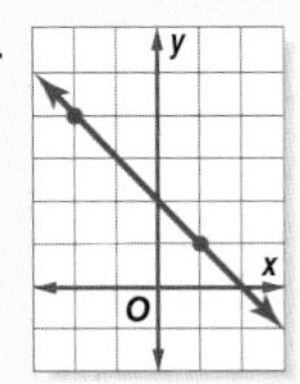

−1

FOLDABLES™ Study Organizer

Linear Functions Make this Foldable to help you organize your notes. Begin with a plain piece of notebook paper.

STEP 1 Fold in Half Fold the paper lengthwise to the holes.

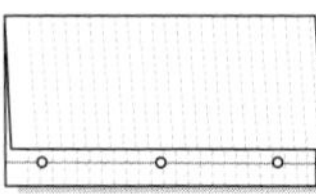

STEP 2 Fold Fold the paper in fourths.

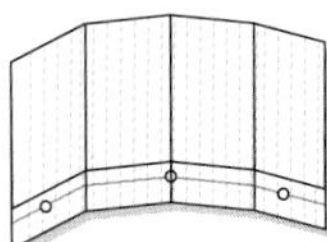

STEP 3 Cut Open. Cut one side along the folds to make four tabs.

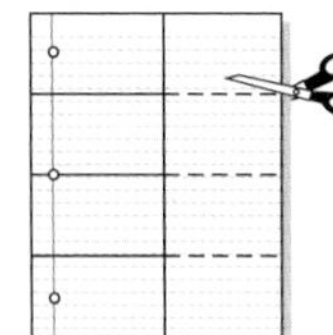

STEP 4 Label Label each tab with the main topics as shown.

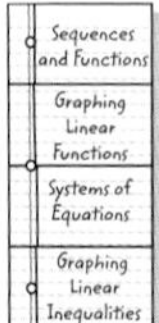

Chapter Notes Each time you find this logo throughout the chapter, use your *Noteables™: Interactive Study Notebook with Foldables™* or your own notebook to take notes. Begin your chapter notes with this Foldable activity.

Math Online **Readiness** To prepare yourself for this chapter with another quiz, visit **msmath3.net/chapter_readiness**

GETTING STARTED

Diagnose Readiness This section provides a review of the basic concepts needed before beginning Chapter 11. Page references are included for additional student help.

Prerequisite Skills review a skill needed in the chapter.

Exercises	Needed for Lesson	Skill
3–6	11-3	Graph Points on a Coordinate Plane
7–10	11-2	Evaluate Expressions
11–14	11-5	Solve Equations
15–16	11-4	Find the Slope of a Line

For more prerequisite skills, see:

- Getting Ready for the Next Lesson at the end of each lesson
- Prerequisite Skills in the Student Handbook on pp. 600–615
- *Math Skills Maintenance Masters*

Answers

3–6. 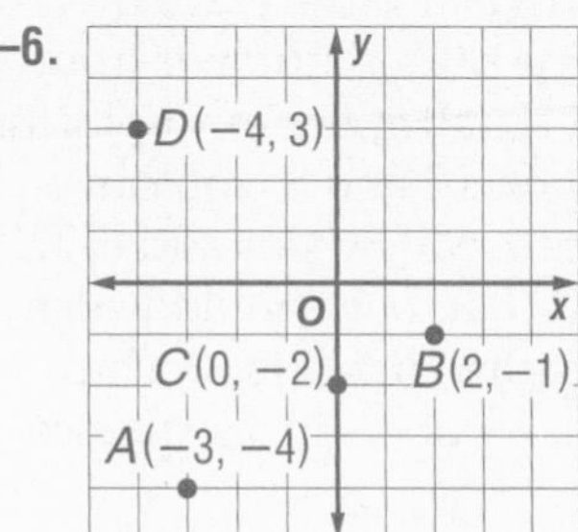

FOLDABLES™ Study Organizer

For more information about Foldables, see *Teaching Mathematics with Foldables.*

Use this Foldable for student writing about linear functions. After students make their Foldables, have them skim through the chapter and write questions in the appropriate sections of their Foldables. As students work through the eight lessons, ask them to record the answers to their questions under the appropriate tabs. During reading, students can use their Foldables to record other questions, take notes, record concepts, define terms, and write examples.

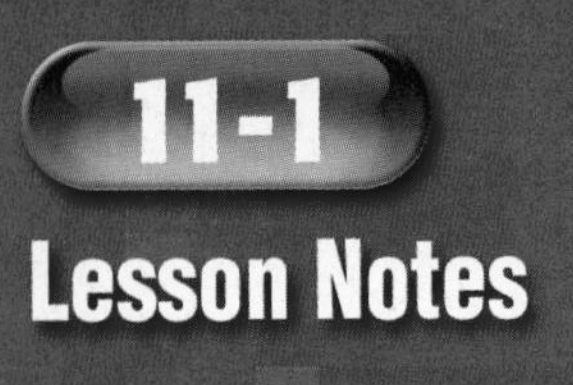

Lesson Notes

Lesson Resources

Chapter 11 Resource Masters
- Study Guide and Intervention, p. 619
- Practice: Skills, p. 620
- Practice: Word Problems, p. 621
- Reading to Learn Mathematics, p. 622
- Enrichment, p. 623

Key Teaching Transparencies, 41
MathPASS Tutorial CD-ROM, 25
Parent and Student Study Guide Online Worksheets, 11-1
Noteables™: Interactive Study Notebook with Foldables™, 11-1

1 Focus

5-Minute Check 11-1
Use as a quiz or review of Chapter 10. (Also available as a transparency)

Bellringer
Problem Solving Write the following on the chalkboard:
2, 8; 21, 3; −9, 36; 5, −15; 28, 7
For each pair, have students explain two or more ways to obtain the second number from the first number. For example, for the numbers 2 and 8, you can either multiply by 4 or add 6. Tell students that they should watch for more than one relationship between numbers in a sequence.

Reading to Learn Mathematics, p. 622 **ELL**

NAME ______ DATE ______ PERIOD ____

11-1 Reading to Learn Mathematics
Sequences

Pre-Activity *Complete the Mini Lab at the top of page 512 in your textbook. Write your answers below.*

1. Continue the pattern for 4, 5, and 6 triangles. How many toothpicks are needed for each case?
9; 11; 13
2. Study the pattern of numbers. How many toothpicks will you need for 7 triangles?
15
3. Continue the pattern for 4, 5, and 6 squares. How many toothpicks are needed for each case?
13; 16; 19
4. How many toothpicks will you need for 7 squares?
22

11-1 Sequences

What You'll LEARN
Recognize and extend arithmetic and geometric sequences.

NEW Vocabulary
sequence
term
arithmetic sequence
common difference
geometric sequence
common ratio

HANDS-ON Mini Lab

Materials
- toothpicks

Work with a partner.
Consider the following pattern.

Number of Triangles	1 triangle	2 triangles	3 triangles
Number of Toothpicks	3 toothpicks	5 toothpicks	7 toothpicks

1. Continue the pattern for 4, 5, and 6 triangles. How many toothpicks are needed for each case? **9; 11; 13**
2. Study the pattern of numbers. How many toothpicks will you need for 7 triangles? **15**

Now, consider another pattern.

Number of Squares	1 square	2 squares	3 squares
Number of Toothpicks	4 toothpicks	7 toothpicks	10 toothpicks

3. Continue the pattern for 4, 5, and 6 squares. How many toothpicks are needed for each case? **13; 16; 19**
4. How many toothpicks will you need for 7 squares? **22**

The numbers of toothpicks needed for each pattern form a sequence. A **sequence** is an ordered list of numbers. Each number is called a **term**.

An **arithmetic sequence** is a sequence in which the difference between any two consecutive terms is the same.

3, 5, 7, 9, 11, ...
+2 +2 +2 +2

To find the next number in an arithmetic sequence, add the common difference to the last term.

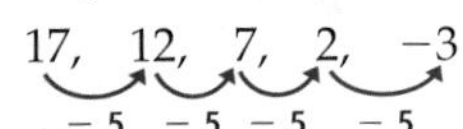

Identify Arithmetic Sequences

1 **State whether the sequence 17, 12, 7, 2, −3, ... is arithmetic. If it is, state the common difference. Write the next three terms of the sequence.**

17, 12, 7, 2, −3 Notice that 12 − 17 = −5, 7 − 12 = −5, and so on.
−5 −5 −5 −5

The terms have a common difference of −5, so the sequence is arithmetic. Continue the pattern to find the next three terms.

−3, −8, −13, −18
(−5, −5, −5)

The next three terms are −8, −13, and −18.

READING Math

And So On The three dots following a list of numbers are read as *and so on.*

A **geometric sequence** is a sequence in which the quotient between any two consecutive terms is the same.

2, 6, 18, 54, 162, …
(×3, ×3, ×3, ×3)

The quotient is called the **common ratio**.

To find the next number in a geometric sequence, multiply the last term by the common ratio.

EXAMPLES Identify Geometric Sequences

State whether each sequence is geometric. If it is, state the common ratio. Write the next three terms of each sequence.

2 **96, −48, 24, −12, 6, …**

96, −48, 24, −12, 6
$\times\left(-\frac{1}{2}\right)$ $\times\left(-\frac{1}{2}\right)$ $\times\left(-\frac{1}{2}\right)$ $\times\left(-\frac{1}{2}\right)$

Notice that $-48 \div 96 = -\frac{1}{2}$, $24 \div (-48) = -\frac{1}{2}$, and so on.

The terms have a common ratio of $-\frac{1}{2}$, so the sequence is geometric.

Continue the pattern to find the next three terms.

6, −3, $\frac{3}{2}$, $-\frac{3}{4}$
$\times\left(-\frac{1}{2}\right)$ $\times\left(-\frac{1}{2}\right)$ $\times\left(-\frac{1}{2}\right)$

The next three terms are −3, $\frac{3}{2}$, and $-\frac{3}{4}$.

TEACHING TIP

Students may have trouble finding the pattern of sequences that are not arithmetic or geometric. Suggest that in these cases students look to see if there is a pattern in the differences between consecutive terms or in the quotients between consecutive terms.

3 **2, 4, 12, 48, 240, …**

2, 4, 12, 48, 240
(×2, ×3, ×4, ×5)

Since there is no common ratio, the sequence is not geometric. However, the sequence does have a pattern. Multiply the last term by 6, the next term by 7, and the following term by 8.

240, 1,440, 10,080, 80,640
(×6, ×7, ×8)

The next three terms are 1,440, 10,080, and 80,640.

Your Turn **State whether each sequence is *arithmetic*, *geometric*, or *neither*. If it is arithmetic or geometric, state the common difference or common ratio. Write the next three terms of each sequence.**

a. 8, 12, 16, 20, 24, …
b. −5, 25, −125, 625, −3,125, …
c. 1, 2, 4, 7, 11, …
d. 243, 81, 27, 9, 3, …

a. arithmetic; 4; 28, 32, 36
b. geometric; −5; 15,625, −78,125, 390,625
c. neither; 16, 22, 29
d. geometric; $\frac{1}{3}$; 1, $\frac{1}{3}$, $\frac{1}{9}$

msmath3.net/extra_examples

2 Teach

Noteables™

As you work the **In-Class Examples,** have students follow along in their *Noteables™: Interactive Study Notebook with Foldables™*, or have students work the examples in their notebooks.

In-Class Examples

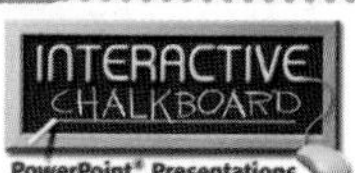

1 State whether the sequence 23, 15, 7, −1, −9, ... is arithmetic. If it is, state the common difference. Write the next three terms of the sequence.
arithmetic; −8; −17, −25, −33

State whether each sequence is geometric. If it is, state the common ratio. Write the next three terms of each sequence.

2 −1, 3, −9, 27, −81, ...
geometric; −3; 243, −729, 2,187

3 6, 12, 13, 26, 27, ... **not geometric; 54, 55, 110**

Intervention Some students can work math problems in their heads, while other students must write out detailed answers. Even if students work problems mentally, remind them that writing out clear answers will help them avoid careless errors.

DAILY INTERVENTION **Differentiated Instruction**

Auditory/Musical Arrange for a student to bring a musical instrument, such as a clarinet or guitar, to class. Have the student play various sequences of notes as the class listens. For example, the student may play the note C, then skip the note D, then play the note E, then skip the note F, and so on. The student should also demonstrate sequences of notes in songs. Students should recognize how sequences affect the sound of the music.

3 Practice/Apply

FOLDABLES™ Follow-Up Before they begin the lesson, encourage students to write a question about sequences under the first tab of their Foldables. As students progress through the lesson, encourage them to take notes and record information that answers their question.

Which One Doesn't Belong? Exercise 3 requires students to classify sequences as arithmetic or geometric. Caution students against looking at only the first two or three terms of a sequence when determining the common difference or ratio for each sequence.

About the Exercises...

Guided Practice Key

Exercises	Examples
4, 7–9	1
6	2
5	3

Assignment Guide

Basic: 11–19 odd, 25, 27–29, 31, 33–44

Average: 11–27 odd, 28, 29, 31, 33–44

Enriched: 10–26 even, 28–40 (Optional: 41–44)

Students practice the same concepts in Exercises 10–27 if they are assigned odd or even problems.

Skill and Concept Check

1. *Writing Math* Explain how to determine whether a sequence is geometric. **See margin.**
2. **OPEN ENDED** Give a counterexample to the following statement. *All sequences are either arithmetic or geometric.* **Sample answer: 1, 4, 9, 16, 25, ...**
3. **Which One Doesn't Belong?** Identify the sequence that is not the same type as the others. Explain your reasoning.

1, 2, 4, 8, 16, ...	125, 25, 5, 1, $\frac{1}{5}$, ...
5, 10, 15, 20, 25, ...	−2, 6, −18, 54, −162, ...

5, 10, 15, 20, 25, ...; It is an arithmetic sequence, and the others are geometric sequences.

GUIDED PRACTICE

State whether each sequence is *arithmetic, geometric,* or *neither*. If it is arithmetic or geometric, state the common difference or common ratio. Write the next three terms of each sequence. **6. geometric; −2; −96, 192, −384**

4. 2, 4, 6, 8, 10, ... **arithmetic; 2; 12, 14, 16**
5. 11, 4, −2, −7, −11, ... **neither; −14, −16, −17**
6. 3, −6, 12, −24, 48, ...

FOOD For Exercises 7–9, use the figure at the right. **8. arithmetic**

7. Make a list of the number of cans in each level starting with the top. **1, 2, 3, 4, 5**
8. State whether the sequence is *arithmetic, geometric,* or *neither*.
9. If the stack of cans had six levels, how many cans would be in the bottom level? **6 cans**

★ indicates increased difficulty

Practice and Applications

HOMEWORK HELP

For Exercises	See Examples
10–31	1–3

Extra Practice See pages 642, 658.

State whether each sequence is *arithmetic, geometric,* or *neither*. If it is arithmetic or geometric, state the common difference or common ratio. Write the next three terms of each sequence. **10–23. See margin.**

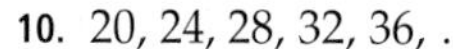

10. 20, 24, 28, 32, 36, ...
11. 1, 10, 100, 1,000, 10,000, ...
12. 486, 162, 54, 18, 6, ...
13. 88, 85, 82, 79, 76, ...
14. 1, 1, 2, 6, 24, ...
15. 1, 2, 5, 10, 17, ...
16. −6, −4, −2, 0, 2, ...
17. 5, −15, 45, −135, 405, ...
18. 189, 63, 21, 7, $2\frac{1}{3}$, ...
19. 4, $6\frac{1}{2}$, 9, $11\frac{1}{2}$, 14, ...
20. ★ 1, $\frac{1}{2}$, $\frac{1}{6}$, $\frac{1}{24}$, $\frac{1}{120}$, ...
21. ★ 16, −4, 1, $-\frac{1}{4}$, $\frac{1}{16}$, ...
22. ★ −1, 1, −1, 1, −1, ...
23. ★ $4\frac{1}{2}$, $4\frac{1}{6}$, $3\frac{5}{6}$, $3\frac{1}{2}$, $3\frac{1}{6}$, ...
24. What are the first four terms of an arithmetic sequence with a common difference of $3\frac{1}{3}$ if the first term is 4? **4, $7\frac{1}{3}$, $10\frac{2}{3}$, 14**
25. What are the first four terms of a geometric sequence with a common ratio of −6 if the first term is 100? **100, −600, 3,600, −21,600**

Answers

1. When the quotient between any two consecutive terms is the same, the sequence is geometric.
10. arithmetic; 4; 40, 44, 48
11. geometric; 10; 100,000, 1,000,000, 10,000,000
12. geometric; $\frac{1}{3}$; 2, $\frac{2}{3}$, $\frac{2}{9}$
13. arithmetic; −3; 73, 70, 67
14. neither; 120, 720, 5,040
15. neither; 26, 37, 50
16. arithmetic; 2; 4, 6, 8
17. geometric; −3; −1,215, 3,645, −10,935
18. geometric; $\frac{1}{3}$; $\frac{7}{9}$, $\frac{7}{27}$, $\frac{7}{81}$
19. arithmetic; $2\frac{1}{2}$; $16\frac{1}{2}$, 19, $21\frac{1}{2}$
20. neither; $\frac{1}{720}$, $\frac{1}{5,040}$, $\frac{1}{40,320}$
21. geometric; $-\frac{1}{4}$; $-\frac{1}{64}$, $\frac{1}{256}$, $-\frac{1}{1,024}$
22. geometric; −1; 1, −1, 1
23. arithmetic; $-\frac{1}{3}$; $2\frac{5}{6}$, $2\frac{1}{2}$, $2\frac{1}{6}$

514 Chapter 11 Algebra: Linear Functions

GEOMETRY For Exercises 26 and 27, use the sequence of squares.

1 unit 2 units 3 units 4 units

26. Write a sequence for the areas of the squares. Is the sequence *arithmetic*, *geometric*, or *neither*? **1, 4, 9, 16, ...; neither**

27. Write a sequence for the perimeters of the squares. Is the sequence *arithmetic*, *geometric*, or *neither*? **4, 8, 12, 16, ...; arithmetic**

SKIING For Exercises 28–32, use the following information. **28. See Ch. 11 Answer Appendix.**
A ski resort advertises a one-day lift pass for \$40 and a yearly lift pass for \$400.

28. Copy and complete the table.

Number of Times At the Ski Resort	1	2	3	4	5
Total Cost with One Day Passes	\$40	\$80			
Total Cost with Yearly Pass	\$400	\$400			

29. Is the sequence formed by the row for the total cost with one day passes *arithmetic*, *geometric*, or *neither*? **arithmetic**

30. Can the sequence formed by the total cost with a yearly pass be considered arithmetic? Explain. **Yes; the common difference is 0.**

31. Can the sequence formed by the total cost with a yearly pass be considered geometric? Explain. **Yes; the common ratio is 1.**

32. Extend each sequence to determine how many times a person would have to go skiing to make the yearly pass a better buy. **more than 10 times**

33. **CRITICAL THINKING** What are the first six terms of an arithmetic sequence where the second term is 5 and the fourth term is 15? **0, 5, 10, 15, 20, 25, ...**

Spiral Review with Standardized Test Practice

34. **MULTIPLE CHOICE** At the beginning of each week, Lina increases the time of her daily jog. If she continues the pattern shown in the table, how many minutes will she spend jogging each day during her fifth week of jogging? **B**

Week	Time Jogging (minutes)
1	8
2	16
3	24
4	32
5	?

(A) 32 min (B) 40 min (C) 48 min (D) 56 min

35. **MULTIPLE CHOICE** Which sequence is geometric? **I**

(F) 5, 5, 10, 30, 120, ... (G) −12, −8, −4, 0, 4, ...

(H) 1, 1, 2, 3, 5, ... (I) −1,280, 320, −80, 20, −5, ...

36. **GEOMETRY** The length of a rectangle is 6 inches. Its area is greater than 30 square inches. Write an inequality for the situation. (Lesson 10-7) $\mathbf{6w > 30}$

Solve each inequality. (Lesson 10-6)

37. $b + 15 > 32$ $\mathbf{b > 17}$ 38. $y - 24 \leq 12$ $\mathbf{y \leq 36}$ 39. $9 \leq 16 + t$ $\mathbf{-7 \leq t}$ 40. $18 \geq a - 6$ $\mathbf{24 \geq a}$

GETTING READY FOR THE NEXT LESSON

PREREQUISITE SKILL Evaluate each expression if $x = 9$. (Lesson 1-2)

41. $2x$ **18** 42. $x - 12$ **−3** 43. $17 + x$ **26** 44. $3x - 5$ **22**

Math Online msmath3.net/self_check_quiz

4 Assess

Open-Ended Assessment

Modeling Have students work in pairs to make models of sequences. Possible materials for the models include balls, blocks, clay, and string. Encourage them to make at least one arithmetic sequence and at least one geometric sequence. For example, one string, three strings, five strings, ...

Study Guide and Intervention, p. 619

NAME ____________ DATE ________ PERIOD ____

11-1 Study Guide and Intervention

Sequences

A **sequence** is an ordered list of numbers. Each number is called a **term**. An **arithmetic sequence** is a sequence in which the difference between any two consecutive terms is the same. This difference is called the **common difference**. To find the next term in the sequence, add the common difference to the last term.

EXAMPLE 1 **State whether the sequence −4, −1, 2, 5, 8, . . . is arithmetic. If it is, state the common difference. Write the next three terms of the sequence.**

−4, −1, 2, 5, 8 (+3 +3 +3 +3) Notice that $-1 - (-4) = 3$, $2 - (-1) = 3$, and so on. The terms have a common difference of 3, so the sequence is arithmetic.

$8 + 3 = \mathbf{11}$, $11 + 3 = \mathbf{14}$, $14 + 3 = \mathbf{17}$. The next three terms are 11, 14, and 17.

A **geometric sequence** is a sequence in which the ratio between any two consecutive terms is the same. This ratio is called the **common ratio**. To find the next term in the sequence, multiply the last term by the common ratio.

EXAMPLE 2 **State whether the sequence −1, 2, −4, 8, −16, . . . is geometric. If it is, state the common ratio. Write the next three terms of the sequence.**

−1, 2, −4, 8 −16 (×(−2) ×(−2) ×(−2) ×(−2)) Notice that $\frac{2}{-1} = -2$, $\frac{-4}{2} = -2$, and so on. The terms have a common ratio of −2, so the sequence is geometric.

$-16 \times -2 = \mathbf{32}$, $32 \times -2 = \mathbf{-64}$, $-64 \times -2 = \mathbf{128}$.
The next three terms are 32, −64, and 128.

Some sequences are neither arithmetic nor geometric. To extend a sequence like this, look for a pattern in the consecutive differences or consecutive ratios. Then apply the pattern to the last term of the sequence.

EXERCISES

State whether each sequence is *arithmetic*, *geometric*, or *neither*. If it is arithmetic or geometric, state the common difference or common ratio. Write the next three terms of the sequence.

1. 0, 3, 6, 9, 12, . . . **arithmetic; 3; 15, 18, 21**
2. 3, 6, 12, 24, 48, . . . **geometric; 2; 96, 192, 384**
3. 6, 11, 16, 21, 26, . . . **arithmetic; 5; 31, 36, 41**
4. 0, 1, 3, 6, 10, . . . **neither; 15, 21, 28**
5. $\frac{1}{9}, \frac{1}{3}$, 1, 3, 9, . . . **geometric; 3; 27, 81, 243**
6. 30, 26, 22, 18, 14, . . . **arithmetic; −4; 10, 6, 2**

Practice: Skills, p. 620

NAME ____________ DATE ________ PERIOD ____

11-1 Practice: Skills

Sequences

State whether each sequence is *arithmetic*, *geometric*, or *neither*. If it is arithmetic or geometric, state the common difference or common ratio. Write the next three terms of the sequence.

1. 1, 5, 9, 13, 17, . . . **arithmetic; 4; 21, 25, 29**
2. −3, −6, −12, −24, −48, . . . **geometric; 2; −96, −192, −384**
3. 2, 5, 8, 11, 14, . . . **arithmetic; 3; 17, 20, 23**
4. 1, 6, 16, 31, 51, . . . **neither; 76, 106, 141**
5. 3, 7, 11, 15, 19, . . . **arithmetic; 4; 23, 27, 31**
6. 4, 9, 14, 19, 24, . . . **arithmetic; 5; 29, 34, 39**
7. 1, −3, 9, −27, 81, . . . **geometric; −3; −243, 729, −2,187**
8. 1, 2, 1, 2, 1, . . . **neither; 2, 1, 2**
9. 7, 4, 1, −2, −5, . . . **arithmetic; −3; −8, −11, −14**
10. −4, 4, −4, 4, −4, . . . **geometric; −1; 4, −4, 4**
11. −5, 10, −20, 40, −80, . . . **geometric; −2; 160, −320, 640**
12. 22, 25, 28, 31, 34, . . . **arithmetic; 3; 37, 40, 43**
13. 0, −2, −5, −9, −14, . . . **neither; −20, −27, −35**
14. 4, 12, 36, 108, 324, . . . **geometric; 3; 972, 2,916, 8,748**
15. −2, 10, −50, 250, −1,250, . . . **geometric; −5; 6,250, −31,250, 156,250**
16. −80, −76, −72, −68, −64, . . . **arithmetic; 4; −60, −56, −52**
17. 448, 224, 112, 56, 28, . . . **geometric; $\frac{1}{2}$; 14, 7, $\frac{7}{2}$**
18. 2, 2, 4, 12, 48, . . . **neither; 240, 1,440, 10,080**
19. 3, $6\frac{1}{2}$, 10, $13\frac{1}{2}$, 17, . . . **arithmetic; $3\frac{1}{2}$; $20\frac{1}{2}$, 24, $27\frac{1}{2}$**
20. 81, 27, 9, 3, 1, . . . **geometric; $\frac{1}{3}$; $\frac{1}{3}, \frac{1}{9}, \frac{1}{27}$**

Practice: Word Problems, p. 621

NAME ____________ DATE ________ PERIOD ____

11-1 Practice: Word Problems

Sequences

GEOMETRY For Exercises 1 and 2, use the sequence of rectangles below.

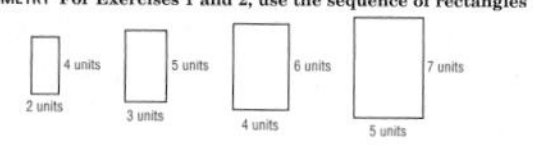

1. Write a sequence for the perimeters of the rectangles. Is the sequence *arithmetic*, *geometric*, or *neither*? Explain how you know. If it is arithmetic or geometric, state the common difference or common ratio. Find the next four terms of the sequence. **12, 16, 20, 24, . . .; Arithmetic; the differences between consecutive terms are all 4; 4; 28, 32, 36, 40.**

2. Write a sequence for the areas of the rectangles. Is the sequence *arithmetic*, *geometric*, or *neither*? If it is arithmetic or geometric, state the common difference or common ratio. Explain how to find the next four terms of the sequence. Then find the next four terms. **8, 15, 24, 35, . . .; Neither; the differences between consecutive terms are consecutive odd integers, 7, 9, and 11, so add 13, 15, 17, and 19 to find four more terms; 48, 63, 80, 99.**

3. **PIZZA** A large pizza at Joe's Pizza Shack costs \$7 plus \$0.80 per topping. Write a sequence of pizza prices consisting of pizzas with no toppings, pizzas with one topping, pizzas with two toppings, and pizzas with three toppings. Is the sequence *arithmetic*, *geometric*, or *neither*? How do you know? **7.00, 7.80, 8.60, 9.40; Arithmetic; you add 0.80 to each term to get the next term.**

4. **SAVINGS** The ending balances in Carissa's savings account for each of the past four years form the sequence \$1,000, \$1,100, \$1,210, \$1,331, ... Is the sequence *arithmetic*, *geometric*, or *neither*? Explain how you know. Find the next two terms of the sequence. **Geometric; the ratios of consecutive terms are all 1.1; \$1,464.10 and \$1,610.51.**

5. **PAYMENT PLAN** A family purchased furniture on an interest-free payment plan with a fixed monthly payment. Their balances after each of the first four payments were \$1,925, \$1,750, \$1,575, and \$1,400. Is the sequence of the balances *arithmetic*, *geometric*, or *neither*? Explain how you know. If it is arithmetic or geometric, state the common difference or common ratio. **Arithmetic; the differences between consecutive terms are all −175; −175.**

6. **MONEY** Continue to find the terms of the sequence of balances in Exercise 5 until you get a term of 0. After how many payments will the balance be \$0? **\$1,225, \$1,050, \$875, \$700, \$525, \$350, \$175, \$0; 12 payments**

11-1b HANDS-ON LAB

Lesson Notes

Lesson Resources

Teaching Mathematics with Manipulatives

- centimeter grid, p. 11
- square dot paper, p. 12
- student recording sheet 11-1b

GETTING STARTED

Teaching Tip Demonstrate the procedures for the lab using a grid drawn on an overhead transparency. Be sure all students understand what is meant by "building a road" using the grid paper bricks.

TEACH

- Discuss with students that if the road length is zero, there is still only one way to not have a road.
- Be sure students understand that their roads must all be 2 units high.
- For kinesthetic learners, use blocks or tiles rather than working with grid paper.

ASSESS

Observe as students solve the **Writing Math** exercises. They should:

- understand the pattern formed by the number of ways to build the road, and
- determine the next term in the sequence by applying the pattern.

11-1b HANDS-ON LAB

A Follow-Up of Lesson 11-1

What You'll LEARN

Determine numbers that make up the Fibonacci Sequence.

Materials

- grid or dot paper
- colored pencils

The Fibonacci Sequence

INVESTIGATE *Work in groups of three.*

Leonardo, also known as Fibonacci, created story problems based on a series of numbers that became known as the *Fibonacci sequence*. In this lab, you will investigate this sequence.

STEP 1 Using grid paper or dot paper, draw a "brick" that is 2 units long and 1 unit wide. If you build a "road" of grid paper bricks, there is only one way to build a road that is 1 unit wide.

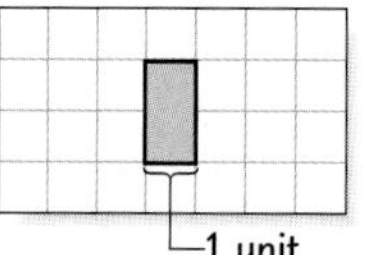

STEP 2 Using two bricks, draw all of the different roads that are 2 units wide. There are two ways to build the road.

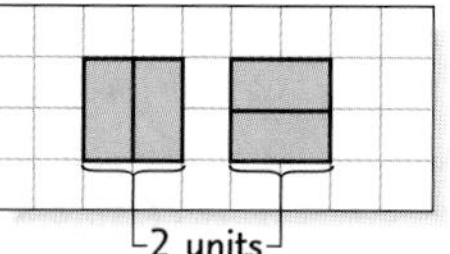

STEP 3 Using three bricks, draw all of the different roads that are 3 units wide. There are three ways to build the road.

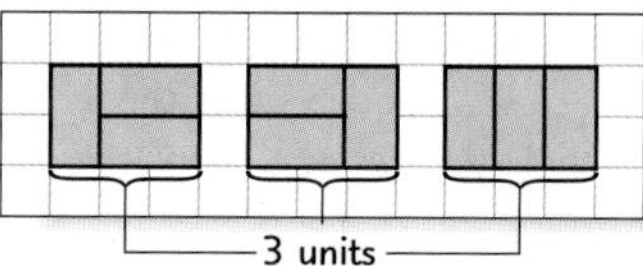

STEP 4 Draw all of the different roads that are 4 units, 5 units, and 6 units long using the brick.

STEP 5 Copy and complete the table.

Length of Road	0	1	2	3	4	5	6
Number of Ways to Build the Road	1	1	2	3	5	8	13

Writing Math

Work with a partner.

1. **Explain** how each number is related to the previous numbers in the pattern. **Each number is the sum of the previous two numbers.**
2. **Tell** the number of ways there are to build a road that is 8 units long. Do not draw a model. **34 ways**
3. **MAKE A CONJECTURE** Write a rule describing how you generate numbers in the Fibonacci sequence.
4. **RESEARCH** Use the Internet or other resource to find how the Fibonacci sequence is related to nature, music, or art.

3. Start with 1, 1. Each number that follows is the sum of the previous two numbers.

4. Sample answer: The number of clockwise spirals and the number of counterclockwise spirals in a pine cone are numbers in the Fibonacci sequence.

11-2 Functions

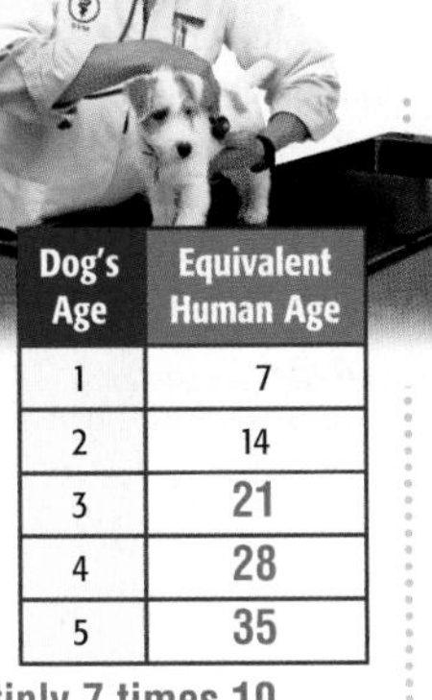

WHEN am I ever going to use this?

ANIMALS Veterinarians have used the rule that one year of a dog's life is equivalent to seven years of human life.

Dog's Age	Equivalent Human Age
1	7
2	14
3	21
4	28
5	35

1. Copy and complete the table at the right.
2. If a dog is 6 years old, what is its equivalent human age? **42 years old**
3. Explain how to find the equivalent human age of a dog that is 10 years old. **Multiply 7 times 10.**

What You'll LEARN

Complete function tables.

NEW Vocabulary

function
function table
independent variable
dependent variable
domain
range

MATH Symbols

$f(x)$ the function of x

TEACHING TIP

Point out that in a function, each input produces one and only one output.

The equivalent human age of a dog depends on, or is a function of, its age in years. A relationship where one thing depends upon another is called a **function**. In a function, one or more operations are performed on one number to get another.

Functions are often written as equations.

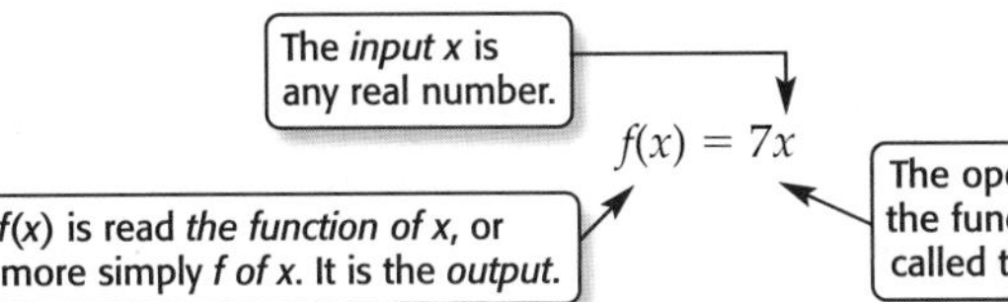

To find the value of a function for a certain number, substitute the number into the function value.

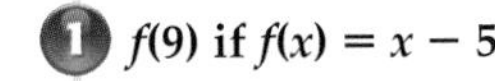

EXAMPLES Find a Function Value

Find each function value.

1 $f(9)$ **if** $f(x) = x - 5$

$f(x) = x - 5$

$f(9) = 9 - 5$ or 4 Substitute 9 for x into the function rule.

So, $f(9) = 4$.

2 $f(-3)$ **if** $f(x) = 2x + 1$

$f(x) = 2x + 1$

$f(-3) = 2(-3) + 1$ Substitute -3 for x into the function rule.

$f(-3) = -6 + 1$ or -5 Simplify.

So, $f(-3) = -5$.

Your Turn Find each function value.

a. $f(2)$ if $f(x) = x - 4$ **−2**

b. $f(6)$ if $f(x) = 2x - 8$ **4**

READING in the Content Area

For strategies in reading this lesson, visit **msmath3.net/reading.**

Math Online msmath3.net/extra_examples

NCLB No Child Left Behind

The goals of the NCLB Act include a stronger emphasis on reading. The **Reading in the Content Area** link helps students become proficient readers.

11-2 Lesson Notes

Lesson Resources

FAST FILE

Chapter 11 Resource Masters

- Study Guide and Intervention, p. 624
- Practice: Skills, p. 625
- Practice: Word Problems, p. 626
- Reading to Learn Mathematics, p. 627
- Enrichment, p. 628

Calculator and Spreadsheet Masters, p. 45

Classroom Math Games, pp. 37–38

Key Teaching Transparencies, 42

Parent and Student Study Guide Online Worksheets, 11-2

Noteables™: Interactive Study Notebook with Foldables™, 11-2

1 Focus

5-Minute Check 11-2

Use as a quiz or review of Lesson 11-1. (Also available as a transparency)

Bellringer

Communication Discuss the terms *dependent* and *independent*. Write students' input on the chalkboard. Then show students the equation $x + 1 = y$. Ask them which variable's value is dependent on the value of the other variable. **y's value depends on x's value.** Students should recognize that x's value is independent of y's value.

Reading to Learn Mathematics, p. 627 ELL

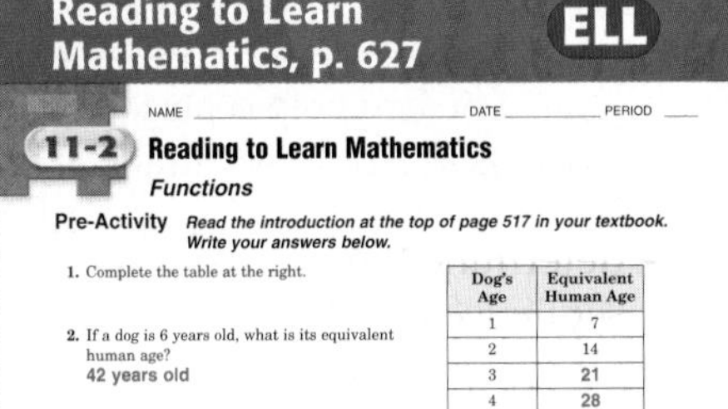

NAME ____________ DATE ________ PERIOD ____

11-2 Reading to Learn Mathematics

Functions

Pre-Activity ***Read the introduction at the top of page 517 in your textbook. Write your answers below.***

1. Complete the table at the right.
2. If a dog is 6 years old, what is its equivalent human age?
42 years old
3. Explain how to find the equivalent human age of a dog that is 10 years old.
Multiply 7 times 10.

Dog's Age	Equivalent Human Age
1	7
2	14
3	21
4	28
5	35

Reading the Lesson

4. If $f(x) = x + 5$, explain how to find $f(2)$. Then find $f(2)$.
Replace x with 2 in $f(x) = x + 5$ and simplify the right side; 7.

2 Teach

In-Class Examples

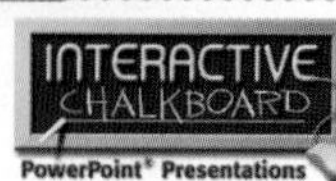

Find each function value.

1. $f(4)$ if $f(x) = x - 8$ **−4**

2. $f(-6)$ if $f(x) = 3x + 4$ **−14**

3. Complete the function table for $f(x) = 4x - 1$.

Input x	Rule $4x - 1$	Output $f(x)$
−3	4(−3) − 1	−13
−2	4(−2) − 1	−9
−1	4(−1) − 1	−5
0	4(0) − 1	−1
1	4(1) − 1	3

PARKING FEES The price for parking at a city lot is $3.00 plus $2.00 per hour.

4. Write a function using two variables to represent the price of parking for h hours. **$p = 3 + 2h$**

5. How much would it cost to park at the lot for 2 hours? **$7.00**

Tips for New Teachers

Intervention Students sometimes have creative ways of misunderstanding math problems. Keep a folder of problems or a journal describing such typical misconceptions. When you teach the subject in future years, you can help other students avoid these pitfalls.

STUDY TIP

Input and Output The variable for the input is called the **independent variable** because it can be any number. The variable for the output is called the **dependent variable** because it *depends* on the input value.

You can organize the input, rule, and output of a function into a **function table**.

EXAMPLE Make a Function Table

3. **Complete the function table for $f(x) = x + 5$.**

Substitute each value of x, or input, into the function rule. Then simplify to find the output.

$f(x) = x + 5$

$f(-2) = -2 + 5$ or 3

$f(-1) = -1 + 5$ or 4

$f(0) = 0 + 5$ or 5

$f(1) = 1 + 5$ or 6

$f(2) = 2 + 5$ or 7

Input	Rule	Output
x	$x + 5$	$f(x)$
−2		
−1		
0		
1		
2		

Input	Rule	Output
x	$x + 5$	$f(x)$
−2	−2 + 5	3
−1	−1 + 5	4
0	0 + 5	5
1	1 + 5	6
2	2 + 5	7

The set of input values in a function is called the **domain**. The set of output values is called the **range**. In Example 3, the domain is {−2, −1, 0, 1, 2}. The range is {3, 4, 5, 6, 7}.

Sometimes functions do not use the $f(x)$ notation. Instead they use two variables. One variable, usually x, represents the input and the other, usually y, represents the output. The function in Example 3 can also be written as $y = x + 5$.

REAL-LIFE CAREERS

How Does a Zookeeper Use Math?

A zookeeper must order the appropriate amount of various foods that will keep their animals healthy.

Math Online Research

For information about a career as a zookeeper, visit msmath3.net/careers

EXAMPLES Functions with Two Variables

ZOOKEEPER The zoo needs 1.5 tons of specially mixed elephant chow to feed its elephants each week.

4. **Write a function using two variables to represent the amount of elephant chow needed for w weeks.**

Words Amount of chow equals 1.5 times the number of weeks.

Function $c \quad = \quad 1.5 \quad \cdot \quad w$

The function $c = 1.5w$ represents the situation.

5. **How much elephant chow will the zoo need to feed its elephants for 12 weeks?**

Substitute 12 for w into the function rule.

$c = 1.5w$

$c = 1.5(12)$ or 18 The zoo needs 18 tons of elephant chow.

DAILY INTERVENTION **Flexible Grouping**

Linear Functions Have students work in pairs to write word problems that can be expressed as functions with two variables. Students can exchange problems with other pairs and write the functions that represent the problems.

Students practice the same concepts in Exercises 9–18 if they are assigned odd or even problems.

Skill and Concept Check

1. **State** the mathematical names for the input values and the output values. **domain; range**

2. **OPEN ENDED** If $f(x) = 2x - 4$, find a value of x that will make the function value a negative number. **Sample answer: 0**

3. **FIND THE ERROR** Mitchell and Tomi are finding the function value of $f(x) = 5x$ if the input is 10. Who is correct? Explain.

Mitchell
$f(x) = 5x$
$10 = 5x$
$\frac{10}{5} = \frac{5x}{5}$
$2 = x$

Tomi
$f(x) = 5x$
$f(10) = 5(10)$ or 50

Tomi; the input is the value of x, not $f(x)$.

GUIDED PRACTICE

Find each function value.

4. $f(4)$ if $f(x) = x - 6$ **−2**
5. $f(-2)$ if $f(x) = 4x + 1$ **−7**

Copy and complete each function table.

6. $f(x) = 8 - x$

x	8 − x	f(x)
−3	8 − (−3)	11
−1	8 − (−1)	9
2	8 − 2	6
4	8 − 4	4

7. $f(x) = 5x + 1$

x	5x + 1	f(x)
−2	5(−2) + 1	−9
0	5(0) + 1	1
1	5(1) + 1	6
3	5(3) + 1	16

8. $f(x) = 3x - 2$

x	3x − 2	y
−5	3(−5) − 2	−17
−2	3(−2) − 2	−8
2	3(2) − 2	4
5	3(5) − 2	13

★ indicates increased difficulty

Practice and Applications

Find each function value.

9. $f(7)$ if $f(x) = 5x$ **35**
10. $f(9)$ if $f(x) = x + 13$ **22**
11. $f(4)$ if $f(x) = 3x - 1$ **11**
12. $f(5)$ if $f(x) = 2x + 5$ **15**
13. $f(-6)$ if $f(x) = -3x + 1$ **19**
14. $f(-8)$ if $f(x) = 3x + 24$ **0**
★ 15. $f\left(\frac{5}{6}\right)$ if $f(x) = 2x + \frac{1}{3}$ **2**
★ 16. $f\left(\frac{5}{8}\right)$ if $f(x) = 4x - \frac{1}{4}$ **$2\frac{1}{4}$**

HOMEWORK HELP

For Exercises	See Examples
9–16	1, 2
17–20	3
21–24	4, 5

Extra Practice
See pages 643, 658.

Copy and complete each function table.

17. $f(x) = 6x - 4$

x	6x − 4	f(x)
−5	6(−5) − 4	−34
−1	6(−1) − 4	−10
2	6(2) − 4	8
7	6(7) − 4	38

18. $f(x) = 5 - 2x$

x	5 − 2x	y
−2	5 − 2(−2)	9
0	5 − 2(0)	5
3	5 − 2(3)	−1
5	5 − 2(5)	−5

19. $f(x) = 7 + 3x$

x	7 + 3x	y
−3	7 + 3(−3)	−2
−2	7 + 3(−2)	1
1	7 + 3(1)	10
6	7 + 3(6)	25

msmath3.net/self_check_quiz

3 Practice/Apply

FOLDABLES™ Follow-Up Before students begin the lesson, encourage them to write a question about functions under the second tab of their Foldables. As students progress through the lesson, encourage them to take notes and record information that answers their question.

DAILY INTERVENTION FIND THE ERROR In Exercise 3, remind students not to think of $f(x)$ as being the same as the variable x.

About the Exercises...

Guided Practice Key

Exercises	Examples
4–5	1, 2
6–8	3

Assignment Guide

Basic: 9–13 odd, 17–25 odd, 26–37

Average: 9–25 odd, 26–37

Enriched: 10–20 even, 21–24, 26–33 (Optional: 34–37)

4 Assess

Open-Ended Assessment

Speaking Have students write a problem in everyday life that can be expressed as a function. Then, have them explain the problem and the function to the class.

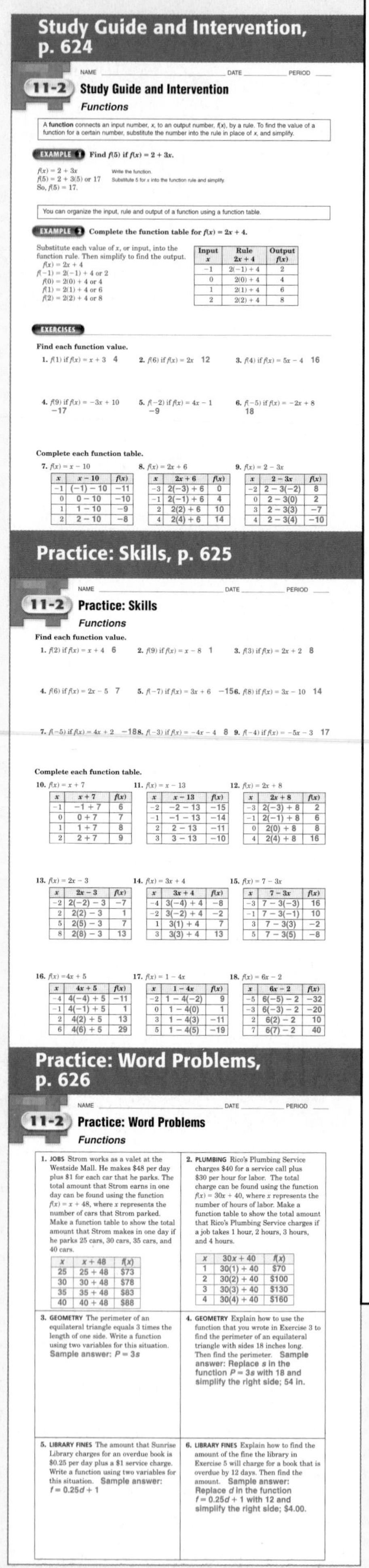

Study Guide and Intervention, p. 624

NAME ________ DATE ________ PERIOD ________

11-2 Study Guide and Intervention

Functions

A **function** connects an input number, x, to an output number, $f(x)$, by a rule. To find the value of a function for a certain number, substitute the number into the rule in place of x, and simplify.

EXAMPLE 1 Find $f(5)$ if $f(x) = 2 + 3x$.

$f(x) = 2 + 3x$ Write the function.
$f(5) = 2 + 3(5)$ or 17 Substitute 5 for x into the function rule and simplify.
So, $f(5) = 17$.

You can organize the input, rule and output of a function using a function table.

EXAMPLE 2 Complete the function table for $f(x) = 2x + 4$.

Substitute each value of x, or input, into the function rule. Then simplify to find the output.
$f(x) = 2x + 4$
$f(-1) = 2(-1) + 4$ or 2
$f(0) = 2(0) + 4$ or 4
$f(1) = 2(1) + 4$ or 6
$f(2) = 2(2) + 4$ or 8

Input x	Rule $2x + 4$	Output $f(x)$
−1	2(−1) + 4	2
0	2(0) + 4	4
1	2(1) + 4	6
2	2(2) + 4	8

EXERCISES

Find each function value.

1. $f(1)$ if $f(x) = x + 3$ 4
2. $f(6)$ if $f(x) = 2x$ 12
3. $f(4)$ if $f(x) = 5x - 4$ 16
4. $f(9)$ if $f(x) = -3x + 10$ −17
5. $f(-2)$ if $f(x) = 4x - 1$ −9
6. $f(-5)$ if $f(x) = -2x + 8$ 18

Complete each function table.

7. $f(x) = x - 10$

x	$x - 10$	$f(x)$
−1	(−1) − 10	−11
0	0 − 10	−10
1	1 − 10	−9
2	2 − 10	−8

8. $f(x) = 2x + 6$

x	$2x + 6$	$f(x)$
−3	2(−3) + 6	0
−1	2(−1) + 6	4
2	2(2) + 6	10
4	2(4) + 6	14

9. $f(x) = 2 - 3x$

x	$2 - 3x$	$f(x)$
−2	2 − 3(−2)	8
0	2 − 3(0)	2
3	2 − 3(3)	−7
4	2 − 3(4)	−10

Practice: Skills, p. 625

NAME ________ DATE ________ PERIOD ________

11-2 Practice: Skills

Functions

Find each function value.

1. $f(2)$ if $f(x) = x + 4$ 6
2. $f(9)$ if $f(x) = x - 8$ 1
3. $f(3)$ if $f(x) = 2x + 2$ 8
4. $f(6)$ if $f(x) = 2x - 5$ 7
5. $f(-7)$ if $f(x) = 3x + 6$ −15
6. $f(8)$ if $f(x) = 3x - 10$ 14
7. $f(-5)$ if $f(x) = 4x + 2$ −18
8. $f(-3)$ if $f(x) = -4x - 4$ 8
9. $f(-4)$ if $f(x) = -5x - 3$ 17

Complete each function table.

10. $f(x) = x + 7$

x	$x + 7$	$f(x)$
−1	−1 + 7	6
0	0 + 7	7
1	1 + 7	8
2	2 + 7	9

11. $f(x) = x - 13$

x	$x - 13$	$f(x)$
−2	−2 − 13	−15
−1	−1 − 13	−14
2	2 − 13	−11
3	3 − 13	−10

12. $f(x) = 2x + 8$

x	$2x + 8$	$f(x)$
−3	2(−3) + 8	2
−1	2(−1) + 8	6
0	2(0) + 8	8
4	2(4) + 8	16

13. $f(x) = 2x - 3$

x	$2x - 3$	$f(x)$
−2	2(−2) − 3	−7
2	2(2) − 3	1
5	2(5) − 3	7
8	2(8) − 3	13

14. $f(x) = 3x + 4$

x	$3x + 4$	$f(x)$
−4	3(−4) + 4	−8
−2	3(−2) + 4	−2
1	3(1) + 4	7
3	3(3) + 4	13

15. $f(x) = 7 - 3x$

x	$7 - 3x$	$f(x)$
−3	7 − 3(−3)	16
−1	7 − 3(−1)	10
3	7 − 3(3)	−2
5	7 − 3(5)	−8

16. $f(x) = 4x + 5$

x	$4x + 5$	$f(x)$
−4	4(−4) + 5	−11
−1	4(−1) + 5	1
2	4(2) + 5	13
6	4(6) + 5	29

17. $f(x) = 1 - 4x$

x	$1 - 4x$	$f(x)$
−2	1 − 4(−2)	9
0	1 − 4(0)	1
3	1 − 4(3)	−11
5	1 − 4(5)	−19

18. $f(x) = 6x - 2$

x	$6x - 2$	$f(x)$
−5	6(−5) − 2	−32
−3	6(−3) − 2	−20
2	6(2) − 2	10
7	6(7) − 2	40

Practice: Word Problems, p. 626

NAME ________ DATE ________ PERIOD ________

11-2 Practice: Word Problems

Functions

1. JOBS Strom works as a valet at the Westside Mall. He makes $48 per day plus $1 for each car that he parks. The total amount that Strom earns in one day can be found using the function $f(x) = x + 48$, where x represents the number of cars that Strom parked. Make a function table to show the total amount that Strom makes in one day if he parks 25 cars, 30 cars, 35 cars, and 40 cars.

x	$x + 48$	$f(x)$
25	25 + 48	$73
30	30 + 48	$78
35	35 + 48	$83
40	40 + 48	$88

2. PLUMBING Rico's Plumbing Service charges $40 for a service call plus $30 per hour for labor. The total charge can be found using the function $f(x) = 30x + 40$, where x represents the number of hours of labor. Make a function table to show the total amount that Rico's Plumbing Service charges if a job takes 1 hour, 2 hours, 3 hours, and 4 hours.

x	$30x + 40$	$f(x)$
1	30(1) + 40	$70
2	30(2) + 40	$100
3	30(3) + 40	$130
4	30(4) + 40	$160

3. GEOMETRY The perimeter of an equilateral triangle equals 3 times the length of one side. Write a function using two variables for this situation. Sample answer: $P = 3s$

4. GEOMETRY Explain how to use the function that you wrote in Exercise 3 to find the perimeter of an equilateral triangle with sides 18 inches long. Then find the perimeter. Sample answer: Replace s in the function $P = 3s$ with 18 and simplify the right side; 54 in.

5. LIBRARY FINES The amount that Sunrise Library charges for an overdue book is $0.25 per day plus a $1 service charge. Write a function using two variables for this situation. Sample answer: $f = 0.25d + 1$

6. LIBRARY FINES Explain how to find the amount of the fine the library in Exercise 5 will charge for a book that is overdue by 12 days. Then find the amount. Sample answer: Replace d in the function $f = 0.25d + 1$ with 12 and simplify the right side; $4.00.

★ 20. Make a function table for $y = 3x + 5$ using any four values for x. **See margin.**

GEOMETRY For Exercises 21 and 22, use the following information.
The perimeter of a square equals 4 times the length of a side.

21. Write a function using two variables to represent the situation. **$P = 4s$**
22. What is the perimeter of a square with a side 14 inches long? **56 in.**

PARTY PLANNING For Exercises 23 and 24, use the following information.
Sherry is having a birthday party at the Swim Center. The cost of renting the pool is $45 plus $3.50 for each person.

23. Write a function using two variables to represent the situation. **$c = 45.00 + 3.50p$**
24. What is the total cost if 20 people attend the party? **$115.00**

25. **WRITE A PROBLEM** Write a real-life problem involving a function. **See margin.**

26. **CRITICAL THINKING** Write the function rule for each function table.

a.

x	$f(x)$
−3	−30
−1	−10
2	20
6	60

$f(x) = 10x$

b.

x	$f(x)$
−5	−9
−1	−5
3	−1
7	3

$f(x) = x - 4$

c.

x	y
−2	−3
1	3
3	7
5	11

$y = 2x + 1$

d.

x	y
−2	−5
1	1
3	5
5	9

$y = 2x - 1$

Spiral Review with Standardized Test Practice

27. **MULTIPLE CHOICE** Which function matches the function table at the right? **A**

x	y
−5	−1
−2	0.2
1	1.4
3	2.2

(A) $y = 0.4x + 1$
(B) $y = 4x - 0.4$
(C) $y = \frac{1}{4}x + 1$
(D) $y = \frac{1}{4}x - 1$

28. **SHORT RESPONSE** A nautical mile is a measure of distance frequently used in sea travel. One nautical mile equals about 6,076 feet. Write a function to represent the number of feet in x nautical miles. **$f(x) = 6{,}076x$**

State whether each sequence is *arithmetic, geometric,* or *neither.* If it is arithmetic or geometric, state the common difference or common ratio. Write the next three terms of each sequence. (Lesson 11-1) **29. geometric; −2; −96, 192, −384**

29. 3, −6, 12, −24, 48, …
30. 74, 71, 68, 65, 62, … **arithmetic; −3; 59, 56, 53**
31. 2, 3, 5, 8, 12, … **neither; 17, 23, 30**

32. **BAND** The school band makes $0.50 for every candy bar they sell. They want to make at least $500 on the candy sale. Write and solve an inequality to find how many candy bars they must sell. (Lesson 10-7) **$0.50x \geq 500$; at least 1,000 candy bars**

33. **ALGEBRA** Solve $\frac{n}{2} + 31 = 45$. (Lesson 10-2) **28**

GETTING READY FOR THE NEXT LESSON

PREREQUISITE SKILL Graph each point on the same coordinate plane. (Page 614)

34. $A(-4, 2)$
35. $B(3, -1)$
36. $C(0, -3)$
37. $D(1, 4)$

34–37. See margin.

Answers

20. Sample answer: $f(x) = 3x + 5$

x	$3x + 5$	y
0	3(0) + 5	5
1	3(1) + 5	8
2	3(2) + 5	11
3	3(3) + 5	14

25. Sample answer: Mr. Jones is traveling on the interstate at an average speed of 55 miles per hour. Write a function to determine the distance he travels in h hours. How far will he travel in 3 hours? $d = 55h$; 165 mi

34–37.

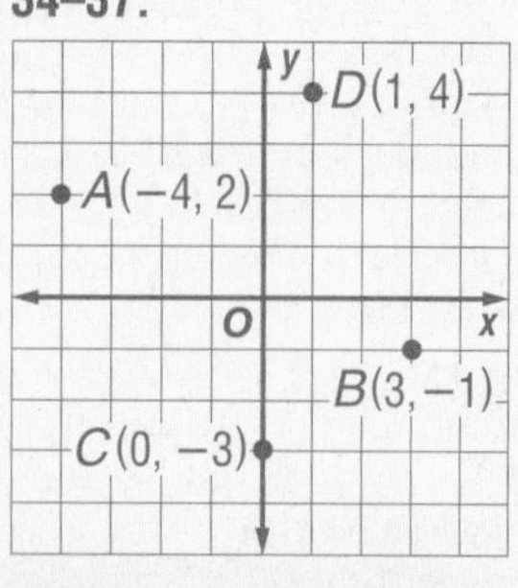

11-3a HANDS-ON LAB

A Preview of Lesson 11-3

Graphing Relationships

What You'll LEARN

Graph relationships.

Materials

- pencil
- paper cup
- 2 paper clips
- large rubber band
- tape
- ruler
- 10 pennies
- grid paper

INVESTIGATE *Work in groups of four.*

In this lab, you will investigate a relationship between the number of pennies in a cup and how far the cup will stretch a rubber band.

STEP 1 Using a pencil, punch a small hole in the bottom of the paper cup. Place one paper clip onto the rubber band. Push the other end of the rubber band through the hole in the cup. Attach the second paper clip to the other end of the rubber band. Place it horizontally across the bottom of the cup to keep it from coming through the hole.

STEP 2 Copy the table at the right.

Number of Pennies x	Distance y

STEP 3 Tape the top paper clip to the edge of a desk. Measure and record the distance from the bottom of the desk to the bottom of the cup. Drop one penny into the cup. Measure and record the new distance from the bottom of the desk to the bottom of the cup.

STEP 4 Continue adding one penny at a time. Measure and record the distance after each addition.

Writing Math

Work with a partner.

1. **Examine** the data. Do you think the number of pennies affects the distance? Explain. **yes; the more pennies, the greater the distance**
2. **Graph** the ordered pairs formed by your data. Do the points resemble a straight line? **See students' work; yes.**
3. **Predict** the distance of the bottom of the cup from the bottom of the desk if 15 pennies are placed in the cup. **See students' work.**
4. **Find** the ratio of each distance to the number of pennies. What do you notice about these ratios?

4. See students' work. They are approximately the same.

11-3a HANDS-ON LAB Lesson Notes

Lesson Resources

Teaching Mathematics with Manipulatives

- pattern for cup, p. 7
- quarter-inch grid, p. 10
- student recording sheet 11-3a

Glencoe Mathematics Classroom Manipulative Kit

- ruler

GETTING STARTED

Teaching Tip Distances will vary depending on the type of rubber band. Test materials prior to the lab to be sure students will obtain reasonable results.

TEACH

- If students are unable to balance the cup vertically, they can make the measurements with the cup tilted as long as they are made the same way each time.
- The line in Exercise 2 may not be straight due to experimental error. Discuss with students possible sources of error such as accuracy of measurements and inconsistent stretching of the rubber band.
- If adding a penny causes the cup to tilt more, the distance measurements will be incorrect.

ASSESS

Observe as students solve the **Writing Math** exercises. They should:

- notice that the distance increases the same amount for each penny added,
- create a graph with distance on the y-axis and the number of pennies on the x-axis, and
- based on the pattern in the data, predict how the distance will change if more pennies are added.

11-3 Lesson Notes

Lesson Resources

Chapter 11 Resource Masters
- Study Guide and Intervention, p. 629
- Practice: Skills, p. 630
- Practice: Word Problems, p. 631
- Reading to Learn Mathematics, p. 632
- Enrichment, p. 633

Calculator and Spreadsheet Masters, p. 46
MathPASS Tutorial CD-ROM, 41
Parent and Student Study Guide Online Worksheets, 11-3
Real-Life Career Masters, p. 37
Noteables™: Interactive Study Notebook with Foldables™, 11-3
Virtual Activities CD-ROM, Graphing Equations with Two Variables

1 Focus

5-Minute Check 11-3

INTERACTIVE CHALKBOARD PowerPoint® Presentations

Use as a quiz or review of Lesson 11-2. (Also available as a transparency)

Bellringer

Communication Have students discuss what they remember about plotting points on a graph. Ask what information they need in order to plot a point. **x-coordinate and y-coordinate** Then draw the graph in the bottom margin on the chalkboard.

(Continued in bottom margin.)

Reading to Learn Mathematics, p. 632 **ELL**

NAME ______ DATE ______ PERIOD ______

11-3 Reading to Learn Mathematics
Graphing Linear Functions

Pre-Activity *Read the introduction at the top of page 522 in your textbook. Write your answers below.*

1. Complete the following function table.

Input x	Rule $1.5x$	Output y	(Input, Output) (x, y)
1	1.5(1)	1.5	(1, 1.5)
2	1.5(2)	3.0	(2, 3.0)
3	1.5(3)	4.5	(3, 4.5)
4	1.5(4)	6.0	(4, 6.0)

2. Graph the ordered pairs on a coordinate plane.

3. What do you notice about the points on your graph?
They appear to be in a straight line.

11-3 Graphing Linear Functions

What You'll LEARN

Graph linear functions by using function tables and plotting points.

NEW Vocabulary

linear function
x-intercept
y-intercept

REVIEW Vocabulary

ordered pair: a pair of numbers used to locate a point on a coordinate plane (Lesson 3-6)

WHEN am I ever going to use this?

ROLLER COASTERS The *Millennium Force* roller coaster has a maximum speed of 1.5 miles per minute. If x represents the minutes traveled at this maximum speed, the function rule for the distance traveled is $y = 1.5x$.

1. Copy and complete the following function table.

Input	Rule	Output	(Input, Output)
x	$1.5x$	y	(x, y)
1	1.5(1)	1.5	(1, 1.5)
2	1.5(2)	3.0	(2, 3.0)
3	1.5(3)	4.5	(3, 4.5)
4	1.5(4)	6.0	(4, 6.0)

2. Graph the ordered pairs on a coordinate plane.
3. What do you notice about the points on your graph?

2. See margin. 3. They appear to be in a straight line.

Ordered pairs of the form (input, output), or (x, y), can represent a function. These ordered pairs can then be graphed on a coordinate plane as part of the graph of the function.

EXAMPLE Graph a Function

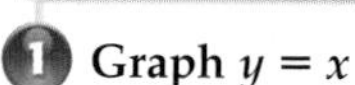

1 Graph $y = x + 2$.

Step 1 Choose some values for x. Make a function table. Include a column of ordered pairs of the form (x, y).

x	$x + 2$	y	(x, y)
0	0 + 2	2	(0, 2)
1	1 + 2	3	(1, 3)
2	2 + 2	4	(2, 4)
3	3 + 2	5	(3, 5)

Step 2 Graph each ordered pair. Draw a line that passes through each point. Note that the ordered pair for any point on this line is a solution of $y = x + 2$. The line is the complete graph of the function.

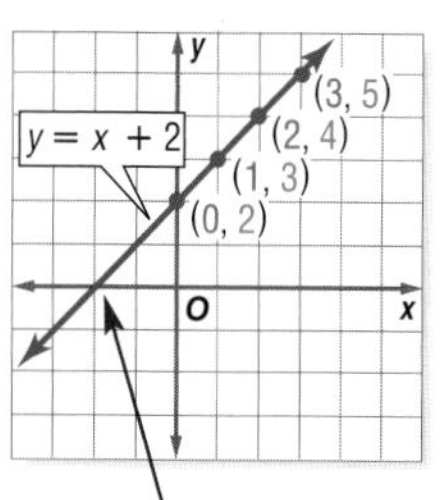

The point where the line crosses the x-axis is the solution to the equation $0 = x + 2$.

Check It appears from the graph that $(-2, 0)$ is also a solution. Check this by substitution.

$y = x + 2$ Write the function.

$0 \stackrel{?}{=} -2 + 2$ Replace x with -2 and y with 0.

$0 = 0$ ✓ Simplify.

TEACHING TIP

Ask students to check $\left(\frac{1}{2}, 2\frac{1}{2}\right)$.

Have students name the ordered pair for each point.

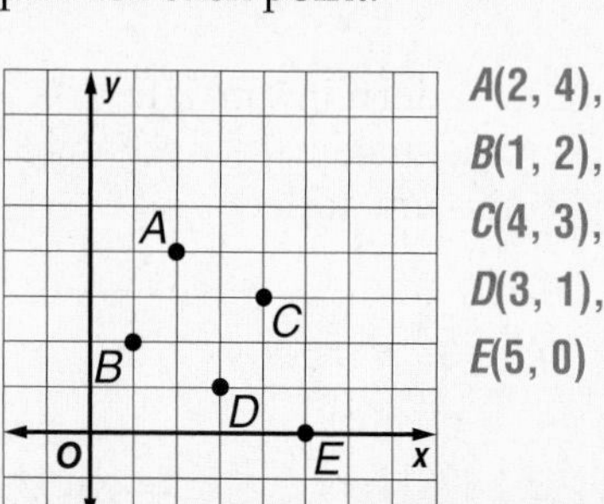

$A(2, 4)$, $B(1, 2)$, $C(4, 3)$, $D(3, 1)$, $E(5, 0)$

Answer (When am I ever going to use this?)

2.

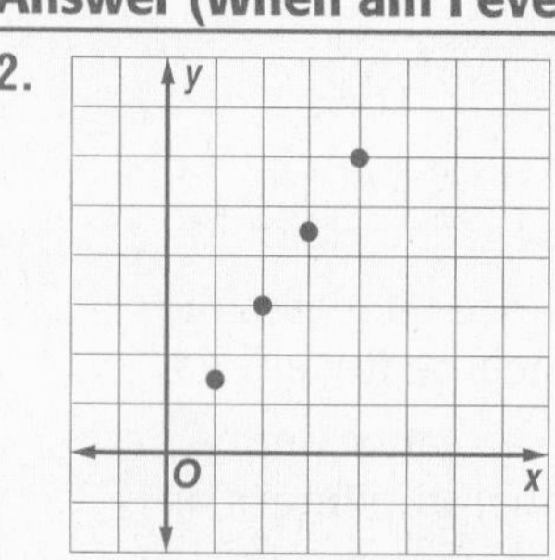

TEACHING TIP
Students will graph nonlinear functions in Chapter 12.

A function in which the graph of the solutions forms a line is called a **linear function**. Therefore, $y = x + 2$ is a *linear equation.*

Concept Summary — **Representing Functions**

Words The value of y is one less than the corresponding value of x.

Equation $y = x - 1$

Ordered Pairs $(0, -1)$, $(1, 0)$, $(2, 1)$, $(3, 2)$

Table

x	y
0	−1
1	0
2	1
3	2

Graph

$y = x - 1$

The value of x where the graph crosses the x-axis is called the **x-intercept**. The value of y where the graph crosses the y-axis is called the **y-intercept**.

EXAMPLE Use x- and y-intercepts

Standardized Test Practice

2 MULTIPLE-CHOICE TEST ITEM Which graph represents $y = 3x - 6$?

A
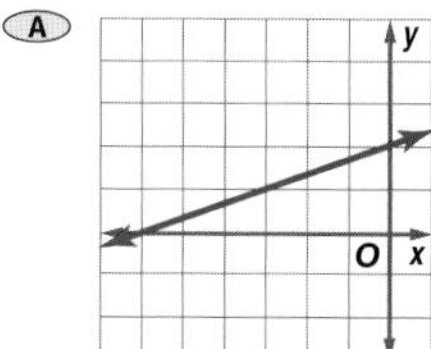

B
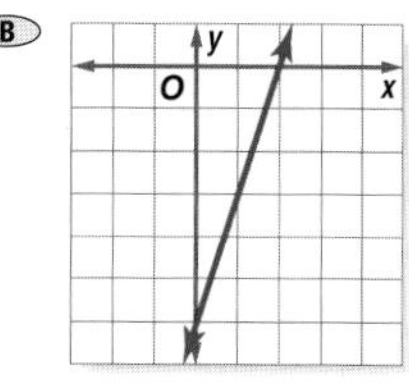

C
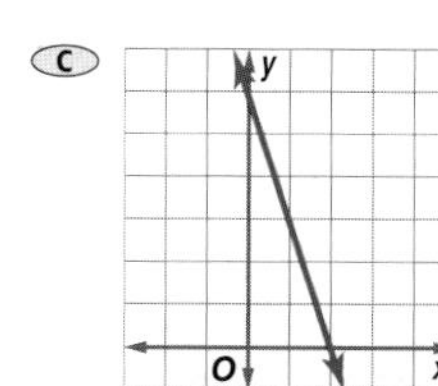

D
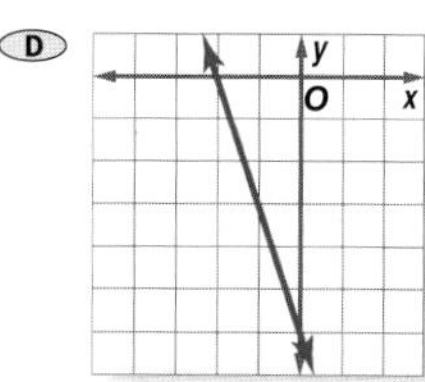

Test-Taking Tip

Use Different Methods
Always work each problem using the method that is easiest for you. You could solve the problem at the right in several ways.

- You could test the coordinates of several points on each graph.
- You could graph the function and see which graph matched your graph.
- You could determine the intercepts and see which graph had those intercepts.

Which method is easiest for you?

Read the Test Item You need to decide which of the four graphs represents $y = 3x - 6$.

Solve the Test Item

The graph will cross the x-axis when $y = 0$.

$0 = 3x - 6$	Let $y = 0$.
$0 + 6 = 3x - 6 + 6$	Add 6.
$6 = 3x$	Simplify.
$\frac{6}{3} = \frac{3x}{3}$	Divide by 3.
$2 = x$	Simplify.

The graph will cross the y-axis when $x = 0$.

$y = 3(0) - 6$	Let $x = 0$.
$y = 0 - 6$	Simplify.
$y = -6$	Simplify.

The x-intercept is 2, and the y-intercept is -6. Graph B is the only graph with both of these intercepts. The answer is B.

msmath3.net/extra_examples

DAILY INTERVENTION — **Differentiated Instruction**

Kinesthetic Have students make a large, 12×12 grid on the floor using masking tape. Each cell should be at least 30 centimeters wide. Draw a large "O" on an index card and place it at the origin. Indicate the axes using the tape. Write the equation $y = 2x + 3$ on the chalkboard. Have students stand at intersections of the cells to indicate points on this line. They should notice that their positions form a straight line. Repeat the activity using other equations.

2 Teach

In-Class Examples

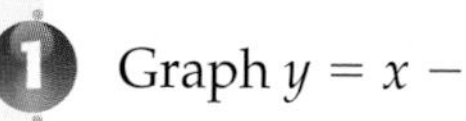

1 Graph $y = x - 3$.

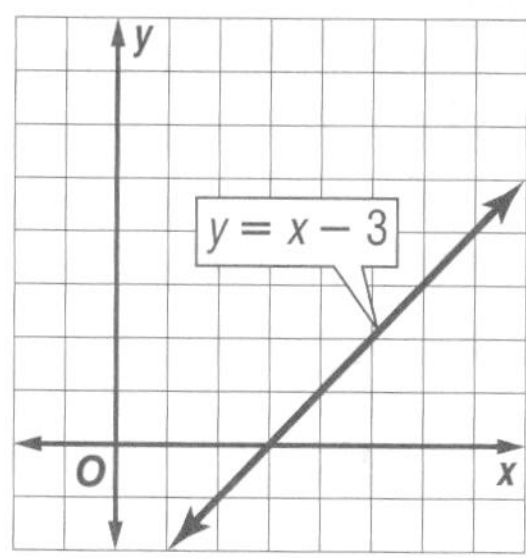

2 MULTIPLE-CHOICE TEST ITEM Which graph represents $y = 2x + 1$? **D**

A.
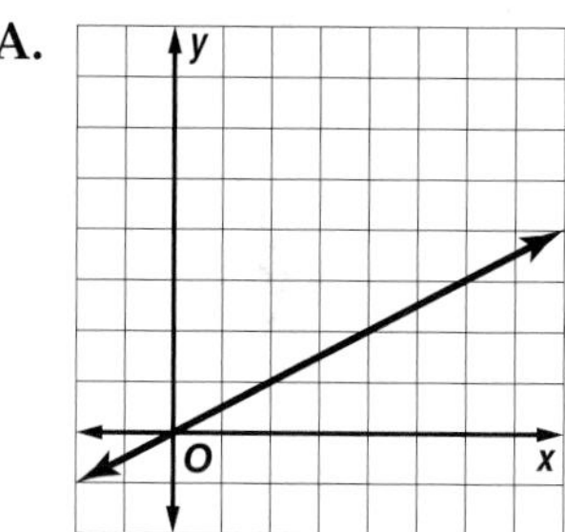

B.
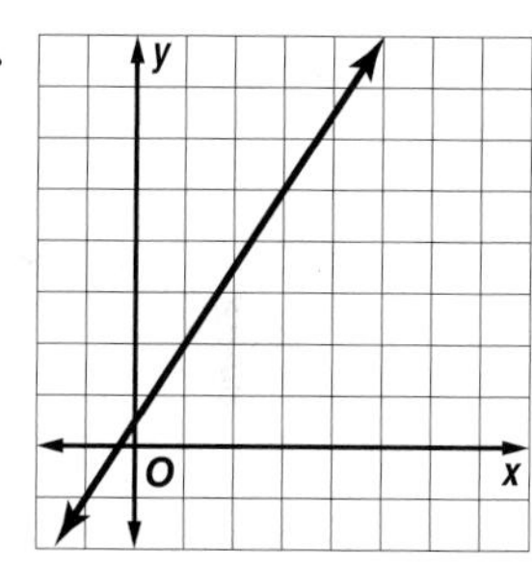

C.
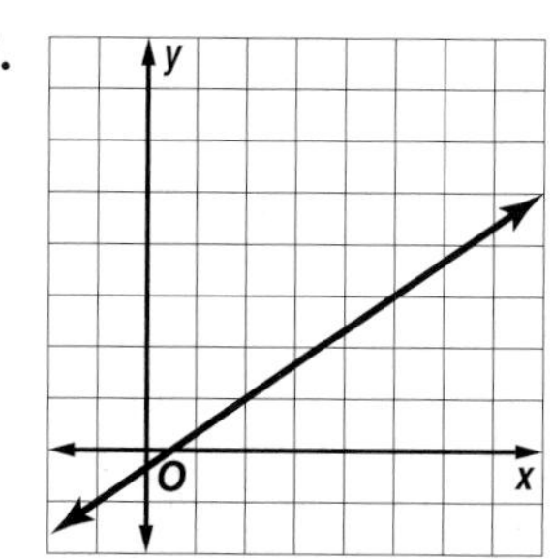

D.
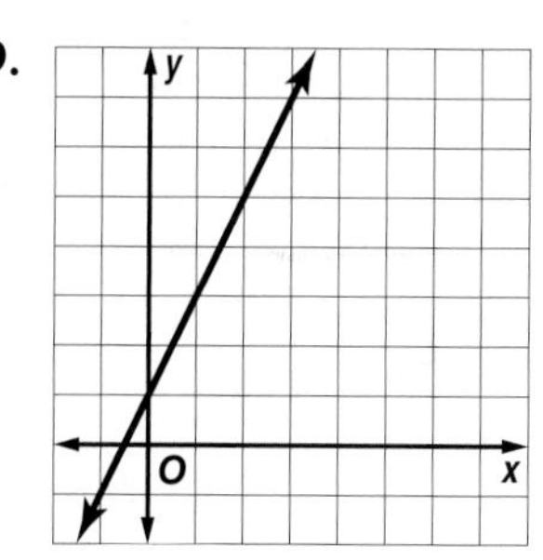

Students practice the same concepts in Exercises 10–21 if they are assigned odd or even problems.

3 Practice/Apply

Which One Doesn't Belong? For Exercise 3, have students graph the four points and see which one is not on the line. Students can also solve using substitution and determine which pair is not a solution.

About the Exercises...

Guided Practice Key

Exercises	Examples
4–8	1
9	2

Assignment Guide

Basic: 11–23 odd, 25–35

Average: 11–23 odd, 24–35

Enriched: 10–22 even, 23–32 (Optional: 33–35)

Skill and Concept Check

1. Writing Math Explain how a function table can be used to graph a function. **1–2. See margin.**

2. **OPEN ENDED** Draw a graph of a linear function. Name the coordinates of three points on the graph.

3. **Which One Doesn't Belong?** Identify the ordered pair that is not a solution of $y = 2x - 3$. Explain your reasoning.

(1, –1) (2, 1) (0, 3) (–2, –7)

(0, 3); 3 does not equal 2(0) – 3 or –3.

GUIDED PRACTICE

4. Copy and complete the function table at the right. Then graph $y = x + 5$. **See margin for graph.**

x	$x + 5$	y	(x, y)
–3	–3 + 5	2	(–3, 2)
–1	–1 + 5	4	(–1, 4)
0	0 + 5	5	(0, 5)
2	2 + 5	7	(2, 7)

Graph each function. 5–7. See margin.

5. $y = 3x$
6. $y = 3x + 1$
7. $y = \frac{x}{2} - 1$

FOOD For Exercises 8 and 9, use the following information.
The function $y = 40x$ describes the relationship between the number of gallons of sap y used to make x gallons of maple syrup.

8. Graph the function. **See Ch. 11 Answer Appendix.**
9. From your graph, how much sap is needed to make to make $2\frac{1}{2}$ gallons of syrup? **100 gal**

Practice and Applications

HOMEWORK HELP

For Exercises	See Examples
10–23	1
27	2

Extra Practice See pages 643, 658.

Copy and complete each function table. Then graph the function.

10. $y = x - 4$

x	$x - 4$	y	(x, y)
–1	–1 – 4	–5	(–1, –5)
1	1 – 4	–3	(1, –3)
3	3 – 4	–1	(3, –1)
5	5 – 4	1	(5, 1)

11. $y = 2x$

x	$2x$	y	(x, y)
–2	2(–2)	–4	(–2, –4)
0	2(0)	0	(0, 0)
1	2(1)	2	(1, 2)
2	2(2)	4	(2, 4)

10–11. See Ch. 11 Answer Appendix for graphs.

Graph each function. 12–21. See Ch. 11 Answer Appendix.

12. $y = 4x$
13. $y = -3x$
14. $y = x - 3$
15. $y = x + 1$
16. $y = 3x - 7$
17. $y = 2x + 3$
18. $y = \frac{x}{3} + 1$
19. $y = \frac{x}{2} - 3$
20. Draw the graph of $y = 5 - x$.
21. Graph the function $y = -\frac{1}{2}x + 5$.
22. **GEOMETRY** The equation $s = 180(n - 2)$ relates the sum of the measures of angles s formed by the sides of a polygon to the number of sides n. Find four ordered pairs (n, s) that are solutions of the equation. **Sample answers: (3, 180), (4, 360), (5, 540), (6, 720)**

Answers

1. Make ordered pairs using the x value and its corresponding y value. Then graph the ordered pairs on a coordinate plane. Draw a line that the points suggest.
2. Sample answer:

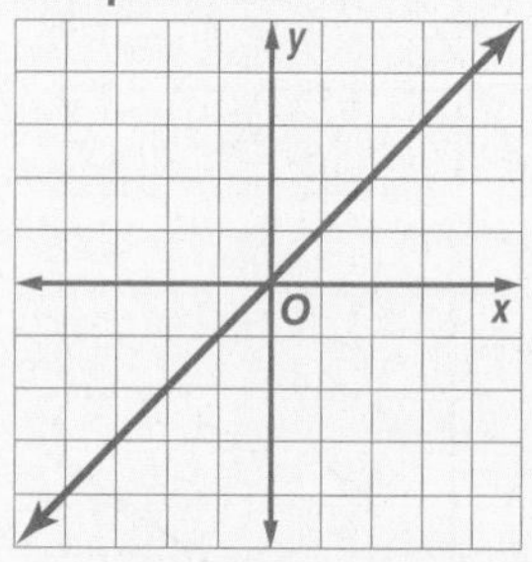

(–2, –2), (0, 0), (2, 2)

4.

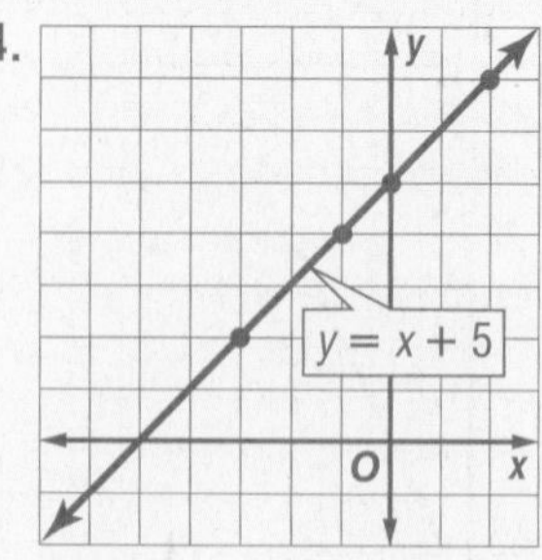

5.

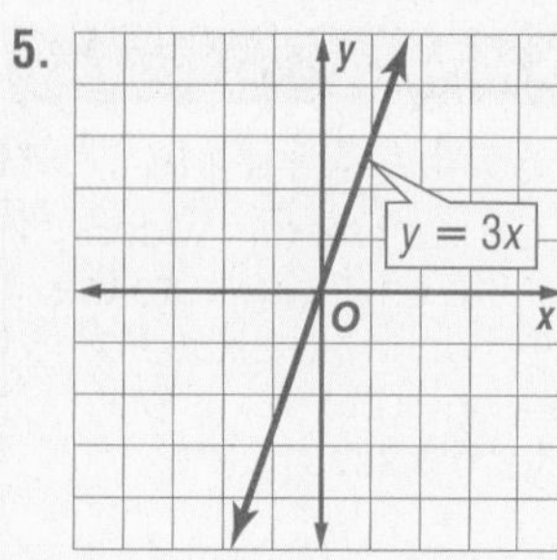

6.

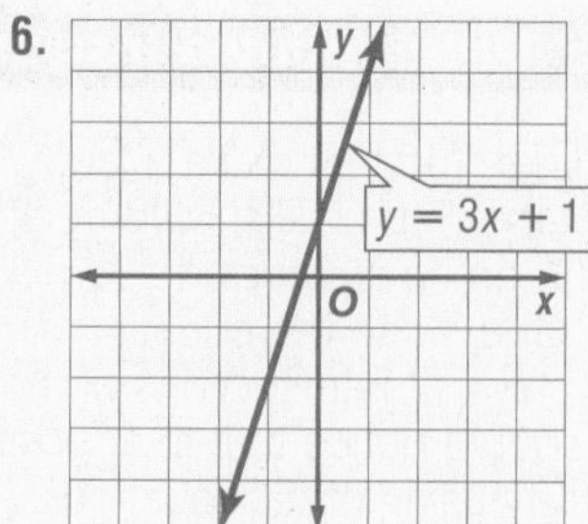

7.

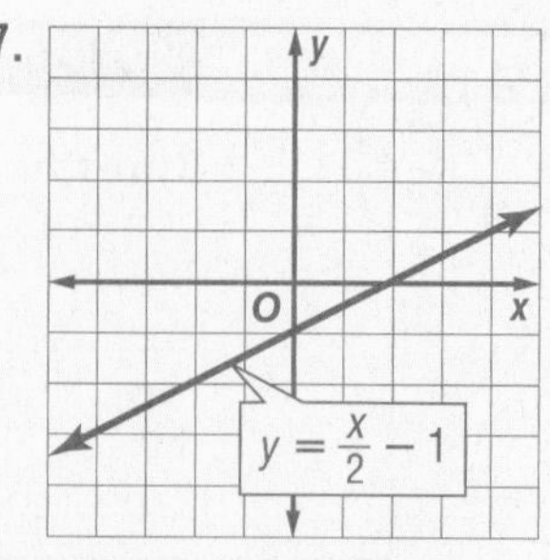

MOUNTAIN CLIMBING **For Exercises 23 and 24, use the following information.**

If the temperature is 80°F at sea level, the function $t = 80 - 3.6h$ describes the temperature t at a height of h thousand feet above sea level.

23. Graph the temperature function. **See Ch. 11 Answer Appendix.**

24. The top of Mount Everest is about 29 thousand feet above sea level. What is the temperature at its peak on a day that is 80°F at sea level? **−24.4°F**

25. **CRITICAL THINKING** Name the coordinates of four points that satisfy each function. Then give the function rule. **a–b. See margin.**

a. 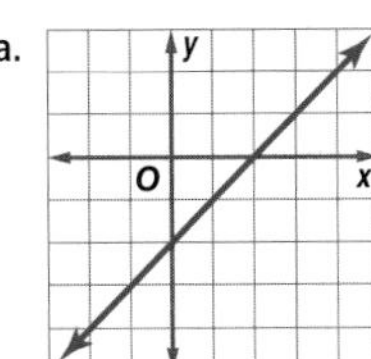

b. 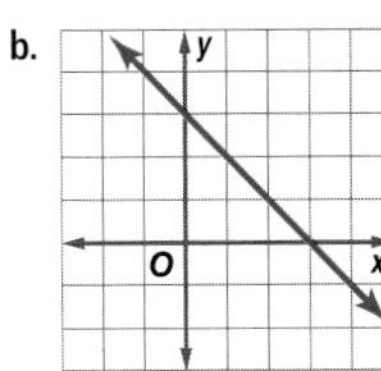

26. **CRITICAL THINKING** The vertices of a triangle are at (−1, −1), (1, −2), and (5, 1). The triangle is translated 1 unit left and 2 units up and then reflected across the graph of $y = x - 1$. What are the coordinates of the image? (*Hint:* Use a ruler.) **(2, −3), (1, −1), (4, 3)**

Spiral Review with Standardized Test Practice

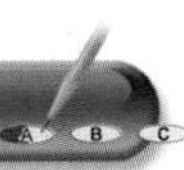

27. **MULTIPLE CHOICE** Which function is graphed at the right? **A**

Ⓐ $y = -2x + 3$ Ⓑ $y = -2x - 3$

Ⓒ $y = 2x + 3$ Ⓓ $y = 2x - 3$

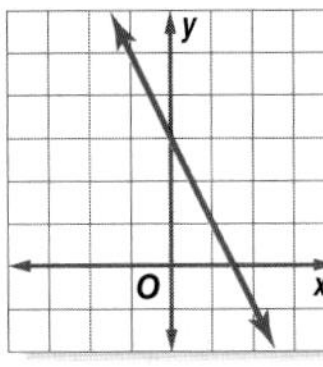

28. **SHORT RESPONSE** An African elephant eats 500 pounds of vegetation a day. Write a function for the amount of vegetation y it eats in x days. Graph the function. **$y = 500x$; See Ch. 11 Answer Appendix.**

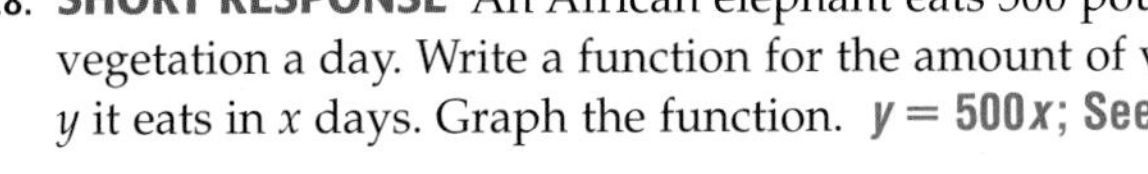

Find each function value. (Lesson 11-2)

29. $f(6)$ if $f(x) = 7x - 3$ **39**

30. $f(-5)$ if $f(x) = 3x + 15$ **0**

31. $f(3)$ if $f(x) = 2x - 7$ **−1**

32. **SCIENCE** Each time a certain ball hits the ground, it bounces up $\frac{2}{3}$ of its previous height. If the ball is dropped from 27 inches off the ground, write a sequence showing the height of the ball after each of the first three bounces. (Lesson 11-1) **18, 12, 8**

GETTING READY FOR THE NEXT LESSON

PREREQUISITE SKILL **Find the slope of each line.** (Lesson 4-3)

33. 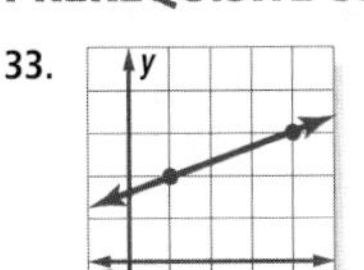 $\frac{1}{3}$

34. 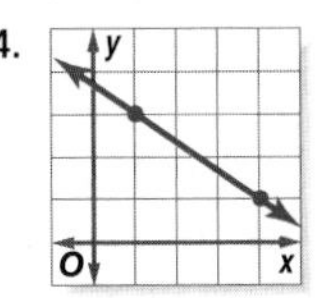 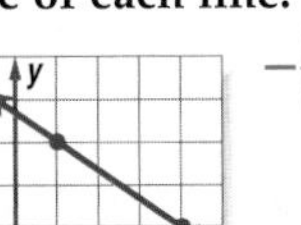 $-\frac{2}{3}$

35. 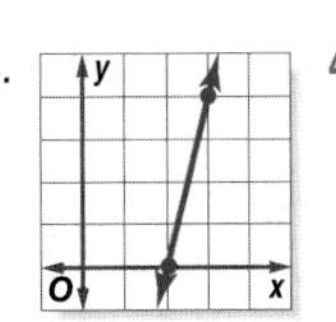 **4**

msmath3.net/self_check_quiz

4 Assess

Open-Ended Assessment

Writing Have students write a description of how to graph the equation $y = 4x - 3$.

Answers

25a. Sample answer: (−2, −4), (0, −2), (2, 0), (4, 2); $y = x - 2$

25b. Sample answer: (−1, 4), (0, 3), (1, 2), (3, 0); $y = 3 - x$

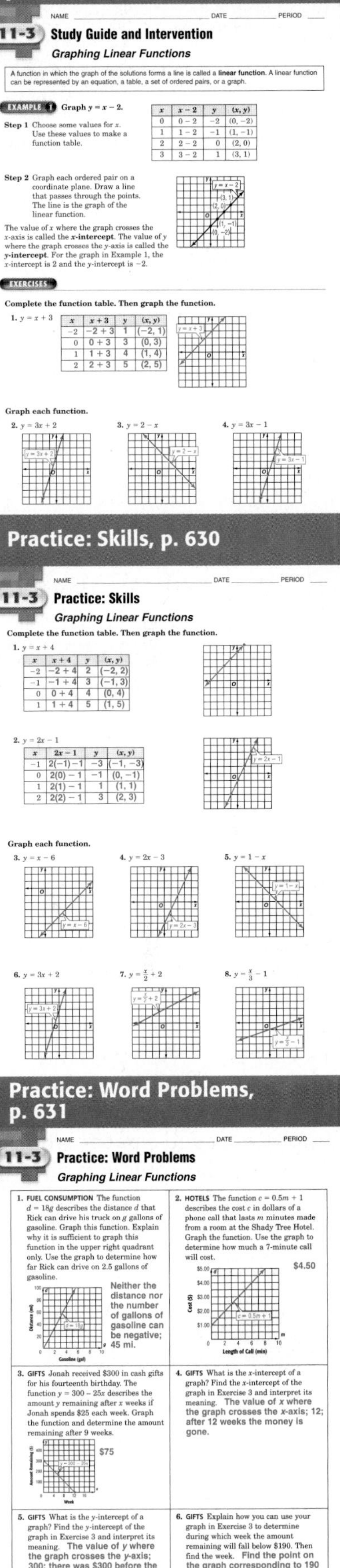

Study Guide and Intervention, p. 629

NAME ________ DATE ________ PERIOD ____

11-3 Study Guide and Intervention

Graphing Linear Functions

A function in which the graph of the solutions forms a line is called a **linear function**. A linear function can be represented by an equation, a table, a set of ordered pairs, or a graph.

EXAMPLE 1 **Graph $y = x - 2$.**

Step 1 Choose some values for x. Use these values to make a function table.

x	$x - 2$	y	(x, y)
0	0 − 2	−2	(0, −2)
1	1 − 2	−1	(1, −1)
2	2 − 2	0	(2, 0)
3	3 − 2	1	(3, 1)

Step 2 Graph each ordered pair on a coordinate plane. Draw a line that passes through the points. The line is the graph of the linear function.

The value of x where the graph crosses the x-axis is called the **x-intercept**. The value of y where the graph crosses the y-axis is called the **y-intercept**. For the graph in Example 1, the x-intercept is 2 and the y-intercept is −2.

EXERCISES

Complete the function table. Then graph the function.

1. $y = x + 3$

x	$x + 3$	y	(x, y)
−2	−2 + 3	1	(−2, 1)
0	0 + 3	3	(0, 3)
1	1 + 3	4	(1, 4)
2	2 + 3	5	(2, 5)

Graph each function.

2. $y = 3x + 2$ 3. $y = 2 - x$ 4. $y = 3x - 1$

Practice: Skills, p. 630

NAME ________ DATE ________ PERIOD ____

11-3 Practice: Skills

Graphing Linear Functions

Complete the function table. Then graph the function.

1. $y = x + 4$

x	$x + 4$	y	(x, y)
−2	−2 + 4	2	(−2, 2)
−1	−1 + 4	3	(−1, 3)
0	0 + 4	4	(0, 4)
1	1 + 4	5	(1, 5)

2. $y = 2x - 1$

x	$2x - 1$	y	(x, y)
−1	2(−1) − 1	−3	(−1, −3)
0	2(0) − 1	−1	(0, −1)
1	2(1) − 1	1	(1, 1)
2	2(2) − 1	3	(2, 3)

Graph each function.

3. $y = x - 6$ 4. $y = 2x - 3$ 5. $y = 1 - x$

6. $y = 3x + 2$ 7. $y = \frac{x}{2} + 2$ 8. $y = \frac{x}{3} - 1$

Practice: Word Problems, p. 631

NAME ________ DATE ________ PERIOD ____

11-3 Practice: Word Problems

Graphing Linear Functions

1. **FUEL CONSUMPTION** The function $d = 18g$ describes the distance d that Rick can drive his truck on g gallons of gasoline. Graph this function. Explain why it is sufficient to graph this function in the upper right quadrant only. Use the graph to determine how far Rick can drive on 2.5 gallons of gasoline. Neither the distance nor the number of gallons of gasoline can be negative; 45 mi.

2. **HOTELS** The function $c = 0.5m + 1$ describes the cost c in dollars of a phone call that lasts m minutes made from a room at the Shady Tree Hotel. Graph the function. Use the graph to determine how much a 7-minute call will cost. $4.50

3. **GIFTS** Jonah received $300 in cash gifts for his fourteenth birthday. The function $y = 300 - 25x$ describes the amount y remaining after x weeks if Jonah spends $25 each week. Graph the function and determine the amount remaining after 9 weeks. $75

4. **GIFTS** What is the x-intercept of a graph? Find the x-intercept of the graph in Exercise 3 and interpret its meaning. The value of x where the graph crosses the x-axis; 12; after 12 weeks the money is gone.

5. **GIFTS** What is the y-intercept of a graph? Find the y-intercept of the graph in Exercise 3 and interpret its meaning. The value of y where the graph crosses the y-axis; 300; there was $300 before the first week.

6. **GIFTS** Explain how you can use your graph in Exercise 3 to determine during which week the amount remaining will fall below $190. Then find the week. Find the point on the graph corresponding to 190 on the vertical axis. This point lies between 4 and 5 on the horizontal axis. The amount falls below $190 during the fifth week.

11-4 Lesson Notes

Lesson Resources

Chapter 11 Resource Masters

- Study Guide and Intervention, p. 634
- Practice: Skills, p. 635
- Practice: Word Problems, p. 636
- Reading to Learn Mathematics, p. 637
- Enrichment, p. 638

Parent and Student Study Guide Online Worksheets, 11-4

Noteables™: Interactive Study Notebook with Foldables™, 11-4

FAST FILE

1 Focus

5-Minute Check 11-4

Use as a quiz or review of Lesson 11-3. (Also available as a transparency)

Bellringer

Hands-On Activity Have students locate a number of different sets of stairs. Suggest that they include a ladder and a garden walk. Have students determine the steepness of the stairs by measuring the vertical increase and dividing by the horizontal measurement. Have students represent the steps on graph paper and compare the steepness. Have students draw a line through each set of steps. Explain that the steepness is the slope for each line.

Reading to Learn Mathematics, p. 637 **ELL**

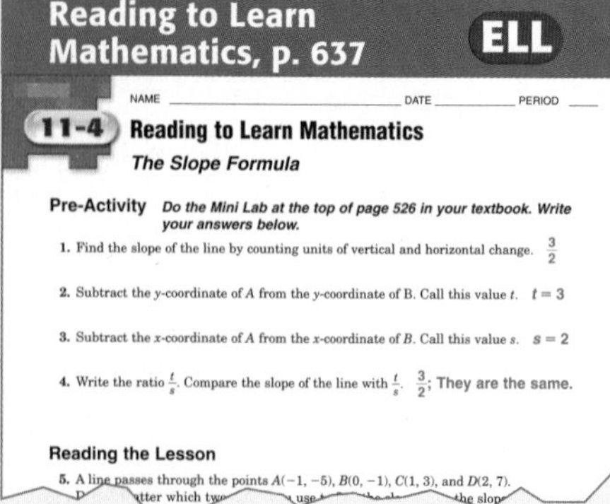

NAME ____________ DATE ____________ PERIOD ____

11-4 Reading to Learn Mathematics

The Slope Formula

Pre-Activity *Do the Mini Lab at the top of page 526 in your textbook. Write your answers below.*

1. Find the slope of the line by counting units of vertical and horizontal change. $\frac{3}{2}$
2. Subtract the y-coordinate of A from the y-coordinate of B. Call this value t. $t = 3$
3. Subtract the x-coordinate of A from the x-coordinate of B. Call this value s. $s = 2$
4. Write the ratio $\frac{t}{s}$. Compare the slope of the line with $\frac{t}{s}$. $\frac{3}{2}$; They are the same.

Reading the Lesson

5. A line passes through the points $A(-1, -5)$, $B(0, -1)$, $C(1, 3)$, and $D(2, 7)$.

11-4 The Slope Formula

What You'll LEARN

Find the slope of a line using the slope formula.

NEW Vocabulary

slope formula

REVIEW Vocabulary

slope: the ratio of the rise, or vertical change, to the run, or horizontal change (Lesson 4-3)

MATH Symbols

x_2 x sub 2

HANDS-ON Mini Lab

Materials

- grid paper

Work with a partner.

On a coordinate plane, graph $A(2, 1)$ and $B(4, 4)$. Draw the line through points A and B as shown.

1. Find the slope of the line by counting units of vertical and horizontal change. $\frac{3}{2}$
2. Subtract the y-coordinate of A from the y-coordinate of B. Call this value t. $t = 3$
3. Subtract the x-coordinate of A from the x-coordinate of B. Call this value s. $s = 2$
4. Write the ratio $\frac{t}{s}$. Compare the slope of the line with $\frac{t}{s}$. $\frac{3}{2}$; They are the same.

You can find the slope of a line by using the coordinates of any two points on the line. One point can be represented by (x_1, y_1) and the other by (x_2, y_2). The small numbers slightly below x and y are called *subscripts*.

Noteables™ **Key Concept: Slope Formula**

Words The slope m of a line passing through points (x_1, y_1) and (x_2, y_2) is the ratio of the difference in the y-coordinates to the corresponding difference in the x-coordinates.

Model

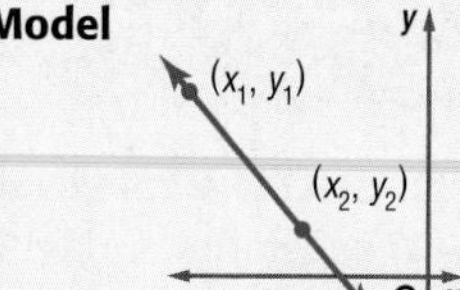

Symbols $m = \frac{y_2 - y_1}{x_2 - x_1}$, where $x_2 \neq x_1$

EXAMPLE Positive Slope

1 Find the slope of the line that passes through $C(-1, -4)$ and $D(2, 2)$.

$m = \frac{y_2 - y_1}{x_2 - x_1}$ Definition of slope

$m = \frac{2 - (-4)}{2 - (-1)}$ $(x_1, y_1) = (-1, -4)$, $(x_2, y_2) = (2, 2)$

$m = \frac{6}{3}$ or 2 Simplify.

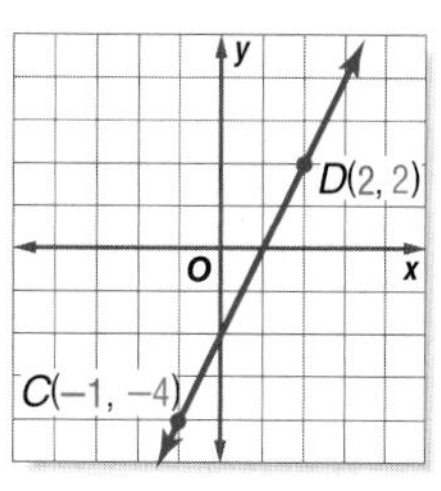

Check When going from left to right, the graph of the line slants upward. This is consistent with a positive slope.

STUDY TIP

Using the Slope Formula

- It does not matter which point you define as (x_1, y_1) and (x_2, y_2).
- However, the coordinates of both points must be used in the same order.

Check In Example 2, let $(x_1, y_1) = (-4, 3)$ and $(x_2, y_2) = (1, 2)$. Then find the slope.

EXAMPLE Negative Slope

2 **Find the slope of the line that passes through $R(1, 2)$ and $S(-4, 3)$.**

$m = \frac{y_2 - y_1}{x_2 - x_1}$ Definition of slope

$m = \frac{3 - 2}{-4 - 1}$ $(x_1, y_1) = (1, 2)$, $(x_2, y_2) = (-4, 3)$

$m = \frac{1}{-5}$ or $-\frac{1}{5}$ Simplify.

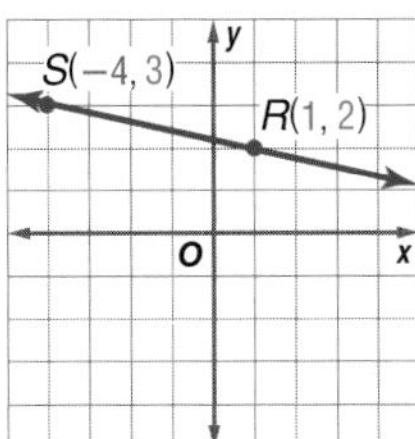

Check When going from left to right, the graph of the line slants downward. This is consistent with a negative slope.

EXAMPLE Zero Slope

3 **Find the slope of the line that passes through $V(-5, -1)$ and $W(2, -1)$.**

$m = \frac{y_2 - y_1}{x_2 - x_1}$ Definition of slope

$m = \frac{-1 - (-1)}{2 - (-5)}$ $(x_1, y_1) = (-5, -1)$, $(x_2, y_2) = (2, -1)$

$m = \frac{0}{7}$ or 0 Simplify.

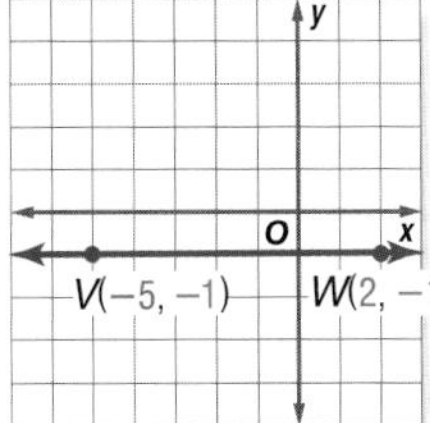

The slope is 0. The slope of any horizontal line is 0.

TEACHING TIP

If students have difficulty understanding that any number divided by 0 is undefined, ask students to set up the following division problem.

$$\begin{array}{r} ? \\ 0\overline{)4} \\ \underline{0} \\ 4 \end{array}$$

0 ← product
4 ← difference

No matter what number they place in the quotient, the product is 0 and the difference is 4. Since 4 is greater than 0, the quotient is not correct.

EXAMPLE Undefined Slope

4 **Find the slope of the line that passes through $X(4, 3)$ and $Y(4, -1)$**

$m = \frac{y_2 - y_1}{x_2 - x_1}$ Definition of slope

$m = \frac{-1 - 3}{4 - 4}$ $(x_1, y_1) = (4, 3)$, $(x_2, y_2) = (4, -1)$

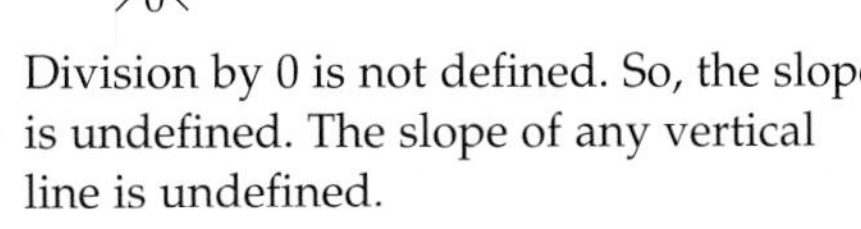

$m = \frac{-4}{0}$ (crossed out) Simplify.

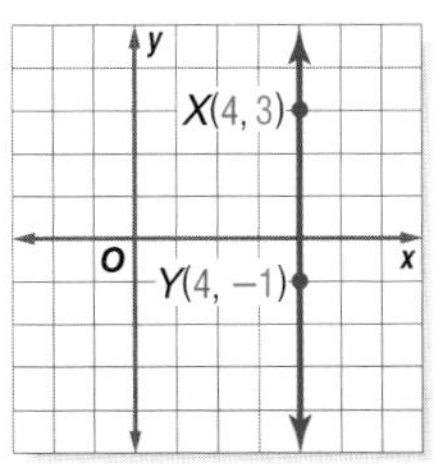

Division by 0 is not defined. So, the slope is undefined. The slope of any vertical line is undefined.

Your Turn **Find the slope of the line that passes through each pair of points.**

a. $M(2, 2)$, $N(5, 3)$ $\frac{1}{3}$

b. $A(-2, 1)$, $B(0, -3)$ **−2**

c. $C(-5, 6)$, $D(-5, 0)$ **undefined**

d. $E(-1, 1)$, $F(3, 1)$ **0**

Math Online msmath3.net/extra_examples

2 Teach

In-Class Examples

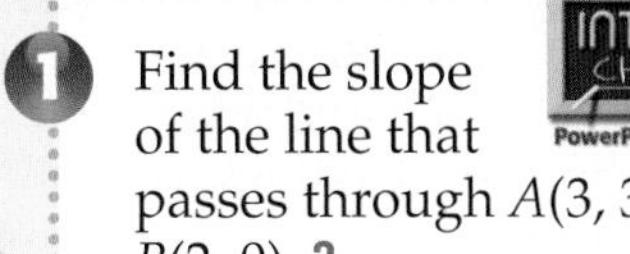

1. Find the slope of the line that passes through $A(3, 3)$ and $B(2, 0)$. **3**

2. Find the slope of the line that passes through $X(-2, 3)$ and $Y(3, 0)$. $-\frac{3}{5}$

3. Find the slope of the line that passes through $P(6, 5)$ and $Q(2, 5)$. **0**

4. Find the slope of the line that passes through $G(2, 4)$ and $H(2, 6)$. **undefined**

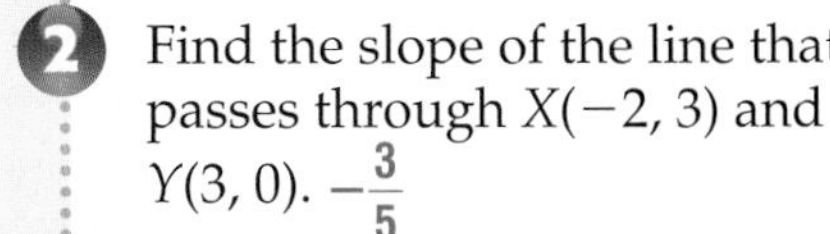

Teaching Strategies To help students remember formulas, it is often helpful for them to have a phrase that is easy to remember. For example, the slope formula is often referred to as *rise over run*. The *rise* is how far up or down it is between the two points, or the difference between *y* values. The *run* is how far side to side it is between the two points, or the difference between *x* values.

DAILY INTERVENTION **Differentiated Instruction**

Visual/Spatial Students can better understand an undefined slope if they observe how the slope increases as a line approaches a vertical position. Begin by positioning a meterstick at about a 45-degree angle against a wall. Have students determine the slope by dividing the height of the triangle by the base. Increase the angle about 10 degrees, and have students determine the slope again. Continue until the meterstick is vertical.

3 Practice/Apply

DAILY INTERVENTION **FIND THE ERROR** In Exercise 3, remind students that they can choose either point to be the starting point, but they must use the same starting point for the x and y values. They can check their answer by using the other point as the starting point.

About the Exercises...

Guided Practice Key

Exercises	Examples
4, 7, 8	1
6	2
5	3

Assignment Guide

Basic: 11–21 odd, 22, 23, 26, 30–40

Average: 11–21 odd, 22, 23, 25, 26, 30–40 (Optional: 27–29)

Enriched: 10–20 even, 22–24, 26–36 (Optional: 37–40)

Answers

1. If $x_2 = x_1$, then $\frac{y_2 - y_1}{x_2 - x_1} = \frac{y_2 - y_1}{0}$ and division by 0 is undefined. Therefore the slope is undefined.
2. Sample answer: (1, 2) and (3, 5); If $(x_1, y_1) = (1, 2)$ and $(x_2, y_2) = (3, 5)$, $m = \frac{5-2}{3-1}$ or $\frac{3}{2}$. If $(x_1, y_1) = (3, 5)$ and $(x_2, y_2) = (1, 2)$, $m = \frac{2-5}{1-3}$ or $\frac{3}{2}$.
3. Martin did not use the x-coordinates in the same order as the y-coordinates.

22.

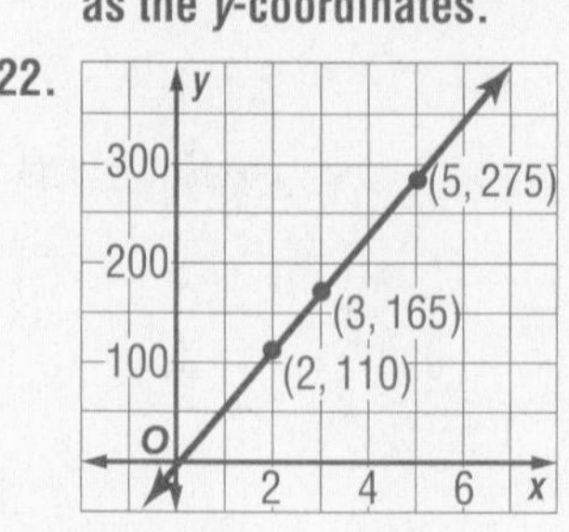

Students practice the same concepts in Exercises 10–23 if they are assigned odd or even problems.

Skill and Concept Check

1. **Writing Math** Explain why the slope formula, which states $m = \frac{y_2 - y_1}{x_2 - x_1}$, says that x_2 cannot equal x_1. **1–2. See margin.**
2. **OPEN ENDED** Write the coordinates of two points. Show that you can define either point as (x_1, y_1) and the slope of the line containing the points will be the same.
3. **FIND THE ERROR** Martin and Dylan are finding the slope of the line that passes through $X(0, 2)$ and $Y(2, 3)$. Who is correct? Explain. **Dylan; see margin.**

Martin

$m = \frac{3-2}{0-2}$

$m = \frac{1}{-2}$ or $-\frac{1}{2}$

Dylan

$m = \frac{3-2}{2-0}$

$m = \frac{1}{2}$

GUIDED PRACTICE

Find the slope of the line that passes through each pair of points.

4. $A(-3, -2), B(5, 4)$ $\frac{3}{4}$
5. $C(-4, 2), D(1, 2)$ **0**
6. $E(-6, 5), F(3, -3)$ $-\frac{8}{9}$

For Exercises 7–9, use the graphic at the right. Note that the years are on the horizontal axis and the second homeownership is on the vertical axis.

7. Find the slope of the line representing the change from 1990 to 2000. $\frac{9}{100}$
8. Find the slope of the line representing the change from 2000 to 2010. $\frac{17}{50}$
9. Which part of the graph shows a greater rate of change? Explain. **The second half; it has a greater slope.**

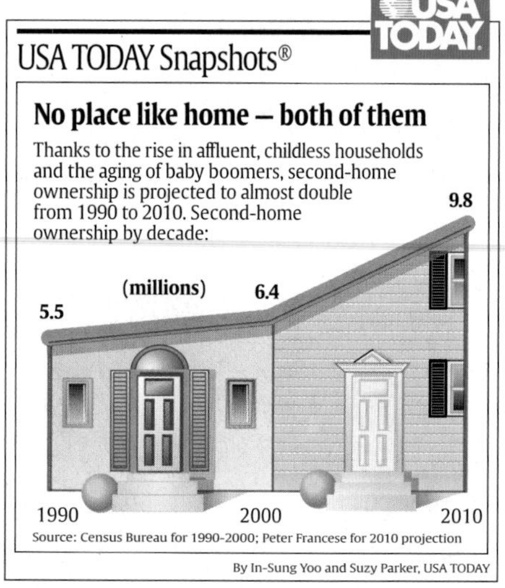

★ indicates increased difficulty **13.** $\frac{1}{5}$ **14.** $-\frac{2}{11}$ **17. undefined** **18. undefined**

Practice and Applications

HOMEWORK HELP

For Exercises	See Examples
10–21	1–4

Extra Practice See pages 643, 658.

Find the slope of the line that passes through each pair of points.

10. $A(0, 1), B(2, 7)$ **3**
11. $C(2, 5), D(3, 1)$ **−4**
12. $E(1, 2), F(4, 7)$ $\frac{5}{3}$
13. $G(-6, -1), H(4, 1)$
14. $J(-9, 3), K(2, 1)$
15. $M(-2, 3), N(7, -4)$ $-\frac{7}{9}$
16. $P(4, -4), Q(8, -4)$ **0**
17. $R(-1, 5), S(-1, -2)$
18. $T(3, -2), U(3, 2)$
19. $V(-6, 5), W(3, -3)$
20. $X(21, 5), Y(17, 0)$
21. $Z(24, 12), A(34, 2)$

19. $-\frac{8}{9}$ **20.** $\frac{5}{4}$ **21.** -1

24. Slope of $\overline{AB}$: $m = \frac{1-0}{9-1}$ or $\frac{1}{8}$

Slope of $\overline{BC}$: $m = \frac{4-1}{10-9}$ or 3

Slope of $\overline{CD}$: $m = \frac{3-4}{2-10}$ or $\frac{1}{8}$

Slope of $\overline{DA}$: $m = \frac{0-3}{1-2}$ or 3

Therefore, $\overline{AB} \parallel \overline{CD}$ and $\overline{BC} \parallel \overline{DA}$, and quadrilateral $ABCD$ is a parallelogram.

25. Slope of $\overline{QR}$: $m = \frac{1-(-2)}{5-(-4)}$ or $\frac{1}{3}$

Slope of $\overline{RS}$: $m = \frac{2-1}{4-5}$ or −1

Slope of $\overline{ST}$: $m = \frac{-1-2}{-5-4}$ or $\frac{1}{3}$

Slope of $\overline{TQ}$: $m = \frac{-1-(-2)}{-5-(-4)}$ or −1

Therefore, $\overline{QR} \parallel \overline{ST}$ and $\overline{RS} \parallel \overline{TQ}$, and quadrilateral $QRST$ is a parallelogram.

TRAVEL For Exercises 22 and 23, use the following information.
After 2 hours, Kendra has traveled 110 miles. After 3 hours, she has traveled 165 miles. After 5 hours, she has traveled 275 miles.

22. Graph the information with the hours on the horizontal axis and miles traveled on the vertical axis. Draw a line through the points. **See margin.**
23. What is the slope of the graph? What does it represent? **55; her average speed**

GEOMETRY For Exercises 24 and 25, use the following information to show that each quadrilateral graphed is a parallelogram.
Two lines that are parallel have the same slope. **24–25. See margin.**

★ 24.

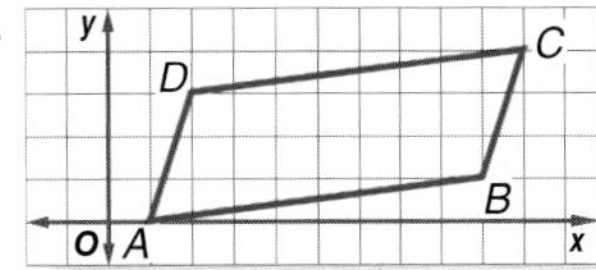

★ 25.

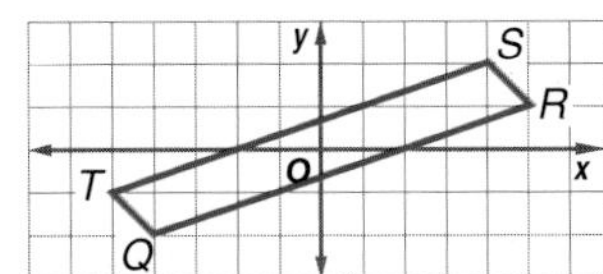

26. **CRITICAL THINKING** Without graphing, determine whether $A(5, 1)$, $B(1, 0)$, and $C(-3, -3)$ lie on the same line. Explain. **No; see margin.**

EXTENDING THE LESSON

For Exercises 27–29, use the graphs at the right. The two lines in each graph are perpendicular.

27. Find the slopes of the lines in graph A. $-2, \frac{1}{2}$
28. Find the slopes of the lines in graph B. $\frac{2}{3}, -\frac{3}{2}$
29. **Make a conjecture** about the slopes of perpendicular lines. **The product of the slopes of two perpendicular lines is −1.**

Graph A

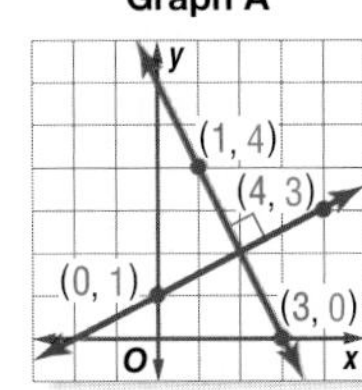

Graph B

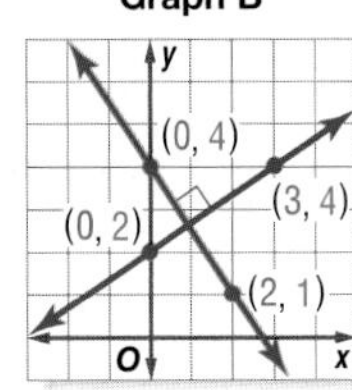

Spiral Review with Standardized Test Practice

30. **MULTIPLE CHOICE** Which graph has a slope of −2? **C**

Ⓐ
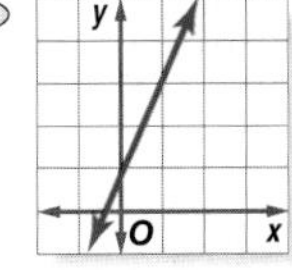

Ⓑ
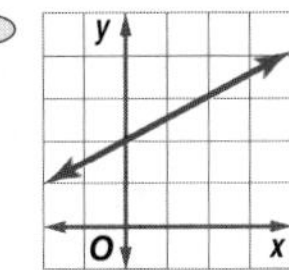

Ⓒ
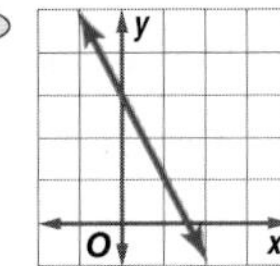

Ⓓ
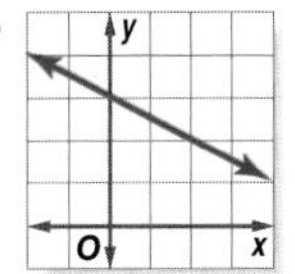

31. **SHORT RESPONSE** Draw a graph of a line with an undefined slope. **See Ch. 11 Answer Appendix.**

Graph each function. (Lesson 11-3) **32–35. See Ch. 11 Answer Appendix.**

32. $y = 5x$
33. $y = x - 2$
34. $y = 2x - 1$
35. $y = 3x + 2$

36. **TEMPERATURE** The function used to change a Celsius temperature (C) to a Fahrenheit temperature (F) is $F = \frac{9}{5}C + 32$. Change 25° Celsius to degrees Fahrenheit. (Lesson 11-2) **77°F**

GETTING READY FOR THE NEXT LESSON

PREREQUISITE SKILL Solve each equation. (Lesson 1-8)

37. $7 + a = 15$ **8**
38. $23 = d + 44$ **−21**
39. $28 = n - 14$ **42**
40. $t - 22 = -31$ **−9**

msmath3.net/self_check_quiz

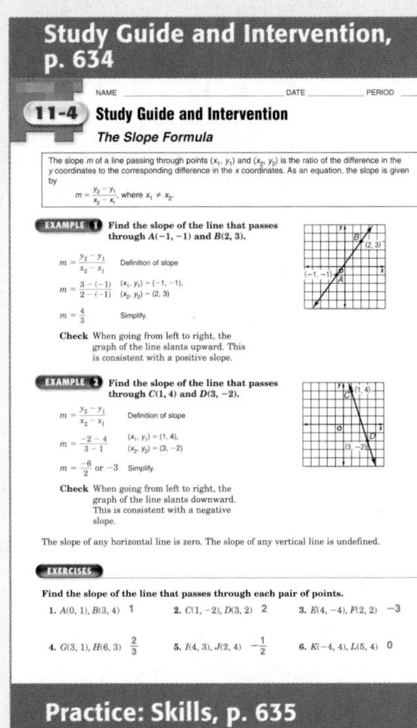

Study Guide and Intervention, p. 634

NAME ______ DATE ______ PERIOD ____

11-4 Study Guide and Intervention

The Slope Formula

The slope m of a line passing through points (x_1, y_1) and (x_2, y_2) is the ratio of the difference in the y coordinates to the corresponding difference in the x coordinates. As an equation, the slope is given by

$$m = \frac{y_2 - y_1}{x_2 - x_1}, \text{ where } x_1 \neq x_2.$$

EXAMPLE 1 **Find the slope of the line that passes through $A(-1, -1)$ and $B(2, 3)$.**

$m = \frac{y_2 - y_1}{x_2 - x_1}$ Definition of slope

$m = \frac{3 - (-1)}{2 - (-1)}$ $(x_1, y_1) = (-1, -1)$, $(x_2, y_2) = (2, 3)$

$m = \frac{4}{3}$ Simplify.

Check When going from left to right, the graph of the line slants upward. This is consistent with a positive slope.

EXAMPLE 2 **Find the slope of the line that passes through $C(1, 4)$ and $D(3, -2)$.**

$m = \frac{y_2 - y_1}{x_2 - x_1}$ Definition of slope

$m = \frac{-2 - 4}{3 - 1}$ $(x_1, y_1) = (1, 4)$, $(x_2, y_2) = (3, -2)$

$m = \frac{-6}{2}$ or -3 Simplify.

Check When going from left to right, the graph of the line slants downward. This is consistent with a negative slope.

The slope of any horizontal line is zero. The slope of any vertical line is undefined.

EXERCISES

Find the slope of the line that passes through each pair of points.

1. $A(0, 1), B(3, 4)$ 1
2. $C(1, -2), D(3, 2)$ 2
3. $E(4, -4), F(2, 2)$ −3
4. $G(3, 1), H(6, 3)$ $\frac{2}{3}$
5. $I(4, 3), J(2, 4)$ $-\frac{1}{2}$
6. $K(-4, 4), L(5, 4)$ 0

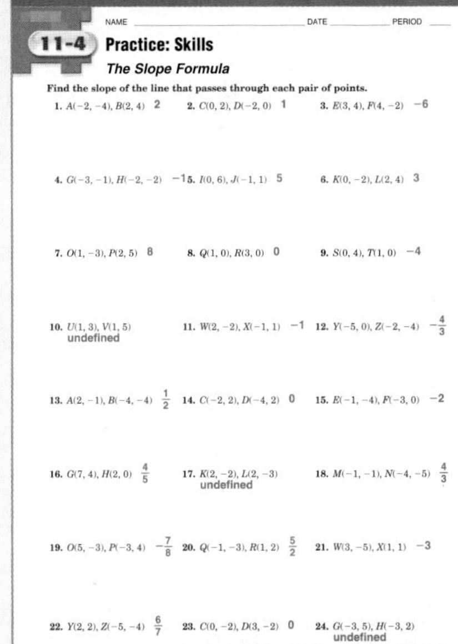

Practice: Skills, p. 635

NAME ______ DATE ______ PERIOD ____

11-4 Practice: Skills

The Slope Formula

Find the slope of the line that passes through each pair of points.

1. $A(-2, -4), B(2, 4)$ 2
2. $C(0, 2), D(-2, 0)$ 1
3. $E(3, 4), F(4, -2)$ −6
4. $G(-3, -1), H(-2, -2)$ −1
5. $I(0, 6), J(-1, 1)$ 5
6. $K(0, -2), L(2, 4)$ 3
7. $O(1, -3), P(2, 5)$ 8
8. $Q(1, 0), R(3, 0)$ 0
9. $S(0, 4), T(1, 0)$ −4
10. $U(1, 3), V(1, 5)$ undefined
11. $W(2, -2), X(-1, 1)$ −1
12. $Y(-5, 0), Z(-2, -4)$ $-\frac{4}{3}$
13. $A(2, -1), B(-4, -4)$ $\frac{1}{2}$
14. $C(-2, 2), D(-4, 2)$ 0
15. $E(-1, -4), F(-3, 0)$ −2
16. $G(7, 4), H(2, 0)$ $\frac{4}{5}$
17. $K(2, -2), L(2, -3)$ undefined
18. $M(-1, -1), N(-4, -5)$ $\frac{4}{3}$
19. $O(5, -3), P(-3, 4)$ $-\frac{7}{8}$
20. $Q(-1, -3), R(1, 2)$ $\frac{5}{2}$
21. $W(3, -5), X(1, 1)$ −3
22. $Y(2, 2), Z(-5, -4)$ $\frac{6}{7}$
23. $C(0, -2), D(3, -2)$ 0
24. $G(-3, 5), H(-3, 2)$ undefined

Practice: Word Problems, p. 636

NAME ______ DATE ______ PERIOD ____

11-4 Practice: Word Problems

The Slope Formula

1. **MOVIES** By the end of its first week, a movie had grossed \$2.3 million. By the end of its sixth week, it had grossed \$6.8 million. Graph the data with the week on the horizontal axis and the revenue on the vertical axis, and draw a line through the points. Then find and interpret the slope of the line.

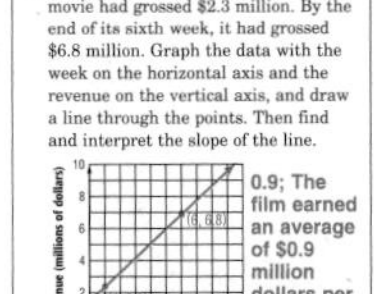

0.9; The film earned an average of \$0.9 million dollars per week for weeks 2–6.

2. **BASKETBALL** After Game 1, Felicia had scored 14 points. After Game 5, she had scored a total of 82 points for the season. After Game 10, she had scored 129 points. Graph the data with the game number on the horizontal axis and the number of points on the vertical axis. Connect the points using two different line segments.

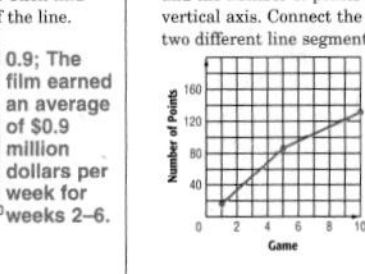

3. **BASKETBALL** Find the slope of each line segment in your graph from Exercise 2 and interpret it. Which part of the graph shows the greater rate of change? Explain. **17; Felicia scored an average of 17 points per game for Games 2–5; 9.4; she scored an average of 9.4 points per game for Games 6–10; the first part; it has a greater slope.**

4. **GEOMETRY** The figure shows triangle ABC plotted on a coordinate system. Explain how to find the slope of the line through points A and B. Then find the slope. **Use the slope formula; $\frac{6}{5}$.**

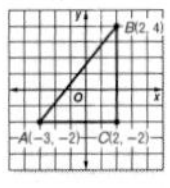

5. Use the figure in Exercise 4. What is the slope of the line through points A and C? How do you know? **0; The line is horizontal.**

6. Use the figure in Exercise 4. What is the slope of the line through points B and C? How do you know? **Undefined; the line is vertical.**

4 Assess

Open-Ended Assessment

Modeling Have students work in small groups to make posters that demonstrate the slope formula. They can use straws or toothpicks glued to the posters to model the slopes.

Answer

26. **The slope of $\overline{AB}$ is $\frac{0-1}{1-5}$ or $\frac{1}{4}$ and the slope of $\overline{BC}$ is $\frac{-3-0}{-3-1}$ or $\frac{3}{4}$. If the points were on the same line, the slopes would be equal.**

Assessment Option

Mid-Chapter Test (Lessons 11-1 through 11-4) is available on p. 675 of the *Chapter 11 Resource Masters.*

ExamView® Pro

Use the networkable ExamView® Pro Testmaker CD-ROM to:

- Create **multiple versions** of tests.
- Create **modified** tests for **inclusion** students with one mouse click.
- **Edit** existing questions and **add** your own questions.
- Build tests aligned with state standards using built-in **state curriculum correlations.**
- Change **English** tests to **Spanish** with one mouse click and vice versa.

FOLDABLES™ Follow-Up Before students complete the Mid-Chapter Practice Test, encourage them to review the notes, definitions, concepts, and main ideas they recorded in their Foldables during the first four lessons of the chapter.

Answers

1. Since this is an arithmetic sequence, add the common difference 3 to the previous term. The next three terms are 17 + 3 or 20, 20 + 3 or 23, and 23 + 3 or 26.
2. Use a function table to find several ordered pairs that satisfy the function. Graph each ordered pair on a coordinate plane. Draw a line that passes through the points on the graph.

Mid-Chapter Practice Test

Vocabulary and Concepts

1. **Explain** how to find the next three terms of the sequence 5, 8, 11, 14, 17, … . (Lesson 11-1) **1–2. See margin.**
2. **Explain** how to graph $y = -2x + 1$. (Lesson 11-3)
3. **Describe** the slopes of a horizontal line and a vertical line. (Lesson 11-4) **A horizontal line has a slope of 0, and a vertical line has an undefined slope.**

Skills and Applications

State whether each sequence is *arithmetic*, *geometric*, or *neither*. If it is arithmetic or geometric, state the common difference or common ratio. Then write the next three terms of the sequence. (Lesson 11-1) **5. geometric; $-\frac{1}{2}$; −2, 1, $-\frac{1}{2}$**

4. 13, 17, 21, 25, 29, … **arithmetic; 4; 33, 37, 41**
5. 64, −32, 16, −8, 4, …
6. 5, 6, 8, 11, 15, … **neither; 20, 26, 33**
7. **PICNICS** Shelby is hosting a picnic. The cost to rent the shelter is \$25 plus \$2 per person. Write a function using two variables to represent the situation. Find the total cost if 150 people attend. (Lesson 11-2) **$c = 25 + 2p$; \$325**

Graph each function. (Lesson 11-3) **8–10. See margin.**

8. $y = -2x$
9. $y = x + 6$
10. $y = 2x - 5$

Find the slope of the line that passes through each pair of points. (Lesson 11-4)

11. $A(2, 5), B(3, 1)$ **−4**
12. $C(-1, 2), D(-5, 2)$ **0**
13. $E(5, 2), F(2, -3)$ **$\frac{5}{3}$**

Standardized Test Practice

14. **MULTIPLE CHOICE** Which equation describes the function represented by the table? (Lesson 11-2) **A**

x	f(x)
−2	−7
0	−3
2	1
4	5

Ⓐ $f(x) = 2x - 3$
Ⓑ $f(x) = x + 4$
Ⓒ $f(x) = n - 3$
Ⓓ $f(x) = 2x + 3$

15. **MULTIPLE CHOICE** Which graph has a negative slope? (Lesson 11-4) **H**

Ⓕ 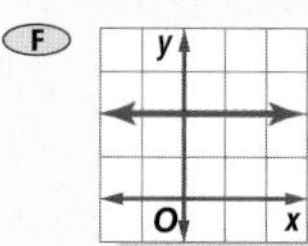

Ⓖ 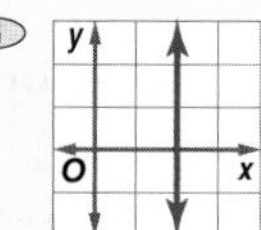

Ⓗ 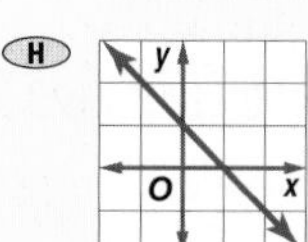

Ⓘ 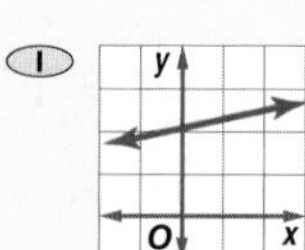

8. 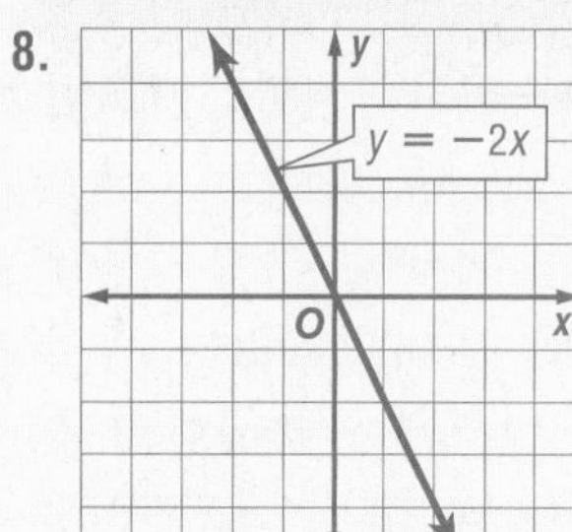

9. 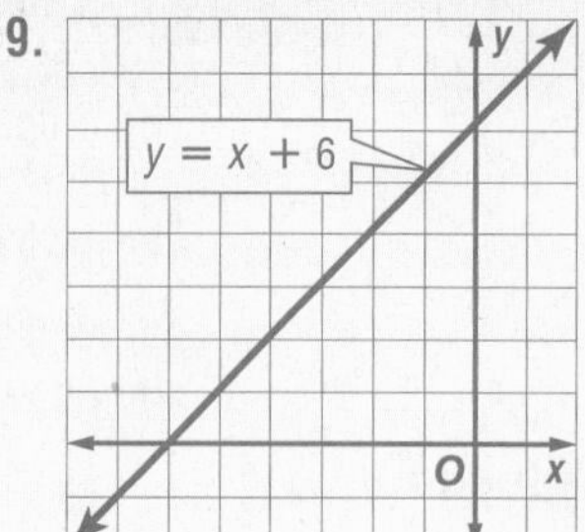

10. 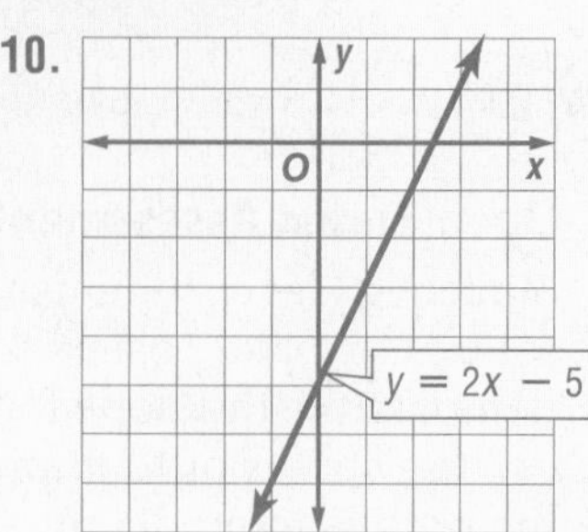

The Game Zone

A Place To Practice Your Math Skills

Math Skill
Graphing Linear Functions

It's a Hit

GET READY!

Players: two
Materials: large piece of paper, marker, grid paper

GET SET!

- Use a marker to list the following functions on a piece of paper.

$y = -2x$	$y = x + 2$	$y = x - 2$
$y = -x + 2$	$y = 3 - x$	$y = 1 - 2x$
$y = 2x$	$y = -x - 1$	$y = x - 1$
$y = x + 1$	$y = 2x - 1$	$y = -x - 2$
$y = x - 3$	$y = 2x + 1$	$y = -x + 1$

- Each player makes two coordinate planes. Each plane should be on a 20-by-20 grid with the origin in the center.

GO!

- Each player secretly picks one of the functions listed on the paper and graphs it on one of his or her coordinate planes.
- The first player names an ordered pair. The second player says *hit* if the ordered pair names a point on his or her line. If not, the player says *miss*.
- Then the second player names an ordered pair. It is either a *hit* or a *miss*. Players should use their second coordinate plane to keep track of their hits and misses. Players continue to take turns guessing.
- **Who Wins?** A player who correctly names the equation of the other player is the winner. However, if a player incorrectly names the equation, the other player is the winner.

The Game Zone

Resources

Math Online For a recording sheet and easy-to-make manipulative for this game, visit: msmath3.net/gamezone

GETTING READY

Objective Graph linear functions.

MANAGEMENT TIPS

Recommended Time
20 minutes

Tips

- Have students use colored pencils when drawing on their coordinate planes so that they can be reused to play the game again.
- Have students change partners to play a second game. Make sure they graph a different function for each game.
- Ask students follow-up questions to check for understanding. For example, after two hits, what do you know? Are some points better to guess, such as the y-intercept? Have students share their strategies.
- You may wish to use the game as an assessment tool for the concepts the students have been learning in Lessons 11-2 through 11-4.

Math Online For an additional game for this chapter, visit: msmath3.net/gamezone

11-5a Graphing Calculator Investigation

GETTING STARTED

Teaching Tip Before students begin the investigation, be sure they understand how to clear existing equations from the memory of their calculators.

TEACH

- Caution students not to confuse the subtraction key, [–], with the opposite or negative key which shows a negative sign in parentheses, [(–)].
- If students work in pairs or small groups for this investigation, be sure they repeat the activity so that everyone has a chance to use the calculator. Remind them to clear the memory before each student begins.

ASSESS

Observe as students solve the **Exercises**. They should:

- understand how to input equations into the calculator and graph them,
- compare and contrast graphs they make on the calculator, and
- realize how changing part of an equation will change the graph.

11-5a Graphing Calculator Investigation

A Preview of Lesson 11-5

What You'll LEARN

Use a graphing calculator to graph families of lines.

Families of Linear Graphs

Families of graphs are graphs that are related in some manner. In this investigation, you will study families of linear graphs.

ACTIVITY

Graph $y = -2x + 4$, $y = -2x + 1$, and $y = -2x - 3$.

STEP 1 Clear any existing equations from the Y= list.

Keystrokes: [Y=] [CLEAR]

TEACHING TIP

Remind students to use the negative key and not the minus key to enter $-2x$.

STEP 2 Enter each equation.

Keystrokes: [(–)] 2 [X,T,θ,n] [+] 4 [ENTER]
[(–)] 2 [X,T,θ,n] [+] 1 [ENTER]
[(–)] 2 [X,T,θ,n] [–] 3 [ENTER]

STEP 3 Graph the equations in the standard viewing window.

Keystrokes: [ZOOM] 6

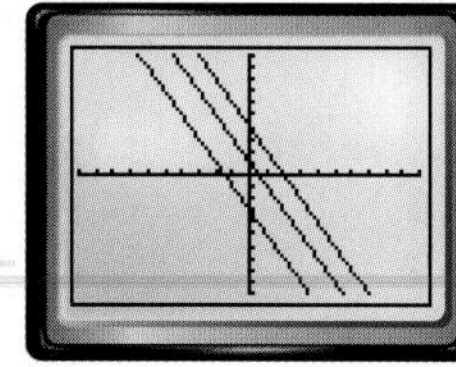

EXERCISES 1 & 5. See margin.

1. **Compare** the three equations.
2. **Describe** the graphs of the three equations.
3. **MAKE A CONJECTURE** Consider equations of the form $y = ax + b$, where the value of a is the same but the value of b varies. What do you think is true about the graphs of the equations?
4. **Use a graphing calculator** to graph $y = 2x + 3$, $y = -x + 3$, and $y = -3x + 3$. See margin.
5. **Compare** the three equations you graphed in Exercise 4.
6. **Describe** the graphs of the three equations you graphed in Exercise 4. They all intersect at (0, 3).
7. **MAKE A CONJECTURE** Consider equations of the form $y = ax + b$, where the value of a changes but the value of b remains the same. What do you think is true about the graphs of the equations? They will all intersect at (0, *b*).
8. **Write** equations of three lines whose graphs are a family of graphs. Describe the common characteristic of the graph. See margin.

2. The graphs are parallel lines.
3. They will be parallel lines.

Math Online msmath3.net/other_calculator_keystrokes

Answers

1. In all three equations, the number multiplied by *x* is -2. However, the numbers added or subtracted to $-2x$ are different.

4.

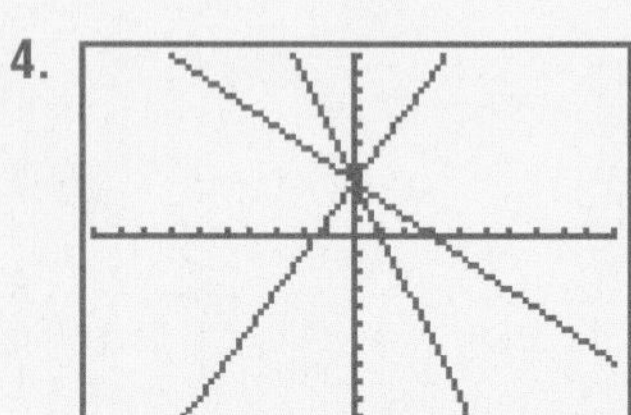

5. In all three equations 3 is added to something involving *x*. However, the numbers multiplied by *x* are all different.
8. Sample answer: $y = 2x - 1$, $y = 2x + 3$, and $y = 2x + 5$; The graphs of the equations are parallel lines.

Slope-Intercept Form

HANDS-ON Mini Lab

Materials
- grid paper

Work with a partner.

Graph each equation listed in the table at the right.

Equation	Slope	y-intercept
$y = 3x + 2$	3	2
$y = \frac{1}{4}x + (-1)$	$\frac{1}{4}$	-1
$y = -2x + 3$	-2	3

1. Use the graphs to find the slope and y-intercept of each line. Copy and complete the table.
2. Compare each equation with the value of its slope. What do you notice? **The slope is the same as the coefficient of x.**
3. Compare each equation with its y-intercept. What do you notice? **The y-intercept is the same as the constant.**

What You'll LEARN

Graph linear equations using the slope and y-intercept.

NEW Vocabulary

slope-intercept form

Link to READING

Everyday Meaning of Intercept: to intersect or cross

All of the equations in the table above are written in the form $y = mx + b$. This is called the **slope-intercept form**. When an equation is written in this form, m is the slope, and b is the y-intercept.

$$y = mx + b$$

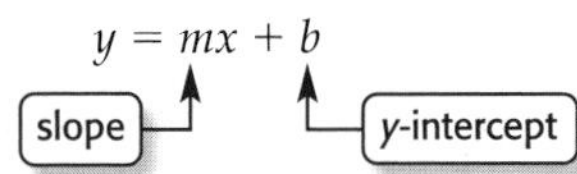

EXAMPLES Find Slopes and y-intercepts of Graphs

State the slope and the y-intercept of the graph of each equation.

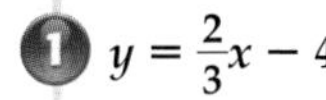

1 $y = \frac{2}{3}x - 4$

$y = \frac{2}{3}x + (-4)$ Write the equation in the form $y = mx + b$.

$y = mx + b$ $m = \frac{2}{3}, b = -4$

The slope of the graph is $\frac{2}{3}$, and the y-intercept is -4.

2 $x + y = 6$

$x + y = 6$ Write the original equation.

$-x \quad -x$ Subtract x from each side.

$y = 6 - x$ Simplify.

$y = -1x + 6$ Write the equation in the form $y = mx + b$. Recall that $-x$ means $-1x$.

$y = mx + b$ $m = -1, b = 6$

The slope of the graph is -1, and the y-intercept is 6.

TEACHING TIP

You may want students to write $y = 6 - x$ as $y = 6 + (-x)$ and then as $y = 6 + (-1x)$ before writing as $y = -1x + 6$.

msmath3.net/extra_examples

11-5 Lesson Notes

Lesson Resources

Chapter 11 Resource Masters
- Study Guide and Intervention, p. 639
- Practice: Skills, p. 640
- Practice: Word Problems, p. 641
- Reading to Learn Mathematics, p. 642
- Enrichment, p. 643

Parent and Student Study Guide Online Worksheets, 11-5

Noteables™: Interactive Study Notebook with Foldables™, 11-5

1 Focus

5-Minute Check 11-5

Use as a quiz or review of Lesson 11-4. (Also available as a transparency)

Bellringer

Communication Given the equation $y = x + 2$, ask students to describe where the line of the equation crosses the x and y axes. Point out to students that substituting 0 for x and then for y in the equation will provide values for the other coordinate.

Reading to Learn Mathematics, p. 642 **ELL**

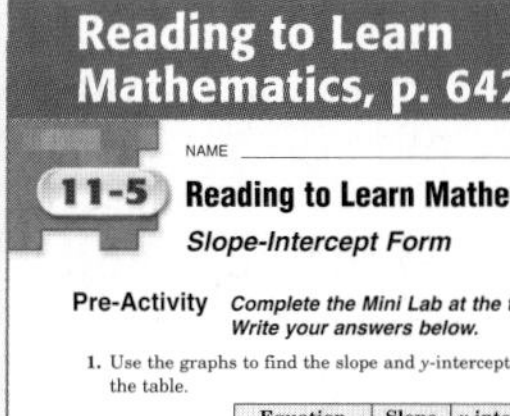

NAME ______ DATE ______ PERIOD ______

11-5 Reading to Learn Mathematics

Slope-Intercept Form

Pre-Activity *Complete the Mini Lab at the top of page 533 in your textbook. Write your answers below.*

1. Use the graphs to find the slope and y-intercept of each line. Complete the table.

Equation	Slope	y-intercept
$y = 3x + 2$	3	2
$y = \frac{1}{4}x + (-1)$	$\frac{1}{4}$	-1
$y = -2x + 3$	-2	3

2. Compare each equation with the value of its slope. What do you notice? The slope is the same as the coefficient of x.
3. Compare each equation with its y-intercept. What do you notice? The y-intercept is the same as the constant.

2 Teach

In-Class Examples

State the slope and the y-intercept of the graph of each equation.

1 $y = \frac{3}{4}x - 5$ **slope $= \frac{3}{4}$, y-intercept $= -5$**

2 $2x + y = 8$ **slope $= -2$, y-intercept $= 8$**

3 Graph $y = \frac{2}{3}x + 2$ using the slope and y-intercept.

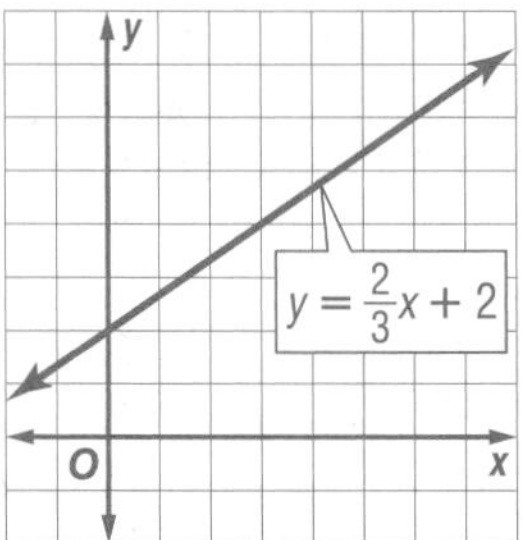

MOVIE RENTAL **A movie rental store charges $4 to rent a movie. If a movie is returned late, the charge is $3 extra per day. The total cost is given by the equation $y = 3x + 4$, where x is the number of days the movie is late.**

4 Graph the equation.

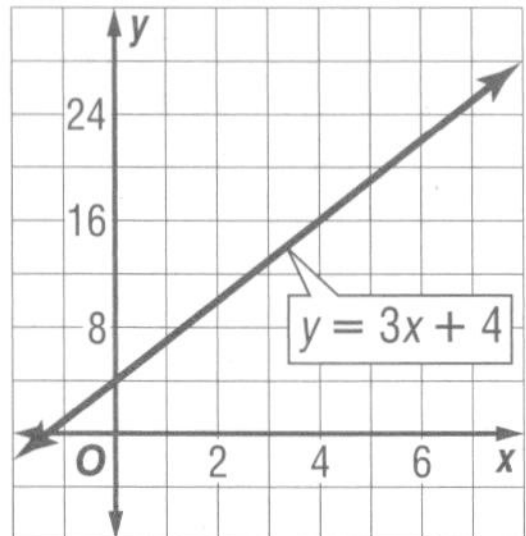

5 Use the graph to find the cost for returning the movie 4 days late. **$16**

6 Describe what the slope and y-intercept represent. **The slope 3 represents the rate of change in price each day a movie is late. The y-intercept 4 is the minimum charge for renting a movie.**

TEACHING TIP

Be sure students understand that $-\frac{3}{2}$ is the same as $\frac{-3}{2}$ or $\frac{3}{-2}$.

REAL-LIFE MATH

ADVERTISING In the year 2000, over $236 billion was spent on advertising in the United States.

Source: McCann-Erickson, Inc.

You can use the slope-intercept form of an equation to graph the equation.

EXAMPLE Graph an Equation

3 Graph $y = -\frac{3}{2}x - 1$ using the slope and y-intercept.

Step 1 Find the slope and y-intercept.

$$y = -\frac{3}{2}x - 1$$

slope $= -\frac{3}{2}$ y-intercept $= -1$

Step 2 Graph the y-intercept $(0, -1)$.

Step 3 Write the slope $-\frac{3}{2}$ as $\frac{-3}{2}$. Use it to locate a second point on the line.

$m = \frac{-3}{2}$ ← change in y: down 3 units
← change in x: right 2 units

Step 4 Draw a line through the two points.

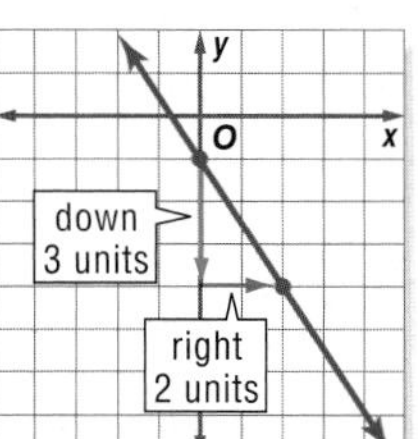

Your Turn **Graph each equation using the slope and y-intercept.** **a–c. See Ch. 11 Answer Appendix.**

a. $y = x + 3$ b. $y = \frac{1}{2}x - 1$ c. $y = -\frac{4}{3}x + 2$

EXAMPLES Graph an Equation to Solve Problems

ADVERTISING **Student Council wants to buy posters advertising the school's carnival. The Design Shoppe charges $15 to prepare the design and $3 for each poster printed. The total cost y can be represented by the equation $y = 3x + 15$, where x represents the number of posters.**

4 Graph the equation.

First find the slope and the y-intercept.

$$y = 3x + 15$$

slope y-intercept

Plot the point (0, 15). Then locate another point up 3 and right 1. Draw the line.

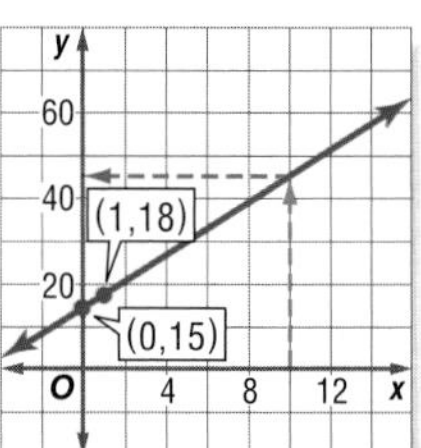

5 Use the graph to find the cost for 10 posters.

Locate 10 on the x-axis. Find the y-coordinate on the graph where the x-coordinate is 10. The total cost is $45.

6 Describe what the slope and y-intercept represent.

The slope 3 represents the cost per poster, which is the rate of change. The y-intercept 15 is the one-time charge for preparing the design.

534 Chapter 11 Algebra: Linear Functions

DAILY INTERVENTION **Unlocking Misconceptions**

Slope-Intercept Form Students may not choose the correct sign for the y-intercept when encountering an equation of the form $y = mx - n$, such as $y = 2x - 4$. Therefore, when the y-intercept is negative, students will have to rewrite the equation. In this case, $y = 2x - 4$ becomes $y = 2x + (-4)$.

Students practice the same concepts in Exercises 13–30 if they are assigned odd or even problems.

Skill and Concept Check

1. **Writing Math** Explain how to graph a line with a slope of $-\frac{5}{4}$ and a y-intercept of -3. **See margin.**
2. **OPEN ENDED** Draw the graph of a line that has a y-intercept but no x-intercept. What is the slope of the line? **See margin; 0.**
3. **Which One Doesn't Belong?** Identify the equation that has a graph with a different slope. Explain your reasoning. **$y = \frac{3}{2}x + 1$; See margin.**

$y = \frac{2}{3}x - 4$	$y = \frac{3}{2}x + 1$	$y = \frac{2}{3}x + 7$	$y = \frac{2}{3}x$

GUIDED PRACTICE

State the slope and the y-intercept for the graph of each equation.

4. $y = x + 2$ **1; 2**
5. $y = -\frac{1}{6}x - \frac{1}{2}$ **$-\frac{1}{6}$; $-\frac{1}{2}$**
6. $2x + y = 3$ **-2; 3**

Graph each equation using the slope and the y-intercept. **7–9. See Ch. 11 Answer Appendix.**

7. $y = \frac{1}{3}x - 2$
8. $y = -\frac{5}{2}x + 1$
9. $y = -2x + 5$

MONEY MATTERS For Exercises 10–12, use the following information.
Lydia borrowed $90 and plans to pay back $10 per week. The equation for the amount of money y Lydia owes after x weeks is $y = 90 - 10x$.

10. Graph the equation. **See Ch. 11 Answer Appendix.**
11. What does the slope of the graph represent? **the amount paid each week**
12. What does the x-intercept of the graph represent? **the number of weeks Lydia will take to pay back her mother**

★ indicates increased difficulty

Practice and Applications

State the slope and the y-intercept for the graph of each equation.

13. $y = 3x + 4$ **3; 4**
14. $y = -5x + 2$ **-5; 2**
15. $y = \frac{1}{2}x - 6$ **$\frac{1}{2}$; -6**
16. $y = -\frac{3}{7}x - \frac{1}{7}$
17. $y - 2x = 8$ **2; 8**
18. $3x + y = -4$ **-3; -4**
19. Graph a line with a slope of $\frac{1}{2}$ and a y-intercept of -3. **See Ch. 11 Answer Appendix.** **16. $-\frac{3}{7}$; $-\frac{1}{7}$**
20. Graph a line with a slope of $-\frac{2}{3}$ and a y-intercept of 0. **See Ch. 11 Answer Appendix.**

★21. Write an equation in slope-intercept form of the line with a slope of -2 and a y-intercept of 6. **$y = -2x + 6$**

★22. Write an equation in slope-intercept form of the line with slope of 4 and a y-intercept of -10. **$y = 4x - 10$**

HOMEWORK HELP

For Exercises	See Examples
13–18, 21–22	1, 2
19–20, 23–30	3
31–36	4–6

Extra Practice See pages 644, 658.

Graph each equation using the slope and the y-intercept. **23–30. See Ch. 11 Answer Appendix.**

23. $y = \frac{1}{3}x - 5$
24. $y = -x + \frac{3}{2}$
25. $y = -\frac{4}{3}x + 1$
26. $y = \frac{3}{2}x - 4$
27. $y = -2x - 3.5$
28. $y = 3x + 1.5$

★29. $y - 3x = 5$

★30. $5x + y = -2$

Math Online msmath3.net/self_check_quiz

3 Practice/Apply

Which One Doesn't Belong?
Students may believe that the last equation in Exercise 3, $y = \frac{2}{3}x$, is different because it does not have a y-intercept. Explain that it does have a y-intercept of 0. The equation could equivalently be written as $y = \frac{2}{3}x + 0$. This problem provides a good opportunity to show students that lines with equal slopes are parallel. Show this to the class by drawing the four lines on a grid on an overhead transparency.

About the Exercises...

Guided Practice Key

Exercises	Examples
4–6	1, 2
7–9	3
10–12	4–6

Assignment Guide

Basic: 13–19 odd, 23–27 odd, 31–33, 37, 39–49

Average: 13–29 odd, 31–35, 37, 39–49

Enriched: 14–30 even, 31–36, 38–45 (Optional: 46–49)

Answers

1. Locate the first point at (0, −3). From this point, go down 5 and right 4 to locate the second point. Draw a line through the two points.
2. Sample answer:

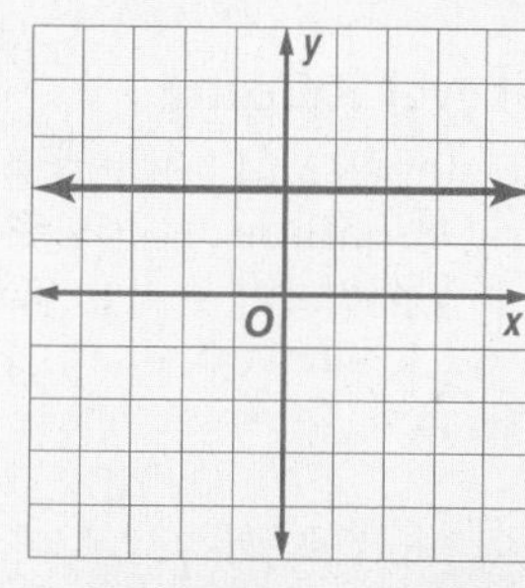

3. The slope of this line is $\frac{3}{2}$, but the slope of each of the other lines is $\frac{2}{3}$.

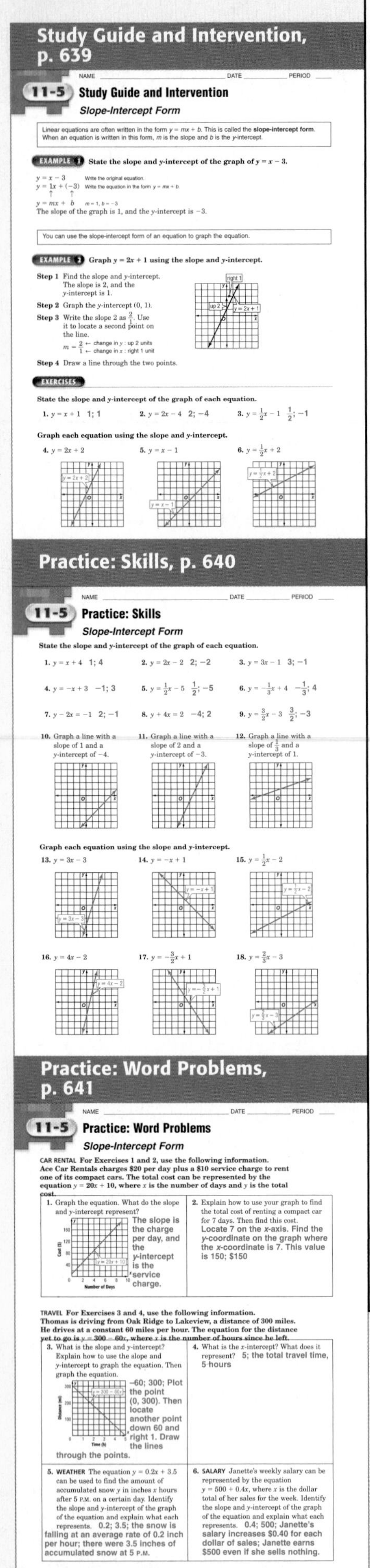
Study Guide and Intervention, p. 639

NAME ______ DATE ______ PERIOD ______

11-5 Study Guide and Intervention

Slope-Intercept Form

Linear equations are often written in the form $y = mx + b$. This is called the slope-intercept form. When an equation is written in this form, m is the slope and b is the y-intercept.

EXAMPLE 1 State the slope and y-intercept of the graph of $y = x - 3$.

$y = x - 3$ Write the original equation.
$y = 1x + (-3)$ Write the equation in the form $y = mx + b$.
$y = mx + b$ $m = 1, b = -3$
The slope of the graph is 1, and the y-intercept is -3.

You can use the slope-intercept form of an equation to graph the equation.

EXAMPLE 2 Graph $y = 2x + 1$ using the slope and y-intercept.

Step 1 Find the slope and y-intercept. The slope is 2, and the y-intercept is 1.
Step 2 Graph the y-intercept (0, 1).
Step 3 Write the slope 2 as $\frac{2}{1}$. Use it to locate a second point on the line.
$m = \frac{2}{1}$ ← change in y: up 2 units; ← change in x: right 1 unit
Step 4 Draw a line through the two points.

EXERCISES

State the slope and y-intercept of the graph of each equation.

1. $y = x + 1$ 1; 1
2. $y = 2x - 4$ 2; −4
3. $y = \frac{1}{2}x - 1$ $\frac{1}{2}$; −1

Graph each equation using the slope and y-intercept.

4. $y = 2x + 2$
5. $y = x - 1$
6. $y = \frac{1}{2}x + 2$

Practice: Skills, p. 640

NAME ______ DATE ______ PERIOD ______

11-5 Practice: Skills

Slope-Intercept Form

State the slope and y-intercept of the graph of each equation.

1. $y = x + 4$ 1; 4
2. $y = 2x - 2$ 2; −2
3. $y = 3x - 1$ 3; −1
4. $y = -x + 3$ −1; 3
5. $y = \frac{1}{2}x - 5$ $\frac{1}{2}$; −5
6. $y = -\frac{1}{3}x + 4$ $-\frac{1}{3}$; 4
7. $y - 2x = -1$ 2; −1
8. $y + 4x = 2$ −4; 2
9. $y = \frac{3}{2}x - 3$ $\frac{3}{2}$; −3
10. Graph a line with a slope of 1 and a y-intercept of −4.
11. Graph a line with a slope of 2 and a y-intercept of −3.
12. Graph a line with a slope of $\frac{1}{3}$ and a y-intercept of 1.

Graph each equation using the slope and y-intercept.

13. $y = 3x - 3$
14. $y = -x + 1$
15. $y = \frac{1}{2}x - 2$
16. $y = 4x - 2$
17. $y = -\frac{3}{2}x + 1$
18. $y = \frac{2}{3}x - 3$

Practice: Word Problems, p. 641

NAME ______ DATE ______ PERIOD ______

11-5 Practice: Word Problems

Slope-Intercept Form

CAR RENTAL For Exercises 1 and 2, use the following information. Ace Car Rentals charges $20 per day plus a $10 service charge to rent one of its compact cars. The total cost can be represented by the equation $y = 20x + 10$, where x is the number of days and y is the total cost.

1. Graph the equation. What do the slope and y-intercept represent? The slope is the charge per day, and the y-intercept is the service charge.
2. Explain how to use your graph to find the total cost of renting a compact car for 7 days. Then find this cost. Locate 7 on the x-axis. Find the y-coordinate on the graph where the x-coordinate is 7. This value is 150; $150

TRAVEL For Exercises 3 and 4, use the following information. Thomas is driving from Oak Ridge to Lakeview, a distance of 300 miles. He drives at a constant 60 miles per hour. The equation for the distance yet to go is $y = 300 - 60x$, where x is the number of hours since he left.

3. What is the slope and y-intercept? Explain how to use the slope and y-intercept to graph the equation. Then graph the equation. −60; 300; Plot the point (0, 300). Then locate another point down 60 and right 1. Draw the lines through the points.
4. What is the x-intercept? What does it represent? 5; the total travel time, 5 hours
5. WEATHER The equation $y = 0.2x + 3.5$ can be used to find the amount of accumulated snow y in inches x hours after 5 P.M. on a certain day. Identify the slope and y-intercept of the graph of the equation and explain what each represents. 0.2; 3.5; the snow is falling at an average rate of 0.2 inch per hour; there were 3.5 inches of accumulated snow at 5 P.M.
6. SALARY Janette's weekly salary can be represented by the equation $y = 500 + 0.4x$, where x is the dollar total of her sales for the week. Identify the slope and y-intercept of the graph of the equation and explain what each represents. 0.4; 500; Janette's salary increases $0.40 for each dollar of sales; Janette earns $500 even if she sells nothing.

GEOMETRY For Exercises 31–33, use the information at the right.

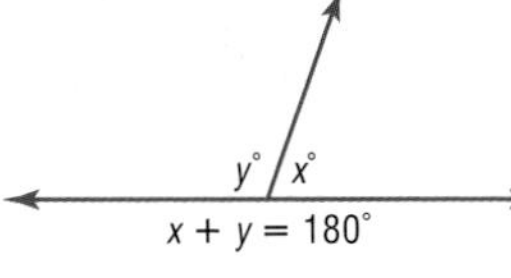

31. Write the equation in slope-intercept form. **$y = -x + 180$**
32. Graph the equation. **See Ch. 11 Answer Appendix.**
33. Use the graph to find the value of y if $x = 70$. **110**

SPACE SCIENCE For Exercises 34–36, use the following information. From 4,074 meters above Earth, the space shuttle Orbiter glides to the runway. Let $y = 4{,}074 - 47x$ represent the altitude of the Orbiter after x seconds.

34. Graph the equation. **See Ch. 11 Answer Appendix.**
35. What does the slope of the graph represent? **the rate of descent**
36. What does the x-intercept of the graph represent? **the time the Orbiter takes to reach ground**
37. **WRITE A PROBLEM** Write a real-life problem that involves a linear equation in slope-intercept form. Graph the equation. Explain the meaning of the slope and y-intercept. **See Ch. 11 Answer Appendix.**
38. Is it *sometimes*, *always*, or *never* possible to draw more than one line given a slope and a y-intercept? Explain. **Never; see margin.**
39. **CRITICAL THINKING** Suppose the graph of a line is vertical. What is the slope and y-intercept of the line? **See margin.**

Spiral Review with Standardized Test Practice

40. **MULTIPLE CHOICE** What is the equation of the graph at the right? **C**

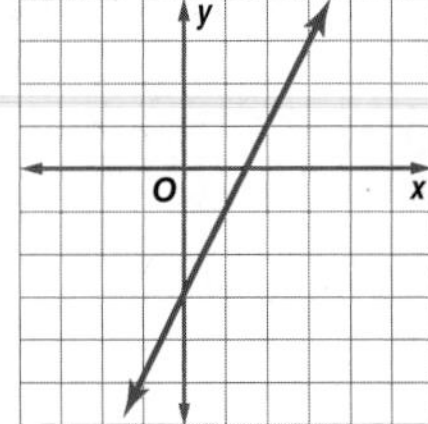

Ⓐ $y = \frac{1}{2}x - 3$ Ⓑ $y = -\frac{1}{2}x - 3$
Ⓒ $y = 2x - 3$ Ⓓ $y = -2x - 3$

41. **MULTIPLE CHOICE** A taxi fare y can be determined by the equation $y = 3x + 5$, where x is the number of miles traveled. What does the slope of the graph of this equation represent? **G**

Ⓕ the distance traveled Ⓖ the cost per mile
Ⓗ the initial fare Ⓘ none of the above

Find the slope of the line that passes through each pair of points. (Lesson 11-4)

42. $M(4, 3), N(-2, 1)$ **$\frac{1}{3}$**
43. $S(-5, 4), T(-7, 1)$ **$\frac{3}{2}$**
44. $X(-9, 5), Y(-2, 5)$ **0**
45. **MEASUREMENT** The function $y = 0.39x$ approximates the number of inches y in x centimeters. Make a function table. Then graph the function. (Lesson 11-3) **See Ch. 11 Answer Appendix.**

GETTING READY FOR THE NEXT LESSON

PREREQUISITE SKILL Graph each point on the same coordinate plane. (Page 614)

46. $A(5, 2)$
47. $B(1.5, 2.5)$
48. $C(2.3, 1.8)$
49. $D(7.5, 3.2)$

46–49. See Ch. 11 Answer Appendix.

4 Assess

Higher-Level Thinking

Find the slopes and y-intercepts of the following equations: $y + x = 3x + 4$ **slope = 2, y-intercept = 4**; $y + 2x + 5 = 0$ **slope = −2, y-intercept = −5**; $y = 3x + 2x - 1$ **slope = 5, y-intercept = −1**

Answers

38. Two lines with the same slope and the same y-intercept are the same line.
39. The slope is undefined. There is no y-intercept unless the graph of the line is the y-axis.

Problem-Solving Strategy

A Preview of Lesson 11-6

Use a Graph

What You'll LEARN

Solve problems by using graphs.

I want to buy a mountain bike. I made a graph with the ratings and the prices of 8 different bikes.

Are the highest rated bikes the most expensive bikes?

Explore	We have a graph. We want to know whether the highest rated bikes are the most expensive. **Mountain Bikes** Price ($): 200, 225, 250, 275, 300, 325, 350, 375 Rating: 0, 5, 10, 15, 20, 25, 30, 35, 40, 45, 50, 55 Higher ratings represent better bikes.
Plan	Let's study the graph.
Solve	The graph shows that the highest rated bike is *not* the most expensive bike. Also the prices of the two bikes with the second highest rating vary considerably.
Examine	Look at the graph. The dot farthest to the right is *not* the highest on the graph.

Analyze the Strategy

1. **Explain** why the bike represented by (48, 300) might be the best bike to buy. **See margin.**
2. **Find** a graph in a newspaper, magazine, or the Internet. Write a sentence explaining the information contained in the graph. **See students' work.**

DAILY INTERVENTION **Differentiated Instruction** **ELL**

Verbal/Linguistic Have each student prepare a small poster showing several types of graphs. Then have students explain how to obtain information from each graph. Students can describe their graphs either to other students in a small group or to the entire class.

11-6a Lesson Notes

1 Focus

Bellringer

Reading Mathematics Remind students that the type of graph used to display data depends on the type of data. A graph like the one shown in this lesson is useful for displaying data that is precise rather than a range. Present various types of graphs and have students read and explain the information on the graphs.

2 Teach

In-Class Example

Solve. Use a graph.

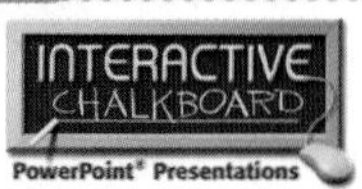

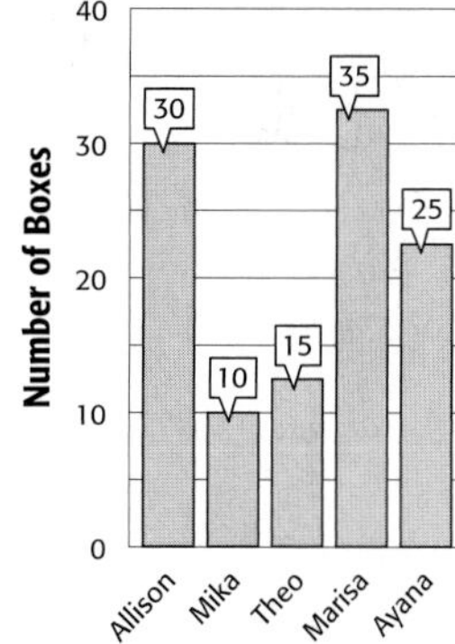

The graph shows how many boxes of cookies were sold by five students for a school fund-raiser. How many boxes did the students sell altogether? **115 boxes**

Answer

1. **Sample answer: It has the second highest rating, but it is the fourth highest price.**

3 Practice/Apply

About the Exercises...

Problem-Solving Strategies
Exercises 5–9 are structured so that students have the opportunity to practice many different problem-solving strategies. You may wish to remind them of some of the strategies they have studied.

- use the four-step plan (p. 6)
- draw a diagram (p. 176)
- use a graph ✓

Answers

4.

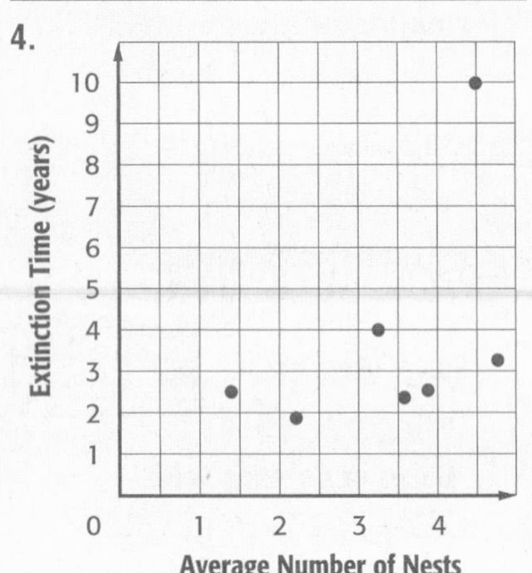

6.

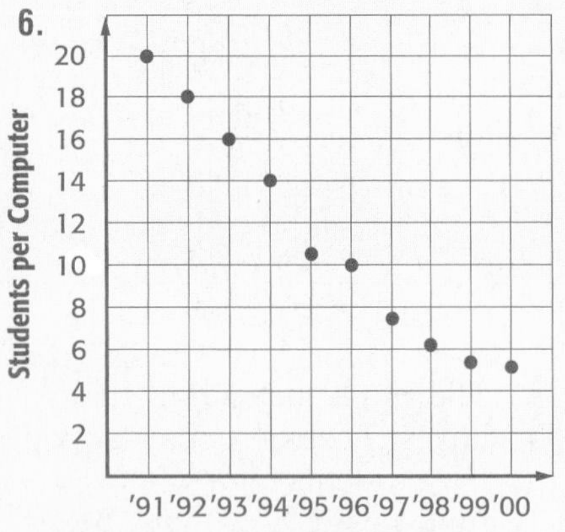

7. The number of students per computer in the U.S. public schools steadily decreased from 1991 to 2000.

Apply the Strategy

Solve. Use a graph.

3. **TECHNOLOGY** Teenagers were asked whether they spent more time using their computer, their video game system, or both equally. The graph shows the results of the survey. How many teenagers were surveyed?

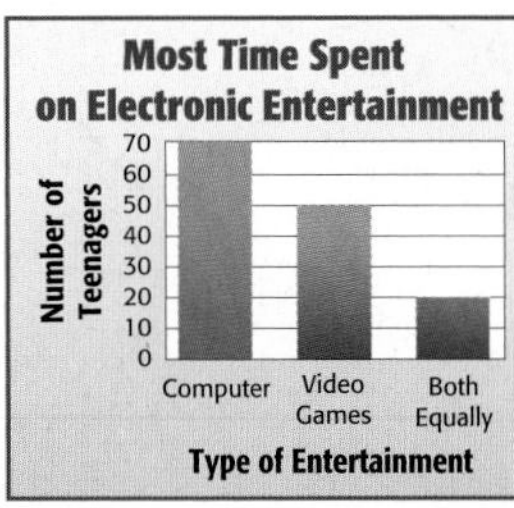

140 teenagers

4. **ZOOLOGY** A zoologist studied extinction times in years of birds on an island. Make a graph of the data. Does the bird with the greatest average number of nests have the greatest extinction time? **See margin; no.**

Bird	Average Number of Nests	Extinction Time (yr)
Cuckoo	1.4	2.5
Magpie	4.5	10.0
Swallow	3.8	2.6
Robin	3.3	4.0
Stonechat	3.6	2.4
Blackbird	4.7	3.3
Tree-Sparrow	2.2	1.9

Mixed Problem Solving

Solve. Use any strategy.

5. **MULTI STEP** Caton's big brother has a full scholarship for tuition, books, and room and board for four years of college. The total scholarship is $87,500. Room and board cost $9,500 per year. His books cost about $750 per year. What is the cost of his yearly tuition? **$11,625**

EDUCATION For Exercises 6 and 7, use the table below. 6–7. See margin.

Year	Students	Year	Students
1991	20	1996	10
1992	18	1997	7.8
1993	16	1998	6.1
1994	14	1999	5.7
1995	10.5	2000	5.4

Students per Computer in U.S. Public Schools

Source: National Center for Education Statistics

6. Make a graph of the data.
7. Describe how the number of students per computer changed from 1991 to 2000.

8. **MONEY MATTERS** Francisco spent twice as much on athletic shoes as he did on a new pair of jeans. The total bill came to $120. What was the cost of his new jeans? **$40**

9. **STANDARDIZED TEST PRACTICE** The blue line shows the cost of producing T-shirts. The green line shows the amount of money received from the sales of the T-shirts. How many shirts must be sold to make a profit? **C**

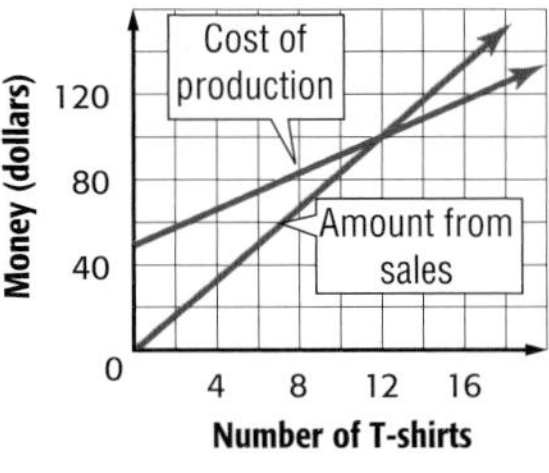

Ⓐ less than 12 T-shirts
Ⓑ exactly 12 T-shirts
Ⓒ more than 12 T-shirts
Ⓓ cannot be determined from the graph

4 Assess

Open-Ended Assessment

Writing Have each student choose one type of graph and write a paragraph explaining the graph and ways it can be used to solve problems. Tell students to imagine they are writing the paragraphs for younger students who are unfamiliar with graphs.

11-6 Statistics: Scatter Plots

HANDS-ON Mini Lab

What You'll LEARN

Construct and interpret scatter plots.

NEW Vocabulary

scatter plot
best-fit line

Work with a partner.

Materials
- tape measure
- grid paper

Measure your partner's height in inches. Then ask your partner to stand with his or her arms extended parallel to the floor. Measure the distance from the end of the longest finger on one hand to the longest finger on the other hand. Write these measures as the ordered pair (height, arm span) on the chalkboard.

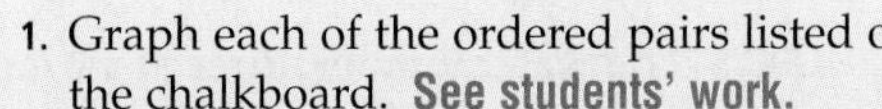

1. Graph each of the ordered pairs listed on the chalkboard. **See students' work.**
2. Examine the graph. Do you think there is a relationship between height and arm span? Explain.

2. yes; the greater the height, the greater the arm span

The graph you made in the Mini Lab is called a scatter plot. A **scatter plot** is a graph that shows the relationship between two sets of data. In this type of graph, two sets of data are graphed as ordered pairs on a coordinate plane. Scatter plots often show a pattern, trend, or relationship between the variables.

Concept Summary — **Types of Relationships**

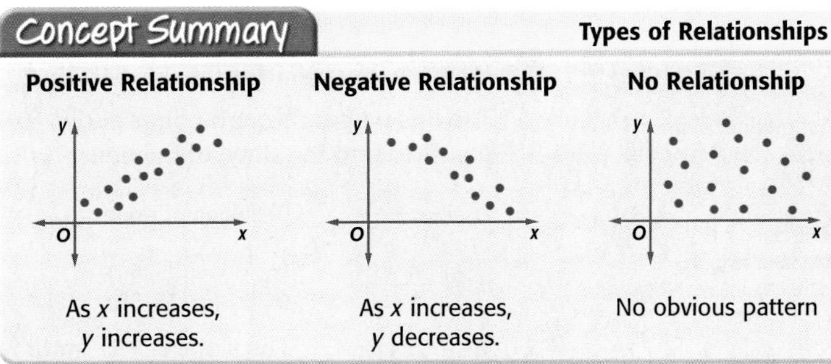

EXAMPLE Identify a Relationship

1 **Determine whether a scatter plot of the data for the hours traveled in a car and the distance traveled might show a *positive*, *negative*, or *no* relationship.**

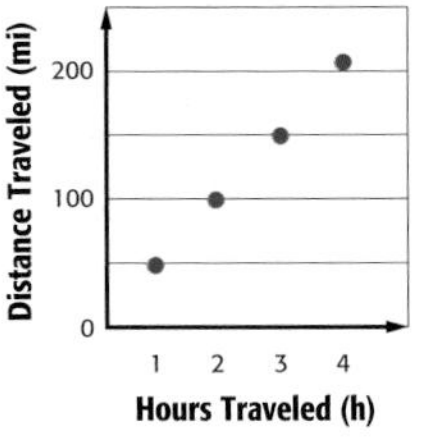

As the number of hours you travel increases, the distance traveled increases. Therefore, the scatter plot shows a positive relationship.

msmath3.net/extra_examples

11-6 Lesson Notes

Lesson Resources

Chapter 11 Resource Masters FAST FILE
- Study Guide and Intervention, p. 644
- Practice: Skills, p. 645
- Practice: Word Problems, p. 646
- Reading to Learn Mathematics, p. 647
- Enrichment, p. 648

Calculator and Spreadsheet Masters, p. 47
Key Teaching Transparencies, 43
Parent and Student Study Guide Online Worksheets, 11-6
Science and Math Lab Masters, pp. 57–60
Teaching Mathematics with Manipulatives, p. 110
Noteables™: Interactive Study Notebook with Foldables™, 11-6

1 Focus

5-Minute Check 11-6 INTERACTIVE CHALKBOARD PowerPoint® Presentations

Use as a quiz or review of Lesson 11-5. (Also available as a transparency)

Bellringer

Problem Solving Tell students that when solving word problems, they should first try to restate the problem in their own words. Write the following question on the chalkboard: Is there a relationship between your study time and your test scores? (Continued in bottom margin.)

Reading to Learn Mathematics, p. 647 **ELL**

NAME ______ DATE ______ PERIOD ______

11-6 Reading to Learn Mathematics
Scatter Plots

Pre-Activity *Complete the Mini Lab at the top of page 539 in your textbook. Write your answers below.*

1. Graph each of the ordered pairs listed on the chalkboard.
   See students' work.
2. Examine the graph. Do you think there is a relationship between height and arm span? Explain.
   yes; the greater the height, the greater the arm span

Reading the Lesson

3. How is a scatter plot different from the graph of a linear function?
   Sample answer: A scatter plot consists of unconnected points, while the graph of a linear function is a continuous line.

Have students restate the problem in their own words and discuss the answer. Make sure students understand that there may be no relationship between two items, and encourage them to give examples of such cases.

2 Teach

In-Class Examples

INTERACTIVE CHALKBOARD PowerPoint® Presentations

Determine whether a scatter plot of the data for the following might show a *positive, negative,* or *no* relationship.

1. cups of hot chocolate sold at a concession stand and outside temperature **negative**

2. birthday and number of sports played **no relationship**

ZOOS The table below shows the average and maximum longevity of various animals in captivity.

Longevity (years)	
Average	**Maximum**
12	47
25	50
15	40
8	20
35	70
40	77
41	61
20	54

Source: *Walker's Mammals of the World*

3. Make a scatter plot using the data above. Then draw a line that seems to best represent the data.

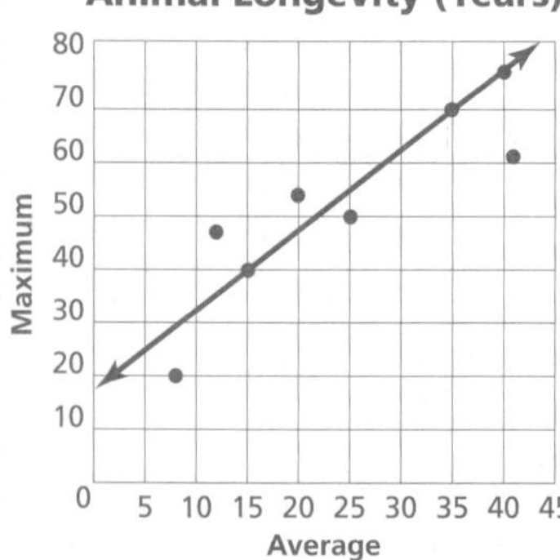

4. Write an equation for this best-fit line. **Sample answer:** $y = \frac{3}{2}x + 17.5$

5. Use the equation to predict the maximum longevity for an animal with an average longevity of 33 years. **about 67 yr**

EXAMPLE Identify a Relationship

2 Determine whether a scatter plot of the data for the month of birth and birth weight show a *positive, negative,* or *no* relationship.

Birth weight does not depend on the month of birth. Therefore, the scatter plot shows no relationship.

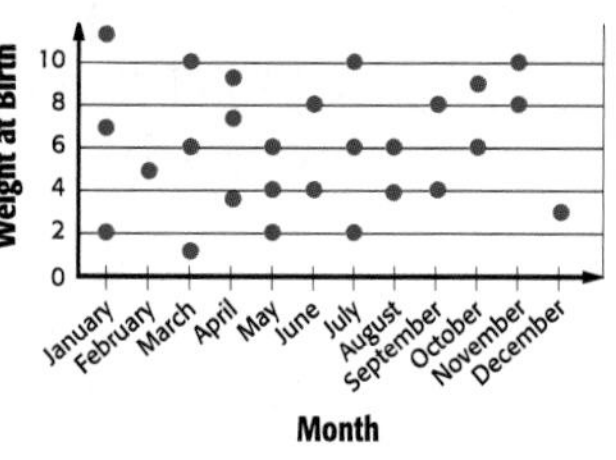

If a scatter plot shows a positive relationship or a negative relationship, a best-fit line can be drawn to represent the data. A **best-fit line** is a line that is very close to most of the data points.

TEACHING TIP
The best-fit line is sometimes called the line of best fit.

REAL-LIFE MATH

LAKES The Great Lakes (Superior, Michigan, Huron, Erie, and Ontario) and their connecting waterways form the largest inland water transportation system in the world.

Source: *The World Book*

EXAMPLES Draw a Best-Fit Line

LAKES The water temperatures at various depths in a lake are given.

Water Depth (ft)	0	10	20	25	30	35	40	50
Temperature (°F)	74	72	71	64	61	58	53	53

3 Make a scatter plot using the data. Then draw a line that seems to best represent the data.

Graph each of the data points. Draw a line that best fits the data.

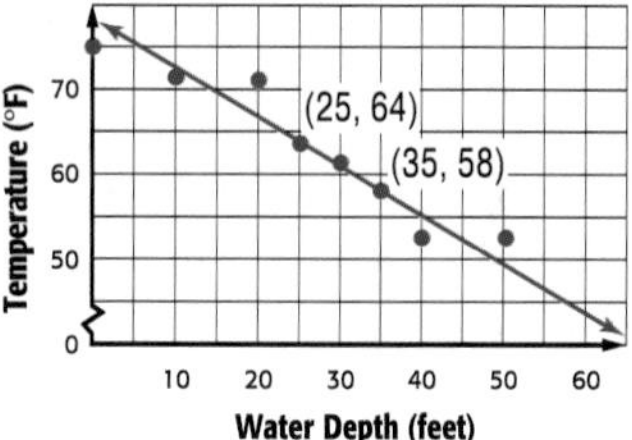

STUDY TIP

Estimation Drawing a best-fit line using the method in this lesson is an estimation. Therefore, it is possible to draw different lines to approximate the same data.

4 Write an equation for this best-fit line.

The line passes through points at (25, 64) and (35, 58). Use these points to find the slope of the line.

$m = \frac{y_2 - y_1}{x_2 - x_1}$ Definition of slope

$m = \frac{58 - 64}{35 - 25}$ $(x_1, y_1) = (25, 64)$, $(x_2, y_2) = (35, 58)$

$m = \frac{-6}{10}$ or $-\frac{3}{5}$ The slope is $-\frac{3}{5}$, and the y-intercept is 79.

Use the slope and y-intercept to write the equation.

$y = mx + b$ Slope-intercept form

$y = -\frac{3}{5}x + 79$ The equation for the best-fit line is $y = -\frac{3}{5}x + 79$.

TEACHING TIP
Point out that although (0, 74) is a data point, the best-fit line passes through (0, 79). The best-fit line does not necessarily pass though any given data point.

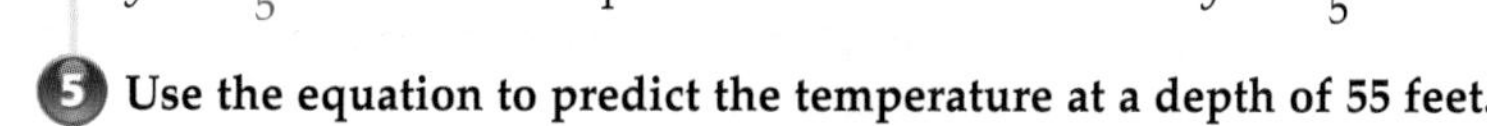

5 Use the equation to predict the temperature at a depth of 55 feet.

$y = -\frac{3}{5}x + 79$ Equation for the best-fit line

$y = -\frac{3}{5}(55) + 79$ or 46 The temperature will be about 46°F.

540 Chapter 11 Algebra: Linear Functions

DAILY INTERVENTION

Unlocking Misconceptions

Best-Fit Line Students sometimes think that the best fit line should be drawn between the first data point and the last data point. Explain to students that they should try to have a line that goes through as many points as possible. They should also try to have the same number of points on either side of the line. Have them draw points and a line on a graph that demonstrates this. Have them model the line with a toothpick or piece of uncooked spaghetti before drawing it.

Students practice the same concepts in Exercises 9–16 if they are assigned odd or even problems.

Skill and Concept Check

1. Writing Math Describe how you can use a scatter plot to display two sets of related data. **1–2. See margin.**
2. **OPEN ENDED** Give an example of data that would show a negative relationship on a scatter plot.
3. **NUMBER SENSE** Suppose a scatter plot shows that as the values of x decrease, the values of y decrease. Does the scatter plot show a *positive*, *negative*, or *no* relationship? **positive**

GUIDED PRACTICE

Determine whether a scatter plot of the data for the following might show a *positive*, *negative*, or *no* relationship.

4. hours worked and earnings **positive**
5. miles per gallon and weight of car **negative**

EDUCATION For Exercises 6–8, use the following table.

Enrollment in U.S. Public and Private Schools (millions)

Year	Students	Year	Students	Year	Students
1900	15.5	1940	25.4	1980	41.7
1910	17.8	1950	25.1	1990	40.5
1920	21.6	1960	35.2	2000	46.9
1930	25.7	1970	45.6		

6. See margin.

6. Draw a scatter plot of the data and draw a best-fit line.
7. Does the scatter plot show a *positive*, *negative*, or *no* relationship? **positive**
8. Use your graph to estimate the enrollment in public and private schools in 2010. **Sample answer: 50 million**

Data Update What is the current number of students in school? Visit msmath3.net/data_update to learn more.

★ indicates increased difficulty

Practice and Applications

Determine whether a scatter plot of the data for the following might show a *positive*, *negative*, or *no* relationship.

9. length of a side of a square and perimeter of the square **positive**
10. day of the week and amount of rain **no relationship**
11. grade in school and number of pets **no relationship**
12. length of time for a shower and amount of water used **positive**
13. outside temperature and amount of heating bill **negative**
14. age and expected number of years a person has yet to live **negative**
15. playing time and points scored in a basketball game **positive**
16. pages in a book and copies sold **no relationship**

HOMEWORK HELP

For Exercises	See Examples
9–16	1, 2
17–20	3–5

Extra Practice See pages 644, 658.

msmath3.net/self_check_quiz

3 Practice/Apply

NUMBER SENSE

In Exercise 3, explain to students that if the x and y values both increase or both decrease, then the relationship is positive. If one increases while the other decreases, then the relationship is negative. If there is no trend for one or the other or both, there is no relationship.

About the Exercises...

Guided Practice Key

Exercises	Examples
4–5, 7	1, 2
6	3
8	4, 5

Assignment Guide

Basic: 9–21 odd, 22–32

Average: 9–15 odd, 17–19, 21–32

Enriched: 10–16 even, 17–20, 22–28 (Optional: 29–32)

Alert! The Data Update following Exercise 8 requires access to the Internet.

Alert! Exercise 21 requires access to the Internet or another resource.

Answers

1. Let one set of data be the x values and the other set of data be the y values. Pair the corresponding x and y values to form ordered pairs. Graph the ordered pairs to form a scatter plot.
2. Sample answer: the number of students passing through the cafeteria line and the amount of food left in the cafeteria
6. 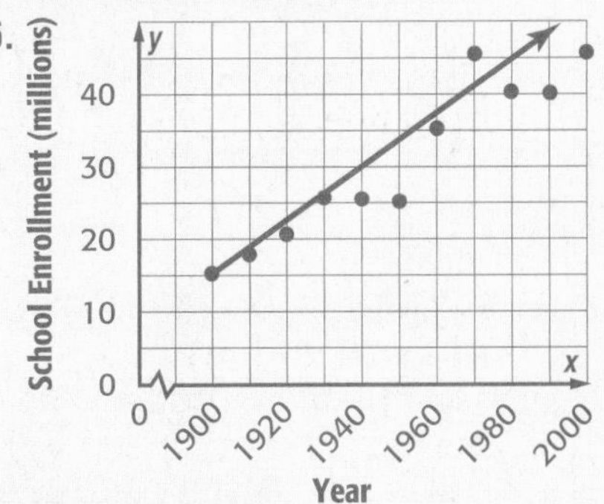

Lesson 11-6 Statistics: Scatter Plots **541**

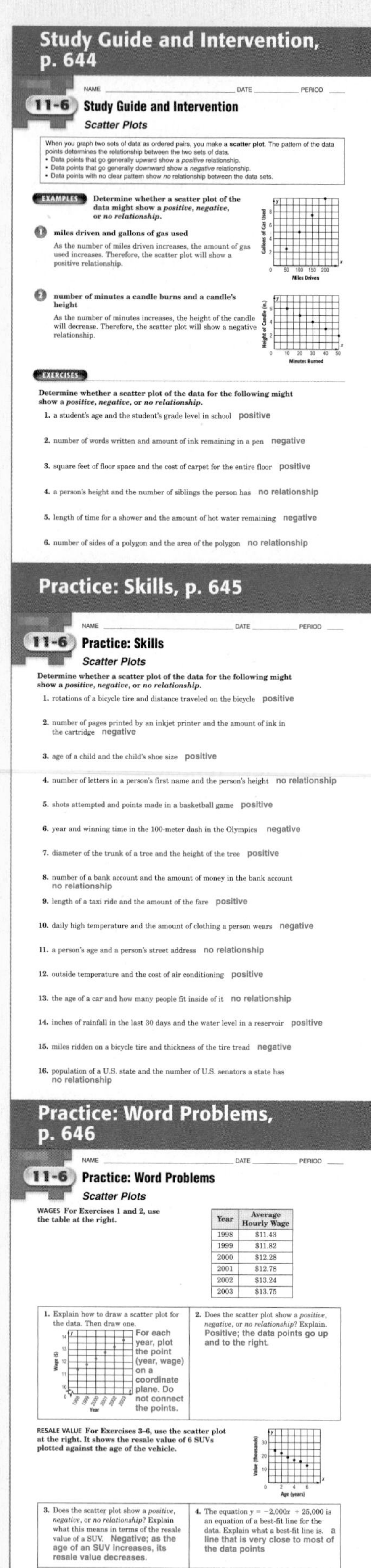

Study Guide and Intervention, p. 644

NAME ______ DATE ______ PERIOD ____

11-6 Study Guide and Intervention

Scatter Plots

When you graph two sets of data as ordered pairs, you make a **scatter plot**. The pattern of the data points determines the relationship between the two sets of data.
- Data points that go generally upward show a *positive* relationship.
- Data points that go generally downward show a *negative* relationship.
- Data points with no clear pattern show *no* relationship between the data sets.

EXAMPLES Determine whether a scatter plot of the data might show a *positive*, *negative*, or *no relationship*.

1. **miles driven and gallons of gas used**
As the number of miles driven increases, the amount of gas used increases. Therefore, the scatter plot will show a positive relationship.

2. **number of minutes a candle burns and a candle's height**
As the number of minutes increases, the height of the candle will decrease. Therefore, the scatter plot will show a negative relationship.

EXERCISES

Determine whether a scatter plot of the data for the following might show a *positive*, *negative*, or *no relationship*.

1. a student's age and the student's grade level in school positive
2. number of words written and amount of ink remaining in a pen negative
3. square feet of floor space and the cost of carpet for the entire floor positive
4. a person's height and the number of siblings the person has no relationship
5. length of time for a shower and the amount of hot water remaining negative
6. number of sides of a polygon and the area of the polygon no relationship

Practice: Skills, p. 645

NAME ______ DATE ______ PERIOD ____

11-6 Practice: Skills

Scatter Plots

Determine whether a scatter plot of the data for the following might show a *positive*, *negative*, or *no relationship*.

1. rotations of a bicycle tire and distance traveled on the bicycle positive
2. number of pages printed by an inkjet printer and the amount of ink in the cartridge negative
3. age of a child and the child's shoe size positive
4. number of letters in a person's first name and the person's height no relationship
5. shots attempted and points made in a basketball game positive
6. year and winning time in the 100-meter dash in the Olympics negative
7. diameter of the trunk of a tree and the height of the tree positive
8. number of a bank account and the amount of money in the bank account no relationship
9. length of a taxi ride and the amount of the fare positive
10. daily high temperature and the amount of clothing a person wears negative
11. a person's age and a person's street address no relationship
12. outside temperature and the cost of air conditioning positive
13. the age of a car and how many people fit inside of it no relationship
14. inches of rainfall in the last 30 days and the water level in a reservoir positive
15. miles ridden on a bicycle tire and thickness of the tire tread negative
16. population of a U.S. state and the number of U.S. senators a state has no relationship

Practice: Word Problems, p. 646

NAME ______ DATE ______ PERIOD ____

11-6 Practice: Word Problems

Scatter Plots

WAGES For Exercises 1 and 2, use the table at the right.

Year	Average Hourly Wage
1998	$11.43
1999	$11.82
2000	$12.28
2001	$12.78
2002	$13.24
2003	$13.75

1. Explain how to draw a scatter plot for the data. Then draw one. For each year, plot the point (year, wage) on a coordinate plane. Do not connect the points.
2. Does the scatter plot show a *positive*, *negative*, or *no relationship*? Explain. Positive; the data points go up and to the right.

RESALE VALUE For Exercises 3–6, use the scatter plot at the right. It shows the resale value of 6 SUVs plotted against the age of the vehicle.

3. Does the scatter plot show a *positive*, *negative*, or *no relationship*? Explain what this means in terms of the resale value of a SUV. Negative; as the age of an SUV increases, its resale value decreases.
4. The equation $y = -2{,}000x + 25{,}000$ is an equation of a best-fit line for the data. Explain what a best-fit line is. a line that is very close to most of the data points
5. Find the slope and *y*-intercept of the best-fit line and explain what each represents. −2,000; 25,000; on average, an SUV is worth $2,000 less each year; the cost of a new SUV is $25,000.
6. Explain how to use the equation in Exercise 4 to estimate the resale value of an 8-year-old SUV. Find the value. Replace *x* in the equation with 8 and simplify; $9,000

FOOD For Exercises 17–20, use the table.

17. Draw a scatter plot of the data. Then draw a best-fit line. **See Ch. 11 Answer Appendix.**
18. Does the scatter plot show a *positive, negative,* or *no* relationship? **positive**
19. Write an equation for the best-fit line. **See margin.**
★20. Use your equation to estimate the number of fat grams in a muffin with 350 Calories. **Sample answer: 12 g**
21. **RESEARCH** Use the Internet or other resource to find the number of goals and assists for the players on one of the National Hockey teams for the past season. Make a scatter plot of the data. **See students' work.**

Nutritional Information of Commercial Muffins

Muffin (brand)	Fat (grams)	Calories
A	2	250
B	3	300
C	4	260
D	9	220
E	14	410
F	15	390
G	10	300
H	18	430
I	23	480
J	20	490

22. **CRITICAL THINKING** A scatter plot of skateboard sales and swimsuit sales for each month of the year shows a positive relationship. **See margin.**
    a. Why might this be true?
    b. Does this mean that one factor caused the other? Explain.

Spiral Review with Standardized Test Practice

23. **MULTIPLE CHOICE** Find the situation that matches the scatter plot at the right. **B**
    - Ⓐ adult height and year of birth
    - Ⓑ number of trees in an orchard and the number of apples produced
    - Ⓒ number of words written and length of pencil
    - Ⓓ length of campfire and amount of firewood remaining

24. **MULTIPLE CHOICE** What type of graph is most appropriate for displaying the change in house prices over several years? **F**
    - Ⓕ scatter plot
    - Ⓖ circle graph
    - Ⓗ bar graph
    - Ⓘ line plot

State the slope and the *y*-intercept for the graph of each equation. (Lesson 11-5)

25. $y = \frac{4}{5}x + 7$ **$\frac{4}{5}$; 7**
26. $y = -\frac{1}{6}x - 4$ **$-\frac{1}{6}$; −4**
27. $4x + y = 2$ **−4; 2**

28. **GEOMETRY** The vertices of a triangle are located at (−2, 1), (1, 7), and (5, 1). Find the slope of each side of the triangle. (Lesson 11-4) **$2, -\frac{3}{2}, 0$**

GETTING READY FOR THE NEXT LESSON

PREREQUISITE SKILL Graph each equation. (Lessons 11-3 and 11-5)

29. $y = -x - 5$
30. $y = \frac{1}{2}x + 3$
31. $y = -\frac{1}{3}x + 1$
32. $y = 5x - 3$

29–32. See Ch. 11 Answer Appendix.

4 Assess

Open-Ended Assessment

Speaking Divide the class into small groups. Then have students in each group determine and describe how to draw a best-fit line for a graph.

Answers

19. Sample answer: $y = 12x + 210$

22a. Sample answer: Both are needed for summer activities, so the sales would increase at the same time.

22b. No; warm weather could be causing the increase in both skateboard and swimsuit sales.

Graphing Calculator Investigation

A Follow-Up of Lesson 11-6

What You'll LEARN

Use a graphing calculator to make a scatter plot.

Scatter Plots

You can use a TI-83/84 Plus graphing calculator to create scatter plots.

ACTIVITY

The following table gives the results of a survey listing the number of vehicles owned by a family and the average monthly gasoline cost in dollars. Make a scatter plot of the data.

Number of Vehicles	1	3	5	2	5	1	2
Monthly Gasoline Cost ($)	19	59	90	55	115	35	58

Number of Vehicles	2	1	3	4	3	3	2
Monthly Gasoline Cost ($)	80	62	77	90	80	112	63

STEP 1 Clear the existing data.
Keystrokes: [STAT] [ENTER] [▲] [CLEAR] [ENTER]

STEP 2 Enter the data.
Input each number of vehicles in L1 and press [ENTER]. Then enter the monthly gasoline cost in L2.

TEACHING TIP

Make sure the students clear all lists already in the calculator.

STEP 3 Turn on the statistical plot.
Select the scatter plot, L1 as the Xlist, and L2 as the Ylist.
Keystrokes: [2nd] [STAT PLOT]

[ENTER] [ENTER] [▼] [ENTER] [▼]

[2nd] [L1] [ENTER] [2nd] [L2]

[ENTER]

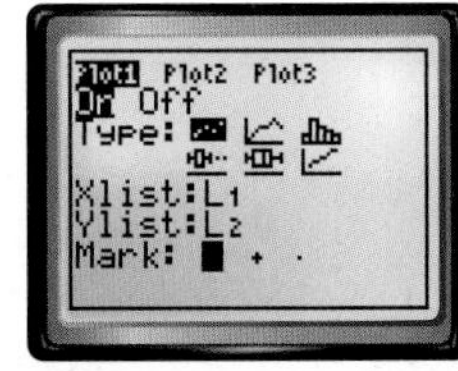

STEP 4 Graph the data.
Keystrokes: [ZOOM] 9

Use the [TRACE] feature and the left and right arrow keys to move from one point to another.

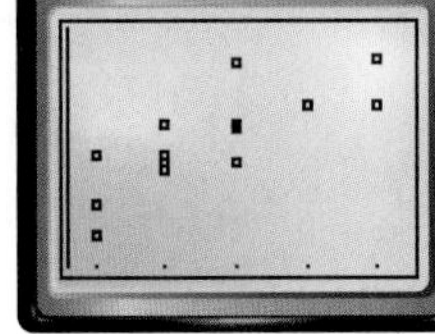

EXERCISES

1. **Describe** the relationship of the data. **positive**
2. **RESEARCH** Find some data to use in a scatter plot. Enter the data in a graphing calculator. Determine whether the data has a *positive*, *negative*, or *no* relationship. **See students' work.**

msmath3.net/other_calculator_keystrokes

11-6b Graphing Calculator Investigation

GETTING STARTED

Teaching Tip Before students begin, encourage them to study the data in the table and try to visualize what a graph of the data might look like. This will help when checking the actual plot.

TEACH

- You may wish to have students practice plotting just a few points before beginning the investigation. This will help them become familiar with the procedures.
- Tell students that they should check the numbers in the L1 and L2 lists to be sure that they have been entered correctly.
- As an extension, students could draw the best-fit line for their scatter plots.

ASSESS

Observe as students solve the **Exercises**. They should:

- study their graphs and describe the data as having a *positive*, *negative*, or *no* relationship, and
- repeat the **Activity** using data they have located themselves.

11-7 Lesson Notes

Lesson Resources

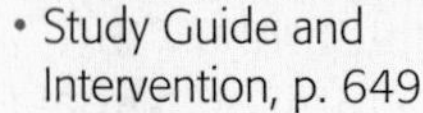

Chapter 11 Resource Masters
- Study Guide and Intervention, p. 649
- Practice: Skills, p. 650
- Practice: Word Problems, p. 651
- Reading to Learn Mathematics, p. 652
- Enrichment, p. 653

Calculator and Spreadsheet Masters, p. 48

Key Teaching Transparencies, 44

Parent and Student Study Guide Online Worksheets, 11-7

Noteables™: Interactive Study Notebook with Foldables™, 11-7

1 Focus

5-Minute Check 11-7

Use as a quiz or review of Lesson 11-6. (Also available as a transparency)

Bellringer

Hands-On Activity Have students graph $y = x + 2$ and $y = -x + 4$ on grid paper. Then have them write the coordinate pair for the point where the lines intersect. **(1, 3)** Tell students that this point is a solution for both equations because it is the only point on both lines. Have them check this by using the point to solve both equations.

(Continued in bottom margin.)

Reading to Learn Mathematics, p. 652 ELL

NAME ______ DATE ______ PERIOD ______

11-7 Reading to Learn Mathematics

Graphing Systems of Equations

Pre-Activity *Read the introduction at the top of page 544 in your textbook. Write your answers below.*

1. Graph both of the equations on a coordinate plane.
2. What are the coordinates of the point where the two lines intersect? What does this point represent? (2, 12); The storm and the ship will meet in 2 hours. At that time the storm will have traveled 12 miles.

Reading the Lesson

3. Explain how to find the solution of a system of two equations by graphing. Graph both equations on the same coordinate plane and locate the point(s) of intersection.
4. Under what conditions will a system of two linear equations have infinitely many solutions? graphs of ...

11-7 Graphing Systems of Equations

What You'll LEARN

Solve systems of linear equations by graphing.

NEW Vocabulary

system of equations
substitution

REVIEW Vocabulary

solution: a value for the variable that makes an equation true (Lesson 1-8)

WHEN am I ever going to use this?

TRAVEL A storm is approaching a cruise ship. If x represents the number of hours, then $y = 6x$ represents the position of the storm, and $y = 5x + 2$ represents the position of the ship.

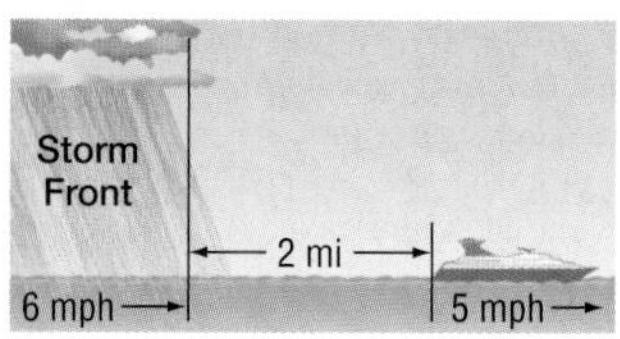

1. Graph both of the equations on a coordinate plane.
2. What are the coordinates of the point where the two lines intersect? What does this point represent?

1. See Ch. 11 Answer Appendix.

2. (2, 12); The storm and the ship will meet in 2 hours. At that time the storm will have traveled 12 miles.

The equations $y = 6x$ and $y = 5x + 2$ form a system of equations. A set of two or more equations is called a **system of equations**.

When you find an ordered pair that is a solution of all of the equations in a system, you have solved the system. The ordered pair for the point where the graphs of the equations intersect is the solution.

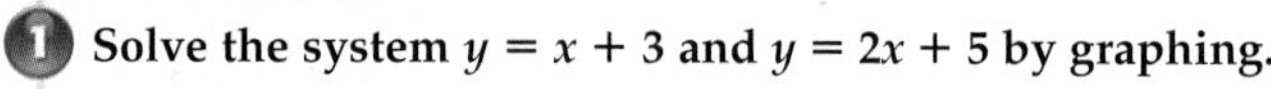

EXAMPLE One Solution

1 **Solve the system $y = x + 3$ and $y = 2x + 5$ by graphing.**

The graphs of the equations appear to intersect at $(-2, 1)$. Check this estimate.

Check	$y = x + 3$	$y = 2x + 5$
	$1 \stackrel{?}{=} -2 + 3$	$1 \stackrel{?}{=} 2(-2) + 5$
	$1 = 1$ ✓	$1 = 1$ ✓

The solution of the system is $(-2, 1)$.

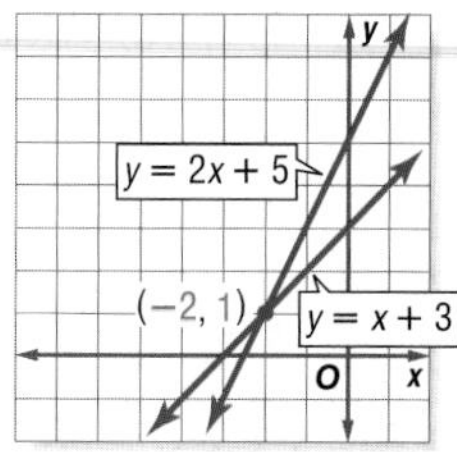

EXAMPLE Infinitely Many Solutions

2 **Solve the system $y = x - 3$ and $y - x = -3$ by graphing.**

Write $y - x = -3$ in slope-intercept form.

$y - x = -3$	Write the equation.
$y - x + x = -3 + x$	Add x to each side.
$y = x - 3$	Both equations are the same.

The solution of the system is all the coordinates of points on the graph of $y = x - 3$.

Next, have students draw $y = x + 2$ and $y = x - 1$ on grid paper. Ask students whether there is any point common to both lines. **no** Therefore, they do not have a common answer.

REAL-LIFE MATH

MONEY MATTERS The amount of online retail spending has been increasing in recent years. It more than doubled from 1999 with \$16.2 billion to 2000 with \$32.5 billion.

Source: BizRate.Com

EXAMPLE No Solution

3 **MONEY MATTERS The Buy Online Company charges \$1 per pound plus \$2 for shipping and handling. The Best Catalogue Company charges \$1 per pound plus \$3 for shipping and handling. For what weight will the shipping and handling for the two companies be the same?**

Let x equal the weight in pounds of the item or items ordered.

Let y equal the total cost of shipping and handling.

Write an equation to represent each company's charge for shipping and handling.

Buy Online Company: $y = 1x + 2$ or $y = x + 2$

Best Catalogue Company: $y = 1x + 3$ or $y = x + 3$

Graph the system of equations.

$y = x + 2$

$y = x + 3$

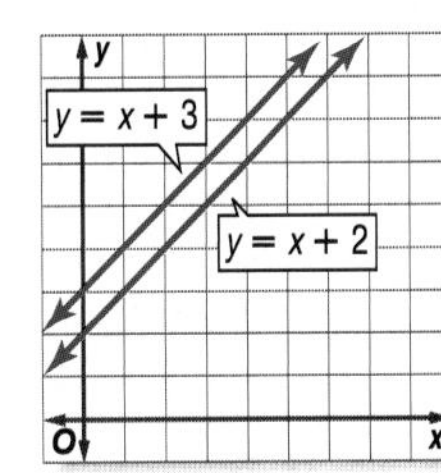

The graphs appear to be parallel lines. Since there is no coordinate pair that is a solution of both equations, there is no solution of this system of equations.

For any weight, the Buy Online Company will charge less than the Best Catalogue Company.

STUDY TIP

Slopes/Intercepts When the graphs of a system of equations have:

- different slopes, there is exactly one solution,
- the same slope and different y-intercepts, there is no solution,
- the same slope and the same y-intercept, there are many solutions.

A more accurate way to solve a system of equations than by graphing is by using a method called **substitution**.

EXAMPLE Solve by Substitution

4 **Solve the system $y = 2x - 3$ and $y = -1$ by substitution.**

Since y must have the same value in both equations, you can replace y with -1 in the first equation.

$y = 2x - 3$	Write the first equation.
$-1 = 2x - 3$	Replace y with -1.
$-1 + 3 = 2x - 3 + 3$	Add 3 to each side.
$2 = 2x$	Simplify.
$\frac{2}{2} = \frac{2x}{2}$	Divide each side by 2.
$1 = x$	Simplify.

The solution of this system of equations is $(1, -1)$. You can check the solution by graphing. The graphs appear to intersect at $(1, -1)$, so the solution is correct.

Your Turn **Solve each system of equations by substitution.**

a. $y = x - 4$, $y = 7$ **(11, 7)**

b. $y = 3x + 4$, $x = 2$ **(2, 10)**

c. $y = -2x - 7$, $y = 1$ **(−4, 1)**

TEACHING TIP

Explain to students that after they substitute a value into one of the equations, they solve the equation using the same methods they have been using in this course.

Math Online msmath3.net/extra_examples

2 Teach

In-Class Examples

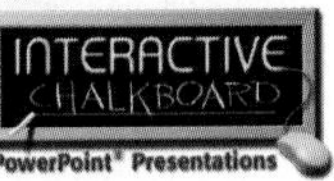

1 Solve the system $y = x - 1$ and $y = 2x - 2$ by graphing. **(1, 0)**

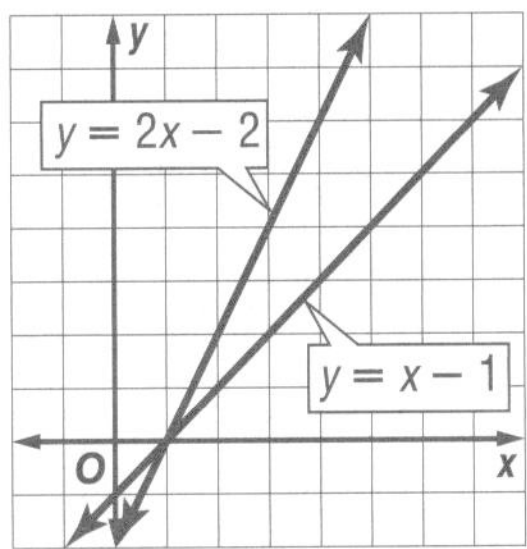

2 Solve the system $y = \frac{1}{2}x + 3$ and $y - \frac{1}{2}x = 3$ by graphing. **The solution is all the coordinates of points on the graph of $y = \frac{1}{2}x + 3$.**

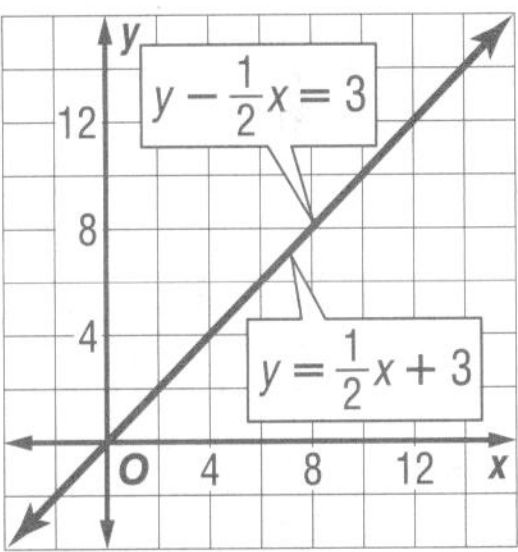

3 **PHONE RATES** One phone company charges \$3 a month plus 10¢ a minute for long-distance calls. Another company charges \$5 a month plus 10¢ a minute for long-distance calls. For how many minutes will the total monthly charges of the two companies be the same? **no solution**

4 Solve the system $y = 3x - 4$ and $y = 5$ by substitution. **(3, 5)**

DAILY INTERVENTION — Flexible Grouping

Graphing Systems of Equations Have students work in pairs to write equations and make graphs of three systems of equations. One system should have one solution, another should have infinitely many solutions, and the third should have no solution.

Tips for New Teachers

Classroom Management Draw a grid on cork board to make a reusable grid students can use for graphing in class. Attach string to two push pins to make lines on the graphs. Numbers on the axes can be attached using small squares of paper.

3 Practice/Apply

FOLDABLES™ Follow-Up Before students begin the lesson, encourage them to write a question about systems of equations under the seventh tab of their Foldables. As students progress through the lesson, encourage them to take notes and record information that answers their question.

NUMBER SENSE
For Exercise 3, students should be able to immediately recognize the slopes and y-intercepts of linear equations. They should understand that equations having the same slope represent either parallel lines or the same line. In this problem, since the y-intercept is different, the lines are parallel.

About the Exercises...

Guided Practice Key

Exercises	Examples
4–6	1, 2
10–12	3
7–9	4

Assignment Guide

Basic: 13, 15, 19–23 odd, 27, 29, 31–33, 35–46

Average: 13–29 odd, 31–33, 35–46

Enriched: 14–28 even, 29–42 (Optional: 43–46)

Students practice the same concepts in Exercises 13–28 if they are assigned odd or even problems.

Skill and Concept Check

1. **Explain** what is meant by a system of equations and describe its solution. **1–3. See margin.**
2. **OPEN ENDED** Draw a graph of a system of equations that has $(-2, 3)$ as its solution.
3. **NUMBER SENSE** Describe the solution of the system $y = \frac{1}{2}x + 1$ and $y = \frac{1}{2}x - 3$ without graphing. Explain.

GUIDED PRACTICE

Solve each system of equations by graphing. **4–6. See Ch. 11 Answer Appendix for graphs.**

4. $y = 2x + 1$, $y = -x + 7$ **(2, 5)**
5. $y = -2x + 4$, $y = 2x$ **(1, 2)**
6. $y = 3x + 1$, $y = 3x - 1$ **no solution**

Solve each system of equations by substitution.

7. $y = 3x - 4$, $y = 8$ **(4, 8)**
8. $y = -2x + 1$, $x = -3$ **(−3, 7)**
9. $y = 0.5x - 4$, $y = 1$ **(10, 1)**

JOBS **For Exercises 10–12, use the information at the right about the summer jobs of Neka and Savannah.**

	Weekly Salary	Starting Bonus
Neka	$300	$200
Savannah	$350	$100

10. Write an equation for Neka's total income y after x weeks. **$y = 300x + 200$**
11. Write an equation for Savannah's total income y after x weeks. **$y = 350x + 100$**
12. When will Neka and Savannah have earned the same total amount? What will that amount be? **2 weeks; $800**

★ indicates increased difficulty **13–18. See Ch. 11 Answer Appendix for graphs.**

Practice and Applications

HOMEWORK HELP

For Exercises	See Examples
13–20	1–3
21–28	4

Extra Practice See pages 644, 658.

Solve each system of equations by graphing. **17. no solution**

13. $y = x - 4$, $y = -2x + 2$ **(2, −2)**
14. $y = 2x - 3$, $y = -x - 6$ **(−1, −5)**
15. $y = 3x - 2$, $y = -\frac{1}{2}x + 5$ **(2, 4)**
16. $y = \frac{1}{3}x + 1$, $y = -2x + 8$ **(3, 2)**
★17. $x + y = -3$, $x + y = 4$
★18. $y - x = 0$, $2x + y = 3$ **(1, 1)**

19. Graph the system $y = x + 8$ and $y = -2x - 1$. Find the solution. **See Ch. 11 Answer Appendix; (−3, 5).**
20. Graph the system $y = -2x - 6$ and $y = -2x - 3$. Find the solution. **See Ch. 11 Answer Appendix; no solution.**

Solve each system of equations by substitution.

21. $y = 3x + 4$, $y = -5$ **(−3, −5)**
22. $y = -2x + 4$, $y = -6$ **(5, −6)**
23. $y = -3x - 1$, $x = -4$ **(−4, 11)**
24. $y = 4x - 5$, $x = 2$ **(2, 3)**
★25. $y = -2x + 9$, $y = x$ **(3, 3)**
★26. $y = 5x - 8$, $y = x$ **(2, 2)**

27. Solve the system $y = -3x + 5$ and $y = 2$ by substitution. **(1, 2)**
28. Solve the system $y = 2x - 1$ and $y = 5$ by substitution. **(3, 5)**

Answers

1. A system of equations is a set of 2 or more equations. The solution of a system of equations is the solution or solutions that solve all the equations in the system.
2. Sample answer:

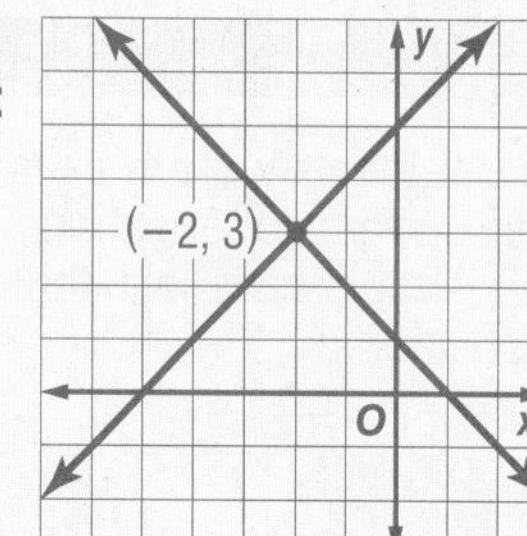

3. The system has no solution. Since the graphs of the equations have the same slope and different y-intercepts, the graphs are parallel lines. Therefore, they do not intersect.

CLUBS For Exercises 29 and 30, use the following information.
The Science Club wants to order T-shirts for their members. The Shirt Shack will make the shirts for a $30 set-up fee and then $12 per shirt. T-World will make the same shirts for $70 set-up fee and then $8 per shirt.

29. For how many T-shirts will the cost be the same? What will be the cost? **10 shirts; $150**
30. If the club wants to order 30 T-shirts, which store should they choose? **T-World**

HOT-AIR BALLOONS For Exercises 31–34, use the information at the right about two ascending hot-air balloons. **33. 4 min**

Balloon	Distance from Ground (meters)	Rate of Ascension (meters per minute)
A	60	15
B	40	20

31. Write an equation that describes the distance from the ground y of balloon A after x minutes. $y = 15x + 60$
32. Write an equation that describes the distance from the ground y of balloon B after x minutes. $y = 20x + 40$
33. When will the balloons be at the same distance from the ground?
34. What is the distance of the balloons from the ground at that time? **120 m**
35. **CRITICAL THINKING** One equation in a system of equations is $y = 2x + 1$. **b. Sample answer:** $y = 2x - 1$
    a. Write a second equation so that the system has (1, 3) as its only solution. **Sample answer:** $y = -x + 4$
    b. Write an equation so that the system has no solutions.
    c. Write an equation so the system has many solutions. **Sample answer:** $y - 2x = 1$

Spiral Review with Standardized Test Practice

36. **MULTIPLE CHOICE** Which ordered pair represents the intersection of lines ℓ and k? **A**

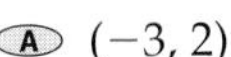 (A) (−3, 2) 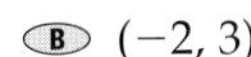 (B) (−2, 3)  (C) (3, −2) (D) (2, −3)

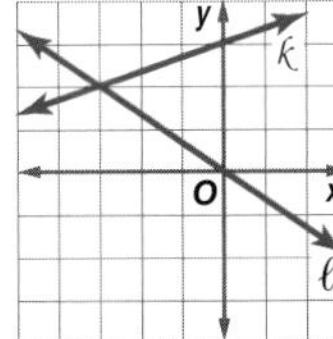

37. **GRID IN** The equation $c = 900 + 5t$ represents the cost c in cents that a long-distance telephone company charges for t minutes. Find the value of t if $c = 1{,}200$. **60**

38. **STATISTICS** Determine whether a scatter plot of the speed of a car and the stopping distance would show a *positive*, *negative*, or *no* relationship. (Lesson 11-6) **positive**

39–41. See Ch. 11 Answer Appendix.

Graph each equation using the slope and the y-intercept. (Lesson 11-5)

39. $y = -\frac{2}{3}x + 2$ 40. $y = \frac{2}{5}x - 1$ 41. $y = 4x - 3$

42. **MULTI STEP** Write an equation to represent *three times a number minus five is 16*. Then solve the equation. (Lesson 10-3) $3n - 5 = 16$; **7**

GETTING READY FOR THE NEXT LESSON **43–46. See Ch. 11 Answer Appendix.**

PREREQUISITE SKILL Graph each inequality on a number line. (Lesson 10-5)

43. $x > -3$ 44. $x \leq 5$ 45. $x < 0$ 46. $x \geq -1$

msmath3.net/self_check_quiz

4 Assess

Higher-Level Thinking

Jamal has 12 coins totaling $2.40. He only has quarters and dimes. Write two equations that represent this data, then solve the system of equations by graphing.

$y = -2.5x + 24$ and $y = -x + 12$; **8 quarters and 4 dimes**

Study Guide and Intervention, p. 649

NAME ______ DATE ______ PERIOD ____

11-7 Study Guide and Intervention
Graphing Systems of Equations

A set of two or more equations is called a **system of equations**. Solving a system of equations means finding an ordered pair that is a solution of all the equations. You can solve a system of equations by graphing. If you graph the equations on the same coordinate plane, the point where the graphs intersect is the solution of the system of equations.

EXAMPLE 1 **Solve the system $y = x - 1$ and $y = -2x + 5$ by graphing.**

Both equations are in slope-intercept form. Use the slope and y-intercept of each equation to graph the two equations. The graphs appear to intersect at (2, 1). Check this by substituting the coordinates into each equation.

Check $y = x - 1$ $\quad$ $y = -2x + 5$
$1 \stackrel{?}{=} 2 - 1$ $\quad$ $1 \stackrel{?}{=} -2(2) + 5$
$1 = 1$ ✓ $\quad$ $1 = 1$ ✓

The solution of the system of equations is (2, 1).

The system of equations in Example 1 had one solution. It is also possible for a system of equations to have no solution. If the lines in the graph are parallel, there is no intersection point, and the system of equations will have no solution.

A system of equations can also be solved by a method called **substitution**.

EXAMPLE 2 **Solve the system $y = x + 4$ and $y = -1$ by substitution.**

$y = x + 4$ Write the first equation.
$-1 = x + 4$ Replace y with −1.
$-1 - 4 = x + 4 - 4$ Subtract 4 from each side.
$-5 = x$ Simplify.

The solution of the system is (−5, −1).

EXERCISES

Solve each system of equations by graphing.

1. $y = x + 1$, $y = 3x - 1$ **(1, 2)**
2. $y = x - 2$, $y = -x + 4$ **(3, 1)**

Solve each system of equations by substitution.

3. $y = 2x + 4$, $y = 6$ **(1, 6)**
4. $y = -3x - 3$, $y = 3$ **(−2, 3)**

Practice: Skills, p. 650

NAME ______ DATE ______ PERIOD ____

11-7 Practice: Skills
Graphing Systems of Equations

Solve each system of equations by graphing.

1. $y = -x + 3$, $y = x - 1$ **(2, 1)**
2. $y = x + 1$, $y = -2x - 2$ **(−1, 0)**
3. $y = 3x + 5$, $y = -x - 3$ **(−2, −1)**
4. $y = -\frac{1}{2}x + 4$, $y = 3x - 3$ **(2, 3)**

Solve each system of equations by substitution.

5. $y = x + 2$, $y = 6$ **(4, 6)**
6. $y = x + 3$, $x = 2$ **(2, 5)**
7. $y = 2x + 6$, $y = 2$ **(−2, 2)**
8. $y = -2x - 5$, $x = -3$ **(−3, 1)**
9. $y = 3x - 7$, $y = -1$ **(2, −1)**
10. $y = -3x + 2$, $x = 5$ **(5, −13)**
11. $y = 4x + 3$, $y = 7$ **(1, 7)**
12. $y = -5x - 2$, $x = -2$ **(−2, 8)**
13. $y = 6x - 5$, $y = 7$ **(2, 7)**

Practice: Word Problems, p. 651

NAME ______ DATE ______ PERIOD ____

11-7 Practice: Word Problems
Graphing Systems of Equations

TAXI SERVICE For Exercises 1–4, use the following information.
A-1 Taxi service charges $5 for pickup plus $1 per mile for a taxi ride.
All-About-Town Taxi service charge $1 for pickup plus $2 per mile.

1. Write an equation for the total charge y for a ride that covers x miles in an A-1 Taxi. $y = x + 5$
2. Write an equation for the total charge y for a ride that covers x miles in an All-About-Town Taxi. $y = 2x + 1$
3. Explain how to solve a system of equations by graphing. Then solve the system by graphing. **Graph both lines on the same coordinate grid and identify the point of intersection; (4, 9).**
4. For what distance is the charge the same for both companies? What is the charge for a ride of this distance? Explain how you know this. **4 miles; $9; the point (4, 9) is a solution of both equations.**
5. **INCOME** Robert and Leta each work at a bicycle shop selling bicycles. Leta makes $150 per week plus $20 for each bicycle she sells, and Robert makes $250 per week. The equations $y = 20x + 150$ and $y = 250$ can be used to represent their weekly salaries. Explain how to solve the system of equations by substitution. Then solve the system by substitution. What does your solution represent? **Substitute 250 for y in the first equation and solve for x; (5, 250); Leta and Robert have the same weekly salary, $250, when Leta sells 5 bicycles.**
6. **FOOD** Antonio's Pizza charges $8.00 for a large pizza and $1.50 for each topping. Zina's Pizzaria charges $10.00 for a large pizza and $1.00 for each topping. Write and solve a system of equations to determine the number of toppings for which the pizzas would cost the same. What is that cost? $y = 8.00 + 1.50x$, $y = 10.00 + 1.00x$; **(4, 14); 4 toppings; $14**

11-8 Lesson Notes

Lesson Resources

Chapter 11 Resource Masters
- Study Guide and Intervention, p. 654
- Practice: Skills, p. 655
- Practice: Word Problems, p. 656
- Reading to Learn Mathematics, p. 657
- Enrichment, p. 658

Parent and Student Study Guide Online Worksheets, 11-8

Noteables™: Interactive Study Notebook with Foldables™, 11-8

FAST FILE

1 Focus

5-Minute Check 11-8

INTERACTIVE CHALKBOARD PowerPoint® Presentations

Use as a quiz or review of Lesson 11-7. (Also available as a transparency)

Bellringer

Communication Draw and label the graph in the bottom margin on the chalkboard. Ask students to explain how to determine which of the three points, $A(-2, 2)$, $B(0, 1)$, or $C(0, 0)$, is a solution of the equation $y = \frac{1}{2}x + 1$. **B** Ask which is a solution to $y < \frac{1}{2}x + 1$. **C** Ask which is a solution of $y > \frac{1}{2}x + 1$. **A** Students should realize they can use substitution to test whether a point on the coordinate plane solves an inequality.

Reading to Learn Mathematics, p. 657 ELL

NAME ____________ DATE ________ PERIOD ____

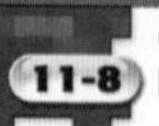

11-8 Reading to Learn Mathematics

Graphing Linear Inequalities

Pre-Activity *Read the introduction at the top of page 548 in your textbook. Write your answers below.*

1. Use the graph to list three different combinations of CDs and books that Sabrina can purchase for \$16. Sample answer: 2 CDs, 12 books; 4 CDs, 8 books; 6 CDs, 4 books
2. Suppose Sabrina wants to spend less than \$16. Substitute (2, 7), (4, 2), (5, 12), and (7, 5) in $2x + y < 16$. Which values make the inequality true? (2, 7), (4, 2)
3. Which region do you think represents $2x + y < 16$? the yellow region
4. Suppose Sabrina can spend more than \$16. Substitute (2, 7), (4, 2), (5, 12), and (7, 5) in $2x + y > 16$. Which values make the inequality true? (5, 12), (7, 5)
5. Which region do you think represents $2x + y > 16$? the blue region

11-8 Graphing Linear Inequalities

What You'll LEARN

Graph linear inequalities.

NEW Vocabulary

boundary
half plane

REVIEW Vocabulary

inequality: a mathematical sentence that contains $>, <, \neq, \leq,$ or $\geq$ (Lesson 10-5)

WHEN am I ever going to use this?

MONEY MATTERS At a sidewalk sale, one table has a variety of CDs for \$2 each, and another table has a variety of books for \$1 each. Sabrina wants to buy some CDs and books.

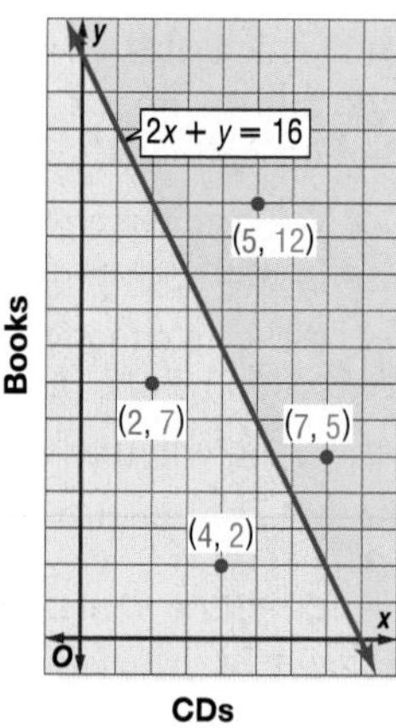

1. Use the graph at the right to list three different combinations of CDs and books that Sabrina can purchase for \$16.
2. Suppose Sabrina wants to spend less than \$16. Substitute (2, 7), (4, 2), (5, 12), and (7, 5) in $2x + y < 16$. Which values make the inequality true? **(2, 7), (4, 2)**
3. Which region do you think represents $2x + y < 16$?
4. Suppose Sabrina can spend more than \$16. Substitute (2, 7), (4, 2), (5, 12), and (7, 5) in $2x + y > 16$. Which values make the inequality true? **(5, 12), (7, 5)**
5. Which region do you think represents $2x + y > 16$?

1. Sample answer: 2 CDs, 12 books; 4 CDs, 8 books; 6 CDs, 4 books

3. the yellow region 5. the blue region

To graph an inequality such as $y < x + 1$, first graph the related equation $y = x + 1$. This is the **boundary**.

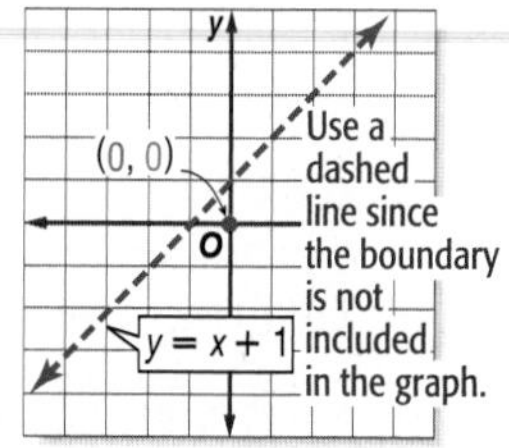

- If the inequality contains the symbol $\leq$ or $\geq$, a solid line is used to indicate that the boundary is included in the graph.
- If the inequality contains the symbol $<$ or $>$, a dashed line is used to indicate that the boundary is not included in the graph.

Next, test any point above or below the line to determine which region is the solution of $y < x + 1$. For example, it is easy to test (0, 0).

$y < x + 1$	Write the inequality.
$0 \overset{?}{<} 0 + 1$	Replace *x* with 0 and *y* with 0.
$0 < 1$ ✓	Simplify.

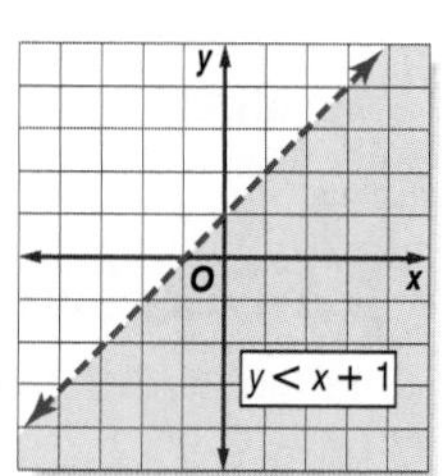

Since $0 < 1$ is true, (0, 0) is a solution of $y < x + 1$. Shade the region that contains this solution. This region is called a **half plane**. All points in this region are solutions of the inequality.

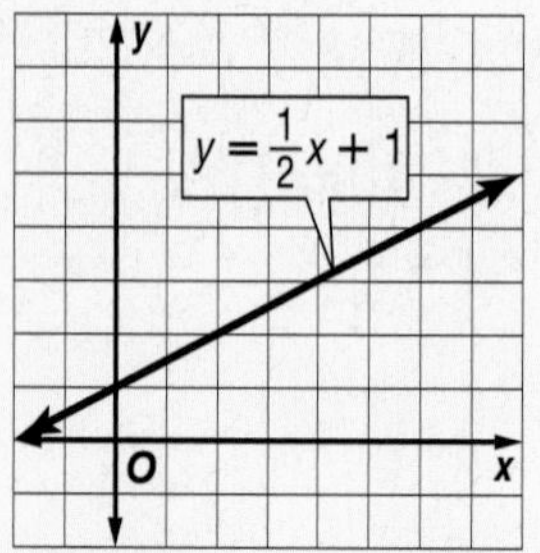

EXAMPLE Graph an Inequality

1 **Graph $y \geq \frac{1}{2}x + 3$.**

Step 1 Graph the boundary line $y = \frac{1}{2}x + 3$. Since $\geq$ is used in the inequality, make the boundary line a solid line.

Step 2 Test a point not on the boundary line, such as (0, 0).

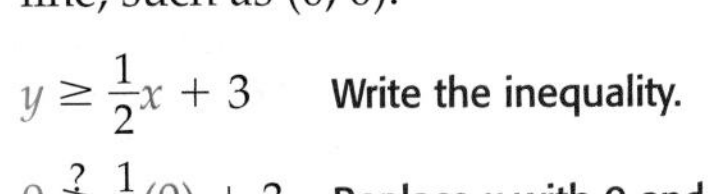

$y \geq \frac{1}{2}x + 3$	Write the inequality.
$0 \overset{?}{\geq} \frac{1}{2}(0) + 3$	Replace *x* with 0 and *y* with 0.
$0 \ngeq 3$	Simplify.

Step 3 Since (0, 0) is not a solution of $y \geq \frac{1}{2}x + 3$, shade the region that does not contain (0, 0).

STUDY TIP

Check You may want to check the graph in Example 1 by choosing a point in the shaded region. Do the coordinates of that point make the inequality a true statement?

The solution of an inequality includes negative numbers as well as fractions. However, in real-life situations, sometimes negative numbers and fractions have no meaning.

EXAMPLE Graph an Inequality to Solve a Problem

2 **FAIRS At the local fair, rides cost \$3 and games cost \$1. Gloria has \$12 to spend on the rides and games. How can she spend her money?**

Let *x* represent the number of rides and *y* represent the number of games. Write an inequality.

Words	Cost of rides	plus	cost of games	is no more than	12.
Inequality	$3x$	$+$	$1y$	$\leq$	12

The related equation is $3x + y = 12$.

$3x + y = 12$	Write the equation.
$3x + y - 3x = 12 - 3x$	Subtract $3x$ from each side.
$y = -3x + 12$	Write in slope-intercept form.

Graph $y = -3x + 12$. Test (0, 0) in the original inequality.

$3x + 1y \leq 12$	Write the inequality.
$3(0) + 1(0) \overset{?}{\leq} 12$	Replace *x* with 0 and *y* with 0.
$0 \leq 12$ ✓	Simplify.

Since Gloria cannot ride or play a negative number of times or a fractional number of times, the answer is any pair of integers represented in the shaded region. For example, she could ride 3 rides and play 2 games.

REAL-LIFE MATH

FAIRS Each year, there are more than 3,200 fairs held in the United States and Canada.

Source: *World Book*

TEACHING TIP

Explain to students that the graph of $3x + y \leq 12$ is the half plane. The entire half plane is not shaded because the negative numbers have no meaning for the real-life situation.

msmath3.net/extra_examples

2 Teach

In-Class Examples

1 Graph $y \leq -x + 3$.

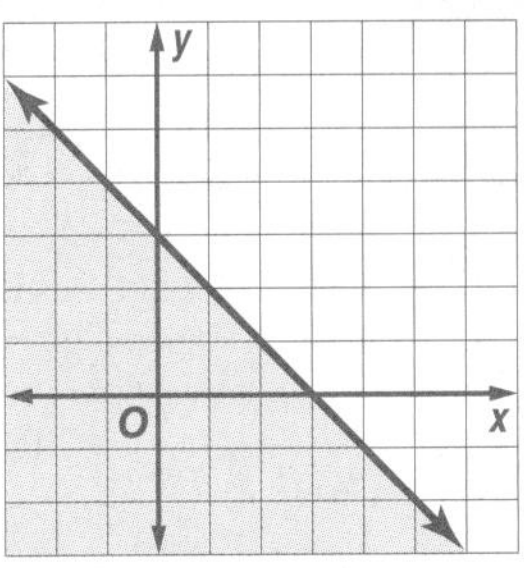

2 **CRAFTS** Sylvia is making items to sell at the school craft sale. Each flower basket takes 15 minutes, and each flower pin takes 1 minute to make. She can spend, at most, 60 minutes making crafts one afternoon. Graph the inequality showing the possible numbers of each item she can make that afternoon. $y \leq -15x + 60$

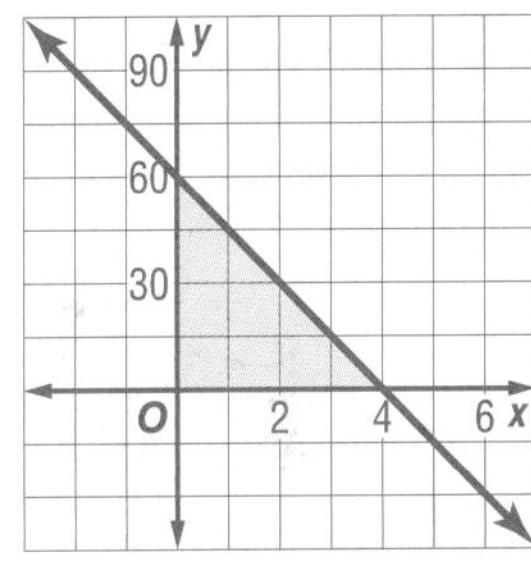

DAILY INTERVENTION

Unlocking Misconceptions

Word Problems When graphing inequalities to solve word problems, students may mistakenly think that any coordinate pair within the shaded region is a possible solution. Remind them that answers may include only integers or only positive numbers.

3 Practice/Apply

DAILY INTERVENTION **FIND THE ERROR** In Exercise 2, remind students that substituting the point (0, 0) in the inequality is usually an easy way to determine which region should be shaded.

About the Exercises...

Guided Practice Key

Exercises	Examples
3–5	1
6–7	2

Assignment Guide

Basic: 9–17 odd, 22–37

Average: 9–21 odd, 22–37

Enriched: 8–20 even, 22–37

Alert! For Exercises 24–25, provide the following pronunciations: khoum (KOOM) and ouguiya (oo-GWEE-uh).

Answers

1. Sample answer: $y > x - 3$

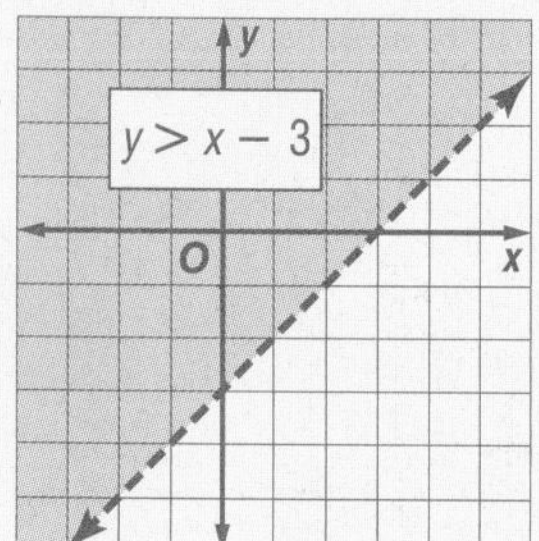

2. Since (0, 0) makes $y \geq \frac{2}{3}x - 2$ true, the region containing (0, 0) should be shaded.

3.

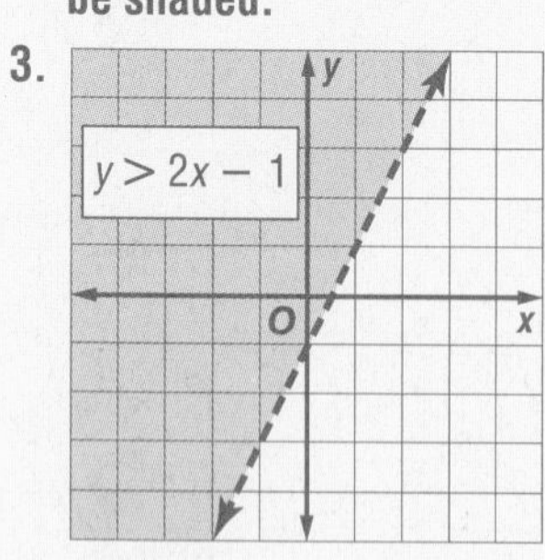

Students practice the same concepts in Exercises 8–21 if they are assigned odd or even problems.

Skill and Concept Check

1. **OPEN ENDED** Write an inequality that has a graph with a dashed line as its boundary. Graph the inequality. See margin.

2. **FIND THE ERROR** Nathan and Micheal are graphing $y \geq \frac{2}{3}x - 2$. Who is correct? Explain. Micheal; see margin.

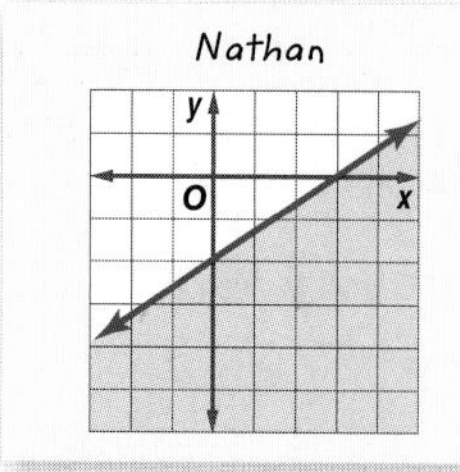

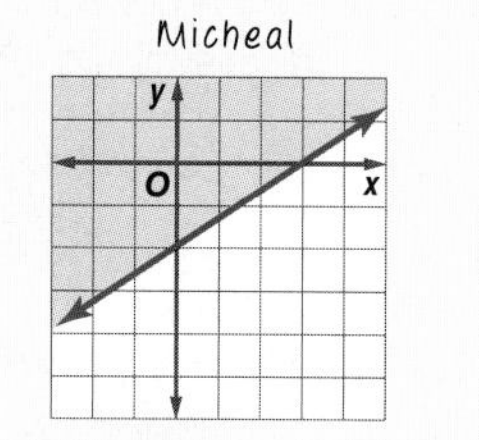

GUIDED PRACTICE

Graph each inequality. 3–5. See margin.

3. $y > 2x - 1$
4. $y \leq \frac{4}{3}x - 2$
5. $y \geq \frac{1}{2}x$

GEOMETRY For Exercises 6 and 7, use the following information.
A formula for the perimeter of an isosceles triangle where x is the length of the legs and y is the length of the base is $P = 2x + y$.

6. Make a graph for all isosceles triangles that have a perimeter greater than 8 units. See margin.

7. Give the lengths of the legs and the base of three isosceles triangles with perimeters greater than 8 units. See margin.

★ indicates increased difficulty

Practice and Applications

HOMEWORK HELP

For Exercises	See Examples
8–21	1
22–25	2

Extra Practice
See pages 645, 658.

Graph each inequality. 8–21. See Ch. 11 Answer Appendix.

8. $y > x - 4$
9. $y \geq x + 5$
10. $y \leq -3x + 3$
11. $y < -x - 2$
12. $y > \frac{5}{2}x + 1$
13. $y < \frac{3}{4}x - 1$
14. $y \leq -\frac{3}{2}x + 2$
15. $y \geq -\frac{2}{5}x - 3$
16. $y < 5x + 3$
17. $y \leq 4x - 1$
★18. $3x + y \geq 1$
★19. $y - 2x > 6$

★20. Graph the inequality *the sum of two numbers is less than 6.*

★21. Graph the inequality *the sum of two numbers is greater than 4.*

SCHOOL For Exercises 22 and 23, use the following information.
Alberto must finish his math and social studies homework during the next 60 minutes. 22–23. See Ch. 11 Answer Appendix.

22. Make a graph showing all the amounts of time Alberto can spend on each subject.

23. Give three possible ways Alberto can spend his time on math and social studies.

4.

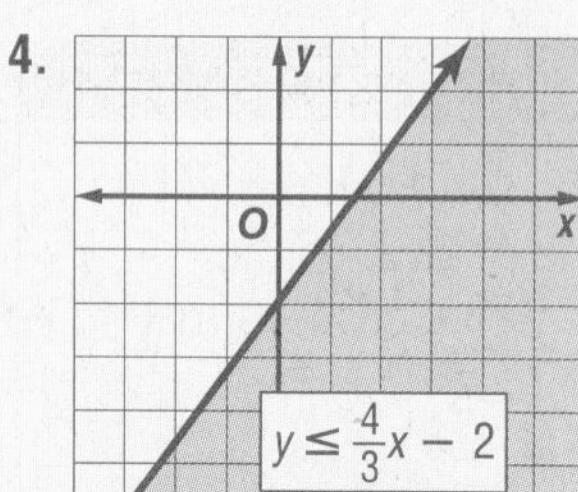

5.

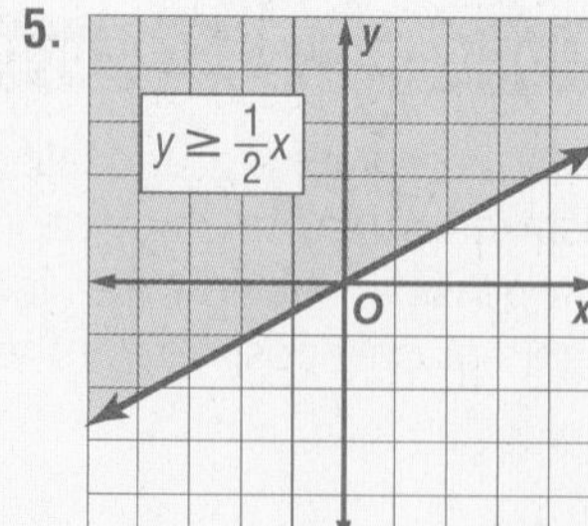

6.

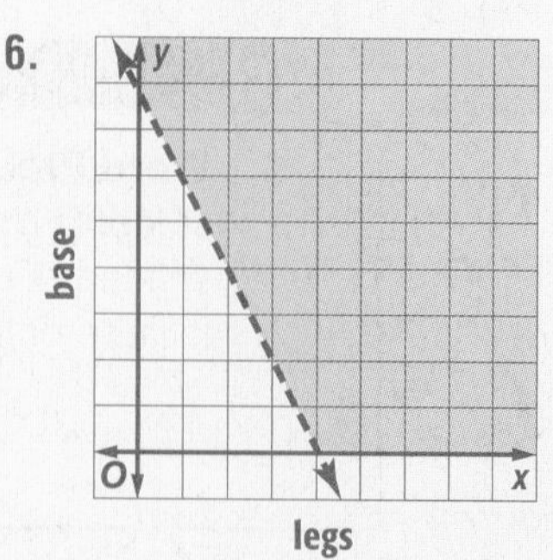

550 Chapter 11 Algebra: Linear Functions

TRAVEL For Exercises 24 and 25, use the information below.
In the monetary system of the African country of Mauritania, five khoums equals one ouguiya. Heather is visiting Mauritania and wants to take at least an amount equal to 30 ouguiyas to the market. The inequality $\frac{1}{5}x + y \geq 30$, where x is the number of khoums and y is the number of ouguiyas, represents the situation.

24. Make a graph showing all the combinations of khoums and ouguiyas Heather can take to the market.
25. Give three possible ways Heather can take an appropriate amount to the market. See margin.
26. **CRITICAL THINKING** Graph the intersection of $y \leq -x - 3$ and $y > x + 2$.

24. See Ch. 11 Answer Appendix. 26. See Ch. 11 Answer Appendix.

Spiral Review with Standardized Test Practice

27. **MULTIPLE CHOICE** Which is the graph of $2x + y > 5$? C

(A) 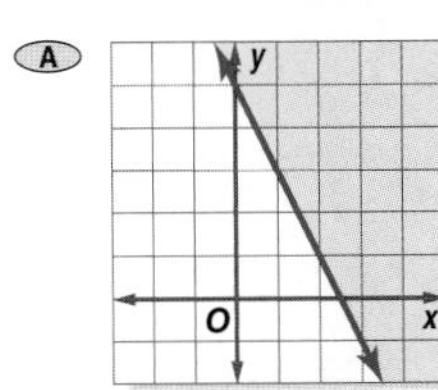

(B) 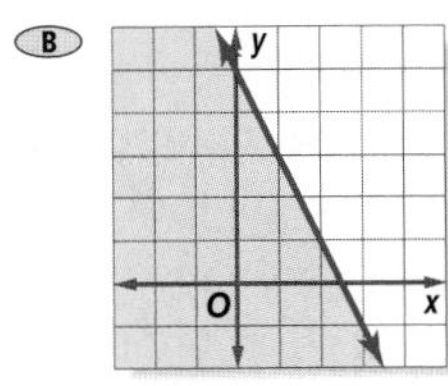

(C) 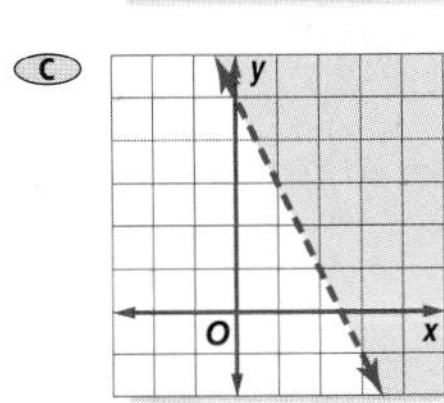

(D) 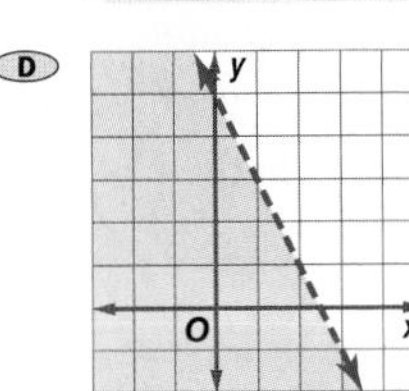

28. **MULTIPLE CHOICE** Which ordered pair is *not* a solution of $y + 3 \leq 2x$? F

(F) (1, 2) (G) (2, 1) (H) (3, −2) (I) (2, −3)

29–32. See Ch. 11 Answer Appendix for graphs.

Solve each system of equations by graphing. (Lesson 11-7)

29. $y = 2x - 5$, $y = -x + 1$ (2, −1)
30. $y = x + 2$, $y = -x$ (−1, 1)
31. $y = -2x + 4$, $y = -2x - 2$ no solution
32. $y = -x + 4$, $y = 2x - 2$ (2, 2)

33. **STATISTICS** Determine whether a scatter plot of the amount of studying and test scores would show a *positive*, *negative*, or *no* relationship. (Lesson 11-6) positive

Find the area of each figure. (Lesson 7-1)

34. 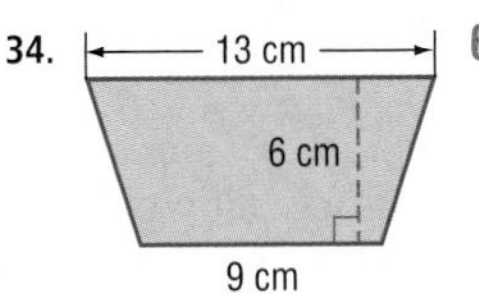

66 cm^2

35. 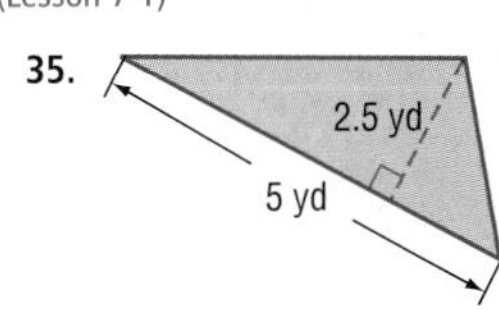

6.25 yd^2

36. 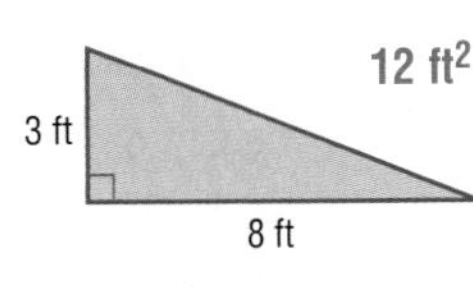

12 ft^2

37. **MULTI STEP** The original price of a jacket is \$58. Find the price of the jacket if it is marked down 25%. (Lesson 5-7) \$43.50

msmath3.net/self_check_quiz

4 Assess

Open-Ended Assessment

Writing Have students write a word problem that can be solved by graphing an inequality. Then, have students exchange problems and solve.

Answers

7. Sample answers: legs: 5 units, base: 2 units; legs: 7 units, base: 5 units; legs: 9 units, base: 1 unit
25. Sample answers: khoums: 5, ouguiyas: 29; khoums: 25, ouguiyas: 30; khoums: 10, ouguiyas: 35

Study Guide and Intervention, p. 654

NAME ______ DATE ______ PERIOD ____

11-8 Study Guide and Intervention
Graphing Linear Inequalities

Graphing a linear inequality takes several steps. First, you must graph the related equation. The related equation is obtained by replacing the inequality symbol with an equals sign. If the inequality symbol is ≤ or ≥, the related equation should be graphed as a solid line. If the inequality symbol is < or >, the related equation should be graphed as a dashed line. This solid or dashed line is the **boundary** of the solution. Next, test any point above or below the line to determine which region is the solution of the inequality. Shade the region that contains the solution. All points in this region are solutions to the inequality.

EXAMPLE 1 Graph $y > 2x - 2$.

Step 1 Graph the boundary line $y = 2x - 2$. Since > is used in the inequality, make the boundary line a dashed line.

Step 2 Test a point not on the boundary line, such as (0, 0).
$y > 2x - 2$ Write the inequality.
$0 \overset{?}{>} 2(0) - 2$ Replace x with 0 and y with 0.
$0 > -2$ ✓ Simplify.

Step 3 Since (0, 0) is a solution of $y > 2x - 2$, shade the region that contains (0, 0).

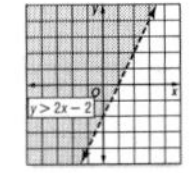

EXERCISES

Graph each inequality.

1. $y < x - 1$ 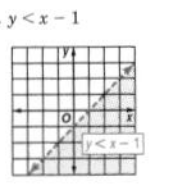
2. $y \leq 4x + 1$
3. $y > -2x + 1$ 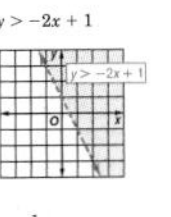
4. $y \leq -x + 2$
5. $y \leq \frac{1}{2}x + 2$ 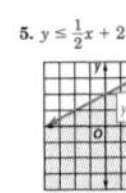
6. $y > \frac{1}{2}x - 1$ 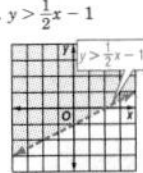

Practice: Skills, p. 655

NAME ______ DATE ______ PERIOD ____

11-8 Practice: Skills
Graphing Linear Inequalities

Graph each inequality.

1. $y > x - 3$
2. $y \leq -x + 2$ 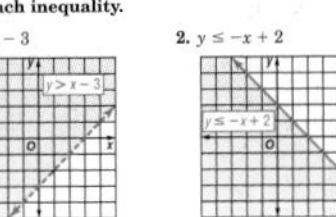
3. $y < 2x + 1$ 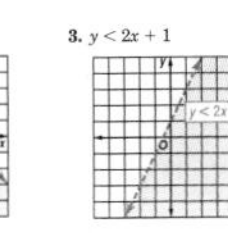
4. $y \geq -2x - 3$ 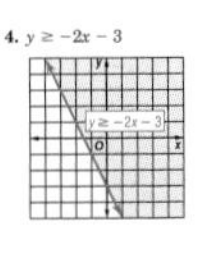
5. $y > 3x + 2$ 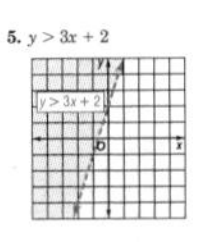
6. $y < -4x - 3$ 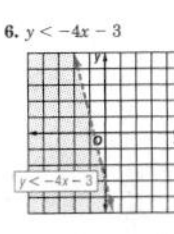
7. $y \geq 5x - 1$ 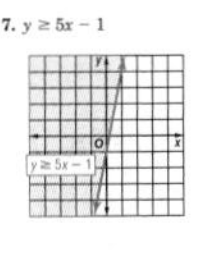
8. $y > \frac{1}{2}x + 1$ 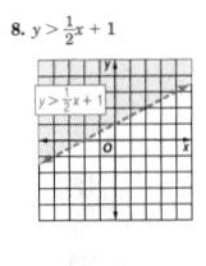
9. $y \leq -\frac{2}{3}x + 3$ 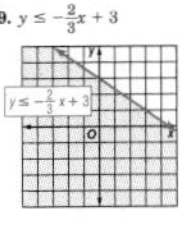
10. $y \leq \frac{1}{2}x - 3$ 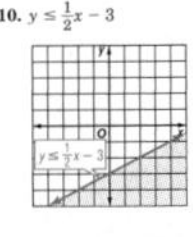
11. $y > -2x - 2$ 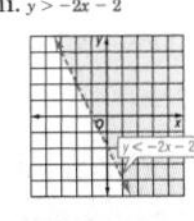
12. $y \geq \frac{1}{4}x + 1$ 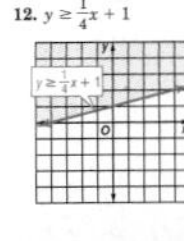

Practice: Word Problems, p. 656

NAME ______ DATE ______ PERIOD ____

11-8 Practice: Word Problems
Graphing Linear Inequalities

NUTRITION For Exercises 1 and 2, use the following information. Carl is making his own sports drink by mixing orange juice and water in a 40 ounce container.

1. Make a graph showing all the different amounts of orange juice and water that Carl can use in his drink.
2. Give three possible amounts of orange juice and water that Carl can use. Sample answers: water 10 oz, OJ 10 oz; water 20 oz, OJ 15 oz; water 30 oz, OJ 10 oz

GEOMETRY For Exercises 3 and 4, use the following information. The formula for the perimeter, P, of a rectangle of length x and width y is $\frac{P}{2} = x + y$.

3. Make a graph for all rectangles that have a perimeter of less than or equal to 20 units.
4. Give three possible measurements for the length and width of a rectangle that has a perimeter of less than or equal to 20 units. Sample answers: length 8 units, width 2 units; length 2 units, width 2 units; length 4 units, width 5 unit

FOOD For Exercises 5 and 6, use the following information. At the local farmer's market, apples are \$2 per pound and blueberries are \$3 per pound. Rene wants to buy at least \$12 worth of apples and blueberries.

5. Make a graph for all the weights of apples and blueberries that Rene can buy.

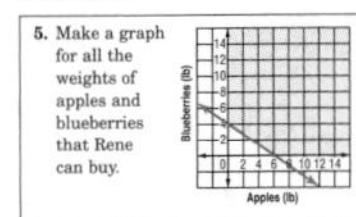

6. Give three possible ways that Rene can buy the amount of fruit she wants. Sample answers: 7 pounds of apples; 5 pounds of apples and 2 pounds of blueberries; 4 pounds of apples and 4 pounds of blueberries

Study Guide and Review

Vocabulary Assessment

- This alphabetical list of vocabulary terms in Chapter 11 includes a page reference where each term was introduced.
- A vocabulary review/test for Chapter 11 is available on p. 672 of the *Chapter 11 Resource Masters*.

Vocabulary PuzzleMaker

ELL The online Vocabulary PuzzleMaker improves students' mathematics vocabulary using four puzzle formats – crossword, scramble, word search using a word list, and word search using clues. Students can work on a computer screen or from a printed handout.

MindJogger Videoquizzes

ELL MindJogger Videoquizzes provide an alternative review of concepts presented in this chapter. Students work in teams in a game show format to gain points for correct answers. The questions are presented in three rounds.

Round 1 Concepts (5 questions)
Round 2 Skills (4 questions)
Round 3 Problem-Solving (4 questions)

ExamView® Pro

Use the networkable ExamView® Pro Testmaker CD-ROM to:

- Create **multiple versions** of tests.
- Create **modified** tests for **inclusion** students with one mouse click.
- **Edit** existing questions and **add** your own questions.
- Build tests aligned with state standards using built-in **state curriculum correlations.**
- Change **English** tests to **Spanish** with one mouse click and vice versa.

Study Guide and Review

Vocabulary and Concept Check

arithmetic sequence (p. 512)	function table (p. 518)	slope formula (p. 526)
best-fit line (p. 540)	geometric sequence (p. 513)	slope-intercept form (p. 533)
boundary (p. 548)	half plane (p. 548)	substitution (p. 545)
common difference (p. 512)	independent variable (p. 518)	system of equations (p. 544)
common ratio (p. 513)	linear function (p. 523)	term (p. 512)
dependent variable (p. 518)	range (p. 518)	*x*-intercept (p. 523)
domain (p. 518)	scatter plot (p. 539)	*y*-intercept (p. 523)
function (p. 517)	sequence (p. 512)	

Choose the correct term or number to complete each sentence.

1. The (domain, range) is the set of input values of a function.
2. The range is the set of (input, output) values of a function.
3. A (sequence, term) is an ordered list of numbers.
4. A geometric sequence has a (common difference, common ratio).
5. A(n) (arithmetic sequence, geometric sequence) has a common difference.
6. The (x-intercept, y-intercept) has the coordinates $(0, b)$.
7. The (half-plane, boundary) is the graph of the equation related to an inequality.
8. The slope formula is $m = \left(\frac{y_2 - y_1}{x_2 - x_1}, \frac{x_2 - x_1}{y_2 - y_1}\right)$.

Lesson-by-Lesson Exercises and Examples

11-1 Sequences (pp. 512–515)

State whether each sequence is *arithmetic*, *geometric*, or *neither*. If it is arithmetic or geometric, state the common difference or common ratio. Write the next three terms of the sequence. **9–12. See margin.**

9. 64, 32, 16, 8, 4, … 10. −7, −4, −1, 2, 5, …
11. 1, 2, 6, 24, 120, … 12. 1, −1, 1, −1, 1, …
13. **SAVINGS** Loretta has \$5 in her piggy bank. Each week, she adds \$1.50. If she does not take any money out of the piggy bank, how much will she have after 6 weeks? **\$14**

Example 1 State whether the sequence is *arithmetic*, *geometric*, or *neither*. If it is arithmetic or geometric, state the common difference or common ratio. Write the next three terms of the sequence.

1, −2, 4, −8, 16, …

1, −2, 4, −8, 16, …
× (−2) × (−2) × (−2) × (−2)

The terms have a common ratio of −2, so the sequence is geometric. The next three terms are 16(−2) or −32, −32(−2) or 64, and 64(−2) or −128.

msmath3.net/vocabulary_review

For more information about Foldables, see *Teaching Mathematics with Foldables.*

Have students look through the chapter to make sure they have included examples in their Foldables for each lesson or topic in the chapter.

Encourage students to refer to their Foldables while completing the Study Guide and Review and to use them in preparing for the Chapter Test.

552 Chapter 11 Algebra: Linear Functions

11-2 Functions (pp. 517–520)

Find each function value.

14. $f(3)$ if $f(x) = 3x + 1$ 10
15. $f(9)$ if $f(x) = 1 - 3x$ −26
16. $f(0)$ if $f(x) = 2x + 6$ 6
17. $f(-11)$ if $f(x) = -2x$ 22
18. $f(-2)$ if $f(x) = x - 1$ −3
19. $f(2)$ if $f(x) = \frac{1}{2}x - 4$ −3

Example 2 Complete the function table for $f(x) = 2x - 1$.

x	$2x - 1$	$f(x)$
−2	2(−2) − 1	−5
0	2(0) − 1	−1
1	2(1) − 1	1
5	2(5) − 1	9

11-3 Graphing Linear Functions (pp. 522–525)

Graph each function. 20–24. See margin.

20. $y = -2x + 1$
21. $y = x - 4$
22. $y = -3x$
23. $y = \frac{1}{2}x - 2$
24. **GEOMETRY** The function $y = 4x$ represents the perimeter y of a square with side x units long. Graph $y = 4x$.

Example 3 Graph $y = 3 - x$.

x	$3 - x$	y	(x, y)
−1	3 − (−1)	4	(−1, 4)
0	3 − 0	3	(0, 3)
2	3 − 2	1	(2, 1)
3	3 − 3	0	(3, 0)

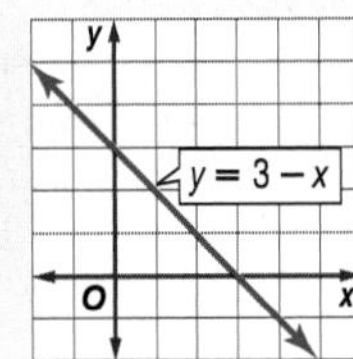

11-4 The Slope Formula (pp. 526–529)

Find the slope of each line that passes through each pair of points.

25. $A(-2, 3), B(-1, 5)$ 2
26. $E(-3, 2), F(-3, 5)$ undefined
27. $G(6, 2), H(1, 5)$ $-\frac{3}{5}$
28. $K(2, 1), L(-3, 1)$ 0

Example 4 Find the slope of the line that passes through $A(-3, 2)$ and $B(5, -1)$.

$m = \frac{y_2 - y_1}{x_2 - x_1}$ Definition of slope

$m = \frac{-1 - 2}{5 - (-3)}$ or $-\frac{3}{8}$ $(x_1, y_1) = (-3, 2)$, $(x_2, y_2) = (5, -1)$

11-5 Slope-Intercept Form (pp. 533–536) 32. −3; −2 33. $-\frac{3}{4}$; 7

State the slope and y-intercept for the graph of each equation.

29. $y = 2x + 5$ 2; 5
30. $y = \frac{1}{2}x - 7$ $\frac{1}{2}$; −7
31. $y = \frac{1}{5}x + 6$ $\frac{1}{5}$; 6
32. $y = -3x - 2$
33. $y = -\frac{3}{4}x + 7$
34. $y = 3x + 7$ 3; 7

Example 5 State the slope and y-intercept of the graph of $y = -\frac{1}{2}x + 3$.

$y = -\frac{1}{2}x + 3$ Write the equation.

$y = mx + b$

The slope of the graph is $-\frac{1}{2}$, and the y-intercept is 3.

Answers (p. 554)

39.

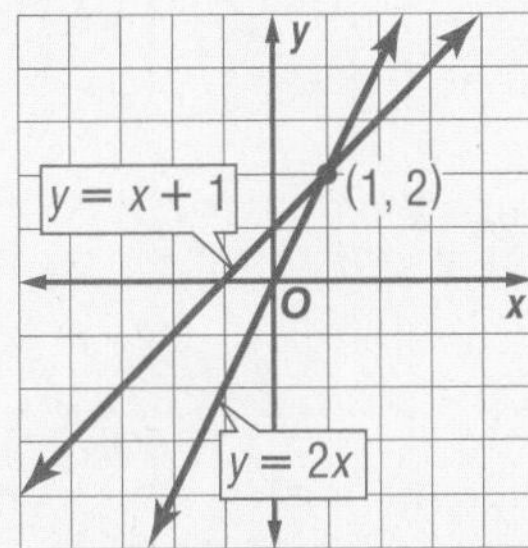

40.

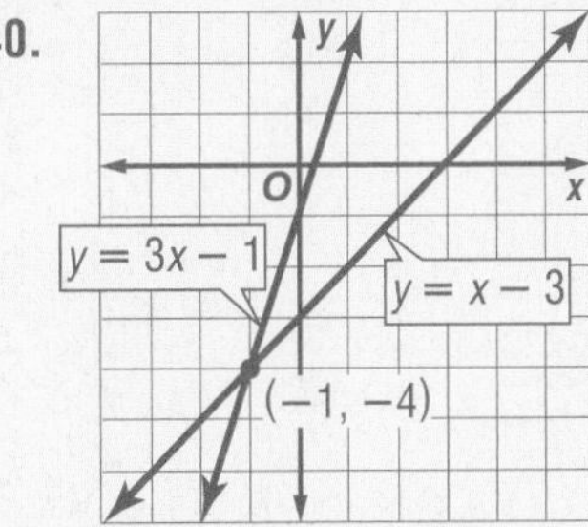

Answers

9. geometric; $\frac{1}{2}$; 2, 1, $\frac{1}{2}$
10. arithmetic; 3; 8, 11, 14
11. neither; 720, 5,040, 40,320
12. geometric; −1; −1, 1, −1

20.

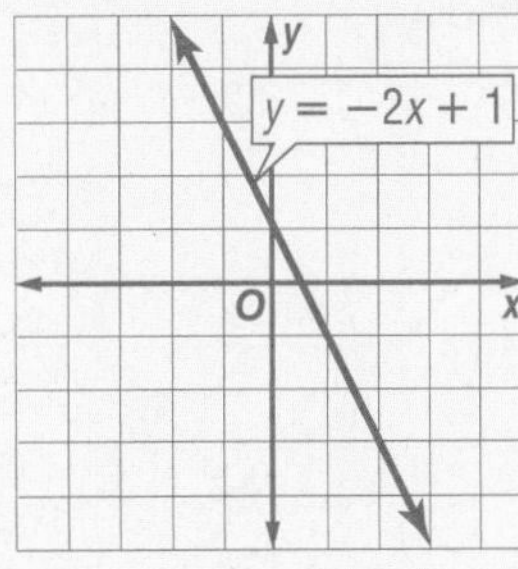

21.

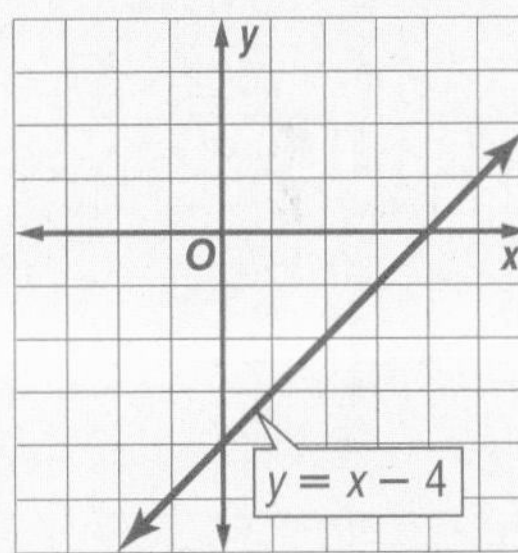

22.

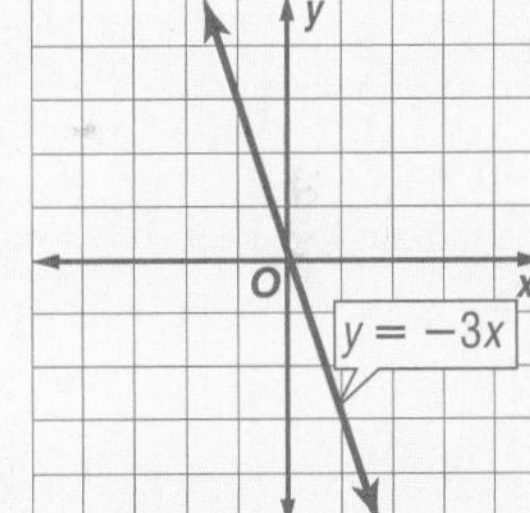

23.

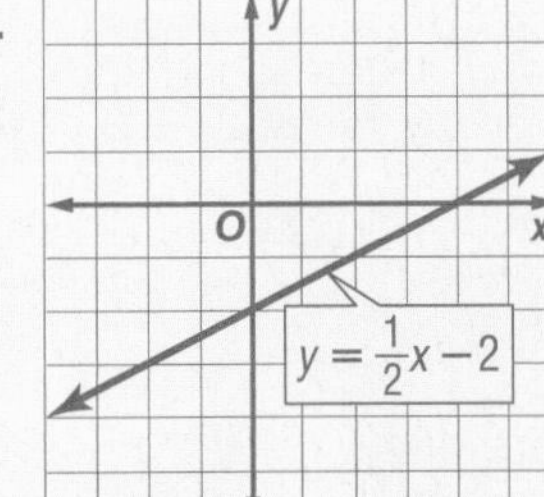

24.

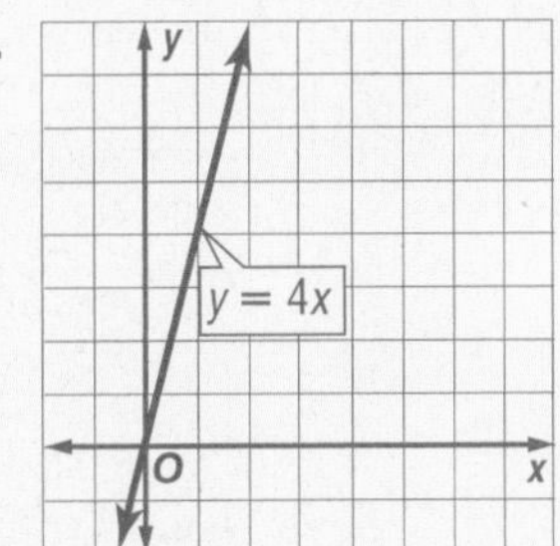

Mixed Problem Solving
For mixed problem-solving practice, see page 658.

Study Guide and Review

Answers

41.

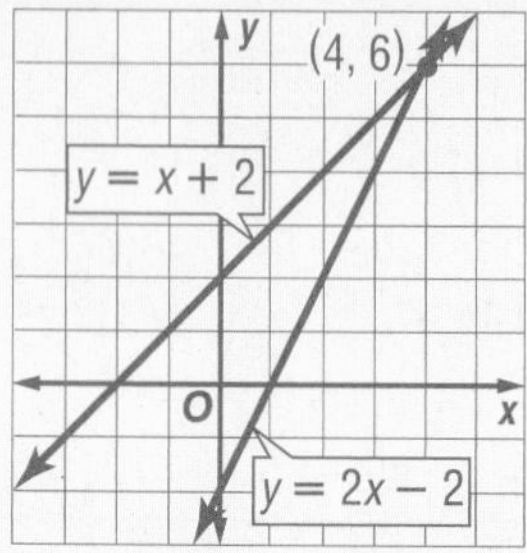

42.

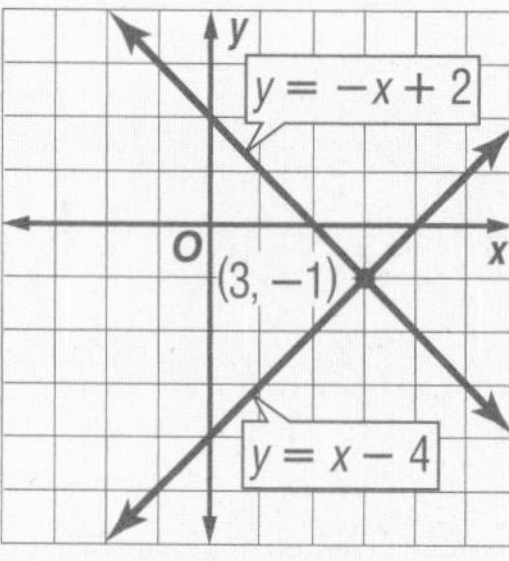

45.

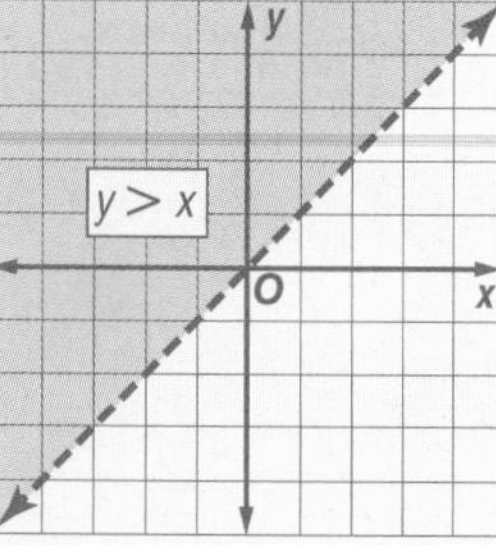

46.

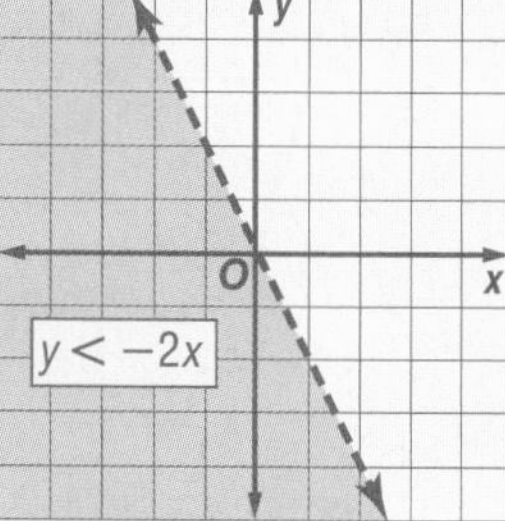

47.

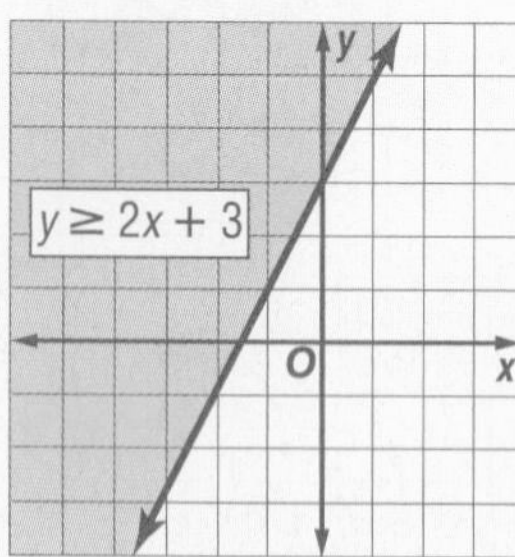

11-6 Statistics: Scatter Plots (pp. 539–542) 36. no relationship 37. positive

Determine whether a scatter plot of the data for the following might show a *positive*, *negative*, or *no* relationship.

35. number of people in the household and the cost of groceries **positive**
36. day of the week and temperature
37. child's age and grade level in school
38. temperature outside and amount of clothing **negative**

Example 6 **Determine whether the graph at the right shows a *positive*, *negative*, or *no* relationship.**

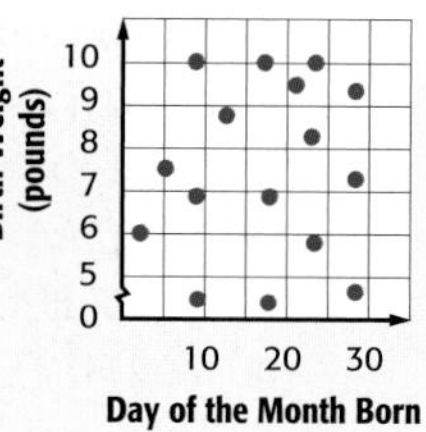

Since there is no obvious pattern, there is no relationship.

11-7 Graphing Systems of Equations (pp. 544–547) 40. (−1, −4)

Solve each system of equations by graphing. **39–42. See margin for graphs.**

39. $y = 2x$ **(1, 2)**
 $y = x + 1$
40. $y = 3x - 1$
 $y = x - 3$
41. $y = 2x - 2$ **(4, 6)**
 $y = x + 2$
42. $y = x - 4$ **(3, −1)**
 $y = -x + 2$

Solve each system of equations by substitution.

43. $y = -2x + 7$
 $x = 3$ **(3, 1)**
44. $y = 3x - 5$
 $x = 4$ **(4, 7)**

Example 7 **Solve the system of equations $y = 2x$ and $y = x - 1$ by graphing.**

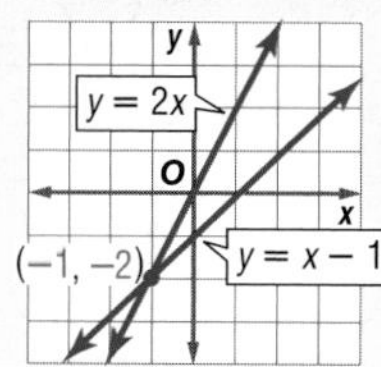

The graphs of the equation appear to intersect at (−1, −2).
Check this estimate.

11-8 Graphing Linear Inequalities (pp. 548–551)

Graph each inequality.

45. $y > x$
46. $y < -2x$
47. $y \geq 2x + 3$
48. $y \leq -x + 5$
49. $y > 3x + 5$
50. $y \leq 2x + 1$

45–50. See margin.

51. **FESTIVALS** At the Spring Festival, games cost $2 and rides cost $3. Nate wants to spend no more than $20 at the festival. Give three possible ways Nate can spend his money. **Sample answers: 3 games, 3 rides; 5 games, 3 rides; 10 games, 0 rides**

Example 8 **Graph $y < 4x - 2$.**

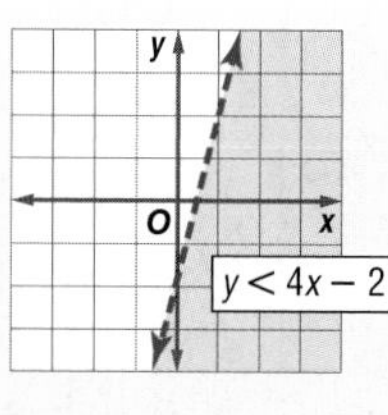

Graph the boundary line $y = 4x - 2$. Since the $<$ symbol is used in the inequality, make the boundary line a dashed line.

Test a point not on the boundary line such as (0, 0). Since (0, 0) is not a solution of $y < 4x - 2$, shade the region that does not contain (0, 0).

48.

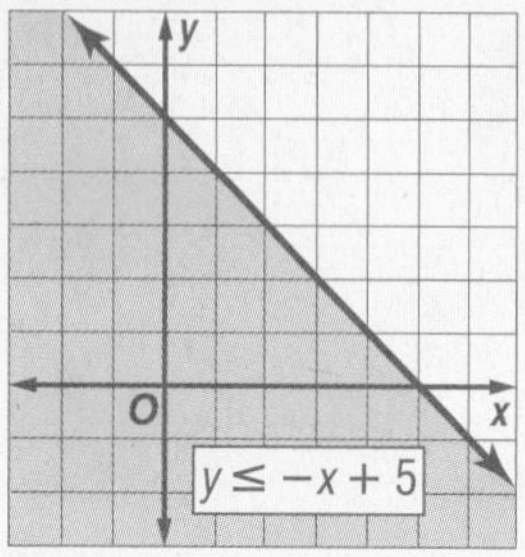

49.

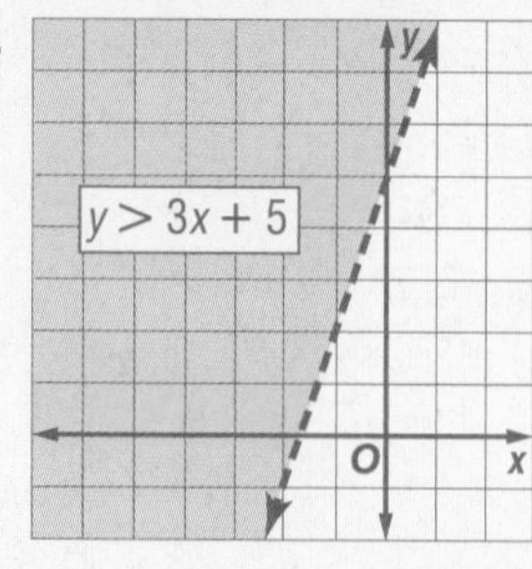

50.

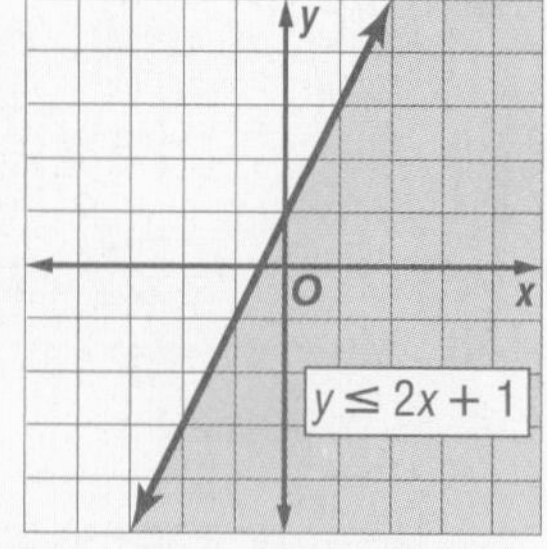

Practice Test

Vocabulary and Concepts

1. **Describe** how you can tell that there is no solution when you graph a system of equations. **The graphs of the two equations are parallel lines.**

2. **Describe** two different ways to graph $y = 2x + 5$. **function table or slope-intercept form**

Skills and Applications

State whether each sequence is *arithmetic, geometric,* or *neither*. If it is *arithmetic* or *geometric,* state the common difference or common ratio. Then write the next three terms of the sequence. **4. geometric; 5; 625, 3,125, 15,625**

3. $-10, -6, -2, 2, 6, \ldots$ **arithmetic; 4; 10, 14, 18**
4. $\frac{1}{5}, 1, 5, 25, 125, \ldots$
5. $61, 50, 40, 31, 23, \ldots$ **neither; 16, 10, 5**

Find each function value.

6. $f(-2)$ if $f(x) = \frac{x}{2} + 5$ **4**
7. $f(3)$ if $f(x) = -2x + 6$ **0**

Graph each function or inequality. **8–11. See Ch. 11 Answer Appendix.**

8. $y = \frac{1}{3}x - 1$
9. $y = -4x + 1$
10. $y < -2x + 3$
11. $y \geq x - 5$

Find the slope of the line that passes through each pair of points.

12. $A(-2, 5), B(-2, 1)$ **undefined**
13. $C(0, 3), D(-5, 2)$ $\frac{1}{5}$
14. $E(2, -1), F(5, -3)$ $-\frac{2}{3}$

CHILD CARE For Exercises 15–17, use the following information. **16. registration fee**
The cost for a child to attend a certain day care center is \$35 a day plus a registration fee of \$50. The cost y for x days of child care is $y = 35x + 50$.

15. Graph the equation.
16. What does the y-intercept represent?
17. What does the slope of the graph represent? **the cost per day**

15. See Ch. 11 Answer Appendix.

18. Solve the system $y = x + 1$ and $y = 2x - 2$ by graphing. **(3, 4); See Ch. 11 Answer Appendix for graphs.**
19. **TRAVEL** Would a scatter plot of data describing the gallons of gas used and the miles driven show a *positive, negative,* or *no* relationship? **positive**

Standardized Test Practice

20. **MULTIPLE CHOICE** Which is the graph of $y = -3x$? **C**

(A) 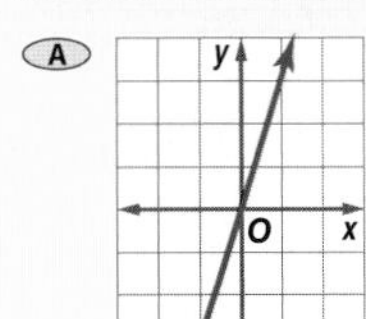

(B) 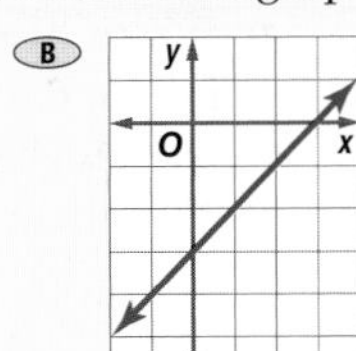

(C) 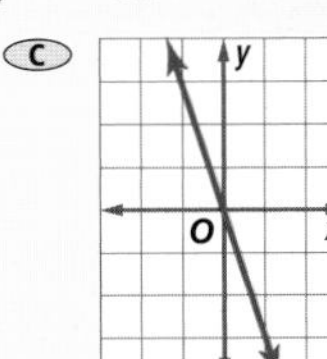

(D) 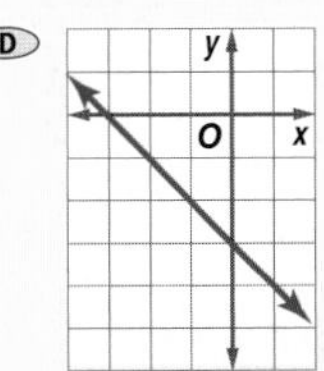

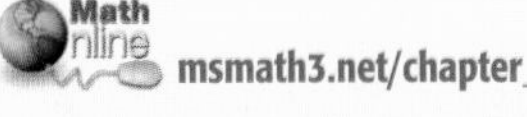

msmath3.net/chapter_test

Practice Test

Assessment Options

Vocabulary Test A vocabulary review/test for Chapter 11 can be found on p. 672 of the *Chapter 11 Resource Masters.*

Chapter Tests There are six Chapter 11 Tests and an Extended Response Assessment task available in the *Chapter 11 Resource Masters.*

Chapter 11 Tests

Form	Type	Level	Pages
1	MC	basic	659–660
2A	MC	average	661–662
2B	MC	average	663–664
2C	FR	average	665–666
2D	FR	average	667–668
3	FR	advanced	669–670

MC = multiple-choice questions
FR = free-response questions

Extended Response Assessment

Extended Response tasks for Chapter 11 can be found on p. 671 of the *Chapter 11 Resource Masters.* A sample scoring rubric for these tasks appears on p. A28.

Portfolio Suggestion

Introduction Various businesses analyze the slopes of graphs to gather information for planning and other business decisions. Market analysts use graphs to try to predict trends. CEOs look at graphs to evaluate how well their companies are performing.

Ask Students to find examples of graphs used in business situations. They can talk to family members, neighbors, or local business owners. Or they can research online or at the library. Students should include brief explanations of the graphs they discover.

Standardized Test Practice

These two pages contain practice questions in the various formats that can be found on the most frequently given standardized tests.

A student recording sheet for these two pages can be found on page A1 of the *Chapter 11 Resource Masters*.

Standardized Test Practice Student Recording Sheet, p. A1

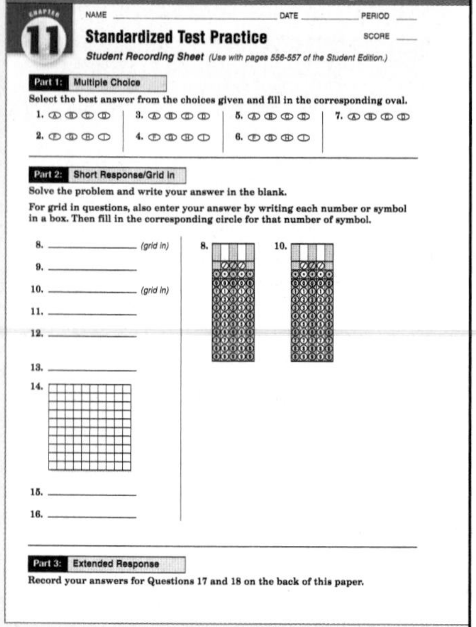

NAME ______ DATE ______ PERIOD ______

Standardized Test Practice SCORE ______

Student Recording Sheet (Use with pages 556–557 of the Student Edition.)

Part 1: Multiple Choice

Select the best answer from the choices given and fill in the corresponding oval.

1. Ⓐ Ⓑ Ⓒ Ⓓ 3. Ⓐ Ⓑ Ⓒ Ⓓ 5. Ⓐ Ⓑ Ⓒ Ⓓ 7. Ⓐ Ⓑ Ⓒ Ⓓ
2. Ⓕ Ⓖ Ⓗ Ⓘ 4. Ⓕ Ⓖ Ⓗ Ⓘ 6. Ⓕ Ⓖ Ⓗ Ⓘ

Part 2: Short Response/Grid In

Solve the problem and write your answer in the blank.

For grid in questions, also enter your answer by writing each number or symbol in a box. Then fill in the corresponding circle for that number of symbol.

8. ______ (grid in)
9. ______
10. ______ (grid in)
11. ______
12. ______
13. ______
14.
15. ______
16. ______

Part 3: Extended Response

Record your answers for Questions 17 and 18 on the back of this paper.

Additional Practice

See pp. 677–678 of the *Chapter 11 Resource Masters* for additional standardized test practice.

Standardized Test Practice

PART 1 Multiple Choice

Record your answers on the answer sheet provided by your teacher or on a sheet of paper.

1. If the following ordered pairs are plotted on a graph, which graph passes through all five points? (Prerequisite Skill, p. 614) **C**

$(-2, 4), (-1, 1), (0, 0), (1, 1), (2, 4)$

Ⓐ 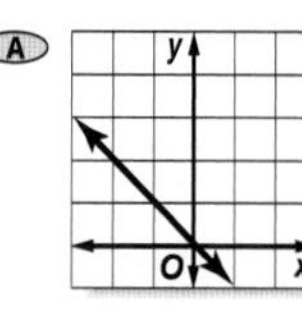

Ⓑ 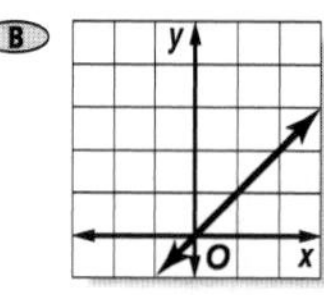

Ⓒ 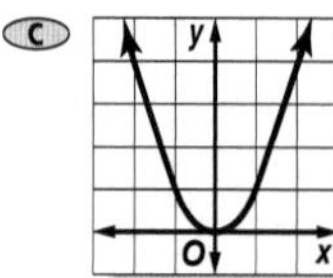

Ⓓ 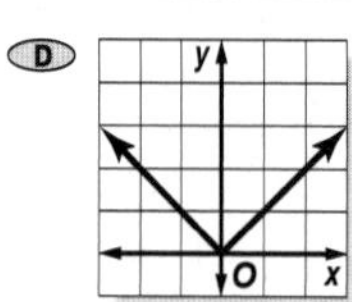

2. Which could be the value of x if $0.6 < x < 68\%$? (Lesson 5-2) **G**

Ⓕ $\frac{3}{5}$ Ⓖ $\frac{2}{3}$

Ⓗ $\frac{5}{7}$ Ⓘ $\frac{6}{8}$

3. Which of the following is *not* a quadrilateral? (Lesson 6-4) **D**

Ⓐ

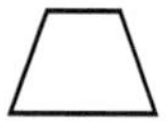

Ⓑ 

Ⓒ 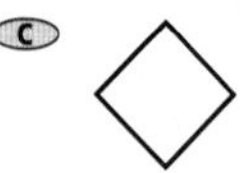

Ⓓ 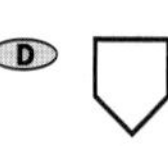

TEST-TAKING TIP

Question 3 Read each question carefully so that you do not miss key words such as *not* or *except*. Then read every answer choice carefully. If allowed to write in the test booklet, cross off each answer choice that you know is not the answer, so you will not consider it again.

4. What is the value of $f(x)$ when $x = 5$? (Lesson 11-1) **G**

x	$f(x)$
0	3
1	4
2	5
5	?

Ⓕ 7 Ⓖ 8

Ⓗ 9 Ⓘ 10

5. Which of the following ordered pairs is a solution of $y = \frac{1}{2}x - 4$? (Lesson 11-2) **D**

Ⓐ $(-2, -3)$ Ⓑ $(4, 2)$

Ⓒ $(6, 1)$ Ⓓ $(8, 0)$

6. The graph shows the distance Kimberly has traveled. What does the slope of the graph represent? (Lesson 11-5) **H**

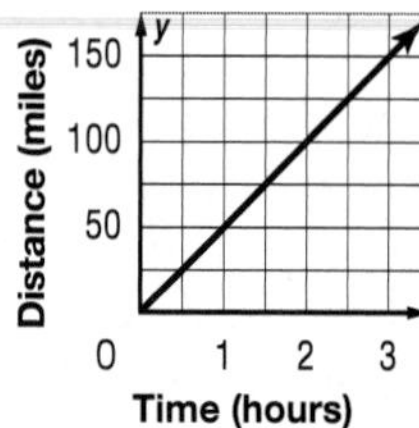

Ⓕ the distance Kimberly traveled

Ⓖ how long Kimberly has traveled

Ⓗ Kimberly's average speed

Ⓘ the time Kimberly will arrive

7. Which display would be most appropriate for the data in a table that shows the relationship between height and weight of 20 students? (Lesson 11-6) **A**

Ⓐ scatter plot Ⓑ line plot

Ⓒ bar graph Ⓓ circle graph

ExamView® Pro

Special banks of standardized test questions similar to those on the TIMSS and NAEP grade 8 tests can be found on this CD-ROM.

Preparing for Standardized Tests
For test-taking strategies and more practice, see pages 660–677.

PART 2 Short Response/Grid In

Record your answers on the answer sheet provided by your teacher or on a sheet of paper.

8. On a number line, how many units apart are -6 and 7? (Lesson 1-3) **13**

9. Find the volume of the pyramid. (Lesson 7-6) **108 cm³**

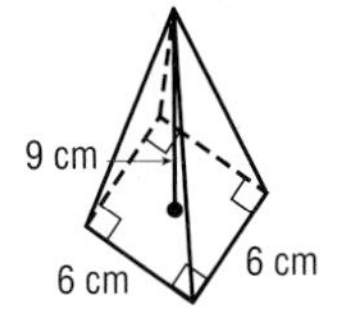

10. Mr. Thomas is drawing names out of a hat in order to create class debating teams. There are 13 girls and 12 boys in the class, and the first name picked is a girl's name. What is the probability that a boy's name will be drawn next? (Lesson 8-5) **1/2**

11. Molly received grades of 79, 92, 68, 90, 72, and 92 on her history tests. What measure of central tendency would give her the highest grade for the term? (Lesson 9-4) **mode**

12. A pair of designer jeans costs \$98, which is \$35 more than 3 times the cost of a discount store brand. The equation to find the cost of the discount store brand d is $3d + 35 = 98$. What is the price of the discount store brand of jeans? (Lesson 10-3) **\$21**

13. Copy and complete the function table for $f(x) = 0.4x + 2$. (Lesson 11-2)

x	y
-5	0
0	2
5	4
10	6

14. Graph $y = \frac{1}{2}x - 2$. (Lesson 11-3)
See Ch. 11 Answer Appendix.

Math Online msmath3.net/standardized_test

15. Describe the relationship shown in the graph. (Lesson 11-6) **The relationship is negative.**

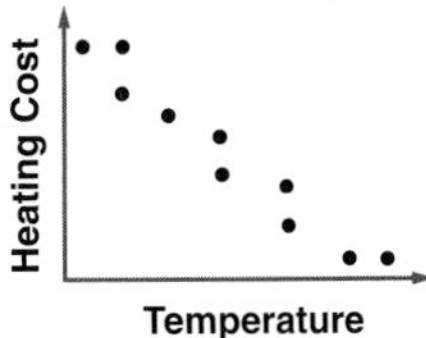

16. What ordered pair is a solution of both $y = 3x - 5$ and $y = x - 7$? (Lesson 11-7) **$(-1, -8)$**

PART 3 Extended Response

Record your answers on a sheet of paper. Show your work.

17. Study the data below. (Lesson 11-6)

Date	Number of Customers	Ice Cream Scoops Sold
June 1	75	100
June 2	125	230
June 3	350	460
June 4	275	370
June 5	175	300
June 6	225	345
June 7	210	325

a. What type of display would be most appropriate for this data? **scatter plot**

b. Graph the data.

c. Describe the relationship of the data.
b–c. See Ch. 11 Answer Appendix.

18. In Major League Soccer, a team gets 3 points for a win and 1 point for a tie. (Lesson 11-8) **b–c. See Ch. 11 Answer Appendix.**

a. Write an inequality for the number of ways a team can earn more than 10 points. **$3x + y > 10$**

b. Graph the inequality.

c. Compare the values graphed and those that actually satisfy the situation.

Standardized Test Practice

Rubrics The following rubrics are sample scoring devices for short response and extended response questions.

Short Response

Points	Description
2	The student demonstrates a thorough understanding of the mathematics of the task. The response may contain minor flaws that do not detract from the demonstration of a thorough understanding.
1	The student has provided a response that is only partially correct.
0	The student has provided a completely incorrect solution or no response at all.

Extended Response

Points	Description
4	The student demonstrates a thorough understanding of the mathematics of the task. The response may contain minor flaws that do not detract from the demonstration of a thorough understanding.
3	The student demonstrates an understanding of the mathematics of the task. The response is essentially correct and demonstrates an essential but less than thorough understanding of the mathematics.
2	The student demonstrates only a partial understanding of the mathematics of the task. Although the student may have used the correct approach to a solution or may have provided a correct solution, the work lacks an essential understanding of the underlying mathematical concepts.
1	The student demonstrates a very limited understanding of the mathematics of the task. The response is incomplete and exhibits many flaws.
0	The student provides a completely incorrect solution or no response at all.

A more detailed 4-point rubric is provided on page A2 of the *Chapter 11 Resource Masters.*

Page 515, Lesson 11-1

28.

Number of Times at the Ski Resort	1	2	3	4	5
Total Cost with One Day Passes	$40	$80	$120	$160	$200
Total Cost with Yearly Pass	$400	$400	$400	$400	$400

Pages 524–525, Lesson 11-3

8.
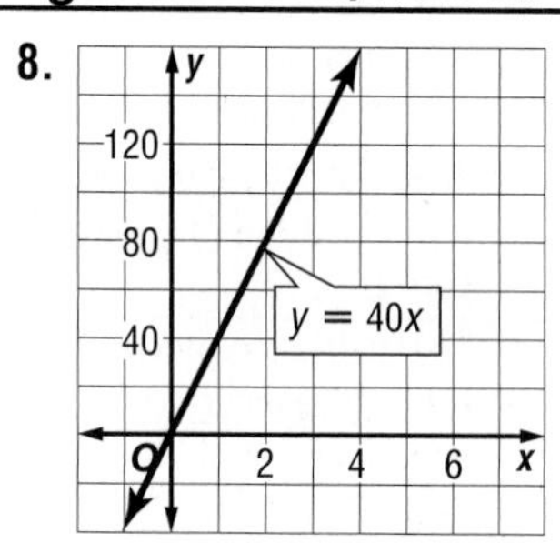

10.
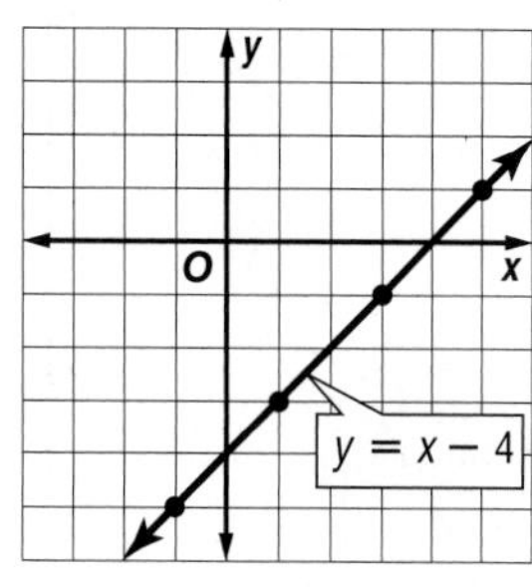

11.
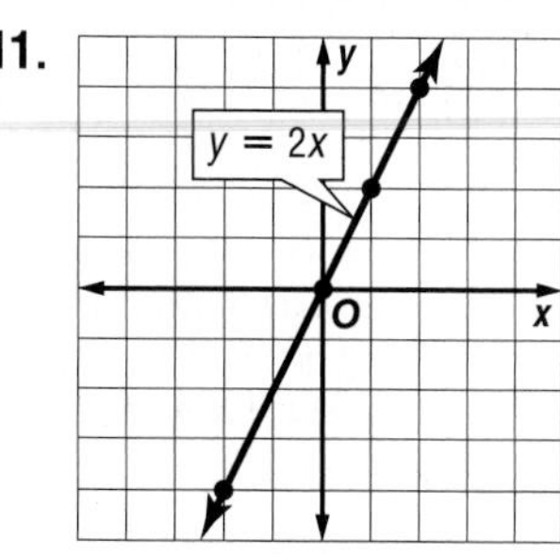

12.
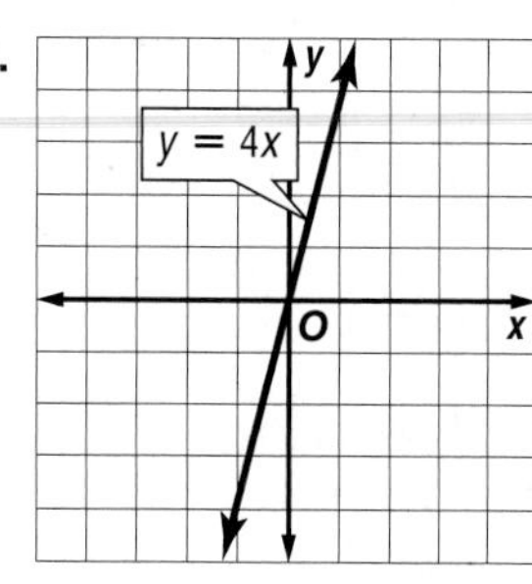

13.
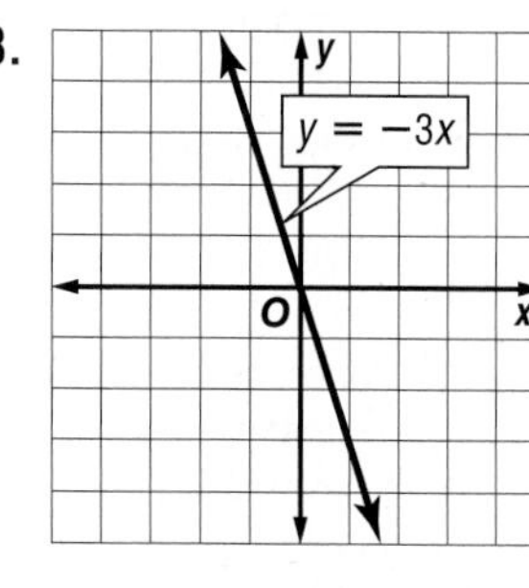

14.
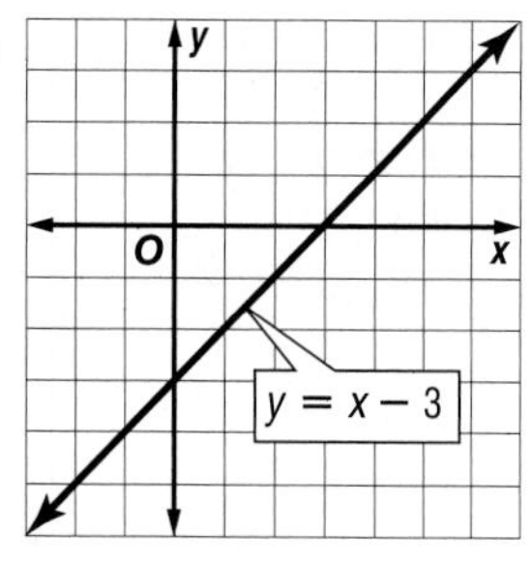

15.
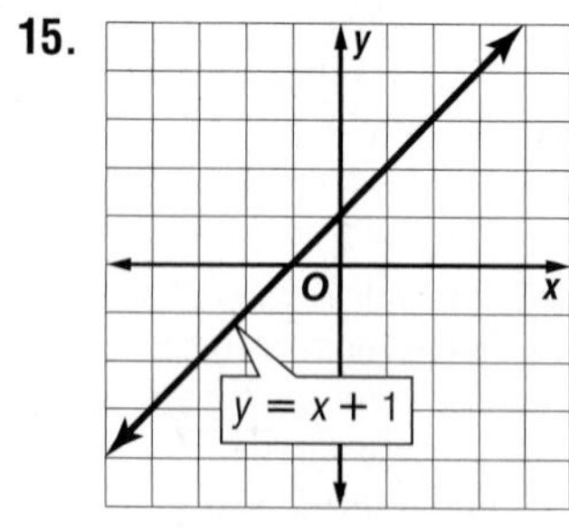

16.
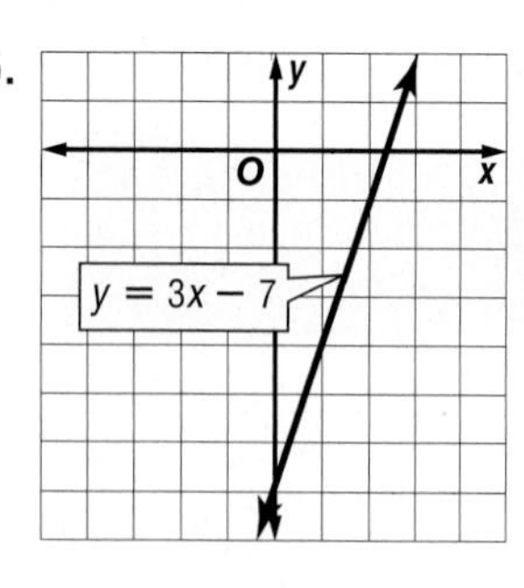

17.
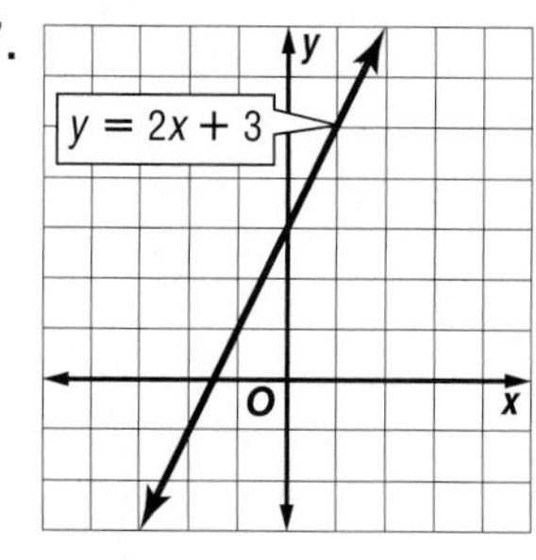

18.
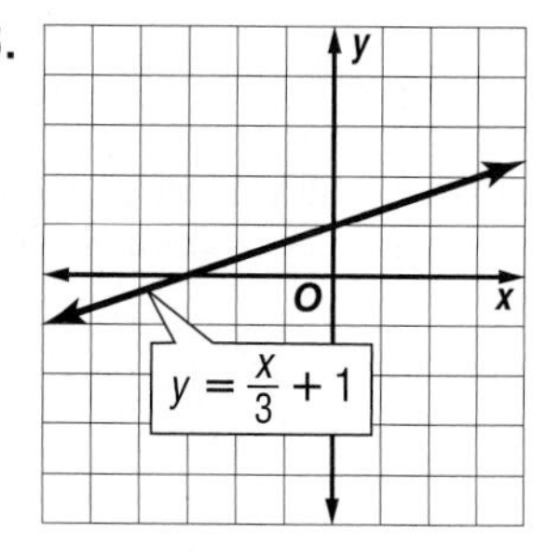

19.
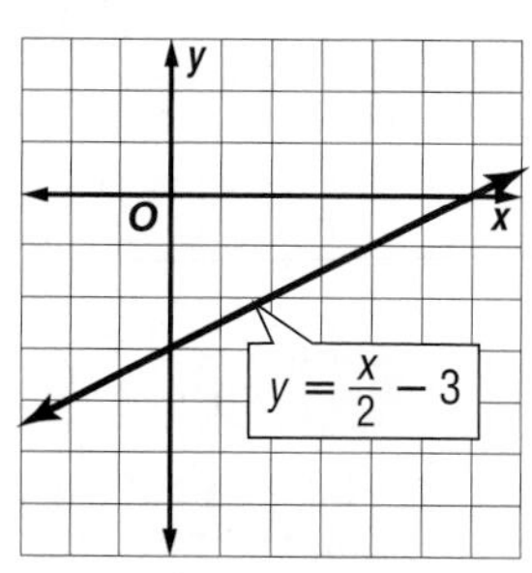

20.
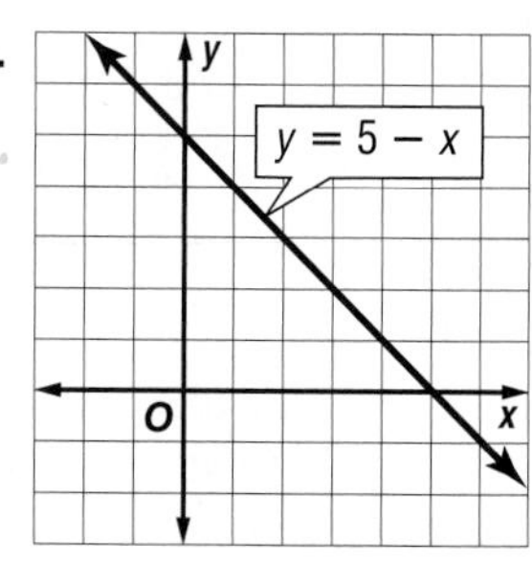

21.
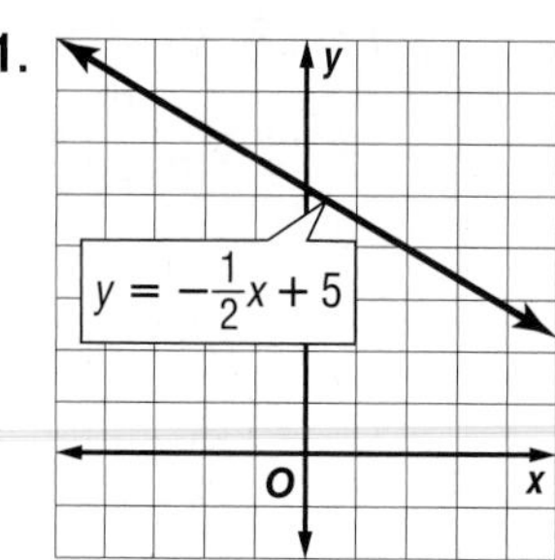

23.
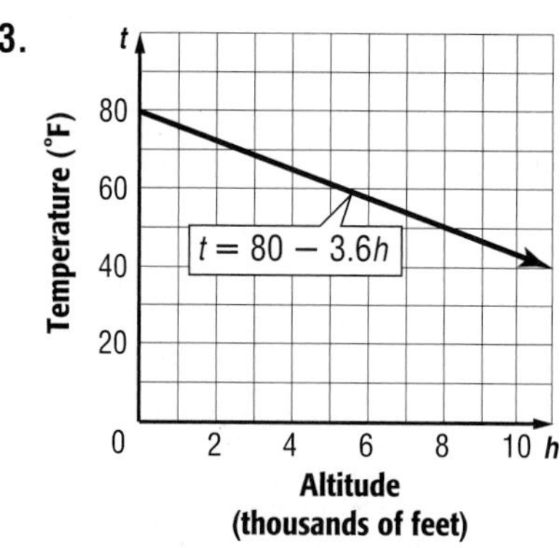

28.
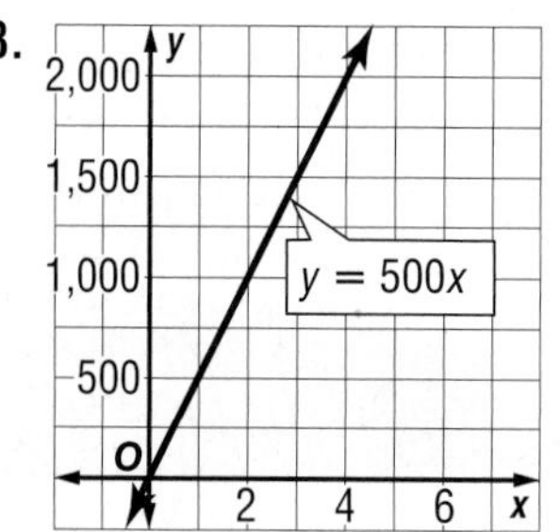

Page 529, Lesson 11-4

31. Sample answer:

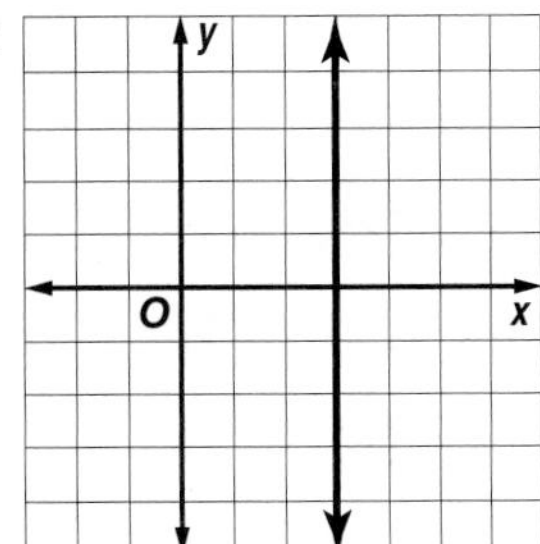

32.

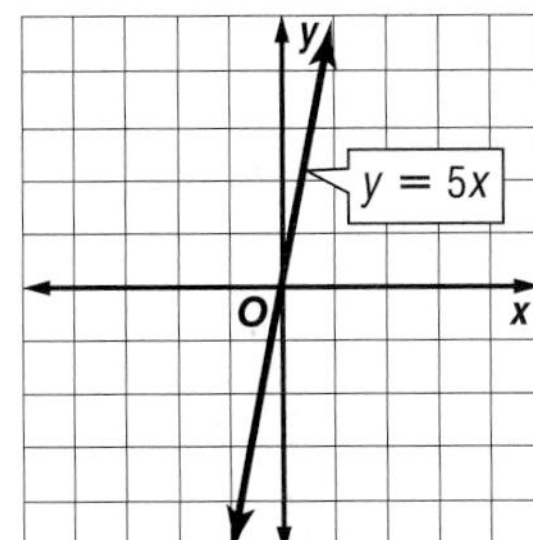

33.

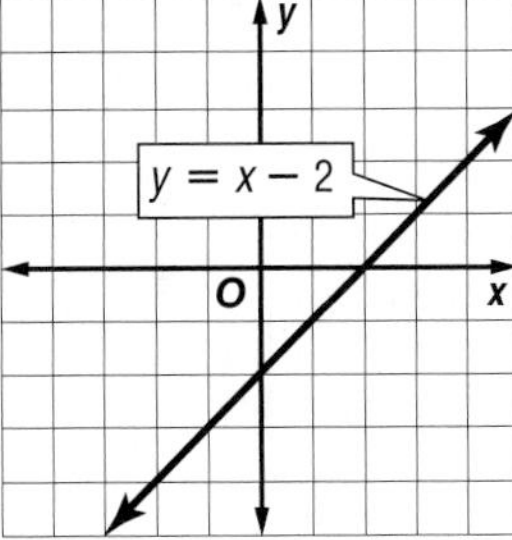

34.

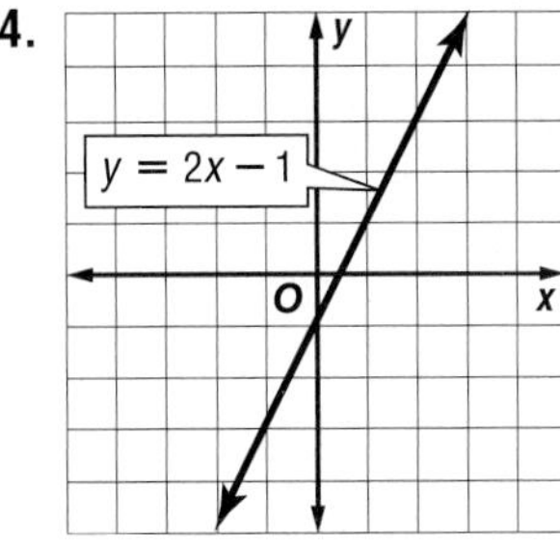

35.

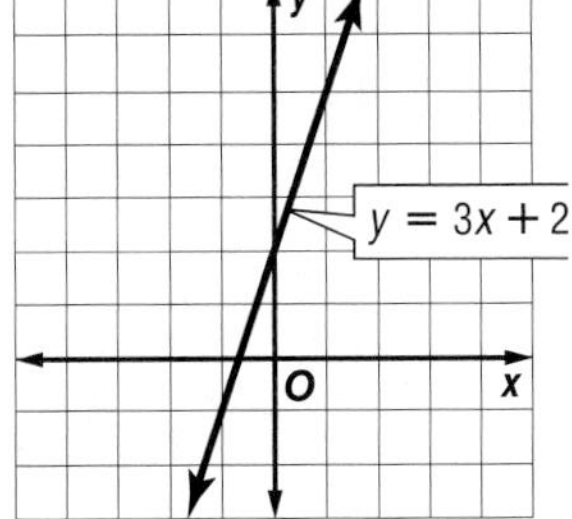

Page 534, Lesson 11-5 (Your Turn)

a.

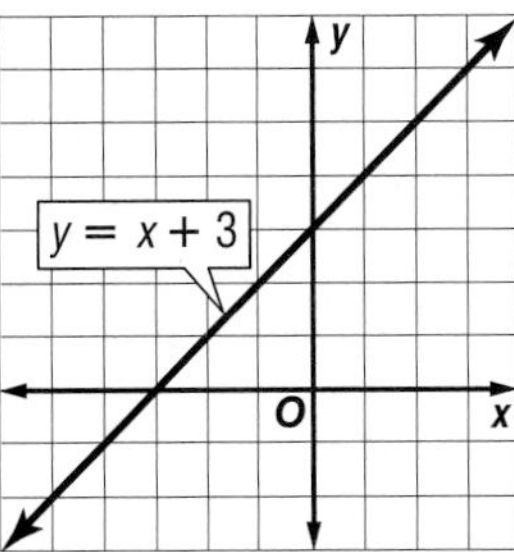

b.

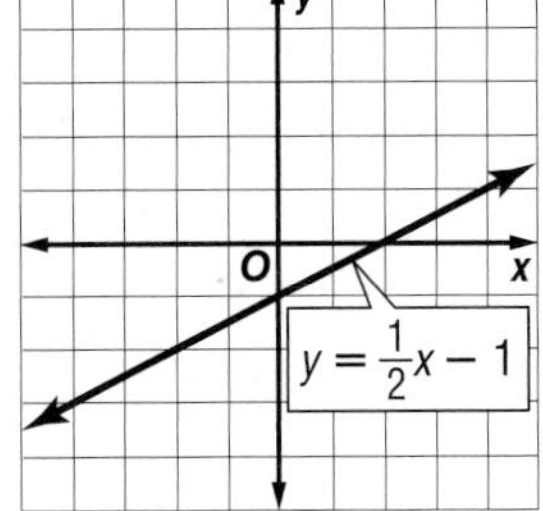

c.

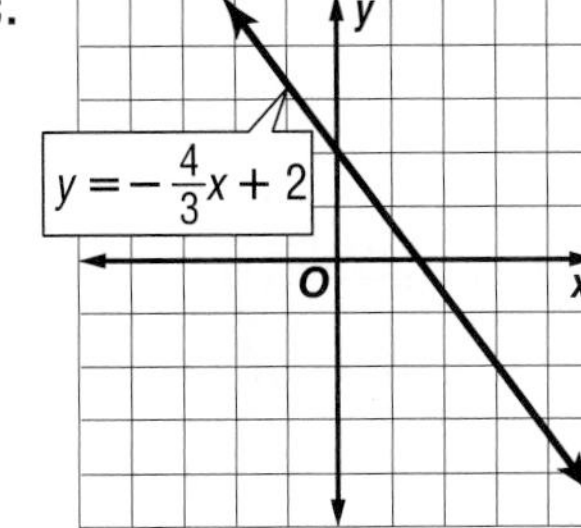

Page 535, Lesson 11-5

7.

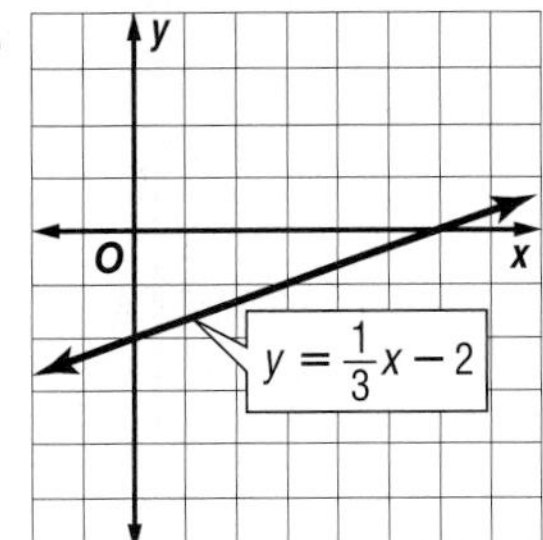

8.

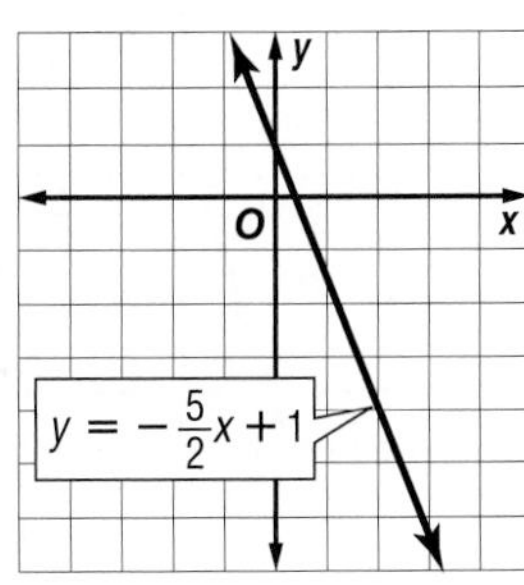

9.

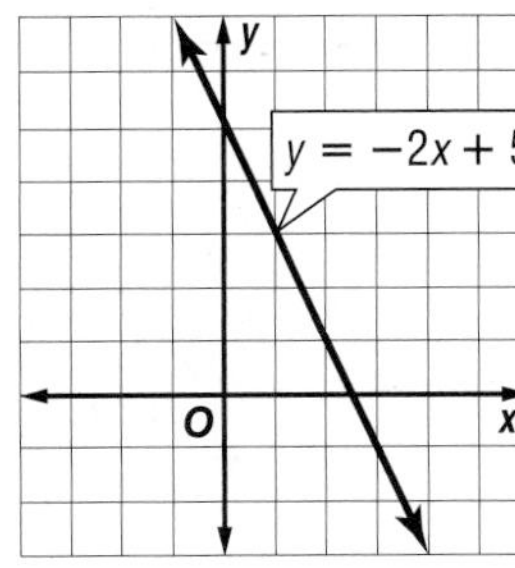

10.

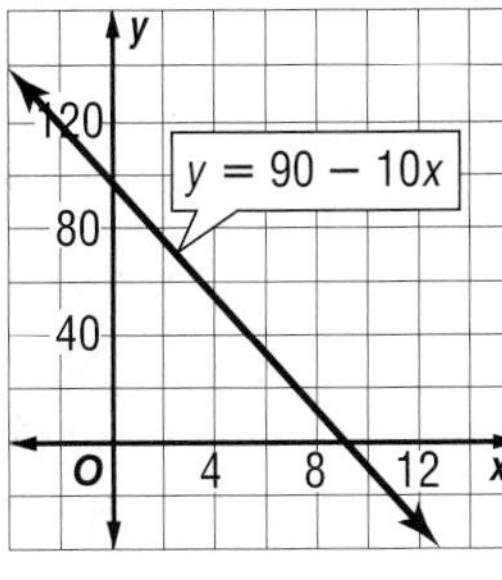

19.

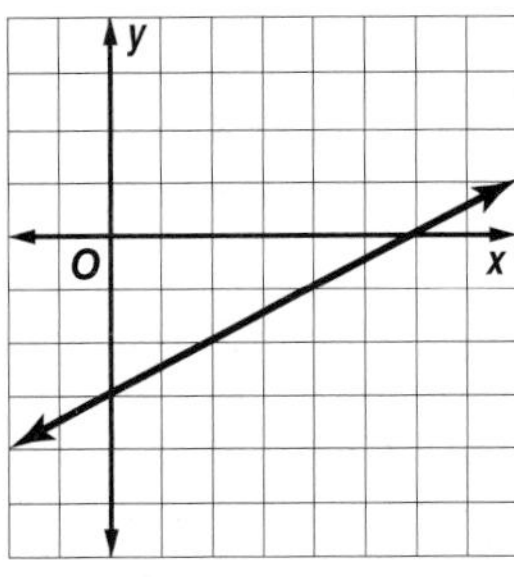

20.

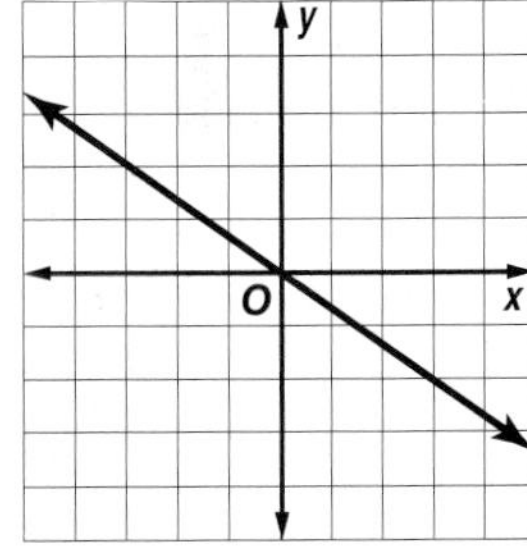

23.

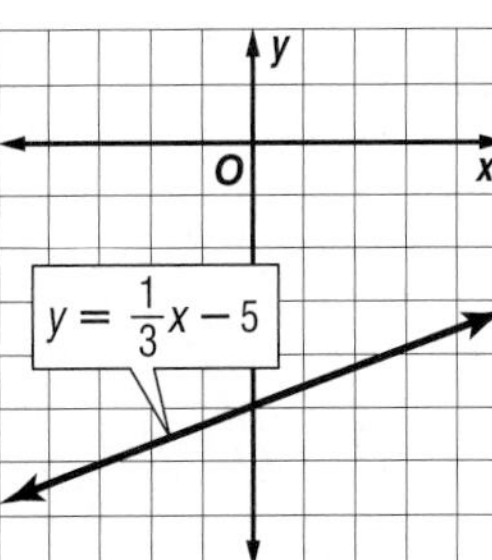

24.

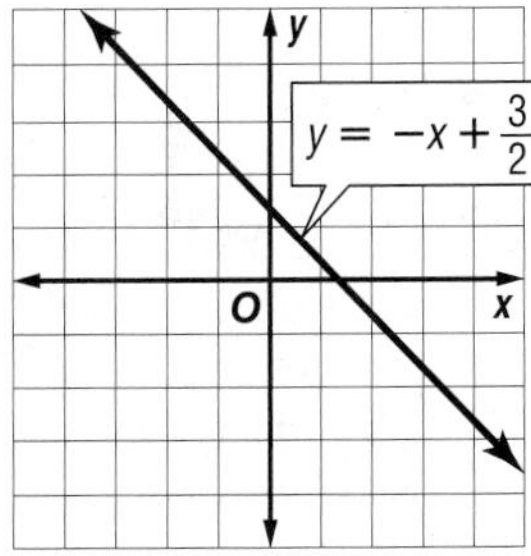

25.

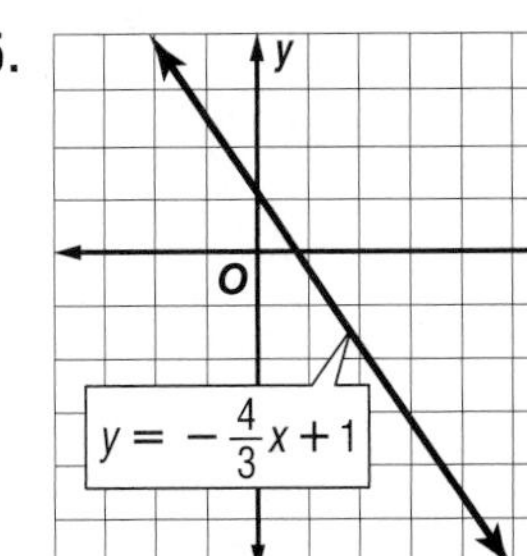

26.

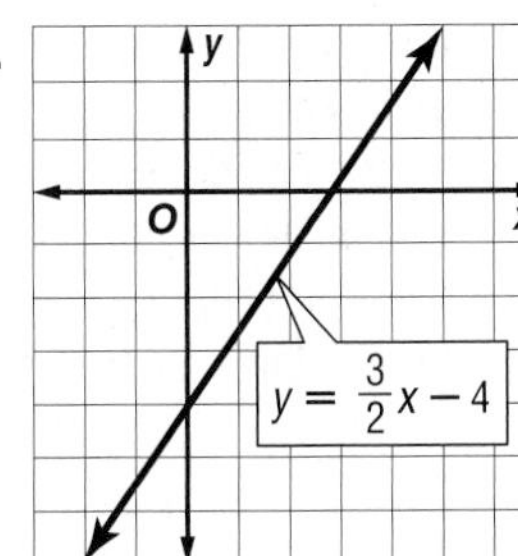

27.

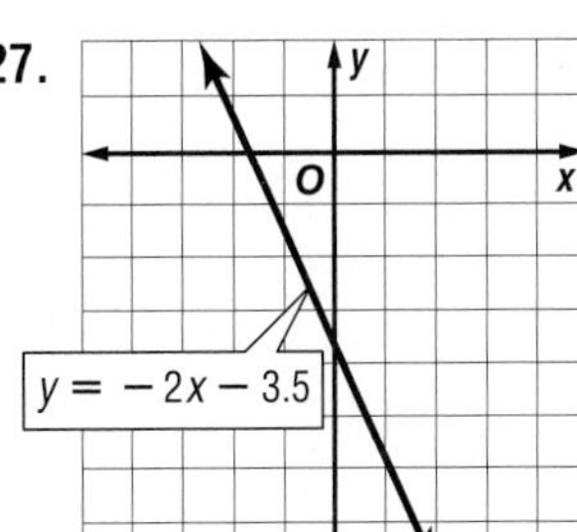

28.

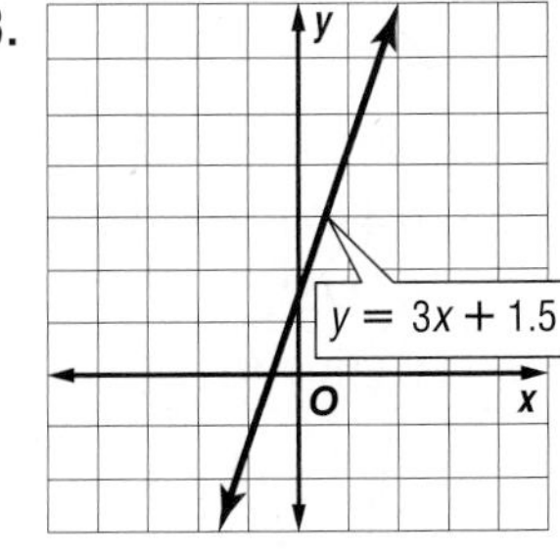

29.

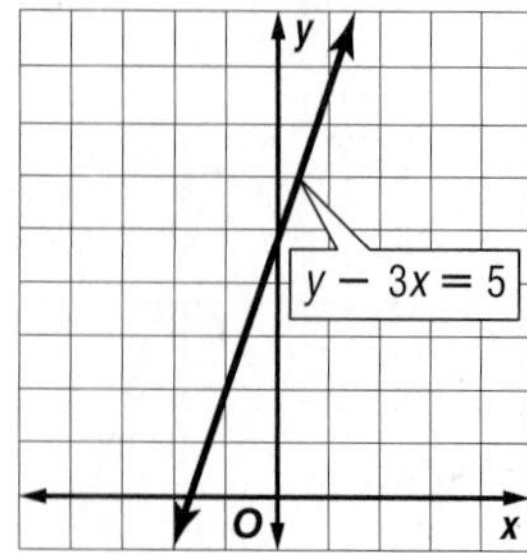

30.

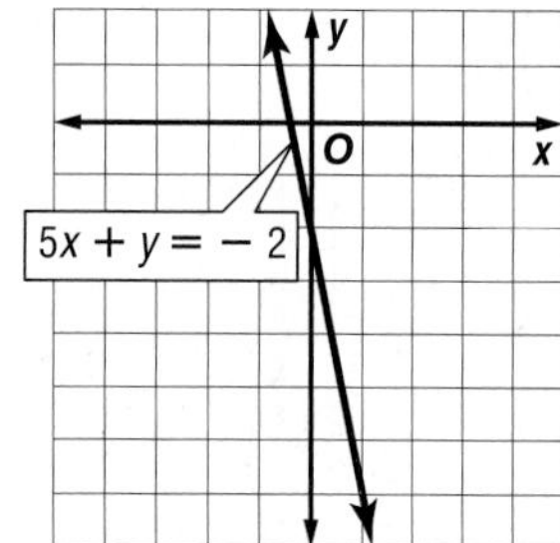

Page 536, Lesson 11-5

32.

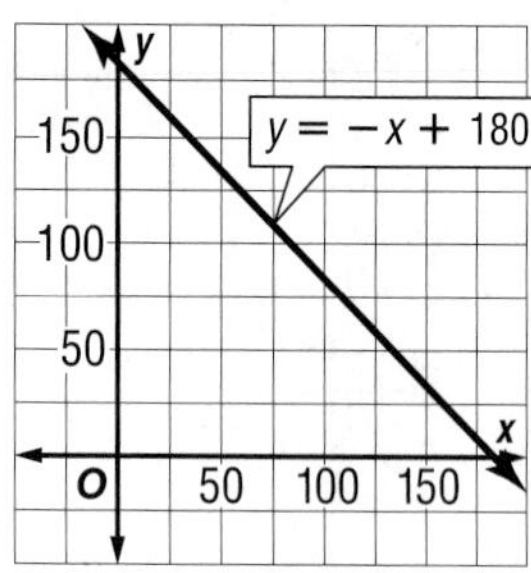

34.

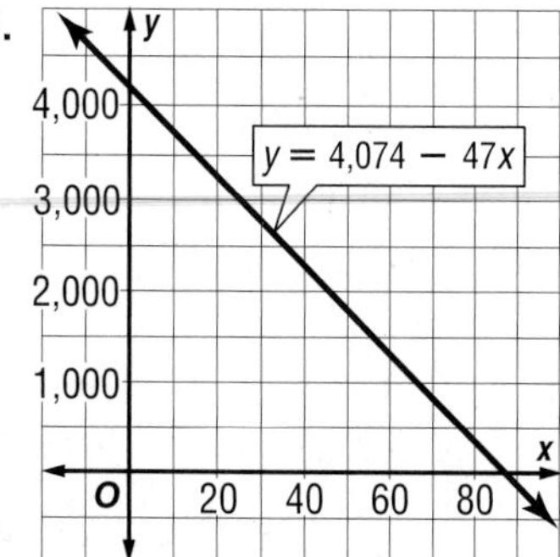

37. Sample answer: Jim is on a long hike. He has already gone 5 miles. He plans to hike 3 miles each hour. The distance y he has traveled in x hours can be determined by $y = 3x + 5$. Draw a graph of the function.
What does the slope represent? (the miles per hour) What does the y-intercept represent? (the distance already traveled)

45.

x	$0.39x$	y	(x, y)
0	0.39(0)	0	(0, 0)
1	0.39(1)	0.39	(1, 0.39)
2	0.39(2)	0.78	(2, 0.78)
3	0.39(3)	1.17	(3, 1.17)
4	0.39(4)	1.56	(4, 1.56)

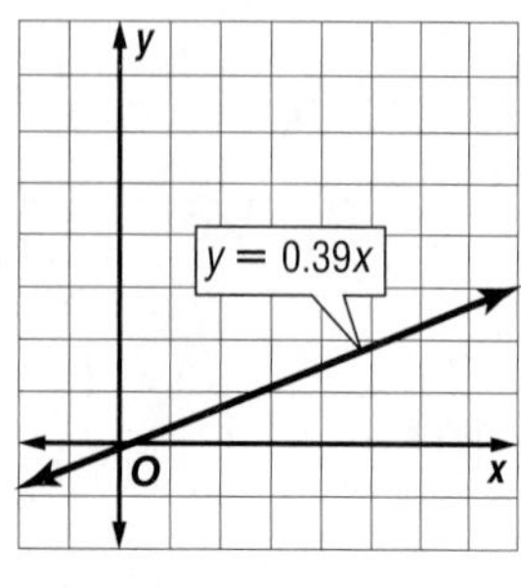

46–49.

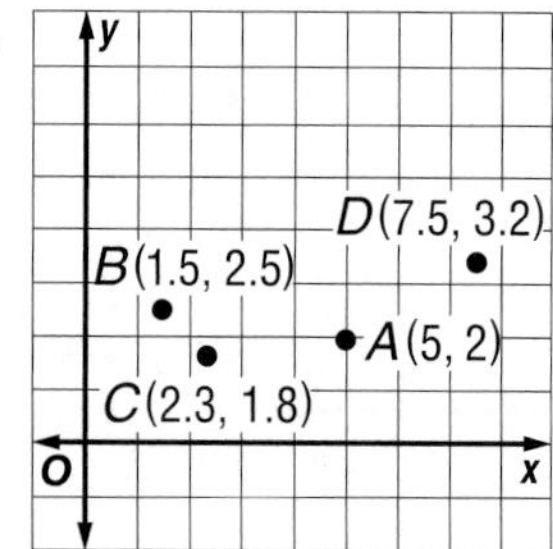

Page 542, Lesson 11-6

17.

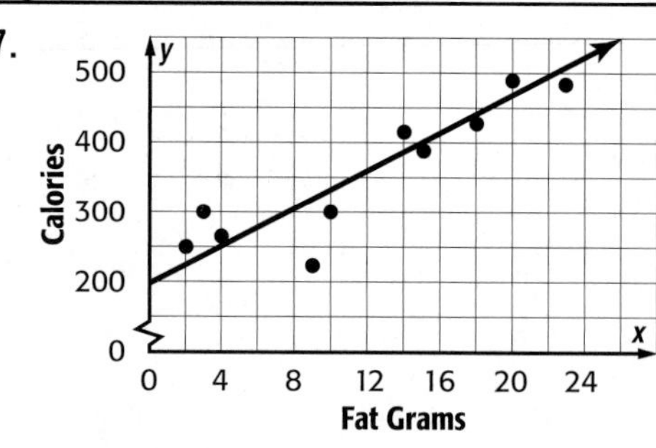

29.

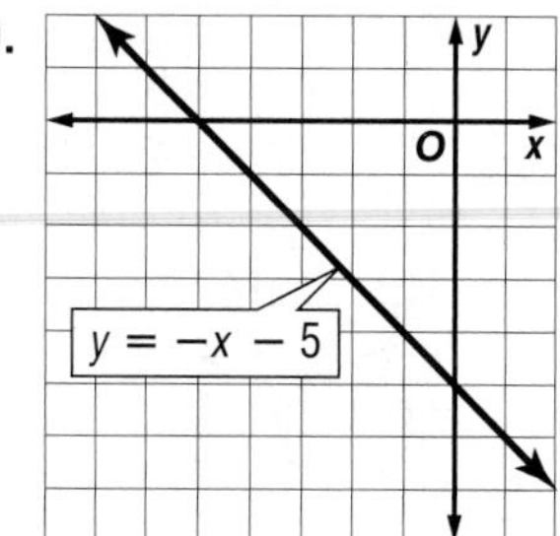

30.

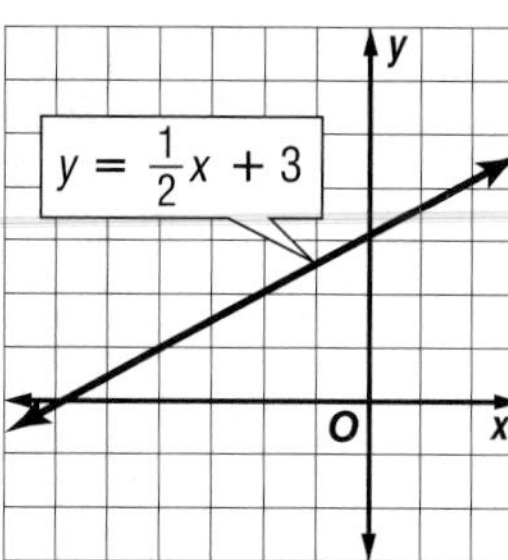

31.

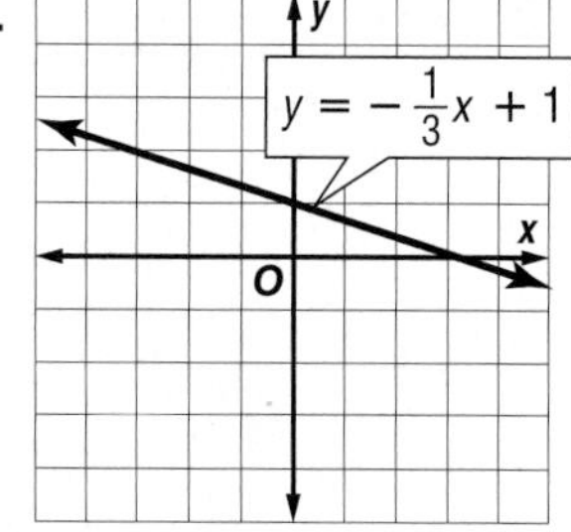

32.

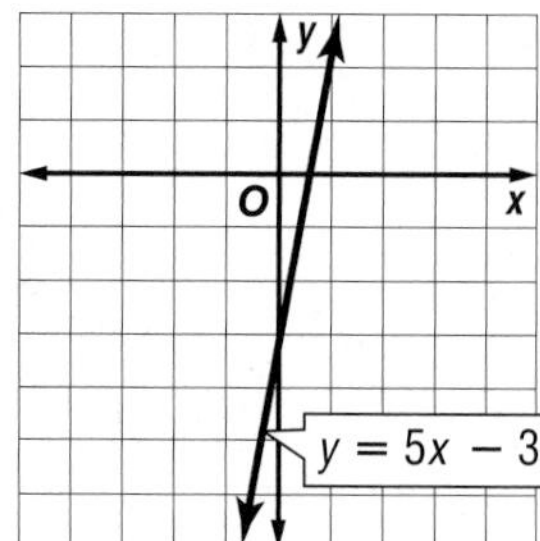

Page 544, Lesson 11-7 (When am I ever going to use this?)

1.

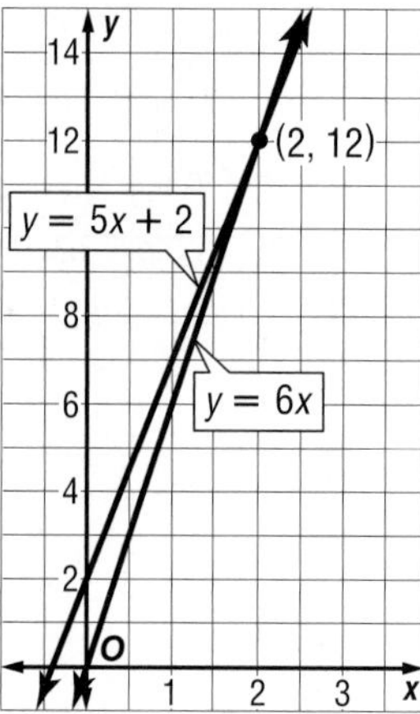

Pages 546–547, Lesson 11-7

4.

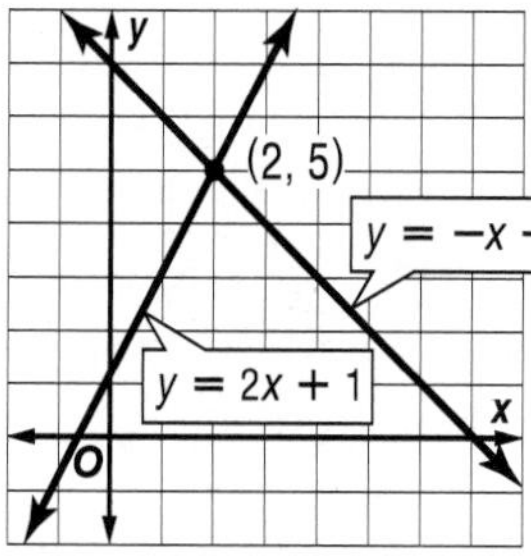

(2, 5)
y = −x + 7
y = 2x + 1

5. 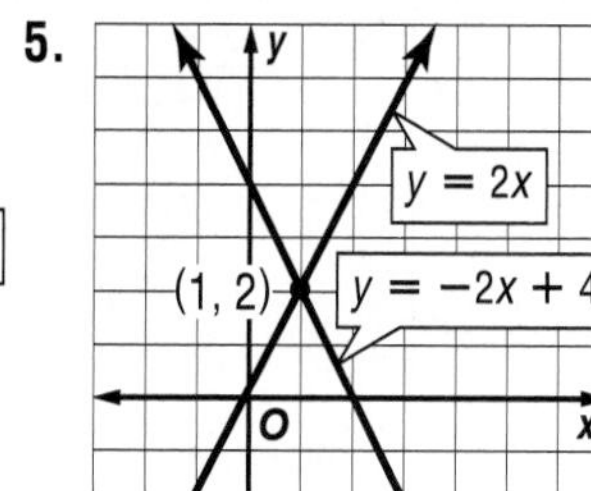

6.

y = 3x + 1
y = 3x − 1

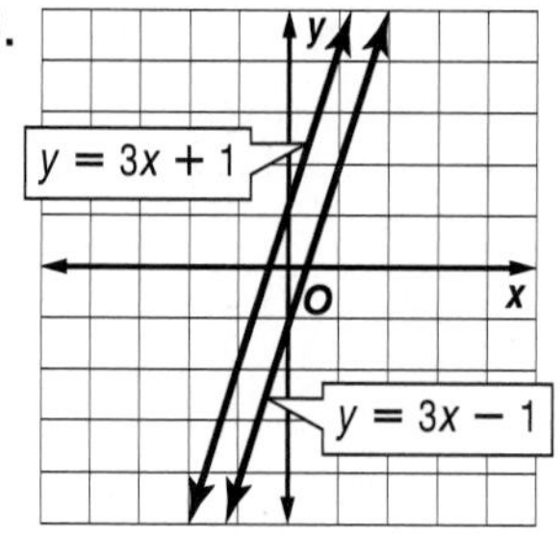

13. 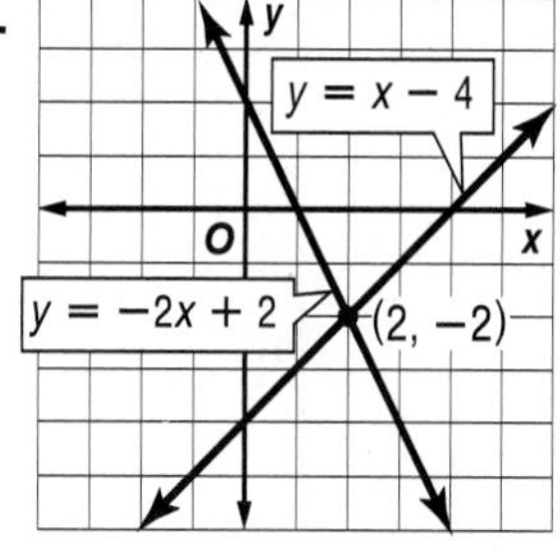

14. 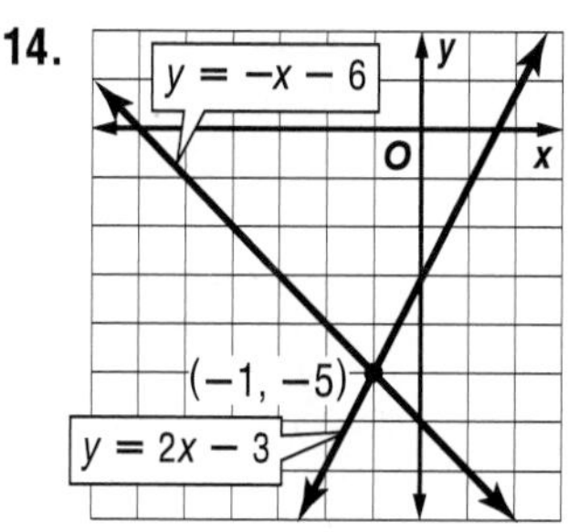

15. 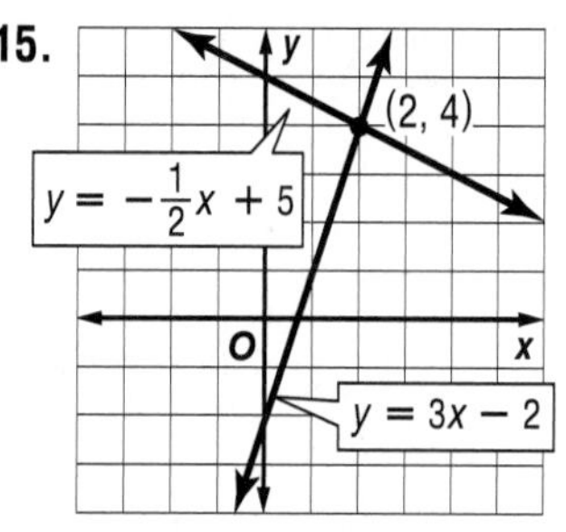

16. 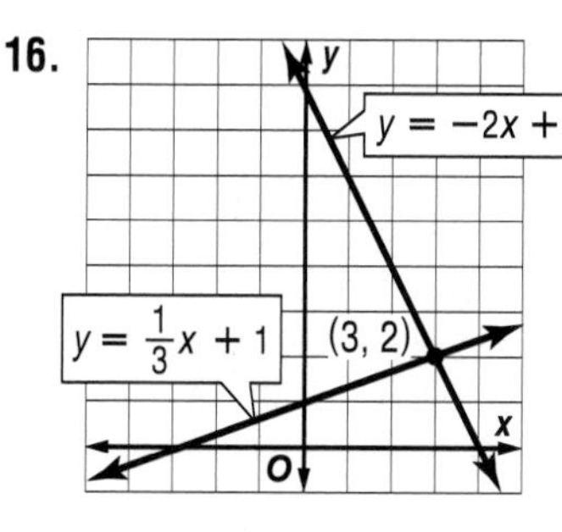

17. 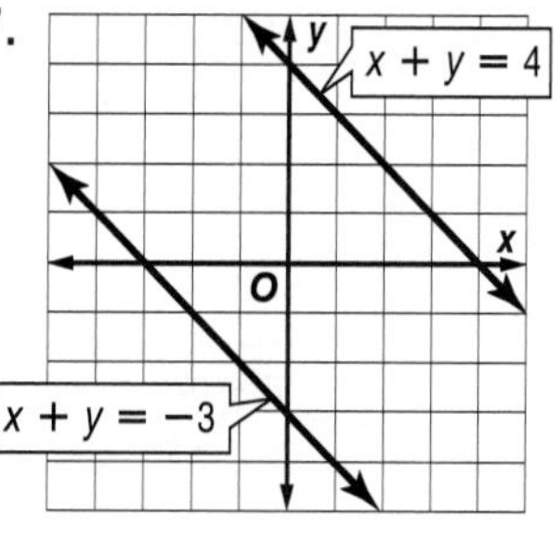

18. 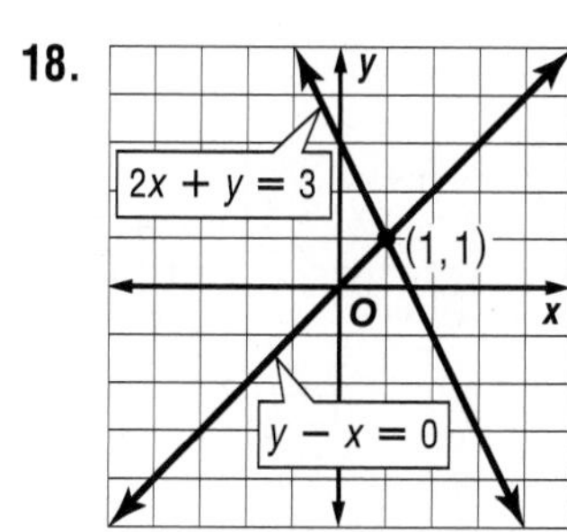

19. 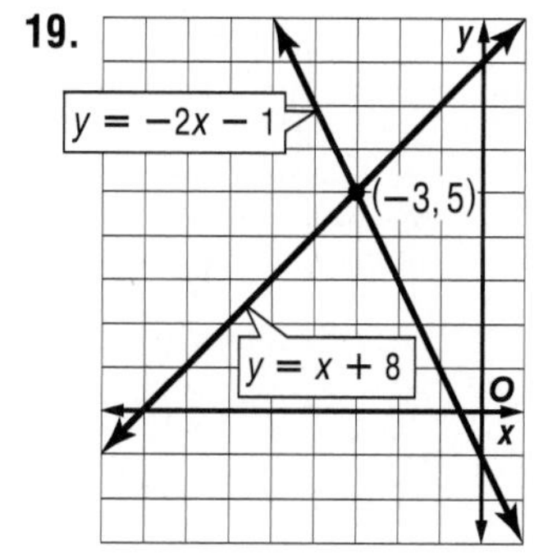

20. 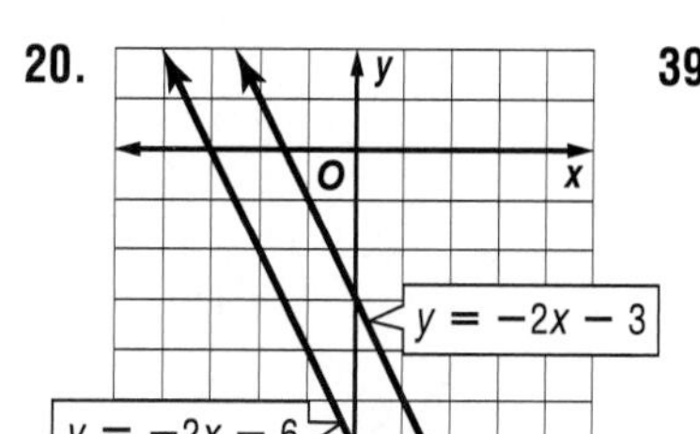

39. 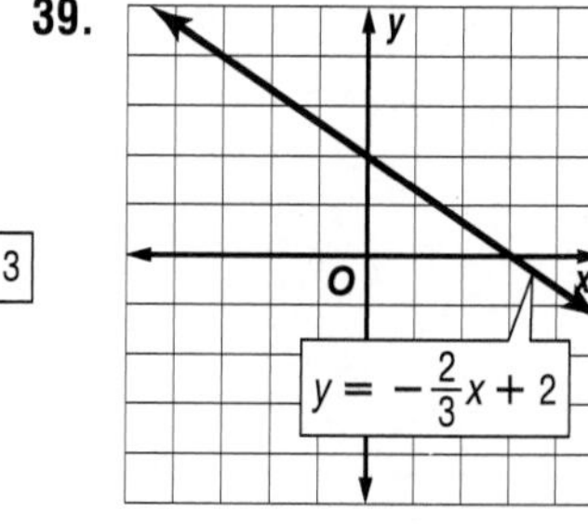

40. 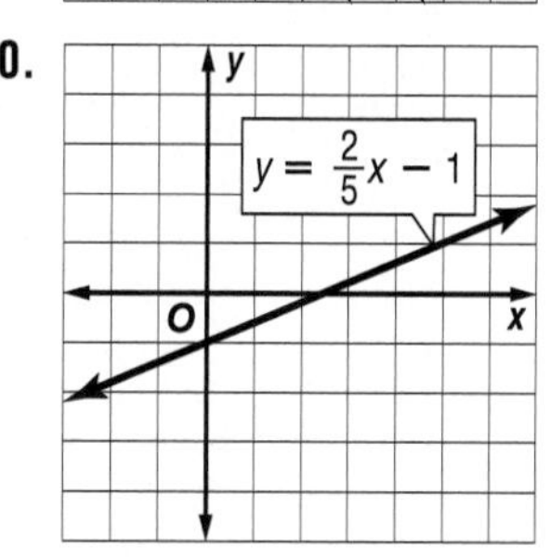

41. 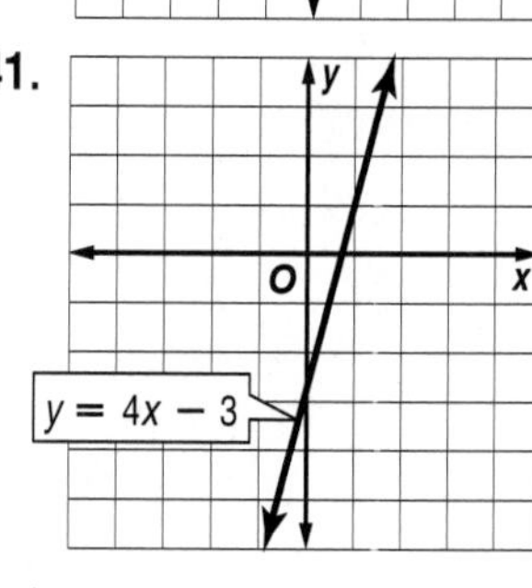

43. 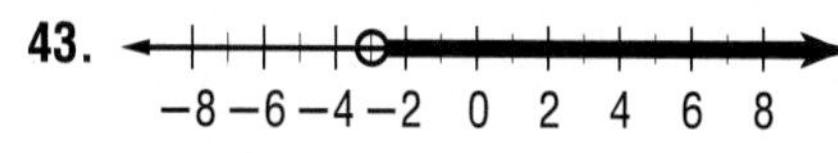

44. 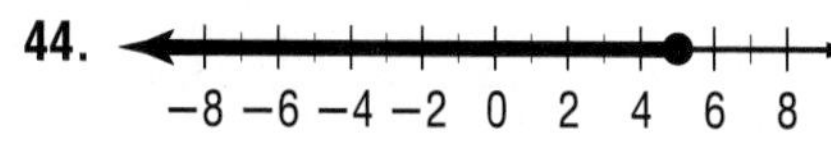

45. 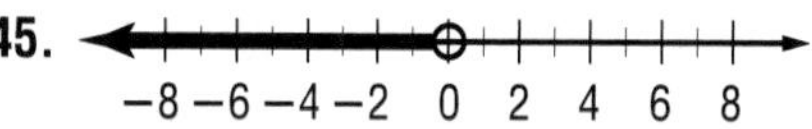

46.

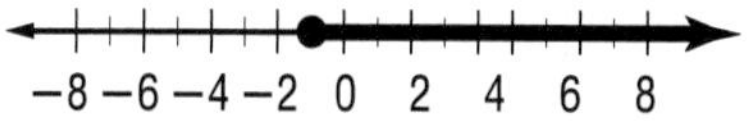

−8 −6 −4 −2 0 2 4 6 8

Pages 550–551, Lesson 11-8

8. 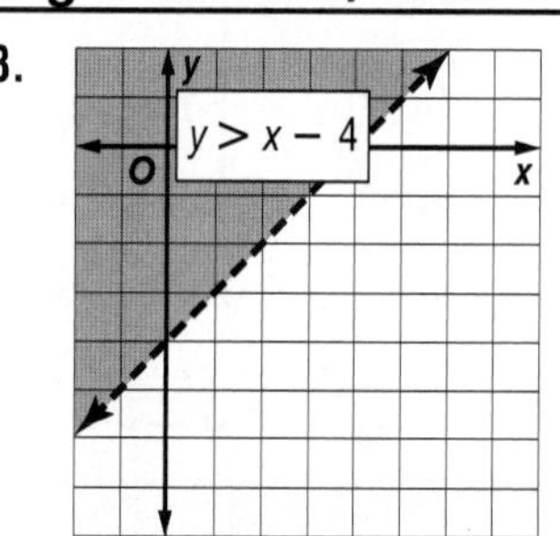

9. 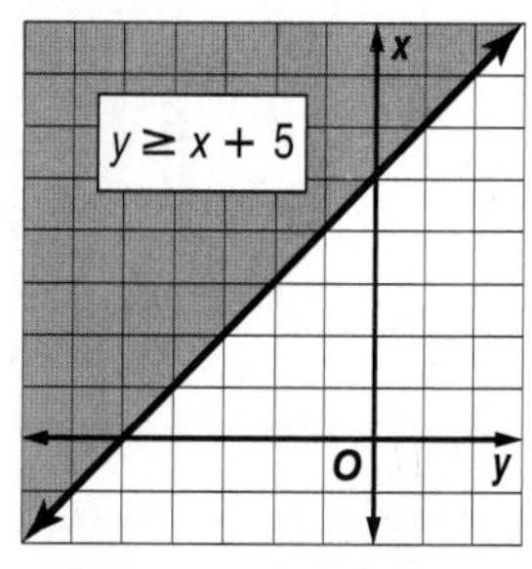

10. 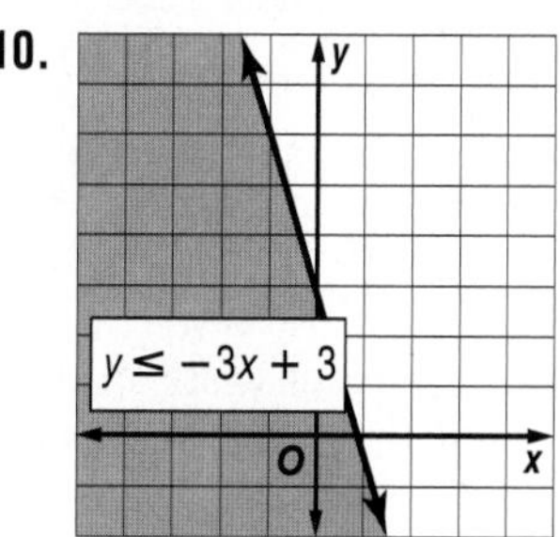

11. 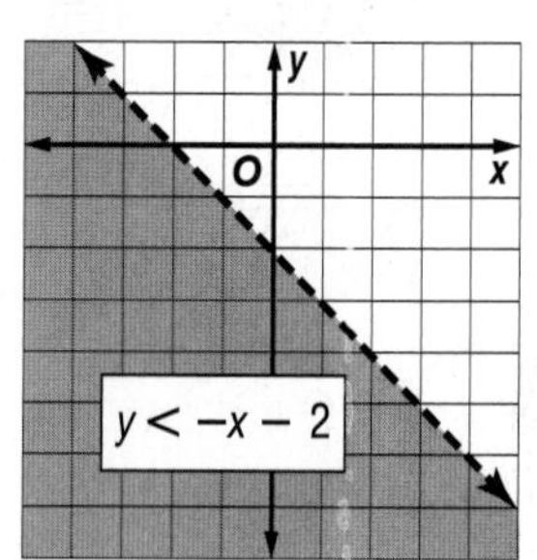

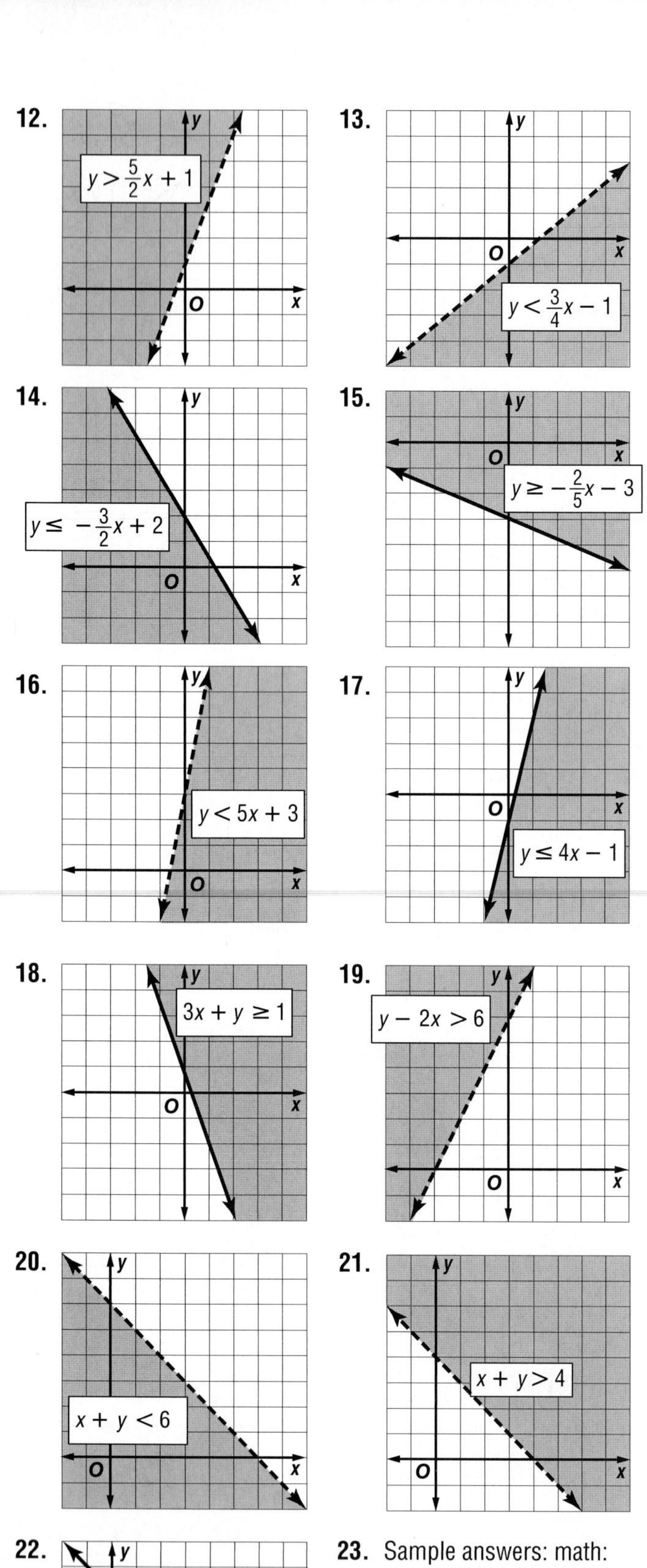

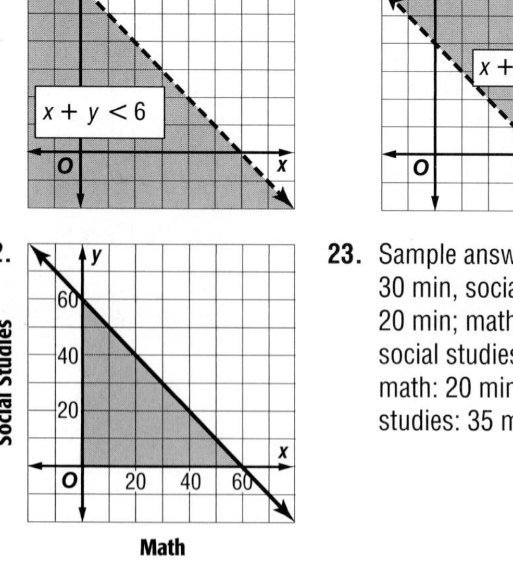

23. Sample answers: math: 30 min, social studies: 20 min; math: 25 min, social studies: 25 min; math: 20 min, social studies: 35 min

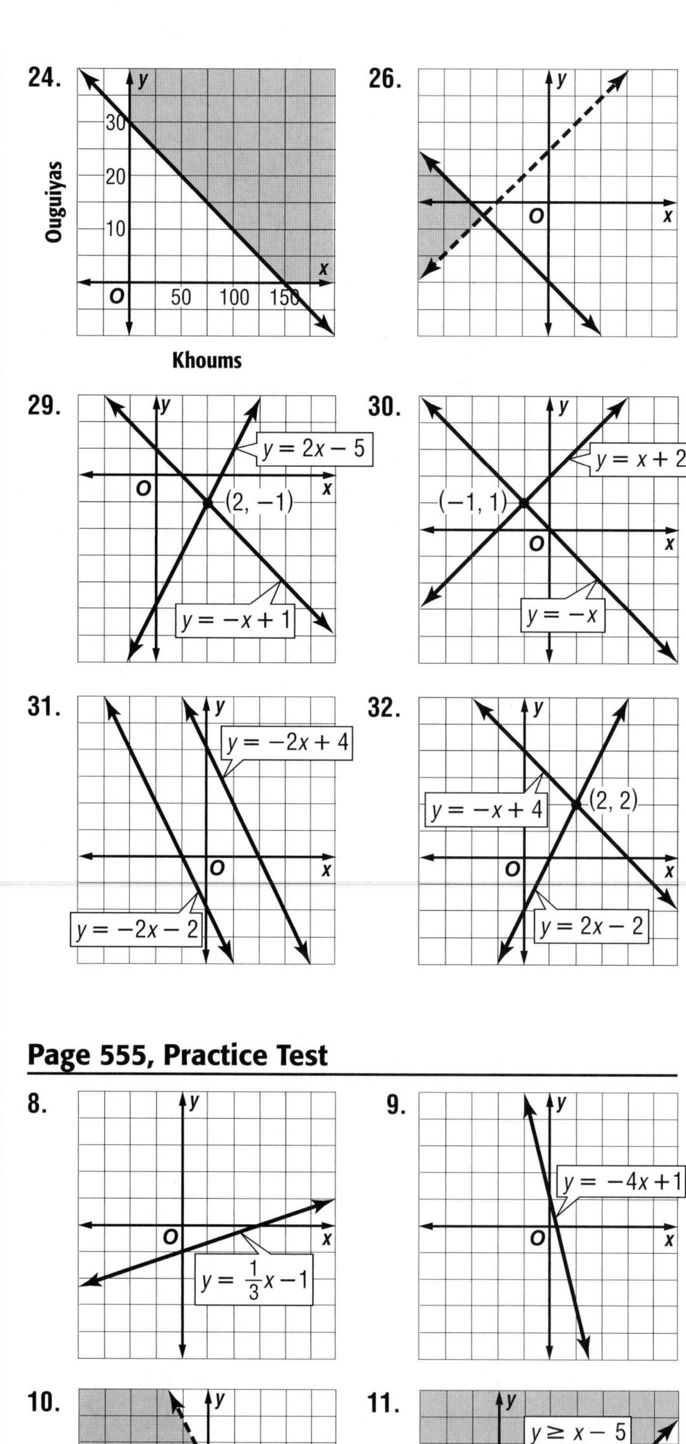

Page 555, Practice Test

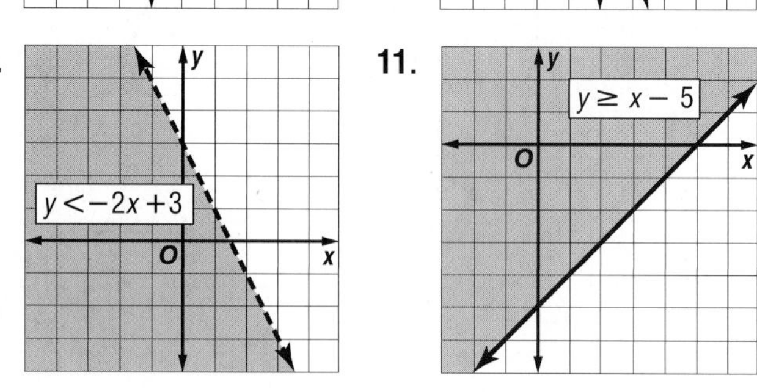

15. 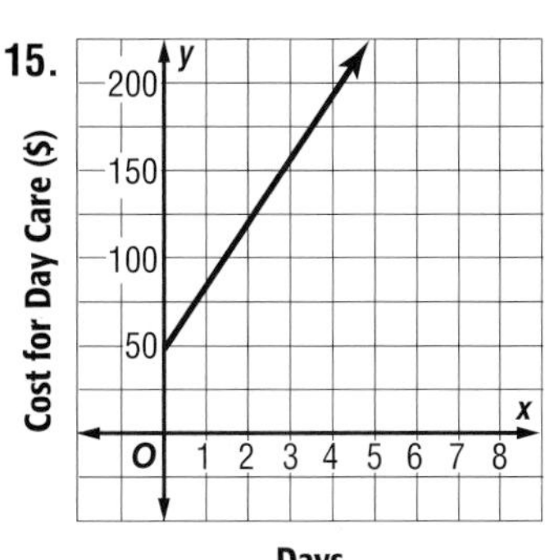

18. 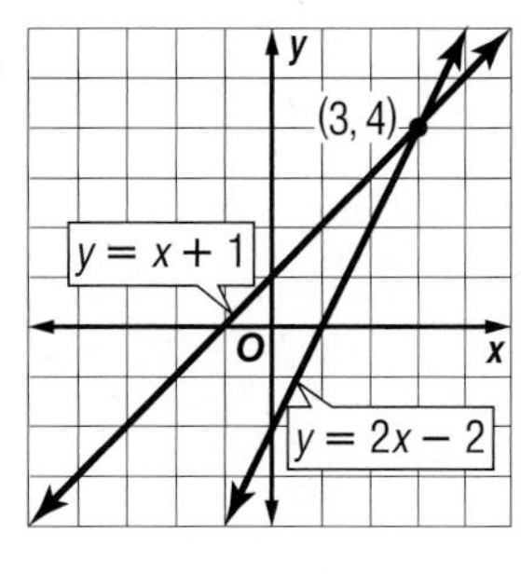

Page 557, Standardized Test Practice

14. 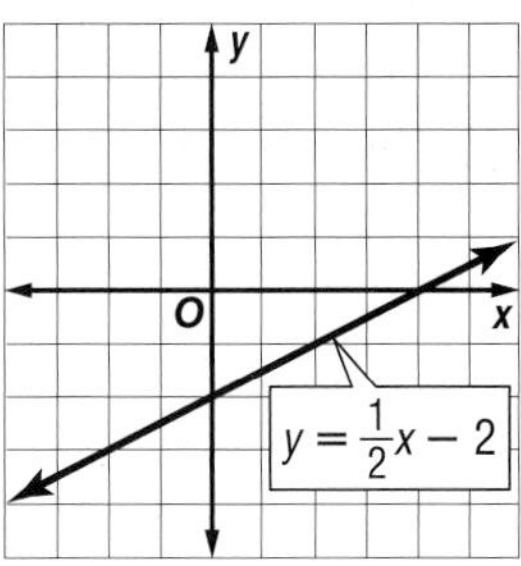

17b. 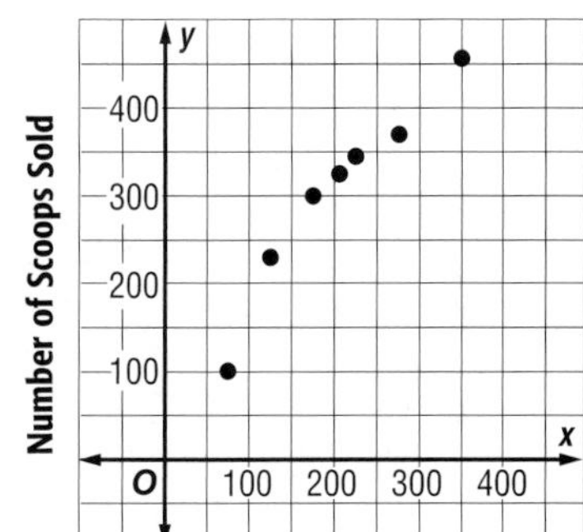

17c. The number of scoops sold increases as the number of customers increases.

18b. 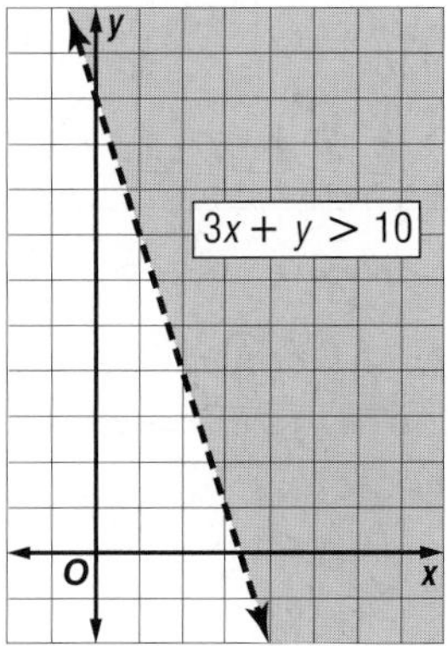

18c. The graph shows all ordered pairs that satisfy the inequality. However, only the ordered pairs that are nonnegative integers satisfy the situation. Also, the sum of the numbers in the ordered pairs cannot exceed the number of games the team plays.

CHAPTER 12

Chapter Overview

Algebra: Nonlinear Functions and Polynomials

	LESSON OBJECTIVES	NCTM Standards	NAEP 2005	State/Local Objectives
12-1	**Linear and Nonlinear Functions** (pp. 560–563) • Determine whether a function is linear or nonlinear.	1, 6, 7, 10	D1a, A2c, A1e, A2g	
12-2	**Graphing Quadratic Functions** (pp. 564–568) **12-2a Graphing Calculator Investigation:** Use a graphing calculator to graph families of quadratic functions. • Graph quadratic functions.	1, 2, 6, 7, 10	A2a, A2c, A2g, A2a, A1e	
12-3	**Simplifying Polynomials** (pp. 569–573) **12-3a Hands-On Lab:** Model expressions using algebra tiles. • Simplify polynomials.	1, 2, 6, 7, 9, 10	A3b, N5e	
12-4	**Adding Polynomials** (pp. 574–577) • Add polynomials.	1, 6, 7, 10	A3b, A3a, A4a, N3f, N5e	
12-5	**Subtracting Polynomials** (pp. 580–583) • Subtract polynomials.	1, 6, 7, 9, 10	A3b, N3f, A3a	
12-6	**Multiplying and Dividing Monomials** (pp. 584–587) • Multiply and divide monomials.	1, 2, 6, 7, 9, 10	A1a, N3f, A3b	
12-7	**Multiplying Monomials and Polynomials** (pp. 588–592) **12-7a Problem-Solving Strategy:** Solve problems by making a model. • Multiply monomials and polynomials.	1, 2, 6, 7, 9, 10	N3f, N5e, A3b, A3a, M1h, G3c	

Key to NCTM Standards:

1=Number & Operations, 2=Algebra, 3=Geometry, 4=Measurement, 5=Data Analysis & Probability, 6=Problem Solving, 7=Reasoning & Proof, 8=Communication, 9=Connections, 10=Representation

NAEP 2005 Standards: See Teacher Resources at math.glencoe.com

Pacing suggestions for the entire year can be found on page T23.

*An electronic version of this chapter is available on **StudentWorks**™. This backpack solution CD-ROM allows students instant access to the Student Edition, lesson worksheet pages, and web resources.*

Chapter Resource Manager

Chapter 12 Resource Masters

Study Guide and Intervention	Practice (Skills and Word Problems)	Reading to Learn Mathematics	Enrichment	Assessment	Applications*	Parent and Student Study Guide Online Worksheets	5-Minute Check Transparencies	Key Teaching Transparencies	MathPASS: Tutorial Plus (lessons)	Teaching Mathematics with Manipulatives	Noteables™: Interactive Study Notebook	Optional Materials
679	680–681	682	683		SM 61–64, 65–68	12-1	12-1				12-1	
684	685–686	687	688	729	SM 69–72 CS 49	12-2	12-2	45			12-2	
689	690–691	692	693		RC 38	12-3	12-3	46	48	112	12-3	
694	695–696	697	698	729, 731	CS 50	12-4	12-4	47			12-4	
699	700–701	702	703			12-5	12-5	48		113	12-5	
704	705–706	707	708	730		12-6	12-6			114–115	12-6	
709	710–711	712	713	715–728, 730, 732–746	CM 39–40	12-7	12-7				12-7	

*** Key to Abbreviations:** *CS = Calculator and Spreadsheet Masters, RC = Real-Life Career Masters, CM = Classroom Math Games (online), SM = Science and Math Lab Manual (online)*

PowerPoint® Presentations

This CD-ROM is a customizable Microsoft® PowerPoint® presentation that includes:

- In-Class Examples
- Links to Online Study Tools
- 5-Minute Check Transparencies
- Your Turn Exercises

Math Skills Maintenance

Use the Math Skills Maintenance Masters to keep your students' basic math skills fresh. Students can review skills one at a time or in a combined format. The Masters are also available online at msmath3.net/maintenance.

CHAPTER 12 Mathematical Content and Teaching Strategies

Continuity of Instruction

Building on Prior Knowledge

Students previously have learned to identify linear equations. They understand that the graph of a linear equation is a straight line. They know that the sum of a number and its additive inverse is zero. They also know how to apply the Distributive Property to algebraic expressions. Students are familiar with exponents.

Learning in This Chapter

In the first part of this chapter, students build on their knowledge of linear functions by comparing them to nonlinear functions, or functions in which the rate of change is not constant. Students learn about monomials, which are single terms in an expression, and sums of monomials, or polynomials. They use what they have learned about additive inverses to add and subtract.

Making Future Connections

Students will extend their skills for simplifying algebraic expressions by learning to divide by polynomials. They will use multiplication and division of monomials in factoring polynomials and in solving quadratic equations. Other future topics that build on skills presented in this chapter include multiplying two binomials and graphing cubic and exponential functions.

Mathematical Background

12-1 Linear and Nonlinear Functions

Students will encounter linear and nonlinear functions throughout their academic careers. In physics, the graph of position vs. time is linear for an object moving at a constant velocity, but nonlinear if the velocity is changing. Graphs used in radioactive dating and graphs showing population changes over time are also nonlinear.

Team Teaching

Inform the other teachers on your team that your students are studying linear and nonlinear functions. Suggestions for curriculum integration are:

Physical Science: the conduction of heat through a material, the acceleration of a moving object

Earth Science: the speed of waves during an earthquake

Social Studies: population growth

12-2 Graphing Quadratic Functions

Functions in which the greatest power of the variable is two are called quadratic functions. The equations $y = -x^2$ and $y = x^2 + 3$ are examples of quadratic functions. Quadratic functions can be used to solve many problems, such as how the surface area of a circular object changes as its radius changes.

12-3 Simplifying Polynomials

Encourage students to use standard form when they write polynomials. A polynomial in standard form is simplified so that the powers of the variable decrease from left to right. Standard form will help students see like and unlike terms, and it will be especially important in later courses when students are factoring and graphing more complex polynomials.

12-4 Adding Polynomials

Students learn two methods for adding polynomials. Encourage them to use either method as they become accustomed to this process. As they become more comfortable, they will probably gravitate toward the horizontal method. When adding polynomials, students can drop the parentheses in order to add like terms.

12-5 Subtracting Polynomials

Subtracting polynomials is similar to subtracting integers. Keep the first expression the same, change subtraction to addition, and take the opposite of the second expression. Then add like terms.

Teacher to Teacher

Dana Schaefer
Coachman Fundamental
Middle School
Clearwater, FL

"I have students use placeholders for terms with a coefficient of zero when performing subtraction problems. This avoids confusion with empty spaces in the problem."

$$\begin{array}{lr} & 6y^2 \quad\quad - 5 \\ (-) & -3y + 4 \\ \hline \end{array} \rightarrow \begin{array}{lr} & 6y^2 + 0y - 5 \\ (-) & -3y + 4 \\ \hline \end{array}$$

Dana Schaefer

12-6 Multiplying and Dividing Monomials

Students may have trouble remembering that the bases must be the same and are not combined when using the Product of Powers and Quotient of Powers rules. Encourage students to write out all the factors represented by an exponent for a few simple problems. For example, writing $a^2 \cdot a^3$ as $(a \cdot a) \cdot (a \cdot a \cdot a)$ will make the answer, $a^2 \cdot a^3 = a^5$, easy to see.

12-7 Multiplying Monomials and Polynomials

If students are confused or overwhelmed by the increasing complexity of polynomials in this chapter, encourage them to regard each step they take in solving a problem individually. For example, using the Distributive Property entails multiplying polynomials to get rid of parentheses. Next, group the like terms. Then, simplify by using addition and subtraction. A systematic approach will help students solve increasingly difficult problems

In-Class Speaker

Functions and polynomials are used almost every day by engineers in various fields. For example, civil engineers use linear equations to describe the forces in the structure of a building. Electrical engineers use linear equations in circuit design and analysis. Invite an engineer to visit the class and describe how functions are used in his or her work. Explain to the engineer ahead of time what the class is studying. Encourage students to think of questions for the engineer before the visit.

What the Research Says

According to Yerushalmy and Schwarz in *Integrating Research on the Graphical Representation of Functions,* graph-plotting technology helps students shift attention from the process of making graphs to analyzing and manipulating the graph itself.

- **In Lesson 12-2a, students use a graphing calculator to explore families of quadratic functions.**

McGraw-Hill Professional Development

Mathematics, YES! is a self-paced, web-based professional development program. Units are based on major mathematical concepts and are standards-based. Actual classroom videos provide a springboard for discussion and activities. Units appropriate for this chapter:

- Patterns and Functions
- Coordinate Pairs and Graphing
- Solving Equations and Inequalities

DAILY INTERVENTION and Assessment

* **Key to Abbreviations:**
TWE = Teacher Wraparound Edition, *CRM* = Chapter Resource Masters

	Type	Student Edition	Teacher Resources	Technology/Internet
INTERVENTION	Ongoing	Prerequisite Skills, pp. 559, 563, 568, 573, 577, 583, 587 Mid-Chapter Practice Test, p. 578	5-Minute Check Transparencies Quizzes 1–4, *CRM*, pp. 729–730 Mid-Chapter Test, *CRM*, p. 731 Study Guide and Intervention, *CRM*, pp. 679, 684, 689, 694, 699, 704, 709	MathPASS: Tutorial Plus msmath3.net/self_check_quiz msmath3.net/extra_examples
	Mixed Review	pp. 563, 568, 573, 577, 583, 587, 592	Cumulative Review, *CRM*, p. 732	
	Error Analysis	Find the Error, pp. 576, 582, 591	Find the Error, *TWE*, pp. 576, 582, 591 Unlocking Misconceptions, *TWE*, pp. 560, 581 Tips for New Teachers, *TWE*, pp. 566, 581	
ASSESSMENT	Standardized Test Practice	pp. 563, 568, 573, 575, 577, 578, 583, 587, 589, 592, 595, 596–597	Standardized Test Practice, *CRM*, pp. 733–734	Standardized Test Practice CD-ROM msmath3.net/standardized_test
	Open-Ended Assessment	Writing Math, pp. 567, 569, 572, 586 Open-Ended, pp. 562, 567, 572, 576, 578, 582, 586, 591 Standardized Test, p. 597	Modeling: *TWE*, pp. 573, 589 Speaking: *TWE*, pp. 568, 583 Writing: *TWE*, pp. 577, 591 Extended Response Assessment, *CRM*, p. 727	
	Chapter Assessment	Study Guide, pp. 593–594 Practice Test, p. 595	Multiple-Choice Tests (Forms 1, 2A, 2B), *CRM*, pp. 715–720 Free-Response Tests (Forms 2C, 2D, 3), *CRM*, pp. 721–726 Vocabulary Test/Review, *CRM*, p. 728	Exam View® Pro Testmaker (see below) MindJogger Videoquizzes msmath3.net/vocabulary_review msmath3.net/chapter_test

For more information on Yearly ProgressPro, see p. 464.

Glencoe Lesson	Yearly ProgressPro Skill Name
12-1	Linear and Non-Linear Functions
12-2	Graphing Quadratic Functions
12-3	Simplifying Polynomials
12-4	Adding Polynomials
12-5	Subtracting Polynomials
12-6	Multiplying and Dividing Monomials
12-7	Multiplying Monomials and Polynomials

ExamView® Pro

Use ExamView® Pro Testmaker CD-ROM to:

- **Create multiple versions of tests.**
- **Create modified tests for inclusion students with one mouse click.**
- **Edit existing questions and add your own questions.**
- **Build tests aligned with state standards using built-in state curriculum correlations.**
- **Change English tests to Spanish with one mouse click and vice versa.**

Reading and Writing in Mathematics

READING in the Content Area

This online worksheet provides strategies for reading and analyzing Lesson 12-3, Simplifying Polynomials. Students are guided through questions about the main idea, subject matter, supporting details, conclusion, clarifying details, and vocabulary of the lesson.

Interactive Study Notebook With Foldables™ is a study organizer that provides helpful steps for students to follow to organize their notes for Chapter 12.

- Students use Noteables to record notes and to complete their Foldables as you present the material in Lessons 12-1 through 12-7.
- Noteables follow the *Teacher Wraparound Edition's* In-Class Examples and *Interactive Chalkboard CD-ROM.*

For more information on Reading and Writing in Mathematics, see pp. T6–T7.

Recommended Outside Reading for Students

Nonfiction

- Thompson, Frances, and Boyd, Cindy. *Hands-On Algebra: Ready-to-Use Games & Activities for Grades 7-12.* Jossey-Bass, ©1998.

  The games and activities in this book help make algebra fun and easy for students. Activities relating to lessons in this chapter include topics on functions and polynomials.

Fiction

- Tumanov, Vladimir. *Jayden's Rescue.* Scholastic, ©2002.

  This story mixes fantasy and suspense to present mathematics in an exciting way. A boy named Alex and his friends must solve math riddles to save the imprisoned queen Jayden and, ultimately, themselves. Perhaps the greatest benefit students will gain from this book is practice in problem-solving skills.

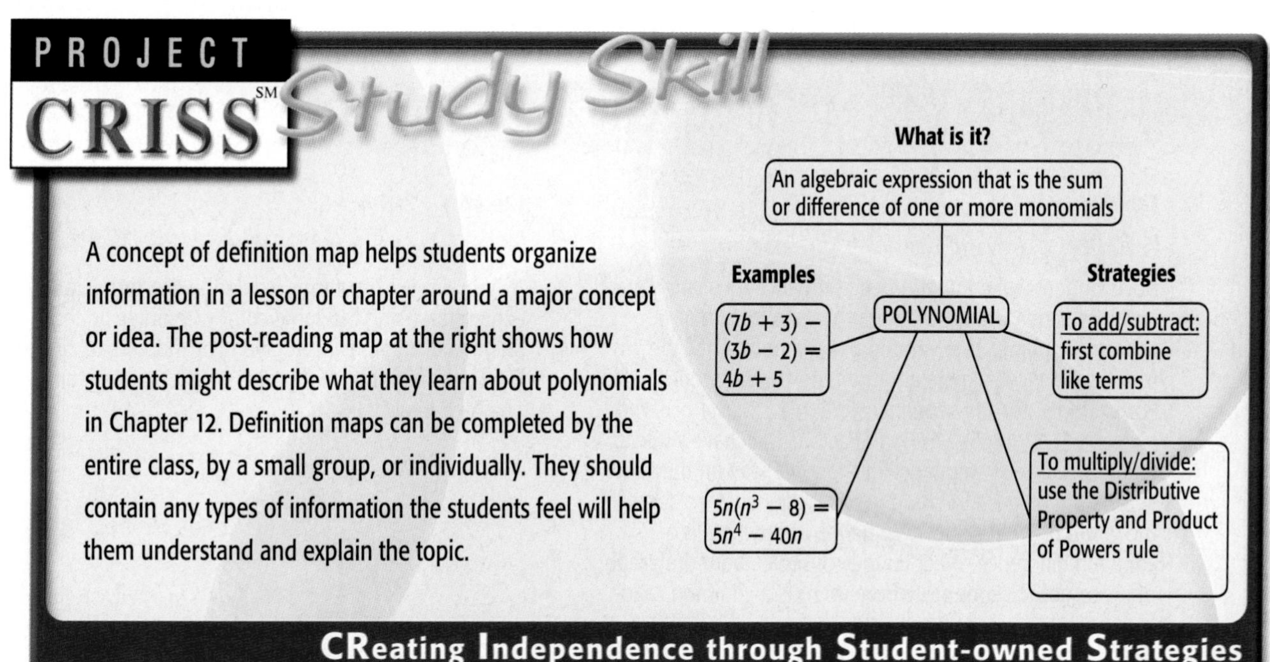

A concept of definition map helps students organize information in a lesson or chapter around a major concept or idea. The post-reading map at the right shows how students might describe what they learn about polynomials in Chapter 12. Definition maps can be completed by the entire class, by a small group, or individually. They should contain any types of information the students feel will help them understand and explain the topic.

For more information on Project CRISS, see p. T8.

CHAPTER 12 Making Connections

School-To-Home

Parent and Student Study Guide

Parents and students may work together to reinforce the concepts and skills of this chapter. These online worksheets are available in English and Spanish at msmath3.net/parent_student. A sample lesson is shown below.

Family Letters and Activities

Send a letter and activity for this chapter home to encourage family members to become active participants in their students' learning. (English: *Chapter 12 Resource Masters*, pp. ix–x; Spanish: log on to msmath3.net/family_letters)

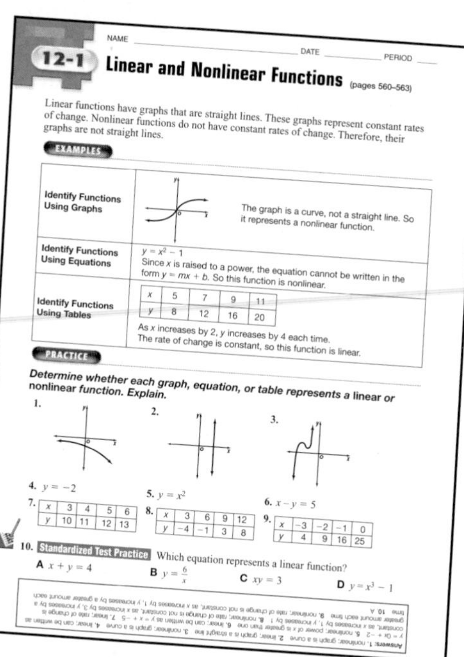

12-1 Linear and Nonlinear Functions (pages 560–563)

Linear functions have graphs that are straight lines. These graphs represent constant rates of change. Nonlinear functions do not have constant rates of change. Therefore, their graphs are not straight lines.

EXAMPLES

Identify Functions Using Graphs	The graph is a curve, not a straight line. So it represents a nonlinear function.
Identify Functions Using Equations	$y = x^2 - 1$ Since x is raised to a power, the equation cannot be written in the form $y = mx + b$. So this function is nonlinear.
Identify Functions Using Tables	x: 5, 7, 9, 11; y: 8, 12, 16, 20 As x increases by 2, y increases by 4 each time. The rate of change is constant, so this function is linear.

PRACTICE

Determine whether each graph, equation, or table represents a linear or nonlinear function. Explain.

1. 2. 3.

4. $y = -2$

5. $y = x^2$

6. $x - y = 5$

7.

x	3	4	5	6
y	10	11	12	13

8.

x	3	6	9	12
y	−4	−1	3	8

9.

x	−3	−2	−1	0
y	4	9	16	25

10. **Standardized Test Practice** Which equation represents a linear function?

A $x + y = 4$ B $y = \frac{6}{x}$ C $xy = 3$ D $y = x^3 - 1$

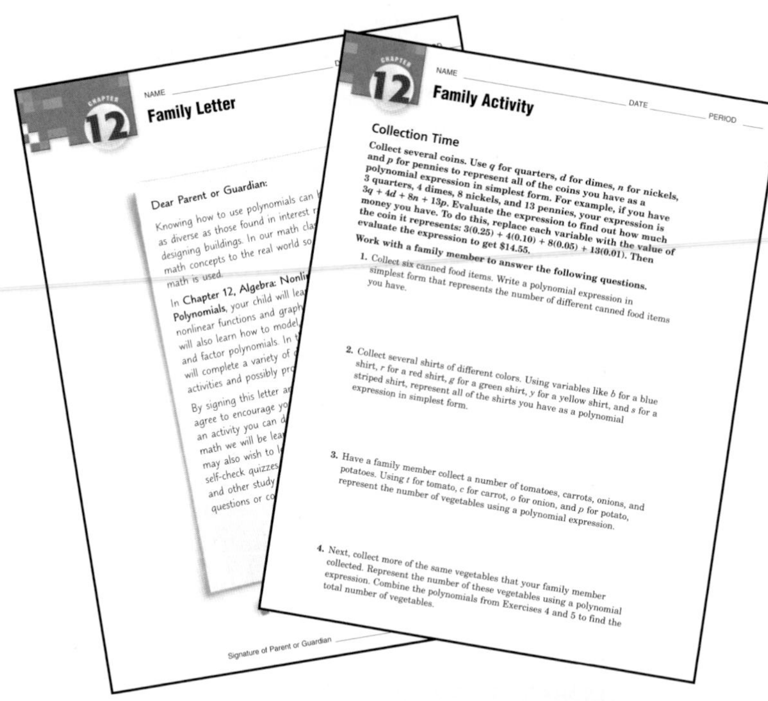

12 Family Letter

Dear Parent or Guardian:

Signature of Parent or Guardian

12 Family Activity

Collection Time

Collect several coins. Use q for quarters, d for dimes, n for nickels, and p for pennies to represent all of the coins you have as a polynomial expression in simplest form. For example, if you have 3 quarters, 4 dimes, 8 nickels, and 13 pennies, your expression is $3q + 4d + 8n + 13p$. Evaluate the expression to find out how much money you have. To do this, replace each variable with the value of the coin it represents: $3(0.25) + 4(0.10) + 8(0.05) + 13(0.01)$. Then evaluate the expression to get $14.55.

Work with a family member to answer the following questions.

1. Collect six canned food items. Write a polynomial expression in simplest form that represents the number of different canned food items you have.

2. Collect several shirts of different colors. Using variables like b for a blue shirt, r for a red shirt, g for a green shirt, y for a yellow shirt, and s for a striped shirt, represent all of the shirts you have as a polynomial expression in simplest form.

3. Have a family member collect a number of tomatoes, carrots, onions, and potatoes. Using t for tomato, c for carrot, o for onion, and p for potato, represent the number of vegetables using a polynomial expression.

4. Next, collect more of the same vegetables that your family member collected. Represent the number of these vegetables using a polynomial expression. Combine the polynomials from Exercises 4 and 5 to find the total number of vegetables.

English Language Learners ELL

Lesson 12-1

Building on Prior Knowledge

Have students take an arithmetic sequence they completed in the previous chapter and graph the points on a coordinate plane. They should use the number of the term as the *x*-coordinate and the term as the *y*-coordinate. For example, for the sequence 3, 5, 7, 9, …, the ordered pairs are (1, 3), (2, 5), (3, 7), and so on. Then have students graph a geometric sequence in the same way on the same coordinate plane. Ask students what they observe about the graph of an arithmetic sequence where there is a common difference. What do they observe about the graph of a geometric sequence where there is a common ratio?

Lesson 12-3

Using Multisensory Activities

As you discuss like terms, circle the like terms in an expression using the same color of marker or chalk. Then have students use crayons or markers to circle the like terms with the same color on their papers and combine them.

MathScape™  This project was supported, in part, by the **National Science Foundation**

MathScape is a mathematics curriculum for grades 6–8 developed by the Seeing and Thinking Mathematically Project at the Education Development Center.

Comparing Function Families
Family Portraits

How to Use *MathScape* with Chapter 12

The unit *Family Portraits* can be used to enhance Lessons 12-1 and 12-7.

- **Enrich** → After you complete **Lesson 12-1,** you can study some nonlinear functions in depth by using the activities on pages 276–277 and 296–297.
- **Introduce** → Before you begin **Lesson 12-2,** you can introduce parabolas by using the activities on pages 290–291.

For other lessons in Chapter 12 that correlate to *MathScape*, see the chart on page T14.

Online Lesson Planner

USA TODAY® Education's Online site offers resources and interactive features connected to each day's newspaper. *Experience Today,* USA TODAY's® daily lesson plan, is available on the site and delivered daily to subscribers. This plan provides instruction for integrating USA TODAY® graphics and key editorial features into your mathematics classroom. Log on to **education.usatoday.com.**

USA TODAY Snapshots® in Chapter 12	
Lesson	**Snapshot**
12-1	We're eating more garlic

Quick Review Math Handbook

is Glencoe's mathematical handbook for students. The Hot Words section includes a glossary of terms while the Hot Topics section consists of explanations of key mathematical concepts. An exercise set is included to check students' understanding of the concepts. This valuable resource can be used as a reference in the classroom or for home study.

Lesson	Hot Topics Section	Lesson	Hot Topics Section
12-1	6-7, 6-8	**12-4,12-5**	3-4, 6-2
12-2	6-7, 9-2	**12-6**	3-4, 6-2
12-3	3-4, 6-2	**12-7**	3-4, 6-2

Notes

Key Chapter Objectives

Lesson 12-1 Determine whether a function is linear or nonlinear.

Lesson 12-2 Graph quadratic functions.

Lessons 12-4 and 12-5 Add and subtract polynomials.

Lesson 12-7 Multiply monomials and polynomials.

"What does racing have to do with math?"

Point out to students that this is only one of many applications of the math that they are studying. Others are provided in the introduction to each lesson.

Vocabulary Builder, pp. vii–viii ELL

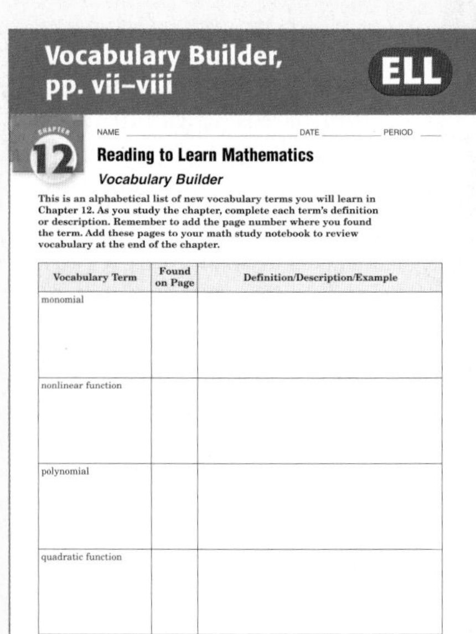

NAME ______ DATE ______ PERIOD ____

12 Reading to Learn Mathematics

Vocabulary Builder

This is an alphabetical list of new vocabulary terms you will learn in Chapter 12. As you study the chapter, complete each term's definition or description. Remember to add the page number where you found the term. Add these pages to your math study notebook to review vocabulary at the end of the chapter.

Vocabulary Term	Found on Page	Definition/Description/Example
monomial		
nonlinear function		
polynomial		
quadratic function		

Chapter 12 Algebra: Nonlinear Functions and Polynomials

"What does racing have to do with math?"

As a race car increases its speed, or accelerates, the distance it travels each second also increases. The relationship between these two quantities, however, is not linear. The distance d that a race car travels in time t, given the rate of acceleration a, can be described by the quadratic function $d = \frac{1}{2}at^2$.

You will solve a problem about racing in Lesson 12-2.

Vocabulary Builder

For a thorough vocabulary list with pronunciations of new words, give students the Vocabulary Builder worksheets from the *Chapter 12 Resource Masters*. Encourage them to complete the definition of each term as they progress through the chapter.

GETTING STARTED

▶ Diagnose Readiness

Take this quiz to see if you are ready to begin Chapter 12. Refer to the lesson number in parentheses for review.

Vocabulary Review

Choose the correct term to complete each sentence.

1. A function in which the graph of the solutions forms a line is called a (straight, linear) function. (Lesson 11-3)
2. The (base, exponent) is the number in a power that is multiplied. (Lesson 2-8)

Prerequisite Skills

Identify the like terms in each expression. (Lesson 10-1)

3. $3x + 5 - x$ **$3x, -x$**
4. $2 - 4n + 1 + 6n$ **2, 1; $-4n$, $6n$**

Rewrite each expression using parentheses so that the like terms are grouped together. (Lessons 1-2 and 10-1)

5. $(a + 2b) + (2a - 5b)$ **$(a + 2a) + (2b - 5b)$**
6. $(8w + 7x) + (3w + 9x)$ **$(8w + 3w) + (7x + 9x)$**

Rewrite each expression as an addition expression by using the additive inverse. (Lessons 1-4 and 1-5)

7. $3 - 5y$ **$3 + (-5y)$**
8. $2m - 7n$ **$2m + (-7n)$**

Write each expression using exponents. (Lesson 2-8)

9. $6 \cdot 6 \cdot 6 \cdot 6$ **6^4**
10. $3 \cdot 7 \cdot 7 \cdot 7 \cdot 3 \cdot 7$ **$3^2 \cdot 7^3$**

Use the Distributive Property to rewrite each expression. (Lesson 10-1)

11. $9(d + 2)$ **$9d + 18$**
12. $-8(f - 3)$ **12. $-8f + 24$**

Nonlinear Functions Make this Foldable to organize your notes. Begin with 7 sheets of $8\frac{1}{2}" \times 11"$ paper.

STEP 1 Fold and Cut Fold a sheet of paper in half lengthwise. Cut a 1" tab along the left edge through one thickness.

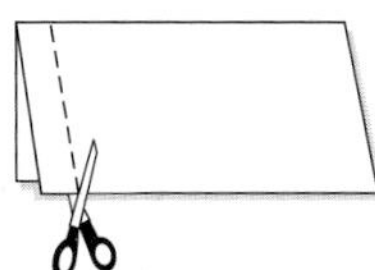

STEP 2 Glue and Label Glue the 1" tab down. Write the title of the lesson on the front tab.

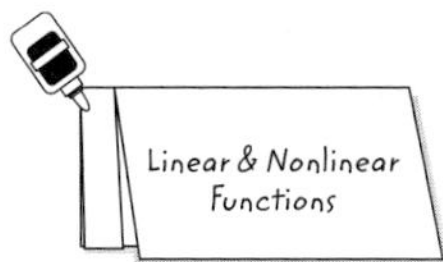

STEP 3 Repeat and Staple Repeat Steps 1–2 for the remaining sheets of paper. Staple together to form a booklet.

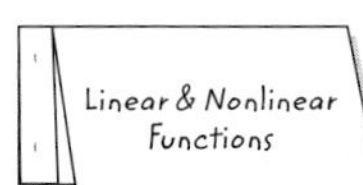

Chapter Notes Each time you find this logo throughout the chapter, use your *Noteables™: Interactive Study Notebook with Foldables™* or your own notebook to take notes. Begin your chapter notes with this Foldable activity.

Readiness To prepare yourself for this chapter with another quiz, visit **msmath3.net/chapter_readiness**

GETTING STARTED

Diagnose Readiness This section provides a review of the basic concepts needed before beginning Chapter 12. Page references are included for additional student help.

Prerequisite Skills review skills needed in this chapter.

Exercises	Needed for Lesson	Skill
3–4	12-3	Identify Like Terms
5–6	12-4	Group Like Terms
7–8	12-5	Use the Additive Inverse
9–10	12-6	Use Exponents
11–12	12-7	Use the Distributive Property

For more prerequisite skills, see:

- Getting Ready for the Next Lesson, at the end of each lesson
- Prerequisite Skills in the Student Handbook on pp. 600–615
- *Math Skills Maintenance Masters*

FOLDABLES™ Study Organizer

For more information about Foldables, see *Teaching Mathematics with Foldables.*

After students make their Foldables, have them label the top of each front page to correspond to the seven lessons in this chapter. Under the tabs of their Foldables, students take notes, define terms, record concepts, and write examples. On the front of each tab, ask students to design a visual (graph, diagram, picture, chart, or concept map) that presents the information introduced in the lesson in a concise, easy-to-study format. Encourage students to clearly label their visuals and write captions as needed.

12-1 Lesson Notes

Linear and Nonlinear Functions

Lesson Resources

Chapter 12 Resource Masters
- Study Guide and Intervention, p. 679
- Practice: Skills, p. 680
- Practice: Word Problems, p. 681
- Reading to Learn Mathematics, p. 682
- Enrichment, p. 683

FAST FILE

Parent and Student Study Guide Online Worksheets, 12-1

Science and Math Lab Masters, pp. 61–68

Noteables™: Interactive Study Notebook with Foldables™, 12-1

1 Focus

5-Minute Check 12-1

Use as a quiz or review of Chapter 11. (Also available as a transparency)

Bellringer

Hands-On Activity Provide students with grid paper and toothpicks. Have them draw an x-axis and a y-axis on the grid. Next, have them lay toothpicks on the grid to represent the lines $y = -3x + 4$, $y = 2x - 3$, $y = 4x + 3$, and $y = -x + 6$. Ask students to state the slope of each line. **−3; 2; 4; −1** Remind students that these are linear functions because they result in a straight line. Explain to students that not all functions are linear.

Reading to Learn Mathematics, p. 682 ELL

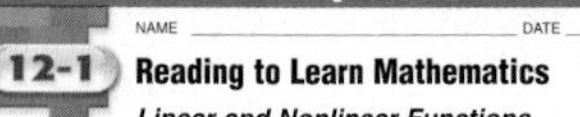

NAME ______ DATE ______ PERIOD ______

Pre-Activity *Read the introduction at the top of page 560 in your textbook. Write your answers below.*

1. During its ascent, did the rocket travel the same distance each second? Explain. No; 38 m the 1st second, 36 m the 2nd second, 32 m the 3rd second, 22 m the 4th second, 10 m the 5th second, and 4 m the 6th second.
2. During its descent, did the rocket travel the same distance each second? Explain. yes; 10 m/s
3. Graph the data whose ordered pairs are (time, height) for the rocket's ascent and descent on separate axes. Connect the points with a straight line or smooth curve. Then compare the two graphs. The graph of the rocket's ascent is curved, while the graph of the rocket's d... is a straight li...

What You'll LEARN

Determine whether a function is linear or nonlinear.

NEW Vocabulary

nonlinear function

REVIEW Vocabulary

function: a relationship where one quantity depends upon another (Lesson 11-2)

WHEN am I ever going to use this?

ROCKETRY The tables show the flight data for a model rocket launch. The first table gives the rocket's height at each second of its ascent, or upward flight. The second table gives its height as it descends back to Earth using a parachute.

Ascent	
Time (s)	Height (m)
0	0
1	38
2	74
3	106
4	128
5	138
6	142

Descent	
Time (s)	Height (m)
7	140
8	130
9	120
10	110
11	100
12	90
13	80

1. During its ascent, did the rocket travel the same distance each second? Explain. **No; 38 m the 1st second, 36 m the 2nd second, 32 m the 3rd second, 22 m the 4th second, 10 m the 5th second, and 4m the 6th second.**
2. During its descent, did the rocket travel the same distance each second? Explain. **yes; 10 m/s**
3. Graph the data whose ordered pairs are (time, height) for the rocket's ascent and descent on separate axes. Connect the points with a straight line or smooth curve. Then compare the two graphs. **See Ch. 12 Answer Appendix.**

In Lesson 11-3, you learned that linear functions have graphs that are straight lines. These graphs represent constant rates of change. **Nonlinear functions** do not have constant rates of change. Therefore, their graphs are not straight lines.

STUDY TIP

Nonlinear Functions The function in Example 1 is a *quadratic function.* The function in Example 2 is an *exponential function.*

TEACHING TIP

Point out that in an exponential function, the variable x is the exponent of a positive number.

EXAMPLES Identify Functions Using Graphs

Determine whether each graph represents a *linear* or *nonlinear* function. Explain.

1

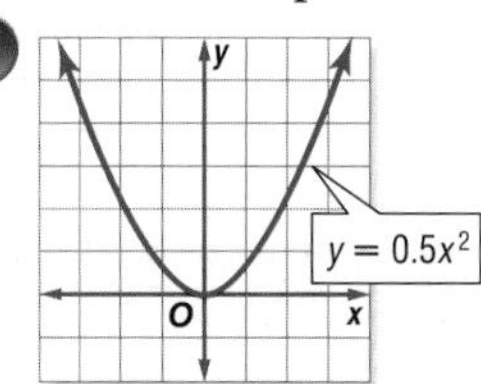

The graph is a curve, not a straight line. So it represents a nonlinear function.

2

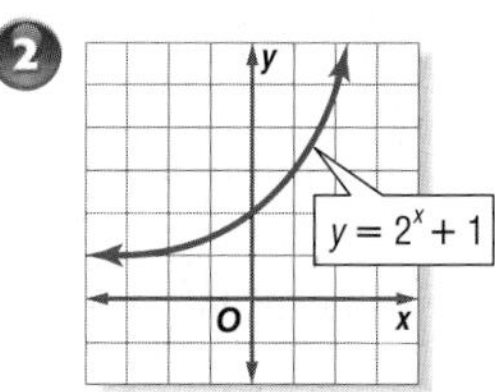

This graph is also a curve. So it represents a nonlinear function.

DAILY INTERVENTION

Unlocking Misconceptions

Linear Equations Students may mistakenly think that only equations written in slope-intercept form, $y = mx + b$, are linear equations. They may have to convert equations like $4y - 3 = 12x$ into the slope-intercept form before they can recognize them as linear. For practice, have them write the following equations in slope-intercept form: $2y + 2x = 10$, $4y - 2x = -24$, $3y + x = 9$, and $-2y + 8x = -2$. $\mathbf{y = -x + 5;}$ $\mathbf{y = \frac{1}{2}x - 6;\ y = -\frac{1}{3}x + 3;\ y = 4x + 1}$

STUDY TIP

Identifying Linear Equations Always examine an equation after it has been solved for y to see that the power of x is 1 or 0. Then check to see that x does not appear in the denominator.

Since the equation for a linear function can be written in the form $y = mx + b$, where m represents the constant rate of change, you can determine whether a function is linear by examining its equation.

EXAMPLES Identify Functions Using Equations

Determine whether each equation represents a *linear* or *nonlinear* function. Explain.

3 $y = x + 4$

Since the equation can be written as $y = 1x + 4$, this function is linear.

4 $y = \frac{6}{x}$

Since x is in the denominator, the equation cannot be written in the form $y = mx + b$. So this function is nonlinear.

A nonlinear function does not increase or decrease at the same rate. You can use a table to determine if the rate of change is constant.

EXAMPLES Identify Functions Using Tables

Determine whether each table represents a *linear* or *nonlinear* function. Explain.

5

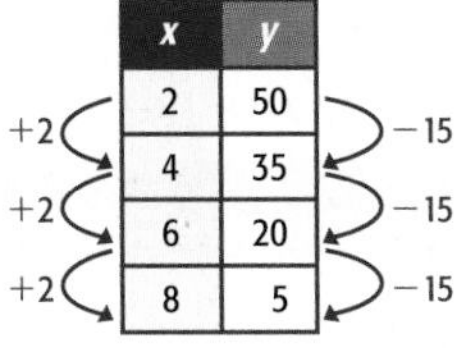

x	y
2	50
4	35
6	20
8	5

As x increases by 2, y decreases by 15 each time. The rate of change is constant, so this function is linear.

6

x	y
1	1
4	16
7	49
10	100

+3, +3, +3; +15, +33, +51

As x increases by 3, y increases by a greater amount each time. The rate of change is not constant, so this function is nonlinear.

TEACHING TIP

Remind students to check to see that the differences between both the x values and the y values are constant before identifying a function as linear.

7 **BASKETBALL** **Use the table to determine whether the number of teams is a linear function of the number of rounds of play.**

Round(s) of play	Teams
1	2
2	4
3	8
4	16
5	32

Examine the differences between the number of teams for each round.

$4 - 2 = 2 \quad 8 - 4 = 4 \quad 16 - 8 = 8 \quad 32 - 16 = 16$

While there is a pattern in the differences, they are not the same. Therefore, this function is nonlinear.

REAL-LIFE MATH

BASKETBALL The NCAA women's basketball tournament begins with 64 teams and consists of 6 rounds of play.

Your Turn **Determine whether each equation or table represents a *linear* or *nonlinear* function. Explain.**

a. $y = 2x^3 + 1$ b. $y = 3x$ c.

x	0	5	10	15
y	20	16	12	8

a. nonlinear; power of x is greater than one

b. linear; can be written as $y = 3x + 0$

c. linear; the rate of change is constant, as x increases by 5, y decreases by 4

Math Online msmath3.net/extra_examples

2 Teach

In-Class Examples

INTERACTIVE CHALKBOARD PowerPoint® Presentations

Determine whether each graph, equation, or table represents a *linear* or *nonlinear* function. Explain.

1

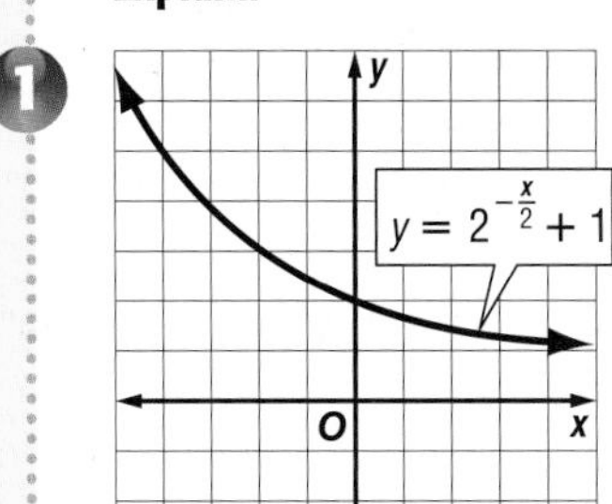

nonlinear; graph is a curve

2

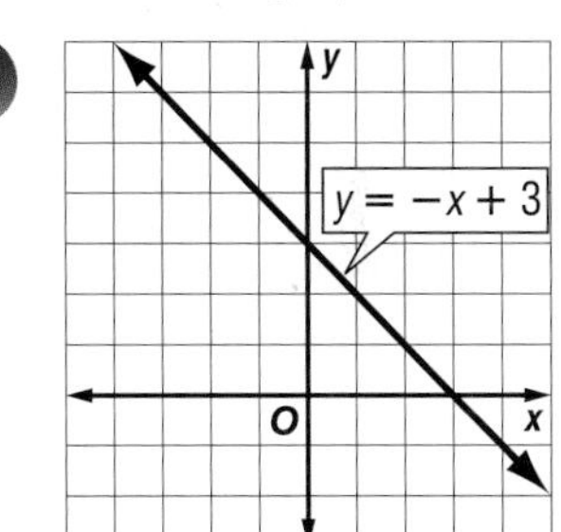

linear; graph is a straight line

3 $y = 5x^2 + 3$ nonlinear; power of x is greater than one

4 $y - 4 = 5x$ linear; can be written as $y = 5x + 4$

5

x	2	4	6	8
y	2	20	54	104

nonlinear; rate of change is not constant

6

x	1	4	7	10
y	0	9	18	27

linear; rate of change is constant, as x increases by 3, y increases by 9

7 **CLOCKS** Use the table in the bottom margin to determine whether or not the number of revolutions per hour that the minute hand on a clock makes is a linear function of the number of hours that pass. linear

TEACHING TIP

Extending the Lesson Inform students that an equation of the form $y = \frac{k}{x}$, where k is a nonzero constant, is an *inverse variation*. The equation in Example 4 is an inverse variation. The graph of an inverse variation is not a straight line, and it does not intersect the x- or y-axis. On page 562, the graph in Exercise 9 is an example of the graph of an inverse variation.

Hour	Minute Hand Revolutions
1	60
2	120
3	180
4	240
5	300

3 Practice/Apply

Which One Doesn't Belong?
In Exercise 2, students should recognize that equations having an exponent greater than one for either x or y are not linear.

About the Exercises...

Guided Practice Key

Exercises	Examples
3–4	1, 2
5–6	3, 4
7–8	5, 6

Assignment Guide

Basic: 9–29 odd, 32–44

Average: 9–29 odd, 31–44

Enriched: 10–28 even, 30–40 (Optional: 41–44)

Alert! The Data Update after Exercise 29 requires access to the Internet.

Students practice the same concepts in Exercises 9–28 if they are assigned odd or even problems.

Skill and Concept Check

1. **OPEN ENDED** Give an example of a nonlinear function using a table of values. See margin.

2. **Which One Doesn't Belong?** Identify the function that is not linear. Explain your reasoning.

$y = 2x$	$y = x^2$	$y - 2 = x$	$x - y = 2$

$y = x^2$; $y = x^2$ cannot be written in the form $y = mx + b$.

GUIDED PRACTICE

Determine whether each graph, equation, or table represents a *linear* or *nonlinear* function. Explain.

3. 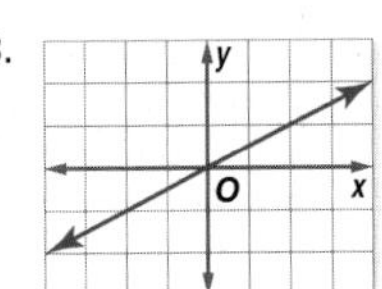
linear; graph is a straight line

4. 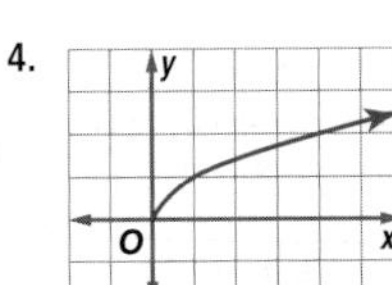
nonlinear; graph is a curve

5. $y = \frac{x}{3}$ linear; can be written as $y = \frac{1}{3}x + 0$

6. $y - x = 1$ linear; can be written as $y = 1x + 1$

7.

x	3	6	9	12
y	12	10	8	6

8.

x	1	2	3	4
y	1	4	9	16

nonlinear; rate of change is not constant

7. linear; rate of change is constant, as x increases by 3, y decreases by 2.

Practice and Applications

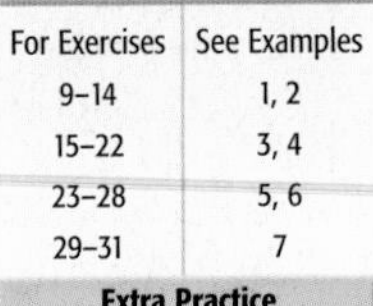

HOMEWORK HELP

For Exercises	See Examples
9–14	1, 2
15–22	3, 4
23–28	5, 6
29–31	7

Extra Practice
See pages 645, 659.

Determine whether each graph, equation, or table represents a *linear* or *nonlinear* function. Explain. 9–28. See margin.

9. 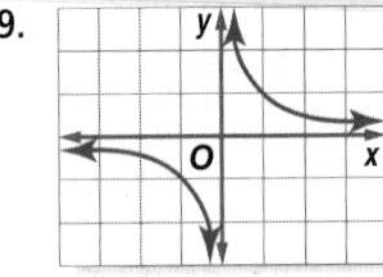

10. 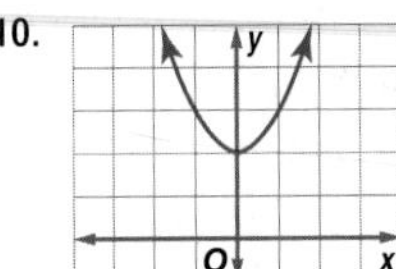

11. 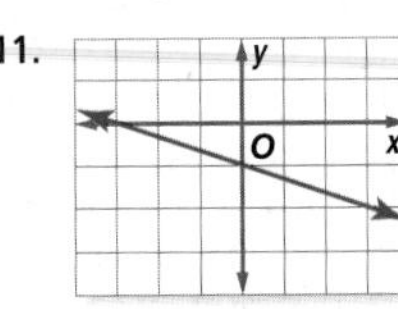

12. 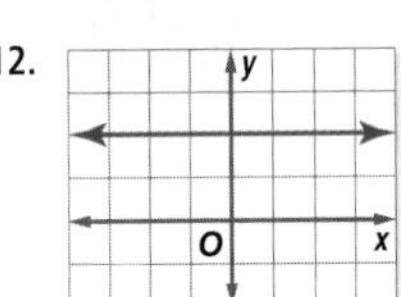

13. 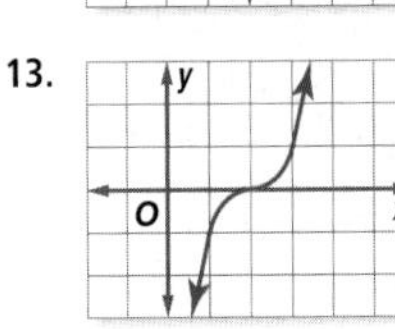

14. 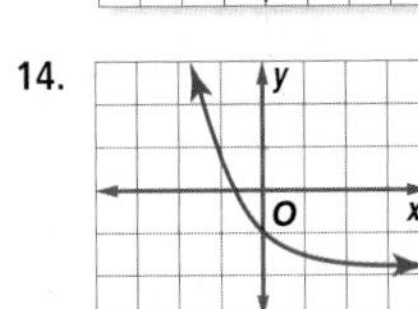

15. $xy = -9$

16. $y = 0.6x$

17. $y = x^3 - 1$

18. $y = 4x^2 + 9$

19. $y = 2^x$

20. $y = \frac{4}{x}$

21. $y = 7$

22. $y = \frac{3x}{2}$

23.

x	1	2	3	4
y	0	2	6	12

24.

x	−1	0	1	2
y	−4	1	6	11

25. 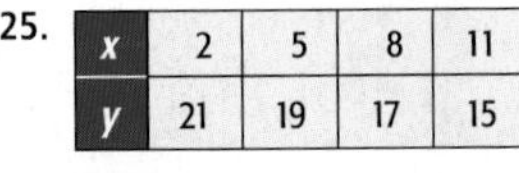

x	2	5	8	11
y	21	19	17	15

26. 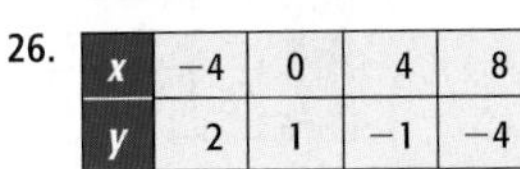

x	−4	0	4	8
y	2	1	−1	−4

27.

x	4	6	8	10
y	4	13.5	32	62.5

28. 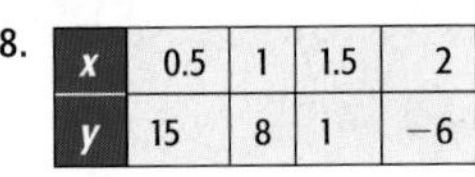

x	0.5	1	1.5	2
y	15	8	1	−6

Answers

1. Sample answer:

x	1	2	3	4
y	3	5	9	15

9. nonlinear; graph is two curves
10. nonlinear; graph is a curve
11. linear; graph is a straight line
12. linear; graph is a straight line
13. nonlinear; graph is a curve
14. nonlinear; graph is a curve
15. nonlinear; when solved for y, x appears in denominator so the equation cannot be written in the form $y = mx + b$
16. linear; can be written as $y = 0.6x + 0$
17. nonlinear; power of x is greater than 1
18. nonlinear; power of x is greater than 1
19. nonlinear; x is an exponent, so the equation cannot be written in the form $y = mx + b$
20. nonlinear; x is in the denominator, so the equation cannot be written in the form $y = mx + b$
21. linear; can be written in the form $y = 0x + 7$
22. linear; can be written in the form $y = \frac{3}{2}x + 0$
23. nonlinear; rate of change is not constant
24. linear; rate of change is constant, as x increases by 1, y increases by 5
25. linear; rate of change is constant, as x increases by 3, y decreases by 2
26. nonlinear; rate of change is not constant
27. nonlinear; rate of change is not constant
28. linear; rate of change is constant, as x increases by 0.5, y decreases by 7

29. **FOOD** The graphic shows the increase in garlic consumption from 1970 to 2000. Would you describe the growth as linear or nonlinear? Explain. **See margin.**

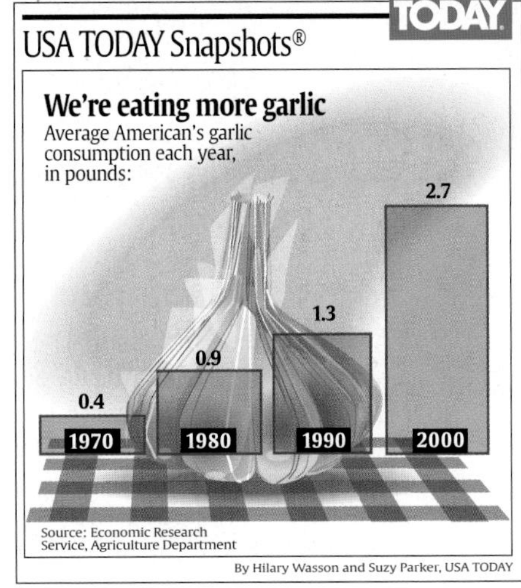

Data Update Is the growth in the consumption of your favorite food linear or nonlinear? Visit msmath3.net/data_update to learn more.

GEOMETRY For Exercises 30 and 31, use the following information. **30. See margin.**
Recall that the circumference of a circle is equal to pi times its diameter and that the area of a circle is equal to pi times the square of its radius.

30. Is the circumference of a circle a linear or nonlinear function of its diameter? Explain.

31. Is the area of a circle a linear or nonlinear function of its radius? Explain.
Nonlinear; the power of r in the function $A = \pi r^2$ is greater than 1.

32. **CRITICAL THINKING** *True* or *False*? All graphs of straight lines are linear functions. Explain your reasoning or provide a counterexample.
False; the graph of a vertical line such as $x = 2$, is not a function.

Spiral Review with Standardized Test Practice

33. **MULTIPLE CHOICE** Which equation represents a nonlinear function? **C**

Ⓐ $y = 3x + 1$ Ⓑ $y = \frac{x}{3}$ Ⓒ $2xy = 10$ Ⓓ $y = 3(x - 5)$

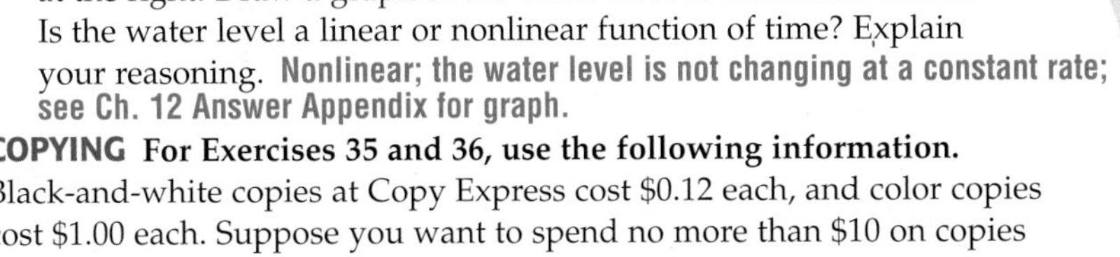

34. **SHORT RESPONSE** Water is poured at a constant rate into the vase at the right. Draw a graph of the water level as a function of time. Is the water level a linear or nonlinear function of time? Explain your reasoning. **Nonlinear; the water level is not changing at a constant rate; see Ch. 12 Answer Appendix for graph.**

COPYING For Exercises 35 and 36, use the following information.
Black-and-white copies at Copy Express cost \$0.12 each, and color copies cost \$1.00 each. Suppose you want to spend no more than \$10 on copies of your club's flyers. (Lesson 11-8)

35. Write an inequality to represent this situation. **$0.12x + y \leq 10$**

36. Graph the inequality and use the graph to determine three possible combinations of copies you could make. **Sample answer: 60 B&W, 2 color; 40 B&W, 5 color; 10 B&W, 8 color; see Ch. 12 Answer Appendix for graph.**

Solve each system of equations by substitution. (Lesson 11-7)

37. $y = 2x + 1$
$y = 3$ **(1, 3)**

38. $y = -4x - 3$
$y = 1$ **(−1, 1)**

39. $y = -5x + 8$
$y = -2$ **(2, −2)**

40. $y = 0.5x - 6$
$y = -4$ **(4, −4)**

GETTING READY FOR THE NEXT LESSON

PREREQUISITE SKILL Graph each function. (Lesson 11-3) **41–44. See Ch. 12 Answer Appendix.**

41. $y = 2x$

42. $y = x + 3$

43. $y = 3x - 2$

44. $y = \frac{1}{3}x + 1$

msmath3.net/self_check_quiz

4 Assess

Higher-Level Thinking

Ask students whether $y = 3$ and $x = 2$ are linear equations. Have them explain their answers. **yes; The graphs of the lines are both straight lines.**

Answers

29. **Nonlinear; the points (year, pounds) would lie on a curved line, not on a straight line and the rate of change is not constant.**

30. **Linear; the function $C = \pi d$ can be written in the form $C = \pi d + 0$.**

Study Guide and Intervention, p. 679

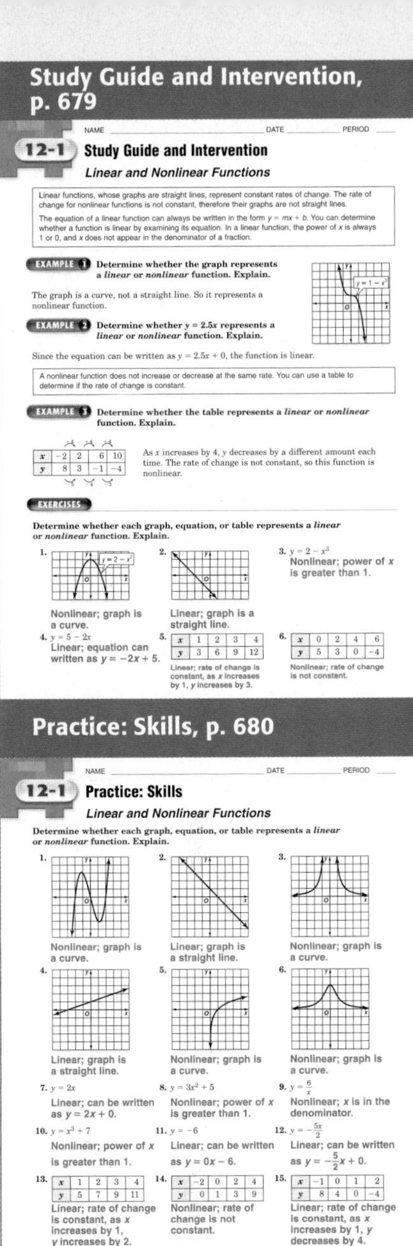

NAME ____________ DATE ______ PERIOD ____

12-1 Study Guide and Intervention

Linear and Nonlinear Functions

Linear functions, whose graphs are straight lines, represent constant rates of change. The rate of change for nonlinear functions is not constant, therefore their graphs are not straight lines.

The equation of a linear function can always be written in the form $y = mx + b$. You can determine whether a function is linear by examining its equation. In a linear function, the power of x is always 1 or 0, and x does not appear in the denominator of a fraction.

EXAMPLE 1 **Determine whether the graph represents a *linear* or *nonlinear* function. Explain.**

The graph is a curve, not a straight line. So it represents a nonlinear function.

EXAMPLE 2 **Determine whether $y = 2.5x$ represents a *linear* or *nonlinear* function. Explain.**

Since the equation can be written as $y = 2.5x + 0$, the function is linear.

A nonlinear function does not increase or decrease at the same rate. You can use a table to determine if the rate of change is constant.

EXAMPLE 3 **Determine whether the table represents a *linear* or *nonlinear* function. Explain.**

x	−2	2	6	10
y	8	3	−1	−4

As x increases by 4, y decreases by a different amount each time. The rate of change is not constant, so this function is nonlinear.

EXERCISES

Determine whether each graph, equation, or table represents a *linear* or *nonlinear* function. Explain.

1. $y = 2 - x^2$ **Nonlinear; graph is a curve.**

2. **Linear; graph is a straight line.**

3. $y = 2 - x^3$ **Nonlinear; power of x is greater than 1.**

4. $y = 5 - 2x$ **Linear; equation can written as $y = -2x + 5$.**

5.

x	1	2	3	4
y	3	6	9	12

Linear; rate of change is constant, as x increases by 1, y increases by 3.

6.

x	0	2	4	6
y	5	3	0	−4

Nonlinear; rate of change is not constant.

Practice: Skills, p. 680

NAME ____________ DATE ______ PERIOD ____

12-1 Practice: Skills

Linear and Nonlinear Functions

Determine whether each graph, equation, or table represents a *linear* or *nonlinear* function. Explain.

1. **Nonlinear; graph is a curve.**

2. **Linear; graph is a straight line.**

3. **Nonlinear; graph is a curve.**

4. **Linear; graph is a straight line.**

5. **Nonlinear; graph is a curve.**

6. **Nonlinear; graph is a curve.**

7. $y = 2x$ **Linear; can be written as $y = 2x + 0$.**

8. $y = 3x^2 + 5$ **Nonlinear; power of x is greater than 1.**

9. $y = \frac{6}{x}$ **Nonlinear; x is in the denominator.**

10. $y = x^3 + 7$ **Nonlinear; power of x is greater than 1.**

11. $y = -6$ **Linear; can be written as $y = 0x - 6$.**

12. $y = -\frac{5x}{2}$ **Linear; can be written as $y = -\frac{5}{2}x + 0$.**

13.

x	1	2	3	4
y	5	7	9	11

Linear; rate of change is constant, as x increases by 1, y increases by 2.

14.

x	−2	0	2	4
y	0	1	3	9

Nonlinear; rate of change is not constant.

15.

x	−1	0	1	2
y	8	4	0	−4

Linear; rate of change is constant, as x increases by 1, y decreases by 4.

16.

x	2	3	4	5
y	3	5	8	12

Nonlinear; rate of change is not constant.

17.

x	−2	1	4	7
y	−4	1	6	11

Linear; rate of change is constant, as x increases by 3, y increases by 5.

18.

x	3	6	9	12
y	10	6	3	1

Nonlinear; rate of change is not constant.

Practice: Word Problems, p. 681

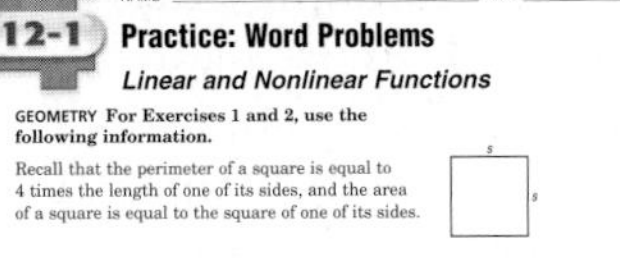

NAME ____________ DATE ______ PERIOD ____

12-1 Practice: Word Problems

Linear and Nonlinear Functions

GEOMETRY For Exercises 1 and 2, use the following information.

Recall that the perimeter of a square is equal to 4 times the length of one of its sides, and the area of a square is equal to the square of one of its sides.

1. Write a function for the perimeter of the square. Is the perimeter of a square a linear or nonlinear function of the length of one of its sides? Explain. **$P = 4s$; linear; the function can be written as $P = 4s + 0$.**

2. Write a function for the area of the square. Is the area of a square a linear or nonlinear function of the length of one of its sides? Explain. **$A = s^2$; nonlinear; the power of s in $A = s^2$ is greater than 1.**

3. **BUSINESS** The Devon Tool Company uses the equation $p = 150t$ to calculate the gross profit p the company makes, in dollars, when it sells t tools. Is the gross profit a linear or nonlinear function of the number of tools sold? Explain. **Linear; the function can be written $p = 150t + 0$.**

4. **GRAVITY** A camera is accidentally dropped from a balloon at a height of 300 feet. The height of the camera after falling for t seconds is given by $h = 300 - 16t^2$. Is the height of the camera a linear or nonlinear function of the time it takes to fall? Explain. **Nonlinear; the power of t in $h = 300 - 16t^2$ is greater than 1.**

5. **LONG DISTANCE** The table shows the charge for a long distance call as a function of the number of minutes the call lasts. Is the charge a linear or nonlinear function of the number of minutes? Explain.

Minutes	1	2	3	4
Cost (cents)	5	10	15	20

Linear; the rate of change is constant.

6. **DRIVING** The table shows the cost of a speeding ticket as a function of the speed of the car. Is the cost a linear or nonlinear function of the car's speed? Explain.

Speed (mph)	70	80	90	100
Cost (dollars)	25	50	150	300

Nonlinear; the rate of change is not constant, as the speed increases by 10 mph, the cost increases by greater and greater amounts.

GETTING STARTED

Teaching Tip Ask students to locate the X,T,θ,n key on their graphing calculators. Tell them that this is a shortcut key for inserting the function variable for whichever mode the calculator is in. If students press this key and get anything other than x, the calculator needs to be returned to Function Mode.

TEACH

- Explain that quadratic functions take the form of $y = ax^2 + c$. Changing the values of a and c affects the shape and position of the graph.
- Have students draw the parabolas on grid paper. Then have them copy one of the parabolas from Step 3 onto tracing paper. Ask them to move the traced parabola over the others as they work Exercise 1.

ASSESS

Discuss the **Exercises**. Students should notice that as a or c changes, the resulting graphs change. Use Exercise 8 to determine whether students have understood how the values of a and c affect quadratic functions.

12-2a Graphing Calculator Investigation

A Preview of Lesson 12-2

What You'll LEARN

Use a graphing calculator to graph families of quadratic functions.

Families of Quadratic Functions

In Lesson 11-5a, you discovered that families of linear functions share the same slope or y-intercept. Families of nonlinear functions also share a common characteristic. You can use a TI-83/84 Plus graphing calculator to investigate families of quadratic functions.

ACTIVITY

Graph $y = x^2$, $y = x^2 + 5$, and $y = x^2 - 3$ on the same screen.

STEP 1 Clear any existing equations from the Y= list.
Keystrokes: Y= CLEAR

STEP 2 Enter each equation.
Keystrokes: X,T,θ,n x^2 ENTER
X,T,θ,n x^2 + 5 ENTER
X,T,θ,n x^2 – 3 ENTER

STEP 3 Graph the equations in the standard viewing window.
Keystrokes: ZOOM 6

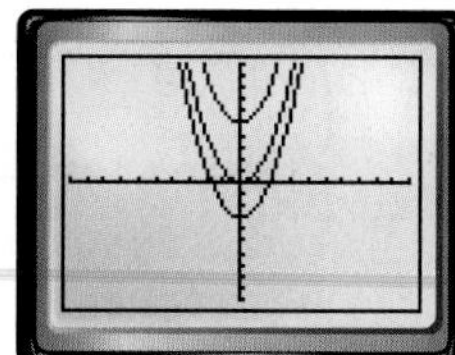

EXERCISES 2, 4, 6. See margin.

1. **Compare and contrast** the three equations you graphed.
2. **Describe** how the graphs of the three equations are related.
3. **MAKE A CONJECTURE** How does changing the value of c in the equation $y = x^2 + c$ affect the graph?
4. **Use a graphing calculator** to graph $y = 0.5x^2$, $y = x^2$, and $y = 2x^2$.
5. **Compare and contrast** the three equations you graphed in Exercise 4.
6. **Describe** how the graphs of the three equations are related.
7. **MAKE A CONJECTURE** How does changing the value of a in the equation $y = ax^2$ affect the graph?
8. **Write** a family of three quadratic functions. Describe the common characteristic of their graphs. See margin.

1. All three equations contain the term x^2. However, the number added to or subtracted from x^2 is different.
3. Changing the value of c changes the vertical position of the graph.
5. All three equations contain the term x^2. However, the number that x^2 is multiplied by is different.
7. Changing the value of a changes the width of the graph.

msmath3.net/other_calculator_keystrokes

Answers

2. The graphs are similar in that they are all in the shape of a "U". However, the graph of $y = x^2$ has its vertex at (0, 0), whereas the graph of $y = x^2 + 5$ has its vertex at (0, 5), and the graph of $y = x^2 - 3$ has its vertex at (0, –3).

4. 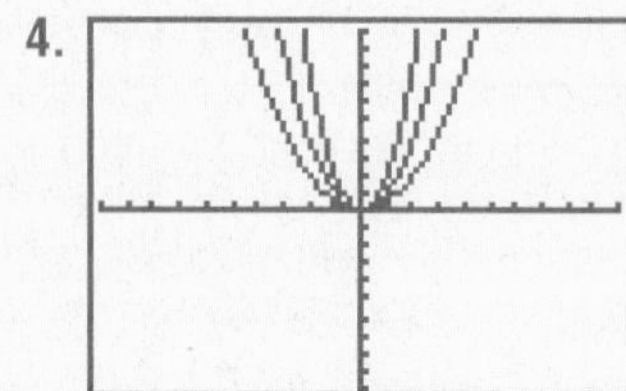

6. The graphs are similar in that they have the same vertex, (0, 0). However, the graph of $y = 0.5x^2$ is wider than the graph of $y = x^2$, and the graph of $y = 2x^2$ is more narrow than the graph of $y = x^2$.
8. Sample answer: $y = 2x^2$, $y = 2x^2 + 5$, $y = 2x^2 - 7$. The graphs have the same width, but are located at different vertical positions on the coordinate plane.

12-2 Graphing Quadratic Functions

What You'll LEARN

Graph quadratic functions.

NEW Vocabulary

quadratic function

HANDS-ON Mini Lab

Materials
- graph paper

Work with a partner.

You know that the area A of a square is equal to the length of a side s squared, $A = s^2$. What happens to the area of a square as its side length is increased?

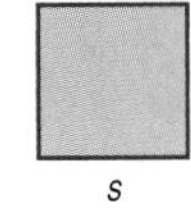

s	s^2	(s, A)
0	0	(0, 0)
1	1	(1, 1)
2	4	(2, 4)
3	9	(3, 9)
4	16	(4, 16)
5	25	(5, 25)
6	36	(6, 36)

STEP 1 Copy and complete the table.

STEP 2 Graph the ordered pairs from the table. Connect them with a smooth curve. **See Ch. 12 Answer Appendix.**

1. Is the relationship between the side length and the area of a square linear or nonlinear? Explain.
2. Describe the shape of the graph.

1. Nonlinear; the graph of the data is not a straight line.

2. Sample answer: It looks like half of the letter U.

A **quadratic function** is a function in which the greatest power of the variable is 2.

EXAMPLES Graph Quadratic Functions: $y = ax^2$

Graph $y = x^2$.

To graph a quadratic function, make a table of values, plot the ordered pairs, and connect the points with a smooth curve.

x	x^2	y	(x, y)
−2	$(-2)^2 = 4$	4	(−2, 4)
−1	$(-1)^2 = 1$	1	(−1, 1)
0	$(0)^2 = 0$	0	(0, 0)
1	$(1)^2 = 1$	1	(1, 1)
2	$(2)^2 = 4$	4	(2, 4)

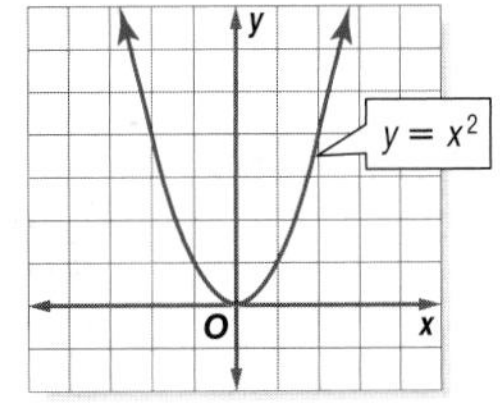

Graph $y = -2x^2$.

x	$-2x^2$	y	(x, y)
−2	$-2(-2)^2 = -8$	−8	(−2, −8)
−1	$-2(-1)^2 = -2$	−2	(−1, −2)
0	$-2(0)^2 = 0$	0	(0, 0)
1	$-2(1)^2 = -2$	−2	(1, −2)
2	$-2(2)^2 = -8$	−8	(2, −8)

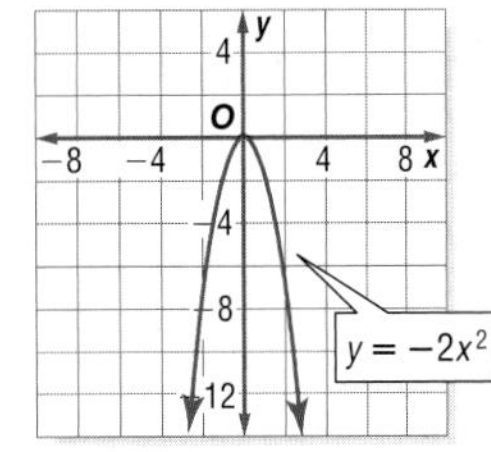

TEACHING TIP

You may wish to have students include fractional values of x such as 1.5 in their table of values so that they can see the shape of the curve they are to draw more clearly.

msmath3.net/extra_examples

DAILY INTERVENTION — Differentiated Instruction

Logical Have students work in small groups to discuss how the sign of the coefficient of x affects the graph of $y = ax^2 + c$. Also, have them discuss how the sign of c affects the graph. Ask them how the graph would change if they interchanged x and y. Would the resulting graph be the graph of a function? Explain. **No; parabolas opening to the left or right have more than one range value for each domain value except at the vertex.**

12-2 Lesson Notes

Lesson Resources

Chapter 12 Resource Masters FAST FILE
- Study Guide and Intervention, p. 684
- Practice: Skills, p. 685
- Practice: Word Problems, p. 686
- Reading to Learn Mathematics, p. 687
- Enrichment, p. 688

Calculator and Spreadsheet Masters, p. 49

Key Teaching Transparencies, 45

Parent and Student Study Guide Online Worksheets, 12-2

Science and Math Lab Masters, pp. 69–72

Noteables™: Interactive Study Notebook with Foldables™, 12-2

1 Focus

5-Minute Check 12-2

Use as a quiz or review of Lesson 12-1. (Also available as a transparency)

Bellringer

Reading Mathematics Tell students that *quadr-* means *square*. Ask them why the greatest power of the variable in a quadratic function is 2. Remind them that a variable with an exponent of 2 is said to be squared and that area is measured in square units. The Hands-On Mini Lab should help them understand that $A = s^2$ describes the area of a square.

Reading to Learn Mathematics, p. 687 ELL

NAME ______ DATE ______ PERIOD ____

12-2 Reading to Learn Mathematics

Graphing Quadratic Functions

Pre-Activity *Complete the Mini Lab at the top of page 565 in your textbook. Write your answers below.*

1. Is the relationship between the side length and the area of a square linear or nonlinear? Explain.
   Nonlinear; the graph of the data is not a straight line.
2. Describe the shape of the graph.
   Sample answer: It looks like half of the letter U.

Reading the Lesson

3. How can you distinguish the equations of quadratic functions from the equations of other functions?
   The highest power in the equations of quadratic functions is 2.

Determine whether each equation represents a quadratic function.

4. $y = 3x - 5$ no
5. $y = 6 - x^2$ yes
6. $y = x^3 + 2$ no
7. $y = \frac{8}{x}$ no

8. Describe the shape of the graph of a quadratic function. What is this ... ample answer ... the ...

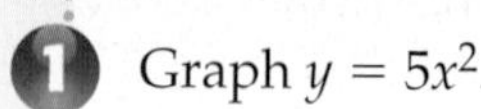

2 Teach

In-Class Examples

1 Graph $y = 5x^2$.

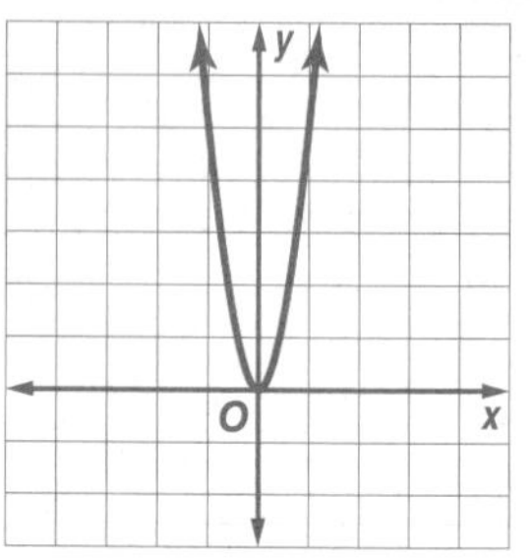

2 Graph $y = -4x^2$.

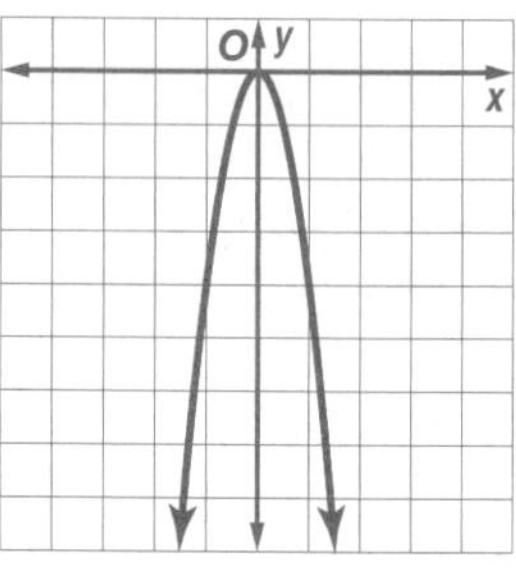

3 Graph $y = 3x^2 + 1$.

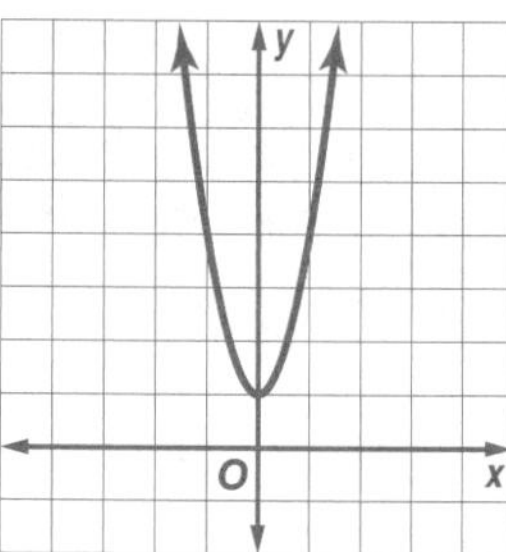

4 Graph $y = -x^2 - 2$.

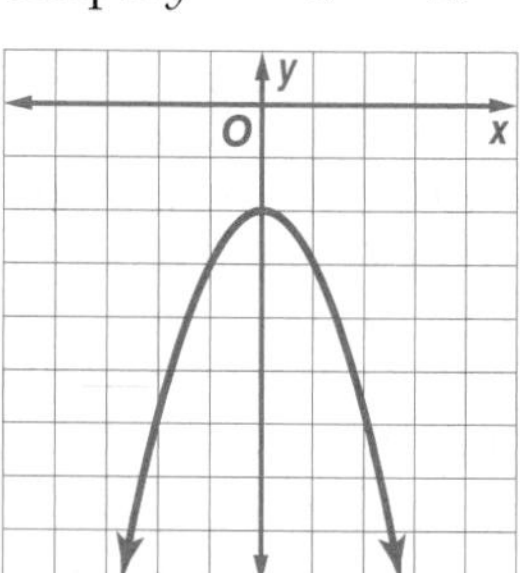

STUDY TIP

Quadratic Functions The graph of a quadratic function is called a *parabola*.

EXAMPLES Graph Quadratic Functions: $y = ax^2 + c$

3 Graph $y = x^2 + 2$.

x	$x^2 + 2$	y	(x, y)
−2	$(-2)^2 + 2 = 6$	6	(−2, 6)
−1	$(-1)^2 + 2 = 3$	3	(−1, 3)
0	$(0)^2 + 2 = 2$	2	(0, 2)
1	$(1)^2 + 2 = 3$	3	(1, 3)
2	$(2)^2 + 2 = 6$	6	(2, 6)

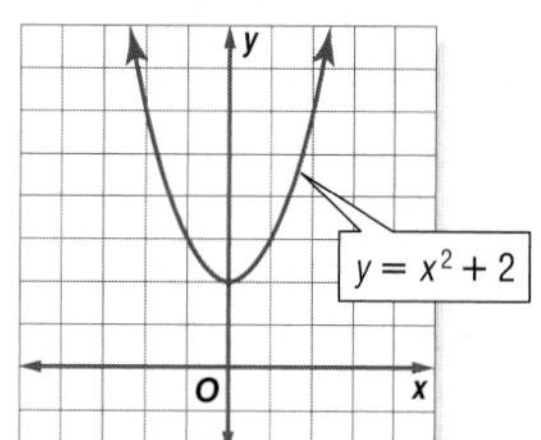

4 Graph $y = -x^2 + 4$.

x	$-x^2 + 4$	y	(x, y)
−2	$-(-2)^2 + 4 = 0$	0	(−2, 0)
−1	$-(-1)^2 + 4 = 3$	3	(−1, 3)
0	$-(0)^2 + 4 = 4$	4	(0, 4)
1	$-(1)^2 + 4 = 3$	3	(1, 3)
2	$-(2)^2 + 4 = 0$	0	(2, 0)

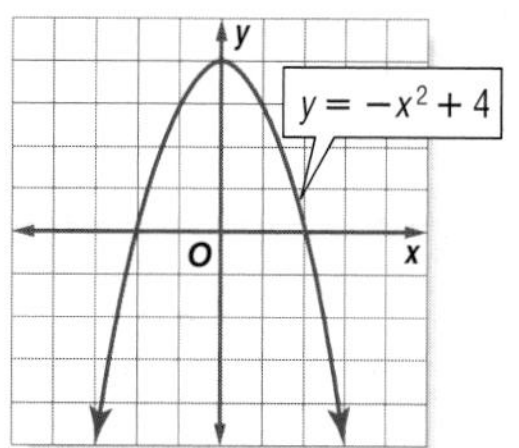

Your Turn Graph each function.

a. $y = x^2 + 1$ b. $y = -2x^2 - 1$ c. $y = -x^2$

a–c. See Ch. 12 Answer Appendix for graphs.

REAL-LIFE MATH

MONUMENTS The Eiffel Tower in Paris, France, opened in 1889 as part of the World Exposition. It is about 986 feet tall.

Source: www.structurae.de

Many real-life situations can be described using quadratic functions.

EXAMPLE Graph a Function to Solve a Problem

5 **MONUMENTS** **The function $h = 0.66d^2$ represents the distance d in miles you can see from a height of h feet. Graph this function. Then use your graph and the information at the left to estimate how far you could see from the top of the Eiffel Tower.**

The equation $h = 0.66d^2$ is quadratic, since the variable d has an exponent of 2. Distance cannot be negative, so use only positive values of h.

d	$h = 0.66d^2$	(d, h)
0	$0.66(0)^2 = 0$	(0, 0)
5	$0.66(5)^2 = 16.5$	(5, 16.5)
10	$0.66(10)^2 = 66$	(10, 66)
15	$0.66(15)^2 = 148.5$	(15, 148.5)
20	$0.66(20)^2 = 264$	(20, 264)
25	$0.66(25)^2 = 412.5$	(25, 412.5)
30	$0.66(30)^2 = 594$	(30, 594)
35	$0.66(35)^2 = 808.5$	(35, 808.5)
40	$0.66(40)^2 = 1,056$	(40, 1,056)

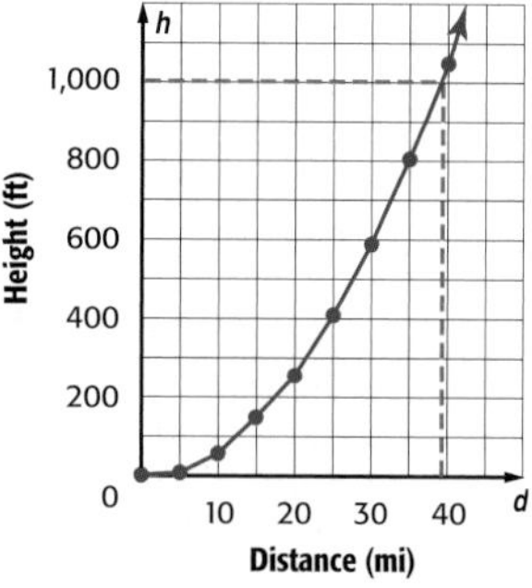

At a height of 986 feet, you could see approximately 39 miles.

Tips for New Teachers

Intervention Some students have trouble determining what the graph of an equation should look like, even after they have plotted some points on the graph. Encourage them to memorize the basic shapes of different types of functions. You may wish to have them keep a list in their math journals showing types of graphs and corresponding functions.

Students practice the same concepts in Exercises 10–29 if they are assigned odd or even problems.

Skill and Concept Check

1. Writing Math Explain how to determine whether a function is quadratic. A function is quadratic if the greatest power of the variable is 2.
2. **OPEN ENDED** Write a quadratic function of the form $y = ax^2 + c$ and explain how to graph it. Sample answer: $y = 2x^2 + 8$; make a table of values, plot the points, and connect them with a smooth curve.
3. **Which One Doesn't Belong?** Identify the function whose graph does not have the same characteristic as the other three. Explain your reasoning.

$y = 2x^2 + 1$	$y = -5x^2$	$y = 7x - 3$	$y = 4x^2 - 2$

$y = 7x - 3$, it is a linear function, while the others are quadratic.

GUIDED PRACTICE

Graph each function. 4–9. See Ch. 12 Answer Appendix.

4. $y = 3x^2$
5. $y = -5x^2$
6. $y = 0.5x^2$
7. $y = x^2 - 2$
8. $y = -x^2 + 1$
9. $y = -2x^2 + 2$

★ indicates increased difficulty

Practice and Applications

Graph each function. 10–21. See Ch. 12 Answer Appendix.

10. $y = 4x^2$
11. $y = -3x^2$
12. $y = -1.5x^2$
13. $y = 3.5x^2$
14. $y = x^2 + 6$
15. $y = x^2 - 4$
16. $y = 2x^2 - 1$
17. $y = 2x^2 + 3$
18. $y = -x^2 + 2$
19. $y = -x^2 - 5$
20. $y = -4x^2 - 1$
21. $y = -3x^2 + 2$

HOMEWORK HELP

For Exercises	See Examples
10–13	1, 2
14–23	3, 4
24–29	5

Extra Practice
See pages 645, 659.

22. Graph the function $y = 0.5x^2 + 1$. 22–23. See Ch. 12 Answer Appendix.
23. Graph the function $y = \frac{1}{3}x^2 - 2$.

RACING For Exercises 24–26, use the following information.

The function $d = \frac{1}{2}at^2$ represents the distance d that a race car will travel over an amount of time t given the rate of acceleration a. Suppose a car is accelerating at a rate of 5 feet per second every second.

24. Graph $d = \frac{1}{2}(5t^2)$. See margin.
25. Find the distance traveled after 10 seconds. 250 ft
26. About how long would it take the car to travel 125 feet? about 7 s

WATERFALL For Exercises 27–29, use the following information.

The quadratic equation $d = -16t^2 + h$ models the distance d in feet a falling object is from the ground or other surface t seconds after it is dropped from a beginning height of h feet. Suppose a drop of water descends from the 182-foot tall American Falls in New York, toward the river below.

27. Graph $d = -16t^2 + 182$. See margin.
28. How high is a drop of water after 2 seconds? 118 ft
29. After about how many seconds will the drop of water reach the river below? about 3.4 s

msmath3.net/self_check_quiz

In-Class Example

GRAVITY The function $d = 4.9t^2$ describes the distance d in meters that a rock falls from a high cliff during time t. Graph this function. Then use your graph to estimate how long it would take a rock to fall 400 meters. about 9 s

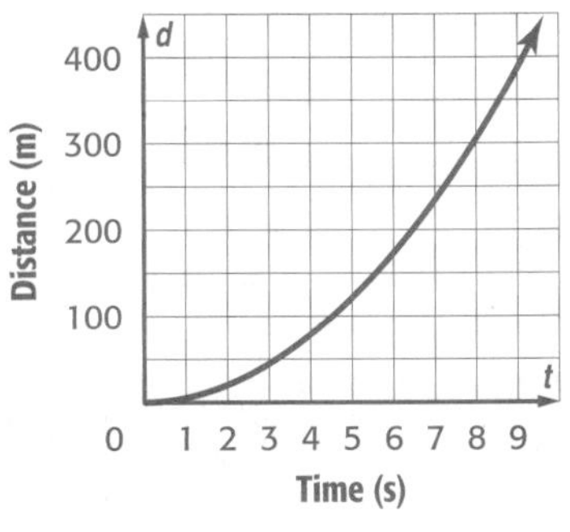

3 Practice/Apply

Which One Doesn't Belong? In Exercise 3, students need to evaluate the characteristics of the function. Be sure they understand that although the function $y = -5x^2$ looks different from the others, it is in the form $y = ax^2 + c$, where $c = 0$. Thus it is quadratic like two of the others.

Answers

24.

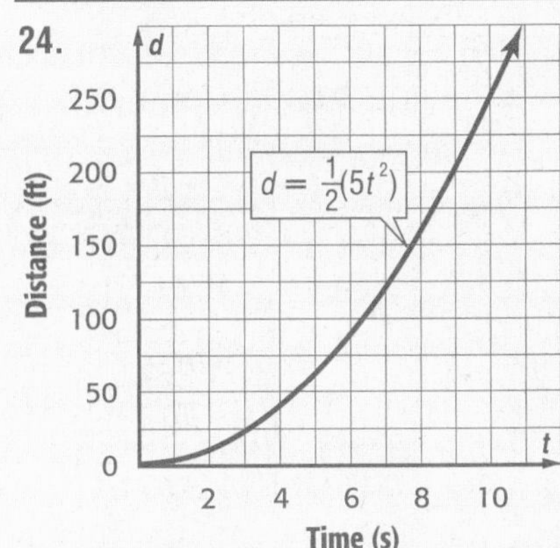

About the Exercises...

Guided Practice Key

Exercises	Examples
4, 6	1
5	2
7	3
8–9	4

Assignment Guide

Basic: 11–23 odd, 24, 25, 27–29, 32–34, 39–52

Average: 11–23 odd, 24, 25, 27–29, 30–34, 39–52 (Optional: 35–38)

Enriched: 10–22 even, 24–48 (Optional: 49–52)

27.

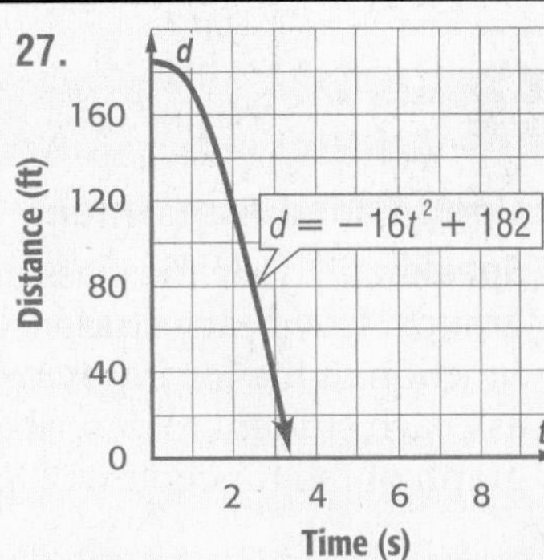

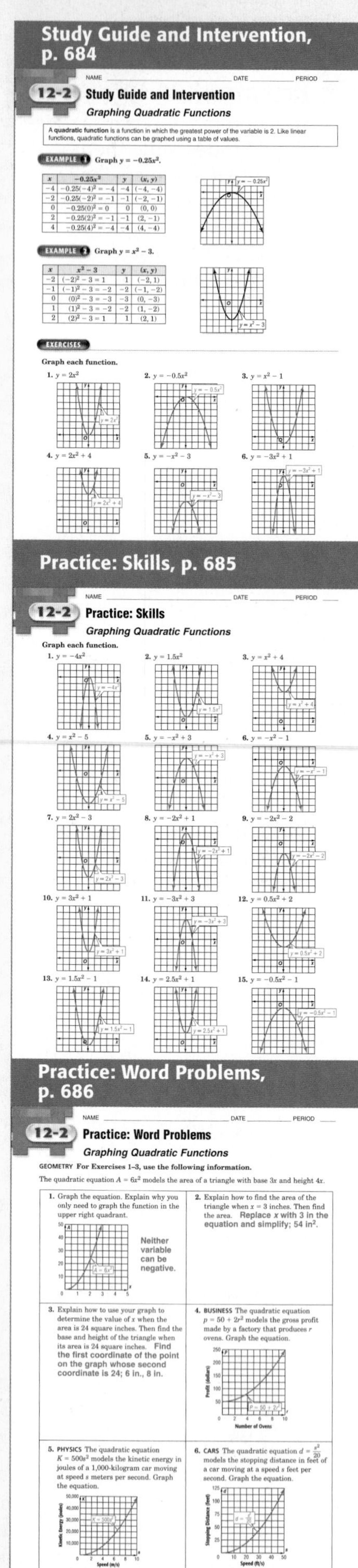

Study Guide and Intervention, p. 684

NAME ______ DATE ______ PERIOD ______

12-2 Study Guide and Intervention

Graphing Quadratic Functions

A **quadratic function** is a function in which the greatest power of the variable is 2. Like linear functions, quadratic functions can be graphed using a table of values.

EXAMPLE 1 Graph $y = -0.25x^2$.

x	$-0.25x^2$	y	(x, y)
−4	$-0.25(-4)^2 = -4$	−4	(−4, −4)
−2	$-0.25(-2)^2 = -1$	−1	(−2, −1)
0	$-0.25(0)^2 = 0$	0	(0, 0)
2	$-0.25(2)^2 = -1$	−1	(2, −1)
4	$-0.25(4)^2 = -4$	−4	(4, −4)

EXAMPLE 2 Graph $y = x^2 - 3$.

x	$x^2 - 3$	y	(x, y)
−2	$(-2)^2 - 3 = 1$	1	(−2, 1)
−1	$(-1)^2 - 3 = -2$	−2	(−1, −2)
0	$(0)^2 - 3 = -3$	−3	(0, −3)
1	$(1)^2 - 3 = -2$	−2	(1, −2)
2	$(2)^2 - 3 = 1$	1	(2, 1)

EXERCISES

Graph each function.

1. $y = 2x^2$ 2. $y = -0.5x^2$ 3. $y = x^2 - 1$
4. $y = 2x^2 + 4$ 5. $y = -x^2 - 3$ 6. $y = -3x^2 + 1$

Practice: Skills, p. 685

NAME ______ DATE ______ PERIOD ______

12-2 Practice: Skills

Graphing Quadratic Functions

Graph each function.

1. $y = -4x^2$ 2. $y = 1.5x^2$ 3. $y = x^2 + 4$
4. $y = x^2 - 5$ 5. $y = -x^2 + 3$ 6. $y = -x^2 - 1$
7. $y = 2x^2 - 3$ 8. $y = -2x^2 + 1$ 9. $y = -2x^2 - 2$
10. $y = 3x^2 + 1$ 11. $y = -3x^2 + 3$ 12. $y = 0.5x^2 + 2$
13. $y = 1.5x^2 - 1$ 14. $y = 2.5x^2 + 1$ 15. $y = -0.5x^2 - 1$

Practice: Word Problems, p. 686

NAME ______ DATE ______ PERIOD ______

12-2 Practice: Word Problems

Graphing Quadratic Functions

GEOMETRY For Exercises 1–3, use the following information.

The quadratic equation $A = 6x^2$ models the area of a triangle with base $3x$ and height $4x$.

1. Graph the equation. Explain why you only need to graph the function in the upper right quadrant. Neither variable can be negative.

2. Explain how to find the area of the triangle when $x = 3$ inches. Then find the area. Replace x with 3 in the equation and simplify; 54 in².

3. Explain how to use your graph to determine the value of x when the area is 24 square inches. Then find the base and height of the triangle when its area is 24 square inches. Find the first coordinate of the point on the graph whose second coordinate is 24; 6 in., 8 in.

4. BUSINESS The quadratic equation $p = 50 + 2r^2$ models the gross profit made by a factory that produces r ovens. Graph the equation.

5. PHYSICS The quadratic equation $K = 500s^2$ models the kinetic energy in joules of a 1,000-kilogram car moving at speed s meters per second. Graph the equation.

6. CARS The quadratic equation $d = \frac{s^2}{20}$ models the stopping distance in feet of a car moving at a speed s feet per second. Graph the equation.

GEOMETRY For Exercises 30 and 31, write a function for each of the following. Then graph the function in the first quadrant.

★30. the volume V of a cube as a function of the edge length a $V = a^3$

★31. the volume V of a rectangular prism as a function of a fixed height of 5 and a square base of varying length s $V = 5s^2$

30–31. See Ch. 12 Answer Appendix for graphs.

CRITICAL THINKING The graphs of quadratic functions may have exactly one highest point, called a *maximum*, or exactly one lowest point, called a *minimum*.

Graph each quadratic equation. Determine whether each graph has a maximum or a minimum. If so, give the coordinates of each point. 32–34. See Ch. 12 Answer Appendix for graphs.

32. $y = 2x^2 + 1$ minimum; (0, 1)
33. $y = -x^2 + 5$ maximum; (0, 5)
34. $y = x^2 - 3$ minimum; (0, −3)

EXTENDING THE LESSON Another type of nonlinear function is graphed at the right. A *cubic function*, such as $y = x^3$, is a function in which the greatest power is 3.

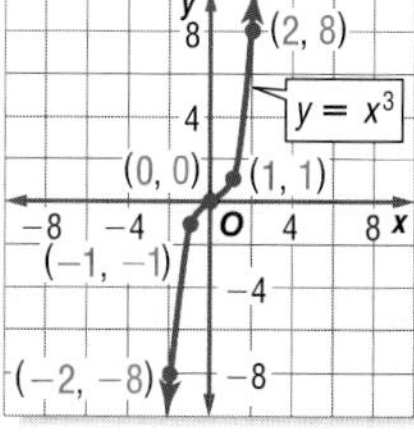

Graph each function. (***Hint***: **You may need to let** x **represent decimal values.**) 35–37. See Ch. 12 Answer Appendix.

35. $y = 2x^3$
36. $y = x^3 + 1$
37. $y = 2x^3 + 2$

38. Graph the equations $y = x^2$ and $y = x^3$ on the same coordinate plane. Describe their similarities and differences. See Ch. 12 Answer Appendix.

Spiral Review with Standardized Test Practice

39. **MULTIPLE CHOICE** Which equation represents the graph at the right? B

(A) $y = 2x^2 - 2$
(B) $y = -0.5x^2 - 2$
(C) $y = -x^2 + 2$
(D) $y = x^2 - 2$

40. **MULTIPLE CHOICE** Which equation represents a quadratic function? I

(F) $y = 2x$
(G) $y = \frac{2}{x}$
(H) $y = x + 2$
(I) $y = -x^2 + 8$

Determine whether each equation represents a ***linear*** **or** ***nonlinear*** **function.** (Lesson 12-1)

41. $y = x - 5$ linear
42. $y = 3x^3 + 2$ nonlinear
43. $x + y = -6$ linear
44. $y = -2x^2$ nonlinear

Graph each inequality. (Lesson 11-8) 45–48. See Ch. 12 Answer Appendix.

45. $y < 2x$
46. $y \geq x + 1$
47. $y > -x - 3$
48. $y \leq -3x + 4$

GETTING READY FOR THE NEXT LESSON

PREREQUISITE SKILL **Identify the like terms in each expression.** (Lesson 10-1)

49. $4a + 1 - 2a$ $4a$ and $-2a$
50. $2x + 3x + 5 - 1$ $2x$ and $3x$; 5 and −1
51. $-1 - 2d + 3 + d$ −1 and 3; $-2d$ and d
52. $x + 2 - 7x + 8$ x and $-7x$; 2 and 8

4 Assess

Open-Ended Assessment

Speaking Divide the class into small groups. Have each student choose a function in the form $y = ax^2 + c$. Then, ask each student to describe what a graph of the function will look like. They should say whether it will point up or down and indicate the location of the vertex.

568 Chapter 12 Algebra: Nonlinear Functions and Polynomials

12-3a HANDS-ON LAB

A Preview of Lesson 12-3

Modeling Expressions with Algebra Tiles

What You'll LEARN

Model expressions using algebra tiles.

Materials

- algebra tiles

In a set of algebra tiles, the integer 1 is represented by a tile that is 1 unit by 1 unit. Notice that the area of this tile is 1 square unit. The opposite of 1, -1, is represented by a red tile with the same shape and size.

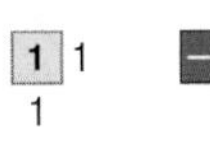

The variable x is represented by a tile that is 1 unit by x units. Notice that the area of this tile is x square units. The opposite of x, $-x$, is represented by a red tile with the same shape and size.

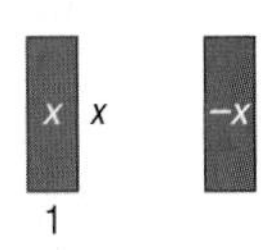

Similarly, the expression x^2 is represented by a tile that is x units by x units. A red tile with the same shape and size is used to represent $-x^2$.

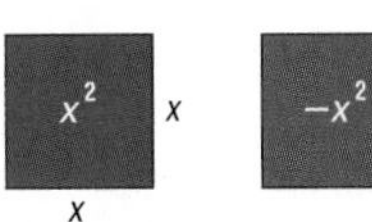

You can use these tiles to model expressions like $2x^2 + 5x - 6$.

ACTIVITY

Use algebra tiles to model $2x^2 + 5x - 6$.

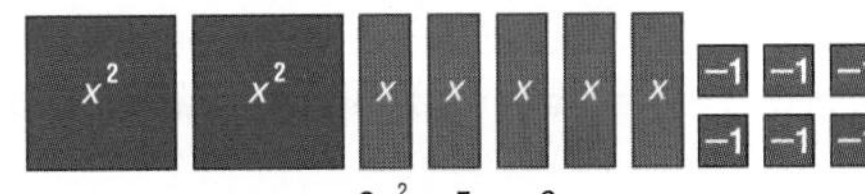

Your Turn **Use algebra tiles to model each expression.**

a. $4x^2$ b. $-3x^2$ c. $3x^2 - 4x$ d. $-x^2 + 2x$

e. $x^2 - x + 1$ f. $-2x^2 + x - 5$ g. $2x^2 - 3x + 2$ h. $-4x^2 + 3x + 8$

a–h. See Ch. 12 Answer Appendix.

Writing Math

1. **Name** the expression modeled below. $-3x^2 + 3x + 4$

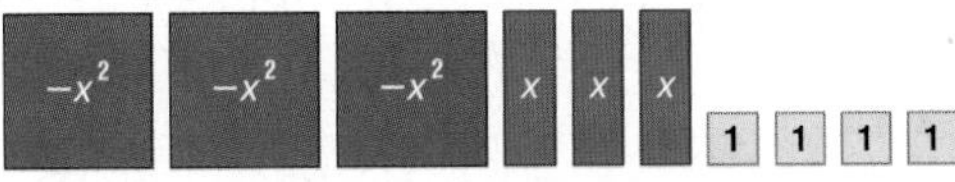

2. **MAKE A CONJECTURE** What might a model of the expression x^3 look like? **a cube with edge length x**

TEACHING TIP

The model for x^3 looks like a thousands cube from base-ten models.

12-3a HANDS-ON LAB Lesson Notes

Lesson Resources

Teaching Mathematics with Manipulatives

- algebra tiles, p. 29
- student recording sheet 12-3a

Glencoe Mathematics Classroom Manipulative Kit

- algebra tiles

Virtual Activities CD-ROM, Area Models of Polynomials

GETTING STARTED

Teaching Tip Before beginning the **Activity**, have students outline an x-units by x-units area, with $x = 6$. Shade one column and point out that the number of units in this column depends on the value of x. Ask students to shade squares to represent $2x + 1$. They should shade two columns and one square.

TEACH

- Using algebra tiles shows students that they can only combine like terms. For example, the x terms cannot be combined with the x^2 terms.

Discuss the **Writing Math** exercises. Use Exercise 1 to determine whether students have become fluent with algebra tiles. For Exercise 2, students should realize three-dimensional objects are represented by cubed terms.

ASSESS

Observe as students solve the **Your Turn** exercises. They should:

- correctly choose the types of tiles needed, and
- relate tiles to corresponding terms in the equation.

12-3 Lesson Notes

Lesson Resources

Chapter 12 Resource Masters
- Study Guide and Intervention, p. 689
- Practice: Skills, p. 690
- Practice: Word Problems, p. 691
- Reading to Learn Mathematics, p. 692
- Enrichment, p. 693

Key Teaching Transparencies, 46
MathPASS Tutorial CD-ROM, 42
Parent and Student Study Guide Online Worksheets, 12-3
Real-Life Career Masters, p. 38
Noteables™: Interactive Study Notebook with Foldables™, 12-3

1 Focus

5-Minute Check 12-3

INTERACTIVE CHALKBOARD
PowerPoint® Presentations

Use as a quiz or review of Lesson 12-2. (Also available as a transparency)

Bellringer
Problem Solving When simplifying polynomials, students must be able to recognize like terms in expressions containing more than one variable. Have them identify each pair of terms in the list in the bottom margin as *like* or *unlike* and explain their answers.

(Continued in bottom margin.)

Reading to Learn Mathematics, p. 692 **ELL**

NAME ______ DATE ______ PERIOD ____

12-3 Reading to Learn Mathematics
Simplifying Polynomials

Pre-Activity *Read the introduction at the top of page 570 in your textbook. Write your answers below.*

1. Let q, d, n, and p represent the value of a quarter, a dime, a nickel, and a penny, respectively. Write an expression for the total amount of money in your backpack. $3q + 5d + 2n + 4p$
2. Write an expression for the total amount of money in your pocket. $2d + 3n$
3. Write an expression for the total amount of money in all. $3q + 7d + 5n + 4p$

Reading the Lesson

4. What is a monomial? a number, a variable, or a product of numbers and/or variables

Determine whether each expression is a monomial. Explain.

5. 8 6. y 7. 5^{-2} 8. $x + 2$

12-3 Simplifying Polynomials

What You'll LEARN
Simplify polynomials.

NEW Vocabulary
monomial
polynomial

REVIEW Vocabulary
like terms: terms that contain the same variable (Lesson 10-1)
simplest form: an algebraic expression that has no like terms or parentheses (Lesson 10-1)

WHEN am I ever going to use this?

MONEY Suppose you need money to buy a drink and a snack. The table shows the number and type of coins you find in your backpack and in your pocket.

Coin Type	Number in Backpack	Number in Pocket
Quarter	3	0
Dime	5	2
Nickel	2	3
Penny	4	0

1. Let q, d, n, and p represent the value of a quarter, a dime, a nickel, and a penny, respectively. Write an expression for the total amount of money in your backpack. $3q + 5d + 2n + 4p$
2. Write an expression for the total amount of money in your pocket. $2d + 3n$
3. Write an expression for the total amount of money in all.

3. $3q + 7d + 5n + 4p$

In Lesson 10-1, you learned that like terms, such as $-5d$ and $2d$, can be combined using the Distributive Property.

$-5d + 2d = (-5 + 2)d$ Distributive Property
$= -3d$ Simplify.

The terms of an expression are also called monomials. A **monomial** is a number, a variable, or a product of numbers and/or variables. An algebraic expression that is the sum or difference of one or more monomials is called a **polynomial**.

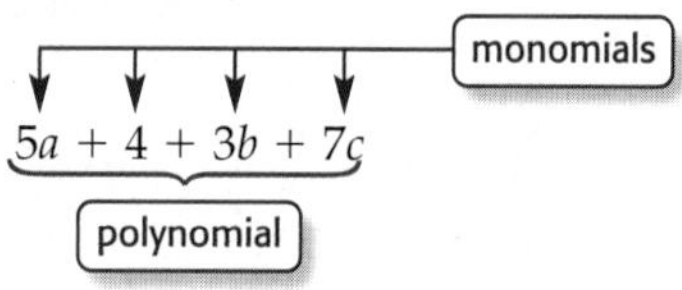

You have already learned how to simplify polynomials like $3x + 4 + 2x - 8$ by combining like terms. You can use the same process to simplify polynomials containing more than one variable.

EXAMPLE Simplify a Polynomial

1 **Simplify $-5d + 2n + 4d - 3n$.**

The like terms in this expression are $-5d$ and $4d$, and $2n$ and $-3n$.

$-5d + 2n + 4d - 3n$ Write the polynomial.
$= -5d + 2n + 4d + (-3n)$ Definition of subtraction
$= (-5d + 4d) + [2n + (-3n)]$ Group like terms.
$= -1d + (-1n)$ or $-d - n$ Simplify by combining like terms.

READING in the Content Area
For strategies in reading this lesson, visit **msmath3.net/reading.**

$3q$ and $4p$ **unlike; different variables**
$4x$ and $3q$ **unlike; different variables**
$6y$ and $8y$ **like**
$8r$ and $8p$ **unlike; different variables**
$2p$ and $9p$ **like**
$8r$ and $-7r$ **like**

The goals of the NCLB Act include a stronger emphasis on reading. The **Reading in the Content Area** link helps students become proficient readers.

The expression $2x^2$ is another example of a monomial, since it is the product of 2, x, and x. You can simplify expressions like $2x^2 + 4 - x^2$ using algebra tiles.

EXAMPLE Simplify Polynomials

2 Simplify $2x^2 + 4 - x^2$.

Use the definition of subtraction to write this polynomial as $2x^2 + 4 + (-x^2)$.

STUDY TIP

Look Back To review zero pairs, see Lesson 1-4.

Method 1 Use models.

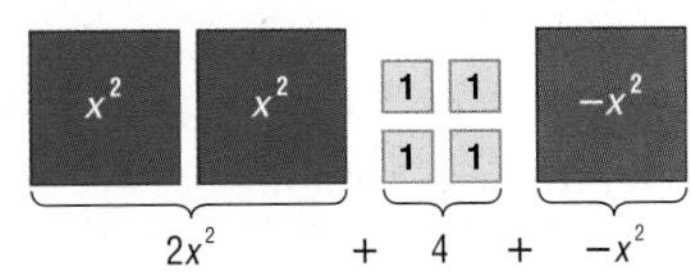

$2x^2 \quad + \quad 4 \quad + \quad -x^2$

Group tiles with the same shape and remove zero pairs.

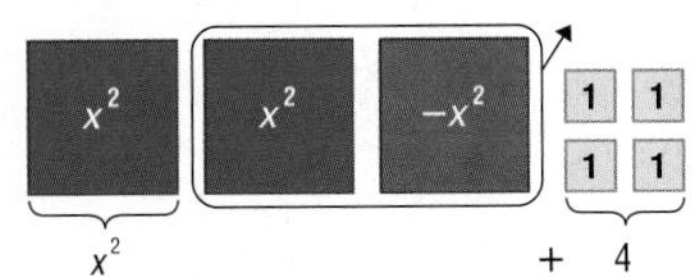

$x^2 \qquad + \quad 4$

Method 2 Use symbols.

Write the polynomial. Then group and add like terms.

$2x^2 + 4 + (-x^2)$

$= [2x^2 + (-x^2)] + 4$

$= [2x^2 + (-1x^2)] + 4$

$= 1x^2 + 4$

$= x^2 + 4$

Thus, $2x^2 + 4 - x^2 = x^2 + 4$.

From these examples, you can see that like terms must have the same variable and the same power. Thus, $2x^2$ and $3x^2$ are like terms, while $4x^2$ and $5x$ are not.

EXAMPLE Simplify Polynomials

3 Simplify $x^2 - 1 - x + 3 + 2x$.

$x^2 - 1 - x + 3 + 2x$ is equal to $x^2 + (-1) + (-1x) + 3 + 2x$.

STUDY TIP

Standard Form When simplifying polynomials, it is customary to write the result in *standard form*; that is, with the powers of the variable decreasing from left to right.
$-5x^2 + 3x + 2$, *not* $3x - 5x^2 + 2$

Method 1 Use models.

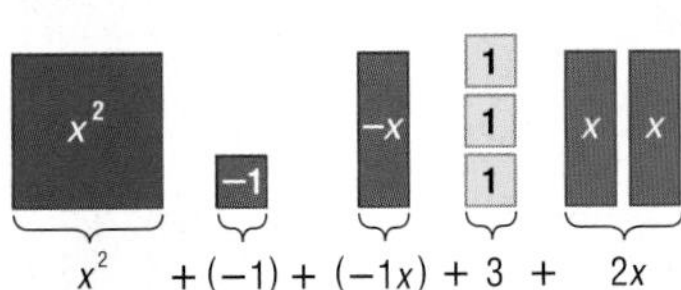

$x^2 \quad + (-1) + (-1x) + 3 + \quad 2x$

Group tiles with the same shape and remove zero pairs.

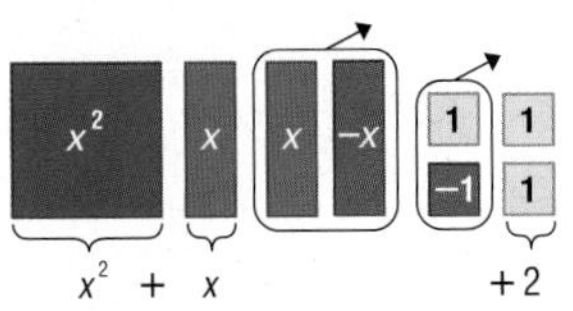

$x^2 + x \qquad +2$

Method 2 Use symbols.

Write the polynomial. Then group and add like terms.

$x^2 + (-1) + (-1x) + 3 + 2x$

$= x^2 + (-1x + 2x) + (-1 + 3)$

$= x^2 + 1x + 2$

$= x^2 + x + 2$

Thus, $x^2 - 1 - x + 3 + 2x = x^2 + x + 2$.

Math Online msmath3.net/extra_examples

2 Teach

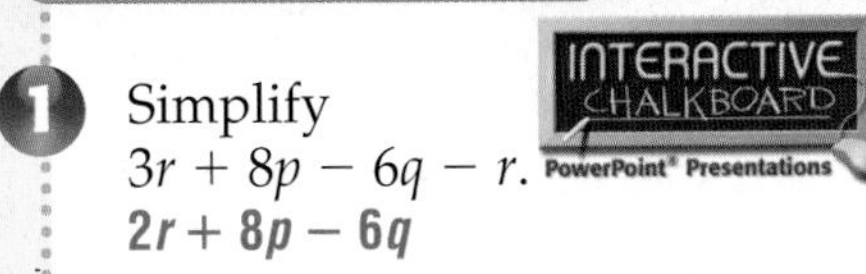

In-Class Examples

INTERACTIVE CHALKBOARD PowerPoint® Presentations

1 Simplify $3r + 8p - 6q - r$. **$2r + 8p - 6q$**

2 Simplify $-6x^2 + 14 + 3x$. **simplest form**

3 Simplify $2x + 8x^2 - 9x + 3 - 2x^2$. **$6x^2 - 7x + 3$**

Tips for New Teachers

Using Manipulatives Craft stores are a good place to obtain useful math manipulatives. For example, plastic quilting squares can be used as durable, reusable grids. Wooden and plastic beads can be used for multiplication and division. You can also find wooden geometric shapes at craft stores.

DAILY INTERVENTION **Differentiated Instruction**

Interpersonal Have students work in groups of four. Tell them to write a polynomial that gives the score of a basketball game as a function of the number of 3-point field goals (t), 2-point field goals (g), and 1-point free throws (f). **score = $3t + 2g + f$** Then find a box score for a basketball game, and tell students the number of each type of score one team had during the game. Students can verify their polynomials by using them to calculate the teams' scores for the game.

Lesson 12-3 Simplifying Polynomials 571

3 Practice/Apply

FOLDABLES™ Follow-Up Remind students to use their Foldables like a journal to record what they learn about simplifying polynomials. For example, they might explain when an expression is in simplest form and how they know it is in simplest form.

Which One Doesn't Belong?
In Exercise 3, students should realize that the variables and the exponents of the variables must match exactly to be considered like terms. Only the coefficient of the terms may be different.

About the Exercises...

Guided Practice Key

Exercises	Examples
4–6	1
7–11	2, 3

Assignment Guide

Basic: 13–19 odd, 23–33 odd, 37–49

Average: 13–37 odd, 38–49

Enriched: 12–36 even, 38–45 (Optional: 46–49)

Answers

12. $-a + 9b$
13. simplest form
14. $-7n + 4p + 5$
15. $8f - 11g$
16. $-4c - d + 2$
17. $2j + k - 2$

Students practice the same concepts in Exercises 12–37 if they are assigned odd or even problems.

Skill and Concept Check

1. **OPEN ENDED** Write a polynomial with four terms that simplifies to $5a - 9b$. **Sample answer: $6a - a + b - 10b$**
2. **Writing Math** Explain why $6x$ and $3x^2$ are not like terms. **The power of x for each term is different; the power of x in $6x$ is 1 and the power of x in $3x^2$ is 2.**
3. **Which One Doesn't Belong?** Identify the expression that is not a like term. Explain your reasoning.

$2y^2$	$-x^2$	$5x^2$	$-4x^2$

$2y^2$; the others are like terms.

GUIDED PRACTICE

Simplify each polynomial. If the polynomial cannot be simplified, write *simplest form.* **4. $5c + 11d$ 5. simplest form**

4. $4c + 5d + 6d + c$
5. $-7x - 8 - 2y$
6. $9g - 9h + 3g + 1$ **$12g - 9h + 1$**
7. $4x + x^2 + 2x$ **$x^2 + 6x$**

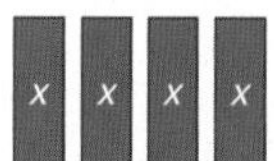

8. $-x^2 + 5 + 3x - 1 + x^2$ **$3x + 4$**

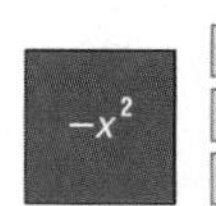
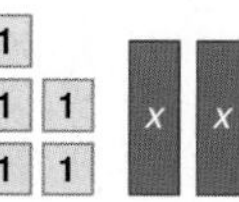

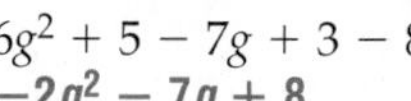

9. $-5w^2 + 3w^2 - 8w$ **$-2w^2 - 8w$**
10. $-9m^2 + 4m - m + 2$ **$-9m^2 + 3m + 2$**
11. $6g^2 + 5 - 7g + 3 - 8g^2$ **$-2g^2 - 7g + 8$**

Practice and Applications

HOMEWORK HELP

For Exercises	See Examples
12–17, 36	1
18–35, 37	2, 3

Extra Practice See pages 646, 659.

Simplify each polynomial. If the polynomial cannot be simplified, write *simplest form.* **12–17. See margin.**

12. $6a + 8b - 7a + b$
13. $5x + 7y + 8 - z$
14. $-n + 4p + 5 - 6n$
15. $3f - 2g - 9g + 5f$
16. $-8c - d + 4c + 2$
17. $2j + 7 + k - 9$
18. $2x^2 - 3x + x$ **$2x^2 - 2x$**

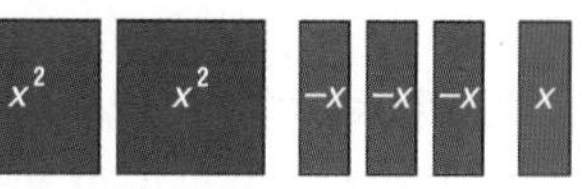
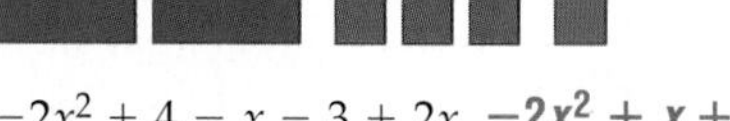

19. $-3x^2 + 2x + x^2$ **$-2x^2 + 2x$**

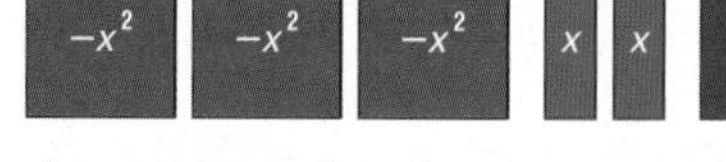

20. $-2x^2 + 4 - x - 3 + 2x$ **$-2x^2 + x + 1$**

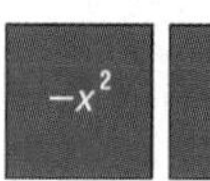

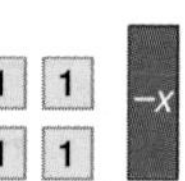
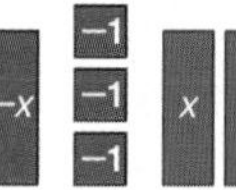

21. $x^2 + x + 2 - x^2 - 3x - 5$ **$-2x - 3$**

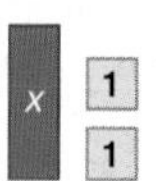

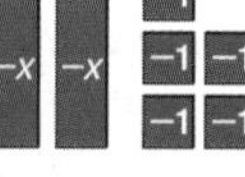

22. $m^2 + m - 3$ **simplest form**
23. $a + 5a^2 - 7a$ **$5a^2 - 6a$**
24. $4 - 3x^2 + 6x + x^2$
25. $2w^2 - 6w - w + 1$
26. $3k^2 + 4 - 8k + k - 2$
27. $y^2 + 8y + 1 + 7y^2 - 4$
28. $a^2 + 3a^2 - 4a + a - 7 - 1$ **$4a^2 - 3a - 8$**
29. $-z^2 + z^2 - 5z + 9z - 2 + 13$ **$4z + 11$**
30. $b^2 + 6b - 9 + b^2 - b + 3$ **$2b^2 + 5b - 6$**
31. $r^2 - 3r + 8 + 2r^2 - 4r + 4$ **$3r^2 - 7r + 12$**
32. $11 - 4n^3 - 8 + n^3 - 4n^3$ **$-7n^3 + 3$**
33. $-5t^3 - 8t^2 + 4t - 6 + 7t^3 + 3t$
34. $1.4x^2 - 3.8x + 1.2x^2 + 4.5x$ **$2.6x^2 + 0.7x$**
35. $\frac{3}{4}y^2 - 5y - \frac{1}{4}y + 5y$ **$\frac{3}{4}y^2 - \frac{1}{4}y$**

24. $-2x^2 + 6x + 4$ 25. $2w^2 - 7w + 1$ 26. $3k^2 - 7k + 2$ 27. $8y^2 + 8y - 3$ 33. $2t^3 - 8t^2 + 7t -$

41.

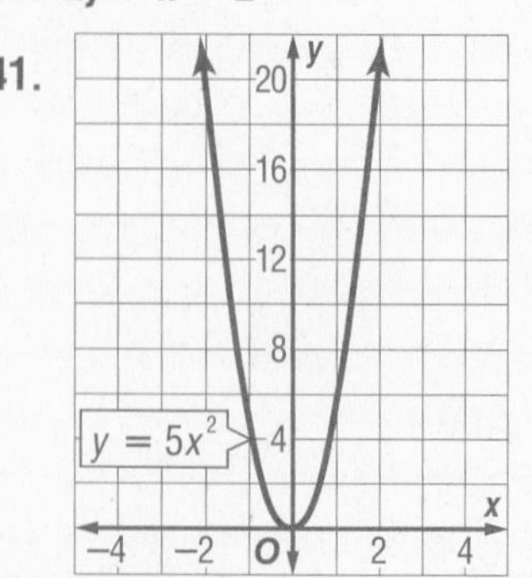

42.

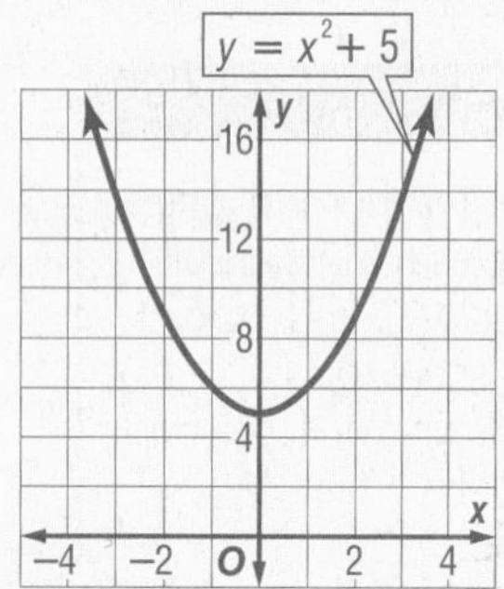

43.

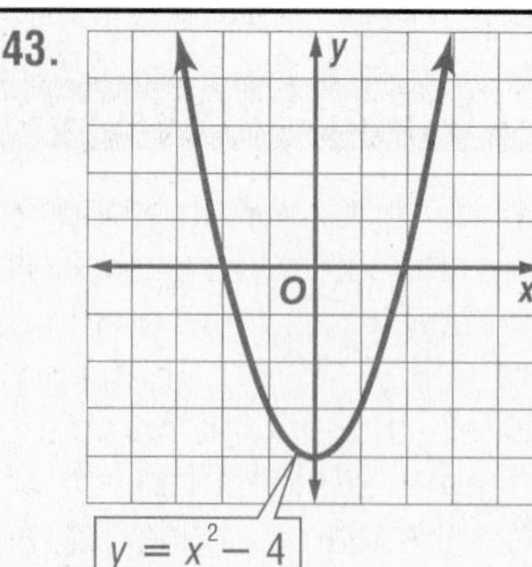

44.

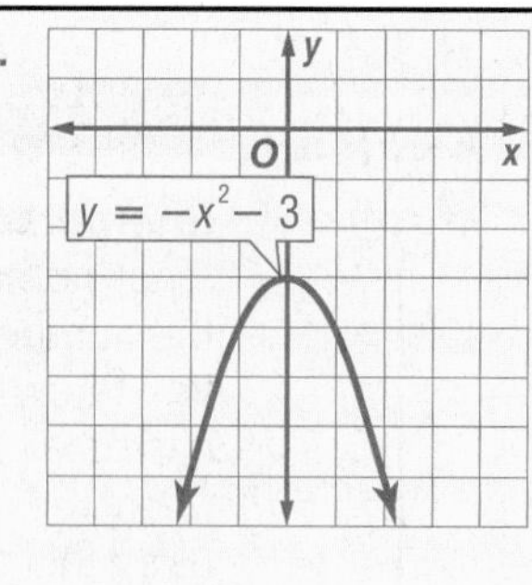

36. **COOKIES** The table shows the number of boxes of each type of cookie Orlando and Emma bought from Science Club members. If m represents the cost of mint cookies, p the cost of peanut butter cookies, and c the cost of chocolate chip cookies per box, write an expression in simplest form for the total amount spent by Orlando and Emma on cookies. **$2m + 3p + 3c$**

Name	Mint	Peanut Butter	Chocolate Chip
Orlando	2 boxes	1 box	0 boxes
Emma	0 boxes	2 boxes	3 boxes

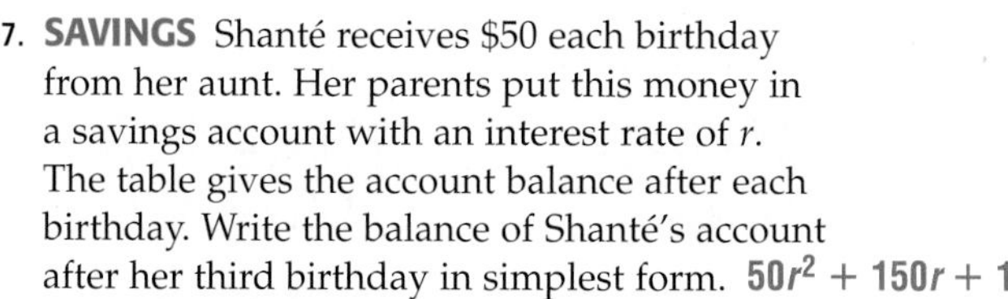

37. **SAVINGS** Shanté receives \$50 each birthday from her aunt. Her parents put this money in a savings account with an interest rate of r. The table gives the account balance after each birthday. Write the balance of Shanté's account after her third birthday in simplest form. **$50r^2 + 150r + 150$**

Birthday	Balance ($)
1	50
2	$(50r + 50) + 50$
3	$(50r^2 + 100r + 50) + (50r + 50) + 50$

38. **CRITICAL THINKING** Determine whether $2x^2 + 3x = 5x^2$ is *sometimes*, *always*, or *never* true for all x. Explain your reasoning. **sometimes; true only if $x = 1$ or 0**

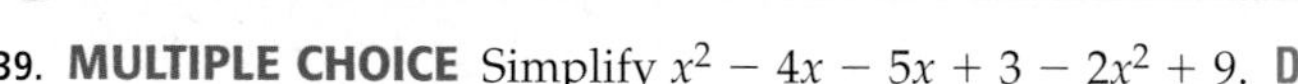

Spiral Review with Standardized Test Practice

39. **MULTIPLE CHOICE** Simplify $x^2 - 4x - 5x + 3 - 2x^2 + 9$. **D**

Ⓐ $3x^2 - 9x + 12$ Ⓑ $2x^2$
Ⓒ $-2x^2 - 9x + 12$ Ⓓ $-x^2 - 9x + 12$

40. **MULTIPLE CHOICE** Write the perimeter of the figure in simplest form. **I**

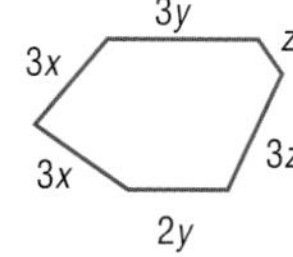

Ⓕ $14xyz$ Ⓖ $15xyz$
Ⓗ $6x + 5y + 3z$ Ⓘ $6x + 5y + 4z$

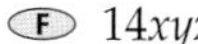

Graph each function. (Lesson 12-2) **41–44. See margin.**

41. $y = 5x^2$ 42. $y = x^2 + 5$ 43. $y = x^2 - 4$ 44. $y = -x^2 - 3$

45. **BIOLOGY** The table shows how long it took for the first 400 bacteria cells to grow in a petri dish. Is the growth of the bacteria a linear function of time? Explain. (Lesson 12-1) **No; the difference between the times varies, so the growth is not constant.**

Time (min)	46	53	57	60
Number of Cells	100	200	300	400

GETTING READY FOR THE NEXT LESSON

PREREQUISITE SKILL Rewrite each expression using parentheses so that the like terms are grouped together. (Lessons 1-2 and 10-1)

46. $(a + 2) + (3a + 4)$ **$(a + 3a) + (2 + 4)$**
47. $(2n + 5) + (5n + 1)$ **$(2n + 5n) + (5 + 1)$**
48. $(c + d) + (7c - 2d)$ **$(c + 7c) + (d - 2d)$**
49. $(x^2 + 4x) + (6x^2 - 8x)$ **$(x^2 + 6x^2) + (4x - 8x)$**

Math Online msmath3.net/self_check_quiz

4 Assess

Open-Ended Assessment

Modeling Divide the class into small groups. Have students write several polynomials that are not simplified. Then have them use algebra tiles to demonstrate to others in their group how to simplify the polynomials.

Study Guide and Intervention, p. 689

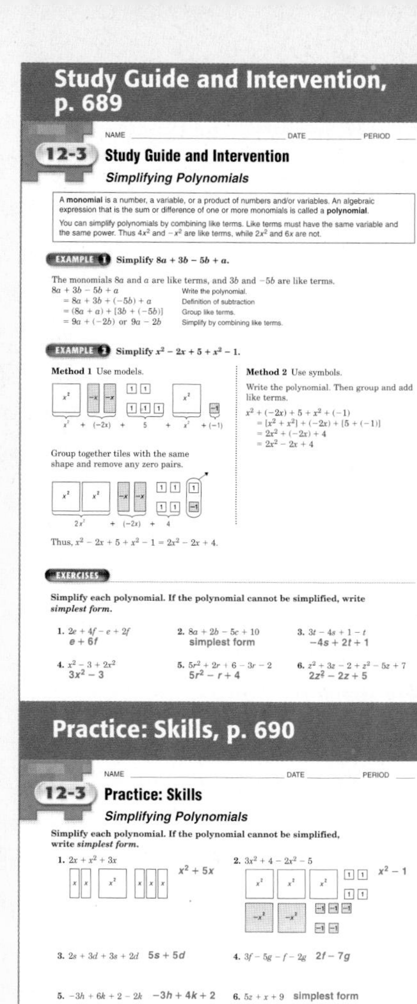

NAME ____ DATE ____ PERIOD ____

12-3 Study Guide and Intervention

Simplifying Polynomials

A **monomial** is a number, a variable, or a product of numbers and/or variables. An algebraic expression that is the sum or difference of one or more monomials is called a **polynomial**.

You can simplify polynomials by combining like terms. Like terms must have the same variable and the same power. Thus $4x^2$ and $-x^2$ are like terms, while $2x^2$ and $6x$ are not.

EXAMPLE 1 Simplify $8a + 3b - 5b + a$.

The monomials $8a$ and a are like terms, and $3b$ and $-5b$ are like terms.

$8a + 3b - 5b + a$ — Write the polynomial.
$= 8a + 3b + (-5b) + a$ — Definition of subtraction
$= (8a + a) + [3b + (-5b)]$ — Group like terms.
$= 9a + (-2b)$ or $9a - 2b$ — Simplify by combining like terms.

EXAMPLE 2 Simplify $x^2 - 2x + 5 + x^2 - 1$.

Method 1 Use models.

$x^2 + (-2x) + 5 + x^2 + (-1)$

Group together tiles with the same shape and remove any zero pairs.

$2x^2 + (-2x) + 4$

Method 2 Use symbols.

Write the polynomial. Then group and add like terms.

$x^2 + (-2x) + 5 + x^2 + (-1)$
$= [x^2 + x^2] + (-2x) + [5 + (-1)]$
$= 2x^2 + (-2x) + 4$
$= 2x^2 - 2x + 4$

Thus, $x^2 - 2x + 5 + x^2 - 1 = 2x^2 - 2x + 4$.

EXERCISES

Simplify each polynomial. If the polynomial cannot be simplified, write *simplest form*.

1. $2e + 4f - e + 2f$ **$e + 6f$**
2. $8a + 2b - 5c + 10$ **simplest form**
3. $3t - 4s + 1 - t$ **$-4s + 2t + 1$**
4. $x^2 - 3 + 2x^2$ **$3x^2 - 3$**
5. $5r^2 + 2r + 6 - 3r - 2$ **$5r^2 - r + 4$**
6. $z^2 + 3z - 2 + z^2 - 5z + 7$ **$2z^2 - 2z + 5$**

Practice: Skills, p. 690

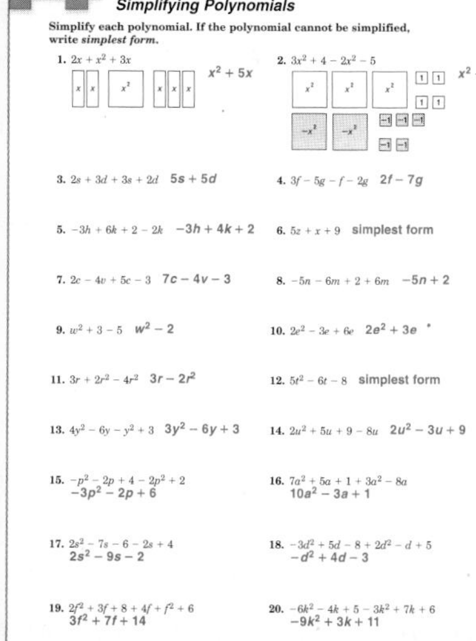

NAME ____ DATE ____ PERIOD ____

12-3 Practice: Skills

Simplifying Polynomials

Simplify each polynomial. If the polynomial cannot be simplified, write *simplest form*.

1. $2x + x^2 + 3x$ **$x^2 + 5x$**
2. $3x^2 + 4 - 2x^2 - 5$ **$x^2 - 1$**
3. $2s + 3d + 3s + 2d$ **$5s + 5d$**
4. $3f - 5g - f - 2g$ **$2f - 7g$**
5. $-3h + 6k + 2 - 2k$ **$-3h + 4k + 2$**
6. $5z + x + 9$ **simplest form**
7. $2c - 4v + 5c - 3$ **$7c - 4v - 3$**
8. $-5n - 6m + 2 + 6m$ **$-5n + 2$**
9. $w^2 + 3 - 5$ **$w^2 - 2$**
10. $2e^2 - 3e + 6e$ **$2e^2 + 3e$**
11. $3r + 2r^2 - 4r^2$ **$3r - 2r^2$**
12. $5t^2 - 6t - 8$ **simplest form**
13. $4y^2 - 6y - y^2 + 3$ **$3y^2 - 6y + 3$**
14. $2u^2 + 5u + 9 - 8u$ **$2u^2 - 3u + 9$**
15. $-p^2 - 2p + 4 - 2p^2 + 2$ **$-3p^2 - 2p + 6$**
16. $7a^2 + 5a + 1 + 3a^2 - 8a$ **$10a^2 - 3a + 1$**
17. $2s^2 - 7s - 6 - 2s + 4$ **$2s^2 - 9s - 2$**
18. $-3d^2 + 5d - 8 + 2d^2 - d + 5$ **$-d^2 + 4d - 3$**
19. $2f^2 + 3f + 8 + 4f + f^2 + 6$ **$3f^2 + 7f + 14$**
20. $-6k^2 - 4k + 5 - 3k^2 + 7k + 6$ **$-9k^2 + 3k + 11$**

Practice: Word Problems, p. 691

NAME ____ DATE ____ PERIOD ____

12-3 Practice: Word Problems

Simplifying Polynomials

1. **BAKING** Mila baked 2 cakes and 3 pies yesterday. Today she baked 4 cakes and 1 pie. Each cake takes c cups of flour, and each pie takes p cups of flour. Write an expression with four terms that represents the total amount of flour Mila used. Then simplify your expression. **$2c + 3p + 4c + p$; $6c + 4p$**

2. **GARDENING** You have 2 bags of potting soil and 1 bag of peat moss. You buy 4 more bags of potting soil and 2 bags of peat moss. Each bag of potting soil weighs s pounds and each bag of peat moss weighs m pounds. Write an expression with four terms that represents the total weight of the bags. Then simplify your expression. **$2s + m + 4s + 2m$; $6s + 3m$**

3. **FOOTBALL** The table shows the numbers of touchdowns, extra points, and field goals earned by each team at a football game. If t represents the number of points for a touchdown, e the points for an extra point, and f the points for a field goal, write an expression with six terms for the total number of points scored during the game. Then simplify your expression.

Team	Touchdowns	Extra Points	Field Goals
Huskies	2	1	1
Hornets	1	1	3

$2t + e + f + t + e + 3f$; $3t + 2e + 4f$

4. **CELL PHONES** The table shows the numbers of anytime minutes and night and weekend minutes that Celia used for three days. If a represents the cost per minute for an anytime minute and n represents the cost per minute for a night and weekend minute, write an expression with four terms for the total cost of Celia's cell phone usage for the three days. Then simplify your expression.

Day	Anytime Minutes	Night and Weekend Minutes
Thursday	25	0
Friday	34	15
Saturday	0	55

$25a + 34a + 15n + 55n$; $59a + 70n$

5. **MONEY** Suppose your coin jar contains 3 rolls of quarters, 2 rolls of dimes, and 5 rolls of nickels. Your sister's coin jar contains 1 roll of quarters, 4 rolls of dimes, and 3 rolls of nickels. Each roll of quarters is worth q dollars, each roll of dimes is worth d dollars, and each roll of nickels is worth n dollars. Write an expression for the total amount of money you and your sister have in your jars. **$4q + 6d + 8n$**

6. **ART** You are making a collage using red triangles, blue squares, and green rectangles. You have 4 squares and 6 triangles on the collage. You plan to add 5 squares, 2 more triangles, and 3 rectangles. Each square has an area of s square inches, each triangle has an area of t square inches, and each rectangle has an area of r square inches. Write an expression in simplest form for the total area of the squares, triangles, and rectangles that will make up your collage. **$9s + 8t + 3r$**

12-4 Lesson Notes

Lesson Resources

Chapter 12 Resource Masters
- Study Guide and Intervention, p. 694
- Practice: Skills, p. 695
- Practice: Word Problems, p. 696
- Reading to Learn Mathematics, p. 697
- Enrichment, p. 698

Calculator and Spreadsheet Masters, p. 50

Key Teaching Transparencies, 47

Parent and Student Study Guide Online Worksheets, 12-4

Noteables™: Interactive Study Notebook with Foldables™, 12-4

FAST FILE

1 Focus

5-Minute Check 12-4

INTERACTIVE CHALKBOARD PowerPoint® Presentations

Use as a quiz or review of Lesson 12-3. (Also available as a transparency)

Bellringer

Communication Write the expression $3x + 8 + 6x + 4$ on the chalkboard. Have students explain how the Associative and Commutative Properties can be applied to this expression in order to group like terms.

Reading to Learn Mathematics, p. 697 ELL

NAME ______ DATE ______ PERIOD ____

12-4 Reading to Learn Mathematics

Adding Polynomials

Pre-Activity *Complete the Mini Lab at the top of page 574 in your textbook. Write your answers below.*

1. Write the polynomial for the tiles that remain. $2x^2 + x - 3$

2. Use algebra tiles to find $(x^2 + x - 2) + (6x^2 - 5x - 1)$. $7x^2 - 4x - 3$

Reading the Lesson

3. When adding two polynomials vertically, how should the terms be arranged? Like terms should be aligned in columns.

Determine whether each vertical addition can be performed as written. Explain.

12-4 Adding Polynomials

What You'll LEARN

Add polynomials.

HANDS-ON Mini Lab

Materials
- algebra tiles

Work with a partner.

Consider the polynomials $3x^2 - 2x + 1$ and $-x^2 + 3x - 4$ modeled below.

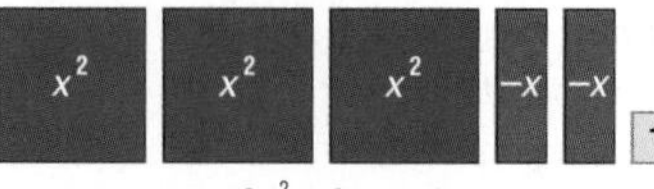

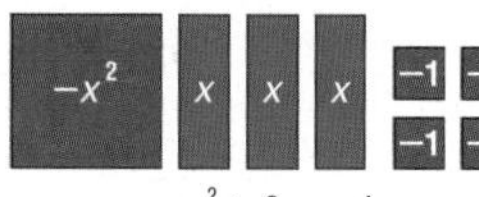

Follow these steps to add the polynomials.

STEP 1 Combine the tiles that have the same shape.

STEP 2 Remove any zero pairs.

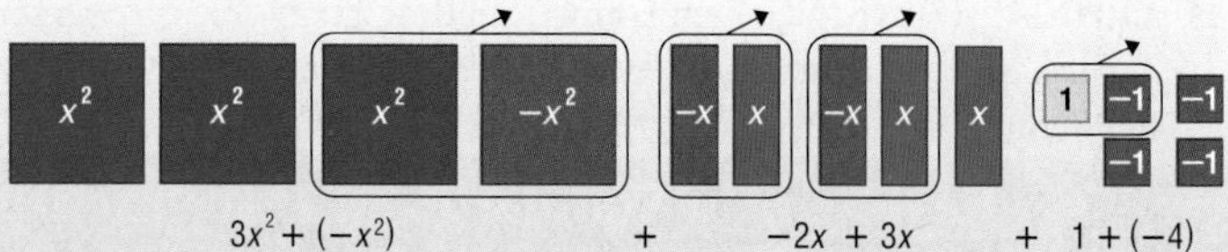

1. Write the polynomial for the tiles that remain. $2x^2 + x - 3$
2. Use algebra tiles to find $(x^2 + x - 2) + (6x^2 - 5x - 1)$.
   $7x^2 - 4x - 3$; See Ch. 12 Answer Appendix for drawing.

You can add polynomials horizontally or vertically by combining like terms.

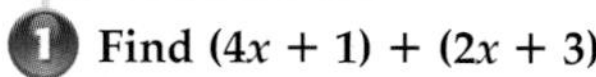

EXAMPLES Add Polynomials

1 **Find $(4x + 1) + (2x + 3)$.**

Method 1 Add vertically.

$$\begin{array}{rl} 4x + 1 & \\ (+)\ 2x + 3 & \text{Align like terms.} \\ \hline 6x + 4 & \text{Add.} \end{array}$$

The sum is $6x + 4$.

Method 2 Add horizontally.

$(4x + 1) + (2x + 3)$
$= (4x + 2x) + (1 + 3)$ Associative and Commutative Properties
$= 6x + 4$

2 **Find $(3x^2 + 5x - 9) + (x^2 + x + 6)$.**

Method 1 Add vertically.

$$\begin{array}{r} 3x^2 + 5x - 9 \\ (+)\ \ x^2 + \ \ x + 6 \\ \hline 4x^2 + 6x - 3 \end{array}$$

Method 2 Add horizontally.

$(3x^2 + 5x - 9) + (x^2 + x + 6)$
$= (3x^2 + x^2) + (5x + x) + (-9 + 6)$
$= 4x^2 + 6x - 3$

The sum is $4x^2 + 6x - 3$.

STUDY TIP

Adding Vertically When adding vertically, be sure to correctly identify the terms of each polynomial. For example, the last term of the polynomial $2x^2 - 3$ is -3, not 3.

EXAMPLES Add Polynomials

3 Find $(7y^2 + 2y) + (-5y + 8)$.

$(7y^2 + 2y) + (-5y + 8) = 7y^2 + (2y - 5y) + 8$ Group like terms.

$= 7y^2 - 3y + 8$ Simplify.

The sum is $7y^2 - 3y + 8$.

4 Find $(6x^2 - x + 5) + (2x^2 - 3)$.

$$\begin{array}{r} 6x^2 - x + 5 \\ (+)\ 2x^2 \quad\ \ - 3 \\ \hline 8x^2 - x + 2 \end{array}$$

Leave a space because there is no other term like $-x$.

The sum is $8x^2 - x + 2$.

Your Turn **Add.** **b. $11a^2 + 5a + 4$**

a. $(4x + 3) + (x - 1)$ **$5x + 2$** b. $(10a^2 + 5a + 7) + (a^2 - 3)$

Polynomials are often used to represent measures of geometric figures.

EXAMPLE Use Polynomials to Solve a Problem

Standardized Test Practice

5 MULTIPLE-CHOICE TEST ITEM Find the measure of $\angle B$ in the figure at the right.

(A) 41° (B) 63° (C) 76° (D) 166°

Read the Test Item The figure is a triangle. The sum of the measures of the angles of a triangle equals 180°. The measure of each angle is determined by the value of x.

Solve the Test Item

Write an equation to find the value of x.

The sum of the measures of the angles	equals	180	
$(2x - 6) + (x + 22) + x$	$=$	180	Write the equation.
$(2x + x + x) + (-6 + 22) = 180$			Group like terms.
$4x + 16 = 180$			Simplify.
$-16 = -16$			Subtract 16 from each side.
$4x = 164$			Simplify.
$\frac{4x}{4} = \frac{164}{4}$			Divide each side by 4.
$x = 41$			Simplify.

Find the measure of angle B.

$m\angle B = 2x - 6$ Write the expression for the measure of angle B.

$= 2(41) - 6$ Replace x with 41.

$= 82 - 6$ or 76 Simplify.

The measure of $\angle B$ is 76°. The answer is C.

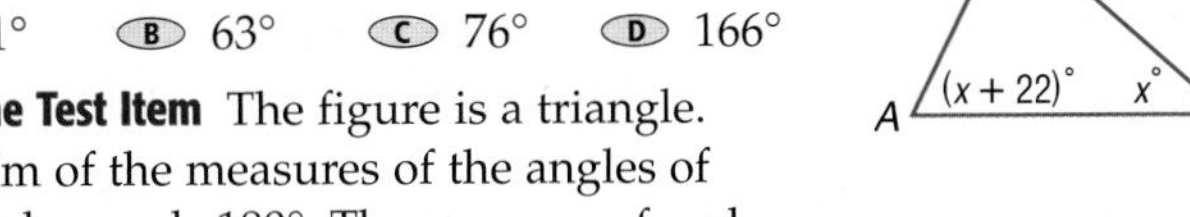

Test-Taking Tip

Many standardized tests provide a list of common geometry facts and formulas. Be sure to find this list before the test begins so you can refer to it easily.

msmath3.net/extra_examples

2 Teach

In-Class Examples

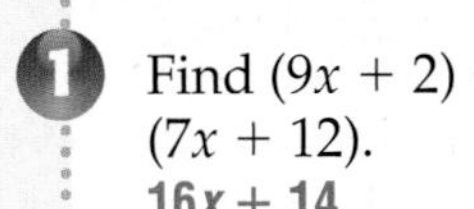

1 Find $(9x + 2) + (7x + 12)$. **$16x + 14$**

2 Find $(4x^2 + 11x - 3) + (-2x^2 + 5x - 7)$. **$2x^2 + 16x - 10$**

3 Find $(15x^2 + 4) + (9x - 13)$. **$15x^2 + 9x - 9$**

4 Find $(3x^2 + 14x - 9) + (-6x + 1)$. **$3x^2 + 8x - 8$**

5 **MULTIPLE-CHOICE TEST ITEM** Find the measure of $\angle A$ in the figure below. **C**

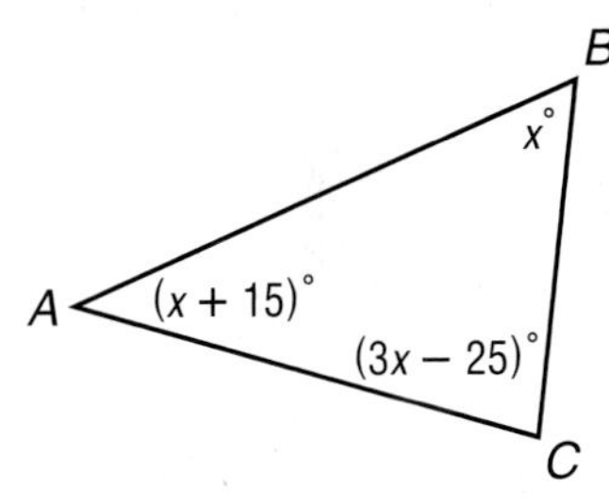

A 13°

B 38°

C 53°

D 109°

DAILY INTERVENTION **Flexible Grouping**

Polynomials Divide the class into small groups. Have students in each group write problems involving the addition of polynomials similar to Example 5 on this page. Encourage them to use other shapes such as squares and pentagons, for which the sum of the interior angles equals 360° and 540°, respectively. Students should take turns drawing a figure, writing the polynomials that define the interior angles, and solving the problem.

Students practice the same concepts in Exercises 11–34 if they are assigned odd or even problems.

3 Practice/Apply

FOLDABLES™ Follow-Up Remind students to use their Foldables like a journal to record what they learn about adding polynomials. For example, they might use words and drawings to describe how to add polynomials.

DAILY INTERVENTION FIND THE ERROR In Exercise 2, you may wish to have students write both polynomials with placeholders. For example, they could write $3a^2 + 2$ as $3a^2 + 0a + 2$.

About the Exercises...

Guided Practice Key

Exercises	Examples
3–7	1–4
8–10	5

Assignment Guide

Basic: 11–39 odd, 41–56

Average: 11–33 odd, 35–37, 39, 41–56

Enriched: 12–34 even, 35–52 (Optional: 53–56)

Answer

48.

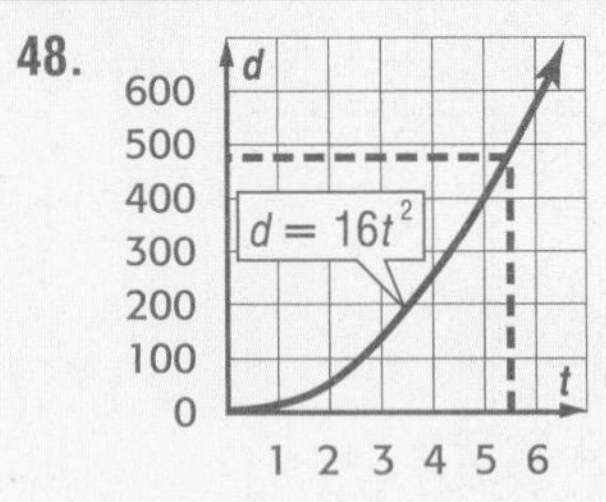

Skill and Concept Check

1. **OPEN ENDED** Write two polynomials whose sum is $4x - 5y$. **Sample answer: $x - 3y$, $3x - 2y$**
2. **FIND THE ERROR** Benito and Cleavon are adding $5a^2 - 7a$ and $3a^2 + 2$. Who is correct? Explain.

Benito

$$\begin{array}{r} 5a^2 - 7a \\ (+)\ 3a^2 + 2 \\ \hline 8a^2 - 5a \end{array}$$

Cleavon

$$\begin{array}{r} 5a^2 - 7a \quad\ \\ (+)\ 3a^2 \qquad + 2 \\ \hline 8a^2 - 7a + 2 \end{array}$$

Cleavon; Benito did not add like terms.

GUIDED PRACTICE

Add.

3. $\begin{array}{r} h + 3 \\ (+)\ 2h + 1 \\ \hline \end{array}$ **$3h + 4$**
4. $\begin{array}{r} 2b^2 + 6b + 9 \\ (+)\ b^2 + 2b - 7 \\ \hline \end{array}$ **$3b^2 + 8b + 2$**
5. $\begin{array}{r} 4t^2 + t + 1 \\ (+)\ 3t^2 \qquad - 5 \\ \hline \end{array}$ **$7t^2 + t - 4$**
6. $(6g^2 - g + 3) + (-2g^2 - 3g + 1)$ **$4g^2 - 4g + 4$**
7. $(8f^2 - 3f) + (5f - 9)$ **$8f^2 + 2f - 9$**

GEOMETRY For Exercises 8–10, use the rectangle at the right.

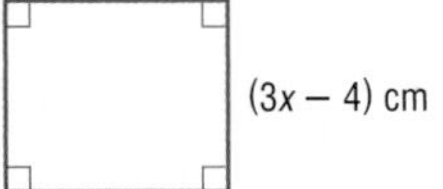

8. Write an expression in simplest form for the perimeter of the rectangle. **$(10x - 2)$ cm**
9. Find the value of x if the perimeter of the rectangle is 48. **5**
10. Find the measure of the length and the width of the rectangle. **13 cm, 11 cm**

Practice and Applications

HOMEWORK HELP

For Exercises	See Examples
11–30	1–4
39–40	5

Extra Practice See pages 646, 659.

Add.

11. $\begin{array}{r} 5y + 6 \\ (+)\ 2y + 4 \\ \hline \end{array}$ **$7y + 10$**
12. $\begin{array}{r} 5p^2 + 3 \\ (+)\ 8p^2 + 1 \\ \hline \end{array}$ **$13p^2 + 4$**
13. $\begin{array}{r} s^2 - s - 4 \\ (+)\ 4s^2 + 2s - 5 \\ \hline \end{array}$ **$5s^2 + s - 9$**
14. $\begin{array}{r} k^2 + 6k - 2 \\ (+)\ 7k^2 - 3k - 1 \\ \hline \end{array}$ **$8k^2 + 3k - 3$**
15. $\begin{array}{r} 4m^2 + m - 5 \\ (+)\ 3m^2 \qquad + 9 \\ \hline \end{array}$ **$7m^2 + m + 4$**
16. $\begin{array}{r} 8x^2 - 6x - 7 \\ (+)\ -4x^2 - 6x \quad\ \\ \hline \end{array}$ **$4x^2 - 12x - 7$**
17. $(2c - 4) + (3c + 3)$ **$5c - 1$**
18. $(9z + 6) + (-5z - 6)$ **$4z$**
19. $(7j^2 + j + 1) + (j^2 - 5j - 2)$ **$8j^2 - 4j - 1$**
20. $(4q^2 - 2q - 1) + (q^2 + 5q + 1)$ **$5q^2 + 3q$**
21. $(5d^2 - 6) + (3d^2 + 5)$ **$8d^2 - 1$**
22. $(-9w^2 + 4) + (4w^2 - 9)$ **$-5w^2 - 5$**
23. $(4n^2 + 8) + (2n^2 - 5n + 1)$ **$6n^2 - 5n + 9$**
24. $(-6r - 2) + (r^2 + 9r + 4)$ **$r^2 + 3r + 2$**
25. $(5v^2 - v + 1) + (v^2 + v + 1)$ **$6v^2 + 2$**
26. $(6x^2 - 5x - 4) + (-x^2 - 8x - 9)$
27. $(5m^2 - 2) + (4m + 6)$ **$5m^2 + 4m + 4$**
28. $(-3g - 10) + (6g^2 + 7g)$ **$6g^2 + 4g - 10$**
29. $(-2b^2 - 3b - 7) + (5b + 2)$
30. $(-3a^2 - 2a - 9) + (-3a^2 - 5a - 3)$ **$-6a^2 - 7a - 12$**

26. $5x^2 - 13x - 13$ 29. $-2b^2 + 2b - 5$

Add. Then evaluate each sum if $x = 6$, $y = 3$, and $z = -5$.

31. $(6x + 2y) + (-4x - y)$ **$2x + y$; 15**
32. $(-3y + 5z) + (10y - 2z)$ **$7y + 3z$; 6**
33. $(-3x + 4z) + (5y - 2z)$ **$-3x + 5y + 2z$; -13**
34. $(4x - 6y - 13z) + (-3x - 4y + 11z)$ **$x - 10y - 2z$; -14**

576 Chapter 12 Algebra: Nonlinear Functions and Polynomials

WORK **For Exercises 35–38, use the following information.**
Wei-Ling works at a grocery store a few hours after school on weekdays and baby-sits on weekends. She makes the same hourly wage for both jobs. During one week, Wei-Ling worked 18 hours at the grocery store, and \$9 was deducted for taxes. She worked 7 hours baby-sitting, and no taxes were deducted. Let x represent her hourly pay.

35. Write a polynomial expression to represent Wei-Ling's grocery store pay. **$18x - 9$**
36. Write a polynomial expression to represent Wei-Ling's pay for baby-sitting. **$7x$**
37. Write a polynomial expression to represent Wei-Ling's total weekly pay. **$25x - 9$**
38. Suppose Wei-Ling makes \$5.50 an hour at both jobs. How much was her weekly pay after taxes? **\$128.50**

GEOMETRY **For Exercises 39 and 40, use the figure at the right.**

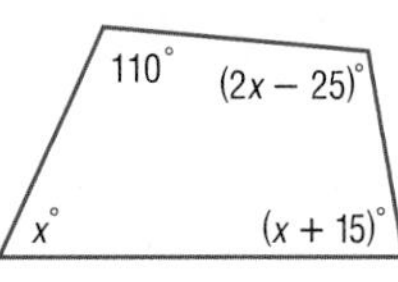

39. Find the sum of the measures of the angles. **$4x + 100$**
40. **MULTI STEP** The sum of the measures of the angles in any quadrilateral is 360°. Find the measure of each angle. **65°, 80°, 105°; 110°**
41. **CRITICAL THINKING** If $(3a - 5b) + (2a + 3b) = 5a - 2b$, then what is $(5a - 2b) - (3a - 5b)$? Explain. **$2a + 3b$; the sum of two numbers minus one of its addends is equal to the other addend.**

Spiral Review with Standardized Test Practice

42. **MULTIPLE CHOICE** What is the sum of $14n + m$ and $n - 9m$? **D**

   Ⓐ $13n - 8m$ Ⓑ $14n - 9m$ Ⓒ $15n - 10m$ Ⓓ $15n - 8m$

43. **SHORT RESPONSE** Find the measure of each angle in the figure at the right. **132°; 48°**

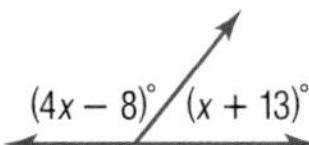

Simplify each polynomial. If the polynomial cannot be simplified, write *simplest form*. (Lesson 12-3)

44. $3t + 2s + s + 8t$ **$3s + 11t$**
45. $7v - 10w + 2$ **simplest form**
46. $6f + 9e - 2e + 16$ **$7e + 6f + 16$**
47. $4q^2 - q - 7 + 6q + 2$ **$4q^2 + 5q - 5$**
48. **SKYDIVING** The distance d a skydiver falls in t seconds is given by the function $d = 16t^2$. Graph this function and estimate how far a skydiver will fall in 5.5 seconds. (Lesson 12-2) **See margin for graph; about 480 ft.**

Find the total amount in each account to the nearest cent. (Lesson 5-8)

49. \$250 at 4% for 2.5 years **\$275**
50. \$760 at 5% for 10 months **\$791.67**
51. \$375 at 9.4% for 14 years **\$868.50**
52. \$1,200 at 2.2% for $3\frac{1}{3}$ years **\$1,288**

GETTING READY FOR THE NEXT LESSON

PREREQUISITE SKILL **Rewrite each expression as an addition expression by using the additive inverse.** (Lessons 1-4 and 1-5)

53. $6 - 7$ **$6 + (-7)$**
54. $a^2 - 8$ **$a^2 + (-8)$**
55. $4x - 5y$ **$4x + (-5y)$**
56. $(c + d) - 3c$ **$(c + d) + (-3c)$**

msmath3.net/self_check_quiz

4 Assess

Open-Ended Assessment

Writing Have students write a step-by-step list of instructions explaining how to add polynomials. Then, have them follow their own instructions as they add the polynomial $(-3x^2 - 3) + (8x^2 - 2x + 15)$. **$5x^2 - 2x + 12$**

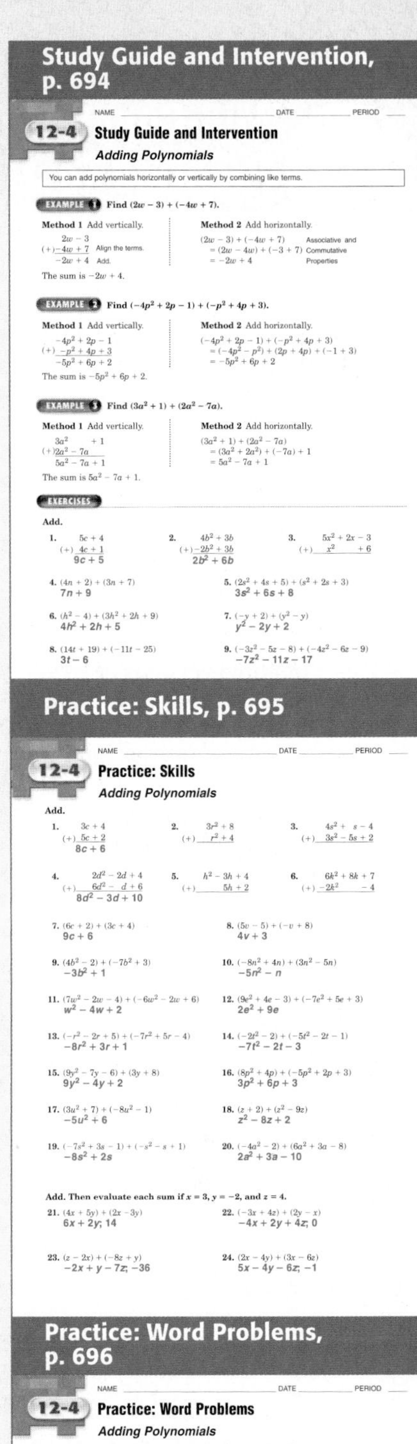

Study Guide and Intervention, p. 694

NAME ______ DATE ______ PERIOD ____

12-4 Study Guide and Intervention
Adding Polynomials

You can add polynomials horizontally or vertically by combining like terms.

EXAMPLE 1 **Find $(2w - 3) + (-4w + 7)$.**

Method 1 Add vertically.

$2w - 3$
$(+)\ -4w + 7$ Align the terms.
$-2w + 4$ Add.

The sum is $-2w + 4$.

Method 2 Add horizontally.

$(2w - 3) + (-4w + 7)$ Associative and
$= (2w - 4w) + (-3 + 7)$ Commutative
$= -2w + 4$ Properties

EXAMPLE 2 **Find $(-4p^2 + 2p - 1) + (-p^2 + 4p + 3)$.**

Method 1 Add vertically.

$-4p^2 + 2p - 1$
$(+)\ -p^2 + 4p + 3$
$-5p^2 + 6p + 2$

The sum is $-5p^2 + 6p + 2$.

Method 2 Add horizontally.

$(-4p^2 + 2p - 1) + (-p^2 + 4p + 3)$
$= (-4p^2 - p^2) + (2p + 4p) + (-1 + 3)$
$= -5p^2 + 6p + 2$

EXAMPLE 3 **Find $(3a^2 + 1) + (2a^2 - 7a)$.**

Method 1 Add vertically.

$3a^2 \quad + 1$
$(+)\ 2a^2 - 7a$
$5a^2 - 7a + 1$

The sum is $5a^2 - 7a + 1$.

Method 2 Add horizontally.

$(3a^2 + 1) + (2a^2 - 7a)$
$= (3a^2 + 2a^2) + (-7a) + 1$
$= 5a^2 - 7a + 1$

EXERCISES

Add.

1. $5c + 4$ $(+)\ 4c + 1$ **$9c + 5$**
2. $4b^2 + 3b$ $(+)\ -2b^2 + 3b$ **$2b^2 + 6b$**
3. $5x^2 + 2x - 3$ $(+)\ x^2 \quad + 6$
4. $(4n + 2) + (3n + 7)$ **$7n + 9$**
5. $(2s^2 + 4s + 5) + (s^2 + 2s + 3)$ **$3s^2 + 6s + 8$**
6. $(h^2 - 4) + (3h^2 + 2h + 9)$ **$4h^2 + 2h + 5$**
7. $(-y + 2) + (y^2 - y)$ **$y^2 - 2y + 2$**
8. $(14t + 19) + (-11t - 25)$ **$3t - 6$**
9. $(-3z^2 - 5z - 8) + (-4z^2 - 6z - 9)$ **$-7z^2 - 11z - 17$**

Practice: Skills, p. 695

NAME ______ DATE ______ PERIOD ____

12-4 Practice: Skills
Adding Polynomials

Add.

1. $3c + 4$ $(+)\ 5c + 2$ **$8c + 6$**
2. $3r^2 + 8$ $(+)\ r^2 + 4$
3. $4s^2 + s - 4$ $(+)\ 3s^2 - 5s + 2$
4. $2d^2 - 2d + 4$ $(+)\ 6d^2 - d + 6$ **$8d^2 - 3d + 10$**
5. $h^2 - 3h + 4$ $(+)\ 5h + 2$
6. $6k^2 + 8k + 7$ $(+)\ -2k^2 \quad - 4$
7. $(6c + 2) + (3c + 4)$ **$9c + 6$**
8. $(5v - 5) + (-v + 8)$ **$4v + 3$**
9. $(4b^2 - 2) + (-7b^2 + 3)$ **$-3b^2 + 1$**
10. $(-8n^2 + 4n) + (3n^2 - 5n)$ **$-5n^2 - n$**
11. $(7w^2 - 2w - 4) + (-6w^2 - 2w + 6)$ **$w^2 - 4w + 2$**
12. $(9e^2 + 4e - 3) + (-7e^2 + 5e + 3)$ **$2e^2 + 9e$**
13. $(-r^2 - 2r + 5) + (-7r^2 + 5r - 4)$ **$-8r^2 + 3r + 1$**
14. $(-2t^2 - 2) + (-5t^2 - 2t - 1)$ **$-7t^2 - 2t - 3$**
15. $(9y^2 - 7y - 6) + (3y + 8)$ **$9y^2 - 4y + 2$**
16. $(8p^2 + 4p) + (-5p^2 + 2p + 3)$ **$3p^2 + 6p + 3$**
17. $(3u^2 + 7) + (-8u^2 - 1)$ **$-5u^2 + 6$**
18. $(z + 2) + (z^2 - 9z)$ **$z^2 - 8z + 2$**
19. $(-7s^2 + 3s - 1) + (-s^2 - s + 1)$ **$-8s^2 + 2s$**
20. $(-4a^2 - 2) + (6a^2 + 3a - 8)$ **$2a^2 + 3a - 10$**

Add. Then evaluate each sum if $x = 3$, $y = -2$, and $z = 4$.

21. $(4x + 5y) + (2x - 3y)$ **$6x + 2y$; 14**
22. $(-3x + 4z) + (2y - x)$ **$-4x + 2y + 4z$; 0**
23. $(z - 2x) + (-8z + y)$ **$-2x + y - 7z$; -36**
24. $(2x - 4y) + (3x - 6z)$ **$5x - 4y - 6z$; -1**

Practice: Word Problems, p. 696

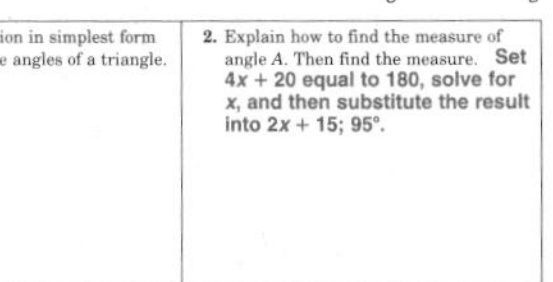

NAME ______ DATE ______ PERIOD ____

12-4 Practice: Word Problems
Adding Polynomials

GEOMETRY **For Exercises 1 and 2, use the figure at the right.**

1. Write an expression in simplest form for the sum of the angles of a triangle. **$4x + 20$**
2. Explain how to find the measure of angle A. Then find the measure. **Set $4x + 20$ equal to 180, solve for x, and then substitute the result into $2x + 15$; 95°.**
3. **GIFTS** For his birthday, Carlos's parents give him \$5 for each year of his age plus \$50. His grandmother gives him \$10 for each year of his age. Let a represent Carlos's age in years. Write a polynomial expression for the amount that Carlos receives from his parents. Then write a polynomial expression for the amount that he receives from his grandmother. **$5x + 50$; $10x$**
4. Write a polynomial expression for the total amount that Carlos receives from his parents and grandmother in Exercise 3. How much will Carlos receive when he is 15 years old? **$15x + 50$; \$275**
5. **TAXIS** Lydia took a taxi from her home to school that charged \$2 plus \$0.50 per mile. Her brother Luke took a taxi the same distance that charged \$3 plus \$0.30 per mile. Let d represent the distance in miles. Write a polynomial expression for the cost of Lydia's taxi. Then write a polynomial expression for the cost of Luke's taxi. **$0.50d + 2$; $0.30d + 3$**
6. Find an expression in simplest form representing the total cost of Lydia and Luke's taxi rides in Exercise 5. What is the total cost if the distance is 20 miles? **$0.80d + 5$; \$21**

Mid-Chapter Practice Test

Assessment Option

Mid-Chapter Test (Lessons 12-1 through 12-4) is available on p. 731 of the *Chapter 12 Resource Masters*.

ExamView® Pro

Use the networkable ExamView® Pro Testmaker CD-ROM to:

- Create **multiple versions** of tests.
- Create **modified** tests for **inclusion** students with one mouse click.
- **Edit** existing questions and **add** your own questions.
- Build tests aligned with state standards using built-in **state curriculum correlations.**
- Change **English** tests to **Spanish** with one mouse click and vice versa.

FOLDABLES™ Follow-Up Before students complete the Mid-Chapter Practice Test, encourage them to review the notes, definitions, concepts, and main ideas they recorded under the tabs of the first four sections of their Foldable study guides.

Answers

1. The graphs of linear functions are straight lines, while the graphs of nonlinear functions are not straight lines.
3. linear; can be written as $y = \frac{1}{3}x$
4. nonlinear; power of x is greater than 1 and the equation cannot be written in the form $y = mx + b$
5. linear; rate of change is constant; as x increases by 2, y decreases by 1
6. nonlinear; rate of change is not constant

CHAPTER 12 Mid-Chapter Practice Test

Vocabulary and Concepts

1. **Describe** the difference between the graphs of linear functions and nonlinear functions. (Lesson 12-1) **See margin.**
2. **OPEN ENDED** Write two polynomials whose sum is $5x - 3y$. (Lesson 12-4) **Sample answer: $3x - 7y$, $2x + 4y$**

Skills and Applications

Determine whether each equation or table represents a *linear* or *nonlinear* function. Explain. (Lesson 12-1) **3–6. See margin.**

3. $3y = x$
4. $y = 5x^3 + 2$

5.

x	1	3	5	7
y	−5	−6	−7	−8

6.

x	−1	0	1	2
y	1	0	1	4

Graph each function. (Lesson 12-2) **7–9. See margin.**

7. $y = 2x^2$
8. $y = -x^2 + 3$
9. $y = 4x^2 - 1$

Simplify each polynomial. If the polynomial cannot be simplified, write *simplest form*. (Lesson 12-3)

10. $3x + 2 - 5x + 1$ **$-2x + 3$**
11. $6a^2 + 5x - 2a$ **simplest form**
12. $y^2 + 3y + 1 + 5y - 2y^2$ **$-y^2 + 8y + 1$**
13. $3x^2 - 6x + 5x + 8$ **$3x^2 - x + 8$**

Add. (Lesson 12-4)

14. $(3a + 6) + (2a - 5)$ **$5a + 1$**
15. $(-3x - 2) + (-2x + 5)$ **$-5x + 3$**
16. $(3q^2 - 5) + (2q^2 - q)$ **$5q^2 - q - 5$**
17. $(a^2 - 2a + 3) + (3a^2 - 5a + 6)$ **$4a^2 - 7a + 9$**
18. **AMUSEMENT PARK RIDES** Your height h above the ground t seconds after being released at the top of a free-fall ride is given by the function $h = -16t^2 + 200$. Graph this function. After about how many seconds will the ride be 60 feet above the ground? (Lesson 12-2) **See Ch. 12 Answer Appendix for graph; about 3 s.**

Standardized Test Practice

19. **MULTIPLE CHOICE** Which expression is *not* a monomial? (Lesson 12-3) **D**

   (A) -6 (B) x^3 (C) $4a$ (D) $\frac{4}{n}$

20. **SHORT RESPONSE** Find the measure of each angle in the figure below. (Lesson 12-4) **50°; 40°**

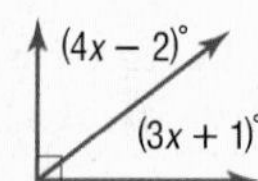

7.

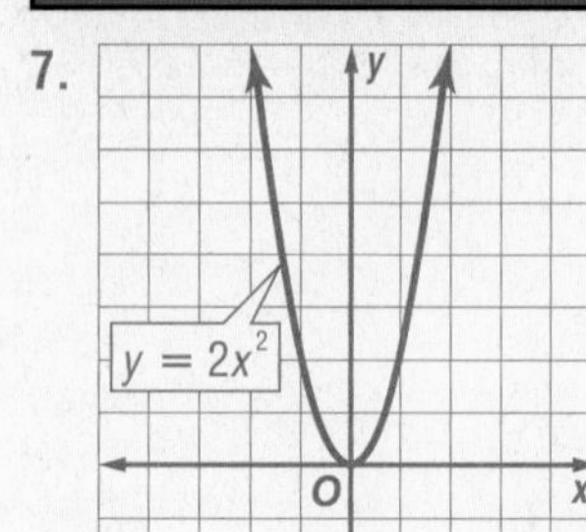

8.

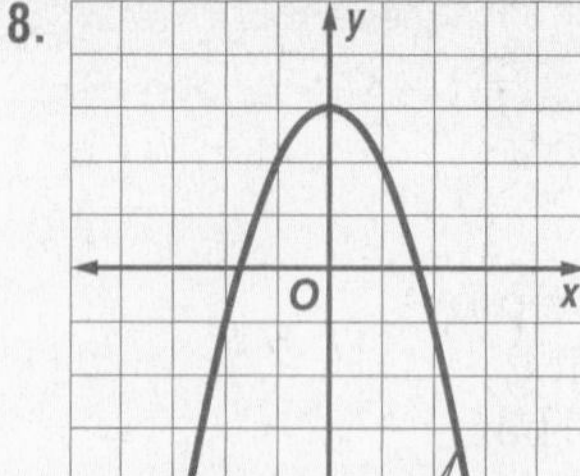

9.

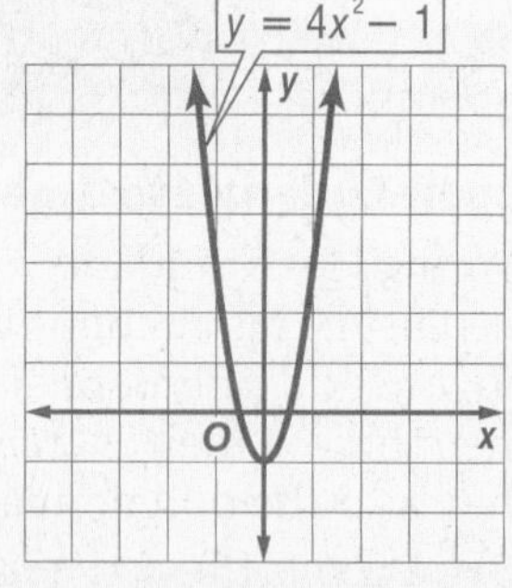

The Game Zone

A Place To Practice Your Math Skills

Polynomial Challenge

GET READY!

Players: four
Materials: stopwatch, algebra tiles, scissors, 10 index cards

GET SET!

- Cut each index card in half to make 20 playing cards.
- Each player should write a polynomial with four or five terms that can be modeled with algebra tiles on each of five cards.
- At least two of the polynomials should contain one or more positive or negative x^2-terms.

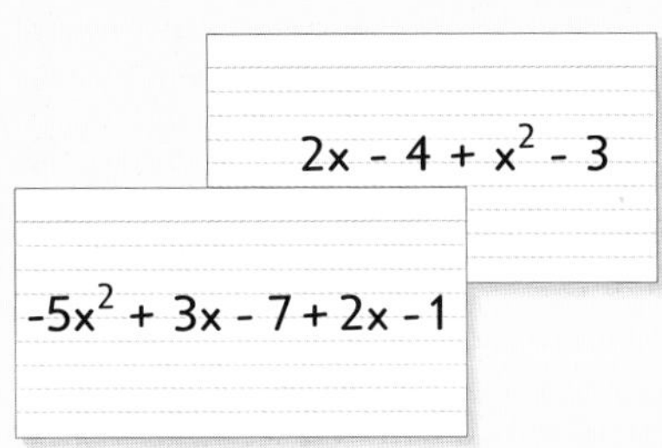

GO!

- Mix the cards and place the stack facedown on the table.
- The first player turns over the top two cards and lays them side-by-side on the table.
- The player then has one minute to model the two polynomials using algebra tiles and find the sum.
- If the player is correct, he or she scores one point. Those cards are then placed in a discard pile and it becomes the next player's turn.
- **Who Wins?** The first player to score 5 points wins.

The Game Zone

Glencoe Mathematics Classroom Manipulative Kit

- stopwatch
- algebra tiles
- scissors

GETTING READY

Objective Add polynomials.

MANAGEMENT TIPS

Recommended Time
30 minutes

Tips

- Write the polynomials ahead of time to save time and ensure a good mix of terms.
- Consider having one student serve as a referee for the game. The referee's job is to verify the sums reported by the players. Students can take turns being the referee.
- You may wish to have students play to 3 points instead of 5 to make the playing time shorter.
- You may wish to use the game as an assessment tool for the concepts the students have been learning in Lessons 12-1 through 12-4.

Math Online For an additional game for this chapter, visit: msmath3.net/gamezone

12-5 Lesson Notes

Lesson Resources

Chapter 12 Resource Masters
- Study Guide and Intervention, p. 699
- Practice: Skills, p. 700
- Practice: Word Problems, p. 701
- Reading to Learn Mathematics, p. 702
- Enrichment, p. 703

Key Teaching Transparencies, 48
Parent and Student Study Guide Online Worksheets, 12-5
Teaching Mathematics with Manipulatives, p. 113
Noteables™: Interactive Study Notebook with Foldables™, 12-5

FAST FILE

Focus

5-Minute Check 12-5

Use as a quiz or review of Lesson 12-4. (Also available as a transparency)

Bellringer

Hands-On Activity Have students demonstrate the process used to subtract integers. Have them use algebra tiles to find the value of the following expressions:

$3 - 5$ **-2**

$-4 - 1$ **-5**

$-3 - (-2)$ **-1**

Reading to Learn Mathematics, p. 702 ELL

NAME ________ DATE ________ PERIOD ____

12-5 Reading to Learn Mathematics
Subtracting Polynomials

Pre-Activity *Complete the Mini Lab at the top of page 580 in your textbook. Write your answers below.*

1. From the tiles that remain, determine the value of $(x + 4) - (-2x + 3)$.
$3x + 1$

2. Use algebra tiles to find $(2x^2 + 3x + 5) - (x^2 - x + 2)$.
$x^2 + 4x + 3$

Reading the Lesson

3. What is the additive inverse of a number or expression? The number or expression that you would add to the original number or expression to get a sum of 0.

12-5 Subtracting Polynomials

What You'll LEARN

Subtract polynomials.

REVIEW Vocabulary

additive inverse: a number and its opposite (Lesson 1-4)

HANDS-ON Mini Lab

Materials
- algebra tiles

Work with a partner.

You can use algebra tiles to find $(x + 4) - (-2x + 3)$.

STEP 1 Model the polynomial $x + 4$.

STEP 2 To subtract $-2x + 3$, you need to remove 2 negative x-tiles and 3 1-tiles.

STEP 3 Since there are no negative x-tiles to remove, add 2 zero pairs of x-tiles. Then remove 2 negative x-tiles and 3 1-tiles.

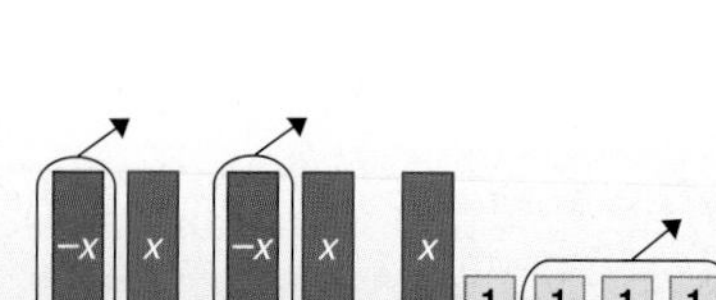

1. From the tiles that remain, determine the value of $(x + 4) - (-2x + 3)$. **$3x + 1$**
2. Use algebra tiles to find $(2x^2 + 3x + 5) - (x^2 - x + 2)$.

2. $x^2 + 4x + 3$; See margin for drawing.

As with adding polynomials, to subtract two polynomials, you subtract the like terms.

EXAMPLES Subtract Polynomials

TEACHING TIP

Point out that the (−) symbol means each term in the expression is to be subtracted, not just the first term.

Subtract.

1 $(7a + 5) - (3a + 4)$

$$\begin{array}{rl} 7a + 5 & \\ (-)\ 3a + 4 & \text{Align like terms.} \\ \hline 4a + 1 & \text{Subtract.} \end{array}$$

The difference is $4a + 1$.

2 $(5x^2 + 3x + 4) - (3x^2 - 2)$

$$\begin{array}{rl} 5x^2 + 3x + 4 & \\ (-)\ 3x^2 \qquad\ - 2 & \text{Align like terms.} \\ \hline 2x^2 + 3x + 6 & \text{Subtract.} \end{array}$$

The difference is $2x^2 + 3x + 6$.

Recall that you can subtract a number by adding its *additive inverse.* You can also subtract a polynomial by adding its additive inverse. To find the additive inverse of a polynomial, find the opposite of each term.

Polynomial	Terms	Opposites	Additive Inverse
$x + 5$	$x, 5$	$-x, -5$	$-x - 5$
$-x^2 - 4x + 2$	$-x^2, -4x, 2$	$x^2, 4x, -2$	$x^2 + 4x - 2$

Answer (Hands-On Mini Lab)

2.

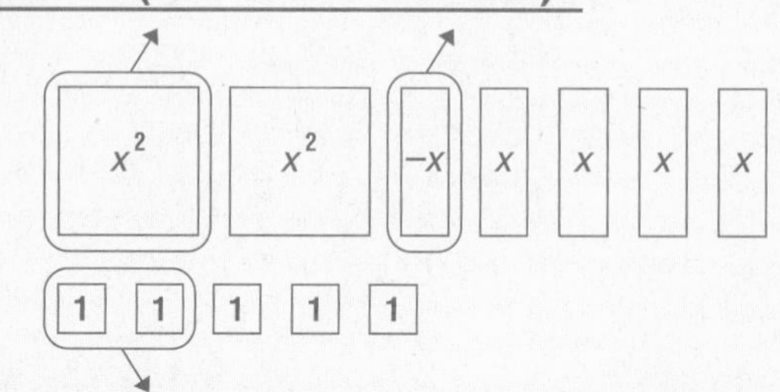

EXAMPLES Subtract Using the Additive Inverse

3 **Find $(4x + 9) - (7x - 2)$.**

The additive inverse of $7x - 2$ is $-7x + 2$.

$(4x + 9) - (7x - 2)$

$= (4x + 9) + (-7x + 2)$ To subtract $(7x - 2)$, add $(-7x + 2)$.

$= (4x - 7x) + (9 + 2)$ Group like terms.

$= -3x + 11$ Simplify by combining like terms.

The difference is $-3x + 11$.

4 **Find $(6y^2 - 5) - (-3y + 4)$.**

The additive inverse of $-3y + 4$ is $3y - 4$.

$$\begin{array}{r} 6y^2 \quad\quad - 5 \\ \underline{(-) \quad -3y + 4} \end{array} \rightarrow \begin{array}{r} 6y^2 \quad\quad - 5 \\ \underline{(+) \quad\quad 3y - 4} \\ 6y^2 + 3y - 9 \end{array}$$

The difference is $6y^2 + 3y - 9$.

Your Turn **Subtract.** b. $-x^2 + x + 5$

a. $(5p + 3) - (12p - 8)$ $-7p + 11$ b. $(x^2 - 6x + 4) - (2x^2 - 7x - 1)$

REAL-LIFE CAREERS

How Does an Automotive Engineer Use Math?

Automotive engineers use polynomials to model a car's speed under different road conditions.

Research

For information about a career as an automotive engineer, visit: msmath3.net/careers

EXAMPLE Use Polynomials to Solve a Problem

5 **CARS Car A travels a distance of $4t^2 + 60t$ feet t seconds after the start of a soapbox derby. Car B travels $5t^2 + 55t$ feet. How far apart are the two cars 8 seconds after the start of the race?**

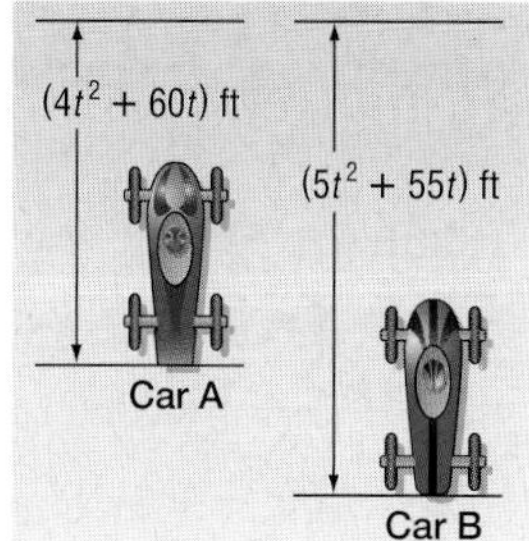

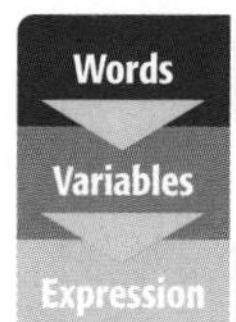

Write an expression for the difference of the distances traveled by each car.

Words	car B's distance minus car A's distance
Variables	t = the time in seconds
Expression	$(5t^2 + 55t) - (4t^2 + 60t)$

$$\begin{array}{r} 5t^2 + 55t \\ \underline{(-)\ (4t^2 + 60t)} \end{array} \rightarrow \begin{array}{r} 5t^2 + 55t \\ \underline{(+)\ (-4t^2 - 60t)} \\ t^2 - \quad 5t \end{array}$$

Now evaluate this expression for a time of 8 seconds.

$t^2 - 5t = (8)^2 - 5(8)$ Replace t with 8.

$= 64 - 40$ or 24 Simplify.

After 8 seconds, the cars are 24 feet apart.

 msmath3.net/extra_examples

2 Teach

In-Class Examples

Subtract.

1 $(8c + 3) - (6c + 2)$
$2c + 1$

2 $(-2d^2 + 6d - 11) - (-3d + 4)$
$-2d^2 + 9d - 15$

3 Find $(6z + 1) - (2z - 5)$.
$4z + 6$

4 Find $(10f^2 - 15) - (-5f + 3)$.
$10f^2 + 5f - 18$

5 **EXPERIMENTS** Students are rolling identical marbles down two side-by-side ramps. The marble on ramp A rolls $3t^2 + 11t$ inches in t seconds. The marble on ramp B rolls $2t^2 + 4t$ inches in t seconds. How far apart are the marbles after 6 seconds?
78 in.

Tips for New Teachers

Intervention Have students keep a journal showing types of problems they miss on math quizzes. Writing out correct solutions will help them learn to solve the problems. They can review the journal periodically to remind themselves of the correct procedures.

DAILY INTERVENTION — Unlocking Misconceptions

Subtracting Polynomials A common problem students have when subtracting polynomials is to apply the negative sign only to the first term in parentheses. For example, they may write $(4x + 3) - (8x - 3)$ as $4x + 3 - 8x - 3$. Review the Distributive Property with students. Have students write polynomials on the chalkboard and show the correct and incorrect way of distributing the negative sign.

3 Practice/Apply

FOLDABLES™ Follow-Up Remind students to use their Foldables like a journal to record what they learn about subtracting polynomials. For example, they might model the subtraction of polynomials.

NUMBER SENSE
In Exercise 1, remind students that the opposite of a term is the same as its additive inverse. Students should remember that adding a term to its additive inverse gives zero.

DAILY INTERVENTION FIND THE ERROR In Exercise 3, students may need to include an intermediate step in which they write the additive inverse by including (−) in front of each term in the second polynomial. Students might write this step $(3a^2 - 3a + 5) + (-)\,2a^2 + (-)\,a - (-)1$. Alternatively, you may wish to show them how to use the Distributive Property. Since $-1(2a^2 + a - 1)$ equals $-2a^2 - a + 1$, students can use this to rewrite the problem without parentheses: $3a^2 - 3a + 5 - 2a^2 - a + 1$. This produces the same result as using the additive inverse but provides an additional justification for students having difficulty accepting such operations.

About the Exercises...

Guided Practice Key

Exercises	Examples
4–11	1–4

Assignment Guide

Basic: 13–37 odd, 41–52

Average: 13–35 odd, 37–39, 41–52

Enriched: 12–32 even, 33–48 (Optional: 49–52)

Students practice the same concepts in Exercises 12–31 if they are assigned odd or even problems.

Skill and Concept Check

1. **NUMBER SENSE** Write the opposite of each term in $4x^2 - 8x + 9$. Then write the additive inverse of this polynomial.
   $-4x^2, 8x, -9; -4x^2 + 8x - 9$
2. **OPEN ENDED** Write two polynomials whose difference is $3x - 8$.
   Sample answer: $7x - 11$ and $4x - 3$
3. **FIND THE ERROR** Karen and Yoshi are finding $(3a^2 - 3a + 5) - (2a^2 + a - 1)$. Who is correct? Explain.

Karen
$(3a^2 - 3a + 5) - (2a^2 + a - 1)$
$= (3a^2 - 3a + 5) + (-2a^2 - a + 1)$
$= a^2 - 4a + 6$

Yoshi
$(3a^2 - 3a + 5) - (2a^2 + a - 1)$
$= (3a^2 - 3a + 5) + (-2a^2 + a - 1)$
$= a^2 - 2a + 4$

Karen; Yoshi did not add the additive inverse of the entire second polynomial.

GUIDED PRACTICE

Subtract. 9. $2n^2 - n - 1$

4. $5z + 2$ minus $(-)\ 3z + 1$ — $2z + 1$
5. $7c^2 + c + 5$ minus $(-)\ 2c^2 + 4$ — $5c^2 + c + 1$
6. $2m^2 + 6m + 8$ minus $(-)\ m^2 + 3m - 1$ — $m^2 + 3m + 9$
7. $(6p + 2) - (p - 1)$ $5p + 3$
8. $(x^2 - x - 4) - (-x + 1)$ $x^2 - 5$
9. $(5n^2 + n - 2) - (3n^2 + 2n - 1)$
10. $(r^2 + r - 1) - (2r^2 - r + 2)$ $-r^2 + 2r - 3$
11. Find the difference of $-4a + 5$ and $a - 1$. $-5a + 6$

Practice and Applications

HOMEWORK HELP

For Exercises	See Examples
12–17	1, 2
18–25	3, 4
32–40	5

Extra Practice See pages 646, 659.

Subtract. 20. $4m^2 + 3m - 10$

12. $3x + 6$ minus $(-)\ 2x + 5$ — $x + 1$
13. $9w + 15$ minus $(-)\ 4w + 12$ — $5w + 3$
14. $8g^2 + 8g + 5$ minus $(-)\ 7g^2 + 5g + 1$ — $g^2 + 3g + 4$
15. $10b^2 - 4b + 9$ minus $(-)\ 5b^2 + b + 3$ — $5b^2 - 5b + 6$
16. $4u^2 + 3u + 2$ minus $(-)\ 2u^2 - 4$ — $2u^2 + 3u + 6$
17. $7y^2 + y + 6$ minus $(-)\ 5y^2 + 1$ — $2y^2 + y + 5$
18. $(10h + 4) - (2h - 3)$ $8h + 7$
19. $(6a + 6) - (-a + 8)$ $7a - 2$
20. $(4m^2 - 8) - (-3m + 2)$
21. $(5k^2 - 7) - (9k + 13)$ $5k^2 - 9k - 20$
22. $(c^2 - 2c + 1) - (c^2 + c - 5)$ $-3c + 6$
23. $(3r^2 + r - 1) - (r^2 - r + 3)$ $2r^2 + 2r - 4$
24. Find the difference of $7x^2 + 12x - 9$ and $4x^2 - 3$. $3x^2 + 12x - 6$
25. What is $-z - 5$ subtracted from $16z - 7$? $17z - 2$

26. $x + 3; -5$ 27. $4y - 8; 12$ 28. $-3x - y - 3; 16$

Subtract. Then evaluate the difference if $x = -8$ and $y = 5$.

26. $(4x + 10) - (3x + 7)$
27. $(6y - 2) - (2y + 6)$
28. $(-3x - 8) - (y - 5)$
29. $(9x + 2y) - (8x - 4)$ $x + 2y + 4; 6$
30. $(x + 5y) - (-4x + 3y)$ $5x + 2y; -30$
31. $(-2x - y) - (-6x - 3y)$ $4x + 2y; -22$
32. **GEOMETRY** The measure of $\angle ABC$ is $(12x - 8)°$. Write an expression in simplest form for the measure of $\angle ABD$. $(7x - 9)°$

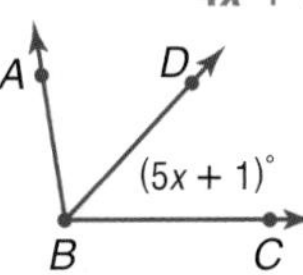

FAST FOOD **For Exercises 33–36, use the following information.** Khadijah ordered 3 burritos and 7 tacos from a fast-food drive through. When Khadijah looked at her receipt, she discovered that she had been charged for 5 burritos and 5 tacos.

Order # 368
5 burritos......$7.95
5 tacos.........$4.95
Total...........$12.90

33. If burritos cost b dollars and tacos cost t dollars, write an expression for the amount Khadijah was charged. **$5b + 5t$**
34. Write an expression for the cost of the food she ordered. **$3b + 7t$**
35. Write an expression for the amount Khadijah was overcharged. **$2b - 2t$**
36. If tacos cost \$0.99 and burritos cost \$1.59, how much was she overcharged? **\$1.20**

FUND-RAISER **For Exercises 37–40, use the following information.** Your club spends \$200 on a pizza fund-raiser kit. Each pizza costs you \$6.50 to make. You sell each pizza for \$10.

37. Write a polynomial that models your total expenses for making x pizzas. **$6.5x + 200$**
38. Write a polynomial that models your income from selling x pizzas. **$10x$**
39. Write a polynomial that models your profit from selling x pizzas. (*Hint*: Profit = Income − Expenses) **$3.5x - 200$**
40. How much profit will you make if you sell 150 pizzas? **\$325**

41. **CRITICAL THINKING** Suppose A and B represent polynomials. If $A + B = 7x + 4$ and $A - B = 3x + 2$, find A and B. **$A = 5x + 3$, $B = 2x + 1$**

Spiral Review with Standardized Test Practice

42. **MULTIPLE CHOICE** Write the additive inverse of $n^2 - 2n + 3$. **B**

    (A) $n^2 + 2n - 3$ (B) $-n^2 + 2n - 3$
    (C) $-n^2 - 2n - 3$ (D) $n^2 + 2n + 3$

43. **SHORT RESPONSE** The perimeter of the triangle is $16x - 7$ units. Write an expression for the missing length. **$5x - 8$ units**

Add. (Lesson 12-4)

44. $(7b + 2) + (-5b + 3)$ **$2b + 5$**
45. $(6v^2 - 4) + (v - 1)$ **$6v^2 + v - 5$**
46. $(t^2 - 8t) + (t^2 + 5)$ **$2t^2 - 8t + 5$**

SCHOOL **For Exercises 47 and 48, use the following information.** The drama club is selling flowers. The sales for the first two weeks are shown in the table. (Lesson 12-3) **47. $119C + 80R$**

Number of Flowers Sold		
Week	Carnations	Roses
1	54	38
2	65	42

47. The selling prices of a carnation and a rose are C and R respectively. Write a polynomial expression for the total sales.
48. If carnations cost \$2 each and roses cost \$5 each, what was the total amount of sales? **\$638**

GETTING READY FOR THE NEXT LESSON

PREREQUISITE SKILL **Write each expression using exponents.** (Lesson 2-8)

49. $3 \cdot 3 \cdot 3 \cdot 3$ **3^4**
50. $5 \cdot 4 \cdot 5 \cdot 5 \cdot 4$ **$4^2 \cdot 5^3$**
51. $7 \cdot (7 \cdot 7)$ **7^3**
52. $(2 \cdot 2) \cdot (2 \cdot 2 \cdot 2)$ **2^5**

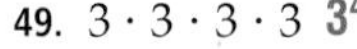

Math Online msmath3.net/self_check_quiz

4 Assess

Open-Ended Assessment

Speaking Provide an opportunity for each student to come to the chalkboard and, while solving a problem, describe the steps for subtracting polynomials.

Study Guide and Intervention, p. 699

NAME ______ DATE ______ PERIOD ____

12-5 Study Guide and Intervention

Subtracting Polynomials

As with adding polynomials, to subtract two polynomials, you subtract like terms.

You can also subtract a polynomial by adding its additive inverse. To find the additive inverse of a polynomial, find the opposite of each term.

EXAMPLE 1 **Find $(8a^2 - 2) - (2a^2 + 3a + 2)$.**

$$\begin{array}{rl} 8a^2 - 2 & \\ (-)\ 2a^2 + 3a + 2 & \text{Align the terms.} \\ \hline 6a^2 - 3a - 4 & \text{Subtract.} \end{array}$$

The difference is $6a^2 - 3a - 4$.

EXAMPLE 2 **Find $(6p - 1) - (-3p - 3)$.**

The additive inverse of $-3p - 3$ is $3p + 3$.

$(6p - 1) - (-3p - 3)$
$= (6p - 1) + (3p + 3)$ To subtract $(-3p - 3)$, add $(3p + 3)$.
$= (6p + 3p) + (-1 + 3)$ Group like terms.
$= 9p + 2$ Simplify.

The difference is $9p + 2$.

EXERCISES

Subtract.

1. $7y + 8$ $(-)\ 2y + 3$
2. $6b^2 - 3b + 2$ $(-)\ 2b^2 + 5b + 1$
3. $6w^2 + 2w + 5$ $(-)\ w^2 + 8$
4. $3z^2 - 2z + 1$ $(-)\ 3z^2 + 6z - 9$
5. $4t^2 - t + 6$ $(-)\ 8t^2 + 2t + 1$
6. $-3a^2 + 3a - 5$ $(-)\ 4a^2 - 6a + 2$ **$-7a^2 + 9a - 7$**
7. $(8m + 6) - (3m + 1)$ **$5m + 5$**
8. $(2x - 1) - (-2x + 2)$ **$4x - 3$**
9. $(10r^2 + 5) - (3r - 7)$ **$10r^2 - 3r + 12$**
10. $(3k^2 + 4k - 5) - (4k^2 + 2k - 3)$ **$-k^2 + 2k - 2$**
11. $(t^2 + 5t + 3) - (5t + 4)$ **$t^2 - 1$**
12. $(4c^2 + c - 6) - (8c^2 - c + 2)$ **$-4c^2 + 2c - 8$**
13. $(9s^2 + 4s) - (2s^2 + 4)$ **$7s^2 + 4s - 4$**
14. $(6v^2 + 3) - (5v - 1)$ **$6v^2 - 5v + 4$**

Practice: Skills, p. 700

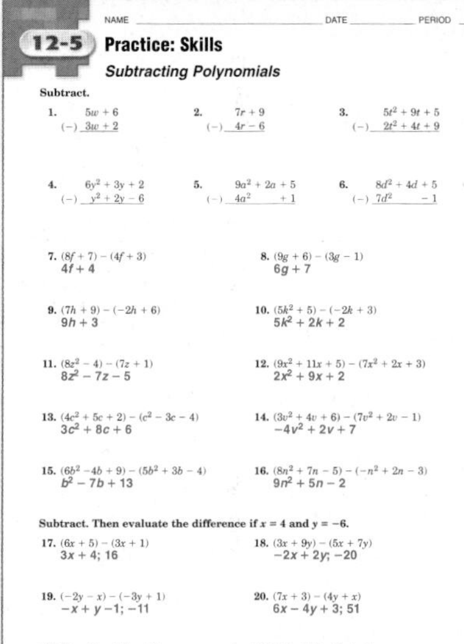

NAME ______ DATE ______ PERIOD ____

12-5 Practice: Skills

Subtracting Polynomials

Subtract.

1. $5w + 6$ $(-)\ 3w + 2$
2. $7r + 9$ $(-)\ 4r - 6$
3. $5t^2 + 9t + 5$ $(-)\ 2t^2 + 4t + 9$
4. $6y^2 + 3y + 2$ $(-)\ y^2 + 2y - 6$
5. $9a^2 + 2a + 5$ $(-)\ 4a^2 + 1$
6. $8d^2 + 4d + 5$ $(-)\ 7d^2 - 1$
7. $(8f + 7) - (4f + 3)$ **$4f + 4$**
8. $(9g + 6) - (3g - 1)$ **$6g + 7$**
9. $(7h + 9) - (-2h + 6)$ **$9h + 3$**
10. $(5k^2 + 5) - (-2k + 3)$ **$5k^2 + 2k + 2$**
11. $(8z^2 - 4) - (7z + 1)$ **$8z^2 - 7z - 5$**
12. $(9x^2 + 11x + 5) - (7x^2 + 2x + 3)$ **$2x^2 + 9x + 2$**
13. $(4c^2 + 5c + 2) - (c^2 - 3c - 4)$ **$3c^2 + 8c + 6$**
14. $(3v^2 + 4v + 6) - (7v^2 + 2v - 1)$ **$-4v^2 + 2v + 7$**
15. $(6b^2 - 4b + 9) - (5b^2 + 3b - 4)$ **$b^2 - 7b + 13$**
16. $(8n^2 + 7n - 5) - (-n^2 + 2n - 3)$ **$9n^2 + 5n - 2$**

Subtract. Then evaluate the difference if $x = 4$ and $y = -6$.

17. $(6x + 5) - (3x + 1)$ **$3x + 4$; 16**
18. $(3x + 9y) - (5x + 7y)$ **$-2x + 2y$; -20**
19. $(-2y - x) - (-3y + 1)$ **$-x + y - 1$; -11**
20. $(7x + 3) - (4y + x)$ **$6x - 4y + 3$; 51**
21. $(5x - 6) - (-8y - 3x)$ **$8x + 8y - 6$; -22**
22. $(-2y + 9) - (6x + y)$ **$-3y - 6x + 9$; 3**

Practice: Word Problems, p. 701

NAME ______ DATE ______ PERIOD ____

12-5 Practice: Word Problems

Subtracting Polynomials

GEOMETRY **For Exercises 1 and 2, use the figures at the right.**

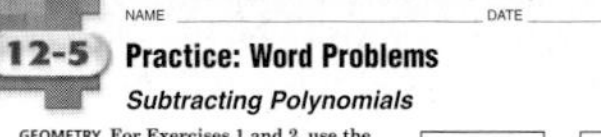

1. Write polynomial expressions in simplest form that represent the perimeters of the two rectangles. Then write a polynomial expression in simplest form that represents the difference between the perimeter of the larger rectangle and the perimeter of the smaller rectangle. **smaller: $2x + 16$; larger: $2x + 24$; 8**
2. Write a polynomial expression in simplest form that represents the difference between the area of the larger rectangle and the area of the smaller rectangle. Then find the difference when $x = 4$. **$2x + 20$; 28 units^2**
3. **SALARY** The polynomial expression $(300 + 0.4s) - (500 + 0.3s)$ represents the difference between two salary options that Chuck has in his new position as a salesperson. Write this difference in simplest form. **$-200 + 0.1s$**
4. **SHOPPING** Maria bought 7 CDs at x dollars each and used a coupon for \$20 off her purchase of more than 5 CDs. Ricky bought 4 CDs at x dollars each and redeemed a coupon for \$10 off his purchase of more than 3 CDs. Write polynomial expressions representing how much each spent after the discount. Then write a polynomial expression in simplest form representing how much more Maria spent than Ricky. **Maria: $7x - 20$; Ricky: $4x - 10$; $3x - 10$**
5. **TESTS** On a test worth 100 points, Jerome missed 3 questions worth p points each but answered a bonus question correctly for an extra 5 points. Suni answered 4 questions incorrectly and did not get the bonus. Write polynomial expressions in simplest form representing each student's score on the test. Then write a polynomial expression in simplest form representing how many more points Jerome scored than Suni. **Jerome; $105 - 3p$; Suni: $100 - 4p$; $5 + p$**
6. **PIZZA** Sal's Pizza Place charges \$8 for a large pizza plus \$0.75 for each topping, while Greco's Cafe charges \$10 for the same size pizza plus \$0.90 for each topping. Write a polynomial in simplest form that represents how much more a pizza with t toppings would cost at Greco's than at Sal's. **$2 + 0.15t$**

12-6

Lesson Notes

Lesson Resources

Chapter 12 Resource Masters

FAST FILE

- Study Guide and Intervention, p. 704
- Practice: Skills, p. 705
- Practice: Word Problems, p. 706
- Reading to Learn Mathematics, p. 707
- Enrichment, p. 708

Parent and Student Study Guide Online Worksheets, 12-6

Teaching Mathematics with Manipulatives, pp. 114–115

Noteables™: Interactive Study Notebook with Foldables™, 12-6

Focus

5-Minute Check 12-6

INTERACTIVE CHALKBOARD
PowerPoint® Presentations

Use as a quiz or review of Lesson 12-5. (Also available as a transparency)

Bellringer

Reading Mathematics Have students review the vocabulary associated with powers, exponents, and bases.

Reading to Learn Mathematics, p. 707 ELL

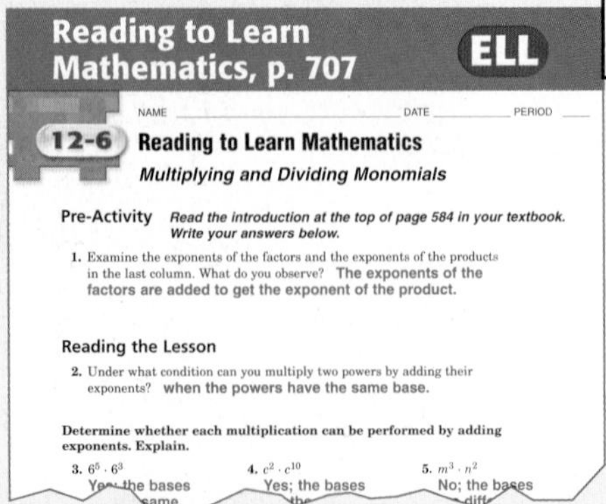

NAME ________ DATE ________ PERIOD ____

12-6 **Reading to Learn Mathematics**

Multiplying and Dividing Monomials

Pre-Activity *Read the introduction at the top of page 584 in your textbook. Write your answers below.*

1. Examine the exponents of the factors and the exponents of the products in the last column. What do you observe? **The exponents of the factors are added to get the exponent of the product.**

Reading the Lesson

2. Under what condition can you multiply two powers by adding their exponents? **when the powers have the same base.**

Determine whether each multiplication can be performed by adding exponents. Explain.

3. $6^5 \cdot 6^3$ Yes; the bases ... same.
4. $c^2 \cdot c^{10}$ Yes; the bases ...
5. $m^3 \cdot n^2$ No; the bases ... diff...

Multiplying and Dividing Monomials

What You'll LEARN

Multiply and divide monomials.

MATH Symbols

x^5 ← exponent; x ← base

x^5 *x* to the fifth power

WHEN **am I ever going to use this?**

SCIENCE The pH of a solution describes its acidity. Neutral water has a pH of 7. Lemon juice has a pH of 2. Each one-unit decrease in the pH means that the solution is 10 times more acidic. So a pH of 8 is 10 times more acidic than a pH of 9.

pH	Times More Acidic Than a pH of 9	Written Using Powers
8	10	10^1
7	$10 \times 10 = 100$	$10^1 \times 10^1 = 10^2$
6	$10 \times 10 \times 10 = 1{,}000$	$10^1 \times 10^2 = 10^3$
5	$10 \times 10 \times 10 \times 10 = 10{,}000$	$10^1 \times 10^3 = 10^4$
4	$10 \times 10 \times 10 \times 10 \times 10 = 100{,}000$	$10^1 \times 10^4 = 10^5$

1. Examine the exponents of the factors and the exponents of the products in the last column. What do you observe?

1. The exponents of the factors are added to get the exponent of the product.

Exponents are used to show repeated multiplication. You can use this fact to help find a rule for multiplying powers with the same base.

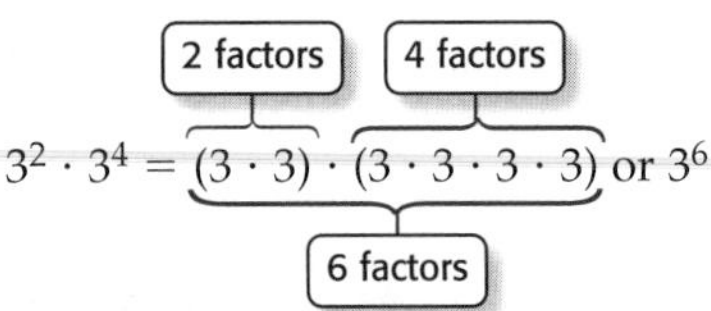

Notice the sum of the original exponents and the exponent in the final product. This relationship is stated in the following rule.

Noteables™ **Key Concept: Product of Powers**

Words To multiply powers with the same base, add their exponents.

Symbols Arithmetic: $2^4 \cdot 2^3 = 2^{4+3}$ or 2^7 Algebra: $a^m \cdot a^n = a^{m+n}$

STUDY TIP

Common Error When multiplying powers, do not multiply the bases. $4^5 \cdot 4^2 = 4^7$, not 16^7.

EXAMPLE **Multiply Powers**

1 Find $5^2 \cdot 5$. Express using exponents.

$5^2 \cdot 5 = 5^2 \cdot 5^1$ $5 = 5^1$

$= 5^{2+1}$ The common base is 5.

$= 5^3$ Add the exponents.

Check $5^2 \cdot 5 = (5 \cdot 5) \cdot 5$

$= 5 \cdot 5 \cdot 5$

$= 5^3$ ✓

EXAMPLE Multiply Monomials

2 **Find $-3x^2(4x^5)$. Express using exponents.**

$-3x^2(4x^5) = (-3 \cdot 4)(x^2 \cdot x^5)$ Commutative and Associative Properties

$= (-12)(x^{2+5})$ The common base is x.

$= -12x^7$ Add the exponents.

Your Turn **Multiply. Express using exponents.**

a. $9^3 \cdot 9^2$ **9^5** b. $y^4 \cdot y^9$ **y^{13}** c. $-2m(-8m^5)$ **$16m^6$**

There is also a rule for dividing powers that have the same base.

Noteables™ **Key Concept: Quotient of Powers**

Words To divide powers with the same base, subtract their exponents.

Symbols Arithmetic: $\frac{3^7}{3^3} = 3^{7-3}$ or 3^4 Algebra: $\frac{a^m}{a^n} = a^{m-n}$, where $a \neq 0$

EXAMPLES Divide Powers

Divide. Express using exponents.

3 $\frac{4^8}{4^2}$

$\frac{4^8}{4^2} = 4^{8-2}$ The common base is 4.

$= 4^6$ Simplify.

4 $\frac{n^9}{n^4}$

$\frac{n^9}{n^4} = n^{9-4}$ The common base is n.

$= n^5$ Simplify.

Your Turn **Divide. Express using exponents.**

d. $\frac{5^7}{5^4}$ **5^3** e. $\frac{x^{10}}{x^3}$ **x^7** f. $\frac{12w^5}{2w}$ **$6w^4$**

REAL-LIFE MATH

SOUND The decibel measure of the loudness of a sound is the exponent of its relative intensity multiplied by 10. A jet engine has a loudness of 120 decibels.

EXAMPLE Divide Powers to Solve a Problem

5 **SOUND The loudness of a conversation is 10^6 times as intense as the loudness of a pin dropping, while the loudness of a jet engine is 10^{12} times as intense. How many times more intense is the loudness of a jet engine than the loudness of a conversation?**

To find how many times more intense, divide 10^{12} by 10^6.

$\frac{10^{12}}{10^6} = 10^{12-6}$ Quotient of Powers

$= 10^6$ Simplify.

The loudness of a jet engine is 10^6 or 1,000,000 times as intense as the loudness of a conversation.

msmath3.net/extra_examples

2 Teach

In-Class Examples

1 Find $7^6 \cdot 7^2$. Express using exponents. **7^8**

2 Find $7x^2(11x^4)$. Express using exponents. **$77x^6$**

Divide. Express using exponents.

3 $\frac{6^{12}}{6^2}$ **6^{10}**

4 $\frac{a^{14}}{a^8}$ **a^6**

5 **UNIT CONVERSION** One centimeter is 10 millimeters, and one kilometer is 10^6 millimeters. How many centimeters are there in one kilometer? **10^5 cm**

Teaching Strategies Students may need more explanation on the subtraction of powers rule stated in the Key Concept box. For example, show students that

$\frac{\cancel{3}\cdot\cancel{3}\cdot\cancel{3}\cdot 3\cdot 3\cdot 3\cdot 3}{\cancel{3}\cdot\cancel{3}\cdot\cancel{3}} = 3^4.$

DAILY INTERVENTION **Differentiated Instruction**

Kinesthetic Provide groups of students with about 150 small objects, such as beads or dried beans. Have students use the objects to model $2^4 \cdot 2^3 = 2^7$. Then, have students use them to model $2^4 \div 2^3 = 2$. Encourage them to model other examples of adding and subtracting exponents until they have verified for themselves that you can multiply or divide powers with the same base by adding or subtracting their exponents, respectively.

3 Practice/Apply

FOLDABLES™ Follow-Up · Remind students to use their Foldables like a journal to record what they learn about multiplying and dividing monomials. Encourage students to draw models when necessary.

NUMBER SENSE
Use Exercise 3 to demonstrate to students how useful adding and subtracting of exponents can be. Suggest that they try to evaluate 2^{100} and 2^{99} before dividing. Students will see that adding or subtracting exponents can quickly solve problems that appear to be very daunting.

About the Exercises...

Guided Practice Key

Exercises	Examples
4–7	1, 2
8–9	3, 4

Assignment Guide

Basic: 11–31 odd, 35, 37, 41, 43, 44–62

Average: 11–37 odd, 38, 39, 41, 43, 44–62

Enriched: 10–38 even, 39, 40, 42, 44–58 (Optional: 59–62)

Students practice the same concepts in Exercises 10–33 and 38–39 if they are assigned odd or even problems.

Skill and Concept Check

1. **Writing Math** Determine whether the following statement is *true* or *false*. *If you change the order in which you multiply two monomials, the product will be different.*
   Explain your reasoning or give a counterexample. **false; $4x(5x^2) = 5x^2(4x) = 20x^3$**
2. **OPEN ENDED** Write a multiplication expression whose product is 4^{15} and a division expression whose quotient is 4^{15}. **Sample answer: $4^7 \cdot 4^8$; $\frac{4^{16}}{4}$**
3. **NUMBER SENSE** Is $\frac{2^{100}}{2^{99}}$ greater than, less than, or equal to 2? **equal**

GUIDED PRACTICE

Multiply or divide. Express using exponents.

4. $4^5 \cdot 4^3$ **4^8**
5. $3^6 \cdot 3$ **3^7**
6. $n^2 \cdot n^9$ **n^{11}**
7. $-2a(3a^4)$ **$-6a^5$**
8. $\frac{7^6}{7}$ **7^5**
9. $\frac{9c^7}{3c^2}$ **$3c^5$**

Practice and Applications

Multiply or divide. Express using exponents.

10. $6^8 \cdot 6^5$ **6^{13}**
11. $7^3 \cdot 7^3$ **7^6**
12. $2^9 \cdot 2$ **2^{10}**
13. $11 \cdot 11^4$ **11^5**
14. $n \cdot n^7$ **n^8**
15. $b^{13} \cdot b$ **b^{14}**
16. $2g \cdot 7g^6$ **$14g^7$**
17. $(3x^8)(5x)$ **$15x^9$**
18. $-4a^5(6a^5)$ **$-24a^{10}$**
19. $(8w^4)(-w^7)$ **$-8w^{11}$**
20. $(-p)(-9p^2)$ **$9p^3$**
21. $-5y^3(-8y^6)$ **$40y^9$**
22. $\frac{3^9}{3^2}$ **3^7**
23. $\frac{4^{10}}{4^5}$ **4^5**
24. $\frac{8^4}{8}$ **8^3**
25. $\frac{10^{12}}{10}$ **10^{11}**
26. $\frac{r^7}{r^2}$ **r^5**
27. $\frac{x^{14}}{x^8}$ **x^6**
28. $\frac{14n^6}{7n}$ **$2n^5$**
29. $\frac{24k^3}{8k^2}$ **$3k$**
30. $xy^2(x^3y)$ **x^4y^3**
31. $4a^2b^3(7ab^2)$ **$28a^3b^5$**
32. $\frac{20a^5b}{4ab}$ **$5a^4$**
33. $\frac{16x^3y^2}{2x^2y}$ **$8xy$**
34. the product of seven to the tenth power and seven cubed **7^{13}**
35. the quotient of n to the sixth power and n squared **n^4**
36. What is the product of 2^6, 2, and 2^3? **2^{10}**
37. Find $x^3 \cdot x^9 \div x^5$. **x^7**

HOMEWORK HELP

For Exercises	See Examples
10–13, 34–35	1
14–21	2
22–33, 36–37	3, 4
38–43	5

Extra Practice See pages 647, 659.

EARTHQUAKES For Exercises 38 and 39, use the information in the table at the right and below.
For each increase on the Richter scale, an earthquake's vibrations, or *seismic waves*, are 10 times greater.

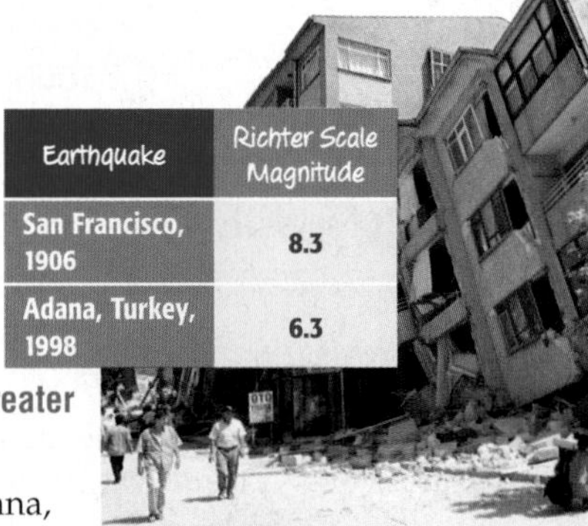

Earthquake	Richter Scale Magnitude
San Francisco, 1906	8.3
Adana, Turkey, 1998	6.3

38. How many times greater are the seismic waves of an earthquake with a magnitude of 6 than an aftershock with a magnitude of 3? **10^3 or 1,000 times greater**
39. How many times greater were the seismic waves of the 1906 San Francisco earthquake than the 1998 Adana, Turkey, earthquake? **10^2 or 100 times greater**

586 Chapter 12 Algebra: Nonlinear Functions and Polynomials

40. **LIFE SCIENCE** A cell culture contains 2^6 cells. By the end of the day, there are 2^{10} times as many cells in the culture. How many cells are there in the culture by the end of the day? **2^{16}**

41. **ASTRONOMY** Venus is approximately 10^8 kilometers from the Sun. The gas giant Saturn is more than 10^9 kilometers from the Sun. About how many times farther away from the Sun is Saturn than Venus? **about 10 times**

42. **GEOMETRY** Find the volume of the rectangular prism. **$315x^3$ in^3**

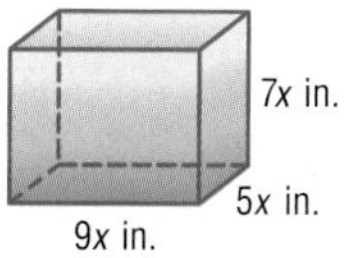

7x in.
5x in.
9x in.

43. **POPULATION** The continent of North America contains approximately 10^7 square miles of land. If the population doubles, there will be about 10^9 people on the continent. At that point, how many people will be on each square mile of land? **10^2 or 100 people/mi^2**

44. **CRITICAL THINKING** What is half of 2^{30}? Write your answer using exponents. **2^{29}**

CRITICAL THINKING Divide. **47. $2x^4y^{-5}$ or $\frac{2x^4}{y^5}$** **49. $a^5b^{-3}c^{-2}$ or $\frac{a^5}{b^3c^2}$**

45. $\frac{a^8}{a^8}$ **1**
46. $\frac{n^2}{n^5}$ **n^{-3} or $\frac{1}{n^3}$**
47. $\frac{6x^7y^4}{3x^3y^9}$
48. $\frac{y^6}{y^{-4}}$ **y^{10}**
49. $\frac{a^8b^{-1}c^{-5}}{a^3b^2c^{-3}}$

Spiral Review with Standardized Test Practice

50. **MULTIPLE CHOICE** Find the product of $-5x^2$ and $-6x^8$. **D**

Ⓐ $-11x^{10}$ Ⓑ $-30x^{16}$ Ⓒ $11x^{10}$ Ⓓ $30x^{10}$

51. **MULTIPLE CHOICE** Find $\frac{(-2)^5}{(-2)^4}$. **G**

Ⓕ $(-2)^9$ Ⓖ -2 Ⓗ 1 Ⓘ 2^9

Subtract. (Lesson 12-5)

52. $(3x + 8) - (5x + 1)$ **$-2x + 7$**
53. $(5a - 2) - (3a - 4)$ **$2a + 2$**
54. $(6y^2 + 3y + 9) - (2y^2 + 8y + 1)$ **$4y^2 - 5y + 8$**

SCHOOL For Exercises 55 and 56, use the following information and the table at the right.

Suppose your total number of grade points for the first semester was 2A + 2B + C and your total for the second semester was A + 3B + D. (Lesson 12-4) **55. 3A + 5B + C + D**

Grade	Grade Points
A	4
B	3
C	2
D	1
F	0

55. Add the polynomials to find your total grade points for the year.

56. Evaluate the sum by substituting the grade point value for each variable. **30**

Find the mean, median, and mode of each set of data. Round to the nearest tenth if necessary. (Lesson 9-4)

57. 52, 57, 52, 33, 39, 43, 53 **47; 52; 52**

58. 19, 28, 25, 64, 64, 76, 18 **42; 28; 64**

GETTING READY FOR THE NEXT LESSON

PREREQUISITE SKILL Use the Distributive Property to write each expression as an equivalent algebraic expression. (Lesson 10-1) **62. $-4p + 24$**

59. $3(x + 4)$ **$3x + 12$**
60. $5(y - 2)$ **$5y - 10$**
61. $-2(n + 8)$ **$-2n - 16$**
62. $-4(p - 6)$

msmath3.net/self_check_quiz

Study Guide and Intervention, p. 704

NAME ____________ DATE ________ PERIOD ____

12-6 Study Guide and Intervention

Multiplying and Dividing Monomials

The Product of Powers Property states that to multiply powers that have the same base, add their exponents: $a^n \cdot a^m = a^{n+m}$.

The Quotient of Powers Property states that to divide powers that have the same base, subtract their exponents: $a^n \div a^m = a^{n-m}$.

EXAMPLES Multiply or divide. Express using exponents.

1. $2^3 \cdot 2^2$

$2^3 \cdot 2^2 = 2^{3+2}$ The common base is 2.
$= 2^5$ Add the exponents.

2. $-2s^6(-7s^7)$

$-2s^6(-7s^7) = (-2 \cdot -7)(s^6 \cdot s^7)$ Commutative and Associative Properties
$= (14)(s^{6+7})$ The common base is s.
$= 14s^{13}$ Add the exponents.

3. $\frac{k^8}{k}$

$\frac{k^8}{k} = k^{8-1}$ The common base is k.
$= k^7$ Subtract the exponents.

4. $\frac{28g^{12}}{-4g^3}$

$\frac{28g^{12}}{-4g^3} = \left(\frac{28}{-4}\right)\left(\frac{g^{12}}{g^3}\right)$ Commutative and Associative Properties
$= (-7)(g^{12-3})$ The common base is g.
$= -7g^9$ Subtract the exponents.

EXERCISES

Multiply or divide. Express using exponents.

1. $3^4 \cdot 3^1$ **3^5**
2. $5^2 \cdot 5^5$ **5^7**
3. $e^2 \cdot e^7$ **e^9**
4. $2a^5 \cdot 6a$ **$12a^6$**
5. $-3t^3 \cdot 2t^8$ **$-6t^{11}$**
6. $4x^2(-5x^6)$ **$-20x^8$**
7. $\frac{2^8}{2^6}$ **2^2**
8. $\frac{7^9}{7^3}$ **7^6**
9. $\frac{v^{14}}{v^6}$ **v^8**
10. $\frac{15w^7}{5w^2}$ **$3w^5$**
11. $\frac{21z^{10}}{7z^9}$ **$3z$**
12. $\frac{10m^8}{2m}$ **$5m^7$**

Practice: Skills, p. 705

NAME ____________ DATE ________ PERIOD ____

12-6 Practice: Skills

Multiplying and Dividing Monomials

Multiply or divide. Express using exponents.

1. $2^7 \cdot 2^2$ **2^9**
2. $4^2 \cdot 4^4$ **4^6**
3. $10^2 \cdot 10^3$ **10^5**
4. $k^8 \cdot k$ **k^9**
5. $t^7 \cdot t^6$ **t^{13}**
6. $2w^2 \cdot 5w^2$ **$10w^4$**
7. $3e^3 \cdot 7e^3$ **$21e^6$**
8. $4r^4(-4r^3)$ **$-16r^7$**
9. $(-6t^7)(5t^2)$ **$-30t^9$**
10. $7y^3 \cdot 6y$ **$42y^4$**
11. $(3u^5)(-9u^6)$ **$-27u^{11}$**
12. $(-2p^7)(-8p^3)$ **$16p^{10}$**
13. $(5c^4)(-7c)$ **$-35c^5$**
14. $(8z^7)(3z^6)$ **$24z^{13}$**
15. $(-3l^2w^3)(2lw^4)$ **$-6l^3w^7$**
16. $\frac{2^9}{2^3}$ **2^6**
17. $\frac{3^8}{3^4}$ **3^4**
18. $\frac{5^9}{5^2}$ **5^7**
19. $\frac{8^7}{8}$ **8^6**
20. $\frac{b^{12}}{b^5}$ **b^7**
21. $\frac{12n^5}{4n^2}$ **$3n^3$**
22. $\frac{14m^3}{7m^2}$ **$2m$**
23. $\frac{9r^8}{3r^4}$ **$3r^4$**
24. $\frac{24t^9}{6t^3}$ **$4t^6$**
25. $\frac{18y^6}{2y}$ **$9y^5$**
26. $a^4c^6(a^2c)$ **a^6c^7**
27. $\frac{15x^8y^4}{3x^5y^2}$ **$5x^3y^2$**
28. $\frac{-21s^6t^3}{3s^2t}$ **$-7s^4t^2$**
29. $\frac{34v^7}{2v^3}$ **$17v^4$**
30. $\frac{4^2q^5}{2q^2}$ **2^3q^3**

Practice: Word Problems, p. 706

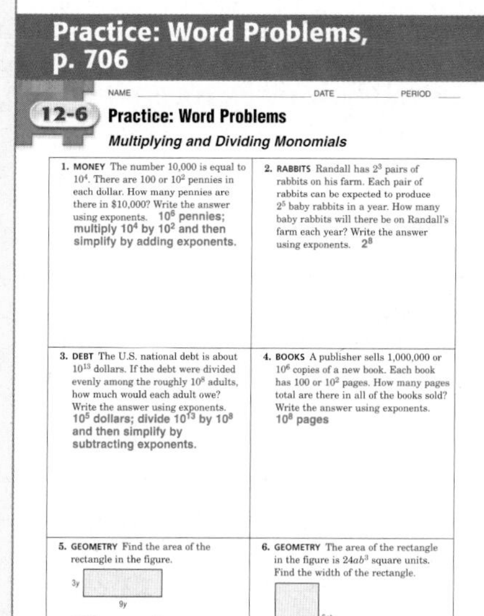

NAME ____________ DATE ________ PERIOD ____

12-6 Practice: Word Problems

Multiplying and Dividing Monomials

1. **MONEY** The number 10,000 is equal to 10^4. There are 100 or 10^2 pennies in each dollar. How many pennies are there in \$10,000? Write the answer using exponents. **10^6 pennies; multiply 10^4 by 10^2 and then simplify by adding exponents.**

2. **RABBITS** Randall has 2^3 pairs of rabbits on his farm. Each pair of rabbits can be expected to produce 2^5 baby rabbits in a year. How many baby rabbits will there be on Randall's farm each year? Write the answer using exponents. **2^8**

3. **DEBT** The U.S. national debt is about 10^{13} dollars. If the debt were divided evenly among the roughly 10^8 adults, how much would each adult owe? Write the answer using exponents. **10^5 dollars; divide 10^{13} by 10^8 and then simplify by subtracting exponents.**

4. **BOOKS** A publisher sells 1,000,000 or 10^6 copies of a new book. Each book has 100 or 10^2 pages. How many pages total are there in all of the books sold? Write the answer using exponents. **10^8 pages**

5. **GEOMETRY** Find the area of the rectangle in the figure. **$27y^2$ square units**

3y
9y

6. **GEOMETRY** The area of the rectangle in the figure is $24ab^3$ square units. Find the width of the rectangle. **$4b^2$ units**

6ab

4 Assess

Higher-Level Thinking

Use $\frac{a^m}{a^n} = a^{m-n}$ to show that a^{-n} is the same as $\frac{1}{a^n}$. **Let $m = 0$. Then $a^{m-n} = a^{-n}$. Since we have $\frac{a^m}{a^n} = a^{m-n}$, then $\frac{a^m}{a^n} = a^{-n}$ or $\frac{a^0}{a^n} = \frac{1}{a^n}$.** Why is it necessary to specify that $a \neq 0$ in this term? **If a were 0, then this would be division by 0, which is undefined in real-number mathematics.**

Lesson 12-6 Multiplying and Dividing Monomials 587

12-7a Lesson Notes

1 Focus

Bellringer
Communication Discuss with students when models are used to solve real-life problems. **Sample answers: architecture, landscaping, city planning, product testing, mural design, and crafts.** Discuss why the model is used rather than the real object in each situation.

2 Teach

In-Class Example

Solve. Use the make a model strategy.

DESKS Caitlyn is responsible for arranging desks in her classroom. There are 32 desks, and she wants to have twice as many desks in each row as she has in each column. Use a model to determine how many desks she should put in each row and how many rows she will need. **4 rows with 8 desks in each row**

Answer

1. **Sample answer: Actually arranging the tables into a 10 by 10 square only to find that you did not have enough tables would waste time and energy. Analyzing a model takes less time and is easier to manipulate.**

12-7a Problem-Solving Strategy

A Preview of Lesson 12-7

Make a Model

What You'll LEARN
Solve problems by making a model.

We need to arrange some of these square tables into a square that is open in the middle and has 10 tables on each side.

We have 35 tables. Do we have enough? Let's **make a model** using these tiles.

Explore	We want to know how many square tables it will take to make the outline of a 10-by-10 square.
Plan	Let's start by making a model of a 4-by-4 square and of a 5-by-5 square. Then, let's look for a pattern.
Solve	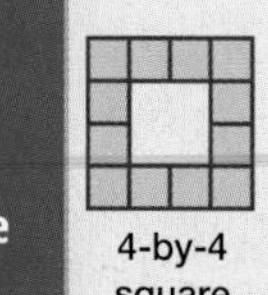 4-by-4 square 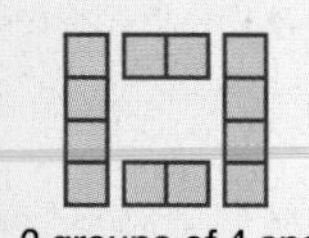 2 groups of 4 and 2 groups of 2 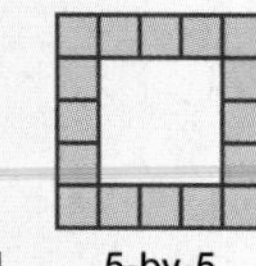 5-by-5 square 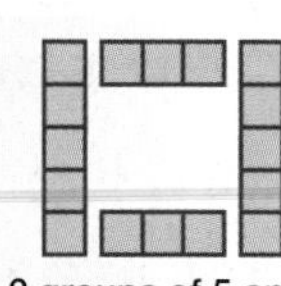 2 groups of 5 and 2 groups of 3 For a 10-by-10 square we need $2 \times 10 + 2 \times 8$ or 36. We have 35 tables, so we need one more.
Examine	We get the same answer when we make 4 groups of tiles. Each group has 1 less tile than the length of the square. Since $4(10 - 1)$ is 36, our answer is reasonable. 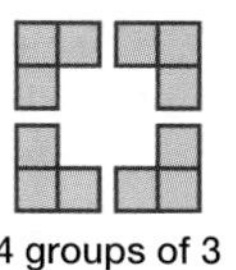 4 groups of 3

Analyze the Strategy

1. **Explain** why building a model is an appropriate strategy for solving the problem. **1–3. See margin.**
2. **Draw a diagram** showing another way the students could have grouped the tiles to solve this problem. Use a 4 by 4 square.
3. **Write** a problem that can be solved by making a model. Describe the model. Then solve the problem.

DAILY INTERVENTION — Differentiated Instruction

Visual/Spatial Have students make a model to solve the following problem. *Find the volume of a prism with a length of 8 centimeters, a width of w centimeters, and a height of 2w.* **$16w^2$**

Apply the Strategy

Solve. Make a model.

4. **STICKERS** In how many different ways can three rectangular stickers be torn from a sheet of such stickers so that all three stickers are attached to each other? Draw each arrangement. **6; See Ch. 12 Answer Appendix.**

5. **GEOMETRY** A 10-inch by 12-inch piece of cardboard has a 2-inch square cut out of each corner. Then the sides are folded up and taped together to make an open box. Find the volume of the box. **96 in^3**

Mixed Problem Solving

Solve. Use any strategy.

6. **PETS** Mrs. Harper owns both cats and canaries. Altogether her pets have thirty heads and eighty legs. How many cats does she have? **10**

TOWER For Exercises 7 and 8, use the figure at the right.

7. How many cubes would it take to build this tower? **25**

8. How many cubes would it take to build a similar tower that is 12 cubes high? **144**

9. **CARS** Yesterday you noted that the mileage on the family car read 60,094.8 miles. Today it reads 60,099.1 miles. Was the car driven about 4 or 40 miles? **about 4 mi**

10. **HOBBIES** Lorena says to Angela, "If you give me one of your baseball cards, I will have twice as many baseball cards as you have." Angela answers, "If you give me one of your cards, we will have the same numbers of cards." How many cards do each of the girls have? **Lorena, 7; Angela, 5**

11. **PARKING** Campus parking space numbers consist of three digits. They are typed on a slip of paper and given to students at orientation. Tara accidentally read her number upside-down. The number she read was 723 more than her actual parking space number. What is Tara's parking space number? **168**

12. **SCIENCE** The light in the circuit will turn on if one or more switches are closed. How many combinations of open and closed switches will result in the light being on? **31**

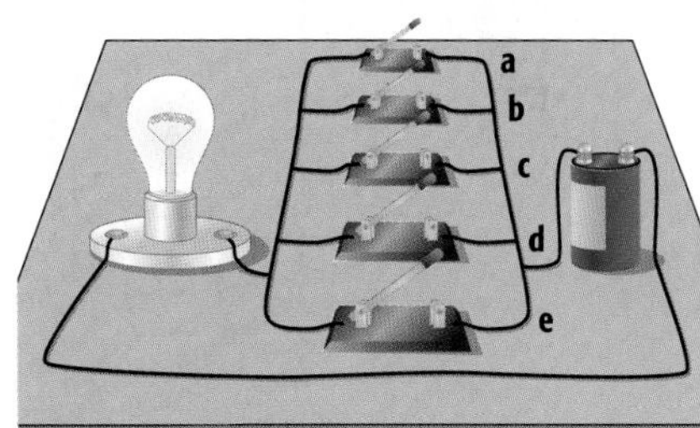

13. **CAMP** The camp counselor lists 21 chores on separate pieces of paper and places them in a basket. The counselor takes one piece of paper, and each camper takes one as the basket is passed around the circle. There is one piece of paper left when the basket returns to the counselor. How many people could be in the circle if the basket goes around the circle more than once? **10, 5, 4, or 2**

14. **STANDARDIZED TEST PRACTICE** In how many different ways can five squares be arranged to form a single shape so that touching squares border on a full side? One arrangement is shown at the right. **B**

    (A) 8 (B) 12
    (C) 16 (D) 20

3 Practice/Apply

About the Exercises...

Problem-Solving Strategies Exercises 6–14 are structured so that students have the opportunity to practice many different problem-solving strategies. You may wish to remind them of some of the strategies they have studied.

- look for a pattern (p. 96)
- draw a diagram (p. 176)
- make an organized list (p. 378)
- make a table (p. 418)
- guess and check (p. 488)
- make a model ✓

4 Assess

Open-Ended Assessment

Modeling Have students work in small groups to brainstorm ways to model the addition and subtraction of polynomials without using algebra tiles. Afterward, have each group demonstrate one method for the class.

Answers

2. 4 groups of 2 and 4 is 12

3. **Sample answer: It could cost 9 cents each time you cut and weld a link of chain. What is the minimum cost to make a length of chain out of 7 separate links? You might use twist ties or strips of paper taped together to model the links; 27 cents.**

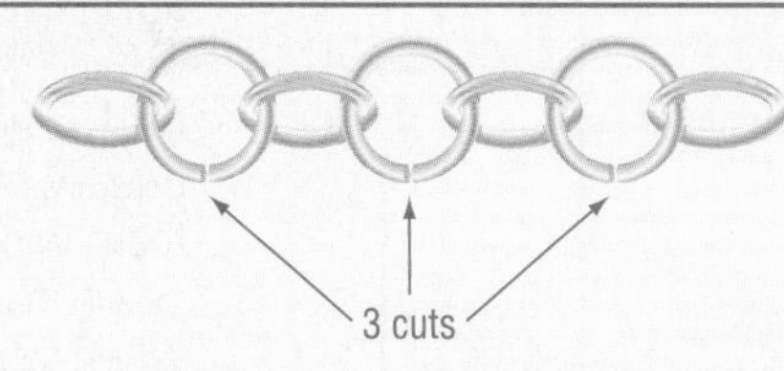

Lesson 12-7a Problem-Solving Strategy: Make a Model **589**

12-7 Lesson Notes

Lesson Resources

Chapter 12 Resource Masters

FAST FILE

- Study Guide and Intervention, p. 709
- Practice: Skills, p. 710
- Practice: Word Problems, p. 711
- Reading to Learn Mathematics, p. 712
- Enrichment, p. 713

Classroom Math Games, pp. 39–40

Parent and Student Study Guide Online Worksheets, 12-7

Noteables™: Interactive Study Notebook with Foldables™, 12-7

Focus

5-Minute Check 12-7

Use as a quiz or review of Lesson 12-6. (Also available as a transparency)

Bellringer

Communication Have students use algebra tiles to determine whether each of the following equations shows a proper use of the Distributive Property.

$3(a + 2) = 3a + 2$ **no; $3(a + 2) = 3a + 6$**

$(6x + 1)x = 6x^2 + 6$ **no; $(6x + 1) = 6x^2 + x$**

$2(y - 9) = 2y - 18$ **yes**

$5x\,(x + 4) = 5x + 20x$ **no; $5x(x + 4) = 5x^2 + 20x$**

$(4p - 8)3 = 12p - 24$ **yes**

Reading to Learn Mathematics, p. 712 ELL

NAME ______ DATE ______ PERIOD ______

12-7 Reading to Learn Mathematics

Multiplying Monomials and Polynomials

Pre-Activity *Complete the Mini Lab at the top of page 590 in your textbook. Write your answers below.*

1. What is $x(x + 3)$ in simplest form? $x^2 + 3x$

Use algebra tiles to find each product. 2–4 See students' models.

2. $x(x + 4)$ $x^2 + 4x$ 3. $x(3x + 1)$ $3x^2 + x$ 4. $2x(x + 3)$ $2x^2 + 6x$

Reading the Lesson

5. Explain how to multiply a polynomial by a monomial. Use the Distributive Property to multiply each term of the polynomial by the monomial.

12-7 Multiplying Monomials and Polynomials

What You'll LEARN

Multiply monomials and polynomials.

HANDS-ON Mini Lab

Materials

- algebra tiles
- product mat

Algebra tiles can be used to form a rectangle whose length and width each represent a polynomial. The area of the rectangle is the product of the polynomials. Use algebra tiles to find $x(x + 3)$.

STEP 1 Use algebra tiles to mark off a rectangle with a width of x and a length of $x + 3$ on a product mat.

STEP 2 Using the marks as a guide, fill in the rectangles with algebra tiles.

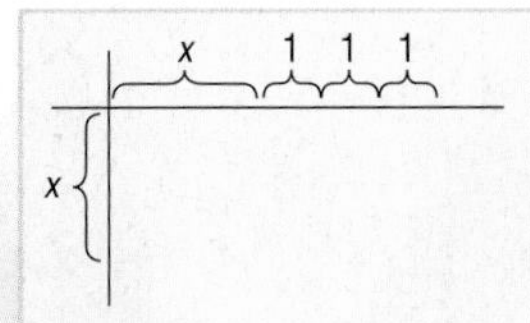

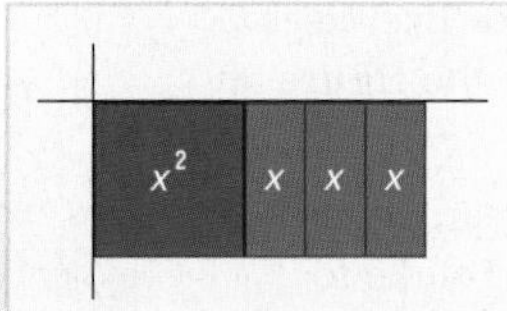

1. What is $x(x + 3)$ in simplest form? **$x^2 + 3x$**

Use algebra tiles to find each product.

2. $x(x + 4)$ **$x^2 + 4x$** 3. $x(3x + 1)$ **$3x^2 + x$** 4. $2x(x + 3)$ **$2x^2 + 6x$**

2–4. See Ch. 12 Answer Appendix for drawings.

In Lesson 10-1, you learned how to rewrite an expression like $4(x + 3)$ using the Distributive Property. This is an example of multiplying a polynomial by a monomial.

monomial → $4(x + 3)$ (polynomial)	$= 4(x) + 4(3)$	Distributive Property
	$= 4x + 12$	Simplify.

Often, the Distributive Property and the definition of exponents are needed to simplify the product of a monomial and a polynomial.

EXAMPLE Use the Distributive Property

1 **Find $x(x + 2)$.**

$x(x + 2) = x(x) + x(2)$	Distributive Property
$= x^2 + 2x$	$x \cdot x = x^2$

DAILY INTERVENTION — **Flexible Grouping**

Multiplying Monomials and Polynomials Divide the class into three equally matched teams to play a mathematical relay race. Provide each team with problems that can be solved by multiplying monomials and polynomials. Begin with one student from each team at the chalkboard. When you say, "Go!" each student begins working the first problem. When the problem is solved, the next person in the team works the next problem. The first team to complete all the problems wins.

EXAMPLE Use the Distributive Property

2 **Find $-5y(y + 8)$.**

$-5y(y + 8) = -5y(y) + (-5y)(8)$	Distributive Property
$= -5y^2 + (-40y)$	$-5 \cdot y \cdot y = -5y^2$
$= -5y^2 - 40y$	Definition of subtraction

Your Turn **Multiply.** b. $40p + 8p^2$ c. $-18x^2 + 12x$

a. $n(n - 9)$ $n^2 - 9n$ b. $(10 + 2p)4p$ c. $-3x(6x - 4)$

Sometimes you may need to use the Product of Powers rule.

EXAMPLES Use the Product of Powers Rule

3 **Find $3n(n^2 - 7)$.**

$3n(n^2 - 7) = 3n[n^2 + (-7)]$	Rewrite $n^2 - 7$ as $n^2 + (-7)$.
$= 3n(n^2) + 3n(-7)$	Distributive Property
$= 3n^3 + (-21n)$	$3n(n^2) = 3n^{1+2}$ or $3n^3$
$= 3n^3 - 21n$	Definition of subtraction

4 **Find $2x(x^2 + 3x - 5)$.**

$2x(x^2 + 3x - 5)$	
$= 2x[x^2 + 3x + (-5)]$	Rewrite $x^2 + 3x - 5$ as $x^2 + 3x + (-5)$.
$= 2x(x^2) + 2x(3x) + 2x(-5)$	Distributive Property
$= 2x^3 + 6x^2 + (-10x)$	Simplify.
$= 2x^3 + 6x^2 - 10x$	Definition of subtraction

d. $20y^3 - 10y^2$
e. $a^3 - 4a^2 + 6a$
f. $-8p^3 + 4p^2 - 12p$

Your Turn **Multiply.**

d. $5y(4y^2 - 2y)$ e. $a(a^2 - 4a + 6)$ f. $-4p(2p^2 - p + 3)$

Students practice the same concepts in Exercises 9–26 if they are assigned odd or even problems.

Skill and Concept Check

1. **OPEN ENDED** Write a polynomial with three terms and a monomial that contains a variable with a power of 1. Then find their product. **Sample answer: $5x^2 + 4x + 1$ and $2x$; $10x^3 + 8x^2 + 2x$**
2. **FIND THE ERROR** Christopher and Stephanie are finding the product of $3x$ and $2x^2 - 3x + 8$. Who is correct? Explain.

Christopher
$3x(2x^2 - 3x + 8)$
$= 6x^2 - 9x + 24$

Stephanie
$3x(2x^2 - 3x + 8)$
$= 6x^3 - 9x^2 + 24x$

Stephanie; Christopher multiplied the polynomial by 3, not by $3x$.

GUIDED PRACTICE

Multiply. 4. $6w^2 - 3w$ 7. $2g^3 - 5g^2 + 9g$

3. $m(m + 5)$ $m^2 + 5m$
4. $(2w - 1)(3w)$
5. $-4x(x + 1)$ $-4x^2 - 4x$
6. $k(k^2 - 7)$ $k^3 - 7k$
7. $g(2g^2 - 5g + 9)$
8. $3z(4z^2 - 6z - 10)$ $12z^3 - 18z^2 - 30z$

Math Online msmath3.net/extra_examples

2 Teach

In-Class Examples

1. Find $y(y + 12)$. $y^2 + 12y$
2. Find $-6x(x + 3)$. $-6x^2 - 18x$
3. Find $7w(w^2 + 6)$. $7w^3 + 42w$
4. Find $9t(t^2 + 6t - 4)$. $9t^3 + 54t^2 - 36t$

3 Practice/Apply

FOLDABLES™ Follow-Up Remind students to use their Foldables like a journal to find similarities and differences between multiplying monomials and polynomials. Students might explain how the Distributive Property helps them multiply a polynomial by a monomial.

DAILY INTERVENTION **FIND THE ERROR** In Exercise 2, tell students to be careful of careless errors when applying the Distributive Property. Stress the importance of checking their work to be sure they have multiplied correctly.

About the Exercises...

Guided Practice Key

Exercises	Examples
3–4	1
5	2
6	3
7–8	4

Assignment Guide

Basic: 9–21 odd, 25, 27–34

Average: 9–25 odd, 27–34

Enriched: 10–26 even, 27–34

4 Assess

Open-Ended Assessment

Writing Have students write four problems that can be solved by multiplying monomials and polynomials. Two of the problems should use the Distributive Property, and two should use the product of powers rule.

Study Guide and Intervention, p. 709

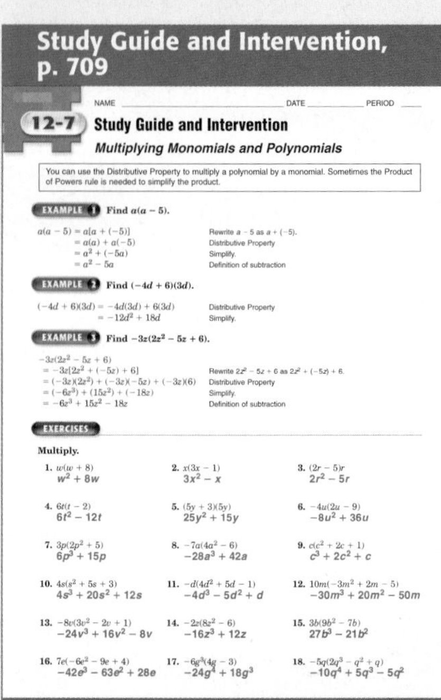
NAME ________ DATE ________ PERIOD ____

12-7 Study Guide and Intervention

Multiplying Monomials and Polynomials

You can use the Distributive Property to multiply a polynomial by a monomial. Sometimes the Product of Powers rule is needed to simplify the product.

EXAMPLE 1 Find $a(a - 5)$.

$a(a-5) = a[a + (-5)]$ — Rewrite $a - 5$ as $a + (-5)$.
$= a(a) + a(-5)$ — Distributive Property
$= a^2 + (-5a)$ — Simplify.
$= a^2 - 5a$ — Definition of subtraction

EXAMPLE 2 Find $(-4d + 6)(3d)$.

$(-4d + 6)(3d) = -4d(3d) + 6(3d)$ — Distributive Property
$= -12d^2 + 18d$ — Simplify.

EXAMPLE 3 Find $-3z(2z^2 - 5z + 6)$.

$-3z(2z^2 - 5z + 6)$
$= -3z[2z^2 + (-5z) + 6]$ — Rewrite $2z^2 - 5z + 6$ as $2z^2 + (-5z) + 6$.
$= (-3z)(2z^2) + (-3z)(-5z) + (-3z)(6)$ — Distributive Property
$= (-6z^3) + (15z^2) + (-18z)$ — Simplify.
$= -6z^3 + 15z^2 - 18z$ — Definition of subtraction

EXERCISES

Multiply.

1. $w(w + 8)$ $w^2 + 8w$
2. $x(3x - 1)$ $3x^2 - x$
3. $(2r - 5)r$ $2r^2 - 5r$
4. $6t(t - 2)$ $6t^2 - 12t$
5. $(5y + 3)(5y)$ $25y^2 + 15y$
6. $-4u(2u - 9)$ $-8u^2 + 36u$
7. $3p(2p^2 + 5)$ $6p^3 + 15p$
8. $-7a(4a^2 - 6)$ $-28a^3 + 42a$
9. $c(c^2 + 2c + 1)$ $c^3 + 2c^2 + c$
10. $4s(s^2 + 5s + 3)$ $4s^3 + 20s^2 + 12s$
11. $-d(4d^2 + 5d - 1)$ $-4d^3 - 5d^2 + d$
12. $10m(-3m^2 + 2m - 5)$ $-30m^3 + 20m^2 - 50m$
13. $-8v(3v^2 - 2v + 1)$ $-24v^3 + 16v^2 - 8v$
14. $-2z(8z^2 - 6)$ $-16z^3 + 12z$
15. $3b(9b^2 - 7b)$ $27b^3 - 21b^2$
16. $7e(-6e^2 - 9e + 4)$ $-42e^3 - 63e^2 + 28e$
17. $-6g^3(4g - 3)$ $-24g^4 + 18g^3$
18. $-5q(2q^3 - q^2 + q)$ $-10q^4 + 5q^3 - 5q^2$

Practice: Skills, p. 710

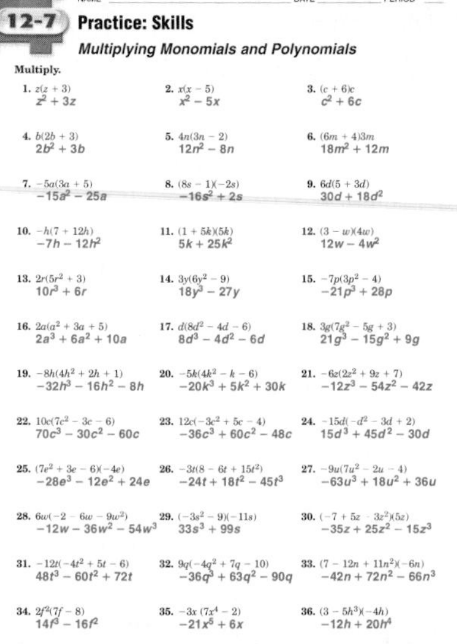
NAME ________ DATE ________ PERIOD ____

12-7 Practice: Skills

Multiplying Monomials and Polynomials

Multiply.

1. $z(z + 3)$ $z^2 + 3z$
2. $x(x - 5)$ $x^2 - 5x$
3. $(c + 6)c$ $c^2 + 6c$
4. $b(2b + 3)$ $2b^2 + 3b$
5. $4n(3n - 2)$ $12n^2 - 8n$
6. $(6m + 4)3m$ $18m^2 + 12m$
7. $-5a(3a + 5)$ $-15a^2 - 25a$
8. $(8s - 1)(-2s)$ $-16s^2 + 2s$
9. $6d(5 + 3d)$ $30d + 18d^2$
10. $-h(7 + 12h)$ $-7h - 12h^2$
11. $(1 + 5k)(5k)$ $5k + 25k^2$
12. $(3 - w)(4w)$ $12w - 4w^2$
13. $2r(5r^2 + 3)$ $10r^3 + 6r$
14. $3y(6y^2 - 9)$ $18y^3 - 27y$
15. $-7p(3p^2 - 4)$ $-21p^3 + 28p$
16. $2a(a^2 + 3a + 5)$ $2a^3 + 6a^2 + 10a$
17. $d(8d^2 - 4d - 6)$ $8d^3 - 4d^2 - 6d$
18. $3g(7g^2 - 5g + 3)$ $21g^3 - 15g^2 + 9g$
19. $-8h(4h^2 + 2h + 1)$ $-32h^3 - 16h^2 - 8h$
20. $-5k(4k^2 - k - 6)$ $-20k^3 + 5k^2 + 30k$
21. $-6z(2z^2 + 9z + 7)$ $-12z^3 - 54z^2 - 42z$
22. $10c(7c^2 - 3c - 6)$ $70c^3 - 30c^2 - 60c$
23. $12c(-3c^2 + 5c - 4)$ $-36c^3 + 60c^2 - 48c$
24. $-15d(-d^2 - 3d + 2)$ $15d^3 + 45d^2 - 30d$
25. $(7e^2 + 3e - 6)(-4e)$ $-28e^3 - 12e^2 + 24e$
26. $-3t(8 - 6t + 15t^2)$ $-24t + 18t^2 - 45t^3$
27. $-9u(7u^2 - 2u - 4)$ $-63u^3 + 18u^2 + 36u$
28. $6w(-2 - 6w - 9w^2)$ $-12w - 36w^2 - 54w^3$
29. $(-3s^2 - 9)(-11s)$ $33s^3 + 99s$
30. $(-7 + 5z - 3z^2)(5z)$ $-35z + 25z^2 - 15z^3$
31. $-12t(-4t^2 + 5t - 6)$ $48t^3 - 60t^2 + 72t$
32. $9q(-4q^2 + 7q - 10)$ $-36q^3 + 63q^2 - 90q$
33. $(7 - 12n + 11n^2)(-6n)$ $-42n + 72n^2 - 66n^3$
34. $2f^3(7f - 8)$ $14f^4 - 16f^3$
35. $-3x(7x^4 - 2)$ $-21x^5 + 6x$
36. $(3 - 5h^3)(-4h)$ $-12h + 20h^4$

Practice: Word Problems, p. 711

NAME ________ DATE ________ PERIOD ____

12-7 Practice: Word Problems

Multiplying Monomials and Polynomials

1. **GEOMETRY** Write an expression in simplest form for the area of the rectangle. What is the area of the rectangle if $c = 5$ units? (rectangle: c by $4c - 5$) $4c^2 - 5c$; 75 units²

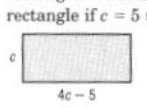

2. **GEOMETRY** Write an expression in simplest form for the area of the triangle. What is the area of the triangle if $z = 2$ units? (triangle: height $4z$, base $5z + 8$) $10z^2 + 16z$; 72 units²

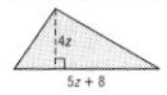

3. **SWIMMING POOLS** The Marshalls' pool is 5 feet longer than twice its width w. Write two expressions for the area of the pool. What is the area of the pool if it is 12 feet wide? $w(2w + 5)$; $2w^2 + 5w$; 348 ft²

4. **BUSINESS** When a factory makes t bicycles in a month, the gross profit on each bicycle is $25 + 2t$ dollars. Write an expression in simplest form for the total gross profit the factory makes in a month that it produces t bicycles. What is the gross profit if the factory makes 40 bicycles? $25t + 2t^2$ dollars; \$4,200

5. **FUND-RAISING** When the Science Club members charged p dollars to wash each car at their car wash, they had $8p$ customers. When they doubled their price, they had 12 fewer customers. Write expressions representing the new price and the new number of customers. Then write an expression in simplest form representing the amount of money they made at the new price. How much money did they raise at the new price if the original price was \$5 for each car? $2p$; $8p - 12$; $16p^2 - 24p$; \$280

6. **GROUP RATES** If Mr. Casey buys t tickets for his class to see a play, each ticket will cost $0.5t - 1$ dollars. If he buys three times as many tickets so that all three eighth grade classes can go, the price for each ticket is 2 dollars less. Write an expression for the total cost of the tickets for all three classes. If there are 20 students in Mr. Casey's class, how much will the tickets for all three classes cost? $1.5t^2 - 9t$; \$420

Practice and Applications

HOMEWORK HELP

For Exercises	See Examples
9–18, 25–26	1, 2
19–24	3, 4

Extra Practice See pages 647, 659.

Multiply. 12. $10x^2 + 2x$ 13. $-6d^2 - 30d$ 15. $24h + 18h^2$

9. $r(r + 9)$ $r^2 + 9r$
10. $t(t - 4)$ $t^2 - 4t$
11. $(3b - 2)(3b)$ $9b^2 - 6b$
12. $(5x + 1)(2x)$
13. $-6d(d + 5)$
14. $-a(7a - 8)$ $-7a^2 + 8a$
15. $6h(4 + 3h)$
16. $8w(1 - 7w)$
17. $11e(2e - 7)$ $22e^2 - 77e$
18. $10a(5a + 5)$
19. $4y(y^2 - 9)$
20. $-6g(2g^2 + 1)$ $-12g^3 - 6g$
21. $t(t^2 + 5t + 9)$ $t^3 + 5t^2 + 9t$
22. $-n(3n^2 - 4n + 13)$ $-3n^3 + 4n^2 - 13n$
23. $-2r(4r^2 - r - 8)$ $-8r^3 + 2r^2 + 16r$
24. $11c(6c^2 - 8c + 1)$ $66c^3 - 88c^2 + 11c$

16. $8w - 56w^2$ 18. $50a^2 + 50a$ 19. $4y^3 - 36y$

25. **GARDENING** A square garden plot measures x feet on each side. Suppose you double the length of the plot and increase the width by 4 feet. Write two expressions for the area of the new plot. $2x(x + 4)$; $2x^2 + 8x$

26. **GEOMETRY** Write an expression in simplest form for the area of the figure. $12x^2 - 15x$

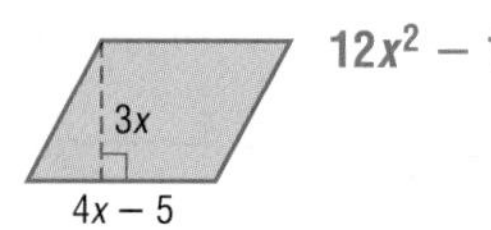

27. **CRITICAL THINKING** Draw a model showing how algebra tiles can be used to find the following product of two *binomials*, or polynomials with two terms: $(x + 2)(x + 3)$. See margin.

Spiral Review with Standardized Test Practice

28. **MULTIPLE CHOICE** What is the product of $4x^2$ and $x^2 + 2x - 3$? C

  (A) $4x^2 + 8x - 12$ (B) $4x^4 + 8x^2 - 12x$
  (C) $4x^4 + 8x^3 - 12x^2$ (D) $5x^2 + 6x + 1$

29. **SHORT RESPONSE** The length of a rectangle is twice its width. If the width is x, write an equation for the area A of the rectangle. Then graph the area as a function of x. $A = 2x^2$; See margin for graph.

Multiply or divide. Express using exponents. (Lesson 12-6)

30. $5^2 \cdot 5$ 5^3
31. $\frac{11^8}{11^5}$ 11^3
32. $3x^3 \cdot 9x^3$ $27x^6$
33. $\frac{21a^5}{3a^4}$ $7a$

34. **BUSINESS** Allison's income from selling x beaded bracelets is $6.50x$. Her expenses are $4x + 35$. Write an expression for her profit. (Lesson 12-5) $2.5x - 35$

INTERDISCIPLINARY PROJECT

Getting Down to Business

Math and Economics It's time to complete your project. Use the information and data you have gathered about the cost of materials and the feedback from your peers to prepare a video or brochure. Be sure to include a scatter plot with your project.

msmath3.net/self_check_quiz

Answers

27.

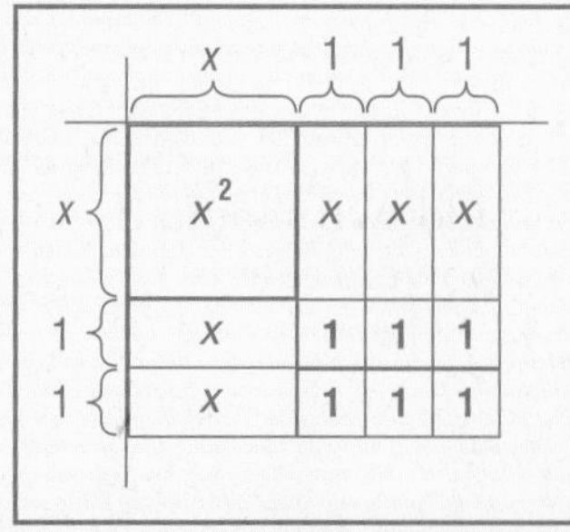

29. (Graph: $A = 2x^2$; A-axis 0, 2, 4, 6, 8; x-axis 1, 2, 3, 4)

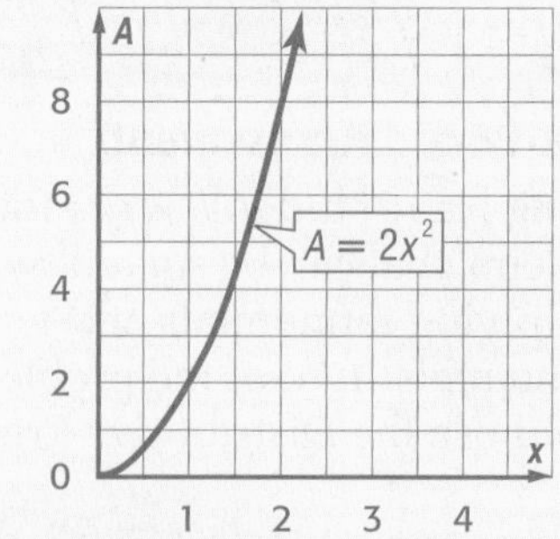

Study Guide and Review

Vocabulary and Concept Check

monomial (p. 570) nonlinear function (p. 560) polynomial (p. 570) quadratic function (p. 565)

State whether each sentence is *true* or *false*. If *false*, replace the underlined word or number to make a true sentence.

1. The expression $x^2 - 3x$ is an example of a monomial. **false; polynomial**
2. A nonlinear function has a constant rate of change. **false; linear**
3. To multiply two polynomials, you combine like terms. **false; add**
4. A quadratic function is a nonlinear function. **true**
5. To divide powers with the same base, subtract the exponents. **true**

Lesson-by-Lesson Exercises and Examples

12-1 Linear and Nonlinear Functions (pp. 560–563)

Determine whether each equation or table represents a *linear* or *nonlinear* function. Explain.

6. $y - 4x = 1$
7. $y = x^2 + 3$
8.

x	2	3	4	5
y	1	3	7	12

nonlinear; rate of change is not constant

Example 1 **Determine whether the table represents a *linear* or *nonlinear* function.**

x	y
−2	−3
−1	−1
0	1
1	3

As x increases by 1, y increases by 2. The rate of change is constant, so this function is linear.

6. linear; can be written as $y = 4x + 1$ 7. nonlinear; power of x is greater than 1

12-2 Graphing Quadratic Functions (pp. 565–568)

Graph each function.

9. $y = -4x^2$
10. $y = x^2 + 4$
11. **SCIENCE** A ball is dropped from the top a 36-foot tall building. The quadratic equation $d = -16t^2 + 36$ models the distance d in feet the ball is from the ground at time t. Graph the function. Then use your graph to find how long it takes for the ball to reach the ground. **See p. 594 margin for graph; 1.5 s**

Example 2 **Graph $y = -x^2 - 1$.**

Make a table of values. Then plot and connect the ordered pairs with a smooth curve.

x	$y = -x^2 - 1$	(x, y)
−2	$-(-2)^2 - 1$	(−2, −5)
−1	$-(-1)^2 - 1$	(−1, −2)
0	$-(0)^2 - 1$	(0, −1)
1	$-(1)^2 - 1$	(1, −2)
2	$-(2)^2 - 1$	(2, −5)

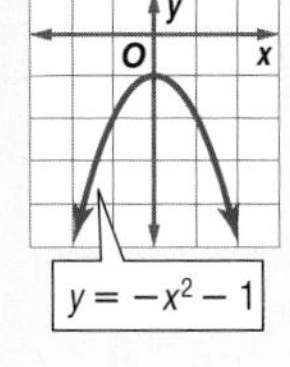

9–10. See p. 594 margin.

msmath3.net/vocabulary_review

Study Guide and Review

Vocabulary Assessment

- This alphabetical list of vocabulary terms in Chapter 12 includes a page reference where each term was introduced.
- A vocabulary review/test for Chapter 12 is available on p. 728 of the *Chapter 12 Resource Masters*.

Vocabulary PuzzleMaker

ELL The online Vocabulary PuzzleMaker improves students' mathematics vocabulary using four puzzle formats — crossword, scramble, word search using a word list, and word search using clues. Students can work on a computer screen or from a printed handout.

MindJogger Videoquizzes

ELL MindJogger Videoquizzes provide an alternative review of concepts presented in this chapter. Students work in teams in a game show format to gain points for correct answers. The questions are presented in three rounds.

Round 1 Concepts (5 questions)
Round 2 Skills (4 questions)
Round 3 Problem Solving (4 questions)

ExamView® Pro

Use the networkable ExamView® Pro Testmaker CD-ROM to:

- Create **multiple versions** of tests.
- Create **modified** tests for **inclusion** students with one mouse click.
- **Edit** existing questions and **add** your own questions.
- Build tests aligned with state standards using built-in **state curriculum correlations.**
- Change **English** tests to **Spanish** with one mouse click and vice versa.

For more information about Foldables, see *Teaching Mathematics with Foldables.*

Have students look through the chapter to make sure they have included examples in their Foldables for each lesson or topic in the chapter.

Encourage students to refer to their Foldables while completing the Study Guide and Review and to use them in preparing for the Chapter Test.

Study Guide and Review

Answers (p. 593)

9.

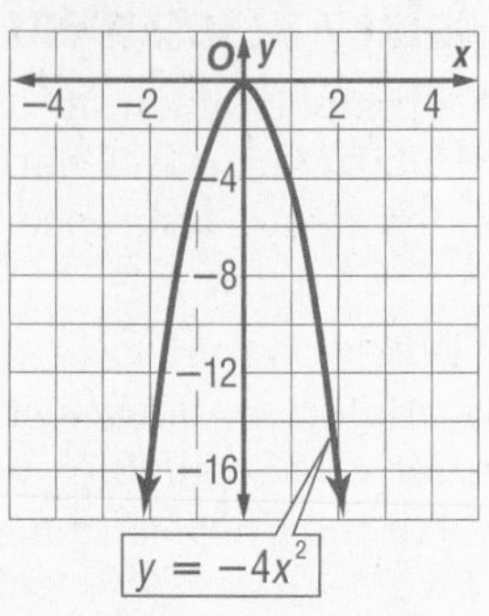

10.

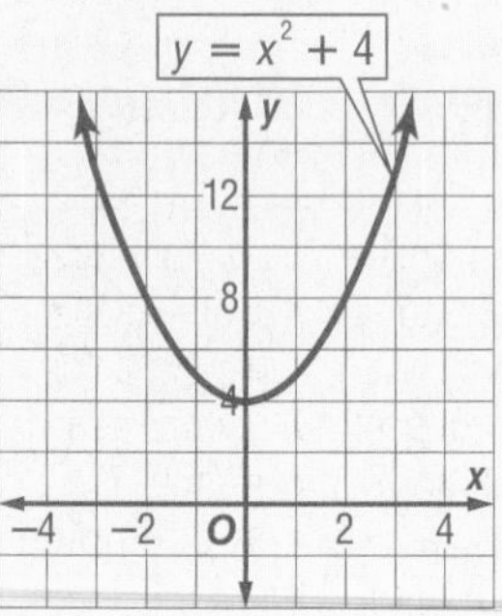

11.

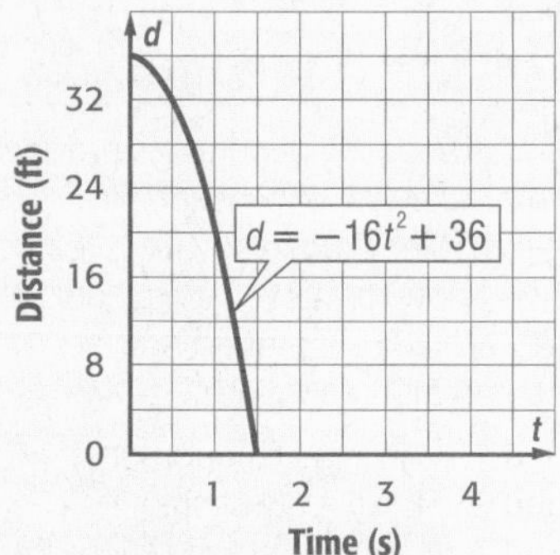

Answers (Practice Test)

1. Sample answer: $2n + 3$ and $6n - 2$
4. linear; graph is a straight line
5. nonlinear; graph is a curve
6. linear; can be written as $y = 2x + 0$
7. linear; can be written as $y = \frac{1}{7}x + 3$
8. linear; rate of change is constant; As x increases by 2, y increases by 8.

Mixed Problem Solving
For mixed problem-solving practice, see page 659.

12-3 Simplifying Polynomials (pp. 570–573)

Simplify each polynomial. If the polynomial cannot be simplified, write *simplest form*.

12. $3a - b - 7a + 2 + 4b$ **$-4a + 3b + 2$**
13. $8x - y + 1$ **simplest form**
14. $3n^2 + 7n - 4n^2 + n$ **$-n^2 + 8n$**

Example 3 Simplify $8a^2 - 5a + 6 - 9a^2 - 6$.

$8a^2 - 5a + 6 - 9a^2 - 6$
$= 8a^2 + (-5a) + 6 + (-9a^2) + (-6)$
$= [8a^2 + (-9a^2)] + (-5a) + [6 + (-6)]$
$= -1a^2 + (-5a) + 0$ or $-a^2 - 5a$

12-4 Adding Polynomials (pp. 574–577)

Add.

15. $(3a^2 + 6a) + (2a^2 - 5a)$ **$5a^2 + a$**
16. $(b^2 - 2b + 4) + (2b^2 + b - 8)$
17. $(10m^2 + 5m - 9) + (-2m + 3)$

16. $3b^2 - b - 4$ 17. $10m^2 + 3m - 6$

Example 4 Find $(3x^2 - 2) + (2x^2 + 5)$.

$(3x^2 - 2) + (2x^2 + 5)$
$= (3x^2 + 2x^2) + (-2 + 5)$ Group like terms.
$= 5x^2 + 3$ Simplify.

12-5 Subtracting Polynomials (pp. 580–583)

Subtract.

18. $(7g + 2) - (5g + 1)$ **$2g + 1$**
19. $(3c - 7) - (-3c + 4)$ **$6c - 11$**
20. $(7p^2 + 2p - 5) - (4p^2 + 6p - 2)$
21. $(6k^2 - 3) - (k^2 - 5k - 2)$ **$5k^2 + 5k - 1$**

20. $3p^2 - 4p - 3$

Example 5 Find $(5x - 1) - (6x + 4)$.

To subtract $6x + 4$, add $-6x - 4$.
$(5x - 1) - (6x + 4)$
$= (5x - 1) + (-6x - 4)$
$= [5x + (-6x)] + [-1 + (-4)]$
$= -1x + (-5)$
$= -x - 5$

12-6 Multiplying and Dividing Monomials (pp. 584–587)

Multiply or divide. Express using exponents.

22. $4 \cdot 4^5$ **4^6**
23. $-9y^2(-4y^9)$ **$36y^{11}$**
24. $\frac{n^5}{n}$ **n^4**
25. $\frac{21c^{11}}{-7c^8}$ **$-3c^3$**

Example 6

Find $3a^3 \cdot 4a^7$.

$3a^2 \cdot 4a^7 = (3 \cdot 4)a^{3+7}$
$= 12a^{10}$

Example 7

Find $\frac{6^8}{6^3}$.

$\frac{6^8}{6^3} = 6^{8-3}$
$= 6^5$

27. $9y^2 + 12y$ 28. $-4n^2 + 8n$ 30. $2x^3 + x^2 - 5x$ 31. $-10k^3 + 6k^2 - 16k$

12-7 Multiplying Monomials and Polynomials (pp. 590–592)

Multiply.

26. $a(a - 7)$ **$a^2 - 7a$**
27. $(3y + 4)(3y)$
28. $-4n(n - 2)$
29. $p(p^2 - 6)$ **$p^3 - 6p$**
30. $x(2x^2 + x - 5)$
31. $-2k(5k^2 - 3k + 8)$

Example 8 Find $-2x(5x + 3)$.

$-2x(5x + 3) = -2x(5x) + (-2x)(3)$
$= -10x^2 + (-6x)$
$= -10x^2 - 6x$

9.

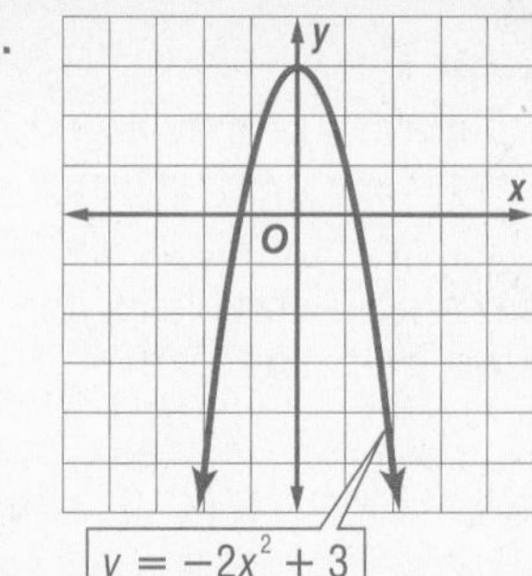

Practice Test

Vocabulary and Concepts

1. **OPEN ENDED** Write two polynomials whose difference is $-4n + 5$. **See margin.**
2. **State** whether the Quotient of Powers rule applies to $\frac{6^5}{3^2}$. Explain. **No; these powers do not have the same base.**
3. **Describe** the function $y = 3x^2$ using two different terms. **nonlinear and quadratic**

Skills and Applications

Determine whether each graph, equation, or table represents a *linear* or *nonlinear* function. Explain. **4–8. See margin.**

4. 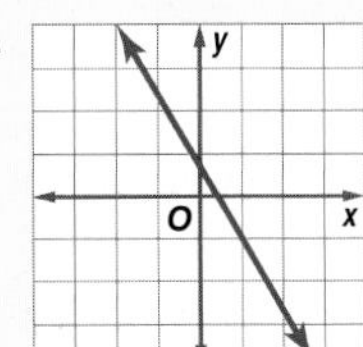

5. 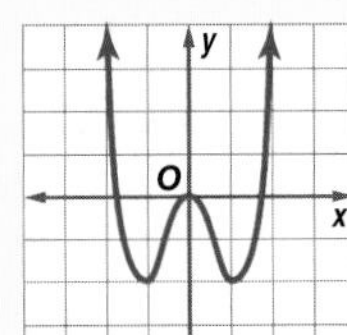

6. $2x = y$

7. $y = \frac{x}{7} + 3$

8.

x	−3	−1	1	3
y	2	10	18	26

9. Graph the function $y = -2x^2 + 3$. **See margin.**

Simplify each polynomial. If the polynomial cannot be simplified, write *simplest form*.

10. $-6x + 4y - 8 + y - 1$ $\mathbf{-6x + 5y - 9}$
11. $2a^2 + 4a + 3a^2 + 5a$ $\mathbf{5a^2 + 9a}$
12. $10p + 7p^2 + 1$ **simplest form**

Add or subtract.

13. $(4c^2 + 2) + (-4c^2 + 1)$ **3**
14. $(-x^2 + 2x - 5) + (4x^2 - 6x)$ $\mathbf{3x^2 - 4x - 5}$
15. $(9z^2 - 3z) - (5z^2 + 8z)$ $\mathbf{4z^2 - 11z}$
16. $(5n^2 - 4n + 1) - (4n - 5)$ $\mathbf{5n^2 - 8n + 6}$

17. **GEOMETRY** Write an expression for the measure of $\angle JKM$. Then find the value of x. $\mathbf{(11x + 4)°; 16}$

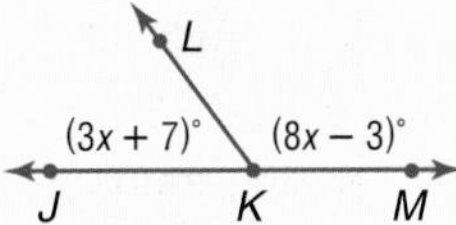

Multiply or divide. Express using exponents.

18. $15^3 \cdot 15^5$ $\mathbf{15^8}$
19. $-5m^6(-9m^8)$ $\mathbf{45m^{14}}$
20. $\frac{3^{15}}{3^7}$ $\mathbf{3^8}$
21. $\frac{-40w^8}{8w}$ $\mathbf{-5w^7}$

Multiply. **24.** $\mathbf{-12x^3 + 24x^2 - 32x}$

22. $8n(n + 3)$ $\mathbf{8n^2 + 24n}$
23. $g^3(6g - 5)$ $\mathbf{6g^4 - 5g^3}$
24. $-4x(3x^2 - 6x + 8)$

Standardized Test Practice

25. **MULTIPLE CHOICE** Find the value of ● in the equation $\frac{x^9}{x^●} = x^3$. **B**

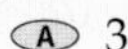 3    6   Ⓒ 12   Ⓓ 27

msmath3.net/chapter_test

Portfolio Suggestion

Introduction In this chapter, students studied nonlinear functions and polynomials.

Ask Students to collect examples of graphs and polynomials that are used in the media and in other classes. For example, students might encounter a graph showing the change in a country's population or a formula that describes linear motion. Have them add these examples to their portfolios.

Practice Test

Assessment Options

Vocabulary Test A vocabulary review/test for Chapter 12 can be found on p. 728 of the *Chapter 12 Resource Masters*.

Chapter Tests There are six Chapter 12 Tests and an Extended Response Assessment task available in the *Chapter 12 Resource Masters*.

Chapter 12 Tests			
Form	Type	Level	Pages
1	MC	basic	715–716
2A	MC	average	717–718
2B	MC	average	719–720
2C	FR	average	721–722
2D	FR	average	723–724
3	FR	advanced	725–726

MC = multiple-choice questions
FR = free-response questions

Extended Response Assessment

Extended Response tasks for Chapter 12 can be found on p. 727 of the *Chapter 12 Resource Masters*. A sample scoring rubric for these tasks appears on p. A26.

Unit 5 Test

A unit test/review can be found on pp. 735–736 of the *Chapter 12 Resource Masters*.

End-of-Year Tests

A **Second Semester Test** for Chapters 7–12 can be found on pp. 737–740 and a **Final Test** for Chapters 1–12 can be found on pp. 741–746 of the *Chapter 12 Resource Masters*.

CHAPTER 12 Standardized Test Practice

These two pages contain practice questions in the various formats that can be found on the most frequently given standardized tests.

A student recording sheet for these two pages can be found on p. A1 of the *Chapter 12 Resource Masters*.

Standardized Test Practice Student Recording Sheet, p. A1

CHAPTER 12 NAME ____ DATE ____ PERIOD ____

Standardized Test Practice SCORE ____

Student Recording Sheet (Use with pages 596-597 of the Student Edition.)

Part 1: Multiple Choice

Select the best answer from the choices given and fill in the corresponding oval.

1. Ⓐ Ⓑ Ⓒ Ⓓ 3. Ⓐ Ⓑ Ⓒ Ⓓ 5. Ⓐ Ⓑ Ⓒ Ⓓ 7. Ⓐ Ⓑ Ⓒ Ⓓ

2. Ⓕ Ⓖ Ⓗ Ⓘ 4. Ⓕ Ⓖ Ⓗ Ⓘ 6. Ⓕ Ⓖ Ⓗ Ⓘ

Part 2: Short Response/Grid In

Solve the problem and write your answer in the blank.

For grid in questions, also enter your answer by writing each number or symbol in a box. Then fill in the corresponding circle for that number of symbol.

8. ____ (grid in)
9. ____ (grid in)
10. ____
11. ____ (grid in)
12. ____
13. ____
14. ____
15. ____ (grid in)

Part 3: Extended Response

Record your answers for Questions 16–20 on the back of this paper.

Additional Practice

See pp. 733–734 in the *Chapter 12 Resource Masters* for additional standardized test practice.

CHAPTER 12 Standardized Test Practice

PART 1 Multiple Choice

Record your answers on the answer sheet provided by your teacher or on a sheet of paper.

1. Nolan wants to make a larger sail for his model boat. How long will the base of the new sail be in inches? (Lesson 4-5) **B**

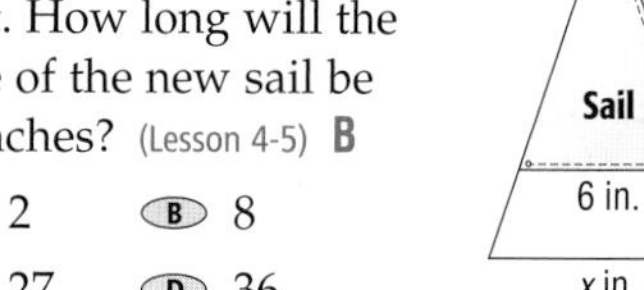

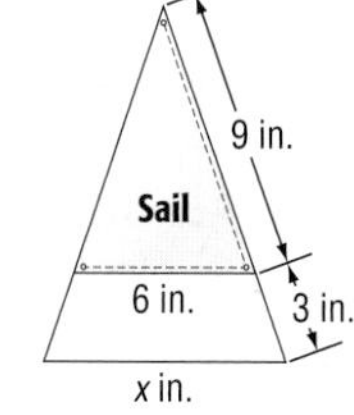

Ⓐ 2 Ⓑ 8 Ⓒ 27 Ⓓ 36

2. Which statement is false? (Lesson 5-5) **G**

Ⓕ 42% of 60 is greater than 24.
Ⓖ 31% of 90 is greater than 30.
Ⓗ 79% of 250 is less than 200.
Ⓘ 3% of 80 is less than 3.

3. A group of dancers form a circle for a routine they are performing. The radius of their circle is 8 yards. If they increase the area of their circle by 4 times, what will be the radius, in yards, of the new circle? (Lesson 7-2) **C**

Ⓐ 2 Ⓑ 12 Ⓒ 16 Ⓓ 32

4. Fourteen dogs are enrolled in dog-training class. All the dogs weigh about 50 pounds, except for Spot, who weighs 35 pounds. How does Spot's weight affect the mean and median weights of the entire class? (Lesson 9-4) **F**

Ⓕ Spot's weight affects the mean more.
Ⓖ Spot's weight affects the median more.
Ⓗ Spot's weight has an equal affect on the mean and median.
Ⓘ Spot's weight has no affect on the mean or median.

5. On the basis of the graph below, what relationship exists between the number of DVDs a person owns and the number of books they own? (Lesson 11-6) **B**

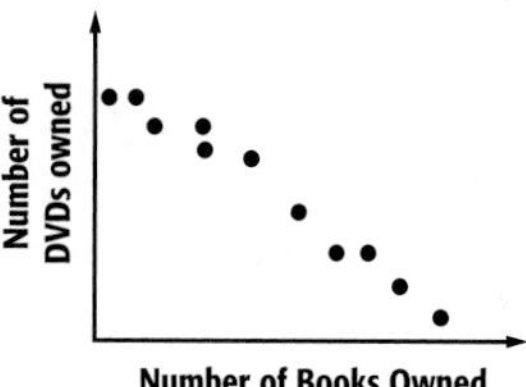

Ⓐ As the number of DVDs owned increases, the number of books owned increases.
Ⓑ As the number of DVDs owned increases, the number of books owned decreases.
Ⓒ There is no relationship between the number of DVDs owned and the number of books owned.
Ⓓ For every DVD owned, there are 3 books owned.

6. Which is the graph of a nonlinear function? (Lesson 12-1) **G**

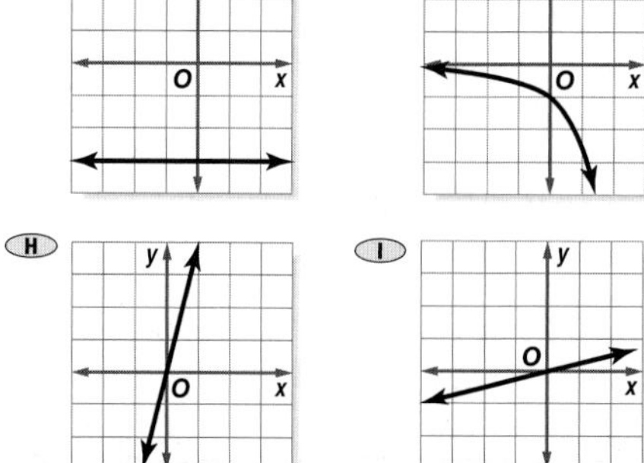

7. If $a = b^4$, which expression is equal to b^8? (Lesson 12-6) **A**

Ⓐ a^2 Ⓑ a^4 Ⓒ a^{12} Ⓓ a^{32}

596 **Chapter 12** Algebra: Nonlinear Functions and Polynomials

ExamView® Pro

Special banks of standardized test questions similar to those on the TIMSS and NAEP grade 8 tests can be found on this CD-ROM.

Preparing for Standardized Tests
For test-taking strategies and more practice, see pages 660–677.

PART 2 Short Response/Grid In

Record your answers on the answer sheet provided by your teacher or on a sheet of paper.

8. A square tile measures 9 inches by 9 inches. What is the least number of tiles needed to cover a rectangular floor measuring 21 feet by 27 feet? (Lesson 1-1) **1,008**

9. There are 240 students in attendance at a student government conference held in Atlanta. Half of these students are from Georgia. Of the remaining students, $\frac{1}{5}$ are from Alabama, and $\frac{1}{4}$ are from Florida. All others are from Tennessee. How many students are from Tennessee? (Lesson 2-3) **66**

10. The block shown below weighs 54 grams. What would be the weight of a block of the same material that measures 6 inches by 6 inches by 6 inches? (Lesson 7-5) **432 g**

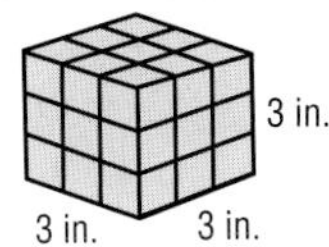

11. Brad's Internet password is a permutation of his initials, B, W, and D, and the numbers 5, 8, and 2. How many different passwords does he have to choose from if no letter or number is used more than once? (Lesson 8-3) **720**

12. What are the coordinates of the point where the graph of $9 + y = 4x$ intercepts the y-axis? (Lesson 11-5) **(0, −9)**

TEST-TAKING TIP

Question 12 Before graphing an equation, determine whether it is necessary to do so in order to answer the question. In Question 12, you can write $9 + y = 4x$ in slope-intercept form and identify its y-intercept to determine where its graph will cross the y-axis.

msmath3.net/standardized_test

13. Copy and complete the table below so that it represents a linear function. (Lesson 12-1) **Sample answer given.**

x	7	5	3	1	−1
y	−4	1	6	11	16

14. Write an expression in simplest form for the perimeter of the figure at the right. (Lesson 12-3) **10a + 4b**

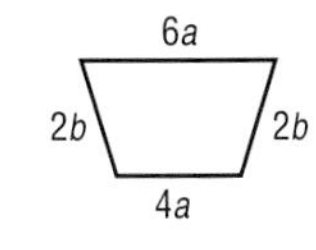

15. Find the measure of the value of x in the figure below. (Lesson 12-4) **17/2 or 8.5**

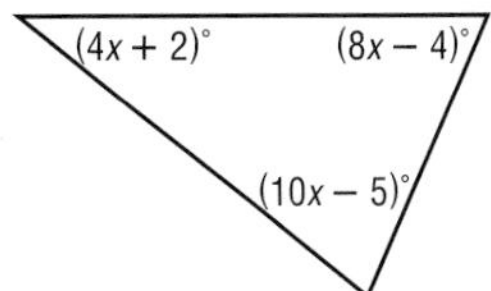

PART 3 Extended Response

Record your answers on a sheet of paper. Show your work.

You have 40 feet of fencing to make a rectangular kennel for your dog. You will use your house as one side. (Lessons 12-2 and 12-7)

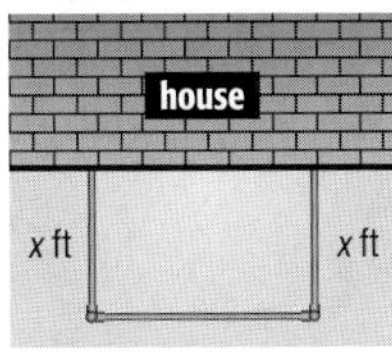

16. Write an algebraic expression for the kennel's length. **40 − 2x**

17. Write an algebraic expression in simplest form for the area of the kennel. **$40x - 2x^2$**

18. Write the area A of the kennel as a function of its width x. **$A = 40x - 2x^2$**

19. Make a table of values and graph the function you wrote in Exercise 18. **See Ch. 12 Answer Appendix.**

20. Use your graph to determine the width that produces a kennel with the greatest area. **10 ft**

Standardized Test Practice

Rubrics The following rubrics are sample scoring devices for short response and extended response questions.

Short Response

Points	Description
2	The student demonstrates a thorough understanding of the mathematics of the task. The response may contain minor flaws that do not detract from the demonstration of a thorough understanding.
1	The student has provided a response that is only partially correct.
0	The student has provided a completely incorrect solution or no response at all.

Extended Response

Points	Description
4	The student demonstrates a thorough understanding of the mathematics of the task. The response may contain minor flaws that do not detract from the demonstration of a thorough understanding.
3	The student demonstrates an understanding of the mathematics of the task. The response is essentially correct and demonstrates an essential but less than thorough understanding of the mathematics.
2	The student demonstrates only a partial understanding of the mathematics of the task. Although the student may have used the correct approach to a solution or may have provided a correct solution, the work lacks an essential understanding of the underlying mathematical concepts.
1	The student demonstrates a very limited understanding of the mathematics of the task. The response is incomplete and exhibits many flaws.
0	The student provides a completely incorrect solution or no response at all.

A more detailed 4-point rubric is provided on page A2 of the *Chapter 12 Resource Masters*.

Page 560, Lesson 12-1 (When am I ever going to use this?)

3.

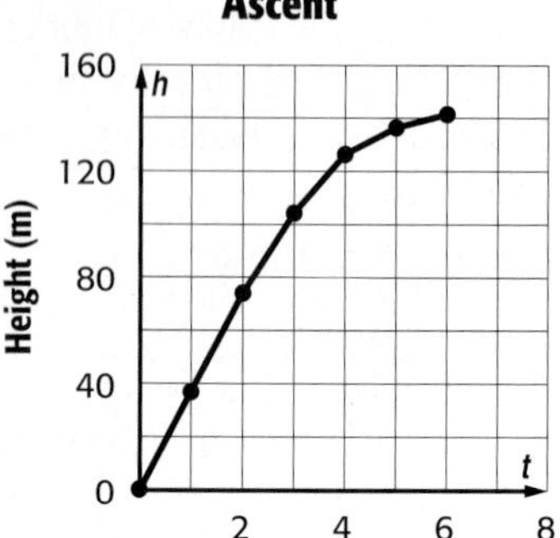

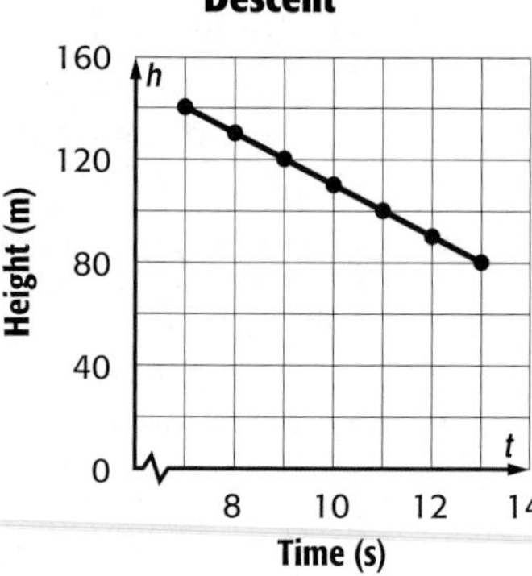

The graph of the rocket's ascent is curved, while the graph of the rocket's descent is a straight line.

Page 563, Lesson 12-1

34.

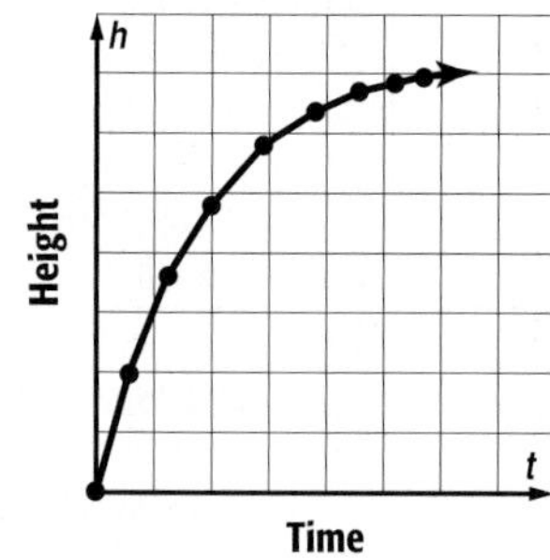

36.

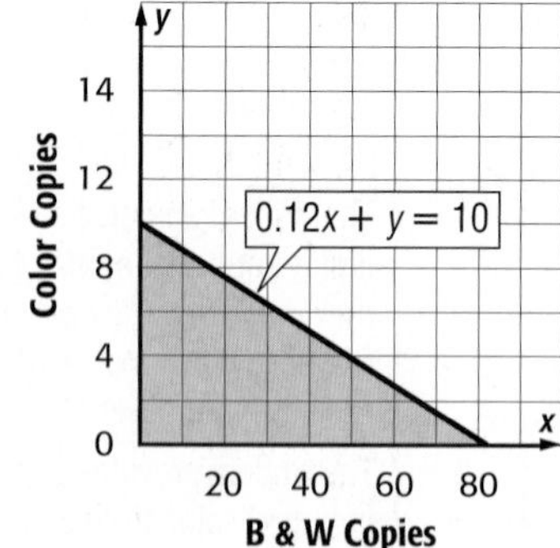

41.

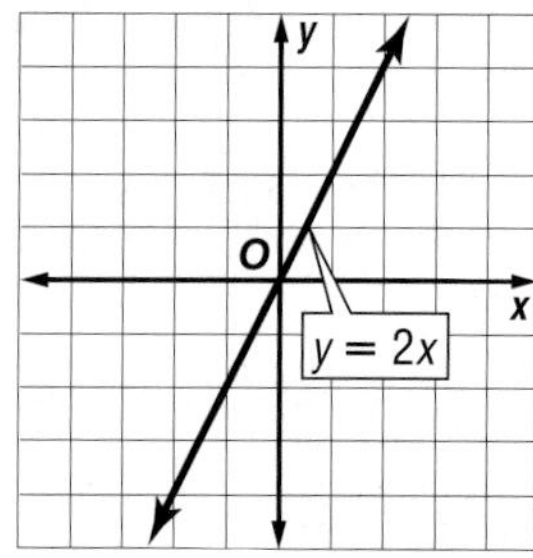

42.

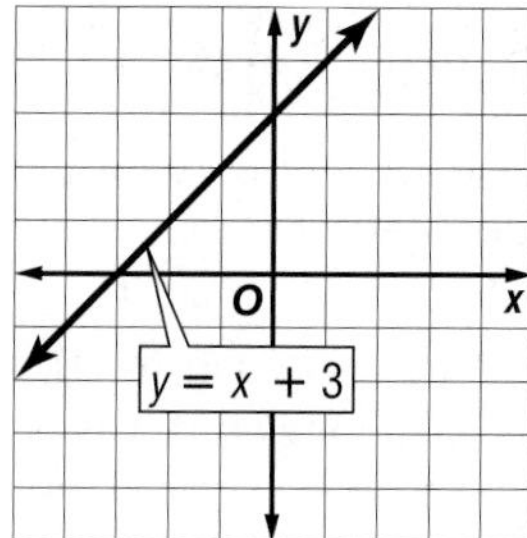

43.

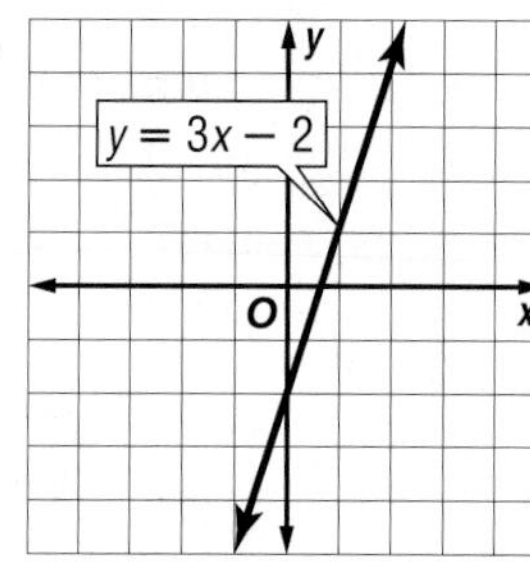

44.

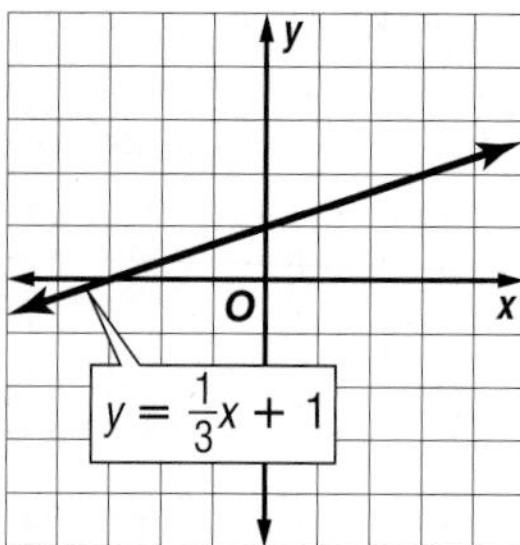

Page 565, Lesson 12-2 (Hands-On Mini Lab)

Step 2.

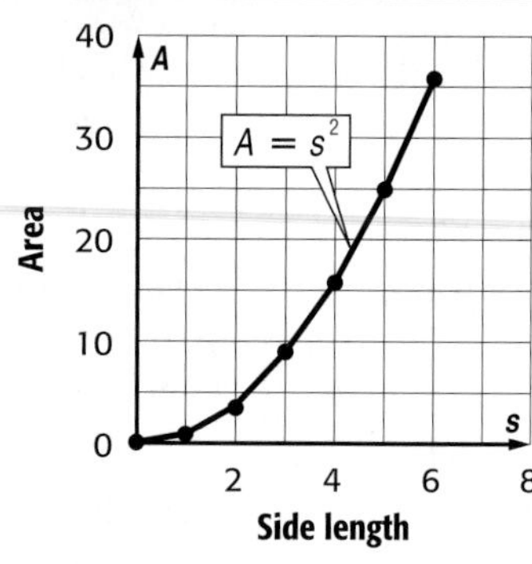

Page 566, Lesson 12-2 (Your Turn)

a.

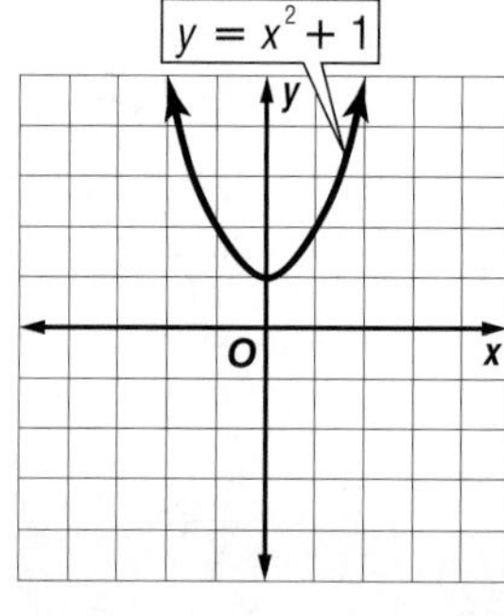

b.

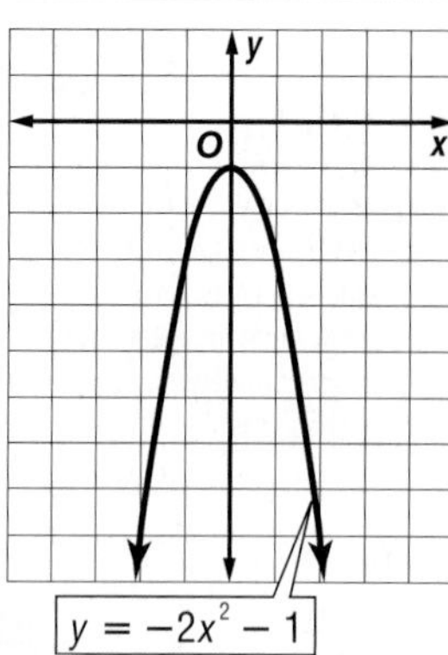

c.

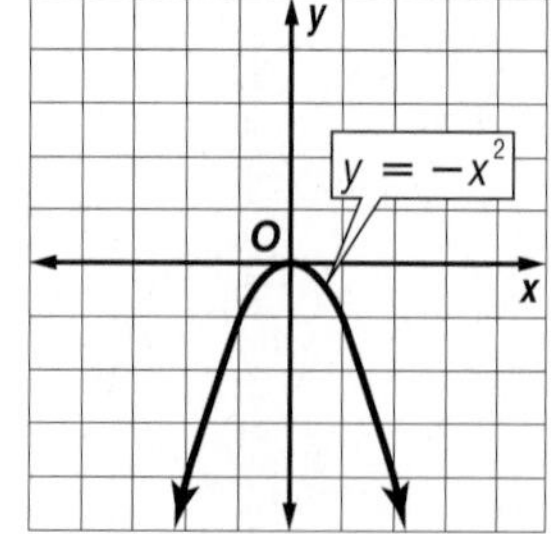

Additional Answers for Chapter 12

Pages 567–568, Lesson 12-2

4.
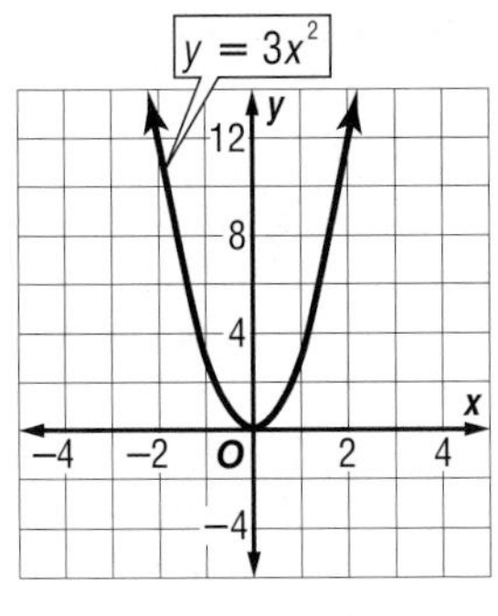

5.
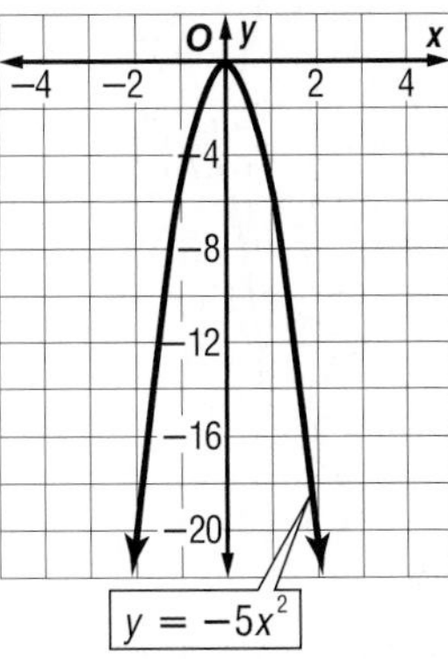

6.
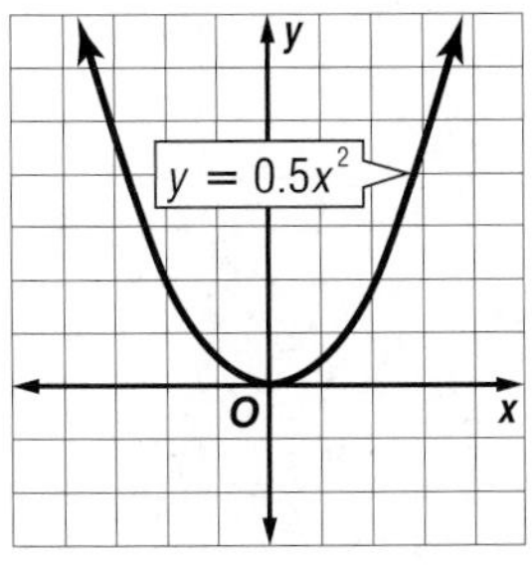

7.
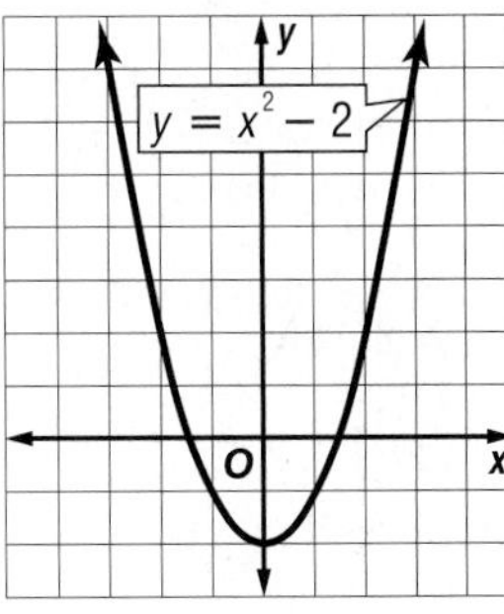

8.
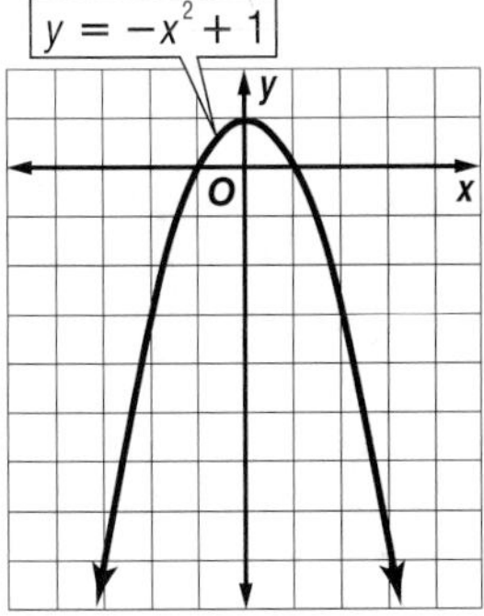

9.
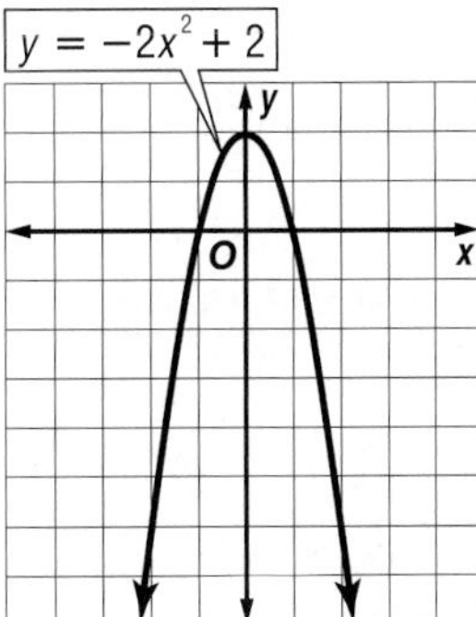

10.
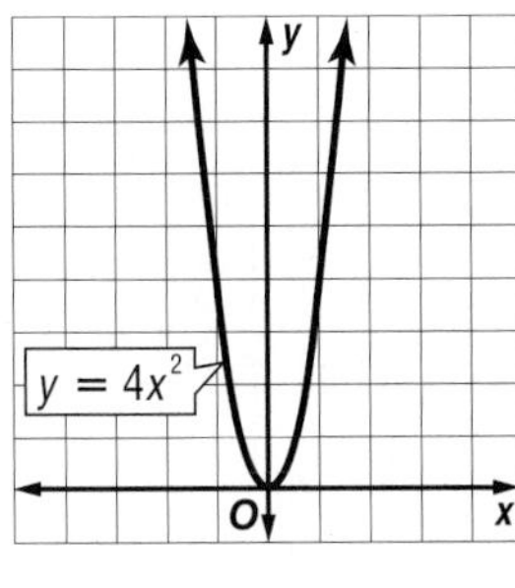

11.
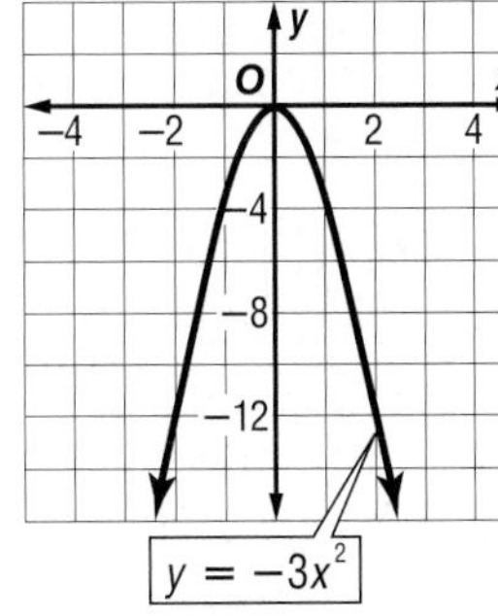

12.
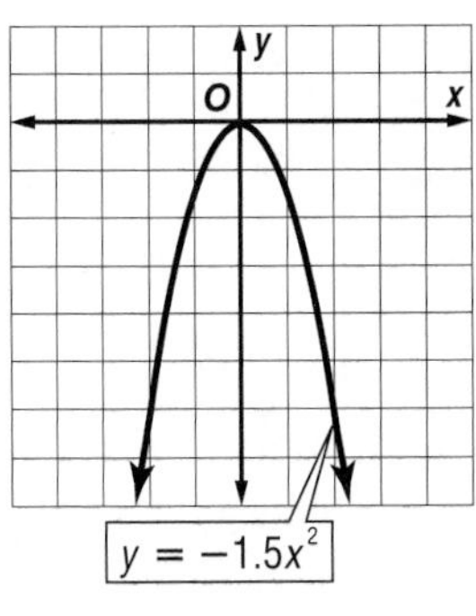

13.
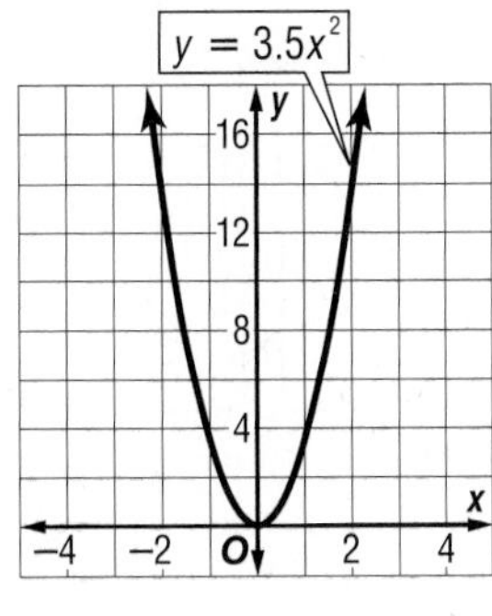

14.
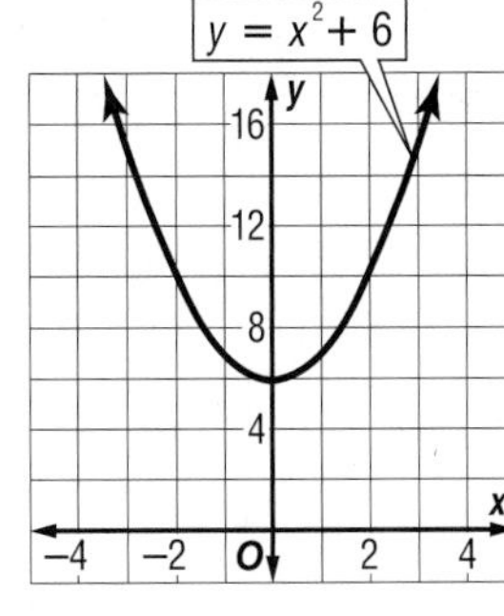

15.
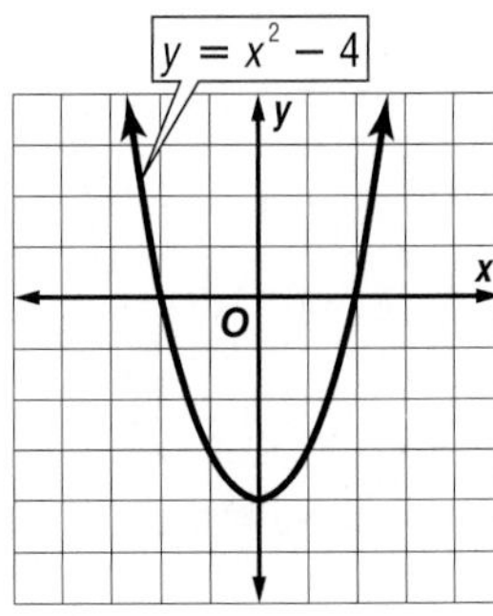

16.
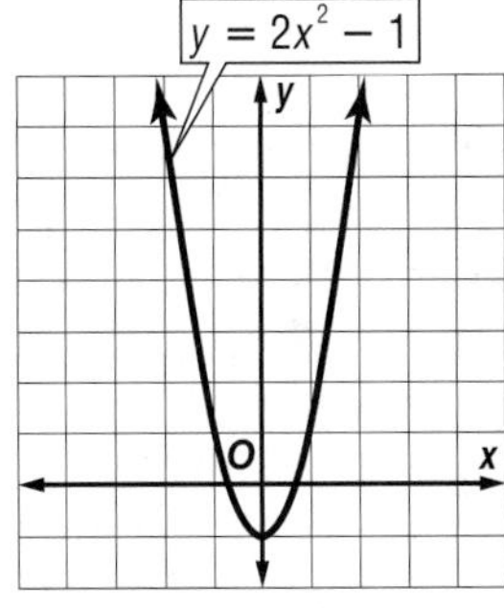

17.
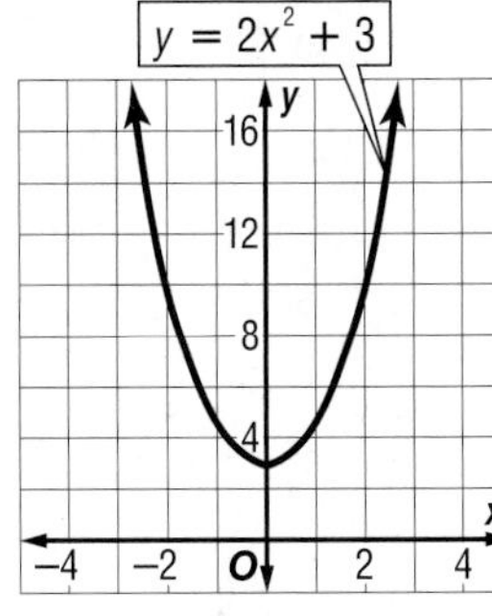

18.
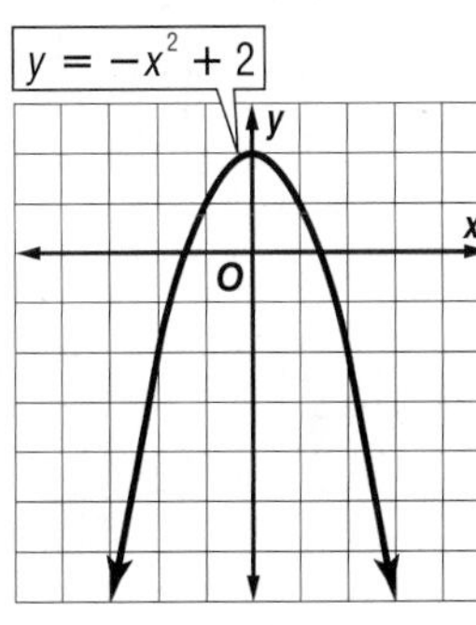

19.
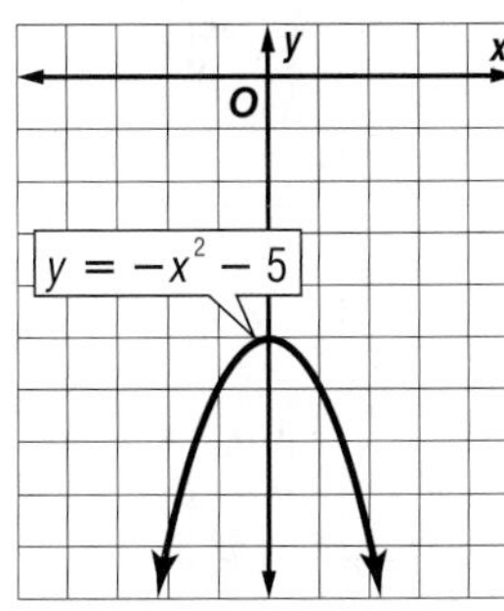

20.
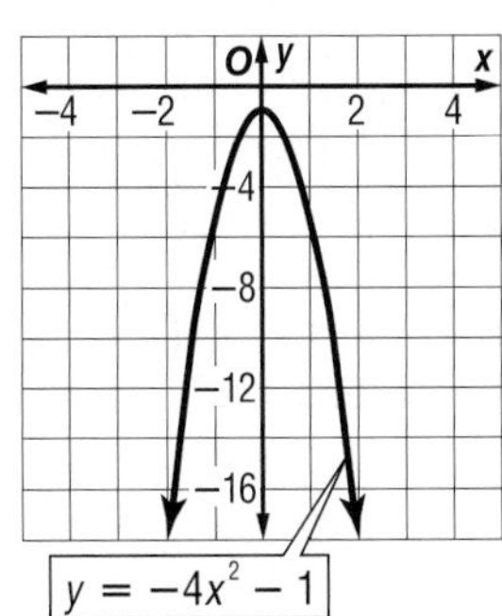

21.
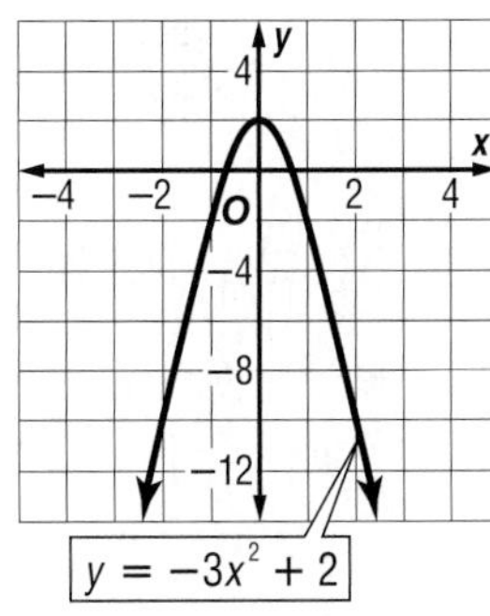

22.
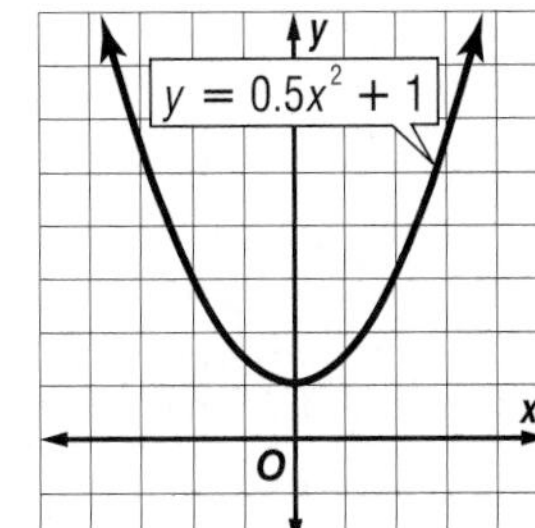

23.
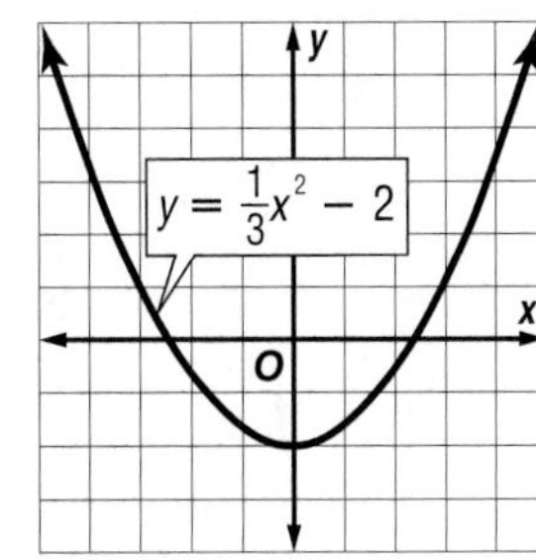

30.

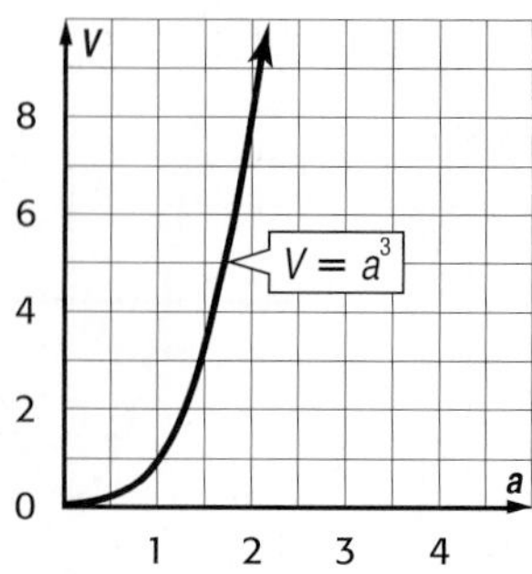

31.

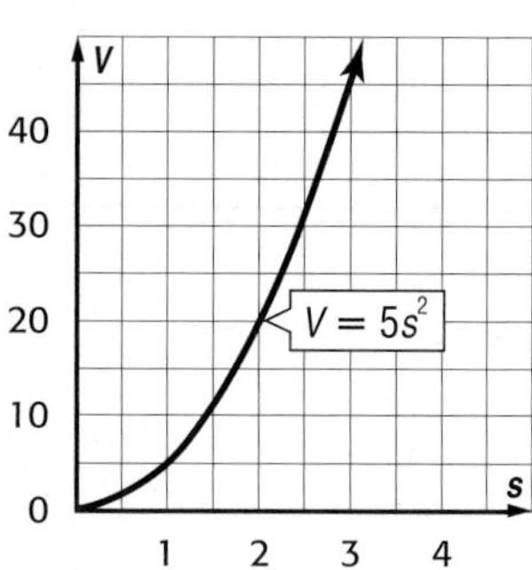

32.

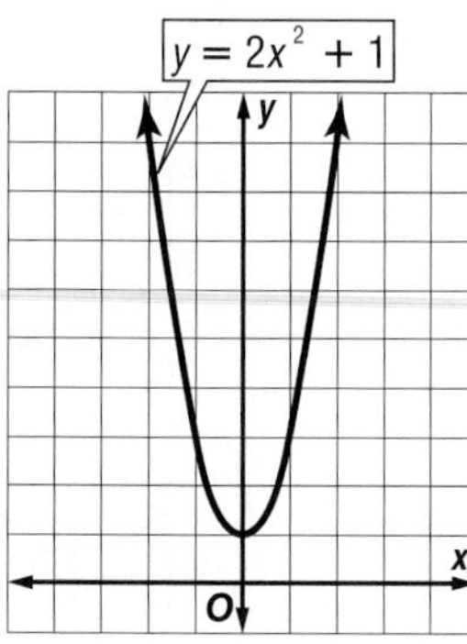

33.

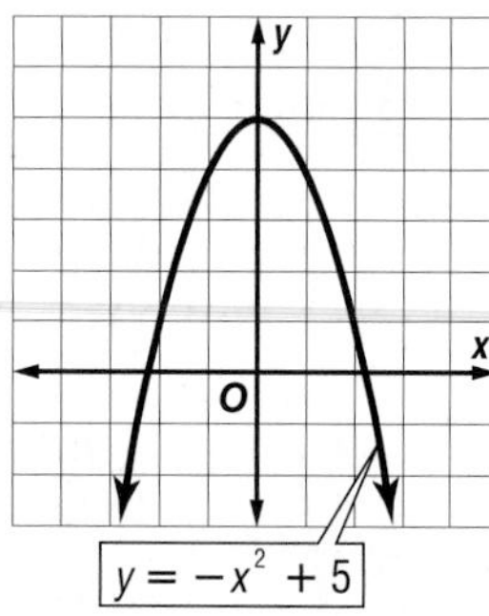

34.

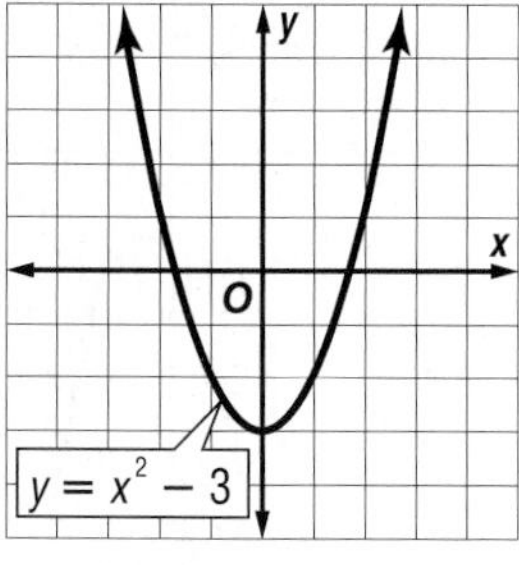

35.

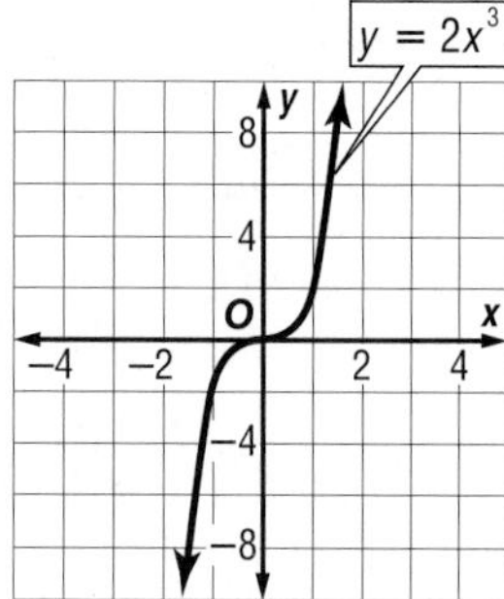

36.

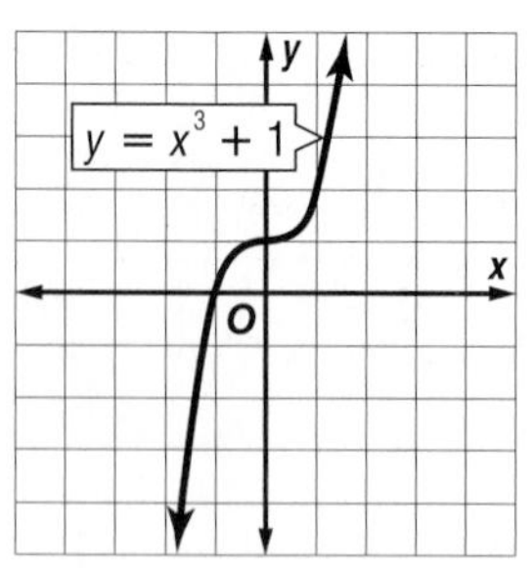

37.

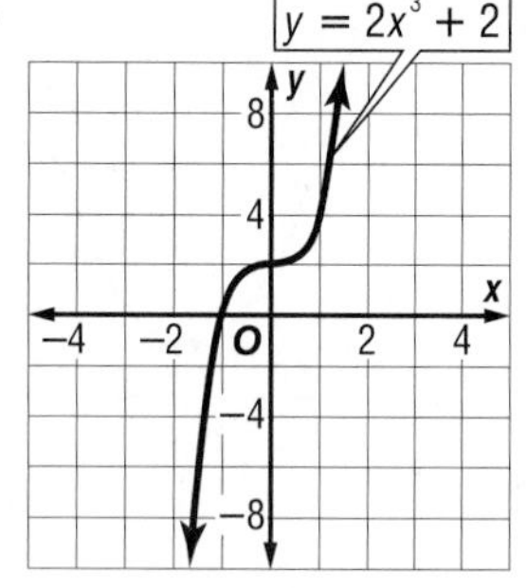

38.

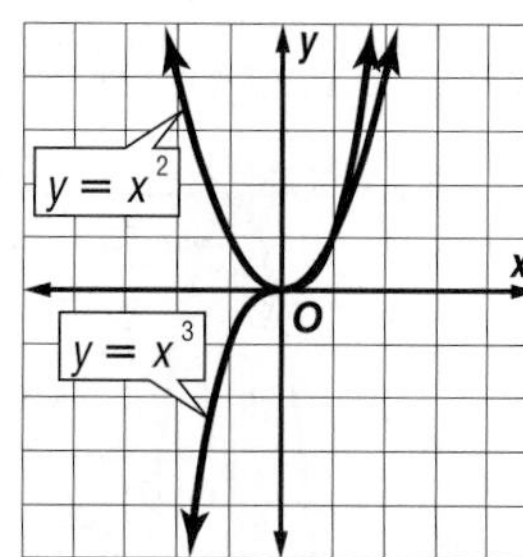

Both graphs cross the y-axis at zero; $y = x^3$ increases at a faster rate and extends below the x-axis.

45.

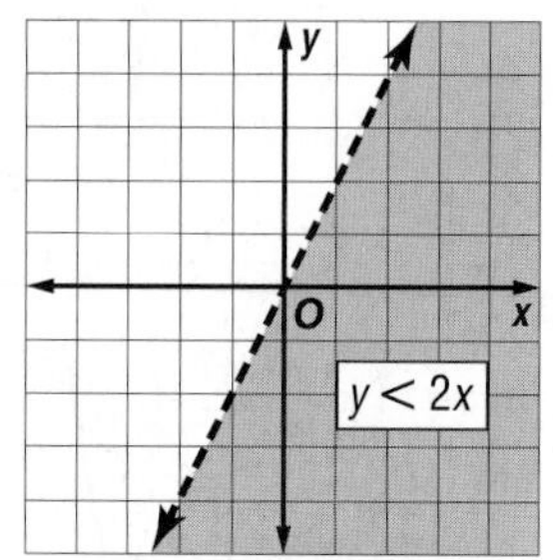

46.

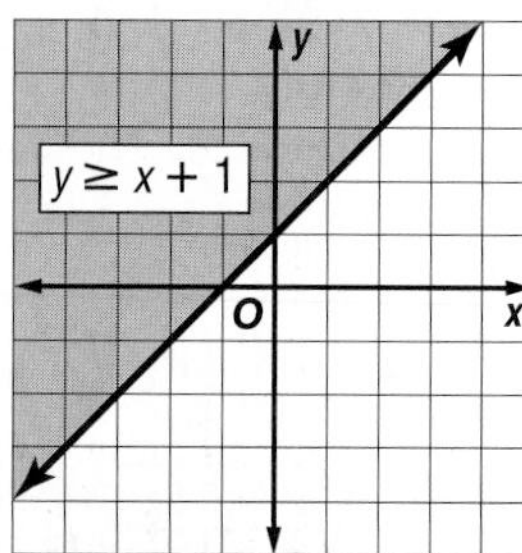

47.

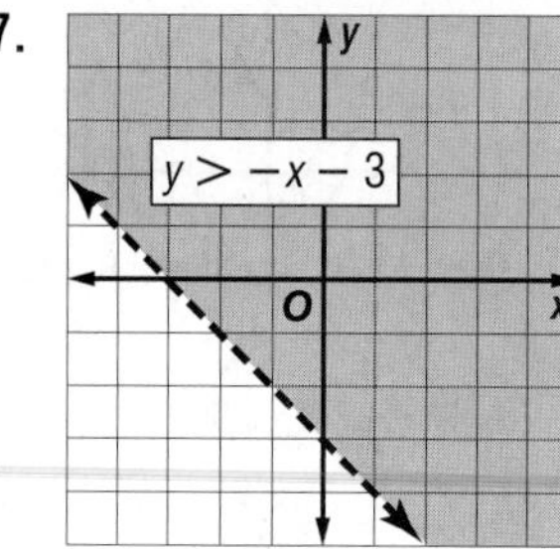

48.

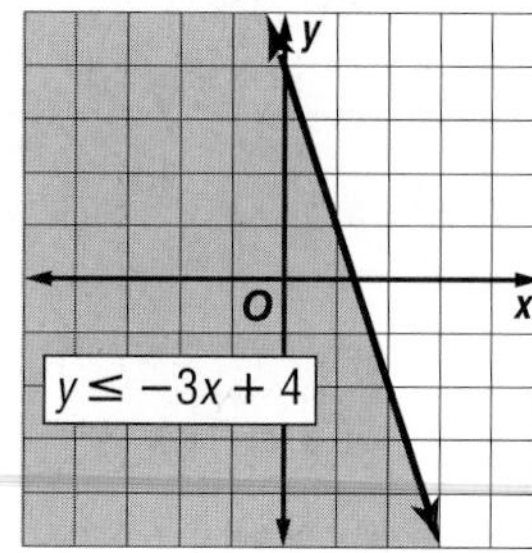

Page 569, Lesson 12-3a

a.

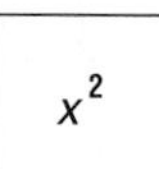

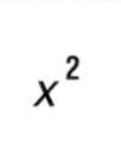

b.

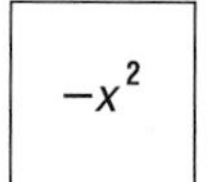
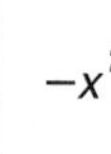
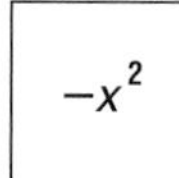

c.

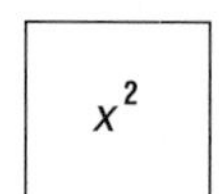
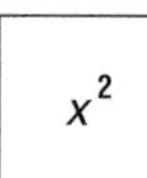
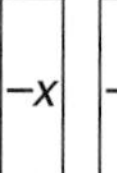

d.

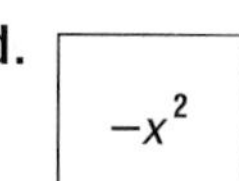
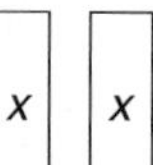
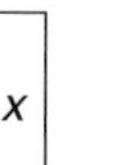

e.

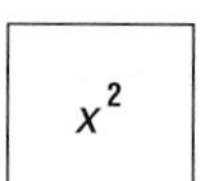
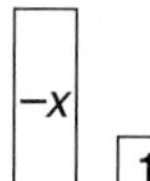

f.

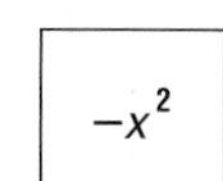
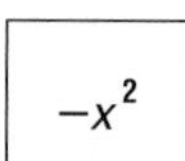
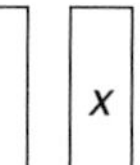
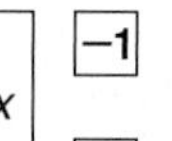
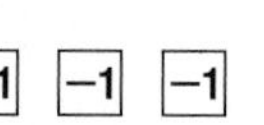

g.

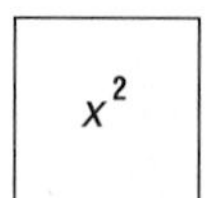
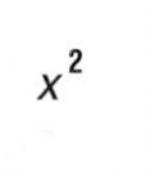
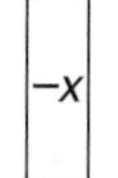
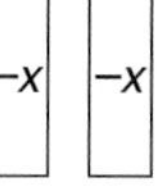

h.

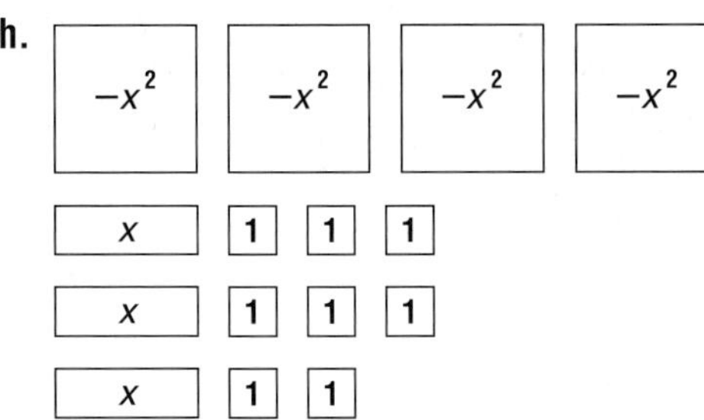

Page 574, Lesson 12-4 (Hands-On Mini Lab)

2.

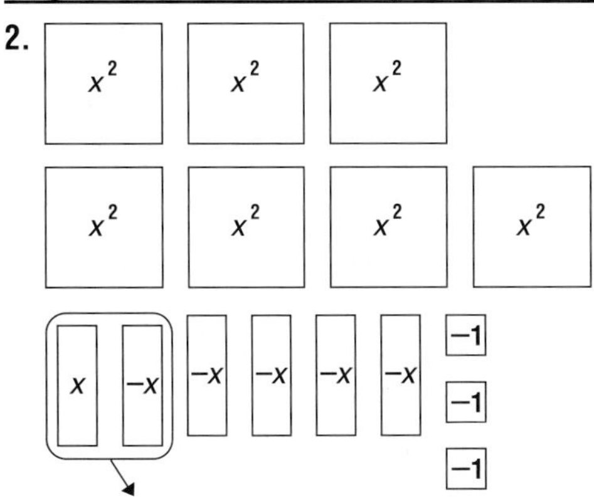

Page 578, Mid-Chapter Practice Test

18.

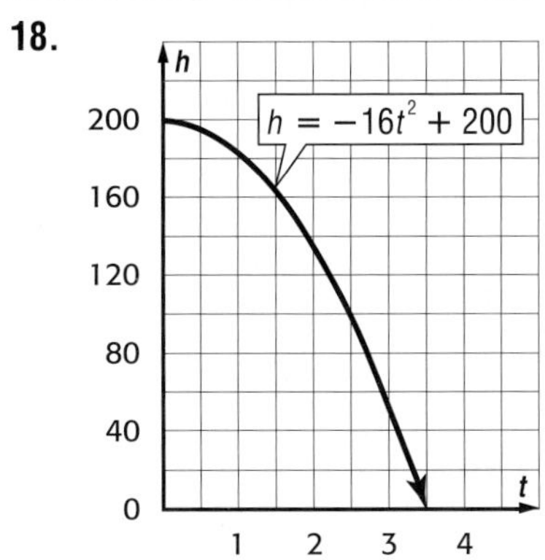

Page 589, Lesson 12-7a

4.

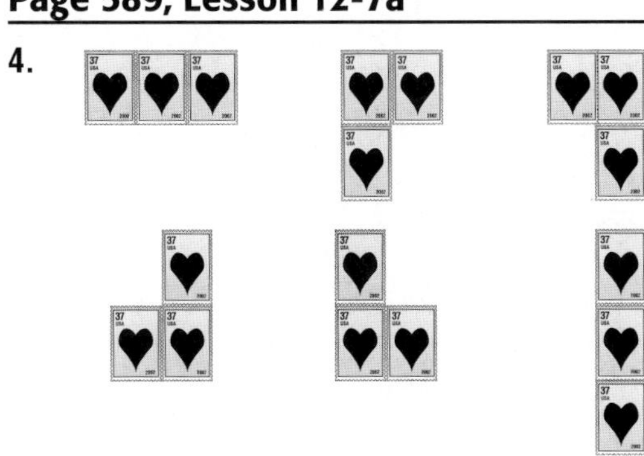

Page 590, Lesson 12-7 (Hands-On Mini Lab)

2.

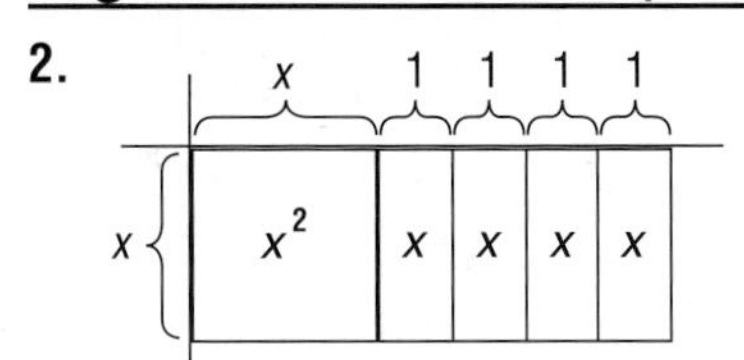

3.

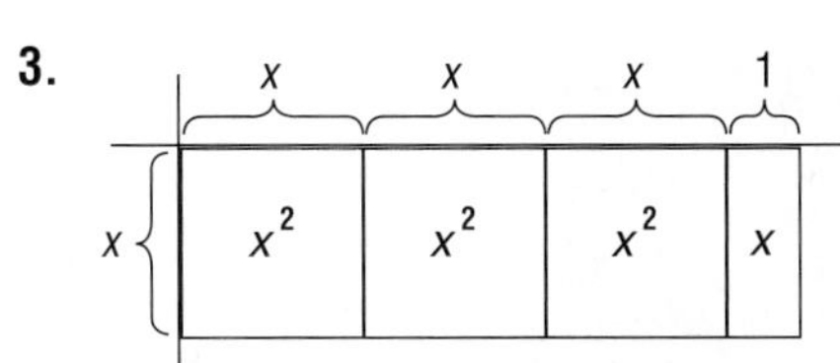

4.

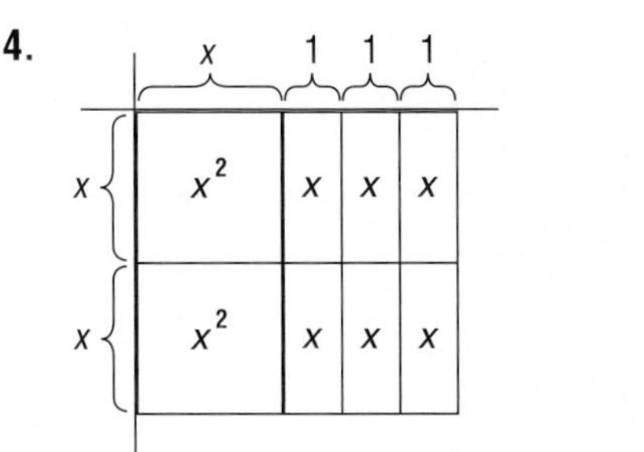

Page 597, Standardized Test Practice

19.

x	$40x - 2x^2$	y	(x, y)
0	$40(0) - 2(0)^2$	0	(0, 0)
2	$40(2) - 2(2)^2$	72	(2, 72)
4	$40(4) - 2(4)^2$	128	(4, 128)
6	$40(6) - 2(6)^2$	168	(6, 168)
8	$40(8) - 2(8)^2$	192	(8, 192)
10	$40(10) - 2(10)^2$	200	(10, 200)
12	$40(12) - 2(12)^2$	192	(12, 192)
14	$40(14) - 2(14)^2$	168	(14, 168)
16	$40(16) - 2(16)^2$	128	(16, 128)
18	$40(18) - 2(18)^2$	72	(18, 72)
20	$40(20) - 2(20)^2$	0	(20, 0)

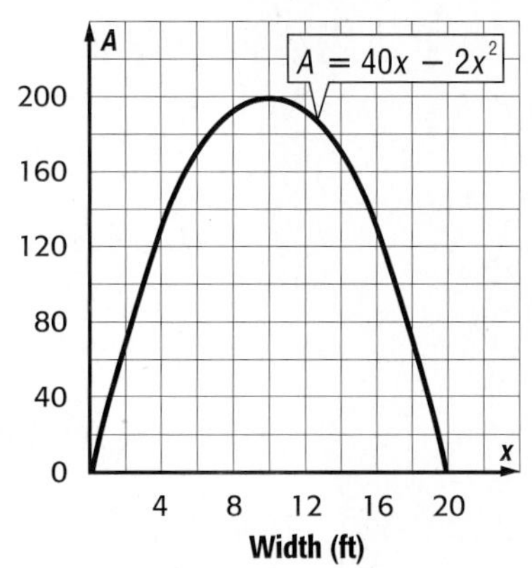

Built-In Workbooks

Skills

Trigonometry

Measurement Conversion

Reference

HOW TO...

USE THE STUDENT HANDBOOK

A Student Handbook is the additional skill and reference material found at the end of books. The Student Handbook can help answer these questions.

What If I Forget What I Learned Last Year?

Use the **Prerequisite Skills** section to refresh your memory about things you have learned in other math classes.

1 Estimation Strategies
2 Displaying Data on Graphs
3 Converting Measurements within the Customary System
4 Converting Measurements within the Metric System
5 Divisibility Patterns
6 Prime Factorization
7 Greastest Common Factor
8 Simplifying Fractions
9 Least Common Multiple
10 Perimeter and Area of Rectangles
11 Plotting Points on a Coordinate Plane
12 Measuring and Drawing Angles

What If I Need More Practice?

The **Extra Practice** section provides additional problems for each lesson.

What If I Have Trouble with Word Problems?

The **Mixed Problem Solving** pages provide additional word problems that use the skills in each chapter.

What If I Need Help on Taking Tests?

The **Preparing for Standardized Tests** section gives you tips and practice on how to answer different types of questions that appear on tests.

What If I Need Practice in Trigonometry and Measurement Conversion?

The **Trigonometry** section gives you more instruction and practice on the sine, cosine, and tangent ratios. The **Measurement Conversion** section gives instruction and practice on converting measures between the metric and customary systems.

What If I Forget a Vocabulary Word?

The **English-Spanish Glossary** provides a list of important, or difficult, words used throughout the textbook. It provides a definition in English and Spanish as well as the page number(s) where the word can be found.

What If I Need to Check a Homework Answer?

The answers to the odd-numbered problems are included in **Selected Answers**. Check your answers to make sure you understand how to solve all of the assigned problems.

What If I Need to Find Something Quickly?

The **Index** alphabetically lists the subjects covered throughout the entire textbook and the pages on which each subject can be found.

What If I Forget a Formula?

Inside the back cover of your math book is a list of **Formulas and Symbols** that are used in the book.

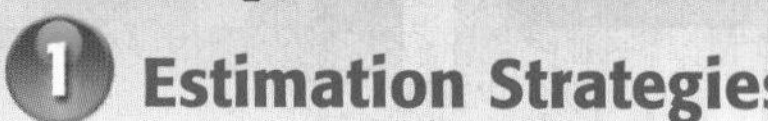

Prerequisite Skills

1 Estimation Strategies

Sometimes you do not need to know the exact answer to a problem, or you may want to check the reasonableness of an answer. In those instances, you can use **estimation**. There are several different methods of estimation. A common method is to use **rounding**.

EXAMPLES Estimate by Rounding

Estimate by rounding.

1 **189.2 × 315.6**

Round each number to the nearest hundred. Then multiply.

$$\begin{array}{rcr} 189.2 & \rightarrow & 200 \\ \underline{\times\ 315.6} & \rightarrow & \underline{\times\ 300} \\ & & 60{,}000 \end{array}$$

The product is about 60,000.

2 $\mathbf{453\frac{1}{5} + 68\frac{2}{3}}$

Round each number to the nearest ten. Then add.

$$\begin{array}{rcr} 453\frac{1}{5} & \rightarrow & 450 \\ \underline{+\ 68\frac{2}{3}} & \rightarrow & \underline{+\ 70} \\ & & 520 \end{array}$$

The sum is about 520.

You can use clustering to estimate sums. **Clustering** works best with numbers that all round to approximately the same number.

EXAMPLES Estimate by Clustering

Estimate by clustering.

3 $\mathbf{13\frac{1}{4} + 16\frac{2}{5} + 14\frac{5}{6} + 15\frac{3}{8}}$

All of the numbers are close to 15. There are four numbers.

The sum is about 4 × 15 or 60.

4 **99.6 + 97.83 + 102.18 + 100.101 + 99.90**

All of the numbers are close to 100. There are five numbers.

The sum is about 5 × 100 or 500.

Compatible numbers are numbers that are easy to compute with mentally.

EXAMPLES Estimate by Using Compatible Numbers

Estimate by using compatible numbers.

5 **76.36 ÷ 24.73**

76.36 is close to 75, and 24.73 is close to 25.

$$24.73\overline{)76.36} \rightarrow 25\overline{)75}^{\,3}$$

The quotient is about 3.

6 $\mathbf{7\frac{3}{8} + 12 + 20\frac{2}{3}}$

The fractions $\frac{3}{8}$ and $\frac{2}{3}$ are close to $\frac{1}{2}$.

$$7\frac{1}{2} + 12 + 20\frac{1}{2} = (7 + 12 + 20) + \left(\frac{1}{2} + \frac{1}{2}\right)$$
$$= 39 + 1 \text{ or } 40$$

The sum is about 40.

600 Prerequisite Skills

A strategy that works well for some addition and subtraction problems is **front-end estimation**. This strategy involves adding or subtracting the left-most column of digits. Then, add or subtract the next column of digits. Annex zeros for the remaining digits.

EXAMPLES Use Front-End Estimation

Use front-end estimation to find an estimate.

7 **5,283 + 3,634**

$$\begin{array}{r} 5{,}283 \\ +\,3{,}634 \\ \hline 8 \end{array} \rightarrow \begin{array}{r} 5{,}283 \\ +\,3{,}634 \\ \hline 8{,}800 \end{array}$$

The sum is about 8,800.

8 **118.1 − 57.5**

$$\begin{array}{r} 118.1 \\ -\,57.5 \\ \hline 6 \end{array} \rightarrow \begin{array}{r} 118.1 \\ -\,57.5 \\ \hline 61.0 \end{array}$$

The difference is about 61.

Exercises

Estimate by rounding. **1–6. Sample answers given.** **2. 80 + 90 + 20 = 190**

1. $42\frac{1}{3} \times 59\frac{3}{4}$ **40 × 60 = 2,400**
2. 78.26 + 90.1 + 18.5
3. $425\frac{2}{3} \times 10\frac{1}{8}$ **426 × 10 = 4,260**
4. 51.68 × 72.31 **50 × 70 = 3,500**
5. $18\frac{3}{4} + 32\frac{2}{5} + 53$ **20 + 30 + 50 = 100**
6. 96.88 × 31.98 **100 × 30 = 3,000**

Estimate by clustering. **7–10. Sample answers given.** **7. 5 × 20 = 100**

7. 19.9 + 17.63 + 21.45 + 20.17 + 18.75
8. $353\frac{1}{3} + 349\frac{2}{5} + 347\frac{3}{4} + 351$ **4 × 350 = 1,400**
9. $74\frac{1}{2} + 72 + 77\frac{2}{3} + 76\frac{3}{5}$ **4 × 75 = 300**
10. 3.12 + 2.75 + 2.89 + 3.25 + 2.9 + 3.05 **6 × 3 = 18**

Estimate by using compatible numbers. **11–16. Sample answers given.**

11. $105\frac{2}{3} \div 26\frac{1}{2}$ **100 ÷ 25 = 4**
12. 69.3 ÷ 34.5 **70 ÷ 35 = 2**
13. $85\frac{2}{5} + 14\frac{1}{3}$ **85 + 15 = 100**
14. $2\frac{3}{5} + 7\frac{1}{2} + 15$ **3 + 7 + 15 = 25**
15. 85.1 ÷ 22.3 **80 ÷ 20 = 4**
16. 12.4 + 19 + 35.6 **10 + 20 + 35 = 65**

Estimate by using front-end estimation. **18. 12,000 + 1,100 = 13,100**

17. 109.67 − 25.88 **80 + 4 = 84**
18. 4,456 + 8,703
19. 625.28 − 400.35 **200 + 20 = 220**
20. $34\frac{5}{8} + 56\frac{1}{3} + 62\frac{3}{7}$ **140 + 12 = 152**
21. $99\frac{3}{8} - 15\frac{1}{2}$ **80 + 4 = 84**
22. 628 + 547 + 432 **1,500 + 90 = 1,590**

Use any method to estimate. **23–34. Sample answers given.** **23. 750 − 50 = 700**

23. 752.6 − 50.1
24. 69.5 × 32 **70 × 30 = 2,100**
25. $88\frac{2}{3} + 2\frac{1}{3}$ **89 + 2 = 91**
26. 99.6 ÷ 18.25 **100 ÷ 20 = 5**
27. 700.45 × 2.1
28. 1,065.6 − 200.8 **1,100 − 200 = 900**
29. 390 ÷ 52 **400 ÷ 50 = 8**
30. 9.5 × 2.3 **10 × 2 = 20**
31. $77\frac{3}{8} - 55\frac{2}{3}$ **77 − 55 = 22**
32. 1,208.85 ÷ 399.1 **1,200 ÷ 400 = 3**
33. $80\frac{1}{5} \div 9\frac{1}{3}$ **81 ÷ 9 = 9**
34. 1,715.3 − 1,399.9 **1,700 − 1,400 = 300**

27. 700 × 2 = 1,400

35. **MONEY MATTERS** At an arts and crafts festival, Lena selected items priced at $5.98, $7.25, $3.25, $8.75, $9.85, $2.50, and $7.25. She has $50 in cash. How could she use estimation to see if she can use cash or if she needs to write a check? **Sample answer: use front-end estimation to estimate the sum at $45, which is less than $50.**

Prerequisite Skills

Prerequisite Skills 601

2 Displaying Data in Graphs

Statistics involves collecting, analyzing, and presenting information, called **data**. Graphs display data to help readers make sense of the information.

- **Bar graphs** are used to compare the frequency of data. The bar graph below compares the average number of vacation days given by countries to their workers.

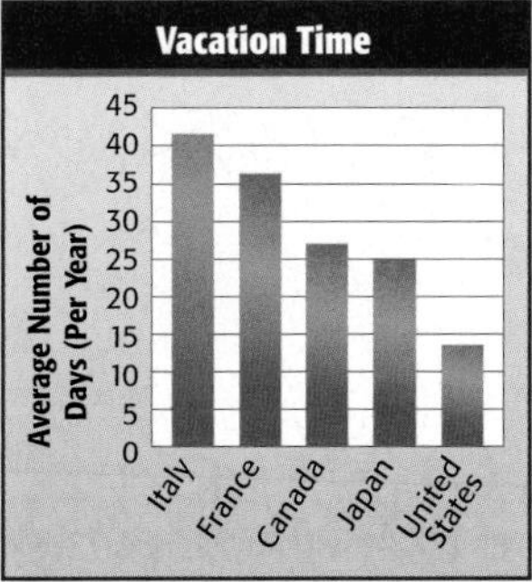

Source: *The World Almanac*

- **Double bar graphs** compare two sets of data. The double bar graph below shows the percent of men and women 65 and older who held jobs in various years.

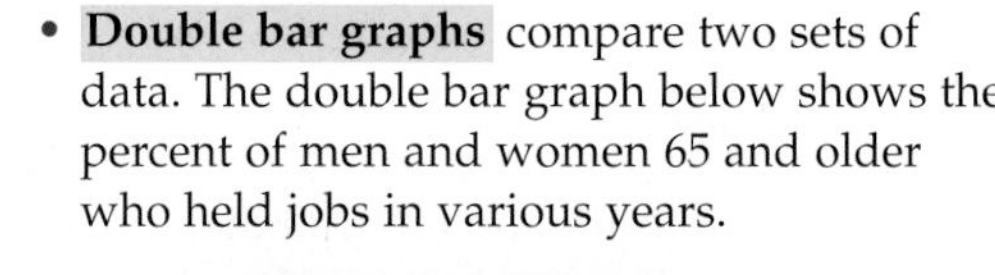

Source: *The World Almanac*

- **Line graphs** usually show how values change over time. The line graph below shows the number of people per square mile in the U.S. from 1800 through 2000.

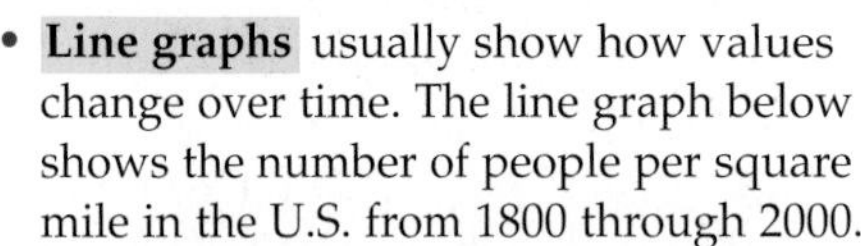

Source: *The World Almanac*

- **Double line graphs**, like double bar graphs, show two sets of data. The double line graph below compares the amount of money spent by both domestic and foreign U.S. travelers.

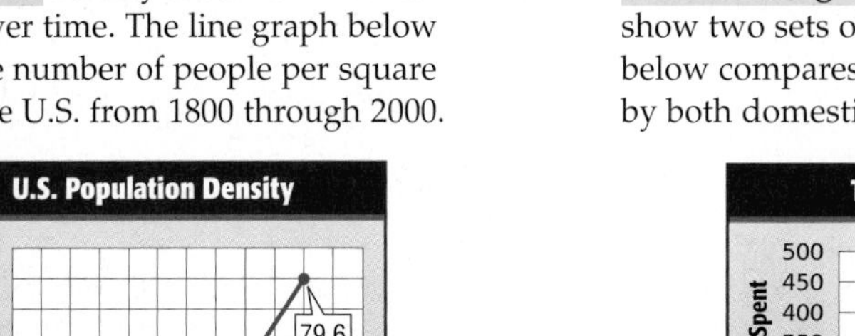
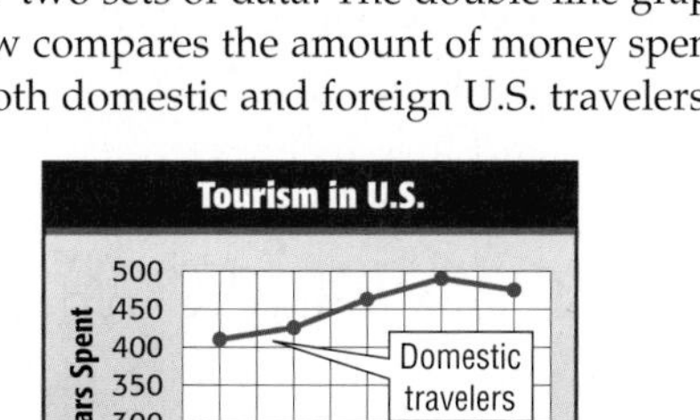

Source: *The World Almanac*

- **Stem-and-leaf plots** are a system used to condense a set of data where the greatest place value of the data is used for the **stems** and the next greatest place value forms the **leaves**. Each data value can be seen in this type of graph.

The stem-and-leaf plot below contains this list of mathematics test scores:

95 76 64 88 93 68 99 96 74 75 92 80 76 85 91 70 62 81

The least number has 6 in the tens place.

The greatest number has 9 in the tens place.

The stems are 6, 7, 8, and 9.

The leaves are ordered from least to greatest.

Stem	Leaf
6	2 4 8
7	0 4 5 6 6
8	0 1 5 8
9	1 2 3 5 6 9

$6 | 2 = 62$

602 Prerequisite Skills

EXAMPLE Choose a Display

1 **Shonny is writing a research paper about the Olympics for her social studies class. She wants to include a graph that shows how the times in the 400-meter run have changed over time. Should she use a line graph, bar graph, or stem-and-leaf plot?**

Since the data would show how the times have changed over a period of time, she should choose a line graph.

Exercises

Determine whether a bar graph, double bar graph, line graph, double line graph, or stem-and-leaf plot is the best way to display each of the following sets of data. Explain your reasoning.

1. how the income of households has changed from 1950 through 2000 **line graph**
2. the income of an average household in six different countries **bar graph**
3. the prices for a loaf of bread in twenty different supermarkets **stem-and-leaf plot**
4. the number of boys and the number of girls participating in six different school sports **double bar graph**

1–4. Sample answers are given. See margin for explanation.

Refer to the bar graph, double bar graph, line graph, double line graph, and stem-and-leaf plot on page 602. **5–9. See margin for sample answers.**

5. Write several sentences to describe the data shown in the graph titled "Vacation Time." Include a comparison of the days worked for Canada and the U.S.
6. Write several sentences to describe the data shown in the graph titled "Older Workers." What other type or types of graphs could you use to display this data? Explain your reasoning.
7. Write several sentences to describe the data shown in the graph titled "Tourism in U.S." What other type or types of graphs could you use to display this data? Explain your reasoning.
8. Write several sentences to describe the data shown in the graph titled "U.S. Population Density." What other type or types of graphs could you use to display this data? Explain your reasoning.
9. Write several sentences to describe the data shown in the stem-and-leaf plot of mathematics test scores. What is an advantage of showing the scores in this type of graph?

For Exercises 10–14, use the stem-and-leaf plot at the right that shows the number of stories in the tallest buildings in Dallas, Texas. **13. about 42 stories**

Stem	Leaf
2	7 9 9
3	0 1 1 1 3 3 4 4 6 6 7
4	0 2 2 5 9
5	0 0 0 0 2 5 6 8
6	0
7	2 2 | 7 = 27

10. How many buildings does the stem-and-leaf plot represent? **29**
11. How many stories are there for the shortest building in the stem-and-leaf plot? the tallest building? **27; 72**
12. What is the median number of stories for these buildings? **40 stories**
13. What is the mean number of stories for these buildings?
14. Explain how the stem-and-leaf plot is useful in displaying the data. **Sample answer: The number of stories in each building can be seen.**

Answers

1. This type of graph is useful for showing changes over a period of time.
2. This type of graph is useful for comparing frequency for several different categories.
3. This type of graph is useful for displaying each data item.
4. This type of graph is useful for comparing frequencies for two sets of data.
5. The U.S. has the fewest vacation days and Italy has the most. The number of days in Canada is about double the number in the U.S.
6. In 1960, about three times more men were employed. The percent for men has decreased and the percent for women has remained about constant. A double line graph could be used to compare the two categories over time.
7. The amount of money spent by domestic travelers has increased at a greater rate than the amount for foreign travelers. A double bar graph could be used to compare the two categories.
8. The population density increased at a much greater rate from 1900 to 2000 than it did from 1800 to 1900. A bar graph could be used to compare the three amounts.
9. There were more scores in the 90s than in any other category. With this type of graph, you can see each score.

Prerequisite Skills

Prerequisite Skills

3 Converting Measurements within the Customary System

The units of length in the customary system are inch, foot, yard, and mile. The table shows the relationships among these units.

- To convert from larger units to smaller units, multiply.
- To convert from smaller units to larger units, divide.

Customary Units of Length
1 mile (mi) = 5,280 feet
1 foot (ft) = 12 inches (in.)
1 yard (yd) = 3 feet

Larger Units → **Smaller Units**

7 ft = 7 × 12 = 84 in.

4 mi = 4 × 5,280 = 21,120 ft

There will be a greater number of smaller units than larger units.

Smaller Units → **Larger Units**

108 in. = 108 ÷ 12 = 9 ft

15 ft = 15 ÷ 3 = 5 yd

There will be fewer larger units than smaller units.

EXAMPLES Convert Customary Units of Length

Complete each sentence.

1 **8 yd = ? ft**

8 yd = (8 × 3) ft
= 24 ft

2 **144 in. = ? ft**

144 in. = (144 ÷ 12) ft
= 12 ft

3 **7.5 mi = ? ft**

7.5 mi = (7.5 × 5,280) ft
= 39,600 ft

The units of weight in the customary system are ounce, pound, and ton. The table at the right shows the relationships among these units. As with units of length, to convert from larger units to smaller units, multiply. To convert from smaller units to larger units, divide.

Customary Units of Weight
1 pound (lb) = 16 ounces (oz)
1 ton (T) = 2,000 pounds

EXAMPLES Convert Customary Units of Weight

Complete each sentence.

4 **12,400 lb = ? T**

12,400 lb = 12,400 ÷ 2,000 or 6.2 T

5 **92 oz = ? lb**

92 oz = 92 ÷ 16 or 5.75 lb

Capacity is the amount of liquid or dry substance a container can hold. Customary units of capacity are fluid ounces, cup, pint, quart, and gallon. The relationships among these units are shown in the table.

Customary Units of Capacity
1 cup (c) = 8 fluid ounces (fl oz)
1 pint (pt) = 2 cups
1 quart (qt) = 2 pints
1 gallon (gal) = 4 quarts

EXAMPLES Convert Customary Units of Capacity

Complete each sentence.

6 **64 fl oz = ? c**

64 fl oz = 64 ÷ 8 or 8 c

7 **4.4 gal = ? qt**

4.4 gal = 4.4 × 4 or 17.6 qt

Prerequisite Skills

604 Prerequisite Skills

EXAMPLE Convert Customary Units Using Two Steps

8 **12 pt = ? gal**

12 pt = (12 ÷ 2) qt First, change pints to quarts.
= 6 qt

6 qt = (6 ÷ 4) gal Then, change quarts to gallons.
= 1.5 gal

So, 12 pints = 1.5 gallons.

Units of time can also be converted. The table shows the relationships between these units

Units of Time	
60 seconds (s) = 1 minute (min)	7 days = 1 week
60 minutes = 1 hour (h)	52 weeks = 1 year
24 hours = 1 day	365 days = 1 year

EXAMPLES Convert Units of Time

Complete each sentence.

9 **84 h = ? days**

84 h = 84 ÷ 24 or 3.5 days

10 **5 weeks = ? days**

5 weeks = 5 × 7 or 35 days

EXAMPLE Adding Mixed Measures

11 **Find the sum of 4 feet 7 inches and 5 feet 10 inches. Simplify.**

4 ft 7 in.
+ 5 ft 10 in. Line up like units and add.
9 ft 17 in. = 9 ft + (12 in. + 5 in.) Separate 17 in. into 12 in. and 5 in.
= 10 ft + 5 in. Replace 12 in. with 1 ft and add like units.

Exercises

Complete each sentence.

1. 2 mi = ? ft **10,560**
2. 48 oz = ? lb **3**
3. 120 min = ? h **2**
4. 8.5 T = ? lb **17,000**
5. 5 days = ? h **120**
6. 63,360 ft = ? mi **12**
7. 150 ft = ? yd **50**
8. 5 gal = ? qt **20**
9. 128 fl oz = ? c **16**
10. 20 weeks = ? days **140**
11. 24 c = ? gal **1.5**
12. 190,080 in. = ? mi **3**
13. 5 T = ? oz **160,000**
14. 36 h = ? days **1.5**
15. 12 oz = ? lb **0.75**
16. 10 pt = ? gal **1.25**
17. 1 mi = ? yd **1,760**
18. 12 gal = ? c **192**
19. 14,080 yd = ? mi **8**
20. 49 days = ? weeks **7**
21. 1 day = ? s **86,400**

Find each sum.

22. 15 ft 2 in. + 32 ft 7 in. = **47 ft 9 in.**
23. 5 gal 1 qt + 10 gal 2 qt = **15 gal 3 qt**
24. 12 h 15 min + 27 h 55 min = **40 h 10 min**
25. 45 lb 14 oz + 62 lb 12 oz = **108 lb 10 oz**
26. 4 yd 2 ft + 16 yd 1 ft = **21 yd**
27. 12 days 7 h + 44 days 20 h = **57 days 3 h**

Prerequisite Skills

Prerequisite Skills 605

Prerequisite Skills

4 Converting Measurements within the Metric System

All units of length in the metric system are defined in terms of the meter (m). The diagram below shows the relationships between some common metric units.

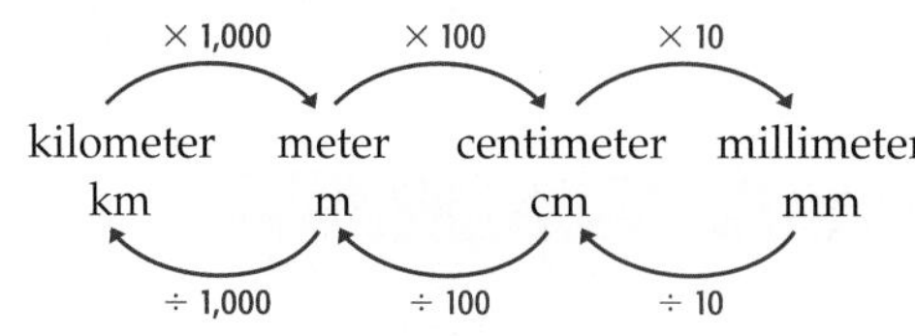

Comparing Metric and Customary Units of Length
1 mm ≈ 0.04 inch (height of a comma)
1 cm ≈ 0.4 inch (half the width of a penny)
1 m ≈ 1.1 yards (width of a doorway)
1 km ≈ 0.6 mile (length of a city block)

- To convert from larger units to smaller units, multiply.
- To convert from smaller units to larger units, divide.

There will be a greater number of smaller units than larger units.

Converting From Larger Units to Smaller Units	Converting From Smaller Units to Larger Units
1 km = 1 × 1,000 = 1,000 m	1 mm = 1 ÷ 10 = 0.1 cm
1 m = 1 × 100 = 100 cm	1 cm = 1 ÷ 100 = 0.01 m
1 cm = 1 × 10 = 10 mm	1 m = 1 ÷ 1,000 = 0.001 km

There will be fewer larger units than smaller units.

EXAMPLES Convert Metric Units of Length

Complete each sentence.

1 7 km = __?__ m

7 km = (7 × 1,000) m
= 7,000 m

2 123 cm = __?__ m

123 cm = (123 ÷ 100) m
= 1.23 m

3 38.9 cm = __?__ mm

38.9 cm = (38.9 × 10) mm
= 389 mm

The basic unit of capacity in the metric system is the liter (L). A liter and milliliter (mL) are related in a manner similar to meter and millimeter.

× 1,000

1 L = 1,000 mL

÷ 1,000

Comparing Metric and Customary Units of Capacity
1 mL ≈ 0.03 ounce (drop of water)
1 L ≈ 1 quart (bottle of ketchup)

EXAMPLES Convert Metric Units of Capacity

Complete each sentence.

4 14.5 L = __?__ mL

14.5 L = 14.5 × 1,000 or 14,500 mL

5 750 mL = __?__ L

750 mL = 750 ÷ 1,000 or 0.75 L

The *mass* of an object is the amount of matter that it contains. The basic unit of mass in the metric system is the kilogram (kg). Kilogram, gram (g), and milligram (mg) are related in a manner similar to kilometer, meter, and millimeter.

1 kg = 1,000 g 1 g = 1,000 mg

Comparing Metric and Customary Units of Mass
1 g ≈ 0.04 ounce (one raisin)
1 kg ≈ 2.2 pounds (six medium apples)

Prerequisite Skills

606 Prerequisite Skills

EXAMPLES Convert Metric Units of Mass

Complete each sentence.

6 **53 kg = __?__ g**

53 kg = 53 × 1,000 or 53,000 g

7 **4,500 g = __?__ kg**

4,500 g = 4,500 ÷ 1,000 or 4.5 kg

Sometimes you need to perform more than one conversion to get the desired unit.

EXAMPLES Convert Metric Units Using Two Steps

Complete each sentence.

8 **35,000 cm = __?__ km**

35,000 cm = 35,000 ÷ 100 m
= 350 m

350 m = 350 ÷ 1,000 km
= 0.35 km

So, 35,000 cm = 0.35 km.

9 **4.5 kg = __?__ mg**

4.5 kg = 4.5 × 1,000 g
= 4,500 g

4,500 g = 4,500 × 1,000 mg
= 4,500,000 mg

So, 4.5 kg = 4,500,000 mg.

Exercises

State which metric unit you would probably use to measure each item.

1. mass of an elephant kg
2. amount of juice in a pitcher L
3. length of a room m
4. distance across a state km
5. mass of a small stone g
6. length of a paper clip cm
7. height of a large tree m
8. amount of water in a medicine dropper mL
9. width of a sheet of paper cm
10. diameter of the head of a pin mm
11. mass of a truck kg
12. cruising altitude of a passenger jet km

Complete each sentence. 28. 0.825 35. 0.425

13. 45 mm = __?__ cm 4.5
14. 2,500 g = __?__ kg 2.5
15. 5,000 m = __?__ km 5
16. 7 L = __?__ mL 7,000
17. 8,000 mg = __?__ g 8
18. 10 km = __?__ m 10,000
19. 25 kg = __?__ g 25,000
20. 450 cm = __?__ mm 4,500
21. 6.4 m = __?__ cm 640
22. 8.25 kg = __?__ g 8,250
23. 655 mL = __?__ L 0.655
24. 982 cm = __?__ m 9.82
25. 79 m = __?__ km 0.079
26. 4,000 mm = __?__ m 4
27. 60,000 mg = __?__ kg 0.06
28. 82,500 cm = __?__ km
29. 5 km = __?__ cm 500,000
30. 12 kg = __?__ mg 12,000,000
31. 8 L = __?__ mL 8,000
32. 72.6 cm = __?__ mm 726
33. 0.45 L = __?__ mL 450
34. 0.625 km = __?__ m 625
35. 425,000 mg = __?__ kg
36. 1 km = __?__ mm 1,000,000
37. **RACES** Priscilla is running a five-kilometer race. How many meters long is the race? 5,000 m
38. **MEDICINE** A large container of medicine contains 0.5 liter of the drug. How many 25-milliliter doses of the drug are in this container? 20 doses

Prerequisite Skills

Prerequisite Skills 607

Answer

23. If $b = 0$, then $a = 2, 5,$ or 8. If $b = 2$, then $a = 0,$ 3, 6, or 9. If $b = 4$, then $a = 1, 4,$ or 7. If $b = 6$, then $a = 2, 5,$ or 8. If $b = 8$, then $a = 0, 3,$ 6, or 9.

5 Divisibility Patterns

If a number is a factor of a given number, you can also say the given number is **divisible** by the factor. For example, 144 is divisible by 9 since $144 \div 9 = 16$, a whole number. A number n is a factor of a number m if m is divisible by n.

A number is divisible by:

- 2 if the ones digit is divisible by 2.
- 3 if the sum of the digits is divisible by 3.
- 4 if the number formed by the last two digits is divisible by 4.
- 5 if the ones digit is 0 or 5.
- 6 if the number is divisible by both 2 and 3.
- 8 if the number formed by the last three digits is divisible by 8.
- 9 if the sum of the digits is divisible by 9.
- 10 if the ones digit is 0.

EXAMPLE Use Divisibility Rules

1 Determine whether 2,418 is divisible by 2, 3, 4, 5, 6, 8, 9, or 10.

2: Yes; the ones digit, 8, is divisible by 2.

3: Yes; the sum of the digits, $2 + 4 + 1 + 8 = 15$, is divisible by 3.

4: No; the number formed by the last two digits, 18, is not divisible by 4.

5: No; the ones digit is not 0 or 5.

6: Yes; the number is divisible by 2 and 3.

8: No; 418 is not divisible by 8.

9: No; the sum of the digits, 15, is not divisible by 9.

10: No; the ones digit is not 0.

So, 2,418 is divisible by 2, 3, and 6, but not by 4, 5, 8, 9, or 10.

Exercises

Determine whether each number is divisible by 2, 3, 4, 5, 6, 8, 9, or 10.

1. 48 **2, 3, 4, 6, 8**
2. 153 **3, 9**
3. 2,470 **2, 5, 10**
4. 56 **2, 4, 8**
5. 165 **3, 5**
6. 323 **none**
7. 918 **2, 3, 6, 9**
8. 1,700 **2, 4, 5, 10**
9. 2,865 **3, 5**
10. 12,357 **3, 9**
11. 16,084 **2, 4**
12. 50,070 **2, 3, 5, 6, 10**
13. 199 **none**
14. 999 **3, 9**
15. 808,080 **2, 3, 4, 5, 6, 8, 10**
16. 117 **3, 9**
17. Is 3 a factor of 777? **yes**
18. Is 5 a factor of 232? **no**
19. Is 6 a factor of 198? **yes**
20. Is 795 divisible by 10? **no**
21. Is 989 divisible by 9? **no**
22. Is 2,348 divisible by 4? **yes**
23. The number $87a{,}46b$ is divisible by 6. What are possible values of a and b? **See margin.**
24. **FLAGS** Each star in the U.S. flag represents a state. If another state joins the Union, could the stars be arranged in a rectangular array? Explain. **Yes; $3 \times 17 = 51$.**

6 Prime Factorization

When a whole number greater than 1 has *exactly* two factors, 1 and itself, it is called a **prime number**. When a whole number greater than 1 has more than two factors, it is called a **composite number**. The numbers 0 and 1 are *neither* prime *nor* composite. Notice that 0 has an endless number of factors and 1 has only one factor, itself.

EXAMPLES Identify Numbers as Prime or Composite

Determine whether each number is *prime*, *composite*, or *neither*.

1 33

The numbers 1, 3, and 11 divide into 33 evenly. So, 33 is composite.

2 59

The only numbers that divide evenly into 59 are 1 and 59. So, 59 is prime.

When a number is expressed as a product of factors that are all prime, the expression is called the **prime factorization** of the number. A **factor tree** is useful in finding the prime factorization of a number.

EXAMPLE Write Prime Factorization

3 **Use a factor tree to write the prime factorization of 60.**

You can begin a factor tree for 60 in several ways.

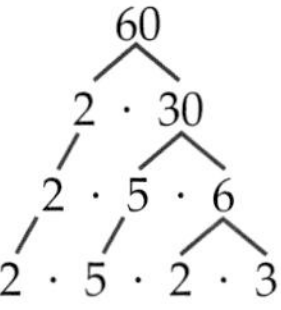

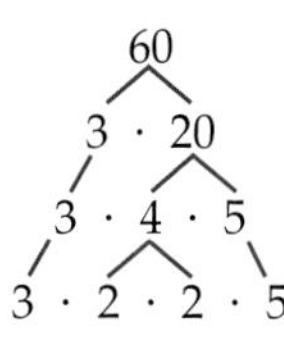

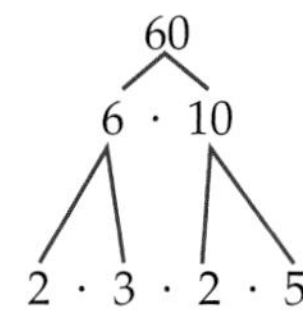

Notice that the bottom row of "branches" in every factor tree is the same except for the order in which the factors are written. So, $60 = 2 \cdot 2 \cdot 3 \cdot 5$ or $2^2 \cdot 3 \cdot 5$.

Every number has a unique set of prime factors. This property of numbers is called the **Fundamental Theorem of Arithmetic**.

Exercises

Determine whether each number is *prime*, *composite*, or *neither*.

1. 45 composite
2. 23 prime
3. 1 neither
4. 13 prime
5. 27 composite
6. 96 composite
7. 37 prime
8. 0 neither
9. 177 composite
10. 233 prime
11. 507 composite
12. 511 composite

Write the prime factorization of each number.

13. 20 $2^2 \cdot 5$
14. 49 7^2
15. 225 $3^2 \cdot 5^2$
16. 32 2^5
17. 25 5^2
18. 36 $2^2 \cdot 3^2$
19. 51 $3 \cdot 17$
20. 75 $3 \cdot 5^2$
21. 80 $2^4 \cdot 5$
22. 117 $3^2 \cdot 13$
23. 72 $2^3 \cdot 3^2$
24. 4,900 $2^2 \cdot 5^2 \cdot 7^2$

Prerequisite Skills

Prerequisite Skills 609

7 Greatest Common Factor

The greatest of the factors common to two or more numbers is called the **greatest common factor (GCF)** of the numbers. One way to find the GCF is to list the factors of the numbers.

EXAMPLE Find the GCF

1 Find the greatest common factor of 36 and 60.

Method 1 List the factors.

factors of 36: 1, 2, 3, 4, 6, 9, (12) 18, 36

factors of 60: 1, 2, 3, 4, 5, 6, 10, (12) 15, 20, 30, 60

Common factors of 36 and 60: 1, 2, 3, 4, 6, 12

The greatest common factor of 36 and 60 is 12.

Method 2 Use prime factorization.

$36 = \boxed{2} \cdot \boxed{2} \cdot \boxed{3} \cdot 3$

$60 = \boxed{2} \cdot \boxed{2} \cdot \boxed{3} \cdot 5$

Common prime factors of 36 and 60: 2, 2, 3

The GCF is $2 \cdot 2 \cdot 3$ or 12.

EXAMPLE Find the GCF

2 Find the greatest common factor of 54, 81, and 90.

Use a factor tree to find the prime factorization of each number.

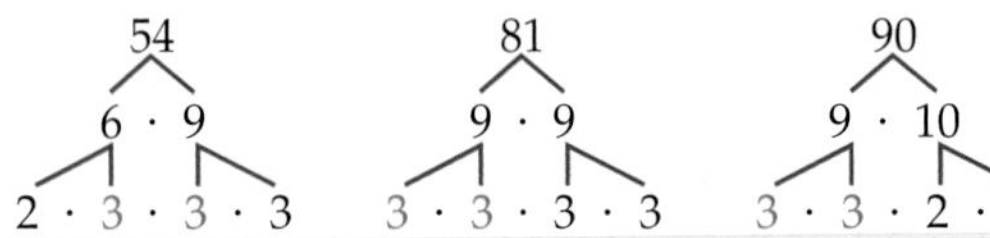

The common prime factors of 54, 81, and 90 are 3 and 3.
The GCF of 54, 81, and 90 is $3 \cdot 3$ or 9.

Exercises

Find the GCF of each set of numbers.

1. 45, 20 **5**
2. 27, 54 **27**
3. 24, 48 **24**
4. 63, 84 **21**
5. 40, 60 **20**
6. 32, 48 **16**
7. 30, 42 **6**
8. 54, 72 **18**
9. 36, 144 **36**
10. 3, 51 **3**
11. 24, 36, 42 **6**
12. 35, 49, 84 **7**
13. **DESIGN** Suppose you are tiling a tabletop with 6-inch square tiles. How many of these squares will be needed to cover a 30-inch by 24-inch table? **20 tiles**
14. **SHELVING** Emil is cutting a 72-inch-long board and a 54-inch-long board to make shelves. He wants the shelves to be the same length while not wasting any wood. What is the longest possible length of the shelves? **18 in.**

Two or more numbers are relatively prime if their greatest common factor is 1. Determine whether each set of numbers is relatively prime.

15. 9, 19 **yes**
16. 7, 21 **no**
17. 3, 51 **no**
18. 4, 28, 31 **yes**

610 Prerequisite Skills

8 Simplifying Fractions

Fractions, mixed numbers, decimals, and integers are examples of **rational numbers**. When a rational number is represented as a fraction, it is often expressed in **simplest form**. A fraction is in simplest form when the GCF of the numerator and denominator is 1.

EXAMPLE Simplify Fractions

1 Write $\frac{30}{45}$ in simplest form.

Method 1 Divide by the GCF.

$30 = \boxed{2} \cdot \boxed{3} \cdot 5$ Factor the numerator.

$45 = \boxed{3} \cdot \boxed{3} \cdot 5$ Factor the denominator.

The GCF of 30 and 45 is $3 \cdot 5$ or 15.

$\frac{30}{45} = \frac{30 \div 15}{45 \div 15}$ Divide numerator and denominator by the GCF, 15.

$= \frac{2}{3}$

Method 2 Use prime factorization.

$\frac{30}{45} = \frac{2 \cdot 3 \cdot 5}{3 \cdot 3 \cdot 5}$ Write the prime factorization of the numerator and denominator.

$= \frac{2 \cdot \cancel{3} \cdot \cancel{5}}{\cancel{3} \cdot 3 \cdot \cancel{5}}$ Divide the numerator and denominator by the GCF, $3 \cdot 5$.

$= \frac{2}{3}$ Simplify.

Exercises

Write each fraction in simplest form. If the fraction is already in simplest form, write *simplest form*.

1. $\frac{8}{72}$ $\frac{1}{9}$
2. $\frac{27}{45}$ $\frac{3}{5}$
3. $-\frac{60}{75}$ $-\frac{4}{5}$
4. $\frac{36}{54}$ $\frac{2}{3}$
5. $-\frac{3}{9}$ $-\frac{1}{3}$
6. $\frac{15}{25}$ $\frac{3}{5}$
7. $\frac{36}{81}$ $\frac{4}{9}$
8. $-\frac{18}{54}$ $-\frac{1}{3}$
9. $\frac{14}{66}$ $\frac{7}{33}$
10. $\frac{24}{54}$ $\frac{4}{9}$
11. $-\frac{15}{24}$ $-\frac{5}{8}$
12. $\frac{48}{72}$ $\frac{2}{3}$
13. $\frac{24}{120}$ $\frac{1}{5}$
14. $-\frac{66}{88}$ $-\frac{3}{4}$
15. $\frac{72}{98}$ $\frac{36}{49}$
16. $-\frac{45}{100}$ $-\frac{9}{20}$
17. $\frac{7}{91}$ $\frac{1}{13}$
18. $\frac{15}{100}$ $\frac{3}{20}$
19. $\frac{15}{60}$ $\frac{1}{4}$
20. $\frac{17}{51}$ $\frac{1}{3}$
21. $-\frac{6}{9}$ $-\frac{2}{3}$
22. $\frac{16}{40}$ $\frac{2}{5}$
23. $-\frac{6}{16}$ $-\frac{3}{8}$
24. $\frac{64}{68}$ $\frac{16}{17}$
25. $\frac{30}{80}$ $\frac{3}{8}$
26. $-\frac{2}{15}$
27. $\frac{90}{120}$ $\frac{3}{4}$
28. $\frac{75}{89}$
29. $-\frac{16}{96}$ $-\frac{1}{6}$
30. $\frac{133}{140}$ $\frac{19}{20}$
31. $\frac{99}{300}$ $\frac{33}{100}$
32. $-\frac{50}{1{,}000}$ $-\frac{1}{20}$
33. $-\frac{90}{6{,}000}$ $-\frac{3}{200}$
34. $-\frac{150}{400}$ $-\frac{3}{8}$
35. $\frac{10}{10{,}000}$ $\frac{1}{1{,}000}$

26. simplest form 28. simplest form

36. Both the numerator and the denominator of a fraction are even. Can you tell whether the fraction is in simplest form? Explain. **See margin.**

37. **WEATHER** The rainiest place on Earth is Waialeale, Hawaii. Of 365 days per year, the average number of rainy days is 335. Write a fraction in simplest form to represent these rainy days as a part of a year. $\frac{67}{73}$ **yr**

38. **OLYMPICS** In the 2000 Olympics, Brooke Bennett of the U.S. swam the 800-meter freestyle event in about 8 minutes. Express 8 minutes in terms of hours using a fraction in simplest form. $\frac{2}{15}$ **h**

Prerequisite Skills

Answer

36. It is not in simplest form because the numerator and denominator have a common factor of 2.

Prerequisite Skills

Answers

1. 0, 7, 14, 21, 28, 35
2. 0, 11, 22, 33, 44, 55
3. 0, 4, 8, 12, 16, 20
4. 0, 5, 10, 15, 20, 25
5. 0, 14, 28, 42, 56, 70
6. 0, 25, 50, 75, 100, 125
7. 0, 150, 300, 450, 600, 750
8. 0, 2, 4, 6, 8, 10
9. 0, 3, 6, 9, 12, 15
10. 0, 6, 12, 18, 24, 30

9 Least Common Multiple

A **multiple** of a number is the product of that number and any whole number.

EXAMPLE List Multiples

1 List the first six multiples of 15.

$0 \cdot 15 = 0, 1 \cdot 15 = 15, 2 \cdot 15 = 30, 3 \cdot 15 = 45, 4 \cdot 15 = 60, 5 \cdot 15 = 75$

The first six multiples of 15 are 0, 15, 30, 45, 60, 75.

The least of the nonzero common multiples of two or more numbers is called the **least common multiple (LCM)** of the numbers. To find the LCM of two or more numbers, you can list the multiples of each number until a common multiple is found, or you can use prime factorization.

EXAMPLE Find the LCM

2 Find the LCM of 12 and 18.

Method 1 List the multiples.

multiples of 12: 0, 12, 24, 36, 48, …
multiples of 18: 0, 18, 36, 72, 90, …

The LCM of 12 and 18 is 36.
Remember that the LCM is a *nonzero* number.

Method 2 Use prime factorization.

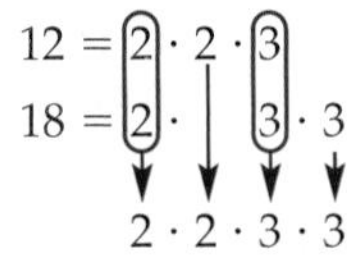

Write the prime factorization of each number.

Multiply the factors, using the common factors only once.

The LCM is $2 \cdot 2 \cdot 3 \cdot 3$ or 36.

Exercises

List the first six multiples of each number. 1–10. See margin.

1. 7
2. 11
3. 4
4. 5
5. 14
6. 25
7. 150
8. 2
9. 3
10. 6

Find the least common multiple (LCM) of each set of numbers.

11. 8, 20 **40**
12. 15, 18 **90**
13. 12, 16 **48**
14. 7, 12 **84**
15. 20, 50 **100**
16. 16, 24 **48**
17. 2, 7, 8 **56**
18. 2, 3, 5 **30**
19. 4, 8, 12 **24**
20. 7, 21, 5 **105**
21. 8, 28, 30 **840**
22. 10, 12, 14 **420**
23. 35, 25, 49 **1,225**
24. 24, 12, 6 **24**
25. 68, 170, 4 **340**
26. 45, 10, 6 **90**
27. 10, 100, 1,000 **1,000**
28. 100, 200, 300 **600**
29. 2, 3, 5, 7 **210**
30. 2, 15, 25, 36 **900**

31. **CIVICS** In the United States, a president is elected every four years. Members of the House of Representatives are elected every two years. Senators are elected every six years. If a voter had the opportunity to vote for a president, a representative, and a senator in 1996, what will be the next year the voter has a chance to make a choice for a president, a representative, and the same Senate seat? **2008**

10 Perimeter and Area of Rectangles

The distance around a geometric figure is called its **perimeter**. The perimeter P of a rectangle is twice the sum of the length ℓ and width w, or $P = 2\ell + 2w$. The measure of the surface enclosed by a figure is its **area**. The area A of a rectangle is the product of the length ℓ and width w, or $A = \ell w$.

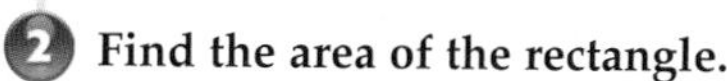

EXAMPLES Find the Perimeter and Area of a Rectangle

1 Find the perimeter of the rectangle.

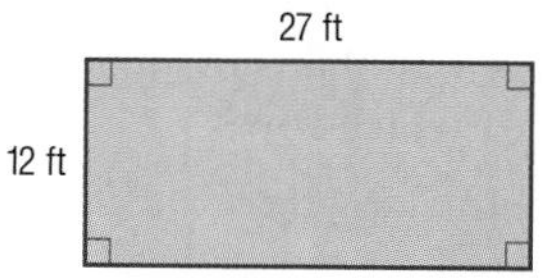

$P = 2\ell + 2w$	Write the formula.
$P = 2(27) + 2(12)$	Replace ℓ with 27 and w with 12.
$P = 54 + 24$	Multiply.
$P = 78$	Add.

27 ft

12 ft

The perimeter is 78 feet.

2 Find the area of the rectangle.

$A = \ell w$	Write the formula.
$A = 27 \cdot 12$	Replace ℓ with 27 and w with 12.
$A = 324$	Multiply.

The area is 324 square feet.

A square is a rectangle whose sides are all the same length. The perimeter P of a square is four times the side length s, or $P = 4s$. Its area A is the square of the side length, or $A = s^2$.

EXAMPLE Estimate the Perimeter and Area of a Square

3 Find the approximate perimeter and area of a square with side length $6\frac{5}{8}$ inches.

$P = 4s$	Write the formula.
$P = 4\left(6\frac{5}{8}\right)$	Replace s with $6\frac{5}{8}$.
$P \approx 4(7)$ or 28	Estimate.

The perimeter is about 28 inches.

$A = s^2$	Write the formula.
$A = \left(6\frac{5}{8}\right)^2$	Replace s with $6\frac{5}{8}$.
$A \approx 7^2$ or 49	Estimate.

The area is about 49 square inches.

Exercises

Find the perimeter and area of each figure.

1. 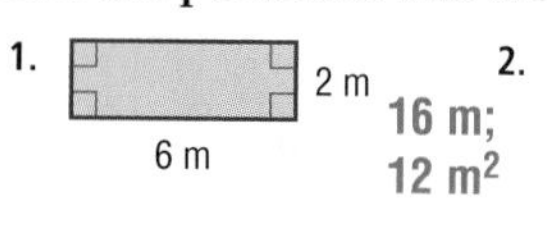

16 m; 12 m^2

2. 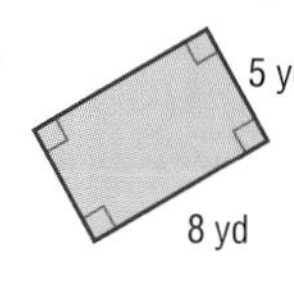

26 yd; 40 yd^2

3. 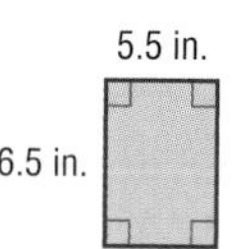

24 in.; 35.75 in^2

4. 

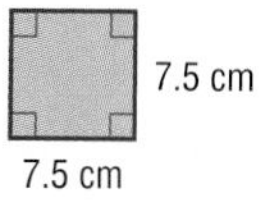

30 cm; 56.25 cm^2

5. rectangle: 3 mm by 5 mm 16 mm; 15 mm^2
6. rectangle: 144 mi by 25 mi 338 mi; 3,600 mi^2
7. square: side length, 75 ft 300 ft; 5,625 ft^2
8. square: side length, 0.75 yd 3 yd; 0.5625 yd^2
9. rectangle: 4.3 cm by 2.7 cm 14 cm; 11.61 cm^2
10. square: side length of 625 m 2,500 m; 390,625 m^2
11. square: side length of 87 km 348 km; 7,569 km^2
12. rectangle: 875.5 mm by 245.3 mm 2,241.6 mm; 214,760.15 mm^2

Prerequisite Skills

Prerequisite Skills 613

11 Plotting Points on a Coordinate Plane

An ordered pair of numbers is used to locate any point on a coordinate plane. The first number is called the *x*-coordinate. The second number is called the *y*-coordinate.

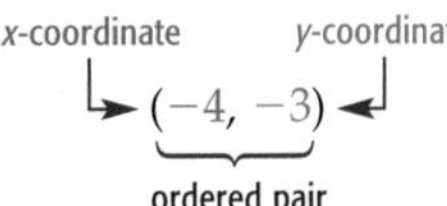

EXAMPLES Identify Ordered Pairs

1 Write the ordered pair that names point *A*.

Step 1 Start at the origin.

Step 2 Move left on the *x*-axis to find the *x*-coordinate of point *A*, which is −1.

Step 3 Move up along the *y*-axis to find the *y*-coordinate which is 4.

The ordered pair for point *A* is (−1, 4).

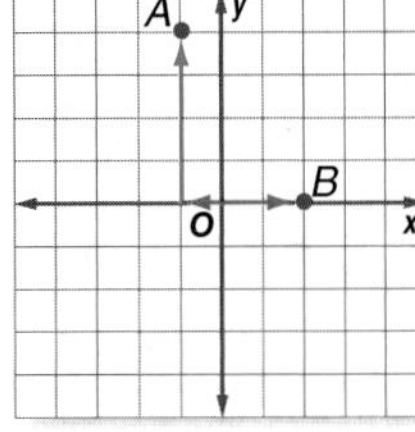

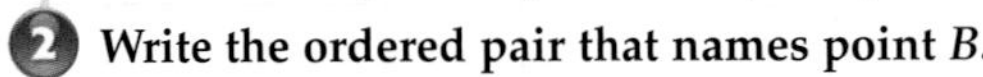

2 Write the ordered pair that names point *B*.

The *x*-coordinate of *B* is 2. Since the point lies on the *x*-axis, its *y*-coordinate is 0.

The ordered pair for point *B* is (2, 0).

EXAMPLE Graph an Ordered Pair

3 Graph and label the point *C*(3, −2) on a coordinate plane.

Step 1 Start at the origin.

Step 2 Since the *x*-coordinate is 3, move 3 units right.

Step 3 Since the *y*-coordinate is −2, move down 2 units. Draw and label a dot.

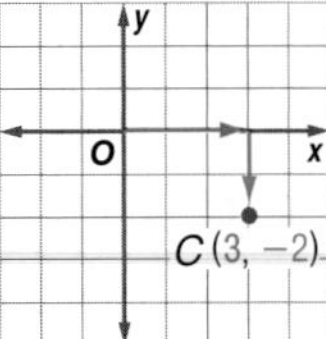

Exercises

Name the ordered pair for the coordinates of each point on the coordinate plane.

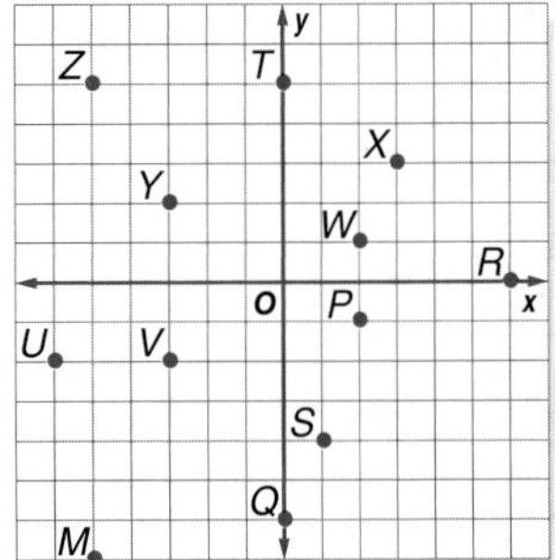

1. *Z* (−5, 5) 2. *X* (3, 3) 3. *W* (2, 1)
4. *Y* (−3, 2) 5. *T* (0, 5) 6. *V* (−3, −2)
7. *U* (−6, −2) 8. *S* (1, −4) 9. *Q* (0, −6)
10. *R* (6, 0) 11. *P* (2, −1) 12. *M* (−5, −7)

13–27. See Answer Appendix.

Graph each point on the same coordinate plane.

13. *A*(4, 7) 14. *C*(1, 0) 15. *B*(0, 7)
16. *E*(−1, −2) 17. *D*(−4, −7) 18. *F*(−10, 3)
19. *G*(9, 9) 20. *J*(7, −8) 21. *K*(−6, 0)
22. *H*(0, −3) 23. *I*(4, 0) 24. *M*(2, 7)
25. *N*(8, −1) 26. *L*(−1, −1) 27. *P*(3, 3)

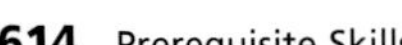

614 Prerequisite Skills

12 Measuring and Drawing Angles

Two rays that have a common endpoint form an **angle**. The common endpoint is called the **vertex**, and the two rays that make up the angle are called the **sides** of the angle.

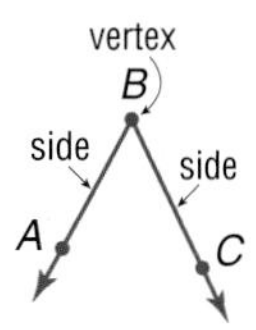

A circle can be divided into 360 equal sections. Each section is one **degree**. You can use a **protractor** to measure an angle in degrees and draw an angle with a given degree measure.

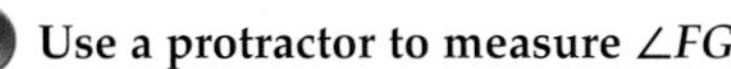

EXAMPLE Measure an Angle

1 Use a protractor to measure $\angle FGH$.

Step 1 Place the center point of the protractor's base on vertex G. Align the straight side with side $\overline{GH}$ so that the marker for 0° is on one of the rays.

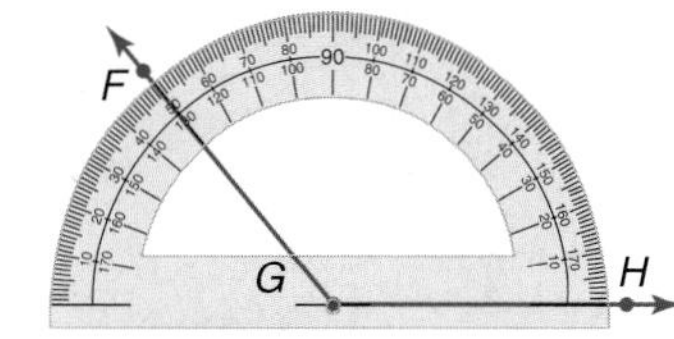

Step 2 Use the scale that begins with 0° at $\overrightarrow{GH}$. Read where the other side of the angle, $\overrightarrow{GF}$, crosses this scale.

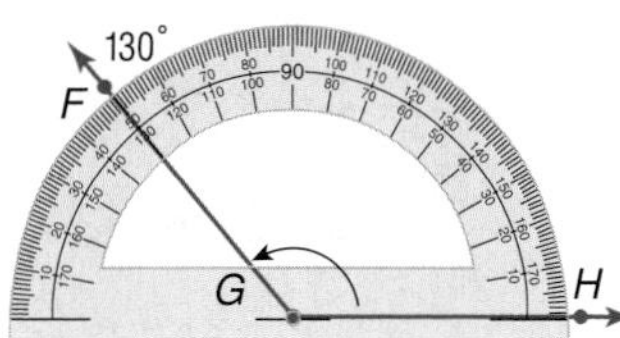

The measure of angle FGH is 130°. Using symbols, $m\angle FGH = 130°$.

EXAMPLE Draw an Angle

2 Draw $\angle X$ having a measure of 75°.

Step 1 Draw a ray. Label the endpoint X.

Step 2 Place the center point of the protractor's base on point X. Align the mark labeled 0 with the ray.

Step 3 Use the scale that begins with 0. Locate the mark labeled 75. Then draw the other side of the angle.

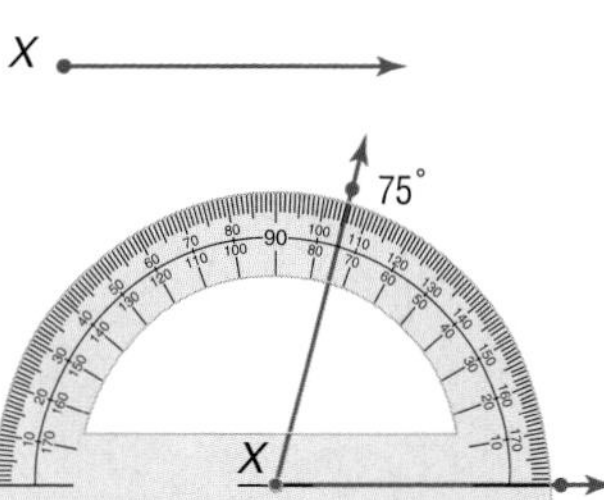

Exercises

Use a protractor to find the measure of each angle.

1. $\angle XZY$ **25°**
2. $\angle SZT$ **15°**
3. $\angle SZY$ **180°**
4. $\angle UZX$ **95°**
5. $\angle TZW$ **125°**
6. $\angle UZV$ **35°**

7–15. See margin.

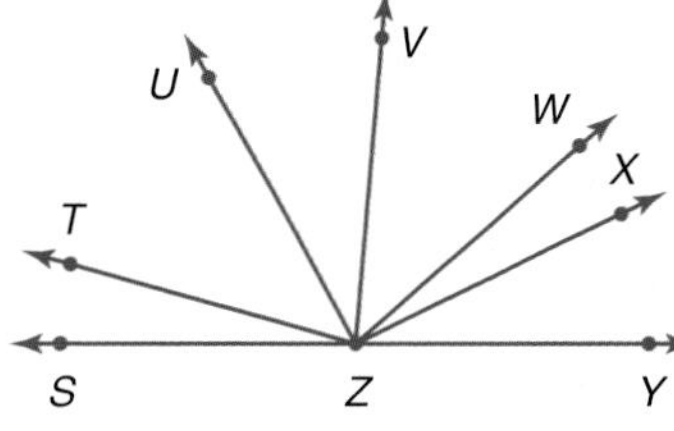

Use a protractor to draw an angle having each measurement.

7. 40°
8. 70°
9. 65°
10. 110°
11. 85°
12. 90°
13. 155°
14. 140°
15. 117°

Answers

7. 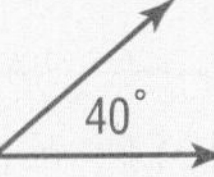

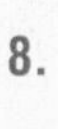

8. 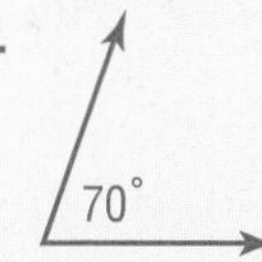

9. 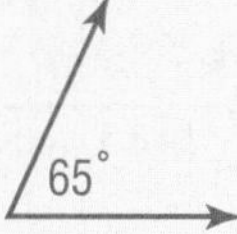

10. 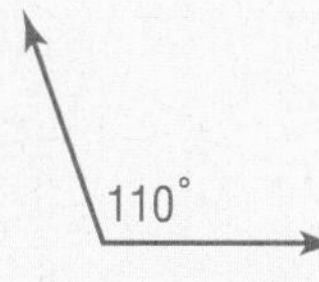

11. 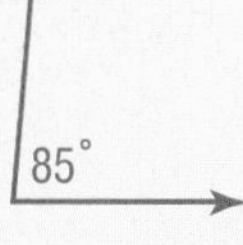

12. 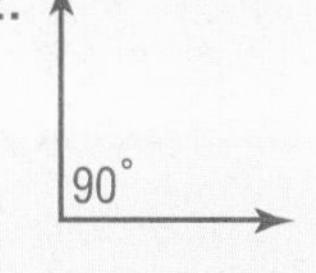

13. 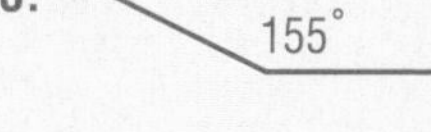

14. 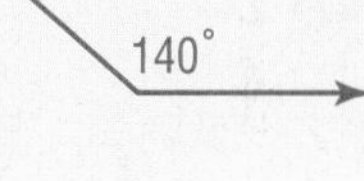

15. 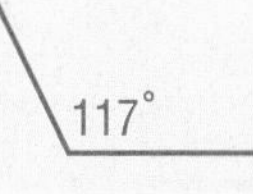

Prerequisite Skills 615

Page 614

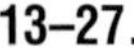

13–27.

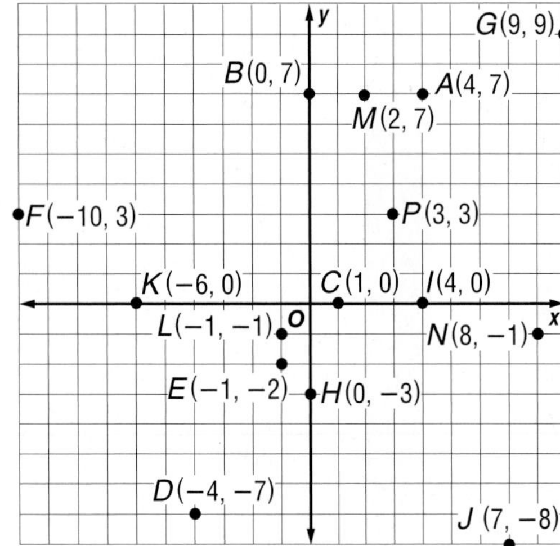

Lesson 1-2

18. Distributive
19. Commutative (×)
20. Associative (+)
21. Commutative (×)
22. Associative (×)
23. Distributive
24. Commutative (×)
25. Additive Identity
26. Multiplicative Identity

Extra Practice

Lesson 1-1

(Pages 6–10)

Use the four-step plan to solve each problem.

1. Joseph is planting bushes around the perimeter of his lawn. If the bushes must be planted 4 feet apart and Joseph's lawn is 64 feet wide and 124 feet long, how many bushes will Joseph need to purchase? **94 bushes**
2. Find the next three numbers in the pattern 1, 3, 7, 15, 31, ... **63, 127, 255**
3. At the bookstore, pencils cost \$0.15 each and erasers cost \$0.25 each. What combination of pencils and erasers can be purchased for a total of \$0.65? **1 pencil, 2 erasers**
4. Cheap Wheels Car Rental rents cars for \$50 per day plus \$0.15 per mile. How much will it cost to rent a car for 2 days and to drive 200 miles? **\$130**
5. Josie wants to fence in her yard. She needs to fence three sides and the house will supply the fourth side. Two of the sides have a length of 25 feet and the third side has a length of 35 feet. If the fencing costs \$10 per foot, how much will it cost Josie to fence in her yard? **\$850**

Lesson 1-2

(Pages 11–15)

Evaluate each expression.

1. $15 - 5 + 9 - 2$ **17**
2. $(5^2 + 2) \div 3$ **9**
3. $12 + 20 \div 4 - 5$ **12**
4. $6 \times 3 \div 9 - 1$ **1**
5. $(4^2 + 2^2) \times 5$ **100**
6. $24 \div 8 - 2$ **1**
7. $\frac{25}{(3^2 - 4)}$ **5**
8. $(15 - 7) \cdot 6 + 2$ **50**
9. $3[15 - (2 + 7) \div 3]$ **36**

Evaluate each expression if $a = 3$, $b = 6$, and $c = 5$.

10. $2a + bc$ **36**
11. ba^2 **54**
12. $\frac{bc}{a}$ **10**
13. $3a + c - 2b$ **2**
14. $(2c + b) \cdot a$ **48**
15. $\frac{2(ac)^2}{b}$ **75**
16. abc **90**
17. $(3b + a)c$ **105**

Name the property shown by each statement. **18–26. See margin.**

18. $2(a + b) = 2a + 2b$
19. $3 \times 5 = 5 \times 3$
20. $(2 + 6) + 5 = 2 + (6 + 5)$
21. $3(4 + 1) = (4 + 1)3$
22. $(7 \times 5)2 = 7(5 \times 2)$
23. $8(2x + 1) = 8(2x) + 8(1)$
24. $5(x + 2) = (x + 2)5$
25. $(3x + 2) + 0 = 3x + 2$
26. $5 \cdot 1 = 5$

Lesson 1-3

(Pages 17–21)

Replace each $\bullet$ with $>$, $<$, or $=$ to make a true sentence.

1. $-3 \bullet 0$ $<$
2. $-1 \bullet -2$ $>$
3. $-5 \bullet -4$ $<$
4. $6 \bullet -7$ $>$
5. $8 \bullet 10$ $<$
6. $-6 \bullet 6$ $<$
7. $-11 \bullet -20$ $>$
8. $-8 \bullet 2$ $<$
9. $-13 \bullet -12$ $<$
10. $|-2| \bullet |5|$ $<$
11. $|13| \bullet |-19|$ $<$
12. $|-6| \bullet |2|$ $>$
13. $|14| \bullet |-14|$ $=$
14. $|0| \bullet |-4|$ $<$
15. $|23| \bullet |-20|$ $>$
16. $|-12| \bullet -12$ $>$

Evaluate each expression.

17. $|-1|$ **1**
18. $|-92|$ **92**
19. $|3|$ **3**
20. $|160 + 32|$ **192**
21. $|80 + 100|$ **180**
22. $|0|$ **0**
23. $|7 - 3|$ **4**
24. $|3| + |-7|$ **10**
25. $|-161|$ **161**
26. $|150|$ **150**
27. $|102| - |-2|$ **100**
28. $|-116|$ **116**

616 Extra Practice

Lesson 1-4

(Pages 23–27)

Add.

1. $-7 + (-7)$ **−14**
2. $-36 + 40$ **4**
3. $18 + (-32)$ **−14**
4. $47 + 12$ **59**
5. $-69 + (-32)$ **−101**
6. $-120 + (-2)$ **−122**
7. $-56 + (-4)$ **−60**
8. $14 + 16$ **30**
9. $-18 + 11$ **−7**
10. $-42 + 29$ **−13**
11. $-13 + (-11)$ **−24**
12. $95 + (-5)$ **90**
13. $-120 + 2$ **−118**
14. $25 + (-25)$ **0**
15. $-4 + 8$ **4**
16. $-9 + (-6)$ **−15**
17. $42 + (-18)$ **24**
18. $-33 + (-12)$ **−45**
19. $7 + (-13) + 6 + (-7)$ **−7**
20. $-6 + 12 + (-20)$ **−14**
21. $4 + 9 + (-14)$ **−1**
22. $-20 + 0 + (-9) + 25$ **−4**
23. $5 + 9 + 3 + (-17)$ **0**
24. $-36 + 40 + (-10)$ **−6**
25. $(-2) + 2 + (-2) + 2$ **0**
26. $6 + (-4) + 9 + (-2)$ **9**
27. $9 + (-7) + 2$ **4**
28. $100 + (-75) + (-20)$ **5**
29. $-12 + 24 + (-12) + 2$ **2**
30. $9 + (-18) + 6 + (-3)$ **−6**

Lesson 1-5

(Pages 28–31)

Subtract.

1. $3 - 7$ **−4**
2. $-5 - 4$ **−9**
3. $-6 - 2$ **−8**
4. $12 - 9$ **3**
5. $0 - (-14)$ **14**
6. $58 - (-10)$ **68**
7. $-41 - 15$ **−56**
8. $-81 - 21$ **−102**
9. $26 - (-14)$ **40**
10. $6 - (-4)$ **10**
11. $63 - 78$ **−15**
12. $-5 - (-9)$ **4**
13. $72 - (-19)$ **91**
14. $-51 - 47$ **−98**
15. $-99 - 1$ **−100**
16. $8 - 13$ **−5**
17. $-2 - 23$ **−25**
18. $-20 - 0$ **−20**
19. $55 - 33$ **22**
20. $84 - (-61)$ **145**
21. $-4 - (-4)$ **0**
22. $-2 - (-3)$ **1**
23. $65 - (-2)$ **67**
24. $0 - (-3)$ **3**
25. $0 - 5$ **−5**
26. $-2 - 6$ **−8**
27. $-4 - 7$ **−11**
28. $-3 - (-3)$ **0**
29. $15 - 6$ **9**
30. $5 - 8$ **−3**

Lesson 1-6

(Pages 34–38)

Multiply.

1. $5(-2)$ **−10**
2. $-11(-5)$ **55**
3. $-5(-5)$ **25**
4. $-12(6)$ **−72**
5. $2(-2)$ **−4**
6. $-3(2)(-4)$ **24**
7. $(-4)(-4)$ **16**
8. $4(21)$ **84**
9. $-50(0)$ **0**
10. $3(-13)$ **−39**
11. $2(2)$ **4**
12. $-2(-2)$ **4**
13. $5(-12)$ **−60**
14. $2(2)(-2)$ **−8**
15. $6(-4)$ **−24**

Divide.

16. $4 \div (-2)$ **−2**
17. $16 \div (-8)$ **−2**
18. $-14 \div (-2)$ **7**
19. $-18 \div 3$ **−6**
20. $-25 \div 5$ **−5**
21. $-56 \div (-8)$ **7**
22. $81 \div 9$ **9**
23. $-55 \div 11$ **−5**
24. $-42 \div (-7)$ **6**
25. $18 \div (-3)$ **−6**
26. $0 \div (-1)$ **0**
27. $-32 \div 8$ **−4**
28. $81 \div (-9)$ **−9**
29. $18 \div (-2)$ **−9**
30. $-21 \div 3$ **−7**

Extra Practice

Extra Practice 617

Lesson 1-7

(Pages 39–42)

Write each verbal phrase as an algebraic expression.

1. 12 more than a number **$12 + n$**
2. 3 less than a number **$n - 3$**
3. a number divided by 4 **$\frac{n}{4}$ or $n \div 4$**
4. a number increased by 7 **$n + 7$**
5. a number decreased by 12 **$n - 12$**
6. 8 times a number **$8n$**
7. 28 multiplied by m **$28m$**
8. 15 divided by a number **$\frac{15}{n}$ or $15 \div n$**
9. 54 divided by n **$\frac{54}{n}$ or $54 \div n$**
10. 18 increased by y **$18 + y$**
11. q decreased by 20 **$q - 20$**
12. n times 41 **$41n$**
13. 5 less than a number **$n - 5$**
14. the product of a number and 15 **$15n$**

Write each verbal sentence as an algebraic equation. **15. $4q - 6 = 18$**

15. 6 less than the product of q and 4 is 18.
16. Twice x is 20. **$2x = 20$**
17. A number increased by 6 is 8. **$n + 6 = 8$**
18. The quotient of a number and 7 is 8. **$\frac{n}{7} = 8$**
19. The difference between a number and 12 is 37. **$n - 12 = 37$**
20. The product of a number and 7 is 42. **$7n = 42$**

Lesson 1-8

(Pages 45–49)

Solve each equation. Check your solution.

1. $g - 3 = 10$ **13**
2. $b + 7 = 12$ **5**
3. $a + 3 = 15$ **12**
4. $r - 3 = 4$ **7**
5. $t + 3 = 21$ **18**
6. $s + 10 = 23$ **13**
7. $9 + n = 13$ **4**
8. $13 + v = 31$ **18**
9. $-4 + b = 12$ **16**
10. $z - 10 = -8$ **2**
11. $-7 = x + 12$ **−19**
12. $7 + g = 91$ **84**
13. $63 + f = 71$ **8**
14. $a + 6 = -9$ **−15**
15. $c - 18 = 13$ **31**
16. $23 = n - 5$ **28**
17. $j - 3 = 7$ **10**
18. $18 = p + 3$ **15**
19. $12 + p = 16$ **4**
20. $25 = y - 50$ **75**
21. $x + 2 = 4$ **2**
22. $r - (-8) = 14$ **6**
23. $m + (-2) = 6$ **8**
24. $5 + q = 12$ **7**
25. $t + 12 = 6$ **−6**
26. $8 + p = 0$ **−8**
27. $12 - x = 8$ **4**
28. $14 + t = 10$ **−4**
29. $x + 5 = 7$ **2**
30. $2 = 3 + x$ **−1**

Lesson 1-9

(Pages 50–53)

Solve each equation. Check your solution.

1. $4x = 36$ **9**
2. $39 = 3y$ **13**
3. $4z = 16$ **4**
4. $\frac{t}{5} = 6$ **30**
5. $100 = 20b$ **5**
6. $8 = \frac{w}{8}$ **64**
7. $10a = 40$ **4**
8. $\frac{s}{9} = 8$ **72**
9. $420 = 5s$ **84**
10. $8k = 72$ **9**
11. $2m = 18$ **9**
12. $\frac{m}{8} = 5$ **40**
13. $\frac{r}{7} = -8$ **−56**
14. $\frac{w}{7} = 8$ **56**
15. $18q = 36$ **2**
16. $9w = 54$ **6**
17. $4 = p \div 4$ **16**
18. $14 = 2p$ **7**
19. $12 = 3t$ **4**
20. $\frac{m}{4} = 12$ **48**
21. $6h = 12$ **2**
22. $-2a = -8$ **4**
23. $0 = 6r$ **0**
24. $\frac{y}{12} = -6$ **−72**
25. $3m = -15$ **−5**
26. $\frac{c}{-4} = 10$ **−40**
27. $-6f = -36$ **6**
28. $81 = -9w$ **−9**
29. $6r = 42$ **7**
30. $\frac{x}{-2} = -15$ **30**

618 Extra Practice

Lesson 2-1

(Pages 62–66)

Write each fraction or mixed number as a decimal.

1. $\frac{2}{5}$ **0.4**
2. $2\frac{3}{11}$ **$2.\overline{27}$**
3. $-\frac{3}{4}$ **−0.75**
4. $\frac{5}{7}$ **$0.\overline{714285}$**
5. $\frac{3}{4}$ **0.75**
6. $-\frac{2}{3}$ **$-0.\overline{6}$**
7. $\frac{7}{11}$ **$0.\overline{63}$**
8. $\frac{1}{2}$ **0.5**
9. $\frac{5}{6}$ **$0.8\overline{3}$**
10. $1\frac{3}{5}$ **1.6**
11. $-2\frac{1}{4}$ **−2.25**
12. $\frac{8}{9}$ **$0.\overline{8}$**

Write each decimal as a fraction or mixed number in simplest form.

13. 0.5 **$\frac{1}{2}$**
14. $0.\overline{8}$ **$\frac{8}{9}$**
15. 0.32 **$\frac{8}{25}$**
16. −0.75 **$-\frac{3}{4}$**
17. $2.\overline{2}$ **$2\frac{2}{9}$**
18. $0.\overline{38}$ **$\frac{38}{99}$**
19. −0.486 **$-\frac{243}{500}$**
20. 20.08 **$20\frac{2}{25}$**
21. −9.36 **$-9\frac{9}{25}$**
22. $10.1\overline{8}$ **$10\frac{17}{90}$**
23. 1.24 **$1\frac{6}{25}$**
24. $-5.\overline{7}$ **$-5\frac{7}{9}$**

Lesson 2-2

(Pages 67–70)

Replace each ● with <, >, or = to make a true sentence.

1. −5.6 ● 4.2 <
2. 4.256 ● 4.25 >
3. 0.233 ● $0.\overline{23}$ >
4. $\frac{5}{7}$ ● $\frac{2}{5}$ >
5. $\frac{6}{7}$ ● $\frac{7}{9}$ >
6. $\frac{2}{3}$ ● $\frac{2}{5}$ >
7. $\frac{3}{8}$ ● 0.375 =
8. $-\frac{1}{2}$ ● 0.5 <
9. 12.56 ● $12\frac{3}{8}$ >
10. −0.25 ● −0.26 >
11. 1.31 ● $1.\overline{31}$ <
12. $\frac{3}{5}$ ● $\frac{2}{3}$ <

Order each set of rational numbers from least to greatest.

13. 0.24, 0.2, 0.245, 2.24, 0.25
14. $0.\overline{3}$, 0.3, $0.3\overline{4}$, $0.\overline{34}$, 0.33
15. $\frac{2}{5}, \frac{2}{3}, \frac{2}{7}, \frac{2}{9}, \frac{2}{1}$ **$\frac{2}{9}, \frac{2}{7}, \frac{2}{5}, \frac{2}{3}, \frac{2}{1}$**
16. $\frac{1}{2}, \frac{5}{7}, \frac{2}{9}, \frac{8}{9}, \frac{6}{6}$ **$\frac{2}{9}, \frac{1}{2}, \frac{5}{7}, \frac{8}{9}, \frac{6}{6}$**
17. 0.25, 0.2, 0.02, 0.251, $\frac{253}{1,000}$
18. $\frac{3}{10}, \frac{3}{2}, \frac{3}{5}, \frac{3}{1}, \frac{3}{8}, \frac{3}{7}, \frac{3}{4}$ **$\frac{3}{10}, \frac{3}{8}, \frac{3}{7}, \frac{3}{5}, \frac{3}{4}, \frac{3}{2}, \frac{3}{1}$**
19. $\frac{3}{5}, \frac{2}{3}$, 0.61, 0.65, $\frac{33}{50}$ **$\frac{3}{5}$, 0.61, 0.65, $\frac{33}{50}, \frac{2}{3}$**
20. $-\frac{3}{5}, -\frac{2}{3}, -\frac{1}{2}, -\frac{3}{4}, -\frac{5}{6}$ **$-\frac{5}{6}, -\frac{3}{4}, -\frac{2}{3}, -\frac{3}{5}, -\frac{1}{2}$**
21. $\frac{4}{9}$, 0.4, 0.44, $\frac{3}{5}$ **0.4, 0.44, $\frac{4}{9}, \frac{3}{5}$**
22. 7.5, $7\frac{2}{3}$, $6\frac{5}{6}$, 6.8 **6.8, $6\frac{5}{6}$, 7.5, $7\frac{2}{3}$**
23. $-\frac{2}{3}, \frac{1}{3}$, 0.1, $\frac{5}{6}$ **$-\frac{2}{3}$, 0.1, $\frac{1}{3}, \frac{5}{6}$**
24. −0.5, 0.5, 0, 0.35, −0.51 **−0.51, −0.5, 0, 0.35, 0.5**

13. **0.2, 0.24, 0.245, 0.25, 2.24** **14.** **0.3, 0.33, $0.\overline{3}$, $0.\overline{34}$, $0.3\overline{4}$** **17.** **0.02, 0.2, 0.25, 0.251, $\frac{253}{1,000}$**

Lesson 2-3

(Pages 71–75)

Multiply. Write in simplest form.

1. $\frac{2}{11} \cdot \frac{3}{4}$ **$\frac{3}{22}$**
2. $4\left(-\frac{7}{8}\right)$ **$-3\frac{1}{2}$**
3. $-\frac{4}{7} \cdot \frac{3}{5}$ **$-\frac{12}{35}$**
4. $\frac{6}{7}\left(-\frac{7}{12}\right)$ **$-\frac{1}{2}$**
5. $\frac{7}{8} \cdot \frac{1}{3}$ **$\frac{7}{24}$**
6. $\frac{3}{4} \cdot \frac{4}{5}$ **$\frac{3}{5}$**
7. $-1\frac{1}{2} \cdot \frac{2}{3}$ **−1**
8. $\frac{5}{6} \cdot \frac{6}{7}$ **$\frac{5}{7}$**
9. $8\left(-2\frac{1}{4}\right)$ **−18**
10. $-3\frac{3}{4} \cdot \frac{8}{9}$ **$-3\frac{1}{3}$**
11. $\frac{10}{21}\left(-\frac{7}{8}\right)$ **$-\frac{5}{12}$**
12. $-1\frac{4}{5}\left(-\frac{5}{6}\right)$ **$1\frac{1}{2}$**
13. $5\frac{1}{4} \cdot 6\frac{2}{3}$ **35**
14. $-8\frac{3}{4} \cdot 4\frac{2}{5}$ **$-38\frac{1}{2}$**
15. $6 \cdot 8\frac{2}{3}$ **52**
16. $\left(\frac{3}{5}\right)\left(\frac{3}{5}\right)$ **$\frac{9}{25}$**
17. $-4\frac{1}{5}\left(-3\frac{1}{3}\right)$ **14**
18. $-8\left(\frac{3}{4}\right)$ **−6**
19. $3\frac{2}{3}\left(-3\frac{1}{2}\right)$ **$-12\frac{5}{6}$**
20. $\left(-\frac{2}{5}\right)\left(-\frac{2}{5}\right)$ **$\frac{4}{25}$**
21. $4\frac{1}{2}\left(-1\frac{1}{3}\right)$ **−6**
22. $-5\left(-3\frac{1}{5}\right)$ **16**
23. $4\frac{1}{3} \cdot 1\frac{1}{2}$ **$6\frac{1}{2}$**
24. $-5\left(3\frac{1}{3}\right)$ **$-16\frac{2}{3}$**
25. $\frac{4}{5} \cdot \frac{7}{6}$ **$\frac{14}{15}$**
26. $-\frac{3}{8} \cdot \frac{7}{9}$ **$-\frac{7}{24}$**
27. $-1\frac{3}{4}\left(-2\frac{1}{7}\right)$ **$3\frac{3}{4}$**
28. $-8\left(5\frac{1}{4}\right)$ **−42**

Extra Practice

Extra Practice 619

Lesson 2-4

(Pages 76–80)

Name the multiplicative inverse of each number.

1. 3 **$\frac{1}{3}$**
2. -5 **$-\frac{1}{5}$**
3. $\frac{2}{3}$ **$\frac{3}{2}$**
4. $2\frac{1}{8}$ **$\frac{8}{17}$**
5. $\frac{1}{15}$ **15**
6. -8 **$-\frac{1}{8}$**
7. $1\frac{1}{3}$ **$\frac{3}{4}$**
8. $-\frac{4}{5}$ **$-\frac{5}{4}$**

Divide. Write in simplest form.

9. $\frac{2}{3} \div \frac{3}{4}$ **$\frac{8}{9}$**
10. $-\frac{4}{9} \div \frac{5}{6}$ **$-\frac{8}{15}$**
11. $\frac{7}{12} \div \frac{3}{8}$ **$1\frac{5}{9}$**
12. $\frac{5}{18} \div \frac{2}{9}$ **$1\frac{1}{4}$**
13. $\frac{1}{3} \div 4$ **$\frac{1}{12}$**
14. $5\frac{1}{4} \div \left(-2\frac{1}{2}\right)$ **$-2\frac{1}{10}$**
15. $-6 \div \left(-\frac{4}{7}\right)$ **$10\frac{1}{2}$**
16. $-6\frac{3}{8} \div \frac{1}{4}$ **$-25\frac{1}{2}$**
17. $\frac{6}{7} \div \frac{3}{5}$ **$1\frac{3}{7}$**
18. $3\frac{1}{3} \div (-4)$ **$-\frac{5}{6}$**
19. $2\frac{5}{12} \div 7\frac{1}{3}$ **$\frac{29}{88}$**
20. $\frac{5}{6} \div 1\frac{1}{9}$ **$\frac{3}{4}$**
21. $\frac{3}{8} \div (-6)$ **$-\frac{1}{16}$**
22. $\frac{5}{8} \div \frac{1}{6}$ **$3\frac{3}{4}$**
23. $4\frac{1}{4} \div 6\frac{3}{4}$ **$\frac{17}{27}$**
24. $4\frac{1}{6} \div 3\frac{1}{8}$ **$1\frac{1}{3}$**
25. $8 \div \left(-1\frac{4}{5}\right)$ **$-4\frac{4}{9}$**
26. $-5 \div \frac{2}{7}$ **$-17\frac{1}{2}$**
27. $\frac{3}{5} \div \frac{6}{7}$ **$\frac{7}{10}$**
28. $4\frac{8}{9} \div \left(-2\frac{2}{3}\right)$ **$-1\frac{5}{6}$**
29. $8\frac{1}{6} \div 3$ **$2\frac{13}{18}$**
30. $-\frac{3}{4} \div 9$ **$-\frac{1}{12}$**
31. $1\frac{11}{14} \div 2\frac{1}{2}$ **$\frac{5}{7}$**
32. $-2\frac{1}{4} \div \frac{4}{5}$ **$-2\frac{13}{16}$**

Lesson 2-5

(Pages 82–85)

Add or subtract. Write in simplest form.

1. $\frac{17}{21} + \left(-\frac{13}{21}\right)$ **$\frac{4}{21}$**
2. $\frac{5}{11} + \frac{6}{11}$ **1**
3. $-\frac{8}{13} + \left(-\frac{11}{13}\right)$ **$-1\frac{6}{13}$**
4. $-\frac{7}{12} + \frac{5}{12}$ **$-\frac{1}{6}$**
5. $\frac{13}{28} - \frac{9}{28}$ **$\frac{1}{7}$**
6. $-1\frac{2}{9} - \frac{7}{9}$ **-2**
7. $\frac{15}{16} + \frac{13}{16}$ **$1\frac{3}{4}$**
8. $2\frac{1}{3} - \frac{2}{3}$ **$1\frac{2}{3}$**
9. $-\frac{4}{35} - \left(-\frac{17}{35}\right)$ **$\frac{13}{35}$**
10. $\frac{3}{8} + \left(-\frac{5}{8}\right)$ **$-\frac{1}{4}$**
11. $\frac{8}{15} - \frac{2}{15}$ **$\frac{2}{5}$**
12. $-2\frac{4}{7} - \frac{3}{7}$ **-3**
13. $-\frac{29}{9} - \left(-\frac{26}{9}\right)$ **$-\frac{1}{3}$**
14. $2\frac{3}{5} + 7\frac{3}{5}$ **$10\frac{1}{5}$**
15. $\frac{5}{18} - \frac{13}{18}$ **$-\frac{4}{9}$**
16. $-2\frac{2}{7} + \left(-1\frac{6}{7}\right)$ **$-4\frac{1}{7}$**
17. $-\frac{3}{10} + \frac{7}{10}$ **$\frac{2}{5}$**
18. $\frac{4}{11} + \frac{9}{11}$ **$1\frac{2}{11}$**
19. $\frac{1}{8} + 1\frac{7}{8}$ **2**
20. $\frac{5}{6} - \frac{7}{6}$ **$-\frac{1}{3}$**
21. $5 - 3\frac{5}{7}$ **$1\frac{2}{7}$**
22. $-3 - 4\frac{5}{8}$ **$-7\frac{5}{8}$**
23. $5\frac{3}{7} + 2\frac{6}{7}$ **$8\frac{2}{7}$**
24. $-9\frac{3}{4} - \left(-2\frac{3}{4}\right)$ **-7**
25. $4\frac{5}{9} - 1\frac{2}{9}$ **$3\frac{1}{3}$**
26. $2\frac{5}{12} - 8\frac{7}{12}$ **$-6\frac{1}{6}$**
27. $-5\frac{1}{4} + 1\frac{3}{4}$ **$-3\frac{1}{2}$**
28. $6\frac{1}{5} - 2\frac{4}{5}$ **$3\frac{2}{5}$**

Lesson 2-6

(Pages 88–91)

Add or subtract. Write in simplest form.

1. $\frac{7}{12} + \frac{7}{24}$ **$\frac{7}{8}$**
2. $-\frac{3}{4} + \frac{7}{8}$ **$\frac{1}{8}$**
3. $\frac{2}{5} + \left(-\frac{2}{7}\right)$ **$\frac{4}{35}$**
4. $-\frac{3}{5} - \left(-\frac{5}{6}\right)$ **$\frac{7}{30}$**
5. $\frac{5}{24} - \frac{3}{8}$ **$-\frac{1}{6}$**
6. $-\frac{7}{12} - \frac{3}{4}$ **$-1\frac{1}{3}$**
7. $-\frac{3}{8} + \left(-\frac{4}{5}\right)$ **$-1\frac{7}{40}$**
8. $\frac{2}{15} + \left(-\frac{3}{10}\right)$ **$-\frac{1}{6}$**
9. $-\frac{2}{9} - \left(-\frac{2}{3}\right)$ **$\frac{4}{9}$**
10. $-\frac{7}{15} - \frac{5}{12}$ **$-\frac{53}{60}$**
11. $\frac{3}{8} + \frac{7}{12}$ **$\frac{23}{24}$**
12. $-2\frac{1}{4} + \left(-1\frac{1}{3}\right)$ **$-3\frac{7}{12}$**
13. $3\frac{2}{5} - 3\frac{1}{4}$ **$\frac{3}{20}$**
14. $\frac{3}{4} + \left(-\frac{4}{15}\right)$ **$\frac{29}{60}$**
15. $-1\frac{2}{3} + 4\frac{3}{4}$ **$3\frac{1}{12}$**
16. $-\frac{1}{8} - 2\frac{1}{2}$ **$-2\frac{5}{8}$**
17. $3\frac{2}{5} - 1\frac{1}{3}$ **$2\frac{1}{15}$**
18. $5\frac{1}{3} + \left(-8\frac{3}{7}\right)$ **$-3\frac{2}{21}$**
19. $\frac{3}{5} - \frac{2}{3}$ **$-\frac{1}{15}$**
20. $1\frac{1}{3} - 2\frac{5}{6}$ **$-1\frac{1}{2}$**
21. $2\frac{1}{2} - \frac{3}{4}$ **$1\frac{3}{4}$**
22. $5\frac{2}{3} + 3\frac{5}{6}$ **$9\frac{1}{2}$**
23. $-5\frac{1}{7} - 3\frac{1}{5}$ **$-8\frac{12}{35}$**
24. $-8\frac{1}{2} + 1\frac{2}{3}$ **$-6\frac{5}{6}$**
25. $5\frac{3}{4} - 8\frac{1}{3}$ **$-2\frac{7}{12}$**
26. $1\frac{3}{4} + 3\frac{5}{8}$ **$5\frac{3}{8}$**
27. $4\frac{1}{2} - \frac{5}{7}$ **$3\frac{11}{14}$**
28. $3\frac{2}{3} + 9\frac{3}{4}$ **$13\frac{5}{12}$**

620 Extra Practice

Lesson 2-7

(Pages 92–95)

Solve each equation. Check your solution.

1. $434 = -31y$ **−14**
2. $6x = -4.2$ **−0.7**
3. $\frac{3}{4}a = -12$ **−16**
4. $-10 = \frac{b}{-7}$ **70**
5. $7.2 = \frac{3}{4}c$ **9.6**
6. $r + 0.4 = 1.4$ **1**
7. $-2.4n = 7.2$ **−3**
8. $7 = \frac{1}{2}d$ **14**
9. $n - 0.64 = -5.44$ **−4.8**
10. $\frac{t}{3} = 2$ **6**
11. $\frac{3}{8} = \frac{1}{2}x$ **$\frac{3}{4}$**
12. $\frac{1}{2}h = -14$ **−28**
13. $k - 1.18 = 1.58$ **2.76**
14. $4\frac{1}{2}s = -30$ **$-6\frac{2}{3}$**
15. $\frac{2}{3}f = \frac{8}{15}$ **$\frac{4}{5}$**
16. $\frac{2}{3}m = 22$ **33**
17. $\frac{2}{3}g = 4\frac{5}{6}$ **$7\frac{1}{4}$**
18. $7 = \frac{1}{3}v$ **21**
19. $\frac{g}{1.2} = -6$ **−7.2**
20. $z - 4\frac{5}{8} = 15\frac{3}{8}$ **20**
21. $-12 = \frac{1}{5}j$ **−60**
22. $a + 3.2 = 6.5$ **3.3**
23. $q - \frac{1}{5} = \frac{2}{3}$ **$\frac{13}{15}$**
24. $3.5z = 7$ **2**
25. $2.5x = \frac{1}{2}$ **$\frac{1}{5}$**
26. $c - 3 = 5\frac{2}{3}$ **$8\frac{2}{3}$**
27. $\frac{2}{3}x = \frac{5}{6}$ **$1\frac{1}{4}$**

Lesson 2-8

(Pages 98–101)

Write each expression using exponents.

1. $4 \cdot 4 \cdot 4 \cdot 4$ **4^4**
2. $3 \cdot 3$ **3^2**
3. $7 \cdot 7 \cdot 7 \cdot 7 \cdot 7 \cdot 7$ **7^6**
4. $4 \cdot 4 \cdot 4 \cdot 4 \cdot 4 \cdot 5 \cdot 5 \cdot 5 \cdot 5 \cdot 5 \cdot 5 \cdot 5 \cdot 5$ **$4^5 \cdot 5^8$**
5. $x \cdot y \cdot y \cdot y \cdot y \cdot x \cdot x \cdot x \cdot y \cdot x$ **$x^5 \cdot y^5$**
6. $b \cdot b \cdot b \cdot b \cdot c \cdot c \cdot c \cdot c \cdot c \cdot c$ **$b^4 \cdot c^6$**
7. $3 \cdot 2 \cdot 5 \cdot 5 \cdot 5 \cdot 2 \cdot 2 \cdot 2 \cdot 3 \cdot 5$ **$2^4 \cdot 3^2 \cdot 5^4$**
8. $a \cdot a \cdot a \cdot b \cdot b \cdot b \cdot a \cdot a \cdot a \cdot b$ **$a^6 \cdot b^4$**
9. $6 \cdot 6 \cdot 6 \cdot 6 \cdot 6 \cdot 6 \cdot 6 \cdot 6$ **6^8**
10. $x \cdot x \cdot x \cdot x \cdot x \cdot x \cdot x \cdot x \cdot x \cdot x$ **x^{10}**
11. $a \cdot b \cdot b \cdot b \cdot b \cdot b \cdot b \cdot b$ **$a \cdot b^7$**

Evaluate each expression.

12. 4^3 **64**
13. 6^2 **36**
14. 2^6 **64**
15. $5^2 \cdot 6^2$ **900**
16. $3 \cdot 2^4$ **48**
17. $10^4 \cdot 3^2$ **90,000**
18. $5^3 \cdot 1^9$ **125**
19. $2^2 \cdot 2^4$ **64**
20. $2 \cdot 3^2 \cdot 4^2$ **288**
21. 7^3 **343**
22. $2^2 \cdot 5^2$ **100**
23. $3^5 \cdot 4^2$ **3,888**
24. $7^2 \cdot 3^4$ **3,969**
25. 3^{-3} **$\frac{1}{27}$**
26. 2^{-4} **$\frac{1}{16}$**
27. 5^{-2} **$\frac{1}{25}$**

Lesson 2-9

(Pages 104–107)

Write each number in standard form.

1. 4.5×10^3 **4,500**
2. 2×10^4 **20,000**
3. 1.725896×10^6 **1,725,896**
4. 9.61×10^2 **961**
5. 1×10^7 **10,000,000**
6. 8.256×10^8 **825,600,000**
7. 5.26×10^4 **52,600**
8. 3.25×10^2 **325**
9. 6.79×10^5 **679,000**
10. 3.1×10^{-4} **0.00031**
11. 2.51×10^{-2} **0.0251**
12. 6×10^{-1} **0.6**
13. 2.15×10^{-3} **0.00215**
14. 3.14×10^{-6} **0.00000314**
15. 1×10^{-2} **0.01**

Write each number in scientific notation.

16. 720 **7.2×10^2**
17. 7,560 **7.56×10^3**
18. 892 **8.92×10^2**
19. 1,400 **1.4×10^3**
20. 91,256 **9.1256×10^4**
21. 51,000 **5.1×10^4**
22. 0.012 **1.2×10^{-2}**
23. 0.0002 **2×10^{-4}**
24. 0.054 **5.4×10^{-2}**
25. 0.231 **2.31×10^{-1}**
26. 0.0000056 **5.6×10^{-6}**
27. 0.000123 **1.23×10^{-4}**

Extra Practice

Extra Practice 621

Lesson 3-3

10. 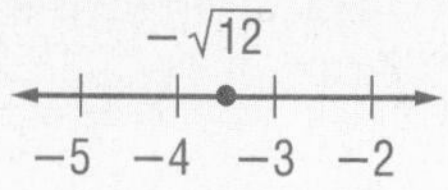

11. 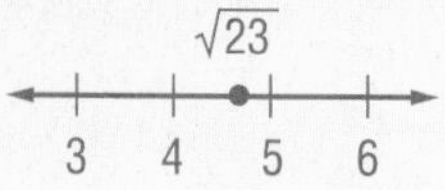

12. 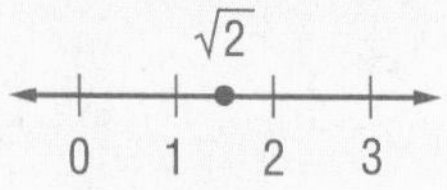

13. 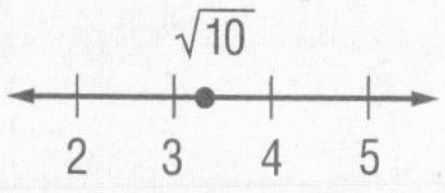

14. 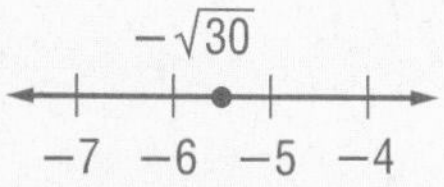

15. 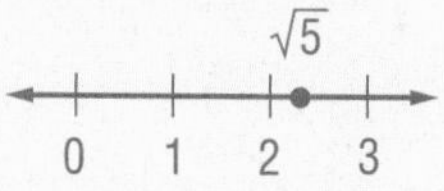

16. 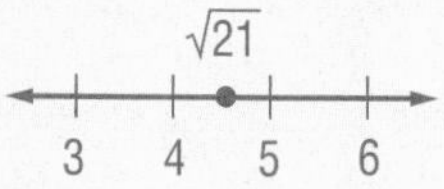

17. 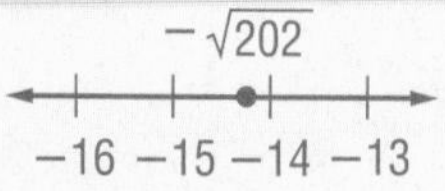

18. 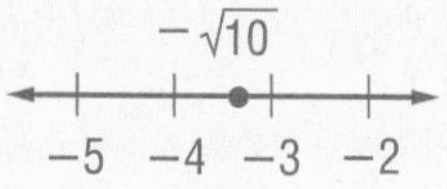

Lesson 3-6

4. 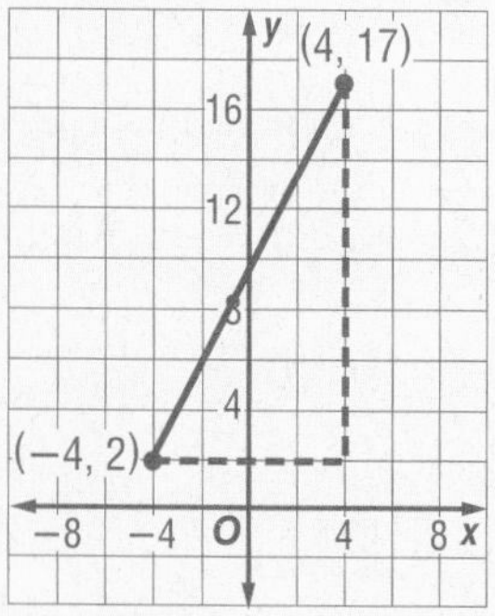

5. 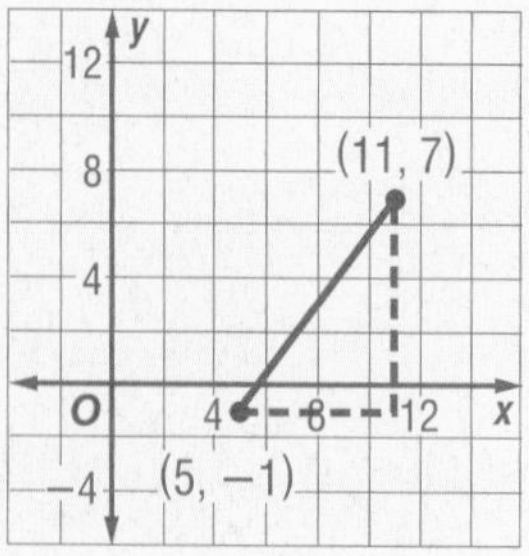

Lesson 3-1

(Pages 116–119)

Find each square root.

1. $\sqrt{9}$ **3**
2. $\sqrt{81}$ **9**
3. $-\sqrt{625}$ **−25**
4. $\sqrt{36}$ **6**
5. $-\sqrt{169}$ **−13**
6. $\sqrt{144}$ **12**
7. $\sqrt{961}$ **31**
8. $\sqrt{324}$ **18**
9. $-\sqrt{225}$ **−15**
10. $-\sqrt{4}$ **−2**
11. $\sqrt{529}$ **23**
12. $-\sqrt{484}$ **−22**
13. $\sqrt{196}$ **14**
14. $\sqrt{729}$ **27**
15. $\sqrt{289}$ **17**
16. $-\sqrt{16}$ **−4**
17. $\sqrt{1,024}$ **32**
18. $\sqrt{0.16}$ **0.4**
19. $\sqrt{0.04}$ **0.2**
20. $\sqrt{2.25}$ **1.5**
21. $\sqrt{0.01}$ **0.1**
22. $-\sqrt{0.09}$ **−0.3**
23. $\sqrt{0.49}$ **0.7**
24. $\sqrt{1.69}$ **1.3**
25. $\sqrt{0.36}$ **0.6**
26. $\sqrt{\frac{289}{10,000}}$ $\mathbf{\frac{17}{100}}$
27. $\sqrt{\frac{169}{121}}$ $\mathbf{\frac{13}{11}}$
28. $-\sqrt{\frac{4}{9}}$ $\mathbf{-\frac{2}{3}}$
29. $-\sqrt{\frac{81}{64}}$ $\mathbf{-\frac{9}{8}}$
30. $\sqrt{\frac{25}{81}}$ $\mathbf{\frac{5}{9}}$

Lesson 3-2

(Pages 120–122)

Estimate to the nearest whole number.

1. $\sqrt{229}$ **15**
2. $\sqrt{63}$ **8**
3. $\sqrt{290}$ **17**
4. $\sqrt{27}$ **5**
5. $\sqrt{333}$ **18**
6. $\sqrt{23}$ **5**
7. $\sqrt{96}$ **10**
8. $\sqrt{19}$ **4**
9. $\sqrt{200}$ **14**
10. $\sqrt{76}$ **9**
11. $\sqrt{17}$ **4**
12. $\sqrt{34}$ **6**
13. $\sqrt{137}$ **12**
14. $\sqrt{540}$ **23**
15. $\sqrt{165}$ **13**
16. $\sqrt{326}$ **18**
17. $\sqrt{52}$ **7**
18. $\sqrt{37}$ **6**
19. $\sqrt{79}$ **9**
20. $\sqrt{89}$ **9**
21. $\sqrt{71}$ **8**
22. $\sqrt{117}$ **11**
23. $\sqrt{410}$ **20**
24. $\sqrt{47}$ **7**
25. $\sqrt{1.30}$ **1**
26. $\sqrt{8.4}$ **3**
27. $\sqrt{18.35}$ **4**
28. $\sqrt{25.70}$ **5**
29. $\sqrt{1.41}$ **1**
30. $\sqrt{15.3}$ **4**

Lesson 3-3

(Pages 125–129)

Name all sets of numbers to which each real number belongs.

1. 6.5 **rational**
2. $\sqrt{25}$ **whole, integer, rational**
3. $\sqrt{3}$ **irrational**
4. −7.2 **rational**
5. $-0.\overline{61}$ **rational**
6. $\frac{1}{2}$ **rational**
7. $\frac{16}{4}$ **whole, integer, rational**
8. −102.1 **rational**
9. $\sqrt{29}$ **irrational**

Estimate each square root. Then graph the square root on a number line. **10–18. See margin for number lines.**

10. $-\sqrt{12}$ **−3.5**
11. $\sqrt{23}$ **4.8**
12. $\sqrt{2}$ **1.4**
13. $\sqrt{10}$ **3.2**
14. $-\sqrt{30}$ **−5.5**
15. $\sqrt{5}$ **2.2**
16. $\sqrt{21}$ **4.6**
17. $-\sqrt{202}$ **−14.2**
18. $-\sqrt{10}$ **−3.2**

Replace each ● with <, >, or = to make a true sentence.

19. $\sqrt{7}$ ● 2.8 $<$
20. $2\frac{1}{3}$ ● $2.\overline{3}$ $=$
21. $\sqrt{121}$ ● 11 $=$
22. 5.6 ● $\sqrt{30}$ $>$
23. 9.45 ● $9.\overline{4}$ $>$
24. $\sqrt{5}$ ● 2.23 $>$
25. $\sqrt{6.25}$ ● $2\frac{1}{2}$ $=$
26. $5\frac{1}{3}$ ● $\sqrt{30}$ $<$
27. $4\frac{2}{3}$ ● $\sqrt{22}$ $<$

622 Extra Practice

6. 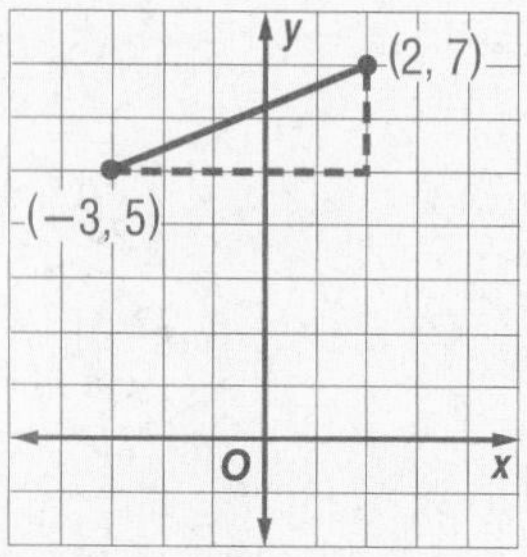

7. 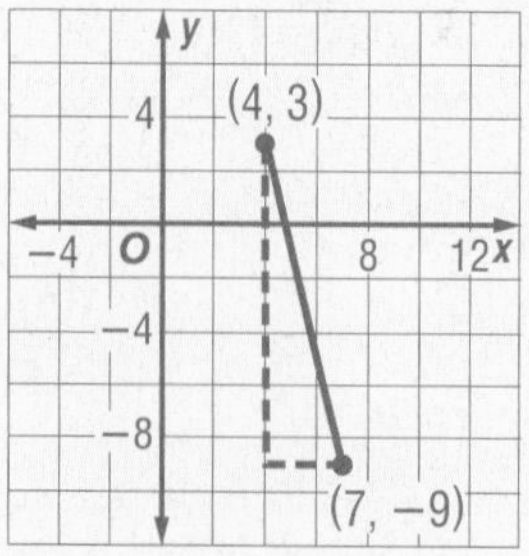

8. 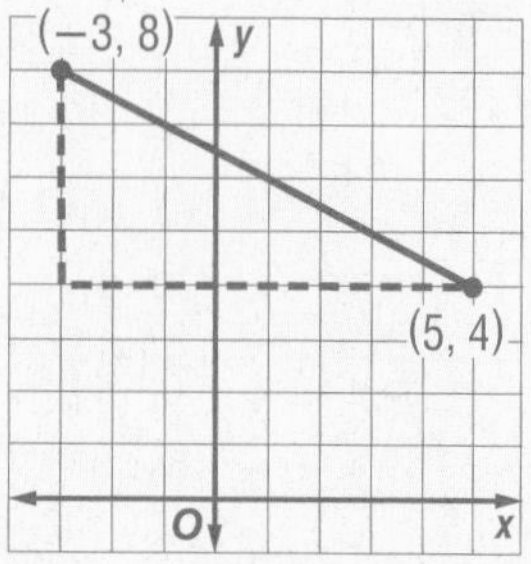

Lesson 3-4

(Pages 132–136)

Write an equation you could use to find the length of the missing side of each right triangle. Then find the missing length. Round to the nearest tenth if necessary. 4. $c^2 = 6^2 + 5^2$; 7.8 cm 5. $c^2 = 12^2 + 12^2$; 17.0 ft 6. $c^2 = 8^2 + 6^2$; 10 in.

1. 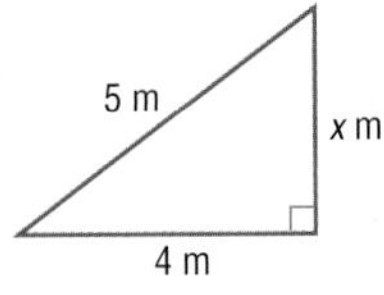

$5^2 = 4^2 + x^2$; 3 m

2. 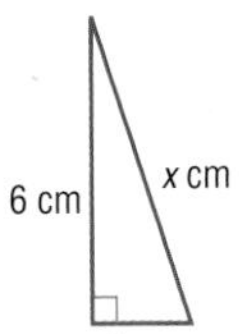 $x^2 = 6^2 + 2^2$; 6.3 cm
6 cm, x cm, 2 cm

3. 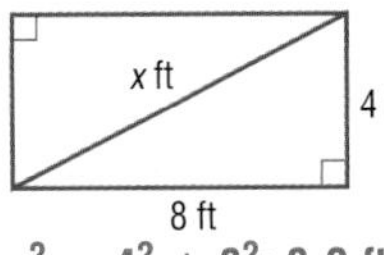 x ft, 4 ft, 8 ft
$x^2 = 4^2 + 8^2$; 8.9 ft

4. a, 6 cm; b, 5 cm
5. a, 12 ft; b, 12 ft
6. a, 8 in.; b, 6 in.
7. a, 20 m; c, 25 m $25^2 = 20^2 + b^2$; 15 m
8. a, 9 mm; c, 14 mm $14^2 = 9^2 + b^2$; 10.7 mm
9. b, 15 m; c, 20 m $20^2 = a^2 + 15^2$; 13.2 m

Determine whether each triangle with sides of given lengths is a right triangle.

10. 15 m, 8 m, 17 m yes
11. 7 yd, 5 yd, 9 yd no
12. 5 in., 12 in., 13 in. yes
13. 9 in., 12 in., 16 in. no
14. 10 ft, 24 ft, 26 ft yes
15. 2 ft, 2 ft, 3 ft no

Lesson 3-5

(Pages 137–140)

Write an equation that can be used to answer each question. Then solve. Round to the nearest tenth if necessary.

1. How far apart are the boats? $d^2 = 7^2 + 3^2$; 7.6 mi

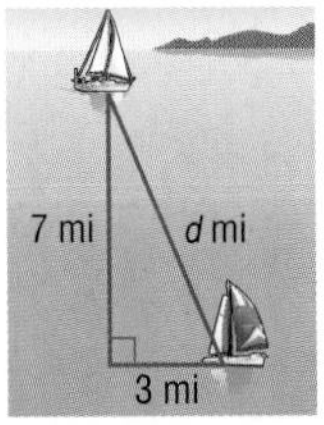

7 mi, d mi, 3 mi

2. How high does the ladder reach?

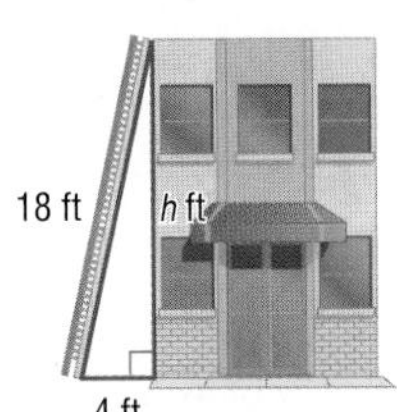

$18^2 = 4^2 + h^2$; 17.5 ft

3. How long is each rafter?

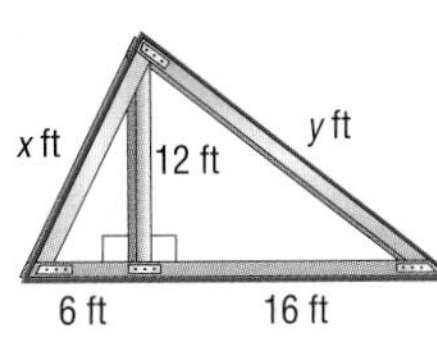

$x^2 = 6^2 + 12^2$; 13.4 ft
$y^2 = 16^2 + 12^2$; 20 ft

Lesson 3-6

(Pages 142–145)

Find the distance between each pair of points whose coordinates are given. Round to the nearest tenth if necessary.

1. 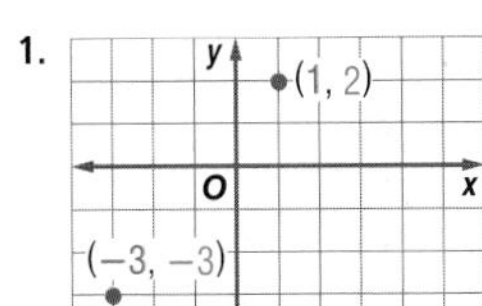

6.4

2. 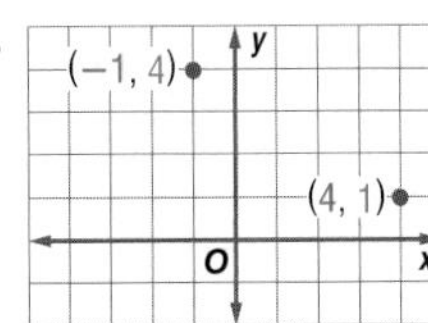

5.8

3. 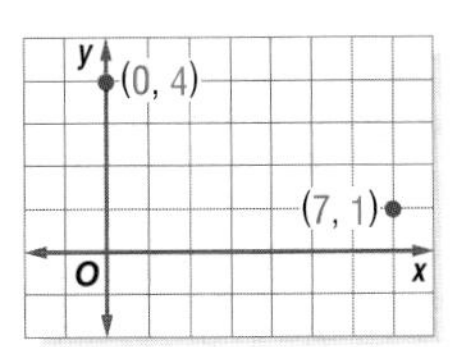

7.6

Graph each pair of ordered pairs. Then find the distance between the points. Round to the nearest tenth. 4–15. See margin for graphs.

4. (−4, 2), (4, 17) 17
5. (5, −1), (11, 7) 10
6. (−3, 5), (2, 7) 5.4
7. (7, −9), (4, 3) 12.4
8. (5, 4), (−3, 8) 8.9
9. (−8, −4), (−3, 8) 13
10. (2, 7), (10, −4) 13.6
11. (9, −2), (3, 6) 10
12. (2, 3), (−1, 6) 4.2
13. (−5, 1), (2, −3) 8.1
14. (0, 1), (5, 2) 5.1
15. (−1, 2), (−2, 3) 1.4

12. 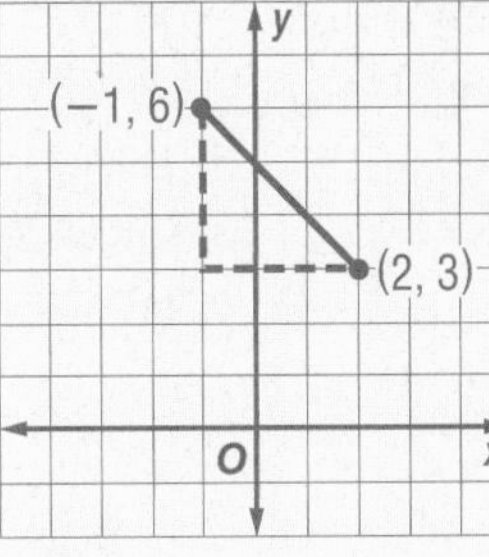

13. 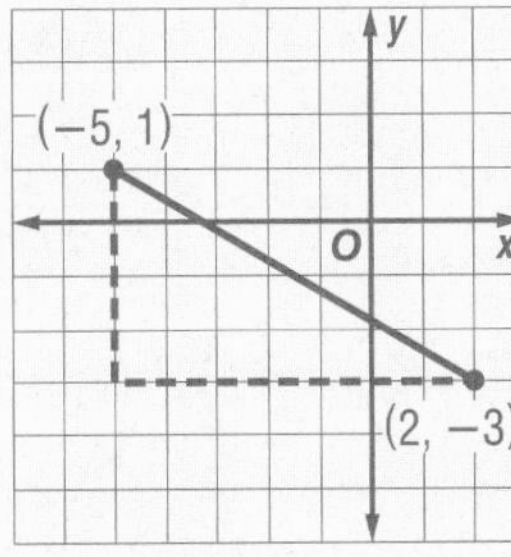

14. 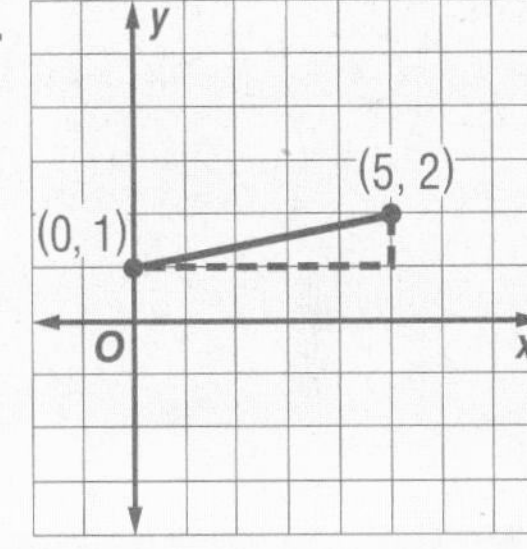

15. 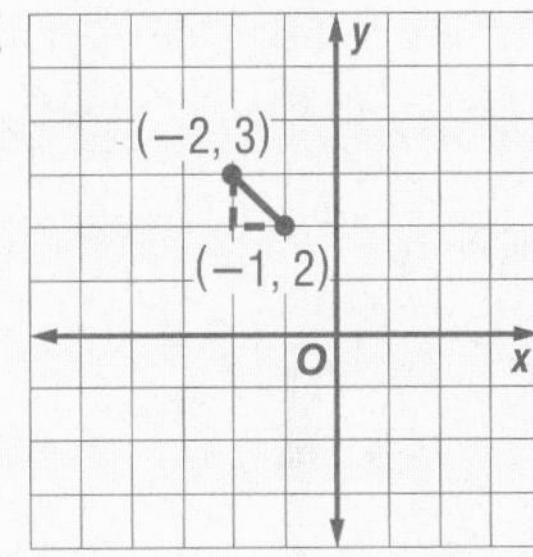

Lesson 3-6

9. 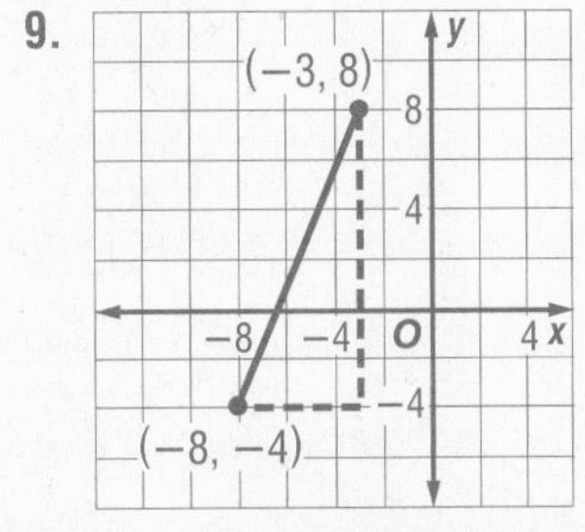

10. 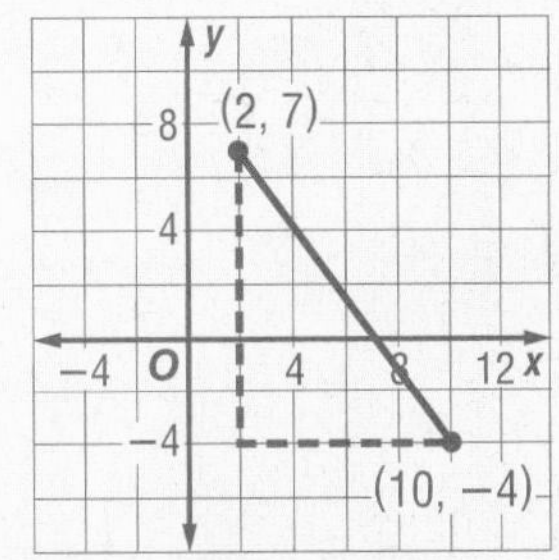

11. 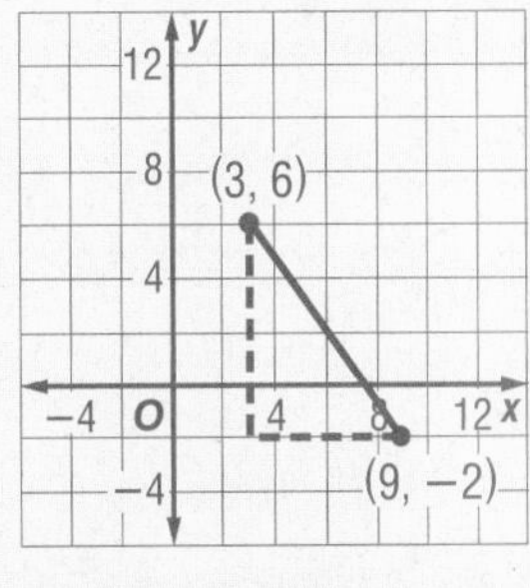

Lesson 4-1

(Pages 156–159)

Express each ratio in simplest form.

1. 27 to 9 **3:1**
2. 4 inches per foot $\frac{1}{3}$
3. 16 out of 48 $\frac{1}{3}$
4. 10:50 **1:5**
5. 40 minutes per hour $\frac{2}{3}$
6. 35 to 15 $\frac{7}{3}$
7. 16 wins to 16 losses $\frac{1}{1}$
8. 7 out of 13 $\frac{7}{13}$
9. 5 out of 50 $\frac{1}{10}$
10. 3 out of 5 $\frac{3}{5}$
11. 20 minutes per hour $\frac{1}{3}$
12. 6 inches per foot $\frac{1}{2}$

Express each rate as a unit rate. **17. 10 preschoolers/teacher**

13. 6 pounds gained in 12 weeks **0.5 lb/week**
14. $800 for 40 tickets **$20/ticket**
15. $6.50 for 5 pounds **$1.30/lb**
16. 6 inches of rain in 3 weeks **2 in./week**
17. 20 preschoolers to 2 teachers
18. 10 inches of snow in 2 days **5 in./day**
19. $500 for 50 tickets **$10/ticket**
20. $360 for 100 dinners **$3.60/dinner**

Lesson 4-2

(Pages 160–164)

For Exercises 1–3, use the following information.

Time	1:00	2:00	2:30	3:00	3:15
Temperature	88°F	89°F	80°F	76°F	76°F

1. Find the rate of change between 2:00 and 2:30. **−18°F/h**
2. Find the rate of change between 1:00 and 3:00. **−6°F/h**
3. Find the rate of change between 3:00 and 3:15. Explain the meaning of this rate of change. **0°F/h; it stopped getting colder.**

For Exercises 4–7, use the following information.

Time	6:00	6:30	6:45	7:00	7:10	7:30	8:00	8:15	8:30
Number of Tickets Sold	2	32	77	137	139	140	142	142	142

4. Find the rate of change between 6:45 and 7:00. **4 tickets/min**
5. Was the rate of change between 8:00 and 8:15 positive, negative, or zero? **zero**
6. Find the rate of change between 6:00 and 8:30. **a little less than 1 ticket/min**
7. During which time period was the greatest rate of change? **6:45–7:00**

Lesson 4-3

(Pages 166–169)

Find the slope of each line.

1. 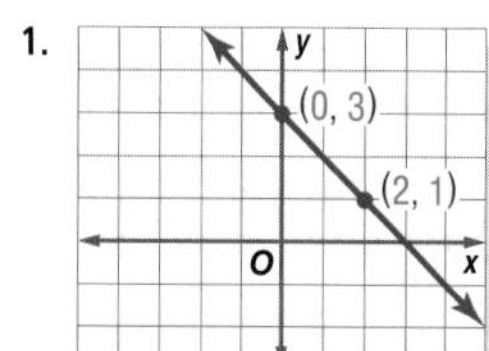

−1

2. 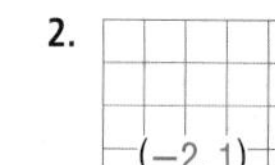
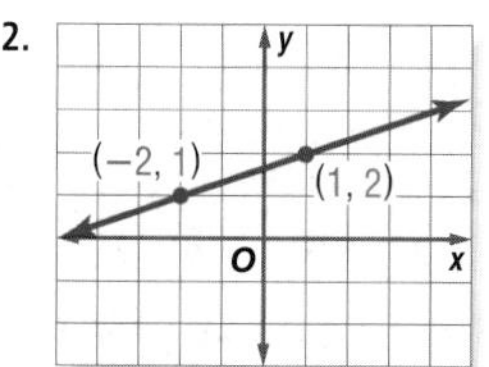

$\frac{1}{3}$

3. 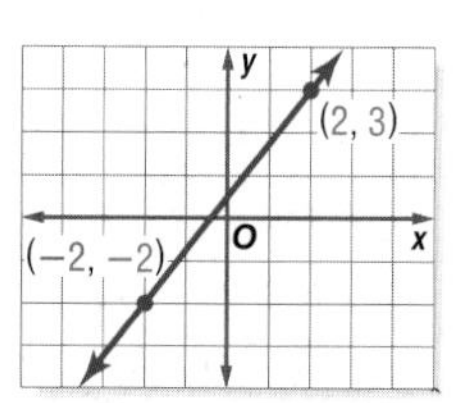

$\frac{5}{4}$

The points given in each table lie on a line. Find the slope of the line.

4. **−1**

x	0	1	2	3
y	1	0	−1	−2

5. $\frac{1}{2}$

x	0	2	4	6
y	0	1	2	3

6. **2**

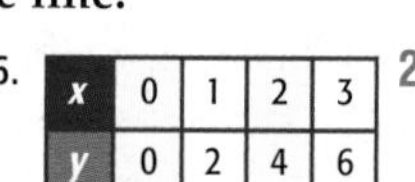

x	0	1	2	3
y	0	2	4	6

Extra Practice

624 Extra Practice

Lesson 4-4

(Pages 170–173)

Determine whether each pair of ratios forms a proportion.

1. $\frac{3}{5}, \frac{5}{10}$ no
2. $\frac{8}{4}, \frac{6}{3}$ yes
3. $\frac{10}{15}, \frac{5}{3}$ no
4. $\frac{2}{8}, \frac{1}{4}$ yes
5. $\frac{6}{18}, \frac{3}{9}$ yes
6. $\frac{14}{21}, \frac{12}{18}$ yes
7. $\frac{4}{20}, \frac{5}{25}$ yes
8. $\frac{9}{27}, \frac{1}{3}$ yes
9. $\frac{2}{3}, \frac{3}{2}$ no
10. $\frac{2}{3}, \frac{14}{21}$ yes
11. $\frac{1}{2}, \frac{5}{10}$ yes
12. $\frac{3}{5}, \frac{15}{9}$ no

Solve each proportion.

13. $\frac{2}{3} = \frac{a}{12}$ 8
14. $\frac{7}{8} = \frac{c}{16}$ 14
15. $\frac{3}{7} = \frac{21}{d}$ 49
16. $\frac{2}{5} = \frac{18}{x}$ 45
17. $\frac{3}{5} = \frac{n}{21}$ 12.6
18. $\frac{5}{12} = \frac{b}{5}$ $2\frac{1}{12}$
19. $\frac{4}{36} = \frac{2}{y}$ 18
20. $\frac{16}{8} = \frac{y}{12}$ 24
21. $\frac{x}{3} = \frac{14}{21}$ 2
22. $\frac{2}{x} = \frac{8}{24}$ 6
23. $\frac{y}{15} = \frac{8}{60}$ 2
24. $\frac{1}{5} = \frac{a}{3}$ 0.6
25. $\frac{27}{8} = \frac{z}{4}$ 13.5
26. $\frac{0.3}{0.2} = \frac{1.5}{c}$ 1
27. $\frac{3}{10} = \frac{z}{36}$ 10.8
28. $\frac{2}{3} = \frac{t}{4}$ $2\frac{2}{3}$

Lesson 4-5

(Pages 178–182)

Determine whether each pair of polygons is similar. Explain your reasoning.

1.
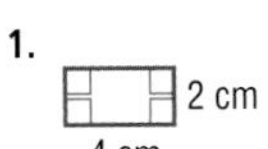

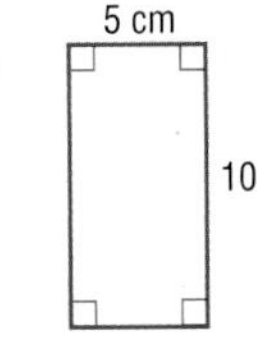

Yes; corresponding angles have same measure, corresponding sides in proportion.

2.
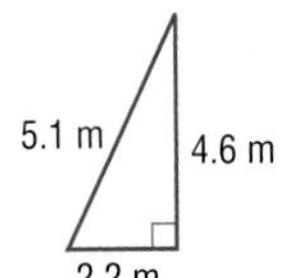

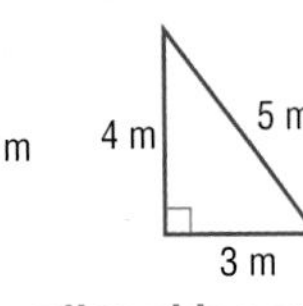

No; corresponding sides are not in proportion.

Each pair of polygons is similar. Write a proportion to find each missing measure. Then solve.

3.
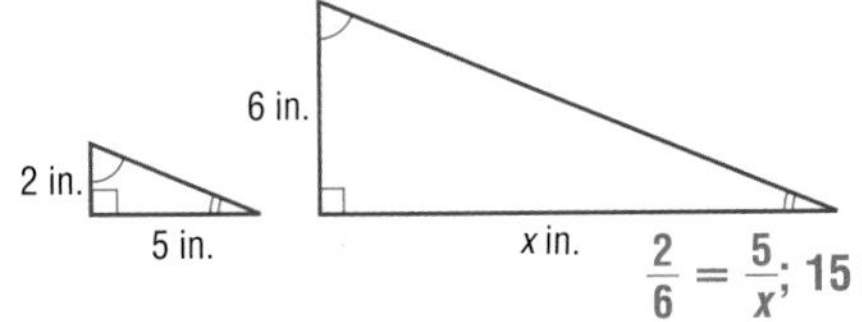

$\frac{2}{6} = \frac{5}{x}$; 15 in.

4.
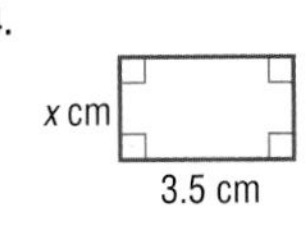

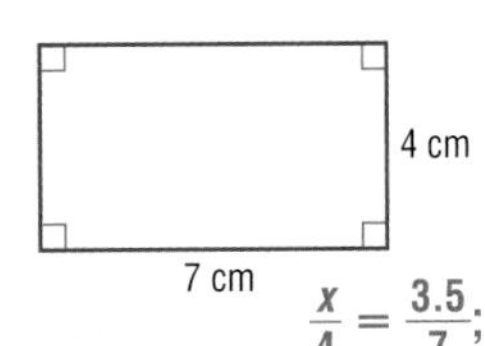

$\frac{x}{4} = \frac{3.5}{7}$; 2 cm

Lesson 4-6

(Pages 184–187)

Solve.

1. The distance between two cities on a map is 3.2 centimeters. If the scale on the map is 1 centimeter = 50 kilometers, find the actual distance between the two cities. 160 km
2. A scale model of the Empire State Building is 10 inches tall. If the Empire State Building is 1,250 feet tall, find the scale of this model. 1 in. = 125 ft
3. On a scale drawing of a house, the dimensions of the living room are 4 inches by 3 inches. If the scale of the drawing is 1 inch = 6 feet, find the actual dimensions of the living room. 24 ft by 18 ft
4. Columbus, Ohio, is approximately 70 miles from Dayton, Ohio. If a scale on an Ohio map is 1 inch = 11 miles, about how far apart are the cities on the map? 6.4 in.

Extra Practice

Extra Practice 625

Lesson 4-8

1. $A'(-2, 0)$, $B'(4, 2)$, $C'(4, -2)$

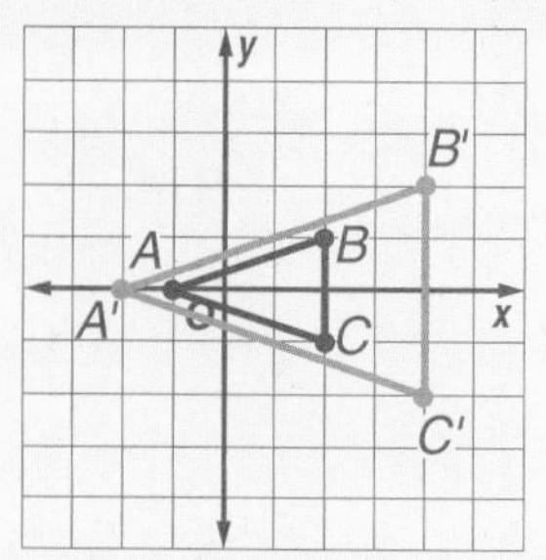

2. $A'(2, 3)$, $B'(0, -1)$, $C'(3, 1)$

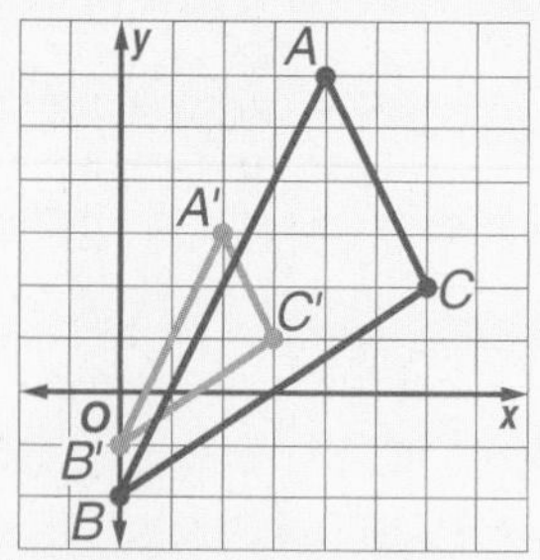

3. $A'(3, -3)$, $B'(3, 6)$, $C'(-3, 3)$

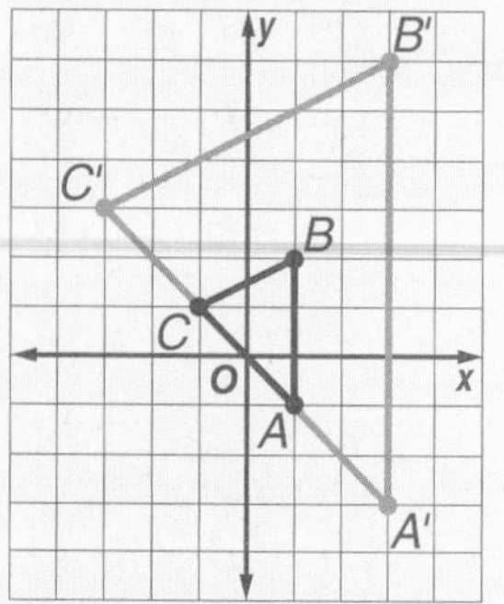

4. $A'(3, 0)$, $B'(0, -6)$, $C'(-3, 6)$

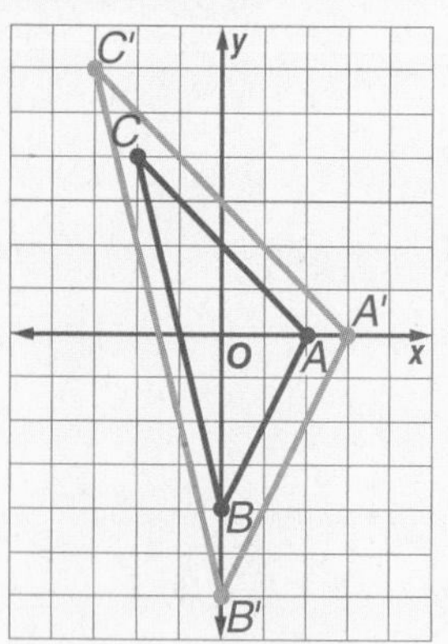

Extra Practice

Lesson 4-7

(Pages 188–191)

Write a proportion. Then determine the missing measure.

1. A road sign casts a shadow 14 meters long, while a tree nearby casts a shadow 27.8 meters long. If the road sign is 3.5 meters high, how tall is the tree? $\frac{3.5}{x} = \frac{14}{27.8}$; 6.95 m
2. Use the map to find the distance across Catfish Lake. Assume the triangles are similar. $\frac{1.2}{4.5} = \frac{0.8}{x}$; 3 km

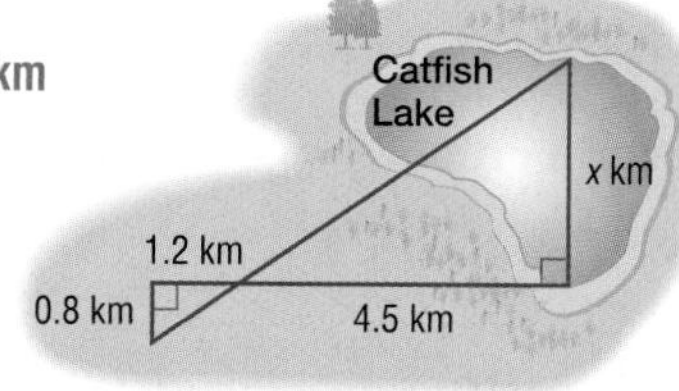

3. A 7-foot tall flag stick on a golf course casts a shadow 21 feet long. A golfer standing nearby casts a shadow 16.5 feet long. How tall is the golfer? $\frac{7}{x} = \frac{21}{16.5}$; 5.5 ft
4. A building casts a shadow that is 150 feet. A tree casts a shadow that is 25 feet. If the tree is 150 feet tall, how tall is the building? $\frac{x}{150} = \frac{150}{25}$; 900 ft
5. A tower casts a shadow that is 120 feet. A pole casts a shadow that is 5 feet. If the tower is 2,400 feet tall, how tall is the pole? $\frac{2{,}400}{x} = \frac{120}{5}$; 100 ft

Lesson 4-8

(Pages 194–197)

Find the coordinates of the vertices of triangle $A'B'C'$ after triangle ABC is dilated using the given scale factor. Then graph triangle ABC and its dilation. 1–4. See margin.

1. $A(-1, 0)$, $B(2, 1)$, $C(2, -1)$; scale factor 2
2. $A(4, 6)$, $B(0, -2)$, $C(6, 2)$; scale factor $\frac{1}{2}$
3. $A(1, -1)$, $B(1, 2)$, $C(-1, 1)$; scale factor 3
4. $A(2, 0)$, $B(0, -4)$, $C(-2, 4)$; scale factor $\frac{3}{2}$

In each figure, the green figure is a dilation of the blue figure. Find the scale factor of each dilation, and classify each dilation as an *enlargement* or as a *reduction*. 5. 3; enlargement 7. 2; enlargement

5.

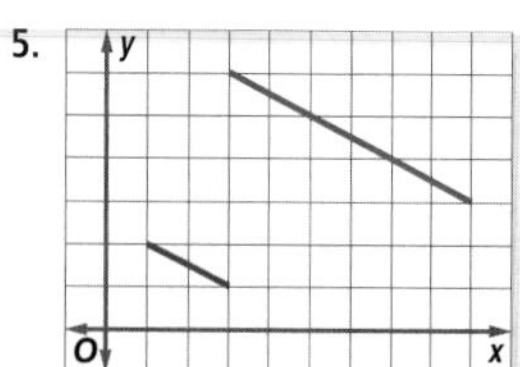

6.

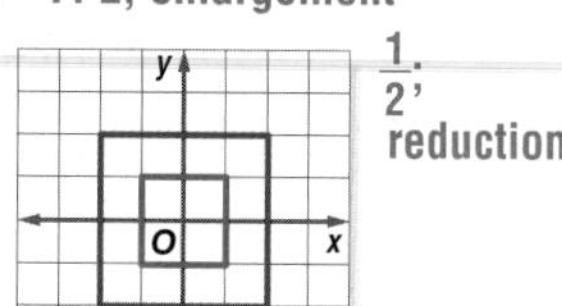

$\frac{1}{2}$; reduction

7.

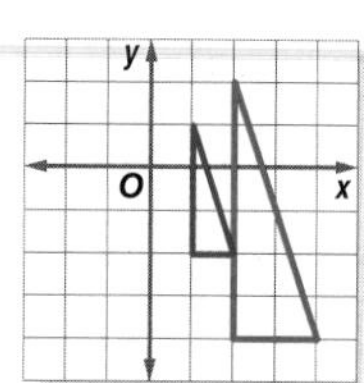

Lesson 5-1

(Pages 206–209)

Write each ratio or fraction as a percent.

1. 3 out of 5 60%
2. $\frac{1}{4}$ 25%
3. $\frac{7}{10}$ 70%
4. 39:100 39%
5. 11 out of 25 44%
6. 72.5:100 72.5%
7. 3 out of 4 75%
8. $\frac{1}{2}$ 50%
9. $\frac{7}{20}$ 35%
10. 93:100 93%
11. 2 out of 8 25%
12. $\frac{9}{20}$ 45%

Write each percent as a fraction in simplest form.

13. 30% $\frac{3}{10}$
14. 4% $\frac{1}{25}$
15. 20% $\frac{1}{5}$
16. 85% $\frac{17}{20}$
17. 3% $\frac{3}{100}$
18. 80% $\frac{4}{5}$
19. 17% $\frac{17}{100}$
20. 55% $\frac{11}{20}$
21. 82% $\frac{41}{50}$
22. 48% $\frac{12}{25}$
23. 32% $\frac{8}{25}$
24. 51% $\frac{51}{100}$

Lesson 5-2

(Pages 210–214)

Write each percent as a decimal.

1. 2% **0.02**
2. 25% **0.25**
3. 29% **0.29**
4. 6.2% **0.062**
5. 16.8% **0.168**
6. 14% **0.14**
7. 23.7% **0.237**
8. 42% **0.42**

Write each decimal as a percent.

9. 0.35 **35%**
10. 14.23 **1,423%**
11. 0.9 **90%**
12. 0.13 **13%**
13. 6.21 **621%**
14. 0.08 **8%**
15. 0.036 **3.6%**
16. 2.34 **234%**

Write each fraction as a percent.

17. $\frac{2}{5}$ **40%**
18. $\frac{49}{50}$ **98%**
19. $\frac{21}{50}$ **42%**
20. $\frac{1}{3}$ **$33\frac{1}{3}\%$**
21. $\frac{81}{100}$ **81%**
22. $\frac{2}{25}$ **8%**
23. $\frac{11}{20}$ **55%**
24. $\frac{9}{75}$ **12%**
25. $\frac{33}{40}$ **$82\frac{1}{2}\%$**
26. $\frac{1}{50}$ **2%**
27. $\frac{41}{50}$ **82%**
28. $\frac{39}{100}$ **39%**

Lesson 5-3

(Pages 216–219)

Write a percent proportion to solve each problem. Then solve. Round answers to the nearest tenth if necessary.

1. 39 is 5% of what number? **$\frac{39}{b} = \frac{5}{100}$; 780**
2. What is 19% of 200? **$\frac{a}{200} = \frac{19}{100}$; 38**
3. 6 is what percent of 30? **$\frac{6}{30} = \frac{p}{100}$; 20%**
4. 24 is what percent of 72? **$\frac{24}{72} = \frac{p}{100}$; 33.3%**
5. 9 is $33\frac{1}{3}\%$ of what number? **$\frac{9}{b} = \frac{33\frac{1}{3}}{100}$; 27**
6. Find 55% of 134. **$\frac{a}{134} = \frac{55}{100}$; 73.7**
7. 8 is what percent of 32? **$\frac{8}{32} = \frac{p}{100}$; 25%**
8. What is 35% of 215? **$\frac{a}{215} = \frac{35}{100}$; 75.3**
9. 62 is 50% of what number? **$\frac{62}{b} = \frac{50}{100}$; 124**
10. 93 is what percent of 186? **$\frac{93}{186} = \frac{p}{100}$; 50%**
11. 90 is 36% of what number? **$\frac{90}{b} = \frac{36}{100}$; 250**
12. 15 is 60% of what number? **$\frac{15}{b} = \frac{60}{100}$; 25**
13. What is 15% of 60? **$\frac{a}{60} = \frac{15}{100}$; 9**
14. 15 is 20% of what number? **$\frac{15}{b} = \frac{20}{100}$; 75**
15. 66 is 75% of what number? **$\frac{66}{b} = \frac{75}{100}$; 88**
16. 31 is what percent of 155? **$\frac{31}{155} = \frac{p}{100}$; 20%**
17. 22 is 25% of what number? **$\frac{22}{b} = \frac{25}{100}$; 88**
18. What is 65% of 150? **$\frac{a}{150} = \frac{65}{100}$; 97.5**
19. 6 is 75% of what number? **$\frac{6}{b} = \frac{75}{100}$; 8**
20. 27 is what percent of 100? **$\frac{27}{100} = \frac{p}{100}$; 27%**

Lesson 5-4

(Pages 220–223)

Compute mentally.

1. 10% of 206 **20.6**
2. 1% of 19.3 **0.193**
3. 20% of 15 **3**
4. 87.5% of 80 **70**
5. 50% of 46 **23**
6. 12.5% of 56 **7**
7. $33\frac{1}{3}\%$ of 93 **31**
8. 90% of 2,000 **1,800**
9. 30% of 70 **21**
10. 40% of 95 **38**
11. $66\frac{2}{3}\%$ of 48 **32**
12. 80% of 25 **20**
13. 25% of 400 **100**
14. 75% of 72 **54**
15. 37.5% of 96 **36**
16. 40% of 35 **14**
17. 60% of 85 **51**
18. 62.5% of 160 **100**
19. 90% of 205 **184.5**
20. 1% of 2,364 **23.64**
21. 20% of 85 **17**
22. 75% of 12 **9**
23. 12.5% of 800 **100**
24. 30% of 90 **27**
25. 1% of 70 **0.7**
26. 40% of 45 **18**
27. 62.5% of 88 **55**

Extra Practice

Extra Practice 627

Lesson 5-5

(Pages 228–231)

Estimate.

1. 33% of 12 $\frac{1}{3} \cdot 12 = 4$
2. 24% of 84 $\frac{1}{4} \cdot 80 = 20$
3. 39% of 50 $\frac{2}{5} \cdot 50 = 20$
4. 19% of 135 $\frac{1}{5} \cdot 135 = 27$
5. 21% of 50 $\frac{1}{5} \cdot 50 = 10$
6. 49% of 121 $\frac{1}{2} \cdot 120 = 60$
7. 72% of 101 $\frac{72}{100} \cdot 100 = 72$
8. 99% of 255 $1 \cdot 255 = 255$
9. 25% of 41 $\frac{1}{4} \cdot 40 = 10$

Estimate each percent. 13. $\frac{25}{270} \approx \frac{25}{250}$ or 10% 14. $\frac{5}{49} \approx \frac{5}{50}$ or 10%

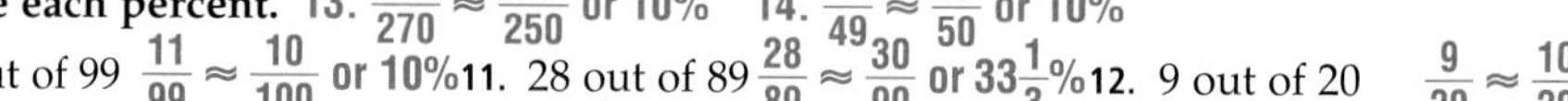

10. 11 out of 99 $\frac{11}{99} \approx \frac{10}{100}$ or 10%
11. 28 out of 89 $\frac{28}{89} \approx \frac{30}{90}$ or $33\frac{1}{3}$%
12. 9 out of 20 $\frac{9}{20} \approx \frac{10}{20}$ or 50%
13. 25 out of 270
14. 5 out of 49
15. 7 out of 57 $\frac{7}{57} \approx \frac{7}{56}$ or 12.5%
16. 2 out of 21 $\frac{2}{21} \approx \frac{2}{20}$ or 10%
17. 12 out of 61 $\frac{12}{61} \approx \frac{12}{60}$ or 20%
18. 7 out of 15 $\frac{7}{15} \approx \frac{7}{14}$ or 50%

Estimate the percent of the area shaded.

19. 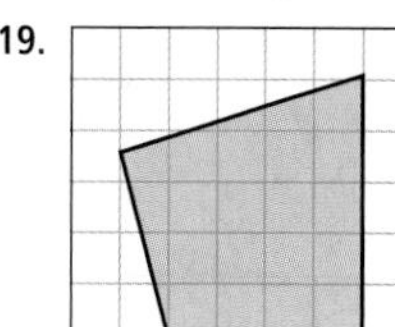 40%

20. 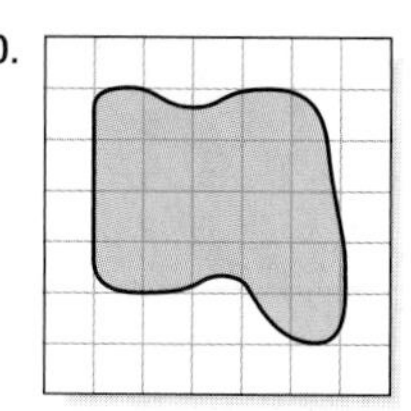 40%

21. 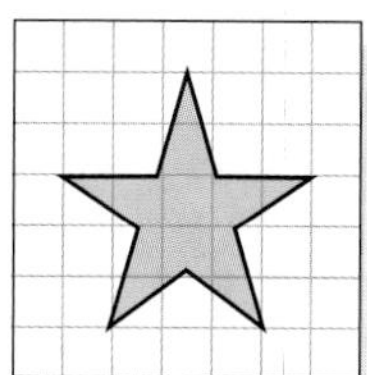 16%

Lesson 5-6

(Pages 232–235)

Solve each equation using the percent equation.

1. Find 5% of 73. 3.65
2. What is 15% of 15? 2.25
3. Find 80% of 12. 9.60
4. What is 7.3% of 500? 36.5
5. Find 21% of 720. 151.20
6. What is 12% of 62.5? 7.5
7. Find 0.3% of 155. 0.465
8. What is 75% of 450? 337.5
9. Find 7.2% of 10. 0.72
10. What is 10.1% of 60? 6.06
11. Find 23% of 47. 10.81
12. What is 89% of 654? 582.06
13. 20 is what percent of 64? 31.25%
14. Sixty-nine is what percent of 200? 34.5%
15. Seventy is what percent of 150? $46\frac{2}{3}$%
16. 26 is 30% of what number? $86\frac{2}{3}$
17. 7 is 14% of what number? 50
18. 35.5 is what percent of 150? $23\frac{2}{3}$%
19. 17 is what percent of 25? 68%
20. 152 is 2% of what number? 7,600

Lesson 5-7

(Pages 236–240)

Find each percent of change. Round to the nearest tenth if necessary. State whether the percent of change is an *increase* or a *decrease*.

1. original: 35
new: 29 17.1%; decrease
2. original: 550
new: 425 22.7%; decrease
3. original: 72
new: 88 22.2%; increase
4. original: 25
new: 35 40%; increase
5. original: 28
new: 19 32.1%; decrease
6. original: 46
new: 55 19.6%; increase

Find the selling price for each item given the cost to the store and markup.

7. golf clubs: $250, 30% markup $325
8. compact disc: $17, 15% markup $19.55
9. shoes: $57, 45% markup $82.65
10. book: $26, 20% markup $31.20

Find the sale price of each item to the nearest cent.

11. piano: $4,220, 35% off $2,743
12. scissors: $14, 10% off $12.60
13. book: $29, 40% off $17.40
14. sweater: $38, 25% off $28.50

628 Extra Practice

Lesson 5-8

(Pages 241–244)

Find the simple interest to the nearest cent.

1. \$500 at 7% for 2 years **\$70**
2. \$2,500 at 6.5% for 36 months **\$487.50**
3. \$8,000 at 6% for 1 year **\$480**
4. \$1,890 at 9% for 42 months **\$595.35**
5. \$760 at 4.5% for $2\frac{1}{2}$ years **\$85.50**
6. \$12,340 at 5% for 6 months **\$308.50**

Find the total amount in each account to the nearest cent.

7. \$300 at 10% for 3 years **\$390**
8. \$3,200 at 8% for 6 months **\$3,328**
9. \$20,000 at 14% for 20 years **\$76,000**
10. \$4,000 at 12.5% for 4 years **\$6,000**
11. \$450 at 11% for 5 years **\$697.50**
12. \$17,000 at 15% for $9\frac{1}{2}$ years **\$41,225**

Lesson 6-1

(Pages 256–260)

Find the value of x in each figure.

1. **132**

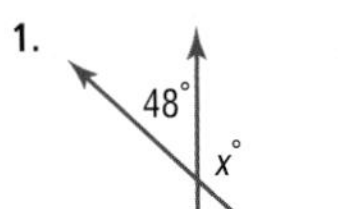

2. **107**

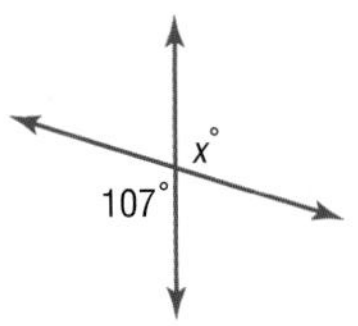

3. **55**

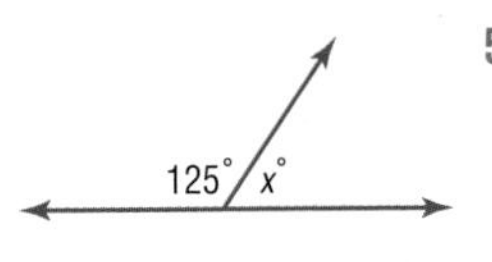

4. 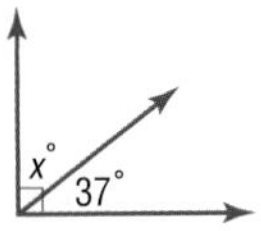 **53**

x°
37°

5. 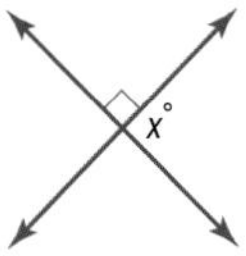 **90**

x°

6. 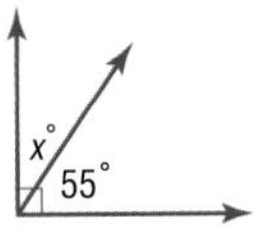 **35**

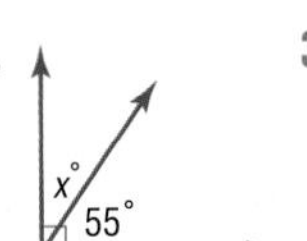

For Exercises 7–10, use the figure at the right.

7. Find $m\angle 6$, if $m\angle 3 = 42°$. **42°**
8. Find $m\angle 4$, if $m\angle 3 = 71°$. **109°**
9. Find $m\angle 1$, if $m\angle 5 = 128°$. **128°**
10. Find $m\angle 7$, if $m\angle 2 = 83°$. **83°**

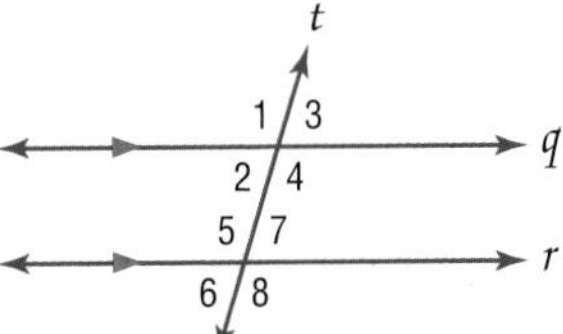

Lesson 6-2

(Pages 262–265)

Find the value of x in each triangle.

1. **50**

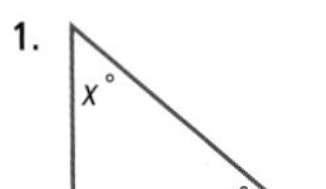

2. **44**

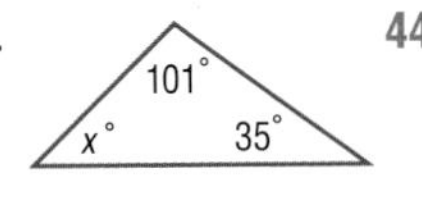

3. **58**

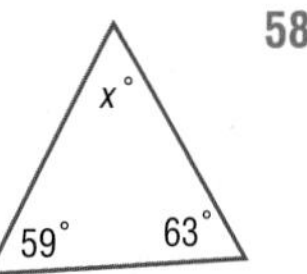

Classify each triangle by its angles and by its sides.

4. **acute, equilateral**

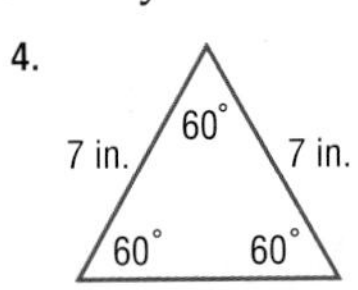

5. **right, scalene**

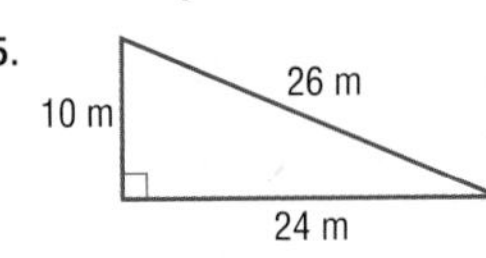

6. **obtuse, isosceles**

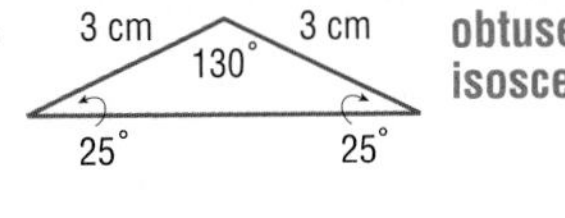

Extra Practice

Extra Practice

Extra Practice 629

Lesson 6-3

(Pages 267–270)

Find each missing length. Round to the nearest tenth if necessary.

1. 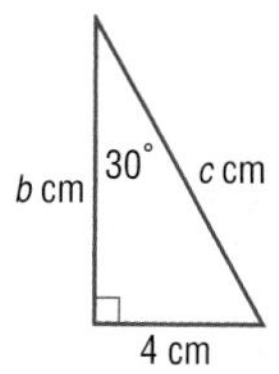 $b \approx 6.9$ cm, $c = 8$ cm

2. 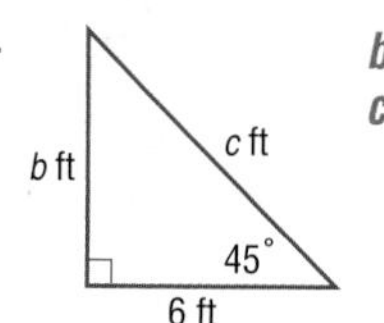

$b = 6$ ft, $c \approx 8.5$ ft

3. 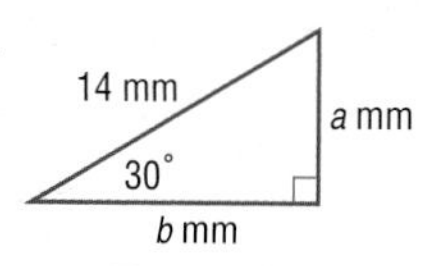

$a = 7$ mm, $b \approx 12.1$ mm

4. 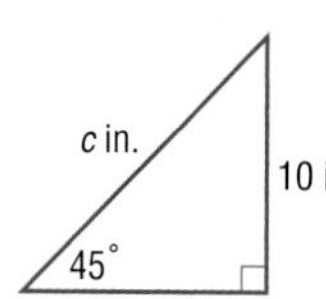

$a = 10$ in., $c \approx 14.1$ in.

5. 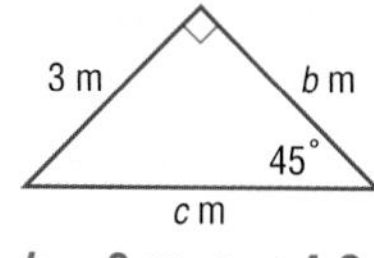

$b = 3$ m, $c \approx 4.2$ m

6. 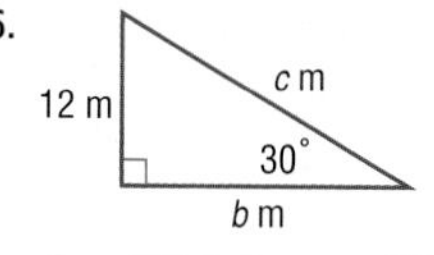

$b \approx 20.8$ m, $c = 24$ m

Lesson 6-4

(Pages 272–275)

Find the value of x in each quadrilateral.

1. 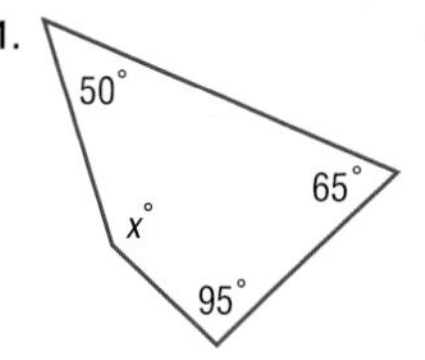

150

2. 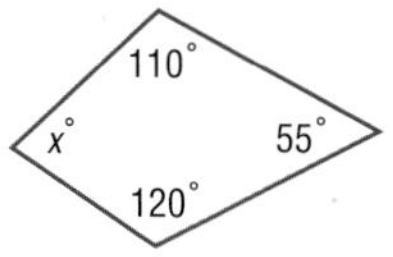 75

3. 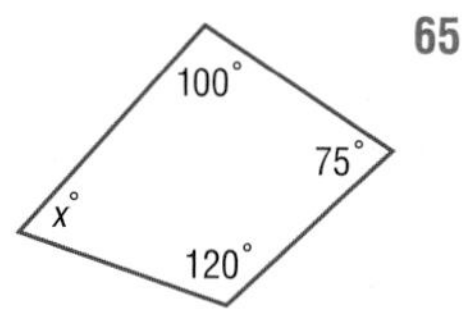

65

Classify each quadrilateral with the name that best describes it.

4. 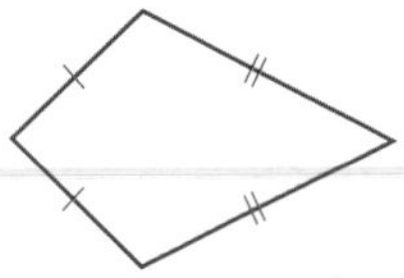 quadrilateral

5. 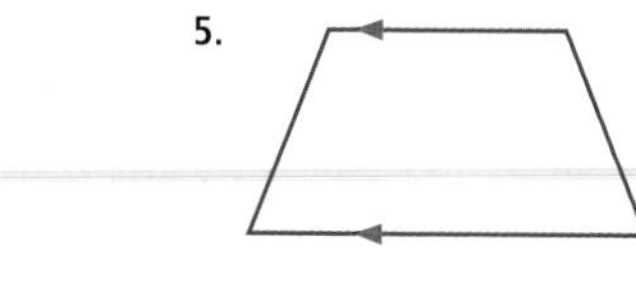
trapezoid

6. 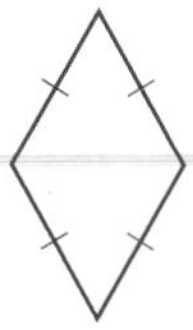 rhombus

Lesson 6-5

(Pages 279–282)

Determine whether the polygons are congruent. If so, name the corresponding parts and write a congruence statement.

1. 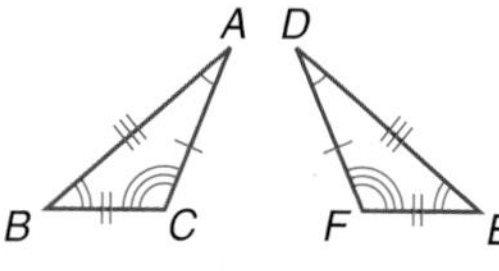

yes; $\angle A \cong \angle D$, $\angle B \cong \angle E$, $\angle C \cong \angle F$, $\overline{AB} \cong \overline{DE}$, $\overline{BC} \cong \overline{EF}$, $\overline{CA} \cong \overline{FD}$; $\triangle ABC \cong \triangle DEF$

2. 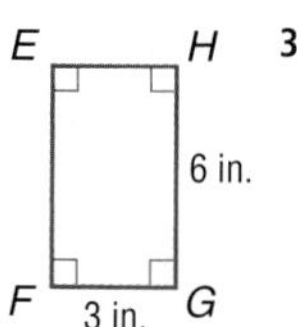

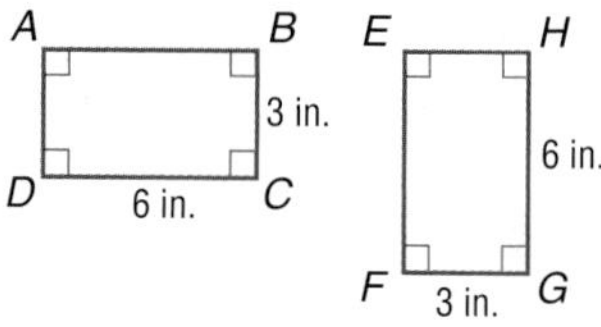

yes; Sample answers: $\angle A \cong \angle E$, $\angle B \cong \angle F$, $\angle C \cong \angle G$, $\angle D \cong \angle H$, $\overline{AB} \cong \overline{EF}$, $\overline{BC} \cong \overline{FG}$, $\overline{CD} \cong \overline{GH}$; $\overline{DA} \cong \overline{HE}$; quadrilateral $ABCD \cong$ quadrilateral $EFGH$

3. 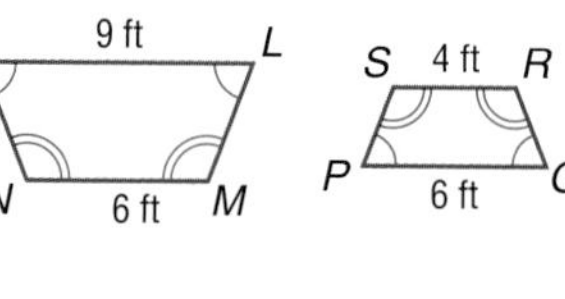

no

In the figure, quadrilateral $ABCD$ is congruent to quadrilateral $EFGH$. Find each measure.

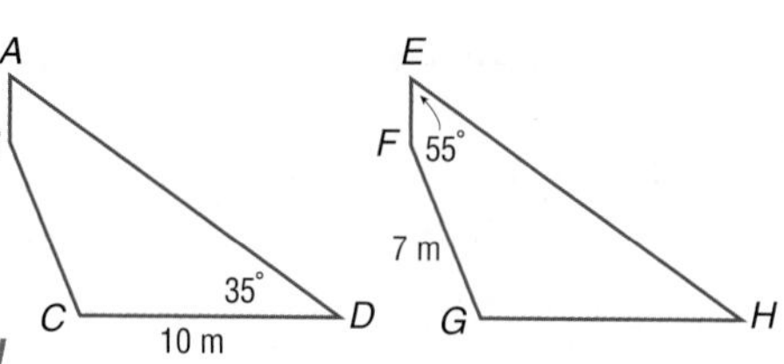

4. $m\angle A$ 55°
5. BC 7 m
6. GH 10 m
7. $m\angle H$ 35°

630 Extra Practice

Lesson 6-6

(Pages 286–289)

Complete parts a and b for each figure.

a. Determine whether the figure has line symmetry. If it does, trace the figure and draw all lines of symmetry. If not write *none*.

b. Determine whether the figure has rotational symmetry. write *yes* or *no*. If *yes*, name the angle(s) of rotation.

1.  yes; 180°

2. 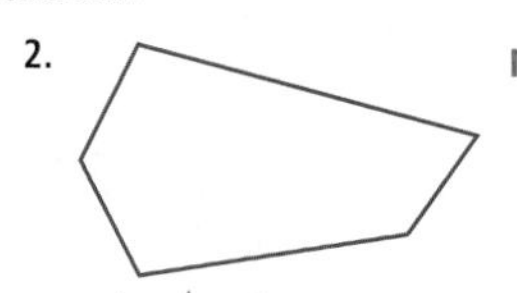 none; no

3. 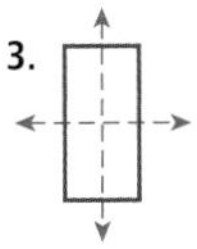 yes; 180°

4. 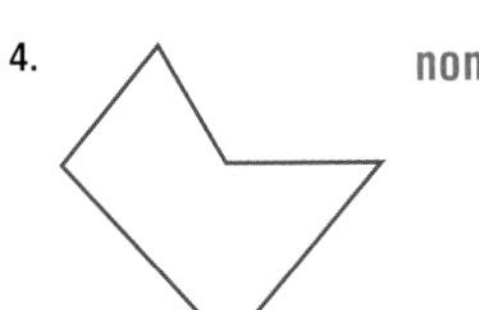 none; no

5. 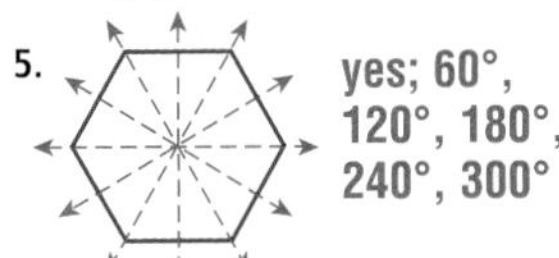 yes; 60°, 120°, 180°, 240°, 300°

6. 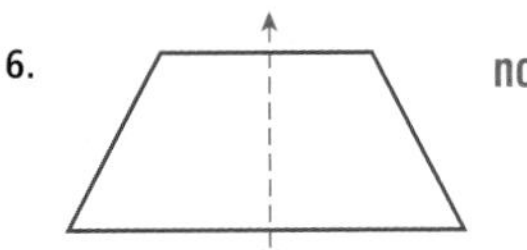 no

Lesson 6-7

(Pages 290–294)

Graph the figure with the given vertices. Then graph the image of the figure after a reflection over the given axis, and write the coordinates of its vertices. 1–2. See margin for graphs. 2. $T'(2, 5)$, $R'(-1, 5)$, $A'(-4, 2)$, $P'(5, 2)$

1. triangle *CAT* with vertices $C(2, 3)$, $A(8, 2)$, and $T(4, -3)$; x-axis $C'(2, -3)$, $A'(8, -2)$, $T'(4, 3)$
2. trapezoid *TRAP* with vertices $T(-2, 5)$, $R(1, 5)$, $A(4, 2)$, and $P(-5, 2)$; y-axis

Name the line of reflection for each pair of figures.

3. 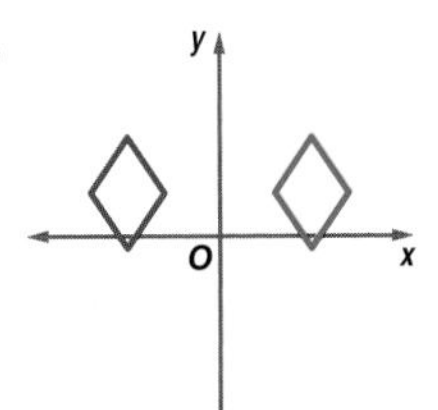

y-axis

4. 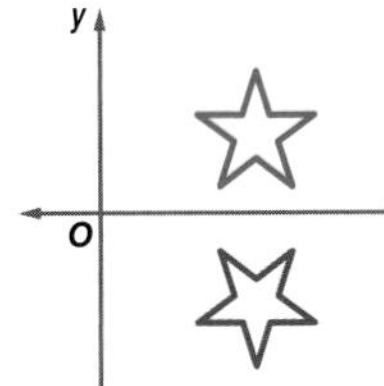

x-axis

5. 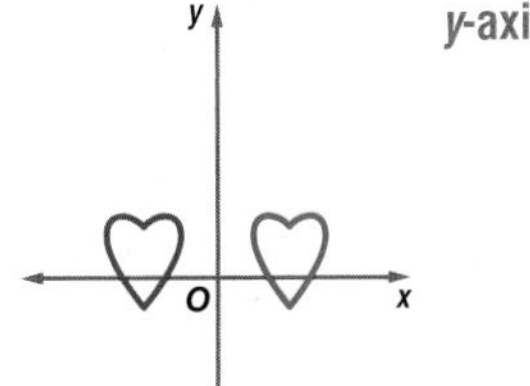

y-axis

Lesson 6-8

(pages 296–299)

Graph the figure with the given vertices. Then graph the image of the figure after the indicated translation, and write the coordinates of its vertices. 1–4. See margin for graphs.

1. rectangle *PQRS* with vertices $P(-7, 6)$, $Q(-5, 6)$, $R(-5, 2)$, and $S(-7, 2)$ translated 9 right and 1 unit down $P'(2, 5)$, $Q'(4, 5)$, $R'(4, 1)$, $S'(2, 1)$
2. pentagon *DGLMR* with vertices $D(1, 3)$, $G(2, 4)$, $L(4, 4)$, $M(5, 3)$ and $R(3, 1)$ translated 5 units left and 7 units down
3. triangle *TRI* with vertices $T(2, 1)$, $R(0, 3)$, and $I(-1, 1)$ translated 2 units left and 3 units down $T'(0, -2)$, $R'(-2, 0)$, $I'(-3, -2)$
4. quadrilateral *QUAD* with vertices $Q(3, 2)$, $U(3, 0)$, $A(6, 0)$ and $D(6, 2)$, translated 3 units left and 1 unit down $Q'(0, 1)$, $U'(0, -1)$, $A'(3, -1)$, $D'(3, 1)$

2. $D'(-4, -4)$, $G'(-3, -3)$, $L'(-1, -3)$, $M'(0, -4)$, $R'(-2, -6)$

Extra Practice

Lesson 6-8

1. 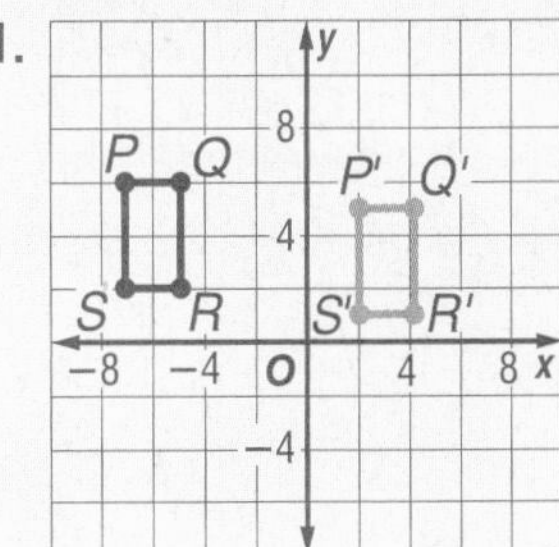

2. 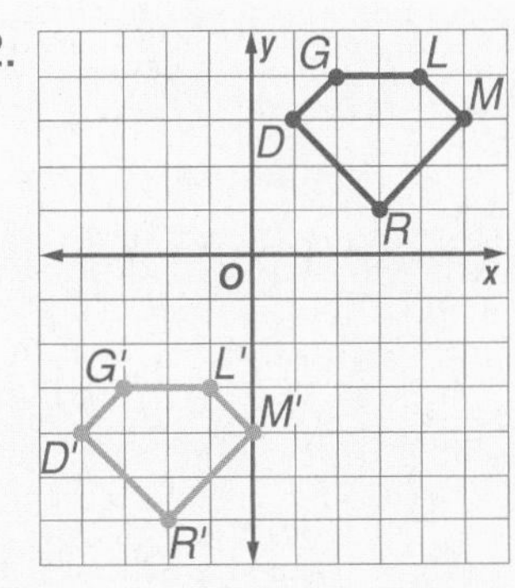

3. 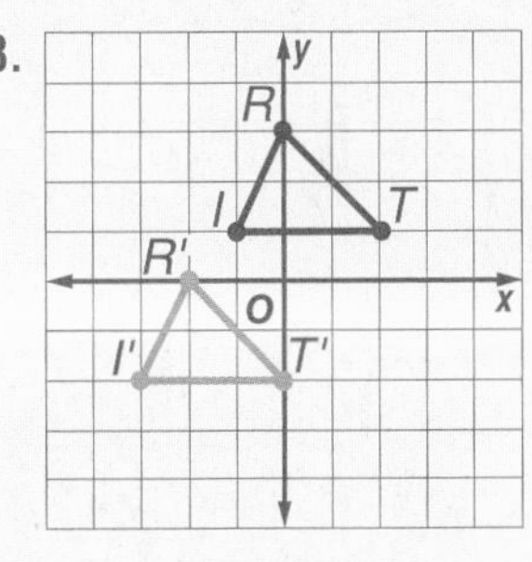

4. 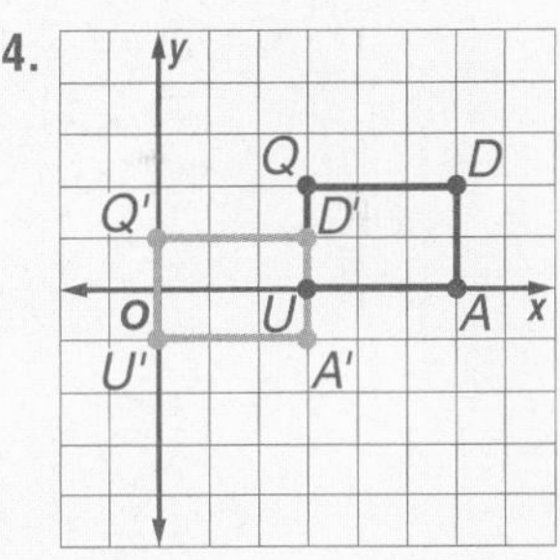

Lesson 6-7

1. 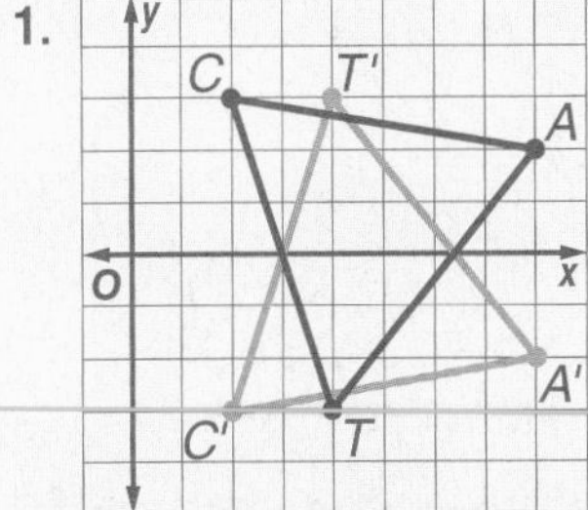

2. 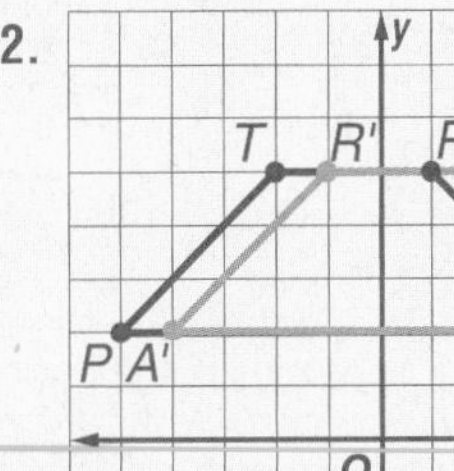

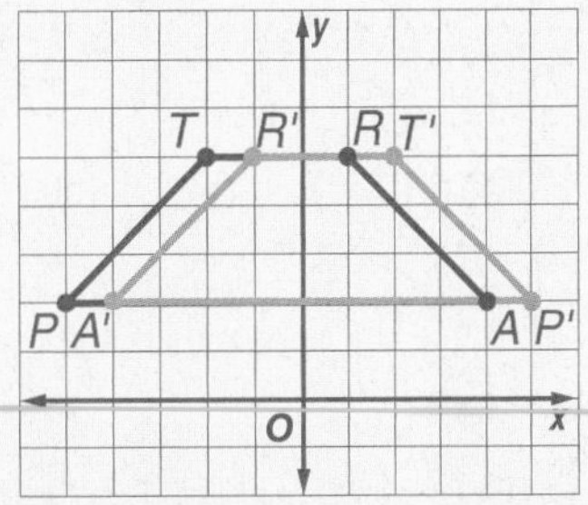

Extra Practice

Lesson 6-9

1.

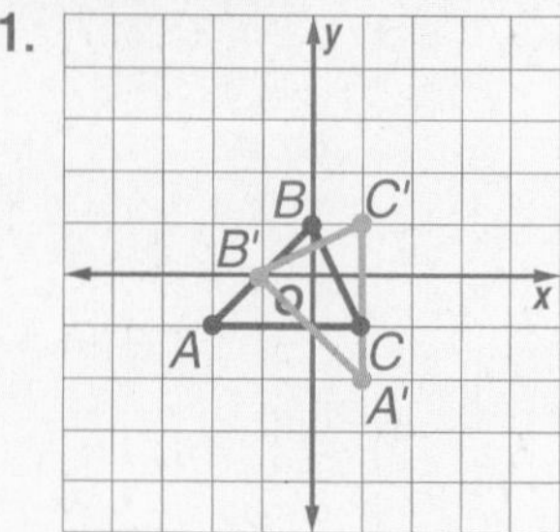

2.

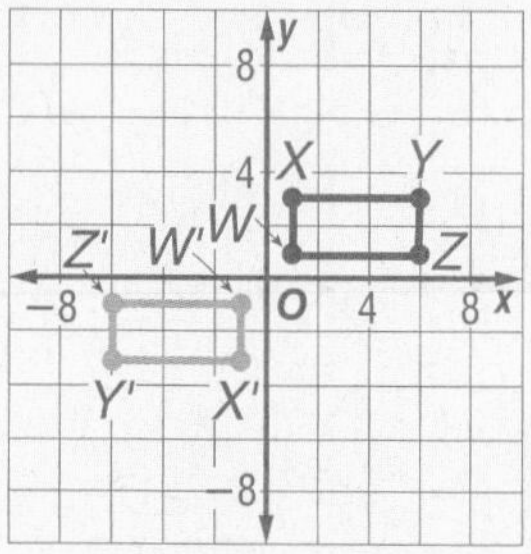

y
8
4
X
Y
Z'
W'
W
Z
−8
O
4
8
x
Y'
X'
−8

3.

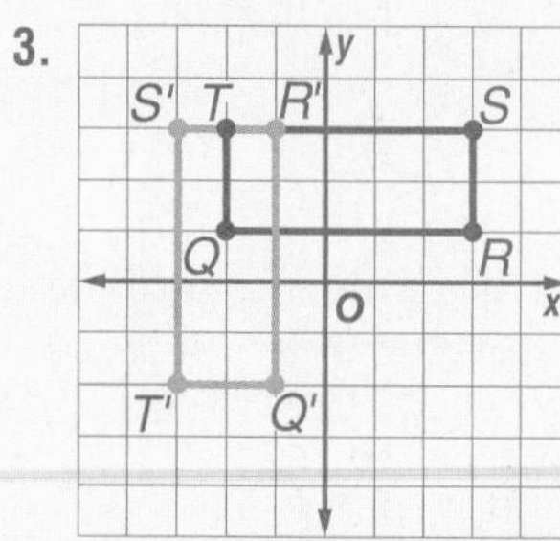

4.

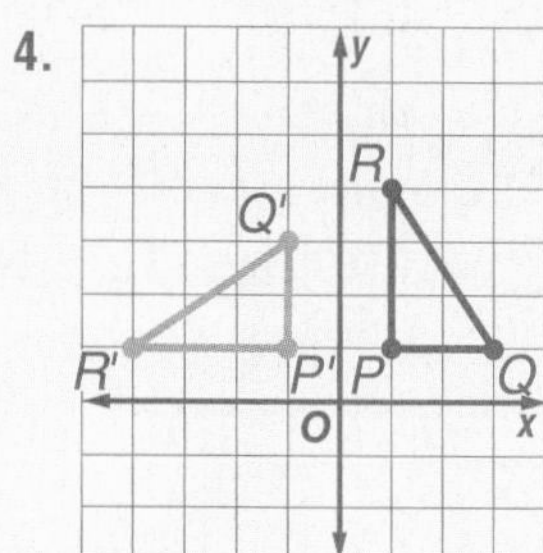

5.

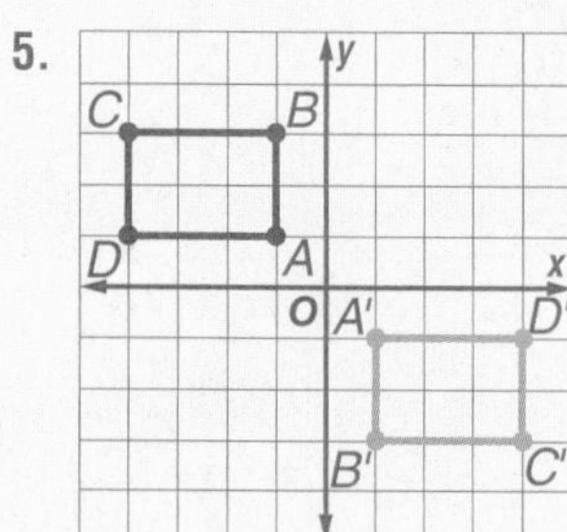

6.

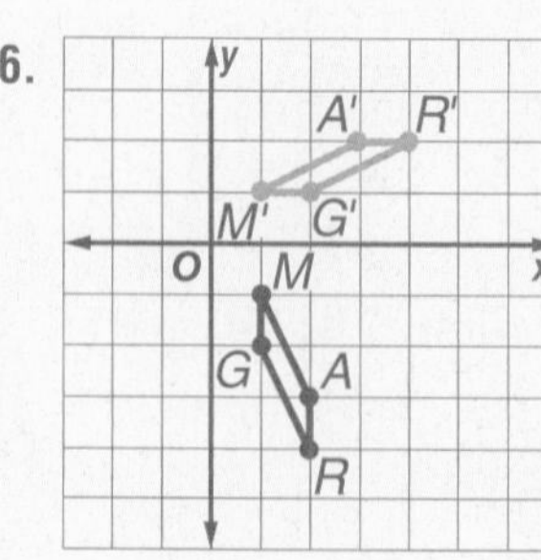

7.

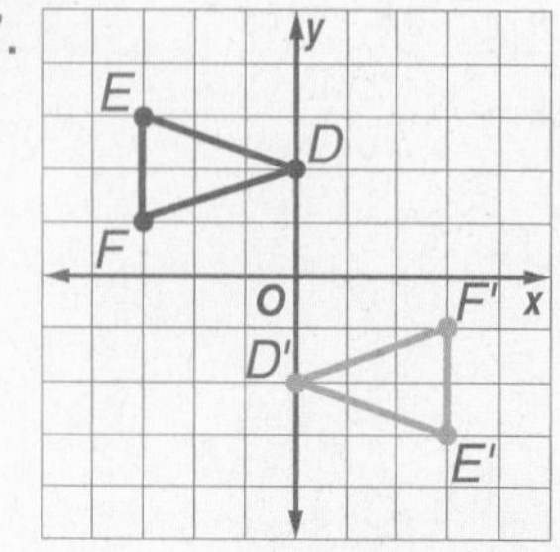

Lesson 6-9 1–7. See margin for graphs.

(Pages 300–303)

Graph the figure with the given vertices. Then graph the image of the figure after the indicated rotation about the origin, and write the coordinates of its vertices. 2. $W'(-1, -1)$, $X'(-1, -3)$, $Y'(-6, -3)$, $Z'(-6, -1)$

1. triangle ABC with vertices $A(-2, -1)$, $B(0, 1)$, and $C(1, -1)$; 90° counterclockwise $A'(1, -2)$, $B'(-1, 0)$, $C'(1, 1)$
2. rectangle $WXYZ$ with vertices $W(1, 1)$, $X(1, 3)$, $Y(6, 3)$, and $Z(6, 1)$; 180°
3. quadrilateral $QRST$ with vertices $Q(-2, 1)$, $R(3, 1)$, $S(3, 3)$, and $T(-2, 3)$; 90° counterclockwise $Q'(-1, -2)$, $R'(-1, 3)$, $S'(-3, 3)$, $T'(-3, -2)$
4. triangle PQR with vertices $P(1, 1)$, $Q(3, 1)$, and $R(1, 4)$; 90° counterclockwise
5. rectangle $ABCD$ with vertices $A(-1, 1)$, $B(-1, 3)$, $C(-4, 3)$, and $D(-4, 1)$; 180°
6. parallelogram $GRAM$ with vertices $G(1, -2)$, $R(2, -4)$, $A(2, -3)$, and $M(1, -1)$; 90° counterclockwise $G'(2, 1)$, $R'(4, 2)$, $A'(3, 2)$, $M'(1, 1)$
7. triangle DEF with vertices $D(0, 2)$, $E(-3, 3)$, and $F(-3, 1)$; 180° $D'(0, -2)$, $E'(3, -3)$, $F'(3, -1)$

4. $P'(-1, 1)$, $Q'(-1, 3)$, $R'(-4, 1)$ 5. $A'(1, -1)$, $B'(1, -3)$, $C'(4, -3)$, $D'(4, -1)$

Lesson 7-1

(Pages 314–318)

Find the area of each figure. 7. $19\frac{3}{8}$ yd²

1. 5 m, 8 m — 20 m² 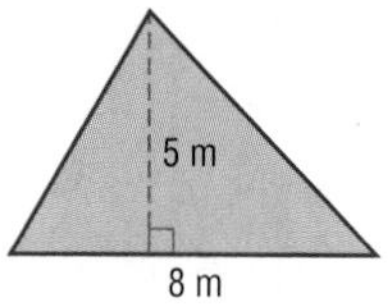
2. 5 in., 6 in. — 15 in² 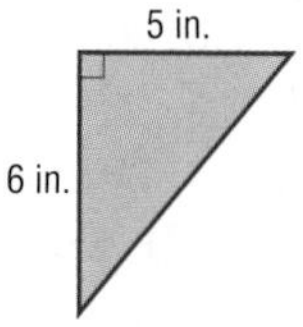
3. 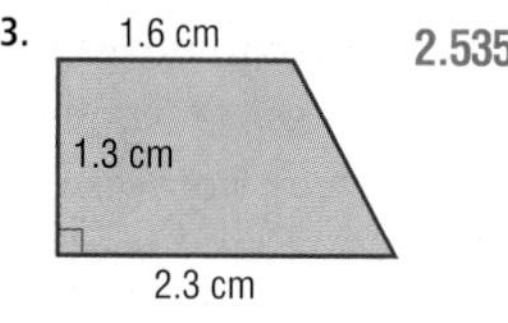

2.535 cm²

4. triangle: base, $2\frac{1}{2}$ in.; height, 7 in. $8\frac{3}{4}$ in²
5. triangle: base, 12 cm; height, 3.2 cm 19.2 cm²
6. trapezoid: bases, 5 ft and 7 ft; height, 11 ft 66 ft²
7. trapezoid: bases, $4\frac{1}{4}$ yd and $3\frac{1}{2}$ yd; height, 5 yd
8. parallelogram: base, 15 cm; height, 3 cm 45 cm²
9. parallelogram: base, 11.2 in.; height, 5 in. 56 in²
10. triangle: base, 7 yd; height, 9 yd 31.5 yd²
11. trapezoid: bases, 9 cm and 10 cm; height, 5 cm 47.5 cm²

Lesson 7-2

(Pages 319–323)

Find the circumference and area of each circle. Round to the nearest tenth.

1. 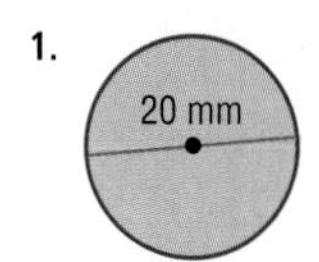

62.8 mm; 314.2 mm²
2. 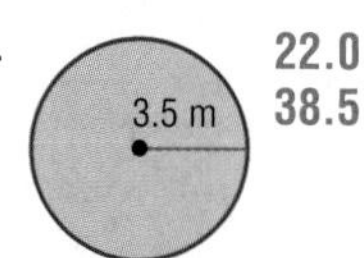

22.0 m; 38.5 m²
3. 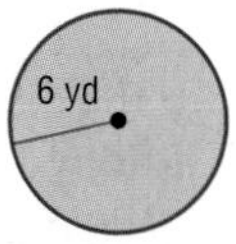 6 yd — 37.7 yd; 113.1 yd²
4. 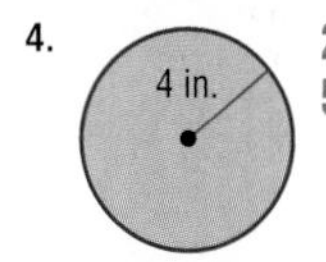

25.1 in.; 50.3 in²
5. 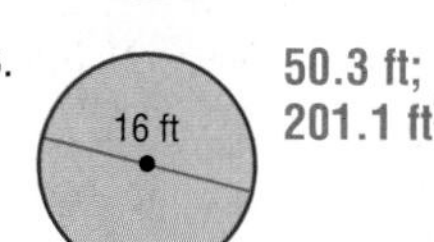

50.3 ft; 201.1 ft²
6. 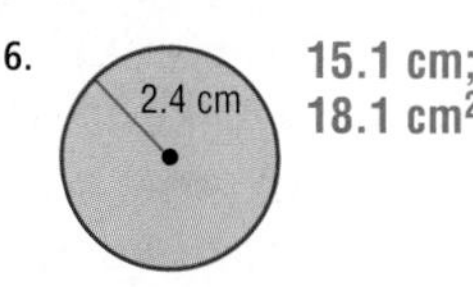

15.1 cm; 18.1 cm²
7. 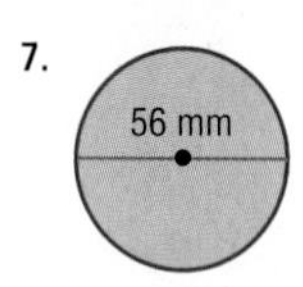

175.9 mm; 2,463.0 mm²
8. 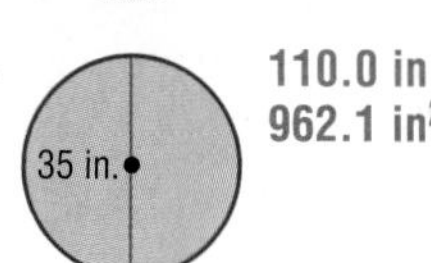

110.0 in.; 962.1 in²
9. 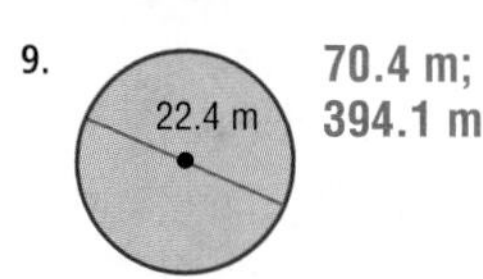

70.4 m; 394.1 m²

Lesson 7-3

(Pages 326–329)

Find the area of each figure. Round to the nearest tenth of necessary.

1. 

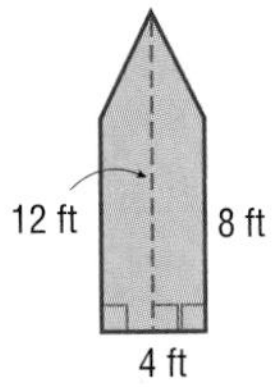

40 ft²

2. 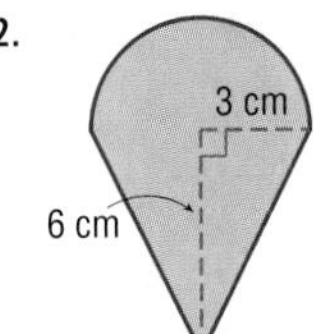

32.1 cm²

3. 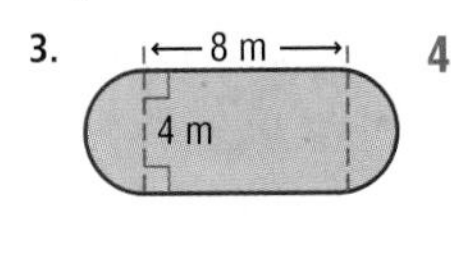

44.6 m²

4. 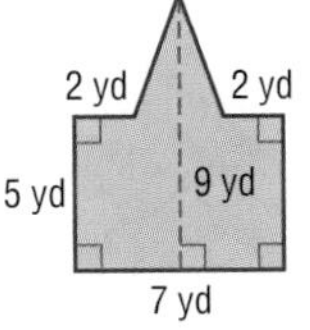

41 yd²

5. 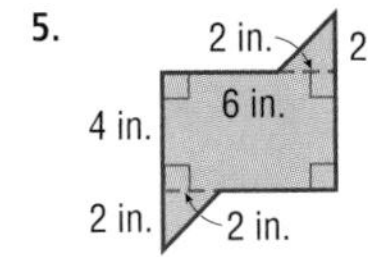

28 in²

6. 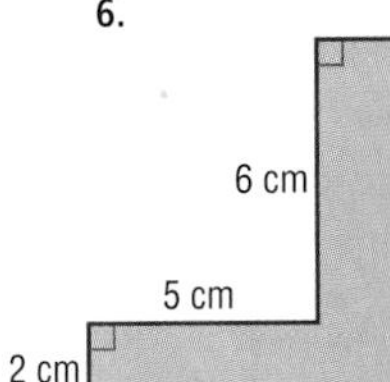

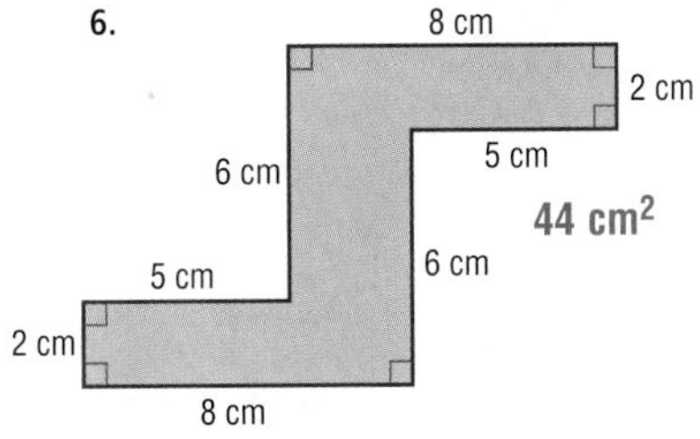

44 cm²

Lesson 7-4

(Pages 331–334)

Identify each solid. Name the number and shapes of the faces. Then name the number of edges and vertices.

1. 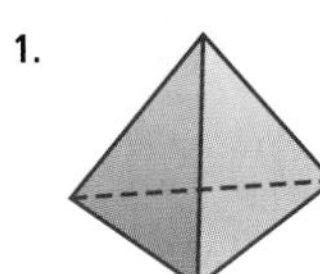
triangular pyramid; 4 faces, all triangles; 6 edges; 4 vertices

2. 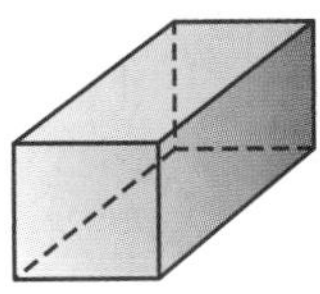
rectangular prism; 6 faces, all rectangles; 12 edges; 8 vertices

3. 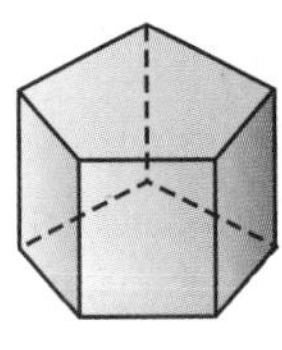
pentagonal prism; 7 faces, 2 pentagons and 5 parallelograms; 15 edges; 10 vertices

4. 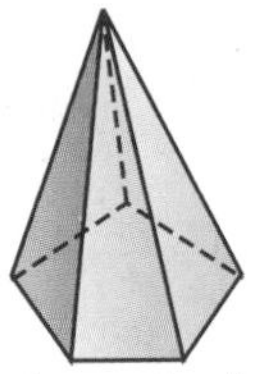 **pentagonal pyramid; 6 faces, 1 pentagon and 5 triangles; 10 edges; 6 vertices**

5. 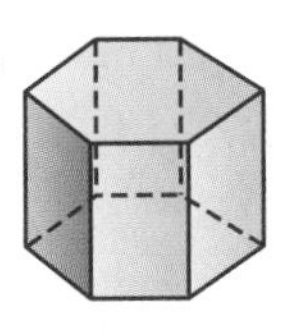
hexagonal prism; 8 faces, 2 hexagons and 6 parallelograms; 18 edges; 12 vertices

6. 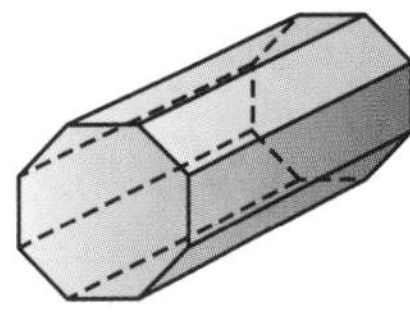

6. octagonal prism; 10 faces, 2 octagons and 8 parallelograms; 24 edges; 16 vertices

Lesson 7-5

(Pages 335–339)

Find the volume of each solid. Round to the nearest tenth if necessary.

1. 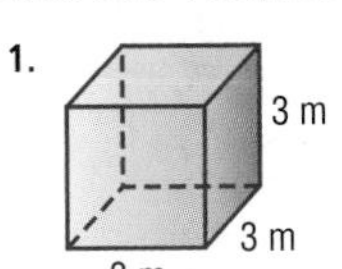

27 m³

2. 

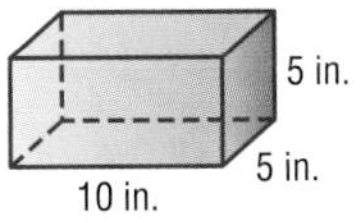

250 in³

3. 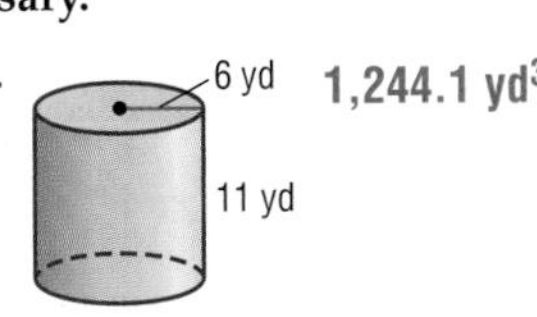

1,244.1 yd³

4. 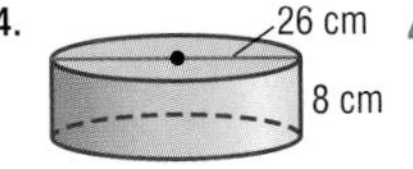

4,247.4 cm³

5. 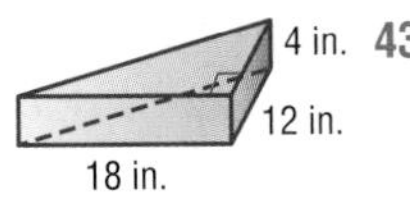

432 in³

6. 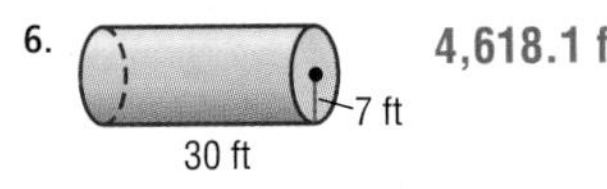

4,618.1 ft³

Extra Practice

Extra Practice 633

Extra Practice

Lesson 7-6

(Pages 342–345)

Find the volume of each solid. Round to the nearest tenth if necessary.

1. 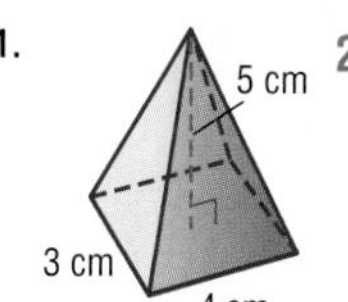

20 cm³

2. 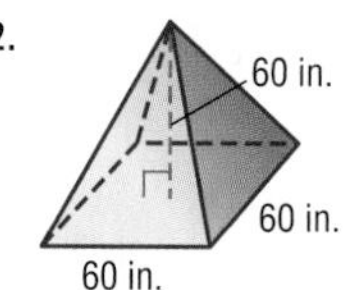

72,000 in³

3. 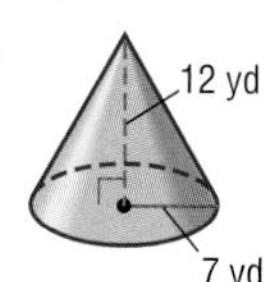

615.8 yd³

4. 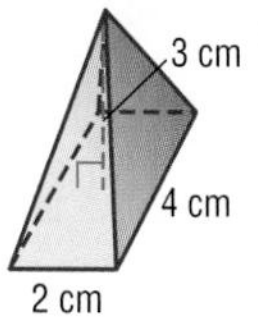 3 cm
4 cm
2 cm
8 cm³

5. 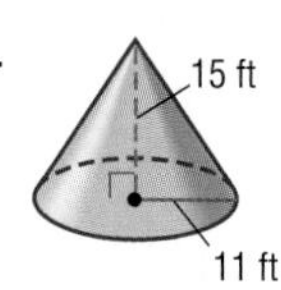

1,900.7 ft³

6. 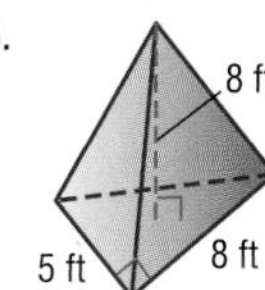

53.3 ft³

Lesson 7-7

(Pages 347–350)

Find the surface area of each solid. Round to the nearest tenth if necessary.

1. 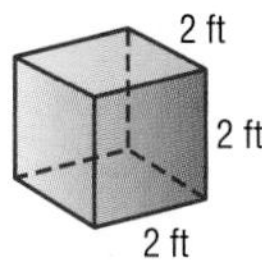

24 ft²

2. 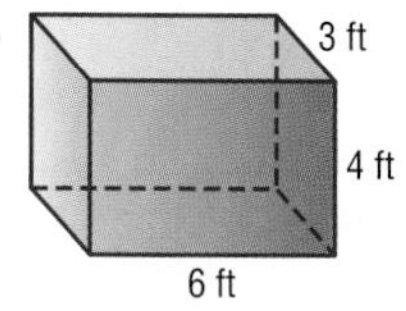

108 ft²

3. 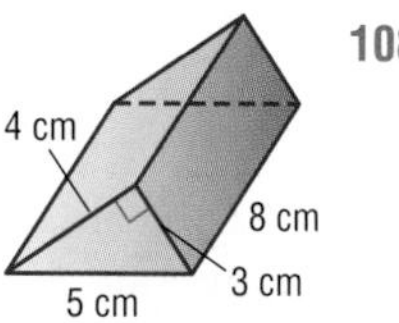

108 cm²

4. 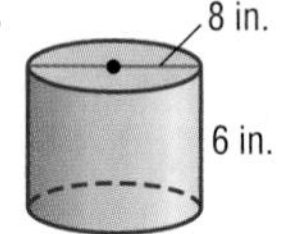

251.3 in²

5. 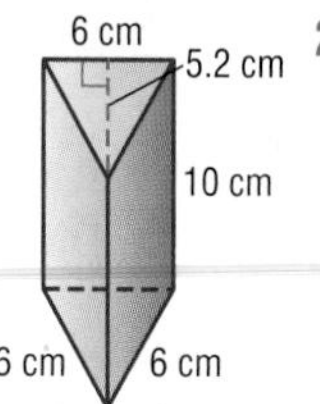

211.2 cm²

6. 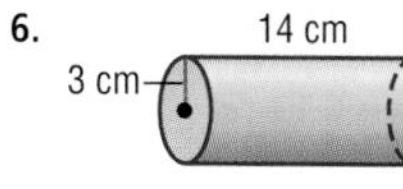

320.4 cm²

Lesson 7-8

(Pages 352–355)

Find the surface area of each solid. Round to the nearest tenth if necessary.

1. 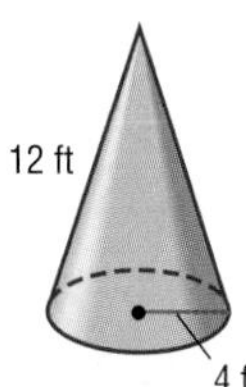

201.1 ft²

2. 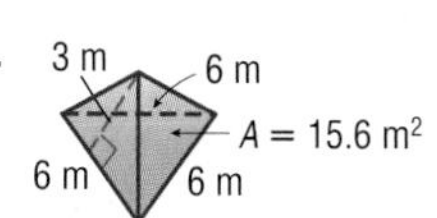

42.6 m²

3. 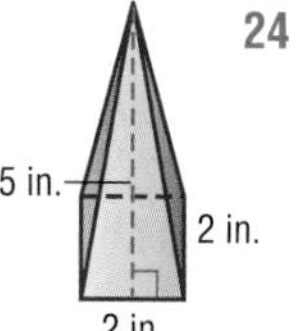

24 in²

4. 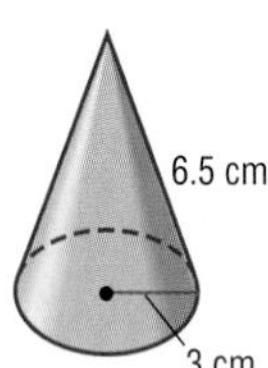

89.5 cm²

5. 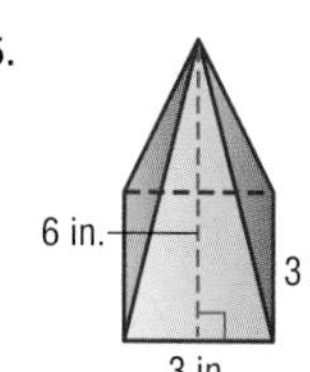

45 in²

6. 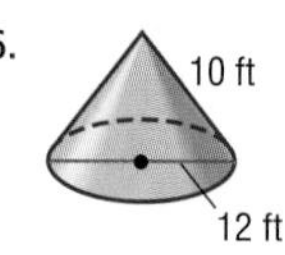

301.6 ft²

634 Extra Practice

Lesson 7-9

(Pages 358–362)

Determine the number of significant digits in each measure.

1. 18 min **2**
2. 7.5 lb **2**
3. 92.46 m **4**
4. 7 ft **1**
5. 0.067 kg **2**
6. 61.7 cm **3**
7. 8 mm **1**
8. 6.02 cm **3**

Find each sum or difference using the correct precision.

9. 9 L + 5.7 L **15 L**
10. 15.27 in. − 3.16 in. **12.11 in.**
11. 3.67 ft + 2.1 ft **5.8 ft**
12. 5.612 m − 3.1 m **2.5 m**
13. 7.1 mi − 5.421 mi **1.7 mi**
14. 0.81 kg + 5.1 kg **5.9 kg**

Find each product or quotient using the correct number of significant digits.

15. 3.257 ft ÷ 0.52 ft **6.3**
16. 3.25 in · 0.2 in **0.7 in^2**
17. 5.7 mm · 3 mm **20 mm^2**
18. 7.1 cm ÷ 2.1 cm **3.4**
19. 18 kg ÷ 3.5 kg **5.1**
20. 3.7 m · 20 m **70 m^2**
21. 1.44 cm · 2.2 cm **3.2 cm^2**
22. 500 mL ÷ 3.5 mL **100**
23. 100 mm · 73.2 mm **7,000 mm^2**

Lesson 8-1

(Pages 374–377)

A date is chosen at random from the calendar below. Find the probability of choosing each date. Write each probability as a fraction, a decimal, and a percent.

1. The date is the thirteenth. **$\frac{1}{30}$; $0.0\overline{3}$; $3.\overline{3}$%**
2. The day is Friday. **$\frac{2}{15}$; $0.1\overline{3}$; $13.\overline{3}$%**
3. It is after the twenty-fifth. **$\frac{1}{6}$; $0.1\overline{6}$; $16.\overline{6}$%**
4. It is before the seventh. **$\frac{1}{5}$; 0.2; 20%**
5. It is an odd-numbered date. **$\frac{1}{2}$; 0.5; 50%**
6. The date is divisible by 3. **$\frac{1}{3}$; $0.\overline{3}$; $33.\overline{3}$%**
7. The day is Wednesday. **$\frac{1}{6}$; $0.1\overline{6}$; $16.\overline{6}$%**
8. It is after the seventeenth. **$\frac{13}{30}$; $0.4\overline{3}$; $43.\overline{3}$%**

November

S	M	T	W	T	F	S
		1	2	3	4	5
6	7	8	9	10	11	12
13	14	15	16	17	18	19
20	21	22	23	24	25	26
27	28	29	30			

Lesson 8-2

(Pages 380–383)

Draw a tree diagram to determine the number of outcomes. **1–4. See Answer Appendix for tree diagrams.**

1. A car comes in white, black, or red with standard or automatic transmission and with a 4-cylinder or 6-cylinder engine. **12 outcomes**
2. A customer can buy roses or carnations in red, yellow, pink, or white. **8 outcomes**
3. A bed comes in queen or king size with a firm or super firm mattress. **4 outcomes**
4. A pizza can be ordered with a regular or deep dish crust and with a choice of one topping, two toppings, or three toppings. **6 outcomes**

Use the Fundamental Counting Principle to determine the number of outcomes.

5. A woman's shoe comes in red, white, blue, or black with a choice of high, medium, or low heels. **12 outcomes**
6. Sandwiches can be made with either ham or bologna, American or Swiss cheese, on wheat, rye, or white bread. **12 outcomes**
7. Sugar cookies, chocolate chip, or oatmeal raisin cookies can be ordered either with or without icing. **6 outcomes**
8. Susan can choose for her outfit a black or tan skirt, a white, pink, or cream shirt, black or tan shoes, and a red or black jacket. **24 outcomes**

Extra Practice

Extra Practice 635

Lesson 8-3

(Pages 384–387)

Find each value.

1. 8! **40, 320**
2. 10! **3,628,800**
3. 0! **1**
4. 7! **5,040**
5. 6! **720**
6. 5! **120**
7. 2! **2**
8. 11! **39,916,800**
9. 9! **362,880**
10. 4! **24**
11. $P(5, 4)$ **120**
12. $P(3, 3)$ **6**
13. $P(12, 5)$ **95,040**
14. $P(8, 6)$ **20,160**
15. $P(10, 2)$ **90**
16. $P(6, 4)$ **360**
17. How many different ways can a family of four be seated in a row? **24 ways**
18. In how many different ways can you arrange the letters in the word *orange* if you take the letters five at a time? **720 ways**
19. How many ways can you arrange five different colored marbles in a row if the blue one is always in the center? **24 ways**
20. In how many different ways can Kevin listen to each of his ten CDs once? **3,628,800 ways**

Lesson 8-4

(Pages 388–391)

Find each value.

1. $C(8, 4)$ **70**
2. $C(30, 8)$ **5,852,925**
3. $C(10, 9)$ **10**
4. $C(7, 3)$ **35**
5. $C(12, 5)$ **792**
6. $C(17, 16)$ **17**
7. $C(24, 17)$ **346,104**
8. $C(9, 7)$ **36**
9. How many ways can you choose five compact discs from a collection of 17? **6,188 ways**
10. How many combinations of three flavors of ice cream can you choose from 25 different flavors of ice cream? **2,300 combinations**
11. How many ways can you choose three books out of a selection of ten books? **120 ways**

Determine whether each statement is a *permutation* or a *combination*.

12. choosing a committee of 3 from a class. **combination**
13. placing 6 different math books in a line **permutation**

Lesson 8-5

(Pages 396–399)

Two socks are drawn from a drawer which contains one red sock, three blue socks, two black socks, and two green socks. Once a sock is selected, it is not replaced. Find each probability.

1. P(a black sock and then a green sock) $\frac{1}{14}$
2. P(a red sock and then a green sock) $\frac{1}{28}$
3. P(two blue socks) $\frac{3}{28}$
4. P(two green socks) $\frac{1}{28}$
5. P(two black socks) $\frac{1}{28}$
6. P(a black sock and then a red sock) $\frac{1}{28}$
7. P(a red sock and then a blue sock) $\frac{3}{56}$
8. P(a blue sock and then a black sock) $\frac{3}{28}$

There are three quarters, five dimes, and twelve pennies in a bag. Once a coin is drawn from the bag it is not replaced. If two coins are drawn at random, find each probability.

9. P(a quarter and then a penny) $\frac{9}{95}$
10. P(a nickel and then a dime) **0**
11. P(a dime and then a penny) $\frac{3}{19}$
12. P(two dimes) $\frac{1}{19}$
13. P(two quarters) $\frac{3}{190}$
14. P(two pennies in a row) $\frac{33}{95}$
15. P(a quarter and then a dime) $\frac{3}{76}$
16. P(a penny and then a quarter) $\frac{9}{95}$

636 Extra Practice

Lesson 8-6

(Pages 400–403)

FOOD For Exercises 1–6, use the survey results at the right.

Favorite Pizza Topping	
Topping	**Number**
pepperoni	45
sausage	25
green pepper	15
mushrooms	5
other	10

1. What is the probability that a person's favorite pizza topping is pepperoni? $\frac{9}{20}$
2. Out of 280 people, how many would you expect to have pepperoni as their favorite pizza topping? **about 126 people**
3. What is the probability that a person's favorite pizza topping is green pepper? $\frac{3}{20}$
4. Out of 280 people, how many would you expect to have green pepper as their favorite pizza topping? **about 42 people**
5. What is the probability that a person's favorite pizza topping is pepperoni or sausage? $\frac{7}{10}$
6. Out of 280 people, how many would you expect to have pepperoni or sausage as their favorite pizza topping? **about 196 people**

1. This is a biased sample, since only voluntary responses are used.

Lesson 8-7

2. This is an unbiased, simple random sample.

(Pages 406–409)

Describe each sample. **3. This is an unbiased, systematic random sample.**

1. To predict who will be the next mayor, a radio station asks their listeners to call one of two numbers to indicate their preferences.
2. To award prizes at a hockey game, four seat numbers are picked from a barrel containing individual papers representing each seat number.
3. To evaluate the quality of the televisions coming off the assembly line, the manufacturer takes one every half hour and tests it.
4. To determine what movies people prefer, people leaving a movie theater showing an action film are asked to give their preference. **This is a biased, convenience sample.**
5. To form a committee to discuss how the cafeteria can be improved, one student is picked at random from each second period class. **This is an unbiased, stratified random sample.**

Lesson 9-1

(Pages 420–424)

ARCHITECTURE For Exercises 1–8, use the histogram at the right. **5. 10 buildings**

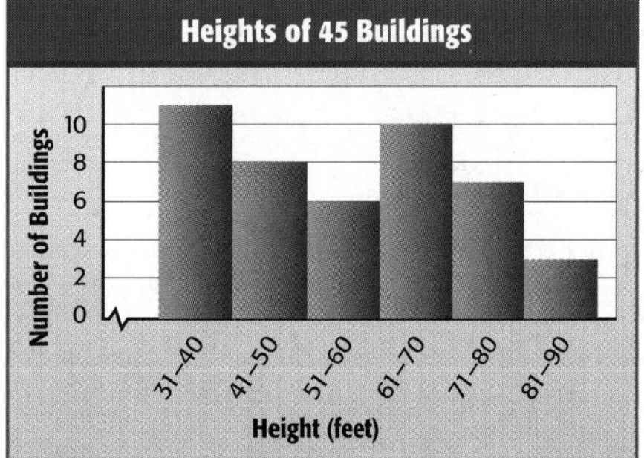

1. How large is each interval? **10 ft**
2. How many buildings are represented in the histogram? **45 buildings**
3. Which interval represents the most number of buildings? **31–40**
4. Which interval represents the least number of buildings? **81–90**
5. How many buildings are taller than 70 feet?
6. How many buildings are less than 51 feet tall? **19 buildings**
7. What is the height of the tallest building? **cannot be determined**
8. How does the number of buildings between 61 and 80 feet tall compare to the number of buildings between 31 and 50 feet tall? **There are 2 more buildings between 31 and 50 feet tall.**

Extra Practice 637

Lesson 9-2

1. Sporting Goods Sales

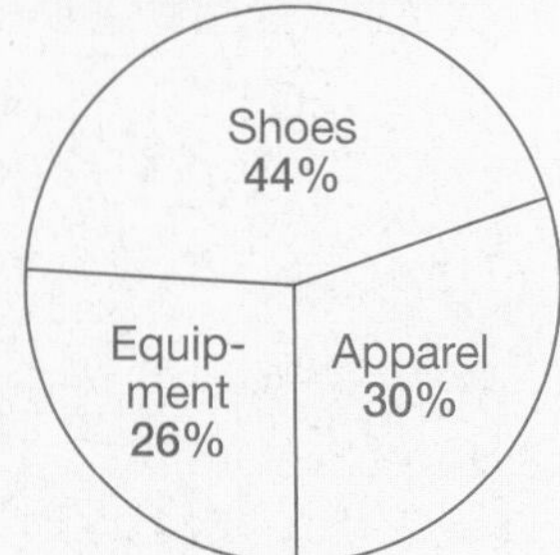

2. Energy Use in Home

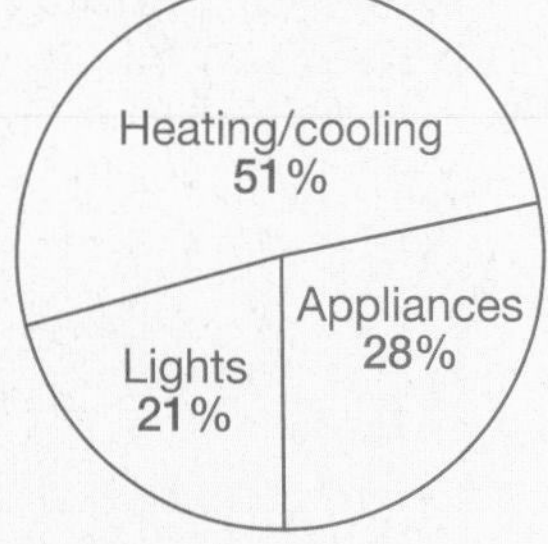

3. Household Income

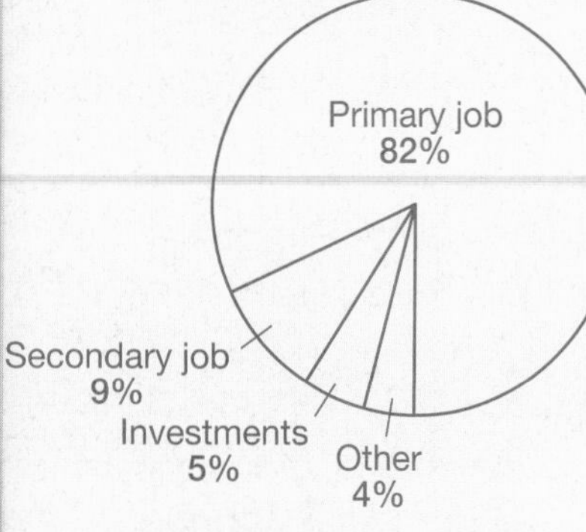

4. Students in North High School

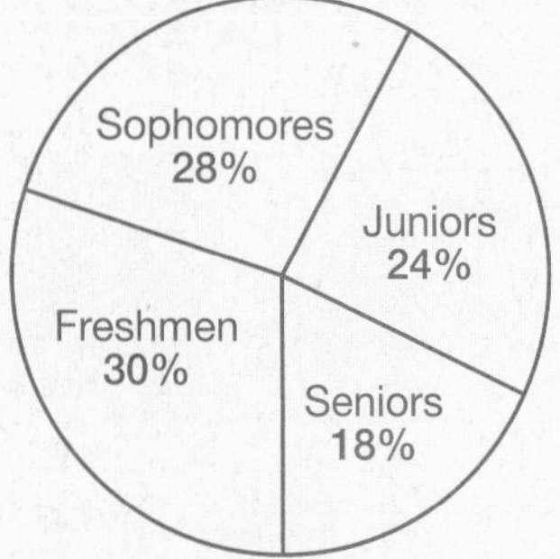

5. Number of Siblings

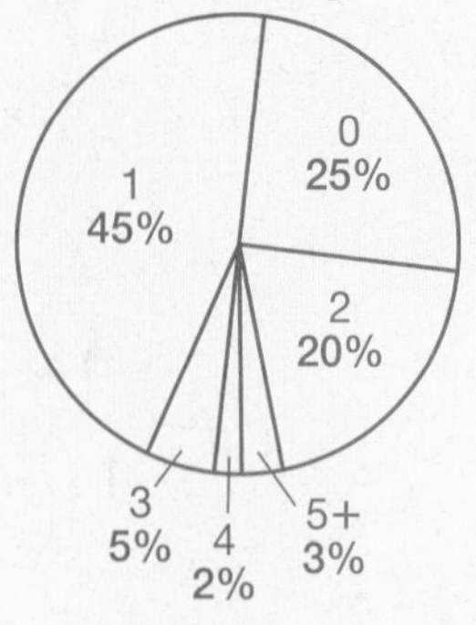

Lesson 9-2 (Pages 426–429)

Make a circle graph for each set of data. 1–6. See margin.

1.

Sporting Goods Sales	
shoes	44%
apparel	30%
equipment	26%

2.

Energy Use in Home	
heating/cooling	51%
appliances	28%
lights	21%

3.

Household Income	
primary job	82%
secondary job	9%
investments	5%
other	4%

4.

Students in North High School	
freshmen	30%
sophomores	28%
juniors	24%
seniors	18%

5.

Number of Siblings	
0	25%
1	45%
2	20%
3	5%
4	2%
5+	3%

6.

Household Expenses	
food	45%
housing	30%
utilities	15%
other	10%

Lesson 9-3 (Pages 430–433)

Choose the most appropriate type of display for each situation. 5. table, bar graph, or pictograph

1. number of televisions in homes compared to the total number of homes in the survey circle graph
2. the amount of sales by different sales people compared to the total sales circle graph
3. ages by intervals of amusement park attendees in marketing information for the park histogram
4. average proficiency test score for five consecutive years line graph
5. numbers of Americans who own motorcycles, boats, and recreational vehicles
6. percent of people who own a certain type of car compared to all car owners circle graph
7. a child's age and his or her height line graph
8. amount of fat grams in intervals in various sandwiches histogram
9. the number of students who have read each of three popular books
10. number of people filing tax returns electronically over the past ten years line graph

9. table, bar graph, or pictogram

Lesson 9-4 (Pages 435–438)

Find the mean, median, and mode for each set of data. Round to the nearest tenth if necessary. 4. 52.1, 54, 56 12. 24.7, 25.5, no mode 13. 99.0; 98.6; no mode

1. 2, 7, 9, 12, 5, 14, 4, 8, 3, 10 7.4, 7.5, no mode
2. 58, 52, 49, 60, 61, 56, 50, 61 55.9, 57, 61
3. 122, 134, 129, 140, 125, 134, 137 131.6, 134, 134
4. 36, 41, 43, 45, 48, 52, 54, 56, 56, 57, 60, 64, 65
5. 3, 9, 14, 3, 0, 2, 6, 11 6; 4.5; 3
6. 6, 3, 1, 8, 7, 2 4.5; 4.5; no mode
7. 11, 15, 21, 11, 6, 10, 11 12.1; 11; 11
8. 21, 20, 19, 20, 18, 21, 23, 25 20.9; 20.5; 20, 21
9. 1, 3, 2, 1, 1, 2, 2, 2, 3 1.9; 2; 2
10. 23, 35, 42, 26, 27, 29, 31, 29, 27 29.9; 29; 27, 29
11. 32.1, 33.5, 31.5, 37.8 33.7; 32.8; no mode
12. 25.5, 26.7, 20.9, 23.4, 26.8, 24.0, 25.7
13. 98.6, 97.9, 98.1, 100.1, 100.2
14. 10.1, 12.3, 11.4, 15.6, 7.3, 10.1 11.1; 10.8; 10.1

6. Household Expenses

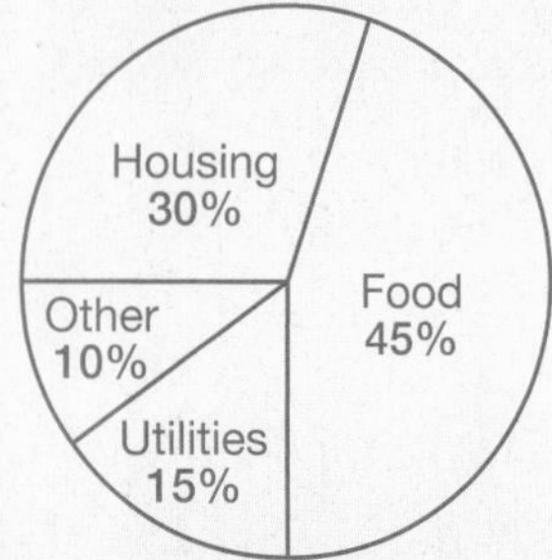

Lesson 9-5 (Pages 442–445)

Find the range, median, upper and lower quartiles, interquartile range, and any outliers for each set of data. 1–14. See margin.

1. 15, 12, 21, 18, 25, 11, 17, 19, 20
2. 2, 24, 6, 13, 8, 6, 11, 4
3. 189, 149, 155, 290, 141, 152
4. 451, 501, 388, 428, 510, 480, 390
5. 22, 18, 9, 26, 14, 15, 6, 19, 28
6. 245, 218, 251, 255, 248, 241, 250
7. 46, 45, 50, 40, 49, 42, 64
8. 128, 148, 130, 142, 164, 120, 152, 202
9. 2, 3, 2, 6, 4, 14, 13, 2, 6, 3
10. 88, 84, 92, 93, 90, 96, 87, 97
11. 2, 3, 5, 4, 3, 3, 2, 5, 6
12. 6, 7, 9, 10, 11, 11, 13, 14, 12, 11, 12
13. 117, 118, 120, 109, 117, 117, 100
14. 12, 14, 17, 19, 13, 16, 17
15. 378, 480, 370, 236, 361, 394, 345, 328, 388, 339 **244; 365.5; 388, 339; 49; 236, 480**
16. 80, 91, 82, 83, 77, 79, 78, 75, 75, 88, 84, 82, 61, 93, 88, 85, 84, 89, 62, 79 **32; 82; 86.5, 77.5; 9; 61 and 62**
17. 195, 121, 135, 123, 138, 150, 122, 138, 149, 124, 149, 151, 152 **74; 138; 150.5, 123.5; 27; 195**

Lesson 9-6 (Pages 446–449)

Draw a box-and-whisker plot for each set of data. 1–10. See Answer Appendix.

1. 2, 3, 5, 4, 3, 3, 2, 5, 6
2. 6, 7, 9, 10, 11, 11, 13, 14, 12, 11, 12
3. 15, 12, 21, 18, 25, 11, 17, 19, 20
4. 2, 24, 6, 13, 8, 6, 11, 4
5. 22, 18, 9, 26, 14, 15, 6, 19, 28
6. 46, 45, 50, 40, 49, 42, 64
7. 2, 3, 2, 6, 4, 14, 13, 2, 6, 3
8. 88, 84, 92, 93, 90, 96, 87, 97
9. 80, 91, 82, 83, 77, 79, 78, 75, 75, 88, 84, 82, 61, 93, 88, 85, 84, 89, 62, 79
10. 195, 121, 135, 123, 138, 150, 122, 138, 149, 124, 149, 151, 152

ZOOS For Exercises 11 and 12, use the following box-and-whisker plot.

Area (acres) of Major Zoos in the United States

0 100 200 300 400 500 600

Source: *The World Almanac*

11. How many outliers are in the data? **2**
12. Describe the distribution of the data. What can you say about the areas of the major zoos in the United States? **The top half of the data is much more spread out than the bottom half of the data. Most major zoos are considerably smaller in area than the few zoos that have very large areas.**

Lesson 9-7 (Pages 450–453)

1. Yes; the values represented by the graph are the same.

FITNESS For Exercises 1 and 2, use the graphs at the right.

1. Do both graphs contain the same information? Explain.
2. Which graph would you use to indicate that many more eighth graders finished the obstacle course than sixth or seventh graders? Explain. **Graph A; since there is a break in the vertical scale of Graph A, the number of eighth graders completing the course seems to be much greater than those who completed the course in the other grades.**

Graph A

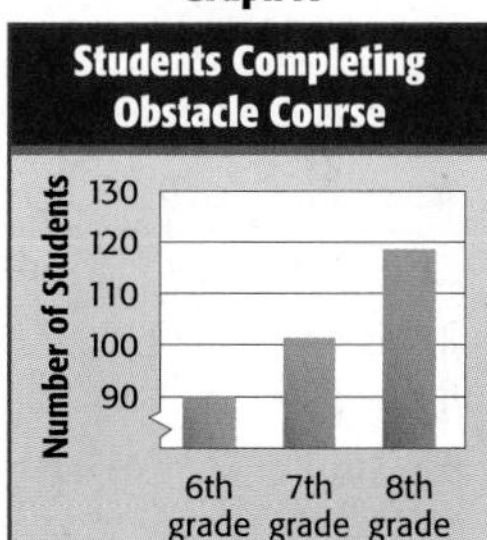

Graph B

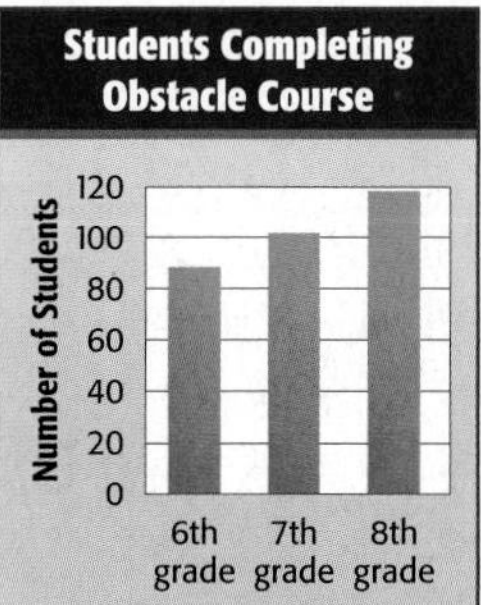

Lesson 9-5

1. 14; 18; 20.5, 13.5; 7; no outliers
2. 22; 7; 12, 5; 7; 24
3. 149; 153.5; 189, 149; 40; 290
4. 122; 451; 501, 390; 111; no outliers
5. 22; 18; 24, 11.5; 12.5; no outliers
6. 37; 248; 251, 241; 10; 218
7. 24; 46; 50, 42; 8; 64
8. 82; 145; 158, 129; 29; 202
9. 12; 3.5; 6, 2; 4; 13, 14
10. 13; 91; 94.5, 87.5; 7; no outliers
11. 4; 3; 5, 2.5; 2.5; no outliers
12. 8; 11; 12, 9; 3; no outliers
13. 20; 117; 118, 109; 9; no outliers
14. 7; 16; 17, 13; 4; no outliers

Extra Practice 639

Extra Practice

Extra Practice

Lesson 9-8

(Pages 454–457)

State the dimension of each matrix. Then identify the position of the circled element.

1. $\begin{bmatrix} 2 \\ \textcircled{3} \\ 1 \end{bmatrix}$ **3 by 1; second row, first column**
2. $\begin{bmatrix} 2 & \textcircled{6} \\ -1 & 0 \end{bmatrix}$ **2 by 2; first row, second column**
3. $[3 \quad 4 \quad \textcircled{-2} \quad 1]$ **1 by 4; first row, third column**
4. $\begin{bmatrix} 6 & 3 & 2 & 1 \\ 0 & \textcircled{1} & -3 & 5 \end{bmatrix}$ **2 by 4; second row, second column**
5. $\begin{bmatrix} \textcircled{6} & 4 & 1 \\ 9 & 0 & 1 \\ 2 & -8 & 11 \end{bmatrix}$ **3 by 3; first row, first column**
6. $\begin{bmatrix} 10 & 9 \\ 2 & 8 \\ 15 & \textcircled{13} \end{bmatrix}$ **3 by 2; third row, second column**

Add or subtract. If there is no sum or difference, write *impossible*.

7. $\begin{bmatrix} 2 & 0 \\ -6 & 4 \end{bmatrix} + \begin{bmatrix} 8 & 6 \\ 1 & -3 \end{bmatrix}$ $\begin{bmatrix} 10 & 6 \\ -5 & 1 \end{bmatrix}$
8. $\begin{bmatrix} 8 & 5 & 2 \\ -1 & 3 & 11 \end{bmatrix} + \begin{bmatrix} -4 & 12 \\ 1 & 8 \\ 6 & -3 \end{bmatrix}$ **impossible**
9. $\begin{bmatrix} 1 & 2 \\ 6 & -3 \\ -5 & 7 \end{bmatrix} - \begin{bmatrix} -2 & 7 \\ 5 & 4 \\ -3 & 9 \end{bmatrix}$ $\begin{bmatrix} 3 & -5 \\ 1 & -7 \\ -2 & -2 \end{bmatrix}$
10. $\begin{bmatrix} 0 & 8 & 6 \\ 7 & -2 & 4 \\ 0 & 0 & 9 \end{bmatrix} - \begin{bmatrix} -6 & 0 & -1 \\ 2 & 4 & 0 \\ -1 & 5 & 8 \end{bmatrix}$ $\begin{bmatrix} 6 & 8 & 7 \\ 5 & -6 & 4 \\ 1 & -5 & 1 \end{bmatrix}$
11. $\begin{bmatrix} 13 & 2 \\ 7 & -1 \end{bmatrix} + \begin{bmatrix} 6 & -5 & 0 \\ 3 & 1 & -2 \\ 2 & 7 & 8 \end{bmatrix}$ **impossible**
12. $\begin{bmatrix} 13 & 5 & 7 \\ -6 & 12 & -1 \end{bmatrix} - \begin{bmatrix} 8 & -6 & 0 \\ -2 & 15 & 2 \end{bmatrix}$ $\begin{bmatrix} 5 & 11 & 7 \\ -4 & -3 & -3 \end{bmatrix}$

Lesson 10-1

(Pages 469–473)

Use the Distributive Property to rewrite each expression.

1. $2(x + 3)$ **$2x + 6$**
2. $3(a + 7)$ **$3a + 21$**
3. $3(g - 6)$ **$3g - 18$**
4. $-2(a + 3)$ **$-2a - 6$**
5. $-1(x - 6)$ **$-x + 6$**
6. $4(a - 5)$ **$4a - 20$**
7. $-6(x - 1)$ **$-6x + 6$**
8. $3(2x + 5)$ **$6x + 15$**
9. $2(3x - 1)$ **$6x - 2$**
10. $-1(2x - 1)$ **$-2x + 1$**
11. $5(-3x + 2)$ **$-15x + 10$**
12. $-7(2x - 2)$ **$-14x + 14$**

Simplify each expression.

13. $3x + 2x$ **$5x$**
14. $6x - 3x$ **$3x$**
15. $2a - 5a$ **$-3a$**
16. $5x - 6x$ **$-x$**
17. $8a - 3a$ **$5a$**
18. $a - 4a$ **$-3a$**
19. $3a + 2a - 6$ **$5a - 6$**
20. $6x + 2x - 3$ **$8x - 3$**
21. $5a - 3 + 2a$ **$7a - 3$**
22. $3x + 7 - 5x$ **$-2x + 7$**
23. $x - 3 + 5x$ **$6x - 3$**
24. $6x - 3x - 2$ **$3x - 2$**
25. $a - 2a + 5$ **$-a + 5$**
26. $6x - 2 + 7x$ **$13x - 2$**
27. $5a - 7a + 2$ **$-2a + 2$**
28. $4a + 2 - 7a - 5$ **$-3a - 3$**
29. $3a - 2 + 5a - 7$ **$8a - 9$**
30. $5x - 3x + 2 - 5$ **$2x - 3$**

Lesson 10-2

(Pages 474–477)

Solve each equation. Check your solution.

1. $2x + 4 = 14$ **5**
2. $5p - 10 = 0$ **2**
3. $5 + 6a = 41$ **6**
4. $\frac{x}{3} - 7 = 2$ **27**
5. $18 = 6q - 24$ **7**
6. $18 = 4m - 6$ **6**
7. $3r - 3 = 9$ **4**
8. $2x + 3 = 5$ **1**
9. $0 = 4x - 28$ **7**
10. $3x - 1 = 5$ **2**
11. $3z + 5 = 14$ **3**
12. $3x - 15 = 12$ **9**
13. $9a - 8 = 73$ **9**
14. $2x - 3 = 7$ **5**
15. $3t + 6 = 9$ **1**
16. $2y + 10 = 22$ **6**
17. $15 = 2y - 5$ **10**
18. $3c - 4 = 2$ **2**
19. $6 + 2p = 16$ **5**
20. $8 = 2 + 3x$ **2**
21. $4b + 24 = 24$ **0**
22. $2x + 3x - 6 = 19$ **5**
23. $-2x - 6 = 14$ **−10**
24. $3x - 9 = -18$ **−3**
25. $2a - 3a + 1 = 15$ **−14**
26. $5x - 3x + 6 = -10$ **−8**
27. $3a - 5a + a = 11$ **−11**
28. $5a - 3a - 5 + 1 = -10$ **−3**
29. $3 = 7a - 6a + 2$ **1**
30. $3y + 5y - 1 = 15$ **2**

640 Extra Practice

Lesson 10-3

(Pages 478–481)

Translate each sentence into an equation. Then find each number.

1. The sum of a number and 7 is 11. $x + 7 = 11$; 4
2. Seven more than the quotient of a number and −2 is 6. $\frac{x}{-2} + 7 = 6$; 2
3. The sum of a number and 6 is 21. $x + 6 = 21$; 15
4. The difference of a number and 2 is 4. $x - 2 = 4$; 6
5. Twice a number plus 5 is −3. $2x + 5 = -3$; −4
6. The product of a number and 3 is 18. $3x = 18$; 6
7. The product of a number and 4 plus 2 is 14. $4x + 2 = 14$; 3
8. Eight less than the quotient of a number and 3 is 5. $\frac{x}{3} - 8 = 5$; 39
9. The difference of twice a number and 3 is 11. $2x - 3 = 11$; 7
10. The sum of 3 times a number and 7 is 25. $3x + 7 = 25$; 6

Lesson 10-4

(Pages 484–487)

Solve each equation. Check your solution.

1. $6x + 10 = 1x$ −2
2. $2a - 5 = -3a$ 1
3. $7a - 5 = 2a$ 1
4. $3a + 7 = 10$ 1
5. $8x + 3 = 2x$ $-\frac{1}{2}$
6. $5x - 3 = -18$ −3
7. $3a - 1 = 2a$ 1
8. $7a - 2 = 12$ 2
9. $3x + 6 = x$ −3
10. $2x + 7 = 11 - 2x$ 1
11. $8x + 10 = 3x$ −2
12. $7a + 4 = 3a$ −1
13. $7x + 8 = 11x$ 2
14. $21x + 11 = 10x$ −1
15. $5x + 5 = 14 + 2x$ 3
16. $7b - 4 = 2b + 16$ 4
17. $2y - 3 = 5 - 2y$ 2
18. $3m = 2m + 7$ 7
19. $9t + 1 = 4t - 9$ −2
20. $-2a + 3 = a - 12$ 5
21. $3x = 9x - 12$ 2
22. $2c + 3 = 3c - 4$ 7
23. $s - 3 = 5 - s$ 4
24. $3w - 5 = 5w - 7$ 1
25. $4x - 7 = 11 + x$ 6
26. $5x + 2 = 10 + x$ 2
27. $3x + 2 = 2x + 5$ 3
28. $8a + 7 = 7a + 8$ 1
29. $3a - 11 = 4a - 12$ 1
30. $2a - 5 = 8a - 11$ 1

Lesson 10-5

(Pages 492–495)

Write an inequality for each sentence.

1. A number is less than 10. $x < 10$
2. A number is greater than or equal −7. $x \geq -7$
3. A number is less than −2. $x < -2$
4. A number is more than 5. $x > 5$
5. A number is less than or equal to 11. $x \leq 11$
6. a number is no more than 8. $x \leq 8$

Graph each inequality on a number line. 7–18. See margin.

7. $x > 5$
8. $y > 0$
9. $z < -2$
10. $a \geq 6$
11. $b \leq 2$
12. $x \geq 1$
13. $a \leq 3$
14. $b \geq 1$
15. $x < -2$
16. $n \geq -3$
17. $t > -1$
18. $y \leq -5$

Lesson 10-5

7. 0 1 2 3 4 5 6 7
8. −3 −2 −1 0 1 2 3 4
9. −5 −4 −3 −2 −1 0 1 2
10. 0 1 2 3 4 5 6 7
11. 0 1 2 3 4 5 6 7
12. −1 0 1 2 3 4 5 6
13. 0 1 2 3 4 5 6 7
14. −2 −1 0 1 2 3 4 5
15. −5 −4 −3 −2 −1 0 1 2
16. −5 −4 −3 −2 −1 0 1 2
17. −4 −3 −2 −1 0 1 2 3
18. −7 −6 −5 −4 −3 −2 −1 0

Extra Practice 641

Lesson 10-7

1.
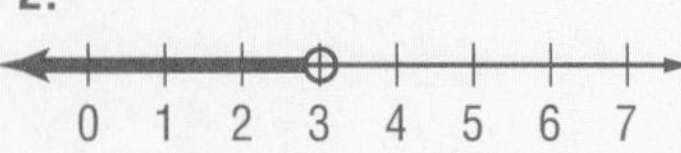

2.
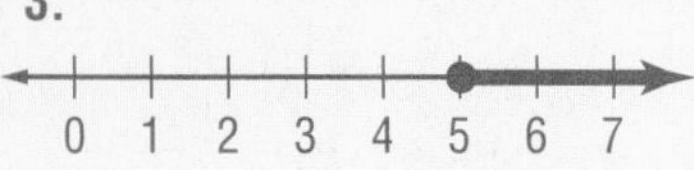

3.
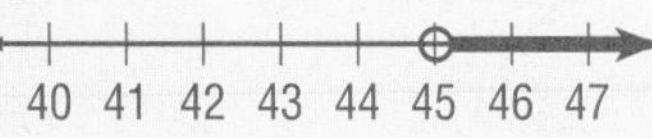

4.
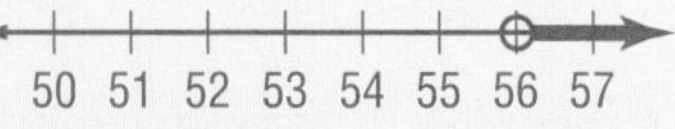

5.
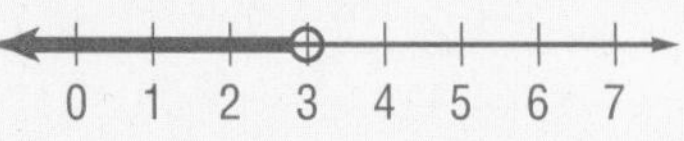

6.
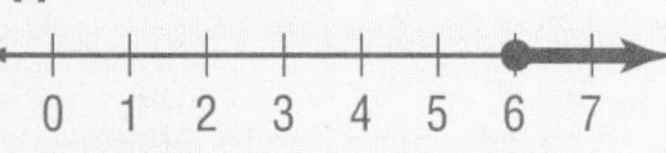

7.
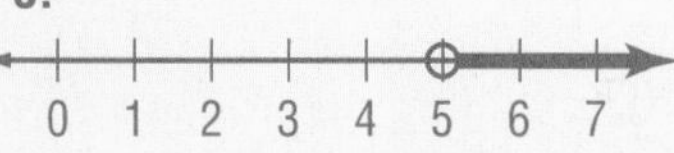

8.

9.
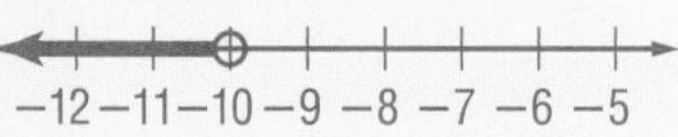

10. −12 −11 −10 −9 −8 −7 −6 −5

11. −7 −6 −5 −4 −3 −2 −1 0

12. 0 1 2 3 4 5 6 7

13. −7 −6 −5 −4 −3 −2 −1 0

14.
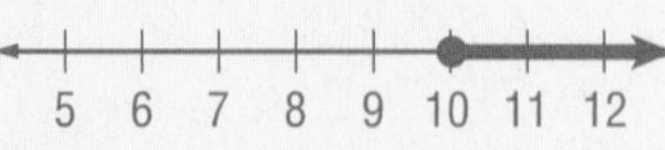

15. −9 −8 −7 −6 −5 −4 −3 −2

Extra Practice

Lesson 10-6

(Pages 496–499)

Solve each inequality. Check your solution.

1. $y + 3 > 7$ **$y > 4$**
2. $c - 9 < 5$ **$c < 14$**
3. $x + 4 \geq 9$ **$x \geq 5$**
4. $y - 3 < 15$ **$y < 18$**
5. $t - 13 \geq 5$ **$t \geq 18$**
6. $x + 3 < 10$ **$x < 7$**
7. $y - 6 \geq 2$ **$y \geq 8$**
8. $x - 3 \geq -6$ **$x \geq -3$**
9. $a + 3 \leq 5$ **$a \leq 2$**
10. $c - 2 \leq 11$ **$c \leq 13$**
11. $a + 15 \geq 6$ **$a \geq -9$**
12. $y + 3 \geq 18$ **$y \geq 15$**
13. $y + 16 \geq -22$ **$y \geq -38$**
14. $x - 3 \geq 17$ **$x \geq 20$**
15. $y - 6 > -17$ **$y > -11$**
16. $y - 11 < 7$ **$y < 18$**
17. $a + 5 \geq 21$ **$a \geq 16$**
18. $c + 3 > -16$ **$c > -19$**
19. $x - 12 \geq 12$ **$x \geq 24$**
20. $x + 5 \geq 5$ **$x \geq 0$**
21. $y - 6 > 31$ **$y > 37$**
22. $a - 6 > 17$ **$a > 23$**
23. $y + 7 > 3$ **$y > -4$**
24. $a + 13 \geq -16$ **$a \geq -29$**
25. $y - 6 > 5$ **$y > 11$**
26. $y + 6 < -5$ **$y < -11$**
27. $x - 17 \geq 34$ **$x \geq 51$**
28. $y + 1 \leq 16$ **$y \leq 15$**
29. $a - 14 \geq 16$ **$a \geq 30$**
30. $x + 14 \leq 20$ **$x \leq 6$**

Lesson 10-7

(Pages 500–504)

Solve each inequality and check your solution. Then graph the solution on a number line. **1–23. See margin for graphs. 24–30. See Answer Appendix.**

1. $5p \geq 25$ **$p \geq 5$**
2. $4x < 12$ **$x < 3$**
3. $15 \leq 3m$ **$5 \leq m$**
4. $\frac{d}{3} > 15$ **$d > 45$**
5. $8 < \frac{r}{7}$ **$56 < r$**
6. $9g < 27$ **$g < 3$**
7. $4p \geq 24$ **$p \geq 6$**
8. $5p > 25$ **$p > 5$**
9. $-4 > \frac{-k}{3}$ **$12 < k$**
10. $\frac{-z}{5} > 2$ **$z < -10$**
11. $-3x \leq 9$ **$x \geq -3$**
12. $-5x > -35$ **$x < 7$**
13. $\frac{a}{-6} < 1$ **$a > -6$**
14. $\frac{x}{-5} \leq -2$ **$x \geq 10$**
15. $-2x < 16$ **$x > -8$**
16. $3p \geq 12$ **$p \geq 4$**
17. $\frac{x}{-2} \leq -2$ **$x \geq 4$**
18. $\frac{y}{6} \leq -5$ **$y \leq -30$**
19. $5p \geq 100$ **$p \geq 20$**
20. $-4x \leq 64$ **$x \geq -16$**
21. $8x \geq 56$ **$x \geq 7$**
22. $-2t < 14$ **$t > -7$**
23. $18 > 3x$ **$6 > x$**
24. $5x > 10$ **$x > 2$**
25. $\frac{a}{3} > 1$ **$a > 3$**
26. $14 \leq 2x$ **$7 \leq x$**
27. $\frac{x}{2} > 0$ **$x > 0$**
28. $2y \geq 22$ **$y \geq 11$**
29. $35 \leq 5d$ **$7 \leq d$**
30. $3x \geq 9$ **$x \geq 3$**

Lesson 11-1

(Pages 512–515)

State whether each sequence is *arithmetic*, *geometric*, or *neither*. If it is arithmetic or geometric, state the common difference or common ratio. Write the next three terms of each sequence. **1–27. See Answer Appendix.**

1. 1, 5, 9, 13, ...
2. 2, 6, 18, 54, ...
3. 1, 4, 9, 16, 25, ...
4. 729, 243, 81, ...
5. 2, −3, −8, −13, ...
6. 5, −5, 5, −5, ...
7. 810, −270, 90, −30, ...
8. 11, 14, 17, 20, 23, ...
9. 33, 27, 21, ...
10. 21, 15, 9, 3, ...
11. $\frac{1}{8}, -\frac{1}{4}, \frac{1}{2}, -1, \ldots$
12. $\frac{1}{81}, \frac{1}{27}, \frac{1}{9}, \frac{1}{3}, \ldots$
13. $\frac{3}{4}, 1\frac{1}{2}, 3, \ldots$
14. 2, 5, 9, 14, ...
15. $-1\frac{1}{4}, -1\frac{3}{4}, -2\frac{1}{4}, -2\frac{3}{4}, \ldots$
16. 9.9, 13.7, 17.5, ...
17. $\frac{1}{2}, 1\frac{1}{2}, 2\frac{1}{2}, 3\frac{1}{2}, \ldots$
18. 2, 12, 32, 62, ...
19. 3, −6, 12, −24, ...
20. 5, 7, 9, 11, 13, ...
21. −0.06, 2.24, 4.54, ...
22. 7, 14, 28, ...
23. −5.4, −1.4, 2.6, ...
24. −96, 48, −24, 12, ...
25. 4, 12, 36, ...
26. 20, 19, 18, 17, ...
27. 768, 192, 48, ...

16. 0 1 2 3 4 5 6 7

17. 0 1 2 3 4 5 6 7

18. −35 −34 −33 −32 −31 −30 −29 −28

19. 15 16 17 18 19 20 21 22

20. −19 −18 −17 −16 −15 −14 −13 −12

21.
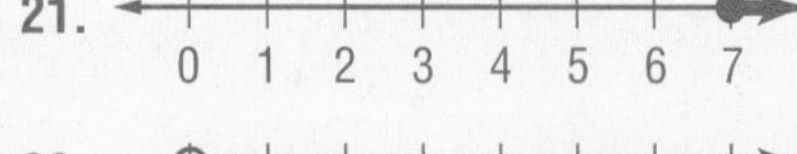

22. −7 −6 −5 −4 −3 −2 −1 0

23.
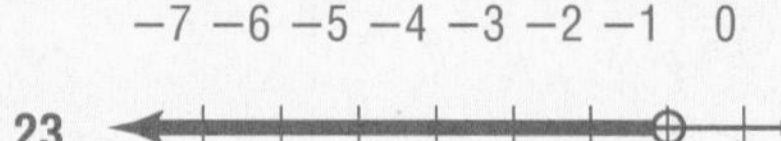

Lesson 11-2

(Pages 517–520)

Find each function value.

1. $f\left(\frac{1}{2}\right)$ if $f(x) = 2x - 6$ **−5**
2. $f(-4)$ if $f(x) = -\frac{1}{2}x + 4$ **6**
3. $f(1)$ if $f(x) = -5x + 1$ **−4**
4. $f(6)$ if $f(x) = \frac{2}{3}x - 5$ **−1**
5. $f(0)$ if $f(x) = 1.6x + 4$ **4**
6. $f(2)$ if $f(x) = 2x - 8$ **−4**
7. $f(-1)$ if $f(x) = -3x + 5$ **8**
8. $f\left(\frac{1}{2}\right)$ if $f(x) = 2x - 1$ **0**
9. $f(6)$ if $f(x) = \frac{2}{3}x + 4$ **8**

Copy and complete each function table.

10. $f(x) = -4x$

x	−4x	f(x)	
−2		8	−4(−2)
−1		4	−4(−1)
0	−4(0)	0	
1	−4(1)	−4	
2	−4(2)	−8	

11. $f(x) = x + 6$

x	x + 6	f(x)
−6	−6 + 6	0
−4	−4 + 6	2
−2	−2 + 6	4
0	0 + 6	6
2	2 + 6	8

12. $f(x) = 3x + 2$

x	3x + 2	f(x)
−3	3(−3) + 2	−7
−2	3(−2) + 2	−4
−1	3(−1) + 2	−1
0	3(0) + 2	2
1	3(1) + 2	5

Lesson 11-3

(Pages 522–525)

Copy and complete the table. Then graph the function. **1–2. See margin for graphs.**

1. $y = 6x + 2$

x	6x + 2	y	(x, y)	
−2	6(−2) + 2	−10		(−2, −10)
−1	6(−1) + 2	−4		(−1, −4)
0	6(0) + 2	2	(0, 2)	
1	6(1) + 2	8	(1, 8)	

2. $y = -2x + 3$

x	−2x + 3	y	(x, y)	
−2		7	(−2, 7)	−2(−2) + 3
−1		5	(−1, 5)	−2(−1) + 3
0	−2(0) + 3	3	(0, 3)	
2	−2(2) + 3	−1	(2, −1)	

Graph each function. **3–9. See margin. 10–18. See Answer Appendix.**

3. $y = -5x$
4. $y = 10x - 2$
5. $y = -2.5x - 1.5$
6. $y = 7x + 3$
7. $y = \frac{x}{4} - 8$
8. $y = 3x + 1$
9. $y = 25 - 2x$
10. $y = \frac{x}{6}$
11. $y = -2x + 11$
12. $y = 7x - 3$
13. $y = \frac{x}{2} + 5$
14. $y = 4 - 6x$
15. $y = -3.5x - 1$
16. $y = 4x + 10$
17. $y = 8x$
18. $y = \frac{x}{3} + 2$

Lesson 11-4

(Pages 526–529)

Find the slope of the line that passes through each pair of points.

1. $A(2, 3), B(1, 5)$ **−2**
2. $C(-6, 1), D(2, 1)$ **0**
3. $E(3, 0), F(5, 0)$ **0**
4. $G(-1, -3), H(-2, -5)$ **2**
5. $I(6, 7), J(11, 1)$ $-\frac{6}{5}$
6. $K(5, 3), L(5, -2)$ **undefined**
7. $M(10, 2), N(-3, 5)$ $-\frac{3}{13}$
8. $O(6, 2), P(1, 7)$ **−1**
9. $Q(5, 8), R(-3, -2)$ $\frac{5}{4}$
10. $S(-1, 7), T(3, 8)$ $\frac{1}{4}$
11. $U(4, -1), V(-5, -2)$ $\frac{1}{9}$
12. $W(3, -2), X(7, -1)$ $\frac{1}{4}$
13. $Y(0, 5), Z(2, 1)$ **−2**
14. $A(6, 5), B(-3, -5)$ $\frac{10}{9}$
15. $C(2, 1), D(7, -1)$ $-\frac{2}{5}$
16. $E(-5, 2), F(0, 2)$ **0**
17. $G(-3, 5), H(-2, 5)$ **0**
18. $I(2, 0), J(3, 5)$ **5**
19. $K(11, 1), L(21, 3)$ $\frac{1}{5}$
20. $M(6, 5), N(-1, 7)$ $-\frac{2}{7}$
21. $O(-2, 3), P(2, -1)$ **−1**
22. $Q(5, 0), R(1, 1)$ $-\frac{1}{4}$
23. $S(0, 0), T(3, -4)$ $-\frac{4}{3}$
24. $U(5, 3), V(5, -2)$ **undefined**

Lesson 11-3

1.
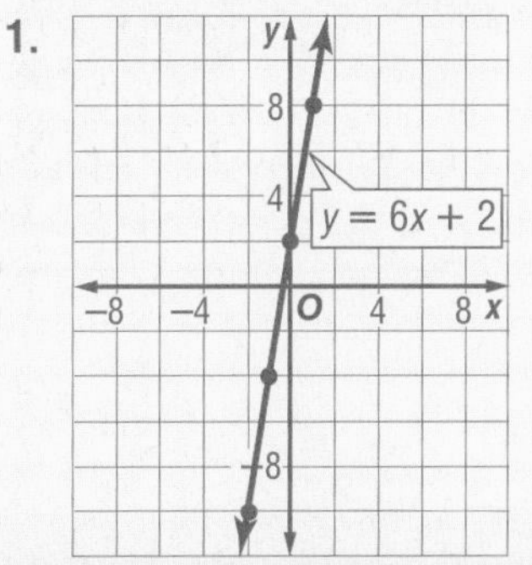

2.
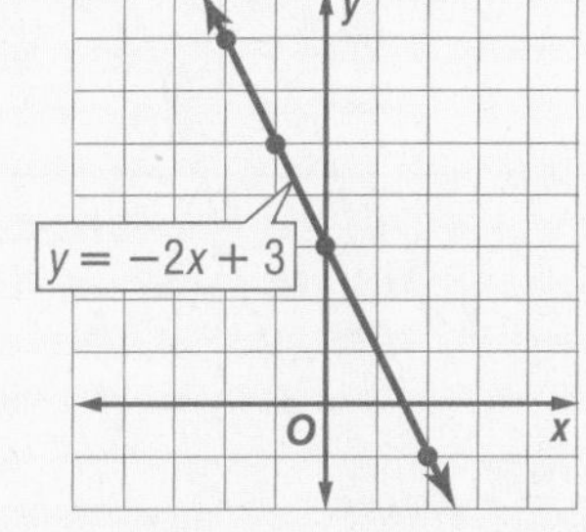

3.
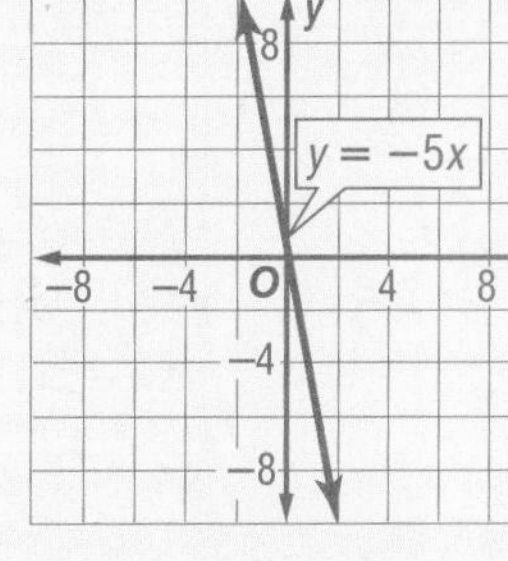

4.
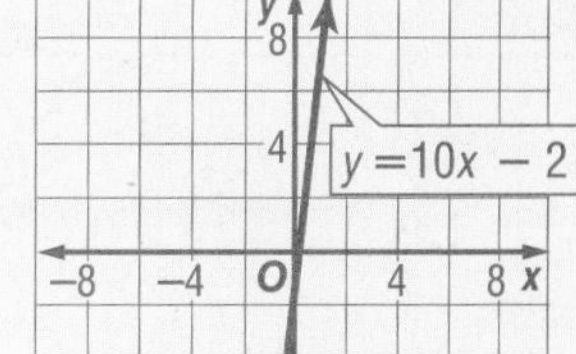

5.
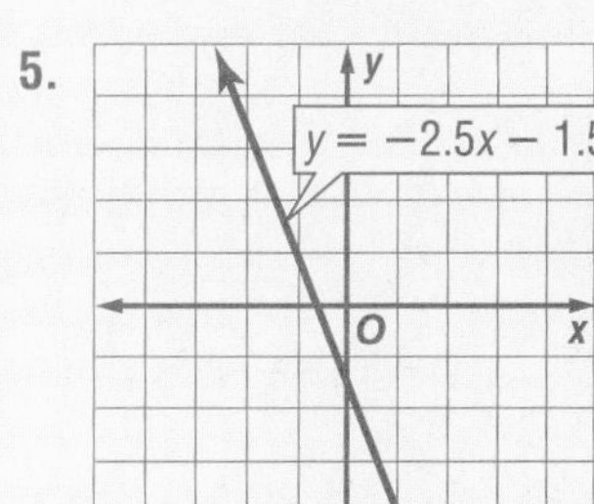

6.
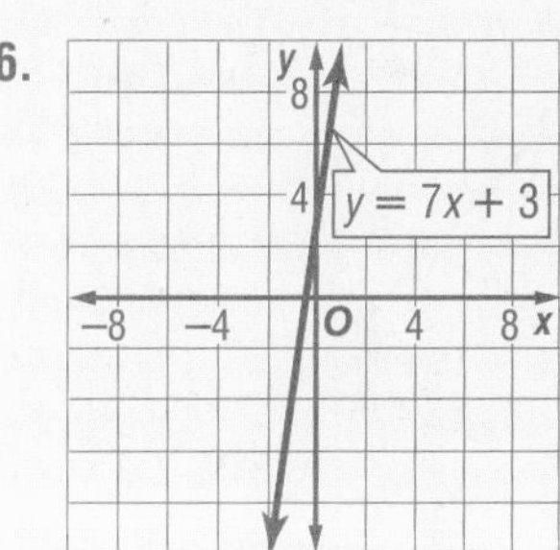

7.
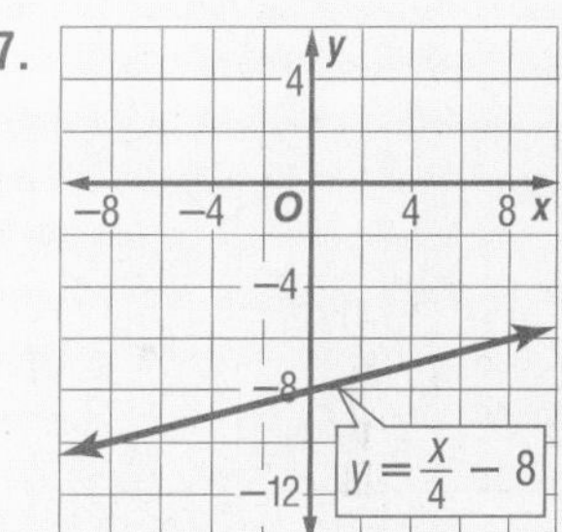

8.
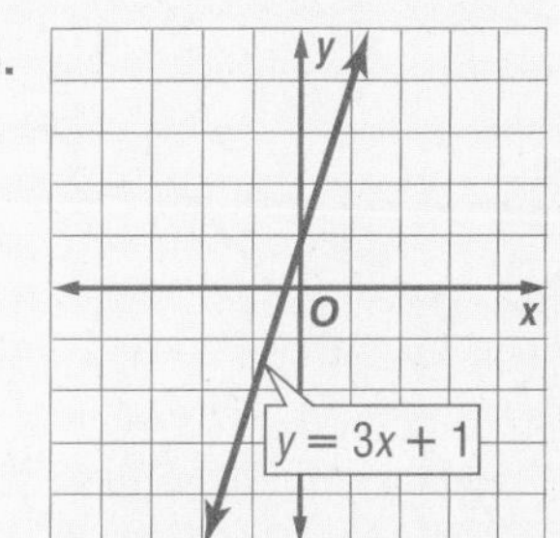

9.
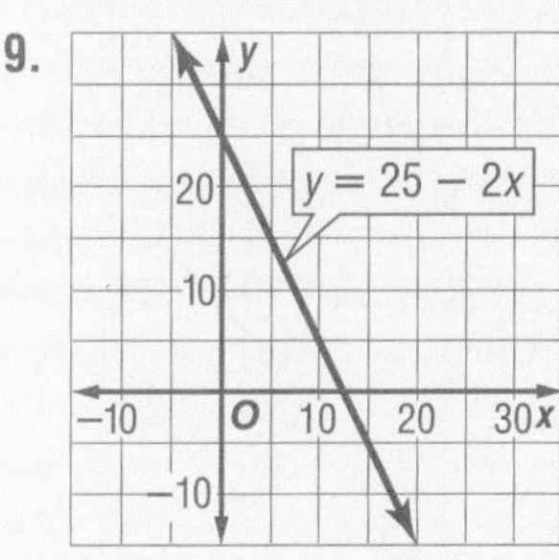

Extra Practice

Lesson 11-5

13.

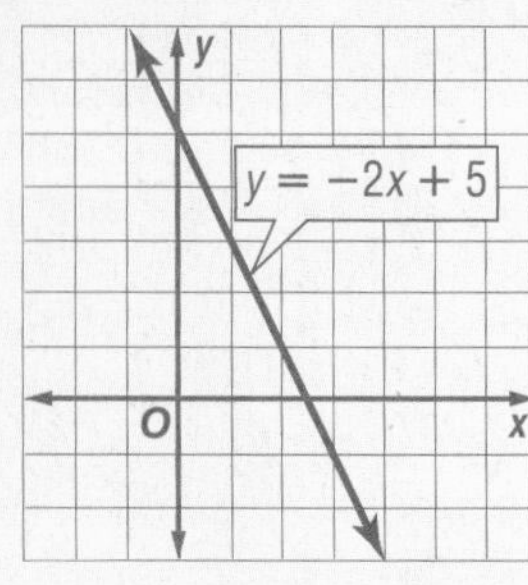

14.

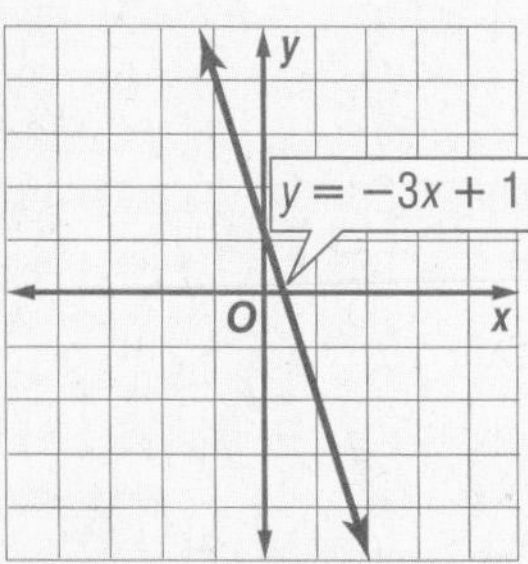

15.

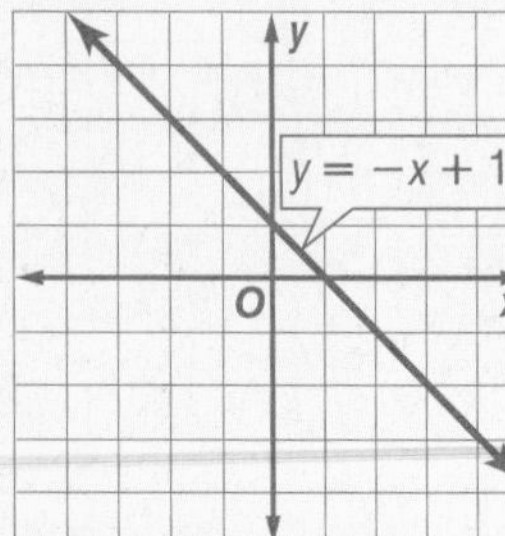

16.

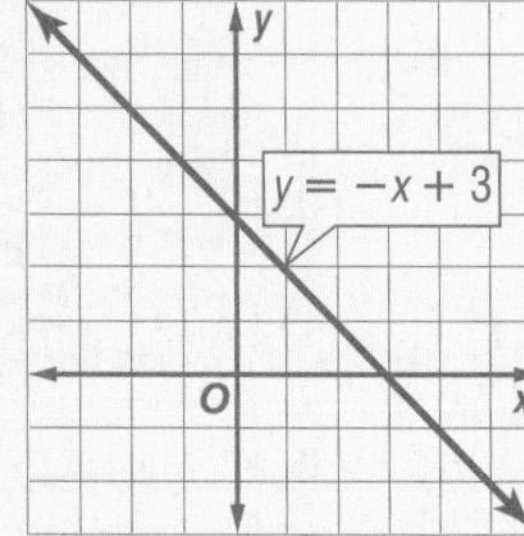

17.

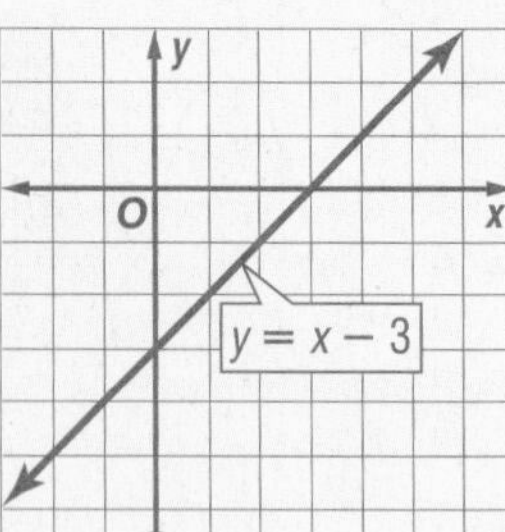

18.

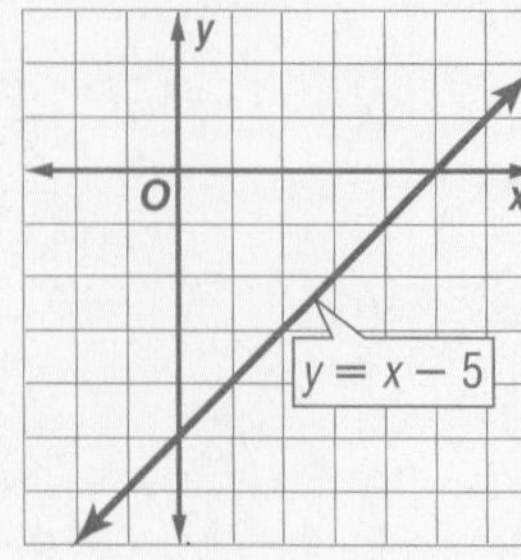

Extra Practice

Lesson 11-5

(Pages 533–536)

State the slope and y-intercept for the graph of each line.

1. $y = 3x - 5$ **3; −5**
2. $y = 2x - 6$ **2; −6**
3. $y = -6x + \frac{1}{2}$ **$-6; \frac{1}{2}$**
4. $y = -7x + \frac{5}{2}$ **$-7; \frac{5}{2}$**
5. $y = \frac{1}{2}x + 7$ **$\frac{1}{2}; 7$**
6. $y = \frac{3}{4}x + 8$ **$\frac{3}{4}, 8$**
7. $y = -\frac{2}{3}x - \frac{1}{3}$ **$-\frac{2}{3}; -\frac{1}{3}$**
8. $y = -\frac{1}{8}x - \frac{3}{8}$ **$-\frac{1}{8}; -\frac{3}{8}$**
9. $y = \frac{2}{3}x + 5$ **$\frac{2}{3}; 5$**
10. $y = -\frac{2}{7}x - 1$ **$-\frac{2}{7}; -1$**
11. $3x + y = 6$ **−3; 6**
12. $y - 4x = 7$ **4; 7**

Graph each equation using the slope and y-intercept. **13–21. See margin. 22–24. See Answer Appendix.**

13. $y = -2x + 5$
14. $y = -3x + 1$
15. $y = -x + 1$
16. $y = -x + 3$
17. $y = x - 3$
18. $y = x - 5$
19. $y = 3x - 6$
20. $y = \frac{5}{2}x - 1$
21. $y = \frac{1}{2}x + 3$
22. $y = -2x - 2$
23. $y - 4x = -1$
24. $2x + y = 3$

Lesson 11-6

(Pages 539–542)

Determine whether a scatter plot of the data for the following might show a *positive, negative,* or *no* relationship. **4. negative 6. negative 9. positive**

1. height and hair color **no relationship**
2. hours spent studying and test scores **positive**
3. income and month of birth **no relationship**
4. price of oranges and number available
5. size of roof and number of shingles **positive**
6. number of clouds and number of stars seen
7. child's age and height **positive**
8. age and eye color **no relationship**
9. number of hours worked and earnings
10. temperature outside and heating bill **negative**
11. length of foot and shoe size **positive**
12. number of candies eaten and number left in a bowl **negative**

13.

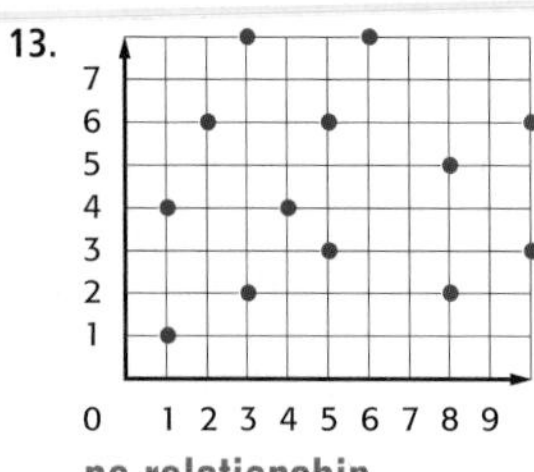

no relationship

14.

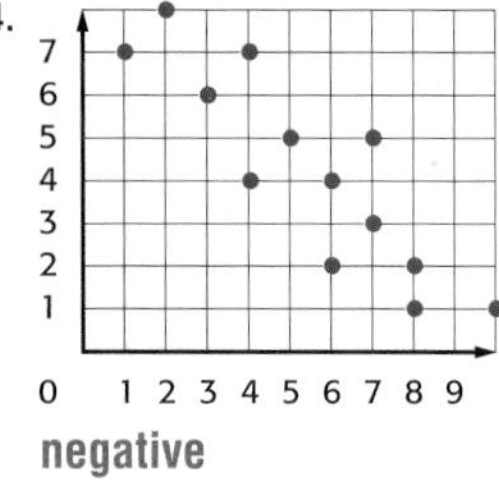

negative

15.

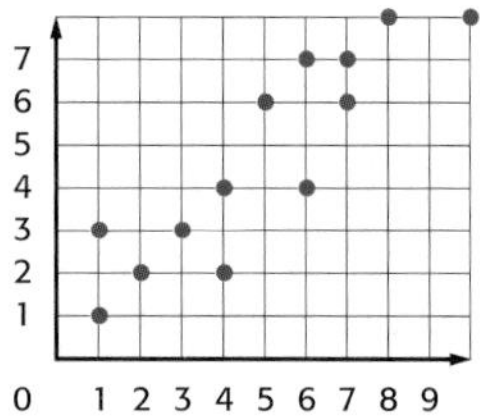

positive

Lesson 11-7

(Pages 544–547)

Solve each system of equations by graphing. **1–12. See Answer Appendix for graphs.**

1. $y = x - 1$, $y = -x + 11$ **(6, 5)**
2. $y = -x$, $y = 2x$ **(0, 0)**
3. $y = -x + 3$, $y = x + 3$ **(0, 3)**
4. $y = x - 3$, $y = 2x$ **(−3, −6)**
5. $y = -x + 6$, $y = x + 2$ **(2, 4)**
6. $y = -x + 2$, $y = x - 4$ **(3, −1)**
7. $y = -3x + 6$, $y = x - 2$ **(2, 0)**
8. $y = 3x - 4$, $y = -3x - 4$ **(0, −4)**
9. $y = 2x + 1$, $y = 3x$ **(1, 3)**
10. $y = -x + 4$, $y = x - 10$ **(7, −3)**
11. $y = -x + 6$, $y = 2x$ **(2, 4)**
12. $y = x - 4$, $y = -2x + 5$ **(3, −1)**

Solve each system of equations by substitution.

13. $y = 2x - 5$, $x = 5$ **(5, 5)**
14. $y = -3x + 5$, $x = -2$ **(−2, 11)**
15. $y = 5$, $y = 2x + 5$ **(0, 5)**
16. $y = -4$, $y = 2x - 6$ **(1, −4)**

19.

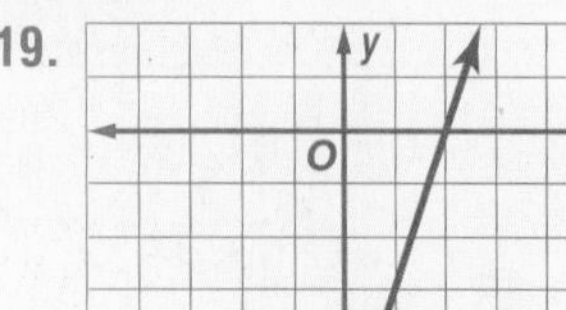

20.

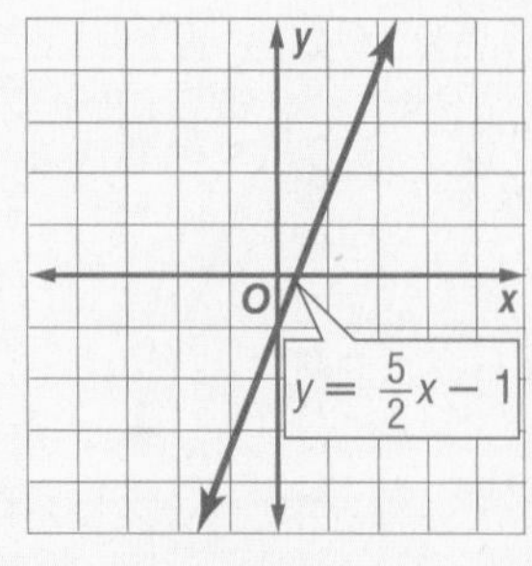

21.

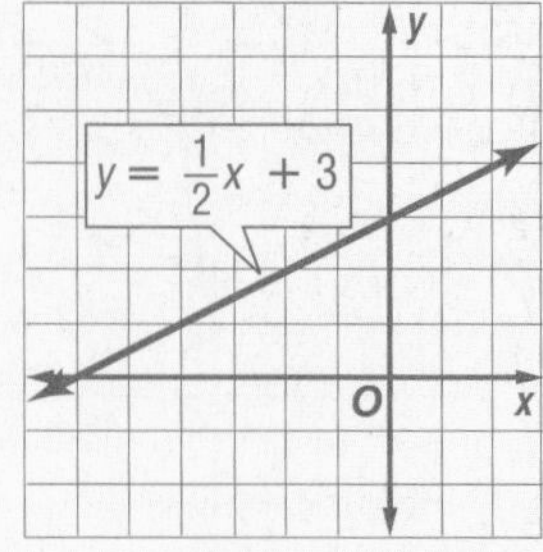

Lesson 11-8

(Pages 548–551)

Graph each inequality. 1–28. See Answer Appendix.

1. $y < 3x$
2. $y < 2x$
3. $y > -2x$
4. $y < -5x$
5. $y \geq 3x + 1$
6. $y \leq 4x + 2$
7. $y \leq -2x$
8. $y \geq -x$
9. $y < x$
10. $y > -x$
11. $y < x + 1$
12. $y \geq -x - 1$
13. $y \leq \frac{1}{2}x + 2$
14. $y \geq \frac{2}{3}x + 5$
15. $y \leq \frac{1}{5}x - 2$
16. $y > \frac{3}{5}x$
17. $y > \frac{7}{8}x$
18. $y \leq -\frac{2}{5}x + 1$
19. $y \geq \frac{1}{4}x$
20. $y < \frac{1}{3}x + 4$
21. $y \geq 2x + 1$
22. $y < x - 3$
23. $y \leq x + 4$
24. $y > -x - 2$
25. $y \geq \frac{1}{2}x - 3$
26. $y < -\frac{1}{2}x + 3$
27. $y > -\frac{1}{3}x - 2$
28. $y \geq \frac{2}{3}x + 1$

Lesson 12-1

(Pages 560–563)

Determine whether each graph, equation, or table represents a *linear* or *nonlinear* function. Explain. 4–18. See margin.

1. 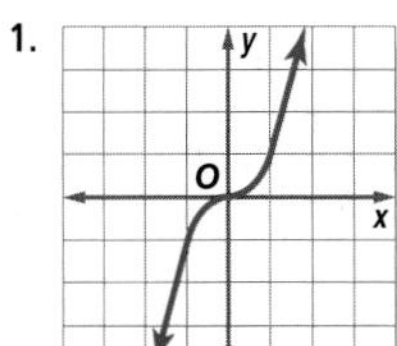

nonlinear; curves

2. 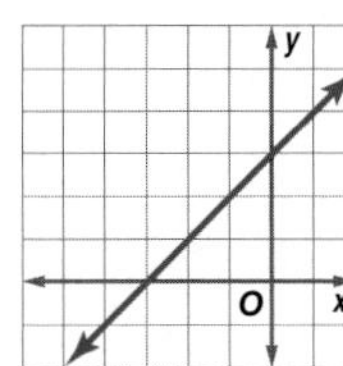

linear; constant rate of change

3. 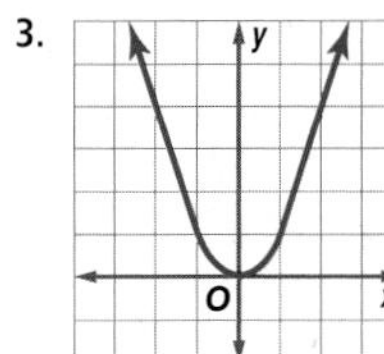

nonlinear; curves

4. $y = 3x$
5. $y = \frac{2}{3}x$
6. $y = x^2 + 5$
7. $y = 4^x$
8. $y = -\frac{3}{x}$
9. $xy = -3$
10. $y = x^3 + 2$
11. $y = 2$
12. $y = 3x + 5$

13.

x	−1	0	1	2
y	2	0	2	8

14. 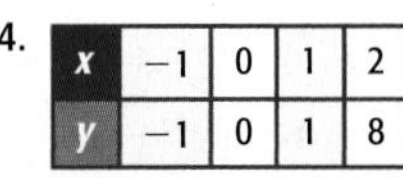

x	−1	0	1	2
y	−1	0	1	8

15. 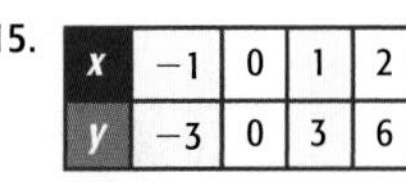

x	−1	0	1	2
y	−3	0	3	6

16. 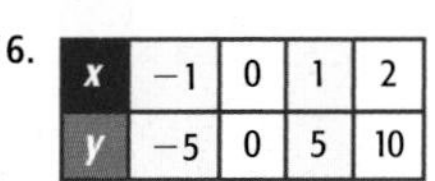

x	−1	0	1	2
y	−5	0	5	10

17.

x	−1	0	1	2
y	−1	0	−1	−4

18.

x	−1	0	1	2
y	1	0	1	16

Lesson 12-2

(Pages 565–568)

Graph each function. 1–28. See Answer Appendix.

1. $y = x^2 - 1$
2. $y = 1.5x^2 + 3$
3. $y = x^2 - x$
4. $y = 2x^2$
5. $y = x^2 + 3$
6. $y = -3x^2 + 4$
7. $y = -x^2 + 7$
8. $y = 3x^2$
9. $y = 3x^2 + 9x$
10. $y = -x^2$
11. $y = \frac{1}{2}x^2 + 1$
12. $y = 5x^2 - 4$
13. $y = -x^2 + 3x$
14. $y = 2.5x^2$
15. $y = -2x^2$
16. $y = 8x^2 + 3$
17. $y = -x^2 + \frac{1}{2}x$
18. $y = -4x^2 + 4$
19. $y = 4x^2 + 3$
20. $y = -4x^2 + 1$
21. $y = 2x^2 + 1$
22. $y = x^2 - 4x$
23. $y = 3x^2 + 5$
24. $y = 0.5x^2$
25. $y = 2x^2 - 5x$
26. $y = \frac{3}{2}x^2 - 2$
27. $y = 6x^2 + 2$
28. $y = 5x^2 + 6x$

Extra Practice

Lesson 12-1

4. linear; constant rate of change
5. linear; constant rate of change
6. nonlinear; 2nd power
7. nonlinear; *x* is a power
8. nonlinear; divided by *x*
9. nonlinear; *x* times *y*
10. nonlinear; 3rd power
11. linear; constant rate of change
12. linear; constant rate of change
13. nonlinear; not a constant rate of change
14. nonlinear; not a constant rate of change
15. linear; constant rate of change
16. linear; constant rate of change
17. nonlinear; not a constant rate of change
18. nonlinear; not a constant rate of change

Extra Practice 645

Lesson 12-3

(Pages 570–573)

Simplify each polynomial. If the polynomial cannot be simplified, write *simplest form*.

1. $2x - x^2 + x - 1$ **$-x^2 + 3x - 1$**

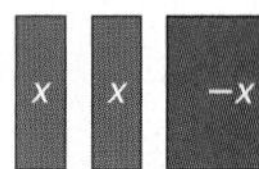
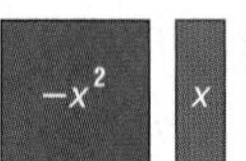

2. $2x^2 + 1 + x^2$ **$3x^2 + 1$**

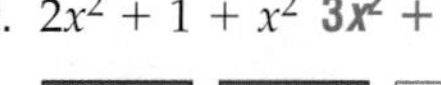

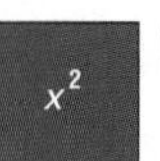

3. $-2y + 3 + x^2 + 5y$
4. $m + m^2 + n + 3m^2$
5. $a^2 + b^2 + 3 + 2b^2$
6. $1 + a + b + 6$ **$a + b + 7$**
7. $x + x^2 + 5x - 3x^2$ **$-2x^2 + 6x$**
8. $-2y + 3 + y - 2$ **$-y + 1$**
9. $6x + 3y - 2x$ **$4x + 3y$**
10. $5a + 2b - 7a - 3b$ **$-2a - b$**
11. $-2x + 5 - 3x + 7$ **$-5x + 12$**
12. $5y - 2z - 6z - 1$ **$5y - 8z - 1$**
13. $x^2 - 3x + 2x^2 - 5x$ **$3x^2 - 8x$**
14. $y^2 + 2y + 1 - 3y^2 - 5y$
15. $4t + 3s - 2t + 7s$ **$2t + 10s$**
16. $4d + 5 - 7d - 8$ **$-3d - 3$**
17. $x^2 - 3x + 4x^2 - 4x + 7$

3. $x^2 + 3y + 3$ 4. $4m^2 + m + n$ 5. $a^2 + 3b^2 + 3$ 14. $-2y^2 - 3y + 1$ 17. $5x^2 - 7x + 7$

Lesson 12-4

(Pages 574–577)

Add.

1. $\begin{array}{r} 2x^2 - 5x + 7 \\ + x^2 - x + 11 \\ \hline \end{array}$ **$3x^2 - 6x + 18$**
2. $\begin{array}{r} 2m^2 + m + 1 \\ + (-m^2) + 2m + 3 \\ \hline \end{array}$ **$m^2 + 3m + 4$**
3. $\begin{array}{r} 2a - b + 6c \\ + 3a - 7b + 2c \\ \hline \end{array}$ **$5a - 8b + 8c$**
4. $\begin{array}{r} 5a + 3a^2 - 2 \\ + 2a + 8a^2 + 4 \\ \hline \end{array}$ **$7a + 11a^2 + 2$**
5. $\begin{array}{r} 3c + b + a \\ + (-c) + b - a \\ \hline \end{array}$ **$2c + 2b$**
6. $\begin{array}{r} -z^2 + x^2 + 2y^2 \\ + 3z^2 + x^2 + y^2 \\ \hline \end{array}$ **$2z^2 + 2x^2 + 3y^2$**
7. $(5x + 6y) + (2x + 8y)$ **$7x + 14y$**
8. $(4a + 6b) + (2a + 3b)$ **$6a + 9b$**
9. $(7r + 11m) + (4m + 2r)$ **$15m + 9r$**
10. $(-z + z^2) + (-2z + z^2)$ **$2z^2 - 3z$**
11. $(3x - 7y) + (3y + 4x + 1)$ **$7x - 4y + 1$**
12. $(5m + 3n - 3) + (8m + 6)$ **$13m + 3n + 3$**
13. $(a + a^2) + (3a - 2a^2)$ **$-a^2 + 4a$**
14. $(3s - 5t) + (8t + 2s)$ **$5s + 3t$**
15. $(3x - 2y) + (5x + 3y)$ **$8x + y$**
16. $(2a - 5b) + (-3a - 6b)$ **$-a - 11b$**
17. $(x + 3) + (x^2 - 3x + 4)$ **$x^2 - 2x + 7$**
18. $(x^2 + 2x - 3) + (3x^2 - 5x - 6)$ **$4x^2 - 3x - 9$**

Lesson 12-5

(Pages 580–583)

Subtract.

1. $\begin{array}{r} 5a - 6m \\ (-)\ 2a + 5m \\ \hline \end{array}$ **$3a - 11m$**
2. $\begin{array}{r} 2a - 7 \\ (-)\ 8a - 11 \\ \hline \end{array}$ **$-6a + 4$**
3. $\begin{array}{r} 9r^2 + r + 3 \\ (-)\ 11r^2 - r + 12 \\ \hline \end{array}$ **$-2r^2 + 2r - 9$**
4. $(9x + 3y) - (9y + x)$ **$8x - 6y$**
5. $(3x^2 + 2x - 1) - (2x + 2)$ **$3x^2 - 3$**
6. $(a^2 + 6a + 3) - (5a^2 + 5)$ **$-4a^2 + 6a - 2$**
7. $(5a + 2) - (3a^2 + a + 8)$ **$-3a^2 + 4a - 6$**
8. $(3x^2 - 7x) - (8x - 6)$ **$3x^2 - 15x + 6$**
9. $(3m + 3n) - (m + 2n)$ **$2m + n$**
10. $(3m - 2) - (2m + 1)$ **$m - 3$**
11. $(x^2 - 2) - (x + 3)$ **$x^2 - x - 5$**
12. $(5x^2 - 4) - (3x^2 + 8x + 4)$ **$2x^2 - 8x - 8$**
13. $(7z^2 + 1) - (3z^2 + 2z - 6)$ **$4z^2 - 2z + 7$**
14. $(2x - 5) - (3x - 6)$ **$-x + 1$**
15. $(5a - 1) - (8a - 3)$ **$-3a + 2$**
16. $(3y^2 - 5) - (5y + 6)$ **$3y^2 - 5y - 11$**
17. $(2x^2 - 6) - (7x - 3)$ **$2x^2 - 7x - 3$**
18. $(x^2 + 5x - 6) - (2x^2 - 3x + 5)$ **$-x^2 + 8x - 11$**
19. $(a^2 - 3a - 5) - (5a^2 - 6a + 2)$ **$-4a^2 + 3a - 7$**

646 Extra Practice

Lesson 12-6

(Pages 584–587)

Multiply or divide. Express using exponents.

1. $2^3 \cdot 2^4$ **2^7**
2. $5^6 \cdot 5$ **5^7**
3. $t^2 \cdot t^2$ **t^4**
4. $y^5 \cdot y^3$ **y^8**
5. $(-3x^3)(-2x^2)$ **$6x^5$**
6. $b^{12} \cdot b$ **b^{13}**
7. $3^5 \cdot 3^8$ **3^{13}**
8. $(-2y^3)(5y^7)$ **$-10y^{10}$**
9. $(6a^5)(-3a^6)$ **$-18a^{11}$**
10. $(-x)(-6x^3)$ **$6x^4$**
11. $(3x^2)(2x^5)$ **$6x^7$**
12. $(-6y^2)(-2y^5)$ **$12y^7$**
13. $(-3a)(-2a^6)$ **$6a^7$**
14. $8a^9(5a^5)$ **$40a^{14}$**
15. $(6x^2)(2x^{11})$ **$12x^{13}$**
16. $\frac{x^{11}}{x^2}$ **x^9**
17. $\frac{a^6}{a^3}$ **a^3**
18. $\frac{b^9}{b^3}$ **b^6**
19. $\frac{7^9}{7^6}$ **7^3**
20. $\frac{2^5}{2^2}$ **2^3**
21. $\frac{11^{10}}{11}$ **11^9**
22. $\frac{16x^3}{4x^2}$ **$4x$**
23. $\frac{25y^5}{5y^2}$ **$5y^3$**
24. $\frac{-48y^3}{-8y}$ **$6y^2$**
25. $\frac{12y^2}{3y^2}$ **4**
26. $\frac{39x^7y^5}{3x^3y}$ **$13x^4y^4$**
27. $\frac{21a^7b^2}{7ab^2}$ **$3a^6$**
28. $\frac{22a^5b^3}{2a^2b}$ **$11a^3b^2$**
29. $\frac{15x^2y}{3xy}$ **$5x$**
30. $\frac{20a^3b^2}{2a^2b}$ **$10ab$**

Lesson 12-7

(Pages 590–592)

Multiply.

1. $a(a + 2)$ **$a^2 + 2a$**
2. $x(2x - 3)$ **$2x^2 - 3x$**
3. $t(3t + 1)$ **$3t^2 + t$**
4. $a(a + 4)$ **$a^2 + 4a$**
5. $m(m - 7)$ **$m^2 - 7m$**
6. $z^2(z + 3)$ **$z^3 + 3z^2$**
7. $6x(x + 10)$ **$6x^2 + 60x$**
8. $3y(5 + y)$ **$15y + 3y^2$**
9. $2d(d^3 + 1)$ **$2d^4 + 2d$**
10. $m^3(m^2 - 2)$ **$m^5 - 2m^3$**
11. $p^5(3p - 1)$ **$3p^6 - p^5$**
12. $b(9 + 4b)$ **$9b + 4b^2$**
13. $4t^3(t + 3)$ **$4t^4 + 12t^3$**
14. $2r^4(5r + 9)$ **$10r^5 + 18r^4$**
15. $3n^2(6 - 7n^3)$ **$18n^2 - 21n^5$**
16. $3x(x^2 + 2)$ **$3x^3 + 6x$**
17. $-2x(x^3 + 2x + 5)$
18. $-3x(-2x - 6)$ **$6x^2 + 18x$**
19. $-2(x - 5)$ **$-2x + 10$**
20. $2x^2(3x + 5)$ **$6x^3 + 10x^2$**
21. $3a^2(2a - 6)$ **$6a^3 - 18a^2$**
22. $5a(7 - 3a)$ **$35a - 15a^2$**
23. $-2a^2(8 - 5a^2)$ **$-16a^2 + 10a^4$**
24. $3x^2(1 + x + 5x^2)$
25. $y(2y^2 + 3y - 1)$
26. $-a(a^2 - 3a + 5)$
27. $2x^2(2x^2 + 2x + 2)$
28. $n(n^2 - n + 3)$ **$n^3 - n^2 + 3n$**
29. $-3t^2(2t^2 - 2t)$ **$-6t^4 + 6t^3$**
30. $-5p^2(4p + 10)$ **$-20p^3 - 50p^2$**

17. $-2x^4 - 4x^2 - 10x$ 24. $3x^2 + 3x^3 + 15x^4$ 25. $2y^3 + 3y^2 - y$ 26. $-a^3 + 3a^2 - 5a$
27. $4x^4 + 4x^3 + 4x^2$

Extra Practice

Extra Practice

Extra Practice 647

Page 635, Lesson 8-2

1. **Color Transmission Engine Outcome**

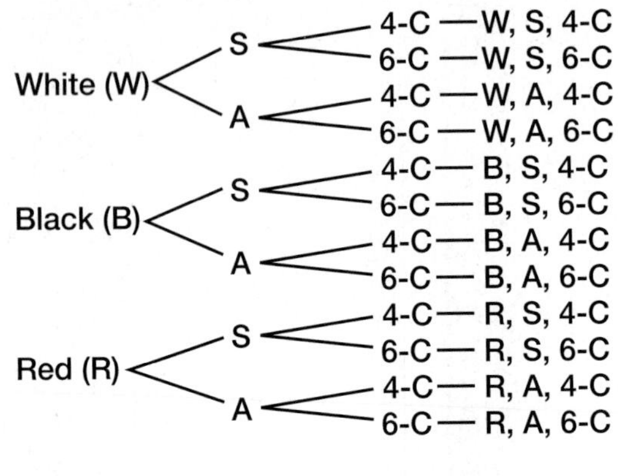

S= standard
A= automatic
4-C = 4-cylinder
6-C = 6-cylinder

2. **Flower Color Outcome**

Roses
- Red — Roses, Red
- Yellow — Roses, Yellow
- Pink — Roses, Pink
- White — Roses, White

Carnations
- Red — Carnations, Red
- Yellow — Carnations, Yellow
- Pink — Carnations, Pink
- White — Carnations, White

3. **Size Mattress Outcome**

Queen
- Firm — Queen, Firm
- Super Firm — Queen, Super Firm

King
- Firm — King, Firm
- Super Firm — King, Super Firm

4. **Crust Number of Toppings Outcome**

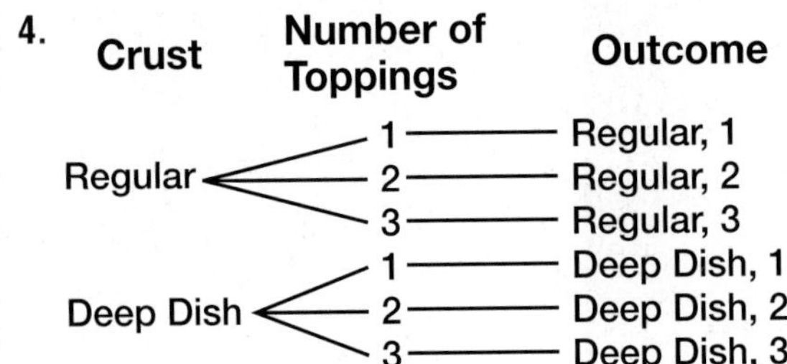

Page 639, Lesson 9-6

1. 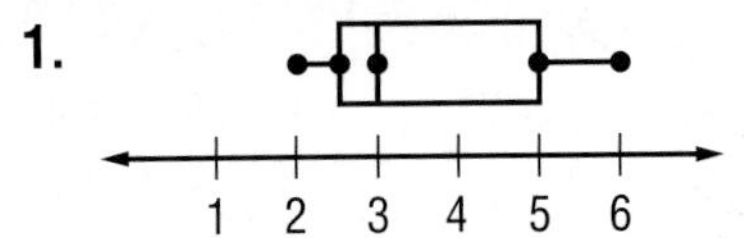

2. 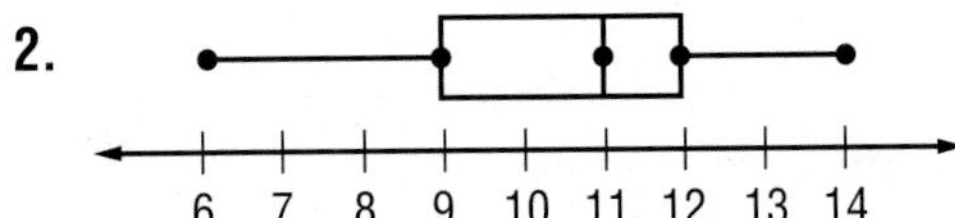

3. 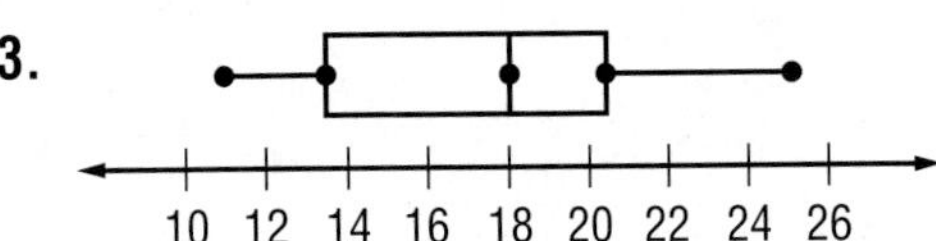

4. 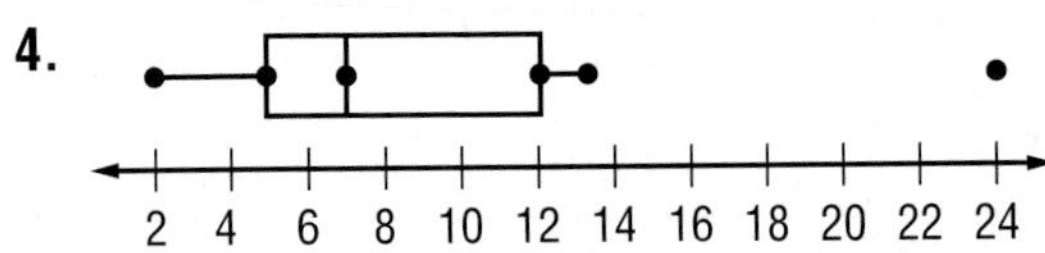

5. 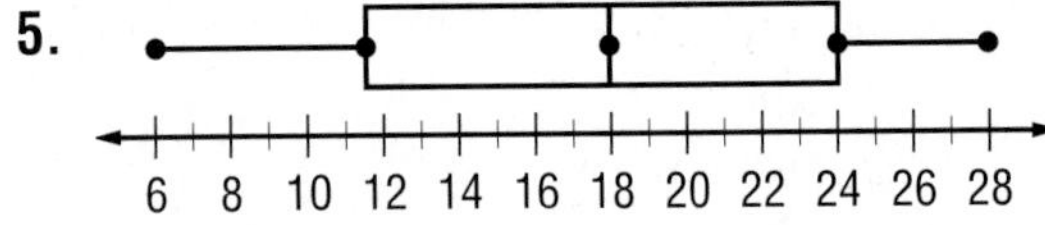

6. 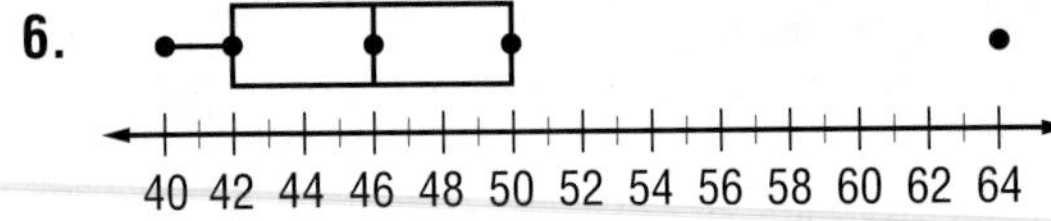

7. 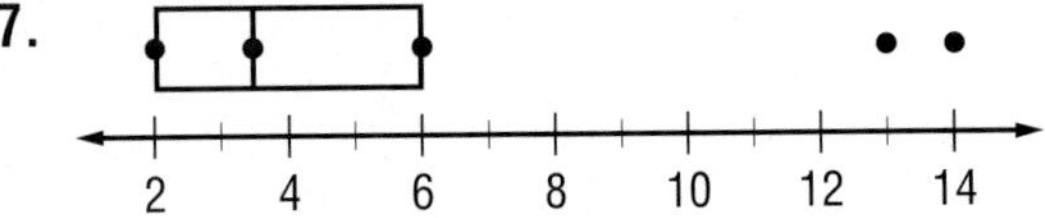

8. 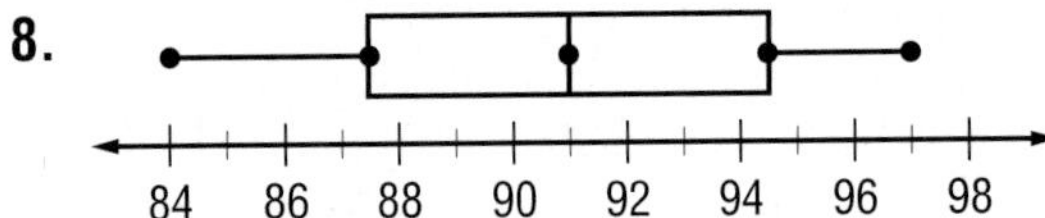

9. 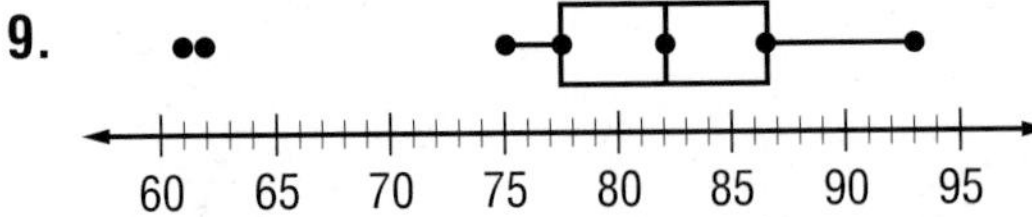

10. 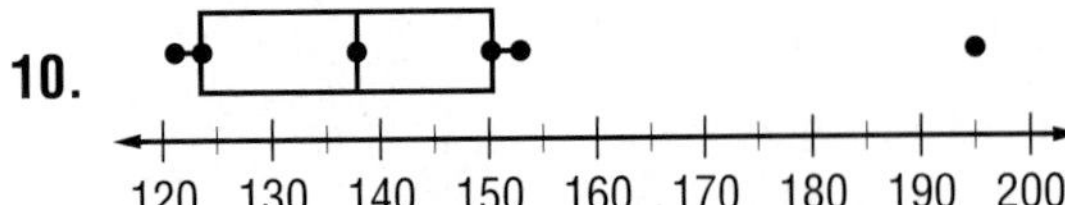

Page 642, Lesson 10-7

24. 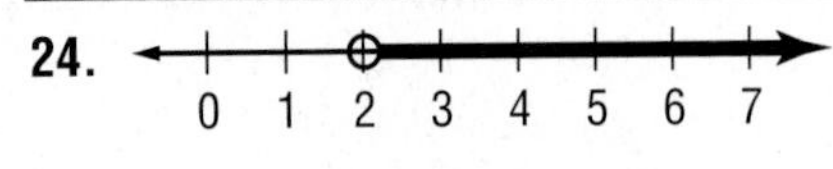

25. 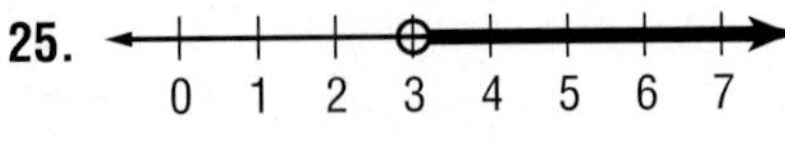

26. 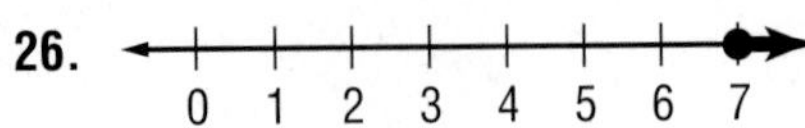

27. 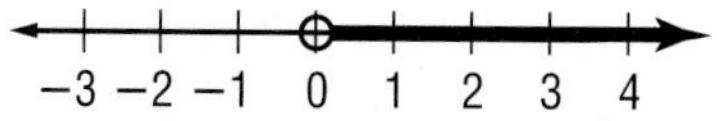 −3 −2 −1 0 1 2 3 4

28. 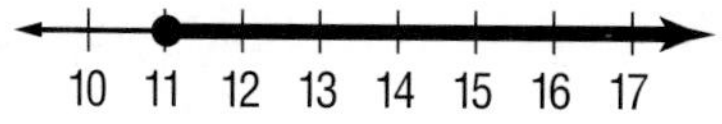 10 11 12 13 14 15 16 17

29. 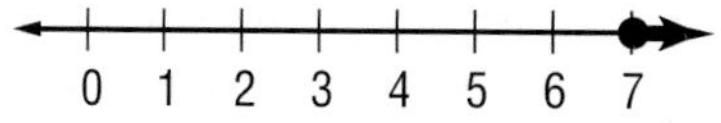 0 1 2 3 4 5 6 7

30. 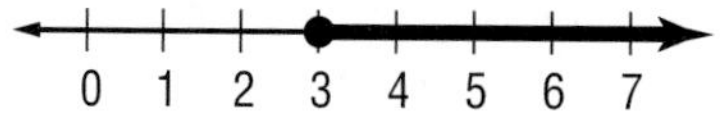 0 1 2 3 4 5 6 7

Page 642, Lesson 11-1

1. arithmetic; 4; 17, 21, 25
2. geometric; 3; 162, 486, 1,458
3. neither; 36, 49, 64
4. geometric; $\frac{1}{3}$; 27, 9, 3
5. arithmetic; −5; −18, −23, −28
6. geometric; −1; 5, −5, 5
7. geometric; $-\frac{1}{3}$; 10, $-3\frac{1}{3}$, $1\frac{1}{9}$
8. arithmetic; 3; 26, 29, 32
9. arithmetic; −6; 15, 9, 3
10. arithmetic; −6; −3, −9, −15
11. geometric; −2; 2, −4, 8
12. geometric; 3; 1, 3, 9
13. geometric; 2; 6, 12, 24
14. neither; 20, 27, 35
15. arithmetic; $-\frac{1}{2}$; $-3\frac{1}{4}$, $-3\frac{3}{4}$, $-4\frac{1}{4}$
16. arithmetic; 3.8; 21.3, 25.1, 28.9
17. arithmetic; 1; $4\frac{1}{2}$, $5\frac{1}{2}$, $6\frac{1}{2}$
18. neither; 102, 152, 212
19. geometric; −2; 48, −96, 192
20. arithmetic; 2; 15, 17, 19
21. arithmetic; 2.3; 6.84, 9.14, 11.44
22. geometric; 2; 56, 112, 224
23. arithmetic; 4; 6.6, 10.6, 14.6
24. geometric; $-\frac{1}{2}$; −6, 3, $-1\frac{1}{2}$
25. geometric; 3; 108, 324, 972
26. arithmetic; −1; 16, 15, 14
27. geometric; $\frac{1}{4}$; 12, 3, $\frac{3}{4}$

Page 643, Lesson 11-3

10.

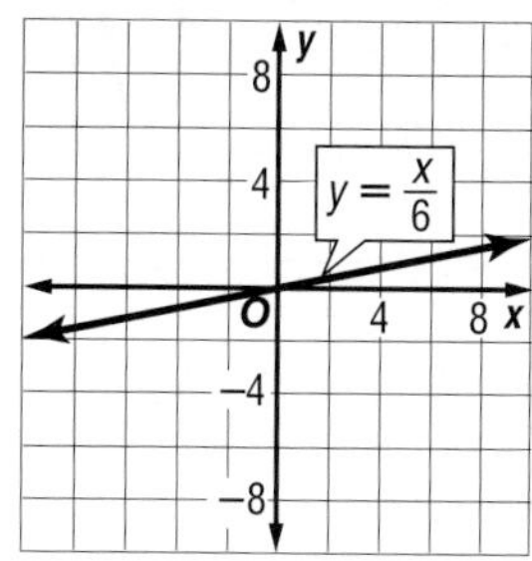

11.

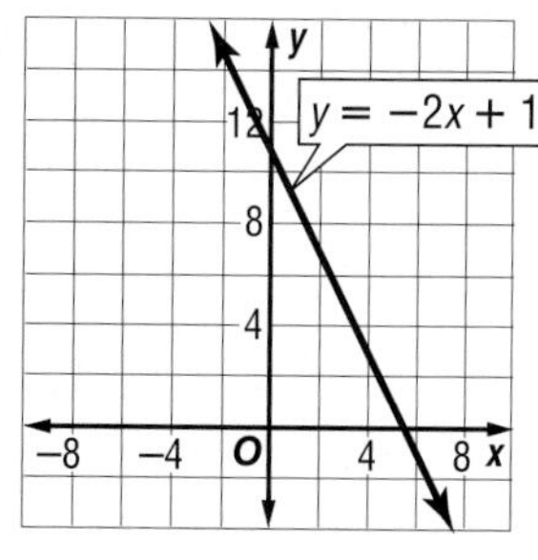

12.

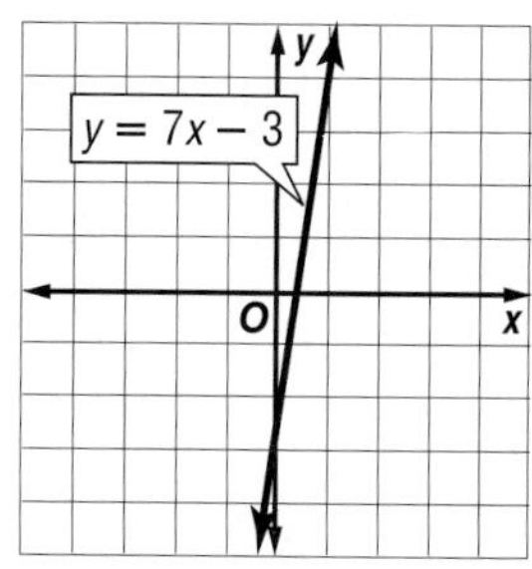

13.

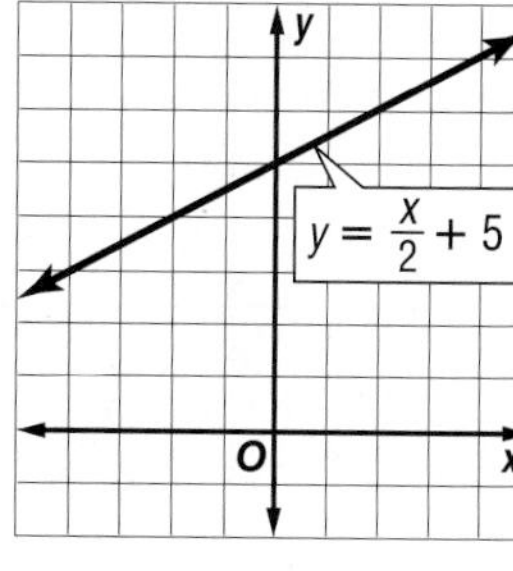

14.

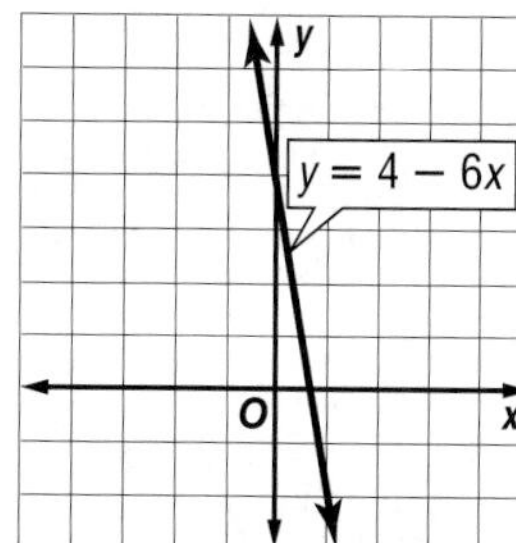

15.

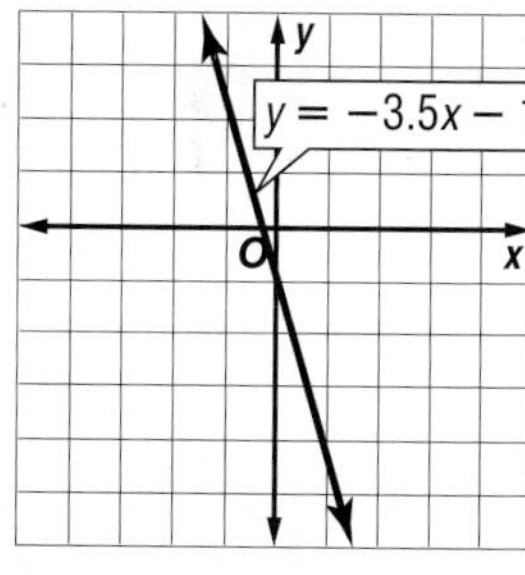

16.

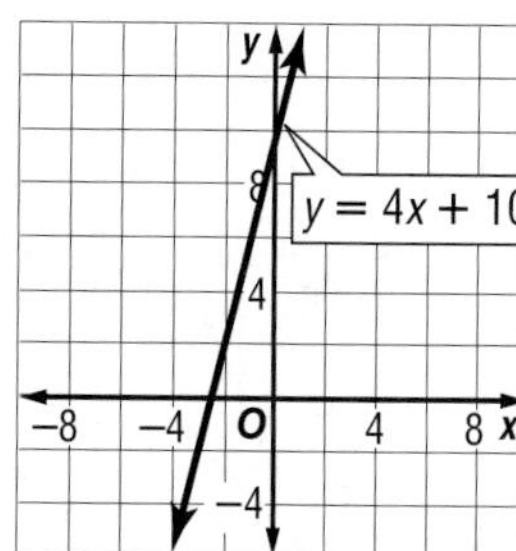

17.

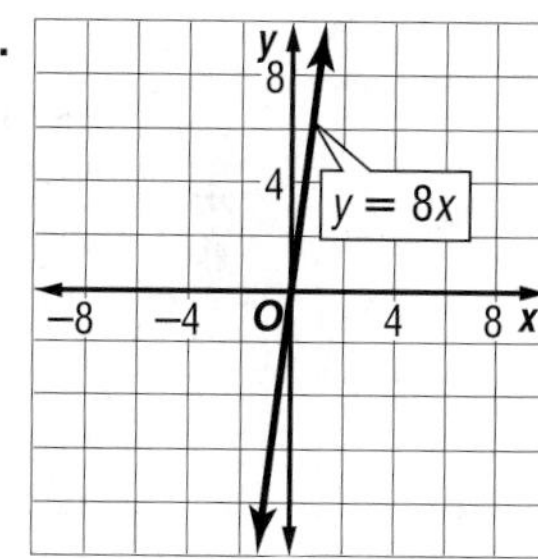

18.

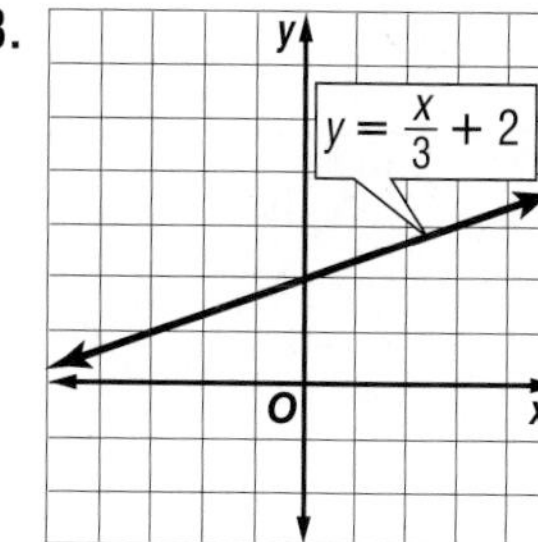

Page 644, Lesson 11-5

22.

$y = -2x - 2$

23. 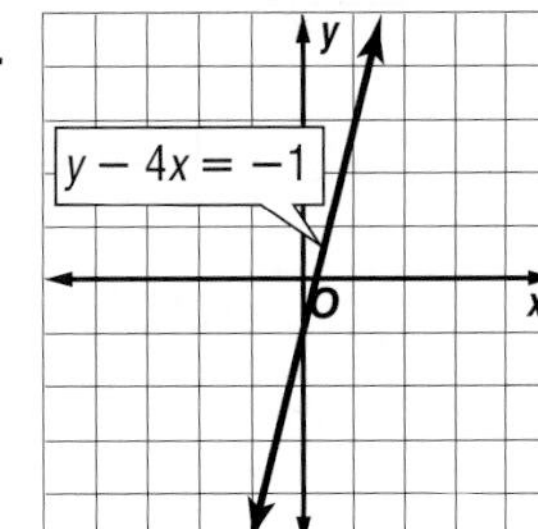

24. 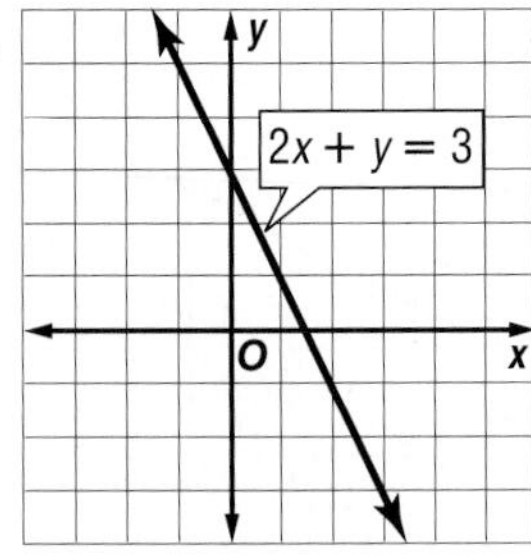

Page 644, Lesson 11-7

1. 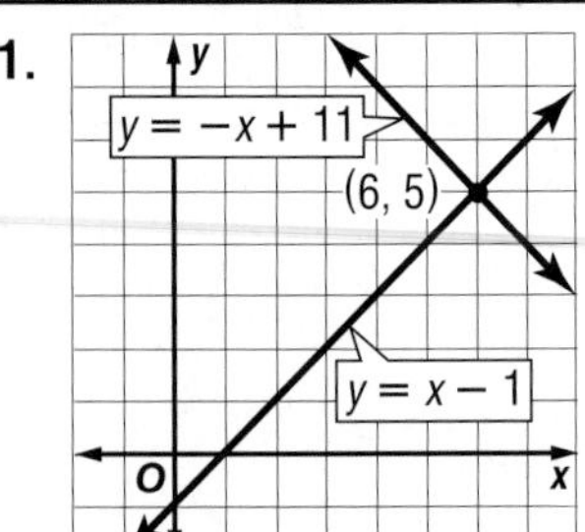

2. 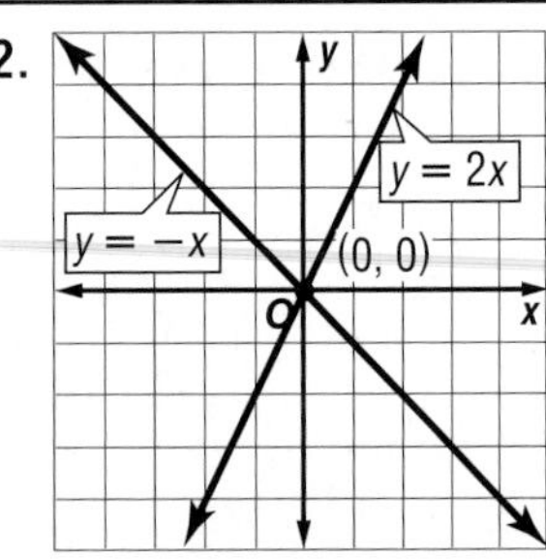

3. 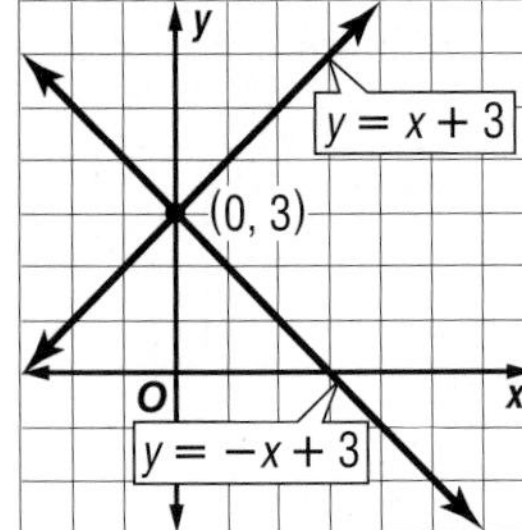

4. 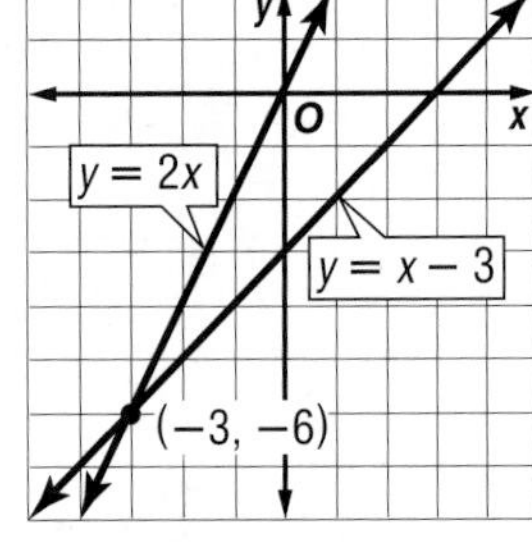

5. 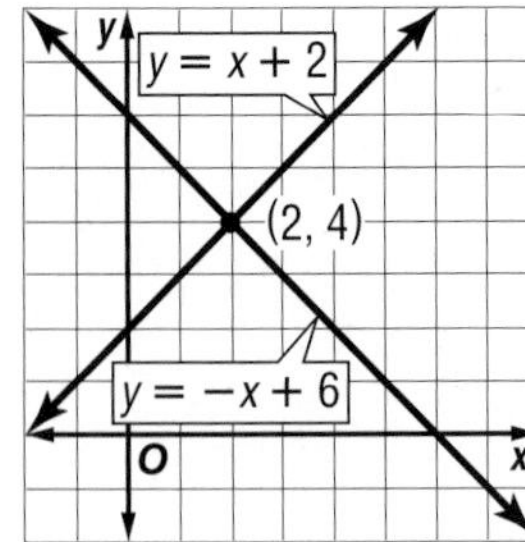

6. 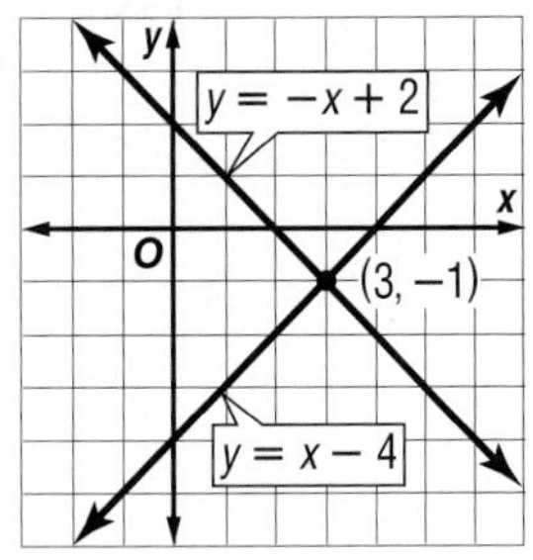

7. 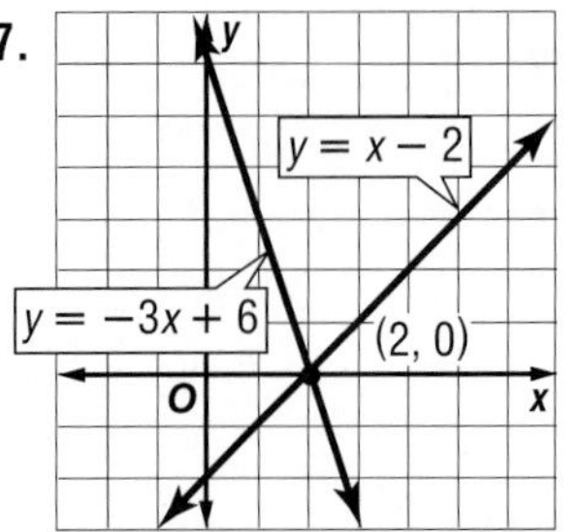

8. 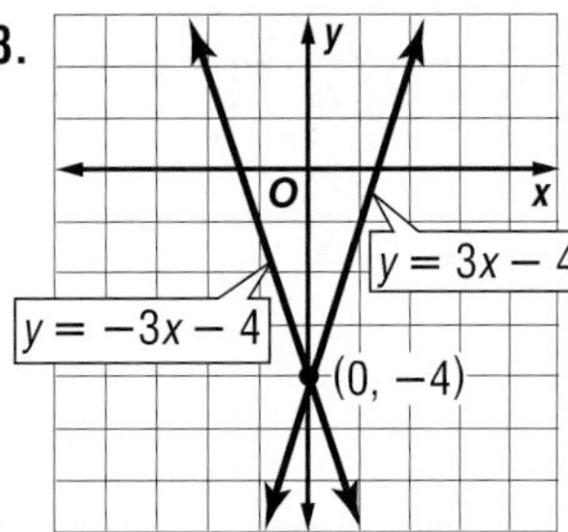

9. 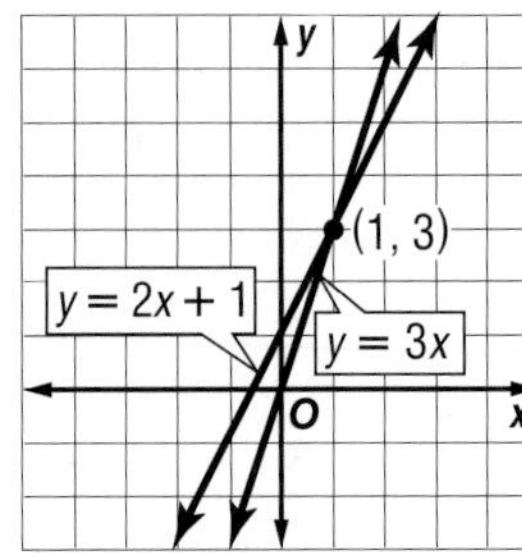

10. 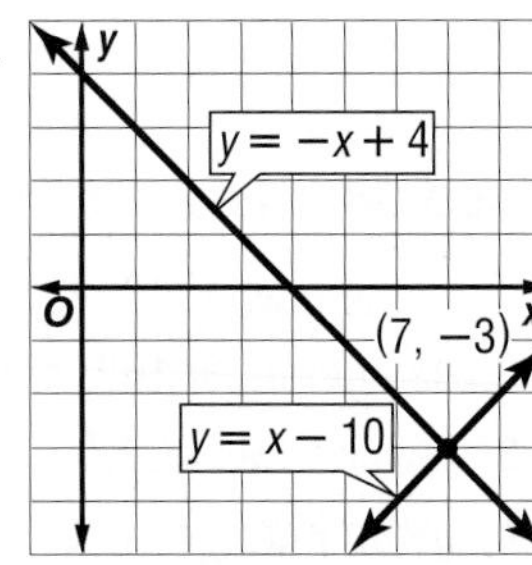

11. 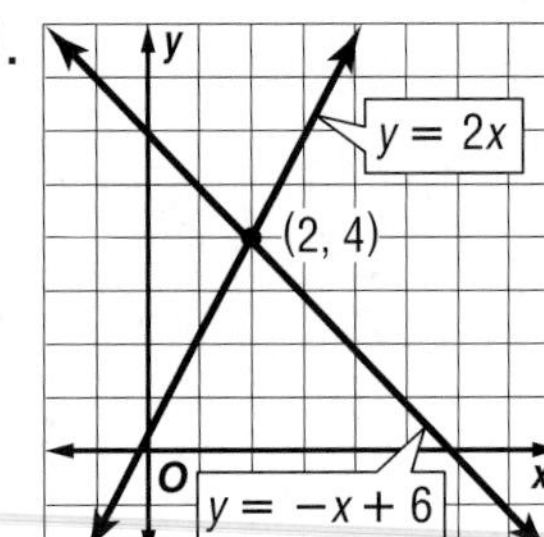

12. 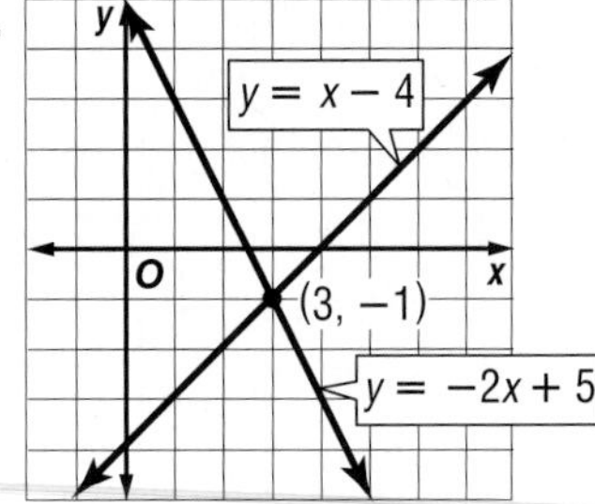

Page 645, Lesson 11-8

1. 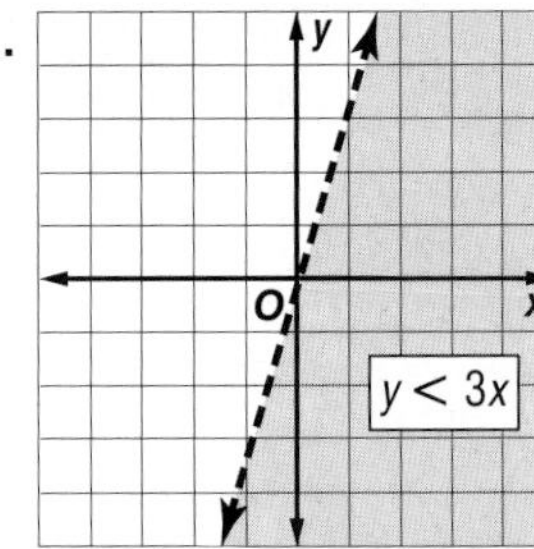

2. 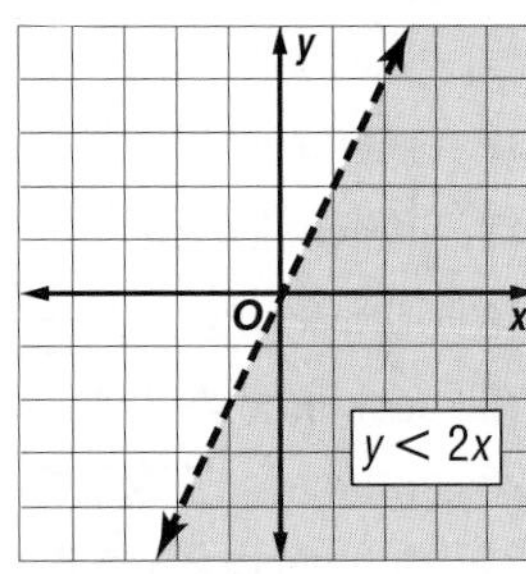

3. 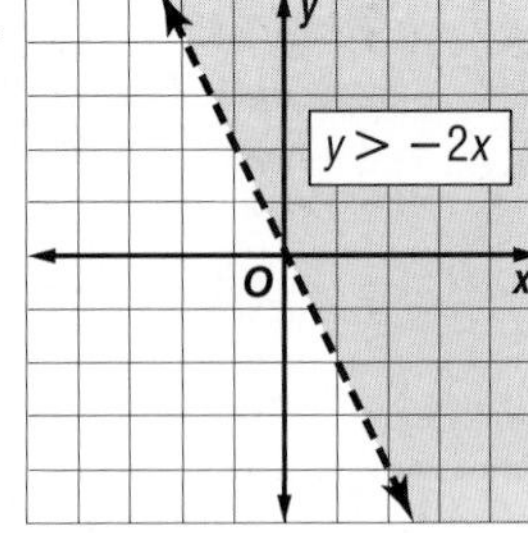

4. 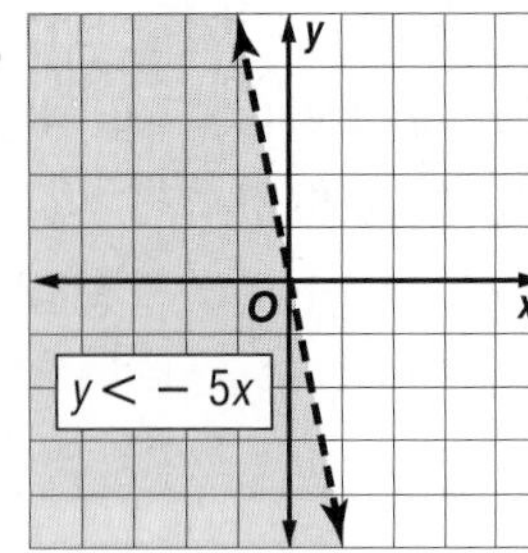

5.
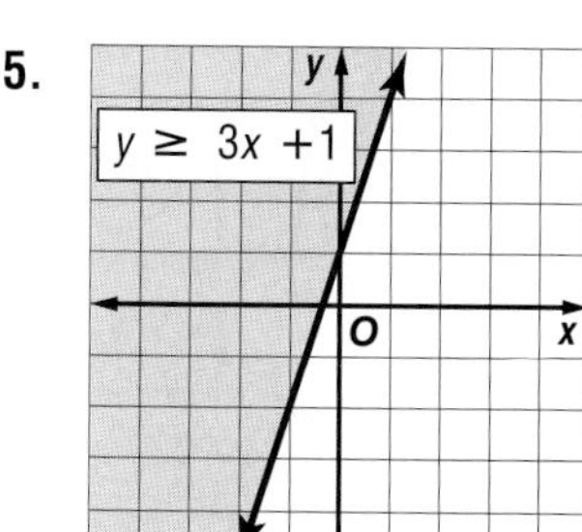

6.
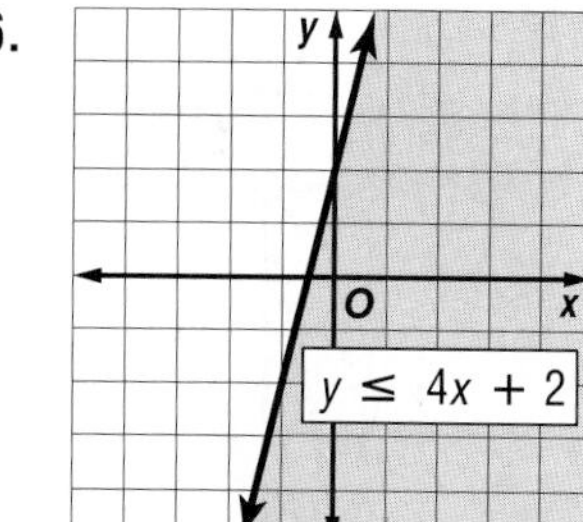

7.
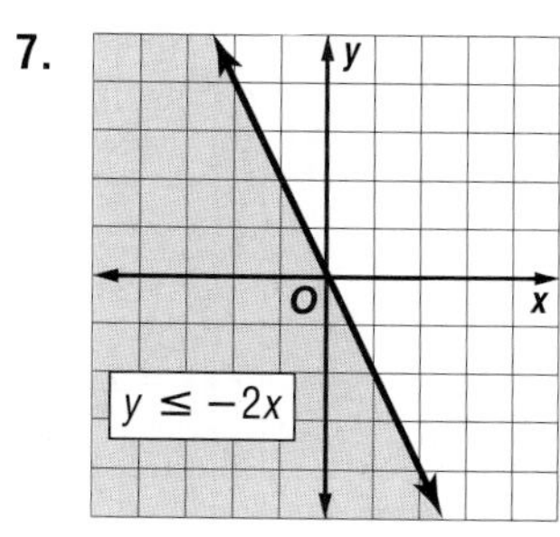

8.
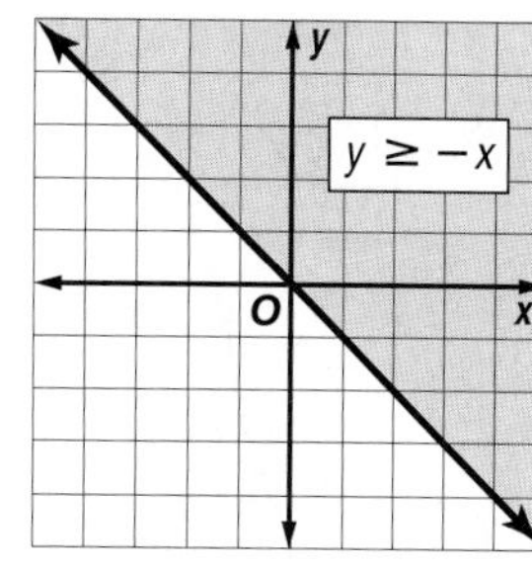

9.
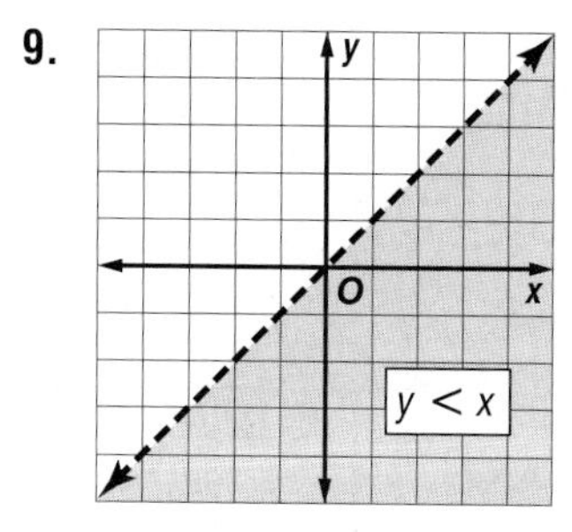

10.
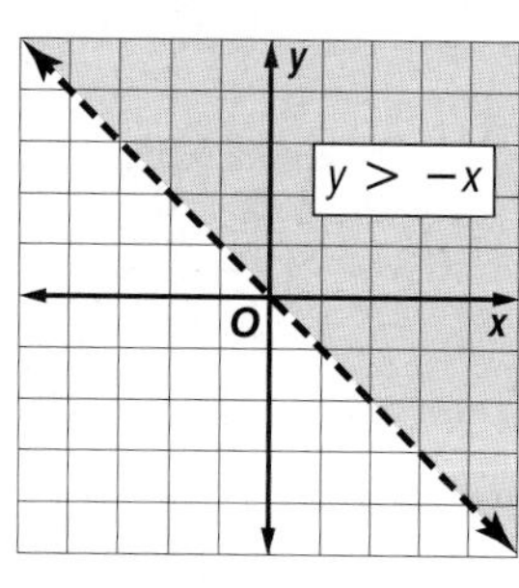

11.
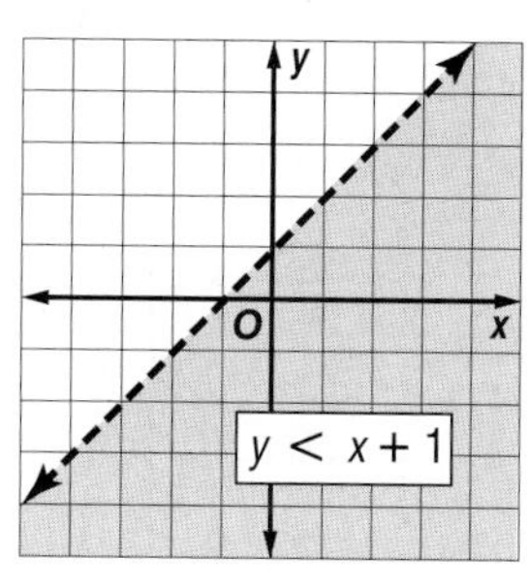

12.
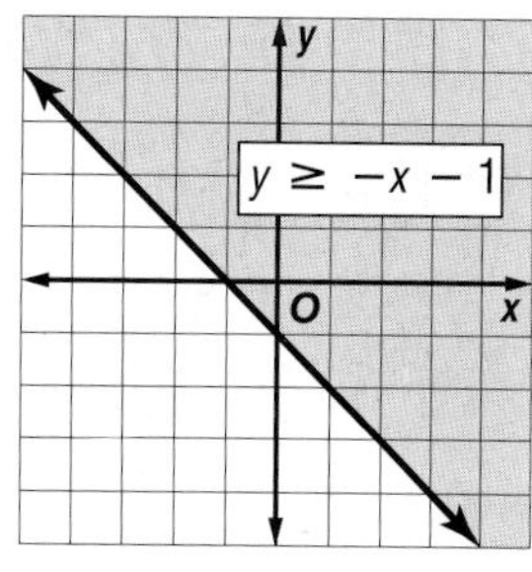

13.
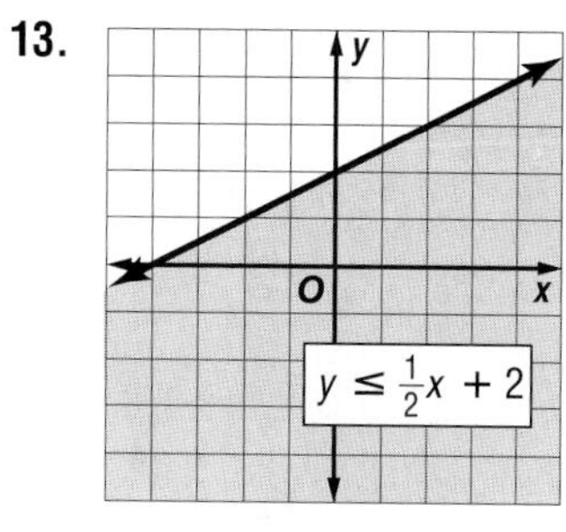

14.
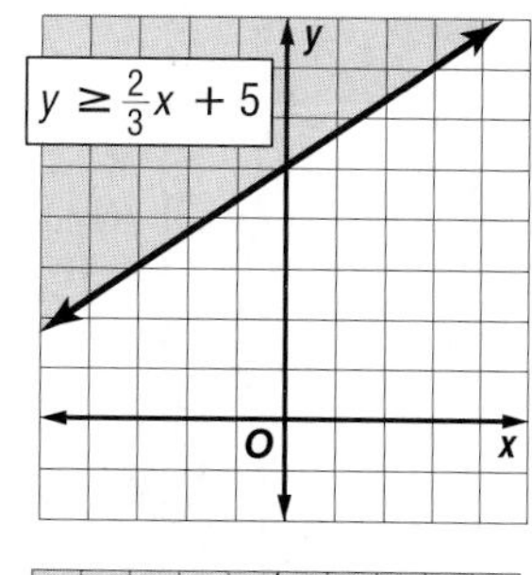

15.
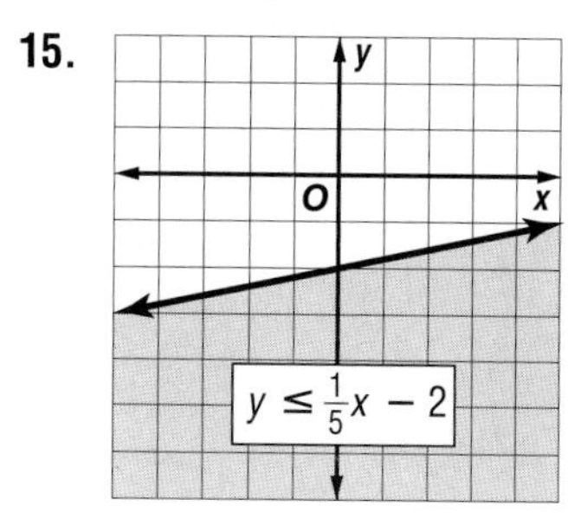

16.
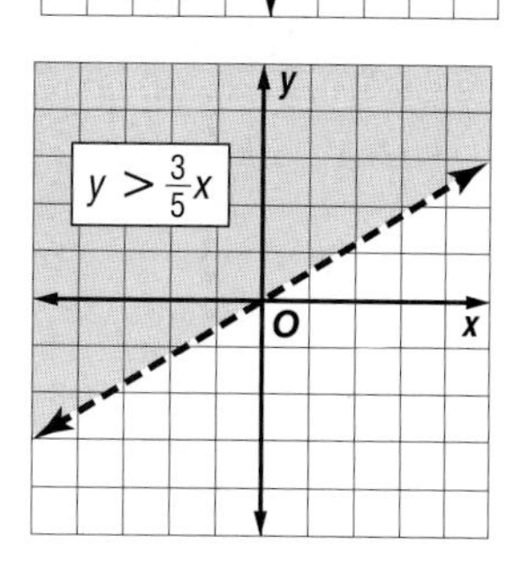

17.
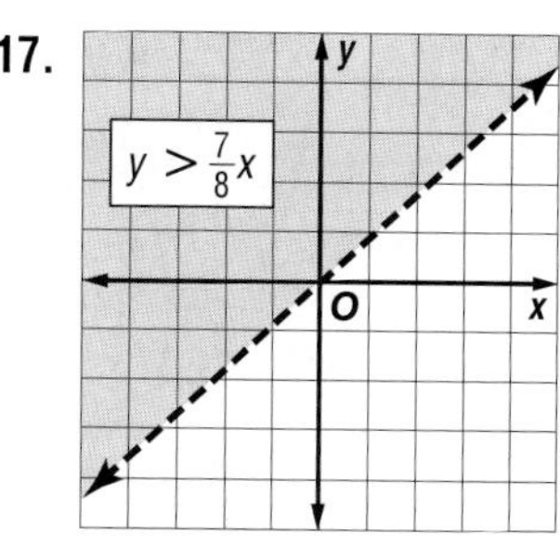

18.
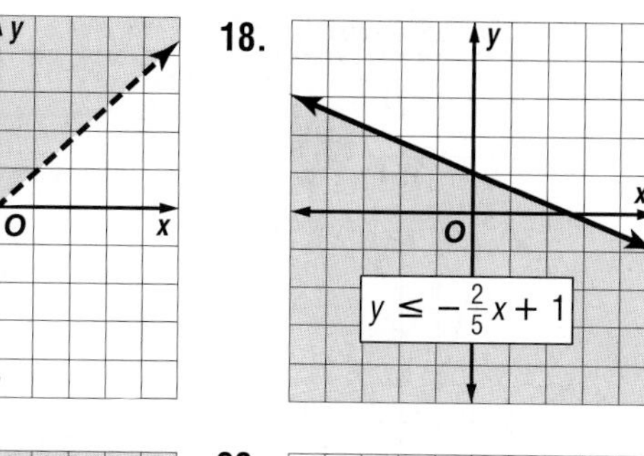

19.
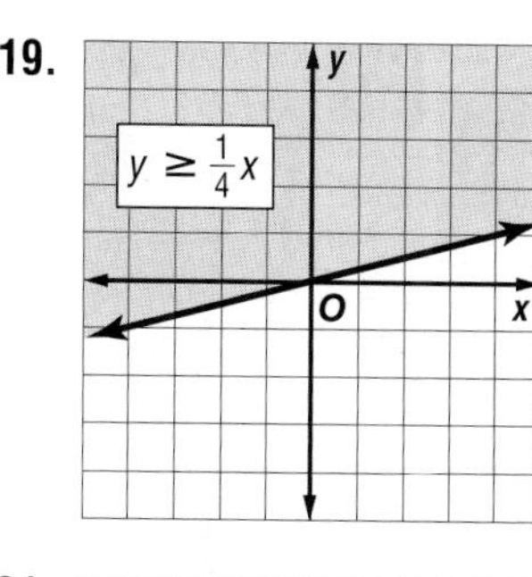

20.
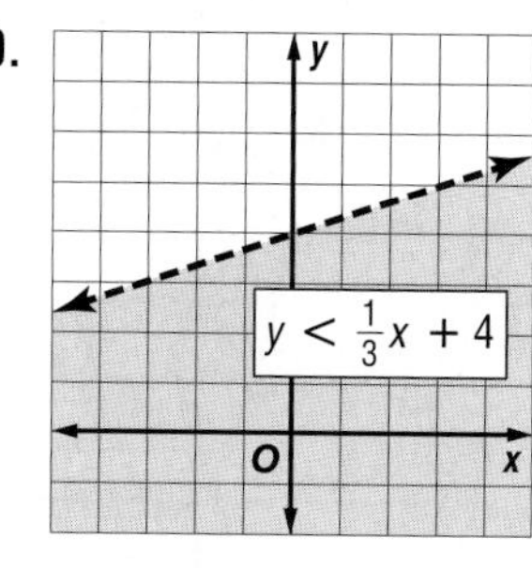

21.
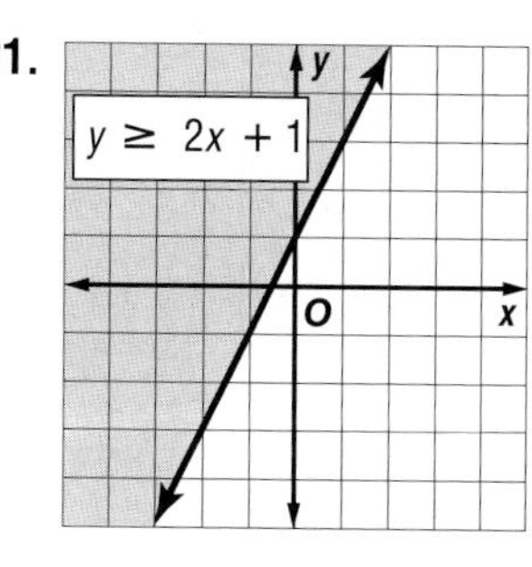

22.
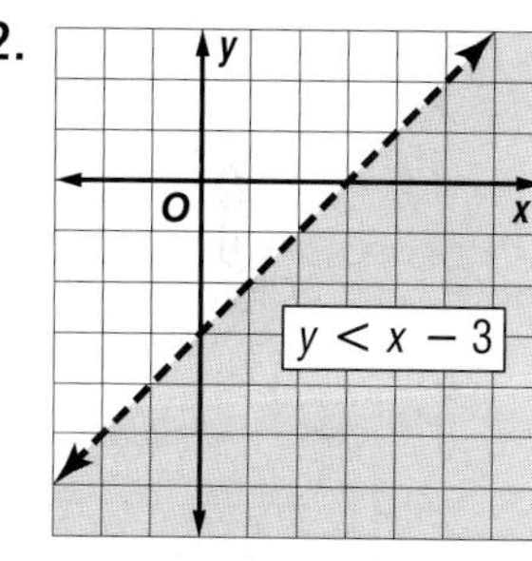

23.
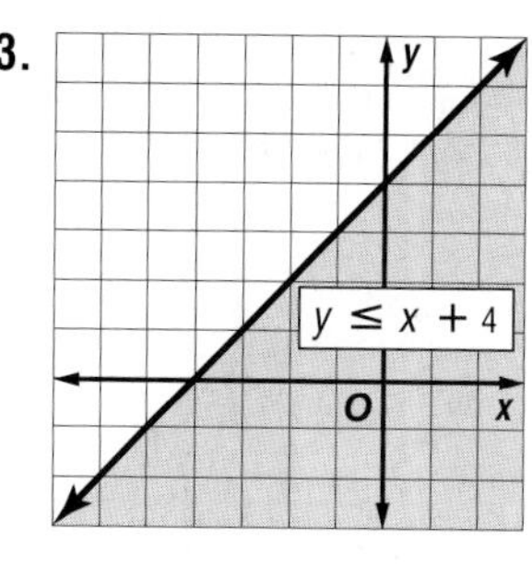

24.
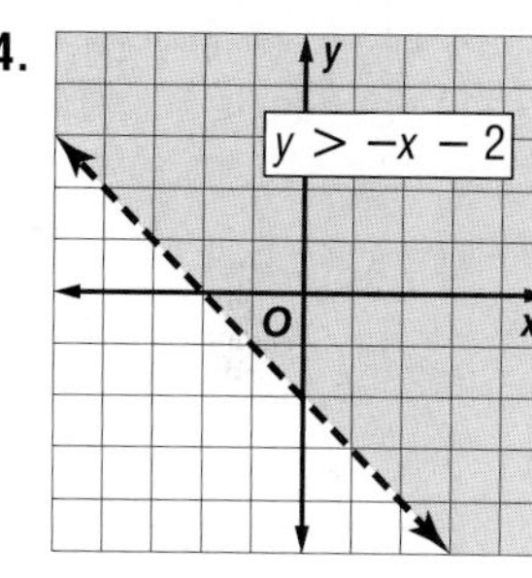

25.
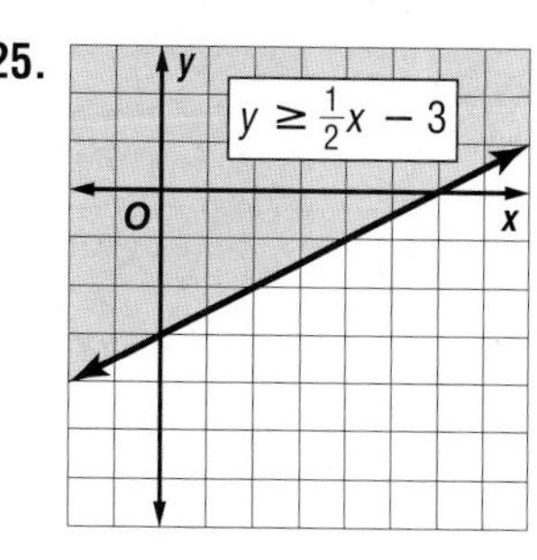

26.
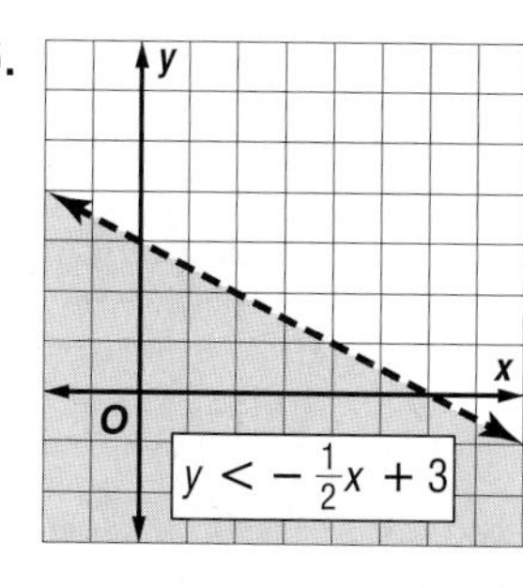

27.
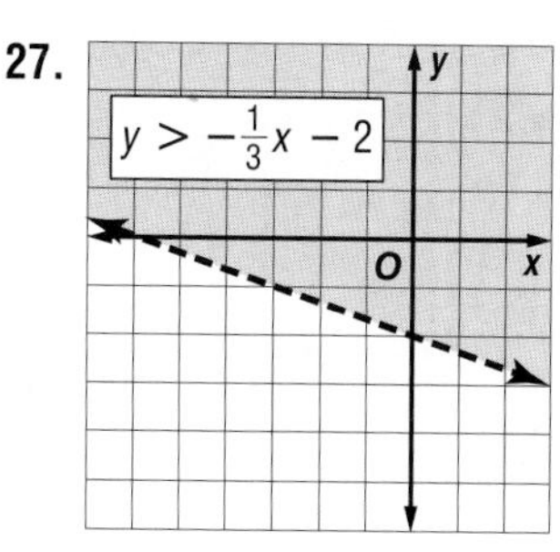

28.
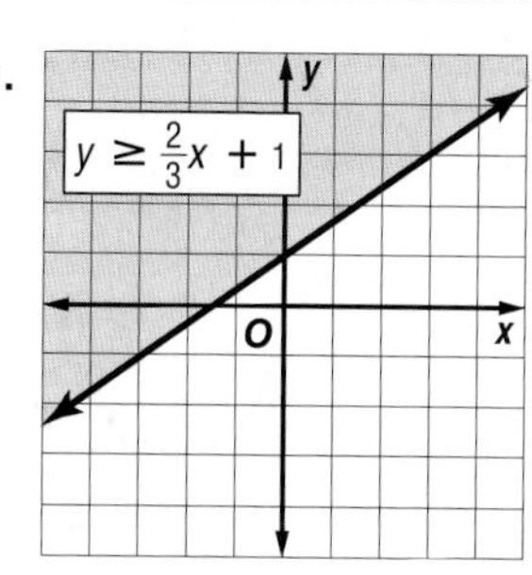

Page 645, Lesson 12-2

1.
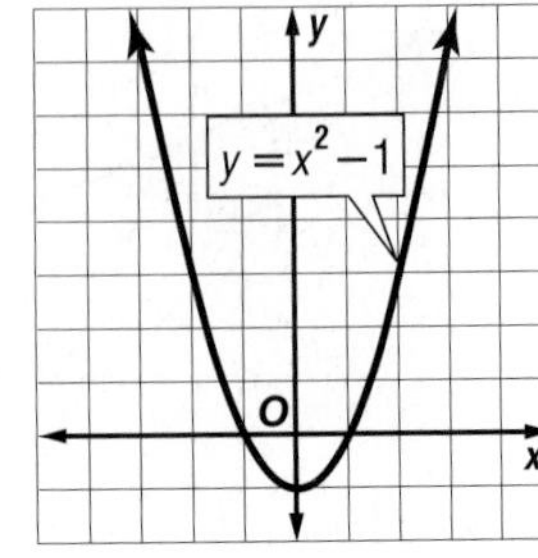

2.
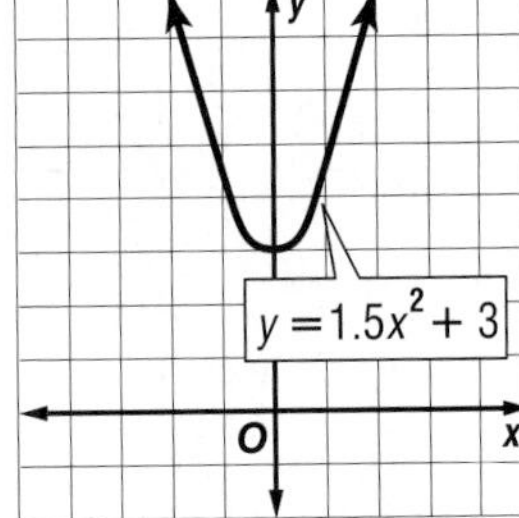

3.
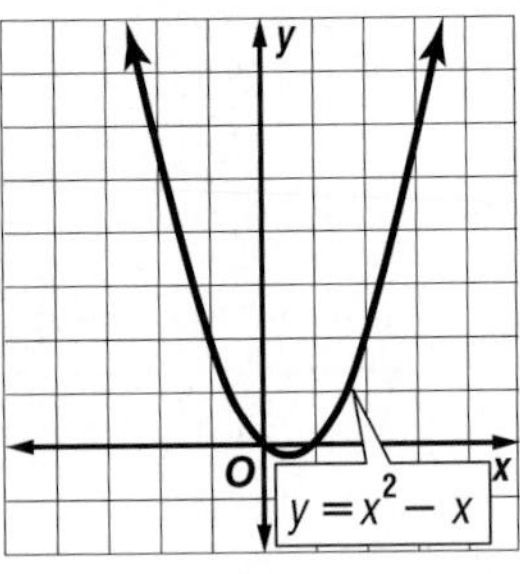

4.
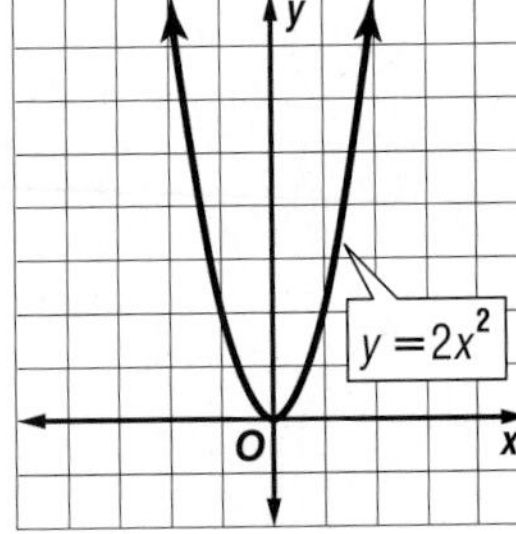

5.
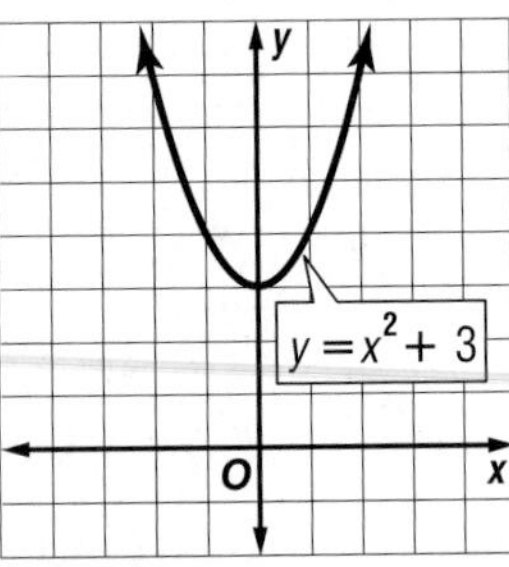

6.
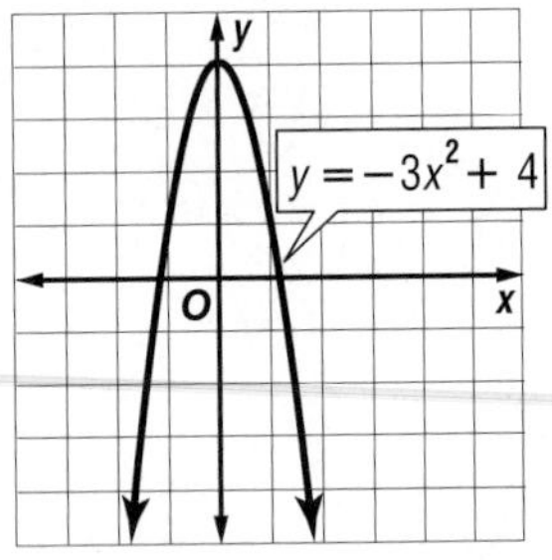

7.
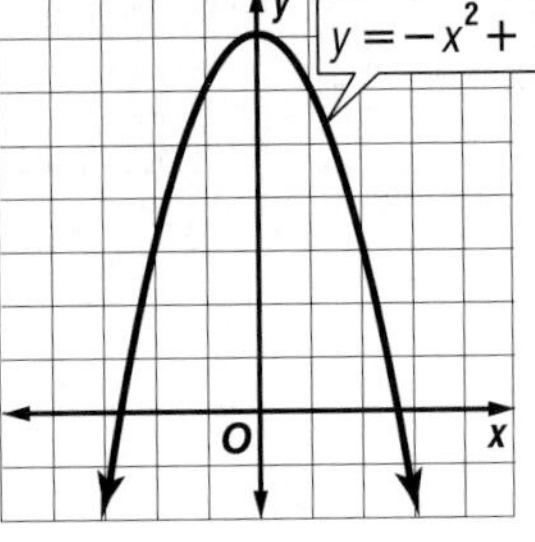

8.
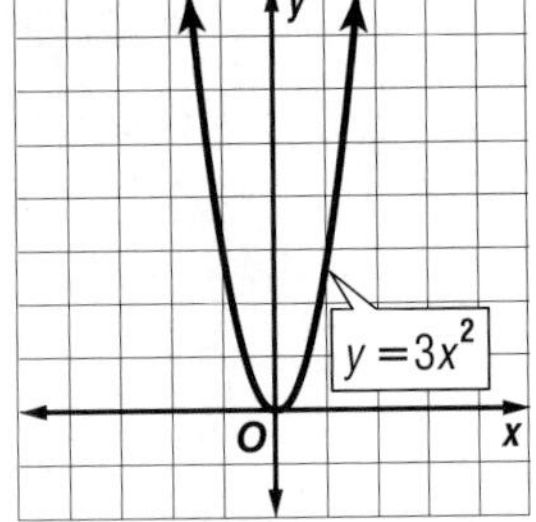

9.
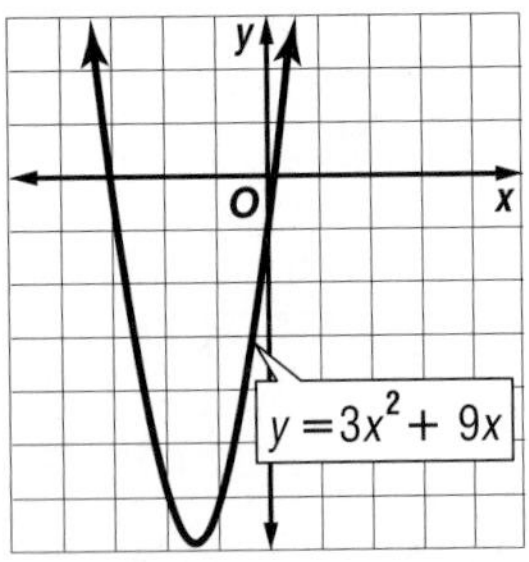

10.
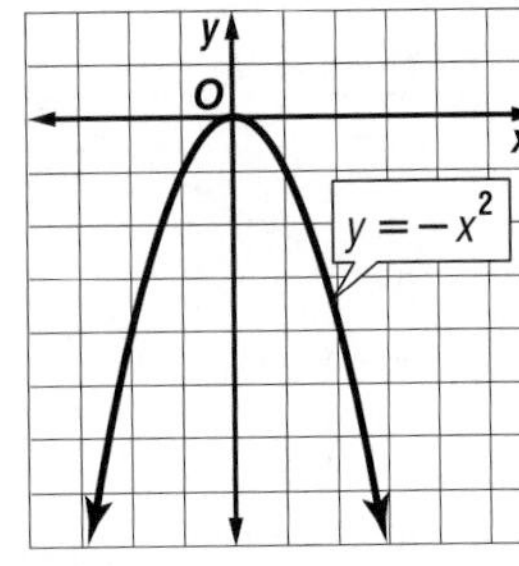

11.
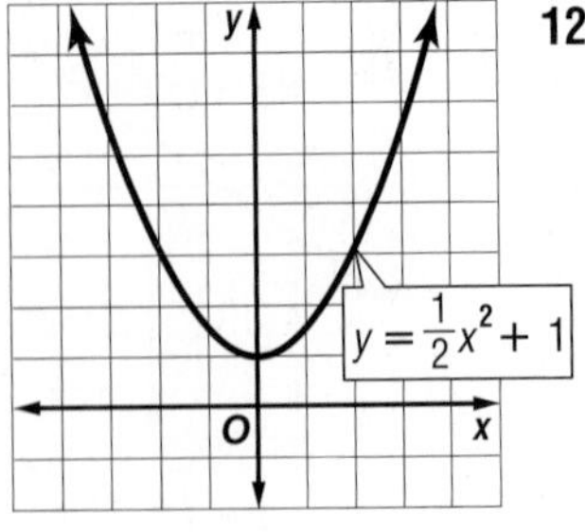

12.
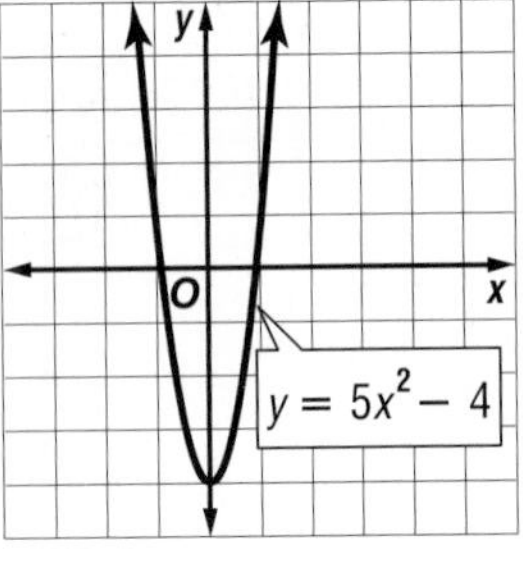

13.
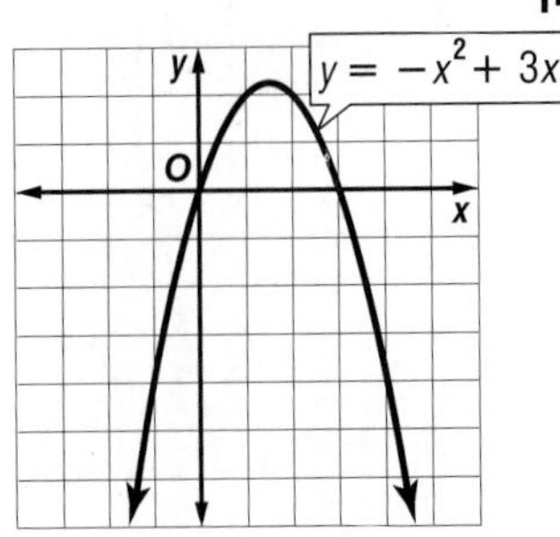

14.
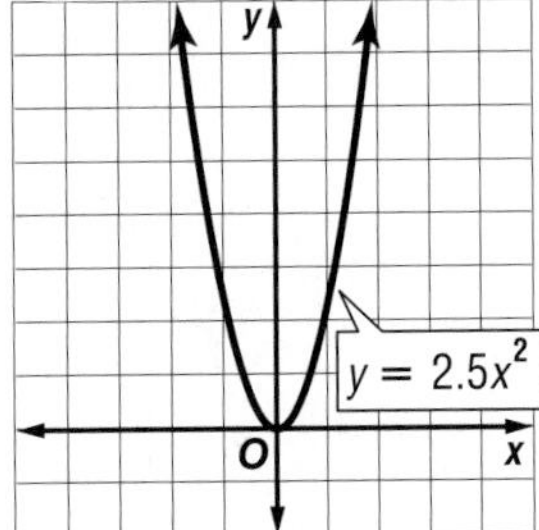

15.
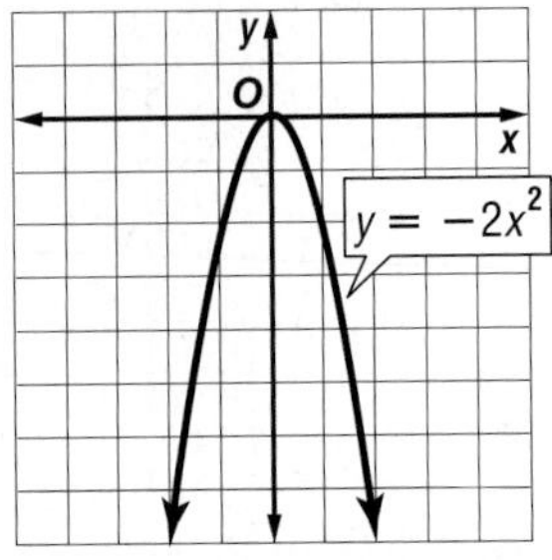

16.
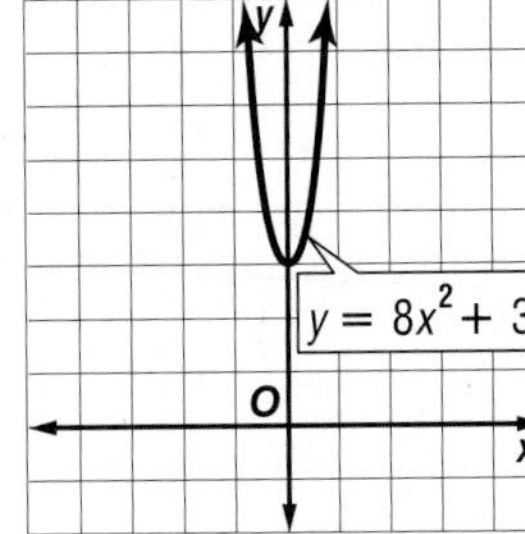

17.
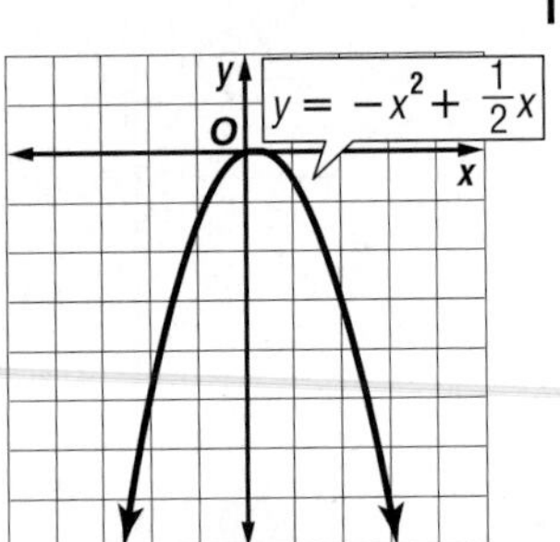

18.
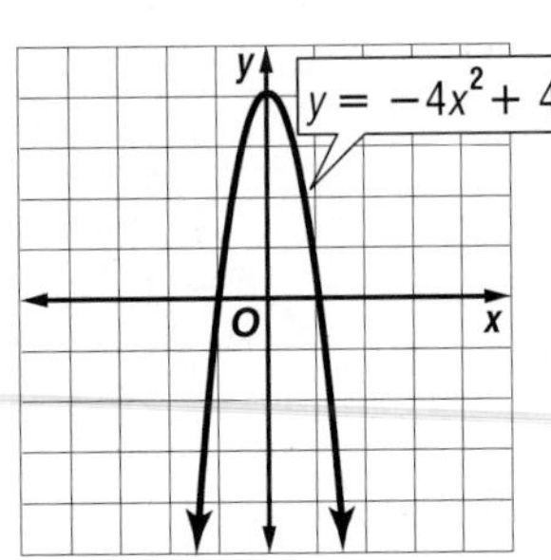

19.
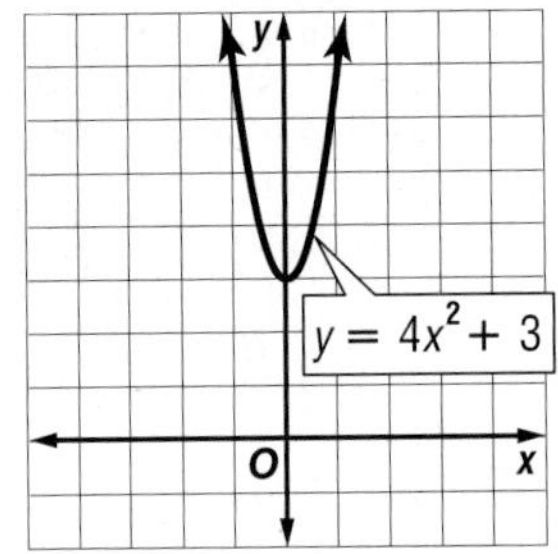

20.
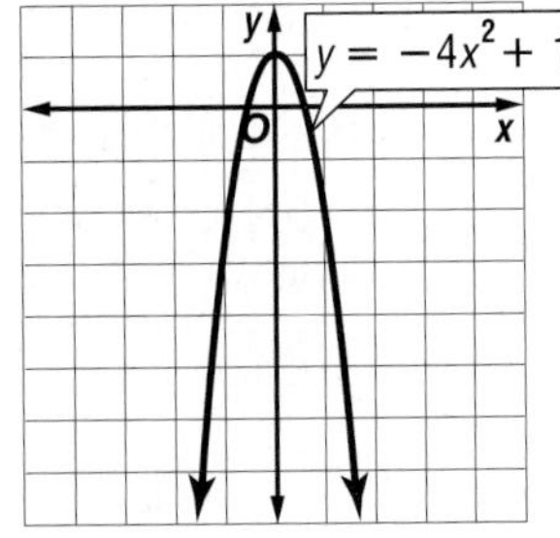

21.
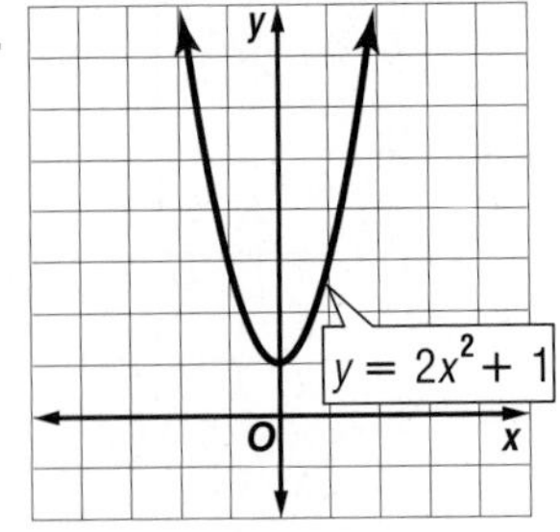

22.
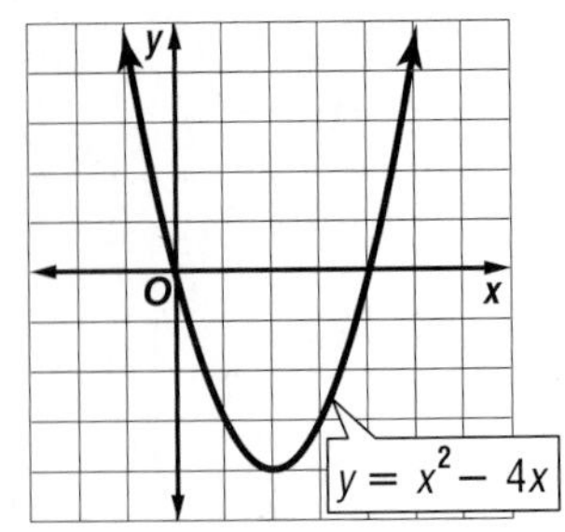

23.
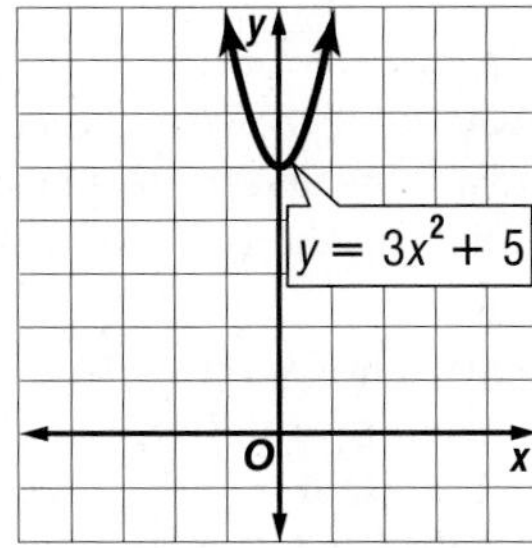

24.
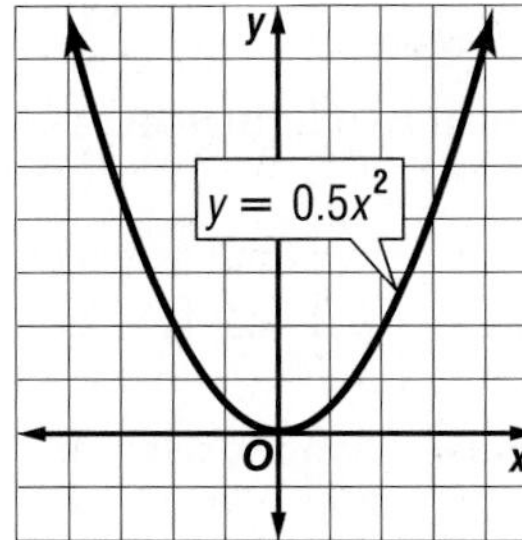

25.
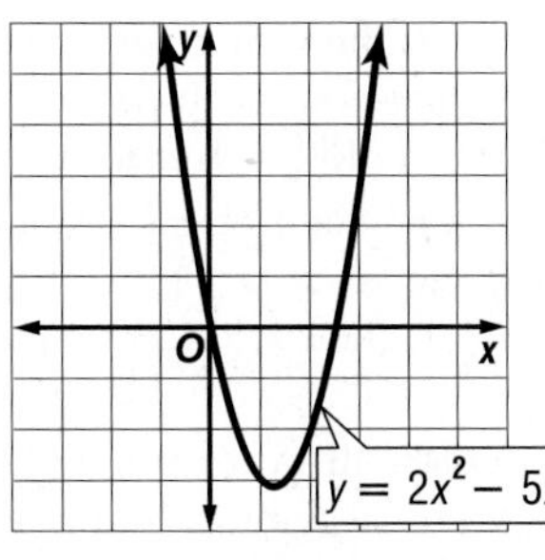

26.
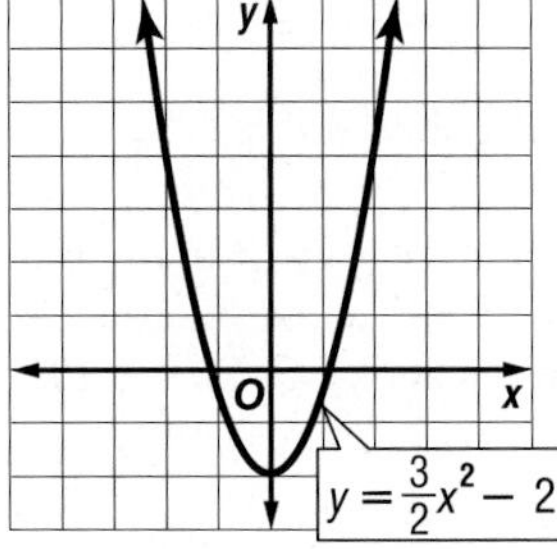

27.
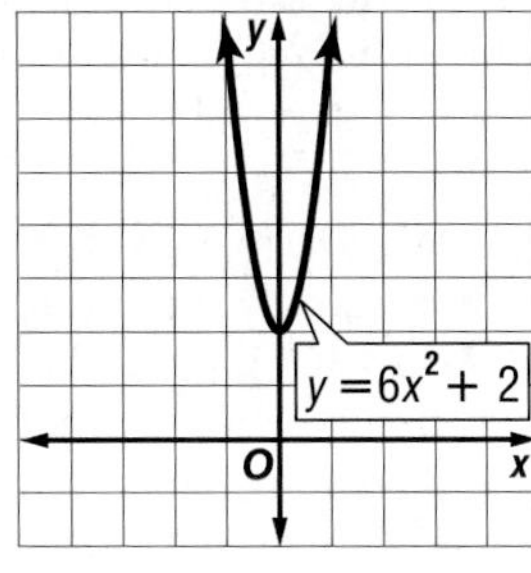

28.
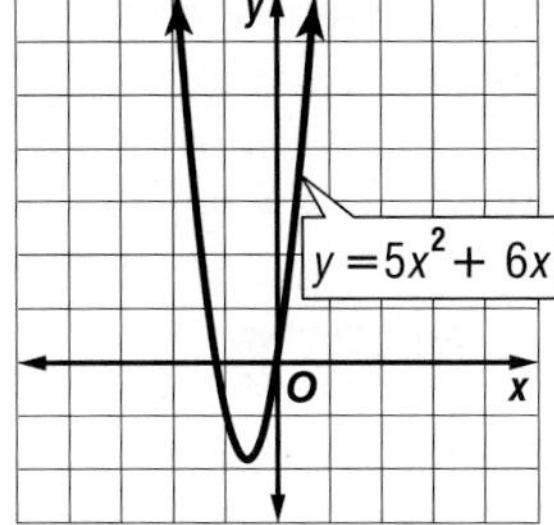

Mixed Problem Solving

Chapter 1 Algebra: Integers

(pages 4–59)

1. **PATTERNS** Draw the next two figures in the pattern below. (Lesson 1-1)

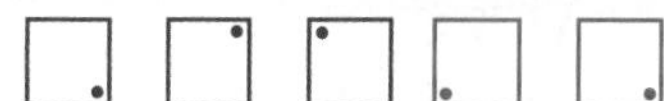

TEMPERATURE For Exercises 2 and 3, use the following information.
The formula $F = \frac{9}{5}C + 32$ is used to convert degrees Celsius to degrees Fahrenheit. (Lesson 1-2)

2. Find the degrees Fahrenheit if it is 30°C outside. **86°F**
3. A local newscaster announces that today is his birthday. Rather than disclose his true age on air, he states that his age in Celsius is 10. How old is he? **50**

4. **SPORTS** In football, a penalty results in a loss of yards. Write an integer to describe a loss of 10 yards. (Lesson 1-3) **−10**

BILLS For Exercises 5 and 6, use the table below. (Lesson 1-4)

Description	Amount ($)
Beginning Balance	435
Gas Company	−75
Electric Company	−75
Phone Company	−100
Deposit	75
Rent	−200

5. How much is in the account? **$60**
6. Kirsten owes the cable company $65. Does she have enough to pay this bill? **no**

7. **WEATHER** For the month of August, the highest temperature was 98°F. The lowest temperature was 54°F. What was the range of temperatures for the month? (Lesson 1-5) **44°F**

8. **WEATHER** During a thunderstorm, the temperature dropped by 5 degrees per half-hour. What was the temperature change after 3 hours? (Lesson 1-6) **−30°**

9. **AGE** Julia is 6 years older than Elias. Define a variable and write an expression for Julia's age. (Lesson 1-7) **s = Elias's age; $s + 6$**

HISTORY For Exercises 10 and 11, use the following information.
To be President of the United States, a person must be at least 35 years old. (Lesson 1-7)

10. If y is the year a person was born, write an expression for the earliest year that he or she could be president. **$y + 35$**
11. If a person became President this year, write an equation to find the latest year he or she could have been born. **$y + 35 = 2004$ (if the year is 2004)**

12. **BANKING** After you withdraw $75 from your checking account, the balance is $205. Write and solve a subtraction equation to find your balance before the withdrawal. (Lesson 1-8) **$a - 75 = 205$; $280**

13. **HEALTH** Dario gained 25 pounds during his junior year. By the end of his junior year, he weighed 160 pounds. Write and solve an addition equation to find out how much he weighed at the beginning of his junior year. (Lesson 1-8) **$w + 25 = 160$; 135 lb**

14. **MONEY** Janelle baby-sits and charges $5 per hour. Write and solve a multiplication equation to find how many hours she needs to baby-sit in order to make $55. (Lesson 1-9) **$5h = 55$; 11 h**

15. **PHYSICAL SCIENCE** Work is done when a force acts on an object and the object moves. The amount of work, measured in foot-pounds, is equal to the amount of force applied, measured in pounds, times the distance, in feet, the object moved. Write and solve a multiplication equation that could be used to find how far you have to lift a 45-pound object to produce 180 foot-pounds of work. (Lesson 1-9) **$180 = 45d$; 4 ft**

1. **HEALTH** A newborn baby weighs $6\frac{3}{4}$ pounds. Write this weight as a decimal. (Lesson 2-1) **6.75 lb**

MEASUREMENT For Exercises 2 and 3, use the figure below. (Lesson 2-1) **2. $6\frac{3}{8}$ in.**

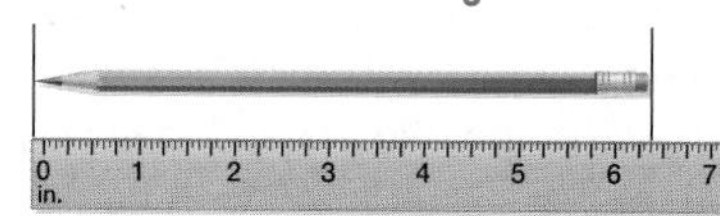

2. Write the length of the pencil as a fraction.
3. Write the length of the pencil as a decimal. **6.375 in.**
4. **SEWING** Which is the smallest seam: $\frac{1}{4}$ inch, $\frac{1}{2}$ inch, or $\frac{1}{8}$ inch? (Lesson 2-2) **$\frac{1}{8}$ in.**

Find the area of each rectangle. (Lesson 2-3)

5. **$\frac{3}{8}$ in²** 6. **$\frac{4}{5}$ yd²**

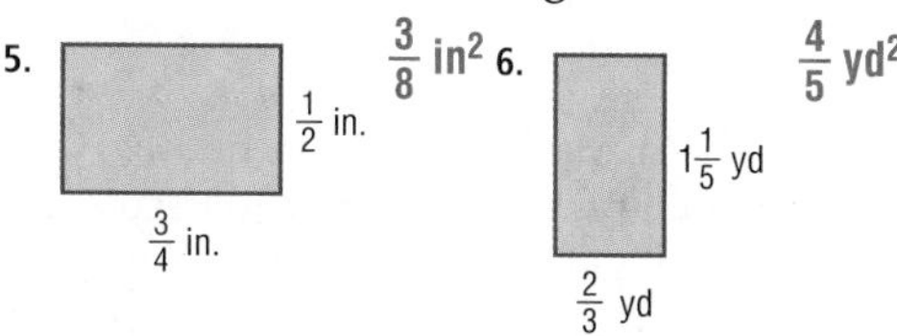

7. **COOKING** Giovanni is increasing his double chocolate chip cookie recipe to $1\frac{1}{2}$ batches. If the original recipe calls for $3\frac{1}{2}$ cups of flour, how much flour does he need for $1\frac{1}{2}$ batches? (Lesson 2-3) **$5\frac{1}{4}$ c**

8. **MEDICINE** A baby gets 1 dropper of medicine for each $2\frac{1}{4}$ pounds of body weight. If a baby weighs $11\frac{1}{4}$ pounds, how many droppers of medicine should she get? (Lesson 2-4) **5 droppers**

9. **LIBRARIES** Lucas is storing a set of art books on a shelf that has $11\frac{1}{4}$ inches of shelf space. If each book is $\frac{3}{4}$ inch wide, how many books can be stored on the shelf? (Lesson 2-4) **15 books**

10. **HEIGHT** Molly is $64\frac{1}{4}$ inches tall. Minya is $62\frac{3}{4}$ inches tall. How much taller is Molly than Minya? (Lesson 2-5) **$1\frac{1}{2}$ in.**

GEOMETRY Find the perimeter of each figure. (Lesson 2-5)

11. **4 ft** 12. **$7\frac{1}{6}$ in.**

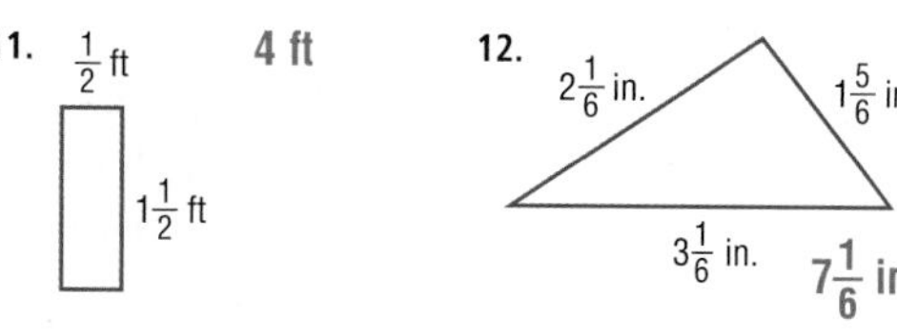

13. **ELECTIONS** In the student council elections, Janie won $\frac{1}{5}$ of the votes, and Jamal won $\frac{2}{3}$ of the votes. What fraction of the votes did the only other candidate receive? (Lesson 2-6) **$\frac{2}{15}$**

14. **CONSTRUCTION** Three pieces of wood are $4\frac{3}{4}$, $5\frac{1}{8}$, and $7\frac{3}{16}$ inches long. If these pieces of wood are laid end to end, what is their total length? (Lesson 2-6) **$17\frac{1}{16}$ in.**

FINANCES For Exercises 15 and 16, use the following information.
Jenna makes \$3.25 per hour delivering newspapers. (Lesson 2-7)

15. Write a multiplication equation you can use to determine how many hours she must work to earn \$35.75. **$3.25h = 35.75$**
16. How many hours does Jenna need to work to earn \$35.75? **11 h**

17. **BIOLOGY** If one cell splits in two every $\frac{1}{2}$ hour, how many cells will there be after $4\frac{1}{2}$ hours? (Lesson 2-8) **512 cells**

18. **EARTH SCIENCE** There are approximately 10^{21} kilograms of water on Earth. Write the number of kilograms of water on Earth in standard form. (Lesson 2-9) **1,000,000,000,000,000,000,000 kg**

19. **HAIR** There are an estimated 100,000 hairs on a person's head. Write this number in scientific notation. (Lesson 2-9) **1×10^5**

20. **LIFE SCIENCE** A petri dish contains 2.53×10^{11} bacteria. Write the number of bacteria in standard form. (Lesson 2-9) **253,000,000,000**

Mixed Problem Solving

Mixed Problem Solving 649

Mixed Problem Solving

1. **GARDENING** A square garden has an area of 576 square feet. What is the length of each side of the garden? (Lesson 3-1) **24 ft**

GEOMETRY The formula for the perimeter of a square is $P = 4s$, where s is the length of the side. Find the perimeter of each square. (Lesson 3-1)

2. Area = 16 square meters **16 m**

3. Area = 144 square inches **48 in.**

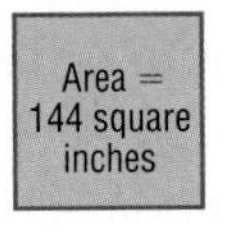

SCIENCE The formula $t = \frac{\sqrt{h}}{4}$ represents the time t in seconds that it takes an object to fall from a height of h feet. (Lesson 3-2)

4. If a ball is dropped from a height of 100 feet, estimate how long it will take to reach the ground. **2.5 s**

5. If a ball is dropped from a height of 500 feet, estimate how long it will take to reach the ground. **5.5 s**

6. **WAVES** The speed s in knots of a wave can be estimated using the formula $s = 1.34\sqrt{\ell}$, where ℓ is the length of the wave in feet. Find the estimated speed of a wave of length 5 feet. (Lesson 3-3) **about 3.0 knots**

7. **GEOMETRY** To approximate the radius of a circle, you can use the formula $r = \sqrt{\frac{A}{3.14}}$, where A is the area of the circle. To the nearest tenth, find the radius of a circle that has an area of 60 square feet. (Lesson 3-3) **4.4 ft**

8. **GEOGRAPHY** In Ohio, a triangle is formed by the cities Cleveland, Columbus, and Toledo. From the distances given below, is this triangle a right triangle? Explain your reasoning. (Lesson 3-4)

no, $120^2 + 99^2 \neq 124^2$

9. **INTERIOR DESIGN** A room is 20 feet by 15 feet. Find the length of the diagonal of the room. (Lesson 3-4) **25 ft**

10. **TRAVEL** Plane A travels north 500 miles. Plane B leaves from the same location at the same time and travels east 250 miles. How far apart are the two planes? (Lesson 3-5) **559.0 mi**

11. **TELEVISION** A television screen has a diagonal measurement of 32 inches and a width of 15 inches. How long is the television? (Lesson 3-5) **28.3 in.**

12. **KITES** A kite string is 25 yards long. The horizontal distance between the kite and the person flying it is 12 yards. How high is the kite? (Lesson 3-5) **21.9 yd**

13. **REPAIRS** Shane is painting his house. He has a ladder that is 10 feet long. He places the base of the ladder 6 feet from the house. How far from the ground will the top of the ladder reach? (Lesson 3-5) **8 ft**

14. **ARCHEOLOGY** A dig uncovers an urn at (1, 1) and a bracelet at (5, 3). How far apart were the two items if one unit on the grid equals 1 mile? (Lesson 3-6) **4.5 mi**

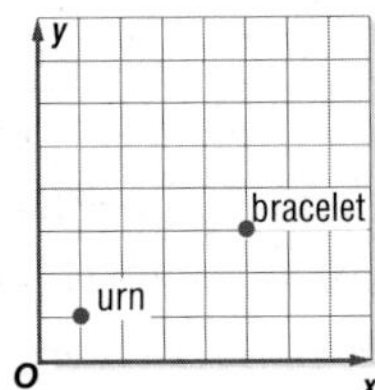

15. **TRAVEL** A unit on the grid below is 0.25 mile. Find the distance from point A to point B. (Lesson 3-6) **about 1.6 mi**

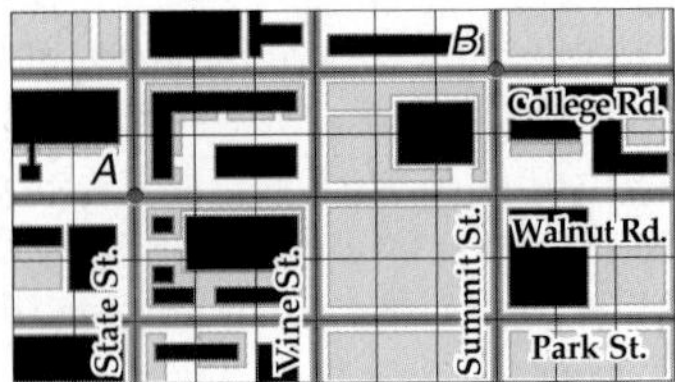

650 Mixed Problem Solving

1. **SHOPPING** You can buy 3 tapes at The Music Shoppe for $12.99, or you can buy 5 of the same tapes for $19.99 at Quality Sounds. Which is the better buy? Explain your reasoning. (Lesson 4-1) **Quality Sounds; see margin for explanation.**
2. **TRAVEL** On a trip, you drive 1,565 miles on 100 gallons of gas. Find your car's gas mileage. (Lesson 4-1) **15.65 mi/gal**
3. **WEATHER** The temperature is 88°F at 2 P.M. and 72°F at 3:30 P.M. What was the rate of change in temperature between these two time periods? (Lesson 4-2) **about −10.7°F/h**

WEIGHTS The table below gives the age and weight of a young child. (Lesson 4-2)

Age (yr)	3	3.5	4	5	7
Weight (lb)	31	34	38	40	45

4. Between which two ages did the child's weight increase at the fastest rate? Explain. **See margin.**
5. Between which two ages did the child's weight increase at the slowest rate? Explain. **between 4 to 5; rate of change is 2 lb/yr**
6. **LOANS** Find the slope of the line below and interpret its meaning as a rate of change. (Lesson 4-3) **See margin.**

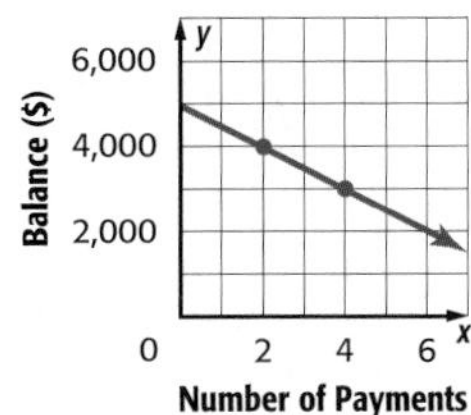

7. **ELECTIONS** About $\frac{2}{3}$ of the eighth grade class voted for Dominic to be Student Council president. If there are 350 students in the eighth grade class, how many voted for Dominic? (Lesson 4-4) **233**
8. **HEALTH** About $\frac{3}{5}$ of the babies born at Memorial Hospital are boys. If there are 250 babies born during the month of September, about how many are boys? (Lesson 4-4) **150**
9. **PHOTOGRAPHY** Eva wants to enlarge the picture below and frame it. The scale factor from the original picture to the enlarged picture is to be 2:5. Find the dimensions of the enlarged picture. (Lesson 4-5) **15 in. by 10 in.**

10. **ARCHITECTURE** The Eiffel Tower is 986 feet tall. If a scale model is 6 inches tall, what is the scale of the model? (Lesson 4-6) **1 in. = $164\frac{1}{3}$ ft**
11. **CARS** A model is being built of a car. The car is 12 feet long and 9 feet wide. If the length of the model is 4 inches, how wide should the model be? (Lesson 4-6) **3 in.**
12. **FLAGPOLE** A 10-foot tall flagpole casts a 4-foot shadow. At the same time, a nearby tree casts a 25-foot shadow. Draw a diagram of this situation. Then write and solve a proportion to find the height of the tree. (Lesson 4-7) **See margin; $\frac{10}{h} = \frac{4}{25}$; $h = 62.5$ ft**
13. **SURVEYING** Write and solve a proportion to find the distance across the river shown in the diagram below. (Lesson 4-7) **See margin.**

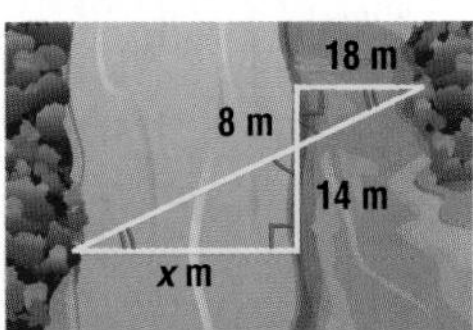

MURAL For Exercises 14 and 15, use the following information.
A design 10 inches long and 7 inches wide is to be enlarged to appear as a wall mural that is 36 inches long. (Lesson 4-8)

14. What is the scale factor for this enlargement? **3.6:1**
15. How wide will the mural be? **25.2 in.**

Mixed Problem Solving

Chapter 4

1. **Quality Sounds is about $4.00 per tape and The Music Shoppe is about $4.33 per tape, so Quality Sounds is the better deal.**
4. **between 3.5 and 4; rate of change is 8 lb/yr**
6. **−500; loan balance decrease $500 per payment**
12.

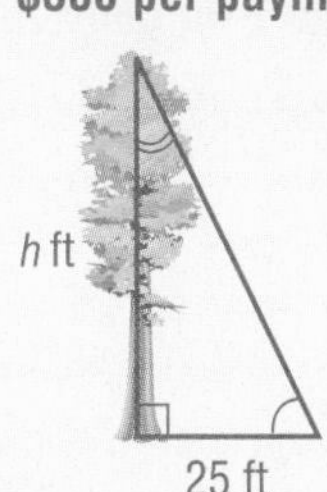

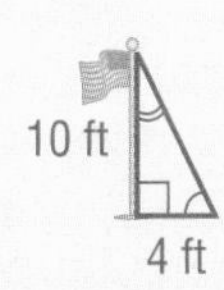

13. $\frac{8}{14} = \frac{18}{x}$; **31.5 m**

Mixed Problem Solving

Chapter 5

13. Sample answer: oxygen, $\frac{3}{5}$ of 120 or 72 lb; carbon, $\frac{1}{5}$ of 120 or 24 lb; hydrogen, $\frac{1}{10}$ of 120 or 12 lb; nitrogen, $\frac{1}{20}$ of 120 or 6 lb; calcium, $\frac{1}{50}$ of 120 or about 2 lb; phosphorus and sulfur, $\frac{1}{100}$ of 120 or about 1 lb

Mixed Problem Solving

Chapter 5 Percent

(pages 204–251)

1. **SCHOOL** Two out of five children entering kindergarten can read. Write this ratio as a percent. (Lesson 5-1) **40%**

2. **ELECTIONS** About 25% of the school voted for yellow and red to be the school colors. Write this percent as a fraction. (Lesson 5-1) $\frac{1}{4}$

3. **FOOD** About $\frac{17}{25}$ of Americans eat fast food at least two times a week. Write $\frac{17}{25}$ as a percent. (Lesson 5-2) **68%**

4. **GEOMETRY** What percent of the area of the rectangle is shaded? (Lesson 5-2) $16\frac{2}{3}\%$

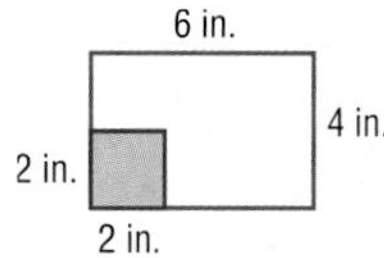

5. **EXAMS** Lexie answered 75% of the questions correctly on an exam. If she answered 30 questions correctly, how many questions were on the exam? (Lesson 5-3) **40**

CANDY For Exercises 6–8, use the table below listing the number of each color of chocolate candies in a jar. (Lesson 5-3)

Color	Number
yellow	4
brown	12
red	2
green	5
orange	1
blue	1

6. What percent of the candies are brown? **48%**
7. What percent of the candies are green? **20%**
8. What percent of the candies are blue? **4%**

9. **RETAIL** Mr. Lewis receives a 10% commission on items he sells. What is his commission on a $35 purse? (Lesson 5-4) **$3.50**

10. **FARMING** A farmer receives 25% of the cost of a bag of flour. Determine the amount of money a farmer receives from a bag of flour that sells for $1.60. (Lesson 5-4) **$0.40**

MOVIES For Exercises 11 and 12, use the following information.
The results of a survey asking children ages 3 to 6 if they liked a recent animated movie are depicted below. (Lesson 5-4)

11. If 120 children were surveyed, how many said they liked the movie? **84**
12. How many said they did not like the movie? **36**

13. **LIFE SCIENCE** The table below lists the elements found in the human body. If Jacinta weighs 120 pounds, estimate how many pounds of each element are in her body. (Lesson 5-5) **See margin.**

Element	Percent of Body
Oxygen	63
Carbon	19
Hydrogen	9
Nitrogen	5
Calcium	1.5
Phosphorus and Sulfur	1.2

Source: *The New York Public Library Science Desk Reference*

14. **RETAIL** A pair of shoes costs $50. If a 5.75% sales tax is added, what is the total cost of the shoes? (Lesson 5-6) **$52.88**

15. **WEATHER** The average wind speed on Mount Washington is 35.3 miles per hour. The highest wind speed ever recorded there is 231 miles per hour. Find the percent of change from the average wind speed to the highest wind speed recorded. (Lesson 5-7) **about 554.4%**

16. **MONEY** Suppose $500 is deposited into an account with a simple interest rate of 5.5%. Find the total in the account after 3 years. (Lesson 5-8) **$582.50**

652 Mixed Problem Solving

FURNITURE For Exercises 1–3, use the following information.
A single piece of wood is used for both the backrest of a chair and its rear legs. The inside angle that the wood makes with the floor is 100°, and the seat is parallel to the floor. (Lesson 6-1)

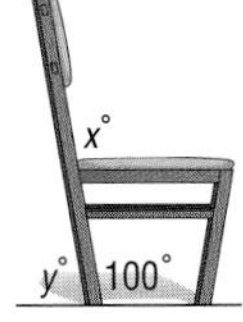

1. Find the values of x and y. **100; 80**
2. Classify the angle measuring $x°$. **obtuse**
3. Classify the angle pair measuring 100° and $y°$ using all names that apply. **adjacent, supplementary**
4. **URBAN PLANNING** Ambulances cannot safely make turns of less than 70°. The proposed site of a hospital's emergency entrance is to be at the northeast corner of Bidwell and Elmwood. Should this site be approved? Explain your reasoning. (Lesson 6-1) **See margin.**

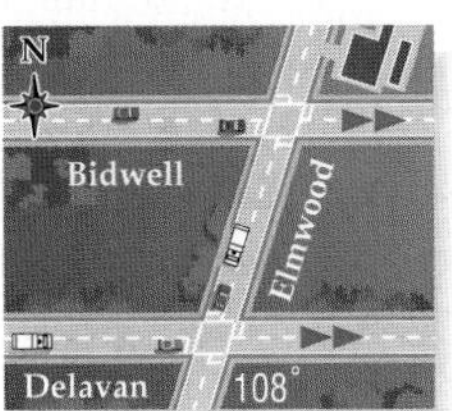

5. **CONSTRUCTION** A 12-foot ladder leans against a house. The base of the ladder rests on level ground and is 4 feet from the house. The top of the ladder reaches 11.3 feet up the side of the house. Classify the triangle formed by the house, the ground, and the ladder by its angles and by its sides. (Lesson 6-2) **right scalene**
6. **MEASUREMENT** At the same time that the sun's rays make a 60° angle with the ground, the shadow cast by a flagpole is 20 feet. To the nearest foot, find the height of the flagpole. (Lesson 6-3) **35 ft**

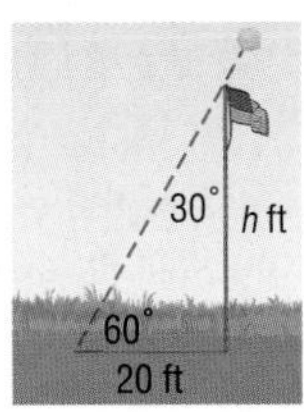

7. **CARPENTRY** Suppose you are constructing a doghouse with a triangular roof. Into what shape will you need to cut the boards labeled A and B in the diagram below? (Lesson 6-4) **trapezoid**

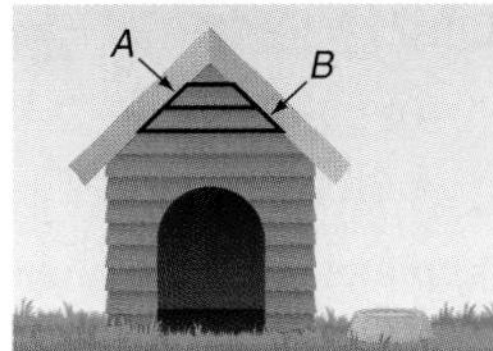

8. **GARDENING** Two triangular gardens have congruent shapes. If 36 bricks are needed to border the first garden how many bricks are needed to border the second garden? Explain your reasoning. (Lesson 6-5) **See margin.**

QUILT PATTERNS For Exercises 9 and 10, use the diagrams below. (Lesson 6-6)

a. 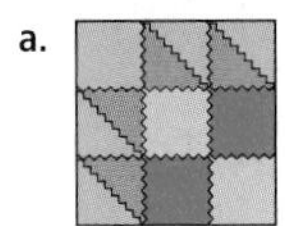

b. 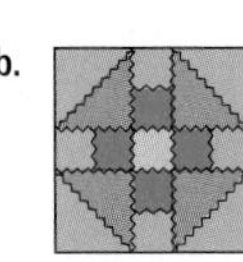

9. Determine whether each pattern has line symmetry. If it does, trace the pattern and draw all lines of symmetry. If not, write *none*. **See margin.**
10. Which pattern has rotational symmetry? Name its angles of rotation. **b.; 90°, 180°, 270°**

ART For Exercises 11–13, copy and complete the design shown at the right so that each finished four-paneled piece of art fits the given description.

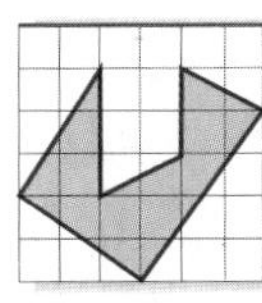
Upper Right Corner

11. The finished art has only a vertical line of symmetry. (Lesson 6-7)
12. The finished art shows translations of the first design to each of the other 3 panels. (Lesson 6-8) **11–13. See margin.**
13. The finished art has rotational symmetry. Its angles of rotation are 90°, 180°, and 270° about the bottom left corner. (Lesson 6-9)

Mixed Problem Solving

11.

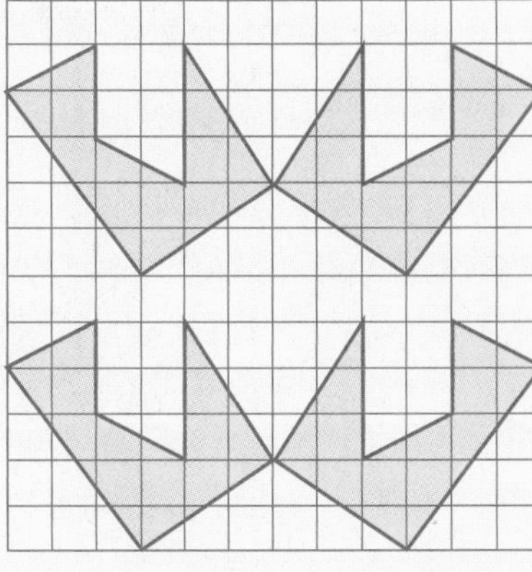

12.

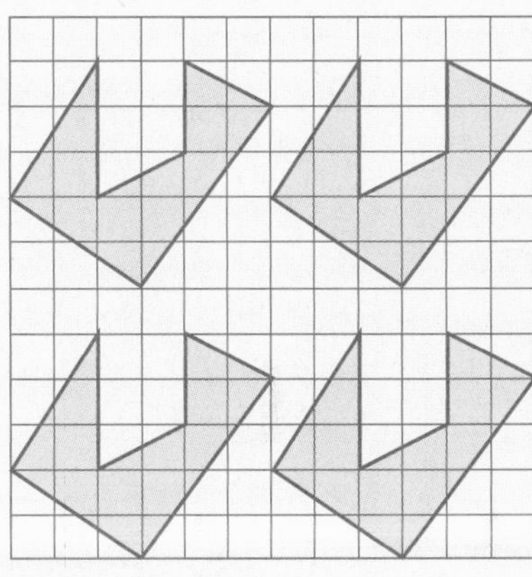

13.

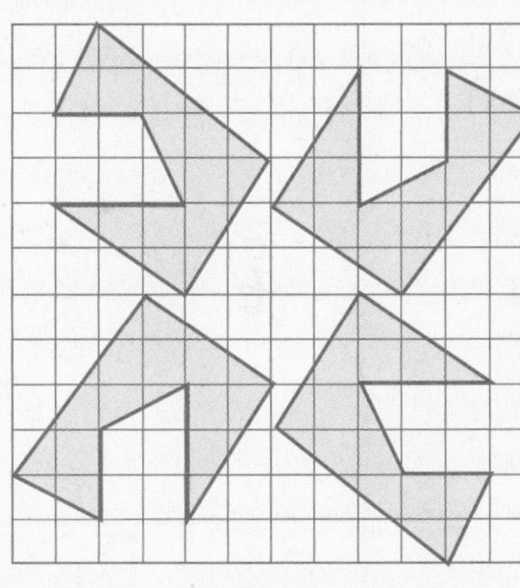

Chapter 6

4. Yes, the two corners at that intersection have measures of 108° and 72°. Therefore, it is just within the safety limits.
8. 36 bricks; congruent sides have equal measure, so their sum will be equal.

9a. yes; 

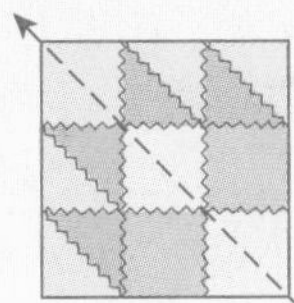

9b. yes;

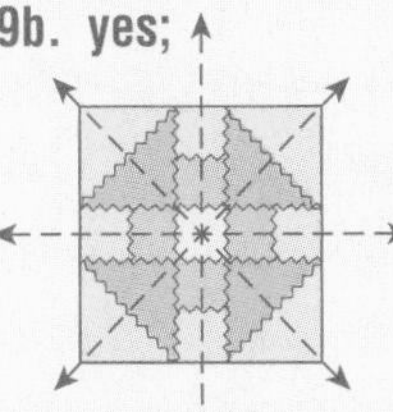

1. **FLOORING** How much will it cost to tile the floor shown if the tile costs \$2.55 per square foot? (Lesson 7-1) **\$408**

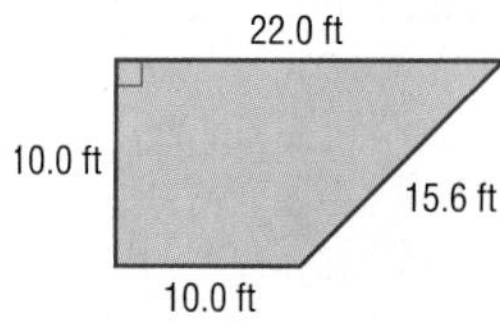

2. **FOOD** An apple pie has a diameter of 8 inches. If 1 slice is $\frac{1}{6}$ of the pie, what is the area of each slice? (Lesson 7-2) **about 8.4 in^2**

3. **MONEY** The diameter of a dime is about 17.9 millimeters. If the dime is rolled on its edge, how far will it roll after one complete rotation? (Lesson 7-2) **about 56.2 mm**

4. **FURNITURE** The top of a desk is shown below. How much workspace does the desktop provide? (Lesson 7-3) **1,488 in^2**

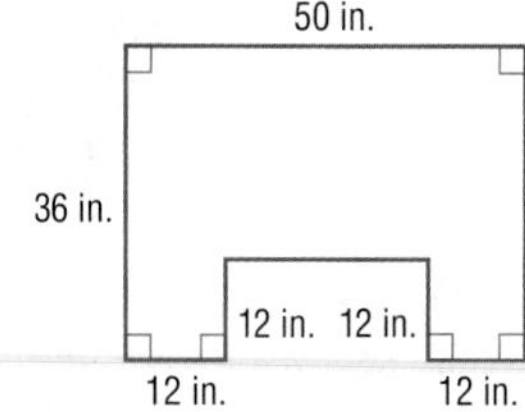

5. **STORAGE** Denise has a hatbox in the shape of a hexagonal prism. How many faces, edges, and vertices are on the hatbox? (Lesson 7-4) **8 faces; 18 edges; 12 vertices**

ANT FARM For Exercises 6 and 7, use the following information.
A 3-foot by 2-foot by 1.5-foot terrarium is to be filled with dirt for an ant farm. (Lesson 7-5)

6. How much dirt will the terrarium hold? **9 ft^3**

7. If each bag from the store holds 3 cubic feet of dirt, how many bags will be needed to fill the terrarium? **3**

8. **BATTERY** A size D battery is cylinder shaped, with a diameter of 33.3 millimeters and a height of 61.1 millimeters. Find the battery's volume in cubic centimeters. (*Hint*: 1 cm^3 = 1,000 mm^3) (Lesson 7-5) **about 53.2 cm^3**

9. **HATS** A clown wants to fill his party hat with confetti. Use the drawing below to determine how much confetti his hat will hold. (Lesson 7-6) **100.5 in^3**

10. **PRESENTS** Viviana wants to wrap a gift in a box that is 5 inches by 3 inches by 3 inches. How much wrapping paper will she need? Assume that the paper does not overlap. (Lesson 7-7) **78 in^2**

11. **PAINTING** A front of a government building has four columns that are each 15 feet tall and 6 feet in diameter. If the columns are to be painted, find the total surface area to be painted. (*Hint*: The tops and bottoms of the columns will not be painted.) (Lesson 7-7) **about 1,131 ft^2**

12. **ICE CREAM** Mr. Snow wants to wrap his ice cream cones in paper. If the radius of the base of the cone is 1.5 inches and the slant height is 5 inches, how much paper will he need to cover one cone? (Lesson 7-8) **23.56 in^2**

13. **FAMOUS BUILDINGS** The front of the Rock and Roll Hall of Fame in Cleveland, Ohio, is a square pyramid made out of glass. The pyramid has a slant height of 120 feet and a base length of 230 feet. Find the lateral area of the pyramid. (Lesson 7-8) **55,200 ft^2**

SURVEYING For Exercises 14 and 15, use the following information.
A surveyor records that Mrs. Smith's yard is 62.5 feet by 30 feet. (Lesson 7-9)

14. Find the perimeter of the yard using the correct precision. **190 ft**

15. What is the area of the yard? Round to the correct number of significant digits. **2,000 ft^2**

654 Mixed Problem Solving

1. **GAMES** To start the game of backgammon, each player rolls a number cube. The player with the greater number starts the game. Ebony rolls a 2. What is the probability that Cristina will roll a number greater than Ebony? (Lesson 8-1) $\frac{2}{3}$

2. **WEATHER** The news reports that there is a 55% chance of snow on Monday. What is the probability that there will be *no* snow on Monday? (Lesson 8-1) **45%**

3. **MONEY** A dime, a penny, a nickel, and a quarter are tossed. How many different outcomes are there? (Lesson 8-2) **16**

4. **PHONE NUMBERS** How many seven-digit phone numbers can be made using the numbers 0 through 9 if the first number cannot be 0? (Lesson 8-2) **9,000,000**

5. **MUSIC** A disc jockey has 12 songs he plans to play in the next hour. How many ways can he pick the next 3 songs? (Lesson 8-3) **1,320 ways**

6. **CONSTRUCTION** A contractor can build 11 different model homes. She only has 4 lots. How many ways can she put a different house on each lot? (Lesson 8-3) **7,920 ways**

7. **GAMES** In the game Tic Tac Toe, players place an X or an O in any of the nine locations that are empty. How many different ways can the first 3 moves of the game occur if X goes first? (Lesson 8-3) **504 ways**

8. **CAPS** Austin wants to take 2 of his 5 baseball caps on his trip. How many different combinations of baseball caps can he take? (Lesson 8-4) **10 combinations**

9. **MEDICINE** There are 8 standard classifications of blood types. An examination for prospective technicians requires them to correctly identify 3 different samples of blood. How many groups of samples can be set up for the examination? (Lesson 8-4) **56 groups**

ELECTRONICS For Exercises 10 and 11, use the following information.
The table below shows the percent of students at Midpark Middle School who have various electronic devices in their bedrooms. (Lesson 8-5)

Electronic Device	Percent
TV	60%
DVD Player	15%
Computer	20%
Game Station	75%

10. What is the probability that a student has both a TV and a computer? **12%**

11. What is the probability that a student has a TV, a DVD player, and a computer? **1.8%**

12. **CARDS** Two cards are drawn from a deck of 20 cards numbered 1 to 20. Once a card is selected, it is not returned. Find the probability of drawing two odd cards. (Lesson 8-5) $\frac{9}{38}$

TELEVISION For Exercises 13 and 14, use the table below. (Lesson 8-6)

Television Show	Number Who Selected as Favorite Show
Show A	35
Show B	25
Show C	20
Show D	10
Show E	10

13. What is the probability a person's favorite prime-time TV show is Show A? $\frac{7}{20}$

14. Out of 320 people, how many would you expect to say that Show A is their favorite prime-time TV show? **about 112**

CONCERTS For Exercises 15 and 16, use the following information.
As they leave a concert, 50 people are surveyed at random. Six people say they would buy a concert T-shirt. (Lesson 8-7) **15. 12%**

15. What percent say they would buy a T-shirt?

16. If 6,330 people attend the next concert, how many would you expect to buy T-shirts? **about 760 people**

Mixed Problem Solving

Mixed Problem Solving

Mixed Problem Solving 655

3. The air is mostly nitrogen. A little over a fifth of the air is oxygen. All other gases and water vapor account for only 1% of the air.
4. Sample answer: circle graph;

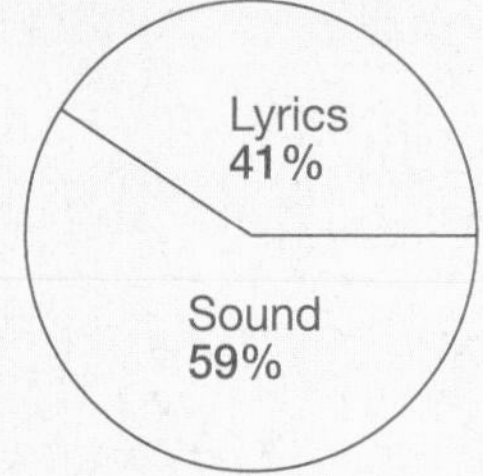

5.

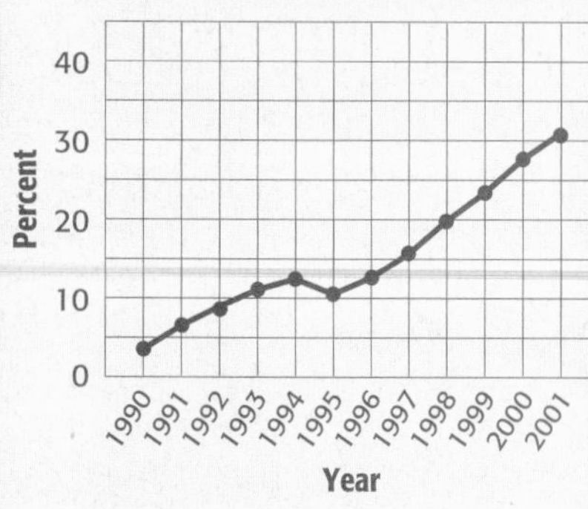

7. 31,344; 18,766
8. 31,693; 10,838; 20,855
9. See bottom margin.
10. Mean; this average of 38.75 is less than either the median or the mode of 45.
11. Median or mode; more than half of the times are greater than the mean time of 38.75 minutes.
12. $\begin{bmatrix} 32 & 4,860 & 12,150.0 \\ 32 & 4,859 & 12,147.5 \\ 28 & 4,726 & 11,815.0 \end{bmatrix}$

ADVERTISING For Exercises 1 and 2, use the histogram below. (Lesson 9-1)

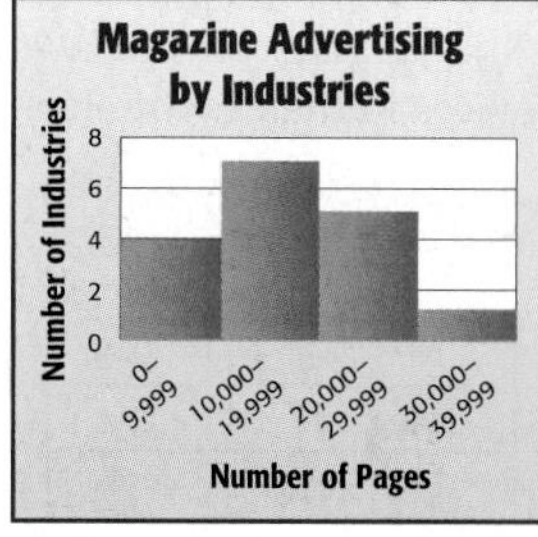

Source: Publisher Information Bureau, Inc.

1. How many industries used 20,000 pages or more of magazine advertising? **6**
2. How many industries used less than 30,000 pages of magazine advertising? **16**
3. **AIR** Use the circle graph below to describe the makeup of the air we breathe. (Lesson 9-2) **See margin.**

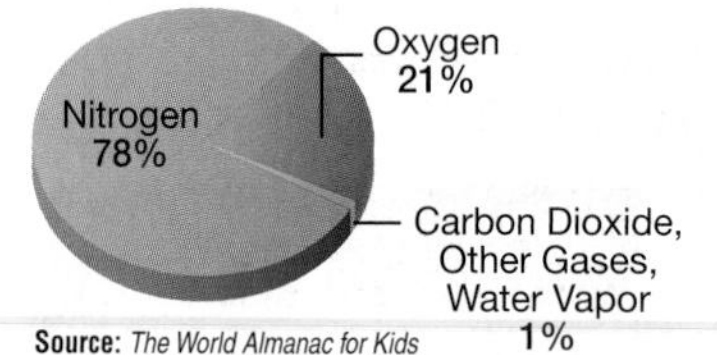

Source: *The World Almanac for Kids*

For Exercises 4 and 5, choose an appropriate type of display for each situation. Then make a display. (Lesson 9-3) **4–5. See margin.**

4. **MUSIC** A survey asked teens what they liked most about a song. 59% said the sound, and 41% said the lyrics.
5. **TAXES**

Tax Returns Filed Electronically

Year	1990	1991	1992	1993
Percent	3.7%	6.6%	9.6%	11.0%
Year	1994	1995	1996	1997
Percent	12.2%	10.5%	12.6%	15.8%
Year	1998	1999	2000	2001
Percent	19.9%	23.3%	27.6%	30.7%

Source: Internal Revenue Service

6. **ANIMALS** What is the mean, median, and mode of the incubation periods of all the birds shown in the table below? (Lesson 9-4)

Bird	Incubation Period (days)
Australian King Parrot	20
Eclectus Parrot	26
Princess Parrot	21
Red Tailed Cockatoo	30
Red-Winged Parrot	21
Regent Parrot	21
Sulphur Crested Cockatoo	30
White Tailed Cockatoo	29
Yellow Tailed Cockatoo	29

Source: www.birds2grow.com

$25.\overline{2}$; 26; 21

POPULATION For Exercises 7–9, use the following information. **7–9. See margin.**
The populations of the smallest countries in 2000 were 860, 10,838, 11,845, 18,766, 26,937, 31,693, and 32,204. (Lessons 9-5 and 9-6)

7. Find the range and median of the data.
8. Find the upper quartile, lower quartile, and interquartile range of the data.
9. Make a box-and-whisker plot for the data.

ENTERTAINMENT For Exercises 10 and 11, use the following information.
The average wait times at each of the major attractions at a theme park are 20, 25, 30, 45, 45, 45, 50, and 50 minutes. (Lesson 9-7)

10. Which measure of central tendancy would the theme park use to encourage people to attend the park? Explain. **10–12. See margin.**
11. Which measure of central tendancy would be more representative of the data?
12. **AUTO RACING** Make a matrix for the following information. (Lesson 9-8)

Daytona 500 Lap and Mileage Leaders

Drivers	Appearances	Laps	Miles
R. Petty	32	4,860	12,150.0
D. Marcis	32	4,859	12,147.5
D. Waltrip	28	4,726	11,815.0

Source: *USA TODAY*

9.

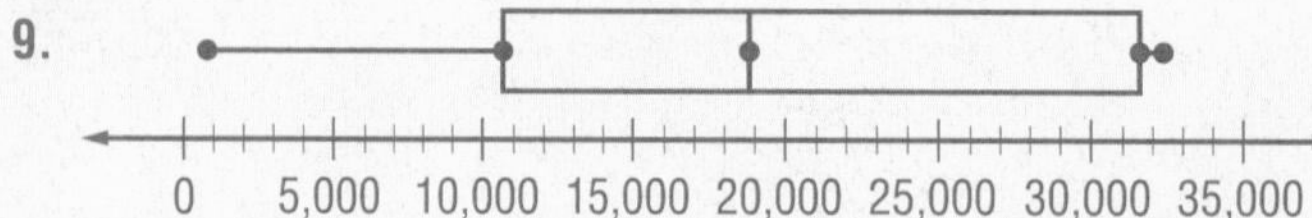

656 Mixed Problem Solving

1. **SCHOOL SUPPLIES** You buy two gel pens for x dollars each, a spiral-bound notebook for \$1.50, and a large eraser for \$1. Write an expression in simplest form for the total amount of money you spent on school supplies. (Lesson 10-1) **$2x + 2.50$**

2. **ENTERTAINMENT** You buy x CDs for \$15.99 each, a tape for \$9.99, and a video for \$20.99. Write an expression in simplest form for the total amount of money you spent. (Lesson 10-1) **$15.99x + 30.98$**

3. **ZOO** Four adults took a trip to the zoo. If they spent \$37 for admission and \$3 for parking, solve the equation $4a + 3 = 37$ to find the cost of admission per person. (Lesson 10-2) **\$8.50**

4. **POOLS** There were 820 gallons of water in a 1,600-gallon pool. Water is being pumped into the pool at a rate of 300 gallons per hour. Solve the equation $300t + 820 = 1{,}600$ to find how many hours it will take to fill the pool. (Lesson 10-2) **2.6 h or 2 h and 36 min**

5. **FOOTBALL** In football, a touchdown and extra point is worth 7 points, and a field goal is worth 3 points. The winning team scored 27 points. The score consisted of two field goals, and the rest were touchdowns with extra points. Write and solve an equation to determine how many touchdowns the winning team scored. (Lesson 10-3) **$7x + 6 = 27$; 3**

6. **DIVING** In diving competitions where there are three judges, the sum of the judges' scores is multiplied by the dive's degree of difficulty. A diver's final score is the sum of all the scores for each dive. The degree of difficulty for Angel's final dive is 2.0. Her current score is 358.5, and the current leader's final score is 405.5. Write and solve an equation to determine what the sum of the judge's scores for Angel's last dive must be in order for her to tie the current leader for first place. (Lesson 10-3) **$2s + 358.5 = 405.5$; 23.5**

7. **GEOMETRY** Write an equation to find the value of x so that each pair of polygons has the same perimeter. Then solve. (Lesson 10-4)

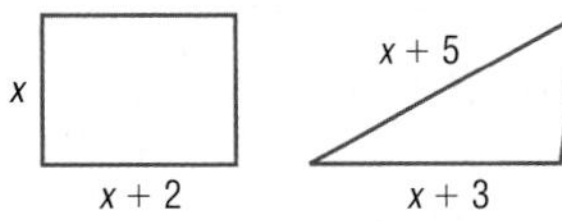

$4x + 4 = 3x + 8$; 4

8. **MUSIC** One music club charges \$35 a month plus \$5 per CD. Another club charges \$7 a month plus \$9 per CD. Write and solve an equation to find the number of CD purchases that results in the same monthly cost. (Lesson 10-4) **$35 + 5x = 7 + 9x$; 7**

For Exercises 9 and 10, write an inequality for each sentence. (Lesson 10-5)

9. **AMUSEMENT PARKS** Your height must be over 48 inches tall to ride the roller coaster. **$h > 48$**

10. **SHOPPING** You can spend no more than \$500 on your vacation. **$d \leq 500$**

11. **GEOMETRY** The base of the rectangle shown is less than its height. Write and solve an inequality to find the possible positive values of x. (Lesson 10-6) **$x + 3 < 12$; $x < 9$**

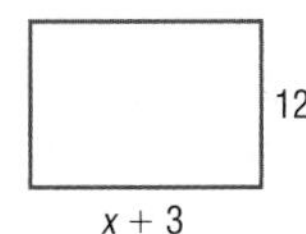

12. **STORMS** A hurricane has winds in excess of 75 miles per hour. A tropical storm currently has wind speeds of 68 miles per hour. Write and solve an inequality to find how much the wind speed must increase to be classified as a hurricane force. (Lesson 10-6) **$68 + x > 75$; $x > 7$; more than 7 mi/h**

13. **SWIMMING** A swimming pool charges \$4 per adult per visit. They also offer a yearly pass for \$112. Write and solve an inequality to find how many times a person must go to the pool so that the yearly pass is less expensive than paying per visit. (Lesson 10-7) **$112 < 4x$; more than 28 times**

Mixed Problem Solving

Mixed Problem Solving

Mixed Problem Solving 657

Chapter 11

4.

x	$x + 30$	$f(x)$
153	153 + 30	183
144	144 + 30	174
161	161 + 30	191
163	163 + 30	193
166	166 + 30	196

6.

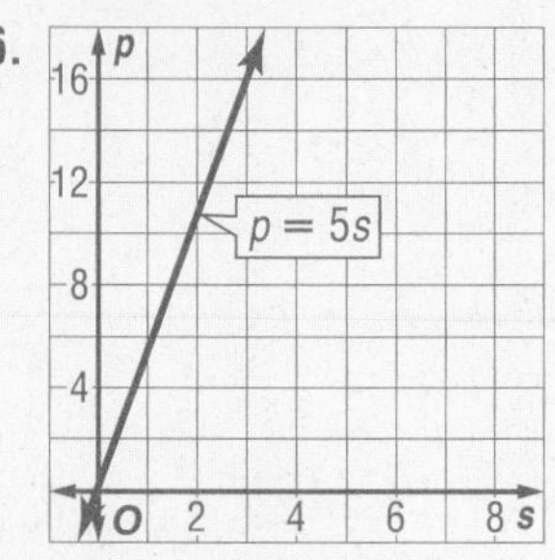

8. **Pool Volume**

Volume (m³): 0, 100, 200, 300, 400, 500 (V); Time (h): 0, 1, 2, 3, 4, 5, 6, 7 (t)

10. The rate at which the pool is being filled in cubic meters of water per hour

11.

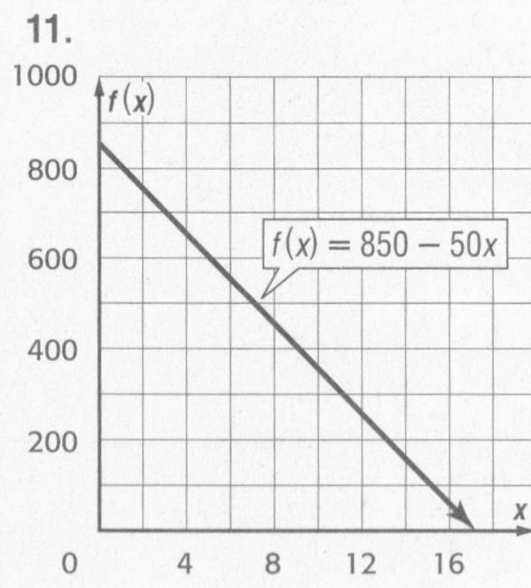

Chapter 11 Algebra: Linear Functions

(pages 510–557)

EARNINGS For Exercises 1–3, use the following information.

Annie earns \$6.50 per hour at her job as a veterinarian's assistant. (Lesson 11-1)

1. Make a list of the total amount of money earned for 1, 2, 3, 4, and 5 hours.
2. State whether the sequence is *arithmetic*, *geometric*, or *neither*. **arithmetic**
3. How much money would she earn for working 7 hours? **\$45.50**

1. \$6.50, \$13, \$19.50, \$26, \$32.50

4. **SPORTS** Tyree's adjusted bowling score can be found using the function $f(x) = x + 30$. In the function, x is his actual score, and 30 is his handicap. Make a function table to show Tyree's adjusted scores if he bowled 153, 144, 161, 163, and 166 in his first five games of the season. (Lesson 11-2) **See margin.**

GEOMETRY For Exercises 5–7, use the following information.

A regular pentagon is a polygon with five sides of equal length. (Lesson 11-3)

5. Write a function for the perimeter of a regular pentagon. $P = 5s$
6. Graph the function. **See margin.**
7. Determine the perimeter of a regular pentagon with sides 3 units long. **15 units**

WATER FLOW For Exercises 8–10, use the following information.

An empty Olympic-sized swimming pool is being filled with water. The table below shows the amount of water in the pool after the indicated amount of time. (Lesson 11-4)

Time (h)	Volume (m³)
2	144
3	216
5	360

8. Graph the information with the hours on the horizontal axis and cubic meters of water on the vertical axis. Draw a line through the points. **See margin.**
9. What is the slope of the graph? **72**
10. What does the slope represent? **See margin.**

For Exercises 11 and 12, use the following information.

Chen is saving for an \$850 computer. He plans to save \$50 each month. The equation $f(x) = 850 - 50x$ represents the amount Chen still needs to save. (Lesson 11-5)

11. Graph the equation. **See margin.**
12. What does the slope of the graph represent? **money saved per month**

LIFE EXPECTANCY For Exercises 13 and 14, use the following table. (Lesson 11-6)

Year Born	Life Expectancy
1900	47.3
1910	50.0
1920	54.1
1930	59.7
1940	62.9
1950	68.2
1960	69.7
1970	70.8
1980	73.7
1990	75.4
2000	77.1

Source: U.S. Census Bureau

13. See margin.

13. Draw the scatter plot for the data.
14. Does the scatter plot show a *positive*, *negative*, or *no* relationship? **positive**

RENTALS For Exercises 15 and 16, use the following information.

Company A charges \$25 plus \$0.10 per mile to rent a car. Company B charges \$15 plus \$0.20 per mile. (Lesson 11-7) **15. See margin.**

15. Write equations for the cost of renting a car from Company A and from Company B.
16. When will the costs be the same? **100 mi**

PACKAGING For Exercises 17 and 18, use the following information.

The weight limit on a certain package is 80 pounds. Two items are to go in this package. (Lesson 11-8)

17. Graph all of the possible combinations of weights for the two items. **See margin.**
18. Give three possible weight combinations. **Sample answer: 10, 60; 25, 50; 40, 40**

13.

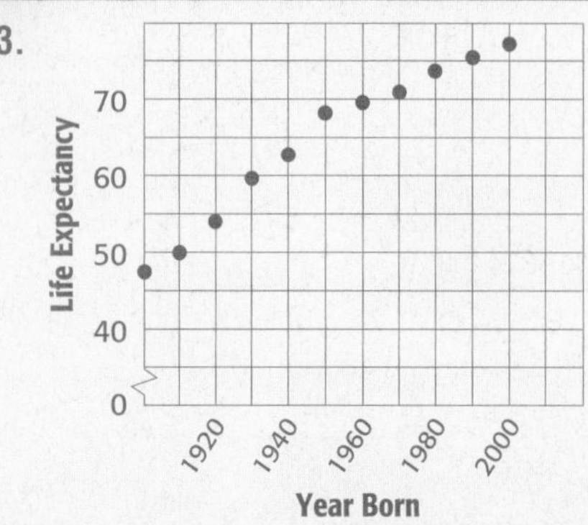

15. $y = 25 + 0.10m$; $y = 15 + 0.20m$

17.

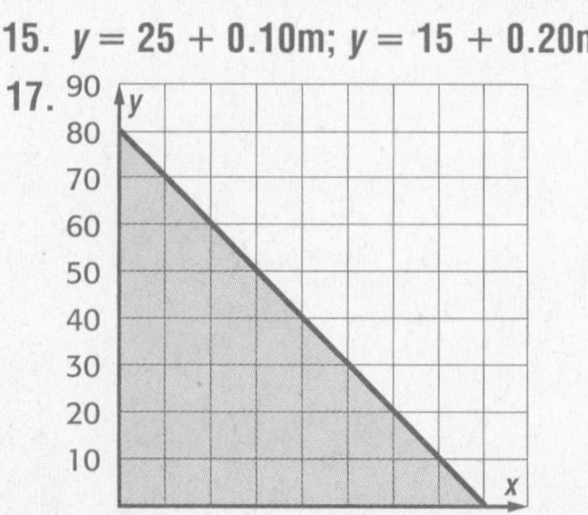

1. **GEOMETRY** Recall that the volume V of a sphere is equal to four-thirds pi times the cube of its radius. Is the volume of a sphere a *linear* or *nonlinear* function of its radius? Explain. (Lesson 12-1) **See margin.**

2. **PRODUCTION** The table lists the cost of producing a specific number of items at the ABC Production Company. Does this table represent a *linear* or *nonlinear* function? Explain. (Lesson 12-1)

Number of Items	Cost ($)
2	2,507
4	2,514
6	2,521
8	2,528

Linear; see margin for explanation.

SCIENCE For Exercises 3–5, use the following information.
A ball is dropped from a 200-foot cliff. The quadratic equation $h = -16t^2 + 200$ models the height of the object t seconds after it is dropped. (Lesson 12-2)

3. Graph the function. **See margin.**
4. How high is the ball after 2 seconds? **136 ft**
5. After about how many seconds will the ball reach the ground? **about 3.5 s**

6. **LANDSCAPING** Write a polynomial that represents the perimeter of the garden below in feet. (Lesson 12-3) **$5x + 6y$**

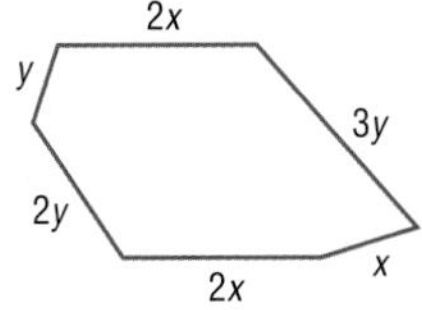

7. **GEOMETRY** Find the measure of each angle in the figure below. (Lesson 12-4) **80°, 65°, 35°**

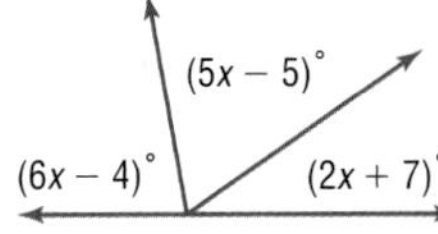

8. **CARPENTRY** To build the top cupboard below, $8x + 6$ square feet of wood is required. The bottom cupboard will require $2x^2 + 12x$ square feet of wood. Find the total square feet of wood required for both cupboards, assuming that there is no waste. (Lesson 12-4) **$2x^2 + 20x + 6$**

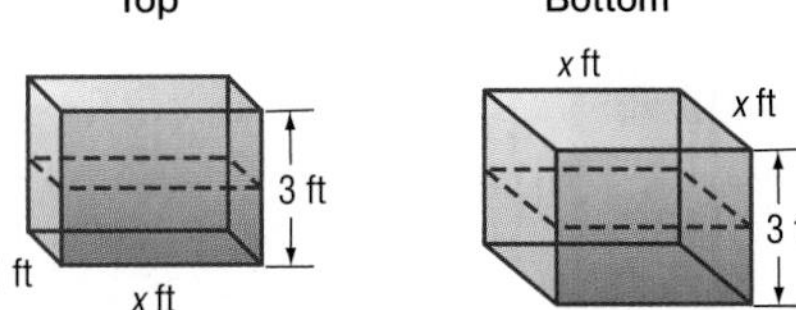

MONEY MATTERS For Exercises 9–11, use the following information.
Alan borrowed $200 each year for college expenses. The amount he owes the bank at the beginning of his second and third years is $(400 + 200r)$ and $(600 + 600r + 200r^2)$ respectively, where r is the interest rate. (Lesson 12-5) **9. $200r^2 + 400r + 200$**

9. Find how much his debt increased between his second and third years.
10. Evaluate the increase for $r = 6\%$. **$224.72**
11. Evaluate the increase for $r = 8\%$. **$233.28**

12. **GEOMETRY** Find the volume of a box that is x inches by $3x$ inches by $5x$ inches. (Lesson 12-6) **$15x^3$ in^3**

13. **LIFE SCIENCE** The number of cells in a petri dish starts at 2^5. By the end of the day, there are 2^{12} cells in the dish. About how many times more cells are in the dish at the end of the day than at the beginning? (Lesson 12-6) **2^7**

HOME IMPROVEMENT For Exercises 14 and 15, use the following information.
A patio's length is to be 6 feet longer than its width. (Lesson 12-7)

14. Write a simplified expression for the area of the patio. **$x^2 + 6x$**
15. Evaluate the expression you wrote in Exercise 14 to find the area of the patio if its width is 24 feet. **720 ft^2**

Chapter 12

1. **Nonlinear; the power of r in the function $V = \frac{4}{3}\pi r^3$ is greater than 1.**
2. **The rate of change is constant, as x the number of items increases by 2, the cost increases by $7.**
3.

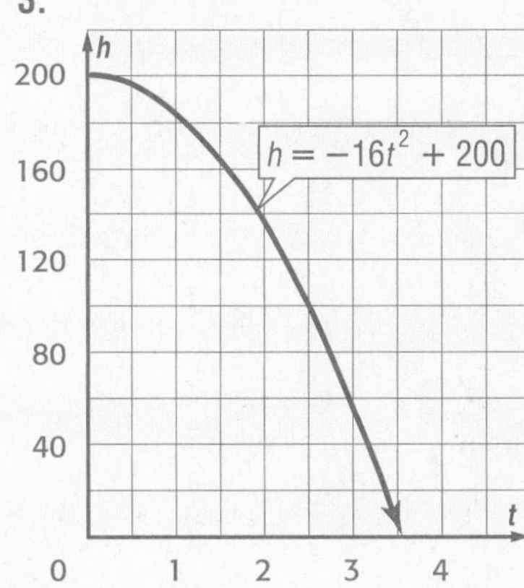

Preparing For Standardized Tests

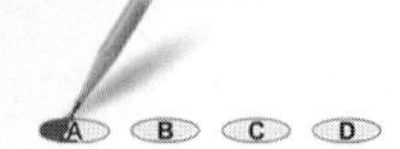

Becoming a Better Test-Taker

At some time in your life, you will probably have to take a standardized test. Sometimes this test may determine if you go on to the next grade level or course, or even if you will graduate from high school. This section of your textbook is dedicated to making you a better test-taker.

TYPES OF TEST QUESTIONS In the following pages, you will see examples of four types of questions commonly seen on standardized tests. A description of each type is shown in the table below.

Type of Question	Description	See Pages
multiple choice	Four or five possible answer choices are given from which you choose the best answer.	662–665
gridded response	You solve the problem. Then you enter the answer in a special grid and shade in the corresponding circles.	666–669
short response	You solve the problem, showing your work and/or explaining your reasoning.	670–673
extended response	You solve a multi-part problem, showing your work and/or explaining your reasoning.	674–677

For each type of question, worked-out examples are provided that show you step-by-step solutions. Strategies that are helpful for solving the problems are also provided.

PRACTICE After being introduced to each type of question, you can practice that type of question. Each set of practice questions is divided into five sections that represent the concepts most commonly assessed on standardized tests.

- Number and Operations
- Algebra
- Geometry
- Measurement
- Data Analysis and Probability

USING A CALCULATOR On some tests, you are permitted to use a calculator. You should check with your teacher to determine if calculator use is permitted on the test you will be taking, and if so, what type of calculator can be used.

If you *are* allowed to use a calculator, make sure you are familiar with how it works so that you won't waste time trying to figure out the calculator when taking the test.

Preparing for Standardized Tests

660 Preparing for Standardized Tests

TEST-TAKING TIPS In addition to the Test-Taking Tips like the one shown at the right, here are some additional thoughts that might help you.

Test-Taking Tip

The units of measure asked for in the answer may be different than the units given in the question. Check that your answer is in the correct units.

- Get a good night's rest before the test. Cramming the night before does not improve your results.
- Watch for key words like NOT and EXCEPT. Also look for order words like LEAST, GREATEST, FIRST, and LAST.
- For multiple-choice questions that ask for the answer choice that is *not* true, check each answer choice, labeling it with the letter T or F to show whether it is true or false.
- Cross out information that is not important.
- Underline key words, and circle numbers in a question.
- Label your answers for open-ended questions.
- Rephrase the question you are being asked.
- Become familiar with common formulas and when they should be used.
- When you read a chart, table, or graph, pay attention to the words, numbers, and patterns of the data.
- Budget your time when taking a test. Don't dwell on problems that you cannot solve. Just make sure to leave that question blank on your answer sheet.

YOUR TEXTBOOK Your textbook contains many opportunities for you to get ready for standardized tests. Take advantage of these so you don't need to cram before the test.

- Each lesson contains two standardized test practice problems to provide you with ongoing opportunities to sharpen your test-taking skills.
- Every chapter contains a completely worked-out Standardized Test Practice Example, along with a Test-Taking Tip to help you solve problems that are similar.
- Each chapter contains two full pages of Standardized Test Practice with Test-Taking Tips. These two pages contain practice questions in the various formats that can be found on the most frequently given standardized tests.

HELP ON THE INTERNET There are many online resources to help you prepare for standardized tests.

- Glencoe's Web site contains Online Study Tools that include Standardized Test Practice. For hundreds of multiple choice practice problems, visit:

  msmath3.net/standardized_test
- Some states provide online help for students preparing to take standardized tests. For more information, visit your state's Board of Education Web site.

Preparing for Standardized Tests

Preparing for Standardized Tests 661

Multiple-Choice Questions

Multiple-choice questions are the most common type of question on standardized tests. These questions are sometimes called *selected-response questions*. You are asked to choose the best answer from four or five possible answers.

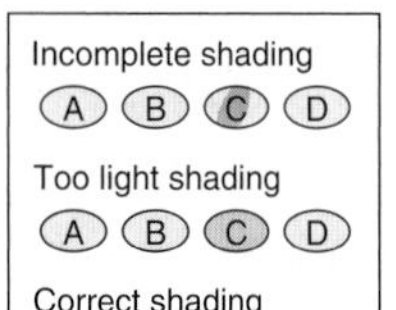

To record a multiple-choice answer, you may be asked to shade in a bubble that is a circle or an oval or just to write the letter of your choice. Always make sure that your shading is dark enough and completely covers the bubble.

The answer to a multiple-choice question may not stand out from the choices. However, you may be able to eliminate some of the choices. Another answer choice might be that the correct answer is not given.

EXAMPLE

1 **Kent places a ladder at a 60° angle against the wall as shown in the diagram. What is the measure of $\angle 1$?**

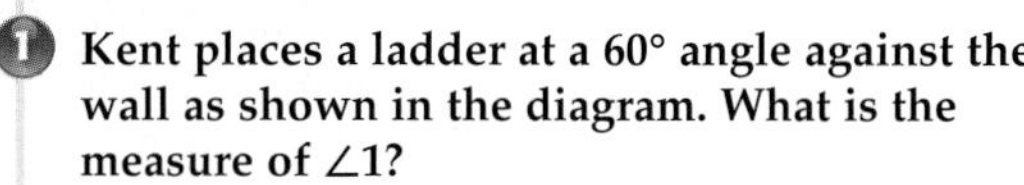

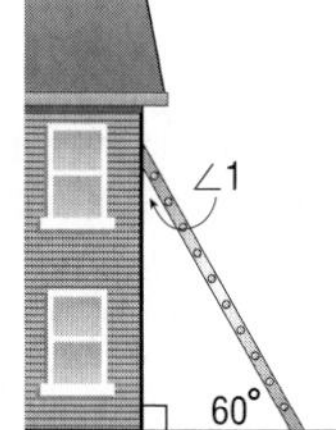

Ⓐ 15° Ⓑ 30° Ⓒ 60°

Ⓓ 90° Ⓔ 180°

STRATEGY

Elimination
Can you eliminate any of the choices?

You know that the ground and wall meet at a 90° angle. You can eliminate choice D because you know that a triangle cannot have two angles measuring 90°. You can also eliminate choice E because the sum of the angles of a triangle is 180°, so just one angle cannot measure 180°. Find the measure of the third angle by subtracting the measures of the two known angles from 180°, the sum of the angles of a triangle.

$180° - 90° - 60° = 30°$ The measure of $\angle 1$ is 30°, and the answer is B.

EXAMPLE

2 **Sam's Super Store sells 8 cans of soup for \$2.25 while Midtown's Mart sells the same soup at 10 cans for \$3.00. Which statement is true?**

Ⓐ **Midtown's Mart has the lower price per can.**
Ⓑ **Sam's Super Store has the lower price per can.**
Ⓒ **Both stores have the same cost per can.**
Ⓓ **None of these can be determined.**

Find the price per can at Sam's Super Store and Midtown's Mart.

Sam's Super Store: $\frac{\$2.25}{8 \text{ cans}} = \$0.28125$ per can

Midtown's Mart: $\frac{\$3.00}{10 \text{ cans}} = \$0.30$ per can

Since $0.28 < 0.30$, Sam's Super Store has the lower cost per can. The answer is B.

Preparing for Standardized Tests

Preparing for Standardized Tests

662 Preparing for Standardized Tests

EXAMPLE

3 **The charges for adult ski passes at Logan Ski Slopes are shown in the table. What is the minimum number of days that an adult must ski in order for the yearly pass to be less expensive than buying daily passes?**

Type of Ski Pass	Cost ($)
Daily	38
Yearly	247

A **4 days**
B **6 days**
C **7 days**
D **8 days**

You need to find the minimum number of daily passes that will cost more than $247.

STRATEGY

Backsolving
Use the answer choices to work backward to find the answer.

Method 1
Multiply each answer choice by $38 to determine which answer choices result in a cost greater than $247.

A $4 \times \$38 = \$152$
B $6 \times \$38 = \$228$
C $7 \times \$38 = \$266$
D $8 \times \$38 = \$304$

Answer choices C and D are both greater than $247. However, the problem asks for the minimum number of days. So answer choice C, 7 days, is correct.

Method 2
Write an inequality comparing the costs of a daily ski pass and a yearly ski pass.

Each daily pass costs $38, so after d days of skiing a person will have spent $38d$.

You want to find when $38d$ is greater than $247, the cost of a yearly pass. Write and solve the inequality.

$38d > 247$	Original inequality
$\frac{38d}{38} > \frac{247}{38}$	Divide each side by 38.
$d > 6.5$	Simplify.

Read the problem a second time just to be sure whether you want the cost to be greater or less than $247.

Since the ski passes are only sold by the day and not by a partial day, the number of days must be a whole number. The next whole number greater than 6.5 is 7. So, 7 days is the minimum number of days in which the yearly pass will be less expensive. The answer is choice C.

Preparing for Standardized Tests

Preparing for Standardized Tests

Preparing for Standardized Tests 663

Preparing for Standardized Tests

Multiple-Choice Practice

Choose the best answer.

Number and Operations

1. Dillon can run at a rate of 9 miles per hour. How many feet per minute is this? **B**

Ⓐ 13.2 Ⓑ 792
Ⓒ 4,752 Ⓓ 47,520

2. Danielle mows lawns for a part-time job in the summer. She charges $8 an hour. If Mrs. Taylor paid Danielle $44, how long did it take Danielle to mow Mrs. Taylor's lawn? **C**

Ⓐ 4.5 h Ⓑ 5 h
Ⓒ 5.5 h Ⓓ 6 h

3. Mario had 18 CDs. On Saturday he bought 4 more CDs. What is the percent of change in the number of CDs he owns? Round to the nearest percent. **B**

Ⓐ 18% Ⓑ 22% Ⓒ 29% Ⓓ 82%

Algebra

4. To raise money for new uniforms, the soccer team is selling shirts that have the team's logo on them. The company making the shirts charges $20 for the design and $5 for each shirt made. The total cost y to the soccer team can be represented by the equation $y = 5x + 20$, where x represents the number of shirts made. Which graph represents this equation? **D**

Ⓐ
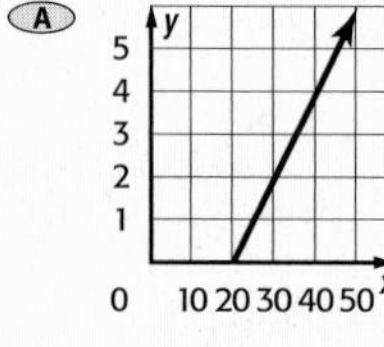

Ⓑ
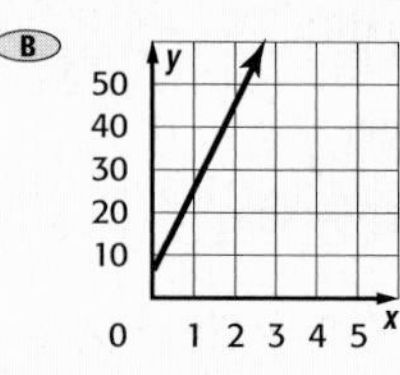

Ⓒ
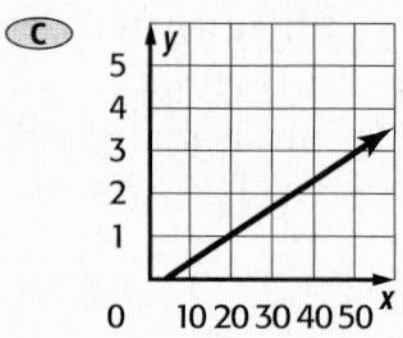

Ⓓ
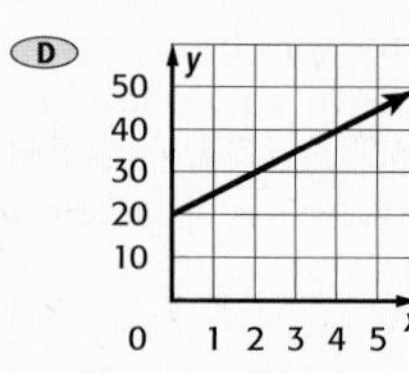

5. Emilia received her allowance on Saturday and took it to the mall. After she spent $5.49 for lunch, she still had $26.51. Which equation could be used to find how much she received for her allowance? **A**

Ⓐ $x - 5.49 = 26.51$ Ⓑ $x + 5.49 = 26.51$
Ⓒ $26.51 - x = 5.49$ Ⓓ $x + 26.51 = 5.49$

6. At the water park you buy your friends a pizza for $15, an order of breadsticks for $3.50, and 4 drinks that cost x dollars each. Which expression represents this situation? **C**

Ⓐ $15 + 7.50x$ Ⓑ $22.50x$
Ⓒ $4x + 18.50$ Ⓓ 22.50

Geometry

7. Sarah is building a kite out of crepe paper and balsa wood. What is the measure of $\angle 1$? **D**

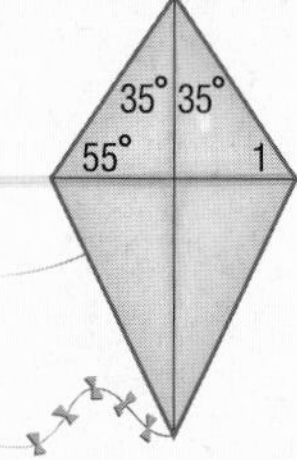

Ⓐ 25° Ⓑ 35° Ⓒ 45° Ⓓ 55°

8. Alysha wants to hang decorative lights diagonally across her ceiling for a party. What should be the minimum length of the light strand? Round to the nearest tenth of a foot if necessary. **C**

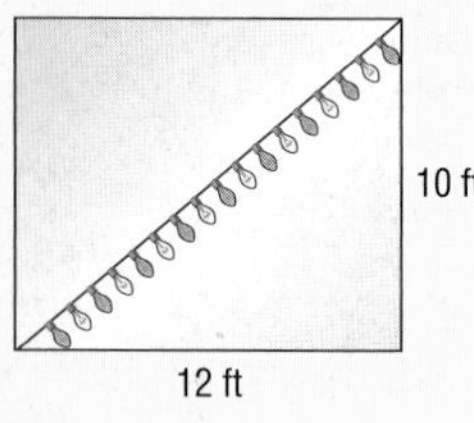

Ⓐ 6.6 ft Ⓑ 12.0 ft
Ⓒ 15.6 ft Ⓓ 22.0 ft

Preparing for Standardized Tests

664 Preparing for Standardized Tests

9. Alonso has a template to make paver bricks for a patio. He needs to enlarge the template by a scale factor of 5. He placed the template on a coordinate grid and labeled the vertices *A*, *B*, *C*, and *D*. What will be the new *x*-coordinate of vertex *A* after the enlargement? **A**

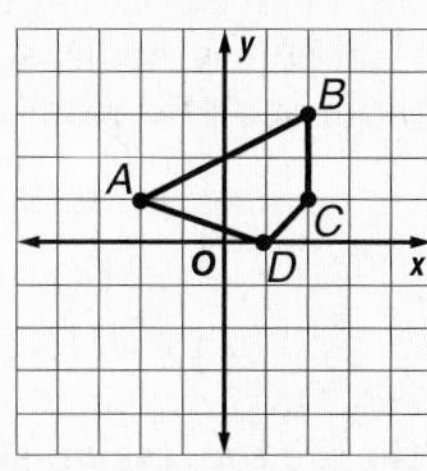

Ⓐ −10 Ⓑ −5 Ⓒ 5 Ⓓ 10

Measurement

10. Keegan rode his bike 49 miles in 3 hours. What was his average speed in miles per hour? Round to the nearest whole number if necessary. **A**

Ⓐ 16 mph Ⓑ 25 mph
Ⓒ 55 mph Ⓓ 147 mph

11. Mr. Myers has a grain bin with the given dimensions. How much grain will the bin hold? Round to the nearest tenth of a cubic foot. **D**

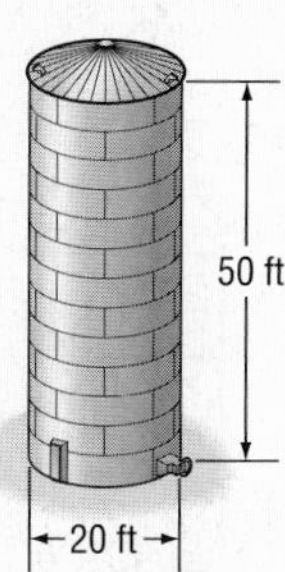

Ⓐ 314.2 ft^3 Ⓑ 1,570.8 ft^3
Ⓒ 3141.6 ft^3 Ⓓ 15,708.0 ft^3

12. One kilogram is approximately 2.2 pounds. If Sara weighs 105 pounds, how many kilograms does she weigh? Round to the nearest tenth of a kilogram. **B**

Ⓐ 40.8 kg Ⓑ 47.7 kg
Ⓒ 209.5 kg Ⓓ 231.0 kg

Data Analysis and Probability

13. Which situation *best* describes the scatter plot? **B**

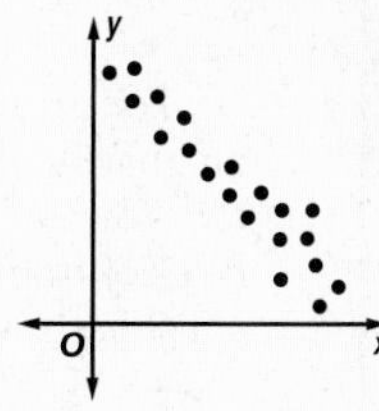

Ⓐ number of hours worked at a job and amount of money earned

Ⓑ number of gallons of water taken out of a swimming pool and height of water in swimming pool

Ⓒ length of hair and age

Ⓓ year of birth and age

Test-Taking Tip

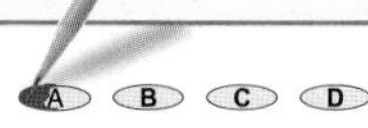

Question 13 When a question asks for the *best* answer, read all the answer choices first and eliminate any unreasonable answer choices.

14. Mileah was comparing the amount of caffeine in six different popular soft drinks. She found that a 12-ounce serving contained the following milligrams of caffeine: 55, 47, 45, 41, 40, and 37. What is the mean of this data set? Round to the nearest milligram. **C**

Ⓐ 37 mg
Ⓑ 43 mg
Ⓒ 44 mg
Ⓓ 55 mg

15. Braden has 32 movies. Eight of these movies are action movies. If he randomly chooses a movie to watch, what is the probability that it is *not* an action movie? **D**

Ⓐ $\frac{1}{4}$ Ⓑ $\frac{1}{3}$
Ⓒ $\frac{1}{2}$ Ⓓ $\frac{3}{4}$

Preparing for Standardized Tests

Preparing for Standardized Tests 665

Gridded-Response Questions

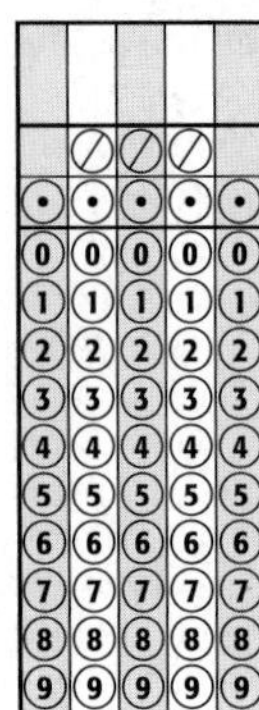

Gridded-response questions are another type of question on standardized tests. These questions are sometimes called *student-produced response* or *grid in*.

For gridded response, you must mark your answer on a grid printed on an answer sheet. The grid contains a row of four or five boxes at the top, two rows of ovals or circles with decimal and fraction symbols, and four or five columns of ovals, numbered 0–9. An example of a grid from an answer sheet is shown.

EXAMPLE

1 Zach is in charge of ordering hot dogs for the concession stand for the home football games. If he needs 70 hot dogs for 2 games, how many will he need for all 8 home games?

What value do you need to find?

You need to find the total number of hot dogs needed for 8 games given the number needed for 2 games.

Write and solve a proportion. Let d represent the number of hot dogs needed for 8 games.

$$\text{hot dogs} \rightarrow \frac{70}{2} = \frac{d}{8} \leftarrow \text{hot dogs} \atop \text{games} \rightarrow \qquad\qquad \leftarrow \text{games}$$

$70 \cdot 8 = 2d$ Find the cross products.

$560 = 2d$ Multiply.

$280 = d$

Zach will need 280 hot dogs for 8 games.

How do you fill in the grid for the answer?

- Print your answer in the answer boxes.
- Print only one digit or symbol in each answer box.
- Do not write any digits or symbols outside the answer boxes.
- You may print your answer with the first digit in the left answer box, or with the last digit in the right answer box. You may leave blank any boxes you do not need on the right or the left side of your answer.
- Fill in only one bubble for every answer box that you have written in. Be sure not to fill in a bubble under a blank answer box.

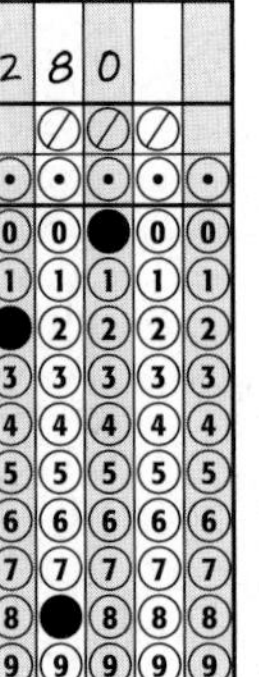

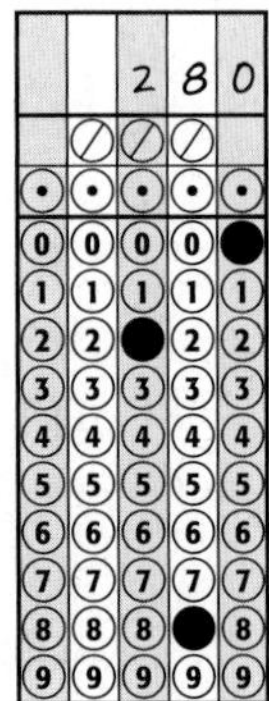

Preparing for Standardized Tests

666 Preparing for Standardized Tests

Many gridded-response questions result in an answer that is a fraction or a decimal. These values can also be filled in on the grid.

EXAMPLE

2 **A plane travels at an average rate of 320 miles per hour. If the plane traveled 80 miles, how many hours has the plane been in flight?**

$r \times t = d$	Use the distance formula.
$320t = 80$	Replace r with 320 and d with 80.
$\frac{320t}{320} = \frac{80}{320}$	Divide each side by 320.
$t = \frac{1}{4}$	Simplify.

The plane has been traveling for $\frac{1}{4}$ of an hour.

How do you fill in the answer grid?

You can either grid the fraction $\frac{1}{4}$, or rewrite it as 0.25 and grid the decimal. The following are acceptable answer responses.

Notice that the question asks for the time in hours, not minutes. So an answer of 15 would be incorrect.

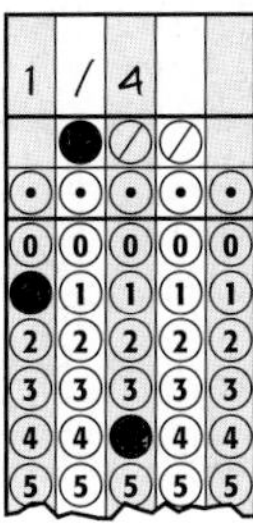

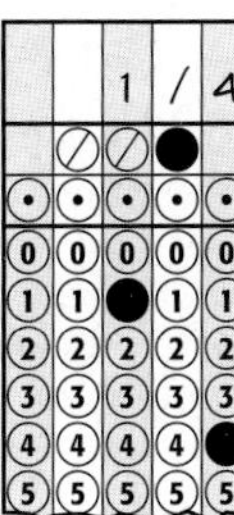

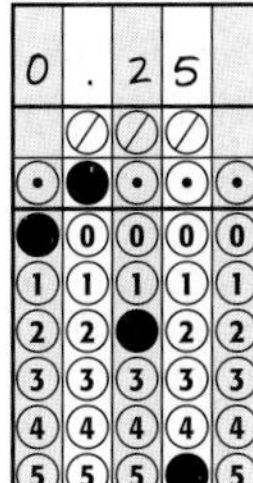

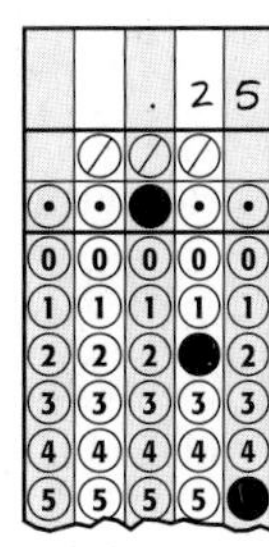

Some problems may result in an answer that is an improper fraction or mixed number. Before filling in the grid, change the mixed number to an equivalent improper fraction or decimal.

EXAMPLE

3 **Triangle ABC is similar to $\triangle QRS$. What is the value of x?**

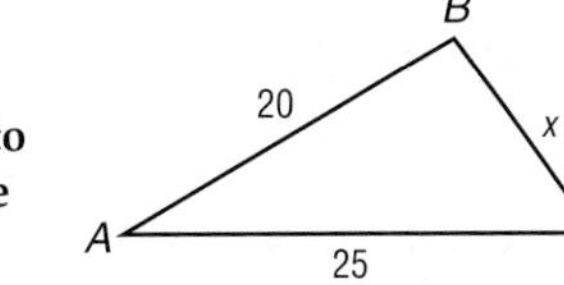

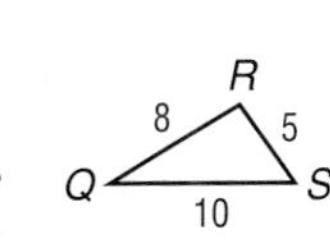

$\frac{BC}{RS} = \frac{AC}{QS}$	Write a proportion.
$\frac{x}{5} = \frac{25}{10}$	$BC = x$, $RS = 5$, $AC = 25$, $QS = 10$
$x \cdot 10 = 5 \cdot 25$	Find the cross products.
$10x = 125$	Multiply.
$\frac{10x}{10} = \frac{125}{10}$	Divide each side by 10.
$x = \frac{25}{2}$ or $12\frac{1}{2}$	

You can either grid the improper fraction $\frac{25}{2}$, or the decimal 12.5. Do not enter 121/2, as this will be interpreted as $\frac{121}{2}$.

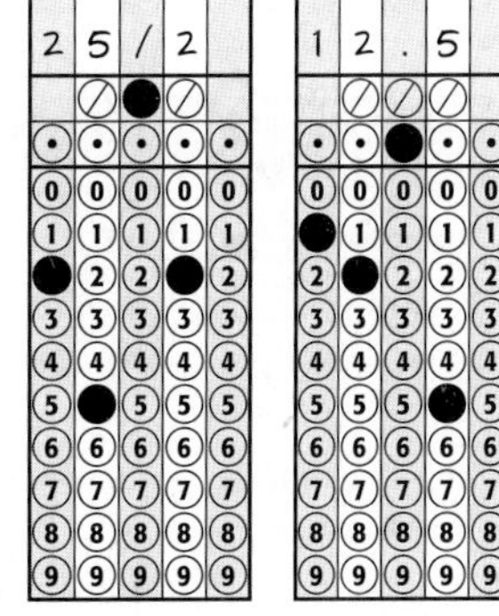

Preparing for Standardized Tests

Preparing for Standardized Tests

Preparing for Standardized Tests 667

Gridded-Response Practice

Solve each problem. Then copy and complete a grid like the one shown on page 666.

Number and Operations

1. John ran $3\frac{1}{2}$ miles on Monday. On Tuesday, he ran $2\frac{1}{4}$ miles. How many more miles did he run on Monday? **5/4**

2. Maria's Fashions is having a sale on shoes. She is discounting every pair of shoes by 35%. If a pair of sandals regularly sell for \$32, what will be the sale price of the sandals in dollars? **20.8**

3. There are approximately 2.54 centimeters in one inch. If the width of a piece of paper is 8 inches, what is the approximate width of the paper in centimeters? **20.32**

4. The atomic weight of iodine is approximately 1.269×10^2. What is iodine's atomic weight written in standard notation? **126.9**

5. Austin's Sandwich Shop offers a lunchtime sandwich special. A customer has a choice of bread, meat, and cheese as shown in the table. How many different sandwich choices are there? **27**

Bread	Meat	Cheese
Sourdough	Turkey	Swiss
Wheat	Ham	American
Rye	Roast Beef	Provolone

Algebra

6. Evaluate $\frac{y^2 - 1}{x + 2}$ if $x = -1$ and $y = 6$. **35**

7. Find $f(-1)$ if $f(x) = 3x + 7$. **4**

8. After a half hour, Kara had walked 1.5 miles. After 1 hour, she had walked 3 miles. If you graph this information with hours on the x-axis and miles on the y-axis, what is the slope of the graph? **3**

9. A video rental store charges \$20 for a membership and \$3 to rent each video. The total cost y can be represented by the equation $y = 3x + 20$, where x represents the number of videos rented. What is the y-intercept of the graph of the equation? **20**

10. The graph shows the enrollment of students grades Pre-K through 8 in thousands from 1970 to 2000. What is the rate of change between 1990 and 2000? **374.4**

Student Enrollment

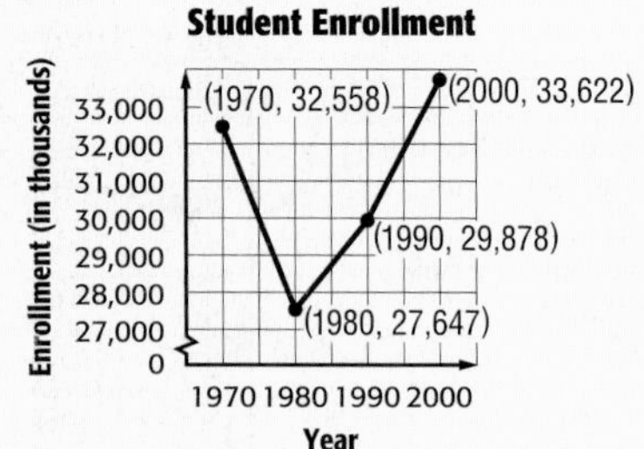

Source: *TIME Almanac*

11. If $\frac{5a^5b^3}{ab}$ is simplified, what is the exponent of a? **4**

Geometry

12. What is the distance between point A and point B? Round to the nearest tenth of a unit. **5.4**

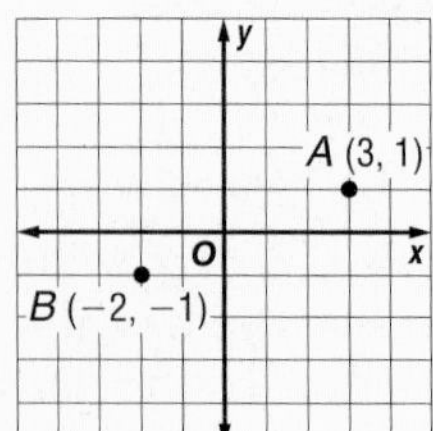

13. What is the measure of $\angle 3$ in degrees? **70**

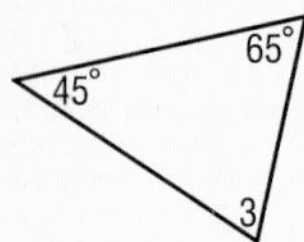

Preparing for Standardized Tests

Preparing for Standardized Tests

668 Preparing for Standardized Tests

14. Triangle *MNO* is dilated with a scale factor of 2. What is the *x*-coordinate of *M* on the dilated image? **5**

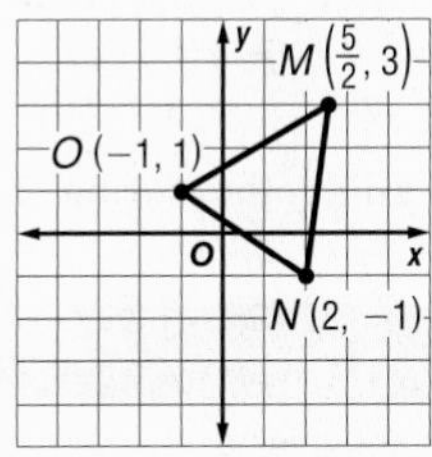

15. If polygon *ABCD* is similar to polygon *RSTU*, what is the measure of $\overline{AB}$? **10.5**

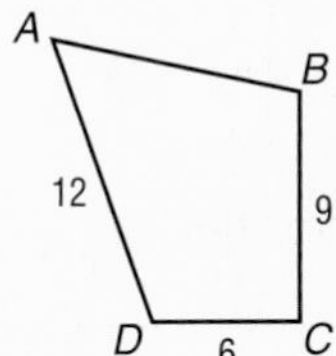

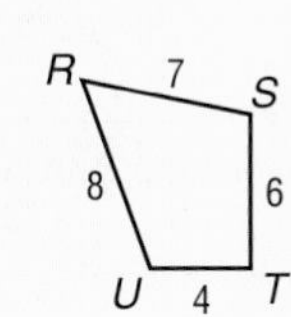

16. Triangle *QRS* is congruent to △*XYZ*. Find the value of *a*. **15**

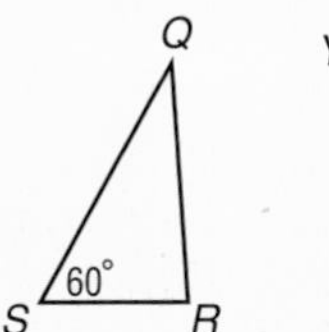

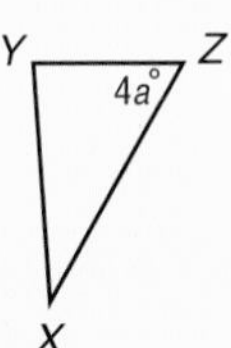

Measurement

17. The distance from Little Rock, Arkansas, to Albuquerque, New Mexico, is 882 miles. What is this distance to the nearest kilometer? (1 kilometer ≈ 0.62 miles) **1423**

18. Giant Value sells 8 bottles of fruit juice for $6.00. Express this as a unit rate in dollars per bottle. **0.75**

19. The Bakers need a cover for their swimming pool. If the swimming pool is round and has a diameter of 15 feet, what will be the area of the cover? Round to the nearest tenth of a square foot. **176.7**

20. What is the surface area of the cone? Round to the nearest square inch. **283**

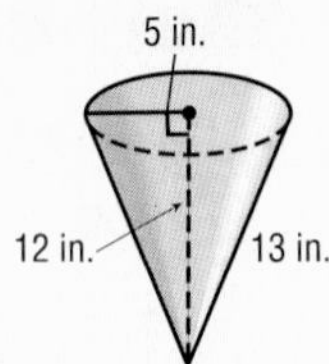

Test-Taking Tip

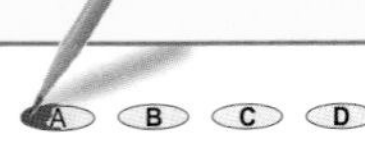

Question 20 A figure may give you more information than you need to solve the problem. Before solving, circle any information in the figure that is needed to find the answer.

Data Analysis and Probability

21. Last week Toya worked the following hours per day: 5, 6, 9, 4, 3, and 9. What is the mean number of hours that she worked per day? **6**

22. The spinner is divided into 8 equal sections. If Megan spins the spinner, what is the probability that the spinner will land on yellow or red? **3/8**

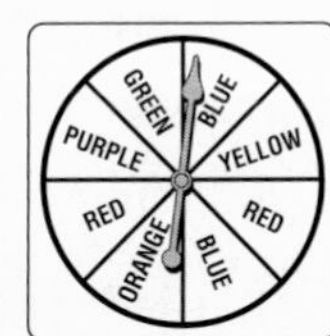

23. The table shows the height in inches of 15 students in Mrs. Garcia's class. What is the interquartile range of the data? **4**

63	62	65	64	69
65	68	68	67	60
64	67	65	70	68

24. A bag contains 2 green marbles, 6 yellow marbles, 5 red marbles, and 9 blue marbles. How many yellow marbles must be added to the bag so that the probability of randomly picking a yellow marble is $\frac{1}{3}$? **2**

25. In Mr. Firewalk's class, 24 of the 30 students said they owned a pet. If the entire school has 890 students, how many of the total students in the school would you expect own pets? **712**

Preparing for Standardized Tests

Preparing for Standardized Tests 669

Short-Response Questions

Short-response questions require you to provide a solution to the problem as well as any method, explanation, and/or justification you used to arrive at the solution. These are sometimes called *constructed-response, open-response, open-ended, free-response*, or *student-produced questions*.

The following is a sample rubric, or scoring guide, for scoring short-response questions.

On some standardized tests, no credit is given for a correct answer if your work is not shown.

Credit	Score	Criteria
Full	2	Full credit: The answer is correct and a full explanation is provided that shows each step in arriving at the final answer.
Partial	1	Partial credit: There are two different ways to receive partial credit. • The answer is correct, but the explanation provided is incomplete or incorrect. • The answer is incorrect, but the explanation and method of solving the problem is correct.
None	0	No credit: Either an answer is not provided or the answer does not make sense.

EXAMPLE

Sophia wants to retile her kitchen floor. If the tiling costs $3.50 per square foot, what will be the cost to tile the entire floor?

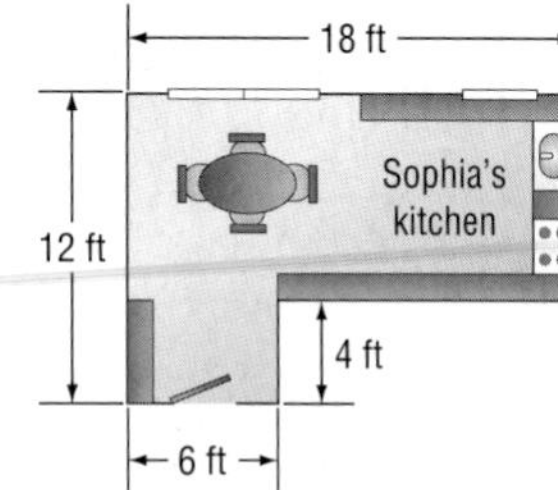

Full Credit Solution

I will break the kitchen into two rectangular regions and find the area of each region.

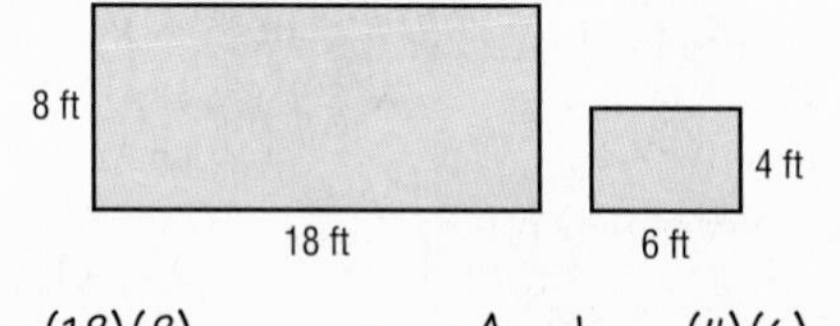

$A = lw = (18)(8)$
$= 144$ square feet

$A = lw = (4)(6)$
$= 24$ square feet

The steps, calculations, and reasoning are clearly stated.

Total area $= 144 + 24 = 168$ square feet

Be sure to complete this final step to answer the question asked.

Since it costs $3.50 for each square foot, I will multiply the total square feet (168) by $3.50.

$168 \times \$3.5 = \$588$

It will cost Sophia $588 to tile her kitchen.

670 Preparing for Standardized Tests

Partial Credit Solution

In this sample solution, there are no explanations for finding the lengths or for the calculations.

There is no explanation of how the lengths were found.

$A = lw$

$= (18)(12) - (4)(12)$

$= 216 - 48$

$= 168$

There are 168 square feet in her kitchen.

$168 \times 3.5 = 588$

It will cost Sophia \$588 to tile her kitchen.

Partial Credit Solution

In this sample solution, the answer is incorrect because the area was calculated incorrectly. However, the process for finding the area and then the cost was correct.

Since the tiling is charged in square feet, I will first find the area of the kitchen in square feet.

The area calculated was incorrect, but an explanation was given for each step.

$A = lw$

$= (18)(12)$

$= 216$

The area of the kitchen is 216 square feet.

Since it costs \$3.50 for each square foot, I will multiply the total square feet (216) by \$3.50.

$216 \times 3.5 = 756$

It will cost Sophia \$756 to tile her kitchen.

No Credit Solution

In this sample solution, there are no explanations, the area is calculated incorrectly, and the cost for the tile was not found.

$A = lw$

$= (18)(12)$

$= 216$

It will cost \$216 to tile the kitchen.

Preparing for Standardized Tests

Preparing for Standardized Tests 671

Answers

7. JR's Landscaping; JR's Landscaping will cost $500 while Great Landscapers will cost $550 for 6 hours.

8.

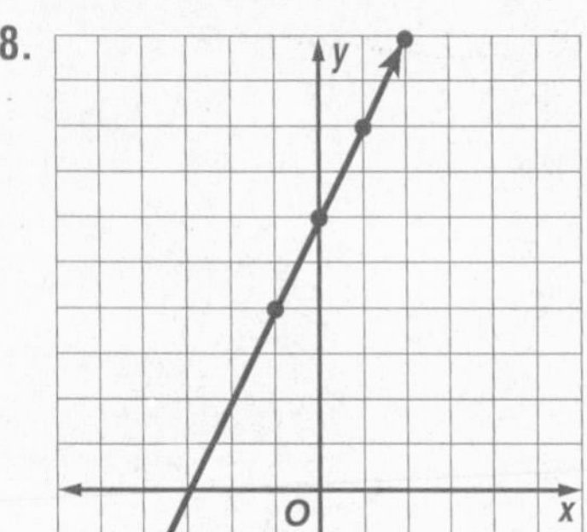

Preparing for Standardized Tests

Short-Response Practice

Solve each problem. Show all your work.

Number and Operations

1. Mr. Collins is the supervisor of the eighth grade basketball league. He has 72 students signed up to play. Each team needs to have the same number of students, but cannot have more than 15 students. What is the greatest number of students that can be on each team? How many teams will Mr. Collins have? **12 players on 6 teams**

2. Mika buys a jacket for $45 plus 6% sales tax. She decided that she didn't want it anymore so she sold it to her friend for $50. How much did she gain or lose from her sale? **she gained $2.30**

3. Karla is baking cookies to take to a bake sale. Her recipe calls for $3\frac{1}{2}$ cups of flour. If she plans on taking $4\frac{1}{2}$ batches to the sale, how much flour will she need? **15.75 c**

4. The Student Council has saved $200 for a field trip to the Discovery Science Museum. If the admission is $8 per student and lunch for each student will cost $5.25, how many students will be able to go? **15 students**

5. Kory is five feet tall. When she stands next to a tree, she casts a 6-foot shadow. How tall is the tree if it casts a 36-foot shadow? **30 ft**

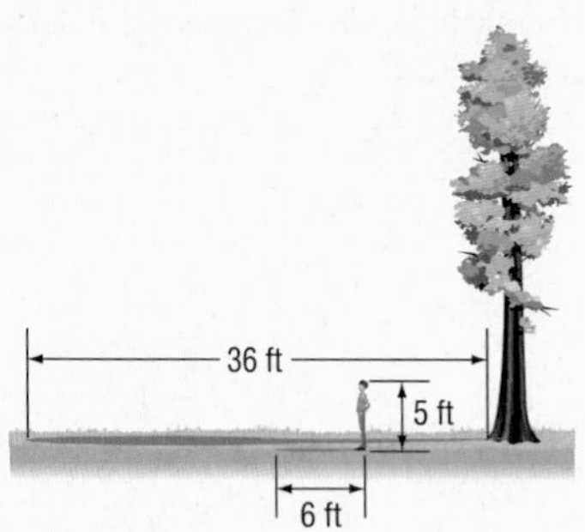

Algebra

6. Miguel has $400. He plans to spend $5 per day on lunch. The equation for the amount of money y Miguel has at any time is $y = 400 - 5x$, where x is the number of days from today. If this equation is graphed, what is the slope? What does the slope mean? **−5; how much he will spend each day**

7. Tyree wants to hire a landscaper. JR's Landscaping Service charges $200 for a design layout and $50 an hour for working on a yard. Great Landscapers charges $400 for a design layout and $25 an hour for working on the yard. If it will take 6 hours to landscape Tyree's yard, which company should he hire? Explain. **See margin.**

8. The points in the table all lie on one line. Find the slope of the line. Then graph the line. **$m = 2$; See margin for graph.**

x	y
−1	4
0	6
1	8
2	10

9. Lucy is helping her father run his campaign for city mayor. If she can make and mail 45 flyers in half an hour, how long will it take her to make and mail 150 flyers? **1 h 40 min**

10. Kyle bought x shirts for $24.99 each, a pair of shoes for $49.99, and a pair of jeans for $51.99. If Kyle spent a total of $201.94, how many shirts did he buy? **4**

Geometry

11. Find the value of x so that the polygons have the same perimeter. **$x = 6$**

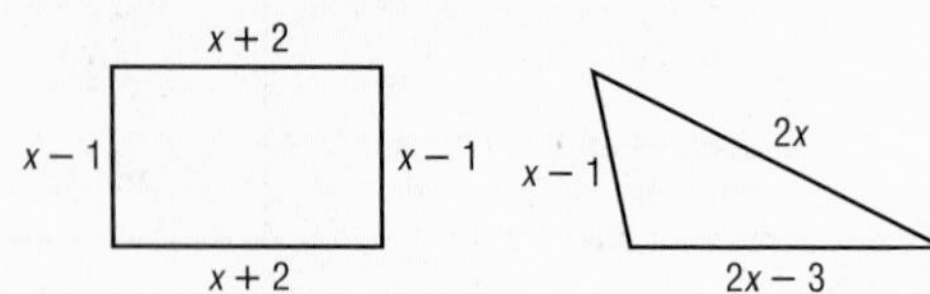

672 Preparing for Standardized Tests

12. Find the measures of a and b. **$a = 70°$, $b = 110°$**

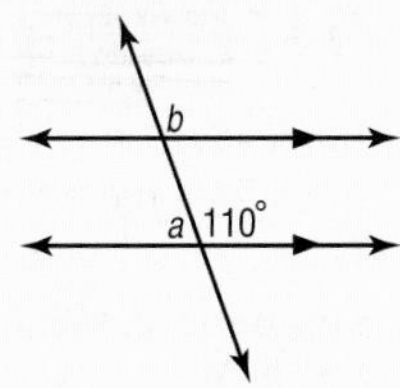

13. From the distances given, do the three cities in Iowa form a right triangle? Explain. **no; $2.5^2 + 4.5^2 \neq 6.5^2$**

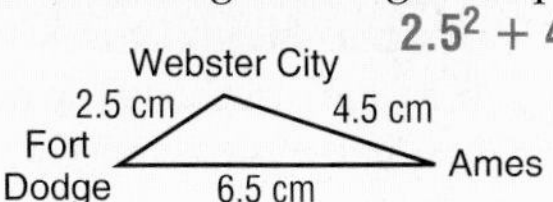

Measurement

14. Find the value of x in the figure. **29°**

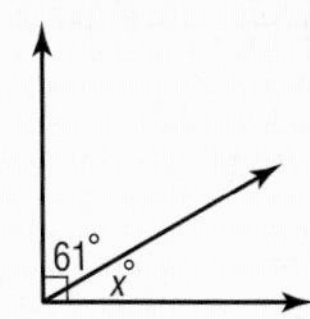

15. What is the ratio of the surface area of the smaller box to the surface of the larger box? **1 to 4**

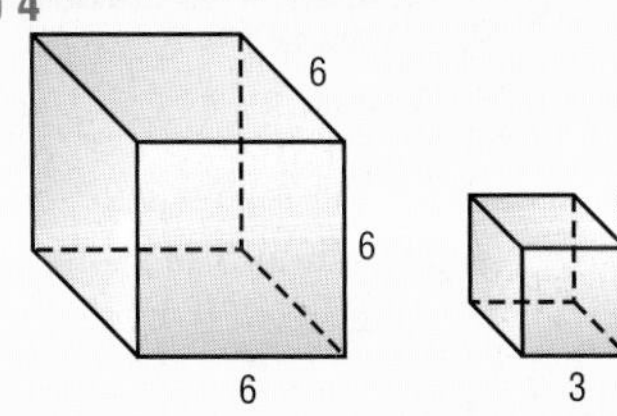

16. Find the area of the figure below. Round to the nearest tenth. **79.3 in^2**

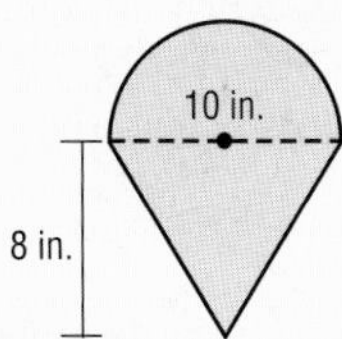

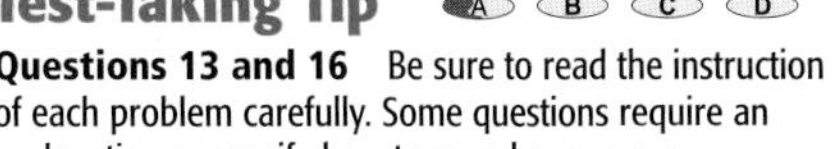

Test-Taking Tip

Questions 13 and 16 Be sure to read the instruction of each problem carefully. Some questions require an explanation or specify how to round answers.

17. The basketball team receives cups of water at every timeout. The cups are shaped as cones as shown below. What is the volume of one cup? Use 3.14 for π. **9.42 in^3**

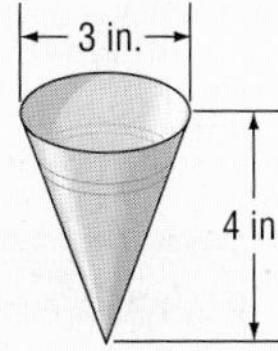

Data Analysis and Probability

18. Lee has 8 pairs of shoes. He is flying to see his brother and can only fit 2 pairs in his suitcase. How many different combinations of 2 pairs of shoes can he take? **28**

19. The table shows a list of favorite sports of the students in Mr. Murray's class.

Sport	Number of Students
swimming	5
basketball	3
golf	2
volleyball	7
football	8
soccer	5
other	5

What is the probability that a randomly selected student has a favorite sport that is swimming or soccer? **2/7**

20. The mean since the mean is $21,000, while the mode and median both equal $12,000.

20. Shari's Boutique has 15 employees. They would like to hire more people since they are expanding their store. The current salaries of the employees are listed in the table.

Position	Yearly Salary	Number of Employees
Manager	$75,000	1
Supervisor	$30,000	4
Clerk	$12,000	10

Which measure of central tendency should Shari use to encourage people to apply? Explain.

Preparing for Standardized Tests

Preparing for Standardized Tests 673

Extended-Response Questions

Extended-response questions are often called *open-ended* or *constructed-response questions*. Most extended-response questions have multiple parts. You must answer all parts to receive full credit.

In extended-response questions you must show all of your work in solving the problem. A rubric is used to determine if you receive full, partial, or no credit. The following is a sample rubric for scoring extended-response questions.

Credit	Score	Criteria
Full	4	Full credit: A correct solution is given that is supported by well-developed, accurate explanations.
Partial	3, 2, 1	Partial credit: A generally correct solution is given that may contain minor flaws in reasoning or computation, or an incomplete solution is given. The more correct the solution, the greater the score.
None	0	No credit: An incorrect solution is given indicating no mathematical understanding of the concept, or no solution is given.

On some standardized tests, no credit is given for a correct answer if your work is not shown.

Make sure that when the problem says to *Show your work*, you show every part of your solution. This includes figures, graphs, and any explanations for your calculations.

EXAMPLE

Lanae owns a music store. The table shows the number of each type of CD that she sold in one weekend.

a. Find the percent of CDs sold for each music type. Round to the nearest percent.

b. Find the number of degrees for each section of a circle graph representing the data. Round to the nearest tenth of a degree. Make a circle graph of the data.

c. If Lanae sells 250 CDs the following weekend, how many would you expect to be Jazz?

Music Type	Number of CDs Sold
Classical	12
Country	9
Hip-Hop	15
Jazz	24
R&B	35

Full Credit Solution

Part a

I will first find the total number of CDs sold.

$15 + 9 + 12 + 35 + 24 = 95$

To find each percent, I will divide the number of CDs in the category by the total number of CDs sold:

Classical: $\frac{12}{95} \approx 13\%$

Country: $\frac{9}{95} \approx 9\%$

Hip-Hop: $\frac{15}{95} \approx 16\%$

Jazz: $\frac{24}{95} \approx 25\%$

R&B: $\frac{35}{95} \approx 37\%$

674 Preparing for Standardized Tests

Part b

I will multiply each percent by 360 to find the number of degrees for each section of the circle.

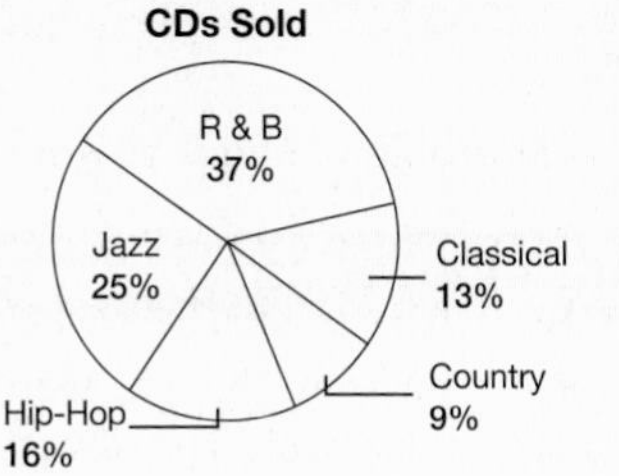

Classical: 13% of 360 $= 0.13 \times 360 = 46.8$

Country: 9% of 360 $= 0.09 \times 360 = 32.4$

Hip-Hop: 16% of 360 $= 0.16 \times 360 = 57.6$

Jazz: 25% of 360 $= 0.25 \times 360 = 90$

R&B: 37% of 360 $= 0.37 \times 360 = 133.2$

Part c

Since 25% of the CDs sold the weekend before were Jazz, you would expect about 25% of the 250 CDs to be Jazz.
25% of 250 $= 0.25 \times 250 = 62.5$.
You should expect about 63 of the CDs sold to be Jazz.

Preparing for Standardized Tests

Partial Credit Solution

Part a This answer includes no explanation of how the percents were found.

Classical: $\approx$ 13% Country: $\approx$ 9% R&B: $\approx$ 37%
Hip-Hop: $\approx$ 16% Jazz: $\approx$ 25%

Part b

To make a circle graph of the data, I first need to find the number of degrees that represent each section.

Classical: 13% of 360 $= 0.13 \times 360$ or 46.8

Country: 9% of 360 $= 0.09 \times 360$ or 32.4

Hip-Hop: 16% of 360 $= 0.16 \times 360$ or 57.6

Jazz: 25% of 360 $= 0.25 \times 360$ or 90

R&B: 37% of 360 $= 0.037 \times 360$ or 133.2

This sample answer only includes part of the answer. The circle graph is missing.

Part c Partial credit is given since no work is shown, but the answer is correct.

About 63 CDs should be Jazz.

No Credit Solution

A student who demonstrates no understanding of how to find the percents, does not make a circle graph, or draws an incorrect graph, and does not understand how to use the information to make predictions receives no credit.

Preparing for Standardized Tests

Preparing for Standardized Tests 675

Answers

3a.

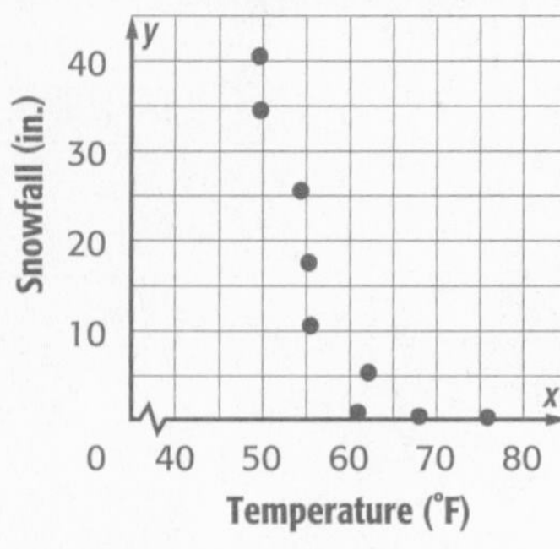

3b. Negative; as the temperature increases, the amount of snowfall decreases.

3c. about 30 in.

4a.

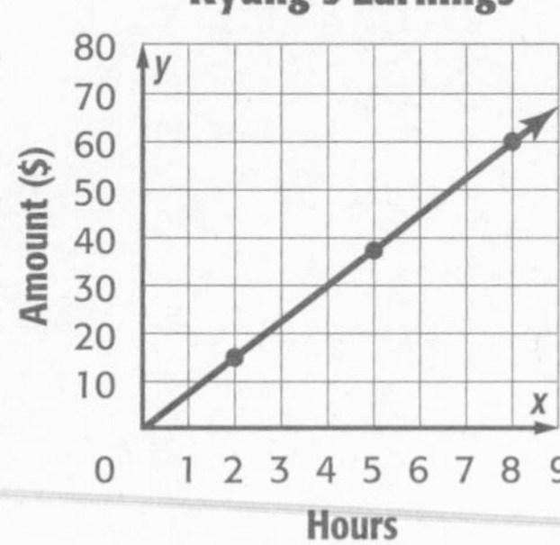

4b. 7.5; It is Kyung's hourly wage.

4c. $255

Extended-Response Practice

Solve each problem. Show all your work.

Number and Operations

1. Ellen has a postcard that she wants to enlarge and hang on her wall. The dimensions of the postcard are 5 inches by 7 inches.
   a. Suppose she enlarges the postcard by a scale factor of 6. What will be the new dimensions? **30 in. by 42 in.**
   b. Ellen found that after enlarging the picture with a scale factor of 6, it still was not the right size. She decided to try to enlarge it so the scale factor from the original picture to the enlarged picture is 3:5. What will be the new dimensions?
   c. Using the dimensions found in Part a, what is the ratio of the area of the smaller picture to the area of the enlarged picture? $\frac{1}{36}$

   b. $8\frac{1}{3}$ in. by $11\frac{2}{3}$ in.

2. The table shows the number of computer users in eight different countries in a recent year.

Country	Computer Users (millions)
United States	168.84
Japan	48.00
Germany	31.59
United Kingdom	25.91
France	21.81
China	21.31
Canada	17.20
Italy	17.17

Source: U.S. Census Bureau

   a. Which country had approximately $\frac{1}{8}$ the number of computer users that the United States had? **China or France**
   b. How many more computer users did Canada have than Italy? **30,000**
   c. If the total number of computer users in the top 15 countries is 420.20 million, what percent of these users are from Germany? Round to the nearest tenth of a percent. **about 7.5%**

Algebra

3. The table shows the annual average temperatures and snowfalls for several cities.

City	Annual Averages	
	Temperature (°F)	Snowfall (in.)
Albuquerque, NM	56.2	10.6
Atlanta, GA	61.3	1.9
Chicago, IL	49.0	40.3
Des Moines, IA	49.9	34.7
Houston, TX	67.9	0.4
Louisville, KY	56.1	17.5
Memphis, TN	62.3	5.5
Miami, FL	75.9	0.0
New York, NY	54.7	26.1

Sources: www.factmonster.com and www.cityrating.com

   a. Draw a scatter plot of the data. Let the x-axis be the average temperature and the y-axis be the average snowfall.
   b. Does the scatter plot show a *positive, negative,* or *no* relationship? Explain.
   c. Use your scatter plot to estimate the amount of annual snowfall you would expect in Cincinnati, Ohio, which has an annual average temperature of 51.7°F.

   a–c. See margin.

4. Kyung works at a golf course for his summer job. The table shows the amount of money that he earns after various number of hours worked. **a–c. See margin.**

Time (h)	Amount ($)
2	15.00
5	37.50
8	60.00

   a. Graph the information with hours on the x-axis and dollars on the y-axis. Draw a line through the points.
   b. What is the slope of the graph? Explain what the slope means.
   c. If Kyung works 34 hours in one week, how much money will he make?

Geometry

5. Chelsea leans a 10-foot ladder on the side of her house. The base of the ladder is 4 feet from the house.

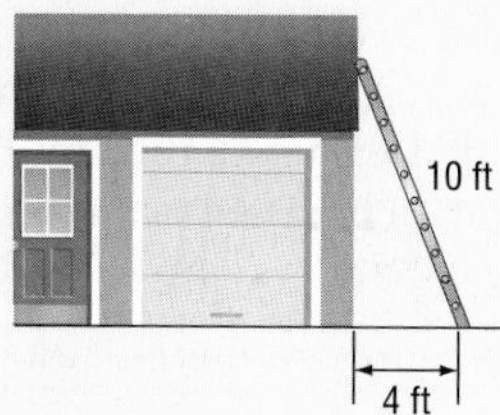

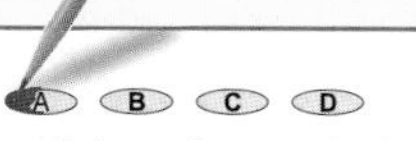

a. How high up the wall does the ladder reach? Round to the nearest tenth of a foot. **9.2 ft**

b. If Chelsea needs the ladder to reach 11 feet up the wall, is this possible? If so, how far from the base of the house should the ladder be? **not possible**

c. Use the diagram to find the measures of the angles in the triangle formed by the ladder, the ground, and the wall. Round to the nearest degree. **90°, 66°, 24°**

Test-Taking Tip

Question 5 After finding the solutions, always go back and read the problem again to make sure your solution answers what the problem is asking.

6. Use $\triangle ABC$ and $\triangle JKL$ in the diagram below.

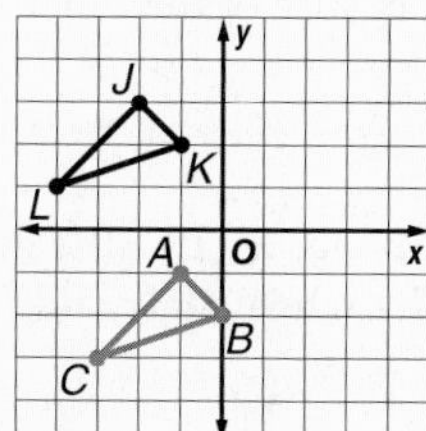

a. Graph the image of $\triangle ABC$ after it is reflected over the y-axis. Write the coordinates of its vertices. **a–c. See margin.**

b. Graph the image of $\triangle JKL$ after it is translated 2 units up. Write the coordinates of its vertices.

c. What translation(s) would transform $\triangle ABC$ to $\triangle JKL$?

Measurement

7. The table shows the winning men's marathon times, rounded to the nearest minute, at five Olympic games.

Year	Runner	Time (min.)
1984	Carlos Lopes	129
1988	Gelindo Bordin	131
1992	Hwang Young-Cho	133
1996	Josia Thugwane	133
2000	Gezahgne Abera	130

Source: *The World Almanac*

a. A marathon is 26.2 miles. What rate did the 2000 winner run the marathon in miles per hour? Round to the nearest tenth. **12.1 mph**

b. If the 1984 winner could keep up his average rate, how long would it take him to run 50 miles? Round to the nearest minute. **246 min**

Data Analysis and Probability

8. The data represent the magnitudes of recent earthquakes. **a–c. See margin.**

6.8	6.4	6.4	7.6
5.9	6.5	5.9	5.0
6.1	7.4	6.5	8.1

Source: *The World Almanac*

a. Make a box-and-whisker plot of the data.

b. What is the interquartile range of the data?

c. What is the median and mean of the data?

9. Forty customers were surveyed as they left Super Slides Water Park. The results are in the table below.

Item	Number Purchased
T-shirt	16
Beverage	36
Food	21

a. What percent of the customers purchased a beverage? **90%**

b. If 215 people attend the park on Monday, about how many of the customers would you expect will purchase food? **113**

c. On Monday, 155 people of the 215 purchased a T-shirt. Would you have expected this? Explain. **See margin.**

Answers

6a. Check students' graph; $A'(1, -1)$, $B'(0, -2)$, $C'(3, -3)$.

6b. Check students' graph; $J'(-2, 5)$, $K'(-1, 4)$, $L'(-4, 3)$.

6c. left 1 unit, up 4 units

8a.

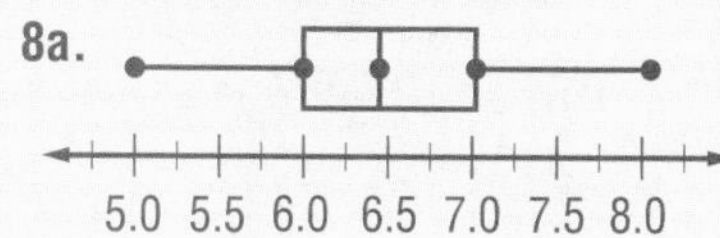

8b. 1.1

8c. 6.45; 6.55

9c. No, because 40% of the people surveyed bought T-shirts, while 72% of the total customers bought T-shirts on Monday.

Preparing for Standardized Tests

The Tangent Ratio

What You'll LEARN

Find the tangent of an angle and find missing measures using the tangent.

NEW Vocabulary

tangent

WHEN am I ever going to use this?

The industrial technology class plans to add a wheelchair ramp to the emergency exit of the auditorium as a class project. They know that the landing is 3 feet high and that the angle the ramp makes with the ground cannot be greater than 6°. They want to find the minimum distance from the landing that the ramp should start.

1. How can you draw a diagram to represent this situation?

1. Draw a right triangle with legs of length 3 ft and *x* ft. Label the angle formed by the ramp and the ground 6°.

Problems like the one above involve a right triangle and ratios. One ratio, called the **tangent**, compares the measure of the leg opposite an angle with the measure of the leg adjacent to that angle. The symbol for the tangent of angle A is tan A.

Key Concept — **Tangent Ratio**

Words If A is an acute angle of a right triangle,

$$\tan A = \frac{\text{measure of the leg opposite } \angle A}{\text{measure of the leg adjacent to } \angle A}.$$

Symbols $\tan A = \frac{a}{b}$

Model

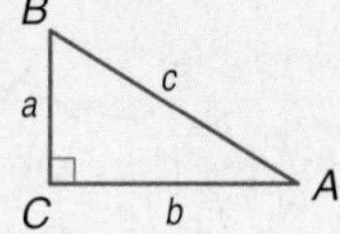

You can also use the symbol for tangent to write the tangent of an angle measure. The tangent of a 60° angle is written as tan 60°. If you know the measures of one leg and an acute angle of a right triangle, you can use the tangent ratio to solve for the measure of the other leg.

EXAMPLE Use Tangent to Solve a Problem

1 CONSTRUCTION In the situation above, what is the minimum distance from the landing that the wheelchair ramp should start?

Use your diagram.

$m\angle A = 6°$

adjacent leg = x feet

opposite leg = 3 feet

$$\tan A = \frac{\text{opposite leg}}{\text{adjacent leg}}$$

$$\tan 6° = \frac{3}{x}$$

$(\tan 6°)(x) = 3$ Multiply each side by x.

$x = \frac{3}{\tan 6°}$ Divide each side by tan 6°.

Trigonometric Table
If your calculator does not have a TAN key, you can use the table on page 685 to estimate answers.

Trigonometry

Trigonometry

Use a calculator to find the value of x.

3 [÷] [TAN] 6 [ENTER] 28.54309336

To the nearest tenth, the ramp should begin about 28.5 feet from the landing.

You can use the TAN^{-1} function on your calculator to find the measure of an acute angle of a right triangle when you know the measures of the two legs.

STUDY TIP

Technology To find TAN^{-1}, press the [2nd] key and then the [TAN] key.

EXAMPLE Use Tangent to Find Angle Measure

2 Find the measure of ∠A to the nearest degree.

From the figure, you know the measures of the two legs. Use the definition of tangent.

C, 10 m, 6 m, A, B

$$\tan A = \frac{\text{opposite leg}}{\text{adjacent leg}}$$

$$\tan A = \frac{6}{10}$$

Now use your calculator to find the measure of ∠A.

[2nd] [TAN^{-1}] 6 [÷] 10 [ENTER] 30.96375653

The measure of A is about 31°.

Skill and Concept Check

1. Writing Math Write a definition of the tangent ratio. **1–2. See margin.**
2. **OPEN ENDED** Explain how to use the tangent ratio to find the measure of a leg of a right triangle.
3. **OPEN ENDED** Explain how to find the measure of an angle in a right triangle when you know the measures of the two legs. **Find the ratio of the opposite side to the adjacent side. Then find TAN^{-1}.**

GUIDED PRACTICE

Find each tangent to the nearest tenth. Find the measure of each angle to the nearest degree.

K, 12 m, R, 20 m, J

4. $\tan J$ **0.6**
5. $\tan K$ **1.7**
6. $m\angle J$ **31°**
7. $m\angle K$ **59°**

8. Find the value of x to the nearest tenth. **3.6**

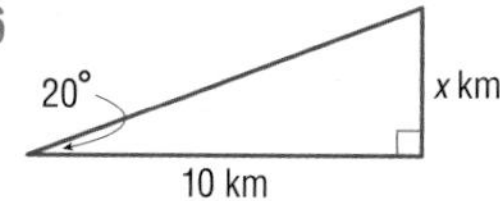

9. **MEASUREMENT** A guyline is fastened to a TV tower 50 feet above the ground and forms an angle of 65° with the tower. How far is it from the base of the tower to the point where the guyline is anchored into the ground? Round to the nearest foot. **107 ft**

Trigonometry

Answers

1. the ratio of the measure of the leg opposite an angle to the measure of the leg adjacent to that angle in a right triangle
2. Substitute the measures that you know into the equation $\tan A = \frac{a}{b}$ and then solve.

Practice and Applications

HOMEWORK HELP	
For Exercises	See Examples
10–11, 14–15, 18–19, 22–26	1
12–13, 16–17, 20–21	2

Complete each exercise using the information in the figures. Find each tangent to the nearest tenth. Find the measure of each angle to the nearest degree.

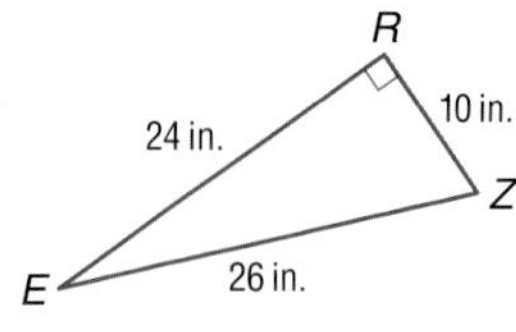

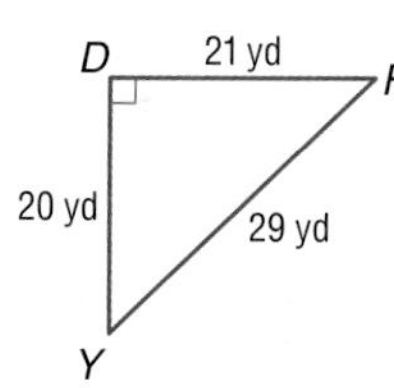

10. $\tan A$ **0.8**
11. $\tan B$ **1.3**
12. $m\angle A$ **37°**
13. $m\angle B$ **53°**
14. $\tan Z$ **2.4**
15. $\tan E$ **0.4**
16. $m\angle Z$ **67°**
17. $m\angle E$ **23°**
18. $\tan F$ **1.0**
19. $\tan Y$ **1.1**
20. $m\angle F$ **44°**
21. $m\angle Y$ **46°**

Find the value of x to the nearest tenth.

22. **6.9**

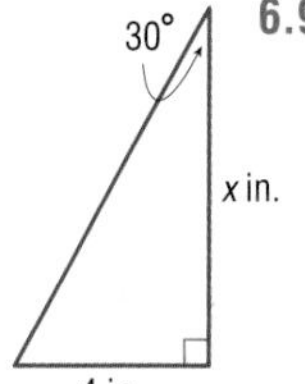

23. **6.7**

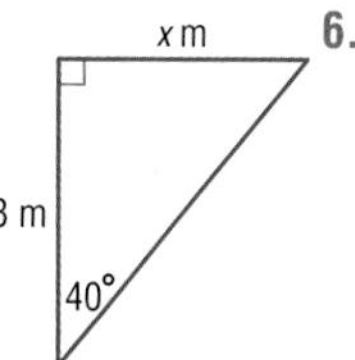

24. **4.3**

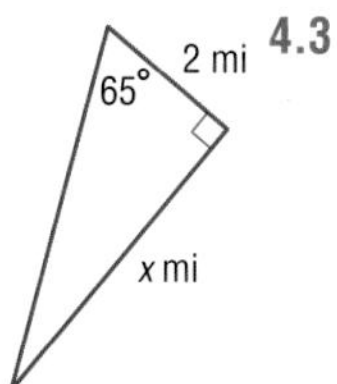

25. If the leg opposite the 53° angle in a right triangle is 4 inches long, how long is the other leg to the nearest tenth? **3.0 in.**

26. If the leg adjacent to a 29° angle in a right triangle is 9 feet long, what is the measure of the other leg to the nearest tenth? **5.0 ft**

27. **MEASUREMENT** A flagpole casts a shadow 25 meters long when the angle of elevation of the Sun is 40°. How tall is the flagpole to the nearest meter? **21 m**

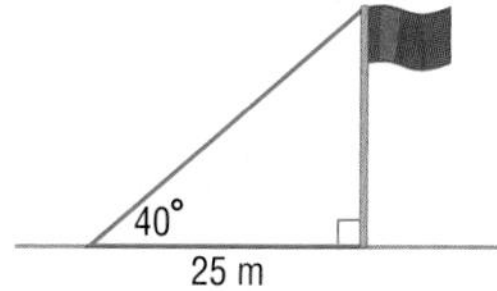

28. **SURVEYING** A surveyor is finding the width of a river for a proposed bridge. A *theodolite* is an instrument used by the surveyor to measure angles. The distance from the surveyor to the proposed bridge site is 40 feet. The surveyor measures a 50° angle to the bridge site across the river. Find the length of the bridge to the nearest foot. **48 ft**

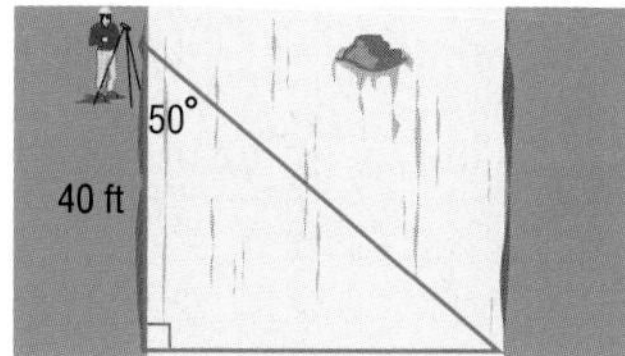

29. **CRITICAL THINKING** In a right triangle, the tangent of one of the acute angles is 1. Describe how the measures of the two legs are related. **They are equal.**

Trigonometry

The Sine and Cosine Ratios

What You'll LEARN

Find the sine and cosine of an angle and find missing measures using sine and cosine.

NEW Vocabulary

trigonometry
sine
cosine
angle of elevation

WHEN am I ever going to use this?

ART Toni decided to make a scale drawing of the Leaning Tower of Pisa for her project in art class. She knows the tower is 177 feet tall and tilts 16.5 feet off the perpendicular.

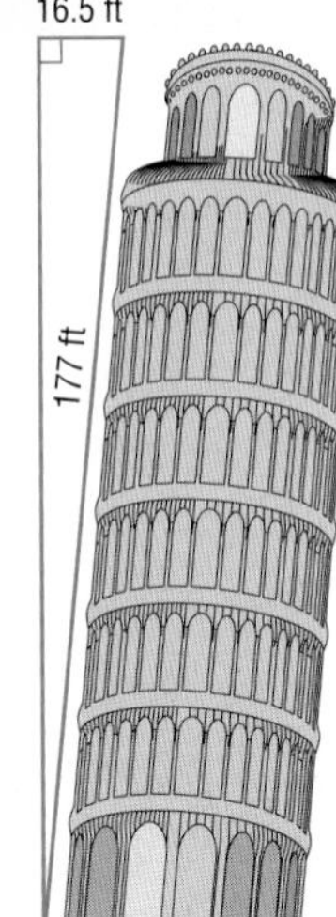

1. In the diagram, what angle describes how much the Tower is leaning?
the angle formed by the hypotenuse and the vertical leg

In the situation above, you know the measures of one leg and the hypotenuse of a right triangle. These are *not* the measures you need to use the tangent ratio. The tangent ratio is only one of several ratios used in the study of the properties of triangles, or **trigonometry**.

Two other ratios are the **sine** ratio and the **cosine** ratio. These can be written as sin A and cos A. They are defined as follows.

Key Concept — **Sine and Cosine Ratios**

Words If A is an acute angle of a right triangle,

$$\sin A = \frac{\text{measure of the leg opposite } \angle A}{\text{measure of the hypotenuse}} \text{ and}$$

$$\cos A = \frac{\text{measure of the leg adjacent to } \angle A}{\text{measure of the hypotenuse}}.$$

Symbols $\sin A = \frac{a}{c}$ $\cos A = \frac{b}{c}$

Model

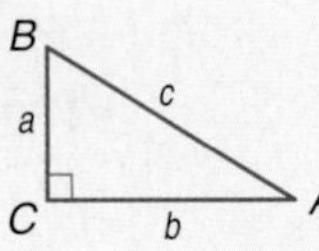

EXAMPLE **Find Sine and Cosine**

1 **Use $\triangle ABC$ to find sin A, cos A, sin B, and cos B.**

$\sin A = \frac{BC}{AB}$
$= \frac{4}{5}$ or 0.8

$\sin B = \frac{AC}{AB}$
$= \frac{3}{5}$ or 0.6

$\cos A = \frac{AC}{AB}$
$= \frac{3}{5}$ or 0.6

$\cos B = \frac{BC}{AB}$
$= \frac{4}{5}$ or 0.8

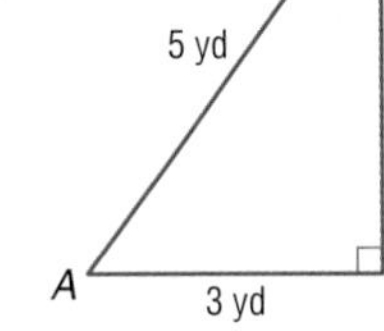

Trigonometry

Trigonometry

You can find the sine and cosine of an angle by using a calculator.

sin 63° → [SIN] 63 0.891006524

cos 63° → [COS] 63 0.4539905

You can use the sine and cosine ratios to find missing lengths of sides or angle measures in a right triangle.

EXAMPLE Use Cosine to Find Side Length

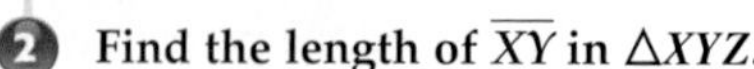

2 Find the length of $\overline{XY}$ in $\triangle XYZ$.

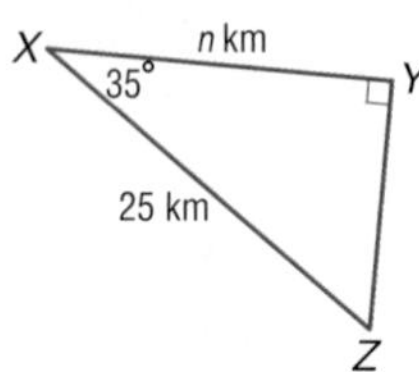

You know the measure of $\angle X$ and the length of the hypotenuse. You can use the cosine ratio.

$\cos X = \frac{XY}{XZ}$ $\frac{\text{adjacent leg}}{\text{hypotenuse}}$

$\cos 35° = \frac{n}{25}$ Replace X with 35°, XY with n, and XZ with 25.

$(25)(\cos 35°) = n$ Multiply each side by 25.

Use a calculator to find the value of n.

25 [×] [COS] 35 [ENTER] 20.47880111

The length of $\overline{XY}$ is about 20.5 kilometers.

EXAMPLE Use Sine to Solve a Problem

3 SCALE DRAWINGS Find the angle that Toni needs to draw for her scale drawing of the Leaning Tower of Pisa.

16.5 ft

177 ft

A

Explore You know the length of the leg opposite the angle and the length of the hypotenuse. You can use sin A.

Plan Substitute the known values into the definition of sine.

$\sin A = \frac{\text{opposite leg}}{\text{hypotenuse}}$

Solve $\sin A = \frac{16.5}{177}$

Use a calculator to find the value of A.

[2nd] [SIN^{-1}] 16.5 [÷] 177 [ENTER] 5.348898164

Toni must draw an angle of about 5°.

Examine Toni knows the angle in her drawing will be very narrow. Since 5° is a very small angle, it is a reasonable answer.

Trigonometry

Trigonometry

Many problems that can be solved using trigonometric ratios deal with angles of elevation. An **angle of elevation** is formed by a horizontal line and a line of sight above it.

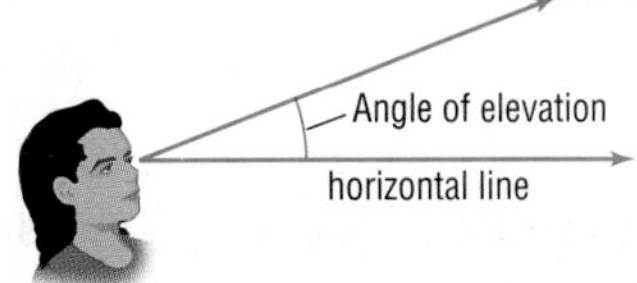

EXAMPLE **Use Angle of Elevation to Solve a Problem**

4 **MEASUREMENT The angle of elevation from a small boat to the top of a lighthouse is 25°. If the top of the lighthouse is 150 feet above sea level, find the distance from the boat to the base of the lighthouse.**

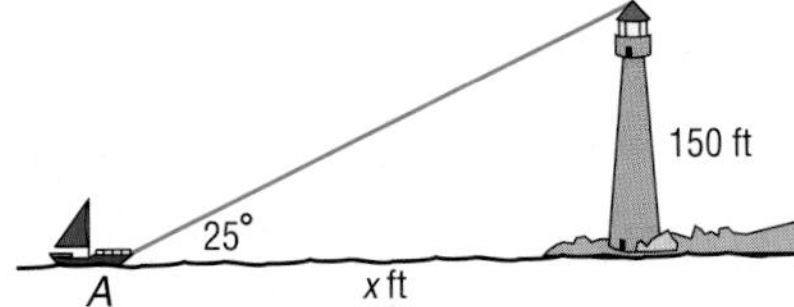

Let x = the distance from the boat to the base of the lighthouse.

$\tan 25° = \frac{150}{x}$ $\quad \frac{\text{opposite leg}}{\text{adjacent leg}}$

$(\tan 25°)\, x = 150$ $\quad$ Multiply each side by x.

$x = \frac{150}{\tan 25°}$ $\quad$ Divide each side by tan 25°.

150 [÷] [TAN] 25 [ENTER] 321.6760381

The boat is about 322 feet from the base of the lighthouse.

Skill and Concept Check

1. *Writing Math* Write a definition for the sine and cosine ratios. **1–2. See margin.**
2. **OPEN ENDED** Show how you could use the sine or cosine to find the missing measure of one of the legs if you know the hypotenuse and an acute angle.

GUIDED PRACTICE

Find each sine or cosine to the nearest tenth. Find the measure of each angle to the nearest degree.

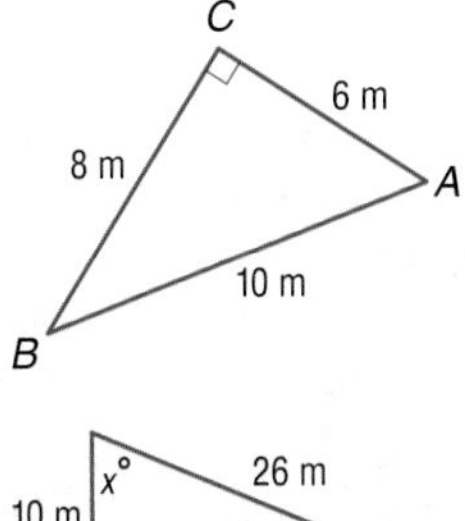

3. cos A **0.6**
4. sin A **0.8**
5. $m\angle A$ **53°**
6. sin B **0.6**
7. cos B **0.8**
8. $m\angle B$ **37°**
9. Find the value of x to the nearest degree. **67°**

$x°$, 26 m, 10 m, 24 m

Trigonometry

Answers

1. sine: ratio of the leg opposite to the hypotenuse; cosine: ratio of the leg adjacent to the hypotenuse
2. Substitute known values into the definition of sine or cosine and then solve.

Trigonometry

10. **TRANSPORTATION** The end of an exit ramp from an interstate highway is 22 feet higher than the highway. If the ramp is 630 feet long, what angle does it make with the highway? Round to the nearest degree. **2°**

Practice and Applications

HOMEWORK HELP	
For Exercises	See Examples
11–14, 19–20, 23–24	1
27, 29	2
15–16, 21–22, 25–26, 28	3
31–32	4

Complete each exercise using the information in the figures. Find each sine or cosine to the nearest tenth. Find the measure of each angle to the nearest degree.

Triangle ABC: AB = 34 ft, BC = 16 ft, AC = 30 ft, right angle at C
Triangle QRS: QR = 12 in., QS = 16 in., RS = 20 in., right angle at Q
Triangle DEF: DF = 20 km, DE = 21 km, FE = 29 km, right angle at D

11. $\sin A$ **0.5**
12. $\sin B$ **0.9**
13. $\cos A$ **0.9**
14. $\cos B$ **0.5**
15. $m\angle A$ **28°**
16. $m\angle B$ **62°**
17. $\sin R$ **0.8**
18. $\cos R$ **0.6**
19. $\sin S$ **0.6**
20. $\cos S$ **0.8**
21. $m\angle R$ **53°**
22. $m\angle S$ **37°**
23. $\sin E$ **0.7**
24. $\cos F$ **0.7**
25. $m\angle E$ **44°**
26. $m\angle F$ **46°**

Find the value of x to the nearest tenth or nearest degree.

27. **12.0 yd** (x yd, 13 yd, 67°)

28. **45°** (x°, 21.2 cm, 15 cm)

29. **30°** (5 km, 10 km, 8.66 km, x°)

30. **HOME IMPROVEMENT** A painter props a 20-foot ladder against a house. The angle it forms with the ground is 65°. To the nearest foot, how far up the side of the house does the ladder reach? **18 ft**

31. **SURVEYING** A surveyor is 85 meters from the base of a building. The angle of elevation to the top of the building is 20°. If her eye level is 1.6 meters above the ground, find the height of the building to the nearest meter. **33 m**

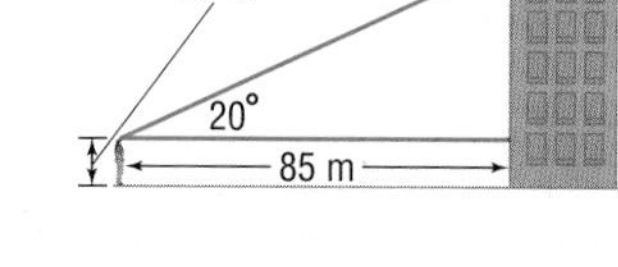

32. **FIRE FIGHTING** A fire is sighted from a fire tower at an angle of depression of 2°. If the fire tower has a height of 125 feet, how far is the fire from the base of the tower? Round to the nearest foot. **3,580 ft**

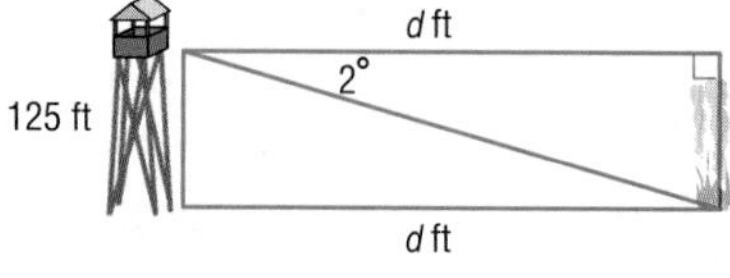

33. **CRITICAL THINKING** Study your answers to Exercises 11–26. Make a conjecture about the relationship between the sine and cosine of complementary angles. **They are equal.**

Table of Trigonometric Ratios

Angle	sin	cos	tan	Angle	sin	cos	tan
0°	0.0000	1.0000	0.0000	45°	0.7071	0.7071	1.0000
1°	0.0175	0.9998	0.0175	46°	0.7192	0.6947	1.0355
2°	0.0349	0.9994	0.0349	47°	0.7314	0.6820	1.0724
3°	0.0523	0.9986	0.0524	48°	0.7431	0.6691	1.1106
4°	0.0698	0.9976	0.0699	49°	0.7547	0.6561	1.1504
5°	0.0872	0.9962	0.0875	50°	0.7660	0.6428	1.1918
6°	0.1045	0.9945	0.1051	51°	0.7771	0.6293	1.2349
7°	0.1219	0.9925	0.1228	52°	0.7880	0.6157	1.2799
8°	0.1392	0.9903	0.1405	53°	0.7986	0.6018	1.3270
9°	0.1564	0.9877	0.1584	54°	0.8090	0.5878	1.3764
10°	0.1736	0.9848	0.1763	55°	0.8192	0.5736	1.4281
11°	0.1908	0.9816	0.1944	56°	0.8290	0.5592	1.4826
12°	0.2079	0.9781	0.2126	57°	0.8387	0.5446	1.5399
13°	0.2250	0.9744	0.2309	58°	0.8480	0.5299	1.6003
14°	0.2419	0.9703	0.2493	59°	0.8572	0.5150	1.6643
15°	0.2588	0.9659	0.2679	60°	0.8660	0.5000	1.7321
16°	0.2756	0.9613	0.2867	61°	0.8746	0.4848	1.8040
17°	0.2924	0.9563	0.3057	62°	0.8829	0.4695	1.8807
18°	0.3090	0.9511	0.3249	63°	0.8910	0.4540	1.9626
19°	0.3256	0.9455	0.3443	64°	0.8988	0.4384	2.0503
20°	0.3420	0.9397	0.3640	65°	0.9063	0.4226	2.1445
21°	0.3584	0.9336	0.3839	66°	0.9135	0.4067	2.2460
22°	0.3746	0.9272	0.4040	67°	0.9205	0.3907	2.3559
23°	0.3907	0.9205	0.4245	68°	0.9272	0.3746	2.4751
24°	0.4067	0.9135	0.4452	69°	0.9336	0.3584	2.6051
25°	0.4226	0.9063	0.4663	70°	0.9397	0.3420	2.7475
26°	0.4384	0.8988	0.4877	71°	0.9455	0.3256	2.9042
27°	0.4540	0.9810	0.5095	72°	0.9511	0.3090	3.0777
28°	0.4695	0.8829	0.5317	73°	0.9563	0.2924	3.2709
29°	0.4848	0.8746	0.5543	74°	0.9613	0.2756	3.4874
30°	0.5000	0.8660	0.5774	75°	0.9659	0.2588	3.7321
31°	0.5150	0.8572	0.6009	76°	0.9703	0.2419	4.0108
32°	0.5299	0.8480	0.6249	77°	0.9744	0.2250	4.3315
33°	0.5446	0.8387	0.6494	78°	0.9781	0.2079	4.7046
34°	0.5592	0.8290	0.6745	79°	0.9816	0.1908	5.1446
35°	0.5736	0.8192	0.7002	80°	0.9848	0.1736	5.6713
36°	0.5878	0.8090	0.7265	81°	0.9877	0.1564	6.3138
37°	0.6018	0.7986	0.7536	82°	0.9903	0.1392	7.1154
38°	0.6157	0.7880	0.7813	83°	0.9925	0.1219	8.1443
39°	0.6293	0.7771	0.8098	84°	0.9945	0.1045	9.5144
40°	0.6428	0.7660	0.8391	85°	0.9962	0.0872	11.4301
41°	0.6561	0.7547	0.8693	86°	0.9976	0.0698	14.3007
42°	0.6691	0.7431	0.9004	87°	0.9986	0.0523	19.0811
43°	0.6820	0.7314	0.9325	88°	0.9994	0.0349	28.6363
44°	0.6947	0.7193	0.9657	89°	0.9998	0.0175	57.2900
45°	0.7071	0.7071	1.0000	90°	1.0000	0.0000	∞

Trigonometry

Converting Measures of Area and Volume

What You'll LEARN

Convert customary and metric units of area and volume.

WHEN am I ever going to use this?

GAMES A Rubik's™ Cube is a puzzle consisting of a cube with colored faces. It can help you understand how to convert measures of area and volume.

1. Look at one face of Rubik's™ Cube. How many cubes are there along each edge? How many squares are there on one face? **3, 9**
2. Suppose the Rubik's™ Cube is made of 3 layers with 9 small cubes in each layer. How many small cubes are there in all? **27**
3. What is the relationship between the number of cubes along each edge and the number of squares on one face? between the number of cubes along each edge and the total number of small cubes?

3. The number of squares is the square of the number of cubes along the edge; the number of small cubes is the cube of the number of cubes along the edge.

TEACHING TIP

You may want to point out that there are 12 inches in 1 foot, and $12^2 = 144$. Also, there are 3 feet in 1 yard, and $3^2 = 9$.

The units of area in the customary system are square inch (in^2), square foot (ft^2), square yard (yd^2), and square mile (mi^2).

Customary Units of Area
$1\ ft^2 = 144\ in^2$
$1\ yd^2 = 9\ ft^2$

Just as when you convert units of length, capacity, or weight:

- to convert from larger units to smaller units, multiply, and
- to convert from smaller units to larger units, divide.

Measurement Conversion

EXAMPLES Convert Customary Units of Area

1 Complete each conversion.

$2\ ft^2 = \underline{\ ?\ }\ in^2$

$2\ ft^2 = (2 \times 144)\ in^2$ To convert from ft^2 to in^2, multiply by 144.

$= 288\ in^2$

2 $48\ ft^2 = \underline{\ ?\ }\ yd^2$

$48\ ft^2 = (48 \div 9)\ yd^2$ To convert from ft^2 to yd^2, divide by 9.

$\approx 5.33\ yd^2$

Your Turn **Complete each conversion.**

a. $1.5\ ft^2 = \underline{\ ?\ }\ in^2$ **216**

b. $45\ ft^2 = \underline{\ ?\ }\ yd^2$ **5**

TEACHING TIP

You may want to point out that there are 12 inches in 1 foot, and $12^3 = 1{,}728$. Also, there are 3 feet in 1 yard, and $3^3 = 27$.

The units of volume in the customary system are cubic inch (in^3), cubic foot (ft^3), and cubic yard (yd^3).

Customary Units of Volume
$1\ ft^3 = 1{,}728\ in^3$
$1\ yd^3 = 27\ ft^3$

Measurement Conversion

STUDY TIP

Alternative Method You can also convert each measurement to yards before finding the volume.

EXAMPLE Convert Customary Units of Volume

3 **BUILDING** **How many cubic yards of concrete will you need for a rectangular driveway that is 44 feet long, 9 feet wide, and 4 inches thick?**

Find the volume in cubic feet, then convert to cubic yards.

$V = \ell wh$

$V = 44 \cdot 9 \cdot \frac{1}{3}$ 4 inches = $\frac{4}{12}$ or $\frac{1}{3}$ foot

$V = 132$ cubic feet

To convert from cubic feet to cubic yards, divide by 27.

$132 \text{ ft}^3 = (132 \div 27) \text{ yd}^3$

$\approx 4.89 \text{ yd}^3$

You need 4.89 cubic yards of concrete.

STUDY TIP

Decimeter A decimeter is a metric unit of length equal to 10 centimeters. One square decimeter is about the size of a computer disk.

The common units of area in the metric system are square millimeter (mm^2), square centimeter (cm^2), square meter (m^2), and square kilometer (km^2). The common units of volume in the metric system are cubic centimeter (cm^3), cubic decimeter (dm^3), and cubic meter (m^3).

Metric Units of Area	Metric Units of Volume
$1 \text{ cm}^2 = 100 \text{ mm}^2$	$1 \text{ dm}^3 = 1{,}000 \text{ cm}^3$
$1 \text{ m}^2 = 10{,}000 \text{ cm}^2$	$1 \text{ m}^3 = 1{,}000 \text{ dm}^3$

EXAMPLES Convert Metric Units

TEACHING TIP

You may want to point out that there are 10 mm in 1 cm, and $10^2 = 100$. Also, there are 100 cm in 1 m, and $100^2 = 10{,}000$. Similarly for volume, there are 10 cm in 1 dm, and $10^3 = 1{,}000$.

Complete each conversion.

4 $16.2 \text{ cm}^2 = \underline{\ ?\ } \text{ mm}^2$

$16.2 \text{ cm}^2 = (16.2 \times 100) \text{ mm}^2$ To convert from cm^2 to mm^2, multiply by 100.

$= 1{,}620 \text{ mm}^2$

5 $1{,}800 \text{ cm}^3 = \underline{\ ?\ } \text{ dm}^3$

$1{,}800 \text{ cm}^3 = (1{,}800 \div 1{,}000) \text{ dm}^3$ To convert from cm^3 to m^3, divide by 1,000.

$= 1.8 \text{ dm}^3$

Your Turn **Complete each conversion.**

c. $3{,}500 \text{ cm}^2 = \underline{\ ?\ } \text{ m}^2$ **0.35**   d. $4.6 \text{ m}^3 = \underline{\ ?\ } \text{ dm}^3$ **4,600**

The metric system is unique in that the measures for length, capacity, and mass are related. When the system was designed, 1 liter was to be the volume of a cube of water one-tenth of a meter on a side, and 1 kilogram was the mass of 1 liter of pure water. (It didn't turn out quite like this, but the actual metric units come very close.) So, if you had a container whose volume was 1.8 cubic decimeters, as in Example 5, it would hold 1.8 liters of water.

Measurement Conversion

Skill and Concept Check

1. Writing Math Explain how to convert 6 cubic yards to cubic feet. **Multiply by 27.**
2. **FIND THE ERROR** Katie and Tyler are converting 288 square inches to square feet. Who is correct? Explain your reasoning.

Tyler	Katie
$288 \div 12 = 24\ ft^2$	$288 \div 144 = 2\ ft^2$

Katie; there are 12 inches in 1 foot, but 144 square inches in 1 square foot.

GUIDED PRACTICE

Complete each conversion. Round to the nearest hundredth if necessary.

3. $3\ ft^2 =$? in^2 **432**
4. $2\ yd^2 =$? ft^2 **18**
5. $15\ ft^2 =$? yd^2 **1.67**
6. $1.5\ ft^3 =$? in^3 **2,592**
7. $4.3\ yd^3 =$? ft^3 **116.1**
8. $40.5\ ft^3 =$? yd^3 **1.5**
9. $10.8\ cm^2 =$? mm^2 **1,080**
10. $148\ mm^2 =$? cm^2 **1.48**
11. $2{,}400\ cm^3 =$? dm^3 **2.4**
12. **BIOLOGY** The total surface area of the average adult's skin is about 21.5 square feet. Convert this measurement to square inches. **about 3,096 in^2**

Practice and Applications

HOMEWORK HELP	
For Exercises	See Examples
13–20	1, 2
21–26	3
27–34	4, 5

Complete each conversion. Round to the nearest hundredth if necessary. **25. 1,720 27. 35.92**

13. $5\ ft^2 =$? in^2 **720**
14. $10.4\ ft^2 =$? in^2 **1,497.6**
15. $288\ in^2 =$? ft^2 **2**
16. $504\ in^2 =$? ft^2 **3.5**
17. $2.4\ yd^2 =$? ft^2 **21.6**
18. $45\ ft^2 =$? yd^2 **5**
19. $70.2\ ft^2 =$? yd^2 **7.8**
20. $2\ ft^3 =$? in^3 **3,456**
21. $0.4\ ft^3 =$? in^3 **691.2**
22. $300\ yd^3 =$? ft^3 **8,100**
23. $15.2\ yd^3 =$? ft^3 **410.4**
24. $28.89\ ft^3 =$? yd^3 **1.07**
25. $17.2\ cm^2 =$? mm^2
26. $0.57\ cm^2 =$? mm^2 **57**
27. $3{,}592\ mm^2 =$? cm^2
28. $15\ mm^2 =$? cm^2 **0.15**
29. $693\ cm^3 =$? dm^3 **0.69**
30. $2\ m^3 =$? dm^3 **2,000**
31. $3.6\ m^3 =$? dm^3 **3,600**
32. **BALLOONS** A standard hot air balloon holds about 2,000 cubic meters of hot air. How many cubic decimeters is this? **2,000,000 dm^3**
33. **REMODELING** Carpet is sold by the square yard. Suppose you have a room that is 18 feet long and 15 feet wide. How many square yards of carpet would cover this room? **30 yd^2**
34. **LANDSCAPING** A landscape architect wants to cover a 40-foot by 12-foot rectangular area with small stones to a depth of 3 inches. Will 100 cubic feet of stones be enough? If not, how many cubic feet are needed? **no; 120 ft^3**
35. **MICROWAVES** The inside of a microwave oven has a volume of 1.2 cubic feet and measures 18 inches wide and 10 inches long. To the nearest tenth, how deep is the inside of the microwave? **11.5 in.**
36. **CRITICAL THINKING** The density of gold is 19.29 grams per cubic centimeter. To the nearest hundredth, find the mass in grams of a gold bar that is 0.75 inch by 1 inch by 0.75 inch. Use the relationship 1 cubic inch $\approx$ 16.38 cubic centimeters. **177.73 g**

Measurement Conversion

Converting Between Measurement Systems

What You'll LEARN

Convert between metric and customary systems of measurement.

REVIEW Vocabulary

dimensional analysis: the process of including units of measurement when you compute (Lesson 2-3)

WHEN am I ever going to use this?

SPORTS One of the most popular and exciting Olympic events is the 100-meter dash. It is also one of the quickest events, lasting less than 10 seconds. **1. a little more than 100 yd**

1. You know that 1 meter is a little longer than 1 yard. Estimate the distance in yards of the 100-meter dash.
2. There are approximately 3.28 feet in 1 meter. What is the distance in feet of the 100-meter dash? **about 328 ft**
3. Compare your answers to Questions 1 and 2. Are they reasonable? Explain.

3. Yes; since there are 3 feet in 1 yard, the answer should be a little more than 3 × 100 or 300. So, 328 ft seems reasonable.

For years you have converted measurements in either the metric system or the customary system. For example, you know that there are 12 inches in 1 foot and 1,000 meters in 1 kilometer.

To convert from larger units to smaller units, multiply.	To convert from smaller units to larger units, divide.
$8\text{ ft} = 8 \times 12 = 96\text{ in.}$	$30\text{ in.} = 30 \div 12 = 2.5\text{ ft}$
$3.9\text{ km} = 3.9 \times 1{,}000 = 3{,}900\text{ m}$	$750\text{ m} = 750 \div 1{,}000 = 0.75\text{ km}$

However, when you convert from one system to the other, it is sometimes difficult to remember which unit is larger. Instead, you can use dimensional analysis and conversion factors. The table below shows conversion factors for units of length.

Key Concept — **Units of Length**

Relationship	Conversion Factors
1 in. ≈ 2.54 cm	$\frac{1\text{ in.}}{2.54\text{ cm}}, \frac{2.54\text{ cm}}{1\text{ in.}}$
1 ft ≈ 0.3048 m	$\frac{1\text{ ft}}{0.3048\text{ m}}, \frac{0.3048\text{ m}}{1\text{ ft}}$
1 yd ≈ 0.9144 m	$\frac{1\text{ yd}}{0.9144\text{ m}}, \frac{0.9144\text{ m}}{1\text{ yd}}$
1 mi ≈ 1.6093 km	$\frac{1\text{ mi}}{1.6093\text{ km}}, \frac{1.6093\text{ km}}{1\text{ mi}}$
1 cm ≈ 0.3937 in.	$\frac{1\text{ cm}}{0.3937\text{ in.}}, \frac{0.3937\text{ in.}}{1\text{ cm}}$
1 m ≈ 1.0936 yd	$\frac{1\text{ m}}{1.0936\text{ yd}}, \frac{1.0936\text{ yd}}{1\text{ m}}$
1 km ≈ 0.6214 mi	$\frac{1\text{ km}}{0.6214\text{ mi}}, \frac{0.6214\text{ mi}}{1\text{ km}}$

TEACHING TIP

Students may ask why there are two equations relating inches to centimeters. Point out that if you start with 1 in. ≈ 2.54 cm and divide each side by 2.54 the result is 0.3937 in. ≈ 1 cm, which is the same as 1 cm ≈ 0.3937 cm. Similarly, there are two equations relating yards to meters and kilometers to miles.

Measurement Conversion

Measurement Conversion

When you use dimensional analysis to convert measurements, choose the conversion factor that allows you to divide out the common units.

EXAMPLE Convert Units of Length

1 Convert 9 centimeters to inches.

Method 1 Use 1 in. ≈ 2.54 cm.

$9 \text{ cm} \approx 9 \cancel{\text{cm}} \cdot \frac{1 \text{ in.}}{2.54 \cancel{\text{cm}}}$

$\approx \frac{9 \text{ in.}}{2.54}$ or 3.54 in.

So, 9 centimeters is about 3.54 inches.

Method 2 Use 1 cm ≈ 0.3937 in.

$9 \text{ cm} \approx 9 \cancel{\text{cm}} \cdot \frac{0.3937 \text{ in.}}{1 \cancel{\text{cm}}}$

$\approx 9 \cdot 0.3937$ in. or 3.54 in.

Your Turn

a. Convert 15 miles to kilometers. **24.14 km**

b. Convert 3 feet to meters. **0.91 m**

Use the conversion factors shown below to convert units of capacity and mass or weight.

TEACHING TIP

You may want to have students derive the following relationships from the ones listed in the table.
1 mL ≈ 0.0338 fl oz
1 L ≈ 2.114 pt
1 L ≈ 1.057 qt
1 L ≈ 0.2642 gal
1 g ≈ 0.0353 oz
1 kg ≈ 2.2046 lb

Measurement Conversion

Measurement Conversion

Key Concept Units of Capacity and Mass or Weight

Relationship	Conversion Factors
1 fl oz ≈ 29.574 mL	$\frac{1 \text{ fl oz}}{29.574 \text{ mL}}, \frac{29.574 \text{ mL}}{1 \text{ fl oz}}$
1 pt ≈ 0.4731 L	$\frac{1 \text{ pt}}{0.4731 \text{ L}}, \frac{0.4731 \text{ L}}{1 \text{ pt}}$
1 qt ≈ 0.9464 L	$\frac{1 \text{ qt}}{0.9464 \text{ L}}, \frac{0.9464 \text{ L}}{1 \text{ qt}}$
1 gal ≈ 3.7854 L	$\frac{1 \text{ gal}}{3.7854 \text{ L}}, \frac{3.7854 \text{ L}}{1 \text{ gal}}$
1 oz ≈ 28.35 g	$\frac{1 \text{ oz}}{28.35 \text{ g}}, \frac{28.35 \text{ g}}{1 \text{ oz}}$
1 lb ≈ 0.4536 kg	$\frac{1 \text{ lb}}{0.4536 \text{ kg}}, \frac{0.4536 \text{ kg}}{1 \text{ lb}}$

EXAMPLE Convert Units Using Two Steps

2 COOKING A recipe for *penne all'arrabbiata* calls for 400 grams of penne pasta. How many pounds of pasta should you use?

You need conversion factors converting grams to ounces and ounces to pounds. Remember, 1 lb = 16 oz.

$400 \text{ g} \approx 400 \cancel{\text{g}} \cdot \frac{1 \cancel{\text{oz}}}{28.35 \cancel{\text{g}}} \cdot \frac{1 \text{ lb}}{16 \cancel{\text{oz}}}$

$\approx \frac{400 \text{ lb}}{453.6}$ or 0.88 lb

You need a little more than $\frac{3}{4}$ pound of pasta.

STUDY TIP

Alternative Method
You can also convert grams to kilograms and then kilograms to pounds.

Skill and Concept Check

1. **Tell** what conversion factor you should use to convert 4.2 kilograms to pounds. $\frac{1 \text{ lb}}{0.4536 \text{ kg}}$
2. **Which One Doesn't Belong?** Identify the measurement that is not the same as the other three. Explain your reasoning.

2 L	2.144 qt	0.528 gal	0.946 pt

0.946 pt; 0.946 pt ≈ 0.45 L and the other measurements convert to 2 L.

GUIDED PRACTICE

Complete each conversion. Round to the nearest hundredth if necessary.

3. 6 in. ≈ __?__ cm 15.24
4. 1.6 cm ≈ __?__ in. 0.63
5. 4 qt ≈ __?__ L 3.79
6. 50 mL ≈ __?__ fl oz 1.69
7. 10 oz ≈ __?__ g 283.5
8. 3.5 kg ≈ __?__ lb 7.72
9. **COOKING** A recipe for apple strudel calls for 250 grams of butter. About how many pounds of butter do you need for the recipe? 0.55 lb or a little more than $\frac{1}{2}$ lb

Practice and Applications

HOMEWORK HELP	
For Exercises	See Examples
10–25	1
26–31	2

Complete each conversion. Round to the nearest hundredth if necessary.

10. 5 in. ≈ __?__ cm 12.7
11. 12 in. ≈ __?__ cm 30.48
12. 15 cm ≈ __?__ in. 5.91
13. 8.2 cm ≈ __?__ in. 3.23
14. 20 mi ≈ __?__ km 32.19
15. 75 mi ≈ __?__ km 120.70
16. 2 L ≈ __?__ qt 2.11
17. 7.2 L ≈ __?__ qt 7.61
18. 25 mL ≈ __?__ fl oz 0.85
19. 10 mL ≈ __?__ fl oz 0.34
20. 16 oz ≈ __?__ g 453.6
21. 30 oz ≈ __?__ g 850.5
22. 5 lb ≈ __?__ kg 2.27
23. 2,000 lb ≈ __?__ kg 907.2
24. 1.8 kg ≈ __?__ lb 3.97
25. 63.5 kg ≈ __?__ lb 139.99
26. 500 g ≈ __?__ lb 1.10
27. 200 g ≈ __?__ lb 0.44
28. 3 lb ≈ __?__ g 1,360.8
29. 5 lb ≈ __?__ g 2,268
30. 16 fl oz ≈ __?__ L 0.47
31. 150 fl oz ≈ __?__ L 4.44
32. **SPORTS** A fund-raising race is 5 kilometers long. About how many miles long is the race? about 3.1 mi
33. **FOOD** A recipe for fruit punch calls for 1 gallon of lemon-lime soda. How many 2-liter bottles of soda should you buy? 2 bottles

35. Top Thrill Dragster, Dodonpa, Silver Star

ROLLER COASTERS For Exercises 34–37, use the table on the fastest and tallest roller coasters on three continents.

34. Convert 120 mph to kph. about 193.1 kph
35. Order the roller coasters from greatest to least speeds.
36. Convert 420 feet to meters. about 128.0 m
37. Order the roller coasters from tallest to shortest.
38. **CRITICAL THINKING** A hectare is a metric unit of area approximately equal to 10,000 square meters or 2.47 acres. The base of the Great Pyramid of Khufu is a 230-meter square. About how many acres does the base cover? about 13 acres

37. Top Thrill Dragster, Thunder Dolphin, Silver Star

Fastest Roller Coasters

Continent	Name	Speed
Asia	Dodonpa	172 kph
Europe	Silver Star	127 kph
North America	Top Thrill Dragster	120 mph

Tallest Roller Coasters

Continent	Name	Height
Asia	Thunder Dolphin	80 m
Europe	Silver Star	73 m
North America	Top Thrill Dragster	420 ft

Source: www.rcdb.com

Measurement Conversion

Measurement Conversion

Glossary/Glosario

A mathematics multilingual glossary is available at www.math.glencoe.com/multilingual_glossary. The glossary includes the following languages.

Arabic	English	Korean	Tagalog
Bengali	Haitian Creole	Russian	Urdu
Cantonese	Hmong	Spanish	Vietnamese

Cómo usar el glosario en español:

1. Busca el término en inglés que desees encontrar.
2. El término en español, junto con la definición, se encuentran en la columna de la derecha.

English / Español

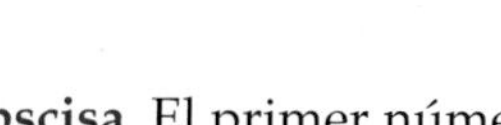

abscissa (p. 142) The first number of an ordered pair; the x-coordinate.

abscisa El primer número de un par ordenado. La coordenada x.

absolute value (p. 19) The distance a number is from zero on the number line.

valor absoluto Número de unidades en la recta numérica que un número dista de cero.

acute angle (p. 256) An angle with a measure greater than 0° and less than 90°.

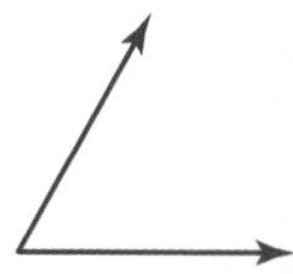

ángulo agudo Ángulo que mide más de 0° y menos de 90°.

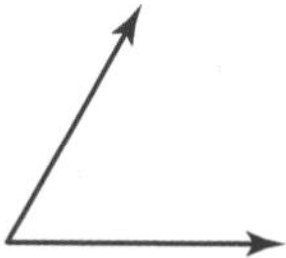

acute triangle (p. 263) A triangle having three acute angles.

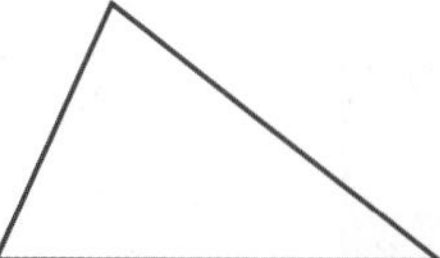

triángulo acutángulo Triángulo que tiene tres ángulos agudos.

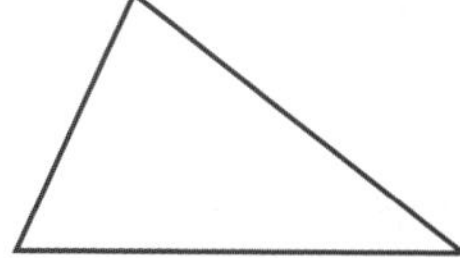

Addition Property of Equality (p. 46) If you add the same number to each side of an equation, the two sides remain equal.

propiedad de adición de la igualdad Si sumas el mismo número a ambos lados de una ecuación, los dos lados permanecen iguales.

additive inverse (p. 25) Two integers that are opposite of each other are called additive inverses. The sum of any number and its additive inverse is zero.

inverso aditivo Dos enteros que son opuestos mutuos reciben el nombre de inversos aditivos. La suma de cualquier número y su inverso aditivo es cero.

adjacent angles (p. 256) Angles that have the same vertex, share a common side, and do not overlap.

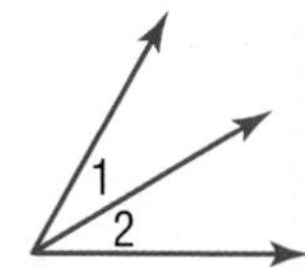

$\angle 1$ and $\angle 2$ are adjacent angles.

ángulos adyacentes Ángulos que comparten el mismo vértice y un común lado, pero no se sobreponen.

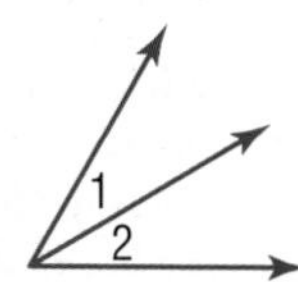

$\angle 1$ y $\angle 2$ son adyacentes.

adjacent side (p. 192) In any right triangle, the side that is not opposite an angle and not the hypotenuse.

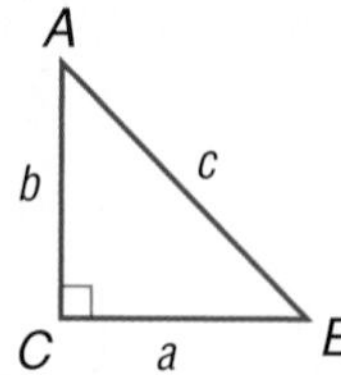

Side b is adjacent to $\angle A$.

lado adyacente En cualquier triángulo rectángulo, el lado que no está opuesto a un ángulo y que no es la hipotenusa.

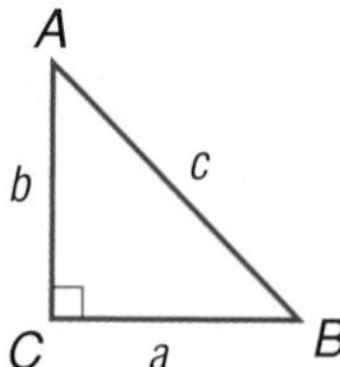

El lado b es adyacente al $\angle A$.

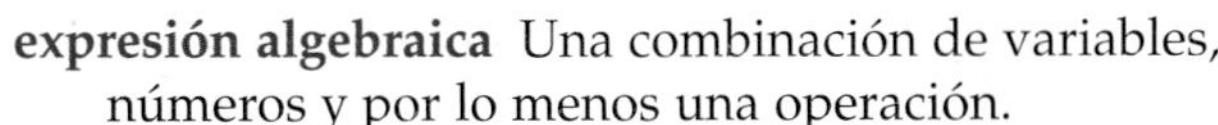

algebraic expression (p. 11) A combination of variables, numbers, and at least one operation.

expresión algebraica Una combinación de variables, números y por lo menos una operación.

alternate exterior angles (p. 258) In the figure, transversal t intersects lines ℓ and m. $\angle 1$ and $\angle 7$, and $\angle 2$ and $\angle 8$ are alternate exterior angles. If lines ℓ and m are parallel, then these pairs of angles are congruent.

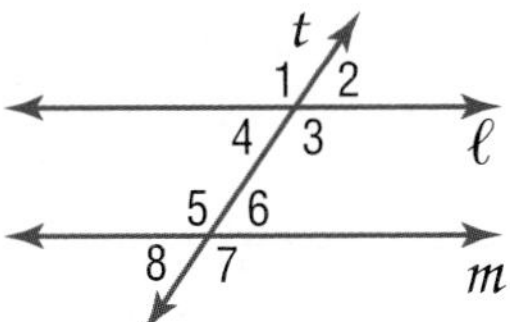

ángulos alternos externos En la figura, la transversal t interseca las rectas ℓ y m. $\angle 1$ y $\angle 7'$ y $\angle 2$ y $\angle 8$ son ángulos alternos externos. Si las rectas ℓ y m son paralelas, entonces estos ángulos son pares de ángulos congruentes.

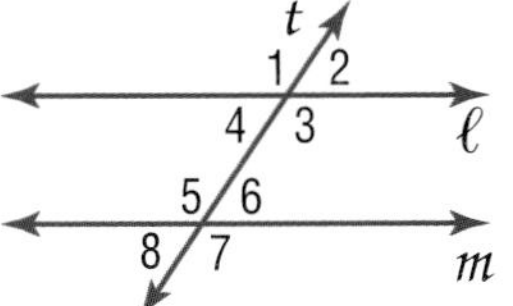

alternate interior angles (p. 258) In the figure above, transversal t intersects lines ℓ and m. $\angle 3$ and $\angle 5$, and $\angle 4$ and $\angle 6$ are alternate interior angles. If lines ℓ and m are parallel, then these pairs of angles are congruent.

ángulos alternos internos En la figura anterior, la transversal t interseca las rectas ℓ y m. $\angle 3$ y $\angle 5$, $\angle 4$ y $\angle 6$ son ángulos alternos internos. Si las rectas ℓ y m son paralelas, entonces estos ángulos son pares de ángulos congruentes.

altitude (p. 314) A line segment perpendicular to the base of a figure with endpoints on the base and the vertex opposite the base.

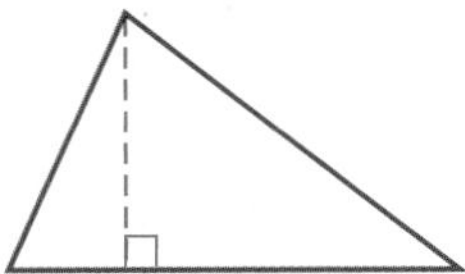

altura Segmento de recta perpendicular a la base de una figura y con extremos en la base y el vértice opuesto a la base.

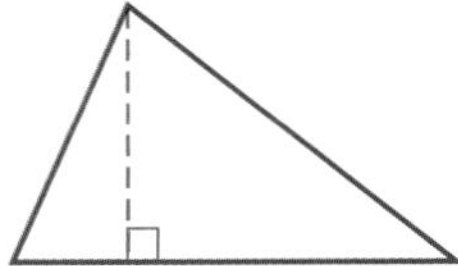

angle of rotation (p. 287) The degree measure of the angle through which a figure is rotated.

ángulo de rotación La medida en grados del ángulo a través del cual se rota una figura.

arithmetic sequence (p. 512) A sequence in which the difference between any two consecutive terms is the same.

sucesión aritmética Sucesión en la cual la diferencia entre dos términos consecutivos es constante.

bar notation (p. 63) In repeating decimals, the line or bar placed over the digits that repeat. Another way to write 2.6363636… is $2.\overline{63}$.

notación de barras En decimales periódicos, la línea o barra que se coloca sobre los dígitos que se repiten. Otra forma de escribir 2.6363636… es $2.\overline{63}$.

base (p. 98) In a power, the number used as a factor. In 10^3, the base is 10. That is, $10^3 = 10 \times 10 \times 10$.

base Número que se usa como factor en un potencia. En 10^3, la base es 10. Es decir, $10^3 = 10 \times 10 \times 10$.

base (p. 216) In a percent proportion, the number to which the percentage is compared.

base En una proporción porcentual, el número con que se compara el porcentaje.

base (p. 314) The base of a parallelogram or a triangle is any side of the figure. The bases of a trapezoid are the parallel sides.

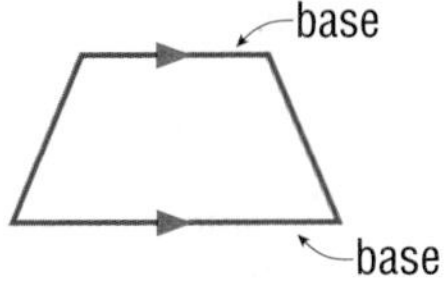

base La base de un paralelogramo o de un triángulo es cualquier lado de la figura. Las bases de un trapecio son sus lados paralelos.

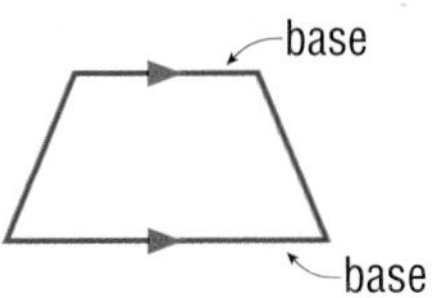

Glossary/Glosario

base (p. 331) The bases of a prism are the two parallel congruent faces.

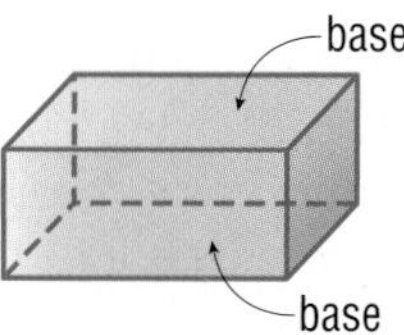

base Las bases de un prisma son las dos caras congruentes paralelas.

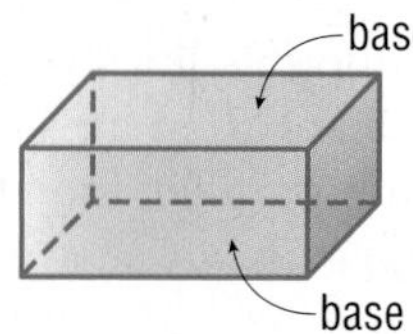

base two numbers (p. 102) Numbers that use only the digits 0 and 1.

números de base dos Números que usan sólo los dígitos 0 y 1.

best-fit line (p. 540) A line that is very close to most of the data points in a scatter plot.

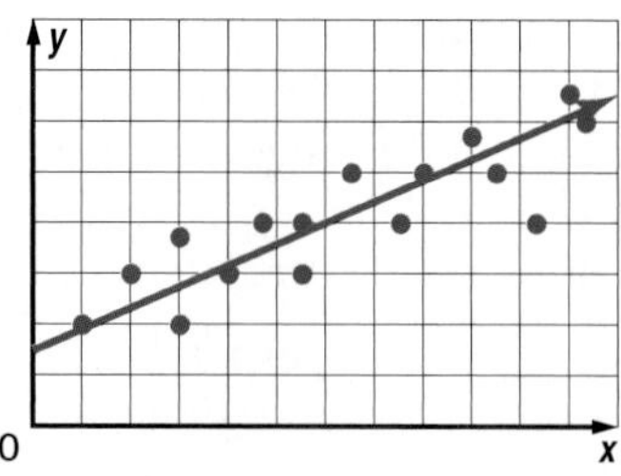

recta de óptimo ajuste Recta que mejor aproxima a los puntos de los datos de una gráfica de dispersión.

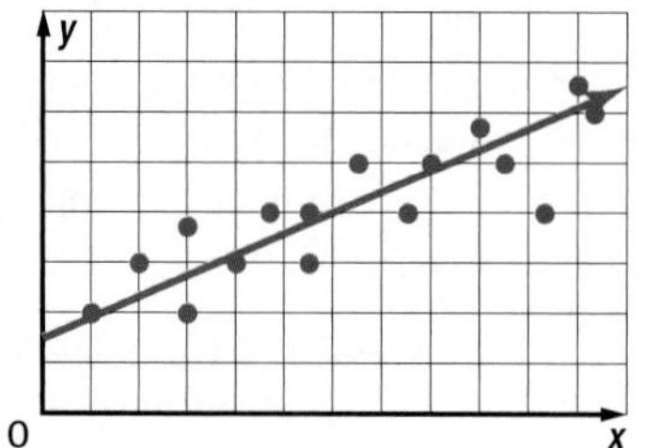

biased sample (p. 407) A sample drawn in such a way that one or more parts of the population are favored over others.

muestra sesgada Muestra en que se favorece una o más partes de una población.

binary numbers (p. 102) Numbers that use only the digits 0 and 1.

números binarios Números que usan sólo los dígitos 0 y 1.

binomial (p. 592) A polynomial with two terms.

binomio Polinomio con dos términos.

boundary (p. 548) A line that separates the solutions from the points that are not solutions in the graph of a linear inequality.

frontera Recta que separa las soluciones de los puntos que no son soluciones en la gráfica de una desigualdad lineal.

box-and-whisker plot (p. 446) A diagram that summarizes data using the median, the upper and lower quartiles, and the extreme values. A box is drawn around the quartile values and whiskers extend from each quartile to the extreme data points.

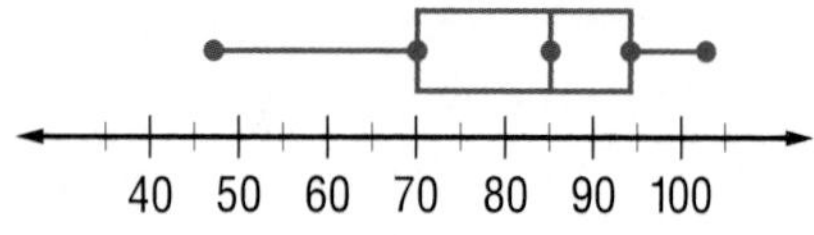

diagrama de caja y patillas Diagrama que resume información usando la mediana, los cuartiles superior e inferior y los valores extremos. Se dibuja una caja alrededor de los cuartiles y se trazan patillas que los unan a los valores extremos respectivos.

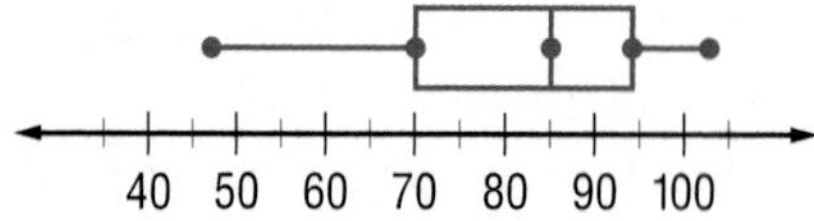

center (p. 319) The given point from which all points on a circle are the same distance.

centro Un punto dado del cual equidistan todos los puntos de un círculo.

center of rotation (p. 300) The fixed point a rotation of a figure turns or spins around.

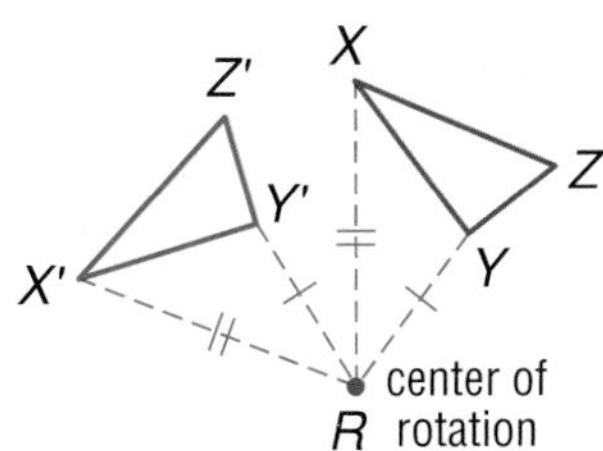

central angle (p. 323) An angle that intersects a circle in two points and has its vertex at the center of the circle.

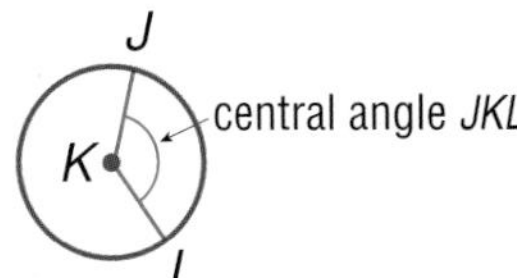

chord (p. 323) A line segment joining two points on a circle.

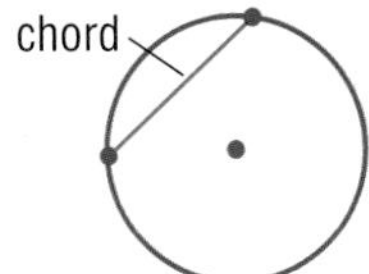

circle (p. 319) The set of all points in a plane that are the same distance from a given point called the center.

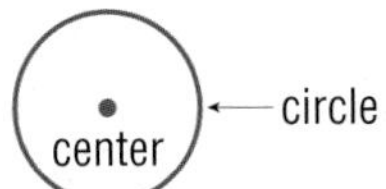

circle graph (p. 426) A type of statistical graph used to compare parts of a whole. The entire circle represents the whole.

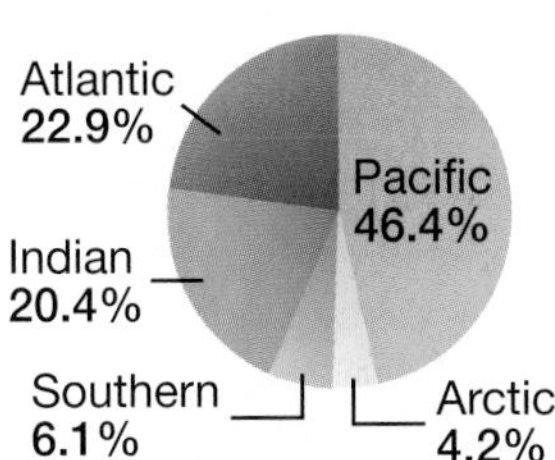

circumference (p. 319) The distance around a circle.

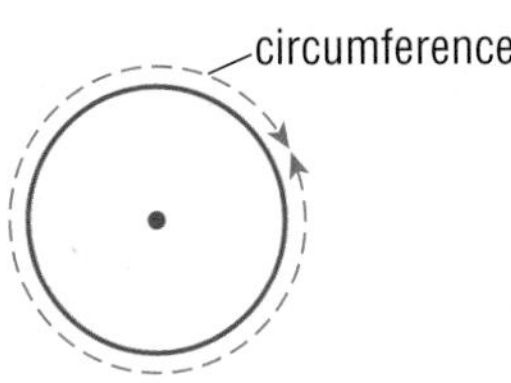

centro de rotación El punto fijo alrededor del cual se lleva a cabo la rotación de un figura.

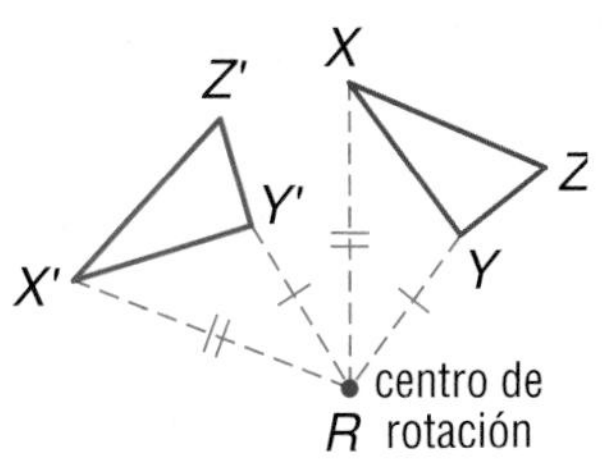

ángulo central Ángulo que interseca un círculo en dos puntos y que tiene su vértice en el centro del círculo.

cuerda Segmento de recta que une dos puntos en un círculo.

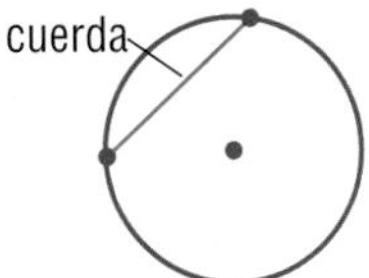

círculo Conjunto de todos los puntos en un plano que equidistan de un punto dado llamado centro.

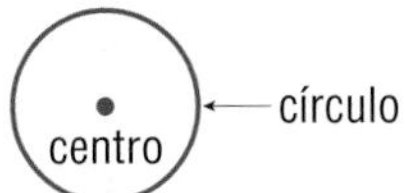

gráfica circular Tipo de gráfica estadística que se usa para comparar las partes de un todo. El círculo completo representa el todo.

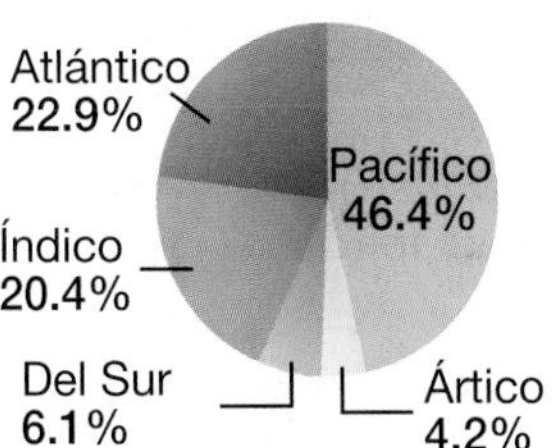

circunferencia La distancia alrededor de un círculo.

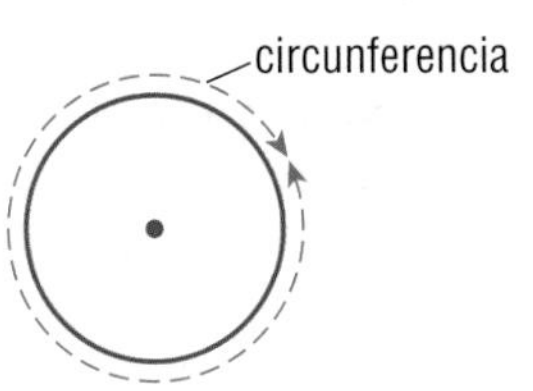

Closure Property (p. 38) A set of numbers is closed under an operation when that operation is performed on any two numbers from that set and the result is always a number in that set of numbers.

coefficient (p. 470) The numerical factor of a term that contains a variable.

column (p. 454) In a matrix, numbers stacked on top of each other in a vertical arrangement form a column.

combination (p. 388) An arrangement or listing in which order is not important.

commission (p. 234) A fee paid to a salesperson based on a percent of sales.

common difference (p. 512) The difference between any two consecutive terms in an arithmetic sequence.

common ratio (p. 513) The quotient between any two consecutive terms in a geometric sequence.

compatible numbers (p. 228) Two numbers that are easy to add, subtract, multiply, or divide mentally.

complementary angles (p. 256) Two angles are complementary if the sum of their measures is 90°.

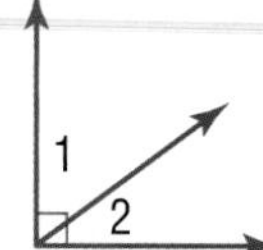

∠1 and ∠2 are complementary angles.

complementary events (p. 375) The events of one outcome happening and that outcome not happening are complementary events. The sum of the probabilities of complementary events is 1.

complex figure (p. 326) A figure that is made up of two or more shapes.

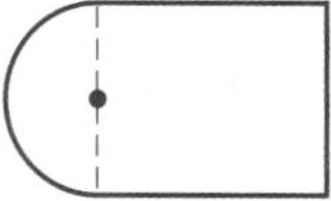

complex solid (p. 337) An object made up of more than one type of solid.

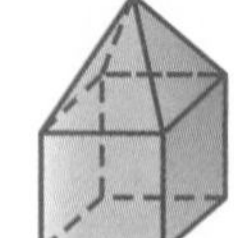

compound event (p. 396) An event that consists of two or more simple events.

compound interest (p. 245) Interest that is paid on the initial principal and on interest earned in the past.

propiedad de clausura Un conjunto de números está cerrado bajo una operación cuando esa operación se realiza en cualquier par de números de ese conjunto y el resultado es siempre un número en el conjunto de números.

coeficiente Factor numérico de un término que contiene una variable.

columna En una matriz, los números colocados uno encima de otro en un arreglo vertical forman una columna.

combinación Arreglo o lista de objetos en que el orden no es importante.

comisión Cantidad que se le paga a un vendedor y la cual se basa en un porcentaje de las ventas.

diferencia común La diferencia entre cualquier par de términos consecutivos en una sucesión aritmética.

razón común El cociente entre cualquier par de términos consecutivos en una sucesión geométrica.

números compatibles Dos números que son fáciles de sumar, restar, multiplicar o dividir mentalmente.

ángulos complementarios Dos ángulos son complementarios si la suma de sus medidas es 90°.

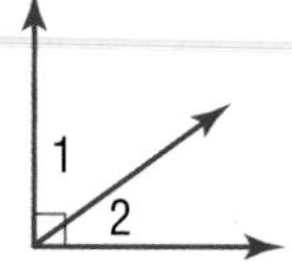

∠1 y ∠2 son complementarios.

eventos complementarios Se dice de los eventos de un resultado que ocurren y el resultado que no ocurre. La suma de las probabilidades de eventos complementarios es 1.

figura compleja Figura compuesta de dos o más formas.

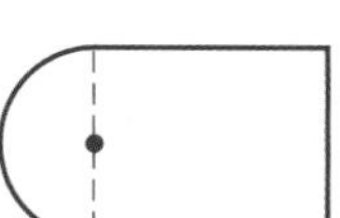

sólido complejo Cuerpo compuesto de más de un tipo de sólido.

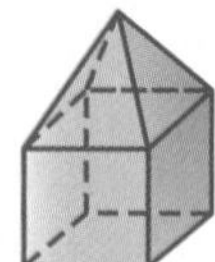

evento compuesto Evento que consta de dos o más eventos simples.

interés compuesto Interés que se paga por el capital inicial y en el interés ganado en el pasado.

cone (p. 343) A three-dimensional figure with one circular base. A curved surface connects the base and the vertex.

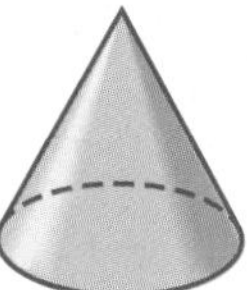

congruent (p. 179) Having the same measure.

congruent polygons (p. 279) Polygons that have the same size and shape.

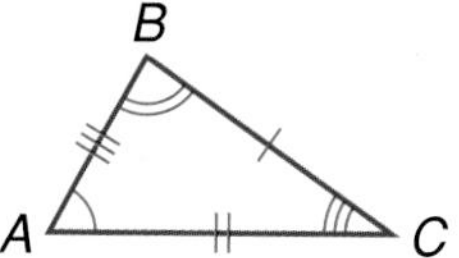

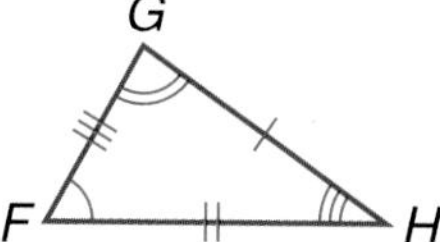

conjecture (p. 7) An educated guess.

constant (p. 470) A term without a variable.

convenience sample (p. 407) A sample which includes members of the population that are easily accessed.

converse (p. 134) The converse of a theorem is formed when the parts of the theorem are reversed. The converse of the Pythagorean Theorem can be used to test whether a triangle is a right triangle. If the sides of the triangle have lengths a, b, and c, such that $c^2 = a^2 + b^2$, then the triangle is a right triangle.

coordinate (p. 18) A number associated with a point on the number line.

coordinate plane (p. 142) A plane in which a horizontal number line and a vertical number line intersect at their zero points.

corresponding angles (p. 258) Angles that have the same position on two different parallel lines cut by a transversal.

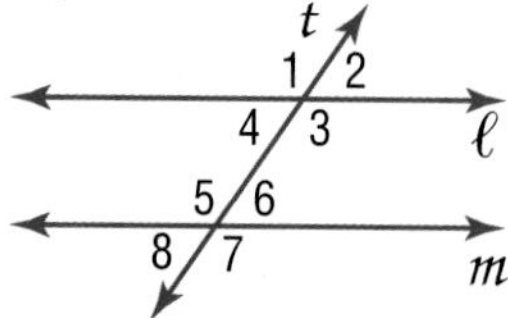

$\angle 1$ and $\angle 5$, $\angle 2$ and $\angle 6$, $\angle 3$ and $\angle 7$, $\angle 4$ and $\angle 8$ are corresponding angles.

cono Figura tridimensional con una base circular. Una superficie curva conecta la base con el vértice.

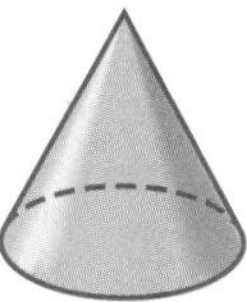

congruente Que tienen la misma medida.

polígonos congruentes Polígonos que tienen la misma medida y la misma forma.

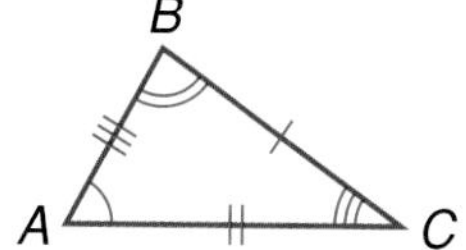

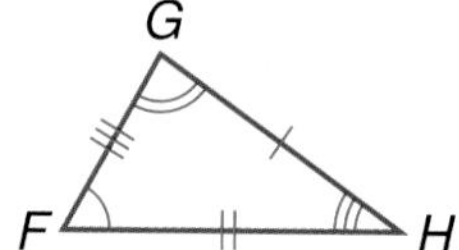

conjetura Suposición informada.

constante Término sin variables.

muestra de conveniencia Muestra que incluye miembros de una población fácilmente accesibles.

recíproco El recíproco de un teorema se forma cuando se invierten las partes del teorema. El recíproco del teorema de Pitágoras puede usarse para averiguar si un triángulo es un triángulo rectángulo. Si las longitudes de los lados de un triángulo son a, b, y c, tales que $c^2 = a^2 + b^2$, entonces el triángulo es un triángulo rectángulo.

coordenada Número asociado con un punto en la recta numérica.

plano de coordenadas Plano en que una recta numérica horizontal y una recta numérica vertical se intersecan en sus puntos cero.

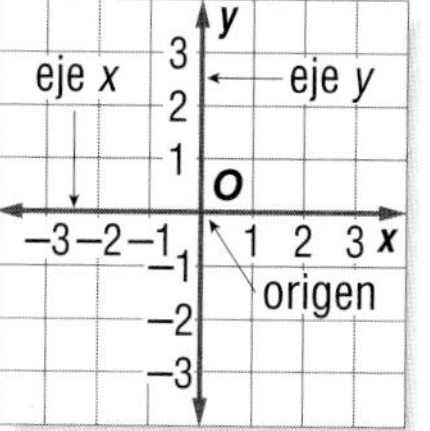

ángulos correspondientes Ángulos que ocupan la misma posición en dos rectas paralelas distintas cortadas por una transversal.

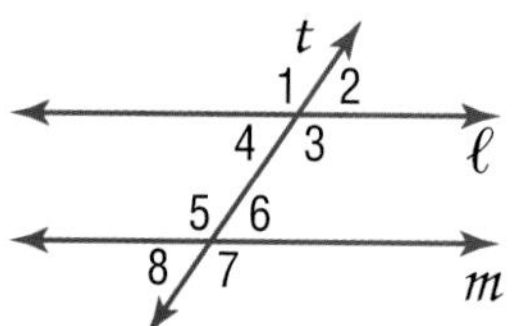

$\angle 1$ y $\angle 5$, $\angle 2$ y $\angle 6$, $\angle 3$ y $\angle 7$, $\angle 4$ y $\angle 8$ son ángulos correspondientes.

corresponding parts (p. 178) Parts of congruent or similar figures that match.

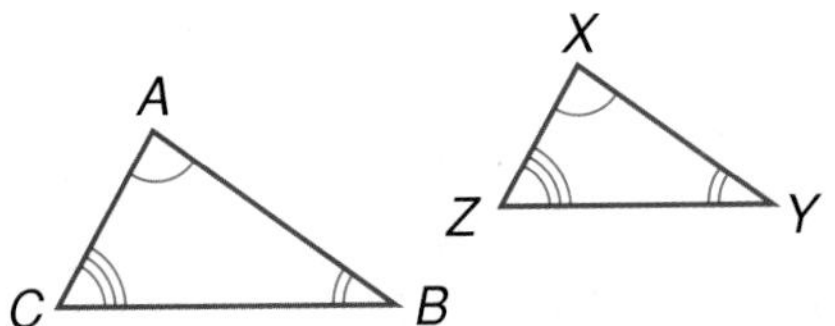

$\overline{AB}$ and $\overline{XY}$ are corresponding sides.
$\angle C$ and $\angle Z$ are corresponding angles.

cosine (p. 681) If A is an acute angle of a right triangle, $\cos A = \frac{\text{measure of the leg adjacent to } \angle A}{\text{measure of the hypotenuse}}$.

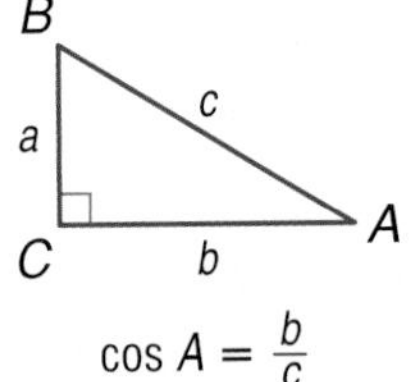

$\cos A = \frac{b}{c}$

counterexample (p. 13) A statement or example that shows a conjecture is false.

cross products (p. 170) The products of the terms on the diagonals when two ratios are compared. If the cross products are equal, then the ratios form a proportion. In the proportion $\frac{2}{3} = \frac{8}{12}$, the cross products are 2×12 and 3×8.

cubic function (p. 568) A function in which the greatest power is 3.

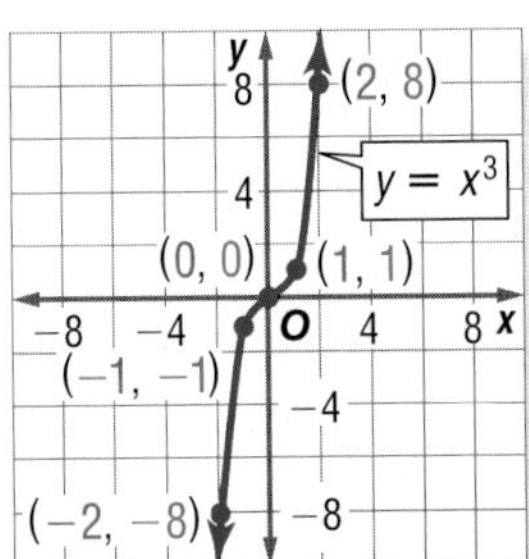

cylinder (p. 336) A solid whose bases are congruent, parallel circles, connected with a curved side.

partes correspondientes Partes de figuras congruentes o semejantes que coinciden.

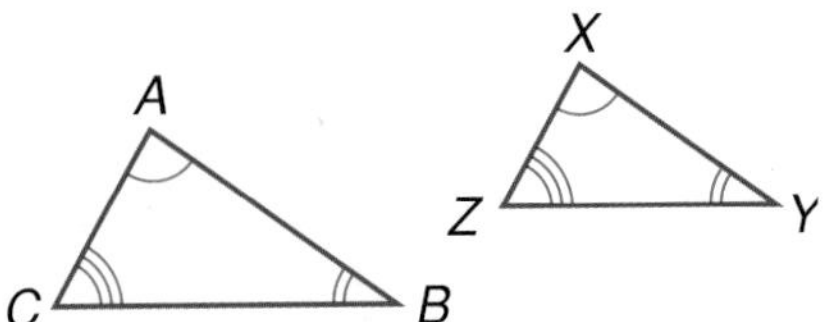

$\overline{AB}$ y $\overline{XY}$ son lados correspondientes.
$\angle C$ y $\angle Z$ son ángulos correspondientes.

cosino Si A es un ángulo agudo de un triángulo rectángulo, $\cos A = \frac{\text{medida del cateto adyacente a } \angle A}{\text{medida de la hipotenusa}}$.

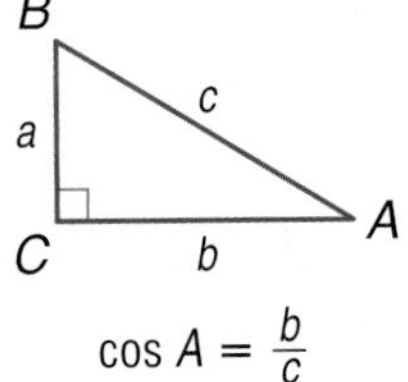

$\cos A = \frac{b}{c}$

contraejemplo Ejemplo o enunciado que demuestra que una conjetura es falsa.

productos cruzados Productos que resultan de la comparación de los términos de las diagonales de dos razones. Si los productos son iguales, las razones forman una proporción. En la proporción $\frac{2}{3} = \frac{8}{12}$, los productos cruzados son 2×12 y 3×8.

función cúbica Función cuya potencia mayor es 3.

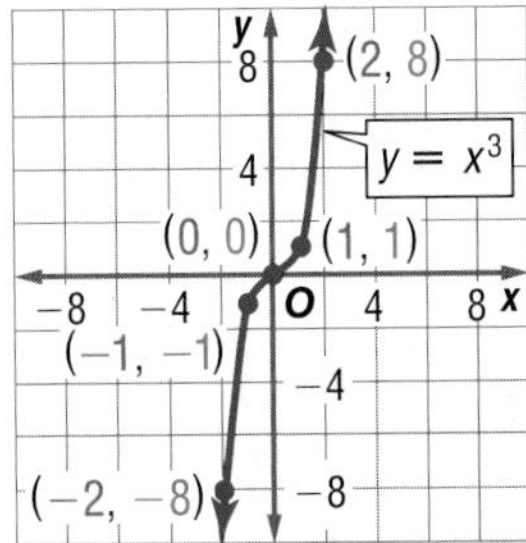

cilindro Sólido cuyas bases son círculos congruentes y paralelos, conectados por un lado curvo.

D

defining a variable (p. 39) Choosing a variable and a quantity for the variable to represent in an expression or equation.

definir una variable El elegir una variable y una cantidad que esté representada por la variable en una expresión o en una ecuación.

dependent events (p. 397) Two or more events in which the outcome of one event does affect the outcome of the other event or events.

dependent variable (p. 518) The variable for the output of a function.

diagonal (p. 334) A segment that joins two vertices of a prism that have no faces in common.

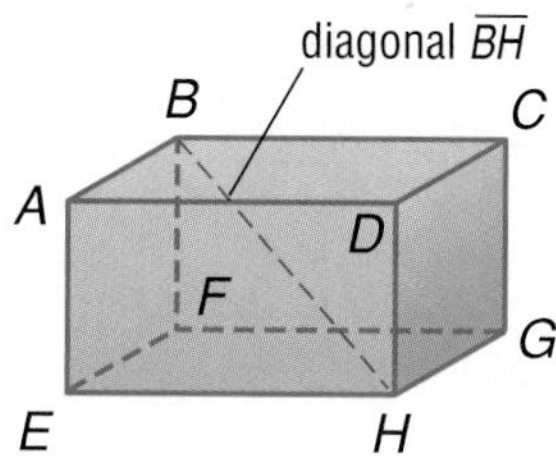

diameter (p. 319) The distance across a circle through its center.

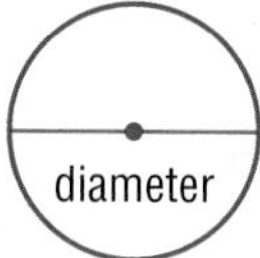

dilation (p. 194) A transformation that results from the reduction or enlargement of an image.

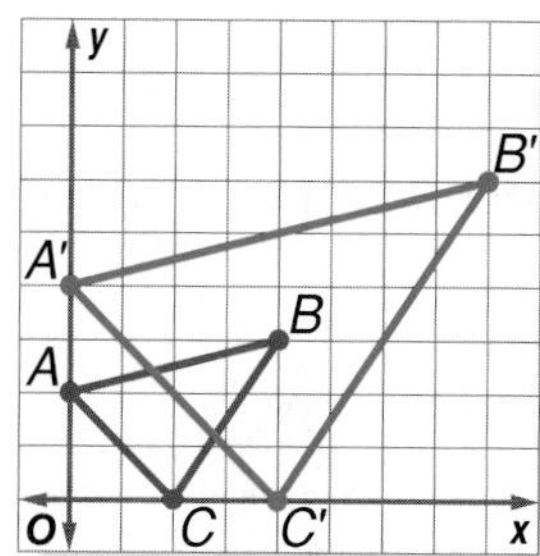

dimensional analysis (p. 73) The process of including units of measurement when you compute.

dimensions (p. 454) A description of a matrix by the number of rows and columns it has. The number of rows is always stated first. For example, a matrix with 3 rows and 5 columns has dimensions 3 by 5.

discount (p. 238) The amount by which a regular price is reduced.

Division Property of Equality (p. 50) If you divide each side of an equation by the same nonzero number, the two sides remain equal.

domain (p. 518) The set of input values in a function.

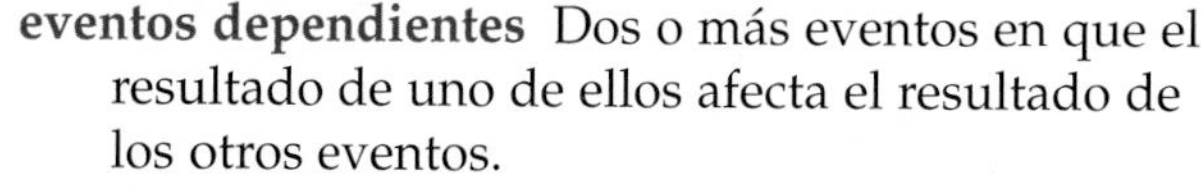

eventos dependientes Dos o más eventos en que el resultado de uno de ellos afecta el resultado de los otros eventos.

variable dependiente La variable para el valor de salida de una función.

diagonal Segmento que une dos vértices de un prisma, los cuales no tienen caras en común.

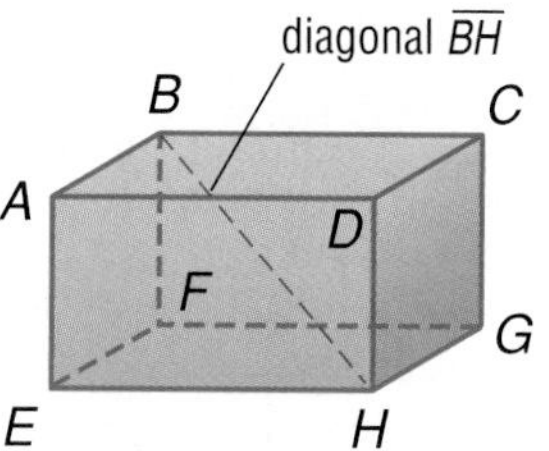

diámetro La distancia a través de un círculo pasando por el centro.

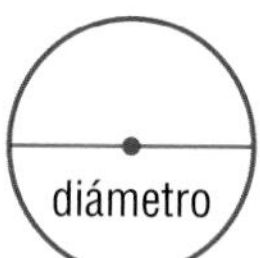

dilatación Transformación que resulta de la reducción o ampliación de una imagen.

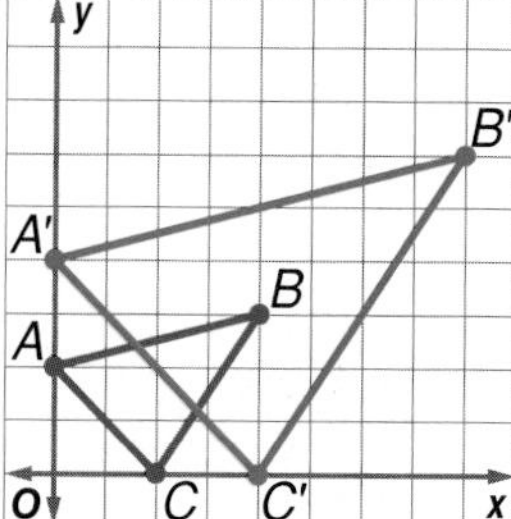

análisis dimensional Proceso que incorpora las unidades de medida al hacer cálculos.

dimensiones Descripción de una matriz según el número de filas y columnas que tiene. El número de filas siempre se escribe primero. Por ejemplo, las dimensiones de una matriz con 3 filas y 5 columnas es 3 por 5.

descuento La cantidad de reducción del precio normal.

propiedad de división de la igualdad Si cada lado de una ecuación se divide entre el mismo número no nulo, los dos lados permanecen iguales.

dominio Conjunto de valores de entrada de una función.

edge (p. 331) The intersection of two faces of a three-dimensional figure.

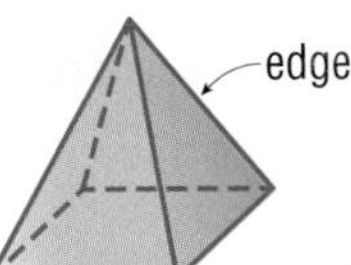

element (p. 454) Each number in a matrix is called an element.

equation (p. 13) A mathematical sentence that contains an equals sign, =.

equiangular (p. 278) A polygon in which all angles are congruent.

equilateral (p. 278) A polygon in which all sides are congruent.

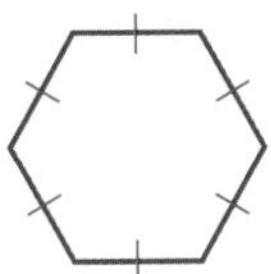

equilateral triangle (p. 263) A triangle that has three congruent sides.

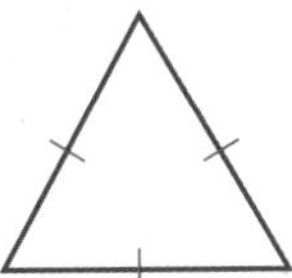

equivalent expressions (p. 469) Expressions that have the same value regardless of the value(s) of the variable(s).

evaluate (p. 11) To find the value of an expression by replacing the variables with numerals.

experimental probability (p. 400) An estimated probability based on the relative frequency of positive outcomes occurring during an experiment.

exponent (p. 98) In a power, the number of times the base is used as a factor. In 10^3, the exponent is 3.

arista La intersección de dos caras de una figura tridimensional.

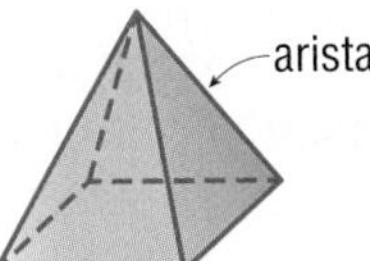

elemento Cada número en una matriz se llama un elemento.

ecuación Un enunciado matemático que contiene un signo de igualdad (=).

equiangular Polígono en el cual todos los ángulos son congruentes.

equilátero Polígono en el cual todos los lados son congruentes.

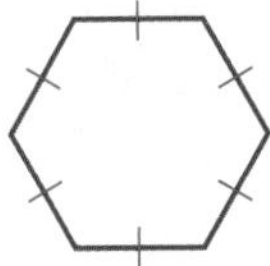

triángulo equilátero Triángulo con tres lados congruentes.

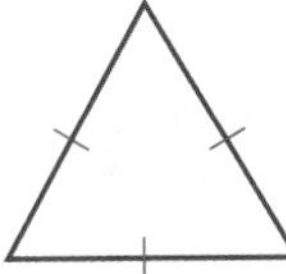

expresiones equivalentes Expresiones que poseen el mismo valor, sin importar los valores de la(s) variable(s).

evaluar Calcular el valor de una expresión sustituyendo las variables por números.

probabilidad experimental Probabilidad de un evento que se estima basándose en la frecuencia relativa de los resultados favorables al evento en cuestión, que ocurren durante un experimento.

exponente En una potencia, el número de veces que la base se usa como factor. En 10^3, el exponente es 3.

face (p. 331) Any surface that forms a side or a base of a prism.

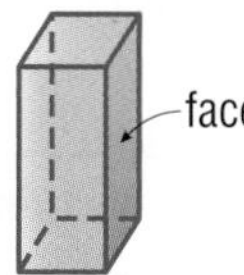

factorial (p. 385) The expression $n!$ is the product of all counting numbers beginning with n and counting backward to 1.

frustum (p. 355) The part of a solid that remains after a top portion of the solid has been cut off by a plane parallel to the base.

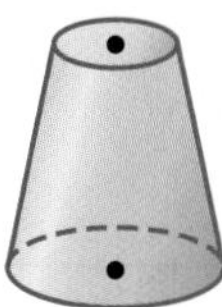

function (p. 517) A relation in which each element of the input is paired with exactly one element of the output according to a specified rule.

function table (p. 518) A table organizing the input, rule, and output of a function.

Fundamental Counting Principle (p. 381) Uses multiplication of the number of ways each event in an experiment can occur to find the number of possible outcomes in a sample space.

cara Cualquier superficie que forma un lado o una base de un prisma.

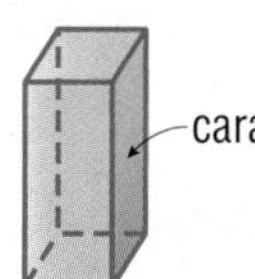

factorial La expresión $n!$ es el producto de todos los números naturales, comenzando con n y contando al revés hasta 1.

cono truncado La parte de un sólido que queda después de que un plano paralelo a la base le corta la parte superior al sólido.

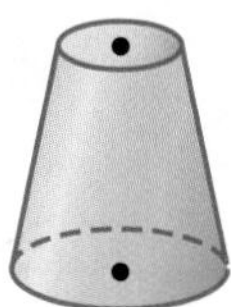

función Relación en que cada elemento de entrada se relaciona con un único elemento de salida, según una regla específica.

tabla de funciones Tabla que organiza las entradas, la regla y las salidas de una función.

principio fundamental de contar Método que usa la multiplicación del número de maneras en que cada evento puede ocurrir en un experimento, para calcular el número de resultados posibles en un espacio muestral.

geometric sequence (p. 513) A sequence in which the quotient between any two consecutive terms is the same.

greatest possible error (p. 362) One-half the precision unit of a measurement.

sucesión geométrica Sucesión en la cual el cociente entre cualquier par de términos consecutivos es la misma.

máximo error posible Una mitad de la precisión de la unidad de medida.

half plane (p. 548) The region that contains the solutions in the graph of a linear inequality.

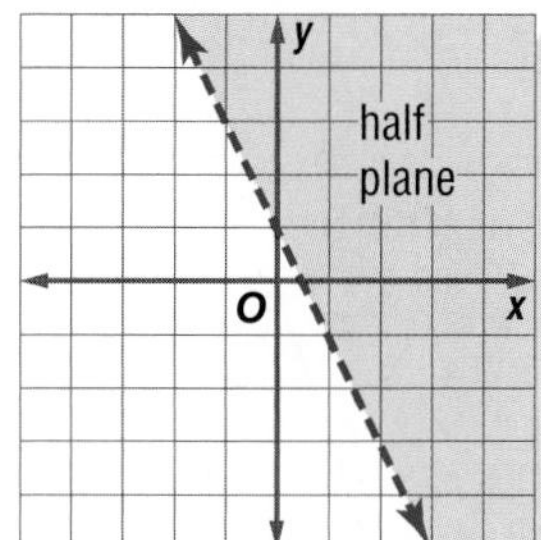

semiplano Región que contiene las soluciones en la gráfica de una desigualdad lineal.

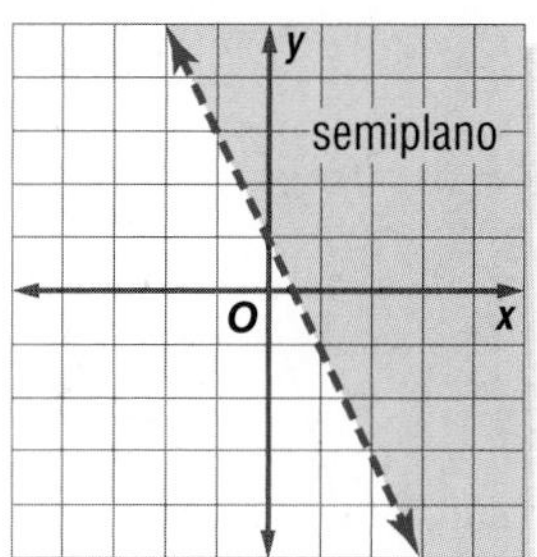

Glossary/Glosario

histogram (p. 420) A special kind of bar graph that displays the frequency of data that has been organized into equal intervals. The intervals cover all possible values of data, therefore, there are no spaces between the bars of the graph.

histograma Tipo especial de gráfica de barras que exhibe la frecuencia de los datos que han sido organizados en intervalos iguales. Los intervalos cubren todos los valores posibles de datos, sin dejar espacios entre las barras de la gráfica.

hypotenuse (p. 132) The side opposite the right angle in a right triangle.

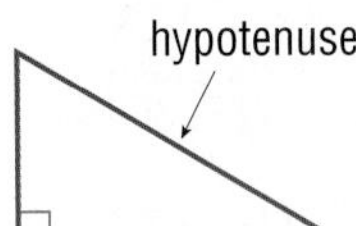

hipotenusa El lado opuesto al ángulo recto de un triángulo rectángulo.

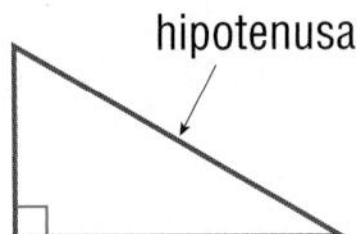

I

independent events (p. 396) Two or more events in which the outcome of one event does not affect the outcome of the other event(s).

eventos independientes Dos o más eventos en los cuales el resultado de uno de ellos no afecta el resultado de los otros eventos.

independent variable (p. 518) The variable for the input of a function.

variable independiente La variable correspondiente al valor de entrada de un función.

indirect measurement (p. 188) A technique using proportions to find a measurement.

medición indirecta Técnica que usa proporciones para calcular una medida.

inequality (p. 18) A mathematical sentence that contains $<$, $>$, $\neq$, $\leq$, or $\geq$.

desigualdad Enunciado matemático que contiene $<$, $>$, $\neq$, $\leq$ o $\geq$.

integers (p. 17) The set of whole numbers and their opposites.
$\ldots, -3, -2, -1, 0, 1, 2, 3, \ldots$

enteros El conjunto de los números enteros y sus opuestos.
$\ldots, -3, -2, -1, 0, 1, 2, 3, \ldots$

interest (p. 241) The amount of money paid or earned for the use of money.

interés Cantidad que se cobra o se paga por el uso del dinero.

interquartile range (p. 442) The range of the middle half of the data. The difference between the upper quartile and the lower quartile.

amplitud intercuartílica El rango de la mitad central de un conjunto de datos. La diferencia entre el cuartil superior y el cuartil inferior.

inverse operations (p. 46) Pairs of operations that undo each other. Addition and subtraction are inverse operations. Multiplication and division are inverse operations.

operaciones inversas Pares de operaciones que se anulan mutuamente. La adición y la sustracción son operaciones inversas. La multiplicación y la división son operaciones inversas.

irrational number (p. 125) A number that cannot be expressed as $\frac{a}{b}$, where a and b are integers and $b \neq 0$.

números irracionales Un número que no se puede expresar como $\frac{a}{b}$, donde a y b son enteros y $b \neq 0$.

isosceles triangle (p. 263) A triangle that has at least two congruent sides.

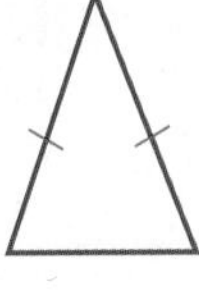

triángulo isósceles Triángulo que tiene por lo menos dos lados congruentes.

lateral area (p. 352) The sum of the areas of the lateral faces of a pyramid.

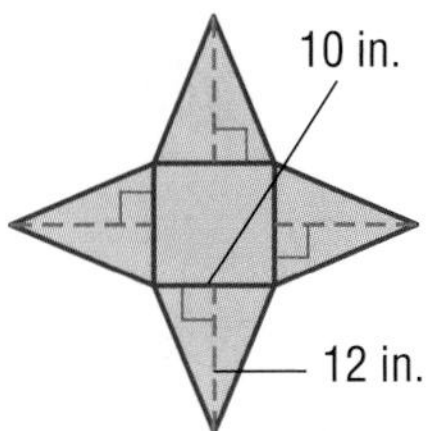

lateral area = $4\left(\frac{1}{2} \times 10 \times 12\right) = 240$ square inches

lateral face (p. 352) A triangular side of a pyramid.

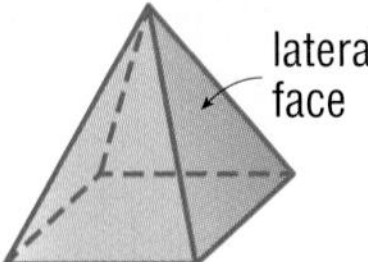

legs (p. 132) The two sides of a right triangle that form the right angle.

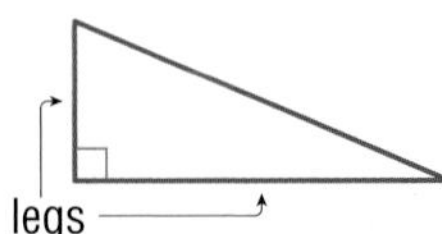

like fractions (p. 82) Fractions that have the same denominator.

like terms (p. 470) Terms that contain the same variable(s).

linear function (p. 523) A function in which the graph of the solutions forms a line.

line of reflection (p. 290) The line a figure is flipped over in a reflection.

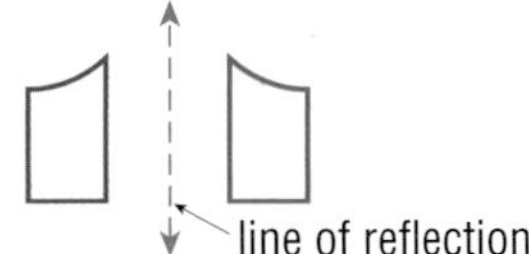

line of symmetry (p. 286) A line that divides a figure into two halves that are reflections of each other.

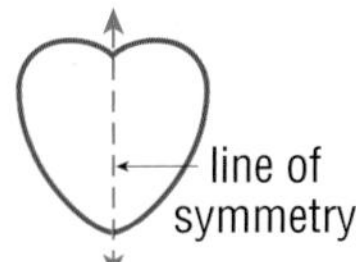

line symmetry (p. 286) Figures that match exactly when folded in half have line symmetry.

lower quartile (p. 442) The median of the lower half of a set of data, represented by LQ.

área lateral La suma de las áreas de las caras laterales de una pirámide.

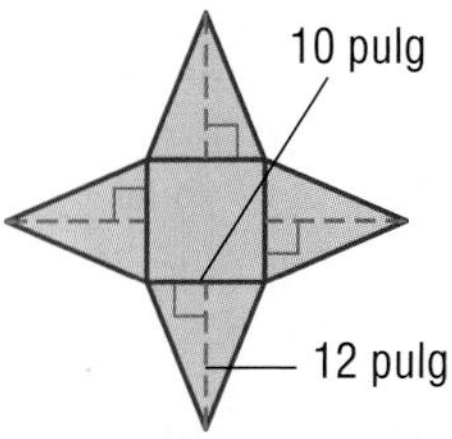

área lateral = $4\left(\frac{1}{2} \times 10 \times 12\right) = 240$ pulgadas cuadradas

cara lateral Un lado triangular de una pirámide.

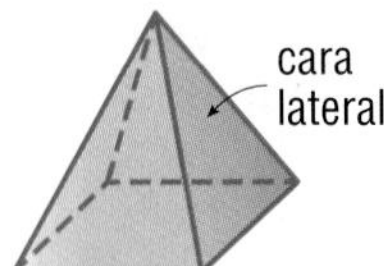

catetos Los dos lados de un triángulo rectángulo que forman el ángulo recto.

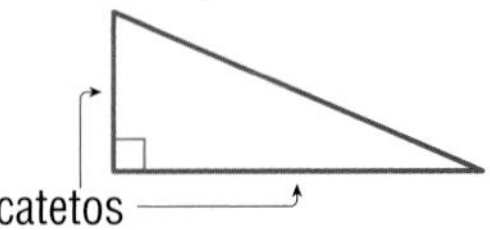

fracciones semejantes Fracciones que tienen el mismo denominador.

términos semejantes Términos que contienen la(s) misma(s) variable(s).

función lineal Función en la cual la gráfica de las soluciones forma un recta.

línea de reflexión Línea a través de la cual se le da vuelta a una figura en una reflexión.

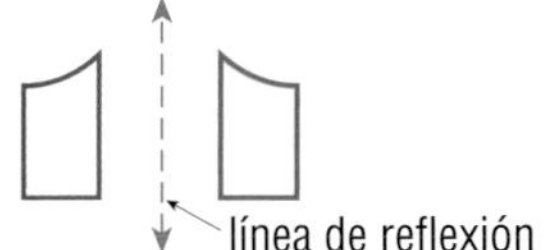

eje de simetría Recta que divide una figura en dos mitades que son reflexiones una de la otra.

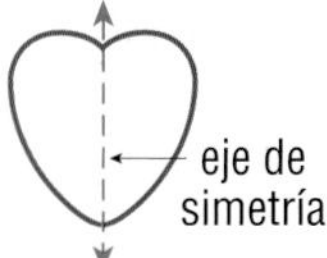

simetría lineal Exhiben simetría lineal las figuras que coinciden exactamente al doblarse una sobre otra.

cuartil inferior La mediana de la mitad inferior de un conjunto de datos, la cual se denota por CI.

M

markup (p. 238) The amount the price of an item is increased above the price the store paid for the item.

matrix (p. 454) A rectangular arrangement of numerical data in rows and columns.

$$\begin{bmatrix} -4 & 2 & -1 \\ 3 & -1 & -7 \end{bmatrix}$$

mean (p. 435) The sum of the numbers in a set of data divided by the number of items in the data set.

measures of central tendency (p. 435) Numbers or pieces of data that can represent the whole set of data.

measures of variation (p. 442) Numbers used to describe the distribution or spread of a set of data.

median (p. 435) The middle number in a set of data when the data are arranged in numerical order. If the data has an even number, the median is the mean of the two middle numbers.

mode (p. 435) The number(s) or item(s) that appear most often in a set of data.

monomial (p. 570) A number, a variable, or a product of a number and one or more variables.

Multiplication Property of Equality (p. 51) If you multiply each side of an equation by the same number, the two sides remain equal.

multiplicative inverse (p. 76) A number times its multiplicative inverse is equal to 1. The multiplicative inverse of $\frac{2}{3}$ is $\frac{3}{2}$.

mutually exclusive (p. 399) Two events that cannot happen at the same time.

margen de utilidad Cantidad de aumento en el precio de un artículo por encima del precio que paga la tienda por dicho artículo.

matriz Arreglo rectangular de datos numéricos en filas y columnas.

$$\begin{bmatrix} -4 & 2 & -1 \\ 3 & -1 & -7 \end{bmatrix}$$

media La suma de los números de un conjunto de datos dividida entre el número total de artículos.

medidas de tendencia central Números o fragmentos de datos que pueden representar el conjunto total de datos.

medidas de variación Números que se usan para describir la distribución o separación de un conjunto de datos.

mediana El número central de un conjunto de datos, una vez que los datos han sido ordenados numéricamente. Si hay un número par de datos, la mediana es el promedio de los dos datos centrales.

moda El número(s) o artículo(s) que aparece con más frecuencia en un conjunto de datos.

monomio Un número, una variable o el producto de un número por una o más variables.

propiedad de multiplicación de la igualdad Si cada lado de una ecuación se multiplica por el mismo número, los lados permanecen iguales.

inverso multiplicativo Un número multiplicado por su inverso multiplicativo es igual a 1. El inverso multiplicativo de $\frac{2}{3}$ es $\frac{3}{2}$.

mutuamente exclusivo Dos eventos que no pueden ocurrir al mismo tiempo.

N

negative number (p. 17) A number that is less than zero.

net (p. 346) A two-dimensional pattern of a three-dimensional figure.

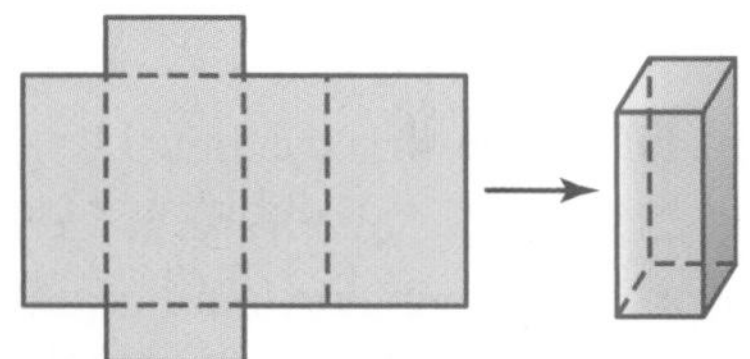

número negativo Número menor que cero.

red Patrón bidimensional de una figura tridimensional.

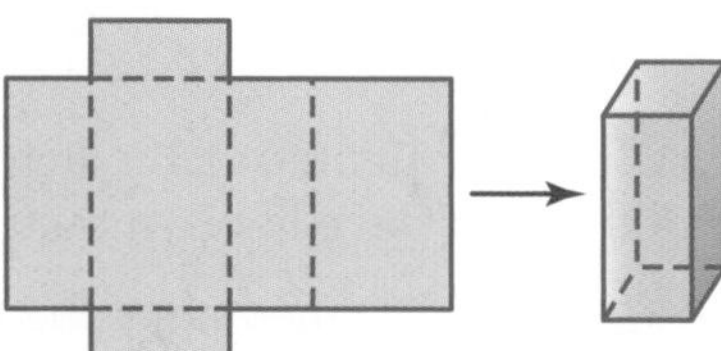

nonlinear function (p. 560) A function that does not have a constant rate of change. The graph of a nonlinear function is not a straight line.

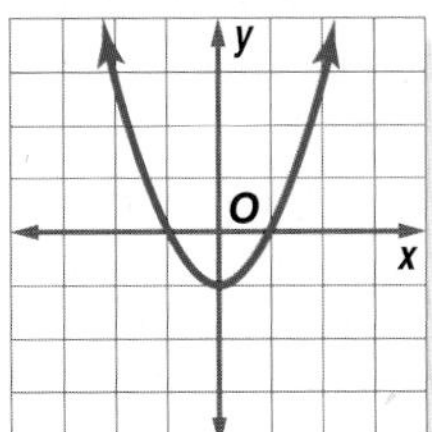

función no lineal Función que no tiene una tasa constante de cambio. La gráfica de una función no lineal no es una recta.

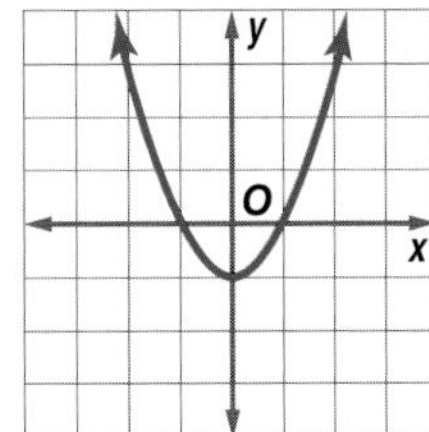

numerical expression (p. 11) A mathematical expression that has a combination of numbers and at least one operation. $4 + 2$ is a numerical expression.

expresión numérica Expresión matemática que tiene una combinación de números y por lo menos una operación. $4 + 2$ es una expresión numérica.

obtuse angle (p. 256) An angle that measures greater than 90° but less than 180°.

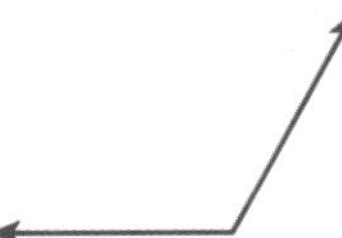

ángulo obtuso Ángulo que mide más de 90° pero menos de 180°.

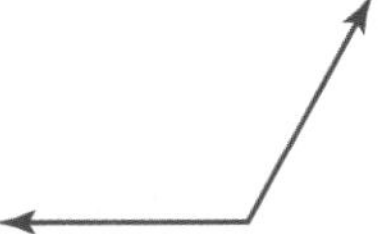

obtuse triangle (p. 263) A triangle having one obtuse angle.

triángulo obtuso Triángulo que tiene un ángulo obtuso.

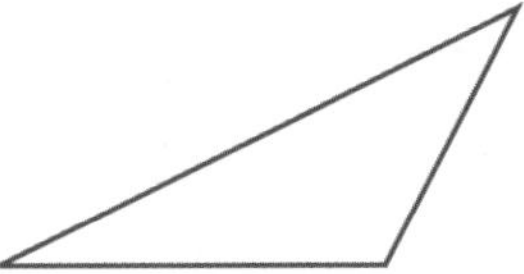

odds (p. 377) A ratio that compares the number of favorable outcomes to the number of unfavorable outcomes.

posibilidad Razón que compara el número de resultados favorables con el número de resultados no favorables.

open sentence (p. 13) An equation that contains a variable.

enunciado abierto Ecuación que contiene una variable.

opposite side (p. 192) In any right triangle, the side opposite an angle is the side that is not part of the angle.

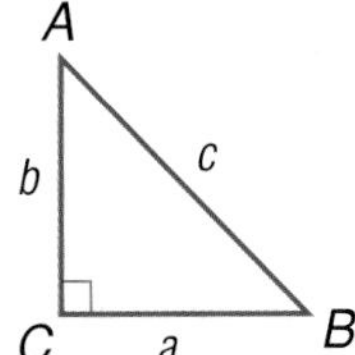

Side a is opposite $\angle A$.

lado opuesto En un triángulo rectángulo, el lado opuesto a un ángulo es el lado que no forma parte del ángulo.

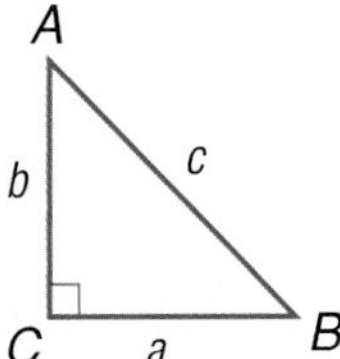

El lado a está opuesto al $\angle A$.

opposites (p. 25) Two numbers with the same absolute value but different signs. The sum of opposites is zero.

opuestos Dos números con el mismo valor absoluto, pero distintos signos. La suma de opuestos es cero.

order of operations (p. 11) The rules to follow when more than one operation is used in an expression.

1. Do all operations within grouping symbols first; start with the innermost grouping symbols.
2. Evaluate all powers before other operations.
3. Multiply and divide in order from left to right.
4. Add and subtract in order from left to right.

orden de las operaciones Reglas a seguir cuando se usa más de una operación en una expresión.

1. Primero ejecuta todas las operaciones dentro de los símbolos de agrupamiento.
2. Evalúa todas las potencias antes que las otras operaciones.
3. Multiplica y divide en orden de izquierda a derecha.
4. Suma y resta en orden de izquierda a derecha.

ordered pair (p. 142) A pair of numbers used to locate a point in the coordinate plane. The ordered pair is written in this form: (x-coordinate, y-coordinate).

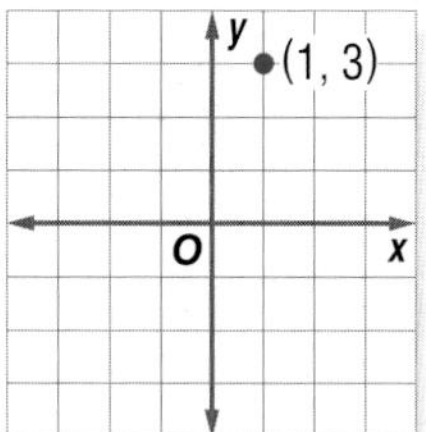

par ordenado Par de números que se utiliza para ubicar un punto en un plano de coordenadas. Se escribe de la siguiente forma: (coordenada x, coordenada y).

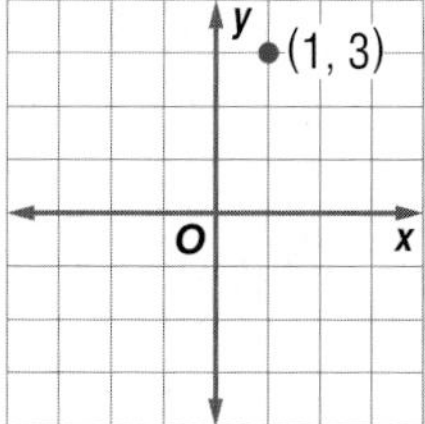

ordinate (p. 142) The second number of an ordered pair; the y-coordinate.

ordenada El segundo número de un par ordenado; la coordenada y.

origin (p. 142) The point of intersection of the x-axis and y-axis in a coordinate plane.

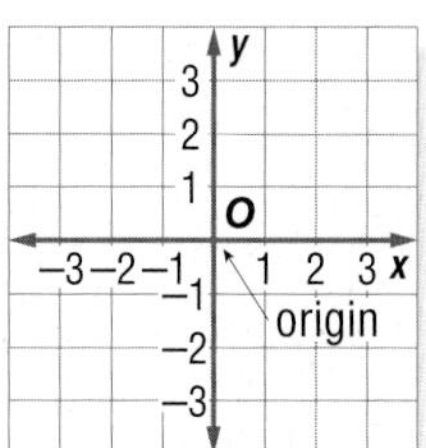

origen Punto en que el eje x y el eje y se intersecan en un plano de coordenadas.

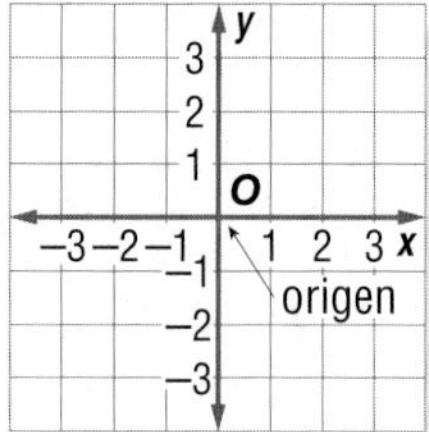

outcome (p. 374) One possible result of a probability event. For example, 4 is an outcome when a number cube is rolled.

resultado Uno de los resultados posibles de un evento probabilístico. Por ejemplo, 4 es un resultado posible cuando se lanza un dado.

outlier (p. 443) Data that are more than 1.5 times the interquartile range from the upper or lower quartiles.

valor atípico Datos que distan de los cuartiles respectivos más de 1.5 veces la amplitud intercuartílica.

P

parallel lines (p. 257) Lines in the same plane that never intersect or cross. The symbol || means parallel.

rectas paralelas Rectas que yacen en un mismo plano y que no se intersecan. El símbolo || significa paralela a.

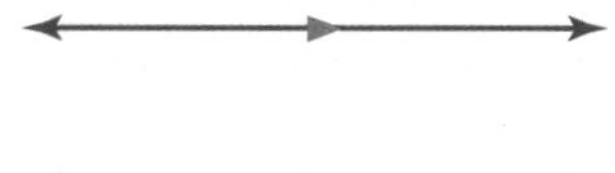

parallelogram (p. 273) A quadrilateral with both pairs of opposite sides parallel and congruent.

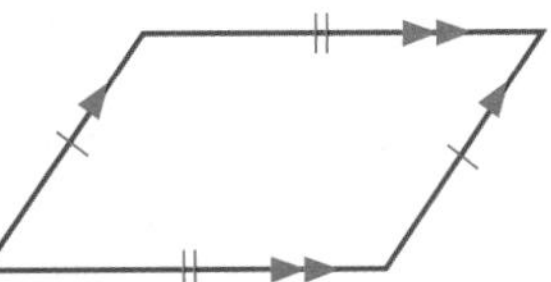

paralelogramo Cuadrilátero con ambos pares de lados opuestos paralelos y congruentes.

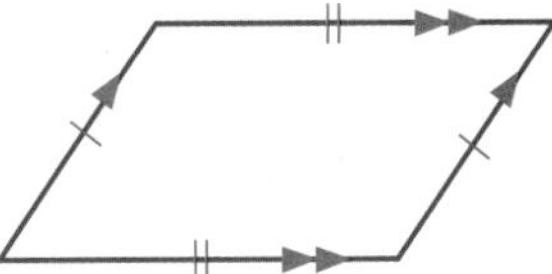

part (p. 216) The number that is being compared to the whole quantity in a percent proportion.

parte El número que se compara con la cantidad total en una proporción porcentual.

percent (p. 206) A ratio that compares a number to 100.

por ciento Razón que compara un número con 100.

percent equation (p. 232) An equivalent form of the percent proportion in which the percent is written as a decimal. Part = Percent · Base

ecuación porcentual Forma equivalente de proporción porcentual en la cual el por ciento se escribe como un decimal. Parte = Por ciento · Base

percent of change (p. 236) A ratio that compares the change in a quantity to the original amount.

porcentaje de cambio Razón que compara el cambio en una cantidad, con la cantidad original.

percent of decrease (p. 237) The percent of change when the new amount is less than the original.

porcentaje de disminución El porcentaje de cambio cuando la nueva cantidad es menos que la cantidad original.

percent of increase (p. 237) The percent of change when the new amount is greater than the original.

porcentaje de aumento El porcentaje de cambio cuando aumenta la nueva cantidad es mayor que la cantidad original.

percent proportion (p. 216) Compares part of a quantity to the whole quantity using a percent. $\frac{\text{part}}{\text{base}} = \frac{\text{percent}}{100}$

proporción porcentual Compara parte de una cantidad con la cantidad total mediante un por ciento. $\frac{\text{parte}}{\text{base}} = \frac{\text{por ciento}}{100}$.

perfect square (p. 116) A rational number whose square root is a whole number. 25 is a perfect square because its square root is 5.

cuadrados perfectos Número racional cuya raíz cuadrada es un número entero. 25 es un cuadrado perfecto porque su raíz cuadrada es 5.

permutation (p. 384) An arrangement or listing in which order is important.

permutación Arreglo o lista donde el orden es importante.

perpendicular bisector (p. 271) A line that passes through the midpoint of a segment and is perpendicular to the segment.

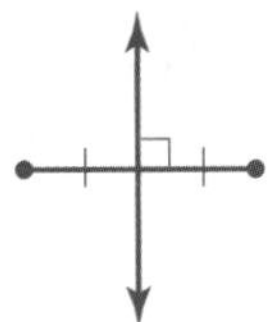

mediatriz Recta que pasa a través del punto medio de un segmento y que es perpendicular al segmento.

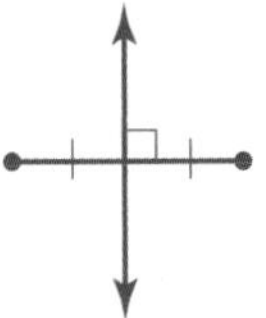

perpendicular lines (p. 257) Two lines that intersect to form right angles.

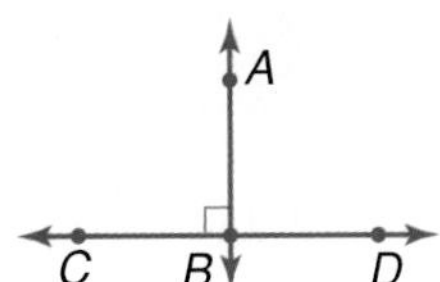

rectas perpendiculares Dos rectas que se intersecan formando ángulos rectos.

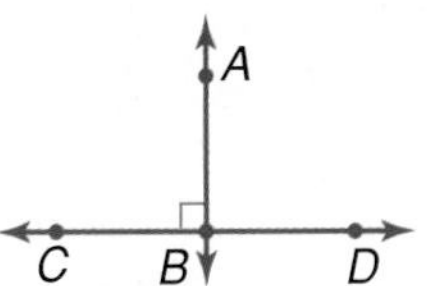

perspective (p. 330) A point of view.

perspectiva Un punto de vista.

Glossary/Glosario

pi (p. 319) The ratio of the circumference of a circle to its diameter. The Greek letter π represents this number. The value of pi is always 3.1415926… .

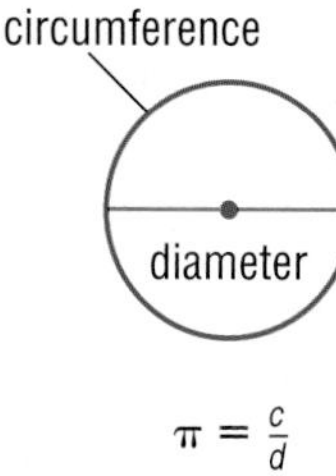

$$\pi = \frac{c}{d}$$

plane (p. 331) A two-dimensional flat surface that extends in all directions.

polygon (p. 178) A simple closed figure in a plane formed by three or more line segments.

polyhedron (p. 331) A solid with flat surfaces that are polygons.

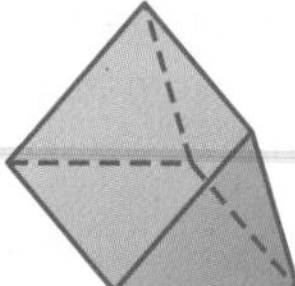

polynomial (p. 570) The sum or difference of one or more monomials.

population (p. 406) The entire group of items or individuals from which the samples under consideration are taken.

powers (p. 12 and p. 98) Numbers written using exponents. Powers represent repeated multiplication. The power 7^3 is read *seven to the third power*, or *seven cubed*.

precision (p. 358) The precision of a measurement depends on the unit of measure. The smaller the unit, the more precise the measurement is.

principal (p. 241) The amount of money invested or borrowed.

principal square root (p. 117) A positive square root.

prism (p. 331) A polyhedron with two parallel, congruent faces called bases.

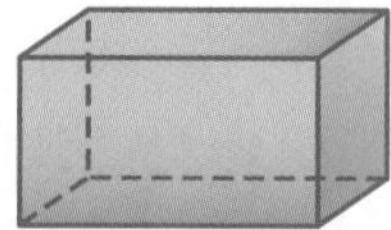

probability (p. 374) The chance that some event will happen. It is the ratio of the number of ways a certain event can occur to the number of possible outcomes.

pi Razón de la circunferencia de un círculo al diámetro del mismo. La letra griega π representa este número. El valor de pi es siempre 3.1415926… .

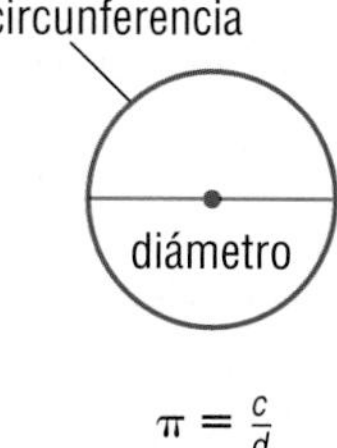

$$\pi = \frac{c}{d}$$

plano Superficie plana bidimensional que se extiende en todas direcciones.

polígono Figura simple y cerrada en el plano formada por tres o más segmentos de recta.

poliedro Sólido cuyas superficies planas son polígonos.

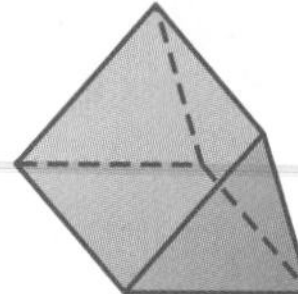

polinomio La suma o la diferencia de uno o más monomios.

población El grupo total de individuos o de artículos del cual se toman las muestras bajo estudio.

potencias Números que se expresan usando exponentes. Las potencias representan multiplicación repetida. La potencia 7^3 se lee *siete a la tercera potencia*, o *siete al cubo*.

precisión El grado de exactitud de una medida, lo cual depende de la unidad de medida. Entre más pequeña es una unidad, más precisa es la medida.

capital Cantidad de dinero que se invierte o que se toma prestada.

raíz cuadrada principal Una raíz cuadrada positiva.

prisma Poliedro con dos caras congruentes y paralelas llamadas bases.

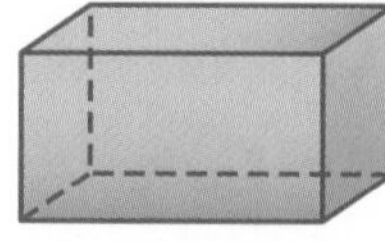

probabilidad La posibilidad de que suceda un evento. Es la razón del número de maneras en que puede ocurrir un evento al número total de resultados posibles.

property (p. 13) An open sentence that is true for any numbers.

proportion (p. 170) A statement of equality of two ratios.

pyramid (p. 331) A polyhedron with one base that is a polygon and faces that are triangles.

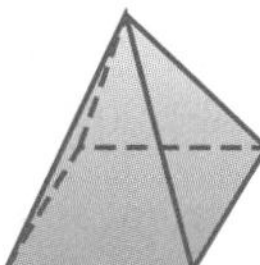

Pythagorean Theorem (p. 132) In a right triangle, the square of the length of the hypotenuse c is equal to the sum of the squares of the lengths of the legs a and b. $c^2 = a^2 + b^2$

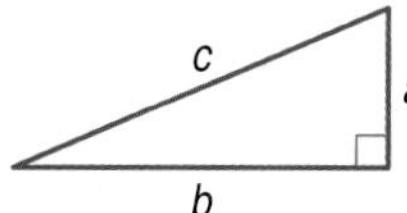

Pythagorean triple (p. 138) A set of three integers that satisfy the Pythagorean Theorem.

propiedad Enunciado abierto que se cumple para cualquier número.

proporción Un enunciado que establece la igualdad de dos razones.

pirámide Poliedro cuya base tiene forma de polígono y caras en forma de triángulos.

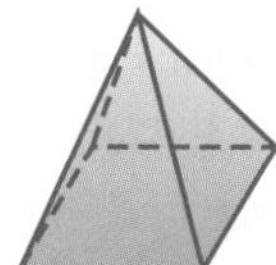

Teorema de Pitágoras En un triángulo rectángulo, el cuadrado de la longitud de la hipotenusa es igual a la suma de los cuadrados de las longitudes de los catetos. $c^2 = a^2 + b^2$

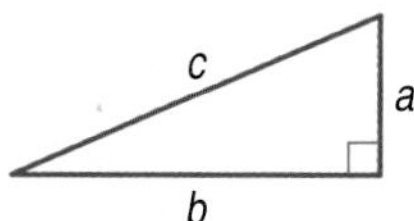

triplete pitagórico Conjunto de tres enteros que satisfacen el Teorema de Pitágoras.

quadrants (p. 142) The four regions into which the two perpendicular number lines of the coordinate plane separate the plane.

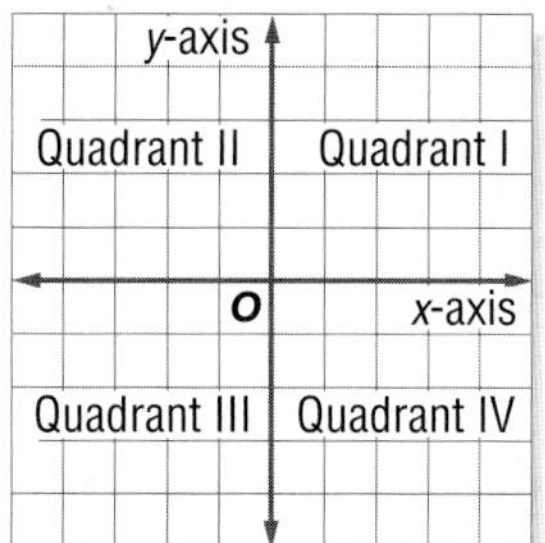

quadratic function (p. 565) A function in which the greatest power of the variable is 2.

quadrilateral (p. 272) A polygon that has four sides and four angles.

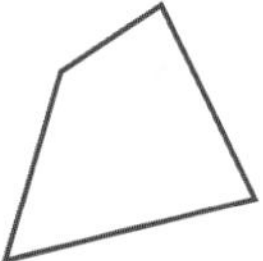

quartiles (p. 442) Values that divide a set of data into four equal parts.

cuadrantes Las cuatro regiones en que las dos rectas numéricas perpendiculares dividen el plano de coordenadas.

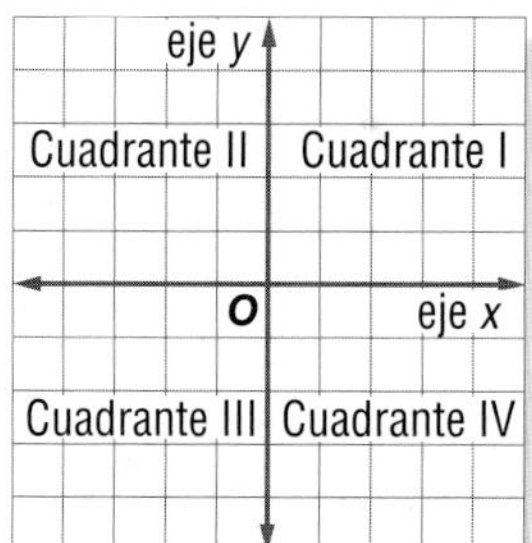

función cuadrática Función en la cual la potencia mayor de la variable es 2.

cuadrilátero Un polígono con cuatro lados y cuatro ángulos.

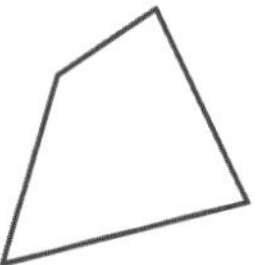

cuartiles Valores que dividen un conjunto de datos en cuatro partes iguales.

radical sign (p. 116) The symbol used to indicate a nonnegative square root, $\sqrt{\ }$.

signo radical Símbolo que se usa para indicar una raíz cuadrada no negativa, $\sqrt{\ }$.

radius (p. 319) The distance from the center of a circle to any point on the circle.

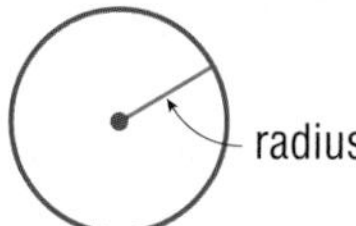

radio Distancia desde el centro de un círculo hasta cualquier punto del mismo.

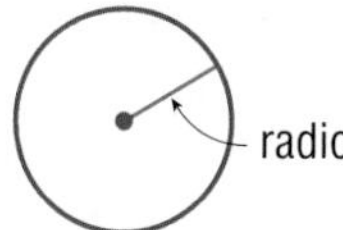

random (p. 374) Outcomes occur at random if each outcome is equally likely to occur.

aleatorio Un resultado ocurre al azar si la posibilidad de ocurrir de cada resultado es equiprobable.

range (p. 442) The difference between the greatest number and the least number in a set of data.

rango La diferencia entre el número mayor y el número menor en un conjunto de datos.

range (p. 518) The set of output values in a function.

rango El conjunto de valores de salida en una función.

rate (p. 157) A ratio of two measurements having different units.

tasa Razón que compara dos cantidades que tienen distintas unidades de medida.

rate of change (p. 160) A rate that describes how one quantity changes in relation to another.

tasa de cambio Tasa que describe cómo cambia una cantidad con respecto a otras.

ratio (p. 156) A comparison of two numbers by division. The ratio of 2 to 3 can be stated as 2 out of 3, 2 to 3, 2:3, or $\frac{2}{3}$.

razón Comparación de dos números mediante división. La razón de 2 a 3 puede escribirse como 2 de cada 3, 2 a 3, 2:3, o $\frac{2}{3}$.

rational number (p. 62) Numbers of the form $\frac{a}{b}$, where a and b are integers and $b \neq 0$.

número racional Números de la forma $\frac{a}{b}$, donde a y b son enteros y $b \neq 0$.

real numbers (p. 125) The set of rational numbers together with the set of irrational numbers.

número real El conjunto de números racionales junto con el conjunto de números irracionales.

reciprocals (p. 76) The multiplicative inverse of a number. The product of reciprocals is 1.

recíproco El inverso multiplicativo de un número. El producto de recíprocos es 1.

rectangle (p. 273) A parallelogram with four right angles.

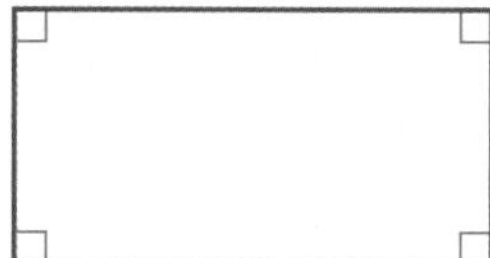

rectángulo Un paralelogramo que tiene cuatro ángulos rectos.

reflection (p. 290) A type of transformation in which a mirror image is produced by flipping a figure over a line.

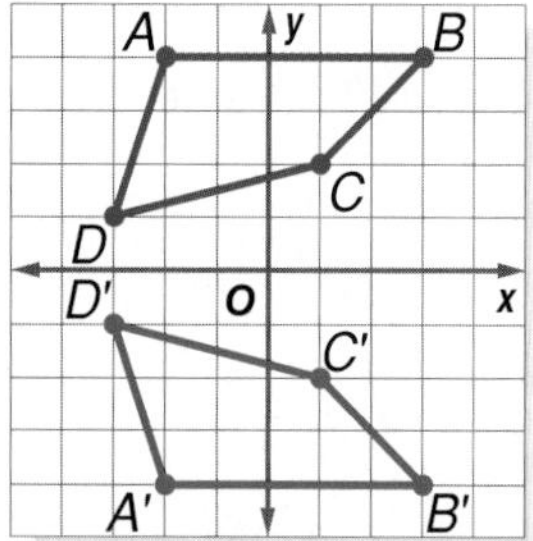

reflexión Tipo de transformación en que se produce una imagen especular al darle vuelta de campana a una figura por encima de una línea.

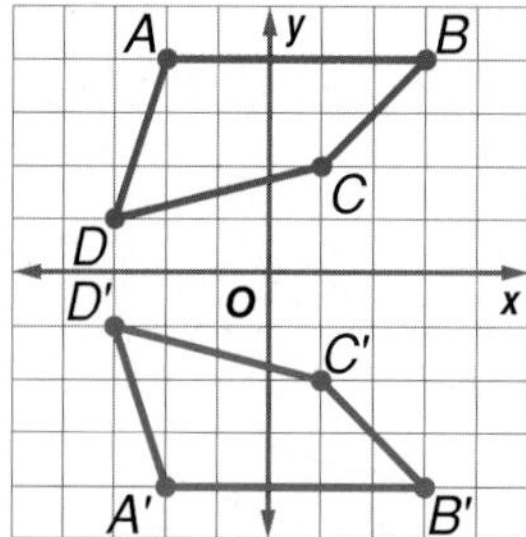

regular polygon (p. 278) A polygon that is equilateral and equiangular.

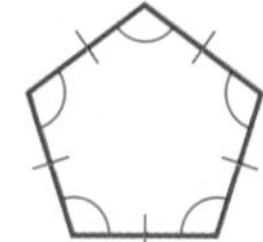

polígono regular Polígono equilátero y equiangular.

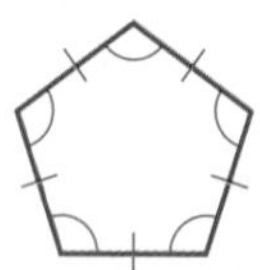

repeating decimal (p. 63) A decimal whose digits repeat in groups of one or more. Examples are 0.181818… and 0.8333… .

rhombus (p. 273) A parallelogram with four congruent sides.

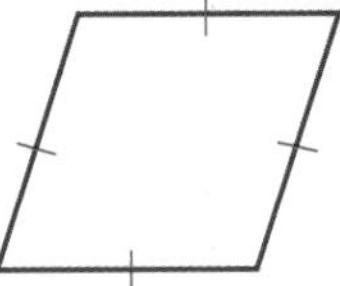

right angle (p. 256 and p. 263) An angle that measures 90°.

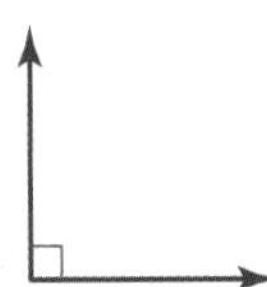

right triangle (p. 132 and p. 263) A triangle having one right angle.

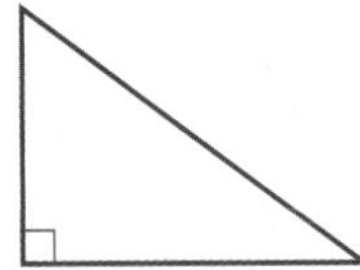

rise (p. 166) The vertical change between any two points on a line.

rotation (p. 300) A transformation involving the turning or spinning of a figure around a fixed point.

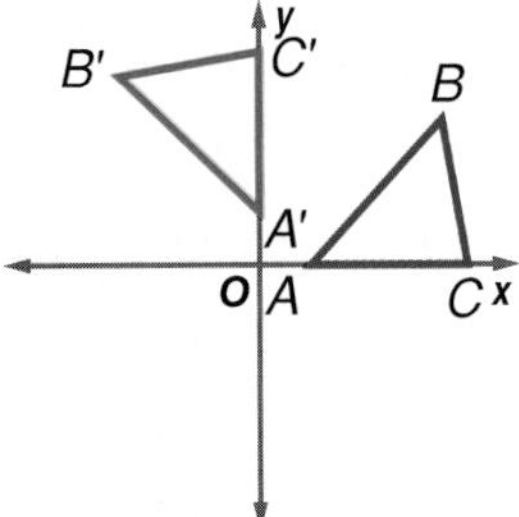

90° rotation about the origin

rotational symmetry (p. 287) A figure has rotational symmetry if it can be turned less than 360° about its center and still look like the original.

row (p. 454) In a matrix, the numbers side by side horizontally form a row.

run (p. 166) The horizontal change between any two points on a line.

decimal periódico Decimal cuyos dígitos se repiten en grupos de uno o más. Por ejemplo: 0.181818… y 0.8333… .

rombo Paralelogramo que tiene cuatro lados congruentes.

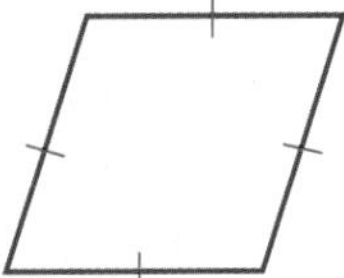

ángulo recto Ángulo que mide 90°.

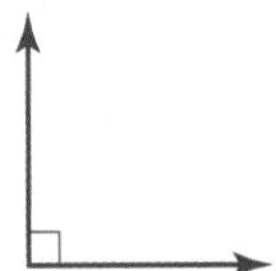

triángulo rectángulo Triángulo que tiene un ángulo recto.

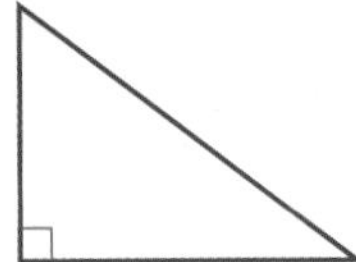

elevación El cambio vertical entre cualquier par de puntos en una recta.

rotación Transformación que involucra girar una figura en torno a un punto central fijo.

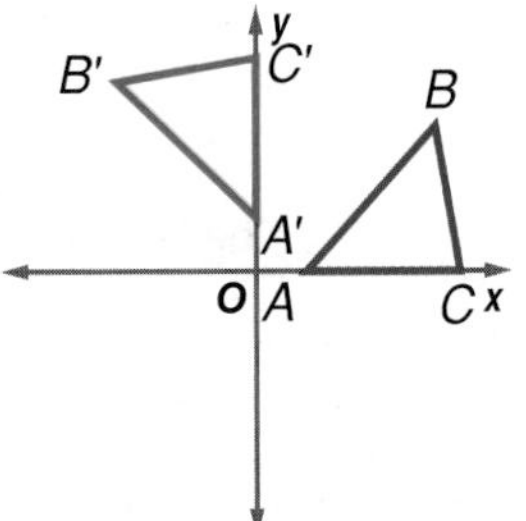

rotación de 90° alrededor del origen

simetría rotacional Una figura posee simetría rotacional si se puede girar menos de 360° en torno a su centro sin que esto cambie su apariencia con respecto a la figura original.

fila En una matriz, los números que están horizontalmente uno al lado del otro.

carrera El cambio horizontal entre cualquier par de puntos en una recta.

S

sample (p. 406) A randomly selected group chosen for the purpose of collecting data.

sample space (p. 374) The set of all possible outcomes of a probability experiment.

scale (p. 184) The ratio of a given length on a drawing or model to its corresponding actual length.

scale drawing (p. 184) A drawing that is similar, but either larger or smaller than the actual object.

scale factor (p. 179) The ratio of the lengths of two corresponding sides of two similar polygons.

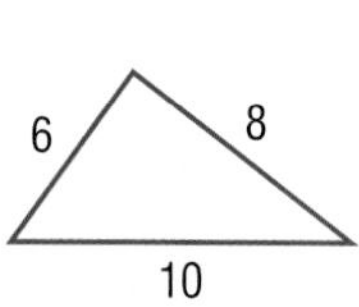

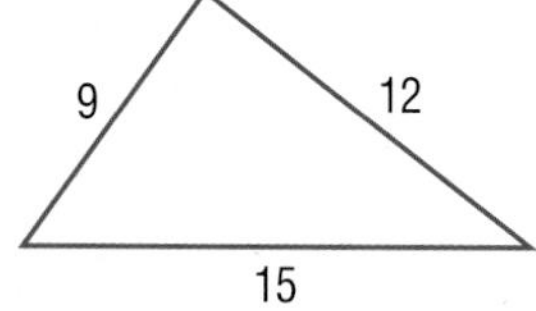

scale factor $= \frac{2}{3}$

scale model (p. 184) A replica of an original object that is too large or too small to be built at actual size.

scalene triangle (p. 263) A triangle with no congruent sides.

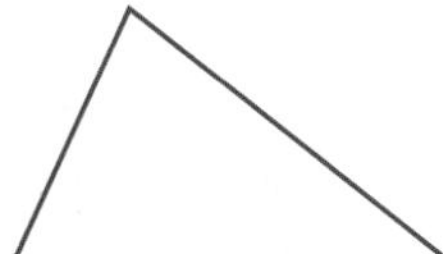

scatter plot (p. 539) A graph that shows the general relationship between two sets of data.

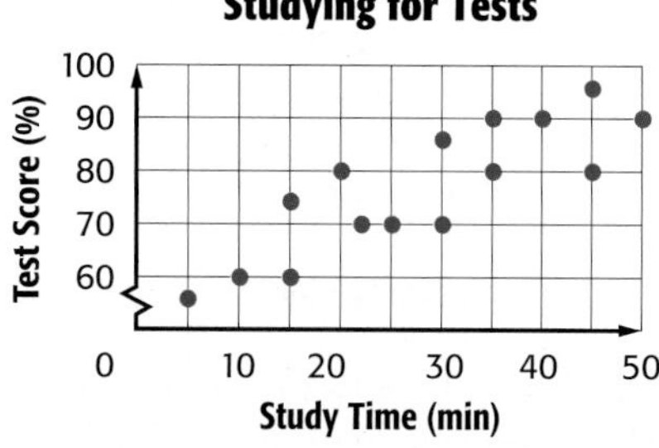

scientific notation (p. 104) A way of expressing numbers as the product of a number that is at least 1 but less than 10 and a power of 10. In scientific notation, 5,500 is 5.5×10^3.

selling price (p. 238) The amount the customer pays for an item.

sequence (p. 512) An ordered list of numbers, such as 0, 1, 2, 3, or 2, 4, 6, 8.

significant digits (p. 358) All of the digits of a measurement that are known to be accurate plus one estimated digit.

muestra Grupo escogido al azar o aleatoriamente que se usa con el propósito de recoger datos.

espacio muestral Conjunto de todos los resultados posibles de un experimento probabilístico.

escala Razón de una longitud dada en un dibujo o modelo a su longitud real correspondiente.

dibujo a escala Dibujo que es semejante, pero más grande o más pequeño que el objeto real.

factor de escala La razón de las longitudes de dos lados correspondientes de dos polígonos semejantes.

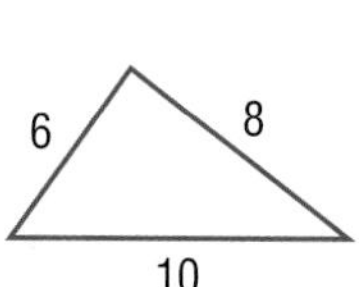

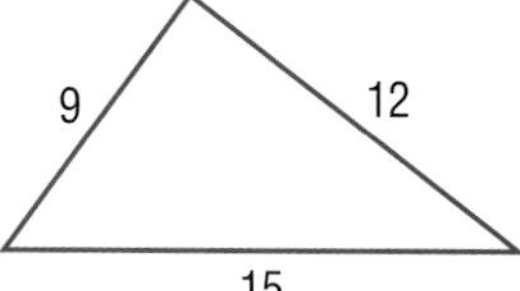

factor de escala $= \frac{2}{3}$

modelo a escala Una replica del objeto original, el cual es demasiado grande o demasiado pequeño como para construirlo de tamaño natural.

triángulo escaleno Triángulo que no tiene lados congruentes.

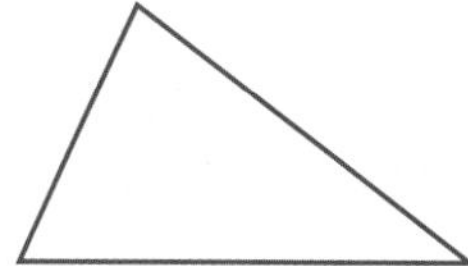

diagrama de dispersión Gráfica que muestra la relación general entre dos conjuntos de datos.

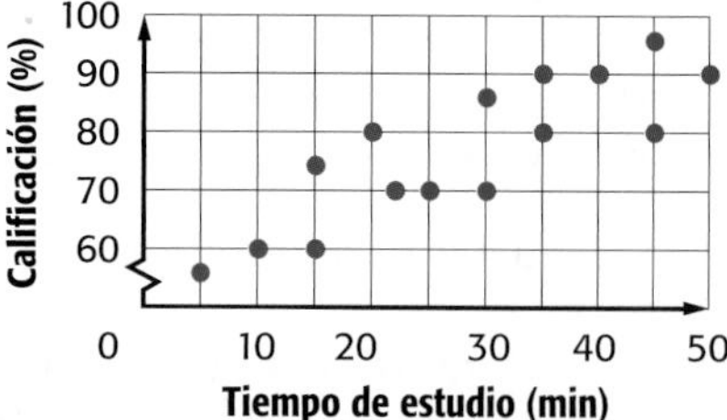

notación científica Manera de expresar números como el producto de un número que es al menos igual a 1, pero menor que 10, por una potencia de 10. En notación científica, 5,500 es 5.5×10^3.

precio de venta Cantidad de dinero que paga un consumidor por un artículo.

sucesión Lista ordenada de números, tales como 0, 1, 2, 3 ó 2, 4, 6, 8.

dígitos significativos Todos los dígitos de una medición que se sabe son exactos, más un dígito aproximado.

similar (p. 178) Polygons that have the same shape are called similar polygons.

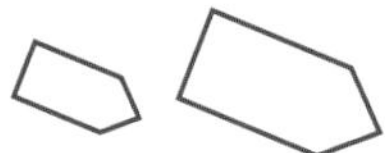

similar solids (p. 356) Solids that have the same shape and their corresponding linear measures are proportional.

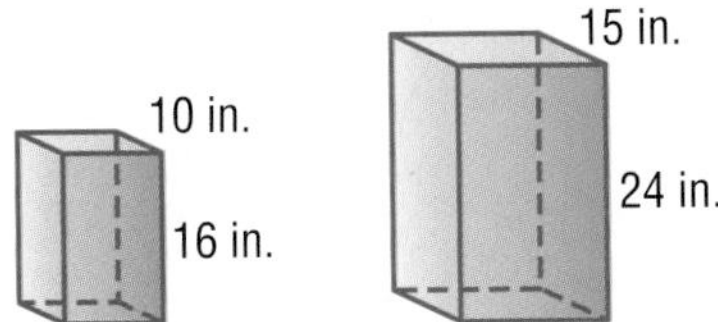

simple event (p. 374) A specific outcome or type of outcome.

simple random sample (p. 406) A sample where each item or person in the population is as likely to be chosen as any other.

simplest form (p. 471) An algebraic expression that has no like terms and no parentheses.

simplifying the expression (p. 471) Using properties to combine like terms.

simulation (p. 404) An experiment that is designed to act out a given situation.

sine (p. 681) If A is an acute angle of a right triangle, $\sin A = \frac{\text{measure of the leg opposite } \angle A}{\text{measure of the hypotenuse}}$.

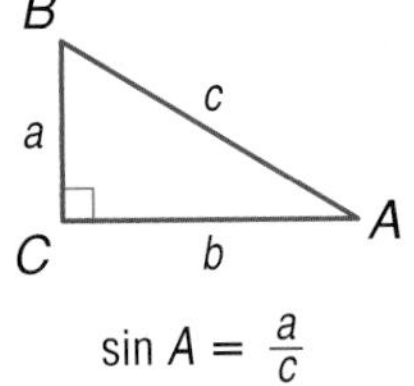

skew lines (p. 334) Lines that do not intersect, but are also not parallel.

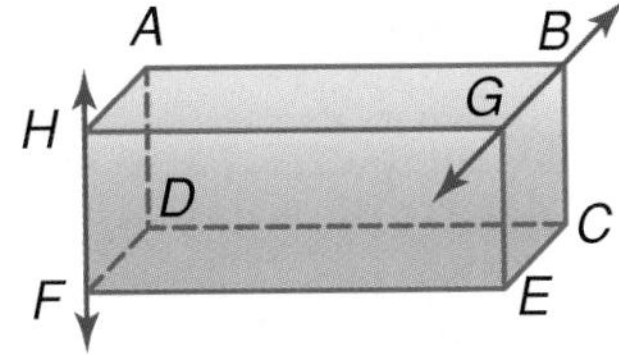

$\overleftrightarrow{HF}$ and $\overleftrightarrow{BG}$ are skew lines.

slant height (p. 352) The altitude or height of each lateral face of a pyramid.

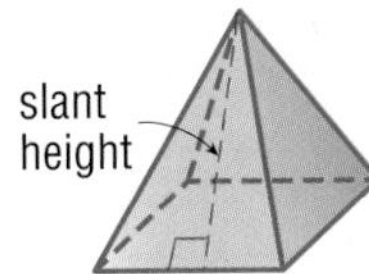

semejante Los polígonos que tienen la misma forma se llaman polígonos semejantes.

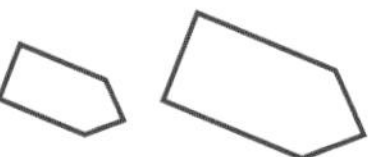

sólidos semejantes Sólidos que tienen la misma forma y cuyas medidas lineales correspondientes son proporcionales.

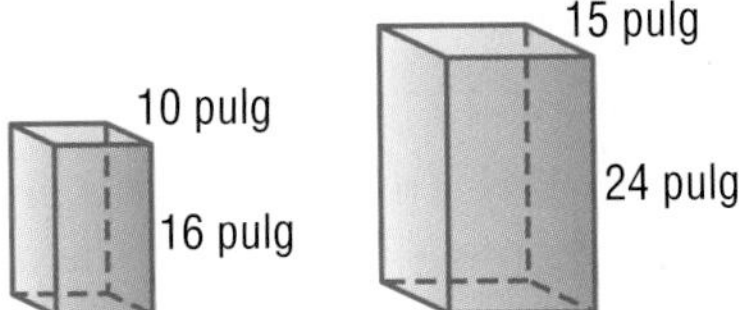

evento simple Un resultado específico o un tipo de resultado.

muestra aleatoria simple Muestra de una población que tiene la misma probabilidad de escogerse que cualquier otra.

forma reducida Expresión algebraica que carece de términos semejantes y de paréntesis.

simplificar una expresión El uso de propiedades para combinar términos semejantes.

simulacro Experimento diseñado para representar una situación dada.

seno Si A es un ángulo agudo de un triángulo rectángulo, sen $A = \frac{\text{medida del cateto opuesto a } \angle A}{\text{medida de la hipotenusa}}$.

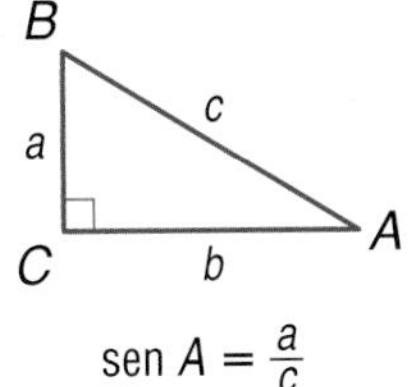

rectas alabeadas Rectas que no se intersecan, pero que tampoco son paralelas.

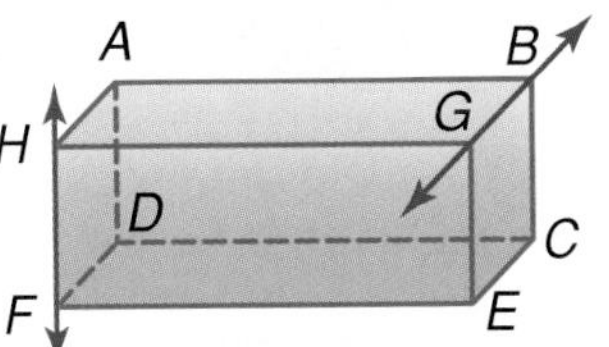

$\overleftrightarrow{HF}$ y $\overleftrightarrow{BG}$ son rectas alabeadas.

altura oblicua La longitud de la altura de cada cara lateral de una pirámide.

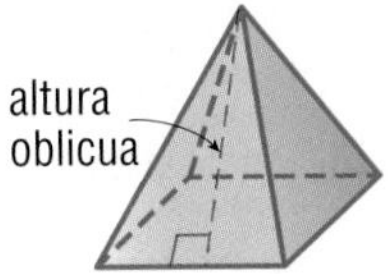

slope (p. 166) The rate of change between any two points on a line. The ratio of vertical change to horizontal change.

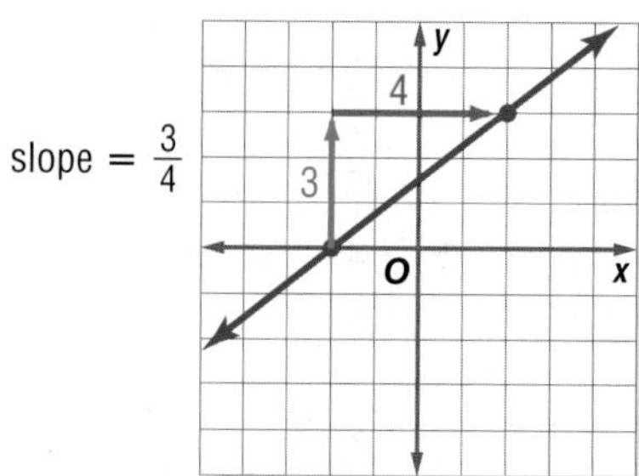

pendiente Razón de cambio entre cualquier par de puntos en una recta. La razón del cambio vertical al cambio horizontal.

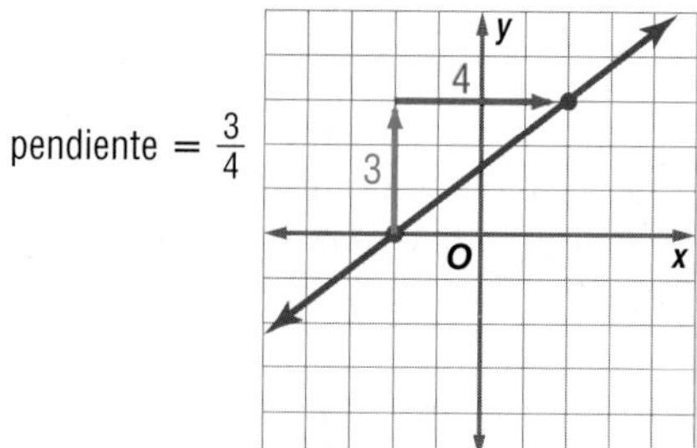

slope formula (p. 526) The slope m of a line passing through two points is the ratio of the difference in the y-coordinates to the corresponding difference in the x-coordinates.
$m = \frac{y_2 - y_1}{x_2 - x_1}$

fórmula de la pendiente La pendiente m de una recta que pasa por dos puntos es la razón de la diferencia en la coordenada y a la diferencia correspondiente en la coordenada x.
$m = \frac{y_2 - y_1}{x_2 - x_1}$

slope-intercept form (p. 533) An equation written in the form $y = mx + b$, where m is the slope and b is the y-intercept.

forma pendiente intersección Ecuación de la forma $y = mx + b$, donde m es la pendiente y b es la intersección y.

solid (p. 331) A three-dimensional figure formed by intersecting planes.

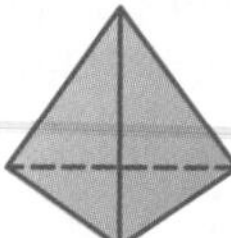

sólido Figura tridimensional formada por planos que se intersecan.

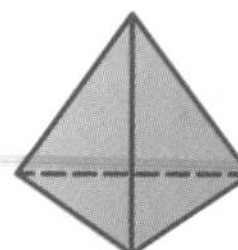

solution (p. 45) The value for the variable that makes an equation true. The solution of $10 + y = 25$ is 15.

solución El valor de la variable de una ecuación que hace que se cumpla la ecuación. La solución de $10 + y = 25$ es 15.

solve (p. 45) Find the value of the variable that makes the equation true.

resolver Proceso de encontrar la variable que satisface una ecuación.

sphere (p. 345) The set of all points in space that are a given distance from a given point, called the center.

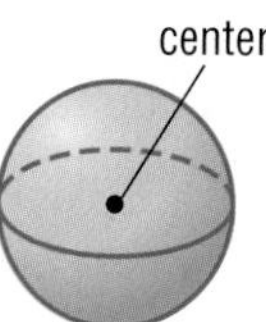

esfera El conjunto de todos los puntos en el espacio que están a una distancia dada de un punto dado, llamado centro.

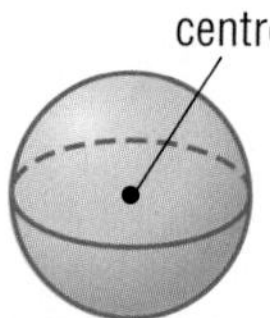

square (p. 273) A parallelogram with four congruent sides and four right angles.

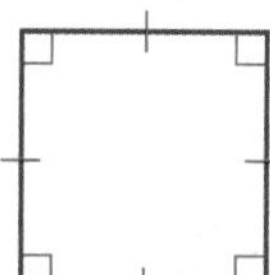

cuadrado Paralelogramo con cuatro lados congruentes y cuatro ángulos rectos.

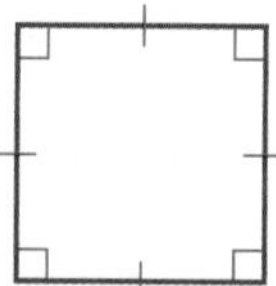

square root (p. 116) One of the two equal factors of a number. If $a^2 = b$, then a is the square root of b. A square root of 144 is 12 since $12^2 = 144$.

raíz cuadrada Uno de dos factores iguales de un número. Si $a^2 = b$, la a es la raíz cuadrada de b. Una raíz cuadrada de 144 es 12 porque $12^2 = 144$.

straight angle (p. 256) An angle that measures 180°.

ángulo llano Ángulo que mide 180°.

stratified random sample (p. 406) A sampling method in which the population is divided into similar, non-overlapping groups. A simple random sample is then selected from each group.

substitution (p. 545) A method used for solving a system of equations that replaces one variable in one equation with an expression derived from the other equation.

Subtraction Property of Equality (p. 45) If you subtract the same number from each side of an equation, the two sides remain equal.

supplementary angles (p. 256) Two angles are supplementary if the sum of their measures is 180°.

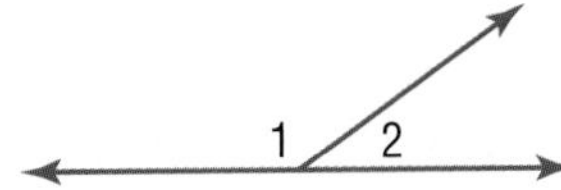

$\angle 1$ and $\angle 2$ are supplementary angles.

surface area (p. 347) The sum of the areas of all the faces of a three-dimensional figure.

3 ft
5 ft
7 ft

$$S = 2(7 \times 5) + 2(7 \times 3) + 2(5 \times 3)$$
$$= 142 \text{ square feet}$$

systematic random sample (p. 406) A sampling method in which the items or people are selected according to a specific time or item interval.

system of equations (p. 544) A set of two or more equations considered together.

muestra aleatoria estratificada Método de muestreo en que la población se divide en grupos semejantes que no se sobreponen. Luego se selecciona una muestra aleatoria simple de cada grupo.

sustitución Método que se usa para resolver un sistema de ecuaciones en que se reemplaza una variable en una ecuación con una expresión derivada de la otra ecuación.

propiedad de sustracción de la igualdad Si sustraes el mismo número de ambos lados de una ecuación, los dos lados permanecen iguales.

ángulos suplementarios Dos ángulos son suplementarios si la suma de sus medidas es 180°.

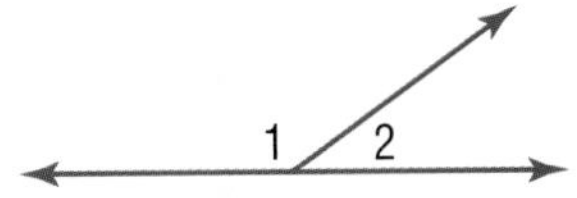

$\angle 1$ y $\angle 2$ son ángulos suplementarios.

área de superficie La suma de las áreas de todas las caras de una figura tridimensional.

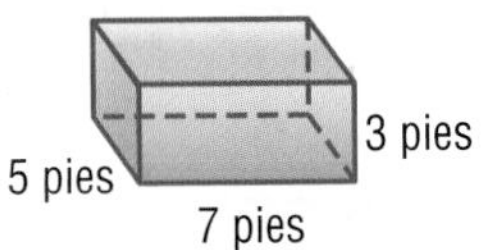

$$S = 2(7 \times 5) + 2(7 \times 3) + 2(5 \times 3)$$
$$= 142 \text{ pies cuadrados}$$

muestra aleatoria sistemática Muestra en que los elementos de la muestra se escogen según un intervalo de tiempo o elemento específico.

sistema de ecuaciones Conjunto de dos o más ecuaciones consideradas juntas.

tangent (p. 678) If A is an acute angle of a right triangle, $\tan A = \frac{\text{measure of the leg opposite } \angle A}{\text{measure of the leg adjacent to } \angle A}$.

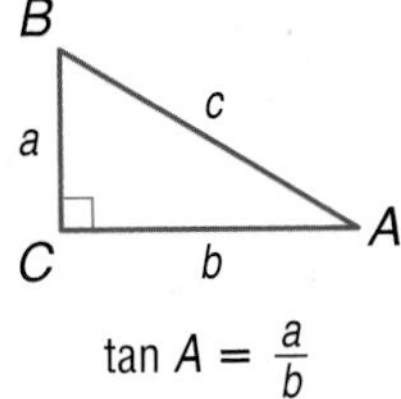

$\tan A = \frac{a}{b}$

term (p. 470) A number, a variable, or a product of numbers and variables.

term (p. 512) A number in a sequence.

terminating decimal (p. 63) A decimal whose digits end. Every terminating decimal can be written as a fraction with a denominator of 10, 100, 1,000, and so on.

tangente Si A es un ángulo agudo en un triángulo rectángulo, $\tan A = \frac{\text{medida del cateto opuesto a } \angle A}{\text{medida del cateto adyacente a } \angle A}$.

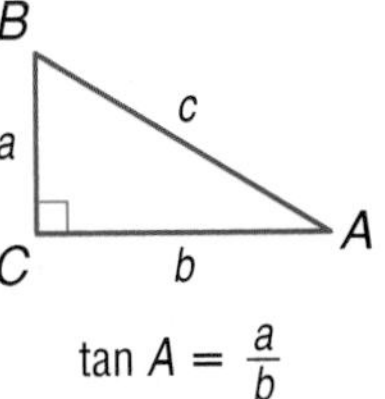

$\tan A = \frac{a}{b}$

término Un número, una variable o un producto de números y variables.

término Un número en una sucesión.

decimal terminal Decimal cuyos dígitos terminan. Todo decimal terminal puede escribirse como una fracción con un denominador 10, 100, 1,000, etc.

theoretical probability (p. 400) Probability based on known characteristics or facts.

transformation (p. 290) A mapping of a geometric figure.

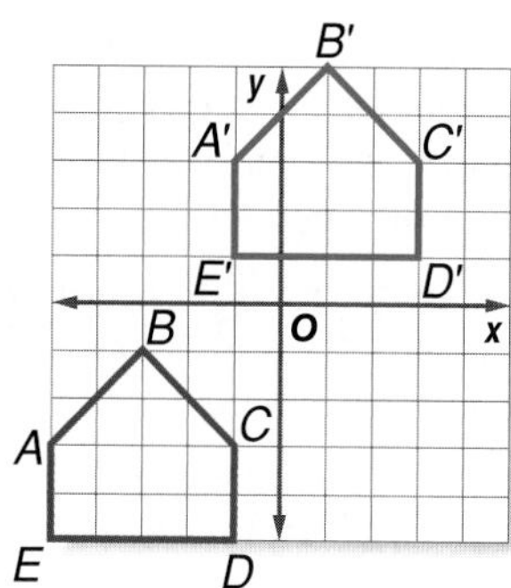

translation (p. 296) A transformation in which a figure is slid horizontally, vertically, or both.

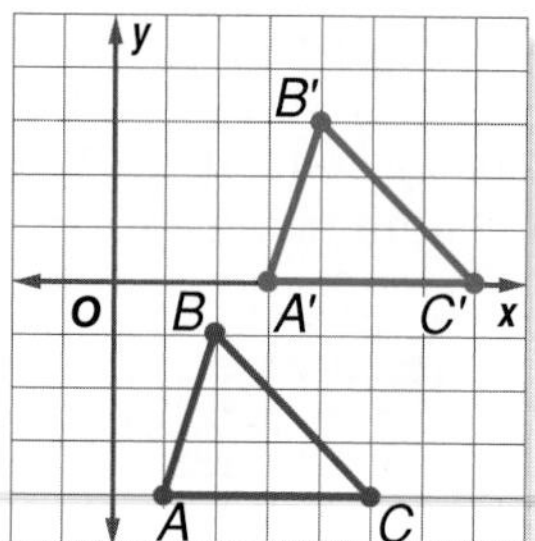

transversal (p. 258) A line that intersects two or more other lines to form eight angles.

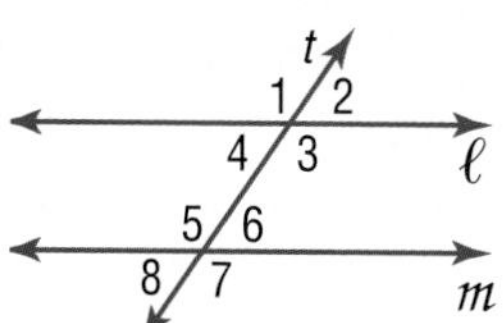

trapezoid (p. 273) A quadrilateral with exactly one pair of parallel opposite sides.

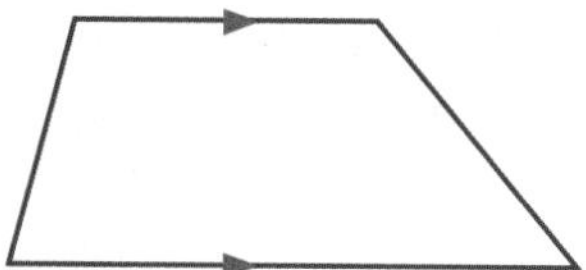

tree diagram (p. 380) A diagram used to show the total number of possible outcomes in a probability experiment.

triangle (p. 262) A figure formed by three line segments that intersect only at their endpoints.

trigonometric ratio (p. 192) The ratio of the lengths of two sides of a right triangle.

probabilidad teórica Probabilidad que se basa en características o hechos conocidos.

transformación Movimiento de una figura geométrica.

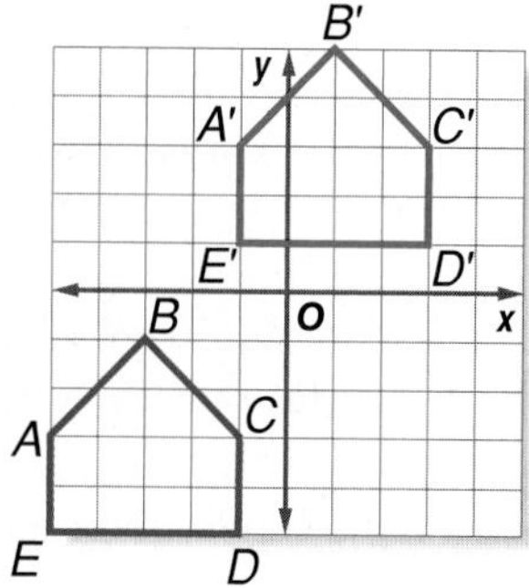

traslación Transformación en que una figura se desliza horizontal o verticalmente o de ambas maneras.

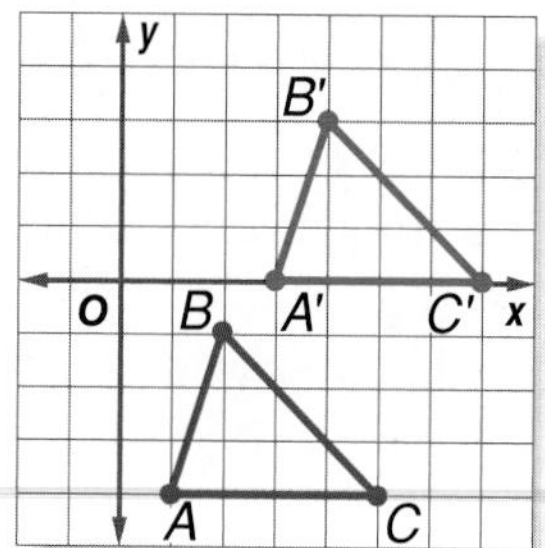

transversal Recta que interseca dos o más rectas formando ocho ángulos.

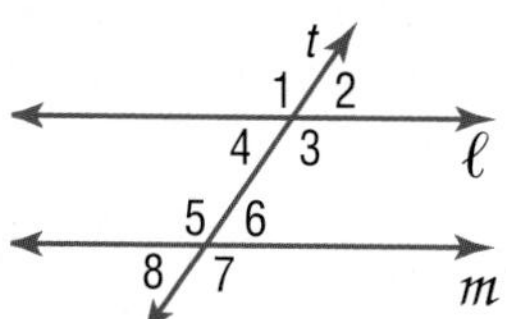

trapecio Cuadrilátero con un único par de lados opuestos paralelos.

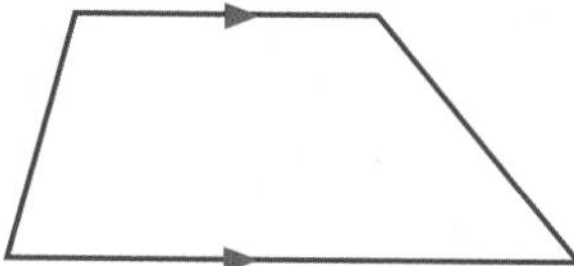

diagrama de árbol Diagrama que se usa para mostrar el número total de resultados posibles en experimento probabilístico.

triángulo Figura formada por tres segmentos de recta que sólo se intersecan en sus extremos.

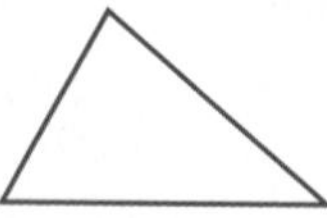

razón trigonométrica La razón de las longitudes de dos lados de un triángulo rectángulo.

trigonometry (p. 192) The study of the properties of triangles.

two-step equation (p. 474) An equation that contains two operations.

trigonometría El estudio de las propiedades de los triángulos.

ecuación de dos pasos Ecuación que contiene dos operaciones.

unbiased sample (p. 406) A sample that is selected so that it is representative of the entire population.

unit fraction (p. 66) A fraction that has 1 as its numerator.

unit rate (p. 157) A rate with a denominator of 1.

unlike fractions (p. 88) Fractions whose denominators are different.

upper quartile (p. 442) The median of the upper half of a set of data, represented by UQ.

muestra no sesgada Muestra que se selecciona de modo que sea representativa de la población entera.

fracción unitaria Fracción cuyo numerador es 1.

razón unitaria Una tasa con un denominador de 1.

fracciones con distinto denominador Fracciones cuyos denominadores son diferentes.

cuartil superior La mediana de la mitad superior de un conjunto de números, denotada por CS.

variable (p. 11) A symbol, usually a letter, used to represent a number in mathematical expressions or sentences.

vertex (p. 331) The vertex of a prism is the point where three or more planes intersect.

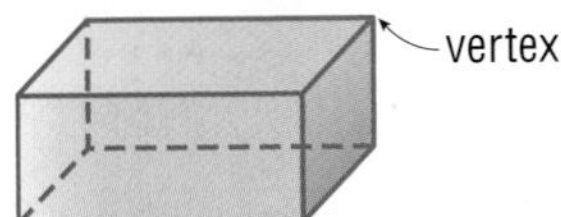

vertical angles (p. 256) Opposite angles formed by the intersection of two lines. Vertical angles are congruent. In the figure, the vertical angles are $\angle 1$ and $\angle 3$, and $\angle 2$ and $\angle 4$.

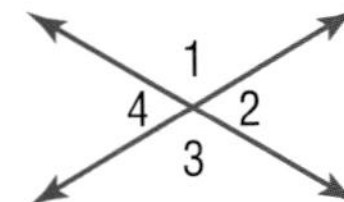

volume (p. 335) The number of cubic units needed to fill the space occupied by a solid.

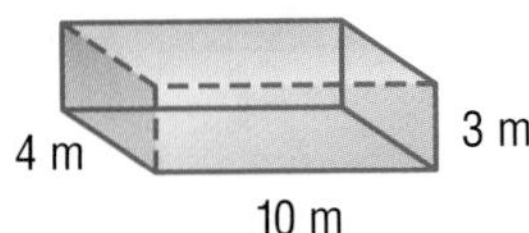

$V = 10 \times 4 \times 3 = 120$ cubic meters

voluntary response sample (p. 407) A sample which involves only those who want to participate in the sampling.

variable Un símbolo, por lo general, una letra, que se usa para representar números en expresiones o enunciados matemáticos.

vértice El vértice de un prisma es el punto en que se intersecan dos o más planos del prisma.

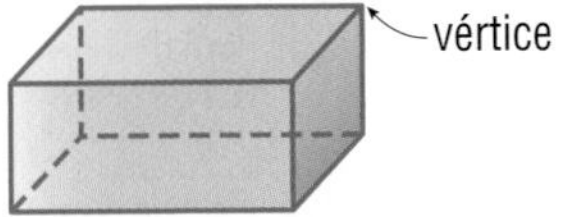

ángulos opuestos por el vértice Ángulos congruentes que se forman de la intersección de dos rectas. En la figura, los ángulos opuestos por el vértice son $\angle 1$ y $\angle 3$, y $\angle 2$ y $\angle 4$.

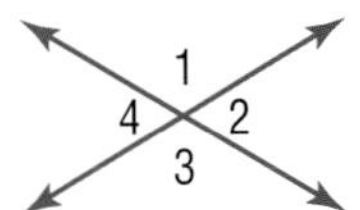

volumen El número de unidades cúbicas que se requieren para llenar el espacio que ocupa un sólido.

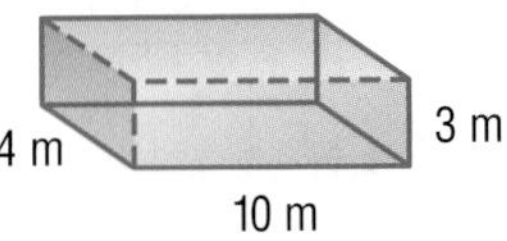

$V = 10 \times 4 \times 3 = 120$ metros cúbicos

muestra de respuesta voluntaria Muestra que involucra sólo aquellos que quieren participar en el muestreo.

***x*-axis** (p. 142) The horizontal number line that helps to form the coordinate plane.

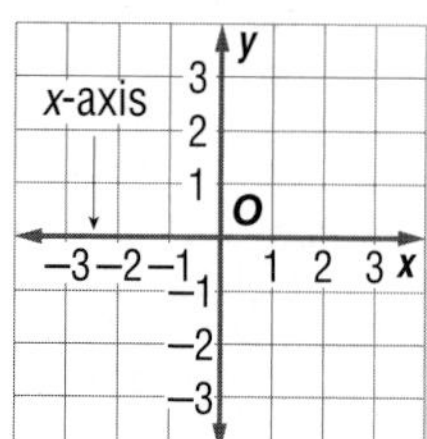

eje *x* La recta numérica horizontal que ayuda a formar el plano de coordenadas.

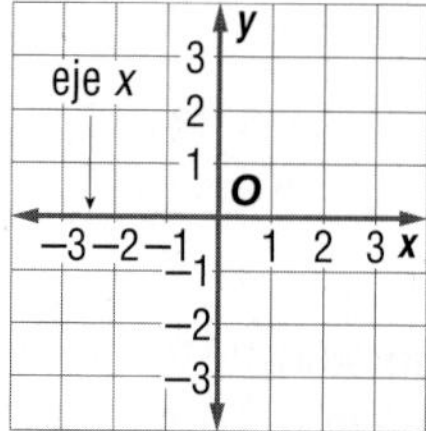

***x*-coordinate** (p. 142) The first number of an ordered pair.

coordenada *x* El primer número de un par ordenado.

***x*-intercept** (p. 523) The value of *x* where the graph crosses the *x*-axis.

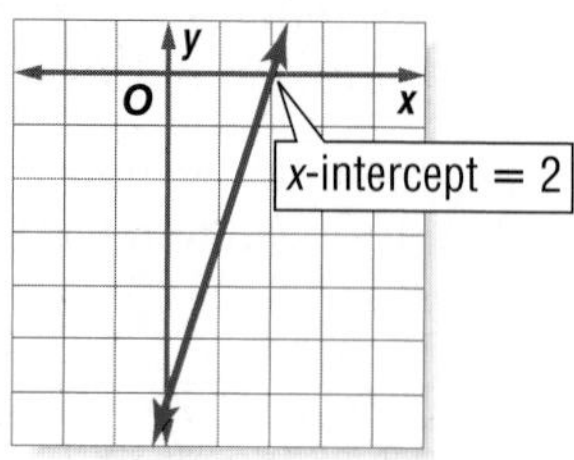

intersección *x* El valor de *x* donde la gráfica cruza el eje *x*.

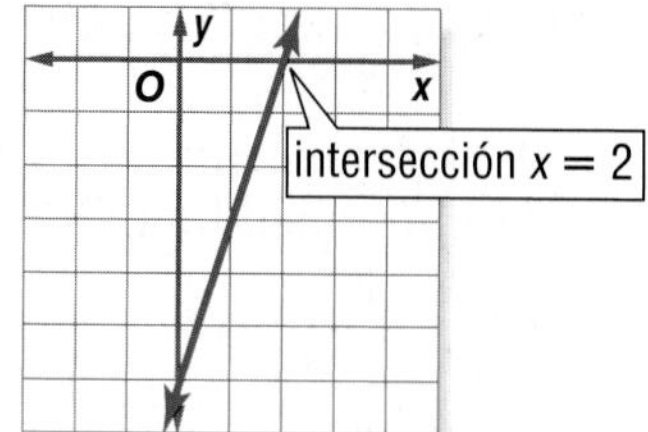

***y*-axis** (p. 142) The vertical number line that helps to form the coordinate plane.

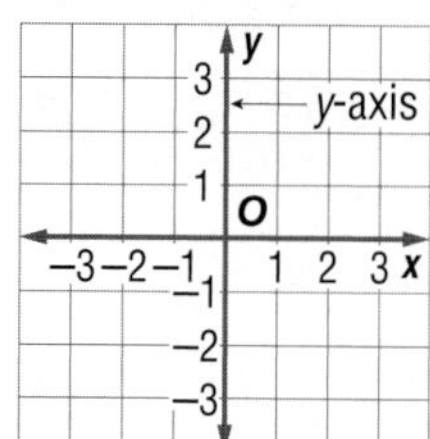

eje *y* La recta numérica vertical que ayuda a formar el plano de coordenadas.

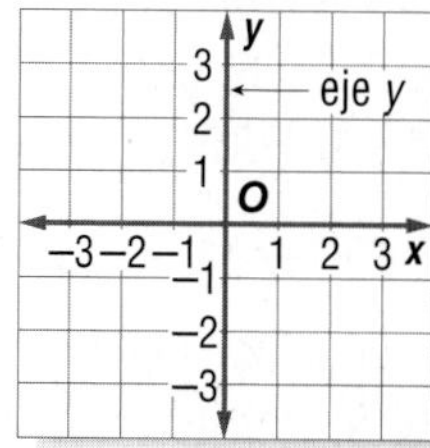

***y*-coordinate** (p. 142) The second number of an ordered pair.

coordenada *y* El segundo número de un par ordenado.

***y*-intercept** (p. 523) The value of *y* where the graph crosses the *y*-axis.

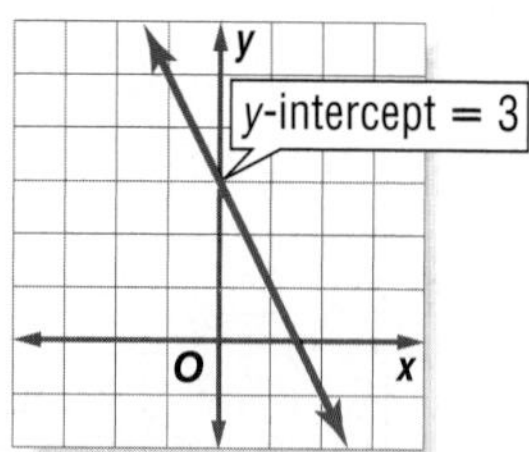

intersección *y* El valor de *y* donde la gráfica cruza el eje *y*.

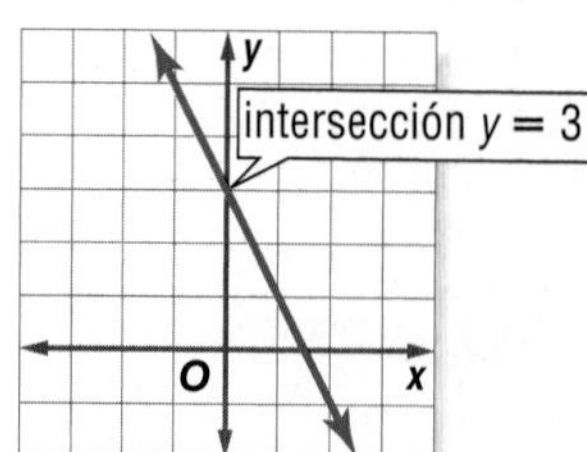

Selected Answers

Chapter 1 Algebra: Integers

Page 5 Chapter 1 Getting Started

1. multiply **3.** 77 **5.** 79.5 **7.** 152 **9.** 2.6 **11.** 30 **13.** 72 **15.** 1,220 **17.** 32 **19.** 0.4 **21.** < **23.** >

Pages 9–10 Lesson 1-1

1. Explore—Identify what information is given and what you need to find. Plan—Estimate the answer and then select a strategy for solving. Solve—Carry out the plan and solve. Examine—Compare the answer to the estimate and determine if it is reasonable. If not, make a new plan. **3.** The numbers increase by 1, 2, 3, and so on; 25. **5.** 6 lb **7.** almost 3 jars/s

9. 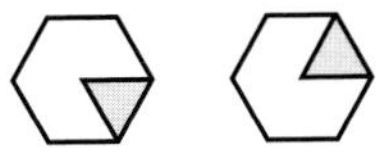

11. 20 **13.** 529,920,000 acres **15.** No; \$8 + \$12 + \$12 > \$30 **17.** \$6 per pair **19.** C **21.** 60 **23.** 14.4

Pages 14–15 Lesson 1-2

1. The everyday meaning of variable is something that is likely to change or vary, and the mathematical meaning of a variable is a placeholder for a value that can change or vary. **3.** Sample answer: $4 \cdot 5 = 5 \cdot 4$ **5.** 12 **7.** 32 **9.** 29 **11.** Commutative (×) **13.** false; $6 + 0 \ngtr 6$ **15.** 22 **17.** 20 **19.** 17 **21.** 22 **23.** 20 **25.** 2 **27.** 57 **29.** 11 **31.** 11 **33.** 144 **35.** 6 **37.** 5 **39.** 35 **41.** about 6,031 **43.** Distributive **45.** Commutative (+) **47.** Identity (+) **49.** 6(4 + 3) **51.** true **53.** false; $(24 \div 4) \div 2 \neq 24 \div (4 \div 2)$ **55.** Sample answer: The equals sign was first introduced by Robert Recorde in 1557. **57.** C **59.** \$4.38 **61.** = **63.** >

Pages 20–21 Lesson 1-3

1. Sample answer: 4 > −5; −5 < 4 **3.** +10

5. 

7. > **9.** 5 **11.** 28 **13.** 4 **15.** −2 **17.** +4 **19.** +60

21. 

23. 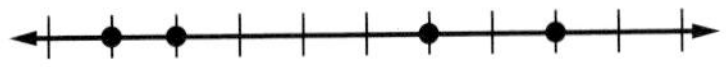

25. < **27.** < **29.** > **31.** =

33. {−37, −23, −12, 0, 45, 55} **35.** {−17, −11, −5, −2, 6} **37.** 14 **39.** 25 **41.** 15 **43.** 3 **45.** −3 **47.** 14 **49.** −4, −3, −1, −1, +1, +1, +2, +4, +4, +5 **51.** helium **53.** 2 **55.** 20 **57.** 11 **59.** Never; the absolute value of a positive number is always positive. **61.** Sometimes; 5 > −4 and $|5| > |-4|$, but −4 > −5 and $|-4| \ngtr |-5|$. **63.** H **65.** 26 **67.** about 2 h **69.** 43 **71.** 65

Pages 26–27 Lesson 1-4

1. To add numbers with different signs, subtract the absolute values of the numbers. Then use the sign of the number with the greater absolute value. **3.** 45 and 54; All of the other numbers are additive inverses. **5.** 4 **7.** −13 **9.** −20 **11.** −26 **13.** 22 **15.** −15 **17.** 15 **19.** 41 **21.** 24 **23.** −30 **25.** −32 **27.** −11 **29.** 8 + (−5); 3 **31.** −1 + 7; 6 **33.** 7 **35.** 2 **37.** −2 **39.** 3 **41.** −6 **43.** Rock: 25, Rap/Hip Hop: 14, Pop: 9, Country: 11 **45.** Sometimes; If x and y have different signs, then $|x + y| \neq |x| + |y|$. If x and y have the same sign, then $|x + y| = |x| + |y|$. **47.** F **49.** > **51.** > **53.** Sample answer: about 500 million. **55.** 17 **57.** 4

Pages 30–31 Lesson 1-5

1. Sample answer: 7 − (−3); 7 + 3 **3.** −5 **5.** −19 **7.** 4 **9.** −7 **11.** 2 **13.** −7 **15.** −12 **17.** −16 **19.** −20 **21.** 14 **23.** 16 **25.** −11 **27.** 7 **29.** −2 **31.** 589 m **33.** Lake Michigan is 37 m deeper than Lake Ontario. **35.** 5 **37.** −23 **39.** 6 **41.** −9 **43.** 10°F **45.** Sample answer: You have \$26 in your checking account. Find the balance in your account after you write a check for \$30. **47.** false; $3 - 2 \neq 2 - 3$ **49.** I **51.** 17 **53.** Identity (+) **55.** 135 **57.** 540

Pages 37–38 Lesson 1-6

1a. positive **1b.** negative **1c.** negative **3a.** Positive; the product of two negative numbers is always a positive number. **3b.** Negative; the product of three negative numbers is always a negative number. **3c.** Positive; the product of four negative numbers is always a positive number. **3d.** Negative; the product of five negative numbers is always a negative number. **5.** 14 **7.** 140 **9.** −4 **11.** −3 **13.** −4 **15.** −56 **17.** 24 **19.** 60 **21.** −72 **23.** 64 **25.** 84 **27.** −125 **29.** −240 **31.** −32 **33.** −35°C **35.** −10 **37.** −20 **39.** 5 **41.** 17 **43.** −9 **45.** 7 **47.** 3 h **49.** −21 **51.** 1 **53.** −6 **55.** −25 **57.** −4 **59.** −25 **61.** If the number of negative factors is odd, then the product is negative. If the number of negative factors is even, then the product is positive. **63.** true **65.** D **67.** −6 **69.** −23 **71.** −11 **73.** Sample answer: in all **75.** Sample answer: of

Pages 41–42 Lesson 1-7

1. Sample answer: the sum of a number and 4; 4 more than a number. **3.** $t - 18$ **5.** $\frac{n}{9}$ **7.** $p \div 5 = 3$ **9.** $n - 6$ **11.** $n + (-9)$ **13.** $\frac{n}{-3}$ **15.** $n - 20$ **17.** $t + 4$ **19.** k = the year Kentucky became a state; $k + 4$ **21.** g = gallons of gasoline; $\frac{260}{g}$ **23.** $150n$ **25.** $n - 8 = 15$ **27.** $-14 = 2n$ **29.** $10 - a = 3.50$ **31.** Sample answer: If the year is 2004, then the equation is $y + 25 = 2004$. **33.** B **35.** −90 **37.** −2 **39.** −\$1,800 **41.** −9 **43.** −27

Pages 47–49 Lesson 1-8

1. If you replace x with 4 in the equation $x + 3 = 7$ you get a true statement, 4 + 3 = 7. **3.** $m - 6 = 4$; this equation can be solved using the Addition Property of Equality, and the others can be solved using the Subtraction Property of Equality. **5.** −5 **7.** 7 **9.** 3 **11.** $n - 20 = -14$; 6 **13.** −2 **15.** −15 **17.** 17 **19.** 18 **21.** 16 **23.** −10 **25.** −59 **27.** 76 **29.** −8 **31.** 8 **33.** $n - 8 = -14$; −6 **35.** $n + 30 = 9$; −21 **37.** $b + 50 = 124$; \$74 **39.** $s - 6 = -5$; 1 or 1 over par **41.** $p = 18.2 - 1.3$; 16.9 **43.** $x + 0.40 = 5.15$; \$4.75 per hour **45.** Sample answer: While playing a computer trivia game, you answer a question correctly and your score is increased by 60 points. If your score is now 20 points, what was your original score? Answer: −40 **47.** B **49.** $7m$ **51.** −940 tigers per year **53.** −36 **55.** −60

Pages 52–53 Lesson 1-9

1. Division Property of Equality; the inverse operation of multiplication is division. **3.** Sample answer: it is greater than 300. **5.** −2 **7.** −5 **9.** −36 **11.** −56 **13.** $\frac{n}{4} = -16$; −64

15. 8 **17.** −2 **19.** 7 **21.** −15 **23.** 70 **25.** −99 **27.** −72 **29.** 60 **31.** 6 **33.** $-3n = 39$; −13 **35.** $\frac{n}{7} = -14$; −98 **37.** $12f = 288$; 24 **39.** $5{,}280m = 26{,}400$; 5 **41.** $500d = 3{,}000$; 6 days **43.** about 114 h **45.** $\frac{d}{r}$ **47.** C **49.** $x + 10 = 4$

Pages 54–56 Chapter 1 Study Guide and Review

1. e **3.** h **5.** a **7.** d **9.** c **11.** 21.4 g **13.** 8 **15.** 1 **17.** 15 **19.** −80 **21.** > **23.** 5 **25.** −33 **27.** −34 **29.** 5 **31.** 3 **33.** −4 **35.** 100 **37.** −60 **39.** 34 **41.** −12 **43.** $n + 7$ **45.** $4x = 48$ **47.** 13 **49.** −22 **51.** 39 **53.** −5 **55.** −13 **57.** −72

Chapter 2 Algebra: Rational Numbers

Page 61 Chapter 2 Getting Started

1. opposites, additive inverses **3.** −9 **5.** 3 **7.** −14 **9.** −28 **11.** −84 **13.** 43 **15.** −12 **17.** 24 **19.** 30 **21.** 48

Pages 65–66 Lesson 2-1

1. Sample answer: $0.\overline{12}$; Since $0.\overline{12} = \frac{4}{33}$, it is a rational number. **3.** $\frac{1}{2}$; It cannot be written as a repeating decimal. **5.** 4.375 **7.** $7.\overline{15}$ **9.** $-1\frac{11}{20}$ **11.** $2\frac{1}{9}$ **13.** 0.875 in. **15.** 0.2 **17.** −0.22 **19.** 5.3125 **21.** $-0.\overline{2}$ **23.** $-0.\overline{54}$ **25.** $7.\overline{24}$ **27.** $0.0\overline{4}$ **29.** $\frac{1}{2}$ **31.** $-\frac{7}{20}$ **33.** $7\frac{8}{25}$ **35.** $-\frac{4}{9}$ **37.** $2\frac{7}{9}$ **39.** $-3\frac{8}{11}$ **41.** $\frac{19}{50}$; $\frac{191{,}919}{500{,}000}$ **43.** $\frac{11}{100}$ oz **45.** $1\frac{5}{8}$ lb **47a.** $\frac{1}{2} = 0.5$, $\frac{1}{4} = 0.25$, $\frac{1}{5} = 0.2$, $\frac{1}{8} = 0.125$ **47b.** $\frac{1}{3} = 0.\overline{3}$, $\frac{1}{6} = 0.1\overline{6}$, $\frac{1}{7} = 0.\overline{142857}$, $\frac{1}{9} = 0.\overline{1}$ **49.** G **51.** −22 **53.** −4 **55.** 15 **57.** 24

Pages 69–70 Lesson 2-2

1. Since 0.28 = 0.28000000 and $0.\overline{28} = 0.28282828\ldots$, 0.28 is less than $0.\overline{28}$. **3.** Greatest to least; since the numerators are the same, the values of the fractions decrease as the denominators increase. **5.** < **7.** < **9.** −0.68, $-\frac{2}{3}$, 0.7, $\frac{3}{4}$ **11.** $\frac{5}{32}, \frac{1}{4}, \frac{3}{8}, \frac{7}{16}, \frac{9}{16}$ **13.** < **15.** > **17.** > **19.** < **21.** < **23.** = **25.** $6\frac{3}{4}$, 6.8, $7\frac{1}{5}$, 7.6 **27.** $-\frac{3}{5}$, −0.5, 0.45, $\frac{4}{7}$ **29.** −2.95, $-2\frac{13}{14}$, −2.9, $-2\frac{9}{11}$ **31.** $\frac{2}{5}$ **33.** $\frac{1}{125}$ s **35.** Florida State University **37.** D **39.** 0.875 in. **41.** −15 **43.** −27 **45.** −96 **47.** 115

Pages 74–75 Lesson 2-3

1. Since $\frac{1}{2} \cdot 1 = \frac{1}{2}$ and $\frac{7}{8}$ is less than 1, $\frac{1}{2} \cdot \frac{7}{8}$ is less than $\frac{1}{2}$. **3.** Enrique; to multiply mixed numbers, you must first rename them as fractions. **5.** $-\frac{1}{18}$ **7.** $\frac{16}{25}$ **9.** $\frac{2}{5}$ **11.** $\frac{1}{21}$ **13.** $-\frac{3}{5}$ **15.** $1\frac{1}{2}$ **17.** $3\frac{1}{2}$ **19.** $-14\frac{1}{6}$ **21.** $\frac{4}{9}$ **23.** $\frac{3}{20}$ **25.** $-\frac{2}{9}$ **27.** $\frac{4}{27}$ **29.** $2\frac{1}{16}$ in. **31.** $\frac{6}{7}$ **33.** 3.78 **35.** C **37.** < **39.** < **41.** $\frac{11}{20}$ **43.** 27 **45.** 15

Pages 79–80 Lesson 2-4

1. If the product of the two numbers is 1, the two numbers are multiplicative inverses. **3.** Sample answer: $\frac{2}{3} \div \frac{5}{6}$ **5.** $\frac{7}{5}$ **7.** $-\frac{4}{11}$ **9.** $-1\frac{1}{4}$ **11.** 7 times longer **13.** $-\frac{8}{5}$ **15.** $\frac{1}{18}$ **17.** $\frac{15}{7}$ **19.** $\frac{8}{33}$ **21.** $\frac{9}{16}$ **23.** $-\frac{4}{5}$ **25.** $\frac{3}{8}$ **27.** $3\frac{4}{7}$ **29.** $-\frac{3}{14}$ **31.** $-3\frac{3}{16}$ **33.** $\frac{8}{9}$ **35.** $\frac{9}{10}$ **37.** $\frac{1}{2}$ **39.** $1\frac{4}{5}$ **41a.** $\frac{43}{76}$ **41b.** $\frac{53}{72}$ **43.** $-a$ **45.** $\frac{1}{3}$ **47.** $2\frac{1}{6}$ **49.** $4x - 8{,}000{,}000$ **51.** 8 **53.** −18

Pages 84–85 Lesson 2-5

1.

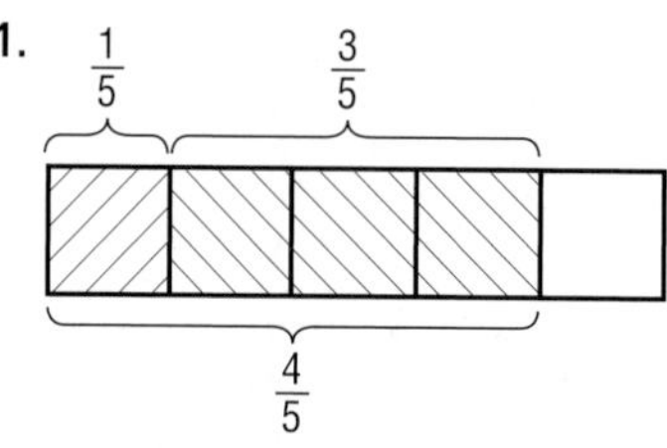

3. Allison; to add like fractions, add the numerators and write the sum over the denominator. **5.** $-\frac{1}{2}$ **7.** $-\frac{1}{2}$ **9.** $\frac{6}{7}$ **11.** $\frac{6}{7}$ **13.** $\frac{1}{6}$ **15.** $-1\frac{3}{4}$ **17.** $-\frac{1}{2}$ **19.** $-1\frac{2}{5}$ **21.** $11\frac{1}{4}$ **23.** $5\frac{1}{5}$ **25.** $-5\frac{2}{3}$ **27.** $1\frac{3}{5}$ **29.** $-4\frac{3}{8}$ **31.** $7\frac{2}{3}$ **33.** Since $\frac{1}{2} \cdot \frac{3}{4} + \frac{1}{2} \cdot \frac{1}{4} = \frac{1}{2}\left(\frac{3}{4} + \frac{1}{4}\right)$ or $\frac{1}{2}(1)$, the answer is $\frac{1}{2}$. **35.** $1\frac{1}{2}$ in. **37.** Since $\frac{2}{3} + \frac{1}{3} = 1$, $\frac{2}{5} + \frac{3}{5} = 1$, and $\frac{1}{6} + \frac{5}{6} = 1$, add 3 to the sum of the whole numbers; 15. **39.** F **41.** $\frac{5}{16}$ **43.** $\frac{3}{4}$ **45.** 42 **47.** 36

Pages 90–91 Lesson 2-6

1. Rename the fractions so they have a common denominator. **3.** Greater than; since both fractions are greater than $\frac{1}{2}$, the sum will be greater than $\frac{1}{2} + \frac{1}{2}$ or 1. **5.** $\frac{1}{8}$ **7.** $-1\frac{7}{30}$ **9.** $-\frac{13}{15}$ **11.** $1\frac{5}{24}$ **13.** $\frac{7}{12}$ **15.** $-\frac{11}{21}$ **17.** $14\frac{13}{14}$ **19.** $-10\frac{3}{8}$ **21.** $4\frac{2}{3}$ **23.** $-5\frac{3}{10}$ **25.** $-3\frac{23}{24}$ **27.** $\frac{421}{1{,}496}$ **29.** $15\frac{1}{4}$ **31.** $-1\frac{1}{8}$ **33.** $12\frac{1}{8}$ **35.** about $\frac{25}{168}$ **37.** $\frac{1}{3}$ **39.** $1\frac{7}{8}$ min **41a.** $\frac{3}{4} \cdot \frac{2}{3} = \frac{1}{2}$ **41b.** $\frac{2}{3} + \frac{3}{4} = 1\frac{5}{12}$ **41c.** $\frac{2}{3} - \frac{3}{4} = -\frac{1}{12}$ **41d.** $\frac{2}{3} \div \frac{3}{4} = \frac{8}{9}$

43.
$$\begin{aligned} &5\tfrac{1}{6} + 4\tfrac{2}{9} \\ &= (5 + 4) + \left(\tfrac{1}{6} + \tfrac{2}{9}\right) \\ &= (5 + 4) + \left(\tfrac{3}{18} + \tfrac{4}{18}\right) \\ &= 9 + \tfrac{7}{18} \\ &= 9\tfrac{7}{18} \end{aligned}$$

45. $-\frac{11}{15}$ **47.** −4 **49.** −15 **51.** −80

Pages 94–95 Lesson 2-7

1. Sample answer: $x + \frac{3}{4} = 1$ **3.** −4.37 **5.** −54 **7.** $\frac{16}{45}$ **9.** $11.9r = 59.5$ **11.** 0.84 **13.** $\frac{1}{6}$ **15.** −28 **17.** 6 **19.** $-1\frac{1}{9}$ **21.** 0.85 **23.** −14.4 **25.** $2\frac{3}{10}$ **27.** $-\frac{1}{4}$ **29.** $-1\frac{3}{5}$ **31.** $5.60 **33.** 4.5 million visitors **35.** A **37.** $\frac{13}{42}$ **39.** $-12\frac{3}{10}$ **41.** $106\frac{3}{16}$ in. **43.** $17 + p$ **45.** 32 **47.** 125

Pages 100–101 Lesson 2-8

1. Sample answer: 3^{-2}; $3^{-2} = \frac{1}{3^2}$ or $\frac{1}{9}$ **3.** 3^6 **5.** $s^3 \cdot r^5$ **7.** 288 **9.** $\frac{1}{216}$ **11.** 300 stars **13.** 30,000 stars **15.** 8^3 **17.** p^6 **19.** $3^2 \cdot 4^3$ **21.** $4^3 \cdot 7^5$ **23.** a^4b^4 **25.** $7^4 \cdot 15^2$ **27.** 8 **29.** 243 **31.** 225 **33.** 4,000 **35.** $\frac{1}{625}$ **37.** $\frac{8}{49}$ **39.** 224 **41.** 64 bacteria **43.** 8 in^3; 216 in^3 **45a.** 10^5 **45b.** $5 \cdot 10^7$ **45c.** $3 \cdot 10^9$ **45d.** $6 \cdot 10^4$ **47.** $(2 \cdot 2 \cdot 2) \cdot (6 \cdot 6)$; 288 **49.** $\frac{11}{18}$ **51.** $2\frac{5}{18}$ **53.** $x + 12$ **55.** 320

Pages 106–107 Lesson 2-9

1. Sometimes; if the decimal is greater than or equal to 1 and less than 10, the value is in scientific notation. If the decimal is less than 1 or greater than or equal to 10, the value is not in scientific notation. **3.** 1.2×10^6; 1.2×10^5 is only 120,000, but 1.2×10^6 is just over one million. **5.** 993,100 **7.** 0.000602 **9.** 8.785×10^9 **11.** 5.24×10^{-1} **13.** 208 **15.** 71,130,000 **17.** 0.0078 **19.** 0.000873 **21.** 1,046,000 **23.** 0.000006299 **25.** 14,000 lb **27.** 6.3×10^5 **29.** 6.7×10^3 **31.** 5.23×10^7 **33.** 3.7×10^{-2} **35.** 7.07×10^{-6} **37.** 1×10^{-24} s **39.** 1×10^{100} **41.** Wrigley Field, Network Associates Coliseum, H.H.H. Metrodome, The Ballpark in Arlington, Yankee Stadium **43.** $\frac{(9 \times 10^4)(1.6 \times 10^{-3})}{(2 \times 10^5)(3 \times 10^4)(1.2 \times 10^{-4})} = 2 \times 10^{-4}$ **45.** Huron **47.** $-\frac{5}{6}$ **49.** 3.12

Pages 108–110 Chapter 2 Study Guide and Review

1. exponent **3.** Like fractions **5.** base **7.** rational number **9.** $1.\bar{3}$ **11.** 5.26 **13.** −2.3 **15.** $\frac{3}{10}$ **17.** $-2\frac{3}{4}$ **19.** $4\frac{1}{3}$ **21.** < **23.** = **25.** $-\frac{3}{4}, -\frac{1}{2}, 0, 0.75$ **27.** $\frac{4}{9}$ **29.** $\frac{5}{11}$ **31.** $2\frac{1}{3}$ **33.** $2\frac{1}{5}$ **35.** 1 **37.** $-\frac{3}{4}$ **39.** $-\frac{1}{15}$ **41.** $-11\frac{1}{6}$ **43.** $11\frac{11}{20}$ **45.** 3.2 **47.** $1\frac{1}{6}$ **49.** 40 **51.** $2^2 \cdot 5^3$ **53.** $4^2 \cdot 9^2$ **55.** 432 **57.** 128 **59.** 67,100 **61.** 0.015 **63.** 3.51×10^{-4} **65.** 7.41×10^6

Chapter 3 Algebra: Real Numbers and the Pythagorean Theorem

Page 115 Chapter 3 Getting Started

1. true

3–6.

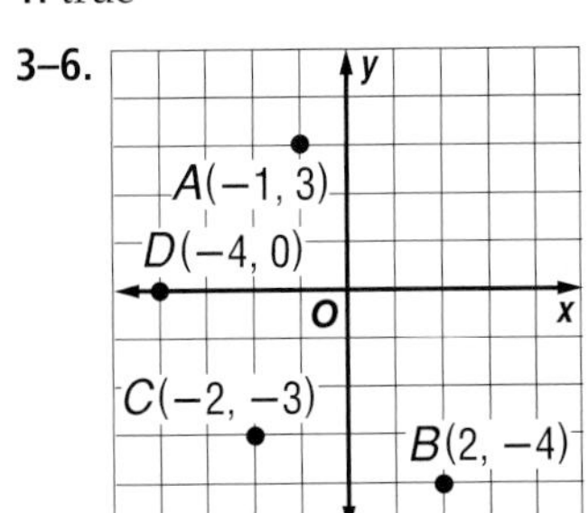

7. 20 **9.** 164 **11.** 32 **13.** 62 **15.** $\frac{2}{3}$ **17.** $\frac{3}{8}$ **19.** 36, 49

Pages 118–119 Lesson 3-1

1. $\sqrt{16} = 4$, which is what golfers yell to warn other players that the ball is coming. **3.** Sample answer: $x^2 = 100$ **5.** 5 **7.** $-\frac{4}{9}$ **9.** 6 or −6 **11.** 30 or −30 **13.** 16 or −16 **15.** 9 **17.** −6 **19.** −12 **21.** 18 **23.** $-\frac{3}{7}$ **25.** 1.2 **27.** −20 **29.** 10 or −10 **31.** 12 or −12 **33.** 50 or −50 **35.** 31 or −31 **37.** $\frac{3}{8}$ or $-\frac{3}{8}$ **39.** 1.1 or −1.1 **41.** 2.01 or −2.01 **43.** 44 in. **45.** 24 m **47a.** 36 **47b.** 81 **47c.** 21 **47d.** x **49.** C **51.** 25,000,000,000,000 mi **53.** $2^4 \cdot 3^2$ **55.** $s^4 \cdot t^3$ **57.** 49, 64 **59.** 25, 36

Pages 121–122 Lesson 3-2

1.

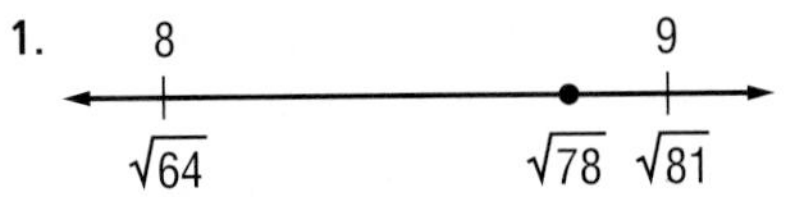

3. Julia; $7^2 = 49$ or about 50, but $25^2 = 625$. **5.** 5 **7.** 12 **9.** 9 or −9 **11.** 4 **13.** 5 **15.** 10 **17.** 7 **19.** 5 **21.** 6 **23.** 13 **25.** 11 **27.** 30 **29.** 28 **31.** 10 or −10 **33.** $5, \sqrt{38}, 7, \sqrt{91}$ **35.** about 3.5 s **37.** B **39.** 90 or −90 **41.** $\frac{3}{20}$ **43.** $\frac{1}{3}$

Pages 128–129 Lesson 3-3

1. Sample answer: $\sqrt{4}$ **3.** $\sqrt{25}$; since $\sqrt{25} = 5$, it is not an irrational number like the others. **5.** integer, rational **7.** rational **9.** −4.2

$-\sqrt{18}$

−6 −5 −4 −3

11. 9.7

$\sqrt{95}$

8 9 10 11

13. = **15.** $\sqrt{30}, 5\frac{1}{2}, 5.\bar{5}, 5.56$ **17.** whole, integer, rational **19.** integer, rational **21.** rational **23.** irrational **25.** rational **27.** rational **29.** Always; an integer can always be written as the integer over 1, so an integer is always a rational number.

31. 2.4

33. −4.7

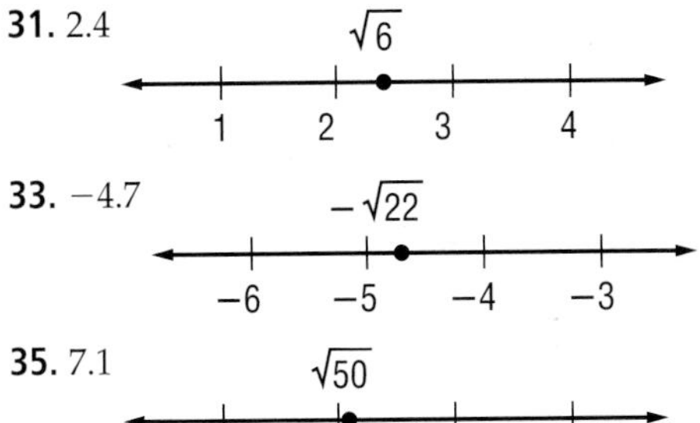

35. 7.1

$\sqrt{50}$

6 7 8 9

37. −10.2

$-\sqrt{105}$

−12 −11 −10 −9

39. < **41.** > **43.** = **45.** $\sqrt{3}, 2.\bar{2}, \sqrt{5}, 2.25$ **47.** $\sqrt{17}$, 4.01, −4.1, $-4.\bar{1}$ **49.** about 53.3 mph **51.** always **53.** 76 ft **55.** 5 or −5 **57.** 0.8 or −0.8 **59.** 34 **61.** 202

Pages 135–136 Lesson 3-4

1.

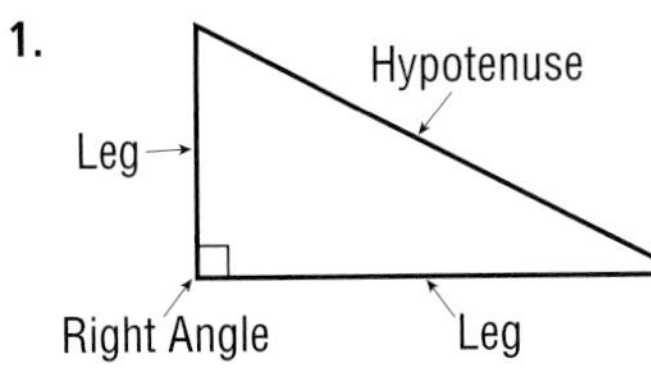

3. Morgan; the hypotenuse (8) and a leg (5) are given. The correct equation to solve the problem is $8^2 = a^2 + 5^2$.

5. $12^2 = a^2 + 8^2$; 8.9 yd **7.** $6^2 = 5^2 + b^2$; 3.3 ft **9.** $10^2 = a^2 + 4^2$; 9.2 yd **11.** yes **13.** $c^2 = 5^2 + 12^2$; 13 in. **15.** $18^2 = 8^2 + b^2$; 16.1 m **17.** $x^2 = 14^2 + 6^2$; 15.2 in. **19.** $c^2 = 48^2 + 55^2$; 73 yd **21.** $c^2 = 23^2 + 18^2$; 29.2 in. **23.** $12.3^2 = a^2 + 5.1^2$; 11.2 m **25.** about 11.5 ft **27.** no **29.** no **31.** no **35.** at knots 3 and 7 from unstaked end

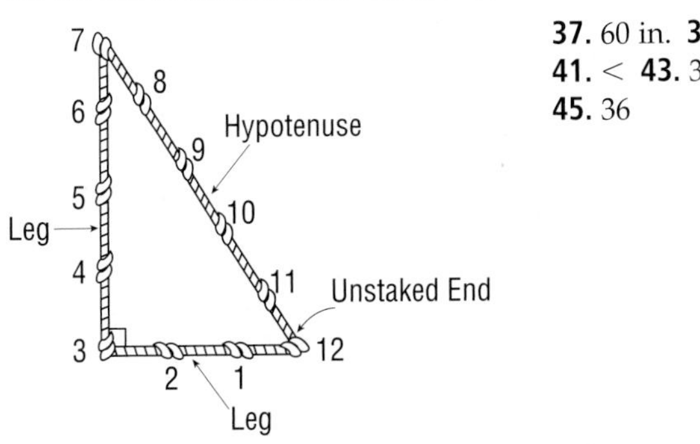

37. 60 in. **39.** > **41.** < **43.** 33 **45.** 36

Pages 138–140 Lesson 3-5

1. The Pythagorean Theorem relates the lengths of the three sides of a right triangle. If you know the lengths of two sides of a right triangle, you can substitute the values into the Pythagorean Theorem and solve for the missing length. **3.** 5-7-9; $9^2 \neq 5^2 + 7^2$ **5.** $d^2 = 7^2 + 10^2$; 12.2 mi **7.** about 5.7 in. **9.** $d^2 = 60^2 + 150^2$; 161.6 yd **11.** $24^2 = 18^2 + \ell^2$; 15.9 mi **13.** $20^2 = 19.5^2 + h^2$; 4.4 m **15.** about 28.5 in. **17.** about 2.6 cm **19.** about 15.3 cm **21.** about 0.5 ft **23.** I **25.** 6.6, 6.7, $\sqrt{45}$, 6.75 **27.** 27 **29.** 1,600,000

31. A (−1, 3)

33. D (−2, −4)

Pages 144–145 Lesson 3-6

1. Pythagorean Theorem **3.** Sample answer: (1, 2) and (4, 6) **5.** 5.7 units

7. (1, 5), (3, 1)

4.5 units

9. (2, 3), (−5, −2)

8.6 units

11. 5.4 units **13.** 6.3 units **15.** 5.8 units

17. (6, 2), (1, 0)

5.4 units

19.

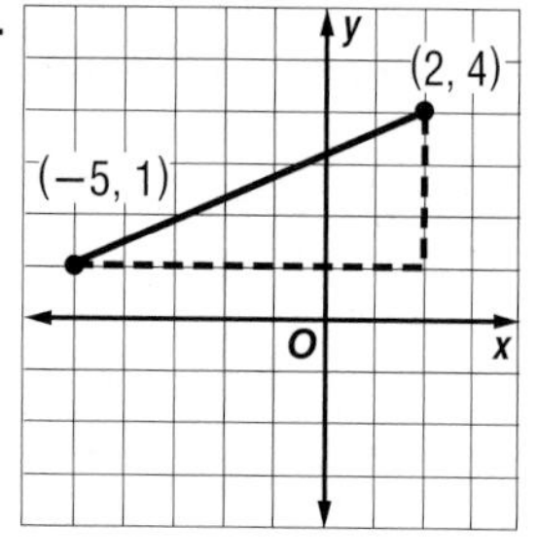

7.6 units

21. (4, −2.3), (−1, −6.3)

6.4 units

23. about 224.9 mi **25.** For horizontal lines, the x-coordinate is half the sum of the x-coordinates of the endpoints and the y-coordinate is the y-coordinate of the endpoints. For vertical lines, the x-coordinate is the x-coordinate of the endpoints and the y-coordinate is half the sum of the y-coordinates of the endpoints. **27.** $c^2 = 4^2 + 2^2$ **29.** 23.4 cm

Pages 146–148 Chapter 3 Study Guide and Review

1. false; cannot **3.** true **5.** false; vertical axis **7.** true **9.** 9 **11.** 8 **13.** $-\frac{2}{3}$ **15.** 17 rows of 17 trees in each row **17.** 6

19. 10 **21.** 3 **23.** 4 **25.** irrational **27.** rational **29.** irrational **31.** $c^2 = 24^2 + 18^2$; 30 in. **33.** $c^2 = 8^2 + 5^2$; 9.4 ft **35.** $6^2 = 5^2 + b^2$; 3.3 in. **37.** $25^2 = 20^2 + h^2$; 15 ft **39.** $\ell^2 = 8^2 + 5^2$; 9.4 ft **41.** about 13.9 m

43. (4, 8), (−1, 2)

7.8 units

45.

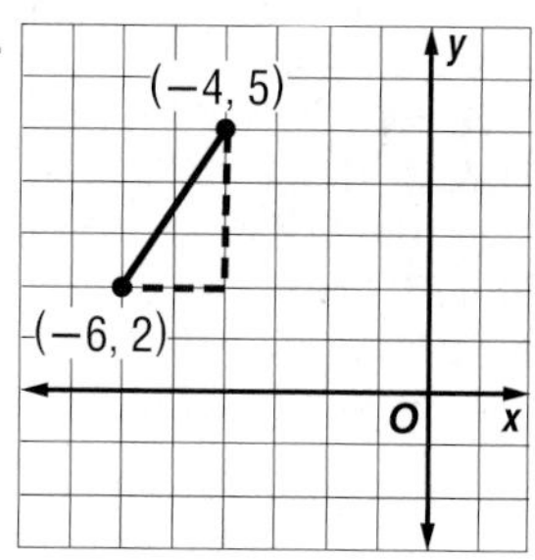

3.6 units

47.

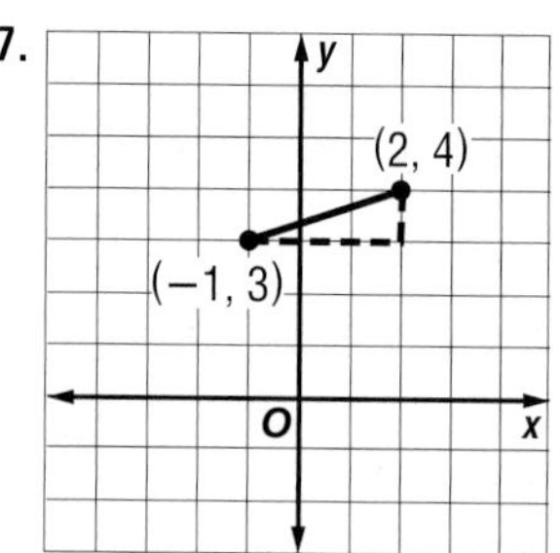

3.2 units

Chapter 4 Proportions, Algebra, and Geometry

Page 155 Chapter 4 Getting Started

1. variable **3.** ordered pair **5.** $\frac{11}{13}$ **7.** $\frac{7}{13}$ **9.** $\frac{3}{4}$ **11.** 6 **13.** −7 **15.** 7 **17.** 1 **19.** 14 **21.** 1.75 **23.** 10.5

Pages 158–159 Lesson 4-1

1. Sample answer: $\frac{16 \text{ yellow}}{10 \text{ red}}$; $\frac{8}{5}$; for every 8 yellow marbles, 5 are red. **3.** 1:15 **5.** 12 to 1 **7.** \$12.50/day **9.** Ben's Mart; the cost at Ben's Mart is about 23.8¢ per apple, while at SaveMost it is about 24.8¢. **11.** 7:8 **13.** $\frac{7}{25}$ **15.** 2 to 9 **17.** 17:2 **19.** \$5.65/h **21.** 1,225 tickets/theater **23.** about 1.8 lb/wk **25.** 6 cans for \$1; 6 for \$1 costs about 16.7¢/can and 10 for \$1.95 cost about 19.5¢/can. **27.** 2 liters for \$1.39; 2 liters for \$1.39 costs about 2.1¢/oz and 12 12-ounce cans for \$3.49 costs about 2.4¢/oz. **29.** 384 **31.** $\frac{1{,}662{,}269}{9}$ **33.** about \$471,000/in² **35.** 18 **37.** Darnell

39.

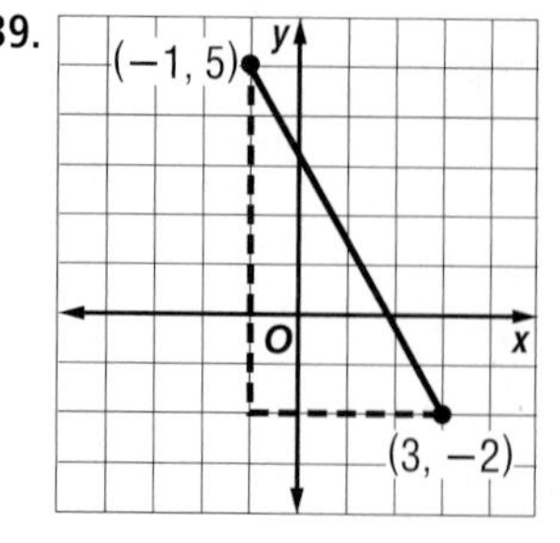

8.1 units

41.

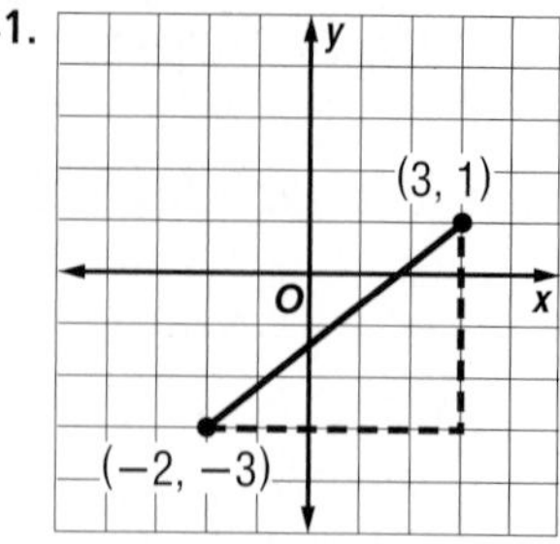

6.4 units

43. 6 **45.** −3

Pages 163–164 Lesson 4-2

1. cost of postage for a 1-oz letter over a period of 4 months in which the cost did not change **3.** 6°/h; about −6.3°/h

5.

7. 4.1 flyers/min **9.** between 1:25 and 1:30 **11.** 100 eagle pairs/yr **13.** between 1984 and 1994

15. Between 2000 and 2002; reading the graph from left to right, the segment connecting 2000 and 2002 is steeper than the segment connecting 1980 and 1990. **17.** $22 billion/yr **19.** 18 **21.** B **23.** 3 to 8 **25.** $\frac{3}{2}$ **27.** $\frac{1}{3}$

Pages 168–169 Lesson 4-3

1. 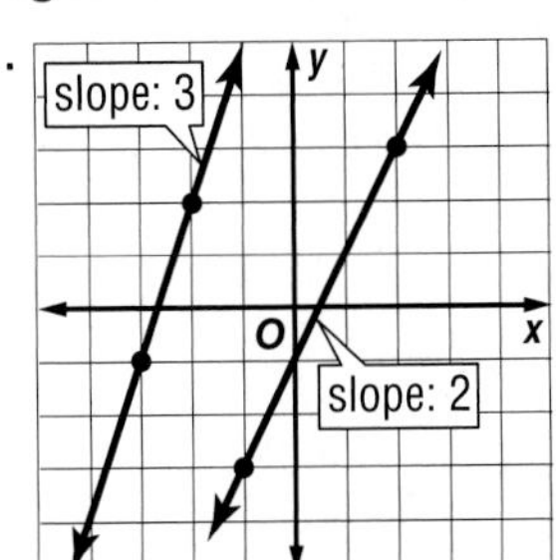

the line with slope 3 **3.** $\frac{4}{3}$

5. 2; 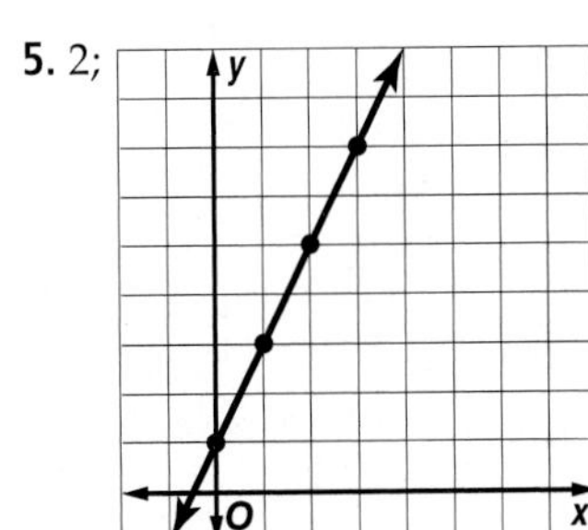

7. $-\frac{3}{4}$ **9.** 0 **11.** $\frac{3}{2}$

13. $\frac{2}{3}$; 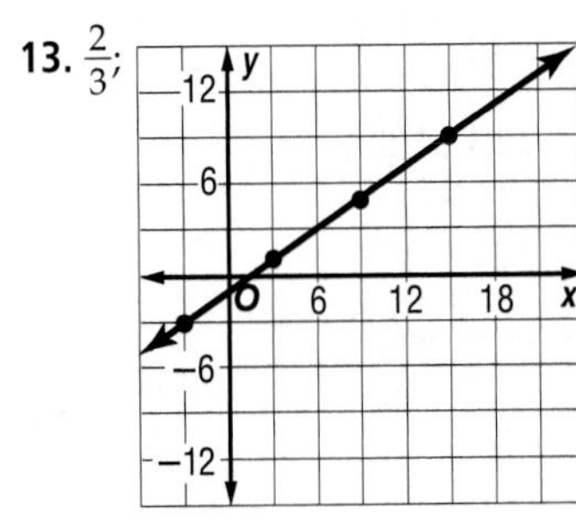

15. 10; $10 increase in cost for each pizza delivered **17.** $\frac{5}{11}$; pressure increases 5 lbs/in^2 for every 11 feet increase in depth **19.** Pedro; he is saving $12.50 per week, while Jenna is only saving $6 per week.

21. 2/3 **23.** 1.8 in./min **25.** 12 **27.** 7.5

Pages 172–173 Lesson 4-4

1. Sample answer: $\frac{3}{10}, \frac{6}{20}, \frac{9}{30}, \frac{24}{80}$ **3.** yes **5.** yes **7.** 16.4 **9.** $\frac{18}{15} = \frac{b}{60}$; 72 **11.** no **13.** yes **15.** yes **17.** yes **19.** 4 **21.** 120 **23.** 7.2 **25.** 1.68 **27.** 1.4 **29.** 22 **31.** $\frac{6}{1} = \frac{96}{p}$; 16 **33.** $\frac{3}{2{,}000} = \frac{x}{3{,}500}$; 5.25 **35.** 24 **37.** about 8.5 in. **39.** $\frac{12}{x} = \frac{1}{2.54}$; 30.48 **41.** $\frac{2}{x} = \frac{3.78}{1}$; 0.53 **43.** Proportional; each statement can be written as a ratio equivalent to 3:2. **45.** D **47.** $\frac{8}{3}$;

49. $\overline{AB}, \overline{BC}, \overline{CA}$ **51.** $\overline{LM}, \overline{MN}, \overline{NP}, \overline{PL}$

Pages 181–182 Lesson 4-5

1. If 2 polygons have corresponding congruent angles and have corresponding sides that are in proportion, then the polygons are similar. **3.** no; $\frac{5}{3} \neq \frac{13}{5}$ **5.** $\frac{x}{6} = \frac{2}{1}$; 12 **7.** Yes; the corresponding angles are congruent and $\frac{3}{5} = \frac{3}{5}$. **9.** No; the corresponding angles are congruent, but $\frac{5}{4} \neq \frac{8}{6}$. **11.** $\frac{x}{4.8} = \frac{5}{4}$; 6 **13.** $\frac{26}{x} = \frac{1.6}{1}$; 16.25 **15.** 46.67 mm **17a.** $\frac{1}{4}$ **17b.** $\frac{1}{9}$ **17c.** $\frac{1}{16}$ **17d.** $\frac{1}{25}$; The ratio of the area is the square of the scale factor. **19.** Always; all corresponding angles between squares are congruent since all four angles in a square are right angles. In addition, all sides in a square are congruent. Therefore, all four ratios of corresponding sides are equal. **21.** $3\frac{3}{4}$ in.

23. 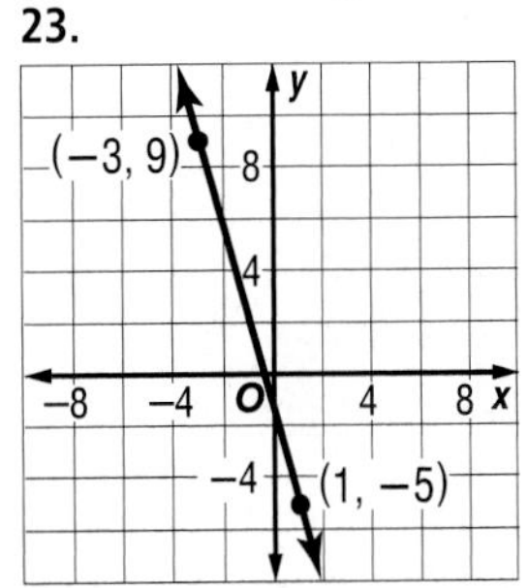

$-\frac{7}{2}$

25. 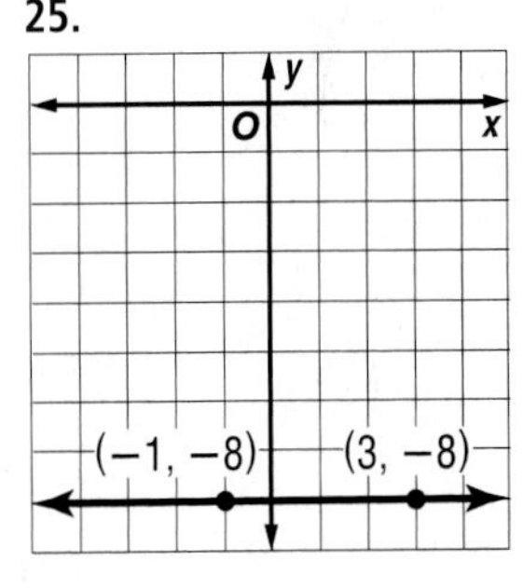

0

27. $\frac{4}{5} = \frac{5}{x}$; 6.25

Pages 186–187 Lesson 4-6

1. Sample answer: 1 in. = 10 ft; 1:120 **3.** 720 mi **5.** 1 in. = 60 ft **7.** 12 ft **9.** 8.4 ft **11.** $13\frac{1}{2}$ ft **13.** $\frac{1}{72}$ **15.** 1 cm = 0.0015 mm **17.** Sample answer: 1 cm = 1.25 m; 11.25 m **19.** A tennis ball; if the circumference of the model is C, then $\frac{C}{11{,}000} = \frac{3}{4{,}000}$, so C = 8.25. **21.** The model built on the 1:75 scale since $\frac{1}{75} > \frac{1}{100}$. **23.** D **25.** Yes; the corresponding angles are congruent, and $\frac{3}{4.8} = \frac{2}{3.2} = \frac{2}{3.2} = \frac{1.5}{2.4}$. **27.** 12.5 **29.** $\angle A \cong \angle D, \angle B \cong \angle E, \angle ACB \cong \angle DCE$

Selected Answers

Pages 189–191 Lesson 4-7

1. $\frac{14}{5} = \frac{h}{6}$

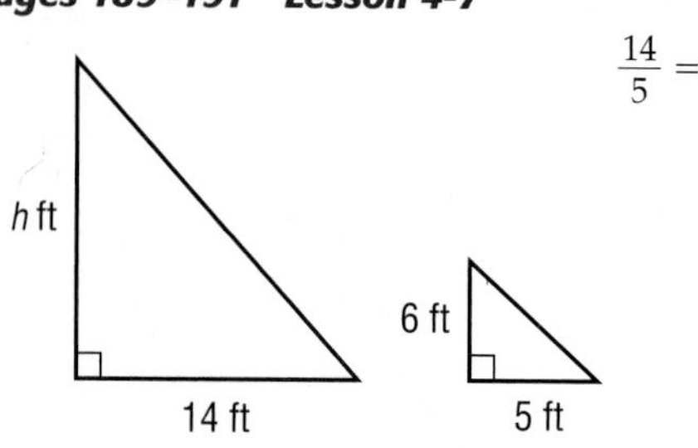

3. $\frac{0.6}{56} = \frac{1.5}{h}$; 140 m

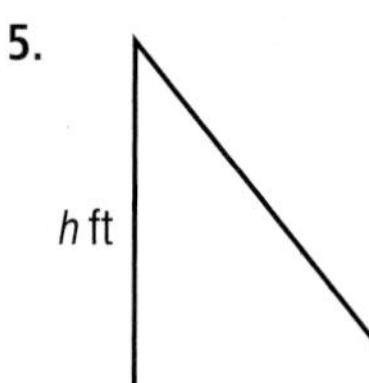

5. $\frac{h}{18.5} = \frac{10}{7}$; about 26 ft

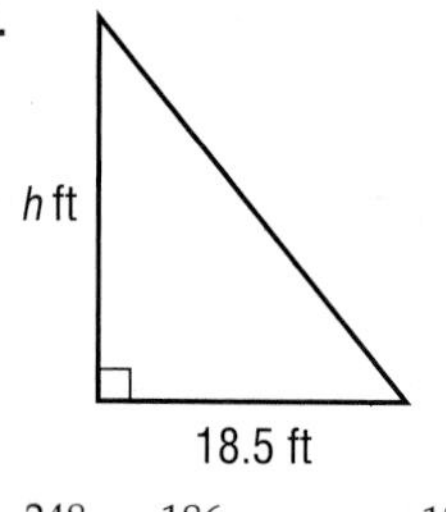

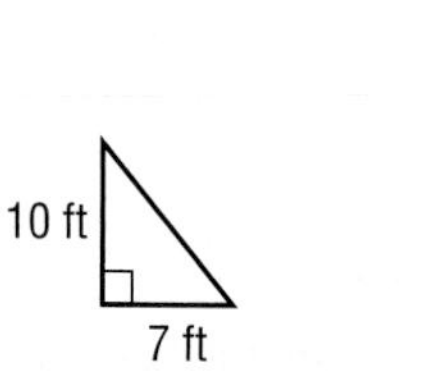

7. $\frac{248}{h} = \frac{186}{9}$; 12 ft **9.** $\frac{135}{252} = \frac{204}{d}$; 380.8 ft

11. $\frac{3}{106} = \frac{h}{212}$; 6 ft

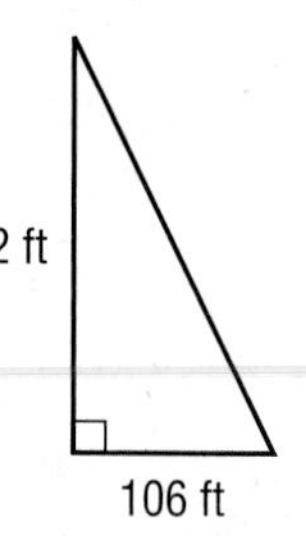

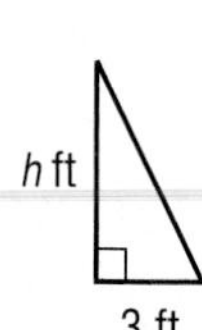

13. $\frac{3}{x} = \frac{5}{62.5}$; 37.5 ft

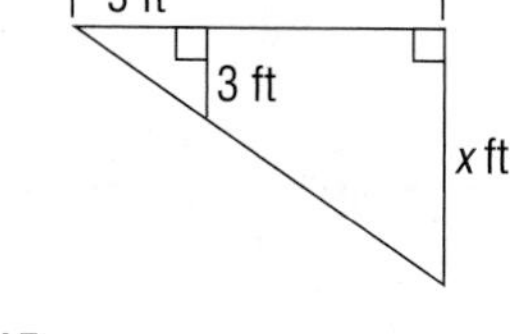

15.

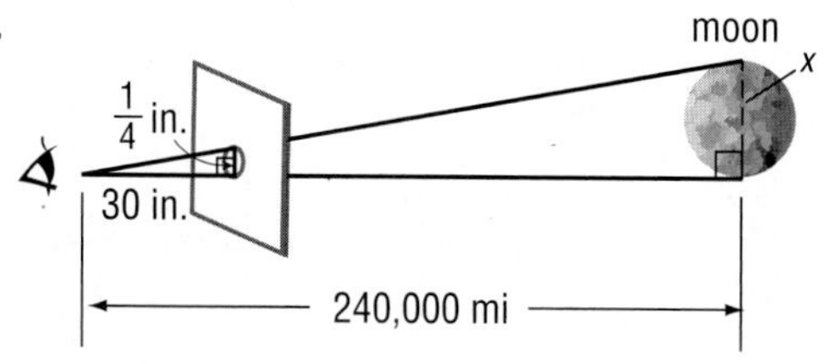

$\frac{\frac{1}{4}}{30} = \frac{x}{240{,}000}$; 2,000 mi

17. $\frac{h}{ED} = \frac{BC}{DC}$ **19.** B **21.** 10 mi **23.** 32.5 mi **25.** $\frac{4.5}{m} = \frac{3}{8}$; 12 **27.** $-4\frac{1}{10}$ **29.** $-1\frac{1}{3}$ **31.** 4.3×10^6 **33.** 2.0×10^{-7}

35. 8 units;

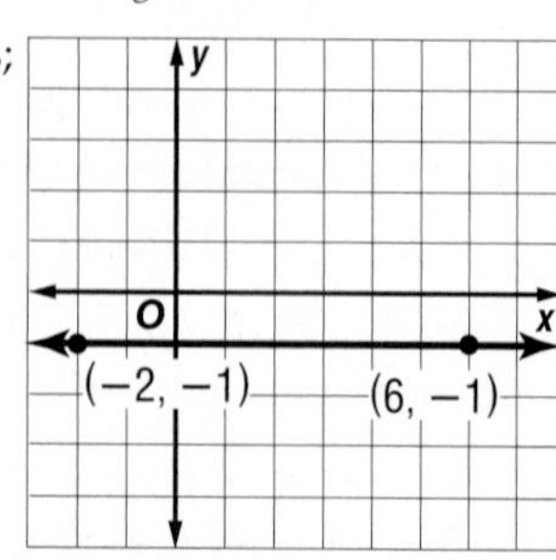

37. 13 units;

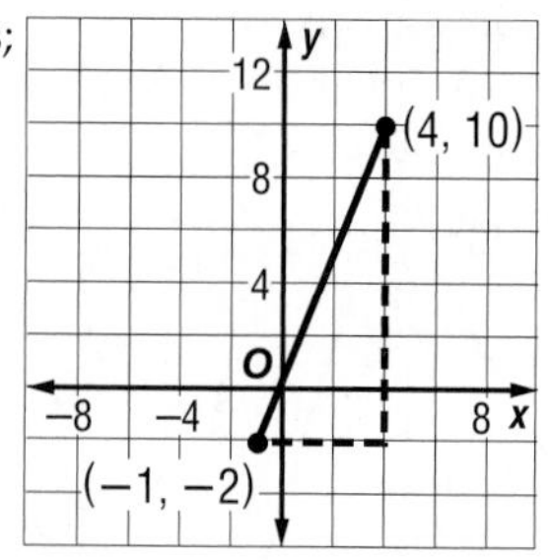

Pages 196–197 Lesson 4-8

1. Sample answer:

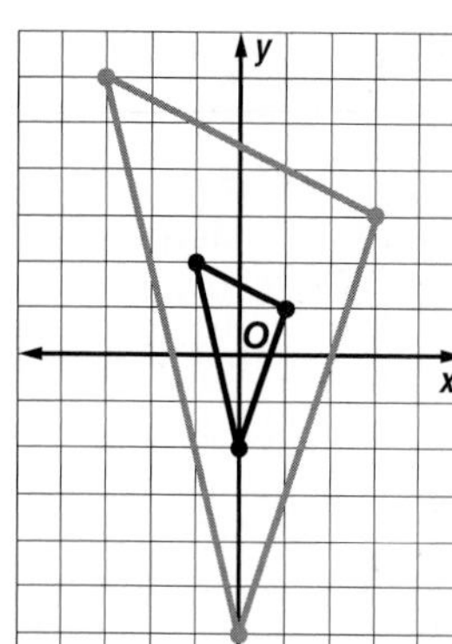

3. $A'(-1, 3)$, $B'\left(-\frac{1}{2}, -1\right)$, $C'\left(2, \frac{3}{2}\right)$;

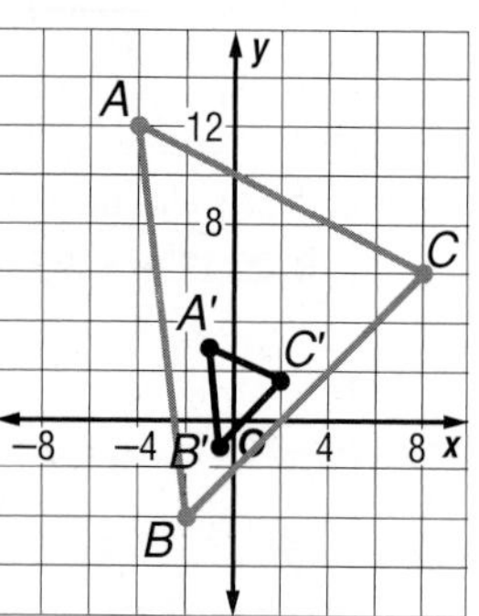

5. $\frac{3}{2}$; enlargement **7.** $H'(0, 6)$, $J'(9, 3)$, $K'(0, -12)$, $L'(-6, -9)$;

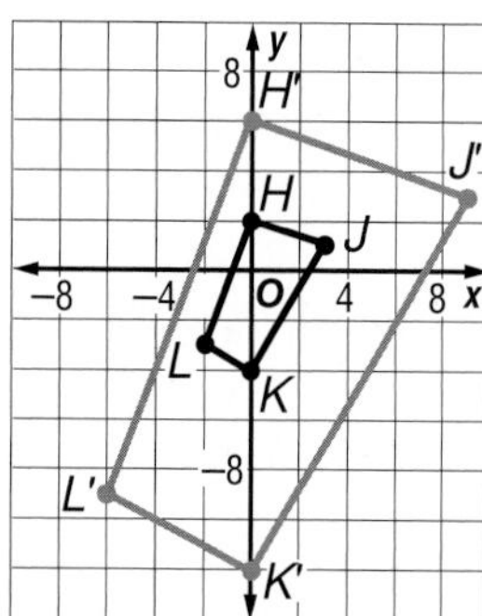

9. $H'(-6, 3)$, $J'\left(4\frac{1}{2}, 3\right)$, $K'\left(4\frac{1}{2}, -3\right)$, $L'(-6, -3)$;

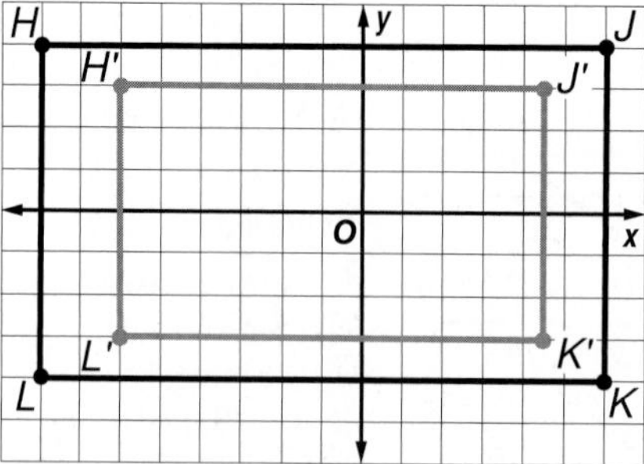

11. $\frac{3}{5}$; reduction **13.** $\frac{4}{3}$; enlargement

15. Sample answer:

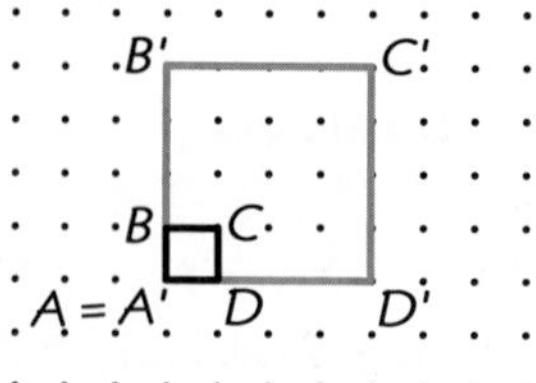

17. 3; enlargement **19.** $\frac{1}{2}$; reduction **21.** 2.5

23.

25. The figure is enlarged and rotated 180°. **27.** G **29.** 5 in. = 7 ft

Pages 198–200 Chapter 4 Study Guide and Review

1. f **3.** a **5.** d **7.** b **9.** 1 for 8 **11.** 1 out of 12 **13.** $\frac{5}{2}$ **15.** $-\frac{3}{4}$;

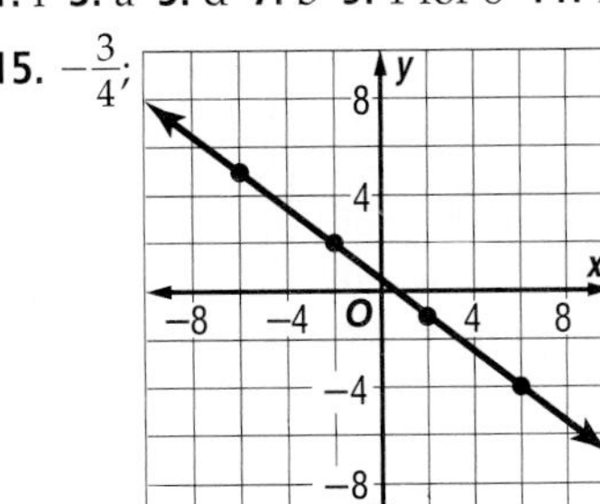

17. 3.5 **19.** 2.85 **21.** $\frac{13}{x} = \frac{5}{1}$; 2.6 **23.** $13\frac{1}{3}$ in. **25.** 22.5 mi **27.** 1 in. = 12 in. or 1 in. = 1 ft **29.** $\frac{5.5}{x} = \frac{2.25}{6}$; $14\frac{2}{3}$ ft **31.** $\frac{2}{5}$; reduction

Chapter 5 Percent

Page 205 Chapter 5 Getting Started

1. equation **3.** proportion **5.** 322 **7.** 32 **9.** 0.875 **11.** 0.375 **13.** 0.25 **15.** 450 **17.** 0.35 **19.** 0.5 **21.** 31.5 **23.** 15.6

Pages 208–209 Lesson 5-1

1. 30%; $\frac{3}{10}$ **3.** $\frac{20}{100}$; All the other numbers equal 40%. **5.** 237% **7.** 45% **9.** $\frac{1}{2}$ **11.** $\frac{1}{250}$ **13.** 23% **15.** 0.3% **17.** 60% **19.** 32% **21.** 34% **23.** 195% **25.** 12% **27.** $\frac{29}{100}$ **29.** $\frac{2}{5}$ **31.** $\frac{9}{20}$ **33.** $\frac{16}{25}$ **35.** $1\frac{1}{4}$ **37.** $\frac{1}{500}$ **39.** $\frac{1}{25}$ **41.** $\frac{9}{20}, \frac{3}{20}, \frac{1}{10}, \frac{2}{25}, \frac{7}{100}$ **43.** 37% **45.** 25% **47.** Since $\frac{43}{50} = \frac{86}{100}$, a student would receive an 86% on the test if he or she answered 43 out of the 50 questions correctly. **49.** H **51.** 4; enlargement **53.** 0.6 **55.** 0.625

Pages 212–214 Lesson 5-2

1. $\frac{13}{25}$; 52%; 0.52 **3.** Aislyn; 0.7 is 7 tenths, not 7 hundredths. **5.** 0.16 **7.** 0.003 **9.** 123% **11.** 72.5% **13.** 87.5% **15.** $83.\overline{3}\%$ **17.** 0.9 **19.** 0.15 **21.** 1.72 **23.** 0.275 **25.** 0.07 **27.** 0.082 **29.** 0.55 **31.** 54% **33.** 37.5% **35.** 0.7% **37.** 40% **39.** 275% **41.** 21% **43.** 85% **45.** 2.5% **47.** 160% **49.** 0.5% **51.** $44.\overline{4}\%$ **53.** 32% **55.** $83.\overline{3}\%$ **57.** > **59.** < **61.** = **63.** 31.25% **65.** 2%, $\frac{3}{20}$, 0.2, $\frac{1}{4}$ **67.** more **69.** $\frac{7}{25}$ **71.** 160% **73.** H **75.** 0.6% **77.** 66% **79.** {−12, −5, −1, 5, 13} **81.** {−65, −61, −58, 57, 64} **83.** 1.6 **85.** 2.4

Pages 218–219 Lesson 5-3

1. Percent means per 100 and p is the number out of 100. **3.** Roberto; the base b is unknown. **5.** $\frac{a}{90} = \frac{60}{100}$; 54 **7.** $\frac{7}{49} = \frac{p}{100}$; 14.3% **9.** $\frac{125}{b} = \frac{30}{100}$; 416.7 **11.** $\frac{16}{64} = \frac{p}{100}$; 25% **13.** $\frac{a}{200} = \frac{35}{100}$; 70 **15.** $\frac{95}{b} = \frac{95}{100}$; 100 **17.** $\frac{120}{360} = \frac{p}{100}$; 33.3% **19.** $\frac{a}{350} = \frac{17.2}{100}$; 60.2 **21.** $\frac{225}{b} = \frac{95}{100}$; 236.8 **23.** $\frac{a}{42} = \frac{5.8}{100}$; 2.4 **25.** $\frac{12}{27} = \frac{p}{100}$; 44.4% **27.** $\frac{57}{b} = \frac{13.5}{100}$; 422.2 **29.** 12.5% **31.** 1,840,000 households **33.** 760,000 households **35.** 680,000 households **39.** Hurt; 7 out of 13 is about 53.8% which is less than 56%. **41.** 75% **43.** 12% **45.** 173.5% **47.** 211 **49.** 72.2

Pages 222–223 Lesson 5-4

1. Since 75% equals $\frac{3}{4}$, find $\frac{3}{4}$ of 40. $\frac{1}{4}$ of 40 is 10. So $\frac{3}{4}$ of 40 is 3 · 10 or 30. **3.** Candace; 10% of 95 = 0.1 · 95 or 9.5. **5.** 20 **7.** 0.52 **9.** 126 **11.** 11 **13.** 8 **15.** 14 **17.** 80 **19.** 5.7 **21.** 0.283 **23.** 3.9 **25.** 120 **27.** 7.2 **29.** $422 **31.** < **33.** = **35.** 5 **37.** 450 Calories **39.** 700 women **41.** Sample answer: $a = 300$, $b = 100$; Since 10% is $\frac{1}{3}$ of 30%, a must equal $3b$. **43.** B **45.** about 22.9% **47.** 87.5% **49.** $22.\overline{2}\%$ **51.** Sample answer: $\frac{2}{3}$ of 90 or 60 **53.** Sample answer: $\frac{2}{7}$ of 70 or 20

Pages 230–231 Lesson 5-5

1. 26% is about 25% or $\frac{1}{4}$. $98.98 is about $100. $\frac{1}{4}$ of 100 is 25. So, 26% of $98.98 is about $25. **3.** 51% of 120; 24% of 240 is less than $\frac{1}{4}$ of 240 or 60. 51% of 120 is greater than $\frac{1}{2}$ of 120 or 60. **5–39. Sample answers given.** **5.** $\frac{2}{3}$ of 21 or 14 **7.** $\frac{6}{35} \approx \frac{7}{35}$ or 20% **9.** $\frac{17.5}{23} \approx \frac{18}{24}$ or 75% **11.** $\frac{3}{10}$ of 50 or 15 **13.** $\frac{1}{5}$ of 75 or 15 **15.** $\frac{1}{5}$ of 70 or 14 **17.** $\frac{1}{2}$ of 160 or 80 **19.** $\frac{2}{3}$ of 9 or 6 **21.** $1\frac{1}{4}$ of 40 or 50 **23.** $\frac{1}{3}$ of 120 or 40 **25.** $\frac{7}{29} \approx \frac{7}{28}$ or 25% **27.** $\frac{4}{21} \approx \frac{4}{20}$ or 20% **29.** $\frac{8}{13} \approx \frac{8}{12}$ or $66\frac{2}{3}\%$ **31.** $\frac{150{,}078}{299{,}000} \approx \frac{150{,}000}{300{,}000}$ or 50% **33.** $\frac{6}{25} \approx \frac{5}{25}$ or 20% **35.** $\frac{13}{36} \approx \frac{12}{36}$ or $33\frac{1}{3}\%$ **37.** $\frac{8{,}084{,}316}{19{,}134{,}293} \approx \frac{8{,}000{,}000}{20{,}000{,}000}$ or 40% **39.** $\frac{2{,}886{,}251}{12{,}586{,}447} \approx \frac{3{,}000{,}000}{12{,}000{,}000}$ or 25% **41.** always **43.** sometimes **45.** G **47.** $\frac{7}{70} = \frac{p}{100}$; 10% **49.** $\frac{42}{b} = \frac{35}{100}$; 120 **51.** 0.4 **53.** 0.1

Pages 234–235 Lesson 5-6

1. $32 = n(40)$ **3.** $80 = n(60)$; The solution of $80 = n(60)$ is $1\frac{1}{3}$, while the solution of each of the others is $\frac{3}{4}$. **5.** 4% **7.** 0.25% **9.** 36 **11.** 30% **13.** 200 **15.** 0.12% **17.** 201.6 **19.** 500 **21.** $2{,}222\frac{2}{9}$ **23.** $133\frac{1}{3}\%$ **25.** 11.5 **27.** 1,131 attempts **29.** New York **31.** B **33.** Sample answer: $\frac{19}{30} \approx \frac{20}{30}$ or $66\frac{2}{3}\%$ **35.** 60 **37.** 90 **39.** 87 **41.** 229

Pages 239–240 Lesson 5-7

1. Find the amount of change. **3.** Sample answer: original: 10, new: 30; The percent of change is 200%. **5.** 20%; decrease **7.** 23.1%; increase **9.** $116.00 **11.** $29.96 **13.** 20%; decrease **15.** 25%; decrease **17.** 53.1%; increase **19.** $144.00 **21.** $17.76 **23.** 50% **25.** $339.15 **27.** $439.08 **29.** 30% **31.** 308 hours or 12 days and 20 hours **33.** Sample answer: There were 25 students in the math class. Two more students enrolled in the class. What is the percent of change? Answer: 8%

35. Sample answer:

$27.9 - 22.4 = 5.5$	Find the difference.
$\frac{a}{b} = \frac{p}{100} \rightarrow \frac{5.5}{22.4} = \frac{p}{100}$	Replace a with 5.5 and b with 22.4.
$5.5 \cdot 100 = 22.4 \cdot p$	Find the cross products.
$550 = 22.4p$	Multiply.
$\frac{550}{22.4} = \frac{22.4p}{22.4}$	Divide each side by 22.4.
$24.6 \approx p$	Simplify.

The percent of change is about 24.6%.

37. about \$0.54 **39.** Sample answer: $\frac{1}{4}$ of 84 or 21 **41.** Sample answer: $\frac{1}{3}$ of 96 or 32 **43.** 3 **45.** 0.04

Pages 243–244 Lesson 5-8

1. In the formula $I = prt$, I represents the interest, p represents the principal, r represents the simple interest rate written as a decimal, and t represents the time in years. **3.** Yes; Yoshiko will earn half of the interest which is 3.5% or 0.035. **5.** \$18.40 **7.** \$421.38 **9.** \$48.75 **11.** \$90.70 **13.** \$187.50 **15.** \$112.50 **17.** \$2,621.25 **19.** \$636.09 **21.** \$14,925.00 **23.** \$1,016.75 **25.** \$72,500 **27.** 14 yr **29.** $540 = 750 \cdot r \cdot 6$; 12% **31.** 25%

Pages 246–248 Chapter 5 Study Guide and Review

1. percent **3.** percent proportion **5.** markup **7.** principal **9.** 4 **11.** 80% **13.** 16.5% **15.** 20% **17.** $1\frac{1}{5}$ **19.** 0.043 **21.** 0.13 **23.** 1.47 **25.** 65.5% **27.** 70% **29.** 1.5% **31.** 87.5% **33.** 96% **35.** $\frac{15}{b} = \frac{30}{100}$; 50 **37.** $\frac{75}{250} = \frac{p}{100}$; 30% **39.** 90 **41.** 16 **43.** 2.43 **45.** Sample answer: $\frac{1}{8}$ of 80 or 10 **47.** Sample answer: $\frac{2}{5}$ of 40 or 16 **49.** Sample answer: $\frac{33}{98} \approx \frac{33}{99}$ or $33\frac{1}{3}$% **51.** 4,620 **53.** 12.3 **55.** 50%; increase **57.** 20%; decrease **59.** 48% **61.** \$17.00 **63.** \$68.25

Chapter 6 Geometry

Page 255 Chapter 6 Getting Started

1. false; $a^2 + b^2 = c^2$ **3.** 86 **5.** 98 **7.** 11.4 ft **9.** 9.5 yd **11.** No; the angles do not have the same measure.

Pages 259–260 Lesson 6-1

1. Sample answer:

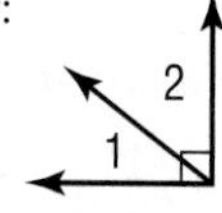

3. straight **5.** adjacent **7.** 153 **9.** 43° **11.** 126° **13.** acute **15.** vertical **17.** adjacent, complementary **19.** 140 **21.** 36 **23.** 45 **25.** 73 **27.** 20 **29.** 70° **31.** 111° **33.** 63° **35.** 59° **37.** 82°

39. They are supplementary. Sample answer: In the diagram, and ∠1 and ∠2 are supplementary. Since ∠1 and ∠3 are alternate interior angles, ∠1 ≅ ∠3. Therefore, replacing ∠1 with ∠3, ∠3 and ∠2 are supplementary.

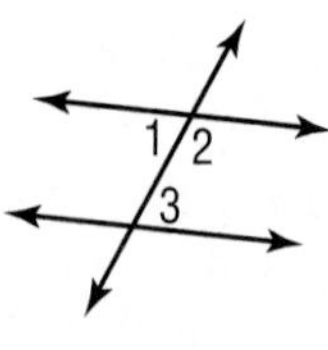

41. A **43.** 35%; increase **45.** 95%; decrease **47.** 81 **49.** 45

Pages 264–265 Lesson 6-2

1. Sample answer: a baseball pennant **3.** 74 **5.** 61 **7.** acute scalene **9.** obtuse isosceles **11.** 40 **13.** 134 **15.** 27 **17.** acute equilateral **19.** right scalene **21.** right isosceles **23.** obtuse isosceles

25. **27.**

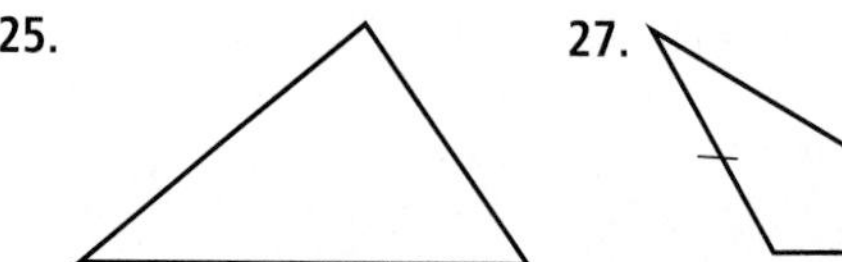

29. not possible **31.** sometimes **33.** The sum of the measures of the angles of a triangle is 180°. If two of the angles of a triangle were greater than or equal to 90°, then the sum of these angles would already be greater than or equal to 180°. **35.** B **37.** 95° **39.** 85° **41.** 9.4 ft **43.** 11.5 in.

Pages 269–270 Lesson 6-3

1. The length of the hypotenuse is twice the length of the leg opposite the 30° angle. **3.** $a = 10$ in., $b \approx 17.3$ in. **5.** $b = 9$ m, $c \approx 12.7$ m **7.** $a = 11$ in., $b \approx 19.1$ in. **9.** $c = 50$ ft, $b \approx 43.3$ ft **11.** $b = 18$ yd, $c \approx 25.5$ yd **13.** 11.6 cm **15.** 7.5 ft, about 10.6 ft **17.** about 3.5 in. **19.** Sample answer: A flowerbed is in the shape of a 45°-45° right triangle. The length of one leg is 6 feet. What is the length of the other two sides of the triangle? 6 ft and about 8.5 ft **21.** B **23.** acute isosceles **25.** acute **27.** alt. exterior **29.** $-\frac{3}{10}$ **31.** -6 **33.** 80

Pages 274–275 Lesson 6-4

1. A square is a parallelogram with four congruent sides. **3.** Trapezoid; the others are all examples of parallelograms. **5.** 30 **7.** square **9.** trapezoid **11.** 95 **13.** 65 **15.** 142 **17.** trapezoid **19.** parallelogram **21.** square **23.** trapezoid **25.** 120 **27.** trapezoid **29.** rhombus, square **31.** true

33. False;

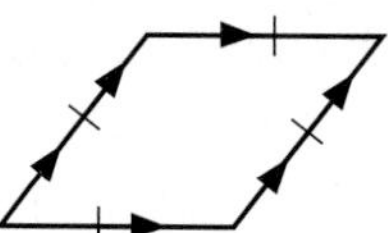

35. C **37.** 13.9 ft **39.** acute, scalene **41.** obtuse, scalene **43.** Yes, the angles have the same measure.

Pages 281–282 Lesson 6-5

1.

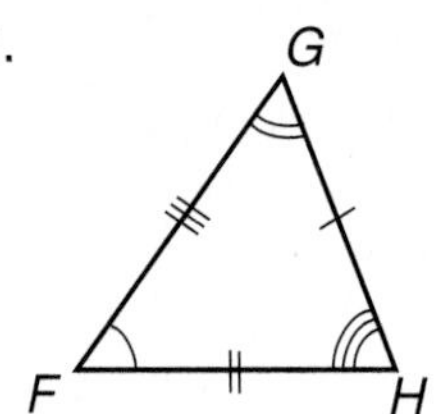

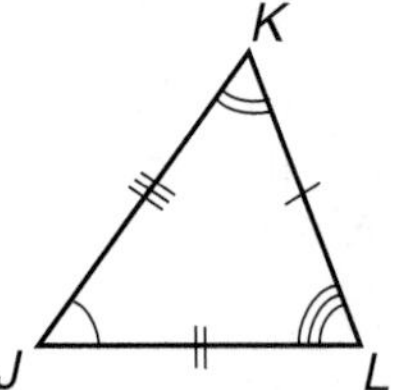

3. yes; $\angle A \cong \angle G$, $\angle C \cong \angle H$, $\angle E \cong \angle F$, $\overline{AC} \cong \overline{GH}$, $\overline{CE} \cong \overline{HF}$, $\overline{AE} \cong \overline{GF}$; $\triangle ACE \cong \triangle GHF$ **5.** 73° **7.** 7 yd **9.** yes; $\angle H \cong \angle P$, $\angle K \cong \angle Q$, $\angle J \cong \angle M$, $\overline{HK} \cong \overline{PQ}$, $\overline{KJ} \cong \overline{QM}$, $\overline{HJ} \cong \overline{PM}$; $\triangle HJK \cong \triangle PMQ$ **11.** no **13.** yes; $\angle A \cong \angle E$, $\angle B \cong \angle D$, $\angle C \cong \angle F$, $\overline{AB} \cong \overline{ED}$, $\overline{BC} \cong \overline{DF}$, $\overline{AC} \cong \overline{EF}$; $\triangle ABC \cong \triangle EDF$ **15.** 6 m **17.** 45° **19.** 90° **21.** 11 in. **23.** 2.5 m **25.** a and d **27.** trapezoid **29.** quadrilateral **31.** A

Pages 288–289 Lesson 6-6

1. Sample answer:

3a. **5a.**

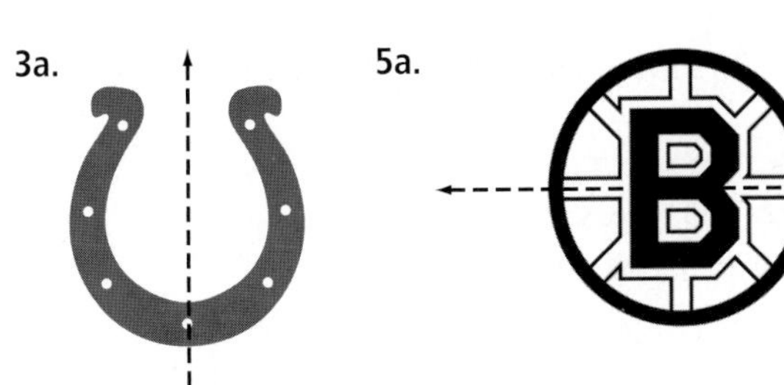

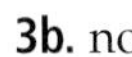

3b. no **5b.** no

7a. **7b.** yes; 180°

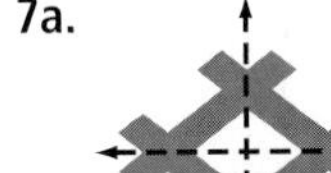

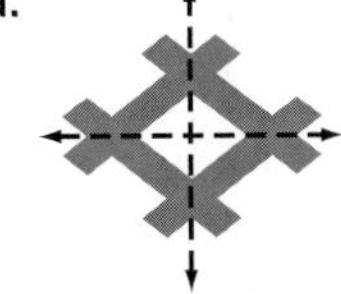

9a. **9b.** yes; 72°, 144°, 216°, 288°

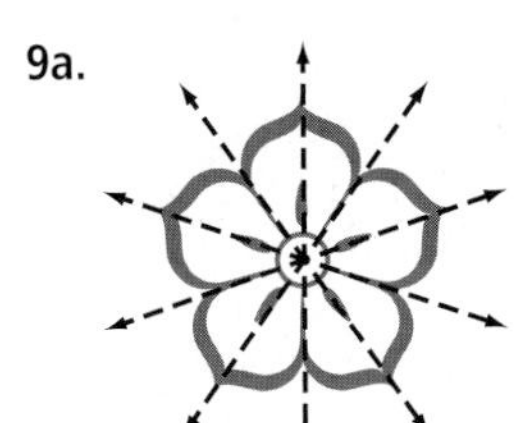

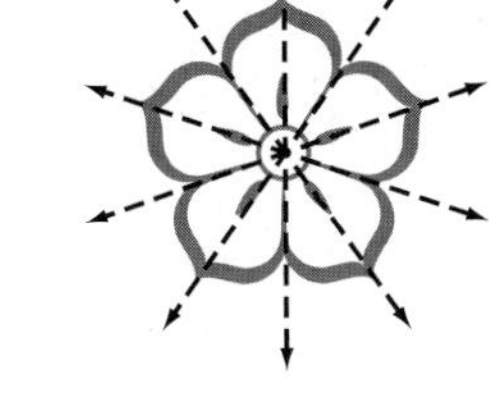

11a. **11b.** no

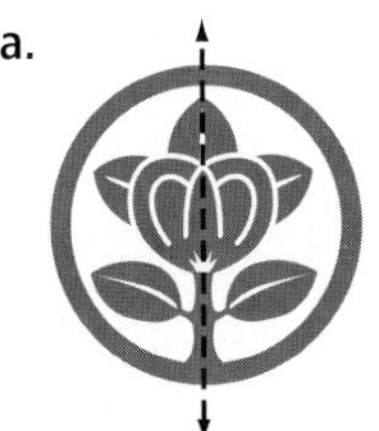

13a. none **13b.** yes; 120°, 240° **15.** Isosceles and equilateral triangles; equilateral triangles

17a. **17b.**

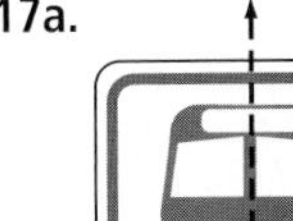

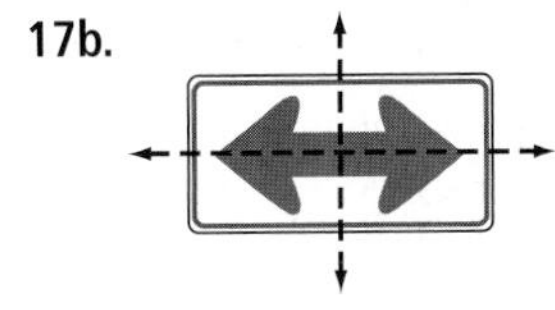

17c. none **17d.** none
19. Sample answers:

line symmetry line symmetry ine and rotationa symmetry

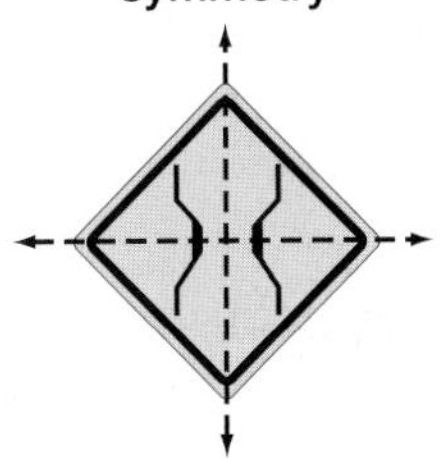

21. true **23.** B **25.** The 4 triangles that form the large triangle in the center appear to be congruent. Three of these smaller triangles are divided into 3 smaller triangles. These smaller triangles appear to be congruent.

27.

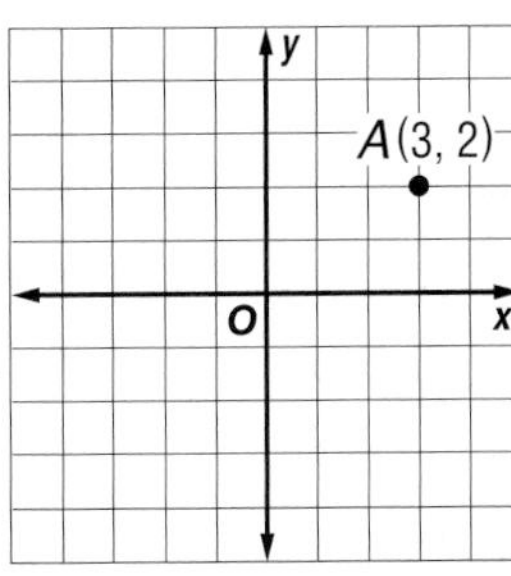

29.

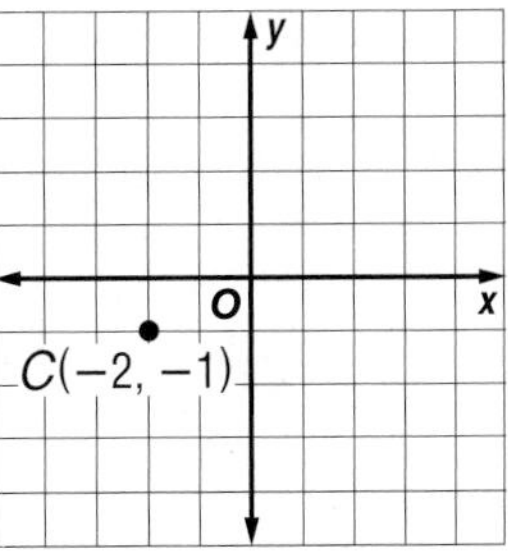

Pages 292–294 Lesson 6-7

1. Sample answer:

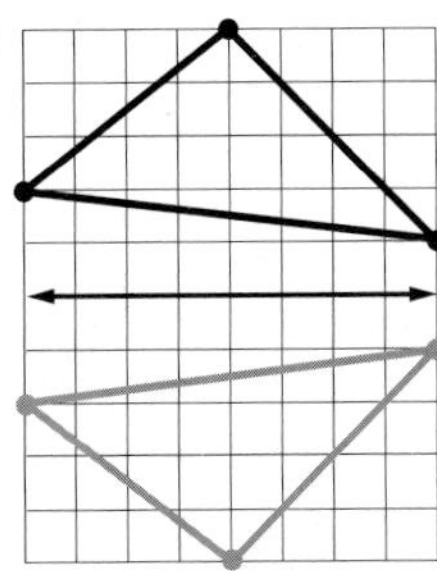

3. The third transformation; all the transformations are reflections of the original figure about the given line. The image of the tip of the dog's tail is not directly across from the tip of the original dog's tail.
5. $Q'(-3, -3)$, $R'(2, -4)$, $S'(3, -2)$, $T'(-2, -1)$;

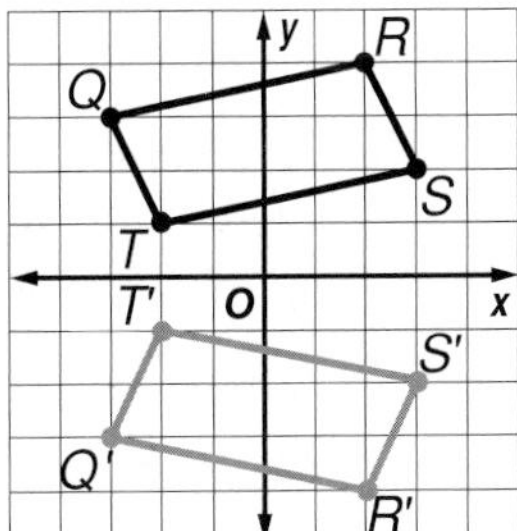

7.

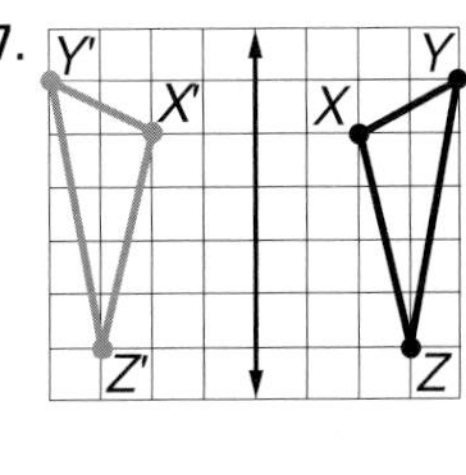

9.

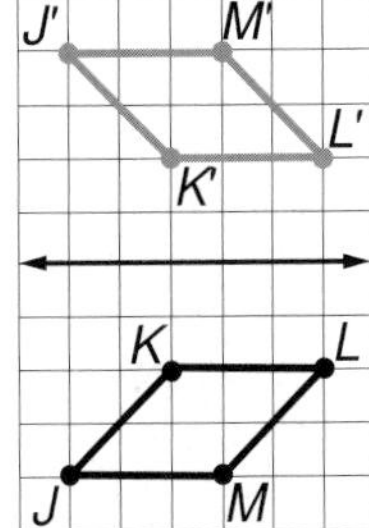

11.

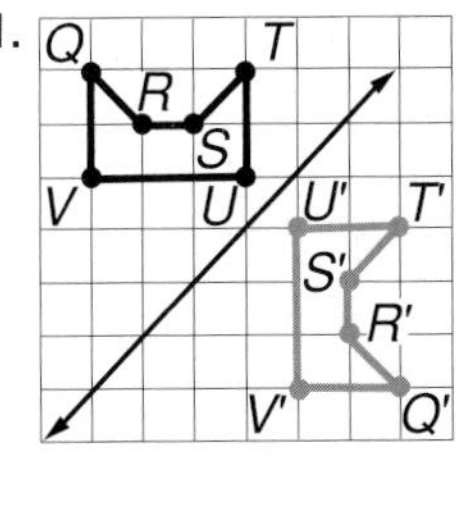

13. No; the image of the tip of the balloon's tail is not directly across from the tip of the original balloon's tail.
15. Yes; each point on the image of the cup is directly across from each corresponding point on the original cup.

17.

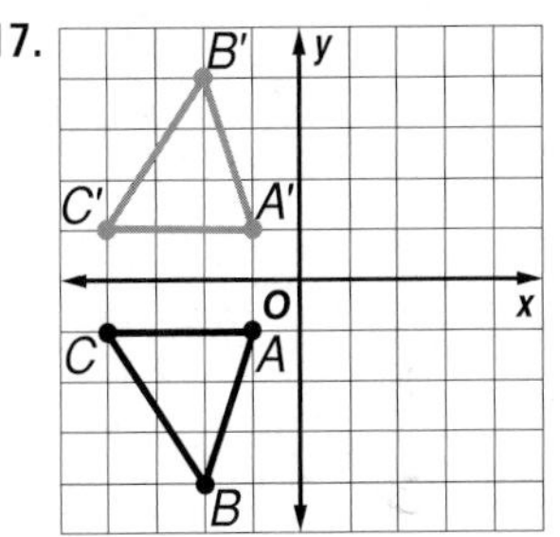

$A'(-1, 1)$, $B'(-2, 4)$, $C'(-4, 1)$

19.

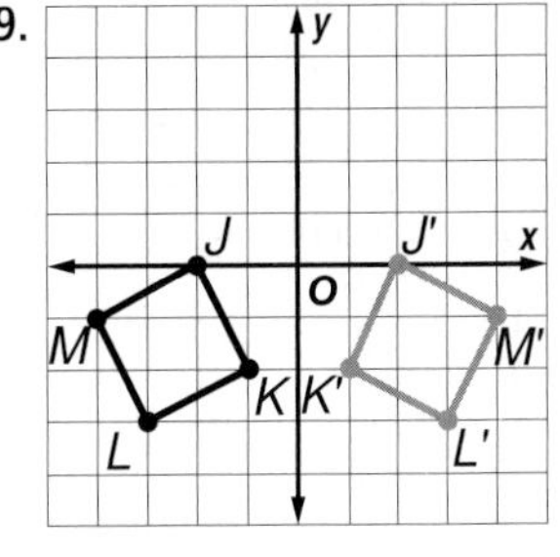

$J'(2, 0)$, $K'(1, -2)$, $L'(3, -3)$, $M'(4, -1)$

21. x-axis 23. y-axis

25. yes;

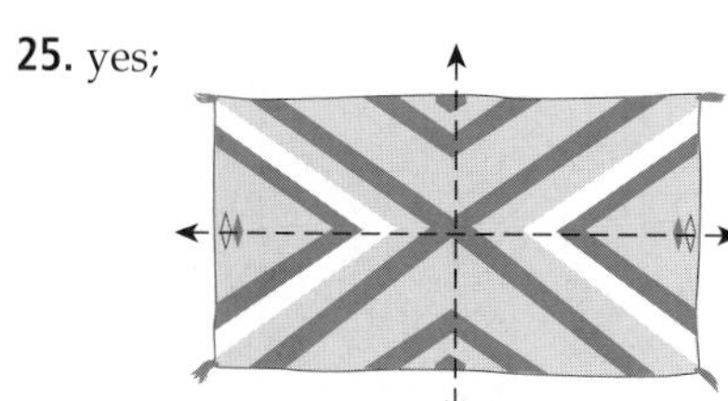

27. H, I, M, O, T, U, V, W, X, Y 29. x-axis; The x-coordinates are the same, but the y-coordinates are opposites.
31. The two pieces are reflections of each other and they are congruent. 33. yes; 180° 35. no 37. 20 39. −2 41. 0

Pages 298–299 Lesson 6-8

1. The fourth transformation; the other transformations are translations, but in the fourth, the figure is turned, so it is not a translation.

3.

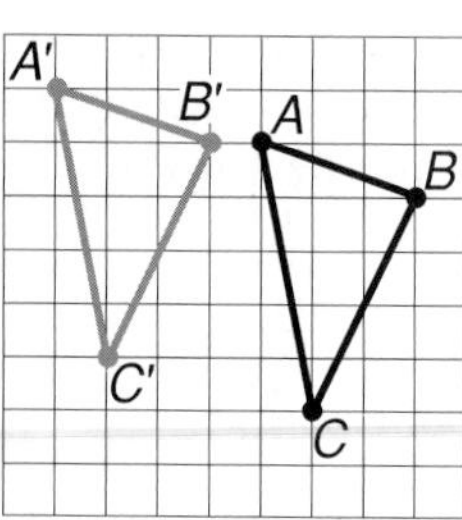

5.

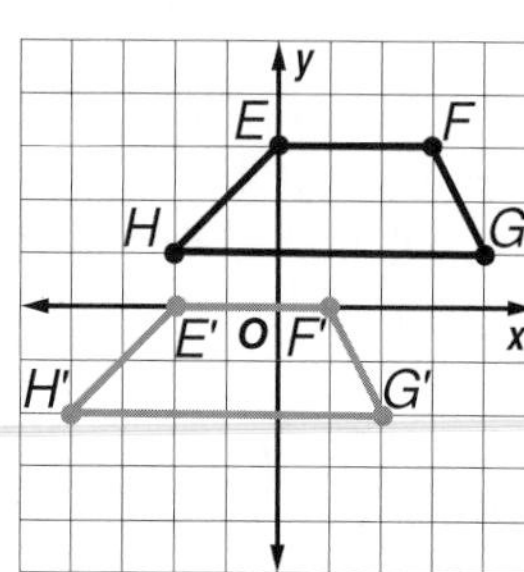

$E'(-2, 0)$, $F'(1, 0)$, $G'(2, -2)$, $H'(-4, -2)$

7.

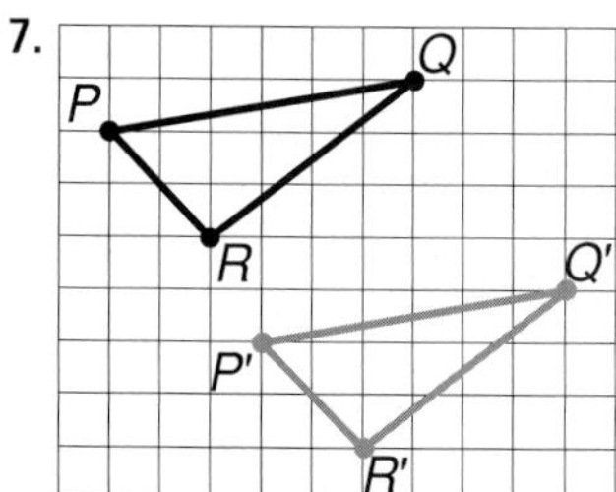

9.

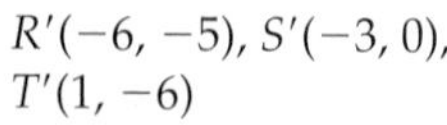

$R'(-6, -5)$, $S'(-3, 0)$, $T'(1, -6)$

11.

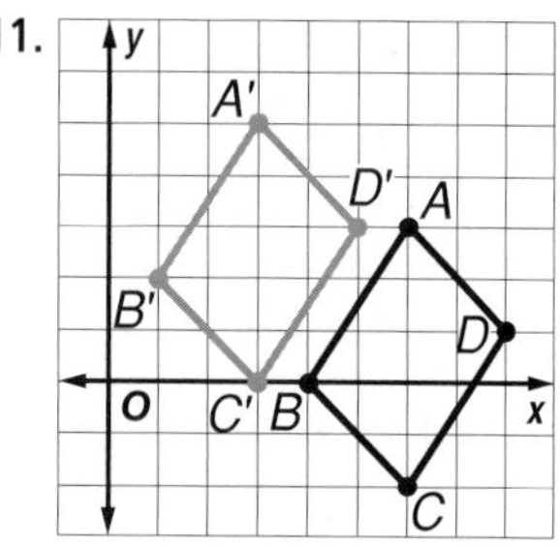

$A'(3, 5)$, $B'(1, 2)$, $C'(3, 0)$, $D'(5, 3)$

13.

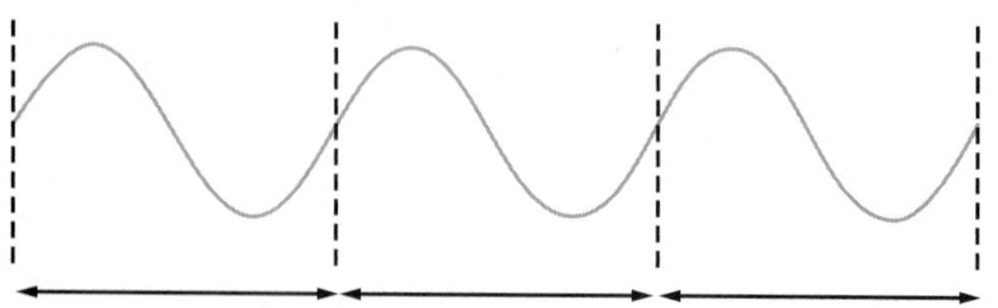

15. $S'(-14, 2)$, $T'(0, 9)$ 17. $(-4, 2)$ 19. yes 21. yes; 180°
23. no

Pages 302–303 Lesson 6-9

1. Sample answer: fan blade, Ferris wheel, car tire

3.

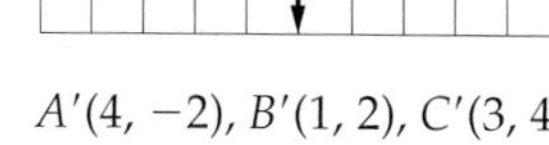

$A'(4, -2)$, $B'(1, 2)$, $C'(3, 4)$

5.

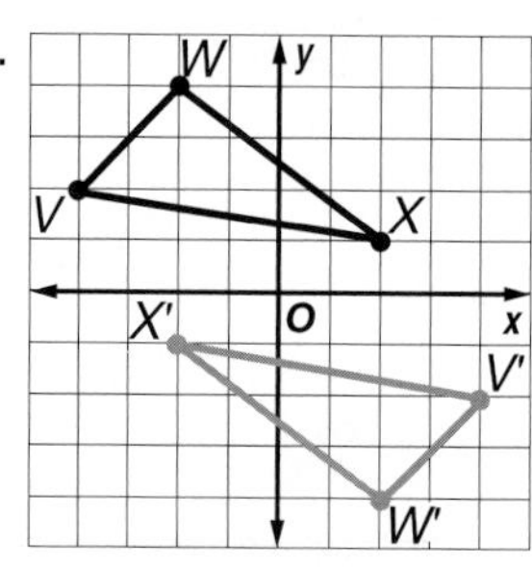

$V'(4, -2)$, $W'(2, -4)$, $X'(-2, -1)$

7.

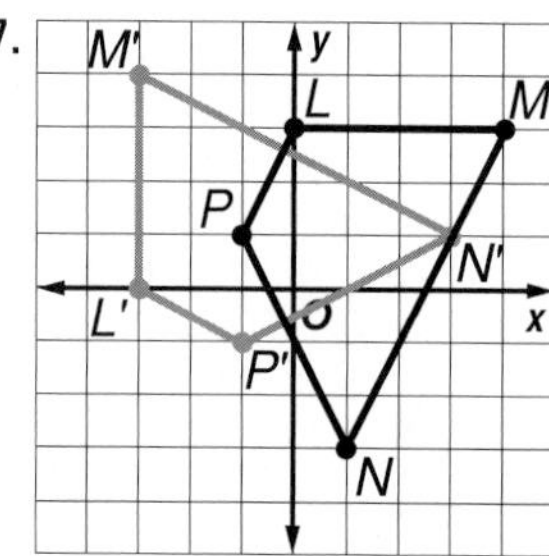

9. Yes; the figure in green is a rotation of the figure in blue 180° about the origin.
11. No; the figure in green is a reflection of the figure in blue over the y-axis.

$L'(-3, 0)$, $M'(-3, 4)$, $N'(3, 1)$, $P'(-1, -1)$

13.

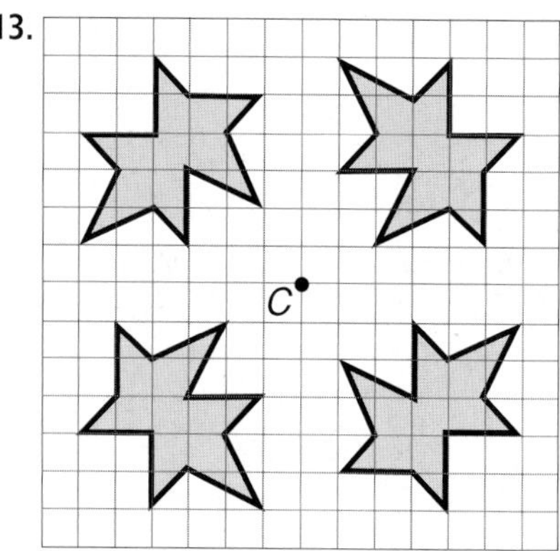

15.

17. rotation 19. reflection 21. The 4 hearts at the bottom of the tie are translations of the first heart at the top of the tie.

23. 25. acute equilateral; yes

Pages 306–308 Chapter 6 Study Guide and Review

1. false; obtuse 3. false; perpendicular 5. true 7. true
9. 137 11. 135° 13. 23 15. $a = 2$ cm, $b \approx 3.5$ cm
17. $b = 10$ ft, $c \approx 14.1$ ft 19. 102° 21. 124° 23. 11 cm

25.

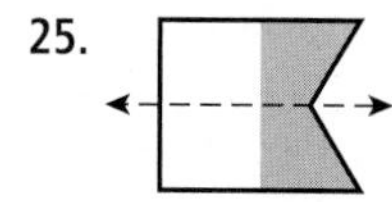

27. none

29.

$Q'(2, -5)$, $R'(4, -5)$, $S'(3, -1)$, $T'(1, -1)$

31.

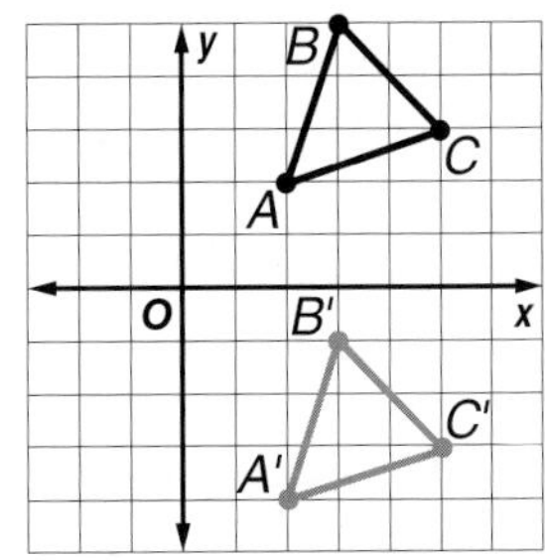

$A'(2, -4)$, $B'(3, -1)$, $C'(5, -3)$

33.

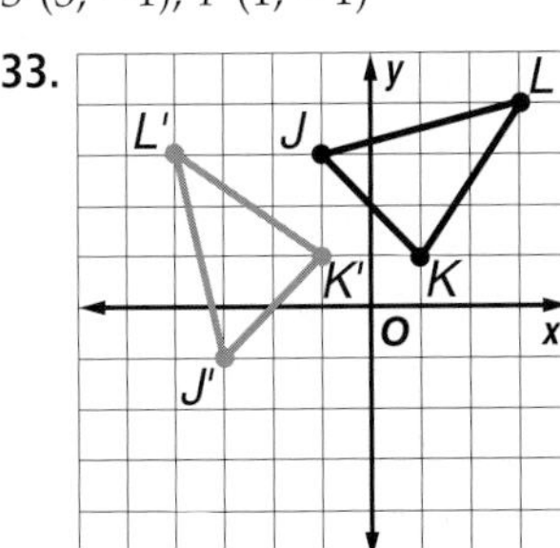

$J'(-3, -1)$, $K'(-1, 1)$, $L'(-4, 3)$

Chapter 7 Geometry: Measuring Area and Volume

Page 313 Chapter 7 Getting Started

1. trapezoid **3.** 32 **5.** 34.0 **7.** 1.8 **9.** 47.1 **11.** 153.9 **13.** quadrilateral

Pages 317–318 Lesson 7-1

1. They are the same; $A = bh$. **3.** Malik; The area of a trapezoid is half the product of the height and the sum of the bases. **5.** 180 m^2 **7.** 25.8 km^2 **9.** 14.04 m^2 **11.** 25 ft^2 **13.** 28 in^2 **15.** 32.4 cm^2 **17.** 14.4 cm^2 **19.** 7 cm **21.** 120,000 km^2 **23.** 112,500 km^2 **25.** Tennessee: 109,158 km^2, Arkansas: 137,741 km^2, Virginia: 109,391 km^2, North Dakota 183,123 km^2 **27.** The area is doubled. **29.** A

31.

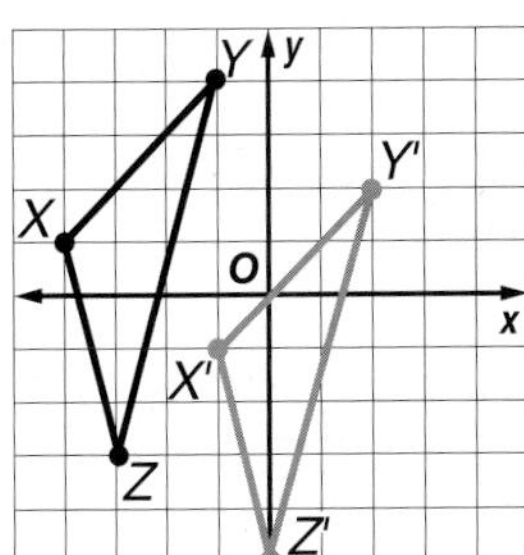

$X'(-1, -1)$, $Y'(2, 2)$, $Z'(0, -5)$

33.

$X'(4, -1)$, $Y'(1, -4)$, $Z'(3, 3)$

35. 58.4 **37.** 176.7

Pages 322–323 Lesson 7-2

1. Sample answer:

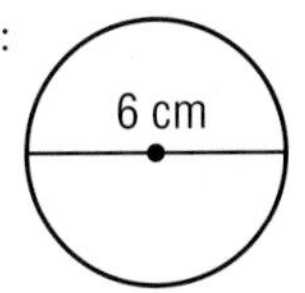

3. 75.4 yd; 452.4 yd^2 **5.** 66.0 ft; 346.4 ft^2 **7.** 16.7 mi; 22.1 mi^2 **9.** 62.8 in.; 314.2 in^2 **11.** 119.4 mi; 1,134.1 mi^2 **13.** 60.9 m; 295.6 m^2 **15.** 22.0 cm; 38.5 cm^2 **17.** 32.6 ft; 84.5 ft^2 **19.** about 7,854 in. or 654.5 feet **21.** about 70,686 yd^2 **23.** 254.5 in^2; 153.9 in^2; 78.5 in^2 **25.** 13.3 ft **27.** 88.0 cm^2 **29.** 18.2 m^2

31. Sample answer: arc *JL*

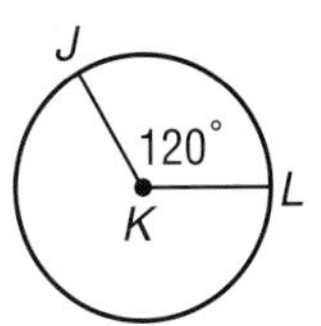

33. C **35.** 17.4 cm^2

37. $W'(3, 1)$, $X'(1, 3)$, $Y'(2, 4)$;

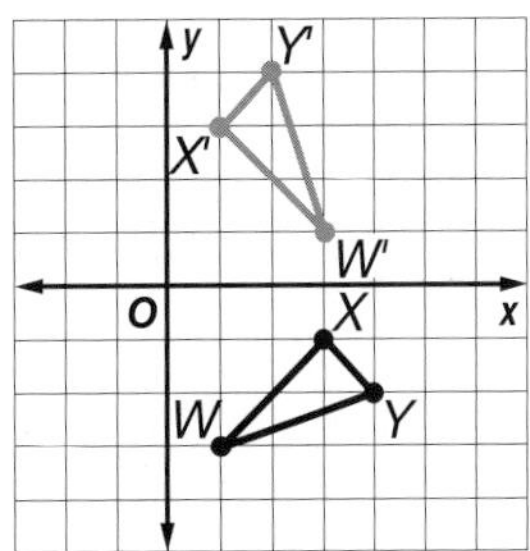

39. 25.1 **41.** 300.15

Pages 328–329 Lesson 7-3

1. Sample answer:

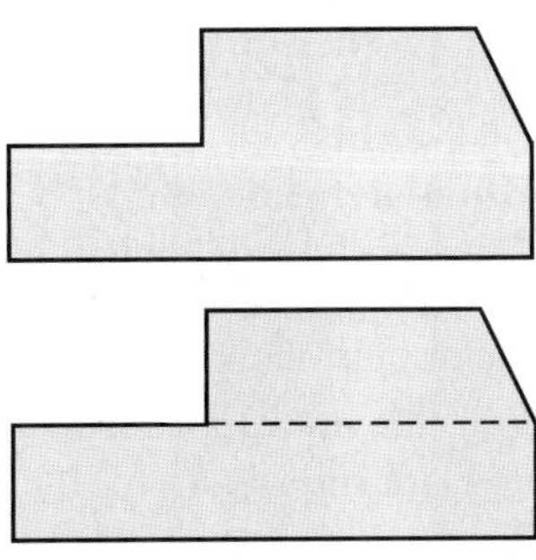

3. 68 cm^2 **5.** 216 in^2 **7.** 240 yd^2 **9.** 87.5 m^2 **11.** 121.2 cm^2 **13.** 103.8 m^2 **15.** about 480.5 units^2 **17.** 3 cans; The area to be painted is 857.5 ft^2, so 857.5 ÷ 350 or about 2.5 cans of paint are needed. Since you cannot buy half a can, you must buy 3 cans.

19. No, the area of the field is about 60,638.3 ft^2, so it will take 60,638.3 ÷ 1,750 or about 35 minutes to mow the field. The grounds crew only has 30 minutes. **21.** C **23.** 95.8 m **25.** 220 ft^2 **27.** quadrilateral **29.** hexagon

Pages 333–334 Lesson 7-4

1. a: vertex; b: face; c: base; d: edge **3.** rectangular prism; 6 faces, all rectangles; 12 edges; 8 vertices **5.** rectangular pyramid; 5 faces, 1 rectangle and 4 triangles; 8 edges; 5 vertices **7.** triangular pyramid; 4 faces, all triangles; 6 edges; 4 vertices **9.** triangular prism; 5 faces, 2 triangles and 3 rectangles; 9 edges; 6 vertices

11a.

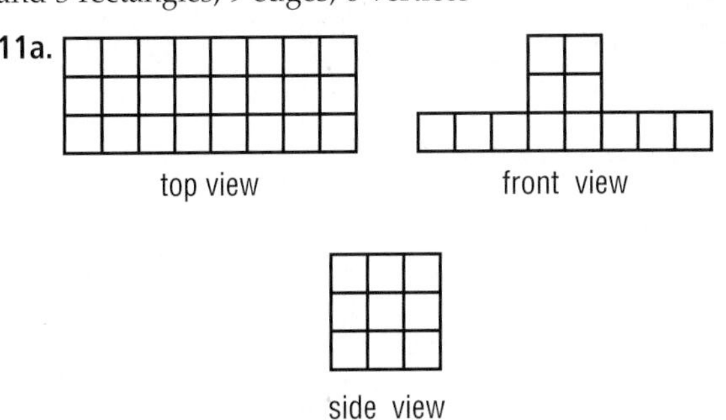

11b. $1\frac{1}{2}$ ft **11c.** $1\frac{1}{2}$ ft^2 **13.** Sometimes; three planes can intersect in a line or not intersect at all if two or more are parallel. **15.** Sometimes; a rectangular prism has 5 vertices, but a triangular prism has 4. **17a.** 2 square pyramids

Selected Answers

17b.

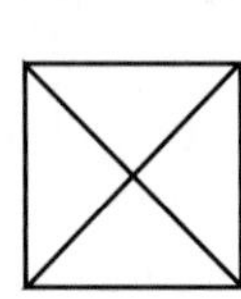

top view

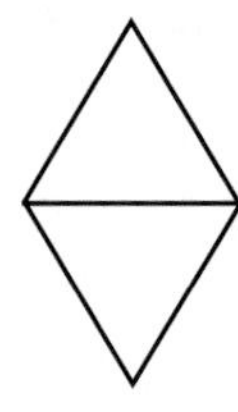

side view

19. $E = 2n$ **21.** $\overline{EF}$ and $\overline{AD}$ **23.** top: rectangular pyramid; bottom: rectangular prism **25.** 146.3 ft^2 **27.** 161.1 in^2 **29.** 15 in^2 **31.** 27.5 cm^2

Pages 337–339 Lesson 7-5

1. The area of the base B of a rectangular prism equals the length ℓ times the width w. Replacing B with ℓw in the formula $V = Bh$, gives another formula for the volume of a rectangular prism, $V = (\ell w)h$ or $V = \ell wh$. **5.** 539 m^3 **7.** 420 ft^3 **9.** 216 mm^3 **11.** 768 m^3 **13.** 55.4 m^3 **15.** 297.5 ft^3 **17.** 576 mm^3 **19.** 14,790 cm^3 **21.** 891.3 yd^3 **23.** 6 in. **25.** 330 ft^3 **27.** 1,728 **29.** 1,000,000 **31.** 40 ft **33.** volume doubles **35.** volume is multiplied by 8 **37.** B **39.** 126 ft^2 **41.** $\frac{3}{2,500}$ **43.** $1\frac{7}{20}$ **45.** 20 **47.** 48

Pages 344–345 Lesson 7-6

1. Doubling its radius; doubling the radius means the volume of the cone is multiplied by 4, while doubling the height multiplies the volume of the cone by 2. **3.** 183.3 m^3 **5.** 14 ft^3 **7.** 1,731.8 mm^3 **9.** 43.3 in^3 **11.** 261.3 m^3 **13.** 230.9 in^3 **15.** 175 cm^3 **17.** 654.5 ft^3 **19.** 13 m^3 **21.** Sample answer: 250 cm^3 **23.** Sample answer: A paper cup is shaped like a cone. If the cup is 6 cm wide and 10 cm tall, find the volume of water the cup will hold; 94.2 cm^3 **25.** 113.1 in^3 **27.** 523.6 m^3 **29.** It multiplies it by 8; replacing r with $2r$ in the formula for the volume of a sphere gives $\frac{4}{3}\pi(2r)^3$ or $8 \cdot \frac{4}{3}\pi r^3$. **31.** 45 cm^3 **33.** trapezoidal prism; 6 faces, 2 trapezoids, 4 rectangles; 12 edges; 8 vertices **35.** 17.3 ft **37.** 23.9 cm

Pages 349–351 Lesson 7-7

1. False; a rectangular prism 2 ft long, 4 ft wide, and 6 ft high has the same volume as a prism 2 ft long, 2 ft wide, and 12 ft high, 48 ft^3. The surface area of the first prism is 88 ft^2, but the surface area of the second prism is 104 ft^2. **3.** Sample answer: 2 ft × 2 ft × 11 ft **5.** 216 in^2 **7.** 467.3 cm^2 **9.** 168.7 cm^2 **11.** 360 ft^2 **13.** 1,154.5 yd^2 **15.** 864 m^2 **17.** 725.7 in^2 **19.** 805 ft^2 **21.** 574.7 in^2 **23.** Double the radius; consider the expression for the surface area of a cylinder, $2\pi r^2 + 2\pi rh$. If you double the height, you will double the second addend. If you double the radius, you will quadruple the first addend and double the second addend. **25.** 12 **27.** 1 **29.** rectangle **31.** triangle **33.** D **35.** 392 m^3 **37.** No; the volume of the refrigerator is 12,852 in^3 or about 7.4 ft^3, which is less than 8 ft^3. **39.** 115 **41.** 35

Pages 354–355 Lesson 7-8

1. The slant height is the height of each lateral face of the pyramid and the height is the perpendicular distance from the vertex to the base of the pyramid. **3.** 64 ft^2 **5.** 115.0 cm^2 **7.** 47.3 ft^2 **9.** 140.4 mm^2 **11.** 659.6 yd^2 **13.** 149.5 cm^2 **15.** 5; The surface area of the roof is 502.7 ft^2. 502.7 ÷ 120 ≈ 4.2. Since you cannot buy a fraction of a roll, 5 rolls of roofing material are needed. **17.** 254.5 in^2 **19.** $\sqrt{18}$ in. **21.** 113.1 m^2 **23.** 804.2 ft^2 **25.** B **27.** 1,278.6 cm^2 **29.** 62.6 **31.** 25.7

Pages 360–362 Lesson 7-9

1. 74.8 oz; 5 lb is measured to the nearest pound, 74 oz is measured to the nearest ounce, and 74.8 oz is measured to the nearest 0.1 oz, therefore 74.8 oz is most precise. **3.** 375.0; all of the other numbers have 3 significant digits, while 375.0 has 4 significant digits. **5.** 2°F **7.** 2 **9.** 5 **11.** 1.5 m **13.** 1.4 **15.** $\frac{1}{8}$ in. **17.** $\frac{1}{4}$ pound **19.** 3 **21.** 2 **23.** 3 **25.** 2 **27.** 9.39 L **29.** 190 m **31.** 5.2 s **33.** 13 ft^2 **35.** 80 **37.** 40 **39.** 10,600 m^2 **41.** 3 **43.** 150 cm^2 **45.** D **47.** 74.6 cm^2 **49.** −3.31 **51.** $\frac{2}{3}$

Pages 363–366 Chapter 7 Study Guide and Review

1. b **3.** d **5.** i **7.** c **9.** g **11.** $140\frac{1}{4}$ in^2 **13.** 106.4 m^2 **15.** 18.8 cm; 28.3 cm^2 **17.** 16.3 m; 21.2 m^2 **19.** 57.5 mm^2 **21.** 200.5 in^2 **23.** hexagonal pyramid; 7 faces, 1 hexagon and 6 triangles; 12 edges; 7 vertices **25.** 660 yd^3 **27.** 163.3 ft^3 **29.** 445.3 yd^3 **31.** 612 m^2 **33.** 95 ft^2 **35.** 520.7 cm^2 **37.** about 175.9 ft^2 **39.** 2 **41.** 3 **43.** 45.3 lb **45.** 16.7

Chapter 8 Probability

Page 373 Chapter 8 Getting Started

1. proportion **3.** $\frac{2}{3}$ **5.** $\frac{7}{33}$ **7.** 7,920 **9.** 3,024 **11.** 35 **13.** 70 **15.** $\frac{1}{2}$ **17.** $\frac{7}{18}$ **19.** 22.4

Pages 376–377 Lesson 8-1

1.

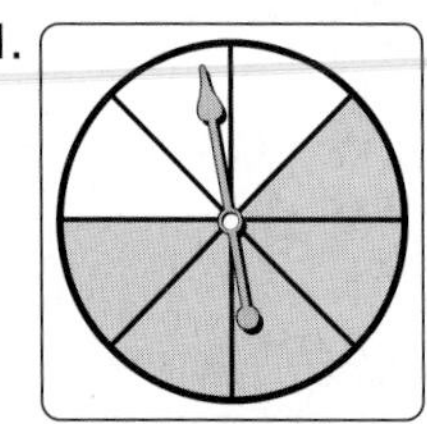

3. Masao; a 2 is only 1 out of 6 possibilities when rolling a number cube. The probability is $\frac{1}{6}$. **5.** $\frac{1}{2}$; 0.5; 50% **7.** $\frac{7}{8}$; 0.875; 87.5% **9.** $\frac{3}{4}$; 0.75; 75% **11.** $\frac{6}{25}$; 0.24; 24% **13.** $\frac{14}{25}$; 0.56; 56% **15.** 1; 1; 100% **17.** $\frac{1}{4}$ **19.** No; $P(\text{greater than } 3) = \frac{1}{2}$ and $P(\text{less than } 3) = \frac{1}{3}$, but $\frac{1}{2} + \frac{1}{3} \neq 1$. **21.** 60% **25.** 0.225 **27.** 17 red crayons **29.** 5:1 **31.** C **33.** The measurement is to the nearest centimeter. There is 1 significant digit. The greatest possible error is 0.5 cm, and the relative error is $\frac{0.5}{8}$ or about 0.063. **35.** The measurement is to the nearest 0.01 m. There are 3 significant digits. The greatest possible error is 0.005 m, and the relative error is $\frac{0.005}{4.83}$ or about 0.0010. **37.** about 267 in^2 **39.** 200 **41.** 112

Pages 382–383 Lesson 8-2

1. With a tree diagram, you can see all the different outcomes. However, with the Fundamental Counting Principle, you only know how many outcomes there are. **3.** 4 more outfits **5.** $\frac{1}{9}$ **7.** 24 pizzas

9.

Penny	Nickel	Dime	Outcome
H	H	H	H, H, H
		T	H, H, T
	T	H	H, T, H
		T	H, T, T
T	H	H	T, H, H
		T	T, H, T
	T	H	T, T, H
		T	T, T, T

H = Heads

T = Tails

8 outcomes

11.

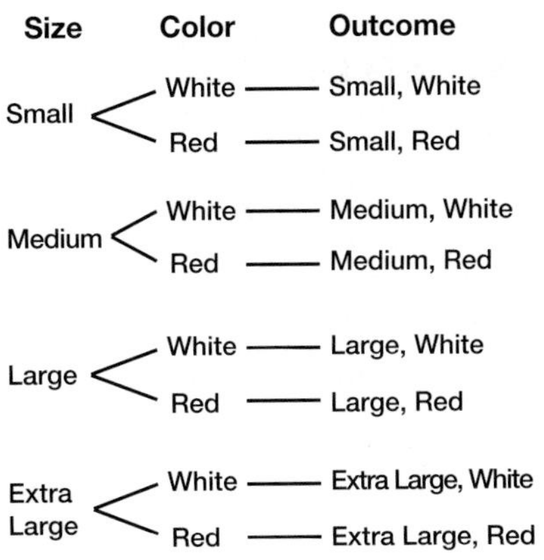

8 outcomes **13.** 42 outcomes **15.** 32 outcomes

17.

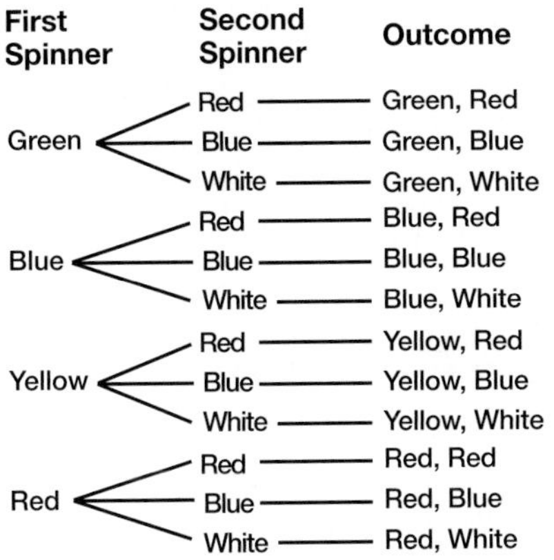

12 outcomes

19. $\frac{1}{2}$ **21.** $\frac{1}{100{,}000}$ **23.** 45,697,600 plates **25.** D **27.** $\frac{2}{11}$ **29.** 1 **31.** 3 significant digits **33.** 5,040 **35.** 1,680

Pages 386–387 Lesson 8-3

1. $9! = 9 \cdot 8 \cdot 7 \cdot 6 \cdot 5 \cdot 4 \cdot 3 \cdot 2 \cdot 1$ and $P(9, 5) = 9 \cdot 8 \cdot 7 \cdot 6 \cdot 5$ **3.** Bailey; $P(7, 3)$ means to start with 7 and use 3 factors. **5.** 840 **7.** 40,320 **9.** 720 ways **11.** 120 **13.** 120 **15.** 240,240 **17.** 303,600 **19.** 2 **21.** 39,916,800 **23.** 24 ways **25.** 3,024 passwords **27.** $\frac{1}{5}$ **29.** 120 ways **31.** 15,600 ways **33.** 3,628,800; $10! = 10 \cdot 9!$ **35.** B **37.** 44 different ways **39.** $\frac{1}{2}$ **41.** $\frac{2}{3}$ **43.** 20 **45.** 190

Pages 390–391 Lesson 8-4

1. Sample answers: selecting a committee of 5 people; selecting a president and vice president of a club **3.** 15 **5.** 7 **7.** permutation **9.** 210 squads **11.** 36 **13.** 9 **15.** 126 **17.** 3,060 **19.** combination **21.** permutation **23.** permutation **25.** 220 pizzas **27.** 6,840 ways **29.** 2,598,960 hands **31.** 259,459,200 ways **33.** Sometimes; they are equal if $y = 1$. **35.** 4,249,575 committees **37.** 32,760 **39.** 5,040 **41.** $\frac{3}{10}$ **43.** $\frac{1}{8}$

Pages 398–399 Lesson 8-5

1. Both independent events and dependent events are compound events. Independent events do not affect each other. Dependent events affect each other. **3.** Evita; spinning the spinner twice represents two independent events. The probability of getting an odd number is $\frac{3}{5}$ each time. **5.** $\frac{1}{4}$ **7.** $\frac{1}{18}$ **9.** $\frac{1}{30}$ **11.** $\frac{1}{10}$ **13.** $\frac{2}{15}$ **15.** $\frac{1}{8}$ **17.** $\frac{1}{19}$ **19.** $\frac{3}{95}$ **21.** $\frac{33}{95}$ **23.** 68.9% **25.** $\frac{4}{13}$ **27.** 4 **29.** 2/17 **31.** 21 **33.** 84 **35.** $\frac{13}{30}$ **37.** $\frac{7}{10}$

Pages 402–403 Lesson 8-6

1. Each experimental probability will be different. Theoretical probability tells you approximately what should happen. **3.** $\frac{13}{25}$ **5.** $\frac{1}{2}$ **7.** The theoretical probability is about the same as the experimental probability. **9.** about 70 cars **11.** about 67 errors **13.** $\frac{4}{15}$ **15.** $\frac{4}{5}$ **17.** about 80 teens **21.** about 200 times **23.** $\frac{3}{2{,}500}$ **25.** The experimental probability is $\frac{15}{75}$ or $\frac{1}{5}$. The theoretical probability is $\frac{1}{4}$. The experimental probability is less than the theoretical probability. **27.** $\frac{5}{44}$ **29.** 31.5 **31.** 16.2

Pages 408–409 Lesson 8-7

1. Taking a survey is one way to determine experimental probability. **3.** This is a biased sample, since people in other states would spend much more than those in Arizona. The sample is a convenience sample since all the people are from the same state. **5.** 48% **7.** This is an unbiased, systematic random sample. **9.** This is a biased sample, since only voluntary responses are used. **11.** This is an unbiased, simple random sample. **13.** Sample answer: Get a list of all the students in the school and contact every 20th student on the list. **15.** about 240 containers **19.** No; the survey should be representative of the whole school. **21.** Sample answer: If the questions are not asked in a neutral manner, the people may not give their true opinion. For example, the question "You really don't like Brand X, do you?" might not get the same answer as the question "Do you prefer Brand X or Brand Y?" Also, the question "Why would anyone like rock music?" might not get the same answer as the question "What do you think about rock music?" **23.** I **25.** $\frac{1}{20}$

Pages 410–412 Chapter 8 Study Guide and Review

1. sample space **3.** multiplying **5.** compound event **7.** Theoretical probability **9.** $\frac{6}{25}$; 0.24; 24% **11.** $\frac{18}{25}$; 0.72; 72% **13.** $\frac{18}{25}$; 0.72; 72% **15.** $\frac{1}{6}$ **17.** $\frac{1}{8}$ **19.** $\frac{3}{8}$ **21.** 6 **23.** 60 **25.** 720 **27.** 120 numbers **29.** 4 **31.** 126 **33.** 21 **35.** $\frac{1}{12}$ **37.** $\frac{1}{6}$ **39.** $\frac{1}{6}$ **41.** $\frac{25}{102}$ **43.** $\frac{4}{15}$ **45.** $\frac{23}{30}$ **47.** This is a biased sample, since only people leaving a concert are surveyed. This is a convenience sample. **49.** about 120 people

Chapter 9 Statistics and Matrices

Page 417 Chapter 9 Getting Started

1. false; biased **3.**

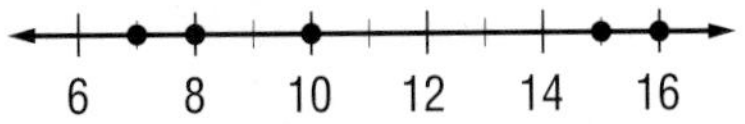

5.

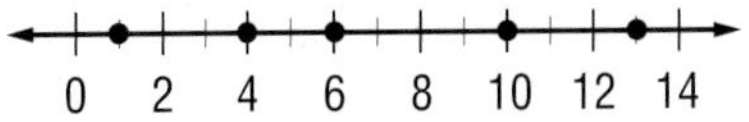

7. −12 **9.** 4 **11.** 0.23, 0.32, 2.03 **13.** 0.01, 0.10, 1.01, 1.10 **15.** 129.6 **17.** 187.2 **19.** 50.4

Pages 422–424 Lesson 9-1

1. Sample answer: 2, 3, 5, 6, 7, 8, 9, 10, 11, 12, 13, 15, 16, 17

Selected Answers

3. **Record High Temperatures for Each State**

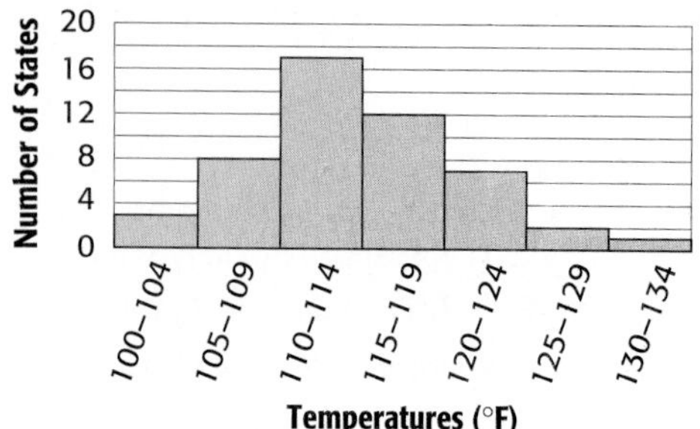

5. **New Broadway Productions for Each Year from 1960-2001**

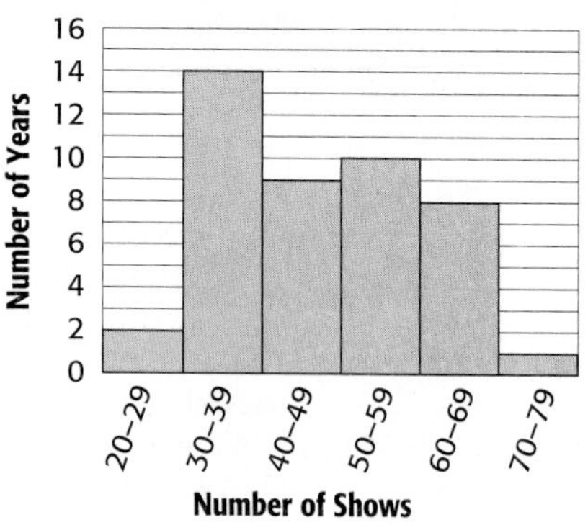

7. Sample answer:

Calories of Various Types of Frozen Bars

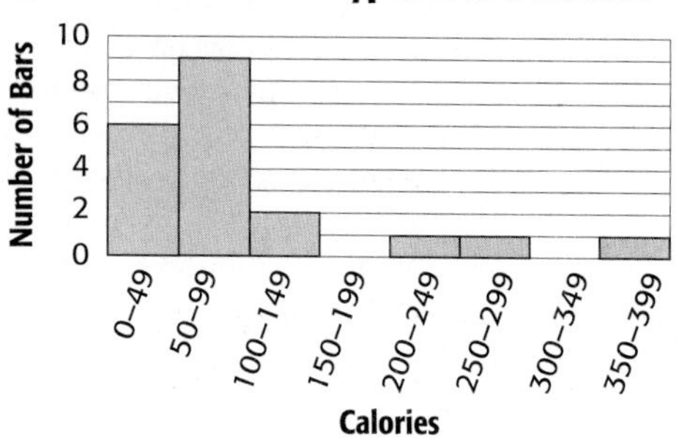

9. 200–399 **11.** 7 states **13.** 37 states **15.** 8 courts **17.** 16 courts **19.** Vermont **21.** 6 counties **25.** G **27.** $\frac{3}{4}$ **29.** $\frac{11}{20}$ **31.** $\frac{33}{50}$ **33.** 5 **35.** 12.6 **37.** 190.8

Pages 428–429 Lesson 9-2

1. Both graphs show how the ages of the signers of the Declaration of Independence were distributed. The bar graph shows how many were in each age interval. The circle graph shows what percent of the signers were in each age interval.

3. Sample answer:

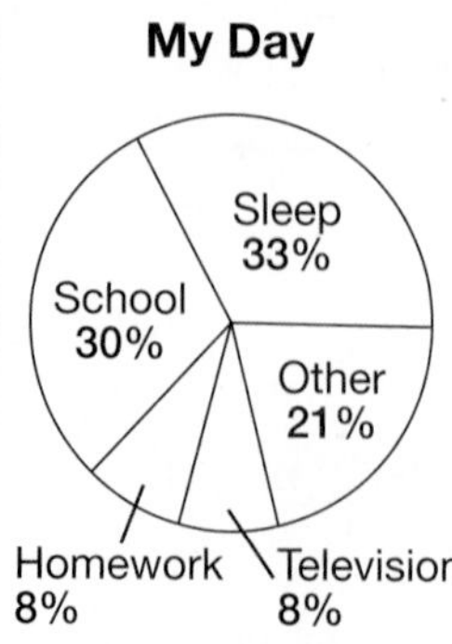

5. **Hawaiian Counties**

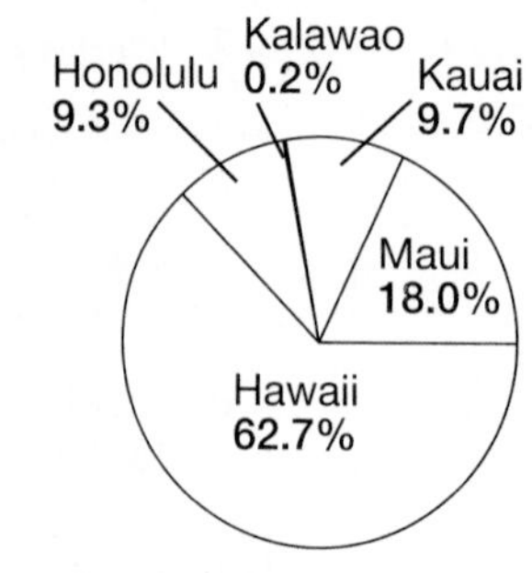

7. **Flowers and Plants Purchased for Mother's Day**

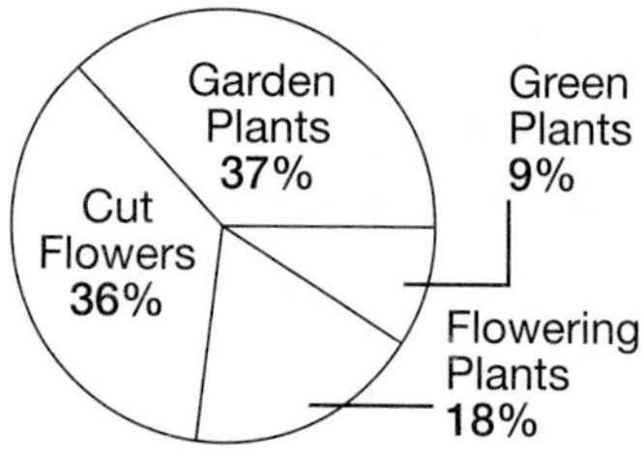

9. U.S. Population by Age

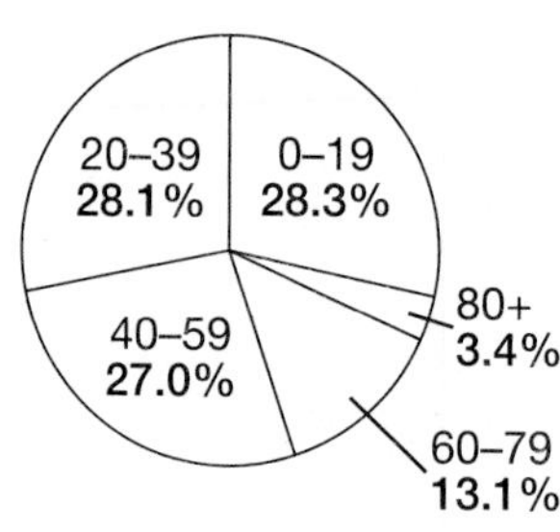

11. Half of the homes are heated with piped gas. About a third of the homes are heated with electricity. The rest of the homes are heated with fuel oil, bottled gas, wood, or something else. **13.** C

15. Sample answer:

Calories of Single Serving, Frozen Pizzas

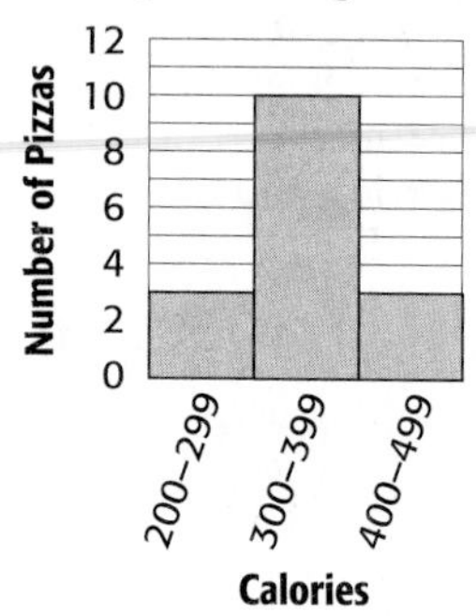

17.

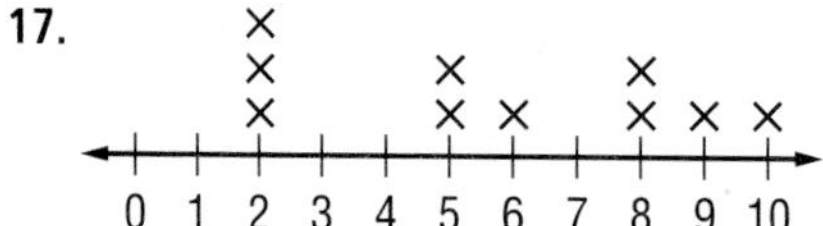

Pages 432–433 Lesson 9-3

1. Both bar graphs and histograms use bars to show how many things are in each category. A histogram shows the frequency of data that has been organized into equal intervals. There is no space between the bars in a histogram.
3. circle graph

5. Sample answer: histogram

Grams of Carbohydrates in a Serving of Various Vegetables

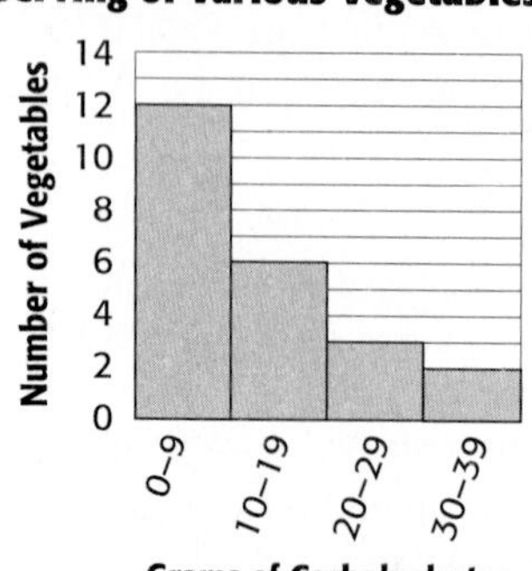

7. table, bar graph, or pictograph **9.** histogram **11.** line graph

13. Sample answer: line graph;

Average Height of Girls

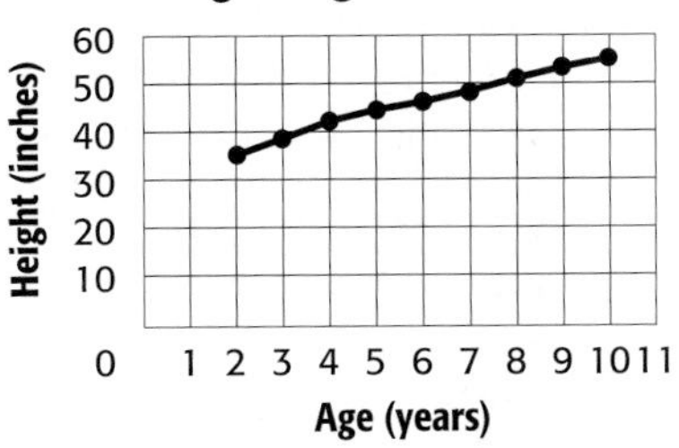

17. Sample answer: **Time Needed to Walk to School**

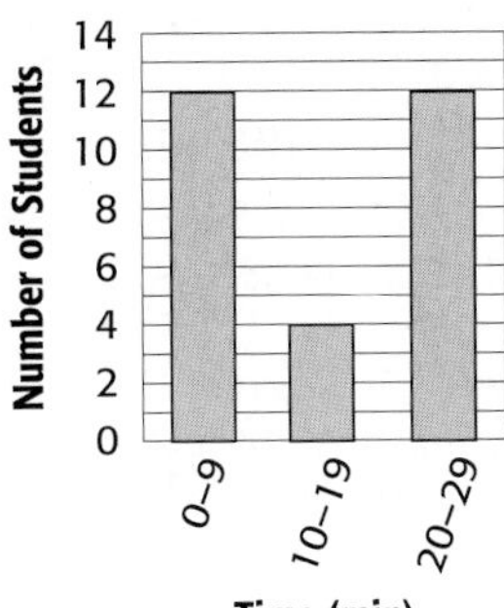

19. 20.5 **21.** 6.5

Pages 437–438 Lesson 9-4

1. No; the mode must always be a member of the set of data, but the mean and median may or may *not* be a member of the set of data. **3.** Erica; you must first order the numbers from least to greatest. **5.** 9; 9; no mode **7.** The median; the mean is affected by the extreme value of 74, and the mode is the least number in the set of data. **9.** 12.8; 14; no mode **11.** 34; 34; 34 **13.** 1.5; 1.6; no mode **15.** 0.5; 0.6; 0.6 **17.** Median; the mode is the least number in the set of data and the mean is affected by the very large number 53. **19.** Sample answer: 1, 1, 1, 1, 14, 15, 18 **21.** G **23.** histogram **25.** 2.89, 2.9, 3.1, 3.2, 3.25 **27.** 15.01, 15.1, 16.79, 16.8, 17.4

Pages 444–445 Lesson 9-5

1. Sample answer: {1, 50, 50, 60, 60, 70, 70, 80} **3.** 9; 59; 62, 58; 4; no outliers **5.** 41.1 million **7.** 33.0 million, 9.1 million **9.** no outliers **11.** 38; 52; 57, 48; 9; 22 **13.** 6.3; 16.6; 18.7, 14.55; 4.15; no outliers **15.** 0.7; 0.55; 0.65, 0.25; 0.4; no outliers **17.** 38; 44, 30 **19.** Philadelphia **21.** 54; 70; 39 **23.** The interquartile range for San Francisco is only 10°F, while the interquartile range for Philadelphia is 31°F. **25a.** Sample answer: {1, 1, 2, 2, 2, 5, 9, 9, 9, 10, 10} and {1, 4, 4, 4, 4, 5, 5, 5, 9, 10, 10} **25b.** Sample answer: {1, 2, 5, 7, 9, 10, 12, 14, 15, 17, 22} and {0, 2, 5, 7, 9, 10, 12, 14, 15, 17, 27} **27.** 1.35 **29.** 7; 7; 3

31. **33.**

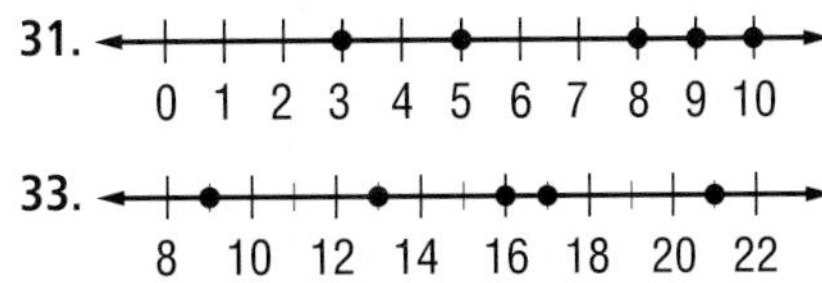

Pages 448–449 Lesson 9-6

1. The box represents the spread of the middle half of the data. **3.** Joseph; 64 is an outlier.

5.

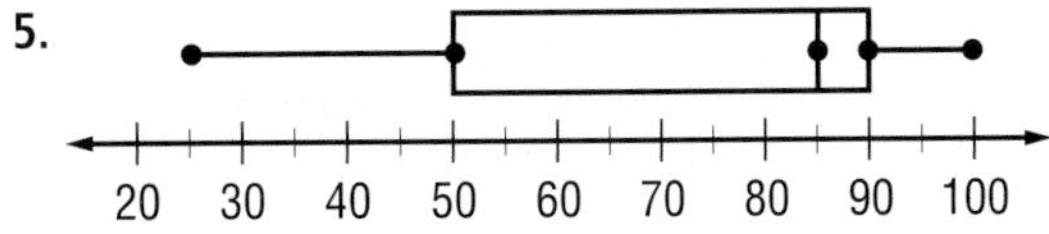

7. 260 **9.** **11.** **13.**

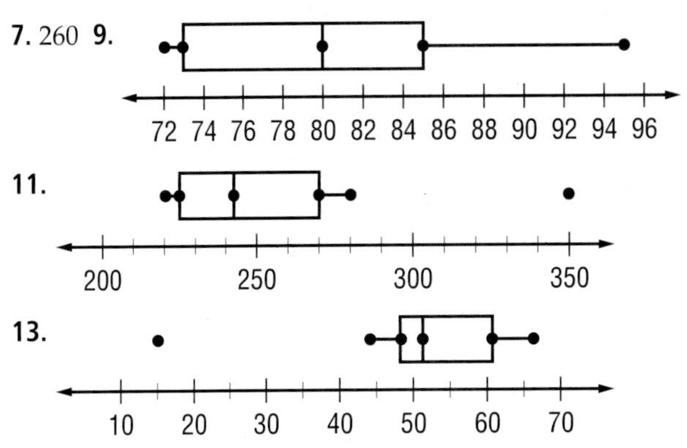

15. domestic **17.** 75% **19.** Sample answer: {20, 20, 20, 30, 35, 40, 50, 60, 70, 70, 70} **21.** 40 **23.** 49; 81; 88, 74; 14; 50 **25.** Since this is a systematic random sample of the entire population concerned with the park, it is an unbiased sample.

Pages 451–453 Lesson 9-7

1. The scale may have a break or may have different sized intervals. The graph may show a larger area than the actual increase. **3.** Graph B; since there is a break in the vertical scale, the number of medals for Norway appears to be much greater than the number of medals for the Soviet Union. **5.** Graph B; the area of the house indicates a much greater median income for the male householder than a female householder. **7.** The advertising is not false. In the last survey, 3 out of 4 people liked Tasty Treats better than Groovy Goodies. However, it is misleading, because combining all the survey results shows only half of the people liked Tasty Treats better than Groovy Goodies. **9.** Mean; it is greater than the median and they will want to appear to pay more money. **11.** Mean; it is greater than the median and they will want to appear to pay more money.

13a. Number of Admissions to Movie Theaters **13b. Number of Admissions to Movie Theaters**

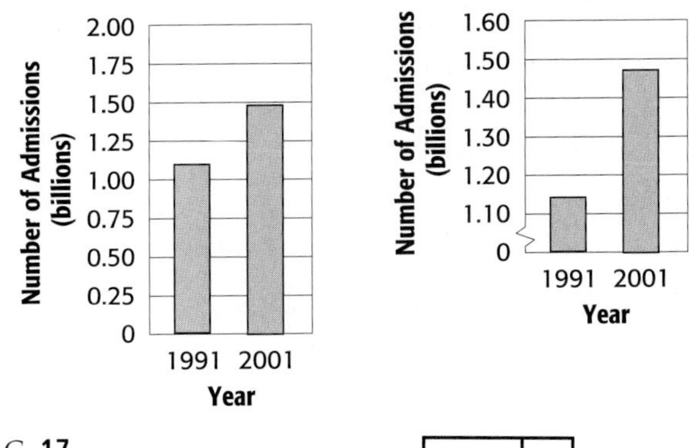

15. G **17.**

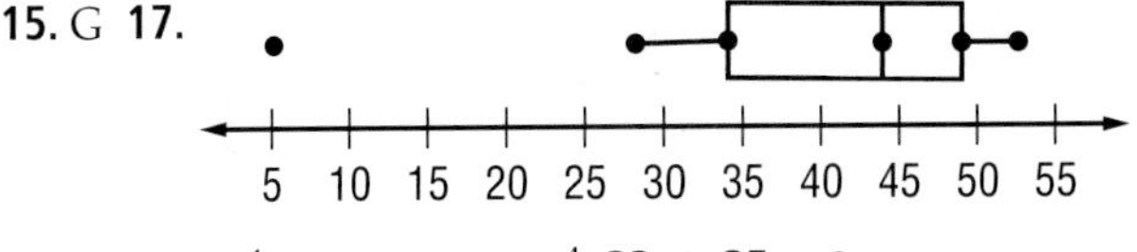

19. 7.02×10^4 **21.** 4.56×10^{-4} **23.** 3 **25.** -2

Pages 456–457 Lesson 9-8

1. A 3-by-2 matrix has 3 rows and 2 columns, and a 2-by-3 matrix has 2 rows and 3 columns. **3.** 3 by 1; third row, first column **5.** 2 by 5; second row, fourth column

7. $\begin{bmatrix} -2 & 13 & -8 \\ 11 & 3 & -18 \\ -5 & -8 & 8 \end{bmatrix}$ **9.** 1 by 3; first row, third column

Selected Answers

11. 3 by 3; third row, first column **13.** 3 by 4; third row, second column

15. $\begin{bmatrix} 2 & 1 & 2 \\ 3 & -5 & -1 \\ 1 & -8 & 8 \end{bmatrix}$ **17.** impossible **19.** $\begin{bmatrix} 12 & 8 & 12 \\ 21 & 17 & 11 \\ 16 & 16 & 15 \end{bmatrix}$

21. C **23.**

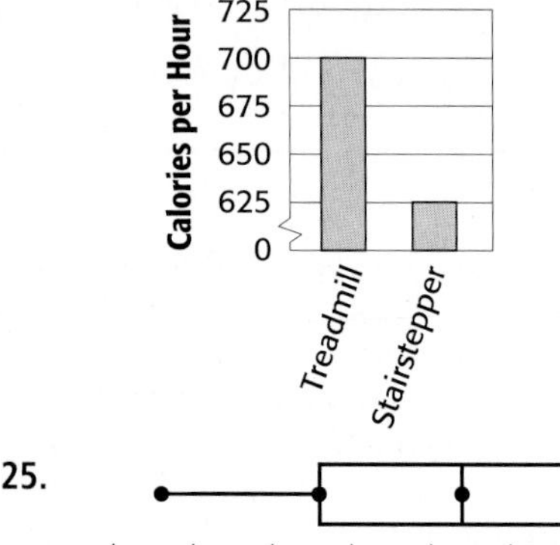

25.

35 40 45 50 55 60 65 70 75

Pages 458–460 Chapter 9 Study Guide and Review

1. true **3.** true **5.** false; median **7.** false; dimensions

9. 10 students

11.

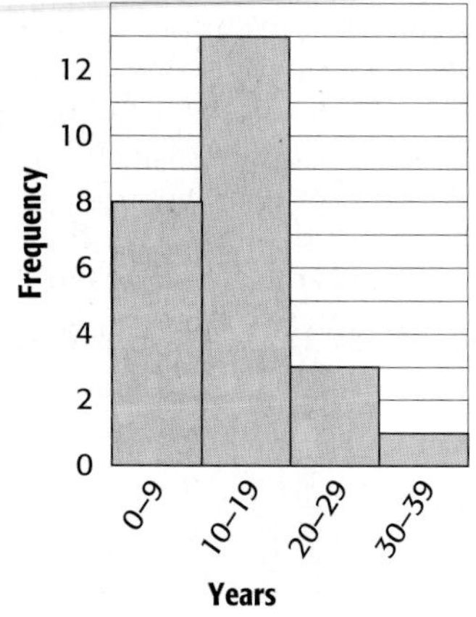

13. circle graph **15.** 16.4, 15, 15 **17.** 7.7, 8, 8 **19.** 11; 3; 5, 2; 3; 12 **21.** 8; 6.5; 8.5, 4.5; 4; no outliers

23.

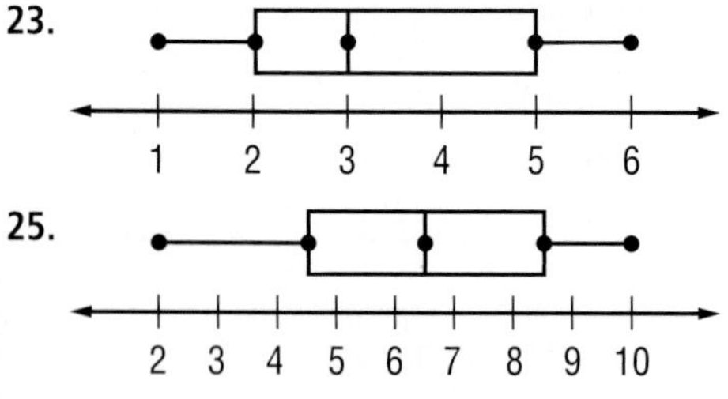

27. median **29.** median **31.** $\begin{bmatrix} 9 & 7 \\ -2 & 2 \end{bmatrix}$ **33.** impossible

Chapter 10 Algebra: More Equations and Inequalities

Page 467 Chapter 10 Getting Started

1. algebraic **3.** true **5.** false **7.** $10 + x = -8$ **9.** $2x - 4 = 26$ **11.** -17 **13.** 19 **15.** 14 **17.** -6 **19.** -32

Pages 472–473 Lesson 10-1

1. terms that contain the same variable or are constants **3.** $5(x - 3)$; $5(x - 3)$ is equivalent to $5x - 15$, while the other three expressions are equivalent to $5x - 3$. **5.** $-3a - 27$ **7.** terms: $8a$, 4, $-6a$; like terms: $8a$ and $-6a$; coefficients: 8, -6; constant: 4 **9.** terms: $5n$, $-n$, 3, $-2n$; like terms: $5n$, $-n$, and $-2n$; coefficients: 5, -1, -2; constant: 3 **11.** $9n$ **13.** $11c$ **15.** $5x - 3$ **17.** $7m + 42$ **19.** $-7n - 14$ **21.** $-8c + 64$ **23.** $-4x + 24$ **25.** $4x - 4y$ **27.** $-12x - 20$ **29.** $12(x - 7)$; $12x - 84$ **31.** $9(x - 3)$; $9x - 27$ **33.** terms: 7, $-5x$, 1; like terms: 7, 1; coefficients: -5; constants: 7, 1 **35.** terms: n, $4n$, $-7n$, -1; like terms: n, $4n$, $-7n$; coefficients: 1, 4, -7; constant: -1 **37.** terms: 9, $-z$, 3, $-2z$; like terms: 9 and 3, $-z$ and $-2z$; coefficients: -1, -2; constants: 9, 3 **39.** $6n$ **41.** $-3k$ **43.** $14x + 4$ **45.** $6 - 3c$ **47.** 7 **49.** -8 **51.** $5\frac{1}{2}y + 100$ **53.** $2t + 24$ **55.** $12x + 6$ **57.** 1 by 2; first row, first column **59.** 3 by 1; third row, first column **61.** Graph B **63.** -6 **65.** -8

Pages 476–477 Lesson 10-2

1. You identify the order in which operations would be performed on the variable, then you undo each operation using its inverse operation in reverse order. **3.** Tomás; Alexis did not undo the operations in reverse order. **5.** 1 **7.** 28 **9.** 8 **11.** -3 **13.** 6 **15.** 3 **17.** -8 **19.** 4 **21.** 27 **23.** 8 **25.** \$6 **27.** -3 **29.** 5 **31.** -9 **33.** -6 **35.** 4 **37.** 4 **39.** -1 **41.** -1 **43.** 7 **45.** Sample answer: $4x + 3 = -17$ **47.** $13 + 3x = 25$; 4 **49.** $-3x - 15$ **51.** $-8p + 56$ **53.** $4n + 5 = 17$

Pages 480–481 Lesson 10-3

1. multiplication by 2 **3.** $3n + 1 = 7$; 2 **5.** $\frac{n}{5} - 10 = 3$; 65 **7.** $5n - 4 = 11$; 3 **9.** $4n + 8 = -12$; -5 **11.** $\frac{n}{3} + 9 = 14$; 15 **13.** $3n - 10 = 17$; 9 **15.** $4x + 25 = 75$; \$12.50 each **17.** $0.07m + 3.95 = 12.63$; 124 min **19.** $4.45s + 100.23 = 216.59$; 26.1 **21.** $n + 2n + (2n + 5) = 200$; \$37, \$74, \$89 **23.** 46 **25.** 9 **27.** -2 **29.** 6 **31.** 2 **33.** 5 **35.** 8 **37.** $3 + 5y$

Pages 486–487 Lesson 10-4

1. Addition Property of Equality **3.** -3 **5.** -4 **7.** 5 **9.** n = number; $3n - 18 = 2n$; 18 **11.** 8 **13.** -9 **15.** 10 **17.** 1 **19.** 5 **21.** 3.6 **23.** -0.25 **25.** -1.8 **27.** 8 **29.** n = number; $4n + 2 = n - 7$; -3 **31.** $60x = 8x + 26$; 0.5 **33.** $14 + 0.8x = x$; \$70 **35.** $5 + 0.10(10x) + 8x = 10x$; 5 mugs **37.** C **39.** $4n + 8 = 60$; 13 **41.** -3 **43.** 18 **45.** false **47.** true

Pages 494–495 Lesson 10-5

1. Sample answer: $n \geq 9$; you will earn at least \$9. **3.** $a < 6$ **5.** false **7.** true

9.

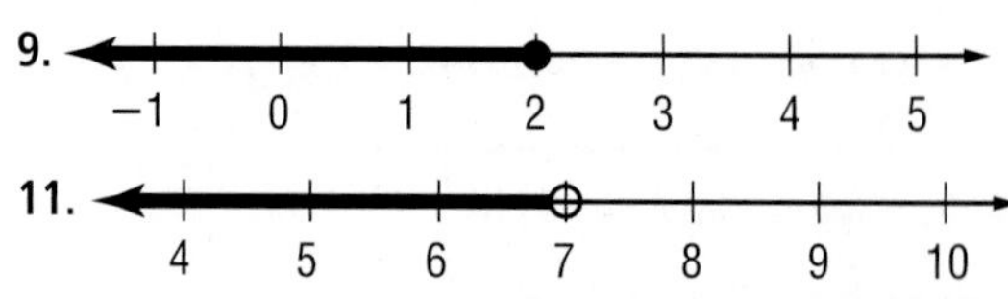

13. $s > 100$ **15.** $\ell \geq 4$ **17.** $c \leq 25$ **19.** true **21.** true **23.** false

25.

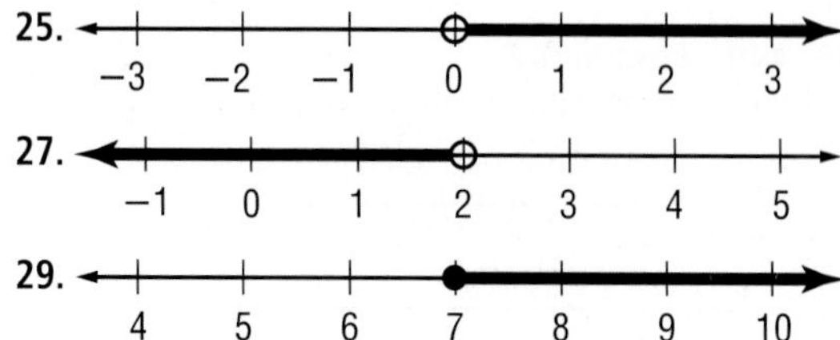

31. 1 2 3 4 5 6 7

33. −6 −5 −4 −3 −2 −1 0

35. $8n \geq 24$ **37.** $n - 4 < 12$ **39.** $t \leq 900$ **41.** $n < -2$
43. Sample answer: These symbols were introduced by the editor of Thomas Harriot's work *Artis Analyticae Praxis ad Aequationes Algebraicas Resolvendas*. **45.** D **47.** 4 **49.** −5
51. $-3 + 6h = 21$; 4 h **53.** −11 **55.** −9

Pages 498–499 Lesson 10-6

1. The same quantity can be subtracted from each side of the equation or inequality without changing the truth of the statement. **3.** $b > 4$ **5.** $g \geq -13$ **7.** $k \geq 7$

9. $c < -2$; −8 −6 −4 −2 0 2

11. $a > 3\frac{1}{2}$; 1 2 3 4 5 6

13. $x \leq 13$ **15.** $k > -10$ **17.** $c < -1$ **19.** $g \geq 17$ **21.** $s \leq 7$
23. $w \geq -2$ **25.** $q \leq -1.3$ **27.** $p > -1.2$ **29.** $f < 3\frac{3}{4}$
31. $n - 11 < 8$; $n < 19$ **33.** $n + 17 \leq 6$; $n \leq -11$

35. $n > 4$; −2 0 2 4 6 8

37. $x \leq -16$;

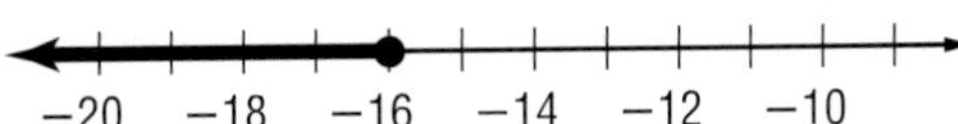

39. $g < -7$; −10 −8 −6 −4 −2 0

41. $h \geq 2$; −4 −2 0 2 4 6

43. $b \leq 7.75$; 5 6 7 8 9 10

45. $w < 4\frac{2}{3}$; 3 4 5 6

47. $99.2 + t > 101$; $t > 1.8$; more than 1.8°F **49.** $15 > x - 3$; $x < 18$; x is less than 18 cm **51.** Never; subtracting x from each side gives $0 > 1$, which is never true. **53.** I **55.** false **57.** true **59.** 133° **61.** 9 **63.** −100

Pages 503–504 Lesson 10-7

1. Sample answer: $\frac{x}{-6} > 3$

3. $x \leq -9$; −14 −12 −10 −8 −6 −4

5. $p \leq 8$; 4 6 8 10 12 14

7. $g > 14$; 8 10 12 14 16 18

9. $a < -8$ **11.** $m \geq 27$

13. $n \leq 5$; −2 0 2 4 6 8

15. $g < -4$; −10 −8 −6 −4 −2 0

17. $y < -11$; −16 −14 −12 −10 −8 −6

19. $r < -3$; −8 −6 −4 −2 0 2

21. $c \leq 1$; −6 −4 −2 0 2 4

23. $a \leq -15$;

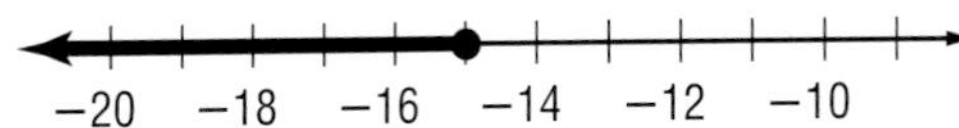

25. $n < -98$;

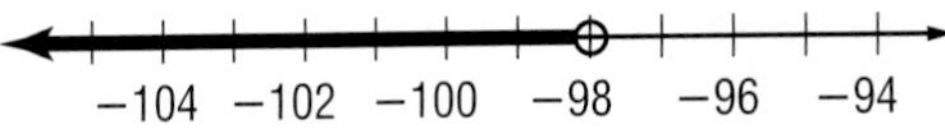

27. $t \geq 10$; 6 8 10 12 14 16

29. $k < 20$; 14 16 18 20 22 24

31. $5.25c \geq 42$; $c \geq 8$; at least 8 h **33.** $4{,}000{,}000 > 8d$; $d < 500{,}000$; less than 500,000 mi **35.** $k \leq -1$ **37.** $n < -9$
39. $c > 28$ **41.** $x \leq -3$ **43.** $\frac{n}{-5} \leq 7$; $n \geq -35$
45. $-2n > -18$; $n < 9$ **47.** D **49.** $y < 2$ **51.** $j \geq -4$
53. $b > 100{,}000$

Pages 505–506 Chapter 10 Study Guide and Review

1. d **3.** a **5.** f **7.** $4a + 12$ **9.** $-7n + 35$ **11.** $7p$ **13.** 6 **15.** −7
17. 35 **19.** $2n + 6 = -4$; −5 **21.** $\frac{x}{8} - 2 = 5$; 56 **23.** −7 **25.** 3

27. $g \geq 92$; 88 90 92 94 96

29. $y \leq -2$ **31.** $d > 14$ **33.** $c \leq -2$ **35.** $m < -3$

Chapter 11 Algebra: Linear Functions

Page 511 Chapter 11 Getting Started

1. false; vertical **3–6.**

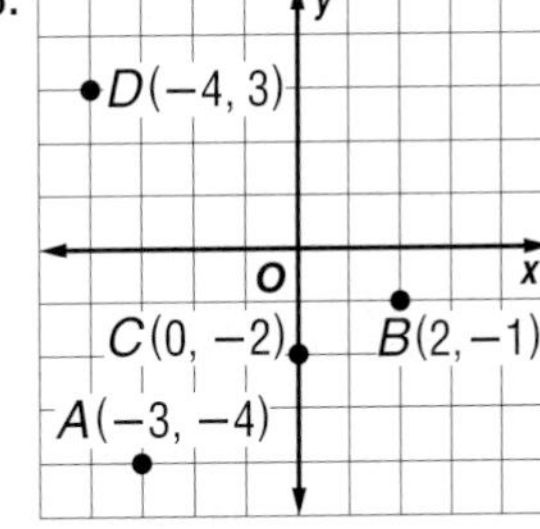

7. 18 **9.** 20
11. 5
13. 4
15. 3

Pages 514–515 Lesson 11-1

1. When the quotient between any two consecutive terms is the same, the sequence is geometric. **3.** 5, 10, 15, 20, 25, …; It is an arithmetic sequence and the others are geometric sequences. **5.** neither; −14, −16, −17 **7.** 1, 2, 3, 4, 5
9. 6 cans **11.** geometric; 10; 100,000, 1,000,000, 10,000,000
13. arithmetic; −3; 73, 70, 67 **15.** neither; 26, 37, 50
17. geometric; −3; −1,215, 3,645, −10,935 **19.** arithmetic; $2\frac{1}{2}$; $16\frac{1}{2}$, 19, $21\frac{1}{2}$ **21.** geometric; $-\frac{1}{4}$; $-\frac{1}{64}$, $\frac{1}{256}$, $-\frac{1}{1{,}024}$
23. arithmetic; $-\frac{1}{3}$; $2\frac{5}{6}$, $2\frac{1}{2}$, $2\frac{1}{6}$ **25.** 100, −600, 3,600, −21,600 **27.** 4, 8, 12, 16, …; arithmetic **29.** arithmetic

31. Yes; the common ratio is 1. **33.** 0, 5, 10, 15, 20, 25, … **35.** I **37.** $b > 17$ **39.** $-7 \leq t$ **41.** 18 **43.** 26

Pages 519–520 Lesson 11-2

1. domain; range **3.** Tomi; the input is the value of x, not $f(x)$. **5.** -7

7.

x	$5x + 1$	$f(x)$
-2	$5(-2) + 1$	-9
0	$5(0) + 1$	1
1	$5(1) + 1$	6
3	$5(3) + 1$	16

9. 35 **11.** 11 **13.** 19 **15.** 2

17.

x	$6x - 4$	$f(x)$
-5	$6(-5) - 4$	-34
-1	$6(-1) - 4$	-10
2	$6(2) - 4$	8
7	$6(7) - 4$	38

19.

x	$7 + 3x$	y
-3	$7 + 3(-3)$	-2
-2	$7 + 3(-2)$	1
1	$7 + 3(1)$	10
6	$7 + 3(6)$	25

21. $P = 4s$ **23.** $c = 45.00 + 3.50p$ **25.** Sample answer: Mr. Jones is traveling on the interstate at an average speed of 55 miles per hour. Write a function to determine the distance he travels in h hours. How far will he travel in 3 hours? $d = 55h$; 165 mi **27.** A **29.** geometric; -2; -96, 192, -384 **31.** neither; 17, 23, 30 **33.** 28

34–37.

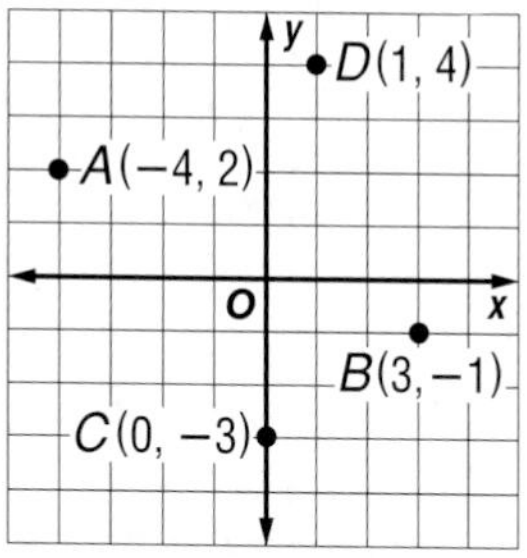

$D(1, 4)$ $A(-4, 2)$ $B(3, -1)$ $C(0, -3)$

Pages 524–525 Lesson 11-3

1. Make ordered pairs using the x value and its corresponding y value. Then graph the ordered pairs on a coordinate plane. Draw a line that the points suggest. **3.** (0, 3); 3 does not equal $2(0) - 3$ or -3.

5.

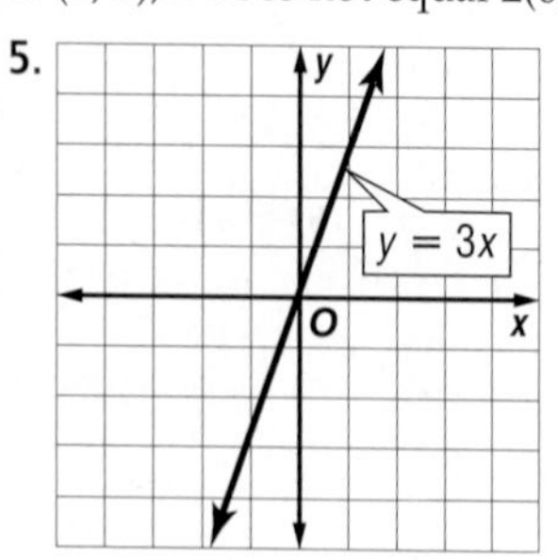

7.

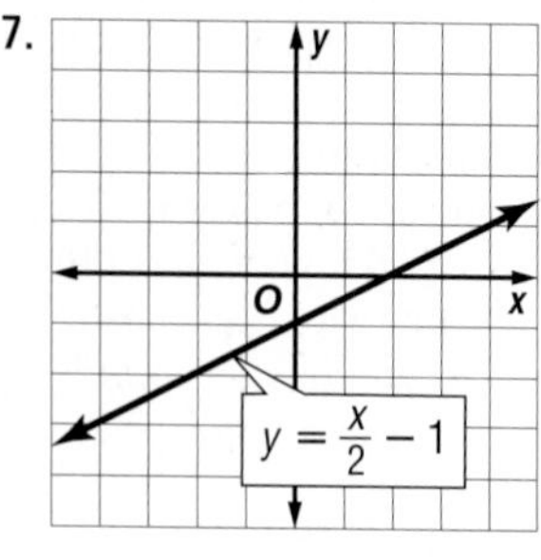

9. 100 gal

11. $y = 2x$

x	$2x$	y	(x, y)
-2	$2(-2)$	-4	$(-2, -4)$
0	$2(0)$	0	(0, 0)
1	$2(1)$	2	(1, 2)
2	$2(2)$	4	(2, 4)

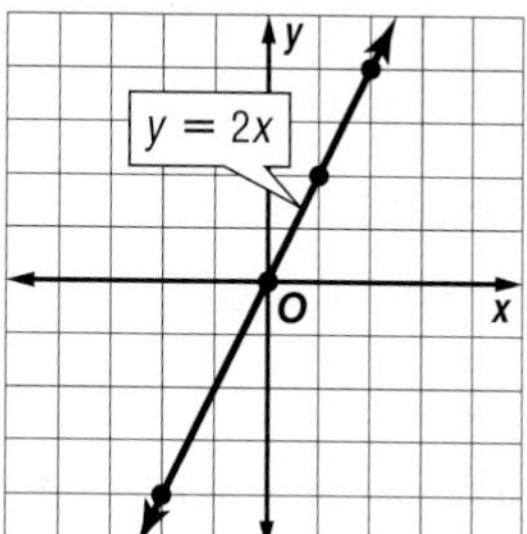

13.

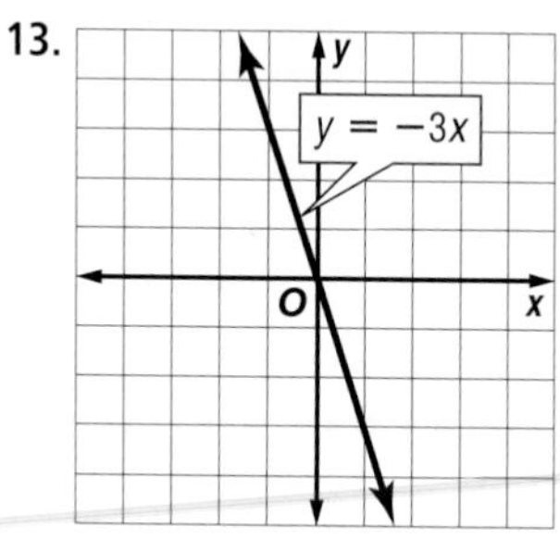

15.

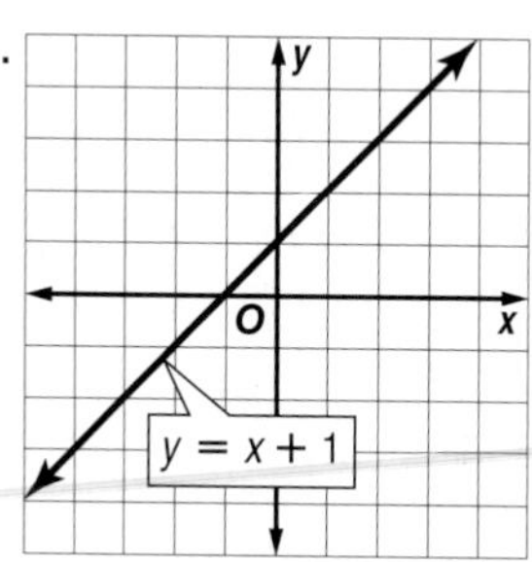

17.

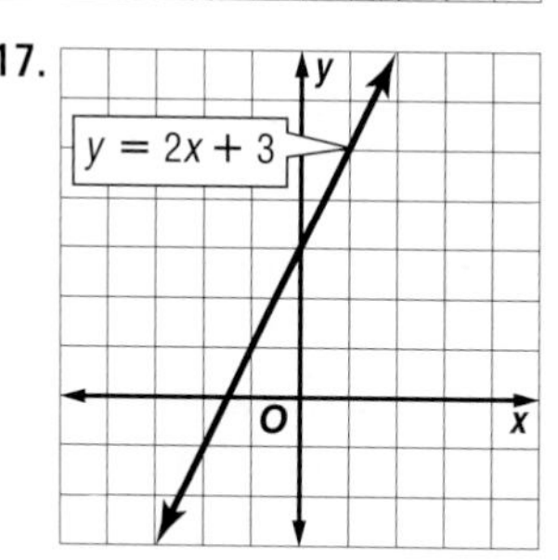

19.

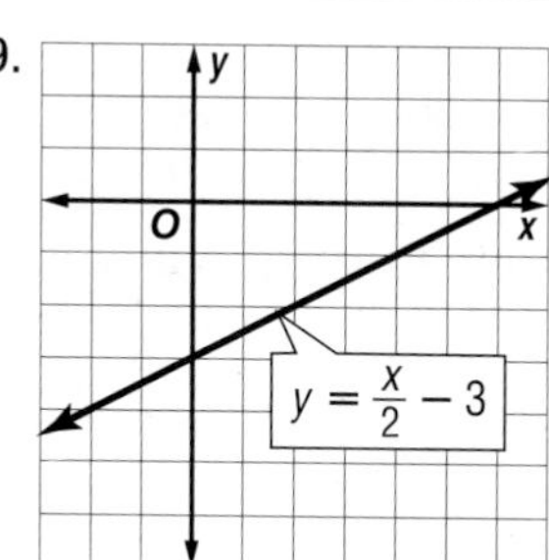

21.

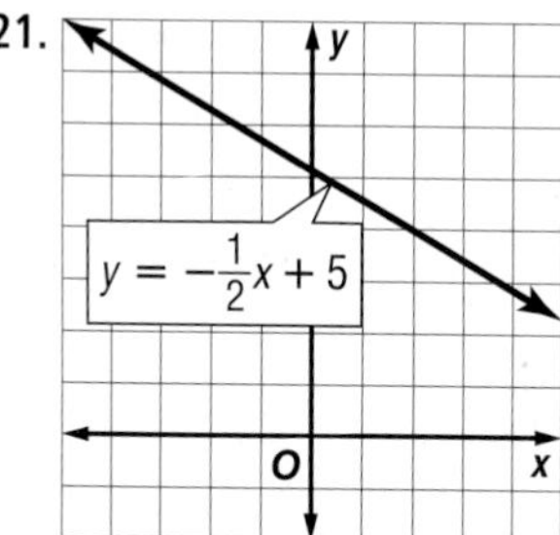

23.

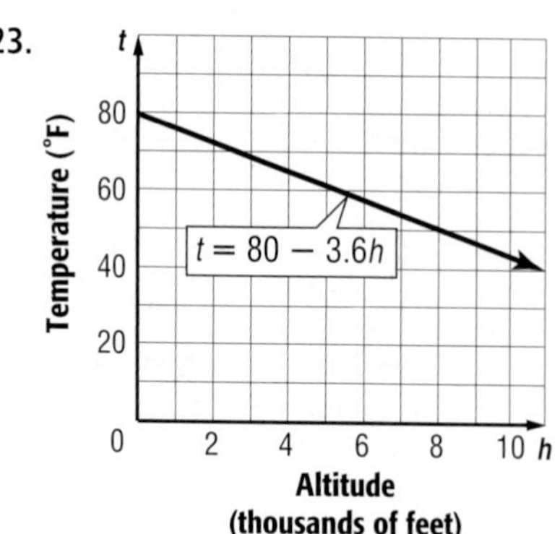

25a. Sample answer: $(-2, -4)$, $(0, -2)$, $(2, 0)$, $(4, 2)$; $y = x - 2$ **25b.** Sample answer: $(-1, 4)$, $(0, 3)$, $(1, 2)$, $(3, 0)$; $y = 3 - x$ **27.** A **29.** 39 **31.** -1 **33.** $\frac{1}{3}$ **35.** 4

Pages 528–529 Lesson 11-4

1. If $x_2 = x_1$, then $\frac{y_2 - y_1}{x_2 - x_1} = \frac{y_2 - y_1}{0}$ and division by 0 is undefined. Therefore the slope is undefined. **3.** Dylan; Martin did not use the x-coordinates in the same order as the y-coordinates. **5.** 0 **7.** $\frac{9}{100}$ **9.** The second half; it has a greater slope. **11.** −4 **13.** $\frac{1}{5}$ **15.** $-\frac{7}{9}$ **17.** undefined **19.** $-\frac{8}{9}$ **21.** −1 **23.** 55; her average speed **25.** Slope of $\overline{QR}$: $m = \frac{1 - (-2)}{5 - (-4)}$ or $\frac{1}{3}$; Slope of $\overline{RS}$: $m = \frac{2 - 1}{4 - 5}$ or −1; Slope of $\overline{ST}$: $m = \frac{-1 - 2}{-5 - 4}$ or $\frac{1}{3}$; Slope of $\overline{TQ}$: $m = \frac{-1 - (-2)}{-5 - (-4)}$ or −1; Therefore, $\overline{QR} \parallel \overline{ST}$ and $\overline{RS} \parallel \overline{TQ}$, and quadrilateral $QRST$ is a parallelogram. **27.** $-2, \frac{1}{2}$ **29.** The product of the slopes of two perpendicular lines is −1.

31. Sample answer:

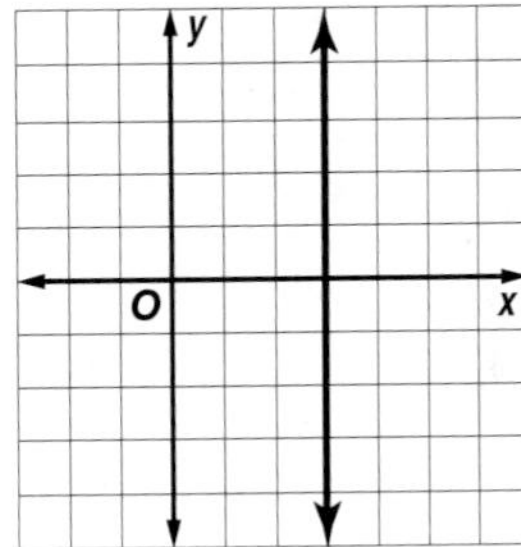

33.

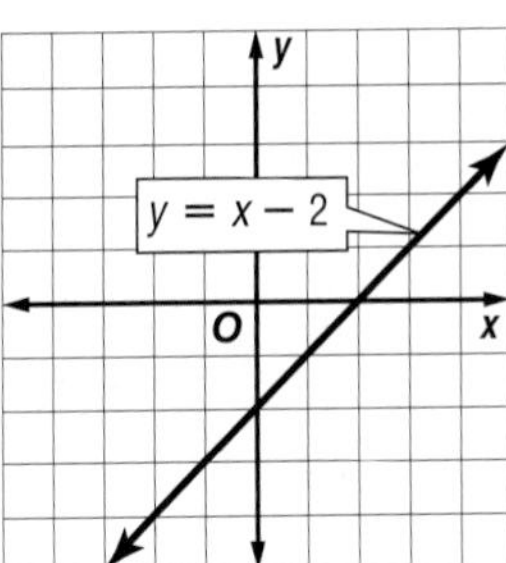

35.

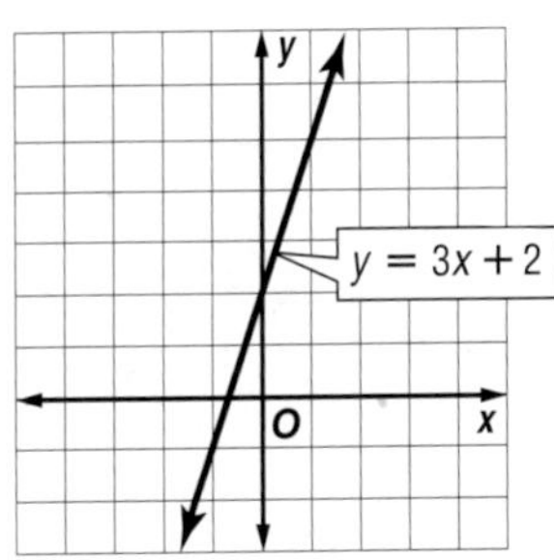

37. 8 **39.** 42

Pages 535–536 Lesson 11-5

1. Locate the first point at (0, −3). From this point, go down 5 and right 4 to locate the second point. Draw a line through the two points. **3.** $y = \frac{3}{2}x + 1$; The slope of this line is $\frac{3}{2}$, but the slope of each of the other lines is $\frac{2}{3}$.

5. $-\frac{1}{6}; -\frac{1}{2}$

7.

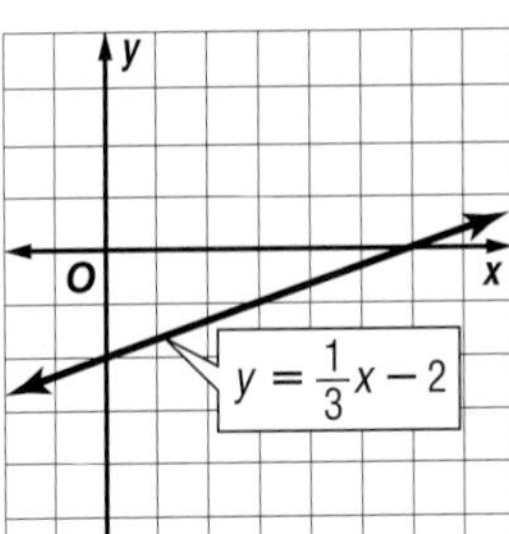

9.

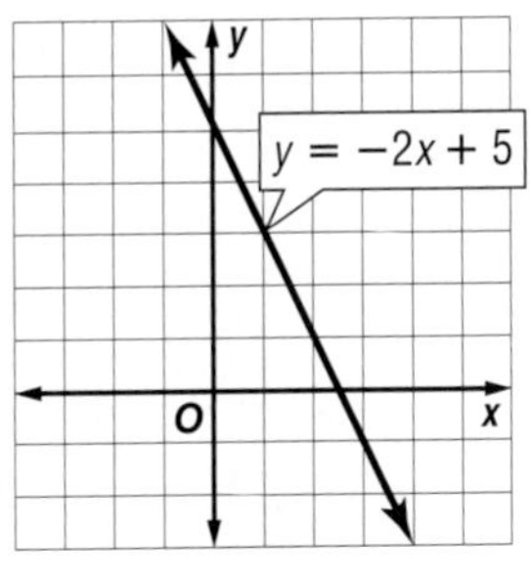

11. the amount paid each week **13.** 3; 4 **15.** $\frac{1}{2}$; −6 **17.** 2; 8

19.

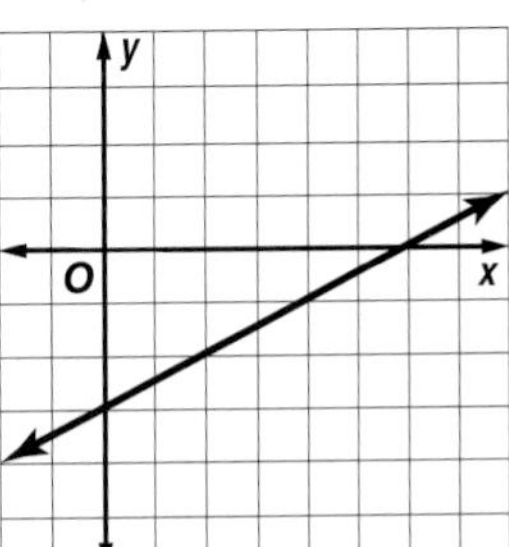

21. $y = -2x + 6$

23.

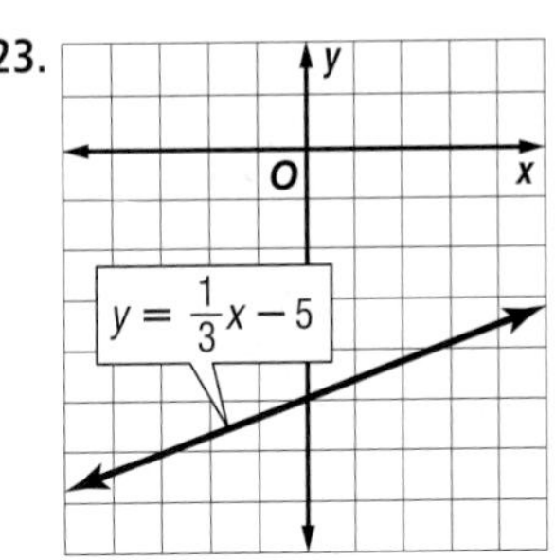

25.

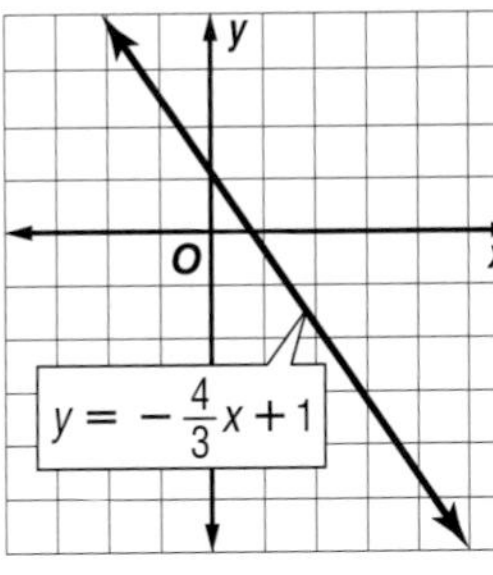

27.

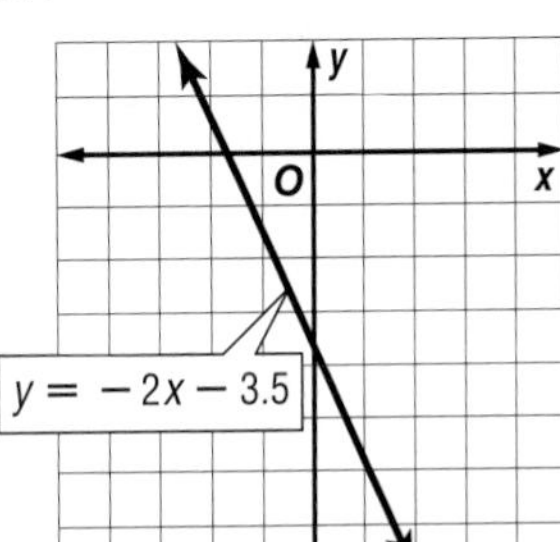

29.

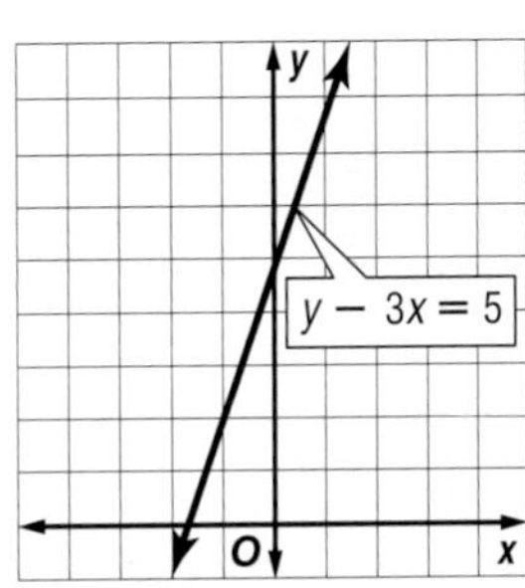

31. $y = -x + 180$ **33.** 110 **35.** the rate of descent **37.** Sample answer: Jim is on a long hike. He has already gone 5 miles. He plans to hike 3 miles each hour. The distance y he has traveled in x hours can be determined by $y = 3x + 5$. Draw a graph of the function.

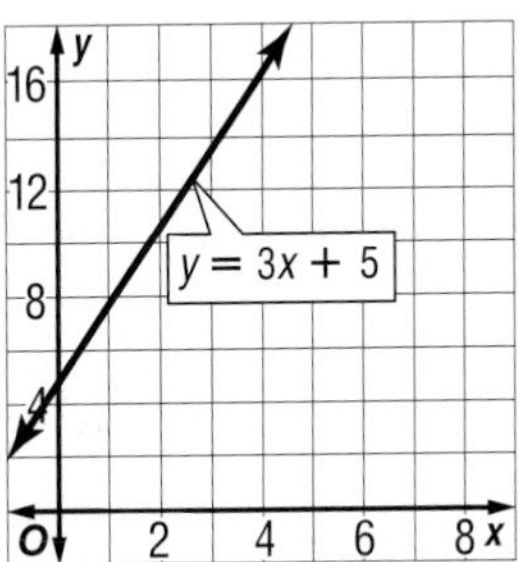

What does the slope represent? (the miles per hour) What does the y-intercept represent? (the distance already traveled) **39.** The slope is undefined. There is no y-intercept unless the graph of the line is the y-axis. **41.** G **43.** $\frac{3}{2}$

45.

x	0.39x	y	(x, y)
0	0.39(0)	0	(0, 0)
1	0.39(1)	0.39	(1, 0.39)
2	0.39(2)	0.78	(2, 0.78)
3	0.39(3)	1.17	(3, 1.17)
4	0.39(4)	1.56	(4, 1.56)

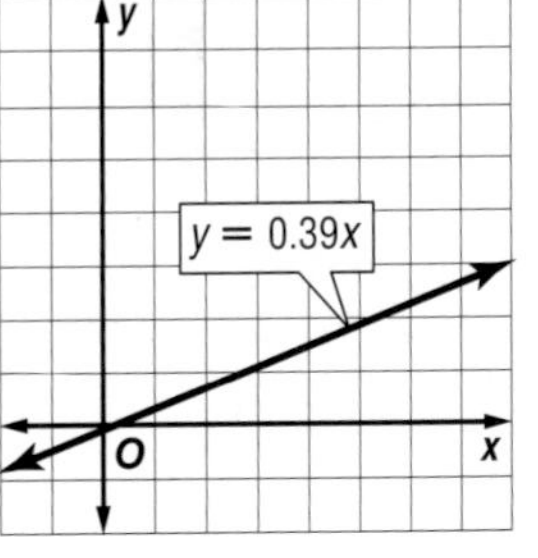

46–49.

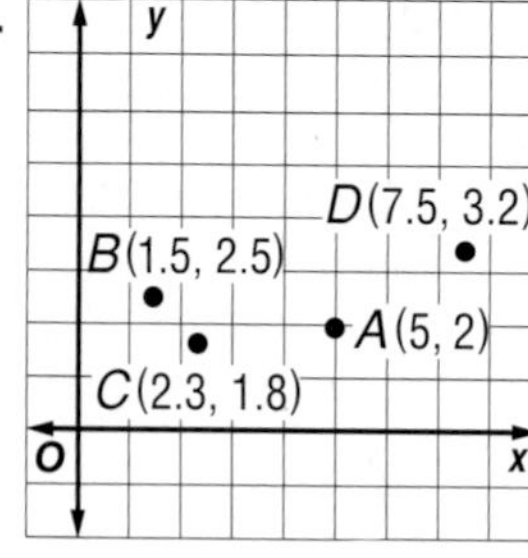

Pages 541–542 Lesson 11-6

1. Let one set of data be the x values and the other set of data be the y values. Pair the corresponding x and y values to form ordered pairs. Graph the ordered pairs to form a scatter plot. **3.** positive **5.** negative **7.** positive **9.** positive **11.** no relationship **13.** negative **15.** positive

17.

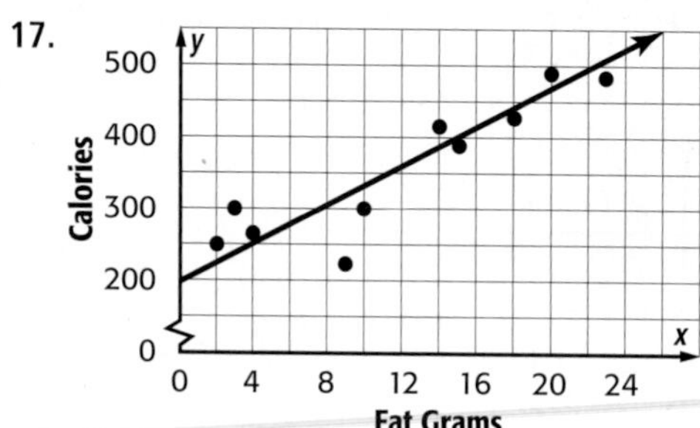

19. Sample answer: $y = 12x + 210$
23. B **25.** $\frac{4}{5}$; 7 **27.** −4; 2

29.

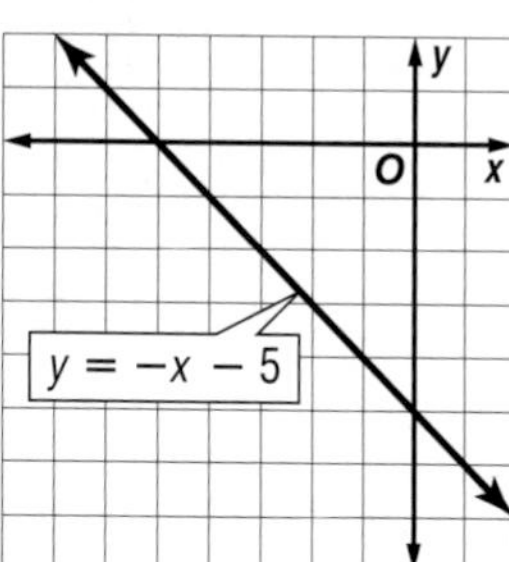

31.

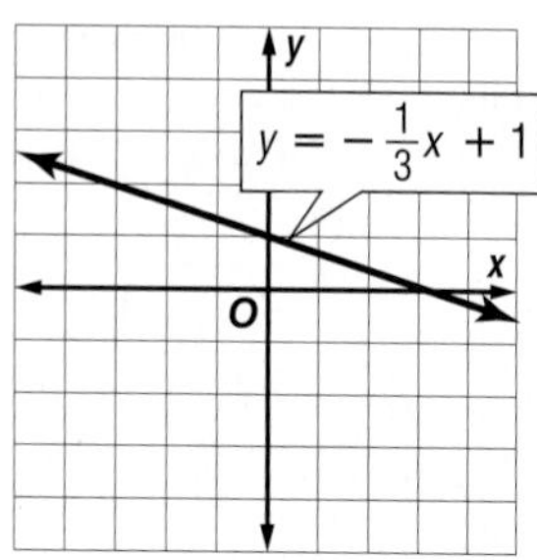

Pages 546–547 Lesson 11-7

1. A system of equations is a set of 2 or more equations. The solution of a system of equations is the solution or solutions that solve all the equations in the system. **3.** The system has no solution. Since the graphs of the equations have the same slope and different y-intercepts, the graphs are parallel lines. Therefore, they do not intersect.

5. (1, 2)

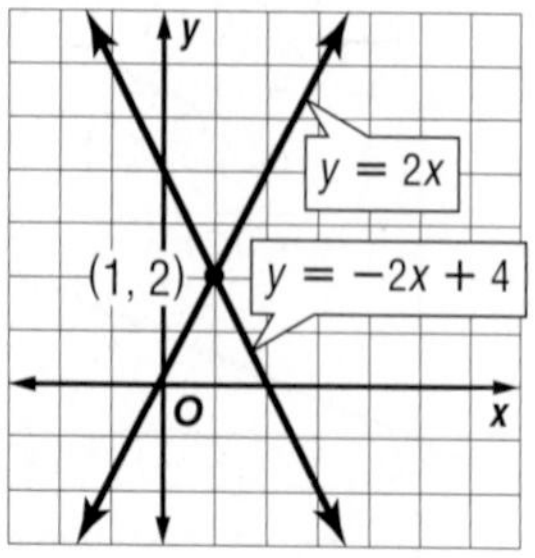

7. (4, 8) **9.** (10, 1) **11.** $y = 350x + 100$

13. (2, −2)

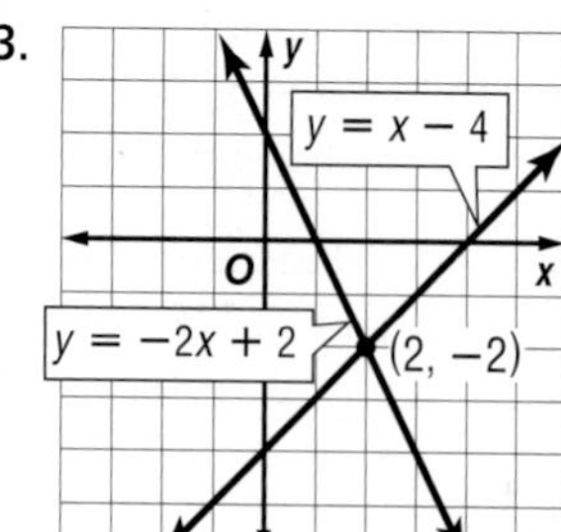

15. (2, 4)

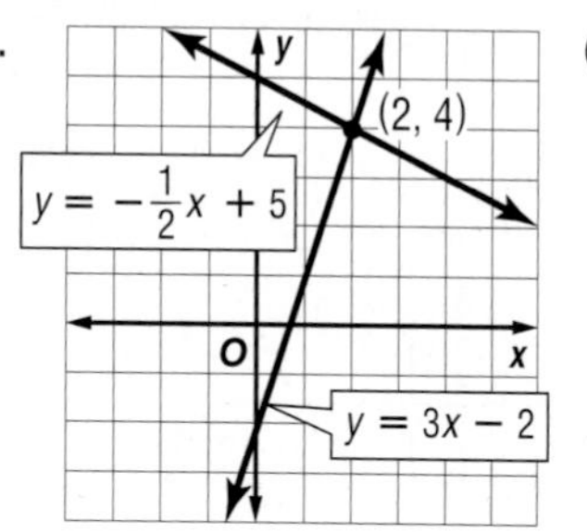

17. no solution

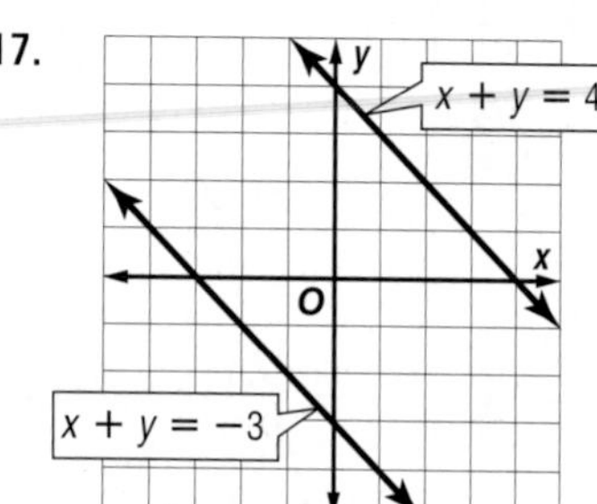

19. (−3, 5)

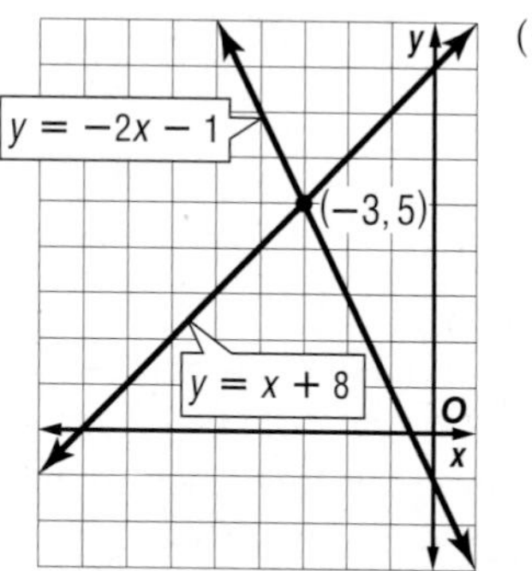

21. (−3, −5) **23.** (−4, 11) **25.** (3, 3) **27.** (1, 2) **29.** 10 shirts; \$150 **31.** $y = 15x + 60$ **33.** 4 min **35a.** Sample answer: $y = -x + 4$ **35b.** Sample answer: $y = 2x - 1$ **35c.** Sample answer: $y - 2x = 1$ **37.** 60

39.

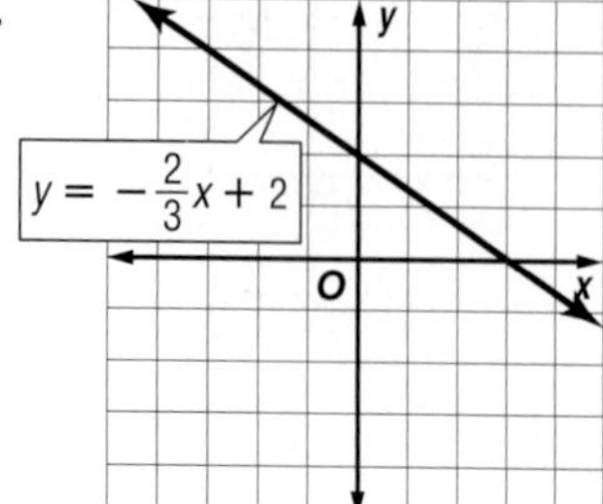

Selected Answers

41.

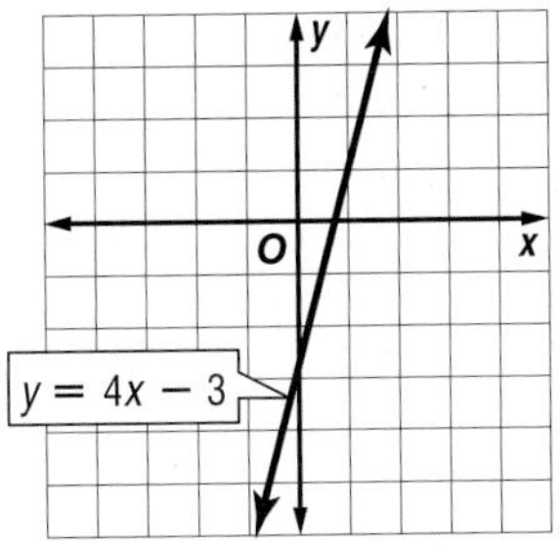

$y = 4x - 3$

43. 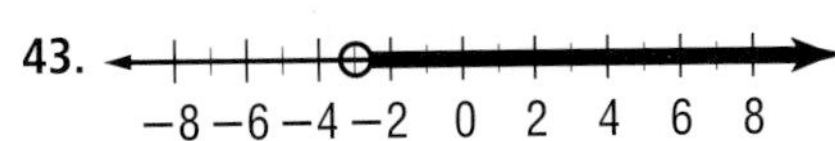

45. −8 −6 −4 −2 0 2 4 6 8

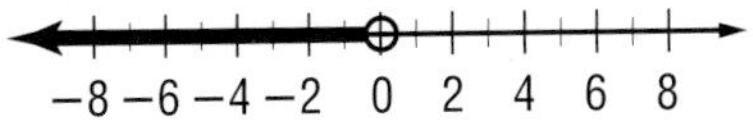

Pages 550–551 Lesson 11-8

1. Sample answer: $y > x - 3$

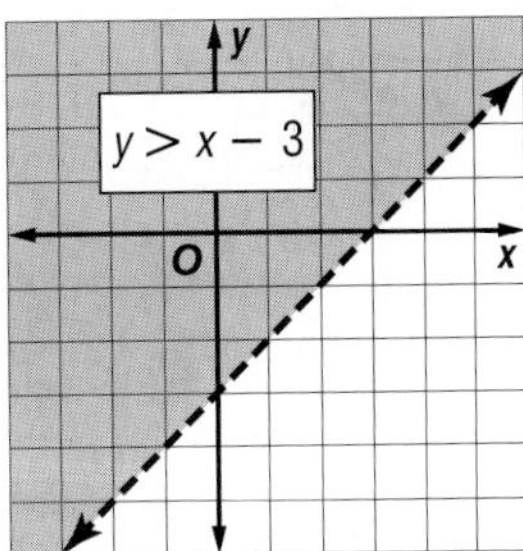

3. $y > 2x - 1$

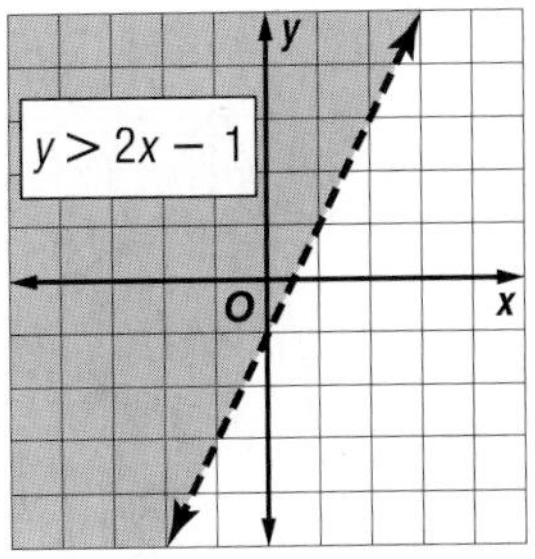

5. 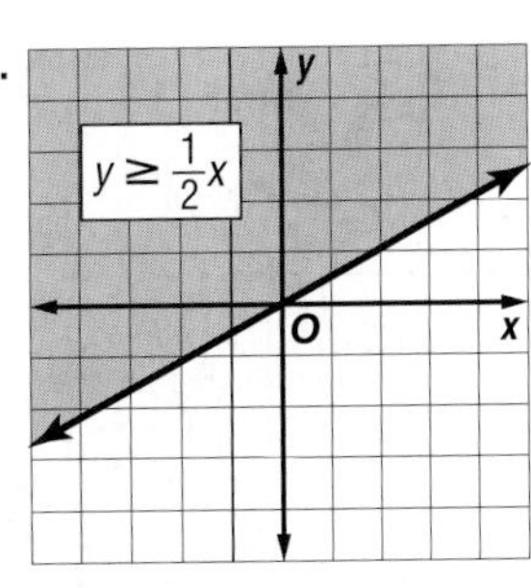

7. Sample answers: legs: 5 units, base: 2 units; legs: 7 units, base: 5 units; legs: 9 units, base: 1 unit

9. 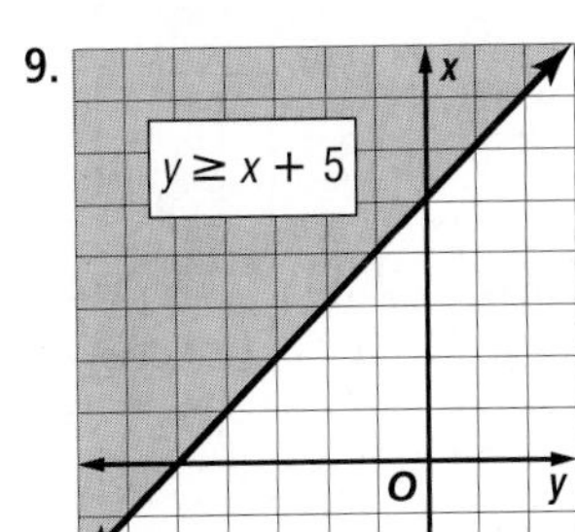

11. $y < -x - 2$

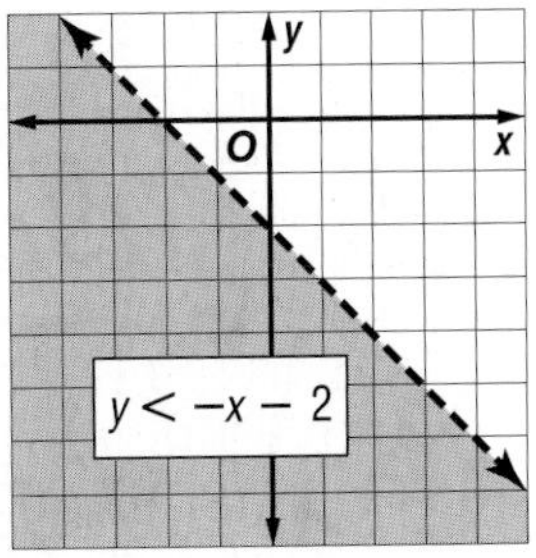

13. 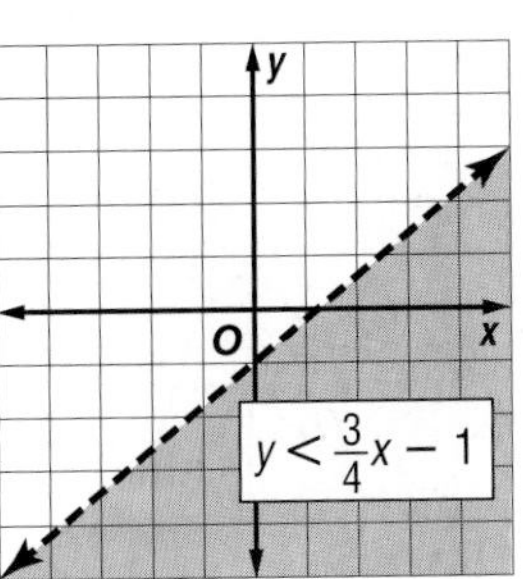

15. 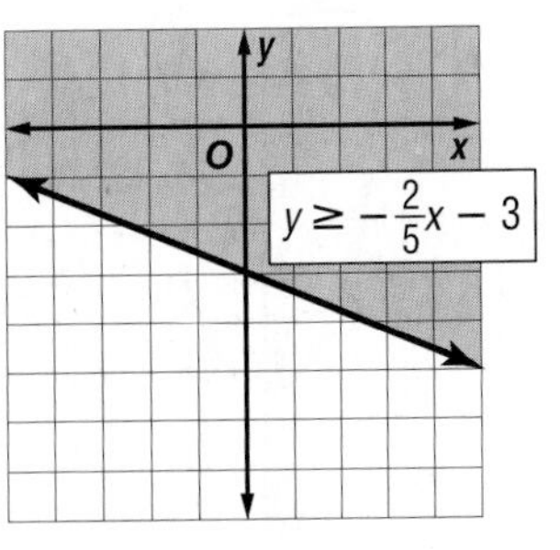

17. 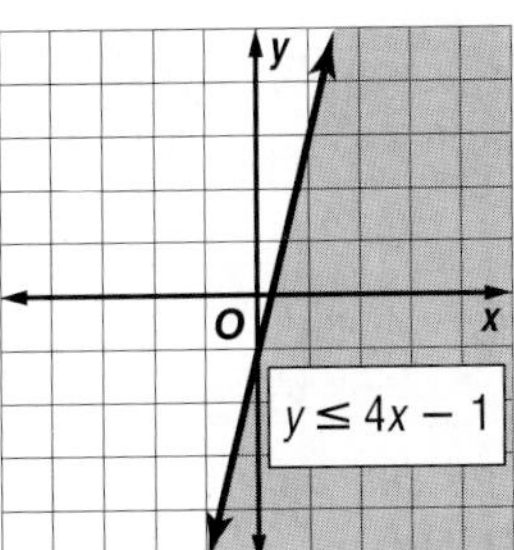

19. 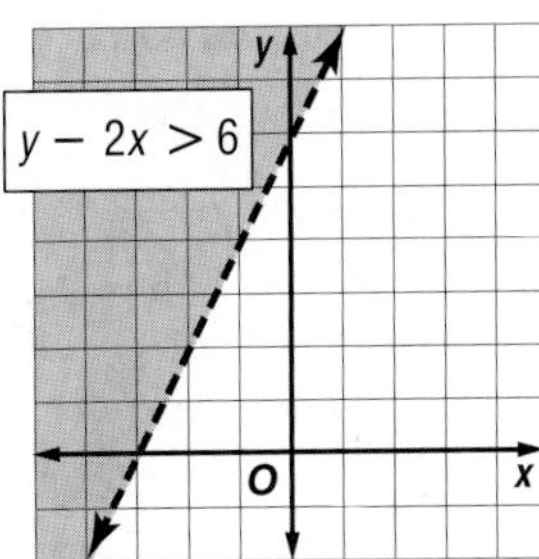

21. 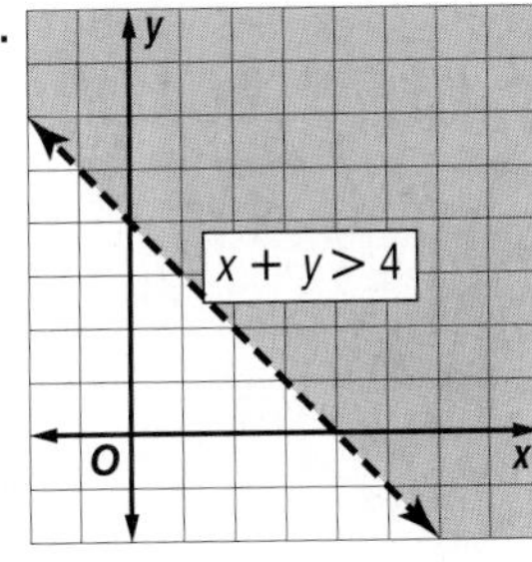

23. Sample answers: math: 30 min, social studies: 20 min; math: 25 min, social studies: 25 min; math: 20 min, social studies: 35 min **25.** Sample answers: khoums: 5, ouguiya: 29; khoums: 25, ouguiya: 30; khoums: 10, ouguiya: 35 **27.** C

29. 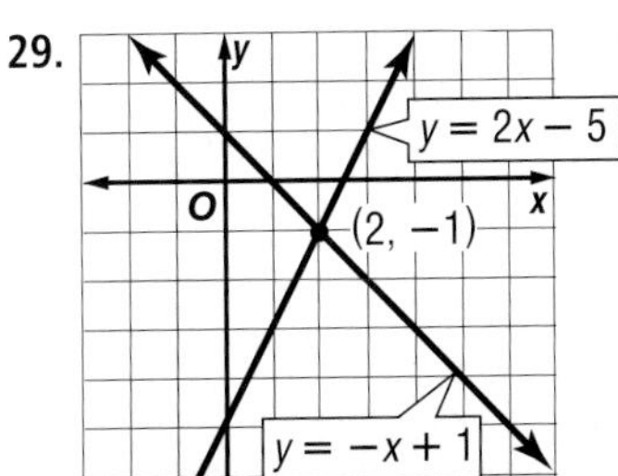

(2, −1)

31. 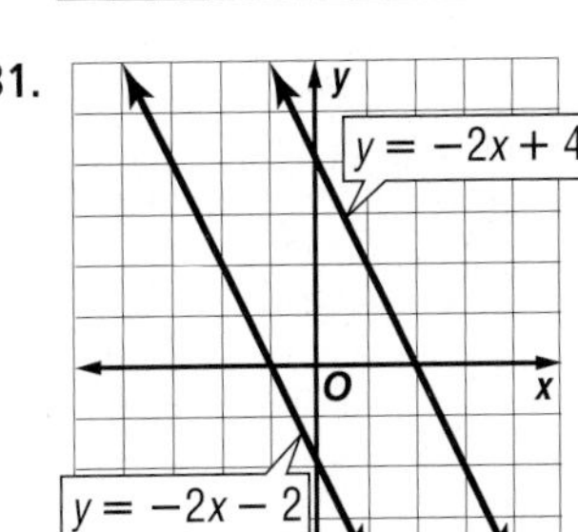

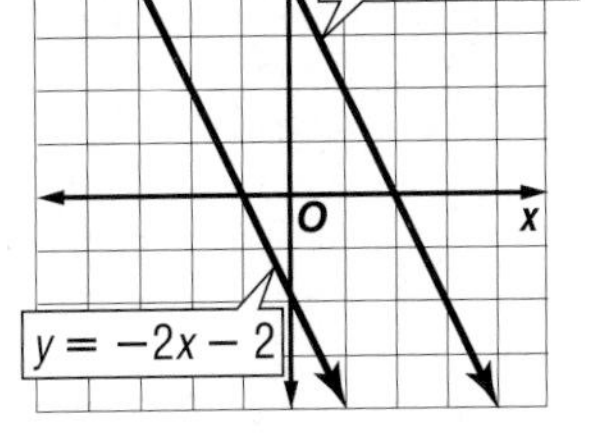

no solution

33. positive **35.** 6.25 yd^2 **37.** \$43.50

Pages 552–554 Chapter 11 Study Guide and Review

1. domain **3.** sequence **5.** arithmetic sequence **7.** boundary **9.** geometric; $\frac{1}{2}$; 2, 1, $\frac{1}{2}$ **11.** neither; 720, 5,040, 40,320 **13.** \$14 **15.** −26 **17.** 22 **19.** −3

21. 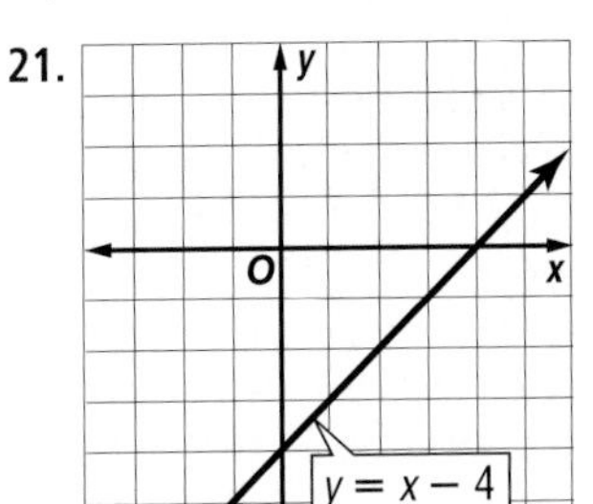

23. $y = \frac{1}{2}x - 2$

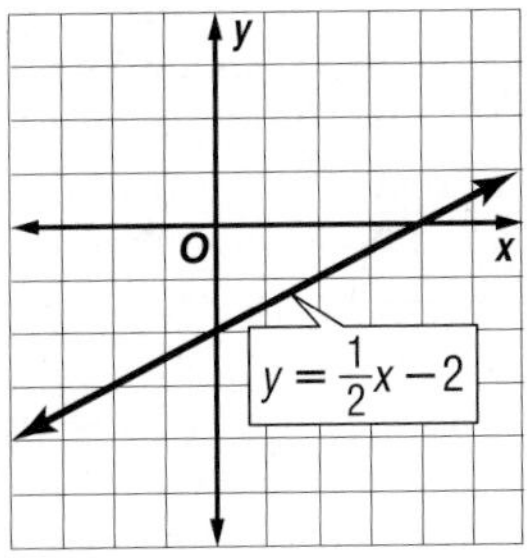

25. 2 **27.** $-\frac{3}{5}$ **29.** 2; 5 **31.** $\frac{1}{5}$; 6 **33.** $-\frac{3}{4}$; 7 **35.** positive **37.** positive

Selected Answers

39.

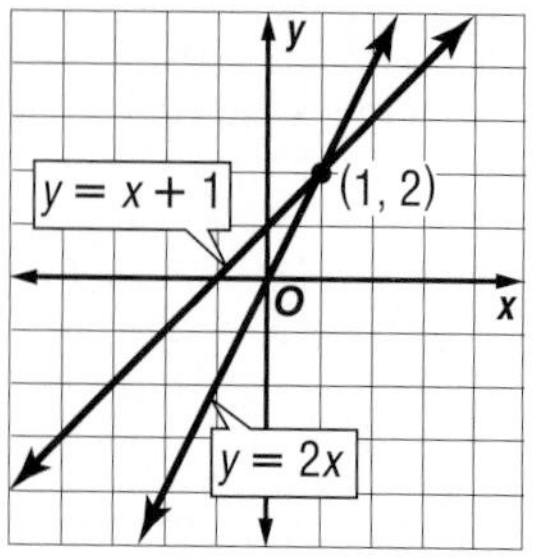

(1, 2)

41.

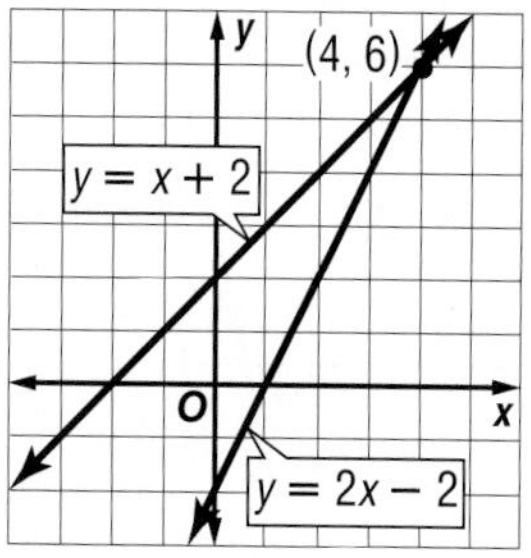

(4, 6)

43. (3, 1)

45.

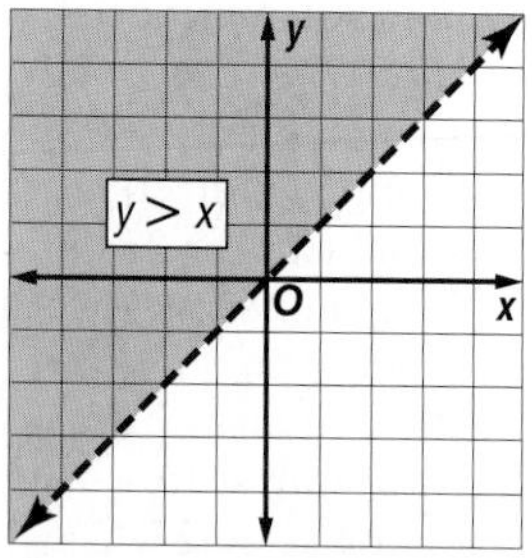

47.

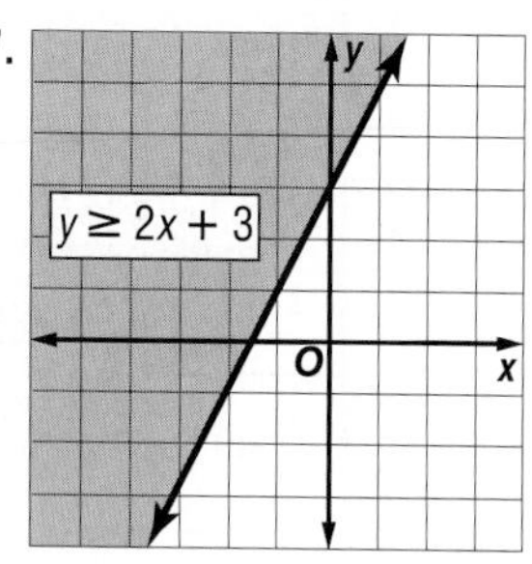

49.

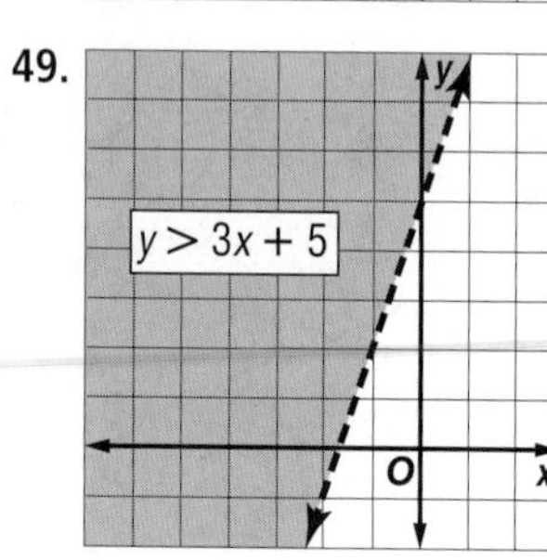

51. Sample answers: 3 games, 3 rides; 5 games, 3 rides; 10 games, 0 rides

Chapter 12 Algebra: Nonlinear Functions and Polynomials

Page 559 Chapter 12 Getting Started

1. linear **3.** $3x, -x$ **5.** $(a + 2a) + (2b - 5b)$ **7.** $3 + (-5y)$ **9.** 6^4 **11.** $9d + 18$

Pages 562–563 Lesson 12-1

1. Sample answer:

x	1	2	3	4
y	3	5	9	15

3. linear; graph is a straight line **5.** linear; can be written as $y = \frac{1}{3}x + 0$ **7.** linear; rate of change is constant, as x increases by 3, y decreases by 2 **9.** nonlinear; graph is two curves **11.** linear; graph is a straight line **13.** nonlinear; graph is a curve **15.** nonlinear; when solved for y, x appears in denominator so the equation cannot be written in the form $y = mx + b$ **17.** nonlinear; power of x is greater than 1 **19.** nonlinear; x is an exponent, so the equation cannot be written in the form $y = mx + b$ **21.** linear; can be written in the form $y = 0x + 7$ **23.** nonlinear; rate of change is not constant **25.** linear; rate of change is constant, as x increases by 3, y decreases by 2 **27.** nonlinear; rate of change is not constant **29.** Nonlinear; the points (year, pounds) would lie on a curved line, not on a straight line and the rate of change is not constant. **31.** Nonlinear; the power of r in the function $A = \pi r^2$ is greater than 1. **33.** C

35. $0.12x + y \leq 10$ **37.** (1, 3) **39.** (2, −2)

41.

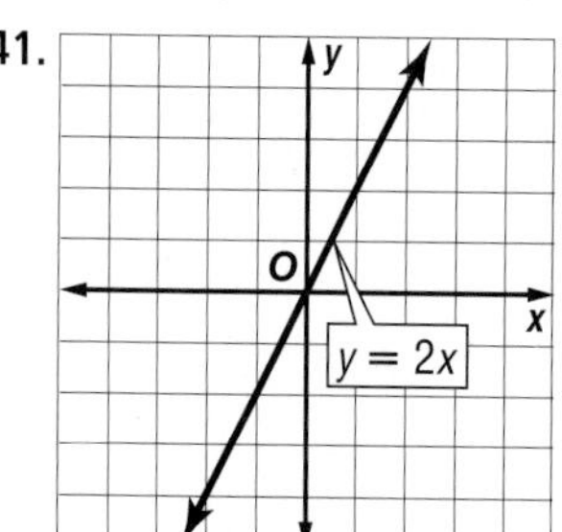

43.

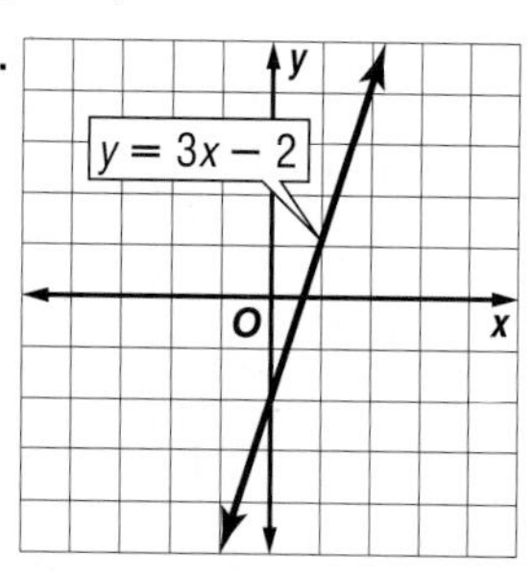

Pages 567–568 Lesson 12-2

1. A function is quadratic if the greatest power of the variable is 2. **3.** $y = 7x - 3$, it is a linear function, while the others are quadratic.

5.

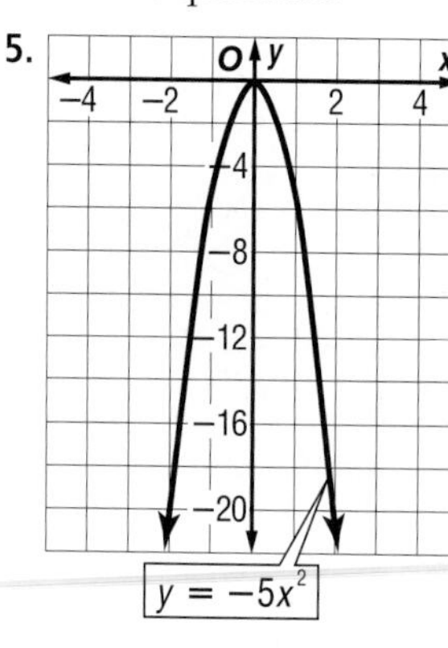

7.

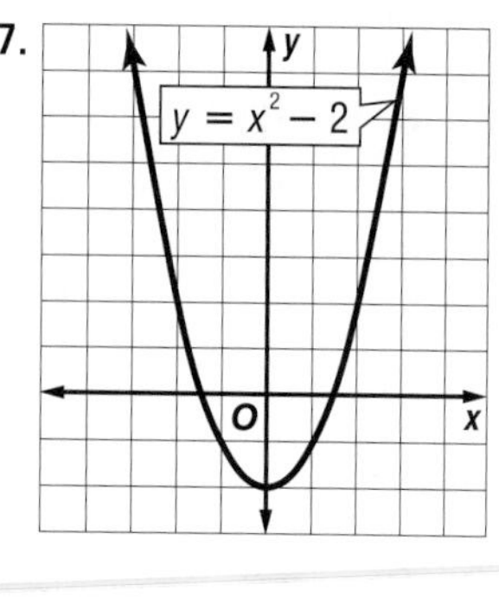

9.

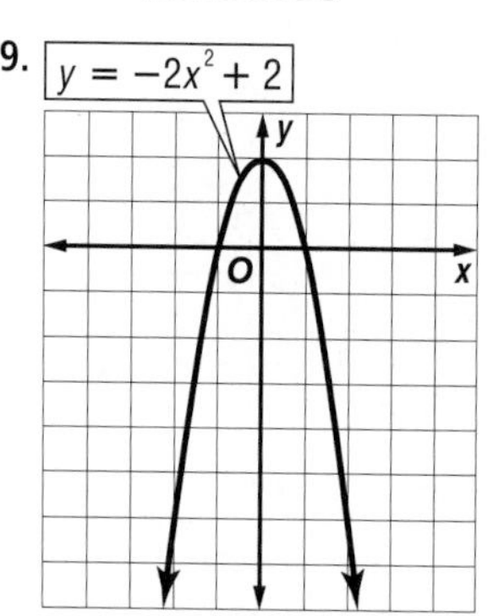

11.

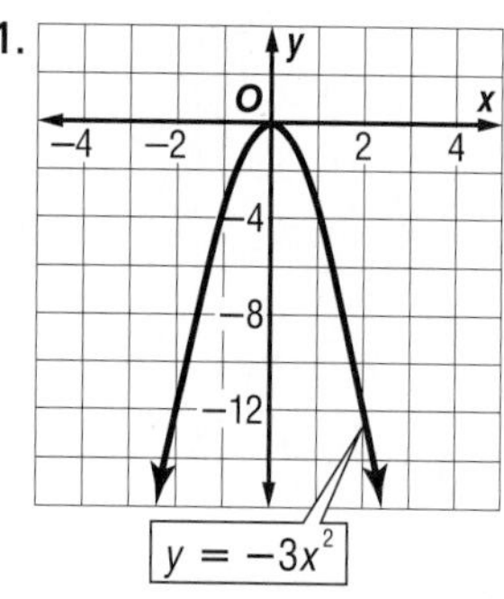

13.

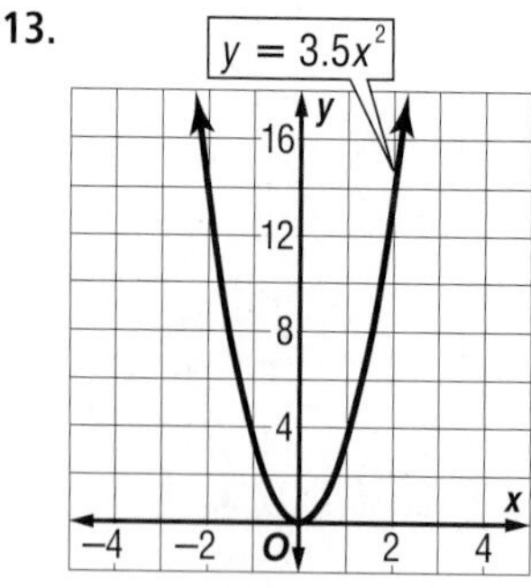

15.

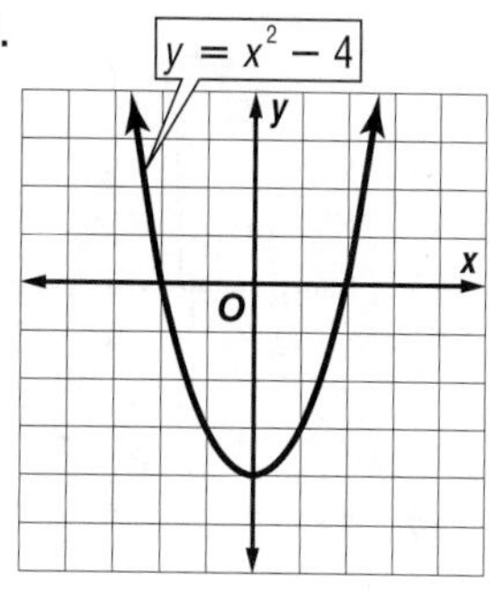

17.

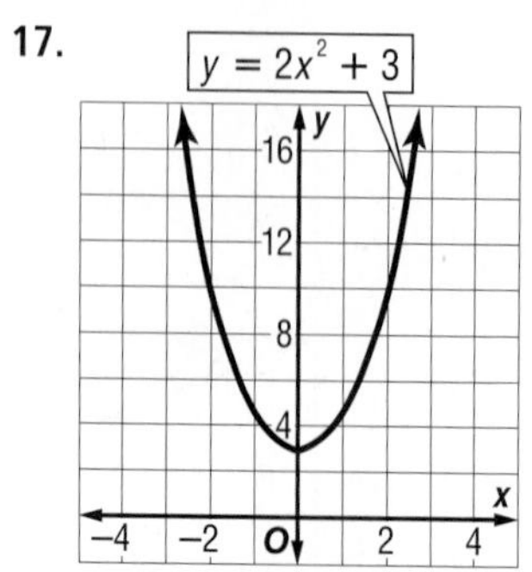

19.

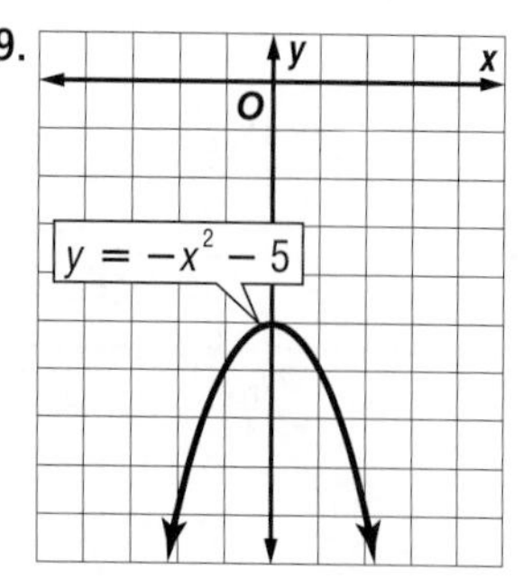

21. 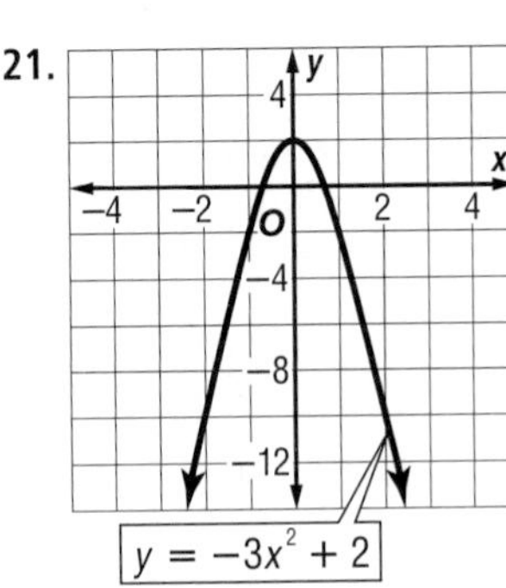

23. 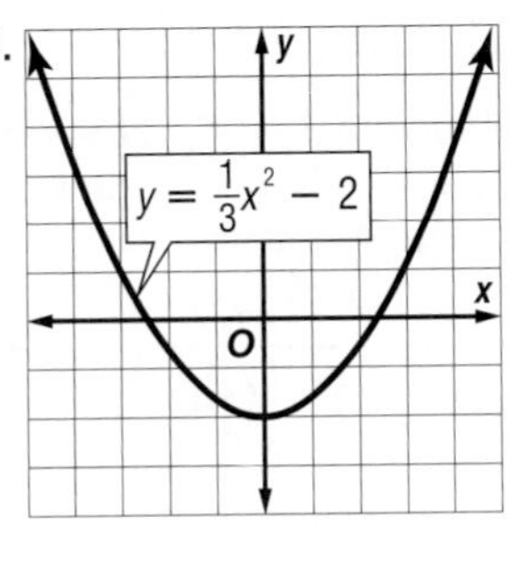

25. 250 ft

27. 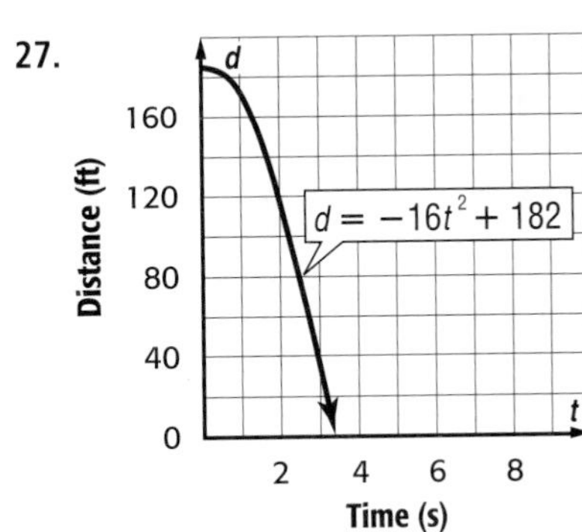

29. about 3.4 s

31. $V = 5s^2$; 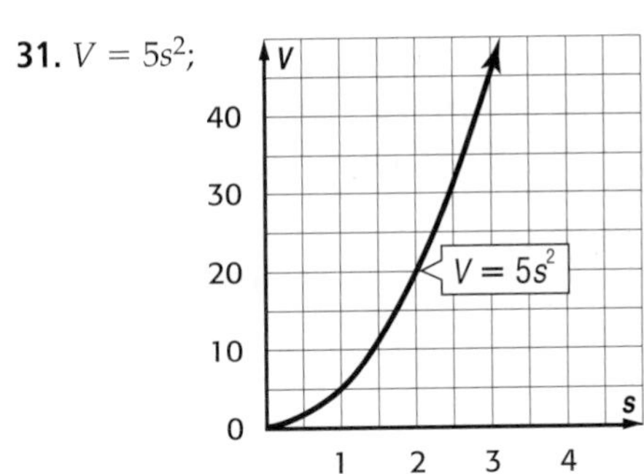

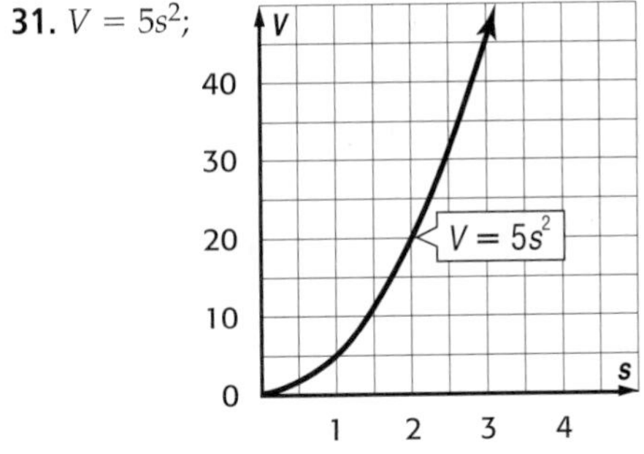

33. 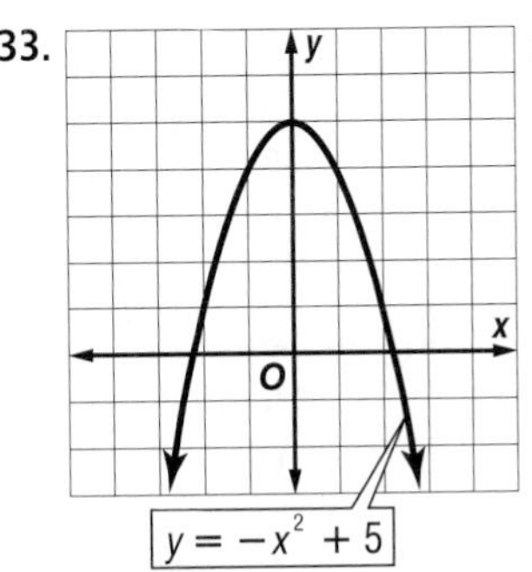

maximum; (0, 5)

35. 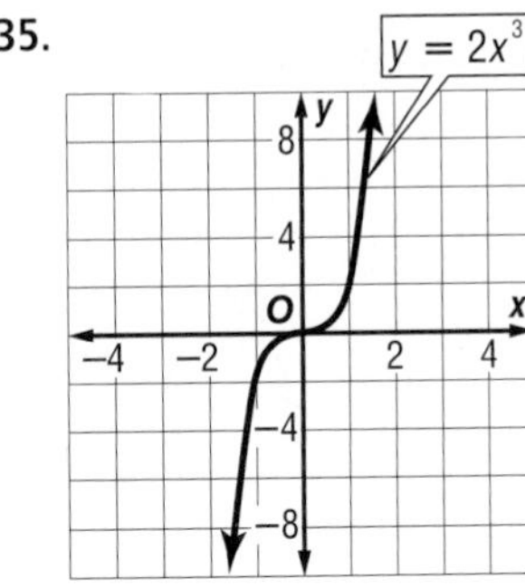

37. $y = 2x^3 + 2$

39. B **41.** linear **43.** linear

45. $y < 2x$

47. 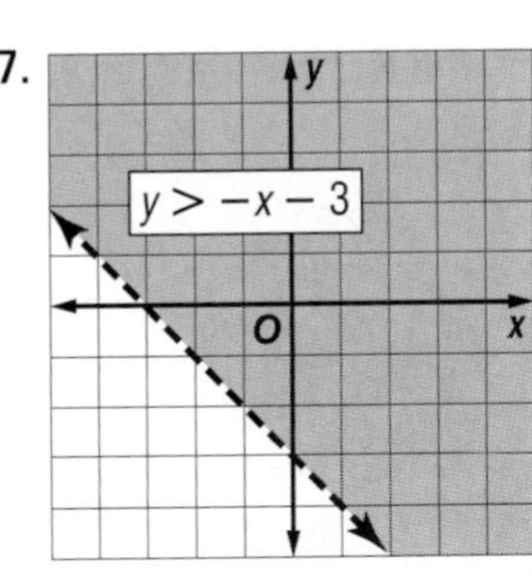

49. $4a$ and $-2a$ **51.** -1 and 3; $-2d$ and d

Pages 572–573 Lesson 12-3

1. Sample answer: $6a - a + b - 10b$ **3.** $2y^2$; the others are like terms. **5.** simplest form **7.** $x^2 + 6x$ **9.** $-2w^2 - 8w$ **11.** $-2g^2 - 7g + 8$ **13.** simplest form **15.** $8f - 11g$ **17.** $2j + k - 2$ **19.** $-2x^2 + 2x$ **21.** $-2x - 3$ **23.** $5a^2 - 6a$ **25.** $2w^2 - 7w + 1$ **27.** $8y^2 + 8y - 3$ **29.** $4z + 11$ **31.** $3r^2 - 7r + 12$ **33.** $2t^3 - 8t^2 + 7t - 6$ **35.** $\frac{3}{4}y^2 - \frac{1}{4}y$ **37.** $50r^2 + 150r + 150$ **39.** D

41. 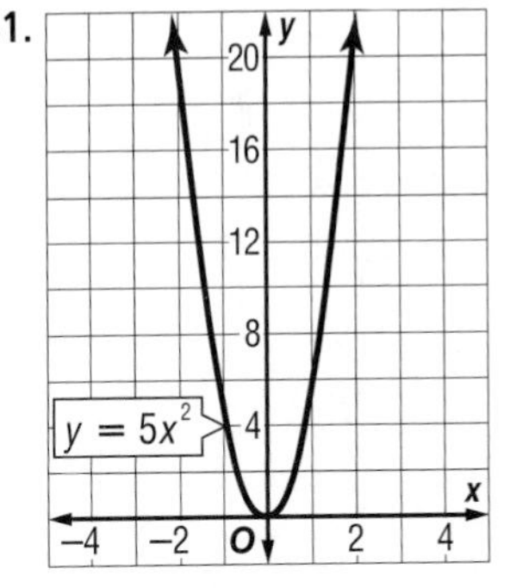

43. 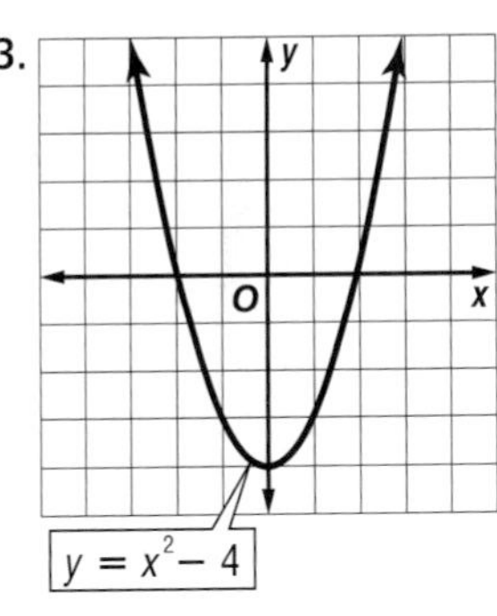

45. No; the difference between the times varies, so the growth is not constant. **47.** $(2n + 5n) + (5 + 1)$ **49.** $(x^2 + 6x^2) + (4x - 8x)$

Pages 576–577 Lesson 12-4

1. Sample answer: $x - 3y$, $3x - 2y$ **3.** $3h + 4$ **5.** $7t^2 + t - 4$ **7.** $8f^2 + 2f - 9$ **9.** 5 **11.** $7y + 10$ **13.** $5s^2 + s - 9$ **15.** $7m^2 + m + 4$ **17.** $5c - 1$ **19.** $8j^2 - 4j - 1$ **21.** $8d^2 - 1$ **23.** $6n^2 - 5n + 9$ **25.** $6v^2 + 2$ **27.** $5m^2 + 4m + 4$ **29.** $-2b^2 + 2b - 5$ **31.** $2x + y$; 15 **33.** $-3x + 5y + 2z$; -13 **35.** $18x - 9$ **37.** $25x - 9$ **39.** $4x + 100$ **41.** $2a + 3b$; the sum of two numbers minus one of its addends is equal to the other addend. **43.** 132°; 48° **45.** simplest form **47.** $4q^2 + 5q - 5$ **49.** \$275 **51.** \$868.50 **53.** $6 + (-7)$ **55.** $4x + (-5y)$

Pages 582–583 Lesson 12-5

1. $-4x^2$, $8x$, -9; $-4x^2 + 8x - 9$ **3.** Karen; Yoshi did not add the additive inverse of the entire second polynomial. **5.** $5c^2 + c + 1$ **7.** $5p + 3$ **9.** $2n^2 - n - 1$ **11.** $-5a + 6$

13. $5w + 3$ **15.** $5b^2 - 5b + 6$ **17.** $2y^2 + y + 5$ **19.** $7a - 2$ **21.** $5k^2 - 9k - 20$ **23.** $2r^2 + 2r - 4$ **25.** $17z - 2$ **27.** $4y - 8$; 12 **29.** $x + 2y + 4$; 6 **31.** $4x + 2y$; -22 **33.** $5b + 5t$ **35.** $2b - 2t$ **37.** $6.5x + 200$ **39.** $3.5x - 200$ **41.** $A = 5x + 3$, $B = 2x + 1$ **43.** $5x - 8$ units **45.** $6v^2 + v - 5$ **47.** $119C + 80R$ **49.** 3^4 **51.** 7^3

Pages 586–587 Lesson 12-6

1. false; $4x(5x^2) = 5x^2(4x) = 20x^3$ **3.** equal **5.** 3^7 **7.** $-6a^5$ **9.** $3c^5$ **11.** 7^6 **13.** 11^5 **15.** b^{14} **17.** $15x^9$ **19.** $-8w^{11}$ **21.** $40y^9$ **23.** 4^5 **25.** 10^{11} **27.** x^6 **29.** $3k$ **31.** $28a^3b^5$ **33.** $8xy$ **35.** n^4 **37.** x^7 **39.** 10^2 or 100 times greater **41.** about 10 times **43.** 10^2 or 100 people/mi^2 **45.** 1 **47.** $2x^4y^{-5}$ or $\frac{2x^4}{y^5}$ **49.** $a^5b^{-3}c^{-2}$ or $\frac{a^5}{b^3c^2}$ **51.** G **53.** $2a + 2$ **55.** 3A + 5B + C + D **57.** 47; 52; 52 **59.** $3x + 12$ **61.** $-2n - 16$

Pages 591–592 Lesson 12-7

1. Sample answer: $5x^2 + 4x + 1$ and $2x$; $10x^3 + 8x^2 + 2x$ **3.** $m^2 + 5m$ **5.** $-4x^2 - 4x$ **7.** $2g^3 - 5g^2 + 9g$ **9.** $r^2 + 9r$ **11.** $9b^2 - 6b$ **13.** $-6d^2 - 30d$ **15.** $24h + 18h^2$ **17.** $22e^2 - 77e$ **19.** $4y^3 - 36y$ **21.** $t^3 + 5t^2 + 9t$ **23.** $-8r^3 + 2r^2 + 16r$ **25.** $2x(x + 4)$; $2x^2 + 8x$

27.

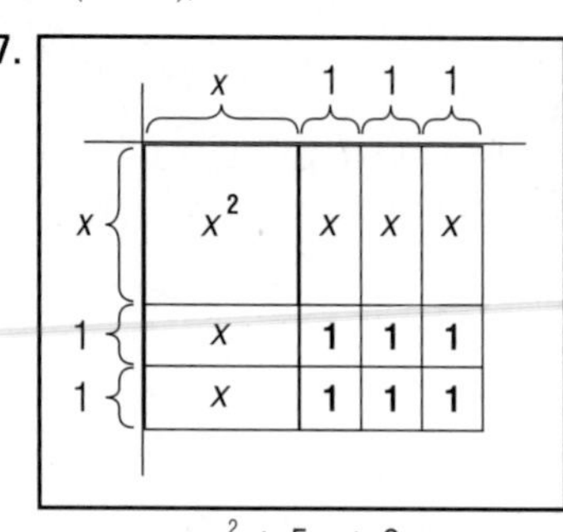

$x^2 + 5x + 6$

29. $A = 2x^2$;

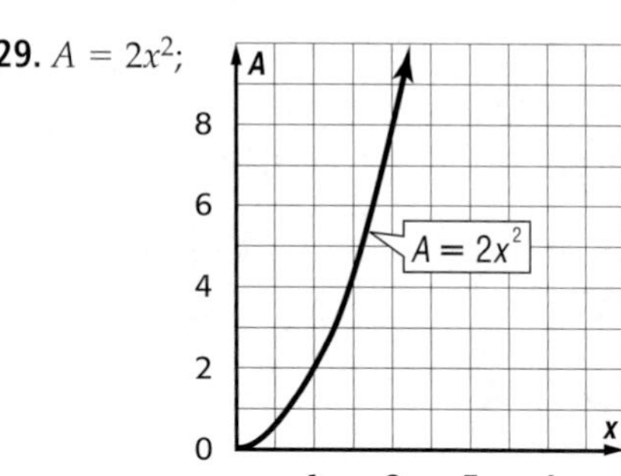

31. 11^3 **33.** $7a$

Pages 593–594 Chapter 12 Study Guide and Review

1. false; polynomial **3.** false; add **5.** true **7.** nonlinear; power of x is greater than 1

9.

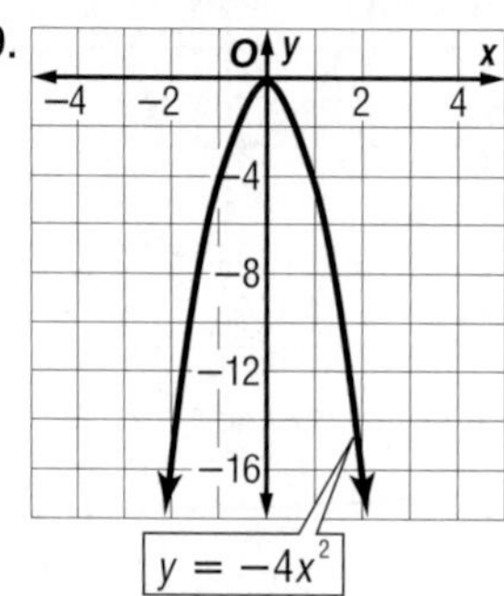

11.

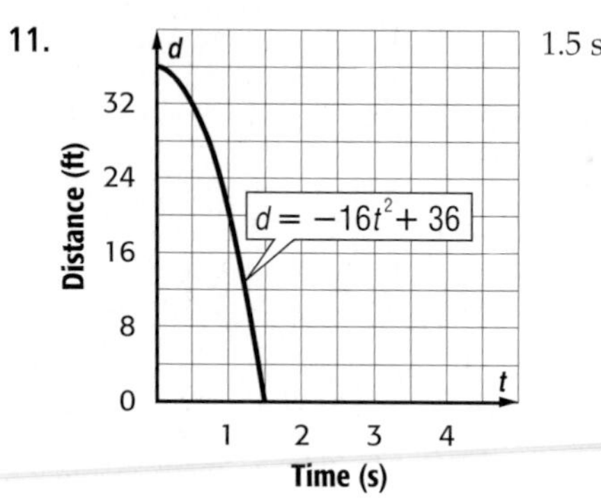

1.5 s

13. simplest form **15.** $5a^2 + a$ **17.** $10m^2 + 3m - 6$ **19.** $6c - 11$ **21.** $5k^2 + 5k - 1$ **23.** $36y^{11}$ **25.** $-3c^3$ **27.** $9y^2 + 12y$ **29.** $p^3 - 6p$ **31.** $-10k^3 + 6k^2 - 16k$

Photo Credits

Cover (tl b)Peter Read Miller/Sports Illustrated, (tr)PhotoDisc; **i** Peter Read Miller/Sports Illustrated; **iv v x** Aaron Haupt; **xi** John D. Norman/CORBIS; **xii** Bob Daemmrich/Stock Boston; **xiii** Paul A. Souders/CORBIS; **xiv** CORBIS; **xv** Cydney Conger/CORBIS; **xvii** Mike Yamashita/Woodfin Camp & Associates; **xviii** Sylvain Grandadam/Getty Images; **xix** Douglas Peebles/CORBIS; **xx** DiMaggio/Kalish/ CORBIS; **xxi** PhotoDisc; **xxiii** John Evans; **xxiv** (t)PhotoDisc, (b)John Evans; **xxv** (t bl)PhotoDisc, (br)John Evans; **xxvi** John Evans; **2–3** Peter Cade/Getty Images; **4–5** Stephen Frink/CORBIS; **7** Ed Bock/CORBIS; **9** W. Cody/CORBIS; **15** (l)Aaron Haupt/Photo Researchers, (r)YVA Momatiuk/Photo Researchers; **18** Skip Comer/Latent Image, (bkgd) Cindy Kassab/CORBIS; **21** Joe Mazzeo/AJGA; **27** David Young-Wolff/PhotoEdit; **30** James Westwater; **33** John Evans; **34** Chris McLaughlin/CORBIS; **36** File Photo; **39** C Squared Studios/PhotoDisc; **40** John D. Norman/CORBIS; **43** (l)PhotoDisc, (r)John Evans; **48** Women's National Basketball Association; **50** Photowood/CORBIS; **51** Aaron Haupt; **60–61** Courtesy Paramount's Kings Island; **62** Bud Lehnhausen/Photo Researchers; **64** Doug Martin; **65** Patricia Fogden/CORBIS; **67** Matt Meadows; **68** Courtesy Paramount Canada's Wonderland, Paramount Parks, Inc.; **70** AP/Wide World Photos; **73** CORBIS; **74** Matt Meadows; **75** Crawford Greenewalt/VIREO; **76** CORBIS; **78** Aaron Haupt; **79** (t)Courtesy Jo McCulty/Ohio State University, (b)Tom Young/CORBIS; **80** (t)George McCarthy/CORBIS, (b)Dennis Johnson/Papilio/CORBIS; **82** Julie Houck/Stock Boston; **87** John Evans; **88** Andy Sacks/Getty Images; **91** CORBIS; **92** Tom Brakefield/CORBIS; **93** Elaine Thompson/AP/Wide World Photos; **96** Matt Meadows; **101** W.H. Freeman & Co.; **104** Flash! Light/Stock Boston; **105** Rafael Macia/Photo Researchers; **106** Bill Amend/Distributed by Universal Press Syndicate; **107** Bob Daemmrich/Stock Boston; **114–115** Michael Howell/Index Stock; **118** Bill Amend/Distributed by Universal Press Syndicate; **121** Charles O'Rear/CORBIS; **123** (l)John Evans, (r)Matt Meadows; **127** Paul A. Souders/CORBIS; **131** John Evans; **133** Wolfgang Kaehler/CORBIS; **143** Aaron Haupt; **152–153** Rob Gage/Getty Images; **154–155** Michael Simpson/Getty Images; **157** Peter Heimsath/Rex USA; **160 162** Doug Martin; **167** Bettmann/CORBIS; **170** Doug Martin; **171** Matt Meadows; **175** John Evans; **176** (l)J. Strange/KS Studios, (r)John Evans; **182** John Evans; **183** Taxi/Getty Images; **185** Doug Martin; **186** M.I. Walker/Photo Researchers; **187** CORBIS; **188** Johnny Hart/Creators Syndicate, Inc.; **190** Reuters/Getty Images News & Sport; **195** Nick Koudis/PhotoDisc; **197** National Gallery of Art/Collection of Mr. & Mrs. Paul Mellon; **204–205** Harry How/Getty Images; **207** Hulton-Deutsch Collection/CORBIS; **210** Cydney Conger/CORBIS; **213** Daryl Benson/Masterfile; **217** Joseph Sohm/Vision of America/CORBIS; **218** Image Bank/Getty Images; **220** Stephen Simpson/Getty Images; **225** John Evans; **226** (l)Laura Sefferlin, (r)Matt Meadows; **229** Laurence Fordyce/Eye Ubiquitous/CORBIS; **231** Alan Schein/CORBIS; **232** David Muench/CORBIS; **235** (l)R. Kord/H. Armstrong Roberts, (r)Steve Vidler/SuperStock; **236** Underwood & Underwood/CORBIS; **238** Matt Meadows; **242** Aaron Haupt; **243** Bettmann CORBIS; **252–253** Flip Chalfant/Getty Images; **254–255** Gary Rhijnsburger/Masterfile; **258** Aaron Haupt; **265** AP/Wide World Photos; **268** (l)Art Resource, NY, (r)Courtesy Greece Cultural Minister; **270** Aaron Haupt; **275** Art Resource, NY; **276** (l)Aaron Haupt, (r)John Evans; **279** Aaron Haupt; **281** Michael & Patricia Fogden/CORBIS; **282** Doug Martin; **284** CORBIS; **285** John Evans; **287** Doug Martin; **288** Courtesy Boston Bruins; **289** (t)Doug Martin, (c)Scott Kim, (b)National Council of Teachers of Mathematics; **290** Darrell Gulin/CORBIS; **293** Art Resource, NY; **299** (t)Burstein Collection/CORBIS, (b)Robert Brons/BPS/Getty Images; **301** Courtesy Ramona Maston/FolkArt.com; **304** Cordon Art-Baarn-Holland; **309** Aaron Haupt; **312–313** Aaron Haupt; **316** David Young-Wolff/PhotoEdit; **321** Jonathan Nourok/PhotoEdit; **322** Aaron Haupt; **324** (l)John Evans, (r)Brent Turner; **328** Doug Martin; **331** Craig Kramer; **332** Doug Martin; **334** (l)Biophoto Associates/Photo Researchers, (c)E.B. Turner, (r)Stephen Frisch/Stock Boston; **339** Inga Spence/Index Stock; **341** John Evans; **343** John Elk III/Stock Boston; **348** Tony Freeman/PhotoEdit; **352** (t)Heathcliff O'Malley/The Daily Telegraph, (b)Biblioteca Ambrosiana, Milan/Art Resource, NY; **54** Mike Yamashita/Woodfin Camp & Associates; **358** (t)King Features Syndicate, (b)Studiohio; **370–371** PhotoDisc; **372–373** DUOMO/CORBIS; **374** Aaron Haupt; **377** James Balog/Getty Images; **378** Laura Sifferlin; **381** Bettmann/CORBIS; **383** PhotoDisc; **384** Aaron Haupt; **386** CORBIS; **387** Ronald Martinez/Getty Images; **389** Andy Sacks/Getty Images; **390** KS Studios; **391** Aaron Haupt; **395** John Evans; **397** Sylvain Grandadam/Getty Images; **401** LWA-Dann Tardif/CORBIS; **402** Mark Thayer; **406** Cooperphoto/CORBIS; **407** Doug Martin; **408** Aaron Haupt; **416–417** Getty Images; **418** Laura Sifferlin; **427** Francis G. Mayer/CORBIS; **431** Getty Images; **432** KS Studios; **437** AFP/CORBIS; **441** John Evans; **442** Matt Meadows; **443** Jacques M. Chenet/CORBIS; **445** PhotoDisc; **447** Geoff Butler; **451** AFP/CORBIS; **454** Martin B. Withers/Frank Lane Picture Library/CORBIS; **456** AFP/CORBIS; **464–465** Lonnie Duka/Index Stock Imagery; **466–467** Bob Winsett/CORBIS; **471** DiMaggio/Kalish/CORBIS; **474** Aaron Haupt; **477** CORBIS; **480** Aaron Haupt; **481** Cris Cole/Allsport/Getty Images; **484** Westlight Stock/OZ Production/CORBIS; **487** Doug Martin; **488 491** John Evans; **492** Doug Martin; **496** John Evans; **499** Aaron Haupt; **500** Doug Martin; **502** Aaron Haupt; **510–511** EyeWire; **514** Aaron Haupt; **515** Ken Redding/CORBIS; **517** Kathi Lamm/Getty Images; **518** Robert Brenner/PhotoEdit, Inc.; **522** Paul M. Walsh/The Morning Journal/AP/Wide World Photos; **531** John Evans; **534** Juan Silva/Getty Images; **537 539** Laura Sifferlin; **540** Phil Schermeister/CORBIS; **541** Barbara Stitzer/PhotoEdit, Inc.; **542** CORBIS; **545** Ron Fehling/Masterfile; **547** PhotoDisc; **549** EyeWire; **551** Banknotes.com; **558–559** DUOMO/CORBIS; **560** Doug Martin; **561** Elise Amendola/AP/Wide World Photos; **566** Lance Nelson/CORBIS; **567** Michael S. Yamashita/CORBIS; **570** CORBIS; **573** Aaron Haupt; **579** John Evans; **581** Doug Martin; **583** Frank Lerner; **584** CORBIS; **585** Mug Shots/CORBIS; **586** Burhan Ozbilici/AP/Wide World Photos; **588** Laura Sifferlin; **598** Peter Read Miller/Sports Illustrated; **686** Jeff Smith/Fotosmith

T1 Doug Martin; **T4 T19** Mark Ransom; **T5** Mug Shots/CORBIS; **T11** Ariel Skelley/CORBIS; **T16** Tim Courlas; **T18** Steve McAlister Productions/Getty Images.

Index

Red type denotes items only in the Teacher Wraparound Edition.

I

N

Index

Index

Index